Contemporary Authors

NEW REVISION SERIES

Contemporary Authors

**A Bio-Bibliographical Guide to
Current Writers in Fiction, General Nonfiction,
Poetry, Journalism, Drama, Motion Pictures,
Television, and Other Fields**

ANN EVORY

Editor

NEW REVISION SERIES volume 3

GALE RESEARCH COMPANY • THE BOOK TOWER • DETROIT, MICHIGAN 48226

EDITORIAL STAFF

Christine Nasso, *General Editor, Contemporary Authors*

Ann Evory, *Editor, New Revision Series*
Peter M. Gareffa and Linda Metzger, *Associate Editors*
Penelope S. Gordon, Denise Gottis, Elaine Guregian, David A. Guy,
James G. Lesniak, Margaret Mazurkiewicz, Catherine Stadelman,
Deborah A. Straub, Thomas Wiloch, and Michaela Swart Wilson, *Assistant Editors*
Ellen Koral, Susan A. Martin, and Susan Salter, *Editorial Assistants*

Frederick G. Ruffner, *Publisher*   James M. Ethridge, *Editorial Director*

Preface

A major change in the preparation of *Contemporary Authors* revision volumes began with the first volume of the newly titled *Contemporary Authors New Revision Series.* No longer are all of the sketches in a given *Contemporary Authors* volume updated and published together as a revision volume. Instead, sketches from a number of volumes are assessed, and only those sketches requiring *significant change* are revised and published in a *Contemporary Authors New Revision Series* volume. This change enables us to provide *Contemporary Authors* users with updated information about active writers on a more timely basis and avoids printing sketches from previous volumes in which there has been little or no change. As always, the most recent *Contemporary Authors* cumulative index continues to be the user's guide to the location of an individual author's listing.

Following are more detailed explanations about the *Contemporary Authors New Revision Series.*

Questions and Answers
About
Contemporary Authors New Revision Series

How do *New Revision Series* volumes differ from previous revision volumes?

Prior to the inception of the *New Revision Series,* all sketches in a given volume of *CA* were revised and published as a unit. For example, *CA* Volumes 41-44, First Revision, the last book published under the previous revision system, contained *all* of the 2,252 sketches listed in the original *CA* Volumes 41-44. The *New Revision Series* differs from previous revisions of individual volumes in two basic ways:

1) The *New Revision Series* lists only those authors whose entries have undergone significant change since their last appearance in *CA*. For example, only 35% or 737 of the sketches in original *CA* Volumes 45-48 (published in 1974) have been revised for the *New Revision Series;* the remaining 65%, or 1,368 sketches, will be updated and placed in future *New Revision Series* volumes *when and if significant change* can be reflected in the entries.

2) *New Revision Series* volumes also contain sketches from several *CA* volumes, including previously revised editions. In addition to sketches drawn from *CA* Volumes 45-48, this volume also contains entries taken from *CA* Volumes 1-4, First Revision (published 1968), *CA* Volumes 5-8, First Revision (published 1969), *CA* Volumes 9-12, First Revision (published 1974), and *CA* Volumes 49-52 (published 1975). The new series name and single-volume numbering system reflect this mixture of sketches and serve to distinguish the *New Revision Series* from earlier revisions.

Why has the *CA* revision system been changed?

While the previous approach to revising *CA* sketches provided complete, accurate, and up-to-date information on all authors in a given volume, we feel the *New Revision Series* even better meets the needs of *CA* users. By employing a selective approach to revisions, we can revise and publish sketches whenever they are out of date. The *New Revision Series* eliminates the need to publish entries with few or no changes.

How are sketches selected for the *New Revision Series*?

Clippings of all sketches in selected *CA* volumes published several years ago are sent to the authors at their last-known addresses. Authors mark material to be deleted or changed, and insert any new personal data, new affiliations, new books, new work in progress, new sidelights, and new biographical/critical sources. All author returns are assessed, additional research is done, if necessary, and those sketches with *significant change* are published in the *New Revision Series*.

If, however, authors fail to reply, or if authors are now deceased, biographical dictionaries are checked for new information (a task made easier through the use of Gale's *Biography and Genealogy Master Index*), as are bibliographical sources, such as *Cumulative Book Index, The National Union Catalog*, etc. Using data from such sources, revision editors select and revise nonrespondents' entries which need *substantial updating*. Sketches not personally reviewed by the authors are marked with a dagger (†) to indicate that these listings have been revised from secondary sources believed to be reliable, but they have not been personally reviewed for this edition by the authors sketched.

In addition, listings for active individual authors from *any* previous volume of *CA* may be included in a volume of the *New Revision Series*. Reviews and articles in major periodicals, lists of prestigious awards, and requests from *CA* users are monitored so that authors on whom new information is in demand can be identified and revised listings prepared promptly.

For example, this volume contains an updated entry for Marilyn French. When her sketch was originally written for *CA* Volumes 69-72 and published in 1978, little critical material was available on her controversial first novel, *The Women's Room*. The completely new sidelights section in her revised sketch reflects the critics' responses to both *The Women's Room* and her second novel, *The Bleeding Heart*.

How much change is likely to occur in a *New Revision Series* entry?

The amount and type of change in any given sketch vary with the author, but all listings in this volume have been revised and/or augmented in various ways. Most entries include *new* degrees, mailing addresses, literary agents, career items, career-related and civic activities, memberships, work in progress, and biographical/critical sources. They may also include the following:

1) Major new awards—The Harry S Truman Award in Civil War History, a Pulitzer Prize, and a National Book Award have been added to historian T. Harry Williams's revised entry. Updated sketches have been prepared for other award-winning authors, including Flannery O'Connor and Anne Sexton.

2) Extensive bibliographical additions—Over thirty-five new titles have been added to Western writer Louis L'Amour's updated sketch, and noted black author James Baldwin's revised entry includes four novels, four essay collections, two plays, and four other works not listed previously.

3) Informative new sidelights—P.G. Wodehouse's revised sidelights section contains not only extensive biographical information but also in-depth discussions about Wodehouse's style and themes. New sidelights for Harold Courlander's sketch describe his successful suit against Alex Haley for copyright infringement in *Roots*.

Other notable people in this volume whose entries have undergone similarly extensive revision include Richard Adams, Margaret Atwood, John Dickson Carr, John Dos Passos, Lawrence Ferlinghetti, Denise Levertov, William Manchester, Marianne Moore, Rosemary Rogers, Lowell Thomas, Pierre Trudeau, Mark Van Doren, and Theodore H. White.

We invite *CA* users to compare original entries with revised listings and provide us with feedback on our revision procedures. To illustrate more specifically the amount and type of change that occurs in a *New Revision Series* entry, Richard Price's original and revised sketches have been reprinted on the following page.

What happens to sketches not included in a *New Revision Series* volume?

Sketches not eligible for a *New Revision Series* volume because the author or a revision editor has verified that no significant change is required will, of course, be available to *CA* users in previously published *CA* volumes. When enough new information is accumulated, either through remailings to the authors or through such sources as reviews, articles, and interviews in periodicals, suggestions from

PRICE, Richard 1949-

PERSONAL: Born October 12, 1949, in New York, N.Y. *Education:* Cornell University, B.S., 1971; Columbia University, graduate study, 1972-74; Stanford University, further graduate study, 1973. *Politics:* None. *Religion:* None. *Home and office:* 325 West End Ave., New York, N.Y. 10023. *Agent:* Carl Brandt, Brandt & Brandt, 101 Park Ave., New York, N.Y. 10017.

CAREER: Hostos Community College, Bronx, N.Y., lecturer in English as a second language, 1973; New York University, New York, N.Y., lecturer in urban affairs, 1973; State University of New York at Stony Brook, Long Island, N.Y., lecturer in creative writing, 1974—. *Awards, honors:* Edith Mirrilees grant in fiction from Stanford University, 1972; Mary Roberts Rinehart Foundation grant, 1973; MacDowell Colony grant, 1973.

WRITINGS: The Wanderers (novel), Houghton, 1974.

WORK IN PROGRESS: Nuns in Trouble, a novel.

PRICE, Richard 1949-

PERSONAL: Born October 12, 1949, in New York, N.Y. *Education:* Cornell University, B.S., 1971; Columbia University, graduate study, 1972-74, M.F.A., 1976; Stanford University, further graduate study, 1973. *Politics:* None. *Religion:* None. *Home and office:* 10 Jones St., New York, N.Y. 10014. *Agent:* Brandt & Brandt, 1501 Broadway, New York, N.Y. 10036.

CAREER: Writer. Lecturer in English as a second language, Hostos Community College, 1973; lecturer in urban affairs, New York University, 1973; lecturer in creative writing, State University of New York at Stony Brook, begining 1974, New York University, 1974 and 1977, State University of New York at Binghamton, 1976, Hofstra University, 1978-79, and Yale University, 1980. *Awards, honors:* Edith Mirrilees grant in fiction from Stanford University, 1972; Mary Roberts Rinehart Foundation grant, 1973; MacDowell Colony grant, 1973; Yaddo fellow, 1977, 1978, and 1980; *Playboy* Magazine Nonfiction Award, 1979; MacDowell fellow, 1979.

WRITINGS—All novels; all published by Houghton: *The Wanderers,* 1974; *Bloodbrothers,* 1976; *Ladies' Man,* 1978.

SIDELIGHTS: Despite his desire not to become known as the "Voice of the Bronx," Richard Price has often had his work compared to that of other writers who have focused on the problems of growing up male in various urban centers of the United States—most notably James T. Farrell (Chicago) and Hubert Selby, Jr. (Brooklyn). Price's grittily realistic portrayal of gang life in the Bronx, *The Wanderers* (published when the author was only 24 years old), was hailed as "an extraordinary first novel" by *Newsweek*'s Charles Michener. Continues the critic: "Like the nerviest of the teen-age gang members who give the novel its title, Price prowls the 1960s jungle of a North Bronx housing project and its environs without fear—or shame. His switchblade prose is not interested in shadows but flesh and blood .... His dialogue has the immediacy of overheard subway conversation. His wit is capable of perceiving the dopey pathos behind adolescent swagger and obscenity as well as capturing the surrealistic exhilaration of mass violence."

Rick Kogan of the *Chicago Sun-Times* calls Price's book "one of the few powerful and worthwhile novels of the year. . . . The language of *The Wanderers* is tough, the gang's actions often crude and vulgar. But it is an important novel for just those reasons. It is real. It is a work that tells its tale in the best

[The remainder of Price's sidelights, too lengthy to reprint here, can be found in his sketch on page 449.]

BIOGRAPHICAL/CRITICAL SOURCES: Chicago Sun-Times, March 31, 1974; *New York,* April 1, 1974; *New York Times Book Review,* April 21, 1974, May 23, 1976, November 12, 1978; *Rolling Stone,* May 9, 1974, May 20, 1976, November 30, 1978; *Newsweek,* May 13, 1974, September 18, 1978; *Village Voice,* May 16, 1974, October 9, 1978; *New Yorker,* May 20, 1974, November 27, 1978; *Contemporary Literary Criticism,* Gale, Volume VI, 1976, Volume XII, 1980; *America,* November 13, 1976; *Saturday Review,* March 20, 1976; *Washington Post Book World,* May 2, 1976, October 15, 1978; *New Statesman,* May 20, 1977; *New York Times,* November 10, 1978, July 22, 1979, August 31, 1979; *New Republic,* January 6, 1979; *New York Review of Books,* January 25, 1979.

—*Sketch by Deborah A. Straub*

CA users, publicity releases, book lists, award lists, etc., these sketches will be revised and placed in a *New Revision Series* volume. Some sketches, however, may never be revised if the existing entries remain accurate. Users should always consult the *CA* cumulative index published in alternate new volumes of *CA* to determine the location of any author's entry.

Can any volumes of *Contemporary Authors* safely be discarded because they are obsolete?

As the chart on the following page indicates, *CA* users who have all First Revision volumes *and* both *Contemporary Authors Permanent Series* volumes can discard corresponding unrevised volumes 1 through 44.

Since the *New Revision Series* does not supersede any specific volumes of *CA*, all of the following must be retained in order to have information on all authors in the series:

- all revised volumes
- the two *Contemporary Authors Permanent Series* volumes
- *CA* Volumes 45-48 and subsequent original volumes

How can information be located on a particular author?

The *CA* cumulative index published in alternate new volumes of *CA* continues to be the user's guide to the location of an individual author's listing. Those authors appearing in the *New Revision Series* are listed in the *CA* index with the designation CANR- in front of the specific volume number. For the convenience of those who do not have *New Revison Series* volumes, the index also notes the specific earlier volume of *CA* in which the sketch appeared. Below is a sample *New Revision Series* index citation:

> Vonnegut, Kurt, Jr. 1922- CANR-1
> Earlier sketch in CA 3R
> See also CLC 1, 2, 3, 4, 5, 8, 12
> See also AITN 1

For the most recent information on Vonnegut, users should refer to Volume 1 of the *New Revision Series,* as designated by "CANR-1"; if that volume is unavailable, refer to *CA* 1-4 First Revision, as indicated by "Earlier sketch in CA 3R," for his 1968 listing. (And if *CA* 1-4 First Revision is unavailable, refer to *CA* 3, published in 1963, for Vonnegut's original listing.)

For the convenience of *CA* users, the *CA* cumulative index also includes references to all entries in three related Gale series—*Contemporary Literary Criticism* (CLC), which is devoted entirely to current criticism on major novelists, poets, playwrights, and other creative writers, *Something About the Author* (SATA), a series of heavily illustrated sketches on juvenile authors and illustrators, and *Authors in the News* (AITN), a compilation of news stories and feature articles from American newspapers and magazines covering writers and other members of the communications media.

Summary

1) *CA* Volumes 41-44, First Revision, marks the end of the previous *CA* revision system.

2) Only authors whose entries have undergone *significant change* since their last appearance in *CA* are listed in the *New Revision Series.*

3) Authors eligible for revised entries in the *New Revision Series* can be drawn from any *CA* volume.

4) Since only active authors are selected for inclusion in the *New Revision Series,* in almost all cases their revised sketches are longer than their previous *CA* entries.

5) The most recent *CA* cumulative index continues to be the user's guide to locating an author's original and revised *CA* entries.

As always, suggestions from users about any aspect of *CA* will be welcomed.

IF YOU HAVE:	YOU MAY DISCARD:
1-4 First Revision (1967)	1 (1962) 2 (1963) 3 (1963) 4 (1963)
5-8 First Revision (1969)	5-6 (1963) 7-8 (1963)
Both 9-12 First Revision (1974) AND *Contemporary Authors Permanent Series,* Volume 1 (1975)	9-10 (1964) 11-12 (1965)
Both 13-16 First Revision (1975) AND *Contemporary Authors Permanent Series,* Volumes 1 and 2 (1975, 1978)	13-14 (1965) 15-16 (1966)
Both 17-20 First Revision (1976) AND *Contemporary Authors Permanent Series,* Volumes 1 and 2 (1975, 1978)	17-18 (1967) 19-20 (1968)
Both 21-24 First Revision (1977) AND *Contemporary Authors Permanent Series,* Volumes 1 and 2 (1975, 1978)	21-22 (1969) 23-24 (1970)
Both 25-28 First Revision (1977) AND *Contemporary Authors Permanent Series,* Volume 2 (1978)	25-28 (1971)
Both 29-32 First Revision (1978) AND *Contemporary Authors Permanent Series,* Volume 2 (1978)	29-32 (1972)
Both 33-36 First Revision (1978) AND *Contemporary Authors Permanent Series,* Volume 2 (1978)	33-36 (1973)
37-40 First Revision (1979)	37-40 (1973)
41-44 First Revision (1979)	41-44 (1974)
45-48 (1974) 49-52 (1975) 53-56 (1975) 57-60 (1976) ↓ ↓ 101 (1981)	NONE: These volumes will not be super-seded by corresponding revised volumes. Individual entries from these and all other volumes appearing in the left col-umn of this chart will be revised and included in the *New Revision Series.*
Contemporary Authors New Revision Series, Volume 1 (1981), Volume 2 (1981), Volume 3 (1981)	NONE: The *New Revision Series* does not replace any single volume of *CA.* All volumes appearing in the left column of this chart must be retained to have in-formation on all authors in the series.

CONTEMPORARY AUTHORS

NEW REVISION SERIES

† Indicates that a listing has been revised from secondary sources believed to be reliable, but has not been personally reviewed for this edition by the author sketched.

A

ABBEY, Merrill R. 1905-

PERSONAL: Born April 19, 1905, in Luverne, Minn.; son of Ray S. and Harriet (Henton) Abbey; married Lucy Marie Robinson, 1927; children: Mary Ruth (Mrs. Richard A. Reading), Stuart Gilbert. *Education:* Hamline University, B.A., 1927; Garrett Theological Seminary (now Garrett-Evangelical Theological Seminary), B.D., 1930; Northwestern University, graduate student, 1930-31. *Home:* 1113 Elm Cove, Luverne, Minn. 56156.

CAREER: Pastor of Methodist churches in Newport, Minn., 1932, Northfield, Minn., 1933-37, Marinette, Wis., 1937-41, Milwaukee, Wis., 1941-46, Madison, Wis., 1946-53, and Ann Arbor, Mich., 1953-59; Garrett-Evangelical Theological Seminary, Evanston, Ill., professor of preaching, 1959-73, professor emeritus, 1973—. Participated in Ecumenical Conferences of the World Methodist Council at Oxford, England, 1951, and Lake Junaluska, N.C., 1956. *Awards, honors:* D.D. from Hamline University, 1942.

WRITINGS: Creed of Our Hope, Abingdon, 1954; *Encounter with Christ,* Abingdon, 1961; *Preaching to the Contemporary Mind,* Abingdon, 1963; *Living Doctrine in a Vital Pulpit,* Abingdon, 1964; *The Word Interprets Us,* Abingdon, 1967; *Man, Media and the Message,* Friendship, 1970; *The Shape of the Gospel,* Abingdon, 1970; *Communication in Pulpit and Parish,* Westminster, 1973; (with O. C. Edwards) *Proclamation: Epiphany, Series A,* Fortress, 1974; *Day Dawns in Fire: America's Search for Meaning,* Fortress, 1976. Contributor to *Religion in Life, Pulpit,* and *Christian Advocate.*

* * *

ABELL, George O(gden) 1927-

PERSONAL: Born March 1, 1927, in Los Angeles, Calif.; son of Theodore Curtis (a Unitarian minister) and Ann (Ogden) Abell; married Lois Everson, June 16, 1951; married Phyllis Fox (an artist), March 10, 1972; children: (first marriage) Anthony Alan, Jonathan Edward. *Education:* California Institute of Technology, B.S., 1951, M.S., 1952, Ph.D., 1957. *Office:* Department of Astronomy, University of California, Los Angeles, Calif. 90024.

CAREER: National Geographic Society, Palomar Observatory Sky Survey, observer, 1953-56; University of California, Los Angeles, associate professor, 1956-67, professor of astronomy, 1967—, chairman of the department, 1968-75.

Lecturer, Griffith Observatory, 1953-57; guest lecturer, Max-Planck Institute fuer Physik und Astrophysik, 1966-67; visiting professor, Royal Observatory, Edinburgh, Scotland, 1976-77. Guest investigator, Mount Wilson and Palomar Observatories, 1957—. Academic director of summer science program for gifted high school seniors, Thacher School, Ojai, Calif., 1960-67. Major presenter and co-producer of television film series, "Understanding Space and Time," BBC-TV, 1979-80. *Military service:* U.S. Army Air Corps, 1945-46; became sergeant. *Member:* International Astronomical Union, American Astronomical Society, Astronomical Society of Pacific (president, 1968-70), American Association for the Advancement of Science.

WRITINGS: (Contributor) *Stars and Galaxies,* Prentice-Hall, 1962, revised edition, University of Chicago Press, 1975; (contributor) *Problems of Extragalactic Research,* Macmillan, 1962; (contributor with Rudolph L. Minkowski) K. A. Strand, editor, *Basic Astronomical Data,* University of Chicago Press, 1963; *Exploration of the Universe,* Holt, 1964, 3rd edition, 1975; *Realm of the Universe,* Holt, 1976, 2nd edition, Saunders, 1980; *Drama of the Universe,* Holt, 1978; (editor with P.J.E. Peebles) *Objects of High Redshift,* Reidel, 1980; (editor with Barry Singer, and contributor) *Science and the Paranormal,* Scribner, 1981. Contributor of articles to journals, including *Astrophysical Journal, Astronomical Journal, New England Journal of Medicine, Skeptical Inquirer, Physics Today, Publications of the Astronomical Society of the Pacific,* and *Nature.* Consulting editor in astronomy, *McGraw-Hill Encyclopedia of Science.*

WORK IN PROGRESS: With Julian Schwinger, a book to accompany television series, "Understanding Space and Time."

AVOCATIONAL INTERESTS: Collecting old operatic and lieder phonograph records dating from 1900.

* * *

ACTON, Harold Mario Mitchell 1904-

PERSONAL: Born July 5, 1904, in Florence, Italy; son of Arthur Mario (an artist) and Hortense (Mitchell) Acton. *Education:* Christ Church, Oxford, B.A., 1926. *Politics:* Conservative Liberal. *Religion:* Roman Catholic. *Home:* Villa La Pietra, Florence, Italy. *Agent:* David Higham Associates Ltd., 5-8 Lower John St., London W1R 4HA, England.

CAREER: Lived in Peking, China, and studied Chinese drama, 1932-39; sometime lecturer in English literature at National University of Peking. *Military service:* Royal Air Force, World War II. *Member:* British Institute of Florence (vice-chairman, 1962), Royal Society of Literature (fellow), Savile Club (London). *Awards, honors:* Knight Commander of the Order of the British Empire; Grand Officer of the Italian Republic.

WRITINGS: Aquarium, Duckworth, 1923; *An Indian Ass,* Duckworth, 1925; *Five Saints and an Appendix,* Robert Holden, 1927; *Cornelian,* Chatto & Windus, 1928; *Humdrum,* Chatto & Windus, 1929; *This Chaos,* The Hours Press, 1930; *The Last Medici,* Faber, 1932; (translator with Chen Shih-Hsiang) *Modern Chinese Poetry,* Duckworth, 1936; (editor and translator with L. C. Arlington) *Famous Chinese Plays,* Vetch, 1937, reprinted, Russell, 1963; (translator with Lee Yi-hsieh) *Glue and Lacquer: Four Cautionary Tales,* Golden Cockerel, 1941; *Peonies and Ponies,* Chatto & Windus, 1941; *Memoirs of an Aesthete,* Methuen, 1948; *Prince Isidore,* Methuen, 1950; *The Bourbons of Naples,* Methuen, 1956; *The Last Bourbons of Naples,* Methuen, 1961; *Florence,* Thames & Hudson, 1961; *Old Lamps for New,* Methuen, 1965; *More Memoirs of an Aesthete,* Methuen, 1970; *Tit for Tat,* Hamish Hamilton, 1972; *Great Houses of Italy: The Tuscan Villas,* Viking, 1973; *Nancy Mitford: A Memoir,* Hamish Hamilton, 1975, Harper, 1976; *The Pazzi Conspiracy: The Plot against the Medici,* Thames & Hudson, 1979.

BIOGRAPHICAL/CRITICAL SOURCES: Saturday Review, October 5, 1968; *Times Literary Supplement,* May 28, 1970; *New York Times,* April 5, 1971; *New Leader,* May 31, 1971; *Washington Post,* December 18, 1973; *New York Times Book Review,* March 28, 1976, September 30, 1979.

*   *   *

ADAMS, Richard (George)   1920-

PERSONAL: Born May 9, 1920, in Newbury, Berkshire, England; son of Evelyn George Beadon (a surgeon) and Lilian Rosa (Button) Adams; married Barbara Elizabeth Acland, September 26, 1949; children: Juliet, Rosamond. *Education:* Worcester College, Oxford, M.A., 1948. *Religion:* Church of England. *Home:* Knocksharry House, Lhergy Dhoo, Peel, Isle of Man, United Kingdom. *Agent:* David Higham Associates Ltd., 5-8 Lower John St., London W1R 4HA, England.

CAREER: British Home Higher Civil Service, 1948-74, serving in Ministry of Housing and Local Government until its amalgamation as part of Department of Environment, Assistant Secretary, Department of Environment, 1968-74; full-time writer, 1974—. Writer-in-residence at University of Florida, 1975, and Hollins College, 1976. *Military service:* British Army, 1940-45. *Member:* Royal Society of Literature (honorary fellow), Royal Society for the Prevention of Cruelty to Animals (vice-president). *Awards, honors:* Guardian Award for children's literature, and Carnegie Medal, both 1972, both for *Watership Down;* California Young Readers' Association Medal, 1977.

WRITINGS—Novels: Watership Down, Rex Collings, 1972, Macmillan, 1974; *Shardik,* Rex Collings, 1974, Simon & Schuster, 1975; *The Plague Dogs,* illustrations by A. Wainwright, Allen Lane, 1977, Knopf, 1978; *The Girl in a Swing,* Knopf, 1980.

Other: (With Max Hooper) *Nature through the Seasons,* illustrations by David A. Goddard and Adrian Williams, Simon & Schuster, 1975; *The Tyger Voyage,* illustrations by

Nicola Bayley, Knopf, 1976; *The Adventures and Brave Deeds of the Ship's Cat on the Spanish Maine: Together with the Most Lamentable Losse of the Alcestis and Triumphant Firing of the Port of Chagres,* illustrations by Alan Aldridge and Harry Willock, Knopf, 1977; (with Max Hooper) *Nature Day and Night,* illustrations by Goddard and Stephen Lee, Viking, 1978; (compiler) *Sinister and Supernatural Stories,* Ward Locke, 1978; (author of introduction) Georgi Vladimov, *Faithful Ruslan,* translation by Michael Glenn, Simon & Schuster, 1979; *The Iron Wolf and Other Stories,* Allen Lane, 1980. Story anthologized in *Kingdoms of Sorcery,* edited by Lin Carter, Doubleday, 1976.

SIDELIGHTS: While still a civil servant in Britain's Department of Environment, Richard Adams began writing *Watership Down.* The story was told originally to amuse his two young daughters; at their insistence, Adams began to write down the tale. The manuscript, which took two years to complete, was rejected by four publishers and three authors' agents. Because he wanted to deliver a book into his daughters' hands, Adams was on the verge of having the novel printed at his own expense when he read of a small publisher who had just reissued an out-of-print animal fantasy; Adams contacted Rex Collings who accepted *Watership Down* for a limited first edition of 2,000 copies. Later reprinted by Penguin as a juvenile, the novel was a surprising success, winning the Guardian Award and Carnegie Medal. The American publisher, Macmillan, marketed the novel as an adult title, and the sales and reviews were again rewarding.

Watership Down relates the adventures of a group of rabbits who must set out in search of a new home because their warren is being razed by a developer who plans to gas all its animal inhabitants. P. S. Prescott of *Newsweek* calls the book "an adventure story of an epic scope. . . . It is a story of exile and survival, of heroism and political responsibility, of the making of a leader and of a community. . . . Adams has constructed a complete civilization, with its own governments, language and mythology." Writing in *New York,* Eliot Fremont-Smith comments: "There are a lot of things that make this book work, including the traditional and here expertly employed device of cliff-hanging chapter endings. But mainly it is Richard Adams's wonderfully rich imagination, together with an extraordinary and totally disarming respect for his material. Tone is all-important in a tale like this, and Adams's is straight, confidently controlled, never maudlin."

Janet Adam Smith writes in the *New York Review of Books* that she believes Adams "is a master of menace and suspense," but she adds: "I much prefer Mr. Adams when he is plain—'where the turf ended, the sky began' conveys in a flash the rabbits' view from the down—or in his high style, as when he meditates on moonlight. . . . Such passages are more than decoration; they (and the chapter headings from Aeschylus, the Psalms, and the Epic of Gilgamesh) dignify the action, making it not just the trek of a bunch of rabbits, but a movement of creatures who are no less part of nature than we are, and whose humble disasters and migrations have a claim to the attention of men, for all the greater scale of *theirs.*"

Smith feels that Macmillan's labeling of the book as simply a novel rather than a juvenile novel "may well encourage readers to go looking for the wrong things. For who would write a novel for adults about rabbits—unless the tale were a fable or a myth? . . . Certainly, it appears at a time when we are becoming increasingly skeptical of our species' ability to live its life decently; there is an inclination to look, if only in fancy, for alternative models in other species, other worlds.... In as much as Mr. Adams has a message for his readers, I'd say it is to make them more sensitive to the complex balance of nature, more aware of the needs and ways of other species (and the effect of human actions on them), more mindful that we are creatures too, and must live in harmony with the others who share our world." Agreeing with Smith is the author himself, who has consistently said that *Watership Down* should not be taken as allegory. As quoted by the *Pittsburgh Press,* Adams comments: "A lot of people have said this is a political fable or even a religious fable or social comment. I promise you it is not a fable or an allegory or a parable of any kind. It is a story about rabbits, that is all."

Despite the reviewers' praise and the public's acceptance, the novel has its critics. An example of negative criticism directed against *Watership Down* comes from the *National Review*'s D. Keith Mano, who questions the complimentary reviews the book has received. Mano writes: "'An exceptional book, a true original.' 'It doesn't fit any known formula, thank goodness.' Nonsense: it fits five or six. This bunny squad could be a John Wayne platoon of GIs. The foresighted, tactful rabbit leader. The fast rabbit. The clever rabbit. The blustery, hard-fighting noncom rabbit. Athos, Porthos, and D'Artagnan on a diet of grass. *Watership Down* is pleasant enough, but it has about the same intellectual firepower as *Dumbo.* 'Refreshes a reader's feeling for the world of man.' Apparently more than one reviewer has been rabbited out of his critical faculties. After all, if your dog started speaking French you'd be loath to criticize his pronunciation. Yet if Hazel and Bigwig and Dandelion were men, they'd make very commonplace characters. What seems a moral, an insight, is just a novelty.... *Watership Down* is an adventure story, no more than that: rather a swashbuckling, crude one to boot. There are virtuous rabbits and bad rabbits: if that's allegory, *Bonanza* is an allegory.... This is an okay book; well enough written. But it is grossly overrated."

Although Mano and others may feel *Watership Down* has been overrated, they cannot question the book's commercial success. Penguin sold more than one and one-quarter million copies of their edition, and the hardcover edition by Macmillan was purchased by more than seven-hundred thousand customers. Alison Lurie of the *New York Review of Books* feels that *Watership Down* has been so successful "not just because it was well written and original. It was attractive also because it celebrated qualities many serious novelists are currently afraid or embarrassed to write about. The heroes and heroines of most contemporary novels (including mine) are sad, bumbling failures; hysterical combatants in the sex war; or self-deceptive men and women of ill-will. What a relief to read of characters who have honor and courage and dignity, who will risk their lives for others, whose love for their families and friends and community is enduring and effective—even if they look like Flopsy, Mopsy, and Benjamin Bunny."

Lurie predicts that Adams's second novel, *Shardik,* will not receive as much acclaim as *Watership Down* partly because in it Adams is "attempting something more difficult." The novel is set in a mythical country and time; the natives worship a giant bear, Shardik. Lurie comments that like *Watership Down, Shardik* can be viewed as "an allegory and history of the relationship of human beings to the physical world." But she believes *Shardik* to be much more than an ecological allegory; she thinks the novel is really a study of how human beings choose and follow their gods. The great bear, Lurie continues, "is not really a magical being; he is not anthropomorphized. All that he does is within the range

of normal animal behavior; only to those who believe in him does it seem symbolical, an Act of God. Because of this belief, however, lives are changed utterly; hundreds of men, women, and children die; a barbaric empire is destroyed and rebuilt and destroyed again, and finally brought a little nearer to civilized humanism.... In *Shardik,* belief causes men to act cruelly and destructively as well as nobly; the bear is a kind of test which brings out hidden strengths and weaknesses, even in those who do not believe in him."

Like Lurie, Bruce Allen believes *Shardik*'s major theme is the effect of religious belief on human beings. He writes in the *Saturday Review:* "[*Shardik* is] a powerfully compelling prose epic that recreates the fortunate fall of unaccommodated man.... Among this book's greatest strengths is its rejection of the modern novel's emphasis on subjective uncertainty. It urges that truth is knowable, and that our intelligences must accept what they recognize for revealed truth—even if it be partial and unsatisfying. Surely, this points to its Christian framework. But isn't there something more, something stretching back still farther? ... In reading *Shardik,* we seem to hear again the old stories that were told to us by old people remembering them from past years, knowing we must be made to hear them, that our survival depends upon them. This is a new story, but it has the satisfying wholeness of the great ones it dares to rival; it should be told, and retold, for many generations."

Newsweek's Arthur Cooper also points to the religious element in *Shardik,* calling the novel "an exploration of the way an incarnate god works on the human psyche.... Beneath the rich vein of allegory and symbolism, Adams is concerned with how a society worships its gods, chooses its values and raises its children. Adams is a splendid descriptive writer whose only flaw—a minor one—is a fondness for the extended Homeric simile.... This is a marvelous novel of epic dimension, more ambitious, deeper, darker and more richly textured than *Watership* [*Down*]."

Praising *Shardik*'s "majestic language, heroic theme and sustained power," Peter Wolf writes in the *New Republic:* "Its achievement is awesome: some of its effects move us so deeply that we're surprised to find them made up of words on a printed page.... No estimate of *Shardik* can overlook how well Adams's firmly cadenced sentences knit with its epical theme, how his style brings to life his uncanny knowledge of bears—their anatomy, feeding and sleeping habits, and reactions to stress. Shardik is both the power of God and a dangerous, wounded animal, half-crazed by hunger, fire and hunters' arrows. Adams makes the great shambling bear a figure of terror and savage grandeur even in his physical ruin."

As with *Watership Down,* the reviewers' praise for *Shardik* was not unanimous. Webster Schott of *Book World* writes: "There is one good thing to say for *Shardik.* Adams writes about nature—trees, plants, animals, stones, bugs—as though he grew in ground next to wild onions. He talks the natural world into life. But there are few of the usual reasons for reading fiction in *Shardik.* We learn nothing about ourselves here; Adams's people belong with Snow White.... The novel is a fake antique, a sexless, humorless, dull facsimile of an epic without historical or psychological relevance. Contrary to Adams's wish, *Shardik* transmits no information we need, want, or can use about how we have chosen or employed our deities. *Shardik* is a long-winded Victorian fantasy, a piece of literary furniture properly destined to be unread by tens of thousands of book-club check writers."

John Skow of *Time* also dislikes the novel; he comments: "There is no iron to this Iron Age fable. The grimness is fake, the fascination with virginity is a naughty bore, and the monstrous figure of Shardik is cheapened by watery supernaturalism.... The author spins out his romance entertainingly, but without dealing seriously with the questions he raises: of belief and its perversion, of authority and its corruption. Good as he is at nature walks, Adams does not venture far into the forests of the mind." The *Listener*'s Kenneth Graham complains that *Shardik* "is too long, and too uneven. There is no real grasp of the inward reaches of character, only of the grand simplicities of archetype." Despite this, Graham adds that "there can be few books on which more loving, energetic inventiveness has been expended than on *Shardik.*... There is enough creative endeavour, careful planning, integrity and sheer multifarious detail in *Shardik* to make a dozen ordinary novels."

Adams's third novel, *The Plague Dogs,* harks back to *Watership Down* in its anthropomorphic use of animals. The novel tells of the adventures of two dogs who have escaped from an animal experimentation laboratory in the English Lake District. In an interview with Jan Rodger of the *Toronto Globe and Mail,* Adams says of the book: "*The Plague Dogs* is not just an attack on animal experimentation.... It is about the way in which, in modern life, almost all of us have a motive for what we do which is other than a simple, direct, honest motive, straightforward hunger or love.... If you are put off by tracts, you are probably not going to like *The Plague Dogs.* But I do feel very indignant about animal experimentation and perhaps my indignation got the better of me."

The *New York Times*'s John Leonard disliked Adams's third novel. "On the one hand, *The Plague Dogs* fairly reeks of literary self-consciousness. In the grand manner of the English novel, it is discursive and coy. It pauses every 12 pages for an afflatus or a tantrum or a pun. It is not above stopping to doggerel and parody, ..." Leonard writes. "On the other hand, *The Plague Dogs* must carry around a big load of philosophical heavy water. It is a polemic on the nature of freedom and illusion, the confusion between objective and subjective states of reality, the meaning of Auschwitz and the iniquities of modern science.... Mr. Adams's oddly sexless world is full of contempt—for science, for politics, for journalism. What is so far missing from that world are the marvelous people who came along with the discursive style in the great English novels he cannibalizes. I finished *Watership Down* in tears at the death of Hazel, the warrior-rabbit. I finished *The Plague Dogs* dry-eyed, having been manipulated."

William Safire takes the opposite point of view in the *New York Times Book Review.* Safire comments that while he disliked *Watership Down,* "in *The Plague Dogs* Richard Adams drags the reluctant reader into his world, entices him into accepting its conventions and atmosphere, and peppers him with hard-to-forget images and messages.... Once hooked by the dogs'-eye view of life, the dogs' fear of 'whitecoats,' and the drama of the chase, the reader is ready for Adams's sermons on animal slavery, on the power of hope to increase endurance, and on the cruelty that freedom demands of fugitives.... Adams is madcap-serious, usually controlled in his outrage, and knows how to evoke a sense of place. It matters not whose ox he allegorizes. *The Plague Dogs* is a savage snarl of a satire, a world created with a purpose clear in the writer's mind. It puts the reader on the scent of himself."

Time's Paul Gray notes that "even Adams's fervent admirers admit that he can be spotty: at best an artful cataloguer of

flora and fauna, at worst a windy sentimentalist.... Adams overwrites almost every scene, but he manages to turn that fault into a virtue. Length can lull disbelief and make the unlikely seem familiar." Joseph McLellan agrees that *The Plague Dogs* is not a perfect novel, but further comments in the *Washington Post:* "By his repeatedly felt presence behind the scenes, manipulating the action and commenting on it, Adams underlines a fact that is already apparent: like them or not, his novels differ from all others being written today.... As the book weathers into a classic (if it does, and it well may) the idiosyncrasies that are a distraction on its first appearance will become part of its charm. And the prospect for the foreseeable future is that its central image—that of two creatures victimized by society, unable to live by its rules but also unable to work out and live by their own outlaw code—is one in which many people will see reflected some part of themselves."

With *The Girl in a Swing,* Adams turns from his former animal heroes to contemporary human characters. The novel relates the meeting and marriage of a young conventional Englishman, Alan Desland, and a beautiful and mysterious German woman named Kathe. As with *Shardik,* this fourth novel involves the supernatural, and here Adams belies the complaint by Leonard and other reviewers that his fictional world is sexless. P. D. James of *Book World* comments: "Two of the most difficult tasks which a novelist can set himself are to write an erotic novel and to deal convincingly with the supernatural, and a writer who attempts both in the same book, particularly when the attempt marks a new direction of his talent, at least deserves an accolade for courage. But Richard Adams ... deserves more. With *The Girl in a Swing* we acclaim success."

James's only complaint about the novel is that she would have liked to know more about Kathe's past and her motivation for marrying Alan Desland. She writes: "The deed which lies at the heart of the book's haunting tragedy is so horrible, at once a symbol of evil and its manifestation, that I felt the need to understand something of the desperation, the moral corruption or the yearning for security from which it sprang." But, she adds: "There may be readers for whom this reticence about Kathe's motives and the details of her past life provides an intensification of the mystery which surrounds her; the horror is rendered more horrible because we can only guess at the psychological springs from which it flows."

Robert Kiely presents no reservations in his complimentary assessment of *The Girl in a Swing.* He writes in the *New York Times Book Review:* "Richard Adams turns his commonplace man into the hero-victim of a tale of fatal passion.... Alan never ceases being the solid, decent chap he was brought up to be. He remains completely believable throughout. The love scenes between him and Kathe are presented with lyrical beauty, a touch of humor and increasing obsessiveness. Kathe's ability to enchant is never in doubt. Finally, the ghost story is absolutely terrifying, as gripping and psychological penetrating as anything in James or Poe. Richard Adams has written, with marvelous tact and narrative power, a strange, beautiful, haunting book."

BIOGRAPHICAL/CRITICAL SOURCES: Times Literary Supplement, December 8, 1972, November 15, 1974, September 30, 1977, October 24, 1980; *New York,* March 4, 1974; *Newsweek,* March 18, 1974, April 28, 1975, March 13, 1978; *Time,* March 18, 1974, April 28, 1975, March 13, 1978; *Pittsburgh Press,* March 20, 1974; *Village Voice,* March 21, 1974; *New Republic,* March 23, 1974, May 3, 1975; *New York Times Book Review,* March 24, 1974, June 30, 1974,

May 4, 1975, March 12, 1978, April 27, 1980; *New York Review of Books*, April 18, 1974, June 12, 1975; *National Review*, April 26, 1974; *Virginia Quarterly Review*, summer, 1974; *Commonweal*, September 27, 1974; *London Times*, November 8, 1974; *Contemporary Literary Criticism*, Gale, Volume IV, 1975, Volume V, 1976; *Listener*, January 2, 1975, September 22, 1977; *Harper's*, May, 1975; *Book World*, May 25, 1975, February 26, 1978, May 11, 1980; *Saturday Review*, May 31, 1975, March 4, 1978; *Los Angeles Times*, July 20, 1975; *Authors in the News*, Gale, Volume I, 1976, Volume II, 1976; *Toronto Globe and Mail*, November 16, 1977; *New York Times*, March 7, 1978; *Atlantic*, April, 1978; *Washington Post*, November 8, 1978.

—*Sketch by Linda Metzger*

* * *

ADAMS, Walter 1922-

PERSONAL: Born August 27, 1922, in Vienna, Austria; son of Edward and Ilona (Schildkraut) Adams; married Pauline Gordon, 1943; children: William James. *Education:* Brooklyn College (now Brooklyn College of the City University of New York), B.A. (magna cum laude), 1942; Yale University, M.A., 1946, Ph.D., 1947. *Home:* 928 Lantern Hill Dr., East Lansing, Mich. *Office:* Economics Department, Michigan State University, East Lansing, Mich.

CAREER: Yale University, New Haven, Conn., instructor in economics, 1945-47; Michigan State University, East Lansing, assistant professor, 1947-51, associate professor, 1951-56, professor, 1956-69, distinguished university professor, 1970—, president of university, 1969-70. Consultant and economic counsel to House and Senate Small Business Committees at various times, 1950-56; member of Attorney General's National Committee to Study Antitrust Laws, 1953-55; consultant, U.S. Senate, Judiciary Committee, 1959, 1961-62; has served as expert witness before U.S. House and Senate committees on numerous occasions since 1949. Made evaluation of American university programs in France, Germany, Italy, Switzerland, Denmark, and Turkey under the auspices of the Carnegie Corp., 1957-58; guest lecturer and visiting professor at universities and institutes in France, Austria, and Switzerland, 1958—; official observer, UNESCO East-West Conference of Economists, Bursa, Turkey, 1958. Member of U.S. Advisory Commission on Educational Exchange, 1961-69. *Military service:* U.S. Army, 1943-45; served in European Theater with 83rd Infantry Division and as aide-de-camp to commanding general of 11th Armored Division; received battlefield commission; became first lieutenant; awarded Bronze Star Medal. *Member:* Association for Social Economics (president, 1980-81), American Economic Association, American Association of University Professors (president, 1972-74), Midwest Economic Association (president, 1978-79).

WRITINGS: (With L. E. Traywick) *Readings in Economics*, Macmillan, 1948; (editor) *The Structure of American Industry*, Macmillan, 1950, 5th edition, 1977; (with H. M. Gray) *Monopoly in America: The Government as Promoter*, Macmillan, 1955; (with J. B. Hendry) *Trucking Mergers, Concentration and Small Business: Analysis of Interstate Commerce Commission Policy, 1950-56*, U.S. Senate, Small Business Committee, 1957; (with John A. Garraty) *From Mainstreet to the Left Bank: Students and Scholars Abroad*, Michigan State University Press, 1959; (with Garraty) *Is the World Our Campus?*, Michigan State University Press, 1960; (with Garraty; introduction by Lyndon B. Johnson) *A Guide to Study Abroad*, Channel Press, 1962; *On the Strategic*

Importance of Western Europe, U.S. House of Representatives, 1964; *The Brain Drain*, Macmillan, 1968; *The Test*, Macmillan, 1971; (with others) *Tariffs, Quotas, and Trade: Problems of the International Economy*, Institute for Contemporary Issues, 1979. Also author of about thirty journal articles and pamphlets published in the U.S. and Europe.

BIOGRAPHICAL/CRITICAL SOURCES: Punch, July 17, 1968; *Saturday Review*, August 16, 1969; *Washington Post*, October 5, 1971.

* * *

ADELMAN, Irma Glicman

PERSONAL: Daughter of Jacob Max (a merchant) and Raissa (Ettinger) Glicman; married Frank L. Adelman (now a physicist), 1950 (divorced, 1979); children: Alexander Mark. *Education:* University of California, Berkeley, B.S. (with honors), 1950, M.A., 1951, Ph.D., 1955. *Office:* Department of Agricultural and Resource Economics, 207 Giannini Hall, University of California, Berkeley, Calif. 94720.

CAREER: University of California, Berkeley, teaching associate, 1955-56, instructor in economics, 1956-57; Mills College, Oakland, Calif., visiting assistant professor, 1958-59; Stanford University, Stanford, Calif., assistant professor, 1959-62; Johns Hopkins University, Baltimore, Md., associate professor, 1962-66; Northwestern University, Evanston, Ill., professor of economics, 1966-72; University of Maryland, College Park, professor of economics, 1972-79; University of California, Berkeley, professor of agricultural and resource economics, 1979—. Senior economist, Development Research Center, International Bank for Reconstruction and Development, 1971-72; held Cleveringa Chair at Leiden University. Consultant to Agency for International Development, U.S. Department of State; former consultant to United Nations Division of Industrial Development, and to Bureau of Labor Statistics. *Member:* American Economic Association (vice-president, 1979-81), National Academy of Sciences (member of social sciences assembly), American Academy of Arts and Sciences (fellow), Econometric Society, American Statistical Association, Phi Beta Kappa. *Awards, honors:* Social Science Research Council faculty research fellowship, 1961-62; Ford Foundation faculty research fellowship, 1965-66; Center for Advanced Study in the Behavioral Sciences fellow, 1970-71; Order of Bronze Tower, Government of South Korea, 1971; Netherlands Institute of Advanced Study fellow, 1977-78.

WRITINGS: (Editor with A. Pepelasis and L. Mears) *Economic Development: Analysis and Case Studies*, Harper, 1961; *Theories of Economic Growth and Development*, Stanford University Press, 1961; (editor with E. Thorbecke) *The Theory and Design of Economic Development*, Johns Hopkins Press, 1966; (with C. T. Morris) *Society, Politics and Economic Development: A Quantitative Approach*, Johns Hopkins Press, 1967; *Practical Approaches to Development Planning: Korea's Second Five Year Plan*, Johns Hopkins Press, 1969; (with Morris) *Economic Growth and Social Equity in Developing Countries*, Stanford University Press, 1973; (with S. Robinson) *Income Distribution Policy in Developing Countries: A Case Study of Korea*, Stanford University Press, 1977. Contributor of articles to professional journals.

* * *

ADLER, Max K(urt) 1905-

PERSONAL: Born June 12, 1905, in Pilsen, Czechoslovakia;

son of Rudolf (a businessman) and Selma (Wiener) Adler; married Janka Steiner, January 4, 1932; children: Eric. *Education:* University of Vienna, Dr.rer.pol., 1932; University of London, B.Sc. (Economics), 1947. *Home:* 793 Finchley Rd., London N.W. 11, England.

CAREER: Started in market research with family firm, Joseph Adler & Sons, Pilsen, Czechoslovakia; continued in same field in London, England, as manager of market research departments of Osborne-Peacock Co. Ltd. for two years, Odhams Press Ltd. for eight years, Hoover Ltd. for three years, and Standard Telephone & Cables Ltd. for three years; with General Electric Co. Ltd., London, as adviser to board on market research; director of studies and business consultant, Institute of Marketing, 1968—. Lecturer, University of London Extra-Mural Department for more than twenty-five years. *Member:* European Society of Market and Opinion Research, Royal Statistical Society, British Sociological Society, British Market Research Society (honorary fellow), Association of Scientific Workers. *Awards, honors:* Silver medal, European Society of Marketing and Opinion Research (one of three medals given in the twenty-five years of the society's existence).

WRITINGS: A Short Course in Market Research, C. E. Fisher & Co., 1951; *Modern Market Research: A Guide for Business Executives,* Crosby Lockwood, 1956, Philosophical Library, 1957; *A Short Guide to Market Research in Europe,* Crosby Lockwood, 1962; *Directory of British Market Research Organisations and Services,* Crosby Lockwood, 1965, 2nd edition, 1967; *Lectures in Market Research,* edited by Jacqueline Marrian, International Publications Service, 1965; *Business Languages of the World,* Marketing House Publishers, 1966; *Market Research and British Industry: A Pilot Study into the Uses of and Attitudes Towards Industrial Market Research at Home and Abroad,* Hallam Press, 1966; *Marketing and Market Research,* Crosby Lockwood, 1967; (editor) *Leading Cases in Market Research,* International Publications Service, 1971; *Collective and Individual Bilingualism: A Sociolinguistic Study,* Buske (Hamburg), 1977; *Pidgins, Creoles and Lingua Francas: A Sociolinguistic Study,* Buske, 1977; *Welsh and the Other Dying Languages in Europe: A Sociolinguistic Study,* Buske, 1977; *Naming and Addressing: A Sociolinguistic Study,* Buske, 1978; *Sex Differences in Human Speech: A Sociolinguistic Study,* Buske, 1978. Also author of *Linguistic Relativity, the Mother Tongue and the Language Community, Non-Vocal Language and Language Substitutes, Marxist Linguistics and Communist Practice,* and *Language Engineering and the Speech Community.* Author of several hundred articles and papers on marketing, market research, economics, and politics.

SIDELIGHTS: Max K. Adler speaks most European languages; his books have been translated into German, French, Dutch, Spanish, Italian, and Portuguese.

*　　*　　*

ADRIAN, Charles R. 1922-

PERSONAL: Born March 12, 1922, in Portland, Ore.; son of Harry R. and Helen (Petersen) Adrian; married Audrey Nelson, 1946; children: Kristin, Nelson. *Education:* Cornell College, B.A., 1947; University of Minnesota, M.A., 1948, Ph.D., 1950. *Office:* Department of Political Science, University of California, Riverside, Calif. 92521.

CAREER: Wayne University (now Wayne State University), Detroit, Mich. 1949-55, began as instructor, became assistant professor; Michigan State University, East Lansing,

assistant professor, 1955-56; administrative assistant in office of the Governor of Michigan, Lansing, 1956-57; Michigan State University, director, Institute for Community Development, 1957-63, professor of political science, 1959-66, chairman of department, 1963-66; University of California, Riverside, professor of political science, 1966—, assistant to the academic vice-president, 1973-74. Has also worked in educational radio and television. *Military service:* U.S. Army Air Forces, 1943-46. *Member:* American Political Science Association, American Society for Public Administration, Phi Beta Kappa.

WRITINGS: Governing Urban America, McGraw, 1955, 5th edition, 1977; *State and Local Governments: A Study in the Political Process,* McGraw, 1960, 4th edition, 1976; (with Oliver P. Williams) *Four Cities: A Study in Comparative Urban Politics,* University of Pennsylvania Press, 1963; (with Charles Press) *The American Political Process,* McGraw, 1965, revised edition, 1969; (with Press) *American Politics Reappraised,* McGraw, 1974; (with Ernest S. Griffith) *History of American City Government, 1775-1870,* Praeger, 1976. Contributor of articles to professional political science and public administration journals, *New Republic, Rotarian,* and others.

*　　*　　*

AGLE, Nan Hayden 1905-

PERSONAL: Born April 13, 1905, in Baltimore, Md.; daughter of Charles Swett and Emily (Spencer) Hayden; married Harold H. Cecil, 1925; married second husband, John N. Agle, 1947; children: (first marriage) Bradford Hayden, Harold Ridgely. *Education:* Attended Goucher College, 1923-24; Maryland Institute of Art, graduate, 1926. *Religion:* Episcopalian. *Home:* 221 Stony Run Lane, Baltimore, Md. 21210.

CAREER: Art teacher in Baltimore, Md., at Friends School for fourteen years and at Baltimore Museum of Art for five years. *Member:* Maryland Mayflower Society, Delta Gamma.

WRITINGS: Princess Mary of Maryland, Scribner, 1956; *Constance the Honeybee,* John C. Winston, 1959; *Makon and the Dauphin,* Scribner, 1961; (with Frances Bacon) *The Lords Baltimore,* Holt, 1962; *Kate and the Apple Tree,* Seabury, 1965; (with Bacon) *The Ingenious John Banvard,* Seabury, 1966; *Joe Bean,* Seabury, 1967; *Kish's Colt,* Seabury, 1968; *Tarr of Belway Smith,* Seabury, 1969; *My Animals and Me,* Seabury, 1970; *Maple Street,* Seabury, 1971; *K. Mouse and Bo Bixby,* Seabury, 1972; *Baney's Lake,* Seabury, 1972; *Susan's Magic,* Seabury, 1973.

(With Ellen Wilson) "Three Boys" series, published by Scribner: *Three Boys and a Lighthouse,* 1951; *... and the Remarkable Cow,* 1952; *... and a Tugboat,* 1953; *... and a Train,* 1953; *... and a Mine,* 1954; *... and a Helicopter,* 1958; *... and Space,* 1962; *... and H2O,* 1968.

AVOCATIONAL INTERESTS: Painting, caring for animals, bridge, reading.

*　　*　　*

AHERN, Barnabas M. 1915-

PERSONAL: Born February 18, 1915, in Chicago, Ill.; son of James and Catherine (Barry) Ahern. *Education:* Passionist Fathers Major Seminaries, Chicago, Ill., and Louisville, Ky., seminarian, 1934-41; Catholic University, S.T.L., 1943; studied at Ecole Biblique, Jerusalem, 1947-48; Pontifical Biblical Commission, Rome, awarded Baccalaureate in Scripture, 1947, Licentiate in Scripture, 1948; Pontifical Biblical Institute, Rome, S.S.D., 1958. *Home:* Padri Passionisti, Pza SS Giovanni E Paolo 13, 00184 Rome, Italy.

CAREER: Entered Roman Catholic Passionist order, 1933, ordained a priest, 1941; Passionist Fathers Major Seminary, Chicago, Ill., professor of scripture, 1943-47, 1948-56; Passionist Fathers Major Seminary, Louisville, Ky., professor of scripture, 1959-62; St. Meinrad Seminary, St. Meinrad, Ind., member of theological faculty, beginning 1962; Gregorian University, Rome, Italy, professor of scripture, 1968—. Peritus (official consultant), Vatican II Council, 1962-65; assistant to secretariat for promoting Christian unity, headed by Augustin Cardinal Bea, 1963—; consultant, Pontifical Biblical Commission, 1966—; member of International Theological Commission, 1969. *Member:* Catholic Biblical Association (president, 1964-65), Mariological Society, Society of Biblical Literature, Liturgical Conference (board of directors). *Awards, honors:* Cardinal Spellman Award of Catholic Theological Society of America, 1964.

WRITINGS: The Epistles to the Galatians and to the Romans, Liturgical Press, 1960; *New Horizons: Studies in Biblical Theology,* Fides, 1963; *Men of Prayer, Men of Action,* Bruce Books, 1971; *The Epistle to the Romans,* Franciscan Herald, 1979. Editor, *New Testament Reading Guide,* Liturgical Press. Scripture editor, *Worship;* member of editorial board, *Bible Today.* Contributor to *New Catholic Encyclopedia,* and to religious journals in United States and Europe.

* * *

AICKMAN, Robert (Fordyce)   1914-

PERSONAL: Born June 27, 1914, in London, England; son of William Arthur (an architect) and Mabel Violet (Marsh) Aickman. *Education:* Attended Highgate School, London, England. *Politics:* Social Credit and Independent. *Home and office:* 12 Gledhow Gardens, London SW5, England. *Agent:* Herbert van Thal, London Management, 235 Regent St., London W1A 2JT, England.

CAREER: Director and chairman, London Opera Society Ltd., 1954-69; chairman of Balmin Productions Ltd. (which administers traveling Ballets Minerva), 1963-68; writer. General director of Market Harborough Festival 1950 of Boats and Arts; director of Thames Tour 1961 of American Wind Symphony Orchestra; director of City of London Festival waterborne concert, 1962. *Member:* National Council on Inland Transport, World Wildlife Fund (member of advisory panel), Inland Waterway Association (founder; past chairman; vice-president), Railway Development Association (vice-president), Lower Avon Navigation Trust (member of council), Upper Avon Navigation Trust (chairman, 1969-75), Stratford-upon-Avon Canal Society (vice-president), Kehnet and Avon Canal Trust (vice-president), Residential Boat Owners Association (president), River Stour Trust (vice-president), Northampton Drama Club (vice-president), Great Ouse Restoration Society (vice-president), Leeds University Waterways Society (vice-president). *Awards, honors:* World Fantasy Award for best short fiction work, 1973-74, for ''Pages from a Young Girl's Diary.''

WRITINGS: (With Elizabeth Jane Howard) *We Are for the Dark,* J. Cape, 1951; *Know Your Waterways,* Temprint, 1954; *The Story of Our Inland Waterways,* Pitman, 1955; *The Late Breakfasters,* Gollancz, 1964; *Dark Entries,* Collins, 1964; (editor) *The Fontana Book of Great Ghost Stories,* eight books, Collins, 1964-72; *The Attempted Rescue* (Volume I of his autobiography), Gollancz, 1966; *Powers of Darkness,* Collins, 1966; *Sub Rosa: Strange Tales,* Gollancz,

1968; *Cold Hand in Mine,* Gollancz, 1975, Scribner, 1978; *Tales of Love and Death,* Gollancz, 1977; *Painted Devils,* Scribner, 1979. Former drama critic, *Nineteenth Century and After;* former film critic, *Jewish Monthly.* Contributor to *The Third Ghost Book, The Fourth Ghost Book,* and of an essay on the Avon to *Portraits of Rivers;* frequent contributor of articles and fiction to newspapers and magazines.

WORK IN PROGRESS: The Model, a tale of old Russia.

AVOCATIONAL INTERESTS: Drama, literature, music, and travel.

* * *

AISTROP, Jack   1916-

PERSONAL: Born August 22, 1916; married Josephine Hunter; children: Jennifer, Josepha. *Home:* 36A Townshend Rd., London N.W. 8, England. *Agent:* James Brown Associates, 25 West 43rd St., New York, N.Y. 10036.

CAREER: Writer. British Information Services, New York, N.Y., director of radio and television divisions, 1947-55; British Broadcasting Corp., London, England, external service, 1946-63, representative in United States, 1963-66, head of production, Gramophone Records and Tapes, London, 1966-76; Omnibus Press, London, editorial consultant, 1976—. *Military service:* British Army, 1939-45. *Member:* Zoological Society (London; fellow). *Awards, honors:* Tom Gallon Award, 1946-47; *Atlantic* award in literature, 1947.

WRITINGS: Backstage with Joe, Farrar, Straus, 1948; *The Lights Are Low,* Roy, 1948; *Pretend I Am a Stranger,* Roy, 1950.

Factual nature books for children: *Every Child's Book of Pets,* Dobson, 1949; *Fun at the Zoo,* Roy, 1951; *Animals around Us,* Dobson, 1953; *Enjoying Pets,* Vanguard, 1955; *Enjoying Nature's Marvels,* Vanguard, 1960; *Pet Lover's Dictionary,* Arco, 1961; *The Mongolian Gerbil,* Dobson, 1970; *Budgerigars and Other Cage Birds,* Arco, 1970.

* * *

AITKEN, Hugh G(eorge) J(effrey)   1922-

PERSONAL: Born October 12, 1922, in Deal, England; son of George Jeffrey and Ellen (Hughes) Aitken; married Janice Hunter, 1955; children: Ellen Bradshaw. *Education:* St. Andrews University, Scotland, M.A., 1947; University of Toronto, M.A., 1948; Harvard University, Ph.D., 1951. *Religion:* Episcopalian. *Home:* 155 Amity St., Amherst, Mass. 01002. *Office:* Department of Economics, Amherst College, Amherst, Mass. 01002.

CAREER: Harvard University, Cambridge, Mass., research fellow, 1951-55; University of California, Riverside, 1955-65, began as instructor, became professor of economics, chairman of division of social sciences, 1961-63, chairman of department of economics, 1963-65; Amherst College, Amherst, Mass., professor of economics, 1965—. *Military service:* Royal Air Force, 1942-46; became leading aircraftsman. *Member:* Economic History Association, Society for the History of Technology.

WRITINGS: The Welland Canal Company, Harvard University Press, 1954; *Canadian Economic History,* Macmillan (Canada), 1956; (editor) *The State and Economic Growth: Papers,* Social Science Research Council, 1959; *Taylorism at Watertown Arsenal,* Harvard University Press, 1960; *American Capital and Canadian Resources,* Harvard University Press, 1961; (editor) *Explorations in Enterprise,* Harvard University Press, 1965; *Did Slavery Pay: Readings in the Economics of Black Slavery in the United States,* Houghton, 1971; *Syntony and Spark—The Origins of Radio,* Wiley-Interscience, 1976. Contributor to professional journals. Editor, *Explorations in Entrepreneurial History,* 1948-54, *Journal of Economic History,* 1966-69.

* * *

ALBERS, Josef 1888-1976

PERSONAL: Born March 19, 1888, in Bottrop, West Germany; came to United States in 1933, naturalized in 1939; died in New Haven, Conn., March 25, 1976; buried in Orange Cemetery, Orange, Conn.; son of Lorenz (a housepainter) and Magdalena (Schumacher) Albers; married Anni Fleischmann (a textile designer), May 9, 1925. *Education:* Teachers Seminar, Buren, West Germany, Teacher Degree, 1908; Royal Art School, Berlin, Art Teacher Degree, 1915; studied at School of Applied Art, Essen, 1916-19, Art Academy, Munich, 1919-20, and Bauhaus, Weimar, 1920-23. *Home:* 808 Birchwood Dr., Orange, Conn. 06477.

CAREER: Teacher in West German public schools, 1908-13, 1915-19, at Bauhaus, Weimar, 1923-25, Dessau, 1925-32, and Berlin, 1932-33; Black Mountain College, Black Mountain, N.C., professor of art, 1933-49; Yale University, New Haven, Conn., professor of art and chairman of department of design, 1950-58, visiting artist, School of Art and Architecture, 1958-60, professor emeritus, 1958-76. Work has been exhibited and published throughout the world; more than 600 exhibitions in United States; work is part of permanent collections of Metropolitan Museum of Art, Guggenheim Museum, Museum of Modern Art, and Whitney Museum of American Art (all New York), and Chicago Art Institute.

MEMBER: National Institute of Arts and Letters, American Academy of Arts and Letters, American Abstract Artists. *Awards, honors:* Awards for painting from Chicago Art Institute, Corcoran Gallery, Carnegie Institute, and other institutions; Yale University, M.A., 1950, D.F.A., 1962; Ada S. Garret Prize, Chicago Art Institute, 1954; William Clark Prize, 1957; Officers Cross of the Order of Merit, West Germany, 1957; Konrad van Soest Preis, West Germany, 1958; Ford Foundation fellowships, 1959, 1964; Graham Foundation Fellowship, 1962; D.F.A., University of Hartford, 1962, California College of Arts and Crafts, 1964, University of North Carolina at Chapel Hill, 1967, University of Illinois, 1969, Minnesota Art School, 1969, Kenyon College, 1969, Washington University, 1971, Maryland Institute, 1972, Pratt Institute, 1975, and Philadelphia College of Art, 1976; American Institute of Graphic Arts gold medal, 1964; LL.D., University of Bridgeport, 1966; Dr. Phil., Ruhr University, 1967; grand prix, Third Arts and Letters Bienal Americana (Chile), 1968; grand prix in painting, Nardrheim-Westfalen (West Germany), 1968; Medal of Fine Arts, American Institute of Architects, 1975.

WRITINGS: Poems and Drawings, Readymade Press, 1958, 2nd edition, Wittenborn, 1961; (with Francois Bucher) *Despite Straight Lines,* Yale University Press, 1961, revised edition, MIT Press, 1977; *Homage to the Square* (poems and drawings), Ives-Stillman, 1962; *Interaction of Color,* Yale University Press, 1963, revised edition, 1975; *Search versus Re-Search* (lectures), Trinity College Press, 1969; *Formulation, Articulation,* Abrams, 1972. Contributor of numerous articles on art education to periodicals in the U.S. and Europe.

SIDELIGHTS: Josef Albers, world-renowned as a teacher and color theorist as well as painter, was best known for "Homage to the Square," a series of several hundred works composed of nested squares of color. Paul Richard of the *Washington Post* wrote that Albers was "less interested in self-expression than in the ways the eye sees colors. . . . [His works] are notable both for the severity of their format and the subtleties of their colors."

"Mr. Albers had a wide influence on several generations of artists here and abroad," said the *New York Times,* "an influence that extended into the realm of sculpture, architecture and industrial design. . . . [His] theories of color relationships became the basis for art courses taught throughout the country." In the 1960's he was hailed as the "Prince of Op," although he did not identify himself with any particular school of geometric abstraction.

"Just putting colors together is the excitement of it," Albers told an interviewer. "The way green submits to blue, for instance, or vice versa. What interests me is the way they marry, interpenetrate and produce the baby, the color that is their product together."

According to the *New York Times,* Albers made clear "in his gnomic, aphoristic writings on art that his static format represented for him a kind of order, an order in which he found not only an esthetic but an ethic as well. . . . 'The reason for esthetics is ethics, and ethics is its aim,' he said. 'When you see how each color helps, hates, penetrates, touches, [or] doesn't, that's parallel to life.'"

In 1971 Albers was honored by a retrospective exhibition at the Metropolitan Museum of Art, "one of the few ever given to a living artist," notes the *Times.*

AVOCATIONAL INTERESTS: With his wife, collecting Pre-Columbian miniatures.

BIOGRAPHICAL/CRITICAL SOURCES: Eugen Gomringer, editor, *Josef Albers,* Wittenborn, 1968; Werner Spies, *Josef Albers,* Abrams, 1970; Jurgen Wissmann, *Josef Albers,* P. Reclam, 1971; *Newsweek,* January 18, 1971; *Art Journal,* spring, 1973; *AIA Journal,* February, 1975; *New York Times,* March 26, 1976; *Washington Post,* March 26, 1976; *Art News,* May, 1976.†

* * *

ALBERTSON, Dean 1920-

PERSONAL: Born August 22, 1920, in Denver, Colo.; married Johnnie Leinbach, 1954 (divorced, 1968); children: Mark Nevins, Constant Kathryn. *Education:* University of California, Berkeley, A.B., 1942, A.M., 1947; Columbia University, Ph.D., 1955. *Office:* Department of History, University of Massachusetts, Amherst, Mass.

CAREER: New York University, New York City, instructor, 1947-48; Columbia University, New York City, assistant director of oral history project, 1948-55; Committee on International Exchange of Persons (Fulbright Awards), Washington, D.C., executive assistant, 1956-59; Brooklyn College (now Brooklyn College of the City University of New York), Brooklyn, N.Y., assistant professor, 1959-64, associate professor of history, 1964-65; University of Massachusetts—Amherst, professor of history, 1965—. *Military service:* U.S. Naval Air Corps, 1943-45, became lieutenant junior grade; received Air Medals. *Member:* American Historical Association, Organization of American Historians, Oral History Association.

WRITINGS: Roosevelt's Farmer, Columbia University Press, 1961; *Eisenhower as President,* Hill & Wang, 1963; (with Howard Quint and Milton Cantor) *Main Problems in American History,* Dorsey, 1964, revised edition, 1978; *American History Visually,* Heath, 1969; (editor and contributor) *The Study of American History*, Dushkin, 1974; *Rebels or Revolutionaries*, Simon & Schuster, 1975.

* * *

ALBION, Robert Greenhalgh 1896-

PERSONAL: Born August 15, 1896, in Malden, Mass.; son of James Francis (a clergyman) and Alice Marion (Lamb) Albion; married Jennie Barnes Pope (a writer), August 16, 1923 (died October 1, 1976). *Education:* Bowdoin College, A.B., 1918; Harvard University, A.M., 1920, Ph.D., 1924. *Politics:* Republican. *Home:* Groton Regency, Groton, Conn. 06340.

CAREER: Princeton University, Princeton, N.J., 1922-49, began as instructor, became professor of history, assistant dean of the faculty, 1929-43, director of the summer session, 1929-42; historian of naval administration and sometime assistant director of naval history, U.S. Navy Department, 1943-50; Harvard University, Cambridge, Mass., first Gardiner Professor of Oceanic History and Affairs, 1949-63, professor emeritus, 1963—. Visiting professor at University of Connecticut, 1964-65, Emory University and Carleton College, 1966, University of Maine, 1966-72, and Bowdoin College, 1971; lecturer at U.S. Naval Academy, U.S. War College, and U.S. Military Academy. Consultant to U.S. War Department, 1943 and Maritime Administration, 1952-53; Munson Institute of Maritime History, Mystic, Conn., coordinator, 1955-66, director, 1966-75. Member, Maine Advisory Committee on Historic Sites, 1960-71; vice-chairman, Maine Archives Committee, 1965-73; member of charter revision and library committees, South Portland, Me. *Military service:* U.S. Army, Infantry, 1917-18; became second lieutenant.

MEMBER: American Military Institute (president, 1941-45), Economic History Association (vice-president), Naval Historical Foundation (trustee, 1946-50), Society for Nautical Research (England; honorary member), Maine Historical Society (member of executive committee, 1958-76; president, 1963-70), Phi Beta Kappa. *Awards, honors:* Litt.D., Bowdoin College, 1948, and Southampton College, 1970; Presidential Certificate of Merit, 1948; L.H.D., University of Maine, 1971.

WRITINGS: Forests and Sea Power: The Timber Problem of the Royal Navy, Harvard University Press, 1926; (with Girard L. McEntee) *Introduction to Military History*, Century, 1929, reprinted, AMS Press, 1971; (editor with L. Dodson) *Journal of Philip V. Fithian*, Princeton University Press, 1931; (with J. B. Pope and W. P. Hall) *History of England and the British Empire*, Ginn, 1937, 4th edition, 1961; *Square-Riggers on Schedule*, Princeton University Press, 1938; *The Rise of New York Port*, Scribner, 1939, published as *The Use of New York Port*, David & Charles, 1971; (with Pope) *Sea Lanes in Wartime: The American Experience*, Norton, 1942, 2nd edition, Shoe String, 1968; (with S.H.P. Read) *The Navy at Sea and Ashore*, U.S. Navy Department, 1947; *Maritime and Naval History: An Annotated Bibliography*, Marine Historical Association, 1955, 4th edition, Mystic Seaport, 1972; *Seaports South of Sahara*, Appleton, 1959; (with Pope and R. H. Connery) *Forrestal and the Navy*, Columbia University Press, 1962; (with W. A. Baker and B. W. Labaree) *New England and the Sea*, Wesleyan University Press, 1972; *Five Centuries of Famous Ships: From the Santa Maria to the Glomar Explorer*, McGraw, 1978; *The Makers of Naval Policy, 1798-1947*, edited by Rowena Reed, Naval Institute Press, 1980. Contributor of articles to encyclopedias, newspapers, and journals. Mem-

ber of editorial board of *Journal of Economic History, Business History Review,* Essex Institute Historical Publications, and of editorial advisory board of *American Neptune;* consultant, *Collier's Encyclopedia, Grolier Encyclopedia.* Editor, *Exploration and Discovery*, 1965.

SIDELIGHTS: Robert Albion pioneered in Harvard's television lectures for extension academic credit, 1959-60, with a course on "Expansion of Europe." He and his wife grew up in Portland, Me., where he developed his interest in maritime history, and they spent part of their time there in Mrs. Albion's old family home. His wife collaborated with him on all his books.

* * *

ALDERMAN, Clifford Lindsey 1902-

PERSONAL: Born August 5, 1902, in Springfield, Mass.; son of Charles Henry and Susie (Lindsey) Alderman; married Mildred Jordan, August 11, 1934. *Education:* U.S. Naval Academy, B.S., 1924. *Home:* 5461 Lemon Tree Lane, Pinellas Park, Fla. 33565.

CAREER: New England Laboratories, Springfield, Mass., assistant chemist, 1925-27; U.S. Bureau of Mines, Pittsburgh, Pa., fuels engineer, 1927-29; *Shipping Digest*, New York City, editor, 1929-40; *Our Navy*, Brooklyn, N.Y., editor, 1940-42, 1945-46; Schenley International Corp., New York City, public relations consultant, 1946-48; Port of New York Authority, New York City, editor, 1948-55; writer. *Military service:* U.S. Navy, 1942-45; became commander. *Member:* Authors Guild.

WRITINGS: The Arch of Stars, Appleton, 1950; *To Fame Unknown*, Appleton, 1954; *The Silver Keys*, Putnam, 1960.

Juveniles: *Joseph Brant*, Messner, 1958; *Samuel Adams: Son of Liberty*, Holt, 1961; *Wooden Ships and Iron Men*, Walker, 1964; *Stormy Knight*, Chilton, 1964; *The Vengeance of Abel Wright*, Doubleday, 1964; *That Men Shall Be Free*, Messner, 1964; *The Way of the Eagles*, Doubleday, 1965; *Liberty, Equality, Fraternity*, Messner, 1965; *The Privateersmen*, Chilton, 1965; *The Story of the Thirteen Colonies*, Random House, 1966; *Devil's Shadow: The Story of Witchcraft in Massachusetts*, Messner, 1967; *Retreat to Victory*, Chilton, 1967; *Death to the King: The Story of the English Civil War*, Messner, 1968; *Flame of Freedom*, Messner, 1969; *The Rhode Island Colony*, Crowell, 1969; *The Great Invasion: The Norman Conquest of 1066*, Messner, 1969; *The Royal Opposition*, Crowell, 1970; *Gathering Storm*, Messner, 1970; *Blood-Red the Roses*, Messner, 1971; *A Cauldron of Witches*, Messner, 1971; *The Golden Age*, Messner, 1972; *Rum, Slaves and Molasses*, Crowell, 1972; *The Wearing of the Green*, Messner, 1972; *Osceola and the Seminole Wars*, Messner, 1973; *The War We Could Have Lost*, Four Winds, 1974; *Witchcraft in America*, Messner, 1974; *The Colony of Connecticut*, F. Watts, 1975; *Colonists for Sale*, Macmillan, 1975; *The Dark Eagle*, Macmillan, 1976; *Symbols of Magic*, Messner, 1977; *Annie Oakley and the World of Her Time*, Macmillan, 1979; *Your Career in Writing*, Messner, in press.

BIOGRAPHICAL/CRITICAL SOURCES: Young Readers' Review, April, 1966, June, 1967, November, 1968; *Best Sellers*, May 1, 1967, June 1, 1969, October 1, 1969, July 16, 1971; *New York Times Book Review*, May 2, 1976.

* * *

ALDRIDGE, John W(atson) 1922-

PERSONAL: Born September 26, 1922, in Sioux City, Iowa;

son of Walter Copher and Nell (Watson) Aldridge; married Leslie Felker, 1954 (divorced, 1968); married Alexandra Bertash, 1968; children: (first marriage) Henry Belden, Stephen Brinson, Leslie Malcolm, Jeremy Watson, Geoffrey Watson. *Education:* Attended University of Chattanooga (now University of Tennessee at Chattanooga), 1940-43; University of California, Berkeley, B.A., 1947; attended Middlebury College, summer, 1942. *Home:* 1050 Wall St., No. 4-C, Ann Arbor, Mich. *Agent:* Gerard McCauley Agency, Inc., 209 East 56th St., New York, N.Y. 10022. *Office:* Department of English, University of Michigan, Ann Arbor, Mich. 48104.

CAREER: University of Vermont, Burlington, lecturer in criticism, 1948-50, assistant professor of English, 1950-53, 1954-55, director, School of Modern Critical Studies, 1950-55; Princeton University, Princeton, N.J., lecturer, Christian Gauss Seminars in Criticism, 1953-54; Sarah Lawrence College, Bronxville, N.Y., visiting professor of English, 1956-57; Queens College of the City of New York (now Queens College of the City University of New York), Flushing, N.Y., visiting professor of English, 1957; New York University, New York, N.Y., Berg Professor of English, 1958; University of Munich, Munich, Germany, Fulbright professor of American literature, 1958-59; Hollins College, Hollins College, Va., writer-in-residence and visiting professor of English, 1960-62; University of Copenhagen, Copenhagen, Denmark, Fulbright professor of American literature, 1962-63; University of Michigan, Ann Arbor, professor of English, 1963—. Member of staff, Bread Loaf Writers Conference, 1968-69; special advisor for American Embassy, Bonn, Germany, 1972-73. *Military service:* U.S. Army, 1943-45; received Bronze Star Medal, five battle stars. *Member:* Modern Language Association of America, P.E.N. National Book Critics Circle. *Awards, honors:* Rockefeller humanities fellowship, 1976-77.

WRITINGS: After the Lost Generation (literary criticism), McGraw, 1951; (editor) *Critiques and Essays on Modern Fiction,* Ronald, 1952; *In Search of Heresy* (literary criticism), McGraw, 1956; (editor) *Selected Stories by P. G. Wodehouse,* Modern Library, 1958; *The Party at Cranton* (novel), McKay, 1960; *Time to Murder and Create: The Contemporary Novel in Crisis,* McKay, 1966; *In the Country of the Young* (social criticism), Harper Magazine Press, 1970; *The Devil in the Fire: Retrospective Essays on American Literature and Culture, 1951-1971,* Harper Magazine Press, 1972.

Contributor: *Twelve Original Essays on Great American Novels,* edited by Charles Shapiro, Wayne State University Press, 1958; *F. Scott Fitzgerald,* edited by Arthur Mizener, Prentice-Hall, 1963; *Contemporary American Novelists,* edited by Harry T. Moore, Southern Illinois University Press, 1964. Contributor of articles to *Harper's, Nation, New Republic, Partisan Review, Virginia Quarterly Review, Saturday Review, New World Writing, New York Times Book Review,* and *New York Herald Tribune Book Review.* Editor, *Discovery* magazine, 1953.

WORK IN PROGRESS: A critical study of the contemporary American novel; a critical biography of Norman Mailer; a critical study of the post World War II American literary generation.

SIDELIGHTS: John Aldridge told *CA:* "I am, and have always wanted to be, a critic of the literature of my own time. With the exception of my novel, *The Party at Cranton,* and an informal sociological study, *In the Country of the Young,* my books have all been studies of current literature, primar-

ily American fiction. I have never considered criticism in any sense a minor or inferior literary form, and one of my ambitions has been to write criticism in such a way that it can be seen to have the qualities of style, structure, and dramatic development which are normally associated with fiction."

*   *   *

ALDRIDGE, Richard Boughton 1930-

PERSONAL: Born November 12, 1930, in New York, N.Y.; son of Albert H. (a physician) and Nancy (Symington) Aldridge; married Josephine Haskell (an artist and author of children's books), October, 1958; children: Abigail Nancy. *Education:* Amherst College, B.A., 1952; Oxford University, M.A., 1957. *Residence:* Sebasco Estates, Me. 04565. *Office:* Department of English, Morse High School, Bath, Me.

CAREER: National Security Agency, Washington, D.C., research analyst, 1952-53; Doubleday & Co., Inc., New York, N.Y., staff member, 1957-58; Morse High School, Bath, Me., member of English department, 1958—, chairman, 1962-69; Hyde School, Bath, Me., teacher, beginning 1970. *Military service:* U.S. Army Counterintelligence Corps, 1953-55. *Awards, honors:* Fulbright fellowships to Oxford University, 1955-57.

WRITINGS: An Apology Both Ways, Indiana University Press, 1957; *Down through the Clouds, the Sea,* Golden Quill, 1963; (editor) *Maine Lines: 101 Contemporary Poems about Maine,* Lippincott, 1970; (with wife, Josephine Aldridge) *Reasons and Raisins,* Parnassus, 1971; (editor) *Poetry Amherst,* Amherst College Press, 1972; *The Wild White Rose,* Crow Hill Press, 1974; *Red Pine, Black Ash* (collected poems), Thorndike Press, 1980.

*   *   *

ALEXANDER, John W(esley) 1918-

PERSONAL: Born April 7, 1918, in Greenville, Ill.; son of John (a college teacher) and Ethel (Cummings) Alexander; married Elizabeth W. Vinson, September 5, 1946; children: John V., Elizabeth Lynne, Mary Elizabeth, Douglas Webb. *Education:* University of Illinois, B.A., 1940, M.A., 1941; University of Wisconsin, Ph.D., 1949. *Religion:* Christian. *Home:* 146 North Prospect Ave., Madison, Wis. 53705. *Office:* 233 Langdon, Madison, Wis. 53703.

CAREER: University of Wisconsin—Madison, instructor, 1947, assistant professor, 1949-52, associate professor, 1952-63, professor of geography, 1963-65, chairman of department, general director of Inter-Varsity Christian Fellowship, 1965—. *Military service:* U.S. Navy, 1942-46; became lieutenant, gunnery officer. *Member:* Association of American Geographers, American Geographical Society, Phi Beta Kappa, Phi Kappa Phi.

WRITINGS: Flight Quarters, Cole-Holmquist, 1946; *Thoughts from the Sea,* Light and Life, 1947; *Economic Geography,* Prentice-Hall, 1963; *Managing Our Work,* Inter-Varsity Press, 1972, 2nd revised edition, 1975; *Scripture Memory One Hundred One,* Inter-Varsity Press, 1975; *Practical Criticism,* Inter-Varsity Press, 1976; (editor) *Believing and Obeying Jesus Christ,* Inter-Varsity Press, 1980. Also author of *What Is Christianity?,* Inter-Varsity Press. Contributor of articles to professional journals.

*   *   *

ALEXANDER, Robert J. 1918-

PERSONAL: Born November 26, 1918, in Canton, Ohio;

son of Ralph S. (a professor) and Ruth (Jackson) Alexander; married Joan Powell, March 26, 1949; children: Anthony, Margaret. *Education:* Columbia University, B.A., 1940, M.A., 1941, Ph.D., 1950. *Politics:* "Socialist, but registered Democrat." *Home:* 944 River Rd., Piscataway, N.J. 08854. *Office:* Department of Economics, Rutgers University, New Brunswick, N.J. 08903.

CAREER: U.S. Government, Washington, D.C., affiliated with Board of Economic Warfare, 1942, and Office of Inter-American Affairs, 1945-46; Rutgers University, New Brunswick, N.J., instructor, 1947-50, assistant professor, 1950-56, associate professor, 1956-61, professor of economics, 1961—. Visiting professor, Columbia University, 1962-63. Visiting summer professor, Atlanta University, 1949, University of Puerto Rico, 1958, 1959, 1962, 1964. Member of Economic Cooperation Administration mission to Spain, 1951-52. Consultant to American Federation of Labor and American Federation of Labor-Congress of Industrial Organizations, 1948—. Member of board of directors, Rand School of Social Sciences, 1953-56, and League for Industrial Democracy, 1955-65; member of national committee, Socialist Party-Social Democratic Federation, 1957-66. *Military service:* U.S. Army Air Forces, 1942-45. *Member:* American Economic Association, American Association of University Professors, Inter-American Association for Democracy and Freedom. *Awards, honors:* Travel grant, U.S. Office of Education, 1945-46; Order of the Condor of the Andes, Government of Bolivia, 1962.

WRITINGS: The Peron Era, Columbia University Press, 1951; *Communism in Latin America,* Rutgers University Press, 1957; *The Bolivian National Revolution,* Rutgers University Press, 1958; (with Charles O. Porter) *The Struggle for Democracy in Latin America,* Macmillan, 1961; *Prophets of the Revolution,* Macmillan, 1962; *Labor Relations in Argentina, Brazil and Chile,* McGraw, 1962; *Today's Latin America,* Doubleday-Anchor, 1962; *A Primer of Economic Development,* Macmillan, 1962; *Latin America,* Scholastic Book Service, 1964; *The Venezuelan Democratic Revolution,* Rutgers University Press, 1964; *Organized Labor in Latin America,* Free Press, 1965; *Latin American Politics and Government,* Harper, 1965; *The Venezuelan Communist Party,* Hoover Institution, 1969; *An Introduction to Argentina,* Praeger, 1969; *Latin American Political Parties,* Praeger, 1973; (editor) *Aprismo: The Ideas and Doctrines of Victor Raul Haya de la Torre,* Kent State University Press, 1973; *Trotskyism in Latin America,* Hoover Institution, 1973; *Agrarian Reform in Latin America,* Macmillan, 1974; *Four Alexander Families of Wayne County, Ohio,* Megaton Press, 1975; *A New Development Strategy,* Orbis, 1976; *Arturo Alessandri: A Biography,* University Microfilms, 1977; *The Tragedy of Chile,* Greenwood Press, 1978; *Juan Domingo Peron: A History,* Westview, 1979. Also author of pamphlets. Contributor of chapters to thirty-eight other books and of several hundred articles to magazines and newspapers.

WORK IN PROGRESS: A biography of Romulo Betancourt.

*   *   *

ALEXANDER, Theron 1913-

PERSONAL: Born August 31, 1913, in Springfield, Tenn.; son of Theron and Mary Helen (Jones) Alexander; married Marie Bailey, August 29, 1936; children: Thomas, Mary. *Education:* Maryville College, Maryville, Tenn., B.A., 1935; University of Tennessee, M.A., 1939; University of Chica-

go, Ph.D., 1949. *Home:* 656 Meadowbrook Ave., Ambler, Pa. 19002.

CAREER: Indiana University, Gary Center, instructor in psychology, 1947-48; Florida State University, Tallahassee, assistant professor of psychology, 1949-54; Child Guidance Clinic, Panama City, Fla., director, 1954-57; U.S. Air Force, Tyndall Field, Fla., lecturer in psychology, 1954-56; University of Iowa, Iowa City, associate professor of psychology in pediatrics, 1957-65; University of Miami, Miami, Florida, professor of psychology in pediatrics, 1965-66; Temple University, Philadelphia, Pa., professor of human development and educational psychology, 1966—, director of Child Development Research Center, 1966-69. Lecturer at international symposium, Sao Paulo, Brazil, 1977. Consultant, Multicultural Consultants International, Inc. *Military service:* U.S. Navy, 1943-45; served in Pacific Theatre, 1943-45; became lieutenant. *Member:* American Psychological Association (fellow), American Association for the Advancement of Science, Sigma Xi.

WRITINGS: Psychotherapy in Our Society, Prentice-Hall, 1963; *Child and Adolescent Psychology,* Atherton, 1969; *Human Development in an Urban Age,* Prentice-Hall, 1973; (contributor) O. G. Johnson and J. W. Bommarito, editors, *Tests and Measurements in Child Development,* Jossey-Bass, 1976; (contributor) Maria Antonietta Dente da Costa Marques, *Alternatives de desenvolvimento: Infra-estrutura e servicos urbanos,* Servico de Documentacao e Biblioteca, 1978; (with others) *Developmental Psychology,* Van Nostrand, 1980. Contributor to professional journals.

WORK IN PROGRESS: A book, *Adult Psychology,* and a monograph, *The Content of Reality.*

SIDELIGHTS: Theron Alexander told *CA:* "The book *Human Development in an Urban Age* took me to Brazil because someone in the government read it and recommended that I be invited to lecture and to participate in their international symposium. Getting to know other cultures not only in Brazil but in other parts of the world has had considerable influence in dealing with questions about human learning and behavior.

"As a student of the 'human condition,' I think four threads have helped me in a search for understanding. One thread is the study of history. For me it is only logical to examine paths that have led us to where we are. A second thread is that of knowledge about other cultures, both primitive and modern. Verities that I accept and value may not appear at all in other parts of the world and this fact helps in looking at my own. A third thread is that of psychotherapy with troubled people. Knowing of the problems they face has increased my own understanding. A fourth thread has been the study and work in relation to biological forces in human behavior. A psychology unrelated to biological forces in human behavior seems to be unsound."

*   *   *

ALLEN, G(eorge) C(yril) 1900-

PERSONAL: Born June 28, 1900, in Kenilworth, England; son of George Henry and Elizabeth (Sharman) Allen; married Eleanora Cameron Shanks, December 21, 1929 (died May, 1972). *Education:* University of Birmingham, B. Com., 1921, M. Com., 1922, Ph.D., 1928. *Religion:* Church of England. *Home:* 15 Ritchie Court, 380 Banbury Rd., Oxford OX2 7PW, England.

CAREER: University of Birmingham, Birmingham, England, research fellow and lecturer, 1925-29; University College, Hull, England, professor of economics, 1929-33; University of Liverpool, Liverpool, England, Brunner Professor of Economy Science, 1933-47; University of London, London, England, professor of political economy, 1947-67. Lecturer, Government College, Japan, 1922-25. Fellow, School of Oriental and African Studies, University of London, and St. Anthony's College, Oxford University. Temporary assistant secretary, Board of Trade, London, 1940-44; temporary counselor, British Foreign Office, 1945-46; member, United Kingdom Monopolies Commission, 1950-62; director, Anglo-Nippon Trust Ltd., 1965-68. Trustee, Institute of Economic Affairs. *Military service:* Royal Air Force, 1918, became second lieutenant. *Member:* British Association (president of economics section, 1950), Royal Economic Society (vice-president, 1933-63), British Academy (fellow), Japan Society. *Awards, honors:* Commander of Order of British Empire; Order of the Rising Sun (third class); Japan Foundation Award, 1980.

WRITINGS: Modern Japan and Its Problems, Allen & Unwin, 1928; *The Industrial Development of Birmingham and the Black Country,* Allen & Unwin, 1929, revised edition, 1966; *British Industries and Their Organisation,* Longmans, Green, 1933, 5th edition, 1970; *Japan: The Hungry Guest,* Allen & Unwin, 1938; (with E. B. Schumpeter) *The Industrial Development of Japan and Manchukuo,* Macmillan, 1940; *A Short Economic History of Modern Japan,* Allen & Unwin, 1946, 4th edition, 1981; (with A. G. Donnithorne) *Western Enterprise in Far Eastern Economic Development,* Allen & Unwin, 1954; (with Donnithorne) *Western Enterprise in Indonesia and Malaya,* Allen & Unwin, 1957; *Japan's Economic Recovery,* Oxford University Press, 1958; *The Structure of Industry in Britain,* Longmans, Green, 1961, 3rd edition, 1970; *Japan's Economic Expansion,* Oxford University Press, 1965; *Japan as a Market and Source of Supply,* Pergamon, 1966; *Economic Fact and Fantasy,* Institute of Economic Affairs, 1967; *Monopoly and Restrictive Practices,* Allen & Unwin, 1968; *The British Disease,* Institute of Economic Affairs, 1976, 2nd edition, 1979; *How Japan Competes,* Institute of Economic Affairs, 1978; *Collected Papers,* two volumes, Macmillan, 1979-80.

WORK IN PROGRESS: Research into Japanese economic questions; research into British industrial questions.

AVOCATIONAL INTERESTS: Literature, especially English and French; water-color painting, gardening, mountain walking, traveling.

*   *   *

ALLEN, Gay Wilson   1903-

PERSONAL: Born August 23, 1903, in Lake Junaluska, N.C.; son of Robert Henry (a carpenter) and Ethel (Garren) Allen; married Evie A. Allison (a librarian), July 15, 1929. *Education:* Duke University, A.B., 1926, A.M., 1929; University of Wisconsin, Ph.D., 1934. *Home:* 454 Grove St., Oradell, N.J. 07649.

CAREER: Bowling Green State University, Bowling Green, Ohio, associate professor, 1935-46; New York University, New York, N.Y., professor of English, 1946-69, professor emeritus, 1969—. Lecturer on tour of Japan with William Faulkner, sponsored by U.S. State Department, 1955. Visiting professor at Harvard University, 1969-70, and Emory University, 1979; summer school teacher at Harvard University, Duke University, and University of Texas. *Member:* Modern Language Association of America, International Association of University Professors of English, P.E.N., Phi Beta Kappa. *Awards, honors:* Rockefeller fellow, 1944-45;

Guggenheim fellow, 1952-53, 1959-60; Tamiment Institute Book Award for the biographical work that best demonstrated the creativity of the free spirit, 1955, for *The Solitary Singer: A Critical Biography of Walt Whitman;* Jay B. Hubbell Medal for contributions to American literature, 1977.

WRITINGS: American Prosody, American Book Co., 1935, reprinted, Octagon Books, 1966; (editor with H. H. Clark) *Literary Criticism: Pope to Croce,* American Book Co., 1941, reprinted, Wayne State University Press, 1961; *Walt Whitman Handbook,* Hendricks House, 1946; (editor with H. A. Pochmann) *Masters of American Literature,* two volumes, Macmillan, 1949; (editor) *Walt Whitman Abroad,* Syracuse University Press, 1955; (editor with C. T. Davis) *Walt Whitman's Poems,* New York University Press, 1955; *The Solitary Singer: A Critical Biography of Walt Whitman,* Macmillan, 1955; (author of introduction) Walt Whitman, *Leaves of Grass,* New American Library, 1958.

Walt Whitman, Grove Press, 1961, revised edition, Wayne State University Press, 1969; *Walt Whitman as Man, Poet, and Legend,* Southern Illinois University Press, 1961, revised and enlarged edition published as *Aspects of Walt Whitman,* Norwood Edition, 1977; (editor with Walter B. Rideout and James K. Robinson) *American Poetry,* Harper, 1965; *William James, a Biography,* Viking, 1967; *A Reader's Guide to Walt Whitman,* Farrar, Straus, 1970; *The World of Herman Melville,* Viking, 1971; (editor) *A William James Reader,* Houghton, 1971; (editor) *Studies in "Leaves of Grass,"* C. E. Merrill, 1972; *The New Walt Whitman Handbook,* New York University Press, 1975; *Waldo Emerson, a Biography,* Viking, 1981. General editor with Sculley Bradley, *The Collected Writings of Walt Whitman,* sixteen volumes, New York University Press, 1961-80.

Contributor to books, including: Frederik Schyberg, *Walt Whitman,* translation by Evie Allison Allen, Columbia University Press, 1951; John C. Broderick, editor, *Whitman, the Poet,* Wadsworth, 1962; Sydney J. Krause, editor, *Essays on Determinism in American Literature,* Kent State University Press, 1964; Francis Murphy, editor, *Discussions of Poetry: Form and Structure,* D. C. Heath, 1964; Marston LaFrance, editor, *Patterns of Commitment in American Literature,* University of Toronto Press, 1967; Clarence Gohdes, editor, *Essays on American Literature in Honor of Jay B. Hubbell,* Duke University Press, 1967; *Memorial Volume to Robert Faner,* Southern Illinois University Press, 1969; (with Charles T. Davis) Edwin Haviland Miller, editor, *A Century of Whitman Criticism,* Indiana University Press, 1969; E. H. Miller, editor, *The Artistic Legacy of Walt Whitman: A Tribute to Gay Wilson Allen,* New York University Press, 1970. Contributor of articles to national and international magazines.

WORK IN PROGRESS: Six more volumes of *The Collected Writings of Walt Whitman.*

SIDELIGHTS: A noted biographer, Gay Wilson Allen has developed a large collection of the writings of Walt Whitman, as well as smaller collections of the work of William James and Ralph Waldo Emerson, for the Hubbell Center for American Historiography at Duke University. The writer for *Kirkus Reviews* calls his biography of Whitman, *Solitary Singer,* a "good biography, the result of twenty-five years work on the part of the biographer. It is sound, sane, accurate, well balanced, neither condemnatory nor unduly adulatory." W. T. Scott of the *New York Herald Tribune Book Review* comments: "His book is admirable not for any charm of style or scintillant penetration—its virtues are the plainer, indispensable ones of scholarship and intelligence.... By his scholarly use of new materials and perspectives he has given us our most thorough and reliable Whitman biography and has told well one of the great stories behind one of our greatest books.'' The *San Francisco Chronicle*'s J. H. Jackson believes *Solitary Singer* "is likely to be the definitive study of Whitman for a long time to come.''

Allen's biography of William James was widely, and for the most part favorably, reviewed. Robert C. LeClair comments in the *Christian Science Monitor:* "What a delightful thing it is to find in a book an alive, palpitating presence, a three-dimensional entity whose reality one continues to feel long after closing the volume! In what may prove to be the definitive as well as the first full-scale biography of William James, Gay Wilson Allen has conjured up the very spirit and substance of the distinguished philosopher, psychologist, teacher, and author. Behind each of his many roles stands the man—the affectionate, witty, spontaneous, understanding son, brother, husband, father, and friend whose capacity for living made him rejoice in his fellow creatures, seeing them as 'unique like himself and forever fascinating.'" The reviewer for *Time* believes that "for all that has been written about William James, psychologist, philosopher, teacher and author, nothing as good as this full-length biography has appeared before. Author Allen ... presents James's complex character with the ease and clarity that distinguished his subject's own style. There is no understanding James's skeptical temperament without understanding his extraordinary family. Using unpublished papers, Allen weaves a rich account of the restless, tightly knit clan.''

The unpublished papers to which Allen had access include much of the correspondence and private writings of several members of the James family. Although William James's letters to his wife are closed to the public until 2023, his grandson described their content to Allen. Quotations from these unpublished works are sprinkled throughout the biography. Stuart Hampshire of the *New York Review of Books* comments: "Allen constructs, principally by quotation, a coherent picture of [James's] greatness as a teacher who inspired independent inquiry and who lent a new dignity to his profession in America.... Professor Allen concentrates attention upon the intricate relationship within the James family, and upon William's efforts to overcome depressions, vacillation, and psychosomatic illnesses. But he is not overemphatic and is content to present the facts from the family papers without thrusting explanation on the reader. He illustrates James's immense charm, his shrewdness, wit, impatience, and integrity by wonderful quotations from letters, and James emerges as an irresistibly amiable and serious man.''

The *New York Times Book Review*'s R.W.B. Lewis feels that "Allen is wise not to impose a rigid order or narrowly interpretive design upon his abundant materials" but adds that "the lack of discrimination is depressing, and amid this cascade of names and addresses and minutiae any clear line of narrative and any clear and significant development of his central figure are for long stretches completely lost.'' T. R. Temple of the *National Observer* agrees with Lewis's assessment, writing that Allen "has based his biography on a lode of revealing family correspondence and memoirs recently made available. The material particularly illuminates the relationship between William and Henry, who were often critical of one another.... This kind of document occasionally makes Mr. Allen's biography fascinating. But such crests are awash in a sea of trivia that mars that total effect; in his anxiety to make full use of the new James material, the author has quoted too much. The James family was addicted to travel and correspondence, and Mr. Allen seemingly records the clan's every observation about food and hotels. He also reserves too much discussion of James's significance in psychology and philosophy for an epilog, making the man's contributions seem almost an afterthought. The layman unfamiliar with James must therefore plow through 494 pages before discovering the full story of why his subject merits attention.''

Robert Sklar of the *Reporter* agrees that James's significance is occasionally lost in the information about his family relations. "For all the pleasure in reading his biography," Sklar writes, "one is hard put to find the whole of William James in it.... The reader of *William James* is surprised to learn from time to time that its bland, slightly baffled, and sickly subject was regarded as a giant by his contemporaries: thousands went to hear him lecture, professional colleagues revered him, followed and debated his work.'' Conversely, Tony Tanner of *London Magazine* writes: "Allen is very good at relating the development of William's thought—moving from art, to science, to medicine, to psychology, finally to philosophy—to the needs, processes and discoveries of his own life. William himself insists that 'a philosophy is the expression of man's intimate character,' and with tact and insight Allen shows how William's own troubles and sicknesses, his neuroses and suicidal depressions, informed the growth of the philosophy through which he both expressed himself and secured himself.''

William H. Gass of *Book Week* believes that Allen "has certainly done as well" with the James biography as the earlier biography of Whitman. "He does not so obviously dote upon his subject; he does not struggle to convince; he does not heap his man with praise," writes Gass. "Nor does he endeavor to give extended accounts of the philosopher's ideas. These discretions, I believe, were wise. Wisest of all, perhaps, was his decision (I think of it as that) to write his history in the tongue of James. There is no more sensitive, resonant, or lively language.... Mr. Allen's own conjectures are modest. He hides himself in his arrangements. Thus this history of James is not so redolent with reference nor so warm with suggestion (Henry might have said) as it might have been, but it is more appropriate to its man for that restraint, and Mr. Allen's careful splicing of quotations into his own considerable account to form one rich and smoothly flowing narrative must be admired by all who have ever attempted the same.''

BIOGRAPHICAL/CRITICAL SOURCES: Kirkus Reviews, December 1, 1954; *Saturday Review,* February 5, 1955, August 12, 1967; *New York Times,* February 6, 1955, June 18, 1969; *New York Herald Tribune Book Review,* February 6, 1955; *Time,* February 7, 1955, December 29, 1967; *San Francisco Chronicle,* February 20, 1955; *American Scholar,* autumn, 1962; *Book Week,* April 2, 1967; *New York Times Book Review,* May 14, 1967; *Newsweek,* May 15, 1967; *Christian Science Monitor,* June 20, 1967, November 3, 1975; *New York Review of Books,* June 29, 1967; *Reporter,* August 10, 1967; *Observer Review,* September 24, 1967; *Yale Review,* October, 1967; *New Statesman,* October 13, 1967; *Listener,* October 19, 1967; *Virginia Quarterly Review,* autumn, 1967; *London Magazine,* December, 1967; *Hudson Review,* spring, 1968; Edwin H. Miller, editor, *The Artistic Legacy of Walt Whitman: A Tribute to Gay Wilson Allen,* New York University Press, 1970.

—*Sketch by Linda Metzger*

ALLISON, R(ichard) Bruce 1949-

PERSONAL: Born May 10, 1949, in San Diego, Calif.; son of Harry B. (a banker) and Dorothy (Buick) Allison. *Education:* Brown University, A.B., 1971. *Home and office:* 2025 Dunn Place, Madison, Wis. 53713.

CAREER: School of Living (SOL) Press, Hinsdale, Ill., director, beginning 1972; currently publisher, Wisconsin Books, Madison.

WRITINGS—Published by School of Living Press, except as indicated: (Editor with Mildred J. Loomis) *Humanizing Our Future*, 1972; (editor) *Toward a Human Future*, 1972; *Democrats in Exile, 1968-1972: The Political Confessions of a New England Liberal*, 1974; *Travel Journal: Europe and North Africa*, 1978; (editor) *Wisconsin's Champion Trees*, Wisconsin Books, 1980. Author of syndicated college newspaper column, "Counter Culture Corner," 1973.

WORK IN PROGRESS: With Robert Gard, *Famous and Historic Trees of Wisconsin*.

*　　*　　*

ALLPORT, Gordon (Willard) 1897-1967

PERSONAL: Born November 11, 1897, in Montezuma, Ind.; died October 9, 1967 of lung cancer in Cambridge, Mass.; son of John Edwards (a physician) and Nellie Edith (Wise) Allport; married Ada Lufkin Gould, 1925; children: Robert Bradlee. *Education:* Harvard University, B.A., 1919, M.A., 1921, Ph.D., 1922; studied in Berlin, Germany, Hamburg, Germany, and Cambridge, England, 1922-24, as holder of Sheldon traveling fellowship. *Home:* 386 School St., Watertown, Mass. *Office:* Department of Social Relations, Harvard University, Cambridge, Mass.

CAREER: Robert College, Istanbul, Turkey, instructor in English, 1919-20; Dartmouth College, Hanover, N.H., assistant professor of psychology, 1926-30; Harvard University, Cambridge, Mass., instructor in social ethics, 1924-26, assistant professor of psychology, 1930-36, associate professor, 1936-42, professor of psychology, 1942-67. Former Director of the National Opinion Research Center; former member of National Commission for UNESCO. Visiting overseas consultant to Institute of Social Research, University of Natal (South Africa), 1956.

MEMBER: American Psychological Association (president, 1939), Eastern Psychological Association (president, 1943), Society for the Psychological Study of Social Issues (president, 1944), Phi Beta Kappa; honorary member of British Psychological Society, Deutsche Gesellschaft fuer Psychologie, Osterreichische Arztegesellschaft fuer Psychotherapie, La Societe Francaise de Psychologie, and other foreign societies. *Awards, honors:* L.H.D., Boston University, 1958, Ohio Wesleyan University, 1962; Gold Medal award, American Psychology Foundation, 1963; D.Sc., Colby College, 1964; D.Litt., Durham University, 1965.

WRITINGS: (With P. E. Vernon) *Studies in Expressive Movement*, Macmillan, 1933, reprinted, Hafner, 1967; (with H. Cantril) *The Psychology of Radio*, Harper, 1935, reprinted, 1971; *Personality: A Psychological Interpretation*, Holt, 1937, reprinted, Constable, 1962; *The Use of Personal Documents in Psychological Science*, Social Science Research Council, 1942; (with L. Postman) *The Psychology of Rumor*, Holt, 1947; *The Individual and His Religion*, Macmillan, 1950; *The Nature of Personality: Selected Papers*, Addison-Wesley, 1950, reprinted, Greenwood, 1975; (contributor) *Cultural Groups and Human Relations* (lectures), Teachers College Press, 1951, reprinted, Books for Libraries, 1970;

The Nature of Prejudice, Beacon, 1954; *Becoming: Basic Considerations for a Psychology of Personality*, Yale University Press, 1955; *Personality and the Social Encounter: Selected Papers*, Beacon Press, 1960; *Pattern and Growth in Personality*, Holt, 1961; *Letters from Jenny*, Harcourt, 1965; *The Person in Psychology: Selected Essays*, Beacon Press, 1968; *Waiting for the Lord: 33 Meditations on God and Man*, Macmillan, 1978. Contributor of over 200 articles to periodicals. Editor, *Journal of Abnormal and Social Psychology*, 1937-49.

SIDELIGHTS: Gordon Allport, a social psychologist whose chief interest was personality theory, studied prejudice, expressive behavior, and religion. His *Personality: A Psychological Interpretation* was a standard textbook in the field and was widely used in classrooms. Allport insisted "that man acts not so much because of universal primordial drives," said *Time*, "but rather as a result of individual characteristics developed over a lifetime. It was once a highly controversial idea, but today more and more psychologists are coming around to this view."

BIOGRAPHICAL/CRITICAL SOURCES: New York Times, October 10, 1967; *Time*, October 20, 1967; Diane Schultz, *Theories of Personality*, Brooks/Cole, 1976.†

*　　*　　*

ALLWARD, Maurice 1923-

PERSONAL: Born February 15, 1923, in London, England; son of Frank Leonard (a lawyer) and Daisy (Webb) Allward; married Alice Proctor, June 1, 1946 (died August, 1977); married June 16, 1979; second wife's maiden name, Furneaux; children: (first marriage) Bruce, Caroline. *Education:* Attended Friends School, Saffron Walden, England, 1938-41. *Politics:* Liberal. *Home:* The Nest, 12 Bearwood Close, Potters Bar, Hertfordshire EN6 5HJ, England.

CAREER: Hawker Aircraft Ltd., Kingston, England, designer, 1941-46; Palmer Tyre Co., London, England, chief draftsman, 1947-56; British Aerospace, Hatfield, England, 1957—, currently deputy manager of technical pulications. Member, Royal Observer Corps. *Military service:* Royal Airforce Volunteer Reserve, 1941-45. *Member:* British Interplanetary Society (associate fellow).

WRITINGS: (With John Taylor) *Spitfire*, Harborough, 1946; (with Taylor) *Wings for Tomorrow*, Ian Allan, 1951; (with J. S. Stevens) *How and Why of Aircraft*, Putnam, 1952; (with Taylor) *Eagle Book of Aircraft*, Longacre, 1954; (with Roy McLeavy) *Farnborough Story*, Fetter, 1956; *The World of Space*, Collins, 1956; (with McLeavy) *London Airport*, Ian Allan, 1957; (with Taylor) *ABC of Missiles and Rockets*, Ian Allan, 1958; *Milestones in Science*, Collins, 1958; (with Taylor) *Every Boy's Book of Flight*, Spring Books, 1959; (with Taylor) *ABC of Satellites and Space Travel*, Ian Allan, 1959.

(With Taylor) *Eagle Book of Rockets and Space Travel*, Longacre, 1961; *Objective—Outer Space*, Collins, 1961; (with McLeavy) *London's Airports*, Ian Allan, 1962; *Do You Know about Spaceflight?*, Collins, 1962; *Do You Know about Aircraft?*, Collins, 1962; *Do You Know about Motor Cars?*, Collins, 1963; *Do You Know about the Earth?*, Collins, 1963; *Air Travel*, Vista, 1963; *Inside a Jet Airliner*, Ian Allan, 1964; *Aircraft*, Wheaton, 1965; (with Taylor) *Westland 50*, Ian Allan, 1965; *Man-Made Miracles*, Golden Pleasure Books, 1966; (co-author) *Great Inventions of the World*, Hamlyn, 1966; *Safety in the Air*, Abelard, 1967; *Triumphs of Flight*, Wheaton, 1968.

Lore of Flight, Tre Tryckare (Gothenburg, Sweden), 1970;

Hurricane Special, Ian Allan, 1975; *F-86 Sabre,* Ian Allan, 1978; *Aircraft—A Picture History,* Ward, Lock, 1979; *What Plane Is That?,* Octopus, 1979. Contributor to *Air Pictorial, Jane's All the World Aircraft,* and to periodicals.

WORK IN PROGRESS: Buccaneer Bomber; Seaplanes and Flying Boats.

SIDELIGHTS: Maurice Allward recalls that he wrote his first book "to relieve boredom while firewatching during the 1939-45 War; it was never published. [My] first article was finally published, for no fee, after being rejected by 29 magazines, selected in descending order of their rates of pay. Writing brings with it a great feeling of personal satisfaction and achievement. It is [my] personal 'safety valve.'"

AVOCATIONAL INTERESTS: Architecture, stamps, ancient monuments, lost civilizations, wildlife, motion picture filming, swimming, and "writing letters offering gratuitous advice to notable persons."

*   *   *

ALPERS, Antony 1919-

PERSONAL: Born September 10, 1919, in Christchurch, New Zealand; son of O.T.J. Alpers; married; children: two sons; one daughter. *Education:* Attended Christ's College, Christchurch, New Zealand. *Agent:* John Johnson, 51-54 Goschen Bldgs., 12-13 Henrietta St., London WC2E 8LF, England. *Office:* Department of English, Queen's University, Kingston, Ontario, Canada K7L 3N6.

CAREER: Journalist in New Zealand for *The Press,* Christchurch, *New Zealand Listener,* Wellington, and *Auckland Star,* Auckland; *Education,* Wellington, editor, 1959-61; University of British Columbia, Vancouver, visiting lecturer, 1962-63; *Local Government,* Christchurch, founding editor, 1965-66; Queen's University, Kingston, Ontario, 1966—, began as assistant professor, currently associate professor of English. Former editor, Caxton Press, Christchurch, New Zealand.

WRITINGS: Katherine Mansfield, Knopf, 1953; *Dolphins: The Myth and the Mammal,* Houghton, 1961; *Maori Myths and Tribal Legends,* Houghton, 1965; *Legends of the South Seas: The World of the Polynesians Seen through Their Myths and Legends, Poetry and Art,* Crowell, 1970; *The Life of Katherine Mansfield,* Viking, 1980.

SIDELIGHTS: In 1953, Knopf published the first book of a young journalist named Antony Alpers. The biography of New Zealand-born short story writer Katherine Mansfield (1888-1923), it was, the author notes in retrospect, "a young man's book; I was twenty-seven when I began it, and still twenty-seven when I finished it four years later, or so I think when forced to look at it." Recalling his limited access to letters and personal papers (most were unavailable to him at the time because the owners were still alive); his timidity, which prevented him from interviewing some of Mansfield's more illustrious friends and contemporaries (such as Bertrand Russell and T. S. Eliot); and his naivete, Alpers reveals in a *Times Literary Supplement* article how he gradually came to realize that a major revision of his biography was in order. "When a dozen years had passed, in the 1960s, the first biography went out of print: and then a great change came over my life," Alpers explains. "Partly on the strength of my book, I was invited in 1966 by Dr. George Whalley to join the Department of English at Queen's University.... Four years later, it was he who suggested that I might 're-vise' it, in the light of new material. I would be eligible for research funds, and for sabbatical leave—unaccustomed privileges for me.

"I set to work, and within a year or so I began to understand what had really happened. Because of deaths in the previous fifteen years, all the 'papers,' or nearly all, had become available, and very great quantities had crossed the Atlantic to North America.... I was to have a second chance."

Alpers found, however, that having a second chance at writing the definitive biography of Mansfield did not necessarily mean that his task was easier. It was, in fact, "very much harder," he reports, "and it took more than twice as long. The 'story' was in fact a different one, at least to me. It was a question partly of dust in the eyes the first time round ...; and partly of mastering all that fresh material, on a vastly greater scale. In 1950 my files and notes and books could all be got into a Rinso carton, which could be slid under a bed, such was life in those days. The equivalent materials for the second biography, collected with the help of Queen's University, the Canada Council, the Xerox Corporation, modern filing equipment, and uncounted airlines, amounted in simple shelf length to twenty times as much."

The Life of Katherine Mansfield appeared in 1980 and was described emphatically by its author as "*not* a revised edition of my first book, but a wholly new biography." In his zeal to discover and record *everything* pertaining to his subject, Alpers leaves "no literary stone unturned," according to the *Times Literary Supplement*'s Rosemary Dinnage. "This is a biography on the mighty twentieth-century scale," she continues. "There may be grumbles that all this biographical machinery is out of proportion to its subject, a girl of slender means, health and output. One answer is that Mansfield's talent was more promising than the work she had time to do.... A more substantial point is that the biography has become a picture of the period as well as of Katherine Mansfield." Furthermore, she notes, Alpers "relate[s] the life to the published work deliberately and successfully.... [He] has most industriously filled in the hitherto mysterious few years before she met [her future husband, John Middleton] Murry at twenty-four."

Commenting in the *Chicago Tribune Book World,* Shirley Ann Grau finds the amount—and type—of detail contained in *The Life of Katherine Mansfield* "frightening," with all the "garish drama of a soap opera." One of the "flaws" Grau points out involves the very technique Dinnage praises: the use of Mansfield's fiction to reconstruct certain events in Mansfield's life. Grau believes that this is "always risky with any writer and totally unreliable with a superior artificer like Mansfield." In addition, Grau states, "Alpers does not write well. His plodding prose is occasionally truly embarrassing.... I was [also] irritated by the fact that there is more here about Katherine Mansfield than I ever wanted to know. Still, when all is said and done, it's an intriguing story."

The *London Times*'s Kay Dick agrees that "as a biographer Mr. Alpers is scrupulous rather than inspired; his approach is often that of a tax inspector, his prose a trifle awkward, his tone sometimes morally patronizing, and he lacks imaginative subtlety." Nevertheless, she declares, "this is in the way of being a definitive biography, and as such utterly engrossing simply because K. M. herself is always engrossing."

Katherine Winton Evans of the *Washington Post Book World* finds the biography to be an "excellent book—fat with details of [Mansfield's] brief, unruly life." Unlike some of her colleagues, Evans praises Alpers for "subtly draw[ing] the connections between her life and work.... [He] writes with grace and scholarly precision about an unfinished—not a minor—writer whose early work is all we have.'' Though he feels the amount of detail contained in *The Life of Katherine Mansfield* is often ''too generous'' and that the author ''can be intrusive,'' the *New York Times Book Review*'s Howard Moss nevertheless admits that Alpers successfully ''places the writer in a larger picture and provides a valuable chronology.'' But the real strength of *The Life of Katherine Mansfield*, Moss concludes, lies in the fact that it ''rescue[s] a complex and heroic woman from the dullness of sanctity.''

BIOGRAPHICAL/CRITICAL SOURCES: New York Times Book Review, March 9, 1980; *Washington Post Book World*, March 23, 1980; *Times Literary Supplement*, March 28, 1980, May 16, 1980; *Chicago Tribune Book World*, March 30, 1980; *London Times*, June 19, 1980.

—*Sketch by Deborah A. Straub*

*   *   *

ALTIZER, Thomas J(onathan) J(ackson)   1927-

PERSONAL: Surname is pronounced *All*-tie-zer; born September 28, 1927, in Cambridge, Mass.; son of Jackson Duncan (a lawyer) and Frances (Greetham) Altizer; married Gayle Pye, July 13, 1961; married second wife, Alma Barker, 1967; children: John Jackson, Katharine Blake. *Religion:* Episcopalian. *Education:* Attended St. John's College, Annapolis, Md., 1944-45; University of Chicago, A.B., 1948, A.M., 1951, Ph.D., 1955. *Home:* 210 Chestnut St., Port Jefferson, N.Y. 11727. *Office:* Department of Religious Studies, State University of New York, Stony Brook, N.Y. 11794.

CAREER: Wabash College, Crawfordsville, Ind., assistant professor of religion, 1954-56; Emory University, Atlanta, Ga., assistant professor, 1956-61, associate professor of Bible and religion, 1961-68; State University of New York at Stony Brook, professor of English and religious studies, 1968—. *Military service:* U.S. Army, 1945-46.

WRITINGS: Oriental Mysticism and Biblical Eschatology, Westminster, 1961; (editor with W.A. Beardslee and Harvey Young) *Truth, Myth, and Symbol*, Prentice-Hall, 1962; *Mircea Eliade and the Dialectic of the Sacred*, Westminster, 1963; (with William Hamilton) *Radical Theology and the Death of God*, Bobbs-Merrill, 1966; *The Gospel of Christian Atheism*, Westminster, 1966; (editor) *Toward a New Christianity*, Harcourt, 1967; *The New Apocalypse: The Radical Christian Vision of William Blake*, Michigan State University Press, 1967; *The Descent into Hell*, Lippincott, 1970; *The Self-Embodiment of God*, Harper, 1977; *Total Presence: The Language of Jesus and the Language of Today*, Seabury, 1980. Contributor to journals in his field.

SIDELIGHTS: As the leader of the Death of God movement of the late 1960's, Thomas Altizer has been characterized by Ray Karras as ''the *enfant terrible* of American theology because, unlike other 'new' theologians, he is directly concerned with the question of God's existence.'' Altizer believes in the death of God as an actual historical event, not a phrase symbolizing a change in one's concept of God. As Daniel Cobb explains, ''The traditional emphasis on God's transcendence has made him irrelevant, indeed antithetical, to the human-historical situation.'' Therefore Altizer says he sees ''no way to true faith apart from an abolition or dissolution of God himself.'' Adherents have been unable to reach a universally acceptable definition of the concept of the death of God. Critic John C. Raines says that to Altizer the death of God signifies ''a revolution in the psyche of man: a loss of any sense of transcendence, the emptying of the cosmos of any Other.''

During the years 1965 to 1968, Altizer's revolutionary position excited a great deal of publicity, hostile and otherwise, for the theological movement (leading to what Altizer has called ''the scandalous success of *Radical Theology and the Death of God*''). As Karras explains in his review for *Motive:* ''Altizer rejoices in the death of the transcendental God. . . . This rejoicing is, I suspect, what so enrages Altizer's hostile critics. . . . It is one thing to tell a man that the conditions of his life are such that he cannot accept a belief in God—you can go along with this and always reserve your options; conditions may change, God may become once again acceptable and you may not have to be alone in the cosmos forever. It is quite another thing to tell a man that there is no transcendental God at all. This is denying human validity as Western man has known it for nearly twenty centuries. It is a revolution that literally overturns the places of God and man.''

While specific criticisms have been made regarding the tone and method of Altizer's writings (a *Times Literary Supplement* reviewer has called his language ''sententious'' and *The Gospel of Christian Atheism* ''by no means a scholarly book''), much of the evaluation of his work has focused on the degree of its relevance or the degree of its optimism/pessimism. Ronald Williams, *Negro Digest* critic, finds the Death of God theologians ''at best irrelevant and at worst deceptive with their precious, sentimental pining.'' Reviewer Cobb concludes, ''As a prophet Altizer catches us where we are all vulnerable, but as a constructive theological thinker he leaves us with little on which to build.'' But as Karras summarized, Altizer is ''hungry enough for the truth to be the atheist that he is, hungry enough for God to be the believer that he also is, and hungry enough for life to be both.''

Writing reviews of his own books for *Christian Century*, Altizer describes his theology as ''the expression of a radical Christian tradition'' having ''the forward and apocalyptic movement of the incarnation, . . . a theology grounded in the sacrificial Christ rather than in the Creator God.'' Some of Altizer's works have been translated into German, Dutch, Italian, Spanish, and Japanese. His work is the subject of numerous doctoral dissertations and scholarly articles.

BIOGRAPHICAL/CRITICAL SOURCES—Books: Kenneth Hamilton, *God Is Dead*, Eerdmans, 1966; Thomas Ogletree, *The Death of God Controversy*, Abingdon, 1966; Jackson Ice and John I. Carey, *The Death of God Debate*, Westminster, 1967; Bernard Murchland, *The Meaning of the Death of God*, Random House, 1967; Glenn R. Wittig, *Radical Theology, Phase Two*, Lippincott, 1968; Langdon Gilkey, *Naming the Whirlwind*, Bobbs-Merrill, 1970; John B. Cobb, Jr., *The Theology of Altizer*, Westminster, 1971; George F. McLean, *Religion in Contemporary Thought*, Alba, 1973; John Senior, *The Death of Christian Culture*, Arlington House, 1978.

Articles: *Christian Century*, March 30, 1966, April 6, 1966, June 1, 1966, August 23, 1967, September 20, 1967, July 22, 1970, May 18, 1977, October 26, 1977, June 7, 1978; *Negro Digest*, March, 1967; *Times Literary Supplement*, July 6, 1967; *Motive*, November, 1967; *Hudson Review*, spring, 1968; *Christian Science Monitor*, June 4, 1970; *Best Sellers*, August, 1977; *Commonweal*, March 3, 1978.

*   *   *

ALVAREZ, A(lfred)   1929-

PERSONAL: Born August 5, 1929, in London, England; son of Bertie and Katie (Levy) Alvarez; married Ursula Graham Barr, 1956 (divorced, 1961); married Audrey Anne Adams,

1966; children: (first marriage) Adam Richard; (second marriage) Luke, Kate. *Education:* Corpus Christi College, Oxford, B.A., 1952, M.A., 1956; Princeton University, visiting fellow, 1953-54. *Agent:* Candida Donadio & Associates, Inc., 111 West 57th St., New York, N.Y. 10019. *Office:* c/o *Observer*, 8 St. Andrew's Hill, London EC4V 5JA, England.

CAREER: Oxford University, Corpus Christi College, Oxford, England, senior research scholar and tutor in English, 1952-55; Rockefeller Foundation, New York, N.Y., visiting fellow, 1955-56, 1958; *Observer*, London, England, 1956—, poetry editor and critic, 1956-66, currently occasional contributor. Gauss Seminarian and visiting lecturer, Princeton University, 1957-58; D. H. Lawrence fellow, University of New Mexico, 1958; drama critic, *New Statesman*, 1958-60; visiting professor at Brandeis University, Waltham, Mass., 1960-61, and State University of New York at Buffalo, 1966; free-lance writer at other periods, and 1956—. *Member:* The Climbers' Club. *Awards, honors:* Vachel Lindsay Prize for Poetry (Chicago), 1961.

WRITINGS: Stewards of Excellence, Scribner, 1958 (published in England as *The Shaping Spirit*, Chatto & Windus, 1958); *The School of Donne*, Chatto & Windus, 1961, Pantheon, 1962; (editor) *The New Poetry*, Penguin, 1962, revised edition, 1966; *Under Pressure: The Writer in Society*, Penguin, 1965; *Lost* (poems), Turret Books, 1968; *Twelve Poems*, The Review, 1968; *Beyond All This Fiddle* (critical essays), Allen Lane, 1968, Random House, 1969; *Penguin Modern Poets 18* (poems), Penguin, 1970; *Apparition* (poems), University of Queensland Press, 1971; *The Savage God: A Study of Suicide*, Weidenfeld & Nicolson, 1971, Random House, 1972; *Samuel Beckett*, Viking, 1973; *Hers* (novel), Weidenfeld & Nicolson, 1974, Random House, 1975; *Autumn to Autumn and Selected Poems, 1953-1976*, Macmillan (London), 1978; *Hunt* (novel), Macmillan, 1978, Simon & Schuster, 1979. Also author of a screenplay, "The Anarchist," 1969. Contributor to *Observer*, *Spectator*, and a number of other American and British periodicals. Advisory editor, "Penguin Modern European Poets" series.

WORK IN PROGRESS: A study of divorce.

SIDELIGHTS: As A. Alvarez summarized himself for *CA*, he "began as a literary critic, but by the end of the 1960s had grown weary of writing books about other people's books, so effectively gave up criticism in order to concentrate on his own creative work." Although his poetry and fiction have been getting a gradually warmer reception, it is as a critic that he has had his greatest success, because of his literary style as well as his conception of the critic's task. His style of criticism is refreshingly contemporary, characterized by a "brisk casualness" and absence of ponderous detail. Alvarez "accepts the full task of criticism. He not only defines and analyzes, but he also assesses and evaluates." Paul Delany writes, "Through his critical essays and *The Savage God* (a study of literature and suicide) Alvarez has become a leading advocate of what he has termed the 'Extremist' poets—Robert Lowell, Anne Sexton, John Berryman, Ted Hughes, Sylvia Plath—who have dared to explore in their art private obsessions with madness, suicide, political terror." The *New York Times*'s John Leonard describes his outlook as "a sensibility fashioned whole out of the bad dreams of the century, pressed upon by what Nabokov called 'the anonymous roller' that leaves a watermark [of paranoia] on every page."

Alvarez's first novel, *Hers*, was not well received. Russell Davies writes that as a critic Alvarez "would have been among the most merciless in pointing out the novel's thin-

ness of texture...." His poems *Autumn to Autumn* fared somewhat better, though were still accused of being "thin not trim, dull not austere" by one reviewer. Derek Stanford of *Books and Bookmen* calls *Autumn to Autumn* "good, very good, strictly minor poetry, much of which poets with bigger names might justifiably be proud...." Stuart Sutherland says of Alvarez's latest work: "*Hunt* is a very good novel, fast-moving and compulsive.... The prosaic is used to offset the sinister. The dialogue is accurate and witty." Even though Leonard points out that Alvarez borrows extensively from the works of other writers (Joseph Conrad, Graham Greene, and Ted Hughes, to name a few), he nevertheless finds *Hunt* to be relatively entertaining, mainly because Alvarez, "besides being well above the norm in intelligence, has a genuine talent for suspense." A *Contemporary Review* critic writes, "Taut, disturbing and expertly constructed, this is a novel not to be missed."

AVOCATIONAL INTERESTS: Rock-climbing, poker, music.

BIOGRAPHICAL/CRITICAL SOURCES: Times Literary Supplement, May 9, 1958, March 3, 1961, February 29, 1968, November 26, 1971, November 8, 1974, April 21, 1978, June 2, 1978; *Poetry*, November, 1959; *Guardian*, February 24, 1961; *Christian Science Monitor*, January 4, 1962, August 2, 1969; *Listener*, February 29, 1968; Ian Hamilton, *The Modern Poet*, Macdonald, 1968; *Observer*, March 3, 1968, December 20, 1970, May 7, 1978; *New Statesman*, March 22, 1968, November 19, 1971, April 14, 1978, June 2, 1978; *Books and Bookmen*, April, 1968, June, 1978; *New York Times*, July 5, 1969, April 7, 1972, March 19, 1975, January 30, 1979; *New York Times Book Review*, July 20, 1969, August 17, 1969, April 16, 1972, March 30, 1975, June 1, 1975, February 11, 1979; *Saturday Review*, August 2, 1969, April 5, 1975; *Book World*, August 10, 1969, April 25, 1972; *Spectator*, December 18, 1971; *New Yorker*, March 31, 1974; *Contemporary Literary Criticism*, Gale, Volume V, 1976, Volume XIII, 1980; *New Review* (London), March, 1978; *Contemporary Review*, July, 1978.

*   *   *

AMACHER, Richard Earl 1917-

PERSONAL: Born December 13, 1917, in Ridgway, Pa.; son of Albert (a foundryman) and Emma (Luchs) Amacher; married Anne Ward, August 26, 1953; children: Alice Marie. *Education:* Attended Oberlin College, 1935-38; Ohio University, A.B., 1939; University of Chicago, additional study, 1939-42; University of Pittsburgh, Ph.D., 1947. *Home:* 515 Auburn Dr., Auburn, Ala. *Office:* English Department, Auburn University, Auburn, Ala.

CAREER: Yale University, New Haven, Conn., instructor in English, 1944-45; Rutgers University, New Brunswick, N.J., 1945-54, began as instructor, became assistant professor; Henderson State College, Arkadelphia, Ark., professor and head of department, 1954-57; Auburn University, Auburn, Ala., associate professor, 1957-65, professor of English, 1965—, Hargis Professor of American Literature, 1978—. Fulbright professor of American literature, University of Wuerzburg in Germany, 1961-62, and Konstanz University, 1969-70; lectured at University of Goettingen and University of Freiburg. *Member:* American Association of University Professors (vice-president, local chapter, 1960-61), Modern Language Association of America, Southeastern American Studies Association (president, 1977-79), Societe Historique d'Auteuil et de Passy (life member). *Awards, honors:* John Billings Fiske Poetry Prize, for "The Cyclotron."

WRITINGS: (Editor) *Franklin's Wit and Folly: The Bagatelles*, Rutgers University Press, 1953; *Practical Criticism*, Henderson State College, 1956; *Benjamin Franklin*, Twayne, 1962; (co-editor) Joseph G. Baldwin, *The Flush Times of California*, University of Georgia Press, 1966; *Edward Albee*, Twayne, 1969; (with Margaret Rule) *Edward Albee at Home and Abroad: A Bibliography*, AMS Press, 1973; (co-editor) *New Perspectives in German Literary Criticism*, Princeton University Press, 1979; *American Political Writers, 1588-1800*, G. K. Hall, 1979. Contributor of short articles and reviews to journals.

*   *   *

AMBROSE, Stephen Edward 1936-

PERSONAL: Born January 10, 1936, in Decatur, Ill.; son of Stephen Hedges (a physician) and Rosepha (Trippe) Ambrose; married former wife, Judith Dorlester, 1957; married Moira Buckley, 1968; children; Stephanie, Barry Halleck, Andrew, Grace, Hugh. *Education:* University of Wisconsin, B.S., 1957, Ph.D., 1963; Louisiana State University, M.A., 1958. *Office:* Department of History, University of New Orleans, New Orleans, La. 70122.

CAREER: Louisiana State University in New Orleans (now University of New Orleans), 1960-64, began as instructor, became associate professor of history; Johns Hopkins University, Baltimore, Md., assistant professor, 1964-66, associate professor of history, 1966-69; U.S. Naval War College, Newport, R.I., Ernest J. King Professor of Maritime History, 1969-70; Kansas State University, Manhattan, Dwight D. Eisenhower Professor of War and Peace, 1970-71; University of New Orleans, professor of history, 1971—. Visiting assistant professor, Louisiana State University, Baton Rouge, 1963-64. *Member:* American Military Institute (member of board of directors), American Committee on the History of the Second World War (member of board of directors), Lewis and Clark Heritage Trail Foundation (member of board of directors), Big Blue Athletic Association (president, 1976-77), Chi Psi.

WRITINGS: (Editor) *A Wisconsin Boy in Dixie*, University of Wisconsin Press, 1961; *Halleck: Lincoln's Chief of Staff*, Lousiana State University Press, 1962; *Upton and the Army*, Louisiana State University Press, 1964; *Duty, Honor, and Country: A History of West Point*, Johns Hopkins Press, 1966; *Eisenhower and Berlin, 1945*, Norton, 1967; (editor) *Institutions in Modern America: Innovation in Structure and Process*, Johns Hopkins Press, 1967; (associate editor) *The Papers of Dwight D. Eisenhower: The War Years*, five volumes, Johns Hopkins Press, 1970; *The Supreme Commander: Eisenhower*, Doubleday, 1970; *Rise to Globalism: American Foreign Policy, 1938-70*, Penguin, 1971, revised edition, 1976; (with James A. Barber, Jr.) *The Military and American Society*, Free Press, 1972; *Crazy Horse and Custer: The Parallel Lives of Two American Warriors*, Doubleday, 1975; *Ike's Spies: Eisenhower and the Espionage Establishment*, Doubleday, 1981. Author of a television documentary, "Eisenhower: Supreme Commander," for BBC-TV, 1973. Author of bi-weekly column, *Baltimore Evening Sun*, 1968—. Contributor of reviews and articles to numerous journals and newspapers, including *American Historical Review, Harvard Magazine, American Heritage*, and *New York Times Book Review*.

WORK IN PROGRESS: A full length biography of Meriwether Lewis.

SIDELIGHTS: Stephen Ambrose's work covers a broad range of American military history, from the fighting between the U.S. Army and the American Indians to American foreign policy during the Cold War years. Reviewers have consistently noted Ambrose's ability to present accounts of complicated historical events in a clear, readable, and stimulating manner. In the *Times Literary Supplement*, the critic writes of *The Supreme Commander* that "Stephen Ambrose's biography of Eisenhower at war provides a full-length-faithfully drawn, and well observed portrait to which he has brought a great deal of new material, together with what must be one of the most lucid accounts of the detailed working of the Allied war machine that we have had so far."

BIOGRAPHICAL/CRITICAL SOURCES: Washington Post, October 10, 1970; *New York Review of Books*, May 6, 1971, September 2, 1971; *Times Literary Supplement*, November 5, 1971; *Contemporary Reviews*, January, 1977.

*   *   *

AMES, Lee J(udah) 1921-
(Jonathan David)

PERSONAL: Name legally changed; born January 8, 1921, in New York, N.Y.; son of Joseph F. and Gertrude (Pascal) Abramowitz; married Jocelyn S. Green (an author and homemaker), June 24, 1945; children: Alison Sally, Jonathan David. *Education:* Attended Columbia University. *Home and office:* 44 Lauren Ave., Dix Hills, N.Y. 11746.

CAREER: Ran one-man advertising agency, 1947-48; taught vocational art, 1947-48; children's book illustrator, 1948—. Artist-in-residence, Doubleday & Co., Inc., New York, N.Y., 1956-61. Has worked on animated films for Walt Disney Studios, written magazine comic strips, and illustrated covers for numerous books. President, Northpoint Civic Association, Commack, N.Y., 1962-63. *Military service:* U.S. Army, 1942-44, became second lieutenant.

WRITINGS—Self-illustrated; published by Doubleday, except as indicated: *Draw, Draw, Draw*, 1962; (with wife, Jocelyn Ames) *City Street Games*, Holt, 1963; *Draw Fifty Animals*, 1974; *Draw Fifty Dinosaurs and Other Prehistoric Animals*, 1977; *Draw Fifty Airplanes, Aircraft, and Spacecraft*, 1977; *Draw Fifty Boats, Trucks, Ships, and Trains*, 1977; *Draw Fifty Famous Faces*, 1978; *Draw Fifty Vehicles*, 1978; *Draw Fifty Famous Cartoons*, 1979; *Draw Fifty Buildings*, 1980; *Make Twenty-Five Crayon Drawings*, 1980; *Make Twenty-Five Felt-Tip Drawings*, 1980; *Draw Fifty Dogs*, 1981.

Illustrator: Shannon Garst, *Three Conquistadors*, Messner, 1948; Jeannette Covert Nolan, *Andrew Jackson*, Messner, 1949; Jim Kjelgaard, *Irish Red, Son of Big Red*, Holiday House, 1951; Garst, *Big Foot Wallace of the Texas Rangers*, Messner, 1951; Samuel Hopkins Adams, *The Santa Fe Trail*, Random House, 1951; Julilly H. Kohler, *The Boy Who Stole the Elephant*, Knopf, 1952; Helen D. Olds, *Christmas-Tree Sam*, Messner, 1952; Kjelgaard, *Outlaw Red*, Holiday House, 1953; Nolan, *Abraham Lincoln*, Messner, 1953; (under pseudonym Jonathan David) M. G. Bonner, *Dugout Mystery*, Knopf, 1953; Adams, *The Pony Express*, 1953; Richard Neuberger, *The Royal Canadian Mounted Police*, Random House, 1953; Nolan, *George Rogers Clark*, Messner, 1954; Phyllis R. Fenner, *Circus Parade*, Knopf, 1954; Kohler, *Crazy As You Look*, Knopf, 1954; Ralph Nading Hill, *Robert Fulton*, Random House, 1954; Fletcher Pratt, *The Civil War*, Doubleday, 1955; Madge Haines and Leslie Morrill, *Wright Brothers, First to Fly*, Abingdon, 1955; Harold McCracken, *Winning of the West*, Doubleday, 1955; Ann Colver, *Yankee Doodle Painter*, Knopf, 1955; Ed Stoddard, *The Story of Power*, Doubleday, 1956; Sterling North, *Abe*

Lincoln, Random House, 1956; *North*, *George Washington*, Random House, 1957; Bruce Lancaster, *The American Revolution*, Doubleday, 1957; McCracken, *Hoofs, Claws and Antlers*, Doubleday, 1958; Roy Gallant, *Exploring the Sun*, Doubleday, 1958; Gallant, *Exploring Chemistry*, Doubleday, 1958; Raymond Holden, *All About Famous Scientific Expeditions*, Random House, 1958.

Pat Lauber, *The Quest of Louis Pasteur*, Doubleday, 1960; Phyllis Fenner, *Kick-Off*, Knopf, 1960; Benjamin Gruenberg and Sidonie Gruenberg, *The Wonderful Story of You*, Doubleday, 1960; Glenn Balch, *Horse in Danger*, Crowell, 1960; Lauber, *All About the Planet Earth*, Random House, 1962; Tad Harvey, *Exploring Biology*, Doubleday, 1963; George Selden, *Sir Arthur Evans*, Macmillan, 1964; Anthony Rowley, *Tool Chest*, L. W. Singer Co., 1967; Enid LaMonte Meadowcroft, *Silver for General Washington*, Crowell, 1967; Alvin Silverstein and Virginia Silverstein, *Life in the Universe*, Van Nostrand, 1967; Sam Elkin, *Search for a Lost City*, Putnam, 1967; John H. Woodburn, *Know Your Skin*, Putnam, 1967; John McNeel, *Brain of Man*, Putnam, 1968; Silverstein, *Origin of Life*, Van Nostrand, 1968; Frank X. Ross, *Stories of the States*, Crowell, 1969; Silverstein, *Carl Linnaeus*, John Day, 1969; Isaac Asimov, *Great Ideas of Science*, Houghton, 1969; Adelaide Holl, *Hide and Seek ABC Book*, Platt, 1971.

WORK IN PROGRESS: Draw Fifty Famous Stars; The Dot, Line and Shape Connection.

*   *   *

AMES, Louise Bates   1908-

PERSONAL: Born October 29, 1908, in Portland, Me.; daughter of Samuel Lewis (a judge) and Annie (Leach) Bates; married Smith Whittier Ames, 1930 (divorced, 1937); children: Joan. *Education:* Attended Wheaton College, 1926-28; University of Maine, A.B., 1930, M.A., 1933; Yale University, Ph.D., 1936. *Office:* 310 Prospect St., New Haven, Conn. 06511.

CAREER: Yale Clinic of Child Development, New Haven, Conn., research assistant, instructor, assistant professor, 1933-50; Gesell Institute of Child Development, New Haven, director of research, 1950-65, associate director, 1965-70, co-director, 1971-76, director, 1977, president, 1977—. Public lecturer; speaker on weekly television program, WBZ, Boston, Mass., 1952-56, WEWS, Cleveland, Ohio, 1960-62; writer of daily syndicated newspaper column, 1951—. *Member:* American Psychological Association, International Council of Women Psychologists, Society for Research in Child Development, Society for Projective Techniques (president, 1969-70), Connecticut State Psychological Association, Sigma Xi. *Awards, honors:* Sc.D., University of Maine, 1954.

WRITINGS: (With Arnold Gesell and others) *The First Five Years of Life*, Harper, 1940; (with Gesell and others) *Infant and Child in the Culture of Today*, Harper, 1943; (with Gesell and others) *The Child from Five to Ten*, Harper, 1946; (with Gesell) *The Story of Child Development in Motion Pictures: A Guide to the Study and Interpretation of the Yale Films of Child Development*, Encyclopaedia Britannica Films, 1947; (with Gesell and others) *Child Development: An Introduction to the Study of Human Growth*, Harper, 1949.

(With Learned, Metraux, and Walker) *Child Rorschach Responses: Developmental Trends from Two to Ten Years*, Hoeber, 1952; (with Learned, Metraux and Walker) *Rorschach Responses in Old Age*, Hoeber, 1954; (with Frances L. Ilg) *Child Behavior*, Harper, 1955; (with Gesell and Ilg)

Youth: The Years from Ten to Sixteen, Harper, 1956; (with Metraux and Walker) *Adolescent Rorschach Responses*, Hoeber, 1959; (with Ilg and others) *The Gesell Institute Party Book*, Harper, 1959; (with Ilg) *Mosaic Patterns of American Children*, Harper, 1962; (with Ilg) *Parents Ask*, Harper, 1962; (with Pitcher) *The Guidance Nursery School*, Harper, 1964; (with Ilg) *School Readiness*, Harper, 1965; *Is Your Child in the Wrong Grade?*, Harper, 1967; *Child Care and Development*, Lippincott, 1970; *Stop School Failure*, Harper, 1972; (with Joan A. Chase) *Don't Push Your Preschooler*, Harper, 1974, revised edition, 1981.

With Ilg; all published by Delacorte: *Your Two Year Old*, 1976; *Your Three Year Old*, 1976; *Your Four Year Old*, 1976; *Your Five Year Old*, 1979; *Your Six Year Old*, 1979. Contributor of numerous articles and reviews to periodicals. Member of editorial board, *Journal of Genetic Psychology*.

SIDELIGHTS: Many of Louise Bates Ames' books have been translated for foreign editions. *Avocational interests:* Traveling, gardening, and reading.

*   *   *

ANASTASIOU, Clifford (John)   1929-

PERSONAL: Born February 24, 1929, in Vancouver, British Columbia, Canada; son of John and Lydia (Stead) Anastasiou; married Joan Diane Barton (a professor), September 20, 1952; children: Melanie Jane, Karen Lea, Roger Barton. *Education:* Attended Victoria College, 1947-50; University of British Columbia, B.A., 1952, M.Ed., 1957; Claremont Graduate School, Ph.D., 1963. *Home:* 3931 Southwest Marine Dr., Vancouver, British Columbia, Canada. *Office:* Department of Education, University of British Columbia, Vancouver, British Columbia, Canada.

CAREER: High school biology teacher in West Vancouver, British Columbia, 1955-57, and Anaheim, Calif., 1957-60; Univeristy of British Columbia, Vancouver, assistant professor, 1962-66, associate professor, 1966-71, professor of education, 1971—. Visiting professor, University of Illinois at Urbana-Champaign, 1976. Staff biologist for Education Development Corp., 1964-65.

WRITINGS: Reading about Science, Book I, Holt, 1968; *Teachers, Children, and Things*, Holt, 1971; *The Stump Book*, Wedge, 1975; *The Creek Book*, Wedge, 1978; *The Estuary Book*, Wedge, 1980; *The Wild Cells*, Canadian Cancer Society, 1980. Author of research studies in mycology. Editor of more than forty-five teachers' guides to environmental, health, and science education.

WORK IN PROGRESS: Research on cancer education and drug education.

*   *   *

ANDERSON, Charles Roberts   1902-

PERSONAL: Born October 17, 1902, in Macon, Ga.; son of Robert Lanier and Gertrude (Roberts) Anderson; married Eugenia Blount, June 1, 1935 (died, 1962); married Mary Pringle, May 3, 1963. *Education:* University of Georgia, A.B. and A.M.; studied at Mercer University Law School for two years; Columbia University, Ph.D. *Home:* 4 Legare St., Charleston, S.C. 29401; and Church Cottage, Cambridge, England (summer).

CAREER: University of Georgia, Athens, instructor, 1927-30; Duke University, Durham, N.C., instructor, associate professor, 1930-41; Johns Hopkins University, Baltimore, Md., beginning 1941, professor, 1946-69, chairman of English department, 1950-56, Caroline Donovan Professor of

American Literature, 1956-69. Visiting professor at Heidelberg University (Germany), 1949, University of Rome, 1952-53, Nagano Seminar (Japan), summer, 1954, University of Torino (Italy), spring, 1960; summer school teacher at Columbia University, Universities of California and Hawaii. Special lecturer, South Carolina Poetry Society, 1940, 1944; Barrow Lecturer, University of Georgia, 1948; Lamar Memorial Lecturer, Wesleyan College, 1957.

MEMBER: Modern Language Association of America (chairman, American literature group, 1957), American Association of University Professors, Melville Society of America (president, 1956), Congress of University Professors of English (international), American Studies Association, Phi Beta Kappa, Phi Delta Theta. *Awards, honors:* Rosenwald fellow, 1938-39; Fulbright fellow in Italy, 1952-53; Huntington Library fellow, 1952; Guggenheim fellow, 1965-66; Christian Gauss Award of Phi Beta Kappa Senate for best book of literary criticism, 1961, for *Emily Dickinson's Poetry: Stairway of Surprise*, and 1978, for *Person, Place and Thing in Henry James' Novels*.

WRITINGS: Journal of a Cruise in the Frigate United States: With Notes on Melville, Duke University Press, 1937; *Melville in the South Seas*, Columbia University Press, 1939; *The Centennial Edition of Sidney Lanier*, ten volumes, Johns Hopkins Press, 1946; *Emily Dickinson's Poetry: Stairway of Surprise*, Holt, 1960; *American Literary Masters*, two volumes, Holt, 1965; *The Magic Circle of Walden*, Holt, 1968; *Thoreau's World*, Prentice-Hall, 1971; *Thoreau's Vision*, Prentice-Hall, 1973; *Person, Place and Thing in Henry James' Novels*, Duke University Press, 1977. Member, editorial board of *American Literature, Modern Language Notes*, and *Journal of American Studies* (Japan).

BIOGRAPHICAL/CRITICAL SOURCES: New Republic, September 14, 1968; *Virginia Quarterly Review*, autumn, 1968; *South Atlantic Quarterly*, winter, 1969; *American Literature*, November, 1971; *Times Literary Supplement*, February 24, 1978.

*　　*　　*

ANDERSON, John Q.　1916-1975

PERSONAL: Born May 30, 1916, in Wheeler, Tex.; died February 19, 1975, in Houston, Tex.; son of Albert S. and Emily Eugenia (Grant) Anderson; married Marie Loraine Epps, August 24, 1946. *Education:* Oklahoma State University, A.B., 1939; Louisiana State University, M.A., 1948; University of North Carolina, Ph.D., 1952. *Religion:* Presbyterian. *Home:* 1106 Dubach, Ruston, La. 71270. *Office:* Department of English, University of Houston, Houston, Tex. 77004.

CAREER: McNeese State College (now University), Lake Charles, La., assistant professor, 1952-53; Texas A & M University, College Station, instructor, 1953-54, assistant professor, 1954-56, associate professor, 1956-59, professor of English, 1959-66, head of department, 1962-66; University of Houston, Houston, Tex., professor of American literature, 1966-74, professor emeritus, 1974-75. Member of editorial board, Paisano Books, 1968-75. Texas delegate, White House Conference on Higher Education in the South, 1967. Lecturer. *Military service:* U.S. Army, 1940-46; Adjutant General's Corps, 1943-46; served in England, France, and Germany; became captain.

MEMBER: Modern Language Association of America, American Studies Association (member of national executive council), American Folklore Society (member of advisory committee), Conference of College Teachers of En-

glish, Western American Literature Association, South-Central Modern Language Association (section chairman, 1955-56, 1956-57), Southwestern American Literature Association (chairman of organizing committee, 1969-70), American Studies Association of Texas (founder; councilor, 1956-58, 1964-65; secretary-treasurer, 1959-62; vice-president, 1962-63; president, 1963-64), Texas Folklore Society (vice-president, 1954-55; president, 1955-56; councilor, 1956-58), North Carolina Folklore Society, Louisiana Folklore Society, Emerson Society, Phi Kappa Phi, Sigma Tau Delta. *Awards, honors:* Faculty Distinguished Achievement Award for teaching, 1961; Outstanding Author, Texas Writer's Roundup, 1967; American Studies Association of Texas Distinguished Fellow, 1974; Texas Folklore Society Distinguished Fellow, 1980.

WRITINGS: (Contributor) *Handbook of Texas*, Texas State Historical Association, 1951; (editor) *Brokenburn: The Journal of Kate Stone, 1861-1868*, Louisiana State University Press, 1955, 2nd edition, 1972; *A Texas Surgeon in the C.S.A.*, Confederate Publishing Co., 1957; *Louisiana Swamp Doctor: The Life and Writings of Henry Clay Lewis*, Louisiana State University Press, 1962; *Tales of Frontier Texas*, Southern Methodist University Press, 1966; *With the Bark On: Popular Humor of the Old South*, Vanderbilt University Press, 1967; (editor) *Campaigning with Parsons' Texas Cavalry Brigade, C.S.A.: The War Journals and Letters of the Four Orr Brothers, Twelfth Texas Cavalry Regiment*, Hill Junior College Press, 1967; *John C. Duval: First Texas Man of Letters*, Steck, 1967; (author of introduction) John C. Duval, *Early Times in Texas*, Steck, 1968; (author of introduction) Owen Wister, *The Virginian*, Dodd, 1968; (contributor) *A Bibliographical Guide to the Study of American Literature*, Louisiana State University Press, 1969; (editor) *Texas Folk Medicine*, Encino Press, 1970; *The Liberating Gods: Emerson on Poets and Poetry*, University of Miami Press, 1971; (contributor) *Notable American Women, 1610-1950: A Biographical Directory*, Harvard University Press, 1971; (with Edwin W. Gaston and James W. Lee) *Southwestern American Literature: A Bibliography*, Swallow Press, 1979. Contributor to journals of literature, folklore, and history. Member of editorial boards, *Mississippi Quarterly*, beginning 1963, and *Computer Studies in Verbal Behavior and the Humanities*, beginning 1966; chairman of editorial board, *Southwestern American Literature Association Journal*, 1969-75.

SIDELIGHTS: John Q. Anderson introduced the study of folklore to both Texas A&M University and the University of Houston. The latter school, as well as Stephen F. Austin State University, Baylor University, Louisiana State University, and Hill Junior College, houses collections of his lectures, unpublished manuscripts, biographical material, research notes, and genealogical compilations. In addition, Anderson's recordings of folksongs are preserved in the archives of various schools, libraries, societies, museums, and radio stations, including the University of North Carolina, the University of Texas, Indiana University, the Library of Congress, the Texas Folklore Society, the Old Courthouse Museum (Vicksburg, Miss.), and stations KUHT (Houston, Tex.) and WGNC (Amarillo, Tex.). Two songs are contained in "A Treasury of Field Recordings," issued by 77 Records (London, England) in 1960.†

*　　*　　*

ANDERSON, Margaret J(ohnson)　1909-

PERSONAL: Born November 5, 1909, in Virginia, Minn.; daughter of Charles J. and Jennie (Helstrom) Johnson; married Clarence D. Anderson (a minister), 1933; children: Lowell, Laurine (Mrs. Elmer Harris). *Education:* Attended Virginia Junior College (now Mesabi State Junior College), 1927-28; Duluth Teacher's College (now University of Minnesota, Duluth), teacher's certificate, 1930; attended Bethel College, St. Paul, Minn., 1956, University of Minnesota, 1953, 1956, University of Oklahoma, 1959-60. *Religion:* Evangelical Covenant Church. *Home:* 1721 Arbor Way, Turlock, Calif. 95380.

CAREER: Elementary school teacher, St. Louis County, Minn., 1928-29, 1931-33; St. Louis County Office, Virginia, Minn., chief clerk, 1930-31. Free-lance writer; frequent speaker at writers' conferences. *Member:* National League of Pen Women, Christian Writer's Guild.

WRITINGS: Ten Talks to Christian Teens, Moody Press, 1957; *Top Secret Bible Quizzes,* Moody Press, 1960; *It's Your Business, Teenager!,* Moody Press, 1960; *Bill and Betty Learn about God,* Zondervan, 1961; *Happy Moments with God,* Zondervan, 1962; "Explore Your Bible" quizbook series, Warner, 1963; *The Christian Writer's Handbook,* Harper, 1974; *Let's Talk about God,* Bethany Fellowship Press, 1975; *Louise,* H. Shaw, 1977; *Looking Ahead: The Realities of Aging–Face Them with Faith,* Concordia, 1978; *Your Aging Parents: When and How to Help,* Concordia, 1979; *Stroke: A Scary Word* (booklet), Concordia, 1980. Contributor to *The Writers Conference Comes to You,* Judson. Contributor of stories and articles to two hundred religious and secular publications.

SIDELIGHTS: Happy Moments with God has been translated into German and Spanish. *Let's Talk about God* has been translated into Norwegian. *Avocational interests:* Crafts, sewing, oil painting, photography.

* * *

ANDERSON, Quentin   1912-

PERSONAL: Born July 21, 1912, in Minnewaukan, N.D.; son of Maxwell (a playwright) and Margaret Elizabeth (Haskett) Anderson; married Margaret Pickett, May 27, 1933 (divorced August, 1946); married Thelma Ehrlich, December 13, 1947; children: (first marriage) Martha; (second marriage) Abraham, Maxwell. *Education:* Attended Dartmouth College, 1931-32; Columbia University, A.B., 1937, Ph.D., 1953; Harvard University, M.A., 1945. *Home:* 29 Claremont Ave., New York, N.Y. 10027. *Office:* 418 Hamilton Hall, Columbia University, New York, N.Y. 10027.

CAREER: Columbia University, New York, N.Y., instructor, 1939-48, associate, 1949-53, assistant professor, 1953-55, associate professor, 1955-61, professor of English, 1961—, Julian Levi Professor in the Humanities, 1978, head of department, Columbia College, 1961-69. Fulbright professor in France, 1962-63; visiting professor, University of Sussex, 1966-67. *Member:* Modern Language Association of America, Authors League, P.E.N. *Awards, honors:* National Endowment for the Humanities senior fellowship, 1973-74; National Humanities Center fellow, 1979-80.

WRITINGS: (Editor and author of introduction) Henry James, *Selected Short Stories,* Rinehart, 1950, revised edition, 1957; *The American Henry James,* Rutgers University Press, 1957; (contributor) Boris Ford, editor, *Pelican Guide to English Literature 6,* Penguin, 1958; (editor with Joseph A. Mazzeo) *The Proper Study: Essays on Western Classics,* St. Martin's, 1962; (editor) Joseph Conrad, *Lord Jim,* Washington Square Press, 1963; *The Imperial Self: An Essay in American Literary and Cultural History,* Knopf, 1971; (editor with others) *Art, Politics and the Will: Essays in Honor*

of Lionel Trilling, Basic Books, 1977. Contributor of essays and reviews to *Virginia Quarterly Review, Partisan Review, Daedalus, American Scholar, Commentary, New York Times Book Review, Times Literary Supplement,* and other publications.

BIOGRAPHICAL/CRITICAL SOURCES: Time, March 22, 1971.

* * *

ANDERSON, Stanley Edwin   1900-1977

PERSONAL: Born in 1900, in Summit, S.D.; died June 18, 1977; son of John and Christine (Person) Anderson; married Inda Johnson, 1926; children: Donald Edwin, Betty Jane Larsen, Eunice Karraker (deceased). *Education:* Union University, Jackson, Tenn., A.B., 1928; Northern Baptist Theological Seminary, B.D., 1947, Th.D., 1948.

CAREER: Pastor of Baptist churches in Minnesota, Washington, Oregon, Tennessee, and Illinois; Northern Baptist Theological Seminary, Chicago, Ill., professor, beginning 1951; former professor, Judson College, Elgin, Ill. *Military service:* U.S. Army, chaplain, 1943-45; became captain; awarded five battle stars and three medals. *Member:* Evangelical Theological Society.

WRITINGS: Every Pastor a Counselor, Van Kampen Press, 1949; *Nehemiah, the Executive,* Baker Book, 1952; *Shepherds to 20,000,000 Service Men,* Higley Press, 1954; *Is Rome the True Church?,* Zondervan, 1958; *Your Baptism Is Important,* Marshall, Morgan & Scott, 1960; *Our Dependable Bible,* Baker Book, 1960; *The First Baptist,* Independent Baptist Publications, 1962; *The First Church,* Independent Baptist Publications, 1964; *Baptists Unshackled,* Fundamental Baptist Press, 1971; *Armstrongism's 300 Errors Exposed by 1300 Bible Verses,* Church Growth Publications, 1973; *The First Communion,* Bogard Press, 1973; *Real Churches or a Fog: A Defense of Real, Local Churches, a Denial of a Foggy, Universal Church,* Bogard Press, 1975; *Our Inerrant Bible,* Bogard Press, 1977. Contributor to magazines.†

* * *

ANDERSON, Verily (Bruce)   1915-

PERSONAL: Born January 12, 1915, in Birmingham, England; daughter of Rosslyn (a clergyman) and Rachel (Gurney) Bruce; married Donald Anderson (chief press officer, Ministry of Information), August, 1940 (deceased); married Paul Paget (sometime surveyor of St. Paul's Cathedral), August, 1971; children: (first marriage) Marian, Rachel, Edward, Janie, Alexandra. *Education:* Attended Royal College of Music, 1931-34. *Religion:* Anglican. *Home:* Templewood, Northrepps, Cromer, Norfolk, England.

CAREER: Variously employed as musician, taxi-driver, secretary, nursemaid, art designer, and shop assistant, 1934-39; served in First Aid Nursing Yeomanry, 1939-43; founder and director of children's holiday home in Sussex, 1954-62; freelance writer. *Member:* Society of Authors, Society of Women Writers and Journalists. *Awards, honors: Spam Tomorrow* named as best book of year, London Literary Festival, 1956; *The Flo Affair* selected as Pick of Publisher, 1963.

WRITINGS: Spam Tomorrow, Hart-Davis, 1956; *Our Square,* Hart-Davis, 1957; *Beware of Children,* Hart-Davis, 1958; *Daughters of Divinity,* Hart-Davis, 1959; *Amanda,* University of London Press, 1960; *Vanload to Venice,* Brockhampton, 1961; *Nine Times Never,* Brockhampton,

1962; *The Golden Hand,* Brockhampton, 1963; *The Flo Affair,* J. Cape, 1963; *The Northrepps Grandchildren,* Hodder & Stoughton, 1968, reprinted, Mallard, 1979; *Scrambled Egg for Christmas,* Hodder & Stoughton, 1968; *The Last of the Eccentrics,* Hodder & Stoughton, 1972; *Friends and Relations: Three Centuries of Quaker Families,* Hodder & Stoughton, 1980. Editor, *Townsend,* 1950-54. Author of plays and scripts for BBC-TV and Anglia-TV. Contributor to *Punch, Observer, Sunday Times, Daily Telegraph, Housewife, Good Housekeeping, Women's Realm, Time and Tide,* and other periodicals. Columnist, *Homes and Gardens* and *Motor Boat and Yachting.*

WORK IN PROGRESS: A biography of Edward de Vere, 17th earl of Oxford, Elizabethan traveller in Europe.

SIDELIGHTS: Beware of Children was made into the motion picture "No Kidding." *Avocational interests:* Music, travel, woodland management.

*   *   *

ANDREWS, Wayne 1913-
(Montagu O'Reilly)

PERSONAL: Born September 5, 1913, in Kenilworth, Ill.; son of Emory Cobb (a businessman) and Helen (Armstrong) Andrews; married Elizabeth Anderson Hodges, June 12, 1948; children: Elizabeth Waties. *Education:* Harvard University, A.B., 1936; Columbia University, graduate study, 1946-48, Ph.D., 1955. *Politics:* Democrat. *Religion:* Episcopalian. *Home:* 521 Neff Rd., Grosse Pointe, Mich. 48230. *Office:* Department of Art and Art History, Wayne State University, Detroit, Mich. 48202.

CAREER: New York Historical Society, New York City, curator of manuscripts, 1948-56; Charles Scribner's Sons, New York City, editor, trade department, 1956-63; Wayne State University, Detroit, Mich., Archives of American Art Professor, 1964—. Architectural photographer. *Member:* Societe Chateaubriand (Paris).

WRITINGS: The Vanderbilt Legend, Harcourt, 1941; *Battle for Chicago,* Harcourt, 1946; (under pseudonym Montagu O'Reilly) *Who Has Been Tampering with These Pianos?,* New Directions, 1948; *Architecture, Ambition and Americans: A Social History of American Architecture,* Harper, 1955, revised edition, Macmillan, 1978; (editor) *Best Short Stories of Edith Wharton,* Scribner, 1958; (editor) Theodore Roosevelt, *Autobiography,* Scribner, 1958; *Architecture in America,* Atheneum, 1960, revised edition, 1979; (editor with Thomas W. Cochran) *Concise Dictionary of American History,* Scribner, 1962; *Germaine: A Portrait of Madame de Stael,* Atheneum, 1963; *Architecture in Michigan: A Representative Photographic Survey,* Wayne State University Press, 1967; *Architecture in Chicago and Mid-America: A Photographic History,* Atheneum, 1968; *Architecture in New York: A Photographic History,* Atheneum, 1969; *Siegfried's Curse: The German Journey from Nietzsche to Hesse,* Atheneum, 1972; *Architecture in New England,* Stephen Greene Press, 1973; *American Gothic,* Random House, 1975; *Pride of the South: A Social History of Southern Architecture,* Atheneum, 1979; *Voltaire,* New Directions, 1981.

WORK IN PROGRESS: A revised edition of *Architecture in Michigan;* a history of surrealism, for New Directions.

BIOGRAPHICAL/CRITICAL SOURCES: Book World, October 13, 1968.

ANGUS, Douglas Ross 1909-

PERSONAL: Born 1909, in Amherst, Nova Scotia, Canada; son of Edgar Ivy and Mabel (Cummings) Angus; married Sylvia Levitt (a writer), 1941; children: Jamie, Christopher. *Education:* Acadia University, B.A., 1934; University of Maine, M.A., 1935; Ohio State University, Ph.D., 1940. *Home:* 31 West Main, Canton, N.Y. *Office:* St. Lawrence University, Canton, N.Y. 13617.

CAREER: George Washington University, Washington, D.C., instructor, 1940-41; University of Tampa, Tampa, Fla., chairman of English department, 1942-45; St. Lawrence University, Canton, N.Y., professor of English, 1947-73, Charles A. Dana Professor of English Literature, 1973-75, professor emeritus, 1975—. Fulbright lecturer at University of Istanbul, 1963-64.

WRITINGS: The Green and the Burning, R. Hale, 1958; *The Lions Fed the Tigers,* Houghton, 1958; *The Ivy Trap,* Bobbs-Merrill, 1959; (editor) *Best Short Stories of the Modern Age,* Fawcett, 1962; *Death on Jerusalem Road,* Random House, 1963; (editor with wife, Sylvia Levitt Angus) *Great Modern European Short Stories,* Fawcett, 1967; (editor with S. L. Angus) *Contemporary American Short Stories,* Fawcett, 1967; (co-editor) *Love Is the Theme,* Fawcett, 1970. Contributor of articles and short stories to *Antioch Review, Esquire, American Scholar,* and other publications.

*   *   *

ANSTEY, Edgar 1917-

PERSONAL: Born March 5, 1917, in Bombay, India; son of Percy L. (an economist) and Vera (Powell) Anstey; married Zoe L. Robertson, June 3, 1939; children: David. *Education:* King's College, Cambridge, M.A., 1938; University College, London, Ph.D., 1949. *Religion:* Anglican. *Home:* Sandrock, Higher Tristram, Polzeath, Cornwall PL27 6TF, England.

CAREER: British Dominions Office, London, England, assistant principal, 1938-40; head of research unit, British Civil Service Commission, 1945-51; principal, British Home Office, 1951-58; British Ministry of Defence, London, senior principal psychologist, 1958-64; British Civil Service Commission, London, chief psychologist, 1964-70; Civil Service Department, London, deputy-chief scientific officer, 1970-77. *Military service:* British War Office, in charge of selection tests for other ranks, 1940-45; became major. *Member:* British Psychological Society (fellow, 1949; member of council 1963; chairman of occupational section, 1963-64).

WRITINGS: (With E. O. Mercer) *Interviewing for the Selection of Staff,* Allen & Unwin, 1956; *Staff Reporting and Staff Development,* Allen & Unwin, 1961; *Committees: How They Work and How to Work Them,* Allen & Unwin, 1962; *Psychological Tests,* Nelson, 1966; *Staff Appraisal and Development,* Allen & Unwin, 1976; *An Introduction to Selection Interviewing,* H.M.S.O., 1977. Contributor to psychology journals.

AVOCATIONAL INTERESTS: Surfing, golf, bridge; enthusiastic fell walker, especially in Lake District of England.

*   *   *

APSLER, Alfred 1907-

PERSONAL: Born November 13, 1907, in Vienna, Austria; son of Herman (an accountant) and Helene (Pasternak) Apsler; married Ernestine Gerson (a college teacher), December 26, 1936; children: Robert G., Ruby Mae. *Education:* University of Vienna, Ph.D., 1930. *Home:* 5565 East Evergreen Blvd., Vancouver, Wash.

CAREER: Clark College, Vancouver, Wash., chairman of social science division and teacher of history, 1956-73; Vienna Teacher's College, Vienna, Austria, coordinator of gerontological programs, beginning 1973, lecturer, 1975. Public speaker; television lecturer; conductor of educational tours, 1961, 1963. *Member:* American Association for United Nations (president, Vancouver chapter, 1957-58), American Association of University Professors (president, Clark College chapter, 1957-58), National Education Association, Northwest Political Science Association, Oregon Historical Association, Oregon Freelance Club, Vancouver Optimist Club (president, 1958-59), Portland City Club. *Awards, honors:* Certificate of Recognition from Freedoms Foundation for editorial writing, 1952; U.S. Office of Education research grant, 1966.

WRITINGS—Published by Messner, except as indicated: *Northwest Pioneer: The Story of Louis Fleischner,* Farrar, Straus, 1960; *Sie Kamen Aus Deutschen Landen* (a German reader), Appleton, 1962; *Fighter for Independence: Jawaharlal Nehru,* 1963; *The Court Factor,* Jewish Publication Society, 1964; *Sun King: Louis XIV of France,* 1965; *Prophet of Revolution: Karl Marx,* 1967; *Iron Chancellor: Otto Von Bismarck,* (Junior Literary Guild selection), 1968; *Introduction to Social Science,* Random House, 1970, 3rd edition, 1980; *Ivan the Terrible,* 1971; *Vive de Gaulle: The Story of Charles de Gaulle,* 1973; *Communes throughout the Ages,* 1974; *From Witchdoctor to Biofeedback,* 1977. Contributor to newspapers and to national youth magazines.

SIDELIGHTS: Alfred Apsler writes: "I was a teacher and a journalist when Austria was swallowed up by the Nazi onslaught. I barely made it across the mountains into Switzerland, and so was saved from almost certain annihilation. Coming to America, I had not only to start a new life, but also do it by using a new language. So it took several years, but eventually I made the way back to my original tasks: teaching and writing.

"I taught history and human relations for many years. So my writing is just an extension of what I do in the classroom, namely: making people and events come to life; trying to convince listeners and readers that the story of man is exciting, colorful, and, also, entertaining."

*   *   *

APTER, David Ernest   1924-

PERSONAL: Born December 18, 1924, in New York, N.Y.; son of Herman and Bella (Steinberg) Apter; married Eleanor Selwyn (a librarian), December 28, 1947; children: Emily, Andrew. *Education:* Antioch College, A.B., 1950; Princeton University, M.A., 1952, Ph.D., 1954. *Politics:* Democrat. *Religion:* None. *Home:* 2800 Ridge Rd., North Haven, Conn. 06473. *Office:* Department of Political Science, Yale University, New Haven, Conn. 06520.

CAREER: Northwestern University, Evanston, Ill., assistant professor of political science, 1954-57; University of Chicago, Chicago, Ill., associate professor, 1957-61; University of California, Berkeley, associate professor, 1961-62, professor of political science, 1962-69, associate director, Institute of International Studies, 1961-64, acting director, 1964-65; Yale University, New Haven, Conn., Henry J. Heinz II Professor of Comparative Political and Social Development, 1969—. Oxford University, Oxford, England, visiting fellow at All Soul's College, 1967-68, senior associate fellow of St. Anthony's College, 1968, Rhodes Visiting Professor at St. Anthony's College, 1972; visiting fellow, Institute for Advanced Study, Princeton University, 1973.

Member of President Kennedy's Task Force on Africa, 1960; director, Peace Corps training program for Ghana, 1961-63; member of Committee on Latin American Studies, Social Science Research Council, 1965-67, and Committee for Comparative Sociological Research, 1968; member of board of directors, International Organizations and Programs, National Academy of Sciences, 1977; member of U.S. national delegation, UNESCO, 1978—. Member of Advisory Committee on African Affairs, U.S. Department of State, 1962-69; consultant to U.S. Department of Health, Education, and Welfare, 1965, to Education in World Affairs, 1969-70, and to Council on Foreign Relations, 1970-71; member of advisory council, Department of Politics, Princeton University, 1973. *Military service:* U.S. Army, 1943-46; became technical sergeant.

MEMBER: International Institute for Differing Civilizations, American Political Science Association, American Sociological Association, American Academy of Arts and Sciences (fellow; member of council, 1971—), American Association for the Advancement of Science, American Society for Legal and Political Philosophy, Council on Foreign Relations, African Studies Association (member of executive board, 1958-61; director, 1963-66), American Society for African Culture (associate member), East African Institute of Social and Economic Research (association fellow), Instituto Di Tella (Argentina; honorary fellow), Century Association, Yale Club (New York), Athenaeum (London). *Awards, honors:* Ford Foundation fellow, Uganda, 1955-56; Center for Advanced Study in the Behavioral Sciences fellow, 1958-59; Guggenheim fellow, 1967-68; Rockefeller Foundation grantee, 1968; Woodrow Wilson Foundation award, 1971, for *Choice and the Politics of Allocation.*

WRITINGS: The Gold Coast in Transition, Princeton University Press, 1955, revised edition published as *Ghana in Transition,* 1972; *The Political Kingdom in Uganda,* Princeton University Press, 1961, revised edition, 1969; (editor with H. Eckstein) *Comparative Politics: A Reader,* Free Press of Glencoe, 1963; (editor) *Ideology and Discontent,* Free Press of Glencoe, 1964; *The Politics of Modernization,* University of Chicago Press, 1965, revised edition, 1971; *Some Conceptual Approaches to the Study of Modernization,* Prentice-Hall, 1968; (editor with James Joll) *Anarchism Today,* Macmillan, 1970; *Choice and the Politics of Allocation: A Developmental Theory,* Yale University Press, 1971; (editor with Charles Andrain) *Contemporary Analytical Theory,* Prentice-Hall, 1972; *Political Change,* Cass (London), 1973; (editor with Louis W. Goodman) *The Multi-National Corporation and Social Change,* Praeger, 1976; *An Introduction to Political Analysis,* Winthrop, 1977. Editor, "Politics of Modernization" series, Institute of International Studies, University of California, Berkeley, 1966-72; contributor to *Encyclopedia of the Social Sciences.* Contributor to professional journals, including *Foreign Policy Bulletin, American Political Science Review,* and *Current History.* Member of editorial board, *Government and Opposition.*

WORK IN PROGRESS: Developmental Socialism in Africa and Latin America; Radicalization and Embourgeoisement.

*   *   *

ARMSTRONG, Charlotte   1905-1969
(Jo Valentine)

PERSONAL: Born May 2, 1905, in Vulcan, Mich.; died July 18, 1969, in Glendale, Calif.; daughter of Frank Hall and Clara (Pascoe) Armstrong; married Jack Lewi, January 21, 1928; children: Jeremy Brett, Jacquelin, Peter Armstrong.

Education: Attended University of Wisconsin, 1922-24; Barnard College, B.A., 1925. *Religion:* Presbyterian. *Agent:* Brandt and Brandt, 101 Park Ave., New York, N.Y. 10017.

CAREER: Worked as classified advertisements taker for the *New York Times*, reporter for *Breath of the Avenue* (fashion buyer's guide), and office assistant for certified public accountants firm, all New York, N.Y., 1925-28; writer. *Member:* Dramatists Guild, Screen Writers Guild; Coronet Club and Dunkers Club (both Glendale, Calif.). *Awards, honors:* *Ellery Queen Mystery Magazine* short story contest award, 1951, for "The Enemy"; Mystery Writers of America Award for best novel of 1956, *A Dram of Poison;* Mystery Writers of America Award, 1958, for short story.

WRITINGS—All published by Coward, except as indicated: *Lay On, Mac Duff*, 1946; *The Case of the Weird Sisters*, 1943; *The Innocent Flower*, 1945, reprinted, Collier, 1965 (published in England as *Death Filled the Glass*, Withy Grove Press, 1945); *The Unsuspected*, 1946; *The Chocolate Cobweb*, 1948, reprinted, Berkley Publishing, 1967; *Mischief* (also see below), 1950; *The Black-Eyed Stranger*, 1951; *Catch-as-Catch-Can*, 1953; (under pseudonym Jo Valentine) *The Trouble in Thor*, 1953, reprinted under real name, Berkley Publishing, 1971; *The Better to Eat You*, 1954; *The Dream Walker* (also see below), 1955, reprinted, White Lion, 1973; *A Dram of Poison*, 1956, reprinted, Berkley Publishing, 1972; *The Albatross* (short stories), 1957; *The Seventeen Windows of Sans Souci*, 1959; *Duo* (contains "The Girl with a Secret" and "Incident at a Corner"), 1959.

A Little Less than Kind, 1963; *The Witch's House* (also see below), 1963; *The Mark of the Hand* [and] *The Dream Walker*, Ace Books, 1963; *The Turret Room*, 1965; *Dream of Fair Woman*, 1966; *I See You* (short stories), 1966; *The Gift Shop* (also see below), 1967; *Lemon in the Basket* (also see below), 1967; *The Balloon Man* (also see below), 1968; *Seven Seats to the Moon*, 1969; *The Protege*, 1970; *The Charlotte Armstrong Reader*, 1970; *The Charlotte Armstrong Treasury* (contains *The Witch's House, Mischief,* and *The Dream Walker*), 1972; *The Charlotte Armstrong Festival* (contains *The Gift Shop, Lemon in the Basket,* and *The Balloon Man*), 1975.

Plays: "The Happiest Days," first produced on Broadway, 1939; *Ring around Elizabeth* (first produced on Broadway, November, 1941), Samuel French, 1942.

Also author of *Something Blue* and *Who's Been Sitting in My Chair?*, both 1962. Author of television scripts and motion picture screenplays. Contributor of poems, short stories, and novelettes to magazines.

SIDELIGHTS: "Maybe we are all potential murderers," Charlotte Armstrong once said, "and reading stories about that crime releases us in some way." Often referred to as the American *grande dame* of the suspense-murder mystery novel, Armstrong was probably best known for her books *The Unsuspected, Mischief,* and *A Dram of Poison*. A *Detroit News* reviewer once characterized her style as "smoothly-flowing, intimately-personal, [and] minutely-perceptive"—a style which ultimately led to the concoction of a tale "which she masterfully spins around the reader until she's got him right over the edge of screeching horror and strung-out nerves."

The Unsuspected was her first real success, though some reviewers criticized her for revealing the identity of the murderer at the beginning of the book (they felt it diminished the story's appeal as a murder "mystery"). Yet in spite of this "flaw," most found the novel entertaining. For example, Isaac Anderson of the *New York Times* commented, "The

mystery element is completely lacking, but there is suspense enough and to spare." A *New Yorker* critic wrote, "Our old friend the suspense formula [is] so expertly handled that one tends to disregard the staggering improbabilities on which it is based." But Howard Haycraft of the *New York World-Telegram* believed that it was Armstrong's writing skill rather than any element of mystery or credibility that made the novel a pleasure to read. Admitting that it was neither a true mystery story nor a psychological study, he concluded that it was an "extraordinarily exciting surface melodrama" characterized by "tight writing and broad, colorful delineation of character and mood." The public's reaction to *The Unsuspected* was not as reserved as that of the critics'; while it was being serialized in the *Saturday Evening Post*, for example, many readers became so involved in the story that they telephoned or wrote Armstrong in order to offer a solution, suggest possible twists to the plot, or guess at the ending.

Mischief enjoyed success among the critics as well as the reading public. In his review in the *New York Times*, Anthony Boucher wrote that Armstrong "has chosen one of the most purely terrifying situations conceivable—that of a teenage baby-sitter whose surface of subnormal placidity conceals a vicious and destructive insanity. Upon this theme she has built, with dazzling virtuosity, in suspense technique, a perfectly constructed melodrama—and more than a melodrama.... The novel is as short as it is rich, packed with meaning and terror in each phrase." A *New Yorker* critic noted that "the story is comparatively simple ... but Miss Armstrong, who is very good at this kind of thing, has managed a fine, chilly combination of terror and suspense." Finally, a *Chicago Sunday Tribune* reviewer felt that "for sheer, crawling horror, this story beats anything of the kind I have ever read. Not that there are no better horror stories, but I know of none that does so well with simple material and plot, such a commonplace setting and an almost casual, matter of fact air."

Though the critics also enjoyed *A Dram of Poison*, they found it very difficult to classify, for it chronicles the sometimes romantic, sometimes suspenseful, and sometimes humorous chain of events leading from an attempted suicide by poison. Christopher Pym of the *Spectator* wrote: "Nobody gets hurt in this pleasantly sentimental, good-natured version of the 'psychological study' sort of crime story, but there is plenty of suspense, and a good chase after the poison bottle. Full marks for the fresh approach." A *Saturday Review* critic noted that "drama turns to gay melodrama as [the] yarn unfolds, but [the] pace is speedy throughout; sprightly is the word." Boucher of the *New York Times*, describing the book as "better simply recommended than written about," was once again full of praise for the author: "[It is enough to say that] this resembles Miss Armstrong's previous novels only in skill and charm, and that reading it is an experience as delightful as it is unclassifiable. You take it from there."

Several of Armstrong's books and stories were made into films. *The Unsuspected* was filmed by Warner Brothers in 1947 and starred Claude Rains (a play adaptation was written by Robert Brome in 1962 and was published by Dramatic Publishing). *Mischief* was filmed by Twentieth Century-Fox Film Corp. in 1952 under the title "Don't Bother to Knock." It starred Marilyn Monroe, Richard Widmark, and Anne Bancroft. "Talk about a Stranger," based on a short story by Armstrong, was also filmed in 1952, and a French production of "The Breakup" ("La Rupture") was filmed in 1970.

BIOGRAPHICAL/CRITICAL SOURCES: New York World-

Telegram, October 3, 1945; *New Yorker*, January 19, 1946, June 24, 1950; *New York Times*, January 20, 1946, June 25, 1950, August 5, 1956, July 20, 1969; *Chicago Sunday Tribune*, June 25, 1950; *Spectator*, July 27, 1956; *Saturday Review*, August 18, 1956; *New York Times Book Review*, May, 1967, October 29, 1967, December 3, 1967, May 26, 1968, April 4, 1969; *Christian Science Monitor*, June 8, 1967, October 5, 1967, August 22, 1968; *National Review*, May 20, 1969; *Washington Post*, July 23, 1969; *Time*, August 1, 1969; *Best Sellers*, January 1, 1970; *Books and Bookmen*, February, 1971; *Detroit News*, June 4, 1972.†

*   *   *

ARMSTRONG, John A(lexander, Jr.) 1922-

PERSONAL: Born May 4, 1922, in St. Augustine, Fla.; son of John Alexander (a commissary superintendent for Pullman Co.) and Maria Virginia (Hernandez) Armstrong; married Annette Taylor, June 14, 1952; children: Janet, Carol, Kathryn. *Education:* University of Chicago, Ph.B., 1948, M.A., 1949; University of Frankfurt, additional study, 1949-50; Columbia University, Ph.D., 1953, Certificate of Russian Institute, 1954. *Politics:* Independent. *Religion:* Roman Catholic. *Home:* 2118 Chamberlain Ave., Madison, Wis. 53705. *Office:* Department of Political Science, University of Wisconsin, Madison, Wis. 53706.

CAREER: U.S. Government, War Documentation Project, Alexandria, Va., research analyst, 1951, 1953-54; University of Denver, Denver, Colo., assistant professor of international relations, 1952; University of Wisconsin—Madison, 1954—, began as assistant professor, became professor of political science, currently Philippe de Commynes Professor of Political Science, executive secretary of Russian Area Studies Program, 1959-63, 1964-65, acting chairman of Western European Studies Program, 1967. Visiting assistant professor of international relations, Columbia University, 1952; consultant, Ford Foundation, 1954-57, Foreign Area Fellowship Program, 1962-63, U.S. Department of State, 1966-69, 1971—, and International Research and Exchanges Board, 1975-78. *Military service:* U.S. Army, 1942-46; served overseas in Ardennes and Rhineland campaigns. *Member:* International Political Science Association (member of council, 1979—), American Association for Advancement of Slavic Studies (president, 1965-67), Conference on European Problems (director, 1972—), Academic Committee on Soviet Jewry, Ukrainian Political Science Association in the U.S., Council on Foreign Relations, American Political Science Association (secretary, conference on Soviet and communist studies, 1961-62), Midwest Conference of Political Scientists, Phi Beta Kappa. *Awards, honors:* Grants from American Council of Learned Societies, National Endowment for the Humanities, and Social Science Research Council; Guggenheim fellow, 1967-68, 1975-76.

WRITINGS: Ukrainian Nationalism, Columbia University Press, 1955, 2nd edition, 1963; *The Soviet Bureaucratic Elite: A Case Study of the Ukrainian Apparatus*, Praeger, 1959, revised edition, 1966; *The Politics of Totalitarianism: The Communist Party of the Soviet Union from 1934 to the Present*, Random House, 1961; *Ideology, Politics, and Government in the Soviet Union: An Introduction*, Praeger, 1962, 3rd edition, 1974; (editor) *Soviet Partisans in World War II*, University of Wisconsin Press, 1964, 4th edition, 1978; *The European Administrative Elite*, Princeton University Press, 1973. Contributor to political and social science journals, including *American Political Science Review*, *American Historical Review*, *Slavic Review*, and *Russian Review*.

WORK IN PROGRESS: A book on evolution of ethnic identity in Europe and the Middle East (from the decline of Rome to the French Revolution).

SIDELIGHTS: John Armstrong told *CA* that the University of Wisconsin "has the unusual and attractive custom" of allowing the holders of some named chairs to name the chair "after a deceased person of some stature. . . . I chose Philippe de Commynes despite the apparent remoteness of his experience. . . . [Commynes had a] keen sense of the practical requirements for political development in Western Europe. . . . Most important to me is Commynes' ultimate rejection of the temptation to adopt the amoral stance his contemporary Machiavelli took a few years later. . . . I believe his words are highly pertinent for every writer who undertakes to give advice, published or otherwise, on the complicated and perilous political decisions of our time."

BIOGRAPHICAL/CRITICAL SOURCES: Wisconsin State Journal, January 28, 1962; *Annals of the American Academy of Political and Social Science*, January, 1974; *American Historical Review*, December, 1974.

*   *   *

ARNHEIM, Rudolf 1904-

PERSONAL: Born July 15, 1904, in Berlin, Germany; came to United States in 1940, naturalized in 1946; son of Georg and Betty (Gutherz) Arnheim; married Mary Frame (a librarian), April 11, 1953; children: Margaret. *Education:* University of Berlin, Ph.D., 1928. *Home:* 1133 South Seventh St., Ann Arbor, Mich. 48103. *Office:* Tappan Hall, University of Michigan, Ann Arbor, Mich. 48109.

CAREER: League of Nations, International Institute of Educational Film, Rome, Italy, associate editor of publications, 1933-38; New School for Social Research, New York, N.Y., member of graduate faculty, lecturer, and visiting professor of psychology, 1943-68; Sarah Lawrence College, Bronxville, N.Y., professor of psychology, 1943-68; Harvard University, professor of psychology of art, 1968-74, professor emeritus, 1974—; University of Michigan, Ann Arbor, visiting professor, 1974—. Fulbright lecturer in psychology, Ochanomizu University, Tokyo, Japan, 1959-60; visiting professor, Harvard University, Carpenter Center for Visual Arts, 1964-65; Mary Duke Biddle Lecturer, Cooper Union, 1975. *Member:* American Society for Aesthetics (past president), American Psychological Association (past president; president, division of psychology and the arts), College Art Association. *Awards, honors:* Guggenheim fellow, 1941-42; Distinguished Service award, National Art Education Association, 1976; D.F.A., Rhode Island School of Design, 1976.

WRITINGS—All published by University of California Press, except as indicated: *Film*, Faber & Faber, 1933; *Radio*, Faber & Faber, 1936, reprinted, Da Capo Press, 1972; (with others) *Poets at Work*, Harcourt, 1948; *Art and Visual Perception*, 1954; *Film as Art*, 1957; *Picasso's Guernica*, 1962; (contributor) Gyorgy Kepes, editor, *Vision and Value*, three volumes, Braziller, 1965-66; *Toward a Psychology of Art*, 1966; *Visual Thinking*, 1969; *Entropy and Art*, 1971; (contributor) C. E. Moorhouse, editor, *Visual Education*, Pitman Australia, 1974; (author of foreword) Mary Henle, editor, *Vision and Artifact*, Springer, 1976; *The Dynamics of Architectural Form* (based on Biddle lectures), 1977.

AVOCATIONAL INTERESTS: Violin, drawing, woodcarving.

BIOGRAPHICAL/CRITICAL SOURCES: New Statesman, April 14, 1967; *Journal of Aesthetics*, spring, 1976.

ARNOLD, Armin H. 1931-

PERSONAL: Born September 1, 1931, in Zug, Switzerland. *Education:* Kant Gymnasium, Zurich, Switzerland, B.A., 1951; University of Fribourg, Lic. es Lettres, 1953, Docteur es Lettres, 1956; additional study at University of Zurich, 1953-54, and University of London, 1955-57. *Politics:* Conservative. *Religion:* Roman Catholic. *Office:* Department of German, McGill University, Montreal, Quebec, Canada.

CAREER: Supported self as professional jazz musician during years of study; University of Fribourg, Fribourg, Switzerland, instructor, 1956-57; College of Fahrwangen, Switzerland, headmaster, 1957-59; University of Alberta, Edmonton, assistant professor of German, 1959-61; McGill University, Montreal, Quebec, assistant professor, 1961-64, associate professor, 1964-65, professor of German, 1965—.

WRITINGS: D. H. Lawrence and America, Linden Press, 1958, Philosophical Library, 1959; *Heinrich Heine in England and America,* International Publications, 1959; (editor) D. H. Lawrence, *The Symbolic Meaning: The Uncollected Versions of Studies in Classic American Literature,* Centaur Press, 1962, Viking, 1964; *James Joyce,* Colloquium-Verlag, 1963, revised and translated edition (with Judy Young), Ungar, 1969; *D. H. Lawrence and German Literature, with Two Hitherto Unknown Essays,* Mansfield Book Mart, 1963; *G. B. Shaw,* Colloquium-Verlag, 1965; *Die Literatur des Expressionismus: Sprachliche und theomatische Quellen,* Kohlhammer, 1966; *Felix Steumpers Abenteurer und Streiche,* Francke (Bern), 1967; (editor) *Kanadische Erzahler der Gegenwart,* Manesse, 1967; *Friedrich Durrenmatt,* Colloquium-Verlag, 1969, 4th edition, 1979, revised and translated edition, Ungar, 1972; *Prosa des Expressionismus,* Kohlhammer, 1972; *D. H. Lawrence,* Colloquium-Verlag, 1972; (with J. Schmidt) *Kriminalromanfuehrer,* Reclam-Verlag, 1978; (editor) *Kriminalerzaehlungen aus drei Jahrhunderten,* Reclam-Verlag, 1979; (editor) *Georg Kaiser,* Klett-Verlag, 1980.

*   *   *

ARNOLD, Edmund C(larence) 1913-

PERSONAL: Born June 25, 1913, in Bay City, Mich.; son of Ferdinand Martin (a mechanic) and Ann (Begick) Arnold; married Viola Burtzlaff, April 19, 1941; children: Kathleen, Bethany, Bruce. *Education:* Bay City Junior College, A.A., 1934; Michigan State University, A.B. (magna cum laude), 1954. *Religion:* Lutheran. *Home:* 3208 Hawthorne Ave., Richmond, Va. 23222. *Office:* Department of Journalism, Virginia Commonwealth University, Richmond, Va.

CAREER: Frankenmuth News, Frankenmuth, Mich., editor, 1940-48, publisher, 1946-69; *Saginaw News,* Saginaw, Mich., picture editor, 1948-52; *State Journal,* Lansing, Mich., night editor, 1952-54; Mergenthaler Linotype Co., director of trade relations, 1954-60, consultant to company's Spanish and Portuguese publications, *Linoticias,* 1960—; Syracuse University, Syracuse, N.Y., professor of journalism and chairman, graphic arts and publishing departments, 1960-75; Virginia Commonwealth University, Richmond, professor of journalism, 1975—. Director, Empire State Seminar for Journalism Teachers, 1962-75; seminar conductor, American Press Institute, 1958—; member, commission on church papers, Lutheran Church in America, 1958—. Consultant to newspapers and magazines; consultant on design to *National Observer, Toronto Star, Boston Globe, Christian Science Monitor,* and others. *Military service:* U.S. Army, 1943-45, combat correspondent, became sergeant; received Bronze Star. *Member:* Inter-American Press

Association, National Editorial Association, New England Press Association, American Academy of Advertising, American Institute of Graphic Arts, New York Deadline Club, Typophiles, Sigma Delta Chi. *Awards, honors:* George A. Polk Award, 1957; special award, National Editorial Association, 1958; Army certificate of appreciation, 1959, 1960, 1971, all for service to "Stars and Stripes"; Elmer Voigt Memorial Award, 1964; George Washington Medal, American Freedoms Foundation, 1969; Journalism Pioneer Medal, 1970; L.H.D., Hartwick College, 1963; Distinguished Teacher in Journalism Award, Society of Professional Journalists; Army Outstanding Civilian Service Medal, 1980; Litt.D., Wagner College, 1980.

WRITINGS: Functional Newspaper Design, Harper, 1956; *Profitable Newspaper Advertising,* Harper, 1960; *Feature Photos That Sell,* Morgan & Morgan, 1960; *Ink on Paper: Handbook of Graphic Arts,* Harper, 1963; (with Hillier Krieghbaum) *The Student Journalist,* New York University Press, 1963; *Tipografia y Diagramatos por Periodicos Latinoamericanos,* Inter American Press, 1965; *Student Journalist and the Yearbook,* Richards Rosen, 1966; *Modern Newspaper Design,* Harper, 1969; *Ink on Paper 2,* Harper, 1971; *Student Journalist and Editing the Yearbook,* Richards Rosen, 1974; (with Krieghbaum) *Handbook of Student Journalism,* New York University Press, 1976; *Arnold's Ancient Axioms,* Ragan Report Press, 1978; *Designing the Total Newspaper,* Harper, 1981; *Editing the Organizational Publication,* Ragan Report Press, 1981. Author of "Graphic Arts" series, International Correspondence Schools, 1966. Contributor of over 1000 articles to journals in his field. Editor, *Linotype News,* 1954—; associate editor, *Printer and Publisher, Offset Newspaper Publishing;* columnist, *Editor and Publisher;* contributing editor, *Random House Dictionary of English Language.*

SIDELIGHTS: "I have been a newspaperman since I edited my first weekly at age seventeen. I consider myself still as such," Edmund Arnold told *CA.* "We are not only the users of the language, but the preservers and guardians thereof. I think language must change to remain vital. But I think that such change should be initiated by the intelligent, not by the rabble."

Arnold explained that "*Functional Newspaper Design* is considered a standard work in the field so I'm considered a specialist in typography and layout. But my interests are far broader. I insist on teaching at least one class outside graphic arts each semester. I fly some 50,000 miles per year. Have helped redesign newspapers in every state and province, Scotland, Iceland, New Zealand, Philippines, Mexico, Argentina, Costa Rica, Ecuador, Chile, and Brazil. I make some seventy-five speeches annually and conduct twenty clinics yearly throughout the United States and Canada on newspaper design and local advertising."

AVOCATIONAL INTERESTS: Calligraphy, water colors, collecting incunabula.

*   *   *

ARNOLD, Richard 1912-
(Coch-y-Bonddhu)

PERSONAL: Born November 7, 1912, in Corstorphine, Scotland; son of Richard (an engineer) and Margaret Marjorie (Sinclair) Arnold; married Trudy Feith, August 13, 1949; children: David James. *Education:* Attended Manchester Grammar School, Manchester, England. *Religion:* Roman Catholic. *Home:* 22 Blenheim Grove, Offord D'Arcy, Huntingdon, Cambridgeshire, England.

CAREER: Wilson Meats Ltd. (branch of Wilson Meats, Inc., Chicago, Ill.), London, England, assistant sales manager, 1953-59; Millard Bros. Ltd. (guns and fishing tackle), London, sales manager, 1959-60; Institute of Physics and The Physical Society, London, exhibitions officer, 1961-65; Steel Sheet Information and Development Association, publicity officer, 1965-69; in own practice as publicity consultant, 1965—. Professional skating coach, 1974—. *Military service:* British Army, with Expeditionary Force to Dunkirk, 1939-40, Commandos, 1940-44, Royal Scots Fusiliers, 1944-46. *Member:* Muzzle Loaders Association of Great Britain (founder).

WRITINGS: *The Shoreshooter,* Seeley Service, 1953; *Come Shooting with Me,* Muller, 1953, Sportshelf, 1956; *Come Sea Fishing with Me,* Muller, 1954, Sportshelf, 1956; *The True Book about the Commandos,* Muller, 1954, Sportshelf, 1958; *The Shooter's Handbook: Gun Care, Minor Gunsmithing, Handloading of Cartridges, Making Decoys, the Law Relating to Firearms and Kindred Matters,* Sweetman, 1955, 4th revised edition, Kaye & Ward, 1981; *Pigeon Shooting,* Faber, 1956, revised edition Kaye & Ward, 1979; *Making and Repairing Fishing Tackle,* W. & G. Foyle, 1956; *Rifle Shooting,* W. & G. Foyle, 1957; *The True Book about David Livingstone,* Muller, 1957, published as *The True Story of David Livingstone, Explorer,* Childrens Press, 1964; (contributor) Jack Thorndike, editor, *Sea Fishing with the Experts,* Allen & Unwin, 1957; *The Complete Sea Angler,* Kaye & Ward, 1957, Sportshelf, 1958, revised edition published as *Modern Sea Angling,* Kaye & Ward, 1970, revised edition, 1981; *Automatic and Repeating Shotguns,* Kaye & Ward, 1958, A. S. Barnes, 1960, revised edition, Kaye & Ward, 1976, published as *The Complete Guide to Shotguns Automatic and Repeating,* Coles Publishing, 1977; *The Book of the .22: A Complete Manual for the .22 Rifleman and the Pistoleer,* A. S. Barnes, 1962, revised edition, Kaye & Ward, 1972; *Modern Camping,* Kaye & Ward, 1963; *The Angler's Handbook,* Arthur Barker, 1967; *Fishing,* Pan Books, 1967; *The Book of Angling,* Arthur Barker, 1969; *Clay Pigeon Shooting,* Kaye & Ward, 1973, 2nd edition, 1980; *Your Book of Sea Fishing,* Faber, 1975; *Better Roller Skating,* Kaye & Ward, 1976, Sterling Publishing, 1977; *Better Ice Skating,* Kaye & Ward, 1976, published as *Ice Skating Made Easy,* Coles Publishing, 1977; *Better Sport Skating,* Kaye & Ward, 1980. Contributor to trade and technical publications as a special correspondent on topical matters and developments, mainly in agricultural and light engineering industries. Contributor of articles to *Angling Times, Field Sports, Shooting Times, Country Sportsman, Hobbies, Motor Cycle News, Lilliput,* and other magazines, mainly in outdoor field. Editor, *Farm Building Digest,* 1969—.

WORK IN PROGRESS: *Artistic Skating.*

SIDELIGHTS: Richard Arnold told *CA:* "I began my writing career as a freelance contributor to local papers at 14 years of age. Earlier I had been writing up notes for local events not usually covered by reporters.

"My working habits when writing are to do nothing at all for a few weeks while the project gathers momentum in my mind. At a sudden moment I then commence writing absolutely non-stop until the work is finished. Sometimes I commence writing as soon as a project is undertaken. On occasions I have been working on one subject, say angling, when having put the first sheet of paper into the typewriter I suddenly start, and finish, a book on an entirely different subject, say skating.

"I have been influenced by noting, in the past, books on cer-

tain subjects which have either been written by experts who could not write, or by competent writers who knew nothing at all about the subject they had chosen. I, therefore, only write about subjects with which I am completely familiar and which I know from practical experience. I have also attempted, and I hope succeeded, in writing in a simple and lucid manner.

"Unfortunately, I feel that we are living in an age of ugliness. Ugly buildings, ugly clothes, ugly music—and I find a lot of contemporary literature possesses a quality of 'ugliness' too.

"I hope to achieve an educational impact upon my readers insofar as they may learn activities from books—not an easy matter I know. But so many practical techniques are passed along by word of mouth and ultimately lost along the line, and too many so-called authoritative writers on subjects in the past have been guilty of copying from earlier writers' works, repeating errors which a knowledge of the subject would have revealed. I am not content to follow other writers and refuse to read any works at all dealing with a subject I am writing about—I prefer to undertake practical work as a research project."

AVOCATIONAL INTERESTS: All aspects of sports, including ice, figure, and dance skating, roller skating, foil and sabre fencing, fresh and salt water fishing, sailing, and ballroom and Scottish dancing (organized ballroom dancing and skating functions and is the proprietor of a mobile disco); natural history and the countryside; photography, including film processing.

*   *   *

ARNOTT, Peter D(ouglas) 1931-

PERSONAL: Born November 21, 1931, in Ipswich, England; son of George William (a civil servant) and Audrey (Smith) Arnott; married Eva Charlotte Schenkel, July 26, 1958; children: Catherine Mary, Christopher Grant, Jennifer Clare. *Education:* University of Wales, B.A., 1952, M.A., 1956, Ph.D., 1958; Oxford University, B.A., 1954. *Home:* 6 Herrick St., Winchester, Mass. 01890. *Office:* Department of Drama, Tufts University, Medford, Mass. 02155.

CAREER: University of Iowa, Iowa City, assistant professor, 1958-61, associate professor, 1961-66, professor of drama, 1966-69; Tufts University, Medford, Mass., professor of drama, 1969—, chairman of department, 1975—. Lecturer on tours throughout United States and England; lecturer in Canada under auspices of Canada Council and Classical Association of Canada, 1960 and 1961. *Member:* Society for Promotion of Hellenic Studies, Classical Association of the Midwest and South, Educational Theatre Association. *Awards, honors:* San Diego State national playwriting award, 1962; D.H.L., Suffolk University, 1978.

WRITINGS—All published by St. Martin's, except as indicated: *An Introduction to the Greek Theatre,* 1959; *Greek Scenic Conventions in the Fifth Centruy B.C.,* Oxford University Press, 1962, reprinted, Greenwood Press, 1978; *Plays without People: Puppetry and Serious Drama,* Indiana University Press, 1964; *An Introduction to the Greek World,* 1967; *The Theatres of Japan,* 1969; *The Romans and Their World,* 1970; *The Ancient Greek and Roman Theatre,* Random House, 1971; *Ballet of Comedians* (novel based on life of J.B.P. Moliere), Macmillan, 1972; *The Byzantines and Their World,* 1973; *An Introduction to the French Theatre,* Rowman & Littlefield, 1977; (editor with Otto Reinert) *Thirteen Plays: An Introduction,* Little, Brown, 1978; (editor with Reinert) *Twenty-Three Plays: An Introductory Antholo-*

gy, Little, Brown, 1978; *The Theater in Its Time: An Introduction*, Little, Brown, 1981.

Editor and translator: *Two Classical Comedies*, Appleton, 1958; Aristophanes, *The Birds* [and] Plautus, *The Brothers Menaechmus*, AHM Publishing, 1958; Sophocles, *Oedipus the King* [and] *Antigone*, Appleton, 1960; *Three Greek Plays for the Theatre*, Indiana University Press, 1961; Aeschylus, *Agamemnon, The Libation Bearers,* [and] *The Eumenides*, Appleton, 1964; Aristophanes, *The Clouds* [and] Plautus, *The Pot of Gold*, AHM Publishing, 1967; Aeschylus, *Seven against Thebes* [and] *Prometheus Bound*, St. Martin's, 1968; Euripedes, *Hecuba* [and] *The Madness of Hercules*, St. Martin's, 1969; Sophocles, *Oedipus at Colonus* [and] *Electra*, AHM Publishing, 1975.

WORK IN PROGRESS: The Theatre in Its Time, for Little, Brown.

BIOGRAPHICAL/CRITICAL SOURCES: Times Literary Supplement, August 24, 1967, September 11, 1970; *Best Sellers,* January 15, 1971; *Economist,* May 7, 1977; *French Review,* May, 1978.

*   *   *

ARNOV, Boris, Jr. 1926-

PERSONAL: Born October 17, 1926, in Los Angeles, Calif.; son of Boris and Helen (Mindlin) Arnov; married, 1955. *Education:* Attended Chicago Medical School, 1944-45; Rollins College, B.S., 1948; University of Miami, Coral Gables, Fla., additional study, 1950-52, M.Ed., 1967; University of California, additional study, 1958-59. *Home:* 650 Northeast Fourth St., Boca Raton, Fla. *Office:* College of Education, Florida Atlantic University, Boca Raton, Fla. 33432.

CAREER: Formerly teacher at Miramonte High School, Orinda, Calif.; currently associate professor of education, Florida Atlantic University, Boca Raton.

WRITINGS: Wonders of the Ocean Zoo, Dodd, 1957; *Wonders of the Deep Sea,* Dodd, 1959; *Inside Our Earth,* Bobbs-Merrill, 1961; *Oceans of the World,* Bobbs-Merrill, 1962; *Bally, the Blue Whale,* Criterion, 1964; *Secrets of Inland Waters,* Little, Brown, 1965; *Homes beneath the Sea,* Little, Brown, 1969; *Fishing for Everyone,* Hawthorne, 1971; *Water: Experiments to Understand It,* Lothrop, 1980. Contributor of articles to fishing magazines and to newspapers.

BIOGRAPHICAL/CRITICAL SOURCES: Commonweal, May 23, 1969.

*   *   *

ASH, Anthony Lee 1931-

PERSONAL: Born October 29, 1931, in Lincoln, Neb.; son of Jesse W. and Virginia (Coleman) Ash; married Barbara Bailey (a secretary), January 31, 1955. *Education:* Attended University of Oregon, 1949-51, and Florida Christian College, 1951-54; Florida State University, B.S., 1956; Abilene Christian College (now University), M.A., 1959; University of Southern California, Ph.D., 1966. *Home:* 1802 Cedar Ridge, Austin, Tex. 78741. *Office:* Institute for Christian Studies, 1908 University Ave., Austin, Tex. 78705.

CAREER: Minister of Church of Christ, 1951—; Pepperdine University, Malibu, Calif., assistant professor of religion and chairman of division, 1972-75; affiliated with Institute for Christian Studies, Austin, Tex., 1975—. *Member:* American Academy of Religion, Society of Biblical Literature.

WRITINGS: Prayer, Sweet, 1964; *The Gospel According to Luke,* Sweet, 1973; *The Word of Faith,* Biblical Research

Society, 1973; *The Psalms,* Sweet, 1980; *The Book of Acts, Volume I,* Sweet, 1980; *Decide to Love,* Sweet, 1980. Contributor to religious periodicals. Editor, *Single Again.*

WORK IN PROGRESS: Commentaries on the books of Jeremiah and Lamentations, for Sweet.

*   *   *

ASHTON, Robert 1924-

PERSONAL: Born July 21, 1924, in Chester, England; son of Joseph and Edith Ashton; married Margaret Alice Sedgwick, 1946; children: Rosalind Helen, Celia Elizabeth. *Education:* University College of Southampton, B.A., 1949; London School of Economics and Political Science, Ph.D., 1953. *Home:* The Manor House, Brundall, Norwich, England. *Office:* University of East Anglia, Norwich NR4 7TJ, England.

CAREER: University of Nottingham, University Park, Nottingham, England, assistant lecturer, 1942-44, lecturer, 1944-61, senior lecturer in economic history, 1961-63; University of East Anglia, Norwich, England, professor of English history, 1963—, dean of School of English Studies, 1964-67. Visiting associate professor of history, University of California, Berkeley, 1962-63; visiting fellow, All Souls College, Oxford University, 1973-74. *Military service:* Royal Air Force, warrant officer, 1943-46. *Member:* Royal Historical Society (fellow).

WRITINGS: The Crown and the Money Market, 1603-40, Oxford University Press, 1960; (contributor) F. J. Fisher, editor, *Essays in the Economic and Social History of Tudor and Stuart England,* Cambridge University Press, 1961; (editor) *James I by His Contemporaries,* Hutchinson, 1969; (contributor) R. H. Parry, editor, *The English Civil War and After, 1642-1658,* Macmillan (London), 1969, University of California Press, 1970; (contributor) D. C. Coleman and A. H. John, editors, *Trade, Government and Economy in Pre-Industrial England,* Weidenfeld & Nicolson, 1976; *The English Civil War: Conservatism and Revolution, 1603-1649,* Weidenfeld & Nicolson, 1978, Norton, 1979; *The City and the Court, 1603-1643,* Cambridge University Press, 1979. Contributor of articles to *Economic History Review, Journal of Economic History,* and others.

WORK IN PROGRESS: Doing research work on the relations between the government and the business world in the seventeenth century.

SIDELIGHTS: Robert Ashton told *CA,* "The most important influence on my development as a historian is that of the late Professor R. H. Tawney, under whom I worked in London."

BIOGRAPHICAL/CRITICAL SOURCES: Observer Review, January 26, 1969.

*   *   *

ASTOR, Mary 1906-

PERSONAL: Original name, Lucile V. Langhanke; born May 3, 1906, in Quincy, Ill.; daughter of Otto and Helen (Vasconcellos) Langhanke; married Kenneth Hawks (a film director), February 28, 1928 (killed in plane crash, 1930); married Franklyn Thorpe, June 29, 1931 (divorced, 1935); married Manuel del Camp, February 18, 1937 (divorced, 1942); married Thomas G. Wheelock, December 24, 1945 (divorced, 1955); children: (second marriage) Marilyn (Mrs. Frank Roh); (third marriage) Anthony. *Education:* Attended schools in Chicago; also studied under private tutors. *Politics:* Republican. *Religion:* Catholic. *Home:* 23388 Mulholland Dr., Woodland Hills, Calif. 91364. *Agent:* Gloria Safier, Inc., 667 Madison Ave., New York, N.Y. 10021.

CAREER: Actress and author; has been in motion pictures, radio, theater, and television. Made film debut in Hollywood, 1920; started in silent pictures, made comeback in sound pictures, and later played character roles. Appeared opposite John Barrymore in "Beau Brummel" and "Don Juan"; other films include "Lost Squadron," "Dodsworth," "The Great Lie," "The Maltese Falcon," "Meet Me in St. Louis," "Cass Timberlane," "Little Women," and "Return to Peyton Place." Stage roles include "Among the Married," "Tonight at 8:30," and "Male Animal." Television performer in many dramatic shows. *Awards, honors:* Motion Picture Academy Award (Oscar) for best supporting actress, 1941, for "The Great Lie."

WRITINGS: My Story (autobiography), Doubleday, 1959; *The Incredible Charlie Carewe* (novel), Doubleday, 1960; *The Image of Kate* (novel), Doubleday, 1962; *The O'Connors* (novel), Doubleday, 1964; *Goodbye Darling, Be Happy* (novel), Doubleday, 1965; *A Place Called Saturday* (novel), Delacorte, 1969; *A Life on Film* (autobiography), Delacorte, 1971.

SIDELIGHTS: Mary Astor's first book, *My Story,* tells of the actress's problems in Hollywood, her marriages and divorces, her scandal-ridden courtroom fight with her second husband for custody of their daughter, and her subsequent bouts with alcoholism and near-suicidal depression. Her comeback from these problems was aided by a Catholic priest and psychologist who encouraged her to write about her life. Comparing the book to other Hollywood confessionals, the *New York Times*'s Lewis Nichols notes the usual inclusion of "fame, sex, alcohol, headlines," but he adds: "There is a difference. Miss Astor seems less interested in standing a reader's hair on end than in getting at the facts about herself." The *Wisconsin Library Bulletin* reviewer calls the book "straightforward, not sensational, and quite well written." Agreeing with these assessments, Hollis Alpert of *Saturday Review* calls the autobiography "an affecting account of a sorely beset and bewildered woman who managed in her maturity to find some serenity and self-sufficiency.... It also happens to be written with distinct literary ability and is thus far superior to (and better written than) the slick ghosted jobs [that are usually written by Hollywood stars.]"

A Life on Film portrays Astor's continued growth after her recovery. Writing in the *New York Times Book Review,* Charles Higham calls the memoir "stimulating, disillusioned and caustic, dealing courageously with a largely wasted career.... There is no escaping the fact that Hollywood largely wasted Mary Astor. But we must be grateful that it supplies the material for her harsh, sad, witty, infinitely likable book." J. A. Avant comments in *Library Journal:* "Astor knows what was good in her life and why and has few illusions about where she's been both personally and professionally.... As autobiography [*A Life on Film*] compares favorably with *An Unfinished Woman,* less intellectually pretentious and somehow more 'finished' than Lillian Hellman's book."

Astor's novels have also received some favorable reviews. Mary Ross of the *New York Herald Tribune Book Review* calls *The Incredible Charlie Carewe* "an exceptional first novel in that, instead of offering lyric subjectivity, it presents an objective and sophisticated portrait of an individual." The reviewer for *Kirkus* believes that this novel is "an engrossing story of a man and those he hurts. The fact of mad-

ness is handled with imagination so that Charlie Carewe emerges as a force of evil almost mystical in proportion, while the struggle of those surrounding him is woven into a pattern of credible and interesting events." And writing in *Book World,* Liz Smith labels *A Place Called Saturday* "an endearing, intriguing, easy-reading tale.... [Astor] is an entertainer. Luckily for us, she is also a gifted and compulsive word-handler. But mostly she is the same talented woman who thrilled us with her incomparable face, voice and acting in 'The Maltese Falcon' [and] who has already told the fascinatingly ruthless story of her life in *My Story....* As a novelist, she loses nothing in the translation of her numerous talents."

BIOGRAPHICAL/CRITICAL SOURCES: Kirkus, November 1, 1958, June 15, 1960, January 15, 1962; *Chicago Sunday Tribune,* January 11, 1959, August 28, 1960; *New York Times,* January 11, 1959; *Newsweek,* January 12, 1959; *Saturday Review,* January 17, 1959; *New York Herald Tribune Book Review,* February 1, 1959, October 23, 1960; *Wisconsin Library Bulletin,* March, 1959; *New York Times Book Review,* September 25, 1960, April 1, 1962, October 17, 1971; *Book World,* December 1, 1968; David Shipman, *Great Movie Stars,* Crown, 1970; Kalton C. Lahue, *Ladies in Distress,* A. S. Barnes, 1971; *Library Journal,* October 15, 1971; Richard Lamparski, *Whatever Became of ... ?,* Crown, 1973; William H. A. Carr, *Hollywood Tragedy,* Fawcett, 1975.

* * *

ATHAS, Daphne 1923-

PERSONAL: Born November 19, 1923, in Cambridge, Mass.; daughter of Pan Constantine and Mildred (Spencer) Athas. *Education:* University of North Carolina, A.B., 1943; Harvard University, additional studies, 1944. *Religion:* Protestant. *Home address:* Box 224, Chapel Hill, N.C. 27514.

CAREER: Perkins School for the Blind, Watertown, Mass., teacher of algebra, 1944-45; U.S. Air Force, London, England, service club director, 1952-58; Durham Technical Institute, Durham, N.C., coordinator of basic education, 1964-66; University of North Carolina at Chapel Hill, lecturer, 1967-73; Tehran University, Tehran, Iran, Fulbright professor of American literature, 1973-74; University of North Carolina at Chapel Hill, lecturer, 1974-79. *Member:* Authors League, Dramatists Guild. *Awards, honors:* Second prize, *London Observer* playwriting contest, 1958, for "Sit on the Earth"; MacDowell fellowship, 1962; National Foundation of Arts and Humanities award, 1969; *Entering Ephesus* was included in *Time*'s ten best fiction books of the year, 1971; Sir Walter Raleigh Cup, Historical Book Club of North Carolina, 1972; National Endowment for the Arts award, 1974-75, and 1979-80; Sir Walter Raleigh Award for fiction, 1979, for *Cora.*

WRITINGS: The Weather of the Heart (novel), Appleton, 1947; *The Fourth World* (novel), Putnam, 1956; (with Gurney Campbell) "Sit on the Earth" (play; produced at Westport Country Playhouse, 1961), published in *London Observer Plays,* Faber, 1957; *Greece by Prejudice* (nonfiction), Lippincott, 1963; *Entering Ephesus* (novel), Viking, 1971; *Cora* (novel), Viking, 1978. Contributor of stories, poems and articles to literary magazines.

WORK IN PROGRESS: A novel.

SIDELIGHTS: With *Entering Ephesus* Daphne Athas "manages to make most practitioners in the crowded coming-of-age field seem calculating and niggardly indeed," writes Martha Duffy. *Saturday Review* critic Muriel Haynes praises

"Athas's astonishingly precise, knowing recall of adolescence. . . . This is a wonderfully loving, pure-spirited book with an exuberant vision. Its secret, of style and attitude, is that the novel refuses to take itself too seriously."

BIOGRAPHICAL/CRITICAL SOURCES: Time, September 13, 1971, January 3, 1972; *New York Times Book Review*, October 3, 1971; *Saturday Review*, October 9, 1971.

*   *   *

ATHEARN, Robert G(reenleaf) 1914-

PERSONAL: Born August 30, 1914, in Kremlin, Mont.; son of Fred D. and Clarinda (Lomen) Athearn; married Claire B. Raney, 1942; children: Frederic James, Dana Leigh. *Education:* University of Minnesota, B.S., 1936, M.A., 1938, Ph.D., 1947. *Home:* 3822 Lakebriar Dr., Boulder, Colo. 80302. *Office:* Department of History, University of Colorado, Boulder, Colo.

CAREER: University of Colorado, Boulder, 1947—, professor of United States history, 1956—. *Military service:* U.S. Coast Guard, 1942-45, became lieutenant junior grade. *Member:* American Historical Association, Organization of American Historians, Western History Association (president, 1964-65). *Awards, honors:* Ford Foundation fellowship, 1954-55; Fulbright fellowship in Great Britain, 1960-61; various awards for *Westward the Briton, High Country Empire,* and *Forts of the Upper Missouri;* award for distinguished career as writer on the American West, American Association for State and Local History, 1971.

WRITINGS: Thomas Francis Meagher: An Irish Revolutionary in America, University of Colorado Press, 1949; *Westward the Briton,* Scribner, 1953; *William Tecumseh Sherman and Settlement of the West,* University of Oklahoma Press, 1956; (editor) *Soldier in the West: The Civil War Letters of Alfred Lacey Hough,* University of Pennsylvania Press, 1957; (with Carl W. Ubbelohde) *Centennial Colorado: Its Exciting Story,* Chambers, 1959; *High Country Empire,* McGraw, 1960; *Rebel of the Rockies: The Denver and Rio Grande Western Railroad,* Yale University Press, 1962; *The American Heritage New Illustrated History of the United States,* sixteen volumes (with foreword by John F. Kennedy, introduction by Allan Nevins), Dell, 1963; (with Robert E. Riegel) *America Moves West,* Holt, 1964; *Forts of the Upper Missouri,* Prentice-Hall, 1967; *Union Pacific Country,* Rand McNally, 1971; *The Coloradans,* University of New Mexico Press, 1976; *In Search of Canaan: Black Migration to Kansas, 1879-80,* Regents Press of Kansas, 1978. Contributor of about 40 articles and 125 reviews to magazines.

BIOGRAPHICAL/CRITICAL SOURCES: Best Sellers, December 15, 1967.

*   *   *

ATKINS, John (Alfred) 1916-

PERSONAL: Born May 26, 1916, in Carshalton, Surrey, England; son of Frank Periam (a broker) and Bertha (Lovell) Atkins; married Dorothy Grey. *Education:* University of Bristol, B.A. (honors), 1938. *Politics:* Liberal Socialist. *Religion:* Agnostic. *Home:* Braeside Cottage, Birch Green, Colchester C02 0NH, Essex, England.

CAREER: Mass Observation, London, England, interviewer, 1939-41; *Tribune,* London, literary editor, 1942-44; Workers' Educational Association, Bristol, England, district organizer, 1948-51; Sudan Government, Ministry of Education, Khartoum, teacher, 1951-55, 1958-68; University of

Lodz, Lodz, Poland, docent, beginning 1970. Rural District Councilor, Dorchester, 1950. *Military service:* Royal Artillery, 1944-46. *Member:* Writers Guild of Great Britain.

WRITINGS: Cat on Hot Bricks (novel), Macdonald & Co., 1948; *The Art of Ernest Hemingway: His Works and His Personality,* Nevill, 1952, published with new introduction, Spring Books, 1964; *George Orwell: A Literary and Biographical Study,* J. Calder, 1953, Ungar, 1965, new edition, J. Calder, 1971; *Arthur Koestler,* Spearman, 1954; *Rain and the River* (novel), Putnam, 1954; *Aldous Huxley: A Literary Study,* J. Calder, 1955, Ungar, 1965, revised edition, J. Calder, 1967, Orion Press, 1968; *Tomorrow Revealed,* Spearman, 1955; *Graham Greene,* J. Calder, 1956, revised edition, 1966, Humanities, 1967; (with J. B. Pick) *A Land Fit for Eros* (novel), Arco, 1956; (contributor) R. O. Evans, editor, *Graham Greene: Some Critical Considerations,* University Press of Kentucky, 1963; *Sex in Literature,* Calder & Boyars, Volume I: *The Erotic Impulse,* 1970, Volume II: *The Classical Experience,* 1973, Volume III: *The Medieval Experience,* 1978; *Six Novelists Look at Society,* J. Calder, 1977; *J. B. Priestley,* J. Calder, 1981. Contributor to *Penguin New Writing* and other collections, and to *Adelphi, Life and Letters Today,* and other periodicals. Compiler of weekly radio magazine in English for European service of Radio Omdurman.

WORK IN PROGRESS: The British Spy Novel, for J. Calder.

SIDELIGHTS: John Atkins told *CA:* "My major pleasure as a writer (and possibly my major drawback, as J. B. Priestley would agree) has always been to write in as many forms and genres as possible. I dislike specialism.

"It is always difficult to know why and how one started writing. Ever since I learnt to read I have written poems and stories. I think it is a delight in self-expression above all else.

"By accident I have become mainly a literary commentator—I never use the word critic. Most criticism sets itself up as an arbiter and there are very few who have the right to do this. In my non-fiction writing I try to help others find their way about the literary jungle, point out paths, give perhaps a different interpretation from some others. I say this has been accidental because I began as a fiction-writer, but my publisher asked me to write another kind of book. He liked it and has asked me to continue ever since.

"My working habits are varied. Much of my work consists of reading and note-taking. When I finally reach the writing stage I like to write three pages per session. Six pages a day if I write morning and afternoon—but a big *if*.

"Nearly all my books these days are written after consultation with my publisher. He regards me as some kind of expert on modern fiction in particular. Some time ago he thought it would be worth while examining the popularity of the supernatural in contemporary fiction. For some time I had wanted to write about the occult. But then this idea cooled off, and my publisher came up with a new one: the spy novel. This appealed to me—like the occult, it forms a genre which one cannot miss if one reads contemporary work. Result: I am contracted to write it. . . .

"George Orwell was once asked for advice and replied: 'Never take advice.' I think this is broadly true. A writer must find his own way because every way is different. He can only learn by his own mistakes. The only area where a little advice might be helpful is in marketing."

Atkins reports that he has had "two books published in French editions: *Tomorrow Revealed* (as *Les memoires du futur*) and the first volume of *Sex in Literature* (as *La sexe dans la litterature*). I have recently written an article on the latter subject for an encyclopaedia which will appear in Spanish.''

BIOGRAPHICAL/CRITICAL SOURCES: Book World, July 14, 1968; *Christian Science Monitor,* July 18, 1968; *Virginia Quarterly Review,* spring, 1969.

* * *

ATWOOD, Margaret (Eleanor) 1939-

PERSONAL: Born November 18, 1939, in Ottawa, Ontario, Canada; daughter of Carl Edmund (an entomologist) and Margaret (Killam) Atwood; divorced; children: Jess. *Education:* University of Toronto, B.A., 1961; Radcliffe College, A.M., 1962; Harvard University, graduate study, 1962-63 and 1965-67. *Politics:* William Morrisite. *Religion:* "Pessimistic Pantheist." *Home address:* Box 1401, Alliston, Ontario, Canada. *Agent:* Phoebe Larmore, 2814 Third St., Santa Monica, Calif. 90405.

CAREER: Worked during her early career as cashier, waitress, market research firm writer, and film script writer; University of British Columbia, Vancouver, lecturer in English literature, 1964-65; Sir George Williams University, Montreal, Quebec, lecturer in English literature, 1967-68; York University, Toronto, Ontario, assistant professor of English literature, 1971-72; University of Toronto, Toronto, writer-in-residence, 1972-73; writer. House of Anansi Press, Toronto, editor and member of board of directors, 1971-73. *Member:* Amnesty International, Writers' Union of Canada (vice-chairman, 1980-81), Canadian Civil Liberties Association (member of board of directors, 1973-75). *Awards, honors:* E. J. Pratt Medal, 1961; President's Medal, University of Western Ontario, 1965; Governor General's Award, 1966, for *The Circle Game;* first prize in Canadian Centennial Commission Poetry Competition, 1967; Union League Civic and Arts Foundation Prize, *Poetry,* 1969; D.Litt., Trent University, 1973; LL.D., Queen's University, 1974; Bess Hokins Prize, *Poetry,* 1974; City of Toronto Book Award, 1977; Canadian Bookseller's Association award, 1977; Periodical Distributors of Canada Short Fiction Award, 1977; St. Lawrence Award for fiction, 1978; Radcliffe Medal, 1980.

WRITINGS: Survival: A Thematic Guide to Canadian Literature, Anansi, 1972; (with others) *Canadian Imagination: Dimensions of a Literary Culture,* Harvard University Press, 1977; *Up in the Tree* (juvenile), McClelland & Stewart, 1978; *Dancing Girls* (short stories), McClelland & Stewart, 1978; (with Joyce Barkhouse) *Anna's Pet,* James Lorimer, 1980.

Poetry: *Double Persephone,* Hawkshead Press, 1961; *The Circle Game,* Contact Press, 1966; *The Animals in That Country,* Oxford University Press (Toronto), 1968, Atlantic-Little, Brown, 1969; *The Journals of Susanna Moodie,* Oxford University Press, 1970; *Procedures for Underground,* Atlantic-Little, Brown, 1970; *Power Politics,* Anansi, 1971, Harper, 1973; *You Are Happy,* Harper, 1974; *Selected Poems,* Oxford University Press, 1976, Simon & Schuster, 1978; *Two-Headed Poems,* Oxford University Press, 1978, Simon & Schuster, 1981.

Novels: *The Edible Woman,* McClelland & Stewart, 1969, Atlantic-Little, Brown, 1970; *Surfacing,* McClelland & Stewart, 1972, Simon & Schuster, 1973; *Lady Oracle,* Simon & Schuster, 1976; *Life before Man,* McClelland & Stewart, 1979, Simon & Schuster, 1980.

Work is represented in more than 100 anthologies, including: *How Do I Love Thee: Sixty Poets of Canada (and Quebec)*

Select and Introduce Their Favourite Poems from Their Own Work, edited by John Robert Colombo, M. G. Gurtig (Edmonton, Alberta), 1970; *Five Modern Canadian Poets,* edited by Eli Mandel, Holt (Toronto), 1970; *72: New Canadian Stories,* edited by David Helwig and Joan Harcourt, Oberon Press, 1972. Contributor of poetry to *Tamarack Review, Canadian Forum, New Yorker, Atlantic, Poetry, Kayak, Quarry, Prism,* and other magazines; contributor of short stories, reviews, and critical articles to *Harper's, Saturday Night, Ellipse,* and other periodicals.

WORK IN PROGRESS: A novel; a book of poetry; a book of essays; a screenplay of *Lady Oracle;* two television scripts with Peter Pearson, "Snowbirds" and "Heaven on Earth."

SIDELIGHTS: "Margaret Atwood," comments Marge Piercy in *American Poetry Review,* "is an extraordinarily good writer who has produced widely different books.... Atwood is a large and remarkable writer. Her concerns are nowhere petty. Her novels and poems move and engage me deeply, can matter to people who read them." Atwood's work has received similar high praise from many critics. For example, Dick Allen, writing in *Poetry,* remarks that *Power Politics* is "a top-flight sequence of poems about a love affair, written with intensity of feeling, careful craft, and harrowing imagery.... [It] is an honest, searching book which touches deeply; it goes about as close to the core of the love struggle as Sylvia Plath did at her very best; we emerge from the experience shaken and at once tough and tender." In *Parnassus,* Rosellen Brown calls it a *"tour de force."* And George Bowering writes that *"Power Politics* is a book of beautiful poetry."

You Are Happy is another book of poetry (among several) which has garnered a very favorable response. Helen Vendler is impressed with the power of Atwood's writing; she observes in the *New York Times Book Review* that the poems in this volume are "guided missiles which have a deadly force of their own, poems so neat and silent that they move in space like an invasion, descend, pierce the mind and leave a wound." In addition, Tom Marshall of the *Ontario Review* discovers evidence of improvement: "The book seems ... to be a turning point in the poet's development. Technically, too, it is an advance over *Power Politics.* Many individual poems from that book tend to lose their force when removed from the context of the whole sequence.... Here there is more technical variety than in the past.... One feels that most poems are autonomous and interesting in and for themselves, ... and yet all contribute to a coherent whole—a human statement, a journey. I think we may be grateful to Margaret Atwood for facing up to the most difficult facts of our existence and for putting the case for joy so minimally and so well."

Not only has Atwood's poetry been acclaimed, but her novels have received much commendation as well. In *Saturday Review,* Benjamin DeMott, for instance, remarks that "on its face Margaret Atwood's *Surfacing* is merely another novelistic go ... at the oldest North American literary theme—that of 'lighting out for the Territory,' finding yourself by losing others, trading culture for nature.... A familiar pattern, to repeat—but the execution is extraordinary.... What is most striking about *Surfacing* is the integrity of the writer's imagination.... Everywhere in the language of this story there are dependencies, associative prefigurings, linkages extending and refining meaning." Moreover, Paul Delany, writing in the *New York Times Book Review,* compares *Surfacing* to Sylvia Plath's *The Bell Jar* and finds that *Surfacing* "avoids the tone of flat, sealed-off resignation on which *The Bell Jar* ends; rather it invigorates by its heroine's resolve to trust herself to the world while refusing, at the same time, to be a victim of it.''

Not all of her books have been unanimously admired. *Lady Oracle* generated some critical debate even among Atwood's fans. In the *New York Times Book Review,* Katha Pollitt argues that Atwood ''seems to have two literary selves. The first, upon which her considerable reputation is based, writes spare, tense poems [and] an extraordinary novel, *Surfacing.* . . . The other Atwood is the author of *Lady Oracle* and an earlier *The Edible Woman.* . . . Both of these books lack the metaphoric and mythic force of the other work while sharing with it a limited interest in individual character. Instead of archtypes and myths, they offer us the stock figures and pat insights of a certain kind of popular feminist-oriented fiction.'' Similarly, Bonnie Lyons, in the *New Orleans Review,* feels that ''*Lady Oracle* is . . . an uneasy mixture of Gothic parody and a comedy of manners . . . [that] never mesh into a unity.'' But what bothers Lyons most ''is its strange closeness and yet distance from *Surfacing.* . . . Many of the same themes and images pervade both works, . . . [but] Lady Oracle seems almost a parody or weird distortion of Atwood's most serious themes.''

On the other hand, some critics are impressed both by the comedy and the way in which *Lady Oracle,* like *Surfacing,* reworks an old theme. Linda Sandler of *Saturday Night,* for instance, notes that ''as a literary genre, growing-up-female-in-the-1950s is as threadbare as a pair of bleached denims, but *Lady Oracle* is utterly unlike any feminist novel I know. For one thing, Atwood has a sense of humour. . . . *Lady Oracle* . . . is an exquisite parody of an obsolete generation. So far, it's been privileged information that Atwood's a brilliant comedian. I vote we make it public.'' In like manner, William McPherson, in the *Washington Post Book World,* points out that Atwood ''writes novels whose pervading theme is—yes—beginning again: old material but freshly and deftly arranged. . . . [*Lady Oracle*] is, in fact, a very funny novel, lightly told with wry detachment and considerable art.''

Unlike *Lady Oracle,* Atwood's next novel, *Life before Man,* has been most favorably compared with her earlier work. In fact, some reviewers see it almost as a culmination of previous efforts. Atwood, observes Roberta Rubenstein in the *Chicago Tribune,* ''has carved out a distinct literary territory: psychic (and physical) survival; the way we are consumed by our consumer society; what it means to be female in times of sexual role upheaval; the inexorability of the past. Now, with *Life before Man,* she has combined all of these dimensions in a novel that chronicles the elaborate minuet between the sexes in a splendid mixture of irony, humor, and realism.'' Rubenstein concludes: ''Moving flawlessly from wit to pathos and back, Atwood constructs a superb living exhibit in which the artifacts are unique (but representative) lives in process. Her dissections of character and situation come from . . . a cave from which 'the past has been vandalized and this is where the loot is stored.' There is ample treasure in this novel.'' In the *New York Times Book Review,* Marilyn French similarly finds that in *Life before Man* Atwood ''combines several talents—powerful introspection, honesty, satire, a taut, limpid style—to create a splendid, fully integrated work.'' ''This novel,'' French continues, ''suggests that we are still living the life before man, before the human . . . has evolved. . . . We may be only a beginning. *Life before Man,* however, is not. It is superb, complete.''

Critics often point to the importance of the Canadian wilderness in Atwood's writing, particularly in *Surfacing.* Her

background perhaps explains the significance of that landscape for her. As she told a *New York Times Book Review* interviewer, ''Six months [after my birth] I was backpacked into the Quebec bush. I grew up in and out of the bush, in and out of Ottawa, Sault Ste. Marie and Toronto. I did not attend a full year of school until I was in grade eight.'' Even after her family settled in Toronto, they passed several months a year in the bush country of northern Canada.

In the same interview, Atwood described her early desire to write and her parents' influence: ''I began writing at the age of 5, but there was a dark period between the ages of 8 and 16 when I didn't write. I started again at 16 and have no idea why, but it was suddenly the only thing I wanted to do. . . . [My parents] didn't encourage me to be a writer, exactly, but they gave me a more important kind of support; that is, they expected me to make use of my intelligence and abilities and they did not pressure me into getting married. . . . Remember that all this was taking place in the 1950's, when marriage was seen as the only desirable goal.'' At the end of the interview, Atwood goes on to speculate about why she writes. She remarks that she does not believe that the desire to write stems from neurosis, because ''if all the art were pearls secreted by the miseries of the oysters, the totally healthy human being would be the one without a creative or joyful bone in her body. Can this be true? . . . Why do I write? I guess I've never felt the necessity of thinking up a really convincing answer to that one. . . . I think the real question is, 'Why doesn't everyone?' ''

BIOGRAPHICAL/CRITICAL SOURCES: Poetry, July, 1972; *West Coast Review,* January, 1973; *New York Times Book Review,* March 4, 1973, April 6, 1975, September 26, 1976, May 21, 1978, February 3, 1980; *Saturday Review,* April, 1973; *New Leader,* September 3, 1973; *American Poetry Review,* November/December, 1973, March/April, 1977; *Contemporary Literary Criticism,* Gale, Volume II, 1974, Volume III, 1975, Volume IV, 1975, Volume VIII, 1978, Volume XIII, 1980, Volume XV, 1980; *Canadian Literature,* spring, 1974; *Ontario Review,* spring-summer, 1975; *Saturday Night,* September, 1976; *Washington Post Book World,* September 20, 1976, January 27, 1980; *Modern Fiction Studies,* autumn, 1976; *Publisher's Weekly,* August 23, 1976; *New York Times,* December 23, 1976, January 10, 1980, February 8, 1980; *New Orleans Review,* Volume V, number 3, 1977; *Christian Science Monitor,* June 12, 1977; *Book Forum,* Volume IV, number 1, 1978; *Chicago Tribune,* January 27, 1980, February 3, 1980; *People,* May 19, 1980.

—*Sketch by David A. Guy*

*   *   *

AUNG, (Maung) Htin   1909-
(The Fourth Brother, U. Htin Aung)

PERSONAL: Born May 18, 1909, in Pegu, Burma; son of U Pein and Daw Mi Mi; married Daw Tin Hla (now an advocate), April 3, 1942. *Education:* University of Rangoon, B.A. (honors), M.A., 1928; University of London, LL.B. (honors), LL.M.; Cambridge University, LL.B. (honors); Trinity College, Dublin, M.Litt., Ph.D., LL.D., 1933; Lincoln's Inn, London, barrister-at-law, 1932; Oxford University, B.C.L., 1968. *Religion:* Buddhist. *Home:* 107 University Ave., Rangoon, Burma.

CAREER: University of Rangoon, Rangoon, Burma, senior lecturer, 1933-36, professor of English, 1936-48, professor of anthropology, 1948-60, rector, 1946-60, vice-chancellor (honorary post), 1959-60; Government of Burma, ambassador of Ceylon, 1959-63; Columbia University, School of International Affairs, New York, N.Y., visiting professor, 1963-64. Secretary, Burma Council of National Education, 1936-46; member of administrative board, International Universities Association, 1950-60; president of Inter-University Board of India, 1954, and Burma Research Society, 1956. Leader of Burmese delegation to UNESCO General Conference, 1950 and 1951. *Military service:* British Army, 1939-45; became captain; honorary colonel and aide-de-camp to President of Burma, 1952-62. *Member:* Rotary Club of Rangoon (president, 1955), Rangoon Chess Club (founder-member). *Awards, honors:* Order of White Elephant (Thailand); honorary LL.D. from Johns Hopkins University, 1951, University College, Dublin, 1956, University of Rangoon, 1961, and University of Ceylon, 1961; D.H.L., Wake Forest University, 1970.

WRITINGS: Burmese Drama, Oxford University Press, 1937; (compiler and editor) *Book of English Verse,* Oxford University Press, 1938; *Burmese Folk Tales,* Oxford University Press, 1948; *Burmese Law Tales,* Oxford University Press, 1962; *Folk Elements in Burmese Buddhism,* Oxford University Press, 1962; *The Stricken Peacock: Anglo-Burmese Relations, 1752-1948,* Nijhoff, 1965; (editor and translator) Sayadaw Thingazar, *Burmese Monks Tales,* Columbia University Press, 1966; *Epistles Written on the Eve of Anglo-Burmese War,* Nijhoff, 1967; *A History of Burma,* Columia University Press, 1968; *Kingdom Lost for a Drop of Honey,* Parent's Magazine Press, 1968; *Burmese History before 1287: Defence of the Chronicles,* Asoka Society Press, 1970. Chairman of editorial committee, Burmese supplement of *Atlantic Monthly.*

WORK IN PROGRESS: Lord Randolph Churchill and the Dancing Peacock: British Conquest of Burma 1886.

BIOGRAPHICAL/CRITICAL SOURCES: Guardian, Rangoon, August, 1958.

*   *   *

AYRTON, Elisabeth Walshe

PERSONAL: Daughter of Douglas and Phyllis Sidney (Johnson) Walshe; married Michael Ayrton (a painter, sculptor, and writer), November, 1951 (died, 1975); children: (previous marriage) three daughters. *Education:* Newnham College, Cambridge, B.A. (honours), M.A. *Politics:* Labour. *Home:* Maze House, Rockhampton, Berkeley, Gloucestershire, England. *Agent:* Nicholas Thompson, Forest House, Havingsham, Warminster, Wiltshire, England.

WRITINGS: The Cooks' Tale, Chatto & Windus, 1957; *Sauce and Sensuality,* Dutton, 1957; *Good Simple Cooking,* Hurst & Blackett, 1958; *Time Is of the Essence,* McGibbon & Kee, 1961; *Doric Temples,* Thames & Hudson, 1961; *The Cretan,* Hodder & Stroughton, 1963, published as *Silence in Crete,* Morrow, 1964; *Royal Favourites,* Folio Society, 1971; *The Cookery of England,* Andre Deutsch, 1974; *Day Eight,* Hutchinson, 1979; *English Provincial Cooking,* Harper, 1980. Also author of *Two Years in My Afternoon,* Secker & Warburg. Contributor to *Reader's Digest Cookery Book* and *Time-Life Cooking.* Contributor of articles and short stories to *Vogue* and other periodicals.

WORK IN PROGRESS: Cookery of the Eighties, for Penguin; a novel on East Africa.

B

BACH, George Leland 1915-

PERSONAL: Born April 28, 1915, in Victor, Iowa; son of James Everett and Ethel (Sies) Bach; married Ruth Jacqueline Bartoo, 1939; children: Christopher, Barbara, Susan, Timothy. *Education:* Grinnell College, B.A., 1936; University of Chicago, Ph.D., 1940. *Home:* 661 Cabrillo Ave., Stanford, Calif. 94305. *Office:* Graduate School of Business, Stanford University, Stanford, Calif.

CAREER: Iowa State University, Ames, instructor, 1939-41; Federal Reserve Board, Washington, D.C., economist and special adviser, 1941-46; Carnegie Institute of Technology (now Carnegie-Mellon University), Pittsburgh, Pa., 1946-66, Falk Professor of Economics and Social Science, 1962-66; Stanford University, Stanford, Calif., Ford Research Professor, 1963-64, Frank E. Buck Professor of Economics, 1966—. Chairman, National Task Force on Economic Education, 1960-62; vice-chairman, Joint Council on Economic Education, 1962—; Federal Reserve Bank of Cleveland, Pittsburgh Branch, director, 1961-66, chairman, 1964-66. *Military service:* U.S. Naval Reserve, 1944-46. *Member:* American Economic Association (member of board of editors, 1952-55; member of executive committee, 1957-60; chairman of committee on graduate study, 1952-53), American Academy of Arts and Sciences (fellow), American Finance Association, Phi Kappa Phi, Phi Beta Kappa. *Awards, honors:* LL.D., Grinnell College, 1956, Carnegie-Mellon University, 1967.

WRITINGS: (Co-author) *Economic Analysis and Public Policy,* Prentice-Hall, 1943, 3rd edition (with M. L. Joseph and N. C. Seeber), 1971; *Federal Reserve Policy Making,* Knopf, 1950; *Economics: Introduction to Analysis and Policy,* Prentice-Hall, 1954, 10th edition, 1980; *Inflation: A Study in Economics, Ethics, and Politics,* Brown University Press, 1958; (editor with M. L. Anshen) *Management and Corporations: 1985,* McGraw, 1961; (co-author) *Economic Education in the Schools,* Committee for Economic Development, 1962; (editor) *The State of Monetary Economics,* National Bureau of Economics, 1963; (with K. Lumsden and R. Attiyeh) *Microeconomics,* Prentice-Hall, 1966; (with Lumsden and Attiyeh) *Macroeconomics,* Prentice-Hall, 1967; *Making Monetary and Fiscal Policy,* Brookings Institution, 1970; *The New Inflation,* Brown University Press, 1972; (with Lumsden and Attiyeh) *Basic Economics: Theory and Cases,* Prentice-Hall, 1972; (co-author) *Improving the Monetary Aggregates,* Federal Reserve Board, 1978.

BACKMAN, Jules 1910-

PERSONAL: Born May 3, 1910, in New York, N.Y.; son of Nathan and Gertrude (Schall) Backman; married Grace Straim, 1935; children: Susan P. Frank, John Randolph. *Education:* New York University, B.C.S. (cum laude), 1931, A.M., 1932, M.B.A., 1933, D.C.S., 1935. *Home:* 59 Crane Rd., Scarsdale, N.Y. 10583. *Office:* Department of Economics, New York University, Washington Sq., New York, N.Y. 10003.

CAREER: New York University, instructor, assistant professor, and associate professor, 1938-50, professor, 1950-60, research professor of economics, 1960-75, professor emeritus, 1975—. Editorial writer, *New York Times,* 1943-48; consultant, Office of Price Administration, Washington, D.C., 1943; consultant to various companies and industries, including steel, railroads, surety, banks and retailing, 1943—; member of board of directors, Scarsdale National Bank, Scarsdale, N.Y., 1959—. New York University Alumni Federation, member of board, 1939—, president, 1954-56; member of board, Jewish Community Center, White Plains, N.Y., 1951—; Hebrew Union College, member of board, 1963—, vice-treasurer, beginning 1965, chairman of board, 1976—; member of New York University Senate, 1962-65. Frequent participant in university conferences on labor problems, growth, and pricing.

MEMBER: Society of Business Advisory Professions (president, 1954; chairman, 1955), American Economic Association, American Statistical Association (honorary fellow), Industrial Labor Relations Association, Beta Gamma Sigma, Alpha Phi Sigma, Lambda Gamma Phi, Omega Sigma Omega, Town Club (Scarsdale, N.Y.; member of board, 1958-64), New York University Club (chairman of board, 1961-65; lifetime honorary chairman, 1972—), Metropolis Country Club. *Awards, honors:* Alumni Meritorious Service Award, 1943, Madden Award, 1960, School of Business Administration Man of the Year Award, 1961, presidential citation, 1964, Great Teacher Award, 1976, all from New York University; American Judaism Award from Reform Jewish Appeal, 1970; Founder's Medal from Hebrew Union College, 1979.

WRITINGS: *Government Price Fixing,* Pitman, 1938; *Price Flexibility and Inflexibility,* New York University Law Quarterly, 1940; *Wartime Price Control,* New York University Law Quarterly, 1940; (with Emanuel Stein) *War Eco-*

nomics, Rinehart, 1942; (with M. R. Gainsbrugh) *Economics of Cotton Textile Industry,* National Industrial Conference Board, 1946; *Surety Rate Making,* Surety Association of America, 1949; *The Economics of Armament Inflation,* Rinehart, 1951; *War and Defense Economics,* Rinehart, 1952; *Economic Data Utilized in Wage Arbitration,* University of Pennsylvania Press, 1952; *Wage Determination,* Van Nostrand, 1959; *Pricing: Policies and Practices,* National Industrial Conference Board, 1961; *The Economics of the Electrical Machinery Industry,* New York University Press, 1962; *Competition in the Chemical Industry,* Manufacturing Chemists Association, 1964; *Foreign Competition in Chemicals and Allied Products,* Manufacturing Chemists Association, 1965; *The Forces Influencing the American Economy,* New York University Press, 1965; *Advertising and Competition,* New York University Press, 1967; *Economics of the Chemical Industry,* Manufacturing Chemists Association, 1970.

Editor: (With others) *War and Defense Economics,* Rinehart, 1952; *Price Practices and Price Policies,* Ronald, 1952; *Business Problems of the Seventies,* New York University Press, 1973; *Multinational Corporations, Trade and the Dollar,* New York University Press, 1974; *Labor, Technology, and Productivity,* New York University Press, 1974; *Social Responsibility and Accountability,* New York University Press, 1975; *Business and the American Economy, 1776-2001,* New York University Press, 1976; *Changing Marketing Strategies in a New Economy,* Bobbs-Merrill, 1977; *Economic Growth or Stagnation?,* Bobbs-Merrill, 1978; *Business Problems of the Eighties,* Bobbs-Merrill, 1980; *Regulation or Deregulation,* Bobbs-Merrill, 1980. Has written about seventy-five pamphlets and more than fifty articles for academic journals. Economics editor, *Trust and Estates,* 1941-46.

SIDELIGHTS: A widely-known public speaker, Jules Backman also has made more than fifty appearances on radio and television. Three of his books have had foreign language editions: *Competition in the Chemical Industry* has been published in Japanese; *Advertising and Competition* has been published in Japanese and German; *Multinational Corporations, Trade and the Dollar* has been published in Spanish. *Avocational interests:* Golf, opera.

*   *   *

BAHM, Archie J(ohn) 1907-

PERSONAL: Surname rhymes with *game;* born August 21, 1907, in Imlay City, Mich.; son of John Samuel (a builder) and Lena (Kohn) Bahm; married Luna Parks Bachelor (an instructor in mathematics), February 13, 1930; children: Raymond John, Elaine Lucia (Mrs. Charles Reed Cundiff). *Education:* Attended Taylor University, 1925-26; Albion College, A.B., 1929; University of Michigan, M.A., 1930, Ph.D., 1933. *Politics:* Democrat. *Religion:* Humanist. *Home:* 1915 Las Lomas Rd. N.E., Albuquerque, N.M. 87106.

CAREER: Royal Oak Daily Tribune, Royal Oak, Mich., staff reporter, summers, 1927 and 1928; Texas Technological College (now Texas Tech University), Lubbock, instructor, 1934-37, assistant professor, 1937-41, associate professor of philosophy and sociology, 1941-46; University of Denver, Denver, Colo., associate professor of philosophy, 1946-48; University of New Mexico, Albuquerque, professor of philosophy, 1948-73, professor emeritus, 1973—, acting chairman of department, 1954-55, 1964-65. Visiting lecturer in philosophy, University of Rangoon, 1955-56, and University of Rhode Island, 1964.

MEMBER: International Metaphysical Society, American Philosophical Association, Metaphysical Society of America, Indian Congress of Philosophy (life member), Southwestern Philosophical Society (organizer, 1935; vice-president, 1946-1947; president, 1948), Mountain-Plains Philosophical Conference (organizer, 1947; chairman, 1953-54; member of executive committee, 1960-61), New Mexico Philosophical Society (organizer, 1949; president, 1949-50; secretary-treasurer for three terms), Phi Beta Kappa, Phi Kappa Phi, Phi Sigma Tau. Member of Tenth, Eleventh, Thirteenth, Fourteenth, Fifteenth, and Sixteenth International Congresses of Philosophy. *Awards, honors:* Fulbright research scholar at University of Rangoon, 1955-56, and at Benares Hindu University, 1962-63; Humanist of the Year award, American Humanist Association (Albuquerque chapter), 1963.

WRITINGS: (Contributor) Elmer Pendell, editor, *Society under Analysis,* Catell Press, 1942; *Philosophy: An Introduction,* Wiley, 1953; (editor) Lao Tzu, *Tao Teh King,* Ungar, 1958; *Philosophy of the Buddha,* Rider & Co., 1958, Harper, 1959; *What Makes Acts Right?,* Christopher, 1958; *Logic for Beginners,* Student Outlines, 1960; *Types of Intuition* (monograph), University of New Mexico Press, 1961; *Yoga: Union with the Ultimate* (new version of the ancient sutras of Patanjali), Ungar, 1961; *The World's Living Religions,* Dell, 1964; *Yoga for Business Executives and Professional People,* Citadel, 1965, published as *Executive Yoga,* Paperback Library, 1970 (published in England as *Yoga for Business Executives,* Stanley Paul, 1967); *The Heart of Confucius: Interpretations of "Genuine Living" and "Great Wisdom,"* Walker & Co., 1969 (published in Japan as *The Heart of Confucius,* Weatherhill, 1969); *Bhagavad Gita: The Wisdom of Krishna,* Somaiya Publications Pvt. Ltd. (Bombay), 1970; *Polarity, Dialectic, and Organicity,* C. C Thomas, 1970; *Ethics as a Behavioral Science,* C. C Thomas, 1974; *Metaphysics: An Introduction,* Harper, 1974; *Comparative Philosophy,* World Books, 1977; *The Specialist,* World Books, 1977; (editor) *Interdependence,* World Books, 1977; *The Philosopher's World Model,* Greenwood Press, 1979; *Why Be Moral?: An Introduction to Ethics,* Munshiram Manoharlal, 1980; *Axiology: The Science of Values,* World Books, 1980; *Ethics: The Science of Oughtness,* World Books, 1980.

Editor and publisher of biennial *Director of American Philosophers,* 1962—. Contributor to *Dictionary of Philosophy,* Philosophical Library, 1942. Contributor of numerous articles and reviews to *Scientific Monthly, Personalist, Journal of Philosophy, International Philosophical Quarterly, Journal of Aesthetics and Art Criticism, Darshana International, Democracy and World Peace, Review of Metaphysics, Philosophy Today,* and other philosophy journals and periodicals. Contributing editor, *Philosophic Abstracts,* 1940-50; associate editor, *Humanist,* 1950-53; editor, *Oriental Philosophy Newsletter,* 1950-51; news editor, *Philosophy East and West,* 1951-62; member of advisory board, *Indian Journal of Philosophic Studies,* 1963-64; associate editor, *Journal of Thought,* 1967-79.

SIDELIGHTS: Archie Bahm told *CA:* "Mankind's doomsday can be postponed if we reduce population, eliminate waste of resources and pollution, overcome obsolete religious fanaticism, and achieve a minimal world government. Growing demoralization may be reversed and loss of direction revitalized by adopting a needed world philosophy informed by a quantum-leap system-gestalt generated by understanding the intricately complicated interdependencies at all levels of existence made obvious by our contemporary crises."

BIOGRAPHICAL/CRITICAL SOURCES: Free Mind, November, 1960.

* * *

BAILEY, Anthony 1933-

PERSONAL: Born January 5, 1933, in England. *Education:* Merton College, Oxford, B.A., 1955, M.A., 1959. *Home:* 16 School St., Stonington, Conn. 06378; and 63 Royal Hill, London S.E. 10, England.

CAREER: New Yorker, New York, N.Y., staff writer, 1956—. *Military service:* British Army, Royal Sussex Regiment, 1950-52; commissioned lieutenant.

WRITINGS: Making Progress, Dial, 1959; *The Mother Tongue,* Macmillan, 1961; *The Inside Passage,* Macmillan, 1965; *Through the Great City,* Macmillan, 1967; *The Thousand Dollar Yacht,* Macmillan, 1968; *The Light in Holland,* Knopf, 1970; *In the Village,* Knopf, 1971; *A Concise History of the Low Countries,* American Heritage, 1972; *Rembrandt's House,* Houghton, 1978; *Acts of Union: Reports on Ireland, 1973-1979,* Random House, 1980; *America, Lost and Found,* Random House, 1981.

SIDELIGHTS: The New York Times Book Review comments: "The threat to American civilization posed by megalopolis ... has been exposed in learned tomes and many frantic magazine articles. [*Through the Great City,*] Anthony Bailey's leisurely ... journey, ... covers much of the same ground, literally and figuratively, but his sane and relaxed approach to the problem is free from professional cant and sensationalism; he views with alarm but not despair."

The Thousand Dollar Yacht is another book that covers familiar ground. According to a reviewer for *The New Yorker,* "Dozens of books describing such matters [as amateur sailing adventures] appear every year.... Mr. Bailey's is different solely because he is a gifted writer who, without dramatics or any heightening of experience, can make everything around him come alive."

This ability to make everything come alive is reflected in Bailey's books on the Netherlands, particularly so in *Rembrandt's House,* which is reconstructed in the minds of Bailey's readers from an inventory of Rembrandt's possessions made by the Insolvency Office of Amsterdam when the artist declared bankruptcy in 1657. Anatole Broyard calls the book "an affectionate meditation on the mood, the texture, and the circumstances of the painter's life and times. Mr. Bailey is as much in love with things as Rembrandt was, and he skillfully mingles his own impressions of Amsterdam today with his subject's. He interprets the town as he does the paintings and drawings, so that we see their reciprocal relationship.... Mr. Bailey moves as Rembrandt did himself, from the tangible to the intangible, the material to the spiritual, the personal to the social. It is an appropriate way to look at an artist who, as much as any in history, immortalized his time and place."

BIOGRAPHICAL/CRITICAL SOURCES: Christian Science Monitor, August 10, 1967; *Newsweek,* August 14, 1967; *New York Times Book Review,* October 15, 1967; *New Yorker,* December 9, 1967, March 30, 1968; *Best Sellers,* September 1, 1970; *New York Times,* May 27, 1978; *Washington Post Book World,* August 3, 1980.

* * *

BAILEY, D(avid) R(oy) Shackleton 1917-

PERSONAL: Surname sometimes listed as Shackleton Bailey; born December 10, 1917, in Lancaster, England; son of J. H. Shackleton (a clergyman and headmaster) and Rosa-

mund Maud (Giles) Bailey; married Hilary Ann Bardwell, 1967 (marriage dissolved, 1974). *Education:* Attended Royal Grammar School, Lancaster, England; Gonville and Caius College, Cambridge, B.A., 1939, M.A., 1943, Litt.D,, 1957. *Office:* Department of Classics, Harvard University, Cambridge, Mass. 02138.

CAREER: Cambridge University, Cambridge, England, university lecturer in Tibetian, 1948-68, Gonville and Caius College, fellow, 1944-55, and 1964-68, senior bursar, 1965-68, Jesus College, fellow and director of studies in classics, 1955-64; University of Michigan, Ann Arbor, professor of Latin, 1968-74; Harvard University, Cambridge, Mass., professor of Greek and Latin, 1975—. Visiting lecturer, Harvard University, 1963; Andrew V. V. Raymond Visiting Professor, State University of New York at Buffalo, 1973-74. *Member:* British Academy (fellow), American Philosophical Association.

WRITINGS: (Editor) *The Satapancasatka of Matrceta,* Cambridge University Press, 1951; *Propertiana,* Cambridge University Press, 1956; *Towards a Text of Cicero ad Atticum,* Cambridge University Press, 1960; (editor) Cicero, *Epistulae ad Atticum,* Volumes IX-XVI, Oxford University Press, 1961; (editor) Cicero, *Letters to Atticus,* seven volumes, Cambridge University Press, 1965-70; *Cicero,* Scribner, 1971; *Two Studies in Roman Nomenclature,* Scholars' Press, 1976; (editor) Cicero, *Epistulae Ad Familiares,* two volumes, Cambridge University Press, 1977, published as *Cicero: Letters to His Friends,* Penguin, 1978. Contributor of articles to *Classical Quarterly, Journal Asiatique,* and other scholarly journals.

AVOCATIONAL INTERESTS: Cats and Wagner.

* * *

BAIRD, J(oseph) Arthur 1922-

PERSONAL: Born June 17, 1922, in Boise, Idaho; son of Jesse H. (a clergyman) and Susanna (Bragstad) Baird; married Mary Harriet Chapman, June 10, 1947; children: Andrew Arthur, Paul Chapman. *Education:* Occidental College, B.A., 1943; San Francisco Theological Seminary, B.D., 1949; University of Edinburgh, Ph.D., 1953; also studied at University of Basel and University of Marburg. *Politics:* Republican. *Religion:* Protestant. *Home:* 1435 Gasche St., Wooster, Ohio 44691. *Office:* College of Wooster, Wooster, Ohio 44691.

CAREER: College of Wooster, Wooster, Ohio, 1954—, currently Synod Professor of Religion. Chairman and member of board of advisors, Lilly Endowment Study on Pre-Seminary Education. *Military service:* U.S. Naval Reserve, 1944-46; served on landing craft; became lieutenant junior grade. *Member:* American Academy of Religion, Society of Biblical Literature, Studiorum Novi Testamenti Societas.

WRITINGS: The Justice of God in the Teaching of Jesus, Westminster, 1963; *Audience Criticism and the Historical Jesus,* Westminster, 1969; *A Critical Concordance of the Synoptic Gospels,* Biblical Research Associates, 1971; (editor with David Noel Freedman) A. Q. Morton and Sidney Michaelson, *A Critical Concordance to the Letter of Paul to the Romans,* Biblical Research Associates, 1977; (editor with Freedman) Francis Andersen and A. Dean Forbes, *A Linguistic Concordance of Jeremiah: Hebrew Vocabulary and Idiom,* Biblical Research Associates, 1978; (editor with Freedman) Joseph B. Tyson and Thomas R. W. Longstaff, *Synoptic Abstract,* Biblical Research Associates, 1978; (editor with Freedman) Yehuda T. Radday and G. M. Leb, *An Analytical, Linguistic, Key-Word-in-Context Concordance to Esther, Ruth, Canticles, Ecclesiastes and Lamentations,* Biblical Research Associates, 1978. General editor, "The Computer Bible" series, Biblical Research Associates. Contributor of articles to professional journals.

WORK IN PROGRESS: The Power of the Kingdom; The Uniqueness of the Gospels; The Holy Word; The New Wine of the Gospels; proto-source analysis and computer-assisted New Testament studies.

AVOCATIONAL INTERESTS: Travel, sailing, golf.

BIOGRAPHICAL/CRITICAL SOURCES: Christian Century, April 30, 1969.

*   *   *

BAKER, Carlos (Heard) 1909-

PERSONAL: Born May 5, 1909, in Biddeford, Me.; son of Arthur E. and Edna (Heard) Baker; married Dorothy T. Scott, August 22, 1932; children: Diane (Mrs. Lansing Wagner), Elizabeth (Mrs. Paul Carter), Brian Arthur. *Education:* Dartmouth College, A.B., 1932; Harvard University, A.M., 1933; Princeton University, Ph.D., 1940. *Politics:* Democrat. *Religion:* Episcopalian. *Home:* 34 Allison Rd., Princeton, N.J. 08540.

CAREER: Princeton University, Princeton, N.J., instructor, 1938-42, assistant professor, 1942-46, associate professor, 1946-51, professor of English, 1951-53, Woodrow Wilson Professor of Literature, 1953-77, professor emeritus, 1977—, chairman of department of English, 1952-58. Fulbright Lecturer in American Literature at Oxford University, Oxford, England, 1957-58, and at Centre Universitaire Mediterraneen, Nice, France, 1958. *Member:* Modern Language Association of America, National Council of Teachers of English, College English Association, American Association of University Professors, Phi Beta Kappa, Century Association, Theta Delta Chi. *Awards, honors:* Litt.D., Dartmouth College, 1957; Guggenheim fellowship, 1965, 1967; D.Hum., University of Maine, 1974; L.H.D., Monmouth College, 1977.

WRITINGS: Shadows in Stone (poetry), Printer's Devil Press (Hanover, N.H.), 1930; *Shelley's Major Poetry: The Fabric of Vision,* Princeton University Press, 1948; *Hemingway: The Writer as Artist,* Princeton University Press, 1952, 4th edition, 1972; *A Friend in Power* (novel), Scribner, 1958; *The Land of Rumbelow* (novel), Scribner, 1963; *A Year and a Day* (poetry), Vanderbilt University Press, 1963; *Ernest Hemingway: A Life Story,* Scribner, 1969; *The Gay Head Conspiracy* (novel), Scribner, 1973; *The Talisman and Other Stories* (short stories), Scribner, 1976.

Editor: (With Willard Thorp and Merle Curti) *American Issues,* Lippincott, 1941; *The American Looks at the World,* Harcourt, 1944; William Wordsworth, *"The Prelude," with a Selection from the Shorter Poems and Sonnets and the 1800 Preface to "Lyrical Ballads,"* Rinehart, 1948; Percy Bysshe Shelley, *Selected Poetry and Prose,* Modern Library, 1951; (with others) *The Major English Romantic Poets: A Symposium in Reappraisal,* Southern Illinois University Press, 1957; *Hemingway and His Critics: An International Anthology,* Hill & Wang, 1961; *Ernest Hemingway: Critiques of Four Major Novels,* Scribner, 1962; John Keats, *Poems and Selected Letters,* Scribner, 1962; Samuel Taylor Coleridge, *Poetry and Prose,* Bantam, 1965; (with others) Wilson Follett, *Modern American Usage,* Hill & Wang, 1966; *Ernest Hemingway: Selected Letters,* Scribner, 1981. Also editor of *Joseph Andrews,* by Henry Fielding, 1959, *Green Mansions,* by William Henry Hudson, 1961, and *The Black Swan,* by Thomas Mann, 1980.

SIDELIGHTS: Carlos Baker took seven years to write his biography *Ernest Hemingway: A Life Story.* He corresponded with hundreds of people who had known Hemingway, and the writer's widow, Mary Hemingway, gave him access to her husband's letters, papers, and unpublished manuscripts. In the resulting biography, Baker does not judge Hemingway's writing; he had already written a critical study, *Hemingway: The Writer as Artist.* Nor does he try to psychoanalyze Hemingway; rather, as Baker explains in the book's preface, he wanted to set the record straight about the facts of Hemingway's life and exploits.

Nation critic James F. Light admits to initial doubts about the validity of a biography authorized by Hemingway's widow. When the book was published, his doubts were dispelled. He calls the book an "admirable study [which] shows no evidence that pressure of any kind has been put upon [the author] to modify his findings or his attitudes about Hemingway. The result is that in *Ernest Hemingway: A Life Story,* Baker portrays the legendary Hemingway, but he also depicts the ordinary man, and if the mythological Hemingway is a giant, the ordinary man, as Baker demonstrates, was at times very human and very, very small. In a study conscientiously avoiding the presentation of anything resembling a 'thesis,' this contrast between the legend and the man becomes especially memorable."

Writing in the *South Atlantic Quarterly,* Lewis Leavy comments: "[Baker] has told [the] story blandly, content to recount what happened and when, not often indulging himself or his reader by explaining why. He remains on the outside of his subject with straightforward statements which can be, and are, documented.... Mr. Baker has retold, sometimes revised, many of the familiar anecdotes; he has omitted some, for reasons which it must be presumed are good; and he has added anecdotes which I, for one, had not heard before. In limiting himself to a style so purposefully declarative, with a minimum of auctorial asides, Mr. Baker takes large risks. His sentences may sometimes seem staccato, so noncommittal and so repetitive in form ... that they lull toward inattention. It can be thought of as a kind of style that Hemingway might admire; but the matter which Mr. Baker presents enlivens it, and as he comes to his final chapters it rises to heights intense and gripping. I can think of no better way of writing about Hemingway as a man.... Mr. Baker accomplishes his task so well that his book will stand as an exemplar beside which many another contemporary biography will seem journeywork: it presents a compelling full-length portrait."

Irving Howe praises Baker's ability as a writer and a biographer. He writes in *Harper's*: "Mr. Baker commands genuine talents. His prose, if rarely glowing, is never clotted. He is seldom the victim of political or psychological preconceptions—indeed, as if to drive virtue into vice, he seems rather innocent of ideas altogether. He doesn't gossip about Hemingway's habits in bed or with booze, nor does he succumb to the Hemingway who devoted a good portion of his later life to self-burlesque. Mr. Baker writes out of entirely decent motives, and these days, when writers can win fame and money by declaring themselves to be morally worse than they are, decency isn't to be sneered at. Mr. Baker also displays certain skills as a biographer. He likes 'action' in the old-fashioned, Western-movie sense. He can turn out a lively set piece, as in his vivid pages about the World War II years.... Through accumulation and shading of detail, Mr. Baker gives us a colorful yet finally commonplace man—at once soft-hearted and tough, finely sensitive and a hopeless braggart, superbly generous and a wretched bully—who had more than his share of adventure, troubles, accidents, and wives.''

Writing in *Saturday Review*, Granville Hicks praises Baker's scholarship, calling the biography ''a superb job of research. He has, moreover, organized his book in such a way that it can be enjoyed by the general reader and at the same time used by scholars: the notes, a hundred pages of them, are in the back of the book, out of the way, and yet so arranged that one can readily discover the source of any statement. The writing is sound and unpretentious. . . . It is good that the writing of the biography was assigned to someone as level-headed and objective as Baker. He fully recognizes Hemingway's faults, but he doesn't get all worked up about them. He is a firm admirer of almost all that Hemingway wrote, but his admiration does not obscure his vision of the man. If I have any criticism of Baker, it is the no doubt unreasonable one that he is too detached. In life Hemingway rarely left people cold; they were either for him or against him, and often first one and then the other. If he had been less dispassionate, Baker might have given his readers, especially his young readers, a stronger sense of the passions Hemingway aroused in so many of his contemporaries.''

Stronger in his reservation about the biography, Jeffrey Hart of the *National Review* finds fault with Baker's method of presenting ''pictures'' from Hemingway's life. ''Baker clearly made a key decision in writing this book,'' Hart comments. ''He would allow the surfaces to imply the depths. If he could assemble enough 'pictures' the reader would sense the inner truth, the seven-eighths of the iceberg below the surface. And so he is ruthlessly objective. He avoids, for the most part, interpretive comment, and he avoids any overt attempt to express the experience behind the pictures. But above all he does not allow the fiction to comment upon the external reality of the life. I do not mean, of course, that he ought to have undertaken a 'biographical' interpretation of the fiction, much less that he should have read the adventures and feelings of the fictional characters back into the life. And I do not mean that he ought to have included literary criticism, repeating what he had written in another book. But as you read this biography (and for all of its undoubted interest) there is a strange lack of congruence between the outer life and the inner psychological reality.''

The *Village Voice*'s James Toback feels that the biography suffers from lack of any thematic control over the material. ''Baker has amassed a densely detailed chronology that shadows Hemingway on a weekly, often a daily, basis from birth to death, naming what must amount to nearly everyone he ever met, every place he ever went, describing childhood schooling, three wars, four wives, omnipresent feuds, recurring physical damage, close friendships, gallons of wine and whiskey, literary struggles, and a seemingly interminable series of hunting and fishing expeditions,'' Toback writes. ''What Baker has failed to do is throw into relief those episodes of Hemingway's life that particularly reveal his character. . . . In a work so dense with fact, there is a need for some kind of emphasis and perspective. As it stands, Baker's dispassionate study is to biography what the noveau roman is to prose fiction. While presenting all the material, Baker fails to delineate or trace any of the striking patterns in Hemingway's life that emerges from it. . . . Keeping in mind Baker's aim ('to make Hemingway live again') and his approach (to amass 'a thousand pictures . . . a thousand scenes in which he was involved'), I would like to suggest that he could have fared better if he had structured his material, looking to connection, pattern, and motif, instead of solely to chronology. Surely there would have been no need for

invention. The material for the biography of a man who epitomized so much of the 20th-century American experience, who was as complex and, finally, as tragic as any fictional hero in modern literature, is all there, waiting to be not just digested, but transformed.''

The *New York Times*'s Christopher Lehmann-Haupt, who calls the biography ''a life-size replica of Ernest Hemingway,'' expresses frustration with the wealth of details, but suggests that part of the problem is with the subject. ''In plain language,'' Lehmann-Haupt writes: ''Reading Carlos Baker's long-awaited biography is hugely exasperating. But then so, apparently, was Ernest Hemingway. And that's the clue to how the whole thing fits together. Reading *Ernest Hemingway* is like spending his life with him. Out of the incredible rubble of detail comes the excitement and the urge to get on with it of the early days in Paris, the 'hair-on-the-chest' bumptiousness after his early novels had made it, the subtle decline into sentimental buffoonery in the late nineteen-thirties and nineteen-forties, the stark and fearsome and chilling tragedy of the final descent into nada y nada. It must have been like that to be with him. And the frustration of wanting Professor Baker to seize the psychological evidence, to say that Hemingway can be explained this way or that—it must have been like that, too. So Baker is probably right when he says that 'even though certain patterns of attitude and behavior emerge clearly from the mosaic of Hemingway's life, no one of them in itself exclusively dominates his psychological life or fully explains the nature and direction of his career as man and artist.' ''

BIOGRAPHICAL/CRITICAL SOURCES: Time, April 18, 1969; *Saturday Review,* April 19, 1969; *New York Times,* April 21, 1969; *Newsweek,* April 21, 1969; *National Review,* April 22, 1969; *New Republic,* April 26, 1969; *New York Times Book Review,* April 27, 1969; *Harper's,* May, 1969; *Commonweal,* May 9, 1969; *New Leader,* May 26, 1969; *Nation,* May 26, 1969; *Atlantic,* June, 1969; *Best Sellers,* June 1, 1969; *Village Voice,* June 19, 1969; *Virginia Quarterly Review,* summer, 1969; *Books and Bookmen,* September, 1969; *New Yorker,* September 13, 1969; *South Atlantic Quarterly,* autumn, 1969; *Commentary,* November, 1969.

—*Sketch by Linda Metzger*

*   *   *

BAKER, (Mary) Elizabeth (Gillette) 1923-

PERSONAL: Born November 14, 1923, in Rochester, N.Y.; daughter of Charles L. and Ruth (Otis) Gillette; married Morton H. Baker, 1947; children: Margaret, Maria, Stephen. *Education:* University of Rochester, A.B., 1945. *Home:* 284 Heath's Bridge Rd., Concord, Mass. 01742.

CAREER: Writer. Houghton Mifflin Co., Boston, Mass., worked in advertising department, 1945-48. *Awards, honors: Weekly Reader* fellowship to Bread Loaf Writers' Conference, 1959.

WRITINGS—All published by Houghton: *Tammy Camps Out,* 1958; *Treasures of Rattlesnake Hill,* 1959; *Fire in the Wind,* 1961; *Tammy Climbs Pyramid Mountain,* 1962; *Tammy Goes Canoeing,* 1966; *Stronger Than Hate,* 1969; *Tammy Camps in the Rocky Mountains,* 1970; *This Stranger, My Son,* 1971.

*   *   *

BAKER, Samm Sinclair 1909-

PERSONAL: Born July 29, 1909, in Paterson, N.J.; son of Simon (a textile manufacturer) and Sara (Carlin) Baker; married Natalie Bachrach (a teacher and professional artist), June 12, 1937; children: Wendy Baker Cammer, Steven Jeffrey. *Education:* University of Pennsylvania, B.S. in Economics, 1929; special courses at Columbia University, New York University, and New School for Social Research. *Home and office:* 1027 Constable Dr. S., Mamaroneck, N.Y. 10543.

CAREER: Part-time and summer work in textile factories, retail stores, and on newspapers prior to 1930; worked with Rauch Associates, Inc. (advertising agency), New York City; Kiesewetter, Baker, Hagedorn & Smith, Inc., 1937-55, began as copy writer, became president; Donahue and Coe, Inc. (advertising agency), New York City, vice-president and member of executive staff, 1955-63; self-employed writer and personal business consultant, 1963—. Consultant to firms in advertising, promotion, merchandising, marketing. Teacher in advanced retail copy writing, New York University. Gardening writer and lecturer for "Flair," American Broadcasting Co. daily network program. *Member:* Mystery Writers of America, Garden Writers of America, Authors Guild, Authors League of America. *Awards, honors:* Awards from U.S. Coast Guard and U.S. Treasury Department for war-time writing activities.

WRITINGS: One Touch of Blood, Graphic, 1955; *Murder, Very Dry,* Graphic, 1956; (contributor) *The Mystery Writer's Handbook,* Harper, 1956; *Miracle Gardening,* Bantam, 1958; *Casebook of Successful Ideas for Advertising and Selling,* Doubleday, 1959.

How to Be an Optimist, and Make It Pay, Doubleday, 1960; *How to Be a Self-Starter,* Doubleday, 1960; *Miracle Gardening Encyclopedia,* Grosset, 1961; *Your Key to Creative Thinking,* Harper, 1962; *Samm Baker's Clear & Simple Gardening Handbook,* Grosset, 1964; (co-author) *1001 Questions and Answers to Your Skin Problems,* Harper, 1965; *Indoor and Outdoor Grow-It Book for Children,* Random House, 1966; (with Irwin M. Stillman) *The Doctor's Quick Weight Loss Diet,* Prentice-Hall, 1967; *Vigor for Men over 30,* Macmillan, 1967; *The Permissible Lie,* World Publishing, 1968; (with Stillman) *The Doctor's Quick Inches-Off Diet,* Prentice-Hall, 1969; (with wife, Natalie Baker) *Introduction to Art,* Abrams, 1969.

How to Protect Yourself Today, Stein & Day, 1970; *Gardening Do's and Don'ts,* Funk, 1970; (with Stillman) *The Doctor's Quick Teenage Diet,* McKay, 1971; (with Stillman) *The Doctor's Quick Weight Loss Diet Cookbook,* McKay, 1972; (with James W. Smith) *"Doctor, Make Me Beautiful!,"* McKay, 1973; (with Stillman) *Dr. Stillman's 14-Day Shape-Up Program,* Delacorte, 1973; *Conscious Happiness,* Grosset, 1975; (with Mary Susan Miller) *Straight Talk to Parents about School,* Stein & Day, 1976; (with Jane Boutelle) *Lifetime Fitness for Women,* Simon & Schuster, 1978; (with Herman Tarnower) *The Complete Scarsdale Medical Diet,* Rawson, Wade, 1979.

(With Leopold Bellak) *Reading Faces,* Holt, 1980. Contributor of articles to *McCall's, This Week, Reader's Digest, Popular Science, Suburbia Today,* and other popular magazines; author of gardening series for King Features syndicate; columnist and contributor of articles for advertising publications; author of radio and television scripts for "Famous Jury Trials," "Lives of Famous Artists," "Medical Horizons," and other programs.

WORK IN PROGRESS: A book on problem-solving; another diet book; a novel.

SIDELIGHTS: Samm Sinclair Baker told *CA:* "'How can I write a Best-Seller?' That's the question I'm *almost* qualified

to answer when it comes to nonfiction (although nobody has a conclusive answer because that's up to the public). I've been fortunate to have all my books sell well, three of them Best Sellers, two of those No. 1 blockbuster Best Sellers. I've been described in the *New York Times* as 'America's Leading Self-Help Author,' and in the *New York Sunday News Magazine* as the 'King of Self-Help.' I can give you at least a partial answer when it comes to self-help or how-to books.

"I learned the key during my years as a successful advertising writer. When I wrote an ad, I would picture myself not as the salesperson on one side of the retail counter, but as the customer on the other side of the counter. I'd ask myself not what I wanted to tell her, but 'what does she want and need to know?' in order to buy the product. The ads worked to make sales.

"Similarly, when I write a self-help book, my focus is not on what I want to tell the reader, but what does she want and need to know about the subject. If I'm writing a diet book, for example, I direct every word to answer what she needs to know in order to lose pounds and inches. I tell the reader how in the clearest, simplest, most understandable words and instructions. I eliminate anything extraneous. I don't allow myself any flowery self-indulgence.

"Furthermore, I have made sure by intensive research and checking that the diet or whatever method I'm telling about *works.* That's why the books work. It's simple to write a Best Seller . . . isn't it?"

BIOGRAPHICAL/CRITICAL SOURCES: Atlantic, September, 1968; *Christian Science Monitor,* September 5, 1968; *Books,* October, 1969; *Christian Century,* January 1, 1969; *New York Times Book Review,* April 15, 1979.

*   *   *

BAKER, Stephen 1921-

PERSONAL: Born April 17, 1921, in Vienna, Austria; married Oleda Freeman, September, 1967; children: Scott, David, *Education:* New York University, B.A., 1941-44; attended Art Students League, 1944-45. *Home:* 5 Tudor City Place, New York, N.Y. 10017; and Hemlock Farms, Hawley, Pa.

CAREER: Cunningham & Walsh, New York City, vice president and art director, 1949-61; Mogul, Baker, Byrne & Weiss, New York City, president, 1964-67; Griswold-Eshleman Co., New York City, executive vice-president, 1967-71; Stephen Baker Associates, Inc., New York City, president, 1971—. Free-lance writer for Columbia Broadcasting System, 1961-64. *Member:* Art Directors Club of New York. *Awards, honors:* Nominated as "Art Director of the Year," 1961, 1967.

WRITINGS: Advertising Layout and Art Direction, McGraw, 1959; *How to Live with a Neurotic Dog,* Prentice-Hall, 1960; *Visual Persuasion,* McGraw, 1961; *How to Play Golf in the Low 120's,* Prentice-Hall, 1962; *How to Look Like Somebody in Business without Being Anybody,* Prentice-Hall, 1963; *How to Live with a Neurotic Wife,* Doubleday, 1970; *How to Live with a Neurotic Husband,* Doubleday, 1970; *How to be Analyzed by a Neurotic Psychoanalyst,* Doubleday, 1971; *Systematic Approach to Advertising Creativity,* McGraw, 1979; *Games Dogs Play,* McGraw, 1979; *Motorist Guide to New York,* Hammond, 1981. Has written about sixty articles for various publications. Columnist for *Advertising Age,* previously for *Art Direction.*

WORK IN PROGRESS: Pictionary; My First Crossword Puzzle; a novel, *The Half Jew; Who's God.*

SIDELIGHTS: Stephen Baker told *CA* that all of his books have been translated into foreign languages, including his advertising textbooks. *How to Live with a Neurotic Dog* has been translated into eighteen languages. Two books have been made into movies. *Avocational interests:* Painting, interior designing, photography.

* * *

BALASSA, Bela 1928-

PERSONAL: Born April 6, 1928, in Budapest, Hungary; son of George and Charlotte Balassa; married Carol Levy, June 12, 1960; children: Mara, Gabor. *Education:* University of Budapest, Doctor Juris rerumque politicarum, 1951; Yale University, Ph.D., 1959. *Home:* 2134 Wyoming Ave. N.W., Washington, D.C. 20008. *Office:* Department of Political Economy, Johns Hopkins University, Baltimore, Md. 21218.

CAREER: Worked for a construction trust in Sztalinvaros, Hungary, as business manager, 1953-56; Yale University, New Haven, Conn., assistant professor, 1959-62, associate professor of economics, 1962-66; Johns Hopkins University, Baltimore, Md., professor of political economy, 1966—. Visiting assistant professor, University of California, Berkeley, 1961-62; visiting associate professor, Columbia University, 1963-64. Consultant to Organization for Economic Cooperation and Development (Paris), 1963, U.S. Department of State, 1963-65, U.N. Economic Commission for Asia and the Far East, 1964, United Nations Conference on Trade and Development, 1966, United States Treasury Department, 1966-67, and International Bank for Reconstruction and Development (World Bank), 1967—. Economic adviser to various governments of developing countries, including the Dominican Republic, 1967, Argentina, 1969, and Korea, 1969.

MEMBER: American Economic Association, Royal Economic Society, Econometric Society, Association for Comparative Economic Studies. *Awards, honors:* Rockefeller Foundation fellowship, 1957-58; Relm Foundation grant, 1958; Ford Foundation dissertation fellowship, 1958-59; John Addison Porter Prize, Yale University, 1959; Social Science Research Council grant, 1963.

WRITINGS: The Hungarian Experience in Economic Planning, Yale University Press, 1959; *The Theory of Economic Integration,* Irwin, 1961; (editor and contributor) *Changing Patterns in Foreign Trade,* Norton, 1964, 3rd revised and expanded edition, 1978; (editor) *Trade Prospects for Developing Countries,* Irwin, 1964; *Trade Liberalization,* McGraw, 1967; (editor) *Studies in Trade Liberalization: Problems and Prospects for the Industrial Countries,* Johns Hopkins Press, 1967; *The Structure of Protection in Developing Countries,* Johns Hopkins Press, 1971; (editor) *European Economic Integration,* North-Holland Publishing, 1975; (editor) *Economic Progress, Private Values and Public Policy: Essays in Honor of William Fellner,* North-Holland Publishing, 1977; *Policy Reform in Developing Countries,* Pergamon Press, 1977; *Development Strategies in Semi-Industrial Countries,* Johns Hopkins Press, 1981; *The Newly Industrializing Countries in the World Economy,* Pergamon, 1981.

Contributor: J. S. Ewing and F. Meissner, editors, *International Business Management,* Wadsworth, 1964; E. S. Phelps and others, editors, *Problems in Modern Economy,* Norton, 1966; R. E. Caves and H. G. Johnson, edi-

tors, *Readings in International Economics,* Irwin, 1968; W. Krause and F. J. Mathis, editors, *International Economics and Business,* Houghton, 1968; R. A. Mundell and A. K. Swaboda, editors, *Monetary Problems and the International Economy,* University of Chicago Press, 1969; Mundell and others, editors, *Trade, Balance of Payments and Growth,* North-Holland Publishing, 1971; P. Robson, editor, *International Economic Integration,* Penguin, 1971; Luis Eugenio Di Marco, editor, *International Economics and Development: Essays in Honor of Raul Prebisch,* Academic Press, 1972; Swoboda, editor, *Europe and the Evolution of the International Monetary System,* [Geneva], 1973; Morris Bornstein, editor, *Plan and Market: Economic Reform in Eastern Europe,* Yale University Press, 1973; Paul Streeten, editor, *Trade Strategies for Development,* Macmillan, 1973; Willy Sellekaerts, editor, *Economic Development and Planning: Essays in Honor of Jan Tinbergen,* Macmillan, 1974; Nancy D. Ruggles, editor, *The Role of the Computer in Economic and Social Research in Latin America,* National Bureau for Economic Research, 1974; Peter B. Kenen, editor, *International Trade and Finance: Frontiers for Research,* Cambridge University Press, 1975; Fritz Machlup, editor, *Economic Integration: Worldwide, Regional, Sectoral,* Macmillan, 1976; Herbert Glejzer, editor, *Quantitative Studies of International Economic Relations,* North-Holland Publishing, 1976; Bertile Ohlin, Per-Ove Hesselborn, and Per Magnus Wijkman, editors, *The International Allocation of Economic Activity,* Macmillan, 1977; Ryan C. Amacher, Gottfried Haberler, and Thomas D. Willett, editors, *Challenges to a Liberal International Economic Order,* American Enterprise Institute for Public Policy Research, 1979; Samuel Katz, editor, *U.S.-European Monetary Relations,* American Enterprise Institute for Public Policy Research, 1979; Edmond Malinvaud, editor, *Economic Growth and Resources,* Macmillan, 1979; Herbert Giersch, editor, *On the Economics of Intra-Industry Trade,* Institut fuer Weltwirtschaft, 1979. Contributor to professional journals, including *American Economic Review, Economic Journal,* and *Journal of Political Economy.*

WORK IN PROGRESS: Research on policy responses to external shocks, the structure of comparative advantage, and industrialization in Western Africa.

* * *

BALCH, Glenn 1902-

PERSONAL: Born December 11, 1902, in Venus, Tex.; son of Glenn Olin (a carpenter) and Edith (Garrison) Balch; married Faula Mashburn; married M. Elise Kendall, 1937; children: Betty Lou Balch Weston, Lynne Balch Stilwell, Mary Birch Balch Cummings, Olin Kendall. *Education:* Baylor University, A.B., 1924; Columbia University, graduate study, 1937; also attended North Texas State University and University of Texas. *Home:* 3890 East Victory Rd., Meridian, Idaho 83642.

CAREER: Worked five years as a newspaper reporter, beginning on *Boise Statesman,* Boise, Idaho; free-lance writer, 1931—. Did publicity, promotion, and advertising to keep fiction and magazine projects going. Began to specialize in children's fiction, which resulted in the "Tack Ranch" stories. *Military service:* U.S. Army Air Forces, World War II; served in Alaska and as commanding officer of the Tenth Combat Camera Unit in the China-Burma-India Theater; awarded Air Medal; transferred to U.S. Army after the war, serving until 1958; became colonel. *Awards, honors:* Boys' Book Clubs of America award, 1950, for *Lost Horse;* George

Washington Memorial Awards from Freedoms Foundation of Valley Forge, 1954, 1956, and 1957.

WRITINGS—Juvenile; all published by Crowell, except as indicated: *Riders of the Rio Grande*, 1937; *Tiger Roan*, 1938; *Hide-Rack Kidnapped*, 1939; *Indian Paint*, 1942, reprinted, Apollo, 1970; *Wild Horse*, 1947; *Viking Dog*, 1949; *Christmas Horse*, 1949; *Lost Horse*, 1950; *Indian Fur*, 1951; *Winter Horse*, 1951; *Squaw Boy*, 1952; *The Midnight Colt*, 1952, reprinted, Apollo, 1970; *Indian Saddle-Up*, 1953; *Wild Horse Tamer*, 1955; *Little Hawk and the Free Horses* (Junior Literary Guild selection), 1957; *The Brave Riders*, 1959; *Horse in Danger*, 1960; *Stallion King*, 1960; *The Spotted Horse*, 1961; *The Runaways*, Doubleday, 1962; *The Book of Horses*, Four Winds, 1967; *Horse of Two Colors*, 1969; *Western Horseback Riding*, Wilshire, 1974; *Buck, Wild* (Junior Literary Guild selection), 1976.

Westerns: *Blind Man's Bullets*, Ace Books, 1957; *Grass Greed*, Ace Books, 1959. Contributor to *American Boy, Boys' Life*, and to adult western and outdoor sports magazines.

WORK IN PROGRESS: A book, tentatively entitled *The Red Petticoat*.

SIDELIGHTS: Glenn Balch told *CA* that his current interests—horses, dogs, exploring, hunting, early-day western history, and Indian life—are the ones he has pursued all his life. His first and most cherished possession was a horse; his early dreams were to be a cowboy, a forest ranger, a roamer of the open spaces, mountains, and forests.

*   *   *

BALDWIN, Gordon C. 1908-
(Gordo Baldwin, Lew Gordon)

PERSONAL: Born June 5, 1908, in Portland, Ore.; son of John A. and Pearl E. (Gibbs) Baldwin; married Pauline Fariss (a high school teacher), May 25, 1935; children: Mrs. Patricia Jane Hutchings, Mrs. Marjorie Louise Clarkson. *Education:* University of Arizona, B.A., 1933, M.A., 1934; University of Southern California, Ph.D., 1941. *Politics:* Republican. *Religion:* Baptist. *Home:* 426 Poppy Pl., Mountain View, Calif. 94043. *Agent:* William Reiss, Paul R. Reynolds, Inc., 12 East 41st St., New York, N.Y. 10017.

CAREER: University of Arizona, Tucson, instructor in archaeology, 1934-37; Arizona State Museum, Tucson, assistant curator, 1937-40; National Park Service, Boulder City, Nev., archaeologist, 1940-48; National Park Service, Omaha, Neb., archaeologist, 1948-53; University of Omaha (now University of Nebraska at Omaha), instructor in anthropology, 1953-54; writer, 1954-74. *Member:* Westerners International (member of board of directors, 1973-79; vice-president, 1974-76), Western Writers of America (member of board of directors, 1962-63, 1968-70; president, 1968-69), Society of Southwestern Authors (member of board of directors, 1972-76), Tucson Corral of the Westerners (sheriff, 1973), Palo Alto Host Lions Club (member of board of directors, 1979—).

WRITINGS: Trail North, Arcadia, 1957; *Trouble Range*, Arcadia, 1959; *Sundown Country*, Arcadia, 1959; *Roundup at Wagonmound*, Arcadia, 1960; *Ambush Basin*, Avalon, 1960; *Brand of Yuma*, Avalon, 1960; *Powdersmoke Justice*, Avalon, 1961; *Wyoming Rawhide*, Avalon, 1961; *America's Buried Past*, Putnam, 1962; *The Ancient Ones*, Norton, 1963; *The World of Prehistory*, Putnam, 1963; *Stone Age Peoples Today*, Norton, 1964; *The Riddle of the Past*, Norton, 1965; *The Warrior Apaches*, Dale Stuart King, 1965;

Race against Time, Putnam, 1966; *Strange People and Stranger Customs*, Norton, 1967; *Calendars to the Past*, Norton, 1967; *How the Indians Really Lived*, Putnam, 1967; *Games of the American Indian*, Norton, 1969; *Indians of the Southwest*, Putnam, 1970; *Talking Drums to Written Word*, Norton, 1970; *Schemers, Dreamers, and Medicine Men*, Four Winds Press, 1970; *Pyramids of the New World*, Putnam, 1971; *Inventors and Inventions of the Ancient World*, Four Winds Press, 1973; *The Apache Indians, Raiders of the Southwest*, Four Winds Press, 1978. Contributor of articles on anthropology to professional journals. Editor, *The Roundup*, 1962-66.

WORK IN PROGRESS: Reviewing western fiction and nonfiction for *The Roundup*.

SIDELIGHTS: Gordon C. Baldwin told *CA:* "During my years as an archeologist in the Southwest and in the high plains area east of the Rocky Mountains, I had collected notes and information and photographs on all phases of western history. I had also written about 60 articles on Indians and archeology and history, all of which were published in technical and non-technical journals. With this background I had little difficulty in writing and selling eight western novels.

"However, in 1960 my agent discovered that I had a Ph.D. degree in anthropology and convinced me that we could both make more money writing nonfiction books for young readers, 10-12 and up. He was right. I also found it a more challenging field and hoped I was helping youngsters as well as older readers by giving them accurate facts about Indians and archeology."

Many of Baldwin's books have also been published in England, Norway, Sweden, Germany, France, and Spain. Some have also been produced as Talking Books for the blind.

AVOCATIONAL INTERESTS: Reading mysteries and spy stories; volunteer work in Mountain View library; walking and sightseeing in the Bay area.

BIOGRAPHICAL/CRITICAL SOURCES: Young Readers' Review, October, 1967.

*   *   *

BALDWIN, James (Arthur) 1924-

PERSONAL: Born August 2, 1924, in New York, N.Y.; son of David (a clergyman) and Berdis (Jones) Baldwin. *Education:* Graduate of De Witt Clinton High School, New York, N.Y., 1942. *Agent:* Edward J. Acton, Inc., 17 Grove St. New York, N.Y. 10014.

CAREER: Variously employed as general handyman, dishwasher, waiter, and office boy in New York, N.Y., and in defense work in Belle Meade, N.J.; writer. Member of national advisory board, Congress on Racial Equality. Director of play, "Fortune and Men's Eyes," in Istanbul, Turkey, 1970, and film, "The Inheritance," 1973. *Member:* Authors League, International P.E.N., Dramatists Guild, Actors' Studio, National Committee for a Sane Nuclear Policy. *Awards, honors:* Eugene F. Saxton fellowship, 1945; Rosenwald fellowship, 1948; Guggenheim fellowship, 1954; National Institute of Arts and Letters grant in literature, 1956; *Partisan Review* fellowship, 1956; Ford Foundation grant-in-aid, 1959; National Conference of Christians and Jews, Brotherhood Award, 1962, for *Nobody Knows My Name;* George Polk Award, 1963; Foreign Drama Critics Award, 1964; National Association of Independent Schools Award, 1964, for *The Fire Next Time;* D.Litt., University of British

Columbia, 1964; American Book Award nomination, 1980, for *Just above My Head.*

WRITINGS—Novels: *Go Tell It on the Mountain,* Knopf, 1953; *Giovanni's Room* (also see below), Dial, 1956, reprinted, Transworld, 1977; *Another Country,* Dial, 1962; *Tell Me How Long the Train's Been Gone,* Dial, 1968; *If Beale Street Could Talk,* Dial, 1974; *Little Man, Little Man: A Story of Childhood* (juvenile), M. Joseph, 1976, Dial, 1977; *Just above My Head,* Dial, 1979.

Essays: *Notes of a Native Son,* Beacon Press, 1955; *Nobody Knows My Name: More Notes of a Native Son,* Dial, 1961; *The Fire Next Time,* Dial, 1963; (with others) *Black Anti-Semitism and Jewish Racism,* R. W. Baron, 1969; (with Kenneth Kaunda) *Menschenwuerde und Gerechtigkeit* (essays delivered at the fourth assembly of the World Council of Churches), edited and introduced by Carl Ordnung, Union-Verl, 1969; *No Name in the Streets,* Dial, 1972; *The Devil Finds Work,* 1976.

Plays, except as indicated: *Blues for Mister Charlie* (first produced on Broadway at ANTA Theatre, April 23, 1964), Dial, 1964; *The Amen Corner* (first produced in Washington, D.C. at Howard University, 1955; produced on Broadway at Ethel Barrymore Theatre, April 15, 1965), Dial, 1968; *One Day, When I Was Lost: A Scenario* (film script; based on *The Autobiography of Malcolm X,* by Alex Haley), M. Joseph, 1972, Dial, 1973; "A Deed from the King of Spain," first produced in New York City at American Center for Stanislavski Theatre Art, January 24, 1974. Also author of dramatization, "Giovanni's Room" (based on novel of same title), for Actors' Studio, 1957.

Other works: *Autobiographical Notes,* Knopf, 1953; (author of text) Richard Avedon, *Nothing Personal* (photography portraits), Atheneum, 1964; *Going to Meet the Man* (short stories), Dial, 1965; *This Morning, This Evening, So Soon* (short story), edited by Johannes Schuetze, Diesterweg, 1967; (with Margaret Mead) *A Rap on Race,* Lippincott, 1971; (with Nikki Giovanni) *A Dialogue,* Lippincott, 1973; (with Francoise Giroud) *Cesar: Compressions d'or,* Hachette, 1973.

Work anthologized in *American Negro Short Stories,* edited by John Henrik Clarke, Hill & Wang, 1966. Contributor to numerous magazines in the United States and abroad, including *Harper's, Nation, Esquire, Partisan Review, Mademoiselle,* and *New Yorker.*

SIDELIGHTS: During the 'fifties and 'sixties, James Baldwin was considered the leading literary spokesman on the issue of racial equality. His masterful re-creations of the experience of being black in a predominately white nation "galvanized a generation of black and white Americans," according to Paul Hendrickson, and as Robert F. Sayre notes, earned Baldwin the designation "prophet, a man who has been able to give a public issue all its deeper moral, historical, and personal significance." According to Martin Fagg, Baldwin, "more than any other writer, . . . can make one begin to feel what it is really like to have a black skin in a white man's world; and he is especially expert at evoking, not merely the brutally overt physical confrontations between black and white, but the subtle unease that lurks beneath all traffic between the colours, distorting the best of intentions on both sides."

Baldwin, the son of a minister from New Orleans and the oldest of nine children, was born in the Harlem section of New York City. The people and scenes of this environment frequently occur in Baldwin's work. Mario Puzo notes that the "alienated, bitterly religious father . . . appears often with slight variations in Baldwin's fiction." Puzo also finds that "in the streets of Harlem, in the dark bedrooms, the dangerous hallways, the chanting churches, Baldwin is at his best."

At the age of fourteen, Baldwin became a preacher at Harlem's Fireside Pentacostal Church. Later, as an adult, he came to "revile" the church for, as Keneth Kinnamon explains, "the historical role of Christianity in the enslavement of black people." In an interview with Judy Bachrach, Baldwin describes himself as being a "holy freak" during his association with the church and offers this explanation: "I . . . was too tormented, and I didn't really understand the gospel. I believed, but I didn't know. Now—now maybe I know, but I don't believe." While Baldwin may now have little use for religion, traces of its effects can still be seen in his work. "This religion," writes Theodore Gross, "has been enormously influential on Baldwin's writing, but it is the music of the religion, the drama of the religion, the fire and excitement that have lingered, and not the essence." Hendrickson speculates that Baldwin's "flight to the church was not so much out of salvation as refuge. It lasted," he adds, "three hysteria-tinged years until he found, or re-found, the fire of literature and the power of rage there with his own voice."

While Baldwin may have found the "fire of literature," he also found it artistically stifling to be a black writer in the United States. In 1948, at the age of twenty-four, Baldwin left the United States for France, "hoping through exile in Europe to escape from a suffocating society that not only seemed to lock every black writer into the crude simplicities of propaganda and protest, but was also peculiarly inimical to a homosexual like himself," Pearl K. Bell writes. His ambition, Irving Howe believes, was "to compose novels in which *the* Negro would be dissolved as a social phantom of hatred-and-condescension, and instead a variety of Negroes, in all their particularity and complexity, would be imagined." While in Paris, where he lived for nearly ten years, Baldwin discovered the distance, and what Bachrach terms "the requisite measure of loneliness and solace," to write what most critics consider three of his most important books: two novels, *Go Tell It on the Mountain* and *Giovanni's Room,* and a collection of essays, *Notes of a Native Son.*

These first works contain the basic themes of Baldwin's later writings. *Go Tell It on the Mountain* and *Notes of a Native Son* are about "the burden of a boy's heritage, his terrifying religion, his ever-expanding, struggling family, and his bleak environment," according to Gross. In addition, as Michel Fabre states, *Go Tell It on the Mountain* "explores all aspects of religion, sexuality, and interracial relations." *Giovanni's Room* concerns a young American who, while living in France, discovers his homosexuality and searches for sexual self-acceptance.

Largely autobiographical, these books center on what Gross defines as "racial distinctions and inequalities, sexual awareness, and the question of national, American identity." The power and eloquence with which Baldwin rendered these themes won him national prominence and the roles of spokesman and prophet. "Many of Baldwin's best insights illuminate our national psychology," writes Robert Emmett Long, "and he is able to do this because his anger is held in poise by his desire to see clearly and to understand justly." Long calls *Notes of a Native Son* and a later essay, *Nobody Knows My Name,* "works of rare distinction in contemporary American writing, expressing a passionate outrage at the social injustice, racial bigotry and ignorance that destroy both the oppressed and the oppressor.'' Although Baldwin was not the only author to deal with these issues, his work was distinguished by ''clarity, subtlety, and vividness,'' Norman Podhoretz comments. More importantly, Baldwin rendered a uniquely ''complex conception of the Negro as a man who is simultaneously like unto all other men and yet profoundly, perhaps irrevocably, different.''

Permeating Baldwin's outrage at racial and sexual injustice is the ''quest for love,'' both on a ''personal level'' and as ''an agent of racial reconciliation and national survival,'' states Kinnamon. This ''search for Love,'' he notes, also involves ''struggle and pain.'' Before this love can be attained one must first face reality and accept the true nature of oneself as well as one's society. Only then, Baldwin proposed in his earlier writings, can man, as well as mankind, overcome hate, bigotry, and fear. ''Baldwin's central theme is the need to accept reality as a necessary foundation for individual identity and thus a logical prerequisite for the kind of saving love in which he places his whole faith,'' C.W.E. Bigsby explains. ''For some this reality is one's racial or sexual nature, for others it is the ineluctable fact of death. . . . Baldwin sees this simple progression as an urgent formula not only for the redemption of individual men but for the survival of mankind.''

In his later work, however, Baldwin doubts mankind's ability to save itself through love. He blames this failure on ''American coldness and callousness that set-up artificial barriers between human beings,'' writes Long. Furthermore, he rejects what George E. Kent terms ''the Western concept of reality, . . . which ignores the uniqueness of the individual and sees reality in terms of its simplifications and categorizations.'' Instead, his work concentrates on acceptance and love between individuals, and he condemns any social or cultural factors that interfere with this process.

The importance of the individual and the negation of social factors that inhibit his development is illustrated in *Another Country* wherein, as Gross describes, ''two people, [a] black [woman] and [a] white [man], have thrown off family and religion and race and country, and alienated from all the institutions surrounding them, depending exclusively on themselves, they seek the reality of each other.'' According to Podhoretz, through the ''interracial and intersexual relations'' evident in *Another Country* and his other novels, ''Baldwin's intention is to deny any moral significance whatever to the categories white and Negro, heterosexual and homosexual.'' Podhoretz continues: ''He is saying that the terms white and Negro refer to two different conditions under which individuals live, but they are still individuals and their lives are still governed by the fundamental laws of being. And he is saying, similarly, that the terms homosexuality and heterosexuality refer to two different conditions under which individuals pursue love, but they are still individuals and their pursuit of love is still governed by the same fundamental laws of being. Putting the two propositions together, he is saying, finally, that the only significant realities are individuals and love, and that anything which is permitted to interfere with the free operation of this fact is evil and should be done away with.''

In general, Baldwin's essays have received a more favorable critical reception than have his novels. J. Mitchell Morse notes that ''Baldwin is one of a number of writers . . . who write excellent expository prose but fall to pieces when they write fiction.'' While reviewers praise Baldwin the essayist for his ''force,'' ''style,'' and ''eloquence,'' they criticize Baldwin the novelist for dealing, as Charles Thomas Samu-

els explains, ''not in experience but in topics, not with characters but with a faceless all-purpose victim.'' Howe credits Baldwin with being ''one of the two or three greatest essayists this country has ever produced,'' and other critics have similar praise. Long elaborates: ''In [his] early essays, Baldwin's intelligence functions brilliantly, coolly, preserving always a sense of proportion. . . . There is first the personal anguish of the writer, 'a confessional' role that is subordinated to the larger issue of all of black America, and its demand for human dignity. Then there is the question of America itself, and its search for identity in its past and present.''

Puzo also comments on Baldwin's status as an essayist and illuminates his novels' shortcomings: ''His essays are as well written as any in our language; in them his thought and its utterance are nothing less than majestical. He has, also, the virtues of passion, serious intelligence and compassionate understanding of his fellow man. Yet it would seem that such gifts . . . are not enough to insure the writing of good fiction. Novelists are born sinners and their salvation does not come so easily, and certainly the last role the artist should play is that of the prosecutor, the creator of a propaganda novel. A propaganda novel may be socially valuable, . . . but it is not art.'' Bell recalls that ''early in his career,'' Baldwin had argued that ''writers with a Cause such as Harriet Beecher Stowe and Richard Wright, . . . are not novelists but pamphleteers, and though their moral sincerity is unexceptionable, they reduce their characters to pawns on a chessboard of social injustice.'' Many critics, however, accuse Baldwin of falling into the same trap by creating what Puzo describes as ''cardboard characters.'' John W. Aldridge notes that ''however sensitive Baldwin may be to the unique quality of the individual human being, he has been generally unsuccessful in creating characters who exist independently of their categorization.''

Baldwin's lapse as a novelist is frequently attributed to his role as spokesman and his celebrity status. Deeply committed, first to the civil rights movement of the 'fifties and 'sixties and, later, to the black power movement of the 'seventies, Baldwin, in the words of Harvey Breit, ''because of his brilliance, his eloquence, his honesty, his courage, his superb intelligence, has become a spokesman, in a sense a captive spokesman, for his people and, as well, a kind of minister without portfolio for both black and white on black-and-white relations.'' As a result, Samuels claims, ''he has fallen back on the vacuities of speechifying'' and his ''fame has increased in proportion to the decline of his art.'' Aldridge offers this assessment of Baldwin's predicament: ''His fame now secure, we have accorded him the highest honor we can bestow upon a public intellectual: We have disarmed him with celebrity, fallen in love with his eccentricities, and institutionalized his outrage into prime-time entertainment.'' In a review of *Tell Me How Long the Train's Been Gone*, Howe finds that Baldwin ''does not know who he is, as writer, celebrity, or black man; so that he now suffers from the most disastrous of psychic conditions—a separation between his feelings and his voice.'' In effect, ''Baldwin is now a writer systematically deceiving himself through rhetorical inflation and hysteria,'' Howe continues, ''whipping himself into postures of militancy and declarations of racial metaphysics which—for him, in *this* book—seem utterly inauthentic.''

However, John Leonard believes that Baldwin ''recovers'' his ''lyric impulse'' in *Just above My Head,* a novel about a gospel singer's ''doomed tryst with pop stardom.'' Leonard claims that Baldwin ''is recapitulating *Go Tell It on the Mountain* and *Giovanni's Room* and those restless, anxious essays.'' He describes the novel as being ''a Sunday in church, and everybody in it sings as if we were running out of Sundays."

Overall, David Littlejohn suggests that "each novel, for Baldwin, has been a stage; a stage to be lived through, transformed into words, then exorcised and transcended. The next novel," he adds, "begins a new stage, and the process goes on." In his interview with Bachrach, Baldwin supports this theory: "The books you've written are the ones that are the worst. It's such a peculiar journey. Once a book is over, you look at it—but one is on the edge of it, everyone is on the edge."

During his career, Baldwin has been labeled "prophet" and "visionary" as well as "propagandist" and "militant." Yet reviewers note that he holds a distinctive position in American literature. "In examining his own emotions and reactions, it is as if he is examining those of the nation," writes Jerry H. Bryant. "This has been his importance to us all. In his excursions into his psyche, delineating with Dostoevskian shamelessness the details of his hurting bruises and wounds, he has often spoken for all of us, has offered himself as a metaphor for our self-inflicted national injury." Sayre echoes this summation of Baldwin's stature when he states: "Certainly one mark of his achievement, whether as novelist, essayist, or propagandist, is that whatever deeper comprehension of the race issue Americans now possess has been in some way shaped by him. And this is to have shaped their comprehension of themselves as well."

BIOGRAPHICAL/CRITICAL SOURCES—Periodicals: *Commonweal*, May 22, 1953, December 8, 1961, October 26, 1962, December 7, 1962; *Commentary*, November, 1953, January, 1957, June, 1968, December, 1979; *New York Times Book Review*, February 26, 1956, July 2, 1961, June 24, 1962, June 2, 1968, June 28, 1968; *Saturday Review*, December 1, 1956, July 1, 1961, February 2, 1963, May 2, 1964, June 15, 1974; *Time*, June 30, 1961, June 29, 1962, November 6, 1964, June 7, 1968; *Atlantic*, July, 1961, July, 1962, March, 1963, July, 1968; *New Republic*, August 7, 1961, August 27, 1962, November 27, 1965; *New Yorker*, November 25, 1961, August 4, 1962; *New York Herald Tribune Book Review*, June 17, 1962; *San Francisco Chronicle*, June 28, 1962; *New Statesman*, July 13, 1962, July 19, 1963; *Nation*, July 14, 1962, November 17, 1962, March 2, 1963, June 10, 1968, July 3, 1976; *Christian Science Monitor*, July 19, 1962; *Newsweek*, February 4, 1963, June 3, 1969; *Harper's*, March, 1963, September, 1968; *America*, March 16, 1963; *Times Literary Supplement*, July 26, 1963, December 10, 1964; *CLA Journal*, Number 7, 1964; *New York Review of Books*, May 28, 1964, December 17, 1964, December 9, 1965; *Book Week*, May 31, 1964, September 26, 1965 *Critique*, winter, 1964-65; *Encounter*, July, 1965.

Partisan Review, winter, 1966; *South Atlantic Quarterly*, summer, 1966; *National Observer*, March 6, 1967, June 3, 1968; *Negro Digest*, April, 1967; *Twentieth Century Literature*, April, 1967; *Western Humanities Review*, spring, 1968; *New York Times*, May 31, 1968, February 2, 1969, May 21, 1971, September 21, 1979; *New Leader*, June 3, 1968, May 27, 1974; *Life*, June 7, 1968, June 4, 1971, July 30, 1971; *Esquire*, July, 1968; *Spectator*, July 12, 1968; *Books and Bookmen*, August, 1968, December, 1979; *Hudson Review*, autumn, 1968; *Listener*, July 25, 1974; *Chicago Tribune*, September 16, 1979, October 10, 1979; *Washington Post*, September 23, 1979, October 15, 1979.

Books: Alfred Kazin, *Contemporaries*, Little, Brown, 1962; Irving Howe, *A World More Attractive: A View of Modern Literature and Politics*, Horizon Press, 1963; Nona Balakian

and Charles Simmons, editors, *The Creative Present: Notes on Contemporary Fiction*, Doubleday, 1963; Norman Podhoretz, *Doings and Undoings*, Farrar, Straus, 1964; Harry T. Moore, editor, *Contemporary American Novelists*, Southern Illinois University Press, 1964; Fern Marja Eckman, *The Furious Passage of James Baldwin*, Evans, 1966; David Littlejohn, *Black on White: A Critical Survey of Writing by American Negroes*, Viking, 1966; Frederick Lumley, *New Trends in 20th Century Drama: A Survey since Ibsen and Shaw*, Oxford University Press, 1967; Warren French, editor, *The Fifties: Fiction, Poetry, Drama*, Everett/Edwards, 1970; M. G. Cook, editor, *Modern Black Novelists: A Collection of Critical Essays*, Prentice-Hall, 1971; *Contemporary Literary Criticism*, Gale, Volume I, 1973, Volume II, 1974, Volume III, 1975, Volume IV, 1975, Volume V, 1976, Volume VIII, 1978, Volume XIII, 1980, Volume XV, 1980; Keneth Kinnamon, editor, *James Baldwin: A Collection of Critical Essays*, Prentice-Hall, 1974.

—*Sketch by Denise Gottis*

*   *   *

BALDWIN, Michael 1930-
(Michael Jesse)

PERSONAL: Born May 1, 1930, in Gravesend, Kent, England; son of Harold Jesse and Elizabeth (Crittenden) Baldwin; married Jean Margaret Bruce, May 22, 1954 (divorced November, 1979); children: Matthew, Adam. *Education:* St. Edmund Hall, Oxford, B.A., 1953, research student, 1954-55. *Home:* 35, Gilbert Rd., Bromley, Kent, England. *Agent:* Anthony Sheil Associates, 52 Floral St., Covent Garden, London WC2E 9DA, England.

CAREER: St. Paul's College, Cheltenham, England, lecturer, 1955; St. Clement Danes Grammar School, London, England, assistant master, 1956-59; Whitelands College, London, senior lecturer, 1959—. Member of advisory committee, *Daily Mirror* children's literary competition. *Military service:* British Army, National Service, 1949-50; became sergeant. Territorial Army, 1950-61; became lieutenant, Royal Artillery. *Member:* Association of School Magazines (member of national advisory committee).

WRITINGS: The Silent Mirror (poems), Fortune Press, 1953; *Voyage from Spring* (poems), Routledge & Kegan Paul, 1957; *Poetry without Tears* (educational), Routledge & Kegan Paul, 1959.

Grandad with Snails (autobiographical), Routledge & Kegan Paul, 1960; *A World of Men* (novel), Secker & Warburg, 1962; *Death on a Live Wire, and On Stepping from a Sixth-Storey Window* (poems), Longmans, Green, 1962; (editor) *Poems by Children, 1950-1961* (educational), Dufour, 1962; (editor) *Billy the Kid, an Anthology of Tough Verse* (educational), Hutchinson, 1963; *Miraclejack* (novel), Secker & Warburg, 1963, Holt, 1967; *In Step with a Goat* (autobiographical), Hodder & Stoughton, 1963; *A Mouthful of Gold* (novel), Secker & Warburg, 1964; *Sebastian and Other Voices*, Secker & Warburg, 1966; *How Chas. Egget Lost His Way in a Creation Myth* (poems), Secker & Warburg, 1967; *The Great Cham*, Secker & Warburg, 1967; *Underneath, and Other Situations* (stories), Secker & Warburg, 1968.

There's a War On, Hodder & Stoughton, 1970; *The Cellar; A Fable*, Hodder & Stoughton, 1972; *Hob* (poems), Chatto & Windus, 1972; *Buried God* (poems), Hodder & Stoughton, 1973.

The Gamecock (novel), Faber, 1980; *Snook* (poems), Phoenix-Springwood, 1980. Author of screenplay, "Miraclejack," based on his novel. Author of a number of dramatic broadcasts.

SIDELIGHTS: Reviewing *Miraclejack*, Peter Buitenhuis writes: "The idea of the story is good; its execution is breathtaking. Baldwin's style is at once terse and poetic. It achieves masterpieces of understatement and splendors of imagery at the same time. His metaphors are reminiscent of the extravagant early phase of Dylan Thomas. . . ." Gillian Tindall expresses enthusiasm for Baldwin's shorter works. "Michael Baldwin's stories are . . . consciously ingenious, carefully planned virtuoso performances by a serious writer who knows just what he wants to do," Tindall comments. "His settings are designedly those of action: a coal-mine, the building trade, the army. I can't think of another writer who conveys the intricate preoccupations and jokes of these traditionally masculine worlds without ever once resorting to a consciously plainman tone in order to do so. Yet perhaps it is this ability of illuminating specialised areas of life without appearing to be involved in them himself that makes Michael Baldwin a slightly sinister writer. He puts distance between himself and his subjects: one story verges on poetry, another is a kind of Gothic comedy, in several apocalyptic judgement seems hovering over the next page, and in one the world ticks to an end in the style of a shooting script."

The dark tone of Baldwin's prose is echoed in his verse. Philip Callow writes: "Michael Baldwin doesn't want poetry that sings, he wants it rheumy, rusty; and it has to rasp. There are as many definitions of poetry as there are blades of grass, but perhaps most poets would agree that a poem is life in concentrated form. These poems are more than concentrated—they are bursting at the seams, splitting at the shoulders, spewing at the mouth. And each time there's an oil slick of ugliness to remind us that the world's a very nasty place but it's all there is at the moment, and it's our own sick mugs we're looking at. Make poetry from that. So, as I see it, these extraordinary buckets slopping over with images, witty and gruesome, gay and grave are poems in the very teeth of that 'contemporary urban existence' of the birth, and its indifference to poetry. . . . Elsewhere he is fast and lusty and apocalyptic and satiric, sometimes all at once, and I began to long for some silence around the words, as you need space in paintings. But that's not his style. He's an awakener, a bull-roarer, and a very talented one."

Baldwin has broadcast extensively for the British Broadcasting Corporation, particularly to schools. He is interested in music, jazz, anything to do with live theatre, and creative writing by children. His favorite occupations are drinking and eating.

A Mouthful of Gold has been made into a film.

BIOGRAPHICAL/CRITICAL SOURCES: Books and Bookmen, September, 1963, August, 1967; *New York Times Book Review*, April 16, 1967; *Book Week*, May 7, 1967; *Times Literary Supplement*, September 14, 1967; *Punch*, January 3, 1968; *Listener*, January 4, 1968, May 23, 1968; *New Yorker*, May 11, 1968; *Observer Review*, May 19, 1968.

*   *   *

BALDWIN, William Lee   1928-

PERSONAL: Born April 12, 1928, in New York, N.Y.; son of William Lee and Mildred (Karnes) Baldwin; married Marcia Diane Hurt; children: Douglas Lee, Ellen Parker. *Education:* Duke University, B.A. (summa cum laude), 1951; Princeton University, M.A., 1953, Ph.D., 1958. *Home:* 8 Rayton Rd., Hanover, N.H. 03755. *Office:* Department of Economics, Dartmouth College, Hanover, N.H. 03755.

CAREER: Princeton University, Princeton, N.J., instructor, 1953-56; Dartmouth College, Hanover, N.H., instructor, 1956-58, assistant professor, 1958-63, associate professor, 1963-67, professor of economics, 1967—, associate chairman, 1965-68, chairman, 1972-74, 1975-78. Visiting assistant professor of economics, Princeton University, 1961-62; Brookings research professor, Brookings Institution (Washington, D.C.), 1963-64; visiting professor of economics, Thammasat University (Bangkok, Thailand), 1968-70. Hanover (N.H.) Consumers Cooperative Society, member, 1956—, treasurer, 1965-66, president, 1966-68. *Military service:* U.S. Army, 1946-48. *Member:* Industrial Organization Society (vice president, 1977-78), American Economic Association, American Association of University Professors, Phi Beta Kappa, Omicron Delta Kappa.

WRITINGS: Antitrust and the Changing Corporation, Duke University Press, 1961; (contributor) H. W. Eldredge, editor, *Taming Megalopolis*, Doubleday, 1967; *The Structure of the Defense Market, 1955-1964*, Duke University Press, 1967; (editor with W. David Maxwell) *The Role of Foreign Financial Assistance to Thailand in the 1980s*, Heath, 1975. Contributor to *Encyclopedia Americana*. Contributor of articles and reviews to professional journals, including *Journal of Law and Economics, Harvard Business Review, Quarterly Review of Economics and Business, Southern Economic Journal, Antitrust Law and Economics Review*, and *Journal of Political Economy*.

*   *   *

BALL, John (Dudley, Jr.)   1911-

PERSONAL: Born July 8, 1911, in Schenectady, N.Y.; son of John Dudley (a scientist) and Alena L. (Wiles) Ball; married Patricia M. Hamilton, August 22, 1942; children: John David. *Education:* Carroll College, B.A., 1934. *Religion:* Lutheran. *Home:* 16401 Otsego St., Encino, Calif. 91316. *Agent:* Carol Brandt, Brandt and Brandt, Inc., 1501 Broadway, New York, N.Y. 10036.

CAREER: Onetime commercial pilot, who also worked in advertising and related fields; Pan American World Airways, Miami, Fla., flight instructor and member of flight crew for U.S. Army Air Transport Command, 1942-46; annotator, Columbia Masterworks Records, 1946-49; *Brooklyn Eagle*, Brooklyn, N.Y., music editor, 1946-50; *New York World Telegram*, New York City, columnist, 1950-51; Radio Station WOL, Washington, D.C., commentator, 1951-52; Institute of Aerospace Sciences, New York City and Los Angeles, Calif., director of public relations, 1958-61; D.M.S., Inc. (publishers), Beverly Hills, Calif., editor-in-chief, 1961-63; writer. Chairman and editor-in-chief, University of California Mystery Library Program. *Member:* Aviation Space Writers Association, Mystery Writers of America, Japan-America Society, Trained Cormorants (scion society of Baker Street Irregulars; president), Judo Black Belt Federation, California Karate Association, Theta Alpha Phi, OX-5 Club, California Akai-Kai. *Awards, honors:* Edgar Award of Mystery Writers of America, 1965, and Crime Writers Association Award (England), 1967, both for *In the Heat of the Night*; D.H.L., Carroll College, 1978.

WRITINGS: The Phonograph Record Industry, Bellman, 1947; *Records for Pleasure*, Rutgers University Press, 1947; *Operation Springboard*, Duell, Sloan & Pearce, 1958; *Spacemaster I*, Duell, Sloan & Pearce, 1960; *Operation Space: An Adventure in Space*, Duell, Sloan & Pearce, 1960; *Edwards: U.S. Air Force Flight Test Center*, Duell, Sloan & Pearce, 1962; *Judo Boy* (Junior Literary Guild selection),

Duell, Sloan & Pearce, 1964; *In the Heat of the Night*, Harper, 1965; *Arctic Showdown*, Duell, Sloan & Pearce, 1966; *Rescue Mission*, Harper, 1966; *The Cool Cottontail* (Mystery Guild selection), Harper, 1966; *Hell for the Angels*, Harper, 1966; *The Passionate Penguin*, Harper, 1966; *Miss 1000 Spring Blossoms*, Little, Brown, 1968; *Dragon Hotel*, Weatherhill (Tokyo), 1968; *Johnny Get Your Gun*, Little, Brown, 1969.

Last Plane Out, Little, Brown, 1970; *The First Team*, Little, Brown, 1971; *Five Pieces of Jade*, Little, Brown, 1972; *The Fourteenth Point*, Little, Brown, 1973; *Mark One–The Dummy*, Little, Brown, 1974; *The Winds of Mitamura*, Little, Brown, 1975; *The Eyes of Buddha*, Little, Brown, 1976; *Phase Three Alert*, Little, Brown, 1977; *Police Chief*, Doubleday, 1977; *The Killing in the Market*, Doubleday, 1978; *The Murder Children*, Dodd, 1979; *Then Came Violence*, Doubleday, 1980.

Editor: *The Mystery Story*, Mystery Library, 1976; *Cop Cade*, Doubleday, 1978. Author of about four hundred magazine articles and short stories in fields of aviation, sociology, astronomy, music, athletics, and travel.

WORK IN PROGRESS: *The Kiwi Target.*

SIDELIGHTS: John Ball first introduced black detective Virgil Tibbs in his novel *In the Heat of the Night*, which was filmed by United Artists in 1967 and starred Sidney Poitier. Subsequent novels by Ball which feature Tibbs are *The Cool Cottontail, Johnny Get Your Gun*, and *Five Pieces of Jade*. The character was also portrayed by Poitier in two other films produced by United Artists, ''They Call Me Mister Tibbs,'' 1970, and ''The Organization,'' 1971.

AVOCATIONAL INTERESTS: Oriental culture, martial arts, flying, travel, music, and book collecting.

BIOGRAPHICAL/CRITICAL SOURCES: *Best Sellers,* April 15, 1965, June 15, 1966, August 15, 1966, October 15, 1969, May 1, 1970, April 1, 1972; *New York Times Book Review,* May 2, 1965, May 22, 1966, August 7, 1966, November 2, 1969, March 12, 1972; *Times Literary Supplement,* January 13, 1966, October 13, 1972; *Book Week,* September 18, 1966; *Books and Bookmen,* August, 1970.

*   *   *

BARKER, A(udrey) L(ilian) 1918-

PERSONAL: Born April 13, 1918, in England; daughter of Harry (an engineer) and Elsie A. (Dutton) Barker. *Education:* Attended county secondary school in England. *Address:* c/o Hogarth Press Ltd., 40-42 William IV St., London WC2N WDF, England.

CAREER: Secretary and sub-editor, British Broadcasting Corp., London, England; free-lance writer. *Member:* Royal Society of Literature (fellow). *Awards, honors:* Atlantic award in Literature, 1946; Somerset Maugham award, 1947, for *Innocents;* Cheltenham Festival Literary award, 1962.

WRITINGS: Innocents: Variations on a Theme (short stories), Hogarth, 1947, Scribner, 1948; *Apology for a Hero,* Scribner, 1950; *Novelette, with Other Stories,* Scribner, 1951; *The Joy-Ride and After,* Hogarth, 1963, Scribner, 1964; *Lost upon the Roundabouts* (short stories), Hogarth, 1964; *A Case Examined* (novel), Hogarth, 1965; *The Middling: Chapters in the Life of Ellie Toms,* Hogarth, 1967; *John Brown's Body,* Hogarth, 1969; *Femina Real* (short stories), Hogarth, 1971; *A Source of Embarrassment* (novel), Hogarth, 1974; *A Heavy Feather* (novel), Hogarth, 1978, Braziller, 1979; *Life Stories* (autobiographical and fictional), Hogarth, in press. Author of television play, ''Pringle.''

BIOGRAPHICAL/CRITICAL SOURCES: *Listener,* October 26, 1967; *Observer Review,* October 29, 1967; *Times Literary Supplement,* November 2, 1967; *Books and Bookmen,* January, 1970.

*   *   *

BARLOW, Frank 1911-

PERSONAL: Born April 19, 1911, in Stoke-on-Trent, England; son of Percy Hawthorn (a schoolmaster) and Margaret Julia (Wilkinson) Barlow; married July 1, 1936; children: John Francis, Michael Edward. *Education:* St. John's College, Oxford, B.A., 1933, M.A., D.Phil., 1937. *Home:* Middle Court Hall, Kenton, Exeter, Devonshire, England.

CAREER: University of London, University College, London, England, assistant lecturer, 1936-40; University College of the South-West, Exeter, England, lecturer, 1946-53, reader, 1949-53; University of Exeter, Exeter, professor of history, 1953-76, dean of faculty of arts, 1955-59, deputy vice-chancellor, 1961-63, public orator, 1974-76. *Military service:* British Army, 1941-46; became major. *Member:* British Academy (fellow), Royal Society of Literature (fellow), Royal Historical Society (fellow; member of council, 1960-63).

WRITINGS: (Editor) *The Letters of Arnulf of Lisieux,* Royal Historical Society, 1939; (editor) *Durham Annals and Documents of the Thirteenth Century,* Surtees Society, 1945; *Durham Jurisdictional Peculiars,* Oxford University Press, 1950; *The Feudal Kingdom of England, 1042-1216,* Longmans, Green, 1955, 3rd edition, 1972; (editor, translator, and author of introduction and notes) *The Life of King Edward, Who Rests at Westminster,* Oxford University Press, 1962; *The English Church, 1000-1066: A Constitutional History,* Shoe String, 1963, 2nd edition, Longman, 1979; *William I and the Norman Conquest,* English Universities Press, 1965, Collier, 1967; (with Dorothy Whitelock, David C. Douglas, and Charles H. Lemmon) *The Norman Conquest: Its Setting and Impact,* Eyre & Spottiswoode, 1966; *Edward the Confessor and the Norman Conquest,* Historical Association, 1966; (editor) *Exeter and Its Region,* University of Exeter, 1969; *Edward the Confessor,* University of California Press, 1970, 2nd edition, Eyre Methuen, 1979; (with Martin Biddle, Olof von Feilitzen, and D. J. Keene) *Winchester in the Early Middle Ages: An Edition and Discussion of the Winton Domesday,* Oxford University Press, 1976; *The English Church, 1066-1154,* Longman, 1979; (contributor) Timothy Reuter, editor, *The Greatest Englishman: Essays on St. Boniface and The Church at Crediton,* Paternoster Press, 1980.

WORK IN PROGRESS: A biography of King William II of England, for Eyre Methuen.

BIOGRAPHICAL/CRITICAL SOURCES: *Observer Review,* November 15, 1970; *Books and Bookmen,* February, 1971.

*   *   *

BARLOW, T(homas) Edward 1931-

PERSONAL: Born April 27, 1931, in McKenzie, Ala.; son of Bertie Edward (a merchant) and Hazel (Parker) Barlow; married Marjorie Dempsey (an elementary school teacher), September 1, 1951; children: David, Cynthia, Thomas, Nancy. *Education:* Graceland College, A.A., 1951; Troy State University, B.S. in Ed., 1952; University of Kansas, graduate study, 1962-64; Tulsa University, M.A., 1969; University of Oklahoma, graduate study, 1970. *Politics:* Republican. *Religion:* Reorganized Latter Day Saints.

CAREER: Teacher in Bay Minette, Ala., 1952-54; minister in Reorganized Latter Day Saints Church, missionary in northern Indiana, 1954-59, district president in Topeka, Kans., 1959-64, district missionary in Tulsa, Okla., 1964-69, Texas-Oklahoma region missionary director in Oklahoma City, Okla., 1969-75, president of British Isles mission in Birmingham, England, beginning 1975. Chairman of Missionary Methods Committee and Quorum of Seventy for Reorganized Latter Day Saints Church.

WRITINGS: Small Group Ministry in the Contemporary Church, Herald House, 1972; *Living Saints Witness at Work,* Herald House, 1976; (editor) *Congregational House Churches,* Herald House, 1978. Contributor to *Saints Herald.*

WORK IN PROGRESS: Witnessing Weekends: Renewal for Churches; Prayer with Meaning.†

* * *

BARNARD, Harry 1906-

PERSONAL: Surname originally Kletzky; born September 5, 1906, in Pueblo, Colo.; son of David (an oculist) and Pauline (Halpern) Kletzky; married Miriam Helstien, June 29, 1929 (divorced, 1942); married Ruth Eisenstat, October 23, 1943; children: (second marriage) Karen, Judith, Ronald, David. *Education:* Attended University of Denver, 1924-25; University of Chicago, Ph.B., 1928; attended John Marshall Law School, 1935-37. *Politics:* Democrat. *Religion:* Judaism. *Home:* 801 Lavergne, Wilmette, Ill. 60091.

CAREER: Chicago Herald-Examiner, Chicago, Ill., member of editorial staff, 1929-35; City of Chicago, Law Department, Chicago, director of research division, 1935-42; University of Chicago, Chicago, director of press relations, 1943-44; *Chicago Times,* Chicago, chief editorial writer, 1944-45; sometime member of editorial staffs of *Chicago Herald-Examiner* and *Chicago Sun,* both Chicago, and *Detroit Times,* Detroit, Mich.; advertising agency writer, 1952-56; free-lance writer, 1957—. Writer-in-residence, Roosevelt University, 1968-69. Chairman, William O. Douglas for Democratic Nomination for President, 1952. Member of boards, Chicago Civil Liberties Committee, National Committee to Abolish House Committee on Un-American Activities, and Onward Neighborhood Settlement House. *Member:* Committee for Sane Nuclear Policy, Committee to Defend Bill of Rights, Committee to Honor Eugene Field. *Awards, honors:* Pontifical Medal of Pope John XXIII, for special edition of encyclical, *Mater et Magistra,* 1962; National Endowment for the Humanities fellow, 1974.

WRITINGS: Eagle Forgotten: The Life of John Peter Altgeld, Bobbs-Merrill, 1938; *Rutherford B. Hayes and His America,* Bobbs-Merrill, 1954; *Independent Man: The Life of Senator James Couzens,* Scribner, 1958; (with Preston Bradley) *Along the Way,* McKay, 1962; (editor and author of preface) *Mater et Magistra,* Discovers Press, 1962; *This Great Triumvarate of Patriots,* Follett, 1971; *The Forging of an American Jew: The Life and Times of Judge Julian W. Mack,* Herzl Press, 1974. Author of syndicated column, "Liberal at Large," in *Chicago Daily News* and other newspapers, 1958-60. Contributor of articles to *Encyclopedia Americana, Dictionary of American Biography, Nation, Saturday Review,* and other publications.

WORK IN PROGRESS: Two biographies, *William O. Douglas* and *Willkie.*

SIDELIGHTS: As a biographer of American political figures, Harry Barnard reports as a major interest "biography

as an illumination of personality and of American history." His biography of Rutherford B. Hayes is considered a landmark for its use of modern psychology. As the critic for *U.S. Quarterly Book Review* notes: "This biography is unique both in its emphasis and in its method. Almost one-half of the book consists of a psychoanalytical study of Hayes' 'endless searching for a father,' his father having died before the boy was born." The *New York Times*'s David Donald comments, "This accurate and detailed volume is certainly the best book yet written on the half-forgotten nineteenth president."

Barnard has donated his manuscripts and other papers as well as an immense collection of his correspondence with many of America's leading political, social, and literary figures to the American Heritage Center of the University of Wyoming.

BIOGRAPHICAL/CRITICAL SOURCES: Saturday Review, January 1, 1955, May 17, 1958; *New York Times,* January 2, 1955, May 18, 1958; *U.S. Quarterly Book Review,* March, 1955; *Editor and Publisher,* May 3, 1958; *Newsweek,* June 16, 1958; *Laramie Daily Boomerang,* January, 1980.

* * *

BARNES, Hazel E(stella) 1915-

PERSONAL: Born December 15, 1915, in Wilkes-Barre, Pa.; daughter of Olin James (a teacher) and May (Petersen) Barnes. *Education:* Wilson College (Chambersburg, Pa.), B.A., 1937; Yale University, Ph.D., 1941; graduate study at Columbia University, 1944, and University of Hawaii, 1951. *Politics:* Democrat. *Home:* 896 Seventeenth St., Boulder, Colo. *Office:* Center for Interdisciplinary Studies, University of Colorado, Boulder, Colo.

CAREER: Woman's College of the University of North Carolina (now University of North Carolina at Greensboro), instructor in classics, 1941-43; Queens College, Charlotte, N.C., associate professor of classics and philosophy, 1943-45; Pierce College, Athens, Greece, teacher, 1945-48, assistant to president, 1948; University of Toledo, Toledo, Ohio, assistant professor of classics and philosophy, 1948-51; Ohio State University, Columbus, assistant professor of philosophy, 1951-53; University of Colorado, Boulder, professor of classics, 1953-77, chairman of department 1965-69, Center for Interdisciplinary Studies, professor, 1977-79, Robert B. Hawkins Distinguished Professor of Humanities, 1979—, director of center, 1979-81. Visiting professor, Yale University, spring, 1974; Phi Beta Kappa, visiting scholar, 1974-75, 1977-78, associate, 1975—, senator, 1979-85. *Member:* American Philosophical Society, American Philological Association, American Society of Aesthetics, Rocky Mountain and Plains States Philosophical Institute, Classical Association of the Middle-West and South, Phi Beta Kappa, Mortar Board. *Awards, honors:* Wilson College, D.Litt., 1965; Teaching Recognition Award, 1967, and University Medal, 1976, both from University of Colorado; Guggenheim fellowship, 1977-78.

WRITINGS: (Translator from the French and author of introduction) Jean-Paul Sartre, *Existential Psychoanalysis* (contains translations of selections from *L'Etre et le Neant*), Philosophical Library, 1953; (translator from the French and author of introduction) Sartre, *Being and Nothingness* (contains translation of full text of *L'Etre et le Neant*), Philosophical Library, 1956; *The Literature of Possibility: A Study in Humanistic Existentialism,* University of Nebraska Press, 1959; (with Donald Sutherland) *Hippolytus in Drama and Myth,* University of Nebraska Press, 1960; (translator from the French and author of introduction) Sartre, *Search for a Method* (contains translation of full text of *Question de Methode*), Knopf, 1963 (published in England as *The Problem of Method,* Methuen, 1964); (editor) Arthur Schopenhauer, *Pessimists' Handbook,* translation from the German by T. Bailey Saunders, University of Nebraska Press, 1964; *An Existentialist Ethics,* Knopf, 1967; *The University as the New Church,* C. A. Watts, 1970; *Sartre,* Lippincott, 1973; *The Meddling Gods: Four Essays on Classical Themes,* University of Nebraska Press, 1974; *Sartre and Flaubert,* University of Chicago Press, 1981.

Author of series, "Week by Week in Greece," for Sunday edition of *National Herald,* 1947-48, and of television series, "Self-Encounter," for National Educational Television, 1962. Contributor to professional journals.

SIDELIGHTS: An Existentialist Ethics, the sequel to *The Literature of Possibility: A Study in Humanistic Existentialism,* is designed to "fill a serious gap in existentialist philosophy," writes Harold A. Durfee. The book "derives its main instrumental ideas from Sartre's early ontology but at the same time situates itself right in the midst of the issues of the current convulsive decade," according to Donald Sutherland, who considers Hazel E. Barnes "a meticulous philosopher with a genuine calling for contemporaneity." The *Virginia Quarterly Review* critic also noted that, while Barnes is well schooled in Sartre's philosophy, she has extended it "in a manner completely her own [and] deftly demonstrates that the existentialist view of life implies an ethical commitment. In this book she spells out the character of that commitment practically as well as theoretically." Sutherland adds that, given a very wide range of choices, "Barnes has written not *the* but *an* existentialist ethics. She chooses to be ethical, she chooses to be active, she chooses the good of humanity as well as the justified individual life. . . . If her choices are limiting and make her ethics not *the* existentialist ethics in full, they still make it extraordinarily broad and more central to the general doctrine than any I can imagine."

The *Choice* reviewer calls the essays in *The Meddling Gods* "rich, penetrating, balanced, [and] felicitious. . . . The range of literary and psychological reference is as apt as it is impressive. . . . The quality and mode of judgment are urbane but never dismissive. . . . This is an important book for the student of literature whose curiosity and sophistication are equal to its demands." According to the critic for the *Virginia Quarterly Review,* the essays "throw revealing light upon characters and situations that are in fact timeless."

BIOGRAPHICAL/CRITICAL SOURCES: New Leader, May 8, 1967; *Christian Century,* July 5, 1967; *Virginia Quarterly Review,* summer, 1967, spring, 1975; *New York Review of Books,* November 9, 1967; *Choice,* March, 1975.

*   *   *

BARON, Samuel H(askell) 1921-

PERSONAL: Born May 24, 1921, in New York, N.Y.; son of James (a clothier) and Dinah (Bader) Baron; married M. Virginia Wilson; children: Sheila, Carla, Laura. *Education:* Cornell University, B.S., 1942; Columbia University, M.A., 1948, Ph.D., 1952. *Home:* 5 Marilyn Lane, Chapel Hill, N.C. 27514. *Office:* University of North Carolina, Chapel Hill, N.C. 27514.

CAREER: University of Tennessee at Knoxville, instructor in history, 1948-50, 1951-53; Grinnell College, Grinnell, Iowa, assistant professor, 1956-57, associate professor, 1957-63, professor of history, 1963-66; University of California, San Diego, professor, 1966-72; University of North Car-

olina at Chapel Hill, alumni distinguished professor, 1972—. Visiting lecturer in history, Northwestern University, 1953-54; visiting assistant professor of history, University of Missouri, 1954-55, and University of Nebraska, 1955-56. *Military service:* U.S. Army, 1942-46; became captain. *Member:* American Historical Association, American Association for the Advancement of Slavic Studies, American Association of University Professors (national council member, 1963-65), American Civil Liberties Union. *Awards, honors:* Harvard fellowship in East Asian studies; grants from Social Science Research Council, American Council of Learned Societies, Guggenheim Foundation, and National Endowment for the Humanities.

WRITINGS: Plekhanov, the Father of Russian Marxism, Stanford University Press, 1963; (editor and translator) Adam Olearius, *The Travels of Olearius in Seventeenth Century Russia,* Stanford University Press, 1967; (co-editor) *Windows on the Russian Past: Essays on Soviet Historiography since Stalin,* American Association for the Advancement of Slavic Studies, 1977; *Muscovite Russia: Collected Essays,* Variorium, 1980.

WORK IN PROGRESS: New Light on G. V. Plekhanov.

*   *   *

BARR, Jene 1900-

PERSONAL: Born July 28, 1900, in Kobrin, Russia; daughter of Joseph and Goldie (Barr) Cohen. *Education:* Graduated from Chicago Normal School of Physical Education, 1920; attended University of Chicago, 1928-29, Chicago Teachers College, 1931, 1933, 1949-50, Art Institute of Chicago, 1932, and Northwestern University, 1935-37. *Politics:* Independent. *Religion:* Jewish. *Home:* 5910 No. Sheridan Rd., Chicago, Ill. 60626; and c/o Bobele, 1085 Tasman Dr., No. 494, Sunnyvale, Calif. 94086.

CAREER: Board of Education, Chicago, Ill., physical education instructor, 1925-35, classroom teacher, 1935-50, teacher-librarian, 1950-64. Teacher of creative writing, Downtown YWCA, Chicago, 1953-56. Educational consultant in the Social Studies, Albert Whitman & Co. *Member:* National Federation of Press Women, Society of Midland Authors (chairman of library committee, 1963—), Children's Reading Round Table (program chairman, 1950; president, 1965-66), Illinois Woman's Press Association (second vice-president, 1957; chairman of student activities committee, 1961—; house chairman, 1961), Illinois Library Association, Chicago Teacher-Librarian's Club (recording secretary, 1962). *Awards, honors:* Midwest Award, Children's Reading Round Table, 1959; National Federation of Press Women awards, including second prize, 1950, for *Little Circus Dog,* first prize, 1951, for *Texas Pete, Little Cowboy,* and second prize, 1955, for *Mr. Mailman;* Mate Palmer Award of Illinois Woman's Press Association, 1950, for *Little Circus Dog,* 1951, for *Texas Pete, Little Cowboy,* 1955, for *Mr. Mailman,* and 1959, for *Baseball for Young Champions.*

WRITINGS: Youth books; published by Whitman, except as noted: *Conrad the Clock,* Wilcox & Follett, 1944; *Little Prairie Dog,* 1949; *Little Circus Dog,* 1949; *Surprise for Nancy,* 1950; *Texas Pete, Little Cowboy,* 1950; *Policeman Paul,* 1952; *Fireman Fred,* 1952; *Mike, the Milkman,* 1953; *Baker Bill,* 1953; *Mr. Mailman,* 1954; *Big Wheels! Little Wheels!,* 1955; *Ben's Busy Service Station,* 1956; *Fast Trains! Busy Trains!,* 1956; *Good Morning, Teacher,* 1957; *Dan the Weatherman,* 1958; (with Catherine Bowers) *Here Is Chicago* (textbook), University Publishing Co., 1958, 4th edition, 1973; *This Is My Country,* 1959; *Miss Terry at the Li-*

brary, 1962; (with others) *How Americans Produce and Obtain Goods and Services* (introductory economics book for young children), Education-Industry Service, 1962; *Mr. Zip and the U.S. Mail*, 1964; *Fire Snorkel Number 7*, 1965; (with Cynthia Chapin) *What Will the Weather Be?*, 1965; *What Can Money Do?*, 1967; *Busy Office, Busy People*, 1968.

"Young Champions" series; with Robert J. Antonacci; published by McGraw: *Baseball for Young Champions*, 1956, 2nd edition, 1977; *Football for Young Champions*, 1958, 2nd edition, 1976; *Basketball for Young Champions*, 1960; *Physical Fitness for Young Champions*, 1962, 2nd edition, 1975. Contributor to *Illinois Libraries. Back of the Yards Journal*, Chicago, Ill., editor of children's column, 1946-48, editor of women's column, 1947-48, 1952.

BIOGRAPHICAL/CRITICAL SOURCES: Chicago Schools Journal, May-June, 1951; *Chicago Daily Tribune*, November 14, 1954; *World Topics Year Book*, 1959.

*   *   *

BAUMANN, Hans 1914-

PERSONAL: Born April 22, 1914, in Amberg, Bavaria; son of Johann (an inspector) and Elisabeth (Kraus) Baumann; married Elisabeth Zoglmann (a violinist), December 17, 1942; children: Veronika. *Education:* Attended University of Berlin. *Home:* 10 Hechendorferstrasse, Murnau, Bavaria, Federal Republic of Germany.

CAREER: Teacher in Bavaria, Germany, 1933-34; worked as manual laborer in postwar period in Germany before becoming full-time writer. *Military service:* German Army, served in Russia and France; taken prisoner in France. *Awards, honors: New York Herald Tribune* Spring Book Festival award for the best juvenile of the year, 1958, for *Sons of the Steppe;* Friedrich Gerstacker Prize, Brunswick, for best children's book of year, 1956; Mildred Batcheldor Award, 1972; Austrian State Prize for translation, 1979.

WRITINGS: Alexander (play), E. Diederichs, 1941; *Atem einer Floete* (poetry), E. Diederichs, 1943; *Der Kreterkoenig* (play), E. Diederichs, 1944.

Der Sohn des Columbus, Ensslin & Laiblin (Reutlingen), 1951, translation by Isabel McHugh and Florence McHugh published as *Son of Columbus*, Oxford University Press, 1957; *Der rote Pull: Abenteuer eines Grossstadtjungen*, Ensslin & Laiblin, 1951; *Das Karussell zur weiten Welt*, Ensslin & Laiblin, 1952; *Die Hoehlen der grossen Jaeger*, Ensslin & Laiblin, 1953, translation by I. McHugh and F. McHugh published as *The Caves of the Great Hunters*, Pantheon Books, 1954, revised edition, 1962; *Steppensoehne: Vom Sieg ueber Dschingis-Khan*, Ensslin & Laiblin, 1954, translation by I. McHugh and F. McHugh published as *Sons of the Steppe: The Story of How the Conqueror Genghis Khan was Overcome*, Walck, 1958; *Die Bruecke der Goetter*, C. Bertelsmann (Guetersloh), 1955; *Penny: Das Geheimnis der Dschunke vom freundlichen Ostwind*, Ensslin & Laiblin, 1956; *Die Barke der Brueder aus der Zeit Heinrichs des Seefahrers*, Ensslin & Laiblin, 1956, translation by I. McHugh and F. McHugh published as *The Barque of the Brothers: A Tale of the Days of Henry the Navigator*, Walck, 1958; *Haenschen in der Grube*, Ensslin & Laiblin, 1957, translation published as *Jackie the Pit Pony*, F. Watts, 1958; (editor) *Russische Gedichte*, Bertelsmann, 1958; *Kleine Schwester Schalbe*, Ensslin & Laiblin, 1958, translation by Katharine Potts published as *Angelina and the Birds*, F. Watts, 1959; *Das Einhorn und der Loewe*, Ensslin & Laiblin, 1959, translation by Potts published as *The Lion and the*

Unicorn, Oxford University Press, 1959; *Die gekraenkte Krokodil*, 1959, translation by Potts published as *The Crotchety Crocodile*, Oxford University Press, 1960.

Die Welt der Pharaonen, S. Mohn (Guetersloh), 1960, translation by Richard Winston and Clara Winston published as *The World of the Pharaohs*, Pantheon, 1960; *Der Baer und sein Brueder*, Ensslin & Laiblin, 1961, translation by Potts published as *The Bear and His Brothers*, Oxford University Press, 1962; *Tina und Nina*, 1963, translation published as *Tina and Nina*, Oxford University Press, 1963; *Boote fuer Morgen* (poems), E. Diederich, 1963; *Gold und Goetter von Peru*, S. Mohn, 1963, translation by Stella Humphries published as *Gold and Gods of Peru*, Pantheon, 1963; *Kasperle hat viele Freunde*, Ensslin & Laiblin, 1965, translation by Joyce Emerson published as *Caspar and His Friends*, Phoenix House, 1967, Walck, 1968.

Loewentor und Labyrinth, S. Mohn, 1966, translation by Humphries published as *Lion Gate and Labyrinth*, Pantheon, 1967; *Der grosse Elefant und der kleine*, Betz (Munich), 1966; *Wer Fluegel hat, kann fliegen*, Ensslin & Laiblin, 1966; (translator) Anna Akhmatova, *Gedichte*, Langewiesche-Brandt (Munich), 1967; *Der Schimmel aus dem Bild*, S. Mohn, 1967; *Das Schiffschaukelschiff*, Ensslin & Laiblin, 1967; *Der grosse Alexanderzug*, Ehrenwirth (Munich), 1967, translation by Humphries published as *Alexander's Great March*, Walck, 1968; *A Tuerl zum Nachbarn*, Ehrenwirth, 1967; *Eduard von Keyserlings Erzaehlungen*, Atlantis (Zurich), 1967; *Der Zirkus ist Da*, Loewes-Verlag, 1967, translation by Michael C. Kitton published as *The Circus Is Here*, Wheaton Publishing, 1967; *Einem Tisch Faellt was Ein*, S. Mohn, 1968; *Fenny; Eine Wuestenfuchsgeschichte*, Betz, 1968, translation by J. J. Aule published as *Fenny, the Desert Fox*, Pantheon, 1970; (compiler) *Ein Fuchs faehrt nach Amerika*, Paulus Verlag, 1968; *Im Lande Ur; die Entdeckung Altmesopotamiens*, Bertelsmann, 1968, translation by Humphries published as *In the Land of Ur: The Discovery of Ancient Mesopotamia*, Pantheon, 1969; *Der Kindermond*, Paulus-Verlag, 1968; *Wolkenreise fuer den Koenig*, Ensslin & Laiblin, 1968; *Das Everl und der Aff*, Ehrenwirth, 1969; *Petja in der Kraehenschule*, Bitter, 1969; *Der Wunderbare Ball Kadalupp*, Betz, 1969, translation by Refna Wilkin published as *Gatalop the Wonderful Ball*, Walck, 1971.

Igel Haben Vorfahrt, Betz, 1970; *Ein Brief nach Buxtehude*, Betz, 1970; *Denkzettel*, Ehrenwirth, 1970; *Dimitri und die Falschen Zaren*, Ehrenwirth, 1970, translation by Anthea Bell published as *Dimitri and the False Tsars*, Walck, 1972; *Kopfkissenbuch fuer Kinder*, Betz, 1972; *Schorschi der Drachentoeter*, Betz, 1972; *Wieviel Uhr ist's Anderswo*, Thienemanns, 1972; *Krokodilvogel und Affenkind*, Betz, 1973; *Eins zu null fuer uns Kinder*, Stalling, 1973; (compiler) *Entscheidung im Labyrinth*, Arena, 1973; *Der Stadt der Tiere*, Stalling, 1974; *Warum Fiffi Fiffi Heisst*, Deutscher Taschenbuch Verlag, 1977; *Katzimir der Groesste*, O. Maier, 1977, translation by Gwen Mrash published as *Katzimir the Greatest*, Dent, 1977; *Fluegel fuer Ikaros*, Thienemanns, 1978, translation by Bell published as *Wings for Icarus*, Dent, 1980; *Reisepass* (poems), Thienemanns, 1978.

Other books translated into English: *The Dragon Next Door*, translation by I. McHugh and F. McHugh, Harrap, 1960; *The Roundabout on the Roof*, Oxford University Press, 1961; *I Marched with Hannibal*, translation by Potts, Oxford University Press, 1961, Walck, 1962; *The Stolen Fire*, translation by Humphries, Pantheon, 1974 (published in England as *Hero Legends of the World*, Dent, 1975); *The Hare's Race*, translation by Elizabeth D. Crawford, Morrow, 1976.

BIOGRAPHICAL/CRITICAL SOURCES: Young Readers Review, February, 1969; *Times Literary Supplement*, October 16, 1969, March 28, 1980; *New York Times Book Review*, November 9, 1969.

*   *   *

BEALS, Carleton   1893-1979

PERSONAL: Born November 13, 1893, in Medicine Lodge, Kan.; died June 26, 1979, in Middletown, Conn., of complications following an operation; son of Leon Eli and Elvina S. (Blickensderfer) Beals; married Carolyn Kennedy (a farmer), June 30, 1956. *Education:* University of California, B.A. (cum laude), 1916; Columbia University, M.A., 1917; additional studies at University of Madrid, 1920, University of Rome, 1922, and University of Mexico, 1923. *Politics:* Independent. *Home:* Killingworth, Firetower Rd., Deep River, Conn. *Agent:* Bertha Klausner International Literary Agency, Inc., 71 Park Ave., New York, N.Y. 10016.

CAREER: American High School, Mexico City, Mexico, principal, 1919-20; instructor of personal staff of President Carranza, 1920; correspondent in Spain and Italy for *Nation* and *Current History*, 1921-23; New York Board of Education, New York City, lecturer, 1924-25; member of expeditions to Indian regions of Mexico, 1926 and 1930-31; correspondent in Central America for *Nation*, 1926-27; National University of Mexico, Mexico City, faculty lecturer, 1927; correspondent in Europe and Middle East, 1929; University of California, Berkeley, faculty lecturer, 1932; correspondent in Cuba, 1932-33 and 1935; North American Newspaper Alliance, New York City, special correspondent in Cuba, 1934; correspondent in South America, 1934 and 1946; *New York Post*, New York City, correspondent in Alabama at Scottsboro Trial, 1935; New School for Social Research, New York City, lecturer, 1936; correspondent in Mexico, 1937, 1946, and 1961; researcher, New Haven Board of Education, New Haven, Conn., 1950-51 and 1956-57, and Fuller F. Barnes Foundation and Bristol Public Library, Bristol, Conn., 1952-53; *Nation*, correspondent in Cuba, 1957, and in Haiti, 1959; Housing Authority of New Haven, New Haven, researcher, 1959-60; *Independent*, New York City, correspondent in Cuba, 1960-61, and in Latin America, 1961. Lecturer at Seminar on Relations with Mexico, 1925-28 and 1930-31, at Conference on the Cause and Cure of War, 1927, and at fourteen Latin American universities, 1961. Chairman, Committee on Jacques Romain, 1935; member of roundtable, Harris Foundation, 1951; member of advisory board, Better Understanding Foundation; member of board of governors, Academy of Foreign Relations. Consultant, Columbia Records, 1964.

MEMBER: American Geographical Society (fellow), Society of American Historians (fellow), P.E.N., Foreign Press Club (Mexico City), Pi Gamma Mu. *Awards, honors:* Bonnheim Award, 1916 and 1917; Bryce History Prize, 1917; Guggenheim fellow, 1931-32; *Arizona Quarterly* Award, 1962, for best article of 1961; National Academy of Recording Arts and Sciences Award, 1965.

WRITINGS: Mexico: An Interpretation, Huebsch, 1923; *Rome or Death: The Story of Fascism*, Century, 1923; *Brimstone and Chili: A Book of Personal Experiences in the Southwest and in Mexico*, Knopf, 1927; *Con Sandino en Nicaragua*, Comite Pro-Sandino, 1928; *Destroying Victor*, Macaulay, 1929; *Mexican Maze* (Book Club of America selection), Lippincott, 1931, reprinted, Greenwood Press, 1971; *Banana Gold*, Lippincott, 1932, reprinted, Arno, 1970; *Porfirio Diaz: Dictator of Mexico*, Lippincott, 1932; *The*

Crime of Cuba, Lippincott, 1933, reprinted, Arno, 1970; *Black River*, Lippincott, 1934; *Fire on the Andes*, Lippincott, 1934; *The Story of Huey P. Long*, Lippincott, 1935, reprinted, Greenwood Press, 1971; *Prologue to Cuban Freedom*, Autenticos, 1935; *The Stones Awake* (novel), Lippincott, 1936; *America South*, Lippincott, 1937; *The New Genius of Roberto de la Selva*, Centro de Estudios Pedagogicos e Hispano Americanos de Mexico, 1937; *The Coming Struggle for Latin America* (*Reader's Digest* Condensed Book selection), Lippincott, 1938, 3rd edition, Halcyon House, 1940; *Glass Houses: Ten Years of Free-Lancing* (autobiography), Lippincott, 1938; *American Earth: The Biography of a Nation*, Lippincott, 1939; *The Great Circle: Further Adventures in Free-Lancing* (autobiography), Lippincott, 1940; *Pan America: A Program for the Western Hemisphere*, Houghton, 1940; *Rio Grande to Cape Horn*, Houghton, 1943; *Dawn over the Amazon* (Literary Guild selection), Duell, Sloan & Pearce, 1943; *Lands of the Dawning Morrow*, Bobbs-Merrill, 1948; *The Long Land: Chile*, Coward, 1949.

Our Yankee Heritage: The Making of Greater New Haven, Bradley & Scoville, 1951, 2nd edition, 1957; *Stephen F. Austin: Father of Texas*, McGraw, 1953; *Our Yankee Heritage: The Making of Bristol*, Bristol Public Library Association, 1954; *Our Yankee Heritage: New England's Contribution to American Civilization*, McKay, 1955, reprinted, Books for Libraries, 1970; *Adventure of the Western Sea: The Story of Robert Gray*, Holt, 1956; *Taste of Glory* (novel), Crown, 1956; *John Eliot: The Man Who Loved the Indians* (Literary Guild selection), Messner, 1958; *House in Mexico*, Hastings House, 1958; *Brass Knuckle Crusade: The Great Know-Nothing Conspiracy*, Hastings House, 1960; *Nomads and Empire Builders: Native Peoples and Cultures of South America*, Chilton, 1961; *Cyclone Carry: The Story of Carry Nation*, Chilton, 1962; (translator) Juan Jose Arivalo, *Anti-Communism in Latin America*, Lyle Stuart, 1963; *Latin America: World in Revolution*, Abelard, 1963; *Eagles of the Andes: South American Struggles for Independence*, Chilton, 1963; *War within a War: The Confederacy against Itself*, Chilton, 1965; *Land of the Mayas: Yesterday and Today*, Abelard, 1967; *The Great Revolt and Its Leaders: The History of Popular American Uprisings in the 1890s*, Abelard, 1968; *Colonial Rhode Island*, Thomas Nelson, 1970; *Great Guerrilla Warriors*, Prentice-Hall, 1970; *The Nature of Revolution*, Crowell, 1970; *Stories Told by the Aztecs before the Spaniards Came*, Abelard, 1970; *The Incredible Incas: Yesterday and Today*, Abelard, 1973.

Contributor: *Genius of Mexico*, Committee on Cultural Relations with Latin America, 1931; *Recovery through Revolution*, Covici, Friede, 1933; *Contemporary Opinion*, Houghton, 1933; *The Writer in a Changing World*, Equinox, 1937; *We Testify*, Smith & Durell, 1941; *Invitation to Learning*, Random House, 1942; *What South America Thinks of Us*, McBride, 1945; *The Price of Liberty*, Harper, 1947; *Exploring Life through Literature*, Scott, Foresman, 1951; *A Treasury of Mississippi River Folk Lore*, Crown, 1955; *Politics U.S.A.*, Macmillan, 1961; *Bits of Silver*, Hastings House, 1961; *The Age of Porfirio Diaz*, University of New Mexico Press, 1977. Also contributor to *Church Problem in Mexico*, 1926.

Author of introduction: *The Under Dogs*, J. Cape, 1930; *Memoirs of Jose Luis Blasio*, Yale University Press, 1939; *J'Accuse*, Dial Press, 1940; *Free Men of America*, Ziff Davis, 1943.

Contributor to numerous books, pamphlets, encyclopedias, magazines, and newspapers in the United States and other countries. Columnist, *Independent*, beginning 1961. Associate editor, *Mexican Folkways*, 1925-37, *Controversy*, 1936, *Living Age*, 1936, and *Modern Monthly*, 1943-46; member of advisory board, *Living Age*, 1933-35; contributing editor, *Common Sense*, 1933-41, *Modern Monthly*, 1935-37, and *Current History*, 1939; president of editorial board, *Latin American Digest*, 1934-36; advisory editor, *Controversy*, 1935.

WORK IN PROGRESS: Several books, including an autobiography.

SIDELIGHTS: The *New York Times* once called Carleton Beals "the dean of correspondents in Latin America. . . . [He] was a colorful, crusading journalist, a native American independent." During his long career, he visited some forty-two countries and covered numerous revolutions and guerrilla uprisings, including four Mexican rebellions, a guerrilla war against the U.S. occupation of Nicaragua (led by General Augusto Sandino), the overthrow of Cuban president Gerado Machado, and the rise of Mussolini's fascist state in Italy. Along the way, Beals said, he managed to meet "some of the world's great leaders, thinkers, writers and artists." As he once told *CA:* "Mine has been a full independent life with the customary number of successes and set-backs, ups and downs. I have witnessed numerous revolutions and governmental turnovers in Latin America, Africa and Europe. My life has covered the downfall of European imperialism and serious setbacks to United States imperialism. I have been gladdened by the independence of India, Pakistan, Indo-China, Indonesia, most of Africa, much of Europe, Mexico, Cuba, Jamaica and other peoples of the Caribbean, the various countries of the Near East, of Morocco, Algiers, Tunis, Lybia and Egypt, the end of the Franco dictatorship (but not his system) in Spain, the new democratic regime in Portugal, the overthrow of Mussolini in Italy. I was present at the time of his march on Rome, and at that time prophesied he would last a quarter of a century. I am saddened by the puppet dictatorships of the United States in Chile, Argentina, Uruguay and Brazil, frightful regimes all of them. But more new independent nations have been born during my life time than any time in the history of the world, and a goodly number of them are examples of human freedom. Not since the collapse of the Spanish empire has the phenomenon of human liberation been more in evidence.

"Being an independent writer . . . is a thorny path. Sooner or later, one steps on everybody's toes. Being an independent writer means having no fixed address; people pin labels on you, and, when the labels don't fit, they hate you. But there is still a large body of independent thinkers in America; there is a large body of tolerant spirits; there is a large body of people seeking knowledge, truth, moral and spiritual understanding. Such as these are my friends and my readers. Sometimes I fail them but not most of the time.

"I have done most of my writing in Spain, Italy, Mexico and Peru, and in this country, chiefly in New York, later in Guilford, Conn., since 1957 in Killingworth, where I have reconditioned one of the village's first schoolhouses as a study, a big barrel-ceiling room, with seven windows, floor to ceiling book shelves, three metal files, a grand piano, good heat, a radio but no television, water colors of Haiti's painter, Joseph Blanchard, neon lights.

"My wife tends to three horses, five goats, a dog and a cat. She gets most of the exercise. When I feel the need for exercise, I usually lie down on my studio couch, and it soon goes away. My working hours are about 9:00 to 2:00, occasionally a few hours in the afternoon, 8:30 p.m. to midnight or maybe 3:00 a.m. I read one book a day (included in work time). Most of my reading is in Spanish."

In addition to his work as a correspondent, Beal often traveled throughout the world as a member of various educational and archaeological expeditions. He spoke Spanish, Italian, and some German, and had a reading knowledge of French, Portuguese, and basic Aztec.

AVOCATIONAL INTERESTS: Chess, horseback-riding.

BIOGRAPHICAL/CRITICAL SOURCES: *Horn Book*, April, 1958; *Nation*, August 20, 1960; *New York Herald Tribune Book Review*, August 28, 1960; *Saturday Review*, December 16, 1961, October 12, 1963; *Yale Review*, December, 1963; *Times Literary Supplement*, March 5, 1964; *Christian Science Monitor*, May 4, 1967; *Spectator*, September 13, 1968; *Best Sellers*, March 1, 1970, March 15, 1971; *Books*, June, 1970; *New York Times*, June 28, 1979; *Time*, July 9, 1979.†

*   *   *

BEATTY, Jerome, Jr. 1918-

PERSONAL: Born December 9, 1918, in New Rochelle, N.Y. *Education:* Dartmouth College, B.A., 1939. *Address:* Box 168, Waquoit, Mass. 02536.

CAREER: *Newark News*, Newark, N.J., reporter, 1940-43; *Coronet*, New York City, associate editor, 1946-49; *Pageant*, New York City, associate editor, 1949-52; *Collier's*, New York City, staff writer, 1952-57; free-lance writer, 1957—. Contributing editor and co-author of "Trade Winds" column, *Saturday Review*, 1957-71; cartoon consultant, *Esquire*, 1957-75. *Military service:* U.S. Army, 1943-46; interpreter attached to Chinese Army. *Member:* Science Fiction Writers of America, American Society of Journalists and Authors, Authors Guild. *Awards, honors:* Massachusetts Children's Honor Award, 1980, for *Matthew Looney's Invasion of the Earth*.

WRITINGS: I Married a Barracks Bag, Kaw River Press, 1944; *Sex Rears Its Lovely Head*, Bantam, 1956; (compiler) *The Saturday Review Gallery*, introduction by John T. Winterich, Simon & Schuster, 1959; *Show Me the Way to Go Home: The Commuter Story*, Crowell, 1959.

Matthew Looney's Voyage to the Earth: A Space Story (juvenile), W. R. Scott, 1961; *Have You Ever Wondered?*, Macfadden, 1962; *Bob Fulton's Amazing Soda Pop Stretcher: An International Spy Story* (juvenile), W. R. Scott, 1963; *The Girls We Leave Behind: A Terribly Scientific Study of American Women at Home*, Doubleday, 1963; *The Clambake Mutiny: An Undersea Story* (juvenile), W. R. Scott, 1964; *One O'Clock in the Button Factory*, Macmillan, 1964; *Matthew Looney's Invasion of the Earth* (juvenile), W. R. Scott, 1965; (editor) Daniel Weston Hall, *Arctic Rovings* (juvenile), W. R. Scott, 1968; *Matthew Looney in the Outback: A Space Story* (juvenile), W. R. Scott, 1969.

Sheriff Stonehead and the Teenage Termites (juvenile), W. R. Scott, 1970; *Blockade!*, Doubleday, 1971; (compiler) *Double Take*, cartoons by Terence Parkes, Greene, 1971; *Matthew Looney and the Space Pirates* (juvenile), W. R. Scott, 1972; *R. J. Reynolds, Our 100th Anniversary*, privately printed, 1975; *From New Bedford to Siberia*, Doubleday, 1977; *Maria Looney on the Red Planet* (juvenile), Avon, 1977; *Maria Looney and the Cosmic Circus* (juvenile), Avon, 1978; *Maria Looney and the Remarkable Robot* (juvenile), Avon, 1979; *Bob Fulton's Terrific Time Machine* (juvenile), Bantam, 1981.

BEATTY, Patricia Robbins 1922-
(Jean Bartholomew)

PERSONAL: Born August 26, 1922, in Portland, Ore.; daughter of Walter M. and Jessie (Miller) Robbins; married John Louis Beatty (a professor of history and humanities), September 14, 1950 (died, 1975); married Carl G. Uhr (a professor of economics); children: (first marriage) Ann Alexandra Beatty Stewart. *Education:* Reed College, B.A., 1944,; graduate study at University of Idaho, 1947-50, and University of Washington, Seattle, 1951. *Politics:* Independent. *Religion:* Protestant. *Residence:* Riverside, Calif.

CAREER: High school teacher of English and history, Coeur d'Alene, Idaho, 1947-50; technical library work, hydrogen bomb project, Wilmington, Del., 1952-53; business and science librarian, Riverside, Calif., 1953-56; teacher of creative writing for young readers, University of California, Riverside, 1967-68, and University of California, Los Angeles, 1968-69. *Awards, honors:* Commonwealth Club of California Medal for best juvenile by California author in 1965, for *Campion Towers;* Southern California Council on Children's and Young People's Literature award for best fiction of the year, 1967, for *The Royal Dirk,* and "Body of Work" award, 1974; Woman of the Year awards from American Association of University Women, 1975, and from Riverside-Magnolia Center Business and Professional Women's Club, 1977.

WRITINGS—Juveniles, published by Morrow, except as indicated: *Indian Canoemaker,* Caxton, 1960; *Bonanza Girl,* 1962; (with husband, John Louis Beatty) *At the Seven Stars,* Macmillan, 1963; *The Nickel Plated Beauty,* 1964; (with J. L. Beatty) *Campion Towers,* Macmillan, 1965; *Squaw Dog,* 1965; (with J. L. Beatty) *The Royal Dirk,* 1966; *The Queen's Own Grove,* 1966; (with J. L. Beatty) *A Donkey for the King,* Macmillan, 1966; *The Lady from Blackhawk,* McGraw, 1967; (with J. L. Beatty) *The Queen's Wizard,* Macmillan, 1967; *Me, California Perkins,* 1968; (with J. L. Beatty) *Witch Dog,* 1968; *Blue Stars Watching,* 1969; (with J. L. Beatty) *Pirate Royal,* Macmillan, 1969.

The Sea Pair, 1970; *Hail Columbia,* 1970; *A Long Way to Whiskey Creek,* 1971; (with J. L. Beatty) *King's Knight's Pawn,* 1971; *O the Red Rose Tree,* 1972; (with J. L. Beatty) *Holdfast,* 1972; *The Bad Bell of San Salvador,* 1973; *Red Rock over the River,* 1973; *How Many Miles to Sundown,* 1974; (with J. L. Beatty) *Master Rosalind,* 1974; (under pseudonym Jean Bartholomew) *The Englishman's Mistress* (adult Gothic novel), Dell, 1974; (with J. L. Beatty) *Who Comes to King's Mountain?,* 1975; *Rufus, Red Rufus,* 1975; *By Crumbs, It's Mine!,* 1976; *Something to Shout About,* 1976; *Billy Bedamned, Long Gone By,* 1977; *I Want My Sunday, Stranger!,* 1977; *Just Some Weeds from the Wilderness,* 1978; *Wait for Me, Watch for Me, Eula Bee,* 1978; *Lacy Makes a Match,* 1979; *The Staffordshire Terror,* 1979; *That's One Ornery Orphan,* 1980.

Also author of materials on English history for Science Research Associates.

SIDELIGHTS: Some of Patricia Beatty's books have been translated into Spanish, Danish, German, and Norwegian. *Avocational interests:* Gardening.

BIOGRAPHICAL/CRITICAL SOURCES: Book World, May 5, 1968, February 23, 1969; *Saturday Review,* April 17, 1971; *Christian Science Monitor,* February 12, 1979.

*   *   *

BECK, Warren

PERSONAL: Born in Richmond, Ind.; son of Wilbur Henry and Lillian (Kemper) Beck; married Carmen Haberman, July 13, 1930 (divorced, 1956); children: James Peter. *Education:* Earlham College, B.A., 1921; Columbia University, M.A., 1926. *Home:* 207 North Park Ave., Appleton, Wis. 54911. *Office:* Department of English, Lawrence University, Appleton, Wis. 54911.

CAREER: Lawrence University, Appleton, Wis., instructor, 1926-29, assistant professor, 1929-32, associate professor, 1932-37, professor of English, 1937-68, professor emeritus, 1968—. Visiting professor at U.S. Army University, Shrivenham, England, 1945, University of Minnesota, 1956, and University of Colorado, 1957; member of faculty of Bread Loaf Graduate School of English, Middlebury College, summers, 1947-55; member of staff of writers' conferences at other colleges and universities. *Member:* Phi Beta Kappa. *Awards, honors:* Friends of American Writers Award, 1945, for *Final Score;* Rockefeller Foundation grant to write fiction and criticism, 1948-59; Ford Foundation fellowship, 1952-53; Lit.D. from Earlham College, 1953; Ehrig Foundation Award for excellence in teaching, 1961; American Council of Learned Societies, fellowship, 1963, grant, 1969; *Joyce's "Dubliners": Substance, Vision, and Art* was chosen by Modern Language Association of America for inclusion in The Scholar's Library, 1970.

WRITINGS: The Blue Sash and Other Stories, Antioch Press, 1941; *Final Score* (novel), Knopf, 1944; *The First Fish and Other Stories,* Antioch Press, 1947; *Pause under the Sky* (novel), Swallow & Morrow, 1947; *The Far Whistle and Other Stories,* Antioch Press, 1951; *Into Thin Air* (novel), Knopf, 1951; *Man in Motion: Faulkner's Trilogy,* University of Wisconsin Press, 1961; *The Rest Is Silence and Other Stories,* Swallow Press, 1963; *Joyce's "Dubliners": Substance, Vision, and Art,* Duke University Press, 1969; *Faulkner: Essays,* University of Wisconsin, 1976.

Also author of monograph, *Huck Finn at Phelps Farm,* published by Archives des Lettres Modernes, 1958. Six short stories have been included in various editions of *Best American Short Stories* and ten in other anthologies. Contributor of stories, critical essays, and reviews to magazines and newspapers.

WORK IN PROGRESS: A novel, *Voices and Silences.*

SIDELIGHTS: Warren Beck told *CA:* "For forty-two years at Lawrence, and elsewhere as visiting professor, I was an 'English teacher,' chiefly of 19th and 20th century literature, English and American, and at times a tutor in literary composition for selected students. Concurrently I have also been a writer of short stories and novels, and, more recently, literary criticism. I'm still trying to apply what I've taught, out of the examples of our betters, both precedent and contemporary. This holds not only in attempts to apply my extracted notions of the arts of fictional composition (my work in progress being a novel), but has held in my literary criticism on Joyce and Faulkner.

"My intention in this latter has been impressionistic rather than scholarly, in that it aims primarily at interpretive explication of the text in hand, and borrows from the learning of others very little except as that may expedite an understanding of the text's particulars at that point. (Conversely, on occasion a scholar quoted by an editor of an anthology or other text may have to be questioned and the student invited to consider whether a less strained, less remotely derived impression, and one nearer in line with the writer's manner and prevalent bent, doesn't give a clearer, more persuasive sense that best harmonizes with the whole passage. Indeed, in textually oriented study, use should be made of whatever exemplifies the words as a continuity of units that structure themselves into larger and larger conceptual entities which coalesce into the complete autonomous work of art.)

"At any rate, in teaching literary works to undergraduates and graduate students, through shared individual attention to the text, I've seen a number, from generations of students in a variety of American institutions, become spontaneously attentive to the particular subject and rapidly progressive in what they were learning to do for themselves as readers of literature. A welcome reassurance for the teacher that they had developed their own tasteful comparative judgments came at term's end when a poll of preferences among ten novels or several poets of a period showed choices scattered all over the list. The total experience didn't surprise me. Nor was I complacent in recalling the anecdote of Toscanini at a culminating rehearsal, when after going straight through the symphony as if in a concert the musicians broke into applause for their conductor, and he cried out, 'Gentlemen, it is not I, it is Beethoven!' But Toscanini, indubitably a genius, was also an eminently learned and severe scholar in music. More humbly, an impressionistic critic can make a similar gesture of deference to any text he feels inclined to promulgate, as teacher or writer, as best he can in its own terms and worth."

* * *

BECKELHYMER, (Paul) Hunter 1919-

PERSONAL: Born November 23, 1919, in Trenton, Mo.; son of Earl Errett (a locomotive engineer) and Corinne (Caffrey) Beckelhymer; married Betty Jane Courtney, August 19, 1951; children: Helen Corinne, Anna Christine, Carolyn Jean. *Education:* Park College, A.B., 1941; University of Chicago, B.D., 1944. *Home:* 5725 Whitman Ave., Ft. Worth, Tex. 76133. *Office:* Brite Divinity School, Texas Christian University, Fort Worth, Tex. 76129.

CAREER: North Shore Christian Church, Chicago, Ill, minister, 1944-46; Church of Christ (Disciples), Kenton, Ohio, minister, 1946-53; Christian Church (Disciples), Hiram, Ohio, minister, 1953-66; Texas Christian University, Brite Divinity School, Forth Worth, associate professor of homiletics, 1966—, member of faculty senate, 1971-73, and 1975-77. Disciples of Christ, member of panel of scholars, 1957-62, and vice-chairman, Board of Higher Education. *Member:* Association for Professional Education of Ministry, American Academy of Homiletics. *Awards, honors:* D.D., Christian Theological Seminary, Indianapolis, Ind., 1959; Alumnus of the Year award, Divinity School, University of Chicago, 1974.

WRITINGS: Meeting Life on Higher Levels, Abingdon, 1956; *Questions God Asks,* Abingdon, 1961; *Hocking Valley Iron Man* (private edition), Bethany Press, 1962; (contributor) W. B. Blakemore, editor, *The Renewal of Church,* three volumes, Bethany Press, 1963; *Dear Connie,* Bethany Press, 1967; (editor) *The Vital Pulpit of the Christian Church,* Bethany Press, 1969; (editor) *The Word We Preach,* Texas Christian University Press, 1970. Contributor of articles to journals. Member of editorial council, *Encounter,* 1959-63.

* * *

BECKER, Stephen (David) 1927-
(Steve Dodge)

PERSONAL: Born March 31, 1927, in Mount Vernon, N.Y.; son of David (a pharmacist) and Lillian (Kevitz) Becker; married Mary Elizabeth Freeburg, December 24, 1947; children: Keir, Julia, David. *Education:* Harvard University,

A.B., 1947; Yenching University, graduate studies, 1947-48. *Politics:* Democrat. *Home and office:* East End, Tortola, British Virgin Islands. *Agent:* Russell & Volkening, Inc., 551 Fifth Ave., New York, N.Y. 10017.

CAREER: Free-lance writer, translator, and editor, 1949—, living in China, France, Alaska, the Guianas, and the United States. Teaching fellow in history, Brandeis University, 1951-52; visiting professor of English, University of Alaska, summer, 1967; teacher in literature, Bennington College, fall, 1971. *Military service:* U.S. Marine Corps, 1945. *Awards, honors:* Guggenheim fellowship in creative writing, 1954.

WRITINGS—Novels, except as indicated: *The Season of the Stranger,* Harper, 1951; *Shanghai Incident,* Gold Medal, 1955; *Juice,* Simon & Schuster, 1959; *Comic Art in America* (history), Simon & Schuster, 1960; *Marshall Field III* (biography), Simon & Schuster, 1964; *A Covenant with Death,* Atheneum, 1965; *The Outcasts,* Atheneum, 1967; *When the War Is Over,* Random House, 1970; *Dog Tags,* Random House, 1972; *The Chinese Bandit,* Random House, 1975; *The Last Mandarin,* Random House, 1979. Author of screenplays, short stories, magazine articles and reviews.

Translator: Romain Gary, *Colors of the Day,* Simon & Schuster, 1953; P. D. Gaisseau, *Sacret Forest,* Knopf, 1954; Louis Carl and Joseph Petit, *Mountains in the Desert,* Doubleday, 1954 (published in England as *Tefedest: Journey to the Heart of the Sahara,* D. Allen, 1954); Andre Dhotel, *Faraway,* Simon & Schuster, 1957; R. Puissesseau, *Someone Will Die Tonight in the Caribbean,* Knopf, 1958; A. Schwarz-Bart, *The Last of the Just,* Atheneum, 1960; Elie Wiesel, *The Town beyond the Wall,* Atheneum, 1964; Andre Malraux, *The Conquerors,* Holt, 1976; Louis-Philippe, *Diary of My Travels in America,* Delacorte, 1978; Agustin Gomez-Arcos, *Ana No,* Secker & Warburg, 1980.

SIDELIGHTS: The *Time* critic calls Stephen Becker "a fiddle-footed traveler with a facile pen." Most critics agree with Stephen Geller of the *New York Times Book Review* who writes that Becker's style is "fluid and graceful," that his language is "acutely and effectively imagistic." If Becker's work has a serious flaw, critics would probably agree that his language isn't always pedestrian enough to be consistent with the characters who speak it. But, as Haskell A. Simpson writes in *Saturday Review,* "Becker's talk . . . shimmers with wit and understanding. . . . The dazzled reader can only wish that Mr. Becker were a playwright or a poet."

The *Time* reviewer states that Becker, like Conrad, is primarily concerned with "the tactical struggles of daily life, the strategic deployments that bring one man success and another failure." And Becker's ability to handle a Conrad-like theme with ease has often been remarked. Reviewing *The Outcasts,* *Harper's* Katherine Gauss Jackson writes: "Mr. Becker is incapable of writing a dull or frivolous book. There is flavor and reason in everything he has to say."

In his review of *The Last Mandarin* in the *Chicago Tribune Book World,* Richard J. Walton agrees that Becker's novels are enjoyable to read. He calls the novel "incredible, but it's such fun—so inventive, fast-paced, and high-spirited—that you more than willingly suspend your disbelief," and adds that "rather than wait for Becker's next book" he "is going to scout out some of his old ones. They must be awfully good."

A Covenant with Death was filmed by Warner Bros. in 1967.

BIOGRAPHICAL/CRITICAL SOURCES: New York Times,

February 16, 1967, November 7, 1969; *Time*, March 17, 1967; *New York Times Book Review*, March 19, 1967, November 9, 1969; *Newsweek*, March 20, 1967; *Harper's*, April, 1967; *Saturday Review*, April 1, 1967; *Chicago Tribune Book World*, May 13, 1979.

* * *

BEGNER, Edith

PERSONAL: Born in New York, N.Y.; daughter of Herrman and Anna (Dorfman) Friedman; married Jacob Anthony Begner, 1938; children: Thomas L. *Education:* Attended Wellesley College, 1937, and Columbia University, 1938-44. *Agent:* Cohn, Glickstein, Lurie, Ostrin & Lubell, 1370 Avenue of the Americas, New York, N.Y. 10019.

CAREER: Writer. *Member:* P.E.N. American Center.

WRITINGS: Just Off Fifth, Rinehart, 1959; *Son and Heir*, Holt, 1960 (published in England as *His Son and Heir*, Secker & Warburg, 1961); *Red in the Morning*, Doubleday, 1963; *A Dark and Lonely Hiding Place*, Bobbs-Merrill, 1968; *Accident of Birth*, Avon, 1977; *Golden Opportunity*, Avon, 1980.

WORK IN PROGRESS: A novel, tentatively entitled *Gerard.*

SIDELIGHTS: Edith Begner comments on the direction her writing has taken: "Right now I seem to be leaning toward the presentation of serious subjects from a humorous point of view in contrast to earlier novels that presented problems within the medical profession with drama and suspense.... One of my favorite writers is Graham Greene.... Among other things, I learned from him to extricate myself from being typecast by publishers into a form they call a 'genre' and to follow my own inclinations no matter how discouraging others may be. I have recently become enamored of children's books in the ten to twelve age group and expect to complete at least one of these in the future." She advises aspiring writers to "write at the same time every day and . . . abandon anything that does not give one joy."

Begner adds: "I believe that the days of the hardcover novel are numbered . . . but I do not believe the paperback companies have yet solved the problem of how to bring forth a good paperback original, nor have the reviewers even begun to address themselves to this new situation [and recognize paperbacks as serious entertainment]. Nevertheless, I remain committed to the principle of the paperback original and will continue to bring out my novels in that form unless someone in the future convinces me of the error of my thinking."

BIOGRAPHICAL/CRITICAL SOURCES: Publisher's Weekly, January 29, 1968; *Best Sellers*, June 1, 1968; *New York Times Book Review*, May 8, 1977.

* * *

BEHR, Edward 1926-

PERSONAL: Born May 7, 1926, in Paris, France; son of Felix and Eugenia (Cade) Behr. *Education:* Magdalene College, Cambridge, M.A., 1950. *Home:* 86 Rue de Monceau, Paris 75008, France. *Office: Newsweek*, 162 Faubourg St. Honore, Paris 75008, France.

CAREER: Reuters (news agency), correspondent in London, England, and Paris, France, 1950-54; European Coal and Steel Community, Luxembourg, information officer, 1955-56; Time Inc., correspondent in Paris, the Middle East, and India, 1957-63; *Saturday Evening Post*, contributing editor, 1963-65; French news-in-depth television program,

"Cinq Colonnes a la Une," reporter-director, 1963-65; *Newsweek*, Paris correspondent, 1965-66, Hong Kong bureau chief, 1966-68, Paris bureau chief, 1968-72, European editor, Paris, 1973—. Frequent contributor to the British Broadcasting Corp. (radio and television). *Military service:* Indian Army, Royal Garhwal Rifles, 1944-48; became acting major. *Member:* Royal Institute on International Affairs (Chatham House), Press Club (both London).

WRITINGS: The Algerian Problem, Norton, 1961, reprinted, Greenwood Press, 1976; (translator, adapter, and editor with Sydney Liu) Lai Ying, *The Thirty-sixth Way: A Personal Account of Imprisonment and Escape from Red China*, Doubleday, 1969; *Bearings: A Foreign Correspondent's Life behind the Lines*, Viking, 1978; *Getting Even* (novel), Harper, 1980. Contributor to *L'Express, Figaro*, and *Nouvel Observateur*.

WORK IN PROGRESS: A second novel.

SIDELIGHTS: Television news assignments have taken Edward Behr to Cuba, Red China, and the United States; his films, "Washington Ville Noire," on the Negro in Washington, and "Enterrements de premiere," about the U.S. mortician, have won awards at a Swiss television festival. *Avocational interests:* Travel, historical research, swimming.

BIOGRAPHICAL/CRITICAL SOURCES: Los Angeles Times, November 19, 1978; *Times Literary Supplement*, October 3, 1980.

* * *

BELFRAGE, Cedric 1904-

PERSONAL: Last syllable of surname is pronounced as in "beverage"; born November 8, 1904, in London, England; son of Sidney Henning (a physician) and Grace (Powley) Belfrage; married Mary Bernick; children: Sally, Nicholas, Anne. *Education:* Attended Corpus Christi College, Cambridge. *Politics:* Socialist. *Home:* Apdo. 630, Cuernavaca, Morelos, Mexico.

CAREER: Hollywood correspondent for British publications, *New York Herald Tribune*, and *New York Sun*, 1927-30; went to London as public relations man for Samuel Goldwyn, 1930, remained as film and theatre critic, waterfront coverer, and roving correspondent for London *Sunday* and *Daily Express*; returned to United States, 1936; *National Guardian*, New York, N.Y., founder and editor, 1948-55; ruled subversive by McCarthy Committee in 1953, twice apprehended by U.S. Immigration and Naturalization Service, and deported to England, 1955; editor-in-exile of *National Guardian* and reporter for various overseas left-wing journals from Europe, Middle East, Africa, Soviet Asia, China, India, Cuba, and South America, 1955-67; settled in Mexico, 1963. *Wartime service:* British Intelligence, New York, 1941-43; Psychological Warfare Division of Supreme Headquarters, Allied Expeditionary Force, France, 1944, Germany (reconstruction of press), 1945. *Awards, honors:* Guggenheim fellow, 1947; Louis M. Rabinowitz Foundation award, 1968.

WRITINGS: Away from It All, Simon & Schuster, 1937; *Promised Land*, Gollancz, 1938; *Let My People Go*, Gollancz, 1940, published as *South of God*, Modern Age, 1941; *They All Hold Swords*, Modern Age, 1941; *A Faith to Free the People*, Dryden Press, 1944; *Abide with Me*, Sloane, 1948; *Seeds of Destruction*, Cameron & Kahn, 1954; *The Frightened Giant*, Secker & Warburg, 1957; *My Master Columbus*, Doubleday, 1961; *The Man at the Door with the Gun*, Monthly Review, 1963; *La Inquisicion democratica* (originally written in English), Siglo Veintiuno (Mexico), 1971, published as *The American Inquisition,* Bobbs-Merrill, 1973; *Something to Guard,* Columbia University Press, 1978.

Translator from the Spanish; all published by Monthly Review Press: *Guatemala: Occupied Country,* 1969; *We the Puerto Rican People,* 1971; *Open Veins of Latin America,* 1973; *Workers' Struggle in Puerto Rico,* 1976; *The Sugarmill,* 1976; *Sandino, General of Free Men,* 1980.

*   *   *

BELTING, Natalia Maree 1915-

PERSONAL: Born July 11, 1915, in Oskaloosa, Iowa; daughter of Paul Everette and Anna Maree (Hanselman) Belting. *Education:* Attended Coe College, 1932-33; University of Illinois, B.S., 1936, M.A., 1937, Ph.D., 1940. *Religion:* Presbyterian. *Home:* R.R. 2, Box 19, The Big Woods, Urbana, Ill. 61801. *Office:* Department of History, University of Illinois, Urbana, Ill. 61801.

CAREER: University of Illinois at Urbana-Champaign, 1942—, began as instructor, associate professor of history, 1973—. Supply preacher in rural Presbyterian churches, Illinois. *Member:* Authors Guild, Wildlife Federation, Delta Zeta, Phi Alpha Theta. *Awards, honors:* Named Illinois Author of the Year by Illinois State Association of Teachers of English, 1979.

WRITINGS: (With P. E. Belting) *The Modern High School Curriculum,* Garrard, 1940; *Kaskaskia under the French Regime,* University of Illinois Press, 1948; *Pierre of Kaskaskia,* Bobbs-Merrill, 1951; *Moon Is a Crystal Ball,* Bobbs-Merrill, 1952; *In Enemy Hands,* Bobbs-Merrill, 1953; *Three Apples Fell from Heaven,* Bobbs-Merrill, 1953; *Cat Tales,* Holt, 1959 (published in England as *King Solomon's Cat: Folk Tales from around the World,* Rapp & Whiting, 1968); *Indy and Mr. Lincoln,* Holt, 1960; *Verity Mullens and the Indian,* Holt, 1960; *Elves and Ellefolk,* Holt, 1961; *The Long-Tailed Bear,* Bobbs-Merrill, 1961; *The Sun Is a Golden Ear Ring,* Holt, 1962; *The Calendar Moon,* Holt, 1964; *The Earth Is on a Fish's Back,* Holt, 1965; *The Stars Are Silver Reindeer,* Holt, 1966; *Christmas Folk,* Holt, 1969; *Winter's Eve,* Holt, 1969; *Summer's Coming In,* Holt, 1970; *The Land of the Taffeta Dawn,* Dutton, 1973; *Our Fathers Had Powerful Songs,* Dutton, 1974; *Whirlwind Is a Ghost Dancing,* Dutton, 1974.

WORK IN PROGRESS: Transcribing and editing a dictionary of Illinois language, compiled by a Jesuit missionary in 1712.

AVOCATIONAL INTERESTS: Baking, gardening, wood carving, the Indians of Illinois.

*   *   *

BENAMOU, Michel J(ean) 1929-1978

PERSONAL: Born December, 1929, in Paris, France; died, 1978; married Gerane Siemering, December, 1951; children: Catherine, Marc, Natalie. *Education:* University of Paris, Sorbonne, licence es lettres, 1951, diplome d'etudes sup., 1952, C.A.P.E.S., 1953, agregation, 1953, doctorat, 1973. *Office:* Department of French, University of Wisconsin—Milwaukee, Milwaukee, Wis. 53201.

CAREER: Lycee, Orleans, France, member of faculty, 1953-54; Ecole Navale, Brest, France, member of faculty, 1954-55; University of Michigan, Ann Arbor, instructor in French, 1956-59; Dartmouth College, Hanover, N.H., assistant professor of French, 1959-63; University of Michigan,

associate professor, 1963-68, professor of French, 1968-69; University of California, San Diego, professor of French and head of French section, 1969-74; University of Wisconsin—Milwaukee, professor of French and director of Center for Twentieth Century Studies, 1974-78. Consultant, U.S. Office of Education, Glastonbury Project, 1959-61; professor in National Defense Education Act summer institutes, University of Georgia, 1959, University of Maine, 1960, University of Colorado, 1961, College of St. Catherine, 1962, and University of Rennes, 1964; coordinator of French language program, Norwich (Vt.) grade school, 1960-63; coordinator of language training, Peace Corps Guinea 2 project, Dartmouth College, 1963; director, Michigan-Wisconsin Junior Year in France, 1965-66. *Military service:* French Navy, 1954-56; became lieutenant. *Member:* Modern Language Association of America, American Association of Teachers of French, International Association of Comparative Literature. *Awards, honors:* Dartmouth College faculty fellowship, 1961-62; Chevalier des palmes academiques, 1975, for services to higher education.

WRITINGS: Vocabulaire Anglais-francais de la Chimie du Petrole, Dunod, 1957; (with others) *French,* Harcourt, 1961; (contributor) *The Achievement of Wallace Stevens,* Lippincott, 1962; (with W. C. Calin and Jean Carduner) *Le Moulin a Paroles,* Ginn, 1963; (editor with Calin) *Aux Portes du Poeme,* Macmillan, 1964; (contributor) *The Act of the Mind,* Johns Hopkins Press, 1965; (with Eugene Ionesco) *Mise en train, Premiere annee de francais,* Macmillan, 1969; *Pour une nouvelle pedagogie du texte litteraire,* Hachette (Paris), 1971; *Wallace Stevens and the Symbolist Imagination,* Princeton University Press, 1972; *L'oeuvre-monde de Wallace Stevens,* H. Champlon (Paris), 1975; (editor with Jerome Rothenberg) *Ethnopoetics: A First International Symposium,* Boston University, 1976. Contributor of articles to French and American professional journals and to *American Oxford Encyclopedia.*†

*   *   *

BENNETT, Norman Robert 1932-

PERSONAL: Born October 31, 1932, in Marlboro, Mass.; son of Norman (a shoe worker) and Viola (Belmore) Bennett; married Ruth Roberts (a university teacher), December 31, 1954 (divorced, 1973); married Jeanne Penvenne, January 20, 1976; children: (second marriage) Jean Norman Bennett. *Education:* Tufts University, A.B. (magna cum laude), 1954; Princeton University, graduate student, 1954-55; Fletcher School of Law and Diplomacy, M.A., 1956; Boston University, Ph.D., 1961. *Politics:* Independent. *Religion:* None. *Office:* African Studies Center, 10 Lenox St., Brookline, Mass. 02146.

CAREER: Boston University, Boston, Mass., instructor, 1960-63, assistant professor, 1963-67, associate professor, 1967-70, professor of history, 1970—. Smith-Mundt Visiting Professor at Kivukoni College, Tanganyika, 1962-63; visiting scholar, Universidade Eduardo Mondlane, Mozambique, 1977. *Member:* American Historical Association, African Studies Association (chairman of archives committee, 1961-63; vice-president, 1979-80; president, 1980-81), American Civil Liberties Union, British Institute of Archaeology and History in East Africa, Tanzania Society, Uganda Society, Nantucket Historical Society, Nantucket Conservation Society. *Awards, honors:* Ford Foundation fellowship, 1958-60; American Philosophical Society award, 1966.

WRITINGS: (Compiler) *Discovering Africa: Source Materials on the Opening of a Great Continent,* [Boston], 1961;

Studies in East African History, Boston University Press, 1963; (editor with George E. Brooks, Jr.) *New England Merchants in Africa: A History Through Documents, 1802 to 1865*, Boston University Press, 1965; (editor with Creighton Gabel) *Reconstructing African Culture History*, Boston University Press, 1967; (editor) *Leadership in Eastern Africa: Six Political Biographies*, Boston University Press, 1968; (compiler) *A Study Guide for Tunisia*, African Studies Center, Boston University, 1968; (compiler) *A Study Guide for Morocco*, African Studies Center, Boston University, 1968; (editor with Daniel F. McCall and Jeffrey Butler) *Eastern African History*, Praeger, 1969; (editor with McCall and Butler) *Western African History*, Praeger, 1969; *From Zanzibar to Ujiji*, African Studies Center, Boston University, 1969; (editor) *Stanley's Despatches to the New York Herald, 1871-1872, 1874-1877*, Boston University Press, 1970; *Mirambo of Tanzania*, Oxford University Press, 1971; (editor with Marguerite Minsaker) *The Central African Journal of Lovell J. Proctor, 1860-1864*, African Studies Center, Boston University, 1971; (editor with McCall) *Aspects of West African Islam*, African Studies Center, Boston University, 1971; (editor) *The Zanzibar Letters of Edward D. Ropes, Jr., 1882-1892*, African Studies Center, Boston University, 1973; *Africa and Europe from Roman Times to the Present*, Africana Publishing, 1975; *A History of the Arab State of Zanzibar*, Methuen, 1978. Contributor to *Tanganyika Notes and Records*, *Journal of African History*, *African Studies Bulletin*, Essex Institute *Historical Collections*, *African Affairs*, and other history and education journals. Editor, *African Studies Bulletin*, 1967-70, *International Journal of African Historical Studies*, 1968—.

WORK IN PROGRESS: Arab versus European in Nineteenth Century East Africa: Americans in East Africa; 19th Century Relations between Zanzibar, Mozambique, and Portugal.

*　　*　　*

BENOIT, Emile 1910-1978

PERSONAL: Born July 14, 1910, in New York, N.Y.; died May 4, 1978. *Education:* Harvard University, B.A., 1932, M.A., 1933, Ph.D., 1938. *Office:* Graduate School of Business, Columbia University, New York, N.Y.

CAREER: Harvard University, Radcliffe College, Cambridge, Mass., tutor, 1934-36; University of Illinois, Urbana, instructor, 1938-39; member of staff, Wells College, Aurora, N.Y., 1939-42; U.S. Government, analyst and economist with War Production Board and Department of Labor, Washington, D.C., 1942-47, attache at U.S. embassies in London and Vienna, 1948-53; McGraw-Hill Publishing Co., New York City, economist, 1954-56; Columbia University, Graduate School of Business, New York City, associate professor, 1956-62, professor of international business, 1962-74, senior research associate, 1974-78. Visiting professor and director of research program on economic adjustments to disarmament, Brookings Institution, 1960-61. Consultant to U.S. Arms Control and Disarmament Agency, and consultant to the U.N. Secretariat, 1961-62; consultant to U.S. Department of Defense, 1964-78; member of board of directors, Bettinger Corp., 1962-63. Member of foreign policy committee, Friends Committee on National Legislation; member of committee on church and economic life, National Council of Churches.

MEMBER: American Economic Association, Americans for Democratic Action (vice-chairman), Phi Beta Kappa. *Awards, honors:* Ford Foundation faculty research fellow-

ship and Carnegie Corp. grant, 1960-61; Ford Foundation research grant, 1962-65.

WRITINGS: Europe at Sixes and Sevens: The Common Market, the Free Trade Association and the United States, Columbia University Press, 1961; (editor with Kenneth Boulding) *Disarmament and the Economy,* Harper, 1963, reprinted, Greenwood Press, 1978; (with P. W. McCracken) *The Balance of Payments and Domestic Prosperity,* University of Michigan Bureau of Business Research, 1963; (consultant) A. H. Smith, *Economics for Our Time,* 4th edition, Webster, 1966; (editor with N. P. Gleditsch) *Disarmament and World Economic Interdependence,* Columbia University Press, 1967; *International Inequality: Is It a Real Issue?* (pamphlet), International Political Science Association, 1971; *Effect of Defense on Developing Economies,* Center for International Studies, Massachusetts Institute of Technology, 1972, published as *Defense and Economic Growth in Developing Countries,* Lexington Books, 1973.

Contributor: *Social Thought from Lore to Science,* Heath, 1938; *United Nations or World Government,* Wilson, 1947; *An Introduction to the History of Sociology,* University of Chicago Press, 1948; *The Sterling Area: An American Analysis,* H.M.S.O., 1951; *Echo der Welt,* Verlag Metz, 1958; Augustus H. Smith, *Economics of Our Times,* McGraw, 1959; *Joint International Business Ventures,* edited by Wolfgang Friedman and George Kalmanoff, Columbia University Press, 1961; *The Liberal Papers,* Anchor Books, 1962; *Preventing World War III,* edited by Quincy Wright, Simon and Schuster, 1962; *The Crossroad Papers,* edited by Hans J. Morgenthau, Norton, 1965. Contributor to *Current History, Challenge, Antioch Review, American Economic Review,* and other economic, political, and social science journals.

AVOCATIONAL INTERESTS: Mountaineering, swimming, chess, music.†

*　　*　　*

BENTLEY, Phyllis Eleanor 1894-1977

PERSONAL: Born November 19, 1894, in Halifax, England; died June, 1977, in Halifax, England; daughter of Joseph Edwin (a textile manufacturer) and Eleanor (Kettlewell) Bentley. *Education:* Attended Cheltenham Ladies' College; University of London, B.A., 1914. *Agent:* A. D. Peters & Co. Ltd., 10 Buckingham St., London WC2N 6BU, England.

CAREER: Former teacher; government secretary during World War I and World War II; library cataloger; free-lance writer. Council and committee member, Royal Literary Fund. Lecturer. *Member:* P.E.N. (vice-president of English centre), Authors Society, Royal Society of Literature (fellow), Halifax Thespians, Halifax Authors' Circle (president), Halifax Antiquarian Society (vice-president), English-Speaking Union Club. *Awards, honors:* D.Litt., University of Leeds, 1949; Order of the British Empire, 1970.

WRITINGS: The World's Bane and Other Stories, Unwin, 1918; *Pedagomania; Or, the Gentle Art of Teaching,* Unwin, 1918; *Environment* (novel), Sidgwick & Jackson, 1922, Hillman-Curl, 1935; *Cat-in-the-Manger* (novel), Sidgwick & Jackson, 1923; *The Spinner of the Years* (novel), Benn, 1928, Rae D. Henkle, 1929; *The Partnership* (novel), Benn, 1928, Little, Brown, 1929, reprinted, Chivers, 1977; *Carr* (biography), Benn, 1929, Macmillan, 1933; *Trio,* Gollancz, 1930, reprinted, Chivers, 1976; *Inheritance* (novel), Macmillan, 1932, reprinted, Pan Books, 1967; *A Modern Tragedy* (novel), Macmillan, 1934; *The Whole of the Story* (short story collection), Gollancz, 1935; *Freedom, Farewell!* (novel),

Macmillan, 1936, reprinted, Gollancz, 1968; *Sleep in Peace* (novel), Macmillan, 1938.

The Power and the Glory (novel), Macmillan, 1940 (published in England as *Take Courage,* Gollancz, 1940); *Manhold,* Macmillan, 1941; *Here Is America* (nonfiction), Gollancz, 1941; *The English Regional Novel* (nonfiction), Allen & Unwin, 1941, reprinted, Arden, 1978; *The Rise of Henry Morcar* (novel), Macmillan, 1946, reprinted, Gollancz, 1967; *Some Observations on the Art of Narrative* (nonfiction), Home & Van Thal, 1946, Macmillan, 1947, reprinted, Arden, 1978; *Colne Valley Cloth from the Earliest Times to the Present Day* (nonfiction), Huddersfield and District Woollen Export Group, 1947; *The Brontes* (nonfiction), Home & Van Thal, 1947, A. Swallow, 1948, reprinted, R. West, 1977, 2nd edition, Arthur Barker, 1966, reprinted, Haskell House, 1975, new edition, Pan Books, 1973; *Life Story* (novel), Macmillan, 1948.

Quorum, Gollancz, 1950, Macmillan, 1951, reprinted, Chivers, 1972; *Panorama: Tales of the West Riding,* Gollancz, 1952, reprinted, Chivers, 1974; *The House of Moreys* (novel), Macmillan, 1953, reprinted, Ace, 1976; *Noble in Reason,* Macmillan, 1955; *Love and Money: Seven Tales of the West Riding,* Macmillan, 1957; *Crescendo* (novel), Macmillan, 1958; *The New Apprentice* (play), Samuel French, 1959.

Kith and Kin: Nine Tales of Family Life, Macmillan, 1960, reprinted, Chivers, 1977; *The Young Brontes* (nonfiction), Roy, 1961; *O Dreams, O Destinations* (autobiography), Macmillan, 1962; *Committees* (nonfiction), Collins, 1962; *Public Speaking* (nonfiction), Collins, 1964; *Enjoy Books: Reading and Collecting* (nonfiction), Gollancz, 1964; *The Adventures of Tom Leigh* (juvenile), Macdonald, 1964, Doubleday, 1966; *Tales of the West Riding,* Gollancz, 1965; *A Man of His Time* (novel), Macmillan, 1966; *Ned Carver in Danger* (juvenile), Macdonald, 1967; *Oath of Silence,* Doubleday, 1967; *Forgery!* (juvenile), Doubleday, 1968 (published in England as *Gold Pieces,* Macdonald, 1968); *Ring in the New,* Gollancz, 1969; *The Brontes and Their World,* Viking, 1969; *Sheep May Safely Graze* (juvenile), Gollancz, 1972; *The New Venturers* (juvenile), Gollancz, 1973; *More Tales of the West Riding,* Gollancz, 1974; (with John Ogden) *Haworth of the Brontes,* Dalton, 1977.

Also author of television plays for children and of various pamphlets for the Bronte Society and the British Council. Contributor of articles and short stories to magazines.

SIDELIGHTS: Phyllis Bentley, a prominent English regional novelist, devoted her career to writing almost exclusively about the West Riding country of Yorkshire, her lifelong home. In particular, her books focused on the rise and fall of the local weaving industry, an occupation she was extremely familiar with due to the fact that both her father and grandfather were textile manufacturers. Within the confines of this strict regionalism, Bentley's literary specialty was the chronicle, a form which allowed her to trace the flow of historical events through several generations of one or more families.

Bentley regarded her trilogy—*Inheritance, The Rise of Henry Morcar,* and *A Man of His Time*—as her most significant accomplishment. Although the first novel in the series (*Inheritance*) was very well-received, the sequels did not meet with as much success. Commenting on *Inheritance,* a *Christian Science Monitor* critic wrote: "The bleak, brusque and raw Yorkshire scene of industrial town and moorland is a fine setting for such an iron drama of the generations. Provincial as the book is, peculiar to their soil as the characters are, these conflicts go to the roots of a sizable part of human

nature, and Miss Bentley presents them with a humanity and a realism not often found with the same resourcefulness among the males. . . . [The book] is generous, powerful, clear-headed without illusions, and most skillfully controlled." A *New Statesman* reviewer felt that "*Inheritance* is written with great intelligence and dramatic power. It cannot be said that [Bentley] breaks new ground, or that she illuminates life for us at unexpected points; but this is perhaps more than one has a right to demand of a novelist who has the courage to be obvious, and the gift of holding one's attention, not only by her narrative skill, but by her own honest absorption in the lives of her *dramatis personae.*"

Some critics, while they enjoyed the book, felt that it tended to "unravel" toward the end. "Miss Bentley's earlier chapters are richer and more realistic than those which bring the recital across the threshold of the twentieth century," observed a *Books* reviewer, "and there is an inevitable loosening of the dramatic fabric. . . . In the scenes of a hundred years ago the author is notably at home. . . . [Nevertheless,] the book has an eloquence which escapes classification." A *New Republic* critic wrote: "If for no other reason, Phyllis Bentley ought to be commended for having gotten new blood out of that terrible old turnip, the English family chronicle. . . . But what is extraordinary about *Inheritance* is the way the story suddenly collapses in the last few chapters, those covering the developments after the War. It is a real collapse. . . . The result is a forced, uncongenial ending tacked on to a work which otherwise has dignity and power."

Bentley's problems with the depiction of more-or-less current events surfaced again in reviewers' comments on *The Rise of Henry Morcar,* the second novel of the trilogy. For example, a *New York Times* critic observed that "Miss Bentley is at her best in the early scenes. . . . Here is a solidity of engrossing detail. . . . [But] the episodes of the recent war . . . have not been assimilated so well. As a lover, Henry Morcar is stilted; as a patriot, he sounds as if his sentiments had been strained through the British Ministry of Information." A *Times Literary Supplement* reviewer also noticed "a rather sudden change of emphasis" (from an examination of Morcar's private life to a more general view of the war years in England) in the second half of the novel, but he feels that the shift "is inherent in the twofold purpose of the story."

Depicting contemporary characters apparently was still a problem for Bentley in the last volume of the trilogy as well, at least according to a *Times Literary Supplement* reviewer. "In this volume Dr. Bentley seems less sure of her characters than in earlier ones. Morcar himself is real enough but the younger generation seems somewhat conceptual, consistent in theory but in practice speaking with no contemporary voice. The background, however, . . . is intimately observed and lovingly described, and the sometimes pedestrian narrative and occasionally sentimental characterization are compensated for by the fact that the problems dealt with are real ones." A *Library Journal* critic agreed with this latter point, but not with the charge that her characters were "sentimental" and lacked a contemporary flavor. "Dr. Bentley's awareness of our time and its difficulties is impressive; her characters compel belief and sympathy. Realistic but never pessimistic, [*A Man of His Time*] should appeal especially to readers tired of sensationalism, absurdity, and futility."

BIOGRAPHICAL/CRITICAL SOURCES: Saturday Review, April 2, 1932, May 12, 1962; *Spectator,* April 2, 1932; *Times Literary Supplement,* April 7, 1932, May 25, 1946, April 13, 1962, March 10, 1966, May 25, 1967; *New States-*

man, April 16, 1932, April 13, 1962, November, 1968; *Christian Science Monitor*, April 16, 1932, November 28, 1969; *Books*, September 18, 1932; *New York Times*, September 18, 1932, December 15, 1946; *New Republic*, October 26, 1932; *Commonweal*, December 28, 1932; *Weekly Book Review*, December 22, 1946; *New Yorker*, December 28, 1946; Phyllis Bentley, *O Dreams, O Destinations* (autobiography), Macmillan, 1962; *New York Herald Tribune Books*, May 13, 1962; *Young Readers' Review*, May, 1966; *Library Journal*, October 1, 1966; *Book World*, May 5, 1968; *Listener*, November 14, 1968.†

*   *   *

BERELSON, Bernard R.   1912-1979

PERSONAL: Born June 2, 1912, in Spokane, Wash.; died September 25, 1979, in North Tarrytown, N.Y.; son of Max and Bessie (Shapiro) Berelson; married Elizabeth Durand, 1941 (divorced, 1945); married Rosalind Kean, 1948 (divorced); married Ruth Palter, August, 1953; children: David, Alice, Lois Ann, William Max, Jenny Bess. *Education:* Whitman College, A.B., 1934; University of Washington, Seattle, B.S., 1936, M.A., 1937; University of Chicago, Ph.D., 1941. *Home:* 7 Ardsley Ter., Irvington-on-Hudson, N.Y.

CAREER: Special analyst, Federal Communications Commission, Foreign Broadcast Intelligence Service, 1941-44; Columbia University, Bureau of Applied Social Research, New York City, research director, 1944-46; University of Chicago, Chicago, Ill., assistant professor, 1946-47, associate professor, 1947-48, professor of library science and social sciences, 1949-51, dean of Graduate Library School and chairman of committee on communication, 1947-51; director of behavioral sciences program, Ford Foundation, 1951-57; University of Chicago, Chicago, professor of behavioral sciences and director of study of graduate education, 1957-59; Columbia University, New York City, director of Bureau of Applied Social Research and professor of sociology, 1960-61; Population Council, New York City, director of communication research program and vice-president, 1962-68, president, 1968-74, president emeritus and senior fellow, 1974-79. *Member:* American Sociological Association, American Association for Public Opinion Research (president, 1951-52), American Academy of Arts and Sciences, National Academy of Sciences (member of committee on population problems). *Awards, honors:* Rockefeller Foundation fellow, 1941.

WRITINGS: (With D. Waples and F. Bradshaw) *What Reading Does to People*, University of Chicago Press, 1940; (with Paul Lazarsfeld and H. Gaudet) *The People's Choice: How the Voter Makes Up His Mind in a Presidential Campaign*, Duell, Sloan & Pearce, 1944, 3rd edition, Columbia University Press, 1968; (with Lester Ansheim) *The Library's Public*, Columbia University Press, 1949, reprinted, Greenwood Press, 1975; (editor) *Education for Librarianship*, University of Chicago Press, 1949, reprinted, Books for Libraries, 1970; (editor with Morris Janowitz) *Reader in Public Opinion and Communication*, Free Press of Glencoe, 1950, revised edition, 1966; *Content Analysis in Communication Research*, Free Press of Glencoe, 1952, reprinted, Hafner, 1971; (with Paul Lazarsfeld and William McPhee) *Voting: A Study of Opinion Formulation in a Presidential Campaign*, University of Chicago Press, 1954; *Graduate Education in the United States*, McGraw, 1960; (with others) *The Social Studies and the Social Sciences*, Harcourt, 1962; (editor) *The Behavioral Sciences Today*, Basic Books, 1963; (with Gary Steiner) *Human Behavior: An Inventory of Scientific*

Findings, Harcourt, 1964, revised edition, 1967; (with others) *Family Planning and Population Programs: A Review of World Developments*, University of Chicago Press, 1966; *Population: Challenging World Crisis*, U.S. Information Agency, 1969; (editor) *National Programmes in Family Planning: Achievements and Problems*, Meenakshi Prakashan (Meerut, India), 1969; (editor) *Family Planning Programs: An International Survey*, Basic Books, 1969; *Population Policy in Developed Countries*, McGraw, 1974; (with others) *World Population: Status Report 1974, a Guide for the Concerned Citizen*, Population Council, 1974; *The Great Debate on Population Policy: An Instructive Entertainment*, Population Council, 1975.

Contributor: Douglas Waples, editor, *Print, Radio and Film in a Democracy*, University of Chicago Press, 1942; Frances Henne, *Communications, Libraries and Youth*, University of Chicago Press, 1948; Wilbur Schramm, editor, *Communications and Modern Society*, University of Illinois Press, 1948; Leonard White, editor, *The State of the Social Sciences*, University of Chicago Press, 1956; *Values in America*, University of Notre Dame Press, 1961. Contributor to *Collier's Encyclopedia*, *Encyclopaedia Britannica*, and to professional journals.†

*   *   *

BERGIN, Thomas Goddard   1904-

PERSONAL: Born November 17, 1904, in New Haven, Conn.; son of Thomas Joseph and Irvinea (Goddard) Bergin; married Florence T. Bullen, December 30, 1929; children: Winifred Mandeville (Mrs. Boyd Hart), Jennifer Mandeville (Mrs. Peter Von Mayrhauser) *Education:* Yale University, B.A., 1925, Ph.D., 1929. *Home:* 48 Wyndybrook Lane, Madison, Conn. 06443. *Office:* Timothy Dwight College, Yale University, New Haven, Conn. 06520.

CAREER: Yale University, New Haven, Conn., instructor in Italian, 1925-30; Western Reserve University (now Case Western Reserve University), Mather College, Cleveland, Ohio, associate professor of Spanish and Italian, 1930-35; State University of New York at Albany, professor of Romance languages, 1935-41; Cornell University, Ithaca, N.Y., professor of Romance languages and curator of Fiske Dante-Petrarch collections, 1941-48, chairman of division of literature and acting chairman of department of English, 1946-48; Yale University, New Haven, professor of Romance languages, 1948-68, Benjamin F. Barge Professor of Romance Languages, 1949-57, Sterling Professor of Romance Languages, 1958—, chairman of department of Italian and Spanish, 1949-58, master of Timothy Dwight College, 1953-68. *Military service:* U.S. Army, 1943-46; became lieutenant colonel; served with Allied Commission in Italy; received Bronze Star, Order of British Empire, Order of Crown of Italy, Order of Sts. Maurice and Lazarus (Italy); special commendation from School of Military Government.

MEMBER: Modern Language Association of America, American Association of Teachers of Italian (president, 1947), Mediaeval Academy of America, American Association of University Professors (president of Yale chapter, 1951-52), Dante Society, Renaissance Society, P.E.N., Phi Beta Kappa, Mory's, Elizabethan Club, Yale Club, Century Association (New York), Savile Club (London). *Awards, honors:* Fulbright scholar in Italy, 1955-56; Litt. D., Hofstra College, 1958; L.H.D., Fairfield University, 1956; Order of Civic Merit (Italy), 1970; Litt.D., Middlebury College, 1976.

WRITINGS: Giovanni Verga, Yale University Press, 1931, reprinted, Greenwood Press, 1969; (editor) *Modern Italian*

Short Stories, Heath, 1938, revised and enlarged edition, 1959.

Luciano Zuccoli, ritratto umbertino, Societa Editrice del Libro Italiano (Rome), 1940; (editor with Raymond Thompson Hill) *Anthology of the Provencal Troubadours,* Yale University Press, 1941; (editor and author of introduction with Theodore Andersson) *French Plays: Brieux, Hervieu, Mirabeau,* American Book Co., 1941; (with George Irving Dale) *Spanish Grammar,* Ronald, 1943; (translator with Max Harold Fisch) *The Autobiography of G. B. Vico,* Cornell University Press, 1944; *Parco Grifeo* (poems), privately printed, 1946; (editor and translator) Machiavelli, *The Prince,* Appleton, 1947; (editor and translator) Dante, *Inferno,* Appleton, 1948; (translator with Fisch) Vico, *The New Science of G. B. Vico,* Cornell University Press, 1948, 2nd edition, 1969; (contributor) *Humanities for Our Times,* University of Kansas Press, 1949.

(Editor and translator) Dante, *Purgatory,* Appleton, 1953; (editor and translator) Dante, *Paradise,* Appleton, 1954; (author of introduction and various translations) *Lyric Poetry of the Italian Renaissance,* edited by Levi Robert Lind, Yale University Press, 1954; (editor) Shakespeare, *The Taming of the Shrew,* Yale University Press, 1954; (editor and translator) Dante, *Divine Comedy,* Appleton, 1955; (translator) Guillaume IX, *The Poems of William of Poitou,* [New Haven], 1955; (editor) Petrarch, *Rhymes: A Selection of Translations,* Oliver & Boyd, 1955; (editor) Raimbaut de Vaqueiras, *Liriche,* Sansoni (Florence), 1956; *Il Canto IX del "Paradiso,"* A. Signorelli (Rome), 1959; Dante, *The Divine Comedy,* Appleton, 1959, revised edition, Grossman Press, 1969.

Almanac for Academics, Yale University Press, 1960; *The Pressure Is Mine,* Printers to Timothy Dwight, 1960; (translator with Sergio Pacifici) Salvatore Quasimodo, *The Poet and the Politician,* Southern Illinois University Press, 1964; (translator) *Italian Sampler: An Anthology of Italian Verse,* M. Casalini (Montreal), 1964; (editor) Bertran de Born, *Liriche,* [Varese], 1964; *Master Pieces from the Files of T.G.B.,* edited by Thomas K. Swing and A. Bartlett Giamatti, Timothy Dwight College Press, 1964; *Dante,* Orion Press, 1965, reprinted, Greenwood Press, 1976; (published in England as *An Approach to Dante,* Bodley Head, 1965); (editor with Ernest Hatch Wilkins) *A Concordance to "The Divine Comedy" of Dante Alighieri,* Belknap Press, 1965; (editor) Petrarch, *Sonnets,* Heritage Press, 1966; (editor) Petrarch, *Selected Sonnets, Odes, and Letters,* Appleton, 1966; (editor) *From Time to Eternity: Essays on Dante's "Divine Comedy,"* Yale University Press, 1967; *Perspectives on "The Divine Comedy"* (essays), Rutgers University Press, 1967; *A Diversity of Dante,* Rutgers University Press, 1969; *Cervantes: His Life, His Times, His Works,* McGraw, 1969; *Dante: His Life, His Times, His Works,* McGraw, 1969.

Petrarch, Twayne, 1970; (translator) Ugo Foscolo, *On Sepulchres,* Bethany Press, 1971; *Invito alla Divina Commedia,* Adriatica editrice, 1971; *Dante's "Divine Comedy,"* Prentice-Hall, 1971; (translator) Petrarch, *Bucolicum Carmen,* Yale University Press, 1972; *Weeds and Transplants,* Picaflor Press, 1976; (translator with A. Wilson) Petrarch, *Africa,* Yale University Press, 1977; *Gridiron Glory,* [New Haven], 1978.

Also contributor to several anthologies, and to *Columbia Dictionary of Modern European Literature, Collier's Encyclopedia,* and *Enciclopedia Bompiani.* Contributor of articles to *Saturday Review, New York Times, New York Herald Tribune, Speculum, Yale Review, Virginia Quarterly Review,* and other periodicals. Former member of editorial

board of Modern Language Association of America; member of editorial board, *Italian Quarterly;* consulting editor, *Books Abroad.*

WORK IN PROGRESS: A monograph on Boccaccio; a Provencal grammar; an autobiography.

SIDELIGHTS: Thomas Bergin's studies of Dante have been praised not only for their scholarly workmanship, but also for their lucid, direct presentation. William John Roscelli praises Bergin's style of writing as "simple and direct, infused with warmth and admiration for the subject." Morris Bishop believes that Bergin avoids the esoteric quality which marks most scholarly literary critics: "Imagination stirs imagination; the reader is moved to join the great journey through the other world."

BIOGRAPHICAL/CRITICAL SOURCES: Book Week, February 14, 1965; *New York Times Book Review,* March 14, 1965; *Christian Science Monitor,* April 20, 1965; *Saturday Review,* May 8, 1965; *National Review,* July 13, 1965; *Yale Review,* October, 1965; *Virginia Quarterly Review,* autumn, 1965; *Times Literary Supplement,* December 2, 1965; *New York Review of Books,* February 17, 1966; *Library Journal,* April 15, 1967, May 15, 1969; *Choice,* June, 1966, March, 1968, December, 1969; *Newsweek,* December 15, 1969; *Atlantic,* February, 1970; *Books Abroad,* autumn, 1970.

*   *   *

BERMOSK, Loretta Sue   1918-

PERSONAL: Born July 17, 1918, in Johnstown, Pa.; daughter of Frank J. and Mary E. Bermosk. *Education:* St. Francis Hospital School of Nursing, Pittsburgh, Pa., R.N., 1939; New York University, B.S.N.Ed., 1949; University of Pittsburgh, M.Litt. in Psychiatric Nursing Education, 1952; University of California, "Research in Social Psychiatry" certificate, 1965. *Politics:* Independent. *Religion:* Roman Catholic. *Home:* 1602 Mikahala Way, Honolulu, Hawaii 96816.

CAREER: University of Michigan, School of Nursing, Ann Arbor, 1952-59, began as instructor, became assistant professor; University of Arizona, College of Nursing, Tucson, associate professor, 1959-63; University of Hawaii, Honolulu, School of Nursing, associate professor and chairman of graduate programs, 1965-72, professor, 1972—, coordinator of master of science program, 1965-75, 1979—, coordinator of health team development program, 1975-79. Visiting professor, University of Tel Aviv, 1972-73, 1980-81. *Military service:* U.S. Army Nurse Corps, 1941-46; became captain. *Member:* American Nurses Association, Mental Health Association, American Association of University Professors, Transcultural Nursing Society, American Academy of Nursing (fellow), Hawaii Association of Women in Science, Hawaii Association, Hawaii Mental Health Association, Sigma Theta Tau. *Awards, honors:* University of Hawaii Excellence in Teaching Award, 1975.

WRITINGS: (With Mary Jane Mordan) *Interviewing in Nursing,* Macmillan, 1964; (with Raymond Corsini) *Critical Incidents in Nursing,* Saunders, 1973; (with Sarah E. Porter) *Women's Health and Human Wholeness,* Appleton, 1979; (with Jeanette Takamura and Lorraine Stringfellow) *Interdisciplinary Health Team Development,* University of Hawaii Press, 1979; (with Robert L. Anders) *Risking: The Self in Group,* F. A. Davis, in press.

Contributor: *Concepts of the Behavioral Sciences in Basic Nursing Education,* National League for Nursing, 1958; *Suggested Core Curriculum for Pre-Service Education of*

Practical Nurses and Psychiatric Attendant Nurses, Michigan League for Nursing, 1959; *Suggestions for Experimentation in the Education of Psychiatric Aides,* National League for Nursing, 1959; *Education and Supervision in Mental Health and Psychiatric Nursing,* National League for Nursing, 1963.

*   *   *

BERNDT, Ronald Murray 1916-

PERSONAL: Born July 14, 1916, in Adelaide, South Australia; son of Alfred Henry Berndt; married, April, 1941; wife's name Catherine (a lecturer in anthropology). *Education:* Sydney University, diploma in anthropology, 1943, B.A., 1950, M.A. (first class honors), 1951; London School of Economics and Political Science, Ph.D., 1955. *Home:* 28 Leake St., Peppermint Grove, Western Australia. *Office:* Department of Anthropology, University of Western Australia, Nedlands, Western Australia.

CAREER: Anthropologist, Northern Territory Pastoral Firm, Australia, 1944-46; University of Sydney, Sydney, Australia, temporary lecturer, 1951-53, lecturer in anthropology, 1954; University of Western Australia, Nedlands, senior lecturer, 1956-58, reader, 1958-63, foundation professor of anthropology, 1963—. Conducted fieldwork in aboriginal Australia, 1939—, and New Guinea, 1951-53. Australian Institute of Aboriginal Studies, Canberra, member of advisory panel on social anthropology, 1961—, member of interim committee, 1962-64, council, 1964—; honorary associate and minister of aboriginal affairs committee, Western Australian Museum, 1962—; adviser on aboriginal affairs, Law Reform Commission, 1979—.

MEMBER: American Anthropological Association (foreign fellow), Royal Anthropological Society of Great Britain and Ireland, Current Anthropology (associate), Australian and New Zealand Association for the Advancement of Science (vice-president, anthropology section, 1959, 1961; president, 1962), Association of Social Anthropologists (British branch), Association of Social Anthropologists (president, Australian branch, 1962-64), Royal Society of Western Australia, Anthropological Society of New South Wales, Anthropological Society of Western Australia (chairman and president, 1959, 1960; vice-president, 1961), University of Western Australia Research Group on Australian Aborigines (chairman, 1961, 1962-63). *Awards, honors:* Nuffield fellow, 1953-54; Carnegie traveling fellow, 1955-56; Wellcome Medal, 1958; University Grants Commission grant, Government of India, 1965; Royal Society of Western Australia Medal, 1979.

WRITINGS: Preliminary Report of Field Work in the Ooldea Region, Western South Australia (monograph), Australian National Research Council, 1945; (with wife, C. H. Berndt, and A. P. Elkin) *Art in Arnhem Land,* University of Chicago Press, 1950; (with C. H. Berndt) *From Black to White in South Australia,* University of Chicago Press, 1951; (with C. H. Berndt) *Sexual Behaviour in Western Arnhem Land,* Viking Fund, 1951; *Kunapipi, A Study of an Australian Aboriginal Religious Cult,* International Universities, 1951; *Djanggawul, an Aboriginal Cult of North-Eastern Arnhem Land,* F. W. Cheshire, 1952, Philosophical Library, 1953; (with C. H. Berndt) *The First Australians,* Ure Smith, 1952, Philosophical Library, 1954; (with C. H. Berndt) *Arnhem Land: Its History and Its People,* F. W. Cheshire, 1954.

Excess and Restraint: Social Control Among a New Guinea Mountain People, University of Chicago Press, 1962; *An Adjustment Movement in Arnhem Land,* Ecole Pratique des

Hautes Etudes, Sorbonne, 1962; (contributor) H. Sheils, editor, *Australian Aboriginal Studies,* Oxford University Press, 1963; (with C. H. Berndt) *The World of the First Australians,* Ure Smith, 1964, University of Chicago Press, 1965; (editor and contributor) *Australian Aboriginal Art,* Macmillan, 1964; (editor with C. H. Berndt, and contributor) *Aboriginal Man in Australia: Festschrift for Professor A. P. Elkin,* Angus & Robertson, 1964; (contributor) F. Alexander, editor, *The Unity of the Humanities,* Cheshire, 1964; (contributor) M. Nimkoff, editor, *Gods, Ghosts, and Men in Melanesia,* Oxford University Press, 1965; (contributor) *Comparative Family Systems,* Houghton, 1965.

(With C. H. Berndt) *Man, Land, and Myth in North Australia,* Ure Smith, 1970; (editor and contributor) *Australian Aboriginal Anthropology,* Australian Institute of Aboriginal Studies, 1970; (editor with P. Lawrence, and contributor) *Politics in New Guinea,* University of Western Australia Press, 1971; (editor with S. Phillips, and contributor) *The Australian Aboriginal Heritage: An Introduction to the Arts,* Australian Society for Education through the Arts, 1973; *Australian Aboriginal Religion,* E. J. Brill, 1974; *Love Songs of Arnhem Land,* Thomas Nelson, 1976; *Three Faces of Love,* Thomas Nelson, 1976; (editor and contributor) *Aborigines and Change: Australia in the Seventies,* Australian Institute of Aboriginal Studies, 1977; (with C. H. Berndt) *Pioneers and Settlers: The Aboriginal Australians,* Pitman, 1978; (editor with C. H. Berndt, and contributor) *Aborigines of the West: Their Past and Their Present,* University of Western Australia Press, 1979.

Contributor to *American People's Encyclopedia, Encyclopaedia Britannica,* and *Encyclopaedia of Papua and New Guinea.* Contributor of more than two hundred articles to journals in Australia and around the world. General editor, *Anthropological Forum.*

WORK IN PROGRESS: Jaraldi Society; Daughters of the Sun; a study of central-west Northern Territory religion; *End of an Era,* concerning pastoral stations in the Northern Territory; *Australian Aboriginal Art.*

*   *   *

BERNSTEIN, Theodore M(enline) 1904-1979

PERSONAL: Born November 17, 1904, in New York, N.Y.; died June 27, 1979, in New York, N.Y.; son of Saul and Sarah (Menline) Bernstein; married Beatrice Alexander, September 2, 1930 (died, 1971); children: Eric M. *Education:* Columbia University, A.B., 1924, B.Litt., 1925. *Home:* 2 Fifth Ave., New York, N.Y. 10011. *Office: New York Times,* Times Square, New York, N.Y.

CAREER: New York Times, New York, N.Y., copy editor, 1925-30, suburban editor, 1930-32, affiliated with foreign desk, 1932-48, foreign editor, 1939-48, assistant night managing editor, 1948-51, news editor, 1951-52, editor of house organ, "Winners and Sinners," 1951-78, assistant managing editor, 1952-69, founding editor of international edition (Paris), 1960, editorial director of book division, 1969-71, executive editor of *Encyclopedic Almanac,* 1969-71, consulting editor, 1972, author of syndicated column, "Bernstein on Words," beginning 1972. School of Journalism, Columbia University, 1925-50, began as instructor, became associate professor. Consultant to U.S. Panel on Educational Research and Development, 1964. *Member:* Overseas Press Club, Sigma Delta Chi.

WRITINGS: (With Robert E. Garst) *Headlines and Deadlines: A Manual for Copy Editors,* Columbia University Press, 1933, 3rd edition, 1961; *Watch Your Language,* Channel Press, 1958; *More Language That Needs Watching*, Channel Press, 1962; *The Careful Writer: A Modern Guide to English Usage*, Atheneum, 1965; *Miss Thistlebottom's Hobgoblins: The Careful Writer's Guide to the Taboos, Bugbears, and Outmoded Rules of English Usage*, Farrar, Straus, 1971; *Bernstein's Reverse Dictionary*, Times Books, 1975; *Dos, Don'ts and Maybes of English Usage*, Times Books, 1977. Contributor to *Saturday Review* and *Reader's Digest*. Member of editorial advisory board, *Columbia University Forum*, 1961-64; consultant on usage, *Random House Dictionary*, beginning 1966, and *American Heritage Dictionary*, beginning 1969.

SIDELIGHTS: Described by *Newsweek* as the "linguistic policeman" of the *New York Times*, Theodore M. Bernstein was the founder and author for over two decades of "Winners and Sinners," an in-house bulletin that proved to be so popular it was eventually distributed (on request) to over 5,000 people outside the *Times*. Designed to call attention to various examples of good and bad usage on the part of the newspaper's writing and editorial staff, the bulletins were characterized by irreverent, pun-filled critiques that amused as well as instructed readers; in addition, they earned Bernstein a reputation as an authority on the English language and formed the basis for two of his books, *Watch Your Language* and *More Language That Needs Watching*. These and several other Bernstein books, including *Headlines and Deadlines*, remain standard texts in many journalism schools throughout the country, prompting University of Michigan professor William E. Porter to comment at the time of Bernstein's death that he was "the ultimate copy editor."

BIOGRAPHICAL/CRITICAL SOURCES: New York Times, November 11, 1977, June 28, 1979; *Washington Post*, June 28, 1979; *Chicago Tribune*, June 29, 1979, July 1, 1979, July 2, 1979; *Newsweek*, July 9, 1979; *A. B. Bookman*, August 6, 1979.

*   *   *

BERRY, Brewton 1901-

PERSONAL: Born August 9, 1901, in Orangeburg, S.C.; son of Joseph A. (an attorney) and Frances Deborah (Pike) Berry; married Margaret Foley Woods, September 11, 1926; children: Margaret (Mrs. F. J. Curtin, Jr.), Deborah (Mrs. Douglas Houser). *Education:* Wofford College, A.B., 1922; Yale University, B.D., 1925; University of Edinburgh, Ph.D., 1930; attended Ohio State University, 1929-31. *Politics:* Independent. *Religion:* Episcopalian. *Home:* 2221 Brixton Rd., Columbus, Ohio 43221. *Office:* Ohio State University, 300 Administration Building, Columbus, Ohio 43210.

CAREER: University of Missouri—Columbia, 1931-45, began as assistant professor, became professor of sociology and anthropology, director of anthropological collection, 1934-45; University of Rhode Island, Kingston, professor of sociology and anthropology and chairman of department, 1945-46; Ohio State University, Columbus, professor of sociology and anthropology, 1946-64, member of editorial board of University press, 1964-78. Director, Archaeological Survey of Missouri, 1933-45. Chairman of refugee resettlement committee, Episcopal diocese of southern Ohio, 1953-56; member of governor's advisory committee on refugees, 1955-62; member of selection committee, Woodrow Wilson National Fellowship Foundation, 1958-61. *Member:* American Anthropological Association, American Sociological Association, Missouri Archaeological Society (honorary life member), Ohio Valley Sociological Society (president, 1955-56), Phi Beta Kappa, Sigma Xi, Faculty Club, Torch Club,

Scioto Country Club (Columbus), Book and Bond Club (Yale University). *Awards, honors:* Julius Rosenwald fellow, 1943-44; Anisfield-Wolf book award, 1952, for *Race Relations*.

WRITINGS: (Co-author) *Archaeological Investigations in Boone County, Missouri*, Missouri Archaeological Society, 1938; (co-author) *Archaeology of Wayne County, Missouri*, Missouri Archaeological Society, 1940; *You and Your Superstitions*, Lucas Brothers, 1940, 2nd edition, 1974; (co-author) *Fundamentals of Sociology*, Crowell, 1950; *Race Relations*, Houghton, 1951, 2nd edition published as *Race and Ethnic Relations*, Houghton, 1958, 4th edition (with Henry Tischler), 1978; *Almost White*, Macmillan, 1963, 2nd edition, 1969; *The Education of American Indians*, U.S. Government Printing Office, 1968; (with others) *The Blending of Races*, Wiley, 1972. Contributor to encyclopedias; contributor of approximately forty articles and twenty-five book reviews to various journals. Editor, *Missouri Archaeologist*, 1935-45, and *Ohio Valley Sociologist*, 1947-53; associate editor, *American Sociological Review*, 1953-56.

WORK IN PROGRESS: The Indians of Ohio.

*   *   *

BETH, Loren Peter 1920-

PERSONAL: Born December 19, 1920, in Evanston, Ill.; son of Leo Peter and Louise (Lucas) Beth; married Carol Ann Koehler, May 25, 1946; children: Janis, Dana Lynn, Karen. *Education:* Attended Northwestern University, 1939-40; Monmouth College, B.A., 1946; University of Chicago, M.A., 1948, Ph.D., 1949. *Politics:* Democrat. *Religion:* Unitarian Universalist. *Home:* 150 Dellwood Dr., Athens, Ga. *Office:* Department of Political Science, University of Georgia, Athens, Ga.

CAREER: Bradley University, Peoria, Ill., 1949-53, began as instructor, became assistant professor of political science; Harding College, Searcy, Ark., assistant professor, 1953-54; University of Florida, Gainesville, 1954-58, began as assistant professor, became associate professor; University of Massachusetts—Amherst, professor of political science, 1958-76; University of Georgia, Athens, professor of political science and head of department, 1976—. Fulbright lecturer, University of Leicester, 1957-58, and Trinity College (Dublin), 1965-66. Member, Amherst Democratic Town Committee, 1960-63; president, Amherst Unitarian Society, 1961-62. *Military service:* U.S. Army, 1942-45, became sergeant. *Member:* American Society for Legal History, American Association of University Professors (chapter vice-president, 1961-62; president, 1973-74), Southern Political Science Association, Northeastern Political Science Association. *Awards, honors:* National Endowment for the Humanities fellow, 1972.

WRITINGS: The American Theory of Church and State, University of Florida Press, 1958; (with W. C. Havard) *Representative Government and Reapportionment*, Public Administration Clearing Service, University of Florida, 1960; *Politics, the Constitution, and the Supreme Court*, Row, Peterson, 1962; (with Havard) *The Politics of Mis-Representation: Rural-Urban Conflict in the Florida Legislature*, Louisiana State University Press, 1962; *The Development of Judicial Review in Ireland, 1937-1966*, Institute of Public Administration (Dublin), 1967; *The Development of the American Constitution, 1877-1917*, Harper, 1971. Contributor to professional journals.

WORK IN PROGRESS: A biography, *John Marshall Harlan, Last of the Tobacco-Spittin' Judges.*

BETHELL, Jean (Frankenberry) 1922-

PERSONAL: Surname is pronounced *Beth*-ell; born February 12, 1922, in Sharon, Pa.; daughter of Thomas Howard (an electrical engineer) and Helen (a teacher; maiden name, Rogers) Frankenberry; married Frederick L. Bethell (a construction executive), August 19, 1955. *Education:* Purdue University, B.S., 1943. *Residence:* New York, N.Y.

CAREER: National Broadcasting Co., New York City, writer for "Dave Garroway Show," 1950-52; Batten, Barton, Durstine and Osborn (advertising firm), New York City, copywriter, 1953; Benton & Bowles (advertising firm), New York City, copywriter, 1954-55; Wieboldt Stores, Inc., Chicago, Ill., advertising copy chief, 1956; Edward H. Weiss Advertising, Chicago, copywriter, 1957; freelance writer, 1960—. *Member:* Pi Beta Phi.

WRITINGS: Herman and Katnip, Wonder Books, 1961; *Baby Huey,* Wonder Books, 1961; *The Monkey in the Rocket,* Grosset, 1962; *The Clumsy Cowboy,* Wonder Books, 1963; *Ollie Bakes a Cake,* Wonder Books, 1964; *A Trick on Deputy Dawg,* Wonder Books, 1964; *How and Why Book of Famous Scientists,* Grosset, 1964; *Muskie and His Friends,* Wonder Books, 1964; *The Tale of Two Ducklings,* Wonder Books, 1964; *Luno the Soaring Stallion,* Wonder Books, 1964; *When I Grow Up,* Wonder Books, 1964; *Barbie Goes to a Party,* Grosset, 1964; *Barbie the Baby-Sitter,* Wonder Books, 1964; *Barbie Adventures to Read Aloud,* Wonder Books, 1964; *Hooray for Henry,* Grosset, 1965; *Petey, the Peanut Man,* Grosset, 1965; *How to Care for Your Dog,* Four Winds, 1967; *Bathtime,* Harper, 1979; *Three Cheers for Mother Jones,* Harper, 1980. Also author of *Elbert Goes Househunting, Touch and Tell Book, Pete's Dragon, The Jungle Book,* and *Playmates.*

"Barney Beagle" series; all published by Grosset: *Barney Beagle,* 1962; *Barney Beagle Plays Baseball,* 1963; *. . . and the Cat,* 1965; *. . . Goes Camping,* 1970.

WORK IN PROGRESS: An adult novel, *Trouble on Townsend Street.*

BIOGRAPHICAL/CRITICAL SOURCES: New York Times Book Review, May 9, 1965, November 5, 1967.

*   *   *

BETTS, Raymond F. 1925-

PERSONAL: Born December 23, 1925, in Bloomfield, N.J.; son of James W. and Cora (Banta) Betts; married Irene E. Donahue, 1956; children: Kenneth L., James W., Susan E. *Education:* Rutgers University, A.B., 1949; Columbia University, M.A., 1950, Ph.D., 1958; post-graduate study at University of Paris, 1954-55; University of Grenoble, D. d'Univ., 1955. *Home:* 311 Mariemont St., Lexington, Ky. 40505. *Office:* Department of History, University of Kentucky, Lexington, Ky. 40506.

CAREER: Hunter College High School, New York, N.Y., teacher, 1955-56; Bryn Mawr College, Bryn Mawr, Pa., assistant professor, 1956-61; Grinnell College, Grinnell, Iowa, assistant professor, 1961-63, associate professor, 1963-65, professor of history, 1965-71; University of Kentucky, Lexington, professor of history, 1971—. *Military service:* U.S. Army, three years; became sergeant first class; received combat infantryman's badge. *Member:* American Historical Association, Society for French Historical Studies (vice-president).

WRITINGS: Assimiliation and Association in French Colonial Theory: 1890-1914, Columbia University Press, 1961; *The Scramble for Africa,* Heath, 1966; *Europe Overseas:*

Phases of Imperialism, Basic Books, 1968; (editor) *The Ideology of Blackness,* Heath, 1971; *The False Dawn: European Imperialism in the Nineteenth Century,* University of Minnesota Press, 1975; *Tricouleur: The French Overseas Empire,* Gordon & Cremonesi, 1978; *Europe in Retrospect: A Brief History of the Past Two Hundred Years,* Heath, 1979.

WORK IN PROGRESS: Uncertain Dimensions: Empire in the Twentieth Century, for University of Minnesota Press.

*   *   *

BEVINGTON, David M(artin) 1931-

PERSONAL: Born May 13, 1931, in New York, N.Y.; son of Merle Mowbray and Helen (Smith) Bevington; married Margaret Bronson Brown, June 4, 1953; children: Stephen Raymond, Philip Landon, Katharine Helen, Sarah Amelia. *Education:* Harvard University, A.B. (cum laude), 1952, A.M., 1957, Ph.D., 1959. *Politics:* Democrat. *Home:* 5747 South Blackstone Ave., Chicago, Ill. 60637. *Office:* Department of English, University of Chicago, Chicago, Ill. 60637.

CAREER: Harvard University, Cambridge, Mass., teaching fellow, 1957-59, instructor, 1959-61; University of Virginia, Charlottesville, assistant professor, 1961-64, associate professor, 1964-66, professor of English, 1966-67; University of Chicago, Chicago, Ill., professor of English, 1967—. *Military service:* U.S. Navy, 1952-55; became lieutenant junior grade. *Member:* American Association of University Professors (acting president, Virginia conference, 1962-63, president, 1963-64), Shakespeare Association of America (president, 1976-77), Renaissance English Text Society (president, 1978—), Modern Language Association of America, Renaissance Society of America.

WRITINGS: From Mankind to Marlowe, Harvard University Press, 1962; (editor) Shakespeare, *I Henry VI,* Penguin, 1966; (editor) *Twentieth-Century Interpretations of "Hamlet,"* Prentice-Hall, 1968; *Tudor Drama and Politics,* Harvard University Press, 1968; (editor) *The Macro Plays,* Johnson Reprint, 1972; (editor) Hardin Craig, *The Complete Works of Shakespeare,* revised edition (Bevington was not associated with earlier editions), Scott, Foresman, 1972, 3rd edition, 1980; (editor) Craig, *An Introduction to Shakespeare,* revised edition (Bevington was not associated with earlier editions), Scott, Foresman, 1975; (editor) *Medieval Drama,* Houghton, 1975; (compiler) *Shakespeare,* AHM Publishing, 1978.

WORK IN PROGRESS: A study of gesture as language in Shakespeare.

AVOCATIONAL INTERESTS: Chamber music and playing the viola.

*   *   *

BEWLEY, Marius 1918-1973

PERSONAL: Born January 23, 1918, in St. Louis, Mo.; died January 24, 1973, in St. George, Staten Island, N.Y.; son of Eugene Hendrix and Lillian (McCune) Bewley. *Education:* St. Louis University, B.A., 1938; Downing College, Cambridge University, B.A., 1940, M.A., D.Phil., 1956. *Home:* 22 Fort Place, St. George, Staten Island, N.Y.

CAREER: Catholic University of America, Washington, D.C., associate professor of English, 1953; Wellesley College, Wellesley, Mass., visiting associate professor, 1959-60; Connecticut College for Women (now Connecticut College), New London, visiting associate professor, 1960-61; Fordham University, New York, N.Y., associate professor, 1961-63, professor, 1963-66; Rutgers University, New

Brunswick, N.J., professor of English, 1966-73. Member of selection committee, Ingram-Merrill Foundation. *Awards, honors:* Fulbright grant; Rockefeller grant; *Hudson Review* fellow; American Council of Learned Societies fellow; Arts and Letters Award, American Academy-National Institute of Arts and Letters, 1973.

WRITINGS: The Complex Fate: Hawthorne, Henry James, and Some Other American Writers, Grove, 1952, reprinted, Gordian Press, 1967; *The Eccentric Design: Form in the Classic American Novel,* Columbia University Press, 1959; (editor and author of introduction) John Donne, *Selected Poetry,* New American Library, 1966, published as *The Selected Poetry of John Donne,* 1979; *Masks and Mirrors: Essays in Criticism,* Atheneum, 1970; (editor) *The English Romantic Poets: An Anthology,* Random House, 1970. Member of editorial board, *Hudson Review,* 1966-73. Contributor to *Spectator, New Statesman, Scrutiny, Partisan Review, Hudson Review,* and *Southern Review.*†

* * *

BIER, Jesse 1925-

PERSONAL: Born July 18, 1925, in Hoboken, N.J.; son of Benjamin Arthur (a bakery owner) and Lenore (Greenberg) Bier; married Laure Darsa, July 21, 1950; children: Ethan, Leslie, Lilian. *Education:* Attended City College of New York (now City College of the City University of New York) and Biarritz American University; Bucknell University, B.A. (summa cum laude), 1949; Princeton University, M.A., 1952, Ph.D., 1956. *Politics:* Democrat. *Home:* Wildcat Rd., Missoula, Mont. *Office:* Department of English, University of Montana, Missoula, Mont.

CAREER: University of Colorado, Boulder, instructor in English, 1952-55; University of Montana, Missoula, assistant professor, 1955-59, associate professor, 1959-65, professor of English, 1965—. Fulbright professor in France, 1957-58; visiting lecturer, Bucknell University, 1965-66; visiting professor, San Diego State University, 1971; held Chair of American Literature, Lausanne University, 1971-72. Consultant to Swiss "Third Cycle" Seminars, 1978. Democratic precinctman, 1962-64. *Military service:* U.S. Army, 1943-46; received Purple Heart. *Member:* American Honor Society (honorary member), Mark Twain Society (honorary member), Phi Beta Kappa. *Awards, honors:* Native Son Award in Fiction of New Jersey State Teachers Association, 1965; Canadian Government study grant, 1979.

WRITINGS: Trial at Bannock (novel), Harcourt, 1963; *A Hole in the Lead Apron* (short stories), Harcourt, 1964; *The Rise and Fall of American Humor,* Holt, 1968; *Year of the Cougar* (novel), Harcourt, 1976. Contributor to *Esquire* and other publications.

WORK IN PROGRESS: After Dying, a play.

AVOCATIONAL INTERESTS: Fishing, reading, travel, music.

* * *

BINDER, Otto O(scar) 1911-1974
(Eando Binder, John Coleridge, Gordon A. Giles, Dean D. O'Brien)

PERSONAL: Born August 26, 1911, in Bessemer, Mich.; died October 14, 1974, in Chestertown, N.Y.; son of Michael (an iron worker) and Marie (Payer) Binder; married Ione Frances Turek (an author of children's books), November 2, 1940; children: Mary Lorine (died, 1967). *Education:* Studied science and chemical engineering at Crane City College,

Northwestern University, and University of Chicago. *Politics:* Independent. *Religion:* Lutheran, Presbyterian.

CAREER: Free-lance writer, 1930-74. Crerar Library, Chicago, Ill., assistant to the science librarian, 1931-32; Otis Kline Literary Agency, New York City, manuscript reader, 1936-38; Spaceways, Inc., New York City, editor-in-chief of *Space World,* 1960-62; Palisade Publications, Inc., New York City, publisher of *Space World,* 1962-63; worked as comic book script writer for eighteen publishing houses, 1939-69. Member of board of directors, Memorial House, Englewood, N.J. *Member:* National Aerospace Education Council, American Institute of Aeronautics and Astronautics, American Rocketry Association (honorary member), National Association of Rocketry (honorary member), Ranger Lunar Capsule Watchers Society (honorary member), Aerospace Writers Association (honorary member), Lunacon Society (honorary member), Aerospace Mail Society (honorary member), Englewood Rocket Club (honorary member).

WRITINGS: (Under pseudonym John Coleridge) *Martian Martyrs,* Columbia, 1940; (under pseudonym John Coleridge) *The New Life,* Columbia, 1940; *Captain Marvel and the Return of the Scorpion,* Fawcett, 1941; *Golden Book of Space Travel,* Golden Press, 1959; *The Moon: Our Neighboring World,* Golden Press, 1959, 2nd edition, 1960; *Planets: Other Worlds of Our Solar System,* Golden Press, 1959, 5th edition, 1965; *Golden Book of Atomic Energy,* Golden Press, 1960; *Golden Book of Jets and Rockets,* Golden Press, 1961; *Victory in Space,* Walker, 1962; *On Tiptoe beyond Darwin,* privately printed, 1962, revised edition (with Max Hugh Flindt) published as *Mankind: Child of the Stars,* Fawcett, 1974; *Careers in Space,* Walker, 1963; *Riddles of Astronomy,* Basic Books, 1964; *The Avengers Battle the Earth-Wrecker,* Bantam, 1967; *What We Really Know about Flying Saucers,* Fawcett, 1967; *Five Steps to Tomorrow,* Curtis Books, 1968.

Editor; all published by Pendulum Press in 1973: Mary Shelley, *Frankenstein;* Jules Verne, *Twenty Thousand Leagues under the Sea;* H. G. Wells, *The Time Machine.*

Under pseudonym Eando Binder (also see *Sidelights* below): *Adam Link, Robot* (stories), Paperback Library, 1965; *Anton York, Immortal* (stories), Belmont Books, 1965; *Enslaved Brains,* Avalon, 1965; *The Impossible World,* Curtis Books, 1967; *Menace of the Saucers,* Belmont Books, 1969; *Secret of the Red Spot,* Curtis Books, 1971; *Night of the Saucers,* Belmont Books, 1971; *Get Off My World,* Curtis Books, 1971; *The Double Man,* Curtis Books, 1971; *Puzzle of the Space Pyramids,* Curtis Books, 1971; *The Mind from Outer Space,* Curtis Books, 1972; *Flying Saucers Are Watching Us,* Belmont Books, 1978.

Work, under pseudonym Eando Binder, has been anthologized in: *The Other Worlds,* Funk, 1941; *From Off This World,* Merlin, 1949; *My Best Science Fiction Story,* Merlin, 1950; *Editor's Choice in Science Fiction,* McBride, 1959; *The Coming of the Robots,* Collier, 1963; *Exploring Other Worlds,* Collier, 1963; *Missing World and Other Stories,* Lerner, 1974.

Also author of booklets for the National Aeronautics and Space Administration (N.A.S.A.). Author of more than three thousand comic book scripts. Author of syndicated cartoon feature "Our Space Age," 1965-68. Contributor of more than three hundred stories, articles, and reviews to *Argosy, New York Times Book Review, Mechanix Illustrated, Fate, Amazing Stories,* and other publications.

SIDELIGHTS: Otto Binder began his writing career in 1932

when he and his brother Earl Binder created their joint pseudonym Eando Binder ("E" for Earl and "O" for Otto). Under that name, they wrote more than one hundred science fiction novels and short stories for the pulp magazines of the thirties. After their writing partnership ended in the early forties, Binder continued to use the pseudonym for some of his own writings. Subsequent book publications under the pseudonym are either by Binder alone or in collaboration with his brother.

Between the years 1939 and 1969, Binder wrote more than three thousand comic book scripts for numerous publishers. His work included a wide variety of stories, ranging from science fiction to mystery, and from "super hero" to horror. It also included writing adventures for such comics characters as Batman, Hawkman, Captain America, Superman, and Captain Marvel.

Although all of his extensive work in the field is highly regarded by comics enthusiasts, Binder is best known as a script writer for the character Captain Marvel. The Captain is unique among "super heroes" in that, although a full-grown adult, his "secret identity" is a young newsboy. Upon saying the secret name "Shazam," the boy magically transforms into Captain Marvel. Because of the character's popularity, "Shazam" has become a part of the English language as a word expressing great surprise and astonishment.

Binder wrote nearly sixty percent of the stories to appear in the *Captain Marvel* comic book, creating many of the secondary characters and most of the villains in the Marvel saga as well. At its peak, *Captain Marvel* had a monthly circulation of two million copies—the highest of any comic book in history—while related books, featuring secondary Marvel characters, enjoyed similar success. Dick Lupoff, in his book *All in Color for a Dime*, praises *Captain Marvel* as "interesting and imaginative, with real suspense, clever gimmicks, legitimate plots, and a delightful air of almost whimsical fantasy to the stories."

Speaking of his life and work in the science fiction field, Binder wrote to *CA*: "I am, admittedly, a 'space crusader.' Not for the sake of space exploration itself but because it represents the greatest challenge facing mankind, in all history. Any nation that fails to forge into its new frontiers of immense knowledge and benefit will ... decline into a second-rate community at best, or fail to survive at worst."

Binder believed that "there are other civilizations in outer space (a minimum of one million 'earths' according to astronomical authority), some wiser than we. Contacting them, even via radio, might benefit us immeasurably.

"Even without gaining direct knowledge or advice from them, the first alien voice or code picked up would instantly revolutionize human thought on earth and bring up the ancient instinct of 'us against the universe.' The end result is obvious—an automatic alliance of all peoples on earth against the (possible) common enemy. Despite its tawdry genesis, this would perhaps bring about the world peace that none of our earth-bound bickerings and thinkings have even come close to.

"Also, contact with (or even contemplation of) millions of other intelligent beings throughout the cosmos will expand human minds to an inconceivable degree. Perhaps it will be the actual beginning of true civilization, for earth and its people must be thought of as only one part of the cosmic community.

"There may be a 'United Worlds' out there, for all we know. The cure for cancer may lie in space also (through efforts of space medics to study the human body far more fully than ever before). Also devising anti-radiation protection (drug perhaps) for astronauts might give us nuclear-fallout protection on earth.

"All my writings in the space field have the purpose of bringing these highly important matters to public attention, and to inspire our young people to join our technological troops."

AVOCATIONAL INTERESTS: Philately (particularly postage stamps commemorating space flights), gardening, playing the accordion, bird-watching, reading.

BIOGRAPHICAL/CRITICAL SOURCES: J. O. Bailey, *Pilgrims Through Space and Time*, Argus, 1947; Sam Moskowitz, *The Immortal Storm: A History of Science Fiction Fandom*, Asfo, 1954; *Editor & Publisher*, September 10, 1960; *Bergen Record* (Bergen, N.J.), March 11, 1961; *New York Journal American*, January 1, 1961; *Analog*, December, 1964; *Galaxy*, April, 1965; *Magazine of Fantasy and Science Fiction*, May, 1966, March, 1968; Dick Lupoff and Don Thompson, editors, *All in Color for a Dime*, Arlington House, 1970; J. Steranko, *The Steranko History of Comics*, two volumes, Crown, 1971; *New York Times*, October 19, 1974; E. Nelson Bridwell, *Shazam: From the Thirties to the Seventies*, Harmony, 1977.†

*   *   *

BISHOP, Donald G. 1907-

PERSONAL: Born May 16, 1907, in Altoona, Pa.; son of Walter M. (a teacher) and Maona (Mason) Bishop; married Iona Fay Maxwell, July 3, 1937. *Education:* University of Akron, A.B., 1928; Princeton University, M.A., 1929; Ohio State University, Ph.D., 1939. *Politics:* Democrat. *Religion:* United Church of Christ. *Home:* 1206 Fordham Dr., Sun City Center, Fla. 33570.

CAREER: University of Akron, Akron, Ohio, instructor in political science, 1931-32; teacher in Akron public schools, 1932-35; Ohio State University, Columbus, graduate assistant in political science, 1935-38; Syracuse University, Syracuse, N.Y., instructor, 1938-42, assistant professor, 1942-46, associate professor, 1946-52, professor of political science, 1952-72, professor emeritus, 1972—, chairman of citizenship program, 1941-48, chairman of international relations program, 1950-65, chairman of department of political science, 1965-66; Slippery Rock State College, Slippery Rock, Pa., professor of political science, 1972-74. Lecturer and news analyst, Chautauqua Institution, 1956-68; adjunct professor, State University of New York at Albany, 1959-63; visiting professor, Tunghai University (Taiwan), 1966-67. Consultant to U.S. government, 1955-70.

WRITINGS: (Co-author with M. J. Fisher) *Municipal and Other Local Governments*, Prentice-Hall, 1950; (editor) *Soviet Foreign Relations*, Syracuse University Press, 1952; *The Future of the New Political System in France*, General Electric Co., 1959; *The Administration of British Foreign Relations*, Syracuse University Press, 1961; *The Roosevelt-Litvinov Agreements: An American View*, Syracuse University Press, 1965; *The Administration of U.S. Foreign Policy through the United Nations*, Oceana, 1967; (contributor) Robert Boardman and A.J.R. Groom, editors, *The Management of Britain's External Relations*, Macmillan (London), 1973. Also contributor to *Approaches to an Understanding of World Affairs*, National Council for the Social Sciences yearbook, 1954. Contributor of articles and reviews to professional journals.

BJORN, Thyra Ferre   1905-1975

PERSONAL: Born September 12, 1905, in Malmberget, Sweden; died February 14, 1975, in Boston, Mass.; came to United States in 1924; daughter of Frans August (a minister) and Maria (Wickman) Ferre; married Robert John Bjorn, June 11, 1927; children: Shirley Ann Bjorn Loveland, Carolyn Elaine (Mrs. C. Jackson Barstow). *Education:* Educated in Sweden. *Religion:* Baptist. *Home:* 568 Williams St., Longmeadow 6, Mass.

CAREER: Writer; lecturer, on tour with Redpath Speaking Bureau, 1953-59; Springfield (Mass.) school system, adult education teacher of creative writing, fall session, 1962-63. *Member:* National League of American Pen Women, Authors Guild, Christian Writers International, International Platform Association, Western Massachusetts Writers Guild, Swedish Historical Foundation, Nordic Club (Springfield, Mass., president, 1955-56), Soroptomist Club, Longmeadow Woman's Club, Longmeadow Maternal Association.

WRITINGS—Published by Holt, except as indicated: *Papa's Wife,* 1955; *Papa's Daughter,* 1958; *Mama's Way,* 1959; *Dear Papa,* 1963; *Once Upon a Christmas Time,* 1964; *This Is My Life,* 1966; *The Home Has a Heart,* 1968; *Then There Grew Up a Generation,* 1970; *The Golden Acre,* Revell, 1975.

SIDELIGHTS: After writing "trunkfuls" of material, Thyra Bjorn published her first book, *Papa's Wife,* and earned a number of honors, including an audience with Queen Louise of Sweden in 1956. That book has been adapted for television, transcribed into Braille for the blind, and translated for publication in the Scandinavian countries. Bjorn wore a traditional Swedish costume for her lectures, which ranged from reminiscences and comical stories about her family to serious talks about prayer and faith. *Avocational interests:* Gardening and everything about home.

BIOGRAPHICAL/CRITICAL SOURCES: New York Times, February 20, 1975; *Publishers Weekly,* March 3, 1975; *AB Bookman's Weekly,* March 17, 1975.†

*   *   *

BLACK, Charles L(und), Jr.   1915-
(Charles Black)

PERSONAL: Born September 22, 1915, in Austin, Tex.; son of Charles L. (a lawyer) and Alzada (Bowman) Black; married Barbara Ann Aronstein (a professor of law), April 11, 1954; children: Gavin Bingley, David Alan, Robin Elizabeth. *Education:* University of Texas, B.A., 1935, M.A., 1938; Yale University, LL.B., 1943. *Office:* Yale Law School, Box 401A, Yale Station, New Haven, Conn. 06520.

CAREER: Davis, Polk, Wardwell, Sunderland & Kiendl (law firm), New York City, associate, 1946-47; Columbia University Law School, New York City, assistant professor, 1947-49, associate professor, 1949-52, professor, 1952-56; Yale University, New Haven, Conn., Henry R. Luce Professor of Jurisprudence, 1956-75, Sterling Professor of Law, 1975—, fellow of Jonathan Edwards College. Visiting professor, University of Texas, 1955; member of faculty, Salzburg Seminar in American Studies, 1956. Legal consultant, NAACP Defense Fund. *Member:* Maritime Law Association, American Association of University Professors, American Academy of Arts and Sciences, Connecticut Academy of Arts and Sciences, Elizabethan Club. *Awards, honors:* Scribes Award, 1961, for *The People and the Court;* Bye fellow, Queen's College, Cambridge, 1966-67; LL.D., Boston

University, 1975; Distinguished Alumnus award, University of Texas at Austin, 1975.

WRITINGS: (With Grant Gilmore) *The Law of Admiralty,* Foundation Press, 1957, 2nd edition, 1975; *The People and the Court,* Macmillan, 1960; *Perspectives in Constitutional Law,* Prentice-Hall, 1963, revised edition, 1970; *The Occasions of Justice,* Macmillan, 1963; *Telescopes and Islands* (poetry), A. Swallow, 1963; *Structure and Relationship in Constitutional Law,* Louisiana State University Press, 1969; *Impeachment: A Handbook,* Yale University Press, 1974; *Capital Punishment: The Inevitability of Caprice and Mistake,* Norton, 1974; (with Bob Eckhardt) *The Tides of Power: Conversations on the American Constitution,* Yale University Press, 1976; (under name Charles Black) *Owls Bay in Babylon* (poetry), Dustbooks, 1980; *Decision according to Law,* Norton, 1981. Contributor to law journals; contributor of articles to national magazines, including *Harper's* and *Saturday Evening Post,* and of poetry (under name Charles Black) to literary magazines.

WORK IN PROGRESS: A second edition of *Capital Punishment;* poetry.

*   *   *

BLACK, Cyril Edwin   1915-

PERSONAL: Born September 10, 1915, in Bryson City, N.C.; son of Floyd Hensen and Zarafinka (Kirova) Black; married Corinne Manning, June 30, 1951; children: James Manning, Christina Ellen. *Education:* Duke University, A.B., 1936; Harvard University, A.M., 1937, Ph.D., 1941. *Home:* 348 Ridgeview Rd., Princeton, N.J. 08540. *Office:* Center of International Studies, Princeton University, Princeton, N.J.

CAREER: Princeton University, Princeton, N.J., instructor, 1939-46, assistant professor, 1946-49, associate professor, 1949-54, professor of history, 1954—, director of Center of International Studies, 1968—. Officer, U.S. Department of State, 1942-46; member of U.S. commission to Greece, 1947, and U.S. delegation to observe Soviet elections, 1958. Lecturer at National War College, 1950; visiting professor at Yale University, 1960. Fellow, Behavioral Studies Center, 1960-61. *Member:* American Historical Association, American Political Science Association, Council on Foreign Relations, Nassau Club (Princeton). *Awards, honors:* Litt.D., Ursinus College, 1978.

WRITINGS: Establishment of Constitutional Government in Bulgaria, Princeton University Press, 1943; (with E. C. Helmreich) *Twentieth Century Europe,* Knopf, 1950, 4th edition, 1972; *Our World History* (based on *World History* by Muzzey, Lloyd, and Smith), Ginn, 1962, revised edition, 1965; *The Dynamics of Modernization,* Harper, 1966; (with R. A. Falk, K. Knorr, and O. R. Young) *Neutralization in World Politics,* Princeton University Press, 1968; (with others) *The Modernization of Japan and Russia,* Free Press, 1975.

Editor: *Challenge in Eastern Europe,* Rutgers University Press, 1954; *Rewriting Russian History,* Praeger, 1956, revised edition, Vintage, 1962; *The Transformation of Russian Society,* Harvard University Press, 1960; (and author of introduction) *Russia on the Eve of War and Revolution,* Vintage, 1961; *Communism and Revolution* (essays resulting from research activity of the Center of International Studies), Princeton University Press, 1964; (with Falk) *The Future of the International Legal Order,* Princeton University Press, Volume I: *Trends and Patterns,* 1969, Volume II: *Wealth and Resources,* 1970, Volume III: *Conflict Manage-*

ment, 1971, Volume IV: *Structure of the International Environment*, 1972; *Comparative Modernization: A Reader*, Free Press, 1975. Contributor to professional journals. Editor, *World Politics*, 1959—.

*   *   *

BLACKER, Irwin R(obert)   1919-

PERSONAL: Born October 6, 1919, in Cleveland, Ohio; son of Louis C. and Sadie (Greenberg) Blacker; married Ethel Marie Handler, 1941; children: Hope, Deborah, Emily. *Education:* Ohio University, B.S.J., 1947; Western Reserve University (now Case Western Reserve University), M.A., 1947, graduate student, 1947-49. *Home:* 3455 Beverly Glen, Sherman Oaks, Calif. *Agent:* Diane Cleaver, Sanford J. Greenburger Associates, Inc., 825 Third Ave., New York, N.Y. 10022.

CAREER: Purdue University, Lafayette, Ind., instructor in English, 1949-50; Central Intelligence Agency, Washington, D.C., employee, 1950-51; Jewish Theological Seminary, New York City, staff director, 1954-56; Columbia Broadcasting System (CBS-TV), New York City, writer, 1956-59; University of Southern California, Los Angeles, 1961-77, became professor of cinema and chairman of graduate studies; free-lance writer, 1977—. Story consultant for CBS-TV and NBC-TV shows; story editor, "Bonanza" and "Greatest Show on Earth." Associate producer-writer of "Brush-Fire," a feature film for Paramount, and "Tear Down the Sky," a feature film for Obelisk Productions. *Military service:* U.S. Army, Engineers, 1941-45; became second lieutenant; awarded Bronze Star and other decorations. *Member:* Writers Guild. *Awards, honors:* Peabody Award; Emerson Poetry Award; American Public Relations Association Trophy.

WRITINGS: (Editor) *Irregulars, Partisans, Guerrillas*, Simon & Schuster, 1954; *Westering*, World Publishing, 1958; *Taos*, World Publishing, 1959, reprinted, Brook House, 1977; *Kilroy Gambit*, World Publishing, 1960; *The Golden Conquistadores*, Bobbs-Merrill, 1960; *The Bold Conquistadores*, Bobbs-Merrill, 1961; *Days of Gold*, World Publishing, 1961; *The Old West in Fiction*, Obolensky, 1961; *The Old West in Fact*, Obolensky, 1962; *Conquest*, Grosset, 1962; (editor) *Prescott's Histories*, Viking, 1964; (editor) *Hakluyt's Voyages*, Viking, 1965; *Cortes and the Aztec Conquest*, American Heritage, 1965; (co-editor) *The Book of Books*, Holt, 1965; *Chain of Command*, Cassell, 1965; *Valley of the Hanoi*, Cassell, 1965; *To Hell in a Basket*, Cassell, 1966; *Search and Destroy*, Random House, 1966; *Standing on a Drum*, Putnam, 1968; *Directors at Work*, Funk, 1970; *The Middle of the Fire*, Scribner, 1971. Also author of some 200 network television plays.

WORK IN PROGRESS: Digs and Documents: The Rediscovery of the Holy Land.

SIDELIGHTS: Although he writes almost as much for films and television as for book publication, Irwin R. Blacker describes himself as "basically an historical novelist and historian." He began writing at the age of twelve and sold his first radio show before reaching the age of twenty.

As a professor at the University of Southern California, Blacker established the largest professional writing program in the country on the graduate level. Students from the cinema division of this program have worked on the screenplays of numerous films, including "Star Wars," "The Sting," "American Graffiti," "Slither," "Sugarland Express," and "Bingo Long." In recognition of his many contributions to the field of literature, the University created the

Irwin R. Blacker Award to be presented to prominent authors living on the West Coast. The first recipients were Will and Ariel Durant, Joan Didion, and Neil Simon.

*   *   *

BLACKING, John (Anthony Randoll)   1928-

PERSONAL: Born October 22, 1928, in Guildford, England; son of William (an architect) and Margaret (Waymouth) Blacking; married Paula Gebers (divorced); children: Caroline (deceased), Jessica, Fiona (deceased), Laura, Valentine. *Education:* King's College, Cambridge, B.A. (honors in social anthropology), 1953, M.A., 1957, Ph.D., 1965, D. Litt., 1972. *Politics:* Socialist. *Religion:* Church of England. *Home:* 18, Cleaver Park, Belfast BT9 5HX, Northern Ireland. *Agent:* Curtis Brown Ltd., 575 Madison Ave., New York, N.Y. 10022. *Office:* Department of Social Anthropology, Queen's University of Belfast, Belfast, Northern Ireland.

CAREER: International Library of African Music, Roodepoort, South Africa, musicologist, 1954-57; field work on anthropological scholarship in northern Transvaal, 1956-58; University of the Witwatersrand, Johannesburg, South Africa, lecturer in social anthropology and African administration, and honorary lecturer in music, 1959-65, professor of social anthropology and chairman of African Studies Programme, 1966-69; Queen's University of Belfast, Belfast, Northern Ireland, professor of social anthropology, 1970—. Visiting professor, Western Michigan University, 1971, Makerere University, and University of Pittsburgh. *Military service:* British Army, commissioned in Coldstream Guards, 1948-49; served in Malayan jungle. *Member:* Royal Anthropological Institute (fellow), Association of Social Anthropologists of the British Commonwealth, International Folk Music Council, Society for Ethnomusicology.

WRITINGS: Black Background: The Childhood of a South African Girl, Abelard, 1964; (editor with Phillip V. Tobias) Antonio de Almeida, *Bushmen and Other Non-Bantu Peoples of Angola: Three Lectures*, Witwatersrand University Press, 1965; *Venda Children's Songs: A Study in Ethnomusicological Analysis*, Witwatersrand University Press, 1967; *Process and Product in Human Society*, Witwatersrand University Press, 1969; *How Musical Is Man?*, University of Washington Press, 1973, 2nd edition, 1976; *Man and Fellowman*, Queen's University of Belfast, 1974; (editor) *The Anthropology of the Body*, Academic Press, 1977; (with Joann W. Kealiinohomoku) *The Performing Arts: Music and Dance*, Mouton, 1979. "Music from Petauke," Album I, a long-playing record issued by Ethnic Folkways Library, 1962, Album II, 1965, Album III, in press. Contributor to scientific journals.

WORK IN PROGRESS: Continuing ethnomusicological and anthropological research; a book on the anthropology of peace.

SIDELIGHTS: John Blacking told *CA:* "I have no hobbies in the true sense of the word, as everything I do is related to my single interest in re-assessing the value of human institutions. [But] I enjoy . . . gardening, playing the piano, taking films and photos, conducting, and composing music." Blacking speaks and writes French, Malay, and Venda.

*   *   *

BLAIR, Walter   1900-

PERSONAL: Born April 21, 1900, in Spokane, Wash.; son of John James and Emma (Merritt) Blair; married Carol Conrad, September 20, 1925; children: Paula (Mrs. Lawrence G. Olinger). *Education:* Yale University, Ph.B., 1923; University of Chicago, M.A., 1926, Ph.D., 1931. *Politics:* Independent. *Home:* 5805 Dorchester Ave., Chicago, Ill. 60637. *Office:* University of Chicago, 1050 East 59th St., Chicago, Ill. 60637.

CAREER: Spokesman-Review, Spokane, Wash., reporter, 1923-25; University of Minnesota, Minneapolis, member of English faculty, 1928-29; University of Chicago, Chicago, Ill., instructor, 1929-30, assistant professor, 1930-39, associate professor, 1939-44, professor of English, 1944-68, professor emeritus, 1968—, chairman of department, 1951-60. Visiting professor, Goethe University, Frankfort, Germany, 1949-50; Mrs. Beckman Lecturer, University of California, Berkeley, 1972; Distinguished Scholar in Residence, University of New Mexico, 1978. *Member:* Modern Language Association of America (member of editorial board, 1945-51; chairman, American Literature division, 1958), American Studies Association, Phi Delta Theta. *Awards, honors:* Society of Midland Authors Thormod Monsen Award, 1961, for *Mark Twain and "Huck Finn,"* and 1978, for *America's Humor;* Jay B. Hubbell Award, 1974; Charles Chaplin Award, American Humor Studies Association, 1975.

WRITINGS: (Editor) *The Sweet Singer of Michigan,* Pascal Covici, 1928; *Two Phases of American Humor,* Duke University Press, 1931; (with F. J. Meine) *Mike Fink, King of Mississippi Keelboatmen,* Holt, 1933, reprinted, Greenwood Press, 1971; (with W. K. Chandler) *Approaches to Poetry,* Appleton, 1935, 2nd edition, 1953; *Native American Humor: 1800-1900,* American Book, 1937, revised edition, Chandler, 1960, reprinted, Arden Library, 1979; *Horse Sense in American Humor,* University of Chicago Press, 1942; *Tall Tale America,* Coward, 1944, 5th edition, 1963; (editor with Theodore Hornberger and Randall Stewart) *Literature of the United States,* Scott, Foresman, 1947, 4th edition, 1966; *Davy Crockett: Truth and Legend,* Coward, 1955; (editor with F. J. Meine) *Half Horse, Half Alligator,* University of Chicago Press, 1956; *Mark Twain and "Huck Finn": 1855-1873,* University of California Press, 1960; (with Hamlin Hill) *The Art of Huckleberry Finn,* Chandler, 1962; (editor) *Selected Shorter Writing of Mark Twain,* Houghton, 1962; (editor with Harrison Hayford) Herman Melville, *Omoo,* Hendricks House, 1966; (with Hornberger, Stewart, and J. Miller) *American Literature: A Brief History,* Scott, Foresman, 1964, revised edition, 1974; (editor) *Mark Twain's Hannibal, Huck, and Tom,* University of California Press, 1969; (with Hill) *America's Humor: From "Poor Richard" to "Doonesbury,"* Oxford University Press, 1978, revised edition, 1980; *James Russell Lowell,* Scribner's, 1979. Also author, with John Gerber, *Reportory,* Scott, Foresman; co-editor of *Better Reading One: Factual Prose,* Scott, Foresman, and *The Literature of the United States,* Scott, Foresman. Contributor to periodicals. Member of editorial board, *American Literature,* 1943-51, and *College English,* 1945-48; member of advisory board, *Encyclopaedia Britannica,* 1951—. Educational consultant, Coronet Films, for "Whitman," 1957, "Mark Twain," 1957, and "Poe," 1958.

WORK IN PROGRESS: Co-editor of "Mark Twain Papers" series and "The Works of Mark Twain" series, for University of California Press; co-editor of *The Mirth of a Nation: America's Great Dialect Humor,* for University of Minnesota Press.

*   *   *

BLAKE, Nelson Manfred 1908-

PERSONAL: Born October 13, 1908, in Island Pond, Vt.; son of Herbert Willard and Gertrude (Nelson) Blake; married Elizabeth May Cox, 1937; children: James Herbert. *Education:* Dartmouth College, A.B., 1930; Brown University, M.A., 1931; Clark University, Ph.D., 1936. *Politics:* Democrat. *Religion:* Methodist. *Home:* 400 Southeast Tenth St., Apt. 218A, Deerfield Beach, Fla. 33441.

CAREER: Gardner High School, Gardner, Mass., teacher of history, 1931-34; Syracuse University, Syracuse, N.Y., instructor, 1936-39, assistant professor, 1939-46, associate professor, 1946-50, professor of history, 1950-71, Maxwell Distinguished Professor of History, 1971-73, professor emeritus, 1973—. *Member:* American Historical Association, Organization of American Historians, American Studies Association, American Association of University Professors.

WRITINGS: (With Oscar T. Barck) *Since 1900: A History of the United States in Our Times,* Macmillan, 1947, 5th edition, 1974; *A Short History of American Life,* McGraw, 1952; *Water for the Cities,* Syracuse University Press, 1956; (with Ralph V. Harlow) *The United States: From Wilderness to World Power,* Holt, 1957, 4th edition, 1964; (with Barck) *The United States in Its World Relations,* McGraw, 1960; *The Road to Reno: A History of Divorce in the United States,* Macmillan, 1962, reprinted, Greenwood Press, 1977; *A History of American Life and Thought,* McGraw, 1963, 2nd edition, 1972; *Novelists' America: Fiction as History, 1910-1940,* Syracuse University Press, 1969; *Land into Water—Water into Land: A History of Water Management in Florida,* University Presses of Florida, 1980. Contributor of articles to various professional journals.

BIOGRAPHICAL/CRITICAL SOURCES: Saturday Review, April 5, 1969; *Books Abroad,* spring, 1970.

*   *   *

BLAKELEY, Thomas J(ohn) 1931-

PERSONAL: Born June 14, 1931, in Cleveland, Ohio; son of Thomas Jefferson and Elizabeth (Lecso) Blakeley; married Janet Stone, August 16, 1957; children: Mary Elizabeth, Damian Andrew, Timothy William. *Education:* Sacred Heart College, Detroit, Mich., B.A., 1953; University of Fribourg, Ph.D., 1960. *Religion:* Roman Catholic. *Home:* 16 Fairmount Way, Quincy, Mass. 02169. *Office:* Department of Philosophy, Boston College, Chestnut Hill, Mass. 02167.

CAREER: University of Fribourg, Fribourg, Switzerland, chief research assistant and director of studies at Institute of East-European Studies, 1960-64; Boston College, Boston, Mass., associate professor, 1964-69, professor of philosophy, 1969—, director of Russian philosophical studies program. *Military service:* U.S. Army, 1953-55. *Member:* Fribourg Philosophical Society (secretary, 1963-64).

WRITINGS: (Compiler, and editor with Joseph M. Bochenski) *Bibliographie der sowjetischen Philosophie,* four volumes, D. Reidel, 1959-63; *Soviet Scholasticism,* Humanities, 1961; (editor with J. M. Bochenski) Innocentius M. Bochenski, *Studies in Soviet Thought,* Volume I, Humanities, 1961; *Soviet Theory of Knowledge,* Humanities, 1964; *Soviet Philosophy: A General Introduction to Contemporary Soviet Thought,* Humanities, 1964; (translator) Helmut Fleischer, *Short Handbook of Communist Ideology,* D. Reidel, 1965; (translator) Guy Planty-Bonjour, *The Categories of Dialectical Materialism: Contemporary Soviet Ontology,* D. Reidel, 1967; (translator) Peter P. Kirschenbaum, *Information and Reflections, on Some Problems of Cybernetics and How Contemporary Dialectical Materialism Copes with Them,* Humanities, 1970; (with others) *Guide to Marxist Philoso-*

phy, Swallow Press, 1972; (with William Gavin) *Russia and America: A Philosophical Comparison*, D. Reidel, 1976; (with J. G. Colbert) *Curso de iniciacion al marxismo: 4 lecciones*, Pamplona, 1977; (with others) *Society, Man, Reality: Marxism and Alternatives*, D. Reidel, 1981. Contributor of more than thirty articles and reviews to learned journals. *Studies in Soviet Thought*, managing editor, 1961-64, editor, 1969—.

WORK IN PROGRESS: Soviet Scientific Atheism.

* * *

BLASSINGAME, Wyatt Rainey 1909-

PERSONAL: Born February 6, 1909, in Demopolis, Ala.; son of Wyatt Childs (a teacher) and Maud (Lurton) Blassingame; married Gertrude Olsen, 1936 (died, 1976); married Lenora Jeanne Toman; children: (first marriage) Peggy Diamant, April Lane. *Education:* Attended Howard College, 1926-28; University of Alabama, A.B., 1930, graduate study, 1931-33; New York University, graduate study, 1951-52. *Politics:* Independent. *Religion:* Protestant. *Home:* Hammoce Rd., Anna Maria, Fla. *Agent:* Lurton Blassingame, 60 East 42nd St., New York, N.Y. 10017.

CAREER: Montgomery Advertiser, Montgomery, Ala., reporter, 1930-31; University of Alabama, University, teaching fellow, 1931-33; Florida Southern College, Lakeland, Fla., instructor, 1948-51; currently a full-time writer. *Military service:* U.S. Navy, 1942-45; received Bronze Star and Presidential Unit Citation. *Awards, honors:* Benjamin Franklin Magazine Award for best short story of 1956, "Man's Courage," in *Harper's;* Outstanding Science Books for Children awards, National Science Teachers Association, for *Wonders of Alligators and Crocodiles, Science Catches the Criminal, Wonders of Raccoons,* and *Thor Heyerdahl.*

WRITINGS—Adult: *For Better, For Worse* (novel), Crowell, 1951; *Live from the Devil* (novel), Doubleday, 1959; *The Golden Geyser* (novel), Doubleday, 1961; *Halo of Spears* (novel), Doubleday, 1962; (with Evans Cottman) *Out-Island Doctor* (nonfiction), Dutton, 1963.

Juvenile nonfiction: *Great Trains of the World*, Random House, 1953; *The French Foreign Legion* (Junior Book-of-the-Month selection), Random House, 1955; *His Kingdom for a Horse* (Junior Literary Guild selection), F. Watts, 1957; *They Rode the Frontier*, F. Watts, 1959; (with Richard Glendinning) *Frontier Doctors*, F. Watts, 1963; *First Book of Florida*, F. Watts, 1963; *The U.S. Frogmen of World War II* (Junior Book-of-the-Month selection), Random House, 1964; *Naturalist-Explorers*, F. Watts, 1964; *Stephen Decatur*, Garrard, 1964; *First Book of the Seashore*, F. Watts, 1964; *First Book of American Expansion*, F. Watts, 1965; *Ponce de Leon*, Garrard, 1965; *Sacagawea: Indian Guide*, Garrard, 1965; (with Glendinning) *Men Who Opened the West*, Putnam, 1966; *Franklin D. Roosevelt: Four Times President*, Garrard, 1966; *Baden-Powell*, Garrard, 1966; *Osceola: Seminole War Chief*, Garrard, 1967; *Navy's Fliers in World War II*, Westminster, 1967; *Combat Nurses of World War II*, Random House, 1967; *Bent's Fort: Crossroads of the Great West*, Garrard, 1967; *Eleanor Roosevelt*, Putnam, 1967; *Look It Up Book of Presidents*, Random House, 1968; *Story of the Boy Scouts*, Garrard, 1968; *Story of the United States Flag*, Garrard, 1969; *Medical Corps Heroes of World War II*, Random House, 1969; *Jake Gaither: Winning Coach*, Garrard, 1969.

William Tecumseh Sherman: Defender of the Union, Prentice-Hall, 1970; *Halsey: Five-Star Admiral*, Garrard,

1970; *Joseph Stalin and Communist Russia*, Garrrard, 1971; *Ernest Thompson Seton*, Garrard, 1971; *Diving for Treasure*, Macrae, 1971; *Dan Beard*, Garrard, 1972; *Wonders of Alligators and Crocodiles*, Dodd, 1973; *Jim Beckwourth: Black Trapper and Indian Chief*, Garrard, 1973; *The Everglades: From Yesterday to Tomorrow*, Putnam, 1974; *Wonders of Frogs and Toads*, Dodd, 1975; *Science Catches the Criminal*, Dodd, 1975; *The Little Killers: Fleas, Lice, and Mosquitos*, Putnam, 1975; *William Beebe: Underwater Explorer*, Garrard, 1976; *Wonders of the Turtle World*, Dodd, 1976; *Wonders of Raccoons*, Dodd, 1977; *Wonders of Crows*, Dodd, 1979; *Thor Heyerdahl: Viking Scientist*, Elsevier-Nelson, 1979; *The Incas and the Spanish Conquest*, Messner, 1980; *Skunks*, Dodd, in press.

Juvenile fiction: *John Henry and Paul Bunyan Play Baseball*, Garrard, 1971; *How Davy Crockett Got a Bearskin Coat*, Garrard, 1972; *Pecos Bill Rides a Tornado*, Garrard, 1973; *Paul Bunyan Fights the Monster Plants*, Garrard, 1974; *Bowleg Bill: Seagoing Cowboy*, Garrard, 1976; *Pecos Bill Catches a Hidebehind*, Garrard, 1977; *Pecos Bill and the Clothesline Snake*, Garrard, 1978.

Contributor of about six hundred stories and articles to national magazines; some stories reprinted in anthologies and textbooks in the United States and abroad.

SIDELIGHTS: Wyatt Blassingame writes *CA:* "The one good thing about writing for a living is you can live wherever you wish. For forty-two years I have lived (most of the time) on Anna Maria, an island joined to the Florida mainland by a bridge. It is a fine place for fishing, swimming, and walking on the beach."

* * *

BLAXLAND, W(illiam) Gregory 1918-

PERSONAL: Born December 7, 1918, in Norwich, Norfolk, England; son of A. J. (a surgeon) and Anna Marion (Andrews) Blaxland; married Elizabeth Finn, October 14, 1953; children: Henry, Lucy. *Education:* Attended Royal Military College at Sandhurst, 1938-39. *Religion:* Church of England. *Home:* Lower Heppington, Street End, Canterbury, Kent, England.

CAREER: British Army, regular officer, Infantry, 1939-55; retired as major after being disabled by poliomyelitis. *Member:* Royal United Service Institute, Mounted Infantry Club, Band of Brothers.

WRITINGS: Tom Glasse and the East Kent Hunt, privately printed, 1958; *The Home Counties Brigade: Its Members and Their Integration*, privately printed, 1960; *The Story of the Queen's Own Buffs, The Royal Kent Regiment*, privately printed, 1963; *J. H. Thomas: A Life for Unity*, Muller, 1964; *Objective Egypt*, Muller, 1966, published as *Egypt and Sinai: Eternal Battleground*, Funk, 1968; *The Farewell Years: The Buffs, 1948-1967*, Regimental Association, 1967; *Amiens, 1918*, Muller, 1968; *A Guide to the Queen's Regiment*, privately printed, 1970; *The Regiments Depart: A History of the British Army, 1945-70*, Kimber, 1971; *The Buffs*, Leo Cooper, 1972; *Golden Miller*, Constable, 1972; *Destination Dunkirk: The Story of Gort's Army*, Kimber, 1973; *The Queen's Own Buffs*, Regimental Association, 1974; *The Plain Cook and the Great Showman: The First and Eighth Armies in North Africa*, Kimber, 1977; *The Middlesex Regiment*, Leo Cooper, 1978; *Alexander's Generals: The Italian Campaign, 1944-1945*, Kimber, 1979. Contributor of articles to *Sunday Express, Country Life, Field,* and *Punch.* Editor, *Baily's Hunting Directory*, 1961-64.

BLEGEN, Theodore C.   1891-1969

PERSONAL: Born July 16, 1891, in Minneapolis, Minn.; died July 18, 1969, in St. Paul, Minn., son of John H. (a professor of Greek) and Anna B. (Olsen) Blegen; married Clara E. Woodward, August 19, 1916; children: Theodore Woodward, Margaret Jane (Mrs. Philip Crum). *Education:* Augsburg College, B.A., 1910; University of Minnesota, B.A., 1912, M.A., 1915, Ph.D., 1925. *Home:* 1588 Northrop St., St. Paul, Minn. *Office:* Minnesota Historical Society, St. Paul, Minn.

CAREER: Hamline University, St. Paul, Minn., assistant professor of history, 1920-22, head of department, 1922-27; University of Minnesota, Minneapolis, professorial lecturer, 1927-29, associate professor, 1929-37, professor of history, 1937-60, dean of graduate school, 1940-60. Minnesota Historical Society, St. Paul, assistant superintendent, 1922-31, superintendent, 1931-39, research fellow, 1960-69. *Member:* Organization of American Historians, (president, 1943-44), American Historical Association, Minnesota Historical Society, Norwegian American Historical Association (editor, 1925-60). *Awards, honors:* L.H.D., St. Olaf College, 1935; honorary doctorate from University of Oslo, 1938; LL.D., Augustana College, 1956, and Carleton College, 1958; Litt. D., Hamline University, 1942, Luther College, 1960, and Macalester College, 1961.

WRITINGS: A Report on the Public Archives, [Madison, Wis.], 1918; *Norwegian Migration to America,* two volumes, Norwegian-American Historical Association, 1931-40, reprinted, Haskell House, 1969; *Minnesota History: A Study Outline,* University of Minnesota Press, 1931; (with Martin B. Ruud) *Norwegian Emigrant Songs and Ballads,* University of Minnesota Press, 1936, reprinted, Arno, 1979; *Minnesota: Its History and Its People,* University of Minnesota Press, 1937; *Building Minnesota,* Heath, 1938; *Grass Roots History,* University of Minnesota Press, 1947, reprinted, Kennikat, 1969; *The Land Lies Open,* University of Minnesota Press, 1949, reprinted, Greenwood Press, 1975; *With Various Voices: Recordings of North Star Life,* Itasca Press, 1949; (with Sarah Davidson) *Iron Face,* Caxton Club, 1950; *The Crowded Boxroom: Sherlock Holmes as Poet,* Sumac, 1951; (editor) *Sherlock Holmes: Master Detective,* Sumac, 1952; *Land of Their Choice,* University of Minnesota Press, 1955; *Minnesota: A History of the State,* University of Minnesota Press, 1963; (editor) Edward D. Neill, *Abraham Lincoln and His Mailbag,* Minnesota Historical Society, 1964; *Lincoln's Secretary Goes West,* Sumac, 1965; *The Voyageurs and Their Songs,* Minnesota Historical Society, 1966; *The Kensington Rune Stone: New Light on an Old Riddle,* Minnesota Historical Society, 1968; *The Saga of Saga Hill,* Minnesota Historical Society, 1970. Also editor of *Ole Rynning's True Account of America,* 1926.

AVOCATIONAL INTERESTS: Study of Sherlock Holmes; collecting ballads of emigration and westward movement.

BIOGRAPHICAL/CRITICAL SOURCES: Henry S. Commager, editor, *Immigration and American History: Essays in Honor of Theodore C. Blegen,* University of Minnesota Press, 1961.†

*   *   *

BLISH, James (Benjamin)   1921-1975
(William Atheling, Jr., Marcus Lyons, Arthur Merlin, Luke Torley; joint pseudonyms: Donald Laverty, John MacDougal)

PERSONAL: Born May 23, 1921, in East Orange, N.J.; died July 30, 1975, in Henley-on-Thames, England; son of Asa Rhodes and Dorothea (Schneewind) Blish; married Mildred Virginia Kidd Emden, May 23, 1947 (divorced, 1963); married Judith Ann Lawrence, November 7, 1964; children: (first marriage) Elisabeth, Charles Benjamin. *Education:* Rutgers University, B.Sc., 1942; attended Columbia University, 1945-46. *Agent:* Robert P. Mills, Ltd., 156 East 52nd St., New York, N.Y. 10022.

CAREER: Trade newspaper editor, New York City, 1947-51; public relations counsel in New York City, and Washington, D.C., 1951-69; writer. *Military service:* U.S. Army, 1942-44. *Member:* Society of Authors, James Branch Cabell Society, History of Science Society, Association of Lunar and Planetary Observers, British Interplanetary Society, Authors League, American Rocket Society, Science Fiction Writers of America (vice-president, 1966-68), Civil Air Patrol. *Awards, honors:* Hugo Award for best science fiction novel, 1958, for *A Case of Conscience;* Eighteenth World Science Fiction Convention Guest of Honor, 1960.

WRITINGS: Jack of Eagles, Greenberg, 1952, published as *Esp-er,* Avon, 1958; (with Fritz Leiber and Fletcher Pratt) *Witches Three,* Twayne, 1952; *The Warriors of Day,* Galaxy, 1953; *Sword of Xota,* Galaxy, 1953; (with Robert Lowndes) *The Duplicated Man,* Avalon, 1959; *Earthman, Come Home* (also see below), Putnam, 1955, reprinted, Hutchinson, 1974; *Year 2018!,* Avon, 1957 (published in England as *They Shall Have Stars* [also see below], Faber, 1957); *The Seedling Stars,* Gnome, 1957; *The Frozen Year,* Ballantine, 1957 (published in England as *Fallen Star,* Faber, 1957, reprinted, Hutchinson, 1976); *A Case of Conscience,* Ballantine, 1958, reprinted, 1979; *VOR,* Avon, 1958; *The Triumph of Time* (also see below), Avon, 1958 (published in England as *A Clash of Cymbals,* Faber, 1958); *Galactic Cluster* (short story collection), New American Library, 1959.

(With Poul Anderson and Thomas N. Scortia) Leo Margulies, editor, *Get Out of My Sky,* Fawcett, 1960; *The Star Dwellers,* Putnam, 1961; *So Close to Home* (short story collection), Ballantine, 1961; (with Virginia Kidd) *Titan's Daughter,* Berkley Publishing, 1961; *A Life for the Stars* (also see below), Putnam, 1962; *The Night Shapes,* Ballantine, 1962; (under pseudonym William Atheling, Jr.) *The Issue at Hand: Studies in Contemporary Magazine Science Fiction,* Advent, 1964, 2nd edition published as *More Issues at Hand: Critical Studies in Contemporary Science Fiction,* 1970; *Doctor Mirabilis: A Novel,* Faber, 1964, revised edition, Dodd, 1971.

Cities in Flight (contains *They Shall Have Stars, A Life for the Stars, Earthman, Come Home,* and *The Triumph of Time*), Faber, 1965, Avon, 1966; *Mission to the Heart Stars,* Putnam, 1965; *Best Science Fiction Stories of James Blish,* Faber, 1965, revised edition, 1973, published as *The Testament of Andros,* Hutchinson, 1977; (editor and author of introduction) *New Dreams This Morning,* Ballantine, 1966; (with Norman L. Knight) *A Torrent of Faces,* Doubleday, 1967; *Welcome to Mars!,* Faber, 1967, Putnam, 1968; *The Vanished Jet* (juvenile), Weybright & Talley, 1968; *Black Easter; or, Faust Aleph-Null,* Doubleday, 1968; (with Robert Silverberg and Jack Zelazny) *Three for Tomorrow: Three Original Novellas of Science Fiction,* Meredith Press, 1969; *Anywhen* (short story collection), Doubleday, 1970, revised edition, Faber, 1971; (editor) *Nebula Award Stories 5,* Doubleday, 1970; *... And All the Stars a Stage,* Doubleday, 1971; *The Day after Judgment,* Doubleday, 1971; *The Quincux of Time,* Dell, 1972; *Midsummer Century,* Doubleday, 1972; (editor) *Thirteen O'Clock and Other Zero Hours: The "Cecil Corwin" Stories of C. M. Kornbluth,* Hale, 1972.

Adapter of scripts based on National Broadcasting Co. television series, except as indicated: *Star Trek* (also see below), Bantam, Volumes I-XI, 1967-75, Volume XII (with J. A. Lawrence), 1977; *Spock Must Die!* (original novel; also see below), Bantam, 1970; *The Star Trek Reader* (contains *Star Trek*, Volumes I-X, Volume XII, and *Spock Must Die!*), four volumes, Dutton, 1976-78.

Also author of television scripts and motion picture screenplays. Contributor of short stories, articles, poetry, and criticism (occasionally under pseudonyms) to numerous magazines. Editor, *Kalki: Studies in James Branch Cabell*, beginning 1967.

WORK IN PROGRESS: A History of Witchcraft, Demonology and Magic; a study of the semantics of music; *The Sense of Music*; another science fiction novel.

SIDELIGHTS: Though known to many readers as the adapter of ''Star Trek'' television scripts into book form, a *Times Literary Supplement* reviewer once referred to James Blish as ''one of the best five or six living writers of science fiction. . . . His ability to convey without undue emphasis the fundamental human link that exists between curious forms of man in exotic surroundings is as faultless as his skill in implying the social and political changes consequent on technological advance.'' A *New York Herald Tribune Book Review* critic wrote: ''A rare Martian orchid to James Blish for giving us science fiction in its purest form; the logical extrapolation of present knowledge and probability so that the reader passes without a quiver from the known to the unknown.''

Blish made a point of including actual scientific and technological detail in his works, for he felt that it was necessary for a science fiction writer to be as accurate as possible in order to convince the reader of the plausibility of the story. He also, at least after the publication of *A Case of Conscience* in 1958, exhibited a fascination with religious themes, especially Christianity and its struggles with satanic powers as perceived by medieval philosophers.

AVOCATIONAL INTERESTS: Music, astronomy, flying.

BIOGRAPHICAL/CRITICAL SOURCES: New York Herald Tribune Book Review, April 13, 1952; *Times Literary Supplement*, September 21, 1967; *Young Readers' Review*, February, 1968; *New York Times*, July 31, 1975; *Washington Post*, August 1, 1975.†

*   *   *

BLISHEN, Bernard Russell   1919-

PERSONAL: Born September 21, 1919, in Harlesdon, England; son of Henry Charles and Lilly (Shipp) Blishen; married Ruth Popkin, 1947; children: Jennifer, Joan, Susan, Peter. *Education:* McGill University, B.A., 1949, M.A., 1950; Columbia University, postgraduate study, 1955-56. *Home:* 531 Hunter St. W., Peterborough, Ontario, Canada. *Office:* Department of Sociology, York University, Downsview, Ontario, Canada.

CAREER: Dominion Bureau of Statistics, Ottawa, Ontario, chief of section, 1950-57; Carleton University, Ottawa, lecturer in sociology, 1956-57; University of British Columbia, Vancouver, lecturer, 1957-61, assistant professor of sociology, 1961-64, director of Institute of Social and Economic Research, 1959-61; Trent University, Peterborough, Ontario, 1964-74, began as associate professor, became professor, dean of graduate studies, 1966-73; York University, Downsview, Ontario, professor of sociology, 1974—, director of Institute for Behavioural Research, 1974-78. Research direc-

tor, Royal Commission on Health Services (Ottawa), 1961-64. *Military service:* Royal Canadian Navy, 1939-45. *Member:* Canadian Political Science Association, Canadian Sociology and Anthropology Association (president, 1977-78), Royal Society of Arts (fellow), American Sociological Association.

WRITINGS: (Editor with others) *Canadian Society*, Free Press of Glencoe, 1961, 3rd edition, Macmillan (Toronto), 1967; *Doctors and Doctrines: The Ideology of Medical Care in Canada*, University of Toronto Press, 1969; (contributor) John Porter and Robin S. Harris, *Towards 2000: The Future of Post-Secondary Education in Ontario*, McClelland & Stewart, 1971. Also co-author of *Does Money Matter?*, Institute for Behavioural Research. Contributor of articles to sociological and other professional journals.

WORK IN PROGRESS: Research on Canadian society, social change in Canada's north, and the quality of life in Canada.

AVOCATIONAL INTERESTS: Sailing, hiking, fishing.

*   *   *

BLOOD, Robert O(scar), Jr.   1921-
(Bob Blood)

PERSONAL: Born August 15, 1921, in Concord, N.H.; son of Robert Oscar and Pauline (Shepard) Blood; married Margaret McKee Cheek, 1944; children: Peter, Alan, Lawrence, Jonathan. *Education:* Dartmouth College, A.B., 1942; Yale Divinity School, B.D., 1945; University of Minnesota, M.A., 1950; University of North Carolina, Ph.D., 1952. *Religion:* Society of Friends. *Home:* 2005 Penncraft Court, Ann Arbor, Mich. 48103.

CAREER: William Penn College, Oskaloosa, Iowa, instructor, 1946-49; Merrill-Palmer Institute, Detroit, Mich., instructor, 1951-52; University of Michigan, Ann Arbor, assistant professor, 1952-57, associate professor, 1957-67; International Christian University, Mitaka, Japan, visiting associate professor, 1967-69; Pendle Hill, Wallingford, Pa., member of faculty, 1969-73; marriage counselor in private practice, 1973—. Fulbright research scholar, Tokyo Educational University, Tokyo, Japan, 1958-59. Consultant, Ann Arbor Institute, Inc., 1977—. *Member:* American Association for Marriage and Family Therapy (fellow), Association for Humanistic Psychology. *Awards, honors:* Burgess research award from National Council on Family Relations.

WRITINGS—All published by Free Press, except as indicated: *Anticipating Your Marriage*, 1955, revised edition published as *Marriage*, 1962, third revised edition (under name Bob Blood, with wife, Margaret Blood), 1978; (with D. M. Wolfe) *Husbands and Wives: The Dynamics of Married Living*, 1960; *Love Match and Arranged Marriage*, 1967; *Northern Breakthrough*, Wadsworth, 1968; *The Family*, 1972.

*   *   *

BLOOM, Alan (Herbert Vawser)   1906-

PERSONAL: Born November 19, 1906, in Over, Cambridgeshire, England; son of Charles Herbert and Katherine (Whitworth) Bloom; married second wife, Flora Elisabeth Mackintosh, October 30, 1956; children: (first marriage) Bridget, Robert, Adrian; (second marriage) Anthea, Jenny. *Education:* Attended schools in England. *Politics:* Liberal. *Religion:* Quaker. *Home:* Bressingham Hall, near Diss, Norfolk, England. *Office:* Blooms Nurseries Ltd., Bressingham, Norfolk, England; and Bressingham Steam Museum, Bressingham, Norfolk, England.

CAREER: Blooms Nurseries Ltd., Bressingham, Norfolk, England, managing director, 1936—. *Member:* Royal Horticultural Society, Royal Agricultural Society, Horticultural Trades Association, Society of Authors, County Landowners Association, various steam engine preservation societies. *Awards, honors:* Victoria Medal of Honour from the Royal Herb Society.

WRITINGS: The Farm in the Fens, Faber, 1944; *The Fens,* R. Hale, 1953; *Hardy Perennials,* Faber, 1957; *The Skaters of the Fens,* Heffer, 1958; *Perennials for Trouble-Free Gardening,* Faber, 1959; *Alpines for Trouble-Free Gardening,* Faber, 1960, Branford, 1961; *The Bressingham Story,* Faber, 1963; *Hardy Plants of Distinction,* Collingridge, 1965; *Moisture Gardening: Hardy Perennials in Their Natural Environment,* Faber, 1966, Branford, 1967; *Alpine Plants of Distinction,* Collingridge, 1968; *Selected Garden Plants,* Jarrolds, 1968; *Selected Garden Plants in Colour,* Jarrolds, 1969; *Steam Engines at Bressingham: The Story of a Live Steam Museum,* Faber, 1970; *Hardy Garden Plants: Sachet Floral,* Faber, 1971; *Perennials for Your Garden,* Floraprint, 1971; *The Best Hardy Perennials,* Faber, 1972; *Prelude to Bressingham,* Dalton, 1975; *Plantsman's Progress,* Dalton, 1977; *Alpines for Your Garden,* Sachet Floriet, 1979; *250 Years of Steam,* World's Work, 1981. Contributor of articles to gardening journals, *Reader's Digest Gardening Guides,* and railway magazines.

SIDELIGHTS: Alan Bloom has an avocational interest in collecting and restoring steam engines. He told *CA:* "This hobby has now become the most comprehensive steam museum in the U.K., with over 40 road and rail locomotives.... Some famous express locomotives are on permanent loan to the museum. Being fully occupied by caring for a five acre garden containing over 5000 kinds of hardy plants, and for the steam museum (which attracts over 150,000 visitors annually), my writing is nearly all done after dark October-April."

*　　*　　*

BLOOM, Samuel William 1921-

PERSONAL: Born September 18, 1921, in Reading, Pa.; son of Hyman (a businessman) and Esther (Knoblauch) Bloom; married Anne Rubinfeld (a psychologist), January 11, 1948; children: Jonathan, Jessica. *Education:* University of Pennsylvania, A.B., 1943; New School for Social Research, M.A., 1950; University of Wisconsin, Ph.D., 1956. *Politics:* Democrat. *Religion:* Jewish. *Home:* 1199 Park Ave., New York, N.Y. 10028. *Office:* Mt. Sinai School of Medicine, City University of New York, 10-46 Annenberg Bldg., New York, N.Y. 10029.

CAREER: Bennington College, Bennington, Vt., instructor in social science, 1951-53; Baylor University, College of Medicine, Houston, Tex., assistant professor of sociology, department of psychiatry, 1956-62; State University of New York Downstate Medical Center, Brooklyn, 1962-68, began as associate professor of sociology in administration, became professor of sociology in psychiatry; City University of New York, Mt. Sinai School of Medicine, New York, N.Y., professor of sociology and community medicine, 1968—. Visiting professor of sociology at Bryn Mawr College and lecturer in sociology and psychiatry at School of Medicine, University of Pennsylvania, 1961-62; visiting professor at Queens College (now Queens College of the City University of New York), 1957, and University of Houston, 1959; visiting professor of social medicine, Hadassah Medical School, Jerusalem, Israel, 1973-74; visiting professor of

behavioral sciences, University of Sydney Medical School, 1978. Consultant in sociology to Veterans Administration Hospital, Houston, Tex., 1959-63, and Texas Institute for Rehabilitation and Research, 1960-62. *Military service:* U.S. Army Air Forces, 1943-46; became staff sergeant. *Member:* American Sociological Association (fellow; secretary-treasurer of section on medical sociology, 1959-62, chairman-elect of section, 1962), American Association for the Advancement of Science, Association of American Medical Colleges, Alpha Kappa Delta.

WRITINGS: (Contributor) E. Gartly Jaco, editor, *Patients, Physicians and Illness,* Free Press of Glencoe, 1958; *The Doctor and His Patient: A Sociological Interpretation,* Russell Sage, 1963, 2nd edition, Free Press Paperbacks, 1965; (contributor) Harold Lief and others, editors, *The Psychological Basis of Medical Practice,* Harper, 1963; (contributor) H. Leideman and David Shapiro, editors, *Psychobiological Approaches to Social Behavior,* Stanford University Press, 1964; *The Medical School as a Social System,* Milbank Memorial Fund Quarterly, 1972; (contributor) Ardi R. Foley, editor, *Challenge to Community Psychiatry,* Beliannal Publications, 1972; *Power and Dissent in the Medical School,* Free Press, 1973; (contributor) Leo Madow, editor, *The Integration of Child Psychiatry into the Basic Residency Program,* Town House Press, 1975; (contributor) M. Sokolowska, editor, *Health and Society,* Reidel Publishing, 1976; (contributor) Y. Nuyens and J. Vansteekiste, editors, *Teaching Medical Sociology,* Nijhoff, 1978; (contributor) E. C. Shapiro and L. M. Lowenstein, editors, *Becoming a Physician,* Ballinger, 1979; (contributor) H. E. Freeman, S. Levine, and L. G. Needer, editors, *The Handbook of Medical Sociology,* Prentice-Hall, 1979.

Contributor of articles and reviews to professional journals. Member of advisory board, *Bulletin on Sociology and the Practice of Medicine,* 1961-63; associate editor of *Journal of Health and Social Behavior,* 1966-68, and *Milbank Memorial Fund Quarterly,* 1969-71.

WORK IN PROGRESS: The History of Medical Sociology, for Free Press.

*　　*　　*

BOARDMAN, Fon Wyman, Jr. 1911-

PERSONAL: Born July 28, 1911, in Bolivar, N.Y.; son of Fon Wyman and Lena (Sternberg) Boardman; married Dorothea Reber, March 11, 1935; children: Constance Mary. *Education:* Columbia University, A.B., 1934. *Home:* 16 West 16th St., New York, N.Y. 10011.

CAREER: Columbia University Press, New York City, copy writer, 1934-42, advertising and publicity manager, 1942-45, sales promotion manager, 1945-51; Oxford University Press, New York City, advertising and publicity manager, 1951-68, secretary, 1960-68, vice-president and marketing director, 1968-72. Lecturer in English, Columbia University, 1954-59. *Military service:* U.S. Army, 1943-46; became master sergeant. U.S. Army Reserve, captain in Military Intelligence. *Member:* Publishers' Adclub (secretary, 1952-54; president, 1954-56), Phi Beta Kappa.

*WRITINGS—*All published by Walck, except as indicated: *Castles,* Oxford University Press, 1957; *Roads,* 1958; *Canals,* 1959; *Tunnels,* 1960; *History and Historians,* 1965; *Economics: Ideas and Men,* 1966; *The Thirties: America and the Great Depression,* 1967; *America and the Jazz Age,* 1968; *America and the Progressive Era,* 1970; *America and the Gilded Age,* 1972; *America and the Virginia Dynasty,* 1974; *Around the World in 1776,* 1975; *America and the Jack-*

sonian Era, 1975; *America and the Civil War Era*, 1976; *Tyrants and Conquerors*, 1977; *Against the Iroquois: The Sullivan Campaign of 1779 in New York State*, 1978; *America and the Robber Barons*, 1979. Contributor to *What Happens in Book Publishing*, edited by Chandler Grannis; also contributor to *Sales on a Shoestring*. Editor of *Columbia University in Pictures*; general editor of "Careers for Tomorrow," a series of twenty-four guidance books for young people, published by Walck; chairman of editorial advisory board, *Columbia University Forum*, 1958-60.

SIDELIGHTS: Fon Wyman Boardman, Jr., told *CA*: "I . . . find [American history] a fascinating subject. On the basis of my experience, though, I have a feeling that it is not being taught as much in the schools as it once was. I regret this because I don't see how anyone can understand present-day America and its problems unless he or she knows something about our unique history."

BIOGRAPHICAL/CRITICAL SOURCES: Young Readers Review, February, 1969; *New York Times Book Review*, February 2, 1969, August 9, 1970.

*   *   *

BOATRIGHT, Mody Coggin   1896-1970

PERSONAL: Born October 16, 1896, in Colorado City, Tex.; died August 20, 1970, in Abilene, Tex.; son of Eldon (a ranchman) and Frances Ann (McAulay) Boatright; married Elizabeth Reck, 1925; married second wife, Elizabeth E. Keefer (an artist), September 12, 1931; children: (first marriage) Frances (Mrs. W. E. Bridges); (second marriage) Mody K. *Education:* West Texas State College (now University), B.A., 1922; University of Texas, M.A., 1923, Ph.D., 1932. *Politics:* Democrat. *Home:* 1419 Newning Ave., Austin, Tex. 78704.

CAREER: University of Texas at Austin, began as instructor, 1926, professor of English, 1950-63, chairman of department, 1952-61. *Military service:* U.S. Army, 1918-19. *Member:* American Folklore Society (fellow; vice-president, 1962), Texas Folklore Society, Texas Institute of Letters, Writers Guild.

WRITINGS: Tall Tales from Texas, foreword by J. Frank Dobie, Southwest Press, 1934; (editor with J. Frank Dobie) *Straight Texas*, Steck, 1937; *Accuracy in Thinking*, Farrar & Rinehart, 1938; (co-editor) *Coyote Wisdom*, Texas Folklore Society, 1938; (co-editor) *In the Shadow of History*, Texas Folklore Society, 1939.

(Co-editor) *Mustangs and Cow Horses*, Texas Folklore Society, 1940; (co-editor) *Freshman Prose Annual*, Houghton, 1940-42; (co-editor) *Texian Stomping Grounds*, Texas Folklore Society, 1941; (with D. R. Long) *Manual and Workbook in English*, Holt, 1943; (co-editor) *Backwoods to Border*, Texas Folklore Society, 1943; (co-editor) *From Hell to Breakfast*, Texas Folklore Society, 1944; (editor) *Mexican Border Ballads, and Other Lore*, Texas Folklore Society, 1946; *Gib Morgan, Minstrel of the Oil Fields*, University Press in Dallas, 1947, reprinted, Southern Methodist University Press, 1965; *Folk Laughter on the American Frontier*, Macmillan, 1949; (editor) *The Sky Is My Tipi*, Texas Folklore Society, 1949.

(Co-editor) *Folk Travelers*, Southern Methodist University Press, 1953; (co-editor) *Texas Folk and Folklore*, Southern Methodist University Press, 1954; (editor with Leo Hughes) *College Prose*, Houghton, 1956; (co-editor) *Mesquite and Willow*, Southern Methodist University Press, 1957; (co-editor) *Madstones and Twisters*, Southern Methodist Univer-

sity Press, 1958; (co-author) *Family Saga and Other Phases of American Folklore*, University of Illinois Press, 1958; (co-editor) *And Horns on the Toads*, Texas Folklore Society, 1959.

(Co-editor) *Singers and Storytellers*, Texas Folklore Society, 1961; (co-editor) *The Golden Log*, Texas Folklore Society, 1962; *Folklore of the Oil Industry*, Southern Methodist University Press, 1963; (co-editor) *A Good Tale and a Bonnie Tune*, Southern Methodist University Press, 1964; (with William A. Owens) *Tales from the Derrick Floor: A People's History of the Oil Industry*, Doubleday, 1970; *Mody Boatright, Folklorist: A Collection of Essays*, edited by Ernest B. Speck, University of Texas Press, 1973.

WORK IN PROGRESS: The Cowboy as Hero.†

*   *   *

BOAZ, Martha (Terosse)

PERSONAL: Born in Stuart, Va.; daughter of James Robert (a county official for the Internal Revenue Service) and Kate (Gilley) Boaz. *Education:* Madison College, B.S., 1935; George Peabody College, B.S. in library science, 1937; University of Michigan, M.A., 1950, Ph.D., 1955. *Politics:* Independent. *Home:* 1849 Campus Rd., Los Angeles, Calif. 90007. *Office:* University of Southern California, Los Angeles, Calif. 90007.

CAREER: Bridgewater High School, Bridgewater, Va., librarian and teacher, 1935-37; Jeffersontown High School, Jeffersontown, Ky., librarian and teacher, 1937-40; Madison College, Harrisonburg, Va., assistant librarian, 1940-49; University of Tennessee, Knoxville, associate professor, 1950-51; University of Michigan, Ann Arbor, instructor, 1951-52; University of Southern California, Los Angeles, associate professor, 1953-55, professor and dean, 1955-79, research associate in Center for Study of American Experience, 1979—. *Member:* American Library Association, Association of American Library Schools (president, 1961-63), American Documentation Institute (president, Southern California chapter, 1962), California Library Association (president, 1962), Beta Phi Mu (president, 1962).

WRITINGS: (Compiler) *Quest for Truth*, two volumes, Scarecrow, 1957; (editor) *A Living Library*, University of Southern California Press, 1957; (with Leroy Merrit and Kenneth Tisdee) *Reviews in Library Book Selection*, Wayne State University Press, 1958; (editor) *Modern Trends in Documentation*, Pergamon, 1959; (with Edwin Castagna) *The Ontario Public Library: A Survey*, [Ontario, Calif.], 1959; *Fervent and Full of Gifts: The Life of Althea Warren*, Scarecrow, 1961; *Strength through Cooperation in Southern California Libraries: A Survey*, [Los Angeles], 1965; *New Directions in Library Service: A Cooperative Library System for Southern California*, Los Angeles Public Library, 1966; *Concepts of Service for the Port Angeles Public Library: A Study with Recommendations*, [Los Angeles], 1967; *Toward the Improvement of Library Education*, Libraries Unlimited, 1973; *Current Concepts in Library Management*, Libraries Unlimited, 1979.

WORK IN PROGRESS: Two books.

AVOCATIONAL INTERESTS: Creative writing, theatre, travel.

*   *   *

BODE, Carl   1911-

PERSONAL: Born March 14, 1911, in Milwaukee, Wis.; son of Paul C. (a civil servant) and Celeste (Schmidt) Bode; married Margaret Lutze, 1938 (died, 1971); married Charlotte Watkins Smith, 1972; children: (first marriage) Barbara, Janet, Carolyn. *Education:* University of Chicago, Ph.B., 1933; Northwestern University, M.A., 1938, Ph.D., 1941. *Politics:* Democrat. *Religion:* Episcopalian. *Home:* 7008 Partridge Pl., College Heights Estates, Hyattsville, Md. 20782. *Office:* Department of English, University of Maryland, College Park, Md. 20742.

CAREER: Teacher at Milwaukee Vocational School, Milwaukee, Wis., 1933-37; University of California, Los Angeles, assistant professor of English, 1946-47; University of Maryland, College Park, professor of English, 1947—, executive secretary of American Civilization Program, 1950-57. Visiting professor, California Institute of Technology, Claremont Colleges, University of Wisconsin, Stanford University, and Northwestern University, 1940-41. Cultural attache, American Embassy to Great Britain, 1957-59; chairman, U.S. Educational Commission in United Kingdom, 1957-59. Consultant to educational and cultural organizations and to United States government. Delegate to American Council of Learned Societies, 1963-73. *Military service:* U.S. Army, 1944-45.

MEMBER: American Studies Association (founder; president, 1952), American Association of University Professors (member of council, 1965-68), Modern Language Association of America, Royal Society of Literature (fellow), American Historical Association, Popular Culture Association (vice-president, 1972-76; president, 1978-80), College English Association (member of board of directors, 1955-57; president, Middle Atlantic section, 1951-52), Thoreau Society of America (director, 1955-57; president, 1960-61), Emerson Society, Mencken Society (founder; president, 1976-79), Maryland Historical Society, Maryland Arts Council (chairman, 1972-76), Phi Beta Kappa, Alpha Tau Omega, Cosmos Club (Washington, D.C.), Hamilton Street Club (Baltimore). *Awards, honors:* Ford Foundation fellowship, 1952-53; Newberry Library fellowship, 1954; Guggenheim fellowship, 1954-55.

WRITINGS: The Sacred Seasons (poems), A. Swallow, 1953; *The American Lyceum: Town Meeting of the Mind,* Oxford University Press, 1956; *The Man behind You* (poems), Heinemann, 1959, Dutton, 1960; *The Anatomy of American Popular Culture, 1840-1861,* University of California Press, 1959, published as *Antebellum Culture,* Southern Illinois University Press, 1970; *The Half-World of American Culture: A Miscellany,* Southern Illinois University Press, 1965; *Mencken,* Southern Illinois University Press, 1969; *Highly Irregular* (a collection of his newspaper columns), Southern Illinois University Press, 1974; *Maryland: A Bicentennial History,* Norton, 1978; *Practical Magic* (poems), Swallow Press/Ohio University Press, 1980.

Editor: *Collected Poems of Henry Thoreau,* Packard, 1943, enlarged edition, Johns Hopkins Press, 1964; *The Portable Thoreau,* Viking, 1947, revised edition, 1964; (co-editor) *American Heritage* (anthology), two volumes, Heath, 1955, revised edition published as *American Literature,* Washington Square Press, Volume I: *The Seventeenth and Eighteenth Centuries,* Volume II: *The First Part of the Nineteenth Century,* Volume III: *The Last Part of the Nineteenth Century,* all 1966; (with Walter Harding) *The Correspondence of Henry David Thoreau,* New York University Press, 1958; (and contributor) *The Young Rebel in American Literature,* Heinemann, 1959, Praeger, 1960; (and contributor) *The Great Experiment in American Literature,* Praeger, 1961; *American Life in the 1840's,* Doubleday, 1967, hardcover edition, 1968; *The Selected Journals of Henry David*

Thoreau, New American Library, 1967, hardcover edition published as *The Best of Thoreau's Journals,* 1971; *Ralph Waldo Emerson: A Profile,* Hill & Wang, 1969; *Midcentury America: Life in the 1850's,* Southern Illinois University Press, 1972; *The Young Mencken,* Dial, 1973; *The New Mencken Letters,* Dial, 1977; (with Malcolm Cowley) *The Portable Emerson,* Viking, 1981.

Columnist, Baltimore *Evening Sun* and *Washington Post.* Contributor to *Encyclopedia Americana* and *Encyclopaedia Britannica;* contributor of poetry and reviews to British and American journals.

WORK IN PROGRESS: Editing and writing an extensive introduction to P. T. Barnum's autobiography, for Penguin.

SIDELIGHTS: "It is seldom that a writer of [Carl] Bode's perception turns his attention to books devoid of any, or almost any, literary merit," comments a reviewer from *Choice,* "but it is perhaps exactly this fact that makes [*The Half-World of American Culture*] . . . so valuable, for Bode does much more than focus his critical eye on the literature of mass culture." Hugh McGovern agrees that "[Bode] is most enlightening and entertaining when he writes of our own popular (low) literature. . . . Here he has Freud off his back and, expressing his own instinctively sound tastes and judgments, appraises something we've all often wondered about."

Reviewing Bode's *Mencken,* C. R. Dolmetsch concedes that "the author has tried to avoid repeating anything that has been said at length in any of the previous [works on Mencken]." In doing so, "he has condensed and compressed a great deal of information from such works . . . producing a kind of shorthand that might well be unintelligible to the reader for whom this book is an introduction to Mencken. . . . [Yet] we are afforded a much more intimate glimpse into Mencken's personal life than we have previously had. . . . We also discover a great deal that was not previously known about Mencken's relationships with . . . important literary personages of the 1920's." Discussing the biography eleven years after its first publication, Ben A. Franklin notes in the *New York Times* that "the Bode book is regarded as the most penetrating look to date at the private Mencken."

Walter Harding comments that Bode's *Ralph Waldo Emerson: A Profile* "is a vivid and vibrant evocation of Emerson, the man, particularly through those sketches by his personal friends. . . . Professor Bode has performed a real service in digging out their almost forgotten essays and in preparing a volume that is a lively biographical introduction to one of our master writers."

Of *Midcentury America,* a *Choice* reviewer writes: "Bode . . . largely succeeds in providing readers with a comprehensive picture of American life during the 1850's. . . . [However] the book has . . . organizational weaknesses. Although the author feels a gap exists on material published by Southern slaves about slavery, he does not fill it with selections drawn from the black presses of that period, from slave songs, or from reminiscences written by such figures as Frederick Douglass. . . . His decision not to include fiction because it is a distortion of history overlooks the idea that writers of fiction often reflect the popular cultural assumptions of their era." In spite of these weaknesses, "Bode has delved deeply into the writing of the pre-war decade," giving the reader refreshingly unfamiliar selections, according to Harold Schwartz. He calls *Midcentury America* "a very entertaining and enlightening book; creative editing of a high order."

Occasionally critics have questioned the relevence of Bode's work. In his review of *The Young Mencken*, Hilton Kramer comments "the criticisms and polemics that won [Mencken] his enormous fame are, for the most part, quite dead.... He is no longer interesting.... The newspaper columns ... have only an antiquarian interest.... I frankly see no excuse for this book." Yet there is enough of an interest in popular culture to assure Bode a receptive, if limited, audience. P. W. Boyntinck writes that in *The Young Mencken*, "the knowing Menckenite will once again encounter downright revivalist gastronomy, colorful popular sociology, and ... mighty truisms."

AVOCATIONAL INTERESTS: Tennis.

BIOGRAPHICAL/CRITICAL SOURCES: Christian Century, November 3, 1965, November 8, 1972; *America,* January 15, 1966; *American Literature,* March, 1966; *Choice,* July, 1966, June, 1969, May, 1973; *Library Journal,* November 15, 1968, March 15, 1973; *New York Times Book Review,* July 16, 1969, September 21, 1969, August 19, 1973; *Washington Post,* September 12, 1969; *Saturday Review,* September 13, 1969; *Best Sellers,* September 15, 1969; *Newsweek,* September 29, 1969; *Nation,* November 10, 1969; *Time,* November 21, 1969; *New Yorker,* December 20, 1969; *Virginia Quarterly Review,* winter, 1970; *New England Quarterly,* June, 1973; *New York Times,* September 4, 1980.

*   *   *

BODSWORTH, (Charles) Fred(erick) 1918-

PERSONAL: Born October 11, 1918, in Port Burwell, Ontario, Canada; son of Arthur John (a tinsmith) and Viola (Williams) Bodsworth; married Margaret Neville Banner, July 8, 1944; children: Barbara (Mrs. Edward Welch), Nancy (Mrs. Richard Hannah), Neville. *Education:* Attended public schools in Canada. *Home and office:* 294 Beech Ave., Toronto, Ontario, Canada M4E 3J2. *Agent:* Curtis Brown, Ltd., 575 Madison Ave., New York, N.Y. 10022.

CAREER: St. Thomas Times-Journal, St. Thomas, Ontario, reporter and copy editor, 1940-43; *Toronto Daily Star* and *Weekly Star,* Toronto, Ontario, reporter, editor, 1943-46; *Maclean's Magazine,* Toronto, staff writer and assistant editor, 1947-55; currently novelist and free-lance writer. *Member:* Writers' Union of Canada, Canadian Authors' Association, Federation of Ontario Naturalists (member of board of directors, 1950—; president, 1964-67), Toronto Field Naturalists' Club (president, 1960-62), Toronto Ornithological Club, Toronto Men's Press Club, Brodie Club (Toronto). *Awards, honors:* Doubleday Canadian Prize Novel Award, 1967, for *The Sparrow's Fall;* Rothman's Merit Award for Literature, 1974.

WRITINGS: Last of the Curlews, Dodd, 1954; *The Strange One* (Literary Guild selection), Dodd, 1960; *The Atonement of Ashley Morden,* Dodd, 1964; *The Sparrow's Fall* (Literary Guild selection), Doubleday, 1967; *The Pacific Coast,* Natural Science of Canada, 1970; (co-author) *Wilderness Canada,* Irwin, 1970. Contributor to *McCall's, Sports Afield, Holiday,* and other magazines and newspapers in Canada and United States.

WORK IN PROGRESS: A book on popular biology and a nature novel.

SIDELIGHTS: Fred Bodsworth is a leader of worldwide naturalist tours. His books have been translated into nine languages. *Avocational interests:* Biology, geology, Indians of northern Canada, canoe trips and camping in the wilderness.

BIOGRAPHICAL/CRITICAL SOURCES: Best Sellers, July 15, 1967.

*   *   *

BOLLENS, John C(onstantinus) 1920-

PERSONAL: Born December 27, 1920, in Pittsburgh, Pa.; son of Constantinus John (a wholesale produce merchant) and Annie (Free) Bollens; married, 1945, wife's name, Virgene; children: Ross, Scott. *Education:* College of Wooster, A.B., 1942; Duke University, A.M., 1948; University of Wisconsin, Ph.D., 1948. *Home:* 14801 Pampas Ricas Blvd., Pacific Palisades, Calif. 90272. *Office:* Department of Political Science, University of California, 405 Hilgard, Los Angeles, Calif. 90024.

CAREER: Municipal League of Seattle, Seattle, Wash., research director, 1945-47; University of California, Berkeley, administrative analyst, Bureau of Public Administration, 1947-50; International City Managers' Association, Chicago, Ill., special assistant to the director, 1950; University of California, Los Angeles, assistant professor, 1950-55, associate professor, 1955-60, professor of political science, 1960—, director of urban studies, Bureau of Governmental Research, 1958-62. Served as director of Metropolitan Areas Study, Council of State Governments, Chicago, 1956; executive officer of Metropolitan St. Louis Survey, 1956-57; executive director of Metropolitan Community Studies, Dayton, Ohio, 1957-59; director, Study of City Charter and Governmental Organization of City of Los Angeles, 1962-63; Youth Opportunities Board of Greater Los Angeles, chairman of research advisory committee, 1963-64, project historian, 1964-65; member of Los Angeles County Citizens Economy and Efficiency Commission, 1964-73, Los Angeles Board of Civil Service Commissioners, 1973-77, Los Angeles American Revolution Bicentennial Committee, 1974-76, and Los Angeles County Civil Service Commission, 1979—; consultant to numerous government and private organizations.

MEMBER: American Political Science Association, American Society for Public Administration (president, Los Angeles metropolitan chapter, 1962-63), National Municipal League, Western Governmental Research Association (executive secretary, 1947-50), Phi Beta Kappa. *Awards, honors:* St. Louis area research work won a Fruin-Colnon award for outstanding contributions to solving metropolitan problems; *American County Government* was selected by the American Library Association as one of the outstanding reference books of 1969; *Governing a Metropolitan Region: The San Francisco Bay Area* won the Governmental Research Association award for the most distinguished research of 1969.

WRITINGS: Problem of Government in San Francisco Bay Region, Bureau of Public Administration, University of California, Berkeley, 1948; (with Stanley Scott) *Local Government in California,* University of California Press, 1951; (with Winston Crouch and others) *State and Local Government in California,* University of California Press, 1952; *Appointed Executive Local Government,* Haynes Foundation, 1952; *Your California Governments in Action,* University of California Press, 1954, revised edition, 1960; (with Crouch and others) *California Government and Politics,* Prentice-Hall, 1956, 7th revised edition, 1981; *The States and the Metropolitan Problem,* Council of State Governments, 1956; *Special District Governments in the United States,* University of California Press, 1957; (with Henry Schmandt) *Path of Progress for Metropolitan St. Louis,* Metropolitan St. Louis Survey, 1957; (with Schmandt) *Back-*

ground for Action, Metropolitan St. Louis Survey, 1957; *Metropolitan Challenge,* Metropolitan Community Studies, 1959; (with Schmandt) *Exploring the Metropolitan Community,* University of California Press, 1961; *A Study of the Los Angeles City Charter,* Town Hall, 1963; (with Schmandt) *The Metropolis: Its People, Politics, and Economic Life,* Harper, 1965, 4th revised edition, 1982; *Communities and Government in a Changing World,* Rand McNally, 1966; (with Scott) *Governing a Metropolitan Region: The San Francisco Bay Area,* Institute of Governmental Studies, University of California, Berkeley, 1968; (with Fletcher Bowron and others) *A Program to Improve Planning and Zoning in Los Angeles,* City of Los Angeles Citizens Committee of Zoning Practices and Procedures, 1969; (with John Bayes and Kathryn Utter) *American County Government,* Sage Publications, 1969; (with John C. Ries) *The City Manager Profession: Myths and Realities,* Public Administrations Service, 1969; (with Burke Roche and others) *Study of the Los Angeles County Charter,* Los Angeles County Citizens Economy and Efficiency Commission, 1970; (with Dale R. Marshall) *A Guide to Participation,* Prentice-Hall, 1973; *Yorty: Politics of a Constant Candidate,* Palisades, 1973; *Jerry Brown: In a Plain Brown Wrapper,* Palisades, 1978; (with Schmandt) *Political Corruption: Power, Money, and Sex,* Palisades, 1979. Contributor to professional journals.

WORK IN PROGRESS: Research on political corruption.

*   *   *

BOLLER, Paul Franklin, Jr. 1916-

PERSONAL: Born December 31, 1916, in Spring Lake, N.J.; son of Paul Franklin (clergyman) and Grace (Hall) Boller. *Education:* Yale University, B.A., 1939, Ph.D., 1947. *Politics:* "Liberal Democrat." *Religion:* "Seeker." *Office:* Department of History, Texas Christian University, Fort Worth, Tex.

CAREER: U.S. Navy Department, Washington, D.C., civilian analyst, 1947-48; Southern Methodist University, Dallas, Tex., 1948-66, began as assistant professor, became professor of history; University of Massachusetts—Boston, professor of history, 1966-76; Texas Christian University, Fort Worth, L.B.J. Professor of History, 1976—. Visiting professor, University of Texas at Austin, 1963-64. Vice-president, Dallas Civil Liberties Union, 1962-63. *Military service:* U.S. Navy, 1942-46; became lieutenant junior grade. *Member:* Organization of American Historians, American Studies Association, American Studies Association of Texas (vice-president, 1960-61; president, 1961-62), Phi Beta Kappa.

WRITINGS: This Is Our Nation, McGraw, 1961; *George Washington and Religion,* Southern Methodist University Press, 1963; (contributor) H. Wayne Morgan, editor, *The Gilded Age,* Syracuse University Press, 1963; *Quotemanship,* Southern Methodist University Press, 1966; *American Thought in Transition, 1865-1900,* Rand McNally, 1969; *American Transcendentalism, 1830-1860,* Putnam, 1974; *Freedom and Fate in American Thought: From Edwards to Dewey,* Southern Methodist University Press, 1978. Contributor to professional journals. Contributing editor, *Southwest Review, Social Science.*

SIDELIGHTS: Paul Franklin Boller, Jr. told *CA:* "Out of the religious turmoil agitating England in the first part of the seventeenth century came two new groups: The Seekers and the Happy Finders. I am something of both: A Happy Seeker. What Thorstein Veblen called 'idle curiosity' has always been powerful in me. My work in the history of American ideas, like all scholarly work, involves fun and

games; but it is also motivated by my wish to learn what unusually gifted people have had to say about the Big Questions in religion, science, philosophy, and ethics. In my books on American thought I have tried to pass on something of what I have learned about these things to other people."

AVOCATIONAL INTERESTS: Music, reading, films, beer parties, jogging, surf-bathing, hiking, and bicycling.

BIOGRAPHICAL/CRITICAL SOURCES: Time, May 26, 1967; *New Yorker,* August 19, 1967.

*   *   *

BONE, Hugh A(lvin) 1909-

PERSONAL: Born January 14, 1909, in Sycamore, Ill.; son of Hugh Alvin (an educator) and Florence (Crowder) Bone; married Elizabeth Purdy (a social worker), June 11, 1938; children: Christopher, James. *Education:* North Central College, B.A., 1931; University of Wisconsin, M.A., 1935; Northwestern University, Ph.D., 1937. *Politics:* Independent. *Religion:* Methodist. *Home:* 6001 51st St. N.E., Seattle, Wash. 98115. *Office:* Department of Political Science, University of Washington, Seattle, Wash. 98105.

CAREER: University of Maryland, College Park, instructor in American government and politics, 1937-39, assistant professor of political science, 1939-42; Queens College (now Queens College of the City University of New York), Flushing, N.Y., assistant professor of political science, 1942-48; University of Washington, Seattle, 1948—, currently professor of political science, chairman of department, 1959-68. Visiting professor, Stanford University, 1949, Columbia University, 1957, University of Hawaii, 1962, and Simon Fraser University, 1978. Director of Washington State-Northern Idaho Citizenship Clearing House (now Center for Education in Politics), 1953-68. Consultant, Battelle Memorial Institute, 1972—. *Military service:* U.S. Army. *Member:* American Political Science Association, Western Political Science Association (president, 1962), Pacific Northwestern Political Science Association (president, 1960), Faculty Men's Club (University of Washington). *Awards, honors:* Ford Foundation fellowship, 1954-55.

WRITINGS: "Smear" Politics: Analysis of 1940 Campaign Literature, American Council on Public Affairs, 1941; (with L. V. Howard) *Current American Government,* Appleton-Century, 1943; *American Politics and the Party System,* McGraw, 1949, 5th edition, 1971; *Grass Roots Party Leadership,* University of Washington Press, 1952; *Viewers Guide to the American Two-Party System,* Political Science Department, University of Washington, 1956; *Party Committees and National Politics,* University of Washington Press, 1958, reprinted with new preface and appendix, 1968; (with David M. Ogden, Jr.) *Washington Politics,* New York University Press, 1960; (with Austin Ranney) *Politics and Voters,* McGraw, 1963, 4th edition, 1976; *The Initiative and the Referendum,* National Municipal Leagues, 1976; (with Ruth Silva, Edward Keynes, and David Adamany) *American Government: Democracy and Liberty in Balance,* Knopf, 1976; (with Cindy Fey) *The People's Right to Know: An Analysis of the Washington State Public Disclosure Law,* Institute for Governmental Research, University of Washington, 1978; (with Robert Pealy and Nand Hart-Nibbrig) *Public Policy-Making Washington Style,* Institute for Governmental Research, University of Washington, 1980.

Contributor: *Public Men,* University of North Carolina Press, 1946; *Presidential Nominating Politics in 1952: The West,* Johns Hopkins Press, 1954; Frank H. Jonas, editor,

Western Politics, University of Utah Press, 1961; *The Grass Roots,* Scott, Foresman, 1968; *Politics in the American West,* University of Utah Press, 1969; Eleanor Bushnell, editor, *The Impact of Reapportionment in the West,* University of Utah Press, 1970. Contributor to professional journals, including *National Municipal Review, American Political Science Review,* and *Western Political Quarterly.*

*   *   *

BONNELL, Dorothy Haworth 1914-

PERSONAL: Born October 12, 1914, in Buffalo, N.Y.; daughter of Lester C. (YMCA and college executive) and Ruby (Peyton) Haworth; married Allen T. Bonnell (president, Community College, Philadelphia), June 14, 1937; children: Annette Peyton, Thomas Haworth, David Wellington, Daniel Churchill. *Education:* Attended Oberlin College, Washington University, and schools in England and Switzerland. *Politics:* Democrat. *Religion:* Society of Friends (Quaker). *Home:* 11 Single Lane, Wallingford, Pa. *Agent:* Robert Lewis Rosen Associates Ltd., 7 West 51st St., New York, N.Y. 10019.

CAREER: American Friends Service Committee, Marseille, France, delegate, 1940-41; United Nations Relief and Rehabilitation Administration, Washington, D.C., administrative assistant, 1944-46; *Personnel Journal,* Swarthmore, Pa., editor, 1950-75. Communications consultant.

WRITINGS: Year of Discovery, Messner, 1962; *She Wore a Star,* Messner, 1964; *Passport to Freedom,* Messner, 1965; *Target Williamstown,* Messner, 1968; *Why Did You Go to College, Linda Warten?,* Messner, 1969. Contributor of short stories, articles and book reviews to periodicals.

WORK IN PROGRESS: A historical romance, tentatively entitled *Between Pride and Passion,* set in Georgia and Virginia during the Civil War.

BIOGRAPHICAL/CRITICAL SOURCES: English Journal, May, 1965; *Young Readers Review,* November, 1967.

*   *   *

BOOTH, Wayne C(layson) 1921-

PERSONAL: Born February 22, 1921, in American Fork, Utah; son of Wayne C. and Lillian (Clayson) Booth; married Phyllis Barnes, 1946; children: Katherine, Richard (deceased), Alison. *Education:* Brigham Young University, B.A., 1944; University of Chicago, M.A., 1947, Ph.D., 1950. *Home:* 5411 South Greenwood Ave., Chicago, Ill. 60615. *Office:* Department of English, University of Chicago, Chicago, Ill. 60637.

CAREER: University of Chicago, instructor, 1947-50; Haverford College, Haverford, Pa., assistant professor, 1950-53; Earlham College, Richmond, Ind., professor of English and chairman of department, 1953-62; University of Chicago, Chicago, Ill., Pullman Professor of English, 1962—, Distinguished Service Professor, 1970—, dean of The College, 1964-69. Member of board of trustees, Earlham College, 1965-75. *Military service:* U.S. Infantry, 1944-46; became staff sergeant. *Member:* Modern Language Association of America (president 1980-82), American Association of University Professors, National Council of Teachers of English, American Academy of Arts and Sciences, Academy of Literary Studies. *Awards, honors:* Ford faculty fellow, 1952-53; Guggenheim fellow, 1956-57, 1969-70; Christian Gauss Award from Phi Beta Kappa, 1962, and David H. Russell Award for Outstanding Research from National Council of Teachers of English, 1966, both for *The Rhetoric of Fiction;*

Quantrell Prize from University of Chicago, 1971, for undergraduate teaching; Distinguished Alumnus Award from Brigham Young University, 1975; National Endowment for the Humanities fellow, 1975-76; Phi Beta Kappa visiting scholar, 1977-78; D.Litt. from Rockford College, 1965, St. Ambrose College, 1971, and University of New Hampshire, 1977.

WRITINGS: The Rhetoric of Fiction, University of Chicago Press, 1961; (editor) *The Knowledge Most Worth Having,* University of Chicago Press, 1967; *Now Don't Try to Reason with Me: Essays and Ironies for a Credulous Age,* University of Chicago Press, 1970; *A Rhetoric of Irony,* University of Chicago Press, 1974; *Modern Dogma and the Rhetoric of Assent,* University of Chicago and University of Notre Dame, 1974; *Critical Understanding: The Powers and Limits of Pluralism,* University of Chicago Press, 1979. Contributor to various professional journals and magazines.

*   *   *

BORAH, Woodrow (Wilson) 1912-

PERSONAL: Born December 22, 1912, in Utica, Miss.; son of Hirsh Hillel (a merchant) and Fannie (Ichkovich) Borah; married Therese Levy, September 8, 1945; children: Jonathan Hillel, Ruth Gail. *Education:* University of California, Los Angeles, A.B. 1935, M.A., 1936; University of California, Berkeley, Ph.D., 1940. *Politics:* Democrat. *Religion:* Jewish. *Home:* 451 Vincente Ave., Berkeley, Calif. *Office:* University of California, Berkeley, Calif.

CAREER: Princeton University, Princeton, N.J., instructor in history, 1941-42; U.S. Office of Strategic Services and Department of State, Washington, D.C., analyst, 1942-47; University of California, Berkeley, 1948—, began as assistant professor, became professor of speech and history, Abraham D. Shepard Professor, 1975-80, professor emeritus, 1980—. *Member:* American Historical Association, Sociedad Mexicana de Antropologia, Academia Mexicana de la Historia (corresponding member).

WRITINGS—All published by University of California Press: *Silk Raising in Colonial Mexico,* 1943; *New Spain's Century of Depression,* 1951; *Early Colonial Trade and Navigation between Mexico and Peru,* 1954; (with S. F. Cook) *Price Trends of Some Basic Commodities in Central Mexico (1531-1570),* 1958; (with Cook) *The Population of Central Mexico in 1548,* 1960; (with Cook) *The Indian Population of Central Mexico, 1531-1610,* 1960; (with Cook) *The Aboriginal Population of Central Mexico on the Eve of the Spanish Conquest,* 1963; (with Cook) *The Population of the Mixiteca Alta,* 1963; (with Cook) *Essays in Population History,* Volumes I and II, *Mexico and the Caribbean,* Volume III, *Mexico and California,* 1970-71. Associate editor, *Western Speech,* 1954-56; member of editorial board, *Hispanic American Historical Review,* 1958-64.

WORK IN PROGRESS: General Indian Court of New Spain.

*   *   *

BORNEMAN, Ernest 1915-
(Cameron McCabe)

PERSONAL: Born April 12, 1915, in Berlin, Germany; son of Curt and Hertha (Blochert) Borneman; married Eva Geisel (an editor and translator); children: Stephen. *Education:* Studied at University of Berlin, 1931-33, School of Oriental and African Studies, London, 1933-35, and Emmanuel College, Cambridge, 1935-37. *Politics:* Liberal. *Home:* A 4612, Scharten, Austria.

CAREER: National Film Board of Canada, Ottawa, Ontario, head of foreign language production, 1941-45, head of international distribution, 1945-47; UNESCO, Paris, France, head of films division, 1947-49; Granada Television Network, London and Manchester, England, head of script department, 1955-58; British Film Institute, London, head of programming, 1959-60; Freies Fernsehen, Frankfurt, Germany, controller of programs and productions, 1960-62; currently teaching at the Universities of Salzburg, Klagenfurt, Bremen, and Marburg.

WRITINGS: (Under pseudonym Cameron McCabe) *The Face on the Cutting Room Floor,* Gollancz, 1937; *A Love Story,* Jarrolds, 1941; *A Critic Looks at Jazz* (originally published as a serial, "An Anthropologist Looks at Jazz" in *Record Changer*), Jazz Music Books, 1946; *Tremolo,* Harper, 1948; *Tomorrow Is Now: The Adventures of Welfare Willy in Search of a Soul,* Neville Spearman, 1959; *Something Wrong,* Four Square, 1961; *The Compromisers,* Deutsch, 1962; *The Man Who Loved Women,* Coward, 1968.

Writings in German: *Lexikon der Liebe,* two volumes, List, 1968, four volume edition, Ullstein, 1979; *Landschaft mit Figuren,* Bertelsmann, 1971; *Sex im Volksmund,* Rowohlt, 1971, two volume pocket edition, 1974; *Psychoanalyse des Geldes,* Suhrkamp, 1973, Urizen Books, 1976; *Unsere Kinder,* Walter, 1973; *Die Umwelt des Kindes,* Walter, 1974; *Das Patriarchat,* S. Fischer, 1975; *Die Welt der Erwachsenen,* Walter, 1976; *Die Ur-Szene,* S. Fischer, 1977; *Sexualitaet,* Beltz, 1979; *Wir machen keinen grossen Mist,* Ullstein, 1980; *Lehrbuch der sexuellen Entwicklungs-psychologie,* Volume I, Jugend & Volk, 1981; *Arbeiterbewegung und Feminismus,* Ullstein, in press.

Motion pictures and feature-length documentaries: "Ulysses," 1949; (with Guy Elmes) "The Flanagan Boy," 1950; (with Elmes) "Bang! You're Dead," 1954; "Face the Music" (musical), 1954; "Double Jeopardy," produced by Republic, 1956; (with Ranveer Singh) "The Long Duel," 1959. Contributor, in one capacity or another, to about two hundred other features, documentaries, and shorts filmed in Canada, United States, and Europe.

Television plays and films: "Tremolo," 1950; "Four O'Clock in the Morning Blues," 1954; (translator and adapter) "Hedda Gabler," 1957; (adapter from radio play) "Sorry Wrong Number," 1957; (adapter) "Break-Up," 1957; (adapter) "Don't Destroy Me," 1957; (adapter) "The Lie," 1957; (with John Hopkins) "After the Party," 1957. Contributor, in one capacity or another, to about seventy other television and radio shows. Also author of stage plays, "The Girl on the Highway" and "The Windows of Heaven."

Contributor of more than one thousand articles to magazines, including *Reader's Digest, Harper's Bazaar, Holiday, Esquire, Playboy,* and *Times Literary Supplement.*

SIDELIGHTS: Ernest Borneman worked his way through school playing in a jazz band and has collected folk music and jazz on four continents. *Avocational interests:* Painting, music.

BIOGRAPHICAL/CRITICAL SOURCES: New York Times Book Review, June 9, 1968.

* * *

BORNING, Bernard C(arl)   1913-

PERSONAL: Born June 19, 1913, in Echo, Minn.; son of B. J. and Bertha (Preuss) Borning; married Coralie J. Hamilton, 1949; children: Alan, Katherine. *Education:* University of

Minnesota, B.A., 1936, Ph.D., 1951. *Home:* 494 Ridge Rd., Moscow, Idaho. *Office:* Department of Political Science, University of Idaho, Moscow, Idaho.

CAREER: Brown & Bigelow, St. Paul, Minn., layout and copywriter, 1937-41; free-lance writer in United States and Latin America, 1937-42; University of Idaho, Moscow, professor of political science, 1949-78, professor emeritus, 1978—, chairman of department, 1959-69. Visiting professor of political science, University of Ife, Nigeria, 1970-71. Member of Moscow School Board, 1954-57; president of Moscow United Fund Board, 1957-60. *Military service:* U.S. Army, Field Artillery; became captain. *Member:* American Association of University Professors, American Political Science Association, Western Political Science Association (member of executive council, 1956-58), Pacific Northwest Political Science Association (member of executive council, 1963-66). *Awards, honors:* Fulbright lectureship, Korea, 1963-64.

WRITINGS: The Political and Social Thought of Charles A. Beard, University of Washington Press, 1962; (with others) *Impact of Reapportionment on the Thirteen Western States,* University of Utah Press, 1970; (editor and contributor) *Nigeria's Path: The First Decade and After,* University of Ife, Nigeria, 1972; (editor and contributor) *The 1976 Presidential Nominating Process in Idaho,* Bureau of Public Affairs Research, University of Idaho, 1976.

* * *

BORTEN, Helen Jacobson   1930-

PERSONAL: Born 1930, in Philadelphia, Pa.; daughter of Joseph and Fay (Riser) Jacobson; married Marvin Borten, 1952 (divorced, 1969); children: Peter Elliot, Laurence Drew. *Education:* Attended Philadelphia Museum College of Art, four years. *Residence:* New York, N.Y.

CAREER: Free-lance artist; illustrator of books, book jackets, record album covers, and greeting cards; writer of children's books. *Awards, honors: Little Big-Feather* was chosen by *New York Times* as one of the ten best-illustrated books of 1956; *Do You See What I See?* was recommended as one of the ten outstanding books of 1959 by the *New York Times,* and included in the American Institute of Graphic Arts Children's Book Show, 1958-60.

WRITINGS—All self-illustrated; published by Abelard, except as indicated: *Do You See What I See?,* 1959; *Do You Hear What I Hear?,* 1960; *A Picture Has a Special Look,* 1961; *Copycat,* 1962; *Do You Move as I Do?,* 1963; *Halloween,* Crowell, 1965; *The Jungle,* Harcourt, 1968; *Do You Know What I Know?,* 1970; *Do You Go Where I Go?,* 1972.

Illustrator: Joseph Longstreth, *Little-Big Feather,* Abelard, 1956; Harold Coy, *First Book of Congress,* F. Watts, 1956; Helen Holland Graham and B. A. Huff, *Taco, The Snoring Burro,* Abelard, 1957; Alma Kehoe Reck, *First Book of Festivals around the World,* F. Watts, 1957; *First Book of the Supreme Court,* F. Watts, 1958; Graham, *Little Don Pedro,* Abelard, 1959; Franklyn Mansfield Branley, *The Moon Seems to Change,* Crowell, 1960; Walter Havighurst, *First Book of the Oregon Trail,* F. Watts, 1960; Branley, *What Makes Day and Night?,* Crowell, 1961; Branley, *The Sun, Our Nearest Star,* Crowell, 1961; *First Book of Language,* F. Watts, 1962; Branley, *Rain and Hail,* Crowell, 1963; Molly Cone, *Purim,* Crowell, 1967.

* * *

BOTHWELL, Jean   d. 1977

PERSONAL: Born in Winside, Neb.; died March 2, 1977, in

Missouri; buried in Lincoln, Neb.; daughter of James Millward (a minister) and Mary Emmeline (Batham) Bothwell. *Education:* Nebraska Wesleyan University, A.B., 1916. *Religion:* Methodist.

CAREER: High school history teacher in Columbus, Neb.; served as business manager and missionary to India for the Methodist church; author in New York, N.Y. *Member:* Society of Women Geographers, Mystery Writers of America, Forum for Writers of Books for Young People, Nebraska Writers Guild, Nebraska State Historical Society, Metropolitan Women's Republican Club. *Awards, honors:* Review Club Poetry Award, 1968; Children's Spring Book Festival Award and New York Herald Tribune award, both in 1946, for *The Thirteenth Stone.*

WRITINGS: Little Boat Boy, Harcourt, 1945; *The Thirteenth Stone,* Harcourt, 1946; *River Boy of Kashmir,* Morrow, 1946; *Star of India,* Morrow, 1947; *The Empty Tower,* Morrow, 1948; *Little Flute Player,* Morrow, 1949; *Onions without Tears* (adult cook book), Hastings House, 1950, published as *The Onion Cookbook,* Dover, 1976; *Peter Holt, P.K.,* Harcourt, 1950; *Sword of a Warrior,* Harcourt, 1951; *Paddy and Sam,* Abelard, 1952; *Story of India,* Harcourt, 1952; *Lost Colony,* Winston, 1953; *Golden Letter to Siam,* Abelard, 1953; *The Wishing Apple Tree,* Harcourt, 1953; *The Borrowed Monkey,* Abelard, 1953; *Hidden Treasure,* Friendship, 1954; *Flame in the Sky,* Vanguard, 1954; *The Red Barn Club,* Harcourt, 1954; *The First Book of Roads,* F. Watts, 1955; *Cal's Birthday Present,* Abelard, 1955; *Ranch of a Thousand Horns,* Abelard, 1955; *Cobras, Cows, and Courage,* Coward, 1956 (published in England as *Men and Monsoons,* Chatto & Windus, 1962); *Search for a Golden Bird,* Harcourt, 1956; *Ring of Fate,* Harcourt, 1957; *Tree House at Seven Oaks,* Abelard, 1957; *Promise of the Rose,* Harcourt, 1958; *The Missing Violin,* Harcourt, 1959.

The Silver Mango Tree, Harcourt, 1960; *The Animal World of India,* F. Watts, 1961; *The Mystery Key,* Dial, 1961; *The Emerald Clue,* Harcourt, 1961; *The Mystery Cargo,* Dial, 1962; *The First Book of Pakistan,* F. Watts, 1962; *The Red Scarf,* Harcourt, 1962; *The Mystery Angel,* Dial, 1963; *Omen for a Princess: The Story of Jahanara,* Abelard, 1963; (with Irene Wells) *Fun and Festival from India,* revised edition, Friendship, 1963; *The White Fawn of Phalera,* Harcourt, 1963; *By Sail and Wind: The Story of the Bahamas,* Abelard, 1964; *The Mystery Gatepost,* Dial, 1964; *Romany Girl,* Harcourt, 1964; *The Dancing Princess,* Harcourt, 1965; *Lady of Roanoke,* Holt, 1965; *The Mystery Egg,* Dial, 1965; *The Mystery Clock,* Dial, 1966; *The First Book of India,* F. Watts, 1966, 2nd revised edition, 1978; *Ride, Zarina, Ride,* Harcourt, 1966; *The Vanishing Wildlife of East Africa,* Abelard, 1967; *The Mystery Box,* Dial, 1967; *The Holy Man's Secret: A Story of India,* Abelard, 1967; *Mystery at the House-of-the-Fish,* Harcourt, 1968; *The Mystery Cup,* Dial, 1968; *The Mystery Tunnel,* Dial, 1969; *The Parsonage Parrot,* F. Watts, 1969; *Defiant Bride,* Harcourt, 1969; *African Herdboy: A Story of the Masai,* Harcourt, 1970; *The Mystery Candlestick,* Dial, 1970; *The Secret in the Wall,* Abelard, 1971.

SIDELIGHTS: A collection of Jean Bothwell's books, papers, and memorabilia is contained at Boston University's Mugar Memorial Library. *Avocational interests:* Collecting antique glass and stamps; historical movies and classical music; interested in studying the effect of the environment on the progress of any given group of people.†

BOURKE, Vernon J(oseph) 1907-

PERSONAL: Born February 17, 1907, in North Bay, Ontario, Canada; became U.S. citizen in 1943; son of Joseph Walter (a prison warden) and Therese (Trudeau) Bourke; married Janet Leahy (a social worker), June 12, 1947; children: Jane (Mrs. Ray Luckhaupt), Thomas, Nancy (Mrs. Vernal Beckmann). *Education:* University of Toronto, B.A., 1928, M.A., 1929, Ph.D., 1937. *Religion:* Catholic. *Office:* St. Louis University, St. Louis, Mo. 63103.

CAREER: University of Toronto, St. Michael's College, Toronto, Ontario, lecturer in philosophy, 1928-31; St. Louis University, St. Louis, Mo., 1931—, started as instructor, became professor of philosophy, professor emeritus, 1975—; University of St. Thomas, Center for Thomistic Studies, Houston, Tex., director, 1978-79, currently research professor. Annual Aquinas Lecturer at some twenty-five centers in United States and Canada. Advisory editor, Musurgia Publishing Co., 1947-50, and Macmillan Co., 1951—. *Member:* World Union of Catholic Philosophical Societies (president, 1963—), Mediaeval Academy of America, American Philosophical Association, American Catholic Philosophical Association (president, 1949; representative at International Congress of Philosophy at Brussels, 1953, Venice, 1958, Mexico City, 1963), American Association of University Professors, Societe Philosophique de Louvain. *Awards, honors:* Aquinas Medal, 1963; Litt.D., Bellarmine College, 1974.

WRITINGS: Augustine's Quest of Wisdom: Life and Philosophy of the Bishop of Hippo, Bruce, 1945; *Thomistic Bibliography, 1920-1940,* St. Louis University Press, 1945; *St. Thomas and the Greek Moralists* (Aquinas lecture), Marquette University Press, 1947; (editor) Thomas Aquinas, *Opera omnia,* Musurgia, 1948-50; *Ethics: A Textbook in Moral Philosophy,* Macmillan, 1951, new edition, 1966; (translator) *Confessions of St. Augustine,* Catholic University of America Press, 1953; *St. Thomas on the Truth of the Catholic Faith,* Book III, Doubleday, 1956, published as *Summa Contragentiles,* Book III, Notre Dame University Press, 1976; *The Pocket Aquinas,* Washington Square, 1960; *Natural Law, Thomism—and Professor Nielsen* (originally published in *Natural Law Forum,* Volume V, 1960), Notre Dame Law School, 1961; *Will in Western Thought: An Historical-Critical Survey,* Sheet, 1964; *Augustine's View of Reality,* Villanova University Press, 1964; (editor and translator) *The Essential Augustine,* Mentor Books, 1964; *Aquinas' Search for Wisdom,* Bruce, 1965; *Ethics,* Macmillan, 1966; *Ethics in Crisis,* Bruce, 1966; (contributor) J. E. Biechler, editor, *Law for Liberty,* Helicon, 1967; (contributor) *Melanges a la memoire de Charles De Koninck,* Press de l'Universite Laval, 1968; *History of Ethics,* Doubleday, Volume I: *Graeco-Roman to Early Modern Ethics,* 1968, Volume II: *Modern and Contemporary Times,* 1968; (contributor) R. Z. Apostol, editor, *Human Values in a Secular World,* Humanities, 1970; *Joy in Augustine's Ethics,* Villanova University Press, 1979; (with T. Miethe) *Thomistic Bibliography 1940-78,* Greenwood Press, 1980.

Contributor of articles on medieval philosophy and ethics to *Collier's Encyclopedia, Runes' Dictionary of Philosophy, New Catholic Encyclopedia, Encyclopedia of Philosophy,* and *Dictionary of Ethics.*

BIOGRAPHICAL/CRITICAL SOURCES: Commonweal, April 30, 1965, November 8, 1968; *Choice,* November, 1968.

BOWIE, Walter Russell 1882-1969

PERSONAL: Born October 8, 1882, in Richmond, Va.; died April 23, 1969, in Alexandria, Va.; son of Walter Russell and Elisabeth H. (Branch) Bowie; married Jean Laverack, September 29, 1909; children: Jean L. Bowie Evans, Beverley Munford, Elisabeth H. Bowie Chapman, Walter Russell, Jr. *Education:* Harvard University, A.B., 1904, A.M., 1905; Virginia Theological Seminary, B.D., 1908. *Office:* Virginia Theological Seminary, Alexandria, Va.

CAREER: Ordained deacon in Protestant Episcopal church, 1908, priest, 1908; rector of Emmanuel Church, Greenwood, Va., 1908-11, St. Paul's Church, Richmond, Va., 1911-23, Grace Church, New York City, 1923-39; Union Theological Seminary, New York City, professor of practical theology, 1939-50, dean of students, 1945-50; Virginia Theological Seminary, Alexandria, professor of homiletics, 1950-55, visiting lecturer, 1955-69. Member of committee which produced the Revised Standard Version of the New Testament. *Military service:* U.S. Army, American Expeditionary Forces; chaplain of base hospital, Toul, France, 1918-19. *Member:* Phi Beta Kappa, Century Club (New York). *Awards, honors:* D.D., University of Richmond, 1915; S.T.D., Syracuse University, 1933; D.D., Virginia Theological Seminary, 1938.

WRITINGS: The Master of the Hill: A Biography of John Meigs, Dodd, 1917; *The Road of the Star*, Revell, 1922; *Some Open Ways to God*, Scribner, 1924; *The Inescapable Christ*, Scribner, 1925; *The Master: A Life of Jesus Christ*, Scribner, 1928, student edition, 1958; *On Being Alive*, Scribner, 1931; *When Christ Passes By*, Harper, 1932; *The Light Shineth in Darkness*, American Bible Society, 1933; *The Heroism of the Unheroic*, Abingdon, 1933; *The Renewing Gospel* (Lyman Beecher lectures), Scribner, 1935; *Great Men of the Bible*, Harper, 1937; *Lift up Your Hearts*, Macmillan, 1939, enlarged edition, Abingdon, 1956.

The Bible, Association Press, 1940; *Remembering Christ*, Abingdon, 1940; *Sunrise in the South: The Life of Mary-Cooke Branch Munford*, Bryd Press, 1942; *Which Way Ahead?*, Harper, 1943; *Preaching*, Abingdon, 1954; *The Story of the Church*, Abingdon, 1955; (editor) Henry Sloane Coffin, *Joy in Believing*, Scribner, 1956; *Christ Be with Me*, Abingdon, 1958; *I Believe in Jesus Christ*, Abingdon, 1959; *The Living Story of the New Testament*, Prentice-Hall, 1959; *Jesus and the Trinity*, Abingdon, 1960; *Men of Fire: Torchbearers of the Gospel*, Harper, 1961; *Women of Light*, Harper, 1963; *The Living Story of the Old Testament*, Prentice-Hall, 1964; *The Compassionate Christ*, Abingdon, 1965; (editor with Kenneth Seeman Giniger) *What Is Protestantism?*, F. Watts, 1965; *Where You Find God*, Harper, 1967; *See Yourself in the Bible*, Harper, 1967; *Learning to Live* (autobiography), Abingdon, 1969.

Children's books: *The Children's Year*, Revell, 1916; *Sunny Windows and Other Sermons for Children*, Revell, 1921; *The Armour of Youth*, Revell, 1923; *Chimes and the Children*, Revell, 1926; *When Jesus Was Born: The Story of Christmas for Little Children*, Harper, 1928; *The Story of Jesus for Young People*, Scribner, 1937; *Bible Story for Boys and Girls*, two volumes, Abingdon-Cokesbury, 1951, 1952.

Pageants: *Christmas Pageant of the Holy Grail*, Abingdon, 1927; *Soldier of Bethlehem*, Abingdon, 1927; *Pageant of the Kings*, Abingdon, 1927; *The Risen Lord: An Easter Pageant*, Abingdon-Cokesbury, 1942. Associate editor, *The Interpreter's Bible*.

BIOGRAPHICAL/CRITICAL SOURCES: Edgar DeWitt Jones, *Royalty of the Pulpit*, Harper, 1951.†

BOYCE, Ronald R(eed) 1931-

PERSONAL: Born January 7, 1931, in Los Angeles, Calif.; son of Reed S. and Martha Fern (Puzey) Boyce; married Norma Rae Loraas, May 6, 1955; (children: Renaye Noreen, Susan Annette. *Education:* University of Utah, B.S., 1956, M.S., 1957; University of Washington, Ph.D., 1960. *Office:* School of Social and Behavorial Sciences, Seattle Pacific University, Seattle, Wash. 98119.

CAREER: Western Washington State College (now Western Washington University), Bellingham, instructor in geography, 1959; Washington University, St. Louis, Mo., research associate, 1960-61; University of Illinois at Urbana-Champaign, assistant professor of planning and director of Wabash Basin Study, 1961-63; University of Iowa, Iowa City, associate professor of geography and research associate, Bureau of Economic and Business Research, 1963-65; University of Washington, Seattle, professor of geography, 1965-76; Seattle Pacific University, School of Social and Behavorial Sciences, Seattle, Wash., professor of urban and regional studies and director, 1976—. *Member:* Association of American Geographers, American Geographical Society, American Institute of Planners, American Association of University Professors, Regional Science Association (chairman, West Lakes Division, 1961), Sigma Xi, Omicron Delta Epsilon. *Awards, honors:* American Council on Education fellow, Baylor University, 1978-79.

WRITINGS: (With Edgar M. Horwood) *Studies of the Central Business District and Urban Freeway Development*, University of Washington Press, 1959; (with Blair T. Bower) *Changing Industrial Patterns in Metropolitan St. Louis and the Demand and Supply of Industrial Land to 1980*, Meramec Basin Research Project, Washington University, 1961; (with E. L. Ullman and Donald J. Volk) *The Meramec Basin Research Project Report*, three volumes, Washington University Press, 1962; (with Seymour Z. Mann) *Urbanism in Illinois: Its Nature, Importance, and Problems*, Public Affairs Research Bureau, Southern Illinois University, 1964; (editor) *Regional Development and the Wabash Basin*, University of Illinois Press, 1964; *The Bases of Economic Geography*, Holt, 1974, 2nd edition, 1978; (editor) *Geography as Spatial Interaction*, University of Washington Press, 1980. Contributor of about twenty articles and reviews to scientific and geographical periodicals.

SIDELIGHTS: Ronald R. Boyce told *CA:* "Writing one's thoughts and findings is a societal obligation to return something of that freely given. It is also a responsible form of accountability and a humbling experience."

*   *   *

BOZEMAN, Adda B(ruemmer) 1908-

PERSONAL: Born December 17, 1908, in Geistershof, Latvia; daughter of Leon and Anna (von Kahlen) von Bruemmer; married second husband, Arne Barkhuus (a physician and senior official of World Health Organization), February 8, 1951; children: (first marriage) Anya Louise Bozeman. *Education:* Ecole Libre Sciences Politiques, Paris, France, diplomee, 1933; Middle Temple Inn of Court, London, England, barrister-at-law, 1936; Southern Methodist University, LL.B., 1937. *Religion:* Protestant. *Home:* 24 Beall Circle, Bronxville, N.Y. 10708.

CAREER: Huberich International Law Offices, associate in Berlin, Germany, in The Hague, Netherlands, and in London, England, 1932-36; Augustana College and Theological Seminary, Rock Island, Ill., associate professor of history, 1943-47; Sarah Lawrence College, Bronxville, N.Y., professor of international relations, 1947-78, professor emerita, 1978—. Visiting professor at Northwestern University and New York University. Visiting professor, New School of Social Research, Graduate School, 1951, 1954, 1962—. Benedict Distinguished Visiting Professor in Political Science, Carleton College, 1978. Seminar director for National Endowment for the Humanities, 1975, 1976, 1978, 1981. *Member:* American Society of International Law, Consortium for the Study of Intelligence (director of academic projects, 1976—), Committee on the Present Danger (member of executive committee), International Society for the Comparative Study of Civilizations (honorary member), International Studies Association, International Sociological Association, American Political Science Association, Armed Forces and Society, Grotius Society, Council on Religion and International Affairs, Columbia Faculty Seminar on Peace (associate). *Awards, honors:* Grants from Carnegie Endowment for International Peace, 1951, for a book on international relations, and from Rockefeller Foundation, 1961, for work on African problems.

WRITINGS: Regional Conflicts around Geneva, Stanford University Press, 1947; *Politics and Culture in International History,* Princeton University Press, 1960; *The Future of Law in a Multicultural World,* Princeton University Press, 1971; *Conflict in Africa: Concepts and Realities,* Princeton University Press, 1976; *How to Think about Human Rights,* National Defence University, 1977; (contributor) *Individual Rights and Social Responsibilities,* University of Southern California Press, 1980. Contributor to journals. Member of editorial board, *ORBIS, Asian Affairs,* and *Review for Comparative Study of Civilization.*

WORK IN PROGRESS: A study of statecraft and intelligence; a study of international order in a multi-cultural world.

* * *

BRAGDON, Henry Wilkinson   1906-1980

PERSONAL: Born September 6, 1906, in Rochester, N.Y.; died March 15, 1980; son of Claude (an architect, stage designer, and author) and Charlotte (Wilkinson) Bragdon; married Katherine Fowler, June 20, 1931 (deceased); married Helen MacDonald Baker (a painter and writer), December 26, 1956; children: (first marriage) David, Peter; (stepchildren) David Baker, Sidney Baker. *Education:* Harvard University, A.B., 1928; Cambridge University, B.A., 1930, M.A., 1934. *Politics:* Mugwump. *Religion:* Episcopalian. *Home:* 171 High St., Exeter, N.H. 03833.

CAREER: Brooks School, North Andover, Mass., head of history department and dean, 1930-45; Phillips Exeter Academy, Exeter, N.H., instructor in history, 1945-63. Chief examiner in social studies, Advanced Placement Commission; trustee, College Entrance Examination Board. *Member:* American Historical Association, Organization of American Historians, American Academy of Political and Social Sciences, New England History Teachers Association (president, 1944-45), New Hampshire Association of Social Studies Teachers (president, 1952-53), New Hampshire Historical Association (trustee), Massachusetts Historical Society, Phi Beta Kappa (honorary member), St. Botolph Club (Boston), Century Association (New York), Examiner Club. *Awards, honors:* Horace Kidger Award, 1954, for services in writing and teaching history.

WRITINGS: (With Alan Blackmer, J. H. Harbison, and McGeorge Bundy) *General Education in School and College,* Harvard University Press, 1952; (with Samuel P. Mc-

Cutchen) *History of a Free People,* Macmillan, 1954, 9th edition, 1978; (with McCutchen and Stuart Gerry Brown) *Frame of Government,* Macmillan, 1962; *Woodrow Wilson: The Academic Years,* Belknap Press, 1967; (with John C. Pittenger) *The Pursuit of Justice: An Introduction to Constitutional Rights,* Crowell, 1969; (with Charles W. Cole and McCutchen) *A Free People: The United States in the Formative Years,* Macmillan, 1970; (editor) *Diary of Claude Fayette Bragdon,* Watertown Daily Times (Watertown, N.Y.), 1974. Also author, with Cole, of *A Free People: The United States in the Twentieth Century,* and, with Thomas H. Eliott, *The Bright Constellation: Documents of American Democracy.* Co-editor, *New Perspectives in American History,* Macmillan. Contributor of articles on testing and teaching to magazines. Editor, *New England Social Studies Bulletin.*

AVOCATIONAL INTERESTS: Gardening, mostly vegetables; camping, wood-chopping.†

* * *

BRANNER, R(obert)   1927-1973

PERSONAL: Born January 13, 1927, in New York, N.Y.; died November 27, 1973, in New York, N.Y.; son of Martin M. (a comic strip artist) and Edith (Fabbrini) Branner; married Shirley Prager (a librarian), January 25, 1953; children: David P. *Education:* Yale University, B.A., 1948, Ph.D., 1953.

CAREER: Yale University, New Haven, Conn., assistant in instruction, art history, 1952-54; University of Kansas, Lawrence, assistant professor, 1954-57; Columbia University, New York, N.Y., assistant professor, 1957-60, associate professor, 1960-66, professor of art history and archaeology, 1966-73. Director of excavations, Bourges Cathedral, Bourges, France, 1951-52. *Member:* Mediaeval Academy of America, College Art Association, Society of Architectural Historians (director, 1960-63), Societe Francaise d'Archeologie, International Center of Romanesque Art (secretary, 1960-62; director, 1962-73), Societe Nationale des Antiquaries de France. *Awards, honors:* Fulbright grant, Paris, 1950-52; American Council of Learned Societies grant-in-aid, 1960; Alice Davis Hitchcock Award, Society of Architectural Historians, 1963, for *La Cathedrale de Bourges;* John Simon Guggenheim fellow, 1963; American Council of Learned Societies fellow, 1966-67; grants from American Philosophical Association, Council on Research in the Humanities, Societe Francaise d'Archeologie, and Societe Nationale des Antiquaires.

WRITINGS: Burgundian Gothic Architecture, Zwemmer, 1960; *Gothic Architecture,* Braziller, 1961; *La Cathedrale de Bourges,* Tardy, 1962; *Saint Louis and the Court Style in Gothic Architecture,* Zwemmer, 1965; *The Painted Medallions in the Sainte-Chapelle in Paris,* American Philosophical Society, 1968; (with David Jacobs) *Master Builders of the Middle Ages,* American Heritage Publishing Co., 1968; *Chartres Cathedral,* Norton, 1969; *Manuscript Painting in Paris during the Reign of St. Louis,* University of California Press, 1977. Editor, *Society of Architectural Historians Journal,* 1964-66. Contributor of articles to professional journals in the United States and abroad.†

* * *

BRAULT, Gerard Joseph   1929-

PERSONAL: Born November 7, 1929, in Chicopee Falls, Mass.; son of Philias Joseph (an insurance agent) and Aline (Remillard) Brault; married Jeanne Lambert Pepin, January

23, 1954; children: Francis, Anne Marie, Suzanne. *Education:* Assumption College, Worcester, Mass., A.B., 1950; Laval University, A.M., 1952; University of Pennsylvania, Ph.D., 1958. *Politics:* Democrat. *Religion:* Roman Catholic. *Home:* 705 Westerly Parkway, State College, Pa. 16801. *Office:* S410 Burrowes, Pennsylvania State University, University Park, Pa. 16802.

CAREER: Bowdoin College, Brunswick, Me., instructor in French, 1957-59, assistant professor of Romance languages, 1959-61; University of Pennsylvania, Philadelphia, associate professor of Romance languages, 1961-65, vice-dean of Graduate School of Arts and Sciences, 1962-65; Pennsylvania State University, University Park, professor of French, 1965—, head of department, 1965-70. Conducted research under U.S. Office of Education contracts, 1960, 1962-63; director of National Defense Education Act special summer institute at Bowdoin College, 1961, 1962, and at Assumption College, 1964. *Military service:* U.S. Army, Counterintelligence Corps, 1951-53; served in France. *Member:* Mediaeval Academy of America (fellow), International Arthurian Society, American Association of Teachers of French, Modern Language Association of America (section secretary, 1961, 1962, 1965; section chairman, 1962, 1963, 1966, 1978), Societe Rencesvals (vice-president, 1973—), Society of Antiquaries of London (fellow), Heraldry Society of London (fellow). *Awards, honors:* Fulbright fellow in France, 1956-57; American Council of Learned Societies grant-in-aid, 1963; Palmes academiques, 1965; Fulbright research scholar and Guggenheim fellow in France, 1968-69; honorary Doctor of Letters degree, Assumption College, 1976.

WRITINGS: (Editor) *Celestine: A Critical Edition of the First French Translations (1527) of the Spanish Classic, La Celestina,* Wayne State University Press, 1963; *Early Blazon: Heraldic Terminology in the Twelfth and Thirteenth Centuries with Special Reference to Arthurian Literature,* Clarendon Press, 1972; *Eight Thirteenth Century Rolls of Arms in French and Anglo-Norman Blazon,* Pennsylvania State University Press, 1973; (editor) *The Song of Roland,* two volumes, Pennsylvania State University Press, 1978. Associate editor, *MLA Abstracts.* Contributor of more than seventy articles to learned journals.

WORK IN PROGRESS: The French-Canadian Heritage in New England.

AVOCATIONAL INTERESTS: Jogging, skiing, swimming.

BIOGRAPHICAL/CRITICAL SOURCES: Worcester Sunday Telegram, January 6, 1963; *Pittsburgh Press,* May 31, 1970.

*   *   *

BRAYBROOKE, David 1924-

PERSONAL: Born October 18, 1924, in Hackettstown, N.J.; son of Walter Leonard (a civil engineer) and Netta Rose (Foyle) Braybrooke; married Alice Boyd Noble, December 31, 1948 (separated, 1978); children: Nicholas, Geoffrey, Elizabeth Page. *Education:* Hobart College, student, 1941-43; Harvard University, B.A., 1948; Cornell University, M.A., 1951, Ph.D., 1953; Oxford University, postgraduate study, 1952-53, postdoctoral study, 1959-60. *Politics:* Independent. *Home:* 6045 Fraser St., Halifax, Nova Scotia, Canada B3H 1R7. *Office:* Arts and Administration Building, Room 365, Dalhousie University, Halifax, Nova Scotia, Canada B3H 4H6; and 1410 Henry St., Dalhousie University, Halifax, Nova Scotia, Canada B3H 4H6.

CAREER: Hobart College (now Hobart and William Smith Colleges), Geneva, N.Y., instructor in history and literature, 1948-50; instructor in philosophy at University of Michigan, Ann Arbor, 1953-54, and Bowdoin College, Brunswick, Me., 1954-56; Yale University, New Haven, Conn., assistant professor of philosophy, 1956-63; Dalhousie University, Halifax, Nova Scotia, associate professor, 1963-65, professor of philosophy and politics, 1965—. Visiting professor of philosophy at University of Pittsburgh, 1965, 1966, and University of Toronto, 1966-67; visiting professor of political science, University of Minnesota, Twin Cities, 1971; visiting professor, School of Social Sciences, University of California, Irvine, 1980. Research assistant, Committee on the Study of Political Behavior, Social Science Research Council, summers, 1957, 1958; part-time dean of liberal arts, Bridgeport Engineering Institute, 1961-63; external examiner, College of Social Studies, Wesleyan University, 1961-64, 1967, 1970. Member of academic advisory panel to the Canada Council, 1968-71; member of the Council for Philosophical Studies, 1974-79. Chairman, Town Democratic Committee, Guilford, Conn., 1961-62. *Military service:* U.S. Army, 1943-46.

MEMBER: American Philosophical Association, American Society for Political and Legal Philosophy, Canadian Philosophical Association (president, 1971-72), Canadian Political Science Association, Royal Institute of Public Administration, Canadian Association of University Teachers (member-at-large of national executive committee, 1970-71; president, 1975-76) National Committee for Sane Nuclear Policy (acting chairman of New Haven branch, 1963), Amnesty International, Phi Beta Kappa. *Awards, honors:* Rockefeller Foundation grant in legal and political philosophy, Oxford University, 1959-60; Guggenheim fellow, 1962-63; Royal Society of Canada fellow, 1980.

WRITINGS: (With Charles E. Lindblom) *A Strategy of Decision: Policy Evaluation as a Social Process,* Free Press, 1963; (editor) *Philosophical Problems of the Social Sciences,* Macmillan, 1965; *Three Tests for Democracy: Personal Rights, Human Welfare, Collective Preference,* Random House, 1968; *Traffic Congestion Goes through the Issue-Machine,* Routledge & Kegan Paul, 1974.

Contributor: Carl J. Friedrich, editor, *The Public Interest,* Atherton, 1962; Nelson W. Polsby, Robert A. Dentler, and Paul A. Smith, editors, *Politics and Social Life,* Houghton, 1963; Nicholas Rescher, editor, *Studies in Moral Philosophy,* Basil Blackwell, 1968; Kurt Baier and Nicholas Rescher, *Values and the Future,* Free Press, 1969; Howard E. Kiefer and Milton K. Munitz, editors, *Mind, Science, and History,* State University of New York Press, 1970; J.R. Pennock and J.W. Chapman, editors, *Participation in Politics,* Lieber-Atherton, 1975; C.A. Hooker and others, editors, *Foundations and Applications of Decision Theory,* Reidel, 1978. Contributor of articles and reviews to *Analysis, Ethics, Journal of Philosophy, Philosophical Review, Review of Metaphysics, Dialogue, American Philosophical Quarterly, History and Theory, Social Research, Canadian Journal of Philosophy, Nous,* and *Philosophical Studies.* Member of board of editors of *American Political Science Review,* 1970-72, *Philosophical Studies,* 1972-76, *Dialogue,* 1974-78, and *Ethics,* 1979—. Editor, *Philosophy in Canada,* 1973-78.

WORK IN PROGRESS: A book on the concept of needs; a book on the history of the concept of justice.

SIDELIGHTS: David Braybrooke told *CA:* "The practical effect of many philosophical inquiries—not to speak of their practical importance—is hard to see. I am ready, even so, to defend carrying them on and to do so vigorously. Yet I am glad that I was trained in a style of philosophy—ordinary language analysis—that works within the reach of unsophisticated serious minds. I am glad, too, that I have been specially concerned with topics—concepts important to social choices—on which philosophy, both in this style and in a more formalistic one, has its best chance to promote human happiness."

*　　*　　*

BRENAN, Gerald 1894-
(George Beaton)

PERSONAL: Born April 7, 1894, on Island of Malta; son of Hugh Gerald and Helen (Graham) Brenan; married Elisabeth Gamel Woolsey, 1931 (died January, 1968); children: Miranda Helen Corre. *Education:* Attended Radley College. *Home:* Alhaurin El Grande, Malaga, Spain.

CAREER: Author. *Military service:* British Army, Infantry, 1914-19; became captain; received Military Cross and Croix de Guerre.

WRITINGS: The Spanish Labyrinth, Cambridge University Press, 1943; *The Face of Spain,* Turnstile Press, 1950; *The Literature of the Spanish People,* Cambridge University Press, 1951; *South from Granada,* Hamish Hamilton, 1957; *A Holiday by the Sea,* Hamish Hamilton, 1961; *A Life of One's Own* (autobiography), Hamish Hamilton, 1962; *The Lighthouse Always Says Yes,* Hamish Hamilton, 1966; *St. John of the Cross,* Cambridge University Press, 1973; *Personal Record* (autobiography), J. Cape, 1974; *Thoughts in a Dry Season,* Cambridge University Press, 1978.

Under pseudonym George Beaton: *Jack Robinson* (picaresque novel), Chatto & Windus, 1933; *Doctor Partridge's Almanack,* Chatto & Windus, 1934.

AVOCATIONAL INTERESTS: Reading, walking.

*　　*　　*

BRENNAN, Joseph Gerard 1910-

PERSONAL: Born November 2, 1910, in Boston, Mass.; son of Joseph and Nora (Sheridan) Brennan; married Mary McLeod, 1938; six children. *Education:* Boston College, A.B., 1933; Harvard University, A.M., 1935; Columbia University, Ph.D., 1942. *Address:* Box 987, Little Compton, R.I. 02837. *Office:* 210 Spruance, U.S. Naval War College, Newport, R.I.

CAREER: College of New Rochelle, New Rochelle, N.Y., 1937-46, began as instructor, became associate professor of philosophy; Barnard College, New York, N.Y., 1946—, began as instructor, became professor of philosophy, professor emeritus, 1976—; U.S. Naval War College, Newport, R.I., professor of philosophy, 1978—. Adjunct professor of philosophy, Hofstra University, 1949-80; visiting professor of philosophy, Sarah Lawrence College, 1965-66. *Military service:* U.S. Naval Reserve; on active duty, 1943-46; became commander. *Member:* American Philosophical Association.

WRITINGS: Thomas Mann's World, Columbia University Press, 1942; *The Meaning of Philosophy,* Harper, 1953, 2nd edition, 1967; *A Handbook of Logic,* Harper, 1957, 2nd edition, 1961; *Three Philosophical Novelists,* Macmillan, 1964; *Ethics and Morals,* Harper, 1973; *The Education of a Prejudiced Man,* Scribner, 1977.

BRETT, Raymond Laurence 1917-

PERSONAL: Born January 10, 1917, in Bristol, England; son of Leonard Stanley and Ellen (Lawrence) Brett; married Kitty Cranmer, 1947; children: John Cranmer, David Lawrence. *Education:* University of Bristol, B.A., 1937; University College, Oxford, B. Litt., 1940. *Home:* The Gables, Station Walk, Cottingham, North Humberside, England. *Office:* Department of English, University of Hull, Hull, England.

CAREER: Secretary to First Lord of Admiralty, London, England, 1940-46; University of Bristol, Bristol, England, lecturer, 1946-52; University of Hull, Hull, England, professor of English, 1952—, dean of Faculty of Arts, 1960-62. Visiting professor, University of Rochester, 1958-59, University of Osnabrueck, Germany, 1976, and University of Baroda and Jadavpur University, India, 1978. *Military service:* Royal Navy, Special Reserve, 1940-46. *Member:* Association of University Teachers, British Association for American Studies.

WRITINGS: The Third Earl of Shaftesbury, Hutchinson, 1951; *George Crabbe,* Longmans, Green, 1958; *Reason and Imagination,* Oxford University Press, 1960; (editor with A. R. Jones) Wordsworth and Coleridge, *Lyrical Ballads,* revised edition, Methuen, 1963; *An Introduction to English Studies,* Edward Arnold, 1965, revised edition, 1977; (editor) *Poems of Faith and Doubt: The Victorian Age,* Edward Arnold, 1965; *Fancy and Imagination,* Methuen, 1969; (editor) *S. T. Coleridge,* Bell & Hyman, 1971; *William Hazlitt,* Longman, 1977; (editor) *Andrew Marvell: Tercentenary Lectures,* Oxford University Press, 1979; (editor) *Barclay Fox's Journal,* Bell & Hyman, 1979.

Contributor: Philip Magnus, editor, *English Essays,* J. Murray, 1949; Basil Willey, editor, *Essays and Studies,* J. Murray, 1958; Sykes Davies and George Watson, editors, *The English Mind,* Cambridge University Press, 1964. Contributor to journals.

*　　*　　*

BREWINGTON, Marion Vernon 1902-1974

PERSONAL: Born June 23, 1902, in Salisbury, Md.; died December 8, 1974, in New London, Conn.; son of Marion Vernon and Margaret (Fulton) Brewington; married Dorothy Riddel, February 14, 1931. *Education:* University of Pennsylvania, B.S., 1925. *Religion:* Episcopalian.

CAREER: Consulting curator of Kendall Whaling Museum, Sharon, Mass.; curator of marine collections, Bostonian Society; curator of Peabody Museum, Salem, Mass.; Mystic Seaport, Mystic, Conn., associate in maritime art, until 1974. *Military service:* U.S. Navy Reserve; became lieutenant commander. *Member:* Massachusetts Historical Society, Maryland Historical Society, Society for Nautical Research, Club of Odd Volumes. *Awards, honors:* Guggenheim fellowship, 1958.

WRITINGS: Chesapeake Bay Log Canoes (also see below), Mariners Museum, 1937; *Chesapeake Bay Bugeyes* (also see below), Mariners Museum, 1941; *Chesapeake Bay, Pictorial Maritime History,* Cornell Maritime Press, 1953, 2nd edition, 1956; *A Checklist of the Paintings, Drawings, and Prints at the Kendall Whaling Museum,* Kendall Whaling Museum, 1957; *Special Exhibition of the Irving S. Olds Collection of American Naval Prints and Paintings,* Peabody Museum, 1959; *Shipcarvers of North America,* Barre, 1962; *Chesapeake Bay Log Canoes and Bugeyes* (revised one-volume edition of *Chesapeake Bay Log Canoes* and

Chesapeake Bay Bugeyes), Cornell Maritime Press, 1963; *Peabody Museum Catalog of Navigating Instruments*, Peabody Museum, 1963; (with wife, Dorothy Brewington) *Kendall Whaling Museum Paintings*, Kendall Whaling Museum, 1965; *Chesapeake Bay Sailing Craft*, Maryland Historical Society, 1966; (with D. Brewington) *The Marine Paintings and Drawings in the Peabody Museum*, Peabody Museum, 1968; (with D. Brewington) *Kendall Whaling Museum Prints*, Kendall Whaling Museum, 1969. Editor, *American Neptune.*†

* * *

BREWSTER, Dorothy 1883-1979

PERSONAL: Born 1883, in St. Louis, Mo.; died April 17, 1979, in Lancaster, Pa.; daughter of William Morris and Lillie (Higbee) Brewster. *Education:* Barnard College, A.B., 1906; Columbia University, A.M., 1907, Ph.D., 1913. *Home:* Creek Dr., Millersville, Pa. 17551.

CAREER: Barnard College, New York City, assistant in English, 1908-11; Bryn Mawr College, Bryn Mawr, Pa., reader in English, 1914-15; Columbia University, New York City, 1915-50, began as instructor, became associate professor of English. *Member:* Modern Language Association of America, Women's Faculty Club (Columbia University), English-Speaking Union (New York).

WRITINGS: Aaron Hill, Columbia University Press, 1913; (with John A. Burrell) *Dead Reckonings in Fiction*, Longmans, Green, 1924; (editor) *Modern Short Stories*, Macmillan, 1928; (with Burrell) *Adventure or Experience: Four Essays on Certain Writers and Readers of Novels*, Columbia University Press, 1930, reprinted, Arno, 1967; (with Burrell) *Modern Fiction*, Columbia University Press, 1934; (editor) *Contemporary Short Stories*, Macmillan, 1937; *East-West Passage*, Allen & Unwin, 1954; *Virginia Woolf's London*, Allen & Unwin, 1959, New York University Press, 1960; *Virginia Woolf*, New York University Press, 1962; (with Burrell) *Modern World Fiction*, Littlefield, 1963; *Doris Lessing*, Twayne, 1965; *Portrait of a Pilgrim: William Brewster of the Mayflower*, New York University Press, 1968.

* * *

BREWTON, John E(dmund) 1898-

PERSONAL: Born December 19, 1898, in Brewton, Ala.; son of John Edmund and Mamie (Solomon) Brewton; married Sara Westbrook, April 12, 1924 (died, April, 1976); children: Betty (Mrs. George M. Blackburn, Jr.). *Education:* Howard College, A.B., 1922; Columbia University, graduate study, 1923; George Peabody College for Teachers, M.A., 1931, Ph.D., 1933. *Politics:* Democrat. *Religion:* Baptist.

CAREER: College instructor, public school teacher, principal, and superintendent, 1922-34; director of research for public schools, Louisville, Ky., 1935-37; George Peabody College for Teachers, Nashville, Tenn., 1937-68, held various positions, including associate director and director of division of surveys and field services, dean of graduate school, acting president, and chairman of English department. Served as director of numerous comprehensive educational surveys on state, county, and local levels. *Member:* National Council of Teachers of English, Tennessee Folklore Society.

WRITINGS: Talks to Young Adventurers, Revell, 1938; (with Lois McMullan and Myriam Page) *Essentials of Communication for High Schools*, Laidlaw Brothers, 1942; (with R. L. Giddings and McMullan) *Learning Essential English*, Laidlaw Brothers, 1947.

Editor: *Under the Tent of the Sky*, Macmillan, 1937; *Gaily We Parade*, Macmillan, 1940, reprinted, 1967; (with Louise Abney, Babette Lemon, and Blanche Wellons) *Excursions in Fact and Fancy*, Laidlaw Brothers, 1949; (with Abney, Lemon, and Wellons) *Your World in Prose and Verse*, Laidlaw Brothers, 1949; (with Abney, Lemon, and Wellons) *Expanding Literary Interests*, Laidlaw Brothers, 1950; (with Abney, Lemon, and Russell Alger Sharp) *Exploring Literary Trails*, Laidlaw Brothers, 1950; (with Abney, Lemon, and Sharp) *Literature of the Americas*, Laidlaw Brothers, 1950; (with Abney, Lemon, and Sharp) *English and Continental Literature*, Laidlaw Brothers, 1950; *Poetry Time*, Upper Room, 1953; (with Lemon and Marie Ernest) *New Horizons through Reading and Literature*, Laidlaw Brothers, 1958; (with McMullan, B. Jo Kinnick, R. Stanley Peterson) *Using Good English*, Laidlaw Brothers, 1961; (with Lorraine A. Blackburn) *They've Discovered a Head in the Box for the Bread, and Other Laughable Limericks*, Crowell, 1978; (with L. A. Blackburn and G. Meredith Blackburn III) *In the Witch's Kitchen: Poems for Halloween*, Crowell, 1980.

Editor with wife, Sara Westbrook Brewton: *Index to Children's Poetry*, H. W. Wilson, 1942, 1st supplement, 1955, 2nd supplement, 1965, 3rd supplement (with G. M. Blackburn III) published as *Index to Poetry for Children and Young People, 1964-1969*, 1972, 4th supplement (with G. M. Blackburn III and L. A. Blackburn) published as *Index to Poetry for Children and Young People, 1970-1975*, 1978; *Bridled with Rainbows: Poems about Many Things of Earth and Sky*, Macmillan, 1949; *Christmas Bells Are Ringing*, Macmillan, 1951; *Sing a Song of Seasons*, Macmillan, 1955; *Birthday Candles Burning Bright*, Macmillan, 1960; *Laughable Limericks*, Crowell, 1965; *America Forever New*, Crowell, 1967; *Shrieks at Midnight: Macabre Poems, Eerie and Humorous*, Crowell, 1969; (and G. M. Blackburn III) *My Tang's Tungled and Other Ridiculous Situations*, Crowell, 1973; (and John B. Blackburn) *Of Quarks, Quasars, and Other Quirks: Quizzical Poems for the Supersonic Age*, Crowell, 1977. Also author of educational survey reports. Editor, *Journal of the Florida Education Association*, 1928-29.

AVOCATIONAL INTERESTS: Gardening.

BIOGRAPHICAL/CRITICAL SOURCES: Young Readers Review, May, 1969.

* * *

BRIGGS, L(loyd) Cabot 1909-1975

PERSONAL: Born June 27, 1909, in Boston, Mass.; died May 14, 1975, in Hancock, N.H.; son of L(loyd) Vernon and Mary Tileston (Cabot) Briggs; married Eleanor M. Livingston, June 29, 1935; married Madeleine Danus, May 8, 1948; children: (first marriage) Eleanor Livingston. *Education:* Harvard University, A.B., 1931, A.M., 1938, Ph.D., 1952; Oxford University, diploma in anthropology, 1932. *Politics:* Independent. *Residence:* Hancock, N.H.

CAREER: Abbott, Proctor & Paine, New York, N.Y., partner in stock brokerage firm, 1938-42; Harvard University, Cambridge, Mass., research associate, 1947-75; Nathaniel Hawthorne College, Antrim, N.H., lecturer in anthropology, beginning 1963; Franklin Pierce College, Rindge, N.H., chairman of anthropology and sociology department, 1967-75. Consultant to the Centre d'Etudes et d'Informations des Problemes Humains dans les Zones Arides, Paris and Algiers, 1960-62. *Military service:* Intelligence and security work, Mediterranean Theater, 1942-47; received U.S. Medal of Freedom and French Officer d'Academie and Ordre du

Merite Saharien. *Member:* American Anthropological Association, American Association of Physical Anthropologists, Royal Anthropological Institute of Great Britain and Ireland, Societe d'Anthropologie de Paris, Societe d'Histore Naturelle de l'Afrique du Nord, Explorers Club.

WRITINGS—Published by Peabody Museum of Archaeology and Ethnology, Harvard University, except as indicated: *Bullterriers: The Biography of a Breed*, Derrydale, 1940; *The Stone Age Races of Northwest Africa*, 1955; *The Living Races of the Sahara Desert*, 1958, reprinted, Kraus Reprint, 1969; *Initiation a l'Anthropologie du Squelette*, Official Press, Algiers, 1958; *Tribes of the Sahara*, Harvard University Press, 1960; *Archaeological Investigations near Tipasa, Algeria*, 1963; (with Norina Lami Guede) *No More For Ever: A Saharan Jewish Town*, 1964; (with Bruce Howe) *The Paleolithic of Tangier, Morocco*, 1967. Contributor of articles and book reviews to professional journals and Science Magazine.

WORK IN PROGRESS: Continuing long range program of anthropological research in the Sahara; *Monteforesta*, with Norina Lami Guede, an exhaustive community study of a North Italian hill village as it was forty years ago.†

*   *   *

BRINITZER, Carl   1907-1974
(Usikota)

PERSONAL: Born January 30, 1907, in Riga, Russia; died October 30, 1974; son of Eugen (a physician) and Jenny (a physician; maiden name, Kaplan) Brinitzer; married Berthe Grossbard (a radio-journalist), July 12, 1939. *Education:* Attended University of Geneva, University of Hamburg, University of Munich, University of Berlin, and University of Kiel; Doctor of Law, 1933. *Office:* British Broadcasting Corp., Bush House, London W.C.2, England.

CAREER: Junior lawyer, Kiel, Germany, 1930-33, public prosecutor, 1933; British Broadcasting Corp., London, England, head of announcer/translator department in German Service, 1938-45, senior scriptwriter in European service, 1945-64, German program organizer, beginning 1964, regular broadcaster in German Service and moderator for B.B.C. in programs arranged with other European networks.

WRITINGS: Strafrechtliche Massnahmen zur Bekaempfung der Prostitution, Kiel University Press, 1933; *Zulu in Germany*, Gollancz, 1938; (editor with Berthe Grossbard) *German versus Hun*, translation by Bernard Miall, Allen & Unwin, 1941; *Cassell's War and Post-War German Dictionary*, Cassell, 1945; *G. C. Lichtenberg: Die Geschichte eines gescheiten Mannes*, Rainer Wunderlich, 1956, translation by Bernard Smith published as *A Reasonable Rebel: Georg Christoph Lichtenberg*, Macmillan, 1960; *Wo die Queen regiert*, Graeber & Olzog, 1956; *Heinrich Heine: Roman seines Lebens*, Hoffmann & Campe, 1960; *Das streitbare Leben des Verlagers Julius Campe*, Hoffmann & Campe, 1962; (author of preface) Johann Christoph Friedrich von Schiller, *Schillers politisches Vermaechtniss*, Hoffmann & Campe, 1962; (editor) *Deutsche Dichter fuhren nach Italien*, F. Kupferberg, 1964; *Liebeskunst ganz prosaisch*, Rowohlt, 1966; *Doktor Johnson und Boswell*, F. Kupferberg, 1968; *Liebeskunst ganz ritterlich*, Hoffmann & Campe, 1968; *Hier spricht London*, Hoffmann & Campe, 1969; *Zwei Loffel Goethe, eine Prise Shaw*, Rowohlt, 1969; (compiler) *Amor's gesammelte Werke*, Rowohlt, 1970; *Wie machte das Cleopatra?*, Deutsche Verlags-Anstalt, 1972; *Immer Arger mit den Frauen*, Claassen Verlag, 1973.

Translator: Desmond Young, *Rommel*, Limes Verlag, 1950;

Rex Stout, *Gast im dritten Stock*, Nes Verlag, 1954; Hugh Cudlip, *Sensationen fur Millionen*, Kindler Verlag, 1955; Stout, *Das zweit Gestandnis*, Nest Verlag, 1956; Stout, *Zu viele Kocke*, Nest Verlag, 1957; Wynant David Hubbard, *Bong Kwe*, Kindler Verlag, 1958; F. E. Halliday, *Shakespeare*, Kindler Verlag, 1961; Stout *Vor Mitternacht*, Nest Verlag, 1962.

Also author of more than one hundred radio plays and documentaries. Contributor to German, English, and Italian newspapers and journals.†

*   *   *

BRINK, Carol Ryrie   1895-

PERSONAL: Born December 28, 1895, in Moscow, Idaho; daughter of Alexander and Henrietta (Watkins) Ryrie; married Raymond W. Brink, July 12, 1918 (deceased); children: David Ryrie, Nora Caroline Brink Hunter. *Education:* Attended University of Idaho, 1914-17; University of California (Berkeley), B.A., 1918. *Religion:* Presbyterian. *Home:* 2404 Loring St., San Diego, Calif. 92109. *Agent:* Caroline Rogers, 1707 Sandpiper, Palm Desert, Calif. 92260.

CAREER: Self-employed author of books for children and adults. Member, Southern California Council on Literature for Children and Young People. *Member:* League of American Penwomen, Authors Guild, Society of Children's Book Writers, P.E.N., Faculty Women's Club (University of Minnesota), Phi Beta Kappa. *Awards, honors:* John Newbery Medal, 1935, for *Caddie Woodlawn;* Friends of American Writers award, 1955, for *The Headland;* D. Litt., University of Idaho, 1965; McKnight Family Foundation medal and National League of American Pen Women award, 1966, both for *Snow in the River;* Southern California Council on Literature for Children and Young People award, 1966; Kerlan Award, 1978.

WRITINGS—All published by Macmillan, except as indicated; juvenile: *Anything Can Happen on the River*, 1934; *Caddie Woodlawn*, 1935; *Mademoiselle Misfortune*, 1936; *Baby Island*, 1937; *All Over Town*, 1939; *Lad with a Whistle*, 1941; *Magical Melons*, 1944; *Caddie Woodlawn, A Play*, 1945; *Narcissa Whitman*, Row, Peterson & Co., 1945; *Lafayette*, Row, Peterson & Co., 1946; *Minty et Compagnie*, Casterman, 1948; *Family Grandstand*, Viking, 1952; *The Highly Trained Dogs of Professor Petit*, 1953; *Family Sabbatical*, Viking, 1956; *The Pink Motel*, 1959; *Andy Buckram's Tin Men*, Viking, 1966; *Winter Cottage*, 1968; *Two Are Better Than One*, 1968; *The Bad Times of Irma Baumlein*, 1972; *Louly*, 1974; *Four Girls on a Homestead*, Latah County (Idaho) Historical Society, 1977.

Adult: *Buffalo Coat*, 1944; *Harps in the Wind*, 1947; *Stopover*, 1951; *The Headland*, 1955; *Strangers in the Forest*, 1959; *The Twin Cities* 1961; *Chateau Saint Barnabe*, 1962; *Snow in the River*, 1964; *The Bellini Look*, Bantam, 1976. Contributor of short stories and poems to magazines. Edited a yearly collection of best short stories for boys and girls, Row, Peterson & Co., 1935-39.

WORK IN PROGRESS: Poetry.

AVOCATIONAL INTERESTS: Traveling, painting, outdoor living, and nature study.

*   *   *

BRINTON, Howard Haines   1884-1973

PERSONAL: Born July 24, 1884, in West Chester, Pa.; died April 9, 1973; son of Edward and Ruthanna (Brown) Brinton; married Anna Shipley Cox (a college professor), July 23,

1921; children: Lydia (Mrs. John Forbes), Edward, Catharine (Mrs. John Cary), Joan Mary (Mrs. Kent Erickson). *Education:* Haverford College, A.B., 1904, A.M., 1905; Harvard University, A.M., 1909; University of California, PhD., 1924. *Politics:* Independent. *Religion:* Quaker. *Home and office:* Pendle Hill, Wallinford, Pa.

CAREER: Pickering College, Newmarket, Ontario, Canada, instructor in mathematics and physics, 1909-15; Guilford College, Guilford College, N.C., professor of mathematics, 1915-1919, acting president, 1917-18, dean, 1918-19; Earlham College, Richmond, Ind., professor of physics, 1922-28; Mills College, Oakland, Calif., professor of religion, 1928-36; Pendle Hill (graduate school), Wallingford, Pa., lecturer and director, 1936-52, lecturer, beginning 1954. American Friends Service Committee representative in Germany, 1919-20, and Japan, 1952-54. Curator of records, Philadelphia early meeting of Friends, beginning 1940. *Member:* American Philosophical Association, Friends Historical Society (president, 1960-63), Phi Beta Kappa. *Awards, honors:* D.Litt., Haverford College, 1950, and Earlham College, 1961.

WRITINGS—Published by Pendle Hill, except as indicated: *The Mystic Will,* Macmillan, 1930; *Creative Worship,* Headley, 1931; *Divine Human Society.* Friends Book Committee, 1938; (editor and contributor) *Children of Light* (essays in honor of Rufus M. Jones), Macmillan, 1938; *Quaker Education,* 1940, 2nd edition, 1949; (editor and contributor) *Byways in Quaker History* (essays in honor of William I. Hull), 1944; *Friends for 300 Years,* Harper, 1952; *Creative Worship, and Other Essays,* 1963; *Ethical Mysticism in the Society of Friends,* 1967; *Quaker Journals: Varieties of Religious Experience among Friends,* 1972; *The Religious Philosophy of Quakerism: The Beliefs of Fox, Barclay, and Penn as Based on the Gospel of John,* 1973.

Booklets; all published by Pendle Hill: *The Quaker Doctrine of Inward Peace,* 1948, reprinted, 1964; *The Pendle Hill Idea,* 1950; *Guide to Quaker Practice,* 1955; *How They Became Friends,* 1961; *Ethical Mysticism in the Society of Friends,* 1967; *The Religion of George Fox,* 1968; *Evolution and the Inward Light: Where Science and Religion Meet,* 1970; *Light and Life in the Fourth Gospel,* 1971; *Meeting House and Farm House,* 1972. Also author of *The Quaker Doctrine of the Holy Spirit.*

Contributor: *Beyond Dilemmas,* Lippincott, 1937; *The Pendle Hill Reader,* Harper, 1950; *The Quaker Approach,* Putnam, 1953.

BIOGRAPHICAL/CRITICAL SOURCES: Survey, June, 1940; *Motive,* May, 1948; *Time,* June 21, 1948.†

*   *   *

BRITTAIN, Frederick   ?-1969

PERSONAL: Born in South Mymms, Hertfordshire, England; died March 15, 1969; son of William and Elizabeth (Daniels) Brittain; married Muriel Cunnington (a pharmacist), 1959. *Education:* Jesus College, Cambridge University, B.A., 1921, M.A., 1925, Litt.D., 1948. *Politics:* Socialist. *Religion:* Anglican.

CAREER: Cambridge University, Cambridge, England, lecturer in medieval Latin literature, 1930-61, proctor or proproctor, 1943-48, fellow of Jesus College, director of studies in modern and medieval languages, librarian, steward, praelector, and keeper of the records. *Member:* Hymn Society of Great Britain and Ireland (vice-president), Footlights Dramatic Club (Cambridge), Alcuin Club, John Mason Neale Society (founder).

WRITINGS: (Translator) F. S. Nitti, *The Decadence of Europe,* Fisher Unwin, 1923; (translator) Nitti, *They Make a Desert,* Dent, 1924; *Saint Radegund,* Heffer, 1925; (editor) *The Lyfe of Saynt Radegunde,* Cambridge University Press, 1926; *The Roosters,* privately printed, 1928; *Saint Giles,* Heffer, 1928; (with H. B. Playford) *The Jesus College Boat Club,* Heffer, Volume I, 1928, Volume II, 1962; *Slowly Forward,* Heffer, 1929; *Oar, Scull, and Rudder: A Bibliography of Rowing,* Oxford University Press, 1930; *South Mymms: The Story of a Parish,* Heffer, 1931; *Latin in Church: The History of Its Pronunciation,* Cambridge University Press, 1934, new edition, Mowbray, 1955; *The Medieval Latin and Romance Lyric to A.D. 1300,* Cambridge University Press, 1937, 2nd edition, 1951, reprinted, Kraus Reprint, 1969; *A Short History of Jesus College, Cambridge,* Heffer, 1940; (with B. L. Manning) *Babylon Bruis'd and Mount Moriah Mended,* Heffer, 1940; *Bernard Lord Manning: A Memoir,* Heffer, 1942; *Arthur Quiller-Couch: A Biographical Study of "Q,"* Cambridge University Press, 1947; *"Q" Anthology,* Dent, 1952 (enlarged edition published under title *Mostly Mymms,* 1954); (with Arthur Gray) *A History of Jesus College, Cambridge,* Heinemann, 1960, revised edition, 1979; *The Penguin Book of Latin Verse,* Penguin, 1962; *Illustrated Guide to Cambridge,* 15th edition, Heffer, 1967; *It's a Don's Life* (autobiography), Heinemann, 1972. Co-author of play, "No More Women," 1933. Editor, *Cambridge Review,* 1942-48. Contributor of articles to *Dictionary of National Biography, Times, Spectator, Classical Review,* and other publications.

AVOCATIONAL INTERESTS: Acting, singing, medieval music, church music, and architecture.

BIOGRAPHICAL/CRITICAL SOURCES: Church Times, February 19, 1954.†

*   *   *

BROEKEL, Rainer Lothar   1923-
(Ray Broekel)

PERSONAL: First syllable of surname rhymes with "rock"; born March 24, 1923, in Dresden, Germany; son of Eugene (a horticulturist) and Hedwig (Hartmann) Broekel; married Margaret McNeely, May 6, 1944; children: Peggy Rae, Randall Ray. *Education:* Illinois College, B.A., 1948; graduate study at Stanford University, 1948-50, and Wesleyan University, 1955. *Religion:* Episcopalian. *Home and office:* 6 Edge St., Ipswich, Mass. 01938.

CAREER: Junior high school science teacher in Murrayville and Jacksonville, Ill., 1950-56; Junior Museum, Jacksonville, Ill., director, 1954-56; Wesleyan University, Middletown, Conn., member of department of school services, 1956-64; American Education Publications, Middletown, science supervisor of "My Weekly Reader" publications, 1956-66; Silver Burdett Co., Morristown, N.J., senior editor, 1966; Addison-Wesley Publishing Co., Reading, Mass., editor-in-chief of juvenile division, 1966-75; author, freelance editor, and educational consultant, 1975—; Institute of Children's Literature, Redding Ridge, Conn., instructor, 1979—; North Shore Community College, Beverly, Mass., instructor, 1980—. *Awards, honors:* L.H.D., Illinois College, 1979.

WRITINGS—Under name Ray Broekel: *The True Book of Tropical Fishes,* Childrens Press, 1956, published as *The Junior True Book of Tropical Fishes,* Muller, 1959; *You and the Science of Plants, Animals, and the Earth,* Childrens Press, 1956; *You and the Sciences of Mankind,* Childrens Press, 1956; *"I Have a Green Nose," Said Zanzibar,* Seale,

1963; *Rodney Bounced Too Much on Monday,* Seale, 1964; *Pangborn, the Peanut Bear, and His Tummy-Drum,* Seale, 1965; *Hugo the Huge,* Doubleday, 1968.

The Saga of Sweet Basil, Doubleday, 1970; (adaptor) *Even the Devil Is Afraid of a Shrew,* Addison-Wesley, 1972; (adaptor) *The Flying Orchestra,* Addison-Wesley, 1974; (adaptor) *The Traffic Stopper,* Addison-Wesley, 1974; (adaptor) *One, Two, Three,* Addison-Wesley, 1974; (adaptor) *The Color Trumpet,* Addison-Wesley, 1974; (adaptor) *Our Bird Friends,* Addison-Wesley, 1974; (translator) *The Painter and the Bird,* Addison-Wesley, 1975; (co-author) *The Underwater Adventure Book,* Random House, 1978; (co-author) *The Trick Book,* Doubleday, 1979; (co-author) *Now You See It,* Little, Brown, 1979; *The Holiday Dragon,* I Discover Books, 1979.

The Mystery of the Funny Money, Carolrhoda, 1980; *The Twist Tie Riddle,* Carolrhoda, 1980; *The President Jackson Case,* Carolrhoda, 1980; *The Shoelace Solution,* Carolrhoda, 1980; *The Moustache Pickpocket,* Carolrhoda, 1980; *The Mystery of the Stolen Base,* Carolrhoda, 1980; *Pack of Fun Facts,* Xerox Paperback Bookclub, 1980; *Volcanoes and Other Disasters,* Xerox Paperback Bookclub, 1980; (co-author) *The Surprise Book,* Doubleday, 1981.

Textbooks and workbooks: *Balloons, Birds, and Balls,* Hayes Book, 1976; *Smiles the Clown,* Hayes Book, 1976; *Meg and the Animals,* Hayes Book, 1976; *The Sunnyside News,* Hayes Book, 1976; *Mystery Island,* Hayes Book, 1976; *Hot Dogs, Pigeons, and Fish That Walk,* Hayes Book, 1976; *Gremlins, Mermaids, and Mousetraps That Fly,* Hayes Book, 1976; *Motorcycles, Swimming, and Dog Dectives,* Hayes Book, 1976; (co-editor) *The Spirit of God,* Sadlier, 1976; (co-author) *Multiple Reading Skills Series,* Lowell & Lynwood, 1976; *Airplanes, Pet Stories, and Fire Trucks,* Hayes Book, 1977; (co-editor) *Earth and Universe,* Cambridge Book Company, 1977; (co-author) *Elementary Science Series,* Addison-Wesley, 1977; *Word Problem Drill, Grade 5,* Hayes Book, 1977; *Word Problem Drill, Grade 6,* Hayes Book, 1977; *Solving Science Mysteries,* Hayes Book, Books 1, 2, and 3, 1977, Book 4, 1979, *Reading: Everyday Survival Skills,* Hayes Book, Book 1, 1978, Books 2, 3, and 4, 1980; (co-author) *Daystreaming,* Economy Company, 1978; (co-author) *Forerunners,* Economy Company, 1978; (co-editor) *Jesus and His Friends,* Sadlier, 1978; (co-editor) *Elementary Science Series,* Houghton, 1979; (editor) *Environmental Education,* Bedford, 1979.

Nature Study, Hayes Book, 1980; *Rhyming Reader,* Hayes Book, 1980; *Something for Everyday,* Hayes Book, 1980; (co-author) *Reading about Science,* seven volumes, McGraw, 1980; (co-author) *Keys to Reading,* Economy Company, 1980; (editor) *Project Business Consultant's Manual,* Junior Achievement, 1980; (editor) *Project Business Student Manual,* Junior Achievement, 1980; (editor) *Project Business Consultant's Binder,* Junior Achievement, 1980; *Environmental Education Evaluation Packet,* Bedford, 1980; *Real Life Math,* six volumes, Instructo Corporation, 1981. Also author of *Science and Language Arts,* 1978. Contributor of over 1,000 stories and articles to children's magazines and other periodicals.

WORK IN PROGRESS: Twenty-six books under contract.

BIOGRAPHICAL/CRITICAL SOURCES: The New York Times Book Review, June 17, 1979.

*   *   *

BRONOWSKI, Jacob   1908-1974

PERSONAL: Surname is pronounced Bron-*off*-ski; born January 18, 1908, in Poland; came to United States in 1964; died August 22, 1974, in East Hampton, N.Y.; son of Abram and Celia (Flatto) Bronowski; married Rita Coblentz, February 17, 1941; children: Lisa Anne, Judith Jill, Nicole Ruth, Clare Beth. *Education:* Jesus College, Cambridge, M.A., 1930, Ph.D., 1933. *Home:* 9438 La Jolla Farms Rd., La Jolla, Calif. 92037. *Office:* Salk Institute for Biological Studies, P.O. Box 9499, San Diego, Calif. 92109.

CAREER: University College, Hull, England, senior lecturer, 1934-42; wartime researcher and head of statistical units dealing with the effects of bombings for British Ministry of Home Security, 1942-45; served with Joint Target Group, Washington, D.C., and as scientific deputy to British Chiefs of Staff mission to Japan, 1945; statistical researcher on economics and industries for British Ministry of Works, 1946-50; National Coal Board of Great Britain, London, England, director of Coal Research Establishment, 1950-59, director-general of Process Development Department, 1959-63; Salk Institute for Biological Studies, San Diego, Calif., research professor, fellow, and director of council for biology in human affairs, 1964-74. Charles Beard Lecturer, Oxford University; Carnegie Visiting Professor, Massachusetts Institute of Technology, 1953; lecturer, American Museum of Natural History, 1965; Eastman Memorial Visiting Professor, University of Rochester, 1965; Condon Lecturer, Oregon State University, 1967; Silliman Lecturer, Yale University, 1967; Bampton Lecturer, Columbia University, 1969; Mellon Lecturer, National Gallery of Art, 1969. Head of projects division, UNESCO, 1948. Commentator on atomic energy and other scientific and cultural subjects for British Broadcasting Corp.; panelist, "Brains Trust" (radio and television program), 1946-59. Lecturer. *Member:* World Academy of Art and Science (fellow), Society for Visiting Scientists, Royal Society of Literature (fellow), American Academy of Arts and Sciences (honorary member), Athenaeum Club (London). *Awards, honors:* Thornton Medal; Italia Prize for best dramatic work broadcast throughout Europe during 1950-51, for "The Face of Violence"; honorary fellow, Jesus College, Cambridge University, 1967.

WRITINGS: The Poet's Defence, Macmillan, 1939, published as *The Poet's Defense: The Concept of Poetry from Sidney to Yeats,* World Publishing, 1966; *Spain 1939: Four Poems,* Andrew Marvell Press, 1939; *William Blake, 1757-1827: A Man without a Mask,* Secker & Warburg, 1943, Transatlantic, 1945, reprinted, Gordon Press, 1976, revised edition, Penguin, 1954, published as *William Blake and the Age of Revolution,* Harper, 1965; *The Common Sense of Science,* Heinemann, 1951, Harvard University Press, 1953, reprinted, 1978; *The Face of Violence: An Essay with a Play* (first produced, 1950), Turnstile Press, 1954, Braziller, 1955, new and enlarged edition, World Publishing, 1967; *Science and Human Values* (also see below), Messner, 1956, revised edition, Penguin, 1964; (editor and author of introduction) *William Blake: A Selection of Poems and Letters,* Penguin, 1958.

(Editor with others) *Science: Chemistry, Physics, Astronomy,* Doubleday, 1960; (with Bruce Mazlish) *The Western Intellectual Tradition: From Leonardo to Hegel,* Harper, 1960; (editor with others) *Technology: Man Remakes His World,* MacDonald, 1963, published as *The Doubleday Pictorial Library of Technology,* Doubleday, 1964, revised edition published under original title, Responsive Environments Corp., 1966; (with others) *Imagination and the University,* University of Toronto Press, 1964; *Insight,* Harper, 1964; (with M. E. Selsam) *Biography of an Atom* (juvenile), Harper, 1965; *The Identity of Man,* Natural History Press, 1965, revised edition, 1971; *Science and Human Values* [and] *The Abacus and the Rose* (radio program; first produced, 1962), Harper, 1965, revised edition, 1972; *On Being an Intellectual,* Smith College, 1968; *Nature and Knowledge: The Philosophy of Contemporary Science,* Oregon State System of Higher Education, 1969.

The Ascent of Man (essays based on television series), British Broadcasting Corp., 1973, Little, Brown, 1974; *A Sense of the Future: Essays in Natural Philosophy,* M.I.T. Press, 1977; *The Visionary Eye: Essays in the Arts, Literature, and Science,* M.I.T. Press, 1978; *Magic, Science, and Civilization,* Columbia University Press, 1978; *The Origins of Knowledge and Imagination,* Yale University Press, 1978.

Also author of radio dramas, including "The Man without a Mask," 1946, "Journey to Japan," 1948, and "The Closing Years," 1951, an opera (with Peter Racine Fricker), "My Brother Died," 1954, several television documentary series, "Science in the Making," 1953-54, "New Horizon," 1958, "Insight," 1960-61, and "The Ascent of Man," 1973, and numerous papers on mathematics. Contributor of articles to newspapers and journals.

SIDELIGHTS: "Jacob Bronowski was a man out of his time," wrote John Lenihan in *Books and Bookmen.* "Superbly wise in mathematics, physical science, biology and literature, he would have been more at ease in Renaissance Italy than in the world of the twentieth century. . . . [He] had the scholar's gift of illuminating the contemporary world obliquely and sharply by telling about the past. . . . Bronowski saw science as a part of man's cultural heritage; to him the progress of science was not an orderly sequence of logical innovations but a shifting pattern which could be appreciated only by recognising the interwoven strands of history, art, literature and philosophy."

A mathematician by training, Bronowski, like many others, was profoundly shaken by the events of World War II; shaken enough, in fact, that he changed the direction of his life. As he once explained to an interviewer: "Hitler's coming struck a most powerful blow at me and my generation. I suddenly realized that being happy, being human, being a scientist, being with friends was not enough. And particularly being an academic, which I was then destined to be, was not going to be enough. Quite suddenly it became clear that whatever one did with one's life after 1932, one had to bear witness for what one believed to be the foundations of human decency. . . . It was no longer enough to be a good person quietly working at your desk. . . . I realized that I was a persuasive person, that coming to England and learning English had given me a gift for the language and for the thought, for the way that English people think about themselves and about eccentrics like me, which was persuasive to other people. And I never looked back. It was then that I began to write about science in general, to address people who were not in university classes, and to go out to do the kind of thing that I became classic for."

The specific turning point in Bronowski's career came in Nagasaki, Japan, at the end of 1945. As a member of a commission assigned to study the effects of atomic bombing, he noted that "of course I had seen all the pictures. I had seen all the aerial surveys, and I had seen all the stereo pictures and I thought I knew what it looked like. But coming into that gloomy valley by the sea, with the ships in the harbor, with the broken railways, was an unforgettable experience. I did not know I was in Nagasaki until we were actually at the side of the ships, because everything was such a tangle of wreckage. . . . [I] knew that we had dehumanized the enemy and ourselves in one blow." Furthermore, he added, "I saw how much deeper the implications of great general actions are. And I came back with a totally different sense of how human beings had to react to one another."

Realizing that scientists could no longer regard themselves as being "wholly withdrawn from public affairs," Bronowski turned more and more towards a study of the relation between art and science. He was firmly convinced that creativity—whether scientific or artistic—springs from the same basic source. "Science and art," he insisted, "are wonderfully human because they both call on imagination and they both require enormous dedication and integrity. When people say to me 'Oh, I do not much care about science; I never could do arithmetic. I am an arts person,' I know they are just telling me a pack of lies. . . . They are against science just because it happens to be the fashionable culture. No, if you care about art or if you care about science you must have a huge sense of involvement with what is human about those things. Now, about science the answer is quite straightforward. The wonder of science is reading the riddle of nature. But the wonder of the arts . . . is reading the riddle of man, reading the riddle of human nature, reading the riddle of *life,* if you like. . . . What makes the arts so wonderfully special and so wonderfully human [is] the ability of the human being to identify himself with someone else and to say 'That is universal humanity, that is what we share and what I try to utter and to invoke at one and the same moment.'"

Science and Human Values was the result of Bronowski's post-World War II soul-searching; it has been widely acclaimed as his best book. In it, Bronowski explained his belief in the link between creative activity in the arts and sciences. A *Christian Science Monitor* critic called it "the best statement I have read of why a scientist loves and values his work and of where his work fits into history." Charles Frankel of the *New York Herald Tribune Book Review* noted that "it offers more information and light about the sciences and their relation to the progress of the human spirit than many books ten times as large." C. P. Snow of the *New Yorker* wrote: "*Science and Human Values* is a remarkable book, and the affirmation of a remarkable man. If I were trying to select six works, in order to explain to an intelligent non-scientist something of the deepest meaning of science, Bronowski's would be one of them."

The Ascent of Man, however, was probably Bronowski's most popular achievement. A collection of essays derived from a thirteen-part BBC-TV series, it was a virtual celebration of the development of man's attempts to understand and control nature from prehistoric times to the present. A *Books and Bookmen* critic, calling it Bronowski's "last and greatest creation," noted that "his enthusiasm and compassion illuminate every page. . . . [This book] will do more for the exaltation of the intellect and the happiness of mankind than any amount of lecture notes or committee minutes." *Time* referred to the series achievement as "an eloquent memorial to one whose singular mission was to democratize 'the aristocracy of the intellect' and help his fellow men strain to hear those thoughts of God."

Throughout the years, in spite of what he had observed in man that discouraged him, Bronowski remained optimistic about the future. Having expressed his conviction that acquiring a thorough understanding of the role of violence in modern society is crucial if one seeks to create a "happy society," he speculated on what the future might hold for mankind: "What violence everywhere shows is that there is a real sense of unease in the tension between people as individuals and the society that they believe fulfills them physically but does not yet fulfill their aspirations as individuals.... [We must understand] that every man has a right to be himself, and no man ... has any more right to speak for the state than that man, or you, or you, or I.... It is not ecology that is threatened. It is not the environment that is threatened. It is the human structure of society which I believe to be at risk.... And happily I am a great optimist. I think we shall win.''

BIOGRAPHICAL/CRITICAL SOURCES: Christian Science Monitor, June 5, 1958, June 25, 1974; New York Herald Tribune Book Review, July 13, 1958; New Republic, August 18, 1958; Choice, July, 1974; New York Times, August 23, 1974; Washington Post, August 23, 1974; Newsweek, September 2, 1974, January 27, 1975; Time, September 2, 1974; Publishers Weekly, September 2, 1974; Books and Bookmen, April, 1975; Jacob Bronowski: Twentieth Century Man (interviews), Salk Institute for Biological Studies, 1976; Los Angeles Times Book Review, March 25, 1979.†

—Sketch by Deborah A. Straub

*   *   *

BROOKES, Edgar Harry 1897-

PERSONAL: Born February 4, 1897; son of Job Harry and Emily Elizabeth (Thomas) Brookes; married Heidi Genevieve Baurquin, 1925; married Edith Constance Moe; children: (first marriage) Arthur, Charles, Rosemary Brookes Rittmann, David, Heidi. Education: University of South Africa, M.A., 1920, D.Litt., 1924. Religion: Anglican. Home: 4 Chapter Close, 6 Taunton Rd., Pietermaritzburg 3201, South Africa. Office: University of Natal, Pietermaritzburg, South Africa.

CAREER: University of Pretoria, Transvaal, South Africa, professor, 1920-33; Adams College, Adams Mission Station, South Africa, principal, 1934-45; Parliament of South Africa, Cape Town, senator, 1937-52; University of Natal, Pietermaritzburg, South Africa, professor of history and political science, 1953-62. Military service: Special Service, 1914-15; became sergeant. Member: South African Institute of Race Relations (president, 1930-31, 1955-56, 1960). Awards, honors: Royal African Society medal for dedicated service in Africa; LL.D., University of Cape Town, 1958, and Queen's University, Kingston, Ontario, 1962; D.Litt., University of Natal, 1966.

WRITINGS: History of Native Policy in South Africa, Nesionale Press, 1924; Colour Problems of South Africa, Lovedale, 1934, reprinted, Negro Universities Press, 1980; South Africa in a Changing World, Oxford University Press, 1954; (with N. Hurwitz) Native Reserves of Natal, Oxford University Press, 1957; (with J. B. Macauly) Civil Liberty in South Africa, Oxford University Press, 1959, Greenwood Press, 1973; The Commonwealth Today, University of Natal Press, 1959; The City of God and the Politics of Crisis, Oxford University Press, 1960; Power, Law, Right and Love: A Study in Political Values, Duke University Press, 1963; (with A. Vandenbosch) The City of God and the City of Man in Africa, University of Kentucky Press, 1964; (with C. Webb) History of Natal, University of Natal Press, 1964; Three Letters from Africa, Pendle Hill, 1965; History of the University of Natal, University of Natal Press, 1965; Freedom, Faith, and the Twenty First Century, Ryerson, 1966; Apartheid: A Documentary Study of Modern South Africa, Routledge & Kegan Paul, 1968; White Rule in South Africa, 1830-1910, revised edition, Verry, 1974; A South African Pilgrimage, Raven Books, 1977.

BROOK-SHEPHERD, (Frederick) Gordon 1918-

PERSONAL: Born March 24, 1918, in England; son of Alfred (an architect) and Doreen (Pearson) Brook-Shepherd; married Baroness Sochor, June, 1948; children: Clive Anthony, Nicola. Education: Cambridge University, B.A. (first class honors), 1939. Politics: Leftwing Conservative. Religion: Church of England. Home: 5 South Ter., Knightsbridge, London S.W. 7, England. Agent: Brandt & Brandt, 101 Park Ave., New York, N.Y. 10017. Office: Sunday Telegraph, 135 Fleet St., London E.C.4, England.

CAREER: Daily Telegraph, London, England, foreign correspondent, 1949-60; Sunday Telegraph, London, diplomatic editor, 1960-65, assistant editor, 1965-75, deputy editor, 1975—. Military service: British Army, General Staff, World War II; became lieutenant colonel. Member: Royal Central Asian Society, Royal Institute of International Affairs, P.E.N.; Travellers Club and Roehampton Club (both London).

WRITINGS: Russia's Danubian Empire, Praeger, 1954; The Austrian Odyssey, St, Martin's, 1957; (with Kurt Peter Karfeld) Austria in Color (includes text by Brook-Shepherd), Oesterreichische Staatsdruckerei, 1957; Where the Lion Trod, St. Martin's, 1960; Dollfuss (biography), St. Martin's, 1961, published as Prelude to Infamy: The Story of Chancellor Dollfuss of Austria, Obolensky, 1962; The Anschluss, Lippincott, 1963 (published in England as Anschluss: The Rape of Austria, Macmillan, 1963); Eagle and Unicorn (novel), Weidenfeld & Nicolson, 1966, published as The Eferding Diaries, Lippincott, 1967; The Last Hapsburg, Weybright & Talley, 1968; Between Two Flags, Putnam, 1973; Uncle of Europe (biography of Edward VII), Harcourt, 1976; The Storm Petrels, Harcourt, 1978; November 1918, Collins, in press. Contributor to Holiday, Atlantic Monthly, Esquire, and other periodicals.

AVOCATIONAL INTERESTS: Shooting, fishing, skiing, tennis, music.

BIOGRAPHICAL/CRITICAL SOURCES: New York Times Book Review, February 5, 1967; Best Sellers, April 1, 1969.

*   *   *

BROPHY, James David, Jr. 1926-

PERSONAL: Born October 5, 1926, in Mt. Vernon, N.Y.; son of James David and Mildred (Stall) Brophy; married Elizabeth Bergen, March 26, 1951; children: Sheila, David, Katharine, Elizabeth, James Mark. Education: Attended Massachusetts Institute of Technology, 1944-45; Amherst College, B.A., 1949; Columbia University, M.A., 1950, Ph.D., 1965; attended University of Dijon, 1950-51. Religion: Roman Catholic. Home: 35 Crystal St., Harrison, N.Y. 10528. Office: Department of English, Iona College, New Rochelle, N.Y. 10801.

CAREER: Iona College, New Rochelle, N.Y., instructor, 1951-58, assistant professor, 1958-64, associate professor, 1964-68, professor of English, 1968—, chairman of department, 1968-71, 1980—. Appointed to Wilton Park Conference, British Foreign Office, 1979. Military service: U.S. Navy, 1945-46; became technician second class. Member: Modern Language Association of America, English Institute. Awards, honors: Fulbright fellowship, 1950-51; New York State Russian study grant, 1962; Ford Foundation Russian language grant, 1963, 1964; New York State faculty scholar, 1965; Iona College faculty fellowships for study in England, 1966-67, 1974-75.

WRITINGS: (Editor with Henry Paolucci) The Achievement

of Galileo, Twayne, 1962; *Edith Sitwell: The Symbolist Order,* Southern Illinois University Press, 1968; *W. H. Auden,* Columbia University Press, 1970; (editor with Raymond Porter) *Modern Irish Literature,* Twayne, 1972. Contributor of articles and reviews to *Modern Age, Renascence, Modern Language Notes, Choice,* and other journals.

WORK IN PROGRESS: A book, tentatively entitled *The Poetry of Thomas Kinsella,* for Twayne.

*   *   *

BROSNAN, James Patrick   1929-
(Jim Brosnan)

PERSONAL: Born October 24, 1929, in Cincinnati, Ohio; son of John Patrick and Rose (Brockhoff) Brosnan; married Anne Stewart Pitcher, June 23, 1952; children: Jamie, Timothy, Kimberlee. *Education:* Attended Xavier University, 1947. *Politics:* Independent. *Home:* 7742 West Churchill St., Morton Grove, Ill. 60053. *Agent:* Max Wilkinson, Littauer & Wilkinson, 500 Fifth Ave., New York, N.Y. 10036. *Office: Chicago Daily News,* 401 North Wabash, Chicago, Ill.

CAREER: Professional baseball player, 1947-63, with Chicago Cubs, St. Louis Cardinals, and Cincinnati Reds; member of research and publicity staff, Arthur Meyerhoff, Inc. (advertising and merchandising), 1949-57; American Broadcasting Co. radio network and station WBKB, Chicago, Ill., sports commentator, 1963-65; *Chicago Daily News,* Chicago, sports columnist, 1965—. *Awards, honors:* National Association of Independent Schools award, 1961, for *The Long Season.*

WRITINGS—Under name Jim Brosnan: *The Long Season,* Harper, 1960; *Pennant Race,* Harper, 1962; *Great Baseball Pitchers,* Random House, 1965; *Great Rookies of Major Leagues,* Random House, 1966; *Little League to Big League,* Random House, 1968; *Ron Santo, 3b,* Putnam, 1974; *Ted Simmons,* Putnam, 1977; (contributor) Irving T. Marsh and Edward Ehre, editors, *Best Sports Stories 1977: A Panorama of the 1976 Sports Year with the Year's Top Photographs,* Dutton, 1977. Contributor of articles to *Sports Illustrated, Life, New York Times Magazine, National Review, St. Louis Post-Dispatch, Atlantic Monthly, MacLean's, Boy's Life, Sport, Playboy,* and *Saturday Evening Post.*

WORK IN PROGRESS: Til the Last Man's Out, a novel about baseball; *The Last Season,* a nonfiction journal about a current major league ball club; *Nine Innings,* a book of short stories; a series of juvenile novels about baseball.

BIOGRAPHICAL/CRITICAL SOURCES: Time, September 5, 1960; *New York Times Book Review,* October 16, 1960; *Saturday Evening Post,* May 13, 1961.

*   *   *

BROUDY, Harry S(amuel)   1905-

PERSONAL: Born July 27, 1905, in Filipowa, Poland; son of Michael and Mollie (Wyzanski) Broudy; married Anne Leve, 1932 (died, 1943); married second wife, Dorothy L. Hogarth, August 15, 1947; children: (second marriage) Richard M. *Education:* Attended Massachusetts Institute of Technology, 1924-25; Boston University, A.B., 1929; Harvard University, M.A., 1933, Ph.D., 1935. *Home:* 406 Sunnycrest Ct., Urbana, Ill. 61801. *Office:* 270 Education, University of Illinois, Urbana, Ill.

CAREER: Milford Daily News, Milford, Mass., reporter, 1929-32; Massachusetts Department of Education, Boston, supervisor, 1936-37; State Teachers College at North Adams

(now North Adams State College), North Adams, Mass., professor of philosophy, 1938-49; Framingham State Teachers College (now Framingham State College), Framingham, Mass., professor of philosophy, 1949-57; University of Illinois at Urbana-Champaign, professor of philosophy of education, 1957-74, professor emeritus, 1974—. Visiting distinguished professor, Memorial University of Newfoundland, 1974, and California State University, Los Angeles, 1978; Kappa Delta Pi Lecturer, 1972; Centennial Lecturer, Peabody College, 1976; Damon Lecturer, 1976; Centennial Professor, Texas A&M University, 1976; Charles DeGarmo Lecturer, 1979; Daniel Powell Lecturer, 1980; lecturer, John Dewey Society, 1980. Consultant to U.S. Agency for International Development (Korea), 1969. *Member:* American Association of University Professors, Philosophy of Education Society (president, 1953), Association for Realistic Philosophy (president, 1954-56), American Philosophical Association, American Psychological Association, American Metaphysical Society, Phi Beta Kappa, Phi Kappa Phi. *Awards, honors:* Fellow, Center for the Advanced Study of the Behavioral Sciences, 1967-68; D.H., Oakland University, 1969; LL.D., Eastern Kentucky University, 1980.

WRITINGS: Building a Philosophy of Education, Prentice-Hall, 1954, 2nd edition, 1961; (with Eugene Freel) *Psychology for General Education,* Longmans, Green, 1956; *Paradox and Promise,* Prentice-Hall, 1961; (with B. O. Smith and Joe R. Burnett) *Democracy and Excellence in American Secondary Education,* Rand McNally, 1964; *The Scholars and the Public Schools* (Boyd H. Bode lecture of 1963), Ohio State University Press, 1964; (with J. R. Palmer) *Exemplars of Teaching Method,* Rand McNally, 1965; *The Real World of the Public Schools,* Harcourt, 1972; *Enlightened Cherishing,* University of Illinois Press, 1972; (editor with Robert Ennis and R. Krimmerma) *Philosophy of Educational Research,* Wiley, 1973; *General Education: The Search for a Rationale,* Phi Delta Kappa, 1974; *Truth and Credibility,* Longman, 1981. Editor, *Educational Forum,* 1964-72.

Contributor: John Wild, editor, *The Return to Reason,* Regnery, 1953; Smith and Ennis, editors, *Language and Concepts in Education,* Rand McNally, 1961; Hobart W. Burns and Charles J. Brauner, editors, *Philosophy of Education,* Ronald, 1962; Stanley Elam, editor, *Education and the Structure of Knowledge,* Rand McNally, 1964; H. R. Ziel, editor, *Education and the Productive Society,* Gage, 1965; R. E. Ohm and William G. Monahan, editors, *Educational Administration: Philosophy in Action,* University of Oklahoma Press, 1965; J. Alan Ross and Ralph Thomson, editors, *Knowledge and the Teacher,* Western Washington State College Press, 1965; James C. Stone and Frederick W. Schneider, editors, *Commitment to Teaching,* Crowell, 1965; Ralph A. Smith, editor, *Aesthetics and Criticism in Art Education,* Rand McNally, 1966; Elam, editor, *Improving Teacher Education in the United States,* Phi Delta Kappa, 1967; Edgar L. Morphet and David L. Jesser, editors, *Planning for Effective Utilization of Technology in Education,* Designing Education for the Future Project, 1968; Christopher J. Lucas, editor, *What Is Philosophy of Education?,* Macmillan, 1968.

George Pappas, editor, *Concepts in Art and Education,* Macmillan, 1970; Sheila Schwartz, editor, *Teaching the Humanities,* Macmillan, 1970; Stan Dropkin, Harold Full, and Ernest Schwarcz, editors, *Contemporary American Education,* Macmillan, 1970; Saul B. Robinsohn, editor, *Curriculum Entwicklung,* Klett-Schwann, 1972; Paul F. Doyle, editor, *Educational Judgements,* Routledge & Kegan Paul, 1973; T. W. Hipple, editor, *The Future of Education,*

Goodyear Publishing, 1974; W. Robert Houston, editor, *Exploring Competency-Based Education*, McCutchan, 1974; Eliot W. Eisner, editor, *The Arts, Human Development, and Education*, McCutchan, 1976; James J. Bosco and Stanley S. Robin, editors, *The Hyperactive Child and Stimulant Drugs*, University of Chicago Press, 1976; R. C. Anderson, editor, *Schooling and Acquisition of Knowledge*, Erlbaum Associates, 1977; Louis Rubin, editor, *The In-Service Education of Teachers*, Allyn & Bacon, 1978; K. Strike and K. Egan, editors, *Ethics and Educational Policy*, Routledge & Kegan Paul, 1978; Ralph Tyler, editor, *From Youth to Constructive Adult Life*, McCutchan, 1978; Stephen M. Dobbs, editor, *Arts Education and Back to the Basics*, National Art Education Association, 1979; Ronald Silverman, editor, *Art, Education, and the World of Work*, National Art Education Association, 1980; Rubin, editor, *Critical Issues in Educational Policy*, Allyn & Bacon, 1980; Douglas Sloan, editor, *Education and Values*, Teachers College Press, 1980. Contributor to National Society for the Study of Education yearbooks, 1958, 1970, and 1971. Contributor to professional journals.

WORK IN PROGRESS: Books on aesthetic education, realism in education, and analysis of content in philosophy of education.

SIDELIGHTS: Harry S. Broudy told *CA*: "I am regarded as a specialist in the philosophy of education. My interests at the moment are in the development and promotion of a unified theory of teacher preparation, a place for aesthetic education more central than it now enjoys, and the uses of knowledge."

*   *   *

BROWN, Alexander (Crosby) 1905-

PERSONAL: Born November 30, 1905, in Rosemont, Pa.; son of James Crosby and Mary Agnes (Hewlett) Brown; married Shirley Baysden, 1942; children: Alexander C., Jr., Benjamin Jarratt, Suzanne Baysden, Johanna Hewlett. *Education:* Yale University, B.A., 1928; College of William and Mary, M.A., 1951. *Religion:* Episcopalian. *Home:* 228 James River Dr., Newport News, Va.

CAREER: Mariners Museum, Newport News, Va., corresponding secretary and chief of publications, 1936-42, 1946-50; Daily Press, Inc., Newport News, literary editor, 1951-73. Corresponding secretary, Newport News Public Library, 1950-75. Member, Friends of the Mariners Museum. *Military service:* U.S. Naval Reserve, 1942-64; retired as commander; active duty, 1942-46. *Member:* Steamship Historical Society of America (former director and publications chief), U.S. Naval Historical Foundation, U.S. Naval Institute, Old Dartmouth Historical Society. *Awards, honors:* Jefferson Davis Medal from Bethel chapter of United Daughters of the Confederacy, 1970, for excellence in historical writing; Certificate of Commendation from American Association for State and Local History, 1971, for *The Dismal Swamp Canal* (1970 edition); Distinguished Service Medal from Christopher Newport College, 1974.

WRITINGS: Horizon's Rim, Dodd, 1936; *The Old Bay Line, 1840-1940*, Dietz, 1940; *The Dismal Swamp Canal*, American Neptune, 1946, revised and enlarged edition, Norfolk County Historical Society, 1970; (editor) *Newport News' 325 Years*, City of Newport News, Va., 1946; *Women and Children Last*, Putnam, 1961; *Steam Packets on the Chesapeake*, Cornell Maritime, 1961; *Life with Grover*, Tidewater, 1962; *The Bugs' Picnic* (juvenile), Spadea, 1966; *Dingle Dinosaur's Good Deed* (juvenile), Spadea, 1967; *Chesapeake Landfalls*, Norfolk County Historical Society, 1974; *Long-*

boat to Hawaii, Cornell Maritime, 1974; *The Good Ships of Newport News*, Tidewater, 1976; *Sea-Lingo: Notes on the Language of Mariners*, Mariners Museum, 1980; *Juniper Waterway: A History of the Albemarle and Chesapeake Canal*, University Press of Virginia, 1981. Also author of *For His Dear Sake: A History of St. Andrew's Parish*, 1969, and *Crosses of Tears: The Miracle of the Fairy Stones* (children's operetta), 1971, with Harold Chapman. Associate editor, *American Neptune: A Quarterly Journal of Maritime History*.

WORK IN PROGRESS: A young adult adventure novel, *Adrift*.

SIDELIGHTS: Alexander Brown established his maritime bent on a twenty-seven month, thirty thousand mile cruise around the world under sail with college classmates in a thirty-three-ton schooner yacht. During World War II he was on the staff of Admiral Samuel Eliot Morison, professor and official historian of U.S. naval operations, and assisted Morison in the preparation of his book *History of U.S. Naval Operations in World War II*.

*   *   *

BROWN, Ashley 1923-

PERSONAL: Born December 19, 1923, in Louisville, Ky.; son of Samuel Ashley and Martha (Stoll) Brown. *Education:* Attended Centre College of Kentucky, 1941-43, and Kenyon College, 1943-44; University of Louisville, B.A., 1945; Vanderbilt University, M.A., 1946, Ph.D., 1958; Yale University, graduate study, 1950-51. *Politics:* Democrat. *Home:* 921 Gregg St., Columbia, S.C. 29201. *Office:* Department of English, University of South Carolina, Columbia, S.C.

CAREER: Washington and Lee University, Lexington, Va., instructor, 1946-53; University of California, Santa Barbara, instructor, 1956-59; University of South Carolina, Columbia, assistant professor, 1959-65, associate professor, 1965-71, professor of English and comparative literature, 1971—. Fulbright professor, Federal University of Rio de Janeiro, 1964-65 and 1971-72. *Member:* South Atlantic Modern Language Association, Southeastern Renaissance Conference, Dante Society of America, Wallace Stevens Society.

WRITINGS: (Editor with Robert S. Haller) *The Achievement of Wallace Stevens*, Lippincott, 1962; (editor with John L. Kimmey) *Satire: An Anthology*, Collins & World, 1967.

Editor, with Kimmey, of "Modes of Literature" series; published by C. E. Merrill, 1968: *Comedy; Romance; Tragedy; Tragicomedy*.

Contributor of articles and translations to *Chicago Review, London Magazine, Ploughshares, Sewanee Review, Shenandoah, Southern Review, Spectator*, and other journals in the United States and England.

WORK IN PROGRESS: A collection of essays and memoirs about thirteen American, British, and Brazilian writers; a collection of translations from the Brazilian poet Joao Cabral de Melo Neto.

AVOCATIONAL INTERESTS: Travel and music.

*   *   *

BROWN, Howard Mayer 1930-

PERSONAL: Born April 13, 1930, in Los Angeles, Calif.; son of Alfred Ralph and Florence (Mayer) Brown. *Education:* Harvard University, B.A. (magna cum laude), 1951, M.A., 1954, Ph.D., 1959. *Home:* 1415 East 54th St., Chicago, Ill. *Office:* Department of Music, University of Chicago, 5835 University Ave., Chicago, Ill.

CAREER: Harvard University, Cambridge, Mass., teaching fellow in music, 1954-58; Wellesley College, Wellesley, Mass., instructor in music, 1958-60; University of Chicago, Chicago, Ill., assistant professor, 1960-63, associate professor, 1963-67, professor of music and director of Collegium Musicum, 1967-72; King's College, London, England, King Edward Professor of Music, 1972-74; University of Chicago, Ferdinand Schevill Distinguished Service Professor of Music, 1976—. Director of the Camerata of the Boston Museum of Fine Arts, 1954-60; curator of musical instruments, Smithsonian Institution, Washington, D.C., 1964-65. *Member:* International Musicological Society, American Musicological Society, Societe francaise de musicologie, Galpin Society, Music Teachers National Association, Phi Beta Kappa. *Awards, honors:* Walter Naumburg travelling fellow, Harvard University, 1951-53, in Vienna, Austria; Huber fellow, Wellesley College, summer, 1959, in Paris, France; grants-in-aid, American Council of Learned Societies, 1961-62; Guggenheim fellow, 1963-64; American Association for the Advancement of Science fellow, 1979—.

WRITINGS: Music in the French Secular Theater: 1400-1550, Harvard University Press, 1963; (editor) *Theatrical Chansons in the Fifteenth and Early Sixteenth Centuries,* Harvard University Press, 1963; *Bibliography of Instrumental Music Printed before 1600,* Harvard University Press, 1965; (with Joan Lascelle) *Musical Iconography: A Manual for Cataloguing Musical Subjects in Western Art before 1800,* Harvard University Press, 1972; *Sixteenth-Century Instrumentation,* American Institute of Musicology, 1973; *Embellishing Sixteenth-Century Music,* Oxford University Press, 1976; *Music in the Renaissance,* Prentice-Hall, 1976. Also editor of "Italian Opera Librettos: 1640-1770" series, sixty volumes, Garland Publishing, 1976-79. Contributor of articles and reviews to professional journals.

WORK IN PROGRESS: A Florentine Chansonnier, two volumes, for University of Chicago Press.

*   *   *

BROWN, Marion Marsh   1908-

PERSONAL: Born July 22, 1908, in Brownville, Neb.; daughter of Cassius Henry and Jenevie (Hairgrove) Marsh; married Gilbert S. Brown (a lawyer), 1937 (deceased); children: Paul Marsh. *Education:* Peru State Teachers College (now Peru State College), Peru, Neb., A.B., 1927; University of Nebraska, M.A., 1930; University of Minnesota, graduate study. *Politics:* Republican. *Religion:* Presbyterian. *Home:* 2615 North 52nd St., Omaha, Neb. 68104.

CAREER: Teacher of English and speech in public high schools in Nebraska, 1928-36; Peru State Teachers College (now Peru State College), Peru, Neb., assistant professor of English, 1935-37; Municipal University of Omaha (now University of Nebraska at Omaha), Omaha, Neb., associate professor, 1953-64, professor of English, 1965-67. Writer, mainly for teen-agers. *Member:* American Association of University Women (past president), National Pen Women, National Council of Teachers of English, Nebraska Council of Teachers of English, Nebraska Writers' Guild (past president), Phi Delta Gamma, Sigma Tau Delta, Kappa Delta Pi, Zeta Tau Alpha. *Awards, honors:* Distinguished Service Award, Peru State College, 1979.

WRITINGS: Young Nathan (Junior Literary Guild selection), Westminster, 1949; *Swamp Fox* (Boys' Clubs of America selection), Westminster, 1950; *Frontier Beacon,* Westminster, 1953; *Broad Stripes and Bright Stars* (Children's Book Club selection), Westminster, 1955; *Prairie Teacher,*

Bouregy, 1957; *Learning Words in Context,* Chandler Publishing, 1961, revised edition, Harper, 1974; *A Nurse Abroad,* Bouregy, 1963; (with Ruth Crone) *The Silent Storm* (Junior Literary Guild selection), Abingdon, 1963; *Stuart's Landing,* Westminster, 1968; (with Crone) *Willa Cather: The Woman and Her Works,* Scribner, 1970; *Marnie,* Westminster, 1971; *The Pauper Prince,* Crescent, 1973; *The Brownville Story,* Nebraska Historical Society, 1974; (with Crone) *Only One Point of the Compass: Willa Cather in the Northeast,* Archer Editions, 1980; *Homeward the Arrow's Flight,* Abingdon, 1980. Contributor of about two hundred short stories and articles to magazines.

SIDELIGHTS: Marion Marsh Brown told *CA:* "One of my editors once said that I write for 'the young in heart, age nine to ninety.' Although I have directed a large portion of my writing to young people in middle school through high school, it is true that adults read and enjoy my books. I hope this says I have something to say which is of value.

"I have always enjoyed young people and believe that I understand some of their growing-up problems. So, through my writing, I have tried to help them confront their problems from a sound value base, and to give them a feeling of continuity with the past which I believe is essential in developing maturity."

*   *   *

BROWN, Myra Berry   1918-

PERSONAL: Born October 27, 1918, in Minneapolis, Minn.; daughter of Louis (a salesman) and Marion (Hosenpud) Berry; married Ned Brown (a literary agent), May 2, 1942; children: Lorna, Elizabeth, Jonathan. *Education:* B.A. from University of California, Los Angeles. *Politics:* Democrat. *Religion:* Jewish. *Home:* 21640 Pacific Coast Hwy., Malibu, Calif. 90265.

CAREER: Paramount Pictures, Hollywood, Calif., secretary, 1939-41; A. and S. Lyons, Beverly Hills, Calif., literary agent, 1942-44; Los Angeles County Department of Health, Los Angeles, Calif., Community discussion leader, 1968-70. Brownie trainer, Los Angeles Council of Girl Scouts; active in Family-School Alliance of University of California, Los Angeles Laboratory Elementary School. *Member:* P.E.N.

WRITINGS—All published by F. Watts, except as indicated: *Company's Coming for Dinner,* 1959; *First Night Away from Home,* 1960; *My Daddy's Visiting Our School Today,* 1961; *Flower Girl,* 1961; *Somebody's Pup,* 1961; *Benjy's Blanket,* 1962; *Ice Cream for Breakfast,* 1963; *Birthday Boy,* 1964; *Casey's Sore Throat Day,* 1964; *Amy and the New Baby,* 1965; *Pip Camps Out,* Golden Gate, 1966; *Sandy Signs His Name,* 1967; *Best Friends,* Golden Gate, 1967; *If You Have a Doll,* 1967; *Pip Moves Away,* Golden Gate, 1967; *Where's Jeremy?,* Golden Gate, 1968; *Best of Luck,* Golden Gate, 1969. Children's book reviewer, *Los Angeles Times,* 1960 and 1961.

*   *   *

BROWNE, Harry   1933-

PERSONAL: Born June 17, 1933, in New York, N.Y.; son of Bradford (a radio announcer and producer and Christian Science practitioner) and Cecil Margaret Browne; married Gloria Maxwell, June 9, 1956 (divorced April, 1964); children: Autumn Lee. *Education:* Attended Los Angeles Valley Junior College. *Agent:* Collier Associates, 280 Madison Ave., New York, N.Y. 10016.

CAREER: James E. Munford Co. (advertising agency), Los

Angeles, Calif., account executive and salesman, 1958-61; John Birch Society, Los Angeles, area manager, 1961-62; American Way Features, Inc. (newspaper feature service), Los Angeles, owner, writer, and editor, 1962-67; Evelyn Wood Reading Dynamics, Los Angeles, marketing manager, 1967; Economic Research Counselors (investment counselors), Los Angeles, member of sales and service staff, 1967-70; writer, 1970—. *Military service:* U.S. Army, 1953-56.

WRITINGS: How You Can Profit from the Coming Devaluation, Arlington House, 1970; *How I Found Freedom in an Unfree World,* Macmillan, 1973; *You Can Profit from a Monetary Crisis,* Macmillan, 1974, revised edition, Bantam, 1975; *The Complete Guide to Swiss Banks,* McGraw, 1976; *New Profits from the Monetary Crisis,* Morrow, 1978. Also author, with Terry Coxon, of *Inflation-Proofing Your Investments,* 1981. Author of newspaper columns, "The American Way" and "Between the Bookends," published in small-town weekly and daily newspapers, 1962-67. Editor of *Freedom* (magazine of Liberty Amendment Committee), 1962-66.

WORK IN PROGRESS: Why People Hate Opera (and What They're Missing).

SIDELIGHTS: When Harry Browne first embarked on a program of self-education, he considered the subject of economics to be the least exciting. By 1964, however, Browne had changed his mind and was offering private courses in the subject. He writes: "I am motivated to write about economics because the subject has been so distorted by economists and politicians—despite its simplicity. I had to be pushed into writing my first book, because I didn't think there was a market for it ... There's a market and a need, and I've grown rich satisfying that need."

Browne continues: "I have no other affiliations because I'm a non-joiner. I went to work for the John Birch Society in 1961 to work against government intervention—but it was a mistake soon rectified."

AVOCATIONAL INTERESTS: Opera, classical music, travel, love, playing with speculative investments, making money, reading, lying on the couch ("not necessarily in that order").

BIOGRAPHICAL/CRITICAL SOURCES: Washington Post Book World, October 29, 1978.

*   *   *

BRUCE, F(rederick) F(yvie) 1910-

PERSONAL: Born October 12, 1910, in Elgin, Scotland; son of Peter Fyvie and Mary (MacLennan) Bruce; married Betty Davidson, 1936; children: Iain Anthony Fyvie, Sheila Davidson. *Education:* University of Aberdeen, M.A., 1932; Cambridge University, B.A., 1934, M.A., 1945; University of Vienna, graduate study, 1934-35. *Home:* The Crossways, Temple Rd., Buxton, Derbyshire SK17 9BA, England.

CAREER: University of Edinburgh, Edinburgh, Scotland, lecturer in Greek, 1935-38; University of Leeds, Leeds, England, lecturer in Greek, 1938-47; University of Sheffield, Sheffield, England, professor of Biblical history and literature, 1947-59; University of Manchester, Manchester, England, Rylands Professor of Biblical Criticism and Exegesis, 1959-78, professor emeritus, 1978—. *Member:* Society for Old Testament Study (president, 1965), Studiorum Novi Testamenti Societas, Victoria Institute (president, 1958-65), British Academy (fellow). *Awards, honors:* D.D., University of Aberdeen, 1957; Burkitt Medal for Biblical studies, British Academy, 1979.

WRITINGS: The Books and the Parchments, Pickering & Inglis, 1950; *Second Thoughts on the Dead Sea Scrolls,* Paternoster, 1956; *The Spreading Flame,* Paternoster, 1958; *The English Bible,* Lutterworth, 1961; *Israel and the Nations,* Paternoster, 1963; *An Expanded Paraphrase of the Epistles of Paul,* Paternoster, 1965; *New Testament History,* Doubleday, 1971; *Paul: Apostle of the Heart Set Free,* Eerdmans, 1978; *Men and Movements in the Primitive Church,* Paternoster, 1979; *In Retrospect: Remembrance of Things Past,* Pickering & Inglis, 1980. Also author of commentaries on various books of the Bible; contributor of articles to philology and theology journals. Editor of *The Evangelical Quarterly,* 1949-80, and *Palestine Exploration Quarterly,* 1957-71; joint editor of *Bible Guides,* published in the United States by Abingdon.

WORK IN PROGRESS: Further Biblical commentaries.

*   *   *

BRUMBAUGH, Robert Sherrick 1918-

PERSONAL: Born December 2, 1918, in Oregon, Ill.; son of Aaron J. and Ruth (Sherrick) Brumbaugh; married Ada Z. Steele, June 5, 1940; children: Robert Conrad, Susan Christianna, Joanna Pauline. *Education:* University of Chicago, A.B., 1938, M.A., 1938, Ph.D., 1942. *Home:* 150 Ridgewood Ave., Hamden, Conn. 06517. *Office:* Department of Philosophy, Yale University, New Haven, Conn. 06520.

CAREER: Bowdoin College, Brunswick, Me., assistant professor of philosophy, 1946-48; Indiana University, Bloomington, assistant professor of philosophy, 1948-50; Yale University, New Haven, Conn., assistant professor, 1951-54, associate professor, 1955-60, professor of philosophy, 1961—. *Military service:* U.S. Army, 1943-46. *Member:* Metaphysical Society of America (counsellor, 1961-65; president, 1965-66), American Philosophical Association, American Association of University Professors (chapter president, 1961-62; member of national council, 1975-78), Society for Ancient Greek Philosophy, Connecticut Academy of Arts and Sciences, Phi Beta Kappa.

WRITINGS: (With N. P. Stallknecht) *The Spirit of Western Philosophy,* Longmans, Green, 1950; (with Stallknecht) *The Compass of Philosophy,* Longmans, Green, 1954; *Plato's Mathematical Imagination,* Indiana University Press, 1954; *Plato on the One: The Hypotheses in the Parmenides and Their Interpretation,* Yale University Press, 1961; (editor with Rulon Wells) *Plato Manuscripts,* [New Haven], 1962, new edition published as *The Plato Manuscripts: A New Index,* Yale University Press, 1968; *Plato for the Modern Age,* Collier, 1962; (with N. M. Lawrence) *Philosophers on Education,* Houghton, 1963; *The Philosophers of Greece,* Crowell, 1965; *Ancient Greek Gadgets and Machines,* Crowell, 1966; (editor) *Six Trials,* Crowell, 1969; (with Lawrence) *Philosophical Themes in Modern Education,* Houghton, 1973; *The Most Mysterious Manuscript: The Voynich Roger Bacon Cipher MS,* Southern Illinois University Press, 1978. Contributor to journals.

SIDELIGHTS: Robert Brumbaugh told *CA:* "One very important thesis that I hope to demonstrate in my writing about philosophy and education is that many of the undesirable features of twentieth century life, which are popularly thought of as 'bad luck,' are rather consequences of bad metaphysics. Given a generally accepted 'common sense' that is out of phase with reality, it is no surprise to find institutions and policy decisions unrealistic and unsuccessful."

BRUSSEL, James Arnold 1905-

PERSONAL: Born April 22, 1905, in New York, N.Y.; son of A. Stanley and Rose (Schwarzwald) Brussel; married Audrey Schuman, March 7, 1957; children: John, Judith. Education: University of Pennsylvania, B.S., 1926, M.D., 1929; postgraduate study at Columbia University and New York Psychiatric Institute. Religion: Hebrew. Home: 175 West 12th St., New York, N.Y. Agent: Oliver G. Swan, Collier Associates, 280 Madison Ave., New York, N.Y. 10016.

CAREER: Beth Israel Hospital, New York City, intern, two years; Department of Mental Hygiene, New York City, employee, 1931-69, assistant commissioner, 1952-69. Certified by American Board of Psychiatry and Neurology in both specialities; certified mental hospital administrator. Consultant, Veterans Administration Hospital, Samson, N.Y., 1946-48, and New York State Social Welfare Department. Military service: U.S. Army, Medical Corps, 1940-46, 1951-52; chief of neuropsychiatric service at various Army hospitals and aboard hospital ship. Member: American College of Physicians (fellow), American Medical Association, American Psychiatric Association, American Association for the Advancement of Science, New York Academy of Medicine, New York State and County Medical Societies. Awards, honors: American Physicians Literary Guild prizes.

WRITINGS: The Rorschach Psychodiagnostic Method, New York State Hospital Press, 1942, revised edition, 1950; Just Murder, Darling, Scribner, 1959; Layman's Guide to Psychiatry, Barnes & Noble, 1961, 2nd edition, 1967; Medical Aid Encyclopedia for the Home, Stravon, 1965; Mother's Encyclopedia, Parents Institute, 1965; Layman's Dictionary of Mental Health, Barnes & Noble, 1965; Casebook of a Crime Psychiatrist, Geis, 1968; The Physician's Concise Handbook of Psychiatry, Brunner, 1969; (with Theodore Irwin) Instant Shrink: How to Become an Expert Psychiatrist in Ten Easy Lessons, Cowles, 1971; (with Irwin) Understanding and Overcoming Depression, Hawthorn, 1973. Contributor to Encyclopedia Americana, 1948-60, and World Encyclopedia. Contributor of articles to New Yorker, Life and Health, Catholic Digest, New York Times, Cosmopolitan, Medical Economics, Daily Telegraph, and other magazines, newspapers, and professional journals.

SIDELIGHTS: James Arnold Brussel is a former tympanist with the New York Doctors' Orchestral Society and the Queens Symphony Orchestra. In addition to his interest in music, Brussel is also a cartoonist; his work has appeared in such publications as Judge and Army.

BIOGRAPHICAL/CRITICAL SOURCES: Atlantic, January, 1969; Antiquarian Bookman, April 19, 1971.

*   *   *

BRYER, Jackson R(obert) 1937-

PERSONAL: Born September 11, 1937, in New York, N.Y.; son of Joseph Jerome (a lawyer) and Muriel (Jackson) Bryer; married Deborah Churchill Chase, August 27, 1960 (divorced April, 1972); children: Kathryn Chase, Jeffrey Russell, Elizabeth Jackson. Education: Friends Seminary, New York, N.Y., diploma, 1955; Amherst College, B.A., 1959; Columbia University, M.A., 1960; University of Wisconsin, Ph.D., 1965. Religion: Congregational. Home: 2254 Georgian Woods Pl., Wheaton, Md. 20902. Office: Department of English, University of Maryland, University College, College Park, Md. 20742.

CAREER: University of Maryland, College Park, instructor in English department, 1964—. Member: Modern Language Association of America.

WRITINGS: (With Samuel French Morse and Joseph N. Riddel) Wallace Stevens Checklist and Bibliography of Stevens Criticism, Alan Swallow, 1963; (with Robert A. Rees) A Checklist of Emerson Criticism, 1951-1961, Transcendental, 1964; The Critical Reputation of F. Scott Fitzgerald: A Bibliographical Study, Shoe String, 1967; (contributor) Irving Malin, editor, Critical Views of Isaac Bashevis Singer, New York University Press, 1969; Fifteen Modern American Authors: A Survey of Research and Criticism, Duke University Press, 1969, revised edition published as Sixteen Modern American Authors: A Survey of Research and Criticism, Norton, 1973; (editor with Matthew J. Bruccoli) F. Scott Fitzgerald in His Own Time: A Miscellany, Kent State University Press, 1971; (editor with John Kuehl) Dear Scott—Dear Max: The Fitzgerald-Perkins Correspondence, Scribner, 1971; (with Eugene Harding) Hamlin Garland and the Critics: An Annotated Bibliography, Whitston Publishing, 1973; Louis Auchincloss and His Critics: A Bibliographical Record, G. K. Hall, 1977; William Styron: A Reference Guide, G. K. Hall, 1978; F. Scott Fitzgerald: The Critical Reception, B. Franklin, 1978; (with M. Thomas Inge and Maurice Duke) Black American Writers: Bibliographical Essays, St. Martin's, 1978; (with Adrian M. Shapiro and Kathleen Field) Carson McCullers: A Descriptive Listing and Annotated Bibliography of Criticism, Garland Publishing, 1980. Contributor to Texas Studies, Modern Drama, Modern Fiction Studies, Books Abroad, Bulletin of Bibliography, New Mexico Quarterly, and other periodicals.

WORK IN PROGRESS: A history of The Little Review.

*   *   *

BUCHANAN, George (Henry Perrott) 1904-

PERSONAL: Born January 9, 1904, in Larne, Northern Ireland; son of Henry and Florence (Moore) Buchanan; married Janet Margesson, August 22, 1952 (died, 1968); married Sandra McCloy, 1974; children: (first marriage) Florence, Emily. Education: Attended Campbell College and University of Belfast. Home: 27 Ashley Gardens, Westminster, London, England.

CAREER: Times, London, England, sub-editor, 1930-35; News Chronicle, London, columnist and drama critic, 1935-38; author and poet. Chairman, Northern Ireland Town and Country Development Committee, 1949-53. Military service: Royal Air Force, Coastal Command, 1940-45; served as operations officer. Member: European Society of Culture (member of executive council, 1954-80), International P.E.N. (member of executive committee, London, 1960-64); Athenaeum and Savile Clubs (both London).

WRITINGS: Passage Through the Present (journal), Constable, 1932, Dutton, 1933; Dance Night (three-act comedy; first produced in London at Embassy Theatre, 1934), Samuel French, 1935; A London Story, Constable, 1935, Dutton, 1936; Words for Tonight (journal), Constable, 1936; Rose Forbes: The Biography of an Unknown Woman (novel), Constable, 1937, augmented edition, Faber, 1950; Entanglement, Constable, 1938, Appleton, 1939; Serious Pleasures: The Intelligent Person's Guide to London, London Transport, 1938, 2nd edition, 1939; The Soldier and the Girl, Heinemann, 1940; A Place to Live (novel), Faber, 1952; Bodily Responses (poems), Gaberbocchus, 1958; Green Seacoast (autobiographical account of childhood in Ireland), Gaberbocchus, 1959, Red Dust, 1968; Conversation with Strangers (poems), Gaberbocchus, 1961; Morning Papers (autobiography), Gaberbocchus, 1965; Annotations (poetry), Carcanet, 1970; Naked Reason (novel), Holt, 1971; Minute-Book of a

City (poems), Carcanet, 1972; *Inside Traffic* (poems), Carcanet, 1976; *The Politics of Culture* (essays), Menard Press, 1977; *Possible Being* (poems), Carcanet, 1980.

Unpublished plays: "A Trip to the Castle," first produced in London at Arts Theatre, 1960; "Tresper Revolution," first produced in London at Arts Theatre, 1961; "War Song," first produced in London at Hampstead Theatre Club, 1965. Book reviewer for *Times Literary Supplement*, 1928-40.

WORK IN PROGRESS: Poems.

*   *   *

BUCHANAN, James McGill   1919-

PERSONAL: Born October 3, 1919, in Murfreesboro, Tenn.; son of James M. and Lila (Scott) Buchanan; married Anne Bakke. *Education:* Middle Tennessee State College (now University), B.S., 1940; University of Tennessee, M.A., 1941; University of Chicago, Ph.D., 1948. *Home:* 207 Eakin St., Blacksburg, Va. *Office:* Center for Public Choice, Virginia Polytechnic Institute, Blacksburg, Va. 24061.

CAREER: University of Tennessee, Knoxville, associate professor of economics, 1948-51; Florida State University, Tallahassee, professor of economics, 1951-56; University of Virginia, Charlottesville, professor of economics, 1956-68; University of California, Los Angeles, professor of economics, 1968-69; Virginia Polytechnic Institute, Blacksburg, University Distinguished Professor, 1969—. *Military service:* U.S. Naval Reserve, 1941-45; awarded Bronze Star. *Member:* American Economic Association (executive committee, 1966-68), Royal Economic Society, Southern Economic Association (president, 1963). *Awards, honors:* Fulbright research scholar, Italy, 1955-56; Fulbright visiting professor, Cambridge University, 1961-62.

WRITINGS: (With C. L. Allen and M. R. Colberg) *Prices, Income, and Public Policy*, McGraw, 1954, 2nd edition, 1959; *Public Principles of Public Debt*, Irwin, 1958; *The Public Finances*, Irwin, 1960, revised edition, 1965; *Fiscal Theory and Political Economy*, University of North Carolina Press, 1960; (with Gordon Tullock) *The Calculus of Consent*, University of Michigan Press, 1962; *Public Finance in Democratic Process*, University of North Carolina Press, 1966; *Demand and Supply of Public Goods*, Rand McNally, 1969; *Cost and Choice*, Markham, 1970; (with Nicos E. Devletoglou) *Academia in Anarchy: An Economic Diagnosis*, Basic Books, 1970; *The Limits of Liberty*, University of Chicago Press, 1975; (with R. Wagner) *Democracy in Deficit*, Academic Press, 1977; *Freedom in Constitutional Contract*, Texas A & M University Press, 1978; *What Should Economists Do?*, Liberty Fund, 1979; (with G. Brennan) *The Power to Tax*, Cambridge University Press, 1980. Contributor to professional journals.

BIOGRAPHICAL/CRITICAL SOURCES: Saturday Review, February 21, 1970; *National Review*, June 30, 1970.

*   *   *

BUCHER, Charles A(ugustus)   1912-

PERSONAL: Born October 2, 1912, in Conesus, N.Y.; son of Grover C. and Elizabeth (Barr) Bucher; married Jacqueline Dubois, August 24, 1941; children: Diana, Richard, Nancy, Gerald. *Education:* Ohio Wesleyan University, A.B., 1937; Columbia University, M.A., 1941; New York University, Ph.D., 1948; Yale University, post-doctoral study. *Home:* 4239 Pinecrest Circle W., Las Vegas, Nev. 89121. *Office:* Department of Physical Education, University of Nevada, Las Vegas, Nev. 89109.

CAREER: Elementary and high school teacher and vice-principal in East Pembroke, N.Y., and Pleasantville, N.Y., 1937-41; taught at New Haven State Teachers College, 1946-50; New York University, New York, N.Y., 1950-80, became professor of education; University of Nevada, Las Vegas, professor of physical education. Consulting editor, Appleton-Century-Crofts, Inc. *Military service:* U.S. Air Force, 1941-46; became captain. *Member:* National Education Association, American Alliance for Health, Physical Education, Recreation, and Dance (fellow), American College of Sports Medicine (fellow), National College Physical Education Association, American School Health Association (fellow), Philippine Association for Health, Physical Education and Recreation (life member). *Awards, honors:* School Bell Award from National Education Association, 1960.

WRITINGS: Foundations of Physical Education, Mosby, 1952, 8th edition, 1979; *Methods and Materials for Physical Education and Recreation: School and Community Activities*, Mosby, 1954; *Administration of School Health and Physical Education Programs*, Mosby, 1955, 4th edition published as *Administration of School and College Health and Physical Education Programs*, 1967, 7th edition published as *Administration of Physical Education and Athletic Programs*, 1979; (with Evelyn Reade) *Physical Education in the Modern Elementary School*, Macmillan, 1958, 2nd edition published as *Physical Education and Health in the Elementary School*, 1964, 3rd edition, 1971; (with Eugene Smith Wilson) *College Ahead!: A Guide for High School Students and Their Parents*, Harcourt, 1958, revised edition published as *College Ahead!: A Guide for High School Students*, 1961; (with Constance Koenig and Milton Barnhard) *Methods and Materials for Secondary School Physical Education*, Mosby, 1961, 5th edition, 1978; *Interscholastic Athletics at the Junior High School Level*, State Education Department, University of the State of New York, 1965; (with Ralph K. Dupree, Jr.) *Athletics in Schools and Colleges*, Center for Applied Research in Education, 1965; (with Elinar A. Olsen and Carl E. Willgoose) *The Foundations of Health*, Appleton, 1967, new edition, 1978; (with Helmuth W. Joel and Gertrude A. Joel) *Guiding Your Child Toward College*, Abingdon, 1967; *Physical Education for Life*, McGraw, 1969; (editor with Myra Goldman) *Dimensions of Physical Education*, Mosby, 1969, new edition, 1974; *Administrative Dimensions of Health and Physical Education Programs, Including Athletic*, Mosby, 1971; *Recreation for Today's Society*, Prentice-Hall, 1974; *Health*, Silver Burdett, 1981; *Physical Education: Change and Challenge*, Mosby, 1981. Contributor of articles to newspapers and magazines, including *Manila Times* and other foreign publications.

BIOGRAPHICAL/CRITICAL SOURCES: Saturday Review, February 15, 1969.

*   *   *

BUCHER, Francois   1927-

PERSONAL: Born June 11, 1927, in Lausanne, Switzerland; son of Alois and Gabrielle (Zundel) Bucher; married Elizabeth R. Ditter, 1954. *Education:* Gymnasium Zurich, B.A., 1947; graduate studies at University of Zurich and University of Rome; University of Bern, Ph.D., 1955. *Office:* Department of Art, Florida State University, Tallahassee, Fla. 32306.

CAREER: University of Bern, Bern, Switzerland, lecturer, 1952; University of Minnesota, Minneapolis, instructor, 1953-54; Yale University, New Haven, Conn., assistant professor, 1954-60; Brown University, Providence, R.I., associate professor, 1960-63; Princeton University, Princeton, N.J., professor, 1963-69; State University of New York at Binghamton, professor, 1970-77; Florida State University, Tallahassee, professor, 1978—. *Member:* College Art Association of America, Mediaeval Academy, International Center for Medieval Art (secretary, 1960-64), Society of Architectural Historians (director), Academy of Spoleto. *Awards, honors:* M.A., Brown University, 1961; Guggenheim fellowship; Institute of Advanced Studies fellowship.

WRITINGS: Notre Dame de Bonmont and the Earliest Cistercian Monasteries of Switzerland, Benteli Ed., 1957; *Josef Albers: Despite Straight Lines,* Yale University Press, 1961; *Pamplona Bibles,* two volumes, Yale University Press, 1971; *Architector,* two volumes, Abaris, 1980. Contributor of articles to professional journals in the United States and abroad. Editor of *Gesta.*

*   *   *

BUCKLEY, Helen E(lizabeth) 1918-

PERSONAL: Born June 6, 1918, in Syracuse, N.Y.; daughter of James F. (an office manager) and Bridget (Horan) Buckley; married Frank E. Simkewicz (a newspaper advertising salesman), January, 1971; children: Niesha (daughter). *Education:* Syracuse University, B.S., 1945, M.S., 1949; Columbia University, Ed.D., 1962. *Home:* 74 West Cayuga St., Oswego, N.Y.

CAREER: Elementary school teacher, Syracuse, N.Y., 1942-49; State University of New York College at Oswego, teacher, 1949-61, professor of English, beginning 1961; part-time teacher, Syracuse University, Syracuse, N.Y. *Member:* National League of American Pen Women, National Education Association, Children's Literature Association, National Council of Teachers of English, New York State Teachers Association, Oswego Art Guild, Friends of Library. *Awards, honors:* Best teacher of the year award, State University of New York at Oswego, 1980.

WRITINGS—All juveniles; all published by Lothrop: *Grandfather and I* (Junior Literary Guild selection), 1959; *Grandmother and I,* 1961; *Where Did Josie Go?,* 1962; *Some Cheese for Charles,* 1963; *My Sister and I,* 1963; *Josie and the Snow,* 1964; *The Little Boy and the Birthdays* (Literary Guild selection), 1965; *Too Many Crackers,* 1966; *Josie's Buttercup,* 1967; *The Little Pig in the Cupboard,* 1968; *The Wonderful Little Boy,* 1970; *Michael Is Brave,* 1971. Contributor of articles to journals.

SIDELIGHTS: Helen E. Buckley's story "The Little Boy" is the basis for the song "Flowers Are Red" by Harry Chapin. Buckley's books have been translated into German and Japanese.

*   *   *

BUCKLEY, Jerome Hamilton 1917-

PERSONAL: Born August 30, 1917, in Toronto, Ontario, Canada; naturalized U.S. citizen, 1948; son of James O. and Madeline (Morgan) Buckley; married Elizabeth Jane Adams, 1943; children: Nicholas, Victoria, Eleanor. *Education:* University of Toronto, B.A., 1939; Harvard University, M.A., 1940, Ph.D., 1942. *Politics:* Democrat. *Religion:* Episcopalian. *Home:* 191 Common St., Belmont, Mass. 02178. *Office:* Widener Library, Harvard University, Cambridge, Mass. 02138.

CAREER: University of Wisconsin—Madison, 1942-54, began as instructor, became professor of English; Columbia

University, New York, N.Y., professor of English, 1954-61; Harvard University, Cambridge, Mass., professor of English, 1961-75, Gurney Professor of English Literature, 1975—. Summer and visiting professor at numerous universities. *Member:* International Association of University Professors of English, Modern Language Association of America, Academy of Literary Studies, American Academy of Arts and Sciences, Tennyson Society (vice-president). *Awards, honors:* Guggenheim fellowship, 1946-47, 1964; Christian Gauss Prize; Phi Beta Kappa book award, 1952.

WRITINGS: William Ernest Henley, Princeton University Press, 1945; *The Victorian Temper,* Harvard University Press, 1951, 2nd edition, 1969; (co-editor) *Poetry of the Victorian Period,* Scott, Foresman, 1955, revised edition, 1965; (editor) *Poems of Tennyson,* Houghton, 1958; *Tennyson: The Growth of a Poet,* Harvard University Press, 1960; (co-editor) *Masters of British Literature,* Houghton, 1962; (editor) Tennyson, *Idylls of the King,* Houghton, 1963; *The Triumph of Time,* Harvard University Press, 1966; *Victorian Poets and Prose Writers,* Appleton, 1966, 2nd edition, AHM Publishing, 1977; (editor) *The Pre-Raphaelites,* Random House, 1968; *Season of Youth,* Harvard University Press, 1974; (editor) *The Worlds of Victorian Fiction,* Harvard University Press, 1975. Also co-editor of *Twelve Hundred Years,* 1949. Contributor to encyclopedias. Contributor of articles and reviews to journals. Advisor to *Victorian Studies, Victorian Poetry, Clio,* and *Review.*

WORK IN PROGRESS: A study of English autobiography.

*   *   *

BUDD, Louis J(ohn) 1921-

PERSONAL: Born August 26, 1921, in St. Louis, Mo.; son of Vincent and Zofia (Kajszo) Budrewicz; married Isabelle Amelia Marx, March 3, 1945; children: Cathy Lou, David Harry. *Education:* University of Missouri, B.A., 1941, M.A., 1942; University of Wisconsin, Ph.D., 1949. *Home:* 2753 McDowell St., Durham, N.C. 27705. *Office:* Department of English, Duke University, Durham, N.C.

CAREER: University of Kentucky, Lexington, 1949-52, began as instructor, became assistant professor of English; Duke University, Durham, N.C., associate professor, 1952-66, professor of English, 1966—, chairman of department, 1973-79. Visiting summer professor at Washington University, St. Louis, Mo., 1953, and Northwestern University, 1961; Fulbright lecturer in India, May, 1966 and October-November, 1972; lecturer at University of Damascus, June, 1978. Chairman of Jay B. Hubbell Center for American Literature Historiography; member of advisory committee, American Studies Research Centre (Hyderabad, India); consultant on English usage, Southern Kraft Div., International Paper Co., summer, 1959. *Military service:* U.S. Army Air Forces, 1942-45; became second lieutenant. *Member:* American Association of University Professors (chapter president, 1971-72), International Association of University Professors of English, American Humor Studies Association (vice-president, 1977-78), Phi Beta Kappa (chapter president, 1963-64). *Awards, honors:* Guggenheim fellow, 1965-66; travel grants from American Philosophical Association, 1956, 1970, 1973.

WRITINGS: (With George K. Smart and Thomas Marshall) *Literature and Society: 1950-1955,* University of Miami Press, 1956; *Mark Twain: Social Philosopher,* Indiana University Press, 1962; *Robert Herrick,* Twayne, 1971; *A Listing of and Selection from Newspaper and Magazine Interviews with Samuel L. Clemens,* ALR Press, 1977; (editor with others) *Toward a New American Literary History: Essays in Honor of Arlin Turner*, Duke University Press, 1980. Contributor to professional journals. Managing editor, *American Literature*, 1979—.

WORK IN PROGRESS: A multi-volume edition of Mark Twain's social and political writings; a book-length study of Mark Twain's public image from 1870 to 1910.

*   *   *

BUDUROWYCZ, Bohdan B(asil) 1921-

PERSONAL: Born September 8, 1921, in Zukow, Poland; son of Ivan and Mary Helen (Lewicki) Budurowycz; married Jean Anne Strazdas, November 29, 1979. *Education:* Attended Philosophic-Theological College, Regensburg, Germany, 1946-48; University of Toronto, B.A., 1952, M.A., 1953, B.L.S., 1955; Columbia University, Ph.D., 1958. *Religion:* Greek Catholic. *Home:* 4 Hazelridge Dr., Toronto, Ontario, Canada M84 4C8. *Office:* Department of Slavic Studies, University of Toronto, Toronto, Ontario, Canada M5S 1A1.

CAREER: Free-lance writer and translator, Toronto, Ontario, Canada, 1949-54; University of Toronto, Toronto, library bibliographer, 1959-65, associate professor, 1965-77, professor of Slavic studies, 1977—. *Member:* Canadian Institute of Ukranian Studies, Polish Institute of Arts and Sciences in America, Canadian Association of Slavists, National Geographic Society, Shevchenko Scientific Society, Beta Phi Mu. *Awards, honors:* Reuben W. Leonard fellowship; Ford Foundation fellowship; fellowship of the program on East Central Europe, Columbia University; Pilsudski Institute of America Anniversary Prize.

WRITINGS: Polish-Soviet Relations, 1932-1939, Columbia University Press, 1963; (contributor) *Soviet Foreign Relations and World Communism*, edited by T. T. Hammond, Princeton University Press, 1965; *Slavic and East European Resources in Canadian Academic and Research Libraries*, National Library of Canada, 1976; (editor) Danuta Irena Bienkowska, *Between Shores: Poetry and Prose*, Poets' & Painters' Press, 1978. Contributor to periodicals.

*   *   *

BUEHR, Walter Franklin 1897-1971

PERSONAL: Born May 14, 1897, in Chicago, Ill.; died January 2, 1971, in Carmel, Calif.; son of Frederick A. and Madeline (Franckle) Buehr; married Camilla Goodwyn, 1938; children: Joan Buehr Hart, Cynthia Buehr Haas, Wendy, Stephen. *Education:* Attended Detroit School of Design, three years, Philadelphia School of Industrial Arts, one and one-half years, and Art Students' League of New York, one year.

CAREER: Clerk with Grand Trunk Railroad and Dodge Brothers, Detroit, Mich., 1913-16; J. L. Hudson Co., Detroit, artist, 1919; Art Students' League, New York, N.Y., instructor, 1943-50; free-lance artist and writer, 1920-71. *Military service:* U.S. Army Engineers, 1917-19; became first sergeant; received active service medal with three battle clasps. *Member:* Hopetown Sailing Club. *Awards, honors:* Gold Medal, Art Directors Club; *Warriors' Weapons* selected by American Library Association as one of 10 best reference library books.

WRITINGS—All juveniles; all self-illustrated; published by Putnam, except as indicated: *Ships and Life Afloat*, Scribner, 1953; *The Story of Locks*, Scribner, 1953; *Through the Locks*, 1954; *Treasure: The Story of Money and Its Safe-*

guarding, 1955; *Harbors and Cargoes*, 1955; *Harvest of the Sea*, Morrow, 1955; *Ships of the Great Lakes*, 1956; *Meat: From Ranch to Table*, Morrow, 1956; *Trucks and Trucking*, 1957; *Knights, Castles, and Feudal Life*, 1957; *Oil: Today's Black Magic*, Morrow, 1957; *Railroads*, 1958; *Underground Riches*, Morrow, 1958; *Cargoes in the Sky*, 1958; *Sending the Word: The Story of Communication*, 1959; *Bread*, Morrow, 1959; *The Crusaders*, 1959; *The Genie and the Word: Electricity and Communication*, 1959.

The Story of the Wheel, 1960; *Timber!: Farming Our Forests*, Morrow, 1960; *Keeping Time*, 1960; *Wonder Worker: The Story of Electricity*, Morrow, 1961; *The World of Marco Polo*, 1961; *The Birth of a Liner*, Little, Brown, 1961; *The French Explorers in America*, 1961; *The Spanish Armada*, 1962; *The Spanish Conquistadores in North America*, 1962; *Volcano!*, Morrow, 1962; *The First Book of Machines*, Watts, 1962; *Westward with American Explorers*, 1963; *Chivalry and the Mailed Knight*, 1963; *Strange Craft*, Norton, 1963; *The Marvel of Glass*, Morrow, 1963; *Warriors' Weapons*, Crowell, 1963; *Rubber: Natural and Synthetic*, Morrow, 1964; *Heraldry: The Story of Armorial Bearings*, 1964; *World beneath the Waves*, Norton, 1964; *Galleys and Galleons*, 1964; *Home Sweet Home in the Nineteenth Century*, Crowell, 1965; *Cloth: From Fiber to Fabric*, Morrow, 1965; *The Magic of Paper*, Morrow, 1966; *Sea Monsters*, Norton, 1966; *Famous Small Boat Voyages*, 1966; *The Portuguese Explorers*, 1966; *Firearms*, Crowell, 1967; *Viking Explorers*, 1967; *Water*, Norton, 1967; *1812: The War and the World*, Rand McNally, 1967; *Plastics: The Man-Made Miracle*, Morrow, 1967; *Automobiles: Past and Present*, Morrow, 1968; *Freight Trains of the Sky*, 1969; *Salt, Sugar, and Spice*, Morrow, 1969; *Food: From Farm to Home*, Morrow, 1970; *Storm Warning: The Story of Hurricanes and Tornadoes*, Morrow, 1972.

Illustrator: William Nephew and Michael Chester, *Moon Base*, Putnam, 1959; Nephew and Chester, *Planet Trip*, Putnam, 1960; Nephew and Chester, *Beyond Mars*, Putnam, 1960; Samuel Epstein and Beryl Williams, *The First Book of the Ocean*, F. Watts, 1961. Contributor of articles to architecture and yachting magazines.

AVOCATIONAL INTERESTS: Sailing; architecture.

BIOGRAPHICAL/CRITICAL SOURCES: Christian Science Monitor, May 5, 1966, May 2, 1968, May 1, 1969; *Book Week*, September 25, 1966; *Instructor*, March, 1967; *Young Readers Review*, May, 1967; *Publishers Weekly*, September 20, 1971.†

*   *   *

BULL, Geoffrey Taylor 1921-

PERSONAL: Born June 24, 1921, in London, England; son of William John (a company director) and Ethel Edith (Taylor) Bull; married Agnes Johnstone Templeton, June 11, 1955; children: Ross Templeton, Geoffrey Peter, Alister William. *Education:* Attended Christ's College, Finchley, England. *Religion:* Christian. *Home:* 4, Bridgegait, Milngavie, Glasgow, Scotland.

CAREER: Worked in banking, 1937-42, and for British national service, 1942-46; missionary evangelical and bible teacher in Great Britain and abroad, 1947—.

WRITINGS—Published by Hodder & Stoughton, except as indicated: *When Iron Gates Yield* (first book in trilogy), Moody, 1955; *God Holds the Key* (second book in trilogy), Moody, 1959; *Coral in the Sand*, 1962, Moody, 1963; *The Sky Is Red* (third book in trilogy), 1965, Moody, 1966; *Ti-*

betan Tales, 1966, published in America as *Forbidden Land: A Saga of Tibet,* Moody, 1967; *A New Pilgrim's Progress: John Bunyan's Classic Imagined in a Contemporary Setting,* 1969; *The City and the Sign: An Interpretation of the Book of Jonah,* 1970, Baker Book, 1972; *Love-Song in Harvest,* Christian Literature Crusade, 1972; *Prisoner from Beyond the River,* 1974; *The Anguish in the Grass,* 1975; *Treasure in My Sack,* H. E. Walter, 1979. Also author of three children's book series published by Pickering & Inglis.

Booklets: *Out of the Low Dungeon* (six broadcast talks), Pickering & Inglis, 1964; *Out of the Mouth of the Lion,* Pickering & Inglis, 1967. Also author of radio and television scripts for British Broadcasting Corp.

SIDELIGHTS: When Iron Gates Yield is a first-hand account of the Communist takeover of eastern Tibet and of Geoffrey Bull's experiences in Chinese prisons. The book has been translated into German, Danish, Swedish, Finnish, Norwegian, and Chinese. *Tibetan Tales* has been translated into German.

* * *

BULLA, Clyde Robert 1914-

PERSONAL: Born January 9, 1914, in King City, Mo.; son of Julian and Sarah (Henson) Bulla. *Education:* "Largely self-educated." *Residence:* Los Angeles, Calif.

CAREER: Professional writer of children's books. Composer of music for children. *Member:* Authors Guild. *Awards, honors:* Boys' Clubs of America Gold Medal, 1955, for *Squanto, Friend of the White Men;* Authors Club of Los Angeles award for outstanding juvenile book by Southern California author, 1961, for *Benito;* Southern California Council on Children's Literature award, 1962, for distinguished contribution to field of children's literature, and 1975, for *Shoeshine Girl;* George F. Stone Center for Children's Books award, 1968, for *White Bird;* Commonwealth Club of California silver medal, 1970, for *Jonah and the Great Fish;* Christopher Award, 1971, for *Pocahontas and the Strangers;* Charlie May Simon Award, 1978, and South Carolina School Children award, 1980, both for *Shoeshine Girl.*

*WRITINGS—*Published by Crowell, except as indicated: *These Bright Young Dreams,* Penn, 1941; *The Donkey Cart,* 1946; *Riding the Pony Express,* 1948; *The Secret Valley,* 1949.

Surprise for a Cowboy, 1950; *A Ranch for Danny,* 1951; *Song of St. Francis,* 1952; *Johnny Hong of Chinatown,* 1952; *Eagle Feather,* 1953; *Star of Wild Horse Canyon,* 1953; *Down the Mississippi,* 1954; *Squanto, Friend of the White Men,* 1954; *White Sails to China,* 1955; *The Poppy Seeds,* 1955; *A Dog Named Penny,* Ginn, 1955; *John Billington: Friend of Squanto,* 1956; *The Sword in the Tree,* 1956; *Old Charlie,* 1957; *Ghost Town Treasure,* 1957; *Pirate's Promise,* 1958; *The Valentine Cat,* 1959; *Stories of Favorite Operas,* 1959.

Three-Dollar Mule, 1960; *A Tree Is a Plant,* 1960; *The Sugar Pear Tree,* 1960; *Benito,* 1961; *The Ring and the Fire,* 1962; *What Makes a Shadow?,* 1962; *Viking Adventure,* 1963; *Indian Hill,* 1963; *St. Valentine's Day,* 1965; *More Stories of Favorite Operas,* 1965; *Lincoln's Birthday,* 1966; *White Bird,* 1966; *Washington's Birthday,* 1967; *Flowerpot Gardens,* 1967; *The Ghost of Windy Hill,* 1968; *Mika's Apple Tree,* 1968; *Stories of Gilbert & Sullivan Operas,* 1968; *New Boy in Dublin,* 1969.

Jonah and the Great Fish, 1970; *Pocahontas and the Strang-*

ers, 1971; *Joseph the Dreamer,* 1971; *Open the Door and See All the People,* 1972; *Noah and the Rainbow* (adapted from a story by Max Bollinger), 1972; *Dexter,* 1973; *The Wish at the Top,* 1974; *Shoeshine Girl,* 1975; *Marco Moonlight,* 1976; *The Beast of Lor,* 1977; (with Michael Syson) *Conquista!,* 1978; *Last Look,* 1979; *Daniel's Duck,* Harper, 1979; *The Stubborn Old Woman,* 1980; *My Friend, the Monster,* 1980.

Also composer of music for song books, with lyrics by Lois Lenski: *We Are Thy Children,* Crowell, 1952; *Songs of Mr. Small,* Oxford University Press, 1954; *Songs of the City,* Edward B. Marks Music Corp., 1956. Composer of librettas for two unproduced operas.

SIDELIGHTS: Clyde Robert Bulla told *CA:* "When young writers ask me for advice, I tell them: 'Read a lot. Write a lot. Keep looking, listening, and wondering.'" *Avocational interests:* Music, painting in oils and water colors, travel.

* * *

BURCHARD, Peter Duncan 1921-

PERSONAL: Born March 1, 1921, in Washington, D.C.; son of Russell Duncan (lawyer) and Ethel (Brokaw) Burchard; married Elizabeth Chamberlain, March 23, 1945 (no longer married); children: Lee, Peter, Jr., Laura. *Education:* Philadelphia Museum School of Art, graduate, 1947. *Politics:* Registered Democrat. *Home:* 901 Powell St., San Francisco, Calif. 94108.

CAREER: Free-lance illustrator, 1947—, free-lance writer, 1956—. Technical illustrator in the aircraft industry, eighteen months, and for the U.S. Navy, 1941-42, 1946. *Military service:* U.S. Army, 1943-46. *Member:* Authors Guild, International P.E.N. *Awards, honors:* Lewis Carroll Shelf Award, 1960, for *Jed;* Guggenheim fellow, 1966-67; *Bimby* named to *Horn Book* honor list, 1968; *Pioneers of Flight* included on Child Study Association book list, 1970; Christopher Award, 1972, for illustrating *Pocahontas and the Strangers.*

WRITINGS: The River Queen, Macmillan, 1957; *The Carol Moran,* Macmillan, 1958; *Balloons from Paper Bags to Skyhooks,* Macmillan, 1960; *Jed,* Coward, 1960; *North by Night,* Coward, 1962; *One Gallant Rush: Robert Gould Shaw and His Brave Black Regiment,* St. Martin's, 1965; *Stranded,* Coward, 1967; *Bimby,* Coward, 1968; *Chito,* Coward, 1969; *Pioneers of Flight,* St. Martin's, 1970; *Rat Hell,* Coward, 1971; *A Quiet Place,* Coward, 1972; *The Deserter,* Coward, 1973; *Harbor Tug,* Putnam, 1974; *Whaleboat Raid,* Coward, 1977; *Ocean Race: A Sea Venture,* Putnam, 1978; *Chinwe,* Putnam, 1979; *Digger,* Putnam, 1980.

Illustrator of over 100 books, including: Marie McSwigan, *Our Town Has a Circus,* Dutton, 1949; Virginia Haviland, *William Penn,* Abingdon, 1952; Hildreth T. Wriston, *Show Lamb,* Abingdon, 1953; Clyde Robert Bulla, *Down the Mississippi,* Crowell, 1954; Grace Tracy Johnson and Harold N. Johnson, *Courage Wins,* Dutton, 1954; Margaret Glover Otto, *Tiny Man,* Holt, 1955; Alf Evers, *Treasure of Watchdog Mountain,* Macmillan, 1955; Marian Cumming, *Clan Texas,* Harcourt, 1955; Bulla, *John Billington: Friend of Squanto,* Crowell, 1956; William L. Brown and Rosalie Moore, *The Boy Who Got Mailed,* Coward, 1957; Bulla, *Pirate's Promise,* Crowell, 1958; Wilma Pitchford Hays, *The Fourth of July Raid,* Coward, 1959; Hays, *Easter Fires,* Coward, 1960; Louisa R. Shotwell, *Roosevelt Grady,* World Publishing, 1963; Earl S. Miers, *Pirate Chase,* Holt, 1965; Peggy Mann, *The Street of Flower Boxes,* Coward, 1966; Lonzo Anderson, *Zeb,* Knopf, 1966; Bulla, *Pocahontas and the Strangers,* Crowell, 1971.

Contributor of stories, articles, and reviews to magazines.

SIDELIGHTS: Peter Burchard told *CA:* "The writers who have helped me most are those who say what they want to say in the simplest, clearest kind of language. Style emerges only as a writer *writes*, not when a writer imitates. Style grows out of passionate thinking, out of a writer's will to convey a thought, a feeling, a picture."

*   *   *

BURDEN, Jean 1914-
(Felicia Ames)

PERSONAL: Born September 1, 1914, in Waukegan, Ill.; daughter of Harry Frederick (real estate man) and Miriam (Biddlecom) Prussing; divorced. *Education:* University of Chicago, B.A., 1936. *Politics:* Democrat. *Home:* 1129 Beverly Way, Altadena, Calif. 91001.

CAREER: Held various positions in advertising and insurance; edited a house organ; West Coast editor of *Faith Today;* West Coast editor of *Yankee* magazine; taught a poetry workshop at Pasadena City College; private teaching, 1960; *Yankee* magazine, Dublin, N.H., poetry editor, 1955—; Meals for Millions Foundation, Los Angeles, Calif., administrative officer, 1956-65; affiliated with Stanford Research Institute, 1965-66; free-lance public relations work, 1966—. *Awards, honors:* First prize of $300 for "Poem Before Departure," appearing in *Best Poems of 1962;* Silver Anvil award, Public Relations Society of America, 1969, for best product publicity program of year.

WRITINGS: Naked as the Glass (poetry), October House, 1963, 2nd edition, 1964; *Journey Toward Poetry* (essays), October House, 1966; *A Celebration of Cats,* Paul Eriksson, 1974; *The Classic Cats,* New American Library, 1975; *The 'Woman's Day' Book of Hints for Cat Owners,* Fawcett, 1980.

Under pseudonym Felicia Ames; pet care books; all published by New American Library: *The Dog You Care For,* 1968; *The Cat You Care For,* 1968; *The Bird You Care For,* 1970; *The Fish You Care For,* 1971.

Work anthologized in "Best Poems" anthologies. Contributor to *Poetry, Atlantic, American Scholar, Trace, Saturday Review, Virginia Quarterly Review, Better Homes and Gardens, Mademoiselle, Prairie Schooner, Southern Review,* and other publications.

WORK IN PROGRESS: Poetry; a book on cats.

SIDELIGHTS: Frances Minturn Howard writes that Jean Burden "lives with two cats, but has a passion for birds. . . . Loves Big Sur, all rocky wild places, and Mozart. Has at times an unexpectedly acid sense of humor." Speaking of her poetry, W. T. Scott of *Saturday Review* writes that Burden "is astringently feminine with a fine economy, a strong delicacy. She always *says* something, often in lovely ways." Burden has recorded some of her poems for the Library of Congress.

BIOGRAPHICAL/CRITICAL SOURCES: Saturday Review, October 26, 1963; *New York Times Book Review,* November 3, 1963; *Yankee,* December, 1963.

*   *   *

BURGESS, Eric 1920-

PERSONAL: Born May 30, 1920, in Stockport, Cheshire, England; son of William (an engineer) and Lily Burgess; married Lilian Slater, August 9, 1947; children: Janis Marie, Stephen Roy, Howard John. *Education:* Attended College of Commerce, Manchester, England, 1934-40, College of Technology, Manchester, 1953-56, and University of California, Los Angeles, 1958-59. *Home and office:* 13361 Frati Lane, Sebastopol, Calif. 95472. *Agent:* Curtis Brown, Ltd., 1 Craven Hill, London W2 3EP, England.

CAREER: Amson Associated Companies, Manchester, England, secretary-accountant, 1946-56; Telecomputing Corp., North Hollywood, Calif., proposal-coordinator in Data Instruments Division, 1956-58, senior member of technical staff in Electronic Systems Division, 1958-60; Mellonics, Inc. (data systems consultants), Tucson, Ariz., vice-president of technical services, 1960-62; Douglas Aircraft, Missiles and Space Systems Division, Santa Monica, Calif., staff assistant in advance programs department, 1962-63; Informatics Inc., Sherman Oaks, Calif., member of senior staff, 1963-65; Wolf Research and Development Corporation, Encino, Calif., deputy director of Los Angeles division, 1965-69; Christian Science Monitor, Boston, Mass., staff correspondent, 1969-72; free-lance writer, 1972—. Science advisor to the film "Moonraker," 1978-79. Lecturer on space flight to technical groups and to lay audiences in Europe and the United States. *Military service:* Royal Air Force, Technical Training Command, 1940-46. *Member:* British Interplanetary Society (fellow; chairman, 1945-46), Royal Astronomical Society (fellow), American Institute of Aeronautics and Astronautics (associate fellow), American Astronautical Society (senior member; chairman, Los Angeles section, 1959-60), Manchester Astronomical Society (honorary member; vice-president, 1952-56). *Awards, honors: Royal Air Force Quarterly* prize, 1945, for essay "Effects of Directed Missiles on Future Warfare and the Defense of the British Commonwealth."

WRITINGS: Rocket Propulsion, Chapman & Hall, 1952; *Frontier to Space,* Chapman & Hall, 1955, Macmillan, 1956; *Rockets and Space Flight,* Hodder & Stoughton, 1956; *Guided Weapons,* Macmillan, 1956; (contributor) *Space Encyclopedia,* Dutton, 1957; *Satellites and Space Flight,* Chapman & Hall, 1957, Macmillan, 1958; (contributor) *Space Weapons,* Praeger, 1959; (with John Herrick) *Rocket Encyclopedia,* Aero, 1959; (editor with H. Jacobs) *Advances in the Astronautical Sciences,* Volume VI, Macmillan, 1960, Volume VII, Plenum, 1961, Volume VIII, Plenum, 1962, (sole editor) Volumes IX, XII, Western Periodicals, 1963; *Long Range Ballistic Missiles,* Chapman & Hall, 1961, Macmillan, 1962; (editor) *On-Line Computing Systems,* American Data Processing, 1965; *Assault on the Moon,* Hodder & Stoughton, 1967; (editor) *The Next Billion Years,* National Aeronautics and Space Administration, 1974; (with R. O. Fimmel and W. Swindell) *Pioneer Odyssey: Encounter with a Giant,* National Aeronautics and Space Administration, 1974, revised edition, 1977; (with Bruce Murray) *Flight to Mercury,* Columbia University Press, 1977; (with James A. Dunne) *The Voyage of Mariner 10,* National Aeronautics and Space Administration, 1978; *To the Red Planet,* Columbia University Press, 1978; (with Fimmel and James Van Allen) *Pioneer: First to Jupiter, Saturn, and Beyond,* National Aeronautics and Space Administration, 1980. General editor, American Astronautical Society's Science and Technology Series, Volumes I-VI, Western Periodicals, 1965, Volumes VII-XII, American Astronautical Society, 1966. Contributor to aeronautical publications in the United States, England, Australia, and Switzerland.

WORK IN PROGRESS: Meteor Red, a novel; *Pioneer Venus,* for the National Aeronautics and Space Administration; *By Jove,* for Columbia University Press.

BIOGRAPHICAL/CRITICAL SOURCES: Los Angeles Citi-

zen News, August 6, 1958; *Los Angeles Mirror News,* August 6, 1958; *Mercury,* October, 1976.

*   *   *

BURKHEAD, Jesse 1916-

PERSONAL: Born November 20, 1916, in Armstrong, Iowa; son of Jesse Verlyn and Florence (Felkey) Burkhead; married Polly Sperry, 1938; children: Susan, Jane. *Education:* Carleton College, B.A., 1938; University of Wisconsin, M.A., 1939, Ph.D., 1942; Harvard University, M.P.A., 1942. *Home:* 5 Pebble Hill Rd. South, Dewitt, N.Y. 13214. *Office:* Department of Economics, Syracuse University, Syracuse, N.Y. 13210.

CAREER: U.S. Bureau of the Budget, Washington, D.C., fiscal analyst, 1942-43, 1946; Lehigh University, Bethlehem, Pa., assistant professor, 1946-48; Syracuse University, Syracuse, N.Y., professor of economics, 1948-68, Maxwell Professor of Economics, 1962—. *Military service:* U.S. Army Air Forces, 1943-46; became second lieutenant. *Member:* American Economic Association, American Society for Public Administration, Society for Public Choice, Phi Beta Kappa. *Awards, honors:* Ford Faculty fellowship in economics, 1959-60; National Tax Association-Tax Institute of America senior scholar, 1977.

WRITINGS: Government Budgeting, Wiley, 1956; (co-author) *River Basin Administration and the Delaware,* Syracuse University Press, 1959; (co-author) *Decisions in Syracuse,* Indiana University Press, 1961; *State and Local Taxes for Public Education,* Syracuse University Press, 1963; *Public School Finance: Economics and Politics,* Syracuse University Press, 1964; (with others) *Input and Output in Large-City High Schools,* Syracuse University Press, 1967; (with John Ross) *Productivity in the Local Government Sector,* Lexington Books, 1974; (co-author) *Public Employment and State and Local Government Finance,* Ballinger, 1980. Contributor of articles to professional journals.

WORK IN PROGRESS: Intergovernmental Relations.

*   *   *

BURNETT, Ben G(eorge) 1924-1975

PERSONAL: Born May 20, 1924, in Seattle, Wash.; died September, 1975; son of Ben H. and Cora (Stocksick) Burnett; married Dorothy Jensen, 1950. *Education:* University of California, Los Angeles, A.B., 1948, Ph.D., 1955. *Home:* 9831 South Cullman Ave., Whittier, Calif. *Office:* Department of Political Science, Whittier College, Whittier, Calif. 90608.

CAREER: University of California, Los Angeles, assistant in political science, 1950-51; Kent State University, Kent, Ohio, instructor, 1951-53; Whittier College, Whittier, Calif., instructor, 1953-54, assistant professor, 1954-57, associate professor, 1957-64, professor of political science and chairman of department, 1964-75. Director and professor, Whittier College in Copenhagen, Denmark, 1960-61; visiting associate professor, University of California, Los Angeles, 1962-63. Research in Mexico, 1958, 1959, in Spain and Portugal, 1961, in Guatemala and Mexico, 1962, and in Chile, 1963-64. *Military service:* U.S. Army, 1943-46; became sergeant; received European Theater ribbon with three battle stars. *Member:* American Political Science Association, Latin American Studies Association, Western Political Science Association, Southern California Political Science Association (secretary-treasurer, 1958-60; member of executive board, 1962). *Awards, honors:* Haynes fellowship, 1956;

University Research Associates fellowship, 1956; Danforth fellowship, 1959; Social Science Research Council fellowship, Chile, 1963-64.

WRITINGS: (With Moises Poblete Troncoso) *The Rise of the Latin American Labor Movement,* A. B. Bookman, 1960; (with Kenneth F. Johnson) *Political Forces in Latin America: Dimensions of the Quest for Stability,* Wadsworth, 1968; *Political Groups in Chile: The Dialogue between Order and Change,* University of Texas Press, 1970. Contributor of articles and reviews to professional journals.†

*   *   *

BURNETT, Collins W.   1914-

PERSONAL: Born March 28, 1914, in Anderson, Ind.; son of Charles and Bertha (Liget) Burnett; married B. Kathryn Kaufman; children: Arlita Jean, Michael Collins. *Education:* Ball State Teachers College, A.B., 1935; Ohio State University, M.A., 1940, Ph.D., 1948. *Politics:* Conservative Democrat. *Religion:* Protestant. *Home:* 947 Edgewater Dr., Lexington, Ky. 40502. *Office:* Department of Higher Education, University of Kentucky, Lexington, Ky. 40506.

CAREER: Ohio State University, Columbus, 1950-68, began as assistant professor, became professor of psychology and assistant dean, professor of higher education, 1963-68; University of Kentucky, Lexington, professor of higher education, 1968—. Consultant to several organizations. *Military service:* U.S. Naval Reserve, 1942—; now commander. *Member:* American Psychological Association (fellow), American Personnel and Guidance Association, Student Personnel Association for Teacher Education (president, 1957; member of professional standards and training committee, 1964-67), American Association of University Professors, National Education Association, Reserve Officers Association. *Awards, honors:* Blue Key, Pi Gamma Mu; Ball State University Distinguished Alumni Service Award, 1966.

WRITINGS: (With Alice Z. Seeman) *Planning for Education,* College of Education, Ohio State University, 1952; (with H. J. Peters and Farwell Peters) *Introduction to Teaching,* Macmillan, 1963; (editor) *The Community Junior College: An Annotated Bibliography with Introductions for School Counselors,* College of Education, Ohio State University, 1968; (editor with Frank W. Badger) *The Learning Climate in the Liberal Arts College: An Annotated Bibliography,* Morris Harvey College, 1970; (editor and contributor) *The Two-Year Institution in American Higher Education,* College of Education, University of Kentucky, 1971; (editor) *Legal Problems in Higher Education,* College of Education, University of Kentucky, 1974; (contributor) S. E. Goodman, editor, *Handbook on Contemporary Education,* Bowker, 1976; (editor and contributor) *The Community and Junior College,* College of Education, University of Kentucky, 1977; (with J. White) *Higher Education Literature in the Seventies as Background for the Eighties: A Selected and Annotated Bibliography,* Oryx, 1981. Contributor to professional journals.

*   *   *

BURTON, David H(enry) 1925-

PERSONAL: Born August 4, 1925, in Oil City, Pa.; son of Henry D. (a fireman) and Isabella E. (DuPlaine) Burton; married Geraldine F. Ferrari (a teacher), August 27, 1960; children: Antoinette, Monica, Victoria Regina. *Education:* University of Scranton, B.A. (magna cum laude), 1949; Georgetown University, M.A., 1950, Ph.D., 1953. *Politics:* Independent. *Religion:* Roman Catholic. *Home:* 163

Wooded Lane, Villanova, Pa. 19085. *Agent:* Shaw Mac-Lean, 11 Rumbold Rd., London S.W.6, England. *Office:* Department of History, St. Joseph's College, Philadelphia, Pa. 19131.

CAREER: U.S. Department of Army, Washington, D.C., intelligence research specialist, 1951-52; Georgetown University, Washington, D.C., lecturer in history, 1954; Duquesne University, Pittsburgh, Pa., assistant professor, 1955-56, associate professor of history, 1956-58; St. Joseph's College, Philadelphia, Pa., professor of history, 1958—. *Military service:* U.S. Army, Infantry, 1943-45; received Bronze Star Medal and Purple Heart. *Member:* American Historical Association, Organization of American Historians, English-Speaking Union, British Association of American Studies. *Awards, honors:* Winston Churchill traveling fellowship from English-Speaking Union, 1972; Pulitzer Prize nomination, 1976, for *American History–British Historians.*

WRITINGS: Theodore Roosevelt: Confident Imperialist, University of Pennsylvania Press, 1968; *Theodore Roosevelt: A Biography,* Twayne, 1972; *Theodore Roosevelt and His English Correspondents,* American Philosophical Society, 1973; *Holmes-Sheehan,* Kennikat, 1976; *American History–British Historians,* Nelson-Hall, 1976; *Oliver Wendell Holmes: What Manner of Liberal?,* Krieger, 1979; *Oliver Wendell Holmes, Jr.,* Twayne, 1980. Contributor to *History Today, Journal of the History of Ideas, Review of Politics, Personalist,* and *History Teacher.*

WORK IN PROGRESS: Holmes-Franklin Ford Letters; Edward Arlington Robinson and the American Artist.

SIDELIGHTS: David H. Burton told *CA:* "Working in biography I become more convinced each year of the wisdom of Disraeli's advice: 'Read no history, only biography, for that is life without theory.'"

* * *

BUTLER, Francelia McWilliams 1913-

PERSONAL: Born April 25, 1913, in Cleveland, Ohio; daughter of Robert William (an educator) and Grace Lucille (Williams) McWilliams; married Jerome Ambrose Butler (a journalist), July 4, 1939 (deceased); children: Susan Ellen Butler Wandell. *Education:* Oberlin College, A.B., 1934; Georgetown University, M.A., 1959; University of Virginia, Ph.D., 1963. *Politics:* Democrat. *Religion:* Congregational. *Home:* Mansfield Hollow Rd., Mansfield Center, Conn. 06250. *Office:* Department of English, University of Connecticut, Storrs, Conn. 06268.

CAREER: Paris Herald, Paris, France, drama critic, 1938; University of Tennessee, Knoxville, assistant professor of English, 1963-65; University of Connecticut, Storrs, 1965—, currently professor of English. Volunteer secretary, Northern Virginia Mental Health Association, 1957. *Member:* Modern Language Association of America, American Studies Association, Children's Literature Association (member of founding board), American Association of University Professors, Bibliographical Society of Virginia. *Awards, honors:* Laurance Rockefeller grant for research and writing on the history of cancer, 1952; University of Tennessee grant for research on Ruskin Commonwealth, 1964; Ford Foundation fellow, Institute of Medieval and Renaissance Studies, University of North Carolina, 1965; Fulbright lecturer, Jagellonian University, Krakow, Poland, 1967-68; University of Connecticut grant for research in England, 1970; National Endowment for the Humanities Award to Africa and South America, 1980.

WRITINGS: James Marion Sims, Pioneer American Cancer Protagonist, Hoeber, 1950; *The Sun Dial,* [Arlington], 1952; *Cancer through the Ages: The Evolution of Hope,* Virginia Press, 1955; (with Gail E. Haley) *The Skip-Rope Book,* introduction by Phyllis McGinley, Dial, 1963; *The Strange Critical Fortunes of Shakespeare's Timon of Athens,* Iowa State University Press, 1966; (editor) Herbert Silvette, *The Doctor on the Stage: Medicine and Medical Men in 17th Century England,* University of Tennessee Press, 1967; *Children's Literature: A Module,* Empire State College, 1974; *Sharing Literature With Children,* Longman, 1977; *Master Works of Children's Literature of the Seventeenth Century,* Stonehill, 1980; *The Lucky Piece* (novel), Stonehill, 1980; (with Jan Bakker) *Marxism, Feminism and Free Love,* Porcupine Press, 1981. Contributor to magazines and journals including *Studies in Philology, Tennessee Historical Quarterly, New York Times Magazine, Antioch Review, Shakespeare Quarterly,* and *Polish Review.* Founding editor, *Children's Literature* (annual), Yale University Press.

WORK IN PROGRESS: The Melted Refrigerator, or The Organic Travel Book.

SIDELIGHTS: Francelia McWilliams Butler told *CA:* "Because of the scorn in which children's literature is held by humanists, I have tried to launch it as a major discipline in the humanities." Among her achievements in this endeavor are the establishment of the first children's literature seminar of the Modern Language Association of America, the first textbook on children's literature designed for classes in the humanities, and the first critical annual of children's literature in the humanities.

AVOCATIONAL INTERESTS: Collecting cookbooks.

BIOGRAPHICAL/CRITICAL SOURCES: Washington Post, September 22, 1963; *Knoxville News Sentinel,* December 29, 1963; *Hartford Times,* January 6, 1971; *New York Times,* September 10, 1974; *Norwich Bulletin,* 1979.

* * *

BYERS, Edward E. 1921-

PERSONAL: Born January 26, 1921, in Pittsburgh, Pa.; son of Edward H. and Flora K. (Anton) Byers; married M. Margaret Baxter, 1950; children: Edward B., Jeanne Ellen, Constance Ann, Robert Douglas. *Education:* University of Pittsburgh, B.S., 1943, Ed.M., 1948; Boston University, Ed.D., 1958. *Home:* 66 Butternut Lane, Stamford, Conn. *Office:* Gregg Division, McGraw-Hill Book Co., 1221 Ave. of the Americas, New York, N.Y. 10020.

CAREER: LaSalle Vocational School, Pittsburgh, Pa., instructor, 1942-43; Fifth Avenue High School, Pittsburgh, teacher, 1946-47; Aspinwall Veterans Administration Hospital, Aspinwall, Pa., acting executive assistant of physical medicine rehabilitation, 1947-48; Simmons College, Boston, Mass., assistant professor, 1948-50, 1952-57, associate professor of secretarial studies, 1957-58; Chandler School for Women, Boston, academic dean, 1958-62; McGraw-Hill Book Co., Gregg Division, New York, N.Y., senior editor, 1963-65, editor-in-chief, business office and management education division, 1966—. *Military service:* U.S. Army, 1943-46, 1950-52, became first lieutenant. *Member:* Eastern Business Education Association, New England Business Educators Association, Kappa Phi Kappa, Phi Delta Kappa, Delta Pi Epsilon.

WRITINGS—Published by McGraw, except as indicated: Dictation for the Medical Secretary, 1952, 3rd edition published as *The Medical Secretary: Terminology and Tran-*

scription, 1967; *Byers First Year Shorthand Aptitude Tests,* Allied, 1959; *Gregg Text-Tapes for Medical Dictation and Transcription,* 1961; *Medical Typing Practice,* 1962, 2nd edition, 1967; *Student's Transcript of the Medical Secretary,* 1967; (with Irene Place and others) *College Secretarial Procedures* (text and study guide), 4th edition, 1972, 5th edition published as *Executive Secretarial Procedures,* 1980; *10,000 Medical Words Spelled and Divided for Quick Reference,* 1972; *Gregg Medical Shorthand Dictionary,* 1976; (with R. Robert Rosenberg and William Mott) *College Business Law* (text and individualized performance guide), 5th edition, 1979.

*   *   *

BYERS, (Amy) Irene   1906-

PERSONAL: Born December 30, 1906, in London, England; married Cyril Martin Byers (a retired Bank of England official); children: Christopher Martin, Jennifer Ann. *Education:* Educated in private school and at business college. *Politics:* Conservative. *Home:* 69 Baldry Gardens, London S.W. 16, England. *Agent:* Winant Towers Ltd., 1 Furnival St., London E.C.4, England.

CAREER: Began as free-lance journalist in Fleet Street, London, England; author specializing in books for boys and girls.

WRITINGS: The Circus, and Other Verses for Children, Muller, 1946; *Mystery at Barber's Reach,* Muller, 1950; *Our Outdoor Friends* (24 leaflets), Meiklejohn & Son, 1949, published in two volumes, 1952-53; *The Adventure of the Floating Flat,* Thomas Nelson, 1952; *The Young Brevingtons,* Parrish, 1953; *Tim of Tamberly Forest,* Parrish, 1954; *Out and About Tales,* Grant Educational, 1954; *The Mystery of Midway Mill,* Hutchinson, 1955; *Adventures at Fairborough's Farm,* Epworth, 1955; *Catherine of Corners,* Parrish, 1955; *Adventure at Dillingdon Dene,* Epworth, 1956; *The Strange Story of Pippin Wood,* Parrish, 1956; *Jewel of the Jungle,* Hutchinson, 1957; *The Missing Masterpiece,* Parrish, 1957; *Adventure at the Blue Cockatoo,* Epworth, 1958; *Flowers for Melissa,* Hutchinson, 1958.

Kennel Maid Sally, Hutchinson, 1960; *Sea Sprite Adventure,* Hulton Educational, 1961; *The Twins' Good Turn,* Hulton Educational, 1961; *Farm on the Fjord,* Hutchinson, 1961; *Tim Returns to Tamberly,* Parrish, 1962; *Silka, the Seal,* Brockhampton Press, 1962; *Two on the Trail,* J. Cape, 1963; *Foresters of Fourways,* Brockhampton Press, 1963; *Mystery at Mappins,* Scribner, 1964 (published in England as *The Merediths of Mappins,* Oliver & Boyd, 1964); *Trouble at Tamberly,* Parrish, 1964; *Joanna Joins the Zoo,* Brockhampton Press, 1964; *Magic in Her Fingers,* Brockhampton Press, 1965; *Half Day Thursday,* J. Cape, 1966; *Foresters Afield,* Brockhampton Press, 1966; *Danny Finds a Family,* Wheaton, 1966; *The House of the Speckled Browns,* Oliver & Boyd, 1967; *The Stage under the Cedars,* Chatto & Windus, 1969; *Cameras on Carolyn,* Chatto & Windus, 1971; *Timothy Tiptoes,* Brockhampton Press, 1975; *Tiptoes Wins Through,* Hodder & Stoughton, 1976; *Tiptoes and the Big Race,* Hodder & Stoughton, 1979. Contributor to (London) *Times* and *Books and Bookmen.*

SIDELIGHTS: Irene Byers's books have been translated into Swedish, Dutch, and Italian; several of them were serialized on British Broadcasting Corp. "Children's Hour." *Avocational interests:* Interior decoration, unusual cookery, and oil painting.

C

CALDERWOOD, James D(ixon)   1917-

PERSONAL: Born September 9, 1917, in Watford, England; American citizen; son of Walter James (a business executive) and Ivy (Dixon) Calderwood. *Education:* London School of Economics and Political Science, B.Com. (honors), 1938; graduate study, University of Geneva, 1939-40, Brookings Institution, 1940-41; Ohio State University, Ph.D., 1943. *Politics:* Independent. *Religion:* Protestant. *Home:* Apartment 203, 6200 Canterbury Drive, Culver City, Calif. *Office:* School of Business Administration, University of Southern California, Los Angeles, Calif. 90007.

CAREER: U.S. Department of Agriculture, Washington, D.C., economist, 1943-44; Ohio State University, Columbus, associate professor of economics, 1946-53; Committee for Economic Development, New York, N.Y., assistant director, Business-Education Division, 1953-55; Pomona College and Claremont Graduate School, Claremont, Calif., professor of economics, 1955-60; University of Southern California, School of Business Administration, Los Angeles, 1960—, currently Joseph A. DeBell Professor of Business Economics and International Trade. Foreign market consultant, Lockheed Aircraft Corp.; West Coast representative, Joint Council on Economic Education; consultant to Federal Reserve Bank of San Francisco, Ford Foundation, California State Department of Education, various businesses and public school systems. Public lecturer. *Military service:* U.S. Army, 1944-45; became sergeant. *Member:* American Economic Association, National Association of Business Economists, National Geographic Society.

WRITINGS: (With Robinson and Morton) *Introduction to Economic Reasoning,* Brookings Institution, 1956, 5th edition, 1980; *Teachers Guide to World Trade,* Joint Council on Economic Education, 1960; (with Mikesell and others) *Problems of Latin American Economic Development,* U.S. Government Printing Office, 1960; *International Economic Problems,* Curriculum Resources, 1961; (with James and Quantius) *Economics: Basic Problems and Analysis,* Prentice-Hall, 1961; (with Bienvenu) *Patterns of Economic Growth,* Curriculum Resources, 1962; *Western Europe and the Common Market,* Scott, Foresman, 1963; *The Problems and Promise of American Democracy,* McGraw, 1964; (with Fersh) *Economics in Action,* Macmillan, 1968; *Economics in the Curriculum,* Wiley, 1970; (with Fersh) *Economics for Decision-Making,* Macmillan, 1974; *The Developing World,* Scott, Foresman, 1976.

SIDELIGHTS: Introduction to Economic Reasoning has been translated into thirteen languages, including Arabic, Iranian, Korean, Hindi. Since World War II James D. Calderwood has made twenty-five trips to Europe, seven to Latin America, seven to Asia, three to Australia, eight to the Middle East, and visited Africa and New Zealand. When he has time to relax, he goes to a beach condominium in Hawaii to "do nothing." He goes to a week-end cottage in the desert to write and "recharge [his] mental batteries."

*   *   *

CALLARD, Maurice (Frederick Thomas)   1912-

PERSONAL: Born December 3, 1912, in Gosport, Hampshire, England; son of James Frederic and Emma (Read) Callard; married Margaret Joan Gouldie, 1947; children: Robert, Margaret. *Education:* Attended schools in Gosport, England. *Home:* 14 Ferrol Rd., Gosport, Hampshire, England.

CAREER: Self-employed in Gosport, England, 1932-38; Auxiliary Fire Service, Gosport, patrol officer, 1938-40; detective sergeant in Palestinian Police Force, 1940-46; full-time writer, 1954—. Lecturer on creative writing and the development of the English novel. *Awards, honors:* Priory Theatre Award for best play, 1973, for "The Devil's Lady."

WRITINGS: The City Called Holy, J. Cape, 1954; *The Splendour and the Havoc,* J. Cape, 1956; *The World and the Flesh,* Hutchinson, 1960; *The End of the Visit,* Doubleday, 1961; *Across the Frontier,* P. Davies, 1964.

Plays: *Sweet Nelly,* New Playwrights' Network, 1972; *Will You Take This Woman?,* New Playwrights' Network, 1974; *A Night in October,* New Playwrights' Network, 1979. Also author of "The Devil's Lady," 1973.

AVOCATIONAL INTERESTS: Painting in oils.

*   *   *

CAMERON, Kenneth Neill   1908-
(Warren Madden)

PERSONAL: Born September 15, 1908, in Barrow in Furness, England; son of Henry Murray (a shipbuilder) and Kathleen Anne (McIntyre) Cameron; married Mary Bess Owen (an associate professor at Hunter College of the City University of New York), April 26, 1946; children: Kathleen Anne. *Education:* McGill University, B.A., 1931; Oxford

University, B.A., B.Litt., and M.A., 1931-34; University of Wisconsin, Ph.D., 1939. *Home:* 4 Washington Square Village, New York, N.Y. 10012. *Office:* English Department, New York University, 19 University Pl., New York, N.Y. 10003.

CAREER: Indiana University at Bloomington, instructor, 1939-43, assistant professor, 1943-47, professor of English, 1947-52; Carl H. Pforzheimer Library, New York City, editor, 1952-67; New York University, New York City, professor of English, 1963-75. *Member:* Modern Language Association of America (chairman, Wordsworth and His Contemporaries section, 1959), P.E.N. *Awards, honors:* Rhodes scholarship, 1931; Modern Language Association—Macmillan Award, 1950, for *The Young Shelley;* Guggenheim fellowship, 1967; D.Litt., McGill University, 1971.

WRITINGS: The Young Shelley: Genesis of a Radical, Macmillan, 1950; (editor and author of introduction and notes) Percy Bysshe Shelley, *Selected Poetry and Prose,* Holt, 1951; (under pseudonym Warren Madden) *The Enormous Turtle,* Bobbs-Merrill, 1954; (editor) *Shelley and His Circle, 1773-1822,* Volumes I and II, Harvard University Press, 1961, Volumes III and IV, Oxford University Press, 1970; (editor) *Shelley, The Esdaile Notebook: A Volume of Early Poems,* Knopf, 1964; *Humanity and Society: A World History,* Indiana University Press, 1973; (editor) *Romantic Rebels: Essays on Shelley and His Circle,* Harvard University Press, 1973; *Shelley: The Golden Years,* Harvard University Press, 1974; *Marx and Engels Today: A Modern Dialogue on Philosophy and History,* Exposition Press, 1976; *Poems for Lovers and Rebels,* privately printed, 1977. Author of sixteen scholarly articles, mostly on Shelley; contributor to *New York Times Book Review* and several professional journals.

WORK IN PROGRESS: Two plays, one on Shelley; *Marxism: A General Survey and Update; Stalin, Mao and Hoxha; Dialectical Materialism.*

BIOGRAPHICAL/CRITICAL SOURCES: New Yorker, May 10, 1969; *Cue,* May 17, 1969.

* * *

CAMPBELL, Alan K. 1923-

PERSONAL: Born May 31, 1923, in Elgin, Neb.; son of Charles E. (a farmer) and Anna (Schneckloth) Campbell; married Linna Jane Owen, March 9, 1945; children: Kimberly Ann, Charles Duncan. *Education:* Whitman College, A.B., 1947; Wayne University (now Wayne State University), M.P.A., 1949; Harvard University, M.P.A., 1950, Ph.D., 1952. *Politics:* Democrat. *Religion:* Protestant. *Home:* Van Ness Center, Veazey Ter. N.W., Washington, D.C. 20008. *Office:* 1900 E St. N.W., Washington, D.C. 20415.

CAREER: Harvard University, Cambridge, Mass., assistant director of summer school, 1950-54, instructor, 1952-54; Hofstra College (now University), Hempstead, N.Y., professor and chairman, political science department, 1954-60; State of New York, Albany, deputy comptroller for administration, 1960-61; Syracuse University, Maxwell Graduate School, Syracuse, N.Y., professor of political science and public administration, 1961-76, director of metropolitan studies program, 1961-68, dean of Maxwell School of Citizenship and Public Affairs, 1969-76; University of Texas at Austin, director of Lyndon B. Johnson School of Public Affairs, 1977; U.S. Civil Service Commission, Washington, D.C., chairman, 1977-78; U.S. Office of Personnel Management, Washington, D.C., director, 1979—. Visiting profes-

sor, Columbia University, 1961-62; visiting lecturer, Harvard University, spring, 1967. Member of state advisory council on continuing higher education, 1966-68; member of advisory committee to the Secretary of Housing and Urban Development, 1967-68. Member of governing council, National Municipal League, 1970-77; member of visiting committee of Harvard Board of Overseers, John F. Kennedy School of Government, 1973-77; member of special committee on state constitutional revision, 1968-70; member of Urban Education Task Force, Department of Health, Education, and Welfare, 1969-70. Member of board of trustees, National Academy of Public Administration, 1971-72. Chairman, state platform committee, 1962. Consultant, Advisory Commission on Intergovernmental Relations, 1969-77, National Academy of Sciences, 1973-74, National Science Foundation, 1973-74, and National Institute of Education, 1975. *Military service:* U.S. Navy, Counter-Intelligence, 1943-46.

MEMBER: Urban America, American Political Science Association, American Society for Public Administration, Inter-University Case Program (member of executive board), New York State Political Science Association (member of executive council), Phi Beta Kappa.

WRITINGS: (Contributor) *Anatomy of a Metropolis,* Harvard University Press, 1959; (editor with Ed Bock) *Case Studies in American Government,* Prentice-Hall, 1962; (with Seymour Sacks) *Metropolitan America: Fiscal Patterns and Governmental Systems,* Free Press, 1967; (editor) *The States and the Urban Crisis,* Prentice-Hall, 1970; (with Joel Berke and R. Goettel) *Financing Equal Educational Opportunity: Alternatives for State Finance,* McCutchan, 1972; (with Roy Bahl and David Greytak) *Taxes, Expenditures, and Economic Base: Case of New York City,* Praeger, 1974; (editor with Bahl) *The Political Economy of State and Local Government Reform,* Free Press, 1976. Contributor to *Watergate: Implications for Responsible Government,* 1974; also contributor of articles dealing with problems of public administration and metropolitan affairs to professional journals.

* * *

CAMPBELL, John Coert 1911-

PERSONAL: Born October 8, 1911, in New York, N.Y.; son of Allan Reuben and Gertrude (DuBois) Campbell; married Mary E. Hillis; children: Allan, Alexander Bruce. *Education:* Harvard University, A.B., 1933, A.M., 1936, Ph.D., 1940. *Home:* 220 South Main St., Cohasset, Mass. 02025. *Office:* Council on Foreign Relations, 58 East 68th St., New York, N.Y. 10021.

CAREER: University of Louisville, Louisville, Ky., instructor, 1940-41; Council on Foreign Relations, New York City, Rockefeller fellow, 1941-42, 1946-49; U.S. Department of State, Washington, D.C., territorial specialist, 1942-46, member, policy planning staff, officer in charge of Balkan affairs, 1949-55; Council on Foreign Relations, New York City, senior research fellow, 1955-78, director of studies, 1977-78. Middle East Institute, member of board of governors, 1964-79, vice-president, 1967-77. U.S. Department of State, member of policy planning council, 1967-68, consultant, 1968-76. *Member:* American Historical Association, American Association for Advancement of Slavic Studies, Middle East Studies Association.

WRITINGS: The United States in World Affairs, 1945-47, Harper, 1947; *The United States in World Affairs, 1947-48,* Harper, 1948; *The United States in World Affairs, 1948-49,*

Harper, 1949; *Defense of the Middle East,* Harper, 1958; *American Policy toward Communist Eastern Europe,* University of Minnesota Press, 1965; *Tito's Separate Road,* Harper, 1967; (with Helen Caruso) *The West and the Middle East,* Council on Foreign Relations, 1972; (editor) *Successful Negotiation: Trieste, 1954,* Princeton University Press, 1976. Reviewer on international subjects for *Foreign Affairs;* contributor to foreign affairs journals.

WORK IN PROGRESS: American Policy in the Middle East.

*   *   *

CAMPBELL, Joseph   1904-

PERSONAL: Born March 26, 1904, in New York, N.Y.; son of Charles William and Josephine (Lynch) Campbell; married Jean Erdman, 1938. *Education:* Attended Dartmouth College, 1921-22; Columbia University, A.B., 1925, M.A., 1927, additional graduate study, 1927-28, 1928-29; graduate study at University of Paris, 1927-28, and University of Munich, 1928-29. *Home:* 136 Waverly Pl., New York, N.Y. 10014. *Agent:* Timothy Seldes, 522 Fifth Ave., New York, N.Y. 10017.

CAREER: Canterbury School, New Milford, Conn., teacher, 1932-33; Sarah Lawrence College, Bronxville, N.Y., member of literature department faculty, 1934-72. Lecturer, Foreign Service Institute, U.S. Department of State, 1956-73; trustee, Bollingen Foundation, 1960-69. *Member:* American Folklore Society, American Oriental Society, American Society for Study of Religion, American Academy of Psychotherapists (honorary member), Century Club, New York Athletic Club. *Awards, honors:* Proudfit fellow, 1927-28, 1928-29; National Institute of Arts and Letters grant in literature, 1949, for *The Hero with a Thousand Faces;* grants-in-aid for editing Zimmer volumes, 1946-55; Distinguished Scholar award, Hofstra University, 1973; D.H.L., Pratt Institute, 1976; Melcher Award for contribution to religious liberalism, 1976, for *The Mythic Image.*

WRITINGS: (With Maud Oakes and Jeff King) *Where the Two Come To Their Father,* Pantheon, 1943; (with Henry Morton Robinson) *A Skeleton Key to "Finnegans Wake,"* Harcourt, 1944, reprinted, Penguin, 1977; *The Hero with a Thousand Faces,* Pantheon, 1949, revised edition, Princeton University Press, 1980; *The Masks of God,* Viking, Volume I: *Primitive Mythology,* 1959, Volume II: *Oriental Mythology,* 1962, Volume III: *Occidental Mythology,* 1964, Volume IV: *Creative Mythology,* 1968; *The Flight of the Wild Gander,* Viking, 1969; *Myths to Live By,* Viking, 1972; *The Mythic Image,* Princeton University Press, 1974; (with Richard Roberts) *Tarot Revelations,* Alchemy Books, 1980.

Editor: Heinrich Robert Zimmer, *Myths and Symbols in Indian Art and Civilization,* Pantheon, 1946, reprinted, Princeton University Press, 1971; Zimmer, *The King and the Corpse: Tales of the Soul's Conquest of Evil,* Pantheon, 1948, reprinted, Princeton University Press, 1971; Zimmer, *Philosophies of India,* Pantheon, 1951, reprinted, Princeton University Press, 1969; *The Portable Arabian Nights,* Viking, 1952; Zimmer, *The Art of Indian Asia,* Pantheon, 1955, second edition (two volumes), Princeton University Press, 1960; *Myths, Dreams, and Religion,* Dutton, 1970; *The Portable Jung,* Viking, 1972; Rato K. Losang, *My Life and Lives: The Story of a Tibetan Incarnation,* Dutton, 1977. General editor of "Papers from the Eranos Yearbooks" series, including *Spirit and Nature,* 1954, *Mysteries,* 1955, *Man and Time,* 1957, *Spiritual Disciplines,* 1960, *Man and Transformation,* 1964, and *The Mystic Vision,* 1969. General

editor, "Myth and Man" series, Thames & Hudson, 1951-54.

Contributor: *The Complete Grimm's Fairy Tales,* Pantheon, 1944, reprinted, Random House, 1972; *James Joyce: Two Decades of Criticism,* Vanguard, 1948; *Psychoanalysis and Culture,* International Universities Press, 1951; *Basic Beliefs,* Sheridan, 1959; *Culture in History,* Columbia University Press, 1960; *Myth and Mythmaking,* Braziller, 1960; *Myths,* McGraw, 1974.

WORK IN PROGRESS: Historical Atlas of World Mythology, for McGraw.

BIOGRAPHICAL/CRITICAL SOURCES: Village Voice, August 1, 1968; *Christian Science Monitor,* October 9, 1969; *Commentary,* December, 1969; *Book World,* November 21, 1971.

*   *   *

CAMPBELL, Robert Wellington   1926-

PERSONAL: Born February 4, 1926, in Wichita, Kan.; son of Robert W. and Kathleen (Payton) Campbell; married Laura M. Mason, 1950; children: Sarah, Andrew, Polly, Benjamin, Emily, Alice. *Education:* University of Kansas, A.B., 1948, M.A. (economics), 1950, M.A. (Russian area studies), 1952; Harvard University, Ph.D., 1956. *Home:* 919 East Hunter, Bloomington, Ind. 47401. *Office:* Department of Economics, Indiana University, Bloomington, Ind. 47405.

CAREER: University of Southern California, Los Angeles, assistant professor, 1955-61; Indiana University at Bloomington, 1961—, currently professor of economics and chairman of department. Visiting associate professor, University of California, Berkeley, 1960-61. Trustee, National Council for Soviet and East European Research. Consultant to Stanford Research Institute, U.S. Department of State, and RAND Corp. *Military service:* U.S. Army, two years. *Member:* American Economic Association, American Association for the Advancement of Slavic Studies (chairman of committee on the current digest of the Soviet press), Association for Comparative Economic Studies (president). *Awards, honors:* Ford Foundation research fellowship for study at Harvard Russian Research Center, 1959; American Council of Learned Societies travel grant to Soviet Union, 1963.

WRITINGS: Soviet Economic Power, Houghton, 1960, 3rd edition published as *The Soviet-type Economies,* 1974; (with Francis P. Hoeber) *Soviet Economic Potential, 1960-1970,* Stanford Research Institute, 1961; *Accounting in Soviet Planning and Management,* Harvard University Press, 1963; *Economics of the Soviet Oil and Gas Industry,* Johns Hopkins Press, 1968; (with John E. Elliott) *Comparative Economic Systems,* Prentice-Hall, 1973; (with Paul Marer) *East-West Trade and Technology Transfer,* International Development Research Center, Indiana University, 1974; *Trends in the Soviet Oil and Gas Industry,* Johns Hopkins Press, 1976; *Soviet Energy Research and Development: Goals, Planning, and Organizations,* RAND Corp., 1978.

Contributor: Robert W. Oliver, *The Role of Small-scale Manufacturing in Economic Development,* Stanford Research Institute, 1957; Gregory Grossman, editor, *Value and Plan: Economic Organization and Calculation in Eastern Europe,* University of California Press, 1960; H. W. Gottinger, editor, *Jahrbuch der Wirtschaft Osteuropas,* Olzog Verlag (Munich), 1960; Wayne A. Leeman, *Capitalism, Market Socialism, and Central Planning,* Houghton, 1963; Harry Shaffer, *The Soviet Economy,* Appleton-Century-Crofts,

1963; Henry Rosovsky, editor, *Industrialization in Two Systems*, Wiley, 1966; John P. Hardt and others, *Soviet Economic Planning*, Yale University Press, 1967.

F. Gehrels and others, editors, *Essays in Economic Analysis and Policy*, Indiana University Press, 1970; V. G. Treml and Hardt, editors, *Soviet Economic Statistics*, Duke University Press, 1971; William D.G. Hunter, editor, *Current Problems of Socialist Economies*, McMaster University, 1971; Morris Bornstein and D. Fusfeld, editors, *The Soviet Economy: A Book of Readings*, 4th edition (Campbell was not associated with earlier editions), Irwin, 1974; Gerard J. Mangone, editor, *Energy Policies of the World*, Volume I, American Elsevier, 1977; C. T. Saunders, editor, *Industrial Policies and Technology Transfers between East and West*, Springer Verlag (Vienna), 1977; W.A.D. Jackson, editor, *Soviet Resource Management and the Environment*, American Association for the Advancement of Slavic Studies, 1978; Elmus Wicker, editor, *Lilly Conference on Recent Developments in Economics*, Indiana University, 1978. Contributor of articles and reviews to professional journals.

WORK IN PROGRESS: Technological Progress and Soviet Energy Policy.

*   *   *

CAPP, Glenn Richard   1910-

PERSONAL: Born September 21, 1910, in Westminster, Tex.; son of Cal W. and Margaret (Middlebrook) Capp; married Thelma Robuck, 1940; children: Glenn Richard, Jr. *Education:* Oklahoma Baptist University, A.B., 1933; Baylor University, LL.B., 1938; University of Southern California, graduate study, 1938; Northwestern University, M.A., 1948. *Politics:* Democrat. *Religion:* Baptist. *Home:* 3000 Cumberland, Waco, Tex. *Office:* Department of Speech, Baylor University, Waco, Tex. 76703.

CAREER: Oklahoma Baptist University, Shawnee, director of debate, 1933-34; Baylor University, Waco, Tex., 1934—, began as instructor, professor of speech 1948—, chairman of department, 1948-78, researcher, 1978—. Director of workshops on communications. *Military service:* U.S. Army Air Forces, 1942-46; became captain. *Member:* American Association of University Professors (president, local chapter, 1961—), Speech Association of America, American Forensic Association, Southern Speech Association (president, 1950), Texas Speech Association, Pi Kappa Delta (president, 1942). *Awards, honors:* Litt.D., Oklahoma Baptist University, 1965; J.D., Baylor University, 1969.

WRITINGS: Practical Debating, Lippincott, 1949; *How to Communicate Orally*, Prentice-Hall, 1961, revised edition, 1966; (editor) *Famous Speeches in American History*, Bobbs-Merrill, 1963; *Principles of Argumentation and Debate*, Prentice-Hall, 1965; *The Great Society: A Sourcebook*, Dickenson, 1967; *Basic Oral Communication*, Prentice-Hall, 1971, revised edition, 1981; *A Student Guide to Oral Communication*, Prentice-Hall, 1971.

WORK IN PROGRESS: A History of Communication at Baylor University, 1845-1980; The Communication Theories and Practices of Glenn R. Capp.

*   *   *

CAPUTI, Anthony (Francis)   1924-

PERSONAL: Born December 22, 1924, in Buffalo, N.Y.; son of Anthony F. and Jessie (Storms) Caputi; married Marjein O'Neill, 1948; children: David, Pauline, Mary, Carol. *Education:* University of Buffalo (now State University of New York at Buffalo), A.B., 1949, M.A., 1951; attended Merton College, Oxford, one year; Cornell University, Ph.D., 1956. *Home:* Gee Hill Rd., Dryden, N.Y. *Office:* Department of English, Cornell University, Ithaca, N.Y. 14850.

CAREER: Cornell University, Ithaca, N.Y., instructor, 1956-59, assistant professor, 1959-63, associate professor, 1963-69, professor of English, 1969—. *Military service:* U.S. Army, 1943-46; became sergeant. *Member:* Modern Language Association of America, Phi Beta Kappa, Phi Kappa Phi.

WRITINGS: John Marston, Satirist, Cornell University Press, 1961; *Modern Drama*, Norton, 1966; (editor) *Masterpieces of World Drama*, six volumes, Heath, 1968; *Loving Evie* (novel), Harper, 1974; *Buffo: The Genius of Vulgar Comedy*, Wayne State University Press, 1978. Contributor to *Journal of English and Germanic Philology*, *Modern Drama*, and *American Literature*.

*   *   *

CARLSON, Dale Bick   1935-

PERSONAL: Born May 24, 1935, in New York, N.Y.; daughter of Edgar M. (an orthopedic surgeon) and Estelle (Cohen) Bick; married Albert W. D. Carlson (an artist-illustrator), November 24, 1962; married second husband, Donald C. Gumbiner, September 17, 1978; children: (first marriage) Daniel Bick, Hannah Bick. *Education:* Wellesley College, B.A., 1957. *Home and office:* 116 East 63rd St., New York, N.Y. 10021. *Agent:* Toni Mendez, Inc., 140 East 56th St., New York, N.Y. 10022.

CAREER: Began as bookseller in Doubleday & Co. store, New York City, 1958; Mel Evans & Co. (editors), New York City, assistant, 1958-59; Thomas Yoseloff, Inc. (publishers), New York City, assistant editor, 1959-60; Parents League of New York, New York City, vice-president and editor-in-chief of *Parents League Bulletin*, 1968-69; free-lance editor for other New York publishing houses. *Awards, honors:* American Library Association Notable Book awards, 1972, for *The Mountain of Truth*, 1973, for *The Human Apes*, and 1974, for *Girls Are Equal Too*.

WRITINGS: Perkins the Brain, Doubleday, 1964; *The House of Perkins*, Doubleday, 1965; *Miss Maloo*, Doubleday, 1966; (editor) *The Brainstormers: Humorous Tales of Ingenious American Boys*, Doubleday, 1966; *Frankenstein* (juvenile adaptation of Mary Shelley's book), Golden Press, 1968; *The Electronic Teabowl*, Golden Press, 1969.

Published by Atheneum, except as indicated: *Dracula* (juvenile adaptation of Bram Stoker's book), Dell, 1970; *Warlord of the Genji*, 1970; *The Beggar King of China*, 1971; *Good Morning, Hannah*, 1972; *Good Morning Danny*, 1972; *The Mountain of Truth*, 1972; *The Human Apes*, 1973; *Girls Are Equal Too*, 1974; *Baby Needs Shoes*, 1974; *Where's Your Head?*, 1977; *Triple Boy*, 1977; *The Plant People*, 1977; *Wild Heart*, 1977; *The Shining Pool*, 1979; *Loving Sex for Both Sexes*, F. Watts, 1979; *Boys Have Feelings Too*, 1980; *Call Me Amanda*, Dutton, 1981.

SIDELIGHTS: Dale Bick Carlson told *CA* that she was prompted to write children's books "because of all the pleasure my books gave me as a child. I continue to write books for children because of the pleasure my own children take in reading good books.... Much of my material comes from my husband's childhood, some from my own, most from watching and living with Danny and Hannah."

CARLSON, Natalie Savage 1906-

PERSONAL: Born October 3, 1906, in Winchester, Va.; daughter of Joseph Hamilton and Natalie (Villeneuve) Savage; married Daniel Carlson (a retired naval officer), December 7, 1929; children: Stephanie Natalie (Mrs. Robert D. Sullivan), Julie Anne McAlpine. *Education:* High school graduate. *Politics:* Republican. *Religion:* Roman Catholic. *Home:* Doral Mobile Home Vilas 17, Clearwater, Fla. 33515.

CAREER: Long Beach Morning Sun, Long Beach, Calif., reporter, 1927-29; writer of children's books. *Member:* Authors Guild, National Association for the Preservation and Perpetuation of Storytelling. *Awards, honors: New York Herald Tribune* Children's Spring Book Festival Awards, 1952, for *The Talking Cat,* and 1954, for *Alphonse, That Bearded One;* Honor Book Awards, 1955, for *Wings against the Wind,* and 1957, for *Hortense: The Cow for a Queen;* Boys' Clubs of America Junior Book Awards, 1955, for *Alphonse, That Bearded One,* and 1956, for *Wings against the Wind;* Newbery Medal runner-up, 1959, for *The Family under the Bridge;* Child Study Association of America Children's Book Award, 1965, for *The Empty Schoolhouse;* nominated U.S. candidate for International Hans Christian Andersen Award, 1966.

WRITINGS: The Talking Cat and Other Stories of French Canada, Harper, 1952; *Alphonse, That Bearded One,* Harcourt, 1954; *Wings against the Wind,* Harper, 1955; *Sashes Red and Blue,* Harper, 1956; *Hortense: The Cow for a Queen,* Harcourt, 1957; *The Happy Orpheline,* Harper, 1957; *The Family under the Bridge,* Harper, 1958; *A Brother for the Orphelines,* Harper, 1959.

The Tomahawk Family, Harper, 1960; *Evangeline: Pigeon of Paris,* Harcourt, 1960; *The Song of the Lop-eared Mule,* Harper, 1961; *A Pet for the Orphelines,* Harper, 1962; *Carnival in Paris,* Harper, 1962; *School Bell in the Valley,* Harcourt, 1963; *Jean-Claude's Island,* Harper, 1963; *The Orphelines in the Enchanted Castle,* Harper, 1964; *The Letter on the Tree,* Harper, 1964; *The Empty Schoolhouse,* Harper, 1965; *Sailor's Choice,* Harper, 1966; *Chalou,* Harper, 1967; *Luigi of the Streets,* Harper, 1967 (published in England as *The Family on the Waterfront,* Blackie & Son, 1969); *Ann Aurelia and Dorothy,* Harper, 1968; *Befana's Gift,* Harper, 1969 (published in England as *A Grandson for the Asking,* Blackie & Son, 1970); *Marchers for the Dream,* Harper, 1969.

The Half-Sisters, Harper, 1970; *Luvvy and the Girls,* Harper, 1971; *Marie Louise and Christophe,* Scribner, 1974; *Marie Louise's Heydey,* Scribner, 1975; *Runaway Marie Louise,* Scribner, 1977; *Jaky or Dodo?,* Scribner, 1978; *Time for the White Egret,* Scribner, 1978; *King of the Cats and Other Tales,* Doubleday, 1980.

SIDELIGHTS: As a Navy wife, Natalie Savage Carlson has been on the move most of her life, which has provided her with numerous opportunities to acquire out-of-the-ordinary background material for her books. As a result, many of her stories describe the lives of children in such diverse locations as an orphanage near Paris, the Arab quarter of Marseilles, and the slums of Rome. Emphasis is placed on local customs, celebrations, and even particularly descriptive foreign words and expressions (defined in a glossary at the end of each book) to add as much authenticity as possible to the story. Furthermore, as a *Saturday Review* critic notes, "There is a fresh quality and original humor in Mrs. Carlson's books which make them as delightful to the adult sharing them with children as they are to the young boys and girls for whom they are intended."

A *Chicago Sunday Tribune* reviewer calls *The Happy Orpheline,* the first in a series of books about the residents of an orphanage near Paris, "a delightfully droll and tender tale," while a *New York Herald Tribune Book Review* critic notes its "charm and pace and fine perceptive details of French life introduced very naturally" as well as its "mood of tender understanding." *The Family under the Bridge,* also set in and near Paris, is cited by the *Chicago Sunday Tribune* reviewer as "a story as wonderfully warm, as unabashedly sentimental as ever tugged at a reader's heart."

A *New York Times Book Review* critic notes that the world of *Luigi of the Streets* (the Arab quarter of Marseilles) is "more exotic, more fantastic to the young reader than all the palaces of Europe and Asia.... Natalie Savage Carlson again exercises her gift for fusing foreign locales and universal values into a strong, realistic story." A *Young Readers' Review* critic, commenting on *Befana's Gift,* writes that "readers of her books can be transplanted to a locale she has written about and feel right at home.... This heartwarming story is simple, truthful and touching.... The colorful New Year's Eve customs in Rome, the unusual Christmas traditions, the feeling of foreign land add spice and interest."

AVOCATIONAL INTERESTS: Working crossword puzzles, making hand puppets of the characters in her books.

BIOGRAPHICAL/CRITICAL SOURCES: Chicago Sunday Tribune, November 17, 1957, November 2, 1958; *New York Herald Tribune Book Review,* November 17, 1957; *Saturday Review,* December 21, 1957, July 25, 1970; *Young Readers' Review,* November, 1966, June, 1968, May, 1969; *Children's Book World,* November 5, 1967; *New York Times Book Review,* November 5, 1967, September 27, 1970; *Book World,* May 5, 1968; *Times Literary Supplement,* August 14, 1970; *Commonweal,* May 21, 1971; *Chicago Tribune Book World,* November 9, 1980.

*   *   *

CARNEY, John Otis 1922-

PERSONAL: Born February 1922, in Chicago, Ill.; son of William Roy and Marie (Murphy) Carney; married Frederika Fly, 1947; children: Thomas R., John Otis, Jr., Peter C. *Education:* Princeton University, B.A., 1946. *Religion:* Roman Catholic. *Home and office:* Cora, Wyo. 82925. *Agent:* Lurton Blassingame, Blassingame, McCauley & Wood, 60 East 42nd St., New York, N.Y. 10017.

CAREER: Louis de Rochemont Associates, New York, N.Y., writer, 1947; *Minneapolis Star,* Minneapolis, Minn., reporter, 1948-49; J. Walter Thompson (advertising agency), Chicago, Ill., writer, 1950-53; free-lance novelist, television and screenwriter, 1954—. *Military service:* U.S. Marine Corps, four years; became captain; awarded five battle stars, Presidential Unit Citation. *Member:* Society of Midland Authors, Screen Writers Guild. *Awards, honors:* Friends of American Writers Best Book Award, 1960, for *Yesterday's Hero;* Christopher Award; Western Heritage Award; Freedoms Foundation Award.

WRITINGS: (With Charles Spalding) *Love at First Flight,* Houghton, 1943; *When the Bough Breaks,* Houghton, 1957; *Yesterday's Hero,* Houghton, 1959; *Good Friday 1963,* Morrow, 1961; *The Paper Bullet,* Morrow, 1966; *New Lease on Life,* Random House, 1970; *Welcome Back Billy Rawls,* Berkley Publishing, 1977; *Chihuahua, 1916,* Prentice-Hall, 1980.

WORK IN PROGRESS: A nonfiction book; a screenplay.

AVOCATIONAL INTERESTS: Hunting, fishing, ranching.

CAROSSO, Vincent Phillip 1922-

PERSONAL: Born March 20, 1922, in San Francisco, Calif., son of Vincent G. (a businessman) and Lucia M. (Barale) Carosso; married Rose Celeste Berti, August 23, 1952; children: Steven Berti. *Education:* University of California, Berkeley, A.B., 1943, M.A., 1944, Ph.D., 1948. *Home:* 375 Riverside Dr., New York, N.Y. 10025.

CAREER: Harvard University, Cambridge, Mass., postdoctoral fellow in American economic and business history, 1948-49; San Jose State College (now University), San Jose, Calif., instructor in history, 1949-50; Carnegie Institute of Technology (now Carnegie-Mellon University), Pittsburgh, Pa., assistant professor of history, 1950-53; New York University, New York, N.Y., assistant professor, 1953-56, associate professor, 1956-61, professor of history, 1962-76, William R. Kenan, Jr. Professor of History, 1976—. Harvard University, visiting associate research professor, 1961-62, visiting research lecturer, 1964-65. *Member:* American Historical Association, Economic History Association, Organization of American Historians. *Awards, honors:* National Endowment for the Humanities senior fellow, 1976-77; American Council of Learned Societies grant-in-aid, 1978; John Simon Guggenheim Memorial fellow, 1980-81.

WRITINGS: California Wine Industry, University of California Press, 1951, reprinted, 1976; (with George Soule) *American Economic History,* Holt, 1957; (with H. B. Parkes) *Recent America: A History,* two volumes, Crowell, 1963; *Investment Banking in America: A History,* Harvard University Press, 1970, reprinted, 1979; (editor) *Wall Street and the Security Markets,* 58 volumes, Arno, 1975; (editor with Stuart Bruchey) *Companies and Men: Business Enterprise in America,* 38 volumes, Arno, 1976; *More Than a Century of Investment Banking: The Kidder, Peabody & Co. Story,* McGraw, 1979; (editor) *The United States in the Twentieth Century,* three volumes, St. Martin's, 1978-80. Contributor of articles and book reviews to professional journals. Associate editor, *Journal of Economic History,* 1955-60; member of editorial board, *Business History Review,* 1957-58, and *Journal of American History,* 1968—.

WORK IN PROGRESS: The Morgans: Private International Bankers.

AVOCATIONAL INTERESTS: Music.

*   *   *

CARPENTER, (John) Allan 1917-

PERSONAL: Born May 11, 1917, in Waterloo, Iowa; son of John Alex and Theodosia (Smith) Carpenter. *Education:* Iowa State Teachers College (now University of Northern Iowa), B.A., 1938. *Politics:* Republican. *Religion:* Presbyterian. *Home:* Suite 4602, John Hancock Bldg., 175 East Delaware Pl., Chicago, Ill. 60611. *Office:* Suite 4601, John Hancock Bldg., 175 East Delaware Pl., Chicago, Ill. 60611.

CAREER: Des Moines (Iowa) public schools, teacher, 1938-40; *Teacher's Digest,* Chicago, Ill., founder, 1938, editor and publisher, 1938-47; *Popular Mechanics,* Chicago, director of public relations, 1943-62; Carpenter Publishing House, Chicago, founder, 1962, president, 1962—; Infordata International, Chicago, founder, 1972, chairman, 1972—. Founder and president of Music Council of Metropolitan Chicago, 1954; Chicago Business Men's Orchestra, principal bassist, chairman of the board, 1957-63. Director of International Speakers Network, Inc. *Member:* American Symphony Orchestra League, American Association for State and Local History, National Association of Corporate Directors, Fine Arts Club of Chicago.

WRITINGS: Between Two Rivers, Klipto, 1940; (with mother, Theodosia Carpenter) *Hi, Neighbor!,* King, 1945; (editor) *Primer for Home Builders,* Windsor Press, 1946; (editor) *Your Guide to Successful Singing,* Windsor Press, 1950; *The Twelve* (poetry) Farcroft, 1955; (compiler and editor) *Home Handyman Encyclopedia and Guide,* sixteen volumes, Little & Ives, 1961, supplement, 1963; (compiler and editor) *Shop Projects,* Popular Mechanics, 1962; *Illinois, Land of Lincoln,* Children's Press, 1968.

Book series; all published by Children's Press: "Enchantment of America" series, fifty-two volumes, 1963-68, revised edition, 1979; "Enchantment of South America" series, thirteen volumes, 1968-71; "Enchantment of Central America" series, seven volumes, 1971; "Enchantment of Africa" series, forty-two volumes, 1972-73.

Also editor of *Index to U.S. Government Periodicals,* 1974—. Contributor to periodicals, including *Reader's Digest* and *Popular Mechanics.*

WORK IN PROGRESS: A complete comprehensive index to *Reader's Digest* beginning with the year 1922 and continuing.

SIDELIGHTS: Allan Carpenter told *CA:* "'What an awesome responsibility!' That was my automatic response the first time I was described as, 'Possibly the most widely read author in the schools today.' Naturally, that thought recurs frequently, sometimes almost frighteningly. When in one way or another nearly every young mind in the country has been or is being influenced to one degree or another by something you have written, it certainly is cause for some serious thought.

"Of the 192 books that have borne my name, 167 titles have been used as supplementary texts. The millions of copies and the nature of their use brings them constantly to the attention of different readers—and each year another generation. Certainly I have no conclusive proof that I have met my responsibility to such numbers of our young people. However, I have a very comforting means of arriving at some subjective conclusions on that score.

"My young readers write to me—voluminously, and their letters not only give me great assurance of the merit of forthcoming generations but also provide me with much gently humorous insight into human nature. Altogether, my correspondence with young readers probably affords more comfort to me than any other evidence concerning the state of the world and whatever part I may have in it. . . . In two sentences, one of my young correspondents sums up my philosophy of nonfiction writing far better than I could: 'It was very interesting. It was true too.' That youngster had more insight than most of the reviewers who have tackled my books."

*   *   *

CARR, John Dickson 1906-1977
(Carr Dickson, Carter Dickson)

PERSONAL: Born November 30, 1906, in Uniontown, Pa.; died February 27, 1977, in Greenville, S.C.; son of Wood Nicholas (a U.S. Congressman and later a postmaster) and Julia Carr; married Clarice Cleaves, 1931; children: Julia, Bonita, Mary. *Education:* Haverford College, graduate, 1928. *Residence:* Greenville, S.C.

CAREER: Writer, 1930-77. Wrote propaganda broadcasts for British Broadcasting Corp. during World War II; initiated "Suspense" radio program. *Member:* Mystery Writers of America (president, 1949), Baker Street Irregulars; Detection Club, Savage Club, and Garrick Club (all London). *Awards, honors:* Edgar Allan Poe Award, Mystery Writers of America, 1949 and 1962; received two Ellery Queen prizes for short stories.

WRITINGS—Fiction, except as indicated: *It Walks by Night,* Harper, 1930; *Castle Skull,* Harper, 1931, reprinted, Berkley Publishing, 1960; *The Lost Gallows,* Harper, 1931, reprinted, Berkley Publishing, 1960; *The Corpse in the Waxworks,* Harper, 1932 (published in England as *Waxworks Murder,* Hamish Hamilton, 1932, new edition, 1967), reprinted, Collier, 1965; *Poison in Jest,* Harper, 1932, reprinted, Hamish Hamilton, 1977; *The Mad Hatter Mystery* (also see below), Harper, 1933, reprinted, Collier, 1965; *Hag's Nook,* Harper, 1933, reprinted, Penguin, 1967, new edition, Collier, 1963, *The Blind Barber,* Harper, 1934, new edition, Collier, 1962; *The Eight of Swords,* Harper, 1934, reprinted, Collier, 1962; *Death-watch* (also see below), Harper, 1935, reprinted, Collier, 1974; *The Three Coffins* (also see below), Harper, 1935 (published in England as *The Hollow Man,* Hamish Hamilton, 1935, reprinted, Remploy, 1977), reprinted, Charter Books, 1980; *The Arabian Nights Murder* (also see below), Harper, 1936, reprinted, Collier, 1965; *The Murder of Sir Edmund Godfrey* (nonfiction), Harper, 1936, reprinted, Hyperion Press, 1975; *The Burning Court* (also see below), Harper, 1937; *The Four False Weapons, Being the Return of Bencolin,* Harper, 1937, reprinted, Collier, 1962; *To Wake the Dead,* Hamish Hamilton, 1937, Harper, 1938, reprinted, Collier, 1965; *The Crooked Hinge* (also see below), Harper, 1938, reprinted, University Extension, University of California, 1976; (with John Rhode [pseudonym of Cecil J. C. Street]) *Fatal Descent,* Dodd, 1939 (published in England as *Drop to His Death,* Heinemann, 1940); *The Problem of the Green Capsule, Being the Psychologists' Murder Case,* Harper, 1939 (published in England as *The Black Spectacles* [also see below], Hamish Hamilton, 1939); *The Problem of the Wire Cage* (also see below), Harper, 1939, reprinted, Severn House, 1977.

The Man Who Could Not Shudder, Harper, 1940, reprinted, Severn House, 1977; *The Case of the Constant Suicides* (also see below), Harper, 1941, reprinted, Hamish Hamilton, 1977; *Death Turns the Tables,* Harper, 1941 (published in England as *The Seat of the Scornful* [also see below], Hamish Hamilton, 1942), reprinted, Berkley Publishing, 1959; *The Emperor's Snuff-box,* Harper, 1942, reprinted, Hamish Hamilton, 1973; *Till Death Do Us Part,* Harper, 1944, reprinted, Hamish Hamilton, 1977; *He Who Whispers,* Harper, 1946, reprinted, Chivers, 1977; *Dr. Fell, Detective, and Other Stories,* edited by Ellery Queen, American Mercury, 1947; *The Sleeping Sphinx,* Harper, 1947; *Below Suspicion,* Harper, 1949; *The Life of Sir Arthur Conan Doyle* (nonfiction), Harper, 1949, reprinted, Vintage Books, 1975.

The Bride of Newgate (historical novel), Harper, 1950, reprinted, Curtis Books, 1972; *The Devil in Velvet,* Harper, 1951, new edition, Bantam, 1960; *The Nine Wrong Answers: A Novel for the Curious,* Harper, 1952, abridged edition, Bantam, 1962; (with Adrian Conan Doyle) *The Exploits of Sherlock Holmes,* Random House, 1954 (published in England as *More Exploits of Sherlock Holmes,* J. Murray, 1964), reprinted, Sphere Books, 1978; *The Third Bullet and Other Stories,* Harper, 1954; *Captain Cut-throat,* Harper, 1955; *Patrick Butler for the Defence,* Harper, 1956; *Fire, Burn!,* Harper, 1957; *The Dead Man's Knock,* Harper, 1958; (editor) Arthur Conan Doyle, *Great Stories,* J. Murray, 1959; *Scandal at High Chimneys,* Harper, 1959.

In Spite of Thunder, Harper, 1960; *The Witch of the Low Tide: An Edwardian Melodrama,* Harper, 1961; *The Demon-*

iacs, Harper, 1962; *The Men Who Explained Miracles* (short stories), Harper, 1963; *Most Secret,* Harper, 1964; *The House at Satan's Elbow,* Harper, 1965, reprinted, Ace Books, 1980; *Panic in Box C,* Harper, 1966; *Dark of the Moon,* Harper, 1967; *Papa La-bas,* Harper, 1968.

The Ghosts' High Noon, Harper, 1970; *Deadly Hall,* Harper, 1971; *The Hungry Goblin: A Victorian Detective Novel,* Harper, 1972; *The Door to Doom,* Harper, 1980.

Under pseudonym Carr Dickson: *The Bowstring Murders,* Morrow, 1933, published under pseudonym Carter Dickson, Heinemann, 1966.

Under pseudonym Carter Dickson: *The Plague Court Murders,* Morrow, 1934; *The White Priory Murders,* Morrow, 1934, reprinted, Berkley Publishing, 1963; *The Unicorn Murders,* Morrow, 1935, reprinted, Tom Stacey Ltd., 1972; *The Red Widow Murders,* Morrow, 1935, reprinted, Heinemann, 1966; *The Magic Lantern Murders,* Heinemann, 1937, reprinted, 1969; *The Peacock Feather Murders,* Morrow, 1937 (published in England as *The Ten Teacups,* Heinemann, 1937); *The Punch and Judy Murders,* Morrow, 1937; *The Judas Window,* Morrow, 1938, published as *The Crossbow Murder,* Berkley Publishing, 1964; *Death in Five Boxes,* Morrow, 1938, reprinted, Belmont Books 1977; *The Reader Is Warned,* Morrow, 1939.

Nine—And Death Makes Ten, Morrow, 1940 (published in England as *Murder in the Submarine Zone,* Heinemann, 1940); *The Department of Queer Complaints* (short stories), Morrow, 1940; *And So to Murder,* Morrow, 1940; *Seeing Is Believing,* Morrow, 1941; *The Gilded Man,* Morrow, 1942; *She Died a Lady,* Morrow, 1943; *He Wouldn't Kill Patience,* Morrow, 1944; *The Curse of the Bronze Lamp,* Morrow, 1945 (published in England as *Lord of the Sorcerers,* Heinemann, 1946); *My Late Wives,* Morrow, 1946; *The Skeleton in the Clock,* Morrow, 1948, reprinted, Belmont Books, 1977; *A Graveyard to Let,* Morrow, 1949, reprinted, Belmont Books, 1978.

Night at the Mocking Widow, Morrow, 1950; *Behind the Crimson Blind,* Morrow, 1952; *The Cavalier's Cup,* Morrow, 1953; *Fear Is the Same,* Morrow, 1956.

Omnibus volumes: *A John Dickson Carr Trio* (contains *The Three Coffins, The Crooked Hinge,* and *The Case of the Constant Suicides*), Harper, 1957; *A Dr. Fell Omnibus* (contains *The Mad Hatter Mystery, Death-watch, The Black Spectacles,* and *The Seat of the Scornful*), Hamish Hamilton, 1959; *Three Detective Novels* (contains *The Arabian Nights Murder, The Burning Court,* and *The Problem of the Wire Cage*), Harper, 1959.

Also author of scripts for weekly radio program, "Appointment with Fear."

SIDELIGHTS: An acknowledged master of a veritable "genre within a genre"—the locked-room murder mystery—John Dickson Carr earned the praise of readers and critics alike throughout his long and prolific writing career. Famous under his real name as well as under the pseudonym Carter Dickson, he specialized in making the seemingly impossible possible without resorting to last-minute plot revelations such as secret passages or hidden trapdoors. Instead, Carr made sure that his story included all the information his readers needed to know to figure out why and how a dead body could be found in a room that was sealed from the *inside.* His philosophy was a simple one: "You don't ever have to mislead the reader. You just state the evidence, and the reader will mislead himself." Nor did he believe that excessive or unwarranted violence was essential to a well-written murder mystery; in short, Carr preferred his "action" to be based on the excitement of discovery through the use of logic and deduction, explaining that "you have got to keep things moving without shooting [your victims] in the guts or pushing them overboard."

Though he was once quoted as saying that "I insisted on loafing 18 hours a day at the typewriter ever since I was old enought to know one letter from another," Carr did not always plan to make a career out of writing. He entered college with the idea of becoming a lawyer but eventually became interested in newspaper work. Soon after graduating, he journeyed to Paris to study at the Sorbonne. Instead of attending classes, however, Carr began writing his first novel, *It Walks by Night.* Appearing in 1930, the book met with favorable reviews and marked the official beginning of Carr's literary career. The next two decades saw him turn out nearly fifty mystery novels and numerous short stories, most of which grew out of the author's fascination with the infinite variations on the locked-room theme.

Besides being credited with introducing attractive female characters to mystery literature, Carr, like many of his colleagues, invented some memorable male characters, most notably two English detectives who made regular appearances in his works. As John Dickson Carr, the author created Dr. Gideon Fell, an eccentric but dignified Oxford don whose physical appearance and personality were modeled after the British journalist and writer G. K. Chesterton. Carter Dickson's favorite sleuth, Sir Henry Merrivale, was, according to the *New York Times,* "a buffoon given to profanity, with a lordly sneer." Carr himself once admitted that "there's a lot of Winston Churchill in him, and even a little of me."

Making use of these two engaging characters, Carr combined elements of farce and the macabre in an effort to solve the apparently insolvable crime. Though some of his later works prompted a few critics to complain about overuse of the locked-room theme and the problems associated with limited characterization (readers of a Carr mystery tended to remember the puzzle rather than the people), Carr's early works earned him a reputation as an impeccable stylist and a thoroughly entertaining storyteller. In a review of *The Arabian Nights Murder,* for example, the *Manchester Guardian* critic wrote that "Mr. Carr conveys admirably the atmosphere of mingled farce and terror, and one can always be sure that through the maze of marvels he constructs he will guide his readers by the thread of logic and sound reasoning." Commenting on *The Crooked Hinge,* a *New York Times* reviewer noted that the author "is an unexcelled master in this field of creepy erudition, swift-moving excitement, and suspense through atmosphere."

The Judas Window led Will Cuppy of *Books* to write: "You may not believe every word of this new Dickson tale, yet you'll probably find it as satisfactory as any thriller you can name, thanks to the author's justly famous skill at plotting and the presence in fine fettle of . . . Sir Henry Merrivale." In a review of this same book, the *New York Time*'s Isaac Anderson agreed with Cuppy, stating that "perhaps you are tired of locked-room murders. . . . But do not condemn the idea until you have read this one, for it is a particularly ingenious one." Finally, as a *National Review* critic observed in a review of a book written near the end of Carr's life, *Deadly Hall:* "The longer Carr writes, the more one appreciates him. And not just as a plotter or stylist, but also as the nearest thing to a moralist currently practicing the noble art of literary detection. . . . What he is . . . is an unapologetic

Tory—an old-fashioned champion of gentility, taste, standards and romance."

Carr, owner of one of the finest crime reference libraries in the world, was an authority of the life and work of Sir Arthur Conan Doyle, the creator of Sherlock Holmes. In 1949, he collaborated with the famed author's son on Conan Doyle's official biography.

Several of Carr's works have been adapted for film presentation. *The Emperor's Snuff-box,* for example, was filmed as "City after Midnight" in 1959. Various short stories and radio scripts have also been made into films, including "Man with a Cloak" in 1951, "Dangerous Crossing" in 1953, and "Colonel March of Scotland Yard" in 1954.

BIOGRAPHICAL/CRITICAL SOURCES: Manchester Guardian, March 6, 1936; *Books,* January 9, 1938; *New York Times,* January 9, 1938, October 16, 1938, March 1, 1977; Howard Haycraft, *Murder for Pleasure: The Life and Times of the Detective Story,* Appleton, 1941; *New Yorker,* September 8, 1951, September 15, 1951; *Publishers Weekly,* June 27, 1960; C. A. Hoyt, editor, *Minor American Novelists,* Southern Illinois University Press, 1970; *National Review,* October 8, 1971; *Contemporary Literary Criticism,* Volume III, Gale, 1975; *Washington Post,* March 2, 1977; *Newsweek,* March 14, 1977; *Time,* March 14, 1977.†

—*Sketch by Deborah A. Straub*

*   *   *

CARRIER, Warren (Pendleton) 1918-

PERSONAL: Born July 3, 1918, in Cheviot, Ohio; son of Burley Warren and Prudence (Alfrey) Carrier; married Marjorie Regan, April 3, 1947 (deceased); married Judy Hall, June 14, 1973; children: (first marriage) Gregory Paul; (second marriage) Ethan Alfrey. *Education:* Attended Wabash College, 1938-40; Miami University, Oxford, Ohio, A.B., 1942; University of North Carolina, graduate study, 1942-44; Harvard University, M.A., 1948; Occidental College, Ph.D., 1962. *Office:* Office of the Chancellor, University of Wisconsin, Platteville, Wis. 53818.

CAREER: University of North Carolina at Chapel Hill, instructor in Romance languages, 1942-44; Boston University, Boston, Mass., instructor, 1945-49; University of Iowa, Iowa City, assistant professor of English, 1949-52; Bard College, Annandale, N.Y., 1953-57, began as assistant professor, became associate professor of literature; Bennington College, Bennington, Vt., member of literature faculty, 1955-58; Deep Springs College, Deep Springs, Calif., professor of language, literature, and philosophy, 1960-62; Portland State College (now University), Portland, Ore., professor of English, 1962-64; Montana State University, Missoula, professor of English and chairman of department, 1964-68; Rutgers University, New Brunswick, N.J., associate dean of Livingstone College, 1968-69; California State University, San Diego (now San Diego State University), dean of College of Arts and Letters, 1969-72; University of Bridgeport, Bridgeport, Conn., vice-president for academic affairs, 1972-75; University of Wisconsin—Platteville, chancellor, 1975—. Visiting professor, Sweet Briar College, 1958-60. *Wartime service:* American Field Service, attached to British Army, 1944-45; served in India-Burma. *Member:* Royal Society of Arts, Poetry Society of America, National Council of Teachers of English, Wisconsin Academy of Arts and Sciences, Phi Beta Kappa. *Awards, honors:* National Endowment for the Arts award, 1970, for "The Image Waits."

WRITINGS: (Translator) *The City Stopped in Time,* New

Directions, 1949; *The Hunt* (novel), New Directions, 1952; (editor with Paul Engle) *Reading Modern Poetry*, Scott, Foresman, 1955, revised edition, 1968; *Bay of the Damned*, John Day, 1957; *Toward Montebello*, Harper, 1966; *Leave Your Sugar for the Cold Morning*, St. Andrew's Press, 1977; (editor) *Guide to World Literature*, National Council of Teachers of English, 1980; (editor with Bonnie Newman) *Literature from the World*, Scribner, 1981. Contributor to *Accent, Los Angeles Times, Perspective, Poetry, Renascence, Prairie Schooner, Virginia Quarterly Review,* and other publications. *Quarterly Review of Literature,* founder, 1943, editor, 1943-44; associate editor, *Western Review,* 1949-50.

WORK IN PROGRESS: A book of poems; a novel, tentatively entitled *The Lobo Affair.*

BIOGRAPHICAL/CRITICAL SOURCES: Poetry, November, 1966.

*   *   *

CARROLL, John B(issell) 1916-

PERSONAL: Born June 5, 1916, in Hartford, Conn.; son of William J. (an insurance underwriter) and Helen M. (Bissell) Carroll; married Mary E. Searle, 1941; children: Melissa (Mrs. F. Stuart Chapin III). *Education:* Wesleyan University, B.A., 1937; University of Minnesota, Ph.D., 1941. *Home:* 409 Elliot Rd., Chapel Hill, N.C. 27514. *Office:* Psychometric Laboratory, University of North Carolina, Chapel Hill, N.C. 27514.

CAREER: Mount Holyoke College, South Hadley, Mass., instructor, 1940-42; Indiana University at Bloomington, instructor, 1942-43; U.S. Department of Defense, Washington, D.C., research psychologist, 1946-49; Harvard University, Cambridge, Mass., 1949-67, began as assistant professor, professor of education, 1956-67; Educational Testing Service, Princeton, N.J., research psychologist, 1967-74; University of North Carolina at Chapel Hill, Kenan Professor of Psychology, 1974—. Committee chairman, College Entrance Examination Board, 1952-65. Member of advisory committee on automatic language processing, National Academy of Science, 1964-67. *Military service:* U.S. Naval Reserve, 1944-46; became lieutenant junior grade. *Member:* American Educational Research Association, American Psychological Association, Psychometric Society (president, 1960-61), Linguistic Society of America, National Academy of Education (founding member; vice-president, 1977—). *Awards, honors:* M.A., Harvard University, 1953; E. L. Thorndike Award for distinguished service to educational psychology, 1970; Diamond Jubilee Medal, Institute of Linguistics, London, 1971; Educational Testing Service award for distinguished service to measurement, 1980.

WRITINGS: The Study of Language, Harvard University Press, 1953; (editor) *Language, Thought, and Reality,* Wiley, 1956; *Modern Language Aptitude Test,* Psychological Corp., 1958; *Language and Thought,* Prentice-Hall, 1964; (with Peter Davies and Barry Richman) *The American Heritage Word Frequency Book,* Houghton, 1971; (editor with Roy Freedle) *Language Comprehension and the Acquisition of Knowledge,* V. H. Winston, 1972; (editor with Jeanne S. Chall) *Toward a Literate Society,* McGraw, 1975; *The Teaching of French as a Foreign Language,* Halsted, 1975. Contributor to language and other journals.

AVOCATIONAL INTERESTS: Music, specifically the piano and composition.

CARROLL, (Archer) Latrobe 1894-

PERSONAL: Born January 5, 1894, in Washington, D.C.; son of Archer Latrobe and Frances Hamilton (Gamble) Carroll; married Ruth Crombie Robinson, 1928. *Education:* Harvard University, A.B., 1918. *Home:* 2 Fifth Ave., Apt. 16-0, New York, N.Y. 10011.

CAREER: The Century Co., New York City, member of editorial staff, 1919; Foreign Press Service, New York City, staff writer, 1920; *Liberty Magazine,* New York City, member of editorial staff, 1924-34; free-lance writer, 1934—. *Military service:* U.S. Army, Corps of Engineers, 1918. *Member:* Authors League of America, Friends of the Library (Asheville; second vice-president, 1960-63), Harvard Club of Western North Carolina. *Awards, honors:* Juvenile Award of American Association of University Women (North Carolina division), 1953, for *Peanut,* and 1955, for *Digby the Only Dog.*

WRITINGS—Juveniles with wife, Ruth Carroll; published by Walck, except as indicated: Luck of the Roll and Go, Macmillan, 1935; *Flight of the Silver Bird,* Messner, 1939; *Scuffles,* 1943; *School in the Sky,* Macmillan, 1945; *The Flying House,* Macmillan, 1946; *Pet Tale,* 1949; *Peanut,* 1951; *Salt and Pepper,* 1952; *Beanie,* 1953; *Tough Enough,* 1954; *Digby the Only Dog,* 1955; *Tough Enough's Trip,* 1956; *Tough Enough's Pony,* 1957; *Tough Enough and Sassy,* 1958.

Tough Enough's Indians, 1960; *Runaway Pony, Runaway Dog,* 1963; *Danny and the Poi Pup,* 1965; *The Picnic Bear,* 1966; *Bumble Pup,* 1968; *The Christmas Kitten,* 1970; *The Managing Hen and the Floppy Hound,* 1972; *Hullabaloo the Elephant Dog,* 1975.

Translator: Camille Flammarion, *Death and Its Mystery: At The Moment of Death,* Century, 1922; Flammarion, *Death and Its Mystery: After Death,* Century, 1923.

AVOCATIONAL INTERESTS: Hiking, travel, and reading.

BIOGRAPHICAL/CRITICAL SOURCES: Richard Walser, *Picturebook of Tar Heel Authors,* North Carolina Department of Archives and History, 1957, 3rd edition, 1966; Muriel Fuller, *More Junior Authors,* H. W. Wilson, 1963.

*   *   *

CASSON, Lionel 1914-

PERSONAL: Born July 22, 1914, in New York, N.Y. *Education:* New York University, A.B., 1934, M.A., 1935, Ph.D., 1939. *Office:* Department of Classics, New York University, New York, N.Y. 10003.

CAREER: New York University, New York, N.Y., instructor, 1936-45, assistant professor, 1945-52, associate professor, 1952-59, professor of classics, 1959—. Director of summer session in classics, American Academy in Rome, 1963—. *Military service:* U.S. Naval Reserve, 1942-46; became lieutenant. *Member:* American Philological Association, American Archaeological Association, Association Internationale des Papyrologues, Society for Nautical Research. *Awards, honors:* Guggenheim fellow, 1952-53, 1959-60; National Endowment for the Humanities fellowship, 1967-68, summer seminar grant, 1978.

WRITINGS: (With E. E. Burriss) *Latin and Greek in Current Use,* Prentice-Hall, 1939, revised edition, 1948; (with E. L. Hettich) *Excavations at Nessana,* Volume II, Princeton University Press, 1950; *The Ancient Mariners: Seafarers and Sea Fighters of the Mediterranean in Ancient Times,* Macmillan, 1959; *Masters of Ancient Comedy,* Macmillan,

1960; (editor and translator) *Selected Satires of Lucian,* Doubleday, 1962; (editor and translator) *Six Plays of Plautus,* Doubleday, 1963; *Illustrated History of Ships and Boats,* Doubleday, 1964; (with the editors of Time-Life books) *Ancient Egypt,* Time, 1965; (editor) *Masterpieces of World Literature: Classical Age,* Dell, 1965; *Ships and Seamanship in the Ancient World,* Princeton University Press, 1971; (editor and translator) *The Plays of Menander,* New York University Press, 1971; (editor and translator) Plautus, *Amphitryon and Two Other Plays,* Norton, 1971; (editor and translator) Plautus, *The Menaechmus Twins, and Two Other Plays,* Norton, 1971; *Travel in the Ancient World,* Allen & Unwin, 1974; *Daily Life in Ancient Rome,* Horizon, 1975; *Daily Life in Ancient Egypt,* Horizon, 1975; (with Robert Claiborne and Brian Fagan) *Mysteries of the Past,* American Heritage, 1977; (contributor) *Discovery of Lost Worlds,* American Heritage, 1979. Member of advisory editorial board, *American Neptune* and *Archaeology.*

*   *   *

CASTANEDA, Hector-Neri   1924-

PERSONAL: Born December 13, 1924, in San Vincente, Zacapa, Guatemala; naturalized U.S. citizen in 1963; son of Ezequiel (a farmer) and Sara (Calderon) Castaneda; married Miriam Mendez, December 24, 1946; children: Xmucane, Kicab, Hector Neri, Omar Sigfrido, Quetzil Eugenio. *Education:* Attended Universidad de San Carlos, Guatemala, 1945-48; University of Minnesota, B.A., 1950, M.A., 1952, Ph.D., 1954; Oxford University, postdoctoral study, 1955-56. *Home:* 2244 Martha St., Bloomington, Ind. 47401. *Office:* Department of Philosophy, Indiana University, Bloomington, Ind. 47405.

CAREER: High school teacher of mathematics and Spanish in Guatemala, 1945-49; University of Minnesota, Minneapolis, instructor in philosophy, 1953-54; Universidad de San Carlos, Guatemala City, Guatemala, assistant professor of philosophy, 1954-55; Duke University, Durham, N.C., visiting assistant professor of philosophy, 1956-57; Wayne State University, Detroit, Mich., assistant professor, 1957-61, associate professor, 1961-64, professor of philosophy, 1963-69, acting chairperson of department, 1965-66, 1968; Indiana University at Bloomington, professor of philosophy, 1969-74, Mahlon Powell Professor of Philosophy, 1974—, dean of Latino affairs, 1978—. Adult education teacher in Ferndale, Mich., 1959-63; University of Texas, visiting lecturer, 1962-63, visiting adjunct professor, 1966; visiting adjunct professor of philosophy at University of Western Ontario, 1968, Wayne State University, 1970, University of Cincinnati, 1970, and University of Pittsburgh, 1972. Indiana University, member of advisory committee for Semiotics Program, 1975-76, committee for research summer fellowships, 1977, Council of Deans, 1978—, Basic Skills Operating Committee, 1978—, advisory committee for the GPOP Program, 1978-79, 1979-80, Committee for Educational Policy, Bloomington Faculty Council, 1979-80, and Committee for Minority Recruitment, Graduate School; National Endowment for the Humanities, director of summer seminars, 1974-76, 1978, director of year-long seminar, 1980-81. Andres Bello Philological Center, Guatemala, founder, president, 1945-47, research director, 1947-48. Has presented papers to several learned societies; referee for journals, including *Critica, Philosophia, American Philosophical Quarterly,* and *Philosophical Studies.* Consultant to National Endowment for the Humanities, National Science Foundation, Canadian Research Council, and to Evaluating Committee, department of philosophy, Lehigh University; consultant to numerous pub-

lishers, including Macmillan Publishing Co., D. Reidel Publishing Co., Princeton University Press, Wayne State University Press, and Indiana University Press.

MEMBER: American Philosophical Association (Western Division; vice-president, 1978-79; president, 1979-80), Society for Exact Philosophy (president, 1972-74), Indiana Philosophical Association (president, 1976-77), Indiana University Concerned Titled Professors Association. *Awards, honors:* British Council fellow, Oxford University, 1955-56; Wayne State University summer grant, 1959; National Science Foundation travel grant, Argentina, 1960; Wayne State Fund Recognition Award in humanities, 1961; American Council of Learned Societies grant, 1962; Oak Ridge Institute of Nuclear Studies fellow, 1963; National Science Foundation grant, 1965-67; Guggenheim fellow, 1967-68; National Endowment for the Humanities independent study grant, 1975-76; American Council of Learned Societies travel grant, France, 1976; Center for Advanced Study in the Behavioral Sciences fellow, 1981-82.

WRITINGS: Funciamentos de la didactica del lenguaje, Publicaciones del Centro Filologico (Guatemala), 1948; *La Dialectica de la Conciencia de Si mismo,* University of San Carlos Press, 1961; (editor with George Nakhnikian and contributor) *Morality and the Language of Conduct,* Wayne State University Press, 1963; *Intentionality, Minds, and Perception,* Wayne State University Press, 1967; *The Structure of Morality,* C. C Thomas, 1974; (editor and contributor) *Action, Knowledge, and Reality,* Bobbs-Merrill, 1974; *La Ontologia de Platon en el Fedon,* University of Mexico Press, 1976; *Thinking and Doing: The Philosophical Foundation of Institutions,* D. Reidel, 1975; *On Philosophical Method,* NOUS Publications, 1980.

Contributor: C. D. Rollins, editor, *Knowledge and Experience,* University of Pittsburgh Press, 1963; Paul Benacerraf, and Hilary Putnam, editors, *Philosophy of Mathematics,* Prentice-Hall, 1963; Paul Edwards, editor, *The Encyclopedia of Philosophy,* Macmillan, 1967; N. Rescher, editor, *The Logic of Decision and Action,* University of Pittsburgh Press, 1967; O. R. Jones, editor, *The Private Language Argument,* St. Martin's, 1971; E. D. Klemke, editor, *Essays on Wittgenstein,* University of Illinois Press, 1971; G. Harman and D. Davidson, editors, *Semantics of Natural Language,* D. Reidel, 1972; J. W. Davis, editor *Value and Valuation: Axiological Studies in Honor of Robert S. Hartman,* University of Tennessee Press, 1972; J. Leach, editor, *Science, Decision and Value,* D. Reidel, 1973; Mario Bunge, editor, *Studies in Exact Philosophy,* D. Reidel, 1973; Boruch Brody, editor, *Readings in the Philosophy of Religion: An Analytic Approach,* Prentice-Hall, 1974; Paul Welsh, editor, *Fact, Value and Perception: Essays in Honor of Charles A. Baylis,* Duke University Press, 1975; H. M. Zellner, editor, *Assassination,* Schenkman, 1974; M. Brand and D. Walton, editors, *Action Theory,* D. Reidel, 1976; Amedo Conte, Risto Hilpinen, and Georg Henrik Von Wright, editors, *Deontische Logik und Semantik,* Athenaion (Wiesbaden), 1977; Peter French, Ted Uehling, and Howard Wettstein, editors, *Contemporary Perspectives in the Philosophy of Language,* University of Minnesota Press, 1979; Peter Van Inwagen, editor, *Time and Cause,* D. Reidel, 1980. Contributor of numerous articles to professional journals. Founder and editor of *NOUS,* 1966—; member of editorial board, *Critica,* 1967—, *Philosophical Archives,* 1975—, and *Manuscrito,* 1976—.

WORK IN PROGRESS: Research on the logic concepts of cognition.

CHAFETZ, Henry   1916-1978

PERSONAL: Born May 2, 1916, in New York, N.Y.; died of cancer January 5, 1978, in New York, N.Y.; son of Benjamin and Frances (Guzman) Chafetz; married. *Education:* Attended New York University, B.A.; also attended New School for Social Research. *Home:* 525 East 86th St., New York, N.Y. *Agent:* McIntosh & Otis, Inc., 475 Fifth Ave., New York, N.Y. 10017. *Office:* Cooper Square Publishers, Inc. and Pageant Bookstore, 59 Fourth Ave., New York, N.Y. 10003.

CAREER: Pageant Bookstore, New York City, co-owner and co-proprietor, 1946-78; Cooper Square Publishers, Inc., New York City, president, 1961-78. *Military service:* U.S. Army Air Forces, 1942-45, became first lieutenant; awarded Air Medal with oak leaf clusters. *Member:* New York Posse of the Westerners.

WRITINGS—Juvenile, except as indicated: The Lost Dream, Knopf, 1955; *The Legend of Befana,* Houghton, 1958; *Play the Devil: A History of Gambling in the United States from 1492-1955* (adult), Bonanga Books, 1960; *Thunderbird and Other Stories,* Pantheon, 1964; *Chanticleer: The Story of a Proud Rooster* (based on the play "Chanticleer" by Edmond Rostand), Pantheon, 1968; (with Ralph Hancock) *The Compleat Swindler* (adult), Macmillan, 1968. Contributor to newspapers, magazines, and television.

AVOCATIONAL INTERESTS: Golf, fishing, literature, American history.†

*   *   *

CHAGALL, David   1930-

PERSONAL: Born November 22, 1930, in Philadelphia, Pa.; son of Harry and Ida (Coopersmith) Chagall; married Juneau Joan Alsin (an artist), November 15, 1956. *Education:* Attended Swarthmore College, 1948-49; Pennsylvania State University, B.A., 1952; Sorbonne, University of Paris, graduate study, 1953-54. *Home address:* P.O. Box 85, Agoura, Calif. 91301.

CAREER: Social case worker for the State of Pennsylvania; teacher in the public schools of Philadelphia, Pa.; staff editor for British science journal in London, England; member of public relations staff of A.E.I.-Hotpoint Ltd. in London; market research analyst for Chilton Company, Philadelphia; research project director for Haug Associates, Los Angeles; currently investigative reporter for *T.V. Guide, Panorama,* and other national magazines; syndicated columnist; lecturer. *Awards, honors:* Poetry prize of University of Wisconsin, 1971; nominee for National Book Award in fiction, 1972, for *Diary of a Deaf Mute;* nominee for Pulitzer Prize in Letters, 1973, for *The Spieler for the Holy Spirit;* Distinguished Health Journalism Award, 1979.

WRITINGS—All novels: Diary of a Deaf Mute, Raben & Sjogren, 1960, Millenium House, 1971; *The Century God Slept,* Sidgwick & Jackson, 1962, Yoseloff, 1963; *The Spieler for the Holy Spirit,* Ashley Books, 1972; (contributor) Barry Cole, editor, *Television Today,* Oxford University Press, 1980; *The New Kingmakers,* Harcourt, 1981. Contributor of short fiction, poetry, articles, and reviews to American and British magazines, journals and newspapers.

WORK IN PROGRESS: A novel about the separatist movement among Mexican-Americans in the southwestern United States, tentatively entitled *Return to Aztlan.*

*   *   *

CHAMBERS, Jonathan David   1898-1970

PERSONAL: Born October 13, 1898, in Underwood, Nottinghamshire, England; died, 1970; son of Edmund and Sarah Ann (Oates) Chambers; married Dorothy Grace Cheston, 1926; children: Dorothy Ann. *Education:* Attended University College, Nottingham; University of London, Ph.D. *Office:* University of Nottingham, Nottingham, England.

CAREER: English master at boys' school in Ashby-de-la-Zouch, England, 1920-22, 1940-47; University College, Nottingham, lecturer, 1924-34, assistant director of adult education, 1934-40, lecturer in economic history, 1947-52, reader in economic and social history, 1952-58, professor of economic history, 1959-64, professor emeritus, 1964-70. *Member:* Nottingham Civic Society (founder), Historical Association (member of council), Thoroton Society (vice-president), Nottinghamshire Local History Council (chairman).

WRITINGS: Nottinghamshire in the Eighteenth Century, Staples, 1932, 2nd edition, Augusta M. Kelley, 1966; *School History of Lincoln,* Lincoln Education Committee, 1938; *Dictators in History,* Nelson, 1940; *Dictators: An Introductory Study in the Sociological Origins of Dictatorship,* Nelson, 1941; *Modern Nottingham in the Making,* Nottingham Journal, 1945; *The Vale of Trent,* Cambridge University Press, 1957; *The Workshop of the World: British Economic History from 1820 to 1880,* Oxford University Press, 1961, 2nd edition, 1968; *Laxton, the Last Open Field Village,* H.M.S.O., 1964; (contributor) D. V. Glass and D.E.C. Eversley, editors, *Population in History,* Edward Arnold, 1965; (with G. E. Mingay) *The Agricultural Revolution, 1750-1880,* Schocken, 1966; (with P. J. Madgwick) *Conflict and Community: Europe since 1750,* George Philip & Son, 1968; (with S. D. Chapman) *The Beginnings of Industrial Britain,* University Tutorial Press, 1970; (with E. I. Abell) *The Story of Lincoln: An Introduction to the History of the City,* S. R. Publishers, 1971; *Population, Economy, and Society in Pre-Industrial England,* edited by W. A. Armstrong, Oxford University Press, 1972. Also editor of *D. H. Lawrence: A Personal Recollection by E. T.*

BIOGRAPHICAL/CRITICAL SOURCES: E. L. Jones and G. E. Mingay, editors, *Land, Labour, and Population in the Industrial Revolution: Essays Presented to J. D. Chambers,* Edward Arnold, 1967, Barnes & Noble, 1968.†

*   *   *

CHARNEY, Maurice (Myron)   1929-

PERSONAL: Born January 18, 1929, in New York, N.Y.; son of A. Benjamin (a business executive) and Sadie A. (Stang) Charney; married Hanna Kurz (a professor of French), June 20, 1954; children: Leopold Joseph, Paul Robert. *Education:* Harvard University, A.B. (magna cum laude), 1949; Princeton University, M.A., 1951, Ph.D., 1952. *Home:* 168 West 86th St., New York, N.Y. 10024. *Office:* English Department, Rutgers University, New Brunswick, N.J. 08903.

CAREER: Hunter College (now Hunter College of the City University of New York), New York, N.Y., instructor in English, 1953-54; Rutgers University, New Brunswick, N.J., instructor, 1956-59, assistant professor, 1959-62, associate professor, 1962-67, professor, 1967-75, distinguished professor of English, 1975—. Fulbright exchange professor at University of Bordeaux and University of Nancy, 1960-61; visiting summer professor at Hunter College, 1963, Harvard University, 1965, Shakespeare Institute of Canada, 1969, Shakespeare Institute of America, 1970, 1971, 1975. Co-chairman, American Civilization Seminar, Columbia University, 1977-79. Member of central executive committee, Folger Institute, 1978-80. Literary adviser, Methuen & Co., 1980—. *Military service:* U.S. Army, 1954-56. *Member:* Academy of Literary Studies (charter member), Modern Language Association of America (chairman of Shakespeare division, 1973, 1976), Shakespeare Association of America, Malone Society, Renaissance Society of America, American Association of University Professors, Phi Beta Kappa.

WRITINGS: Shakespeare's Roman Plays, Harvard University Press, 1961; (editor and author of introduction) *Discussions of Shakespeare's Roman Plays,* Heath, 1964; (editor) Shakespeare, *Timon of Athens,* Signet, 1965; (editor) *The Tragedy of "Julius Caesar,"* Bobbs-Merrill, 1969; *Style in "Hamlet,"* Princeton University Press, 1969; *How to Read Shakespeare,* McGraw, 1971; *Comedy High and Low,* Oxford University Press, 1978; (editor) *Comedy: New Perspectives,* New York Literary Forum, 1978; (editor) *Shakespearean Comedy,* New York Literary Forum, 1980; *Sexual Fiction,* Methuen, 1981. Contributor of articles and reviews to twenty-five journals; member of editorial board, *Shakespeare Quarterly, Review of Psychoanalytic Books,* and *New York Literary Forum.*

WORK IN PROGRESS: A critical book on Joe Orton for Macmillan; a collection of essays on *Hamlet;* a book on Shakespeare and his contemporary dramatists tentatively entitled *Shakespeare—and the Others.*

SIDELIGHTS: Maurice Charney told *CA:* "I have always been much impressed by Anthony's words for the dead Caesar: 'You all did love him once, not without cause.' That would make a perfect epitaph for a writer, who imagines his career as a form of flirtation and seduction of an unknown public. The writer hopes that his works will enlist him in the magic circle of humanity, what Hawthorne called 'catching hold of the magnetic chain' of humanity. This is a strange, remote, and audacious attempt to sign on to the human race. Its mental and oneiric quality endows it with special properties set apart from daily life. The writer as thaumaturge can transcend his other roles as father, husband, teacher, and ritual clown that characterize his daily life."

* * *

CHATTERJEE, Margaret (Gantzer) 1925-

PERSONAL: Born September 13, 1925, in London, England; Indian citizen; daughter of Norman (a civil servant) and Edith (Hickman) Gantzer; married N. N. Chatterjee (formerly joint secretary in the ministry of labor and employment in the Indian government), 1946; children: Malay Kumar (son), Nilima (daughter), Amala (daughter). *Education:* Somerville College, Oxford University, B.A. (with honors), 1946, M.A., 1956; University of Delhi, Ph.D., 1961; University of London, postdoctoral study, 1961. *Home:* D2, 29-31 Chhatra Marg, Delhi 110007, India. *Office:* Department of Philosophy, University of Delhi, Delhi, India.

CAREER: University of Delhi, Delhi, India, lecturer in philosophy at Miranda House, University College for Women, 1956-62, reader in philosophy, 1962-76; Visva-Gharati, Santini Ketan, India, professor of comparative religion, 1976-77; University of Delhi, professor of philosophy, 1977—, chairman of department, 1979—. Music critic for *Statesman* (Delhi). Broadcaster of philosophical talks and piano and lieder recitals on All India Radio. *Member:* International Society for Metaphysics (vice-president).

WRITINGS: Our Knowledge of Other Selves, Asia Publishing House, 1963; *Philosophical Enquiries,* New Age (Calcutta), 1967; *The Spring and the Spectacle* (poems), Writer's

Workshop (Calcutta), 1967; *Towards the Sun* (poems), Writer's Workshop, 1970; *The Sandalwood Tree* (poems), Writer's Workshop, 1972; *At the Homeopaths* (short stories), Writer's Workshop, 1973; *The Existentialist Outlook,* Orient Longman, 1974; (editor) *Contemporary Indian Philosophy,* Allen & Unwin, 1974; *The Sound of Wings* (poems), Arnold-Heinemann, 1978; *The Language of Philosophy,* Allied, in press. Translator with Kshitis Roy, Bibhuti Bhusan Banarji, *Pather Panchali,* abridged edition. Poems have appeared in five anthologies, including *Span.* Contributor of articles, poetry, and short stories to magazines and professional journals. Member of board of editorial consultants, *Religious Studies* (London) and *Religious Traditions* (Australia).

WORK IN PROGRESS: Gandhian Religious Thought; a fifth collection of poems.

SIDELIGHTS: Margaret Chatterjee told *CA:* "As a writer of both philosophy and poetry I am fascinated by the different ways in which each of these distils experience. Born and brought up in the United Kingdom, having lived most of my life in India, I do not believe in frontiers—whether between people or between disciplines. My poetry is fed by my knowledge of many cultures, my short stories by what I hope is a somewhat Dickensian eye, and my philosophy by my insistence that the philosopher is first and foremost a writer and not a professional technical performer. In this respect I am closer to the French than the Anglo-Saxon tradition. My book *The Language of Philosophy* has a lot to say about metaphor. In other words, my work in philosophy and poetry is not kept in separate compartments."

AVOCATIONAL INTERESTS: Gardening, baroque music, Hungarian culture, Jewish studies, comparative theology.

* * *

CHERRY, Kelly

PERSONAL: Born in Baton Rouge, La.; daughter of J. Milton (a violinist and professor of music theory) and Mary (a violinist and writer; maiden name, Spooner) Cherry; married Jonathan Silver, December 23, 1966 (divorced, 1969). *Education:* Mary Washington College, B.A., 1961; University of Virginia, graduate study, 1961-63; University of North Carolina at Greensboro, M.F.A., 1967; also attended New Mexico Insitute of Mining and Technology, Virginia Polytechnic Institute (now Virginia Polytechnic Institute and State University), Richmond Professional Institute (now Virginia Commonwealth University), University of Richmond, and University of Tennessee. *Residence:* Madison, Wis. *Agent:* Scott Meredith Literary Agency, Inc., 845 Third Ave., New York, N.Y. 10022. *Office:* Department of English, University of Wisconsin, Madison, Wis.

CAREER: Behrman House, Inc. (publishers), New York City, editor and writer, 1970-71; Charles Scribner's Sons, New York City, editor, 1971-72; John Knox Press, Richmond, Va., editor, 1973; Southwest Minnesota State College (now Southwest State University), Marshall, writer-in-residence, 1974-75; University of Wisconsin—Madison, associate professor and writer-in-residence, 1977—. Has also worked as editorial assistant, copy editor, tutor, and teacher to emotionally disturbed teenagers. *Awards, honors:* Canaras Award for fiction from St. Lawrence University Writers Conference, 1974; Bread Loaf fellow, 1975; Yaddo fellow, 1979; National Endowment for the Arts grant, 1980.

WRITINGS: (Contributor and author of teacher's guide) Jules Harlow, editor, *Lessons from Our Living Past,* Behrman, 1972; *Sick and Full of Burning* (novel), Viking, 1974; *Lovers and Agnostics* (poems), Red Clay, 1975; *Relativity: A*

Point of View, Louisiana State University Press, 1977; *Augusta Played*, Houghton, 1979; *Conversion*, Treacle Press, 1979; *Songs for a Soviet Composer*, Singing Wind Press, 1980. Work is represented in numerous anthologies, including *Best American Short Stories*, edited by Martha Foley, Houghton, 1972, and *Pushcart Prize II*, edited by Bill Henderson, Avon, 1977.

Contributor of stories and poems to magazines, including *Commentary, Southern Review, Georgia Review, Esquire, Anglican Theological Review, Southern Poetry Review, Carolina Quarterly, Fiction*, and *Western Humanities Review*.

WORK IN PROGRESS: Another novel.

SIDELIGHTS: Kelly Cherry once wrote *CA:* "Philosophy rightly comprehended is the becoming-aware-of abstraction in real life, since in order to abstract, you must have something to abstract from. Why, just to get from Tuesday to Thursday, you have to solve the problem of free will.

"My novels, then, deal with moral dilemmas and the shapes they create as they reveal themselves in time. My poems seek out the most suitable temporal or kinetic structure for a given emotion.

"I think that the crucial unit of the poem is the line; in the story, it's sentence; and in the novel, it's the scene. I know that these sentiments run counter to the American tradition, or too much of it, but I think that much of the American literary tradition is dull, anti-intellectual, and unmusical, and furthermore, easily embarrassed by emotional honesty. This of course is not to deny those American writers who are exciting, wise, and beautiful, but too many of them are dead."

K. M. Purnell believes Cherry's opinions concerning the importance of the line, the sentence, and the scene are reflected in her writings and offers Cherry's *Relativity: A Point of View* as an example. Purnell writes in the *Library Journal* that this "collection is organized into sections neatly prefaced by a quotation which draws together and offers insights into the poems in that section. That technique is characteristic of the poet's work: the language is firm and down-to-earth, form and rhyme are carefully manipulated.... A woman's point of view is present, but it is spoken, not shouted."

Cherry more recently told an interviewer for *Library Journal* that "if anyone asks what my dominant theme is—the one that overrides all my work—I still have to say it's structure. Like other sentimentalists, I would like to restore the unity that we lost when we split the atom. But of course it doesn't count if the restoration isn't one of reality. Sand castles amuse but don't intrigue. I choose instead to dig in my own backyard, in which there is, necessarily, a certain amount of dirt. But playing where I do, I see my neighbor's linen on the line, and observe how structure and sun gladden the heart—and bemuse the mind. Birds flying south stop here overnight."

AVOCATIONAL INTERESTS: Paleontology, cosmology, Russian literature from the pre-Revolutionary period, Latin, music, C. S. Pierce, and Joyce Cary.

BIOGRAPHICAL/CRITICAL SOURCES: Library Journal, October 1, 1974, June 15, 1977; *Authors in the News*, Volume I, Gale, 1976; *Chicago Tribune*, April 1, 1979.

*　　*　　*

CHILDRESS, Alice 1920-

PERSONAL: Born in 1920, in Charleston, S.C.; married Nathan Woodard (a musician); children: Jean (Mrs. Richard Lee). *Education:* Attended public schools in New York, N.Y.; Radcliffe Institute for Independent Study, graduate, 1968. *Residence:* Roosevelt Island, N.Y. 10044. *Agent:* Flora Roberts, Inc., 65 East 55th St., New York, N.Y. 10022.

CAREER: Actress and director with American Negro Theatre, New York, N.Y., for eleven years; writer. Has made several appearances on Broadway and television. Lecturer at universities and schools. *Member:* P.E.N., Dramatists Guild (member of council), Writers East (member of council), Harlem Writers Guild. *Awards, honors:* Obie Award for best original Off-Broadway play, *Village Voice*, 1956, for "Trouble in Mind"; John Golden Fund for Playwrights grant, 1957; Woodward School Book Award, 1975; Jane Addams Honor Award for young adult novel, 1974, National Book Award nomination, 1974, and Lewis Carroll Shelf Award, University of Wisconsin, 1975, all for *A Hero Ain't Nothin' but a Sandwich;* named honorary citizen of Atlanta, Ga., 1975, for opening of "Wedding Band"; achievement award, National Association for Negro Business and Professional Women's Clubs, 1975; Virgin Islands film festival award for best screenplay, 1977, for "A Hero Ain't Nothin' but a Sandwich"; Paul Robeson Award for outstanding contributions to the performing arts, Filmmakers Hall of Fame, 1977; "Alice Childress Week" officially observed in Charleston, S.C. and Columbia, S.C., 1977, to celebrate opening of "Sea Island Song."

WRITINGS: Like One of the Family: Conversations from a Domestic's Life, Independence Press, 1956; (editor) *Black Scenes: Collections of Scenes from Plays Written by Black People about Black Experience*, Doubleday, 1971; *A Hero Ain't Nothin' but a Sandwich* (novel; also see below), Coward, 1973; *A Short Walk* (novel), Coward, 1979.

Plays: "Florence" (one-act), first produced at American Negro Theatre, directed by Childress, 1949; (adaptor) Langston Hughes, "Just a Little Simple" (based on Hughes's novel, *Simple Speaks His Mind*), first produced in New York City at Club Baron Theatre, September, 1950; "Gold through the Trees," first produced in New York City at Club Baron Theatre, 1952; "Trouble in Mind," first produced Off-Broadway at Greenwich Mews Theatre, directed by Childress, November 3, 1955 (published in *Black Theatre: A Twentieth-Century Collection of the Work of Its Best Playwrights*, edited by Lindsay Patterson, Dodd, 1971); *Wedding Band* (also see below; first produced in Ann Arbor, Mich. at University of Michigan, December 7, 1966; produced Off-Broadway at New York Shakespeare Festival Theatre, directed by Childress and Joseph Papp, September 26, 1972), Samuel French, 1973; "String" (one-act; also see below), first produced Off-Broadway at St. Mark's Playhouse, March 25, 1969; *When the Rattlesnake Sounds* (juvenile), Coward, 1975; *Let's Hear It for the Queen* (juvenile), Coward, 1976; "Sea Island Song," produced in Charleston, S.C., 1977; *Mojo* [and] *String* (two one-act plays; produced in Los Angeles at Inner City Cultural Center, 1978), Dramatists Play Service, 1971.

Screenplays: *Wine in the Wilderness* (first produced in Boston by WGBH-TV, 1969), Dramatists Play Service, 1970; "Wedding Band," ABC-TV, 1973; "A Hero Ain't Nothin' but a Sandwich" (based on novel of same title), New World Pictures, 1978.

Also author of plays "The World on a Hill" (published in *Plays to Remember*, Macmillan, 1968), "Martin Luther King at Montgomery, Alabama," music by husband, Nathan

Woodard, 1969, "A Man Bearing a Pitcher," 1969, "The African Garden," music by Woodard, 1971, and "The Freedom Drum," music by Woodard. Work represented in numerous anthologies, including *The Best Short Plays of 1972*, edited by Stanley Richards, Chilton, 1972, *The Young American Basic Reading Program*, Lyons & Carnaham, 1972, *Success in Reading*, Silver Burdette, 1972, and *Best Short Plays of the World Theatre, 1968-1973*, edited by Richards, Crown, 1973. Author of column, "Here's Mildred," *Baltimore Afro-American*, 1956-58. Contributor of plays, articles, and reviews to *Masses and Mainstream, Black World, Freedomways, Essence*, and other publications.

SIDELIGHTS: Alice Childress's work is noted for its frank treatment of racial issues, its compassionate yet discerning characterizations, and its universal appeal. Because the subject matter (such as miscegenation and teenage drug addiction) of her books and plays is often controversial, Childress's work has been banned in certain locations. She told *CA* that some affiliate stations refused to carry the nationally televised broadcasts of "Wedding Band" and "Wine in the Wilderness"; and, in the case of the latter play, the entire state of Alabama banned the telecast. Moreover, Childress notes that as late as 1973 the novel *A Hero Ain't Nothin' but a Sandwich* "was the first book banned in a Savannah, Georgia school library since *Catcher in the Rye*, which the same school banned in the fifties." Despite such regional resistance, Childress has won much critical praise and respect for writings that a *Variety* reviewer terms "powerful and poetic."

Doris E. Abramson calls Childress "a crusader and a writer who resists compromise. She tries to write about Negro problems as honestly as she can." The problems Childress tackles most often are racism and its effects. "Trouble in Mind," for example, is a play within a play that focuses on the anger and frustration experienced by a troupe of black actors as they try to perform stereotyped roles in a play that has been written, produced, and directed by whites. As Sally R. Sommer of the *Village Voice* explains, "The plot is about an emerging rebellion begun as the heroine, Wiletta, refuses to enact a namby-Mammy, either in the play or for her director." The *New York Times*'s Arthur Gelb finds that Childress "has some witty and penetrating things to say about the dearth of roles for Negro actors in the contemporary theatre, the cut-throat competition for these parts and the fact that Negro actors often find themselves playing stereotyped roles in which they cannot bring themselves to believe." And of "Wedding Band," a play about an interracial relationship that takes place in South Carolina during World War I, Clive Barnes writes, "Miss Childress very carefully suggests the stirrings of black consciousness, as well as the strength of white bigotry."

Critics Sommer and the *New York Times*'s Richard Eder find that Childress's treatment of the themes and issues in "Trouble in Mind" and "Wedding Band" gives these plays a timeless quality. "Writing in 1955, . . . Alice Childress used the concentric circles of the play-within-the-play to examine the multiple roles blacks enact in order to survive," Sommer remarks. She finds that viewing "Trouble in Mind" years later enables one to see "its double cutting edge: It predicts not only the course of social history but the course of black playwrighting." Eder states: "The question [in "Wedding Band"] is whether race is a category of humanity or a division of it. The question is old by now, and was in 1965, [when the play was written,] but it takes the freshness of new life in the marvelous characters that Miss Childress has created to ask it."

The strength and insight of Childress's characterizations have been widely commented upon; critics contend that the characters who populate her plays and novels are believable and memorable. Eder praises the "rich and lively characterization" of "Wedding Band." The *Nation*'s Harold Clurman is similarly impressed with this aspect of the play. "There is an honest pathos in the telling of this simple story," he comments, "and some humorous and touching thumbnail sketches reveal knowledge and understanding of the people dealt with." In the novel *A Short Walk*, Childress chronicles the life of a fictitious black woman, Cora James, from her birth in 1900 to her death in the middle of the century, illustrating, as James McLellan describes it, "a transitional generation in black American society." McLellan notes that the story "wanders considerably" and that "the reader is left with no firm conclusion that can be put into a neat sentence or two." What is more important, he asserts, is that "the wandering has been through some interesting scenery, and instead of a conclusion the reader has come to know a human being—complex, struggling valiantly and totally believable." And of Childress's novel about teenage heroin addiction, *A Hero Ain't Nothin' but a Sandwich*, the *Lion and the Unicorn*'s Miguel Oritz states, "The portrait of whites is more realistic in this book, more compassionate, and at the same time, because it is believable, more scathing."

Some criticism has been leveled at what reviewers, such as Abramson and Edith Oliver, believe to be Childress's tendency to speechify, especially in her plays. "A reader of the script is very much aware of the author pulling strings, putting her own words into a number of mouths," Abramson says of "Trouble in Mind." According to Oliver of the *New Yorker*, "The first act [of 'Wedding Band'] is splendid, but after that we hit a few jarring notes, when the characters seem to be speaking as much for the benefit of us eavesdroppers out front . . . as for the benefit of one another."

For the most part, however, Childress's work has been acclaimed for its honesty, insight, and compassion. In his review of *A Hero Ain't Nothin' but a Sandwich*, Oritz writes: "The book conveys very strongly the message that we are all human, even when we are acting in ways that we are somewhat ashamed of. The structure of the book grows out of the personalities of the characters, and the author makes us aware of how much the economic and social circumstances dictate a character's actions." John T. Gillespie agrees with this assessment and points to the book's wide-ranging appeal. "*Hero* is not just a family of blacks and their problems," he remarks. "It deals with themes and experiences that are universal, such as rejection, love, the importance of family ties, poverty, and the problem of growing old." Finally, Loften Mitchell of *Crises* concludes: "Miss Childress writes with a sharp, satiric touch. Character seems to interest her more than plot. Her characterizations are piercing, her observations devastating."

Alice Childress comments: "Books, plays, tele-plays, motion picture scenarios, etc., I seem caught up in a fragmentation of writing skills. But an idea comes to me in a certain form and, if it stays with me, must be written out or put in outline form before I can move on to the next event. I sometimes wonder about writing in different forms; could it be that women are used to dealing with the bits and pieces of life and do not feel as [compelled to specialize]? The play form is the one most familiar to me and so influences all of my writing—I think in scenes.

"My young years were very old in feeling, I was shut out of so much for so long. [I] soon began to embrace the low-profile as a way of life, which helped me to develop as a writer.

Quiet living is restful when one's writing is labeled 'controversial.'

"Happily, I managed to save a bit of my youth for spending in these later years. Oh yes, there are other things to be saved [besides] money. If we hang on to that part within that was once childhood, I believe we enter into a new time dimension and every day becomes another lifetime in itself. This gift of understanding is often given to those who constantly battle against the negativities of life with determination."

BIOGRAPHICAL/CRITICAL SOURCES: New York Times, November 5, 1955, February 2, 1969, October 26, 1972, February 3, 1978, January 11, 1979; *Crises,* April, 1965; *Negro Digest,* April, 1967, January, 1968; Doris E. Abramson, *Negro Playwrights in the American Theatre: 1925-1959,* Columbia University Press, 1969; *Show Business,* April 12, 1969; *Washington Post,* May 18, 1971; *New Yorker,* November 4, 1972; *Nation,* November 13, 1972; *Variety,* December 20, 1972; John T. Gillespie, *More Juniorplots: A Guide for Teachers and Librarians,* Bowker, 1977; *Lion and the Unicorn,* fall, 1978; *Los Angeles Times,* November 13, 1978; *Village Voice,* January 15, 1979; *New York Times Book Review,* November 11, 1979; *Washington Post Book World,* December 28, 1979; *Contemporary Literary Criticism,* Gale, Volume XII, 1980, Volume XV, 1980.

—Sketch by Denise Gottis

*　　　*　　　*

CHRISTIAN, Reginald Frank 1924-

PERSONAL: Born August 9, 1924, in Liverpool, England; son of Herbert Alexander and Jessie (Scott) Christian; married March 29, 1952; children: Jessica Ilott, Giles Nicholas. *Education:* Queen's College, Oxford University, B.A., 1949, M.A., 1950. *Home:* The Roundel, St. Andrews, Fife, Scotland. *Office:* Department of Russian, St. Salvator's College, University of St. Andrews, St. Andrews, Scotland KY16 9AL.

CAREER: British Embassy, Moscow, Russia, member of staff, 1949-50; University of Liverpool, Liverpool, England, lecturer in Russian, and head of department, 1950-55; University of Birmingham, Birmingham, England, senior lecturer, 1956-63, professor of Russian language and literature, 1963-66, head of department, 1956-63; University of St. Andrews, St. Andrews, Scotland, professor and head of department of Russian, 1966—, dean of graduate students, 1972-73, dean of Faculty of Arts, 1975-78. Visiting professor of Russian, McGill University, 1961-62; visiting lecturer, Moscow Institute of Foreign Languages, 1964-65. *Military Service:* Royal Air Force, 1943-46; became flying officer. *Member:* British Universities Association of Slavists (treasurer, 1959-61; president, 1967-70); Association of Teachers of Russian (honorary vice-president).

WRITINGS: Korolenko's Siberia, Liverpool University Press, 1954; (with F. M. Borras) *Russian Syntax,* Oxford University Press, 1959, 2nd revised edition, 1971; *Tolstoy's War and Peace: A Study,* Oxford University Press, 1962; (with Borras) *Russian Prose Composition,* Oxford University Press, 1963, 2nd revised edition, 1973; *Tolstoy: A Critical Introduction,* Cambridge University Press, 1969; (editor and translator) *Legend: Tolstoy's Letters,* Scribner, 1978, Volume I: *1828-1879,* Volume II: *1880-1910.* Contributor of articles and reviews to European and American professional journals.

WORK IN PROGRESS: An edition of Tolstoy's diaries.

AVOCATIONAL INTERESTS: Hill-walking, music (playing the violin), squash.

*　　　*　　　*

CHURCH, Richard 1893-1972

PERSONAL: Born March 26, 1893, in London, England; died March 4, 1972, in Kent, England; son of Thomas John and Lavina Annie (Orton) Church; married Caroline Parfett, 1915; married second wife, Catherine Anna Schimmer, 1928 (died, 1965); married Dorothy Beale, 1967; children: three daughters, one son. *Education:* Attended public schools in England. *Home:* Scotney Castle, Lamberhurst, Kent, England. *Agent:* Laurence Pollinger, Ltd., 11 Long Acre, London WC2E 9LH, England.

CAREER: Civil servant, Whitehall, London, England, 1909-33; J. M. Dent & Sons, Ltd. (publishers), London, editor, 1933-51. Former director, English Festival of Spoken Poetry. Lecturer for British Council throughout Europe, India, and Africa. *Member:* Royal Society of Literature (fellow; vice-president, 1968), Royal Society of Art (fellow, 1970), English Association (former president), Society of Authors, Society of Bookmen, P.E.N. (president, 1958-59), Athenaeum Club, Savile Club, Canterbury Literary Club (past president, Kent and Sussex Poetry Society (president, 1962). *Awards, honors:* Femina Vie Heureuse Prize, 1938; *Sunday Times* gold medal, 1955, for *Over the Bridge;* Foyle Poetry Prize, 1957; commander, Order of the British Empire, 1957.

WRITINGS—Novels: Oliver's Daughter: A Tale, Dent, 1930; *High Summer,* Dent, 1931, Smith & Durrell, 1932; *The Prodigal Father,* John Day, 1933; *The Apple of Concord,* Dent, 1935; *The Porch,* Dent, 1937, reprinted, New Portway Reprints, 1976; *The Stronghold,* Dent, 1939; *The Room Within,* Dent, 1940, reprinted, New Portway Reprints, 1977; *A Squirrel Named Rufus* (juvenile), Dent, 1941, John C. Winston, 1947; *The Sampler,* Dent, 1942; *The Cave* (juvenile), Dent, 1950, revised edition, 1953, published as *Five Boys in a Cave,* John Day, 1951; *The Nightingale,* Hutchinson, 1952; *Dog Toby: A Frontier* (juvenile), Hutchinson, 1952; *The Dangerous Years,* Heinemann, 1956; *Down River* (juvenile), Heinemann, 1958; *The Crab-Apple Tree,* Heinemann, 1959; *The Bells of Rye* (juvenile), Heinemann, 1960, John Day, 1961; *Prince Albert,* Heinemann, 1963; *The White Doe* (juvenile), Heinemann, 1968, John Day, 1969; *Little Miss Moffatt: A Confession,* Heinemann, 1969; *The French Lieutenant: A Ghost Story for Young Readers,* John Day, 1971.

Poetry: *The Flood of Life,* Fifield, 1917; *Hurricane,* Selwyn & Blount, 1919; *The Dream,* Benn, 1922; *Philip,* Blackwell, 1923; *The Portrait of the Abbot,* Benn, 1926; *Theme with Variations,* Benn, 1928; *Glance Backward,* Dent, 1930; *News from the Mountain,* Dent, 1932; *Twelve Noon,* Dent, 1936; *The Solitary Man,* Dent, 1941; *Twentieth Century Psalter,* Dent, 1943; *The Lamp,* Dent, 1946; *Collected Poems,* Dent, 1948, published as *The Collected Poems of Richard Church,* AMS Press, 1976; *Selected Lyrical Poems,* Staples, 1951; *The Prodigal* (verse play), Staples, 1953; *The Inheritors,* Heinemann, 1957; *North of Rome,* Hutchinson, 1960; *The Burning Bush: Poems, 1958-1966,* Heinemann, 1967; *Twenty-five Lyrical Poems,* Heinemann, 1967.

Editor: (And author of introduction) Algernon C. Seinburne, *Poems and Prose,* Dutton, 1940; *John Keats: An Introduction and a Selection,* Phoenix House, 1948; Percy Bysshe Shelley, *Poems,* Cassell, 1949; *Poems for Speaking,* Dent, 1950; Phoebe Hesketh, *Out of the Dark: New Poems,* Heinemann, 1954; *The Spoken Word* (anthology), Collins, 1955;

(with M. M. Bozman) *Poems of Our Time, 1900-1960*, Dent, 1959; *The Little Kingdom: Essays by Divers Hands*, Oxford University Press, 1965.

Autobiographies: *Over the Bridge*, Heinemann, 1955, Dutton, 1956; *The Golden Sovereign*, Dutton, 1957; *The Voyage Home*, Heinemann, 1964, John Day, 1966.

Other: *Mood without Measure*, Heinemann, 1927; *Mary Shelley*, Howe, 1928, reprinted, Norwood Editions, 1975; *Calling for a Spade*, Dent, 1939; *Eight for Immortality*, Dent, 1941, reprinted, Books for Libraries, 1969; *Plato's Mistake*, Allen & Unwin, 1941; *British Authors*, Longmans, Green, 1943, revised edition, 1948, reprinted, Arno, 1974; *Green Tide*, Country Life, 1945; *Kent*, Hale, 1948, revised edition, 1966; *A Window on a Hill*, Hale, 1949; *Growth of the English Novel*, Methuen, 1951, Barnes & Noble, 1961; *A Portrait of Canterbury*, Hutchinson, 1953; *Small Moments*, Hutchinson, 1957, Dutton, 1958; *A Country Window*, Heinemann, 1958; *Calm October*, Heinemann, 1961; *A Stroll before Dark*, Heinemann, 1965; *A Look at Tradition*, Oxford University Press, 1965; (with I. Hofbauer) *London: Flower of Cities All*, John Day, 1966; *Speaking Aloud*, Heinemann, 1968; *A Harvest of Mushrooms, and Other Sporadic Essays*, Heinemann, 1970; *The Wonder of Words*, Hutchinson, 1970; *London in Colour*, Batsford, 1971; *Kent's Contribution*, Baths, Adams and Dart, 1972; *My England*, Heinemann, 1973. Also author of monthly essay for home forum page of the *Christian Science Monitor* for over forty years. Also contributor to magazines, newspapers, and other periodicals including *Spectator* and *New Statesman*.

SIDELIGHTS: Richard Church once told *CA:* "I have been writing since boyhood, that is, over sixty years, and have readers all over the world. Many of my books have been translated into European languages, and Japanese.

"The half dozen books for children have been written for my own children and grandchildren. One, *Five Boys in a Cave*, was not even written. It was dictated to a secretary at the urgent command of my first grandson. It is now translated into many languages; is a schoolbook in Japan, U.S.A., Britain, and is reprinted annually. Usually, however, I write in longhand in bound manuscript books, making few changes, and my secretary takes the finished manuscript and types it in her office. Both in my verse and prose, I am concerned to make the words musical, and the sense immediately clear, thus giving both body and soul to the work. My books are intended for Everyman and Everywoman, this includes Every Child."

AVOCATIONAL INTERESTS: Music and gardening.

BIOGRAPHICAL/CRITICAL SOURCES: Christian Science Monitor, July 19, 1968; *New York Times*, March 5, 1972; *Time*, March 20, 1972.†

*   *   *

CICELLIS, Kay 1926-

PERSONAL: Born 1926, in Marseilles, France; daughter of Gerasimos and Vassilia (Saliari) Cicellis; married Nicholas Paleologos, 1957; children: Michael-Emmanuel, Anna-Francesca. *Home:* 6 Hatzikostas St., Athens 602, Greece. *Agent:* Curtis Brown Group Ltd., 1 Craven Hill, London W2 3EW, England.

CAREER: United Nations Relief and Rehabilitation Administration, Athens, Greece, translator, 1945-47; Greek Broadcasting Institute, Athens, writer-adaptor, 1953-55.

WRITINGS: The Easy Way (short story collection), Grove, 1950; *No Name in the Steet* (novel), Grove, 1952; *Death of a Town* (short story collection), Grove, 1954; *Ten Seconds from Now* (novel), Grove, 1956; *The Way to Colonos* (novellas), Secker & Warburg, 1960; (translator) Stratis Tsirkas, *Drifting Cities*, Knopf, 1974; (translator) Manolis Chatzidakis, *Benaki Museum*, C B Publishers, 1975; (translator) Vassos Karageorhais, *Cyprus Museum and Archaelogical Sites of Cyprus*, C B Publishers, 1975; (translator) Manolis Andronikos, *Delphi*, C B Publishers, 1975; Andronikos, *Olympia*, C B Publishers, 1975; Andronikos, *Pella Museum*, C B Publishers, 1975; Andronikos, *Thessalonike Archaeological Museum*, C B Publishers, 1975; (translator) Zissimos Lorenzatos, *The Lost Center*, Princeton University Press, 1980. Contributor of articles and reviews to *Harper's Bazaar, Mademoiselle, Paris Review*, and *London Magazine*. Author of several feature programs produced by British Broadcasting Corporation, and a libretto for an opera composed by A. Kounadis.

WORK IN PROGRESS: "A series of loosely-connected texts on the problems of language."

SIDELIGHTS: Several of Kay Cicellis' books have been published in Germany, Spain, Portugal, and France. *Avocational interests:* The cinema, gastronomy, linguistics, psychology.

*   *   *

CLEARY, Jon 1917-

PERSONAL: Born November 22, 1917, in Sydney, Australia; son of Matthew and Ida (Brown) Cleary; married Constantine Joy Lucas, September 6, 1946; children: Catherine, Jane. *Education:* Left school at end of second year of high school in Sydney, Australia. *Home:* 71 Upper Pitt St., Kirribilli, New South Wales, Australia. *Agent:* John Farquharson Ltd., 8 Bell Yard, London WC2A 2JU, England.

CAREER: Prior to World War II worked at "too many jobs to be listed," including commercial artist, salesman, delivery man, laundry worker, bush worker, and sign painter; full-time writer, 1945—, except for a year in London, England, as journalist with Australian Government Bureau, and two years in New York, N.Y., with the Australian Bureau. *Military service:* Australian Army, 1940-45; served in Middle East, New Guinea, and New Britian campaigns; became lieutenant. *Awards, honors:* Australian Broadcasting Commission National Play Award, co-winner of first prize, 1944; *Sydney Morning Herald* National Novel Contest, second prize, 1946; Crouch gold medal for best Australian novel of 1950; *New York Herald Tribune* World Story Contest, co-winner of Australian section; Edgar Allan Poe Award, 1974.

WRITINGS—All published by Morrow, except as indicated: *These Small Glories*, Angus & Robertson, 1946; *You Can't See around Corners*, Scribner, 1947, 4th edition, Horwitz, 1965; *The Long Shadow*, Laurie, 1950, reprinted, Severn House, 1976; *Just Let Me Be*, Laurie, 1951; *The Sundowners*, Scribner, 1952; *The Climate of Courage*, Collins, 1954; *Justin Bayard*, 1955; *The Green Helmet*, 1958; *Back of Sunset*, 1959; *North from Thursday*, 1961; *The Country of Marriage*, 1962; *Forests of the Night*, 1963; *A Flight of Chariots*, 1963; *The Fall of an Eagle*, 1964; *The Pulse of Danger*, 1966; *The High Commissioner*, 1966; *The Long Pursuit*, 1967; *Season of Doubt*, 1968; *Remember Jack Hoxie*, 1969; *Helga's Web*, 1970; *The Liberators*, 1971 (published in England as *Mask of the Andes*, Collins, 1971); *The Ninth Marquess*, 1972 (published in England as *Man's Estate*, Collins, 1972); *Ransom*, 1973; *Peter's Pence*, 1974; *The Safe House*, 1975; *A Sound of Lightning*, Collins, 1975, Morrow, 1976; *High Road to China*, 1977; *Vortex*, 1978; *The Beaufort Sisters*,

1979; *A Very Private War*, 1980; *The Golden Sabre*, 1981. Also author of film scripts for Warner Brothers, Inc., Metro-Goldwyn-Mayer, Inc., Paramount Pictures Corp., and Ealing Films; author of television scripts for productions in the United States and England.

SIDELIGHTS: Although Jon Cleary's permanent home is in Australia, he and his family spend more than half of the time traveling. They have lived in the United States, England, Spain, Italy, and Austria, and have traveled in Europe, Africa, Asia, South America, and throughout Australia and its neighboring islands.

Six of Cleary's novels have been filmed: *Justin Bayard* in 1958 by Southern Pacific, *The Green Helmet* in 1960 by Metro-Goldwyn-Mayer, *The Sundowners* in 1961 by Warner Bros., *The High Commissioner* in 1968 by Rank, *You Can't See around Corners* in 1969 by Universal, and *Helga's Web* in 1976 by Kingscroft.

AVOCATIONAL INTERESTS: Cricket, squash, tennis.

BIOGRAPHICAL/CRITICAL SOURCES: New York Times Book Review, July 9, 1967, July 7, 1968, September 14, 1969, June 2, 1974; *Best Sellers*, May 1, 1969, March 15, 1971, May 1, 1974; *Books & Bookmen*, July, 1969; *Times Literary Supplement*, July 17, 1969, March 16, 1973; *Books*, October, 1969.

*   *   *

CLEM, Alan L(eland) 1929-

PERSONAL: Born March 4, 1929, in Lincoln, Neb.; son of Remey Leland (a clergyman and school administrator) and Bernice (Thompson) Clem; married Mary Louise Burke, October 24, 1953; children: Andrew, Christopher, Constance, John, Daniel. *Education:* University of Nebraska, B.A., 1950; American University, M.A., 1957, Ph.D., 1960. *Politics:* Republican. *Religion:* Episcopalian. *Home:* 902 Valley View Dr., Vermillion, S.D. 57069. *Office:* Department of Political Science, University of South Dakota, Vermillion, S.D. 57069.

CAREER: Ayres Advertising Agency, Lincoln, Neb., copywriter, then research director, 1950-52; press secretary in Washington, D.C., for U.S. Representative Carl Curtis, 1953-54, and Representative R. D. Harrison, 1955-58; U.S. Department of Agriculture, Foreign Agricultural Service, Washington, D.C., information specialist, 1959-60; University of South Dakota, Vermillion, associate professor, 1960-64, professor of government, 1964-76, professor of political science, 1978—, Governmental Research Bureau, assistant director, 1960-64, associate director, 1964-76, chairman of department of political science, 1976-78. Partner, Opinion Survey Associates, 1964—. Television election analyst, KELO-TV. *Member:* American Political Science Association, Midwest Political Science Association (member of executive council), Alpha Tau Omega, Sigma Delta Chi, Phi Beta Kappa, Phi Alpha Theta, Pi Sigma Alpha.

WRITINGS: The U.S. Agricultural Attache: His History and His Work, Foreign Agricultural Service, U.S. Department of Agriculture, 1960; *Spirit Mound Township in the 1960 Election: A Study of Rural Attitudes Toward Issues, Candidates, and Campaign Appeals*, Governmental Research Bureau, University of South Dakota, 1961; *South Dakota Political Almanac: A Presentation and Analysis of Election Statistics, 1889-1960*, Governmental Research Bureau, University of South Dakota, 1962, 2nd edition, Dakota Press, 1970; *The Nomination of Joe Bottum: Analysis of a Committee Decision to Nominate a United States Senator*,

Governmental Research Bureau, University of South Dakota, 1963; *Precinct Voting: The Vote in Eastern South Dakota, 1940-1960*, Governmental Research Bureau, University of South Dakota, 1963; (editor) *Proceedings of the Fifth Annual Conference for South Dakota Assessing Officers*, Governmental Research Bureau, University of South Dakota, 1963; *Political Attitudes of South Dakota High School Students*, Governmental Research Bureau, University of South Dakota, 1963.

West River Voting Patterns: The Vote in Western South Dakota, 1940-1960, Governmental Research Bureau, University of South Dakota, 1965; (compiler with George M. Platt) *A Bibliography of South Dakota Government and Politics*, Governmental Research Bureau, University of South Dakota, 1965; *Popular Representation and Senate Vacancies*, Governmental Research Bureau, University of South Dakota, 1966; *Roll Call Voting Behavior in the South Dakota Legislature*, Governmental Research Bureau, University of South Dakota, 1966; *Prairie State Politics: Popular Democracy in South Dakota*, Public Affairs Press, 1967; (editor) *Contemporary Approaches to State Constitutional Revision*, Governmental Research Bureau, University of South Dakota, 1969.

(Contributor) *Explaining the Vote*, Social Science Research Center, University of North Carolina, 1973; *The Making of a Congressman: Seven Campaigns of 1974*, Duxbury Press, 1976; *Measuring Legislative Committee Performance*, Governmental Research Bureau, 1977; *American Electoral Politics: Strategies for Renewal*, Van Nostrand, 1981. Contributor to history, law, and political science journals.

SIDELIGHTS: Alan Clem told *CA:* "I wrote *American Electoral Politics: Strategies for Renewal* because I felt it was high time for someone to pull together and integrate the sensible, long overdue ideas for simplifying and opening up the party and electoral structures of our political system. There is no good excuse for our electoral processes and institutions to be so complicated and inconsistent. Renewal will require persistent effort at many levels across the nation, and I hope this book will contribute to that effort."

AVOCATIONAL INTERESTS: Bridge, golf, heraldry, old road maps, church history, game theory, and Edmund Burke.

*   *   *

CLERY, (Reginald) Val(entine) 1924-
(Janus)

PERSONAL: Surname is pronounced like "Cleary"; born January 26, 1924; son of Claude Valentine (an engineer) and Dora Frances (Reilly) Clery; married Susan Salaman, October 4, 1960 (divorced, 1971); children: Emma, Daniel, Louisa. *Education:* Attended school in Ireland. *Home and office:* 40 Huntley St., Apt. 1, Toronto, Canada M4Y 1L2.

CAREER: Puppet Opera Co., Dublin, Ireland, stage manager, 1954-55; Canadian Broadcasting Corp. (CBC), London, England, producer, 1959-65, executive producer in Toronto, Ontario, 1965-70; *Books in Canada*, Toronto, editor, 1971-73. *Military service:* British Army, Royal Artillery and Commandos, 1941-46; served as lance-bombardier. *Awards, honors: Irish Writing* story award, 1947; story award from *Observer*, 1955.

WRITINGS: Promotion and Response: Report on Canadian Book Promotion, Canadian Book Publishers Council, 1971; *Canada in Colour*, Hounslow Press, 1972; *Windows*, Penguin, 1978; *Doors*, Penguin, 1978; *Canada from the News-*

stand, Macmillan (Canada), 1978; *A Day in the Woods,* Greey de Pencier Books, 1978; *Seasons of Canada,* Hounslow Press, 1979; (with Richard Hogarth) *Dragons,* Penguin, 1979. Also translator of *Eskimo Diary* and editor of *Cities.* Author of column, appearing under pseudonym Janus, in *Quill and Quire.* Contributor to *Globe, Globe and Mail, Toronto Star, Maclean's,* and *Weekend.*

WORK IN PROGRESS: Angels, Jonathon James Books; *The Canadian Feast,* Clarke, Irwin; *Solo Chief,* Madison Press; a political satire with the working title, *Gulliver in Canada.*

*   *   *

CLEWES, Dorothy (Mary)   1907-

PERSONAL: Born July 6, 1907, in Beckenham, Kent, England; daughter of Frank and Annie Gertrude Parkin; married Winston David Armstrong Clewes (a writer), 1932 (died July 26, 1957). *Education:* Attended University of Nottingham. *Religion:* Church of England. *Home:* Soleic, King's Ride, Alfriston, Sussex, England. *Agent:* Curtis Brown Ltd., 575 Madison Ave., New York, N.Y. 10022.

CAREER: Secretary and dispenser to Nottingham physician, 1924-32; professional writer. Speaker at schools and libraries in England, United States. *Member:* P.E.N. (executive committee), Society of Authors, National Book League. *Awards, honors:* Junior Literary Guild Award, 1957.

WRITINGS: The Rivals of Maidenhurst, Nelson, 1925; *She Married a Doctor,* Jenkins, 1943, published as *Stormy Hearts,* Arcadia, 1944; *Shepherd's Hill,* Low, 1945; *To Man Alone,* Arcadia, 1945; *The Cottage in the Wild Wood* (also see below), Faber, 1945; *The Stream in the Wild Wood* (also see below), Faber, 1946; *Treasure in the Wild Wood,* Faber, 1947; *The Wild Wood* (contains *The Cottage in the Wild Wood* and *The Stream in the Wild Wood*), Coward, 1948; *Stranger in the Valley,* Harrap, 1948; *The Fair in the Wild Wood,* Faber, 1949; *Blossom on the Bough,* Harrap, 1949.

Henry Hare's Boxing Match, Coward, 1950; *Summer Cloud,* Harrap, 1951; *Henry Hare's Earthquake,* Coward, 1951; *Henry Hare, Painter and Decorator,* Chatto & Windus, 1951; *Henry Hare and the Kidnapping of Selina Squirrel,* Chatto & Windus, 1951; (contributor) *The Eleanor Farjeon Giftbook,* Hamilton, 1965; *Guide Dogs for the Blind,* Hamilton, 1966.

Teen-age, young adult, adventure; all published by Coward, except as indicated: *The Adventure of the Scarlet Daffodil,* Chatto & Windus, 1952, published as *The Mystery of the Scarlet Daffodil,* 1953; *The Mystery of the Blue Admiral,* 1954; *Adventure on Rainbow Island,* Collins, 1956, published as *Mystery on Rainbow Island,* 1957; *The Mystery of the Jade Green Cadillac,* 1958; *The Mystery of the Lost Tower Treasure,* 1960; *The Mystery of the Singing Strings,* 1961; *The Purple Mountain,* Collins, 1962; *The Golden Eagle,* 1962; *Operation Smuggle,* Collins, 1964; *The Midnight Smugglers,* 1964; *Guide Dog,* 1965.

Children's books; all published by Coward, except as indicated: *The Secret,* 1956; *The Runaway,* 1957; *The Happiest Day,* 1958; *The Old Pony,* 1960; *Hide and Seek,* 1960; *The Hidden Key,* 1961; *All the Fun of the Fair,* 1962; *The Birthday,* 1963; *Boys and Girls Come out to Play,* Hamish Hamilton, 1964; *The Holiday,* 1965; *Roller Skates, Scooter, and Bike,* 1966; *A Boy Like Walt,* 1967; *A Bit of Magic,* Hamish Hamilton, 1967; *Adopted Daughter,* 1968; *Upside-down Willie,* Hamish Hamilton, 1968; *A Girl Like Cathy,* Collins, 1968; *Special Branch Willie,* Hamish Hamilton, 1969; *Fire*

Brigade Willie, Hamish Hamilton, 1970; *Library Lady,* Chatto, Boyd & Oliver, 1970, published as *The Library,* Coward, 1971; *Peter and the Jumbie,* Hamish Hamilton, 1970; *The End of Summer,* 1971; *Two Bad Boys,* Hamish Hamilton, 1971; *Storm over Innish,* Heinemann, 1972, Thomas Nelson, 1973; *Hooray for Me,* Heinemann, 1972; *The Secret of the Sea,* Heinemann, 1973; *Ginny's Boy,* Heinemann, 1973; *A Skein of Geese,* Chatto, Boyd & Oliver, 1973; *Wanted: A Grand,* Chatto & Windus, 1974; *Missing from Home,* Heinemann, 1975, Harcourt, 1978; *Nothing to Declare,* Heinemann, 1976; *The Testing Year,* Heinemann, 1977; *Merry-go-round,* White Lion, 1977. Contributor to children's magazines and annuals.

Fantasy: *Wilberforce and the Slaves,* Hutchinson, 1961; *Skyraker and the Iron Imp,* Hutchinson, 1962; *The Branch Line,* Hamish Hamilton, 1963; *Red Rover and the Combine Harvester,* Hutchinson, 1966.

WORK IN PROGRESS: An adult novel, period, semi-biographical.

*   *   *

CLIFFORD, Mary Louise Beneway   1926-

PERSONAL: Born August 15, 1926, in Ontario, N.Y.; married Robert L. Clifford, July 14, 1951; children: Christopher, Joan Candace. *Education:* Cornell University, A.B., 1948; College of William and Mary, M.A., 1978. *Home:* 109 Shellbank Dr., Williamsburg, Va. 23185. *Office:* National Center for State Courts, 300 Newport Ave., Williamsburg, Va.

CAREER: Worked for the American Legation, Beirut, Lebanon, 1949-51; National Center for State Courts, Williamsburg, Va., staff associate, 1977—. *Member:* Phi Beta Kappa.

WRITINGS: Bisha of Burundi, Crowell, 1973; *Salah of Sierra Leone,* Crowell, 1975.

"The Land and People" series; all published by Lippincott: *The Land and People of Afghanistan,* 1962; *. . . of Malaysia,* 1968; *. . . of Liberia,* 1971; *. . . of Sierra Leone,* 1974; *. . . of the Arabian Peninsula,* 1977.

The Noble & Noble African Studies Program, Noble & Noble, 1971: Volume I: *The African Environment: Portrait of a Continent,* Volume II: *The Voices of Africa: The People,* Volume III: *Creeds and Cultures in Modern Africa: Belief, Tradition, and Change,* Volume IV: *Echoes from the African Past: Hunting and Fishing Peoples,* Volume V: *The Timeless Search: The Pastoral People of Africa,* Volume VI: *Master of the Soil: The Farming People of Africa,* Volume VII: *The Creative Africans: Artists and Craftsmen,* Volume VIII: *Challenge of the City: The Urban African,* Volume IX: *Stone and Steel: The Builders of Africa,* Volume X: *Africa: The Beginning of Tomorrow–Government, Statesmen, and African Unity.*

WORK IN PROGRESS: A novel about the Virginia Indians between 1560 and 1622.

*   *   *

CLOETE, Stuart   1897-1976

PERSONAL: Born July 23, 1897, in Paris, France; died March 20, 1976; son of Laurence and Edith (Park) Cloete; married Florence Eileen Horsman, 1918 (divorced, 1940); married Mildred E. Ellison, 1940. *Education:* Attended Bilton Grange and Lancing College in England. *Address:* Box 37, Hermanus, South Africa. *Agent:* William Morris Agency, 1350 Ave. of the Americas, New York, N.Y. 10019.

CAREER: Rancher in South Africa, 1926-35; professional

writer, 1935-76. Trustee, South Africa Foundation. *Military service:* British Army, Coldstream Guards, 1914-18; became acting captain. *Member:* National Arts Club, Overseas Press Club (New York), Guards Club, Savage Club (London), Explorers Club. *Awards, honors:* National Institute of Arts and Letters fellowship, 1957.

*WRITINGS—*Novels; all published by Houghton, except as indicated: *The Turning Wheels* (Book-of-the-Month Club selection), 1937; *Watch for the Dawn,* 1939; *The Hills of Doves,* 1941; *Christmas in Mantabeleland,* Doubleday, 1942; *Congo Song* (Literary Guild selection), 1943; *The Curve and the Tusk: A Novel of Change among Elephants and Men,* 1952; *Mamba,* 1956; *The Mask,* 1957; *Gazella,* 1958; *The Fiercest Heart,* 1960; *Rags of Glory,* Doubleday, 1963; *The Thousand and One Nights of Jean Macaque,* Trident, 1965; *How Young They Died,* Trident, 1969; *The Abductors,* Trident, 1970.

Collected short stories; all published by Collins, except as indicated: *The Soldiers' Peaches and Other African Stories,* Houghton, 1959; *The Silver Trumpet,* 1961; *The Looking Glass and Other African Stories,* 1963, new edition published as *Land of the Eagle and Other African Stories,* Fontana Books, 1971; *The Honey Bird and Other African Stories,* 1964; *The Writing on the Wall and Other African Stories,* 1967, published as *Chetoko, and Other African Stories,* 1976; *Three White Swans and Other Stories,* 1971; *The Company with the Heart of Gold and Other Stories,* 1973; *More Nights with Jean Macaque,* 1975; *Canary Pie,* 1976.

Other: *Yesterday Is Dead,* Smith & Durrell, 1940; *The Young Men and the Old* (poems), Houghton, 1941; *Against These Three: A Biography of Paul Kruger, Cecil Rhodes, and Lobengula, Last King of the Matabele,* Houghton, 1945, published as *African Portraits: A Biography of Paul Kruger, Cecil Rhodes, and Lobengula, Last King of the Matabele,* Collins, 1946; *The Third Way,* Houghton, 1947; *The African Giant: The Story of a Journey,* Houghton, 1955; *Storm over Africa: A Study of the Mau Mau Rebellion, Its Causes, Effects, and Implications in Africa South of the Sahara,* Culemborg, 1956; *West with the Sun,* Doubleday, 1962; *South Africa: The Land, It's People and Achievements,* Da Gama, 1969; *A Victorian Son: An Autobiography, 1897-1922,* Collins, 1972; *The Gambler: An Autobiography, 1920-1939,* Collins, 1973. Contributor to *Life, Saturday Evening Post, Esquire, Vogue, Town and Country,* and other magazines.

SIDELIGHTS: Stuart Cloete once told *CA:* "My life has been divided into three parts. I have been successively a soldier, a cattle rancher, and a writer. Early I learned about the mystery of battle, as a soldier I saw death. I have always been interested in the mystery of love or as it is now called sex. Life is the story of birth, love, and death. These are what concern a novelist."

Many of Cloete's novels were not well received in his home country of South Africa due to the recurring theme of interracial love and religious disillusionment. As the *New York Times* reported, the publication of *The Turning Wheels* "began a series of novels covering a South African family from 1812 to 1930. In it there were interracial love affairs and in 1937, it was, like four of his later books banned in South Africa. The ban was not lifted until 1974," two years before Cloete died.

As Jean Stubbs once wrote: "Stuart Cloete belongs to the ancient tradition of story-tellers, who hold the attention of their audiences with brilliant word-pictures and dramatic incidents compulsively from beginning to end.... Mr. Cloete emerges as a man's man in a man's country: the white hunter

who places courage and pride first on the lift of virtues. He has a marvellous eye for detail: copper nails in wood spurting green flame, a black boy cleaning stained spear heads back to brightness with sand and spittle, the red eyes of white rates glimmering like 'a thousand rubies' in the firelight.''

The Fiercest Heart was made into a motion picture by Twentieth Century-Fox in 1969. *The Hill of Doves* was also made into a motion picture in 1969. The film rights to *Rags of Glory* and *The Turning Wheels* were sold, but the films were never made.

AVOCATIONAL INTERESTS: Farming, painting, gardening.

BIOGRAPHICAL/CRITICAL SOURCES: Manchester Guardian, December 10, 1957; *New Yorker,* October 25, 1958; *New York Times Book Review,* August 25, 1963; *Books and Bookmen,* February, 1968; *New York Times,* March 21, 1976; *Washington Post,* March 23, 1976; *Time,* April 5, 1976.†

*   *   *

COGSWELL, Fred(erick William) 1917-

PERSONAL: Born November 8, 1917, in East Centreville, New Brunswick, Canada; son of Walter Scott (a farmer) and Florence (White) Cogswell; married Margaret Hynes, July 3, 1944; children: Carmen Patricia, Kathleen Mary. *Education:* University of New Brunswick, B.A. (with honours), 1949, M.A., 1950; University of Edinburgh, Ph.D., 1952. *Politics:* New Democratic Party. *Religion:* Christian. *Home:* 769 Reid St., Fredericton, New Brunswick, Canada. *Office:* University of New Brunswick, Fredericton, New Brunswick, Canada.

CAREER: University of New Brunswick, Fredericton, assistant professor, 1952-57, associate professor, 1957-61, professor of English, 1961—. Editor and publisher, *Fiddlehead* magazine, 1952-66, and Fiddlehead Books, 1967—. *Military service:* Canadian Army, 1940-45; became staff sergeant; was decorated. *Member:* Association of Canadian Teachers of English, Canadian Association of University Teachers, Canadian Humanities Association, Institute of International Affairs, Canadian Authors' Association, Canadian Poets Guild, Association of Canadian and Quebec Literatures (president, 1978-80), Atlantic Publishers Association (president, 1978-80). *Awards, honors:* I.O.D.E. Scholar for New Brunswick, 1950-52; Nuffield Fellow, 1959-60; Gold Medal of Poets Laureate International presented by Republic of the Phillipines, 1965; Canada Council senior fellowship, 1967-68.

*WRITINGS—*All published by Fiddlehead, except as indicated: *The Stunted Strong,* 1954; *The Haloed Tree,* Ryerson, 1956; (translator) *The Testament of Cresseid,* Ryerson, 1957; *Descent from Eden,* Ryerson, 1959; *Lost Dimension,* Outposts Publications, 1960; (editor) *A Canadian Anthology,* 1960; (editor and contributor) *Five New Brunswick Poets,* 1962; (editor with Robert Tweedie and S. W. MacNutt) *The Arts in New Brunswick,* [Fredericton], 1966; (editor with T. R. Lower) *The Enchanted Land,* Gage, 1967; *Star People,* 1968; *Immortal Plowman,* 1969; *In Praise of Chastity,* New Brunswick Chapbooks, 1970; (editor and translator) *One Hundred Poems of Modern Quebec,* 1970; (editor and translator) *A Second Hundred Poems of Modern Quebec,* 1971; *The House without a Door,* 1973; *Light Bird of Life,* 1974; (editor) *The Poetry of Modern Quebec,* Harvest, 1976; *Against Perspective,* 1977. Also author of *The Chains of Liliput,* 1971, and *A Long Apprenticeship* (collected poems), 1980.

Contributor of poems to over one hundred periodicals, as well as articles to *Dalhousie Review, Trace, Queen's, Canadian Forum,* and other journals. Editor, *Humanities Association Bulletin,* 1967-72.

WORK IN PROGRESS: Translating the complete poems of Emile Nelligan.

SIDELIGHTS: Fred Cogswell told *CA:* "I have lived, counting my wartime experience, upwards of eight years in Europe (principally Scotland). I have a fluent reading knowledge of French. I am interested quite literally in everything in the universe and I am a monist. As a poet, anthologist, critic, editor, and biographer, I have been most concerned with sincerity, accuracy, imagination and empathy. I also prefer the plain to the ornate and feel art ought to simplify—it is a training in grasping, expressing and communicating essentials."

BIOGRAPHICAL/CRITICAL SOURCES: Quill and Quire, July, 1980.

*　　*　　*

COLE, John P(eter)   1928-

PERSONAL: Born December 9, 1928, in Sydney, New South Wales, Australia; son of Philip (an artist) and Marjorie (Pickford) Cole; married Isabel Urrunaga, June 21, 1952; children: Francis John, Richard Philip. *Education:* University of Nottingham, B.A., M.A., Ph.D.; additional study, Pavia University, 1950-51. *Home:* 10, Ranmore Close, Bramcote, Nottinghamshire, England. *Office:* Department of Geography, University of Nottingham, Nottingham, England.

CAREER: University of Reading, Reading, England, assistant lecturer in geography, 1955-56; University of Nottingham, Nottingham, England, lecturer, 1956-69, reader, 1969-75, professor of regional geography, 1975—. *Military service:* Royal Navy, two years; became sub-lieutenant. *Member:* Institute of British Geographers.

WRITINGS: La Geografia urbana de la gran Lima, National Planning Office of Peru, 1957; *Geography of World Affairs,* Penguin, 1959, 5th edition, 1979; (with F. C. German) *A Geography of the U.S.S.R.,* Butterworth, 1961, 2nd edition published as *A Geography of the U.S.S.R.: The Background of a Planned Economy,* 1970, Rowman & Littlefield, 1971; *Italy,* Chatto & Windus, 1964, published as *Italy: An Introductory Geography,* Praeger, 1966; *Latin America: An Economic and Social Geography,* Butterworth, 1965, revised edition, 1970, 2nd revised edition, 1975; *A Geography of the U.S.S.R.,* Penguin, 1967; (with C.A.M. King) *Quantitative Geography: Techniques and Theories in Geography,* Wiley, 1968; (with N. J. Beynon) *New Ways in Geography,* Blackwell, 1968; *Situations in Human Geography: A Practical Approach,* Blackwell, 1975; (with P. M. Mather) *Peru, 1940-2000: Performance and Prospects,* Department of Geography, University of Nottingham, 1978; *The Development Gap,* Wiley, 1980.

WORK IN PROGRESS: Research on world development.

*　　*　　*

COLES, Robert (Martin)   1929-

PERSONAL: Born October 12, 1929, in Boston, Mass.; son of Philip Winston (an engineer) and Sandra (Young) Coles: married Jane Hallowell (a teacher), July 4, 1960; children: Robert Emmet, Daniel Agee, Michael Hallowell. *Education:* Harvard University, A.B., 1950; Columbia University, M.D., 1954. *Politics:* Independent. *Religion:* Episcopalian.

Home address: Coolidge Rd., Concord, Mass. 01742. *Office:* Harvard University Health Services, 75 Mt. Auburn St., Cambridge, Mass. 02138.

CAREER: University of Chicago clinics, Chicago, Ill., intern, 1954-55; Massachusetts General Hospital, Boston, resident in psychiatry, 1955-56; McLean Hospital, Belmont, Mass., resident in psychiatry, 1956-57; Judge Baker Guidance Center—Children's Hospital, Roxbury, Mass., resident in child psychiatry, 1957-58, fellow in child psychiatry, 1960-61; Massachusetts General Hospital, member of psychiatric staff, 1960-62; Harvard University, Cambridge, Mass., clinical assistant in psychiatry at Medical School, 1960-62, research psychiatrist in Health Services, 1963—, lecturer in general education, 1966—, professor of psychiatry and medical humanities at Medical School, 1978—. Member of alcoholism clinic staff, Massachusetts General Hospital, 1957-58; supervisor in children's unit, Metropolitan State Hospital (Boston), 1957-58; psychiatric consultant, Lancaster Industrial School for Girls (Lancaster, Mass.), 1960-62; research psychiatrist, Southern Regional Council (Atlanta, Ga.), 1961-63. Consultant to Ford Foundation, Southern Regional Council, and Appalachian Volunteers. Member of board of trustees, Robert F. Kennedy Memorial. Member of board of Field Foundation, Institute of Current World Affairs, Reading is Fundamental, American Freedom from Hunger Foundation, National Rural Housing Coalition, and Twentieth Century Fund. Member of National Sharecroppers Fund and National Advisory Committee on Farm Labor. *Military service:* U.S. Air Force, 1958-60; chief of neuropsychiatric service, Keesler Air Force Base, Biloxi, Miss.

MEMBER: American Psychiatric Association, American Orthopsychiatric Association, Group for the Advancement of Psychiatry, American Academy of Arts and Sciences (fellow), Phi Beta Kappa, Harvard Club (New York and Boston). *Awards, honors:* Atlantic grant, 1965, in support of work on *Children of Crisis;* National Educational Television award, 1966, for individual contribution to outstanding programming; Family Life Book Award from Child Study Association of America, Ralph Waldo Emerson Award from Phi Beta Kappa, Anisfield-Wolf Award in Race Relations from *Saturday Review,* Four Freedoms Award from B'nai B'rith, and *Parents' Magazine* Medal, all in 1968, all for *Children of Crisis;* Hofheimer Prize for Research from American Psychiatric Association, 1968; Pulitzer Prize, 1973, for Volumes II and III of *Children of Crisis;* McAlpin Award from National Association of Mental Health, 1973.

WRITINGS: Children of Crisis, Little, Brown, Volume I: *A Study in Courage and Fear,* 1967, Volume II: *Migrants, Sharecroppers, Mountaineers,* 1971, Volume III: *The South Goes North,* 1971, Volume IV: *Eskimos, Chicanos, Indians,* 1978, Volume V: *Privileged Ones: The Well-Off and the Rich in America,* 1978; *Dead End School,* illustrated by Norman Rockwell, Little, Brown, 1968; *Still Hungry in America,* introduction by Edward M. Kennedy, World Publishing, 1969; *The Grass Pipe* (juvenile), Little, Brown, 1969; *The Image Is You,* edited by Donald Erceg, Houghton, 1969; (with Maria W. Piers) *The Wages of Neglect,* Quadrangle, 1969.

Uprooted Children: The Early Lives of Migrant Farmers (Horace Mann lecture, 1969), University of Pittsburgh Press, 1970; (with Joseph H. Brenner and Dermot Meagher) *Drugs and Youth: Medical, Psychiatric, and Legal Facts,* Liveright, 1970; *Erik H. Erikson: The Growth of His Work,* Little, Brown, 1970; *The Middle Americans* (photographs by Jon Erikson), Little, Brown, 1971; (with Daniel Berrigan) *The Geography of Faith* (conversations between Berrigan and Coles), Beacon Press, 1971; *Saving Face,* Little, Brown,

1972; (editor with Jerome Kagan) *Twelve to Sixteen: Early Adolescence* (essays), Norton, 1972; *Farewell to the South*, Little, Brown, 1972; *A Spectacle Unto World*, Viking, 1973; *Riding Free*, Atlantic-Little, Brown, 1973; *The Old Ones of New Mexico*, University of New Mexico Press, 1973; *The Darkness and the Light*, Aperture, 1974; *The Busses Roll*, Norton, 1974; *Irony in the Mind's Life: Essays on Novels by James Agee, Elizabeth Bowen and George Eliot*, University of Virginia Press, 1974; *Headsparks*, Little, Brown, 1975; *William Carlos Williams: The Knack of Survival in America*, Rutgers University Press, 1975; *Mind's Fate: Ways of Seeing Psychiatry and Psychoanalysis*, Little, Brown, 1975; *A Festering Sweetness: Poems of American People*, University of Pittsburgh Press, 1978; (with wife, Jane Hallowell Coles) *Women of Crisis*, Delacorte, Volume I: *Lives of Struggle and Hope*, 1978, Volume II: *Lives of Work and Dreams*, 1980; *The Last and First Eskimos*, New York Graphic Society, 1978; *Walker Percy: An American Search*, Atlantic-Little, Brown, 1978; *Flannery O'Conner's South*, Louisiana State University Press, 1980.

Contributor: Charles Rolo, editor, *Psychiatry in American Life*, Little, Brown, 1963; Erik H. Erikson, editor, *Youth: Change and Challenge*, Basic Books, 1963; Talcott Parsons and Kenneth Clark, editors, *The Negro American*, Houghton, 1966; Jules Masserman, editor, *Science and Psychoanalysis*, Volume IX, Grune, 1966; James L. Sundquist, *On Fighting Poverty*, Basic Books, 1969; Philip Kelley and Ronald Hudson, editors, *Diary by E.B.B.: The Unpublished Diary of Elizabeth Barrett Browning, 1831-1832*, Ohio University Press, 1969; John H. Fandberg, editor, *Introduction to the Behavioral Sciences*, Holt, 1969.

Author of introduction: Barbara Field Bensiger, *The Prison of My Mind*, Walker & Co., 1969; *What Is a City?: A Multi-Media Guide on Urban Living*, Boston Public Library, 1969; *A Letter to a Teacher*, Random House, 1970.

Contributor to periodicals and professional journals, including *Atlantic Monthly, New Yorker, New Republic, New York Review of Books, Book Week, Partisan Review, Harper's, Saturday Review, Massachusetts Review, New York Times Book Review, Yale Review, American Journal of Psychiatry, Daedalus, Dissent, Appalachian Review, Harvard Educational Review, Contemporary Psychoanalysis*, and *Commonweal*. Contributing editor, *New Republic*, 1966—; member of editorial board, *American Scholar*, 1968—, *Contemporary Psychoanalysis*, 1969-70, and *Child Psychiatry and Human Development*, 1969—.

WORK IN PROGRESS: Coles is "presently working in Northern Ireland and South Africa, looking into the process of 'political socialization' in those countries."

SIDELIGHTS: Robert Coles is often described as one of the leading authorities on the issues of poverty and racial discrimination in the United States. He has devoted much of his time to studying, observing, and researching the effects of integration and poverty on young children and has spent many years studying the psychiatric aspects of school desegregation in the South, in such cities as Atlanta, New Orleans, Asheville, Charlotte, Burnsville, Clinton, Oak Ridge, and Little Rock. His research also encompasses the anxieties that confront civil rights activists upon entering college.

Best known for his massive multi-volume study of children in various stressful situations, *Children of Crisis*, Coles is often asked to give expert testimony before Congressional committees. J. H. Katz of the *Library Journal* notes: "Coles's work demonstrates his compassion and understanding of the human condition. He is able to be sensitive to the anguish, pain, and experience of all children.... His book provides a conscience and consciousness raiser for teachers, educators, and social scientists.... As Coles states, it is his 'wish that soon, and in every one of our states, boys and girls . . . get to meet and know one another.' Hopefully, the reader too will get to know these children and have a better insight into their experiences." H. M. Caudill of the *New York Review of Books* notes that "perhaps only a psychiatrist could enable the reader to glimpse so clearly the meaning of the poverty and rootlessness that mark the lives of so many people in our society. In [Coles's] books, poverty, drug addiction, welfarism, urban rioting, lawlessness, and racism cease to be abstractions. They are attached to living people and their emotions and insights become real and are shared. Suddenly one realizes what the 'urban crisis' is about, above all because Coles ... has followed the rural poor from the ravaged countryside to the cities they flee to; and he understands what it means to make that trip."

Donna Joy Newman feels that Coles's research methods set him apart from most others in his field. As Newman explains: "Although he is affiliated with Harvard University, he remains a maverick in the academic and medical fields. He eschews traditional academic research in favor of drawing his observations from long hours spent with children, talking with them, playing games with them, taking them for walks, having them draw pictures for him."

Coles believes these methods are far more successful in discovering the true feelings of children. As he explained to a *Chicago Tribune* interviewer: "What I'm doing in my work is tapping that depth of feeling. . . . You see this in their artwork. At eight and ten their art is very rich and fluid, creative, resourceful, and imaginative. And then suddenly, at twelve or thirteen, they lose all interest in art. They might tell their art teacher they can't draw. What's that about? Well, they're turning off a great part of their creative lives."

His technique, H. J. DuBois of the *Library Journal* feels, makes Coles's books so popular and well-read: "Basic to the success of his studies has been the liberal use of quotations from taped interviews—quotations which capture better than a straight narrative ever could the convictions, personal tragedies, prejudices, frustrations, hopes, and spirit of dignity and pride of his subject." Agreeing with DuBois, Leslie Dunbar of the *Saturday Review* writes: "Coles is one of the very few scholars who has managed the surpassingly difficult and complicated task of remaining a scholar while personally participating in the civil rights and anti-poverty movement. . . . But if as a person he is committed, as a scholar he is characteristically tentative and cautious. 'My conclusions,' he points out, 'are not sweeping, categorical, or easily translated into one or another program.'"

AVOCATIONAL INTERESTS: Tennis, skiing.

BIOGRAPHICAL/CRITICAL SOURCES: Christian Science Monitor, May 2, 1968; *Saturday Review*, November 21, 1970; *Time*, February 14, 1972, July 15, 1974; *Library Journal*, January 1, 1972, March 1, 1978; *New York Review of Books*, March 9, 1972; *New York Times Book Review*, June 11, 1978; *New York Times*, January 10, 1979; *Chicago Tribune*, April 24, 1979; *Washington Post Book World*, June 29, 1980; *Chicago Tribune Book World*, November 9, 1980; *Times Literary Supplement*, November 21, 1980.

*   *   *

COLLIE, Michael (John) 1929-

PERSONAL: Born August 8, 1929, in England; son of Leslie Grant and Elizabeth (Robertson) Collie; married second wife, Joanne L'Heureux, 1960. *Education:* Cambridge University, B.A., 1952, M.A., 1956. *Home:* 150 Farnham Ave., Toronto M4V 1H5, Ontario, Canada. *Office:* Winters College, York University, Toronto, Ontario, Canada.

CAREER: University of Manitoba, Winnipeg, assistant professor of English, 1957-61; Exeter University, Exeter, England, staff tutor, 1961-62; Mount Allison University, Sackville, New Brunswick, assistant professor of English, 1962-65; York University, Winters College, Toronto, Ontario, associate professor, 1965-67, professor of English literature, 1967—, dean of graduate studies, 1969-73. *Military service:* British Intelligence Corps, 1947-49. *Member:* International Association of University Professors of English, Modern Language Association of America, Modern Humanities Research Association, Association of Canadian University Teachers of English, Canadian Association of University Teachers.

WRITINGS: Poems, Ryerson, 1959; *Skirmish with Fact,* Ryerson, 1960; *Laforgue,* Oliver & Boyd, 1964; *Jules Laforgue derniers vers,* University of Toronto Press, 1965; *The House* (poems), Macmillan, 1967; *Kerdruc Notebook,* Rampant Lions Press, 1972; *New Brunswick,* Macmillan, 1974; *George Meredith: A Bibliography,* University of Toronto Press, 1974; *George Gissing: A Bibliography,* University of Toronto Press, 1975; *George Gissing: A Biography,* Shoe String, 1977; *Jules Laforgue,* Athlone Press, 1977; *The Alien Art,* Shoe String Press, 1979.

WORK IN PROGRESS: George Borrow Eccentric, a biography; *The Life and Work of Alfred Sisley.*

*   *   *

COLLIER, Zena   1926-
(Zena Shumsky; pseudonym: Jane Collier)

PERSONAL: Born January 21, 1926, in London, England; married Lou Shumsky (a photographer), May 3, 1945 (divorced, 1967); married Thomas M. Hampson (a lawyer), December 30, 1969; children: (first marriage) Jeffrey, Paul. *Home:* 83 Berkeley St., Rochester, N.Y. 14607. *Agent:* Curtis Brown, 575 Madison Ave., New York, N.Y. 10022.

CAREER: Free-lance writer. Resident fellow, Yaddo writer's colony, 1978 and 1980. *Member:* Women in Communications, Mystery Writers of America, American Civil Liberties Union (director, New York State chapter, 1966-67; director, Genesee Valley chapter, 1974-76), Friends of the University of Rochester Libraries, Friends of the Rochester Public Library (member of board of directors, 1967-70, 1979—).

WRITINGS: (Under pseudonym Jane Collier) *The Year of the Dream,* Funk, 1962; (under name Zena Shumsky, with Lou Shumsky) *First Flight,* Funk, 1962; (under name Zena Shumsky) *Shutterbug,* Funk, 1963; (under pseudonym Jane Collier) *A Tangled Web,* Funk, 1967; *Seven for the People: Public Interest Groups at Work,* Messner, 1979. Work anthologized in *Alfred Hitchcock Presents Stories to Be Read with the Lights On,* Random House, 1973, and *Best Detective Stories,* Dutton, 1979. Contributor of short stories and articles to *McCall's, Woman's Day, Canadian Home Journal, Literary Review, Publishers Weekly, Family Circle, Alfred Hitchcock's Mystery Magazine,* and other periodicals.

*   *   *

COLTON, Harold S(ellers)   1881-1970
PERSONAL: Born August 29, 1881, in Philadelphia, Pa.;

died December 29, 1970; son of Sabin Woolworth, Jr. and Jessie (Sellers) Colton; married Mary Russell Ferrell, May 23, 1912; children: Joseph Ferrell, Sabin Woolworth IV (deceased). *Education:* University of Pennsylvania, B.S., 1904, A.M., 1906, Ph.D., 1908.

CAREER: University of Pennsylvania, Philadelphia, assistant, 1909-12, instructor, 1912-18, assistant professor, 1918-26, professor, 1926-54, professor emeritus, 1954-70. Museum of Northern Arizona, Flagstaff, director, 1928-58, director emeritus, 1958-70; director, San Francisco Mountain Zoological Station, Flagstaff, 1929-54. Member, Archeological Commission of Arizona, 1929-31. Trustee, Arizona State Teachers College at Flagstaff (now Northern Arizona University), 1929-31, and Santa Fe Laboratory of Anthropology, 1934-53. *Military service:* Military Intelligence, 1918-19; became captain. Officers Reserve Corps, 1919-26.

MEMBER: American Association for the Advancement of Science (president of southwest division, 1935-36), American Geographic Society (fellow), American Society of Zoologists, American Society of Naturalists, American Anthropological Association, Ecological Society of America, American Microscopic Society, Society for American Archaeology, American Genetic Association, Northern Arizona Society of Science and Art, Philadelphia Academy of Natural Science, Sigma Xi, University of Pennsylvania Faculty Club, Flagstaff Rotary Club (president, 1936-37). *Awards, honors:* LL.D., University of Arizona, 1955; D.Sc., Arizona State College, 1958; U.S. Department of the Interior Conservation Service Award, 1959.

WRITINGS: (With Frank C. Baxter) *Days on the Painted Desert and in the San Francisco Mountains: A Guide,* Museum of Northern Arizona, 1927, 2nd edition, 1932; *A Survey of Prehistoric Sites in the Region of Flagstaff, Arizona,* U.S. Government Printing Office, 1932, reprinted, Scholarly Press, 1977; (with L. L. Hargrave) *Handbook of Northern Arizona Pottery Wares,* Northern Arizona Society of Science and Art, 1937, reprinted, AMS Press, 1977; *Prehistoric Culture Units and Their Relationships in Northern Arizona,* Northern Arizona Society of Science and Art, 1939; *The Sinagua: A Summary of the Archaeology of the Region of Flagstaff, Arizona,* Northern Arizona Society of Science and Art, 1946; *Hopi Kachina Dolls,* University of New Mexico, 1949, revised edition, 1959, published as *Hopi Kachina Dolls with a Key to Their Identification,* 1971; *Potsherds: An Introduction to the Study of Prehistoric Southwestern Ceramics and Their Use in Historic Reconstruction,* Northern Arizona Society of Science and Art, 1953; *Black Sand: Prehistory in Northern Arizona,* University of New Mexico Press, 1960; *North of Market Street: Biography of Jessie S. and Sabin W. Colton, Jr.,* [Flagstaff], 1961; *The Couth Little World of Haddie Colton* (poetry and prose collection), [Flagstaff], 1961; *Hopi History and Ethnobotany* (bound with *The Hopi: Their History and Use of Their Lands* by Florence H. Ellis), Garland Publishing, 1974. Also author, with wife, Mary Russell Ferrell Colton, of *The Little-Known Small House Ruins in the Coconino Forest;* author of numerous bulletins and articles, most published by the Museum of Northern Arizona.†

*   *   *

COMBER, Lillian   1916-
(Lillian Beckwith)

PERSONAL: Born April 25, 1916, in Wirral, Cheshire, England; daughter of Robert and Lillian (Beckwith) Lloyd; married Edward Comber; children: Geoffrey, Elizabeth

Ann. *Home:* Ballyre House, Kirk Michael, Isle of Man, United Kingdom. *Agent:* Curtis Brown Ltd., 25 West 43rd St., New York, N.Y. 10036.

CAREER: School teacher, 1936-38; crofter (operator of a small farm), 1943-60. *Member:* Society of Authors, P.E.N.

WRITINGS—All under pseudonym Lillian Beckwith: *The Hills Is Lonely*, Hutchinson, 1959, Dutton, 1963; *The Sea for Breakfast*, Hutchinson, 1961, Dutton, 1962; *The Loud Halo*, Hutchinson, 1964, Dutton, 1965; *Green Hand*, Hutchinson, 1967; *A Rope—In Case*, Hutchinson, 1968, Dutton, 1969; *About My Father's Business*, Hutchinson, 1971; *Lightly Poached*, Hutchinson, 1973; *The Spuddy*, Delacorte, 1974; *Beautiful Just!*, Hutchinson, 1975; *Hebridean Cookbook*, Hutchinson, 1976; *Bruach Blend*, Hutchinson, 1978. Contributor of numerous short stories to magazines.

WORK IN PROGRESS: A Small Party.

SIDELIGHTS: Lillian Beckwith told *CA:* "Going to the Hebrides and taking over a croft (a small farm) proved the awakening of a desire to write. Intrigued by the simple way of life and by the toughness and humour of the islanders I felt compelled to record my experiences. What was initially intended to be only a chronicling of daily events grew into several books and, finding the publishers and the public liked them, I continued with other forms of writings, viz, novels and short stories. Most of my work has been translated into many different languages.

"When I am asked for advice by aspiring writers I usually reply: 'Put a blank sheet of paper in your typewriter and threaten it with words.'"

AVOCATIONAL INTERESTS: Amateur theatricals, giving children's parties, walking, and beachcombing.

*   *   *

CONKLIN, Groff   1904-1968

PERSONAL: Born September 6, 1904, in Glen Ridge, N.J.; died July 19, 1968, in Pawling, N.Y.; son of William Bogart and Sarah Hogate (Groff) Conklin; married Lucy Tempkin, October 1, 1937 (died November 7, 1954); married Florence Alexander Wohlken, June 5, 1958. *Education:* Attended Dartmouth College, 1923-25, and Harvard University, 1925-26; Columbia University, A.B., 1927.

CAREER: Doubleday & Co., Inc., New York City, assistant manager of book stores, 1930-34; University of Chicago Press, Chicago, Ill., assistant editor, 1934-36; editor, Robert M. McBride Company, 1937; U.S. Bureau of the Census, Washington, D.C., information consultant, 1939; Federal Home Loan Bank Board, Washington, D.C., information specialist, 1940; Tauxemont Home Builders, Tauxemont, Va., president, 1941-42; Office of Strategic Services, Washington, D.C., presentation specialist, 1943-45; U.S. Senate, Subcommittee on Wartime Health and Education, Washington, D.C., senior writer, 1945-46; U.S. Department of Commerce, Office of Technical Services, Washington, D.C., deputy chief of Information Division, 1946-47; National Institutes of Health, National Cancer Institute, Bethesda, Md., senior information specialist, 1947-48; American Diabetes Association, New York City, director of publications, 1950-52; *Living for Young Homemakers* (magazine), New York City, associate editor, 1959-60; senior researcher, Scientific Advisory Board, N. W. Ayer & Son, 1960-61; American Diabetes Association, senior writer, 1961-64; American Heritage Publishing Co., New York City, science editor, *American Heritage Dictionary*, 1965-68. Free-lance writer and editor, with specialties in fields of architecture, building

materials, medicine, and science fiction, 1930-68. *Member:* Authors Guild, Authors League of America, National Association of Science Writers.

WRITINGS: How to Run a Rental Library, Bowker, 1934, 2nd edition, 1947; *All About Subways* (juvenile), Messner, 1938; *All About Houses*, Messner, 1940; (contributor) *Home Repairs Made Easy*, Doubleday, 1949; (with Arthur Watkins) *Insulate and Air Condition Your Home*, Arco, 1955; *The Weather Conditioned House*, Reinhold, 1958; (with N. D. Fabricant) *The Dangerous Cold: Its Cures and Complications*, Macmillan, 1965.

Editor: (With Burton Rascoe) *The Smart Set Anthology*, Reynal, 1934; *The New Republic Anthology, 1915-1935*, F. W. Dodge, 1936; (with Rascoe) *Bachelor's Companion: A Smart Set Collection*, Grayson, 1944; *Best of Science Fiction*, Crown, 1946, revised edition, 1963; *Treasury of Science Fiction*, Crown, 1948.

Big Book of Science Fiction, Crown, 1950; *The Science Fiction Galaxy*, Permabooks, 1950; *Possible Worlds of Science Fiction*, Vanguard, 1951, revised edition, Berkley Publishing, 1960; *Invaders of Earth*, Vanguard, 1952; *Omnibus of Science Fiction*, Crown, 1952; *Science Fiction Adventures in Dimension*, Vanguard, 1953; (with wife, Lucy Conklin) *The Supernatural Reader*, Lippincott, 1953, 2nd edition, 1962; *Crossroads in Time*, Permabooks, 1953; *Six Great Short Novels of Science Fiction*, Dell, 1954; *Science Fiction Thinking Machines: Robots, Androids, Computers*, Vanguard, 1954 (also see below); *Strange Adventures in Science Fiction*, Grayson, 1954; *Strange Travels in Science Fiction*, Grayson, 1954.

Science Fiction Terror Tales, Gnome, 1955; Theodore Sturgeon, *Way Home: Stories of Science Fiction and Fantasy*, Funk, 1955; *Operation Future*, Permabooks, 1955; *Science Fiction Adventures in Mutation*, Vanguard, 1956; *Science Fiction Omnibus*, Berkley Publishing, 1956, revised edition, 1963; Sturgeon, *Thunder and Roses*, M. Joseph, 1957; *The Graveyard Reader*, Ballantine, 1958; *Four for the Future*, Pyramid Publications, 1959; *Br-r-r!: Ten Chilling Tales*, Avon, 1959.

Thirteen Great Stories of Science Fiction, Fawcett, 1960; *Great Science Fiction by Scientists*, Collier, 1962; *Twisted*, Belmont-Tower, 1962; *Worlds of When: Five Short Novels*, Pyramid Publications, 1962; (with Isaac Asimov) *Fifty Short Science Fiction Tales*, Collier, 1963; (with N. D. Fabricant) *Great Science Fiction about Doctors*, Collier, 1963; *Great Stories of Space Travel*, Grosset, 1963; *Seventeen x Infinity*, Dell, 1963; *Twelve Great Classics of Science Fiction*, Fawcett, 1963; *Dimension Four*, Pyramid Publications, 1964; *Five Odd*, Pyramid Publications, 1964; *Selections from "Science Fiction Thinking Machines"* (contains stories originally published in *Science Fiction Thinking Machines: Robots, Androids, Computers*), Bantam, 1964.

Five Unearthly Visions, Fawcett, 1965; *Giants Unleashed*, Grosset, 1965; *Great Detective Stories about Doctors*, Collier, 1965; *Thirteen above the Night*, Dell, 1965; *Another Part of the Galaxy*, Fawcett, 1966; *Science Fiction Oddities*, Berkley Publishing, 1966; *Elsewhere and Elsewhen*, Berkley Publishing, 1968; *Seven Trips through Time and Space*, Fawcett, 1968; *Ten Great Mysteries by Edgar Allan Poe*, Scholastic Book Services, 1968; *Possible Tomorrows*, Sidgwick & Jackson, 1972.

Also author of pamphlets; contributor to several encyclopedias. Book reviewer, *Time*, 1942. Contributor to over twenty magazines, including *American Mercury, Better Homes and Gardens, Science Illustrated, Infantry Journal, Harper's*, and *Look*.†

CONROY, John Wesley 1899-
(Jack Conroy; pseudonyms: Tim Brennan, Hoder Morine, John Norcross)

PERSONAL: Born December 5, 1899, in a coal mining camp near Moberly, Mo.; son of Thomas Edward (one-time Catholic priest in Canada who later organized and led a miners union) and Eliza Jane (McCollough) Conroy; married Elizabeth Gladys Kelly, June 30, 1922; children: Margaret Jean (Mrs. James Tillery; deceased), Thomas Vernon (deceased), John Wesley, Jr. *Education:* Attended University of Missouri, 1920-21. *Politics:* Democrat. *Religion:* Methodist. *Home:* 701 Fisk Ave., Moberly, Mo. 65270. *Agent:* Porter, Gould & Dierks, 215 West Ohio St., Chicago, Ill. 60610.

CAREER: Toured United States, mostly by boxcar, as migratory worker in 1920's; editor of *Rebel Poet*, 1931-32, *Anvil*, 1933-37, *New Anvil*, 1939-41; associate editor of *Nelson's Encyclopedia* and *Universal World Reference Encyclopedia*, 1943-47; Standard Education Society, Chicago, Ill., senior associate editor of *New Standard Encyclopedia*, 1947-66, director of Standard Information Service, 1949-55. Creative writing instructor, Columbia College, Chicago, 1962-66; lecturer on folklore at University of Chicago, University of Illinois, Northwestern University, University of Washington, and University of Oregon. *Member:* International Platform Association, Society of Midland Authors (vice-president for Missouri). *Awards, honors:* Guggenheim fellowship for creative writing, 1935; joint recipient of James L. Dow Award of the Society of Midland Authors, 1967, for *Anyplace but Here;* Literary Times Award, 1967; Louis M. Rabinowitz Foundation grant, 1967; L.H.D. from University of Missouri—Kansas City, 1975; literary award from Missouri Library Association, 1977; National Endowment for the Arts grant, 1978.

WRITINGS: (Editor with Edward R. Cheyney) *Unrest, 1929* (verse anthology), Stockwell, 1929; (editor with Cheyney) *Unrest, 1930*, Studies Publications, 1930; (editor with Cheyney) *Unrest, 1931*, Henry Harrison, 1931; *The Disinherited*, Covici, Friede, 1933, 2nd edition, with introduction by Daniel Aaron, Hill & Wang, 1963; *A World to Win*, Covici, Friede, 1935; (with Arna Bontemps) *The Fast Sooner Hound* (juvenile), Houghton, 1942; *They Seek a City: A Study of Negro Migration*, Doubleday, 1945; (with Bontemps) *Slappy Hooper, the Wonderful Sign Painter* (juvenile), Houghton, 1946; (editor) *Midland Humor*, Wyn, 1947; (with Bontemps) *Sam Patch, the High, Wide and Handsome Jumper* (juvenile), Houghton, 1951; (contributor) Frank Luther Mott, editor, *Missouri Reader*, University of Missouri Press, 1964; (with Bontemps) *Anyplace but Here*, Hill & Wang, 1966; (contributor) Harvey Swados, editor, *American Writers and the Great Depression*, Bobbs-Merrill, 1966; (editor with Curt Johnson) *Writers in Revolt: The Anvil Anthology, 1933-1940*, Lawrence Hill, 1973; *The Jack Conroy Reader*, edited by Jack Salzman and David Ray, B. Franklin, 1980. Stories have been anthologized in *A Treasury of American Folklore*, edited by B. A. Botkin.

Literary editor of *Chicago Defender*, 1946-47, *Chicago Globe*, 1949, and *Foolkiller*, 1973—. Book reviewer for *Chicago Tribune, Kansas City Star*, and *Chicago Sun-Times;* former reviewer for *Chicago Daily News* and *St. Louis Post-Dispatch*. Contributor to *American Mercury, Esquire*, and *New Republic*.

WORK IN PROGRESS: A book on oral folklore of the Ozarks; a collection of sentimental songs and poems, 1865-1910, titled *The Rosewood Casket: A Garland of Rue and Lavender;* research for autobiography.

SIDELIGHTS: Revival of Jack Conroy's social novel of the thirties, *The Disinherited,* caused a number of critics around the country to take a backward look at a book that sold only 2,700 copies in its day, yet caused more than a ripple in the literary world. The book was hailed then as a "proletarian novel," one which Margaret Wallace of the *New York Times* describes as "written with impressive simplicity, in language which is brutal and uncompromising, as homely and expressive, as his subject demands." Wallace continues, "In [Conroy's] very rejection of special pleading, on the one hand, and of literary artifice, on the other, lies the strength of his story."

Daniel Aaron, professor of English at Smith College, in his introduction to the new edition calls *The Disinherited* "a good example of the American picaresque novel." How does a manuscript written thirty years ago read today? Will Wharton's opinion in the *St. Louis Post-Dispatch:* "Our verdict is, it's still swingin' prose, as H. L. Mencken thought when he printed portions of it in the old *American Mercury....* Much of Conroy's time has been devoted to helping younger writers ... and some discerning readers of *The Disinherited* may sense that its author is an individual who rates service to fellow man higher than space in the bookshelf."

In his early years as a novelist Conroy was praised by Louis Adamic of *Saturday Review of Literature* as "a writer of great energy and promise ... [who] with some luck, is almost bound to be increasingly noteworthy." Although many of his colleagues have changed their politics over the years, Conroy has not. As *Los Angeles Times Book Review*'s Ben Pleasants comments in his review of *The Jack Conroy Reader*, "It is refreshing to look back on one radical writer who has retained his angry integrity and dwells in the world of reality."

As editor of the *Rebel Poet, Anvil*, and *New Anvil*, Conroy published the early work of a number of writers later well known, among them Richard Wright, Frank Yerby, Nelson Algren, and Kenneth Patchen.

BIOGRAPHICAL/CRITICAL SOURCES: Harry R. Warfel, *American Novelists of Today*, American Book, 1951; Walter B. Rideout, *The Radical Novel in the United States, 1900-1954*, Harvard University Press, 1956; *Chicago Daily News*, March 23, 1963; *San Francisco Chronicle*, April 2, 1963; *St. Louis Post-Dispatch*, April 13, 1963; *Chicago Sun-Times*, April 14, 1963, March 2, 1980; *Cleveland Press*, April 26, 1963; *Magazine of Books*, May 12, 1963; *Atlantic Monthly*, June, 1963; *New York Times*, April 10, 1966; David Madden, editor, *Proletarian Writers of the Thirties*, Southern Illinois University Press, 1968; *Missouri Library Association Quarterly*, March, 1968; *New Letters*, winter, 1972, fall, 1972; *Journal of Popular Culture*, winter, 1973; *Newsletter of the Society for the Study of Midwestern Literature*, summer, 1974; *Triquarterly* magazine, 1978; *Midwestern Miscellany VIII*, Midwestern Press, 1980; *New Republic*, March 1, 1980; *Chicago Tribune*, March 16, 1980; *Los Angeles Times Book Review*, June 8, 1980.

*   *   *

COOK, Fred J(ames) 1911-

PERSONAL: Born March 8, 1911, in Point Pleasant, N.J.; son of Frederick P. (a hardware store employee and tax collector) and Huldah (Compton) Cook; married Julia Barbara Simpson, June 5, 1936 (died, 1974); married Irene Fine, June 22, 1976; children: (first marriage) Frederick P. II, Barbara Jane. *Education:* Rutgers University, B.Litt., 1932. *Politics:* "Mugwump, New Dealish." *Home:* 722 Fernmere

Ave., Interlaken, N.J. *Agent:* Peter Shepherd, Harold Ober Associates, 40 East 49th St., New York, N.Y. 10017.

CAREER: Asbury Park Press, Asbury Park, N.J., reporter, 1933-36; *New Jersey Courier*, Toms River, editor, 1936-37, assistant editor, then city editor, 1938-44; *New York World Telegram and Sun*, New York, N.Y., rewriteman, 1944-59; free-lance writer, 1959—. *Awards, honors:* New York Newspaper Guild Page One Award for best city reporting, 1958, best magazine feature, for "The FBI," 1959, best magazine reporting, for "The Shame of New York," 1960, and for crusading journalism, for series on the energy crisis in *Nation*, 1980; Sidney Hillman Award, 1960, for magazine article in *Nation*, "Gambling, Inc."

WRITINGS: The Girl in the Death Cell (on the Snyder Gray case), Gold Medal Books, 1953; *The Girl on the Lonely Beach* (on the Starr Faithful case), Fawcett, 1954; (with Robert Hendrickson) *Youth in Danger*, Harcourt, 1956; *The Unfinished Story of Alger Hiss*, Morrow, 1958; *What Manner of Men: Forgotten Heroes of the Revolution*, Morrow, 1959; (editor) Bruce Lancaster, *The Golden Book of the American Revolution* (teen-age book), introduction by Bruce Catton, Golden Press, 1959.

(Editor) *The Second World War* (edition for young readers), Golden Press, 1960; *Rallying a Free People: Theodore Roosevelt*, Kingston House, 1961; *A Two-Dollar Bet Means Murder*, Dial, 1961; *John Marshall, Fighting for Justice*, Kingston House, 1961; *Entertaining the World: P. T. Barnum*, Encyclopaedia Britannica, 1962; *The Warfare State*, foreword by Bertrand Russell, Macmillan, 1962; *Building the House of Labor: Walter Reuther*, Encyclopaedia Britannica, 1963; *The FBI Nobody Knows*, Macmillan, 1964; *Barry Goldwater: Extremist of the Right*, Grove, 1964; *The Corrupted Land: The Social Morality of Modern Americans*, Macmillan, 1966; *The Secret Rulers: Criminal Syndicates and How They Control the U.S. Underworld*, Duell, Sloan & Pearce, 1966; *The Plot against the Patient*, Prentice-Hall, 1967; *What So Proudly We Hailed*, Prentice-Hall, 1968; *Franklin D. Roosevelt, Valiant Leader* (juvenile), Putnam, 1968; *The New Jersey Colony* (juvenile), Collier, 1969.

The Nightmare Decade: The Life and Times of Senator Joe McCarthy, Random House, 1971; *The Army-McCarthy Hearings, April-June, 1954: A Senator Creates a Sensation Hunting Communists*, F. Watts, 1971; *The Rise of American Political Parties*, F. Watts, 1971; *The Cuban Missile Crisis, October, 1962: The U.S. and Russia Face a Nuclear Showdown*, F. Watts, 1972; *The Demagogues* (juvenile), Macmillan, 1972; *The Muckrakers: Crusading Journalists Who Changed America*, Doubleday, 1972; *Mafia*, Fawcett, 1973; *American Political Bosses and Machines*, F. Watts, 1973; *Lobbying in American Politics*, F. Watts, 1976; *Privateers of '76*, Bobbs-Merrill, 1976; *Julia's Story: The Tragedy of an Unnecessary Death*, Holt, 1976; *Mob, Inc.*, F. Watts, 1977; *Storm before Dawn* (novel), Condor, 1978; *City Cop* (juvenile), Doubleday, 1979; *The Ku Klux Klan: America's Recurring Nightmare*, Messner, 1980.

Contributor to *Reader's Digest, American Heritage, Saturday Review, New York Times, True Detective*, and other publications.

WORK IN PROGRESS: A fact-juvenile book on the Watergate scandal.

SIDELIGHTS: Sean Cronin called *What So Proudly We Hailed* "a lively, provocative but, above all, a relevant book. [Fred J. Cook's] insight is sharp, his comment always to the point. He is a great one to prick bubble reputations and to explode myths."

"I am essentially a questioner, a critic of our times," Cook has written. "A major concern is the increasing tendency of our mass society to build massive power structures in which the individual becomes increasingly lost and helpless."

Cook told *CA* that he feels the apprehension expressed in that statement "has been more than vindicated by recent events." He explains, "[When an oil company can earn three billion dollars in clear profit in the first half of 1980] and when at the same time the American homeowner is being victimized by heating oil prices that the major companies have refused to justify, you have a graphic example of greedy corporate power whose only concern is the bottom line of profits, no matter what happens to the individual. This is a situation that I thoroughly exposed in the articles for *Nation* that won the Newspaper Guild of New York's 1980 Page One Award for crusading journalism in magazines."

AVOCATIONAL INTERESTS: Reading, fishing, swimming, big league baseball, and the fortunes of the Rutgers football team.

BIOGRAPHICAL/CRITICAL SOURCES: Time, December 7, 1959; *Christian Science Monitor*, July 3, 1968; *Nation*, September 2, 1968, April 26, 1971.

*   *   *

COOK, Olive 1916-

PERSONAL: Born February 20, 1916, in Cambridge, England; daughter of Arthur Hugh (a librarian, Cambridge University Library) and Kate (Webb) Cook; married Edwin Smith (a photographer and painter), September 7, 1954 (died December, 1971). *Education:* Newnham College, Cambridge University, M.A. (with honors), 1937. *Home:* The Coachhouse, the Vineyard, Saffron Walden, Essex, England.

CAREER: National Gallery, London, England, supervisor of publications, 1937-45; Carnegie Institute of Technology (now Carnegie-Mellon University), Pittsburgh, Pa., English representative, 1951-63; Denman College, visiting tutor in painting, history of painting and architecture, 1956—. *War service:* Air raid warden, Hampstead, London, England, 1939-45. *Member:* Women's International Art Club (London). *Awards, honors:* Second prize, Premio Agrigento, awarded by the Italian Government for a painting of Agrigento, 1952.

WRITINGS: Suffolk, Elek, 1948; *Collectors' Items*, Hutchinson, 1952; *Cambridgeshire*, Blackie, 1953; (with husband, Edwin Smith) *English Cottages and Farmhouses*, Thames & Hudson, 1954; *Breckland*, Robert Hale, 1956, reprinted, 1980; *The Kingdom above the Clouds*, Blackie, 1960; (with E. Smith) *English Abbeys and Priories*, Thames & Hudson, 1961; *Movement in Two Dimensions*, Hutchinson, 1963; *Parish Churches in Britain*, Studio Vista Books, 1964; (with E. Smith) *Prospect of Cambridge*, Batsford, 1965; (with E. Smith) *The Wonders of Italy*, Thames & Hudson, 1965; *The English House through Seven Centuries*, Thomas Nelson, 1968; (with E. Smith) *Ireland*, Thames & Hudson, 1966; *The Staensted Affair*, Pan Books, 1967; (with E. Smith) *England*, Thames & Hudson, 1971; *The English Country House: An Art or a Way of Life*, Thames & Hudson, 1974; (with Hutton) *English Parish Churches*, photographs by E. Smith, Thames & Hudson, 1976. Also author of libretto for "The Split Goose Feather," 1979. Contributor to *Saturday Book, Heathside Book, City*, and other publications.

WORK IN PROGRESS: English Farmsteads and Cottages, for Thames & Hudson.

SIDELIGHTS: Olive Cook's paintings are exhibited in museums, art galleries, and private collections. She exhibited a one-man show in Cambridge, 1979.

* * *

COOLEY, Lee Morrison 1919-

PERSONAL: Born October 3, 1919, in New York, N.Y.; daughter of Harry (a machinist) and Ann (Rosan) Morrison; married Leland Frederick Cooley (a writer), August 6, 1956. *Education:* Attended Straubenmuller Textile School, New York, N.Y., 1938, New York School of Applied Design for Women, 1939, and University of California, Irvine. *Address:* 541 Alta Vista Way, Laguna Beach, Calif. 92651.

CAREER: Former dancer, appearing with Metropolitan Opera Co. and in Broadway shows and films; Columbia Broadcasting System, New York, N.Y., choreographer for "Perry Como Show," "Vic Damone Show," and "Peggy Lee Show," 1950-57; currently affiliated with department of fine arts, University of California, Irvine. *Member:* Screen Actors Guild, Actors Equity.

WRITINGS—All with husband, Leland F. Cooley: *The Simple Truth about Western Land Investment,* Doubleday, 1964, revised edition, 1968; *The Retirement Trap,* Doubleday, 1965; *How to Avoid the Retirement Trap,* Nash Publishing, 1972; *Land Investment, U.S.A.,* Nash Publishing, 1973; *Pre-Medicated Murder,* Chilton, 1975.

WORK IN PROGRESS: An original screenplay, tentatively entitled *Girl in Yellow;* a screenplay of L. F. Cooley's *The Art Colony;* a novel, tentatively entitled *The Ashcroft Woman.*

* * *

COONEY, Barbara 1917-

PERSONAL: Born August 6, 1917, in Brooklyn, N.Y.; daughter of Russell Schenck (a stockbroker) and Mae Evelyn (Bossert) Cooney; married Guy Murchie, December, 1944 (divorced March, 1947); married Charles Talbot Porter (a physician), July, 1949; children: Gretel Goldsmith, Barnaby, Charles Talbot, Jr., Phoebe. *Education:* Smith College, B.A., 1938. *Politics:* Independent. *Home and office:* Pepperell, Mass. 01463.

CAREER: Free-lance author and illustrator, 1938—. *Military service:* Women's Army Corps, World War II; became second lieutenant. *Awards, honors:* Caldecott Medal for the year's best illustrated book for children, 1958, for *Chanticleer and the Fox,* and 1980, for *Ox-Cart Man;* silver medallion, University of Southern Mississippi, 1975; medal from Smith College, 1976.

WRITINGS—All self-illustrated: *King of Wreck Island,* Farrar & Rinehart, 1941; *The Kellyhorns,* Farrar & Rinehart, 1942; *Captain Pottle's House,* Farrar, 1943; (adapter) Geoffrey Chaucer, *Chanticleer and the Fox,* Crowell, 1958; (adapter) *The Little Juggler,* Hastings House, 1961; *Cock Robin,* Scribner, 1965; (adapter) Jacob and Wilhelm Grimm, *Snow White and Rose Red,* Delacorte, 1966; *Christmas,* Crowell, 1967.

Illustrator: Carl Malmberg, *Ake and His World,* Farrar & Rinehart, 1940; Frances M. Frost, *Uncle Snowball,* Farrar & Rinehart, 1940; Oskar Seidlin, *Green Wagons,* Houghton, 1943; Anne Molloy, *Shooting Star Farm,* Houghton, 1946; Phyllis Crawford, *The Blot: Little City Cat,* Holt, 1946; Nancy Hartwell, *Shoestring Theater,* Holt, 1947; L. L. Bein, *Just Plain Maggie,* Harcourt, 1948; Lee Kingman, *Rocky Summer,* Houghton, 1948; Ruth C. Seeger, *American Folk*

Songs for Children, Doubleday, 1948; Child Study Association of America, *Read Me Another Story,* Crowell, 1949; Rutherford Montgomery, *Kildee House,* Doubleday, 1949; Kingman, *The Best Christmas,* Doubleday, 1949.

Phyllis Krasilovsky, *The Man Who Didn't Wash His Dishes,* Doubleday, 1950; Ruth C. Seeger, *Animal Folk Songs for Children,* Doubleday, 1950; Nellie M. Leonard, *Graymouse Family,* Crowell, 1950; Child Study Association of America, *Read Me More Stories,* Crowell, 1951; Elisabeth C. Lansing, *The Pony That Ran Away,* Crowell, 1951; Lansing, *The Pony That Kept a Secret,* Crowell, 1952; Mary M. Aldrich, *Too Many Pets,* Macmillan, 1952; Barbara Reynolds, *Pepper,* Scribner, 1952; Miriam E. Mason, *Yours, with Love, Kate,* Houghton, 1952; Margaret W. Brown, *Christmas in the Barn,* Crowell, 1952; Seeger, *American Folk Songs for Christmas,* Doubleday, 1953; Leonard, *Grandfather Whiskers, M.D.,* Crowell, 1953; Lee Kingman, *Peter's Long Walk,* Doubleday, 1953; Lansing, *A Pony Worth His Salt,* Crowell, 1953; Jane Quigg, *Fun for Freddie,* Oxford University Press, 1953; Margaret Sidney, *The Five Little Peppers,* Doubleday, 1954; Brown, *Little Fir Tree,* Crowell, 1954; Margaret G. Otto, *Pumpkin, Ginger, and Spice,* Holt, 1954; Helen Kay, *Snow Birthday,* Farrar, Straus, 1955; Louisa May Alcott, *Little Women,* Crowell, 1955; Louise A. Kent, *The Brookline Trunk,* Houghton, 1955; Catherine S. McEwen, *Away We Go: One-Hundred Poems for the Very Young,* Crowell, 1956; Catherine Marshall, *Friends with God,* Whittlesey House, 1956; Kay, *City Springtime,* Hastings House, 1957; Neil Anderson, *Freckle Face,* Crowell, 1957; Henrietta Buckmaster, *Lucy and Loki,* Scribner, 1958; Harry Behn, *Timmy's Search,* Seabury, 1958; Rutherford Montgomery, *Hill Ranch,* Doubleday, 1959; Otto, *Little Brown Horse,* Knopf, 1959.

Le Hibou et la Poussiquette (French adaptation of *The Owl and the Pussycat* by Edward Lear), translated by Francis Steegmuller, Little, Brown, 1961; Walter De La Mare, *Peacock Pie,* Knopf, 1961; Margaret G. Otto, *Three Little Dachshunds,* Holt, 1963; Margeret W. Brown, *Where Have You Been?,* Hastings House, 1963; Sarah O. Jewett, *White Heron,* Crowell, 1963; Virginia Haviland, *Favorite Fairy Tales Told in Spain,* Little, Brown, 1963; *Papillot, Clignot, et Dodo* (French adaptation of *Wynken, Blynken, and Nod* by Eugene Field), translated by Steegmuller and Norbert Guterman, Farrar, Straus, 1964; Hugh Latham, *Mother Goose in French,* Crowell, 1964; Anne Molloy, *Shaun and the Boat,* Hastings House, 1965; Jane Goodsell, *Katie's Magic Glasses,* Houghton, 1965; Samuel Morse, *All in a Suitcase,* Little, Brown, 1966; Aldous Huxley, *Crowns of Pearblossom,* Random House, 1967; Alastair Reid and Anthony Kerrigan, *Mother Goose in Spanish,* Crowell, 1968; Natalia M. Belting, *Christmas Folk,* Holt, 1969.

William Wise, *The Lazy Young Duke of Dundee,* Rand McNally, 1970; Homer, *Dionysus and the Pirates,* translated and adapted by Penelope Proddow, Doubleday, 1970; Felix Salten, *Bambi: A Life in the Woods,* Simon & Schuster, 1970; *Book of Princesses,* Scholastic Book Services, 1971; Homer, *Hermes, Lord of Robbers,* translated and adapted by Proddow, Doubleday, 1971; Homer, *Demeter and Persephone,* translated and adapted by Proddow, Doubleday, 1972; May Garelick, *Down to the Beach,* Four Winds, 1973; Robin Supraner, *Would You Rather Be a Tiger?,* Houghton, 1973; Edna Mitchell Preston, *Squawk to the Moon, Little Goose,* Viking, 1974; E. L. Horwitz, *When the Sky Is Like Lace,* Lippincott, 1975; M. J. Craig, *Donkey Prince,* Doubleday, 1977; Donald Hall, *Ox-Cart Man,* Viking, 1980; *I Am Cherry Alive,* Harper, 1980.

BIOGRAPHICAL/CRITICAL SOURCES: Illustrators of Children's Books: 1744-1945, Horn Book, 1947; *Illustrators of Children's Books: 1946-1956,* Horn Book, 1958; *Publishers Weekly,* March 23, 1959; *American Library Association Bulletin,* April, 1959; *More Junior Authors,* edited by Muriel Fuller, H. W. Wilson, 1963; *Newbery and Caldecott Medal Books: 1956-1965,* edited by Lee Kingman, Horn Book, 1965; Diana Klemin, *The Art of Art for Children's Books,* C. N. Potter, 1966; Jean Poindexter Colby, *Writing, Illustrating and Editing Children's Books,* Hastings House, 1967; *Illustrators of Children's Books 1957-1966,* Horn Book, 1968; Elinor W. Field, *Horn Book Reflections,* Horn Book, 1969; Lee Bennett Hopkins, *Books Are by People,* Citation Press, 1969; Constantine Georgiou, *Children and Their Literature,* Prentice-Hall, 1969.

*   *   *

COOPER, Emmanuel 1938-
(Jonathan Sidney)

PERSONAL: Born December 12, 1938, in Derbyshire, England; son of Frederick (a butcher) and Kate Elizabeth (Cooke) Cooper. *Education:* Attended Dudley College, 1958-60, and Bournemouth Art School, 1960-61. *Home and office:* 38 Chalcot Rd., London NW1, England. *Agent:* Towers Winant Ltd., 14 Cliffords Inn, London EC4 1DA, England.

CAREER: Potter. Part time lecturer at Middlesex Polytechnic and Cambernoll Art School, 1971—. *Military service:* Royal Air Force, 1956-58. *Member:* Craftsmen Potters Association (member of council, 1969—), Federation of British Craft Society (member of council, 1972-74).

WRITINGS: Handbook of Pottery, Longmans, Green, 1970; *Taking Up Pottery,* Arthur Barker, 1972; *A History of Pottery,* St. Martin's, 1972; (editor with Eileen Lewenstein) *New Ceramics,* Van Nostrand, 1974; *Glazes for the Studio Potter,* Scribner, 1978; *The Studio Potter's Book of Glaze Recipes,* Scribner, 1980; *Potter: A World History,* St. Martin's, 1981. Contributor, occasionally under pseudonym Jonathan Sidney, to *Morning Star, Gay News,* and *Art and Artists.* Co-editor, *Ceramic Review,* 1969—.

WORK IN PROGRESS: Reseach in homosexuality in Western art, 1450 to the present.

*   *   *

COOVER, Robert (Lowell) 1932-

PERSONAL: Born February 4, 1932, in Charles City, Iowa; son of Grant Marion and Maxine (Sweet) Coover; married Marie del Pilar Sans-Mallafre, June 3, 1959; children: Diana Nin, Sara Chapin, Roderick Luis. *Education:* Attended Southern Illinois University at Carbondale, 1949-51; Indiana University at Bloomington, B.A. 1953; University of Chicago, M.A., 1965. *Residence:* London, England. *Agent:* Georges Borchardt, Inc., 136 East 57th St., New York, N.Y. 10022.

CAREER: Writer of fiction and poetry. Has taught at Bard College, Annandale-on-Hudson, N.Y., 1966-67, University of Iowa, Iowa City, 1967-69, Princeton University, Princeton, N.J., 1972-73, Columbia University, New York, N.Y., 1972, and Virginia Military Institute, Lexington, 1976. Producer and director of film "On a Confrontation in Iowa City," 1969. *Military service:* U.S. Naval Reserve, 1953-57; became lieutenant. *Awards, honors:* William Faulkner Award for best first novel, 1966, for *The Origin of the Brunists;* Rockefeller Foundation grant, 1969; Guggenheim fellowships, 1971 and 1974; citation in fiction from Brandeis University, 1971; Academy of Arts and Letters award, 1975; National Book Award nomination, 1977, for *The Public Burning.*

WRITINGS: The Origin of the Brunists (novel; also see below), Putnam, 1966; *The Universal Baseball Association, Inc., J. Henry Waugh, Prop.* (novel), Random House, 1968; *Pricksongs & Descants* (collected short fiction), Dutton, 1969; *The Water-Pourer* (chapter from *The Origin of the Brunists*), Bruccoli Clark, 1972; *The Public Burning* (novel), Viking, 1977.

Plays: *A Theological Position* (contains "A Theological Position," "The Kid," [produced Off-Broadway at American Place Theatre, November 17, 1972], "Love Scene," [produced in Paris as "Scene d'amour," 1973, produced in New York City, 1974], and "Rip Awake"), Dutton, 1972.

Work represented in many anthologies, including *New American Review 4,* New American Library, 1968, *New American Review 14,* Simon & Schuster, 1972, and *American Review,* Bantam, 1974. Contributor of short stories, poems, essays, and translations to numerous periodicals, including *Evergreen Review, Cavalier, Esquire, Tri-Quarterly, Harper's, Antioch Review, Quarterly Review of Literature, Playboy,* and *Fiddlehead.*

WORK IN PROGRESS: "Several narratives, short and long, in various media."

SIDELIGHTS: Robert Coover's work has generated much attention, especially among college audiences and critics, who contend that Coover, by mixing the actual with illusion, creates another, alternative world. Amazing, fantastic, and magic are among the words used to describe the effect of his fiction. *Time's* Paul Gray notes that Coover has won a "reputation as an avant-gardist who can do with reality what a magician does with a pack of cards: Shuffle the familiar into unexpected patterns." Coover begins his novels with ordinary subjects and events, then introduces elements of fantasy and fear which, left unhindered, grow to equal, if not surpass, what is real within the situation. Michael Mason of the *Times Literary Supplement* believes that Coover structures his novels around the idea of "an American superstition giving rise to its appropriate imaginary apocalypse."

The Origin of the Brunists, Coover's first and most conventional novel, chronicles the rise and fall of a fictitious religious cult. This cult arises when the sole survivor of a mining disaster, Giovanni Bruno, claims to have been visited by the Virgin Mary and rescued via divine intervention. As the cult grows in numbers and hysteria, it is exploited and inflamed by the local newspaper editor until the situation reaches what Philip Callow of *Books and Bookmen* terms "apocalyptic proportions." Although some critics, such as Callow, find the novel's conclusion disappointing and anticlimactic, others, such as the *New Statesman's* Miles Burrows, describe the book as being "a major work in the sense that it is long, dense, and alive to a degree that makes life outside the covers almost pallid."

In a *New Republic* review of Coover's second novel, *The Universal Baseball Association, Inc.,* Richard Gilman writes, "What this novel summons to action is our sense . . . of the possible substitution of one world for another, of the way reality implies alternatives." The book's protagonist, Henry Waugh, is bored with his job and his life. To alleviate his boredom, Waugh creates, within his imagination, an entire baseball league, complete with statistics and team and player names and histories. Plays, players, and fates are determined by dice, and Waugh, according to Gilman, presides "over this world of chance with a creator's calm dignity." When the dice rule that a favored player must die during a game, both Waugh's imaginary and real worlds fall apart. Waugh could, of course, choose to ignore the dice's decision, but to do so would be in violation of "the necessary laws that hold the cosmos together," a *Time* reviewer explains. At the novel's end, Waugh disappears from the story, leaving his players to fashion their own existence, myths, and rituals. The *National Observer*'s Clifford A. Ridley comments: "[This] is a novel about continuity, about order, about reason, about God, and about the relationships between them. Which is to say that it is a parable of human existence, but do not feel put off by that; for it is a parable couched in such head-long, original prose and set down in a microcosmos of such consistent fascination that it is far too busy entertaining to stop and instruct."

Red Smith, however, disagrees. In a *Book World* review, Smith remarks: "A little fantasy goes a long way, though, and after an imaginary beanball kills an imaginary player . . . , the author never finds the strike zone again. It all becomes a smothering bore." Ronald Sukenick of the *New York Review* shares Smith's assessment of the novel's second-half: "Baseball has already been made to carry a heavy cargo in this book but now it gets heavier. With the plausibility of the actual game lost, the philosophical freight begins to take over. Mythy echoes and allusions fall thick as snow."

Pricksongs & Descants, Coover's collection of short fiction pieces, has been widely praised. Coover's experimental forms and techniques produce "extreme verbal magic," according to the *New York Times*' Christopher Lehmann-Haupt. "Nothing in Mr. Coover's writing is quite what it seems to be," the critic continues. "In the pattern of the leaves there is always the smile of the Cheshire Cat." And Marni Jackson in *Critique* explains: "An innocent situation develops a dozen sinister possibilities, sprouting in the readers imagination while they are suspended, open-ended, on the page. . . . Every disturbing twist the story might take is explored; all of them could have happened, or none. . . . Like a good conjurer, even when you recognize his gimmicks, the illusion continues to work."

Reaction to *The Public Burning,* Coover's "factional" account of the conviction and execution in 1953 of alleged spies Julius and Ethel Rosenberg, has been mixed. A satire on the mood and mentality of the nation at the time of the execution, the novel loosely combines fact and fiction. Coover sets the site of the Rosenbergs' electrocutions in Times Square, adds surrealistic parodies of various personalities and events of the era, and provides then Vice-President Richard Nixon as the narrator-commentator. Most critics admire Coover's effort but criticize the book for being excessive and undisciplined. Piers Brendon of *Books and Bookmen* describes the novel as a "literary photo-montage" and "a paean of American self-hatred, a torrid indictment of the morally bankrupt society where for so long Nixon was the one." Lehmann-Haupt, in a later *New York Times* review, states that he was "shocked and amazed" by the book; he explains: "*The Public Burning* is an astonishing spectacle. It does not invite us to participate. . . . It merely allows us to watch, somewhat warily, as its author performs."

In the *New York Times Book Review,* Thomas R. Edwards notes that "horror and anger are the governing feelings in *The Public Burning.*" He comments: "As a work of literary art, *The Public Burning* suffers from excess. . . . But all vigorous satire is simplistic and excessive, and this book is an extraordinary act of moral passion." Brendon was similarly impressed by the novel's scope and also aware of its ultimate shortcomings: "*The Public Burning* is an ambitious failure. It is a huge, sprawling, brilliant, original excercise in literary photo-montage. It combines fact and fiction, comedy and terror, surrealism and satire, travesty and tragedy. [But it] is too overblown, too undisciplined, too crude, too lurid."

Overall, most critics agree that Coover is among the more notable new writers of the past two decades. Noting Coover's experimental approach to fictional forms and his originality and versatility as a prose stylist, they frequently compare his work to that of John Barth's, Donald Barthelme's, and Thomas Pynchon's. In his review of *Pricksongs & Descants,* Lehmann-Haupt calls Coover "among the best we now have writing." And Joyce Carol Oates comments in the *Southern Review:* "Coover . . . exists blatantly and brilliantly in his fiction as an authorial consciousness. . . . He will remind readers of William Gass, of John Barth, of Samuel Beckett. He is as surprising as any of these writers, and as funny as Donald Barthelme; both crude and intellectual, predictable and alarming, he gives the impression of thoroughly enjoying his craft."

Film rights to "The Baby Sitter," a story from *Pricksongs & Descants,* and *The Universal Baseball Association, Inc.* have been sold.

BIOGRAPHICAL/CRITICAL SOURCES: New Statesman, April 14, 1967, June 16, 1978; *Books and Bookmen,* May, 1967, August, 1978; *New Republic,* August, 17, 1967; *New York Times,* June 13, 1968, October 22, 1969, November 18, 1972, September 7, 1977; *Time,* June 28, 1968, August 8, 1977; *Book World,* July 7, 1968, November 2, 1969; *New York Times Book Review,* July 7, 1968, August 14, 1977; *National Observer,* July 29, 1968; *Saturday Review,* August 31, 1968; *New York Review,* March 13, 1969; *Critique,* Volume XI, number 3, 1969; *Newsweek,* December 1, 1969; *Nation,* December 8, 1969; *Village Voice,* July 30, 1970; *Esquire,* December, 1970; William Gass, *Fiction and the Figures of Life,* Knopf, 1971; *Cue,* November 25, 1972; Max Schulz, *Black Humor Fiction of the 1960s,* Ohio University Press, 1973; *Contemporary Literary Criticism,* Gale, Volume III, 1975, Volume VII, 1977, Volume XV, 1980; *Atlantic,* November, 1977; *Times Literary Supplement,* June 16, 1978.

—*Sketch by Denise Gottis*

* * *

COPELAND, E(dwin) Luther 1916-

PERSONAL: Born January 24, 1916, in Drennen, W. Va.; son of Luther Lowell (a lumberman) and Nannie (Hurt) Copeland; married Louise E. Tadlock, June 5, 1946; children: Judith Carol, Joy Marie, Sarah Elizabeth, Rebecca Louise, John Luther. *Education:* Mars Hill College, A.A., 1942; Furman University, B.A., 1944; Southern Baptist Theological Seminary, Th.M., 1946; Yale University, Ph.D., 1949. *Home:* 3701 Pembrook Pl., Raleigh, N.C. 27612. *Office:* Southern Baptist Theological Seminary, Louisville, Ky.

CAREER: Baptist minister. Southern Baptist Convention, Foreign Mission Board, missionary to Japan, 1948-56; Seinan Gakuin University, Fukuoka, Japan, professor of Christian history, 1949-56, chancellor, 1952-55; Southeastern Baptist Theological Seminary, Wake Forest, N.C., professor of missions, 1956-72, distinguished professor of missions, 1972-75; Southern Baptist Convention, Foreign Mission Board, missionary to Japan, 1975-81; Seinan Gakuin University, professor of Christian history, 1976-80, chancellor, 1976-80; Southern Baptist Theological Seminary, Louisville, Ky., senior professor of missions, 1981—. Visiting professor of missions at Southern Baptist Theological Seminary, Louisville, Ky., 1953-54; visiting research professor of comparative religion, Banaras Hindu University, Varanasi, India, 1963-64; Fletcher Visiting Professor of Missions, Southeastern Baptist Theological Seminary, 1980-81. *Member:* American Society of Missiology, International Association for Mission Studies, Association of Missions Professors. *Awards, honors:* Fulbright research scholarship in comparative religion, India, 1963-64; American Association of Theological Schools faculty fellowship, 1969-70.

WRITINGS: The Japanese Government and Protestant Christianity, 1889-1900 (pamphlet), Foreign Affairs Association of Japan, 1954; *Christianity and World Religions,* Convention Press, 1963; (contributor) G. Allen West, editor, *Christ for the World,* Broadman, 1963; *Frontiers of Advance,* Convention Press, 1964; (contributor) F. Russell Bennett, Jr., editor, *The Mission of the Suburban Church,* Home Mission Board, Southern Baptist Convention, 1971; (contributor) Ralph Herring and others, editors, *How to Understand the Bible,* Broadman, 1974; (contributor) Roger S. Greenway, editor, *Discipling the City,* Baker Book, 1979. Contributor of articles to mission and religious periodicals.

WORK IN PROGRESS: Church Growth in the New Testament.

AVOCATIONAL INTERESTS: Beekeeping and hiking.

*   *   *

CORBIN, Richard 1911-

PERSONAL: Born November 4, 1911, in Schenectady, N.Y.; son of Charles Mosher (an accountant) and Lillian (Haddow) Corbin; married Marjorie Kennedy, June 25, 1938; children: R. Jonathan, Geoffrey C., Christopher W. *Education:* Colgate University, B.A., 1933; Columbia University, M.A., 1939. *Home:* 50 Oakridge, Peekskill, N.Y.

CAREER: Bay Shore (N.Y.) High School, teacher, 1933-37; Peekskill (N.Y.) High School, chairman of department of English, 1937-60; Hunter College High School, New York, N.Y., chairman of department of English, 1960-72. Visiting lecturer at Appalachian State College (now University), Cornell University, Colgate University, University of Colorado, University of Missouri, Columbia University. Consultant, Educational Testing Service, NDEA Institutes, U.S. Office of Education. *Member:* National Council of Teachers of English (first vice-president, 1964; president, 1965; co-director of task force on language programs for the disadvantaged), New York State English Council (former president), Phi Beta Kappa.

WRITINGS: (With Porter Perrin) *Guide to Modern English, Upper Years,* Scott, Foresman, 1955; (with Vander Beek and Blough) *Guide to Modern English, Books Nine and Ten,* Scott, Foresman, 1960; (editor) *Poetry I,* Macmillan, 1962, revised edition published as *Currents in Poetry,* 1968; (with Perrin) *Guide to Modern English, Books Eleven and Twelve,* Scott, Foresman, 1963; *What Parents Should Know about the Teaching of Writing in Our Schools,* Macmillan, 1966; (with Smiley and Marcatante) *Stories in Song and Verse,* Macmillan, 1966; (editor with Ned Hoopes) *Surprises: Twenty Stories by O. Henry,* Dell, 1966; (editor with Miriam Balf) *Twelve American Plays: 1920-1960,* Scribner, 1969, revised edition, 1973; (with son, Jonathan Corbin) *Research Papers: A Guided Writing Experience for Senior High School Students,* 2nd revised edition, New York State English Council, 1978. Contributor of articles to education journals. Special advisory editor on usage for *Thorndike-Barn-*

hart *High School Dictionary;* chairman of advisory committee for vocabulary section of *World Book Encyclopedia Dictionary.* Editor and reader of long-play recordings of poems, Macmillan, 1963.

*   *   *

CORLEY, Robert N(eil) 1930-

PERSONAL: Born March 21, 1930, in Oak Park, Ill.; son of Paul R. (a railway mail clerk) and Vera M. (Hoobler) Corley; married Elinor A. McAloon, October 5, 1952. *Education:* University of Illinois, B.S., 1952, J.D., 1956. *Politics:* Republican. *Religion:* Methodist. *Home:* 1 South Stratford Dr., Athens, Ga. 30605. *Office:* University of Georgia, Athens, Ga. 30602.

CAREER: Practicing attorney in Illinois; University of Illinois at Urbana-Champaign, assistant professor, 1957-61, associate professor, 1961-68, professor of business law and business administration, 1968-75; University of Georgia, Athens, distinguished professor of legal studies, 1975—. *Military service:* U.S. Army Reserve, Finance Corps, 1952-59; became first lieutenant.

WRITINGS: (With Robert L. Black) *The Legal Environment of Business,* McGraw, 1963, 5th edition (with Black and O. Lee Reed), 1981; (with Black and O. E. Adams) *Outlines of Commercial Law,* Stipes, 1963; (editor with others) Essel Ray Dillavou and C. G. Howard, *Principles of Business Law,* 7th edition, Prentice-Hall, 1964, 11th edition (with William J. Robert), 1979; *Materials and Cases for Use in Estate Planning,* Stipes, 1964; (contributor) *Handbook of Business Administration,* McGraw, 1967; (with Robert) *Fundamentals of Business Law,* Prentice-Hall, 1974, 2nd edition, 1978; (with Floyd W. Windal) *The Accounting Profession: Ethics, Responsibility, and Liability,* Prentice-Hall, 1980; (with Charles F. Floyd and Peter J. Shedd) *Real Estate and the Law,* Random House, 1981. Contributor to *Illinois Bar Journal.* Editor of case comments in *American Business Law Journal.*

*   *   *

CORSINI, Raymond J. 1914-

PERSONAL: Born June 1, 1914, in Rutland, Vt.; son of Joseph and Evelyn (Lavaggi) Corsini; married Lucy Yula, 1941; married second wife, Kleona Rigney, 1966; children: (first marriage) Evelyn Anne. *Education:* City College (now City College of the City University of New York), B.S., 1939, M.S., 1941; University of Chicago, Ph.D., 1955. *Home and office:* 140 Niuiki Cir., Honolulu, Hawaii 96821.

CAREER: Psychologist with state prison systems in New York, 1942-47, California, 1947-50, and Wisconsin, 1950-53; University of Chicago, Chicago, Ill., psychologist, 1955-59; Daniel D. Howard Associates, Chicago, industrial psychologist, 1959-64; University of California, Berkeley, lecturer in School of Criminology, 1964-65; clinical psychologist in private practice, 1965—. Counselor, Family Education Centers of Hawaii, 1965—; research associate, School of Public Health, University of Hawaii, 1966—; consultant and supervisor of individual education, Our Lady of Sorrows School, 1971—. *Member:* American Psychological Association, North American Society of Adlerian Psychology, American Academy of Psychotherapists.

WRITINGS: Methods of Group Psychotherapy, McGraw, 1957; (co-editor) *Critical Incidents in Psychotherapy,* Prentice-Hall, 1959; (co-author) *Roleplaying in Business and Industry,* Free Press of Glencoe, 1961; *Critical Incidents in*

Teaching, Prentice-Hall, 1964; (with Samuel Cardone) *Role-playing in Psychotherapy,* Aldine, 1966; (with Vincent Calia) *Critical Incidents in School Counseling,* Prentice-Hall, 1972; (editor with Loretta S. Bermosk) *Critical Incidents in Nursing,* Saunders, 1973; (with Genevieve Painter) *The Practical Parent: The ABC's of Child Discipline,* Harper, 1973; (editor) *Current Psychotherapies,* F. E. Peacock, 1973, 2nd edition, 1979; *The Family Council,* Regnery, 1974; (editor) *Current Personality Theories,* F. E. Peacock, 1977; (editor) *Readings in Current Personality Theories,* F. E. Peacock, 1978; (with Edward Ingas) *Alternative Educational Systems,* F. E. Peacock, 1979; (co-editor) *Great Cases in Psychotherapy,* F. E. Peacock, 1979; *Role-Playing: A Manual for Group Leaders,* University Associates, 1980; (co-editor) *Theories of Learning,* F. E. Peacock, 1980. Contributing editor, *Journal of Individual Psychology* and *Group Psychotherapy.*

WORK IN PROGRESS: Mama Mia, a life-with-mother type book; *Prison Psychologist,* fourteen years of prison reminiscences; *Educational Systems around the World* and *Individual Psychology: Theory and Practice,* both for F. E. Peacock; *Handbook of Innovative Psychotherapies,* for Wiley; *Give In or Give Up,* for Nelson-Hall.

* * *

COULTER, E(llis) Merton 1890-

PERSONAL: Surname is pronounced *Coal*-ter; born July 20, 1890, in Catawba County, N.C.; son of John Ellis (a farmer, lumberman, and stockman) and Lucy Ann (Propst) Coulter. *Education:* University of North Carolina, A.B., 1913; University of Wisconsin, M.A., 1915, Ph.D., 1917. *Politics:* Independent Democrat. *Religion:* Lutheran. *Home address:* P.O. Box 587, Athens, Ga. 30601.

CAREER: Marietta College, Marietta, Ohio, member of history faculty, 1917-19; University of Georgia, Athens, associate professor, 1919-23, professor of history, 1923-58, Regents' Professor Emeritus of History, 1958—. Visiting professor at University of Texas, 1929-30, 1942-45, Louisiana State University, 1934-35, Hebrew University of Jerusalem, 1952; visiting summer professor at Harvard University, Ohio State University, University of Chicago, Duke University, National University of Mexico, and six other U.S. universities. *Member:* American Historical Association, Organization of American Historians, Southern Historical Association (former president), Georgia Historical Society. *Awards, honors:* Litt.D., Marietta College, 1948; LL.D., University of North Carolina, 1952.

WRITINGS: (With W. E. Connelley) *History of Kentucky,* two volumes, American Historical Society, 1922; *The Civil War and Readjustment in Kentucky,* University of North Carolina Press, 1926; *College Life in the Old South,* Macmillan, 1928, published as *College Life in the Old South as Seen at the University of Georgia,* University of Georgia Press, 1973.

Short History of Georgia, University of North Carolina Press, 1933, published as *Georgia: A Short History,* 1947, revised edition, 1960; (editor) *Georgia's Disputed Ruins,* University of North Carolina Press, 1937; *William G. Brownlow: Fighting Parson of the Southern Highlands,* University of North Carolina Press, 1937; (editor) *The Other Half of Old New Orleans,* Louisiana State University Press, 1939; (editor) *The Course of the South to Secession: An Interpretation by Ulrich Bonnell Phillips,* Appleton, 1939.

Thomas Spalding of Sapelo, Louisiana State University Press, 1940; *John Jacobus Flournoy, Champion of the*

Common Man in the Antebellum South, Georgia Historical Society, 1942; *The South During Reconstruction, 1865-1877,* Louisiana State University Press, 1947; *Travels in the Confederate States: A Bibliography,* University of Oklahoma Press, 1948; (editor with A. B. Saye) *A List of the Early Settlers of Georgia,* University of Georgia Press, 1949, 2nd edition, 1967.

The Confederate States of America, 1861-65, Louisiana State University Press, 1950; *Wormsloe: Two Centuries of a Georgia Family,* University of Georgia Press, 1955; *Lost Generation: The Life and Death of James Barrow, C.S.A.,* Confederate, 1956; *Auraria: The Story of a Georgia Gold-Mining Town,* University of Georgia Press, 1956; *The Myth of Dade County's Seceding from Georgia in 1860,* Georgia Historical Society, 1957; (editor) *The Journal of William Stephens,* University of Georgia Press, Volume I: *1741-43,* 1958, Volume II: *1743-45,* 1959.

(Editor) *Confederate Receipt Book,* University of Georgia Press, 1960; *James Monroe Smith, Georgia Planter, Before Death and After,* University of Georgia Press, 1961; *John Ellis Coulter, Small-Town Businessman of Tarheelia,* privately printed, 1962; (editor) *The Journal of Peter Gordon, 1732-35,* University of Georgia Press, 1963; *Joseph Vallence Bevan, Georgia's First Official Historian,* University of Georgia Press, 1964; *Old Petersburg and the Broad River Valley of Georgia: Their Rise and Decline,* University of Georgia Press, 1965; *Georgia Waters: Tallulah Falls, Madison Springs, Scull Shoals, and the Okefenokee Swamp,* Georgia Historical Quarterly, 1965; *The Toombs Oak, the Tree That Owned Itself, and Other Chapters of Georgia,* University of Georgia Press, 1966; (editor) Warren Grice, *Georgia through Two Centuries,* Lewis Historical Publishing, 1966; *William Montague Brown, Versatile Anglo-Irish American,* University of Georgia Press, 1967; *Negro Legislators in Georgia during the Reconstruction Period,* Georgia Historical Quarterly, 1968.

Daniel Lee, Agriculturist: His Life North and South, University of Georgia Press, 1971; *The Last Visit of Jefferson Davis to Georgia and Other Topics in the History of the State,* Georgia Historical Quarterly, 1971; *George Walton Williams: The Life of a Southern Banker, 1820-1903,* Hibriten Press, 1976; *Abraham Baldwin: Yale College Leader, University of Georgia Founder, States' Rights Nationalist, 1754-1807,* Cherokee Publishing, 1981. Editor, *Georgia Historical Quarterly,* 1924-74.

AVOCATIONAL INTERESTS: E. Merton Coulter has pursued his hobbies—walking, color photography, and mountain climbing—in travel on four continents. He is also interested in music.

* * *

COULTER, John (William) 1888-

PERSONAL: Born February 12, 1888, in Belfast, North Ireland; son of Francis and Annie (Clements) Coulter; married Olive Clare Primrose (a writer), July 4, 1936; children: Primrose (Mrs. John T. Pemberton, Jr.), Clare Elizabeth Crieve. *Education:* Attended Municipal Technical Institute and School of Art, both in Belfast, Northern Ireland, and University of Manchester. *Home:* 484 Avenue Rd., Apt. 702, Toronto, Ontario, Canada. *Agent:* International Copyrights Bureau, 26 Charing Cross Rd., London W.C.2, England.

CAREER: Teacher of art and English at Coleraine Academical Institution, Coleraine, Ireland, 1913-14, Wesley College, Dublin, Ireland, 1914-19; writer. *Member:* (Honorary member) Canadian Association for Theatre History, Arts and

Letters Club (Toronto). *Awards, honors:* D.Litt., York University, 1979.

WRITINGS: The House in the Quiet Glen (play), Macmillan (Canada), 1937; *The Family Portrait* (play), Macmillan (Canada), 1937; *Radio Drama Is Not Theatre*, Macmillan (Canada), 1937; *Transit through Fire* (opera libretto), Macmillan (Canada), 1942; *Deirdre of the Sorrows* (opera libretto), Macmillan (Canada), 1944, abridged version published as *Deirdre*, 1965; *Churchill* (biography), Ryerson, 1944; *Turf Smoke* (novel), Ryerson, 1945; *The Blossoming Thorn* (verse), Ryerson, 1946; *The Trial of Louis Riel* (play), Oberon Press, 1960; *Riel* (play; first produced in 1950, later revised for radio), Ryerson, 1962; *The Crime of Louis Riel* (play), Players Co-Op, 1966; "Capful of Pennies," first produced in Toronto, Ontario, at Central Library Theatre, 1967, revised version entitled "Mr. Kean of Drury Lane," 1980; *The Drums Are Out* (play; first produced in Dublin, Ireland, at Abbey Theatre), St. Paul University, 1971; "God's Ulsterman" (radio play; adapted from stage play), first produced by Canadian Broadcasting Co., 1974; *Francois Bigot* (play), Hounslow Press, 1978; *Prelude to a Marriage* (autobiography), Oberon Press, 1979; *In My Day* (autobiography), Hounslow Press, 1980.

Other plays produced: "Mr. Oblomov," "Holy Manhattan," "The Fiddling Hind," "Sleep My Pretty One," "Clogherbann Fair." Also author of plays, as yet unpublished and unproduced: "While I Live," 1966; "Highlights," 1979; "Living Together," 1979. Editor, *Ulster Review*, 1926; assistant editor, *New Adelphi*, 1927-30. Contributor of plays, feature programs, criticism, and reviews to British Broadcasting Corp., Canadian Broadcasting Co., and Radio Eireann. Contributor to journals and newspapers in England, Ireland, Canada, and United States.

WORK IN PROGRESS: Writing general and individual play prefaces for projected volumes of his selected plays.

*   *   *

COURLANDER, Harold   1908-

PERSONAL: Born September 18, 1908, in Indianapolis, Ind.; son of David (a primitive painter) and Tillie (Oppenheim) Courlander; married Emma Meltzer, June 18, 1949; children: Erika, Michael, Susan. *Education:* University of Michigan, B.A., 1931. *Home and office:* 5512 Brite Dr., Bethesda, Md. 20034.

CAREER: Farmer in Romeo, Mich., 1933-1938; Douglas Aircraft Co., Eritrea (now Ethiopia), historian, 1942-43; U.S. Office of War Information, New York City, and Bombay, India, editor, 1943-45; U.S. Information Agency, Voice of America, New York City, editor, 1945-54, Washington, D.C., senior political analyst, 1960-74. United Nations, New York City, press officer for U.S. Mission, 1954, writer and editor, *United Nations Review*, 1956-59. *Awards, honors:* Avery Hopwood Award, 1931, 1932; Franz Boas Fund research grant for folklore study in Dominican Republic, 1939; American Council of Learned Societies grants for research in Haiti, 1939, 1940; American Philosophical Society grants for studies in New World Negro cultures, 1946, 1954, 1955; Wenner-Gren Foundation grants for work in United States and West Indian Negro folk music, 1946, 1954, 1955, 1956, 1962; Guggenheim fellowships for studies in African and Afro-American cultures, 1948, 1955.

WRITINGS: Swamp Mud, Blue Ox Press, 1936; *Home to Langford County*, Blue Ox Press, 1938; *Haiti Singing*, University of North Carolina Press, 1939, Cooper Square, 1973; *The Caballero*, Farrar & Rinehart, 1940; (contributor) *Mis-*

celanea de estudios dedicados a Fernando Ortiz, [Havana], 1955; *The Drum and the Hoe: Life and Lore of the Haitian People*, University of California Press, 1960, new edition, 1980; *Shaping Our Times: What the United Nations Is and Does*, Oceana, 1960, revised edition, 1962; *On Recognizing the Human Species*, Anti-Defamation League of B'nai B'rith, 1960; *Negro Songs from Alabama*, Oak, 1960; *The Big Old World of Richard Creeks*, Chilton, 1962; *Negro Folk Music U.S.A.*, Columbia University Press, 1963; (with Remy Bastien) *Religion and Politics in Haiti*, Institute for Cross-Cultural Research, 1966; *Vodounin Haitian Culture*, Institute for Cross-Cultural Research, 1966; *The African*, Crown, 1967; *The Fourth World of the Hopis*, Crown, 1971; *Tales of Yoruba Gods and Heroes*, Crown, 1973; *The Son of the Leopard*, Crown, 1974; *A Treasury of African Folklore*, Crown, 1975; *A Treasury of Afro-American Folklore*, Crown, 1976; *The Mesa of Flowers*, Crown, 1977; (with Albert Yava) *Big Falling Snow*, Crown, 1978.

Folk tale collections: *Uncle Bouqui of Haiti*, Morrow, 1942; (with George Herzog) *The Cow-Tail Switch, and Other West African Stories*, Holt, 1947; (with Robert Kane) *Kantchil's Lime Pit, and Other Stories from Indonesia*, Harcourt, 1950; (with Wolf Leslau) *The Fire on the Mountain, and Other Ethiopian Stories*, Holt, 1950; *Ride with the Sun*, Whittlesey House, 1955; *Terrapin's Pot of Sense*, Holt, 1957; (with Albert K. Prempeh) *The Hat Shaking Dance, and Other Tales from the Gold Coast*, Harcourt, 1957; *The Tiger's Whisker, and Other Tales and Legends from Asia and the Pacific*, Harcourt, 1959; *The King's Drum, and Other African Folk Tales*, Harcourt, 1962; *The Piece of Fire, and Other Haitian Tales*, Harcourt, 1964; (with Ezekiel A. Eshugbayi) *Olode the Hunter, and Other Tales from Nigeria*, Harcourt, 1968 (published in England as *Ijapa the Tortoise, and Other Nigerian Tales*, Bodley Head, 1969); *People of the Short Corn: Tales and Legends of the Hopi Indians*, Harcourt, 1970.

Albums, compiled and edited from own field recordings: "Cult Music of Cuba," Ethnic Folkways Library, 1949; "Meringues," Folkways Records, 1950; "Drums of Haiti," Ethnic Folkways Library, 1950; "Folk Music of Haiti," Ethnic Folkways Library, 1950; "Folk Music of Ethiopia," Ethnic Folkways Library, 1951; "Songs and Dances of Haiti," Ethnic Folkways Library, 1952; "Haitian Piano," Folkways Records, 1952. Compiler and editor of other collections for Ethnic Folkways Library, including "Caribbean Folk Music," "Folk Music, U.S.A.," "African and Afro-American Drums," and "Afro-American Folk Music."

Contributor of articles to *Saturday Review, Musical Quarterly, New Republic, Journal of Negro History, Opportunity, African Arts, Chicago Sun-Times, Village Voice,* and other periodicals.

WORK IN PROGRESS: Heroes of Segou: The Oral Literature of the Bamana of the Upper Niger; Hopi Texts (transcriptions of Hopi oral literature); *The Crest and the Hide, and Other African Stories.*

SIDELIGHTS: Harold Courlander told *CA:* "Although my work has been with both fiction and nonfiction (often scholarly), I think of myself primarily as a narrator. I have always had a special interest in using fiction and nonfiction narration to bridge communications between other cultures and our own. While a number of my publications seem to be mere 'folklore,' I consider them to be fragments of a large body of oral literature. Folk tales as such have no special meaning for me unless they convey human values, philosophical outlook, cultural heritage and, hopefully, literary essence. I am equally motivated to create a narration of my own, which I hope will last a while, and to set down, for example, an African epic which already has shown its power to endure."

With the knowledge of forty years of folklore research behind him, Courlander wrote his novel *The African*. While in itself his most successful book, it has the added distinction of being the subject of a successful copyright infringement suit against *Roots* author Alex Haley. Haley's book, the result of twelve years of family research, was first published ten years after Courlander's. In the settlement of the suit, Haley acknowledged that portions of *Roots* had been taken from *The African*. *The African*, however, was not as enthusiastically received by publishers, nor did it have the benefit of media hype to boost its appeal. According to Jacqueline Trescott's 1978 *Washington Post* article, at the time the suit was settled Courlander's book had earned him $28,000 in royalties, while Haley had earned $2.6 million from hardcover sales alone.

BIOGRAPHICAL/CRITICAL SOURCES: New York Times Book Review, April, 28, 1968; *Book World*, May 5, 1968; *National Observer*, September 22, 1968; *Times Literary Supplement*, October 16, 1969; *Washington Post*, December 16, 1978.

*   *   *

COWLEY, Malcolm 1898-

PERSONAL: Born August 24, 1898, in Belsano, Pa.; son of William (a homeopathic physician) and Josephine (Hutmacher) Cowley; married Marguerite Frances Baird, July, 1919 (divorced, 1932); married Muriel Maurer, June 18, 1932; children: Robert William. *Education:* Harvard University, B.A. (cum laude), 1920; Universite de Montpellier, diplome, 1922. *Politics:* Democrat. *Home:* Church Rd., Sherman, Conn. 06784. *Office:* Viking Press, 625 Madison Avenue, New York, N.Y. 10022.

CAREER: Writer, editor, lecturer. Worked for *Sweet's Architectural Catalogue*, New York City; free-lance writer and translator, 1925-29; *New Republic*, New York City, literary editor, 1929-44; Office of Facts and Figures, Washington, D.C., member of staff, 1942; Viking Press, New York City, literary adviser, 1948—. Visiting professor, University of Washington, 1950, Stanford University, 1956, 1959, 1960-61, 1965, University of Michigan, 1957, University of California, 1962, Cornell University, 1964, Hollins College, 1968, 1970, University of Minnesota, 1971, and University of Warwick, 1973. Helped organize first American Writers Congress in 1935, and was active in League of American Writers which grew out of the Congress; director of Corporation of Yaddo. Chairman of zoning board, Sherman, Conn., 1945-68. *Wartime service:* American Field Service, 1917; served in France. U.S. Army, artillery officers' training school, 1918. *Member:* National Institute of Arts and Letters (president, 1956-59, 1962-65), American Academy of Arts and Letters (chancellor, 1967-76), Club des Bibliophages, Phi Beta Kappa, Century Association and Harvard Club (both New York). *Awards, honors:* Levinson Prize, 1928, and Harriet Monroe Memorial Prize, 1939, both for verse published in *Poetry;* National Institute of Arts and Letters grant in literature, 1946; National Endowment for the Arts grant, 1967; Signet Society Medal, 1976; Hubbell Medal for service to the study of American letters, 1979. Litt.D. from Franklin and Marshall College, 1961, Colby College, 1962, University of Warwick, 1975, University of New Haven, 1976, and Monmouth College, 1978.

WRITINGS—Published by Viking, except as indicated: *Exile's Return* (literary history of the 1920's), Norton, 1934,

revised edition, Viking, 1951; *The Literary Situation* (literary history), 1954; (with Daniel Pratt Mannix) *Black Cargoes: A History of the Atlantic Slave Trade, 1518-1865*, 1962; *The Faulkner-Cowley File*, 1966; *Think Back on Us: A Contemporary Chronicle of the 1930's* (literary history), edited and with an introduction by Henry Dan Piper, Southern Illinois University Press, 1969; *A Many-Windowed House: Collected Essays on American Writers and American Writing*, Southern Illinois University Press, 1970; (with Howard Hugo) *The Lesson of the Masters* (criticism), Scribner, 1971; *A Second Flowering: Works and Days of the Lost Generation* (literary history), 1973; *And I Worked at the Writer's Trade* (memoirs), 1978; *The Dream of the Golden Mountains: Remembering the 1930s* (memoirs), 1980; *The View from Eighty* (essay), 1980.

Poetry: *Blue Juniata*, Cape & Smith, 1929; *The Dry Season*, New Directions, 1941; *Blue Juniata: Collected Poems*, Viking, 1968.

Editor: Brantz Mayer, *Adventures of an African Slaver: Being a True Account of the Life of Captain Theodore Canot*, Garden City, 1928; *After the Genteel Tradition: American Writers since 1910*, Norton, 1937, revised edition, Southern Illinois University Press, 1964; (with Bernard Smith) *Books That Changed Our Minds*, Doubleday, 1940; *The Portable Hemingway*, Viking, 1944; (with Hannah Josephson) *Aragon: Poet of the French Resistance*, Duell, Sloan & Pearce, 1945 (published in England as *Aragon: Poet of Resurgent France*, Pilot Press, 1946); *The Portable Faulkner*, Viking, 1946, revised edition, 1966; *The Portable Hawthorne*, Viking, 1948, revised edition, 1969; *The Complete Poetry and Prose of Walt Whitman*, Pellegrini, 1948, published as *The Works of Walt Whitman*, Funk, 1968; *Stories by F. Scott Fitzgerald*, Scribner, 1951; Fitzgerald, *Tender Is the Night*, Scribner, 1951; (with Edmund Wilson) *Three Novels by F. Scott Fitzgerald*, Scribner, 1953; *Great Tales of the Deep South*, Lion Press, 1955; *Writers at Work: The "Paris Review" Interviews*, Viking, 1958; Walt Whitman, *Leaves of Grass: The First (1855) Edition*, Viking, 1959; Sherwood Anderson, *Winesburg, Ohio*, Viking, 1960; (with son, Robert Cowley) *Fitzgerald and the Jazz Age*, Scribner, 1966.

Translator from the French: Pierre MacOrlan, *On Board the Morning Star*, A. & C. Boni, 1924; Joseph Delteil, *Joan of Arc*, Minton, 1926; Paul Valery, *Variety*, Harcourt, 1927; Marthe Lucie Bibesco, *Catherine-Paris*, Harcourt, 1928; Bibesco, *The Green Parrot*, Harcourt, 1929; Maurice Barres, *The Sacred Hill*, Macaulay, 1929; Raymond Radiguet, *The Count's Ball*, Norton, 1929; Andre Gide, *Imaginary Interviews*, Knopf, 1944; (with James R. Lawler) Valery, *Leonardo Poe Mallarme*, Princeton University Press, 1972.

Associate editor, *Broom*, 1928, and *Cessation;* associate editor and book critic, *New Republic*, 1929-44.

SIDELIGHTS: In 1934 Malcolm Cowley published an autobiographical literary history, *Exile's Return*, and established himself as an important writer. In 1965 the editor of *Literary Times* wrote, "Malcolm Cowley is, next to Edmund Wilson, the finest literary historian and critic alive in America today."

In the early thirties, Cowley's name was frequently associated with the political left. But, as Murray Kempton notes, "even then, Cowley's was a commitment primarily literary. He remained a spectator and he confessed in 1934 that, as 'a petty bourgeois critic,' he was debarred from complete involvement." Daniel Aaron adds: "Few writers identified with the left during this period managed better than Cowley did to remain on speaking terms with literary acquaintances to the right and left of him." Aaron believes that it was Cowley's intention, in advocating leftist principles, to "mediate between the 'art as a weapon' school of literary judgement and ivory-tower subjectivism," and he believed that Communist ideology proposed an environment in which the artist could function most effectively. Kempton outlines his argument: "Malcolm Cowley [was not a Communist, but he] believed that the young writer was wise to be one and could give him better reasons than he could give himself. . . . The revolution could give a man, Cowley indicated, the gift of prophecy. 'It gives the sense of human life, not as a medley of accidents, but as a connected and continuous process. . . . It gives the values, the unified interpretation without which one can neither write good history nor good tragedy.' Cowley was not one of the committed and he was there mainly as an ornament. He confessed himself unable by condition and vestiges of class heritage to contest for the glories of this vision; they belonged to the young and the plebian." Cowley thought that the revolution provided a "new source of strength" for the writer who could derive inspiration from the potential greatness of a rising class. Kempton continues: "For Cowley and his friends social rebellion was a new turn and the passion they brought to it seems more rhetorical now than they knew then. Cowley was the most articulate historian of their highly complicated state of mind, and his *Exile's Return* . . . is their best testament."

Reviewers frequently note that Cowley's most important achievement as a critic has been his treatment of William Faulkner's fiction. The *Literary Times* editor writes: "Probably more than any single person, Cowley is responsible for the entrenchment of . . . Faulkner as a major American writer with his brilliant introduction and presentation of *The Portable Faulkner* in 1946."

But Cowley is most often recognized as a literary historian and his *Exile's Return,* if not the definitive chronicle of the 1920's, is certainly one of the most widely read. When the book was first published, Isabel Paterson of *Books* called it "touching, interesting, amusing; it reveals a likable soul and, therefore, should appeal to a much wider audience than the literary group with which it is concerned." In a *New York Post* review, Herschel Brickell stated that "the writing in the book is a good deal better than the thinking," but went on to say that it was "undeniably an important contribution to American literary history of our times." And J. D. Adams of the *New York Times* wrote: "As the sincere attempt of a writer of our time to explain himself and his generation, to trace the flux of ideas and other influences to which he was subjected during his formative years, Mr. Cowley's book is a valuable document. It should interest the literary historian of the future no less than it must interest Mr. Cowley's contemporaries, however hard some of them may find it to grant him all his premises and to agree with all his deductions from them." When *Exile's Return* was revised in 1951, the new edition sparked further critical commentary. Lloyd Morris, in a *New York Herald Tribune Book Review* article, called it "the most vivacious of all accounts of literary life during the fabulous 1920s" and said that the book "offers an intimate realistic portrait of the era that produced a renaissance in American fiction and poetry." J. W. Krutch of the *Saturday Review of Literature* noted that "Mr. Cowley's estimate of his most successful elder contemporaries, including Joyce, Eliot, and Proust, is cool and on the whole rather remarkably far this side of idolatry. But these evaluations do not seem

unjust, and his picture of life on the Left Bank and in Greenwich Village is highly colored without being exaggerated."

Another literary history for which Cowley has received considerable praise is *A Second Flowering,* a book dealing with eight literary figures: Fitzgerald, Hemingway, Dos Passos, Cummings, Wilder, Faulkner, Wolfe, and Hart Crane. William Styron, in a *New York Times Book Review* article, writes: "It is testimony to Cowley's gifts both as a critic and a literary chronicler that the angle of vision seems new; that is, not only are his insights into these writers' works almost consistently arresting, but so are his portraits of the men themselves. . . . Cowley can be as rough and relentless as an old mill-wheel in his judgments, whether it be upon some odious personal quality, such as Hemingway's unregenerate and infantile competitiveness, or on a matter of literature. Either way, the critic cuts close to the bone." P. S. Prescott of *Newsweek* agrees that the essays in this book are "a skillful blend of criticism and biography" and adds that the pieces "on the individual writers, all of whom have been over-observed and overanalyzed, remain fresh and perceptive." Prescott concludes, "Cowley's book, I think, may be—and may remain—the best brief introduction to the generation."

Writing in the *Sewanee Review,* Lewis P. Simpson expresses his opinion that *A Second Flowering* "represents a part of a long struggle on Cowley's part to redeem the American writer from his condition of alienation. It would be misleading to say that this struggle has dominated Cowley's wide-ranging work as a literary critic. It is hardly too much to say that it provides a strong unifying theme in his complex and varied achievement. But in the same breath we must observe that it is a struggle Cowley has never intended to win. When we add to his criticism Cowley's small but important body of poetry, we see running through the whole range of his work as a twentieth-century poet, critic, and literary and cultural historian a basic motive of alienation. As both a creator and an interpreter of the literature of the lost generation, Cowley is a contributor to one of its leading aspects: a myth or a legend of creativity which is definable as a poetics of exile. He apprehended first the American writer's exile from childhood, second his exile from society, and finally his exile from what may be termed the sense of being in the wholeness of the self. The first two revelations are stated in Cowley's best-known book, *Exile's Return;* the third—of which the first two are stages—is nowhere, so far as I know, set down explicitly by Cowley. It does not lend itself to overstatement. Implied in the first edition of *Exile's Return,* it is significantly modified or even repudiated in the second, a reversal which carries over strikingly in a remarkable essay entitled 'A Natural History of the American Writer.' But on the other hand its implication is strong in three of Cowley's most significant essays, those on Frost, Hawthorne, and Whitman. Its major appearance may be discerned in *Blue Juniata: Collected Poems.'*

In an interview with Allen Geller, Cowley compared contemporary literature to the work produced in the twenties and thirties. "I think there is a very interesting group of writers today," he said mentioning Saul Bellow and John Cheever among those he considered most important. "[Literary taste] has become more sophisticated. Whether it's better or not is always the question, but it has more knowledge, more points of reference." He added, "The great change from the 1930s is that nobody any longer believes in his duty or ability to any extent or in any manner whatever to reshape or alter conditions."

In a *Southern Review* interview with Diane U. Eisenberg,

Cowley commented on the state of free-lance writing today in comparison to when he began working: "The trade of free lance is harder today. I don't think there are so many free-lance fiction writers. There are not many magazines that publish their work. As late as the 1920s and 1930s there were dozens of magazines that published short stories and paid for them. The *Saturday Evening Post* paid Scott Fitzgerald $4000 per story a while in the early thirties. On that, Fitzgerald could live like a spendthrift prince. And I think there were others who were paid up to $5000 by the *Post* at that time. That doesn't exist now; there's one magazine that pays well for stories and that is the *New Yorker*. I don't think there's another one. Many magazines pay well for articles and so most free lancers you meet today are article writers, not fiction writers. On the other hand, at the popular top of the profession it is novelist fiction writers who hit the jackpot."

Eisenberg asked, "Are you satisfied with what you've accomplished?" In reply, Cowley said: "No! Distinctly dissatisfied! It goes back to a long and bad error that I made during my twenties. That is, partly influenced by French friends, I decided, 'Well, I just have to keep at this thing honestly and if I make any great success in my twenties or thirties I'm not going to keep at it honestly,' so I actually *tried* not to make a success. I was the anticareerist at that time for myself. And a part of the result was that I didn't drive myself to write some big work that was really expected of me. I had chances, too, but I didn't drive myself to finish it. And the fact that I didn't drive myself hard enough in my twenties is the big error I made. I should have been looking much more at the big overall pattern . . . keeping at producing bigger books."

In his final statement to Eisenberg, Cowley concluded: "The writer's trade is a laborious, tedious but lovely occupation of putting words into patterns. I love that trade, profession, vocation. And that is something that persists over time."

AVOCATIONAL INTERESTS: Gardening, pine trees.

BIOGRAPHICAL/CRITICAL SOURCES—Books: Philip Rahv, editor, *Discovery of Europe*, Houghton, 1947; Murray Kempton, *Part of Our Time*, Simon & Schuster, 1955; Harvey Breit, *The Writer Observed*, World Publishing, 1956; Daniel Aaron, *Writers on the Left*, Harcourt, 1961; Kenneth Rexroth, *Assays*, New Directions, 1961; Howard Nemerov, *Poetry and Fiction: Essays*, Princeton University Press, 1963; Diane U. Eisenberg, *Malcolm Cowley: A Checklist of His Writings, 1915-1973*, Southern Illinois University Press, 1975.

Periodicals: *Bookman*, October, 1930; *Saturday Review of Literature*, January 16, 1934, June 30, 1951; *Books*, May 27, 1934; *New York Times*, May 27, 1934, June 10, 1951, February 13, 1962, August 17, 1977, April 28, 1978, March 26, 1980, October 1, 1980; *New York Herald Tribune Book Review*, May 28, 1934, June 24, 1951, October 7, 1951; *New York Post*, June 2, 1934; *Nation*, July 4, 1934, June 5, 1967; *Booklist*, June 15, 1951; *New Yorker*, June 30, 1951, June 23, 1973; *New York Times Book Review*, July 8, 1951, February 12, 1967, November 17, 1968, May 6, 1973; *Literary Times*, April, 1965; *New Republic*, March 11, 1967; *Saturday Review*, March 11, 1967; *Canadian Forum*, January, 1968; *Choice*, September, 1973; *Sewanee Review*, spring, 1976; *Southern Review*, spring, 1977; *Washington Post Book World*, September 7, 1980.

—*Sketch by Peter M. Gareffa*

COWLING, Maurice John 1926-

PERSONAL: Born September 6, 1926, in London, England; son of Reginald Frederick (a chartered patent agent) and May Cowling. *Education:* Attended Jesus College, Cambridge University. *Office:* Peterhouse, Cambridge, England.

CAREER: Jesus College, Cambridge University, Cambridge, England, fellow, 1951-53, 1961-63; affiliated with British Foreign Office, 1954; *London Times*, London, England, leader writer, 1955-56; worked for *Daily Express*, London, 1956-57; Cambridge University, lecturer in history, 1961-75, reader in modern English history, 1975—, fellow of Peterhouse, 1963—. Conservative parliamentary candidate for Bassetlaw in British general election, 1959. Member of Cambridgeshire and Isle of Ely County Council, 1966.

WRITINGS—All published by Cambridge University Press, except as indicated: *Nature and Limits of Political Science*, 1963; *Mill and Liberalism*, 1963; *1867: Disraeli, Gladstone, and Revolution*, 1967; *The Impact of Labour*, 1971; *The Impact of Hitler*, 1975; (editor) *Conservative Essays*, Cassell, 1978; *Religion and Public Doctrine in Modern England I*, 1980.

BIOGRAPHICAL/CRITICAL SOURCES: Observer Review, July 23, 1967, April 25, 1971, July 27, 1975; *Listener*, August 3, 1967, July 13, 1978; *Times Literary Supplement*, August 31, 1967, July 25, 1975, September 29, 1978; *Cambridge Review*, May 7, 1971, October, 1975.

*   *   *

CRANE, Caroline 1930-

PERSONAL: Born October 30, 1930, in Chicago, Ill.; daughter of Roger Alan (a foundation executive) and Jessie Louise (a social worker; maiden name, Taft) Crane; married Yoshio Kiyabu (a travel agent), July 11, 1959; children: Crane Ryo, Laurel Rei. *Education:* Bennington College, A.B., 1952; Columbia University, graduate study, 1952-53. *Politics:* Democrat. *Home:* 317 West 93rd St., New York, N.Y. 10025. *Agent:* Muriel Fuller, P.O. Box 193, Grand Central Station, New York, N.Y. 10017.

CAREER: United Nations Children's Fund, U.S. Committee, New York, N.Y., writer, 1957-60; author. *Member:* Authors Guild of Authors League of America.

WRITINGS—Young adult novels, except as indicated: *Pink Sky at Night*, Doubleday, 1963; *Lights Down the River*, Doubleday, 1964; *A Girl Like Tracy*, McKay, 1966; *Wedding Song*, McKay, 1967; *Don't Look at Me That Way*, Random House, 1970; *Stranger on the Road*, Random House, 1971; *Summer Girl* (adult novel), Dodd, 1979; *The Girls Are Missing* (adult novel), Dodd, 1980; *Coast of Fear* (adult novel), Dodd, 1981.

WORK IN PROGRESS: Four suspense novels; two historical novels set in Russia.

SIDELIGHTS: Caroline Crane writes *CA:* "It seems sometimes as though I have had not one, but two or three writing careers. As a stagestruck teenager, I wrote plays for the sole purpose of producing and acting in them. Years later, when I turned to novels, enough of the teenager must have been left in me so that she was the one who defined my writing. The first six books I wrote, which spanned a publication period of eight years, are novels for young adults. Of those, the first two deal with the theatre. The rest are 'problem' novels, that is, they are concerned with the subjects of teenage marriage, alcoholic parents, and mental retardation.

"Suddenly, everything changed; I was no longer interested

in writing for young people. The transition, however, was long and painful. Apparently, my writing style and way of thinking had not caught up with my interests. It was another eight years, and almost as many unpublished manuscripts, before I finally broke through with my first adult suspense novel, *Summer Girl*.

"The only things that kept me going during that discouraging era were the knowledge that I *had* published before and, therefore, could probably do it again and the fact that, no matter what else I tried, from office work to running a home typing service, I could not stop writing. It is an addiction. It colors my whole life. Whatever I do, whatever places I visit, always seems to bear a tag that reads: How can I use this in my writing? In 1978, a friend persuaded me to join her on a train trip through France. I took notes along the way and used that trip as chapter one of *Coast of Fear*.

"*Summer Girl* was inspired by a magazine article about women who summer at the Long Island beaches, taking with them live-in teenage babysitters to share the work load. A nubile adolescent, a harried mother perhaps lacking in self-confidence, a susceptible husband—what a dynamite situation. *The Girls Are Missing* was born of reflections on the case of Jack the Ripper. Didn't the man have a family, friends, neighbors? Did any of them have any idea of his double identity? What would it be like to wonder?

"For me, writing is a kind of sharing of emotions, experiences, and ideas. I love reading other people's suspense novels, and hope I can bring the same pleasure and excitement to my own readers."

AVOCATIONAL INTERESTS: Travel, history, ballet, opera, reading suspense novels.

* * *

CRANSTON, Maurice (William) 1920-

PERSONAL: Born May 8, 1920, in London, England; son of William (a theatrical manager) and Catherine (Harris) Cranston; married Baroness Maximilana von und zu Franberg, November 11, 1958; children: Nicholas, Stephen. *Education:* Attended Birkbeck College, 1945; St. Catherine's Society, Oxford University, B.A., 1948, M.A., 1950, B. Litt, 1951. *Politics:* Liberal. *Home:* One a, Kent Ter., Regents Park, London N.W. 1, England. *Agent:* A. D. Peters, 10 Buckingham St., London WC2N 6BU, England; and Harold Matson Co., Inc., 22 East 40th St., New York, N.Y. 10016. *Office:* London School of Economics and Political Science, University of London, Aldwych, London W.C. 2, England.

CAREER: University of London, London, England, lecturer in social philosophy, 1950-59, professor of political science in London School of Economics and Political Science, 1959—. Visiting professor of government, Harvard University, 1965-66; professor of political science, Institut Universitaire Europeen, Florence, Italy, 1979-81. Literary adviser, Methuen & Co., Ltd., 1959—. *Member:* International P.E.N., Institut International de Philosophie Politique (president), Societe Europeen de Culture (Venice; member of executive council), Royal Society of Literature (fellow), Book Society (member of selection committee, 1957-59), Royal Literary Fund, Society of Authors, American Academy of Arts and Sciences (foreign member), Alliance Francaise (vice-president), Political Science Society, Mind Association, Association of University Teachers, Garrick Club. *Awards, honors:* Tom Gallon Prize, 1953; Society of Authors' traveling scholarship, 1954; James Tait Black Memorial Prize for best biography published in United Kingdom, 1958, for *John Locke*.

WRITINGS: Freedom, Longmans, Green, 1953; *John Locke: A Biography,* Macmillan, 1957; *Human Rights Today,* Ampersand Press, 1962; *Jean-Paul Sartre,* Grove, 1962; *What Are Human Rights?,* Basic Books, 1963; (editor) *Western Political Philosophers,* Bodley Head, 1964; *Glossary of Political Terms,* Bodley Head, 1966; *Political Dialogues,* Basic Books, 1969; (editor) *The New Left: Six Critical Essays,* Bodley Head, 1970, Library Press, 1971; *The Mask of Politics,* Basic Books, 1974. Regular contributor of literary features to British Broadcasting Corp.'s "Third Programme."

* * *

CROMIE, Alice Hamilton 1914-
(Alice Hamilton, Vivian Mort)

PERSONAL: Born May 29, 1914, in Chariton, Iowa; daughter of James Albert and Margaret (Bertrand) Hamilton; married Robert Allen Cromie (the host of television show, "The Cromie Circle"), May 22, 1937; children: Michael Allen, Richard Allen, Barbara Allen, James Allen. *Education:* Attended Kansas City Junior College, 1932-33, and University of Missouri, 1934; University of Texas, A.B., 1937. *Politics:* Independent. *Religion:* Protestant. *Home address:* Route 1, Box 42, Grayslake, Ill. 60030; and 82 Misciano, Camaiore (Lucca), Italy. *Agent:* Hilda Lindley, 128 East 56th St., New York, N.Y. 10022.

CAREER: Free-lance writer and lecturer; work has included promotional advertising and greeting card verses. *Member:* Mystery Writers of America, Critics Circle, Society of American Travel Writers, Travel Journalist Guild, American Society of Journalists and Authors, Authors Guild, Women in Communications (North Shore chapter), The Writers, Western Writers of America, Midwest Travel Writers Association, Midland Authors, Civil War Round Table of Chicago.

WRITINGS: (Editor) *A Tour Guide to the Civil War,* Quadrangle, 1965, revised edition, Dutton, 1975; (author of preface) *The Charlotte Armstrong Reader,* Coward, 1970; *Nobody Wanted to Scare Her,* Doubleday, 1974; *A Tour Guide to the Old West,* Times Books, 1977; *Lucky to Be Alive?,* Simon & Schuster, 1979. Work is anthologized in *Post Scripts,* McGraw, 1943. *Chicago Tribune,* author, under pseudonym Vivian Mort, of mystery review column, "Crime on My Hands," 1963-66, weekly book reviewer, 1966—, currently author of suspense column; author of column, *North Shore* (magazine). Contributor of fiction, light verse, and humorous verse to *Saturday Evening Post, Reader's Digest, Ladies' Home Journal, Collier's, Look,* and *American.* Contributing editor, *Suburbia, Mississippi* (magazine).

WORK IN PROGRESS: With Janine Warsaw, *House for Sale,* a mystery; *To See the Elephant,* a Civil War novel.

BIOGRAPHICAL/CRITICAL SOURCES: Chicago Tribune Book World, February 4, 1979.

* * *

CROSSER, Paul K. 1902-1976

PERSONAL: Born August 11, 1902, in Windau, Latvia; died May 19, 1976; son of Julius and Rose (Kossovski) Crosser; married Frances Schiller, 1943. *Education:* University of Berlin, Doctor of Economics, 1932; Columbia University, Ph.D., 1942. *Address:* Box 32, 139th and Convent Ave., New York, N.Y.

CAREER: Public Housing Bank, Berlin, Germany, economist, 1930-33; U.S. Project on Technological Unemployment, Washington, D.C., economist, 1936-39; Columbia University, Teachers College, New York, N.Y., research associate, 1939-41; Adelphi University, Garden City, N.Y., professor of economics, 1956-68, professor emeritus, 1968-76. Lecturer, City College of the City University of New York, beginning, 1945. Speech writer, New York municipal mayoral campaign for the election of Robert Wagner, 1953; speech writer, presidential campaign for the reelection of Dwight D. Eisenhower, 1956, and election of Lyndon B. Johnson, 1964. *Wartime service:* U.S. War Department, Services of Supply, 1941-45. *Member:* American Association for the Advancement of Science, American Philosophical Association, Royal British Institute of Philosophy, American Economic Association, British Economic History Society, American Sociological Association, Pi Gamma Mu, Phi Delta Kappa.

WRITINGS: Ideologies and American Labor, Oxford University Press, 1941; *The Nihilism of John Dewey,* Philosophical Library, 1955; *Economic Fictions: A Critique of Subjectivistic Economic Theory,* Philosophical Library, 1957; *State Capitalism in the Economy of the United States,* Bookman Associates, 1960; *War Is Obsolete,* Humanities, 1966; (with others) *East-West Dialogues: Foundations and Problems of Revolutionary Praxis,* Humanities, 1973; *Prolegomena to All Future Metaeconomics: Formation and Deformation of Economic Thought,* Warren Green, 1974. Contributor to professional journals.

WORK IN PROGRESS: The Transformation of Medieval Christian Ethics.

SIDELIGHTS: Several of Paul Crosser's books have been translated into foreign languages. *Avocational interests:* Travel in foreign countries.†

* * *

CROUZET, Francois Marie-Joseph 1922-

PERSONAL: Born October 20, 1922, in Monts-sur-Guesnes, France; son of Maurice (a historian) and Henriette (Pactat) Crouzet; married former wife, Francoise Dabert, March 27, 1947; married present wife, J. P. Dalem; children: Marie-Anne, Denis, Joel. *Education:* Sorbonne, Universite de Paris, licence es-lettres, 1943, diplome d'etudes superieures, 1944, agregation d'histoire, 1945, doctorat eslettres, 1956; London School of Economics and Political Science, graduate study, 1946-49. *Home:* 6 rue Benjamin-Godard, 75116 Paris, France. *Office:* Universite de Paris-Sorbonne, 1 rue Victor-Cousin, 75005 Paris, France.

CAREER: Lycee de Beauvais, Beauvais, France, instructor, 1945; research fellow in Great Britain, 1945-46; research associate, Centre national de la recherche scientifique, France, 1947-49; Universite de Paris, faculte des lettres, Paris, France, assistant lecturer, 1949-53; instructor, Lycee Janson-de-Sailly, 1953-56; Universite de Bordeaux, Bordeaux, France, associate professor of history, 1956-58; Universite de Lille, Lille, France, professor of contemporary history, 1958-64; Universite de Paris, Nanterre, France, professor of economic and social history, 1964-69; Universite de Paris, Sorbonne, Paris, professor of northern European history, 1969—. Visiting professor, Columbia University, spring, 1961, University of California, Berkeley, summer, 1964, and University of Geneva, 1969-72; visiting fellow, University College, Cambridge University, autumn, 1969, and All Souls College, Oxford University, autumn, 1976. Chairman of committee for modern history, Centre national de la recherche scientifique, 1976-80; director, Centre de recherches sur la civilisation de l'Europe moderne, 1977—.

MEMBER: Corps universitaires (member of consulting committee and conseil superieur, 1969—), British Academy (corresponding fellow), Royal Historical Society (corresponding fellow), Association francaise des historiens economists (president, 1974-77). *Awards, honors:* Bronze medal, Centre national de la recherche scientifique, 1957; Prix G. Maugin, Academie des science morales et politiques, 1959; honorary doctorate, University of Birmingham, 1977.

WRITINGS: L'Economie du commonwealth, Presses universitaires de France, 1950; *L'Economie britannique et le blocus continental, 1806-1813,* Presses universitaires de France, 1958; *Le Conflict de Chypre, 1946-1959,* E. Bruylant, 1973; *L'Economic de la Grande-Bretazne victorienne,* S.E.D.E.S., 1978.

Editor: (With Guy S. Metraux) *The Nineteenth-Century World: Readings from the History of Mankind,* New American Library, 1963; (with Metraux) *The Evolution of Science: Readings from the History of Mankind,* New American Library, 1963; (with Metraux) *The New Asia,* New American Library, 1965; (with Metraux) *Religions and the Promise of the Twentieth Century,* New American Library, 1965; (with Metraux) *Studies in the Cultural History of India,* Verry, 1965; (with W. H. Chaloner and W. M. Stern) *Essays in European Economic History, 1789-1914,* Edward Arnold, 1969, St. Martin's, 1970; (and author of introduction) *Capital Formation in the Industrial Revolution,* Barnes & Noble, 1972; (with P. Leon) *L'Industrialisation en Europe au xix 'siecle,* Centre national de la recherche scientifique, 1972; (and author of introduction) *Les Hommes d'etat celebres,* Volume V, Mazenod, 1975; (with F. Bedarida and D. Johnson) *De Guillaume le conquerant au Marche commun: Dix siecles d'histoire frances-britannique,* Albin Michel, 1979. Contributor of articles and book reviews to economic history journals. Member of editorial board, *Business History Review, Explorations in Economic History, Revue historique,* and *Revue d'histoire economique t sociale.*

WORK IN PROGRESS: Books on the British industrialists during the Industrial Revolution, for Hachette; a study of the Industrial Revolution.

SIDELIGHTS: Francois Marie-Joseph Crouzet's main field of interest and research is the economic and social history of Britain and France in the late eighteenth and early nineteenth centuries, with a secondary interest in recent British history and Anglo-French relations.

* * *

CROZIER, Brian (Rossiter) 1918-

PERSONAL: Born August 4, 1918, in Kuridala, Queensland, Australia; son of Robert Henry (a mining engineer) and Elsa (McGillivray) Crozier; married Mary Lillian Samuel, September 7, 1940; children: Kathryn-Anne, Isobel (Mrs. C. J. Colbourn), Michael, Caroline. *Education:* Attended Peterborough College, 1930-35, and Trinity College of Music, London, 1935-36. *Home:* 112 Bridge Lane, Temple Fortune, London NW11 9JS, England.

CAREER: Reporter or sub-editor for various provincial and suburban newspapers, 1940-41; free-lance art and music critic in London, England, 1941-43; Reuters (news agency), London, sub-editor, 1943-44; *News Chronicle,* London, sub-editor, 1944-48; *Sydney Morning Herald,* Sydney, Australia, feature writer, 1948-51; Reuters-Australian Associated Press, correspondent in Melbourne, Australia, and Southeast Asia, 1951-52; features editor, *Straits Times,* Singapore, 1952-53; *Foreign Report* (confidential bulletin published by *Economist*), London, editor, 1954-64; British Broadcasting

Corp., London, political commentator, 1954-65; Forum World Features, London, chairman, 1965-74; Institute for the Study of Conflict, London, founder and director, 1970-79; columnist and consultant, *Now!*, London, and *National Review*, New York, N.Y., 1979—. Lecturer. Painter; work has been exhibited in London and Sydney. *Member:* Royal United Institute for Defence Studies, U.S. Strategic Institute, International Institute for Strategic Studies; Royal Commonwealth Society and Royal Automobile Club (both London).

WRITINGS: The Rebels: A Study of Post-War Insurrections, Beacon Press, 1960; *The Morning After: A Study of Independence*, Oxford University Press (New York), 1963; *Neo Colonialism: A Background Book*, Dufour, 1964; *South-East Asia in Turmoil*, Penguin, 1965, 3rd edition, 1968; *The Struggle for the Third World*, Dufour, 1966; *Franco: A Biographical History*, Eyre & Spottiswoode, 1967, published as *Franco*, Little, Brown, 1968; *The Masters of Power*, Little, Brown, 1969; (editor and contributor) *"We Will Bury You,"* Stacey, 1970; *Since Stalin: An Assessment of Communist Power*, Coward, 1970 (published in England as *The Future of Communist Power*, Eyre & Spottiswoode, 1970); *De Gaulle: The First Full Biography*, Scribner, 1973 (published in England in two volumes as *De Gaulle*, Eyre Methuen, Volume I: *The Warrior*, 1973, Volume II: *The Statesman*, 1974); *A Theory of Conflict*, Scribner, 1974; (with Eric Chou) *The Man Who Lost China: The First Full Biography of Chiang Kai-shek*, Scribner, 1976; *Strategy of Survival*, Arlington House, 1978; *The Minimum State*, Hamish Hamilton, 1979; *Franco: Crepusculo de un hombre*, Planeta, 1980.

Contributor: Evan Luard, editor, *The Cold War*, Thames & Hudson, 1964; Sibnarayan Ray, editor, *Vietnam: Seen from East and West*, Nelson (Melbourne), 1966; Alastair Buchan, editor, *Problems of Modern Strategy*, Chatto & Windus, 1970; Hugh Thomas, editor, *Our Twentieth Century World*, Weidenfeld & Nicolson, 1970; Philip Toynbee, editor, *The Distant Drum*, Sidgwick & Jackson, 1976; *Book of the Year*, Encyclopaedia Britannica, 1976; Duncan and Weston-Smith, editors, *Lying Truths*, Pergamon, 1979.

Also author of pamphlets and reports and editor of *Annual of Power and Conflict*, 1971-79. Contributor to publications in England, the United States, and other countries.

WORK IN PROGRESS: This War Called Peace, with Drew Middleton and Jeremy Murray-Brown, for Jonathon James Books.

SIDELIGHTS: Brian Crozier comments: "As a foreign correspondent in Southeast Asia from 1951 to 1952, and on the staff of the *Straits Times*, I studied terrorism and insurgency in Indonesia, Malaya, and Vietnam. Later, for the *Economist* and other publications, and for the BBC, I reported violent situations in Cyprus, Algeria, the ex-Belgian Congo, and Latin America. With the publication of *The Rebels* in 1960, I pioneered the systematic study of political violence; this work became mandatory reading at Fort Bragg, the U.S. Army War College, the Israel Defence College, and many other military institutions. These experiences led me to found, with Professor Leonard Schapiro, Sir Robert Thompson, and others, the Institute for the Study of Conflict."

Crozier notes that as a political commentator and foreign correspondent he has interviewed "many heads of state or government," including Ho Chi Minh, Ngo Dinh Diem, Chiang Kai-shek, and Francisco Franco. He concludes: "As a political writer, I have tried to provide a reliable and unsentimental guide to world conflict. As a biographer, I have concentrated on three major military statesmen: Franco, de Gaulle, and Chiang Kai-shek."

Crozier's biography of Charles de Gaulle has garnered much critical attention. Robert O. Paxton in the *New York Times Book Review* calls it "a well-informed narrative of rich detail." *Newsweek*'s Arthur Cooper expresses a similar view, stating that "Crozier has produced not only the first truly complete biography of *le grand Charles* but what is likely to be the best we shall have for some time." The critic continues: "The de Gaulle who emerges from these pages is a paradox, a man who adored his wife and, until she died at 19, his mentally retarded daughter, but who also was 'cold and aloof,' a political animal of 'overweening vanity' who 'had a few intimates but no friends.'"

Furthermore, Cooper notes that "Crozier has managed to put de Gaulle in human perspective, [which] is no small achievement, but what really distinguishes this biography is its sober, penetrating assessment of the general's career." Paxton, citing the fact that de Gaulle's "theatrical sense and his myth-making skill were the best of his time," explains: "Mr. Crozier, in a final summation, concludes that de Gaulle accomplished few of the great things he set out to do. Mr. Crozier believes that de Gaulle fully succeeded only as a showman."

Reaction to *The Man Who Lost China*, Crozier's biography of Chiang Kai-shek, has been mixed. O. Edmund Clubb of the *New York Times Book Review*, for example, comments: "It is evident that the author has consulted his sources and had his interviews with important Chinese political figures. . . . But it also becomes apparent that some of the assembled material has not been properly verified; the work contains numerous errors of fact." In the *New Republic*, James Thompson contends that the book's major drawback is its contradictory approach to Chiang: "Crozier's view of Chiang is so confused, so ambivalent . . . as to suggest that two authors of totally opposing viewpoints were writing under the same name. Half the time Chiang's flaws and errors make him patently incompetent for the job of running China. The rest of the time he is a hero of very grand proportions—but betrayed by Communist agents, fellow travelers, bad luck and FDR. As a result, both the book's title and the book's subject remain, at the end, an enigma."

Taking such faults into account, Clubb nevertheless praises Crozier's "portrait of Chiang Kai-shek" for presenting "intimate and interesting detail" concerning the late leader's military and political career, as well as his personal life. Clubb concludes: "The Crozier . . . work is imperfect history; but it contributes to our knowledge of that Chinese machiavellian Chiang Kai-shek who, in a turbulent era, played the balance-of-power game in the East Asian arena and survived—but lost China."

BIOGRAPHICAL/CRITICAL SOURCES: Observer Review, October 29, 1967; *Spectator*, November 24, 1967, October 18, 1969; *Listener*, December 21, 1967; *New York Times*, April 1, 1968; *Book World*, April 21, 1968; *Best Sellers*, May 1, 1968, January 15, 1974; *New Republic*, May 4, 1968, February 2, 1974, January 22, 1977; *National Observer*, May 20, 1968; *New York Times Book Review*, June 28, 1968, January 27, 1974, October 24, 1976; *L'Express*, November 10-16, 1969; *New Yorker*, February 7, 1970; *Times Literary Supplement*, October 5, 1973, May 3, 1974; *Harper*, December, 1973; *Washington Post Book World*, January 13, 1974, October 31, 1976; *National Review*, January 18, 1974, January 5, 1979; *Newsweek*, January 21, 1974; *Commonweal*, April 5, 1974; *Virginia Quarterly Review*, summer, 1974; *Political Science Quarterly*, summer, 1977; *New Statesman*, March 17, 1978; *Encounter*, August, 1978.

CRUMP, Fred H., Jr. 1931-

PERSONAL: Born June 7, 1931, in Houston, Tex.; son of Fred H. and Carol Crump. *Education:* Sam Houston State Teachers College (now Sam Houston State University), B.S., 1953, M.S., 1961. *Home:* 94 Santa Anita, Rancho Mirage, Calif. 92270.

CAREER: Junior high school art teacher, formerly in Orange, Tex., in Palm Springs, Calif., 1960—; author and illustrator of children's books.

WRITINGS—Self-illustrated: *Marigold and the Dragon*, Steck, 1964; *The Teeny Weeny Genie*, Steck, 1966; *Missy and the Duke*, Blaine Ethridge, 1977. Also author-illustrator of *Trigger the Trouser Mousie and Other Stories.*

Illustrator of books by Garry Smith and Vesta Smith; published by Steck, except as indicated: *Creepy Caterpillar*, 1961; *Flagon the Dragon*, 1962; *Mitzi*, 1963; *Jumping Julius*, 1964; *Leander Lion*, 1966; *Florabelle*, 1968; *Crickety Cricket*, 1969; *Poco*, Prism Press, 1975.

WORK IN PROGRESS: "A very small 'space epic' and a very large hippo book."

SIDELIGHTS: Fred H. Crump, Jr. comments, "I am still muddling along teaching junior high school art in Palm Springs, drawing bugs and dragons on weekends, and going to every movie that hits town."

*   *   *

CUDDON, John Anthony 1928-

PERSONAL: Born June 2, 1928, in Southsea, Hampshire, England; son of Philip Basil and Gladys (Cummings) Cuddon. *Education:* Brasenose College, Oxford, M.A., 1956, B. Litt, 1958. *Politics:* Socialist. *Religion:* Roman Catholic. *Home:* 43 Alderbrook Rd., London S.W.12, England.

CAREER: Schoolmaster and author. *Military service:* British Army, 1947-49; became lieutenant.

WRITINGS—Novels; published by Barrie & Rockliff, except as indicated: *A Multitude of Sins*, 1961; *Testament of Iscariot*, 1962; *The Acts of Darkness*, 1963; *The Six Wounds*, 1964; *The Bride of Battersea*, Hodder & Stoughton, 1967.

Nonfiction: *The Owl's Watchsong* (study of Istanbul), Barrie & Rockliff, 1960; *The Companion Guide to Jugoslavia*, Harper, 1968, 2nd edition, Collins, 1974; *Dictionary of Literary Terms*, Deutsch, 1977; *Dictionary of Sports and Games*, Macmillan, 1980.

Also author of play "The Triple Alliance," produced in London, 1961. Contributor to newspapers and magazines.

WORK IN PROGRESS: The Field of Blackbirds, a travel book; a series of books on sports; *Shellback*, a novel.

SIDELIGHTS: John Anthony Cuddon's books have been translated into Dutch, German, French, and Polish. *Avocational interests:* Natural sciences, art, theater, ball games, and religion.

BIOGRAPHICAL/CRITICAL SOURCES: Observer, July 2, 1967; *New Statesman*, July 14, 1967; *Books & Bookmen*, August, 1967.

*   *   *

CUMING, Geoffrey John 1917-

PERSONAL: Born September 9, 1917, in Gilston, Hertfordshire, England; son of Gordon and Winifred Mary (Johnston) Cuming; married Ann Rachel Lucas, July 5, 1952; children: Mark Alexander, Rachel Mary. *Education:* Attended Eton College, 1930-36; Oriel College, Oxford, B.A., 1940, M.A.,

1943, D.D., 1962. *Politics:* Liberal. *Home and office:* St. Mary's Vicarage, Humberstone, Leicester, England.

CAREER: Anglican curate in Burnley, England, 1947-50; St. John's College, Durham, England, vice-principal, 1950-55; vicar in Billesdon, England, 1955-62, and Humberstone, England, 1963-74. Marriage guidance counselor. Member, Church of England Liturgical Commission, 1965-80. *Wartime service:* British Non-Combatant Corps, 1941-44. *Member:* Ecclesiastical History Society, Overseas Club.

WRITINGS: (With Francis F. Clough) *The World's Encyclopaedia of Recorded Music*, Sidgwick & Jackson, 1952, 3rd supplement, 1957; (editor) *The Durham Book*, Oxford University Press, 1961; (with others) *The English Prayer Book, 1549-1662*, S.P.C.K., 1963; (editor) *Studies in Church History*, Volume II, Thomas Nelson, 1965, Volume III, E. J. Brill, 1966, Volume IV, E. J. Brill, 1967, Volume V: *The Church and Academic Learning*, E. J. Brill, 1969, Volume VI: *The Mission of the Church and the Propagation of the Faith*, Cambridge University Press, 1970, Volume VII (with Derek Baker): *Councils and Assemblies*, Cambridge University Press, 1971, Volume VIII (with Baker): *Popular Belief and Practice*, Cambridge University Press, 1972; *A History of Anglican Liturgy*, Macmillan (London), 1969, revised and enlarged edition, 1980; (editor with Ronald C. Jasper) *Prayers of the Eucharist: Early and Reformed*, Collins, 1975, 2nd edition, enlarged, Oxford University Press, 1979; *Hippolytus: A Text for Students*, Grove Books, 1976. Contributor to *Music and Letters, Gramophone*, and to religious journals.

AVOCATIONAL INTERESTS: Gramophone records and music in general.

*   *   *

CURLEY, Daniel 1918-

PERSONAL: Born October 4, 1918, in East Bridgewater, Mass. *Agent:* John Schaffner Literary Agency, 425 East 51st St., New York, N.Y. 10022.

CAREER: Writer and teacher. Associate, University of Illinois Center for Advanced Study, 1968. *Awards, honors:* Guggenheim fellowship in fiction, 1958; National Council on the Arts award, 1971, for *In The Hands of Our Enemies;* Illinois Arts Council award for fiction, 1975.

WRITINGS: That Marriage Bed of Procrustes (stories), Beacon Press, 1957; *How Many Angels?* (novel), Beacon Press, 1958; *A Stone Man, Yes* (novel), Viking, 1964; *In the Hands of Our Enemies* (stories), University of Illinois Press, 1970; *Love in the Winter* (stories), University of Illinois Press, 1976; *Ann's Spring* (children's book), Crowell, 1977; *Billy Beg and the Bull* (children's book), Crowell, 1978; *Hilarion* (children's book), Houghton, 1979. Also author of several plays produced on college campuses.

Work represented in anthologies, including *Best American Short Stories*, 1955 and 1964, and *O. Henry Prize Short Stories*, 1965. Contributor of short stories, poetry, and criticism to *Kenyon Review, Epoch, Modern Fiction Studies*, and other literary periodicals. Member of editorial board, *Accent*, 1955-60; editor, *Ascent*, 1975—.

*   *   *

CUSHMAN, Dan 1909-

PERSONAL: Born June 9, 1909, in Marion, Mich.; son of Sumner Davis and Rose Ann (Blaisdell) Cushman; married Elizabeth Louise Loudon, 1940; children: Mary Louise, Robert Loudon, Stephen James, Matthew George. *Education:* University of Montana, B.S., 1934. *Address:* 1500

Fourth Ave. N., Great Falls, Mont. *Agent:* H. N. Swanson, Inc., 8523 Sunset Blvd., Los Angeles, Calif. 90069; and Lena Gedin, Linnegatan 38, Stockholm, Sweden.

CAREER: Variously employed as correspondent and writer for several magazines and newspapers, prospector, assayer and geologist, radio announcer and writer, and newspaper reporter; novelist. Founder, Stay Away, Joe Publishers, Great Falls, Mont. *Awards, honors:* Spur Award for best historical novel, Western Writers of America, 1958, for *The Silver Mountain;* National Association of Independent Schools selected *The Grand and the Glorious* as one of the ten best books for pre-college readers, 1963.

WRITINGS: Montana, Here I Be!, Macmillan, 1950; *Naked Ebony,* Fawcett, 1951; *Jewel of the Java Sea,* Fawcett, 1951; *Badlands Justice,* Macmillan, 1951; *The Ripper from Rawhide,* Macmillan, 1952; *Stay Away, Joe* (Book-of-the-Month Club selection; also see below), Viking, 1953; *The Fabulous Finn,* Fawcett, 1954; *Tongking,* Ace Books, 1954; *The Fastest Gun,* Dell, 1955; *The Old Copper Collar,* Ballantine, 1957; *The Silver Mountain,* Appleton, 1957; *Tall Wyoming,* Dell, 1957; *Goodbye, Old Dry,* Doubleday, 1959; *Brothers in Kickapoo,* McGraw, 1962 (published in England as *Boomtown,* Arthur Barker, 1962); *Adventure in Laos,* Bantam, 1963; *Four for Texas,* Bantam, 1963; *The Grand and the Glorious,* McGraw, 1963; *The Great North Trail,* McGraw, 1966; *Cow-Country Cookbook,* Stay Away, Joe Publishers, 1967; *Montana—The Gold Frontier,* Stay Away, Joe Publishers, 1973; *Plenty of Room and Air,* Stay Away, Joe Publishers, 1975. Also author of musical "Whoop-Up" (based on Cushman's book *Stay Away, Joe*), produced on Broadway. Contributor of articles and stories to national magazines and newspapers.

SIDELIGHTS: "Stay Away, Joe," a film adaptation of Dan Cushman's book of the same title, was produced by Metro-Goldwyn-Mayer in 1960 and starred Elvis Presley.

* * *

CUTSHALL, Alden 1911-

PERSONAL: Born April 12, 1911, in Olney, Ill. *Education:* Eastern Illinois State Teachers College (now Eastern Illinois University), B.Ed., 1932; University of Illinois, M.A., 1935; Ohio State University, Ph.D., 1940. *Religion:* Methodist. *Home:* 667 North Elizabeth, Lombard, Ill. 60148. *Office:* University of Illinois at Chicago Circle, Chicago, Ill. 60680.

CAREER: Teacher in Illinois public schools, 1932-34, and 1937-39; University of Illinois at Urbana-Champaign and Chicago Circle, 1940—, began as instructor, professor of geography, beginning 1955, professor emeritus, 1972—, head of department, Chicago Circle campus, 1964-69, associate member of Center for Advanced Study, 1962-63. Fulbright lecturer to the Philippines, 1957-58. Principal research analyst, Far East Division, U.S. Office of Strategic Services and Department of State, 1944-46. *Member:* American Association for the Advancement of Science, Association of American Geographers, National Council for Geographic Education, Philippine Geographic Society, Illinois Geographic Society (president, 1963-64), Illinois State Academy of Science, Chicago Geographic Society (president, 1975-77). *Awards, honors:* Fulbright research grant, Philippines, 1950-51.

WRITINGS: (Co-author) *World Political Geography,* Crowell, 1948, revised edition, 1957; *The Philippines: Nation of Islands,* Van Nostrand, 1964; (co-author) *Focus on Southeast Asia,* Praeger, 1972; *Southeast Asia: Realms and Contrast,* Kendall/Hunt, 1974; *Illinois: Land and Life in the Prairie State,* Kendall/Hunt, 1978. Contributor to encyclopedias, including *Encyclopaedia Britannica* and *Encyclopedia Americana,* and of about ninety articles to scientific journals. Associate editor, *Philippine Geographic Journal.*

WORK IN PROGRESS: Continuing research into the economic geography of Southeast Asia, especially the Philippines, and the historical and economic geography of Illinois.

SIDELIGHTS: Alden Cutshall comments: "The titles of my writings, whether book, chapter, article, or newsletter, sound technical and possibly uninteresting, but all of them contain something in a lighter vein. They can be read with interest by the layman as well as the professional. I believe very strongly that writing is a craft and an art. For me it is hard work, but enjoyable."

D

da CRUZ, Daniel, Jr. 1921-
(John Ballantine, T. T. Cross)

PERSONAL: Born November 17, 1921, in Oxford, Ohio; son of Daniel (a professor and author) and Lenore (a registered nurse; maiden name, Rager) da Cruz; married Leila Shaheen (the general manager of a publishing company in Beirut, Lebanon), June 6, 1958; children: Lina Lenore, Daniel Nicholas. *Education:* Attended Miami University, Oxford, Ohio, 1939-41, Colorado College, 1949-50, George Washington University, 1950-51, American University of Beirut, 1952, University of Oklahoma, 1956, Johns Hopkins University, and University of Michigan; Georgetown University, B.S.L. (magna cum laude), 1957. *Home and office:* 55 Cairo St., Beirut, Lebanon.

CAREER: Texas Co. (oil), New York City, public relations writer, 1947-48; U.S. Department of State, editor in Washington, D.C., 1950-52, press attache at U.S. Embassy in Baghdad, Iraq, 1952-53; American University of Beirut, Beirut, Lebanon, instructor in languages, 1957-59; representative in the Middle East for Harper & Row Publishers, Inc., John Wiley & Sons, Inc., and other U.S. publishers, 1959-61; chief correspondent in the Middle East for McGraw-Hill World News, Beirut, 1963-72; Miami University, Oxford, Ohio, adjunct professor of anthropology, 1977—; vice-president of Doremus & Co. (advertising and public relations) in New York City and deputy managing director and regional director in the Mideast of Doremus International, 1978-79. Editorial consultant, Arabian-American Oil Co., 1963-66. *Military service:* U.S. Marine Corps, 1941-47. *Awards, honors:* Special Edgar Award, Mystery Writers of America, 1977, for *The Captive City.*

WRITINGS: A Provisional Analysis of Segmental Phonemes in Caddo (monograph), Georgetown University Press, 1957; *Men Who Made America–The Founders of a Nation,* Crowell, 1962; *Men Who Made America–A Nation Comes of Age,* Crowell, 1964; *Vulcan's Hammer,* New American Library, 1967; *Double Kill,* Gold Medal, 1972; *Deep Kill,* Gold Medal, 1974; *Sky Kill,* Gold Medal, 1974; *Landfall,* Ballantine, 1975; *Pipedream,* Ballantine, 1975; *Fire Kill,* Gold Medal, 1976; *The Captive City,* Ballantine, 1976.

Contributor of about 200 feature articles on Mideast politics, economics, culture, and military affairs to American newspapers and magazines and of promotional sections on Leba-

non, Jordan, and Kuwait to *Newsweek* and *Time.* Editor-in-chief, *Middle East Express* (English-language weekly of McGraw-Hill World News), 1963-72; guest editor, *Middle East Forum,* 1972; Middle East editor, *Middle East Enterprise,* 1975.

AVOCATIONAL INTERESTS: Running, judo.

* * *

DAHRENDORF, Ralf 1929-

PERSONAL: Born May 1, 1929, in Hamburg, Germany. *Education:* University of Hamburg, Dr. phil., 1952; University of London, Ph.D., 1956. *Office:* University of London, School of Economics, Houghton St., London WC2A 2AE, England.

CAREER: University of Saarbruecken, Saarbruecken, Germany, assistant, 1954-57, Privatdozent, 1957-58; University of Hamburg, Hamburg, Germany, professor, 1958-60; University of Tuebingen, Tuebingen, Germany, professor of sociology, 1960-65; University of Constance, Constance, Germany, professor of sociology, 1965-69, currently on leave; University of London, London, England, director of School of Economics, 1974—. Member of German Parliament, 1969-70. Center for Advanced Study in the Behavioral Sciences, Palo Alto, Calif., fellow, 1957-58. Visiting professor at Columbia University, 1960. Trustee, Ford Foundation, 1976—. Member of numerous commissions. *Member:* International Sociological Association, German Sociological Society (president, 1967-70), Anglo-German Society, American Academy of Arts and Sciences (honorary member), National Academy of Sciences (foreign associate), American Philosophical Society, P.E.N., Rotary Club. *Awards, honors:* Journal Fund Award for learned publication, 1959, 1966; Grand Prix de l'Ordre du Merite du Senegal, 1971; D.Litt., University of Reading, 1973; LL.D., University of Manchester, 1973; D.Sc., New University of Ulster, 1973; fellow, London School of Economics, 1973; fellow, Imperial College of Science and Technology, 1974; D.Univ., Open University, 1974; D.H.L., Kalamazoo College, 1974; Grand Croix de l'Ordre du Merite du Luxembourg, 1974; Grosses Bundesverdienstkreuz mit Stern und Schulterband, 1974; fellow, St. Anthony's College, 1975; Litt.D., Trinity College, Dublin, 1975; Grosses goldenes Ehrenzeichen am Bande, 1975; Grand Croix de l'Ordre de Leopold II, 1975; doctorate, Universite Catholique de Louvain, 1977; LL.D., Wagner College, 1977; D.Sc., University of Bath, 1977; fellow, British Academy, 1977; D.H.L., University of Maryland, 1978; D.Univ., University of Surrey, 1978; LL.D., University of York, 1979.

WRITINGS: Marx in Perspektive, J.H.W. Dietz, 1953, 2nd edition, 1971; *Industrie und Betriebssoziologie,* De Gruyter, 1956, 2nd edition, 1962; *Soziale Klassen und Klassenkonflikt in der industriellen Gesellschaft,* F. Enke, 1957, translated, revised and expanded by author as *Class and Class Conflict in Industrial Society,* Stanford University Press, 1959; *Homo Sociologicus,* Westdeutscher Verlag, 1958; *Sozialstruktur des Betriebes,* T. Gabler, 1959; *Gesellschaft und Frieheit,* Piper Verlag, 1961; *Ueber den Ursprung der Ungleichheit unter den Menschen,* Mohr, 1961; *Die angewandte Aufklaerung,* Piper Verlag, 1963; *Gesellschaft und Democratie in Deutschland,* Piper Verlag, 1965, translation published as *Society and Democracy in Germany,* Doubleday, 1967; *Bildung ist Buergerrecht,* Nannen, 1965; *Das Mitbestimmungsproblem in der deutschen Sozialforschung,* Piper Verlag, 1965; *Essays in the Theory of Society,* Stanford University Press, 1968; *Die angewandte Aufklarung,* Fischer-Bucherei, 1968; *Fur eine Erneuerung der Demokrati in der Bundesrepublik,* Piper Verlag, 1968; *Konflikt end Freiheit,* Piper Verlag, 1972; *Pladoyer fur die Europaische Union,* Piper Verlag, 1973; *The New Liberty: Survival and Justice in a Changing World,* Stanford University Press, 1975; *Life Chances,* Stanford University Press, 1980.

*   *   *

DALE, Celia (Marjorie)

PERSONAL: Born in London, England; daughter of James (an actor) and Marguerite (Adamson) Dale; married Guy Ramsey (a journalist and critic), October 30, 1937 (died 1959); children: Simon James. *Education:* Educated in England. *Home:* 44 Talbot Rd., London N6, England. *Agent:* Curtis Brown Ltd., 1 Craven Hill, London W2 3EP, England; and James Brown Assos., Inc., 25 West 43rd St., New York, N.Y. 10036.

CAREER: Held various secretarial positions, including secretary to Arthur Christiansen, editor of *London Daily Express,* until 1944; reader for various London publishers, columnist, and novelist, 1959—. *Member:* International P.E.N. (member of executive committee, 1962-66); Crime Writers Association (member of executive committee, 1978-80).

WRITINGS: The Least of These, Hurst & Blackett, 1943, Macmillan, 1944; *To Hold the Mirror,* Hurst & Blackett, 1946; *The Dry Land,* J. Cape, 1952; *The Wooden O,* J. Cape, 1953; *Trial of Strength,* J. Cape, 1955; *A Spring of Love,* Cassell, 1960, Walker & Co., 1967; *Other People,* Cassell, 1964, Walker & Co., 1970; *A Helping Hand,* Walker & Co., 1966; *Act of Love,* Walker & Co., 1969; *A Dark Corner,* Macmillan (London), 1971, Walker & Co., 1972; *The Innocent Party,* Walker & Co., 1973; *Deception,* Harper, 1979 (published in England as *Helping with Inquiries,* Macmillan, 1979). Short stories represented in anthologies. Book review columnist and contributor, *Homes and Gardens.*

WORK IN PROGRESS: A novel.

SIDELIGHTS: According to John D. Foreman, "[Celia] Dale's forte lies in her development of the characters in her little novels; she can touch upon tiny frustrations and moments of loneliness and abandonment with skill and compassion, register with great happiness the small moments of triumph of her characters."

Several of Dale's novels have been serialized for British radio and television programs, and some of her short stories have been read on the radio. Screen rights to *A Dark Corner* have been sold.

AVOCATIONAL INTERESTS: Travel, reading, people.

BIOGRAPHICAL/CRITICAL SOURCES: Best Sellers, March 15, 1967, June 1, 1969, April 1, 1970; *Times Literary Supplement,* June 12, 1969.

*   *   *

DALE, Margaret J(essy) Miller   1911-
(Margaret J. Miller)

PERSONAL: Born August 27, 1911, in Edinburgh, Scotland; daughter of James (a professor of pathology) and Margaret (Clare) Miller; married C. R. Dale, September 3, 1938 (divorced); children: Anna Clare, Richard, Diana. *Education:* Lady Margaret Hall, Oxford, B.A. (second class honours), 1933. *Home:* 26 Greys Hill, Henley, Oxon, England. *Agent:* John Johnson, Clerkenwell House, 45-47 Clerkenwell Green, London EC1R 0HT, England.

CAREER: Associated Screen News, Montreal, Quebec, scenario writer, 1935-36; Asiatic Petroleum Co., London, England, assistant editor of *Shell* magazine, 1937-39; writer. *Member:* International P.E.N.

WRITINGS—Under name Margaret J. Miller; children's books: *Seven Men of Wit,* Hutchinson, 1960; *Gunpowder Treason,* Macdonald & Co., 1968; *Plot for the Queen,* Macdonald & Co., 1969; *Emily: The Story of Emily Bronte,* Lutterworth, 1969; *King Robert the Bruce,* Macdonald & Co., 1970; *The Fearsome Road,* Abelard, 1974; *The Fearsome Island, the Fearsome Tide,* Abelard, 1975; *The Far Castles,* Blackie & Son, 1978; *The Big Brown Teapot,* Hodder & Stoughton, 1980.

Published by Brockhampton Press, except as indicated: *The Queen's Music,* 1961; *The Powers of the Sapphire,* 1962; *Dr. Boomer,* 1964; (contributor) Margery Fisher, editor, *Open the Door* (anthology), 1965; *Mouse Tails,* 1967; *Willow and Albert,* 1968; (editor) *Knights, Beasts and Wonders: Tales and Legends from Mediaeval Britain,* 1968, David White, 1969; *Willow and Albert Are Stowaways,* 1970.

Also author of about 200 scripts for Schools Broadcasting and of several scripts for Schools Television. Contributor to *London Times* and *Times Educational Supplement.*

WORK IN PROGRESS: Another children's book, *A Life of Roald Amundsen,* for Hodder & Stoughton.

SIDELIGHTS: Margaret J. Miller Dale gathers the material for her children's fantasies from her travels to remote parts of Scotland. Dale has also traveled to Rhodesia, South Africa, and Portuguese East Africa and has written about these countries in an historical and educational manner. *Avocational interests:* Music, especially choral singing, boating and fishing, travel, especially in the western islands of Scotland, historical and literary research, and folklore.

*   *   *

DALLY, Ann Mullins   1926-
(Ann Mullins)

PERSONAL: Born March 29, 1926, in London, England; daughter of Claud (a metropolitan magistrate, barrister, and author) and Gwendolen (a designer and weaver; maiden name, Brandt) Mullins; married Peter John Dally (a psychiatrist), April 1, 1950 (divorced, 1969); married Phillip Wellsted Egerton, June 29, 1979; children: (first marriage) Simon, Mark, Emma, Jane, John, Adam. *Education:* Somerville College, Oxford, B.A. (with honours), 1946,

M.A., 1950; St. Thomas's Hospital, M.B., B.S., 1953, D.Obst.R.C.O.G., 1955. *Home:* 13 Devonshire Place, London W.1., England. *Agent:* A. D. Peters & Co. Ltd., 10 Buckingham St., London WC2N 6BU, England.

CAREER: War Office, London, England, lecturer to His Majesty's Forces overseas, 1946-47; St. James's Hospital, Balham, England, house physician and surgeon in obstetrics and gynaecology, 1954-55; Weir research fellow, Wandsworth Hospital Group, 1956-59; currently in private practice. *Member:* British Medical Association, Royal Society of Medicine (fellow), Queen's Club. *Awards, honors:* British Medical Association research scholar, 1955-56; Southwest Metropolitan Regional Hospital Board research prize, 1956, for paper describing research into chest diseases; Royal Society of Medicine, Nichols research fellow, 1956-57.

WRITINGS: Slim for Health, Parrish, 1960; *A-Z of Babies,* Parrish, 1961; (with others) *How Parents Can Help,* Home Education Centre, 1961; (with Ronald Sweeney) *A Child Is Born,* P. Owen, 1965; *The Intelligent Person's Guide to Modern Medicine,* Gollancz, 1966, published as *A Reader's Guide to Modern Medicine,* Harper, 1968; *Cicely: The Story of a Doctor,* Gollancz, 1968; *Mothers: Their Power and Influence,* Weidenfeld & Nicolson, 1976; *The Morbid Streak: Destructive Aspects of the Personality,* Wildwood House, 1978; *Why Women Fail: Change and Choice in Modern Women,* Wildwood House, 1979. Contributor of numerous articles to newspapers and journals, including *Observer, Sunday Telegraph, Family Doctor, Lancet,* and *Sunday Times.* Editor, *Maternal and Child Care* and *Weekend Telegraph.*

WORK IN PROGRESS: Two books, with the "provisional titles" *Motherhood and Modern Women* and *The Open Cage: Male Response to Modern Feminism.*

AVOCATIONAL INTERESTS: Country life, tennis, riding, reading, cinema and theatre-going.

*   *   *

DANIELL, Albert Scott   1906-1965
(Richard Bowood, David Scott Daniell, John Lewesdon)

PERSONAL: Born July 1, 1906, in London, England; died August 29, 1965; married Elizabeth Mary Thirlby, June 3, 1939; children: Richard John Scott. *Education:* Attended Bedford Modern School. *Politics:* "Tentative Conservative." *Religion:* Protestant. *Home:* Bridport, Dorset, England.

CAREER: Professional writer. *Military service:* British Army, Royal Engineers, 1941-46; served in Sicily and Italy; became captain; mentioned in dispatches. *Member:* Authors' Club, Society of Authors, Royal United Services Institution (all London).

WRITINGS—Under pseudonym Richard Bowood; published by Wills & Hepworth, except as indicated: *Story of Flight,* 1960; *Great Inventions,* 1961; *Story of Railways,* 1961; *Story of Ships,* 1962; (with F. E. Newing) *The Weather,* 1962; (with Newing) *Magnets, Bulbs and Batteries,* 1962; (with Newing) *Lights, Mirrors and Lenses,* 1962; (with Newing) *Levers, Pulleys and Engines,* 1963; (with Newing) *Air, Wind and Flight,* 1963; *Story of Houses and Homes,* 1963; *Naples Ahead,* Macmillan, 1963; *Story of Clothes and Costume,* 1964; *The Story of Our Churches and Cathedrals,* 1964; *Soldiers, Soldiers,* Hamlyn, 1965; (with Newing) *Animals and How They Live,* 1965; (with Newing) *Plants and How They Grow,* 1965; *Horsey and Company and the Bank*

Robbers, Golden Pleasure Books, 1965; *Red Gaskell's Gold,* Macmillan, 1966; (with Newing) *Birds and How They Live,* 1966; (with R. Lampitt) *Our Land in the Making,* 1966, Book I: *Earliest Times to Norman Conquest,* Book II: *Norman Conquest to Present Day; Underwater Exploration,* 1967.

Under pseudonym David Scott Daniell, except as indicated; *Young English: The Story of a School Boy,* J. Cape, 1931; *Mornings at Seven,* J. Cape, 1940; *The Time of the Singing,* J. Cape, 1941; *Nicholas Wilde,* J. Cape, 1948; *Children's Theatre Plays,* Harrap, 1949; *More Children's Theatre Plays,* Harrap, 1951; *Cap of Honour: The Story of the Gloucestershire Regiment, 1694-1950,* Harrap, 1951, new edition, White Lion Publishers, 1976; *Mission for Oliver,* J. Cape, 1953, reprinted, Atlantic Book Publishing, 1968; *Royal Hampshire Regiment, 1918-1950,* Gale & Polden, 1953; *Polly and Oliver,* J. Cape, 1954; *Costume Plays for Schools,* Harrap, 1955; *The Dragon and the Rose,* J. Cape, 1955; *History of the East Surrey Regiment, 1920-1952,* foreword by G.R.P. Roupell, Benn, 1957; *Hideaway Johnnie,* Brockhampton, 1958, reprinted, White Lion Publishers, 1976; *Hunt Royal,* J. Cape, 1958; *4th Hussar: The Story of the British Cavalry Regiment,* Gale & Polden, 1959; *The Boy They Made King,* J. Cape, 1959.

Fifty Pounds for a Dead Parson, J. Cape, 1960; *The Rajah's Treasure,* Duell, Sloan & Pearce, 1960 (published in England as *Polly and Oliver at Sea,* J. Cape, 1960); *Battles and Battlefields,* Batsford, 1961, reprinted, Beaver Books, 1977; (under pseudonym John Lewesdon) *Ladybird Book of London,* Wills & Hepworth, 1961; (with G. W. H. Lampe) *Faith of Our Fathers,* University of London Press, 1961; (with Lampe) *Sandro's Battle,* J. Cape, 1962; *Explorers and Exploration,* Batsford, 1962; *By Jiminy* (also see below), Brockhampton, 1962; *Saved by Jiminy,* Brockhampton, 1963; *Polly and Oliver Besieged,* J. Cape, 1963; *Golden Pomegranate,* Brockhampton, 1963; *By Jiminy Ahoy,* Brockhampton, 1963; *By Jiminy in the Jungle,* Brockhampton, 1964; *Polly and Oliver Pursued,* J. Cape, 1964; *Discovering the Army,* University of London Press, 1965; *World War I: An Illustrated History,* Benn, 1965; *Sea Fights,* Batsford, 1966; *By Jiminy in the Highlands,* Brockhampton, 1966; *World War II: An Illustrated History,* Benn, 1966; *Your Body,* Wills, & Hepworth, 1967.

"Ladybird Book of Travel Adventure" series; published by Wills & Hepworth: *Flight One: Australia,* 1958; *Flight Two: Canada,* 1959; *Flight Three: U.S.A.,* 1959; *Flight Four: India,* 1960; *Flight Five: Africa,* 1961; *Flight Six: Holy Land,* 1962.

Also author of screenplay "By Jiminy" (based on book of same title), produced by British Children's Film Foundation, and over six hundred radio and television plays for children and adults. Contributor of essays to newspapers.

SIDELIGHTS: Albert Scott Daniell once told *CA* that he enjoyed writing for young people by whom "vivacity and verve are appreciated" and that he lived in the country "for the sake of the wider vista and slower passage of time."

Some of Daniell's books have been translated into French and Swedish.

AVOCATIONAL INTERESTS: Bridge, travel in France and Italy.†

*   *   *

D'ARCY, Martin C(yril)   1888-1976

PERSONAL: Born June 15, 1888, in Bath, Somerset, England; died November 20, 1976, in London, England; son of

Martin Valentine and Madoline (Keegan) D'Arcy. *Education:* Oxford University, Litterae Humaniores (with first class honours), 1916, M.A., 1919; Gregorian University, D.D., 1924. *Home:* 114 Mount St., London W. 1, England.

CAREER: Entered Society of Jesus, 1906; ordained Roman Catholic priest, 1921; Stonyhurst College, Lancashire, England, teacher, 1916-19, 1923-24; Oxford University, Oxford, England, lecturer in philosophy, 1926-45, master of Campion Hall, 1932-45. Visiting professor at Fordham University, 1939-40, University of Notre Dame, 1952, Georgetown University, 1956-57, 1959-60, and Boston College, 1962-63; Danforth Lecturer, Cornell University, 1958; British Council on the Humanities Lecturer to Italy, Spain, Portugal, and Malta. English provincial of the Society of Jesus, 1945-50; conventual chaplain of Knights of Malta, beginning 1954. Roman Catholic religious representative for British Broadcasting Corp., 1937-45. *Member:* Royal Society of Literature (fellow, beginning 1959), American Academy of Arts and Sciences (honorary member), Athenaeum Club. *Awards, honors:* D. Litt., Georgetown University, 1935, Fordham University, 1940, Marquette University, 1955, National University of Ireland, 1957, and Laval University, 1962.

WRITINGS: The Mass and the Redemption, Burns, 1926; *Spirit of Charity,* Burns, 1929; *Christ as Priest and Redeemer,* Burns, 1930; *The Nature of Belief,* Sheed, 1931, new edition, Herder, 1958, reprinted, Greenwood Press, 1976; *Mirage and Truth,* Macmillan, 1931; *Thomas Aquinas,* Oxford University Press, 1932; *The Problem of Evil,* Longmans, Green, 1940; *Death and Life,* Longmans, Green, 1942; *The Mind and Heart of Love: Lion and Unicorn, a Study in Eros and Agape,* Faber, 1946, World Publishing, 1956, 2nd edition, Collins, 1962; *Communism and Christianity,* Penguin, 1958; *The Meeting of Love and Knowledge: Perennial Wisdom,* Harper, 1957, reprinted, Greenwood Press, 1979; *The Meaning and Matter of History: A Christian View,* Farrar, Straus, 1959 (published in England as *The Sense of History: Secular and Sacred,* Faber, 1959).

No Absent God: The Relations between God and the Self, Harper, 1962; *Literature as a Christian Comedy,* St. Joseph's College, 1962; *Of God and Man: Thoughts on Faith and Morals,* Dimension Books, 1964; (editor) Thomas Aquinas, *Selected Writings,* Dutton, 1964; *Facing God,* Catholic Book Club, 1964; *Dialogue with Myself,* Trident, 1966; *Facing the People,* Dimension Books, 1968; (editor) Maisie Ward, *The English Way,* Books for Libraries Press, 1968; *Facing the Truth,* Dimension Books, 1969; *Humanism and Christianity,* New American Library, 1969; (editor with others) *A Monument to Saint Augustine,* World Publishing, 1969; *Revelation and Love's Architecture,* Charles River Books, 1976.

BIOGRAPHICAL/CRITICAL SOURCES: Vogue, July, 1950; *Life,* January 28, 1952; *Modern Catholic Thinkers,* Burns & Oates, 1958.†

*   *   *

DARLING, Edward 1907-1974

PERSONAL: Born June 19, 1907, in Roxbury, Mass.; died December 12, 1974, in Dennis, Mass.; son of Charles Balfour and Effie (MacNaughton) Darling; married Dorothea Dane Parker, July 11, 1932; children: Nancy Joan (Mrs. Carl Hard, Jr.). *Education:* Dartmouth College, A.B., 1929; Harvard University, graduate study, 1930-31. *Politics:* Independent. *Religion:* Unitarian Universalist. *Address:* Box 333, Dennis, Mass. 02638. *Agent:* McIntosh & Otis, Inc., 475 Fifth Ave., New York, N.Y. 10017.

CAREER: Held various jobs, 1931-34; Yarmouth High School, Bass River, Mass., head of English department, 1934-39; Belmont (Mass.) Junior High School, head of social sciences department, 1939-45; Unitarian Universalist Association, Boston, Mass., sales manager, Beacon Press, Inc., 1945-58, director, 1958-62, director of department of publications, Unitarian Universalist Association, 1958-69, general editor, 1969-72; Cape Cod Community College, West Barnstable, Mass., instructor in creative writing, beginning 1972.

WRITINGS: Three Old-Timers: Sandwich-Barnstable-Yarmouth (documentary novel), Wayside Studio, 1936, published as *Three Old Timers of Cape Cod,* Wake-Brook, 1974; (with Chester Howland) *Thar She Blows,* Funk, 1951; *How We Fought for Our Schools,* Norton, 1954; *Old Quotes at Home,* Beacon Press, 1958; (with Ashley Montagu) *The Prevalence of Nonsense,* Harper, 1968; (with Hugo J. Hollerorth) *Freedom and Responsibility,* Beacon Press, 1969; (with Montagu) *The Ignorance of Certainty,* Harper, 1970; *When Sparks Fly Upward,* Washburn, 1970. Also author of *They Cast Long Shadows,* 1969.

WORK IN PROGRESS: Deja Vu: So What Else Is New?; People in Trouble.

SIDELIGHTS: Edward Darling once wrote *CA:* "It seems to me that mankind is in trouble, but that circumstances have never been otherwise and that most of the trouble can be traced to irrational behavior or belief. Since the bizarre so often puts human behavior under the microscope, my focus has been on popular error—particularly the error of utter certainty when the best we can hope for is the highly probable. I like to prick the pompous and expose the folly; and I claim no immunity from inaccuracy myself."†

*   *   *

DARLING, Lois MacIntyre 1917-

PERSONAL: Maiden name originally spelled McIntyre; born August 15, 1917, in New York, N.Y.; daughter of Malcolm (a mechanical engineer) and Grace (Hamilton) McIntyre; married Louis Darling, Jr. (a writer and illustrator), June 3, 1946 (died January 21, 1970). *Education:* Attended Grand Central School of Art, 1935-40, and Columbia University, 1947-51; studied privately with artists Frank Reilly and Frank V. DuMond, 1938-41. *Home and office:* 4 Smith Neck Rd., Rte. 5, Old Lyme, Conn. 06371.

CAREER: Riverside Yacht Club, Riverside, Conn., sailing instructor and head of junior program, 1940-41; Boucher Manufacturing Co., New York City, maker of ship models for war effort, 1942-43; free-lance illustrator, 1946—; American Museum of Natural History, New York City, staff artist, department of paleontology, 1951-53; writer and illustrator, 1953—. Treasurer, Connecticut Conservationists, Inc., 1955-56. *Military service:* U.S. Navy, WAVES, 1943-45. *Member:* American Institute of Biological Sciences, Nature Conservancy, National Audubon Society, Authors Guild, Society of Illustrators, Thames Science Center, Valley Shore Audubon Society, Westport Audubon Society (conservation chairman, 1953-60), Catboat Association. *Awards, honors:* National woman's sailing championship, 1941.

WRITINGS—Author and illustrator with husband, Louis Darling, Jr., except as indicated: Before and after Dinosaurs, Morrow, 1959; *Sixty Million Years of Horses,* Morrow, 1960; *The Science of Life,* World Publishing, 1961; *Bird,* Houghton, 1962; *Turtles,* Morrow, 1962; *Coral Reefs,* World Publishing, 1963; *The Sea Serpents around Us,* Little, Brown, 1965; *General Ecology,* Morrow, 1967; *A Place in the Sun: Ecology and the Living World, Morrow, 1968; Worms, Morrow, 1972. Sole author and illustrator of H.M.S. Beagle: Further Research, or Twenty Years a-Beagling, 1977, and The Mariner's Mirror, 1978.

Illustrator of numerous books, including: Llewellyn Howland, Sou'west and by West, Harvard University Press, 1948; Edwin H. Colbert, Evolution of the Vertebrates, Wiley, 1955, 3rd edition, 1980; (with L. Darling, Jr.) Rachel Carson, Silent Spring, Houghton, 1962; (with L. Darling, Jr.) Roger Tory Peterson, Birds, Life Nature Library, 1963; (with L. Darling, Jr.) Niko Tinbergen, Animal Behavior, Life Nature Library, 1965; (with L. Darling, Jr.) Maurice Brooks, The Appalachians, Houghton, 1965; Corey Ford, Where the Sea Breaks Its Back, Little, Brown, 1966.

WORK IN PROGRESS: A book on ponds and streams, for Houghton; a book on ecology, for Morrow; a children's book.

SIDELIGHTS: Lois Darling comments: "My husband, Louis, and I first started writing and illustrating our own books in an effort to help both child and adult to become better aware of our absolute dependence on the world's ecosystems. We were young, innocent, and enthusiastic in those days, and we liked to feel that we were adding a molecule to the drop in the bucket of human knowledge, truth, and beauty.

"Louis died of cancer at 53; to a certain extent, I have carried on our work since then, but I have also been drawing and painting simply because this is what I like to do. For many a year, Louis and I did our share—both in the early conservation battles and with our writings and illustrations (our worst, we always felt, in the most important book, Rachel Carson's Silent Spring). Now I believe that it is up to future generations to do what they must, if indeed this sad world can be saved from human ignorance and greed."

AVOCATIONAL INTERESTS: Sailing, walking.

*   *   *

DARLING, Louis, Jr.   1916-1970

PERSONAL: Born April 26, 1916, in Stamford, Conn.; died January 21, 1970, of cancer, in Norwich, Conn.; son of Louis and Llanceley (Lockwood) Darling; married Lois MacIntyre (a writer and illustrator), June 3, 1946. Education: Attended Grand Central School of Art, 1936-37; studied privately with artists Frank V. DuMond and Frank Reilly, 1938-40. Politics: Democrat. Residence: Old Lyme, Conn.

CAREER: Writer and illustrator. Conservationist. Military service: U.S. Army Air Forces, 1942-45; became staff sergeant. Member: American Association for the Advancement of Science, American Ornithological Society, National Audubon Society, Authors Guild of Authors League of America, Ecological Society of America, British Ornithological Society, Nature Conservancy, Animal Behavior Society, Catboat Association, Coffee House Club (New York). Awards, honors; John Burroughs Medal, 1966, for The Gull's Way.

WRITINGS—Self-illustrated; published by Morrow: Greenhead, 1954; Chickens, 1955; Seals and Walruses, 1955; Penguins, 1956; Kangaroos and Other Animals with Pockets, 1958; The Gull's Way, 1965.

With wife, Lois MacIntyre Darling: Before and after Dinosaurs, Morrow, 1959; Sixty Million Years of Horses, Morrow, 1960; The Science of Life, World Publishing, 1961; Turtles, Morrow, 1962; Bird, Houghton, 1962; Coral Reefs, World Publishing, 1963; The Sea Serpents around Us, Little,

Brown, 1965; General Ecology, Morrow, 1967; A Place in the Sun: Ecology and the Living World, Morrow, 1968; Worms, Morrow, 1972.

Illustrator of over 60 books, including: Margaret E. Bell, Watch for a Tall White Sail, Morrow, 1948; Elizabeth Howard, North Winds Blow Free, Morrow, 1949; Ruth Dudley, Hank and the Kitten, Morrow, 1949; Beverly Cleary, Henry Huggins, Morrow, 1950; E. Howard, Peddler's Girl, Morrow, 1951; Jerrold Beim, Swimming Hole, Morrow, 1951; Cleary, Ellen Tebbits, Morrow, 1951; Cleary, Henry and Beezus, Morrow, 1952; Beim, Country Garage, Morrow, 1952; Cleary, Otis Spofford, Morrow, 1953; Beim, Erick on the Desert, Morrow, 1953; Carl L. Biemiller, Magic Ball from Mars, Morrow, 1953; Cleary, Henry and Ribsy, Morrow, 1954; Beim, Shoeshine Boy, Morrow. 1954; Cleary, Beezus and Ramona, Morrow, 1955; Beim, Country School, Morrow, 1955; Beim, Thin Ice, Morrow, 1956; Delia Goetz, Deserts, Morrow, 1956; Oliver Butterworth, The Enormous Egg, Little, Brown, 1956; Cleary, Henry and the Paper Route, Morrow, 1957; Beim, Time for Gym, Morrow, 1957; Goetz, Tropical Rain Forests, Morrow, 1957; Eleanor Cameron, Mister Bass's Planetoid, Atlantic-Little, Brown, 1958; Goetz, Arctic Tundra, Morrow, 1958; Lucy Gallup, Independent Bluebird, Morrow, 1959; Goetz, Grasslands, Morrow, 1959; Alberta W. Constant, Miss Charity Comes to Stay, Crowell, 1959; Robert M. McClung, Shag, Last of the Plains Buffalo, Morrow, 1960; Goetz, Swamps, Morrow, 1961; Goetz, Mountains, Morrow, 1962; (with L. M. Darling) Rachel Carson, Silent Spring, Houghton, 1962; Cleary, Henry and the Clubhouse, Morrow, 1962; (with L. M. Darling) Roger Tory Peterson, Birds, Life Nature Library, 1963; Cleary, Ribsy, Morrow, 1964; Goetz, Islands of the Ocean, Morrow, 1964; Cleary, Mouse and the Motorcycle, Morrow, 1965; (with L. M. Darling) Niko Tinbergen, Animal Behavior, Life Nature Library, 1965; (with L. M. Darling) Maurice Brooks, The Appalachians, Houghton, 1965; Cleary, Ramona the Pest, Morrow, 1968; Cleary, Runaway Ralph, Morrow, 1970.

BIOGRAPHICAL/CRITICAL SOURCES: New York Herald Tribune, April 4, 1966; New York Times, April 5, 1966.†

*   *   *

DARYUSH, Elizabeth   1887-1977

PERSONAL: Born December 5, 1887, in London, England; died April 7, 1977; daughter of Robert Seymour (a poet) and Mary Monica (Waterhouse) Bridges; married Ali Akbar Daryush, December 29, 1923. Education: Privately tutored. Home: Stockwell, The Ridgeway, Boar's Hill, Oxford, England.

WRITINGS: Charitessi, Bowes, 1911; Verses, Blackwell Booksellers, 1916; Selected Poems, Macmillan (London), 1935; Sixth Book Verses, Alden Press, 1938; Selected Poems, foreword by Yvor Winters, Morrow, 1947, revised and enlarged edition, Carcanet Press, 1972; Seventh Book Verses, Carcanet Press, 1971; Selected Poems, Carcanet Press, 1972; Collected Poems, introduction by Donald Davies, Carcanet Press, 1976; (contributor) L. P. Smith, Robert Bridges (biography), Norwood, 1978.

Published by Oxford University Press: Sonnets from Hafez and Other Verses, 1921; First Book Verses, 1930; Second Book Verses, 1932; Third Book Verses, 1933; Fourth Book Verses, 1934; The Last Man and Other Verses (Fifth Book Verses), 1936.

Contributor of poems to Southern Review and other periodicals.

SIDELIGHTS: In comparing the poetry of Elizabeth Daryush to that of her contemporaries, John Matthias once offered this analogy: "Elizabeth Daryush . . . [appears] rather like someone who has suddenly stepped out of the wrong century to find herself at the wrong party wearing the wrong clothes. There she stands in her brocades speaking her *o'ers* and *'twixts* and *'tweens* in her very proper accent. . . . But the effect of her presence is curious," Matthias continued. "Suddenly everyone's language sounds indecorous, full of improprieties and vulgarities."

Jan Schreiber of the *Southern Review* agreed that Daryush's "diction is often that of ladies' magazines of the nineteenth century." However, Schreiber found that the poet's "best writing is independent of [this characteristic]. It comes," the critic explained, "from a kind of moral vision attainable by the poet only in response to a fairly clear-cut situation. . . . When the theme is undisguised and of straightforward human concern, the words come right and confound criticism."

BIOGRAPHICAL/CRITICAL SOURCES: American Review, January, 1937; *Southern Review,* summer, 1973; *Poetry,* April, 1974; *Contemporary Literary Criticism,* Volume VI, Gale, 1976; *Times Literary Supplement,* April 9, 1977.†

*   *   *

DAUTEN, Carl Anton   1913-1976

PERSONAL: Born June 2, 1913, in St. Louis, Mo.; died, 1976; son of Paul Martin (a minister) and Louise (Heyer) Dauten; married Dorothea Hoeman, July 18, 1942; children: Thomas, Jane, Mary. *Education:* Washington University, A.B., 1936, A.M., 1939, Ph.D., 1944. *Religion:* Lutheran. *Home:* 720 Cranbrook Dr., Kirkwood, Mo. 63122. *Office:* Washington University, St. Louis, Mo. 63130.

CAREER: National Lead Co., St. Louis, Mo., production control chemist, 1937-38; Shurtleff College, Alton, Ill., professor of business administration, 1940-44; Missouri Valley College, Marshall, professor of economics and business, acting treasurer, and business manager, 1944; University of Arkansas, Fayetteville, assistant professor of statistics, 1944-45; Washington University, St. Louis, Mo., beginning 1945, professor of finance and banking, beginning 1952, director of doctoral program, Graduate School of Business, 1960-63, associate provost, 1962-64, 1967-1969, vice-chancellor for administration, 1964-69, executive vice-chancellor, beginning 1969. Senior administrative assistant, U.S. Civil Service Commission, Detroit, Mich., 1942; consultant on management development to Southwestern Bell Telephone Co., and the Lutheran Church—Missouri Synod; member of board of directors and chairman of Education Commission, Council of Lutheran Churches of Greater St. Louis, 1961-65; member of advisory board, Concordia Seminary Research Center, 1963-69; Concordia Publishing House, member of board of directors, beginning 1965, chairman, 1971. *Member:* American Finance Association, National Bureau of Economic Research American Economic Association, Artus, Beta Gamma Sigma, Phi Beta Kappa, Omicron Delta Kappa.

WRITINGS: Business Finance, Prentice-Hall, 1948, 2nd edition, 1956; *Business Fluctuations and Forecasting,* South-Western, 1954, 2nd edition published as *Business Cycles and Forecasting,* 1961, 5th edition (with L. M. Valentine), 1978; *Financing the American Consumer,* American Investment Co., 1956; (with Merle Welshans) *Principles of Finance,* South-Western, 1958, 4th edition, 1975; *Consumer Finance Companies in a Dynamic Economy,* Washington University Press, 1960. Associate editor, *Journal of Finance,* 1958-60.†

DAVIDSON, Eugene (Arthur)   1902-

PERSONAL: Born September 22, 1902, in New York, N.Y.; son of William and Bertha (Passarge) Davidson; married Louise Keil, April 6, 1928 (divorced); married Suzette M. Zurcher, November, 1968; children: (first marriage) Eugene, Lisa. *Education:* Yale University, B.A., 1927, graduate study, 1927-28. *Home:* 780 River Rock Rd., Santa Barbara, Calif.

CAREER: Yale University Press, New Haven, Conn., editor, 1929-59; *Modern Age,* Chicago, Ill., editor, 1960-70. President, Foundation for Foreign Affairs, 1957-70; chairman, Committee on European Problems. Lecturer in Germany and at U.S. colleges, 1947, and 1962. *Member:* P.E.N., Arts Club (Chicago), Graduates Club and Elizabethan Club (both New Haven). *Awards, honors:* Litt.D., Park College, 1977.

WRITINGS: The Death and Life of Germany, Knopf, 1959; *The Trial of the Germans,* Macmillan, 1966; *The Nuremburg Fallacy,* Macmillan, 1973; *The Making of Adolf Hitler,* Macmillan, 1977. Contributor of book reviews, articles, and poetry to magazines, including the *Yale Review, Freeman, Saturday Review of Literature,* and *Progressive.*

SIDELIGHTS: Eugene Davidson was a reporter at the 1961 Eichmann trial in Jerusalem.

BIOGRAPHICAL/CRITICAL SOURCES: New York Times Book Review, November 20, 1977.

*   *   *

DAVIES, David W(illiam)   1908-

PERSONAL: Born May 23, 1908, in Winnipeg, Manitoba, Canada; son of Owen Henry (a customs official) and Catherine (McCaffery) Davies; married Thelma E. Stengel, November 11, 1936. *Education:* University of California, Los Angeles, B.A., 1932; University of California, Berkeley, B.L.S., 1934, M.A., 1940; University of Chicago, Ph.D., 1947. *Home:* 524 West 10th St., Claremont, Calif. 91711. *Office:* SAI Comsystems, 300 South Park, Pomona, Calif.

CAREER: Huntington Library, San Marino, Calif., staff member, 1936-38; University of California, Berkeley, Bancroft Library, in charge of rare books and manuscripts, 1938-41; Utah State University, Logan, librarian, 1941-43; University of Vermont, Burlington, director of libraries, 1946-47; Claremont Colleges, Claremont, Calif., librarian, 1947-67; senior lecturer, College of Librarianship, Wales, 1967-68; Immaculate Heart College, Los Angeles, Calif., professor of library science, 1968-70; California State University, Fullerton, lecturer in library science, 1970-73; Lloyd Corp., Beverly Hills, Calif., staff writer, 1973-75; Elsevier Publishing Co., Amsterdam, Netherlands, project writer, beginning 1975; currently affiliated with SAI Comsystems, Beverly Hills, Calif. Professor of library science, University of Southern California, summers, 1970, 1972. *Military service:* U.S. Army, 1943-45; became first sergeant. *Member:* Renaissance Society of America, Society for British Studies, California Library Association, Zamorano Club (president, 1963—), Grolier Club. *Awards, honors:* Guggenheim fellow, 1963-64.

WRITINGS: The World of the Elseviers, 1580-1712, Nijoff, 1954; *A Primer of Dutch 17th Century Overseas Trade,* Nijoff, 1961; *Dutch Influences on English Culture, 1558-1625,* Cornell University Press, 1964; (editor) Roger Williams, *The Actions of the Low Countries,* Cornell University Press, 1964; *Elizabethans Errant: The Strange Fortunes of Sir Thomas Sherley and His Three Sons,* Cornell University

Press, 1967; *An Enquiry into the Reading of the Lower Classes,* Castle Press, 1970; *The Evergreen Tree,* Castle Press, 1971; (editor with Elizabeth S. Wrigley) *Concordance to the Essays of Francis Bacon,* Gale, 1973; *Public Libraries as Culture and Social Centers,* Scarecrow, 1974; *Sir John Moore's Last Campaign, 1808-1809,* Nijoff, 1974. Contributor to magazines and journals.

BIOGRAPHICAL/CRITICAL SOURCES: New York Times Book Review, October 29, 1967.

* * *

DAVIES, Rupert Eric 1909-

PERSONAL: Born November 29, 1909; son of Walter Pierce and Elizabeth Miriam (Everett) Davies; married Margaret Price Holt, August 7, 1937; children: Mary Elizabeth, John Pierce, Stephen Holt and Judith Margaret (twins). *Education:* Balliol College, Oxford, B.A., 1932, M.A., 1936; Wesley House, Cambridge, B.A., 1934, B.D., 1946; also attended University of Tuebingen. *Home:* 6 Elm Tree Dr., Bishopsworth, Bristol BS13 8LY, England.

CAREER: Ordained Methodist minister; Kingswood School, Bath, England, chaplain and classics master, 1935-47; Bedminster Circuit, Bristol, England, minister, 1947-50; Bristol Ebenezer Circuit, Bristol, minister, 1950-52; Didsbury College, Bristol, lecturer in church history and history of doctrine, 1952-67; Wesley College, Bristol, principal, 1967-73; John Wesley's Chapel, Bristol, warden, 1976—. World Methodist Council, member of executive committee, 1951-76, convener of faith and order committee, 1955-69; member, Anglican-Methodist Unity Commission, 1965-69; World Council of Churches, member of Faith and Order Commission, 1966-74, and Faith Assembly, 1968; president, Methodist Conference, 1970-71. Board of governors, Kingswood School, secretary, 1948-70, chairman, 1975—; chairman of council, Redland High School, 1976-80. *Member:* Oxford Society, Mastermind Club, Old Pauline Club.

WRITINGS—Published by Epworth, except as indicated: *The Problems of Authority in the Continental Reformers: A Study of Luther, Zwingli, and Calvin,* 1946, reprinted, Greenwood Press, 1978; *Reading Your Bible,* 1950; (editor with R. N. Flew) *The Catholicity of Protestantism,* Lutterworth, 1951; *The Sunday School Today,* Methodist Youth Department, 1952; *Praying Together,* 1953; (editor) *Approach to Christian Education,* 1954, Philosophical Library, 1956; (editor) *John Scott Lidgett,* 1957; *Why I Am a Protestant,* 1958; *Studies in I Corinthians,* 1962; *Methodists and Unity,* Mowbray, 1962; *Methodism,* 1963, new revised edition, 1976; (editor with E. Gordon Rupp) *History of the Methodist Church in Great Britain,* Volume I, 1966, Volume II, 1979; *Religious Authority in an Age of Doubt,* 1968; *A Christian Theology of Education,* N.C.E.C., 1975; *What Methodists Believe,* Mowbray, 1977; *The Church in Our Times: An Ecumenical History from a British Perspective,* 1979.

* * *

DAVIN, D(aniel) M(arcus) 1913-

PERSONAL: Born September 1, 1913, in Invercargill, New Zealand; son of Patrick (a railway worker) and Mary (Sullivan) Davin; married Winifred Gonley (an editor), July 22, 1939; children: Anna, Delia Davin Morgan, Brigid Sanford-Smith. *Education:* Attended Sacred Heart College, Auckland, New Zealand; Otago University, M.A., 1934, Dip. M.A., 1935; Balliol College, Oxford, B.A., 1939, M.A., 1945. *Home:* 103 Southmoor Rd., Oxford OX2 6RE, En-

gland. *Agent:* David Higham Associates Ltd., 5-8 Lower John St., Golden Square, London W1R 4HA, England.

CAREER: Affiliated with Clarendon Press, Oxford, England, 1945-78. Oxford University Press, Oxford, England, assistant secretary to the delegates, 1948-70, deputy secretary to the delegates, 1970-78. *Military service:* British Army, 1939-45; served with New Zealand Division, 1940-45; became major; mentioned in dispatches; received the Order of the British Empire. *Member:* P.E.N., Authors Society, Royal Society of Arts (fellow).

WRITINGS—Novels, except as indicated: *Cliffs of Fall,* Nicholson & Watson, 1945; *For the Rest of Our Lives,* Nicholson & Watson, 1947, reprinted, M. Joseph, 1965; *The Gorse Blooms Pale* (short stories), M. Joseph, 1947; *Roads from Home,* M. Joseph, 1949; *The Sullen Bell,* M. Joseph, 1956; *No Remittance,* M. Joseph, 1959; *Not Here, Not Now,* R. Hale, 1970; *Brides of Price,* R. Hale, 1972, Coward, 1973; *Breathing Spaces* (short stories), R. Hale, 1975.

Nonfiction: (With John Mulgan) *Introduction to English Literature,* Clarendon Press, 1947; *Crete* (official history), War History Branch, Department of Internal Affairs, Wellington, New Zealand, 1953; (with W. K. Davin) *Writing in New Zealand: The New Zealand Novel,* Parts I and II, School Publications Branch, Department of Education, Wellington, 1956; *Katherine Mansfield in Her Letters,* School Publications Branch, Department of Education, Wellington, 1959; *Closing Times* (literary memoirs), Oxford University Press, 1975.

Editor: (And author of introduction) *New Zealand Short Stories,* Oxford University Press, 1953; *English Short Stories of Today: Second Series,* Oxford University Press, 1958; (and author of introduction) Katherine Mansfield, *Selected Stories,* Oxford University Press, 1963.

* * *

DAVINSON, Donald E(dward) 1932-

PERSONAL: Born July 20, 1932, in Middlesbrough, Yorkshire, England; son of Henry (an estimator) and Isabel (Johnson) Davinson; married Ann Kennedy, July 6, 1957; children: Roger, Joanna, Deborah. *Education:* University of London, B.Sc.; Newcastle School of Librarianship, D.P.A., F.L.A., 1959. *Politics:* Conservative. *Religion:* Church of England. *Home:* 14 Albion Rd., Scarborough, North Yorks Y011 2BT, England. *Office:* School of Librarianship, Leeds Polytechnic, Becketts Park, Leeds, Yorkshire, England.

CAREER: Middlesbrough Public Library, Middlesbrough, England, branch librarian, 1949-56; Warrington Public Library, Warrington, England, chief assistant, 1956-58; Dukinfield Public Library, Dukinfield, England, chief librarian, 1958-59; Belfast City Library, Belfast, Northern Ireland, business librarian, 1959-62; Leeds Polytechnic, School of Librarianship, Leeds, England, lecturer, 1962-64, principal lecturer, 1965-68, head of school, 1968—. Council for National Academic Awards, chairman of librarianship board, 1971-80, member of council, 1976—; member, Library Advisory Council, 1978—. Editorial advisor, Clive Bingley Ltd., 1964-78. *Military service:* British Army, 1950-52. *Member:* Library Association, Association of Assistant Librarians (member of council, 1956-59).

WRITINGS: Periodicals: A Manual of Practice for Librarians, Grafton & Co., 1960, 2nd edition, Deutsch, 1964; *Commercial Information: A Source Handbook,* Pergamon, 1965; *Academic and Legal Deposit Libraries: An Examination Guidebook,* Shoe String, 1965, 2nd edition, revised, 1969; *The Periodicals Collection: Its Purposes and Uses in*

Libraries, British Book Center, 1970, 2nd edition, West-view, 1978; *Bibliographic Control*, Shoe String, 1975; *Theses and Dissertations as Information Sources*, Shoe String, 1977; *Reference Service*, Bingley, 1980. Also author, with A. Thompson, of *Technical College Libraries*, 1971. General editor, "Examination Guide" series, Bingley, 1964-72. Contributor to *Chambers's Biographical Dictionary* and to professional journals. Editor, *Norbrala*, 1955-56, *Northern Ireland Libraries*, 1961-62.

WORK IN PROGRESS: Controlled Circulation Periodicals; Higher Education in Britain.

AVOCATIONAL INTERESTS: Spectator sports.

*   *   *

DAVIS, Christopher   1928-

PERSONAL: Born October 23, 1928, in Philadelphia, Pa.; son of Edward (a lawyer) and Josephine (Blitzstein) Davis; married Sonia Fogg, June 6, 1953; children: Kirby Gray, Katherine Hart, Emily Fogg, Sarah Baldwin. *Education:* University of Pennsylvania, A.B., 1955. *Home:* 6436 Overbrook Ave., Philadelphia, Pa. 19151. *Agent:* Wallace & Sheil Agency, Inc., 177 East 70th St., New York, N.Y. 10021; and Curtis Brown Ltd., 575 Madison Ave., New York, N.Y. 10022.

CAREER: Free-lance writer. Lecturer in creative writing, University of Pennsylvania, 1958-69, Bowling Green State University, 1970, Drexel University, Indiana University of Pennsylvania, and Bryn Mawr College. *Member:* Authors Guild, P.E.N., Phi Beta Kappa. *Awards, honors:* National Endowment for the Arts fellow, 1967-68; Guggenheim fellowship, 1972-73; National Book Award nomination for *A Peep into the Twentieth Century;* recipient of National Arts Council fellowships.

WRITINGS: Lost Summer, Harcourt, 1958; *First Family*, Coward, 1961; *A Kind of Darkness*, Hart-Davis, 1962; *Belmarch: A Legend of the First Crusade*, Viking, 1964; *Sad Adam, Glad Adam* (juvenile), Crowell, 1966; *The Shamir of Dachau*, New American Library, 1966; *Ishmael: A Self Portrait*, Cassell, 1967, Harper, 1969; *A Peep into the Twentieth Century* (novel), Harper, 1971; *The Producer* (nonfiction), Harper, 1972; *The Sun in Mid-Career*, Harper, 1975; *Suicide Note*, Harper, 1977; *Waiting for It* (nonfiction), Harper, 1980. Work represented in anthologies, including *O'Henry Prize Stories*, 1966, and *Best Magazine Articles*, 1968. Contributor of stories, poems, and essays to *Philadelphia Bulletin, Saturday Evening Post, Esquire, Los Angeles Times, Travel and Leisure, Pennsylvania Gazette*, and *Holiday*.

WORK IN PROGRESS: A novel.

SIDELIGHTS: Characterized by a *Time* reviewer as "a painstaking craftsman," Christopher Davis is also credited by Robert Steiner of *Nation* as having the "ability to write boldly of moral matters without ever losing sight of fiction as art." Edmund Fuller describes *Ishmael: A Self Portrait* as "a book of beauty and fascination that does not yield its meanings or intentions easily, or at one reading."

Davis's novel *A Peep into the Twentieth Century* has also been well received by critics. D. K. Mano calls it a "brawny, hard, enlightening book—truthful and sad," and D. W. McCullough believes that it is "a novel that demands serious attention. It never entertains, but it is as sparse, as unblinking, even as cruel as an unfaded daguerrotype."

BIOGRAPHICAL/CRITICAL SOURCES: Best Sellers, September 15, 1966, November, 1977; *Saturday Review*, September 24, 1966, September 4, 1971; *New York Times*

Book Review, October 2, 1966, December 21, 1969, May 30, 1970, September 11, 1977; *Book Week*, November 13, 1966; *Times Literary Supplement*, May 4, 1967; *Book World*, November 23, 1969; *Atlantic*, January, 1970; *Nation*, June 21, 1970; *Time*, July 19, 1971; *New York Times*, February 7, 1972, March 15, 1980.

*   *   *

DAVIS, Elwood Craig   1896-

PERSONAL: Born March 20, 1896, in Cheney, Wash.; son of Wilson Stuart and Lena (Craig) Davis; married Kathleen W. Skalley, 1931. *Education:* University of Washington, B.A. 1924; University of Chicago, M.A., 1926; Columbia University, Ph.D., 1932. *Home:* 1114 Pacific Ave., No. 301, Everett, Wash. 98201.

CAREER: Washington State Normal School (now Western Washington University), Bellingham, director of physical education and athletics, 1924-25, 1927, 1929; Pennsylvania State College (now University), University Park, professor of physical education, 1931-40; University of Pittsburgh, Pittsburgh, Pa., director of health and physical education, 1940-42; University of Louisville, Louisville, Ky., dean of men, 1945-47; University of Southern California, Los Angeles, chairman of division of health, physical education, and therapies, 1947-64, professor emeritus, 1964—; California State University, Northridge, lecturer, 1964-76. *Military service:* U.S. Navy, observer-bombardier, 1917-19; awarded Bronze Star; U.S. Naval Reserve, 1942-45; became commander.

MEMBER: American Association for Health, Physical Education, Recreation and Dance (fellow; national vice-president, 1942; president of Southwest District, 1952; archivist, 1970-73), College Physical Education Association (national president, 1942; president of western branch, 1958), American Association of University Professors, American Academy of Physical Education (fellow), National Education Association, American Association for the Advancement of Science, Phi Kappa Sigma, Phi Epsilon Kappa, Phi Delta Kappa, Kappa Delta Pi, Rotary International (local president, 1938), Masons. *Awards, honors:* Four honor awards from American Association for Health, Physical Education, Recreation and Dance and its branches; W. G. Anderson Award, 1954; Hetherington Award and Publication Award, both from American Academy of Physical Education, both 1965; Phi Epsilon Kappa National Honor Award, 1965; Luther Halsey Gulick Medal, 1965.

WRITINGS: Methods and Techniques Used in Surveying Health and Physical Education in City Schools: An Analysis and Evaluation, Teachers College, Columbia University, 1932, reprinted, AMS Press, 1972; (with John D. Lawther) *Successful Teaching in Physical Education*, Prentice-Hall, 1941, 2nd edition, 1948; (with Earl Wallis) *Toward Better Teaching in Physical Education*, Prentice-Hall, 1961; *The Philosophic Process in Physical Education*, Lea & Febiger, 1961, 2nd edition (with Donna Mae Miller), 1967, 3rd edition (with William A. Harper, Roberta J. Park, and others), 1977; (with Gene A. Logan) *Biophysical Values of Muscular Activity*, W. C. Brown, 1961, 2nd edition (with Logan and Wayne C. McKinney), 1965, 3rd edition (with George J. Holland) published as *Values of Physical Activity*, 1975; (with Robert Downey and others) *Exploring Physical Education*, Wadsworth, 1962; (editor) *Philosophies Fashion Physical Education*, W. C. Brown, 1963; (with Virginia Lindblad Nance) *Golf*, W. C. Brown, 1966, 4th edition, 1980; (with Miller and others) *Quality of Living*, W. C. Brown, 1967. Editor with

Miller, *American Academy of Physical Education Papers,* 1967-70. Contributor to professional journals and to *Esquire* and *Foil.* Co-editor, *Quest,* 1963-66.

WORK IN PROGRESS: Health Education.

SIDELIGHTS: Commenting on the nature and value of motivation in his life and career, Elwood Craig Davis told *CA:* "A motivating force—whether a carrot just beyond the donkey's nose, or a stick at the other end in the form of a master value or a great purpose—seems to be one personal absolute in a life of worth. You'll recall that even giants like Albert Schweitzer spent years searching for such a personal absolute to replace the one which no longer pushed or pulled. Then, suddenly, there it was, his *Reverence for Life!* But, as many know, such a force does not always appear full-blown. It comes gradually like knock-down parts or a jigsaw puzzle.

"The key concept in Lecomte du Nouey's *Human Destiny,* 'It is the effort that counts,' at the time it first jumped out from the page, filled precisely a major and initial part of a much-needed master motivator in my personal as well as my professional life. Not long thereafter it became, '*You* must make the effort.' Then, a short time later, 'You must make the effort *to improve.*' Shortly, came, 'But what *is* your best? *What* is your best? What is your *best?*' And, finally, so far, 'What is *your* best?'"

AVOCATIONAL INTERESTS: Readings in anthropology and philosophy, golf, salt-water fishing.

*   *   *

DAVIS, Jerome   1891-1979

PERSONAL: Born December 2, 1891, in Kyoto, Japan; died October 19, 1979, in Olney, Md.; son of Jerome Dean (a missionary) and Frances (a missionary; maiden name, Hooper) Davis; married Mildred Rood, July 20, 1920 (deceased); children: Frances Elizabeth (deceased), Helen Patricia Davis Platt, Wilfred G. *Education:* Oberlin College, A.B., 1913; Columbia University, M.A., 1919, Ph.D., 1922; Union Theological Seminary, B.D., 1920. *Religion:* United Church of Christ and Society of Friends. *Residence:* Olney, Md. *Agent:* (Lectures) Howard Higgins, Redpath Bureau, 507 Rockingham, Rochester, N.Y.

CAREER: Secretary to Wilfred Grenfell, Labrador, 1915; war work in Russia for world's committee of Young Men's Christian Association, 1916-18; Columbia University, New York, N.Y., Gilder fellow, 1920-21; Dartmouth College, Hanover, N.H., assistant professor of sociology, 1921-24; Yale University, Divinity School, New Haven, Conn., Gilbert L. Stark Chair of Practical Philanthropy, 1924-37; public and university lecturer, beginning 1937; world's committee of Young Men's Christian Association, director of prisoner-of-war camps in Canada, 1940-43; correspondent in Russia, 1943-44; Promoting Enduring Peace, Inc., Woodmont, Conn., founder and executive director, 1952-60. Visiting professor at Hiram College, 1946-47, University of Colorado, 1950, Fisk University, 1954, International Christian University, Tokyo, 1965; lecturer at Japanese universities, 1955. Leader of peace missions, special investigation groups, and goodwill tours to Europe, the Soviet Union, and the Peoples Republic of China. Chairman, Connecticut Legislative Commission on Jails, 1931-39; delegate to Democratic National Convention, 1940; vice-president, speakers research committee for the United Nations. Trustee, Oberlin College, 1945-57.

MEMBER: American Federation of Teachers (president, 1936-39), American Sociological Society, American Economic Association, American Association of University Professors, Eastern Sociological Society (former president), Military Order of Loyal Legion, Alpha Chi Rho, Cosmos Club (Washington, D.C.). *Awards, honors:* D.D., Oberlin College and LL.D., Hillsdale College, both 1933; D.Litt., Florida Southern College, 1947; Gandhi Peace Award, 1967.

WRITINGS: Russians and Ruthenians in America, Doran, 1921; *The Russian Immigrant,* Macmillan, 1922, reprinted, Arno, 1969; *Adventuring in World Cooperation,* United Society of Christian Endeavor, 1925; (with Roy Chamberlain) *Christian Fellowship among the Nations,* Pilgrim, 1925; (editor) *Business and the Church,* Century, 1926; (editor with Harry E. Barnes) *Readings in Sociology,* 1927; (editor with Barnes) *Introduction to Sociology,* Heath, 1927, revised edition, 1931; (editor) *Christianity and Social Adventuring,* Century, 1927; (editor and author of introduction) *Labor Speaks for Itself on Religion,* Macmillan, 1929; *Contemporary Social Movements,* Century, 1930; (editor) *The New Russia: Between the First and Second Five-Year Plans,* introduction by Edward M. House, John Day, 1933, reprinted, Books for Libraries Press, 1968; *The Jail Population of Connecticut,* State of Connecticut, 1935; *Capitalism and Its Culture,* Farrar, Straus, 1935, revised edition, 1941; (editor with E. Stein) *Labor Problems in America,* Farrar, Straus, 1940; *Behind Soviet Power,* introduction by Joseph E. Davies, Readers Press, 1946; *Character Assassination,* Philosophical Library, 1950; *Peace, War and You,* Schuman, 1952; *Religion in Action,* Philosophical Library, 1956; (with Hugh B. Hester) *On the Brink,* Lyle Stuart, 1959; *Citizens of One World,* Citadel, 1961; *World Leaders I Have Known,* Citadel, 1963; (editor) *Disarmament: A World View* (symposium), Citadel, 1964; *A Life Adventure for World Peace: An Autobiography,* foreword by James A. Pike, Citadel, 1967; (editor) *Peace or World War III: A Symposium,* Greenwich Book Publishers, 1968. Contributor to *Atlantic, Christian Century, Nation, Forum, Harper's, Survey, Century,* and other magazines.

SIDELIGHTS: Jerome Davis's lifelong interest in the subject of world peace began during World War I when, sent by the Young Men's Christian Association, he visited prisoners of war in Russia. Davis, who was in Russia at the time of the Bolshevik revolution, became a friend of Nikolai Lenin and was invited to the Kremlin on several occasions. On subsequent trips to the Soviet Union, Davis met with Joseph Stalin, Nikita Khrushchev, and Alexi Kosygin. Due to his social and political views and his association with the above Soviet leaders, Davis was frequently accused of sympathizing with Communist and radical ideologies. In 1943, Davis initiated a libel suit against writer Benjamin Stohlberg and the Curtis Publishing Company for one such accusation. Stohlberg, Davis charged, "had falsely portrayed him as 'a Communist and a Stalinist,'" Walter H. Waggoner reported in the *New York Times.* Davis was awarded an $11,000 settlement.

BIOGRAPHICAL/CRITICAL SOURCES: A Life Adventure for Peace: An Autobiography, foreword by James A. Pike, Citadel, 1967; *New York Times,* October 24, 1979.†

*   *   *

DAVIS, Paxton   1925-

PERSONAL: Born May 7, 1925, in Winston-Salem, N.C.; son of James Paxton (a tobacco executive) and Emily (McDowell) Davis; married Wylma Elizabeth Pooser, June 6, 1951 (divorced, 1971); married Peggy Painter Camper, July 21, 1973; children: (first marriage) Elizabeth Keith, Anne Beckley, James Paxton III. *Education:* Virginia Military Institute, cadet, 1942-43; Johns Hopkins University, B.A., 1949. *Politics:* Democrat. *Religion:* Presbyterian. *Address:* P.O. Box 33, Fincastle, Va. 24090. *Agent:* Curtis Brown Ltd., 575 Madison Ave., New York, N.Y. 10021.

CAREER: Reporter for *Winston-Salem Journal,* Winston-Salem, N.C., 1949-51, *Richmond Times Dispatch,* Richmond, Va., 1951-52, and *Twin City Sentinel,* Winston-Salem, 1952-53; Washington and Lee University, Lexington, Va., assistant professor, 1953-58, associate professor, 1958-63, professor of journalism, 1963-76, head of department, 1968-74. *Military service:* U.S. Army, 1943-46, served two years in China-Burma-India Theater; became sergeant; received two battle stars for Burma campaigns of 1944-45. *Awards, honors:* First place award for interpretive reporting, Virginia Press Association, 1951; Bread Loaf Writers' Conference fellow, 1956; Shenandoah Award for distinguished writing, 1956.

WRITINGS: Two Soldiers: Two Short Novels, Simon & Schuster, 1956; *The Battle of New Market: A Story of VMI,* Little, Brown, 1963; *One of the Dark Places,* Morrow, 1965; *The Seasons of Heroes,* Morrow, 1967; *A Flag at the Pole: Three Soliloquies,* Atheneum, 1976; *Ned,* Atheneum, 1978; *Three Days,* Atheneum, 1980. Contributing editorial columnist, *Roanoke Times* and *World News,* beginning 1976. Contributor of short stories, poems, and articles to *New York Times, New York Times Book Review, Playboy, Hopkins Review, Bluebook, Shenandoah,* and *Lyric.* Book editor, *Roanoke Times,* 1961—.

WORK IN PROGRESS: A novel.

BIOGRAPHICAL/CRITICAL SOURCES: Best Sellers, September 15, 1967; *New York Times Book Review,* September 17, 1967, April 27, 1980.

*   *   *

DAVIS, Robert P. 1929-
(Joe Brandon)

PERSONAL: Born October 8, 1929, in New York, N.Y.; son of Joseph L. (a jewelry dealer) and Almina Davis. *Education:* Syracuse University, B.A., 1951; Yale University, Ph.D. *Politics:* Republican. *Religion:* Roman Catholic. *Home:* 241 Tradewind Dr., Palm Beach, Fla. 33480.

CAREER: Member of television production departments of Batten, Barton, Durstine & Osborn, New York City, N.Y., 1951-53, and Ogilvy, Benson & Mather, New York City, 1953-55; free-lance writer. *Member:* American Water Color Society, Authors Guild, Writers Guild of America, East. *Awards, honors:* Academy Award for best short film, 1960, for "Day of the Painter"; San Francisco Film Festival award for best fiction short film, 1961; Claude Bellanger Grand Prix; Cine Gold Eagle.

WRITINGS: Apes on a Tissue Paper Bridge, Fleet, 1963; *Goodby Bates McGee,* Macfadden, 1967; *The Dingle War,* Prentice-Hall, 1968; (under pseudonym Joe Brandon) *Cock-a-Doodle Dew,* Macfadden, 1972; (under pseudonym Joe Brandon) *Paradise in Flames,* Pocket Books, 1976; *The Pilot* (Reader's Digest Book Club selection; also see below), Morrow, 1976; *Cat Five,* Morrow, 1977 (published in England as *Hurricane,* Sphere Books, 1977); *Control Tower* (Reader's Digest Book Club selection), Putnam, 1980; *The Divorce,* Morrow, 1980.

Also author of screenplays "Day of the Painter," Walt Disney Productions, 1960, "The Pilot," based on novel of same title, 1980, "Come Thursday," and "The Tin Tiger." Contributor of numerous articles to *Sports Afield, Good House-*

keeping, *Town and Country, New York Times, Irish Times,* and other publications.

WORK IN PROGRESS: A novel, *The Ashburton Castle.*

*   *   *

DAVISON, Peter 1928-

PERSONAL: Born June 27, 1928, in New York, N.Y.; son of Edward (a poet) and Natalie (Weiner) Davison; married Jane Auchincloss Truslow (a writer), March 7, 1959; children: Edward Angus, Lesley Truslow. *Education:* Harvard University, A.B. (magna cum laude), 1949; Fulbright Scholar, St. John's College, Cambridge University, 1949-50. *Office:* Atlantic Monthly Press, 8 Arlington St., Boston, Mass. 02116.

CAREER: Harcourt, Brace, Jovanovich, Inc. (publishers), New York, N.Y., editorial assistant, 1950-51, assistant editor, 1953-55; Harvard University Press, Cambridge, Mass., assistant to director, 1955-56; Atlantic Monthly Press, Boston, Mass., associate editor, 1956-59, executive editor, 1959-64, director, 1964-79, senior editor, 1979—, poetry editor, *Atlantic.* Lecturer. *Military service:* U.S. Army, 1951-53. *Member:* Phi Beta Kappa; Harvard Club, Century Association (both New York); Examiner Club, St. Botolph Club, Signet Society (all Boston). *Award, honors:* Yale Series of Younger Poets prize, 1963; National Institute of Arts and Letters award, 1972; National Book Critics Circle Award in poetry, 1979, for *Hello Darkness: The Collected Poems of L. E. Sissman.*

WRITINGS: The Breaking of the Day, and Other Poems, Yale University Press, 1964; *The City and the Island,* Atheneum, 1966; *Pretending to Be Asleep* (poems), Atheneum, 1970; *Half Remembered: A Personal History* (autobiography), Harper, 1973; *Walking the Boundaries* (selected poems), Atheneum, 1974; *A Voice in the Mountain* (poems), Atheneum, 1977; (editor) L. E. Sissman, *Hello Darkness: The Collected Poems of L. E. Sissman,* Atlantic-Little, Brown, 1978; *Barn Fever, and Other Poems,* Atheneum, 1981. Also author of *Dark Houses,* 1971, and editor of *The World of Farley Mowat: A Selection from His Work,* 1980. Work represented in numerous anthologies, including *A Controversy of Poets,* edited by Paris Leary and Robert Kelly, Doubleday, 1965, *Understanding Poetry,* and several volumes of *Borestone Mountain Poetry Awards.* Contributor of poems and critical essays to *Encounter, Kenyon Review, Partisan Review, Atlantic, New Yorker, Hudson Review, Harper's, Poetry,* and many other publications.

WORK IN PROGRESS: Poems.

SIDELIGHTS: In a review of *Pretending to Be Asleep,* Victor Howes states that Peter Davison succeeds in his work "because he is a poet with something to say." Howes explains: "Unlike the parrot, or the parodist, who deals only in echoes of things overheard, Peter Davison reads like a man talking to men. He writes about life-and-death concerns, about being aware (awake), and about being unaware (asleep), and about pretending to be asleep when you are really awake. . . . [His] third book of poems is the virtuoso performance of a man trying on a variety of poetic hats in an effort to find one that fits. Fits, that is, for everyday and for all days in all kinds of weathers." Phoebe Adams also praises Davison's works, adding: "[His] poems are the loot of a borderer's raids into the territory between wish and truth, imagination and reality, dream and waking, and they display what is normally half-understood or willfully forgotten."

Davison writes *CA:* "I must be one of the few poets of my

generation who has never either taken or given a creative writing class, but I cannot suggest what to make of that fact. Poetry for me is not work but pleasure, not a career but a second life—a play within a play.''

BIOGRAPHICAL/CRITICAL SOURCES: New York Times Book Review, December 11, 1966; Contemporary Literature, winter, 1968; Atlantic, May, 1970; Christian Science Monitor, June 4, 1970.

*   *   *

DAWE, Roger David 1934-

PERSONAL: Born September 15, 1934, in Bristol, England; son of Charles Vivian and Louisa (Butler) Dawe; married Kerstin Wallner, November 12, 1961. *Education:* Attended Clifton College; Gonville and Caius College, Cambridge, B.A., 1957, M.A., 1961, Ph.D., 1962. *Office:* Trinity College, Cambridge University, Cambridge, England.

CAREER: Cambridge University, Cambridge, England, research fellow in classics at Gonville and Caius College, 1957-63, fellow in classics at Trinity College, 1963—. *Awards, honors:* Litt.D., Gonville and Caius College, Cambridge University, 1974.

WRITINGS: Investigation and Collation of Manuscripts of Aeschylus, Cambridge University Press, 1964; *Repertory of Conjectures on Aeschylus,* E. J. Brill, 1965; *Studies on the Text of Sophocles,* E. J. Brill, Volumes I and II, 1973, Volume III, 1978; *Sophocles Tragoediae,* Tuebner, Volume I, 1975, Volume II, 1979; (co-editor) *Dionysiaca,* privately printed, 1978; *Sophocles' "Oedipus Rex,"* Cambridge University Press, 1982. Contributor of articles to scholarly publications.

WORK IN PROGRESS: Literary work on Homer.

*   *   *

DAY, Beth (Feagles) 1924-
(Elizabeth Feagles)

PERSONAL: Born May 25, 1924, in Fort Wayne, Ind.; daughter of Ralph L. (an engineer) and Mary A. (West) Feagles; married Donald Day, 1945 (divorced, 1960); married Harry Padva, June 15, 1962 (deceased); married Carlos P. Romulo (foreign minister of the Philippines). *Education:* University of Oklahoma, B.A., 1945. *Home:* 74 McKinley Rd., Forbes Park, Makati, Philippines. *Agent:* Paul R. Reynolds, Inc., 12 East 41st St., New York, N.Y. 10017. *Office:* 35 East 38th St., New York, N.Y. 10016.

CAREER: Member of staff, magazine of Douglas Aircraft; editorial assistant, *Southwest Review,* Dallas, Tex.; freelance writer and speaker on international affairs. *Member:* American Society of Journalists and Authors, Authors League, Society of Women Geographers, Chaine des Rotisseurs. *Awards, honors:* Honorary doctorate, Philippine Women's University, 1975; citation for "furthering Philippine-American understanding," University of Pangasinan.

WRITINGS: Little Professor of Piney Woods: The Story of Professor Laurence Jones, Messner, 1955; *Grizzlies in Their Back Yard* (also see below), Messner, 1956; *Glacier Pilot: The Story of Bob Reeve and the Flyers Who Pushed Back Alaska's Air Frontiers,* Holt, 1957; *No Hiding Place* (also see below), Holt, 1957; *A Shirttail to Hang To: The Story of Cal Farley and His Boys Ranch,* preface by J. Edgar Hoover, Holt, 1959; *This Was Hollywood: An Affectionate History of Filmland's Golden Years,* Doubleday, 1960; *Passage Perilous,* Putnam, 1962; (with Helen Klaben) *Hey, I'm Alive,*

McGraw, 1964; (with Tom Pyle) *Pocantico: Fifty Years on the Rockefeller Domain,* Duell, Sloan & Pearce, 1964; (with Frank Wilson) *Special Agent,* Holt, 1965; (with Helen Margaret Liley) *Modern Motherhood: Pregnancy, Childbirth and the Newborn Baby,* Random House, 1967, revised edition, 1969; (with Louanne Ferris) *I'm Done Crying,* M. Evans, 1969; *My Name Is Dr. Rantzau,* Fayard, 1970; (with Jacqui Schiff) *All My Children,* M. Evans, 1971; *Sexual Life between Blacks and Whites: The Roots of Racism,* introduction by Margaret Mead, World Publishing, 1972; *The Philippines: Shattered Showcase of Democracy in Asia,* introduction by husband, Carlos P. Romulo, M. Evans, 1974; *The Manila Hotel,* National Media, 1979.

Children's books: (With former husband, Donald Day) *Will Rogers, the Boy Roper,* Houghton, 1950; (with Jessie Joyce) *Joshua Slocum, Sailor,* Houghton, 1953; *Gene Rhodes, Cowboy,* Messner, 1954; *America's First Cowgirl, Lucille Mulhall,* introduction by Charles Mulhall, Messner, 1955; (under name Elizabeth Feagles) *Talk Like a Cowboy: A Dictionary of Real Western Lingo for Young Cowboys and Cowgirls,* Naylor, 1955; (with Liley) *The Secret World of the Baby,* Random House, 1969; *The World of the Grizzlies* (based on adult nonfiction book *Grizzlies in Their Backyard*), Doubleday, 1969; *Life on a Lost Continent: A Natural History of New Zealand,* Doubleday, 1971.

Also author of television plays "The Man Nobody Wanted" and "No Hiding Place," based on book of same title. Contributor of articles to magazines in the United States and abroad, including *Ladies' Home Journal, McCall's, Reader's Digest, Cosmopolitan, Good Housekeeping, Catholic Digest, Parents, Woman's Day, Redbook,* and *New York Times Magazine.*

WORK IN PROGRESS: Articles on Southeast Asia.

SIDELIGHTS: Beth Day's work covers a variety of subject matter, such as sociology, history, biography, medicine, and current socio-political events. Day told *CA,* "I have always viewed my work as serving as a sort of translator or bridge between my readers and either specialized information or unique knowledge of an interesting personality." Day adds that for the past few years her work has focused on promoting "new understanding between the Philippines and Southeast Asia and the American public," and that she employs a dual approach to the matter by "explaining Asian things to Americans and American custom and thinking to Asians."

Day's books have been translated into French, Italian, and German. *Hey, I'm Alive* has been adapted for television.

BIOGRAPHICAL/CRITICAL SOURCES: New York Times Book Review, April 21, 1968, November 3, 1968; Saturday Review, February 22, 1969; Best Sellers, February 15, 1971; Writer's Digest, March, 1971.

*   *   *

DEAL, William S(anford) 1910-

PERSONAL: Born April 9, 1910, near Taylorsville, N.C.; son of Virgil M. V. and Lacy Eva (Miller) Deal; married Myrna Clara Allen; children: Evangeline Sue. *Education:* McKinley-Roosevelt College, Chicago, Ill., Th.B., 1942; National Bible College, Wichita, Kan., Th.M., 1946; Taylor University, A.B., 1950; Northern Baptist Theological Seminary, graduate study, 1951-56; Burton Seminary, Colorado Springs, Colo., Th.D., 1957; Pasadena College, M.A., 1965. *Home and office:* 11326 Ranchito St., El Monte, Calif. 91732.

CAREER: Pastor at Pilgrim Holiness churches in North

Carolina, 1930-37; evangelist in the eastern United States and in the West Indies, 1937-42; district superintendent, Pilgrim Holiness church, North Carolina Conference, 1942-49, Pacific Northwest Conference (Salem, Ore.), 1950-58, and California Conference, 1963-64; Western Pilgrim College, El Monte, Calif., president, 1958-60; evangelist and writer, 1960—; counselor, 1964—; California State licensed counselor in family, marriage, and child counseling, 1966—. Publisher, Deal Publications.

WRITINGS: The Unpardonable Sin Explained, Pilgrim Publishing House, 1940, revised edition, Beacon Hill, 1963; *Problems of Modern Youth,* West Publishing, 1952; *The Victorious Life,* Eerdmans, 1954; *Living Christian in Today's World,* Pilgrim Publishing House, 1958; *Problems of the Spirit-Filled Life,* Beacon Hill, 1961; *The Soul Winner's Guide,* Zondervan, 1961; *A Happy Married Life and How to Live It,* Zondervan, 1963; *Happiness and Harmony in Marriage,* Beacon Hill, 1969; *John Bunyon: Tinker of Bedford,* Good News Publishers, 1976; *March of Holiness through the Centuries,* Beacon Hill, 1979; *God's Answer for the Unequally Yoked,* Good News Publishers, 1980.

Published by Revivalist Press, except as indicated: *Faith, Facts and Feelings,* 1931; *Letters to New Converts,* 1933; *The Furnace of Affliction,* 1935, new edition, Zondervan, 1959; *Messages for Modern Youth,* 1937; *Heart Talks on the Deeper Life,* 1938, revised edition, Higley Huffman Press, 1964.

Published by Deal Publications: *Can Christianity Survive the Coming World Crisis?,* 1952; *Stepping Heavenward,* 1953; *What a Young Christian Ought to Know,* 1956; *Where in the World Are You Going?,* 1980; *The Adventures of Jonah,* 1980; *Battling with the Devil and Depression,* 1980.

Published by Baker Book: *The Christian's Daily Guide,* 1957; *Daily Christian Living,* 1962; *What Every Sunday School Teacher Should Know,* 1963; *Baker's Pictorial Introduction to the Bible,* 1967; *Daily Christian Manna,* 1974.

Contributor of articles, features, and stories to magazines. Contributing editor, *Christian Life;* editorial consultant, *Christian Inquirer.*

SIDELIGHTS: William S. Deal told *CA* that he first experienced the "call of God to writing" as a teenager, and that he wrote his first book at the age of eighteen with the hope of "encouraging other young people to better religious understanding." He adds that since his initial effort, "all my books have been written to bless and inspire people to higher, more godly living." Deal believes that all would-be authors should seek some professional training and offers this advice: "If you feel the urge or call to write, set to the task and keep writing."

Baker's Pictorial Introduction to the Bible has been translated into German.

*   *   *

de ANGELI, Marguerite 1889-

PERSONAL: Born March 14, 1889, in Lapeer, Mich.; daughter of Shadrach George (a representative for Eastman-Kodak) and Ruby (Tuttle) Lofft; married John Dailey de Angeli, April 2, 1910 (deceased); children: John, Arthur, Harry E., Nina (Mrs. Alfred Kuhn), Maurice Bower. *Education:* Attended public schools in Lapeer, Mich., and Philadelphia, Pa. *Religion:* Protestant. *Home:* Cathedral Village, No. F 506, East Cathedral Rd., Philadelphia, Pa. 19128.

CAREER: Concert and church soloist from 1906 to the 1920's; illustrator of articles for *Country Gentleman;* writer

and illustrator of children's books, 1935—. *Member:* Philadelphia Art Alliance, Pennsylvania Historical Society, Philadelphia Bookseller's Association (honorary member). *Awards, honors: Bright April* cited as an "honor book" by *New York Herald Tribune,* 1946; John Newbery Medal, 1950, and Lewis Carroll Shelf Award, 1961, both for *The Door in the Wall;* named Distinguished Daughter of Pennsylvania, 1958; Lit Brothers Good Neighbor Community Service Award, 1963; awarded citation for "distinguished and lasting contribution to the world of children's books," Graduate School of Library Science, Drexel Institute of Technology, 1963; Regina Medal, Catholic Library Association, 1968.

WRITINGS—Self-illustrated children's books, except as indicated; published by Doubleday, except as indicated: *Ted and Nina Go to the Grocery Store* (also see below), 1935; *Ted and Nina Have a Happy Rainy Day* (also see below), 1936; *Henner's Lydia,* 1936; *Petite Suzanne,* 1937; *Skippack School,* 1938; *A Summer Day with Ted and Nina* (also see below), 1940; *Thee, Hannah!,* 1940; *Elin's Amerika,* 1941; *Copper-Toed Boots,* 1943; *Yonie Wondernose,* 1944; *Turkey for Christmas,* Westminster, 1944; *Bright April,* 1946; *Jared's Island,* 1947; *The Door in the Wall,* 1949; *Just Like David,* 1951; *Book of Nursery and Mother Goose Rhymes,* 1954; *Black Fox of Lorne,* 1956.

The Old Testament, edited by Samuel Terrien, 1960; *A Pocket Full of Posies,* 1961; *Marguerite de Angeli's Book of Favorite Hymns,* 1963; *The Goose Girl,* 1964; *The Ted and Nina Story Book* (contains *Ted and Nina Go to the Grocery Store, Ted and Nina Have a Happy Rainy Day,* and *A Summer Day with Ted and Nina*), 1965; (with son, Arthur Craig de Angeli) *The Empty Barn,* Westminster, 1966; *The Old Testament* (Bible stories), 1967; *Butter at the Old Price* (autobiography), 1971; *Fiddlestrings,* 1974; *The Lion in the Box,* 1975; *Whistle for the Crossing,* 1977. Also author of *Up the Hill,* 1942.

BIOGRAPHICAL/CRITICAL SOURCES: Authors in the News, Volume II, Gale, 1976; *Children's Literature Review,* Volume I, Gale, 1976.

*   *   *

DeBOER, John James 1903-1969

PERSONAL: Born October 12, 1903, in Chicago, Ill.; died May 21, 1969; buried in Fairmount Cemetery, Willow Springs, Ill.; son of James and Maria (Wezeman) DeBoer; married Henrietta Anne Geerdes, September 3, 1931; children: Fredrik. *Education:* Attended Calvin College, 1919-21; Wheaton College, A.B., 1923; University of Chicago, A.M., 1927, Ph.D., 1938. *Office:* Department of Education, University of Illinois, Urbana, Ill.

CAREER: Chicago Christian High School, Chicago, Ill., teacher of English, 1923-31; Chicago Teachers College (now Chicago State University), Chicago, professor of education, 1931-45; Herzl Junior College, Chicago, teacher of English, 1945-47; University of Illinois at Urbana-Champaign, professor of education, 1947-69. *Member:* National Council of Teachers of English (past president), National Conference on Research in English (past president), American Educational Research Association, Phi Delta Kappa. *Awards, honors:* Susan Colver Rosenberg Award; Hatfield Award.

WRITINGS: (Editor with Ida T. Jacobs) *Educating for Peace,* Appleton-Century, 1940; (editor) *Subject Fields in General Education,* Appleton-Century, 1942; (with Ruth G. Strickland) *Design for Elementary Education,* Hinds, Hayden & Eldredge, 1945; *Creative Reading,* Graessle-Mercer,

1950; (with Walter V. Kaulfers and Helen Rand Miller) *Teaching Secondary English*, McGraw, 1951, reprinted, Greenwood Press, 1970; (with Paul B. Hale and Esther Landin) *Reading for Living: An Index to Reading Materials for Use in Human Relations Programs in Secondary Schools*, Illinois Department of Public Instruction, 1953; (with Martha Dallmann) *The Teaching of Reading*, Holt, 1960, 4th edition, 1974.

Contributor to *Cyclopedia of Modern Education*. Contributor to professional journals. Editor, *Elementary English Review;* assistant editor, *English Journal;* co-editor, *Secondary Education*, 1966.

WORK IN PROGRESS: Reading in the High School.

AVOCATIONAL INTERESTS: Chess.†

*　　*　　*

De CRISTOFORO, R(omeo) J(ohn)   1917-
(R. J. Cristy, Cris Williams)

PERSONAL: Born April 28, 1917, in New York, N.Y.; son of Nicholas and Rosina (Capella) De Cristoforo; married May A. Ferrari (a writer and artist), June 7, 1942; children: Daniel Taft, David, Ronald John. *Education:* Attended various universities. *Home:* 27861 Natoma Rd., Los Altos Hills, Calif. 94022.

CAREER: Variously employed as inspector of experimental aircraft, director of education materials for Magna Engineering Corp., and teacher of arts and crafts; free-lance writer on manual arts, 1946—. *Awards, honors:* Short story award, *Writer's Digest* contest.

WRITINGS: Power Tool Woodworking for Everyone, McGraw, 1953, published as *Modern Power Tool Woodworking*, Magna Publications, 1967; *The New Handyman's Carpentry Guide*, Fawcett, 1959; *Plywood Projects You Can Build*, Fawcett, 1959; *Handyman's Concrete and Masonry Handbook*, Arco, 1960; *Home Carpentry Handbook*, Fawcett, 1960; *How to Choose and Use Power Tools*, Arco, 1960, published as *Mechanix Illustrated: How to Choose and Use Power Tools*, Fawcett, 1960; *Fun with a Saw*, McGraw, 1961; *New Carpentry Handbook*, Fawcett, 1962; *Concrete and Masonry Ideas for the Homeowner*, Fawcett, 1962; *Mechanix Illustrated: The How-to Book of Carpentry*, Fawcett, 1963, published as *The How-to Book of Carpentry*, Arco, 1966; *How-to Book of Concrete and Masonry*, Fawcett, 1964; *How to Build Your Own Furniture*, Harper, 1965; *The Practical Book of Carpentry*, Arco, 1969.

De Cristoforo's Complete Book of Power Tools, Popular Science, 1972; (contributor) *Woodworking Projects for the Home*, Harper, 1973; (contributor) *Homeowners Handbook*, Popular Science, 1974; *Concrete and Masonry: Techniques and Design*, Reston, 1975; *Hand Tool Woodworking*, H. P. Books, 1977; *De Cristoforo's House Building Illustrated*, Harper, 1977. Also author of *Woodworking Techniques: Joints and Their Applications*, Reston. Contributor to encyclopedias, including *The Practical Handyman's Encyclopedia* and *Popular Science Homeowner's Encyclopedia*. Contributor of poetry, fiction, and over one thousand how-to articles to *Popular Science*, *Popular Mechanics*, *Better Homes and Gardens*, and other magazines.

AVOCATIONAL INTERESTS: Photography and art, including charcoal nudes and portraits.

*　　*　　*

DEGLER, Carl N(eumann)   1921-

PERSONAL: Born February 6, 1921, in Orange, N.J.; son of Casper (a fireman) and Jewell (Neumann) Degler; married Catherine Grady (a teacher), November 19, 1948; children: Paul Grady, Suzanne Catherine. *Education:* Upsala College, A.B., 1942; Columbia University, M.A., 1947, Ph.D., 1952. *Politics:* Democrat. *Home:* 907 Mears Ct., Stanford, Calif. 94305. *Office:* Department of History, Stanford University, Stanford, Calif. 94305.

CAREER: Hunter College (now Hunter College of the City University of New York), New York City, instructor in history, 1947-48; New York University, Washington Square College, New York City, instructor in history, 1947-50; Adelphi University, Garden City, N.J., instructor in history, 1950-51; Vassar College, Poughkeepsie, N.Y., 1952-68, began as instructor, became professor of history, chairman of department, 1966-68; Stanford University, Stanford, Calif., professor of history, 1968—, Margaret Byrne Professor of American History, 1972—. Visiting summer professor of history at Ripon College, 1959, and Stanford University, 1964; visiting professor of history, Columbia University, 1963-64; Harmsworth Professor of American History, Oxford University, 1973-74. *Military service:* U.S. Army Air Forces, Weather Service, 1942-45.

MEMBER: Society of American Historians, American Academy of Arts and Sciences, American Historical Association, American Studies Association (president, Pacific Coast branch, 1971-72), Organization of American Historians (member of executive board, beginning 1970; president, 1979-80), Economic History Association, American Association of University Professors, Southern Historical Association. *Awards, honors:* American Council of Learned Societies fellow, 1964-65; Bancroft Prize, Columbia University, Beveridge Prize, American Historical Association, National Book Award nomination, and Pulitzer Prize in history, all 1972, for *Neither Black nor White;* Guggenheim fellowship, 1972-73; National Endowment for the Humanities senior fellow, 1976-77; Center for Advanced Studies in the Behavioral Sciences fellow, 1979-80; recipient of honorary degrees from Upsala College, Ripon College, Oxford University, and Colgate University.

WRITINGS: Out of Our Past: The Forces That Shaped Modern America, Harper, 1959, revised edition, 1970; (with others) *The Democratic Experience*, Scott, Foresman, 1963; (editor) *Pivotal Interpretations in American History* (anthology), two volumes, Harper, 1966; (editor and author of introduction) Charlotte Perkins Gilman, *Women and Economics*, Harper, 1966; *The Age of the Economic Revolution, 1876-1900*, Scott, Foresman, 1967, revised edition, 1977; *Affluence and Anxiety*, Scott, Foresman, 1968, revised edition, 1975; (editor) *The New Deal*, Quadrangle, 1970; *Neither Black nor White: Slavery and Race Relations in Brazil and the United States*, Macmillan, 1971; *The Other South: Dissenters in the Nineteenth Century South*, Harper, 1974; *Place over Time: The Continuity of Southern Distinctiveness*, Louisiana State University Press, 1977; *At Odds: Women and the Family in America from the Revolution to the Present*, Oxford University Press, 1980.

Contributor: Sidney Hook, editor, *Philosophy and History*, New York University Press, 1963; William Nelson, editor, *Theory and Practice in the American Political Tradition*, University of Chicago Press, 1964; Robert Jay Lifton, editor, *The Woman in America*, Houghton, 1965, Alfred F. Young, editor, *Dissent: Explorations in the History of American Radicalism*, Northern Illinois University Press, 1968; Stanley Cohen and Lorman Ratner, editors, *The Development of an American Culture*, Prentice-Hall, 1970.

Contributor of articles and reviews to popular magazines and scholarly journals, including *American Quarterly, New York Times Magazine, American Heritage,* and *Yale Review.* Member of editorial advisory board, *Signs: Journal of Women and Culture,* 1977—, *Journal of Family History,* 1978—, and *Plantation Society,* 1979—.

WORK IN PROGRESS: A book on the role of biological thought on social policy in the twentieth century.

SIDELIGHTS: Until the publication of Carl N. Degler's *Neither Black nor White,* many scholars were perplexed by the fact that although Brazil and the United States had been the largest slave-holding nations in the Western world, "Brazil never developed a system of rigid segregation of the sort that replaced slavery in this country," according to Willie Lee Rose in the *New York Review of Books;* "and blacks of Latin countries retained much more of their African culture." In his Pulitzer Prize-winning study of this dilemma, Degler refutes the theory proposed by Giberto Freyre and Frank Tannenbaum in 1946: that because of religious and legal precedents, Brazil's Portuguese settlers were more inclined to recognize the humanity of the slave; thus, Freyre and Tannenbaum contend, upon emancipation Brazil's slaves were easily absorbed into society, while this country's slaves, as well as their descendents, faced continued hostility and fear.

Degler states that in fact Brazilian slavery was as harsh, if not harsher, than its North American counterpart. He argues that Brazil's successful assimilation of its freed slaves was due to demographic, economic, and cultural factors rather than humane attitudes and treatment. Degler points to the fact that in Brazil, unlike in the United States, blacks and mulattos were a majority. Moreover, the Portuguese settlers were not attracted to the physical labor involved in skilled trades and crafts, making it possible for blacks to move freely into these areas. As a result, blacks were able to improve their economic status. "The work is good history and good sociology," Rose comments, "in that it explores the contemporary facts and ambiguities of Brazilian race relations more thoroughly than others have done." The critic continues: "Degler succeeds admirably in bringing logic and common sense to the main question that has dominated historians for . . . years. His synthesis of the Latin scholarship with what is now known about slavery in this country is lucid, and stands up to several close readings."

Degler writes *CA:* "I have always written about those historical subjects or problems that have seemed important to me, and which I thought, if properly expressed, would prove useful for nonacademic people to know about. Throughout my writing career, my primary interest has been to communicate with the public about history without losing contact with my professional colleagues and their standards and concerns. In short, I have tried to write for both audiences."

BIOGRAPHICAL/CRITICAL SOURCES: Library Journal, June 15, 1971; *American Anthropologist,* August, 1972; *Journal of Negro History,* January, 1973; *Journal of American History,* June, 1973; *Americas,* January, 1974; *New Republic,* February 16, 1974, May 10, 1980; *Virginia Quarterly Review,* spring, 1974, *New York Times Book Review,* March 10, 1974, April 20, 1980; *National Review,* April 26, 1974; *New York Review of Books,* October 17, 1974; *New York Times,* May 19, 1980; *Washington Post Book World,* June 29, 1980.

DEINDORFER, Robert Greene 1922-
(Jay Bender, Jay Dender, Robert Greene)

PERSONAL: Born July 3, 1922, in Galena, Ill.; son of Charles Robert (a dentist) and Marion (Greene) Deindorfer; married Joan Brown (in public relations work), May 4, 1963; children: Scott Greene. *Education:* Attended University of Missouri, 1940-43. *Politics:* Democrat. *Religion:* Episcopalian. *Home:* 114 East 71st St., New York, N.Y. 10021. *Agent:* Knox Burger Associates Ltd., 39½ Washington Sq. S., New York, N.Y. 10012.

CAREER: Free-lance magazine writer, 1949—; New York Stock Exchange, New York City, book, newspaper feature, and magazine manager, 1955-70; Booke & Co., New York City, N.Y. magazine director of media, 1970-73. Taught course in magazine writing, New York University, 1960-61. Consultant, Peace Corps, 1961-65, and Office of Economic Opportunity, 1965-67; public relations advisor, City of New York. *Military service:* U.S. Marine Corps, 1942-43. U.S. Merchant Marine, 1944-45. *Member:* Society of Magazine Writers, National Press Club, New York University Faculty Club.

WRITINGS: The Great Gridiron Plot, Whitman, 1946; *True Spy Stories,* Crest Books, 1961; (with George Ratterman) *Confessions of a Gypsy Quarterback,* Coward, 1962; (with Richard Wilmer Rowan) *Secret Service: 33 Centuries of Espionage,* revised edition (Deindorfer was not associated with earlier edition), Hawthorn, 1967; (editor) *The Spies,* Fawcett, 1969; *Life in Lower Slaughter,* Dutton, 1975; *The Incompleat Angler: Fishing Walten's Water,* Dutton, 1977; *Tall Tales,* Workman Publishing, 1980. Contributor to *Redbook, Ladies' Home Journal, Life, Look, Reader's Digest, Good Housekeeping, This Week, Cosmopolitan, Nation's Business, Pageant, Saturday Review, Parade, Saturday Evening Post, True, Argosy.*

WORK IN PROGRESS: Two books on espionage; magazine articles.

SIDELIGHTS: Research for articles has taken Robert Greene Deindorfer to Europe a number of times, to the Middle East, and to Africa (once for an eighteen-month period).

*   *   *

DeLAET, Sigfried J(an) 1914-

PERSONAL: Born June 15, 1914, in Ghent, Belgium; son of Leopold (a teacher) and Louise (Joski) DeLaet. *Education:* University of Ghent, Litt. Dr., 1937. *Office:* University of Ghent, 2 Blandyenberg, B-9000, Ghent, Belgium.

CAREER: Athenaeum, Alost, Belgium, teacher, 1937-42; University of Ghent, Ghent, Belgium, assistant professor, 1942-47, lecturer, 1947-51, professor of archaeology, 1951—. Member of archaeological excavation expeditions. *Member:* International Union of Prehistoric and Protohistoric Sciences (secretary, 1952—), Royal Flemish Academy of Sciences of Belgium, Prehistoric Society of Great Britain (honorary corresponding member), Society of Antiquaries of Scotland (honorary fellow), Deutsches Archaeologisches Institut, Jysk Arkaeologisk Selskap, Istituto Italiano de Preistoria and Protostoria, Schweizerische Gesellschaft fuer Urgeschichte, Maatchappy der Nederlandse Letterkunde te Leiden, Society of Antiquaries of London (honorary fellow). *Awards, honors:* Commander, Order of Leopold; Great Officer, Order of the Crown.

WRITINGS: De Samenstelling van den Romeinschen Senaat, De Sikkel, 1941; *Aspects de la vie sociale et economique sous Auguste et Tibere,* Office de Publicite (Brussels),

1949; *Portorium, l'organisation Douaniere chez les Romains*, De Tempel, 1949, reprinted Arno 1975; *L'Archeologie et ses problemes*, Latomus, 1954, translation published as *Archaeology and Its Problems*, Macmillan, 1957; *Geschiedenis van Belgie*, De Vlam, 1955, 5th edition, 1976; *The Low Countries*, Praeger, 1958; *La Civilisation des Champs d'Urnes en Flandre*, De Tempel, 1958; (with W. Glasbergen) *De Voorgeschiedenis der Lage Landen*, Wolters, 1959; *Encyclopedie der Geschiedenis (Prehistorie, Oudheid)*, Scientia, 1963; (with J. Dhondt) *Voorgeschiedenis, Oudheid en Vroege Middeleeuwen*, De Vlam, 1963; *La Prehistoire de l'Europe*, Meddens, 1967; *La Necropole gallo-Romaine de Blicquy*, De Tempel, 1972; *Voorhistorische Kulturen in het Zuiden der Lage Landen*, Universa, 1974, 2nd edition, 1979; *Acculturation and Continuity in Atlantic Europe*, De Tempel, 1976; *Le Gue du plantin*, De Tempel, 1977. Editor, *Dissertationes archaeologicae Gandenses* and *Helinium*.

SIDELIGHTS: L'Archeologie et ses problemes has been translated into Dutch, Danish, Swedish, Italian, Spanish, and Polish, as well as into English.

* * *

de LAUNAY, Jacques F(orment) 1924-

PERSONAL: Born January 28, 1924, in Roubaix, France; son of Jean (an industrialist) and Maria (Herman) de Launay; married December 21, 1950, wife's maiden name, Delcroix; children: Marie-Christine. *Education:* University of Lille, Licence en Droit; University of Paris, additional study. *Religion:* Roman Catholic. *Home:* Souverain 209, Brussels, Belgium. *Office:* Helene Boucher, 2, Marcq-en-Baroeul, 59 700, France.

CAREER: French Government, Paris, France, attached to Office of Minister of Public Health, 1946-47; European Movement, Brussels, Belgium, deputy secretary, 1948-51; European Bureau for Youth and Childhood, Brussels, general manager, 1950-63; Transassim-France, Marcq-en-Baroeul, general manager, 1960—. Administrator, Congovoa, Kinshasa, Zaire, 1968-72. *Military service:* French Army, volunteer, 1944-45. *Member:* International Association for the Teaching of History (secretary-general, 1957-72). *Awards, honors:* Medaille de la Resistance.

WRITINGS: Le Monde en guerre, 1939-1945, J. B. Janin, 1945; (with Claude Murat) *Jeunesse d'Europe*, introduction by Andre Gide, France-Empire, 1948; *Fascisme rouge: Contribution a la defense de l'Europe*, Editions Montana, 1954; *The Vocational Training of Young Agricultural Workers in the Member Countries of the E.O.E.C.*, European Bureau for Youth and Childhood, 1954; *European Resistance Movements*, two volumes, Pergamon, 1960; *L'Education professionnelle en Europe meridionale*, H. & M. Schaumans, 1960; *La Formation des formateurs*, Societe d'Etudes et d'Expansion, 1961; (editor) Louis Loucheur, *Carnets secrets, 1908-1932*, Brepols, 1962; *Secrets diplomatiques*, Brepols, 1963, Volume I: *1914-1918*, Volume II, *1939-1945*, translation by Edouard Nadier published as *Secret Diplomacy of World War II*, Simmons-Boardman, 1963; (with Henri Bernard, Georges-Andre Chevallaz, and Roger Gheysens) *Les Dossiers de la seconde guerre mondiale*, Marabout Universite, 1964; *Les Grandes controverses de l'histoire contemporaine*, Editions Recontre, Volume I: *1914-1945*, 1964, translation by J. J. Buckingham published as *Major Controversies of Contemporary History*, Pergamon, 1965, Volume II: *1789-1914*, 1973; *Le Congres de Vienne et l'Europe*, Brepols, 1964, translation by J. Granger published as *The Congress of Vienna and Europe*, Pergamon, 1964.

Histoire contemporaine de la diplomatie secrete, 1914-1945, Editions Rencontre, 1965; *Emile Mayrisch et la politique du patronat europeen, 1926-1933*, P. de Meyere, 1965; *Napoleon III and Europe*, Pergamon, 1965; *Les Deux guerres mondiales*, Brepols, 1965, translation by J. Granger published as *Two World Wars*, Pergamon, 1965; *Histoire de la diplomatie secrete, 1789-1914*, Editions Rencontre, 1966; *Le Dossier de Vichy*, Julliard, 1967; *Les Grandes controverses du temps present, 1945-1965*, Editions Rencontre, 1967; *Les Derniers jours du fascisme*, Dargaud, 1968; *Napoleon: Un Portrait psychopolitique*, P. de Meyer, 1968; *De Gaulle et sa France*, Dargaud, 1968, translation by Dorothy Albertyn published as *De Gaulle and His France: A Political and Historical Portrait*, Julian Press, 1968; *Les Derniers jours de nazisme*, Dargaud, 1969; (with Gheysens) *Histoire de la guerre psychologique et secrete, 1939-1963*, Editions Rencontre, 1970; (with M. Kajima, V. Pons, and A. Zurcher) *Coudenhove-Kalergi*, Centre de Recherches Europeenes, 1971; *La France de Petain* (also see below), Nachette, 1972; *Les Morts mysterieuses de l'histoire contemporaine*, Editions Rencontre, 1973; (with Gheysens) *Les Grands espions de notre temps*, Editions Rencontre, 1973; *Psychologie et sexualite des grands contemporains*, Editions Rencontre, 1973; (editor) *Dictionnaire biographique d'histoire contemporaine*, Editions Rencontre, 1973; *Les grandes decisions de la 2e guerre mondiale*, introductions by G. A. Craig, G. A. Chevallaz, and G. Vedovato, Edito-Service, 1973.

Histoires secretes de la Belgique, A. Moreau, 1975; *Hitler en Flandres*, Byblos, 1975; *Titulescu et l'Europe*, Byblos, 1976; *Polices secretes et secrets de police*, Editions de l'Esperance, 1976; *La Belgique a l'heure allemande*, P. Legrain, 1977; *Les Derniers jours du fascisme en Europe*, Albatros, 1977; *Eva Hitler, nee Braun* (also see below), La Table Ronde, 1978. Also author of screenplays "Le Temps des Doryphores," with D. Remy (based on book *La France de Petain*), produced by Actualites francaises, 1967, and "Eva Hitler, nee Braun," with J. M. Charlier (based on book of same title), produced by Technisonor, 1978.

WORK IN PROGRESS: Grandes controverses de l'histoire: De la Genese a 1789; Histoires secretes de la Scandinavie, 1939-1945; Psychologie et sexualite des grandes contemporaines, 1789-1989.

* * *

DeLEEUW, Cateau 1903-1975
(Kay Hamilton, Jessica Lyon)

PERSONAL: Born September 22, 1903, in Hamilton, Ohio; died June 2, 1975; daughter of Adolph Lodewyk (a consulting engineer) and Katherine (Bender) DeLeeuw. *Education:* Attended Metropolitan Art School, 1920-21, and Art Students' League, 1924-25. *Home:* 1763 Sleepy Hollow Lane, Plainfield, N.J. 07060.

CAREER: Illustrator and writer. *Member:* Pen and Brush Club, American Artists Professional League, Ohio Historical Society, New York State Historical Association, Plainfield Art Association (founder; first president; honorary member), Listentome Club. *Awards, honors:* Joint citation with Adele DeLeeuw from Martha Kinney Cooper Ohioana Library Association, 1958, for "outstanding work over the years for children."

WRITINGS: The Dutch East Indies and the Philippines, Holiday House, 1943; *Hurricane Heart*, Arcadia, 1943; *A Day to Come*, Arcadia, 1944; *William Tyndale*, Association Press, 1955; *One Week of Danger*, Thomas Nelson, 1959; *Give Me Your Hand* (Junior Literary Guild selection), Little,

Brown, 1960; *Fear in the Forest* (*Weekly Reader* Children's Book Club selection), Thomas Nelson, 1960; *The Turn in the Road*, Thomas Nelson, 1961; *Against All Others*, Ward, Lock, 1961; *The Proving Years*, Thomas Nelson, 1962; *Determined to be Free*, Thomas Nelson, 1963; *Roald Amundsen*, Garrard, 1965; *Truth to Tell*, Whitman Publishing, 1965; *Benedict Arnold*, Putnam, 1970.

With sister, Adele DeLeeuw: *Anim Runs Away*, Macmillan, 1938; *Mickey the Monkey*, Little, Brown, 1952; *Make Your Habits Work For You* (Executive Book Club selection), Farrar, Straus, 1952; *Hideaway House*, Little, Brown, 1953; *The Expandable Browns*, Little, Brown, 1955; *Showboat's Coming!*, World Publishing, 1956; *The Caboose Club*, Little, Brown, 1957; *Breakneck Betty*, World Publishing, 1957; *The Strange Garden*, Little, Brown, 1958; *Apron Strings*, World Publishing, 1959; *Where Valor Lies* (Catholic Youth Book Club selection), Doubleday, 1959; *Love Is the Beginning*, World Publishing, 1960; *Nurses Who Led the Way*, Whitman Publishing, 1961; *The Salty Skinners*, Little, Brown, 1964; *Anthony Wayne: Washington's General*, Westminster, 1974.

Under pseudonym Kay Hamilton; all published by Macrae, except as indicated: *The Doctor on Elm Street*, 1947; *Love Is Where You Find It*, 1947; *Young Doctor Glenn*, 1948; *The Gentle Heart*, 1949; *Doctor Alice's Daughter*, 1950; *Portrait by Kathie*, 1951; *The Loves of Holly Bennett*, Foulsham, 1953; *A Home for Doctor T.*, Ward, Lock, 1960.

Under pseudonym Jessica Lyon; all published by Macrae, except as indicated: *Betty Loring—Illustrator* (Junior Literary Guild selection), Messner, 1948; *For a Whole Lifetime*, 1949; *From This Day Forward*, 1951; *This My Desire*, 1952; *Bright Gold*, 1953; *To Have and Not Hold*, 1954; *Not For One Alone*, 1955; *The Proud Air*, 1956; *The Given Heart*, 1957.

SIDELIGHTS: Cateau DeLeeuw told *CA* that she began as a portrait painter, then illustrated her sister Adele's stories before taking up writing herself. *Avocational interests:* Original needlepoint and making jewelry.†

*   *   *

de LONGCHAMPS, Joanne (Cutten) 1923-

PERSONAL: Born January 7, 1923, in Los Angeles, Calif.; daughter of Alfred Beverly (a building contractor) and Ruth (Avery) Cutten; married Galen Edward de Longchamps (a teacher), January 21, 1941; children: Galen Dare. *Education:* Attended Los Angeles City College, 1939-40, and University of Nevada, 1941-47, 1956-62. *Politics:* Democrat. *Home:* 821 North Center St., Reno, Nev. 89501. *Office address:* P.O. Box 2526, Reno, Nev. 89505.

CAREER: Poet and painter. Has taught classes in poetry; lecturer at University of Nevada, 1962, 1971, 1972, and 1973. Paintings and collages exhibited at local and regional shows, 1941—. *Member:* Poetry Society of America. *Awards, honors:* Reynolds Lyric Award, Poetry Society of America, 1954; *Carolina Quarterly* annual award, University of North Carolina, 1959.

WRITINGS—Poems: *And Ever Venus*, Wagon & Star, 1944; *Eden under Glass* (Book Club for Poetry selection), Golden Quill, 1957; *The Hungry Lions*, Indiana University Press, 1963; *The Wishing Animal*, Vanderbilt University Press, 1970; *The Schoolhouse Poems*, West Coast Poetry Review, 1975; *One Creature*, West Coast Poetry Review, 1977; *Warm-Bloods, Cold Bloods*, West Coast Poetry Review, 1981. Poetry represented in several anthologies, including *Southern Poetry Review: A Decade of Poems*, edited by Guy

Owen, Southern Poetry Review Press, 1969, and *The New York Times Book of Verse*, edited by Thomas Lask, Macmillan, 1970. Contributor of poems to *Accent*, *American Scholar*, *Antioch Review*, *Contact*, *Poetry*, *Prairie Schooner*, *San Francisco Review*, *Sparrow*, *Trace*, *Voices*, and other publications. Associate editor, *Destinies*, 1944.

WORK IN PROGRESS: A new book of poems.

SIDELIGHTS: Joanne de Longchamps writes *CA:* "'There is no intensity without rules, limits, and artifice.' This quotation is a jotting in my current workbook. It reflects my feelings about poem-making, past and present. I have always suggested that one cannot successfully break rules, innovate, unless the rules are known. The mystery of art is the presence of form; and new forms are waiting to be made.

"It is a cliche that there can be no freedom without discipline. How that word can rankle, implying as it does restriction, even punishment. I propose positive definitions for discipline: It can be the liberating factor; it is choosing to know, to learn; it is the capacity for paying attention, for sensing a saving order in the chaos of living and the clutter of words."

*   *   *

DEMING, Richard 1915-
(Max Franklin)

PERSONAL: Born April 25, 1915, in Des Moines, Iowa; son of Fred Kemp (a history teacher) and Erva Pearl (Smyers) Deming; married Ruth Lorraine DuBois; children: Tracey Lou, Barbara, Patricia. *Education:* Attended Central Methodist College, Fayette, Mo., two years; Washington University, A.B., 1937; University of Iowa, M.A., 1939. *Religion:* Unitarian. *Address:* P.O. Box 3129, Ventura, Calif. 93003. *Agent:* Scott Meredith Literary Agency, Inc., 845 Third Ave., New York, N.Y. 10022.

CAREER: Social worker in St. Louis, Mo., 1939-41; American National Red Cross, Dunkirk, N.Y., chapter manager, 1945-50; free-lance writer, 1946—. *Military service:* U.S. Army, 1941-45; served in European theater; became captain. *Member:* Mystery Writers of America, American Legion, Masons, Elks. *Awards, honors:* Distinguished alumni citation from Central Methodist College, 1958.

WRITINGS: *The Gallows in My Garden*, Rinehart, 1952; *Tweak the Devil's Nose*, Rinehart, 1953; *Whistle Past the Graveyard*, Rinehart, 1954; *Dragnet* (juvenile), Whitman Publishing, 1957; *Dragnet: The Case of the Courteous Killer*, Pocket Books, 1958; *Dragnet: The Case of the Crime King*, Pocket Books, 1959; *Fall Girl*, Zenith, 1959; *Walk a Crooked Mile*, Boardman, 1959; *Hit and Run*, Pocket Books, 1960; *Kiss and Kill*, Zenith, 1960; *American Spies* (juvenile), Whitman Publishing, 1960; *Edge of the Law*, Berkley Publishing, 1960; *This Is My Night*, Monarch Books, 1961; *Vice Cop*, Belmont Books, 1961; *Body for Sale*, Pocket Books, 1962; *The Careful Man*, W. H. Allen, 1962; *Anything but Saintly*, Pocket Books, 1963; *She'll Hate Me Tomorrow*, Monarch Books, 1963; *Famous Investigators* (juvenile), Whitman Publishing, 1963; *Death of a Pusher*, Pocket Books, 1964; *This Game of Murder*, Monarch Books, 1964; *The Police Lab at Work*, Bobbs-Merrill, 1967; *Heroes of the International Red Cross*, Meredith Press, 1969; *Man and Society: Criminal Law at Work*, Hawthorn, 1970; *Big Jake*, Paperback Library, 1971; *What's the Matter with Helen?*, Beagle Books, 1971; *Man against Man: Civil Law at Work*, Hawthorn, 1972; *Sleep: Our Unknown Life*, Thomas Nelson, 1972; *Vida*, Lancer, 1972; *Man and the World: International Law at Work*, Hawthorn, 1974; *Metric Power: Why and How We Are Going Metric*, Thomas Nelson, 1974; *Women: The*

New Criminals, Thomas Nelson, 1977; *The Paralegal*, Elsevier/Nelson, 1980.

"The Mod Squad" series; published by Pyramid Publications, except as indicated: *The Mod Squad: The Greek God Affair*, 1968; . . . *A Groovy Way to Die*, 1968; . . . *The Sock-It-to-Em-Murders*, 1969; . . . *Spy-In*, 1969; . . . *Assignment, the Arranger*, Whitman Publishing, 1969; . . . *The Hit*, 1970; . . . *Assignment, the Hideout*, Whitman Publishing, 1970.

Under pseudonym Max Franklin: *Justice Has No Sword*, Rinehart, 1953; *Hell Street*, Rinehart, 1954; *99 44/100% Dead*, Award, 1974; *The Destructors*, Ballantine, 1974; *The Fifth of November*, Ballantine, 1975; *Baby Blue Marine*, New American Library, 1976; *The Last of the Cowboys*, New American Library, 1977; *Good Guys Wear Black*, New American Library, 1978; *The Dark*, New American Library, 1978; *Vega$*, Ballantine, 1978.

"Starsky and Hutch" series; published by Ballantine: *Starsky and Hutch*, 1975; *Starsky and Hutch #2: Kill Huggy Bear*, 1976; . . . *#3: Death Ride*, 1976; . . . *#4: Bounty Hunter*, 1977; . . . *#5: Terror on the Docks*, 1977; . . . *#6: The Psychic*, 1977; . . . *#7: The Setup*, 1978; . . . *#8: Murder on Playboy Island*, 1978.

"Charlie's Angels" series; published by Ballantine: *Charlie's Angels*, 1977; *Charlie's Angels #2: The Killing Kind*, 1977; . . . *#3: Angels on a String*, 1977; . . . *#4: Angels in Chains*, 1977; . . . *#5: Angels on Ice*, 1978.

Has written for television and films. Work represented in mystery, crime, western, and science fiction anthologies, including seven editions of *Best Detective Stories of the Year*, published by Dutton. Contributor of several hundred short stories and short novels to numerous magazines.

AVOCATIONAL INTERESTS: Swimming, fishing, bowling, and travel.

* * *

DERRY, John W(esley) 1933-

PERSONAL: Born January 27, 1933, in Gateshead, Durham, England; son of Hugh McDonald (a vanman) and Sarah Isabella (Turner) Derry. *Education:* Emmanuel College, Cambridge, B.A., 1954, M.A., 1958, Ph.D., 1961. *Politics:* Independent. *Religion:* United Reformed Church. *Home:* 116 Wingate Rd., Newcastle-upon-Tyne, England. *Agent:* Bolt & Watson Ltd., 8-12 Old Queen St., Storey's Gate, London SW1H 9HP, England. *Office:* Department of History, University of Newcastle-upon-Tyne, Newcastle-upon-Tyne NE4 9BT, England.

CAREER: London School of Economics and Political Science, London, England, assistant lecturer in political science, 1961-63, lecturer in political science, 1963-65; Cambridge University, Downing College, Cambridge, England, fellow in and assistant director of studies in history, 1965-70; University of Newcastle-upon-Tyne, Newcastle-upon-Tyne, England, lecturer, 1970-73, senior lecturer, 1973-77, reader in history, 1977—.

WRITINGS: William Pitt, Batsford, 1962; *A Short History of 19th Century England, 1793-1868*, New American Library, 1963; *The Regency Crisis and the Whigs, 1788-1789*, Cambridge University Press, 1963; *The Radical Tradition*, St. Martin's, 1967; *Parliamentary Reform*, Macmillan, 1966; *Political Parties*, Macmillan, 1968; *Bobbett's England*, Folio, 1968; *Charles James Fox*, Batsford, 1972; *Castlereagh*, Lane, 1976; *English Politics and the American Revolution*, Dent, 1976.

WORK IN PROGRESS: A biography, *Earl Arey of the Reform Bill*.

AVOCATIONAL INTERESTS: Music, especially Wagner, Mozart, Strauss, and Britten; literature, drama and poetry, especially Shakespeare, Donne, T. S. Eliot, and W. B. Yeats; the theological writings of P. T. Forsyth; cricket as a spectator sport.

* * *

DEWEY, Ariane 1937-
(Ariane Aruego)

PERSONAL: Born August 17, 1937, in Chicago, Ill.; daughter of Charles S. Dewey, Jr. and Marjorie (Goodman) Graff; married Jose E. Aruego, Jr. (an author and illustrator), 1961 (divorced, 1973); married Claus Dannasch, 1976; children: (first marriage) Juan. *Education:* Sarah Lawrence College, B.A., 1959. *Residence:* New York, N.Y.

CAREER: Harcourt, Brace & World, Inc., New York, N.Y., researcher and art editor for children's textbooks, 1964-65; free-lance writer and illustrator of children's books, 1969—. Performer with "Artists in Process Improvisational Dance Group," 1973-74.

AWARDS, HONORS: A Crocodile's Tale was named to the American Institute of Graphic Arts' (AIGA) list of children's books of the year, 1972, and was a Children's Book Council Showcase title, 1973; *The Chick and the Duckling* was a Children's Book Council Showcase title, 1973; *Milton the Early Riser* was an American Library Association (ALA) Notable Book of 1972 and received a citation of merit from the Society of Illustrators; *Mushroom in the Rain* was an ALA Notable Book of 1974, was named to the AIGA list of children's books of the year, 1974, was an International Reading Association-Children's Book Council (IRA-CBC) Classroom Choice, 1974, and received a Gold Medal at the Internationale Buchkunst-Ausstellung (Leipzig), 1977; *Marie Louise and Christophe* was named to the AIGA list of children's books of the year, 1974, and was an IRA-CBC Classroom Choice, 1974; *Herman the Helper* was a *Boston-Globe*-Horn Book Honor Book, 1974, and an IRA-CBC Classroom Choice, 1974; *Owliver* was an IRA-CBC Classroom Choice, 1974, an ALA Notable Book of 1974, a Children's Book Council Showcase title, 1975, and received a citation of merit from the Society of Illustrators; *Two Greedy Bears* was an IRA-CBC Classroom Choice, 1977; *The Strongest One of All* was an IRA-CBC Classroom Choice, 1978; *Rum Pum Pum* was an IRA-CBC Classroom Choice, 1979; *We Hide, You Seek* was an ALA Notable Book of 1979 and an IRA-CBC Classroom Choice, 1980.

WRITINGS—Self-illustrated: The Fish Peri: A Turkish Folk Tale, Macmillan, 1979; *The Thunder God's Son: A Peruvian Folk Tale*, Greenwillow, 1981.

Self-illustrated with Jose Aruego; all under name Ariane Dewey, except as indicated: *The King and His Friends*, Scribner, 1969; *Juan and the Asuangs: A Tale of Philippine Ghosts and Spirits*, Scribner, 1970; *Symbiosis: A Book of Unusual Friendships*, Scribner, 1970; *Pilyo the Piranha*, Macmillan, 1971; *Look What I Can Do*, Scribner, 1971; (under name Ariane Aruego) *A Crocodile's Tale*, Scribner, 1972; *We Hide, You Seek*, Greenwillow, 1979.

Illustrator; all with Jose Aruego; all under name Ariane Dewey, except as indicated: Robert Kraus, *Whose Mouse Are You?*, Macmillan, 1970; Kay Smith, *Parakeets and Peace Pies*, Parents' Magazine Press, 1970; Jack Prelutsky, *Toucans Two and Other Poems*, Macmillan, 1971; Charlotte

Pomerantz, *The Day They Parachuted Cats on Borneo*, Young Scott Books, 1971; Kraus, *Leo the Late Bloomer*, Windmill Books, 1971; Christina Rossetti, *What Is Pink?*, Macmillan, 1971; Elizabeth Coatsworth, *Good Night*, Macmillan, 1972; (under name Ariane Aruego) Mirra Ginsburg, *The Chick and the Duckling*, Macmillan, 1972; (under name Ariane Aruego) Kraus, *Milton the Early Riser*, Windmill Books, 1972; Ginsburg, *Mushroom in the Rain*, Macmillan, 1974; Natalie Savage Carlson, *Marie Louise and Christophe*, Scribner, 1974; Kraus, *Herman the Helper*, Windmill Books, 1974; Kraus, *Owliver*, Windmill Books, 1974.

Ginsburg, *How the Sun Was Brought Back to the Sky*, Macmillan, 1975; Dorothy O. Van Woerkom, *Sea Frog, City Frog*, Macmillan, 1975; Carlson, *Marie Louise's Heyday*, Scribner, 1975; Kraus, *Three Friends*, Windmill Books, 1975; Ginsburg, *Two Greedy Bears*, Macmillan, 1976; Kraus, *Boris Bad Enough*, Windmill Books, 1976; Ginsburg, *The Strongest One of All*, Greenwillow, 1977; Carlson, *Runaway Marie Louise*, Scribner, 1977; David Kherdian, editor, *If Dragon Flies Made Honey* (poetry collection), Greenwillow, 1977; Kraus, *Noel the Coward*, Windmill Books, 1977; Maggie Duff, *Rum Pum Pum*, Macmillan, 1978; Marjorie Weinman Sharmat, *Mitchell Is Moving*, Macmillan, 1978; Mitchell Sharmat, *Gregory the Terrible Eater*, Four Winds, 1980; Kraus, *Another Mouse to Feed*, Windmill Books, 1980; Ginsburg, *Where Does the Sun Go at Night?*, Greenwillow, 1980; Kraus, *Mert the Blurt*, Windmill Books, 1980; George Shannon, *Lizard's Song*, Greenwillow, 1981.

WORK IN PROGRESS: Illustrating, with Jose Aruego, George Shannon's *Dance Away* and Natalie Savage Carlson's *Marie Louise and Christophe at the Carnival*, as well as new books by Robert Kraus; doing research on folk tales to retell and illustrate.

*   *   *

Di CESARE, Mario A(nthony)   1928-

PERSONAL: Born August 21, 1928, in New York, N.Y.; son of Donato (a tailor) and Virginia (DiPleco) Di Cesare; married Emily Bell, June 13, 1954 (divorced, 1969); married Carol-Lee Hoskins, 1969; children: nine. *Education:* St. Mary's Seminary, Techny, Ill., B.A., 1952; Indiana University, graduate study, 1953-54; Columbia University, M.A., 1954, Ph.D., 1960. *Politics:* Liberal. *Religion:* Roman Catholic. *Home:* 69 Bennett Ave., Binghamton, N.Y. 13905. *Office:* Department of English, State University of New York, Binghamton, N.Y. 13901.

CAREER: Duquesne University, Pittsburgh, Pa., instructor in English, 1954-55; Pratt Institute, Brooklyn, N.Y., instructor, 1955-59; State University of New York at Binghamton, instructor, 1959-61, assistant professor, 1961-64, associate professor of English, 1964-68, professor of English and comparative literature, 1968—, co-director, Program in Comparative Literature, 1966-67, chairman of English department, 1968-73. Lecturer at Rutgers University, 1957-58, summer, 1961, and Brooklyn College of the City University of New York, summers, 1959, 1960, and 1961; visiting associate professor at New York University, summer, 1965, and University of Pittsburgh, summer, 1969. *Member:* Modern Language Association of America, American Association of University Professors, Renaissance Society of America, Consumers Union. *Awards, honors:* Fellowships from State University of New York Research Foundation, 1962, 1963, 1965, and 1966, Guggenheim Foundation, 1963-64, Robert Frost Library, Amherst College, 1976, and National Endowment for the Humanities, 1976-77.

WRITINGS: Vida's Christiad and Vergilian Epic, Columbia University Press, 1964; (translator with Rigo Mignani) Juan Ruiz, *The Book of Good Love*, State University of New York Press, 1970; *Bibliotheca Vidiana: A Complete Bibliography*, Sansoni, 1974; *The Alter and the City: A Reading of Vergil's "Aeneid,"* Columbia University Press, 1974; (editor with Mignani) *A Concordance to the Complete Writings of George Herbert*, Cornell University Press, 1977; (editor with Ephim Fogel) *A Concordance to the Poems of Ben Johnson*, Cornell University Press, 1978; *George Herbert and Seventeenth-Century Religious Poets*, Norton, 1978. Also editor of a concordance to the works of Juan Ruiz, for State University of New York Press, 1977. Director and general editor, "Medieval and Renaissance Texts and Studies" series.

WORK IN PROGRESS: A book, *The Poetics of Epic; Concordance to Christopher Marlowe*, with Robert Fehrenbach and Lea Ann Boone; a reference work, *Vergil in the Renaissance*, with G. N. Knauer.

AVOCATIONAL INTERESTS: Reading occasional mystery stories; "spasmodic do-it-yourself household repairs."

*   *   *

DICKINSON, Patric Thomas   1914-

PERSONAL: Born December 26, 1914, in Nasirabad, India; son of Arthur Thomas (an army officer) and Eileen (Kirwan) Dickinson; married Sheila Shannon (an editor and anthologist), December 19, 1947; children: David Dunbar, Virginia Kirwan. *Education:* St. Catharine's College, Cambridge, B.A. (with honors), 1936. *Home:* 38 Church Square, Rye, Sussex, England.

CAREER: Schoolmaster, 1936-39; British Broadcasting Corp., London, England, producer, Transcription Service, 1942-45, poetry editor, Home Service and Third Programme, 1945-48; free-lance writer, broadcaster, and critic, 1948—. Gresham Professor of Rhetoric, City University, London, 1964-67; lecturer and reader. Director, Poetry Festival, Royal Court Theater, 1963. *Member:* Savile Club. *Awards, honors:* Atlantic award in literature, 1948; Cholmondeley Award, 1973.

WRITINGS—Poems, except as indicated: The Seven Days of Jericho, Andrew Dakers, 1944; *Theseus and the Minotaur, and Poems* (also see below), J. Cape, 1946; *Stone in the Midst, and Poems* (also see below), Methuen, 1948; *A Round of Golf Courses: A Selection of the Best Eighteen* (guide), Evans Brothers, 1951; *The Sailing Race, and Other Poems*, Chatto & Windus, 1952; *The Scale of Things*, Chatto & Windus, 1955;

The World I See, Chatto & Windus, 1960, Dufour, 1962; *This Cold Universe*, Chatto & Windus, 1964; *The Good Minute: An Autobiographical Study*, Gollancz, 1965; *Selected Poems*, Chatto & Windus, 1968; *More Than Time*, Chatto & Windus, 1970, Wesleyan University Press, 1971; *A Wintering Tree*, Chatto & Windus, 1973; *The Bearing Beast*, Chatto & Windus, 1976; *Our Living John*, Chatto & Windus, 1979; *Poems from Rye*, Martello Bookshop, 1980.

Editor, except as indicated: *Soldier's Verse* (anthology), Muller, 1945; (and author of introduction) Byron, *Poems*, Grey Walls Press, 1949; (with wife, Sheila Shannon) *Personal Portraits*, Parrish, 1950; (with Erica Marx and J. C. Hall) *New Poems 1955*, M. Joseph, 1955; *Poetry Supplement*, Poetry Book Society, 1958; (with Shannon) *Poems to Remember: A Book for Children* (anthology), Harvill, 1958; (translator) Virgil, *The Aeneid*, New American Library,

1962; (with Shannon) *Poets' Choice: An Anthology of English Poetry from Spenser to the Present Day*, Evans Brothers, 1967; (and author of introduction and notes) C. Day Lewis, *Selections from His Poetry*, Chatto & Windus, 1967.

Plays: *Stone in the Midst* (first produced in London at Mercury Theatre, 1951), published in *Stone in the Midst, and Poems*, Methuen, 1948; (adaptor) Jules Supervielle, "Robinson," produced in London, 1953; "The Golden Touch," first produced in Wolverhampton, England, 1956; (translator) Aristophanes, *Aristophanes against War: Three Plays* (contains "The Acharnians," "The Peace," and "Lysistrata"), Oxford University Press, 1957; *A Durable Fire* (first produced in Canterbury, England at Canterbury Festival, 1962), Chatto & Windus, 1962; (adaptor) Plautus, "Pseudolus," produced in Stoke on Trent, England, 1966; (translator) Aristophanes, *The Complete Plays*, two volumes, Oxford University Press, 1970. Also author or adaptor of radio plays *Theseus and the Minotaur*, 1945 (published in *Theseus and the Minotaur, and Poems*, J. Cape, 1946), "The First Family," 1960, "Wilfred Owen," 1970, and "The Pensive Prisoner," 1970, and of television play "Lysistrata," 1964.

Librettos: (With Bernard Rose) "Ode to St. Catherine," produced in Cambridge, England, 1973; (with Alan Ridout) "Creation," produced in Ely, England, 1973; (with Stephen Dodgson) "The Miller's Secret," produced in Cookham, England, 1973. Also author of "The Return of Odysseus," with Malcolm Arnold, and "Good King Wenceslaus," with Ridout.

AVOCATIONAL INTERESTS: Collecting Sunderland lustre pottery and playing golf.

BIOGRAPHICAL/CRITICAL SOURCES: Times Literary Supplement, August 24, 1967, April 4, 1980; *New Statesman*, February 28, 1969, September 25, 1970; *Poetry*, September, 1969; *London Magazine*, October, 1969.

* * *

DICKINSON, Robert Eric 1905-

PERSONAL: Born February 9, 1905, in Manchester, England; son of William and Mary (Jones) Dickinson; married Mary Winwood, 1941. *Education:* University of Leeds, B.A. and M.A. (with honors in geography), 1926; University of London, Ph.D., 1932. *Religion:* Church of England. *Home:* 636 Roller Coaster Rd., Tucson, Ariz. 85705.

CAREER: University College (now University of Exeter), Exeter, England, assistant lecturer, 1926-28; University of London, University College, London, England, 1928-47, began as lecturer, became reader; Syracuse University, Syracuse, N.Y., professor of geography, 1947-58; University of Leeds, Leeds, England, professor and head of department, 1958-67; affiliated with University of Arizona, Tucson, 1967-75. Visiting professor at University of California, Berkeley, 1960-61, University of Washington, Seattle, summer, 1961, and 1964, University of Minnesota, 1963, and University of Nebraska, 1963-64. *Military service:* Royal Air Force, Intelligence Service, 1941-45; became squadron leader. *Member:* Association of American Geographers, Royal Geographical Society (fellow), American Geographical Society (fellow). *Awards, honors:* Rockefeller Foundation traveling fellowships, 1931-32 and 1936-37; Guggenheim fellowship, 1957-58.

WRITINGS: (With O.J.R. Howarth) *Making of Geography*, Oxford University Press, 1932, reprinted, Greenwood Press, 1976; *Regions of Germany*, Routledge & Kegan Paul, 1943; *The German Lebensraum*, Penguin, 1943; *City, Region and Regionalism*, Routledge & Kegan Paul, 1947; *West Euro-*pean City*, Routledge & Kegan Paul, 1951, 2nd edition, Humanities, 1963; *Germany: A General and Regional Geography*, Methuen, 1953; *The Population Problem of Southern Italy: An Essay in Social Geography*, Syracuse University Press, 1955, reprinted, Greenwood Press, 1977; *City and Region: A Geographical Interpretation*, Humanities, 1964, abridged edition published as *City Region in Western Europe*, 1967; *Makers of Modern Geography*, Praeger, 1969; *Regional Ecology: The Study of Man's Environment*, Wiley, 1970; *Environments of America*, Vantage, 1974; *The Regional Concept: Anglo-American Leaders*, Routledge & Kegan Paul, 1976.

* * *

DIETZ, Lew 1907-

PERSONAL: Born May 22, 1907, in Pittsburgh, Pa.; son of Louis Andrew (an engineer) and Bertha Anne (Staiger) Dietz; married Denny Winters (a painter). *Education:* Attended New York University, 1927-30. *Politics:* Democrat. *Residence:* Rockport, Me. *Agent:* Curtis Brown Ltd., 575 Madison Ave., New York, N.Y. 10022.

CAREER: Crowell Publishing Co., New York, N.Y., copywriter, 1930-33; *Camden Herald*, Camden, Me., editor, 1948-49; writer. Past member, Maine State Commission on the Arts and Humanities. Chairman, Rockport Conservation Committee.

WRITINGS—Published by Little, Brown, except as indicated: *Jeff White: Young Woodsman*, 1949; *Jeff White: Young Trapper*, 1950; *Jeff White: Young Guide*, 1952; *Jeff White: Young Lumberjack*, 1954; *Jeff White: Forest Fire Fighter*, 1956; *Pines for the King's Navy*, 1958; *Full Fathom Five*, 1959; *Wilderness River*, 1961; *Savage Summer*, 1964; *The Allagash*, Holt, 1968; *Touch of Wildness: A Maine Woods Journal*, Holt, 1970; *The Year of the Big Cat*, 1970; (with Harry Goodridge) *A Seal Called Andre*, Praeger, 1975; *Night Train at Miscasset Station*, Doubleday, 1978. Assistant editor, *Maine Coast Fisherman*, 1959-61, and *Outdoor Maine*, 1961-62.

WORK IN PROGRESS: The Stranger.

SIDELIGHTS: "The Return of the Big Cat," a film adaptation of Lew Dietz's *The Year of the Big Cat*, was produced by Walt Disney Studios. *Avocational interests:* Hunting and fishing, and studying natural history and marine biology.

BIOGRAPHICAL/CRITICAL SOURCES: Popular Writing in America, Oxford University Press, 1974.

* * *

DILLARD, Annie 1945-

PERSONAL: Born April 30, 1945, in Pittsburgh, Pa.; daughter of Frank and Pam (Lambert) Doak; married Richard Henry Wilde Dillard (a poet and novelist), June 5, 1965 (divorced, 1975); married Gary Clevidence (a novelist), April 12, 1980. *Education:* Hollins College, B.A., 1967, M.A., 1968. *Agent:* Blanche Gregory, 2 Tudor City Place, New York, N.Y. 10017.

CAREER: Writer. Teacher of poetry and creative writing, Western Washington State University; distinguished visiting professor, Wesleyan University, 1979-81. Member of board of advisors, Ossabaw Island Project. *Member:* Authors Guild, P.E.N., Poetry Society of America, Phi Beta Kappa. *Awards, honors:* Pulitzer Prize for general nonfiction, 1974, for *Pilgrim at Tinker Creek;* Washington State Governor's Award for Literature, 1978.

WRITINGS: Tickets for a Prayer Wheel (poems), University of Missouri Press, 1974; *Pilgrim at Tinker Creek,* Harper's Magazine Press, 1974; *Holy the Firm,* Harper, 1978. Columnist, *Living Wilderness,* 1973-75. Contributor to *Atlantic Monthly, Prose, American Scholar, Poetry, Harper's, Chicago Review, Antaeus,* and other periodicals. Contributing editor, *Harper's,* 1973—.

SIDELIGHTS: Few young writers know the pleasure of having their first published prose receive widespread critical acclaim. Fewer still are awarded a major literary prize for this same work. Annie Dillard's *Pilgrim at Tinker Creek,* however, inspired several favorable comparisons with no less than Thoreau's *Walden* and also won a Pulitzer Prize in 1974.

Describing herself as "a poet and a walker with a background in theology and a penchant for quirky facts," Dillard reveals early in the book her intention to present "what Thoreau called 'a meteorological journal of the mind'"; that is, a detailed account of a period of solitude spent in communion with nature and in deep meditation. As a *Commentary* critic observes, *Pilgrim at Tinker Creek* belongs "squarely in the American tradition of essayistic narratives in which one person, unencumbered by *idees recues,* stripped of conventional prejudices, tries to 'front the essential facts,' to make sense of the universe starting from degree zero."

Continues the critic: "One of the most pleasing traits of the book is the graceful harmony between scrutiny of real phenomena and the reflections to which that gives rise. Anecdotes of animal behavior become so effortlessly enlarged into symbols by the deepened insight of meditation. Like a true transcendentalist, Miss Dillard understands her task to be that of full alertness, of making herself a conscious receptacle of all impressions. She is a connoisseur of spirit, who knows that seeing, if intense enough, becomes vision."

Furthermore, states the critic, Dillard's meditations appear even more attractive to the reader due to the beauty of her language, "which is scrupulously precise, unpretentiously lyrical, and sometimes charged with power of concentrated perception. Most of the natural lore which she chooses to relate is fascinating enough in itself, and Miss Dillard has a good eye for its most dramatic elements. . . . She has the rare ability to recreate the emotional tone of experience without abandoning accuracy or specificity of detail."

Eleanor B. Wymard of *Commonweal* sees strains of existentialism rather than transcendentalism in *Pilgrim at Tinker Creek.* After pointing out that Dillard is firmly convinced that "beauty and violence are equal parts of the mystery of creation," she notes: "As her narrative develops, [the author] grows comfortable with ambiguity, accepting the senseless ways of nature while scrupulously describing it. Fidelity to horrible detail makes her celebration of life startling, for her style is so careful of the minute that her theme, in comparison, borders on the irrational. How can one be a believer while portraying honestly the chaotic ways of nature? . . . Dillard is exploring, in truth, not merely the woodland of Tinker Creek, but, more profoundly, what it means to be a believer in God. . . . By insisting that human beings have the visionary capacity to see both the beauty and the violence of the world with new eyes, Dillard is different from the traditional Transcendentalist. Although the 'anchorhold' at Tinker Creek reminds one inevitably of Walden Pond, Dillard is closer to Melville than to Thoreau. Her awareness of both light and darkness is profound. . . . [She] witnesses to the existential condition as nature reveals it, begging us to see it with her, for freedom to Annie Dillard lies in acute awareness of the terms of life. She does not intend her hermitage at Tinker Creek to stand as a political statement nor to inspire ethical behavior or social reform. If she has a mission, it is purely that of the Christian artist: to offer new insight into human existence. For Annie Dillard, it is significant to feel nature profoundly, for then she is close to asking the ultimate question about being, and, for her, to do this is everything."

Melvin Maddocks of *Time* observes in his review of *Pilgrim at Tinker Creek* that "at first she seems to fit into a pattern as predictable as a wildlife calendar, this Annie Dillard, . . . who looks out of her cottage window on nature and, sure enough, starting right on schedule with January, records the seasons as they come and go at Tinker Creek in Virginia. . . . [But] reader, beware of this deceptive girl. . . . Here is no gentle romantic twirling a buttercup, no graceful inscriber of 365 inspirational prose poems. . . . To an age hooked on novelty, variety and pluralism, her message is as clear as William Blake's: 'See a world in a grain of sand'—if you dare. Allying herself to leeched turtles, she sums up herself and perhaps her species thus: 'I am a frayed and nibbled survivor in a fallen world.' But what she has done is bear witness to her mystery as no leeched turtle (and few living writers) could—in a remarkable psalm of terror and celebration."

Several reviewers, though they admit that *Pilgrim at Tinker Creek* has its virtues, also find certain aspects of it silly or annoying. Charles Deemer of the *New Leader,* for example, claims that "if Annie Dillard had not spelled out what she was up to in this book, I don't think I would have guessed. . . . Her observations are typically described in overstatement reaching toward hysteria, and the lessons she would impart are at best sophomoric, at worst pompous twaddle. Still, there is enough fun and good will in *Pilgrim at Tinker Creek* that I cannot dismiss it altogether. . . . I must confess that I, too, enjoy moments beside creek and pond, and I, too, have seen and thought things which have changed my life. But if Annie Dillard wants to change lives, she had better talk sense or breath spiritual fire. . . . She only demonstrates once again how terribly self-centered the species can be, with respect both to its place in nature and to its place among fellow humans. Call this book a meteorological journal of an egomaniac. . . . There is not one genuine ecological concern voiced in the entire book. The focus is on the silly notion that insects and plants should behave like people. . . . But Dillard isn't really so naive. Her style simply gets away from her."

Muriel Haynes of *Ms.* is somewhat more charitable in her assessment of *Pilgrim at Tinker Creek.* Calling it "a passionate vision [that] will console many," she writes: "[Dillard's] style slides in and out of the colloquial and the everyday to the reverential and the celebratory. Her imaginative flights have the special beauty of surprise. . . . No one could fail to find her facts enthralling. She has read and quotes or paraphrases scores of writings about natural phenomena, marvelous tales told by travelers to regions hidden from most of us. Her own experiences are less exotic but meticulously graphic. She writes with appreciation and respect for all living creatures." Nevertheless, Haynes concludes, "Dillard is susceptible to fits of rapture. From time to time her prose reaches a school-girlish pitch. At moments of ecstasy she tends to become overwrought; reeling, staggering, gasping for death, she surrenders to self-dramatization. Yet in control she can soar with words of moving purity."

Eudora Welty, commenting in the *New York Times Book Review,* feels that "a reader's heart must go out to a young writer with a sense of wonder so fearless and unbridled. . . .

There is ambition about [Dillard's] book that I like, one that is deeper than the ambition to declare wonder aloud. It is the ambition to feel. This is a guess. But if this is what she has at heart, I am not quite sure that in writing this book she wholly accomplished it.'' After quoting a particularly confusing paragraph, for example, Welty states, ''I honestly do not know what she is talking about at such times. The only thing I could swear to is that the writing here leaves something to be desired.'' Furthermore, continues Welty, ''[the] author is given to changing style or shifting moods with disconcerting frequency and abruptness.... You might be reading letters home from camp, where the moment before you might have though you were deep in the Book of Leviticus.''

In a somewhat different vein, the critic questions the advisability of making the book so self-oriented. She remarks: ''Annie Dillard is the only person in her book, substantially the only one in her world; I recall no outside human speech coming to break the long soliloquy of the author. Speaking of the universe very often, she is yet self-surrounded, and, beyond that, book-surrounded. Her own book might have taken in more of human life without losing a bit of the wonder she was after. Might it not have gained more?''

Despite these faults, however, Welty concludes that the book has merit. ''Is the Pilgrim on her right road?,'' she asks. ''That depends on what the Pilgrim's destination is. But how much better, in any case, to wonder than not to wonder, to dance with astonishment and go spinning in praise, than not to know enough to dance or praise at all; to be blessed with more imagination than you might know at the given moment what to do with than to be cursed with too little to give you—and other people—any trouble.''

On the other hand, Hayden Carruth, writing in the *Virginia Quarterly Review,* says *Pilgrim at Tinker Creek* is a ''dangerous'' and ''subversive'' book due to its obvious affection for nostalgia. He writes: ''In many respects Annie Dillard's book ... is so ingratiating that even readers who find themselves in fundamental disagreement with it may take pleasure from it, a good deal of pleasure.... [She] has done what many would like but few are able to do. She has organized her life, there in her primarily natural habitat, so that she has plenty of time to spend not only in the field but in the library and laboratory as well.... And she uses her knowledge well.... Inevitably, however, she does more than this: she asks what it all means.... Out of these quandaries Annie Dillard always contrives to emerge with a statement of spiritual affirmation, a statement which is, moreover, though expressive of her own sensibility, conventional in substance.... In essence her view in plain old-fashioned optimistic American transcendentalism, ornamented though it may be with examples from quantum physics and biochemistry.... [She also] devotes many pages to what can only be called rhapsody, evocation in words of her own epiphanies. Unfortunately, much of this writing is confused, exaggerated, sentimental, and unconvincing.... [Furthermore,] Annie Dillard's book is a work done in 'the deep affection of nostalgia' (her words) for an abstract past, with little reference to life on this planet at this moment, its hazards and misdirections, and to this extent it is a dangerous book, literally a subversive book, in spite of its attractions. To my mind the view of man and nature held by any honest farmer ... is historically more relevant and humanly far more responsible than the atavistic and essentially passive, not to say evasive, view held by Annie Dillard.''

America's Mike Major does not subscribe to this view of Dillard and her work. Commenting on her writing in general, he notes: ''Dillard brings to her work an artist's eye, a scien-

tist's curiosity, a metaphysician's mind, all woven together in what might be called, essentially, a theologian's quest.... [She] is not so much an aging hippie doing her own precious little thing, or even a detached, observing scientist, as an intellectual sculptress, painstakingly constructing a huge, objective scaffolding capable of encompassing ultimate meanings, a penetrating vision into the realities of nature, man and God. Unambitious the woman is not.... [Her] nonfiction reads like poetry because, in fact, it is. Her forging together of these two disparate forms was accomplished not without some travail.... The reason for her extraordinary efforts lies in her passion to charge her prose with such inner cohesiveness that it fulfills the function of poetry. She constructs her nonfiction as carefully as a sonnet.... [But] more than artist, scientist, thinker or even theologian, Dillard is primarily a mystic, bruising her soul against the Absolute.''

Dillard herself takes issue with those who regard her work as the result of anything less than hard work. Fearful of being categorized as a sort of untutored free spirit who chose to commune with nature for a year and then just happened to write a prize-winning book about the experience, she explained to Major that ''people want to make you into a cult figure because of what they fancy to be your life style, when the truth is your life is literature! You're writing consciously, off of hundreds of index cards, often distorting the literal truth to achieve an artistic one. It's all hard, conscious, terribly frustrating work! But this never occurs to people. They think it happens in a dream, that you just sit on a tree stump and take dictation from some little chipmunk! ... If you're going to think or write seriously, you have to be intelligent. You have to keep learning or die on your feet.'' Recalling the grueling ordeal of working on *Pilgrim at Tinker Creek*—an eight-month, seven-days-a-week, fifteen-to-sixteen-hour-a-day project, accomplished not in the great outdoors, but in a library study carrel—Dillard concludes, ''I rarely write, I hate to write!''

BIOGRAPHICAL/CRITICAL SOURCES: Time, March 18, 1974; October 10, 1977; *New York Times Book Review,* March 24, 1974; *New Republic,* April 6, 1974; *America,* April 20, 1974, February 11, 1978, May 6, 1978; *New Leader,* June 24, 1974; *Ms.,* August, 1974; *Virginia Quarterly Review,* autumn, 1974; *Commentary,* October, 1974; *Commonweal,* October 24, 1975, February 3, 1978; *New York Times,* September 21, 1977; *Washington Post Book World,* October 16, 1977; *Best Sellers,* December, 1977; *Contemporary Literary Criticism,* Volume IX, Gale, 1978.

—*Sketch by Deborah A. Straub*

*   *   *

DISNEY, Doris Miles   1907-1976

PERSONAL: Born December 22, 1907, in Glastonbury, Conn.; died March 8, 1976, in Fredericksburg, Va.; daughter of Edward Lucas and Elizabeth (Malone) Miles; married George J. Disney, June 19, 1936 (deceased); children: Elizabeth Miles. *Education:* Attended public schools in Glastonbury, Conn. *Religion:* Roman Catholic. *Residence:* Fredericksburg, Va.

CAREER: Affiliated with publicity departments of social agencies and other organizations; full-time writer. *Member:* Woman's Club of Plainville, Civil War Round Table (West Hartford, Conn.)

WRITINGS—Suspense novels; published by Doubleday, except as indicated: *A Compound for Death,* 1943; *Murder on a Tangent,* 1945; *Who Rides a Tiger?,* 1946; *Dark Road,*

1946; *Appointment at Nine*, 1947; *Enduring Old Charms*, 1947; *Testimony by Silence*, 1948; *That Which Is Crooked*, 1948; *Family Skeleton*, 1949; *Count the Ways*, 1949; *Fire at Will*, 1950, reprinted, Manor, 1976; *Look Back on Murder*, 1951, reprinted, Ace Books, 1976; *Straw Man*, 1951 (published in England as *The Case of the Straw Man*, Foulsham, 1958); *Heavy, Heavy Hangs*, 1952; *Do unto Others*, 1953; *Prescription: Murder*, 1953; *The Last Straw*, 1954 (published in England as *Driven to Kill*, Foulsham, 1957); *Room for Murder*, 1955; *Trick or Treat*, 1955; *Unappointed Rounds*, 1956 (published in England as *Post Office Case*, Foulsham, 1957); *Method in Madness*, 1957; *My Neighbor's Wife*, 1957; *Dead Stop*, Dell, 1957; *Too Innocent to Kill*, 1957; *Black Mail*, 1958; *Quiet Violence*, Foulsham, 1959; *No Next of Kin* (Detective Book Club selection), 1959; *Did She Fall or Was She Pushed?*, 1959.

Dark Lady, 1960 (published in England as *Sinister Lady*, R. Hale, 1962); *Mrs. Meeker's Money*, 1961; *Should Auld Acquaintance* (Detective Book Club selection), 1962; *Find the Woman* (Detective Book Club selection), 1962; *Here Lies*, 1963; *The Departure of Mr. Gaudette* (Detective Book Club selection), 1964 (published in England as *Fateful Departure*, R. Hale, 1965); *The Hospitality of the House*, 1964; *Unsuspected Evil*, R. Hale, 1965; *Shadow of a Man*, 1965; *At Some Forgotten Door*, 1966; *The Magic Grandfather*, 1966; *Night of Clear Choice* (Detective Book Club selection), 1967; *Money for the Taking*, 1968; *Voice from the Grave*, 1968; *Two Little Children and How They Grew*, 1969; *Do Not Fold, Spindle, or Mutilate*, 1970 (published in England as *Death by Computer*, R. Hale, 1971); *The Chandler Policy*, Putnam, 1971; *The Day Miss Bessie Lewis Disappeared* (Detective Book Club selection), 1972; *Only Couples Need Apply* (Detective Book Club selection), 1973; *Don't Go into the Woods Today*, 1974; *Cry for Help*, 1975; *Winifred*, 1976.

SIDELIGHTS: Three of Doris Miles Disney's books have been adapted for films. "Stella," produced by Twentieth Century Fox in 1950, was based on *Family Skeleton*. In 1953, United Artists released "The Straw Man," and in 1971 ABC-TV premiered the made-for-television movie, "Do Not Fold, Spindle, or Mutilate"; both films were based on Disney's novels of the same titles.

BIOGRAPHICAL/CRITICAL SOURCES: Wilson Library Bulletin, June, 1954.†

*　　*　　*

DIVINE, Robert A(lexander) 1929-

PERSONAL: Born May 10, 1929, in Brooklyn, N.Y.; son of Walter E. and Emily (Mable) Divine; married Barbara Christine Renick, August 6, 1955; children: John Douglas, Elisabeth Terry, Richard Lawrence, Kirk MacLennan. *Education:* Yale University, B.A., 1951, M.A., 1952, Ph.D., 1954. *Religion:* Methodist. *Home:* 2402 Rockingham Circle, Austin, Tex. 78704. *Office:* Department of History, University of Texas, Austin, Tex. 78712.

CAREER: University of Texas at Austin, instructor, 1954-57, assistant professor, 1957-61, associate professor, 1961-63, professor of history, 1963—, chairman of department, 1965-68. *Member:* American Historical Association, Organization of American Historians. *Awards, honors:* Center for Advanced Study in the Behavioral Sciences fellow in Stanford, Calif., 1962-63.

WRITINGS: American Immigration Policy, 1924-1952, Yale University Press, 1957; (editor) *American Foreign Policy*, Meridian, 1960; *The Illusion of Neutrality*, University of Chicago Press, 1962; *The Reluctant Belligerent: American

Entry into World War II, Wiley, 1965; *Second Chance: The Triumph of Internationalism in America during World War II*, Atheneum, 1967; *Foreign Policy and U.S. Presidential Elections*, two volumes, F. Watts, 1974; *Since 1945*, Wiley, 1975; *Blowing on the Wind*, Oxford University Press, 1978.

*　　*　　*

DIXON, John W(esley), Jr. 1919-

PERSONAL: Born August 18, 1919, in Richmond, Va.; son of John Wesley (a minister) and Margaret Collins (Denny) Dixon; married Vivian Slagle, January 9, 1943; children: Susan, Judith, Miriam. *Education:* Attended University of Bristol, 1938-39; Emory and Henry College, B.A., 1941; Columbia University, graduate study, 1950; University of Chicago, Ph.D., 1953. *Politics:* Democrat. *Religion:* Episcopalian. *Home:* 216 Glenhill Lane, Chapel Hill, N.C. 27514. *Office:* 101 Saunders Hall, University of North Carolina, Chapel Hill, N.C. 27514.

CAREER: Michigan State College of Agriculture and Applied Science (now Michigan State University), East Lansing, instructor in literature and fine arts, 1950-52; Emory University, Atlanta, Ga., assistant professor of humanities and art history, 1952-57; Dickinson College, Carlisle, Pa., associate professor of art history, 1957-60; Florida Presbyterian College, St. Petersburg, associate professor of humanities and art history, 1960-63; University of North Carolina at Chapel Hill, associate professor, 1963-68, professor of religion and art, 1968—. Executive director, Faculty Christian Fellowship, National Council of Churches, 1955-57. *Military service:* U.S. Army, Medical Administrative Corps, 1941-46; became first lieutenant. *Member:* American Academy of Religion, College Art Association.

WRITINGS: Form and Reality: Art as Communication (study book), Methodist Student Movement, 1957; (contributor) Finley Eversole, editor, *Christian Faith and the Contemporary Arts*, Abingdon, 1962; *Nature and Grace in Art*, University of North Carolina Press, 1964; (contributor) Howard Hunt, editor, *Humanities, Religion and the Arts Tomorrow*, Holt, 1972; (contributor) F. W. Dillistion and James Waddell, editors, *Art and Religion as Communication*, John Knox, 1974; *The Hale Lectures*, Seabury-Western Seminary, 1976; (contributor) Ruth Tiffany Barnhous and Urban T. Holmes, Jr., editors, *Male and Female*, Seabury, 1976; *Art and the Theological Imagination*, Seabury, 1978; *The Physiology of Faith*, Harper, 1979.

Also author of papers for American Academy of Religion and College Art Association. Work represented in anthology *Religion and Contemporary Western Culture*, edited by Edward Cell, Abingdon, 1967. Contributor of articles and reviews to scholarly publications.

WORK IN PROGRESS: Continued studies on the relation between religion and art.

*　　*　　*

DODSON, Daniel B. 1918-

PERSONAL: Born March 21, 1918, in Portland, Ore.; son of William Daniel Boone (a businessman) and Besse E. (Krum) Dodson; married Judith Ware, August, 1943; children: Dorian, Elizabeth. *Education:* Attended University of Vienna, 1937-38; Reed College, B.A., 1941; Columbia University, M.A., 1947, Ph.D., 1954. *Politics:* Democrat. *Home:* 1 Sparkill Ave., Sparkill, N.Y. 10976. *Agent:* Harold Ober Associates, Inc., 40 East 49th St., New York, N.Y. 10022. *Office:* English Department, Columbia University, New York, N.Y. 10027.

CAREER: Columbia University, New York, N.Y., instructor, 1948-54, assistant professor, 1954-59, associate professor, 1959-70, professor of English, 1970—. *Military service:* U.S. Army Air Forces, 1942-46; became first lieutenant; received Distinguished Flying Cross, Air Medal with oak-leaf cluster. *Member:* Modern Language Association of America.

WRITINGS: *The Man Who Ran Away*, Dutton, 1961; (editor) *Eight Russian Short Stories*, Fawcett, 1962; (editor and author of introductions) *Twelve Modern Plays*, Wadsworth, 1970; *Malcolm Lowry*, Columbia University Press, 1970; (with M. S. Barranger) *Generations: An Introduction to Drama*, Harcourt, 1971; *The Dance of Love* (novel), Mason & Charter, 1974; *Scala Dei* (novel), Mason & Charter, 1975; *On a Darkling Plain* (novel), Mason & Charter, 1976; *Looking for Zoe* (novel), Dodd, 1981. Contributor of short fiction to *Esquire* and *Story*, and of articles to scholarly journals.

WORK IN PROGRESS: A novel; a study of the modern theatre.

*   *   *

DOMJAN, Joseph (Spiri) 1907-

PERSONAL: Born March 15, 1907, in Budapest, Hungary; naturalized U.S. citizen; married March 13, 1944; wife's name, Evelyn (a graphic artist); children: Alma, Michael Paul, Daniel George. *Education:* Attended Royal Academy of Fine Arts, Budapest, Hungary, 1935-42. *Residence:* Tuxedo Park, N.Y. 10987.

CAREER: Hungarian Royal Academy of Fine Arts, Budapest, assistant professor of fine arts, 1941-42; self-employed woodcut artist in Budapest, 1942-56, Switzerland, 1956-57, and the United States, 1957—. Work exhibited at 425 one-man shows on four continents and contained in permanent collections of more than 175 museums, including Victoria and Albert Museum, Metropolitan Museum of Art, Bibliotheque National, Smithsonian Institution, and Library of Congress. Lecturer and author.

MEMBER: Metropolitan Museum of Art (life fellow), Print Council of America, American Color Print Society, Silvermine Guild of Artists, Goetheanum (Switzerland), Society of Illustrators, Society of American Graphic Artists, Societe d'encouragement au progres, National Academy of Design. *Awards, honors:* National Salon prize, 1936; Fine Arts Hall prize, 1941; Nemes Marcell prize, 1942; Purchase Awards, Johansen Abstract Collection, 1948, International Color Woodcut Exhibition, Victoria and Albert Museum, 1950, and International Exhibition of Graphic Arts, 1952; Mihaly Zichy Prize for graphic arts, 1952; Munkacsy Prize of fine arts and "Master of the Color Woodcut" (China), both 1955; Kossuth Prize of fine arts, 1956; Rockefeller Foundation grant, 1957; named "printmaker of 1961," Print Club of Albany, 1961; book awards from National Educational Society and American Institute of Graphic Arts, both 1964; award of faithfulness, Washington-Kossuth Historical Society, 1966; Sonia Watter Award, American Color Print Society and award of merit, Society of Illustrators, both 1967; award of excellence, Society of Illustrators, 1968; silver medal and diploma, Societe d'encouragement au progres, 1969; medal of honor, Hungarian Helicon Society, George Washington Award, American Hungarian Studies Foundation, and silver medal and diploma, International Academy of Literature, Arts and Science, all 1970; Chapelbrook Foundation grant, 1972; Rakoczi award (Hungary), 1976; Rakoczi Foundation award (Toronto), 1980.

WRITINGS: (Fine arts editor) *Hunyadi* (album), [Budapest],

1956; (illustrator) Evelyn A. Domjan, *The Edge of Paradise*, Domjan Studio, 1980; (illustrator) E. A. Domjan, *Eternal Wool*, Domjan Studio, 1980.

Self-illustrated and designed: *Wildflowers*, Medimpex (Budapest), 1954; *32 Color Woodcuts*, Corvina (Budapest), 1956; *Ungarische Legende*, Atlantis Verlag (Zurich), 1957; *Henry Hudson of the River*, Art Edge, 1959; *Janos Hunyadi: 10 Woodcuts*, Art Edge, 1960; *Hungarian Heroes and Legends*, Van Nostrand, 1963; *Peacock Festival*, Art Edge, 1964; *The Proud Peacock*, Holt, 1965; *The Little Princess Goodnight*, Holt, 1966; *Domjan the Woodcutter* (monograph), Art Edge, 1966; *The Fifteen Decisive Battles of the World*, Limited Editions Club, 1969; *The Little Cock*, Lippincott, 1969; *Hungarian Song*, American—Hungarian Literary Guild, 1969; *Domjan Portfolio*, Art Edge, 1970; *I Went to the Market*, Holt, 1970; *The Joy of Living*, Holt, 1971; *The Artist and the Legend: A Visit to China Is Remembered and the Legends Unfold*, Opus Publications, 1975; *Wing Beat* (collection of eagle woodcuts) introduction by G. E. Pogany, Domjan Studio, 1976; *Pacatus: A Trademark from Antiquity*, Domjan Studio, 1979. Also illustrator for *Bellringer*, a collection of poems by Ruth Laurene, 1975.

SIDELIGHTS: Joseph Domjan writes *CA:* "I live in nature. True, you can't see me carrying an easel into the woods or painting outdoors, but I look and preserve an impression. I may walk out into the garden in the middle of the night. I look at the summer stars, the deep velvet-blue sky, the silver moon. [At dawn there is] the sunrise, pale pink-orange in the far distance over the lake and hills, trees and flowers brushed lightly with morning glow.

"Nothing happens just by chance in my life, although it seems that I came to make woodcuts by chance. The first series was born as a result of a misunderstanding: I was told to fill the rooms of an exhibition hall with woodcuts, which I did. As I look back and compare these early works (key-blocks in red with underprintings of red) to my present works (all color), I can say that it was a miracle. I am a painter, but I am very happy that I have the woodcut as my tool. I love black-and-white woodcuts, but when the time comes to make them into color it will be a holiday; for such holidays it is worthwhile to live."

BIOGRAPHICAL/CRITICAL SOURCES: John R. Biggs, *Woodcuts*, Bradford Press, 1958.

*   *   *

DONNELLY, Dorothy (Boillotat) 1903-

PERSONAL: Born September 7, 1903, in Detroit, Mich.; daughter of Alexander and Theresa (Ferstl) Boillotat; married Walter A. Donnelly (a former editor of University of Michigan Press), September 1, 1931; children: Stephen, Jerome, Denis. *Education:* University of Michigan, B.A., 1931, M.A., 1932. *Politics:* Independent. *Religion:* Roman Catholic. *Home:* 612 Lawrence St., Ann Arbor, Mich. 48104.

CAREER: Writer. *Member:* Phi Beta Kappa, Kappa Phi. *Awards, honors:* Union League Civic prize for poem, "Three-Toed Sloth," and Harriet Monroe Memorial Award for poem, "People," both from *Poetry* magazine; Arts Foundation prize, 1954; Longview Foundation award for "People"; gold medal, Assumption University, 1976.

WRITINGS: *The Bone and the Star*, Sheed, 1944; *The Golden Well*, Sheed, 1950; (contributor) *Faith, Reason, and Modern Psychiatry*, Kenedy, 1955; *Trio in a Mirror* (poems), University of Arizona Press, 1960; (contributor) *Christianity and Culture*, Helicon, 1961; (contributor) *The Various Light* (poems), Aurora Press, 1964; (contributor) *The New Yorker Book of Poems* (anthology), Viking, 1969; *God and the Apple of His Eye,* Prow Books, 1973; (contributor) *New Coasts and Strange Harbors* (poetry anthology), Crowell, 1974; *Kudzu: New and Selected Poems,* Pourboire Press, 1979. Contributor of poems and articles to *transition* (Paris), *Pylon* (Rome), *Blackfriars* (England), *Commonweal, New Yorker, Poetry, Hudson Review, Spectrum, Chicago Choice, Burning Deck,* and other publications.

*   *   *

DONOHUE, John W(aldron) 1917-

PERSONAL: Born September 17, 1917, in New York, N.Y.; son of John H. (a plumbing contractor) and Cecilia (Waldron) Donohue. *Education:* Fordham University, A.B., 1939; St. Louis University, M.A. and Ph.L., 1944; Woodstock College, S.T.L., 1951; Yale University, Ph.D., 1955. *Office:* America Press, 106 West 56th St., New York, N.Y. 10019.

CAREER: Entered Society of Jesus, 1939, ordained Roman Catholic priest, 1950; Canisius High School, Buffalo, N.Y., instructor in Latin and English, 1944-47; Fordham University, New York City, instructor, 1955-58, assistant professor, 1958-61, associate professor, 1961-63, 1966-67, professor of history and philosophy of education, 1967-69, adjunct professor, 1969—, dean of Thomas More College, 1963-66; *America* (weekly journal), New York City, associate editor, 1972—. Adjunct member of faculty, St. Joseph's Seminary, 1961-68; director of studies, Society of Jesus (New York province), 1968-71. Member of committee for examination in history, American education, New York College Proficiency Examination Program, New York State Department of Education, 1964-70. Trustee of St. Louis University and Fordham University. *Member:* Philosophy of Education Society, Religious Education Association.

WRITINGS: Christian Maturity, Kenedy, 1955; *Work and Education: The Role of Technical Culture in Some Distinctive Theories of Humanism,* Loyola University Press, 1959; (contributor) John Blewett, editor, *John Dewey: His Thought and Influence,* Fordham University Press, 1960; (contributor) Joseph E. O'Neill, editor, *A Catholic Case against Segregation,* Macmillan, 1961; *Jesuit Education: An Essay on the Foundations of Its Idea,* Fordham University Press, 1963; (contributor) A. M. Kazamias, P. Nash, and H. J. Perkinson, editors, *The Educated Man: Studies in the History of Educational Thought,* Wiley, 1965; (contributor) V. F. Daues, M. R. Holloway, and L. Sweeny, editors, *Wisdom in Depth: Essays in Honor of Henri Renard,* Bruce (Milwaukee), 1966; *St. Thomas Aquinas and Education,* Random House, 1968; (contributor) Henry Ehlers, editor, *Crucial Issues in Education,* 4th edition (Donohue was not associated with earlier editions), Holt, 1969; *Catholicism and Education,* Harper, 1973.

Contributor to proceedings and to *The Catholic Encyclopedia for School and Home, Westminster Dictionary of Christian Education, The New Catholic Encyclopedia,* and *Sacramentum Mundi: An Encyclopedia of Theology.* Contributor of articles to religious journals.

*   *   *

DORST, Jean (Pierre) 1924-
(Pierre d'Urstelle)

PERSONAL: Born August 7, 1924, in Mulhouse, Haut-Rhin, France; son of Joseph V. and Gabrielle M. (Rusch) Dorst. *Education:* University of Besancon, baccalaureate; University of Paris, Licence de sciences naturelles, Doctorat es sci-

ences. *Religion:* Roman Catholic. *Home:* 114 ter avenue de Versailles, Paris 75016, France. *Office:* Museum National d'Histoire Naturelle, 55 rue de Buffon, Paris 75005, France.

CAREER: Museum National d'Histoire Naturelle, Paris, France, assistant director, 1949-62, professor and director of zoological laboratories, 1963—, director general, 1976—. Member, Academie des sciences, Institut de France, 1973—, and Academie des sciences d'outre-mer, 1980—; member of council, Institut oceanographique, 1975, Radio-France, 1978, Conseil superieur de l'education nationale, 1978, Ecole pratique des hautes etudes, 1980, and Conservatoire national des arts et metiers, 1980; president, Conseil national de la protection de la nature, 1976; past president and member of council, Charles Darwin Foundation for the Galapagos Islands. Member of jury, J. Paul Getty Conservation Prize. *Member:* Societe Orinthologique de France, American Ornithologists' Union, Deutsche Ornithologen Gesellschaft (honorary member), British Ornithologists' Union, Sociedad Espanola de Ornitologia, Sociedade Portuguesa de Ornitologia, Zoological Society of London, Explorers Club (New York; corresponding member).

WRITINGS: Les Migrations des oiseaux, Payot, 1956, 2nd edition, 1962, published as *The Migrations of Birds,* Houghton, 1962; *Les Oiseaux,* Hachette, 1957; (with Mandahl-Barth) *Oiseaux de cage,* Nathan, 1958; *Le Monde des oiseaux,* Hachette, 1962; *Birds Everywhere* (juvenile), Whitman, 1963; *Les Animaux voyageurs,* Hachette, 1964; *Avant que nature meure,* Delachaux & Niestle, 1965; *L'Homme de-nature,* Le Seuil, 1970; *A Field Guide to the Larger Mammals of Africa,* Collins, 1970; *Central and South America,* Chanticleer, 1970; *La Vie des oiseaux,* two volumes, Recontre, 1972; *Les Oiseaux dans leur milieu,* Recontre, 1972; *L'Univers de la vie,* Imprimerie Nationale, 1975; *La Force du vivant,* Flammarion, 1979. Contributor of about 400 articles to magazines and professional journals. Editor, *Mammalia,* a journal.

WORK IN PROGRESS: Le Temps des colchiques, for Stock; *A Life of Charles Darwin,* for Flammarion.

SIDELIGHTS: Jean Dorst has travelled to all parts of the world on twenty scientific expeditions. He is competent in French, English, German, and Spanish. *Avocational interests:* Music, painting, other fine arts.

*   *   *

DOS PASSOS, John (Roderigo) 1896-1970

PERSONAL: Born January 14, 1896, in Chicago, Ill.; died of an apparent heart attack September 28, 1970, in Baltimore, Md.; buried in Westmoreland Co., Va.; son of John Randolph Dos Passos (an attorney) and Lucy Addison Sprigg; married Katherine F. Smith, September, 1929 (died, 1947); married Elizabeth Hamlin Holdridge, August, 1949; children: (second marriage) Lucy Hamlin. *Education:* Harvard University, B.A. (cum laude), 1916. *Politics:* Began left-wing, shifting to conservative in his later years. *Residence:* Westmoreland, Va. *Agent:* Brandt & Brandt Literary Agents, 1501 Broadway, New York, N.Y. 10036.

CAREER: Volunteered for ambulance duty in France with Norton-Harjes Ambulance Unit, 1917, in Italy with Red Cross, 1918, and with U.S. Army Medical Corps, 1918-19; traveled to Near East with Near East Relief, 1921; *New Masses,* founder, 1926, executive board member, beginning 1926; correspondent in Central America, 1932; correspondent for *Life* magazine in the Pacific, 1945, and in South America, 1948. Treasurer, National Committee for Defense of Political Prisoners, 1932. *Member:* American Academy of

Arts and Letters, American Academy of Arts and Sciences, Authors League, Virginia Committee on Constitutional Government. *Awards, honors:* Guggenheim fellowships, 1939, 1940, 1942; National Institute of Arts and Letters Gold Medal Award for fiction, 1957; Antonio Feltrinelli Prize from Italian Academia Nazionale dei Lincei, 1967, for innovation in narrative.

WRITINGS: (Contributor) *Eight Harvard Poets*, Laurence J. Gomme, 1917; *One Man's Initiation—1917*, Allen & Unwin, 1919, Doran, 1922, published with new introduction, Cornell University Press, 1969, published as *First Encounter*, Philosophical Library, 1945; *Three Soldiers*, Doran, 1921, reprinted, Houghton, 1964; *Rosinante to the Road Again*, Doran, 1922; *A Pushcart at the Curb*, Doran, 1922; *Streets of Night*, Doran, 1923; *Manhattan Transfer*, Harper, 1925, reprinted, Bentley, 1980; *Orient Express*, Harper, 1927, reprinted, Octagon, 1976; *Facing the Chair*, Sacco-Vanzetti Defense Committee, 1927, reprinted, DaCapo Press, 1970; *In All Countries*, Harcourt, 1934; (contributor) Henry Hart, editor, *American Writers Conference*, International Publishers, 1935; *The Villages Are the Heart of Spain*, Esquire-Coronet, 1937; *Journeys between Wars*, Harcourt, 1938, reprinted, Octagon, 1980; *The Living Thoughts of Tom Paine, Presented by John Dos Passos*, Longmans, Green, 1940, reprinted, Fawcett, 1964; *The Ground We Stand On*, Harcourt, 1941, reprinted, Kraus Reprints, 1970; (contributor) Herman Ould, editor, *Writers in Freedom*, Hutchinson, 1942; *State of the Nation*, Houghton, 1944, reprinted, Greenwood Press, 1973; *Tour of Duty*, Houghton, 1946, reprinted, Greenwood Press, 1974.

The Prospect before Us, Houghton, 1950, reprinted, Greenwood Press, 1973; *Life's Picture History of World War II*, Time Inc., 1950; *Chosen Country*, Houghton, 1951; *The Head and Heart of Thomas Jefferson*, Doubleday, 1954; *Most Likely to Succeed*, Prentice-Hall, 1954; *The Theme Is Freedom*, Dodd, 1956, reprinted, Arno, 1971; *The Men Who Made the Nation*, Doubleday, 1957; (contributor) *Essays on Individuality*, University of Pennsylvania Press, 1958; *The Great Days*, Sagamore, 1958; *Prospects of a Golden Age*, Prentice-Hall, 1959.

Midcentury: A Contemporary Chronicle, Houghton, 1961; *Mr. Wilson's War*, Doubleday, 1962; *Brazil on the Move* (travel), Doubleday, 1963; *Occasions and Protests* (essays, 1936-1964), Regnery, 1964; *Thomas Jefferson: The Making of a President*, Houghton, 1964; (contributor) Allan Nevins, editor, *Lincoln and the Gettysberg Address*, University of Illinois Press, 1964; *Shackles of Power: Three Jeffersonian Decades, 1801-1826*, Doubleday, 1966; *The World in a Glass: A View of Our Century Selected from the Novels of John Dos Passos*, Houghton, 1966; *The Best Times* (reminiscences), New American Library, 1966; *The Portugal Story: Three Centuries of Exploration and Discovery*, Doubleday, 1969.

Easter Island: Island of Enigmas, Doubleday, 1971; *The Fourteenth Chronicle: Letters and Diaries of John Dos Passos*, edited by Townsend Ludington, Gambit, 1973; *Century's Ebb: The Thirteenth Chronicle*, Gambit, 1975; *Promise of U.S.A.: John Dos Passos' Thumbnail Biographies*, edited by Edgar Stanton, Hwong Publishing, 1975.

Trilogies: *The 42nd Parallel*, Harcourt, 1930, reprinted, New American Library, 1969, *1919*, Harcourt, 1932, reprinted, New American Library, 1969, *The Big Money*, Harcourt, 1936, reprinted, New American Library, 1966 (trilogy published as *U.S.A.*, Harcourt, 1937); *Adventures of a Young Man*, Houghton, 1939, reprinted, Queens House, 1977, *Number One*, Houghton, 1943, reprinted, Queens House, 1977, *The Grand Design*, Houghton, 1949, reprinted, Queens House, 1977 (trilogy published as *District of Columbia*, Houghton, 1952).

Plays: *The Garbage Man* (produced, 1926; also see below), Harper, 1926; *Airways, Inc.* (also see below), Macaulay, 1928; *Three Plays* (contains "The Garbage Man," "Airways, Inc.," and "Fortune Heights"; "Fortune Heights" produced in U.S.S.R., 1933), Harcourt, 1934; (with Paul Shyre) *U.S.A.: A Dramatic Revue*, Samuel French, 1963.

Translator from the French, and illustrator, of B. Cendrar's *Panama*. Contributor to *Nation, New Republic, New Masses, Common Sense, Esquire, Partisan Review, National Review*, and other periodicals.

SIDELIGHTS: Jean-Paul Sartre once called John Dos Passos "the best novelist of our time." Nevertheless, Gore Vidal noted that although he was "admired extravagantly in the '20's and '30's, Dos Passos was largely ignored in the '40's and '50's, his new works passed over either in silence or else noted with that ritual sadness we reserve for those whose promise to art has not been kept."

Reviews of his earlier works reflect the expectations that Dos Passos raised in the literary world. Sinclair Lewis heralded *Manhattan Transfer* as "a novel of the very first importance; a book which the idle reader can devour yet which the literary analyst must take as possibly inaugurating, at long last, the vast and blazing dawn we have awaited. It may be the foundation of a whole new school of novel-writing. Dos Passos may be, more than Dreiser, Cather, Hergesheimer, Cabell, or Anderson the father of humanized and living fiction . . . not merely for America but for the world! . . . I regard *Manhattan Transfer* as more important in every way than anything by Gertrude Stein or Marcel Proust or even the great white boar, Mr. Joyce's *Ulysses*." Mary Ross wrote of *1919*: "Mr. Dos Passos's writing is always distinguished by a remarkable sensuous perception, but more than that, he has a directness, independence and poignancy of thought and emotion that seems to me unexcelled in current fiction. . . . *1919* will disturb or offend some of its readers. Their recoil will be in itself a mark of its force. No novel . . . with which I am familiar seems to me to have surpassed it in power, range, and beauty."

After the completion of the *U.S.A.* trilogy, Theodore Spencer declared: "No one concerned with the health of the novel as a living form can fail to . . . regard his achievement with respect. He writes from a wise and comprehending point of view; his construction is firm; his narrative is swift, realistic, and interesting. There are few novelists in this country today whose craftsmanship is as secure, and whose sense of American life as understanding and awake." However, Alfred Kazin noted that while *U.S.A.* became an epic, "it is a history of defeat. There are no flags for the spirit in it, and no victory save the mind's silent victory that integrity can acknowledge to itself. It is one of the saddest books ever written by an American." Even so, Kazin added, "what Waldo Frank said of Mencken is particularly relevant to Dos Passos: he brings energy to despair."

Viewed from the perspective of thirty years later, Peter Meinke's review of *The Fourteenth Chronicle* found Dos Passos "to be in that main American tradition beginning with Whitman that seeks to grasp the American experience by accumulation of detail, by great width and scope, by swallowing America whole, as it were, rather than carving out deep chunks from certain sections as his friends Hemingway, Fitzgerald, Faulkner and Cummings did. . . . While the book is ultimately sad, with the elderly out-of-step writer exclaiming that 'the rank idiocy of the younger generation is more than I can swallow' . . . the main impression one gets from reading it is that of a decent and generous man of boundless enthusiasm and energy." D. J. Stewart's review of *Occasions and Protests* noted the "startling emphasis on vision, on seeing clear, rounded, individual *shapes* of things . . . provides a kind of touchstone wherewith to reread and better understand what these pieces are about. For they are . . . essentially the reactions to life of a man who uses his eyes intensely and voraciously, one who lives with and through his vision." Dos Passos sees things with the coolness and the clarity of the camera's eye, which accounts for one of his most frequently-mentioned faults: his two-dimensional vision tends to create types, defeating the creation of characters with any true individuality.

Don Gifford offered a possible explanation for these types: "At its core, Dos Passos's 'settled theory' is bitterly anti-intellectual—it postulates a 'natural man' who shares 'certain simple realities which are universal to all men.'" Walter Allen, however, believed that Dos Passos did not become a reactionary in his later years, but that "he [continued] to attack, in the name of individual freedom, power that he [believed had] become monolithic. He remains essentially an anarchist." A *Time* reviewer grants that "politics . . . helped to undermine [Dos Passos's] reputation." Nevertheless, "the most consistent theme in his life was a vaguely anarchic impulse, a craving for individuality which no ideology could permanently satisfy."

According to Gifford, Dos Passos explained his philosophy in *Occasions and Protests*—that "personal freedom and individual liberty constitute the highest good, and that this good is under attack by evil in the form of institutional authority in mass society (big government, big labor, big business, etc.) and in the form of 'the prescriptions of doctrine' (Communism, liberalism, conformism, etc.)." However, this philosophy does not produce an optimistic view of his characters. Edmund Wilson asserted many years ago that Dos Passos's "disapproval of capitalistic society becomes distaste for all the human beings who compose it." This same view was expressed in 1939 by Alfred Kazin, who wrote: "For Dos Passos irony itself has become the supreme style; the cold, methodical ferocity of his prose, with its light, bitter thrust, its extraordinary pliability and ease, becomes a cackling solemnity. [*Adventures of a Young Man*] really trembles with an internal disgust. Dos Passos has always disliked most of his characters, but here his characteristic repugnance and exasperation yield to pure hatred."

The effects of these emotions were examined by Sartre. "Dos Passos's hate, despair, and lofty contempt are real," he commented. "But that is precisely why his world is not real; it is a created object. I know of none—not even Faulkner's or Kafka's—in which the art is greater or better hidden. I know of none that is more precious, more touching or closer to us. This is because he takes his material from our world. And yet, there is no stranger or more distant world. Dos Passos has invented only one thing, an art of story-telling. But that is enough to create a universe." A reviewer for *Christian Century* detailed the disintegration of such a universe when he wrote: "Great was the fall of novelist Dos Passos from the ideological summit he had assumed in the leftist movements of the 1930's. His style, his provocativeness, his sense of the current—none of these has left him. But he has become a rather weary and repetitive recaller of an American past most of which never existed." Maxwell Geismar continues the discussion, commenting that "the

decline of Dos Passos's work is another tragedy in contemporary letters. But if the trouble with the later Hemingway or the later Faulkner is that they are not really serious any more, perhaps the trouble with Dos Passos is that he has become much too serious."

R. A. Fraser lamented that, in *Occasions and Protests,* "nothing is left of the Dos Passos style but his habit of omitting the hyphen. His prose could once—perhaps will again—slap life into the cheeks of the most commonplace landscape, the most banal event; here . . . it's rouge that's being applied, slowly, laboriously and inaccurately. Even his ear has betrayed him." John Gross wrote in his review of *Midcentury,* "All one can do for the sake of the man who once wrote *Manhattan Transfer* and *The Big Money* is look the other way." H. M. Robinson seems similarly inclined. He recalled: "Time was, when the publication of a novel by John Dos Passos called for the lighting of bonfires on promontories. But no triumphant flare will greet the appearance of his latest work. . . . Kindly reviewers may regard the book as a temporary lapse of energy. . . . But Mr. Dos Passos deserves something more constructive than mercy. . . . The weakness of *The Grand Design* proceeds not so much from the waning of Mr. Dos Passos's creative powers—though there is a marked decline here—as from the exhaustion of the genre in which he is working." "Yet," Vidal noted, "there is something about Dos Passos which makes a fellow writer unexpectedly protective, partly out of compassion for the man himself, and partly because the fate of Dos Passos is a chilling reminder of those condemned to write for life that this is the way it almost always is in a society which, to put it tactfully, has no great interest in the development of writers, a process too slow for the American temperament. As a result our literature is rich with sprinters but significantly short of milers."

"Decline is probably a merely conventional way to characterize the shift in Dos Passos's approach to interpreting American life," Herbert Gold commented. "He was more consistent than we realized. His first radical work is animated by boyish bitterness and anger—combined with the youthful ambition to make a literary mark. The later conservative or right-wing work is animated by aging bitterness and anger—combined with the older man's desire to take a few revenges on a time that has passed him by. What remains constant, and of constant value in a writer who never quite achieved his ambitions, is a passion that might be derived from both the paltriest and the deepest of sources: the sense of his unique self." To this, Granville Hicks conceded that "Dos Passos . . . cannot now reach the height he reached in *U.S.A.* but *Midcentury* shows how much there is that he can still do well. . . . And, tired and hopeless as he may be, Dos Passos is still a man of solid integrity, saying exactly what he thinks."

Examination of the decline in Dos Passos's popularity yields several conjectures as to what went wrong. Vance Bourjaily claimed: "Dos Passos, through the years, has become a better and better writer; but the appeal of his point of view has grown narrower and narrower. For a work of literature at its best, is a creation; and *The Grand Design,* with its caricatures and its atmosphere of intangible bias, is merely an interpretation." Early in Dos Passos's career Henry Hazlitt foresaw such difficulties. "Mr. Dos Passos is a writer of extraordinary talent," he wrote in his review of *The 42nd Parallel.* "He knows American cities, he knows a great deal about life, he has a shrewd insight into men and women. . . . But it leaves one wondering whether [his] present method is not more a handicap than a help to him. This kaleidoscopic shaking of the fragments of several novels into one no longer has the attraction of novelty, and its other advantages are not always clear.'' In 1961, John Wrenn demonstrated the validity of Hazlitt's misgivings. He explained: ''Dos Passos has been admired for characteristics which today, with a perspective of twenty years, appear to be superficial: for his success in the novel of protest; for his brilliant technical innovations in such a work as *U.S.A.*; for his contemporaneity—his grasp of the problems and events of the time as they related to individual characters in his fiction. When the novel of protest became all too familiar, the innovations of *U.S.A.* no longer new, and the events of his major novels no longer *current* ones, even his best work seemed to become no longer relevant.''

One of Dos Passos's loyal admirers, James T. Farrell, wrote in 1958: ''John Dos Passos writes with great ease and he is technically inventive. . . . From *Three Soldiers* to *The Great Days,* we can see in Dos Passos the effort of one man of talent and sensibility to take hold of this changing play of forces in our life.'' But Wrenn observed that contemporary Americans were no longer his audience, principally because he had been stereotyped as ''rebel of the twenties, ex-communist, political novelist, disillusioned social critic,'' and writers so labeled were out of fashion. Robie Macaulay felt that much of Dos Passos's work was ''bound to taste rather stale to this generation, a spectacle not current enough to be news and not quite old enough to be history. . . . But, given enough distance, Dos Passos will have his day again. How he will be read in another time is hard to say. . . . I should say that it will be less as a social interpreter than as a primitive portraitist of American lives during a certain time.'' To this Thomas Lask added: ''Dos Passos may become known as the author of one book, but in its range and reach, in its willingness to meet head on the possibilities of American life, it is large enough to be considered a life's work.''

Arthur Mizener noted that, in spite of his faults, ''Dos Passos is the only major American novelist of the twentieth century who has had the desire and the power to surround the lives of his characters with what Lionel Trilling once called 'the buzz of history'—the actual, homely, everyday sounds of current events and politics, of social ambitions and the struggle for money, of small pleasures and trivial corruptions, amidst which we all live. He has given us a major aspect of our experience that has hardly been touched by any other novelist of our time.'' Kazin echoed these sentiments when he wrote: ''It is often assumed that Dos Passos was a 'left-wing' novelist in the Thirties who, like other novelists of the period, turned conservative and thus changed and lost his creative identity. . . . But [*U.S.A.*] is not simply a 'left-wing' novel, and its technical inventiveness and freshness of style are typical of the Twenties rather than the Thirties. In any event, Dos Passos has always been so detached from all group thinking that it is impossible to understand his development as a novelist by identifying him with the radical novelists of the Thirties. He began earlier. . . . In all periods he has followed his own perky, obstinately independent course. . . . It is not his values but the loss by many educated people of a belief in 'history' that has caused Dos Passos's relative isolation in recent years. . . . Alone among his literary cronies, Dos Passos managed to add this idea of history as the great operative force to their enthusiasm for radical technique, the language of Joyce, and 'the religion of the world.'''

AVOCATIONAL INTERESTS: Travel, sailing, canoeing, gardening, painting watercolors.

BIOGRAPHICAL/CRITICAL SOURCES—Books: Alfred

Kazin, *On Native Grounds,* Reynal, 1942; Maxwell Geismar, *Writers in Crisis,* Houghton, 1942; Edmund Wilson, *The Triple Thinkers,* revised edition, Oxford University Press, 1948; Jack Potter, *A Bibliography of John Dos Passos,* Normandie House, 1950; Henry Steele Commager, *The American Mind,* Yale University Press, 1950; W. M. Frohock, *The Novel of Violence in America: 1920-1950,* University Press in Dallas, 1950; Malcolm Cowley, *Exile's Return,* revised edition, Viking, 1951; Edmund Wilson, *The Shores of Light,* Farrar, Straus, 1952; Mark Eastman and others, *John Dos Passos: An Appreciation,* Prentice-Hall, 1954; Jean-Paul Sartre, *Literary and Philosophical Essays,* Rider, 1955; Geismar, *American Moderns: From Rebellion to Conformity,* Hill & Wang, 1958; Joseph Warren Beach, *American Fiction: 1920-1940,* Russell & Russell, 1960; John H. Wrenn, *John Dos Passos,* Twayne, 1961; Chester E. Eisinger, *Fiction of the Forties,* University of Chicago Press, 1963; John Brantley, *The Fiction of John Dos Passos,* San Antonio College, 1964; Walter Allen, *The Modern Novel in Britain and the United States,* Dutton, 1965; Arthur Mizener, *Twelve Great American Novels,* New American Library, 1967; Allen Belkind, editor, *Dos Passos, the Critics, and the Writer's Intention,* Southern Illinois University Press, 1972; Melvin Landsberg, *Dos Passos Path to U.S.A.: A Political Biography, 1912-1936,* Colorado Associated University Press, 1972; Stephen Longstreet, *We All Went to Paris,* Macmillan, 1972; *Contemporary Literary Criticism,* Gale, Volume I, 1973, Volume IV, 1975, Volume VIII, 1978, Volume XI, 1979, Volume XV, 1980; Malcolm Cowley, *Second Flowering,* Viking, 1973; George J. Becker, *John Dos Passos,* Ungar, 1974; John Dos Passos, *Fourteenth Chronicle: Letters and Diaries,* edited by Townsend Ludington, Deutsch, 1974; Andrew Hook, editor, *Dos Passos: A Collection of Critical Essays,* Prentice-Hall, 1974; G. A. Knox and H. M. Stahl, *Dos Passos and the Revolting Playwrights,* Folcroft, 1976; Francis M. Rogers, *The Portuguese Heritage of John Dos Passos,* Portuguese Continental Union of the U.S.A., 1976.

Periodicals: *Nation,* November 15, 1922, March 12, 1930, June 3, 1939, April 14, 1956; *Bookmen,* December, 1922; *Saturday Review of Literature,* December 5, 1925, May 5, 1934, September 2, 1944, January 8, 1949; *Atlantic Bookshelf,* June 30, 1930; *Spectator,* September 27, 1930; *Nation and Athenaeum,* November 1, 1930; *Books,* March 13, 1932, April 29, 1934, July 1, 1934, June 4, 1939; *Springfield Republican,* March 13, 1932; *New Statesman and Nation,* June 11, 1932; *New York Times,* May 6, 1934, May 20, 1934, August 31, 1941, July 23, 1944, September 29, 1970; *Review of Reviews,* September, 1936; *Forum,* September, 1936; *Atlantic,* October, 1936; *Commonweal,* June 2, 1939, March 5, 1943, January 28, 1949, October 8, 1954; *New Yorker,* June 3, 1939, August 24, 1946, March 18, 1961; *New Republic,* June 14, 1939, September 1, 1941, July 24, 1944, September 2, 1946, September 27, 1954, April 28, 1958; *Times Literary Supplement,* June 17, 1939, October 27, 1950, January 28, 1965; *Living Age,* September, 1939; *Atlantic,* April, 1943, March, 1961; *Yale Review,* summer, 1943; *New York Herald Tribune Weekly Book Review,* January 2, 1949; *San Francisco Chronicle,* January 9, 1949, February 26, 1961; *Catholic World,* February, 1949.

Time, September 27, 1954, March 3, 1961, October 12, 1970; *Saturday Review,* December 12, 1959, February 25, 1961, March 15, 1969; *New York Times Book Review,* December 20, 1959, December 25, 1960, April 7, 1963, January 10, 1965; *New York Herald Tribune Lively Arts,* February 26, 1961; *Christian Science Monitor,* March 2, 1961; *Esquire,*

May, 1961; *New Statesman,* October 27, 1961; *Christian Century,* November 28, 1962, November 4, 1964; *New York Herald Tribune Books,* December 2, 1962; *National Review,* December 1, 1964, October 20, 1970; *New Leader,* March 15, 1965; *Book Week,* March 28, 1965; *Social Education,* April, 1965; *South Atlantic Quarterly,* spring, 1966; *Twentieth Century Literature,* October, 1967; *Statesman,* March 1, 1968; *Paris Review,* spring, 1969; *Newsweek,* October 12, 1970; *Saturday Review/World,* September 11, 1973; *Washington Post Book World,* October 28, 1973.†

—Sketch by Penelope S. Gordon

[Sketch approved by wife, Elizabeth H. Dos Passos]

*   *   *

DOUGLASS, Paul F(ranklin) 1904-

PERSONAL: Born November 7, 1904, in Corinth, N.Y.; son of George C. (a clergyman) and Mabel (Parker) Douglass. *Education:* Wesleyan University, A.B., 1926; University of Chicago, graduate study, 1928; University of Cincinnati, M.A., 1929, Ph.D. (Taft fellow), 1931; University of Berlin, postdoctoral study, 1931-33. *Politics:* Democrat. *Religion:* Methodist. *Home:* PAR Farm, Inc., Granville, N.Y. 12832. *Office address:* Folger Bldg., P.O. Box 199, West Fawlet, Vt. 05775.

CAREER: Cincinnati Post, Cincinnati, Ohio, reporter, 1926-27, educational editor, 1927-28; Chicago Bureau correspondent, *Christian Science Monitor,* 1928-30; director of study, courts of limited jurisdiction and Cincinnati Municipal Court, for Johns Hopkins University, Institute of Law, in Ohio, 1930-31; ordained to Methodist ministry, 1933; pastor in Poultney, Vt., 1933-41; American University, Washington, D.C., president, 1941-52; advisor to the president and counsel to Ministry of Foreign Affairs, Republic of Korea, 1952-55; Rollins College, Winter Park, Fla., professor of government and director of Center for Practical Politics, 1956-71; National League of Postmasters, Washington, D.C., general counsel, 1971—. Admitted to Vermont State Bar, 1937, the Bar of U.S. Supreme Court, 1941, and the Bar of District of Columbia; member of Vermont House of Representatives, 1937-39, 1939-41, and Vermont Senate, 1941-43. Chairman, Task Force on Leisure, National Council of Churches, 1965-67. Director, Management Corporation of America. Trustee, National Recreation and Park Association, 1965-67.

MEMBER: Association of Urban Universities (president, 1949-50), American Recreation Foundation (vice-chairman, 1958-62), American Bar Association, Federal Communications Bar Association, American Society of International Law, American Political Science Association, National Press Club, Cosmos Club. *Awards, honors:* LL.D., Wesleyan University, 1946; Order of Ascending Star with Rosetta, Republic of China, 1948; Haakon VII Cross, Norway, 1948; Order of Taiguk, Republic of Korea, 1950.

WRITINGS: The Newspaper and Responsibility, Caxton, 1929; *Justice of Peace Courts,* Johns Hopkins Press, 1932; *The Organization of the Press at the Disarmament Conference,* American Academy of Political and Social Science, 1932; *Mayors' Courts of Hamilton County, Ohio,* Johns Hopkins Press, 1933; *Practice and Procedure in Ohio Courts of Limited Jurisdiction,* Baldwin-Banks, 1934; *The Economic Independence of Poland,* Ruter Press, 1934; *God among the Germans,* University of Pennsylvania Press, 1935; (editor) *Consumer Credit* (annals), American Academy of Political and Social Science, 1938; *The Story of German Methodist,* Methodist Book, 1939; *The Yankee Tradition,*

Free Press of Glencoe, 1941; *Spiritual Experiences in Administration,* American University Press, 1944; *Wesleys at Oxford,* Bryn Mawr Press, 1953; *Six upon the World,* Little, Brown, 1954; *The Group Workshop Way,* Association Press, 1957; (editor) *Recreation in the Age of Automation,* American Academy of Political and Social Science, 1957; *Communication through Reports,* Prentice-Hall, 1958; *Teaching for Self-Education: As a Life Goal,* Harper, 1960; *How to Be an Active Citizen,* University of Florida Press, 1960; *Government: Principles and Concepts,* World Publishing, 1967; *Black Apostle to Yankeeland,* Sullivan, 1972; *Guide to Planning the Farm Estate: With Checklists and Forms,* Institute for Business Planning, 1978, 2nd edition, 1979. Also author of *The ABC of Industrial Parks,* 1960, *New Towns,* 1970, and *Inside Isthmus America,* 1971. Contributor to *Encyclopedia Americana;* contributor of articles to professional journals.

WORK IN PROGRESS: The Political Behavior of Syngman Rhee; The Reuthers and the Rewarding Society; The Theory of Leisure Experience; The Successions: Korea, 1880-1980.

AVOCATIONAL INTERESTS: Work on his farm; raising registered Holsteins; dairying.

*   *   *

DOUTY, Esther M(orris) 1909-1978

PERSONAL: Born March 24, 1909, in Mount Vernon, N.Y.; died December 13, 1978, in Washington, D.C.; daughter of John Charles and Rosalie (Bien) Morris; married Harry M. Douty (an associate commissioner, U.S. Bureau of Labor Statistics), August 16, 1930; children: Christopher Morris (died, 1970), Harriet Taylor. *Education:* Duke University, A.B., 1930; University of North Carolina, graduate study, 1933-34. *Politics:* Independent. *Religion:* Unitarian Universalist. *Residence:* Washington, D.C. *Agent:* McIntosh & Otis, Inc., 475 Fifth Ave., New York, N.Y. 10017.

CAREER: Social worker in Orange County, N.C., 1934-36. Director of workshop in junior biography, Writers' Conference, Georgetown University, 1960-68; lecturer in junior biography, Writers' Institute, George Washington University, 1961. *Member:* Children's Book Guild (president, 1961-62), Phi Beta Kappa. *Awards, honors:* Boys' Clubs of America certificate award, 1957, for *Ball in the Sky;* American Library Association "notable book" citation, 1968, for *Forten the Sailmaker.*

WRITINGS—Juvenile: *Story of Stephen Foster,* Grosset, 1954; *Ball in the Sky: John Wise, America's Pioneer Balloonist,* Henry Holt, 1956; *Patriot Doctor: The Story of Benjamin Rush,* Messner, 1959; *America's First Woman Chemist–Ellen Richards,* Messner, 1961; *Under the New Roof: Five Patriots of the Young Republic,* Rand McNally, 1965; *Forten the Sailmaker: Pioneer Champion of Negro Rights,* Rand McNally, 1968; *Mr. Jefferson's Washington,* Garrard, 1970; *Charlotte Forten: Free Black Teacher,* Garrard, 1971; *The Brave Balloonists: America's First Airmen,* Garrard, 1974; *Hasty Pudding and Barbary Pirates: A Life of Joel Barlow,* Westminster, 1975. Contributor to various publications, including *American Heritage, New Republic,* and *Reporter.*

AVOCATIONAL INTERESTS: Collecting and coloring antique engravings relating to the American scene, and experimenting with the old art of transferring them to glass.

BIOGRAPHICAL/CRITICAL SOURCES: Young Readers' Review, October, 1968; *New York Times Book Review,* October 27, 1968; *Children's Book World,* November 3, 1968; *New Yorker,* December 14, 1968.†

DOWDEN, Anne Ophelia 1907-
(Anne Ophelia Todd)

PERSONAL: Born September 17, 1907, in Denver, Colo.; daughter of James Campbell (the chairman of department of clinical pathology at University of Colorado) and Edith (Brownfield) Todd; married Raymond Baxter Dowden (a teacher and administrator), April 1, 1934. *Education:* Attended University of Colorado, 1925-26; Carnegie Institute of Technology (now Carnegie-Mellon University), B.A., 1930; additional study at Art Students League of New York and Beaux Arts Institute of Design. *Religion:* Protestant. *Home:* 205 West 15th St., New York, N.Y. 10011.

CAREER: Pratt Institute, Brooklyn, N.Y., instructor in drawing, 1930-33; Manhattanville College, Purchase, N.Y., teacher of art and chairman of department, 1932-53; freelance textile designer, 1935-55; botanical illustrator, 1950—. Paintings, textile designs, and botanical water colors have been exhibited at Carnegie Institute of Technology (now Carnegie-Mellon University), Whitney Museum, Metropolitan Museum of Art, Newark Museum, Silvermine Artists Guild, Cooper Union Museum, Brooklyn Botanic Garden, and Hunt Botanical Library. *Awards, honors:* Tiffany Foundation fellow, 1929, 1930, and 1932; *Wild Green Things in the City* chosen as Children's Book Showcase Title, 1973; *Look at a Flower* named "notable book" by the American Library Association.

WRITINGS—Self-illustrated: The Little Hill: A Chronicle of Flora on a Half Acre at the Green Camp, Ringwood, New Jersey, Cooper Union Art School, 1961; (under name Anne Ophelia Todd) *Cooper Union Art School 8,* Cooper Union Art School, 1961; *Look at a Flower,* Crowell, 1963; *The Secret Life of the Flowers,* Odyssey, 1964; (with Richard Thomson) *Roses,* Odyssey, 1965; *Wild Green Things in the City: A Book of Weeds,* Crowell, 1972; *The Blossom on the Bough: A Book of Trees,* Crowell, 1975; *State Flowers,* Crowell, 1978; *This Noble Harvest: A Chronicle of Herbs,* Collins & World, 1979.

Illustrator: Jessica Kerr, *Shakespeare's Flowers,* Crowell, 1969; Hal Borland, *Plants of Christmas,* Golden Press, 1969; Louis Untermeyer, editor, *Roses,* Golden Press, 1970; Untermeyer, *Plants of the Bible,* Golden Press, 1970; Borland, *The Golden Circle,* Crowell, 1977; Phyllis Busch, *Wildflowers and the Stories behind Their Names,* Scribner, 1977. Botanical illustrations published in four issues of *Life,* 1952-57, in *House Beautiful, Natural History,* and *Audubon.*

WORK IN PROGRESS: Illustrating *The Lore and Legend of Flowers* by Robert Crowell, for Crowell.

*   *   *

DRACKETT, Phil(ip Arthur) 1922-
(Paul King)

PERSONAL: Born December 25, 1922, in London, England; son of Arthur Ernest (a builder) and Mary Jane (King) Drackett; married Joan Isobel Davies, June 19, 1948. *Education:* University of London, general schools certificate. *Home:* 9 Victoria Rd., Mundesleg, Norfolk, England.

MEMBER: Institute of Journalists, Guild of Motoring Writers, Sports Writers Association.

WRITINGS: Fighting Days, A-American, 1944; *Come Out Fighting,* A-American, 1945; *Speedway,* W. & G. Foyle, 1951; *Motor Racing,* W. & G. Foyle, 1952; *Motoring,* W. & G. Foyle, 1955; (with Leslie Webb) *You and Your Car,* W. & G. Foyle, 1957; (with A. Thompson) *You and Your Motor Cycle,* W. & G. Foyle, 1958; *Great Moments in Motoring,*

Roy, 1958; *Automobiles Work Like This,* Phoenix House, 1958, Roy, 1960; *Veteran Cars,* W. & G. Foyle, 1961; *The Young Car Driver's Companion,* Sportshelf, 1961; *Vintage Cars,* W. & G. Foyle, 1962; *Motor Rallying,* W. & G. Foyle, 1963; *Driving Your Car: Passing the Test, and After,* Sportshelf, 1964; *Taking Your Car Abroad,* W. & G. Foyle, 1965; *International Motor Racing Book,* four volumes, Souvenir Press, 1967-70; *Let's Look at Cars,* Muller, 1967; *Slot Car Racing,* Souvenir Press, 1968; *Like Father, Like Son: The Story of Malcolm and Donald Campbell,* Clifton Books, 1969; *Rally of the Forests: The Story of the RAC International Rally of Great Britain,* Pelham Books, 1970; *Motor Racing Champions,* two volumes, Purnell Books, 1971-72; *The Book of the Veteran Car,* Pelham Books, 1973; *The Book of Great Disasters,* Purnell Books, 1978; *The Book of Dangerman,* Purnell Books, 1979; *The Encyclopedia of the Motor Car,* Octopus, 1979; *The All-Colour World of Cars,* Octopus, 1979; *Inns and Harbours of North Norfolk,* Royal Automobile Club, 1980; *Car Makers,* Macdonald Educational, 1980; *Vintage Cars,* Octopus, 1980; *The Story of the RAC International Rally,* Haynes, 1980. Contributor to programs of British Broadcasting Corp. and Independent Television; contributor of articles to many periodicals and newspapers.

*   *   *

DRESSEL, Paul L(eroy) 1910-

PERSONAL: Born November 29, 1910, in Youngstown, Ohio; son of David Calvin (a carpenter) and Aura Olive (Jacobs) Dressel; married Wilma Frances Sackett, September 18, 1933; children: Carol Ann, Linda Kathleen, Jeana Lynn. *Education:* Youngstown College (now Youngstown State University), A.A., 1929; Wittenberg University, A.B., 1931; Michigan State College of Agriculture and Applied Science (now Michigan State University), M.A., 1934; University of Michigan, Ph.D., 1939. *Religion:* Protestant. *Home:* 235 Maplewood Dr., East Lansing, Mich. 48823. *Office:* Office of Institutional Research, Michigan State University, East Lansing, Mich. 48223.

CAREER: Michigan State University, East Lansing, instructor and assistant professor of mathematics, 1934-42, professor and director of Office of Evaluation Services, 1954-59, professor of university research, 1959—, director of Orientation Office, 1940-44, director of counseling and chairman of board of examiners, 1944-54, Office of Institutional Research, director, 1959-75, assistant provost, 1959-76. Director, Cooperative Study of Evaluation in General Education, American Council on Education, 1949-53. *Member:* American Association for the Advancement of Science (fellow), American Psychological Association (fellow), American Educational Research Association, National Education Association, National Council for Measurement in Education (president, 1961-62), American Association for Higher Education (president, 1970-71), National Society for the Study of Education, Association for Institutional Research, Association for General and Liberal Studies. *Awards, honors:* LL.D., Wittenberg University, 1966; Distinguished Faculty Award, Michigan State University, 1975.

WRITINGS: (With others) *Comprehensive Examinations in a Program of General Education,* Michigan State College Press, 1949; (with John Schmid) *An Evaluation of the Tests of General Educational Development,* American Council on Education, 1951; (with Raymond Hatch) *Guidance Services in the Secondary School,* W. C. Brown, 1953; (with Lewis B. Mayhew) *General Education: Explorations in Evaluation,* American Council on Education, 1954; (with Mayhew) *Handbook for TheeAnalysis,* W. C. Brown, 1954; (with

Mayhew) *Science Reasoning and Understanding,* W. C. Brown, 1954; (with Mayhew) *Critical Thinking in the Social Sciences,* W. C. Brown, 1954; *Research in General Education Instruction,* Association for Higher Education, Volume I, 1955, Volume II (with Margaret F. Lorimer), 1957; (with Clarence H. Nelson) *Test Item Folios,* Educational Testing Service, 1956; (with Mayhew) *Critical Analysis and Judgement in the Humanities,* W. C. Brown, 1956; (with Mayhew and Earl J. McGrath) *The Liberal Arts as Viewed by Faculty Members in Professional Schools,* Institute of Higher Education, Teachers College, Columbia University, 1959; *A Report of Differential Prediction and Placement in Colleges and Universities,* [East Lansing], 1959; (with Irvin J. Lehmann) *Critical Thinking, Attitudes and Values in Higher Education,* Michigan State University, 1959.

Liberal Education and Journalism, Institute of Higher Education, Teachers College, Columbia University, 1960; (with Lorimer) *The Attitudes of Liberal Arts Faculty Members toward Liberal and Professional Education,* Teachers College, Columbia University, 1960; *The Undergraduate Curriculum in Higher Education,* Center for Applied Research in Education, 1963; (with Jeannette A. Lee) *Liberal Education and Home Economics,* Teachers College, Columbia University, 1963; *College and University Curriculum,* McCutchan, 1968, 2nd edition, 1971; (with Frances DeLisle) *Undergraduate Curriculum Trends,* American Council on Education, 1969; (with F. Craig Johnson and Philip Marcus) *The Confidence Crisis,* Jossey-Bass, 1970; (with others) *Institutional Research in the University,* Jossey-Bass, 1971; (with Sally B. Pratt) *The World of Higher Education,* Jossey-Bass, 1971; (with William H. Faricy) *Return to Responsibility: Higher Constraints on Autonomy in Higher Education,* Jossey-Bass, 1972; (with DeLisle) *Blueprint for Change: Doctoral Programs for College Teachers* (monograph), American College Testing Program, 1972; (with Mary Magdala Thompson) *Independent Study,* Jossey-Bass, 1973; (with Thompson) *College Teaching: Improvement by Degrees,* American College Testing Program, 1974; *Handbook of Academic Evaluation,* Jossey-Bass, 1976; (with Lou Anna Simon) *Allocating Resources among Departments* (monograph), Jossey-Bass, 1976; (with Thompson) *A Degree for College Teachers: The Doctor of Arts,* Carnegie Council on Policy Studies in Higher Education, 1977; (with Thomas M. Freeman and Albert B. Lynd) *The Autonomy of Public Colleges,* Jossey-Bass, 1980; *Improving Degree Programs: A Guide to Curriculum Development, Administration and Review,* Jossey-Bass, 1980.

Editor: (And contributor) *Evaluation in General Education,* W. C. Brown, 1954; (with Nelson) *Questions and Problems in Science,* Educational Testing Service, 1956; (and contributor) *Evaluation in the Basic College of Michigan State University,* Harper, 1958; (with Horace T. Morse) *General Education for Personal Maturity,* W. C. Brown, 1960; (and contributor) *Evaluation in Higher Education,* Houghton, 1961; *The New Colleges: Toward an Appraisal* (monograph), American College Testing Program and American Association for Higher Education, 1971.

Contributor: C. E. Erickson, editor, *A Basic Text for Guidance Workers,* Prentice-Hall, 1947; Ralph F. Berdie, editor, *Concepts and Programs of Counseling,* University of Minnesota Press, 1951; William G. Tyrrell, editor, *Social Studies in the College Program for the First Two Years,* National Council for the Social Studies, 1953; Sidney J. French, editor, *Accent on Teaching,* Harper, 1954; Berdie, editor, *Counseling and the College Program,* University of Minnesota Press, 1954; Thomas H. Hamilton, editor, *The Basic*

College of Michigan State College, Michigan State College Press, 1955; Melvene Hardee, editor, *Counseling and Guidance in General Education,* World Book, 1955; Mayhew, editor, *General Education: An Account and Appraisal,* Harper, 1960; McGrath, editor, *Cooperative Long-Range Planning in Liberal Arts Colleges,* Institute of Higher Education, Teachers College, Columbia University, 1964; Herman A. Estrin and Delmer M. Goode, *College and University Teaching,* W. C. Brown, 1964; Morris Keeton and Conrad Hilberry, *Struggle and Promise: A Future for Colleges,* McGraw, 1969; Asa S. Knowles, editor, *Handbook of College and University Administration,* McGraw, 1970.

Contributor to encyclopedias, education association yearbooks, and published conference reports; contributor of almost one hundred monographs, articles, and book reviews to education journals.

WORK IN PROGRESS: A book on college and university administration; a book on college teaching.

*   *   *

DRINAN, Robert F(rederick)   1920-

PERSONAL: Born November 15, 1920, in Boston, Mass.; son of James J. and Anne (Flanagan) Drinan. *Education:* Boston College, A.B., 1940, M.A., 1947; Georgetown University, LL.B., 1949, LL.M., 1950; Gregorian University, Th.D., 1954. *Home:* Boston College, 140 Commonwealth Ave., Chestnut Hill, Mass. 02167.

CAREER: Entered Society of Jesus (Jesuits), 1942; ordained Roman Catholic priest, 1953. Admitted to District of Columbia Bar, 1950, Bar of U.S. Supreme Court, 1955, and Massachusetts State Bar, 1956; Boston College, Law School, Chestnut Hill, Mass., 1956-70, became professor of law, assistant dean, 1955-56, dean, 1957-70; U.S. House of Representatives, Washington, D.C., Democratic Congressman from Massachusetts' Fourth District, 1970-80, member of House Judiciary Committee, 1971-80 (chairman, Subcommittee on Criminal Justice, 1979-80), House Internal Security Committee, 1971-74, House Government Operations Committee, 1975-80, and House Select Committee on Aging, 1977-80, member of official congressional delegations to numerous Asian nations, including Vietnam, Thailand, Indonesia, the People's Republic of China, and Japan, member of executive or steering committees of various congressionally affiliated conferences, study groups, and caucuses. Visiting professor, Law School, University of Texas at Austin, 1966-67; visiting lecturer, Andover-Newton Theological Seminary, 1966-68; member of visiting committee, Divinity School, Harvard University. Chairman of advisory committee for Massachusetts, U.S. Commission on Civil Rights, 1962-70. Founder, National Interreligious Task Force on Soviet Jewry; chairman of international committee for the release of Anatoly Shcharansky; member of board of directors, Bread for the World.

MEMBER: American Bar Association (chairman of section on family law, 1966-67), American Judicature Society (member of national executive committee, 1962-64), Association of American Law Schools (member of executive committee, 1967-69), American Civil Liberties Union (member of national advisory council), Americans for Democratic Action (vice-president), National Conference of Christians and Jews (member of national board of trustees), American Academy of Arts and Sciences (fellow), Massachusetts Bar Association (vice-president, 1961-64; chairman of committee on the administration of justice, 1962-69), Boston Bar Association (chairman of committee on family law, 1960-64).

Awards, honors: Honorary degrees from Worcester State College and Long Island University, both 1970, Rhode Island College, 1971, St. Joseph's College (Philadelphia), 1975, Syracuse University and Villanova University, both 1977, Framingham State College, 1978, and University of Santa Clara, 1980.

WRITINGS: Federal Aid to Education, Clergy Conference, Archdiocese of Chicago, 1962; *Religion, the Courts and Public Policy,* McGraw, 1963; *New Dimensions in the Professional Responsibilities of the Bar,* Maine Bar Association, 1963; (contributor) Dallin H. Oaks, editor, *The Wall between Church and State,* University of Chicago, 1963; *The Changing Order of the Lawyer in an Era of Non-Violent Action,* Congress of Racial Equality, 1964; *The Constitution, Governmental Aid and Catholic Higher Education,* National Catholic Educational Association, 1968; (editor) *The Right to Be Educated,* foreward by Arthur J. Goldberg, Corpus Books, 1968; *Democracy, Dissent and Disorder: The Issues and the Law,* Seabury, 1969; *Vietnam and Armageddon: Peace, War and the Christian Conscience,* Sheed, 1970; *Honor the Promise: America's Commitment to Israel,* Doubleday, 1977. Contributor to several law journals and reviews. Contributing editor, *America,* 1958-70; editor-in-chief, *Family Law Quarterly,* 1967-70.

WORK IN PROGRESS: A book on legal-moral problems in America, tentatively titled *Law and Morality in America.*

SIDELIGHTS: Congressman Robert F. Drinan spent the first half of 1980 quietly campaigning for re-election. A popular and respected five-term incumbent, he was expected to win a sixth term with "no significant opposition," according to *Time.* Thus it came as a shock when Drinan, a Roman Catholic priest, announced in May of that election year that he would relinquish his congressional seat and abandon his political career. "I'm not running for re-election," he explained. "I've been forbidden to do so by the pope."

A flurry of anger and speculation greeted the priest's disclosure. Ostensibly, the pope's decision was prompted by his belief in the separation of church and state and was based on church law. "Article 139 of the church's canon law forbids priests to hold elective office," *Time* reports, "though the provision does allow local church authorities to make exceptions if they decide a priest's involvement in politics would be for the good of the community." However, *Newsweek*'s Kenneth L. Woodward points to the fact that "these standards have not always been enforced. Drinan regularly received permission to run in the past, and many other priests in the United States and abroad also have won elective office." The reason, then, behind the pope's order? "The angry suspicion in many congressional offices and among Drinan's constituents was that John Paul II was particularly offended by Drinan's liberal views," Woodward explains. "A keen advocate of civil liberties and social services, Drinan supports federal funding of abortions for poor women."

According to commentators, this view is grounded in more than "angry suspicion." In the *New Republic,* Richard P. McBrien, a professor of theology at the University of Notre Dame, contends that "it is difficult to avoid the conclusion that the papal order was directed explicitly at Father Drinan, and that the reason was not the broader theoretical question of priests in politics but the specific question of abortion." And a *Commonweal* observer notes: "Drinan has been attacked by the church before; in 1972 an article in *L'Osservatore Romano* appeared to single him out for criticism, misrepresenting his position on abortion legislation along the way. It is quite possible that Drinan has been on a Vatican 'list' for some time."

Initially, there had been some concern that the pope's decree would ultimately effect politically active priests in troubled Latin America. The Vatican quickly denied this supposition. However, it is less clear just how the Drinan decision will apply to the many nuns who hold elective office in the United States. The Vatican states that "the 'spirit' of the ban against Drinan does apply to nuns," *Time* notes. "But several of the nuns [questioned] say they will stay in office unless the pope specifically orders them to quit."

Most of the anger and controversy surrounding Drinan's case has been directed at the Vatican's handling of the matter. "In this instance, Rome erred, both in what it did and how it did it," the *Commonweal* reporter opines. McBrien elaborates: "The decision and its manner of execution are in some conflict with two principles of Catholic theology: The principle of subsidiarity (which requires, among other things, that decisions should be made as closely as possible to the point where they will have their impact) and the principle of collegiality (which requires, among other things, that decisions should be made in light of local circumstances, experiences, traditions, and cultures)." The *National Review*'s William F. Buckley, Jr. chastizes the Vatican for its lack of diplomatic aplomb. Buckley states that "the pope's general position is eminently defensible." Nevertheless he contends: "Everything about the Vatican's order . . . was clumsy. . . . The resulting picture was that of a Polish pope, living in Rome, traveling in Africa, reaching into the politics of Boston . . . to tell the people there, in effect, whom they could not send to Congress. The diplomacy of the episode was inept."

Despite what others have to say regarding the church's action, Drinan himself "obeyed the pope's decision without question," *Time* reports. Buckley finds that the priest and former politician "has borne his cross with grace, reminding his constituents that, notwithstanding the many temptations of the world, his hierarchy of loyalties survives." In *Newsweek,* Drinan's campaign manager suggests that as far as the ex-congressman is concerned the decision to resign was a simple one: "The church is his life, his heart. He never once considered defiance."

BIOGRAPHICAL/CRITICAL SOURCES: Christian Century, February 4, 1970; *America,* May 17, 1980, May 24, 1980; *Newsweek,* May 19, 1980; *Time:* May 19, 1980; *Commonweal,* May 23, 1980; *New Republic,* June 14, 1980; *National Review,* June 27, 1980.

*   *   *

DRURY, Clifford Merrill 1897-

PERSONAL: Born November 7, 1897, in Early, Iowa; son of William (a farmer) and Mae Charity (Dell) Drury; married Miriam Leyrer, November 17, 1922; children: Robert Merrill, Patricia, Philip Edward (deceased). *Education:* Buena Vista College, B.A., 1918; San Francisco Theological Seminary, B.D., 1922, S.T.M., 1928; University of Edinburgh, Ph.D., 1932. *Politics:* Republican. *Home:* 2889 San Pasqual St., Pasadena, Calif. 91107.

CAREER: Ordained to Presbyterian ministry, 1922; Community Church (American), Shanghai, China, pastor, 1923-27; First Presbyterian Church, Moscow, Idaho, pastor, 1928-38; San Francisco Theological Seminary, San Anselmo, Calif., professor of church history, 1938-63. *Military service:* U.S. Army, 1918. U.S. Naval Reserve, 1933-58, on active duty, 1941-46, official historian of U.S. Navy Chaplain Corps, 1944-56; became captain; received Secretary of Navy Commendation with medal. *Member:* Church History Society,

Phi Beta Kappa. *Awards, honors:* D.D., Buena Vista College, 1941; Litt.D., Whitworth College, 1955; Distinguished Service Award, Presbyterian Historical Society, 1960; D.H.L., Whitman College, 1964; first recipient of Captain Robert Gray Medal, Washington State Historical Society, 1968.

WRITINGS: Nicodemus: A Three-act Religious Drama Based upon the Three New Testament References to Nicodemus, the Pharisee, privately printed, 1934; *Pioneer of Old Oregon: Henry Harmon Spalding,* Caxton, 1936; *Marcus Whitman, M.D.: Pioneer and Martyr,* Caxton, 1937; *Elkanah and Mary Walker: Pioneers among the Spokanes,* Caxton, 1940; (contributor) Ward Willis Long, editor, *Ninetieth Anniversary, March 17, 1940, First Presbyterian Church, Stockton, California,* Simarel Printing Co., 1940; *United States Navy Chaplains, 1778-1945,* U.S. Government Printing Office, 1945; (compiler) *The History of the Chaplain Corps, United States Navy,* five volumes, U.S. Government Printing Office, 1948-57; *A Tepee in His Front Yard: A Biography of H. T. Cowley, One of the Four Founders of the City of Spokane, Washington,* Binfords, 1949; *Presbyterian Panorama: One Hundred and Fifty Years of National Missions History,* Westminster, 1952; (editor) *Diary of Titian Ramsay Peale: Oregon to California, Overland Journey, September and October, 1841,* G. Dawson, 1957; *The Beginnings of Talmak's "Galloping over the Butte"* (address), privately printed, 1958; *A Bibliography of California Religious Imprints, 1846-1876,* California Historical Society, 1970.

Published by Arthur Clark: (Editor and author of introduction) *The Diaries and Letters of Henry H. Spalding and Asa Bowen Smith Relating to the Nez Pearce Mission, 1838-1842,* 1958; (editor) *First White Women over the Rockies: Diaries, Letters, and Biographical Sketches of the Six Women of the Oregon Mission Who Made the Overland Journey in 1836 and 1838,* three volumes, 1963-66; *San Francisco YMCA: 100 Years by the Golden Gate, 1853-1963,* 1963; *William Anderson Scott, "No Ordinary Man,"* 1967; *Rudolph James Wig: Engineer, Pomona College Trustee, Presbyterian Layman,* 1968; *California Imprints, 1846-1876: Pertaining to Social, Educational, and Religious Subjects,* 1970; *Marcus and Narcissa Whitman, and the Opening of Old Oregon,* two volumes, 1973; (editor) *Nine Years with the Spokane Indians: The Diary, 1838-1848, of Elkanah Walker,* 1976; *Chief Lawyer of the Nez Perce Indians, 1796-1870,* 1979. Contributor of forty articles to history journals. Editor, *Army-Navy Chaplain,* 1945-46.

* * *

DUDDEN, Arthur P(ower) 1921-
(Arthur Power)

PERSONAL: Born October 26, 1921, in Cleveland, Ohio; son of Arthur Clifford and Kathleen Florence (Bray) Dudden; married Millicent Ruth Hancock, April 24, 1943 (divorced, August 31, 1964); married Adrianne Churchill Onderdenk, June 5, 1965; children: (first marriage) Kathleen Hancock, Candace Louise; (second marriage) Alexis Bray. *Education:* Wayne University (now Wayne State University), A.B., 1942; University of Michigan, A.M., 1947, Ph.D., 1950. *Politics:* Democrat. *Home:* 829 Old Gulph Rd., Bryn Mawr, Pa. 19010. *Office:* Department of History, Bryn Mawr College, Bryn Mawr, Pa. 19010.

CAREER: Ford Motor Co., Ypsilanti, Mich., veterans counselor, 1946; Bryn Mawr College, Bryn Mawr, Pa., assistant professor, 1950-56, associate professor, 1956-65, professor of history, 1965—, chairman of department, beginning 1968.

Instructor, City College (now City College of the City University of New York), summer, 1950; University of Pennsylvania, member of faculty, Institute of Humanistic Studies for Executives, 1953-59, educational coordinator, special program in American civilization, 1956, visiting associate professor of history, summers, 1958, 1962, and 1965; visiting associate professor of history, Princeton University, 1958-59, and Haverford College, 1962-63; distinguished lecturer to Denmark and Sweden, U.S. Department of State, 1963; visiting professor of history, Trinity College, Hartford, Conn., 1965. Member, Bicentennial Commission on International Conferences of Americanists, 1973-76. Consultant, Peace Corps, 1962-66. Has appeared on television programs, including "Documents of American History," WFIL, "Dateline Yesterday," WCAU, and "The Longer View." *Military service:* U.S. Naval Reserve, 1942-45.

MEMBER: American Historical Association, Organization of American Historians, Economic History Association, American Studies Association (secretary-treasurer, Middle Atlantic States chapter, 1956-59; treasurer, 1969, 1972; executive secretary, 1969-72), Fellows in American Studies (secretary-treasurer; president, 1956-62), Fulbright Alumni Association (president, 1976-80; executive director, 1980—). *Awards, honors:* Senior Fulbright research scholar to Denmark, 1959-60; four research grants from American Philosophical Society.

WRITINGS: (Editor with Peter Bachrach) *Abstracts of Completed Doctoral Dissertations, 1950-1951,* U.S. Department of State, 1952; (editor) *Woodrow Wilson and the World of Today,* University of Pennsylvania Press, 1957; (author of teacher's manual) Richard Hofstadter, William Miller, and Daniel Aaron, *The American Republic,* Prentice-Hall, Volume I, 1959, Volume II, 1960, 2nd edition, 1970; *Understanding the American Republic,* Prentice-Hall, Volume I, 1961, 2nd edition, 1970, Volume II, 1962, 2nd edition, 1971; *Objective Tests: The American Republic,* Prentice-Hall, 1962; (editor and author of introduction) *The Assault of Laughter: A Treasury of American Political Humor,* A. S. Barnes, 1962, revised and enlarged edition published as *Pardon Us, Mr. President!: American Humor on Politics,* 1975; *The United States of America: A Syllabus of American Studies,* University of Pennsylvania Press, 1963, Volume I: *Literature, Language, and the Arts,* Volume II: *History and Social Sciences;* (author of instructor's and student's guides) Hofstadter, Miller, and Aaron, *The United States,* 2nd edition (Dudden was not associated with earlier edition), Prentice-Hall, 1967; (contributor) Herbert Shapiro, editor, *The Muckrakers and American Society,* Heath, 1968; (contributor) Hennig Cohen, editor, *Landmarks of American Writing,* Basic Books, 1969; *Joseph Fels and the Single-Tax Movement,* Temple University Press, 1971.

Also contributor to Bobbs-Merrill's reprint series in history. Contributor of articles on humor (under pseudonym Arthur Power) and history to journals in the United States and abroad.

WORK IN PROGRESS: Coordinating a special *American Quarterly* issue on American humor.

SIDELIGHTS: Arthur P. Dudden told *CA:* "My zest for history in general and American history in particular dates from my undergraduate days. I have wondered more than once if, as the American-born son of English immigrants, my fixation for the history of this country is subconsciously rooted in a drive to establish myself in my parents' uneasily adopted land.

"My interest in chronicling social responses to industrial

change springs naturally from growing-up next door to the automobile industry and its workers in Detroit. My doctoral dissertation on the popular turmoil against monopoly in the late nineteenth century followed suit, as did my biography of Joseph Fels, who was determined to eradicate unemployment and poverty from society. My growing involvement in the new interdiscipline of American studies reflects a recognition that literature, the arts, sociology, and other fields of study have a great deal to offer toward understanding the United States.

"Along the way I have added an avocation—the study of humor, specifically, political humor; I have converted my sideline into a popular culture study." Dudden adds: "My study of history reinforces my sense of humor, and my writings on humor reinforce my insights into history. Together they produce a working equilibrium."

*   *   *

DUKERT, Joseph M(ichael)   1929-

PERSONAL: Born September 19, 1929, in Baltimore, Md.; son of Andrew Joseph (an auto mechanic) and Margaret (Przybyl) Dukert; married Virginia Linthicum, April 14, 1952 (died November 12, 1967); married Betty Cole, May 19, 1968. Education: University of Notre Dame, B.A. (magna cum laude), 1951; graduate study at Georgetown University, 1951-52, Johns Hopkins University, 1955, 1957, and Johns Hopkins School of Advanced Study, Bologna, Italy, 1955-56. Politics: Republican. Religion: Roman Catholic. Home and office: 4709 Crescent St., Washington, D.C. 20016. Agent: Marilyn Marlow, Curtis Brown Ltd., 575 Madison Ave., New York, N.Y. 10022.

CAREER: Baltimore News Post, Baltimore, Md., copyreader, late news editor, reporter, and feature writer, 1953-55; Martin Co. (division of Martin-Marietta), Baltimore, Md., member of information services staff, 1956-59, director of public relations, Nuclear Division, 1960-62, and Research Institute for Advanced Studies, 1962-65; currently energy consultant and author. Executive producer of film "Power for Continent 7"; member of original steering group, national committee on public understanding of the atom. Republican National Convention, delegate, 1960 and 1968, alternate delegate, 1964; member, G.O.P. national committee, 1967-68; chairman, Maryland Republican state central committee, 1966-69. Vice-president, Baltimore Junior Chamber of Commerce, 1960-61; officer, Baltimore City Jail Board, 1963-68; member of board, Baltimore Civic Opera, 1965-68. Military service: U.S. Air Force, Psychological Warfare, 1951-53; became lieutenant. Member: National Association of Science Writers, Atomic Industrial Forum, Cosmos Club. Awards, honors: "Cindy" award, Industrial Film Producers Association, 1962, for film "Power for Continent 7"; Antarctic Service Medal, Department of Defense, 1965; Golden Eagle Award, 1979, for film "Fly Faster, Fly Longer."

WRITINGS: Atompower, Coward, 1962; This Is Antarctica, Coward, 1965, 2nd edition, 1971; Nuclear Ships of the World, Coward, 1973; Energy History of the United States, 1776-1976, U.S. Government Printing Office, 1976; (consulting editor) Energy in America's Future: The Choices before Us, Johns Hopkins Press, 1979. Also author of film documentaries on various scientific subjects, including "Fly Faster, Fly Longer," and contributor to "Decision Makers Bookshelf" series, 1980. Contributor of articles to Labor Law Journal, Catholic Digest, Space Aeronautics, Foreign Affairs, Smithsonian, and other publications.

WORK IN PROGRESS: A book on chemical elements; a thesis on guidelines for a new Isthmian canal treaty; an energy history of the United States based on ideas outlined in the "Decision Makers Bookshelf" series.

*   *   *

DULLES, Avery (Robert)   1918-

PERSONAL: Born August 24, 1918, in Auburn, N.Y.; son of John Foster (the U.S. Secretary of State, 1953-59) and Janet (Avery) Dulles. Education: Harvard University, A.B., 1940, graduate study, 1940-41; Woodstock College, Ph.L., 1950, S.T.L., 1957; Gregorian University, S.T.D., 1960. Office: Department of Theology, Catholic University of America, Washington, D.C. 20064.

CAREER: Entered Society of Jesus (Jesuits), 1946; ordained Roman Catholic priest, 1956; Fordham University, New York, N.Y., instructor in philosophy, 1951-53; Woodstock College, Woodstock, Md., assistant professor, 1960-62, associate professor, 1962-69, professor of systematic theology, 1969-74; Catholic University of America, Washington, D.C., professor of systematic theology, 1974—. Visiting lecturer at Fordham University, spring, 1970, Weston College School of Theology, Boston College, spring, 1971, Union Theological Seminary (New York), spring and fall, 1971-74, Princeton Theological Seminary, fall, 1972, Pontifical Gregorian University (Rome), spring, 1973, Episcopal Theological Seminary (Alexandria, Va.), spring, 1975, and Lutheran Theological Seminary at Gettysburg, fall, 1978; member of board of trustees, Fordham University, 1969-72; member of academic council, Irish School of Ecumenics, 1971-78; Woodstock Theological Center (Washington, D.C.), research associate, 1974—, member of board of directors, 1974-79; member of advisory board, Ethics and Public Policy Program, Kennedy Institute, Georgetown University, 1977-80. Member of Catholic Commission on Intellectual and Cultural Affairs, 1967—, Catholic Bishops' Advisory Council, 1969-74, and U.S. Lutheran-Roman Catholic Dialogue, 1972—. Military service: U.S. Naval Reserve, 1942-46; became lieutenant; received Croix de Guerre.

MEMBER: Catholic Theological Society of America (member of board of directors, 1970-72, 1974-77; vice-president, 1974-75; president, 1975-76), American Theological Society (vice-president, 1977-78; president, 1978-79), Gustave Weigel Society (member of board of consultants, 1966—). Awards, honors: LL.D., St. Joseph's College (Philadelphia), 1969, and Iona College, 1980; Cardinal Spellman Award for distinguished achievement in theology, 1970; Christopher Award, 1972, for The Survival of Dogma; Presidential Bicentennial Award, Boston College, 1976; Woodrow Wilson International Center for Scholars fellow, 1977; L.H.D., Georgetown University, 1977; Th.D., University of Detroit, 1978.

WRITINGS: Princeps Concordiae, Harvard University Press, 1941; A Testimonial to Grace, Sheed, 1946; (with James M. Demske and Robert J. O'Connell) Introductory Metaphysics, Sheed, 1955; Apologetics and the Biblical Christ, Newman Press, 1963; The Dimensions of the Church, Newman Press, 1967; Revelation and the Quest for Unity, foreword by Robert McAfee Brown, Corpus Books, 1968; Revelation Theology: A History, Herder, 1969; (with Wolfhart Pannenberg and Carl E. Braaten) Spirit, Faith, and Church, Westminster, 1970; A History of Apologetics, Corpus Books, 1971; The Survival of Dogma, Doubleday, 1971; Models of the Church, Doubleday, 1974; Church Membership as a Catholic and Ecumenical Problem, Marquette University Press, 1974; The Resilient Church, Doubleday, 1977.

Contributor to numerous books, including: *Protestant Churches and the Prophetic Office*, Woodstock College Press, 1961; *The Ignatian Experience as Reflected in the Spiritual Theology of Karl Rahner*, Program to Promote the Spiritual Exercises, 1965; *Toward a Theology of Christian Faith: Readings in Theology*, Kenedy, 1968; *Biblical Revelation and Christ*, Corpus Books, 1969. Author of column "Theology for Today," *America*, 1967-68. Contributor to *New Catholic Encyclopedia, Encyclopaedia Britannica*, and to theological journals, including *Theological Studies, Thought, Worship*, and *American Ecclesiastical Review*. Associate editor of ecumenism, *Concilium*, 1963—; member of editorial advisory board, *Mid-Stream: An Ecumenical Journal*, 1974—.

BIOGRAPHICAL/CRITICAL SOURCES: Christian Century, January 22, 1969, February 10, 1971; *Commonweal*, December 19, 1969.

*   *   *

DUNNETT, Dorothy   1923-
(Dorothy Halliday)

PERSONAL: Born August 25, 1923, in Dunfermline, Scotland; daughter of Alexander and Dorothy E. (Millard) Halliday; married Alastair M. Dunnett (an editor, author, playwright, and company chairman), September 17, 1946; children: Ninian M., Mungo H. *Home:* 87 Colinton Rd., Edinburgh, Scotland.

CAREER: British Civil Service, Scottish Government Departments, Edinburgh, assistant press officer, 1940-46; professional portrait painter, 1950—; director, Scottish Television, Ltd., 1979—; writer. Executive officer, Board of Trade, Glasgow, Scotland, 1946-55. Portraits are exhibited in Royal Scottish Academy. Trustee, Scottish National War Memorial, 1962—. *Member:* P.E.N., Crime Writers' Association, Renaissance Society of America, Scottish Society for Northern Studies, Scottish Society of Women Artists, Glasgow Art Institute, New Club (Edinburgh), Caledonian Club (London). *Awards, honors:* Scottish Arts Council Award, 1976, for *Checkmate*.

*WRITINGS—*All novels, except as indicated: *Game of Kings*, Putnam, 1961; *Queen's Play*, Putnam, 1964; *The Disorderly Knights*, Putnam, 1966; *The Photogenic Soprano*, Houghton, 1968 (published in England under name Dorothy Halliday as *Dolly and the Singing Bird*, Cassell, 1968); *Pawn in Frankincense*, Putnam, 1969; *Murder in the Round*, Houghton, 1970 (published in England under name Dorothy Halliday as *Dolly and the Cookie Bird*, Cassell, 1970); *The Ringed Castle*, Cassell, 1971, Putnam, 1972; *Match for a Murderer*, Houghton, 1971 (published in England under name Dorothy Halliday as *Dolly and the Doctor Bird*, Cassell, 1971); (contributor) *Scottish Short Stories* (anthology), Collins, 1973; *Murder in Focus*, Houghton, 1973 (published in England under name Dorothy Halliday as *Dolly and the Starry Bird*, Cassell, 1973); *Checkmate*, Putnam, 1975; (under name Dorothy Halliday) *Dolly and the Nanny Bird*, M. Joseph, 1976.

WORK IN PROGRESS: King Hereafter, a novel set in 11th century Europe during the reign of Scotland's King Macbeth.

AVOCATIONAL INTERESTS: Travel ("abroad a good deal, largely in the United States"), sailing ("have done a lot around Hebridean Islands off Scotland"), music and ballet ("keen supporter of Scottish opera, Scottish Theatre Ballet, and the Edinburgh International Festival of Music and the Arts").

BIOGRAPHICAL/CRITICAL SOURCES: New York Times Book Review, December 8, 1968; *Times Literary Supplement*, October 23, 1969; *Harper's*, October, 1971; Francis Russell Hart, *The Scottish Novel: From Smollett to Spark*, Harvard University Press, 1978.

*   *   *

DUPLESSIS, Yvonne   1912-
(Yves Duplessis)

PERSONAL: Born January 26, 1912, in Paris, France; married December 22, 1936; husband's surname, Tuchmann (a professor at La Faculte de Medecine); children: Evelyne, Alain. *Education:* Institut Catholique, Sorbonne, Paris, Diplome d'Etudes Superieures de Philosophie, 1932; Faculte des Lettres de Paris, Certificate d'Ethnologie, 1935; Faculte des Lettres de Montpellier, Doctorat d'Universite, 1945. *Religion:* Catholic. *Home:* 67 avenue Raymond-Poincare, Paris 75116, France.

CAREER: Affiliated with Centre National de Tele-Enseignement, Vanves, Seine, France, 1960-69; currently president, Commission d'Etude de la Sensibilite Dermo-Optique, Centre d'Information de la Couleur. *Member:* Institut Metapsychique International. *Awards, honors:* First prize, Schweizerisches Vereinigung fuer Parapsychologie, 1976, for work on color telepathy and dermo-optic sensitivity.

*WRITINGS—*All under name Yves Duplessis: *Le Surrealisme*, Presses Universitaires de France, 1950, 11th edition, 1978, translation by Paul Capon published as *Surrealism*, Walker & Co., 1962; *La Vision para-psychologique des Couleurs*, Epi, 1974, translation by Paul van Toal published as *The Paranormal Perception of Color*, Parapsychology Foundation (New York), 1975. Contributor to professional journals in Europe, Asia, and the United States.

WORK IN PROGRESS: Further investigation into dermo-optic perception, "with the help of the Parapsychology Foundation of New York."

SIDELIGHTS: Yvonne Duplessis told *CA* that she "has participated for many years in the telepathy experiments of the Institut Metapsychique International" and that her "researches and experiments have, in recent years, been concerned particularly with dermo-optic perception." Duplessis adds that she employs volunteers, both sighted and blind, as subjects in her research.

*   *   *

DUPRE, Louis

PERSONAL: Born in Veerle, Belgium; son of Clemens Vincent and Francisca (Verlinden) Dupre; married Edith Cardoen; children: (previous marriage) Christian. *Education:* Berchmanianum Nijmegen, Holland, Licence (philosophy), 1950; University of Louvain, Ph.D., 1952; graduate study in Denmark, 1957; Berchmanscollege Louvain, Belgium, Licence (theology), 1958. *Religion:* Catholic. *Home:* 67 Racebrook Rd., Woodbridge, Conn. 06525. *Office:* Department of Religious Studies, Yale University, New Haven, Conn. 06520.

CAREER: Georgetown University, Washington, D.C., 1958-72, became professor of philosophy; Yale University, New Haven, Conn., 1973—, currently member of department of religious studies. *Member:* Hegel Society (president, 1973-74), American Council of Learned Societies (fellow), American Catholic Philosophical Association (president, 1970-71).

WRITINGS: Het Vertrekpunt der Marxistische wijsbegeerte: De kritiek op Hegels staatsrecht (title means "The

Starting Point of Marxist Philosophy''), Standaard-Boekhandel, 1954; *Kierkegaard's Theologie: De Dialectiek van het Christen-worden*, Spectrum, 1958, translation published as *Kierkegaard as Theologian: The Dialectic of Christian Existence*, Sheed, 1963; *Contraception and Catholics: A New Appraisal*, Helicon, 1964; *The Philosophical Foundations of Marxism*, Harcourt, 1966; (editor and author of introduction) *Faith and Reflection: A Selection from the Writings of Henry Dumery*, Herder, 1969; *The Other Dimension: A Search for the Meaning of Religious Attitudes*, Doubleday, 1971; *Transcendent Selfhood*, Seabury, 1976; *A Dubious Heritage*, Newman Books, 1978. Also author of *Marx's Critique of Culture*, 1981. Contributor of about 100 articles to theosophical and theological publications.

WORK IN PROGRESS: Books on the early philosophy of Marx and on the philosophy of religion.

* * *

DUROSELLE, Jean-Baptiste Marie Lucien Charles 1917-

PERSONAL: Born November 17, 1917, in Paris, France; son of Albert and Jeanne (Peronne) Duroselle; married Christiane Viant, October 1, 1940; children: Henri, Genevieve, Dominique, Michel. *Education:* Attended Lycee Louis-le-Grand, 1935-38; Ecole Normale Superieure, Agrege d'histoire et geographie, 1943, Docteur es lettres, 1949. *Religion:* Catholic. *Home:* 15, rue Laurent-Gaudet, Le Chesnay, Yvelines 78, France. *Office:* Sorbonne, University of Paris, 17 rue de la Sorbonne, Paris V, France.

CAREER: Lycee de Chartres, Chartres, France, history teacher, 1943-45; University of Paris, Sorbonne, Paris, France, assistant professor of contemporary history, 1945-49; Lycee Hoche, Versailles, France, history teacher, 1949-50; University of Sarre, Saarbruecken, Germany, professor, 1950-56, titular professor, 1953—, dean of faculty of letters, for two years; University of Lille, Lille, France, professor of contemporary history, 1957-58; Fondation nationale des sciences politiques, Paris, professor and director, Centre d'etude des relations internationales, 1958-64; University of Paris, Sorbonne, professor of contemporary history and director of Institut d'histoire des relations internationales contemporaines, 1964—. Visiting professor at University of Notre Dame, 1951, 1953, Brandeis University, 1958, Harvard University, 1959, Colegio de Mexico, 1963, University of Seattle, 1970, and New York University, 1978; taught at Johns Hopkins School of Advanced International Studies, Bologna, Italy, 1955-66. Director, U.S. Educational Commission for France, 1964-69. *Military service:* French Army, artillery reserve officer, 1939-40. *Member:* Societe des gens de lettres (co-chairman, committee on French-Italian modern history), Academie des sciences morales et politiques, American Historical Association (honorary member), American Philosophical Society (foreign member), Societe d'histoire moderne (honorary president). *Awards, honors:* Chevalier de la legion d'honneur; Chevalier des palmes academiques; Officer, l'Ordre national du merite; honorary doctorates from University of Notre Dame and University of Liege.

WRITINGS: Histoire du catholicisme, Presses universitaires de France, 1949, 3rd edition, 1967; *Les Debuts du catholicisme social en France (1822-1870)*, Presses universitaires de France, 1951; *Histoire diplomatique de 1919 a nos jours*, Dalloz, 1953, 7th edition, 1978; *De l'utilisation des sondages d'opinion en histoire et en science politique*, Institut universitaire d'information sociale et economique, 1957;

Les Relations internationales, 1871-1918: Les Hommes d'etat, Centre de documentation universitaire, 1958; *De Wilson a Roosevelt: Politique exterieure des Etats-Unis de 1913-1945*, A. Colin, 1960, translation by Nancy Lyman Roelker published as *From Wilson to Roosevelt: Foreign Policy of the United States, 1913-1945*, Harvard University Press, 1963; *Histoire: Le Monde contemporain*, Fernand Nathan, 1960; (with Pierre Gerbet) *Histoire, 1848-1914*, Fernand Nathan, 1961; *L'Europe de 1815 a nos jours: Vie politique et relations internationales*, Presses universitaires de France, 1964, 2nd edition, 1967; (with Pierre Renouvin) *Introduction a l'histoire des relations internationales: Forces profondes et hommes d'etat*, A. Colin, 1964, 2nd edition, 1966, translation by Mary Ilford published as *Introduction to the History of International Relations*, Praeger, 1967.

L'Idee d'Europe dans l'histoire, preface by Jean Monnet, Denoel, 1965; *La Politique exterieure de la France de 1914 a 1945*, Centre de documentation universitaire, 1965; *Le Conflit de Trieste, 1945-1954*, Dotation Carnegie, 1966; *Les Relations franco-allemandes de 1918 a 1950*, Centre de documentation universitaire, 1966; *Les Relations internationales de l'Allemagne et de l'Italie de 1919 a 1939*, Centre de documentation universitarie, 1967; *Les Relations franco-allemandes de 1914 a 1939*, Centre de documentation universitaire, 1967; *Le Drame de l'Europe*, two volumes, Richelieu, 1969; *Le Monde dechire, 1945-1970*, two volumes, Richelieu, 1970; *La France et les francais*, Richelieu, 1972, Volume I: *1900-1914*, Volume II: *1914-1920; La France et les Etats-Unis: Des Origines a nos jours*, Senil, 1976, translation by Derek Coltman published as *France and the United States: From the Beginnings to the Present*, University of Chicago Press, 1978; *La Decadance, 1932-1939*, Imprimerie nationale, 1979.

Editor; published by A. Colin: *La Politique etrangere et ses fondements*, 1954; *Les Relations germano-sovietiques de 1933 a 1939*, 1954; *Les Frontieres europeennes de l'U.R.S.S., 1917-1941*, 1957; (with Jean Meyriat) *Les Nouveaux Etats dans les relations internationales*, 1962; (with Meyriat) *La Communaute internationale face aux jeunes Etats*, 1964; (with Meyriat) *Politiques nationales envers les jeunes Etats*, 1964.

Also editor of ''Politique etrangere de la France, 1871-1969'' series and ''Notre siecle'' series, both for Imprimerie nationale. Contributor to *Encyclopedie francaise*, and of articles to periodicals in France, the United States, the Soviet Union, and other countries. Chairman of editorial board, *Publications de la Sorbonne* and *Comite pour la publication des documents diplomatiques francais;* honorary editor, *Revue d'histoire moderne et contemporaine;* co-editor, *Relations internationales.*

WORK IN PROGRESS: Tout empire pervia: Theorie des relations internationales.

SIDELIGHTS: Jean-Baptiste Duroselle wrote *CA* that he is a former ''disciple of the great French historian Pierre Renouvin and his successor at the Sorbonne.'' Duroselle explains that he has devoted his career to the development of ''a global view of international relations founded upon history'' and that he has pursued his goal via writing history texts and theoretical essays. Moreover, the author states that he and Professor Jacques Freymond of Geneva have created ''a 'Franco-Swiss School of International Relations,''' which led to the founding of *Relations internationales.*

E

ECKELS, Jon
(Askia Akhnaton)

PERSONAL: Born in Indianapolis, Ind.; son of Thomas Arthur and Anna (Harris) Eckels; children: Jon David Malcolm. *Education:* Indiana Central College, B.A., 1961; Pacific School of Religion, B.D., 1966; Stanford University, Ph.D., 1975. *Politics and religion:* Christian Animist. *Home:* 1925 Miller, Indianapolis, Ind. *Agent:* Tarun Bedi, Via Halo Ticcagli 9, Rome 00189, Italy. *Office:* Firesign International Communications, 131-29 Farmers Blvd., Jamaica, N.Y. 11434.

CAREER: Ordained minister, 1966; pastor of United Methodist churches in Oakland and San Francisco, Calif., 1964-68; Mills College, Oakland, instructor in English, 1968; Merrit College, Oakland, instructor in English, 1969-70; Firesign International Communications, Jamaica, N.Y., publisher and editor, 1973—; Stanford University, Stanford, Calif., member of English department staff, 1974-75; minister, Shattuck Avenue United Methodist Church, Oakland, 1975-78, and Springfield Gardens United Methodist Church, Jamaica, N.Y., 1978—. Teacher and board member, Martin Luther King Jr., In-Community School, Oakland, 1966-68, and New Community School, Berkeley, Calif., 1967-69; founder, Act III Freedom School, 1967-68. Chairman, Anti-Poverty Commission, Oakland; vice-president, Opportunities Industrialization Committee; chairman, Cultural Development Center, 1967-68.

WRITINGS—Poetry: *This Time Tomorrow,* Julian Richardson, 1966; *Black Dawn,* privately printed, 1966; *Home Is Where the Soul Is,* Broadside Press, 1969; *Black Right On,* Julian Richardson, 1969; *Our Business in the Streets: Black Poetry,* Broadside Press, 1971; *Firesign: Poetry for the Free and Will Be,* Firesign Press, 1973; *Stone Spirit Space,* Firesign Press, 1975; *Crystal Flame,* Firesign Press, 1976; *Pursuing the Pursuit: The Black Plight in White America,* Exposition Press, 1977.

WORK IN PROGRESS: Back to Basics, poetry; *The Spiritual Rage,* an autobiography.

SIDELIGHTS: Jon Eckels told *CA:* "In my writings, both poetry and prose, I attempt to combine and reflect political radicalism and deep spirituality. I believe in personal and political freedom and responsibility. Although I feel most especially called to struggle . . . for the Third World generally and Black people specifically, I recognize my human obligation to all peoples. I believe in loving people, having faith in God, and completely working to renew and re-create. . . . I believe love is more than we know."

BIOGRAPHICAL/CRITICAL SOURCES: Time, April 4, 1970; *Phylon,* winter, 1972.

*   *   *

EIBL-EIBESFELDT, Irenaeus   1928-

PERSONAL: Born June 15, 1928, in Vienna, Austria; son of Anton and Maria (von Hauninger) Eibl-Eibesfeldt; married Eleonore Siegel, February 10, 1950; children: Bernolf, Roswitha. *Education:* University of Vienna, Ph.D. *Home:* Soecking, Fichtenweg, West Germany. *Office:* Max-Planck-Institut fuer Verhaltensphysiologie, 8131 Seewiesen, West Germany.

CAREER: Biological Station Wilhelminenberg, near Vienna, Austria, zoologist, 1946-49; Max-Planck-Institut fuer Verhaltensphysiologie, research associate in Percha near Starnberg, West Germany, 1951-69, head of independent research unit on human ethology in Seewiesen, West Germany, 1970—. University of Munich, Munich, West Germany, docent, 1963-69, professor of zoology, 1969—. Member of skin-diving expeditions to the Galapagos Islands, the Caribbean Sea, the Indian Ocean, Africa, and South America. *Member:* Gesellschaft fuer Anthropologie und Human-genetik, Deutsche Akademie der Naturforscher, Deutsche Zoologische Gesellschaft, Senckenbergische Naturforschende Gesellschaft, International Society for Research on Aggression, Society for Human Ethology, Animal Behavior Society, American Association for the Advancement of Science, Charles Darwin Foundation, Australian Academy for Forensic Sciences.

WRITINGS: Das Verhalten der Nagetiere, W. DeGruyter, 1958; *Survey on the Galapagos Islands,* UNESCO (Paris), 1960; *Galapagos: Die Arche Noah im Pazifik,* Piper Verlag, 1960, 5th edition, 1977, translation by Alan Houghton Brodrick published as *Galapagos: The Noah's Ark of the Pacific,* Doubleday, 1960; *Im Reich der tausend Atolle: Als Tierpsychologe in den Korallenriffen der Malediven und Nikobaren,* Piper Verlag, 1964, translation by Gwynne Vevers published as *Land of a Thousand Atolls: A Study of Marine Life in the Maldive and Nicobar Islands,* MacGibbon & Kee, 1965, World Publishing, 1966; *Haie: Angriff, Abwehr, Arten,* Kosmos, 1965; *Ethologie: Die Biologie des Verhaltens,*

Akademische Verlagsgesellschaft Athenaion, 1966, published as *Grundriss der vergleichenden Verhaltensforschung*, Piper Verlag, 1967, 6th edition, 1980, translation by Erich Klinghammer published as *Ethology: The Biology of Behavior*, Holt, 1970, 2nd edition, 1975.

Liebe und Hass, Piper Verlag, 1970, 5th edition, 1972, translation by Geoffrey Strachan published as *Love and Hate: The Natural History of Behavior Patterns*, Holt, 1972; *Die! Ko Buschmann-Gesellschaft*, Piper Verlag, 1972; *Der vorprogrammierte Mensch*, Molden Verlag, 1973; *Krieg und Frieden*, Piper Verlag, 1975, translation published as *The Biology of Peace and War*, Viking, 1979; *Menschenforschung auf neuen Wegen*, Molden Verlag, 1976; *Der Hai: Legende eines Moerder*, C. Bertelsmann Verlag, 1977.

Author of scripts for scientific and educational films. Contributor of over 200 articles to scientific journals and handbooks.

SIDELIGHTS: Irenaeus Eibl-Eibesfeldt told *CA* that the first fifteen years of his career were "devoted to animal behavior studies, in particular the process of ritualization, communicative behavior, and the studies of phylogenetic adaptation in behavior. Since 1963," he continues, "[my] interest has focused increasingly on the study of human behavior by the biological approach (human ethology). The studies include documentation of human behavior in tribal societies. The focal points of these studies are the bushman of the central Kalahari, the Eipo in West Irian, the Yanomami of the upper Orinoko, the Himba in South West Africa, and the Balenese."

Eibl-Eibesfeldt's books have been translated into several languages. *Liebe und Hass* and *Der vorprogrammierte Mensch* were best-sellers in Germany.

* * *

EISENBERG, Ralph 1930-1973

PERSONAL: Born May 17, 1930, in Newark, N.J.; died August 16, 1973; son of Jacob Joseph and Jane (Zackin) Eisenberg; married Ruth Phyllis Bennett, August 31, 1952; children: Andrea Sara, Jay Joseph. *Education:* Attended Rutgers University, 1948-49; University of Illinois, A.B., 1952, A.M., 1953; Princeton University, M.A., 1957, Ph.D., 1961. *Religion:* Jewish. *Home:* 2006 Greenbrier Dr., Charlottesville, Va.

CAREER: Research associate, New Jersey Government Institutes and Agencies Commission, 1957-58; University of South Carolina, Columbia, assistant professor of political science, 1958-60; University of Virginia, Charlottesville, assistant professor of political science, 1960-65, associate professor of government and foreign affairs, 1965-73, assistant director, Institute of Government, 1965-69, associate director, 1969-71, assistant provost of the university, 1971-73. Visiting professor, University of Sussex, fall, 1970. Staff member, Virginia Commission on Redistricting, 1961. *Military service:* U.S. Air Force, 1955-57; became first lieutenant. U.S. Air Force Reserve, beginning 1957; became captain. *Member:* American Political Science Association, American Association of University Professors, Virginia Social Science Association, Phi Beta Kappa, Pi Sigma Alpha.

WRITINGS: Conflicts of Interest among Public Officers and Employees in Great Britain, New Jersey Legislative Services Commission, 1957; (with Paul T. David) *Devaluation of the Urban and Suburban Vote*, two volumes, Bureau of Public Administration, University of Virginia, 1961, 1962;

(contributor) *Cases in State and Local Government*, Prentice-Hall, 1961; (with David) *State Legislative Redistricting: Major Issues in the Wake of Judicial Decision*, Public Administration Service (Chicago), 1962; (contributor) Rocco Tresolini and R. T. Frost, editors, *Cases in American National Government and Politics*, Prentice-Hall, 1966; (editor) *Perspectives on State and Local Finance: A Seminar*, Southern Regional Education Board, 1967; (contributor) *State Legislatures in American Politics*, Duke University, 1968; *Guide to County Redistricting*, Institute of Government, University of Virginia, 1970; *Virginia Votes, 1924-1968*, Institute of Government, University of Virginia, 1971; (contributor) William Havard, editor, *The Changing Politics of the South*, Louisiana State University Press, 1972. Contributor to professional journals. *Newsletter* (University of Virginia), assistant editor, 1965-69, associate editor, 1969-71.†

* * *

ELDER, Glen(nard) H(oll), Jr. 1934-

PERSONAL: Born February 28, 1934, in Cleveland, Ohio; son of Glennard Holl (a chiropractor) and Norma (Johnson) Elder; married Karen Elwell Bixler, August 30, 1958; children: Brent, Rod, Jeffrey. *Education:* Pennsylvania State University, B.S., 1957; Kent State University, M.A., 1958; University of North Carolina, Ph.D., 1961. *Politics:* Democrat. *Religion:* Protestant. *Home:* 115 Cayuga Park Cir., Ithaca, N.Y. 14580. *Office:* Department of Sociology, Uris Bldg., Cornell University, Ithaca, N.Y.

CAREER: University of California, Berkeley, assistant professor of sociology, 1962-65, assistant research sociologist at Institute of Human Development, 1962-67; University of North Carolina at Chapel Hill, associate professor, 1967-71, professor of sociology, 1971-79; Cornell University, Ithaca, N.Y., professor of sociology and human development, 1979—. Co-director, Committee on the Life Course, Social Science Research Council, 1979—. Research associate, Institute of Human Development, University of California, Berkeley; senior fellow, Boys' Town Research Center. *Member:* International Sociological Association, American Sociological Association, Sociological Research Association, Social Science History Association, Society for Research in Child Development. *Awards, honors:* National Institute of Mental Health postdoctoral fellowship, 1962; Center for Advanced Study in the Behavioral Sciences fellow invitation, 1978; National Council on Family Relations Ernest A. Burgess Award, 1979.

WRITINGS: Adolescent Achievement and Mobility Aspirations, Institute for Research in Social Science, University of North Carolina, 1962; (contributor) Edgar Borgatta and William Lambert, editors, *The Handbook of Personality Theory and Research*, Rand McNally, 1968; *Age Groups, Status Transitions, and Socialization*, U.S. Government Printing Office, 1968; *Adolescent Socialization and Personality Development*, Rand McNally, 1971; (editor) *Linking Social Structure and Personality*, Sage Publications, 1973; *Children of the Great Depression*, University of Chicago Press, 1974; (editor with Sigmund Dragastin and contributor) *Adolescence in the Life Cycle*, Hemisphere Press, 1975; (contributor) Tamara Hareven, editor, *Transitions: The Family and Life Course in Historical Perspective*, Academic Press, 1978; (contributor) Sarane Boocock and John Demos, editors, *Turning Points: Historical and Sociological Essays on the Family*, University of Chicago Press, 1978; (contributor) Joseph Adelson, editor, *Handbook of Adolescent Psychology*, Wiley, 1980; *Family Structure and Socialization*, Arno,

1980. Also contributor to *Biography and Society,* edited by Daniel Bertaux, 1980; contributor to *Annual Review of Sociology.* Contributor of articles to sociology and education journals, including *International Journal of Behavioral Development, American Behavioral Scientist, International Social Science Journal, Merrill-Palmer Quarterly of Behavior and Development, Sociometry,* and *American Journal of Sociology.*

WORK IN PROGRESS: Families in Depression and War; Rural Change and Family Change, a comparative and historical study of the farm family and family farming in New York; *History and the Life Course,* critical and analytical essays on the life course as a theoretical perspective in sociological, psychological, and historical studies; *Social Change in Women's Lives,* a three generation study of social roles and health, and a long-term study of social change in the family and life course, both based on longitudinal archives from the Institute of Human Development, Berkeley, Calif.

*   *   *

ELLACOTT, S(amuel) E(rnest) 1911-

PERSONAL: Born May 20, 1911, in Winkleigh, Devon, England; son of Ernest (an estate worker) and Emily (Ford) Ellacott; married Kathleen Abbott, July 12, 1937. *Education:* Attended Royal Albert Memorial School of Art, 1927-32, Barnstaple School of Science and Art, 1932-36, Exmouth Training College, 1946-47, University of Southampton, 1965-66, and Portsmouth College of Education. *Politics:* Conservative. *Religion:* Protestant. *Home:* Pendennis, 8 Willand Rd., Braunton, North Devon, England.

CAREER: Teacher of English, history, and art at secondary schools in Braunton, Devon, England, 1947-53, and Barnstaple, Devon, 1953-71; author and illustrator, 1952—. *Military service:* British Army, Devon Home Guard, 1940-44; became sergeant. *Member:* Arms and Armour Society, Devonshire Association. *Awards, honors:* Carnegie Medal runner-up and Library Association "honours book" citation, both 1962, for *Armour and Blade.*

WRITINGS: Golden Hammer, privately printed, 1961; *Ships under the Sea,* Hutchinson, 1961; *Armour and Blade,* Abelard (London), 1962; *Collecting Arms and Armour,* Arco, 1964; *Spearman to Minuteman,* Abelard (London), 1965, Abelard (New York), 1966; *Conscripts on the March,* Abelard (London), 1965, Abelard (New York), 1966; *The Norman Invasion,* Abelard, 1966; *A History of Everyday Things in England,* Volume V, Putnam, 1968; *The Seaman,* Books I and II, Abelard, 1970; *Until You Are Dead* (historical novel), Abelard (London), 1972, published as *Fight until You Die,* Coronet Books, 1973; *Braunton Story* (local history), Quest Publications, Volume I: *Here Is Braunton,* 1979, Volume II: *Braunton Ships and Seamen,* 1980.

Published by Methuen, except as indicated: *The Story of Ships,* 1952, 2nd edition, 1958; *The Story of Aircraft,* 1952, 5th edition, 1962; *Wheels on the Road,* 1952, 2nd edition, 1956; *The Story of the Kitchen,* 1953, 2nd edition, 1960; *Forge and Foundry,* 1955; *Guns,* 1955; *Spinning and Weaving,* 1956; *Rockets,* 1959, revised edition, Criterion, 1961.

Illustrator; all by R. R. Sellman, except as indicated; published by Methuen, except as indicated: *Castles and Fortresses,* 1954; *The Crusades,* 1955; *The Elizabethan Seaman,* 1957; *Civil War and Commonwealth,* 1958; John Laffin, *The Face of War,* Abelard, 1963.

WORK IN PROGRESS: A historical novel; a history of agri-

culture, *The Years and the Land;* a history of costume, *Clothes and Centuries; Braunton Farming.*

AVOCATIONAL INTERESTS: Rifle and pistol shooting, antique arms, historical costumes, rowing, walking, cycling, art, and village life.

*   *   *

ELLIOTT, John H(uxtable) 1930-

PERSONAL: Born June 23, 1930, in Reading, England; son of Thomas Charles and Janet Mary (Payne) Elliott; married Oonah Sophia Butler, March 22, 1958. *Education:* Attended Eton College, 1943-48; Trinity College, Cambridge, B.A., 1952, Ph.D., 1955. *Home:* 14 Newlin Rd., Princeton, N.J. *Office:* School of Historical Studies, Institute for Advanced Study, Princeton, N.J. 08540.

CAREER: Cambridge University, Cambridge, England, assistant lecturer in history, 1958-62, lecturer, 1962-67; King's College, University of London, London, England, professor of history, 1968-73; Institute for Advanced Studies, Princeton, N.J., School of Historical Studies, professor, 1973—. Fellow, British Academy, 1972, and American Academy of Arts and Sciences, 1977. *Military service:* British Army, 1948-49.

WRITINGS: The Revolt of the Catalans, Cambridge University Press, 1963; *Imperial Spain, 1469-1716,* St. Martin's, 1963; *Europe Divided, 1559-1598,* Collins, 1968; *The Old World and the New, 1492-1650,* Cambridge University Press, 1970; (with Jose F. de la Pera) *Memoriales y Cartas del Conde Duque de Olivares,* two volumes, Alfaguara, 1978 and 1980; (with Jonathon Brown) *A Palace for a King: The Buen Retiro and the Court of Philip IV,* Yale University Press, 1980.

WORK IN PROGRESS: A biography of the Count-Duke of Olivares.

AVOCATIONAL INTERESTS: Looking at buildings and pictures; travel.

*   *   *

ELLIOTT, Lawrence 1924-

PERSONAL: Born January 18, 1924, in Brooklyn, N.Y.; son of Samuel (the owner of a plate glass and mirror factory) and Gussie (Goldsmith) Edelstein; married Gisele Suzanne Kayser, July 19, 1969; children: (previous marriage) Jain Susan, Elizabeth Ann, Barbara Lee; (present marriage) Nicholas Samuel. *Education:* City College (now City College of the City University of New York), B.S.S., 1950. *Residence:* Aix-en-Provence, France. *Office: Reader's Digest,* European Editorial Office, 216 boulevard St. Germain, Paris 75007, France.

CAREER: Coronet, New York City, associate editor, 1948-54; *Lifetime Living,* New York City, articles editor, 1954-55; free-lance writer, 1955-60; *Reader's Digest,* staff writer, covering Alaska and western Canada, 1960-70, roving editor and European correspondent, 1970—. Co-producer and co-host of radio program "In Touch," WHUC, Hudson, N.Y. Trustee, West Islip Public Library, 1963-67. *Military service:* U.S. Army, Infantry, 1942-46; became first lieutenant. *Member:* Overseas Press Club (New York), Anglo-American Press Club (Paris). *Awards, honors:* Freedoms Foundation Medal, 1950, for article in *Coronet,* "This Is Our Flag"; Best Book Award in nonfiction, Alaska Press Club, 1966, for *On the Edge of Nowhere;* Jugendbuchpreis (Germany) for best biography, 1971, for *George Washington Carver.*

WRITINGS: *A Little Girl's Gift,* Holt, 1963; *George Washington Carver: The Man Who Overcame,* Prentice-Hall, 1966; (with James Huntington) *On the Edge of Nowhere,* Crown, 1966; (with Daniel K. Inouye) *Journey to Washington* (biography), Prentice-Hall, 1967; *The Legacy of Tom Dooley,* World Publishing, 1969; *I Will Be Called John* (biography of Pope John XXIII), introduction by Edward M. Kennedy, Reader's Digest Press, 1972; *The Long Hunter* (biography of Daniel Boone), Reader's Digest Press, 1974. Contributor to magazines.

WORK IN PROGRESS: *The Last Insurgent: Fiorello La Guardia in His Time.*

* * *

ELLIS, John M(artin) 1936-

PERSONAL: Born May 31, 1936, in London, England; son of John Albert (an engineer) and Emily (Silvey) Ellis; married Caroline Ayre Hails, July 3, 1959 (divorced May, 1978); married Barbara Rhoades, June 28, 1978; children: (first marriage) Richard, Andrew, Katherine, Jill. *Education:* University of London, B.A. (first class honors), 1959, Ph.D., 1965. *Home:* 105 Meadow Rd., Santa Cruz, Calif. 95060. *Office:* Department of German, Crown College, University of California, Santa Cruz, Calif. 95060.

CAREER: University of Wales, Aberystwyth, tutorial assistant in German, 1959-60; University of Leicester, Leicester, England, assistant lecturer in German, 1960-63; University of Alberta, Edmonton, assistant professor of German, 1963-66; University of California, Santa Cruz, associate professor, 1966-70, professor of German literature, 1970, dean of Graduate Division, 1977—. *Military service:* British Army, Royal Artillery, 1954-56.

MEMBER: Modern Language Association of America, American Association of Teachers of German, American Association for Aesthetics, Modern Humanities Research Association, American Association of University Professors (president of local chapter, 1972-75) English Goethe Society, Kleist-Gesellschaft. *Awards, honors:* Guggenheim fellow, 1970-71; National Endowment for the Humanities senior fellow, 1975-76.

WRITINGS: *Schiller's "Kalliasbriefe" and the Study of His Aesthetic Theory,* Mouton, 1969; *Kleist's "Prinz Friedrich von Homburg": A Critical Study,* University of California Press, 1970; *Narration in the German Novelle: Theory and Interpretation,* Cambridge University Press, 1974; *The Theory of Literary Criticism: A Logical Analysis,* University of California Press, 1974; *Heinrich von Kleist: Studies in the Character and Meaning of His Writings,* University of North Carolina, 1979.

Contributor: C. Russ, editor, *Der Schriftsteller Siegfried Lenz,* Hoffman & Campe (Hamburg), 1973; *The University in the Seventies: The Impact of Changing Circumstances,* University of California Press, 1973; Angel Flores, editor, *Eleven Approaches to Kafka's Story,* Gordian, 1977; C. P. Magill, Brian A. Rowley, and Christopher J. Smith, editors, *Tradition and Creation: Essays in Honour of Elizabeth Mary Wilkinson,* W. S. Maney, 1978; Paul Hernadi, *What Is Criticism?,* Indiana University Press, 1980.

Contributor of about sixty articles and reviews to journals, including *Twentieth Century, Seminar: A Journal of Germanic Studies, Modern Language Journal, Modern Language Review, Word, New Literary History, German Life and Letters,* and *German Quarterly.*

WORK IN PROGRESS: A book on the theory of language.

ELMAN, Robert 1930-

PERSONAL: Born November 14, 1930, in New York, N.Y.; son of Dave (an instructor in medical hypnosis) and Pauline (Reffe) Elman; married Loris R. Harrington (a medical secretary), March 4, 1957; children: Natalie, Thomas. *Education:* Attended Rollins College, 1948-49, and Carnegie Institute of Technology (now Carnegie-Mellon University), 1949-51; Columbia University, B.S., 1953. *Home and office:* 410 Central Park W., New York, N.Y. 10025. *Agent:* Paul R. Reynolds, Inc., 12 East 41st St., New York, N.Y. 10017.

CAREER: *Guns and Hunting* (magazine), New York City, managing editor, 1960-68, editor-in-chief, 1968-69; Maco Publishing Co. (magazine publisher), New York City, editor-in-chief, 1968-69; *American Sportsman* (magazine), New York City, editor, 1969-70; Ridge Press, New York City, outdoor editor and consultant, 1970-71; free-lance writer, 1971—; Winchester Press, New York City, associate editor, 1974—. History consultant to publishers and arms manufacturers. *Military service:* U.S. Army, 1953-55. *Member:* Authors Guild, Authors League of America, Outdoor Writers Association of America, National Rifle Association, Wilderness Society, Environmental Defense Fund, National Wildlife Federation, New England Outdoor Writers Association, New York State Rifle and Pistol Association.

WRITINGS: *Fired in Anger: The Personal Handguns of American Heros and Villains,* Doubleday, 1968; *Discover the Outdoors* (juvenile), Lion Press, 1969; (with Harold L. Peterson) *The Great Guns,* Grosset, 1971; *The Great American Shooting Prints,* Knopf, 1972; (with Jerry Gibbs) *Outdoor Tips,* Rutledge Books, 1972; *The Atlantic Flyway,* Winchester Press, 1972; *The Hiker's Bible,* Doubleday, 1973; *The Hunter's Field Guide to the Game Birds and Animals of North America* (Outdoor Life Book Club selection), Knopf, 1974; (editor) *Hunting America's Game Animals and Birds,* Winchester Press, 1975; (editor) *All about Deer Hunting in America,* Winchester Press, 1976; (editor with others) Lawrence R. Koller, *How to Shoot: A Complete Guide to the Use of Sporting Firearms—Rifles, Shotguns, and Handguns—on the Range,* new revised edition (Elman was not associated with earlier edition), Doubleday, 1976; *The Living World of Audubon Mammals,* Country Life Books, 1976; *First in the Field: America's Pioneering Naturalists,* Mason/Charter, 1977; *1001 Hunting Tips,* Winchester Press, 1978; *The Fisherman's Field Guide to the Freshwater and Saltwater Gamefish of North America,* Knopf, 1978.

Work represented in anthologies, including: *The American Sportsman Treasury,* edited by Jerry Mason and Adolph Suehsdorf, Knopf, 1971; *Gun Talk,* edited by Dave Moreton, Winchester Press, 1973; *Hunting Moments of Truth,* edited by Eric Peper and James Rikhoff, Winchester Press, 1973. Contributor to national periodicals.

WORK IN PROGRESS: *New York City's Wildlife* (tentative title).

AVOCATIONAL INTERESTS: Hiking, camping, fishing, hunting, travel (has visited Italy, Greece, Egypt, India, Mexico, Canada, Bahamas, Galapagos Islands, Ecuador, Jamaica, and Iceland).†

* * *

ELSON, Edward L(ee) R(oy) 1906-

PERSONAL: Born December 23, 1906, in Monongahela, Pa.; son of Leroy (a locomotive engineer) and Pearl (Edie) Elson; married Frances Sandys, May, 1928 (died December, 1933); married Helen Chittick, February 8, 1937; children:

Eleanor (Mrs. Erland Heginbotham), Beverly Lynn (Mrs. Frank M. Gray, Jr.), Mary Faith (Mrs. Duncan MacRae), David Edward. *Education:* Asbury College, A.B., 1928; University of Southern California, M.Th., 1931. *Home:* 4000 Cathedral Ave. N.W., Washington, D.C. 20016. *Office:* U.S. Senate, No. 220, Old Senate Office Bldg., Washington, D.C. 20510.

CAREER: Ordained to Presbyterian ministry, 1930; First Presbyterian Church, La Jolla, Calif., minister, 1931-41; National Presbyterian Church, Washington, D.C., minister, 1946-72, served as pastor to former President and Mrs. Eisenhower and other government officials; U.S. Senate, Washington, D.C., chaplain, 1969—. Moderator, Los Angeles Presbytery, 1938, and Washington, D.C. Presbytery, 1966; western regional director, Presbyterian Post-War Fund, 1946; United Presbyterian Church of the United States, member of board of pensions, 1948-57, has served as commissioner to the General Assembly; national chaplain, Disabled American Veterans, 1950-51; president, Washington Federation of Churches, 1952-54. Member of advisory council, Center for the Study of the Presidency, 1975—; member of board of visitors, graduate department of library and information services, Catholic University of America, 1978—; member of board of directors, Freedoms Foundation; vice-president, Religious Heritage of America; member of advisory committee on the arts, John F. Kennedy Center for the Performing Arts. Trustee, Walter H. Judd National Scholarship Fund and Institute, 1978—; founding trustee, National Thanksgiving Foundation of Dallas, 1978—. *Military service:* U.S. Army Reserve, 1930-61; on active duty, 1941-46, served as chaplain of XXI Corps and 7th Army in Europe; became colonel.

MEMBER: Washington Federation of Churches (president, 1952-54), Military Chaplains Association (president, 1957-59), International Platform Association (chaplain, 1978—), Military Order of the World Wars (chaplain, Washington, D.C. chapter, 1952—), American Society of Church History, Academy of Religion and Mental Health, Church Service Society, Phi Chi Phi, Theta Sigma, Chi Alpha, Kiwanis Club (La Jolla, Calif.; honorary life member; former president); Young Men's Christian Association, Cosmos Club, and St. Andrew's Society (all Washington, D.C.). *Awards, honors*—Military: Legion of Merit; Bronze Star; Army Commendation Medal; Croix de Guerre avec palme (France); Medal of Freedom (France); Silver Star of Jordan First Class; Gold Medal, Lebanese Order of Merit First Class; Arms of the City of Colmar (France); German Occupation Medal; Reserve Officers Medal with three clusters; Chief of Army Chaplains Silver Medallion; National Defense Medal; American Theatre Medal; European Theatre Medal. Civilian: D.D., Wheaton College, 1934, and Occidental College, 1947; Litt.D., Centre College of Kentucky, 1953, Lafayette College, 1958, and Gettysburg College, 1960; L.L.D., Norwich University, 1953, Davis and Elkins College, 1955, Asbury College, 1958, and Hope College, 1961; L.H.D., University of Southern California, 1954, College of Wooster, 1960, and Washington and Jefferson College, 1960; D.Hum., Parson College, 1955; S.T.D., College of Emporia, 1956; D.Min., Salem College, 1974. Named "clergy churchman of the year," Religious Heritage of America and Washington Pilgrimage of American Churchmen, 1954; Freedoms Foundation awards for sermons, 1951, 1954, 1957, 1958, 1959, 1960, 1962, 1964, 1971, 1972, and 1974; Honor Medal, 1954, for *America's Spiritual Recovery;* Freedoms Foundation principal sermon awards, 1964 and 1971; in 1971, the National Presbyterian Church in Washington, D.C. dedicated

the Edward L. R. Elson Monumental Wall; named honorary citizen, Dallas, Tex., Charlotte, N.C., and Alliance, Ohio.

WRITINGS: One Moment with God, Doubleday, 1951; *America's Spiritual Recovery,* Revell, 1954; (author of introduction) *A Treasury of Faith,* Dell, 1957; *And Still He Speaks,* Revell, 1960; *The Inevitable Encounter,* Eerdmans, 1962; *Senate Prayers,* U.S. Government Printing Office, 1972—.

Contributor: G. Paul Butler, editor, *Best Sermons,* Volume VI, McGraw, 1955; *Great Addresses of 1958,* University of Iowa, 1958; *Representative American Speeches,* H. W. Wilson, Volume XXX, number 4 (edited by A. C. Baird): *1957-1958,* 1958, Volume XLIV, number 4 (edited by Waldo W. Braden): *1971-1972,* 1972; *The Minister's Handbook,* Revell, 1960; H. D. Moore and others, editors, *And Our Defense Is Sure,* Abingdon, 1964; Ralph G. Turnbull, editor, *If I Had Only One Sermon to Preach,* Baker Book, 1966; *Vietnam: The Christian-the Gospel-the Truth,* Office of the General Assembly, United Presbyterian Church of the United States, 1967; *Family Heritage Bible,* World Publishing, 1968; Charles L. Wallis, editor, *Our American Heritage,* Harper, 1970; *Great Preaching,* Word Books, 1970; Wallis, editor, *The Ministers' Manual,* Harper, 1971. Contributor to periodicals.

*   *   *

ELSTON, Allan Vaughan   1887-1976

PERSONAL: Born July 28, 1887, in Kansas City, Mo.; died October 21, 1976; son of John William (a surgeon and cattle rancher) and Sarah (Gentry) Elston; married Kathleen Chastain, 1919; children: Allan V., Jr., Magene Elston Corwin, John William. *Education:* University of Missouri, B.S. in Civil Engineering, 1909. *Politics:* Democrat. *Religion:* Methodist. *Agent:* Paul R. Reynolds, Inc., 12 East 41st St., New York, N.Y. 10017.

CAREER: Worked as transitman for railroads in the West and Midwest, 1909-13; Chile Copper Co., Chuquicamata, Chile, resident engineer, 1913-15; cattle rancher in Barela, Colo., 1915-17; Wood, Elston & Witten, Tulsa, Okla., consulting engineer, 1918-19; Elston, Axon & Russell, Springfield, Mo., consulting engineer, 1920-24; free-lance fiction writer, 1924-76. *Military service:* U.S. Army, Corps of Engineers, 1917-18; became captain; Tank Destroyers, 1942-45; became lieutenant colonel. *Member:* Western Writers of America, Kappa Sigma.

WRITINGS—Published by Lippincott, except as indicated: *Come Out and Fight,* Doubleday, 1941; *Guns on the Cimarron,* Macrae, 1943; *Hit the Saddle,* Macrae, 1947; *The Sheriff of San Miguel,* 1949; *Ranch of the Roses,* Ward, Lock, 1949; *Deadline at Durango,* 1950; *Grass and Gold,* 1951; *Round-up on the Picketwire,* 1952; *Saddle Up for Sunlight,* 1952; *Stage Road to Denver,* 1953; *Wagon Wheel Gap,* 1954; *Long Lope to Lander,* 1954; *Forbidden Valley,* 1955; *The Wyoming Bubble,* 1955; *The Marked Men,* 1956; *Last Stage to Aspen,* 1956; *Grand Mesa,* 1957; *Rio Grande Deadline,* 1957; *Wyoming Manhunt,* 1958; *Montana Masquerade,* 1959; *Gun Law at Laramie,* 1959; *Beyond the Bitterroots,* 1960; *Sagebrush Serenade,* 1960; *Timberline Bonanza,* 1961; *Treasure Coach from Deadwood,* 1962; *Roundup on the Yellowstone,* 1962; *The Seven Silver Mountains,* Berkley Publishing, 1964; *The Landseekers,* 1964; *Montana Passage,* Berkley Publishing, 1967; *Arizona Skyline,* Berkley Publishing, 1969; *Paradise Prairie,* Berkley Publishing, 1971.

Contributor of sixteen stories to anthologies, including *Famous Mysteries,* Scott, Foresman, 1954. Contributor of over three hundred short stories, novelettes, and serials to national magazines, including *American Magazine, Collier's, Cosmopolitan, Woman's Home Companion,* and *This Week.*

WORK IN PROGRESS: The Lawless Border; The Big Pasture, Montana Manhunt.

SIDELIGHTS: Historical research on the American West was Allan Vaughan Elston's greatest interest. According to his publisher, the author always did on-the-scene research for a story before writing it; he also pored over old newspapers and maps to familiarize himself with the news of the day and the geography of the setting.

Most of his books ran as serials in the New York Daily News Syndicate of newspapers before their publication in book form. A dozen of his stories have been made into motion pictures, and many were televised on such programs as "Alfred Hitchcock Presents," "The Robert Montgomery Show," and "Playhouse of the Air."

BIOGRAPHICAL/CRITICAL SOURCES: James Strode Elston, *The Elston Family in America,* Tuttle, 1942.†

*   *   *

ELTON, Geoffrey R(udolph) 1921-

PERSONAL: Original surname, Ehrenberg; born August 17, 1921, in Tuebingen, Germany; son of Victor L. (a classical scholar) and Eva (Sommer) Ehrenberg; married Sheila Lambert (a historian), August 30, 1952. *Education:* Attended Rydal School, Colwyn Bay, Wales, 1939-40; University of London, B.A., Ph.D.; Cambridge University, M.A., Litt.D. *Office:* Clare College, Cambridge University, Cambridge, England.

CAREER: University of Glasgow, Glasgow, Scotland, assistant in history, 1948-49; Cambridge University, Cambridge, England, 1949—, began as assistant lecturer, lecturer in history, 1949-63, reader in Tudor studies, Clare College, 1963-67, professor of English constitutional history, 1967—, fellow and director of studies in history, 1954-67, syndic, Cambridge University Press, 1960-73. *Military service:* British Army, Infantry and Intelligence, during World War II; became sergeant. *Member:* British Academy (fellow), Royal Historical Society (fellow; president, 1973-77), American Academy of Arts and Sciences (foreign member).

WRITINGS: The Tudor Revolution in Government: Administrative Changes in the Reign of Henry VIII, Cambridge University Press, 1953; *England under the Tudors,* Putnam, 1955; *Star Chamber Stories,* Methuen, 1958; (editor) *New Cambridge Modern History,* Volume II, Cambridge University Press, 1958; (editor) *The Reformation, 1520-1559,* Cambridge University Press, 1958; (editor) *The Tudor Constitution: Documents and Commentary,* Cambridge University Press, 1960; *Henry VIII: An Essay in Revision,* Routledge & Kegan Paul, 1962; (editor) *Ideas and Institutions: Renaissance and Reformation,* Macmillan, 1963, 2nd edition, 1968; (with George Kitson Clark) *Guide to Research Facilities in History in the Universities of Great Britain and Ireland,* Cambridge University Press, 1963, 2nd edition, 1965; *Reformation Europe, 1517-1559,* Collins, 1963, Meridian Books, 1964; (editor) Albert Frederick Pollard, *Wolsey,* Collins, 1965; *The Practice of History,* Methuen, 1967, Crowell, 1968; *The Future of the Past: An Inaugural Lecture,* Cambridge University Press, 1968; *The Body of the Whole Realm: Parliament and Representation in Medieval and Tudor England,* University Press of Virginia, 1969; *England, 1200-1640,* Cornell University Press, 1969.

Political History: Principles and Practice, Basic Books, 1970; *Modern Historians on British History, 1485-1945: A Critical Bibliography, 1945-1969,* Methuen, 1970, Cornell University Press, 1971; *Twenty-Five Years of Modern British History: A Bibliographical Survey, 1945-1969,* British Book Centre, 1971; *Policy and Police: The Enforcement of the Reformation in the Age of Cromwell,* Cambridge University Press, 1972; *Reform and Renewal: Thomas Cromwell and the Commonweal,* Cambridge University Press, 1973; *Studies in Tudor and Stuart Politics and Government,* two volumes, Cambridge University Press, 1974; *Reform and Reformation: England, 1509-1558,* Harvard University Press (London), 1977. Contributor to history journals.

WORK IN PROGRESS: Studies on parliament during the reign of Queen Elizabeth I.

BIOGRAPHICAL/CRITICAL SOURCES: Listener, January 11, 1968; *South Atlantic Quarterly,* summer, 1968; *Books and Bookmen,* June 1969; *Spectator,* September 27, 1969; *Observer,* November 16, 1969; *New Statesman,* September 18, 1970; *Times Literary Supplement,* October 16, 1970.

*   *   *

EMBRY, Margaret Jacob 1919-1975

PERSONAL: Born August 28, 1919, in Salt Lake City, Utah; died December, 1975; daughter of Clarence Cecil and Florence C. (Johnson) Jacob; married Alvin Leon Embry (an engineer), 1939; children: Kristin, Susan, Patricia, Alan, Meredith, Jonathan. *Education:* University of Utah, B.A., 1940. *Home:* La Matriz, Mountain Rte., Box 8, Jemez Springs, N.M. 87025.

CAREER: Storyteller on children's radio program, KRSN, 1957-59. *Member:* American Association of University Women, National Writers Club.

WRITINGS—All juveniles; all published by Holiday House: *The Blue Nosed Witch,* 1956; *Kid Sister,* 1958; *Mr. Blue,* 1963; *Peg-leg Willy,* 1966; *My Name Is Lion* (Junior Literary Guild selection), 1970; *Shadi,* 1971. Author of column "Minutiae," *Los Alamos Times,* 1951.†

*   *   *

EPP, Margaret A(gnes) 1913-
(Agnes Goossen)

PERSONAL: Born August 1, 1913, in Waldheim, Saskatchewan, Canada; daughter of Henry (a missionary) and Agnes (a missionary; maiden name, Goossen) Epp. *Education:* Graduate of Bethany Bible Institute, Hepburn, Saskatchewan, Canada; additional study at Prairie Bible Institute, Three Hills, Alberta, Canada. *Address:* P.O. Box 178, Waldheim, Saskatchewan, Canada.

CAREER: Writer, mainly for children and teenagers, 1949—.

WRITINGS—Published by Moody, except as indicated: *Peppermint Sue,* 1955; *North to Sakitawa,* 1955; *Light on Twin Rocks* [and] *Music in the Wapawekkas,* 1956; *The Long Chase* [and] *Budworms and Tepees,* 1956; *Vicki Arthur,* 1956; *The Sign of the Tumbling T,* 1956; *Come Back, Jonah* [and] *The Secret of Larrabie Lake,* 1956; *Sap's Running,* 1956; *Thirty Days Hath September* (story collection), 1956; *Canadian Holiday,* 1956; *Shades of Great Aunt Martha,* 1956; *Anita and the Driftwood House,* 1957; *All in the April Evening* (story collection), 1959; *No Hand Sam* (missionary stories), Mennonite Press, 1959.

(Under pseudonym Agnes Goossen) *Mystery at Pony*

Ranch, 1963; *But God Hath Chosen; The Story of John and Mary Dyck*, Mennonite Press, 1963; *Come to My Party* (nonfiction), Zondervan, 1964; *A Fountain Sealed*, Zondervan, 1965; *The Brannans of Bar Lazy B*, 1965; *Trouble on the Flying M*, 1966; *The North Wind and the Caribou*, 1966; *Search Down the Yukon*, 1967; *Walk in My Woods* (autobiography), 1967; *Prairie Princess*, 1967, published as *Sarah and the Magic Twenty-Fifth*, Victor, 1977; *No Help Wanted*, 1968; *The Princess and the Pelican*, 1968, published as *Sarah and the Pelican*, Victor, 1977; *This Mountain Is Mine* (biography), 1969; *The Princess Rides a Panther*, 1970, published as *Sarah and the Lost Friendship*, Victor, 1979; *Call of the Wahoo and Other Adventures*, 1971; *Great Frederick and Friends*, 1971; *Runaway at the Running K*, 1972; *Into All the World* (adult nonfiction), Prairie Press, 1973; *The Earth Is Round* (historical novel), Christian Press, 1974; *Proclaim Jubilee!* (adult nonfiction), Bethany Press, 1977; *Sarah and the Mystery of the Hidden Boy*, Victor, 1978; *Tulpengasse* (adult nonfiction), Christian Press, 1979; *Sarah and Those Darnley Boys*, Victor, 1980.

SIDELIGHTS: Margaret Epp comments: "From the age of seven, I 'knew' I would one day write books. The intuition came in a sudden flash of awe and excitement to me, an MK (missionary kid) attending a boarding school in Shantung, China. Many events and obstacles intervened before the dream could even begin to take shape, but I never lost it entirely.

"The great rivals for my writing time—from spring thaw to winter freeze—are my yard and garden. The gardener occupies the Boss's seat then, no doubt about it. The writer, biding her time with hard-held patience, waits for the first killing frost. Any night now!"

*   *   *

ERICKSON, Phoebe

PERSONAL: Born in Baileys Harbor, Wis.; daughter of Axel Eric and Emily (Anderson) Erickson; married Arthur Blair, 1947. *Education:* Attended Chicago Art Institute, 1931-33.

CAREER: Free-lance artist, author, and illustrator of children's books. Paintings have been exhibited in jury shows at Metropolitan and Whitney Museums, New York, N.Y., and at Art Institute, Chicago, Ill. Archaeology researcher in Europe, 1960. *Member:* American Museum of Natural History, American Swedish Historical Foundation, Wisconsin Academy of Sciences, Ridges Wildflower Sanctuary. *Awards, honors:* William Allen White Children's Book Award, 1957, for *Daniel 'Coon;* Dorothy Canfield Fisher Children's Book Award, 1960, for *Double or Nothing.*

WRITINGS—All self-illustrated: *Slip, The Story of a Little Fox*, Childrens Press, 1945; *Cattail House*, Childrens Press, 1949, new edition, 1962; *Black Penny*, Knopf, 1951; *The True Book of Animals of Small Pond*, Childrens Press, 1953; *Daniel 'Coon: The Story of a Pet Raccoon*, Knopf, 1954; *Baby Animal Friends*, Wonder Books, 1954; *Double or Nothing*, Harper, 1958; *Wildwing*, Harper, 1959; *Just Follow Me*, Follett, 1961; *Uncle Debunkel: Or, the Barely Believable Bear*, Knopf, 1964; *Who's in the Mirror?* Knopf, 1965.

Illustrator: Thornton Waldo Burgess, *Baby Animal Stories*, Grosset, 1949; Burgess, *Nature Almanac*, Grosset, 1949; Burgess, *Stories Around the Year*, Grosset, 1955; Johanna Dewitt, *Littlest Reindeer*, Childrens Press, 1957; Caroline Kramer, *Read-Aloud Nursery Tales*, Random House, 1957; Burgess, *Adventures of Peter Cottontail*, Grosset, 1958.

WORK IN PROGRESS: A book researched in Mexico.

SIDELIGHTS: Phoebe Erickson was born and grew up on a farm in the Door County of Wisconsin. Her parents came from Sweden in 1880 and reared a family of thirteen children, of whom she was the twelfth. She remembers evenings when her father read aloud and she "covered yards of brown paper or birchbark with drawings of strange looking horses and even stranger looking people." She told *CA:* "Much of early education I owe to my parents, the rest to public libraries. As a child I wanted to be a cowboy, an artist, a poet and a musician. Using 'do-it-yourself' methods, I have had some small degree of success. Nature and all wildlife are my chief interests. So far, all of my books have been for children, and since much of the joy in my life has come from the natural world, I seek to share that realization with others, especially children."†

*   *   *

ERLICH, Victor   1914-

PERSONAL: Born November 22, 1914, in Petrograd, Russia; son of Henryk and Sophie (Dubnov) Erlich; married Iza Sznejerson (a social worker), February 27, 1940; children: Henry Anthony, Mark Leo. *Education:* Free Polish University, M.A., 1937; Columbia University, Ph.D., 1951. *Office:* Yale University, New Haven, Conn. 06520.

CAREER: New Life, Warsaw, Poland, assistant literary editor, 1937-39; *Yiddish Encyclopedia*, New York, N.Y., research writer, 1942-43; University of Washington, Seattle, 1948-62, began as assistant professor, professor of Slavic languages and literature, 1958-62, assistant director of Far Eastern and Russian Institute, 1961-62; Yale University, New Haven, Conn., visiting professor of Slavic literature, 1962-63, Bensinger Professor of Russian Literature, 1963—. *Military service:* U.S. Army, 1943-45; received Purple Heart. *Member:* International Association of Slavonic Languages and Literatures (member of executive council), Modern Language Association of America (member of executive council), American Association for the Advancement of Slavic Studies (member of board of directors), American Society for Aesthetics, American Council of Learned Societies. *Awards, honors:* Ford Foundation fellow, 1953-54; Guggenheim fellow, 1957-58, 1964; M.A., Yale University, 1963.

WRITINGS: Russian Formalism: History, Doctrine, Mouton, 1955, 4th edition, 1980; (contributor) *For Roman Jakobson*, Mouton, 1956; (contributor) *Stil- und Formprobleme in der Literatur*, [Heidelberg], 1959; (contributor) *Russia under Khrushchev*, Praeger, 1962; *The Double Image: Concepts of the Poet in Slavic Literatures*, Johns Hopkins Press, 1964; *Gogol*, Yale University Press, 1969; (contributor) *Approaches to Poetics*, Columbia University Press, 1973; (editor) *Twentieth-Century Russian Criticism* (anthology), Yale University Press, 1975; *Pasternak: Twentieth-Century Views*, Prentice-Hall, 1979. Contributor to *Comparative Literature, Studies in Romanticism, Slavic Review*, and other periodicals.

BIOGRAPHICAL/CRITICAL SOURCES: Virginia Quarterly Review, spring, 1970.

*   *   *

ETMEKJIAN, James   1915-

PERSONAL: Born January 12, 1915, in Harpoot, Turkey; son of Garabed (a businessman) and Araxi (Bagdasarian) Etmekjian; married Lillian Krikorian, June 29, 1952; children: Charles, Roxanne. *Education:* Harvard University, A.B., 1939, A.M., 1942; additional study at Middlebury

Spanish School, 1945, Boston University, 1946, 1952, and 1953, and Sorbonne, University of Paris, 1947; Brown University, Ph.D., 1958. *Religion:* Armenian Apostolic Church. *Home:* 35 Llewellyn Rd., West Newton, Mass. 02165. *Office:* Department of Modern Foreign Languages and Literatures, Boston University, Boston, Mass.

CAREER: Dana Hall School, Wellesley, Mass., head of department of French and Spanish, 1941-50; employed as high school teacher, head of foreign language department, extension lecturer, and French instructor, 1950-61; Queens College of the City University of New York, Flushing, assistant professor of education and Romance languages, 1961-64; Southern Illinois University at Edwardsville, associate professor of Romance languages, 1964-65; University of Bridgeport, Bridgeport, Conn., professor of French and chairman of department of foreign languages, 1965-72; Boston University, Boston, Mass., lecturer in Armenian studies and Romance languages, 1972—. Professor and assistant director of National Defense Education Act, Foreign Language Institutes, University of Maine, 1959, 1961, and 1962, Michigan State University, 1960, and University of Massachusetts in Aracachon, France, 1964 and 1965. *Member:* National Association for Armenian Studies and Research, Armenian Literary Society, Society for Armenian Studies, Phi Beta Kappa. *Awards, honors:* American Council of Learned Societies grant for preparation of Armenian reader; traveling fellowship from French Government; Brown University fellow; Health, Education, and Welfare grant.

WRITINGS: (With Raymond Caefer and Frances O'Brien) *Speaking French,* Allyn & Bacon, 1963; *A Graded West Armenian Reader,* National Association for Armenian Studies and Research, 1963; *French Influence on the Western Armenian Renaissance,* Twayne, 1964; (with Caefer and O'Brien) *Le Francais Courant I,* Allyn & Bacon, 1964; *Le Francais Courant II,* Allyn & Bacon, 1965; *Pattern Drills in Language Teaching,* New York University Press, 1967; (with Caefer) *Spoken and Written French in Review,* Bobbs-Merrill, 1972; (editor) *An Anthology of Western Armenian Literature,* Caravan Books, 1980. Contributor to language education and literary journals.

WORK IN PROGRESS: History of Armenian Literature.

SIDELIGHTS: James Etmekjian writes *CA:* "I write because on given occasions I feel the need to write. The motivation is not financial (of the nine volumes I have authored, co-authored, or edited, only one has been done with the specific aim of financial gain), but rather a desire to comment, to suggest, to improve, or to make a small contribution to the social, educational, or cultural scene. The outcome has been four French textbooks, one book on language methodology, one Armenian provincial history, two anthologies of Armenian literature, and one scholarly study in comparative literature, supplemented by many articles on Armenian community issues, Armenian history, and Armenian literature. The last two categories have received increasingly greater emphasis during the past few years. I consider it an obligation to make Armenian history and literature better known to the outside world as a small but significant part of our humanistic heritage."

F

FAIRBANK, John K(ing) 1907-

PERSONAL: Born May 24, 1907, in Huron, S.D.; son of Arthur Boyce and Lorena C. V. (King) Fairbank; married Wilma Cannon, June 29, 1932; children: Laura, Holly. *Education:* Attended University of Wisconsin, 1925-27; Harvard University, A.B.; Rhodes Scholar, Balliol College, Oxford, 1929-31, and College of Chinese Studies, Peking, 1932; Oxford University, Ph.D., 1936. *Home:* 41 Winthrop St., Cambridge, Mass. 02138. *Office:* East Asian Research Center, Harvard University, 1737 Cambridge St., Cambridge, Mass. 02138.

CAREER: Tsing Hua University, Peking, China, lecturer, 1933-34; Harvard University, Cambridge, Mass., 1936—, professor of history, beginning 1946, Francis Lee Higginson Professor of History, 1959-76, professor emeritus, 1977—, director of East Asian Research Center, 1955-73. Served with coordinator of Information and Office of Strategic Services, Washington, D.C., 1941-42; special assistant to American ambassador, Chungking, China, 1942-43; acting deputy director in charge of Far Eastern operations, Office of War Information, Washington, D.C., 1944-45; director, United States Information Service in China, 1945-46. Lecturer; has made appearances on numerous radio and television shows.

MEMBER: Asia Society (honorary chairman of China council), National Committee on United States-China Relations, Far Eastern Association (vice-president, 1950-51), Council on Foreign Relations, Association for Asian Studies (president, 1959), American Historical Association (president, 1968), American Academy of Arts and Sciences, American Philosophical Society, American Council of Learned Societies, Massachusetts Historical Society, Phi Beta Kappa, Beta Theta Pi. *Awards, honors:* Rockefeller Foundation fellowship in the humanities, 1934-36; Guggenheim fellow in Japan, 1952-53, and in Asia and the Soviet Union, 1960; American Council of Learned Societies award in the humanities, 1964; LL.D., Korea University, 1964, University of Toronto, 1967, Swarthmore College, 1968, Harvard University, 1970, Oberlin College, 1971, and University of Cincinnati, 1973; L.H.D., University of Wisconsin, 1969, University of Massachusetts, 1974, and Middlebury College, 1975; honorary degree, Northwestern University, 1978, and Brandeis University, 1979.

WRITINGS: The United States and China, Harvard University Press, 1948, 4th revised edition, 1979; (co-author) *The*

Next Step in Asia, Harvard University Press, 1949; (with K. C. Liu) *Modern China: A Bibliographical Guide to Chinese Works, 1898-1937,* Harvard University Press, 1950; (with Conrad Brandt and Benjamin Schwartz) *A Documentary History of Chinese Communism, 1921-1950,* Harvard University Press, 1952; *Trade and Diplomacy on the China Coast,* two volumes, Harvard University Press, 1954, reprinted, Stanford University Press, 1967; (with S. Y. Teng) *China's Response to the West,* two volumes, Harvard University Press, 1954; (with Masataka Banno) *Japanese Studies of Modern China,* Tuttle, 1955, reprinted, Harvard University Press, 1971; (editor and contributor) *Chinese Thought and Institutions,* University of Chicago Press, 1957.

A History of East Asian Civilization, Houghton, Volume I: (with Edwin O. Reischauer) *East Asia: The Great Tradition,* 1960, Volume II: (with Reischauer and Albert Craig) *East Asia: The Modern Transformation,* 1965, revised edition published in one volume as *East Asia: Tradition and Transformation,* 1973; *China: The People's Middle Kingdom and the U.S.A.,* Harvard University Press, 1967; (editor and contributor) *The Chinese World Order: Traditional China's Foreign Relations,* Harvard University Press, 1968; (editor and contributor) *Chinese Ways in Warfare,* Cambridge University Press, 1974; *China Perceived: Images and Policies in Chinese-American Relations,* Knopf, 1974; (editor and author of introduction) *The Missionary Enterprise in China and America,* Harvard University Press, 1974; (with Noriko Kamachi and Chuzo Ichiko) *Japanese Studies of Modern China since 1953: A Bibliographical Guide to Historical and Social-Science Research on the Nineteenth and Twentieth Centuries,* East Asian Research Center, Harvard University, 1975; *Chinese-American Interactions: A Historical Summary,* Rutgers University Press, 1975; (editor with K. F. Bruner and E. M. Matheson) *The I.G. in Peking: Letters of Robert Hart, Chinese Maritime Customs, 1868-1907,* two volumes, Belknap Press, 1975; (editor) *Our China Prospects: Symposium on Chinese-American Relations,* American Philosophical Society, 1977.

General editor, with Denis Twitchett, and contributor to Volumes X, XI, and XII of the series "The Cambridge History of China." Has recorded lectures, "China Talks," Harvard University Press, 1974, and commentaries to accompany filmstrip series, "China Old and New," Harvard University Press, 1975. Contributor of articles to professional journals, magazines, and newspapers, including

American Historical Review, Journal of Asian Studies, Atlantic, Foreign Affairs, New Republic, and *Life*.

* * *

FAIRBROTHER, Nan 1913-1971

PERSONAL: Born December 23, 1913, in Coventry, England; died November 24, 1971, in London, England; daughter of Arthur and Lily (Dickenson) Fairbrother; married William McKenzie, 1939; children: Dan Peter, John Stewart. *Education:* University of London, B.A. (with honors in English), 1933.

CAREER: Writer and landscape architect.

WRITINGS—Published by Knopf, except as indicated: *An English Year* (autobiography), 1954 (published in England as *Children in the House,* Hogarth, 1954); *Men and Gardens,* 1956; *The Cheerful Day* (autobiography), 1960; *The House in the Country* (autobiography), 1965 (published in England as *The House,* Hogarth, 1965); *New Lives, New Landscapes: Planning for the Twenty-First Century,* foreword by Walter Muir Whitehill, 1970; *Shelter: Environments and Human Needs,* Penguin, 1972; *The Nature of Landscape Design: As an Art Form, a Craft, a Social Necessity,* foreword by F. Fraser Darling, 1974.†

* * *

FAULKNER, Peter 1933-

PERSONAL: Born July 10, 1933, in Eastbourne, England; son of Howard Bertram and Dorothy Edith (Todd) Faulkner; married Pamela Watkinson, March 30, 1959; children: Jacqueline Kay, John Howard. *Education:* Trinity Hall, Cambridge, B.A., 1956, M.A., 1961; University of Birmingham, M.A., 1961. *Politics:* Socialist. *Religion:* Humanist. *Home:* Glacis, Belvidere Rd., Exeter, Devon EX4 4RU, England. *Office:* School of English, University of Exeter, Exeter, Devon EX4 Q11, England.

CAREER: Fircroft College, Selly Oak, Birmingham, England, tutor in English, 1957-63; University of Durham, Durham, England, lecturer in English, beginning 1963; currently affiliated with School of English, University of Exeter, Exeter, England. Visiting senior lecturer, Fourah Bay College, Sierra Leone, 1965-66. *Member:* Fabian Society, William Morris Society, Rationalist Press Association. *Awards, honors:* Peter Floud Memorial Essay Competition, William Morris Society, second prize, 1961, for essay on Morris and Yeats, first prize, 1963, for essay on Morris and Gill.

WRITINGS: William Morris and W. B. Yeats, Dolmen Press (Dublin), 1962; *Yeats and the Irish Eighteenth Century* (Yeats Centenary Papers), Dolmen Press, 1965; (editor) Thomas Holcroft, *Anne St. Ives,* Oxford University Press, 1971; *William Morris: The Critical Heritage,* Routledge & Kegan Paul, 1973; *Humanism in the English Novel,* Pemberton-Elek, 1976; *Modernism,* Methuen, 1977; *Robert Bage,* Twayne, 1979; *Angus Wilson: Mimic and Moralist,* Secker & Warburg, 1980. Contributor of articles to literary journals in Ireland, England, and the United States.

WORK IN PROGRESS: Against the Age: An Introduction to William Morris.

BIOGRAPHICAL/CRITICAL SOURCES: Georgia Review, spring, 1971; *Times Literary Supplement,* July 11, 1980; *New York Times Book Review,* November 16, 1980.

FELTON, Ronald Oliver 1909-
(Ronald Welch)

PERSONAL: Born December 14, 1909, in Aberavon, Glamorganshire, Wales; son of Oliver (an accountant) and Alice (Thomas) Felton; married Betty Llewellyn Evans, 1934; children: Mary Felton Simmons. *Education:* Attended Berkhamsted School, 1922-28; Clare College, Cambridge, M.A. (with honors), 1931. *Religion:* Church of England. *Home:* Carreg Cennen, Okehampton, Devonshire, England.

CAREER: Okehampton Grammar School, Okehampton, Devonshire, England, headmaster, 1947-64; writer of historical books for children. *Military service:* Territorial Army, 1933-39. Welch Regiment, during World War II; served in Normandy and Germany; became major. *Awards, honors:* Carnegie Medal, Library Association, 1954, for *Knight Crusader.*

WRITINGS—Children's books: *Sker House,* Hutchinson, 1954.

Under pseudonym Ronald Welch: *The Black Car Mystery,* Pitman, 1950; *The Clock Stood Still,* Pitman, 1951; *The Gauntlet,* Oxford University Press (New York), 1951; *Knight Crusader,* Oxford University Press, 1954; *Mohawk Valley,* Criterion, 1958; *Nicholas Carey,* Criterion, 1963; *Tank Commander,* Thomas Nelson, 1972; *Zulu Warrior,* David & Charles, 1975.

Published by Oxford University Press (London), except as indicated: *Ferdinand Magellan* (biography), 1955, Criterion, 1956; *Captain of Dragoons,* 1956; *Captain of Foot,* 1959; *Escape from France,* 1960, Criterion, 1961; *For the King,* 1961, Criterion, 1962; *Bowman of Crecy,* 1966, Criterion, 1967; *The Hawk,* 1967, Criterion, 1969; *Sun of York,* 1970; *The Galleon,* 1971; *Ensign Carey,* 1976.

AVOCATIONAL INTERESTS: Military history, collecting model soldiers, motoring on the continent, photography.

BIOGRAPHICAL/CRITICAL SOURCES: Times Literary Supplement, May 25, 1967; *Books and Bookmen,* June, 1967; *Book World,* October 8, 1967.

* * *

FENNEMA, Owen Richard 1929-

PERSONAL: Born January 23, 1929, in Hinsdale, Ill.; son of Nick (a dairy plant owner) and Fern (First) Fennema; married Ann Elizabeth Hammer (a professor), August 22, 1948; children: Linda Gail, Karen Elizabeth, Peter Scott. *Education:* Kansas State University, B.S., 1950; University of Wisconsin—Madison, M.S., 1951, Ph.D., 1960. *Religion:* Congregational. *Home:* 5010 Lake Mendota Dr., Madison, Wis. 53705. *Office:* Department of Food Science, University of Wisconsin, Madison, Wis. 53706.

CAREER: University of Wisconsin—Madison, assistant professor, 1960-64, associate professor, 1964-69, professor of food chemistry, 1969—. *Member:* Institute of Food Technologists, Society for Cryobiology, American Chemical Society, Phi Tau Sigma, Gamma Sigma Delta.

WRITINGS: Low Temperature Preservation of Foods and Living Matter, Dekker, 1973; *Principles of Food Science,* Dekker, Volume I: *Food Chemistry,* 1975, Volume II: *Physical Methods of Food Preservation,* 1976; *Proteins at Low Temperatures,* American Chemical Society, 1979. Contributor to *Journal of Food Science* and *Journal of Agriculture and Food Chemistry.* Member of editorial board, Society for Cryobiology, 1966—, Institute of Food Technologists, 1974-77, *Journal of Food Processing and Preservation,* 1977—, and *Journal of Food Biochemistry,* 1977-80; consulting editor, *Food Science Monographs,* 1967-75.

* * *

FENNER, Carol Elizabeth 1929-

PERSONAL: Born September 30, 1929, in New York, N.Y.; daughter of Andrew J. and Esther (Rowe) Fenner; married Jiles B. Williams (a retired U.S. Air Force major). *Home:* 190 Rebecca Rd., Battle Creek, Mich. 49015.

CAREER: Writer and illustrator. *Awards, honors: Gorilla, Gorilla* was cited as a "notable book" by the American Library Association.

WRITINGS: Tigers in the Cellar (juvenile), Harcourt, 1963; *Christmas Tree on the Mountain,* Harcourt, 1966; *Lagalag, the Wanderer,* Harcourt, 1968; *Gorilla, Gorilla,* Random House, 1973; *The Skates of Uncle Richard,* Random House, 1978, published as *Ice Skates,* Scholastic Book Services, 1980; (contributor) *The Third Coast: Contemporary Michigan Fiction,* Wayne State University Press, 1980.

WORK IN PROGRESS: A collection of stories concerning one family, tentatively entitled *The Alma Stories,* for Random House.

SIDELIGHTS: Carol Elizabeth Fenner comments: "In my writing, I am either plodding or flying; there seems to be no middle ground. I believe that most people are capable of writing interestingly and well, but that few have the temperament or desire to plod along far enough for their wings to open, to knock on formidable doors, or to organize the chaos of sensation received through the mind and to build with it ideas and experiences, shaped and held by words, that will bridge to other minds.

"A writer must have a certain compulsion to write; and perhaps it is also necessary to receive physical satisfaction from the pressure of pen against paper, fingers against keys.

"I do not believe in 'gifted' abilities, only in fortunate ones."

AVOCATIONAL INTERESTS: Printing and reproduction methods, tennis, horses, swimming, cooking, and rose gardening.

* * *

FERGUSON, Peter R(oderick) I(nnes) 1933-

PERSONAL: Born December 30, 1933, in Bromley, Kent, England; son of Roderick I(nnes) and Kathleen Mary (Harwood) Ferguson; married Constance Patricia Woodmanery, 1967. *Education:* Balliol College, Oxford, B.A., 1958. *Home:* 74 West Riding Bricket Wood, St. Albans, Hertfordshire, England. *Agent:* A. D. Peters & Co. Ltd., 10 Buckingham St., London WC2N 6BU, England. *Office:* Department of English, Herts College of Higher Education, Hertfordshire, England.

CAREER: Teacher of Latin, English, and games at a co-educational grammar school in Middlesex, England, 1961-70; Herts College of Higher Education, Hertfordshire, England, lecturer in English, 1970—. *Military service:* British Army, Intelligence Corps, 1952-54; became lieutenant.

WRITINGS: Autumn for Heroes (novel), J. Cape, 1959; *Monster Clough* (novel), Hodder & Stoughton, 1962; *A Week before Winter* (novel), Hodder & Stoughton, 1971; *A Week by the Sea* (textbook), Longmans, 1976; *It Never Snows in England* (reader), Longmans, 1979. Contributor of poems, stories, articles, reviews, and translations to various periodicals.

WORK IN PROGRESS: A novel, *The Fretters Barsman.*

SIDELIGHTS: Peter Ferguson writes *CA:* "I need two things to write a novel: a metaphor and a structure. Metaphors are given, structures emerge. Metaphors are few and precious and not to be confused with images, which can often be indulgently entertained and seem to offer the lineaments of an emergent structure but which, in the end, prove to lack real substance, leaving you with a whole lot of faking to do." The author remarks that such "faking" brings with it either the "attendant loss of artistic self-respect, or the decision to discard some twenty thousand or so words (leaving sufficient flashes here and there to make this act not the instant and ruthless one it should be)." Ferguson continues: "I once spent more than two years working on a novel whose centrepiece was the North Circular Road in London; and somehow or other—probably because it is pleasant to be writing and in constant production—I managed to conceal from myself the fact that the North Circular Road was merely an image, suitable enough to be a credible background, but not of itself generating any of the universal applications one must derive from a foregrounded metaphor.

"My best metaphor is Huffrey Badger, a holy innocent or *tabula rasa* fun-person, through whom I can view the whole of life, as I know it, anew and the whole of life, as he sees it, with undiminishable pleasure. Not so long ago, a publisher returned a Huffrey Badger manuscript to me with the comment that she hoped I would find someone with more courage than herself to publish the book. It is the nicest put-down I have ever received. So it goes."

* * *

FERGUSSON, Francis 1904-

PERSONAL: Born February 21, 1904, in Albuquerque, N.M.; son of Harvey Butler (a lawyer) and Clara (Huning) Fergusson; married Marion Crowne, January 16, 1931 (died, 1959); married Peggy Watts, July 26, 1962; children: (first marriage) Harvey, Honora. *Education:* Attended Harvard University, 1921-23; Queen's College, Oxford, B.A., 1926. *Address:* Box 143, Kingston, N.J. 08528. *Office:* Princeton University, Princeton, N.J. 08540.

CAREER: American Laboratory Theatre, New York City, associate director, 1926-30; *Bookman,* New York City, theater critic, 1930-32; New School for Social Research, New York City, lecturer and executive secretary, 1932-34; Bennington College, Bennington, Vt., professor of literature and drama, 1934-47; Princeton University, Princeton, N.J., member of Institute for Advanced Study, 1948-49, director of Gauss Seminars in criticism, 1949-52; Rutgers University, New Brunswick, N.J., professor of comparative literature, 1952-73; Princeton University, professor, 1973—. Indiana University at Bloomington, fellow, School of Letters, 1950, visiting professor, 1952-53. *Member:* Modern Language Association of America, National Institute of Arts and Letters, P.E.N. *Awards, honors:* Rhodes scholar, Oxford University; Christian Gauss Award, Phi Beta Kappa, 1953, for *Dante's Drama of the Mind;* National Institute of Arts and Letters grant in literature, 1953; D.Litt., University of New Mexico, 1955; *Kenyon Review* fellow in criticism, 1957.

WRITINGS—Criticism, except as indicated: (Editor and author of introduction) James Joyce, *Exiles,* New Directions, 1945; *The Idea of a Theater: A Study of Ten Plays,* Princeton University Press, 1949; (author of introduction) *Plays of Moliere,* Modern Library, 1950; *Dante's Drama of the Mind: A Modern Reading of the "Purgatorio",* Princeton University Press, 1953; *The Human Image in Dramatic Literature* (essays), Doubleday, 1957; (author of introduc-

tion) Paul Valery, *Plays*, Pantheon, 1960; (author of intro-
duction) Aristotle, *Poetics*, Hill & Wang, 1961; (editor and
author of introduction) William Shakespeare, *Tragedies of
Monarchy: Hamlet* [and] *Macbeth* [and] *King Lear*, Dell,
1962; *Poems, 1929-1961* (collection of the author's verse),
Rutgers University Press, 1962; *Dante Alighieri: Three Lectures*, Gertrude Clarke Whittall Poetry and Literature Fund,
U.S. Library of Congress, 1965; *Dante*, Macmillan, 1966;
Shakespeare: The Pattern in His Carpet, Delacorte, 1970;
*Literary Landmarks: Essays on the Theory and Practice of
Literature*, Rutgers University Press, 1976; *Trope and Alle-
gory: Themes Common to Dante and Shakespeare*, Univer-
sity of Georgia Press, 1977.

Plays: (Translator and adaptor) Sophocles, *Electra: A Version for the Modern Stage, with Notes on Production and
Critical Bibliography*, William R. Scott, 1938; "The King
and the Duke: A Melodramatic Farce from Huckleberry
Finn" (with music; produced Off-Broadway, June, 1955),
published in *From the Modern Repertoire: Series Two*, edited by Eric Bentley, University of Denver Press, 1952;
(translator) Sophocles, *Electra*, Dell, 1965.

General editor, "Laurel Shakespeare" series, Dell, 1958-68.
Member of editorial board, *Comparative Literature*, 1952-
60, and *Sewanee Review*.

SIDELIGHTS: Unlike the majority of modern critics, Francis Fergusson is most concerned with the action of a poem or
play rather than its language. Fergusson's concept of action
does not involve plot or the sequence of events, but the extent to which a play or poem represents a shared vision of
the whole of the human situation. In a *Southern Review* article entitled "Francis Fergusson: The Pattern in His Criticism," Ashley Brown comments: "He tries to see the literary work as a complete object. I must remark, somewhat
parenthetically, that he has managed to stay aloof from the
literary fashions and quarrels of the last forty years. One
feels, in reading his books or even his reviews, that he has
never concerned himself with things which are not of permanent interest."

BIOGRAPHICAL/CRITICAL SOURCES: Stanley Edgar
Hyman, *The Armed Vision*, Vintage, 1955; *Saturday Re-
view*, May 5, 1962; *Poetry*, September, 1962; *Book Week*,
July 24, 1966; *New York Times Book Review*, November 20,
1966; *New York Review of Books*, November 19, 1970; Alan
Cheuse and Richard Koffler, editors, *The Rarer Action:
Essays in Honor of Francis Fergusson*, Rutgers University
Press, 1971; *New Yorker*, April 19, 1976; *Southern Review*,
January, 1978; *Sewanee Review*, July, 1978.

*   *   *

FERLINGHETTI, Lawrence (Monsanto) 1919(?)-
(Lawrence Ferling)

PERSONAL: Born Lawrence Ferling; restored original fam-
ily name, 1954; born March 24, 1919(?), probably in Yon-
kers, N.Y.; son of Charles S. (an auctioneer) and Clemence
(Monsanto) Ferling; married Kirby Selden Smith, April,
1951; children: Julie, Lorenzo. *Education:* University of
North Carolina, A.B.; Columbia University, M.A., 1948;
Sorbonne, University of Paris, Doctorat de l'Universite,
1951. *Politics:* "Now an enemy of the State." *Religion:*
"Catholique manque." *Residence:* Big Sur, Calif. *Office:*
City Lights Books, 1562 Grant Ave., San Francisco, Calif.
94133.

CAREER: Poet, playwright, and editor; worked for *Time*
magazine after World War II; taught French in an adult education program in San Francisco, Calif., 1951-53; City Lights

Pocket Bookshop (now City Lights Books), San Francisco,
co-owner, 1953—, founder and editor of City Lights Books
(publishing house), 1955—. Participated with Allen Ginsberg
in a Pan-American cultural conference at the University of
Concepcion, Chile, 1960. *Military service:* U.S. Naval Reserve, 1941-45; became lieutenant commander; was command officer during Normandy invasion.

WRITINGS: (Translator) Jacques Prevert, *Selections from
Paroles*, City Lights, 1958; *Her* (novel), New Directions,
1960; *Howl of the Censor* (trial proceedings), edited by J. W.
Ehrlich, Nourse Publishing, 1961, reprinted, Greenwood
Press, 1976; (with Jack Spicer) *Dear Ferlinghetti*, White
Rabbit Press, 1962; *The Mexican Night: Travel Journal*,
New Directions, 1970; *Northwest Ecolog*, City Lights, 1978;
(with Nancy J. Peters) *Literary San Francisco: A Pictorial
History from the Beginning to the Present*, Harper, 1980.

Poetry: *Pictures of the Gone World*, City Lights, 1955, reprinted, Kraus Reprint, 1973; *Tentative Description of a
Dinner Given to Promote the Impeachment of President Eisenhower*, Golden Mountain Press, 1958; *A Coney Island of
the Mind*, New Directions, 1958; *Berlin*, Golden Mountain
Press, 1961; *One Thousand Fearful Words for Fidel Castro*,
City Lights, 1961; *Starting from San Francisco*, with record-
ing of poems, New Directions, 1961, revised edition without
recording, 1967; (with Gregory Corso and Allen Ginsberg)
Penguin Modern Poets 5, Penguin, 1963; *Thoughts of a Con-
certo of Telemann*, Four Seasons Foundation, 1963; *Where
Is Vietnam?*, City Lights, 1965; *To F—— Is to Love Again,
Kyrie Eleison Kerista; or, The Situation in the West, Fol-
lowed by a Holy Proposal*, F—— You Press, 1965; *Christ
Climbed Down*, Syracuse University, 1965; *An Eye On the
World: Selected Poems*, MacGibbon & Kee, 1967; *Moscow
in the Wilderness, Segovia in the Snow*, Beach Books, 1967;
After the Cries of the Birds, Dave Haselwood Books, 1967;
Fuclock, Fire Publications, 1968; *The Secret Meaning of
Things*, New Directions, 1969; *Tyrannus Nix?*, New Direc-
tions, 1969; *Back Roads to Far Places*, New Directions,
1971; *Love Is No Stone on the Moon*, ARIF Press, 1971; *The
Illustrated Wilfred Funk*, City Lights, 1971; *Open Eye, Open
Heart*, New Directions, 1973; *Who Are We Now?*, City
Lights, 1976; *Landscapes of Living and Dying*, New Direc-
tions, 1979; *A Trip to Italy and France*, New Directions,
1980.

Plays: *Unfair Arguments with Existence: Seven Plays for a
New Theatre* (contains "The Soldiers of No Country" [first
produced in London, 1969], "Three Thousand Red Ants"
[first produced in New York City, 1970; also see below],
"The Alligation" [first produced in San Francisco, 1962;
also see below], "The Victims of Amnesia" [first produced
in New York City, 1970; also see below], "Motherlode,"
"The Customs Collector in Baggy Pants" [first produced in
New York City, 1964], and "The Nose of Sisyphus"), New
Directions, 1963; *Routines* (contains thirteen short plays,
including "The Jig Is Up," "His Head," "Ha-Ha," and
"Non-Objection"), New Directions, 1964; "3 by Ferlingh-
etti: Three Thousand Red Ants, The Alligation, [and] The
Victims of Amnesia," first produced in New York City,
1970.

Editor; all published by City Lights: *Beatitude Anthology*,
1960; Pablo Picasso, *Hunk of Skin*, 1969; Charles Upton,
Panic Grass, 1969; *City Lights Anthology*, 1974.

Author of introduction: Diane Di Prima, *This Kind of Bird
Flies Backward*, Totem Press, 1958; Michael McClure, *Meat
Science Essays*, City Lights, 1963; Bob Kaufmann, *Soli-
tudes*, Union General d'Editions (Paris), 1966; Ray Bremser,

Angel, Tompkins Square Press, 1967; Tom Picard, *High on the Walls,* Fulcrum, 1967.

Contributor: *New Directions in Prose and Poetry 16,* New Directions, 1957; Ralph J. Gleason, editor, *Jam Session: An Anthology of Jazz,* Putnam, 1958; Seymour Krim, editor, *The Beats,* Fawcett, 1960; Elias Wilentz, *The Beat Scene,* Corinth, 1960; Donald M. Allen, editor, *The New American Poetry: 1945-1960,* Grove, 1960; Alain Bosquet, editor and translator, *Trente-cinq jeunes poetes americains,* Gallimard, 1960; Lyle E. Linville, editor, *Tiger,* Linville-Hansen Associates, 1961; Ursule Spier Erickson and Robert Pearsall, editors, *The Californians,* Hesperian House, 1961; Thomas Parkinson, editor, *A Casebook on the Beat,* Crowell, 1961; Gregory Corso and Walter Hollerer, editors, *Junge Amerikanische Lyrik,* Carl Hanser (Munich), 1961; Gene Baro, editor, *Beat Poets,* Vista Books (London), 1961; J. Laughlin, editor, *New Directions in Prose and Poetry 17,* New Directions, 1961; Markku Lahtela and Anselm Hollo, translators, *Idan Ja Lannen Runot,* Weilin & Goos (Helsinki), 1962; *Poetry Festival,* Poetry Center, San Francisco State College, 1962; *Nuestra Decada,* Universidad Nacional Autonoma de Mexico, 1964; Laughlin, editor, *New Directions in Prose and Poetry 18,* New Directions, 1964; Paris Leary and Robert Kelly, editors, *A Controversy of Poets,* Doubleday, 1965; Chad Walsh, editor, *Garlands for Christmas,* Macmillan, 1965; Louis Dudek, editor, *Poetry of Our Time,* Macmillan (Toronto), 1965; (contributor of translation) Willis Barnstone, editor, *Modern European Poetry,* Bantam, 1966; Harriet W. Sheridan, *Structure and Style,* Harcourt, 1966; Walter Lowenfels, editor, *Where Is Vietnam?,* Doubleday, 1967.

Recordings: (With Kenneth Rexroth) "Poetry Readings in 'The Cellar'," Fantasy, 1958; "Tentative Description of a Dinner to Impeach President Eisenhower, and Other Poems," Fantasy, 1959; "Tyrannus Nix? and Assassination Raga," Fantasy, 1971; (with Corso and Ginsberg) "The World's Greatest Poets 1," CMS, 1971.

Also author of narration for film "Have You Sold Your Dozen Roses?," California School of Fine Arts Film Workshop, 1957. Contributor to numerous publications, including *San Francisco Chronicle, Nation, Evergreen Review, Liberation, Chicago Review, Transatlantic Review,* and *New Statesman.* Editor, *Journal for the Protection of All Beings, Interim Pad,* and *City Lights Journal.*

SIDELIGHTS: Lawrence Ferlinghetti was a prominent figure in the Beat poetry movement of the 1950's, a movement whose primary purpose was to bring poetry back to the people. Often concerned with political or social issues, Beat poetry was written in a common language owing more to the patterns of ordinary speech than to traditional poetic structures. Many literary critics greeted the movement with stiff resistance. As Peter Collier notes, however, the Beat poets have won "a grudging respect even from the literary elite whose definitions of the world, of art and the artist's role, they originally set out to dispute. Beginning as renegades, they have had a considerable impact on their times. They have made poetry public, and made it vital." Ferlinghetti's City Lights Bookstore served as a meeting place for Beat writers while his press published and promoted Beat writings. His publication of Allen Ginsberg's poetry collection *Howl* in 1956 led to his arrest on obscenity charges. The subsequent trial, during which he was acquitted of the charges in a landmark decision, drew national attention to the Beat movement.

Ferlinghetti's own poetry has been both praised and condemned. M. L. Rosenthal writes in the *Nation* that Ferlin-

ghetti is "a deft, rapid-paced, whirling performer. He has a wonderful eye for meaning in the commonplace." Kathleen Wiegner notes in the *American Poetry Review* that "what is always delightful about Ferlinghetti is the good time he has at what is often a deadly serious business—telling people what is good for them." Kenneth Rexroth is of the opinion that Ferlinghetti's *A Coney Island of the Mind* "nudges *Howl* for first place as the most popular poetry book of the [1950's]." Noting that Ferlinghetti has been grouped with other Beat poets and criticized accordingly, Crale D. Hopkins writes: "His poetry cannot be dismissed either as protest polemic or as incoherently personalized lyric. His craftsmanship, thematics, and awareness of the tradition justify a further consideration." On the more negative side, Vernon Young describes Ferlinghetti as "one of those spiritual panhandlers bred of our age who has been *infected* by poetry." Jonathan Williams thinks Ferlinghetti's poetry is "real jivy, real groovy, all that—but ultimately kind of stupid." Nevertheless, F. Moramarco of *World Literature Today* describes Ferlinghetti as "one of America's most popular poets."

Although most closely identified with his poetry, Ferlinghetti's single novel *Her* has been well-received. Described by the author as "a surreal semi-autobiographical blackbook of a semi-mad period of my life," the book deals with a young man's search for his identity. Pierre Lepape calls it "a masterpiece of the young American novel." Vincent McHugh of the *San Francisco Chronicle* considers *Her* "the most important American prose work I've seen in the last 20 years and decidedly one of the pleasantest."

A less favorable response has greeted Ferlinghetti's dramatic work. Writing in the *New York Times* of the three-play performance "Three by Ferlinghetti," Clive Barnes states: "Lawrence Ferlinghetti is a poet for whom I have considerable respect. But as a playwright he does not, so far, even begin to make dramatic sense or theatrical logic." Speaking of the same work, John Simon comments in *New York* that "Ferlinghetti tends to be unfocused, diffuse (quite an achievement, considering the brevity of the pieces), [and] bereft of a genuine dramatic impulse and pulsation." On a more positive note, the reviewer for *Cue* concludes that "the most impressive thing about [the three plays] is the intensity of their themes and the depth of Ferlinghetti's commitment to the gut-issue of man's destruction of man."

In all of his work, Ferlinghetti has displayed a continuing concern with political expression. His poetry often addresses political subjects, as in *Where Is Vietnam?* and *Tyrannus Nix?,* while the work he publishes through City Lights Books often exhibits both literary and political concerns.

As a publisher, Ferlinghetti is particularly sensitive to matters of government censorship. He holds that government grants to writers constitute a subtle form of control. Speaking to Ben Pleasants of the *Los Angeles Times,* Ferlinghetti declares: "Officially, [writers receiving grants] can say anything they want and still get the grant. Nevertheless, there's an ... influence at work, unspoken, that says, 'Don't Bite the Hand That Feeds You.'" Comparing censorship in other countries to that in the United States, Ferlinghetti believes there is "very real censorship in Russia.... There's no comparison between the U.S. and Russia. Here it's more innocuous, it's a self-imposed censorship, really an *abdication* of freedom of speech."

Ferlinghetti is well aware of his position as social-dissident-turned-successful-publisher. "Herbert Marcuse once noted," he tells Pleasants, "the enormous capacity of society to ingest its own most dissident elements. As soon as you become a successful dissident you get on TV and you're writing books for publishers and living in a beach community in Los Angeles. . . . It happens to everyone successful within the system. I'm ingested myself.''

Ferlinghetti's poem ''Autobiography'' was choreographed by Sophie Maslow in 1964. ''A Coney Island of the Mind'' was adapted for the stage by Steven Kyle Kent, Charles R. Blaker, and Carol Brown and produced at the Edinburgh Festival in Scotland in 1966. Another adaptation of the poem was presented by Ted Post on the television program ''Second Experiment in Television'' in 1967.

BIOGRAPHICAL/CRITICAL SOURCES: New York Times Book Review, September 2, 1956, September 7, 1958, April 29, 1962, July 21, 1968, September 8, 1968, September 21, 1980; *Life*, September 9, 1957; *Saturday Review*, October 5, 1957, September 4, 1965; *Commentary*, December, 1957; *Reporter*, December 12, 1957; *Wilson Library Bulletin*, June, 1958; *Nation*, October 11, 1958; *Poetry*, November, 1958, July, 1964, May, 1966; *Liberation*, June, 1959; *Observer*, November 1, 1959, April 9, 1967; *New York Times*, April 14, 1960, April 15, 1960, April 16, 1960, April 17, 1960, February 26, 1967, February 27, 1967, September 13, 1970; *Library Journal*, November 15, 1960; Donald M. Allen, editor, *The New American Poetry: 1945-1960*, Grove, 1960; *Commonweal*, February 3, 1961; *San Francisco Chronicle*, March 5, 1961; *Minnesota Review*, July, 1961; Kenneth Rexroth, *Assays*, New Directions, 1961; *Carleton Miscellany*, spring, 1965; *Sunday Times* (London), June 20, 1965; David Kherdian, *Six Poets of the San Francisco Renaissance: Portraits and Checklists*, Giligia Press, 1967; *San Francisco Oracle*, February, 1967; *New Statesman*, April 14, 1967; *Punch*, April 19, 1967; *Times Literary Supplement*, April 27, 1967; *Wisconsin Studies in Contemporary Literature*, summer, 1967; *Books and Bookmen*, November, 1967; *Listener*, February 1, 1968; *Ramparts*, March, 1968; *Los Angeles Times*, July 20, 1969, March 18, 1980; *Virginia Quarterly Review*, autumn, 1969, spring, 1974.

Cue, October 3, 1970; *New York*, October 5, 1970; Ruby Cohn, *Dialogue in American Drama*, Indiana University Press, 1971; Samuel Charters, *Some Poems/Poets: Studies in American Underground Poetry since 1945*, Oyez, 1971; *Contemporary Literary Criticism*, Gale, Volume II, 1974, Volume VI, 1976, Volume X, 1979; *Parnassus: Poetry in Review*, spring/summer, 1974; *Sewanee Review*, fall, 1974; *Prairie Schooner*, fall, 1974, summer, 1978; *Italian Americana*, autumn, 1974; *Midwest Quarterly* autumn, 1974; *New Republic*, February 22, 1975; *World Literature Today*, summer, 1977; *America*, August 20, 1977; *San Francisco Review of Books*, September, 1977; *American Poetry Review*, September/October, 1977; *San Francisco Bay Guardian*, October 6, 1977; *Critique: Studies in Modern Fiction*, Volume XIX, Number 3, 1978; Neeli Cherkovski, *Ferlinghetti: A Biography*, Doubleday, 1979.

—*Sketch by Thomas Wiloch*

*　　　*　　　*

FERNANDEZ de la REGUERA, Ricardo 1914-

PERSONAL: Born April 27, 1914, in Barcelona, Spain; son of Angel and Concepcion (Ugarte) Fernandez de la Reguera; married Susana March (a writer), April 3, 1940; children: Alfredo. *Education:* Universidad de Barcelona, license in philosophy and letters, 1946. *Home:* Av. Gral. Mitre, 144, Barcelona, Spain.

CAREER: Writer, 1933—. *Military service:* Served with Batallion ''C'' de Cazadores de Cerinola, 1936-39. *Member:*

P.E.N., Socio del Comes. *Awards, honors:* Ciudad de Barcelona, for *Cuando voy a morir;* Internacional Club Espana award for *Perdimos el paraiso;* Concha Espina, for *Bienaventurados los que aman;* Pensiones Fundacion March, 1961 and 1962, for *Episodios nacionales contemporaneos.*

WRITINGS: Cuando voy a morir, Destino, 1951, translation published as *In the Darkness of My Fury*, O. Wolff, 1959; *Cuerpo a tierra*, Garbo, 1954, translation published as *Reach for the Ground*, Schuman, 1964; *Perdimos el paraiso*, Planeta, 1955; *Bienaventurados los que aman*, Planeta, 1956; *Espionaje-cuentos*, Taurus, 1963; (with wife, Susana March Fernandez de la Reguera) *Episodios nacionales contemporaneos*, Planeta, Volume I: *Heroes de Cuba*, 1963, Volume II: *Heroes de Fillipinas*, 1963, Volume III: *Fin de unda regencia*, 1964, Volume IV: *La Boda de Alfonso XIII*, 1965, Volume V: *La Semana Tragica*, 1966, Volume VI: *Espana neutral*, 1967, Volume VII: *El Desastre de annual*, 1968, Volume VIII: *La Dictadura I*, 1969, Volume IX: *La Dictadura II*, 1970, Volume X: *La Caida de un rey*, 1972, Volume XI: *La Republica I*, 1979. Also author of radio and television scripts. Contributor to periodicals and literary reviews.

WORK IN PROGRESS: Further volumes of *Episodios nacionales contemporaneos*, in collaboration with wife, S. M. Fernandez de la Reguera.

SIDELIGHTS: As a writer, Ricardo Fernandez de la Reguera is primarily interested in human values. He writes, ''I am preoccupied with the solitude of man and the absurdity of life.'' His works are concerned with the poor and humble, and with ''our common indefensibility and our bitter and irrevocable destiny.'' Fernandez de la Reguera adds that he encloses his social commentary in an ''intense narrative river bed which conceals the message without making concessions to the gallery.''

*　　　*　　　*

FERRIS, Paul (Frederick) 1929-

PERSONAL: Born February 15, 1929, in Swansea, Wales; son of Frederick Morgan (an engineer) and Olga (Boulton) Ferris; married Gloria Moreton, December 29, 1953; children: Jonathan Moreton, Virginia Ann. *Education:* Attended grammar school in Swansea, Wales. *Agent:* Curtis Brown Ltd., 1 Craven Hill, London W2 3EP, England.

CAREER: South Wales Evening Post, Swansea, Wales, member of editorial staff, 1949-52; *Woman's Own* (weekly magazine), London, England, member of editorial staff, 1953; *Observer* (Sunday newspaper), London, assistant in foreign news service, 1953, radio columnist, 1954—, news editor, 1962. *Military service:* Royal Air Force, 1947-49.

WRITINGS: A Changed Man (novel), Hutchinson, 1958; *The City*, Gollancz, 1960, Random House, 1961; *Then We Fall* (novel), Hutchinson, 1960; *The Church of England*, Gollancz, 1962, Macmillan, 1963; *A Family Affair* (novel), Hutchinson, 1963; *The Destroyer* (novel), Hutchinson, 1965; *The Doctors* (nonfiction), Gollancz, 1965; *The Nameless: Abortion in Britain Today*, Hutchinson, 1966; *The Dam* (novel), Hutchinson, 1967; *Men and Money: Financial Europe Today*, Hutchinson, 1968, published as *The Money Men of Europe*, Macmillan, 1969; *The House of Northcliffe: A Biography of an Empire*, World Publishing, 1972; *Very Personal Problems*, Weidenfeld & Nicolson, 1973; *The Cure* (novel), Dial, 1974; *The Detective*, Weidenfeld & Nicolson, 1976; *Dylan Thomas*, Coward, 1977; *High Places* (novel), Coward, 1977; *Talk to Me about England* (novel), Coward, 1979. Also author of television and radio scripts. Contributor to *Punch*, *Town*, *Queen*, *Harper's Bazaar*, *Observer*, and *Spectator*.

BIOGRAPHICAL/CRITICAL SOURCES: Saturday Review, March 29, 1969; *Detroit News,* May 7, 1972; *Washington Post Book World,* October 3, 1979.

* * *

FEUER, Lewis S(amuel) 1912-

PERSONAL: Born December 7, 1912, in New York, N.Y.; son of Joseph and Fannie (Weidner) Feuer; married Kathryn Jean Beliveau (a college professor), October 13, 1946; children: Robin Kathryn. *Education:* City College (now City College of the City University of New York), B.S., 1931; Harvard University, A.M., 1932, Ph.D., 1935. *Politics:* Independent. *Religion:* Jewish. *Home:* 1519 Dairy Rd., Charlottesville, Va. 22903. *Office:* Department of Sociology, Abell Hall, University of Virginia, Charlottesville, Va. 22903.

CAREER: City College (now City College of the City University of New York), New York, N.Y., instructor in philosophy, 1939-42; Vassar College, Poughkeepsie, N.Y., associate professor of philosophy, 1946-51; University of Vermont, Burlington, professor of philosophy, 1951-57; University of California, Berkeley, professor of philosophy and social science, 1957-66; University of Toronto, Toronto, Ontario, professor of sociology, 1966-76; University of Virginia, Charlottesville, university professor of sociology and humanities, 1976—. American Council of Learned Societies exchange scholar to the Soviet Academy of Science, 1963. *Military service:* U.S. Army, 1942-46; became sergeant. *Member:* American Association of University Professors (president, Vermont chapter, 1955-56), American Philosophical Association, American Sociological Association, American Association for the Sociological Study of Jewry, American Jewish Historical Society. *Awards, honors:* Bowdoin Prize, Harvard University, 1935.

WRITINGS: Psychoanalysis and Ethics, C. C Thomas, 1955; *Spinoza and the Rise of Liberalism,* Beacon, 1958, revised edition, 1965; (editor) Karl Marx and Friedrich Engels, *Basic Writings on Politics and Philosophy,* Doubleday, 1959; *The Scientific Intellectual,* Basic Books, 1963; *The Conflict of Generations: The Character and Significance of Student Movements,* Basic Books, 1968; *Marx and the Intellectuals,* Doubleday, 1969; *Einstein and the Generation of Science,* Basic Books, 1974; *Ideology and the Ideologists,* Harper, 1975. Contributor of articles to *New York Times Magazine* and to professional journals.

SIDELIGHTS: In *The Conflict of Generations,* Lewis S. Feuer contends that the campus demonstrations of the 1960's were chiefly motivated by an ancient conflict, "the rebellion of idealistic sons against their . . . fathers," a *Virginia Quarterly Review* critic explains. Published shortly after such student activities began to wane, the book nevertheless generated a flurry of controversy. While some reviewers, such as George Woodcock in the *New Leader,* praise the work for its "sanity and . . . essential fairness," others, such as *Commonweal's* Norman Birnbaum, chide, "The book takes into account no ambiguities, and few complexities."

George Keller begins his *Book World* review by stating, "This may be the most controversial book of the year on the subject of student activism." According to Keller, after chronicling the "student movements, tactics and causes" that have occurred over the centuries and throughout the world, Feuer proposes "that since the beginning of life on earth, young people have been at odds with whatever social system they are born into and have been hostile to the older

people who run the order." A *Time* critic reports that Feuer's "general thesis" is that "[student activists] are simply acting out their hostility toward Father. Student movements, as Feuer sees them, are history's proof of the Oedipus complex." While the critic finds that "the theory is, at best, debatable," the book "makes fascinating reading as a partial compilation of the games a great many young people play."

Other critics have taken a less charitable view. Robert Paul Wolff notes that Feuer "succeeds brilliantly" in tracing the history of student rebellions. "His theory is coherent, his narrative fascinating, his catalogue of confirmatory evidence impressive," Wolff writes in the *New York Times Book Review.* However, he adds: "Then [the author] turns to the United States, and his book falls apart. Instead of historical perspective and sociological insight, we get partisan bickering, debater's point-scoring and a serious distortion of events." In *Atlantic,* Dan Wakefield voices similar complaints: "In the guise of cool, 'objective' scholarship, Feuer uses the cheapest kind of Freudian mumbo jumbo to seek to discredit almost everything about the student movement and to ignore what he can't discredit. . . . Professor Feuer psychoanalyzes away the most idealistic and sincere actions, seeing always neurosis instead of nobility, complexes rather than commitments."

Like Wakefield, Woodcock criticizes Feuer's "reliance on Freudian concept." Yet overall he believes that *The Conflict of Generations* "stands out as the best analysis written so far of the movements that have swept over our world from end to end." And Keller, though he cites Feuer's "failure to grant clearly" that some of the students' grievances were justified, also draws a favorable conclusion. "In a curious way I can't help liking a sociologist who reminds us, as novelists and good clergymen used to, of the torment, idealism, ambition, love and envy that feed the roots of human action, even the most seemingly noble."

BIOGRAPHICAL/CRITICAL SOURCES: New York Times, June 16, 1963; *Scientific American,* August, 1963; *Atlantic,* September, 1966, June, 1969; *Book World,* March 9, 1969; *New York Times Book Review,* March 23, 1969; *Time,* April 4, 1969; *Commonweal,* May 9, 1969; *New Leader,* May 26, 1969; *Christian Science Monitor,* June 5, 1969; *Virginia Quarterly Review,* autumn, 1969.

* * *

FIENNES, Ranulph (Twisleton-Wykeham) 1944-

PERSONAL: Surname is pronounced Fines; born third baronet, March 7, 1944, in Windsor, England; son of Ranulph Twisleton-Wykeham (second baronet; lieutenant colonel and regimental commander in the Royal Scots Greys) and Audrey Joan (Newson) Fiennes; married Virginia Pepper, 1970. *Education:* Attended Eton College. *Home:* St. Peter's Well, Lodsworth, Petworth, West Sussex, England.

CAREER: Explorer, author, and lecturer. Spent childhood in South Africa. British Army, 1965-70, began as lieutenant, became captain of Royal Scots Greys; served with Special Air Service, 1966-68, and Sultan of Muscat's Armed Forces, 1968-70. Leader of British expeditions to White Nile, 1969, Jostedalsbre Glacier, 1970, and Headless Valley, British Columbia, 1971, and of polar expeditions in 1977 and 1980. Has appeared on television and in documentary films; broadcasts over BBC. *Awards, honors:* Sultan's Bravery Medal, 1970; Krug Award of Excellence, 1980.

*WRITINGS—*All published by Hodder & Stoughton: *A Talent for Trouble,* 1970; *Ice Fall in Norway,* 1972; *The Head-*

less Valley, 1973; *Where Soldiers Fear to Tread,* 1975; *Hell on Ice,* 1979.†

* * *

FILBY, P(ercy) William 1911-

PERSONAL: Born December 10, 1911, in Cambridge, England; came to United States in 1957, naturalized in 1961; son of William Lusher (a builder) and Florence Ada (Stanton) Filby; married Nancie Elizabeth Giddens, Aug. 20, 1936 (divorced, 1957); married Vera Ruth Weakliem (a U.S. Government research analyst), May 23, 1957; children: (first marriage) Ann Veronica (Mrs. Ward Chesworth), Jane Vanessa (Mrs. Anthony Maisey), Roderick, Guy. *Education:* Attended Cambridge University, 1928-29. *Politics:* Democrat. *Religion:* Church of England. *Home:* 8944 Madison St., Savage, Md. 20863.

CAREER: Cambridge University, Cambridge, England, member of library staff, 1930-37, Cambridge Philosophical Library (natural science), director, 1937-40; British Foreign Office, London, England, senior archivist, 1946-57; Peabody Institute Library, Baltimore, Md., assistant director, 1957-65; Maryland Historical Society, Baltimore, librarian and assistant director, 1965-72, director, 1972-78; professional appraiser of literary material, 1978—. Secretary to Sir James G. Frazer, 1935-40. Lecturer at universities on calligraphy, fine printing, genealogy, heraldry, and Sir James G. Frazer. *Military service:* British Army, Intelligence Corps, 1940-46; became captain. *Member:* American Library Association, Special Libraries Association (president, Baltimore chapter), Bibliographical Society of America, Manuscript Society (director, 1972-75; president, 1976-78), Baltimore Bibliophiles (president, 1963-65), Typophiles, Grolier Club (member of library committee, beginning 1965).

WRITINGS—Editor: Cambridge Papers, Cambridge University Library, 1935; *Calligraphy and Handwriting in America, 1710-1962,* Italimuse, 1963; (with others) *Two Thousand Years of Calligraphy,* American Library Association, 1965; *American and British Genealogy and Heraldry: A Selected List of Books,* American Library Association, 1970, 2nd edition, 1975, with supplement, 1980; (with Edward G. Howard) *Star Spangled Books: Books, Sheet Music, Newspapers, Manuscripts, and Persons Associated with the Star-Spangled Banner,* Maryland Historical Society, 1972; (with Mary K. Meyer) *Passenger and Immigration Lists Index,* Gale, three volumes, 1980, 2nd series, 1981; *Bibliography of Ship Passenger Lists,* Gale, 1980; (with Meyer) *Who's Who in Genealogy and Heraldry,* Gale, 1981; *Bibliography of American County Histories,* Genealogical Publishing, 1981. Also contributor to *American Reference Books Annual.*

AVOCATIONAL INTERESTS: Researching genealogy and heraldry, particularly British sources.

* * *

FISHER, Michael John 1933-

PERSONAL: Born November 26, 1933, in England; son of John Greenwood and Gillian Lois (Manlove) Fisher. *Education:* University of Capetown, M.B., Ch.B., 1956. *Agent:* Harold Matson Co., Inc., 22 East 40th St., New York, N.Y. 10016.

CAREER: Bethnal Green Hospital, London, England, intern, 1957-58; Doctors' Hospital, New York, N.Y., resident, 1958-60; American Hospital, Paris, France, resident, 1960-61; director of product communications, Geigy Pharmaceuticals, 1962-66; full-time writer, Corfu, Greece, 1967-71; offi-

cer for United Kingdom Medical Research Council, 1972—. *Member:* British Medical Association.

WRITINGS: The Sharp Edge of the Sun, Cassell, 1960; *Bethnal Green,* Holt, 1961; *In Pluto's Kingdom,* Cassell, 1963; *The Executive,* Constable, 1969; *The Captives,* Constable, 1970; *Of Love and Violence,* Constable, 1971; *The Voyager,* Constable, 1972; *The Dam,* Constable, 1973. Contributor of short stories to *Atlantic Monthly, Mademoiselle,* and *London Magazine.*

WORK IN PROGRESS: A novel, *The Hostage.*

AVOCATIONAL INTERESTS: Ocean racing, painting.

* * *

FITZGIBBON, Theodora (Joanne Eileen Winifred) Rosling 1916-

PERSONAL: Born October 21, 1916, in London, England; daughter of John Archibald (an engineer) and Alice (Hodgkins) Rosling; married Constantine FitzGibbon (an author), 1943 (divorced, 1960); married George Morrison (a film archivist and director), 1960. *Education:* Educated in convents in England and Belgium. *Politics:* "Very liberal." *Home:* Atlanta, Coliemore Rd., Dalkey, County Dublin, Ireland. *Agent:* Harold Ober Associates, Inc., 40 East 49th St., New York, N.Y. 10017; and David Higham Associates Ltd., 5-8 Lower John St., Golden Sq., London W1R 4HA, England.

CAREER: Stage and film actress in London, England, Paris, France, and Rome, Italy, for twelve years; society editor, *Mid-Ocean News,* Bermuda, for one year. *Awards, honors:* Awarded bronze medals, Frankfurt International Food Fair literary section, 1956, for *Cosmopolitan Cookery in an English Kitchen,* and 1960, for *High Protein Diet and Cookery Book* and *The Young Cook's Book.*

WRITINGS: Cosmopolitan Cookery in an English Kitchen, Verschoyle, 1952; *Weekend Cookery,* Deutsch, 1956; (with Michael Hemans) *High Protein Diet and Cookery Book,* Deutsch, 1957; *Country House Cooking,* Deutsch, 1958; *The Young Cook's Book,* Deutsch, 1958; *Game Cooking,* Deutsch, 1963, Transatlantic, 1965; *The Art of British Cooking,* Doubleday, 1965; *Flight of the Kingfisher* (fiction), Phoenix House, 1967; *A Taste of Ireland,* Dent, 1968, Houghton, 1969.

A Taste of Scotland, Dent, 1970; *A Taste of Wales,* Dent, 1971; (with Robert Wilson) *Eat Well and Live Longer,* Dent, 1972; *A Taste of England: The West Country,* Dent, 1972; *Cookery Book,* Gill & Macmillan, 1972; *A Taste of London,* Dent, 1973, Houghton, 1974; *A Taste of Paris,* Dent, 1974, Houghton, 1975; *A Taste of Rome,* Houghton, 1975; *A Taste of the Sea,* David & Charles, 1976, A. S. Barnes, 1977; *The Food of the Western World,* Hutchinson, 1976, Quadrangle, 1977; *Making the Most of It,* Hutchinson, 1978, Arrow, 1980; *Crockery Pot Cookbook,* Pan Books, 1978; *A Taste of Yorkshire,* Pan Books, 1979; *Traditional Scottish Cookery,* Fontana Books, 1979; *A Taste of the Lake District,* Pan Books, 1980.

Also author of a play and a children's program for the British Broadcasting Corp. Work represented in anthologies, including *Scotch Whiskey,* Macmillan (London), 1974, and *The Pleasures of the Table,* Oxford University Press, 1981. Contributor to *Cheshire Life.* Cookery editor, *Irish Times* and *Image.*

WORK IN PROGRESS: Irish Food, for Gill & Macmillan; *Traditional West Country Cookery,* for Fontana Books.

FLEISCHMAN, Harry 1914-

PERSONAL: Born October 3, 1914, in New York, N.Y.; son of Abraham and Rachel (Cohn) Fleischman; married Natalie Wiencek, June 18, 1937; children: Martha Emily, Peter Norman, Maria Louise. Education: Attended City College (now City College of the City University of New York), 1931-33. Home: 11 Wedgewood Lane, Wantagh, N.Y. 11793.

CAREER: Organizer, Amalgamated Clothing Workers, Michigan, 1937-38; Socialist Party, Indiana-Illinois regional director, 1939-42, national secretary in New York City, 1942-50, served as campaign manager for Norman Thomas' presidential campaigns, 1944 and 1948; U.S. Department of State, "Voice of America," New York City, labor editor, 1951-53; American Jewish Committee, National Labor Service, New York City, director, 1953-69, labor and race relations director, 1963-79, president of Professional Staff Organization, 1967-72; organizer, Long Island Progressive Coalition, 1979. Member of executive board, Post-War World Council, 1942-67, Religion and Labor Council, 1953-65, and Workers Education Local 189, American Federation of Teachers, 1958-64; League for Industrial Democracy, chairman of executive committee, 1962-76, currently member of national board; vice-president, Workers Defense League, 1963—; executive director, National Alliance for Safer Cities, 1970-79; member of national board, Democratic Socialist Organizing Committee, 1974—; member of board of directors, Institute for Democratic Socialism, 1976—. Organizer of first labor television workshop; instructor at various union summer institutes. President and trustee, Levittown Public Library, 1967-73; co-chairman, Friends of Norman Thomas High School, 1975—.

MEMBER: Adult Education Association (chairman of labor education section, 1964-65), Americans for Democratic Action, National Association of Human Rights Officials, Association of Jewish Communal Relations Workers (member of executive board, 1968-72), American Civil Liberties Union, National Association for the Advancement of Colored People, American Arbitration Association (member of national panel), Workmen's Circle. Awards, honors: Fund for the Republic grant, 1958, for We Open the Gates; J. M. Kaplan Fund grant, 1960, for Norman Thomas; American Heritage Award, John F. Kennedy Library for Minorities, 1972.

WRITINGS: (Contributor) What Can Social Democracy Do for World Freedom?, Universitas, 1949; Let's Be Human, Oceana, 1960; Norman Thomas: A Biography, Norton, 1964, 3rd edition, 1969; (contributor) Donald B. King and Charles W. Quick, editors, Legal Aspects of the Civil Rights Movement, Wayne State University Press, 1965; (contributor) Warren Marr II and Maybelle Ward, editors, Minorities and the American Dream: A Bicentennial Perspective, Arno, 1976.

Author of pamphlets and monographs for the National Labor Service, including Security, Civil Liberties and Unions, with Ben Segal and Joyce L. Kornbluh, 1956, We Open the Gates: Labor's Fight for Equality, with James Rorty, 1958, Is Labor Color Blind?, 1960, Labor and the Civil Rights Revolution, 1960, Equality and the Unions, 1961, Epitaph for Jim Crow, 1963, Is Robert Welch a Secret Communist?, 1965, Norman Thomas: Leader at Large, 1966, The Civil Rights Story: A Year's Review, 1966, How to Combat Racism and Bigotry, 1975, Steps to Safer Neighborhoods and Schools, 1979, and Brown and Intergroup Relations, 1979. Author of column, "Let's Be Human," published in more than one hundred labor, religious, and black journals. Contributor to Encyclopedia Yearbook and to labor and liberal journals. Editor, Socialist Call, 1947-50.

WORK IN PROGRESS: A volume of memoirs; an "oral history book based on interviews with about 100 people who, [having been] active in the Socialist Party in the 1930's and 1940's, discuss what brought them into the movement and what impact it had on their lives."

BIOGRAPHICAL/CRITICAL SOURCES: Long Island Press, April 10, 1960.

*   *   *

FLESCH, Rudolf (Franz) 1911-

PERSONAL: Born May 8, 1911, in Vienna, Austria; came to United States in 1938, naturalized in 1944; son of Hugo (a lawyer) and Helene (Basch) Flesch; married Elizabeth Terpenning, September 6, 1941; children: Anne (Mrs. Peter Wares), Hugo, Gillian, Katrina, Abigail, Janet. Education: University of Vienna, Jur.D., 1933; Columbia University, B.S., 1940, M.A., 1942, Ph.D., 1943. Home: 24 Belden Ave., Dobbs Ferry, N.Y. 10522.

CAREER: Free-lance writer.

WRITINGS—All published by Harper, except as indicated: Marks of Readable Style: A Study in Adult Education, Teachers College, Columbia University, 1943; The Art of Plain Talk, 1946; (with A. H. Lass) The Way to Write, 1947, 2nd edition, McGraw, 1955; The Art of Readable Writing, 1949, revised and enlarged edition, 1974; How to Test Readability, 1951; The Art of Clear Thinking, 1951; (editor) Best Articles: Most Memorable Articles of the Year, Hermitage House, 1953; How to Make Sense, 1954; Why Johnny Can't Read–And What You Can Do about It, 1955; Teaching Johnny to Read, Grosset, 1956; (with others) How You Can Be a Better Student, Sterling, 1957; The Book of Unusual Quotations, 1957, published as The New Book of Unusual Quotations, 1966; A New Way to Better English, 1958; How to Write, Speak and Think More Effectively, 1960; How to Be Brief: An Index to Simple Writing, 1962, published as How to Express Yourself Clearly and Briefly, Citadel, 1968; The ABC of Style: A Guide to Plain English, 1964; (editor) The Book of Surprises, 1965; Say What You Mean, 1972; Look It Up, 1977; How to Write Plain English, 1979; Why Johnny Still Can't Read, 1981.

BIOGRAPHICAL/CRITICAL SOURCES: Los Angeles Times Book Review, November 4, 1979.

*   *   *

FLEW, Antony G(arrard) N(ewton) 1923-

PERSONAL: Born February 11, 1923, in London, England; son of Robert Newton (a minister) and Alice Winifred (Garrard) Flew; married Annis Ruth Harty Donnison (a school teacher); children: Harriet Rebecca, Joanna Naomi. Education: St. John's College, Oxford, M.A. (with first class honors), 1948. Politics: Conservative. Home: 26 Alexandra Rd., Reading RG1 5PD, England. Office: Department of Philosophy, University of Reading, Whiteknights, Reading, England.

CAREER: Oxford University, Christ Church, Oxford, England, lecturer in philosophy, 1949-50; University of Aberdeen, Aberdeen, Scotland, lecturer in moral philosophy, 1950-54; University of Keele, Keele, England, professor of philosophy, 1954-71; University of Calgary, Calgary, Alberta, professor of philosophy, 1972-73; University of Reading, Reading, England, professor of philosophy, 1973—. Visiting professor at New York University, 1958, Swarthmore College, 1961, University of Pittsburgh, 1965, University of Malawi, 1967, University of Maryland, 1970, State University of New York at Buffalo, 1971, and University of California, San Diego, 1978-79; Gavin David Young Lecturer, University of Adelaide, 1963. Has participated in talks and discussions on radio and television. *Military service:* Royal Air Force, Intelligence (Japanese), 1943-45; became flight officer. *Member:* Mind Association, Aristotelian Society, Rationalist Press Association (vice-president), Freedom Association (member of council), Voluntary Euthanasia Society (chairman of executive committee, 1976-79). *Awards, honors:* John Locke Prize, Oxford University, 1948; D.Litt., University of Keele, 1974.

WRITINGS: A New Approach to Psychical Research, C. A. Watts, 1953; *Hume's Philosophy of Belief,* Humanities, 1961; *God and Philosophy,* Hutchinson, 1966, Harcourt, 1967, new edition, Hutchinson, 1975; *Evolutionary Ethics,* St. Martin's, 1967; *An Introduction to Western Philosophy,* Bobbs-Merrill, 1971; *Crime or Disease?,* Barnes & Noble, 1973; *Thinking about Thinking,* Collins, Sons & Co., 1975, published as *Thinking Straight,* Prometheus Books, 1977; *The Presumption of Atheism* (philosophical essays), Barnes & Noble, 1976; *Sociology, Equality and Education* (philosophical essays), Barnes & Noble, 1976; (with T. B. Warren) *The Warren-Flew Debate,* National Christian Press, 1977; *A Rational Animal* (philosophical essays), Clarendon Press, 1978; *Philosophy: An Introduction,* Hodder & Stoughton, 1979; *The Procrustean Ideal* (philosophical essays), Temple Smith, in press.

Editor: (And author of introduction) *Logic and Language,* Humanities, Volume I, 1951, Volume II, 1953; (with A. C. MacIntyre) *New Essays in Philosophical Theology,* Macmillan, 1955; *Essays in Conceptual Analysis,* Macmillan (London), 1956; (and author of introduction) *Hume on Human Nature and the Understanding,* Collier, 1962; (and author of introduction) *Body, Mind and Death,* Macmillan (New York), 1964; (and author of introduction and notes) *Malthus: An Essay on the Principle of Population,* Penguin, 1971; (and contributor) *A Dictionary of Philosophy,* Macmillan (London), 1979.

Contributor: W. P. Alston, editor, *Religious Belief and Philosophical Thought,* Harcourt, 1963; A. Sesonke and N. Fleming, editors, *Human Understanding: Studies in the Philosophy of David Hume,* Wadsworth, 1965; P. Edwards and A. Pap, editors, *A Modern Introduction to Philosophy,* revised edition, Free Press, 1965; T. M. Penelhum, editor, *Immortality,* Wadsworth, 1974; W. D. Hudson, editor, *New Studies in Ethics,* Volume II, Macmillan, 1974; M. Goldinger, editor, *Punishment and Human Rights,* Schenkman, 1974; J. K. Ludwig, editor, *Philosophy and Parapsychology,* Prometheus Books, 1977; A. L. Caplan, editor, *The Sociobiology Debate,* Harper, 1979.

Contributor to encyclopedias, including *Encyclopaedia of Philosophy, Encyclopaedia Britannica,* and *Collier's Encyclopaedia.* Contributor to professional journals in England, Germany, Australia, and the United States. Member of editorial board, *Sociological Review,* 1954-71; member of editorial advisory board, *Question,* 1958—; consulting editor, *Humanist,* 1972—, *Journal of Critical Analysis,* 1974—, *Hume Studies,* 1976—, and *Journal of Libertarian Studies,* 1976—.

WORK IN PROGRESS: The Politics of Procrustes, for Temple Smith.

SIDELIGHTS: Various books and articles by Antony Flew have been translated into German, Italian, Spanish, Thai, Portuguese, and Hebrew. *Avocational interests:* Travel, walking.

*   *   *

FLORA, Fletcher   1914-1969

PERSONAL: Born May 20, 1914, in Parsons, Kan.; died May 5, 1969; son of Harrison and Addie (Turner) Flora; married Betty Ogden, 1940; children: Harrison, Timothy, Susan. *Education:* Parsons Junior College, A.A., 1934; Kansas State College, B.S., 1938; University of Kansas, graduate study, summers 1938, 1939, 1940. *Agent:* Scott Meredith Literary Agency, Inc., 845 Third Ave., New York, N.Y. 10022.

CAREER: Teacher in public schools in Golden City, Mo., 1939-41 and St. Louis County, Mo., 1941-42; U.S. Department of Army (civil service), Fort Leavenworth, Kan., education advisor, 1945-63. *Military service:* U.S. Army, 1943-45; became staff sergeant. *Awards, honors:* Cock Robin Mystery Award, Macmillan, 1960.

WRITINGS: Strange Sisters, Lion Books, 1954; *Desperate Asylum,* Lion Books, 1955; *The Brass Bed,* Lion Books, 1956; *The Hot Shot,* Avon, 1956; *Wake up with a Stranger,* New American Library, 1959; *Killing Cousins,* Macmillan, 1960; *The Seducer,* Monarch, 1961; *The Irrepressible Peccadillo,* Macmillan, 1962; *Skuldoggery,* Belmont, 1967; (with Stuart Palmer) *Hildegarde Withers Makes the Scene,* Random House, 1969. Work has appeared in Ellery Queen anthologies, Random House, 1963 and 1964, and in Alfred Hitchcock anthologies, Dell, 1962, 1963, 1964, and 1965.†

*   *   *

FLORA, James (Royer)   1914-

PERSONAL: Born January 25, 1914, in Bellefontaine, Ohio; son of James Bernard (a barber) and Laura (Royer) Flora; married Jane Sinnickson (a painter and illustrator), March 1, 1941; children: Roussie, Joel, Caroline, Robert, Julia. *Education:* Attended Urbana University, 1931-33, Art Academy of Cincinnati, 1934-39, and Atelier 17, two years. *Politics:* Independent. *Home and office:* St. James Pl., Bell Island, Rowayton, Conn. 06853.

CAREER: Little Man Press, Cincinnati, Ohio, co-founder and co-publisher, 1939-42; Columbia Recording Corp., New York, N.Y. and Bridgeport, Conn., art director and sales promotion manager, 1942-50; free-lance writer, illustrator, and art director, 1950—. Consulting art director and member of board, Benwill Publishing Corp., 1957-62; art director, Computer Design Publishing Co., 1962—. *Member:* Authors Guild, Rowayton Art Center, Thursday Club.

WRITINGS—Self-illustrated children's books, except as indicated; published by Harcourt, except as indicated: *The Fabulous Fireworks Family* (also see below), 1955; *The Day the Cow Sneezed,* 1957; *Charlie Yup and His Snip-Snap Boys,* 1959; (illustrator) *The Talking Dog and the Barking Man,* F. Watts, 1960; *Leopold, the See-through Crumbpicker* (also see below), 1961; *Kangaroo for Christmas,* 1962; *My Friend Charlie,* 1964; *Grandpa's Farm,* 1965; *Sherwood Walks Home,* 1966; *Fishing with Dad,* 1967; *The Joking Man,* 1968; *Little Hatchy Hen,* 1969.

Published by Atheneum: *Pishtosh, Bullwash, and Wimple,* 1972; *Stewed Goose,* 1973; *The Great Green Turkey Creek Monster,* 1976; *Grandpa's Ghost Stories,* 1978; *Wanda and the Bumbly Wizard,* 1980.

Also author of *New Orleans Wood Engravings in Portfolio* (adult nonfiction), Little Man Press. Author of script and designer of animated films, "The Fabulous Fireworks Family" (based on Flora's book of same title), 1959, "Leopold, The See-through Crumbpicker" (based on Flora's book of same title), 1973, and "Weston Woods."

SIDELIGHTS: James Flora told *CA:* "It grieves me that many children never discover the joys of reading and the great world that is available in books. I try in all of my stories to give children a rollicking, joyous experience which will encourage them to acquire the reading habit."

Flora has traveled and painted in Mexico and Europe.

BIOGRAPHICAL/CRITICAL SOURCES: American Artist, January, 1955; *New York Times Book Review,* November 9, 1969.

* * *

FLOREN, Lee 1910-
(Brett Austin, R. V. Donald, Lisa Fanchon, Claudia Hall, Wade Hamilton, Matt Harding, Matthew Whitman Harding, Felix Lee Horton, Stuart Jason, Mark Kirby, Grace Lang, Marguerite Nelson, Lew Smith, Maria Sandra Sterling, Sandra Sterling, Lee Thomas, Len Turner, Will Watson, Dave Wilson)

PERSONAL: Born March 22, 1910, in Hinsdale, Mont.; divorced; children: Adriana, Roberto. *Education:* Attended Montana State University, two years; Santa Barbara State Teacher's College (now University of California, Santa Barbara), B.A.; Occidental College, teaching certificate; Texas Western College (now University of Texas at El Paso), M.A., 1964. *Residence:* Mexico.

CAREER: Teacher of woodshop and science in California, 1942-45; has taught creative writing at San Bernardino Valley College; full-time free-lance writer, 1945—.

WRITINGS—Published by Phoenix Press, except as indicated: *Cottonwood Pards,* 1944; *The Gun-Slammer,* 1945; *The Long S,* 1945; *Bonzana at Wishbone,* 1946; *Gunsmoke Holiday,* 1947; *Hangman's Range,* 1947; *Guns of Powder River,* 1947; *Milk River Range,* 1949; *Riders in the Night,* 1950; *Rail North,* Foulsham, 1950.

Published by Arcadia House, except as indicated: *Pinon Mesa,* 1952; *Guns of Wyoming,* 1952; *Rifles on the Rimrock,* 1952; *Troubled Grass: A Story of the Old Southwest,* Abelard, 1952; *Freight for the Little Snowies,* World's Work, 1953; *Hell's Homestead,* World's Work, 1953; *Shadow of My Gun,* 1953; *Sonora Stage,* 1953; *Wild Border Guns,* 1953; *Wyoming Rustlers,* Foulsham, 1953; *Blackleg Bullets,* 1954; *Border Gold,* 1954; *Broken Horn,* Quality, 1954; *Law of the West,* W. H. Allen, 1954; *Pistol Partners,* W. H. Allen, 1954; *Rifles on the Rattlesnake,* 1954; *Four Texas North,* Ace Books, 1955; *Guns along the Pecos,* World's Work, 1955; *Hot Gun Holiday,* World's Work, 1955; *Riders in the Storm,* 1955; *Winchester Wages,* 1955; *Way of the Gun,* R. Hale, 1955; *Gunsmoke Range,* R. Hale, 1956; *Bitter Is the Land,* World's Work, 1956.

Published by Wright & Brown, except as indicated: *Gunsmoke Lawyer,* 1957; *Guns along the Arrowhead,* 1957; *Cow-Thief Trail,* 1958; *Thunder in the Gunsmoke,* 1958; *Hard Riders,* R. Hale, 1958; *Winchester War,* 1960; *Renegade Gamblers,* R. Hale, 1961; *Guns on Circle S,* R. Hale, 1962; *High Thunder,* R. Hale, 1962; *Montana Maverick,* R. Hale, 1962; *The Last Freighter,* 1962; *John Wesley Hardin, Texas Gunfighter,* Macfadden, 1962; *Two Guns North,* Avon, 1963; *Rifles for Fort Hall,* Consul Books, 1963; *Mad*

River Guns, Macfadden, 1965; *Wyoming Gun War,* Lancer Books, 1965; *West of Barbwire,* Bouregy, 1967; *Tall Texan,* Bouregy, 1967; *Wolf Dog Range,* Macfadden, 1967; *Black Gunsmoke,* Paperback Library, 1968; *Rustler's Trail,* Paperback Library, 1968.

Published by Lancer Books, except as indicated: *Rustlers of Cyclone Pass,* Avalon, 1968; *Wyoming Justice,* Avalon, 1969; *Trail to Latigo,* Avalon, 1970; *Roll the Wagons,* 1970; *Legacy of the Lost,* 1970; *Ben Thompson: Gambler with a Gun,* 1970; *Frontier Lawman,* 1970; *The Last Gun,* 1971; *Bloody Rifles,* 1971; *Female Feud,* Associated Press, 1971.

Published by Manor, except as indicated: *Law of the West,* Tower Books, 1977; *Callahan Rides Alone,* Tower Books, 1977; *The Saddle Tramps,* 1978; *Gunlords of Stirrup Basin,* 1978; *Gun to Gun,* 1978; *Wyoming Saddles,* 1978; *This Grass, This Gun,* 1978; *Rails West to Glory,* 1978; *Gun Wolves of Lobo Basin,* 1978; *Gunpowder Grass,* 1979; *Renegade Rancher,* 1979; *High Trail to Rawhide,* 1979; *The Bushwhackers,* Tower Books, 1979; *Gunpowder Mesa,* 1980; *Scattergun Grass,* Tower Books, 1980; *This Trail to Gunsmoke,* 1980; *The Rawhide Men,* 1980; *High Border Riders,* 1980; *The High Gun,* 1980.

Under pseudonym Brett Austin: *Rawhide Summons,* Phoenix Press, 1947; *Gambler's Gun Luck,* Wright & Brown, 1949; *Gun-Doc of the Ambush Trail,* Wright & Brown, 1949; *Black Boulder Ranch,* Phoenix Press, 1950; *Burnt Wagon Ranch,* Phoenix Press, 1950; *Rolling River Range,* Phoenix Press, 1950; *Call to Montana,* World's Work, 1953; *Rimrock Rifles,* W. H. Allen, 1954; *Two Sons of Satan,* Ward, Lock, 1956; *Texans Ride North,* Avalon, 1968; *Sagebrush Saga,* Avalon, 1969.

Under pseudonym Brett Austin; published by Arcadia House: *Lobo Valley,* 1951; *Broomtail Basin,* 1952; *Guns of Montana,* 1952; *When a Renegade Rides,* 1952; *Coyotes of Willow Brook,* 1952; *Wind River Range,* 1953; *Arizona Saddles,* 1954; *Circle M Triggers,* 1954; *Hammerhead Range,* 1955; *Roll the Wagons,* 1956.

Under pseudonym R. V. Donald: *The Arab Captors,* Lastimas Books, 1968; *I, Coxswain,* Lastimas Books, 1970.

Under pseudonym Lisa Fanchon: *The Kidnapped Virgin,* P.E.C. Books, 1968; *Sex Club of Don Pedro,* Lastimas Books, 1969; *The Gay Girls,* Lastimas Books, 1969; *Palace of Sin,* Greenleaf Classics, 1969; *Palace of Lust,* Greenleaf Classics, 1969; *Naked When I Fled,* Lastimas Books, 1969; *Scandalous Confessions of an English Traveler,* Lastimas Books, 1970; *All Woman,* Macfadden, 1971; *Man Trap,* Macfadden, 1971.

Under pseudonym Claudia Hall: *Wait for the Day,* Arcadia House, 1955.

Under pseudonym Wade Hamilton; published by Arcadia House, except as indicated: *Rimrock Renegade,* Phoenix Press, 1951; *Gun Lobos,* 1952; *Sagebrush,* 1952; *The Longhorn Brand,* 1952; *Cougar Basin,* 1953; *Muddy Wheels,* 1953; *Gun Luck,* 1954; *Trail's End,* 1954; *Saddle Wolves,* Ward, Lock, 1956; *They Ride with Rifles,* Ward, Lock, 1956; *Trail to High Pine,* 1956; *Saddles North,* Avalon, 1968; *Gunsmoke Law,* Avalon, 1969; *Ride the Wild Country,* Tower Books, 1977; *Gunsmoke,* Tower Books, 1977; *Ride against the Rifles,* Manor, 1979.

Under pseudonym Matt Harding; published by Lastimas Books, except as indicated: *The Dancing Diva,* 1968; *Plundered Virgin,* Greenleaf Classics, 1968; *Women of Lust,* 1968; *I, Margo,* 1968; *Rap Softly, Lover,* 1969; *Boy and Woman,* 1969; *Las Vegas Madame,* Lancer Books, 1970; *I,*

Jonathon Richardson, 1970; *They Couldn't Say No*, Macfadden, 1970; *The Office Game*, Lancer Books, 1972; *Edge of Gunsmoke*, Manor, 1979.

Under pseudonym Matthew Whitman Harding: *Muskets on the Mississippi*, Popular Library, 1972.

Under pseudonym Felix Lee Horton: *With Long Knife and Musket*, Popular Library, 1972.

Under pseudonym Stuart Jason: *Valley of Death*, Pinnacle Books, 1973; *The Deadly Doctor*, Pinnacle Books, 1973.

Under pseudonym Grace Lang: *Love a Hostage*, Avalon, 1969; *The Singing Pines*, Avalon, 1969.

Under pseudonym Marguerite Nelson; published by Avalon, except as indicated: *Forever This Love*, 1957; *Jill's Hollywood Assignment*, 1958; *Nancy's Dude Ranch*, 1958; *Air Stewardess*, Bouregy, 1961; *Far Are the Hills*, Bouregy, 1961; *Hollywood Nurse*, Arcadia House, 1963; *High Pines Singing*, 1969; *Doctor Wilson's Dilemma*, 1969; *Tropic Nurse*, 1969; *Mercy Nurse*, Manor, 1979.

Under pseudonym Lew Smith; published by Arcadia House, except as indicated: *Raiders of White Pine*, Boardman, 1951; *Smoky River*, 1953 (published under author's real name, G. K. Hall, 1979); *Boothill Court*, 1954; *Powdersmoke Canyon*, 1954; *Riders of Rifle Range*, World's Work, 1954; *Rimrock Raiders*, 1954; *Dusty Wheels*, 1955; *Ramrod*, Ward, Lock, 1955.

Under pseudonym Maria Sandra Sterling: *War Drum*, Popular Library, 1972.

Under pseudonym Sandra Sterling: *Strickland's Women*, Lastimas Books, 1968; *Love Cult*, Lastimas Books, 1968; *The Tortured Virgin*, Lastimas Books, 1969.

Under pseudonym Lee Thomas; published by Phoenix Press, except as indicated: *Texas Talbert*, 1945; *The Circle W*, 1945; *Smokestack Iron*, 1947; *Texas Cowman*, 1947; *Dusty Boots*, 1950; *Broken Creek*, Arcadia House, 1952; *The Ambush Trail*, Arcadia House, 1952; *Gambler's Guns*, Arcadia House, 1953; *Wolf Dog Town*, Arcadia House, 1953.

Under pseudonym Len Turner: *Texas Medico*, Arcadia House, 1954; *Winter Kill*, Arcadia House, 1954.

Under pseudonym Will Watson; published by Phoenix Press, except as indicated: *Wolf Dog Range*, 1946; *Saddle Pals*, 1947; *Double Cross Ranch*, 1950; *North to Wyoming*, World's Work, 1953; *War on Alkali Creek*, 1951.

Under pseudonym Dave Wilson: *Puma Pistoleers*, Arcadia House, 1951.

Also author, under various pseudonyms, of other western, Gothic, juvenile, detective, and biographical novels and novelettes, as well as "case study books on medical and psychological subjects." Contributor of about 1,000 short stories and articles, also under various pseudonyms, to popular publications.

SIDELIGHTS: Lee Floren told *CA* that he intends to semi-retire from writing in order to concentrate on selling the reprint rights to his considerable, already published, works. Floren notes that he is the author of some three hundred novels and feels that "three hundred is enough." He continues: "I've deforested too many trees already. Let some young buck pick up where I am leaving off, which seems to be a natural law of something or other."

Floren remarks that "when not writing, my favorite pastime is reading," and he offers this appraisal of the quality of contemporary popular fiction in the United States: "I honestly believe that never before in the history of the English language have there been so many poor authors. The quality of a book seemingly no longer counts. What counts is the advertising budget and the amount of propaganda put out, not the book's contents. In my opinion, the United States is being 'blessed' with the sorriest out-put of 'literature' to date. Let's pray it gets no worse, if such is possible." Yet Floren also states that his own motivation for writing is strictly a monetary one: "I write for one thing and that is *money.* If the money stopped coming in from my writing, I'd stop writing. I am a firm believer in Doc Johnson's 'Nobody but a blockhead writes for anything but money.' And I feel sure that in the original statement the good doctor used a stronger word than *blockhead.*"

*   *   *

FLORY, Jane Trescott 1917-

PERSONAL: Born June 29, 1917, in Wilkesbarre, Pa.; daughter of Leroy Charles (an engineer) and Hazel (Nixon) Trescott; married Arthur Louis Flory (an artist and college instructor), September 29, 1941 (died, 1972); married Barnett R. Freedman, July 6, 1980; children: (first marriage) Cynthia Jane, Christine Kate, Erika Susan. *Education:* Philadelphia Museum School of Industrial Art (now Philadelphia College of Art), diploma, 1939. *Home:* 1814 Beech Ave., Melrose Park, Philadelphia, Pa. 19126.

CAREER: Free-lance writer and illustrator of children's books, 1939—; Philadelphia College of Art, Philadelphia, Pa., director of evening division, 1958-74.

WRITINGS—Children's books; all self-illustrated, except as indicated: *Snooty, the Pig Who Was Proud*, Whitman Publishing, 1944; *How Many?*, Holt, 1944; *What Am I?*, Domesday, 1945; *The Wide Awake Angel*, Grosset, 1945; (illustrator) Laura Harris, *Away We Go*, Garden City Books, 1945; *The Hide-Away Ducklings*, Grosset, 1946; (with husband, Arthur Flory) *The Cow in the Kitchen*, Lothrop, 1946; *Fanny Forgot*, Whitman Publishing, 1946; *Once upon a Windy Day*, Whitman Publishing, 1947; *Toys*, Whitman Publishing, 1948; *The Powder Puff Bunny Book*, Capitol Publishing Co., 1948; *The Lazy Lion*, Whitman Publishing, 1949; *Timothy, the Little Brown Bear*, Rand McNally, 1949; *ABC*, Whitman Publishing, 1949; *Farmer John*, Whitman Publishing, 1950; *Mr. Snitzel's Cookies*, Rand McNally, 1950; *The Too-Little Fire Engine*, Wonder Books, 1950; *The Pop-up Runaway Train*, Avon, 1951; *Count the Animals*, Loew, 1952; *Surprise in the Barn*, Whitman Publishing, 1955; *Jeremy's ABC Book*, Behrman, 1957.

Published by Houghton: *Peddler's Summer*, 1960; *A Tune for the Towpath*, 1962; *One Hundred and Eight Bells*, 1963; *Clancy's Glorious Fourth*, 1964; *Mist on the Mountain*, 1966; *Faraway Dream*, 1968; *Ramshackle Roost*, 1972; *We'll Have a Friend for Lunch*, illustrated by Carolyn Croll, 1974; *The Liberation of Clementine Tipton*, 1974; *The Golden Venture*, 1976; *The Unexpected Grandchildren*, illustrated by Croll, 1977; *The Lost and Found Princess*, 1979; *It Was a Pretty Good Year*, 1979; *The Bear on the Doorstop*, illustrated by Croll, 1980.

WORK IN PROGRESS: A juvenile novel, set in the 1920's; research on a book about Puerto Rico.

BIOGRAPHICAL/CRITICAL SOURCES: Young Readers' Review, May, 1966.

*   *   *

FONER, Philip (Sheldon) 1910-

PERSONAL: Born December 14, 1910, in New York, N.Y.;

son of Abraham (a garage owner) and Mary (Smith) Foner; married Roslyn Held (a technical editor), 1939; children: Elizabeth (Mrs. Robert S. Van der Paer), Laura. *Education:* City College (now (City College of the City University of New York), B.A., 1932; Columbia University, M.A., 1933, Ph.D., 1940. *Home:* 250 South 13th St., Philadelphia, Pa. 19107. *Office:* Department of History, Lincoln University, Lincoln University, Pa. 19352.

CAREER: City College (now City College of the City University of New York), New York City, instructor in history, 1932-41; International Fur and Leather Workers, New York City, educational director, 1941-45; Citadel Press, New York City, 1945-67, became publisher; Lincoln University, Lincoln University, Pa., professor of history, 1967-79, professor emeritus, 1980—. *Member:* American Historical Association, Organization of American Historians, Association for the Study of Negro Life and History, Phi Beta Kappa.

WRITINGS: Business and Slavery: The New York Merchants and the Irrepressible Conflict, University of North Carolina Press, 1941, reprinted, Russell, 1968; *Morale Education in the American Army: War for Independence, War of 1812, Civil War,* International Publishers, 1944; *The Jews in American History, 1645-1865,* International Publishers, 1946; *History of the Labor Movement in the United States,* International Publishers, Volume I: *From Colonial Times to the Founding of the American Federation of Labor,* 1947, Volume II: *From the Founding of the American Federation of Labor to the Emergence of American Imperialism,* 1956, 2nd edition, 1975, Volume III: *The Policies and Practices of the American Federation of Labor, 1900-1909,* 1964, Volume IV: *The Industrial Workers of the World, 1905-1917,* 1966, Volume V: *The American Federation of Labor in the Progressive Era, 1910-1915,* 1980; *The Fur and Leather Workers Union: A Story of Dramatic Struggles and Achievements,* Nordan Press, 1950; *The Life and Writings of Frederick Douglass,* five volumes, International Publishers, 1950-75; *Mark Twain: Social Critic,* International Publishers, 1958, 2nd edition, 1966.

A History of Cuba and Its Relations with the United States, International Publishers, Volume I: *From the Conquest of Cuba to la Escalera, 1492-1845,* 1962, Volume II: *From the Annexationist Era to the Second War for Independence,* 1963; *Frederick Douglass: A Biography,* Citadel, 1964, 2nd edition, 1969; *The Case of Joe Hill,* International Publishers, 1966; *The Bolshevik Revolution: Its Impact on American Radicals, Liberals, and Labor,* International Publishers, 1967; *American Labor and the Indo-china War: The Growth of Union Opposition,* International Publishers, 1971; *The Spanish-Cuban-American War and the Birth of American Imperialism, 1895-1902,* two volumes, Monthly Review Press, 1971; *Organized Labor and the Black Worker, 1619-1973,* Praeger, 1974; *History of Black Americans,* Volume I: *From Africa to the Emergence of the Cotton Kingdom,* Greenwood Press, 1975; *Labor and the American Revolution,* Greenwood Press, 1976; *Blacks in the American Revolution,* Greenwood Press, 1976; *The Democratic–Republican Societies, 1790-1800,* Greenwood Press, 1976; *American Socialism and Black Americans: From the Age of Jackson to World War II,* Greenwood Press, 1977; *Antonio Maceo: The 'Bronze Titan' of Cuba's Struggle for Independence,* Monthly Review Press, 1977; *The Great Labor Uprising of 1877,* Monad Press, 1977; *Women and the American Labor Movement,* Free Press, Volume I: *From Colonial Times to the Eve of World War I,* 1979, Volume II: *From World War I to the Present,* 1980.

Editor: (And author of introduction) *Thomas Jefferson:*

Selections from His Writings, International Publishers, 1943; *Basic Writings of Thomas Jefferson,* University of North Carolina Press, 1944; (and author of introduction) *Abraham Lincoln: Selections from His Writings,* International Publishers, 1944; *George Washington: Selections from His Writings,* International Publishers, 1944; (and author of introduction) *Frederick Douglass: Selections from His Writings,* International Publishers, 1945; (and author of biographical essay, notes, and introduction) *The Complete Writings of Thomas Paine,* two volumes, Citadel, 1945, reprinted, 1969, published as *The Life and Major Writings of Thomas Paine,* 1961; *Franklin Delano Roosevelt: Selections from His Writings,* International Publishers, 1947; *Jack London: American Rebel,* Citadel, 1947, revised edition, 1964; (and author of notes) *The Letters of Joe Hill,* Oak Publications, 1965; (and author of introduction) *Helen Keller: Her Socialist Years,* International Publishers, 1967; (and author of introduction) *The Autobiographies of the Haymarket Martyrs,* Humanities, 1969.

The Black Panthers Speak, Lippincott, 1970; *W.E.B. Du Bois Speaks: Speeches and Addresses,* two volumes, Pathfinder, 1970; (and author of commentary) *The Voice of Black America: Major Speeches by Negroes in the United States, 1797-1971,* Simon & Schuster, 1972, updated edition published as *The Voice of Black America: Major Speeches by Negros in the United States, 1797-1973,* Capricorn Books, 1973; *When Karl Marx Died: Comments in 1883,* International Publishers, 1973; (and author of introduction) Jose Marti, *Inside the Monster: Writings on the United States and American Imperialism,* translated by Elinor Randall and others, Monthly Review Press, 1975; *American Labor Songs of the Nineteenth Century,* University of Illinois Press, 1975.

Frederick Douglass on Women's Rights, Greenwood Press, 1976; (and author of introduction and notes) *We, the Other People: Alternative Declarations of Independence by Labor Groups, Farmers, Women's Rights Advocates, Socialists, and Blacks,* University of Illinois Press, 1976; *The Formation of the Workingmen's Party of the United States, 1876,* American Institute for Marxist Studies, 1976; *The Factory Girls: A Collection of Writings on Life and Struggles in the New England Factories of the 1840's,* University of Illinois Press, 1977; (and author of introduction) Marti, *Our America: Writings on Latin America and the Struggle for Cuban Independence,* translated by Randall and others, Monthly Review Press, 1977; (with Brewster Chamberlin, and author of introduction) *Friedrich A. Sorge's Labor Movement in the United States: A History of the American Working Class from Colonial Times to 1890,* translated by B. Chamberlin and Angela Chamberlin, Greenwood Press, 1977; *Paul Robeson Speaks: Writings, Speeches, Interviews,* Brunner/Mazel, 1978; (with Ronald L. Lewis) *The Black Worker: A Documentary History from Colonial Times to the Present,* four volumes, Temple University Press, 1978-80; *Jose Marti on Education,* Monthly Review Press, 1979; (with George Walker) *Proceedings of the Black State Convention, 1840-1865,* Temple University Press, Volume I, 1979, Volume II, 1980. Member of board of editors, *Journal of Negro History* and *Pennsylvania History.*

WORK IN PROGRESS: Volumes two through four of *History of Black Americans;* volumes six through ten of *History of the Labor Movement in the United States.*

AVOCATIONAL INTERESTS: Tennis, sailing, swimming, mountain climbing, opera and music in general.

FOOT, M(ichael) R(ichard) D(aniell) 1919-

PERSONAL: Born December 14, 1919, in London, England; son of Richard Cunningham (a merchant) and Nina (Raymond) Foot; married former wife, Elizabeth King, April 1, 1960; children: Sarah, Richard. *Education:* Attended New College, Oxford, 1938-39, M.A., 1945, B.Litt., 1950. *Politics:* Radical. *Religion:* Agnostic. *Office:* 88 Heath View, London N2, England.

CAREER: Oxford University, Oxford, England, lecturer at various colleges and university lecturer, 1947-67, resident senior member in research and teaching, 1947-59; University of Manchester, Manchester, England, professor of modern history, 1967-73; deputy chairman, European Discussion Centre, 1973-74; historian, 1974—. *Military service:* British Army, parachutist, 1939-45; became major; awarded French Croix de Guerre. *Member:* Royal Historical Society (fellow).

WRITINGS: (With J. L. Hammond) *Gladstone and Liberalism,* English Universities Press, 1952, Collier Books, 1966; *British Foreign Policy since 1898,* Hutchinson's University Library, 1956; *Men in Uniform,* Praeger, 1961; *SOE in France,* H.M.S.O., 1966; (editor) W. E. Gladstone, *The Gladstone Diaries,* Oxford University Press, Volumes I and II, 1968, Volumes III and IV (with H.C.G. Matthew), 1974; (editor) *War and Society,* Elek, 1973; *Resistance,* Eyre Methuen, 1976; *Six Faces of Courage,* Eyre Methuen, 1978; (with J. M. Langley) *MI9,* Bodley Head, 1979, Little, Brown, 1980. Contributor to *New Cambridge Modern History,* 1960, *Encyclopaedia Britannica,* and *Dictionary of National Biography.* Contributor of articles to *English Historical Review, Economist,* and other publications.

WORK IN PROGRESS: A history of England from 1875 to 1916.

AVOCATIONAL INTERESTS: "Reading and trying to write good English"; following contemporary English and international politics; travel.

*   *   *

FOOTE, Shelby 1916-

PERSONAL: Born November 17, 1916, in Greenville, Miss.; son of Shelby Dade (a business executive) and Lillian (Rosenstock) Foote; married Gwyn Rainer, September 6, 1956; children: Margaret Shelby, Huger Lee. *Education:* Attended University of North Carolina, 1935-37. *Home and office:* 542 East Parkway S., Memphis, Tenn. 38104.

CAREER: Novelist, historian, and playwright. Novelist-in-residence, University of Virginia, Charlottesville, 1963; playwright-in-residence, Arena Stage, Washington, D.C., 1963-64; writer-in-residence, Hollins College, Hollins College, Va., 1968. Judge, National Book Award in history, 1979. *Military service:* U.S. Army, Artillery, 1940-44; became captain. U.S. Marine Corps, 1944-45. *Awards, honors:* Guggenheim fellowships, 1958, 1959, and 1960; Ford Foundation grant, 1963; Fletcher Pratt Award, 1964, for *The Civil War: A Narrative;* named distinguished alumnus, University of North Carolina, 1974.

WRITINGS—Novels, except as indicated; published by Dial, except as indicated: *Tournament,* 1949; *Follow Me Down* (also see below), 1950, reprinted, Random House, 1978; *Love in a Dry Season* (also see below), 1951; *Shiloh,* 1952, reprinted, Random House, 1976; *Jordan County* (also see below), 1954; *The Civil War: A Narrative* (history), Random House, Volume I: *Fort Sumter to Perryville,* 1958, Volume II: *Fredericksburg to Meridian,* 1963, Volume III: *Red River to Appomattox,* 1974; *Three Novels* (contains "Follow

Me Down," "Love in a Dry Season," and "Jordan County"), 1964; *September, September,* Random House, 1979. Also author of play, "Jordan County: A Landscape in the Round," produced in Washington, D.C., 1964.

WORK IN PROGRESS: A novel, *Two Gates to the City.*

SIDELIGHTS: Although his novels have been favorably received, Shelby Foote is best known for his three-volume narrative history of the Civil War. Originally envisioned as a one-volume work, Foote's effort grew into what critics call a "monumental" project that took some twenty years to complete. In the *New York Times Book Review,* Nash K. Burger explains: "After writing five novels, one of which, *Shiloh,* dealt with the Civil War, Mississippi-born Shelby Foote was asked by a New York publisher to write a short, one-volume history of that conflict. Foote agreed. It seemed a nice change of pace before his next novel. Now, 20 years later, the project is completed: Three volumes . . . , 2,934 pages, a million and a half words." Burger follows his account of the writing of *The Civil War: A Narrative* with this assessment, "It is a remarkable achievement, prodigiously researched, vigorous, detailed, absorbing."

Other reviewers have voiced similar praise. *Newsweek*'s Peter S. Prescott states that "the result [of Foote's labor] is not only monumental in size, but a truly impressive achievement." He reports that "Foote the novelist cares less for generalizations about dialectics, men and motives than for creating 'the illusion that the observer is not so much reading a book as sharing an experience.'" According to M. E. Bradford in the *National Review,* in this endeavor the author has succeeded: "There is, of course, a majesty inherent in the subject [of the Civil War].... [And] the credit for recovering such majesty to the attention of our skeptical and unheroic age will hereafter belong . . . to Mr. Foote."

Foote's account of the war is strictly a military one, detailing the battles, men, and leaders on both sides of the conflict. "The War itself . . . is indeed Foote's subject," Bradford remarks. "The *war,* the *fighting*—and not its economic, intellectual, or political causes." Lance Morrow echoes this summation in a *Time* review: "[Foote's] attention is focused on the fighting itself—fortification, tactics, the strange chemistries of leadership, the workings in the generals' minds. Foote moves armies and great quantities of military information with a lively efficiency."

Critics note that though such military histories concerning the Civil War are not uncommon, Foote's is one of the most comprehensive, covering as it does the Union and Confederate Armies in both the eastern and western theaters of the war. Moreover, they express admiration for the author's balanced and objective view of the conflict. C. Vann Woodward of the *New York Review of Books* contends that "in spite of his Mississippi origins, Foote . . . attempts to keep an even hand in giving North and South their due measure of praise and blame." Burger agrees and adds that although Foote's chronicle begins and ends with reports on the activities of Jefferson Davis, this "is not indicative of any bias in favor of the South or its leader.... The complete work," the critic continues, "is a monumental, even-handed account of this country's tragic, fratricidal conflict."

In discussing Foote's concentration on the war itself and "therefore the persons who made, died in, or survived that conflict," Bradford asserts that it is not "an exaggeration to speak of the total effect produced by this emphasis as epic." Prescott concludes: "To read Foote's chronicle is an awesome and moving experience. History and literature are rarely so thoroughly combined as here; one finishes [the last] volume convinced that no one need undertake this particular enterprise again.''

BIOGRAPHICAL/CRITICAL SOURCES: New York Times, September 25, 1949, September 23, 1951, April 6, 1952, April 25, 1954, November 16, 1958; *Saturday Review,* November 19, 1949, June 5, 1954, December 13, 1958; *Time,* July 3, 1950, January 27, 1975; *New York Herald Tribune Book Review,* July 16, 1950, October 21, 1951, April 6, 1952, May 2, 1954, November 23, 1958; *Atlantic,* May, 1952, December, 1963; *Chicago Sunday Tribune,* November 16, 1958; *San Francisco Chronicle,* November 28, 1958; *Commonweal,* January 9, 1959; *New York Times Book Review,* December 1, 1963, December 15, 1974, March 5, 1978; *Christian Science Monitor,* December 4, 1963; *Book Week,* December 15, 1963; *Newsweek,* December 2, 1974, January 30, 1978; *National Review,* February 14, 1975; *New York Review of Books,* March 6, 1975.

*   *   *

FORDE-JOHNSTON, James (Leo) 1927-

PERSONAL: Born May 7, 1927, in Liverpool, England; son of James and Elsie (Thompson) Forde-Johnston; married Kathleen Mary Healy, September 8, 1962; children: James, Kathleen, Richard, Andrew. *Education:* University of Liverpool, B.A., 1952, M.A., 1954. *Home:* 6 Greystoke Ave., Sale, Cheshire, England.

CAREER: Liverpool Museum, Liverpool, England, assistant keeper of archaeology, 1954-56; investigator on archaeological field work, Royal Commission on Historical Monuments, England, 1956-58; University of Manchester Museum, Manchester, England, keeper of ethnology and general archaeology, 1958-70, keeper of ethnology, 1970—. *Military service:* British Army, 1946-48; became sergeant. *Member:* Society of Antiquaries (fellow), Royal Archaeological Institute, Royal Anthropological Institute, Prehistoric Society, Lancashire and Cheshire Antiquarian Society (member of council).

WRITINGS: Neolithic Cultures of North Africa: Aspects of One Phase in the Development of African Stone Age Culture, Liverpool University Press, 1959, Humanities, 1960; *History from the Earth,* Phaidon Press, 1974; *Hillforts of the Iron Age in England and Wales,* Liverpool University Press, 1976; *Prehistoric Britain and Ireland,* Dent, 1976; *Castles and Fortifications in Britain and Ireland,* Dent, 1977; *Hadrian's Wall,* Book Club Associates, 1977; *Great Medieval Castles of Britain,* Book Club Associates, 1979; *Guide to the Castles of England and Wales,* Constable, 1981. Contributor of articles to archaeological and antiquarian journals.

WORK IN PROGRESS: The King's Castles; Castles and Town Halls in France.

*   *   *

FRANCIS, Marilyn 1920-

PERSONAL: Born January 26, 1920, in Columbus, Ohio; daughter of Roy Brooke (a sales manager) and Ruth (Needles) Francis; married Alvin V. Wetmore, Jr. (a sales manager), October 18, 1961 (divorced, 1968). *Education:* Ohio University, B.S., 1941. *Politics:* Republican. *Religion:* Protestant. *Address:* P.O. Box 263, Cottonwood, Ariz. 86326.

CAREER: Western Electric Co., Kearny, N.J., employment interviewer, 1941-45; Retail Credit Co., Newark, N.J., insurance investigator, 1945-51; free-lance writer, 1951—. Director, Phoenix Poetry Workshop, 1957-60; Sedona Art Center, Sedona, Ariz., member of board of directors, 1961-72, vice-

president, 1971-72; director, Winged Arts Gallery, Sedona, 1969-73. Chairman, Arizona State Behavioral Health Advisory Council, 1979-80. Sedona Public Library, member of board of trustees, 1963-66, president, 1964-65. Publicity chairman, Sedona-Oak Creek Chamber of Commerce, 1965-66. Conducted twenty-week radio program on poetry, KELE-FM, Phoenix.

MEMBER: Poetry Society of America, National Writers Club, American Poets Fellowship Society, National League of American Pen Women (president, Phoenix branch, 1959-61, Sedona branch, 1976-78), Soroptomist International, Centro studie scambi (Rome; honorary vice-president, 1975-76, 1980), Sedona Soroptomists (president, 1964-65), Alpha Xi Delta (national finance chairman, 1952-57). *Awards, honors:* Arizona State Poetry Contest, first place, 1955, 1956; Emerson Poem Contest, Ohio University, second place, 1956; National Writers Club, Poetry Contest award for narrative poem, *Thunder in the Superstitions,* and certificate of achievement for meritorious literary work published during 1958, both 1959; Southwest Writers Conference, first place manuscript award, 1960, for collection of verse, *Tangents at Noon;* Ohio University Alumni Association certificate of merit, 1961, for ''distinguished attainments in the field of literature''; Phoenix Arts Council award, 1968, for ''distinguished contribution to the arts''; New York Poetry Forum prize, 1978.

WRITINGS—Poems: *Thunder in the Superstitions,* Firebird, 1959; *Tangents at Noon,* Naylor, 1961; *Space for Sound,* Naylor, 1962; *Mirror without Glass,* Northland Press, 1964; *Symbols for Instants,* Naylor, 1965; *Radius: Red Rocks,* Publishers Press, 1972; *Rivers of Remembrance* (performed as verse drama, music by D'Esta Williams, in Phoenix at Phoenix Theatre Center, 1967), Quality Publications, 1980.

Work represented in anthologies, including *Avalon,* Different Press, 1955, 1957, and 1958, and *Poems Southwest,* edited by Wilbur Stevens, Prescott College, 1968. Author of column, ''Sedona Viewpoints,'' 1962-64. Contributor of poetry and articles to *Saturday Evening Post, Christian Science Monitor, Red Rock News, Arizona Republic, Arizona Highways,* and other publications. Editor of poetry column ''Sandtracks,'' in *Arizonian,* 1958-63; Sedona editor, *Verde Independent* (newspaper), 1973-74.

WORK IN PROGRESS: A musical comedy about the pre-Civil War ''camel experiment'' in Arizona; research on the ''interaction and contribution of the Spanish-Mexican and Austrian-Jew to [Arizona's] early territorial days''; a series of philosophical poems.

SIDELIGHTS: Marilyn Francis told *CA* that with the publication of her seventh book, *Rivers of Remembrance,* ''I guess I can say with some feeling of authority that I prefer structure in poetry to amorphous verse because of the discipline required of the author.'' Francis continues: ''It tends to hone one's thinking and execution to a fine point of communication. Compression—making a work carry all the freight it can—is important to me, and I deplore the aimless looseness so extant; it has its place only if used for effect. It is not, to me, an end in itself. And, of course, music is paramount in any kind of poetry. The rhythm, the dynamics, must underlie any effective poetry. With that conviction, it has pleased me mightily that composers often ask if they may set my works to music.

''Of course, I have always had to do other things to keep the dollars coming in. My poetry has sold well, but not well enough to keep all the economics together. I squirm to avoid the nine to five routine so that there is still creative time, and that creative time is the heart of my existence. This is a private heart—my neighbors do not understand what a poet is or does—but they accept me now with my typewriter and are more comfortable when they can see an article with my byline. So be it! Perhaps it is necessary to be an outsider in order to have the perspective for poetry.''

A number of Francis' sonnets have been set to music by D'Esta Williams. *Thunder in the Superstitions* has also been adapted and performed as a "music with poetry production."

*   *   *

FRANK, Jerome D(avid) 1909-

PERSONAL: Born May 30, 1909, in New York, N.Y.; son of Jerome W. and Bess (Rosenbaum) Frank; married Elizabeth Kleeman, January 4, 1948; children: Deborah, David, Julia, Emily. *Education:* Harvard University, A.B. (summa cum laude), 1931, A.M., 1932, Ph.D., 1934, M.D. (cum laude), 1939. *Religion:* American Ethical Union. *Home:* 603 West University Parkway, Baltimore, Md. 21210.

CAREER: Johns Hopkins University, School of Medicine, Baltimore, Md., instructor in psychiatry, 1942-46; Veterans Administration, Washington, D.C., research associate on group psychotherapy research project, 1946-49; Washington School of Psychiatry, Washington, D.C., instructor, 1947-49; Howard University, Washington, D.C., clinical associate professor of psychiatry, 1948-49; Johns Hopkins University, School of Medicine, associate professor of psychiatry, 1949-59, professor of psychiatry, 1959-74, professor emeritus, 1974—, psychiatrist-in-charge, psychiatric out-patient department, Johns Hopkins Hospital, 1951-63. H. B. Williams Travelling Professor in Psychiatry to Australia and New Zealand, 1971; Litchfield Lecturer, Oxford University, 1977; honorary professor, Universidad Nacional Mayor de San Marcos, 1978. Member of various advisory committees, National Institute of Mental Health, 1951-55, 1957-61, 1968-69, and 1974-78. Member of advisory committee to the Psychiatry and Neurology Service, department of medicine and surgery, central office of Veterans Administration, 1960-64. Consultant to Veterans Administration and National Institute of Mental Health. *Military service:* U.S. Army, Medical Corps, 1943-46; became major.

MEMBER: Society for the Psychological Study of Social Issues (member of council, 1962-64; president, 1965-66), American College of Psychiatrists (fellow), Council for a Livable World (member of board of directors, 1963—), American Psychiatric Association (fellow), American Psychological Association (fellow), American Group Psychotherapy Association (fellow), American Psychopathological Association (president, 1963-64), Group for the Advancement of Psychiatry, American Medical Association, American Association of University Professors, SANE (member of national board, 1963—), Physicians for Social Responsibility (member of board of directors, 1979—), Patuxent Institution (member of advisory board, 1954-58), Metropolitan Baltimore Association for Mental Health (member of board of directors, 1952—), Phi Beta Kappa, Alpha Omega Alpha, Sigma Xi. *Awards, honors:* Emil A. Gutheil Award, Association for the Advancement of Psychotherapy, 1970; Kurt Lewin Memorial Award, Society for the Psychological Study of Social Issues, 1972; honorary doctorate, Universidad Peruana, 1978; Blanche Ittleson Award, American Orthopsychiatric Association, 1979.

WRITINGS: (With Florence Powdermaker) *Group Psycho-*

therapy: Studies in Methodology of Research and Therapy, Harvard University Press, 1953; *Persuasion and Healing: A Comparative Study of Psychotherapy,* Johns Hopkins Press, 1961, 2nd edition, 1973; *Sanity and Survival: Psychological Aspects of War and Peace,* introduction by J. W. Fulbright, Random House, 1967; (with Rudolph Hoehn-Saric, Stanley D. Imber, Bernard L. Liberman, and Anthony R. Stone) *Effective Ingredients of Successful Psychotherapy,* Brunner, 1978; *Psychotherapy and the Human Predicament: A Psychosocial Approach,* edited by Park E. Dietz, Schocken, 1978. Contributor of general articles to *Harper's* and *Atlantic,* and of scientific articles to professional journals.

WORK IN PROGRESS: Enjoying the Sunset.

SIDELIGHTS: Jerome D. Frank writes *CA:* "My writings fall naturally into two categories, differing in content and motivated by quite different concerns. The first, which is best represented by *Persuasion and Healing,* reports to professional colleagues and interested laymen my views as to the healing components shared by all forms of psychological healing." Frank refers to this book as "the natural outgrowth of my professional work" and comments, "Writing it was an enjoyable experience, and I am pleased with the recognition it has received.

"The other category, exemplified by *Sanity and Survival,* has its roots in a lifelong concern with human problems. This was a strictly private preoccupation until the atom bomb was dropped on Hiroshima. I was on Army duty in the nearby Philippines at the time, which for me may have heightened the impact of this event. In any case, I have been obsessed ever since with the prospect of a nuclear holocaust. I have spent the past twenty-five years writing and speaking in an effort to apply insights gained from my professional background to an understanding of this appalling problem. Needless to say, this has been a frustrating and depressing experience. It has made vivid to me the gross inadequacy of our knowledge of the sociopsychological forces determining international conflict.

"Although my efforts have received some recognition—Senator J. W. Fulbright wrote an introduction to *Sanity and Survival*—they have, of course, not had the slightest practical effect. In fact, the combined efforts of professionals from all relevant fields, as well as those of laymen, have failed to delay even slightly the accelerating march to nuclear disaster. These gloomy realizations are somewhat tempered by the thought that at least I have tried."

Persuasion and Healing has been translated into Spanish and Japanese, and *Sanity and Survival* has been translated into German.

BIOGRAPHICAL/CRITICAL SOURCES: Book World, February 18, 1968; *New York Times Book Review,* March 3, 1968; *Commonweal,* April 19, 1968; *New York Review of Books,* October 10, 1968.

*   *   *

FRANK, Ronald E(dward) 1933-

PERSONAL: Born September 15, 1933, in Chicago, Ill.; son of Raymond and Ethel (Lundquist) Frank; married Iris Donner, June 14, 1958; children: Linda, Lauren, Kimberly. *Education:* Attended University of Illinois, Navy Pier Branch, 1951-53; Northwestern University, B.S. and B.A., 1955, M.B.A., 1956; University of Chicago, Ph.D., 1960. *Politics:* Independent. *Religion:* Protestant. *Home:* 219 Comrie Dr., Villanova, Pa. 19085. *Office:* Wharton School, University of Pennsylvania, Philadelphia, Pa. 19104.

CAREER: Northwestern University, School of Business, Evanston, Ill., instructor in business statistics, 1956-57; Harvard University, Graduate School of Business Administration, Cambridge, Mass., assistant professor of business administration, 1960-65; University of Pennsylvania, Wharton School, Philadelphia, associate professor, 1965-68, professor of marketing, 1968—, chairman of department, 1971-74, vice dean and director of research and Ph.D. programs, 1974-76. Assistant professor of business administration, Graduate School of Business, Stanford University, 1963-65; co-director or member of faculty of executive development programs and seminars for General Foods, Miles Laboratories, and other companies and organizations. Member of research board of review, Consumer Research Institute. Consultant to Market Research Corporation of America, Hills Brothers Coffee, Inc., Prentice-Hall, Inc., National Broadcasting Company (NBC), and other corporations; consultant to numerous law firms.

MEMBER: American Marketing Association (member of board of directors, 1968-70; vice-president, Marketing Education Division, 1972-73), American Statistical Association (chairman, subsection on marketing, 1975), Institute of Management Science, Association for Consumer Research, American Association for Public Opinion Research, American Economic Association, Beta Gamma Sigma.

WRITINGS: (With Alfred Kuehn and William Massy) *Quantitative Techniques in Marketing Analysis,* Irwin, 1962; (with John Matthews, Robert Buzzell, and Theodore Levitt) *Marketing: An Introductory Analysis,* McGraw, 1964; (with Massy) *Computer Programs for the Analysis of Consumer Panel Data,* Graduate School of Business, Stanford University, 1965; (with Paul Green) *Manager's Guide to Marketing Research,* Wiley, 1967; (with Green) *Quantitative Methods in Marketing,* Prentice-Hall, 1967; (contributor with Massy) Patrick J. Robinson, editor, *Promotional Decisions Using Mathematical Models,* Allyn & Bacon, 1967; (with Massy and Thomas Lodahl) *Purchasing Behavior and Personal Attributes,* University of Pennsylvania Press, 1968; (with Massy) *An Econometric Approach to a Marketing Decision Model,* M.I.T. Press, 1971; (with Massy and Yoram Wind) *Market Segmentation,* Prentice-Hall, 1972; (contributor with Leonard Lodish and Henry Claycamp) Steuart Britt, editor, *Marketing Handbook,* Dartnell Corp. (Chicago), 1974; (contributor with Massy) John Farley and John Howard, editors, *Control Error in Market Research Data,* Lexington Books, 1975; (with Marshall Greenberg) *The Public's Use of Television,* Sage Publications, Inc., 1980; (contributor) Robert Ferber, editor, *Handbook of Marketing Research,* McGraw, in press.

Also author, with Greenberg, of *Audience Segmentation Analysis for Public Television Program Development, Evaluation and Promotion: A Demonstration Project,* for John and Mary Markle Foundation, 1976. Contributor to proceedings. Contributor of articles on marketing to professional journals. Member of editorial board, *Journal of Marketing Research,* 1972-75; founding editor, *Journal of Consumer Research,* 1973-76.

WORK IN PROGRESS: A book on the public's use of public television.

*   *   *

FRANKEL, J(oseph)   1913-

PERSONAL: Born May 30, 1913, in Lwow, Poland; son of I. and R. (Roseenzweig) Frankel; married Elizabeth A. Kyle, May 22, 1944; children: Inge D. *Education:* University of

Lwow, LL.B., 1935; University of Western Australia, LL.M., 1948; University of London, Ph.D., 1950. *Home:* The Old Rectory, Avington, Winchester, Hampshire SO21 1DD, England. *Office:* Department of Politics, University of Southampton, Southampton, England.

CAREER: University of London, University College, London, England, assistant lecturer in international relations, 1951-52; University of Aberdeen, Aberdeen, Scotland, lecturer in politics, 1952-60, head of department, 1960-63; University of Southampton, Southampton, England, professor of politics, 1964-78, professor emeritus, 1978—, dean of faculty of social sciences, 1965-68. *Member:* Political Science Association, Royal Institute for International Affairs, British International Studies Association.

WRITINGS—Published by Oxford University Press, except as indicated: *The Making of Foreign Policy,* 1963; *International Relations,* 1964, 2nd edition, 1969; *International Politics: Conflict and Harmony,* Lane, 1969; *National Interest,* Praeger, 1970; *Contemporary International Theory and the Behavior of States,* 1970; *British Foreign Policy, 1945-1974,* 1974; *International Relations in a Changing World,* 1979.

WORK IN PROGRESS: A book on argument and explanation in international relations.

*   *   *

FRANKLIN, John Hope   1915-

PERSONAL: Born January 2, 1915, in Rentiesville, Olka.; son of Buck Colbert (an attorney; also the first Negro judge to sit in chancery in Oklahoma district court) and Mollie (Parker) Franklin; married Aurelia Whittington, June 11, 1940; children: John Whittington. *Education:* Fisk University, A.B., 1935; Harvard University, A.M., 1936, Ph.D., 1941. *Home:* 5805 South Blackstone Ave., Chicago, Ill. 60637. *Office:* Department of History, University of Chicago, Chicago, Ill. 60637.

CAREER: St. Augustine's College, Raleigh, N.C., instructor in history, 1938-43; North Carolina College, Durham, instructor in history, 1943-47; Howard University, Washington, D.C., professor of history, 1947-56; Brooklyn College of the City University of New York, Brooklyn, N.Y., professor of history and chairman of department, 1956-64; University of Chicago, Chicago, Ill., professor of history, 1964—, John Matthews Manly Distinguished Service Professor, 1969—, chairman of history department, 1967-70. Visiting professor at University of California, Harvard University, University of Wisconsin, Cornell University, University of Hawaii, Australia National University, Salzburg (Austria) Seminar, and other institutions; Pitt Professor of American History and Institutions, Cambridge University, 1962-63. Board of Foreign Scholarships, member, 1962-69, chairman, 1966-69. Member of board of directors, Legal Defense and Educational Fund, National Association for the Advancement of Colored People (NAACP). Member of board of trustees, Fisk University, 1947—. Member of board, Illinois Bell, Chicago (Ill.) Public Library, and Museum of Science and Industry (Chicago).

MEMBER: American Historical Association (member of executive council, 1959-62; president, 1979), Organization of American Historians (president, 1975), Association for Study of Negro Life and History, American Studies Association, Southern Historical Association (life member; president, 1970). *Awards, honors:* LL.D. from Morgan State College (now University), 1960, Lincoln University, 1961, Virginia State College, 1961, Hamline University, 1965, Lincoln College, 1965, Fisk University, 1965, Columbia University, 1969, and University of Notre Dame, 1970; A.M., Cambridge University, 1962; L.H.D. from Long Island University, 1964, University of Massachusetts, 1964, and Yale University, 1977; Litt.D., Princeton University, 1972; recipient of other honorary degrees.

WRITINGS: The Free Negro in North Carolina, 1790-1860, University of North Carolina Press, 1943, reprinted, Russell, 1969; *From Slavery to Freedom: A History of Negro Americans,* Knopf, 1947, 5th edition, 1980; *The Militant South, 1800-1860,* Belknap Press, 1956; *Reconstruction after the Civil War,* University of Chicago Press, 1961; *The Emancipation Proclamation,* Doubleday, 1963; (with John W. Caughey and Ernest R. May) *Land of the Free,* Benziger, 1965, revised edition, 1970; (with the editors of Time-Life Books) *Illustrated History of Black Americans,* Time-Life, 1970; *Racial Equality in America,* University of Chicago Press, 1976; *A Southern Odyssey: Travelers in the Antebellum North,* Louisiana State University Press, 1976.

Editor: *The Civil War Diary of J. T. Ayers,* Illinois State Historical Society, 1947; Albion Tourgee, *A Fool's Errand,* Belknap Press, 1961; T. W. Higginson, *Army Life in a Black Regiment,* Beacon Press, 1962; *Three Negro Classics,* Avon, 1965; (with Isadore Starr) *The Negro in Twentieth Century America,* Random House, 1967; *Color and Race,* Houghton, 1968; W.E.B. Du Bois, *The Suppression of the African Slave Trade,* Louisiana State University Press, 1969; John R. Lynch, *Reminiscences of an Active Life: The Autobiography of John R. Lynch,* University of Chicago Press, 1970.

Contributor: Arthur S. Link and Richard Leopold, editors, *Problems in American History,* Prentice-Hall, 1952, 2nd revised edition, 1966; Rayford W. Logan, editor, *The Negro Thirty Years Afterward,* Howard University Press, 1955; *The Americans: Ways of Life and Thought,* Cohen & West, 1956; Charles Frankel, editor, *Issues in University Education,* Harper, 1959; Ralph Newman, editor, *Lincoln for the Ages,* Doubleday, 1960; Charles G. Sellars, Jr., editor, *The Southerner as American,* University of North Carolina Press, 1960; Herbert Hill, editor, *Soon One Morning,* Knopf, 1963; H. V. Hodson, editor, *The Atlantic Future,* Longmans, Green, 1964; John C. McKinney and Edgar T. Thompson, editors, *The South in Continuity and Change,* Duke University Press, 1965; John P. Davis, editor, *The American Negro Reference Book,* Prentice-Hall, 1966; Harold Hyman, editor, *New Frontiers of the American Reconstruction,* University of Illinois Press, 1966; Kenneth Clark and Talcott Parsons, editors, *The Negro American,* Houghton, 1966; Daniel J. Boorstein, editor, *The American Primer,* [Chicago], 1966; C. Vann Woodward, editor, *The Comparative Approach to American History,* Basic Books, 1968. Also contributor to *American History: Recent Interpretations,* edited by A. S. Eisentstadt, 1962, *William Wells Brown: Author and Reformer,* by William E. Farrison, 1969, *Henry Ossawa Turner: American Artist,* by Marcia M. Mathews, 1969, and *Crusade for Justice: The Autobiography of Ida B. Wells,* edited by Alfreda M. Duster, 1970.

Author of pamphlets for U.S. Information Service. General editor, "Zenith Books" series on secondary education, Doubleday, 1965—, and "Negro American Biographies and Autobiographies" series, University of Chicago Press, 1969—; also co-editor of series in American history for Crowell and AHM Publishing, 1964—. Contributor of articles to numerous journals and periodicals.

FRANTZ, Charles 1925-

PERSONAL: Born April 22, 1925, in Rocky Ford, Colo.; son of Osee C. (a hatchery owner) and Blanche (Talhelm) Frantz; married Charlotte Stutzman, June 8, 1950; children: Marina, Trevor Kelly, Corinne. *Education:* Attended Colorado State College (now University), 1943-44; Earlham College, A.B., 1950; Haverford College, A.M., 1951; University of Chicago, Ph.D., 1958. *Office:* Department of Anthropology, State University of New York, Buffalo, N.Y. 14261.

CAREER: Worked in U.S. Civilian Public Service Camps, 1944-46; University of Chicago, Chicago, Ill., research associate in anthropology, 1958-60; Portland State College (now University), Portland, Ore., 1953-64, began as instructor, became professor, executive officer in department of anthropology, 1960-64; University of Toronto, Toronto, Ontario, visiting professor, 1964-65; Howard University, Washington, D.C., professor and director of African Studies, director of research program, 1965-67; State University of New York at Buffalo, professor of anthropology, 1968—. Head of department of sociology, Ahmadu Bello University, Zaria, Nigeria, 1970-72. Program chairman, Northwestern Anthropological Conference, 1963-64. Has done field work in South Dakota, 1951, British Columbia, 1956-57, Southern Rhodesia, 1958-60, Nigeria, 1970-72, 1974, and 1976, and Cameroun, 1977, 1980.

MEMBER: American Anthropological Association (fellow; executive secretary, 1966-68), African Studies Association (fellow), American Ethnological Society, Society for Applied Anthropology (fellow), Association of Social Anthropologists of the Commonwealth, International African Institute, American Sociological Association, Northeastern Anthropological Association (president, 1975-76), Sigma Xi. *Awards, honors:* Mary Campbell Award, American Friends Service Committee, 1956-58; grants from Wrenner-Gren Foundation, 1960, and American Council of Learned Societies, 1964-65.

WRITINGS: (With Cyril A. Rogers) *Racial Themes in Southern Rhodesia,* Yale University Press, 1962; *The Student Anthropologist's Handbook,* Schenkman, 1972; *Pastoral Societies, Stratification, and National Integration in Africa,* Scandinavian Institute of African Studies, 1975. Contributor of chapters to scholarly books. Contributor of articles to professional journals.

WORK IN PROGRESS: A book on pastoral/nomadic societies; a book on the utopian Doukhobors of Canada; a book on the history of anthropology in the United States; research on cultural ecology, cultural and racial pluralism, and African urbanism.

AVOCATIONAL INTERESTS: Travel, books, and chamber music.

*   *   *

FRANZMANN, Martin H. 1907-1976

PERSONAL: Born January 29, 1907, in Lake City, Minn.; died March 28, 1976, in Cambridge, England; son of William and Else (Griebling) Franzmann; married Alice Bentzin, July 6, 1933; children: John William, Peter Bentzin, Alice Louise. *Education:* Northwestern College, A.B., 1928; University of Chicago, 1931-33, 1946, 1950; Thiensville Seminary, diploma, 1936. *Religion:* Lutheran.

CAREER: Northwestern College, Watertown, Wis., instructor in classics, 1936-46; Concordia Seminary, St. Louis, Mo., professor, 1946-69, chairman of department of exegetical theology, 1957-67. Instructor in theology, Westfield

House, Cambridge, England, 1969-71; lecturer, Concordia Seminary, 1972-73. Member of committee on doctrinal unity, Missouri Synod of Lutheran Church, beginning 1950; secretary, Synodical Conference, 1952-56. *Awards, honors:* D.D., Concordia Seminary, 1958.

WRITINGS—All published by Concordia, except as indicated: *Follow Me,* 1961; *The Word of the Lord Grows,* 1961; *New Courage for Daily Living,* 1963; *Ha! Ha! Among the Trumpets,* 1966; (with F. Dean Lueking) *Grace under Pressure: The Way of Meekness in Ecumenical Relations,* 1966; *Concordia Commentary: Romans,* 1968; *Pray for Joy,* 1970; (editor and author of introduction, notes, and references) *Concordia Bible with Notes: The New Covenant,* 2nd edition (Franzmann was not associated with earlier edition), Collins & World, 1971; *The Revelation to John: A Commentary,* 1976. Also author of *Art of Exegesis* (cassette), 1972, *Alive with the Spirit,* 1973, and *Introduction to the New Testament* (correspondence course study outline and syllabi). Contributor to *Concordia Theological Monthly.*†

*   *   *

FRASCA, John (Anthony) 1916-1979

PERSONAL: Born May 25, 1916, in Lynn, Mass.; died December 4, 1979, in Tampa, Fla.; son of Michele Angelo (a contractor) and Maria (Gordan) Frasca; married Louise Cummings, December 20, 1948; children: Charlotte (Mrs. Eugene Krupa), Sydney (Mrs. Vincent Giovenco), Karen, Michele (Mrs. John Krentzman), John, Jr. *Education:* Attended Holmes Junior College, 1936-38; Mississippi College, B.A., 1940. *Politics:* Democrat. *Religion:* Roman Catholic. *Home and office:* 4517 Vasconia St., Tampa, Fla. 33609.

CAREER: Reporter in Hattiesburg, Miss., beginning 1940; *Boston Record-American,* Boston, Mass., rewriter, 1948-53; *Philadelphia Daily News,* Philadelphia, Pa., rewriter, 1953-57; Pennsylvania Democratic Party, Harrisburg, publicity director, 1957-58; *Sons of Italy Times,* Philadelphia, editor, 1959-63; *Tampa Tribune,* Tampa, Fla., investigative writer and columnist, 1964-68; free-lance writer, 1968-79. Press secretary to Pennsylvania Governor David L. Lawrence, 1958; publicity director for senatorial campaign of Supreme Court Justice Michael Musmano of Pennsylvania, 1964. Political analyst, consultant to weekly newspapers, and radio commentator, 1958-64. *Military service:* U.S. Marine Corps, 1942-45; became first lieutenant. *Member:* American Newspaper Guild (chairman of *Philadelphia Daily News* unit, 1954-57).

AWARDS, HONORS: Award from Texas Associated Press, 1954, for best feature of the year; award from Philadelphia Press Association, 1956, for best writing of the year; Mental Health Bell Award from Pennsylvania Mental Health Association, 1956; Philadelphia Good Citizenship Award, 1956; second prize from Pennsylvania Newspaper Publishers Association, 1956, for "My Ten Days in a Mental Hospital"; first prize from Pennsylvania Newspaper Publishers Association, 1957, for "Children Who Walk Alone"; best feature award from Pennsylvania Newspaper Publishers Association, 1957, for "Inside Israel"; second prize for court coverage from Pennsylvania Newspaper Publishers Association, 1957, for "Injustice for Our Kids"; Pennsylvania Optimist Club Award, 1957; Heywood Broun Memorial Award for Journalism from American Newspaper Guild, 1965, and Pulitzer Prize, 1966, for series on Robert Lamar Watson; Edgar Allan Poe Award from Mystery Writers of America, 1968, for *The Mulberry Tree.*

WRITINGS: The Mulberry Tree, Prentice-Hall, 1967; *Con*

Man or Saint?, Droke House, 1969; *A Sharecropper's Best Short Stories,* Koscot, Inc., 1970; *The Unstoppable Glenn Turner,* Marlborough House, 1971; (editor) *GWT Changed the World for Me: The Story of Glenn W. Turner, Motivational Genius,* Pyramid Publications, 1972; (with Michael Harris) *The Sun Rose Late,* House of Collectibles, 1974. Columnist, *La Gaceta.*

WORK IN PROGRESS: A biography of millionaire entrepreneur Charles Woods, tentatively entitled *From the Himalayas to Valley Forge.*

SIDELIGHTS: Toward the end of his life, John Frasca's primary concern was the "monstrous injustice perpetrated against people by prosecutors seeking headlines—with the result that the victims are found innocent and left broke." He proposed that the branch of government (Federal or state) responsible for indictments be required to reimburse people found innocent by the court or jury for the cost of their legal defense.

In 1961, Frasca was commissioned by Jewish newspapers across the United States to cover the Adolf Eichmann trial in Jerusalem.

BIOGRAPHICAL/CRITICAL SOURCES: Best Sellers, May 1, 1968.†

*   *   *

FRATCHER, William F(ranklin) 1913-

PERSONAL: Born April 4, 1913, in Detroit, Mich.; son of Vernon Claude (a trust company officer) and Ethel Stuart (Thomas) Fratcher; married Elsie Florene Briscoe, August 22, 1941; children: Agnes Ann. *Education:* Wayne University (now Wayne State University), A.B. (with distinction), 1933, A.M., 1938; University of Michigan, J.D. (with distinction), 1936, LL.M., 1951, S.J.D., 1952; Command and General Staff College, graduate, 1944; additional study at Sorbonne, University of Paris, 1945. *Religion:* Presbyterian. *Home:* 1812 Cliff Dr., Columbia, Mo. 65201. *Office:* School of Law, Tate Hall, University of Missouri, Columbia, Mo. 65211.

CAREER: Admitted to Michigan State Bar, 1936, and to Missouri State Bar; Lewis & Watkins, Detroit, Mich., attorney-at-law, 1936-41; University of Missouri—Columbia, associate professor, 1947-49, professor of law, 1949—, R. B. Price Distinguished Professor of Law, 1971—. Visiting professor of law at University of Michigan, summer, 1952, New York University, 1954-55, 1963, and 1965, and Hastings College of the Law, University of California, 1976; research associate, University of Michigan, summer, 1953; University of London, Ford Foundation law faculty fellow in international studies and honorary member of King's College faculty of law, 1963-64. Member of research council, New York Temporary State Commission on Estates, 1963. Reporter for Uniform Probate Code, 1963-70, *International Encyclopedia of Comparative Law,* 1966-74, Missouri Probate Law Revision Project, 1973-80, Missouri Guardianship Law Revision Project, 1975—, and Missouri Trust Law Revision Project, 1980—. *Military service:* U.S. Army, Judge Advocate General's Department, 1941-47; served as U.S. commissioner and chairman, International Commission for Control of the Central Registry of War Criminals and Security Suspects, 1946; held other posts in Berlin, Paris, and Frankfurt; became lieutenant colonel; received Legion of Merit, Commendation Ribbon. U.S. Army Reserve, 1947-71; retired as colonel.

MEMBER: American Bar Association, Reserve Officers

Association of the United States (chapter president; secretary), Selden Society (state correspondent), Boone County Bar Association, Pipe Roll Society, Scabbard and Blade, Pi Sigma Alpha, Delta Theta Phi, Delta Sigma Rho. *Awards, honors:* Order of the Coif, 1936; research grants from National Conference of Commissioners on Uniform State Laws, University of Michigan, 1966, American Bar Foundation, University of Colorado, 1967, and International Association of Legal Science, Oxford University, 1969; American College of Probate Counsel, academic fellow, 1971.

WRITINGS: The National Defense Act, U.S. Government Printing Office, 1945; *Perpetuities and Other Restraints,* University of Michigan Press, 1955; (with Lewis M. Simes) *Cases and Materials on the Law of Fiduciary Administration,* 2nd edition, Callaghan, 1956; *Trusts and Estates in England,* Pageant, 1968; *Cases and Materials on Veterinary Jurisprudence,* University of Missouri, 1968; (contributor) Arthur I. Winard, editor, *Landmark Papers on Estate Planning, Wills, Estates and Trusts,* Prentice-Hall, 1968; (contributor) *Planning Large Estates Workshops,* Practising Law Institute (New York), 1968; (with others) *Uniform Probate Code,* West Publishing, 1970; (contributor) Robert R. Wright, editor, *Uniform Probate Code Practice Manual,* American Law Institute, 1972, 2nd edition, edited by Richard V. Wellman, 1977; (contributor) *International Encyclopedia of Comparative Law,* Teubingen, 1974; (contributor) Edward C. Halbach, Jr., editor, *Death, Taxes and Family Property,* West Publishing, 1977; *The Law Barn,* University of Missouri, 1978; *The Luncheon Guest,* Exposition, 1979. Also editor, with others, of *Manual for Courts-Martial,* published by the U.S. Army, 1949, and author of "pocket parts" for *The Law of Future Interests* by Simes and Allan F. Smith, 1961, 1965-79. Contributor to *Encyclopaedia Britannica.* Contributor of over sixty articles and reviews to legal publications.

WORK IN PROGRESS: A revision of the Missouri guardianship and trust law; "keeping up Simes' and Smith's *The Law of Future Interests*"; "preparing a new edition of a leading treatise on a related field of law," for Little, Brown.

*   *   *

FREDERICK, Robert Allen 1928-

PERSONAL: Born February 3, 1928, in Mishawaka, Ind.; son of Ralph L. (a design engineer) and Garnet Frederick; married Mary Swartz, November 23, 1950 (divorced, 1967); married Saradell Ard (a professor of art), September 10, 1969; children: (first marriage) Carol Heren, John Billington, Peter Carey. *Education:* Hanover College, A.B., 1950; Indiana University, M.S., 1951, Ph.D., 1960. *Office:* Alaska Historical Commission, Office of the Governor, College of Arts and Sciences, University of Alaska, 3211 Providence Ave., Anchorage, Alaska 99504.

CAREER: Texas Technological College (now Texas Tech University), assistant to dean of students, 1951-53; U.S. Naval Academy Preparatory School, Annapolis, Md., instructor in history, 1953-56; Alaska Methodist University, Anchorage, 1960-76, began as associate professor, became professor of history; Alaska Historical Commission, Anchorage, executive director, 1973—. Executive director of Alaska Humanities Task Force, 1971-72; vice-chairman of board of advisers and Alaskan adviser, National Trust for Historic Preservation, 1970-79. *Military service:* U.S. Naval Reserve, 1953-56; became lieutenant. *Member:* American Historical Association, Organization of American Historians, American Association for State and Local History,

Alaska Historical Society (member of board, 1967-75; president, 1968-69). *Awards, honors:* Indiana University Foundation research grant, 1962-63; National Endowment for the Humanities and American Historical Association grants, 1967, for directing Conference on Alaskan History.

WRITINGS: (Editor and contributor) *Frontier Alaska: Historical Interpretation and Opportunity,* Alaska Methodist University Press, 1968; (editor) *Proceedings of American Association for State and Local History,* American Association for State and Local History, 1969; (editor and contributor) *Writing Alaska's History: A Guide to Research,* Alaska Historical Commission, 1974; (contributor) *Alaska Native Land Claims,* Alaska Native Foundation, 1976. Contributor to *Alaska Review.* Editorial advisor, *Alaska Journal,* 1970—.

WORK IN PROGRESS: Richard Lieber and the Preservation of American Landscape, a conservation biography.†

*   *   *

FREEDMAN, Morris 1920-

PERSONAL: Born October 6, 1920, in New York, N.Y.; son of Boris (a bookbinder) and Anna (Katz) Freedman; married Charlotte Kopelman (an elementary teacher), 1945 (divorced, 1975); children: Paul, Iris. *Education:* City College (now City College of the City University of New York), B.A. (with honors), 1941; Columbia University, M.A., 1950, Ph.D., 1953. *Religion:* Jewish. *Home:* 4007 Clagett Rd., College Heights, Md. 20782. *Office:* Department of English, University of Maryland, College Park, Md. 20740.

CAREER: City College (now City College of the City University of New York), New York City, instructor and lecturer, 1945-54; *Commentary,* New York City, associate editor, 1954-55; University of New Mexico, Albuquerque, 1955-66, began as assistant professor, became professor of English; University of Maryland, College Park, professor of English, 1966—, head of department, 1967-73. Free-lance magazine writer, 1945-54. *Military service:* U.S. Army Air Forces, 1943-45. *Member:* Milton Society of America, Phi Beta Kappa.

WRITINGS: Confessions of a Conformist, Norton, 1961; *Chaos in Our Colleges,* McKay, 1962; (editor) *Fact and Object,* Harper, 1963; (editor) *Essays in Modern Drama,* Heath, 1964; *Compact English Handbook,* McKay, 1965; (editor with Paul B. Davis) *Contemporary Controversy,* Scribner, 1965; (contributor) *American Theatre,* Edward Arnold, 1967; *The Moral Impulse: Modern Drama from Ibsen to the Present,* Southern Illinois University Press, 1967; (editor with Davis) *Controversy in Literature,* Scribner, 1968; (editor) *Tragedy: Texts and Commentary,* Scribner, 1968; *American Drama in Social Context,* Southern Illinois University Press, 1971; (with former wife, Charlotte K. Freedman) *Into America: An Introduction to American Literature,* Macmillan, 1972; (with Carolyn Banks) *American Mix,* Lippincott, 1972. Work represented in anthologies. Contributor of articles, essays, and stories to general magazines and professional journals.

WORK IN PROGRESS: An American Life; Savage Emptiness: Drama since Beckett.

*   *   *

FREEMAN, Gillian 1929-

PERSONAL: Born December 5, 1929, in England; daughter of Jack (a dental surgeon) and Freda (Davids) Freeman; married Edward Thorpe, September 12, 1955; children: Harriet Amelia, Matilda Helen Rachel. *Education:* University of

Reading, B.A. (with honors), 1951. *Home:* 42 Jacksons Lane, London N.6, England. *Agent:* Curtis Brown Ltd., 1 Craven Hill, London W2 3EP, England.

CAREER: C. J. Lytle Ltd., London, England, copywriter, 1951-52; London County Council, London, teacher, 1952-53; *North London Observer,* London, reporter, 1953; Louis Golding, London, literary secretary, 1953-55; author, 1955—.

WRITINGS: The Liberty Man, Longmans, Green, 1955; *Fall of Innocence,* Longmans, Green, 1956; *Jack Would Be a Gentleman,* Longmans, Green, 1959; *The Story of Albert Einstein,* Vallentine, Mitchell, 1960; *The Leather Boys* (also see below), Anthony Blond, 1961; *The Campaign,* Longmans, Green, 1963; *The Leader* (novel), Anthony Blond, 1965, Lippincott, 1966; *The Undergrowth of Literature* (nonfiction), Thomas Nelson, 1967; *The Alabaster Egg* (novel), Viking, 1970; *The Marriage Machine* (novel), Stein & Day, 1975; *The Schoolgirl Ethel* (biography), Penguin, 1976; *The Confessions of Elisabeth Von S.: The Story of a Young Woman's Rise and Fall in Nazi Society,* Dutton, 1978 (published in England as *Nazi Lady,* Anthony Blond, 1978).

Author of one-act play "Pursuit," produced by the National Theatre Co., 1969, and of scenario for the ballet "Mayerling," produced by the Royal Ballet, 1978. Also author of screenplays, including "The Leather Boys" (based on Freeman's novel of same title), 1963, "That Cold Day in the Park" (based on a novel by Richard Miles), 1965, "I Want What I Want" (based on a novel by Geoff Brown), 1973, and "Girl on a Motorcycle."

Contributor of stories and fiction reviews to *Spectator, London Magazine, Courier, Books and Bookmen, Sunday Times, Times Literary Supplement,* and other publications.

WORK IN PROGRESS: An Easter Egg Hunt; the scenario for Kenneth Macmillan's ballet, "Isadora."

AVOCATIONAL INTERESTS: Theatre, ballet, and cinema techniques.

BIOGRAPHICAL/CRITICAL SOURCES: London Magazine, May, 1963, December, 1967; *Books and Bookmen,* May, 1963; Brigid Brophy, *Don't Never Forget,* J. Cape, 1966; *Observer Review,* October 29, 1967; *Listener,* November 2, 1967; *New York,* June 9, 1969; *Times Literary Supplement,* October 16, 1970; *New York Times,* February 26, 1972; *Los Angeles Times,* October 5, 1979.

*   *   *

FREEMAN, Lucy (Greenbaum)   1916-

PERSONAL: Born December 13, 1916, in New York, N.Y.; daughter of Lawrence Samuel (a lawyer) and Sylvia (Sobel) Greenbaum; married William Freeman (a newspaperman), October 5, 1946 (divorced). *Education:* Bennington College, B.A., 1938. *Politics:* Democrat. *Home and office:* 210 Central Park S., New York, N.Y. 10019. *Agent:* Mary Yost Associates, Inc., 75 East 55th St., New York, N.Y. 10022.

CAREER: New York Times, New York, N.Y., reporter, 1941-52; free-lance writer, 1952—. *Member:* National Association of Science Writers, P.E.N., American Society of Journalists and Authors, Mystery Writers of America, Authors Guild. *Awards, honors:* Writers Award for "outstanding contribution to public understanding of psychiatry," American Psychiatric Association, 1976.

WRITINGS: Fight against Fears, Crown, 1951; *Hope for the Troubled,* Crown, 1953; *Before I Kill More,* Crown, 1955; *Hospital in Action,* Rand McNally, 1956; *Search for Love,* World Publishing, 1957; *So You Want to Be Psychoanalyzed!,* Holt, 1958; *The Story of Psychoanalysis,* Pocket Books, 1960; (with Ted Atkinson) *All the Way!,* Paxton-Slade, 1961; (with Harold Greenwald) *Emotional Maturity in Love and Marriage,* Harper, 1961; *The Abortionist,* Doubleday, 1962; *Children Who Kill,* Berkley Publishing, 1962; (with Edwina Williams) *Remember Me to Tom,* Putnam, 1963; (with Lewis L. Robins) *Chastise Me with Scorpions,* Putnam, 1964; (with Hyman Spotnitz) *The Wandering Husband,* Prentice-Hall, 1964; *Why People Act That Way,* Crowell, 1965; (with Renatus Hartogs) *The Two Assassins,* Crowell, 1965; (editor) *The Mind,* Crowell, 1967; *Lords of Hell,* Dell, 1967; *Farewell to Fear,* Putnam, 1969; *The Cry for Love,* Macmillan, 1969.

(With Lisa Hoffman) *The Ordeal of Stephen Dennison,* Prentice-Hall, 1970; (with Anita Stevens) *I Hate My Parents,* Cowles Book Co., 1970; *The Dream,* Arbor House, 1971; *The Story of Anna O.,* Walker & Co., 1972; *Betrayal,* Stein & Day, 1976; *Who Is Sylvia?,* Arbor House, 1979; *Friend Rediscovered,* Arbor House, 1980; *Too Deep for Tears,* Dutton, 1980. Contributor of articles to *Cosmopolitan, McCall's, New York Times,* and other publications.

AVOCATIONAL INTERESTS: Golf, dancing, swimming, going to the racetrack.

*   *   *

FREEMAN-GRENVILLE, Greville Stewart Parker   1918-

PERSONAL: Born June 29, 1918, in Hook Norton, Oxfordshire, England; married Lady Kinloss, August 29, 1950; children: Bevil, Teresa, Hester. *Education:* Attended Eastbourne College; Worcester College, Oxford, B.Litt., 1940, M.A., 1943, D.Phil., 1957. *Religion:* Roman Catholic. *Home:* North View House, Sheriff Hutton, Yorkshire, England.

CAREER: Abadan Technical Institute, Abadan, Iran, lecturer, 1947-48; Dar Al-Mualamin Al-Aliya, Baghdad, Iraq, lecturer, 1948-49; Her Majesty's Overseas Civil Service, education officer in Tanganyika, 1950-60, education adviser in Aden, 1961-64; University of Ghana, Institute of African Studies, Accra, senior research fellow in African history, 1964-66; University of York, York, England, senior teaching and research fellow in Swahili, 1966-69; professor of African history, State University of New York, 1969-74. Visiting professor of history, Columbia University, 1965-66. Member of historical committee, East African Swahili Committee, 1958-64, 1972—. *Military service:* British Army, Royal Berkshire Regiment, 1939-46; became captain. *Member:* Royal Numismatic Society (fellow), Society of Antiquaries (fellow), Royal Asiatic Society (fellow), Royal Commonwealth Society (fellow), British Academy (member of Fontes Historias Africanae committee, 1972—). *Awards, honors:* British Academy European Exchange grant, 1976; *Chronology of World History* named "one of outstanding reference books of 1976" by the American Library Association.

WRITINGS: The Medieval History of the Coast of Tanganyika, Oxford University Press, 1962; (compiler) *The East African Coast: Select Documents,* Clarendon Press, 1962, 2nd edition, Collings, 1975; (contributor) *History of East Africa,* Volume I, Clarendon Press, 1962; *Muslim and Christian Calendars,* Oxford University Press, 1963, 2nd edition, Collings, 1977; *The French at Kilwa Island,* Clarendon Press, 1965.

Chronology of African History, Oxford University Press, 1973; *Chronology of World History: A Calendar of Principal*

Events from 3100 B.C. to A.D. 1976, Collings, 1976, 2nd edition, 1978; A Modern Atlas of African History, Collings, 1976; The Queen's Lineage, Collings, 1977; Atlas of British History: From Prehistoric Times to 1978, Collings, 1979; The Mourbasa Rising of 1631 against the Portuguese, Oxford University Press, 1980; (editor and translator) The Book of the Wonders of India, East-West Publications, in press; (editor) Memories of an Arabian Princess, East-West Publications, in press; The Beauties of Cairo: A Guide to the Chief Christian and Islamic Monuments, East-West Publications, in press.

Contributor to Encyclopaedia Britannica, Encyclopaedia of Islam, and to Numismatic Chronicle, Man, Uganda Journal, Tanganyika Notes and Records, Swahili, African Ecclesiastical Review, Studi Medievali, and other publications.

WORK IN PROGRESS: Cairo, the Victorious and Beautiful City: A History of the Islamic Monuments, East-West Publications; editing Description of Egypt, 1825-1828, by Edward Lane, East-West Publications; Atlas of Middle Eastern History.

SIDELIGHTS: Freeman-Grenville's primary interests are in the study of pre-colonial Africa from African sources, the Indian Ocean, and the Middle East. Competent in Latin, Greek, Arabic, Swahili, French, and Portuguese, he has traveled extensively in Europe, Africa, and the Middle East.

*   *   *

FRENCH, Dorothy Kayser 1926-

PERSONAL: Born February 11, 1926, in Milwaukee, Wis.; daughter of Paul (in public relations) and Gertrude (Ament) Kayser; married Louis N. French (a patent attorney for Phillips Petroleum Co.), July 2, 1948; children: Nancy, Laura. Education: University of Wisconsin, B.A., 1948. Home: 2136 Starlight Ct., Bartlesville, Okla. 74003.

CAREER: Shorewood Herald, Shorewood, Wis., society editor, 1947; Wisconsin State Journal, Madison, women's editor, 1948-50; Bartlesville Record, Bartlesville, Okla., society editor, 1951; free-lance writer, 1951—. Member: American Association of University Women (branch secretary, 1950-52), Theta Sigma Phi, Mortar Board, Kappa Delta.

WRITINGS: Mystery of the Old Oil Well, F. Watts, 1963; Swim to Victory, Lippincott, 1969; A Try at Tumbling, Lippincott, 1970; Pioneer Saddle Mystery, Lantern Press, 1975; I Don't Belong Here, Westminster, 1980; Wish upon a Par, New Reader's Press, in press. Contributor of short stories and articles to magazines.

WORK IN PROGRESS: Hi/Lo books for teenagers who read at a third or fourth-grade level.

*   *   *

FRENCH, Marilyn 1929-
(Mara Solwoska)

PERSONAL: Born November 21, 1929, in New York, N.Y.; daughter of E. Charles and Isabel (Hazz) Edwards; married Robert M. French, Jr. (a lawyer), June 4, 1950 (divorced, 1967); children: Jamie, Robert M. III. Education: Hofstra College (now University), B.A., 1951, M.A., 1964; Harvard University, Ph.D., 1972. Agent: Charlotte Sheedy Literary Agency, 145 West 86th St., New York, N.Y. 10024.

CAREER: Writer. Hofstra University, Hempstead, N.Y., instructor in English, 1964-68; College of the Holy Cross, Worcester, Mass., assistant professor of English, 1972-76; Harvard University, Cambridge, Mass., Mellon fellow in English, 1976—. Artist-in-residence at Aspen Institute for Humanistic Study, 1972. Lecturer. Member: Modern Language Association of America, Society for Values in Higher Education, Virginia Woolf Society, James Joyce Society, Phi Beta Kappa.

WRITINGS: The Book as World: James Joyce's "Ulysses", Harvard University Press, 1976; The Women's Room (novel), Summit Books, 1977; The Bleeding Heart, Summit Books, 1980; Shakespeare's Division of Experience, Summit Books, 1981; (author of introduction) Edith Wharton, House of Mirth, Jove Books, 1981; (author of introduction) Wharton, Summer, Jove Books, 1981. Also author of two unpublished novels. Contributor of articles and stories, sometimes under pseudonym Mara Solwoska, to journals, including Soundings and Ohio Review.

WORK IN PROGRESS: A book of essays, Marilyn French: On Women, Men, and Morals.

SIDELIGHTS: "I wanted to tell the story of what it is like to be a woman in our country in the middle of the twentieth century," Marilyn French remarked to a New York Times interviewer in explanation of her reasons for writing the controversial novel The Women's Room. If there is one point of agreement among the critics reviewing this novel, however, it is the fact that it certainly triggers emotional responses from its readers, whether they be negative or positive reactions.

Acknowledging French's skill in eliciting and provoking response from her readers, Brigitte Weeks writes in the Washington Post Book World that "the reader, a willing victim, becomes enmeshed in mixed feelings. Perhaps that is why I resented The Women's Room in a way I have never resented a novel before. It is a novel that lacks grace, restraint, good manners, an acceptance of the realities and pleasantries of life. It forces confrontations on the reader mercilessly." But Weeks also adds: "As a polemic the book is brilliant, forcing the reader to accept the reactions of the women as the only possible ones; closing firmly every loophole that might lead to a better understanding of women by men."

Christopher Lehmann-Haupt of the New York Times writes of The Women's Room: "The best compliment I can pay it is that I kept forgetting that it was fiction. It seized me by my preconceptions and I kept struggling and arguing with its premises. Men can't be that bad, I kept wanting to shout at the narrator. There must be room for accommodation between the sexes that you've somehow overlooked.... And the damnable thing is, she's right. Her story is true. At least it seems true. If it doesn't imitate a truth in the real world, it created a real world of its own."

One reason for this strong response might be found in French's characterizations. The characters seem to draw the readers in, to hold their attention. As the Washington Post Book World points out in a review of The Women's Room: "Its characters are engaged in demonstrating a premise most of us are unable and unwilling to accept, yet we care for them, sympathize with them and give them our support.... Most important, in its ungainly groping way it touches a painful chord, extracts an unwilling realization that its women speak at least a part of the truth about themselves and how our society has treated them."

Lehmann-Haupt agrees and writes: "So when Miss French has finished, we have glimpsed almost every type of unhappy woman imaginable.... It is as if Miss French were reconstituting cliches. Yet all of her women pulse with life and individuality. And this makes it all the more painful to the reader when all her men turn out to be part of a single rampant ego."

However, one critic who does not agree that *The Women's Room* draws readers into its characters' lives is V. K. Musmann. The *Library Journal* reviewer feels "the novelist slogs dutifully through the details of Mira's [the main character and narrator] early life, but is unable to create an interesting character or a sense of dramatic tension.... The women become the focus of the novel. Like a thin person trapped in a fat body, the story of Mira is hidden by excessive details and extraneous events. The novel skims surfaces and never probes deeply into lives or feelings."

Disagreeing with Musmann, a *Virginia Quarterly Review* critic writes: "Enthusiastic reviewers in the daily and weekly press have called Marilyn French's polemic the major novel of the women's liberation movement, and they have a point. The book does have an impact; this male reviewer found himself embarrassed for his sex. It is scarcely a surprise that women have suffered indignities for generations just because they are women, but it takes works like Ms. French's to make us realize just why that has got to stop. For those women who do not submit in a male-dominated society, life can be hellish, as Ms. French's heroines (she would reject the term) prove."

Critics occasionally charge that in French's novels the male characters are portrayed as "stick figures," "empty men," and "cardboard villains." Richard Phillips writes in the *Chicago Tribune* that "to read one of her novels—either the best selling *The Women's Room,* or her latest, *The Bleeding Heart*—means wincing through hundreds of pages of professed revulsion over the male species of human kind. Man means power, control, rage. Even the nice guys finish last. Men are bastards. Women suffer. It is a message written with all the subtlety of a sledgehammer, but one that, French argues, is only a mirror reflection of what men themselves are taught from birth: Contempt for women."

Anne Tyler writes in her review of *The Women's Room* in the *New York Times Book Review* that "there is no 'equal time' offered; the men are given no chance to tell their side of the story. Compared to the women—each separate and distinct, each rich in character—the men tend to blur together. They're all villains, and cardboard villains at that. But this narrowness is, I believe (or hope), intentional. The bias of *The Women's Room* is a part of the novel. It's almost the whole point.... The problem, she feels, is that the white middle-class male is really hollow: a sort of walking uniform, making the expected jokes, maintaining the expected postures. No wonder it's hard to describe him."

To readers like Tyler who do not realize her purpose in creating one-sided male characters, French responds in the *New York Times:* "That infuriates me. Every time I see that I see orange. The men are there as the women see them and feel them—impediments in women's lives. That's the focus of the book. Aristotle managed to build a whole society without mentioning women once. Did anyone ever say: 'Are there women in (Joseph Conrad's) *Nigger of the Narcissus?*'"

However, Alice Adams feels this one-sided characterization only serves to disenfranchise many readers who might otherwise read and learn from French's literature. Adams writes of *The Bleeding Heart* in the *Chicago Tribune Book World:* "The core problem though, is the persistently belligerent anti-male bias. (In fact, at some point reading this novel, I decided that it must be a put-on, a spoofing exercise in feminist self-criticism.) There is something radically wrong with a radical feminist novel, polemically so, in which one's sympathies continuously lurch away from the heroine and toward her lover, a man whom one perceives as being treated with great injustice."

But in fact, Lehmann-Haupt suggests in his recent review of *The Bleeding Heart:* "One is driven ... to contemplating Miss French's ideology. Are all industrialists incapable of understanding human love and aesthetic beauty because they are locked into a power-grid that obliterates sensitivity and compassion? Well, possibly most of them are, but I happen to know personally one or two who are not. Are all wives of corporation executives emotionally starved because they are part of a system that denies their true natures? Again, I know a couple of exceptions. The fact that I do destroys Miss French's case, because instead of writing about specific people, as a novelist ought to do, she has tried to create generalities. And if her generalities aren't true, then nothing about her novel is real."

A number of critics and readers are astonished at the amount of bitterness and anger that French has unleashed in her novels *The Women's Room* and *The Bleeding Heart.* Disappointed with French's second novel, *The Bleeding Heart,* Adams writes: "My own view is that French is simply too angry to write well or to think clearly, and that only a profound change in the world would change or pacify her. A commendable stance, surely, but not one that makes for very good novels. Which is to say that her politics are superior to her fiction."

Publishers Weekly's Barbara Bannon explains that "French's own life, widely publicized when *The Women's Room* was published, began in a poor family of Polish descent. It included marriage before she finished college; a son and daughter now adults; and a determination to go back on her own and finish her education—involving B.A. and M.A. degrees from Hofstra and a Ph.D. from Harvard. The marriage was a disaster and desperately hard to break out of. Now she says of her ex-husband, 'I saw him at my daughter's wedding, and that was enough to last for ten years. When I think of living with a man again I have the same nightmare of being back living with my husband, and I think, "O God, I've married him again".'"

In 1956, French read Simone de Beauvoir's *The Second Sex,* a book considered by many to be the first text of the current feminist movement with its basic theme that women must be true to themselves and not live through men. This book greatly impressed and influenced her, especially, French told *CA,* "the sections on women writers who kept postponing doing their literary work." It was soon after this that she began to write short stories herself in order to express her own feelings and frustrations.

Although French insists her novels are not necessarily autobiographical, she is quick to add as she did for *People* magazine's Gail Jennes that "there is nothing in [*The Women's Room*] I've not felt."

And when asked why she continues "to deal with men, especially if her own novels are not autobiographical, as she insists" French told Phillips that "whatever my inclinations were, and however I lead my life, I would still be writing about women and men, because women and men live on this Earth. And I assume that the Earth is going to go on being peopled."

In an interview with Nan Robertson of the *New York Times,* French remarks: "Men believe men are central to women's lives and they're not—even when they become economically central, even psychologically, when we have to please them. Children are the center of a woman's life. Work is always central. When you have children, they become your work, your opus. . . . Viewed by men, a woman peeling potatoes is funny. A woman hanging clothes on a line is automatically funny. If men don't trivialize our lives they make them comic.''

French explains this premise in greater detail to Phillips. She tells him: "Contempt for women is not an accident, it is not a by-product of our culture. It is the heart. The culture is founded on it. It is the essential central core; without it, the culture would fall apart.''

Although many readers might disagree, Phillips feels French has faith that someday things might change in the area of man and woman relationships. Phillips writes: "French rejects male biology as the reason for such sexual separation today, and thus holds out a hope that whatever was done can someday be undone. It just takes some shock treatment, like maybe *The Women's Room* and *The Bleeding Heart*.''

Suzanne Fields writes in the *Detroit News* that "just as feminists have identified and denounced misogyny in books written by men, it behooves us all to arraign those books which exude a destructive hatred of men. Such feelings can infect and calcify in dangerous ways. To intersperse torrid sex scenes with tirades against men for the imagined crime of being men merely allows villains and victims to exchange places. The rules of the game, weighted as they are to create those villains and victims, go unchallenged.''

Weeks is one critic who disagrees with Phillips' statement about French's novel and others of the same genre. As she comments in her review in the *Washington Post Book World*: "The trouble with feminist novels is that politics gets in the way of fiction, and sorting out the resulting reactions is like extracting Brer Rabbit from the briar patch. In this respect *The Women's Room* is no exception. The novel's basic thesis—that there is little or no foreseeable future for coexistence between men and women—is powerfully stated, but still invokes a lonely chaos repellent to most readers. In almost every other way, though, the novel is exceptional; and despite its length, for a novel of ideas it is easy to read.''

Although the reviews of French's *The Women's Room* seem truly mixed, the reader response has been tremendous. Over four million copies have been sold since its original publication in 1977, and the book was on the best-seller list for nearly a year in hardcover and another year in paperback. In addition, countless women readers have written to French to say that what she wrote in the book is their truth.

Bannon feels that it is this "genuine sympathy for other women caught in life situations, trivial or deadly serious, for which they were never prepared that made Marilyn French's first novel, *The Women's Room*, such a breakthrough bestseller in hardcover and paperback.'' And in a previous issue of *Publishers Weekly*, another reviewer writes that this book "speaks from the heart to women everywhere. It is as if French had been taking notes for twenty years. Her dialogue, her characterizations, her knowledge of the changing relationships, sexual and otherwise, between men and women in a complex world of shifting values, are all extraordinary. . . . It is, French says, women who best support women in crisis times.''

In her interview with Jennes, French explains the reader's reaction this way: "Books, movies, TV teach us false images of ourselves. We learn to expect fairy-tale lives. Ordinary women's daily lives—unlike men's—have not been the stuff of literature. I wanted to legitimize it and I purposely chose the most ordinary lives [for the characters in the book]—not the worst cases. . . . I wanted to break the mold of conventional women's novels.''

Bannon suggests still another reason for French's popularity: "In both of French's novels women's commitment to raising children as one of the most important elements in their lives is clearly recognized and accepted as fact, and it is her understanding of this, her refusal to look down on such a traditional women's role, that makes her novels accessible to many women who might not relate to a more formalized 'feminist' position.''

French's more recent novel, *The Bleeding Heart*, is receiving the same mixed reviews as French's first novel. According to Phillips, the book "has so far been subjected to ruthless surgery by critics, who dismiss it as more polemics than passion, boxed with cardboard characters, and not especially well written at that.'' French explains to the *Chicago Tribune* that while she is a bit surprised, she is not worried. "I thought it would be loved,'' French confessed. "The criticism was hard to take the first week or so. Then I remembered that *The Women's Room* got the same criticism initially.''

French told Phillips she feels that because of the types of books she writes and often the reaction that they receive, many "people think I cause divorces because women are reading my books. A lot of men like to think that it's all *me*, that it is all my doing. They don't understand where women are coming from—because they don't listen to women, ever.''

Phillips writes that "Marilyn French seems neither concerned nor likely to moderate her vilification of men simply to heal the wounds of ostracism. . . . Mankind is the enemy, after all, and French cannot give up an inch in her crusade against male supremacy. Never.''

The Women's Room was produced as a "made-for-TV-movie,'' 1980.

AVOCATIONAL INTERESTS: Amateur musician; parties, cooking, travel.

BIOGRAPHICAL/CRITICAL SOURCES: Times Literary Supplement, February 18, 1977, April 21, 1978, May 9, 1980; *Publishers Weekly*, August 29, 1977, August 21, 1978, March 7, 1980; *Washington Post Book World*, October 9, 1977, March 9, 1980; *New York Times Book Review*, October 16, 1977, November 13, 1977; *New York Times*, October 27, 1977, March 9, 1980, March 10, 1980; *Library Journal*, November 15, 1977; *Ms.*, January, 1978, April, 1979; *People*, February 20, 1978; *Virginia Quarterly Review*, Volume 54, number 2, 1978; *Contemporary Literary Criticism*, Volume X, Gale, 1979; *Chicago Tribune Book World*, March 9, 1980; *Detroit News*, April 20, 1980; *Chicago Tribune*, May 4, 1980; *Washington Post*, May 7, 1980.

—*Sketch by Margaret Mazurkiewicz*

*   *   *

FRIEDMAN, B(ernard) H(arper) 1926-

PERSONAL: Born July 27, 1926, in New York, N.Y.; son of Leonard and Madeline (Uris) Friedman; married Abby Noselson, 1948; children: Jackson, Daisy. *Education:* Cornell University, B.A., 1948. *Home:* 435 East 52nd St., New York, N.Y. 10022. *Agent:* Gunther Stuhlmann, P.O. Box 276, Becket, Mass. 01223.

CAREER: University Place Apartments, New York City, residential manager, 1948-49; Cross & Brown Co., New York City, real estate broker, 1949-50; Uris Buildings Corp., New York City, vice-president and director, 1950-63; full-time writer, 1963—; Cornell University, Ithaca, N.Y., lecturer in creative writing, 1966-67; Fine Arts Work Center,

Provincetown, Mass., director and staff consultant, 1968—. Trustee of Whitney Museum of American Art, 1961—. Member of advisory council, Cornell University College of Arts and Sciences, 1968—, and Herbert F. Johnson Museum, 1972—. Founding member, Fiction Collective, 1973—. *Military service:* U.S. Navy, 1944-46. *Awards, honors:* Fels Award, Coordinating Council of Literary Magazines, for "Moving in Place."

WRITINGS—Novels: *Circles*, Fleet, 1962, published as *I Need to Love*, Macfadden Books, 1963; *Yarborough*, World Publishing, 1964; *Whispers*, Ithaca House, 1972; *Museum*, Fiction Collective, 1974; *Almost a Life*, Viking, 1975; *The Polygamist*, Atlantic-Little, Brown, 1981.

Biographies: (Editor) *School of New York: Some Younger Artists*, Grove, 1959; (with Barbara Guest) *Robert Goodnough*, Musee de Poche, 1962; *Lee Krasner*, Whitechapel Gallery, 1965; *Jackson Pollock: Energy Made Visible*, McGraw, 1972; *Alfonso Ossorio*, Abrams, 1973; *Salvatore Scarpitta*, Contemporary Arts Museum (Houston), 1977; *Gertrude Vanderbilt Whitney*, Doubleday, 1978; *Myron Stout*, Whitney, 1980.

WORK IN PROGRESS: Coming Close, a collection of "autobiographical fictions."

SIDELIGHTS: B. H. Friedman's writings frequently concern the fine arts and those who are involved in them. His novels *Circles* and *Museum* are based upon his own experiences in the art world while his biographies and monographs are of prominent artists. As Irving Malin writes in his review of *Museum*, "Friedman's knowledge of art (and the art world) is apparent on every page. [He] gives us an insider's novel."

Friedman told *CA* that during the fifteen years he was in the real estate business he contributed many articles to literary and art magazines. "When I left business to write full time," he says, "I discovered that I did not write any more than previously but that the quality of the writing improved with greater concentration and more time for contemplation."

BIOGRAPHICAL/CRITICAL SOURCES: Detroit News, August 6, 1972; *Saturday Review*, September 9, 1972; *Observer*, February 11, 1973; *New Statesman*, February 16, 1973; *Times Literary Supplement*, November 9, 1973; *New York Times Book Review*, October 13, 1974, August 24, 1975, December 24, 1978; *New Republic*, October 19, 1974; *Christian Science Monitor*, July 9, 1975; *New Yorker*, September 8, 1975; *Hudson Review*, winter, 1975; *Carolina Quarterly*, spring, 1976; *Contemporary Literary Criticism*, Volume VII, Gale, 1977; *New York Times*, December 8, 1978.

*   *   *

FRIEDMAN, Irving S(igmund) 1915-

PERSONAL: Born January 31, 1915, in New York, N.Y.; son of Sigmund and Sara (Tobor) Friedman; married Edna M. Edelman, September 27, 1938; children: Barbara Ellen (Mrs. Reid Peyton Chambers), Kenneth Sigmund, John Stephen. *Education:* City College (now City College of the City University of New York), A.B., 1935; Columbia University, M.A., 1937, Ph.D., 1940. *Home:* 6620 Fernwood Ct., Bethesda, Md. 20034; and 860 UN Plaza, New York, N.Y. *Office:* 399 Park Ave., New York, N.Y. 10022.

CAREER: Assistant to trade commissioner, Government of India, 1940-41; U.S. Department of Treasury, Office of the Secretary, Washington, D.C., economist in the Middle East, China, India, and other locations, 1941-45, assistant director

of monetary research, 1946; International Monetary Fund, Washington, D.C., head of research department in United States-Canada Division, 1946-48, policy assistant to deputy managing director, 1948-51, director of exchange restrictions department, 1951-64; International Bank for Reconstruction and Development (World Bank), Washington, D.C., economic adviser to president, chairman of Economic Committee, and member of president's council, 1964-70, professor-in-residence, 1971-74, consultant, 1974—; First National City Bank, New York, N.Y., senior advisor for international operations, 1974—. Visiting fellow at Yale University and All Souls College, Oxford University, 1970-71; guest lecturer, Vatican University. Special responsibility for staff work, National Advisory Council on International Monetary and Financial Problems; chairman, Center of Concern, beginning 1971. *Member:* Society for International Development (vice-president and treasurer), American Economic Association. *Awards, honors:* M.A., Oxford University.

WRITINGS: British Relations with China: 1931-1939, Institute of Pacific Relations (New York), 1940, reprinted, AMS Press, 1976; (with Margaret M. Garritsen) *Foreign Economic Problems of Postwar United States*, American Institute of Pacific Relations, 1947; *Foreign Exchange Control and the Evolution of the International Payments System*, International Monetary Fund (Washington, D.C.), 1958; *Inflation: A World-Wide Disaster*, Houghton, 1973, published as *Inflation: A Growing World-Wide Disaster*, Anchor Press, 1975; *The Emerging Role of Private Banks in the Developing World*, Citicorp (New York), 1977. Contributor to *Encyclopaedia Britannica;* contributor of articles on finance and economics to numerous publications, including *World Development, World Today, Canadian Political Science Quarterly, Colorado Quarterly*, and *National Bank of Belgium Bulletin.†*

*   *   *

FRIEDMAN, (Eve) Rosemary (Tibber) 1929- (Rosemary Tibber; Robert Tibber)

PERSONAL: Born February 5, 1929, in London, England; daughter of Maurice (a businessman) and Priscilla (Deyong) Tibber; married Dennis Friedman (a medical practitioner); children: Susan Caroline, Louise Antoinette, Charlotte Eve, Emma Pandora. *Education:* Attended Queen's College and University College, London. *Religion:* Jewish. *Home:* 2 St. Katherine's Precinct, Regents Park NW1 4HH, England. *Agent:* Debbie Owen, 78 Narrow St., London E.14, England.

CAREER: Fiction writer. *Member:* Society of Authors, P.E.N., White House Club.

WRITINGS: (Under name Rosemary Tibber) *Practice Makes Perfect*, Hodder & Stoughton, 1969; *The Life Situation*, Barrie & Jenkins, 1977; *The Long Hot Summer*, Hutchinson, 1980.

Under pseudonym Robert Tibber; published by Hodder & Stoughton, except as indicated: *No White Coat*, 1957; *Love on My List*, 1959, reprinted, Chivers, 1976; *We All Fall Down*, 1960; *Patients of a Saint*, 1961, reprinted, Chivers, 1976; *The Fraternity*, 1963; *The Commonplace Day*, 1964; *Aristide* (children's book), Hutchinson, 1966, Dial, 1967; (contributor) Philip Longworth, editor, *Confrontations with Judaism* (symposium), Anthony Blond, 1967.

Contributor of short stories to *Woman's Journal, Housewife, Good Housekeeping, Ladies' Home Journal, Woman and Beauty*, and *Cosmopolitan*.

AVOCATIONAL INTERESTS: Swimming.

FRIEDRICH, Otto (Alva) 1929-

PERSONAL: Born February 3, 1929, in Boston, Mass.; son of Carl Joachim (a professor) and Lenore (Pelham) Friedrich; married Priscilla Boughton, April 13, 1950; children: Elizabeth, Margaret, Nicholas, Amelia, Charles Anthony. *Education:* Harvard University, A.B. (magna cum laude), 1948. *Politics:* Independent. *Home:* 569 Bayville Rd., Locust Valley, N.Y. *Office:* Time, Time, Inc., Time and Life Bldg., New York, N.Y. 10020.

CAREER: Stars and Stripes, Darmstadt, Germany, copy editor, 1950-52; United Press, reporter and copy editor in London, England, and Paris, France, 1952-54; *New York Daily News,* New York City, copy editor, 1954-57; *Newsweek,* New York City, assistant foreign editor, 1957-62; *Saturday Evening Post,* New York City, foreign editor, 1962-63, assistant managing editor, 1963-65, managing editor, 1965-69; *Time,* New York City, senior editor, 1971—, national editor, 1978—. *Awards, honors:* George Polk Memorial Award for best book on journalism, Long Island University, 1971, for *Decline and Fall.*

WRITINGS: The Poor in Spirit, Little, Brown, 1952; *The Loner,* Crown, 1964; *Ring Lardner,* University of Minnesota Press, 1965; *Decline and Fall,* Harper, 1970; *Before the Deluge: A Portrait of Berlin in the 1920's,* Harper, 1972; *The Rose Garden,* Lippincott, 1972; *Going Crazy,* Simon & Schuster, 1976; *Clover: The Tragic Love of Clover and Henry Adams and Their Brilliant Life in America's Gilded Age,* Simon & Schuster, 1979.

Children's books; with wife, Priscilla B. Friedrich; published by Lothrop, except as indicated: *The Easter Bunny That Overslept,* 1957; *Clean Clarence,* 1959; *Sir Alva and the Wicked Wizard,* 1960; *The Marshmallow Ghosts,* 1961; *Noah Shark's Ark,* A. S. Barnes, 1961; *The Wishing Well in the Woods,* 1962; *The Christmas Star,* A. S. Barnes, 1962; *The April Umbrella,* 1963; *The League of Unusual Animals,* Steck, 1965.

Contributor to *Esquire, McCall's, Reader's Digest, Harper's, Yale Review,* and other publications.

WORK IN PROGRESS: The End of the World.

SIDELIGHTS: In *Decline and Fall,* Otto Friedrich recounts the demise of the *Saturday Evening Post,* a venerated weekly magazine that was, in the words of *Esquire*'s Malcolm Muggeridge, "an institution." Muggeridge adds that "for a publication with such a record to founder attracted more than the usual amount of attention. It was front-page news, a story ardently covered." From first-hand experience (Friedrich was an editor at the *Post* from 1962 to its collapse in 1969), the author details the financial struggles and corporate infighting and mismanagement that characterized the publication's last years. "I had come to the *Post* in 1962 in the mistaken belief that it would be a quiet and congenial place to work," Friedrich writes in *Harper's,* "and I soon found that its leading executives were engaged in a ferocious struggle for power."

Throughout his account of the futile and often comic corporate attempts to salvage the *Post,* Friedrich displays "extraordinary success at characterization of his colleagues," John Brooks comments in the *New York Times Book Review.* "His portraits of his fellow-editors and executives are as vivid and living as they are sardonic." A *Newsweek* critic asserts, "Friedrich's achievement is to have captured the entire rogue's gallery and turned them into characters in a kind of novel." In *Best Sellers,* William H. Archer offers a similar assessment, "Adding a definite human dimension to

the portrait of every participant in the drama, Mr. Friedrich makes this primarily a story of people . . . as well as a record of loans, statistics, fast bucks and lawsuits."

Before the Deluge, Friedrich's chronicle of the political and cultural events in Berlin between the World Wars, has won similar acclaim. According to Russell Barnes in the *Detroit News:* "Berlin in the 1920's was probably the most exciting city culturally and politically that the world had seen since Renaissance Florence and Rome. Its music, theatre, night life, films and science outshone Paris, London or New York. . . . But beneath the glittering upper levels of society, the masses of ordinary people were hungry, miserable, and desperate. Few realized it, but Germany was having its last big fling. The stage was being set for World War II." Barnes and others praise Friedrich for providing a vivid and informative account of this dramatic period in history. "In novelistic fashion, he intersperses his account of political events with cultural ones and tidbits about life, sin and scandal in this wicked city," the *Washington Post*'s Wolf Von Eckardt explains. The reviewer adds that "Friedrich paints his portrait of the city . . . with bold, vivid dabs of anecdote" which make the book come "alive."

On the other hand, Christopher Lehmann-Haupt of the *New York Times* finds "something disappointing about [*Before the Deluge*]." While he agrees that Friedrich's "account of the familiar political events is unusually vivid," he argues that "most of what is here has been told before, and can be read in well-known books on the period." However, Von Eckardt remarks that although "the history is familiar, . . . Friedrich brings to it all much fascinating new detail and plausible insights."

Critical reaction to *Clover* has been mixed. In this biography of the wife of author Henry Adams, Friedrich attempts to dispel the mystery surrounding her suicide. Katherine Winton Evans of the *Washington Post Book World* notes, "Except for Clover's published letters (out of print and hard to come by) and the . . . statue at her unmarked grave (hard to find in Rock Creek Cemetary), all that survive are questions." Edmund Morris outlines the questions in the *New York Times Book Review:* "Why, after 13 years of brilliant social life and outwardly happy marriage, did Clover kill herself? Why did Adams refuse ever to speak of her again, even to the extent of leaving a 20-year gap in his autobiography?"

Evans and Morris find that although Friedrich explores these questions, he fails to provide any solutions. Morris suggests that "Friedrich is a prisoner of his material. The fact is that, for all his prodigious industry, there is very little documentary evidence of how Clover looked, thought, loved and suffered." He explains: "She left no children and did no enduring work. . . . Even the letters to her father, which chronicle every week of her married life, concern themselves almost entirely with details of dress, decoration and society gossip."

However, Jane Majeski believes the "dismal story" of the Adamses' marriage and Clover's suicide is "no more than a framework" upon which Friedrich creates "a thoroughly enjoyable portrait of American society during the late 19th century." She continues, "The substance [of Friedrich's work] is to be found in his entertaining and informative descriptions of important events and personalities of the age, of which the Adamses were close observers by virtue of their birth and wealth." In this context, the somewhat frivolous information contained in Clover's letters to her father takes on new significance as "Friedrich judiciously mixes serious and weighty historical matters with gossip and trivia of the time.'' Majeski concludes that "*Clover* is a sympathetic and compelling evocation of the spirit of an age.''

BIOGRAPHICAL/CRITICAL SOURCES: Harper's, December, 1969; *New York Times Book Review,* May 31, 1970, October 28, 1979; *Best Sellers,* July 1, 1970; *Newsweek,* July 6, 1970; *Nation,* September 14, 1970; *Esquire,* October, 1970; *Washington Post,* May 4, 1972; *New York Times,* May 5, 1972, October 19, 1979; *Detroit News,* May 30, 1972; *Washington Post Book World,* November 4, 1979; *Chicago Tribune Book World,* November 18, 1979.

—*Sketch by Denise Gottis*

*   *   *

FROELICH, Robert E.   1929-

PERSONAL: Born July 24, 1929, in St. Louis, Mo.; son of Edwin J. (a physician) and M. G. (Hastings) Froelich; married F. Marian Bishop (a professor), September 5, 1954; children: Edwin, Krisan. *Education:* Washington University, A.B., 1951, M.D., 1955. *Office address:* Department of Psychiatry, School of Primary Medical Care, University of Alabama, P.O. Box 1247, Huntsville, Ala. 35807.

CAREER: Medical College of Georgia School of Medicine, Augusta, resident, 1958-61; University of Missouri, Columbia, assistant professor of psychiatry, 1961-67; University of Southern California, Los Angeles, assistant professor, 1967-68; University of Missouri, associate professor, 1968-69; University of Oklahoma, College of Medicine, Norman, associate professor, 1969-72, professor of psychiatry and behavioral science, beginning 1972; currently member of faculty, department of psychiatry, School of Primary Medical Care, University of Alabama, Huntsville. *Military service:* U.S. Army Air Force, Medical Corps, 1956-58; became captain.

WRITINGS: (With wife, F. Marian Bishop) *Medical Interviewing: A Programmed Manual,* Mosby, 1969, 3rd edition published as *Clinical Interviewing Skills: A Programmed Manual for Data Gathering, Evaluation, and Patient Management,* 1977; (editor) *Handbook for the Psychiatry Clerkship,* [Columbia, Mo.], 1969; (editor) *Film Reviews in Psychiatry, Psychology, and Mental Health: A Descriptive and Evaluative Listing of Educational and Instructional Films,* Pierian, 1974; (with others) *Communication in the Dental Office: A Programmed Manual for the Dental Professional,* Mosby, 1976.†

*   *   *

FRYE, Richard N(elson)   1920-

PERSONAL: Born January 10, 1920, in Birmingham, Ala.; son of Nels and Lillie (Hagman) Frye; married Barbara York, May 29, 1948 (divorced, 1973); married Eden Naby, 1975; children: (first marriage) Jeffrey Lawrence, Rebecca, Robert Granger. *Education:* University of Illinois, A.B., 1939; Harvard University, M.A., 1940, Ph.D., 1946; School of Oriental and African Studies, postdoctoral study, 1946-47. *Home:* 86 Beech St., Belmont, Mass. *Office:* 546 Widener Library, Harvard University, Cambridge, Mass. 02138.

CAREER: Harvard University, Cambridge, Mass., Aga Khan Professor of Iranian, 1957—. Visiting professor at Frankfurt University, Frankfurt, Germany, 1958-59, and University of Hamburg, 1968-69. Director of Asia Institute, Pahlavi University, Shiraz, Iran, 1969-74. Has lectured in France, the Soviet Union, Iran, and Afghanistan, and conducted expeditions to Iran, Afghanistan, and Soviet Central Asia. *Military service:* U.S. Army, Office of Strategic Ser-

vices, 1941-45. *Member:* American Academy of Arts and Sciences.

WRITINGS: Notes on the Pre-Islamic Coinage of Transoxiana, American Numismatic Society, 1949; (editor) *The Near East and the Great Powers,* Harvard University Press, 1950; (translator from the Armenian with R. P. Blake) *History of the Nation of the Archers,* Harvard University Press, 1952; *History of Bukhara,* Mediaeval Society of America, 1954; *Iran,* Holt, 1954; (editor) *Islam and the West,* Harvard University Press, 1957; *Persia,* Allen & Unwin, 1962, published as *The Heritage of Persia,* World Publishing, 1963; *Medieval Bukhara,* University of Oklahoma Press, 1967; *The Sasanian Remains of Qasr-iAbu Nasr,* Harvard University Press, 1973; *The Golden Age of Persia,* Weidenfeld & Nicolson, 1975; *Islamic Iran and Central Asia,* Variorum, 1979.

Contributor of more than 120 articles to English, German, Russian, and Iranian journals. Member of editorial board, *Journal of the Asia Institute* (Iran).

*   *   *

FULLER, Reginald H(orace)   1915-

PERSONAL: Born March 24, 1915, in Horsham, England; came to the United States in 1955; son of Horace (an agricultural engineer) and Cora (Heath) Fuller; married Ilse Barda (formerly a coordinator of Christian education), June 17, 1942; children: Caroline (Mrs. Robert E. Sloat), Rosemary (Mrs. John G. Bazuzi), Sarah. *Education:* Peterhouse, Cambridge, B.A. (first class honors), 1937, M.A., 1941; Evangelisches Stift, additional study, 1938-39. *Home and office:* Virginia Theological Seminary, Alexandria, Va. 22304.

CAREER: Ordained deacon of Church of England, 1940, priest, 1941; curate in Bakewell, England, 1940-43, Ashbourne-W-Mapleton, England, 1943-45, and Birmingham, England, 1945-50; Queen's College, Birmingham, lecturer in theology, 1946-50; St. David's College, Lampeter, Wales, professor of theology, 1950-55; Seabury-Western Theological Seminary, Evanston, Ill., professor of New Testament languages and literature, 1955-66; Union Theological Seminary, New York, N.Y., Baldwin Professor of Sacred Literature, 1966-72; Virginia Theological Seminary, Alexandria, professor of New Testament, 1972—. Adjunct professor, Columbia University, 1969-72; visiting professor at Graduate Theological Union (Berkeley, Calif.), 1975, and College of Emmanuel and St. Chad (Saskatoon, Sask.), 1978. Examining chaplain to the Bishop of Monmouth, 1950-55; canon theologian of British Honduras, 1968—; Bishop's commissary for the United States, 1968—. Member of Study Commission, World Council of Churches, 1957—; member of Episcopal-Lutheran Conversations, 1969-73, Anglican-Lutheran Conversations, 1970-73, 1977—, and Lutheran-Catholic Dialogue Task Force, 1971-73, 1975-78. *Awards, honors:* Schofield Prize and Crosse Studentship, Cambridge University, 1938; S.T.D., General Theological Seminary, 1960, and Philadelphia Divinity School, 1962; American Association of Theological Schools fellowship, 1961.

WRITINGS: (With Richard P. C. Hanson) *The Church of Rome: A Dissuasive,* S.C.M. Press, 1948, revised edition, Seabury, 1960; *The Mission and Achievement of Jesus: An Examination of the Presuppositions of New Testament Theology,* Allenson, 1954; (with G. E. Wright) *The Book of the Acts of God: Christian Scholarship Interprets the Bible,* Doubleday, 1957, published as *The Book of the Acts of God: Contemporary Scholarship Interprets the Bible,* 1960; *What Is Liturgical Preaching?,* S.C.M. Press, 1957, 2nd edition, 1960; *Luke's Witness to Jesus Christ,* Association Press,

1958; *The New Testament in Current Study,* Scribner, 1962; *Interpreting the Miracles,* Westminster, 1963; *The Foundations of New Testament Christology,* Scribner, 1965; (with B. Rice) *Christianity and the Affluent Society,* Hodder & Stoughton, 1966, Eerdmans, 1967; *A Critical Introduction to the New Testament,* Duckworth, 1966; *Lent with the Liturgy,* S.P.C.K., 1968; *The Formation of the Resurrection Narratives,* Macmillan, 1971; *Preaching the New Lectionary,* Liturgical Press, 1974; *The Use of the Bible in Preaching,* Bible Reading Fellowship, 1980.

Translator: Dietrich Bonhoeffer, *The Cost of Discipleship,* Macmillan, 1948; *Kerygma and Myth I: A Theological Debate,* Macmillan, 1953, revised edition, Harper, 1961; Bonhoeffer, *Prisoner for God,* Macmillan, 1954; Rudolf K. Bultmann, *Primitive Christianity in Its Contemporary Setting,* Longmans, Green (Toronto), 1956; Joachim Jeremias, *Unknown Sayings of Jesus,* Macmillan, 1957; Walther von Loewenich, *Modern Roman Catholicism,* Macmillan (London), 1959; Bonhoeffer, *Letters and Papers from Prison,* Macmillan (New York), 1959; *Kerygma and Myth II,* S.P.C.K., 1962; (with wife, Ilse Fuller) Helmut Flender, *St. Luke, Theologian of Redemptive History,* Fortress, 1967; (and author of introduction with I. Fuller) J. Moltmann and J. Weissbach, *Two Studies in the Theology of Bonhoeffer,* Scribner, 1967; (with I. Fuller) Albert Schweitzer, *Reverence for Life,* Harper, 1969; (with I. Fuller) G. Bornkamm, *The New Testament: A Guide to Its Writings,* Fortress, 1973; (with I. Fuller) E. Schweizer, *The Holy Spirit,* Fortress, 1980.

Contributor: *Evangelische Weihnachten,* Furch Verlag, 1949; *A Theological Wordbook of the Bible,* S.C.M. Press, 1950; *The Place of Bonhoeffer,* Association Press, 1962; *Conflicting Images of Man,* Seabury, 1966. Contributor to *Encyclopaedia Britannica,* 1960, *Hastings Dictionary of the Bible,* 1963, and to theological and church journals.

BIOGRAPHICAL/CRITICAL SOURCES: Times Literary Supplement, March 23, 1967.

*   *   *

FUSSELL, G(eorge) E(dwin)   1889-

PERSONAL: Born September 10, 1889, in Weymouth, Dorset, England; son of George William (a brewer) and Emma Maria (Pragnell) Fussell; married Kathleen Rosemary Turner (a part-time librarian), November 22, 1939; children: Helen Rosemary. *Education:* Attended London School of Economics and Political Science. *Home:* 55 York Rd., Sudbury, Suffolk C010 6NF, England.

CAREER: British War Office, Whitehall, London, England, clerk, 1906-09; affiliated with Ministry of Agriculture, Whitehall, London, 1909-49. *Member:* Royal Historical Society (fellow), Economic History Society, Agricultural History Society (United States), German Agricultural History Society, British Agricultural History Society (founder; three-term

member of executive committee), Suffolk Local History Society. *Awards, honors:* D.Litt., University of Exeter, 1972.

WRITINGS: Chronological List of Early Agricultural Books in the Ministry of Agriculture Library, H.M.S.O., 1930; *The Exploration of England: A Select Bibliography of Travel and Topography, 1570-1815,* Mitre Press, 1935; (editor) *Robert Loder's Farm Accounts, 1610-1620,* Royal Historical Society, 1936; *Farming Systems from Elizabethan to Victorian Days in the North and East Ridings of Yorkshire,* City of York, 1944; *The Old English Farming Books,* Crosby Lockwood, Volume I: *Fitzherbert to Tull, 1523-1730,* 1947, reprinted, Aberdeen Rare Books, 1978, Volume II: *Tull to Board of Agriculture, 1731-1792,* 1950; *Village Life in the 18th Century,* Littlebury & Co., 1947; *Tolpuddle to T.U.C.: A Century of Farm Labourer's Politics,* Windsor Press, 1948; (editor with wife, Kathleen R. Fussell, and author of two introductions) Hugh Plat, *Delightes for Ladies,* Crosby Lockwood, 1948; *The English Rural Labourer: His Home, Furniture, Clothing and Food from Elizabethan to Victorian Days,* Batchworth Press, 1949, reprinted, Greenwood Press, 1975.

(Contributor) *Bibliography of British History: The 18th Century, 1714-1789,* Clarendon Press, 1951; *The Farmer's Tools, 1500-1900,* Melrose, 1952; (with K. R. Fussell) *The English Countrywoman: A Farmhouse Social History, 1500-1900,* Melrose, 1953, reprinted, Benjamin Blam, 1971; (with K. R. Fussell) *The English Countryman: His Life and Work, 1500-1900,* Melrose, 1955; (author of introduction) *English Farming Past and Present,* 6th edition (Fussell was not associated with earlier editions), Quadrangle, 1961; *Farming Technique from Prehistoric to Modern Times,* Pergamon, 1966; *The English Dairy Farmer, 1500-1900,* Cass & Co., 1966; (contributor) Melvin Kranzberg, editor, *Technology in Western Civilization,* Oxford University Press, 1967; *The Story of Farming,* Permagon, 1969.

Crop Nutrition: Science and Practice before Liebig, Coronado Press, 1971; *The Classical Tradition in West European Farming,* David & Charles, 1972; *Jethro Tull: His Influence on Mechanized Agriculture,* Osprey Publishing, 1973; *James Ward, R.A., Animal Painter, 1769-1859, and His England,* M. Joseph, 1974; *Farms, Farmers and Society: Systems of Food Production and Population Numbers,* Coronado Press, 1976. Also contributor to volumes four and five of *A History of Technology,* edited by Charles Singer, 1958, to the new edition of *Chambers's Encyclopaedia,* and to *Encyclopaedia Britannica.* Contributor of several articles to learned and professional periodicals in England, Germany, and the United States.

WORK IN PROGRESS: Old English Farming Books, Volume III: *1792-1838,* Volume IV: *1839-1900.*

AVOCATIONAL INTERESTS: Walking in rural districts and travel in foreign countries.

G

GADNEY, Reg 1941-

PERSONAL: Born January 20, 1941, in Cross Hills, England; son of Bernard C. (a school teacher) and Margaret A. M. (Lilley) Gadney; married Annette Kobak (a writer), July 16, 1966; children: Guy, Amy. *Education:* St. Catharine's College, Cambridge, M.A., 1966. *Office:* Royal College of Art, London, England.

CAREER: Massachusetts Institute of Technology, Cambridge, instructor in architecture and research fellow at School of Architecture and Planning, 1966-67; National Film Theatre, London, England, deputy controller, 1967-69; Royal College of Art, London, tutor, 1969—. Consultant to American Arts Documentation Centre; editorial advisor to Paladin Books, Granada Publishing, and Lion & Unicorn Press. *Military service:* British Army, Coldstream Guards, assistant to naval, military, and air attache at British Embassy in Oslo, 1959-62; became lieutenant. *Member:* Marylebone Cricket Club.

WRITINGS—Novels, except as indicated: *Drawn Blanc,* Heinemann, 1970, Coward, 1971; *Somewhere in England,* St. Martin's, 1971; *Seduction of a Tall Man,* Heinemann, 1972; *Something Worth Fighting For,* Heinemann, 1974; *Victoria,* Coward, 1975; *The Last Hours before Dawn,* Heinemann, 1976; *Constable and His World* (nonfiction), Norton, 1976; *The Champagne Marxist,* Hutchinson, 1977; *The Cage,* Coward, 1977.

Also author of museum catalogues and of a television film, "Forgive Our Foolish Ways," British Broadcasting Corp., 1970. Contributor to *Granta, Image, Broadsheet, Mosaic, Vou, Cambridge Review, London, Spectator,* and *Leonardo.* Editor, *Granta;* honorary editor, *Leonardo.*

* * *

GAFFNEY, (Merrill) Mason 1923-

PERSONAL: Born October 18, 1923, in White Plains, N.Y.; son of Matthew Page and Laura (Clarke) Gaffney; married Estelle Pao An Lau, March 8, 1952 (divorced, 1968); married Ruth Letita Atwood, September 22, 1973; children: (first marriage) Bradford Clarke, Ann Reed, Stuart Morgan; (second marriage) Laura Atwood, Patricia Mason, Matthew Rollin. *Education:* Attended Harvard University, 1941-43, and University of Virginia, 1943-44; Reed College, B.A., 1948; University of California, Berkeley, Ph.D., 1956. *Home:* 3040 Tyler St., Riverside, Calif. 92503. *Office:* Department of Economics, University of California, Riverside, Calif.

CAREER: University of Oregon, Eugene, instructor in economics, 1953-54; North Carolina State College (now North Carolina State University at Raleigh), Raleigh, instructor, 1954-55, assistant professor of economics, 1955-58; University of Missouri—Columbia, associate professor, 1958-61, professor of agricultural economics, 1961-62; University of Wisconsin—Milwaukee, professor of economics, 1962-71, chairman of department, 1963-65; Resources for the Future, Inc., Washington, D.C., visiting scholar, 1969-71, senior research associate, 1971-73; Economic Policy Analysis Institute of British Columbia, Victoria, director, 1973-76; University of California, Riverside, professor of economics, 1976—. Visiting professor, University of California, Los Angeles, 1967-68. *Military service:* U.S. Army Air Forces, 1943-46.

MEMBER: American Economic Association, Phi Beta Kappa. *Awards, honors:* Ford Foundation faculty research fellowship, 1957-58; Jesse H. Neal Award for business journalism, 1960; grants from Lincoln Foundation, 1963-64, and Robert Schalkenbach Foundation, 1967, 1968, and 1968-69.

WRITINGS: Concepts of Financial Maturity of Timber and Other Assets, Department of Agricultural Economics, North Carolina State College, 1957; (editor and contributor) *Extractive Resources and Taxation,* University of Wisconsin Press, 1967.

Contributor: Alfred Steffund, editor, *Yearbook of Agriculture,* U.S. Government Printing Office, 1958; Marion Clawson and others, editors, *Land Economics Research,* Johns Hopkins Press, 1962; Richard Stauber, editor, *Approaches to the Study of Urbanization,* Governmental Research Center, University of Kansas, 1964; James Dixon, editor, *Air Conservation,* American Association for the Advancement of Science, 1965; Henry Jarrett, editor, *Environmental Quality in a Growing Economy,* Resources for the Future, 1966.

Daniel Holland, editor, *The Assessment of Land Value,* University of Wisconsin Press, 1970; R. G. Putnam, F. J. Taylor, and P. G. Kettle, editors, *A Geography of Urban Places,* Methuen, 1970; Robert S. Ross and William C. Mitchell, editors, *Readings on Public Choice in America,* Markham, 1971; Richard Andrews, editor, *Urban Land Use Policy: The Central City,* Free Press, 1972; Clawson and Harvey S. Perloff, editors, *Modernizing Urban Land Policy,* Johns Hopkins Press, 1973; Robert D. Hamrin and Robert H. Haveman, editors, *The Political Economy of Federal Policy,* Harper, 1973; George Peterson, editor, *Property Tax*

Reform, Urban Institute, 1973; Arthur Lynn, Jr., editor, Property Taxation, Land Use, and Public Policy, University of Wisconsin Press, 1976; George Rohrlich, editor, Environmental Management: Economic and Social Dimensions, Ballinger, 1976; Paul Downing, editor, Local Service Pricing Policies and Their Effect on Urban Spatial Structure, University of British Columbia Press, 1977; Andrew Thompson and Michael Crommelin, editors, Mineral Leasing As an Instrument of Public Policy, University of British Columbia Press, 1977; Richard Lindholm and Lynn, editors, One Hundred Years after Progress and Poverty, University of Wisconsin Press, 1979; R. A. Andelson, editor, Critics of Henry George, Fairleigh Dickinson University Press, 1979. Also contributor to Water Resource Management, edited by Charles J. Meyers and Dan Tarlock.

Also author of government reports; contributor to government reports and proceedings. Contributor to professional journals and to Reader's Digest, Nation, Challenge, Christian Science Monitor, and other publications.

WORK IN PROGRESS: Full Employment on a Small Planet and Full Employment through Active Use of Land and Capital.

*   *   *

GALE, Robert L(ee) 1919-

PERSONAL: Born December 27, 1919, in Des Moines, Iowa; son of Erie Lee (a sales manager) and Miriam (Fisher) Gale; married Maureen Dowd, November 18, 1944; children: John, James, Christine. Education: Dartmouth College, B.A., 1942; Columbia University, M.A., 1947, Ph.D., 1952. Home: 131 Techview Ter., Pittsburgh, Pa. 15213. Office: University of Pittsburgh, Pittsburgh, Pa. 15213.

CAREER: University of Delaware, Newark, instructor, 1949-52; University of Mississippi, University, assistant professor, 1952-56, associate professor, 1956-59; University of Pittsburgh, Pittsburgh, Pa., assistant professor of English, 1959-60, associate professor, 1960-65, professor of American literature, 1965—. Fulbright professor at Oriental Institute, Naples, Italy, 1956-58, and University of Helsinki, 1975. Military service: U.S. Army, Counter Intelligence Corps, 1942-45; became second lieutenant. Member: Modern Language Association of America, Phi Beta Kappa.

WRITINGS: The Caught Image: Figurative Language in the Fiction of Henry James, University of North Carolina Press, 1964; Thomas Crawford, American Sculptor, University of Pittsburgh Press, 1964; Barron's Simplified Approach to Thoreau's "Walden," Barron's, 1965; Plots and Characters in the Fiction of Henry James, Archon, 1965; Barron's Simplified Approach to Ralph Waldo Emerson and Transcendentalism, Barron's, 1966; Barron's Simplified Approach to Crane's "The Red Badge of Courage," Barron's, 1966; Barron's Simplified Approach to "The Grapes of Wrath" by John Steinbeck, Barron's 1966; A Critical Study Guide to James' "The American," Littlefield, 1966.

A Critical Study Guide to James' "The Ambassadors," Littlefield, 1967, published as Pennant Key-Indexed Study Guide to Henry James' "The Ambassadors," Educational Research Associates and Bantam, 1967; A Critical Study Guide to James' "The Turn of the Screw," Littlefield, 1968; A Critical Study Guide to Dreiser's "Sister Carrie," Littlefield, 1968; Plots and Characters in the Fiction and Sketches of Nathaniel Hawthorne, Archon, 1968; Barron's Simplified Approach to Edgar Allan Poe, Barron's, 1969; Plots and Characters in the Fiction and Narrative Poetry of Herman Melville, Archon, 1969; Richard Henry Dana, Jr., Twayne, 1969; A Critical Study Guide to Twain's "Tom Sawyer," Littlefield, 1969; Barron's Simplified Approach to Edith Wharton's "Ethan Frome," Barron's, 1969.

Plots and Characters in the Fiction and Poetry of Edgar Allan Poe, Archon, 1970; (contributor) James Woodress, editor, Eight American Authors, Norton, 1971; Francis Parkman, Twayne, 1973; Plots and Characters in Works of Mark Twain, two volumes, Archon, 1973; Charles Warren Stoddard, Boise State University, 1977; John Hay, G. K. Hall, 1978; Charles Marion Russell, Boise State University, 1979. Editor, "Plots and Characters" series, Archon, 1976—. Contributor, American Literary Scholarship: An Annual, 1977—.

WORK IN PROGRESS: Luke Short, for G. K. Hall; "Ernest Haycox," for Greenwood Press; Henry Wilson Allen, for Popular Culture Press; Theodore Roosevelt, for Boise State University.

*   *   *

GALLAHER, Art, Jr. 1925-

PERSONAL: Born March 22, 1925, in Duncan, Okla.; son of Art and Mildred (Dunnaway) Gallaher; married Dixie Ann Clower, 1950; children: Erin Brynn, Kell Darren. Education: University of Oklahoma, B.A., 1950, M.A., 1951; University of Arizona, Ph.D., 1956. Office: Department of Anthropology, University of Kentucky, Lexington, Ky.

CAREER: University of Houston, Houston, Tex., 1956-62, began as instructor, became associate professor; University of Nebraska, Lincoln, associate professor of anthropology, 1962-63; University of Kentucky, Lexington, associate professor, 1963-67, professor of anthropology and behavioral science, 1967—, chairman of department of anthropology, 1970-72, dean of College of Arts and Sciences, 1972-80, vice-president for academic affairs, 1980—, deputy director of Center for Developmental Change, 1966-70. Military service: U.S. Coast Guard, 1943-46. Member: American Anthropological Association (fellow), American Ethnological Society (councillor, 1968-71), Society for Applied Anthropology (fellow; secretary-treasurer, 1966-71; treasurer, 1971-75; president, 1977-78), Central States Anthropological Society.

WRITINGS: Plainville Fifteen Years Later, Columbia University Press, 1961; (editor) Perspectives in Developmental Changes, University of Kentucky Press, 1968; (editor with Harland Padfield) The Dying Community, University of New Mexico Press, 1980.

Contributor: Philip Olson, editor, America as a Mass Society, Free Press of Glencoe, 1963; A. Vidich, J. Bensman, and M. Stein, editors, Reflections on Community Studies, Wiley, 1964; Wes Meierhenry, editor, Media and Educational Innovation, University of Nebraska, 1966; W. J. Gores and L. C. Hodapp, editors, Cultural Relevance and Educational Issues, Little, Brown, 1973; J. Culbertson, R. Farquhar, B. Fogarty, and Mark Shibles, editors, The Preparation of Educational Administrators: Social Science Perspectives, Merrill Co., 1973; Thomas Weaver, editor, To See Ourselves, Scott, Foresman, 1973; Frank Riddel, editor, Appalachia: It's People, Heritage, and Problems, Kendall/Hunt, 1974; Susan Abbott and John van Willigen, editors, Predicting Culture Change, University of Georgia, 1979.

WORK IN PROGRESS: Co-editing a book "on the problems of studying in one's own culture"; a book on sociocultural change among Irish peasants; co-authoring a volume on education in a developing society.

GAMORAN, Mamie (Goldsmith) 1900-

PERSONAL: Born January 17, 1900, in Long Island, N.Y.; daughter of Nathan Israel (a food broker) and Mamie (Aronson) Goldsmith; married Emanuel Gamoran (a religious educator), December 17, 1922 (died November, 1962); children: Abraham Carmi, Nathaniel Hillel, Judith Reena (Mrs. Eli Chernin). *Education:* Attended Columbia University, 1921-22; Jewish Theological Seminary of America, teacher's certificate, 1922; University of Cincinnati, additional study, 1923-24. *Politics:* Democrat. *Religion:* Jewish. *Home:* 229 West 78th St., New York, N.Y. 10024.

CAREER: Bureau of Jewish Education, commerical secretary, 1918-20, and secretary director, 1920-22, in New York, N.Y., teacher in Cincinnati, Ohio, 1931-33; vice-president, Jewish Community Council, 1940-41, 1943-44; Congregation of Adath Israel, Cincinnati, supervisor of religious school, 1945-47. Member of board, Hebrew Arts School for Music and Dance, 1955-65; secretary, American committee, Israel White House Library Fund for Children, 1963-70. *Member:* Hadassah (president, Cincinnati chapter, 1938-40; regional vice-president, 1942-44; member of national board, 1950—), Federation of Jewish Women's Organizations (former president, Cincinnati branch), Hebrew Federation of America (vice-president, 1973-74; secretary 1979—).

WRITINGS—Published by Union of American Hebrew Congregations, except as indicated: *The Voice of the Prophets*, 1929; *With Singer and Sage*, 1930; *Hillel's Happy Holidays*, 1939; *Days and Ways*, 1941; *Funways to Holidays*, 1951; *The New Jewish History*, with activity books, Volume I, 1953, Volume II, 1955, Volume III, 1957; *Hillel's Calendar*, 1960; *The Story of Dr. Benderly*, Jewish Education Press, 1963; (with husband, Emanuel Gamoran) *Talks to Jewish Teachers*, 1966; *The Jewish Times*, 1975; *The Hebrew Spirit in America*, 1975; (editor with Samuel Grand) *Emanuel Gamoran–His Life and Work*, 1979. Contributor of short stories, poems, and articles to various publications, including *Liberal Judaism*, *Christian Home*, *Jewish Education*, and *Reconstructionist*.

SIDELIGHTS: Mamie Gamoran told *CA:* "It seems to me that I have always written—in high school, for clubs, mostly fun pieces, until I was lucky enough to have the opportunity to write textbooks and storybooks for children in Jewish and non-Jewish religious schools. This led to other assignments. I often hear from grown men and women who say that they used my books in their youth and are now getting the same books for their children. So, in many cases, a third generation has been touched by my work. I am very grateful."

*   *   *

GANN, L(ewis) H(enry) 1924-

PERSONAL: Name originally Ludwig Hermann Ganz; born January 28, 1924, in Mainz, Germany; son of Hermann Friedrich (a merchant) and Charlotte (Fromberg) Ganz; married Rita Herta Niesler, September 6, 1950; children: Margarita Herta Charlotte, Thomas Michael. *Education:* Oxford University, B.A., 1950, M.A., 1954, B.Litt., 1955, D.Phil., 1964. *Office:* Hoover Institution, Stanford University, Stanford, Calif. 94305.

CAREER: Rhodes-Livingstone Institute, Lusaka, Northern Rhodesia (now Zambia), historian, 1951-52; University of Manchester, Manchester, England, assistant lecturer, 1952-54; National Archives of Rhodesia and Nyasaland, Salisbury, Rhodesia, archivist and editor, 1954-63; Stanford University, Hoover Institution, Stanford, Calif., 1964—, began as research associate, became deputy curator of African

collection, currently senior fellow. *Military service:* British Army, Royal Fusiliers and Intelligence, 1944-47; became sergeant. *Member:* African Studies Association (Great Britain and United States), Royal Historical Society (fellow), American Historical Association, Conference on British Studies, Leo Baeck Institute.

WRITINGS: The Birth of a Plural Society: The Development of Northern Rhodesia under the British South Africa Company, 1894-1914, University of Manchester Press, 1958; (contributor) V. W. Brelsford, editor, *Handbook to the Federation of Rhodesia and Nyasaland*, Cassell, 1960; (with Peter Duignan) *White Settlers in Tropical Africa*, Penguin, 1962; *A History of Northern Rhodesia: Early Days to 1953*, Chatto & Windus, 1964; (with Michael Gelfand) *Huggins of Rhodesia: The Man and His Country*, Allen & Unwin, 1964; *A History of Southern Rhodesia: Early Days to 1934*, Chatto & Windus, 1965; (with Duignan) *Burden of Empire: An Appraisal of Western Colonalism in Africa South of the Sahara*, Praeger, 1967; (editor with Duignan and contributor) *Colonialism in Africa, 1870-1960*, Cambridge University Press, Volume I: *The History and Politics of Colonialism, 1870-1914*, 1969, Volume II: *The History and Politics of Colonialism, 1914-1960*, 1970, Volume V: *A Bibliographic Guide to Colonialism in Sub-Saharan Africa*, 1973, Volume IV: *The Economics of Colonial Rule*, 1975.

Central Africa: The Former British States, Prentice-Hall, 1971; *Guerrillas in History*, Hoover Institution, Stanford University, 1971; (with Duignan) *Africa and the World at Large: An Introduction to the History of Sub-Saharan Africa from Antiquity to 1840*, Chandler Publishing, 1972; (with Duignan) *A Bibliographical Guide to Colonialism in Sub-Saharan Africa*, Cambridge University Press, 1973; (with Duignan) *The Rulers of German Africa, 1884-1914*, Stanford University Press, 1977; (with Duignan) *The Rulers of British Africa, 1884-1914*, Stanford University Press, 1978; (editor with Duignan) *African Proconsuls*, Free Press, 1978; *The Rulers of Belgian Africa, 1884-1914*, Princeton University Press, 1979; (with Duignan) *South Africa: War, Revolution, or Peace?*, Hoover Institution, Stanford University, 1979; (with Duignan) *Why South Africa Will Survive*, Croom Helm, 1981. Contributor of articles to newspapers, magazines, and journals.

*   *   *

GANTT, Fred, Jr. 1922-197(?)

PERSONAL: Born November 12, 1922, in Foreman, Ark.; deceased; son of Fred (a banker-accountant) and Margaret Elizabeth (Taaffe) Gantt. *Education:* Southern Methodist University, B.A., 1943, M.A., 1948; University of Texas, Ph.D., 1962. *Politics:* Democrat. *Religion:* Methodist. *Office:* Department of Political Science, North Texas State University, Denton, Tex. 76203.

CAREER: Southern Methodist University, Dallas, Tex., instructor in government, 1947-52; Lone Star Ordnance Plant, Texarkana, Tex., assistant to personnel director, 1952-55; Texarkana College, Texarkana, Tex., instructor in social science and dean of adult education, 1955-58; University of Texas, Main University (now University of Texas at Austin), research associate of Institute of Public Affairs, 1959-61; Agricultural and Mechanical College of Texas (now Texas A & M University), College Station, instructor in government, 1961-62; North Texas State University, Denton, assistant professor, 1962-64, associate professor, 1964-66, professor of government, 1966-69, chairman of department of political science, beginning 1969. Visiting professor of government, University of Texas, 1968, 1973, and 1974. Consultant, Texas Constitutional Revision Commission, 1968, National Governors' Conference study committee on constitutional revision and general government organization, 1968, Dallas County Commissioner's Court, 1972, and University of Houston's project on Texas constitutional revision, 1972-73. Delegate to Democratic State Convention, 1964. *Military service:* U.S. Army, 1944-46; became sergeant. *Member:* American Political Science Association, American Association of University Professors, Southern Political Science Association, Southwestern Social Science Association, Southwestern Political Science Association (president, 1970-71), Texas Association of College Teachers, Academy of Political Science of Columbia University, Pi Sigma Alpha, Psi Chi, Phi Theta Kappa. *Awards, honors:* Named "outstanding professor," North Texas State University, 1970.

WRITINGS: The Texas Constitutional Amendments of 1960, Institute of Public Affairs, University of Texas, 1960; *The Chief Executive in Texas: A Study in Gubernatorial Leadership,* University of Texas Press, 1964; (editor with others and contributor) *Governing Texas: Documents and Readings,* Crowell, 1966, 3rd edition, 1974; *The Governor's Veto in Texas: An Absolute Negative?,* Institute of Public Affairs, University of Texas, 1969; *Special Legislative Sessions in Texas: The Governor's Bane or Blessing,* Institute of Public Affairs, University of Texas, 1970; *The Impact of the Texas Constitution on the Executive,* Institute for Urban Studies, University of Houston, 1973. Also co-author of *The Use of Land Resources in Dallas County, Texas,* 1972. Contributor of articles to professional journals.

WORK IN PROGRESS: A monograph, *Legislative Perceptions of the Executive's Role in Lawmaking Process,* for Institute of Public Affairs, University of Texas.†

* * *

GARDNER, Lloyd C(alvin) 1934-

PERSONAL: Born November 9, 1934, in Delaware, Ohio; son of Lloyd Calvin (a government employee) and Hazel (Grove) Gardner; married Nancy Wintermute, June 3, 1956; children: Rebecca, Erin, Timothy. *Education:* Ohio Wesleyan University, A.B., 1956; University of Wisconsin, M.S., 1957, Ph.D., 1960. *Home:* 15 Redcoat Dr., East Brunswick, N.J. 08816. *Office:* Department of History, Rutgers University, New Brunswick, N.J. 08903.

CAREER: Lake Forest College, Lake Forest, Ill., instructor in history, 1959-60; Rutgers University, New Brunswick, N.J., assistant professor, 1963-64, associate professor, 1964-67, professor of history, 1967—, chairman of department, 1970-73. Fulbright lecturer, 1975-76. *Military service:* U.S. Air Force, 1960-63; now captain, U.S. Air Force Reserve. *Awards, honors:* Guggenheim fellow, 1973-74.

WRITINGS: Economic Aspects of New Deal Diplomacy, University of Wisconsin Press, 1964; (editor and author of introduction) *A Different Frontier: Selected Readings in the Foundations of American Economic Expansion,* Quadrangle, 1966; *Architects of Illusion: Men and Ideas in American Foreign Policy, 1941-1949,* Quadrangle, 1970; (with others) *Origins of the Cold War,* Blaisdell, 1970; (editor and author of introduction) *The Korean War,* Quadrangle, 1972; (with others) *Creation of the American Empire,* Rand McNally, 1973; (editor) *The Great Nixon Turn-Around,* New Viewpoints, 1973; (co-author) *Looking Backward: A Reintroduction to American History,* McGraw, 1974; (editor) *American Foreign Policy, Present to Past,* Collier-MacMillan, 1974;

(editor) *Wilson and Revolutions: 1913-1921,* Lippincott, 1976; *Imperial America: American Foreign Policy in the Twentieth Century,* Harcourt, 1976.

WORK IN PROGRESS: Anglo-American Reactions to Revolution, 1913-1921: The Wilson-Lloyd George Era; Anglo-American Reactions to Revolution, 1931-1945: The World War II Era.

BIOGRAPHICAL/CRITICAL SOURCES: Virginia Quarterly Review, summer, 1970.

* * *

GARDNER, William Earl 1928-

PERSONAL: Born October 11, 1928, in Hopkins, Minn.; son of William Henry and Ida (Swenson) Gardner; married Marcia F. Anderson, November 4, 1950; children: Mary, Bret, Anne, Eric. *Education:* University of Minnesota, B.S., 1950, M.A., 1959, Ph.D., 1961. *Home:* 2631 Burd Pl., St. Louis Park, Minn. 55426. *Office:* 104 Burton Hall, University of Minnesota, Minneapolis, Minn. 55455.

CAREER: Teacher at Balaton (Minn.) High School, 1950-51, Rockford (Minn.) Public Schools, 1951-53, and New Ulm (Minn.) Public Schools, 1953-54; University High School, Minneapolis, Minn., instructor in history, 1954-61; University of Minnesota, College of Education, Minneapolis, assistant professor, 1961-64, associate professor of secondary education, 1964-67; York University, York, England, visiting professor, 1967-68; University of Minnesota, College of Education, professor of secondary education and chairman of department, 1968-69, assistant dean, 1969-70, associate dean, 1970-76, acting dean, 1976-77, dean, 1977—. Minnesota National Laboratory, director of social studies section, 1962-64, acting director, 1965-67. *Member:* National Council for the Social Studies, National Society for the Study of Education, North Central Association of Schools and Colleges (member of evaluating teams), Minnesota Council for the Social Studies (member of board of directors, 1962-67; executive secretary, 1964-67), Phi Delta Kappa, Alpha Sigma Pi.

WRITINGS: (Contributor) Helen M. Robinson, editor, *Materials for Reading,* University of Chicago Press, 1957; *Story of Our Country* (textbook), Allyn & Bacon, 1959; *New World's Foundations in the Old* (history text), Allyn & Bacon, 1962; (with Everett Keach and Robert Fulton) *Education and Social Crisis,* Wiley, 1968; (contributor) Robert Irving Smith, editor, *Men and Societies,* Heinemann, 1969; (contributor) D. B. Heater, editor, *The Teaching of Politics,* Methuen, 1969; (editor with Fred A. Johnson) *Social Studies in Secondary Schools: A Book of Readings,* Allyn & Bacon, 1970; (contributor) Richard E. Gross and Raymond H. Muessig, editors, *Problem-Centered Social Studies Instruction,* National Council for the Social Studies, 1971. Contributor to yearbooks and to professional journals. Editor, *Bulletin* of Minnesota Council for the Social Studies 1963-65.

* * *

GARRETT, Thomas S(amuel) 1913-1980
(Tom Garrett)

PERSONAL: Born September 29, 1913, in Gorakhpur, United Provinces, India; died April 10, 1980; son of Stephen (a clergyman) and Anna (Cross) Garrett; married Lilian Holdsworth, 1941; children: Elizabeth. *Education:* Christ's College, Cambridge, B.A., 1936, M.A., 1938; attended Ridley Hall, Cambridge, 1936-37. *Home and office:* The Rectory, Hallaton, Market Harborough, Liecestershire LE16 8TY, England.

CAREER: Church of England, Diocese of London, ordained deacon, 1937, priest, 1938; Parish of St. Mary, Stoke Newington, London, curate, 1937-39; Church Missionary Society, London, missionary to India, beginning 1940; lecturer, St. John's College, Palayamkottai, Tirunelveli Diocese, India, 1940-42; Tamilnad Theological College, Tirumaraiyur, Nazareth, South India, vice-principal, 1946-63; Church Missionary Society, Tirunelveli Diocese, secretary, 1951-63; senior chaplain and advisor on church union to archbishop of West Africa, 1963-65; University of Nigeria, Nsukka, lecturer, 1965, head of department of religion, 1966-68; Tamil Nadu Theological Seminary, Madurai, India, professor of theology, 1969-71; bishop of Tirunelveli, Church of South India, 1971-74; assistant bishop of Diocese of Leicester and rector of Hallaton with Horninghold and Allexton, Liecester, England, 1975-80. Church of South India, presbyter, 1947-63, and member of liturgy committee and theological commission; member of Church of South India-Lutheran interchurch commission, working toward union of the two churches, 1950-63, and Nigerian Church Union liturgy committee, beginning 1965; chairman, Tamil Theological Literature Committee, 1961-80; lecturer, Theological Study Institute of the Association of Theological Colleges of Southeast Asia, 1965. *Military service:* Indian Army, Chaplains' Department, 1942-46. *Member:* Society for African Church History, Evangelical Fellowship for Theological Literature (United Kingdom), Indian Christian Theological Association. *Awards, honors:* Wordsworth Student, Cambridge University.

WRITINGS: *The Liturgy of the Church of South India,* Oxford University Press, 1952; *Worship in the Church of South India,* Lutterworth Press, 1958, revised edition, 1965; *Christian Worship: An Introductory Outline,* Oxford University Press, 1961, 2nd edition, Oxford University Press, 1963; *Signposts to Theological Study,* Indian Christian Students' Library, 1964; (translator) Cyprian, *De Unitate,* Indian Christian Students' Library, 1964; *Unity in Nigeria,* Edinburgh House Press, 1965; *'Who is My Mother': In Quest of the Virgin Mary,* Christian Literature Society (India), 1974. Also contributor to *The Book of Common Worship* of the Church of South India.

Books in Tamil include a commentary on St. Mark's gospel, studies in early Old Testament personalities, and contributions to the *Tamil Theological Dictionary of the Bible.* Contributes articles and reviews to theological journals.

SIDELIGHTS: Thomas Garrett told *CA:* "I rather hope that posterity will accord me a small niche in the history of the development of worship in the latter part of the 20th century. Though I have received scant recognition for it so far, I rather think that my most important work has been my contributions to *The Book of Common Worship* of the Church of South India. I drafted several of the services contained therein . . . and piloted them through the stages leading to their acceptance by the Church of South India. I also contributed prayers to other parts of this prayer book which, since its publication in the early 1960's, has influenced other modern prayer books. It has been particularly gratifying to me that the ordination services, which I first worked out while studying in an Indian ashram in 1955-56, were accepted as models for liturgical revision by the Anglican Consultative Council (a worldwide representative body of the Anglican Communion). The result is that . . . the Church of England and an increasing number of provinces of the Anglican Communion now follow Thomas Garrett rather than Thomas Cramner in their mode of ordaining their clergy."

AVOCATIONAL INTERESTS: Bird watching.

GARTEN, Hugh F(rederick)   1904-1975

PERSONAL: Surname originally Koenigsgarten; born April 13, 1904, in Brno, Czechoslovakia; died, 1975; son of Fritz (a manufacturer) and Elizabeth (Brueck) Koenigsgarten; married Anne Leonard Smith (a teacher), March 7, 1952. *Education:* University of Heidelberg, D.Phil., 1930; Oxford University, D.Phil., 1944. *Politics:* Conservative. *Religion:* Church of England. *Home:* 10 Priory Mansions, Drayton Gardens, London S.W.10, England. *Agent:* Peter Janson-Smith, 42 Great Russell St., London W.C. 1, England.

CAREER: Writer and journalist in Berlin, Germany, 1928-33, and Vienna, Austria, 1933-38; Oxford University, New College, Oxford, England, teacher, 1940-45; Westminster School, London, England, teacher of German language and literature, 1947-65; British Broadcasting Corp., London, editor and producer, 1965-66; University of Surrey, Guildford, England, lecturer in London, beginning 1965. *Member:* P.E.N. (English center), Gerhart Hauptmann Society (Germany), Goethe Society (England).

WRITINGS: *Georg Kaiser,* G. Kiepenheuer, 1928; *Gerhart Hauptmann,* Yale University Press, 1954; *Modern German Drama,* Essential Books, 1959, revised edition, Methuen, 1964; (translator with J. M. Ritchie) *Seven Expressionist Plays: Kokoschka to Barlach,* Calder & Boyars, 1968; (editor) Georg Kaiser, *Von Morgens bis Mitternachts,* Methuen, 1968; (editor) Gerhart Hauptmann, *Die Ratten: Berliner Tragikomoedie,* Methuen, 1969; *Wagner the Dramatist,* J. Calder, 1977, Rowman & Littlefield, 1978.

Also librettist for operas "Tyll," 1928, and "Lord Spleen," 1930, editor of school editions of Zuckmayer's *Der Hauptmann von Koepenick,* Duerrenmatt's *Romulus der Grosse,* and Frisch's *Andorra,* and translator of Kaiser's plays "The Raft of the Medusa" and "The Protagonist." Contributor to *Encyclopaedia Britannica, Grolier Encyclopedia,* and *Encyclopedie de la Pleiade* and to periodicals, including *Drama, German Life and Letters,* and *Times Literary Supplement.*

AVOCATIONAL INTERESTS: Music.†

                    *   *   *

GASKELL, (John) Philip (Wellesley)   1926-

PERSONAL: Born January 6, 1926, in London, England; son of John Wellesley Gaskell (an engineer) and Olive (Baker) Gaskell Braithwaite; married Margaret Bennett (a librarian), October 5, 1948; children: Luke Wellesley, Roger Philip, Kate Matilda. *Education:* King's College, Cambridge, B.A., 1949, M.A., 1954, Ph.D., 1956. *Home:* 2 Park Parade, Cambridge CBS 8AL, England.

CAREER: Cambridge University, King's College, Cambridge, England, fellow, 1953-60, dean, 1954-56, tutor, 1956-58; Oundle School, Northampton, England, head of English department and librarian, 1960-62; University of Glasgow, Glasgow, Scotland, keeper of special collections in university library, 1962-66, warden of Maclay Hall, 1962-64, and Wolfson Hall, 1964-66; Cambridge University, fellow and librarian, Trinity College, 1967—, tutor, 1973—, Sanders Reader in Bibliography, 1978-79. *Military service:* British Army, Royal Artillery, 1943-47. *Member:* Society of Authors.

WRITINGS: *The First Editions of William Mason,* Cambridge Bibliographical Society, 1951; *John Baskerville: A Bibliography,* Cambridge University Press, 1958, revised edition, 1973; *Caught!* (novel), Hart-Davis, 1960; *A Bibliography of the Foulis Press,* Hart-Davis, 1965; *Morvern Transformed,* Cambridge University Press, 1968, revised edition,

1980; (with R. Robson) *The Library of Trinity College, Cambridge,* Trinity College, Cambridge University, 1971; *A New Introduction to Bibliography,* Oxford University Press, 1972, 3rd revised edition, 1979; (editor and translator with P. Bradford) *Orthotypographia of Heironymus Hornschuch,* Cambridge University Library, 1972; *From Writer to Reader,* Oxford University Press, 1978; *Trinity College Library: The First 150 Years,* Cambridge University Press, 1980. Contributor to journals and periodicals. Editor, *Book Collector,* 1952-54. Contributor to periodicals and journals.

WORK IN PROGRESS: A book about authorship and book production since 1950.

AVOCATIONAL INTERESTS: Music, flying, photography.

*   *   *

GASSNER, John Waldhorn   1903-1967

PERSONAL: Born January 30, 1903, in Maramaros-Sziget, Hungary; came to United States, 1911; died April 2, 1967, of a heart ailment in New Haven, Conn.; son of Abraham Waldhorn (a furrier) and Fannie (Weinberger) Gassner; married Mollie Kern, December 1, 1926; children: Caroline. *Education:* Columbia University, B.A., 1924, M.A., 1925, additional study, 1925-26, 1928-29. *Home:* 100 York St., New Haven, Conn. *Agent:* William Morris Agency, 1350 Ave. of the Americas, New York, N.Y. 10019. *Office:* School of Drama, Yale University, New Haven, Conn.

CAREER: New York Herald-Tribune, New York City, member of staff and book reviewer, 1926-28; Theatre Guild, New York City, play editor, translator, adaptor, and head of play department, 1929-44; Dramatic Workshop, New York City, chairman of drama department, 1940-49; Columbia Pictures Industries, Inc., Hollywood, Calif., and New York City, manager of play department, 1944-47; Columbia University, New York City, lecturer in dramatic arts, 1949-56; Queens College (now Queens College of the City University of New York), Flushing, N.Y., professor of English, 1951-56; Yale University, New Haven, Conn., Sterling Professor of Playwriting and Dramatic Literature, 1956-67. Lecturer on the dramatic arts at universities throughout the United States. Independent producer on Broadway, 1947-49. Member of Pulitzer Prize drama jury, 1957-63. Member of board of directors, John Golden Foundation, 1961-67; member of board of overseers for theatre arts, Brandeis University, 1965. Trustee, National Theatre Conference, 1961.

MEMBER: Shaw Society of London (vice-president, 1954-67), Outer Circle (president, 1961-67), New York Drama Critics Circle, Modern Language Association of America, Renaissance Society, John Milton Society, American Society for Theatre Research, Speech Association of America, American Educational Theatre Association, Shakespeare Society, Friends of Columbia Libraries, Friends of Paul Klapper Library (Flushing, N.Y.), Phi Beta Kappa, Society for Ethical Culture, Yale Club of New Haven, Columbia University Faculty Club, Yale University Faculty Club. *Awards, honors:* Guggenheim fellowship; M.A., Yale University, 1956; American Educational Theatre Association award of merit, 1959; Centenary gold medal, Boston College, 1963; D.H., Eastern Michigan University, 1963; Kelsey Allen Award, 1965, and other awards.

WRITINGS: Masters of the Drama, Random House, 1940, 3rd revised edition, Dover, 1954; *Theatre and the Social Scene: A Bibliography,* American Educational Theatre Association, 1946; *Human Relations in the Theatre,* Freedom Pamphlet, 1949; *The Theatre in Our Times: A Survey of the Men, Materials and Movements in the Modern Theatre,*

Crown, 1954; *Form and Idea in Modern Theatre,* Dryden Press, 1956, revised edition published as *Directions in Modern Theatre and Drama,* Holt, 1965; *Theatre at the Crossroads,* Holt, 1960; (contributor) *Varieties of Literary Experience,* New York University Press, 1962; (editor and contributor) *Ideas in the Drama,* Columbia University Press. 1964; *Eugene O'Neill* (pamphlet), University of Minnesota Press, 1965; (contributor) Angel Flores, editor, *Spanish Drama,* Bantam, 1968; (contributor) Clive Barnes, editor, *Fifty Best Plays of the American Theatre,* Crown, 1969.

Editor: (With Burns Mantle) *A Treasury of the Theatre,* Simon & Schuster, 1935, revised edition (sole editor) published in three volumes, 1951, 4th edition, 1967, college edition (sole editor) published in two volumes, Volume I, Holt, 1959, 3rd edition, 1967, Volume II, Dryden, 1950, 4th edition (with revisions by Bernard F. Dukore), Holt, 1970; *Twenty Best Plays of the Modern American Theatre,* Crown, 1939; (with Philip Barber) *Producing the Play,* Dryden, 1941, revised edition, 1953; (with Stith Thompson) *Our Heritage of World Literature,* Dryden, 1942, Book 1: *Literature in Translation,* Book 2: *Literature in Our Own Tongue;* (with Dudley Nichols) *Twenty Best Film Plays,* two volumes, Crown, 1943, reprinted, Garland Publishing, 1977; *English Comedies,* Book League of America, 1944; (with Nichols) *Best Film Plays of 1943-44,* Crown, 1945, reprinted, Garland Publishing, 1977; *Best Plays of the Modern American Theatre,* Crown, 1945; *Comedies of Moliere,* Book League of America, 1945; (with Nichols) *Best Film Plays of 1945,* Crown, 1946, reprinted, Garland Publishing, 1978; *Twenty-Five Best Plays of the Modern American Theatre,* Crown, 1949.

Selected Plays of Sean O'Casey, Braziller, 1954; *Twenty Best European Plays on the American Stage,* Crown, 1957; *Four Great Elizabethan Plays,* Bantam, 1959; (with Nichols, and author of introduction) *Great Film Plays,* Crown, 1959; William Archer, *Playmaking,* Dover, 1960; *Five Plays of Gerhart Hauptmann,* Bantam, 1961; *Seven Plays by August Strindberg,* Bantam, 1961; *Last Plays of Henrik Ibsen,* Bantam, 1962; *Medieval and Tudor Drama,* Bantam, 1963; *Ideas in the Drama,* Columbia University Press, 1963; *Eight Expressionist Plays by Strindberg,* Bantam, 1963; (with Morris Sweetkind) *Intruducing the Drama,* Holt, 1963; (and contributor) *O'Neill: A Collection of Critical Essays,* Prentice-Hall, 1964; (with Sidney Thomas) *The Nature of Art,* Crown, 1964; (with William Green) *Elizabethan Drama,* Bantam, 1966; *The World of Contemporary Drama* (pamphlet), Public Affairs Association, 1966; *Best Plays of the Early American Theatre,* Crown, 1966; (with Ralph G. Allen) *Theatre and Drama in the Making,* Houghton, 1964; *Four New Yale Playwrights,* Crown, 1965; (with Frederick H. Little) *Reading and Staging the Play: An Anthology of One-Act Plays,* Holt, 1967; (with Morris Sweetkind) *Tragedy, History, and Romance,* Holt, 1968; *Dramatic Soundings,* Crown, 1968; (and compiler with wife, Mollie Gassner) *Fifteen International One-Act Plays,* Washington Square Press, 1969. Editor and author of introduction, "Best American Plays" series, Crown, 1947-71. Also editor, with Edward Quinn, *Readers' Encyclopedia of World Drama,* Crowell, 1969.

Author of introduction: Aristotle, *Theory of Poetry and Fine Art,* translated by S. H. Butcher, Dover, 1951; *Playwrights on Playwriting,* Hill & Wang, 1960; Thornton Wilder, *The Long Christmas Dinner and Other Plays in One Act,* Harper, 1963; *Drama Was a Weapon,* Rutgers University Press, 1963; *Strindberg: The Origin of Psychology in Modern Drama,* Citadel, 1964; *Three Plays from the Yale School of Drama,* Dutton, 1964; *Four New Yale Playwrights,* Crown,

1965. Adaptor of several British plays for the American stage, including "A Nativitie Play," and Stefan Zweig's "Jeremiah." Contributor to encyclopedias and yearbooks, *Oxford Companion to the Theatre, Enciclopedia dello spettacolo,* and other publications.

Drama critic for *New Theatre Magazine,* 1935-37, *Forum,* 1937-38, and 1943-48, *Time,* 1938, *Direction,* 1939-43, and *Current History,* 1943-48. Senior contributing editor, *Theatre Arts,* 1951-54; contributing editor, *Drama Critique, Theatre Workshop, Theatre Time,* and *Tulane Drama Review.*

WORK IN PROGRESS: Drama books.

SIDELIGHTS: John Gassner was a great supporter and promoter of American theatre. According to a reporter for the *New York Times,* Gassner, "for many years, devoted much of his time and energies to the discovery, encouragement and guidance of American playwrights, including Tennessee Williams and Arthur Miller."

Gassner once remarked that "what really matters in art is the transfiguration of reality into the manifestation of essential truth, spirit and vision. . . . So long as the theatre exists at all there will always be two standards, the absolute standard of the litterateurs who can live a comfortable distance from the stage, and the relative one of those compelled by profession or inclination to live with the stage and come to terms with it."

Gassner also felt that the theatre was "a mirror of history." He believed that the lesson learned from three thousand years of drama was "that man will somehow survive—probably to blunder but to seek again and perhaps find a way of life that the spirit can some day regard without a shudder."

AVOCATIONAL INTERESTS: Music, art, and book collecting.

BIOGRAPHICAL/CRITICAL SOURCES: New York Times, April 3, 1967; *Publishers Weekly,* April 17, 1967; *Tulane Drama Review,* summer, 1967; *Books Abroad,* spring, 1968.†

*   *   *

GATNER, Elliott S(herman) M(ozian)   1914-

PERSONAL: Born October 24, 1914, in New York, N.Y.; son of Abraham Elliott (a newspaper reporter) and Tillie (Sherman) Gatner; married Shirley V. Golden (a schoolteacher), July 13, 1941; children: Alice Roberta, Deborah Ann. *Education:* Long Island University, B.A., 1936; City College (now City College of the City University of New York), M.S., 1939; Columbia University, B.S. in L.S., 1947. *Home:* 81-07 248th St., Bellerose, N.Y. 11426.

CAREER: Long Island University, Brooklyn, N.Y., instructor in English, 1938-47, instructor in history, 1948-52, assistant professor, 1953-56, associate professor, 1956-63, professor of history and government, 1963—, assistant director of libraries, 1961-65, assistant to the provost, 1964-65, associate director of libraries, exhibitions, and Long Island University Press, 1965-75, director, 1975—. Lecturer. Library consultant; research consultant to industry. *Military service:* U.S. Army, 1941-46, 1950-52; received Bronze Star, Combat Infantryman Badge. U.S. Army Reserve; became major. *Member:* College English Association, National Council of Teachers of English, American Historical Association, American Association of University Professors, American Library Association, Modern Language Association of America, American Society for Legal History, Organization

of American Historians, Phi Delta Kappa. *Awards, honors:* Ed.D., Columbia University, 1975; recipient of Conspicuous Service Cross, New York.

WRITINGS: Analytical Survey of Cooperative Agreements among Institutions of Higher Education in the Metropolitan Area of New York City, Long Island University Alumni Association, 1940; (with Francesco Cordasco and N. Resnick) *Study Guide to English Literature,* two volumes, Lamb, 1947-48; *University Handbook for Research and Report Writing,* Lamb's Book Exchange, 1946, 3rd edition published as *Handbook for Research and Report Writing,* Barnes & Noble, 1948, 4th edition published as *Research and Report Writing,* 1955, 10th edition, Harper, 1971; (contributor) Cordasco, *A Brief History of Education,* Littlefield, 1963; (editor) Paul Kosok, *Life, Land and Water in Ancient Peru,* Long Island University Press, 1965; *College Level English Composition Course,* Future Resources and Development, Inc., 1971; (editor with Albert Fein) *University and Community,* Long Island University Press, 1971; (contributing editor) Cordasco and William Brickman, editors, *A Bibliography of American Educational History,* AMS Press, 1975. Book reviewer for *Brooklyn Daily Eagle* and *Educational Studies.*

WORK IN PROGRESS: A census of eighteenth-century American libraries; literary antecedents of the American constitution.

AVOCATIONAL INTERESTS: Mass communications, philately, photography, and painting.

*   *   *

GAUNT, Leonard   1921-

PERSONAL: Born March 26, 1921; married Jean Anne Stewart, March 26, 1955. *Home and office:* 44 Hatherop Rd., Hampton, Middlesex, England.

CAREER: Croner Publications Ltd. (reference book publisher), London, England, assistant editor, 1948-53; *British Export Gazette,* London, assistant editor, 1953-61; Focal Press Ltd. (photography book publisher), London, technical editor, 1962-77; writer. *Military service:* Royal Air Force, 1939-46.

WRITINGS—Published by Focal Press, except as indicated: *The Carriage and Insurance of Cargoes.* Witherby, 1955; *Ilford Book of Colour,* 1963; *How to Choose and Use Your Thirty-Five Millimeter Camera,* 1963, 2nd edition, 1966; *How to Choose the Camera You Need,* 1963; *How to Make Your Own Enlargements,* 1964; *Lens Guide,* 1967, revised edition, 1972; *Electronic Flash Guide,* 1967, 2nd edition, 1970; (editor with Paul Petzold) *Pictorial Encyclopedia of Photography,* A. S. Barnes, 1968, revised edition, Focal Press, 1979; *Take Color,* 1969; *Commonsense Photography,* 1969, 4th edition, 1979; *Praktica Way,* 1972, 4th edition, revised, 1978; *Focalguide to Thirty-Five Millimeter SLR,* 1974; *Canon Reflex Way,* 1974, revised edition, 1979; *Praktica Book,* 1975, 2nd edition, 1979; *Focalguide to Thirty-Five Millimeter,* 1975; *Olympus OM1 and OM2 Book,* 1975; *Zorki and Fed Book,* 1976; *Focalguide to Lenses,* 1977; *Canon SLR Book,* 1978; *Focalguide to the Darkroom,* 1978; *Fujica ST Book,* 1978; *Focalguide to Camera Accessories,* 1979.

WORK IN PROGRESS: Books on photography subjects.

*   *   *

GEBLER, Ernest   1915-

PERSONAL: Born January 1, 1915, in Dublin, Ireland; son of Adolphe (a Czech musician) and Margaret (Wall) Gebler;

married Leatrice Gilbert, 1950 (divorced, 1952); married Edna O'Brien (an author), 1953 (divorced, 1967); married Jane Incott, 1968; children: (first marriage) John Carl. *Residence:* Dublin, Ireland.

CAREER: Novelist, playwright, and screenwriter.

WRITINGS—Novels: *He Had My Heart Scalded*, Low, 1946; *The Plymouth Adventure: The Voyage of the Mayflower* (Literary Guild selection), Doubleday, 1950; *A Week in the Country*, Doubleday, 1957; *The Love Investigator*, Doubleday, 1960; *The Old Man and the Girl*, Doubleday, 1968; *Hoffman*, Doubleday, 1969.

Also author of plays "She Sits There Smiling," "The Spaniard in Galway," "The Painted Woman," "Kingdom Come," "Call Me Daddy," and "A Cry for Help," produced by Irish National Theatre; author of screenplays, including "The Girl with Green Eyes," with Edna O'Brien (based on O'Brien's novel *The Lonely Girl*), "The Love Investigator" (based on novel of same title), and "Hoffman" (based on novel of same title), EMI, 1970, and of numerous television plays.

WORK IN PROGRESS: Two novels, *A Civilized Life* and *The Mushroom Eaters;* compiling *A Handbook for Survival.*

SIDELIGHTS: Ernest Gebler writes *CA:* "Publishers and others usually complain that I follow no recognizable line, expecially in my novels. The only answer I have to that is too many authors write the same book over and over again. While writing is a profession, like medicine or bridge building, it gives a secure livelihood to very few of us. I'm grateful that the six novels I've published over the last thirty years have given me a more than generous livelihood, due to wide sales, foreign translations, film and television rights.

"Writing is also a profession of deep and lasting satisfaction, whether you make a living by it or not. You may never come across anyone reading one of your books on a train or in a park, but you know your are getting into the minds of lots of people; and if you are doing no more than entertaining or getting someone through a difficult time, it is still worthwhile. A young woman once wrote me that, upon returning from the library one evening, she decided she'd come to the end, drew the curtains, blanketed the door, and stuffed the chimney in her little room. Then she lay down on the hearth rug and turned the gas fire on without lighting it. Always a hungry reader, she picked up [one of my novels] and began reading—that would be the way to go out, reading. 'But I got so interested,' [she told Gebler,] 'I turned off the gas and all that and opened the window. I just had to know what was going to happen [in the book.]' She thanked me, most touchingly. It was a book I had deliberately written as an entertainment. Whatever it did for her, it taught me a lesson: Writing may be a part of living for me, but reading is a part of being able to go on, a part of living for untold millions. We [writers] function in a peculiar way, rarely if ever seeing or hearing from those we service. Being able to read is necessary to a civilized life."

BIOGRAPHICAL/CRITICAL SOURCES: Saturday Review of Literature, April 29, 1950.

* * *

GELFAND, Lawrence Emerson 1926-

PERSONAL: Born June 20, 1926, in Cleveland, Ohio; son of Maurice H. (an attorney) and Rachel (an attorney; maiden name, Shapiro) Gelfand; married Miriam Ifland (an instructor in Russian), June 14, 1953; children: Julia, Daniel, Ronald. *Education:* Western Reserve University (now Case Western Reserve University), B.A., 1949, M.A., 1950; University of Washington, Ph.D., 1958. *Home:* 1437 Oakcrest St., Iowa City, Iowa 52240. *Office:* Department of History, University of Iowa, Iowa City, Iowa 52242.

CAREER: Assistant professor of history at University of Hawaii, Honolulu, 1956-58, University of Washington, Seattle, 1958-59, and University of Wyoming, Laramie, 1959-62; University of Iowa, Iowa City, assistant professor, 1962-64, associate professor, 1964-66, professor of history, 1966—. Visiting associate professor of history, University of Oregon, summer, 1966; visiting professor of history, University of Montana, 1970, and University of Washington, 1974. *Military service:* U.S. Army, 1944-46; became sergeant; awarded Purple Heart. *Member:* American Historical Association, Organization of American Historians, Society for Historians of American Foreign Relations. *Awards, honors:* American Council of Learned Societies grant in Korean studies, 1951; Rockefeller Foundation research fellowship, 1964-65.

WRITINGS: The Inquiry: American Preparations for Peace, 1917-1919, Yale University Press, 1963; (editor with Robert Skotheim) W. Stull Holt, *"Historical Scholarship in the United States" and Other Essays,* University of Washington Press, 1967; (editor) Lewis Einstein, *A Diplomat Looks Back* (memoirs), Yale University Press, 1968; (editor) *Herbert Hoover: The Great War and Its Aftermath, 1914-1923,* University of Iowa Press, 1979.

WORK IN PROGRESS: The American Commission to Negotiate Peace, 1918-1920; American Diplomats and World Politics.

* * *

GELLIS, Roberta L(eah Jacobs) 1927-
(Leah Jacobs)

PERSONAL: Born September 27, 1927, in New York, N.Y.; daughter of Morris B. (a chemist) and Margaret (Segall) Jacobs; married Charles Gellis (a teacher), April 14, 1946; children: Mark Daniel. *Education:* Hunter College (now Hunter College of the City University of New York), B.A., 1946; Brooklyn Polytechnic Institute, M.S., 1951; New York University, graduate study, 1954-59. *Politics:* Democrat ("vaguely"). *Religion:* Jewish. *Home:* 119 Princeton St., Roslyn Heights, Long Island, N.Y. 11577. *Agent:* Lyle Kenyon Engel Book Creations, Inc., Schillings Crossing Rd., Canaan, N.Y. 12029.

CAREER: Foster D. Snell, Inc., New York City, chemist, 1947-54; McGraw-Hill Book Co., New York City, editor, 1954-56; New York University, New York City, teaching assistant in English, 1956-58; Hudson Laboratories, New York City, bacteriologist, 1961-63. Freelance editor for Macmillan Publishing Co., Inc., Interscience, John Wiley & Sons, Inc., and other publishers. *Member:* Authors Guild, Pen and Brush Club.

WRITINGS: Knights' Honor, Doubleday, 1964; *Bond of Blood,* Doubleday, 1965; (under name Leah Jacobs) *The Psychiatrist's Wife,* New American Library, 1966; *Sing Witch, Sing Death,* Bantam, 1975; *The Dragon and the Rose,* Playboy Press, 1977; *The Sword and the Swan,* Playboy Press, 1977; *The English Heiress,* Dell, 1980; *The Cornish Heiress,* Dell, 1981; *Siren Song,* Playboy Press, 1981.

"Roselynde Chronicle" series; published by Playboy Press: *Roselynde,* 1978; *Alinor,* 1978; *Joanna,* 1978; *Gilliane,* 1979; *Rhiannon,* 1981.

WORK IN PROGRESS: Sequels to the novels *The Cornish Heiress* and *Siren Song;* further volumes in the "Roselynde

Chronicle" series; research on American spies during the Revolution.

SIDELIGHTS: Roberta L. Gellis writes *CA:* "My major interests are both vocational and avocational—science and literature. I hope that the scientific training has given me a sufficient taste for exactness to make my historical novels accurate, and that my devotion to literature (particularly medieval and eighteenth-century) has taught me to use my imagination in the application of scientific principles." She adds that "I hope to give my readers a feeling for history—a thing lived and made by people, not a string of dry dates and facts."

AVOCATIONAL INTERESTS: Animals, English and European history.

* * *

GHURYE, G(ovind) S(adashiv) 1893-

PERSONAL: Born December, 1893, in Malvan, Maharashtra, India; son of Sadashi and Parvati Ghurye; married; children: Sudhish, Mrs. Kumud S. Desai. *Education:* University of Bombay, B.A., 1916, M.A., 1918; Cambridge University, Ph.D., 1923. *Politics:* "Unattached intellectual." *Religion:* Hindu. *Home:* Prasad, 17th Rd., Khar, Bombay 52, Maharashtra, India.

CAREER: University of Bombay, Bombay, India, assistant to the lecturer in Sanskrit, Elphinstone College, beginning 1918, reader in sociology, 1924-34, professor of sociology, 1935-59, professor emeritus, 1960—, chairman of department of sociology, 1924-59. *Member:* Indian Sociological Society (founder and president, 1951—).

WRITINGS: Caste, Class and Occupation, Popular Book Depot, 1932, 5th edition published as *Caste and Race in India,* Popular Prakashan, 1971; *The Scheduled Tribes,* Popular Book Depot, 1943, 2nd edition, 1959; *Culture and Society,* Oxford University Press, 1947; (editor with others) *Papers in Sociology,* University of Bombay, 1947; *Occidental Civilization,* International Book House, 1948; *Indian Costume,* Popular Book Depot, 1950, 2nd edition, Popular Prakashan, 1964; *Race Relations in Negro Africa,* Asia Publishing House, 1952; (with L. N. Chapekar) *Indian Sadhus,* Popular Book Depot, 1954, 2nd edition, Popular Prakashan, 1964; *Family and Kin in Indo-European Culture,* Popular Book Depot, 1956, 2nd edition, 1962; *Sexual Behavior of the American Female,* Current Book House, 1957; *Mahadev Kolis,* Popular Book Depot, 1957; *Vidyas,* Popular Book Depot, 1957; *Bharatanatya and Its Costume,* Popular Book Depot, 1958.

After a Century and a Quarter, Popular Book Depot, 1960; *Gods and Men,* Popular Book Depot, 1962; *Cities and Civilisation,* Popular Book Depot, 1963; *Anatomy of a Rururban Community,* Popular Book Depot, 1963; *Anthropo-Sociological Papers,* Popular Book Depot, 1963; *Religious Consciousness,* Popular Book Depot, 1965; *Shakespeare on Conscience and Justice,* Popular Book Depot, 1965; *Rajput Architecture,* Popular Prakashan, 1968; *Two Brahmanical Institutions,* Popular Prakashan, 1972; *I and Other Explorations,* Popular Prakashan, 1973; *Whither India,* Popular Prakashan, 1974.

Also author of *Social Tensions in India,* 1968, *Indian Acculturation: Agastga and Skanda,* 1977, *India Reasserts Democracy,* 1978, *Vedic India,* 1979, *The Legacy of the Romayana,* 1979, and *The Burning Caldron of Northeast India,* 1980. Contributor to professional journals. Former chief editor, *Sociological Bulletin.*

GILES, Janice Holt 1909-1979

PERSONAL: Born March 28, 1909, in Altus, Ark.; died June 1, 1979, in Knifley, Ky.; daughter of John Albert (a teacher) and Lucy (a teacher; maiden name, McGraw) Holt; married Otto Moore, 1927 (divorced, 1939); married Henry Giles, October 11, 1945; children: (first marriage) Elizabeth Moore Hancock. *Education:* Attended University of Arkansas and Transylvania College (now University). *Politics:* Democrat. *Religion:* Presbyterian. *Home and office:* Spout Springs, Knifley, Ky. 42753. *Agent:* Paul R. Reynolds, Inc., 12 East 41st St., New York, N.Y. 10017.

CAREER: Worked as director of religious education for Pulaski Heights Community Church, Little Rock, Ark., and as director of children's work for Arkansas-Louisiana Board of Missions, Disciples of Christ, Little Rock; Presbyterian Seminary, Louisville, Ky., assistant to dean, 1941-50; full-time free-lance writer, 1950-79. Member of board of directors, Adair County (Ky.) Arts and Crafts Corp. *Member:* Authors League of America, National League of American Pen Women.

WRITINGS—Published by Houghton, except as indicated: *The Enduring Hills,* Westminster, 1950, revised edition, with new foreword by the author, Houghton, 1971; *Miss Willie,* Westminster, 1951, revised edition, with new foreword by the author, Houghton, 1971; *Tara's Healing,* Westminster, 1951, reprinted, Houghton, 1972; (with husband, Henry E. Giles) *Harbin's Ridge,* 1951, reprinted, 1977; *Forty Acres and No Mule* (nonfiction), Westminster, 1952, 2nd edition, 1967; *The Kentuckians,* 1953, reprinted, Avon, 1976; *The Plum Thicket,* 1954, reprinted, Fawcett, 1978; *Hannah Fowler,* 1956, reprinted, Avon, 1977; *The Believers,* 1957, reprinted, Avon, 1976; *The Land beyond the Mountains,* 1958, revised edition, 1974; *Johnny Osage,* 1960, reprinted, G. K. Hall, 1980; *Savanna,* 1961; *Voyage to Santa Fe,* 1962; (with H. E. Giles) *A Little Better Than Plumb* (nonfiction), 1962; *Run Me a River,* 1964.

(With H. E. Giles) *The G.I. Journal of Sgt. Giles* (nonfiction), 1965; *Time of Glory,* 1966; *Special Breed,* 1966; *The Great Adventure,* 1966; *Shady Grove,* 1968; *Six-Horse Hitch,* 1969; *The Damned Engineers,* 1970; (with H. E. Giles) *Around Our House,* 1971; *The Kinta Years,* 1973; *Wellspring,* 1975. Contributor of short stories to periodicals, including *McCall's, Good Housekeeping,* and *Woman's Day.*

BIOGRAPHICAL/CRITICAL SOURCES: Louisville Courier-Journal Magazine, June 18, 1950, September 23, 1951, March 8, 1959; *Wilson Library Bulletin,* February, 1958; *State Library System,* Frankfort, Ky., 1963; *Bulletin* of Kentucky Association of School Librarians, spring, 1965.†

* * *

GILL, Joseph 1901-

PERSONAL: Born November 8, 1901, in Killamarsh, England; son of Daniel (a coal mining official) and Charlotte (Roddis) Gill. *Education:* University College, London, B.A., 1924, B.A. (honors in Greek and Latin), 1938, Ph.D. 1949; Gregorian University, Ph.D., 1926, S.T.L., 1933. *Home:* 10 Albert Rd., Harborne, Birmingham B17 0AN, England.

CAREER: Entered Society of Jesus (Jesuits), 1918, ordained Roman Catholic priest; Pontifical Oriental Institute, Rome, Italy, professor of Byzantine history and Byzantine Greek, 1938-39, 1946-66, rector, 1962-67; Gregorian University, Rome, Italy, professor of Anglican theology, 1948-66; Heythrop College, Chipping Norton, England, professor,

1968—; Campion Hall, Oxford, England, tutor, 1970-80. *Military service:* Royal Air Force, chaplain, 1940-46; mentioned in dispatches.

WRITINGS: La Chiesa Anglicana, Instituto Editoriale Galileo, 1948; (editor) *Quae supersunt Actorum graecorum Concilii Florentini,* Pontificium Institutum Orientalium Studiorum, 1953; *The Council of Florence,* Cambridge University Press, 1959, 2nd edition, 1961; *Eugenius IV, Pope of Christian Union,* Newman, 1961; (with Edmund Flood) *The Orthodox: Their Relations with Rome,* Paulist Press, 1964; *Personalities of the Council of Florence, and Other Essays,* Basil Blackwell, 1964, Barnes & Noble, 1965; *Orationes Georgii Scholarii in Concilio Florentino habitae,* Pontificium Institutum Orientalium Studiorum, 1964; *Constance et Bale-Florence* (history of the 9th Ecumenical Council), l'Orante, 1965; *Church Union: Rome and Byzantium (1204-1453),* Variorum Reprints, 1979; *Byzantium and the Papacy, 1198-1400,* Rutgers University Press, 1979.

Contributor: A. Piolanti, *Il Protestantesimo ieri e oggi,* F. Ferrari, 1958; C. Boyer, *Il Problema ecumenico oggi,* Editrice Queriniana, 1960; *Le Concile et les conciles,* Editions du Cerf, 1960; *L'Unita della Chiesa,* Vita e Pensiero, 1962; Wilhelm de Vries, *Rom und die Patriarchate des Ostens,* Karl Alber, 1963; Ivanka, Tyciak, and Wiertz, editors, *Handbuch der Ostkirchenkunde,* Patmos-Verlag, 1970; *Miscellanea Marciana di Studi Bessarionea,* Padova, 1976; P. Whitting, editor, *Byzantium: An Introduction,* 2nd edition, Basil Blackwell, 1978; J.T.A. Koumoulides, editor, *Hellenic Prospectives: Essays in the History of Greece,* University Press of America, 1980. Contributor of articles to encyclopedias and historical journals.

WORK IN PROGRESS: John V. Palaeologus.

*   *   *

GILLETT, Eric (Walkey) 1893-1978

PERSONAL: Born August 24, 1893, in Bowdon, Cheshire, England; died December 8, 1978; son of Samuel Walkey and Edith Suzette (Barlow) Gillett; married Joan Edwards, August 12, 1926 (deceased); married Nancy Emmy Miller, October 8, 1962 (deceased); children: (first marriage) John Anthony Cecil Walkey, Anthea Carol (deceased). *Education:* Lincoln College, Oxford, B.A. (with honors), M.A. *Religion:* Anglican. *Home:* Flat 4, 29 Brunswick Sq., Hove, East Sussex BN3 1EJ, England. *Agent:* A. P. Watt & Son, 26/28 Bedford Row, London WC1R 4HL, England.

CAREER: University of Birmingham, Birmingham, England, lecturer in English literature and warden of Chancellor's Hall, 1922-27; Raffles College, Singapore, Johore Professor of English Language and Literature, 1927-32; literary adviser to Chapman & Hall Ltd., 1932-34, Longmans, Green & Co., 1935-51, and George G. Harrap & Co., 1952-58; general editor, Royal National Institute for the Blind, 1958-61; member of staff, Royal College of Music, 1961-71. Extension lecturer, University of London, Oxford University, and Cambridge University. Celebrity lecturer throughout England, in Holland and Sweden; speaker on more than two thousand radio programs. *Military service:* British Army, 1914-19; became captain; invalided. *Member:* Royal Society of Literature (fellow), Royal Automobile Club, Regency Society of Brighton and Hove (vice-chairman), United Oxford Club, Cambridge University Club, Hove Club, Marylebone Cricket Club, Vincent's Club (Oxford).

WRITINGS: Books and Writers, Malaya Publishing House, 1930; (editor) *Anthology for Children,* Malaya Publishing House, 1930; (editor) *Poets of Our Time,* Nelson, 1932;

Maria Jane Jewsbury, Oxford University Press, 1932; (with T. Earle Welby) *Normal English Prose,* Oxford University Press, 1934; (editor and author of introduction) *Elizabeth Ham by Herself, 1783-1820,* Faber, 1942; (with W. J. Entwistle) *The Literature of England, A.D. 500-1942,* Longmans, Green, 1943, 4th edition, 1961; (editor) *Junior Film Annual,* Low, 1946; *Eric Gillett's Film Book,* Low, 1947; (editor) *Film Fairyland,* Low, 1948; (editor) *Collins Film Book* (annual publication), Collins, 1948-51; (editor) J. B. Priestley, *All about Ourselves,* Heinemann, 1956. Also author of children's books and of scripts for British Broadcasting Corp.; general editor of guides issued by British Government to U.S. Armed Forces in Britain during World War II. Drama critic, *Yorkshire Post.* Contributor of articles and reviews to periodicals.

WORK IN PROGRESS: A Short History of English Literature.†

*   *   *

GINIGER, Kenneth Seeman 1919-

PERSONAL: Born February 18, 1919, in New York, N.Y.; son of Maurice Aaron and Pearl (Triester) Giniger; married Carol Virginia Wilkins (comptroller of American Ethical Union), September 27, 1952. *Education:* Attended University of Virginia, 1935-39, New York Law School, 1940-41. *Politics:* Republican. *Religion:* Episcopalian. *Home:* 1045 Park Ave., New York, N.Y. 10028. *Office:* K. S. Giniger Co., Inc., 235 Park Ave. S., New York, N.Y. 10003.

CAREER: Partner, Signet Press, 1939-40; Prentice-Hall, Inc., New York City, director of public relations, 1946-49, editor-in-chief of trade book division, 1949-52; Hawthorn Books, Inc., New York City, vice-president and general manager, 1952-61, president, 1961-65; K. S. Giniger Co., Inc., New York City, president, 1965—. President, Consolidated Book Publishers division of Processing & Books, Inc., Chicago, Ill., 1969-74, Tradewinds Group division of IPC Ltd., Sydney, Australia, 1974-76. Lecturer, New School for Social Research, 1948-49, New York University, 1979—. Member of national advisory board, Foundation for Religious Action, 1956—; Laymen's National Bible Committee, 1957—, first vice-president, 1960-63, president, 1963-71. Assistant to the director, Central Intelligence Agency, 1951-52. *Military service:* U.S. Army, 1941-45, 1952-53; became major. *Member:* P.E.N. (member of executive board, 1970-73), Overseas Press Club and Players (both New York), National Press Club and Army and Navy Club (both Washington, D.C.), Author's Club and Garrick Club (both London). *Awards, honors:* Brotherhood Week Award from National Conference of Christians and Jews for *The Compact Treasury of Inspiration,* 1956; chevalier, French Legion of Honor, 1966.

WRITINGS—Editor: *The Compact Treasury of Inspiration,* Hawthorn, 1955; *America, America, America,* F. Watts, 1957; *A Treasury of Golden Memories,* Doubleday, 1958; (with Walter Russell Bowie) *What Is Protestantism?,* F. Watts, 1965; *The Sayings of Jesus,* Golden Press, 1967; *A Little Treasury of Hope,* Collins, 1968; *A Little Treasury of Comfort,* Collins, 1968; *A Little Treasury of Healing,* Collins, 1968; *A Little Treasury of Christmas,* Collins, 1968; (with Will Yolen) *Heroes for Our Times,* Stackpole, 1969; *The Family Advent Book,* Doubleday, 1979. Contributor of articles to magazines and newspapers. Associate editor of *Arts and Decoration* and *Spur,* 1940-41; member of editorial board, *RAM Reports,* 1977—, *Communications and the Law,* 1978—.

GIOSEFFI, Daniela 1941-

PERSONAL: Surname is pronounced Gee-o-*sef*-ee; born February 12, 1941, in Orange, N.J.; daughter of Daniel Donato (a chemical engineer) and Josephine (Buzesky) Gioseffi; married Richard J. Kearney (a theatrical designer), September 5, 1965 (separated); children: Thea D. *Education:* Montclair State College, B.A., 1963; Catholic University of America, M.F.A., 1965. *Politics:* "Humane." *Religion:* "All and therefore none." *Home address:* P.O. Box 197, Brooklyn Heights, N.Y. 11202. *Agent:* Scott Meredith Agency, 845 Third Ave., New York, N.Y. 10022.

CAREER: Professional actress playing in stock resident and touring companies, 1964-69. Has given poetry readings at colleges, universities, and theatres throughout the United States and Europe and on radio and television programs in the United States and England. Creator of "Brooklyn Bridge Poetry Walk," sponsored by New York State Council on the Arts and New York City Cultural Affairs Department, June 25, 1972; founder of Walt Whitman/Hart Crane Memorial Poetry Series at Long Island Historical Society, fall, 1973. *Member:* Poetry Society of America, Actors Equity Association, SANE, Mobilization for Survival, Shad Alliance, Friends of the Earth, Planetary Citizens. *Awards, honors:* Creative Arts Public Service grants, New York State Council on the Arts, 1972, for multi-media, 1977, for poetry.

WRITINGS: "Care of the Body" (multi-media poems), first produced Off-Off Broadway at Cubiculo Theatre, May 3, 1970; "The Birth Dance of Earth" (multi-media presentation), first produced in New York, 1972; "The Golden Daffodil Dwarf and Other Works" (poem-plays), first produced Off-Broadway at St. Clement's Theatre, January 4, 1973; "Fathers and Sons" (play; based on novel by Ivan Turgenev), produced at the Classic Theatre in New York and for WBAI-Radio, November, 1973; *The Great American Belly Dance* (novel), Doubleday, 1977; *Eggs in the Lake* (poems), Boa Editions, 1979; *Earth Dancing: Mother Nature's Oldest Rite* (nonfiction), Stackpole, 1980.

Poetry and short stories represented in anthologies, including: *Contemporaries,* edited by Jean Malley, Viking, 1972; *Rising Tides: Twentieth Century American Women Poets,* edited by Laura Chester, Washington Square Press, 1973; *We Become New: Contemporary American Women Poets,* edited by Lucille Iverson, Bantam, 1973; *The Ardis Anthology of New American Poetry,* Ardis, 1978; *Seasons of Women,* edited by Penelope Washburn, Harper, 1979. Contributor of poems to *Nation, Chelsea, Ambit* (England), *Quadrant* (Australia), *Dialog* (Canada), *Choice, Paris Review, Antaeus, New York Quarterly, Minnesota Review, Ms.,* and *Modern Poetry Studies.*

SIDELIGHTS: Daniela Gioseffi told *CA:* "I write in all forms, poetry, plays, stories, novels, sing poems to the lyre, and dance, because I aspire to healing some of the rifts in the twentieth century American psyche. In the beginning poetry, music, dance, drama were all part of the same ritualistic aspiration."

*   *   *

GIPSON, Fred(erick Benjamin) 1908-1973

PERSONAL: Born February 7, 1908, in Mason, Tex.; died August 14, 1973, at his home near Mason, Tex.; son of Beckton and Emma (Dieshler) Gipson; married Tommie Eloise Wynn, 1940 (divorced, 1964); children: Philip Michael (deceased), Thomas Beckton. *Education:* Attended University of Texas, 1933-37. *Politics:* Democrat. *Agents:* (Books) Maurice Crain, 18 East 41st St., New York, N.Y.; (motion

pictures) H. N. Swanson, 8523 Sunset Blvd., Hollywood, Calif. 90009.

CAREER: Corpus Christi Caller-Times, Corpus Christi, Tex., reporter, 1938-40; free-lance writer, 1940-73. *Member:* Texas Institute of Letters (president, 1960), Headliners Club (Austin, Tex.). *Awards, honors:* McMurray Bookshop (Dallas, Tex.) award, 1949, for *Hound-Dog Man,* and 1950, for *Recollection Creek;* Cokesbury Book Store (Dallas, Tex.) award for children's book by Texas writer on Texas subject, 1956, for *The Trail Driving Rooster;* Maggie Award for Western book, 1958, for *Old Yeller;* William Allen White Children's Book Award, 1959, for *Old Yeller;* First Sequoyah Award, Oklahoma, 1959; Northwest Pacific Award, 1959.

WRITINGS—Nonfiction: *Fabulous Empire: Colonel Zack Miller's Story,* Houghton, 1946 (published in England as *Circles Round the Wagon,* M. Joseph, 1949); (with J. Oscar Langford) *Big Bend: A Homesteader's Story,* University of Texas Press, 1952, 2nd edition, 1973; *Cowhand: The Story of a Working Cowboy,* Harper, 1953, reprinted, Texas A&M University Press, 1977; *The Cow Killers: With the Aftosa Commission in Mexico,* University of Texas Press, 1956; *An Acceptance Speech,* Harper, 1960.

Fiction; published by Harper, except as indicated: *Hound-Dog Man* (Book-of-the-Month Club selection), 1949, reprinted, University of Nebraska Press, 1980; *The Home Place,* 1950, abridged edition published as *Return of the Texan,* Oliver & Boyd, 1962; *Recollection Creek,* 1955, revised edition for juveniles, 1959; *The Trail-Driving Rooster* (juvenile), 1955; *Old Yeller* (juvenile), 1956; *Savage Sam* (juvenile), 1962; *Little Arliss* (juvenile), 1978; *Curly and the Wild Boar,* 1980.

Author of screen adaptations of *Old Yeller* for Walt Disney Productions, 1957, *Hound-Dog Man* for Twentieth Century-Fox, 1959, and *Savage Sam,* with William Tunberg, for Walt Disney Productions, 1963. Also author of a television play "Brush Roper." Contributor to periodicals, including *Reader's Digest, Liberty,* and *Collier's.*†

*   *   *

GIPSON, Lawrence Henry 1880-1971

PERSONAL: Born December 7, 1880, in Greeley, Colo.; died September 26, 1971, in Bethlehem, Pa.; son of Albert Eugene (an editor) and Lina Maria (West) Gipson; married Jeannette Reed, October 8, 1909 (died, 1967). *Education:* University of Idaho, A.B., 1903; Oxford University, B.A., 1907; Yale University, Ph.D., 1918. *Religion:* Congregationalist. *Residence:* Bethlehem, Pa. *Office:* 405, The Library, Lehigh University, Bethlehem, Pa. 18015.

CAREER: University of Idaho, Moscow, instructor, 1903-04; College of Idaho, Caldwell, professor of history, 1907-10; Wabash College, Crawfordsville, Ind., professor of history, 1911-17, professor of history and political science, 1918-24; Lehigh University, Bethlehem, Pa., professor of history and head of department of history and government, 1924-46, research professor of history, 1946-52, research professor emeritus, 1952-71. Oxford University, Harmsworth Professor of American History, 1951-52, fellow of Queen's College, 1951-52, honorary fellow of Lincoln College, 1965-71; visiting professor of history at Indiana University, University of Pennsylvania, and Columbia University. Honorary consultant in American history, Library of Congress, 1965-67. *Military service:* Helped organize first Officers Training Camp at Fort Benjamin Harrison, Indianapolis, Ind., during World War I; served as adjutant, North Central Military District, Chicago Headquarters.

MEMBER: American Antiquarian Society, American Academy of Political and Social Science, American Historical Association, Royal Historical Society, Conference on British Studies (president, 1959-61), Conference on Early American History (founder), American Rhodes Scholar Association, Institute of Early American History and Culture (member of executive council, 1956-58), Massachusetts Historical Society (corresponding member), Mississippi Historical Association, Pennsylvania Historical Association (past president; past council member), Historical Society of Pennsylvania, Clements Library Associates, Colonial Williamsburg, Friends of Huntington Library, Phi Beta Kappa, Phi Alpha Theta, Franklin Inn Club (Philadelphia).

AWARDS, HONORS: Justin Winsor Prize of American Historical Association for *Jared Ingersoll,* 1921; Loubat Prize, Columbia University, for first six volumes of "The British Empire before the American Revolution," 1948; Bancroft Prize, Columbia University, for seventh volume, *Great War for the Empire: The Victorious Years,* 1950; Philadelphia Anthenaeum Literary Award for eighth volume, *Great War for the Empire: The Culmination,* 1954; Pulitzer Prize in history for tenth volume, *The Triumphant Empire: Thunder Clouds Gather in the West,* 1962. Rhodes Scholar, Oxford University, 1904; American Council of Learned Societies research grants, 1927, 1929; Social Science Research Council grant, 1929; Rockefeller Foundation grants, 1951-1963. D. Litt., Temple University 1947; M.A., Oxford University, 1951; L.H.D., Lehigh University, 1951, Yale University, 1955, and Kenyon College, 1961; LL.D., University of Idaho, 1953, Moravian College, 1961, and Wabash College, 1963.

WRITINGS: *Jared Ingersoll: A Study of American Loyalism in Relation to British Colonial Government,* Yale University Press, 1920, published as *American Loyalist: Jared Ingersoll,* 1971; (editor) *The Moravian Indian Mission on White River,* Indiana Historical Bureau, 1938; *Lewis Evans,* Historical Society of Pennsylvania, 1939; *The Coming of the Revolution, 1763-1775,* Harper, 1954. Also author of numerous monographs and other short publications.

"The British Empire before the American Revolution" series; published by Knopf, except as indicated: *The British Isles and the American Colonies,* Caxton, 1936, Volume I: *Great Britain and Ireland, 1748-1754,* revised edition, Knopf, 1954, Volume II: *The Southern Plantations, 1748-1754,* revised edition, Knopf, 1960, Volume III: *The Northern Plantations, 1748-1754,* revised edition, Knopf, 1960; *Zones of International Friction,* Volume IV: *North America South of the Great Lakes Region, 1748-1754,* 1940, Volume V: *The Great Lakes Frontier, Canada, the West Indies, India, 1748-1754,* 1942; *The Great War for the Empire,* Volume VI: *The Years of Defeat, 1754-1757,* 1946, Volume VII: *The Victorious Years, 1758-1760,* 1949, Volume VIII: *The Culmination, 1760-1763,* 1954; *The Triumphant Empire,* Volume IX: *New Responsibilities within the Enlarged Empire, 1763-1766,* 1956, Volume X: *Thunder Clouds Gather in the West, 1763-1766,* 1961, Volume XI: *The Rumbling of the Coming Storm, 1766-1770,* 1965, Volume XII: *Britain Sails into the Storm, 1770-1776,* 1965, Volume XIII: *The Empire beyond the Storm,* 1967; *A Bibliographical Guide to the History of the British Empire, 1748-1776,* 1968; *A Guide to Manuscripts Relating to the History of the British Empire, 1748-1776,* 1970.

Contributor: *The Expansion of the Anglo-Saxon Nations,* [London], 1920; *Essays . . . Presented to Charles McLean Andrews,* [New Haven], 1931; *Essays . . . in Honor of Wilbur Cortez Abbott,* [Cambridge, Mass.], 1941. Also contribu-

tor to *Writings on Pennsylvania History: A Bibliography,* 1946, *Principles and Functions of Government in the United States,* 1948, and *The American Story,* 1956; contributor to dictionaries and encyclopedias, including *Dictionary of American Biography,* 1930-35, *Dictionary of American History,* 1940, *New Century Cyclopedia of Names,* 1954, and *Encyclopaedia Britannica,* 1956. Contributor of articles to professional journals. Member of board of editors, *American Historical Review,* 1946-52; founder and member of board of editors, *Pennsylvania History;* member of board of advisers, *Journal of British Studies.*

SIDELIGHTS: Lawrence Henry Gipson was best known for his comprehensive "The British Empire before the American Revolution" series which C. F. Mullett of *Political Science Quarterly* called "a definitive account of an important era published in a form fitting so magisterial an achievement." *Library Journal's* R. R. Rea said that Gipson "stands in the forefront of American historians. His exhaustive . . . study of the British Empire is the greatest single-author multi-volume project of this generation."

The series is noteworthy for several reasons, the first of which is its historical scholarship. In a *Saturday Review* article, R. B. Morris wrote, "In the long process of revising our estimates of the old British Empire, no scholar, either here or abroad, has explored so widely and researched so prodigiously as Lawrence Henry Gipson." And Mullett made the point that "Mr. Gipson has not been content to paraphrase and reset other men's pages. Time and again he has gone back to the sources, even remote sources. The consequence is rather solidity than novelty, rather substance than interpretation."

Another outstanding feature, particularly in a technical work of this magnitude, is the writing quality and popular appeal of the series. A. L. Burt of the *Canadian Historical Review* wrote: "Professor Gipson, who is personally as modest as his work is ambitious, would be the last to claim a style such as has distinguished some of the classics, but there is no denying that his writing has literary quality. It flows with an easy grace, though sometimes it runs too long without reaching a period; and it occasionally develops a positive beauty, particularly in descriptive passages." In a *Christian Science Monitor* review, Crane Brinton said that even though Gipson "will not capture the interest of those who like their history highly seasoned and above all brief, he ought to have an audience beyond the specialists. For this is in many ways the kind of book to interest the cultivated layman." And J. T. Adams of the *New York Times* found that Gipson had "a humane touch and a flair for selecting arresting and fascinating quotations from the authorities, manuscript and others which he has consulted."

Finally "The British Empire before the American Revolution" is unique for its distinctive outlook on the American colonies. Gipson studied and taught extensively in Great Britain and as a result of this experience was able to present his series from the British point of view. But, as *New York Times* reviewer T. J. Wertenbaker explained, "since there has been so much written from the American point of view this adds to rather than detracts from the value of this scholarly, well-written book." Morris, the *Saturday Review* critic, called Gipson "unabashedly an admirer of the British empire" and said that he "paints a sympathetic canvas" where England is concerned; yet he feels that the author maintained "a considerable measure of objectivity" in the series.

AVOCATIONAL INTERESTS: Horticulture, meetings of learned societies.

BIOGRAPHICAL/CRITICAL SOURCES: *Christian Science Monitor*, September 30, 1936; *Spectator*, December 11, 1936; *New York Times*, April 14, 1940, March 3, 1946, November 14, 1954, October 7, 1956; *Saturday Review*, August 31, 1940, September 24, 1949, December 18, 1965; *Canadian Historical Review*, December, 1942, December, 1949, June, 1959, June, 1962; *Political Science Quarterly*, September, 1946, September, 1962; *New York Herald Tribune Book Review*, October 2, 1949, November 28, 1954; *New York Herald Tribune*, January 17, 1954; *Chicago Sunday Tribune*, August 29, 1954, December 9, 1956; *Library Journal*, October 1, 1958; *New England Quarterly*, December, 1962, March, 1968, June, 1971; *Book Week*, January 2, 1966; *Times Literary Supplement*, September 28, 1967, April 2, 1971; *Journal of American History*, December, 1967; *American Historical Review*, February, 1968.†

*   *   *

GIRDLESTONE, Cuthbert Morton 1895-1975

PERSONAL: Born September 17, 1895, in Bovey Tracey, Devonshire, England; died December 10, 1975, in France; son of James Hammond le Breton (a clergyman) and Edith Margaret (Coles) Girdlestone; married Anne Marie Micheletti, June 21, 1923; children: Magdalen Winefride, Ann Edith Girdlestone Kretz. *Education:* Attended private schools in England and France; Sorbonne, University of Paris, Licence es Lettres, 1915; Trinity College, Cambridge, B.A., 1926, M.A., 1923. *Politics:* Liberal. *Home:* 1, Parc de la Berengere, St. Cloud, S. et O., France.

CAREER: Cambridge University, Cambridge, England. lecturer in French, 1922-26; University of Durham, Newcastle-upon-Tyne, England, professor of French, 1926-60. *Military service:* British Army, Norfolk Regiment, 1918-19. *Awards, honors:* Chevalier de la Legion d'Honneur, 1955.

WRITINGS: *Dreamer and Striver: The Poetry of Frederic Mistral,* Methuen, 1936; *Mozart et ses Concertos pour piano,* Fischbacher, 1939, translation published as *Mozart's Piano Concertos,* Cassell, 1948, 3rd edition, 1978, published as *Mozart and His Piano Concertos,* Dover, 1964; *Jean-Philippe Rameau: His Life and Work,* Cassell, 1957, revised edition, Dover, 1969; (co-editor) *Claudel: L'Announce faite a Marie,* Cambridge University Press, 1945; (editor) *Racine: Bajazet,* Basil Blackwell, 1956; (translator) Marcel Aubert and Simone Goubet, *Romanesque Cathedrals and Abbeys of France,* Vane, 1966; *Louis-Francois Ramond, 1755-1827: Sa Vie, son oeuvre litteraire et politique,* Lettres Modernes (Paris), 1968; *La Tragedie en musique, 1673-1750: Consideree comme Genre litteraire,* Droz (Geneva), 1972. Contributor of articles on music, architecture, and French literature to journals.†

*   *   *

GITTINGS, Jo (Grenville) Manton 1919- (Jo Manton)

PERSONAL: Born July 28, 1919, in Hertfordshire, England; daughter of Grenville Manton; married Robert Gittings (a poet and biographer), January, 1949; children: two stepsons, two daughters. *Education:* Girton College, Cambridge University, B.A. (first class honors), 1941, M.A., 1946. *Religion:* Anglican. *Home:* The Stables, East Dean, Chichester, Sussex, England.

CAREER: British Broadcasting Corp., London, England, planner, writer, and producer of history broadcasts to schools, 1942-49. Vice-chairman of governors, Chichester High School for Girls and Chichester Lancastrian School for Girls, 1955—. *Member:* Society of Authors. *Awards, honors:* Junior Book Award from Boys Clubs of America, for *The Story of Albert Schweitzer.*

WRITINGS: *The Enchanted Ship,* Oxford University Press, 1950; *The Peach Blossom Forest,* Oxford University Press, 1951; *The Story of Albert Schweitzer,* Methuen, 1955; *A Portrait of Bach,* Methuen, 1957; *Elizabeth Garrett Anderson, M.D.,* A. & C. Black, 1958, published in America as *Elizabeth Garrett, M.D.,* Abelard, 1960; (with husband, Robert Gittings) *Windows on History* (five volumes), Hulton, 1959-65; (with R. Gittings) *The Story of John Keats,* Methuen, 1962; *Sister Dora,* Methuen, 1971; *Gods, Beasts, and Men,* Hulton, 1974; *Mary Carpenter and the Children of the Streets,* Heinemann, 1976; (with R. Gittings) *The Flying Horses,* Methuen, 1977; (with R. Gittings) *The Second Mrs. Hardy,* Heinemann, 1979. Also author of scripts on British and European history for broadcasts to schools, 1949—.

*   *   *

GLANVILLE, Brian (Lester) 1931-

PERSONAL: Born September 24, 1931, in London, England; son of James Arthur and Florence (Manches) Glanville; married Elizabeth Pamela de Boer Manasse, March 19, 1959; children: Mark Brian James, Toby John and Elizabeth Jane (twins), Josephine Sarah. *Education:* Attended Charterhouse School, 1945-49. *Home:* 160 Holland Park Ave., London W. 11, England. *Agent:* John Farquharson Ltd., 8 Bell Yard, London WC2A 2JU, England.

CAREER: Journalist and writer, 1949—. Sports columnist, *Sunday Times,* London, 1958—; soccer columnist, *New York Times.* Manager of football (soccer) club, the Chelsea Casuals, in London. Literary adviser, The Bodley Head Ltd., London, 1958-62. *Awards, honors:* First prize at Berlin Film Festival for script of British Broadcasting Corp. television documentary, "European Centre Forward," 1963.

WRITINGS: *The Reluctant Dictator,* Laurie, 1952; *Henry Sows the Wind,* Secker & Warburg, 1954; *Soccer Nemesis,* Secker & Warburg, 1955; *Along the Arno,* Secker & Warburg, 1956; *The Bankrupts,* Doubleday, 1958; *After Rome, Africa* (suspense novel), Secker & Warburg, 1959.

A Bad Streak (stories), Secker & Warburg, 1961; *Diamond,* Farrar, Straus, 1962; *The Director's Wife* (stories), Secker & Warburg, 1963; *The Rise of Gerry Logan,* Secker & Warburg, 1963, Delacorte, 1965; *Goalkeepers Are Crazy: A Collection of Football Stories,* Secker & Warburg, 1964; *The King of Hackney Marshes, and Other Stories,* Secker & Warburg, 1965; *A Second Home,* Delacorte, 1966; *A Roman Marriage* (short novel), Coward, 1967; *The Artist Type,* J. Cape, 1967, Coward, 1968; *People in Sport,* Secker & Warburg, 1967; *Soccer,* Crown, 1968; *The Olympian* (novel), Coward, 1969; *A Betting Man* (stories), Coward, 1969.

A Cry of Crickets (novel), Coward, 1970; *Money Is Love,* Doubleday, 1972 (published in England as *The Financiers,* Secker & Warburg, 1972); *Goalkeepers Are Different* (juvenile), Crown, 1972; *The Thing He Loves* (stories), Secker & Warburg, 1973; *The Comic,* Stein & Day, 1975; *The Dying of the Light,* Secker & Warburg, 1976; *A Book of Soccer,* Oxford University Press (New York), 1979; *Never Look Back,* M. Joseph, 1980. Original contributor to British Broadcasting Corp. television program, "That Was the Week That Was"; author of commentary for film of 1966 World Cup matches, "Goal!" Contributor of short stories and articles to *Mademoiselle, Gentleman's Quarterly,* and other magazines.

SIDELIGHTS: Brian Glanville's best-known novel is probably *The Olympian*, the story of the making of an Olympic runner. The book has been exceptionally well received by critics, many of whom believe that it is the author's finest work. Bill Perkins of the *National Observer* calls it "one of the best sports novels of all time" and goes on to say that Glanville "tells his story with a variety of techniques, all of which work wonderfully. Parts are told by Ike [the runner] in his simple Cockney style, parts in third person, parts through newspaper clippings and sports announcers, and parts by an articulate friend who serves as the drama's Greek chorus." Pete Axthelm, in his *Newsweek* review, explains that as a sportswriter Glanville "has spent years around athletes and their world and he is a keen observer of all its large and small ironies, hypocrisies and tensions. *The Olympian* is full of the pompous athletic officials, petty and dictatorial coaches and other characters familiar to anyone who has spent much time around major track competitions; Glanville's satirical gifts in themselves make the book a worthwhile portrait of a fascinating and little-understood field. But he provides much more. His tale is brilliantly told.... And it is also as serious an effort as anyone has made to explore the tortures and indecisions of the totally dedicated athlete."

Thomas Lask of the *New York Times* writes that *The Olympian* "takes a median position, equidistant from the mythic, fantasy-serving character of Bernard Malamud's *The Natural* and from the hard-line naturalism of Budd Schulberg's *The Harder They Fall*." And he feels that Glanville "can pace and plan a sub-four-minute mile better than most coaches, and he knows what goes into the training and making of these runners from the tedious cross-country runs to the final 250-yard kick that may make the difference between a winning or losing race. There are enough of these details, of the mechanics of the expense-paid tour, club politics and coaching rivalries to satisfy every track and field buff, and enough close-run races to stir a kinetic response in the most torpid reader." Richard Schickel, in a review for *Harper's*, calls *The Olympian* "a sober, suspenseful, carefully crafted and controlled work that penetrates to the center of the athletic enigma. Which is this: you ask a quite ordinary personality who has, by chance, been endowed with some extraordinary physical capacity ... and ask him to develop it, arduously, painfully, at the expense of life's ordinary amenities to absolutely freakish levels." Schickel continues: "Every four years, as I watch the athletes line up for the start of some Olympic event or other the same scary thought always strikes me: four years of effort, four years of these lives will be judged successes or failures by what happens in the next few seconds or minutes.... And Mr. Glanville makes you see and feel how a rather simple man can slowly, without ever quite realizing what is happening to him, be drawn to this mad moment, how his spirit is corrupted by it even as his flesh is purified in preparation for it."

AVOCATIONAL INTERESTS: Playing soccer.

BIOGRAPHICAL/CRITICAL SOURCES: London Magazine, April, 1961; William Walsh, *A Human Idiom*, Chatto & Windus, 1964; *Punch*, October 18, 1967; *New Statesman*, November 17, 1967; *New York Times*, May 22, 1969, June 13, 1969; *Newsweek*, June 23, 1969; *New York Times Book Review*, June 29, 1969; *Times Literary Supplement*, July 17, 1969, October 24, 1980; *National Observer*, July 21, 1969; *Harper's*, August, 1969; *Books*, October, 1969, April, 1970; *New York*, April 18, 1970; *Best Sellers*, May 1, 1970; *Contemporary Literary Criticism*, Volume VI, Gale, 1976.

GLANZ, Rudolf 1892-1978

PERSONAL: Born December 21, 1892, in Vienna, Austria; died July 17, 1978; came to United States in 1938, naturalized citizen; son of David (an artisan) and Regine (Graeber) Glanz; married Rose Levi, November 29, 1921 (died, 1941); married Charlotte Brandes (a clerk), March 12, 1950; children: Ruth (Mrs. Alfred Michaels). *Education:* Attended Beth Hamidrash, 1910-14; University of Vienna, Dr. juris utriusque, 1918. *Religion:* Jewish. *Home:* 620 West 171st St., New York, N.Y. 10032.

CAREER: Admitted to bar, Vienna, Austria, 1928; Yivo Institute for Jewish Research, New York, N.Y., research historian, 1938-56, member of advisory research council, 1940, member of board of directors, beginning 1945; author and lawyer. Chairman of law committee, member of executive committee, and member of board of directors, Vienna Jewish Community, 1924. *Military service:* Austrian Army, 1914-18. *Member:* American Historical Association, American Jewish Historical Society, Labor Zionist Organization of America-Poale Zion, Conference on Jewish Studies. *Awards, honors:* Committee for Displaced Scholars research grant, 1940.

WRITINGS—Published by Ktav, except as indicated: *Jews in Relation to the Cultural Milieu of Germans in America Up to the 1880's*, [New York], 1947; *The Jews of California: From the Discovery of Gold until 1880*, 1960; *The Jew in the Old American Folklore*, 1961; *German Jewish Names in America*, [New York], 1961; *Jew and Mormon: Historical Group Relations and Religious Outlook*, 1963; *Jew and Irish: Historical Group Relations and Immigration*, 1966; *Geschichte des niederen Juedischen Volkes in Deutschland: Eine Studie ueber historisches Gaunertum, Bettelwesen und Vagantentum*, [New York], 1968; *The German Jew in America: An Annotated Bibliography Including Books, Pamphlets, and Articles of Special Interest*, 1969; *Studies in Judaica Americana*, 1970; *Jew and Italian: Historic Group Relations and the New Immigration (1881-1924)*, 1971; *The Jew in Early American Wit and Graphic Humor*, 1973; *The Jewish Woman in America: Two Female Immigrant Generations*, Volume I: *The Eastern European Jewish Woman*, 1976, Volume II: *The German Jewish Woman*, 1977.

Also author of *Yiddish Elements in German Thief Jargon*, 1928, *Lower Classes of German Jewry in the 18th Century*, 1932, *Immigration of German Jews Up to 1880*, 1947, *Source Material: History of Jewish Immigration to U.S.*, 1951, *Jews and Chinese in America*, 1960, *The Rothschild Legend in America*, 1960, *German Jews in New York City in the 19th Century*, 1960, and *Aspects of the Social, Political, and Economic History of the Jews in America*, for Ktav.

Contributor to English and Yiddish publications. Editor, *Juedische Arbeiter*, 1924.

WORK IN PROGRESS: Research on immigration, historic group relations, American social history, history of the lower classes, historic folklore, and European history.†

*   *   *

GLASKOWSKY, Nicholas A(lexander), Jr. 1928-

PERSONAL: Born August 27, 1928, in Springfield, Mass.; son of Nicholas Alexander (a chemist) and Marian (Cook) Glaskowsky; married Elizabeth Pope, June 13, 1953; children: Peter Nicholas, Alexandra Elizabeth. *Education:* Harvard University, A.B., 1948; Stanford University, M.B.A., 1954, Ph.D., 1960. *Home:* 13421 Southwest 69th Ct., Miami, Fla. 33156. *Office:* School of Business Administration, University of Miami, Coral Gables, Fla. 33124.

CAREER: Menlo College, Menlo Park, Calif., instructor, 1954-55; Stanford University, Graduate School of Business, Stanford, Calif., case editor, 1955-56, lecturer, 1956-57; University of Minnesota, School of Business Administration, Minneapolis, lecturer, 1957-58, assistant professor, 1958-61, associate professor, 1961-64, professor, 1964-71, associate dean, 1966-70; National Distribution Services, Inc., Atlanta, Ga., president and chief executive officer, 1971-74; University of Miami, School of Business Administration, Coral Gables, Fla., professor, 1974—, associate dean of graduate programs and research, 1980—. Consultant to business firms. *Military service:* U.S. Army, 1948-52. *Member:* Academy of Management, Society of Logistics Engineers (member of advisory board), American Society of Traffic and Transportation.

WRITINGS: Management for Tomorrow, Graduate School of Business, Stanford University, 1958; *The Development of Coordinated Air-Truck Transportation,* School of Business Administration, University of Minnesota, 1962; (with G. E. Germane and J. L. Heskett) *Highway Transporation Management,* McGraw, 1963; (with Heskett and R. M. Ivie) *Business Logistics,* Ronald, 1964, revised edition, 1973; (with Heskett, Ivie, and L. Schneider) *Case Problems in Business Logistics,* Ronald, 1973; (with Germane, Heskett, and R. T. Davis) *The Logistics of Furniture Distribution,* Educational Research, 1975; (with B. F. O'Neil and D. R. Hudson) *Motor Carrier Regulation,* A.T.A. Foundation, 1976; (with L. R. Batts and R. D. Roth) *Motor Carrier Regulatory Environments,* A.T.A. Foundation, 1978. Author of monthly column, "Computer Applications to Problems of Transportation and Distribution Management," in *Transportation and Distribution Management,* 1963-66. Associate editor and referee, *Transportation and Logistics Review.*

*   *   *

GLIAUDA, Jurgis 1906-

PERSONAL: Born July 4, 1906, in Tobolsk, Siberia; son of Stasys (a government employee) and Maria Gliauda; married Maria Yankus; children: Jurgis-George. *Education:* University of Lithuania, law degree. *Home:* 946 East Herring Ave., West Covina, Calif. 91790.

CAREER: Has been a government executive in Lithuania and an attorney in Kaunas, Lithuania.

WRITINGS: Ave America (poetry), Friends', 1950; *Namai ant smelio* (novel), Draugas Co-workers' Club, 1952, published as *House upon the Sand,* Manyland Books, 1963; *Ora Pro Nobis* (novel), Draugas Co-workers' Club, 1953; *Gestanti Saule* (short stories; title means "The Setting Sun"), Lithuanian Book Club, 1954; *Raidziu Paseliai* (novel; title means "The Sowing of Letters"), Lithuanian Book Club, 1955; "Ciurlionis" (play), first produced 1959; *Siksnospar-niu Sostas* (novel; title means "The Throne of Bats"), Lithuanian Book Club, 1960; *Ikaro Sonta* (novel), Nida Book Club, 1961, published as *Sonata of Icarus,* Maryland Books, 1967; *Agonija* (novel; title means "Agony"), Nida Book Club, 1965; *Delfino zenkle* (novel; title means "Under the Sign of the Dolphin"), Draugas Co-workers' Club, 1966; *Liepsnos ir Apmaudo Asociai* (novel; title means "The Amphorae of Flame and Dispair"), Lithuanian Book Club, 1969; *Aitvarai ir Giria* (novel; title means "The Goblins and the Forest"), Revival of Lithuania Association, 1970; *Simas* (documentary), Viltis Club, 1971; *Taikos Rytas* (short stories; title means "A Peaceful Morning"), Nida Book Club, 1972; *Breksmes Nasta* (novel; title means "The Burden of Twilight"), Lithuanian Book Club, 1972; *Sunkiausiu Keliu*

(novel; title means "The Most Difficult Way"), Grinius Fund, 1972; *Kompiuterine Santuoka* (title means "The Wedding by Computer"), Nida-Pradalge, 1972; "Naktis" (play; title means "The Night"), first produced 1974; *Pa-gaire* (novel; title means "The Windy Spot"), Lithuanian Book Club, 1975; *Narsa Gyventi* (novel; title means "Daring to Live"), Lithuanian Book Club, 1978; *Perlojos Respublika* (novel; title means "The Republic of Perloja"), Dzukai Society, 1979; *Bausme* (short stories; title means "The Punishment"), Nida Book Club, 1980. Editor, *Lietuvis Teisininkas (The Lithuanian Lawyer),* 1949-52.

SIDELIGHTS: Jurgis Gliauda told *CA* that through his writings, he searches for "the sense of living the awful disillusions and hopes, the meeting of illusions and reason, the crisscrossing of sunny emotions and scepticism." He feels that "the process of creativity is a never-ending incarnation of the author into his drastically conflicting personalities, and adventurous travels through a labyrinth of dramatic or lyrical situations." He adds that writing is not a fiction but an essence of his life. *Avocational interests:* "Travel and reading, and an 'acute feeling' for contemporary problems of literature and of naked life."

BIOGRAPHICAL/CRITICAL SOURCES: Time, June 28, 1963; King Features Syndicate, July 6, 1963; *B'nai B'rith Messenger,* September 13, 1963; *Lithuanian Writers in the West,* Loyola University Press, 1979.

*   *   *

GOLD, Ivan 1932-

PERSONAL: Born May 12, 1932, in New York, N.Y.; son of Murray Arthur (a businessman) and Syd (Hartman) Gold; married Vera Cochran (a writer), 1968; children: Ian Matthew. *Education:* Columbia University, B.A., 1953; School of Oriental and African Studies, London, B.A., 1959; University of Barcelona, graduate study, 1959-60. *Home:* 96 Bay State Rd., Boston, Mass. 02215. *Agent:* Georges Borchardt, Inc., 136 East 57th St., New York, N.Y. 10022.

CAREER: Writer. Lecturer in creative writing, School of General Studies, Columbia University, 1964-67; visiting professor of English, Bard College, 1971-72; Boston University, special lecturer in graduate program in creative writing, 1974-76, teacher in fiction workshop, summers, 1975-80, teacher in Metropolitan College, 1979; visiting lecturer in English and creative writing, Brandeis University, 1976-77. *Military service:* U.S. Army, 1953-55. *Awards, honors:* Second prize, O. Henry Memorial Awards, 1961, for "The Nickel Misery of George Washington Carver Brown," originally published in *Esquire;* Guggenheim fellowship, 1963-64; Ingram-Merrill Foundation fellowship, 1964; Rosenthal Award, National Institute of Arts and Letters, 1964; National Endowment for the Arts grant, 1966; New York State Council on the Arts award, 1973.

WRITINGS: (Translator with Shozaburo Miyamoto) *Flower and Bird Painting of the Sung Period,* Faber, 1962; *Nickel Miseries* (collection of two novellas, three short stories), Viking, 1963; *Sick Friends* (novel), Dutton, 1969.

Contributor of short stories to anthologies: *The Best American Short Stories,* Houghton, 1954, revised edition, 1961; *The Love-Makers,* Pyramid Publications, 1956; *The Esquire Reader,* Dial, 1961; *Prize Stories: The O'Henry Awards,* Doubleday, 1961; *Breakthrough,* McGraw, 1964; *The World of Modern Fiction,* Simon & Schuster, 1966; *How We Live,* Macmillan, 1968; *The Single Voice,* Collier, 1969; *Fifty Years of the American Short Story,* Doubleday, 1970; *Writers as Teachers, Teachers as Writers,* Holt, 1970; *The*

Shapes of Fiction, Open and Closed, Holt, 1971; *Travelers,* Macmillan, 1972; *The Myth of American Manhood,* Dell, 1978; *Sex Roles in Literature,* Longman, 1980.

Contributor of fiction to periodicals, including *Esquire, Playboy, Cavalier,* and *Genesis West;* contributor of nonfiction to newspapers and magazines, including *New York Times, Village Voice, Washington Post, Nation, Commonweal, Harper's,* and *Newsday.*

WORK IN PROGRESS: A novel.

SIDELIGHTS: Ivan Gold's first book, a collection entitled *Nickel Miseries,* was very well received by critics. George Adelman, in a *Library Journal* review, says that "the stories are violent, humorous, shocking, even repellent; but despite Gold's extreme pessimism about his generation, not without hope. A fine new writer with a remarkably keen ear." A *Virginia Quarterly Review* critic writes: "Three old and two new short stories, dazzling in their brilliance, are enough to establish without further question Mr. Gold's cleverness and technical facility.... [He] has a fine satirical sense; he understands the value of understatement; and he knows precisely how to achieve his effects." And William Peden of the *New York Times Book Review* feels that "whether he is writing of the jungles of Manhattan or the off-limits back streets of Japan, Mr. Gold displays an intimate knowledge of both his people and their backgrounds. He creates his stories with skill and understanding; *Nickel Miseries* is a solid achievement."

Many critics see some of the positive elements of *Nickel Miseries* in Gold's novel, *Sick Friends,* but in general the book has not been reviewed as generously as the earlier work. The book tells the story of Jason Sams, author of a highly-praised book of short stories, and the obsession he develops for artists' groupie Christa Sarkassian. Leonard Kriegel of *Commonweal* notes the autobiographical nature of the novel and writes: "What we demand of the writer of autobiographical fiction is that he make his ghosts ours as he lays them to rest, that his choice of jungle, to use a much-overused word, be *relevant* to our time and terror. And this, it seems to me, is exactly what Gold has managed to do in *Sick Friends,* for what he says about the relationships created by those in their mid-thirties is not only depressing but may go a long ways towards explaining why we feel so much guilt about those who follow us (for some of us, including Jason Sams, our students)." R. V. Cassill, in a *Book World* review, calls Gold "a master of the vernacular appropriate to his particular scene. The idioms of dialogue and the narrator's randy ramblings flawlessly recreate the small vanities, evasions, coppings out, the conditional generosities, the genuine but limited tolerances, the subsidized anxieties, the ploys and counterploys of the friends' non-mercenary trade in women."

One common criticism of the book is that it is too long for the story it tells. Clive Jordan of the *New Statesman,* for instance, says that "any old-time troubadour would have compressed these hundreds of wallowing pages into one brief quatrain about the pain of loving." *Sick Friends* has also drawn a good deal of criticism for its explicit sexual detail. In a *Best Sellers* article, Paul Kiniery writes: "A more fitting title for this book would be: 'Sex: What Fun!' New York writer Jason Sams and visiting Californian Christa Sarkissian evidently believe that they are the first to discover sex. They proceed to exploit it within an hour after their first meeting and continue to do so for the following 343 pages. One wonders why the author wrote the book; one wonders why the publisher published it.... The book

should be a likely competitor for the greatest literary mistake of 1969." Cassill adds that "if Gold has left anything out in his cataloguing of the utterances, gestures, secretions, durations, smells, clothing disposal or texture of the supporting surface in the serial intercourse of Jason and Christa, I can't readily guess what it might be."

Richard Stern of the *New York Times Book Review,* however, explains that both the length and sexual content are vital to the integrity of Gold's story: "It may be that the depth of Jason's involvement with Christa needs all the trips to the grocery, the letters from friends, the sharp business of the street. (Most of these are intelligent and funny anyway.) It surely needs the sexual detail. Jason knows Christa the way Jacob knew Leah, but it turns out that that's most of what he knows about her and that's his enthrallment and his book. It's important then to make their sexual congress vivid.... There's none of the poetic slime of *Couples,* nor, on the other hand, none of *Portnoy's* stony farce. We have love's labors won and lost, and in the process see how Christa's sexual power is the source of her ruinous liquidity. No small trick."

AVOCATIONAL INTERESTS: Socializing, fathering.

BIOGRAPHICAL/CRITICAL SOURCES: Library Journal, April 1, 1963; *New York Herald Tribune Book Review,* May 5, 1963; *New York Times Book Review,* May 5, 1963, October 12, 1969; *Virginia Quarterly Review,* autumn, 1963; *Book World,* September 21, 1969; *New York Times,* September 30, 1969; *Best Sellers,* October 1, 1969; *Commonweal,* November 28, 1969.

*　　*　　*

GOLDBERG, Carl 1938-

PERSONAL: Born January 21, 1938, in Brooklyn, N.Y.; son of Samuel L. and Mollie (Hecht) Goldberg; married Merle Ann Cantor (a psychiatric social worker), July 3, 1959. *Education:* American International College, B.A., 1960; University of Wyoming, M.A., 1961; University of Oklahoma, Ph.D., 1966; Washington School of Psychiatry, certificate in analytic group psychotherapy, 1970. *Home:* 2650 East 13th St., Brooklyn, N.Y. 11238.

CAREER: Certified psychologist by Maryland Board of Professional Examiners Psychologists, 1970; licensed psychologist in District of Columbia, 1973. New York University, New York, N.Y., psychometrist, 1961-62; Hawthorne Cedar Knolls School, Hawthorne, N.Y., research psychologist, 1964-66; Kings County Hospital, Brooklyn, N.Y., postdoctoral clinical psychology intern, 1966-67; St. Elizabeth's Hospital, Washington, D.C., supervisory and training clinical psychologist, 1967-71; Laurel Comprehensive Community Mental Health Center, Prince George's County, Md., director, 1971—. Instructor, University of Virginia, 1968; lecturer, Psychiatric Institute Foundation, 1971-73; member of teaching staff of Washington School of Psychiatry, 1973, and of several psychotherapy institutes in Virginia, New York, and Montreal; guest lecturer on transatlantic voyages of S.S. *France,* associate clinical professor, George Washington University, 1974. Private practice in psychotherapy, Washington, D.C., 1968. Director, Northern Prince George's County Mental Health Team, 1971—, and Crossroads Institute (center for group psychotherapy service, training, and research) 1974. Consultant to National Drug Training Center, 1973, and to St. Elizabeth's Hospital Overholser Training Division and East Side Division.

MEMBER: American Psychological Association, American Group Psychotherapy Association, Prince George's County

Mental Health Association (professional adviser), District of Columbia Psychological Association, Psi Chi.

WRITINGS: (With H. W. Polsky and D. S. Claster) *Dynamics of Residential Treatment,* University of North Carolina Press, 1968; (with Polsky and Claster) *Social System Perspectives in Residential Institutions,* Michigan State University Press, 1970; *Encounter: Group Sensitivity Training Experience* (Psychiatry and Social Science Book Club selection), Science House, 1970; (with wife, Merle Cantor Goldberg) *The Human Circle: An Existential Approach to the New Group Therapies,* Nelson-Hall, 1973; *Therapeutic Partnership: Ethical Concerns in Psychotherapy,* Springer Verlag, 1973; *In the Defense of Narcissism: The Creative Self in Search of Meaning,* Gardner Press, 1980.

Contributor: D. A. Evans and W. L. Claiborn, editors, *Mental Health Issues and the Urban Poor,* Pergamon, 1974; J. Bradt, editor, *Systems, Science and the Future of Health,* Groome Center, 1976; L. R. Wolberg and M. L. Aronson, editors, *Group Therapy 1976,* Stratton Intercontinental Medical Books Corp., 1976; H. Grayson and C. Loew, editors *Changing Approaches to Psychotherapy,* Spectrum, 1977; Wolberg and Aronson, editors, *Group Therapy 1978,* Stratton Intercontinental Medical Books Corp., 1978; Wolberg and Aronson, editors, *Group Therapy and Family Therapy 1981,* Brunner, 1981; D. Halperin, editor *The New Religions,* SPI Publications, in press.

Contributor to *Proceedings of the International Group Psychotherapy Congress.* Author of column on mental health in *Laurel News Leader,* 1971-72. Contributor to professional journals, including *Group Psychotherapy and Psychodrama, Hospital and Community Psychiatry, Canada's Mental Health, Psychotherapy and Social Science Review,* and *International Journal of Psychiatry.*

WORK IN PROGRESS: Courage in the Modern World.

* * *

GOLDFRANK, Helen Colodny 1912-
(Helen Kay)

PERSONAL: Born October 27, 1912, in New York, N.Y.; daughter of Hyman and Tessie (Herman) Colodny; married Herbert Goldfrank, December 7, 1933; children: Lewis, Deborah, Joan. *Home:* 375 Nannyhagen Rd., Thornwood, N.Y. 10594.

CAREER: Writer. Member of board, "Learning to Read through the Arts," Guggenheim Museum. *Member:* Authors League of America, P.E.N., Society of Children's Book Writers, International Brancusi Society (vice-president).

WRITINGS—All under pseudonym Helen Kay: *Apple Pie for Lewis,* Alladin Books, 1951; *One Mitten Lewis* (Junior Literary Guild selection), Lothrop, 1955; *Snow Birthday* (Junior Literary Guild selection), Farrar, Straus, 1955; *City Springtime,* Hastings House, 1957; *Lincoln, A Big Man,* Hastings House, 1958; *The Magic Mitt,* Hastings House, 1959; *Pony for the Winter* (Junior Literary Guild selection), Farrar, Straus, 1959; *Summer to Share,* Hastings House, 1960; *Kendy's Monkey Business,* Farrar, Straus, 1961; *Cats on Pier #56,* Reilly & Lee, 1961; *Abe Lincoln's Hobby,* Reilly & Lee, 1961; *A Duck for Keeps* (Lucky Book Club selection), Abelard, 1962; *How Smart Are Animals?,* Basic Books, 1962; *House of Many Colors,* Abelard, 1963; *The Secrets of the Dolphin,* Macmillan, 1964; *A Stocking for a Kitten,* Abelard, 1965; *Picasso's World of Children,* Doubleday, 1965; *Henri's Hands for Pablo Picasso,* Abelard, 1965; *Man and Mastiff,* Macmillan, 1967; *An Egg Is for Wishing* (Junior Literary Guild selection), Abelard, 1966; *A Name for Little No Name,* Abelard, 1968; *A Lion for a Sitter,* Abelard, 1969; *Apron On, Apron Off,* Scholastic Book Services, 1968; *Apes,* Macmillan, 1970; *A Day in the Life of a Baby Gibbon,* Abelard, 1972.

WORK IN PROGRESS: A story on the boyhood of Rumanian sculptor Constantin Brancusi, entitled *The Staff of the Shepherd.*

SIDELIGHTS: Although Helen Colodny Goldfrank cites *The Secrets of the Dolphin* as her favorite among her many books, she considers *Picasso's World of Children* to be a personal triumph of sorts in light of her five-year struggle to get it published. As she explains to *CA:* "No one would believe me when I said that Picasso had done more work on childhood than any other artist, or that his output was an encyclopedia of childhood. I had to try to reach out from a farm in Thornwood to Mougins and Paris, in some frenzied way, to get the rights, to do the book, and to prove that it existed. . . . [It] grew out of the need for quality illustrations in children's books, and while it was a book for the whole family, it is used as a basic text and introduction to the works of Pablo Picasso."

Goldfrank was assisted in her efforts by Daniel Henry Kahnweiler, an art entrepreneur and backer of Picasso. Upon learning what she wished to do, he put all the resources of the Galerie Louise Leiris (the gallery that represented Picasso in France and throughout the world) at her disposal. Goldfrank continues: "In the 1967 comprehensive Picasso show at the Louvre, Paris, France, *Picasso's World of Children* was chosen from among hundreds as a reference in the catalogue, and stands among seventeen listed there. . . . Victor D'Amico, a former educational director of the Museum of Modern Art wired me on the publication of the book: 'Congratulations! How did you manage to get a children's book on an adult list?' To me that was one of the highest compliments—for all children's books should and must be adult material, too."

* * *

GOOD, I(rving) John 1916-
(K. Caj Doog)

PERSONAL: Born December 9, 1916, in London, England; son of Morris Edward (an antique dealer, sculptor, and author under pseudonym Mosheh Oved) and Sophia (Polikoff) Good. *Education:* Jesus College, Cambridge University, B.A., 1938, Ph.D., 1941, M.A., 1943, Sc.D., 1963, D.Sc., 1964. *Religion:* "Scientific Methodist." *Office:* Department of Statistics, Virginia Polytechnic Institute and State University, Blacksburg, Va. 24061.

CAREER: Served in British Foreign Office, Bletchley, England, 1941-45; University of Manchester, Manchester, England, lecturer in mathematics with responsibility for the electronic computer, 1945-48; Government Communication Headquarters, Cheltenham, England, deputy chief scientific officer, 1948-58; Admiralty Research Laboratory, Teddington, England, deputy chief scientific officer, 1959-62; affiliated with Institute for Defense Analyses, Communications Research Division, Princeton, N.J., 1962-64; Oxford University, Trinity College, Oxford, England, fellow in computer science and on Science Research Council, 1964-67; Virginia Polytechnic Institute and State University, Blacksburg, University Distinguished Professor of Statistics, 1967—. Research associate professor, Princeton University, 1955. Consultant to International Business Machines Corp., 1958.

MEMBER: Royal Statistical Society, Mind Association,

Institute of Mathematical Statistics (fellow), British Society for the Philosophy of Science, American Statistical Association (fellow), International Statistical Institute, British Association, Mathematical Association of America, General Systems, Mensa, Ratio Club, Institut International de Statistique, Classification Society, Paraphysical Research Association, London Mathematical Society, Cambridge Philosophical Society. *Awards, honors:* Mathematical Association of America prize for expository writing of high quality in *American Mathematics Monthly*, April, 1962; Horsley Prize from Virginia Academy of Science, 1972.

WRITINGS: Probability and the Weighing of Evidence, Hafner, 1950; (general editor) *The Scientist Speculates: An Anthology of Partly-Baked Ideas,* Basic Books, 1963; *The Estimation of Probabilities: An Essay on Modern Bayesian Methods,* M.I.T. Press, 1965; (with D. B. Osteyee) *Information, Weight of Evidence . . . ,* Springer, 1974.

Contributor: *Uncertainty and Business Decisions,* Liverpool University Press, 2nd edition, 1957; *Information Theory, Fourth London Symposium,* Butterworth, 1961; *Logic, Methodology, and Philosophy of Science,* Stanford University Press, 1962; *Theories of the Mind,* Free Press of Glencoe, 1962; *Time Series Analysis,* Wiley, 1963; *New Perspectives in Organization Research,* Wiley, 1964; *Advances in Computers,* Academic Press, 1965; *Machine Intelligence 2,* American Elsevier, 1967; *International Encyclopedia of the Social Sciences,* Macmillan, 1968; *Pattern Recognition,* Institution of Electrical Engineers/National Physical Laboratory, 1968; *Encyclopedia of Linguistics, Information, and Control,* Pergamon, 1969; *Multivariate Analysis II,* Academic Press, 1969; *Machine Intelligence 4,* Edinburgh University Press, 1969; *Induction, Physics, and Ethics,* Reidel, 1970; *Cybernetics, Art and Ideas,* Studio Vista, 1971; *Foundations of Statistical Inference,* Holt, 1971; *Computers in Number Theory,* Academic Press, 1971; *Cybernetics, Simulation, and Conflict Resolution,* Spartan, 1971; *Interdisciplinary Investigation of the Brain,* Plenum Press, 1972; *Science, Decision, and Value,* Reidel, 1973; *A Companion to Medical Studies,* Blackwell Scientific Publications, 1974; *PSA 1972,* Reidel, 1974; *Foundations of Probability Theory, Statistical Inference, and Statistical Theories of Science,* Reidel, 1976; *Machine Intelligence 8,* Horwood, 1977; *Classification and Clustering,* Academic Press, 1977; *International Encyclopedia of Statistics,* Free Press, 1978; *Bayesian Analysis in Econometrics and Statistics: Essays in Honor of Harold Jeffries,* North-Holland Publishing, 1980; *Philosophical Foundations of Economics,* Reidel, 1980; *A History of Computing in the Twentieth Century,* Academic Press, 1980; *Encyclopedia of Statistical Sciences,* Wiley, 1981. Contributor to *McGraw-Hill Encyclopaedia of Science and Technology;* contributor of 220 papers and 450 reviews to scientific and mathematical journals in England and the United States, some under pseudonym K. Caj Doog.

WORK IN PROGRESS: A book on clinical decisions, with W. I. Card; *Probability Density Estimation and Bump Hunting,* for Decker; other research on probability estimation.

SIDELIGHTS: I. John Good told *CA:* "I wrote my first book because I believed the world needed more rationality, which to me meant the use of probability judgements. At that time nearly all statisticians were kidding themselves into thinking that subjective probability judgements were not necessary in scientific work.

"When I was in high school, I lived in Hendon, London, which had a good public library. There I found books by F. P. Ramsey and J. M. Keynes which influenced my philos-

ophy of probability. This philosophy was useful in my work during World War II on German ciphers. At that time my thinking was further influenced by A. M. Turing.

"When I was nine years of age I had diptheria and, while in the hospital, I discovered that the square root of two could not be expressed as the ratio of two whole numbers. G. H. Hardy later described this in his book, *A Mathematician's Apology,* as the greatest discovery of the ancient Greeks —whom he also described as 'fellows of another college.'

"My earliest post-natal memory that anyone will believe was finding it necessary to scream because I did not know what to call my mother, I have much earlier memories but they will not be believed so it is pointless to mention them. Some of my memories of my early childhood would make some readers blush."

*   *   *

GOODHEART, Eugene   1931-

PERSONAL: Born June 26, 1931, in New York, N.Y.; son of Samuel and Miriam (Oxenhorn) Goodheart; married Patricia Carol Somer, July 23, 1960 (divorced, January, 1974); married Joan Bamberger, July 8, 1977; children: Eric, Jessica. *Education:* Columbia University, A.B., 1953, Ph.D., 1961; University of Virginia, M.A., 1954; additional study at Sorbonne, University of Paris, 1956-57. *Home:* 25 Bernard Ave., Watertown, Mass. *Office:* Department of English, Boston University, Boston, Mass.

CAREER: City College (now City College of the City University of New York), instructor in English, 1955-56, 1957-58; Bard College, Annandale-on-Hudson, N.Y., instructor, 1958-60, assistant professor, 1960-62; University of Chicago, Chicago, Ill., assistant professor of English, 1962-66; Mt. Holyoke, South Hadley, Mass., associate professor in English, 1966-67; Massachusetts Institute of Technology, Cambridge, 1967-74, began as associate professor, became professor; Boston University, Boston, Mass., professor of English and chairman of department, 1974-80. Visiting assistant professor at Wesleyan University, Middletown, Conn., summer, 1963. *Member:* Phi Beta Kappa. *Awards, honors:* Fulbright scholarship to Paris; fellowships from University of Virginia, Dupont, 1953-54, Columbia University, 1957-58, American Council of Learned Societies, 1965-66, Guggenheim Foundation, 1970-71, and National Endowment for the Humanities, 1980-81.

WRITINGS: The Utopian Vision of D. H. Lawrence, University of Chicago Press, 1963; *The Cult of the Ego,* University of Chicago Press, 1968; *Culture and the Radical Conscience,* Harvard University Press, 1973; *The Failure of Criticism,* Harvard University Press, 1978. Contributor of essays and reviews to numerous periodicals.

WORK IN PROGRESS: Book on the artist as hero.

*   *   *

GOODLAD, John I.   1920-

PERSONAL: Born August 19, 1920, in North Vancouver, British Columbia, Canada; married Evalene M. Pearson, August 23, 1945; children: Stephen John, Mary Paula. *Education:* University of British Columbia, B.A. (first class honors), 1945, M.A., 1946; University of Chicago, Ph.D., 1949. *Home:* 3235 Rambla Pacifico, Malibu, Calif. *Office:* Graduate School of Education, University of California, Los Angeles, Calif. 90024.

CAREER: Teacher and principal at schools in Surrey, British Columbia, Canada, and director of education at British

Columbia Provincial Industrial School for Boys; Emory University, Atlanta, Ga., associate professor, 1949-50, professor and director of division of teacher education, and director of Agnes Scott College-Emory University teacher education program, 1950-56; University of Chicago, Chicago, Ill., professor and director of Center for Teacher Education, 1956-60; University of California, Los Angeles, professor of education and director of University Elementary School, 1960—, dean of Graduate School of Education, 1967—. Director of research and development division, Institute for Development of Educational Activities, 1966—. Member of board of directors, Council for the Study of Mankind, 1965-71 (chairman, 1969-71), National Foundation for the Improvement of Education, 1970-74, Longview Foundation, 1972—, and Global Perspectives in Education, Inc. (founding member), 1974—; National Humanities Faculty, member of board of trustees, 1972-76, vice-chairman, 1973-74; UNESCO Institute for Education, member of governing board, 1972-79, vice-chairman, 1974-75. Chairman of educational advisory board, Encyclopaedia Britannica Educational Corp., 1966-69; member of educational advisory board, Science Research Associates, 1974—; Lamplighter School, member of educational advisory council, 1976—, chairman, 1979—; International Learning Cooperative, chairman of professional advisory council and member of governing board, 1978—. Member of President's Task Force on Early Education, 1966-67, and President's Task Force on Education of the Gifted, 1967-68; member of national advisory council, Institute for Studies in Education, University of Notre Dame, 1970-75; member of National Council on Foreign Language and International Studies, 1980—.

MEMBER: National Society for the Study of Education (member of board, 1961—; chairman, 1972-73), Association for Supervision and Curriculum Development, American Council on Education (chairman of Council on Cooperation in Teacher Education, 1959-62), National Society of College Teachers of Education (president, 1962-63), American Educational Research Association (president, 1967-68), National Academy of Education (founding member; secretary-treasurer, 1971-77). *Awards, honors:* Fund for the Advancement of Education postdoctoral fellowship.; L.H.D., National College of Education, 1967, University of Louisville, 1968; LL.D., Kent State University, 1974, Pepperdine University, 1976.

WRITINGS: (With Herrick, Estvan, and Eberman) *The Elementary School,* Prentice-Hall, 1956; (with Spain and Drummond) *Educational Leadership and the Elementary School Principal,* Holt, 1956; (with R. H. Anderson) *The Nongraded Elementary School,* Harcourt, 1959, revised edition, 1963; *Planning and Organizing for Teaching,* National Education Association, 1963; *School Curriculum Reform in the United States,* Fund for the Advancement of Education, 1964; (editor) *The Changing American School,* National Society for the Study of Education, 1966; *The Development of a Conceptual System for Dealing with Problems of Curriculum and Instruction,* University of California Press, 1966; (with others) *The Changing School Curriculum,* Fund for the Advancement of Education, 1966; (with O'Toole and Tyler) *Computers and Information Systems in Education,* Harcourt, 1966; *School, Curriculum, and the Individual,* Blaisdell, 1966; (with Klein and others) *Behind the Classroom Door,* Charles A. Jones Publishing, 1970, revised edition published as *Looking behind the Classroom Door,* 1974; (editor and contributor) *Schooling for the Future: Toward Quality and Equality in American Precollegiate Education,* President's Commission on School Finance, 1971; (editor with

Harold G. Shane) *The Elementary School in the United States,* University of Chicago Press, 1973; (with Klein, Novotney, and others) *Early Schooling in the United States,* McGraw, 1973; (with Feshbach and Lombard) *Early Schooling in England and Israel,* McGraw, 1973; (editor) Carmen Culver and Gary J. Hoban, *Power to Change: Issues for the Innovative Educator,* McGraw, 1973; (with Klein, Novotney, Tye, and others) *Toward a Mankind School: An Adventure in Humanistic Education,* McGraw, 1974; (with others) *The Conventional and the Alternative in Education,* McCutcheon, 1975; *The Dynamics of Educational Change: Toward Responsive Schools,* McGraw, 1975; *Facing the Future: Issues in Education and Schooling,* McGraw, 1976; *What Schools Are For* (monograph), Phi Delta Kappa, 1979. Also author of *The Uses of Alternative Theories of Educational Change,* 1976, and *Curriculum Inquiry: The Study of Curriculum Practice,* 1979.

Contributor: *Viewpoints on Educational Issues and Problems,* University of Pennsylvania Press, 1952; Vincent J. Glennon, editor, *Frontiers of Elementary Education III,* Syracuse University Press, 1956; *How to Live with Your Children,* Young Mothers Study Club, Inc., 1956; Frederick Gruber, editor, *The Good Education of Youth,* University of Pennsylvania Press, 1957; Helen M. Robinson, editor, *Materials for Reading,* University of Chicago Press, 1957; *The Education of Teachers: New Perspectives,* National Commission on Teacher Education and Professional Standards, 1958; Francis S. Chase and Harold A. Anderson, editors, *The High School in a New Era,* University of Chicago Press, 1958; Robinson, editor, *Reading Instruction in Various Patterns of Grouping,* University of Chicago Press, 1959.

Gruber, editor, *Education in Transition,* University of Pennsylvania Press, 1960; *Tomorrow's Teaching,* Frontiers of Science Foundation of Oklahoma, 1962; William A. Jenkins, editor, *The Nature of Knowledge,* University of Wisconsin Press, 1962; Elmer R. Smith, editor, *Teacher Education: A Reappraisal,* Harper, 1962; Robert Ulich, editor, *Education and Mankind,* Harcourt, 1964; J. B. Conant, *Education of American Teachers,* McGraw, 1963; Eliezer Krumbein, editor, *Innovation in Teacher Education,* Northwestern University Press, 1965; *New Approaches to Individualizing Instruction,* Educational Testing Service, 1965; *Curriculum Change: Direction and Process,* Association for Supervision and Curriculum Development, 1966; Edgar L. Morphet and Charles O. Ryan, editors, *Implications for Education of Prospective Changes in Society,* Designing Education for the Future, 1967; *Education Parks,* U.S. Commission on Civil Rights, 1967; Otto Bird, editor, *Great Ideas Today,* 1969, Encyclopaedia Britannica, 1969; Dwight W. Allen and Eli Seifman, editors, *The Teacher's Handbook,* Scott, Foresman, 1971; John F. Kneller, editor, *Foundations of Education,* 3rd edition, Wiley, 1971; I. Keith Tyler and Catherine M. Williams, editors, *Educational Communication in a Revolutionary Age,* Charles A. Jones Publishers, 1973; Stephen M. Dobbs, editor, *Arts Education and Back to Basics,* National Art Education Association, 1979; Jerome J. Housman, editor, *Arts and the Schools,* McGraw, 1980. Contributor to *Encyclopaedia Britannica* and *Encyclopedia of Educational Research;* contributor of more than 150 articles to education journals and yearbooks.

Contributing editor, *Progressive Education,* 1955-58; member of editorial advisory board, *Child's World,* 1952-75, *Education Digest,* 1968-70, *Educational Forum,* 1969-71, *Educational Technology,* 1970-72, *International Review of Education,* 1972—, *Learning,* 1972—, *Tech Journal of Education,* 1974-77, *Review of Education,* 1974—, *Journal of*

Aesthetic Education, 1976-78, and *Educational Horizons,* 1978—; chairman of editorial advisory board, *New Standard Encyclopedia,* 1953-75; chairman of publications committee, Association for Supervision and Curriculum Development, 1955-57; member of board of editors, *School Review,* 1956-58, *Journal of Teacher Education,* 1958-60, and *American Educational Research Journal,* 1964-66; editorial consultant, *Journal of Curriculum Studies,* 1967-75; member of board of reviewers, *Journal of Research and Development in Education,* 1979.

WORK IN PROGRESS: A study of schooling in the United States.

*　　*　　*

GORDIMER, Nadine 1923-

PERSONAL: Born November 20, 1923, in Springs, South Africa; daughter of Isidore (a jeweler) and Nan (Myers) Gordimer; married Reinhold H. Cassirer (director of Johannesburg branch of Sotheby Parke Bernet), January 29, 1954; children: Oriane Cassirer Gavron, Hugo. *Education:* Attended private schools and, for one year, University of Witwatersrand. *Home:* 7 Frere Rd., Parktown West, Johannesburg, Transvaal, South Africa. *Agent:* Russell & Volkening, Inc., 551 Fifth Ave., New York, N.Y. 10017.

CAREER: Writer. Ford Foundation visiting professor, under auspices of Institute of Contemporary Arts, Washington, D.C., 1961. *Member:* International P.E.N. (vice-president), American Academy of Arts and Sciences (honorary member), American Academy of Literature and Arts (honorary member), Comunita Europea Degli Scrittora. *Awards, honors:* W. H. Smith Literary Award, 1961, for short story collection, *Friday's Footprint;* James Tait Black Award, 1969; Booker Prize, 1974; Grand Aigle d'Or, 1975; D.Litt., University of Leuven, 1980.

WRITINGS—Published by Viking, except as indicated: *The Soft Voice of the Serpent, and Other Stories,* Simon & Schuster, 1952; *The Lying Days* (novel), Simon & Schuster, 1953; *Six Feet of the Country,* Simon & Schuster, 1956; *A World of Strangers* (novel), Simon & Schuster, 1958; *Friday's Footprint, and Other Stories,* 1960; *Occasion for Loving,* 1963; *Not for Publication, and Other Stories,* 1965; *The Late Bourgeois World* (novel), 1966; *South African Writing Today,* Penguin, 1968.

A Guest of Honour (novel), 1970; *Livingstone's Companions* (stories), 1971; *The Conservationist* (novel), 1975; *Selected Stories,* 1976; *Burger's Daughter* (novel), 1979; *A Soldier's Embrace* (stories), 1980. Contributor to periodicals, including *New Yorker, Atlantic, Harper's, Holiday, Kenyon Review,* and *Encounter.*

SIDELIGHTS: Nadine Gordimer is well known as both a novelist and short story writer. Her work centers on life in her native South Africa and is particularly notable for its sensitive probing of apartheid and its effect on the people of that politically troubled country. Maxwell Geismar, in a *Saturday Review* article on Gordimer's novel *The Conservationist,* says that the author possesses an understanding of South African blacks that few whites have achieved. Speaking of her portrayal of black farm workers, Geismar writes: "She has a fine grasp of the language they speak—both among themselves and to their masters. She knows their customs, habits, superstitions, holiday ceremonials, and tribal rituals. And she sees right through the deceptive masks they wear for their dealings with the whites and even with the Indian settlers in South Africa.... I am not suggesting that *any* white South African writer can really penetrate the black

African consciousness. For that we may have to await the native black artists of that continent, who are historically about to emerge and tell their story.... [But] as things stand, Nadine Gordimer is one of the very few links between white and black in South Africa. She is a bearer of culture in a barbaric society. And she is a luminous symbol of at least one white person's understanding of the black man's burden."

When Gordimer's first book, a short-story collection entitled *Soft Voice of the Serpent, and Other Stories,* was published in 1952, Sylvia Stallings of the *New York Herald Tribune Book Review* said that "Miss Gordimer has reduced confusion to simplicity. The symbols she holds up are good for all times and all places, reminding us of our universal humanity. South Africa pervades all her writing, and yet these tales are never over-weighted with their local color. Africa is there, but it seems familiar to us, already our own; no more than a point of departure." Commenting on the lack of sensationalism in these stories, John Barkham of the *Saturday Review* wrote: "Readers who seek in these score or so tales any direct reflection of the headlines will not find them there. Miss Gordimer is a subtle writer who makes her points delicately and obliquely." And in a review for *Commonweal,* Richard Hayes said: "Nadine Gordimer works a vein of quiet but intensely perceptive observation. Her stories, limned against a background of a well-known and loved South Africa, carry their own spatial and material authenticity. Miss Gordimer is, indeed, so much a mistress of this time and place, so verbally dextrous, so mercilessly accurate in her sensory responses, that one anticipates the performance of a potentially major writer."

Gordimer's first novel, *The Lying Days,* was equally well received. In a *New York Times* review, James Stern wrote that the book "is in many respects as mature, as packed with insight into human nature, as void of conceit and banality, as original and as beautifully written as a novel by Virginia Woolf. This name springs to one's mind because Miss Gordimer is a writer who can not only capture but express in the lives of human beings those moments which are so fleeting, so impalpable, as well as so common that they are overlooked by all but a very rare artist. I can think of no modern first novel superior to Miss Gordimer's." Sylvia Stallings said that the book "gives a picture of South Africa as fascinating and tragic as the fiction of Alan Paton. But whereas Mr. Paton writes of adults, men and women who realize only in their maturity the extent of the tensions among which they live, Miss Gordimer is concerned with the young, trying to come to terms in their late adolescence with what history and injustice have bequeathed them."

Some critics had problems with Gordimer's second novel, *A World of Strangers.* Irving Howe of the *New Republic* found the book "sadly flawed by Miss Gordimer's literary self-consciousness. She spins her sentences immaculately; she never drops into anger or vital passions; the satiny flow of similes and metaphors, modestly calling attention to themselves, survives every pressure of her subject.... The subject of *A World of Strangers* may indicate that Miss Gordimer lives in Johannesburg, that very hell of our world; but her style suggests that she is really an inhabitant of the *New Yorker.*" In a *New Statesman* review, P. H. Johnson wrote that "her work is somewhat lacking in real inner power. The characters are well enough drawn; yet not one of them has the stature which propels a novelist's creation into an area of the reader's own experience." And in a *Library Journal* article, P. G. Anderson said: "*The Lying Days* showed promise; *A World of Strangers* doesn't live up to that promise even though the writing is good throughout. There are quotable, discerning phrases, but the plot is thin and an atmosphere of 'So what?' hangs over the whole.'' Edmund Fuller of the *Chicago Sunday Tribune,* however, disagreed that this book suffers in comparison to Gordimer's earlier work. He found that *A World of Strangers* ''reveals the rewarding steady development of the notable talent previously displayed in the earlier novel and her two volumes of short stories. She is an artist of marked skill and control, with perceptive insights into character and moral dilemmas.'' William Peden of the *New York Times* also liked the novel, saying that the author ''throughout, writes with insight and skill commensurate with the significance of her subject-matter. *A World of Strangers,* I believe, is the most impressive book of her already distinguished career.'' And Virginia Peterson, in a review for the *New York Herald Tribune Book Review,* made the point that this novel ''contains no arch-sized figures, no peaks of actions, no clarion words. Rather, it is a skillful and tender chiaroscuro to hang in your memory and remind you that all faces—no matter what their pigment—are merely windows, and that what lies behind those windows is the only thing that counts.''

In a *Christian Science Monitor* review of *Occasion for Loving,* John Hughes wrote: ''The strength of Miss Gordimer's writing is in her graphic characterizations, the gentle accuracy of her settings, and that intangible spell of reality which she weaves about all her work.... This is a mature and sophisticated book and there is a handful of tough words sprinkled among the shebeens and dives of Johannesburg. But this for the most part is Nadine Gordimer in the fine style we have come to expect of her: deeply honest and sensitive.'' *Harper's* critic K. G. Jackson noted that ''her perceptions are so penetrating and thought-provoking on little things and big that one reads slowly, marking passages, stopping sometimes for argument but more often for agreement.... The book is full of searching questions and honest answers in the framework of an absorbing story.'' But Hoke Norris of the *Saturday Review,* while admitting that ''throughout there is a splendid feel for character and for the delicate balance among human beings caught in relationships ordinary and extraordinary,'' felt that ''if there were only more living and less interior talk about living, ... then we would have a novel that really moves as good fiction must, and not merely a series of static (if seething) rationalizations. Unfortunately, the total effect here is one of stasis.''

Gordimer's next novel, *The Late Bourgeois World,* also met with somewhat mixed reviews. *Newsweek's* reviewer criticized: ''In this slim, nervous novel about tensions in racially torn South Africa, Miss Gordimer—usually so cool and distant—bristles openly with angry frustration.'' The reviewer found that ''a gloomy sense of insoluble problems permeates the novel—the race dilemma, wars, the bomb; even Miss Gordimer's lush South African sunsets are somehow altered so that they exist like faded postcards from a former world.... The pall of heavy gloom has finally invaded Miss Gordimer's stoic fiction.'' On the other hand, a *Times Literary Supplement* writer wrote: ''Miss Gordimer improves steadily and excitingly from book to book. [This] is probably her finest yet.'' The reviewer noted that ''there is very little plot and what there is is simply seen in retrospect. There is only the situation, and the beautifully created characters who are engaged in it.... Despite its background of the horror of life under an oppressive regime, this is in no sense a political novel. Only incidentally, and after one has put down the book, does one reflect on the situation out of which so

fine, compassionate, and exquisitely written a work has emerged.''

Gordimer's best-known work—and the one for which she has received the most praise from critics—is probably the 1970 novel, *A Guest of Honour.* Thomas Lask of the *New York Times* called it ''a long, spacious, comprehensive work of fiction'' and went on to say that ''it has all the lineaments of a traditional story. It is leisurely and detailed in narrative, melodramatic in its ending, exhaustive and superbly successful in its evocation of landscape and background. It lacks the restless energy and off-beat psychological probing of much current fiction. In fact, there's something Olympian, something magnificently confident in the way in which this South African writer goes about her work.... *A Guest of Honour* is a perceptive and a persuasive political novel that has the challenge and inevitability of history itself. It is political in that the major figures think and act in the light of their politics. It is free of that romantic and sentimental softness that made Robert Boldt's *A Man for All Seasons* and Jean Anouilh's *Becket* such conspicuous failures. As in Malraux's *Man's Fate,* and Koestler's *Darkness at Noon,* the fascination of the book derives from the dialectical play of its ideas.''

In a *Best Sellers* review, Carolyn Riley calls the novel ''one of those no-nonsense books for which the terms 'entertaining,' 'informative,' and 'well-written' are almost irrelevant. More than a novel, more than a 'history' of the new African nation which it presents, *A Guest of Honour* is more like a delimited *experience* of a time and a place—complex, confusing, straightforward, exciting, dull, stimulating, appalling, joyful. As a novelist, Miss Gordimer almost presupposes good plot, competent structuring, and fine writing. She aspires to, and achieves, success at a much higher—more 'real'—level.'' Reviewing the book for the *Nation,* Jose Yglesias wrote: ''The literary cliche that a good writer creates a whole world in his novels is true in Miss Gordimer's case. By the end of its 504 pages you know the country so well—its landscape, its weather, its people and social and political movements—that it comes as a shock to discover, when you start to write about it, that it was never given a name. It does not exist, any more than the political leaders in its story, but you cannot, after finishing this novel, read about the new African nations without finding teasing similarities.... Anyone who has read Miss Gordimer knows how superb a craftsman she is, how beautifully she bends the language to her needs, how acute an observer she is of even the quietest moment. It is well to emphasize these qualities of hers once more: if they cannot by themselves make *A Guest of Honour* the novel of first rank that it is, they give to the narrative its glittering surface and its flying urgency and—no contradiction here—make the reader continually remind himself that he must come back once more to savor this detail and to wring all the nuances from that scene. I know of no one in contemporary literature of whom this can be said except Solzhenitsyn in his major works.''

In *The Conservationist,* according to *Newsweek* reviewer Peter S. Prescott, Gordimer ''develops her story's physical and moral landscapes simultaneously. Her narrative advances by means of interior monologues interrupted by dialogue, by remembered conversations poking through present perceptions, by imagined scenes and confrontations. Symbols germinate and multiply.'' In his *New Statesman* review, Paul Theroux called the book ''a triumph of style'' and said that it ''is the clearest expression I have ever read of the state of the union, an evocation of the whole South African nightmare. It is not often that lyrical intelligence and political purpose are combined in so effective a way.... This book makes practically every other novel I've reviewed in the past few years look like indulgent trifling." The book, written in the first person, tells the story of Mehring, a wealthy white South African industrialist and land owner. Jonathan Raban, in an *Encounter* review, said that the author "has taken on Mehring's contemptuous, powerful sexuality and has felt the world through the stirrings of his genitals as well as simply watched it through his eyes. On this level alone, there has been no novel with which to compare it since Angus Wilson's *The Middle Age of Mrs. Eliot*.... [Gordimer] writes about being a man with more curiosity, passion and intelligence than any man could bring to the subject." Raban found that "the extraordinary thing is that Mehring is so complete and powerful a fictional character that he survives all of Miss Gordimer's efforts to trip him up. He only stops his prose when his brains are blown out. And he, not Miss Gordimer, finally dominates the novel." Not all critics were happy with the book, however. W. H. Archer wrote in a *Best Sellers* article: "The picture of the man which emerges very slowly from [these pages is] over-diluted with much that is tiresomely irrelevant. An inordinate amount of space is devoted to Mehring's casual feminine pickups, as unrewarding for the reader as most of this story; it is populated by two-dimensional names which hardly come alive as they drift through a setting that, as described—or more often suggested—arouses little curiosity concerning the South African countryside. For these busy times this fictional fantasy seems unrewarding in relation to the time spent on it."

Gordimer's 1979 novel, *Burger's Daughter*, according to Anatole Broyard of the *New York Times*, "is both a political novel and a love story, one that suggests that there is no politics without love or love without politics. Neither side of Nadine Gordimer's book is sacrificed to the other. Here is a democracy of passions.... Miss Gordimer evokes geographies of ironies, large as landscapes, as lifetimes. The last thing we see in Africa is a drunken old black man on a cart, insanely whipping a donkey that, insanely, refuses to move." Anthony Sampson, in a *New York Times Book Review* article, wrote: "No one has better described the vigor and humor, as well as the misery, of Soweto. Yet the political moments are always illuminated by the intense observation of people and places—tiny details precisely and lovingly described—that brings every incident to life and that gives Miss Gordimer's writing such universality. People, landscapes and politics are blended together in this evocative style, and through the eyes of the young, bewildered daughter the wide arc of South African politics comes into sudden focus. It is an integration reminiscent of the great Russian prerevolutionary novels. It remains extraordinary that such a novel should come out of a country so uncompromising and so increasingly brutalized, where the image of the flogged donkey has such fearful relevance; and it might seem equally surprising that an author of such sensitivity could live there. But this, too, was a Russian phenomenon. The very bleakness of the political predicament and the closeness to suffering seem able not only to provide insights into the political crisis, but to give a heightened awareness of the richness and values of life."

Eric Redman of the *Washington Post Book World* said: "I don't know a living writer who's even in a class with this enchanting and adroit South African. Many small delights distinguish Gordimer's fiction. Her prose is meticulous yet earthily sensual, a blend of metaphor and minute detail.... She has an unerring sense of scene, an ability to build force as if each chapter were one of her luminous short stories.

And while her writing is oblique, it is never obscure." Redman continues: "The technical mastery of Gordimer's craft is subordinate, however, to her literary purpose: to capture the many nuances of desire and perception without losing their emotional intensity. This is no small task; contemporary writing often achieves intensity only through the clash of bloodless stereotypes, or else sacrifices intensity in order to explore every nook and cranny of the human psyche. Gordimer's gift is to combine power with intricacy."

The *Chicago Tribune*'s Dolores Barclay calls Nadine Gordimer "a thorn in the side of the South African government." She says that Gordimer's novels "have stirred the foes of *apartheid* with words that slash at the system" and notes that three of these books have been banned in South Africa, for periods of up to twelve years. Lee Lescaze of the *Washington Post* reports that Gordimer refused to appeal the banning of these books because, she says, "I didn't want to recognize [the board of censors'] authority. I'm its victim, but I'm not going to recognize its mechanism." These three books were all released from the ban eventually, but Gordimer says that the government still regards her as a "very disloyal South African." She responds: "I consider myself an intensely loyal South African. I care deeply for my country. If I didn't, I wouldn't still be there."

BIOGRAPHICAL/CRITICAL SOURCES: Saturday Review, May 24, 1952, October 3, 1953, September 13, 1958, January 16, 1960, May 8, 1965, August 20, 1966, December 4, 1971, March 8, 1975; *New York Herald Tribune Book Review,* May 25, 1952, October 4, 1953, October 21, 1956, September 21, 1958, January 10, 1960, April 7, 1963; *San Francisco Chronicle,* May 26, 1952, November 9, 1953, January 24, 1960; *New Yorker,* June 7, 1952, November 21, 1953, November 29, 1958, May 12, 1975; *New York Times,* June 15, 1952, October 4, 1953, October 7, 1956, September 21, 1958, May 23, 1965, October 30, 1970, September 19, 1979, August 20, 1980; *New Republic,* July 7, 1952, November 10, 1958, May 8, 1965, September 10, 1966, September 13, 1975; *Commonweal,* October 23, 1953, July 9, 1965, November 4, 1966; *Times Literary Supplement,* October 30, 1953, July 13, 1956, June 27, 1958, February 12, 1960, March 1, 1963, July 22, 1965, July 7, 1966, May 14, 1971, May 26, 1972, January 9, 1976, July 9, 1976, April 25, 1980; *New Statesman and Nation,* August 18, 1956; *Time,* October 15, 1956, September 22, 1958, January 11, 1960, November 16, 1970, July 7, 1975; *New Statesman,* May 24, 1958, May 14, 1971, November 8, 1974, November 28, 1975; *Library Journal,* September 1, 1958; *Chicago Sunday Tribune,* September 21, 1958; *Booklist,* October 1, 1958, January 10, 1960.

New York Times Book Review, January 10, 1960, September 11, 1966, October 31, 1971, April 13, 1975, April 18, 1976, August 19, 1979, August 24, 1980; *Spectator,* February 12, 1960; *Christian Science Monitor,* January 10, 1963, November 4, 1971, May 19, 1975; *Harper's,* February, 1963, April, 1976; *Newsweek,* May 10, 1965, July 4, 1966, March 10, 1975, April 19, 1976; Martin Tucker, *Africa in Modern Literature: A Survey of Contemporary Writing,* Ungar, 1967; *Best Sellers,* December 15, 1970, November 15, 1971, March 15, 1975; *Nation,* June 18, 1971, August 18, 1976; *Encounter,* August, 1971, February, 1975; *Washington Post Book World,* November 28, 1971, April 6, 1975, August 26, 1979, September 7, 1980; *Contemporary Literary Criticism,* Gale, Volume III, 1975, Volume V, 1976, Volume VII, 1977, Volume X, 1979; *London Magazine,* April/May, 1975; *New York Review of Books,* June 26, 1975, July 15, 1976; *Ms,* July, 1975; *America,* April 17, 1976; *Sewanee Review,* spring, 1977; *Detroit News,* September 2, 1979; *Chicago Tribune*

Book World, September 9, 1979; *Washington Post,* December 4, 1979; *Chicago Tribune,* May 18, 1980.

—*Sketch by Peter M. Gareffa*

* * *

GOULD, Jean R(osalind) 1919-

PERSONAL: Born May 25, 1919, in Greenville, Ohio; daughter of Aaron J. and Elsie (Elgutter) Gould; divorced. *Education:* Attended University of Michigan for two years; University of Toledo, A.B., 1937. *Politics:* Reform Democrat.

CAREER: Amalgamated Clothing Workers Union, National Education Office, New York, N.Y., editorial and rewrite work, part-time, 1952-62; National Opinion Research Center, Princeton, N.J., research and public opinion work. County committeewoman, Democratic Party. Member of advisory board, Virginia Center for the Creative Arts, 1978—. *Member:* Authors Guild, Authors League of America, International P.E.N., Phi Kappa Phi. *Awards, honors:* Thomas A. Edison Award and prize for special excellence in contributing to character development of children, 1959, for *That Dunbar Boy;* fellowships at MacDowell Colony and Huntington Hartford Foundation, the latter in 1962 for work on Robert Frost book; fellowship at Yaddo, 1964, and Huntington Hartford Foundation, 1965, both for biographical studies of American playwrights; Ossabaw Island Foundation fellowships, 1968 and 1976; Radio Network Book Reviews "Oppie" Award for best biography of the year, 1969, Ohioana Library Association award, 1969, and American Association of University Women special award, 1970, all for *The Poet and Her Book: A Biography of Edna St. Vincent Millay;* National Book Award nomination, 1975, for *Amy: The World of Amy Lowell;* Virginia Center for the Creative Arts fellowships, 1978 and 1979, for studies of American women poets.

WRITINGS—Youth books: Fairy Tales, Whitman, 1944; *Miss Emily* (biography of Emily Dickinson), Houghton, 1946; *Jane* (biography of Jane Austen), Houghton, 1947; *Young Thack* (biography of William Makepeace Thackeray), Houghton, 1949; *Sidney Hillman,* Houghton, 1952; *Fisherman's Luck,* Macmillan, 1954; *That Dunbar Boy* (biography of Paul Laurence Dunbar), Dodd, 1958.

Adult books; all published by Dodd: (Editor and contributor) *Homegrown Liberal,* 1954; *Young Mariner Melville* (Literary Guild selection), 1956; *A Good Fight: F.D.R.'s Conquest of Polio,* 1960; *Winslow Homer: A Portrait,* 1962; *Robert Frost: The Aim Was Song,* 1964; *Modern American Playwrights,* 1966; *The Poet and Her Book: A Biography of Edna St. Vincent Millay,* 1969; *Walter Reuther: Labor's Rugged Individualist,* 1972; *Amy: The World of Amy Lowell and the Imagist Movement,* 1975; *American Women Poets: Pioneers of Modern Poetry,* 1980. Member of editorial board, *National Forum,* 1978.

WORK IN PROGRESS: Research for *American Women Poets in Contemporary Poetry.*

SIDELIGHTS: Jean R. Gould told *CA:* "To use an old phrase, which will surely date me, I was injected, if not born, with 'printer's ink in my veins.' My family was in the minor publishing business from the time I was six years old. They printed [or] published theater programs for years, plus an entertainment guide and a weekly paper. My mother wrote poetry and editorials; my aunt was a newspaperwoman for fifty years. So quite naturally, I began writing when I was about ten years old. My first effort was a play which I not only wrote, but directed and played the lead. My first writing

'job' was as assistant editor to my mother. A creative urge resulted in short stories, fairy tales, and plays for children. Several of the last were included in *Best Plays for Young Readers* in various years of the fifties. I always thought I would write novels and plays, but became known as a biographer instead. [This was] quite by accident.

"Because I wrote poetry, I loved reading it, and through a rare, truly literary professor [of] both seventeenth-century and contemporary poetry, I came under the spell of Emily Dickinson. A good many books had already been written about the New England mystic-poet, but none for young readers. So I wrote *Miss Emily,* which, after some hesitation, Houghton accepted and published. It was unexpectedly successful and stayed in print a long time. Since publishers, like movie producers, always want more of a successful [genre], I became a biographer. As might be expected, I have written more biographies of poets that of other figures of note; but my collective work *Modern American Playwrights* proved very successful and led to [my] present project on modern American poets, which at first was to have dealt with both sexes. However, since 'women's lib' and the E.R.A. have become so prominent, it was suggested by my publishers that I confine my subjects to women responsible for the evolution of modern poetry. Then I discovered the vast number of women writing poetry today and being recognized for their work on the same level as men. So two books became necessary instead of a single volume."

AVOCATIONAL INTERESTS: Politics, gardening, watercolor painting, and cooking.

BIOGRAPHICAL/CRITICAL SOURCES: New York Times, April 28, 1946; *Saturday Review of Literature,* September 28, 1946; *New York Herald Tribune Weekly Book Review,* May 11, 1947; *New York Herald Tribune Book Review,* May 11, 1952; *Villager,* April 20, 1961; *New York Times Book Review,* September 20, 1964; *Book World,* May 18, 1969; *Saturday Review,* June 7, 1969; *Best Sellers,* July 1, 1972, January, 1976; *New Republic,* December 6, 1975; *Choice,* March, 1976.

* * *

GRAMATKY, Hardie 1907-1979

PERSONAL: Born April 12, 1907, in Dallas, Tex.; died April 29, 1979, in Westport, Conn.; son of Bernhard August and Blanche (Gunner) Gramatky; married Dorothea Cooke, 1932; children: Linda Anne Smith. *Education:* Attended Stanford University, two years, and Chouinard Art School, two years. *Home and office:* 60 Roseville Rd., Westport, Conn. 06880.

CAREER: Walt Disney Productions, Hollywood, Calif., head animator, 1930-36; *Fortune,* New York City, pictorial reporter, 1937-40; U.S. Army Air Forces, New York City and Hollywood, supervisor of training film, 1942-44; freelance writer and artist, 1944-79. Lecturer on children's literature in schools and colleges. Member of Connecticut Committee for the Gifted, 1953-55. *Member:* National Academy of Design, American Watercolor Society (secretary, 1946-48), Society of Illustrators (member of board, 1941-42), Westport Artists, Salmagundi Club (New York). *Awards, honors:* Forty top watercolor awards, including Chicago International Award, 1942, and American Water Color Society High Winds Medal, 1979.

WRITINGS—All published by Putnam: Little Toot, 1939; *Hercules,* 1940, published as *Hercules: The Story of an Old Fashioned Fire Engine,* 1980; *Loopy,* 1941; *Creeper's Jeep,* 1948; *Sparky,* 1952; *Homer and the Circus Train,* 1957; *Boli-*

var, 1961; *Nikos and the Sea God*, 1963; *Little Toot on the Thames*, 1964; *Little Toot on the Grand Canal*, 1968; *Happy's Christmas*, 1970; *Little Toot on the Mississippi*, 1973; *Little Toot through the Golden Gate*, 1975. Also author, with Osmond Molarsky, of "Ellsworth Elephant" series in *Family Circle* magazine, 1959-62.

WORK IN PROGRESS: Little Toot and Loch Ness.

SIDELIGHTS: Hardie Gramatky's *Little Toot*, rated as one of the all-time greats in children's literature by the Library of Congress, has been read and enjoyed by countless children around the world since it first appeared in 1939. Though the sequels have also been fairly popular, none has quite matched the success of the original story of the saucy little tugboat who unexpectedly becomes a hero. It has, for example, been featured in a movie by Walt Disney called "Melody Time" (1942) and has been adapted for television and records, including one produced in 1977 by Caedmon Records entitled "All the Little Toot Stories" (as read by Hans Conried). In addition, all bookmobiles in the Los Angeles area have nameplates designating them as "Little Toots," and, in 1978, a "Little Toot" poster was published. "Little Toot" has even been a float in the Pasadena (Calif.) Tournament of Roses Parade.

Gramatky strongly believed that the success of children's books depends primarily on the pictures. As a result, he usually began his books by drawing the pictures first and then building a story around them. Nevertheless, he felt that his main mission was to get children to read; he regarded his illustrations as a way of making them extend their imaginations. As he explained to *CA:* "My work with children consists of 'chalk-talk' lectures.... [It] appeals to them to do more creative work [and] to use their great imaginations. I have talked at schools and libraries all over America and the result has been most heartening and surprising. Children have great creative ability—and their imaginations are tremendous!"

Aside from his illustrations for children's books, Gramatky painted many award-winning watercolors. His work is represented in many private and permanent public collections, including those at the Chicago Art Institute, Brooklyn Museum, Frye Museum (Seattle), Toledo Museum of Art, Marietta College (Ohio), and many others.

BIOGRAPHICAL/CRITICAL SOURCES: Annis Duff, *Bequest of Wings*, Viking, 1944; May Hill Arbuthnot, *Children and Books*, Scott, Foresman, 1947; Elizabeth Rider Montgomery, *The Story behind Modern Books*, Dodd, 1949; Cornelia Meigs and others, editors, *A Critical History of Children's Literature*, Macmillan, 1953; *Elementary English*, October, 1960; *American Artist*, May, 1962; *Books Are by People*, Citation Press, 1969; *Hartford Courant*, Hartford, Conn., December 9, 1973; *Christian Science Monitor*, May 1, 1974; *Authors in the News*, Volume I, Gale, 1976; *New York Times*, May 1, 1979; *AB Bookman's Weekly*, May 21, 1979.

*   *   *

GRAY, Dulcie

PERSONAL: Born in Kuala Lumpur, Malaysia; daughter of Arnold Savage (a lawyer) and Kate Edith Clulow (Gray) Bailey; married Michael Denison (an actor), April 29, 1939. *Education:* Educated in England and Malaya. *Religion:* Anglican. *Home:* Shardeloes, Amersham, Buckinghamshire, England. *Agent:* Douglas Rae Management, Ltd., 28 Charing Cross Rd., London WC2H 0DB, England.

CAREER: Actress, 1939—; writer. Has starred in about twenty-eight London plays, including Shaw's "Candida" and "Heartbreak House," and played on tour in South Africa, Australia, Hong Kong, Berlin; most recent London roles were in Agatha Christie's "A Murder Is Announced," at the Vaudeville Theatre, 1979, and Alan Ayckbourn's "Bedroom Farce," at the Prince of Wales Theatre, 1979. Films include "They Were Sisters," with James Mason, and "The Glassy Mountain," with her husband as co-star. Also has made more than five hundred radio and television appearances. *Member:* Crime Writers Association, Mystery Writers of America, British Actors Equity. *Awards, honors:* Queen's Silver Jubilee Medal, 1977; Times Educational Supplement Senior Information Award, 1979, for *Butterflies on My Mind*.

WRITINGS—All published by Macdonald & Co., except as indicated: *Love Affair* (play), Samuel French, 1957; *Murder on the Stairs*, Arthur Barker, 1957; *Murder in Melbourne*, Arthur Barker, 1958; *Baby Face*, Arthur Barker, 1959; *Epitaph for a Dead Actor*, Arthur Barker, 1960; *Murder on a Saturday*, Arthur Barker, 1961; *Murder in Mind*, 1963; *The Devil Wore Scarlet*, 1964; *Quarter for a Star*, 1964; (with husband, Michael Denison) *The Actor and His World*, Gollancz, 1964; *The Murder of Love*, 1967; *Died in the Red*, 1967; *Murder on Honeymoon*, 1969; *For Richer, for Richer*, 1970; *Deadly Lampshade*, 1971; *Understudy to Murder*, 1972; *Dead Give-Away*, 1974; *Ride on a Tiger*, 1975; *Stage Door Fright* (short stories), 1977; *Death in Denims* (juvenile), Everest Books, 1977; *Butterflies on My Mind*, Angus & Robertson, 1978; *Dark Calypso*, 1979. Short stories included in *The Girl on the Bus* (anthology of love stories), Pan Books, 1966, and eleven anthologies of horror stories published by Pan Books. Author of radio plays for British Broadcasting Corp. and of musical play, "Love a la Carte." Contributor of articles to *Sunday Express, Daily Sketch, Tatler*, short stories to *Evening Standard, Evening News*.

WORK IN PROGRESS: A detective novel set in Wales; a book on three generations of a theatrical family.

*   *   *

GREEN, John Alden   1925-

PERSONAL: Born November 4, 1925, in Cardston, Alberta, Canada; son of John Henry Forbes and Olivia M. (Thornhill) Green; married Michele-Therese Jugant, August 27, 1954; children: John Scott, Jeffrey Paul, Evan Curtis, Alan Merrill, Kerry Anne, Cammie Suzanne, Nicole Renee, Brent Eric, Richard Derrin. *Education:* Brigham Young University, B.A., 1954, M.A. 1955; University of Washington, Seattle, Ph.D., 1960. *Religion:* Church of Jesus Christ of Latter-day Saints (Mormon). *Home:* 623 South 590 E., Orem, Utah. *Office:* Department of French, Brigham Young University, Provo, Utah.

CAREER: University of North Dakota, Grand Forks, assistant professor, 1960-62, associate professor of French, 1962-63; University of Wichita, Wichita, Kan., associate professor and chairman of department of French, 1963-64; Brigham Young University, Provo, Utah, 1964—, began as associate professor, currently professor of French. *Military service:* Royal Canadian Army, Signal Corps, 1944-46; announcer-producer for British Forces Network, Hamburg, Germany. *Member:* American Association of Teachers of French, Modern Language Association of America, Rocky Mountain Modern Language Association, Phi Kappa Phi. *Awards, honors:* KSL announcing award, 1953; professor of the year, Brigham Young University, College of Humanities, 1979-80.

WRITINGS—Published by Brigham Young University Press, except as indicated: (With others) *Research on Language Teaching: An Annotated International Bibliography for 1945-61,* University of Washington Press, 1962; *That's the Spirit!,* 1968; (translator) Moliere, *The Miser,* 1975; *Liberty vs. Authority: The Gallant Assault on France,* 1976; *A Remarkable Discovery,* 1977; (translator) Moliere, *The Would-Be Gentleman,* 1978; (translator) Moliere, *Tartuffe,* 1979; *Marcel Schwob,* Droz, 1980. Also translator of *Prophecy in Music,* 1975. Author of motion picture scripts: "Earn and Learn on the Farm," "The Happy City," and "The Story of Chamber Music." Contributor of articles and reviews to *Modern Language Quarterly, French Reviews, New Era, Perspective,* and other periodicals.

*   *   *

GREEN, Paul (Eliot) 1894-

PERSONAL: Born March 17, 1894, near Lillington, N.C.; son of William Archibald (a farmer) and Betty (Byrd) Green; married Elizabeth Atkinson Lay, July 6, 1922; children: Paul E., Jr., Byrd Green Cornwell, Betsy Green Moyer, Janet Green Catlin. *Education:* Buie's Creek Academy (now Campbell College), graduate, 1914; University of North Carolina, A.B., 1921; Cornell University, graduate study, 1922-23. *Home:* Old Lystra Rd., Chapel Hill, N.C. 27514. *Agent:* Samuel French, Inc., 25 West 45th St., New York, N.Y. 10036.

CAREER: University of North Carolina at Chapel Hill, 1923-63, began as instructor in philosophy, professor of dramatic art, 1939-44, professor of radio, television, and motion pictures, 1962-63. President, American Folk Festival, 1934-45, National Theatre Conference, 1940-42. U.S. National Committee for UNESCO, member of executive commission, 1950-52, delegate to UNESCO conference in Paris, 1951; Rockefeller Foundation lecturer, in Asia, on arts (music, drama, and literature) in the American theater, 1951; delegate, International Conference on the Performing Arts, Athens, 1962. *Military service:* U.S. Army, Engineers, 1918-19; served in Belgium and France; became second lieutenant.

MEMBER: National Institute of Arts and Letters, American Society of Composers, Authors and Publishers, American National Theater Academy (director, 1959-61), Southern Regional Council, American Educational Theater Association, Southeastern Theatre Conference, North Carolina State Literary and Historical Association (president, 1942-43), Phi Beta Kappa.

AWARDS, HONORS: Belasco Cup, 1925, for *The No 'Count Boy;* Pulitzer Prize in drama, 1927, for *In Abraham's Bosom;* Guggenheim fellow for study of European drama, 1928-30; Claire M. Senie Drama Study Award, 1937, for *Johnny Johnson;* Freedom Foundation Medal, 1951, for "Faith of Our Fathers," 1956, for *Wilderness Road,* and 1967, for *Texas;* the Southeastern Theatre Conference named a "Paul Green Year" in 1956-57; Fortieth Anniversary Award, Yale Drama School, 1965; Theta Alpha Phi Medallion of Honor, 1965; North Carolina Achievement Award, 1965; Distinguished Alumnus Award, University of North Carolina, 1973, and Campbell College, 1975; National Theatre Conference citation, 1974; Distinguished Citizen Award, State of North Carolina, 1976; First North Caroliniana Award, 1978; the Paul Green Theatre of the University of North Carolina at Chapel Hill was dedicated in 1978; award for distinguished service to theatre, American Theatre Association, 1978; named Dramatist Laureate of North Carolina, 1979. Litt.D., Western Reserve University, 1941,

Davidson College, 1948, University of North Carolina at Chapel Hill, 1956, Berea College, 1957, University of Louisville, 1957, Campbell College, 1969, North Carolina School of the Arts, 1976, Moravian College, 1976, and Duke University, 1980.

WRITINGS—Plays: (Adapter) Otto Ludwig, "The Forest Warder," published in *Poet Lore,* summer 1913; "The Long Night," published in *Carolina Magazine,* 1920; "Granny Boling," published in *Drama,* August-September, 1921; "Sam Tucker," published in *Poet Lore,* summer, 1923, revised edition entitled "Your Fiery Furnace" (also see below); *Old Christmas,* McBride, 1928; *In Abraham's Bosom* (also see below; first produced in Provincetown, Mass., at Provincetown Playhouse, December 30, 1926; produced Off-Broadway at Garrick Theatre, February 14, 1927), Allen & Unwin, 1929; "Potter's Field" (also see below), first produced in Boston, Mass., 1934, revised edition published as *Roll Sweet Chariot* (first produced on Broadway at Cort Theatre, October 2, 1934), Samuel French, 1935; *Shroud My Body Down* (first produced in Chapel Hill, N.C., 1934), Clio Press, 1935, revised edition published as *The Honeycomb,* Samuel French, 1972; *People* (also see below; first produced in New York, 1934), music by Dolphe Martin, Samuel French, 1935.

Johnny Johnson: The Biography of a Common Man (first produced in New York at Forty-fourth Street Theatre, November 19, 1936), Samuel French, 1937, revised edition, 1972; *The Enchanted Maze: The Story of a Modern Student in Dramatic Form* (first produced in Chapel Hill, N.C., 1935), Samuel French, 1939; *Franklin and the King,* Dramatists Play Service, 1939; (adapter with Richard Wright) *Native Son* (adapted from Wright's novel of the same title; first produced on Broadway at St. James Theatre, March 24, 1941), Harper, 1941; (adapter) Henrik Ibsen, *Peer Gynt* (first produced on Broadway at ANTA Theatre, January 28, 1951), Samuel French, 1951; *Trumpet in the Land* (first produced in New Philadelphia, Ohio, at Tuscarawas Amphitheatre, 1970), Samuel French, 1972.

One-act plays; all published by Samuel French: *The Last of the Lowries* (also see below; first produced in Chapel Hill, N.C., 1920), 1925; *The Lord's Will* (also see below; first produced in Chapel Hill, 1922), 1925; *In Aunt Mahaly's Cabin* (first produced in Baltimore, Md., 1925), 1925; *The Man Who Died at Twelve O'Clock* (first produced in Thermopolis, Wyo., 1925), 1927; *The No 'Count Boy* (also see below; first produced in Dallas, Tex., 1925; produced on Broadway at Belasco Theatre, May 6, 1925), 1928, revised ("white") edition, 1953; (with Erma Green) *Fixin's* (first produced in Chapel Hill, 1924), 1934; *White Dresses* (also see below; first produced in White Plains, N.Y., 1923), 1935; *Hymn to the Rising Sun* (also see below; first produced in New York at Civic Repertory Theatre, January 12, 1936), 1936; *The Southern Cross* (first produced in Dallas, 1936), 1938; *The Critical Year: A One-act Sketch of American History and the Beginning of the Constitution,* 1939; *This Declaration,* 1954.

Symphonic dramas: *The Lost Colony* (first produced at Roanoke Island, N.C., 1937), University of North Carolina Press, 1937; *The Highland Call: A Symphonic Play of American History* (first produced in Fayetteville, N.C., 1939), University of North Carolina Press, 1941; *The Common Glory: A Symphonic Drama of American History* (first produced in Williamsburg, Va., at Matoaka Lake Amphitheatre, 1947), University of North Carolina Press, 1948, revised edition, Samuel French, 1975; "Faith of Our Fathers," first produced in Washington, D.C., at Carter Barron Amphitheatre, 1950; *Wilderness Road: A Symphonic Outdoor*

Drama (first produced in Berea, Ky., at Indian Fort Amphitheatre, 1955), Samuel French, 1956; *The Founders: A Symphonic Outdoor Drama* (first produced in Williamsburg at Cove Amphitheatre, 1957), Samuel French, 1957; *The Confederacy: A Symphonic Outdoor Drama Based on the Life of General Robert E. Lee* (first produced in Virginia Beach, Va., at Robert E. Lee Amphitheatre, 1959), Samuel French, 1959; *The Stephen Foster Story: A Symphonic Drama Based on the Life of the Composer* (first produced in Bardstown, Ky., at J. Dan Talbott Amphitheatre, 1959), Samuel French, 1960; *Cross and Sword: A Symphonic Drama of the Spanish Settlement of Florida* (first produced in St. Augustine, Fla., at St. Augustine Amphitheatre, 1965), Samuel French, 1966; *Texas: A Symphonic Outdoor Drama of American Life* (first produced in Palo Duro Canyon, Tex., at Pioneer Amphitheatre, 1966), Samuel French, 1967; "Drumbeats in Georgia: A Symphonic Drama of the Founding of Georgia by James Edward Oglethorpe," first produced at Jekyll Island, Ga., at Jekyll Island Amphitheatre, 1973; "Louisiana Cavalier: A Symphonic Drama of the Eighteenth-Century French and Spanish Struggle for the Settling of Louisiana," first produced in Natchitoches, La., 1976; "We the People: A Symphonic Drama of George Washington and the Establishment of the United States Government," first produced in Columbia, Md., 1976. Also author of "The Lone Star," produced in 1977.

Unpublished plays: "Surrender to the Enemy," first produced in Chapel Hill, N.C., 1917; "Old Wash Lucas" (also see below), produced in Chapel Hill, 1921; "The Old Man of Edenton" (also see below), produced in Chapel Hill, 1921; (with wife, Elizabeth Lay Green) "Blackbeard" (also see below), first produced in Chapel Hill, 1922; "Wrack P'int," first produced in Chapel Hill, 1923; "Quare Medicine" (also see below), first produced in Chapel Hill, 1925; "The Field God" (also see below), first produced in New York at Greenwich Village Theatre, April 21, 1927; "The House of Connelly" (also see below), first produced on Broadway at Martin Beck Theatre, September, 28, 1931; "Tread the Green Grass" (also see below), music by Lamar Stringfield, first produced in Iowa City, Iowa, 1931; "Unto Such Glory" (also see below), first produced in New York at Civic Repertory Theatre, January 12, 1936; (with Josefina Niggly) "Serenata," first produced in Santa Barbara, Calif., 1953; "The Seventeenth Star," first produced in Columbus, Ohio, 1953; (adapter) H. Meilhac and L. Halevy, "Carmen," music by Georges Bizet, first produced in Central City, Colo., at Central City Opera Festival, 1954; "Supper for the Dead" (also see below), first produced Off-Broadway at Theatre De Lys, July 6, 1954; "The Goodbye" (also see below), first produced in New York, 1954; "Sing All a Green Willow," produced by the Carolina Playmakers, 1969; "The Thirsty Heart" (also see below), first produced in Orangeburg, N.C., 1971; "The Hot Iron" (also see below), revised edition produced in Berea, Ky., as "Lay This Body Down" (also see below), 1972.

Play collections: *The Lord's Will and Other Carolina Plays* (includes "The Lord's Will," "Blackbeard," "Old Wash Lucas," "The No 'Count Boy," "The Old Man of Edenton," and "The Last of the Lowries"), Holt, 1925; *Lonesome Road: Six Plays for the Negro Theatre* (contains "In Abraham's Bosom," "White Dresses," "The Hot Iron," "The Prayer Meeting," "The End of the Row," and "Your Fiery Furnace"), McBride, 1926; *In the Valley and Other Carolina Plays* (includes "Quare Medicine," "Supper for the Dead," "Saturday Night," "The Man Who Died at Twelve O'Clock," "In Aunt Mahaly's Cabin," "The No

'Count Boy," "The Man on the House," "The Picnic," "Unto Such Glory," and "The Goodbye"), Samuel French, 1928; *The House of Connelly and Other Plays* (includes "The House of Connelly," "Potter's Field," and "Tread the Green Grass"), Samuel French, 1931; *Out of the South: The Life of a People in Dramatic Form* (includes "The House of Connelly," "The Field God," "In Abraham's Bosom," "Potter's Field," "Johnny Johnson," "The Lost Colony," "The No 'Count Boy," "Saturday Night," "Quare Medicine," "The Hot Iron," "Unto Such Glory," "Supper for the Dead," "The Man Who Died at Twelve O'Clock," "White Dresses," and "Hymn to the Rising Sun"), Harper, 1939; *Salvation on a String* (includes "The Goodbye," "Chair Endowed," "Supper for the Dead," and "The No 'Count Boy"), Harper, 1946; *Wings for to Fly: Three Plays of Negro Life, Mostly for the Ear but Also for the Eye* (contains "The Thirsting Heart," "Lay This Body Down," and "Fine Wagon"), Samuel French, 1959; *Five Plays of the South* (contains "The House of Connelly," "In Abraham's Bosom," "Johnny Johnson," "Hymn to the Rising Sun," and "White Dresses"), Hill & Wang, 1963.

Novels and short stories: *Wide Fields* (short stories), McBride, 1928; *The Laughing Pioneer: A Sketch of Country* (novel), McBride, 1932; *This Body the Earth* (novel), Harper, 1935; *Salvation on a String and Other Tales of the South* (short stories), Harper, 1946; *Dog on the Sun: A Volume of Stories*, University of North Carolina Press, 1949; *Words and Ways: Stories and Incidents from My Cape Fear Valley Folklore Collection*, North Carolina Folklore Society, 1968; *Home to My Valley* (short stories), University of North Carolina Press, 1970: *Land of Nod and Other Stories: A Volume of Black Stories*, University of North Carolina Press, 1976.

Essays: *The Hawthorn Tree*, University of North Carolina Press, 1943; *Forever Growing*, University of North Carolina Press, 1945; *Dramatic Heritage*, Samuel French, 1953; *Drama and the Weather*, Samuel French, 1958; *Plough and Furrow*, Samuel French, 1963.

Music: (Compiler) *The Lost Colony Song Book*, Fischer, 1938; *The Highland Call Song Book*, University of North Carolina Press, 1941; (author of lyrics) *Song of the Wilderness*, University of North Carolina Press, 1947; (author of lyrics) *The Common Glory Song Book*, Fischer, 1951; *Texas Song Book*, Samuel French, 1967; *Texas Forever*, Samuel French, 1967.

Film scripts: "Cabin in the Cotton," Warner Bros., 1932; "State Fair," Fox Film Corp., 1932; "Dr. Bull," Fox Film Corp. 1933; "Voltaire," Warner Bros., 1933; "David Harum," Fox Film Corp., 1934; "Black Like Me," Film Features, 1963. Contributor to many other feature film scripts.

Contributor of radio plays to *The Free Company Presents*, Dodd, 1941. Contributor of articles and stories to periodicals, including *Theatre Arts, Dramatists, Guild Bulletin, New York Times Magazine, Atlantic,* and *Esquire.* Editor of *Reviewer*, 1925.

WORK IN PROGRESS: A folk history of the Cape Fear Valley people in several volumes; a volume of short stories; a full-length play.

SIDELIGHTS: In a *Denver Post* article, Robert Downing refers to Paul Green as "the dean of American dramatics." Green has been very successful in theatre; in one season he had two plays produced on Broadway: *The Field God* and his Pulitzer Prize-winning *In Abraham's Bosom.* He has also achieved great success with film scripts (including "State Fair" and "Black Like Me") and radio plays. But he is best known for his innovative "symphonic dramas"—outdoor plays derived from the life and history of people in a particular locale and produced in huge amphitheatres.

These outdoor dramas started with *The Lost Colony*. Originally presented at Roanoke Island, N.C. with a cast of 150, it has been repeated every summer since. *The Common Glory* was produced in Williamsburg, Va., for twenty-eight seasons beginning in 1947. Several other outdoor plays are presented every summer season, including *Wilderness Road, The Stephen Foster Story, Cross and Sword, Texas,* "Louisiana Cavalier," and "The Lone Star." Although he obviously enjoys this medium and continues to write symphonic dramas, Green is somewhat concerned with the future of outdoor productions. He told Downing: "It costs about $500,000 to mount an outdoor show. Here I am worrying about better technical solutions for some of our theatres, trying to get directors to use light like music to help delineate characters—and what I really have to think about is gasoline for people to get to us. What good is a show without an audience?"

Green has been active in the movement to abolish capital punishment, outspoken in opposition to racial injustice, and a lecturer on world peace and understanding.

AVOCATIONAL INTERESTS: Fishing, gardening, music.

BIOGRAPHICAL/CRITICAL SOURCES: Barrett H. Clark, *Paul Green*, Samuel French, 1928; Agatha B. Adams, *Paul Green of Chapel Hill*, University of North Carolina Press, 1951; John Gassner, *The Theatre in Our Times*, Crown, 1954; David W. Sievers, *Freud on Broadway*, Hermitage, 1955; Gassner, *Theatre at the Crossroads*, Holt, 1960; *Reader's Digest*, July, 1960; Charles Lower and William Free, *History into Drama: A Casebook on Paul Green's "The Lost Colony,"* Odyssey, 1962; Walter S. Lazenby, *Paul Green*, Steck, 1970; Vincent S. Kenny, *Paul Green*, Twayne, 1972; *Denver Post*, February 24, 1974.

*   *   *

GREENBERG, Sidney 1917-

PERSONAL: Born September 27, 1917, in Brooklyn, N.Y.; son of Morris (a presser) and Sadie (Armel) Greenberg; married Hilda Weiss, October 31, 1942; children: Shira Beth, Reena Keren, Adena Joy. *Education:* Yeshiva University, A.B., 1938; Jewish Theological Seminary, Rabbi, 1942, Doctor of Hebrew Literature, 1947. *Home:* 300 Old Farm Rd., Wyncote, Pa. 19095.

CAREER: Temple Sinai, Philadelphia, Pa., rabbi, 1942—. *Military service:* U.S. Army, chaplain, 1944-46; became captain. *Member:* Zionist Organization of America, Jewish Chaplains Association, Rabbinical Assembly of America (president, Philadelphia branch, 1954-56), B'nai B'rith.

WRITINGS: (Editor) *A Treasury of Comfort*, Crown, 1954, new edition, Wilshire, 1967; (editor with Abraham Rothberg) *The Bar Mitzvah Companion*, Behrman, 1959; *Adding Life to Our Years*, J. David, 1959; (editor) *A Modern Treasury of Jewish Thoughts*, Yoseloff, 1960; (compiler and editor with Morris Silverman) *Our Prayer Book: A New and Original Siddur Text for Religious Schools*, Prayer Book Press, 1961; *A Jew for All Seasons* (cantata), [Philadelphia], 1963; *A Treasury of the Art of Living*, Hartmore House, 1963; *Finding Ourselves: Sermons on the Art of Living*, J. David, 1964; *High Holiday Services for Children*, Prayer Book Press, 1968; (with S. Allan Sugarman) *Sabbath and Festival Services for Children*, Prayer Book Press, 1970; (with Sugarman) *A Contemporary High Holiday Service for Teenagers and . . .* , Prayer Book Press, 1970; *Hidden Hungers: High*

Holiday Sermons on the Art of Living, Hartmore House, 1972; *Likrat Shabbat: Worship, Study, and Song for Shabbath and Festival Services and for the Home*, Prayer Book Press, 1973; *The New Mahzor for Rosh Hashanah and Yom Kippur*, Prayer Book Press, 1977. Member of editorial board, *Reconstructionist* and *Jewish Digest*.

*   *   *

GREENE, Jack P(hillip) 1931-

PERSONAL: Born August 12, 1931, in Lafayette, Ind.; son of Ralph B. (an agricultural engineer) and Nellie (Miller) Greene; married Sue Neuenswander, June 27, 1953; children: Megan, Granville. *Education:* University of North Carolina, A.B., 1951; Indiana University, M.A., 1952; graduate study at University of Nebraska, 1952-55, and University of Bristol, 1953-54; Duke University, Ph.D., 1956. *Politics:* Democratic. *Religion:* Protestant. *Residence:* Baltimore, Md. *Office:* Department of History, Johns Hopkins University, Baltimore, Md. 21218.

CAREER: Michigan State University, East Lansing, instructor in history, 1956-59; Western Reserve University (now Case Western Reserve University), Cleveland, Ohio, associate professor of history, 1959-65; University of Michigan, Ann Arbor, associate professor of history, 1965-66; Johns Hopkins University, Baltimore, Md., professor of history, 1966-75, Andrew W. Mellon Professor of Humanities, 1975—, chairman of history department, 1970-72. Visiting associate professor, Johns Hopkings University, 1964-65; Harmsworth Professor of American History, Oxford University, 1975-76; Fulbright Professor, Hebrew University of Jerusalem, 1979. Member of Institute for Advanced Study, 1970-71. *Military service:* U.S. Army Reserve, Military Intelligence, 1956-63. *Member:* American Historical Association, Organization of American Historians, Conference on British Studies, American Antiquarian Society, Royal Historical Society, Royal Society for the Arts, Southern Historical Association, Massachusetts Historical Society. *Awards, honors:* Fulbright fellow, United Kingdom, 1953-54; Guggenheim fellow, 1964-65; Woodrow Wilson International Center for Scholars fellow, 1974-75; Center for Advanced Study in the Behavioral Sciences fellow, 1979-80.

WRITINGS: The Quest for Power: The Lower Houses of Assembly in the Southern Royal Colonies, 1689-1776, published for Institute of Early American History and Culture by University of North Carolina Press, 1963; *The Reappraisal of the American Revolution in Recent Historical Literature*, Service Center for Teachers of History, 1967; (compiler with Edward C. Papenfuse, Jr.) *The American Colonies in the Eighteenth Century, 1689-1763*, Appleton, 1969; *The Nature of Colony Constitutions*, University of South Carolina Press, 1970; *All Men Are Created Equal*, Oxford University Press, 1976.

Editor: (And author of introduction) *The Diary of Colonel Landon Carter of Sabine Hall, 1752-1778*, two volumes, published for Virginia Historical Society by University Press of Virginia, 1965, revised introduction published separately as *Landon Carter: An Inquiry into the Personal Values and Social Imperatives of the Eighteenth-Century Virginia Gentry*, University Press of Virginia, 1967; *Settlements to Society, 1584-1763*, Norton, 1966; *Colonies to Nation, 1763-1789*, Norton, 1967; *The Ambiguity of the American Revolution*, Harper, 1968; (and author of introduction) *The Reinterpretation of the American Revolution, 1763-1789*, Harper, 1968; *Great Britain and the American Colonies, 1606-1763*, Harper, 1970; (with Robert Forster and author of introduction)

Preconditions of Revolution in Early Modern Europe, Johns Hopkins Press, 1970, 2nd edition, 1972; (with David W. Cohen) *Neither Slave nor Free: The Freedmen of African Descent in the Slave Societies of the New World*, Johns Hopkins Press, 1972; (and author of introduction) *The First Continental Congress: A Documentary History*, U.S. Government Printing Office, 1974; (with Pauline Maier) *Interdisciplinary Studies of the American Revolution*, Sage Publications, 1976.

Contributor of chapters to several books. Contributor to journals, including *Journal of Southern History, South Atlantic Quarterly, American Historical Review, Journal of Social History*, and *Political Science Quarterly*. Visiting editor, *William and Mary Quarterly*, 1961-62.

WORK IN PROGRESS: Paradise Defined: Studies in the Formation of Corporate Identity in Plantation America, 1650-1815; The Causal Pattern of the American Revolution.

*   *   *

GREGORY, Horace (Victor)   1898-

PERSONAL: Born April 10, 1898, in Milwaukee, Wis.; son of Henry Bolton (president of a bakery supply and machinery firm) and Anna Catherine (Henckel) Gregory; married Marya Zaturenska (a poet; Pulitzer prize winner, 1938), 1925; children: Joanna Elizabeth (Mrs. S. H. Zeigler), Patrick Bolton. *Education:* Attended German-English Academy, Milwaukee, Wis., 1914-19; University of Wisconsin, B.A., 1923; summer art student at Milwaukee School of Fine Arts, 1913-16. *Religion:* Episcopalian. *Home:* Palisades, Rockland County, N.Y. *Agent:* Mavis MacIntosh, 30 East 60th St., New York, N.Y.

CAREER: Poet and critic; writer in New York and Europe, 1923—. Sarah Lawrence College, Bronxville, N.Y., lecturer in poetry and critical theory and instructor in advanced writing, 1934-60, professor emeritus, 1960—. *Member:* National Institute of Arts and Letters. *Awards, honors: Poetry's* Lyric Prize, 1928; Levinson Prize for group of poems, 1934; Levinson Award, 1936; Russell Loines Award for Poetry, from National Institute of Arts and Letters, 1942; Guggenheim fellowship, 1951; Union League Civic and Arts Foundation prize, 1951; Academy of American Poets fellowship, 1961; Bollingen Prize, 1965, for *Collected Poems;* honorary doctor of letters from University of Wisconsin, 1977.

WRITINGS: Pilgrim of the Apocalypse, Viking, 1933, 2nd augmented edition published as *D. H. Lawrence: Pilgrim of the Apocalypse*, Grove, 1957; *Shield of Achilles: Essays on Beliefs in Poetry*, Harcourt, 1944; (with wife, Marya Zaturenska) *A History of American Poetry, 1900-1940*, Harcourt, 1946; (with Jeanette Covert Nolan and James T. Farrell) *Poet of the People: An Evaluation of James Whitcomb Riley*, Indiana University Press, 1951; *Amy Lowell: Portrait of the Poet in Her Time*, Thomas Nelson, 1958; *The World of James McNeill Whistler*, Thomas Nelson, 1959; *The Dying Gladiators, and Other Essays*, Grove, 1961; *Dorothy Richardson: An Adventure in Self-Discovery*, Holt, 1967; *The House on Jefferson Street: A Cycle of Memories*, Holt, 1971; *The Spirit of Time and Place* (collected essays), Norton, 1972.

Poetry: *Chelsea Rooming House*, Covici, Friede, 1930; *No Retreat*, Harcourt, 1933; *Wreath for Margery*, Modern Editions Press, 1933; *Chorus for Survival*, Covici, Friede, 1935; *Poems, 1930-1940*, Harcourt, 1941; *Selected Poems*, Viking, 1951; *Medusa in Gramercy Park*, Macmillan, 1961; *Alphabet for Joanna* (juvenile), Holt, 1963; *Collected Poems*, Holt, 1964; *Another Look*, Holt, 1976.

Translator: Catullus, *Poems*, Covici, Friede, 1931; Catullus, *Poems, Translated*, Grove, 1956 (published in England as *The Poems of Catullus*, Thames & Hudson, 1956); Ovid, *The Metamorphoses*, Viking, 1958; *The Love Poems of Ovid*, New American Library, 1964.

Editor: (With Eleanor Clark) *New Letters in America*, Norton, 1937; *Critical Remarks on the Metaphysical Poets*, Golden Eagle, c. 1943; (and author of introduction) *The Triumph of Life* (anthology of elegiac and devotional verse), Viking, 1943; *The Portable Sherwood Anderson*, Viking, 1949; Violet Paget, *Snake Lady*, Grove, 1954; (with wife, Marya Zaturenska) *The Mentor Book of Religious Verse*, New America Library, 1956; Robert Browning, *Selected Poetry*, Rinehart, 1956; (with others) *Riverside Poetry, 4: An Anthology of Student Poetry*, Twayne, 1962; (with M. Zaturenska) *The Crystal Cabinet: An Invitation to Poetry*, Holt, 1962; (with M. Zaturenska) *The Silver Swan: Poems of Romance and Mystery*, Holt, 1966. Associate editor, *The Tiger's Eye.*

Also author of introduction to *Columbia Poetry, 1940*, Columbia University Press, 1940, afterword to Thomas Hardy's *The Return of the Native*, New American Library, 1959, introduction to Lewis Carroll's *Alice's Adventures in Wonderland, [and] Through the Looking-Glass*, New American Library, 1960, and introduction to *e. e. cummings: A Selection of Poems*, Harvest Books, 1966.

Contributor of poetry to anthologies, and of poetry and critical articles to magazines and journals, including *New Republic, Nation, Vanity Fair, Books, Atlantic Monthly*, and *New Verse* (London).

SIDELIGHTS: By 1933 Horace Gregory had established himself as an important poet. At that time, E. L. Walton called him "a poet who has a long view of history and literature, and a passionate conviction concerning the beauty of human life.... Here is an intense but disciplined creative talent. Mr. Gregory has an authentic lyric gift, a strong sense of the dramatic, and a knowledge of the robustly humorous in the common man's life.... He is here, taking part in America's radical thought. Fixed in today, he views the past as part of the present. The result is no Wasteland, no frustration, but a picture of a violent, somehow heroic land of great power misused."

Gregory, it is true, was one of the best poets of the American Left, yet he never lost his lyric-elegiac voice. His work has always been contemporary, but at the same time it possesses "a learned awareness of the past," writes W. T. Scott. Gregory, he adds, "is a classicist who has employed his spirit not to avoid the confusing modern world but to clarify and enrich it." While having been accused of borrowing, as Donne was, he has, according to Raymond Larsson, borrowed "only what is rightly his—by temperament." He possesses, writes Herbert Gorman, "sensitivity of a high order, intuitive intelligence and a nostalgic cadence that is peculiarly his own.... There is brilliant phrasing in [his] poems, atmosphere, aroma, whatever it may be called, that seizes upon the reader's mind and permeates it and is that indescribable thing called poetry."

Elizabeth Drew praises his emotional range as "perhaps the most comprehensive among modern poets.... As a craftsman, he is equally varied, commanding a precision of phrase and purity of line which can evoke effects of concentrated and sinewy intensity, of emotional warmth and vigor, and of disciplined, formal grace." His poems also contain, as G. F. Whicher notes, "a depth of terror and a depth of tenderness for the human lot. These things are not modern but timeless." John Frederick Nims also finds in these poems a certain "quality of hauntedness." Gregory can, says Theodore Weiss, "turn a beggar, say, into something mythical by the fundamental, terrible power—a power by his merely being—housed in him and shining through. . . . Much more than skill, his work is a generous air, brooding over hallucinated, nightmared multitudes, an air listening, absorbing, and singing it all forth, transformed, somehow fulfilled in its very failures."

There are in his poems echoes of the classicists, of Browning, T. S. Eliot, and D. H. Lawrence (of whose work he wrote the first important critical study). M. L. Rosenthal believes that Gregory was early haunted "by the Laurentian plunge into darkness . . . [and attempted] to merge that motif with the Marxian ideas of the rebirth of society through revolutionary change. When . . . he shakes off the tendentiousness implicit in this mode of thought, . . . he is seen to be a poet of the elusiveness of the self." W. R. Benet finds that his elusiveness makes Gregory's poems "at times unintelligible," and he believes that Gregory "affects a most impressionistic manner" as well. Larsson finds some of Gregory's poetry opaque and lacking strict fastidiousness. J. L. Sweeney does not agree, believing instead that Gregory "deals with each situation ironically but gently. Human experience is his material, but he does not patronize or poeticize it. He simply extracts its essence, adding nothing which might artificially dignify it. The inherent dignity of the essential is the beauty of Gregory's poetry."

Allen Tate writes of *No Retreat:* "No American poet writing today surpasses Gregory in mastery of rhythm and image. His finest passages, though obviously produced with great labor, have all the look of inevitable ease. The image is never elaborated beyond the span of a manageable rhythm, which follows precisely the complexity of image. . . ." In 1962 Dudley Fitts welcomed *Medusa in Gramercy Park,* saying: "We need to be reminded, every once in a while, of the poet's responsibility to his art, to his audience, and to himself. *Medusa in Gramercy Park* is a paradigm of responsibility. . . . There are two great debts, or influences: the classical tradition, specifically Latin, and Robert Browning. Both . . . have been wholly assimilated into what can only be called the Gregorian style. . . . [This book reinforces the stature] of one of the surest and proudest artistic reputations of our day."

Gregory writes: "Since 1934 (during the summer) I have made frequent journeys . . . to Europe, returning often to London, Edinburgh, and Venice. In these cities I have done considerable writing and research. My book of poems, *Chorus for Survival,* was written in Dublin and in London. My version of Ovid's *Metamorphoses* was started in Rome."

A Horace Gregory Fund has been established to support the creative efforts of retired scholars, educators, poets, and writers.

AVOCATIONAL INTERESTS: Music, painting, reading in philosophy, history, and the classics.

BIOGRAPHICAL/CRITICAL SOURCES: Saturday Review, March 4, 1933, March 13, 1971; *New York Times Book Review,* March 26, 1933, May 24, 1964, August 27, 1967; *Nation,* April 5, 1933; *Books,* May 4, 1941; *Atlantic,* June, 1941; *Yale Review,* summer, 1941; *Chicago Sunday Tribune,* September 16, 1951; *Poetry,* September, 1962, November, 1964; *Reporter,* September 10, 1964; M. L. Rosenthal, *The Modern Poets,* Oxford University Press, 1965; *New York Times,* January 27, 1971; *Time,* February 8, 1971; *Best Sellers,* March 15, 1971; *Modern Poetry Studies* (special Horace Gregory issue), spring, 1973.

GRICE, Frederick 1910-

PERSONAL: Born June 21, 1910, in Durham, England; son of Charles Oliver (a miner) and Mary Jane (Hewitt) Grice; married Gwendoline Simpson, April 8, 1939; children: Gillian (Mrs. C. G. Clarke), Erica (Mrs. N. Johnson). *Education:* King's College, London, B.A. (honors); Hatfield College, Durham, D.Th.P.T. *Religion:* Anglican. *Home:* 91 Hallow Rd., Worcester, England.

CAREER: City of Worcester Training College, Worcester, England, head of English department, 1946-72. *Military service:* Royal Air Force, 1941-46; became flight lieutenant.

WRITINGS: Folk Tales of the North Country, Drawn from Northumberland and Durham, Thomas Nelson, 1944; *Folk Tales of the West Midlands,* Thomas Nelson, 1952; *Folk Tales of Lancashire,* Thomas Nelson, 1953; *Night Poem, and Other Pieces,* Peter Russell, 1955; *Aidan and the Strolling Players,* Duell, Sloan & Pearce, 1960 (published in England as *Aidan and the Strollers,* J. Cape, 1960); *The Bonny Pit Laddie,* Oxford University Press (London), 1960, published as *Out of the Mines: The Story of a Pit Boy,* F. Watts, 1961; *The Moving Finger,* Oxford University Press (Toronto), 1962, published as *The Secret of the Libyan Caves,* F. Watts, 1963; *Rebels and Fugitives,* Batsford, 1963, Norton, 1964; *A Northumberland Missionary,* Oxford University Press, 1963; *Jimmy Lane and His Boat,* F. Watts, 1963; *The Rescue* [and] *The Poisoned Dog* (two tales), F. Watts, 1963; *Bill Thompson's Pigeon,* Oxford University Press (London), 1963, F. Watts, 1968; *A Severnside Story,* Oxford University Press, 1964; (with Dora Saint) *The Lifeboat Haul* [and] *Elizabeth Woodcock* (the former by Grice, the latter by Saint), Oxford University Press, 1965; *The Luckless Apple,* Oxford University Press, 1966; *The Oak and the Ash,* Oxford University Press, 1968; *Dildrum, King of the Cats, and Other English Folk Stories* (includes "Dildrum, King of the Cats," "Black Vaughan," "The Magic Ointment," "The Iron Gates," "The Boy and the Fairies," "The Three Rivers," "The Pedlar of Swaffham," and "The Well at the World's End"), F. Watts, 1968; *The Courage of Andy Robson,* Oxford University Press, 1969; *The Black Hand Gang,* Oxford University Press, 1971; *Young Tom Sawbones,* Oxford University Press, 1972; *Francis Kilvert: Priest and Diarist,* Kilvert Society, 1974; *Nine Days Wonder,* Oxford University Press, 1976; *Johnny Head in Air,* Oxford University Press, 1978. Author of textbooks for slow readers. Contributor to periodicals and to British Broadcasting Corp. feature and poetry programs.

WORK IN PROGRESS: Francis Kilvert and His World.

SIDELIGHTS: Frederick Grice told *CA:* "I am deeply interested in France. Passionately fond of Provence. Would like to be an artist as well as a writer—or a collector."

BIOGRAPHICAL/CRITICAL SOURCES: Books and Bookmen, July, 1968, June, 1969.

* * *

GRIFFIN, Susan 1943-

PERSONAL: Born January 26, 1943, in Los Angeles, Calif.; daughter of Walden and Sarah (Colvin) Griffin; married John Levy, June 11, 1966 (divorced, 1970); children: Rebecca Siobhain. *Education:* Attended University of California, Berkeley, 1960-63; San Francisco State College (now University), B.A. (cum laude), 1965; California State University, San Francisco (now San Francisco State University), M.A.,1973. *Politics:* "Radical, feminist." *Religion:* None. *Home:* 1008 Euclid Ave., Berkeley, Calif. 94708. *Agent:* Julie Fallowfield, McIntosh & Otis, Inc., 475 Fifth Ave., New York, N.Y. 10017.

CAREER: Poet. Has worked as a waitress, switchboard and teletype operator, and housepainter; Hamilton Recreation Center, San Francisco, Calif., drama teacher, 1964-65; *Ramparts* (magazine), San Francisco, assistant editor, 1966-68; San Francisco State College (now University), San Francisco, instructor in English, 1970-71; Poetry in the Schools program, teacher of poetry in Oakland, Calif. high schools, 1972-73; University of California, Berkeley, instructor in English and women's studies in extension school, 1973-75; San Francisco State University, instructor, 1974-75. Visiting writer, Delta College of San Joaquin and Cazenovia College. *Awards, honors:* Ina Coolbrith Prize in Poetry, 1963; Emmy Award, 1975, for *Voices;* National Endowment for the Arts grant, 1976.

WRITINGS: Dear Sky (poetry), Shameless Hussy Press, 1971; *Le Viol,* L'Etincelle (Canada), 1972; *Let Them Be Said,* Mama Press, 1973; *Letters,* Twowindows Press, 1973; *The Sink,* Shameless Hussy Press, 1973; *Voices* (a play in poetry; first produced in San Francisco in 1974), Feminist Press, 1975; *Like the Iris of an Eye* (poetry), Harper, 1976; *Woman and Nature: The Roaring Inside Her,* Harper, 1978; *Rape: The Power of Consciousness,* Harper, 1979. Work represented in numerous anthologies including: *Women: Feminist Stories by New Fiction Authors,* Eakins, 1971; *No More Masks: An Anthology of Poems by Women,* edited by Florence Howe and Ellen Bass, Doubleday, 1973. Contributor to many periodicals including *Ramparts, Sundance, Shocks, Ms,* and *Aphra.*

WORK IN PROGRESS: Pornography and Silence, for Harper.

SIDELIGHTS: Library Journal reviewer A. B. Eaglen writes of Susan Griffin's collection of poetry, *Like the Iris of an Eye:* "If there is a stronger, better, more forceful feminist poem than Griffin's 'An Answer to a Man's Question, "What Can I Do About Women's Liberation?"'" I'd like to see it—and that is only one excellent poem in a uniformly excellent collection by one of the most-quoted feminist poets writing today. A fine anthology of work that has been available before this only in anthologies and small press offerings, for collections serving women and/or lovers of good contemporary poetry."

Valerie Miner writes in *Ms* of Griffin's more recent book: "*Woman and Nature* is feminist philosophy written in poetic prose. Susan Griffin explores woman's traditional identification with the earth—both as sustenance for humanity and victim of male ravage. The book is cultural anthropology, visionary prediction, literary indictment, and personal claim. Griffin's testimony about the lives of women throughout Western civilization reveals extensive research from Plato to Galileo to Freud to Emily Carr to Jane Goodall to Adrienne Rich. . . . Griffin moves us from pain to anger to communion with and celebration of the survival of woman and nature."

Summing up her philosophy of writing, Susan Griffin wrote *CA:* "As a woman, I struggle to write from my life, to reflect all the difficulties, angers, joys of my existence in a culture that attempts to silence women, or that does not take our work, or words or our lives seriously. In this, I am a fortunate woman, to be published, to be read, to be supported, and I live within a cultural and social movement aiming toward the liberation of us all. And within and also beyond all this I experience the transformations of my soul through the holy, the ecstatic, the painfully born or joyously mode *word.* I know now that never when I begin to write will I truly know what or how my vision will become."

Voices was adapted for television and networked in 1974.

BIOGRAPHICAL/CRITICAL SOURCES: Library Journal, December 1, 1976; *Ms,* April, 1978; *Publishers Weekly,* August 28, 1978.

*   *   *

GRIMALDI, J(ohn) V. 1916-

PERSONAL: Born September 6, 1916, in New York, N.Y.; son of Ottavio V. and Ernestine (Lima) Grimaldi; married T. Joan Formichella, 1942; children: Jacqueline Anne, John Gardner. *Education:* New York University, B.S., 1939, M.A., 1941, Ph.D., 1955; Polytechnic Institute of Brooklyn, B.Ch.E., 1951. *Home:* 13044 Mindanao Way, Marina Del Rey, Calif. 90291. *Office:* University of Southern California, Institute of Safety and Systems Management, University Park, Los Angeles, Calif. 90007.

CAREER: Began career with Scully Steel Products Co.; Grumman Aircraft Engineering Corp., Bethpage, N.Y., safety director, 1941-44; New York University, New York City, research associate, 1944-45; Association of Casualty and Surety Companies, New York City, research engineer, 1945-46, director of research and engineering division, 1946-56, director of industrial division, National Conservation Bureau, 1945-56; General Electric Co., New York City, consultant on health, safety, and plant protection, 1956-67; New York University, lecturer on safety education, 1951-61, adjunct assistant professor, 1961-64, adjunct associate professor, 1964-67, professor, 1967—, director of the Center for Safety, 1967-77; University of Southern California, Los Angeles, currently professor and interim executive director of Institute of Safety and Systems Management. Consultant to other industries on control of hazards. Member of board of directors of New York Safety Council, 1959, President's Committee on Employment of the Physically Handicapped, 1948-56, National Safety Council, 1960, U.S. Department of Labor Business Research Advisory Council Policy, Planning Committee of Industrial Hygiene Foundation, National Advisory Committee on Occupational Safety and Health, U.S. Department of Health and Human Services National Institute for Occupational Safety and Health (chairman of study section, 1980—), and U.S. Department of Interior Coal Mine Safety Research Committee. Speaker at professional and technical conferences.

MEMBER: American Society of Safety Engineers (chairman, Metropolitan Chapter, 1947; president, 1961-62), American Society of Mechanical Engineers (chairman of executive committee, safety division, 1950-51), American Chemical Society, American Institute of Chemists. *Awards, honors:* Twice awarded the Arthur Williams Memorial Research fellowship from American Museum of Safety; Founders Day Award from New York University; Medal of the Associacao Nacional de Medicina de Trabalho; Centennial Medal of the American Society of Mechanical Engineers.

WRITINGS: The Physically Impaired: A Guide to Their Employment, Association of Casualty and Surety Companies, 1946; (co-author) *Ground Safety in Aviation Operations,* New York University Press, 1950; *Safety Management-Accident Cost and Control,* Irwin, 1956, 2nd revised edition, 1975; (contributor) *Safety and Accident Prevention in Chemical Operations,* Wiley, 1965; *Production Handbook,* Ronald, 1972. Contributor to *World Book Encyclopedia,* 1977, and to professional journals.

WORK IN PROGRESS: A chapter for inclusion in *Occupational Medicine.*

GRIMSLEY, Ronald 1915-

PERSONAL: Born October 19, 1915, in Leicester, England; son of Herbert and Frances M. (Parkinson) Grimsley; married Valerie Owen Davies, July 7, 1956; children: Amanda Gay, Adrienne Clare, Nigel Mark. Education: University College, Leicester, England, B.A. (honors in French), 1937; Sorbonne, University of Paris, Licence es Lettres, 1948; Keble College, Oxford University, M.A., 1948, D.Phil., 1948. Religion: Church of England. Office: Department of French, University of Bristol, 17/19 Woodland Rd., Bristol BS8 1TE, England.

CAREER: University College of North Wales, Bangor, began as instructor, became reader in French; University of Bristol, Bristol, England, professor of French, 1964—. Military Service: British Army, Royal Artillery and Intelligence Corps, 1940-45; became sergeant.

WRITINGS: Existentialist Thought, University of Wales Press, 1955, 2nd edition, 1960; Jean-Jacques Rousseau: A Study in Self-Awareness, University of Wales Press, 1961; Jean d'Alembert (1717-83), Clarendon Press, 1963; Soren Kierkegaard and French Literature: Eight Comparative Studies, University of Wales Press, 1966; Rousseau's Religious Writings, Clarendon Press, 1970; Rousseau: Du Contrat Social, Clarendon Press, 1972; The Philosophy of Rousseau, Oxford University Press, 1973; Kierkegaard: A Biographical Introduction, [London], 1973; From Montesquieu to Laclos: Studies on the French Enlightenment, Droz, 1974. Contributor of articles on literature, philosophy, and comparative literature to professional journals.

WORK IN PROGRESS: Research on aspects of French Enlightenment thought.

AVOCATIONAL INTERESTS: Music and foreign travel.

*   *   *

GRINSELL, Leslie Valentine 1907-

PERSONAL: Born February 14, 1907, in London, England; son of Arthur John and Janet (Tabor) Grinsell. Education: Attended Highgate School, London, England. Religion: Anglican. Home: 32 Queen's Ct., Bristol, England.

CAREER: Officer, Barclays Bank Ltd., 1925-41, 1945-49; member of staff, Victoria County History of Wiltshire, 1949-52; Bristol City Museum, Bristol, England, curator of archaeology, 1952-72. Military service: Royal Air Force, 1941-45; served in Egypt; became flight lieutenant. Member: Society of Antiquaries (fellow), Prehistoric Society (treasurer, 1947-70), British Association (recorder, anthropology and archaeology section, 1955-58). Awards, honors: M.A., Bristol University, 1971; Order of the British Empire, 1972.

WRITINGS: The Ancient Burial-Mounds of England, Methuen, 1936, 2nd edition, 1953, published with new introduction and bibliography, Greenwood Press, 1975; White Horse Hill and the Surrounding Country, St. Catherine Press, 1939; Egyptian Pyramids, John Bellows, 1947; (contributor) Studies in the History of Swindon, Swindon (England) Borough Council, 1950; (contributor) Victoria History of Wiltshire, published for University of London Institute of Historical Research by Oxford University Press, 1957; The Archaeology of Wessex: An Account of Wessex Antiquities from the Earliest Times to the End of the Pagan Saxon Period, with Special Reference to Existing Field Monuments, Methuen, 1958; Dorset Barrows, Dorset Natural History and Archaeological Society, 1959; A Brief Numismatic History of Bristol: Being a Guide to Bristol Coins, Tokens, and Medals in the City Museum, Bristol and in Other Collections, Bristol City

Museum 1962; (editor) A Survey and Policy Concerning the Archaeology of the Bristol Region, two volumes, Bristol Archaeological Research Group, 1964-66; Prehistoric Sites in the Mendip, South Cotswold and Bristol Region, Bristol Archaeological Research Group, 1966; (with Philip Rahtz and Alan Warhurst) The Preparation of Archaeological Reports, 2nd edition, Bristol Archaeological Research Group, 1962, revised edition (with Philip Rahtz and David Price Williams), John Baker, 1974; Guide Catalogue to the South Western British Prehistoric Collections, Bristol City Museum, 1968; (with Max Hebditch) Roman Sites in the Mendip, Cotswold, Wye Valley and Bristol Region, Bristol Archaeological Research Group, 1968; Archaeology of Exmoor: Bideford Bay to Bridgwater, Augustus M. Kelley, 1970; Regional Archaeology: South Western England, International Publications Service, 1970; Guide-Catalogue to the Collections of Ancient Europe, Bristol City Museum, 1972; (with C.E. Blunt and Michael Dolley) Sylloge of Coins of the British Isles, Bristol and Gloucester Museums, British Academy, 1973; The Bath Mint, Spink & Son, 1973; Barrow, Pyramid and Tomb, Thames & Hudson, 1975, revised edition published in Italian as Piramidi, Necropoli e Mondi Sepolti, Newton Compton Editori, 1978; Folklore of Prehistoric Sites in Britain, David & Charles, 1976; Barrows in England and Wales, Shire Archaeologies, 1979.

WORK IN PROGRESS: Dorset Barrows Supplement, for Dorset Natural History and Archaeological Society; research on prehistoric sepulchral monuments, and on the later history of archaeological sites, especially their folklore.

*   *   *

GROHSKOPF, Bernice

PERSONAL: Born in Troy, N.Y.; daughter of Philip A. and Jenny (Jacobs) Appelbaum; married Herbert Grohskopf (a chemical engineer), September 2, 1952 (separated, 1978); children: Peggy. Education: Columbia University, B.S., 1948, M.A., 1954; New York University, additional study, 1960-66. Home: 10 Crestmont Rd., Montclair, N.J. 07042.

CAREER: Columbia University Press, New York, N.Y., assistant to manager of publications department, 1946-48; magazine editor, Dell Publishing Co., 1948-50; free-lance editor, Frederick Ungar Publishing Co.; Sweet Briar College, Sweet Briar, Va., writer-in-residence, 1980-81. Member: Authors Guild, P.E.N., American Association of University Women. Awards, honors: Seeds of Time appeared on the American Library Association's list of Notable Children's Books for 1963; New Jersey State Teachers of English Award, 1970, for The Treasure of Sutton Hoo; MacDowell Colony fellowships, 1976, 1978, 1980; Virginia Center for the Creative Arts fellowships, 1977, 1979; Karolyi Foundation fellowships, 1979, 1980; New Jersey State Council on the Arts fellowship, 1980.

WRITINGS—All published by Atheneum, except as indicated: Seeds of Time (introduction to Shakespeare for young readers), 1963; From Age to Age, 1968; The Treasure of Sutton Hoo, 1970; Shadow in the Sun, 1975; Notes on the Hauter Experiment, 1975; Children in the Wind, 1977; Blood and Roses, 1979; Tell Me Your Dream, Scholastic, in press; End of Summer, Avon, in press. Contributor to Random House Encyclopedia, 1978; contributor of short stories to Folio, Phylon, Woman's Day, and other periodicals.

BIOGRAPHICAL/CRITICAL SOURCES: Montclair Times, May 16, 1963.

GROSS, Seymour L. 1926-

PERSONAL: Born January 28, 1926, in New York, N.Y.; son of Joseph L. and Henrietta (Weinreb) Gross; married Elaine Linford, 1951; children: Thelma Lee, Thomas Linford, James Linford. *Education:* University of Denver, A.B., 1949, A.M., 1950; University of Illinois, Ph.D., 1954. *Home:* 19519 Shrewsbury Rd., Detroit, Mich. 48221. *Office:* Department of English, University of Detroit, 4001 West McNichols, Detroit, Mich. 48221.

CAREER: University of Illinois at Urbana-Champaign, instructor, 1954-55; South Bend-Mishawaka Center of Indiana University (now Indiana University at South Bend), instructor, 1955-57; University of Notre Dame, Notre Dame, Ind., assistant professor, 1957-60, associate professor, 1960-66, professor of English, 1966-69; University of Detroit, Detroit, Mich., Burke O'Neill Professor of American Literature, 1969—. Professor extra-ordinary, University of Skopje, Skopje, Yugoslavia, 1962-63. *Member:* Modern Language Association of America, American Association of University Professors (secretary-treasurer of Notre Dame chapter, 1961), American Studies Association, Phi Beta Kappa.

WRITINGS: A "Scarlet Letter" Handbook, Wadsworth, 1960; *Eudora Welty: A Bibliography of Criticism and Comment,* University of Virginia Press, 1960; (editor with Milton R. Stern) *American Literature Survey,* four volumes, Viking, 1962, 3rd edition, 1975; (editor) *A "Benito Cereno" Handbook,* Wadsworth, 1965; (editor with John Edward Hardy) *Images of the Negro in American Literature,* University of Chicago Press, 1966; (editor) Nathaniel Hawthorne, *The House of the Seven Gables,* Norton, 1966; (editor) Hawthorne, *The Blithedale Romance,* Norton, 1979; (editor) Hawthorne, *The Scarlet Letter,* Norton, 1979. Contributor of articles to *American Literature, Modern Fiction Studies, South Atlantic Quarterly,* and other professional journals.

AVOCATIONAL INTERESTS: The history of medicine.

BIOGRAPHICAL/CRITICAL SOURCES: New Leader, April 10, 1967; *Contemporary Literature,* winter, 1968.

*   *   *

GUNSTON, William Tudor 1927-
(Bill Gunston)

PERSONAL: Born March 1, 1927, in London, England; son of William John (a professional soldier and linguist) and Stella Hazelwood (Cooper) Gunston; married Margaret Anne Jolliff, October 10, 1964; children: Jeannette Christina, Stephanie Elaine Tracy. *Education:* University of Durham, Inter-B.Sc., 1946; attended Northampton College of Advanced Technology (now The City University), London, 1948-51. *Politics:* Conservative. *Religion:* Church of England. *Home and office:* High Beech, Kingsley Green, near Haslemere, Surrey GU27 3LL, England. *Agent:* Donald Copeman Ltd., 46 Bedford Row, London WC1R 4LR, England.

CAREER: Iliffe & Sons, London, England, member of editorial staff of *Flight International,* 1951-54, technical editor, 1955-64, technology editor of *Science Journal,* 1964-70; freelance writer, 1970—. *Military service:* Royal Air Force, flying instructor, 1945-48. *Member:* Association of British Science Writers, Circle of Aviation Writers (chairman, 1956, 1961).

WRITINGS—All under name Bill Gunston: *Your Book of Light* (juvenile), Faber, 1968; *Hydrofoils and Hovercraft,* Doubleday, 1968; *Flight Handbook,* Iliffe, 1968; (with John

W. R. Taylor, Kenneth Munson, and John W. Wood) *The Lore of Flight,* Time-Life, 1970.

The Jet Age, Arthur Barker, 1972; *Transport Problems and Prospects,* Dutton, 1972; *Transport Technology,* Crowell-Collier, 1972; (contributor) Edward de Bono, editor, *Technology Today,* Routledge & Kegan Paul, 1972; (with Frank Howard) *The Conquest of the Air,* Random House, 1973; *Bombers of the West,* Scribner, 1973.

Shaping Metals (young adult), Macdonald & Co., 1974; *Attack Aircraft of the West,* Scribner, 1974; *Philatelist's Companion,* David & Charles, 1974; (contributor) *Encyclopedia of Air Warfare,* Salamander, 1974; *Our World Encyclopedia,* Volumes VI and VII, Macmillan, 1975; *Man and Materials* (juvenile), six volumes, Macmillan, 1975-76; *Transport,* Macmillan, 1975; *F-4 Phantom,* Scribner, 1975; *Supersonic Fighters of the West,* Scribner, 1975; *Fighters 1914-1915,* Hamlyn Publishing, 1975; *Aircraft,* Macdonald & Co., 1975; *Fabulous Facts in Transport,* Theorem, 1975; *Submarines,* Arcos, 1975; *Encyclopedia of Combat Aircraft,* Salamander, 1975; *Fighters since 1945,* Hamlyn Publishing, 1975.

Minimacs (juvenile), six volumes, Macmillan, 1976; *Night Fighters,* Patrick Stephens, 1976; *Helicopters 1900-1960,* Hamlyn Publishing, 1976; *Helicopters since 1960,* Hamlyn Publishing, 1976; *World Land Speed Record,* Hamish Hamilton, 1976; *World Air Speed Record,* Hamish Hamilton, 1976; *Finding out about Railways,* Purnell, 1976; (co-author) *The Soviet War Machine,* Salamander, 1976; *Modern Military Aircraft,* Salamander, 1976; (co-author) *Coal: Technology for Britain's Future,* Macmillan, 1976; (contributor) *The International Book of Wood,* Mitchell Beazley, 1976; *The F-111,* Ian Allan, 1977; *Combat Aircraft of World War II,* Salamander, 1977; (co-author) *Hitler's Luftwaffe,* Salamander, 1977; (co-author) *Soviet Airpower,* Salamander, 1977; (contributor) *World War 3,* Hamlyn Publishing, 1977.

Finding out about Aircraft, Purnell, 1978; *Bombers,* Hamlyn Publishing, 1978; *Fighters,* Hamlyn Publishing, 1978; *By Jupiter* (biography of Sir Roy Fedden), Royal Aeronautical Society, 1978; (editor and contributor) *St. Michael Encyclopedia of Aviation,* Sundial Press, 1978; (consulting editor and contributor) *The Flyer's Handbook,* Marshall Editions, 1978; (contributor) *Encyclopedia of Aviation,* Octopus, 1978; *Encyclopedia of Missiles and Rockets,* Salamander, 1979; (contributor) *Encyclopedia of World Air Forces,* Salamander, 1979; (contributor) *The Chinese War Machine,* Salamander, 1979; (contributor) *The U.S. War Machine,* Salamander, 1979.

Tornado, Ian Allan, 1980; *Aircraft of World War 2,* Octopus Books, 1980; *The Planemakers,* New English Library, 1980; (editor and contributor) *St. Michael Encyclopedia of General Knowledge,* Sundial Press, 1980; *Water,* Macdonald Educational, 1980; *Jane's Aerospace Dictionary,* Jane's Publishing Co., 1980; *Fighters of the 1950's,* Patrick Stephens, 1980; *Aircraft* (juvenile), Usborne West, 1980; (editor and contributor) *World Air Power,* Aerospace Publishing, 1980; (contributor) *Jane's Encyclopedia of Aviation,* Jane's Publishing, 1980; (consulting editor) *The Colour Encyclopedia of Aviation,* Octopus Books, 1980.

Also author of *World War II,* Bison Books, and *Technology at Work,* Doubleday; consultant and contributor to *The Joy of Knowledge Encyclopedia,* Mitchell Beazley. Writer of materials for industry, business, government, and education and research institutions, including Nuffield Foundation, Ford Foundation, UNESCO, the British Government, Rutherford High Energy Laboratory, British Broadcasting Corp., Hughes Aircraft, and Rolls-Royce.

Contributor to encyclopedias and yearbooks, including *National Encyclopedia, Junior Encyclopedia, Brassey's Annual and Defence Yearbook, Aircraft Annual, Young Scientist's Annual,* and *Look and Learn Annual.* Contributor to magazines, juvenile periodicals, and newspapers all over the world, including *New Scientist, Aircraft* (Australia), *Speed and Power, Battle,* and *Aeroplane Monthly.* Aviation Editor, *Weapons and Warfare;* consulting editor, *The Illustrated International Encyclopedia of Aviation.*

WORK IN PROGRESS: "Despite a supposed recession in publishing, 22 major tasks at present under contract."

SIDELIGHTS: Bill Gunston writes: "I left my old firm in 1970 . . . and cast around looking for a job (and the best offers were all outside the United Kingdom), but first I had to clear a vast backlog of free-lance work. I am still trying to clear it, but the pile is now twice as large. I have a golden rule for authors: if you are daunted at the size of the task, or the amount of research needed, just sit down and write the book. When it is finished you will wonder why you were worried."

*   *   *

GUTNIK, Martin J(erome) 1942-

PERSONAL: Born December 1, 1942, in Winnipeg, Manitoba, Canada; son of Max and Sally (Kaminsky) Gutnik; married second wife, Natalie Browne, September 14, 1978; children: Max Michael, Anne Felisha, Liza Michelle, Andrew Benjamin. *Education:* University of Wisconsin—Milwaukee, B.S., 1966, M.S., 1972. *Office:* Atwater School, 2100 East Capitol Dr., Shorewood, Wis. 53211.

CAREER: Atwater School, Shorewood, Wis., elementary science teacher, 1970—. Director of Atwater Environmental Science Center; member of Wisconsin State Science Curriculum Committee. *Military service:* U.S. Army, 1966-69. *Member:* National Science Teachers Association, National Wildlife Federation, Wisconsin Elementary, Kindergarten, Nursery Education Association, Shorewood Education Association.

WRITINGS—Published by Childrens Press, except as indicated: *Ecology and Pollution: Air,* 1973; *Ecology and Pollution: Water,* 1973; *Ecology and Pollution: Land,* 1973; *Energy: Its Past, Present, and Future,* 1975; *What Plants Produce,* 1976; *How Plants Make Food,* 1976; *How Plants Are Made,* 1976; *How to Do a Science Project and Report,* F. Watts, 1980; *The Science of Classification,* F. Watts, 1980.

WORK IN PROGRESS: The Cadmus Society, a novel of intrigue; *The Glastor Council.*

H

HAAS, Dorothy F.
(Dee Francis)

PERSONAL: Born in Racine, Wis.; daughter of Allen L. (a pharmacist) and Elizabeth (Sweetman) Haas. *Education:* Marquette University, B.S., 1955. *Home:* 336 West Wellington Ave., Chicago, Ill. 60657. *Office address:* Rand McNally & Co., P.O. Box 7600, Chicago, Ill. 60680.

CAREER: Whitman Publishing Division, Western Publishing Co., Racine, Wis., 1955-68, became senior editor; Worldbook Childcraft, Chicago, senior editor, 1968-70; Rand McNally & Co., Chicago, 1970—, currently senior editor, trade division, books for children and young adults. *Awards, honors:* Children's Reading Round Table Award, 1979.

*WRITINGS—*Published by Whitman, except as indicated: *Little Joe's Puppy,* 1957; *Mimi, the Merry-go-Round Cat,* 1958; *Christopher John's Fuzzy Blanket,* 1959; *That Puppy!,* 1960; *Soda Pop,* 1960; *Oh, Look!,* 1961; *A Penny for Whiffles,* 1962; *Patrick and the Duckling,* 1963; *Especially from Thomas,* 1965; *Grandpapa and Me,* 1966; *A Special Place for Johnny,* 1966; *Maria, Everybody Has a Name,* 1966; *This Little Pony,* 1967; *The Bears Upstairs,* Greenwillow Press, 1978; *Poppy and the Outdoors Cat,* 1980.

Original stories based on television or movie series; some under pseudonym Dee Francis: *Corky and White Shadow,* 1956; *Rinty and Pals for Rusty,* 1957; *Captain Kangaroo and the Too-Small House,* 1958; *Fury,* 1958; *Sir Lancelot,* 1958; *Quick Draw McGraw: Badmen Beware,* 1960; *National Velvet,* 1962; *Tom and Jerry: Goody Go-Round,* 1967.

Adaptations of movie scripts; under pseudonym Dee Francis: *Pinocchio,* 1961; *Babes in Toyland,* 1961; *The Sword in the Stone,* 1963.

Biography: *Men of Science,* 1959.

Editor of "Tween-Age Books" (fiction for pre-teens): "Tell-a-Tale Books," "Big Tell-a-Tale Books," and "Tiny Tot Tales."

AVOCATIONAL INTERESTS: Music, art, travel.

* * *

HAGEE, John C(harles) 1940-

PERSONAL: Born April 12, 1940, in Baytown, Tex.; son of Bythel (a minister) and Vada (Swick) Hagee; married second wife, Diana Castro, April 12, 1976; children: (first marriage) Letitia Kirsten, John Christopher; (second marriage) Chris-

tina Rose, Matthew Charles. *Education:* Southwestern Bible Institute, Th.B., 1960; Trinity University, B.S., 1964; North Texas State University, M.Ed., 1969. *Home:* 2719 Oak Bluff, San Antonio, Tex. 78230. *Office:* Church of Castle Hills, 214 Roleto, San Antonio, Tex. 78213.

CAREER: Protestant clergyman; Trinity Church, San Antonio, Tex., founder and pastor, 1966-1975; Church of Castle Hills, San Antonio, pastor, 1975—. President of Global Evangelism, Inc., 1973—, and Global Evangelism Television, Inc.

WRITINGS: Invasion of Demons, Revell, 1973; *Like a Cleansing Fire,* Revell, 1974; *Scandalous Saint,* Whitaker House, 1974.

WORK IN PROGRESS: The Last Church Will Be Like the First Church.

AVOCATIONAL INTERESTS: Sports; singing; playing piano, saxophone, and bass guitar.

* * *

HAHN, Hannelore

PERSONAL: Born in Dresden, Germany; daughter of Arthur and Helen (Brach) Hahn; children: Tina Stoumen. *Education:* Attended Black Mountain College, 1945-47, and Whittier College, 1947; University of Southern California, B.A., 1952. *Home and office address:* Box 810, Gracie Station, New York, N.Y. 10028. *Agent:* Denise Marcil, 316 West 82nd St., New York, N.Y. 10024.

CAREER: Atlantis Productions, Inc. (educational films), Hollywood, Calif., research assistant, 1956-57; U.S. Information Service, New York City, coordinator for two U.S. Department of State exhibits, 1958-59; American Institute of Physics, New York City, historical and biographical research, 1962-65; Chermayeff & Geismar Associates, New York City, exhibit research for U.S. Pavilion at Expo 67, Montreal, 1965-66; New York City Department of Parks, New York City, consultant, doing research on design of play equipment and nature conservation, beginning 1966; president and publisher, Tenth House Enterprises, Inc., 1978—. Producer and director of Women's Writing Conference retreats, 1976—. *Member:* International Women's Writing Guild (founder and director, 1976—). *Awards, honors:* Prix de Paris finalist, *Vogue,* 1952.

WRITINGS: Take a Giant Step, Little, Brown, 1960; (translator) *The Scientific Correspondence of Albert Einstein,* Institute for Advanced Studies, 1975. Poetry has appeared in numerous anthologies, including *For Neruda, for Chile,* edited by Volker Braun, Beacon Press, 1975. Contributor to *Saturday Book, Mademoiselle,* and *New York Quarterly.* Editor of *Places* (annual directory), Tenth House, 1978, 1979, 1980.

SIDELIGHTS: "I think a writer catches fish," notes Hannelore Hahn in an essay written for the International Women's Writing Conference, 1977. "A writer catches thoughts and impressions quickly before they swim back into the deep ocean. In this way a writer is a collector of data, which, when connected to other data, fills the unbearable void. Yes, [the writer is] a catcher of fish, a knotter of nets, a spinner of yarn. And also, the writer is a weaver. Because the writer connects one piece of information with another and weaves a tapestry by tying together hundreds and thousands of threads. Our thoughts dart back and forth like shuttles, but they are invisible shuttles. And our looms are invisible, too. To passionately pursue and nurture that which is invisible requires faith."

*   *   *

HALL, Kathleen M(ary) 1924-

PERSONAL: Born January 28, 1924, in England; daughter of Frank Gardner and Mary Constance (Whyatt) Hall. *Education:* St. Hilda's College, Oxford, B.A., 1946, M.A., 1949, Ph.D., 1953. *Home:* 44 Bassett Green Rd., Southampton, England. *Office:* Department of French, University of Southampton, Southampton, England.

CAREER: British Ministry of Supply, London, England, temporary assistant, 1944-45, assistant principal, 1945-46; Queen's University, Belfast, Northern Ireland, assistant lecturer in French, 1953-55; University of Southampton, Southampton, England, lecturer, 1955-69, senior lecturer in French, 1969—. *Member:* Society for French Studies, Society for Renaissance Studies.

WRITINGS: Pontus de Tyard and His Discours Philosophiques, Oxford University Press, 1963; (editor with K. Cameron and F. Higman) Theodore de Beze, *Abraham Sacifiant* [Geneva; Switzerland], 1967; (editor with C. N. Smith) Jean de la Taille, *Dramatic Works,* Athlone, 1972; (editor) Estienne Jodelle, *Cleopatre Captive,* Exeter University Texts, 1980. Contributor to *Encyclopaedia Britannica* and language journals.

WORK IN PROGRESS: Studies of French Renaissance drama, Marguerite de Navarre, Rabelais, DuBellay, and Montaigne.

AVOCATIONAL INTERESTS: Embroidery.

*   *   *

HALL, Oakley (Maxwell) 1920-
(O. M. Hall, Jason Manor)

PERSONAL: Born July 1, 1920, in San Diego, Calif.; son of Oakley M. and Jessie (Sands) Hall; married Barbara Edinger, June 28, 1945; children: Oakley III, Mary Barbara Sands, Tracy Elizabeth, Sara Brett. *Education:* University of California, Berkeley, B.A., 1943; State University of Iowa, M.F.A., 1950. *Home address:* P.O. Box 2101, Olympic Valley, Calif. 95730. *Agent:* Harold Matson & Co., 22 East 40th St., New York, N.Y. 10016.

CAREER: State University of Iowa Writer's Workshop, staff member, 1950-52; University of California, Irvine, professor of English, 1968—, director of graduate program in

writing, 1968-78. *Military service:* U.S. Marine Corps, 1939-45. *Awards, honors:* Pulitzer Prize nomination, 1958, for *Warlock.*

WRITINGS: (Under name O. M. Hall) *Murder City,* Farrar, Straus, 1949; *So Many Doors,* Random House, 1950; *Corpus of Joe Bailey,* Viking, 1953; *Mardios Beach,* Viking, 1955; *Warlock,* Viking, 1958; *The Downhill Racers,* Viking, 1963; *The Pleasure Garden,* Viking, 1966; *A Game for Eagles,* Morrow, 1970; *Report from Beau Harbor,* Morrow, 1971; *The Adelita,* Doubleday, 1975; *The Bad Lands,* Atheneum, 1978. Also author of libretto for *Angle of Repose,* an opera based on the book by Wallace Stegner, 1976.

Under pseudonym Jason Manor: *Too Dead to Run,* Viking, 1953; *The Red Jaguar,* Viking, 1954; *The Pawns of Fear,* Viking, 1955; *The Tramplers,* Viking, 1956.

Contributor of short stories to *Western Review, Epoch, Antioch Review,* and other little magazines.

SIDELIGHTS: In a review of *The Pleasure Garden,* Wirt Williams writes: "[Oakley Hall] . . . has always had an X-ray penetration of social orders, big and little, and the keenest sensitivity to their nuances and subtleties. And he has always had a skill with plot that was absolutely dangerous.

"His great and manifest growth here is in the range and intensity of language and imagery. The dimension that the edited image creates was in the past his most serious lack: the absence of poetry was almost all that kept his *Warlock* from being the culminating, *fin de series* work in a century of fiction about the American West. Now he has that dimension."

In *Report from Beau Harbor* Hall again displays his skill and understanding. Bernard Weinstein notes in his *Best Sellers* article that the book "never sacrifices the humanity of its characters to shallow opportunism." The critic explains that Hall "perceives this country in depth as well as in breadth. For this is a book that cuts deeply into the marrow of upper-middle-class America with the scalpel of skepticism." Martin Levin of the *New York Times Book Review* echoes Williams's earlier review: "[Hall] establishes a painfully recognizable social climate, . . . bound together with a storyteller's sense and an adhesive of bitter humor." *Book World's* Sara Blackburn finds the resulting characterizations uncannily real. "It pleases me to report that no one lives happily ever after," she adds. "Hall . . . has a rare gift for depicting those moments during which people grow and change."

One of Hall's more recent books does not always fare as well with critics. *The Bad Lands,* set in Dakota Territory during the 1880's, deals with range wars and the influx of the small farmers and ranchers into the territory. Ross Thomas of the *Washington Post* writes: "It's obvious . . . that a considerable amount of diligent research has gone into this book. . . . Although he tries very hard indeed, Hall does not quite capture either the essence or the flavor of the time and place about which he writes." That does not bother *Newsweek's* P. S. Prescott at all. The reviewer comments: "You will not hear me breathe a word against this story. I loved every predictable page of it. The great pleasure . . . of any mythic fiction is that we already know the story before we have begun it: We read for confirmation."

Warlock was filmed by Twentieth Century-Fox in 1959, *The Downhill Racers* by Paramount in 1969 as "Downhill Racer."

BIOGRAPHICAL/CRITICAL SOURCES: Hudson Review, spring, 1967; *Kenyon Review,* Volume 30, number 1, 1968; *Variety,* December 24, 1969; *Best Sellers,* December 1, 1970,

November 1, 1971; *New York Times Book Review,* October 17, 1971, May 14, 1978; *Book World,* January 2, 1972; *Washington Post,* May 20, 1978; *Newsweek,* June 5, 1978.

* * *

HALL, Vernon, Jr. 1913-

PERSONAL: Born November 30, 1913, in Atlanta, Ga.; son of Vernon and Anne (Webb) Hall; married Marie-Louise Michaud, June 17, 1938 (deceased); children: Anne-Marie (Mrs. Walter M. Doolittle). *Education:* Attended Amherst College, 1932-34; New York University, A.B. (summa cum laude), 1936, M.A., 1937; University of Wisconsin, Ph.D., 1940. *Residence:* Madison, Wis. *Office:* Department of Comparative Literature, 924 Van Hise Hall, 1220 Linden Dr., University of Wisconsin, Madison, Wis. 53706.

CAREER: Teacher at University of Wisconsin—Madison, 1937-40; Pueblo Junior College, Pueblo, Colo., instructor, 1940-41; Dartmouth College, Hanover, N.H., assistant professor, 1941-46, associate professor, 1946-50, professor of comparative literature, 1950-64; University of Wisconsin—Madison, professor of comparative literature, 1964—, chairman of department, 1970-71. Visiting professor at City College of New York (now City College of the City University of New York), 1940-41, New York University, 1950, 1964, University of New Mexico, 1961, University of Wisconsin, 1962, University of Aix-Marseilles, 1965-66, and Ewha Women's University, 1980. *Member:* Renaissance Society of America, American Association of University Professors, Modern Language Association of America (past secretary and chairman of groups and sections), Soceite des Sciences et des Arts d'Agen (honorary). *Awards, honors:* M.A. from Dartmouth College.

WRITINGS: Renaissance Literary Criticism: A Study of Its Social Content, Columbia University Press, 1945; *Life of Julius Caesar Scaliger,* American Philosophical Society, 1950; (with J. B. Stearns) *Byzantine Gold Coins in the Dartmouth Collection,* Dartmouth College Press, 1953, (editor with J. W. Bennett and O. Cargill) *Studies in the England Renaissance Drama,* New York University Press, 1959; *A Short History of Literary Criticism,* New York University Press, 1963; *Literary Criticism: Plato to Johnson,* Appleton, 1970; *The Vernon Hall Collection of European Medals,* Elvehjem Museum of Art, 1978. Also author of *A History of Western Criticism* (in Korean). Book reviewer, *New York Herald Tribune.* Assistant editor of *Renaissance News,* 1948-50; foreign language editor of *Explicator,* 1948—; editorial adviser of *College English,* 1952-54.

SIDELIGHTS: Vernon Hall, Jr. is competent in French, Italian, and Latin.

* * *

HALLGARTEN, Siegfried Fritz 1902-

PERSONAL: Born June 6, 1902, in Winkel, Rheingau, Germany; son of Arthur (a wine merchant) and Frieda (Heyum) Hallgarten; married Friedel L. Liebmann; children: Peter Alexander, Anthony Bernard Richard. *Education:* University of Frankfurt, Referandar, 1926, Assessor, 1929; University of Heidelberg, Dr.jur.utr., 1927. *Religion:* Jewish. *Home:* 20 Bracknell Gardens, London N.W. 3, England.

CAREER: Court of Justice, Frankfurt, Germany, auxiliary judge, 1930; Marxheimer-Hallgarten (law firm), Wiesbaden, Germany, lawyer, 1931-33; S. F. Hallgarten (later Hallgarten Wines Ltd.), London, England, wine importer, 1933-73; lawyer, 1973—. Managing director of Arthur Hallgarten,

Winkel, Germany, and Savermo Ltd. and L. Rosenheim & Sons, both of London. Member of board, Association of Jewish Refugees. *Member:* P.E.N., K.C. Fraternity of Jewish Graduates of German Universities (member of board).

WRITINGS: Rhineland-Wineland, Elek Books, 1951, 4th edition, Arlington Books, 1965; *Alsace and Its Wine Gardens,* Deutsch, 1957, published as *Alsace, Wine Gardens, Cellars and Cuisine,* 1978; (with Andre Simon) *The Great Wines of Germany,* McGraw, 1963; *Guide to the Vineyards, Estates and Wines of Germany,* Publivin, 1974; *German Wines,* Faber, 1976, revised edition, 1981; (with wife, F. L. Hallgarten) *The Wine Gardens of Austria,* Argus, 1979. Also author of *Fiddlers in the Cellar,* 1980, (with F. L. Hallgarten) *Viticulture in the Holy Land,* 1981, and (with F. L. Hallgarten) *Wines of the Loire,* 1981. Contributor to newspapers and to wine trade journals.

SIDELIGHTS: Siegfried Hallgarten told *CA:* "Having been brought up in a viticultural region, wine was my hobby. When I lost my profession as a lawyer in 1933 through Nazi legislation, I made my hobby my profession. I became a wine importer in England and started to lecture and write about wine and wine law. When I retired from business in 1973 I got involved in a battle with German viticultural authorities and knew that that battle could only be won if I became a fully fledged lawyer again. This is the reason I rejoined the German bar, specializing in wine law, law of unfair trading and trade marks."

* * *

HALLINAN, Nancy 1921-

PERSONAL: Born February 5, 1921, in London, England; daughter of Charles T. (a journalist) and Hazel (Hunkins) Hallinan; divorced; children: Rosalind Addison Goethals. *Education:* Vassar College, B.A., 1942; graduate study at Columbia University, 1946-47, and New School for Social Research, 1947-48. *Politics:* Registered Democrat. *Religion:* Episcopal. *Home and office:* 276 Riverside Dr., New York, N.Y. 10025. *Agent:* Shirley Fisher, McIntosh & Otis, 475 Fifth Ave., New York, N.Y. 10017.

CAREER: Reporter for newspapers in Newburgh, N.Y., and Binghamton, N.Y., 1942-44; Office of War Information, New York, N.Y., editorial assistant, 1944-45; free-lance writer. Has taught creative writing at Pace University, Ethical Culture School of Adult Education, Elizabeth Seton College, and Mount St. Vincent College. Reader for Harper & Row and Book-of-the-Month Club. *Awards, honors:* Writing fellowships at Yaddo, Edward MacDowell Artists' Colony, and Rhode Island Creative Arts Center; winner of Creative Artists Public Service Program, 1979-80; second prize, O. Henry Awards, 1980.

WRITINGS: Rough Winds of May, Harper, 1955; *A Voice from the Wings,* Knopf, 1965; *Night Swimmers,* Harper, 1976. Contributor of short stories to *Cornhill, New Voices, American Writing Today, Touchstone, American Vanguard, Cosmopolitan, Harper's,* and other periodicals. Fiction editor, *The Smith.*

Collaborator: Susan Peterson, *The Living Tradition of Maria Martinez,* Kodansha, 1977; Linnea Pearson and Ruth Purtilo, *Separate Paths,* Harper, 1977; Beatrice Lydecker, *What the Animals Tell Me,* Harper, 1977; Mario Capelli, *The Great Drake,* Harper, 1977.

WORK IN PROGRESS: A biography tentatively entitled *Sasakawa, Man for All Nations.*

SIDELIGHTS: Nancy Hallinan told *CA:* "I believe I write

fiction as a way of sorting experiences, making sense out of mystery, creating form and order out of existential disorder. I write nonfiction as an assignment for money, and I end up learning a great deal and enjoying myself in the process. The work-in-progress biography has been pure adventure from the very beginning, and it also included a trip to Japan. Writing is hellishly hard work. Yet it's not a bad life, and it's too late now for me to be anything else but a writer.''

AVOCATIONAL INTERESTS: Theatre, ballet and modern dance, good movies, painting, sculpture, travel.

*   *   *

HALPER, Albert   1904-

PERSONAL: Born August 3, 1904, in Chicago, Ill.; son of Isaac and Rebecca (Alpert) Halper; married Lorna Blaine Howard (an artist), December 28, 1956; children: (prior marriage) Thomas. *Education:* Attended Northwestern University, 1924-25. *Home address:* RD2, Pawling, N.Y. 12564.

CAREER: Novelist. *Awards, honors:* Guggenheim fellowship in creative writing, 1934.

WRITINGS: Union Square (Literary Guild selection), Viking, 1933, reprinted, Belmont-Tower, 1962; *On the Shore,* Viking, 1934; *The Foundry,* Viking, 1934, reprinted, AMS Press, 1974; *The Chute,* Viking, 1937, reprinted, AMS Press, 1974; *Sons of the Fathers,* Harper, 1940; *The Little People,* Harper, 1942, reprinted, AMS Press, 1976; *Only an Inch from Glory,* Harper, 1943; (editor) *This Is Chicago,* Holt, 1952; *The Golden Watch,* Holt, 1953; *Atlantic Avenue,* Dell, 1956; *The Fourth Horseman of Miami Beach,* Norton, 1966; (editor) *The Chicago Crime Book,* World Publishing, 1967; *Good-Bye, Union Square,* Quadrangle, 1970; *Post War,* Rapoport Press, 1975. Contributor of stories and articles to *New Yorker, Harper's, Atlantic, Holiday, Yale Review,* and other periodicals.

Plays: (With Joe Schrank) "My Aunt Daisy," 1954; "Top Man," 1955.

WORK IN PROGRESS: A novel.

SIDELIGHTS: Albert Halper wrote *CA:* "Why [do] I write? Knut Hamsum, one of my favorite authors, was asked the same question in the 1930's, a question directed toward notable European writers. His reply, which won first prize, was: 'I write to kill time.' Those words have been buried inside my mind for decades. I cannot improve upon his reply, but I can try. So here goes: I write because I must.''

*   *   *

HALPERIN, Morton H.   1938-

PERSONAL: Born June 13, 1938, in Brooklyn, N.Y.; son of Harry (a lawyer) and Lillian (Neubart) Halperin; children: David, Mark, Gary. *Education:* Columbia University, A.B., 1958; Yale University, M.A., 1959, Ph.D., 1961. *Religion:* Jewish. *Office:* 122 Maryland Ave. N.E., Washington, D.C. 20002.

CAREER: Harvard University, Cambridge, Mass., research associate, Center for International Affairs, 1960-66, instructor, 1961-63, assistant professor of government, 1964-66; Office of the Assistant Secretary of Defense, Washington, D.C., special assistant, 1966-67, deputy assistant secretary of defense, 1967-69; member of senior staff, National Security Council, 1969; Brookings Institution, Washington, D.C., senior fellow, 1969-73; director of research project, Twentieth Century Fund, 1974-75; director of project on national security and civil liberties, 1975-77; director of Center for

National Security Studies, 1978—. Consultant to RAND Corp. *Member:* American Political Science Association, American Civil Liberties Union, Council on Foreign Relations, Institute for Strategic Studies. *Awards, honors:* Rockefeller Foundation grant for research on China's military and foreign policy.

WRITINGS: (With Sheldon Raab) *The Columbia College Student, 1956-57: A Study of the Whole Man,* Columbia College, 1957; *Nuclear Weapons and Limited War,* Center for International Affairs, Harvard University, 1960; (with Thomas C. Schelling) *Strategy and Arms Control,* Twentieth Century Fund, 1961; *Limited War: An Essay on the Development of the Theory and an Annotated Bibliography,* Center for International Affairs, Harvard University, 1961; *A Proposal for a Ban on the Use of Nuclear Weapons,* Institute for Defense Analysis, 1961; *Arms Control and Inadvertent General War,* Institute for Defense Analysis, 1962; *The Limiting Process in the Korean War,* Center for International Affairs, Harvard University, 1962; *Limited War in the Nuclear Age,* Wiley, 1963; *China and the Bomb,* Praeger, 1965; (with Dwight Perkins) *Communist China and Arms Control,* Praeger, 1965; *Chinese Nuclear Strategy: The Early Post Detonation Period,* Institute for Strategic Studies, 1965; *Is China Turning In?,* Center for International Affairs, Harvard University, 1965; *China and Nuclear Proliferation,* Center for Policy Study, University of Chicago, 1966; *Contemporary Military Strategy,* Little, Brown, 1967, revised edition published as *Defense Strategy for the Seventies,* 1971; (editor) *Sino-Soviet Relations and Arms Control,* M.I.T. Press, 1967.

(Editor with Arnold Kantor) *Readings in American Foreign Policy: A Bureaucratic Perspective,* Little, Brown, 1973; (with Priscilla Clapp and Kantor) *Bureaucratic Politics and Foreign Policy,* Brookings Institution, 1974; (editor with Clapp) *United States-Japanese Relations: The 1970's,* Harvard University Press, 1974; *National Security and Policy-Making: Analyses, Cases, and Proposals,* Lexington Books, 1975; (with others) *The Lawless State: The Crimes of the U.S. Intelligence Agencies,* Penguin, 1976; (with Daniel Hoffman) *Top Secret: National Security and the Right to Know,* New Republic Books, 1977; (with Hoffman) *Freedom vs. National Security,* Chelsea House, 1977. Contributor to professional journals. Member of editorial board, *Foreign Policy.*

*   *   *

HALPERN, Joel M.   1929-

PERSONAL: Born April 8, 1929; son of Carl and Nettie Halpern; married Barbara Kerewsky, 1952; children: Kay, Susannah, Carla. *Education:* University of Michigan, A.B., 1950; Columbia University, Ph.D., 1956. *Office:* Department of Anthropology, University of Massachusetts, Amherst, Mass. 01002.

CAREER: Columbia University, New York, N.Y., lecturer in anthropology, 1955; anthropological abstractor, Arctic Bibliography, 1956; Human Relations Area Files, Washington, D.C., research associate, 1956; International Cooperation Administration, Community Development Division, Luang Prabang, Laos, field service officer, 1956-58; University of California, Los Angeles, assistant professor of anthropology, 1958-63; Brandeis University, Waltham, Mass., associate professor of anthropology, 1963-65; Harvard University, Russian Research Center, Cambridge, Mass., associate, 1965-67; University of Massachusetts—Amherst, associate professor, 1967-69, professor of anthropology,

1969—. Visiting professor, Albert Ludwigs-Universitat and Arnold Bergstrasser-Institute, 1970-71; resident fellow, Massachusetts Institute of Technology-Harvard Joint Center for Urban Studies, 1969-70; senior research fellow, Center for Urban and Community Studies, University of Toronto, summer, 1974. Consultant, RAND Corp., 1959-61.

MEMBER: American Anthropological Association, Society for Applied Anthropology, Association for Asian Studies, American Association for the Advancement of Slavic Studies. *Awards, honors:* Council on Economic and Cultural Affairs grant, 1958; University of California faculty fellowship, 1959; American Council of Learned Societies summer grant, 1960, travel grants, 1966, 1979, research grant, 1972; National Science Foundation grants, 1961-62, 1963, 1964, 1965-67, 1974-77, 1979-81, travel grant, 1973; University of California Center for Slavic studies grant, 1963; Golden Bruin Award from University of California, Los Angeles, 1963, for outstanding teaching and university service; National Institute of Mental Health research grant, 1968, special fellowship, 1969-70; Southeast Asia Development Advisory Group research grant, 1969; Center for a Voluntary Society research grant, 1973; National Endowment for the Humanities research grant, 1973-77; grants from National Institute of Child Health and Human Development, 1974-77, and Institute of Comparative Education and Culture, Kyushu University, Japan, 1976-77; Biomedical Sciences research grant from University of Massachusetts, 1977; American Philosophical Society research grant, 1978.

WRITINGS: (With wife, Barbara Kerewsky Halpern) *Yugoslavia,* Doubleday, 1956; *Social and Cultural Change in a Serbian Village,* Columbia University Press, 1956, condensed edition published as *A Serbian Village,* 1958, revised edition, Harper, 1967; *Aspects of Village Life and Culture Change in Laos,* Council on Economic and Cultural Affairs, 1958; (editor with John A. McKinstry and Dalip Saund) *Bibliography of Anthropological and Sociological Publications on Eastern Europe and the U.S.S.R.,* Russian and East European Studies Center, University of California, 1961; *The Rural and Urban Economies of Laos,* Bell & Howell, 1961; *The Natural Economy of Laos,* Bell & Howell, 1961; *Economy and Society of Laos: A Brief Survey,* Southeast Asia Studies, Yale University, 1964; *Government, Politics and Social Structure in Laos: A Study of Tradition and Innovation* (monograph), Yale University, 1964; *The Changing Village Community,* Prentice-Hall, 1967; *Bibliography of English Language Sources on Yugoslavia,* edited by Stanley Radosh, Department of Anthropology, University of Massachusetts, 1969.

(With B. K. Halpern) *A Serbian Village in Historical Perspective,* Holt, 1972; (with J. Hafner and W. Haney) *Mekong Basin Development: Laos and Thailand: Selected Bibliographies,* Centre d'Etude du Sud-Est Asiatique et de l'Extreme-Orient, 1974; (editor with B. K. Halpern and contributor) Joseph Orebski, *The Changing Peasantry of Eastern Europe,* Schenkman, 1976; (editor with B. K. Halpern and contributor) *Selected Papers on a Serbian Village: Social Structure as Reflected by History, Demography and Oral Tradition,* Department of Anthropology, University of Massachusetts, 1977; (editor with William Turley) *The Training of Vietnamese Communist Cadres in Laos,* Centre d'Etude du Sud-Est Asiatique et de l'Extreme-Orient, 1977. Also author, *Laos and Mekong Basin Development,* 1972.

Contributor: *Laos: Its People, Its Society, Its Culture,* Human Relations Area Files, 1960; J. G. Peristiany, editor, *Acts of the Mediterranean Sociological Conference,* Social Sciences Centre, 1963; Raymond Firth and B. S. Yamey,

editors, *Capital, Savings, and Credit in Peasant Societies,* Allen & Unwin, 1964; Jerzy Karcz, *Soviet and East European Agriculture,* University of California Press, 1967; P. Kunstadter, editor, *Southeast Asian Tribes, Minorities, and Nations,* Princeton University Press, 1967; H. J. Benda and J. A. Larkin, editors, *The World of Southeast Asia,* Harper, 1967; Peristiany, editor, *Contributions to Mediterranean Sociology, Mediterranean Rural Communities, and Social Change,* Mouton, 1968; R. M. French, editor, *The Community: A Comparative Perspective,* Peacock, 1969; Wayne Vucinich, editor, *Contemporary Yugoslavia: Twenty Years of Socialist Experiment,* University of California Press, 1969; R. C. Tilman, editor, *Man, State, and Society in Contemporary Southeast Asia,* Praeger, 1969; Paul Horecky, editor, *Southeastern Europe: A Guide to Basic Publications,* University of Chicago Press, 1969.

W. A. Fairservis, Jr., *Costumes of the East,* Chatham, 1971; (with B. K. Halpern) *People in States,* Addison-Wesley, 1972; Peter Laslett, editor, *Household and Family in Past Time,* Cambridge University Press, 1972; John T. McAllister, editor, *Southeast Asia: The Politics of National Integration,* Random House, 1973; D. Smith, editor, *Sister-City Programs: An Evaluation,* Center for a Voluntary Society, 1973; Brian DuToit and Helen T. Safa, editors, *Migration and Urbanization: Models and Adaptive Strategies,* Aldine, 1975; Jean Cuisenier, editor, *Family Life Cycle in European Societies,* Mouton, 1977; *Ethnicity and Cultural Pluralism in the U.S.A.,* Japan Broadcasting Corp., 1978; Cuisenier, editor, *Europe as a Culture Area,* Mouton, 1979; Ivan Volgyes and others, editors, *The Process of Rural Transformation: Eastern Europe, Latin America, and Australia,* Pergamon Press, 1980. Also contributor to *Biennial Review of Anthropology,* 1967, *American Peoples Encyclopedia,* 1969, *Encyclopedia Americana,* 1969, and *Harvard Encyclopedia of American Ethnic Groups;* contributor to scholarly journals and magazines.

SIDELIGHTS: Joel M. Hapern told *CA:* "As a professional anthropologist I have never considered myself an author as such. Over the years, however, it has become increasingly apparent to me that scholarly concerns can never exist totally apart from their social context. While I do not think that scholarship should be directly linked with political advocacy I do believe that it should be conducted with sensitivity to the world in which we live. Thus, for example, while having studied Yugoslavia for almost 30 years I do not perceive my role as an advocate of the political philosophy of its government but rather see my function as one of helping Americans understand another culture, a society, a political system in all of its fascinating complexity. [From] the mail received I am also aware that my writings have helped Americans of Serbian background understand a bit more of their rich traditions.

"As my materials have begun to be widely used in school texts, I have been concerned that the data gathered and published through my efforts be presented accurately even if they must be simplified for younger audiences. It has also been of increasing concern to me that the people about whom I write be presented as full human beings possessed of their own dignity and having an integral value system. As I have begun to write more about the results of my computer based demographic researches I feel even more strongly that quantitative approaches not obscure this vision.

"This notion of about the full humanity of seemingly exotic peoples very much applies to my researches and writings about the peoples of Laos whose current revolutionary experiences are full of tragic overtones. No anthropologist or writer ever lives totally apart from the people whom he describes. Our fates are intertwined. This feeling was also brought home to me on a visit I recently made to Iowa. In a bookstore there I came across a book of photographs of rural life in that state during the 1930's. These were taken by photographers of the Farm Security Administration of the Department of Agriculture. Examining these photographs carefully I was struck by their similarity to those of rural Polesie, then in pre-war eastern Poland, which I had published in *The Changing Peasantry of Eastern Europe.* In performing this task, I did not then realize fully that this seemingly distant way of life also related very much to the experiences of people in our own country during the same period. Details of the technology differed, as did aspects of the physical settings, but the family groupings and the expressions on the faces spoke strongly of a common experience. I hope that it will be possible for me to continue to pursue these points of view in the future. By reinterpreting the past and integrating it with a cross-cultural perspective projected against present and future problems I think that those with anthropological training can write meaningfully for a broad audience.''

BIOGRAPHICAL/CRITICAL SOURCES: Humanities, June, 1977.

*   *   *

HALVERSON, Richard C.   1916-

PERSONAL: Born February 4, 1916, in Pingree, N.D.; son of LeRoy Arthur and Edna (Nielson) Halverson; married Doris Seaton, 1943; children: Richard C., Jr., Stephen, Debbie. *Education:* Wheaton College, B.S., 1939; Princeton Theological Seminary, B.Th. *Home:* 5876 Marbury Rd., Bethesda, Md. *Office:* Fourth Presbyterian Church, 5500 River Rd., Washington, D.C. 20016.

CAREER: Forest Home Christian Conference, Grounds, Calif., managing director, 1942; Lynwood Presbyterian Church, Kansas City, Mo., assistant minister, 1942-44; Forest Home Christian Conference, director, 1944; First Presbyterian Church, Coalinga, Calif., minister, 1944-47; First Presbyterian Church, Hollywood, Calif., minister of new life, 1947-56; Fourth Presbyterian Church, Washington, D.C., minister, 1958—. Associate executive director, International Christian Leadership, Washington, D.C., 1956; president, Concern Ministries, Inc. (charitable foundation); chairman of board of directors, World Vision, Inc., Los Angeles, Calif.; member of advisory board, Navigators and Orient Crusades Mission. Active in prayer breakfast movement, 1956—. *Member:* Sertoma Club International (life). *Awards, honors:* LL.D., Wheaton College, 1958; Valley City State College Distinguished Alumnus Award, 1977; Religious Heritage of America Clergyman of the Year Award, 1978.

WRITINGS: Christian Maturity, Cowman, 1956, published as *Be Yourself–and God's,* 1971; *Perspective,* Cowman, 1957, reprinted, Zondervan, 1973; *Man to Man: A Devotional Book for Men,* Cowman, 1961; (editor) *The Quiet Men,* Cowman, 1963; *Gospel for the Whole of Life,* Cowman, 1964; *Walk with God between Sundays,* Zondervan, 1965; *Relevance,* Word Books, 1968; *Manhood with Meaning,* Zondervan, 1972; *How I Changed My Thinking about the Church,* Zondervan, 1972, published as *A Living Fellowship-A Dynamic Witness,* 1974; *A Day at a Time: Devotions for Men,* Zondervan, 1974.

SIDELIGHTS: Richard C. Halverson has made a number of trips to the Orient in connection with his duties as chairman of the board of directors of World Vision, Inc.; pastor's con-

ferences have taken him to Burma, Thailand, the Fiji Islands, and several other countries.

*   *   *

HALVORSON, Arndt L(eroy)   1915-

PERSONAL: Born March 3, 1915, in Dell Rapids, S.D.; son of Leonhard Ahnfeldt and Agnes (Solie) Halvorson; married Kaia Emily Elvestrom, June 17, 1940; children: Karen (Mrs. John Hedland), Richard, Gretchen, Sara, Martha, Leonard. *Education:* Augustana College, Sioux Falls, S.D., B.A., 1936; Luther Theological Seminary, B.Th., 1940; graduate study at Columbia University, 1944-46, University of Washington, Seattle, 1948, and University of Edinburgh, 1958-59. *Politics:* Democrat. *Home:* 2360 Como Ave., St. Paul, Minn. *Office:* Luther Theological Seminary, 2375 Como Ave. W., St. Paul, Minn. 55108.

CAREER: Ordained Lutheran minister; pastor of churches in Casper, Wyo., 1940-44, Forest City, Iowa, 1946-51, Minneapolis, Minn., 1951-58; Waldorf College, Forest City, Iowa, president, 1950-51; Luther Theological Seminary, St. Paul, Minn., professor of homiletics, 1958—. Guest preacher, Columbia Broadcasting System Radio, 1949—; weekly preacher, "Seminary Hour." Member of board of higher education, Evangelical Lutheran Church; president, Minnesota Lutheran Welfare Society. *Member:* Association of Seminary Professors in the Practical Fields, Lions International. *Awards, honors:* Distinguished alumnus award, 1962, and D.D., 1974, both from Augustana College.

WRITINGS—All published by Augsburg: *Take Up Thy Cross,* 1949; *One Life to Live,* 1963; *In Communion* (for teen-agers), 1965; *All Things New,* 1974; *Reality in the Pulpit,* 1981; *A Touch of Newness,* 1981. Contributor of chapters to educational books and books of sermons, and articles to religious journals.

*   *   *

HAMBURGER, Michael J(ay)   1938-

PERSONAL: Born September 27, 1938, in Bronx, N.Y.; son of Max and Rose (Rosenberg) Hamburger; married Janice Fine, June 12, 1960; children: Beth, Abby. *Education:* Syracuse University, B.S., 1959; Carnegie-Mellon University, M.S., 1962, Ph.D., 1964. *Office:* Federal Reserve Bank of New York, 33 Liberty St., New York, N.Y. 10045.

CAREER: University of Pennsylvania, Philadelphia, assistant professor of economics, 1963-66; Federal Reserve Bank of New York, New York, N.Y., special assistant, 1966-72, senior economist, 1972-74, advisor, 1974—. Visiting professor at New School for Social Research, 1972-77, Rutgers University, 1977-79, and New York University, 1979—. Economic adviser to Bank of England, 1970. *Member:* American Economic Association, Econometric Association, Alpha Kappa Psi, Beta Alpha Psi, Beta Gamma Sigma, Phi Kappa Phi.

WRITINGS: (With M. E. Polakoff and others) *Financial Institutions and Markets,* Houghton, 1970; (with Edwin Mansfield, John Rapoport, Jerome Schnee, and Samuel Wagner) *Research and Innovation in the Modern Corporation,* Norton, 1971; (contributor) R. S. Thorn, editor, *Monetary Theory and Policy,* Praeger, 1976; (contributor) K. Brunner and A. H. Meltzer, editors, *Institutions, Policies and Economic Performance,* North-Holland, 1976; (contributor) R. L. Teigen, editor, *Readings in Money, National Income and Stabilization Policy,* Irwin, 1978; (contributor) Brunner and M. Neumann, editors, *Inflation, Unemployment and*

Monetary Control, Dunker & Homblot, 1979; (contributor) F. Edwards, editor, *Key Issues in Financial Regulation,* McGraw, 1979. Contributor to journals in his field.

* * *

HAMILTON, Charles 1913-

PERSONAL: Born December 24, 1913, in Ludington, Mich.; son of Charles and Ethel Louise (Carr) Hamilton; married Diane Brooks, March 21, 1962; children: Carolyn, Charles, Cynthia, Brooks. *Education:* University of California, Los Angeles, B.A., 1937, M.A., 1939. *Home:* 166 East 63rd St., New York, N.Y. 10021.

CAREER: Prentice-Hall, Inc. (publishers), New York City, sales correspondent, 1940-41; William H. Wise & Co., New York City, office manager, 1941-42, 1946-47; Ben Sackheim, New York City, copywriter, 1948; Bibliotherapy, Inc., New York City, president, 1951-62; Charles Hamilton Autographs, Inc., New York City, president, 1953—; also founder and president of Charles Hamilton Galleries, Inc. (first auction house in America devoted exclusively to autographs), 1963—. Consultant on manuscripts and rare documents. *Military service:* U.S. Army Air Corps, 1942-45; became technical sergeant; awarded Bronze Star and six battle stars. *Awards, honors:* Civil War Round Table of New York Prize for best book on Lincoln, 1963, *Lincoln in Photographs.*

WRITINGS: Cry of the Thunderbird: The American Indian's Own Story, Macmillan, 1950; *Men of the Underworld: The Professional Criminal's Own Story,* Macmillan, 1952 (published in England as *Crime U.S.A.,* 1956); (editor) *Braddock's Defeat,* University of Oklahoma Press, 1959; *Collecting Autographs and Manuscripts,* University of Oklahoma Press, 1961; (with Lloyd Ostendorf) *Lincoln in Photographs,* University of Oklahoma Press, 1963; *The Robot That Helped Make a President,* privately printed, 1965; *Scribblers and Scoundrels,* Paul Eriksson, 1968; (with wife, Diane Hamilton) *Big Name Hunting: A Beginner's Guide to Autograph Collecting,* Simon & Schuster, 1973; *The Book of Autographs,* Simon & Schuster, 1978; *The Signature of America: A Fresh Look at Famous Handwriting,* Harper, 1979; (contributor) *Book of Lists,* Morrow, Volume I: 1979, Volume II, 1980; *Great Forgers and Famous Fakes: The Manuscript Forgers of America and How They Fooled the Experts,* Crown, 1980; *American Autographs: Revolutionary War Leaders and Presidents,* University of Oklahoma Press, 1981. Contributor of more than fifty articles on autographs in *Hobbies,* 1948-58; also contributor of numerous other articles on autographs and manuscripts in other periodicals. Also author of two privately printed pamphlets of poems.

WORK IN PROGRESS: A Scalpel for the Stars, with James Camner; *The Anatomy of Evil: A Study of Nazi Handwriting; The Art of the Illustrated Letter; Great American Letters; Association Books; Inside Auctions: The Revelations of a New York Auctioneer; The Watercolor Paintings of Adolf Hitler.*

SIDELIGHTS: Charles Hamilton began his autograph collection as a boy, when he sent Rudyard Kipling his week's allowance—ten cents—in exchange for his signature. Today his auction gallery in Manhattan holds all the world's records for top prices. Hamilton told *CA:* "When I first started to write professionally more than three decades ago, I turned out books on a variety of subjects. During the past few years I've confined myself to the subject of philography in the hope that I can set down for future generations the experiences of more than half a century as an autograph collector and dealer."

During his career, Hamilton has helped send fifteen thieves and manuscript forgers to prison. Nevertheless, he continues, "I've been savagely criticized for selling Nazi documents and relics at auction and [have] even been threatened by bombs and grenades. But after investing four years of my life in fighting Hitler and his henchmen, I feel he 'owes me' and I don't hesitate to make money out of the Nazis."

AVOCATIONAL INTERESTS: Collecting old guns, swords, and books on snakes, birds, insects, and witchcraft.

BIOGRAPHICAL/CRITICAL SOURCES: New York Herald Tribune, May 19, 1963; *American Weekly,* May 19, 1963; *Time,* April 2, 1965, May 28, 1965; *National Insider,* September 12, 1965, November 14, 1965; *Americana,* May-June, 1978; *People,* July 31, 1978; *Esquire,* October, 1979; *Philatelic Review,* January, 1980.

* * *

HAMILTON, Edmond 1904-1977
(Alexander Blade, Robert Castle, Hugh Davidson, Will Garth, Brett Sterling, Robert Wentworth)

PERSONAL: Born October 21, 1904, in Youngstown, Ohio; died February 1, 1977, in Lancaster, Pa.; son of Scott B. and Maude (Whinery) Hamilton; married Leigh Brackett (a science fiction writer), December 31, 1946 (died March 18, 1978). *Education:* Attended Westminster College, New Wilmington, Pa., 1919-21. *Home and office:* Rural Delivery 2, Kinsman, Ohio.

CAREER: Free-lance writer, primarily of science fiction, 1926-77. *Member:* Authors Guild of America. *Awards, honors:* Guest of honor at 22nd World Science Fiction Convention, 1964; elected to First Fandom Science Fiction Hall of Fame, 1967.

WRITINGS: The Horror on the Asteroid, Ian Allan, 1936, reprinted, Gregg, 1975; *Murder in the Clinic,* Utopian, 1945; *Tiger Girl,* Utopian, 1945; *The Monsters of Juntonheim,* Pemberton, 1950; *Tharkol, Lord of the Unknown,* Pemberton, 1950; *City at World's End,* Fell, 1951; *The Star of Life,* Torquil Press, 1959; *The Sun Smasher* (bound with *Starhaven,* by Ivar Jorgenson), Ace Books, 1959; *The Haunted Stars,* Torquil Press, 1960; *Battle for the Stars,* Torquil Press, 1961; (contributor) Larry Shaw, editor, *Great Science Fiction Adventures,* Lancer Books, 1963; *The Valley of Creation,* Lancer Books, 1964; *Fugitive of the Stars* (bound with *Land beyond the Map,* by Kenneth Bulmer), Ace Books, 1965; *Doomstar,* Belmont-Tower, 1966; *The Harpers of Titan* (bound with *Dr. Cyclops,* by Henry Kuttner and *Too Late for Eternity,* by Bruce Walton), Popular Library, 1967; *A Yank at Valhalla,* Ace Books, 1973; *What's It Like Out There?* (short story collection), Ace Books, 1974; *The Best of Edmond Hamilton,* edited and introduced by wife, Leigh Brackett, Ballantine, 1977.

"John Gordon" series: *The Star Kings,* Fell, 1949; *Beyond the Moon,* Signet, 1950; *Return to the Stars,* Lancer Books, 1970.

"Interstellar Patrol" series; published by Ace Books: *Outside the Universe,* 1964; *Crashing Suns,* 1965.

"Starwolf" series; published by Ace Books: *The Weapon from Beyond,* 1967; *The Closed Worlds,* 1968; *World of the Starwolves,* 1968.

"Captain Future" series; published by Popular Library: (Under pseudonym Brett Sterling) *Danger Planet,* 1967; *Calling Captain Future,* 1967; *Galaxy Mission,* 1967; *Captain Future and the Space Emperor,* 1967; *Outlaw World,* 1968; *The Magician of Mars,* 1968; *Quest beyond the Stars,*

1968; *Outlaws of the Moon*, 1969; *The Comet Kings*, 1969; *Planets in Peril*, 1969; *Captain Future's Challenge*, 1969.

Also author of scripts, *Black Terror* (comic strip), 1941-45. Contributor of more than 400 short stories to science fiction publications.

SIDELIGHTS: "Out of the twenties into the early thirties came [Edmond] Hamilton," writes Donald A. Wolheim, "—and a sudden spark that was momentarily to light up the greatest concept of the world of science-fiction ideas: the galactic civilization. . . . A civilization of intelligent beings, in contact with each other, trading with each other, banded together in some sort of Federation of the Stars to assist, to enlighten, to defend." As a young author of science fiction, Hamilton primarily wrote for the "pulp" publications of the period. His most noted stories centered on the exploits of the Interstellar Patrol, "a patrol ship of the stars traveling many hundreds of times the speed of light," Wolheim explains. "And crewed by one being each of a dozen or two dozen intelligent cooperating civilized worlds."

Within this realm, Hamilton helped to introduce many innovative and widely imitated concepts. The notion that Earth is controlled by aliens from outer-space has been credited to Hamilton, as has the idea of programming robots to perform specific tasks. Hamilton was also one of the first science fiction writers to explore the concept of devolution, a kind of evolution in reverse, in which cosmic radiation causes higher life forms to regress with each successive generation until, finally, they reach their lowest and most primitive state.

Hamilton wrote hundreds of stories during his lifetime. His later writings, according to Wolheim, proved Hamilton to be "a far more sophisticated, far more able and skilled a storyteller than the youth who pounded out those tales of the Patrol." However, although the quality of his work improved, Wolheim suggests that Hamilton could not "hope to surpass that concept which for one moment pushed the borders of science fiction ahead."

BIOGRAPHICAL/CRITICAL SOURCES: Analog, December, 1950, August, 1951, November, 1959, November, 1960, June, 1962, September, 1965; *Galaxy,* April, 1963; Samuel Moskowitz, *Seekers of Tomorrow,* World Publishing, 1966; *New Worlds,* June, 1969; *Luna Monthly,* August, 1969; *Science Fiction Review,* January, 1971; Donald A. Wolheim, *The Universe Makers,* Harper, 1971; *Contemporary Literary Criticism,* Volume I, Gale, 1973; *Publishers Weekly,* March 14, 1977.†

*   *   *

HAMMOND, Norman   1944-

PERSONAL: Born July 10, 1944, in England. *Education:* Cambridge University, B.A., 1966, diploma in classical archaeology, 1967, M.A., 1970, Ph.D., 1972. *Office:* Archaeology Program, Douglas College, Rutgers University, New Brunswick, N.J. 08903.

CAREER: Cambridge University, Cambridge, England, research fellow in Centre of Latin American Studies, 1967-71, Leverhulme Trust fellow in New World archaeology, 1972-75, fellow of Fitzwilliam College, 1973-75; University of Bradford, School of Archaeological Sciences, West Riding, England, senior lecturer, 1975-77; Rutgers University, New Brunswick, N.J., member of faculty, 1977—, director of archaeology program, 1980—. Visiting professor, University of California, Berkeley, 1977. Director of television film for British Broadcasting Corp., 1970; reviewer for BBC radio. *Member:* Royal Asiatic Society (fellow), Society for Libyan

Studies, Society for Afghan Studies, American Anthropological Association (foreign fellow), Society for American Archaeology, American Association for the Advancement of Science, Prehistoric Society, Society of Antiquaries of London (fellow).

WRITINGS: The British Museum in British Honduras: Lubaantun 1926-1970, British Museum, 1972, published as *Lubaantun 1926-1970: The British Museum in British Honduras,* Farrar, Straus, 1978; (editor) *South Asian Archaeology,* Duckworth, 1973; (editor) *Mesoamerican Archaeology: New Approaches,* University of Texas Press, 1974; *Lubaantum: A Classic Maya Realm,* Peabody Museum, Harvard University, 1975; (editor) *Social Process in Maya Prehistory,* Academic Press, 1977; (co-editor) *The Archaeology of Afghanistan,* Academic Press, 1978; (editor with Gordon R. Willey) *Maya Archaeology and Ethnohistory,* University of Texas Press, 1979. Contributor to *Antiquity, American Antiquity, Man, Science, Archaeology,* and *East and West.* Archaeological correspondent for *Times* (London), 1967—.

WORK IN PROGRESS: Research on Maya cultures; numerous articles and reviews.

SIDELIGHTS: Norman Hammond has led expeditions to North Africa, Afghanistan, and Central America. He has also done archaeological work in Greece and Ecuador.

*   *   *

HANFF, Helene

PERSONAL: Born in Philadelphia, Pa.; daughter of Arthur Joseph (a salesman) and Miriam (Levy) Hanff. *Education:* Attended Temple University, one year. *Politics:* Democrat. *Religion:* Jewish. *Home and office:* 305 East 72nd St., New York, N.Y. 10021. *Agent:* Flora Roberts, Inc., 65 East 55th St., New York, N.Y. 10022.

CAREER: Paramount Pictures, New York City, manuscript reader, 1946-52; free-lance writer of dramatic shows for Columbia Broadcasting System and National Broadcasting Co. television, 1952-58; free-lance writer, 1958—. Democratic county committeewoman, New York City. Also broadcasts a monthly "Women's Hour" over B.B.C. radio. *Member:* Writers Guild of America East (member of executive council of Television and Screen Writers union, 1961-63), MacDowell Colonists Association, Lenox Hill Democratic Club (president, 1970). *Awards, honors:* Columbia Broadcasting System grant-in-aid for work on historic scripts for television.

WRITINGS: Underfoot in Show Business, Harper, 1962, reprinted, Little, Brown, 1980; *84, Charing Cross Road,* Grossman, 1970; *The Duchess of Bloomsbury Street,* Lippincott, 1973; *Apple of My Eye,* Deutsch, 1977, Doubleday, 1978.

Juvenile, except as indicated: *The Day the Constitution Was Signed,* Doubleday, 1961; *The Battle for New Orleans,* Doubleday, 1961; *Terrible Thomas,* Harper, 1964; *More Terrible Thomas,* Harper, 1964; (with L. L. Smith) *Early Settlers in America: Jamestown, Plymouth and Salem,* Grosset, 1965; *Religious Freedom,* Grosset, 1966; *Good Neighbors: The Peace Corps in Latin America,* Grosset, 1966; *John F. Kennedy, Young Man of Destiny,* Doubleday, 1966; *Our Nation's Capitol,* Doubleday, 1967, 2nd edition, 1973; *The Unlikely Twins: Paraguay and Uruguay,* Doubleday, 1967; *Elizabeth I,* Doubleday, 1967; *The Movers and Shakers* (young adult) S. G. Phillips, 1969; *Butch Elects a Mayor,* Parents' Magazine Press, 1969. Also author of thirty scripts for television's "Hallmark Hall of Fame" and "Matinee

Theater'', as well as scripts for eight U.S. Army training films. Contributor of articles to *Harper's*, *New Yorker*, and *Reader's Digest*.

SIDELIGHTS: Although the bulk of her work is aimed at children and young adults, Helene Hanff is better known for the four books she has written for the general adult audience. The first of these, *Underfoot in Show Business*, was published in 1962 and more recently in 1980 as a result of revived interest in her work. Hanff described the book for *CA* as the story of ''my misspent youth trying to crash the Broadway theatre as a playwright way back in the days of the Lunts and the Theatre Guild.'' It has been praised as a ''wonderfully zany, funny memoir'' by a *Publisher's Weekly* reviewer, while Chris Wall of the *Los Angeles Times* comments: ''This thoroughly entertaining book testifies it's better to try and fail than to not try at all. More enjoyable as well.'' Although *Times Literary Supplement*'s Craig Brown suggests that Hanff's affections are limited to the fame the arts offer and the colorful characters they attract, he points out that such ''scepticism towards art and its practitioners is in few places more necessary than in New York, and many of Miss Hanff's wisecracks are laudable.'' He finds her ability to ''encapsulate the characters of her fellow strugglers in a few words with wit and charity'' particularly praiseworthy.

Hanff's best-known book is probably *84, Charing Cross Road*, a collection of twenty years' correspondence between the author and a British bookstore with which she did business. A reviewer for *Best Sellers* offers this description of it: ''Pleasant, easy, cheerful, and literate.'' Thomas Lask of the *New York Times* calls it ''a nineteenth-century book in a twentieth-century world. It will beguile an hour of your time and put you in tune with mankind . . . provide an emollient for the spirit and the sheath for the exposed nerve. And . . . restore your vanishing faith that something can be done against the encroachments of the computerized society.'' *Saturday Review*'s Haskel Frankel senses a similar aura about the book. He writes: ''Somewhere here, for those who can feel, there is a love story . . . between a woman and the world. . . . It is the treasure of the year.''

Departing from these memoirs and *The Duchess of Bloomsbury Street* (a sequel to *84, Charing Cross Road* in which Hanff actually visits England and meets the people behind the letters she'd received), *Apple of My Eye* takes the form of a diary-guidebook. Thomas Lask's *New York Times* review approaches it with affection, calling it ''a book every bibliophile cherishes as he would a lost love. . . . It's personal, informal, idiosyncratic, and it sometimes growls in anger. But it is full of those bits of information a visitor should have and often does not. . . . [Other books] are fuller and more pointedly factual, but none is more juicy or flavorsome.''

84, Charing Cross Road was produced for Public Broadcasting Service in 1976. Hanff describes her monthly broadcast on BBC radio as telling an English audience what's going on ''not just in my town but in my neighborhood and my apartment house (which is a very chummy building; a kind of small town in itself).''

AVOCATIONAL INTERESTS: Theater, classical music, baseball (as a spectator), cooking, reading nonfiction.

BIOGRAPHICAL/CRITICAL SOURCES: New York Times, September 11, 1970, June 23, 1978; *Best Sellers*, October 15, 1970; *Harper*, November, 1970; *Saturday Review*, November 7, 1970; *Los Angeles Times*, August 24, 1980; *Publishers Weekly*, September 3, 1980; *Times Literary Supplement*, December 19, 1980.

HANLEY, Clifford 1922-
(Henry Calvin)

PERSONAL: Born October 28, 1922, in Glasgow, Scotland; son of Henry and Martha (Griffiths) Hanley; married Anna Easton Clark, January 10, 1948; children: Clifford, Jane, Joanna. *Education:* Attended schools in Glasgow, Scotland. *Home:* 36 Munro Rd., Glasgow, Scotland. *Agent:* Curtis Brown Ltd., 1 Craven Hill, London W2 3EW, England.

CAREER: Scottish Newspaper Services (news agency), Glasgow, reporter, 1941-46; *Daily Record*, Glasgow, columnist, 1946-57; *TV Guide*, Glasgow, columnist, 1957-58; *Evening Citizen*, Glasgow, columnist, 1958-60; *Spectator*, London, England, television critic, 1963. Director, Glasgow Films Ltd., 1957-63. Appears regularly on television in Scotland ''as subversive social commentator.'' Lecturer. *Member:* National Union of Journalists, P.E.N. (member of Glasgow council, 1962—), Glasgow Literary and Philological Society (president, 1962-63), Screenwriters Guild, Scottish Arts Council, Inland Waterways Advisory Council.

WRITINGS: Dancing in the Streets (autobiography), Hutchinson, 1958; *Love from Everybody*, Hutchinson, 1959, published as *Don't Bother to Knock*, Brown, Watson, 1961; *The Taste of Too Much*, Hutchinson, 1960, revised edition, edited by Vincent Whitcombe, Blackie & Son, 1967; *Second Time Around*, Houghton, 1964 (published in England as *Nothing but the Best*, Hutchinson, 1964); *A Skinful of Scotch*, Houghton, 1965; *The Hot Month*, Houghton, 1967; *The Redhaired Bitch*, Houghton, 1969; *Prissy*, Collins, 1978; *The Scots*, David & Charles, 1980.

Under pseudonym Henry Calvin: *The System*, Hutchinson, 1962; *It's Different Abroad*, Harper, 1963; *The Italian Gadget*, Hutchinson, 1966; *The DNA Business*, Hutchinson, 1967; *A Nice Friendly Town*, Hutchinson, 1967; *Miranda Must Die*, Hutchinson, 1968; *Boka Lives!*, Harper, 1969; *The Chosen Instrument*, Hutchinson, 1969; *The Poison Chasers*, Hutchinson, 1971; *Take Two Popes*, Hutchinson, 1974.

Plays: ''The Durable Element,'' produced in Dundee, 1961; ''Saturmacnalia'' (musical), produced at Glasgow Citizens Theatre, 1962; ''Dear Boss'' (television play), produced in England, 1962; ''Oh for an Island'' (musical), produced at Glasgow Citizens Theatre, 1963; ''Dick McWhitty'' (musical), produced in 1964; ''Oh Glorious Jubilee'' (musical), produced at Leeds Playhouse Theatre, December 10, 1970; ''Down Memory Lane,'' networked by STV, 1971. Song lyrics include unofficial national anthem, ''Scotland the Brave.'' Contributor of several hundred articles to newspapers in Great Britain.

AVOCATIONAL INTERESTS: Music and talk, brewing own beer, sailing in self-built boat.

BIOGRAPHICAL/CRITICAL SOURCES: Clifford Hanley, *Dancing in the Streets*, Hutchinson, 1958; *Times Literary Supplement*, March 9, 1967, June 29, 1967, September 21, 1967; *Books and Bookmen*, May, 1967, September, 1968, June, 1969; *Punch*, March 15, 1969, April 23, 1969, September 3, 1969; *Book World*, May 18, 1969; *New York Times Book Review*, July 20, 1969.

*   *   *

HANNAN, Joseph F(rancis) 1923-

PERSONAL: Born February 26, 1923, in Paterson, N.J.; son of Frank and Alice (O'Neill) Hannan; married Margaret M. Condon, April 13, 1944; children: Joseph, Kathleen, Frank, Matthew, Eileen. *Education:* Rutgers University, A.B., 1955, graduate study; Seton Hall University, M.A., 1960;

additional graduate study at Princeton University, Montclair State College, Stevens Institute of Technology, and Newark State College. *Religion:* Catholic. *Home:* 80 Perrin Ave., Pompton Lakes, N.J. 07742.

CAREER: Semi-skilled worker before entering teaching profession; elementary and secondary school teacher of social studies and English in Wayne, N.J., 1955-60; Anthony Wayne Junior High School, Wayne, guidance counselor, 1960-63; Wayne Valley High School, Wayne Valley, N.J., guidance director, 1963-69; Fair Lawn High School, Fair Lawn, N.J., guidance counselor, 1969—. *Military service:* U.S. Coast Guard, 1941-45. *Member:* National Education Association, American Personnel and Guidance Association, Authors Guild, Authors League of America, New Jersey Guidance Association, New Jersey Education Association, Wayne Education Association.

WRITINGS: Never Tease a Dinosaur: Tales of a Man in a Woman's World, Holt, 1962; (contributor) *The Best in Books,* Doubleday, 1963; *Killing Time,* Holt, 1964; (contributor) Dorothy Peterson, *The Elementary School Teacher,* Appleton-Century-Crofts, 1964; (contributor) John R. Lee and Jonathon C. McLendon, *Readings on Elementary Social Studies,* Allyn & Bacon, 1965; (contributor) M. Jerry Weiss, editor, *Tales out of School,* Dell, 1967; (contributor) Jan Miller, editor, *Kid Stuff,* Hallmark, 1969. Also author of *The Webster Weeks Reader, At War on Ellis Island,* and *The Ancient Mariner.* Contributor of humorous articles to magazines.

WORK IN PROGRESS: A novel.

AVOCATIONAL INTERESTS: Bowling, golf, fishing, and playing banjo.

*   *   *

HANSEN, Gary B(arker)   1935-

PERSONAL: Born October 4, 1935, in Ogden, Utah; son of Clarence James (a teacher) and Lena (Barker) Hansen; married Helen Ure, September 7, 1962; children: Mark Gary, Ann Marie, Janet Kay, Karen Alice. *Education:* Utah State University, B.S., 1957, M.S., 1963; Cornell University, Ph.D., 1971. *Home:* 1950 North 1050 East, Logan, Utah 84321. *Office:* Department of Economics, Utah State University, Logan, Utah 84322.

CAREER: London School of Economics and Political Science, London, England, Fulbright scholar, 1965-66; Utah State University, Logan, assistant professor, 1967-73, associate professor, 1973-77, professor of economics, 1977—, director of center for Productivity and Quality of Working Life, 1976—. *Military service:* U.S. Army, 1957-59; became first lieutenant. *Member:* Industrial Relations Research Association, American Economic Association, American Society for Training and Development, Society for Professionals in Dispute Resolution.

WRITINGS: (With Leonard J. Arrington) *The Richest Hole on Earth: The History of the Bingham Copper Mine,* Utah State University Press, 1963; *Britain's Industrial Training Act: Its History, Development and Implications for America,* National Manpower Policy Task Force, 1967; *Dropouts and Completers in the Utah Apprenticeship System, 1969-1974: Causes and Consequences,* Utah State University, 1975; *Manpower Advisory Services in the Workplace: A Missing Link in National Manpower Policy,* two volumes, Utah State University, 1976; *Shutdown: A Case Study of Displaced Rural Workers,* Utah State University Center for Productivity and Quality of Working Life, 1978; *Hard Rock*

Miners in a Shutdown, Utah State University Center for Productivity and Quality of Working Life, 1980. Contributor to *Labor Law Journal, Personnel Management* (Great Britain), *Training and Development Journal,* Industrial Relations Research Association *Proceedings, Comparative Education Review, Utah Historical Quarterly,* and *Journal of European Training.*

WORK IN PROGRESS: Studies of industrial training and the CETA manpower system, worker and community impacts of plant shutdowns, apprenticeship dropouts, and comparative manpower and training systems in developed and developing countries.

AVOCATIONAL INTERESTS: Travel, camping, music, reading.

*   *   *

HARDT, J(ohn) Pearce   1922-

PERSONAL: Born June 16, 1922; son of Sydney Burk and Muriel (Pearce) Hardt; married Mary Elena Scapellati, 1953; children: John, Anthony, Daniel, Michael, Richard. *Education:* University of Washington, B.A., 1945, M.A., 1948; Columbia University, A.M., 1950, Ph.D., 1955. *Home:* 8028 Cindy Lane, Bethesda, Md. *Office:* Congressional Research Service, Library of Congress, Washington, D.C.

CAREER: Ford Foundation, New York, N.Y., consultant, 1951-52; Air University, Maxwell Air Force Base, Montgomery, Ala., consultant, 1953-55; Corporation for Economics and Industrial Research, Washington, D.C., staff specialist on Soviet economy, 1956-59; affiliated with Operations Research Office, Johns Hopkins University, and Research Analysis Corp., 1959-71; Library of Congress, Congressional Research Service, Washington, D.C., senior specialist in Soviet economics and associate director for senior specialists, 1971—. Adjunct professor of economics, Institute of Sino-Soviet Studies, George Washington University, 1966. Lecturer in economics, University of Maryland, 1956-65. Consultant to Secretary of Defense, 1968—. *Military service:* U.S. Army, 1942-46; became captain, received European and Asiatic Theater ribbons with three battle stars, Philippine Liberation ribbon, and Unit Citation. *Member:* American Economic Association, American Association for the Advancement of Slavic Studies (president of Washington, D.C. chapter), Association for Comparative Economic Studies (member of executive committee, 1977—), Delta Upsilon, Cosmos Club. *Awards, honors:* Rockefeller fellowship, 1949; Old Master Award, Purdue University, 1975.

WRITINGS: Economics of the Soviet Electric Power Industry, Air University Press, 1955; *Shortage of Soviet Electric Power: A Brake on Industrial Growth, 1955-1960,* Air University Press, 1956; *Dispersal of the Soviet Electric Power Industry,* Air University Press, 1957; (with C. Darwin Stolzenbach and Martin J. Kohn) *The Cold War Economic Gap: The Increasing Threat to American Supremacy,* Praeger, 1961; (editor with Herbert Levine, Norman Kaplan, and Marvin Hoffenberg) *Mathematics and Computers in Soviet Economic Planning,* Yale University Press, 1967; (editor with V. G. Treml) *Soviet Economic Statistics,* Duke University Press, 1972.

Contributor: *The Development of the Soviet Economy: Plan and Performance,* Praeger, 1968; *Soviet Union: Fifty Years of Communism,* Johns Hopkins University Press, 1968; *Interest Groups in Soviet Politics,* Princeton University Press, 1971; Michael McGwire, editor, *Soviet Naval Policy: Objectives and Constraints,* Praeger, 1975; Robert Bauer, editor, *The Interaction of Economics and Foreign Policy,* University of Virginia Press, 1975; F. Fleron, editor, *Technology and Commercial Culture: The Socio-Cultural Impact of Technology under Socialism,* Praeger, 1977; *The Soviet Threat: Myths and Realities,* The Academy of Political Science, 1978; *Soviet Foreign Policy toward Western Europe,* Praeger, 1978. Also author of numerous government publications. Editor, Association for Comparative Economic Studies *Bulletin.*

* * *

HARDWICK, Elizabeth 1916-

PERSONAL: Born July 27, 1916, in Lexington, Ky.; daughter of Eugene Allen and Mary (Ramsey) Hardwick; married Robert Lowell (a poet), July 28, 1949 (divorced October, 1972); children: Harriet. *Education:* University of Kentucky, A.B., 1938, M.A., 1939; Columbia University, additional study, 1939-41. *Home:* 15 West 67th St., New York, N.Y. 10023.

CAREER: Writer. Adjunct associate professor of English, Barnard College, New York, N.Y. *Member:* American Academy and Institute of Arts and Letters. *Awards, honors:* Guggenheim fellowship in fiction, 1948; George Jean Nathan Award for dramatic criticism (first woman recipient), 1967; National Book Critics Circle award nomination, 1980, for *Sleepless Nights.*

WRITINGS: The Ghostly Lover (novel), Harcourt, 1945; *The Simple Truth* (novel), Harcourt, 1955; (editor) *The Selected Letters of William James,* Farrar, Straus, 1960; *A View of My Own* (essays), Farrar, Straus, 1962; *Seduction and Betrayal: Women and Literature* (essays), Random House, 1974; *Sleepless Nights* (novel), Random House, 1979. Contributor to periodicals, including *Partisan Review, New Yorker,* and *Harper's.* Founder and advisory editor, *New York Review of Books.*

SIDELIGHTS: "In certain ways," writes Joan Didion, "the mysterious and somnabulistic 'difference' of being a woman has been, over thirty-five years, Elizabeth Hardwick's great subject, the topic to which she has returned incessantly: it colored both of her early novels, *The Ghostly Lover* in 1945 and *The Simple Truth* in 1955, as well as many of the essays collected in 1962 as *A View of My Own* and all of those published in 1974 as *Seduction and Betrayal: Women and Literature.* She has chronicled again and again the undertow of family life, the awesome torment of being a daughter—an observer in the household, a constant reader of the domestic text—the anarchy of sex. She has illuminated lives traditionally misrepresented as tragic instances of the way all women live." Didion continues: "Perhaps no one has written more acutely and poignantly about the ways in which women compensate for their relative physiological inferiority, about the poetic and practical implications of walking around the world deficient in hemoglobin, deficient in respiratory capacity, deficient in muscular strength and deficient in stability of the vascular and autonomic nervous systems. 'Any woman who has ever had her wrist twisted by a man recognizes a fact of nature as humbling as a cyclone to a frail tree branch,' she observed in an essay on Simone de Beauvoir some years ago, an assertion of 'woman's difference' at once so explicit and so obscurely shameful that it sticks like a burr in one's capacity for wishful thinking."

Edmund White of the *Washington Post Book World* calls *Sleepless Nights* "a novel written in the purest style imaginable. Americans are people easily embarrassed—by unearned emotion and unconversational rhetoric. Nothing in *Sleepless Nights* will embarrass its readers. Even its experi-

mentalism is quiet, unobtrusive, growth rings secreted around a core that remains invisible." In a *Chicago Tribune Book World* review, Roberta Rubenstein says that the tone of the book "is cool, controlled, cerebral. One is reminded of the striking poetic images of Virginia Woolf and of Lillian Hellman's lucid portraiture of people and places. Yet, while the images and vignettes are often brilliant in themselves, their limits are those of the narrator: Holding herself aloft from feeling, she produces a sense of detachment in the reader, making it difficult for one to develop an emotional connection to her experience.... The effect is a kind of fictional scrapbook rather than a novel—one that captures a poignant, unsentimental nostalgia. Jewel-like but distant, *Sleepless Nights* may cure more insomnia than it records."

John Leonard writes: "In the middle of *Sleepless Nights,* I was thinking of Rilke's *Notebooks.* I was also thinking of Renata Adler's *Speedboat* and Joan Didion's *Play It as It Lays.* These are sad books, redeemed by language. The fragments, the shards, they pile up—as though in the aftermath of a shattering explosion, an irreparable loss—gleam, like diamonds or steel, and if you touch them they draw blood.... Elizabeth [the narrator] of *Sleepless Nights* is a much more interesting mind than the Maria Wyeth of *Play It as It Lays,* and we come to know her far better than we were allowed to know the Gen Fain of *Speedboat.*" Leonard goes on: "Like Miss Hardwick, Elizabeth is a writer, and a reader. She pauses in her remembering to cite something apposite from Goethe, Nietzsche, Borges, Ibsen, Pasternak, Flaubert, Dostoevsky, Casanova, the Goncourts. These citations are themselves fragments, pieces of the ruins. What is astonishing, though, is that, again and again, Miss Hardwick's prose compares favorably with the prose of the masters."

BIOGRAPHICAL/CRITICAL SOURCES: New York Times Book Review, April 29, 1979; *New York Times,* May 4, 1979; *Washington Post Book World,* May 6, 1979; *Chicago Tribune Book World,* May 13, 1979; *Contemporary Literary Criticism,* Volume XIII, Gale, 1980.

* * *

HARKNESS, David J(ames) 1913-

PERSONAL: Born April 19, 1913, in Jellico, Tenn.; son of David Alexander and Jessie (Jones) Harkness. *Education:* University of Tennessee, B.A., 1934; Columbia University, M.A., 1939, postgraduate summer study, 1946, 1951. *Politics:* Republican. *Religion:* Presbyterian. *Home:* 1411 Kenesaw Ave., Knoxville, Tenn. 37919. *Office:* University of Tennessee Extension Division, Knoxville, Tenn. 37916.

CAREER: Parkdale High School, Parkdale, Ore., English teacher, 1934-35; English teacher and principal in Jellico (Tenn.) schools, 1935-40, 1943-46; Lincoln Memorial University, Harrogate, Tenn., English instructor, 1940-43; East Tennessee State College, Johnson City, director of training school, 1946-47; University of Tennessee, Extension Division, Knoxville, director of program planning and library services, 1947—. *Member:* Adult Education Association of U.S.A., American Library Association, American Studies Association, National University Extension Association, Speech Association of Tennessee (president, 1953-55), Tennessee Education Association, Tennessee Library Association, East Tennessee Historical Society, Phi Kappa Phi, Phi Delta Kappa, Pi Kappa Alpha, Masons.

WRITINGS: (With R. Gerald McMurtry) *Lincoln's Favorite Poets,* University of Tennessee Press, 1959.

Brochures; all published by Division of University Extension, University of Tennessee: *Tennessee in Literature,* 1949; *Tennessee in Recent Books, Music and Drama,* 1950; *The Biographical Novel: A Bibliography with Notes,* 1950; *Famous Women of Tennessee and Literary Landmarks of the Volunteer State,* 1951; *Music and Legends for American Holidays: A Manual for Program Planners,* 1951; *Some First Facts about Tennessee: A Manual for School and Club Programs,* 1952; *Literary Profiles of the Southern States: A Manual for Schools and Clubs,* 1953; *The American Heritage in Historical Fiction,* 1953; *The Southwest and West Coast in Literature: A Manual for Schools and Clubs,* 1954; *Literary Trails of the Western States,* 1955; *Literary New England: A Manual for Schools and Clubs,* 1956; *The Bible in Fiction and Drama: A Bibliography with Notes,* 1956; *Literary Mideast U.S.A.,* 1957; *Legends of the Holidays: A Manual for Program Planners,* 1957; *The Literary Midwest: A Manual for Schools and Clubs,* 1958; *Arts and Letters in Fiction and Drama: A Bibliography with Notes,* 1958; *The Great Lakes States and Alaska and Hawaii in Literature: A Manual for Schools and Clubs,* 1959; *Abraham Lincoln and Cumberland Gap,* 1959.

Heroines of the Blue and Gray: A Civil War Centennial Program Manual, 1960; *Heroines of the American Revolution,* 1961; (compiler) *Legends and Lore: Southern Indians, Flowers, Holidays,* 1961; *Southern Heroes, Heroines and Legends,* 1962; *Lincoln and the Land-Grant Idea,* 1962; *Southern Heroines of Colonial Days,* 1963; (compiler) *The Dogwood in Legend and Literature,* 1964; *Tennessee–The Most Interesting State,* 1965, revised edition, 1968; *Kentucky and Tennessee,* 1966; (compiler) *Tennessee and Mississippi: Where the Old South Meets the New,* 1967; *Forgotten Heroes of the American Revolution,* 1968; *Tennessee and Arkansas,* 1968; *Tennessee and North Carolina,* 1969; *Tennessee and Virginia,* 1970; *Tennessee and Alabama,* 1971; *Tennessee Heritage,* 1971; *Tennessee and Missouri,* 1972; *Tennessee and Georgia,* 1973; *Northeastern Heroines of the American Revolution,* 1974; *Colonial Heroines of Tennessee, Kentucky and Virginia,* 1974; *New England Heroines of Colonial Days,* 1975; *Indian Legends of the Southern Mountains,* 1976; *Legends of Southern Indians,* 1976; *Legends of Christmas,* 1977; *Legends of Easter,* 1978; *Southern Indian Legends III,* 1979; *Happy Holidays: Legends and Music,* 1980.

*   *   *

HARRELL, John G(rinnell)   1922-

PERSONAL: Born May 24, 1927, in Los Angeles, Calif.; son of Orville Jones (a real estate developer) and Charlotte (Grinnell) Harrell; married Mary Jane Pyburn, June 6, 1959. *Education:* Occidential College, A.B., 1944; attended Virginia Theological Seminary, 1944-45; Church Divinity School of the Pacific, M.Div., D.D., 1947. *Home and office:* 148 York Ave., Berkeley, Calif. 94708.

CAREER: Ordained Episcopal priest, 1947. National Council of Episcopal Church, Greenwich, Conn., executive secretary for audio-visual education, 1957-62; St. Margaret's House (Episcopal graduate school for women), Berkeley, Calif., lecturer in communications, 1962-66; independent producer of multimedia materials, 1966—.

WRITINGS: (Editor and translator) *Selected Writings of Richard Rolle,* S.P.C.K., 1963; *Teaching Is Communicating: An Audio-Visual Handbook for Church Use,* Seabury, 1965; *Hello in Exile* (poem), privately printed, 1965; *Basic Media in Education,* St. Mary's College Press, 1974; *To Tell of Gideon,* privately printed, 1975; *A Storyteller's Treasury,*

privately printed, 1977. Also author of *Daybreak: A Performance Piece for Reader and Musicians,* 1977. Contributor to *Christian Century, Theology Today, Motive, Liturgy, Religion Teachers Journal,* and other religious journals.

Television and films: "Let Us Pray," an experimental jazz liturgy presented by Columbia Broadcasting System; "Jazz Evensong," also presented by Columbia Broadcasting System and first performed by Modern Jazz Quartet at International Jazz Festival, Washington, D.C. Also author of educational films, including "Here and Now" and the "CoCo" series of nature films for young children. With wife, Mary Harrell, creator and producer of multimedia productions, including "The Fire and the Mind," "Lord, Come!," "Communicating the Gospel Today," and "Time Being."

WORK IN PROGRESS: The Quest of the Storyteller and *The Man on a Dolphin.*

SIDELIGHTS: John Harrell told *CA:* "What is not readily apparent in the bibliographic data is my life-long struggle with the problems of communication. Some of my writing and teaching has been in communications theory, but far more important have been my experiences in experimenting with new forms of communication, whether with poetry and music, six-screen projection, or creating happenings in the 60's. Surprisingly, my next move during the 70's was back to the ancient art of storytelling.

"I find it valuable occasionally to be published by an established house, but my greatest delight is in designing my own books. A book is not just the alphabet all mixed up. It is a visual and tactile experience, perhaps even an oral one as we convert the print into the imagined sound of speech. When the creator of the book is both author and designer, there is chance for a unity of experience that industrial bookpublishing cannot achieve."

*   *   *

HARRIS, Leon A., Jr.   1926-

PERSONAL: Born June 20, 1926, in New York, N.Y.; son of Leon A. (a merchant) and Lucile (Herzfeld) Harris; married Marina Svetlova (a ballerina), September 10, 1963 (divorced February, 1970). *Education:* Harvard University, B.A., 1947. *Home:* 4512 Fairfax, Dallas, Tex. 75205. *Agent:* Julian Bach Literary Agency, Inc., 747 Third Ave., New York, N.Y. 10017.

CAREER: A. Harris & Co. (department store), Dallas, Tex., executive vice-president, 1947-60; Empire State Bank, Dallas, director, 1962—; Trammell Crow Realty Trust, Dallas, chairman, 1963-69. Trustee of Dallas Museum of Fine Arts, Dallas Public Library, and St. Mark's School; member of board of directors of Dallas Community Chest, Dallas Symphony, Friends of the Dallas Public Library, and Friends of the Texas Libraries. *Military service:* U.S. Naval Reserve, 1944-46. *Member:* American Society of Composers, Authors, and Publishers, Dallas Historical Society (trustee), Dallas Association for the United Nations (member of board of directors); Century Association and Harvard Club (both New York). *Awards, honors:* Italian Order of the Star of Solidarity.

WRITINGS: The Night before Christmas in Texas, Lothrop, 1952; *The Great Picture Robbery,* Atheneum, 1963; *Young France: Children of France at Work and at Play,* Dodd, 1964; *The Fine Art of Political Wit: Being a Lively Guide to the Artistic Invective, Elegant Epithet, and Polished Impromptus as Well as the Gallant and Graceful Worldly Wit of Various British and American Politicians from the 18th Cen-*

tury through Our Own Days of Grace, Dutton, 1964; *Only to God: The Extraordinary Life of Godfrey Lowell Cabot*, Atheneum, 1967; *Maurice Goes to Sea*, Norton, 1968; *Young Peru: Children of Peru at Work and at Play*, Dodd, 1969.

The Moscow Circus School, Atheneum, 1970; *Yvette*, McGraw, 1970; *The Russian Ballet School*, Atheneum, 1970; (self-illustrated with photographs) *Behind the Scenes in a Car Factory*, Lippincott, 1972; (self-illustrated with photographs) *Behind the Scenes in a Department Store*, Lippincott, 1972; (self-illustrated with photographs) *Behind the Scenes of Television Programs*, Lippincott, 1972; *Upton Sinclair: American Rebel*, Crowell, 1975; *Merchant Princes: An Intimate History of Jewish Families Who Built Great Department Stores*, Harper, 1979. Contributor to periodicals, including *New York*, *Cosmopolitan*, *Good Housekeeping*, and *New York Times*.

SIDELIGHTS: A *New York Times Book Review* writer calls *Merchant Princes* "a friendly account of the origins of such emporia as Macy's, Neiman-Marcus, and Sears, Roebuck.... Mr. Harris does not, however, shrink from disclosing plenty of dirt: avarice, adultery and vulgarity.... He also tucks quite a lot of fascinating social history into the various family chronicles." Christopher Lehmann-Haupt asks: "How can Leon Harris tell the story of some twelve different Jewish merchandising families without boringly repeating himself? ... Colorful these various families may have been, but can their hues have varied enough to sustain a book of over 350 pages?" Lehmann-Haupt says that Harris gets around the problem of repetition by using the family chronicles as "springboards to generalities." In this way he is able to launch into discussions of politics, philanthropy, history, and into a variety of amusing anecdotes about the department store founders. "On the whole," says Lehmann-Haupt, "the tactic works. Not only is repetition avoided, but a solid structure is erected—sturdy enough to hold regional history, gossip, personal reminiscenses and a history of the art and science of department-store merchandising."

BIOGRAPHICAL/CRITICAL SOURCES: *Times Literary Supplement*, May 25, 1967; *New York Times Book Review*, November 15, 1967, May 12, 1968, March 29, 1970, December 30, 1979, December 28, 1980; *New Yorker*, December 2, 1967; *Young Readers' Review*, October, 1968; *New York Times*, December 27, 1979.

*   *   *

HARRISON, G(eorge) B(agshawe) 1894-

PERSONAL: Born July 14, 1894, in Hove, Sussex, England; came to the United States, 1949; son of Walter and Ada (Bagshaw) Harrison; married Dorothy Agnes Barker, April 9, 1919; children: Leslie Michael (deceased), Anthony Francis (deceased), Joan Cicely McIntosh. *Education:* Attended Brighton College, Cambridge; Queens' College, Cambridge, B.A., 1919, M.A., 1922; King's College, London, Ph.D., 1928. *Home:* 36A Manson St., Palmerston North, New Zealand.

CAREER: Assistant master, Felsted School, 1920-22; St. Paul's Training College, Cheltenham, England, senior lecturer in English, 1922-24; University of London, King's College, London, England, assistant lecturer, 1924-27, lecturer, 1927-29, reader in English literature, 1929-43; Queen's University, Kingston, Ontario, professor of English and head of department, 1943-49; University of Michigan, Ann Arbor, professor of English, 1949-64, professor emeritus, 1964—. Frederic Ives Carpenter Visiting Professor of English, University of Chicago, 1929; lecturer at Sorbonne, University of

Paris, 1933, and in Holland, 1940; Alexander Lecturer, University of Toronto, 1947. Member, International Committee for English in the Liturgy, beginning 1965. *Military service:* British Army, Infantry, 1914-19, served in India and Mesopotamia; became captain; Royal Army Service Corps and Intelligence Corps, 1940-43. *Member:* Modern Language Association of America, American Association of University Professors. *Awards, honors:* Litt.D. from Villanova University, 1960, Holy Cross College, 1961, and Marquette University, 1963; LL.D. from Assumption College, 1962; L.H.D. from Fairfield University, 1964; Campion Award for long and eminent service in the cause of Christian literature, 1970.

WRITINGS: (With E.A.G. Lamborn) *Shakespeare: The Man and His Stage*, Oxford University Press, 1923, Haskell House, 1977; (contributor of essay) *Willobie His Avisa, 1594*, Dutton, 1926, reprinted, Barnes & Noble, 1966; *Shakespeare's Fellows*, John Lane, 1923, Folcroft, 1978; *The Story of Elizabethan Drama*, Cambridge University Press, 1924, Folcroft, 1978; *The Genius of Shakespeare*, Harper, 1927; *An Elizabethan Journal: Being a Record of Those Things Most Talked about during the Years 1591-1594* (also see below), Constable, 1928, Cosmopolitan Book Corp., 1929, Routledge & Kegan Paul, (Boston), 1974; *John Bunyan*, Doubleday, 1928, reprinted, Folcroft, 1973.

Elizabethan England, Benn, 1930, Norwood, 1975; *A Second Elizabethan Journal: Being a Record of Those Things Most Talked of during the Years 1595-1598* (also see below), Constable, 1931, Routledge & Kegan Paul, 1974; *A Last Elizabethan Journal: Being a Record of Those Things Most Talked of during the Years 1599-1603* (also see below), Constable, 1933, Routledge & Kegan Paul, 1974; *Shakespeare under Elizabeth*, Holt, 1933 (published in England as *Shakespeare at Work, 1592-1603*, Routledge & Kegan Paul, 1933, University of Michigan Press, 1958); *Digging for History*, Thomas Nelson, 1937; *The Life and Death of Robert Devereux*, Holt, 1937, reprinted, Folcroft, 1973; *The Wanderings of Ulysses*, Thomas Nelson, 1937; *The Day before Yesterday*, Cobden-Sanderson, 1938; *The Elizabethan Journals* (contains *An Elizabethan Journal*, and *A Last Elizabethan Journal*), Routledge & Kegan Paul, 1938, revised three volume edition, Macmillan, 1939, reprinted, Routledge & Kegan Paul (Boston), 1974, abridged two volume edition, Doubleday, 1965; *New Tales from Shakespeare*, Thomas Nelson, 1938; *New Tales from Malory*, Thomas Nelson, 1939; *Introducing Shakespeare*, Penguin (London), 1939, Penguin (New York), 1947, 15th edition (London), 1978; *More New Tales from Shakespeare*, Thomas Nelson, 1939; *Elizabethan Plays and Players*, Routledge & Kegan Paul (London), 1940, University of Michigan Press, 1956; *New Tales from the Old Testament*, Thomas Nelson, 1940; *More New Tales from the Old Testament*, Thomas Nelson, 1940; *New Tales of Troy*, Thomas Nelson, 1940; *A Jacobean Journal: Being a Record of Those Things Most Talked of during the Years 1603-1606*, Macmillan, 1941; *Shakespeare's Tragedies*, Routledge & Kegan Paul, 1951, Oxford University Press (New York), 1952; *A Second Jacobean Journal: Being a Record of Those Things Most Talked of during the Years 1607-1610*, University of Michigan Press, 1958; *Profession of English*, Harcourt, 1962; *The Fires of Arcadia*, Harcourt, 1965. Also author of *Shakespeare*, 1927.

Editor: *The Church Book of Bunyan Meeting, 1650-1821*, Dutton, 1928; *England in Shakespeare's Day*, Methuen, 1928, Richard West, 1978, 2nd edition, Methuen, 1949, Books for Libraries Press, 1970; *The Wonderful Discoverie of Witches in the Countie of Lancaster: The Trial of the Lan-*

cashire Witches, A.D. 1612, P. Davies, 1929, reprinted, Muller, 1972; *Narrative of the Persecution of Agnes Beaumont in 1674,* Constable, 1929; *Henry P. Northumberland, Advice to His Son,* Benn, 1930; (and translator with R. A. Jones) Andre Hurault sieur de Maisse, *De Maisse: A Journal of All That Was Accomplished by Monsieur de Maisse, Ambassador in England from King Henri IV to Queen Elizabeth,* Random House, 1931, reprinted, Norwood, 1977; (with Harley Granville-Barker) *A Companion to Shakespeare Studies,* Cambridge University Press, 1934, Doubleday, 1960; *A Book of English Poetry, Chaucer to Rosetti,* Famous Books, 1938, revised edition, Penguin, 1958; John Bunyan, *Pilgrim's Progress,* Limited Editions, 1941, revised edition, Dent, 1954; Bunyan, *Grace Abounding to the Chief of Sinners and the Life and Death of Mr. Badman,* two volumes, Dutton, 1953; *Major British Writers,* two volumes, Harcourt, 1954, enlarged edition, 1959, abridged edition, 1967; *Julius Caesar in Shakespeare, Shaw and the Ancients,* Harcourt, 1960; (author of introduction) *The Bible for Students of Literature and Art,* Doubleday, 1964; (with Arthur M. Eastman) *Shakespeare's Critics: From Jonson to Auden,* University of Michigan Press, 1964; *Elizabethan and Jacobean Quartos* (also see below; based on "Bodley Head Quartos" series, 1922-26), fifteen volumes, Barnes & Noble, 1966.

All by William Shakespeare; all published by Harcourt, except as indicated: *The Taming of the Shrew,* Harrap, 1929; (with F. H. Pritchard) *As You Like It,* Holt, 1932; (with Pritchard) *Hamlet,* Holt, 1932; (with Pritchard) *Macbeth,* Holt, 1932; (with Pritchard) *The Merchant of Venice,* Holt, 1932; *23 Plays and Sonnets,* 1948, published as *Major Plays and Sonnets,* 1958; *Six Plays of Shakespeare,* 1949; *The Complete Works,* 1952; *Four Plays,* 1954; *King Lear,* 1962; (and author of introduction) *Twelfth Night, Or What You Will,* 1962; (and author of introduction) *King Henry the Fourth, Parts I and II,* 1963; (and author of introduction) *The Tragedy of Hamlet, Prince of Denmark,* 1963; (and author of introduction) *The Tragedy of Macbeth,* 1963.

All by Shakespeare; all published by Shakespeare Recording Society: *Richard the Second,* 1961; *Romeo and Juliet,* 1961; *As You Like It,* 1962; *Antony and Cleopatra,* 1962; *Cymbeline,* 1962; *The Tragedy of Troylus and Cressida,* 1962; *The Comedy of Errors,* 1962; *Hamlet,* 1963; *The Merchant of Venice,* 1963; *Henry the Fourth, Part Two,* 1964; *Julius Caesar,* 1964; *King John,* 1964; *A Midsummer Night's Dream,* 1964; *The Tragedy of King Lear,* 1965; *The Two Gentlemen of Verona,* 1965; *King Richard III,* 1965; *The Merry Wives of Windsor,* 1966.

Also editor of numerous sixteenth- and seventeenth-century texts, including: Robert Greene, *The Black Bookes Messenger, 1592,* 1924; Thomas Nash, *Pierce Penilesse, His Supplication to the Divell, 1592,* 1924; John Marston, *The Scourge of Villanie, 1599,* 1925; *The Letters of Queen Elizabeth I,* 1935. Also editor of "The Penguin Shakespeare" series, Penguin, 1937-59. Editor, "Bodley Head Quartos" series (also see above), Dutton, 1922-26.

*   *   *

HARRISON, K(enneth) C(ecil) 1915-

PERSONAL: Born April 29, 1915, in Hyde, Cheshire, England; son of Thomas and Anne (Wood) Harrison; married Doris Taylor, August 26, 1941; children: David John, Timothy Michael. *Education:* Attended schools in Hyde, Cheshire, England. *Home:* 50 West Hill Way, Totteridge, London N20 8QS, England. *Office:* c/o Library Association, 7 Ridgmount St., London WC1E 7AE, England.

CAREER: Assistant librarian in Hyde, Cheshire, England, 1931-36; branch librarian in Coulsdon, England, 1936-39; borough librarian in Hyde, England, 1939-47, in Hove, Sussex, England, 1947-50, in Eastbourne, Sussex, England, 1950-58, and in Hendon, London, England, 1958-61; city librarian of Westminster, London, England, 1961-80. Chairman of joint organizing committee, National Library Week, 1964-69. Governor, Westminster Technical College. Lecturer on librarianship, travel and literary subjects. *Military service:* British Army, Infantry, 1940-46; served in North Africa, Sicily, France, Belgium, Holland, took part in D-Day landing; became major; awarded Order of British Empire.

MEMBER: International Association of Metropolitan Libraries (vice-president), Commonwealth Library Association (president, 1972-75; executive secretary, 1980—), National Central Library (chairman of executive committee), Central Music Library Council, National Book League (council member), Library Association (council member; president, 1973), Westminster Arts Council (honorary secretary, 1965-80; vice-president, 1980—), Eastborne Rotary Club (president, 1956-57), Marylebone Cricket Club. *Awards, honors:* Made Knight (first class) of the Order of the Lion of Finland.

WRITINGS: First Steps in Librarianship: A Student's Guide, Grafton & Co., 1950, 5th revised edition, Deutsch, 1980; *Sixty Years of Service: The Diamond Jubilee of the Eastbourne Public Libraries, 1896-1956,* Eastbourne Public Libraries, 1956; *Libraries in Scandinavia,* Grafton & Co., 1961, International Publications, 1962, 2nd edition, revised, Deutsch, 1969; *The Library and the Community,* Deutsch, 1963, 3rd revised edition, 1977; *Public Libraries Today,* Philosophical Library, 1963; *Facts at Your Fingertips: Everyman's Guide to Reference Books,* Mason Publications, 1964, 2nd edition, 1967; (with S. G. Berriman) *British Public Library Buildings,* Deutsch, 1966; *Libraries in Britain,* Longmans, Green, for British Council, 1968; *Libraries and the Three Cultures,* George Peabody College for Teachers, 1969; *Public Relations for Librarians,* Deutsch, 1976; (editor) *Prospects for British Librarianship,* Library Association, 1976; (editor) *Public Library Policy,* K. G. Saur, 1981. Contributor to *Times* (London), *Listener, UNESCO Bulletin for Libraries,* and to library journals in United States, Europe, and India. Editor, *Library World,* 1961-71.

AVOCATIONAL INTERESTS: Reading, travel, motoring, holidays in the sun, and watching cricket and football.

*   *   *

HASSAN, Ihab Habib 1925-

PERSONAL: Born October 17, 1925, in Cairo, Egypt; came to United States in 1946, naturalized in 1956; son of Habib and Faika (Hamdi) Hassan; married Alida Koten, April 18, 1949 (divorced); married Sarah Margaret Greene, 1966; children: (first marriage) Geoffrey. *Education:* University of Cairo, B.Sc., 1946; University of Pennsylvania, M.S., 1948, M.A., 1950, Ph.D., 1953. *Home:* 2137 North Terrace Ave., Milwaukee, Wis. 53202.

CAREER: Rensselaer Polytechnic Institute, Troy, N.Y., instructor in English, 1952-54; Wesleyan University, Middletown, Conn., instructor, 1954-55, assistant professor, 1955-58, associate professor, 1958-62, professor of English, 1962-63, Benjamin L. Waite Professor of English, 1963-70, chairman of department, 1963-64, 1968-69, director of College of Letters, 1964-66, director of Center for Humanities, 1969-70; University of Wisconsin—Milwaukee, Vilas Research Professor, 1970—. Tutor, American Seminars at Salzburg, 1965 and 1975. Fulbright lecturer, Grenoble, France, 1966-67 and Nice, France, 1974-75; Distinguished Fulbright lecturer, Kyoto Seminars in American studies, summer, 1974. Visiting fellow, Woodrow Wilson International Center for Scholars, 1972; senior fellow, Camargo Foundation, 1974-75; visiting scholar, Rockefeller Bellagio Study and Conference Center, 1978. Member of editorial board, Wesleyan University Press, 1963-66. *Member:* Modern Language Association of America, American Studies Association, International Comparative Literature Association, Sigma Xi. *Awards, honors:* Guggenheim fellow, 1958-59 and 1962-63; fellow, School of Letters, Indiana University, 1964.

WRITINGS: Radical Innocence: The Contemporary American Novel, Princeton University Press, 1961; *Aspects du Hero Americain Contemporain,* Lettres Modernes, 1963; *The Literature of Silence: Henry Miller and Samuel Beckett,* Knopf, 1968; (editor) *Liberations: New Essays on the Humanities in Revolution,* Wesleyan University Press, 1971; *The Dismemberment of Orpheus: Toward a Postmodern Literature,* Oxford University Press, 1971; *Contemporary American Literature: 1945-1972,* Ungar, 1973; *Paracriticisms,* Illinois University Press, 1975; *The Right Promethean Fire,* Illinois University Press, 1980.

Contributor to journals and newspapers, including *Saturday Review, New York Times Book Review, American Scholar, Critique, Nation, Book Week.* Member of editorial board, *American Quarterly,* 1965-67. Member of advisory board, *Diacritios,* 1973—, *Humanities in Society,* 1978—, and *PMLA,* 1979-83.

SIDELIGHTS: In her review of *The Literature of Silence: Henry Miller and Samuel Beckett,* Sue Wienhorst writes in *Encounter* of Ihab Hassan's ability or talent as a literary critic: "As a combination of cultural analysis and genre description that focuses upon the interior logic of the contemporary spirit and the literary form in which this logic is reflected, Mr. Hassan's criticism has great power. In his adept and sensitive hand, this approach convinces us of the seriousness and the integrity of anti-literature as an *avant-garde* genre and illumines a broad range of contemporary art and thought."

BIOGRAPHICAL/CRITICAL SOURCES: Encounter, summer, 1968.

*   *   *

HAUGAARD, Erik Christian 1923-

PERSONAL: Born April 13, 1923, in Frederiksberg, Denmark; son of Gotfred Hans Christian (a professor of biochemistry) and Karen (Pedersen) Haugaard; married Myrna Seld (a writer), December 23, 1949; children: Mikka Anja, Mark. *Education:* Attended Black Mountain College, 1941-42, and New School for Social Research, 1947-48. *Home:* Toad Hall, Ballydehob, County Cork, Ireland.

CAREER: Author of youth books, drama, and poetry. Worked as farm laborer in Fyn, Denmark, 1938-40, and later as a sheep herder in Wyoming. *Military service:* Royal Canadian Air Force, 1943-45; became flight sergeant; received War Service Medal from Christian X of Denmark. *Awards, honors:* John Golden Fund fellowship for play, "The Heroes," 1958; honorable mention, *New York Herald Tribune* Children's Spring Book Festival, 1962, for *Hakon of Rogen's Saga,* and 1967, for *The Little Fishes;* American Library Association Notable Book Awards, 1963, for *Hakon of Rogen's Saga,* 1965, for *A Slave's Tale,* and 1971, for *The Untold Tale;* Boston *Globe*-Horn Book Award, 1967, Jane Addams Award, 1968, and Danish Cultural Minister's Prize, 1970, all for *The Little Fishes.*

WRITINGS: Twenty-Five Poems, Squire Press, 1957; *Hakon of Rogen's Saga* (youth book), Houghton, 1963; *A Slave's Tale* (youth book), Houghton, 1965; *Orphans of the Wind* (youth book), Houghton, 1966; *The Little Fishes* (youth book), Houghton, 1967; *The Rider and His Horse,* Houghton, 1968; *The Untold Tale,* Houghton, 1971; (translator) *Complete Fairy Tales and Stories of Hans Christian Andersen,* Doubleday, 1973; *Portrait of Poet: Hans Christian Andersen* (pamphlet), Library of Congress, 1974; *A Messenger for Parliament,* Houghton, 1976; (translator) *Hans Christian Andersen: His Classical Fairy Tales,* Doubleday, 1978; *Cromwell's Boy,* Houghton, 1978; *Chase Me! Catch Nobody!,* Houghton, 1980.

Plays: "The Heroes"; "The President Regrets"; "An Honest Man." Translator of Eskimo poetry, collected by Knud Rasmussen, for *American Scandinavian Review.*

WORK IN PROGRESS: The Last Vikings, based on research now in progress in Greenland.

SIDELIGHTS: Erik Haugaard wrote *CA:* "When I was a little boy, I used to tell myself stories, and in all of them I was the hero. I paid little attention to my own size, time, place, or even ideas. In the morning I could lead the French Revolution and in the afternoon be an aristocrat making a fine speech before my head was chopped off. But time catches all children in his net; some day they must grow up and lose their wings.

"Although I grew up and learned to distinguish between dreams and reality, the wish to tell stories remained. I was no longer the hero and a note of sadness had crept into my stories, for the purpose of telling them had changed. The stories I had told myself as a child had been dreams trying to explain an unknown world; now my stories dealt with a known world. I had grown up, been through a war, married and had children of my own, I had lived, experienced my share of happiness and sorrow, tested my strength and learned of my weakness.

"Man is forever lonely; but he has two friends whom he cannot lose, for though he may be unfaithful to them, they will never desert him. Nature and Art: ageless and eternal, they were there before we were born and will remain when we are gone. We are a part of nature which no end of scientific development can change, though it can distance us from it. Art: literature, music, painting, sculpture are the immortal parts of mortal man. This, too, we can deny; but only at the cost of greater loneliness. Hans Christian Andersen died long ago; but the fairy tales he wrote remain; if we do not read them the loss is not his but ours.

"No author can know whether his stories have enough truth in them to make them live forever. But if this is not his ambition, then I would not call him a humble man but a fraud. Once words are printed they take on a far greater importance than when they are spoken; therefore, especially when we write for children, we must only write what we consider to be the truth. Platitudes and lies are not harmless when they are disguised as truth and served to that audience which has the least experience with which to expose them."

BIOGRAPHICAL/CRITICAL SOURCES: Book World, September 7, 1969; *Times Literary Supplement,* October 16, 1969; *Books and Bookmen,* December, 1969.

*   *   *

HAWES, Gene R(obert) 1922-

PERSONAL: Born May 14, 1922, in Chicago, Ill.; son of Addison Eugene and Ariadne (Palmer) Hawes; married

Betty L. Peterson, December 17, 1949; children: Mark, Elizabeth, Roberta. *Education:* Columbia University, A.B., 1949. *Home:* 34 Aldridge Rd., Chappaqua, N.Y. 10514.

CAREER: Columbia Alumni News, New York City, editor, 1951-55; College Entrance Examination Board, New York City, editor, 1955-60; Science Research Associates (educational publishers), Chicago, Ill., director of information, 1960-62; Columbia University, New York City, editor of *Columbia Research News* and consultant to Columbia University Press, 1962-68; free-lance author. Founding principal and member of board of directors, The Hudson Group, Inc., 1971—. Consultant to Time, Inc., 1963. *Military service:* U.S. Navy, 1944-46. *Member:* Authors Guild.

WRITINGS: The New American Guide to Colleges, New American Library, 1959, 4th edition, New American Library and Columbia University Press, 1972; *Educational Testing for the Millions: What Tests Really Mean for Your Child,* McGraw, 1964; (with R. M. Friedberg) *Careers in College Teaching,* Walck, 1965; *To Advance Knowledge,* American University Press Services, 1967; (with Ewald B. Nyquist) *Open Education,* Bantam, 1972; (with David M. Brownstone) *How to get the Money to Pay for College,* McKay, 1978; (with Gail Thain Parker), *College On Your Own,* Bantam, 1978; *Hawes Comprehensive Guide to Colleges,* New American Library, 1978; *Careers Tomorrow in Leading Growth Fields for College Graduates,* New American Library, 1979; (with Helen Weiss and Martin Weiss) *How to Raise Your Child to Be a Winner,* Rawson, Wade, 1980; (with David M. Brownstone), *The Complete Career Guide,* Simon & Schuster, 1980. Contributor to *This Week, Esquire, Saturday Review, Ladies' Home Journal,* and other magazines. Editor-in-chief of monthly newsletter, *Compress-Gases and Cryogenics Report,* 1980—.

WORK IN PROGRESS: Various books and articles.

*   *   *

HAYES, Carlton J(oseph) H(untley) 1882-1964

PERSONAL: Born May 16, 1882, in Afton, N.Y.; died September 3, 1964; son of Philetus A. and Permelia Mary (Huntley) Hayes; married Mary Evelyn Carroll, September 18, 1920; children: Mary Elizabeth Hayes Tucker, Carroll J. *Education:* Columbia University, A.B., 1904, A.M., 1905, Ph.D., 1909. *Religion:* Catholic. *Home and office:* 88 Morningside Dr., New York, N.Y.

CAREER: Columbia University, New York, N.Y., lecturer, 1907-10, assistant professor, 1910-15, associate professor, 1915-19, professor of history, 1919-35, Seth Low Professor, 1935-50, professor emeritus, 1950-64. U.S. Ambassador to Spain, 1942-45. *Military service:* U.S. Army, Military Intelligence, 1918-19; became captain. Officers Reserve Corps, 1919-25; became major. *Member:* American Historical Association (former president), American Catholic Historical Association (former president), New York State Historical Association, Columbia University Club, Alpha Chi Rho. *Awards, honors:* Laetare Medal, 1946; Cardinal Gibbons Medal, 1949; Alexander Hamilton Medal, 1952; Knight of Malta, Grand Cross Order of Alfonso the Wise. L.H.D., Marquette University, 1929, Williams College, 1939, University of Detroit, 1950, and Georgetown University, 1953; LL.D., University of Notre Dame, 1921, Niagara University, 1936, Fordham University, 1946, and Michigan State University, 1955; Litt.D., Columbia University, 1929.

WRITINGS—All published by Macmillan, except as indicated: *An Introduction to the Sources Relating to the Germanic Invasions,* Longmans, Green, 1909, reprinted, AMS

Press, 1967; (with Robert Livingston Schuyler) *A Syllabus of Modern History,* Columbia University Press, 1912, 3rd edition, 1916; *British Social Politics: Materials Illustrating Contemporary State Action for the Solution of Social Problems,* Ginn, 1913, reprinted, Books for Libraries Press, 1972; *A Brief History of the Great War,* 1920; (with Parker T. Moon) *Modern History,* 1923, 4th edition, 1941, reprinted, 1959; *A Political and Social History of Modern Europe,* two volumes, 1924; *Essays on Nationalism,* 1926, reprinted, Russell & Russell, 1966; (with Moon) *Ancient History,* 1929; (with Moon) *Ancient and Medieval History,* 1929.

France: A Nation of Patriots, Columbia University Press, 1930, reprinted, Octagon, 1974; *The Historical Evolution of Modern Nationalism,* R. R. Smith, 1931, reprinted, Russell & Russell, 1968; (with Moon and John W. Wayland) *World History,* 1932, 3rd edition, 1955; *A Political and Cultural History of Modern Europe,* Volume I: *Three Centuries of Predominantly Agricultural Society, 1500-1830,* revised edition, 1932, Volume II: *A Century of Predominantly Industrial Society, 1830-1935,* 1939; *Outline of the History of Modern Europe, 1500-1932,* Part I: *1500-1830,* Eckhardt, 1935; (editor with Newton Baker) *American Way,* Willett, 1936; *Analytical Survey of Modern European History,* revised edition, 1938.

A Generation of Materialism, 1871-1900, Harper, 1941; *Wartime Mission in Spain, 1942-1945,* 1945, reprinted, Da Capo Press, 1976; (with Marshall W. Baldwin and Charles W. Cole) *History of Europe,* 1949, 3rd edition published as *History of Western Civilization,* 1962; *The United States and Spain: An Interpretation,* Sheed, 1951, reprinted, Greenwood Press, 1970; *Modern Europe to 1870,* 1953; *Contemporary Europe since 1870,* 1953, revised edition, 1958; *Christianity and Western Civilization,* Stanford University Press, 1954; *Nationalism: A Religion,* 1960; (with Margareta Faissler) *Modern Times: The French Revolution to the Present,* 1965; (with Frederick F. Clark) *Medieval and Early Modern Times: The Age of Justinian to the Eighteenth Century,* 1966; (with James H. Hanscom) *Ancient Civilizations: Prehistory to the Fall of Rome,* 1968. Author of pamphlets. Contributor to *Encyclopaedia Britannica, Encyclopedia of Social Sciences,* and journals.†

*   *   *

HAYES, Samuel P(erkins) 1910-

PERSONAL: Born January 28, 1910, in South Hadley, Mass.; son of Samuel P. (psychologist) and Agnes (Stone) Hayes; married Alice Mary Cable, March 25, 1937; children: Susan, Jonathan. *Education:* Amherst College, A.B., 1931; Yale University, Ph.D., 1934; University of Chicago, postdoctoral fellow of Social Science Research Council, 1937-38. *Politics:* Democrat. *Home:* 2122 California St. N.W., Apt. 652, Washington, D.C. 20008. *Office:* Committee on Agriculture, U.S. House of Representatives, 3363 House Office Bldg. Annex 2, Washington, D.C. 20515.

CAREER: Mt. Holyoke College, South Hadley, Mass., instructor in psychology, 1934-37; Sarah Lawrence College, Bronxville, N.Y., member of economics faculty, 1938-40; Young & Rubicam, Inc., New York City, member of economics and market research staff, 1940-42; U.S. Government, Lend-Lease Administration and Foreign Economic Administration, held various positions in Washington, D.C., Algiers, London, Oslo, Copenhagen, 1942-45; Dun & Bradstreet, Inc., New York City, associate director of marketing and research service, 1945-48; U.S. Government, held various positions in State Department, Economic Cooperation

Administration, and Mutual Security Administration in Washington, D.C. and Indonesia, 1948-53; Foundation for Research on Human Behavior, Ann Arbor, Mich., director, 1953-60; University of Michigan, Ann Arbor, professor of economics and director of center for research on economic development, 1959-62; Foreign Policy Association, New York City, president, 1962-74; U.S. House of Representatives, Washington, D.C., staff consultant, Committee on Agriculture, 1979—. Lecturer, Salzburg Seminar in American Studies, 1965. Senior specialist, East-West Center, 1968; resident scholar, Villa Serbelloni, 1971; director of New York region, Campaign for Yale, 1975-76. Member of advisory committee on political organization, Democratic National Committee, 1955-60. Institute of International Education, member of committee on educational interchange policy, 1960-64, chairman, 1963-64. Member of Washington Institute of Foreign Affairs. Consultant to UNESCO, on evaluation of development projects, 1954-59, University of Kansas City, and University of Pittsburgh, 1957-58, President's Task Force on Foreign Economic Assistance, 1961, Peace Corps, 1961-62, and World Bank, 1976-78.

MEMBER: American Statistical Association (fellow; member of committee on committees, 1955-57), American Psychological Association (fellow), American Association for the Advancement of Science (fellow), American Economic Association (member of sub-committee on undergraduate economics, 1946-48), Council on Foreign Relations, Society for International Development, Amateur Chamber Music Players (chairman), Cosmos Club (Washington, D.C.), Phi Beta Kappa, Sigma Xi, Chi Phi. *Awards, honors:* Moore fellowship in philosophy, Amherst College; L.H.D., Amherst College, 1966.

WRITINGS: (Co-author) *Industrial Conflict: A Psychological Interpretation*, Cordon Press, 1939; (co-author) *Towards World Prosperity*, Harper, 1947; (co-author) *The Progress of Underdeveloped Areas*, University of Chicago Press, 1952; (co-editor with Rensis Likert) *Some Applications of Behavioral Research*, UNESCO, 1957; *Measuring the Results of Development Projects*, UNESCO, 1959, revised edition published as *Evaluating Development Projects*, 1966; *An International Peace Corps*, Public Affairs Institute, 1961; (editor) *The Beginning of American Aid to Southeast Asia*, Heath, 1971. Contributor of numerous articles to professional journals. Member of editorial committee, *American Statistician*, 1947-51.

AVOCATIONAL INTERESTS: Chamber music (viola) and tennis.

BIOGRAPHICAL/CRITICAL SOURCES: New York Times, October 18, 1953, August 16, 1962; *Ann Arbor News,* Ann Arbor, Mich., October 18, 1953, August 16, 1962; *Christian Science Monitor,* October 27, 1962.

*   *   *

HAYWOOD, H(erbert) Carl(ton)   1931-

PERSONAL: Born July 2, 1931, in Taylor County, Ga.; married 1951 (divorced, 1971); children: Carlton, Terry, Elizabeth, Kristen. *Education:* Attended West Georgia College, 1948-50; San Diego State College (now University), A.B., 1956, M.A., 1957; University of Illinois, Ph.D., 1961. *Home:* 857 Stirrup Dr., Nashville, Tenn. 37221. *Office:* Box 40, George Peabody College for Teachers of Vanderbilt University, Nashville, Tenn. 37203.

CAREER: Veterans Administration Hospital, Danville, Ill., clinical psychology trainee, 1957-61; Eastern Illinois Mental Health Unit, Danville and Watseka, Ill., clinical psycholo-

gist, 1959-61; Veterans Administration Hospital, Danville, staff psychologist, 1961-62; George Peabody College for Teachers of Vanderbilt University, Nashville, Tenn., assistant professor, 1962-65, associate professor, 1965-66, Kennedy Associate Professor, 1966-69, Kennedy Professor of Psychology, 1969-75, professor of psychology, 1975—, director of John F. Kennedy Center for Research on Education and Human Development, 1971—; Vanderbilt University, School of Medicine, professor of neurology, 1971—. Visiting professor at University of Toronto, 1965-66. Tennessee Department of Mental Health and Mental Retardation, consultant, 1964—, chairman of research committee, 1977—. Consultant to National Institutes of Health, President's Committee on Mental Retardation, and various institutions and government bodies. *Military service:* U.S. Navy, 1950-54.

MEMBER: American Association on Mental Deficiency (fellow; vice-president for psychology, 1975-77; president, 1980-81), American Psychological Association (president, Division on Mental Retardation, 1978-79; member of council of representatives, 1980-82), American Association for the Advancement of Science, Psychonomic Society, Society for Research in Child Development, Institute of Medicine (National Academy of Sciences), Midwestern Psychological Association, Southeastern Psychological Association, Sigma Xi.

WRITINGS—Editor: (And contributor) *Brain Damage in School Age Children*, Council for Exceptional Children, 1968; *Social-Cultural Aspects of Mental Retardation*, Appleton, 1970; (with M. J. Begab and H. Garber) *Prevention of Retarded Development in Psychosocially Disadvantaged Children*, University Park Press, in press; (with J. R. Newbrough) *Living Environments for Developmentally Retarded Persons*, University Park Press, in press.

Contributor: Joseph Zubin and George Jervis, editors, *Psychopathology of Mental Development*, Grune, 1967; H. I. Day, D. E. Berlyne, and D. E. Hunt, editors, *Intrinsic Motivation: A New Direction in Intelligence*, Holt, 1971; (with J. W. Filler, Jr., M. A. Shifman, and G. Chatelanat) P. McReynolds, editor, *Advances in Psychological Assessment*, Jossey-Bass, 1975; N. Hobbs, editor, *The Futures of Children*, Jossey-Bass, 1975; M. Kindred, J. Cohen, D. Penrod, and T. Shaffer, editors, *The Mentally Retarded Citizen and the Law*, Free Press, 1976; (with W. P. Burke) I. C. Uzgiris and F. Weizmann, editors, *The Structuring of Experience*, Plenum, 1977; P. Mittler, editor, *Research to Practice in Mental Retardation*, University Park Press, 1977; Mittler, editor, *Frontiers of Knowledge in Mental Retardation*, University Park Press, 1980.

Contributor to *Encyclopaedia Britannica*. Contributor to numerous proceedings; contributor of over fifty articles and occasional reviews to scientific journals. *Abstracts of Peabody Studies in Mental Retardation*, co-editor, 1965, editor, 1968; *American Journal of Mental Deficiency*, consulting editor, 1966-69, editor, 1969-79.

*   *   *

HAZLITT, Henry   1894-

PERSONAL: Born November 28, 1894, in Philadelphia, Pa.; son of Stuart Clark and Bertha (Zauner) Hazlitt; married Frances S. Kanes, July, 1936. *Education:* Attended City College (now City College of the City University of New York), 1912. *Home:* 65 Drum Hill Rd., Wilton, Conn. 06897.

CAREER: Editor and writer, New York, N.Y., 1913—. *Wall Street Journal*, reporter, 1913-16; *New York Evening Post,* member of financial staff, 1916-18; Mechanics and Metals National Bank, writer of monthly financial letter, 1919-20; *New York Evening Mail,* financial editor, 1921-23; *New York Herald,* editorial writer, 1923-24; *New York Sun,* editorial writer, 1924-25, literary editor, 1925-29; *Nation,* literary editor, 1930-33; *American Mercury,* editor, 1933-34; *New York Times,* member of editorial staff, 1934-46; *Freeman,* co-founder and co-editor, 1950-52, president and editor-in-chief, 1953; *Newsweek,* writer of "Business Tides" column, 1946-66; syndicated columnist for Los Angeles Times Syndicate, 1966-69. Lecturer at colleges and universities in the United States, Mexico, Peru, Netherlands, and Austria. Radio and television panelist and debater with government officials on national issues. Trustee, Foundation for Economic Education. *Military service:* U.S. Aviation Service, World War I. *Member:* Authors Club (London); Century Association, Dutch Treat Club (all New York). *Awards, honors:* Twice received the George Washington Honor Medal from Freedom Foundation; Litt.D. from Grove City College, 1958; LL.D. from Bethany College, Bethany, W.Va., 1961; S. Sc. D. from Universidad Francisco Marroquin, 1976.

WRITINGS: Thinking as a Science, Dutton, 1916, reprinted, Nash Publishing, 1969; *The Way to Will Power,* Dutton, 1922; (editor) *A Practical Program for America* (essays), Harcourt, 1932, reprinted, Books for Libraries, 1967; *The Anatomy of Criticism,* Simon & Schuster, 1933; *A New Constitution Now,* McGraw, 1942, reprinted, Arlington House, 1974; *Economics in One Lesson,* Harper, 1946, revised edition, Arlington House, 1979; *Will Dollars Save the World?,* Foundation for Economic Education, and Appleton, 1947; *Illusions of Point Four,* Foundation for Economic Education, 1950; *The Great Idea* (novel), Appleton, 1951, reprinted as *Time Will Run Back,* Arlington House, 1966; *The Free Man's Library,* Van Nostrand, 1956; *The Failure of the "New Economics": An Analysis of the Keynesian Fallacies,* Van Nostrand, 1959; *What You Should Know about Inflation,* Van Nostrand, 1960, 2nd edition, 1965; (editor) *The Critics of Keynesian Economics,* Van Nostrand, 1960, reprinted, Arlington House, 1977; *The Foundations of Morality,* Van Nostrand, 1964, 2nd edition, 1972; *Man vs. the Welfare State,* Arlington House, 1969; *The Conquest of Poverty,* Nash Publishing, 1973; *The Inflation Crisis and How to Resolve It,* Arlington House, 1978. Publications include pamphlets on government and economics. Member of editorial board, *American Scholar,* 1941-44.

WORK IN PROGRESS: A book, tentatively entitled *Is Politics Insoluble?*

SIDELIGHTS: Henry Hazlitt wrote *CA:* "I have written sixteen full-length books. I think I have been extremely fortunate, for many reasons, in having been a newspaper man. A journalist forms the habit of writing often several thousand words a week. When he has become accustomed to this, he never has a 'writing block,' which some of my non-journalistic friends used to complain about. One reason he never has it is that he never fears it. More important, habit and necessity have solved that problem for him."

Sales of *Economics in One Lesson* long ago passed the 600,000 mark, and the book has been translated into eight languages. Another of Hazlitt's books, *The Failure of the "New Economics,"* has been translated into German, Japanese, Swedish, and Spanish.

HEINEY, Donald (William) 1921-
(MacDonald Harris)

PERSONAL: Born September 7, 1921, in South Pasadena, Calif.; son of William Thomas and Hazel F. (Lemon) Heiney; married Ann Borgman, 1948; children: Paul Adrian, Conrad James. *Education:* U.S. Merchant Marine Academy, B.S., 1943; University of Redlands, B.A., 1947; University of Southern California, A.M., 1948, Ph.D., 1952. *Agent:* Virginia Barber Literary Agency, Inc., 44 Greenwich Ave., New York, N.Y. 10011.

CAREER: Member of Merchant Marine, 1942-43; University of Southern California, Los Angeles, lecturer in comparative literature, 1949-53; University of Utah, Salt Lake City, instructor, 1953-54, assistant professor, 1954-59, associate professor of English, 1959-65; University of California, Irvine, professor of comparative literature and director of Program in Comparative Literature, 1965-70, currently co-director of fiction, Program in Writing; writer. Fulbright professor, Universities of Bologna and Venice, 1959-60; visiting lecturer, University of Paris, 1972-73. *Military service:* U.S. Naval Reserve, officer on tanker in European and South Pacific zones, 1943-46; became lieutenant junior grade. *Member:* Phi Beta Kappa. *Awards, honors:* First place story award, Utah State Institute of Fine Arts, 1959, for "Behold, the Abundance of the Lord"; grants from American Council of Learned Societies, 1962-63, 1966; American Philosophical Society grant, 1962-63; National Book Award nomination, 1976, for *The Balloonist.*

WRITINGS: Contemporary Literature, Barron's 1954; *Recent American Literature,* Barron's, 1958; *America in Modern Italian Literature,* Rutgers University Press, 1964; *Three Italian Novelists,* University of Michigan Press, 1968.

Under pseudonym MacDonald Harris; all novels, except as indicated: *Private Demons,* Houghton, 1961; *Mortal Leap,* Norton, 1964; *Treploff,* Gollancz, 1968, Holt, 1969; *They Sailed Alone* (juvenile nonfiction), Houghton, 1972; *Bull Fire,* Random House, 1973; *The Balloonist,* Farrar, Straus, 1976; *Yukiko,* Farrar, Straus, 1977; *Pandora's Galley,* Harcourt, 1979; *The Treasure of Sainte Foy,* Atheneum, 1980; *Herma,* Atheneum, 1981.

Work anthologized in *Prize Stories, 1959,* edited by Paul Engle, Doubleday, 1959, and *The Best American Short Stories,* edited by Martha Foley, Houghton, 1967. Contributor of short stories to *Atlantic, Saturday Evening Post, Cosmopolitan, Esquire, Harper's,* and to numerous literary quarterlies.

WORK IN PROGRESS: Fiction.

SIDELIGHTS: Donald Heiney told *CA:* "My recent fiction, while based on a fundamentally realistic view of life, has tended toward the form known in Latin-American literature as 'magic realism'; that is, it has come to incorporate elements of the fabulous, the unreal, and the magic, while at the same time it presents these in an utterly flat and factual technique. This tendency, which is first noticeable in *Bull Fire,* is particularly evident in my more recent books, *Yukiko, The Treasure of Sainte Foy,* and *Herma.* Another recurring note in my work is that I often use popular forms—the historical novel in *Pandora's Galley,* the war-adventure novel in *Yukiko,* and the crime-thriller in *The Treasure of Sainte Foy*—as frameworks for what are fundamentally serious and personal novelistic statements. Yet I use the term 'serious' only with qualifications; there is a note of irony, satire, or humor, in all my work, since I regard laughter—if one is able to laugh; if not a wry smile—as the only appropriate response to the essentially tragic quality of the human condition."

BIOGRAPHICAL/CRITICAL SOURCES: Observer, December 15, 1968; *Punch,* December 18, 1968; *Saturday Review,* December 20, 1969; *New Yorker,* December 27, 1969, June 30, 1980; John J. White, *Mythology in the Modern Novel: A Study of Prefigurative Techniques,* Princeton University Press, 1971; *Esquire,* May, 1973; *Spectator,* September 29, 1973; *Atlantic,* October, 1976; *New York Times Book Review,* November 7, 1976, October 9, 1977, July 13, 1980; *New Statesman,* May 13, 1977, April 14, 1978; *Times Literary Supplement,* May 13, 1977, April 21, 1978, August 22, 1980; *National Review,* November 25, 1977; *West Coast Review of Books,* January, 1978; (under pseudonym MacDonald Harris) *Contemporary Literary Criticism,* Volume IX, Gale, 1978; *Chicago Tribune Book World,* July 1, 1979.

* * *

HELM, P(eter) J(ames) 1916-

PERSONAL: Born June 16, 1916, in Waterfoot, Lancashire, England; son of James Edgar (a doctor) and Marjorie (Ashworth) Helm; married October 7, 1942 (wife's name, Joan Ellen); children: Ann. *Education:* Magdalene College, Cambridge, B.A., 1938, M.A., 1946. *Home:* The Croft, Bradford-on-Tone, Taunton, Somerset, England. *Agent:* John Johnson, Clerkenwell House, 45/7 Clerkenwell Green, London EC1R 0HT, England. *Office:* Department of History, Queen's College, Taunton, Somerset, England.

CAREER: Queen's College, Taunton, Somerset, England, senior history master, 1946-73, second master, 1952-73.

WRITINGS: Dead Men's Fingers, John Long, 1960, published as *A Walk into Murder,* Scribner, 1961; *History of Europe, 1450-1660,* G. Bell, 1961, Ungar, 1964; *Death Has a Thousand Entrances* (Mystery Book Guild selection), John Long, 1962; *Alfred the Great,* R. Hale, 1963; *Modern British History, 1815-1964,* G. Bell, 1965; *The Man with No Bones,* John Long, 1966; *Jeffreys,* R. Hale, 1966, published as *Jeffreys: A New Portrait of England's Hanging Judge,* Crowell, 1967; *England under the Yorkists and Tudors, 1471-1603,* G. Bell, 1968, Humanities, 1969.

Discovering Prehistoric England, R. Hale, 1971; *Exploring Roman Britain,* R. Hale, 1975; *Exploring Saxon and Norman England,* R. Hale, 1976; *Exploring Tudor England,* R. Hale, 1981; *The Brainpicker,* R. Hale, 1981. Contributor to *Time and Tide, Outposts, Archaeological Journal,* and other periodicals.

WORK IN PROGRESS: John Dee: His Life and Times.

AVOCATIONAL INTERESTS: Travel, painting, poetry.

BIOGRAPHICAL/CRITICAL SOURCES: Times Literary Supplement, January 26, 1967; *Virginia Quarterly Review,* autumn, 1967.

* * *

HENDRIE, Don(ald Franz), Jr. 1942-

PERSONAL: Born May 28, 1942, in Plainfield, N.J.; son of Donald Franz (a lawyer) and Helen Marie (Pennywitt) Hendrie; married Susan Niebling (a painter), June 17, 1966; children: Nathan Zed, Arden Wing. *Education:* Attended Tulane University, 1961-62; Stanford University, B.A., 1965; State University of Iowa, M.F.A., 1967. *Politics:* "Ironic socialist." *Residence:* Nottingham, N.H.

CAREER: Nathaniel Hawthorne College, Antrim, N.H., instructor in English, 1967-69; Mount Holyoke College, South Hadley, Mass., instructor, 1970-71, assistant professor of English, 1971-77; Instituto Allende, School of Writing, San

Miguel de Allende, Mexico, director, 1978-80; State University of Iowa, Writers' Workshop, Iowa City, visiting lecturer in writing, 1980-81. *Awards, honors:* National Endowment for the Arts fellowship in creative writing, 1978; William Sloane fellow in prose, Bread Loaf Writers' Conference, 1978.

WRITINGS: Boomkitchwatt (novel), John Muir, 1973; *Scribble, Scribble, Scribble* (short stories), Lynx, 1977; (contributor) Bill Henderson, editor, *The Pushcart Prize III* (anthology), Avon, 1979; *Blount's Anvil* (novel), Lynx, 1980. Contributor of short stories, articles, and reviews to *Lynx, Mercury Book Review, Silo II, Iowa Review, Confluence, Viva,* and *New England Review.*

WORK IN PROGRESS: A novel, *A Criminal Journey.*

* * *

HERNTON, Calvin C(oolidge) 1932-

PERSONAL: Born April 28, 1932, in Chattanooga, Tenn.; son of Magnolia Jackson; married Mildred Webster, May 28, 1958; children: Antone. *Education:* Talladega College, B.A., 1954; Fisk University, M.A., 1956; attended Columbia University, 1961. *Office:* Department of Afro-American Studies, Oberlin College, Oberlin, Ohio 44074.

CAREER: Writer. Benedict College, Columbia, S.C., instructor in history and sociology, 1957-58; Edward Waters College, Jacksonville, Fla., instructor in sociology, 1958-59; Alabama Agricultural and Mechanical College (now University), Normal, instructor in social sciences, 1959-60; Southern University and Agricultural and Mechanical College, Baton Rouge, La., instructor in sociology, 1960-61; New York State Department of Welfare, New York, N.Y., social worker, 1961-62; currently faculty member at Oberlin College, Oberlin, Ohio.

WRITINGS: The Coming of Chronos to the House of Nightsong: An Epical Narrative of the South (poetry), Interim 1963; *Sex and Racism in America,* Doubleday, 1965 (revised edition published in England as *Sex and Racism,* Deutsch, 1969); *White Papers for White Americans,* Doubleday, 1966; *Coming Together: Black Power, White Hatred, and Sexual Hangups,* Random House, 1971; *Scarecrow* (novel), Doubleday, 1974; (with Joseph Berke) *The Cannabis Experience,* P. Owen, 1974; *Medicine Man* (poetry), Reed, Cannon, 1976. Work anthologized in *Beyond the Blues,* edited by Rosey E. Pool, Hand & Flower Press, 1962, and in other publications. Also author of plays. Contributor to *Negro Digest, Freedomways,* and other periodicals.

SIDELIGHTS: In a review of *White Papers for White Americans,* Brooks Johnson writes in *Negro Digest:* "It is virtually impossible to bring something new to the area of race, but, infrequently, the very gifted see and are able to express the centuried problems with something that approaches creativity because of the sensitivity and forcefulness with which they relate the old truths. Calvin C. Hernton's work is an example of such a process. He has the ability to tell, narrate, and explain, which he does at varying tempos and moods—in the manner of a good, highly polished jazz group. I don't mean to imply that his technique is slick—it isn't. Mr. Hernton is smooth because he is a man who knows his subject matter and has mastered the delicate balance between what observation and honesty dictate and what natural talent makes possible. The product in this case is a book that knows no time."

BIOGRAPHICAL/CRITICAL SOURCES: Saturday Review, February 12, 1966; *Negro Digest,* May 1967.

HERRMANNS, Ralph 1933-

PERSONAL: Born January 31, 1933, in Berlin, Germany; now Swedish citizen; son of Otto (a chief justice) and Edith (Jacoby) Herrmanns. *Education:* University of Uppsala, B.A., 1953. *Religion:* Jewish. *Home:* Braennkyrkagatan 77, Stockholm 117 23, Sweden. *Office address:* Box 10148, Stockholm 100 55, Sweden.

CAREER: Journalist for Swedish newspapers and foreign correspondent, 1953-62; Ediciones Albon Medillin, Colombia (affiliate of Bonnier Group, Stockholm, Sweden), editor-in-chief and publisher, 1962-64; Ahlen & Akerlunds Foerlag (Bonnier Magazine Group), Stockholm, editor-in-chief, 1964-66; served in China for Time-Life Books and Life International, 1966-67; writer, 1967—. *Military service:* Royal Swedish Horse Guards Reserve. *Member:* International P.E.N.; Publicistklubben and Svenska Journalistfoerbundet (both Stockholm). *Awards, honors:* Film on Joan Miro represented Swedish Broadcasting Corp. at film festivals in Cannes, France, Milan, Italy, and Brno, Czechoslovakia, 1970.

WRITINGS: Lee an, Hing och draken, Bonnier, 1961, translation by Annabelle Macmillan published as *Lee Lan Flies the Dragon Kite,* Harcourt, 1963; *Barnen vid Nordpolen,* Bonnier, 1963, translation by Macmillan published as *Children of the North Pole,* Harcourt, 1964; *Bilen Julia,* Bonniers, 1963, translation by Macmillan published as *Our Car Julia,* Harcourt, 1964; *Pojken och floden,* Bonnier, 1964, translation by Joan Tate published as *River Boy: Adventure on the Amazon,* Harcourt, 1965; *Flickan som hade braatom,* Bonnier, 1967; (with Don Almquist) *Den foertrollade laedan,* Bonnier, 1967; (contributor) *Asia: A Natural History,* Random House, 1968; (contributor) *The Cooking of China,* Time-Life 1968; *Den foerskraecklige snoemannen,* Bonnier, 1969, translation published as *In Search of the Abominable Snowman,* Doubleday, 1970; *Pojken som vile maala vaerldens vackraste tavla,* Bonnier, 1970, translation published as *The World's Most Beautiful Painting,* Wheaton, 1972; *Joan Miro: Liljevalchs,* [Stockholm], 1972; *Natten och droemmen: Att maala som Miro,* Bonnier, 1972; *Posters by Miro,* Wahlstroem & Widstrand, 1974; *Carl Gustaf von Rosen* (biography), Wahlstroem & Widstrand, 1975; *The Royal Palace of Stockholm* (translation of *Det levande slottet*), Bonnier, 1978; *The Archipelago of Stockholm,* Askild & Kaernekull, 1980; *Isaac Gruenewald–en fest foer oegat,* Askild & Kaernekull, 1980.

Also author and producer of film on Joan Miro and of radio play on Pablo Picasso, both for Swedish Broadcasting Corp., and of other films for Nordisk Tonefilm. Contributor of chapters to books.

WORK IN PROGRESS: A political novel set in the Middle East; an art book on the Swedish painter Goesta Werner; a film for Swedish television on the painter Ernst Josephson.

AVOCATIONAL INTERESTS: Modern paintings, antique Chinese bronzes, dogs, and horses.

*   *   *

HERSEY, Jean 1902-

PERSONAL: Born September 29, 1902; daughter of John Jay and Mary (Mattocks) McKelvey; married Robert Wilson Hersey, December 5, 1924; children: Joan Carr, Robert Huntington, Timothy Wilson. *Education:* Attended Brearley School. *Religion:* New Thought. *Home address:* Box 45, Crosslands, Kennett Square, Pa. 19348. *Agent:* McIntosh & Otis, Inc., 475 Fifth Ave., New York, N.Y. 10017.

MEMBER: Tryon Garden Club. *Awards, honors:* Asta award for best garden writing of the year, 1962.

WRITINGS: I Like Gardening, Hale, Cushman & Flint, 1941; *Halfway to Heaven: Guatemala Holiday,* Prentice-Hall, 1947; *Garden in Your Window,* Prentice-Hall, 1949; *Carefree Gardening: New and Easier Ways to Have an Abundance of Flowers and Vegetables,* Van Nostrand, 1961; *Wild Flowers to Know and Grow,* Van Nostrand, 1964; *A Sense of Seasons,* Dodd, 1964; *A Woman's Day Book of House Plants,* Simon & Schuster, 1965; *The Shape of a Year,* Scribner, 1967; (with husband, Robert Hersey) *These Rich Years: A Journal of Retirement,* Scribner, 1969; (with R. Hersey) *Cooking with Herbs,* Scribner, 1972, revised edition, 1977; (with R. Hersey) *Growing Herbs Indoors,* Scribner, 1972; (with R. Hersey) *Change in the Wind,* Scribner, 1972; *Woman's Day Book of Wildflowers,* Simon & Schuster, 1976; *Woman's Day Book of Annuals and Perennials,* Simon & Schuster, 1977; *A Widow's Pilgrimage,* Simon & Schuster, 1979; *The Touch of the Earth,* Simon & Schuster, 1981.

Also author of series of booklet-inserts on wild flowers, houseplants, flowering shrubs, and trees, and other subjects, each with two hundred color paintings, introductory article, and identifications for *Woman's Day* magazine. Contributor of several hundred articles to *House and Garden, Flower Grower, House Beautiful,* and other magazines.

AVOCATIONAL INTERESTS: Traveling in Europe, particularly Switzerland; camping in a tent trailer in the North Carolina mountains and on the southern beaches; water color painting.

*   *   *

HIBBS, Douglas A(lbert), Jr. 1944-

PERSONAL: Born July 17, 1944, in Miami Beach, Fla.; son of Douglas Albert and Lillian (Carter) Hibbs; married Giustina Mastrangelo (a teacher), October 31, 1965 (divorced, 1976); married Eva Bernbro, January 12, 1980; children: (first marriage) Christina. *Education:* Southern Connecticut State College, B.A. (with honors), 1966; University of Wisconsin, M.A., 1968, Ph.D., 1972. *Home:* 12 Francis Ave., Cambridge, Mass. 02138. *Office:* Department of Government, Littauer M-35, Harvard University, Cambridge, Mass. 02138.

CAREER: Massachusetts Institute of Technology, Cambridge, instructor, 1970-71, assistant professor, 1971-76, associate professor of political science, 1976-78; Harvard University, Cambridge, professor of government, 1978—. Consultant to John Wiley & Sons, Northwestern University Press, and National Science Foundation. *Member:* American Political Science Association, American Statistical Association, American Economic Association, Econometric Society. *Awards, honors:* Ford Foundation research grant for Center for International Studies, 1971; National Science Foundation research grants, 1972, 1975, 1976, 1977, 1978, 1979, 1980; National Institute of Mental Health research grant, 1974; A.M., Harvard University, 1978; Center for Advanced Study in the Behavioral Sciences fellowship; German Marshall Fund research grant.

WRITINGS: Mass Political Violence: A Cross-National Causal Analysis, Wiley, 1973; (contributor) H. L. Costner, editor, *Sociological Methodology: 1973-1974,* Jossey-Bass, 1974; (contributor) D. Heise, editor, *Sociological Methodology,* Jossey-Bass, 1977; (editor and contributor) *Contemporary Political Economy,* North-Holland, 1980. Contributor of articles to *American Political Science Review, American*

Journal of Political Science, British Journal of Political Science, and *World Politics.* Consultant-reader for journals, including *American Sociological Review, American Political Science Review, Political Methodology, Journal of Conflict Resolution, Journal of Interdisciplinary History,* and *Psychological Bulletin.*

* * *

HIGDON, Hal 1931-

PERSONAL: Born June 17, 1931, in Chicago, Ill.; son of H.J. (an editor) and Mae (O'Leary) Higdon; married Rose Musacchio, April 12, 1958; children: Kevin, David, Laura. *Education:* Carleton College, B.A., 1953. *Home:* 2815 Lake Shore Dr., Michigan City, Ind. 46360. *Agent:* Ben Kamsler, H.N. Swanson, Inc., 8523 West Blvd., Los Angeles, Calif. 90069.

CAREER: Kiwanis Magazine, Chicago, Ill., assistant editor, 1957-59; free-lance magazine writer, 1959—. Partner of travel company, Roadrunner Tours. *Military service:* U.S. Army, 1954-56. *Member:* Society of Magazine Writers, Road Runners Club of America.

WRITINGS: The Union Versus Dr. Mudd, Follett, 1964; *Heroes of the Olympics,* Prentice-Hall, 1965; (editor) *Pro Football, U.S.A.,* Putnam, 1968, abridged edition published as *Inside Pro Football,* Grosset, 1970; *The Horse that Played Center Field,* Holt, 1969; *The Business Healers,* Random House, 1970; *On the Run from Dogs and People,* Regnery, 1971; *Thirty Days in May: The Indy 500,* Putnam, 1971; *Champions of the Tennis Court,* Prentice-Hall, 1971; *The Electronic Olympics,* Holt, 1971; *Finding the Groove,* Putnam, 1973; *The Crime of the Century,* Putnam, 1976; *Fitness After Forty,* World Publishing, 1977; *The Marathoners,* Putnam, 1980. Senior writer, *The Runner.*

SIDELIGHTS: Hal Higdon competes as a long distance runner and was the first American to finish in the 1964 Boston Marathon.

In 1975 and again in 1977 Higdon won gold medals for winning the 3000 meter steeplechase at the World Veterans Games (for runners over forty) in Canada and Sweden. He told *CA:* "One of the ways to become a success is to have your hobby suddenly become a national fad."

* * *

HIGGINS, Rosalyn (Cohen) 1937-
(Rosalyn Cohen)

PERSONAL: Born June 2, 1937, in London, England; daughter of Lewis (a company director) and Fay (Inberg) Cohen; married Terence Langley Higgins (an economist). *Education:* Girton College, Cambridge, B.A. (first class honors), 1958, LL.B. (first class honors), 1959; Yale University, J.S.D., 1962. *Religion:* Jewish. *Home:* 18 Hallgate, Blackheath Park, London S.E.3, England. *Office:* London School of Economics and Political Sciences, University of London, London, England.

CAREER: United Kingdom intern at United Nations, 1958; University of London, London School of Economics and Political Science, London, England, junior fellow in international studies, 1961-63; Royal Institute of International Affairs, London, international lawyer, 1963-74; University of Kent at Canterbury, Canterbury, England, held Chair of International Law, 1978-81; University of London, London School of Economics and Political Science, Chair of International Law, 1981—. Visiting fellow, Brookings Institution, 1960, and London School of Economics, 1974-78. Occa-

sional lecturer. *Member:* International Law Association, American Society of International Law (vice-president), Oxford and Cambridge Club. *Awards, honors:* Commonwealth Fund fellowship to Yale, 1959-61; Rockefeller Foundation award for research on United Nations, 1961-63; annual award, American Society of International Law, 1971; honorary doctorate, University of Paris, 1980.

WRITINGS: The Development of International Law Through the Political Organs of the United Nations, Oxford University Press, 1963; (contributor) Ronald Segal, editor, *Sanctions against South Africa,* Penguin, 1964; (with others) *United Nations Forces: A Legal Study,* Stevens & Sons, 1964, Praeger, 1968; *Conflict of Interests: International Law in a Divided World,* Dufour, 1965; *The Administration of United Kingdom Foreign Policy Through the United Nations,* edited by Gerard J. Mangone, Maxwell School of Citizenship and Public Affairs, Syracuse University, 1966; *South West Africa: The Court's Judgment,* International Commission of Jurists, 1967; (compiler) *United Nations Peacekeeping, 1946-1967: Documents and Commentary,* Oxford University Press, Volume I: *The Middle East,* 1969, Volume II: *Asia,* 1970, Volume III: *Africa,* 1980, Volume IV: *Europe,* 1981. Contributor of articles to *World Today, International Affairs,* and of articles and reviews to yearbooks and journals of law and politics, some under name Rosalyn Cohen.

WORK IN PROGRESS: Procedure under the European Convention on Human Rights.

* * *

HILL, Hamlin (Lewis) 1931-

PERSONAL: Born November 7, 1931, in Houston, Tex.; son of Hamlin Lewis and Marguerite (Courtin) Hill; married Arlette Crawford, December 27, 1952; children: Cynthia, Scott, Sondra, William. *Education:* University of Texas, 1949-51, M.A., 1954; University of Houston, B.A., 1953; University of Chicago, Ph.D., 1959. *Office:* Department of English, University of New Mexico, Albuquerque, N.M. 87131.

CAREER: University of New Mexico, Albuquerque, instructor in English, 1959-61; University of Wyoming, Laramie, assistant professor of English, 1961-63; University of New Mexico, assistant professor, 1963-65, associate professor of English, 1965-68; University of Chicago, Chicago, Ill., professor of English, 1968-75; University of New Mexico, professor of English, 1975—, chairman of department, 1979—. Visiting professor at Stanford University, 1972-73. Summer lecturer at University of Nebraska, 1960, and University of Wyoming, 1968. Visiting lecturer at University of California, Berkeley, spring, 1965; Fulbright lecturer, University of Copenhagen, 1966-67, and University of Wuerzburg, 1980. Seminar director, National Endowment for the Humanities, summers, 1977-80. *Military service:* U.S. Army, 1954-56. *Member:* Modern Language Association of America, American Studies Association, National Council of Teachers of English, American Association of University Professors. *Awards, honors:* Grant-in-aid, American Council of Learned Societies, 1963, 1965, and 1967; Guggenheim fellow, 1971-72.

WRITINGS: Mark Twain's Book Sales, privately printed, c. 1961; (editor with Walter Blair) *The Art of Huckleberry Finn,* Chandler Publishing, 1962, revised edition, 1969; (editor) Mark Twain, *The Adventures of Huckleberry Finn: A Facsimile of the First Edition,* Chandler Publishing, 1962; (editor) Mark Twain, *A Connecticut Yankee in King Arthur's*

Court: A Facsimile of the First Edition, Chandler Publishing, 1963; *Mark Twain and Elisha Bliss*, University of Missouri Press, 1964; (editor) *Mark Twain's Letters to His Publishers, 1867-1894*, University of California Press, 1967; *Mark Twain: God's Fool*, Harper, 1975; (with Walter Blair) *America's Humor from Poor Richard to Doonesbury*, Oxford University Press, 1978. Contributor of articles to professional periodicals.

WORK IN PROGRESS: Second volume of *Mark Twain's Collected Letters*.

BIOGRAPHICAL/CRITICAL SOURCES: Book Week, March 5, 1967; *New Statesman*, June 23, 1967; *New York Times Book Review*, July 30, 1967; *Times Literary Supplement*, August 24, 1967; *South Atlantic Quarterly*, summer, 1968.

* * *

HILL, Kathleen Louise 1917-
(Kay Hill)

PERSONAL: Born April 7, 1917, in Halifax, Nova Scotia; daughter of Henry and Margaret Elizabeth (Ross) Hill. *Education:* Attended schools in Halifax, Nova Scotia. *Religion:* Protestant. *Residence:* Ketch Harbour, Nova Scotia, Canada.

CAREER: Secretary and court reporter before becoming full-time free-lance writer, 1957—. *Member:* Association of Canadian Television and Radio Artists, Writers Federation of Nova Scotia. *Awards, honors:* "Best Juvenile Book in Canada" award, Canadian Library Association, 1969, for *And Tommorrow the Stars;* Nickey Metcalfe Award, 1971.

WRITINGS—Under name Kay Hill: Glooscap and His Magic: Legends of the Wabanaki Indians, Dodd, 1963; *Badger, the Mischief Maker*, Dodd, 1965; *And Tomorrow the Stars: The Story of John Cabot*, Dodd, 1968; *More Glooscap Stories: Legends of the Wabanaki Indians*, Dodd, 1970; *Joe Howe: The Man Who Was Nova Scotia*, McClelland & Stewart, 1980.

Plays: *Three to Get Married* (three-act comedy), Samuel French, 1964; *Cobbler: Stick to Thy Last* (one-act play; produced in Ottawa, Canada at the National Arts Centre, July 5, 1969), Dramatic Publishing, 1967; "The Lady in Black" (television play), 1969.

Work represented in numerous anthologies, including: *Beyond the Footlights*, edited by Hugh Duncan McKellar, Macmillan, 1963; *Encounter*, Methuen, 1973; *Transitions II*, Methuen, 1978. Children's stories and plays have also been represented in numerous anthologies. Also author of series of thirteen television dramas, "Byng's Boarders," 1956, and of series of twenty-six television dramas, "Indian Legends." Also author of numerous radio and television plays. Contributor of articles, short stories, serials, and documentaries for numerous periodicals.

WORK IN PROGRESS: A children's book on the modern Indian, for Dodd.

SIDELIGHTS: Kathleen Louise Hill told *CA:* "I've always liked writing, especially fiction, and had pieces published in Sunday school and school magazines to begin with. For years I wrote spasmodically, selling nothing, then I found a market in radio and later in television, and one television show for children "Indian Legends" led to the writing of *Glooscap and His Magic*.

"When I haven't been writing, I've been an office worker, private secretary and court stenographer in various busi-

nesses—oil company, trust company, rubber manufacturer, piblic library and an historic site. Whenever I could, I gave up my office job and took a few months or a year off just to write. When the money ran out, I went back to stenography. Gradually I was able to write full time.

"I write to earn my living in the way that I find most enjoyable—and I write to communicate, to make people laugh and cry (I hope) especially children. I use everyday experiences as well as history, present and past, for ideas and background. I read philosophy sometimes to get myself started on something—it works for some reason. I find that unless I am moved, even a little, by what I am writing, I cannot move others—so I wait for that little jolt in the interior that says 'Yes, this is it—keep on.'"

AVOCATIONAL INTERESTS: Oil painting, Scottish country dancing.

* * *

HILLIER, Jack R(onald) 1912-

PERSONAL: Born August 29, 1912, in London, England; son of Charles Edward (a civil servant) and Minnie (Davies) Hillier; married Mary Palmer, May 28, 1938; children: Bevis, Mary Alison. *Education:* Attended schools in London, England. *Home:* 27 Whitepost Hill, Redhill, Surrey, England.

CAREER: Wood-engraver and water-colorist; writer. *Military service:* Royal Air Force, 1940-45; became flight sergeant. *Member:* Ukiyo-e Society of America, Society for Protection of Ancient Buildings.

WRITINGS: Old Surrey Water-Mills, Skeffington, 1951; *Japanese Masters of the Colour-Print*, Phaidon, 1954; *Hokusai*, Phaidon, 1955; *Landscape Prints of Old Japan* (Grabhorn Collection), Book Club of California, 1960; *The Japanese Print: A New Approach*, G. Bell, 1960, reprinted, Tuttle, 1975; *Utamaro: Color Prints and Drawings*, Phaidon, 1961, 2nd edition, Dutton, 1979; *Japanese Drawings*, Shorewood, 1965; *Hokusai Drawings*, Phaidon, 1966; *Japanese Colour Prints*, Phaidon, 1966, New York Graphic Society, 1967.

Catalogue of the Gale Collection of Japanese Paintings and Prints, two volumes, Minneapolis Institute of Arts, 1970; *Suzuki Harunobu*, Philadelphia Museum of Art, 1970; *The Uninhibited Brush: Japanese Art in the Shijo Style*, Hugh Moss, 1974; *Japanese Prints and Drawings from the Vever Collection*, three volumes, Sotheby Parke Bernet, 1977; *The Art of Hokusai in Book Illustration*, University of California Press, 1980; *Japanese Drawings of the Eighteenth and Nineteenth Centuries*, International Exhibitions Foundation, 1980; *Exhibition Catalogue of the Hillier Collection*, British Museum Publications, 1980. Also author of *Catalogue of the Harari Collection of Japanese Paintings and Drawings*. Contributor to *Connoisseur, Oriental Art*, and other periodicals.

AVOCATIONAL INTERESTS: Gardening, music, other arts.

* * *

HINES, Robert Stephan 1926-

PERSONAL: Born September 30, 1926, in Kingston, N.Y.; son of Harry Jacob (a businessman) and Gertrude (Payne) Hines; married Germaine Marie Lahiff, December 9, 1950. *Education:* Juilliard School of Music, B.S., 1952; University of Michigan, M. Mus., 1956. *Religion:* Lutheran. *Home:* 55 University Ave., Honolulu, Hawaii 96822.

CAREER: Choral director of General Motors Corp. and director of music, Our Saviour Lutheran Church, Detroit, Mich., 1952-57; Southern Illinois University at Carbondale, assistant professor of music, 1957-61; Wichita State University, Wichita, Kan., 1961-71, began as associate professor, became professor of music and chairman of choral-voice department; University of Miami, Miami, Fla., visiting professor of music, 1971-72; University of Hawaii at Manoa, Honolulu, professor of music, 1972-80, chairman of department, 1980—. Visiting professor, University of Michigan, summer, 1960; visiting lecturer, Northwestern University, summer, 1960, and University of Texas, summer, 1968. *Military service:* U.S. Navy, Construction Battalion, 1944-46. *Member:* American Choral Directors Association (life member), American Association of University Professors, American Federation of Musicians, National Education Association, Music Teachers National Association, Phi Kappa Lambda.

WRITINGS: (Editor) *The Composer's Point of View: Essays on Twentieth-Century Choral Music by Those Who Wrote It,* University of Oklahoma Press, 1963; (co-editor) *Selected Lists of Choral Music,* Music Educators National Conference, 1968; (editor) *The Orchestral Composer's Point of View: Essays on Twentieth-Century Music by Those Who Wrote It,* University of Oklahoma Press, 1970; *Singer's Manual of Latin Diction and Phonetics,* Schirmer Books, 1975; (co-author) *Ear Training and Sight-Singing,* two volumes, Schirmer Books, 1979. Editor or arranger of over 125 choral works for Belwin-Mills, Concordia, Elkan-Vogel, Lawson-Gould, Marks, G. Schirmer, and Schmitt, Hall & McCreary. Contributor to *Choral Journal.*

WORK IN PROGRESS: The Craft of Choral Composition.

SIDELIGHTS: Robert Hines told *CA:* "Except for the early years, my entire life in the art of music has been in the role of an educator-performer. Whatever books and choral editions or arrangements I have produced in the past twenty years have been a direct result of student-classroom experiences wherein I saw a hole in the fabric of scholarship or music and tried to plug it."

AVOCATIONAL INTERESTS: Collecting art, investments, travel.

BIOGRAPHICAL/CRITICAL SOURCES: Antiquarian Bookman, yearbook, 1970.

*   *   *

HINMAN, Charlton (Joseph Kadio)   1911-1977

PERSONAL: Born February 10, 1911, in Fort Collins, Colo.; died March 16, 1977, in Bethesda, Md.; son of Claude H. and Ethel (Charlton) Hinman; married Jane van Meter, November 8, 1936 (divorced September, 1966); married Myra Mahlow, February 22, 1968; children: (first marriage) Barbara. *Education:* Cornell University, B.A., 1933; Oxford University, B.A., 1936, M.A., 1939; University of Virginia, Ph.D., 1941. *Politics:* Democrat. *Home:* 1020 Crestline Dr., Lawrence, Kan. *Office:* Department of English, University of Kansas, Lawrence, Kan.

CAREER: Folger Shakespeare Library, Washington, D.C., research fellow, 1941-42, honorary fellow, 1953-59; Johns Hopkins University, Baltimore, Md., assistant professor, 1946-50; University of Kansas, Lawrence, professor of English, 1960-63, University Distinguished Professor, 1963-77. *Military service:* U.S. Navy, 1942-46, 1950-52; became commander. *Member:* Modern Language Association of America, Shakespeare Association of America, Malone So-

ciety (Oxford), Bibliographical Society (London), Bibliographical Society of the University of Virginia. *Awards, honors:* Rhodes scholar; Guggenheim fellow, 1954-55; Bollingen research fellow, 1956-58; Byron Caldwell Smith award for outstanding scholarly writing, 1963.

WRITINGS: The Printing and Proofreading of the First Folio of Shakespeare, two volumes, Oxford University Press, 1963; *The First Folio of Shakespeare,* Norton, 1968; (with Fredson Bowers) *Two Lectures on Editing: Shakespeare and Hawthorne,* Ohio State University Press, 1969.

Editor; all written by William Shakespeare: *Timon of Athens,* Penguin, 1964; *Richard II,* Shakespeare Quarto Facsimile Series, 1966; *Henry IV,* Shakespeare Quarto Facsimile Series, 1966; *Much Ado about Nothing,* Clarendon Press, 1971; *Othello,* Oxford University Press, 1975. Contributor to professional journals.

WORK IN PROGRESS: Editions of other Shakespeare plays; continuing research on textual programs in Elizabethan drama.

SIDELIGHTS: Charlton Hinman was the inventor of the Hinman Collating Machine, an optical instrument for making detailed comparisons of theoretically identical documents. It is used for finding variants in literary texts and for detecting fakes and forgeries. About twenty-five such instruments may be found in the United States in various university libraries, including Harvard University, the University of Virginia, Yale University, the University of Illinois, and the University of Kansas. One machine is in the British Museum in London.

BIOGRAPHICAL/CRITICAL SOURCES: Sunday Telegraph, London, England, May 26, 1963; *Newsweek,* January 6, 1969; *New York Times,* March 18, 1977; *Publishers Weekly,* March 28, 1977.†

*   *   *

HOBSBAUM, Philip (Dennis)   1932-

PERSONAL: Born June 29, 1932, in London, England; son of Joseph (an engineer) and Rachel (Sapera) Hobsbaum; married Hannah Kelly, August 7, 1957 (marriage dissolved, 1968); married Rosemary Phillips Singleton, July 20, 1976. *Education:* Downing College, Cambridge, B.A., 1955, M.A., 1960; Royal Academy of Music, licentiate, 1956; Guildhall School of Music, licentiate, 1957; research at University of Sheffield, 1959, Ph.D., 1968. *Home:* 156 Wilton St., Glasgow 920, Scotland. *Office:* Department of English, University of Glasgow, Glasgow 912, Scotland.

CAREER: Writer, 1955—; part-time lecturer and teacher, 1955-59; Queen's University, Belfast, Northern Ireland, lecturer in English, 1962-66; University of Glasgow, Glasgow, Scotland, lecturer in English, 1966-72, senior lecturer, 1972-79, reader, 1979—. Member of Northern Ireland Civic Theatre Committee, 1963-64. *Member:* Association of University Teachers, BBC Club (Glasgow).

WRITINGS: (Editor with Edward Lucie-Smith) *A Group Anthology,* Oxford University Press, 1963; *The Place's Fault, and Other Poems,* St. Martin's, 1964; *Snapshots,* Festival Publications, 1965; *In Retreat, and Other Poems,* Macmillan, 1966, Dufour, 1968; *Coming Out Fighting* (poems), Dufour, 1969; *Ten Elizabethan Poets,* Longmans, Green, 1969; *A Theory of Communication,* Macmillan, 1969, published in America as *A Theory of Criticism,* Indiana University Press, 1970; *A Readers' Guide to Charles Dickens,* Thames & Hudson, 1972; *Women and Animals,* Macmillan, 1972; *Tradition and Experiment in English Poetry,* Macmillan, 1979; *A Reader's Guide to D. H. Lawrence,* Thames & Hudson, 1981.

Work represented in several anthologies, including *Happenings,* edited by Maurice Wollman and David Grugeon, Harrap, 1964, *Young Commonwealth Poets,* edited by Peter L. Brent, Heinemann, 1965, and *The Pattern of Poetry,* edited by William K. Seymour and John Smith, F. Watts, 1967. Contributor to *Listener, Spectator, Encounter, Scottish International, Transatlantic Review, Encore, The Review, Times Literary Supplement, Twentieth Century, Outposts, Poetry Review, New York Times, London Magazine, Ambit, Priapus,* and *Texas Quarterly.* Editor, *Delta,* 1954-55; co-editor, *Poetry from Sheffield,* 1959-61; member of editorial board, *Northern Review,* 1964-66.

WORK IN PROGRESS: An introduction to criticism; poems for several voices.

SIDELIGHTS: Alan Brownjohn of the *New Statesman* explains in his review of *Coming Out Fighting* that "Hobsbaum writes with . . . honesty, but the confessional rawness of [this book] is pretty difficult to take; and one hopes that it is only an interim stage in an enterprising poet's progress. . . . The content of most of the love poems is curiously untender and crude, the manner brutally banal. . . . He is rather better (though much too indulgently anecdotal) when he is being stridently rancorous and hearty in the pub verses."

Encounter critic Colin Falck writes of Hobsbaum's *In Retreat, and Other Poems* that "the trouble with Hobsbaum's poetry is not that he relies on the abstractions of the educated mind but that he exercises them always on the same dismal subject-matter—himself and the latest signs of his decrepitude. . . . His latest book has some satisfyingly angry moments. The best are his satirisings of academia . . . focusing on that institution's contempt for human spontaneity and on the warped energy which can spring from it with a kind of Lawrentian hatred. . . . Hobsbaum's worst fault, apart from his obviousness . . . is a self-indulgent need to remind us that his own sensitivity really puts him beyond all this spiritual squalor when that is precisely what it doesn't seem to have done. He writes like a man who knows he has lost, but after so much concentrated self-pity the reader is unlikely to believe that he ever tried very hard in the first place."

Hobsbaum founded "The Group," a creative writing seminar in 1955, which has since become a movement in contemporary poetry. He appears regularly on British Broadcasting Corp. "Third Programme."

AVOCATIONAL INTERESTS: Walking, music, theatre, arguing, and cooking.

BIOGRAPHICAL/CRITICAL SOURCES: Twentieth Century, June, 1960; G. S. Fraser, *The Writer and the Modern World,* Penguin, 1964; *Encounter,* March, 1967; *Kenyon Review,* Volume 30, number 5, 1968; *New Statesman,* April 25, 1969, September 18, 1970; *Poetry,* July, 1969; *Times Literary Supplement,* July 24, 1969, October 20, 1972; *Hudson Review,* summer, 1972; *Books and Bookmen,* December, 1972; *Review of English Studies,* February, 1973.

*   *   *

HOBSBAWM, Eric J(ohn Ernest) 1917-
(Francis Newton)

PERSONAL: Born June 9, 1917, in Alexandria, Egypt; son of Leopold Percy and Nelly (Gruen) Hobsbawm; married Marlene Schwarz; children: Andrew John, Julia Nathalie. *Education:* Cambridge University, B.A., 1939, M.A., 1943,

Ph.D., 1951. *Office:* Department of History, Birkbeck College, University of London, London W.C.1, England.

CAREER: Cambridge University, King's College, Cambridge, England, fellow in history, 1949-55; University of London, Birkbeck College, London, England, lecturer in history, 1947-59, reader in history, 1959-70, professor of economic and social history, 1970—. Andrew D. White Professor-at-Large, Cornell University, 1976—. Honorary fellow, King's College, Cambridge University, 1973—. *Military service:* British Army, 1940-46; became sergeant. *Member:* Economic History Society (council, 1951—), Society for the Study of Labour History (chairman, 1966-72), British Academy (fellow, 1976—), American Academy of Arts and Sciences (honorary foreign member), Hungarian Academy of Sciences. *Awards, honors:* D. Phil. from University of Stockholm, 1970; D.C.L. from University of Chicago, 1976.

WRITINGS: (Editor) *Labour's Turning Point, 1880-1900,* Lawrence & Wishart, 1948; *Social Bandits and Primitive Rebels,* Free Press, 1959 (published in England as *Primitive Rebels,* Manchester University Press, 1959); (under pseudonym Francis Newton) *The Jazz Scene,* MacGibbon & Kee, 1959, Monthly Review Press, 1960.

The Age of Revolution, 1789-1848, World Publishing, 1962, revised edition, 1977; *Labouring Man,* Weidenfeld & Nicolson, 1964, Basic Books, 1965; (author of introduction) Karl Marx, *Pre-Capitalist Economic Formations,* Lawrence & Wishart, 1964; *Industry and Empire: The Making of Modern English Society,* Pantheon, 1968 (published in England as *Industry and Empire: An Economic History of Britain since 1750,* Weidenfeld & Nicolson, 1968); (with George F. E. Rude) *Captain Swing,* Lawrence & Wishart, 1969, Norton, 1975; *Bandits,* Delacorte, 1969; *Revolutinaries,* Pantheon, 1973; *The Age of Capital, 1848-1875,* Scribner, 1975; (with Giorgio Napolitano) *En torno a los origenes de la revolucion industrial,* Siglo, 1971, translation published as *Italian Road to Socialism,* Lawrence Hill, 1977. Contributor to *New Statesman, Times Literary Supplement, Economic History Review, Past and Present,* and other professional and general journals.

SIDELIGHTS: Eric Hobsbawm has long been considered one of the leading European experts on the history of working classes. "Hobsbawm is a most accomplished historian," A.J.P. Taylor writes in the *Observer Review.* Taylor feels that "as an historian of economic and social developments [Hobsbawm] has two special gifts. He has taken to heart Lenin's dictum's 'patiently explain.' At each stage of his narrative he seeks to provide full and precise explanation for what happened. . . . Hobsbawm's other virtue is to be always aware of the British people. Most historians, by a sort of occupational disease, are interested only in the upper classes and assume that they themselves would have been numbered among the privileged if they had lived a century or two ago—a most unlikely assumption. Mr. Hobsbawm places his loyalty firmly on the other side of the barricades."

Asa Briggs cites in *Book World* a reason why Hobsbawm's approach is appealing to many readers of history. Briggs writes in his review of *Captain Swing* that Hobsbawm and his co-author George Rude "ask different questions and, as Marxists, they give different answers. They are less concerned with literary evidence, more concerned with seeking to relate economic and social structure to the pattern of agitation."

Agreeing with Briggs, *New Statesman* reviewer James Joll explains that "Hobsbawm writes extremely well: his description of the lot of the proletariat has an eloquence worthy of Marx himself. . . . Hobsbawm is very successful in retaining a world-wide perspective while necessarily concentrating on conditions in Europe, the cradle of the middle class and of capitalism. . . . It is exceptional to read a work of general history which it is hard to put down."

AVOCATIONAL INTERESTS: Jazz, urban culture.

BIOGRAPHICAL/CRITICAL SOURCES: Observer Review, May 5, 1968; *Book World,* May 4, 1969; *Economist,* December 27, 1969; *New Statesman,* November 21, 1975.

*   *   *

HODGE, Jane Aiken   1917-

PERSONAL: Born December 4, 1917, in Watertown, Mass.; daughter of Conrad (the poet) and Jessie (McDonald) Aiken; married Alan Hodge (editor of *History Today*), January 3, 1948 (died, 1979); children: Jessica Mary, Joanna Margaret Marrack. *Education:* Somerville College, Oxford, B.A. (with honors), 1938; Radcliffe College, A.M., 1939. *Politics:* Democrat. *Home:* 23 Eastport Lane, Lewes, East Sussex BN7 1TL, England. *Agent:* Harold Ober Associates, 40 East 49th St., New York, N.Y. 10017.

CAREER: In government service, Washington, D.C., 1941-44; Time, Inc., New York, N.Y., researcher, 1944-47; *Life,* researcher in London, England, 1947-48; novelist. *Member:* Authors League of America, Society of Authors.

WRITINGS—Novels; all published by Doubleday: *Maulever Hall,* 1964; *The Adventurers,* 1965; *Watch the Wall, My Darling,* 1966; *Here Comes a Candle,* 1967; *The Winding Stair,* 1968; *Marry in Haste,* 1970; *Greek Wedding,* 1970; *Savannah Purchase,* 1971.

All published by Coward, except as indicated: *Strangers in Company,* 1973; *Shadow of a Lady,* 1974; *One Way to Venice,* 1975; *Rebel Heiress,* 1975; *Runaway Bride,* Fawcett, 1976; *Judas Flowering,* 1976; *Red Sky at Night,* 1978; *Last Act,* 1979. Also author of nonfiction work, *The Double Life of Jane Austen,* Coward, 1972.

SIDELIGHTS: In an article for *Writer,* Jane Aiken Hodge explains her technique and philosophy on the writing of historical novels. She writes: "Historical novels are like icebergs. There is (or should be) more to them than meets the eye. A dear friend, and eminent literary agent, once told me that the secret of success was to do a vast amount of research, and then let practically none of it show. I think this is very sound advice to the beginner in the field, or to anyone else, for that matter. The reader does not want to be bothered with learned disquisitions on the customs or events of the period in which the story is set, but he must have confidence that you, the author, know all about them. And the only way to achieve this, is, quite simply, to do so. Then you can slide in the casual little detail that makes for conviction, and it will work."

Hodge continues to describe her feelings on the subject in *Books and Bookmen:* "I write historical novels, where there is room for characters to breathe and live, and change the story if necessary. I once had a hero turn villain halfway through a book, though it is only fair to add that it was never published. But it was fun while it lasted. Historical novels have all kinds of advantages. First, they free one, completely, from the insidious snares of the first person. People ask me, from time to time, when I am going to write a modern novel, and I usually answer, 'Never'. A more truthful reply would be that I wrote one years ago, and learned my lesson. The personal would keep breaking through, and I disliked the result very much. I then moved, logically, to the detec-

tive story; discovered that, for me, it too had its limitations; and retired, with a contented sigh, into the early 19th century, where I intend to stay."

BIOGRAPHICAL/CRITICAL SOURCES: Books and Bookmen, June, 1969; *The Writer,* June, 1972.

*   *   *

HODSON, Henry V(incent)   1906-

PERSONAL: Born May 12, 1906; son of Thomas Callan and Kathleen (Manly) Hodson; married Margaret Elizabeth Honey, March 28, 1933; children: Nicholas Jeremy, Anthony Edward, Daniel Houghton, Henry Charles. *Education:* Balliol College, Oxford, B.A., 1928, M.A., 1934. *Religion:* Anglican. *Home:* 23, Cadogan Lane, London SW1X 9DP, England. *Office: Annual Register of World Events,* 18 Northumberland Ave., London WC2N 5BJ, England.

CAREER: British Economic Advisory Council, London, England, staff member, 1930-31; *Round Table,* London, assistant editor, 1931-34, editor, 1934-39; British Ministry of Information, London, director of Empire Division, 1939-41; Government of India, New Delhi and Simla, constitutional adviser to viceroy, 1941-42; British Ministry of Production, London, principal assistant secretary, 1942-45; *Sunday Times,* London, assistant editor, 1945-50, editor, 1950-61; Ditchley Foundation, Oxford, England, provost, 1961-71; Hodson Consultants, London, partner, 1971—; *Annual Register of World Events,* London, editor, 1973—. Fellow of All Souls College, Oxford University, 1928-35. Mercer Company of City of London, warden, 1962-64, master, 1964-65. Governor of Royal Shakespeare Theatre, City University, and Abingdon School. *Member:* Royal Statistical Society (fellow), Royal Institute of International Affairs (member of council, 1942-50), Royal Commonwealth Society, Society of Authors, Institute of Journalists (fellow).

WRITINGS: Economics of a Changing World, Faber, 1933; (with Thomas Cook and B. K. Long) *The Empire in the World,* Oxford University Press, 1937; *Slump and Recovery, 1929-1937,* Oxford University Press, 1938; (editor) *The British Commonwealth and the Future,* Oxford University Press, 1939; *Twentieth-Century Empire,* Faber, 1948; *The Anatomy of Anglo-American Relations,* Ditchley Foundation, 1962; *Problems in Anglo-American Relations,* Ditchley Foundation, 1963; *The Great Divide: Britain, India, Pakistan,* Hutchinson, 1971; *The Diseconomics of Growth,* Angus & Robertson, 1972. British advisory editor, *Encyclopedia Americana.* Contributor to *Sunday Times,* and other periodicals. Consultant editor, *International Foundation Directory* and *Who's Who in Business.*

WORK IN PROGRESS: An autobiography.

*   *   *

HOFFMANN, Banesh   1906-

PERSONAL: Born September 6, 1906, in Richmond, Surrey, England; son of Maurice and Leah (Brozel) Hoffmann; married Doris Marjorie Goodday, July 10, 1938; children: Laurence David, Deborah Ann. *Education:* Oxford University, B.A. (first class honours), 1929; Princeton University, Ph.D., 1932. *Home:* 43-17 169th St., Flushing, N.Y. 11358. *Office:* Queens College of the City University of New York, Flushing, N.Y. 11367.

CAREER: University of Rochester, Rochester, N.Y., research associate, 1932-35; Institute for Advanced Study, Princeton, N.J., member, 1935-37, 1947-48; Queens College of the City University of New York, Flushing, N.Y., instructor, 1937-40, assistant professor, 1941-48, associate professor, 1949-52, professor of mathematics, 1953-77, professor emeritus, 1977—. Visiting professor, University of London, 1959. Research associate, Harvard University, 1966-67. Engineer, Federal Telegraph and Telephone Laboratory, World War II. Former consultant, Westinghouse Science Talent Search and National Consortium on Testing. Has appeared on numerous radio and television programs. Lecturer. *Member:* American Physical Society (fellow), American Mathematical Society, American Association for the Advancement of Science (fellow), National Energy Foundation (member of advisory council), New York Academy of Sciences, Baker Street Irregulars. *Awards, honors:* Distinguished Teacher of the Year, Queens College of the City University of New York Alumni Association, 1963; Gravity Research Foundation prize ($1,000), 1964, for essay "Negative Mass as a Gravitational Source of Energy in the Quasi-Stellar Radio Sources"; science writing award, American Institute of Physics and U.S. Steel Foundation, 1973, for *Albert Einstein: Creator and Rebel.*

WRITINGS: The Strange Story of the Quantum, Harper, 1947, 2nd edition, Dover, 1959; *About Vectors,* Prentice-Hall, 1966; *The Tyranny of Testing,* Crowell, 1962; (editor) *Perspectives in Geometry and Relativity,* Indiana University Press, 1966; (translator from the French) O. Costa de Beauregard, *Precis of Special Relativity,* Academic Press, 1966; (with Helen Dukas) *Albert Einstein: Creator and Rebel,* Viking, 1972; (with Dukas) *Albert Einstein: The Human Side,* Princton University Press, 1979. Co-author with Einstein and L. Infeld of a research paper on the theory of relativity. Contributor to technical journals, and to *American Scholar, American Scientist, National Observer, Baker Street Journal, London Mystery Magazine,* and other periodicals. Member of editorial advisory board, *The Writings of Albert Einstein.* Former member of editorial board, *Journal of Mathematics and Mechanics.*

WORK IN PROGRESS: Relativity and Its Roots.

SIDELIGHTS: Thomas Lask writes in the *New York Times* of Banesh Hoffmann's book *Albert Einstein: Creator and Rebel* that "this new life of Einstein concentrates on that aspect of Einstein that made him renowned: the theoretical physicist. Unlike so many other authors who neglect the scientist for Einstein the quaint character or the involved pacifist or the victim of Nazism, Hoffmann and his collaborator, Helen Dukas, Einstein's former secretary, write about the originality of his thought, his contribution to our conception of the universe, his place in world science."

Lask continues his review by explaining that Hoffmann "is especially successful in conveying what it is like to rethink one's view of the universe and what it means to have that fresh view confirmed. One can feel, almost share, the excitement and deep satisfaction that must have come to Einstein, Sir Arthur Eddington and those who worked with him when the results of the 1919 eclipse of the sun confirmed Einstein's prediction of the perihelion of Mercury. It is breathtaking to think that an idea so vast and so remote could prove out so accurately in fact."

A critic for *Saturday Review* remarks that Albert Einstein's life "is a story that has been told before, of course, but rarely with such warmth and undisguised respect. And in the end Hoffmann's technique proves its worth: By taking us step by step through the intricacies of Einstein's work, Hoffmann gives us a far more illuminating portrait of the man than any catalogue of residence changes and domestic quarrels could."

Library Journal reviewer Laurie Tynan writes of Hoffmann's second Einstein book, *Albert Einstein: The Human Side,* that "this modest volume illuminated Einstein's character rather than his scientific theories. Einstein received numerous fan letters from young and old and earnest requests from journalists to explain scientific and personal views. His replies thoughtfully expound on science, morality, religion, Zionism, Nazism, music, and fame."

AVOCATIONAL INTERESTS: Playing the piano.

BIOGRAPHICAL/CRITICAL SOURCES: Saturday Review, October 28, 1972; *New York Times,* November 4, 1972; *Library Journal,* March 15, 1979.

*   *   *

HOLBROOK, David (Kenneth)   1923-

PERSONAL: Born January 9, 1923, in Norwich, Norfolk, England; son of Kenneth Redvers and Elsie (Grimmer) Holbrook; married Margot Davies-Jones, April 23, 1949; children: Susan Magdalen, Kate Cressida, Jonathan Benedict, Thomas Simeon David. *Education:* Downing College, Cambridge, B.A., 1947, M.A., 1952. *Politics:* "Existentialist, follower of Polanyi." *Religion:* Agnostic. *Home:* Denmore Lodge, Brunswick Gardens, Cambridge CBJ 8DQ, England.

CAREER: Bureau of Current Affairs, London, England, assistant editor, 1947-51; Workers' Educational Association, East Anglia, England, tutor, 1951-54; Cambridgeshire Village College, Bassingbourn, England, tutor, 1954-61; Cambridge University, King's College, Cambridge, England, fellow, 1961-65. Author, poet, and critic. Consultant on National Defense Education Act English programs in United States, 1966. *Military service:* British Army, Tank Regiment, 1942-45; served in Normandy invasion; became lieutenant. *Awards, honors:* First writer to receive fellowship from Cambridge University Press (in collaboration with King's College) to write poetry and educational books 1961-65; Leverhulme senior research fellowship, 1965; Arts Council Writer's grants, 1970, 1976, and 1979.

WRITINGS: English for Maturity, Cambridge University Press, 1961, 2nd edition, 1967; *Imaginings* (poems; Poetry Book Society choice), Putnam, 1961; *Lights in the Sky* (short stories), Putnam, 1962; *Llareggub Revisited: Dylan Thomas and the State of Modern Poetry* (criticism), Bowes, 1962, published as *Dylan Thomas and Poetic Dissociation,* with an introduction by Harry T. Moore, Southern Illinois University Press, 1964; *Against the Cruel Frost* (poems), Putnam, 1963; *The Secret Places* (on education), preface by Naomi Mitchison, Methuen, 1964, University of Alabama Press, 1965; (with Raymond O'Malley and others) *English in the C.S.E.,* Cambridge University Press, 1964; *English for the Rejected,* Cambridge University Press, 1964; *The Quest for Love* (criticism), Methuen, 1964, University of Alabama Press, 1965.

Flesh Wounds (novel), Methuen, 1966; *The Exploring Word: Creative Disciplines in the Education of Teachers of English,* Cambridge University Press, 1967; *Object Relations* (poems), Methuen, 1967; *Children's Writing: Problems of Sincerity and Realism,* Cambridge University Press, 1967; (author of introduction) T. F. Powys, *Mr. Weston's Good Wine,* Heinemann, 1967; *Old World, New World* (poems), Rapp & Whiting, 1969.

Human Hope and the Death Instinct, Pergamon, 1971; *Sex and Dehumanization,* Pitman, 1972; *The Masks of Hate,* Pergamon, 1972; *Dylan Thomas: The Code of Night,* Athlone Press, 1972; *The Pseudo-Revolution,* Tom Stacey, 1972;

English in Australia Now, Cambridge University Press, 1972; *Gustav Mahler and the Courage to Be,* Vision Press, 1975; *Sylvia Plath: Poetry and Existence,* Athlone Press, 1976; (co-author) *The Apple Tree,* Cambridge University Press, 1976; *Lost Bearings in English Poetry,* Barnes & Noble, 1977; *Education, Nihilism and Survival,* Darton, Longman & Todd, 1977; *A Chance of a Lifetime* (poems), Anvil Press, 1978; *Moments in Italy,* Keepsake Press, 1978; *A Play of Passion* (novel), W. H. Allen, 1978; *English for Meaning,* National Foundation for Educational Research, 1980; *Selected Poems,* Anvil Press, 1980.

Compilations; published by Cambridge University Press, except as indicated: *Children's Games,* Gordon Fraser, 1957; *Iron, Honey, Gold* (verse anthology), 1961, published in four volumes under same title, 1965; *People and Diamonds* (short story anthology), 1962; *Thieves and Angels* (anthology of dramatic pieces), 1963; *Visions of Life* (prose anthology), 1964; *I've Got to Use Words* (four texts in creative English for less able children), 1966; (with Elizabeth Poston) *The Cambridge Hymnal,* 1966; *Plucking the Rushes: An Anthology of Chinese Poetry,* translated by Arthur Waley, Heinemann, 1968; *The Case against Pornography,* Open Court, 1972; *The Honey of Man,* Thomas Nelson, 1973.

Contributor: Denys Thompson, editor, *Discrimination and Popular Culture,* Pelican, 1965; Thomas Blackburn, editor, *Understanding Poetry,* Methuen, 1966; Edward Blishen, *The World of the Child,* Hamlyn, 1966.

Other: "The Borderline" (opera for children), music by Wilfred Mellers, produced in London, 1959; (editor) "The Broadstream Books" series (shortened editions of literary works for school use, with first series including *Oliver Twist, My Childhood, Roughing It,* and *Pudd'nhead Wilson*), Cambridge University Press, 1965; (with John Joubert) *The Quarry* (opera for children), Novello, 1967. Also has written librettos for a dramatic cantata and play-in-music, and songs. Contributor to *Penguin New Poets No. 4, Pelican Guide to English Literature,* and numerous journals and newspapers. Member of editorial board, *New Universities Quarterly.*

WORK IN PROGRESS: A number of novels, two about childhood; a critical study of the "Narnia" books of C. S. Lewis; and introduction to phenomenology and existenitalism and a collection of love poems.

SIDELIGHTS: David Holbrook wrote *CA:* "All my writing is of a piece. In poetry and novels I try to make some kind of sense of my existence, and I have deliberately chosen to write about normal quotidian life, feeling that if we can't find meaning there, there is no hope. My educational writings are an attempt to uphold the disciplines of the imagination and of being in a utilitarian world. My critical studies try to show that there is a true way to tackle the problems of life, in the search to realise the potentialities of the self; but also false solutions based on hate, and the positives of the false self. . . . I believe the need to symbolise is a primary need, and is everywhere neglected and abused. Alas, the penalties for pointing out the falsities of contemporary culture are severe—one is ignored, or one's books are not reviewed. English culture is too much in the hands of fashionable nihilists and moral inversionists, and this new establishment shows itself bigoted and censorious. However, the only real answer is to patiently go on with one's creative work in hope, and in this I am grateful to the few readers who appreciate what one is trying to do."

AVOCATIONAL INTERESTS: Painting, music.

BIOGRAPHICAL/CRITICAL SOURCES: Guardian, March 28, 1963; *Time,* August 14, 1964; *Times Literary Supplement,* April 6, 1967, May 25, 1967, June 22, 1967, July 13, 1967; *Observer,* May 14, 1967; *Punch,* July 5, 1967; *Listener,* July 6, 1967; *Journal of Moral Education,* February, 1973; *Human World,* May, 1973; *Books and Bookmen,* September, 1973.

*   *   *

HOLLES, Robert Owen   1926-

PERSONAL: Born October 11, 1926, in London, England; married, 1952; children: Christopher, John, Anneliese. *Education:* Attended grammar school in Marlow, Buckinghamshire, England. *Religion:* Church of England. *Home:* Ware House, Stebbing, Essex, England. *Agent:* Oliver G. Swan, Paul R. Reynolds, Inc., 12 East 41st St., New York, N.Y. 10017.

CAREER: Left school at fourteen to serve as career soldier in British Army, 1941-57; attended Army Apprentice School, 1941-45; became armourer sergeant and served with Gloucester Regiment in Korea, later in Nigeria. Journalist and author, 1957-59; author and playwright, 1960—.

WRITINGS: Now Thrive the Armourers, Harrap, 1952; *The Bribe Scorners,* Harrap, 1956; *Captain Cat,* Macmillan, 1960; *The Seige of Battersea,* Macmillan, 1962; *Religion and Davey Peach,* M. Joseph, 1962; *The Nature of the Beast,* Heinemann, 1965; *Spawn,* Doubleday, 1979; *I'll Walk Beside You,* Hamish Hamilton, 1979. Also author of scenario of *The Seige of Battersea* for a film with the same title; author of over thirty television plays; contributor of articles and short stories to British and Canadian magazines.

WORK IN PROGRESS: A new novel for Doubleday.

AVOCATIONAL INTERESTS: Cricket, playing the autoharp, taping bird songs, and looking at women.

*   *   *

HOLLISTER, Bernard C(laiborne)   1938-

PERSONAL: Born March 17, 1938, in Chicago, Ill.; son of Joseph (a newspaperman) and Mildred (Pillinger) Hollister; married Edna Rozanski, August 10, 1963 (divorced November, 1975); married Roberta S. Anderson, July 20, 1979; children: (first marriage) Suzanne. *Education:* Roosevelt University, B.A., 1962; Northern Illinois University, M.A., 1967; Illinois Institute of Technology, M.S.T., 1971; also attended Universtiy of Chicago, summer, 1966, 1966-67, and Rutgers University, summer, 1967. *Home:* 321 Grand View, Glen Ellyn, Ill. 60137. *Office:* Willowbrook High School, 1250 South Ardmore, Villa Park, Ill. 60181.

CAREER: Cook County Department of Public Aid, Chicago, Ill., caseworker, 1962-63; Willowbrook High School, Villa Park, Ill., teacher of sociology, 1963—; National College of Education, Evanston, Ill., teacher, 1972—. Consultant to Media Basics, Coronet Multimedia, Doubleday Multimedia, Films, Inc., and other companies. Has conducted workshops and clinics. *Awards, honors:* National Science Foundation grant in sociology, 1970-71; John Hay summer fellowship.

WRITINGS: (With Deane Thompson) *Grokking the Future: Science Fiction in the Classroom,* Pflaum-Standard, 1973; (editor) *Another Tomorrow: A Science Fiction Anthology,* Pflaum-Standard, 1974; *You and Science Fiction: A Humanistic Approach to Tomorrow,* with teacher's guide, National Textbook, 1976; *Teacher's Guide to Eric Sloane,* Ballantine, 1976; *Program Guide to Reading Science Fiction,* Coronet, 1978; (author of study guide) H. G. Wells, *The Island of Dr.*

Moreau, Media Basics, 1980; *The Mass Media Workbook: Learning Activities Involving Today's Media,* with teacher's guide, National Textbook, 1981. Contributor to *Chicago Tribune, Futures Conditional, Social Education, Media and Methods, Opt,* and *English Journal.*

*   *   *

HOLLOWAY, John 1920-

PERSONAL: Born August 1, 1920; son of George (a stoker at Queen's Hospital, Hackney) and Evelyn (Astbury) Holloway; married Audrey Gooding, 1946; married second wife, Joan Black, 1978; children: (first marriage) Emily, Benjamin. *Education:* New College, Oxford, M.A., 1945, D.Phil., 1947. *Address:* Queen's College, Cambridge University, Cambridge, England.

CAREER: Oxford University, All Souls College, Oxford, England, fellow, 1946-60; University of Aberdeen, Aberdeen, Scotland, lecturer in English, 1949-54; Cambridge University, Queen's College, Cambridge, England, lecturer in English, 1954-66, reader in modern English, 1966-72, professor of modern English, 1972—. Byron Professor of English, University of Athens, Athens, Greece, 1961-63; Alexander White Professor, University of Chicago, 1966. Visiting professor, Johns Hopkins University, 1972. Lecturer on tour of Ceylon, India, Pakistan, 1958, and Middle East, 1964. Delivered the Virginia Lectures, University of Virginia, 1979. *Military service:* British Army, Artillery and Intelligence, 1939-45. *Member:* Royal Society of Literature (fellow). *Awards, honors:* D.Litt., University of Aberdeen, 1954; Litt.D., Cambridge University, 1970.

WRITINGS: Language and Intelligence, Macmillan, 1951, reprinted, Shoe String, 1974; *The Victorian Sage,* St. Martin's, 1953; (editor) *Poems of the Mid-Century,* Harrap, 1957; (editor) Percy Bysshe Shelley, *Selected Poems,* Heinemann, 1959; *The Charter Mirror* (essays), Routledge & Kegan Paul, 1960, Horizon, 1962; *The Story of the Night: Studies in Shakespeare's Major Tragedies,* Routledge & Kegan Paul, 1961, University of Nebraska Press, 1963; *The Colours of Clarity* (essays), Shoe String, 1964; *The Lion Hunt* (essays), Shoe String, 1964; *A London Childhood,* Routledge & Kegan Paul, 1966, Scribner, 1968; *Widening Horizons in English Verse,* Routledge & Kegan Paul, 1966, Northwestern University Press, 1967; (editor) Charles Dickens, *Little Dorrit,* Penguin, 1967; *Blake: The Lyric Poetry,* Edward Arnold, 1968; *The Establishment of English,* Cambridge University Press, 1972; (editor with Joan Black) *Later English Broadside Ballads,* Routledge & Kegan Paul, Volume I, 1975, Volume II, 1979; *The Proud Knowledge: Poetry and the Self, 1620-1920,* Routledge & Kegan Paul, 1977; *Narrative and Structure,* Cambridge University Press, 1979.

Poetry; published by Routledge & Kegan Paul, except as indicated: *The Minute, and Longer Poems,* Marvell Press, 1956, Macmillan, 1959; *The Fugue,* 1960; *The Landfallers,* 1962; *Wood and Windfall,* 1965; *New Poems,* Scribner, 1970; *Planet of Winds,* 1977.

WORK IN PROGRESS: A comparative study of twentieth-century European poetry.

SIDELIGHTS: John Holloway is often considered to be one of the few British poets who writes in a "traditional" style. According to a reviewer for *Choice,* "mostly traditional in meter and rhyme, the poems are subtle, witty, and interesting—intellectual, but concerned with what Holloway calls 'the stranger realities that spread all around intellectuality's narrow circle.' One hopes that more of this first-rate craftsman's work will appear in this country where so little good 'traditional' poetry is published."

Agreeing, Jerome Cushman writes in *Library Journal* that he believes the key to Holloway's poetry is "the unabashed use of regular rhyme scheme in many poems [that] gives the poetry an old-fashioned aura, and yet the sound is contemporary, quietly intellectual in contradistinction to the noise and flash of much of today's product. The poems are leisurely simple in theme and archaic in tone. . . . Holloway universalizes small things and common places."

Another critic for *Choice* feels that "Holloway writes with a mind that combines the sensuousness of living with the cold, hard realities of modern relationships. [*Planet of Winds*] continues the vein established in *New Poems.* The works are varied in style and structure, they are colloquial in tone, yet lyrical, gentle, meditative. The play with language in its richness and sparsity is perhaps his most outstanding gift."

However, *Times Literary Supplement* reviewer, Robert Gittings, theorizes that it is the strong sense of humanity apparent in Holloway's poems that attracts many of his followers. "Over all, in his poems, there is a gentle, resigned, yet acute perception of problems posed by life: no solutions, but a constant and often humorous awareness. . . . Sometimes the association of ideas may seem a little cloudy; but at other times it is sharp, flashing and clear."

R. D. Spector of *Saturday Review* believes that Holloway's strong point is his wit. He writes: "It is not with any sense of derogation that I emphasize the quality of wit in John Holloway's [poems] although he himself seems rather defensive about it. Whether about nature, love, or language, his poems strike their best notes when they combine his sharp perception with an equally sharp expression. . . . [Holloway] has a fine ear for how voices sound, a good sense of the rhythms of ordinary conversation. Though not lacking in appropriate feeling, his poems still impress most with their wit, and that is no small asset."

BIOGRAPHICAL/CRITICAL SOURCES: New Statesman, January 27, 1967; *Library Journal,* March 1, 1968, July, 1970; *Saturday Review,* December 26, 1970; *Choice,* October, 1971, February, 1978; *Times Literary Supplement,* October 21, 1977.

*   *   *

HOLMAN, Felice 1919-

PERSONAL: Born October 24, 1919, in New York, N.Y.; daughter of Jac C. (an engineering consultant) and Celia (an artist; maiden name, Hotchner) Holman; married Herbert Valen, April 13, 1941; children: Nanine Elisabeth. *Education:* Syracuse University, B.A., 1941. *Home:* 158 Hillspoint Rd., Westport, Conn.

CAREER: Author. Worked as an advertising copywriter in New York, N.Y., 1944-50. *Awards, honors:* Austrian Book Prize, Lewis Caroll Shelf Award, and American Library Association Notable Book Award, all 1978, for *Slake's Limbo.*

WRITINGS: Elisabeth, The Birdwatcher, Macmillan, 1963; *Elisabeth, The Treasure Hunter,* Macmillan, 1964; *Silently, the Cat and Miss Theodosia,* Macmillan, 1965; *Victoria's Castle,* Norton, 1966; *Elisabeth and the Marsh Mystery,* Macmillan, 1966; *Professor Diggin's Dragons,* Macmillan, 1966; *The Witch on the Corner,* Norton, 1966; *The Cricket Winter,* Norton, 1967; *The Blackmail Machine,* Macmillan, 1968; *A Year to Grow,* Norton, 1968; *At the Top of My Voice: Other Poems,* Norton, 1969; *The Holiday Rat and the Utmost Mouse,* Grosset, 1969; *Solomon's Search,* Grosset, 1970; *The Future of Hooper Toote,* Scribner, 1972; *I Hear*

You Smiling, and Other Poems, Scribner, 1973; *The Escape of the Giant Hogstalk,* Scribner, 1974; *Slake's Limbo,* Scribner, 1974; (with daughter, Nanine Valen) *The Drac: French Tales of Dragons and Demons,* Scribner, 1975; *The Murderer,* Scribner, 1978.

SIDELIGHTS: Felice Holman wrote *CA:* "When people ask why or how I happened to write for young people, I sometimes give a sort of flip answer because I am not really sure. It must have been a combination of things. I know I didn't sit down and say 'Now I am going to write a story for young people.' I had always been writing *something* from the time I was a child and I just kept on writing. Since I like to talk with young people and I like to hear what they have to say, it is only natural that I would like them to hear what I have to say, too. One of the ways to have people listen to you is to write.

"I have a lot of respect for the intelligence of young readers and I don't write to them in different ways than I would speak with them. Since young people are going to be the grown up people very soon, I think they are probably the most important people around. It gives me a lot of satisfaction to be talking to the most important people around, the people who are going to help fix up a lot of the things we know are wrong.

"My books are sometimes spin-offs from real experiences. *The Witch on the Corner* lives on my corner. I took it over from there. I knew a man like Professor Diggins. And sometimes ideas can come from newspaper stories as in *The Holiday Rat and the Utmost Mouse.* And then sometimes they just seem to come out of my head like daydreams that settle themselves onto pages of a book. Sometimes it's fun and sometimes it's hard work. But there is always the good thought that at the end of the fun or work there will be a book."

*   *   *

HOOPER, William Loyd 1931-

PERSONAL: Born September 16, 1931, in Sedalia, Mo.; son of George Francis (a paint contractor) and Mary Evelyn (McNabb) Hooper; married Doris Jean Wallace. *Education:* Southwest Baptist College, certificate, 1951; William Jewell College, B.A., 1953; University of Iowa, M.A., 1956; George Peabody College for Teachers, Ph.D. *Politics:* Republican. *Religion:* Baptist. *Home:* 10-A Essex Rd., Gravesend, Kent, England. *Office:* Emmanuel Baptist Church, Windmill St., Gravesend, Kent, England.

CAREER: Public School teacher in Essex, Iowa, 1953-55 and Atalissa, Iowa, 1955-56; Southwest Baptist College, Bolivar, Mo., professor, 1956-60; First Baptist Church, Old Hickory, Tenn., minister of music, 1960-62; New Orleans Baptist Theological Seminary, New Orleans, La., dean of school of church music, 1962-74; Newstead Wood School for Girls, Orpington, England, head of music department, 1974-79; Emmanuel Baptist Church, Gravesend, England, pastor, 1979—. Chief examiner in music, Southeast Regional Examinations Board, 1976—. Member of board of directors, Community Concert Association, Bolivar, Mo. *Member:* Hymn Society of America, National Association of Teachers of Singing, American Guild of Organists, Music Educators National Conference.

WRITINGS—Published by Broadman, except as indicated: *Church Music in Transition,* 1963; *His Saving Grace Proclaim* (cantata), 1964; *Music Fundamentals,* 1966; *Jubilee* (cantata), Carl Fischer, 1968; *Litany of Praise* (cantata), Carl Fischer, 1972; *And He Shall Come* (cantata), 1978. Contribu-

tor to *Church Musician.* Choral arrangements and compositions published by five publishers.

WORK IN PROGRESS: The Teachers' Survival Kit, a manual for in-service training of church school teachers; *Before the Knot Is Tied,* a marriage guidance manual for pastoral use in pre-marriage counselling.

*   *   *

HOPE, Ronald (Sidney) 1921-

PERSONAL: Born April 4, 1921, in London, England; son of George William (a laborer) and Martha (Turrell) Hope; married Marion Whittaker, December 20, 1947; children: Marion Elizabeth, Ronald Anthony. *Education:* New College, Oxford, B.A., 1941, M.A., 1946, D. Phil., 1949. *Home:* 207 Balham High Rd., London S.W., England. *Office:* The Marine Society, 202 Lambeth Rd., London SE1 7JW, England.

CAREER: Oxford University, Brasenose College, Oxford, England, fellow and lecturer in economics, 1946-47; Seafarers' Education Service and College of the Sea, London, England, director, 1947-76; The Marine Society, London, director, 1976—. Justice of the Peace, 1963-70; chairman, London Nautical School; former chairman of Social Workers Pension Fund and of Social Service Supplies. *Military service:* Royal Naval Volunteer Reserve, 1941-45; became lieutenant. *Awards, honors:* Officer, Order of the British Empire.

WRITINGS: Spare Time at Sea, Maritime Press, 1954, 2nd edition, 1974; *Economic Geography,* Philip & Son, 1956, 5th edition, 1969; *Dick Small in the Half-Deck,* Chatto & Windus, 1958; *Ships,* Macmillan, 1958.

(Editor) *The Harrap Book of Sea Verse,* Harrap, 1960, Books for Libraries, 1969; (editor) *The Shoregoer's Guide to World Ports,* Maritime Press, 1963; *Introduction to the Merchant Navy,* Seafarers' Education Service, 1965, 3rd edition, 1967; (editor) *Seamen and the Sea: A Collection of New Sea Stories by Merchant Seamen,* Harrap, 1965; *In Cabined Ships at Sea: Fifty Years of the Seafarer's Education Service,* Harrap, 1969.

(Editor) *Voices from the Sea,* Harrap, 1977; (editor) *Twenty Singing Seamen,* Stanford Maritime, 1979; *The Merchant Navy,* Stanford Maritime, 1980. Regular contributor to *Fairplay* and *Seafarer.*

BIOGRAPHICAL/CRITICAL SOURCES: Seafarer, spring, 1964.

*   *   *

HOPPE, Art(hur Watterson) 1925-

PERSONAL: Surname rhymes with "sloppy"; born April 23, 1925, in Honolulu, Hawaii; son of Arthur Scrivener (an attorney) and Margaret (Watterson) Hoppe; married Gloria Nichols, April 27, 1946; children: Leslie, Andrea, Arthur N., Prentiss. *Education:* Harvard University, B.A. (cum laude), 1949. *Office: San Francisco Chronicle,* San Francisco, Calif.

CAREER: San Francisco Chronicle, San Francisco, Calif., reporter, 1949-59, author of column, "The Innocent Bystander," 1960—, currently syndicated by Chronicle Features to about one hundred newspapers. *Military service:* U.S. Navy, 1942-46; served as pharmacist's mate second class on destroyers in Pacific.

WRITINGS: The Love Everybody Crusade, Doubleday, 1963; *Dreamboat* (novel), Doubleday, 1964; *The Perfect Solution to Absolutely Everything* (collection of Hoppe's columns), Doubleday, 1968; *Mr. Nixon and My Other Problems*, Chronicle Books, 1971; *Miss Lollipop and the Doomsday Machine* (novel), Doubleday, 1973; *The Tiddling Tennis Theorem* (novel), Viking, 1977. Contributor to *New Yorker, Harper's, Esquire, Playboy, Nation, Yachting,* and other periodicals.

SIDELIGHTS: Arthur Hoppe covered a variety of assignments (including posing as a Skid Row derelict) before he became a nationally-known columnist, considered by former Presidential Press Secretary Pierre Salinger as "the best political humorist in the country." His own characteristic blend of satire, sarcasm, and whimsey, however, is applied irreverently to a great many subjects only faintly—or not at all—political.

Marvin Kitman writes in *Book World* that "Art Hoppe is the humorist's humorist." In his review of Hoppe's *The Perfect Solution to Absolutely Everything,* Kitman reports that "it's the best collection of pure Hoppe since the last [book] in 1962. In recent memory there hasn't been a book by an American humorist with four children which completely ignores them—except in a brief acknowledgment thanking them for 'keeping quiet.' It's a portfolio of columns worthy of a Pulitzer Prize for humorous writing, something the Pultizer jurors have never intentionally given an award for."

BIOGRAPHICAL/CRITICAL SOURCES: Newsweek, June 24, 1963; *Book World,* October 20, 1968.

* * *

HORNBERGER, Theodore 1906-1975

PERSONAL: Born January 13, 1906, in Northville, Mich.; died March 14, 1975; buried in Ann Arbor, Mich.; son of John Jacob (a teacher) and Katharine (Watson) Hornberger; married Marian Louise Welles, February 7, 1929; children: Jean Alice (Mrs. Roland Cleveland), Katharine Watson (Mrs. Allen Denenberg). *Education:* University of Michigan, B.S., 1927, M.A., 1929, PH.D., 1934; King's College, London, additional study, 1927-28. *Politics:* Democrat. *Religion:* Protestant. *Office:* English Department, University of Pennsylvania, Philadelphia, Pa.

CAREER: University of Michigan, Ann Arbor, instructor, 1928-36, assistant professor of English, 1936-37; Huntington Library, San Marino, Calif., research fellow, 1936-37; University of Texas, Main University (now University of Texas at Austin), professor, 1937-46; University of Minnesota, Minneapolis, professor of English, 1946-60, chairman of department, 1950-58; University of Pennsylvania, Philadelphia, professor of English, 1960-75, John Welsh Centennial Professor of History and English Literature, 1968-75, acting chairman of English department, 1968-69. Visiting summer lecturer, Harvard University, 1938, Northwestern University, 1940, Duke University, 1941, 1942, 1950, Ohio State University, 1945, and University of Colorado, 1966. Visiting professor, University of Brazil, 1952. Guggenheim fellow, 1967-68; Thord-Gray Lecturing fellow, Uppsala University, 1973. *Member:* Modern Language Association of America (chairman, American Literature Group, 1956), American Historical Association, American Studies Association, History of Science Society (council, 1947-50), National Council of Teachers of English (chairman, college section, 1951-52), American Dialect Society, College English Association, Colonial Society of Massachusetts.

WRITINGS: (Editor) *Compendium Physicae,* Colonial Society of Massachusetts, 1940; *Scientific Thought in the American Colleges, 1638-1800,* University of Texas Press, 1945, reprinted, Octagon, 1968; (editor with Walter Blair and

Randall Stewart) *The Literature of the United States,* Scott, Foresman, 1946, 3rd edition, 1965; (editor) *William Cullen Bryant and Isaac Henderson: New Evidence on a Strange Partnership,* Haskell House, 1950, reprinted, 1972; *Benjamin Franklin,* University of Minnesota Press, 1962. Editorial board, *American Literature,* 1958-65; book review editor, *American Quarterly,* 1962-66.

WORK IN PROGRESS: Puritanism and Science; Benjamin Franklin as a Writer.†

* * *

HORTON, John (William) 1905-

PERSONAL: Born October 22, 1905, in Nottingham, England; son of John Henry (a factory manager) and Sarah (Nixon) Horton; married Olwen Morfydd Griffiths, August 16, 1937; children: John Nicholas, Sarah Catherine, Jane Elizabeth. *Education:* University of London, B.A., 1931; University of Durham, B. Mus., 1935; F.R.C.O., A.R.C.M. *Home:* The Cottage, Burland Rd., Brentwood, Essex, England.

CAREER: Teacher of music and other subjects, 1925-37; program assistant, 1937-47, Schools Department, British Broadcasting Corp.; Ministry of Education, H.M. inspector of schools, 1947-59, staff inspector, 1959-67; part-time college lecturer, free-lance examiner, author, broadcaster, 1967—.

WRITINGS: Stories of Great Music, Thomas Nelson, 1943; *The Chamber Music of Mendelssohn,* Oxford University Press, 1946; *Legends in Music,* Thomas Nelson, 1948; *Cesar Franck,* Oxford University Press, 1948; (contributor) G.E.H. Abraham, editor, *Grieg: A Symposium,* Lindsay Drummond, 1948; *Approach to Music,* Allen & Unwin, 1950; *Grieg: A Biography,* Dufour, 1950; *Some Nineteenth Century Composers,* Oxford University Press, 1950; *Scandinavian Music: A Short History,* Norton, 1963; *Brahms Orchestral Music,* BBC Publications, 1968, University of Washington Press, 1969; *Mendelssohn Chamber Music,* University of Washington Press, 1972; *Music in British Primary Schools,* Scholastic Book Services, 1972; *The Music Group,* six volumes, Schott, 1969-72; *Grieg,* Biblio Distribution, 1974; *A Book of Christmas Music,* Schott, 1975; *A Book of Early Music,* Schott, in press; *Songs, Signs and Stories,* three volumes, Schott, in press.

* * *

HOUGH, Richard (Alexander) 1922-
(Bruce Carter)

PERSONAL: Born May 15, 1922, in Brighton, Sussex, England; son of George (a banker) and Margaret (Esilman) Hough; married Helen Charlotte Woodyatt (a writer and illustrator of children's books), July 17, 1943; married second wife, Judy Taylor (publisher and editor of children's books), 1980; children: (first marriage) Sarah Hough Garland, Alexandra, Deborah, Bryony. *Education:* Attended schools in England. *Home:* 7/217 Sussex Gardens, London W.2, England. *Agent:* James Brown Associates, 25 West 43rd St., New York, N.Y. 10036.

CAREER: The Bodley Head Ltd. (publishers), London, England, 1947-55, began as editor, became manager; Hamish Hamilton Ltd. (publishers), London, editor of children's books, 1955-70. *Military service:* Royal Air Force, pilot, 1941-46.

WRITINGS: The Fleet that Had to Die, Viking, 1958; *Admirals in Collision,* Viking, 1959; *The Potemkin Mutiny,* Pantheon, 1960, reprinted, Greenwood Press, 1975; (editor) *Great Auto Races*, Harper, 1961; *A History of the World's Sports Cars*, Harper, 1961; (with Michael Frostick) *A History of the World's Classic Cars*, Harper, 1963; *Death of the Battleship*, Macmillan, 1963; (editor) *First and Fastest*, Harper, 1963; *Dreadnought: A History of the Modern Battleship*, Macmillan, 1964, 3rd edition, 1974; (with Frostick) *A History of the World's Racing Cars*, Harper, 1965; (editor) *The Motor Car Lover's Companion*, Harper, 1965; *The Big Battleship*, Harper, 1966; (with L.J.K. Setright) *A History of the World's Motorcycles*, Harper, 1966, revised edition, 1973; *The Great Dreadnought: The Strange Story of H.M.S. Agincourt*, Harper, 1967; *A History of the World's High Performance Cars*, Harper, 1967; *The Long Pursuit*, Harper, 1969.

Admiral of the Fleet: The Life of John Fisher, Macmillan, 1970; *The Blind Horn's Hate*, Norton, 1971; *Captain Bligh and Mr. Christian*, Dutton, 1973; *The Mountbattens*, Dutton, 1975; *One Boy's War*, Heinemann, 1975; (editor) *Advice to My Granddaughter: Letters from Queen Victoria to Princess Victoria of Hesse*, Simon & Schuster, 1976; *The Great Admirals*, Morrow, 1977; *Man O'War: The Fighting Ship in History*, Scribner, 1979; *The Last Voyage of Captain James Cook*, Morrow, 1979; *Wings against the Sky* (novel), Morrow, 1979; *The Fight of the Few* (novel), Morrow, 1979; *Wings to Victory* (novel), Morrow, 1981; *Mountbatten: Hero of Our Time*, Random House, 1981.

Under pseudonym Bruce Carter: *Into A Strange Lost World*, Crowell, 1953; *Speed Six*, Harper, 1956; *Target Island*, Harper, 1957, 2nd edition, Hamish Hamilton, 1967; *The Kidnaping of Kensington*, Harper, 1958; *Four-wheel Drift*, Harper, 1960; *Fast Circuit*, Harper, 1962; *Nuvolari and the Alpha Romeo*, Coward, 1968; *Jimmy Murphy and the White Duesenberg*, Coward, 1968; *The Airfield Man*, Coward, 1966; *Galapagos: The Enchanted Islands*, Addison, 1975; *Buzzbugs*, Warne, 1977.

SIDELIGHTS: Richard Hough wrote *CA*: "In my rare moments of retrospection, being a 'workaholic,' it occurs to me that my pleasure and total commitment to writing, whether for children or adults, is founded on the enthusiasms of my childhood and adolescence and young manhood, with all the many varied colours and experiences with which they provided me: a staid, conservative home life with few events of note, during which my imagination may have beaten about ineffectually like a moth against the window pane of a brightly-lit room. My wife and her mother opened the window when I was seventeen, and then the war swept me away, in the midst of which we married. The colours were very vivid and various in those years, 1941-45. And then we had children, three rather quickly and one much later, and it was hard going to pay the bills, until about 1958, when I had my first big seller, and a long *New Yorker* serial which pumped me full of unaccumstomed wealth and much needed self-confidence."

BIOGRAPHICAL/CRITICAL SOURCES: Washington Post Book World, July 22, 1979; *London Times*, September 1, 1980.

*   *   *

HOUGH, S(tanley) B(ennett) 1917-
(Rex Gordon, Bennett Stanley)

PERSONAL: Born February 25, 1917, in Preston, Lancashire, England; son of Simeon and Eva (Bennett) Hough; married Justa Elisabeth Cecilia Wodschow, 1938. *Politics:* Social Democrat. *Home and office:* 1 Albion Pl., Ponsa-

nooth, Truro, Cornwall, England. *Agent:* A. M. Heath & Co. Ltd., 40-42 William IV St., London WC2N 4DD, England; Brandt & Brandt Literary Agents, Inc., 1501 Broadway, New York, N.Y. 10036.

CAREER: Marconi Radio Co., radio operator, 1936-38; International Marine Radio Co., radio officer in wartime service, 1939-45; self-employed in yachting business, 1946-51; full-time writer of fiction and travel books, 1951—. *Awards, honors:* Infinity Award for best science fiction novel of year, 1957.

WRITINGS—Published by Hodder & Stoughton, except as indicated: *Frontier Incident*, 1951; *Moment of Decision*, 1952; *Mission in Guemo*, 1953, Walker & Co., 1964; *The Seas South*, 1953; *The Primitives*, 1954; *Extinction Bomber*, Lane, 1956; *A Pound a Day Inclusive* (travel), 1957; *The Bronze Persues*, Secker & Warburg, 1959; *Expedition Everyman*, 1959; *Beyond the Eleventh Hour*, 1961; *Mission in Guemo*, Walker & Co., 1964; *Where?: An Independent Report on Holiday Resorts in Britain and the Continent*, 1964; *Dear Daughter Dead*, Gollancz, 1965, Walker & Co., 1966; *Sweet Sister Seduced*, Gollancz, 1968; *Fear Fortune, Father*, Gollancz, 1974.

Under pseudonym Rex Gordon: *Utopia 239*, Heinemann, 1955; *No Man Friday*, Heinemann, 1956, published as *First on Mars*, Ace Books, 1957; *First to the Stars*, Ace Books, 1959 (published in England as *The Worlds of Eclos*, Consul, 1969); *First through Time*, Ace Books, 1962 (published in England as *The Time Factor*, Gibbs & Phillips, 1967); *Utopia Minus X*, Ace Books, 1967 (published in England as *The Paw of God*, Library 33, 1967); *The Yellow Fraction*, Ace Books, 1969.

Under pseudonym Bennett Stanley: *The Alscott Experiment*, Hodder & Stoughton, 1954; *Sea to Eden*, Hodder & Stoughton, 1954; *Government Contract*, Hodder & Stoughton, 1955.

SIDELIGHTS: S. B. Hough wrote *CA*: "One of the most frequent questions an author is asked is why, not content with his own name, he invents new names to write under. What is his sinister purpose? What is he hiding? Does he also write pure pornography and subversion under still other names? Of course the questioner does not usually ask the latter few questions, but they are in his mind.

"Unfortunately, the answer is much more prosaic. . . . Some writers at some periods of their lives write faster, and a wider variety of books, than their publisher is willing to print. Very often, since writers are often not very good with money, they have to. But publishers do not like a writer to change his character or his spots either. If Book Publishers Incorporated have spent a fortune building up a writer for her heart-throbs they don't like her next book to turn out to be a treatise on mathematics, or still less a first-person male account of adventures in brothels. So the answer is obvious. Stick to one line with one publisher, put a new name on the title page of anything different, and, if he's willing, let a different publisher, who specialises in that kind of thing, have it.

"In fact, this has worked well for me, and, more important, it represents a convenience to readers. Pick up a book by S. B. Hough and you know that you are going to get an odd kind of thriller in which the characters have not all been computer pre-programmed, so they have been known to stop themselves if what they are doing is right on occasion. True, this isn't the most popular line to take in a thriller, it slows down the book. But if you don't like it, you can try a Rex Gordon.

"Rex Gordon writes science-fiction ('hard' science-fiction, not anti-science supernatural nonsense), and the pace is a lot faster, and it is a *genre* that is much more demanding. Science-fiction readers know everything. Make a passing reference to Dostoevsky or Mozart, the atmosphere of Jupiter or a philosophic concept like Occams Razor, and they will know what you mean. It is useful to know this, but there is something interesting too.''

*   *   *

HOULE, Cyril O(rvin) 1913-

PERSONAL: Born March 26, 1913, in Sarasota, Fla.; son of John Louis (a realtor) and Annie M. (Hescock) Houle; married Bettie Carr Eckhardt Totten, May 15, 1947; children: David Eckhardt. *Education:* University of Florida, B.A.E., 1934, M.A.E., 1934; University of Chicago, Ph.D., 1940. *Home:* 5510 Woodlawn Ave., Chicago, Ill. *Office:* University of Chicago, 5835 Kimbark Ave., Chicago, Ill.

CAREER: University of Chicago, Chicago, Ill., instructor, 1939-42, assistant professor, 1942-45, associate professor and dean of university college, 1945-52, professor of education, 1952-79, professor emeritus, 1979—. Visiting professor at University of California, Berkeley, University of Wisconsin, and University of Washington, Seattle. Director of UNESCO seminar, Sweden, 1950. Senior program consultant, W. K. Kellogg Foundation, 1976—. *Awards, honors:* Fulbright fellow, Great Britain, 1950-51; D.H.L. from Rutgers University, DePaul University, and Roosevelt University; LL.D. from Florida State University and Syracuse University.

WRITINGS: (With Floyd W. Reeves and Thomas Fansler) *Adult Education,* McGraw, 1938; (with others) *The Armed Services and Adult Education,* American Council on Education, 1947; *Libraries and Adult Education,* UNESCO, 1951; (with Charles A. Nelson) *The University, the Citizen, and World Affairs,* American Council on Education, 1956; *The Effective Board,* Association Press, 1961; *The Inquiring Mind,* University of Wisconsin Press, 1962; *Continuing Your Education,* McGraw, 1964; *Residential Continuing Education,* Syracuse University, 1971; *The Design of Education,* Jossey-Bass, 1972; *The External Degree,* Jossey-Bass, 1973. Also author of *Continuing Learning in the Professions,* 1980. Contributor of articles to yearbooks, symposiums, and periodicals.

WORK IN PROGRESS: "Four volumes bringing together previous writings in adult education"; a revision of *The Effective Board.*

*   *   *

HOUSTON, John Porter 1933-

PERSONAL: Born April 21, 1933, in Wilmar, Calif.; son of William Bascom (a manufacturer) and Sappho (Davis) Houston; married Mona Tobin (a professor), July 6, 1959; children: Natalie Melissa. *Education:* University of California, Berkeley, B.A., 1954; University of Aix-Marseilles, graduate study, 1954-55; Yale University, Ph.D., 1959. *Office:* French Department, Indiana University, Bloomington, Ind., 47401.

CAREER: Yale University, New Haven, Conn., instructor in French, 1958-62; Indiana University at Bloomington, assistant professor, 1962-65, associate professor, 1965-70, professor of French, 1970—. *Member:* Modern Language Association of America. *Awards, honors:* Morse fellowship, Yale University, 1961-62.

WRITINGS: The Design of Rimbaud's Poetry, Yale University Press, 1963; (editor with wife, Mona Tobin Houston) *Francois Mauriac, Genitrix,* Prentice-Hall, 1966; *The Demonic Imagination: Style and Theme in French Romantic Poetry,* Louisiana State University Press, 1969; *Fictional Technique in France, 1802-1927,* Louisiana State University Press, 1972; *Victor Hugo,* Twayne, 1974; *Fundamentals of Learning,* Academic Press, 1976; *The Traditions of French Prose Style: A Rhetorical Study,* Louisiana State University Press, in press. Also author of *French Symbolism and the Modernist Movement* and *French Symbolist Poetry,* both published by Louisiana State University Press.

*   *   *

HOUSTON, W(illiam) Robert, Jr. 1928-

PERSONAL: Born June 13, 1928, in Port Arthur, Tex.; son of William Robert (minister) and Bernice (Strickland) Houston; married Elizabeth Craig, July 22, 1950; children: John Robert, Elizabeth Ann, Alan Craig. *Education:* Paris Junior College, A.A., 1947; North Texas State College (now University), B.S., 1949, M.Ed., 1952; University of Texas, Ed.D., 1961. *Home:* 9831 Vogue, Houston, Tex. 77080. *Office:* College of Education, University of Houston, Houston, Tex. 77004.

CAREER: Public schools, Albuquerque, N.M., teacher, 1949-51; public schools, Midland, Tex., teacher, 1951-52, dean, 1952-55, elementary school principal, 1955-59; University of Texas, Main University (now University of Texas at Austin, supervisor of student teachers, 1959-60, research associate, 1960-61; Michigan State University, East Lansing, assistant professor of elementary education, 1961-63, associate professor of education, 1963-66, professor, 1967-70; University of Houston, Houston, Tex., professor of education, 1970—, associate dean, 1973—. *Member:* Association of Teacher Educators, National Council of Teachers of Mathematics, National Society for the Study of Education, National Council for the Social Studies, Phi Delta Kappa.

WRITINGS: (With M. Vere DeVault) *Sir Isaac Newton,* Steck, 1960; (with Roger Osborn, DeVault, and Claude Boyd) *Extending Mathematics Understanding,* C. E. Merrill, 1961, revised edition, 1969; (contributor) DeVault, editor, *Improving Mathematics Programs,* C. E. Merrill, 1961; (with DeVault and Boyd) *Television and Consultant Services as Methods of In-Service Education for Elementary School Teachers of Mathematics,* University of Texas Press, 1962; (contributor) Hugo David, editor, *Handbook for Student Teaching,* Brown, 1964; (with Frank Blackington and Horton Southworth) *Professional Growth through Student Teaching,* C. E. Merrill, 1965; (contributor) *New Directions in Mathematics,* Association for Childhood Education International, 1965; *Teaching in the Modern Elementary School,* Macmillan, 1967; (editor) *Improving Mathematics Education for Elementary School Teachers,* Macmillan, 1967; (with William W. Joyce, W. R. Gross, and S. D. Lee) *Exploring Regions of Latin America and Canada,* Follett, 1968, revised edition published as *Exploring Our World: Latin America and Canada,* 1977; (with R. Osborn, M. V. DeVault, and C. Boyd) *Understanding the Number System,* C. E. Merrill, 1969.

(With W. V. Hicks, R. Cheney, and R. Marquard) *The New Elementary School Curriculum,* Van Nostrand, 1970; (compiler with Joyce, and R. G. Oana) *Elementary Education in the Seventies,* Holt, 1970; *Strategies and Resources for Developing a Competency-Based Teacher Education Program,* Multi-State Consortium on Performance-Based Education, 1972; (editor with Robert B. Howsam) *Competency-Based Teacher Education: Progress, Problems, and Prospects*, Science Research Associates, 1972; (with Loye Hollis) *Acquiring Competencies to Teach Mathematics in Elementary Schools*, Professional Educators Publications, 1973; (with others) *Resources for Performance-Based Education*, Multi-State Consortium on Performance-Based Education, 1973; (with Wilford A. Weber and James M. Cooper) *A Guide to Competency-Based Teacher Education*, Competency-Based Instructional Systems, 1973; (editor) *Competency Assessment, Research, and Evaluation*, Multi-State Consortium on Performance-Based Education, 1973; (editor) *Exploring Competency-Based Education*, McCutchan, 1974.

(With others) *Criteria for Describing and Assessing Competency-Based Programs*, Multi-State Consortium on Performance-Based Education, 1975; (with Joyce, Gross, and Lee) *Exploring World Regions*, Follett, 1975; (contributor) *Modern Elementary Education: Teaching and Learning*, Macmillan, 1976; (editor with L. Marshall, and H. J. Freiberg) *Staff Development for Alternative Schools*, Government Printing Office, 1977; (with Karl Massanari and William H. Drummond) *Emerging Professional Roles for Teacher Educators*, American Association of Colleges for Teacher Education, 1978; (with others) *Assessing School/College/Community Needs*, Center for Urban Education, University of Nebraska at Omaha, 1978; (contributor) *Focus on the Future: Implications for Education*, University of Houston, 1978; (with others) *Designing Short-term Instructional Programs*, Association of Teacher Educators, 1979.

Contributor to professional journals; also contributor of chapters to books on student teaching, teacher education, needs assessment, competency-based education, and mathematics education.

*   *   *

HOVDA, Robert W(alker)   1920-

PERSONAL: Surname is pronounced *Hahv*-da; born April 10, 1920, in Clear Lake, Wis.; son of Leslie Raymond and Helma Regina (Lohn) Hovda. *Education:* Attended Hamline University, 1938-41; St. John's University, Collegeville, Minn., B.A., 1945; St. John's Seminary, seminarian, 1945-49; Catholic University of America, S.T.L., 1960. *Politics:* "Democrat (left wing)." *Home and office:* St. Joseph's Church, 371 Sixth Ave., New York, N.Y. 10014.

CAREER: Ordained Roman Catholic priest, 1949; Diocese of Fargo, Fargo, N.D., parish priest, 1949-59; Catholic University of America, Washington, D.C., instructor in theology, 1959-62; North Dakota State University, Fargo, chaplain of St. Paul's Student Center, 1963-65; Liturgical Conference, Washington, D.C., editor, 1965-78; Jesuit School of Theology, Chicago, Ill., instructor, 1978-80; St. Joseph's Church, New York, N.Y., pastoral associate, 1980—. *Wartime service:* Conscientious objector serving in Civilian Public Service Camp. *Member:* American Civil Liberties Union, National Association for the Advancement of Colored People, Congress of Racial Equality, North American Academy of Liturgy, Catholic Peace Fellowship, Democratic Socialist Organizing Committee, Dignity, Societas Liturgica, Women's Ordination Conference.

WRITINGS—All published by Liturgical Conference, except as indicated: (Editor, author of introduction, and contributor) *Sunday MoEning Crisis: Renewal in Catholic Worship*, Helicon, 1963; (editor) *Church Architecture: The Shape of Reform*, 1965; (editor) *Jesus Christ Reforms His Church*, 1966; *Manual of Celebration*, 1970; (with Gabe Huck) *There's No Place Like People: Planning Small Group Liturgies*, 2nd edition (Hovda was not associated with earlier edition), Argus, 1971; *Celebrating Baptism*, 1970; *Dry Bones: Living Worship Guides to Good Liturgy*, 1973; *There Are Different Ministries*, 1975; *Strong, Loving and Wise: Presiding in Liturgy*, 1976.

Contributor; all published by Liturgical Conference except as indicated: *Problems before Unity*, Helicon, 1962; *The Layman in the Church, and Other Essays*, Alba, 1963; F.R. McManus, editor, *The Revival of the Liturgy*, Herder & Herder, 1963; *Liturgy Committee Handbook*, 1971; *Children's Liturgies*, 1971; *Parishes and Families*, 1973; *Signs, Songs and Stories*, 1974; *This Far by Faith*, 1977; *It Is Your Own Mystery*, 1977; *Touchstones for Liturgical Ministers*, 1978. Contributor of essays and book reviews to religious and educational periodicals.

WORK IN PROGRESS: Essays under the general rubric of ecclesial and liturgical renewal.

*   *   *

HOWARD, Helen Addison   1904-

PERSONAL: Born August 4, 1904, in Missoula, Mont.; daughter of Albert A. and Helena (Cullenan) Howard; married Ben Overland, April 24, 1946. *Education:* State University of Montana (now University of Montana), A.B., 1927; University of Southern California, M.A., 1933. *Home and office:* 410 South Lamer St., Burbank, Calif. 91506.

CAREER: Daily Missoulian, Missoula, Mont., special reporter and feature writer, 1923-29; U.S. Department of Agriculture, survey work in Los Angeles, Calif., 1943; Radio Reports, Inc., Los Angeles, radio-television monitor and editor, 1943-56; Los Angeles Police Department, clerk-typist in records and identification division, 1950-51. Member of cavalry unit, Women's Ambulance and Defense Corps of America, 1942-45; member of board of directors, Equestrian Trails, Inc., 1954; troop captain, California Rangers (youth cavalry organization), 1954-56. Public speaker at women's civic and church groups, 1966. *Member:* P.E.N. International, Montana Historical Society, Montana Mountaineer Club (publicity manager, 1922-24), General Alumni Association of University of Southern California, Alumni Association of University of Montana, Equestrian Trails (Corral 15).

WRITINGS: War Chief Joseph, Caxton, 1941, revised and updated edition published as *Saga of Chief Joseph*, 1965; (contributing editor) *Frontier Omnibus*, Montana State University Press, 1962; *Northwest Trail Blazers*, Caxton, 1963; *American Indian Poetry*, Twayne, 1979—; *American Frontier Tales*, Mountain Press, 1980—. Contributor to *Dictionary of Indian Tribes of America*. Contributor of short stories and historical articles to such periodicals as *Washington Historical Quarterly, Writer, Frontier and Midland, Historical Bulletin, Journal of the West, Pacific Northwest Quarterly, Catholic Digest*, and *Real West*; contributor of horse articles to such periodicals as *Equestrian Trails, Arabian Horse News, Horseman, Western Horseman*, and *Saddle Action. Journal of the West*, book reviewer, 1969—, member of editorial advisory board, 1978—.

SIDELIGHTS: Helen Addison Howard wrote *CA:* "An inborn love of horses is my first love, inherited from my paternal 'Johnny Reb' grandfather, William A. Howard. Since age eight, I wanted to be an 'author' and to own a purebred Arabian horse. Through the years, a few editors and publishers kindly accepted me as an 'author' with a driving urge to contribute works of substance to the world's store of educational knowledge. At the age 'when life begins at forty' I was able to buy and keep my first Arab horse, a uniquely understanding animal who one day (hopefully) will be the subject of his own book revealing extraordinary intelligent, untrained examples of equine behavior.''

War Chief Joseph was dramatized as "Hear Me, My Chiefs" for radio presentation by National Broadcasting Co. in 1949 in commemoration of American Indian Day.

*   *   *

HOWE, Doris Kathleen
(Mary Munro, Kaye Stewart; Newlyn Nash, a joint pseudonym)

PERSONAL: Daughter of George William and Agnes (Hepworth) Howe. *Education:* Educated in England. *Home:* Middle Brig How, Skelwith Bridge, Ambleside, Cumbria, England.

CAREER: Novelist and short story writer.

WRITINGS—All published by Ward, Lock: *I Must Go Back: A Kootenay Romance,* 1946; *The Eager Heart: A Kootenay Story,* 1947; *All Vigil Ended: A Kootenay Tale,* 1947; *On Eagle's Wings: A Kootenay Incident,* 1948; *Three O'Clock,* 1949; *The Unknown Road,* 1949; *The Year of Decision,* 1951; *Second Chances,* 1951; *Deep in My Memory,* 1952; *The Happy Pilgrim,* 1953; *I Give You My Heart,* 1955; *Somewhere My Love,* 1955; *Winter Jasmine,* 1956; *Goodbye Summer,* 1957; *Trial for Love,* 1957; *The Shores of Love,* 1958; *Island Destiny,* 1958; *Forever Mine,* 1959; *Sweet Life,* 1959; *Some Other Door,* 1960; *The Waters of Time,* 1960.

Under pseudonym Mary Munro; all published by R. Hale: *The Wheel of Life,* 1958; *Moon Light,* 1958; *A Dream Came True,* 1958; *The Bargain,* 1959; *The Golden Vase,* 1959; *A Red Rose,* 1960; *Whispering Sands,* 1961; *The Honey Pot,* 1962; *Second Love,* 1962; *The Singing House,* 1974; *Shadow across the Desert,* 1976; *Hotel by the Loch,* 1977; *From March to September,* 1977; *This Girl Is Mine,* 1978.

Under pseudonym Kaye Stewart: *The Touchstone,* Jenkins, 1945.

With sister, Muriel Howe, under joint pseudonym Newlyn Nash; all published by John Gresham: *Beach of Dreams,* 1961; *Dance of Destiny,* 1962; *Magic of Love,* 1962; *Wild Garlic,* 1962; *The Affair at Claife Manor,* 1963; *The Pearl,* 1963.

Contributor of over a hundred short stories to magazines.

*   *   *

HOYLE, Fred 1915-

PERSONAL: Born June 24, 1915, in Bingley, Yorkshire, England; son of Ben and Mabel Hoyle; married Barbara Clark, December 28, 1939; children: Geoffrey, Elizabeth Jeanne (Mrs. N. J. Butler). *Education:* Emmanuel College, Cambridge, M.A., 1939. *Office:* St. John's College, Cambridge University, Cambridge, England.

CAREER: Cambridge University, Cambridge, England, research fellow of St. John's College, 1939-72, honorary fellow, 1973—, university lecturer in mathematics, 1945-58, Plumian Professor of Theoretical Astronomy and Experimental Philosophy, 1958-73, director of Institute of Theoretical Astronomy, 1966-72. California Institute of Technology, visiting professor of astrophysics, 1953 and 1954, visiting associate in physics, 1963—, and Sherman Fairchild Distinguished Scholar, 1974-75. Professor of astronomy, Royal

Institution, 1969-72; Andrew D. White Professor-at-Large, Cornell University, 1972-78. Honorary research professor, University of Manchester, 1972—, and University of Cardiff, 1975—. Member of staff, Mount Wilson and Palomar Observatories in California, 1956-58. Senior exhibitioner of the Royal Commission of the Exhibition of 1851, 1939; member of science research council, 1967-72. *Wartime service:* British Admiralty, wartime research, 1940-45.

MEMBER: Royal Astronomical Society (fellow; president, 1971-73), Royal Society (fellow; vice-president, 1970-71), American Academy of Arts and Sciences (honorary member), American Philosophical Society, National Academy of Sciences (foreign associate). *Awards, honors:* Smith Prize, 1939; received Gold Medal from Royal Astronomical Society, 1968; Kalinga Prize, 1968; Bruce Medal, Astronomical Society of the Pacific, 1970; knighted, 1972; Royal Medal from Royal Society, 1974; Dorothea Klumpke-Roberts Award, Astronomical Society of the Pacific, 1977. Academic: D.Sc. from University of Norwich, 1967, University of Leeds, 1969, University of Bradford, 1975, and University of Newcastle, 1976.

WRITINGS: Some Recent Researches in Solar Physics, Cambridge University Press, 1949; *The Nature of the Universe,* Harper, 1951, revised edition, 1960; *A Decade of Decision,* Heinemann, 1953, published as *Man and Materialism,* Harper, 1956; *Frontiers of Astronomy,* Heinemann, 1955, New American Library, 1957; *Astronomy,* Doubleday, 1962; *Star Formation,* H.M.S.O., 1963; *Of Men and Galaxies,* University of Washington Press, 1964; *Encounter with the Future,* Trident, 1965; *Galaxies, Nuclei, and Quasars,* Harper, 1965; *Man in the Universe,* Columbia University Press, 1966; *From Stonehenge to Modern Cosmology,* W. H. Freeman, 1972; *Copernicus,* Harper, 1973; *The Relation of Physics and Cosmology,* W. H. Freeman, 1973; (with J. V. Narlikar) *Action-at-a-Distance in Physics and Cosmology,* W. H. Freeman, 1974; *Astronomy and Cosmology,* W. H. Freeman, 1975; *Highlights in Astronomy,* W. H. Freeman, 1975 (published in England as *Astronomy Today,* Heinemann, 1975); *Ten Faces of the Universe,* W. H. Freeman, 1977; *Stonehenge: A High Peak of Prehistoric Culture,* W. H. Freeman, 1977; *On Stonehenge,* W. H. Freeman, 1977; *Energy or Extinction,* Heinemann, 1977; (with Chandra Wickramasinghe) *Lifecloud,* Harper, 1978; *The Cosmogony of the Solar System,* Enslow, 1978; (with Wickramasinghe) *Diseases from Space,* Harper, 1979; (with son, Geoffrey Hoyle) *Commonsense in Nuclear Energy,* Heinemann, 1979, W. H. Freeman, 1980; (with J. Norlikar) *The Physics-Astronomy Frontier,* W. H. Freeman, 1980.

Science fiction; all published by Harper, except as indicated: *The Black Cloud,* 1957; *Ossian's Ride,* 1959; (with John Elliott) *A for Andromeda,* 1962; (with G. Hoyle) *Fifth Planet,* 1963; (with Elliott) *Andromeda Breakthrough,* 1964; *October the First Is Too Late,* 1966; *Element 79,* New American Library, 1967; (with G. Hoyle) *Rockets in Ursa Major,* Heinemann, 1969; (with G. Hoyle) *Seven Steps to the Sun,* Heinemann, 1970; (with G. Hoyle) *The Molecule Man: Two Short Novels,* Heinemann, 1971; (with G. Hoyle) *The Inferno,* Heinemann, 1973; (with G. Hoyle) *Into Deepest Space,* 1974; (with G. Hoyle) *The Westminster Disaster,* 1978. Also author with G. Hoyle, *The Incandescent Ones,* 1976. Author of libretto, "The Alchemy of Love." Contributor of numerous articles to scientific and professional journals.

WORK IN PROGRESS: Research in steady-state theory of cosmology and nucleosynthesis in stars and supernovae, and on the relation of biology to astronomy, with particular reference to the origin of life, and to evolution.

SIDELIGHTS: Fred Hoyle is an internationally eminent astronomer and professor who is almost equally as well-known as an author of science fiction chronicles as for his more traditional scientific treatises.

Many critics feel it is this highly technical and scientific background that make Hoyle's science fiction so enjoyable and believable. For example, Robert Garioch writes in his review of Seven Steps to the Sun in Listener that "this is a remarkable story, well-told, and too credible for comfort.... The science in Seven Steps to the Sun is correct, as a middle-aged reviewer many learn by consulting his 15-year-old son. The main interest, however, is in the anthropology.... It is not at all far-fetched."

Jeanne Cavallini agrees with Garioch and explains in Library Journal that "Fred Hoyle is considered one of the world's foremost astrophysicists and has recently been knighted; his distinguished scientific background is evident in [The Molecule Men: Two Short Novels]. Science fiction buffs who like their science fiction to take place in the present and to have the stamp of scientific accuracy will enjoy these stories."

Hoyle's fascination with mathematics and astronomy surfaced at an early age. He taught himself the multiplication tables before he was six and would often stay up all night looking through a telescope he received as a gift.

In 1951, Hoyle published The Nature of the Universe in which he stated and explained theories that he and a number of other scientists at Cambridge University held concerning the origin and the character of the universe. One of these hypotheses is termed the "Steady-State Theory." Hoyle contends that the universe is endlessly expanding, with no beginning and no center. He believes that new stars and galaxies are continually being formed and are perpetually moving through space.

These theories caused a considerable stir in the scientific community, for this particular theory disputed the long-standing and more traditional "Explosion Theory" or the "Expansion-Contraction Theory".

Rockets in Ursa Major was produced as a Christmas pantomime for children. A for Andromeda and The Andromeda Breakthrough were the basis for two space serials for television.

BIOGRAPHICAL/CRITICAL SOURCES: Nature, March 15, 1958; Listener, June 18, 1970; Library Journal, December 15, 1972; Scientific American, December, 1975; Best Sellers, July, 1977; Choice, November, 1978; Times Literary Supplement, January 25, 1980.

*   *   *

HUGGETT, Frank E(dward)   1924-

PERSONAL: Born March 25, 1924, in London, England; son of Hubert George and Caroline (Cant) Huggett; married Renee Bell (a writer), May 25, 1924; children: Diana Tarrant. Education: Attended Emanuel School; Wadham College, Oxford, B.A., 1948. Home: Ashdown, Great Green, Thurston, Bury St. Edmunds, Suffolk, England.

CAREER: Reporter, Westminster Press Provincial Newspapers, 1949-52; Daily Telegraph, London, England, sub-editor, 1952-55; Look and Listen, London, editor, 1956-57; Regent Street Polytechnic, London, lecturer in journalism, 1958-65; Ministry of Defence, London, lecturer, 1966-68. Lecturer in Britain and Europe.

WRITINGS: The Coal Miner, Ward, Lock, 1955; The True Book about Newspapers, Muller, 1955; South of Lisbon:

Winter Travels in Southern Portugal, Gollancz, 1960; Farming, Dufour, 1963; The Newspapers, Heinemann, 1968; Modern Belgium, Praeger, 1969.

A Short History of Farming, Macmillan, 1970; What They've Said about Nineteenth Century Reformers, Oxford University Press, 1971; The Modern Netherlands, Praeger, 1971; How It Happened, Basil Blackwell, 1971, Barnes & Noble, 1972; Travel and Communications, Harrap, 1971; What They've Said about Nineteenth Century Statesmen, Oxford University Press, 1972; A Day in the Life of a Victorian Farm Worker, Allen & Unwin, 1972; The Battle for Reform, Lutterworth, 1973; Factory Life and Work, Harrap, 1973; The Dutch Today, Dutch Government Publishing Office, 1974, 2nd edition, 1977; Housing the People, Thomas Nelson, 1974; Life and Work at Sea, Harrap, 1975; (editor) A Dictionary of British History, Basil Blackwell, 1975; The European Countryside, Thomas Nelson, 1975, 2nd edition, 1979; The Land Question and European Society, Harcourt, 1975; Slaves and Slavery, Lutterworth, 1975; Farming in Britain, A. & C. Black, 1975, 3rd edition published as Farming, 1980; The Netherlands, Macdonald, 1976; Life below Stairs: Domestic Servants in England from Victorian Times, Scribner, 1977; (editor and compiler) Victorian England as Seen by "Punch", Sidgwick & Jackson, 1978; Goodnight Sweetheart, W. H. Allen, 1979; Carriages at Eight, Lutterworth, 1979. Contributor to various journals.

SIDELIGHTS: Frank E. Huggett wrote CA: "I write to live and because writing is my life. I need the continual stimulus of new topics to interest me, so I have covered a great range of subjects in my writing; but for me there is still a central theme. I am always trying to probe behind the facade of social history to discover what people in the past really thought and felt. Occasionally, I feel that I succeed."

*   *   *

HUGHES, Philip Edgcumbe   1915-

PERSONAL: Born April 30, 1915, in Sydney, New South Wales, Australia; son of Randolph William (an author) and Muriel (Stanley-Hall) Hughes; married Margaret Byers, April 22, 1945; children: Marion. Education: University of Cape Town, B.A., 1937, M.A., 1939, D.Litt., 1955; University of London, B.D., 1946. Home: 1565 Cherry Lane, Rydal, Pa. 19046.

CAREER: Clergyman, Church of England; Tyndale Hall, Bristol, England, lecturer, 1947-52, vice-principal, 1951-52; University of Bristol, Bristol, lecturer in theology, 1948-52; Churchman (quarterly of Anglican theology), London, England, editor, 1959-68; Conwell School of Theology, Philadelphia, Pa., professor of historical theology, 1968-70. Guest professor of New Testament exegesis at Columbia Theological Seminary, Decatur, Ga., 1964; visiting professor of New Testament, Westminster Theological Seminary, Philadelphia, Pa., 1970—. Lecturer and preacher in Europe, United States, and Canada. Member: Studiorum Novi Testamenti Societas, Renaissance Society of America, American Society for Reformation Research.

WRITINGS: Revive Us Again, Marshall, Morgan & Scott, 1947; The Divine Plan for Jew and Gentile, Tyndale Press, 1949; (translator) Pierre Marcel, The Biblical Doctrine of Infant Baptism: Sacrament of the Covenant of Grace, James Clarke, 1953; (editor) Canon Law and the Church of England: An Examination of the Present Revision, Church Book Room Press for the Church Society, 1955; Scripture and Myth: An Examination of Rudolf Bultmann's Plea for Demythologization, Tyndale Press, 1956; The Position of the

Celebrant at the Service of Holy Communion, Church Book Room Press, 1957; *The Revision of Canon Law: Where Is It Leading Us?,* Church Book Room Press, 1957; (translator with P. J. Allcock and others) J. J. von Allmen, editor, *Companion to the Bible,* Oxford University Press, 1958 (published in England as *Vocabulary of the Bible,* Lutterworth, 1958); *The Public Baptism of Infants,* Church Book Room Press, 1959.

(Editor) Edward Arthur Litton, *Introduction to Dogmatic Theology,* new edition, James Clarke, 1960; *Paul's Second Epistle to the Corinthians,* Eerdmans, 1962; *Christianity and the Problem of Origins,* Presbyterian & Reformed, 1964; *But for the Grace of God: Divine Initiative and Human Need,* Hodder & Stoughton, 1964, Westminster, 1965; (with James Atkinson) *Anglicanism and the Roman Church,* Church Book Room Press, 1964; *Theology of the English Reformers,* Hodder & Stoughton, 1965, Eerdmans, 1966; (editor and translator) *The Register of the Company of Pastors of Geneva in the Time of Calvin,* Eerdmans, 1966; (editor and contributor) *Creative Minds in Contemporary Theology: A Guidebook to the Principal Teachings of Karl Barth, G. C. Berkouwer, Dietrich Bonhoeffer, Emil Brunner, Rudolf Bultmann, Oscar Cullman, James Denney, C. H. Dodd, Herman Dooyeweerd, P. T. Forsyth, Charles Gore, Reinhold Niebuhr, Pierre Teilhard de Chardin, and Paul Tillich,* Eerdmans, 1966, 2nd edition, 1969; (editor and author of foreword) *Churchmen Speak: Thirteen Essays,* Marcham Manor Press, 1966; *The Control of Human Life,* Presbyterian & Reformed, 1971; *Confirmation in the Church Today,* Eerdmans, 1973; *Interpreting Prophecy: An Essay in Biblical Perspectives,* Eerdmans, 1976; *Hope for a Despairing World: The Christian Answer to the Problem of Evil,* Baker Book, 1977; *A Commentary on the Epistle to the Hebrews,* Eerdmans, 1977. Contributor to other theological works and symposia. Contributor of articles to philosophical and theological journals in England, United States, France and the Netherlands. Editor, *Christian Foundations,* Hodder & Stoughton, 1964-67.

*   *   *

HUGO, Richard F(ranklin)   1923-

PERSONAL: Born December 21, 1923, in Seattle, Wash.; son of Herbert F. (in the U.S. Navy) and Esther (Monk) Hugo; married Barbara Williams, August 3, 1951 (divorced February 10, 1966); married Ripley Schemm, July 12, 1974; stepchildren: Melissa Hansen, Matthew Hansen. *Education:* University of Washington, Seattle, B.A., 1948, M.A., 1952. *Home:* 2407 Wylie, Missoula, Mont. 59801. *Office:* Department of English, University of Montana, Missoula, Mont. 59801.

CAREER: Employed in various positions at Boeing Co., Seattle, Wash., 1951-63; University of Montana, Missoula, 1964—, began as visiting lecturer, currently professor of English. *Military service:* U.S. Army Air Forces, 1943-45; served in Mediterranean theater; became first lieutenant; received Distinguished Flying Cross and Air Medal. *Awards, honors:* Northwest Writers award, 1966; Rockefeller Foundation creative writing grant, 1967-68; Guggenheim fellowship, 1977-78; Theodore Roethke Prize and Helen Bullis Award, both from *Poetry Northwest.*

*WRITINGS—*Poems, except as indicated: *A Run of Jacks,* University of Minnesota Press, 1961; (with others) *Five Poets of the Pacific,* edited by Robin Skelton, University of Washington Press, 1964; *Death of the Kapowsin Tavern,* Harcourt, 1965; *Good Luck in Cracked Italian,* World Publishing, 1969.

Published by Norton: *The Lady in Kicking Horse Reservoir,* 1973; *What Thou Lovest Well, Remains American,* 1975; *31 Letters and 13 Dreams,* 1977; *Selected Poems,* 1979; *The Triggering Town: Lectures and Essays on Poetry and Writing* (prose), 1979; *White Center,* 1980; *The Right Madness on Skye,* 1980.

WORK IN PROGRESS: West Marginal Way, an autobiographical work.

SIDELIGHTS: Of *The Lady in Kicking Horse Reservoir, Poetry's* Dick Allen writes: "It is the sense of the man which compels our admiration for Richard Hugo's poetry. Reading [this work] we are forever at the side of the poet: Having fun, fishing, driving through Montana, constantly participating in the life about which he writes. Hugo illuminates the almost lost places in America and in our own lives."

For the most part, Hugo is what Marjorie G. Perloff of *Book World* calls "a regional poet." She explains that "the region he celebrates is the Pacific Northwest, specifically his home state, Montana." In *31 Letters and 13 Dreams,* Hugo continues this regional celebration. The book is comprised of poems "addressed to other poets, 'sent' from various cities or small towns," Charles Molesworth of the *Georgia Review* comments. He adds: "Many are charming and humorous—not in any sharply witty way, but with the humor of common sense that draws back from satire of corrosive irony. They are confessional . . . and ramblingly obsessive, . . . but they become distinctive by being thoroughly centered in Hugo's sensibility. They're riddled with nostalgia, and tinged with self-pity; they want to be grand without grandiloquence, and to be vast without losing touch with local detail."

The University of Montana holds the collection of Hugo's manuscripts.

BIOGRAPHICAL/CRITICAL SOURCES: Washington Post Book World, September 16, 1973; *Poetry,* May, 1974; *Contemporary Literary Criticism,* Volume VI, Gale, 1976; *New York Times Book Review,* May 14, 1978, March 25, 1979; *Georgia Review,* fall, 1978; *Prairie Schooner,* fall, 1978; *Los Angeles Times Book Review,* September 16, 1979; *Best Sellers,* April, 1980.

*   *   *

HUMPHREYS, Emyr Owen   1919-

PERSONAL: Born April 15, 1919, in Prestatyn, Wales; son of William and Sarah (Owen) Humphreys; married Elinor Myfanwy Jones, April 25, 1946; children: Dewi, Mair, Sion, Robyn. *Education:* University College of Wales, University of Wales, B.A.; additional study at University College of North Wales. *Home:* Penyberth, 13 Llangors Rd., Cyncoed, Cardiff, Wales. *Agent:* Richard Scott Simon Ltd., 32 College Cross, London N1 1PR, England.

CAREER: Onetime schoolmaster; producer of drama for British Broadcasting Corp. radio and television until 1962; novelist. *Awards, honors:* Somerset Maugham Award for *Hear and Forgive,* 1953; Hawthornden Prize for *A Toy Epic,* 1959; Welsh Arts Council Prize, 1972 and 1975; Gregynog Arts fellow, 1975; Society of Authors Prize, 1979.

WRITINGS: The Little Kingdom, Eyre & Spottiswoode, 1947; *The Voice of a Stranger,* Eyre & Spottiswoode, 1949; *A Change of Heart,* Eyre & Spottiswoode, 1951; *Hear and Forgive,* Gollancz, 1953; *A Man's Estate,* Eyre & Spottiswoode, 1955; *The Italian Wife,* Eyre & Spottiswoode, 1957; *Y Tri Llais,* Llyfrau'r Dryw, 1958; *A Toy Epic,* Eyre & Spottiswoode, 1959.

The Gift, Eyre & Spottiswoode, 1963; *Outside the House of Baal*, Eyre & Spottiswoode, 1965; *Natives* (stories), Secker & Warburg, 1968; *Ancestor Worship* (poetry), Gee, 1970: (with W. S. Jones) *Dinhs*, Llyfrau'r Dryw, 1970; *National Winner* (novel), Macdonald & Co., 1971; *Flesh and Blood* (novel), Hodder & Stoughton, 1974; *Landscapes* (poetry), Oxford University Press, 1976; *The Best of Friends* (novel), Hodder & Stoughton, 1978; *The Kingdom of Bran* (poetry), Ragged Robin Press, 1979; *The Anchor Tree*, Hodder & Stoughton, 1980.

WORK IN PROGRESS: A history of the development of the Welsh identity; another novel.

* * *

HUMPHRIES, (George) Rolfe 1894-1969

PERSONAL: Born November 20, 1894, in Philadephia, Pa.; died April 22, 1969; son of John Henry and Florence L. (Yost) Humphries; married Helen W. Spencer, June 26, 1925; children: John III (deceased). *Education:* Attended Stanford University, 1912-13; Amherst College, A.B. (cum laude), 1915. *Home:* 25 Jeffrey Lane, Amherst, Mass. *Office:* Department of English, Amherst College, Amherst, Mass.

CAREER: Teacher and athletic coach at Potter School for Boys, San Francisco, Calif., 1914-23, and Browning School for Boys, New York, N.Y., 1923-24; Woodmere Academy, Woodmere, N.Y., teacher of Latin, 1925-57; Hunter College (now Hunter College of the City University of New York), New York, N.Y., professor of Latin, 1957; Amherst College, Amherst, Mass., lecturer in English, 1957-65, professor emeritus, 1965-69. Visiting Walker-Ames Professor of English, University of Washington, 1966. Member of summer faculty at writers' conferences at University of New Hampshire, Indiana University, University of Colorado, University of Utah, Portland State University. *Military service:* U.S. Army, 1917-19; became first lieutenant. *Member:* National Institute of Arts and Letters, American Association of University Professors. *Awards, honors:* Guggenheim fellow in poetry, 1938-39; Shelley Memorial Award for poetry, 1947; honorary A.M., Amherst College, 1950; Borestone Mountain Poetry Award for *The Wind of Time*, 1951, for *Poems, Collected and New*, 1956; Academy of American Poets $5,000 fellowship, 1955; Winterfest Poetry Award ($500), 1966.

WRITINGS—Published by Scribner, except as indicated: *Out of the Jewel*, 1942; *The Summer Landscape*, 1944; *Forbid Thy Ravens*, 1947; (editor) *New Poems by American Poets*, Arno, Volume I, 1953, Volume II, 1957; *The Wind of Time*, 1950; *Poems, Collected and New*, 1954, *Green Armour on Green Ground*, 1956; *Collected Poems of Rolfe Humphries*, Indiana University Press, 1965; (editor) *Wolfville Yarns of Alfred Henry Lewis*, Kent State University Press, 1968; *Coat of a Stick: Late Poems*, Indiana University Press, 1969.

Translator: Federico Garcia Lorca, *Poet in New York*, Norton, 1940; Virgil, *Aeneid*, Scribner, 1951; Garcia Lorca, *Gypsy Ballads*, Indiana University Press, 1953; Ovid, *Metamorphoses*, Indiana University Press, 1955; Juvenal, *Satires*, Indiana University Press, 1958; Ovid, *Art of Love*, Indiana University Press, 1958; Martial, *Selected Epigrams*, Indiana University Press, 1963; Garcia Lorca, *Five Plays: Comedies and Tragicomedies*, Indiana University Press, 1963; Lucretius, *The Way Things Are* (translation of *De Rerum Natura*), Indiana University Press, 1968; (and editor) *Nine Thorny Thickets: Selected Poems of Dafydd Ap Gwilym*, Kent State University Press, 1970.

BIOGRAPHICAL/CRITICAL SOURCES: Nation, August 28, 1967; *New York Times*, April 24, 1969; *Washington Post*, April 24, 1969; *Newsweek*, May 5, 1969.†

* * *

HUNT, Hugh 1911-

PERSONAL: Born September 25, 1911, in Camberley, Surrey, England; son of Cecil Edwin (an army officer) and Ethel (Crookshank) Hunt; married Janet Gordon, November 8, 1941; children: Caroline, Simon. *Education:* Attended Marlborough College, Wilts, England; Sorbonne University, diploma, 1930; Heidelberg University, diploma, 1930; Magdalen College, Oxford, B.A., 1933, M.A., 1960. *Religion:* Church of England. *Home:* Cae Terfyn, Criccieth, Gwynedd LL52 0SA, Wales.

CAREER: Maddermanket Theatre, Norwich, England, director, 1933-34; Abbey Theatre, Dublin, Ireland, director, 1934-38; Bristol Old Vic Theatre, Bristol, England, director, 1946-49; Old Vic Theatre, London, England, director, 1949-53; Australian Elizabeth Theatre Trust, Sydney, director, 1954-61; University of Manchester, Manchester, England, professor of drama, 1961-74, professor emeritus, 1974—. Arts Council of Great Britain, member of drama panel, 1949-53, 1963-66, member of the Independent Television Authority, 1965-70; director of Sadlers Wells Trust, 1965-70; member of drama panel, Welsh Arts Council, 1979—. *Military service:* His Majesty's Forces, 1939-46; became major. *Member:* Garrick Club (London). *Awards, honors:* Commander of the Order of the British Empire.

WRITINGS: Old Vic Prefaces, Routledge & Kegan Paul, 1954, reprinted, Greenwood Press, 1973; *The Director in the Theatre*, Routledge & Kegan Paul, 1954; *The Making of Australian Theatre*, Cheshire, 1960; *The Live Theatre*, Oxford University Press, 1962; *The Revels History of Drama in English*, Volume VII, Methuen, 1978; *The Abbey: Ireland's National Theatre, 1904-1979*, Columbia University Press, 1979; *Sean O'Casey*, Columbia University Press, 1980. Contributor of articles to periodicals.

Plays: (With Frank O'Connor) "In the Train" (one act); "The Invincibles."

* * *

HUNT, Raymond G(eorge) 1928-

PERSONAL: Born July 1, 1928, in Buffalo, N.Y.; son of William R. (in automotive services) and Florence (Elkington) Hunt; married Viola C. Wannenwetsch, June 3, 1949; children: Gregory W., Karen S. *Education:* University of Buffalo (now State University of New York at Buffalo), B.A., 1952, Ph.D., 1958. *Politics:* Democrat. *Home:* 487 Brantwood Rd., Snyder, N.Y. 14226. *Office:* School of Management, State University of New York, Buffalo, N.Y. 14214.

CAREER: Washington University, St. Louis, Mo., assistant professor of psychology, 1958-61; State University of New York at Buffalo, 1961—, began as assistant professor of psychology, now professor of organization and human resources. Consultant in social psychology, U.S. Veterans Administration. *Military service:* U.S. Army, 1945-48. *Member:* American Psychological Association, American Sociological Association, Academy of Management, American Society for Public Administration, Phi Beta Kappa. *Awards, honors:* Co-recipient of Helen M. DeRoy Award, Society for Study of Social Problems, 1960, for research and writing in the field of social problems.

WRITINGS: (Editor with E. P. Hollander) *Current Perspectives in Social Psychology,* Oxford University Press, 1963, 4th edition, 1976; (with others) *Nurses, Patients and Social Systems,* University of Missouri Press, 1967; (editor with Hollander) *Classic Perspectives in Social Psychology,* Oxford University Press, 1972; *Interpersonal Strategies for System Management,* Brooks-Cole, 1974; (editor with B. Bowser) *Impact of Racism on White Americans,* Sage Publications, in press. Regular contributor to psychological, sociological, and management journals.

WORK IN PROGRESS: Research in organizational behavior and management, and in social policy.

*   *   *

HUNT, William 1934-

PERSONAL: Born May 21, 1934; married second wife, Elisabeth, 1976; children: (first marriage) Phillip Devin; (second marriage) Katherine, Damon Michael. *Education:* University of Chicago, B.A., 1964. *Home:* 1024 Eleventh St., Wilmette, Ill. 60091. *Office:* Esperanza School for Retarded Children, 520 North Marshfield Ave., Chicago, Ill. 60622.

CAREER: Poet. Labor organizer, 1953-58; community organizer, 1963-66; *Chicago Review,* Chicago, Ill., poetry editor, 1963-67; Department of Human Resources, Chicago, director of information, 1970-73; director of community affairs, Bureau of Employment Security, Illinois Department of Labor, 1974-75; director of public services, Model Cities and Chicago Committee on Urban Opportunity, 1975-76; Esperanza School for Retarded Children, Chicago, administrator, 1976—. Poet-in-residence, Northeastern Illinois University, 1979-81. *Awards, honors:* National Endowment for the Arts grant, 1967-68; Langston Hughes Memorial Prize of *Poetry Magazine* for poems in February, 1970, issue.

WRITINGS: Of the Map That Changes (poems), Swallow Press, 1973; *Oceans and Corridors of Orpheus* (long poem), Elpenor Books, 1979.

WORK IN PROGRESS: Revising a second collection of poems.

SIDELIGHTS: William Hunt told *CA:* "My interest in expressing passionate states of mind or of mood in a clear or dramatic context fluctuates. Perhaps it is a sign of only spasmodic concern for the common reader's interests. My interests, my path, in so far as these terms can be used to describe what is arriving from the future, focuses more on love of the activity than on the results.

"There has been a numerical proliferation of poets in recent years but with it a waning of active intelligence. In many spheres of life today this is also true. So-called scientists of all sorts substitute the results of enumeration and quantification for forms of thinking. Whether they have microscopes, telescopes or polling pads in hand, little active attempt is made to consider changing phenomena. Too many 'thinkers' are unable to convincingly bridge controversy, to see that the old forms upon which society situated itself no longer exist, that an inner activity of heartfelt thought will be required to renew those areas of life which we share with others. Despite my expression of this being the case, I do not experience my knowledge of it as an abstract picture of modern day life. Like Hansel and Gretel we simply must proceed to find our way home. My working in poetry proceeds out of this apprehension."

*   *   *

HUNTER, Alan (James Herbert) 1922-

PERSONAL: Born June 25, 1922, in Hoveton St. John, Norwich, England; son of Herbert Ernest (a poultry farmer) and Isabella (Andrew) Hunter; married Adelaide Cubitt (an antique dealer), March 6, 1944; children: Helen. *Religion:* Zen Buddhist. *Home:* 3 St. Laurence Ave., Brundall, Norwich NR13 5QH, England.

CAREER: Poultry farmer, Hoveton St. John, Norwich, England, 1936-40; bookseller in Norwich, 1946-57; full-time writer, 1957—. *Military service:* Royal Air Force, 1940-46; became leading aircraftsman. *Member:* Society of Authors, Crime Writers Association, Norwich Writer Circle (vice-president, 1955—), Yare Valley Sailing Club (rear commodore, 1961-62; vice commodore, 1962-63; commodore, 1963—).

WRITINGS: The Norwich Poems, 1943-44, Soman Wherry Press, 1945; *Gently Does It,* Rinehart, 1955; *Gently by the Shore,* Rinehart, 1956; *Gently Down the Stream,* Cassell, 1957, Roy, 1960; *Landed Gently,* Cassell, 1957, Roy, 1960; *Gently through the Mill,* Cassell, 1958; *Gently in the Sun,* Cassell, 1959, Berkley Publishing, 1964.

Gently with the Painters, Cassell, 1960, Macmillan, 1976; *Gently to the Summit,* Cassell, 1961, Berkley Publishing, 1965; *Gently Go Man,* Cassell, 1961, Berkley Publishing, 1964; *Gently Where the Roads Go,* Cassell, 1962; *Gently Floating,* Cassell, 1963, Berkley Publishing, 1964; *Gently Sahib,* Cassell, 1964; *Gently with the Ladies,* Cassell, 1965, Macmillan, 1974; *Gently North-West,* Cassell, 1967; published as *Gently in the Highlands,* Macmillan, 1975; *Gently Continental,* Cassell, 1967; *Gently Coloured,* Cassell, 1969; *Gently with the Innocents,* Cassell, 1970, Macmillan, 1974; *Gently at a Gallop,* Cassell, 1971; *Vivienne: Gently Where She Lay,* Cassell, 1972; *Gently French,* Cassell, 1973; *Gently in Trees,* Cassell, 1974, published as *Gently through the Woods,* Macmillan, 1975; *Gently with Love,* Cassell, 1975; *Gently Where the Birds Are,* Cassell, 1976; *Gently Instrumental,* Cassell, 1977; *Gently to a Sleep,* Cassell, 1978; *The Honfleur Decision,* Constable, 1980; *Gabrielle's Way,* Constable, 1980.

Omnibus volumes: *Gently in an Omnibus: Three Complete Novels* (contains *Gently Does It, Gently through the Mill,* and *Gently in the Sun*), Cassell, 1966, St. Martin's, 1972; *Gently in Another Omnibus* (contains *Gently Go Man, Gently Where the Roads Go,* and *Gently Floating*), Cassell, 1969, St. Martin's, 1972.

Also author of several plays. Contributor of reviews of crime books; contributor of humorous short stories to BBC Publications.

WORK IN PROGRESS: Fields of Heather.

SIDELIGHTS: Alan Hunter wrote *CA:* "I work with a pipe in my mouth, mostly at a typewriter, though I have had spells of manuscript writing. I switched to manuscript for a while to free me from being tied to a desk. Instead I drove out to some quiet spot and worked there on a clipboard—but since I write my books in the autumn and winter, the practice was limited by weather. I write comparatively slowly. For me narrative tempo/flavour is critical and I need to get it right as I proceed; I have never been able to rough-draft a book for later redaction. My early books were all first-draft, with a few manuscript emendations, and it was not until I began writing books in manuscripts that I used a second draft. Now I continue the second draft practice, though often there is little difference between the two drafts: just here and there a minor adjustment.

"In my experience there is no effective advice that one can offer on creative writing. Those with the knack don't need advice, those without the knack can't use it. Only the latter send you manuscript to criticise, and you will be wise to stop at praise. The former can be told nothing, except by themselves. They take their teaching from the example of others, embodying what they need and learning at length to jettison their redundancies. If I had to teach creative writing to my son I would simply point to a box of stationery.

"Every writer I have ever read has influenced me, down to copywriters for produce cartons. Simenon, Lawrence, Proust, Chandler are writers I have found unusually compatible. In their attitudes, principally: their examples of mental stance. But one learns everywhere, continuously, it may be from the next commerical. Perhaps most likely from the next commercial.

"The eye cannot see itself, the sword cannot cut itself, and I doubt if any author knows in truth why he writes. I am conscious of an audience who enjoys what I enjoy, who will find disturbing what I find disturbing, enlightening what I find enlightening, and is urgent to share these things with me. We have a direction together which I have the task of making manifest. Whence? Towards some good not possible to define. I think this is the situation of every author above the level of simple commerce. Or even below it."

Gently Does It was adapted for the stage and was produced under the title "That Man Gently" in Harlow, England, November, 1961. Many of Hunter's books have been published in Germany, Sweden, Norway, France, Italy, Spain, and Yugoslavia.

BIOGRAPHICAL/CRITICAL SOURCES: Books and Bookmen, April, 1970, March, 1971; *Punch,* June 14, 1967, April 16, 1969.

*   *   *

HUPPE, Bernard F.   1911-

PERSONAL: Born August 1, 1911, in New York, N.Y.; son of Bernard F. and Irma (Honthumb) Huppe; married Marian Lois McMaster, August 13, 1943; children: Anne McMaster, B. F. Alexander II, Geoffrey McMaster. *Education:* Amherst College, B.A.; New York University, Ph.D., 1940. *Home address:* Box 406, Castine, Me. 04421. *Office:* Department of English, Harpur College, State University of New York, Binghamton, N.Y.

CAREER: Duke University, Durham, N.C., assistant in English, 1934-35; Washington Square College, New York, N.Y., instructor, 1935-41; Princeton University, Princeton, N.J., assistant professor of English, 1946-50; State University of New York at Binghamton, Harpur College, associate professor, 1950-53, professor of English, 1953-75, Distinguished Service Professor, 1975-80, professor emeritus, 1980—, chairman of division of humanities, 1952-54, chairman of English department, 1963-70, director of Center for Medieval and Early Renaissance, 1970-75. Visiting professor, University of Southampton, 1970-71, and University of Aarhus, 1980. Fulbright lecturer, University of Vienna, 1955-56. Board of Foreign Scholars, member of selection board for Austria, 1958-60, chairman, 1961; fellowship review committee, National Foundation on the Arts and Humanities, 1966. *Military service:* U.S. Army, Corps of Engineers, 1942-46; became captain; awarded Bronze Star. *Member:* Modern Language Association of America.

WRITINGS: (With D. W. Robertson *Piers Ploughman and Scriptural Tradition,* Princeton University Press, 1950; (with R. W. Rafuse) *The Liberal Arts,* State University of New York Press, 1954; (with Jack Kaminsky) *Logic and Lan-*

guage, Knopf, 1956; *Doctrine and Poetry,* State University of New York Press, 1959; (with D. W. Robertson, Jr.) *Fruyt and Chaf,* Princeton University Press, 1963; *A Reading of the Canterbury Tales,* State University of New York Press, 1964; *Web of Words,* State University of New York Press, 1969; (with P. Szarmach) *The O. E. Homily,* State University of New York Press, 1978. Contributor of articles on medieval literature to periodicals. Member of publications committee, State University of New York.

WORK IN PROGRESS: Four Old English Poems: Translations and Studies of Vainglory, Creation, Dream of the Road, Judith.

*   *   *

HUTCHINGS, Margaret (Joscelyne)   1918-

PERSONAL: Born December 18, 1918, in Brentwood, Essex, England; daughter of William Jabez (a draper) and Marjorie Winifred (Golding) Howard; married Sidney Alfred Hutchings (a consulting optician), June 1, 1939; children: Richard John, Christopher William, David George. *Education:* Educated in England. *Religion:* Church of England. *Home:* Mimosa House, South Weald, Brentwood, Essex, England.

CAREER: Free-lance writer; toymaker; designer. Chairman, Bon Marche Ltd. Demonstrator of toymaking on British Broadcasting Corp. television. Past president, Ongar Women's Institute. *Member:* British Toy Makers' Guild. *Awards, honors:* International Handicrafts Exhibition (Olympia, London, England) awards for Father Christmas and sledge, 1956, for giant monkey, 1957, and for toy village, 1958.

WRITINGS: Glove Toys, Studio Books, 1958; *Modern Soft Toy Making,* Mills & Boon, 1959, Branford, 1960; (self-illustrated) *Toying with Trifles,* Mills & Boon, 1960; (contributor) The Marchioness of Anglesey, editor, *The Country Woman's Year,* M. Joseph, 1960; *Hints on Soft Toys,* Mills & Boon, 1961; (self-illustrated) *Patchwork Playthings,* Branford, 1961; *Dolls and How to Make Them,* Branford, 1963; *What Shall I Do with This?,* Mills & Boon, 1963, Taplinger, 1965; *The Book of the Teddy Bear,* Mills & Boon, 1964, Branford, 1965; *What Shall I Do Today?,* Mills & Boon, 1965, Taplinger, 1966; *What Shall I Do This Month?,* Mills & Boon, 1965, Taplinger, 1966; *What Shall I Do: From Scandinavia,* Mills & Boon, 1966, Taplinger, 1967.

Making New Testament Toys, Taplinger, 1972; *Making Old Testament Toys,* Taplinger 1972; *Making and Using Finger Puppets,* Mills & Boon, 1973; *Toys from the Tales of Beatrix Potter,* Mills & Boon, 1973, Warne, 1974; *Modelling in Hessian,* Mills & Boon, 1975; *Sculpting in Burlap,* Taplinger, 1975; *Nature's Toyshop,* Transatlantic, 1976; *Button-Box Book,* Transatlantic, 1976; *Wool-Bag Book,* Transatlantic, 1976. Contributor of articles to newspapers and magazines, including *Home and Country, Housewife, Sunday Times, She,* and *Good Housekeeping.*

SIDELIGHTS: Margaret Hutchings hates insincerity, indecision, two-faced people, procrastination, cold weather, eggs, and cocktail parties. She loves babies, old people, small animals (except mice), sunshine, the music of a roundabout, deserted seashores, fruit, and spaghetti.

*   *   *

HUTCHINSON, Ray Coryton   1907-1975

PERSONAL: Born January 23, 1907, in Finchley, Middlesex, England; died July 3, 1975, in London, England; buried at St. Katherines Church, Merstham, Surrey, England; son of Harry and Lucy Mabel (Coryton) Hutchinson; married Margaret Owen Jones, April 2, 1929; children: Ann Coryton, Jeremy Olpherts, Elspeth Owen Hutchinson Welldon, Piers Evelyn. *Education:* Oriel College, Oxford, M.A. 1927. *Religion:* Church of England. *Home:* Dysart, Blechingley, Redhill, Surrey, England. *Agent:* Curtis Brown, Ltd., 575 Madison Ave., New York, N.Y. 10022.

CAREER: Colman Ltd., Norwich, England, assistant advertising manager, 1927-35; novelist, 1935-75. *Military service:* British Army, 1940-45; became major. *Member:* Royal Society of Literature (fellow). *Awards, honors:* Gold Medal Award from *London Sunday Times*, 1938, for novel, *Testament;* W. H. Smith Literature Award, 1966.

WRITINGS—All published by Farrar & Rinehart, except at indicated: *The Answering Glory,* 1932; *The Unforgotten Prisoner,* 1934; *One Light Burning,* 1935; *Shining Scabbard* (Book-of-the-Month Club selection), 1936, reprinted, Duckworth, 1968; *Testament,* 1938; *The Fire and the Wood,* 1940, reprinted, Duckworth, 1970; *Interim,* 1945; *Elephant and Castle* (Book-of-the-Month Club selection), Rinehart, 1947, reprinted, Greenwood Press, 1971; *Journey with Strangers,* Rinehart, 1952; *The Stepmother,* Rinehart, 1955, reprinted, White Lion, 1973; *March the Ninth,* Rinehart, 1957; *The Inheritor,* Harper, 1962; *A Child Possessed,* Bles, 1964, Harper, 1965; *Johanna at Daybreak,* M. Joseph, 1969; *Origins of Cathleen: A Diversion,* M. Joseph, 1971; *Recollection of a Journey,* White Lion, 1974; *Rising,* M. Joseph, 1976; *Two Men of Letters: Correspondence between R. C. Hutchinson, Novelist, and Martyn Skinner, Poet, 1957-74,* edited by Rupert Hart-Davis, M. Joseph, 1979. Also author of play, "Last Train South," produced at St. Martin's Theatre, London, 1938. Contributor of short stories to British magazines.

AVOCATIONAL INTERESTS: Motoring, gardening, occasional broadcasting.†

I

ILLINGWORTH, Ronald Stanley 1909-

PERSONAL: Born October 7, 1909, in Harrogate, England; son of Herbert Edward (an architect) and Ellen (Brayshaw) Illingworth; married Cynthia-Mary Redhead (a pediatrician); children: Andrea, Robin, Corinne. *Education:* University of Leeds, M.B., Ch.B., 1934, M.D., 1936, Diploma in Public Health (with distinction), 1938; Diploma in Child Health, 1938. *Politics:* Conservative. *Religion:* Baptist. *Home:* 8 Harley Rd., Sheffield, England. *Office:* Children's Hospital, Sheffield, England.

CAREER: University of Sheffield, Sheffield, England, professor of child health, 1947—. Pediatrician at Children's Hospital and United Sheffield Hospitals. *Military service:* Royal Army, Medical Corps, served in Middle East, 1941-45; became lieutenant colonel. *Member:* Royal Photographic Society (fellow), Royal College of Physicians (fellow), American Academy of Pediatrics, Soviet Academy of Pediatricians. *Awards, honors:* Spence Medal from British Paediatric Association; Aldrich Award from American Academy of Pediatrics; Dawson Williams Prize from British Medical Association.

WRITINGS: Some Aspects of Child Health, University of Sheffield, 1949; *The Normal Child: Some Problems of the First Three Years and Their Treatment,* Little, Brown, 1953, 2nd edition published as *The Normal Child: Some Problems of the First Five Years and Their Treatment,* 1957, 7th edition, 1979; (with wife, Cynthia-Mary Illingworth) *Babies and Young Children: Feedings, Management and Care,* Churchill, 1954, 6th edition, Churchill Livingstone, 1977; *Children and Sleep,* Family Health Publications, 1956; (editor) *Recent Advances in Cerebral Palsy,* Little, Brown, 1958; *Common Ailments in Babies,* British Medical Association, 1959, published as *Common Ailments in Toddlers,* 1960.

The Development of the Infant and Young Child, Normal and Abnormal, Livingstone, 1960, 7th edition, Churchill Livingstone, 1980; *Your Child from Five to Twelve,* British Medical Association, 1962; *An Introduction to Developmental Assessment in the First Year,* Education and Information Unit, National Spastics Society, 1962; *The Normal School Child: His Problems, Physical and Emotional,* Heinemann, 1964; (with C. M. Illingworth) *Lessons from Childhood: Some Aspects of the Early Life of Unusual Men and Women,* Williams & Wilkins, 1966; *All about Feeding Your Baby,* British Medical Association, 1966; *Common Symptoms of*

Disease in Children, F. A. Davis, 1967, 6th edition, Churchill Livingstone, 1979; (with D. Egan and R. C. MacKeith) *Developmental Screening,* Heinemann, 1969, 2nd edition, Blackwell Scientific Publications, 1977; *Treatment of the Child at Home,* F. A. Davis, 1971; *The Child at School: A Pediatricians Guide for Teachers,* Blackwell Scientific Publications, 1975. Contributor of chapters to over fifty textbooks, thirteen encyclopedias, and to over 400 medical papers. Contributor of articles to medical and photographic journals.

WORK IN PROGRESS: Infections in Children: Prevention and Immunisation, for Churchill Livingstone; *Your Child's Development: Physical, Emotional, and Intellectual, and How to Help It,* for Churchill Livingstone.

*　　　*　　　*

ILSLEY, Velma (Elizabeth) 1918-

PERSONAL: Born August 6, 1918, in Edmonton, Alberta, Canada; daughter of Rowland Sutherland and Lily E. (Thomas) Ilsley; married James W. Ledwith (a physician), May 1, 1962. *Education:* Studied at Rutgers University, 1936-38, Moore Institute of Art, 1938-40, Art Students League, Sculpture Center, New School for Social Research, and Hunter College of the City University of New York. *Politics:* Independent. *Home:* 59 East Shore Rd., Huntington, N.Y.

CAREER: Writer and illustrator of children's books, painter, and sculptor. Began career as a fashion illustrator. *Member:* Society of Illustrators, Authors League of America.

WRITINGS—All self-illustrated: The Pink Hat, Lippincott, 1956; *A Busy Day for Chris,* Lippincott, 1957; *The Long Stocking,* Lippincott, 1959; *Once upon a Time* (baby record book in verse), C. R. Gibson, 1960; *M Is for Moving,* Walck, 1966.

Illustrator: Elizabeth Honness, *Mystery of the Doll Hospital,* Lippincott, 1955; Gladys Adshead, *Brownies, It's Christmas,* Oxford University Press, 1955; Mabel Leigh Hunt, *Miss Jellytot's Visit,* Lippincott, 1955; Hunt, *Stars for Cristy,* Lippincott, 1956; Joan Lowery Nixon, *Mystery of Hurricane Castle,* Abelard, 1956; Honness, *Mystery in the Square Tower,* Lippincott, 1957; Sybil Conrad, *Enchanted Sixteen,* Holt, 1957; Emma Atkins Jacob, *For Each a Dream,* Holt, 1958; Hunt, *Cristy at Skippinghills,* Lippincott, 1958; Norma Simon, *My Beach House,* Lippincott, 1958; Adshead, *Brownies, Hurry,* Walck, 1959.

Rebecca Caudhill, *Time for Lisa*, Thomas Nelson, 1960; Alice P. Miller, *The Heart of Camp Whipporwill*, Lippincott, 1960; Molly Cone, *Only Jane*, Thomas Nelson, 1960; Adshead, *The Smallest Brownie's Fearful Adventure*, Walck, 1961; *What's a Cousin*, Knopf, 1962; Alma Powers, *Waters, the Giving Gift*, Farrar, Straus, 1962; Duane Bradley, *Mystery at the Shoals*, Lippincott, 1962; Beman Lord, *Our New Baby's ABC*, Walck, 1964; Nan Hayden Agle, *Kate and the Apple Tree*, Seabury, 1965; Agle, *Joe Bean*, Seabury, 1966; Margaret Hodges, *Sing Out Charley*, Farrar, Straus, 1968; Anne Houston, *The Cat across the Way*, Seabury, 1968.

Rosalie K. Fry, *Mungo*, Farrar, Straus, 1972; Dorothy Crayder, *She, the Adventuress*, Atheneum, 1973; Tanith Lee, *Princess Hynchatti and Some Other Surprises*, Farrar, Straus, 1973; Crayder, *She and the Dubious Three*, Atheneum, 1974; Anne Alexander, *To Live a Lie*, Atheneum, 1975. Has illustrated more than twenty jacket covers.

SIDELIGHTS: Velma Ilsley wrote *CA*: "*M Is for Moving*, the title of my alphabet book, could have been the title for the first five years of my childhood. In 1920, my father died and we moved from British Columbia to Nova Scotia, then to California and finally to Lakewood, New Jersey where I had most of my schooling. I have very few memories of my early years. The highlights were gathering hailstones in San Bernardino and 'sailing over our sea lawn' in a rocking wash-tub.

"My interest in the arts started in Lakewood. My father, formerly a teacher and owner of a men's clothing store, had come from a family of artists. Our small apartment was full of my mother's paintings; though now being the sole supporter of three daughters, she spent most of her time sewing. My older sister and I made up stories and illustrated them for our own amusement. All of us drew. With a small jigsaw we cut out wooden dolls that we later painted, shellacked and sold. We also spent hours dancing to Ned Wayburn records and were usually on the school entertainment programs either as acrobatic, toe or tap dancers: my mother, the choreographer. Though not a professional dancer, it was through her dancing graces and some wonderful, influential friends (namely, Caroline Fuller, an author, and Katherine Hinsdale, the librarian) that made it possible for us to spend enjoyable hours on some of the loveliest estates in Lakewood. I remember playing games and having lunch with the Arthur Brisbane children, to whom my mother taught dancing, having tea with Mrs. Charles Lathrop Pack in her garden and dining with John D. Rockefeller, Sr. It was because of these friends that we were able to vacation in Nova Scotia on the Bay of Fundy where my father had spent his boyhood.

"After college and art school I became a fashion artist in Philadelphia, then Miami and eventually New York, where I continued in that career as free-lancer until I lost the Saks Fifth Avenue children's account. This was a turning point in my life—I decided to be an illustrator of children's books. Eunice Blake, then children's editor at Lippincott, gave me my first chance, and a short time later Ursula Nordstrom of Harper & Row suggested I write my own picture books. It was thanks to some severe criticism from the poet Horace Gregory, who was teaching a course I took at The New School, that prompted me to analyze the drawing style of my as yet unsold picture book, *The Pink Hat*, rewrite it completely, except for the opening two lines, and sell it to Lippincott. The children who had been models for my fashion drawings became models for my stories, illustrations and paintings for many years. Now, I mostly create my own.

"The subjects of my books are usually based on personal feelings, experiences, habits or chance happenings. *The Pink Hat* resulted from paintings I had done of my models in a hat; *A Busy Day for Chris* from a drawing I had made of a little girl contentedly lying in a meadow and my own love for the outdoors—whether it was 'opening windows wide' to look out on the green parks in Tudor City where I lived, or riding through the Connecticut countryside in an old M.G. with the windshield down. *M Is for Moving* was written after my marriage and more moving, culminating in our present nineteenth-century house in Huntington Harbor. Here, I paint, sculpture and fill a 'LONG STOCKING' with stories, just begun, half finished or being revised.''

* * *

IRELAND, Norma Olin 1907-

PERSONAL: Born March 27, 1907, in Wadsworth, Ohio; daughter of Carl Leroy (a farmer) and Jessie (a musician; maiden name, Latimer) Olin; married David E. Ireland (an industrial engineer), August 15, 1931. *Education:* University of Akron, B.A., 1928; Western Reserve University (now Case Western Reserve University), B.S. in L.S., 1929. *Politics:* Republican. *Religion:* Congregationalist. *Home:* 2237 Brooke Rd., Fallbrook, Calif. 92028.

CAREER: University of Akron, Akron, Ohio, reference and reserve room librarian in Bierce Library, 1929-36, night school instructor, 1936; Pomona College Library, Claremont, Calif., acting head of loan department, 1936-37; Glendale Public Library, Glendale, Calif., acting head of reference department and assistant to librarian, 1937-38; University of Southern California, Los Angeles, associate professor in Library School, 1938, acting head of education library, 1938; Ireland Book and Library Service, Altadena, Calif., co-owner, 1938—; Ireland Indexing Service, Altadena and Spring Valley, Calif., director, 1938—; free-lance technical indexer and researcher, 1956—; certified genealogy records researcher, 1969—. *Member:* American Library Association (national chairman, 1938-39), American Society of Indexers, Society of Mayflower Descendants, Daughters of the American Revolution, National Contesters Association (president, 1953-54), Junior Members Round Table, Connecticut Society of Genealogists, Fallbrook Art Association, Phi Mu, Chi Delta Phi, Alpha Phi Gamma, Pi Gamma Mu, Fallbrook Woman's Club.

WRITINGS—Published by Faxon, except as indicated: *Historical Biographies for Junior and Senior High Schools, Universities, and Colleges: A Bibliography*, McKinley Publishing, 1933; *The Picture File in School, College, and Public Libraries*, 1935, revised edition, 1952; *The Pamphlet File in School, College, and Public Libraries*, 1937, revised edition, 1954; (with husband, David E. Ireland) *An Index to Monologs and Dialogs*, 1939, revised edition, 1949; *An Index to Indexes: A Subject Bibliography of Published Indexes*, 1942; (editor) *Local Indexes in American Libraries*, 1947.

(Editor) *N.C.A. Handbook*, A. D. Freese, 1954; (with John Mead Atwater) *Long Word Books*, Book 1, A. D. Freese, 1956; *An Index to Skits and Stunts*, 1958; *Index to Scientists of the World, from Ancient to Modern Times: Biographies and Portraits*, 1962; *Index to Full-Length Plays, 1944-1964*, 1965.

Index to Women, from Ancient to Modern Times: Biographies and Portraits, 1970; *Index to Fairy Tales, 1949-1972*, 1970; *Index to Inspiration: A Thesaurus of Subjects for Speakers and Writers*, 1976; *Index to America: Eighteenth-Century Life and Customs*, 1976; *Index to America: Seventeenth-Century Life and Customs*, 1978; *Index to*

Fairy Tales, 1973-1977, 1979. Columnist, *Fallbrook Enterprise.* Contributor to *Encyclopedia of Education;* also contributor of over 130 articles to periodicals. Editor of junior librarians' section, *Wilson Library Bulletin,* 1936-37; editor, *NCA Bulletin, 1953-54;* editor, "Practical Contester" section, *Contest,* 1954-59.

WORK IN PROGRESS: Index to America: Nineteenth-Century Life and Customs, a supplement to *Index to Women; Index to American Twentieth Century, 1900-1980.*

SIDELIGHTS: Norma Ireland wrote *CA:* "God and serendipity have combined to make my writing possible. My first book was suggested after I had compiled a bibliography for a library patron (when I was a reference librarian) who said: 'This should be published as there is nothing like it in print, and it is much needed in schools.' I sent it, therefore, to a historical magazine whose editor replied: 'If you will expand it, we'll publish it as a book.' Later, I saw the need for many reference books, both manuals and indexes for use in libraries, schools, and universities.

"I was born and raised on a farm, the youngest of three sisters. Every Christmas brought at least one book, and thus we had a sizable home library—much needed because the small town only had a inadequate library in the school. Moving to the city when a junior in high school was an exciting but traumatic experience, but I survived and graduated as valedictorian of my large class. Perhaps I had a heritage of survival and accomplishment because I was the descendant of American pioneers: two Mayflower pilgrims and nine revolutionary ancestors. My choice of career was three-fold: journalism, law, or library science, in that order. After a college pre-law course and much journalism, combined with five years part-time work in the local library (while in high school and college), I finally decided on going to library school. Reason: Getting a job as a librarian seemed the best possibility for a woman in those early-depression years.

"At the present time I am writing two columns for the local newspaper.... I have a small genealogy business, a 'service' for amateur genealogical workers, mostly photocopy work of old and rare newspapers, magazines, and books I own. I hope to compile my family 'pedigree' book, eventually."

AVOCATIONAL INTERESTS: Genealogy, philately, contesting, book collecting, travel, music (plays organ and piano), tape recording, oil painting, jewelry making and repair, pets, needlepoint, reading, miniatures.

BIOGRAPHICAL/CRITICAL SOURCES: Contest, October, 1953; *American,* June, 1954; *Fallbrook Enterprise,* June 14, 1979.

*   *   *

ISAACS, Alan 1925-

PERSONAL: Born January 14, 1925, in London, England; son of Stanley (a company director) and Regina (Hiller) Isaacs; married Pauline Elliott, 1948 (died, 1952); married Fleur Richmond, May 21, 1955 (died, 1964); married Jacqueline Boulting, 1966; children: (first marriage) Amanda Valentine, Penelope Ann; (second marriage) Lucy, Joanna, Emma (stepdaughters). *Education:* Attended St. Paul's School, London, England, 1938-42; Imperial College of Science and Technology, London, B.Sc., Ph.D. *Politics:* Labor. *Religion:* Agnostic. *Home:* Heathbourne Lodge, Bushey Heath, Hertfordshire, England.

CAREER: University of London, Imperial College of Science and Technology, London, England, research assistant in physical chemistry, 1946-50; Polish University College, London, part-time lecturer, 1947-49; Alfred Isaacs & Sons (raw material suppliers), London, director, 1951-55; freelance writer, lexicographer, and publisher, 1970—. Associate, City and Guilds of London Institute. Technical adviser to Constable & Co. (publishers).

WRITINGS—Published by Penguin, except as indicated: *Introducing Science,* 1961, Basic Books; 1962, revised edition, 1971; (with E. B. Uvarov and D. R. Chapman) *Penguin Dictionary of Science,* 1964, revised edition, 1979; *Survival of God in the Scientific Age,* 1966.

Editor: (With H. J. Gray) *New Dictionary of Physics,* 2nd edition (Isaacs was not associated with previous edition), Longman, 1975; *The Multilingual Commercial Dictionary,* Facts on File, 1980; *The Macmillan Encyclopedia,* Macmillan, 1981.

Editor of series; all published by Pan Books, 1976—: "Dictionary of Physical Sciences"; "Dictionary of Life Sciences"; "Dictionary of Earth Sciences"; "Dictionary of Economics and Commerce"; "Dictionary of Philosophy." Contributor to journals. Scientific editor of *Hamlyn World Dictionary,* 1971; advisory scientific editor, *CBS Almanac,* 1974—.

SIDELIGHTS: Introducing Science has been translated into Dutch, Spanish, German, Portuguese, Hebrew, and Japanese. *Avocational interests:* Music, painting.

J

JACK, Donald Lamont 1924-

PERSONAL: Born December 6, 1924, in Radcliffe, Lancashire, England. *Education:* Attended Marr College (Scotland), Royal Academy of Fine Arts (Belgium), and Canadian Theatre School. *Home:* 14 Russell St. E., Lindsay, Ontario, Canada.

CAREER: Berlin Air Line (Royal Air Force weekly), Berlin, Germany, music critic, 1945-46; worked in Canada as salesman, freight checker, department store packer, oil-field surveyor, typist, proof-machine operator, and script writer, 1951-57; free-lance writer, 1957—. *Military service:* Royal Air Force, radio operator, 1943-47. *Awards, honors: Toronto Globe and Mail*-Stratford Shakespearean Festival Play Competition First Prize, 1959, for "The Canvas Barricade"; National Safety Congress (Chicago, Ill.) Award for best safety film, 1960, for "The Broken Doll"; Leacock Medal for humor, 1962, for *Three Cheers for Me,* and 1973, for *That's Me in the Middle;* Periodical Distributors of Canada Author's Award, 1977, for *It's Me Again;* Leacock Medal, 1979, for *Me Bandy, You Cissie.*

WRITINGS: Three Cheers for Me (also see below), Macmillan, 1962; *The Journals of Bartholomew Bandy,* Volume I: *Three Cheers for Me,* revised edition, Doubleday, 1973, Volume II: *That's Me in the Middle,* Doubleday, 1973, Volume III: *It's Me Again,* two parts, Doubleday, 1975, Volume IV: *Me among the Ruins* (originally published as part 2 of *It's Me Again*), PaperJacks, 1976, Volume V: *Me Bandy, You Cissie,* Doubleday, 1979; *Sinc, Betty, and the Morning Man: The Story of CFRB,* Macmillan (Toronto), 1977; *The Story of Canadian Medicine,* Doubleday, 1981. Also author of four stage plays, thirty-nine television plays, eighteen radio plays, fifty film scripts, and one novelette, "Where Did Rafe Madison Go?," *Macleans,* 1958. Contributor of articles to magazines.

WORK IN PROGRESS: Two novels.

BIOGRAPHICAL/CRITICAL SOURCES: Toronto Globe and Mail, November 14, 1959; *Hamilton Spectator,* November 14, 1959, May 5, 1962; *CBC Radio and TV Writer,* winter, 1959.

*　　*　　*

JACK, R(obert) Ian 1935-

PERSONAL: Born March 12, 1935, in Dunfries, Scotland; son of Robert (a banker) and Janet Wilson (Swan) Jack; married Sybil Milliner Thorpe (a university lecturer), February, 1961 (divorced, 1978); married Stella Gwendolen Charman, May, 1979; children: Adrian Laurence Robert, Christopher James Edmund, Antony Ronald Geoffrey. *Education:* University of Glasgow, M.A., 1957; University of London, Ph.D., 1961. *Office:* St. Andrew's College, University of Sydney, Sydney, New South Wales 2042, Australia.

CAREER: University of London, London, England, research fellow, Institute of Historical Research, 1959-61; University of Sydney, Sydney, New South Wales, Australia, lecturer, 1961-64, senior lecturer, 1965-69, associate professor of history, 1970—, acting dean of Faculty of Arts, 1972, sub-dean, 1972-73, dean, 1974-77. *Member:* Royal Historical Society (fellow), Australian Society for Historical Archaeology (president, 1972-77), History Teachers Association of New South Wales (chairman, 1969-70).

WRITINGS: The Grey of Ruthin Valor, Sydney University Press, 1965; *Medieval Wales,* Cornell University Press, 1972; (contributor) R. A. Griffiths, editor, *Boroughs of Mediaeval Wales,* University of Wales Press, 1978; (with J. M. Birmingham and D. N. Jeans) *Australian Pioneer Technology: Sites and Relics,* Heinemann Educational, 1979; *A Colonial Scene: The Hawkesbury-Nepean Valley,* University of Sydney Press, 1980; (contributor) H. E. Hallam, editor, *The Agrarian History of England and Wales,* Cambridge University Press, 1981.

General editor: "Topics in Modern History" series, five books, Rigby, 1973, and "Monographs on Historical Archaeology" series, published by Australian Society for Historical Archaeology, 1973—.

WORK IN PROGRESS: A second volume of *Australian Pioneer Technology,* for Heinemann Educational; various projects on colonial archaeology in Australia.

*　　*　　*

JACKSON, Percival Ephrates 1891-1970

PERSONAL: Born June 16, 1891, in New York, N.Y.; died August 22, 1970; son of Solomon Henry and Belle (Bloch) Jackson; married Irma Weinstock, October 15, 1921 (deceased); children: Jean Von Sternberg, Muriel Emsheimer. *Education:* New York University, L.L.B., 1912.

CAREER: Admitted to New York State Bar, 1912; attorney. Special counsel to McAdoo Senate Committee investigating bankruptcy and receivership in the U.S. courts, 1936. Director of several manufacturing and utility firms, including United Gas Improvement Co., Long Island Lighting Co., and Missouri Public Service Co. *Military service:* U.S. Army Air Forces, 1917-18; became lieutenant. *Member:* American Bar Association, Bankers Club of America, Nassau County Lawyers Association, New York County Lawyers Association, Association of the Bar of the City of New York, North Shore Country Club.

WRITINGS: Law of Cadavers, Prentice-Hall, 1937, 2nd edition, 1950; *Look at the Law,* Dutton, 1940; *What Every Corporation Director Should Know,* William-Frederick, 1949; *Corporate Management,* Michie Co., 1955; *Justice and the Law,* Michie Co., 1960; (editor) *The Wisdom of the Supreme Court,* University of Oklahoma Press, 1962; *Dissent in the Supreme Court: A Chronology,* University of Oklahoma Press, 1969.

Poetry: *Odds and Ends,* Peter Pauper Press, 1953; *Candor and Conclusion,* Peter Pauper Press, 1954; *Triptych,* Peter Pauper Press, 1955; (editor) *Justice and the Law: An Anthology of American Legal Poetry and Verse,* Michie Co., 1960.†

*   *   *

JACKSON, Wes 1936-

PERSONAL: Born June 15, 1936, in Topeka, Kan.; son of Howard T. (a farmer) and Nettie (Stover) Jackson; married Dana Lee Percival, December 22, 1957; children: Laura, Scott, Sara. *Education:* Kansas Wesleyan University, B.A., 1958; University of Kansas, M.A., 1960; North Carolina State University, Ph.D., 1967. *Religion:* Unitarian Universalist. *Home and office:* Route 3, Salina, Kan. 67401.

CAREER: Welder, farm hand, ranch hand; high school teacher of biology in the public schools of Olathe, Kan., 1960-62; Kansas Wesleyan University, Salina, assistant professor, 1962-64, associate professor of biology, 1967-71; California State University, Sacramento, associate professor, 1971-73, professor of environmental studies, 1973-75; currently co-director of Land Institute, Salina, Kan.

WRITINGS: Man and the Environment, W. C. Brown, 1971, 3rd edition, 1978; *New Roots for Agriculture,* Friends of the Earth, 1980.

WORK IN PROGRESS: Research toward an ecological ethic, back-to-the-land experiments in the development of alterations of life styles and technology assessment, and on development of alternative perennial crops in polyculture; Great Plains studies on energy, water, and agriculture; a review article on the promise of herbaceous perennial seed-producing polycultures.

*   *   *

JACOB, Ernest Fraser 1894-1971

PERSONAL: Born September 12, 1894, in Leeds, Yorkshire, England; died October 7, 1971, in England; son of Ernest Henry and Emma L. (Fraser) Jacob. *Education:* Oxford University, M.A., D.Phil.; University of Manchester, M.A. *Office:* All Souls College, Oxford University, Oxford, England.

CAREER: University of London, King's College, London, England, lecturer in medieval history, 1922-24; Oxford University, Christ Church, Oxford, England, tutor, 1924-29; University of Manchester, Manchester, England, professor of medieval history, 1929-45; Oxford University, Chichele Professor of Modern History, 1950-61, Chichele Professor Emeritus 1961-71, fellow and librarian of All Souls College.

Church commissioner, Church of England, beginning 1948. *Member:* British Academy (fellow), Athenaeum Club (London). *Awards, honors:* D.Litt., University of Manchester.

WRITINGS: (With W.R.L. Rowe) *Illustrations to the Life of St. Alban,* Clarendon Press, 1924; *Studies in the Period of Baronial Reform and Rebellion: 1258-1267,* Clarendon Press, 1925, reprinted, Octagon, 1974; *The Holy Roman Empire,* Benn, 1929; *The Renaissance,* Benn, 1930, reprinted, Folcroft Library Editions, 1974; (translator) Charles Bemont, *Simon de Montfort, Earl of Leicester, 1208-1265,* Clarendon Press, 1930, reprinted, Greenwood Press, 1974; *Essays in the Conciliar Epoch,* Manchester University Press, 1943, 3rd edition, University of Notre Dame Press, 1963; *Henry V and the Invasion of France,* English Universities Press, 1947, Macmillan, 1950, revised edition, Collier, 1966; *The Fifteenth Century: 1399-1485,* Clarendon Press, 1961; *Archbishop Henry Chichele,* Thomas Nelson (London), 1967.

Editor: (With C. G. Crump and contributor) *The Legacy of the Middle Ages,* Clarendon Press, 1926, reprinted, 1962; (with V. H. Galbraith and J. G. Edwards and contributor) *Essays in Honour of James Tait,* Manchester University Press, 1933; *The Register of Henry Chichele, Archbishop of Canterbury, 1414-1443,* four volumes, Oxford University Press, 1937-47; *What We Defend: Essays in Freedom by Members of the University of Manchester,* Oxford University Press, 1942; (and author of introduction) *Italian Renaissance Studies: A Tribute to the Late Cecilia M. Ady,* Barnes & Noble, 1960, published as *Italian Renaissance Studies,* Faber, 1966; Herbert Henry Edmund Craster, *The History of All Souls College Library,* Faber, 1971.

Contributor: E. Prestage, editor, *Chivalry,* [London], 1928; *Studies in Medieval History Presented to F. M. Powicke,* Clarendon Press, 1948; R. W. Seton-Watson, editor, *Prague Essays,* Clarendon Press, 1949; *Medieval Studies Presented to Dr. Rose Graham,* Clarendon Press, 1950; *Medieval Studies Presented to Aubrey Gwynn, S.J.,* [Dublin], 1962; *Medieval Records of the Archbishops of Canterbury,* [London], 1962; *Essays in British History Presented to Sir Keith Feeling,* [London], 1964; *Medieval Miscellany Presented to Eugene Vinaver,* Manchester University Press, 1965.

Contributor to *New Catholic Encyclopedia.* Contributor of articles to professional journals. Chairman of advisory committee, *Journal of Ecclesiastical History,* beginning 1950.

WORK IN PROGRESS: The Council of Constance.

BIOGRAPHICAL/CRITICAL SOURCES: Books and Bookmen, October, 1967.†

*   *   *

JACOBSON, Harold Karan 1929-

PERSONAL: Born June 28, 1929, in Detroit, Mich.; son of Harold Kenneth (a businessman) and Maxine A. (Miller) Jacobson; married Merelyn Jean Lindbloom, August 25, 1951; children: Harold Knute, Eric Alfred, Kristoffer Olaf, Nils Karl. *Education:* University of Michigan, A.B., 1950; Yale University, M.A., 1952, Ph.D., 1955. *Politics:* Democrat. *Religion:* Episcopal. *Home:* 2174 Delaware Dr., Ann Arbor, Mich. 48103. *Office:* Center for Political Studies, Institute for Social Research, University of Michigan, Ann Arbor, Mich. 48106.

CAREER: University of Houston, Houston, Tex., assistant professor of political science, 1955-57; University of Michigan, Ann Arbor, assistant professor, 1957-61, associate professor, 1961-65, professor of political science, 1965—, chairman of department, 1972-74, program director of Institute for Social Research, 1977—. Visiting professor, University of Geneva, 1965-66, 1970-71, and 1977-78. *Military service:* U.S. Army Reserve, 1951-62; became lieutenant. *Member:* International Political Science Association, International Studies Association (president of midwest division, 1969-70), American Political Science Association, Political Science Association, Society for Values in Higher Education, American Association for the Advancement of Science, Phi Beta Kappa, Phi Eta Sigma, Phi Kappa Phi. *Awards, honors:* Fellow, World Affairs Center, 1959-60; University of Michigan, Press Award for Diplomats, Scientists, and Politicians, 1968, and Distinguished Faculty Achievement Award, 1978.

WRITINGS: (Editor) *America's Foreign Policy,* Random House, 1960, 2nd edition, 1965; *The USSR and the UN's Economic and Social Activities,* University of Notre Dame Press, 1963; (with Eric Stein) *Diplomats, Scientists and Politicians: The United States and the Nuclear Test Ban Negotiations,* University of Michigan Press, 1966; (editor with William Zimmerman) *The Shaping of Foreign Policy,* Atherton, 1969; (with Robert W. Cux and others) *The Anatomy of Influence: Decision Making in International Organization,* Yale University Press, 1973; *Networks of Interdependence: International Organizations and the Global Political System,* Knopf, 1979. Contributor of articles to *Foreign Affairs* and other professional journals. Member of board of editors, *International Organization;* member of editorial board, *Journal of Conflict Resolution, American Journal of International Law,* and *International Studies Quarterly.*

*   *   *

JACOBSON, Morris K(arl) 1906-

PERSONAL: Born December 29, 1906, in Memel, Germany; son of George (a salesman) and Minna (Jakobsohn) Jacobson; married Lena Schechter, July 14, 1929; children: John Ernest. *Education:* New York University, B.S., 1928; Columbia University, A.M., 1930. *Politics:* Democrat. *Religion:* Jewish. *Home:* 865 Southeast Capon St., Palm Bay, Fla. 32905.

CAREER: John Adams High School, New York City, teacher of German, 1937-53; Andrew Jackson High School, New York City, chairman of department of foreign languages, 1953-70. Associate in malacology, American Museum of Natural History. *Member:* American Malacological Union (president, 1955), New York Shell Club (president, 1949-51), Astronaut Trail Shell Club. *Awards, honors:* National Science Foundation grant, 1966, to write on land shells of Cuba.

WRITINGS: (With William K. Emerson) *Shells of the New York City Area,* Argonaut, 1961; (with Emerson) *Shells from Cape Cod to Cape May,* Dover, 1971; (with Emerson) *Wonders of the World of Shells,* Dodd, 1971; (with Emerson) *American Museum of Natural History Guide to Shells,* Knopf, 1976; (with Rosemary Pang) *Wonders of Sponges,* Dodd, 1976; (with Emerson) *Wonders of Starfish,* Dodd, 1977; (with David R. Franz) *Wonders of Jellyfish,* Dodd, 1978; (with Franz) *Wonders of Coral and Coral Reefs,* Dodd, 1979; (with Franz) *Wonders of Snails and Slugs,* Dodd, 1980. Also editor of *How to Study and Collect Shells* and author of numerous monographs. Contributor of articles on shells to journals. Editor of *Bulletin of American Malacological Union,* 1965-72, and *New York Shell Club Notes,* 1970—.

WORK IN PROGRESS: A translation of J. W. Abalos' novel, *Shunko;* studies on the helicinid snails of Cuba; research on the life of Charles Wright, a botanist.

SIDELIGHTS: Morris K. Jacobson told *CA:* "I write because I like to write. I must be one of the people whom Dr. Samuel Johnson so deeply despised—those who write without the prospect of financial reward. Thus if I do happen to earn some money with my writing, it is a case of pure serendipity.

"My first published (unpaid) writing had to do with scientific articles on the subject of malacology (study of mollusks). I have written a great many, popular and scientific, since then. This was good training because it forced me to be direct, short-winded, and clear. Editors of scientific periodicals don't have room for artistic prolixity.

"I cannot compose on a typewriter; everything has to be written out in longhand first. Revision takes place ten days to two weeks later and frequently there is a third revision. I write a little every day even when I am not engaged on a specific writing task. This daily routine helps structure my day, and a structured day is essential for a retired school teacher."

*   *   *

JARRETT, H(arold) Reginald 1916-

PERSONAL: Born May 6, 1916, in Salford Priors, Evesham, Warwickshire, England; son of Thomas Reginald (a gardener) and Amy (Whyborn) Jarrett; married Edna Smith, February 5, 1944 (died, 1971); children Diana Reed Ayodele, Valerie Reed. *Education:* University of Birmingham, B.A. (with honors), 1938, diploma in education, 1939; University of London, B.Sc. (with honors), 1945, M.Sc., 1946, Ph.D., 1951. *Home:* 42 Roslin Rd. S., Talbot Woods, Bournemouth BH3 7EG, England.

CAREER: Methodist missionary, Bathurst, Gambia, 1941-45; Fourah Bay University College, Freetown, Sierra Leone, senior lecturer in geography, 1950-56; University College, Ibadan, Nigeria, senior lecturer in geography, 1957-58; Newcastle University College, New South Wales, Australia, senior lecturer in geography, 1963-67. *Member:* Royal Geographical Society (fellow), Geographical Association, Institute of Economic Affairs.

WRITINGS: A Geography of Sierra Leone and Gambia, Longmans, Green, 1954, 2nd edition, 1964; *A Geography of West Africa,* Dent, 1956, 2nd edition published as *A Geography of West Africa, Including the French Territories, Portuguese Guinea, and Liberia,* 1957, 7th edition, Evans Brothers, 1980; *Physical Geography for West Africa,* Longmans, Green, 1958, 2nd edition, 1968; *A General World Geography for African Schools,* Methuen, 1958; *An Outline Geography of Africa,* Methuen, 1962, 3rd edition, 1971; *Africa,* Macdonald & Evans, 1962, 5th edition, 1979; *Land and Landscape,* University of London Press, 1965; *Landscape and Livelihood,* University of London Press, 1967; *A Geography of Manufacturing,* Macdonald & Evans, 1969, 2nd edition, 1977; (with J. J. Branigan) *The Mediterranean Lands,* Macdonald & Evans, 1969, International Publications Service, 1970; *Topical Geography,* Macdonald & Evans, 1977. Contributor to *Encyclopaedia Britannica, Book of Knowledge, American Peoples Encyclopedia.* Contributor of other articles to geographical journals.

WORK IN PROGRESS: Further research on west Africa, and tropical geography.

SIDELIGHTS: H. Reginald Jarrett wrote *CA:* "I first began to write geography textbooks to meet a need—the lack of suitable teaching material for West African schools. As the taste for writing grew, I enlarged my canvas to include schools and colleges in other parts of the world, aiming especially to tell students something of the African landscape and peoples which I had grown to love. In the back of my mind I viewed this (and still do) as part of my missionary outreach, hoping that my books would help to bring greater knowledge; that the greater knowledge would bring greater understanding, and the greater understanding greater tolerance and forbearance among the people of the world.''

* * *

JOHNSON, B(urdetta) F(aye) 1920-
(B[urdetta] F[aye] Beebe)

PERSONAL: Born February 4, 1920, in Marshall, Okla.; daughter of Alfred Khlar and Beulah B. (Thurlow) Beebe; married James Ralph Johnson (a Marine Corps officer, writer and illustrator), October 11, 1961. *Education:* Attended schools in Andover, Ohio, and Marshall, Okla. *Religion:* Protestant. *Home and office address:* P.O. Box 5295, Santa Fe, N.M. 87501.

CAREER: Oklahoma Employment Security Commission, Oklahoma City, recording stenographer for Appeals Tribunal, 1941-48; Carver Chiropractic College, Oklahoma City, office manager, 1948-52; Love and Law Food Brokers, Oklahoma City, secretary, 1952-55; Caston Lumber Co., Oklahoma City, secretary to owner, 1955-56; National Food Brokers Association, Washington, D.C., convention manager, 1957-64; full-time writer in Santa Fe, N.M., 1964—. *Member:* Order of the Amaranth, Order of the Eastern Star. *Awards, honors:* Boys' Clubs of America award, 1963, for *Coyote, Come Home.*

WRITINGS—All juveniles published by McKay, except as indicated; co-authored and illustrated by husband, James Ralph Johnson: *American Wild Horses*, 1964; *American Bears*, 1965.

Under name B. F. Beebe; illustrated by J. R. Johnson, except as indicated: *Run, Light Buck, Run!* (Junior Literary Guild selection), 1962; *Appalachian Elk*, 1962; *Coyote, Come Home*, illustrated by Larry Toschile, 1963; *American Lions and Cats*, 1963; *Chestnut Cub*, 1963; *American Wolves, Coyotes and Foxes*, 1964; *Assateague Deer*, 1965; *Coyote for Keeps*, Follett, 1965; *American Desert Animals*, 1966; *Ocelot* (Junior Literary Guild selection), 1966; *Yucatan Monkey*, 1967; *Animals South of the Border*, 1968; *African Elephants*, 1968.

WORK IN PROGRESS: More animal books, fact and fiction, and books on outdoor recreation.

SIDELIGHTS: Natural history, photography, travel, camping and hiking in the Appalachian Mountains are interests B. F. Johnson shares with her husband. The inspiration for *Run, Light Buck, Run!* came from a trip photographing antelope in the Southwest, and from a trip into the Grand Canyon. The Johnsons have also traveled through Africa and hiked in Arizona's Sunset Crater, Painted Desert, and Petrified Forest. *Run, Light Buck, Run!* and *Coyote, Come Home* were made into Walt Disney television features.

''Before I'm through,'' Johnson says, ''I intend to introduce boys and girls to every American animal family and describe its way of life. Today is a happy time for wild animals and people who study them. Wise conservation and game management are bringing back the wilderness. . . . Several sightings of mountain lions were made on farms less than twenty miles from our nation's capital.''

JOHNSON, Elmer Douglas 1915-

PERSONAL: Born August 2, 1915, in Durham, N.C.; son of Ulysses S. (a farmer and merchant) and Nancy M. (Smith) Johnson; married Rosa Shepherd, November 7, 1936; children: Eric Shepherd, Lynn Douglas, Elaine Carol, Giles Kerry. *Education:* University of North Carolina, B.A., 1936, M.A., 1942, Ph.D., 1951. *Religion:* Presbyterian. *Home:* 718 Baywood Cir., Sanford, Fla. 32771.

CAREER: Tennessee Valley Authority, Guntersville, Ala., camp librarian, 1936-40; U.S. War Department, Arlington, Va., research analyst, 1942-44; Limestone College, Gaffney, S.C., librarian and professor of history, 1944-53; University of Southwestern Louisiana, Lafayette, director of libraries, 1954-63; Radford College, Radford, Va., librarian and professor of history, 1963-80. *Member:* American Library Association, Bibliographical Society of America, American Historical Association, Organization of American Historians, Virginia Social Science Association, Phi Beta Kappa, Phi Alpha Theta.

WRITINGS: Communication: A Concise Introduction to the History of the Alphabet, Writing, Printing, Books, and Libraries, Scarecrow, 1955, 4th edition, 1973; *Of Time and Thomas Wolfe: A Bibliography, with a Character Index of His Works*, Scarecrow, 1959; *History of Libraries in the Western World*, Scarecrow, 1965, 3rd edition (with Michael H. Harris), 1976; *Thomas Wolfe: A Checklist*, Kent State University Press, 1970; (with Katherine Sloan) *South Carolina: A Documentary Profile of the Palmetto State*, University of South Carolina Press, 1971; *Radford Then and Now: A Pictorial History*, Radford Bicentennial Commission, 1975. Contributor to *Biographical Dictionary of North Carolinians* and *Encyclopedia of the South*, both 1980. Contributor of articles and reviews to history and library journals. Editor of *Southwestern Louisiana Journal*, 1957-60 and *Louisiana Library Association Bulletin*, 1956, 1958; editor of index, *Louisiana Schools*, 1924-63. Managing editor, *Journal of Sport History*, 1973-76.

WORK IN PROGRESS: People Named Johnson, a historical work.

SIDELIGHTS: Elmer Johnson wrote *CA:* ''Most of my research and writing has been concerned with the relationship of books and people. The impact of graphic communication, in all its phases, has been and continues to be the most significant factor in the civilization of man. Much more work needs to be done on this subject.

''Right now I am personally involved in the trauma of retirement. What does it mean? What is a 'senior citizen'? What can I do and what can't I do? I plan to continue writing, but probably in a lighter vein. Facetiously I tell my friends that I'm working on a book entitled: 'What's Wrong with Everything—and Why!' ''

AVOCATIONAL INTERESTS: Collecting works by and about Thomas Wolfe, gardening, flower photography.

* * *

JOHNSON, Hildegard Binder 1908-

PERSONAL: Born August 20, 1908, in Berlin, Germany; daughter of Albert Wilhelm and Emma (Gartenschlaeger) Binder; married Palmer Oliver Johnson (a professor; died January 24, 1960); children: Gisela Charlotte, Karin Luise. *Education:* Attended University of Rostock, University of Marburg, and University of Innsbruck, 1928-30; University of Berlin, M.A., 1933, Ph.D., 1934. *Home:* 3312 Edmund Blvd., Minneapolis, Minn. 55406. *Office:* Department of Geography, Macalester College, St. Paul, Minn. 55105.

CAREER: Assistant at high school in England, 1934-35; Mills College, Oakland, Calif., assistant instructor, 1935-36; Macalester College, St. Paul, Minn., 1947—, began as assistant professor in department of geography, professor and chairman of department, currently professor emerita, 1975—. Visiting professor at University of Minnesota, University of Georgia, University of Washington, and University of California, Berkeley. *Member:* Association of American Geographers, American Geographical Society, National Council for the Social Studies, National Council for Geographic Education (fellow), Society of Women Geographers, Minnesota Historical Society, Minnesota Council for the Social Studies (president, 1957-59). *Awards, honors:* Social Science Research Council grants, 1940, 1946; Izaac Walton League award, 1950, for conservation education; Association of American Geographers award, 1958, for meritorious contribution to geography; Thomas Jefferson Award, 1971; D.H.L., Macalester College, 1975.

WRITINGS: (Contributor) Adolf Eduard Zucker, editor, *The Forty-Eighters: Political Refugees of the German Revolution of 1848,* Columbia University Press, 1950; (contributor) *Forschungen zu Staat und Verfassung,* Duncker & Humblot (Berlin), 1958; *A Comparative Study of an Introductory Geography Course on ETV and in the Classroom,* Department of Geography, Macalester College, 1960; *Carta Marina: World Geography in Strassburg, 1525,* University of Minnesota Press, 1963; *An Introduction to the Geography of the Twin Cities,* Department of Geography, Macalester College, 1970; *Order upon the Land,* Oxford University Press, 1976; *The Orderly Landscape,* University of Minnesota Press, 1977; (contributor) *This Land of Ours,* Indiana Historical Society, 1978. Contributor of approximately fifty articles to professional journals in United States, Canada, and Germany, Editor, *Minnesota Geographer,* 1950-62.

WORK IN PROGRESS: Contributing a chapter to *Minnesota Historical Society Ethnic Project,* and *Progress in Human Geography.*

SIDELIGHTS: Hildegard Binder Johnson wrote *CA:* ''After twenty-eight years as 'scholar-teacher' at Macalester I became an author-lecturer after mandatory retirement in 1975. Inspiration derived from a compulsive urge to observe the out-of-doors rather than from reading books. The rural scene forever invites questions that can be answered only by searching its wider context. My general humanistic education led to an interest in many topics rather than specialization. Whatever the mind perceives through our eyes fascinates me: hence my publications range from German settlements in the Midwest, the location of mission stations in Africa, the tragic erosion in gullied fields, to the United States land survey that is the basis for America's cultural landscape.

''I believe with William James that 'a large acquaintance with particulars makes us wiser than the possession of abstract formulas' and with Bertrand Russell that the knowledge of different countries and peoples 'diminishes the tyranny of familiar surroundings over imagination.' Indeed, the diversity of places and the variety of people in their relationship to their surroundings is a condition of the human enterprise and of the dignity of man. I would like to believe that I taught my students to observe intelligently what there is to see in America.''

*   *   *

JONES, G(eorge) Curtis 1911-

PERSONAL: Born October 18, 1911, in Dundas, Va.; son of George Edward (a farmer and businessman) and Rosa Ella (Singleton) Jones; married Sybil Nettleton, August 28, 1935; children: G. Curtis, Jr., David and DeWitt (twins), Peter and Paul (twins). *Education:* Lynchburg College, A.B., 1933; Yale University, B.D., 1936. *Home:* 111 Mt. Hermon Rd., Ashland, Va. 23005.

CAREER: Minister of Christian Church (Disciples of Christ); pastor of churches in Tazewell, Va., Washington, N.C., Detroit, Mich., Richmond, Va., Nashville, Tenn., St. Louis, Mo., Des Moines, Iowa, and Macon, Ga.; currently lecturer and consultant to congregations, colleges and universities, and church agencies. Christian Church, chairman of stewardship committee, Home and State Mission Planning Council, 1954, chairman of board of directors, Unified Promotion, 1954-56, member of committee on program and arrangements, World Convention in Edinburgh, Scotland, 1955-60, member of executive board, Disciples Council of Greater St. Louis, 1956-63, member of committee on nominations, International Convention, 1963, member of new study committee, World Convention in Puerto Rico, 1965, member of North American section of program committee, World Convention in Adelaide, Australia, 1970, former member of Georgia Regional Board. National Council of Churches, member of commission on religion and health, 1955-63, member of department of stewardship and benevolence, 1956-63. Member of board of directors, Children's Family Service, 1954-55, Y.M.C.A., 1961-62, Southern Christian House, 1970-71, and Vineville Christian Towers (retirement home); member of Mayor's Committee, 1961-62; member of board of trustees, Drake University, 1964—. Has done numerous broadcasts on radio and television. Member of clergymen's national advisory council, Planned Parenthood Federation of America, 1960-63; member of advisory council, Culver-Stockton College, 1963.

MEMBER: International Mark Twain Society, Mental Health Association (member of executive board, 1955-56), Iowa Society of Christian Churches (chairman of committee on ministry, 1966-68), Tennessee Anti-Tuberculosis Association (member of board of directors, 1953-55), Metropolitan Church Federation of Greater St. Louis (president, 1962), Des Moines Ministerial Association (president, 1967-68). *Awards, honors:* D.D., Lynchburg College, 1948.

WRITINGS: Repairing Our Religion, Christopher, 1945; *On Being Your Best,* Macmillan, 1950; *Which Way Is Progress?,* Bethany Press, 1954; *What Are You Worth?,* Bethany Press, 1954; *In Their Light We Walk,* Bethany Press, 1954; *What Are You Doing?,* Bethany Press, 1955; *Youth Deserves to Know,* Macmillan, 1958; *March of the Year,* Bethany Press, 1959; *Parents Deserve to Know,* Macmillan, 1960; *Handbook of Church Correspondence,* Macmillan, 1962; *Patterns of Prayer,* Bethany Press, 1964; *The Church Parking Lot,* Fortress, 1967; *A Man and His Religion,* Bethany Press, 1967; *Strongly Tempted,* World Publications, 1968; *I Met a Man,* Word, Inc., 1971; *Candles in the City,* Word, Inc., 1973; *How Come We're Alive?,* Word, Inc., 1976; *The Good Life,* United Church Press, 1976; *We Knew His Power,* Abingdon, 1976; *The Naked Shepherd,* Word, Inc., 1979. Former weekly columnist for *Macon Telgraph and News.* Contributor of numerous articles to periodicals.

*   *   *

JONES, (Morgan) Glyn 1905-

PERSONAL: Born February 28, 1905, in Merthyr Tydfil, Wales; son of William Henry (a government clerk) and Margaret (a school teacher; maiden name, Williams) Jones; married Doreen Jones, August, 1935. *Education:* Attended St. Paul's College, Cheltenham, England. *Home:* 158 Manor Way, Whitchurch, Cardiff CF4 1RN, Wales. *Agent:* Laurence Pollinger Ltd., 18 Madox St., London W.1, England.

CAREER: Former schoolmaster and English teacher in Cardiff, Wales. Reviewer, interviewer, and translator (from Welsh) for radio. *Member:* Yr Academi Gymreig (vice-president, English language section). *Awards, honors:* Welsh Arts Council award, 1968, for *The Dragon Has Two Tongues.*

WRITINGS: The Blue Bed, and Other Stories, J. Cape, 1937, Dutton, 1938; *Poems,* Fortune Press, 1939; *The Water Music, and Other Stories,* Routledge & Kegan Paul, 1944; *The Dream of Jake Hopkins* (poems), Fortune Press, 1945; (translator and adapter with T. J. Morgan) *The Saga of Llywarch the Old,* Golden Cockerel Press, 1955; *The Valley, the City, the Village* (novel), Dent 1956, reprinted, Severn House, 1980; *The Learning Lark* (novel), Dent, 1960; *The Island of Apples* (novel), John Day, 1965; *The Dragon Has Two Tongues* (essays on Anglo-Welsh writers and writing), Dent, 1968; *Selected Short Stories,* Dent, 1971; *The Beach of Falesa* (verse libretto), Oxford University Press, 1974; *Selected Poems,* Gomer, 1975; *Welsh Heirs* (short stories), Gomer, 1977; (editor and contributor) *The Oxford Book of Welsh Verse in English,* Oxford University Press, 1977.

Short stories and poems have appeared in anthologies, including: *Welsh Short Stories,* Faber, 1937; *Best Short Stories,* 1938 and 1940; *Modern Welsh Poetry,* edited by Keidrych Rhys, Faber, 1944; *New British Poets,* edited by Kenneth Rexroth, New Directions, 1949; *Poetry of the Present,* edited by Geoffrey Griason, Phoenix House, 1949; *Romantic Anthology,* edited by Shimanski and Treece, Grey Walls Press, 1949; *Quite Early One Morning,* edited by Dylan Thomas, New Directions, 1954; *Images of Tomorrow,* edited by John Heath-Stubbs, S.C.M. Press, 1954; *Worlds Classics,* Oxford University Press, 1956; *Presenting Welsh Poetry,* Faber, 1959; *Welsh Voices,* Dent, 1967; *This World of Wales,* edited by Gerald Morgan, University of Wales Press, 1968; *The Lilting House,* Dent, 1969; *The Shining Pyramid,* 1971; *British Poetry since 1960,* edited by Schmidt and Lindop, Carcanet Press, 1972; *New Poems* (P.E.N. anthologies), 1958, 1961, and others. Reviewer for periodicals in Wales and England, including *Western Mail* (Wales) and *Times* (London).

WORK IN PROGRESS: Essays on twentieth-century literature in Wales, tentatively entitled *Profiles;* translations of traditional Welsh poems, tentatively entitled *When the Rosebush Brings Forth Apples.*

*   *   *

JONES, Peter d'Alroy   1931-

PERSONAL: Born June 9, 1931, in Hull, England; son of Alfred and Margery (Rutter) Jones; married Beau Fly, June 10, 1961 (divorced); children: Kathryn, Barbara. *Education:* University of Manchester, B.A. (honors), 1952, M.A., 1953; London School of Economics and Political Science, University of London, additional study, 1953-56, Ph.D., 1963. *Office:* Trinity College, Hartford, Conn. 06106.

CAREER: Worked in England at various times as free-lance editor, school teacher, farm assistant, and factory worker; University of Manchester, Manchester, England, assistant lecturer in American studies, 1957-58; Tulane University, New Orleans, La., visiting assistant professor of economics and history, 1959-60; Smith College, Northampton, Mass., 1960-68, began as assistant professor, became professor of

history; University of Illinois at Chicago Circle, Chicago, professor of history, 1968-80; Trinity College, Hartford, Conn., W. R. Kenan, Jr. Professor of American Institutions and Values, 1980—. Visiting professor, University of Warsaw, Poland, 1973-74; guest professor, University of Dusseldorf, Germany, 1974-75. Consultant and lecturer in American studies, U.S. Department of State, 1973—; co-director, Project for the Study of American Mayors, 1978—. *Military service:* Royal Air Force, 1956-57. *Member:* American Association of University Professors, American Economic Association, Economic History Association, American Historical Association, Conference on British Studies, Economic History Society (England), British Association for American Studies, Authors Guild of the Authors League of America.

WRITINGS: An Economic History of the United States since 1783, Routledge &, Kegan Paul, 1956, 2nd edition, 1964; (with A. N. Simons) *The Story of the Saw,* Newman Neame, 1960; *America's Wealth,* Macmillan, 1963; *Robert Hunter's "Poverty": Social Conscience in the Progressive Era,* Harper, 1965; *The Consumer Society,* Penguin, 1965; *The Christian Socialist Revival, 1877-1914: Religion, Class and Social Conscience in Late-Victorian Britain,* Princeton University Press, 1968; (editor) *The Robber Barons Revisited,* Heath, 1968; *The U.S.A.: A History of Its People and Society,* two volumes, Dorsey, 1976; *Since Columbus: Pluralism and Poverty in the History of the Americas,* Heinemann, 1977; (editor with M. G. Holli) *The Ethnic Frontier: Group Survival in Chicago and the Midwest,* Eerdmans, 1978; (with M. G. Holli) *Biographical Dictionary of American Mayors, 1820-1980,* Greenwood Press, 1981. Contributor of articles and reviews to scholarly journals and the general press.

WORK IN PROGRESS: A study of the convergence of modern societies.

AVOCATIONAL INTERESTS: Travel, music, the theater, squash, fiction writing.

*   *   *

JONGEWARD, Dorothy   1925-

PERSONAL: Surname sounds like *Young*-word; born November 10, 1925, in Spokane, Wash.; daughter of Joseph E. (a candy maker) and Grace (Gibbs) Kolander; married Wallace Jongeward (a sales representative), May 31, 1949; children: Mark, Jill, Sherri. *Education:* Washington State University, B.S., 1949, B.Ed., 1950, M.Ed., 1952. *Home and office:* 724 Ironbark Ct., Orinda, Calif. 94563.

CAREER: Licensed marriage, child, and family counselor, 1964—. Member of faculty at University of California, Berkeley, Extension Division, 1965—; president of Transactional Analysis Management Institute, Inc., 1974—. Professor of human behavior and transactional analysis, California America University; has also taught at University of Idaho, Washington State University, University of Colorado, University of Richmond, University of California, California State University, Laymen's School of Religion, Cabrillo Junior College, and Diablo Valley College; has conducted workshops and seminars and given lectures; has developed programs for continuing education of women and affirmative action programs for organizations. Consultant in human resource development and interpersonal relations and communications. Testified before California Advisory Committee on the Status of Women, 1966. Member of board of regents, John F. Kennedy University. Has appeared on television and radio programs. *Member:* International Transactional Analysis Association (teaching member), Association for

Humanistic Psychology, California Marriage and Family Counseling Association (life member), Phi Beta Kappa, Phi Kappa Phi.

WRITINGS—All published by Addison-Wesley, except as indicated: (With Muriel James) *Born to Win: Transactional Analysis with Gestalt Experiments*, 1971; (with James) *Winning with People: Group Exercises in Transactional Analysis*, 1973; (with others) *Everybody Wins: Transactional Analysis Applied to Organizations*, 1973, revised edition, 1976; (with Dru Scott) *Affirmative Action for Women: A Practical Guide*, 1973, revised edition, 1975; (with James) *The People Book: Transactional Analysis for Students*, 1975; (with Scott) *Women as Winners: Transactional Analysis for Personal Growth*, 1976; (with Philip C. Seyer) *Choosing Success: Transactional Analysis on the Job*, Wiley, 1978; (with James) *Winning Ways in Health Care: Transactional Analysis for Effective Communication*, 1980. Contributor to *Marriage Counseling Quarterly*, *P.S. for Secretaries*, and *Transactional Analysis Journal*.

SIDELIGHTS: Dorothy Jongeward has been a pioneer and leader in the fields of family life education, sex education, adult education, continuing education for women, and the applications of transactional analysis to business, industry, and government. *Avocational interests:* Travel, painting, swimming, hiking, dancing.

BIOGRAPHICAL/CRITICAL SOURCES: Transactional Analysis Bulletin, July, 1970, July, 1979; *Bank American*, July-August, 1972; *Business Week*, January 12, 1974; *Family Circle*, June, 1975.

*   *   *

JUNKER, Karin Stensland 1916-

PERSONAL: Born October 7, 1916, in Lidingo, Stockholm, Sweden; daughter of Josef Gottfrid (a publisher and translator) and Elisabet M. (Samuelsson) Jonsson; married Bengt Junker, March 2, 1940 (died, 1970); children: Sten, Lena, Boel, Riken, Anders. *Education:* Attended University of Stockholm, 1935-37, 1954-58, Phil.D., 1968. *Politics:* Liberal (moderate). *Religion:* Lutheran. *Home:* Asogatan 211, S-116 32 Stockholm, Sweden. *Office:* Department of Pediatrics, Karolinska Institutet, S-104 01 Stockholm; and Norrtull's Hospital, S-113 45 Stockholm, Sweden.

CAREER: Writer, 1944—. Editor, Swedish State Institute for Building Research, 1947-53. Committee member of Royal Board of Education, 1957-58, of Department of Social Work, 1958-59. Associate professor of medical science, University of Stockholm, Stockholm, Sweden, 1973. President, Wenner-Gren Research Laboratory, 1978—. Member of board of Swedish Scouts' and Guides' Association foundations for handicapped children, of Swedish National Association for Retarded Children, and of other foundations and boards for handicapped youth. *Wartime service:* Special service in Security Guard, 1941-44. *Member:* International College of Pediatrics (vice-president, 1974-78), Kungliga Saells-Kapet Pro Patria, Saells-Kapet Barnavaard (presi-

dent, 1974—), First-of-May-Flower National Association, Stockholm Committee.

WRITINGS: Du kanner mig icke (novel; title means "You Don't Know Me"), Fahlcrantz & Gumaelius, 1944; *Det okuvliga hjaertat* (title means "The Unsubduable Heart"), Fahlcrantz & Gumaelius, 1945; *Building Production Methods of Scandinavia*, State Institute of Building Research, 1950; *Auditory Training of Deaf and Hard of Hearing*, Scout Association Publication, 1952; (with Lennart Holmgren) *Hoerseltraening och fostran av doeva smaabarn*, 2nd edition, Scoutfoerlaget, 1952; *What Shall We Do with Ture?*, Scout Association Publication, 1956; *De ensamma*, Natur & Kultur, 1961, 5th edition, 1980; translation by Gustaf Lannestock published as *The Child in the Glass Ball*, Abingdon, 1964; *Samhallets samvetsbarn* (title means "Community's Conscience Children"), Natur & Kultur, 1964; (with Bengt Barr) *Children with Speech Disorders*, Kooperativa foerb (Stockholm), 1964; (contributor) *Annorlunda barn* (title means "Otherwise Children"), 1965; *Paralinguistics and Kinesics in Pathological Speech Development*, University of Stockholm, 1965; *On the Behavioral Pattern in Infants at Sound Perception Against the Background of Later Developed Speech and Communicative Behavior*, University of Stockholm, 1968; (contributor) *Foeraeldraboken* (title means "Parents' Book"), Bernce's, 1968; *Den Lilla Maenniskan: Kontakt och stimulans livets foersta Villkor* (title means "The Small Human Being: Contact and Stimulation: The First Prerequisites of Life"), Natur & Kultur, 1975, 2nd edition, 1980.

Also author: (With Evy Blid) *How a "Lekotek" Was Started, and How It Works*, 1969; (with Barr) *Functional Contact Test for Babies as a Screening Method*, 1970; (with Holmgren) *Auditory Training and Education of Small Deaf Children*, 1971; *Lekoteket paa Blockhusudden* (title means "A Program for Training through Systematic Play Activity"), 1971.

WORK IN PROGRESS: Haer slutar allmaen vaeg (title means "End of the General Highway"), a sequel to *The Child in the Glass Ball; Solo Part for Cello*, a novel, completed and awaiting publication.

SIDELIGHTS: Karin Stensland Junker told *CA:* "As the mother of two children mentally retarded (in different ways), I switched over my interests to the field of child development in 1953 ... and thus left the field of building research.... I want to keep the door open to artistic writing, though." During journeys in Europe, Asia, Africa, and United States, Junker says that she has found the problems of the mentally handicapped much the same: "Too little is done to employ and occupy them; much more could be done to fight prejudice against them." She is now focusing on the early diagnosis of handicaps in children, and has developed a screening test for 7-to-9-month-old infants (BOEL), which has been applied to all Swedish babies since 1971. The test has also been introduced in Denmark, Finland, Norway, Italy, and the Netherlands.

K

KALINA, Sigmund 1911-1977

PERSONAL: Born September 28, 1911, in Brooklyn, N.Y.; died, 1977; son of Victor and Bessie (Fram) Kalina; married Gertrude Lee Tendler (a personnel manager); children: Daniel, Susan Kalina Krenitsky. *Education:* Attended University of Arkansas, 1930-31; Long Island University, B.S., 1935; Hofstra University, M.S., 1965; State University of New York at Potsdam, graduate study, 1965-67. *Residence:* Valley Stream, Long Island, N.Y. *Office:* Berner High School, Massapequa, Long Island, N.Y.

CAREER: Lifeguard at public beaches of New York, N.Y., 1930-40; teacher of biology at Berner High School, Massapequa, Long Island, N.Y. Adult education instructor in Valley Stream, Long Island; nature counselor at Shibley Camp. Science consultant to Filmstrip House, Inc. *Wartime service:* U.S. Merchant Marine, 1943-47; senior ammunition inspector in New York and New Jersey, and supervisor at ports of embarkation.

WRITINGS—Juvenile; published by Lothrop: *The House That Nature Built*, 1972; *Your Bones Are Alive*, 1972; *About Blood*, 1973: *Your Nerves and Their Messages*, 1973; *Air: The Invisible Ocean*, 1973; *Your Blood and Its Cargo*, 1974; *Three Drops of Water*, 1974; *How to Sharpen Your Study Skills*, 1975; *How to Make a Dinosaur*, 1976. Also author of filmstrips.

WORK IN PROGRESS: A book on pollution as it relates to flora and fuana of a developing stream.†

* * *

KALLMAN, Chester (Simon) 1921-1975

PERSONAL: Born January 7, 1921, in Brooklyn, N.Y.; died January 7, 1975. *Education:* Brooklyn College (now Brooklyn College of the City University of New York), B.A.; graduate study at University of Michigan. *Home:* Democharous 23, Marasleiou, Athens 601, Greece.

CAREER: Poet and librettist. *Awards, honors:* American Academy of Arts and Letters grant, 1955; Ingram Merrill Foundation grant, 1964; Morton Dauwen Zabel Prize, *Poetry* magazine, 1970.

WRITINGS: Elegy (poetry), Gotham Book Mart, 1951; *Storm at Castelfianco*, Grove, 1956; (editor with W. H. Auden and Noah Greenberg) *An Elizabethan Song Book: Lute Songs, Madrigals and Rounds*, Doubleday, 1956, published as *An Anthology of Elizabethan Lute Songs, Madrigals and Rounds*, Norton, 1970; (translator) Milton J. Cross, editor, *Favorite Arias from the Great Operas*, Doubleday, 1960; *Absent and Present*, Wesleyan University Press, 1963; *The Sense of Occasion* (poetry), Braziller, 1971; *The Rise and Fall of the City of Mahagonny*, David R. Godine, 1976.

Librettos and lyrics: (With Auden) *The Rake's Progress* (music by Igor Stravinsky; first produced in Venice, 1951, produced in New York, 1953), Boosey & Hawkes, 1951; *Bluebeard's Castle* (adaptation of libretto by Bela Balazs; music by Bela Bartok), Boosey & Hawkes, 1952; *Falstaff* (adaptation of libretto by Arrigo Boito; music by Boito), G. Ricordi, 1954; (with Auden) *The Magic Flute* (adaptation of libretto by Emanuel Schikaneder and C. L. Giesecke; music by Mozart), Random House, 1956; "The Abduction from the Seraglio" (adaptation of libretto by C. F. Bretzner; music by Mozart), first produced in Statford, Conn., 1956; "Panfilo and Lauretta" (originally entitled "The Tuscan Players"; music by Cesar Chavez), first produced in New York, 1957; *Anne Boleyn* (adaptation of libretto by Felice Romani; music by Gaetano Donizeti), G. Ricordi, 1959; (with Auden) "The Seven Deadly Sins of the Lower Middle Class" (adaptation of ballet-cantata by Bertolt Brecht; music by Kurt Weill), first produced in New York at New York City Center, 1959; (with Auden) *Elegy for Young Lovers* (music by Hans Werner Henze; first produced in Glyndebourne, Sussex, 1961), Schott (Mainz), 1961; *Don Giovanni* (adaptation of libretto by Lorenzo da Ponte; music by Mozart), E. C. Schirmer, 1961; (with Auden) *The Bassarids* (based on Euripides' "The Bacchae"; first produced in German translation in Salzburg, at Salzburg Festival, 1966; produced in Santa Fe, N.M. at Santa Fe Opera, 1968), Schott (Mainz), 1966; (with Auden) *The Entertainment of the Senses* (music by John Gardner; first produced in London, 1974), Schott (Mainz), 1966; (with Auden) "Love's Labour's Lost" (musical adaptation of Shakespeare; music by Nicholas Nabokov), first produced at Twenty-fifth Edinburgh International Festival, 1971. Also with Auden, adapted "Arcifanfano, King of Fools," which was performed for the first time since 1778, in New York, November, 1965. Also translator of numerous librettos.

SIDELIGHTS: Chester Kallman was often admired for his observance of poetic form. Robert Mazzocco of the *New York Review of Books* once wrote that Kallman "is a poet who knows most of what there is to know about meter and form. . . . And here is a poet who knows most of what there is to know about rhetoric. . . . It is a small-scale virtuosity, but virtuosity nonetheless.''

This lyrical sense was always present in Kallman's writings. W. J. Smith explained in *Harper's* that "Kallman wastes no time: his poems go directly always to the heart of the matter. He writes clearly, and with a subtle ear trained by years of writing for opera. . . . At times, when writing of childhood sharply observed and recalled, he presents skillfully the distortion of nightmare (he has a real talent for the grotesque); at others, he is delicately lyrical and often very funny.''

Besides being considered a master of poetic form and technique, many critics believed Kallman was also very talented in his use of metaphors. W. H. Auden, Kallman's collaborator on many librettos, believed that "the final section [of *The Sense of Occasion*], "The African Ambassador," is a very remarkable achievement indeed. To begin with, it is a technical tour de force. . . . Secondly, Mr. Kallman has succeeded in what is one of the most difficult of all tasks, namely, in inventing a myth, or rather, perhaps, a metaphor, that does not remain private to the author but is accessible to all. . . . I have no hesitation in saying that, in my opinion, "The African Ambassador" is one of the most original and significant poems written in the past twenty years.''

Michael Mesic was equally as lavish with his praise of Kallman's writing ability. In his review in *Poetry* he wrote: "Some will say [Kallman's] poems are out of date, for verses that do not tell their age are out of fashion, as not strictly of the moment. But unlike checks that must be cashed upon receipt, this is currency good for all occasions and worth more than the paper it is printed on. Mr. Kallman is a coiner, in the highest sense, an adept at that artistic counterfeit which is more valuable than the gold standard of the present. The medals from his mint are stamped not with the image of the time but with personality and personal knowledge which shine through and are enforced by a precision little practised nowadays. Chester Kallman's sense of occasion and his art are both practised and inspired.''

Although recognized and respected as a poet, Chester Kallman was also looked upon as an excellent librettist. Kallman collaborated with fellow poet W. H. Auden on many librettos. In 1975, the *New York Times* reprinted a 1953 review of Kallman's first libretto, *The Rake's Progress*, which was based on the famous Hogarth engravings. Olin Downes, the *New York Times* music critic at that time, wrote: "We were wholly unprepared for the quality of the libretto by W. H. Auden and Chester Kallman. . . . It is in essence a morality play. It has certain psychological undercurrents, with Freudian twists and symbolisms of which Hogarth never dreamed.''

BIOGRAPHICAL/CRITICAL SOURCES: Harper's, September, 1963, March, 1972; *New York Times Book Review,* September 1, 1963; *Poetry,* April, 1972; *New York Review of Books,* June 15, 1972; *Contemporary Literary Criticism,* Volume II, Gale, 1974; *New York Times,* January 19, 1975; *AB Bookman's Weekly,* February 3, 1975; *Opera News,* July, 1975.†

*   *   *

KANDEL, I(saac) L(eon) 1881-1965

PERSONAL: Born January 22, 1881, in Rumania; died June 14, 1965; son of Abraham and Fanny (Manales) Kandel; married Jessie S. Davis, July 27, 1915 (died August, 1949); children: Alan Davis, Helen Kandel Hyman. *Education:* University of Manchester, B.A., 1902, M.A., 1905; Columbia University, Ph.D., 1910.

CAREER: Royal Academical Institution, Belfast, Ireland, master, 1906-08; Columbia University, Teachers College, New York, N.Y., instructor, 1913-15, associate in education, 1915-23, professor of education and associate in International Institute, 1923-47, professor emeritus, 1947-65; University of Manchester, Manchester, England, professor, 1947-50. Visiting professor, Johns Hopkins University, University of Pennsylvania, University of California, Yale University, and City College (now City College of the City University of New York). Staff member, Carnegie Foundation, 1914-23, and Committee for a Free Europe, beginning 1952. Trustee, Finch Junior College. *Member:* National Academy of Education (charter member), National Education Association, Society of College Teachers of Education, American Council of Learned Societies, American Association of University Professors, Phi Delta Kappa, Kappa Delta Pi (Laureate chapter). *Awards, honors:* Litt.D., University of Melbourne, 1937; Chevalier de la Legion d'Honneur, 1937; L.L.D., University of North Carolina, 1946.

WRITINGS: Training of Elementary School Teachers in Germany, Teachers College, Columbia University, 1910, reprinted, AMS Press, 1972; *Elementary Education in England with Special Reference to London, Liverpool, and Manchester,* U.S. Government Printing Office, 1914; *Federal Aid for Vocational Education,* Carnegie Foundation, 1917; *The Reform of Secondary Education in France,* Teachers College, Columbia University, 1924; (editor) *Twenty-five Years of American Education,* Macmillan, 1924, reprinted, Books for Libraries, 1966; *Essays in Comparative Education,* Teachers College, Columbia University, 1930; *History of Secondary Education: A Study in the Development of Liberal Education,* Houghton, 1930; *Comparative Education,* Houghton, 1933, reprinted, Greenwood Press, 1970; (with Lester Wilson) *Introduction to the Study of American Education,* Ronald, 1934, reprinted, Arden Library, 1979; *The Making of Nazis,* Teachers College, Columbia University, 1935, reprinted, Greenwood Press, 1970; *Examinations and Their Substitutes in the United States,* Carnegie Foundation, 1936, reprinted, Arno, 1971; *Types of Administration with Particular Reference to the Educational Systems of New Zealand and Australia,* New Zealand Council for Educational Research, 1938; *Conflicting Theories of Education,* Macmillan, 1938, reprinted, Russell & Russell, 1967.

Professional Aptitude Tests in Medicine, Law, and Engineering, Teachers College, Columbia University, 1940; *The End of an Era,* Teachers College, Columbia University, 1941; *The Cult of Uncertainty,* Macmillan, 1943, reprinted, Arno, 1971; *Intellectual Cooperation: National and International,* Teachers College, Columbia University, 1944; *United States Activities in International Cultural Relations,* American Council on Education, 1945; *The Impact of the War upon American Education,* University of North Carolina Press, 1948, reprinted, Greenwood Press, 1974; *Raising the School-Leaving Age,* UNESCO, 1951; *The New Era in Education: A Comparative Study,* Houghton, 1955; (contributor) John Sargent, editor, *Education and Society: Some Studies of Education Systems in Europe and America,* Batchworth Press, 1955; *American Education in the Twentieth Century,* Harvard University Press, 1957; *William Chandler Bagley: Stalwart Educator,* Teachers College, Columbia University, 1961. Editor, *Educational Yearbook of the International Institute of Teachers College,* Columbia University, 1924-44. Contributor to professional journals. Editor, *School and Society,* 1946-53.

SIDELIGHTS: I. L. Kandel traveled extensively in most

European countries, as well as in New Zealand, Australia, Latin America, and South Africa.†

*   *   *

KANY, Charles E(mil) 1895-1968

PERSONAL: Born July 6, 1895, in Dolgeville, N.Y.; died, 1968; son of Julius and Josephine (Miller) Kany. *Education:* University of Michigan, A.B., 1917; Harvard University, M.A., 1918, Ph.D., 1920.

CAREER: Bryn Mawr College, Bryn Mawr, Pa., associate, 1921-22; University of California, Berkeley, 1922-66, began as instructor, became professor of Spanish. *Member:* American Association of Teachers of Spanish, Hispanic Society of America (corresponding member). *Awards, honors:* Guggenheim fellowship, 1928-29.

WRITINGS: Life and Manners in Madrid, 1750-1800, University of California Press, 1932, reprinted, AMS Press, 1970; *The Beginnings of the Epistolary Novel in France, Italy, and Spain,* University of California Press, 1937, reprinted, Porcupine Press, 1979; *American-Spanish Syntax,* University of Chicago Press, 1945, 2nd edition, 1951, reprinted, 1975; (with M. Dondo) *Spoken French for Students and Travelers,* Heath, 1946, 2nd edition (with Bernard F. Uzan), 1978; *Spoken Italian for Travelers and Tourists,* Little, Brown, 1946; *Practical Spanish Grammar,* Heath, 1951; (with C. F. Melz) *Spoken German for Travelers and Tourists,* Little, Brown, 1954; *American-Spanish Semantics,* University of California Press, 1960; *American-Spanish Euphemisms,* University of California Press, 1960; *Spoken Spanish for Students and Travelers,* Heath, 1961, 3rd edition (with Manuel Duran), 1978. Contributor of chapter on American-Spanish language to *Handbook of Latin American Studies,* Library of Congress, 1945-51.

AVOCATIONAL INTERESTS: Music, particularly piano.†

*   *   *

KARL, Frederick R(obert) 1927-

PERSONAL: Born April 10, 1927, in Brooklyn, N.Y.; son of Louis and Edith (Sablow) Karl; married Dolores Mary Oristaglio (a banker), June 8, 1951; children: Deborah Laura, Rebecca Elizabeth, Judith Leah. *Education:* Columbia College, B.A., 1948; Stanford University, M.A., 1949; Columbia University, Ph.D., 1957. *Home:* 140 West 86th St., New York, N.Y. 10024. *Office:* Department of English, City College of the City University of New York, New York, N.Y. 10031.

CAREER: City College of the City University of New York, New York, N.Y., member of English department faculty, 1957—. *Military service:* U.S. Navy, World War II. *Member:* Modern Language Association of America. *Awards, honors:* Fulbright grant in American literature; Guggenheim fellowship; National Endowment for the Humanities senior research grant.

WRITINGS: A Reader's Guide to Great Twentieth Century English Novels, Noonday, 1959; *A Reader's Guide to Joseph Conrad,* Farrar, Straus, 1960; *The Quest,* Heinemann, 1961; *The Contemporary English Novel,* Farrar, Straus, 1962; *C. P. Snow: The Politics of Conscience,* Southern Illinois University Press, 1963; (co-editor) *The Existential Imagination,* Fawcett, 1963; (co-editor) *Short Fiction of the Masters,* Putnam, 1963; *A Century of Fiction: The British Novel in the Nineteenth Century,* Farrar, Straus, 1965; *The Adversary Literature; the English Novel in the Eighteenth Century: A Study in Drama,* Farrar, Straus, 1974; *Joseph Conrad: The Three Lives* (biography), Farrar, Straus, 1979. Contributor of book reviews and articles to literary publications.

WORK IN PROGRESS: Editing *The Collected Letters of Joseph Conrad,* to be published in eight volumes by Cambridge University Press.

SIDELIGHTS: In a review of *Joseph Conrad: The Three Lives* for the *Los Angeles Times Book Review,* Robert Kirsch writes: "Short of the discovery of any new mass of material, this meticulous and detailed work, based on extensive research and the Conrad letters (which Karl is preparing for publication), is likely to be the standard biography as to the facts of Conrad's life and it should be indispensable to any future criticism of Conrad's work." James R. Mellow, in his *Chicago Tribune Book World* article, says that "Karl brings to his biography of the writer all the essential resources of Conrad's public and private lives; this is a sane, thorough, and psychologically perceptive study. At his best, Karl nails down the paradoxical distinctions between Conrad's maritime career where 'tasks were defined, status and roles determined by rank, change shackled by custom and tradition,' and the anarchy of his literary life which had 'no fixed standards except those posed from within.' The 'third' life of the title concerns Conrad's childhood in subjugated Poland, as the son of a Polish poet and dissident, Apollo Korzeniowski, who was sent into Russian exile—along with his tubercular wife and four-year-old son—for his anti-czarist activities."

However, Mellow finds that "the overriding problem with *Joseph Conrad: The Three Lives* is length—an unwieldy 1,008 pages with extensive footnotes and too much shuttling back and forth in the narrative past-present-and-future, resulting in needless repetition.... There are a number of distracting but fashionable literary allusions—to Kafka, Beckett, Jung, Mallarme, Herbert Marcuse, and to Conrad's Orphic and Promethean tendencies, his 'marginality,' existentialist leanings. There are, too, the usual reverential references to Erik Erikson and his psychohistory of Mahatma Gandhi. Evidently it is impossible, nowadays, to write a biography without a great deal of bowing and scraping in that direction."

Nicholas Guild, writing in the *Washington Post Book World,* makes the point that "Conrad poses a number of problems for his biographers. His published recollections are demonstrably unreliable, and he seems in all respects to have been secretive and untrustworthy about his past. Direct evidence for his youth in Poland and his career at sea is neither extensive nor particularly revealing. The scholar must do a very judicious job of sifting. Karl, however, too often abandons that caution which becomes the biographer of so slippery a subject to indulge in speculations more appropriate to the novelist." Guild believes that this problem is most pronounced in the early part of the biography, "dealing with periods of Conrad's life for which there is little direct evidence. Once he takes up his literary career, and has the letters to work with, Karl is much better." Anatole Broyard of the *New York Times* disagrees. "Even here," he writes, Karl "tends to take Conrad too much at his word, for in his letters Conrad was fond of melodramatic and nihilistic pronouncements about the condition of man, statements that his work exposed as posturing or mere surface irritation." Guild concludes that "taken as a whole ... *The Three Lives* is simply too flawed, too poorly argued as a work of conjectural psychology, too prone to the fanciful analogy presented as the discovery of some arcane truth, to replace Jocelyn

Baines' critical biography as the standard life of this most interesting of our great modern novelists.''

In a *Publishers Weekly* article, interviewer Joseph Barbato notes that ''for Karl, the book represents, quite literally, a lifetime of scholarship in the work and life of Conrad.'' But Karl admits that from the start, he wanted to write a ''novelistic treatment'' of the author's life rather than a straightforward biography. He told Barbato that he tried to make the book ''a reading experience rather than a scholarly experience. My aim was to create a full narrative of Conrad's life and, in a sense, to disguise the scholarship and the referential work that went into it.''

BIOGRAPHICAL/CRITICAL SOURCES: Publishers Weekly, January 29, 1979; *New York Times Book Review,* February 11, 1979; *New York Times,* February 17, 1979; *Los Angeles Times Book Review,* February 18, 1979; *Washington Post Book World,* February 18, 1979; *Chicago Tribune Book World,* February 25, 1979; *Times Literary Supplement,* November 23, 1979.

* * *

KARP, Abraham J. 1921-

PERSONAL: Born April 5, 1921, in Indura, Poland; son of Aaron (a furrier) and Rachel (Shor) Karp; married Deborah Burstein, June 17, 1945; children: Hillel Judah, David Jacob. *Education:* Yeshiva University, B.A., (magna cum laude), 1942; Jewish Theological Seminary of America, rabbi, 1945, M.H.L., 1949, D.D., 1971; additional study at Columbia University. *Home:* 240 Cobbs Hill Dr., Rochester, N.Y. 14610. *Office:* Department of History, University of Rochester, Rochester, N.Y. 14627.

CAREER: Rabbi, Temple Israel, Swampscott, Mass., 1948-51, Beth Shalom, Kansas City, Mo., 1951-56, and Temple Beth El, Rochester, N.Y., 1956-72; University of Rochester, Rochester, N.Y., professor of history and religious studies, 1972—, Philip S. Bernstein Professor of Jewish Studies, 1975—. Visiting professor, Dartmouth College, 1967, Jewish Theological Seminary of America, 1967, 1971, and Hebrew University, 1970. Corresponding member, Institute of Contemporary Jewry, Hebrew University, 1973—. Fellow, Institute of Talmudic Ethics. *Member:* Rabbinical Assembly of America (member of executive council, 1959-62), American Jewish Historical Society (member of executive council, beginning 1960; president, 1972-75), Jewish Publication Society, Phi Beta Kappa. *Awards, honors:* Lee M. Friedman Medal.

WRITINGS: When Your Child Asks about God, United Synagogue, 1954; *Our December Dilemma,* United Synagogue, 1958; *The Jewish Way of Life,* Prentice-Hall, 1962, revised edition published as *The Jewish Way of Life and Thought,* Ktav, 1980; *A History of the United Synagogue of America, 1913-1963,* United Synagogue, 1963; (editor and author of introduction) *The Jewish Experience in America,* American Jewish Historical Society, 1969, Volume I: *The Colonial Period,* Volume II: *In the Early Republic,* Volume III: *The Emerging Community,* Volume IV: *The Era of Immigration,* Volume V: *At Home in America;* (author of epilogue) Rufus Learsi, *The Jews in America,* Ktav, 1972; (author of introduction) *Beginnings: Early American Judaica,* eleven volumes, Jewish Publication Society of America, 1975; (editor) *Golden Door to America: The Jewish Immigrant Experience,* Viking, 1976; *To Give Life,* Schocken, 1980.

WORK IN PROGRESS: Haven and Home: A History of the Jew in America.

AVOCATIONAL INTERESTS: Book collecting in fields of Hebraica and early American Judaica.

* * *

KEEGAN, Mary Heathcott 1914-
(Mary Heathcott, Mary Raymond)

PERSONAL: Born September 30, 1914, in Manchester, England; daughter of Edward and Ada (Webb) Heathcott; married Eric A. Keegan (a business executive), September 10, 1938; children: Sara Lou, Mark. *Education:* Attended private school in London, England. *Home:* Cockenskell, Blawith, near Ulverston, England. *Agent:* Harvey Unna Ltd., 79 Baker St., London W.1, England.

CAREER: Began career as journalist, working as general reporter, columnist, writer for women's pages; member of staff of *Evening News,* London, England, 1934-40, *Straits Times,* Singapore, 1940-42, Ministry of Information, Delhi, India, 1942-43, *Time and Tide,* London, 1945, *John Herling's Labor Letter,* Washington, D.C., 1951-54; free-lance writer and novelist, 1954—.

*WRITINGS—*Under psuedonym Mary Raymond; published by Collins except as indicated: *Paradise Is Here,* 1953; *If Today Be Sweet,* 1956; *Island of the Heart,* 1957; *Love Be Wary,* 1958; *The Day of Return,* 1959; *Her Part of the House,* 1960; *Hide My Heart,* 1961; *Thief of My Heart,* 1962; *Never Doubt Me,* 1962; *Shadow of a Star,* 1963; *Change of Heart,* 1964, *Take-Over,* 1965; *Girl in a Mask,* 1965; *The Divided House,* 1966; *The Long Journey Home,* 1967; *I Have Three Sons,* 1968; *That Summer,* 1970; *Surety for a Stranger,* 1971; *The Pimpernel Project,* 1972; *The Silver Girl,* 1973; *Villa of Flowers,* 1976; *April Promise,* R. Hale, 1980. Short story under name Mary Heathcott anthologized in *Short Story No. 4,* edited by Whit Burnett, Wyn, 1953. Contributor to British and American magazines and newspapers.

* * *

KELLER, Thomas F(ranklin) 1931-

PERSONAL: Born September 22, 1931, in Greenwood, S.C.; son of Alonzo (an entrepreneur) and Helen (Seago) Keller; married Margaret Query, June 15, 1956; children: Thomas Crafton (died March, 1980), Neel McKay, John Caldwell. *Education:* Duke University, A.B., 1953; University of Michigan, M.B.A., 1957, Ph.D., 1960. *Home:* 1024 West Markham Ave., Durham, N.C. 27701. *Office:* Graduate School of Business Administration, Duke University, Durham, N.C. 27706.

CAREER: Peat, Marwick, Mitchell & Co., Charlotte, N.C., auditor, 1953; University of Michigan, Ann Arbor, instructor, 1958-59; Duke University, Durham, N.C., 1959—, began as assistant professor, now professor of accounting. Visiting associate professor, University of Washington, 1963-64, and Carnegie-Mellon University, 1966-67. *Military service:* U.S. Army, 1953-55. *Member:* American Institute of Certified Public Accountants, American Accounting Association (vice-president, 1968-69), Financial Executives Institute, North Carolina Association of Certified Public Accountants, Beta Alpha Sigma, Phi Kappa Sigma, Alpha Kappa Psi, Beta Gamma Sigma. *Awards, honors:* Ford Foundation summer research fellowship, 1960, 1961.

WRITINGS: Accounting for Corporate Income Taxes, School of Business Administration, University of Michigan, 1961; (with Walter Meigs and Charles Johnson) *Intermediate Accounting,* McGraw, 1963, revised edition, 1968; (editor with Stephen Zeff) *Financial Accounting Theory: Issues and*

Controversies, two volumes, McGraw, 1964-69; (contributor) Morton Backer, editor, *Modern Accounting Theory*, Prentice-Hall, 1966; (with Meigs and Johnson) *Advanced Accounting*, McGraw, 1966; (editor with Stephen A. Zeff) *Financial Accounting Theory II*, McGraw, 1969; (contributor) Sidney Davidson, editor, *Handbook of Modern Accounting*, McGraw, 1970; (editor with A. Rashad Abdel-Khalik) *Financial Information Requirements for Security Analysis*, Duke University, 1977; (editor with Abdel-Khalik) *The Impact of Accounting Research on Practice and Disclosure*, Duke University Press, 1978; (with Abdel-Khalik) *Earnings or Cash Flows: An Experiment on Functional Fixation and the Valuation of the Firm*, American Accounting Association, 1979. Contributor to *Journal of Accountancy*, *Accounting Review*, *Cooperative Accountant*, *Management Accounting*, *Hospital Administration*, and *Law and Contemporary Problems*.

WORK IN PROGRESS: Revisions of *Financial Accounting Theory I* and *Handbook of Modern Accounting*.

*   *   *

KENNEDY, Richard S(ylvester)   1920-

PERSONAL: Born October 13, 1920, in St. Paul, Minn.; son of William W. (a chemist) and Ellen (Foley) Kennedy; married Ella Dickinson, March 31, 1943; children: Elizabeth, Catherine, James. *Education:* Attended University of Southern California, 1938-39; University of California, Los Angeles, B.A., 1942; University of Chicago, M.A., 1947; Harvard University, Ph.D., 1953. *Politics:* Democrat. *Religion:* Unitarian Universalist. *Home:* 120 Merbrook Lane, Merion, Pa. *Office:* Department of English, Temple University, Philadelphia, Pa.

CAREER: Harvard University, Cambridge, Mass., teaching fellow, 1948-50; University of Rochester, Rochester, N.Y., assistant professor of English, 1950-57; University of Wichita, Wichita, Kan., associate professor, 1957-63, professor of English 1963-64; Temple University, Philadelphia, Pa., professor of English, 1964—. *Military service:* U.S. Navy, 1942-46; became lieutenant; awarded Bronze Star Medal, Purple Heart. *Member:* Modern Language Association of America, American Studies Association, National Association for the Advancement of Colored People.

WRITINGS: The Window of Memory: The Literary Career of Thomas Wolfe, University of North Carolina Press, 1962; *The Notebooks of Thomas Wolfe*, two volumes, University of North Carolina Press, 1970; *Dreams in the Mirror: A Biography of E. E. Cummings*, Liveright, 1980. Contributor to *Dictionary of American Biography* and to professional journals.

WORK IN PROGRESS: The early career of Robert Browning; a history of twentieth-century American fiction; a study of Thomas Hardy.

SIDELIGHTS: Richard S. Kennedy's biographies have drawn strong praise from several critics. C. H. Holman of the *Virginia Quarterly Review* calls Kennedy's first book, *The Window of Memory*, "a work of impressive scope and critical importance, the first fully detailed, exhaustive, and truly first-rate study of a major writer the unevenness and seeming formlessness of whose work has been a serious challenge to American criticism." Although a *Times Literary Supplement* reviewer differs with Holman on the grounds that the critical aspect of the book falls short of his expectations, he still affirms that of all the books available on Thomas Wolfe, "Kennedy's is certainly the most painstaking, consistently enlightening and elegant." *Saturday Re-*

view's R. E. Spiller agrees, noting that "never before has the evidence [of Thomas Wolfe's creative processes] been so carefully sifted and presented. This is the scholar's workbook for all future study of Wolfe."

Similarly, Kennedy's biography of E. E. Cummings, *Dreams in the Mirror*, does not rely heavily on what critics have said for its emphasis. As Richard Holmes, writing for the London *Times*, points out, Kennedy's "warmhearted and psychologically acute biography is content to leave the larger literary questions alone, and locate Cummings vividly within his American inheritance.... The success of Kennedy's biography is shown most distinctly in the places where he links ... psychological interpretation with Cummings' uniquely established literary identity."

Dreams in the Mirror, unlike earlier biographies of Cummings that were closely controlled by the poet, includes "tastefully but in satisfying detail" information that had previously been suppressed, writes Joseph McLellan in the *Washington Post*. "Kennedy handles his subject with an understanding and sympathy that could not automatically be expected," the reviewer continues. "Besides providing a wealth of previously unpublished biographical detail, he ventures discreetly and convincingly into psychological analysis, and his examination of some of the poems uncovers details that might have been missed previously even by avid admirers."

Kennedy told *CA* that his strong interest in biography has influenced his work in progress as well. What he originally intended to be a history of twentieth-century American fiction, "may turn out to be 'The Lives of the Modern American Novelists'" instead.

AVOCATIONAL INTERESTS: Pottery-making, photography.

BIOGRAPHICAL/CRITICAL SOURCES: Wichita Eagle and Beacon, November 14, 1962; *Wichita Sunday Eagle*, November 25, 1962; *Virginia Quarterly Review*, winter, 1963; *Saturday Review*, January 12, 1963; *Times Literary Supplement*, July 26, 1963; *Los Angeles Times*, January 27, 1980; *Washington Post*, February 3, 1980; *London Times*, June 5, 1980.

*   *   *

KENT, Allen   1921-

PERSONAL: Born October 24, 1921, in New York, N.Y.; son of Samuel and Anne (Begun) Kent; married Rosalind Kossoff, January 24, 1943; children: Merryl Frances, Emily Beth, Jacqueline Diane, Carolyn May. *Education:* City College (now City College of the City University of New York), B.S., 1942. *Office:* University of Pittsburgh, Pittsburgh, Pa. 15260.

CAREER: Essex Chemicals, Inc., Chester, Conn., chief chemist, 1946-47; Interscience Publishers, New York, N.Y., associate editor, 1947-51; Massachusetts Institute of Technology, Cambridge, research associate, 1951-53; Battelle Memorial Institute, Columbus, Ohio, principal documentation engineer, 1953-55; Western Reserve University (now Case Western Reserve University), Cleveland, Ohio, associate director, Center for Documentation of Communication Research, and professor of library science, 1955-63; University of Pittsburgh, Pittsburgh, Pa., director of Knowledge Availability Systems Center, and professor of library and information sciences, beginning 1963, currently Distinguished Service Professor of Library and Information Sciences, director of communications programs, 1969—. Allen

Kent Associates (consultants), Pittsburgh, Pa., president, 1961—. Consultant on information retrieval to Special Assistant to the President, and to several government agencies, 1955—. Lecturer in Europe and South America.

MEMBER: American Institute of Chemists (fellow), American Association for the Advancement of Science (fellow), International Committee on Information Retrieval and Machine Translation (general secretary), American Chemical Society (chairman, committee on chemical documentation, 1956-57), Special Libraries Association (chairman, advisory council, 1956-57), American documentation Institute, American Library Association.

WRITINGS: Literature Research as a Tool for Creative Thinking, Western Reserve University, 1956; (editor with Jess H. Shera and James W. Perry) *Documentation in Action,* Reinhold, 1956; (with others) *Machine Literature Searching,* Interscience, 1956; (with Helen Loftus) *Automation in the Library: An Annotated Bibliography,* American Documentation, 1956; *Automation in Literature Research: A Report on the ASM Mechanized Literature Searching Project,* Metals Division, Special Libraries Association, 1956; (with Perry) *The Western Reserve University Searching Selector: Summary of Functions and Capabilities,* [Cleveland], 1956; (with Perry) *New Indexing-Abstracting System for Formal Reports, Development and Proof Services,* privately printed, 1957; (editor with Shera and Perry) *Information Systems in Documentation,* Interscience, 1957; (with Perry) *Documentation and Information Retrieval: An Introduction to Basic Principles and Cost Analysis,* Western Reserve University Press, 1957; (editor with others) *Information Resources,* Western Reserve University Press, 1957; (with Perry and Robert E. Booth) *Machine Searching of Metallurgical Literature,* [Cleveland], 1957; (with T. H. Rees) *The Jargon of Machine Literature Searching,* Center for Documentation and Communication Research, Western Reserve University, 1957; (with Booth) *Trend in Information Services: U.S. versus U.S.S.R. Developments in Scientific and Engineering Fields,* privately printed, 1957; (with T. H. Rees and Perry) *A Demonstration in Automation Correlation for Purposes of Commercial Intelligence,* School of Library Science, Western Reserve University, 1957.

(Editor with Perry) *Tools for Machine Literature Searching: Semantic Code Dictionary, Equipment, Procedure,* Interscience, 1958; (editor with Perry and Gilbert Peaks) *Progress Report in Chemical Literature Retrieval,* Interscience, 1958; (with Perry) *Centralized Information Services, Opportunities and Problems,* Western Reserve University Press, 1958; (editor with others) *Punched Cards,* Reinhold, 1958; (with Perry and T. H. Rees) *Machine Documentation Equipment,* School of Library Science, Western Reserve University, 1958; *Non-conventional Retrieval Systems in Documentation: Preliminary Comparative Analysis,* School of Library Science, Western Reserve University, 1958; (with Janet Rees) *Mechanized Searching Experiments Using the WRU Searching Selector: Preliminary Report,* Western Reserve University, 1958; *Minimum Criteria for a Coordinated Information Service,* U.S. Air Force, 1959; (with Perry) *The Storage and Retrieval of Nonnumerical Data in Large and Complex Documentation Systems,* Western Reserve University, 1959.

Exploitation of Recorded Information, privately printed, 1960; (editor with others) *Information Retrieval and Machine Translation,* Interscience, 1960; (contributor) *Searching and Chemical Literature,* American Chemical Society, 1961; (contributor) *Dissemination and Implementation,* Indiana University Press, 1962; *Textbook on Mechanized Infor-*

mation Retrieval, Interscience, 1962, 3rd edition, 1971; (editor) Lev I. Gutenmakher, *Electronic Information-Logic Machines,* Wiley, 1963; (editor with Orrin E. Taulbee) *Electronic Information Handling,* Spartan, 1965; (editor) *Library Planning for Automation,* Spartan, 1965; (with John Canter) *Specialized Information Centers,* Spartan, 1965; (editor with others) *Electronic Handling of Information, Testing and Evaluation,* Thompson Book Co., 1967; (editor with Harold Lancour) *Encyclopedia of Library and Information Science,* 29 volumes, Dekker, 1968-80.

Information Analysis and Retrieval, Becker & Hayes, 1971; (editor with Lancour) *Copyright: Current Viewpoints on History, Laws, Legislation,* Bowker, 1972; (with Edward M. Arnett) *Computer Based Chemical Information,* Dekker, 1973; (contributor) A. Debons, editor, *Information Science: A Search for Indentity,* Dekker, 1974; (editor) *Resource Sharing in Libraries,* Dekker, 1974; (editor with J. Belzer and A. G. Holzman) *Encyclopedia of Computer Science and Technology,* Dekker, fifteen volumes, 1975-80; (editor with Thomas Galvin) *Library Resource Sharing,* Dekker, 1977; (editor with Galvin) *The On-Line Revolution in Libraries,* Dekker, 1978; (editor with Galvin) *The Structure and Governance of Library Networks,* Dekker, 1979; *Use of Library Materials: The University of Pittsburgh Study,* Dekker, 1979.

*   *   *

KENT, Homer A(ustin), Jr. 1926-

PERSONAL: Born August 13, 1926, in Washington, D.C.; son of Homer Austin (a professor and clergyman) and Alice (Wogaman) Kent; married Beverly Jane Page, August 1, 1953; children: Rebecca Anne, Katherine Ruth, Daniel Arthur. *Education:* Attended American University, 1945; Bob Jones University, A.B., 1947; Grace Theological Seminary, B.D., 1950, Th.M., 1952, Th.D., 1956. *Home:* 305 Sixth St., Winona Lake, Ind. 46590. *Office:* Grace Theological Seminary, Wooster Rd., Winona Lake, Ind. 46590.

CAREER: Minister, Fellowship of Grace Brethren Churches; Grace Theological Seminary, Winona Lake, Ind., professor of New Testament, 1951—, dean, 1962-76, president, 1976—. *Member:* Evangelical Theological Society.

WRITINGS: The Pastoral Epistles: Studies in I and II Timothy and Titus, Moody, 1958; (contributor) *Wycliffe Bible Commentary,* Moody, 1962; *Ephesians: The Glory of the Church,* Moody, 1971; *Jerusalem to Rome: Studies in the Book of Acts,* Baker Book, 1972; *The Epistle to the Hebrews: A Commentary,* Baker Book, 1972; *Light in the Darkness: Studies in the Gospel of John,* Baker Book, 1974; *The Freedom of God's Sons: Studies in Galatians,* Baker Book, 1976; *Treasures of Wisdom: Studies in Colossians and Philemon,* Baker Book, 1978; (contributor) *Expositor's Bible Commentary,* Zondervan, 1978. Contributor of articles to *Bibliotheca Sacra* and *Baker's Dictionary of Theology.* Editor, *Grace Journal.*

*   *   *

KENYON, J(ohn) P(hilipps) 1927-

PERSONAL: Born June 18, 1927, in Sheffield, England; son of William Houston and Edna Grace (Philipps) Kenyon; married Angela Jane Ewert, September 26, 1962; children: Charlotte Clare, Daniel Louis. *Education:* University of Sheffield, B.A., 1948; Cambridge University, Ph.D., 1954. *Office:* Department of Modern History, University of St. Andrews, St. Andrews, Fife KY16 9AJ, Scotland.

CAREER: Cambridge University, Cambridge, England, fellow of Christ's College, 1954-62, assistant lecturer in history, 1955-60, lecturer, 1960-62; University of Hull, Hull, England, professor of history, 1962-80; University of St. Andrews, St. Andrews, Scotland, professor of modern history, 1981—. Visiting associate professor, Columbia University, 1959-60; Ford's Lecturer in English History, Oxford University, 1975-76. *Military service:* Royal Air Force, 1948-50; became flying officer. *Member:* Historical Association. *Awards, honors:* Litt.D., University of Sheffield, 1980.

WRITINGS: Robert Spencer, Earl of Sunderland, 1641-1702, Longmans, Green, 1958; *The Stuarts: A Study in English Kingship,* Batsford, 1958, Macmillan, 1959, 2nd edition, Wiley, 1967; *The Nobility in the Revolution of 1688,* University of Hull, 1963; (editor) Samuel Pepys, *Diary,* revised and abridged edition, Macmillan, 1963; (editor) *The Stuart Constitution, 1603-1688: Documents and Commentary,* Cambridge University Press, 1966; (editor and author of introduction) George Savile Halifax, *Complete Works,* Penguin, 1969; *The Popish Plot,* St. Martin's, 1972; *Revolution Principles,* Cambridge University Press, 1977; *Stuart England,* Pelican, 1978. Contributor to historical journals, including *English Historical Review.*

WORK IN PROGRESS: Research on English historiography.

*   *   *

KERSHAW, Alister (Nasmyth) 1921-

PERSONAL: Born December 19, 1921, in Melbourne, Australia; son of Alton and Frances (Thomson) Kershaw; married Sheila Sanders, October 18, 1957; children: Sylvain, Solange. *Education:* Attended Wesley College, Melbourne, Australia. *Home:* Maison Salle, Sury-en-Vaux, Cher, France. *Agent:* Rosica Colin, 4 Hereford Sq., London SW7 4TU, England.

CAREER: Affiliated with Australian Broadcasting Commission, Melbourne, 1941-47; private secretary to author Richard Aldington in the south of France, 1947-51; U.S. Information Service, Paris, France, head of western press analysis, 1951-53; Australian Broadcasting Commission, currently Paris correspondent.

WRITINGS: The Lonely Verge, Warlock Press, 1943; *Excellent Stranger,* Reed & Harris, 1944; *Bibliography of the Works of Richard Aldington,* Quadrant Press, 1950; *Accent and Hazard,* Stramur Presse, 1951; *Murder in France,* Constable, 1955; *A History of the Guillotine,* J. Calder, 1958; (editor with Jacques Temple) *Richard Aldington: An Intimate Portrait,* Southern Illinois University Press, 1965; *No-Man's-Land,* La Murene, 1969; (editor) *Critical Writings of Richard Aldington,* Southern Illinois University Press, 1970; *Opera Comique,* La Murene, 1979. Also author of a biography of Leon Daudet.

AVOCATIONAL INTERESTS: Wine, French politics.

*   *   *

KEYES, Ralph 1945-

PERSONAL: Surname rhymes with "eyes"; born January 12, 1945, in Cincinnati, Ohio; son of Scott (a regional planner) and Charlotte (a writer; maiden name, Shachmann) Keyes; married Muriel Gordon (a health counselor), February 13, 1965; children: one son. *Education:* Antioch College, B.A., 1967; London School of Economics and Political Science, graduate study, 1967-68. *Home:* 537 Westdale Ave., Swarthmore, Pa. 19081. *Agent:* Donald Cutler, Sterling Lord Agency, Inc., 660 Madison Ave., New York, N.Y. 10021.

CAREER: Newsday, Long Island, N.Y., assistant to publisher and staff writer, 1968-70; free-lance writer, 1970—. Visiting assistant professor, Prescott College, 1971 and 1974; lecturer, Temple University, 1979—. Fellow, Center for Studies of the Person, La Jolla, Calif., 1970-79.

WRITINGS: We, the Lonely People: Searching for Community, Harper, 1973; *Is There Life after High School?,* Little, Brown, 1976; *The Height of Your Life,* Little, Brown, 1980. Contributor to *Newsweek, Nation, Playboy, Mademoiselle, Human Behavior, Popular Psychology, Car and Driver, Change, West, Parade, Esquire, New York, Reader's Digest, Publishers Weekly,* and *Cosmopolitan.*

WORK IN PROGRESS: Compiling writing by sons about fathers and a collection of contemporary quotes; a book about risk-taking.

SIDELIGHTS: "My attitude is to want to confront directly anything I think might stand in my way in life," Ralph Keyes once told a *Los Angeles Times* interviewer. For Keyes, these obstacles have ranged from learning how to deal with loneliness in an increasingly dehumanized and mobile society to the obvious (and not so obvious) difficulties associated with being unusually tall or short. Relying on statistical information, results from questionnaires, and comments obtained during personal interviews, the author blends a touch of humor (and occasional sadness) with his factual findings to come up with highly readable and entertaining "studies" of various inadequacies and neuroses which plague not only him, but countless other American adults as well. But why, he is often asked, does he choose to dwell almost exclusively on the negative aspects of human existence? The answer, notes Keyes, is simple: "Failure is more interesting than Bruce Jenner. Failure is much more universal than success and I'm looking for universal subjects. I'm much more interested in exploring areas where I feel room for growth."

One of Keye's most popular endeavors in this field focuses on what he believes to be the ultimate American experience—high school. Although his *Is There Life after High School?* covers some fairly familiar territory, most readers, once they have gotten over the pain of recalling those traumatic years, have found the book a delight. With his customary blend of facts and humor, and a certain nostalgia as well, Keyes recounts the trials and tribulations of adolescence as seen through the eyes of various celebrities and non-celebrities. According to some reviewers, this method is especially appealing when dealing with a subject such as high school, for it always comes as a relief to know that Henry Kissinger was the fat kid nobody would eat lunch with and that the bully who used to push Mike Nichols's head underwater and stand on it is now a used-car salesman.

Taking into account these stories and other types of information, Keyes concludes that the most significant factor in determining the future course of a person's life is whether the person was an "innie" or an "outie" in high school, with the "in" group consisting of male jocks and their female equivalents—cheerleaders—and the "out" group consisting of everyone who is *not* a jock or a cheerleader. In short, he offers some comfort to the "outies" of the world; he claims that they are better off in the long run, for the "innies" almost always, in the words of the *Washington Post Book World's* L. J. Davis, "suffer from an encore problem when it comes to facing the great world. . . . [They] tend to wonder why the cheering stopped." "Outies," on the other hand, never forget what it means to fail and usually end up getting a second chance to succeed later in life.

Lois Gould, commenting in the *New York Times Book Review,* calls Keyes's book a "painstaking—and pain-inducing—autopsy on high school." She continues: "High school, like youth itself, is best appreciated from a safe distance—say, 20 years. Even then, it hurts when you laugh. And if you stop laughing, it hurts worse. Ralph Keyes knows all this only too well. He is, like most of us, a lifelong sufferer from high school dis-ease. . . . Painful as it is to revive these horrors by publishing them, it is, for some, the only thing that helps. . . . Keyes is fond of quoting rock star Frank Zappa, to the effect that 'high school isn't a time or place; it's a state of mind.' And in Keyes's mind, the state remains peopled by raunchy Doby Gillises, Archies and Jugheads, all wearing letter sweaters, and by Gidgets doing maddeningly sexy cartwheels knowing full well their underpants are showing."

For Francis H. Curtis of *Best Sellers,* the book falls somewhat short of expectations, for "while [it] does make a valid point or two, Keyes has tried to capitalize on research to give it authenticity and on sex and foul language to make it a seller. This turns an interesting topic and a valuable contribution to the literature on adolescence into a treatise that fails to be much of either."

The *Christian Science Monitor's* R. J. Cattani, however, disagrees with Curtis, perhaps choosing not to take the author's "study" quite so seriously. Admitting that Keyes is "a high school fan, a reunion buff" who "writes more with nostalgia than irony," the reviewer nevertheless concludes that *Is There Life after High School?* "roars with adolescent enthusiasm and apprehension. . . . [The author] should find many readers among those who now and then take out their senior yearbooks."

Finally, the *Washington Post Book World's* Davis observes: "Reading this thoroughly engaging little study is like finding your adoption papers; we always knew it was true. High school in America is a universal but singularly worthless social experience that spectacularly rewards the meaningless skills of a few, traumatizes the majority, and marks us for life. . . . Keyes doesn't tell us what to do about it, but it is nice to know that we aren't alone."

BIOGRAPHICAL/CRITICAL SOURCES: Library Journal, May 15, 1976; *Washington Post Book World,* May 30, 1976; *New York Times Book Review,* June 13, 1976; *Christian Science Monitor,* July 21, 1976; *Best Sellers,* September, 1976; *New York Times,* April 14, 1980; *Los Angeles Times,* May 8, 1980; *Newsweek,* May 19, 1980.

—*Sketch by Deborah A. Straub*

*   *   *

KIDD, J(ames) R(obbins) 1915-
(J. Roby Kidd)

PERSONAL: Born May 4, 1915, in Wapella, Saskatchewan, Canada; son of John (an automobile dealer) and Muriel (Robbins) Kidd; married Margaret Easto, August 24, 1943; children: Bruce, Ross, Alice, David, Dorothy. *Education:* Sir George Williams University, B.A., 1938; McGill University, M.A., 1943; Columbia University, Ed.D., 1947. *Home address:* R.R. 1, Kendall, Ontario, Canada. *Office:* Ontario Institute for Studies in Education, 252 Bloor St. West, Toronto, Ontario, Canada M5S 1V6.

CAREER: Young Men's Christian Association, secretary for adult program or boys' work program in Montreal, Quebec, Ottawa, Ontario, and New York, N.Y., 1935-47; Canadian Association for Adult Education, Toronto, Ontario, direc-

tor, 1947-61; Social Science Research Council and Humanities Research Council, Ottawa, secretary-treasurer, 1961-65; Overseas Institute of Canada, Ottawa, director of Canada-India Colombo Plan (adult education project) at University of Rajasthan, Jaipur, India, 1965-66; Ontario Institute for tudies in Education, Toronto, chairman of department of adult education, 1966-72, professor, 1972—. International Council for Adult Education, secretary general, 1973-79, treasurer, 1979—. Instructor in adult education at Ontario College of Education, University of British Columbia, and Columbia University; consultant to University College of the West Indies, 1954, 1957-58, and University of Alaska, 1961-62. Chairman of adult education committee, World Confederation of the Organizations of the Teaching Profession, 1959-61; president, World Conference on Adult Education, 1960; chairman, UNESCO International Committee for the Advancement of Adult Education; executive secretary, Overseas Institute of Canada; treasurer, Canada Foundation; member of national board, Canadian Centenary Council. *Member:* Arts and Letters Club (Toronto), Cercle Universitaire (Ottawa). *Awards, honors:* L.L.D., University of British Columbia, 1961, Concordia University, 1968, Trent University, 1972, McGill University, 1979, and Laurentian University, 1980; member, Order of Canada, 1975; William Pearson Tully Medal, Syracuse University, 1976.

WRITINGS: (With L. H. Strauss) *Look, Listen and Learn,* Association Press, 1947; (editor) *Adult Education in Canada,* Canadian Association for Adult Education, 1950; *Adult Education in the Canadian University,* Canadian Association for Adult Education, 1956; *How Adults Learn,* Association Press, 1958; *Adult Education in the Caribbean,* Canadian Association for Adult Education, 1958; (editor under name J. Roby Kidd) *Adult Education in a Free Society,* Guardian Bird Publications, 1958; *Continuing Education,* Canadian Conference on Education, 1961; *Eighteen to Eighty,* Toronto Board of Education, 1961; *Continuing Education in Alaska,* University of Alaska, 1962; *Financing Continuing Education,* Scarecrow, 1962; (editor) *Learning and Society,* Canadian Association for Adult Education, 1963; *The Implications of Continuous Learning,* Gage, 1966; *Education for Perspective,* Indian Adult Education Association, 1969; (editor with Robert M. Smith and George F. Aker) *Handbook of Adult Education,* Macmillan, 1970; (editor with Anil Bordia and J. A. Draper) *Adult Education in India: A Book of Readings,* Nachiketa Publications, 1973; *Whilst Time Is Burning,* I.R.D.C., 1973; (editor under name J. Roby Kidd, with Clif Bennett and Jindra Kulich) *Comparative Studies in Adult Education,* Syracuse University Publications in Continuing Education, 1975; (editor under name J. Roby Kidd with George R. Selman) *Coming of Age: Canadian Adult Education in the 1960's,* Canadian Association for Adult Education, 1978; (editor with Budd L. Hall) *Adult Education: A Design for Development,* Pergamon, 1978; *The World of Literacy,* I.D.R.C., 1979. Also editor, with Hall, of *Structures of Adult Education,* UNESCO. General editor, "Democratic Way" series and "Community Organization" series, published by Canadian Citizenship Council. Writer of manuals on camping, film utilization, and group discussion, and of pamphlets. Contributor to *Encyclopaedia Canadiana, Encyclopaedia Britannica, Encyclopedia Americana.* Editor, *Convergence,* 1968-74.

*   *   *

KIDNEY, Dorothy Boone 1919-

PERSONAL: Born February 4, 1919, in Presque Isle, Me.; daughter of Frank R. (a blacksmith) and Bertha (Libby)

Boone; married Milford L. Kidney (a calculating machine salesman). *Education:* Gorham State Teachers College (now University of Maine at Gorham), B.S., 1960. *Religion:* Church of the Nazarene. *Home address:* Box 394, Washburn, Me. 04786.

CAREER: Teacher of English in Maine schools, 1960-75.

WRITINGS: Come and See, Moody, 1963; *Lively Youth Meetings,* Moody, 1964; *Away from It All,* A. S. Barnes, 1969; *I Like,* Moody, 1971; *That Upside Down Feeling,* Moody, 1971; *Portrait of Debec,* Moody, 1972; *Speaking of Miracles,* Beacon Hill, 1974; *A Home in the Wilderness,* A. S. Barnes, 1976; *No Secrets,* Beacon Hill, 1978; *A Time to Live,* Logos International, 1980; *Wilderness Journal,* Gannett Publishing, 1980; *Mystery of the Old Clock Shop,* Beacon Hill, 1981. Contributor of short stories, articles, and poems to newspapers and magazines, including *Down East, Seventeen, Charm,* and religious periodicals (almost exclusively since 1947). Former columnist, "Glimpses of the Allagash," in *Moosehead Gazette.*

* * *

KIEV, Ari 1933-

PERSONAL: Born December 30, 1933, in New York, N.Y.; son of I. Edward (a librarian) and Mary (a librarian; maiden name, Nover) Kiev; married Phylliseve Kovens (a concert pianist), March 27, 1960; children: Jonathan, Marshall. *Education:* Harvard University, A.B., 1954; Cornell University, M.D., 1958; University of London, postdoctoral study at Institute of Psychiatry, 1961-62. *Office:* 150 East 69th St., New York, N.Y. 10021.

CAREER: Diplomate, American Board of Psychiatry; Kings County Hospital Center, Kings County, N.Y., intern, 1958-59; Johns Hopkins Hospital, Baltimore, Md., resident, 1959-61; Columbia University, New York City, College of Physicians and Surgeons, research associate in psychiatry, 1964-67; field station director, Psychiatric Epidemiology Research Unit, 1966-67; New York State Psychiatric Institute, New York City, assistant attending psychiatrist, 1964-67; Cornell University Medical College, New York City, clinical associate professor of psychiatry and head of program in social psychiatry, 1967—; New York Hospital, New York City, associate attending psychiatrist, 1967—. Visiting professor of anthropology, Brandeis University, 1967-68. Director of Social Psychiatry Research Institute and of Life Strategy Workshops. Member of U.S. Olympic Council on Sports Medicine, 1978. *Member:* International Committee Against Mental Illness (medical director), American Psychiatric Association, American Medical Association, Society for Applied Anthropology, Royal Medico-Psychological Association.

WRITINGS: (Editor) *Magic, Faith and Healing: Studies in Primitive Psychiatry Today,* Free Press, 1964; (contributor) Joseph Zubin, editor, *Comprehensive Psychopathology: Animal and Human,* Grune, 1967; (contributor) Joseph Zubin and George A. Jervis, editors, *Psychopathology of Mental Development,* Grune, 1967; (author of introduction) L. M. Epstein, *Sex Laws and Customs in Judaism,* Ktav, 1967; *Curanderismo: Mexican-American Folk Psychiatry,* Free Press, 1968; (editor) *Psychiatry in the Communist World,* Science House, 1968; (editor) *Social Psychiatry,* Volume I, Science House, 1969; (contributor) E. Mansell Pattison, editor, *Clinical Psychiatry,* Volume V, Little, Brown, 1969; (contributor) Jules H. Masserman, editor, *Transcultural Psychiatric Approach,* Grune, 1969; (contributor) Stanley C. Plog and Robert B. Edgerton, editors,

Changing Perspectives in Mental Illness, Holt, 1969; (contributor) Raymond Prince, editor, *Trance and Possession States,* 1969; (contributor) *Multidisciplinary Conference on Identifying Suicide Potential,* Columbia University Press, 1970; *Transcultural Psychiatry,* Free Press, 1972; (with Mario Argandona) *Mental Health in a Developing World: A Case Study in Latin America,* Free Press, 1972; *A Strategy for Daily Living,* Free Press, 1973; *Handling Executive Stress,* Nelson-Hall, 1973; *The Drug Epidemic,* Free Press, 1973; *A Strategy for Success,* Macmillan, 1977; *The Suicidal Patient,* Nelson-Hall, 1977; *The Courage to Live,* Crowell, 1979; *Active Loving,* Crowell, 1979; (with Vera Kohn) *Executive Stress: An A.M.A. Survey Report,* A.M.A. Publishers, 1979; *Conference on the Future of Mental Health Services in Kenya,* Excerpta Medica, 1980; *Riding through the Downers, Hassles, Snags and Funks,* Dutton, 1980.

Contributor of articles to neurology, psychiatry, and anthropology journals. Member of editorial board, *Transcultural Psychiatric Research Review and Newsletter* and *Journal of Pastoral Counselling;* member of editorial advisory board, *International Journal of Social Psychiatry;* associate editor, *International Journal of Psychiatry,* 1965—; editor, *Attitude.*

* * *

KILLAM, (Gordon) Douglas 1930-

PERSONAL: Born August 26, 1930, in New Westminster, British Columbia, Canada; son of Harry (a clerk) and Margaret (Currie) Killam; married Helen Shelagh Ann Anderson, August 20, 1959; children: Christopher, Sarah. *Education:* University of British Columbia, B.A. (honors), 1955; University of London, Ph.D., 1964. *Politics:* None. *Religion:* Protestant. *Home:* 108 Glasgow St. N., Guelph, Ontario, Canada. *Office:* Department of English, University of Guelph, Guelph, Ontario, Canada N1G 2W1.

CAREER: Canadian Broadcasting Corp. (CBC), Vancouver, British Columbia, television producer, 1956-60; Fourah Bay College, Freetown, Sierra Leone, lecturer in English literature, 1963-65; University of Alberta, Edmonton, assistant professor of English, 1965-66; University of Ibadan, Ibadan, Nigeria, lecturer in English, 1966-67; University of Lagos, Yaba Lagos, Nigeria, senior lecturer in English, 1967-68; York University, Downsview, Ontario, assistant professor, 1968-69, associate professor of English, 1969-73, master of Bethune College, 1971-73; Acadia University, Wolfville, Nova Scotia, professor of English and head of department, 1973-76, dean of arts; University of Guelph, Guelph, Ontario, head of department of English, 1977—. Visiting lecturer, University of British Columbia, summer, 1965; professor and chairman of department of literature, University of Dar Es Salaam (Tanzania), 1970-71; external examiner, University of Nairobi, 1971-72, University of Alberta, 1974, and University of Ottawa, 1977.

MEMBER: Association of Commonwealth Literature and Language Studies (chairman, 1980-83), Canadian Association of African Studies (vice-president, 1973-74; president, 1974-75), Association of Canadian University Teachers of English, American Sociological Association, Modern Language Association of America. *Awards, honors:* Canada Council research grants, 1967, for study of J. M. Stuart-Young, and 1971, for compiling bibliography of English fiction presenting Africa; Rockefeller Foundation research and teaching fellowship, 1970-71.

WRITINGS: Africa in English Fiction: 1874-1939, Ibadan University Press, 1967; *The Novels of Chinua Achebe,*

Heinemann, 1969, revised edition published as *The Writings of Chinua Achebe*, 1977; (contributor) B. A. King, editor, *Introductions to Nigerian Literature*, Evans Brothers, 1971; (contributor) E. D. Jones, editor, *African Literature*, Volume V, Heinemann, 1971; (editor) *African Writers on African Writing*, Heinemann, 1973; (author of introduction) Margaret Laurence, *A Jest of God*, McLelland & Stewart, 1974; (contributor) King, editor, *Ten English Literatures*, Routledge & Kegan Paul, 1977; *The Writing of Ngugi Wa Thiongo*, Heinemann, 1980; (editor) *Critical Perspectives on Ngugi Wa Thiongo*, Heinemann, 1980.

Contributor of about twenty articles and reviews to academic journals, including *Black Academy Review, Sewanee Review, Twentieth Century Literature, Black Orpheus, Insight,* and *Journal of the Historical Society of Nigeria*. Guest editor, *Journal of the Canadian Association of African Studies*, 1975; editor, *World Literature Written in English*; co-editor, *Canadian Journal of African Studies*.

WORK IN PROGRESS: The Writing of Margaret Laurence: The Iniquitous Coaster; a biography of John Moray Stuart-Young; *A Bibliography of English Fiction Presenting Africa: 1865-1980;* research on the theme of imperialism in nineteenth-century writing, based on *The Imperial Idea and Its Enemies,* by A. P. Thornton; editing *East African Literatures Written in English,* for Heinemann, and a second volume of *African Writers on African Writing*.

*   *   *

KIMMEL, Eric A.   1946-

PERSONAL: Born October 30, 1946, in Brooklyn, N.Y.; son of Morris N. (a certified public accountant) and Anne (an elementary school teacher; maiden name, Kerker) Kimmel; married Elizabeth Marcia Sheridan (a professor of education), April 7, 1968 (divorced, 1975); married Doris Ann Blake, June 16, 1978; children: Bridgett (stepdaughter). *Education:* Lafayette College, A.B., 1967; New York University, M.A., 1969; University of Illinois, Ph.D., 1973. *Politics:* Democrat. *Religion:* Jewish. *Home:* 2525 Northeast 35th Ave., Portland, Ore. 97212. *Office:* Department of Education, Portland State University, P.O. Box 751, Portland, Ore. 97207.

CAREER: Indiana University at South Bend, assistant professor of education, 1973-78; Portland State University, Portland, Ore., associate professor of education, 1978—. *Member:* National Council of Teachers of English, American Association of University Professors, Phi Beta Kappa, Phi Delta Kappa, Kappa Delta Pi.

WRITINGS: The Tartar's Sword, Coward, 1974; *Mishka, Pishka and Fishka and Other Galician Tales,* Coward, 1976; *Why Worry?,* Pantheon, 1979; *Nicanor's Gate,* Jewish Publication Society, 1980; *Hershel of Ostropol,* Jewish Publication Society, 1981. Also author of quarterly column reviewing children's books in *Interchange*. Contributor to *Horn Book, Elementary English, Response, Ripples, Highlights for Children, Cricket,* and other periodicals.

WORK IN PROGRESS: The Jungle Adventure; Rose's Story.

SIDELIGHTS: Eric A. Kimmel wrote *CA:* "Two years ago I fulfilled a lifelong dream and moved to the West Coast. Oregon is an inspiring place to live and work. Mountains, oceans and deserts are never more than a few hours drive away. I love horses and would happily abandon the driver's seat for a saddle anytime. With such temptations it often requires a great deal of willpower to sit and write, but fortunately the Oregon rain that falls incessantly from September to March keeps me indoors and busy.

"At this point my writing appears to be spreading into new dimensions. I enjoy writing for children. However many of my best stories have been turned down as too 'adult,' though the children I have read them to enjoy them. I often wonder how much real contact editors have with children and why certain books are published as 'juveniles' that no child will ever read. If all my wishes come true, I will be able to live on my writing and retire to a ranch where I can spend days on horseback. Who knows? It may happen yet."

*   *   *

KIRZNER, Israel M(ayer)   1930-

PERSONAL: Born February 13, 1930, in London, England; naturalized U.S. citizen; son of E. Wulf and Annie (Bloch) Kirzner; married Charlotte Nussbaum, 1957; children: Pinchas E., Sarah R., Isaac E. *Education:* Brooklyn College (now Brooklyn College of the City University of New York), B.A., 1954; New York University, M.B.A., 1955, Ph.D., 1957. *Office:* Department of Economics, New York University, New York, N.Y. 10003.

CAREER: New York University, New York, N.Y., assistant professor 1957-61, associate professor, 1961-68, professor of economics, 1968—. *Member:* American Economic Association, Royal Economic Society, Econometric Society, American Statistical Association, Phi Beta Kappa. *Awards, honors:* Volker Fund fellow, 1956-57; Earhart Foundation fellow, 1957.

WRITINGS: The Economic Point of View: An Essay in the History of Economic Thought, Van Nostrand, 1960, 2nd edition, Cato Institute, 1976; *Market Theory and the Price System,* Van Nostrand, 1963; *An Essay on Capital,* Augustus M. Kelley, 1966; *Competition and Entrepreneurship,* University of Chicago Press, 1978; *Perception, Opportunity and Profit: Studies in the Theory of Entrepreneurship,* University of Chicago Press, 1979; *Perils of Regulation: A Market Process Approach,* University of Miami, 1979.†

*   *   *

KLINEFELTER, Walter   1899-

PERSONAL: Born November 3, 1899, near Glen Rock, Pa.; son of Edwin F. (a farmer) and Sophia (Bricker) Klinefelter; married Mildred Rosenkrans, 1926 (deceased); married Edna McCollough, 1939; children: Mildred Klinefelter Druck, Nancy. *Education:* Gettysburg College, A.B., 1920. *Home address:* R.D. 1, Dallastown, Pa. 17313.

CAREER: For thirty years, worked in a variety of positions, including teacher and store manager, in the Commonwealth of Pennsylvania. *Member:* Arthur Machen Society, Baker Street Irregulars, Cartophilatelists.

WRITINGS: Maps in Miniature: Notes Critical and Historical on Their Use on Postage Stamps, Hawthorn, 1936; *Christmas Books* (essay), Southworth-Anthoesen Press, 1936; (editor and author of introduction) *A Bibliographical Checklist of Christmas Books,* Southworth-Anthoesen Press, 1937; *Books about Poictesme: An Essay in Imaginative Bibliography,* Black Cat Press, 1937; (editor) *More Christmas Books,* Southworth-Anthoesen Press, 1938; *Ex Libris A. Conan Doyle: Sherlock Holmes,* Black Cat Press, 1938; *Illustrations in Miniature: Postal Designs from Books and Manuscripts,* Black Cat Press, 1939; *The Fortsas Bibliohoax,* Carteret Book Club, 1941.

(Translator and author of commentary) Rabelais, *Catalogue*

of the Choice Books Found by Pantagruel in the Abbey of Saint Victor, William P. Wreden, 1952; *The World Minutely Mapped*, privately printed, 1953; *A Small Display of Old Maps and Plans*, Prairie Press, 1962; *Sherlock Holmes in Portrait and Profile*, Syracuse University Press, 1963; *A Packet of Sherlockian Bookplates*, privately printed, 1964; *Twenty-five Years of Service*, York Junior College, 1968; *The Case of the Conan Doyle Crime Library*, Sumac Press, 1968; *A Further Display of Old Maps and Plans*, Sumac Press, 1969; (contributor) Richard K. Doud, editor, *Portfolio 6*, Winterthur Museum, 1970; *Lewis Evans and His Maps*, American Philosophical Society, 1971; *A Third Display of Old Maps and Plans*, Sumac Press, 1973; *York's Liberty Bell*, Sumac Press, 1975; *John Klinefelter, Colonial Settler*, privately printed, 1977; *A Fourth Display of Old Maps and Plans*, Sumac Press, 1978. Contributor to publications of the Pennsylvania German Society.

WORK IN PROGRESS: A Catalog of Catalogs, a translation, with commentary, of Johan Fischart's *Catalogus Catalogorum*.

*   *   *

KNIGHT, Damon (Francis) 1922-
(Donald Laverty, a joint pseudonym)

PERSONAL: Born September 19, 1922, in Baker, Ore.; son of Frederick Stuart and Leola (Damon) Knight; married Gertrud Werndl; married Helen Schlaz; married Kate Wilhelm (a writer), February 23, 1963; children: Valerie, Christopher, Leslie, Jonathan. *Education:* Attended high school in Hood River, Ore. *Home:* 1645 Horn Lane, Eugene, Ore. 97404.

CAREER: Science fiction writer and editor. Milford Science Fiction Writers' Conference, co-founder, 1956, director, 1956-76; visiting lecturer, Clarion Workshop, 1968—; adjunct professor, Michigan State University, 1979. *Member:* Science Fiction Writers of America (founding president, 1965-67). *Awards, honors:* Hugo Award from World Science Fiction Convention, 1956, for best science fiction criticism; Pilgrim Award, 1975, for contributions to science fiction; Jupiter Award, 1976, for short story "I See You."

WRITINGS—Novels: Hell's Pavement, Lion Press, 1955, published as *Analogue Men*, Berkley Publishing, 1962; *Masters of Evolution*, Ace Books, 1959; *The People Maker*, Zenith Books, 1959, published as *A for Anything*, Berkley Publishing, 1965; *The Sun Saboteurs* (bound with *The Light of Lilith* by Wallis G. McDonald), Ace Books, 1961; *Beyond the Barrier*, Doubleday, 1964; *Mind Switch*, Berkley Publishing, 1965, published as *The Other Foot*, Whiting & Wheaton, 1965, M-B Publishing, 1971; *The Rithian Terror*, Ace Books, 1965; *Three Novels: Rule Golden, Natural State*, [and] *The Dying Man*, Doubleday, 1967.

Short story collections, except as indicated: *In Search of Wonder: Essays on Modern Science Fiction*, Advent, 1956, 2nd edition, 1967; *Far Out: 13 Science Fiction Stories*, Simon & Schuster, 1961; *In Deep*, Berkley Publishing, 1963; *Off Center: A Scintillating Science Fiction Collection*, Ace Books, 1965; *Turning On: Thirteen Stories*, Doubleday, 1966 (published in England as *Turning On: Fourteen Stories*, Gollancz, 1967); *World without Children* [and] *The Earth Quarter*, Lancer Books, 1970; *The Best of Damon Knight*, Pocket Books, 1974; *Rule Golden and Other Stories*, Avon, 1979.

Editor of anthologies: *A Century of Science Fiction*, Simon & Schuster, 1962; *First Flight*, Lancer Books, 1963, published as *Now Begins Tomorrow*, 1969; *A Century of Great Short Science Fiction Novels*, Dial, 1964; *Tomorrow x 4*, Fawcett, 1964; *The Shape of Things*, Popular Library, 1965;

(and translator) *Thirteen French Science-Fiction Stories*, Bantam, 1965; *The Dark Side*, Doubleday, 1965; *Beyond Tomorrow: Ten Science Fiction Adventures*, Harper, 1965; *Cities of Wonder*, Doubleday, 1966; *Nebula Award Stories 1965*, Doubleday, 1966; *Worlds to Come: Nine Science Fiction Adventures*, Harper, 1967; *Science Fiction Inventions*, Lancer Books, 1967; *Toward Infinity: Nine Science Fiction Tales*, Simon & Schuster, 1968 (published in England as *Towards Infinity: Nine Science Fiction Adventures*, Gollancz, 1970); *One Hundred Years of Science Fiction*, Simon & Schuster, 1968; *The Metal Smile*, Belmont Books, 1968.

Dimension X: Five Science Fiction Novellas, Simon & Schuster, 1970 (published in England as *Elsewhere x 3*, Coronet, 1974); *First Contact*, Pinnacle Books, 1971; (and contributor) *A Pocketful of Stars*, Doubleday, 1971; *Perchance to Dream*, Doubleday, 1972; *A Science Fiction Argosy*, Simon & Schuster, 1972; *Tomorrow and Tomorrow: Ten Tales of the Future*, Simon & Schuster, 1973; *A Shocking Thing*, Pocket Books, 1974; *The Golden Road*, Simon & Schuster, 1974; *Happy Endings: 15 Stories by the Masters of the Macabre*, Bobbs-Merrill, 1974; *Best Stories from Orbit, Volumes 1-10*, Putnam, 1975; *Science Fiction of the Thirties*, Bobbs-Merrill, 1975; *Westerns of the Forties*, Bobbs-Merrill, 1977; (and contributor) *Turning Point* (essays), Harper, 1977; *Western Classics from the Great Pulps*, Barnes & Noble, 1978. Also editor of "Orbit" series, Volumes 1-13, Putnam, 1966-73, Volumes 14-21, Harper, 1974-80.

Other: (Translator) Rene Barjavel, *Ashes, Ashes*, Doubleday, 1967; *Charles Fort: Prophet of the Unexplained* (biography), Doubleday, 1970; *The Futurians* (biography), John Day, 1977. Editor, *Worlds Beyond*, 1950-51, and *If*, 1958-59; book editor, *Science Fiction Adventures*, 1953-54, and *Magazine of Fantasy and Science Fiction*, 1959-60; founding editor, *Science Fiction Writers of America Bulletin*, 1965-67.

SIDELIGHTS: Damon Knight's science fiction criticism has received high praise from writers in the field. Spider Robinson writes in *Analog* that *In Search of Wonder*, a collection of Knight's criticism, "is generally considered a classic. . . . I enjoyed the book immensely with two reservations. First, I disagreed with Knight about 50 percent of the time. . . . Second, I was made distinctly uneasy by the ferocity (and *constancy*) with which Knight went for the jugular. [Nonetheless, it is] one of the most stimulating and provocative books about SF I've ever read." James Blish, writing in *More Issues at Hand* under the pseudonym William Atheling, Jr., remembers when Knight first began "to publish a series of reviews of science fiction books so uncompromising in tone, and so well grounded in literary experience and taste, as to raise howls of scrub-brushing among the unwashed. . . . Historically, Knight's criticisms promptly made the mutual-admiration-society or notice-of-availability kind of review look fatuous, and encouraged several other practitioners toward greater severity."

BIOGRAPHICAL/CRITICAL SOURCES: Galaxy, September, 1955; Basil Davenport, editor, *The Science Fiction Novel: Imagination and Social Criticism*, Advent, 1959; Kingsley Amis, *New Maps of Hell: A Survey of Science Fiction*, Harcourt, 1960; *Amazing Stories*, August, 1961; William Atheling, Jr., *The Issue at Hand*, Advent, 1964; *Analog*, June, 1964, November, 1979; *Magazine of Fantasy and Science Fiction*, November, 1964, December, 1967; *New Worlds*, January, 1965; *New York Times Book Review*, November 14, 1965, April 24, 1977; Atheling, *More Issues at Hand*, Advent, 1970; *National Review*, March 10, 1970, January 19, 1973; *Science Fiction Review*, October, 1970, November/December, 1978; *Times Literary Supplement*,

June 11, 1971, October 13, 1972, March 7, 1975; *Luna Monthly,* April/May, 1972; *Books and Bookmen,* June, 1972, September, 1973; Brian W. Aldiss and Harry Harrison, editors, *Hell's Cartographers: Some Personal Histories of Science Fiction Writers,* Harper, 1976; *America,* April 23, 1977; *Psychology Today,* June, 1977.

*   *   *

KNIGHTS, L(ionel) C(harles) 1906-

PERSONAL: Born May 15, 1906, in Grantham, Lincolnshire, England; son of C. E. and Lois M. (Kenney) Knights; married Elizabeth Mary Barnes, October 31, 1936; children: Charles Benjamin, Christine Frances. *Education:* Cambridge University, B.A., 1928, M.A., 1931, Ph.D., 1936. *Office:* 57 Jesus Lane, Cambridge CB5 8BS, England.

CAREER: University of Manchester, Manchester, England, 1933-47, began as temporary assistant lecturer in English, became senior lecturer in English; University of Sheffield, Sheffield, England, professor of English literature, 1947-52; University of Bristol, Bristol, England, Winterstoke Professor of English, 1953-64; Cambridge University, Cambridge, England, King Edward VII Professor of English Literature, 1965-73, professor emeritus, 1973—. Visiting Andrew Mellon Professor of English, University of Pittsburgh, 1961-62; Beckman Visiting Professor, University of California, Berkeley, 1970; lecturer for British Council in Germany, Austria, and India. *Awards, honors:* Doct. de l'univ., University of Bordeaux, 1964; honorary doctorates from University of York, 1969, University of Manchester, 1974, University of Sheffield, 1978, and University of Warwich, 1979; honorary fellow, Selwyn College, Cambridge University, 1974.

WRITINGS: How Many Children Had Lady Macbeth, Minority Press, 1933, reprinted, Haskell House, 1973; *Drama and Society in the Age of Jonson,* Chatto & Windus, 1937, Norton, 1968; *Explorations: Essays in Criticism,* Chatto & Windus, 1946, reprinted, New York University Press, 1964; *Shakespeare's Politics* (annual Shakespeare lecture), British Academy, 1957; *Some Shakespearean Themes,* Chatto & Windus, 1959; *An Approach to Hamlet,* Chatto & Windus, 1960 (preceding two books published in one volume, Stanford University Press, 1966); (editor with Basil Cottle) *Metaphor and Symbol,* Butterworth & Co., 1960; *Further Explorations,* Stanford University Press, 1965; *Public Voices: Literature and Politics,* Chatto & Windus, 1971, Rowman & Littlefield, 1972; *Explorations III,* University of Pittsburgh Press, 1976. Member of editorial board, *Scrutiny,* 1932-53.

*   *   *

KOHOUT, Pavel 1928-

PERSONAL: Born July 20, 1928, in Prague, Czechoslovakia; son of Otomar and Ludvika (Talska) Kohout; married second wife, Jelena Masinova (a student), January 31, 1971; children: (first marriage) Ondrej, Katherina, Thereza. *Education:* Attended University of Prague, four years. *Residence:* Vienna, Austria. *Address:* c/o Reich Verlag AG, Zinggentorstrasse 4, 6006 Lucerne, Switzerland.

CAREER: Cultural attache in Moscow, U.S.S.R., for government of Czechoslovak Socialist Republic, 1949-50; journalist, radio-reporter, playwright, stage and motion picture producer, and television editor. *Military service:* CSR Army; became captain, demoted to "soldier," 1971. *Awards, honors:* Czokor-Award (Austria), 1971, for literary and dramatic works; Austrian State Award for European Literature, 1978.

WRITINGS: Verse a pisne z let 1945-1952, Mlada fronta, 1952; (with Antonin Pelc) *Antonin Pelc v boji za mir,* Statni nakl., 1954; (with Erich Einhorn and Pravoslav Sovak) *Marianske Lazne,* Krajske nakl., 1960; (with Guenter Grass) *Briefe ueber die Grenze: Versuch eines Ost-West-Dialogs,* C. Wegner, 1968; *Aus dem Tagebuch eines Konterrevolutionaers* (autobiography; translation from the original Czech by Gustav Solar and Felix R. Bosonnet), C. J. Bucher, 1969, translation from the original Czech by George Theimer published as *From the Diary of a Counterrevolutionary,* McGraw-Hill, 1972; *Weissbuch in Sachen Adam Juracek, Professor fuer Leibeserziehung und Zeichnen an der Paedagogischen Lehrenstalt in K., kontra Sir Isaac Newton, Professor fuer Physik an der Universitaet Cambridge . . .* (translation from the original Czech by Alexandra Baumrucker and Gerhard Baumrucker), C. J. Bucher, 1970, translation by Alex Page published as *White Book: Adam Juracek, Professor of Drawing and Physical Education at the Pedagogical Institute in K., vs. Sir Isaac Newton, Professor of Physics at the University of Cambridge . . . ,* Braziller, 1977; (with Jan Neruda) *Geschichten von der Prager Kleinseite,* G. Lentz, 1974; *Die Henkerin* (translation from the original Czech by A. Baumrucker and G. Baumrucker), Reich Verlag, 1978, translation published as *The Hangwoman,* Putnam, 1980; *Jolana und der Zauberer* (children's book; translated from the Czech manuscript "Jolana a kouzelnik" by Jitka Bodlakova), Kinderbuchverlag Reich, 1980. Also author of children's book, *Die Amsel,* translated from the Czech manuscript "Rikali mu frkos," Annette Betz (Munich).

Published plays: "Zarijove Noci" (title means "September Nights"), first produced in Prague, 1955, published as *Zarijove Noci: komedie o sesti obrazech,* Orbis, 1956, new version with F. Daniel and V. Jasny published as *Zarijove Noci: filmovy scenar na motivy divadelni hry Pavla Kohouta,* Nase vojsko, 1957; "Takova laska" (title means "Such a Love"), first produced in Prague at Realisticke divadlo, October 13, 1957, published as *Takova laska: hra v dvoch castiach,* Osveta, 1958, translation from the original Czech by A. Baumrucker and G. Baumrucker published as *So Eine Liebe,* C. J. Bucher, 1969.

"Treti Sestra" (title means "The Third Sister"), first produced in Prague at Realisticke divadlo, 1960, published as *Treti Sestra: nova variace na stare tema, vytesana z domovniho schodu, o dvou dilech,* Orbis, 1961; (adapter) Jules Verne, *Cesta kolem sveta za 80 dni* (title means "Journey around the World in 80 Days"; first produced in Prague at Divadlo S. K. Neumanna, 1961), Orbis, 1962; "Dvanact" (title means "Twelve"), first produced in Prague at DISC, published as *Dvanact: Dvanact obrazu ze zivota dvanacti mladych hercu,* Orbis, 1963; (adapter) Karel Capek, "Valka s Mloky" (title means "Salamander War"), first produced in Prague at Divadlo na Vinohradech, published as *Valka s Mloky: musical-mystery,* Orbis, 1963; (with Jaroslav Hasek) "Josef Svejk," first produced in Prague at Divadlo na Vinohradech, published as *Josef Svejk: aneb, Tak nam zabili Ferdinanda a jine citaty z Osudu dobreho vojaka Svejka,* Orbis, 1964; *August, August, August* (first produced in Prague at Divadlo na Vinohradech, 1967), Dilia, 1967, translation from the original Czech by A. Baumrucker and G. Baumrucker published under same title, C. J. Bucher, 1969.

Krieg im Dritten Stock [and] *Evol: Zwei Einakter* (two one-act plays, translated from the original Czech; "Evol" first produced in Graz at Vereinigte Buehen, 1970; "Krieg im Dritten Stock" first produced in Vienna at Akademietheater, 1971), translation from the original Czech by A. Baumrucker and G. Baumrucker, C. J. Bucher, 1971; *Armer Moerder* (translation from the Czech manuscript "Ubohy vrah", first produced in Duesseldorf at Duesseldorfer Schauspielhaus, 1972), translation from the original Czech by A. Baumrucker and G. Baumrucker, C. J. Bucher, 1972, translation by Herbert Berghof and Laurence Luckinbill published as *Poor Murderer: A Play* (first produced on Broadway at Ethel Barrymore Theater, October 20, 1976), Viking, 1975; *Roulette* (translation from the original Czech first produced in Lucerne at Stadttheater, 1975), translation from the original Czech by A. Baumrucker and G. Baumrucker, Reich Verlag, 1975.

Other plays: "Das gute Leid," 1951; "Zwoelf," 1963; "Pech unterm Dach" (first produced in Ingolstadt, Germany, at Stadttheater, 1974), 1972; "Brand im Souterrain" (first produced in Ingolstadt at Stadttheater, 1974), 1973; "Attest," translation from the original Czech first produced in Vienna at Akademietheater, 1979.

Collections of plays include *Tri hry: Zarijove Noci, Sbohem smutku, Takova laska,* Mlada fronta, 1958, and *So Eine Liebe, Reise um die Erde in 80 Tagen, August, August, August: Drei Theaterstuecke,* C. J. Bucher, 1969. Also author of ten television and motion picture scripts. Work is represented in anthologies. Editor-in-chief, *Dikobraz,* 1950-52.

WORK IN PROGRESS: A novel, tentatively entitled *Reise nirgendwohin* ("Trip to Nowhere"); a play; a continuation of *From the Diary of a Counterrevolutionary.*

SIDELIGHTS: According to *Modern Drama*'s Marketa Goetz Stankiewicz, Pavel Kohout "has evoked more praise and more abuse than any other contemporary Czechoslovak writer." As a result of his support for the 1968 "Spring in Prague" movement and the "Charter 77" human rights petition, Kohout was expelled from the Writers' Union and the Communist Party; he soon came to be regarded as a "nonperson" in Czechoslovakia and was eventually expatriated in late 1979. Though his works are no longer published or produced in his native country, they are increasingly coming to the attention of Western readers and critics.

Known primarily as a playwright, Kohout had been writing for some twenty years before one of his works, "Poor Murderer," appeared in an English-language version. Set in 1905, it tells the story of Anton Ignatyevich Kerzhentsev, an actor who has been playing Hamlet and who, during the course of a performance, imagines he has really murdered the actor playing the part of Polonius because he recently married the girl Kerzhentsev loves. Confined to a mental institution, Kerzhentsev is granted permission to stage an autobiographical play in order to prove he is indeed sane and therefore guilty of a passion-inspired murder. Though it is not an obviously political play, some observers have detected subtle political overtones in the concept of an artist being forcibly confined to an asylum while he struggles to prove that he is not a passionless creature. Thus, in light of the Soviet practice of confining dissidents to mental hospitals, Kerzhentsev can be regarded as a metaphor for the physical restraints placed on human dignity and, of course, on freedom of expression.

Yet the major controversy surrounding "Poor Murderer" (and a number of other Kohout plays as well) does not concern the presence or absence of any political overtones. Due to the fact that a great deal of Kohout's work is derivative in the sense that he relies heavily on borrowing or adapting themes and stylistic devices from other writers and their works, questions often arise as to just how successfully he integrates his material and makes it his own. Kohout himself certainly makes no secret of his preference for working on adaptations rather than on original projects: "I admit, I have more fun with adaptations for the stage than with my own plays. Writing is like a game of solitaire, the author plays against himself. An adaptation, on the other hand, is like a duel. You must force the picture to leave its frame and become alive. You must breathe life even into a collection of newspaper clippings." In short, as Stankiewicz summarizes, "Kohout's attitude [is] that the main task of the playwright-adapter is to add 'a third dimension' to a two-dimensional work of art."

Numerous reviewers cite the unmistakable influence of Pirandello, Peter Weiss's "Marat/Sade," and Tom Stoppard's "Rosencrantz and Guildenstern Are Dead" on Kohout's "Poor Murderer"; the plot itself is based on a short story by Leonid Andreyev. Critics who have nothing but praise for the play believe Kohout has shown a great deal of skill in adapting such diverse material, while those who do not like "Poor Murderer" point out that it is outdated, haphazardly executed, and, above all, lifeless and boring.

John Simon, for example, commenting in the *New Leader,* writes: "Pavel Kohout's 'Poor Murderer' makes me doubly sorry for its author. Bad enough to be physically restrained in Czechoslovakia by refusal of a travel visa; how much worse to be intellectually sequestered from what goes on in the free world, so that you write as if Pirandello, Giraudoux and Anouilh were the reigning dramatists and concoct a pale pastiche of their manner." During the course of his summary of the plot, Simon notes that the audience is "meant to wonder whether [the actor Kerzhentsev] is really mad, or merely, like Hamlet, feigning madness, but—since he is a garrulous, self-important dullard—it is unfortunately rather hard to care. As for the romantic triangle underlying the tale, it is so limply passionless as to make it sublimely unimportant who ends up with whom." Observing that the audience is also meant to wonder about the outcome of the play, the critic concludes that he "wouldn't give a kopek to know [what happens], even if the playwright had deigned to shed some of that ambiguity he wraps himself in."

Others, too, find it difficult to care what happens in "Poor Murderer." Describing it as "an earnest, serious and intellectual play, more mental than theatrical," the *New York Post*'s Martin Gottfried nevertheless declares that Kohout "is so concerned with examining his hero that he seems to have forgotten what he was examining him for." A *Newsweek* reviewer, noting the influence of Pirandello, remarks that "Kohout's juggling of illusion and reality badly lacks the precision of the Italian master's. . . . The result is something that's empty and ponderous at the same time." Harold Clurman of the *Nation* agrees, stating: "It is clear that the author has borrowed the Pirandellian pharmacopoeia of 'Henri IV.' The dose that he has imbibed has acted on him like a cathartic. The result is windy, pretentious and dull. Nothing comes to life."

In contrast to these views, the *New York Times*'s Clive Barnes calls "Poor Murderer" "a strange, dazzling and intellectual play that zigzags across the stage and ricochets across the mind. . . . [Kohout represents] European writing at its best and most imaginative. This present play is a variation upon many themes. . . . Its literary allusions . . . are exquisitely contrived. But what is important about the play—and I recommend the work most strongly—is the manner in which, by using the metaphor of acting as a symbol for madness, it leads the spectator quite hypnotized into the antechambers, rooms and dungeons of madness. . . . To call a play an intellectual exercise can sometimes be merely to damn it with faint huzzahs, but this play is an intellectual exercise well worth taking. . . . This is a Hamlet play worthy of consideration with Tom Stoppard's 'Rosencrantz and Guildenstern Are Dead.'"

Brendan Gill of the *New Yorker* finds "Poor Murderer" to be "highly accessible in its wit, in its unflagging energy, and in its nimble, crisscrossing cat's cradle of a plot, which throws off pleasing little surprises from first line to last. . . . Far from disowning [its] distinguished ancestors, 'Poor Murderer' pays open tribute to them. . . . For the thousandth time and with the usual delight, we observe how the artist, out of a past laboriously mastered, fashions with seeming ease something indisputably new."

Stankiewicz also defends and praises Kohout's decision to draw on the old in order to fashion something new. In comments made before the Broadway production of "Poor Murderer," she states that Kohout's dramatic adaptations of other writers' works "have proved to be among the most highly demanded items of Czechoslovak literary export" even though "his theatre seems to have developed apart from general theatre repertory; in response to the general public's need to be offered topical entertainment, it draws its subject matter from their familiar contemporary scene." As a result, Stankiewicz concludes, "the author's somewhat uneven literary talent may lay itself open to criticism because of its very richness and many-sidedness. But one thing is certain: Kohout uses every aspect of the stage with unfailing intuition and to the delight of any audience. He is, one might say—entirely without irony—truly a playwright of the people. For the world outside watching the ups and downs of the rich theatre life of this small country, Pavel Kohout emerges as an outstanding, colourful sample of Czechoslovakia's dramatic culture and as a barometer of Czechoslovak theatre."

Soon after "Poor Murder"'s run on Broadway, Kohout's first novel (the first major work to deal with the Soviet invasion of Czechoslovakia), *White Book,* finally appeared in an English translation. An absurdist, thinly-veiled critique of Soviet oppression, *White Book* tells the story of Adam Juracek, a professor who, through sheer willpower, defies Newton's law of gravity and begins walking on ceilings. Naturally, his accomplishment creates a panic in the government, which concludes that "the breaking of such a well-known law was liable to shake confidence in laws generally." A national emergency is declared and Juracek is imprisoned, tried, and sent to a mental institution for treatment. While doctors there fail to identify the source of his power, they do manage to brainwash him into a state of total apathy. Years later, when a general amnesty is granted to all prisoners, Juracek is allowed to re-enter society, remembering only his identification number and unable to participate in one of the day's most common pastimes—defying gravity by walking on ceilings.

Many reviewers have hailed *White Book* as brilliant satire; the *New York Times Book Review*'s David Binder, for example, calls it an "ingenious tale" by an author who is both "comic and profoundly earnest, as perhaps only the Czechs can be. . . . [*White Book* is the product] of a most original mind." Peter Z. Schubert of *World Literature Today* believes that it "can be read as a profound work dense with allusions or as a humorous fiction. In either case the book is well worth reading." *Saturday Review*'s Peter Gardner agrees, stating that *White Book* is "a major literary comment on the present Czech government in particular and on socialist irrationalism in general, too dense with allusions and ironies for easy reading, but richly worthwhile."

Notes Josef Skvorecky, also of *World Literature Today:* "The author's theatrical experience is clearly noticeable: the book uses techniques essentially similar to those employed by writers who, in the sixties, read their stories from the stages of the 'small theatres' of Prague; these 'text-appeal' stories too were predominantly satirical, and, more often than not, of an absurdist nature. But *White Book* is a fine novel, well shaped and absorbing, to which—as to the works of Kafka—history has added another dimension. . . . There are numerous allusions to the events of 1968, but in the last analysis the entire grimly black joke can stand as a metaphorical judgment of a Marxism that can no longer cope with new facts, except in a (pseudo) legal and psychiatric fashion. . . . *White Book* convincingly demonstrates that its author is one of those versatile writers who feel at home in all literary forms and in several genres."

Some critics, however, occasionally find *White Book* to be a chore to read. A *Choice* reviewer, attributing the difficulty to Kohout's "peculiar style," concludes that *White Book* is "at times quite entertaining, at other times rather boring." The *New Statesman*'s Jeremy Treglown has no quarrel with Kohout's style; the difficulty as he sees it is that "satire rarely translates well. It depends not only on common assumptions (no sweat in the particular case of Pavel Kohout's critique of Soviet oppression) but, more problematically, on a common shock threshold. So *White Book* presents a dilemma. I wanted to find it a courageously funny act of protest by this Czech author against a regime whose response to such acts is (as the fiction reminds us) notably humourless. But after a few pages it reads predictably, a story that suffers in translation by comparison with the Western satiric fantasies it emulates." Admitting that "we're in a particularly bad position to enjoy communist anti-establishment irony because the capitalist variety is—in proportion to the deviousness of its targets—so much subtler," Treglown concludes that everything in *White Book* "seems under-realised: you need your own idiom . . . to being the situation home in anything other than documentary terms."

Unlike Treglown, Enoch Brater of the *Nation* believes Kohout is more than able to "bring the situation home." After contrasting the blatantly political theme of *White Book* to the more subtle and ominous "Poor Murderer," Brater writes: "Because Kohout moves us so swiftly from methods of political satire to questions of fundamental morality, his novel becomes something more impressive than an item for systematic review. . . . [*White Book*] comes from behind the barricades [of 1968] to document the shift in political winds which seemed so inexplicably brutal 'under Western eyes.' . . . [In *White Book,*] fiction masquerades as history with fantasy rendered as primary source material. . . . Through it all Kohout presents a man dedicated to science trying to maintain his humanity. But Adam is ultimately undone by science itself: the strange new science of the mind."

In some concluding remarks on Kohout's work as a whole, Brater observes: "What [Westerner audiences] have seen of Kohout's work sparkles with ingenuity and life. Rising above all political considerations, Kohout writes about individuals caught up in a system beyond their control. For him absurdity is not so much the relatively safe metaphysical fantasy it has become for so many of our best writers but a practical matter of everyday life and death. It is not a problem of coping but of questioning itself. . . . Pavel Kohout makes of political satire a matter of universal conscience, calling our attention to the still unaccomplished goal of making laws protecting human rights as sacred and irrefutable as the law of gravity itself."

BIOGRAPHICAL/CRITICAL SOURCES: Saturday Review, July 29, 1972, September 3, 1977; New Republic, September 6, 1975; New York Times, October 21, 1976; New York Post, October 21, 1976; Newsweek, November 1, 1976; New Yorker, November 1, 1976; Nation, November 13, 1976, September 24, 1977; New Leader, November 22, 1976; New York Times Book Review, August 7, 1977; Modern Drama, September, 1977; World Literature Today, spring, 1978, autumn, 1978, summer, 1979; Choice, April, 1978; New Statesman, August 25, 1978; Contemporary Literary Criticism, Volume XIII, Gale, 1980.†

—Sketch by Deborah A. Straub

*   *   *

KOTKER, Zane 1934-

PERSONAL: Born January 2, 1934, in Waterbury, Conn.; daughter of Edward S. (a clergyman) and Jean (Cadwallader) Hickcox; married Norman Richard Kotker (a writer and editor), June 7, 1965; children: David, Ariel. Education: Middlebury College, B.A., 1956; Columbia University, M.A., 1960. Home: 45 Lyman Rd., Northampton, Mass. 01060.

CAREER: Waterbury Republican-American, Waterbury, Conn., reporter, 1957-58; New England Review, New Haven, Conn., co-editor and publisher, 1960-63; Silver Burdett Co., Morristown, N.J., editor, 1963-66; Harcourt Brace Jovanovich, Inc., New York, N.Y., department head, 1966-69; writer, 1969—. Awards, honors: Fellowship from National Endowment for the Arts, 1974; MacDowell Colony fellow, 1979.

WRITINGS—All novels; all published by Knopf: Bodies in Motion, 1972; A Certain Man, 1976; White Rising, 1981. Contributor of short stories and articles to Redbook, New York, Galaxy, and Savvy.

WORK IN PROGRESS: A fourth novel.

BIOGRAPHICAL/CRITICAL SOURCES: Saturday Review, May 27, 1972; New Republic, February 19, 1977; Best Sellers, April, 1977; Commonweal, April 29, 1977.

*   *   *

KOTZWINKLE, William 1938-

PERSONAL: Born November 22, 1938, in Scranton, Pa.; son of William John (a printer) and Madolyn (Murphy) Kotzwinkle; married Elizabeth Gundy (a writer). Education: Attended Rider College and Pennsylvania State University.

CAREER: Writer. Awards, honors: World Fantasy Award for best novel, 1977, for Doctor Rat; recipient of two National Magazine Awards for fiction; Breadloaf Writer's Conference scholarship.

WRITINGS—Novels, except as indicated: Elephant Bangs Train (short story collection), Pantheon, 1971; Hermes 3000, Pantheon, 1972; The Fan Man, Avon, 1974; Swimmer in the Secret Sea, Avon, 1975; Night-book, Avon, 1974; Doctor Rat, Knopf, 1976; Fata Morgana, Knopf, 1977; Herr Nightingale and the Satin Woman, Knopf, 1978; Jack in the Box, Putnam, 1980.

Juvenile: The Fireman, Pantheon, 1969; The Ship That Came Down the Gutter, Pantheon, 1970; Elephant Boy: The Story of the Stone Age, Farrar, Straus, 1970; The Day the Gang Got Rich, Viking, 1970; The Oldest Man, and Other Timeless Stories, Pantheon, 1971; The Return of Crazy Horse, Farrar, Straus, 1971; The Supreme, Superb, Exalted, and Delightful, One and Only Magic Building, Farrar, Straus, 1973; Up the Alley with Jack and Joe, Macmillan,

1974; The Leopard's Tooth, Seabury, 1976; The Ants Who Took Away Time, Doubleday, 1978; Dream of Dark Harbor, Doubleday, 1979; The Nap Master, Harcourt, 1979.

Work represented in anthologies, including O. Henry Prize Stories, 1975, and All Our Secrets Are the Same, published by Esquire magazine.

SIDELIGHTS: William Kotzwinkle's work is known for its humorous imagery; the author of adult novels as well as children's literature, Kotzwinkle is "a writer with an original bent for wildly funny imagery," writes a New York Times Book Review critic. In the New Republic, William Kennedy finds that The Fan Man is an "artfully structured, supremely insane novel about a freaky quasi-Hindu-shmindu brahman who is one with the ridiculously filthy worn-out world. It is Buddha's story turned inside out . . . and set in Manhattan." Other novels, such as Fata Morgana and Doctor Rat, have generated similar comments.

Jerome Charyn states in the New York Times Book Review that Fata Morgana is "a curious mingling of genres: detective story and fairy tale. It manages to pull the reader in because William Kotzwinkle, who has written for both children and adults, is able to move from the mundane to the grotesque, from magic to hard-nosed fact, without bruising his story." Set in Paris in 1861, the novel concerns a police detective's investigation of a conjurer who, according to Charyn, "seems to be mesmerizing Paris with a fortune-telling machine." The Saturday Review's Hollis Alpert remarks that by mixing the elements of suspense and sorcery, Kotzwinkle succeeds in showing that the "overly familiar" suspense form "allows for wit, cleverness, displays of arcane knowledge, daring invention, and . . . good writing." And a New Yorker critic comments, "Gaudy, decadent, smoothly polished, this beguiling novel is perhaps less a fata morgana [mirage] than a feat of stage magic, well rehearsed and well performed by a fine craftsman."

In Doctor Rat, Kotzwinkle employs the animal fable to illustrate his theme of man's cruelty and destructiveness. Set in a cancer research laboratory, the novel is narrated from the animals' point of view and offers graphically detailed accounts of what Anne Larsen of the Village Voice calls "the atrocities of human experimentation on animals." A Listener reviewer comments: "There is a faint but authentic Blakeian echo in Mr. Kotzwinkle's rage, and it gives his book the voltage necessary to bypass insulating ideas and strike right into the emotions. If it is not a criticism of life, it is certainly a savage review of it."

Other critics, however, argue that the novel offers an overly sentimental, shallow, and distorted view of man's nature. "[Kotzwinkle's] humans are purely, wholly, and simplistically villainous; his 'good' animals are the essence of the passive, mind-blown counterculture, housed in the skins of hippopotami and chipmunks," according to Larsen. In the New York Times Book Review, Richard P. Brickner attacks Doctor Rat for being "recklessly sentimental in its argument." He continues: "It did not persuade me, as it seems to have meant to, that laboratory research, using animals, into the causes of cancer is the equivalent of Dr. Mengele's experiments at Auschwitz." Thomas LeClair in the Saturday Review echoes Brickner's assessment of the novel when he states that although he was impressed by the book's beginning, "alternating between shrillness and sentiment, Doctor Rat ultimately cancels itself out." Similarly, Robert Stone of Harper's admires the intention of Doctor Rat and its author but finds that the novel fails because of its one-sided, sentimental approach: "Doctor Rat is a very contemporary novel by a writer who knows what the contemporary novel is for, and it tries to deliver what the times demand—an examination of modern society and a little conscience-forging for the race. It's an unashamed moral statement which upends verismo to get at basic truths. . . . But, taken on its own terms, *Doctor Rat* does not deliver. . . . It's too contrived, too ingratiating, too soft at the center to carry the weight of its own intentions.''

AVOCATIONAL INTERESTS: Folk guitar.

BIOGRAPHICAL/CRITICAL SOURCES: New York Times Book Review, January 10, 1974, November 2, 1975, May 30, 1976, May 1, 1977, November 9, 1980; *New Republic,* March 2, 1974; *Atlantic,* May, 1974; *Village Voice,* September 15, 1975, June 28, 1976; *Contemporary Literary Criticism,* Gale, Volume V, 1976, Volume XIV, 1980; *Saturday Review,* May 29, 1976, April 30, 1977; *Harper's,* June, 1976; *Listener,* July 22, 1976; *New Yorker,* July 25, 1977; *Observer,* January 8, 1978.

*   *   *

KRASNER, Jack Daniel   1921-1978

PERSONAL: Born June 10, 1921, in Atlanta, Ga.; died October 6, 1978; son of Samuel (a merchant) and Dora (Gershman) Krasner; married Selma Levine (a travel agent), June 18, 1948; children: Stephen, Michael. *Education:* Attended Atlanta Junior College, 1940-41; University of Georgia, B.S., 1945; New York University, M.A., 1950, Ph.D., 1952. *Politics:* Independent. *Religion:* Jewish. *Home and office:* 388 Lydecker St., Englewood, N.J. 07631.

CAREER: Mount Sinai Hospital, New York City, intern in psychology, 1948-50, assistant clinical psychologist, 1950-53; Postgraduate Center for Mental Health, New York City, fellow-in-training, 1952-55, psychologist, 1955-57, senior psychologist, 1957-61, associate supervisor, 1961-63, senior supervisor and lecturer, beginning 1963. Fairleigh Dickinson University, adjunct associate professor, 1965-67, assistant professor of psychology, 1967-71; associate professor of pastoral counseling, Iona College, beginning 1968. Consulting psychologist, Stony Lodge, Ossining, N.Y., 1948-53; private practice of psychoanalysis in Englewood, N.J., beginning 1956; attending clinical psychologist, Englewood Hospital, 1956-60; director of group psychotherapy, New Jersey Center for Psychotherapy, 1961-64; member of staff, Group Psychotherapy Program for Adolescents and Mothers, Bergen Pines Hospital, 1963-71. President and member of board of directors, Group Psychotherapy Foundation, beginning 1970. *Military service:* U.S. Army Air Forces, 1942-43.

MEMBER: American Psychological Association (secretary of Division 29, 1972-75), American Group Psychotherapy Association (fellow; chairman of social issues committee, 1972), American Academy of Psychotherapy, American Geriatric Society, New Jersey Psychotherapy Association (president, 1970-71), New York Society of Clinical Psychologists. *Awards, honors:* Gralnick Award of Postgraduate Center for Mental Health, 1957.

WRITINGS: (Contributor) P. H. Hoch and Joseph Zubin, editors, *Relationship of Psychological Tests to Psychiatry,* Grune, 1952; (with Asya L. Kadis and others) *A Practicum of Group Psychotherapy,* Harper, 1963; (contributor) J. L. Moreno, editor, *The International Handbook of Group Psychotherapy,* Philosophical Library, 1966; (with Jules Barron and Benjamin Fabrikant) *Psychotherapy: A Psychological Perspective,* Selected Academic Readings, 1971; (with Martin R. Protell) *Psychodynamics in Dental Practice,* C. C Thomas, 1975; (with Fabrikant) *To Enjoy Is to Live,* Nelson-

Hall, 1977. Contributor to journals. Editor, *New Jersey Psychologist.*†

*   *   *

KRISLOV, Samuel   1929-

PERSONAL: Born October 5, 1929, in Cleveland, Ohio; son of Isaak and Gertrude (Hutner) Krislov; married Donna Carol Taylor (a pianist), September 15, 1951 (divorced); children: Sharon Lee, Diana Beth, Daniel Robert, Melanie Bathsheba, Lee Shalom. *Education:* Attended Western Reserve University (now Case Western Reserve University), 1947-48; New York University, B.A., 1951, M.A., 1952; Princeton University, Ph.D., 1955. *Politics:* Democrat. *Religion:* Jewish. *Home:* 1718 Oliver Ave., South Minneapolis, Minn. 55405. *Office:* Department of Political Science, University of Minnesota, Minneapolis, Minn.

CAREER: University of Vermont, Burlington, instructor in political science, 1955; Hunter College (now Hunter College of the City University of New York), New York, N.Y., instructor in political science, 1955-56; University of Oklahoma, Norman, assistant professor, 1956-60, associate professor of political science, 1960-61; Michigan State University, East Lansing, visiting assistant professor, 1959-61, associate professor of political science and research associate of School of Labor and Industrial Relations, 1961-64; University of Minnesota, Minneapolis, associate professor, 1964-65, professor of political science, 1965—, chairman of department, 1969-72, 1975-78. Visiting professor, Columbia University, 1966, Brandeis University, 1978-79. Research assistant, New York Joint Legislative Committee on Interstate Cooperation, 1955-56; delegate to Michigan Democratic conventions, 1962-64; member of Ingham County (Mich.) Democratic Committee, 1962-64; member of Minnesota Committee on Judicial Standards, 1971-73; chairman, Committee on Research on Law Enforcement and Criminal Justice, 1975-80. Fellow, National Institute of Justice, 1980. *Member:* American Political Science Association, American Association of University Professors, Law and Society Association (president, 1974-77), Midwest Political Science Association (president, 1975-76), Midwest Conference of American Society for Legal History, Midwest Conference of Political Scientists, Phi Beta Kappa. *Awards, honors:* Social Science Research Council grants, 1958, 1961; Ford Foundation International Relations grant, 1963; National Institute of Mental Health grants, 1963, 1967, 1969, 1971; American Philosophical Society grant, 1964; Russell Sage fellow, 1966-67; Ford faculty fellowship, 1972-73; Guggenheim fellow, 1979-80.

WRITINGS: (With T. S. Sinclair and Lloyd Wells) *The Politics of Judicial Review, 1937-1957* (monograph), Arnold Foundation, 1957; (editor with James A. Burkhart and others) *American Government: The Clash of Issues,* Prentice-Hall, 1960, 4th edition, 1972; (editor with Lloyd D. Musolf) *The Politics of Regulation: A Reader,* Houghton, 1964; (contributor) Gottfried Dietze, editor, *Essays on the American Constitution: A Commemorative Volume in Honor of Alpheus T. Mason,* Prentice-Hall, 1964; (contributor) Donald Cameron Rowat, editor, *The Ombudsman, Citizens Defender,* Allen & Unwin, 1965; *The Supreme Court in the Political Process,* Macmillan, 1965; *The Politics of Legal Advice: Michigan and the ADCU Controversy,* McGraw, 1965; *The Negro in Federal Employment: The Quest for Equal Opportunity,* University of Minnesota Press, 1967; *The Supreme Court and Political Freedom,* Free Press, 1968; *The Judicial Process and Constitutional Law,* Little, Brown, 1972; (editor with others) *Compliance and the Law: A Multi-Discipli-*

nary Approach, Sage Publications, 1972; Representative Bureaucracy, Prentice-Hall, 1975; (author and editor with Susan White) Knowing about Crime, National Academy of Science, 1977; Projecting Legislative Impact on the Courts, National Academy of Science, 1980. Contributor to political science and law periodicals.

* * *

KUEHNELT-LEDDIHN, Erik (Maria) Ritter von 1909-
(Francis Stuart Campbell, Chester F. O'Leary, Tomislav Vitezovic)

PERSONAL: Born July 31, 1909, in Tobelbad, Austria; son of Erik Ritter von Kuehnelt-Leddihn and Isabella (von Leddihn); married Countess Marie-Christiane Goess, July 3, 1937; children: Erik, Isabel, Gottfried. Education: Theresianic Academy, Vienna, Austria, B.A., 1927; University of Budapest, M.A., 1934, Dr. Pol. Sc., 1937; additional study in law and theology, University of Vienna. Politics: Liberal Monarchist. Religion: Catholic. Home: A-6072, Lans, Tyrol, Austria. Agent: Mrs. Anthony Gran, 506 La Guardia, New York, N.Y. 10012.

CAREER: Beaumont College, Old Windsor, England, master, 1935-36; Georgetown University, Washington, D.C., assistant professor of political geography, 1937-38; St. Peter's College, Jersey City, N.J., chairman of history department, 1938-43; Fordham University, New York, N.Y., lecturer in Japanese, 1942-43; Chestnut Hill College, Philadelphia, Pa., professor of history and sociology, 1943-47. Member: Sovereign Order of Knights of Malta. Awards, honors: Literary prize, Entr'aide Sociale, Paris, 1936.

WRITINGS: (Under pseudonym Tomislav Vitezovic) Die Anderen, Amalthea, 1931; Jesuiten, Spiesser, Bolschewiken, Anton Pustet, 1933, translation by I. J. Collins published as Gates of Hell, Sheed, 1934; Ueber dem Osten Nacht, Anton Pustet, 1935, translation by Edwin Muir and Willa Muir published as Night over the East, Sheed, 1936; Moscow, Sheed, 1940, revised edition published as Moscow, 1979, 1946; (under pseudonym Francis Stuart Campbell) The Menace of the Herd; or, Procrustes at Large, Bruce, 1943; (under pseudonym Chester F. O'Leary) Mord im Blaulicht, Amandus, 1948; (under pseudonym Chester F. O'Leary) Die Urvaeter Amerikas, Amandus, 1949; Liberty or Equality?: The Challenge of Our Time, edited by John P. Hughes, Caxton, 1952; Black Banners, Forty-five Press, 1952, Caxton, 1954; Freiheit oder Gleichheit?: Die Schicksalsfrage des Abendlandes (incorporating part of Liberty or Equality), Otto Mueller, 1953; El Nuevo conservatismo y el nuevo liberalismi en Europe y Norte-america, Ateneo, 1955.

Zwischen Ghetto und Katakombe: Von Christlicher Existenz heute, Otto Mueller, 1960; Libertad o Igualdad (containing parts of Liberty or Equality), Rialp, 1962; Die Gottlosen, Berglandbuch, 1962; Democracy Revisited, Intercollegiate Society of Individualists, 1962; Christliche Sozialromantiker, Foerderung der schweizerischen Wirtschaft, 1964; Las Estados Unidos y Europa: El Problema de la comprension, Instituto de Estudios Politicos, 1965; Lateinamerika: Geschichte eines Scheiterns?, Fromm, 1967; Hirn, Herz und Rueckgrat: Der Zeitlose Christ, Gedanken zu seiner Anatomie, Fromm, 1968, translation published as The Timeless Christian, Herald Press, 1969.

Amerika: Leitbild im Zwielicht, Johannes Verlag, 1971; Luftschloesser, Luegen und Legenden, Herold, 1972; Leftism: From Sade and Marx to Hitler and Marcuse, Arlington House, 1974; Das Raetsel Liebe: Materialien fuer eine Ges-

chlechter theologie, Herold, 1975; Narrenschiff auf Linkskurs, Styria, 1977; The Intelligent American's Guide to Europe, Arlington House, 1979; Rechts, wo das Herz Schlaegt, Styria, 1980.

Contributor: F. J. Sheed, editor, Born Catholics, Sheed, 1954; Catholicism in America, Harcourt, 1954; Handbuch der Weltgeschichte, Otto Walter, 1956; Dan Herr and Lane Clement, editors, Realities, Bruce, 1958; Gendaiderwege: Festschrift fuer Ida Friederike Goerres, Thomas Verlag, 1961; Between Two Cities: God and Man in America, Loyola University Press (Chicago), 1962; A. Hunold, editor, Lateinamerika: Land der Sorge, Land der Zukunft, Eugen Rentsch, 1963; Rafael Lopez Jordan, editor, Levando el Ancla, Ediciones Studium, 1964; Moskau-Peking, Walter, 1965; Seeds of Anarchy, Argus, 1969; Der Adel in Oesterreich, Kremayr & Scherian, 1971.

Also contributor to The Book of Catholic Authors, 3rd series, 1945, and to Ordo Jahrbuch, X and XIII, 1958, 1962. Contributor to periodicals on four continents. European correspondent, National Review, 1954—.

WORK IN PROGRESS: San Schimon; Rudolf and Clarissa; Idiotenfuehrer durch die moderne Geschichte.

SIDELIGHTS: Erik Ritter von Kuehnelt-Leddihn told CA that he sees his main task as interpreting the Old and the New World to each other. He lectures annually in the United States. His books have been translated for publication in five European countries, Chile, and Brazil. He held the first exhibition of his paintings in 1971. Avocational interests: Painting, philately, photograpy.

BIOGRAPHICAL/CRITICAL SOURCES: Books, May 13, 1934, November 3, 1940; America, May 16, 1936; Catholic World, July, 1943; Annual of American Academicians, November, 1943; Commonweal, December 17, 1954; National Review, August 25, 1970, September 28, 1979.

* * *

KUHN, Alfred   1914-
PERSONAL: Born December 22, 1914, in Reading, Pa.; son of Alvin Boyd (an author) and Mary G. (Leippe) Kuhn; married Nina de Angeli, October 18, 1941; children: David, Jeffrey, Henry. Education: Albright College, B.A., 1935; University of Pennsylvania, M.A., 1941, Ph.D., 1951. Home: 574 U.S. 52, New Richmond, Ohio 45157. Office: University of Cincinnati, Cincinnati, Ohio 45221.

CAREER: University of Pennsylvania, Philadelphia, instructor in industry, 1946-49; University of Cincinnati, Cincinnati, Ohio, 1949—, began as assistant professor, currently David Sinton Professor of Economics and Sociology. Labor arbitrator. Member: American Economic Association, Industrial Relations Research Association, Society for General Systems Research, American Association of University Professors, American Civil Liberties Union, Academy of Management, Academy of Independent Scholars, Association for Integrative Studies, American Sociological Association, Social Science Education Consortium.

WRITINGS: Study of Racial Discrimination in Cincinnati, Wilder Foundation, 1952; Arbitration in Transit: An Evaluation of Wage Criteria, University of Pennsylvania Press, 1952; Labor: Institutions and Economics, Rinehart, 1956, revised edition, Harcourt, 1967; The Study of Society: A Unified Approach, Irwin, 1963 (published in England as The Study of Society: A Multidisciplinary Approach, Tavistock Publications, 1966); (with Kenneth Boulding and Lawrence Senesh) System Analysis and Its Use in the Classroom, Social Science Education Consortium, 1973; *The Logic of Social Systems,* Jossey-Bass, 1974; *Unified Social Science,* Dorsey, 1975; (with Edward Herman) *Collective Bargaining and Industrial Relations,* Prentice-Hall, 1981. Contributor of articles on wage theory, systems theory, and philosophy to professional journals.

WORK IN PROGRESS: The Logic of Organization: A System-Based Synthesis of Organization Theory.

* * *

KURELEK, William 1927-1977

PERSONAL: Surname is pronounced Coo-*reh*-lehk; born March 3, 1927, in Whitford, Alberta, Canada; died November, 1977, in Toronto, Ontario, Canada; son of Metro and Mary (Hululak) Kurelek; married Jean Andrews, October 8, 1962; children: Catherine, Stephen, Barbara, Thomas. *Education:* University of Manitoba, B.A., 1949. *Religion:* Roman Catholic. *Address:* Isaacs Gallery, 832 Yonge St., Toronto, Ontario, Canada M4W 2H1.

CAREER: Picture framer in Toronto, Ontario, 1959-71; artist in Toronto, 1960-77. Work has appeared in more than fifty one-man and group exhibitions in galleries throughout Canada, Great Britain, and the United States, including the Isaacs Gallery, Toronto, 1960, 1962-64, 1966, 1968, 1970, 1972-74, 1976, 1978, and 1980, J. B. Speed Art Museum, Louisville, Ky., 1962, Banfer Gallery, New York, 1963, Montreal Museum of Fine Arts, 1963, Rochester Memorial Art Gallery, New York, 1963, National Gallery of Canada, Ottawa, 1963, 1965, and 1968, Commonwealth Gallery, London, England, 1963, Edmonton Art Gallery, 1965 and 1970, Winnipeg Art Gallery, 1965, Yellowstone Art Center, Montana, 1967, Cornell University, 1971, Burnaby Art Gallery, British Columbia, 1973, and Canada House Gallery, London, 1978; paintings are also represented in various permanent collections, including Museum of Modern Art, New York, and National Gallery of Canada. *Member:* Royal Canadian Academy of Art. *Awards, honors:* Canada Council senior arts grant, 1969; *New York Times* Best Illustrated Children's Book Award, 1973, for *A Prairie Boy's Winter,* and 1974, for *Lumberjack;* Canadian Association of Children's Librarians Illustrators Award, for *A Prairie Boy's Summer;* honorary Doctor of Law, University of Windsor, 1976; Christian Culture Award, 1977; Order of Canada, 1977.

WRITINGS—All self-illustrated: *A Prairie Boy's Winter* (juvenile), Houghton, 1973; *O Toronto,* New Press, 1973; *Someone with Me* (autobiography), Center for Improvement of Undergraduate Education, Cornell University, 1973, revised edition, McClelland & Stewart, 1980; *Lumberjack* (juvenile), Houghton, 1974; *The Passion of Christ According to St. Matthew,* Niagara Falls Art Gallery and Museum, 1975; *Kurelek Country,* Houghton, 1975, published as *Kurelek's Canada,* Pagurian Press (Scarborough, Ont.), 1975; *Fields,* Tundra Books (Plattsburgh, N.Y.), 1975; *A Prairie Boy's Summer* (juvenile), Houghton, 1975; (with Abraham Arnold) *Jewish Life in Canada,* Hurtig, 1976; *The Last of the Arctic,* Pagurian Press, 1976; *A Northern Nativity: Christmas Dreams of a Prairie Boy* (juvenile), Tundra Books (Montreal), 1976; *The Ukrainian Pioneer,* Niagara, 1980.

Illustrator: Mary Paximadas, *Look Who's Coming,* Maracle Press, 1976; W. O. Mitchell, *Who Has Seen the Wind,* Macmillan (Toronto), 1976; Ivan Franko, *Fox Mykyta,* Tundra Books (Montreal), 1978.

SIDELIGHTS: Described by a *Saturday Night* critic as "one of the most distinctive Canadian painters of this century," William Kurelek was a self-taught artist who learned his craft by trial and error while apprenticed to a picture framer. His books for children, *A Prairie Boy's Winter, Lumberjack, A Prairie Boy's Summer,* and *A Northern Nativity,* combine rich colors and simple, solid, peasant-like human figures with a deceptively spare and subdued writing style to evoke powerful scenes of Depression-era Canada. Enhanced by illustrations reminiscent of the work of Brueghel and Diego Rivera, Kurelek's stories recall the author's own childhood as a farmboy in the prairie provinces as well as his later stints as a lumberjack in Canadian logging camps. All have been praised for their "homely honesty" and warmly affectionate and nostalgic atmosphere.

In a particularly descriptive analysis of *Lumberjack,* for example, the *New York Times Book Review*'s Robert Newton Peck, though he found Kurelek's characters to be "as wooden as their logs, little more than general store mannequins who pose silently in checkerboard shirts," nevertheless declared: "I like this book.... Wisely perhaps, all frills of literature have been hacked off by a craftsman who cuts as well with a pen as he trims his lumber with an axe.... Kurelek is no poet. Still, so earnestly does he wade into his work and revere its sanctity, pleasing images often fall as cones from a white pine.... On every page, you will be rewarded by paintings in color, as plain as the prose, drawn with a heavy hand; yet in a compelling and manly style that complements its words.... [They are] clumsy words, thick and cold and weary with work. You almost have to heft up each one with a woodhook and haul it from the hills by the grit and grunt of your own gut. But if you want my opinion, spit on your hands and do the job."

Three films have been produced dealing with William Kurelek's life and work: "Kurelek," released by the National Film Board of Canada, 1967; "Pacem in Terris," a film based on his paintings and drawings, 1971; and "The Maze," a psychological film study of his struggle to overcome mental illness, Cornell University, 1971.

BIOGRAPHICAL/CRITICAL SOURCES: New York Times Book Review, December 9, 1973, November 3, 1974, December 12, 1976; *Horn Book,* December, 1974; *Time,* December 23, 1974; *Children's Literature Review,* Volume II, Gale, 1976; *Saturday Night,* May, 1980; *Quill and Quire,* June, 1980; *Books in Canada,* June/July, 1980.†

* * *

KWANT, Remigius C(ornelis) 1918-
(R. C. Kwant, Remy C. Kwant)

PERSONAL: Born January 14, 1918; son of Antonius and Catherina (Stam) Kwant. *Education:* Institutum Angelicum, Rome, Italy, Phil. Dr., 1945; additional study at Sorbonne, University of Paris, and at Higher Institute of Philosophy, Louvain, Belgium, 1952-54. *Home and office:* Hezer Enghweg 34, Den Dolder, The Netherlands.

CAREER: Agostinian Seminary, Eindhoven, Netherlands, professor of philosophy, 1945-61; University of Utrecht, Utrecht, Netherlands, professor of philosophy, 1961—. Visiting professor, Duquesne University, Pittsburgh, Pa., 1959, 1965, University of Natal, South Africa, 1965, Manhattanville College, 1968. *Member:* Association for Thomistic Philosophy, Association for Scientific Philosophy, Dutch Association for Philosophy.

WRITINGS: De Gradibus entis, H. J. Paris, 1946; *Idelisme en Christendom,* Het Spectrum, 1948; *Het Arbeidsbestel: Een Studie over de geest van onze samenleving,* Het Spectrum, 1956, 4th edition (under name R. C. Kwant), 1962; *Ontmoeting van wetenschap an arbeid,* Het Spectrum, 1958;

Wijsbegeerte van de Ontmoeting, Het Spectrum, 1959, revised edition (under name R. C. Kwant), 1966, translation by Robert C. Adolphs published as *Encounter,* Duquesne University Press, 1960; *De Ontwikkeling van het sociale denken: Tekst van de rede uitgesproken voor het congres ter herdenking van het derde lustrum,* Central Staatkundige Vorming, 1960; *Philosophy of Labor,* Duquesne University Press, 1960.

De Wijsbergeerte van Karl Marx, Het Spectrum, 1961, 4th edition (under name R. C. Kwant), 1966; *De Fenomenologie van Merleau-Ponty,* Het Spectrum, 1962, revised edition (under name R. C. Kwant) published as *Die Wijsbegeerte van Merleau-Ponty,* 1968, translation by Henry J. Koren published as *The Phenemenological Philosophy of Merleau-Ponty,* Duquesne University Press, 1963; *Fenomenologie van de taal,* Het Spectrum, 1963, 3rd edition (under name R. C. Kwant), 1967, translation by Koren published (under name Remy C. Kwant) as *Phenomenology of Language,* Duquesne University Press, 1965; *Sociale filosofie,* Het Spectrum, 1963, 2nd edition (under name R. C. Kwant), 1967, translation by Koren published (under name Remy C. Kwant) as *Phenomenology of Social Existence,* Duquesne University Press, 1965; *De Christen en de wereld,* Bigot en Van Rossum, 1963; *Filosofie van de arbeid,* Nederlandsche Boekhandel, 1964.

De Stemmen van de stilte: Merleau-Ponty's analyse van de schilderkunst, Paul Brand, 1966; (under name Remy C. Kwant) *From Phenomenology to Metaphysics: An Inquiry into the Last Period of Merleau-Ponty's Philosophical Life,* Duquesne University Press, 1966; *Apartheidspolitiek als structureel geweld,* Paul Brand, 1969; (with S. Ijsseling) *Filosoferen: Gangbare vormen van wijsgerig denken,* Samsom, 1978; (with J. Frenken) *Gemengde gevoelens,* Van Loghum Slaterus, 1980.

Under name R. C. Kwant: *Mens en kritiek: Een Analyse van de functie van de kritiek in het menselijke bestaan,* Het Spectrum, 1962, translation by Koren published (under name Remy C. Kwant) as *Critique: Its Nature and Function,* Duquesne University Press, 1967; *Mens en expressie in het licht van de wijsbegeerte van Merleau-Ponty,* Het Spectrum, 1968, translation by Koren published (under name Remy C. Kwant) as *Phenomenology of Expression,* 1969; *Een Nieuwe vrijheid,* Samsom, 1970; *Persoon en structuur,* Samsom, 1971; *Gevangen in eigen net: het vraagstuk van het medium-determinisme,* Samsom, 1972; *Mensbeelden: Filosofie in een pluriforme Samenleving,* Samsom, 1973; *Gedrang rondom het podium: problemen van het publiciteitsveld,* Wetenschapplijke Uitgeverij, 1975; *De visie van Marx,* Boom, 1975, revised edition, 1978; *Waarheidscrisis: eternalisering, kapitalisering en afschrijving van weten,* De Toorts, 1975; (with D. J. van Houten) *Maatschappijkritiek, Verkenning van het verschijnsel maatschappijkritiek,* Samsom, 1976; *Structuralisten en structuralisme,* Samsom, 1979.

L

LAMB, Karl A(llen) 1933-

PERSONAL: Born January 24, 1933, in Worland, Wyo.; son of Lawrence (a realtor) and Floribel (Krueger) Lamb; married Sally Ann Walker, July 12, 1959; children: Steven B., Amy, Martin, Cynthia. *Education:* Yale University, B.A., 1954; Oxford University (Rhodes scholar, 1954-57), D.Phil., 1958. *Politics:* Independent. *Residence:* Santa Cruz, Calif. *Office:* Cowell College, University of California, Santa Cruz, Calif.

CAREER: University of Michigan, Ann Arbor, 1958-63, began as instructor, became assistant professor of political science; University of California, Santa Cruz, academic assistant to the chancellor, 1963-65, fellow of Cowell College, 1965—, associate professor of government, 1966-69, professor of politics, 1970—, associate dean of graduate division, 1966-69, acting provost of Cowell College, 1978-79. Director, Michigan Citizenship Clearing House, 1959-61. Member of staff, Republican National Convention, 1960; faculty intern, Republican National Committee, 1964. *Military service:* U.S. Army Reserve, Artillery; active duty, 1958; present rank, captain. *Member:* American Political Science Association, Association of American Rhodes Scholars, Western Political Science Association, Northern California Political Science Association (president, 1971), Santa Cruz Yacht Club.

WRITINGS: (Contributor) *The Politics of Reapportionment,* Atherton, 1962; (contributor) *Inside Politics: The National Conventions, 1960,* Oceana, 1962; (with W. J. Pierce and J. P. White) *Apportionment and Representative Institutions: The Michigan Experience,* Institute for Social Science Research, 1963; (with N. C. Thomas) *Congress: Politics and Practice,* Random House, 1964; (with P. Smith) *Campaign Decision-Making,* Wadsworth, 1968; *The People, Maybe,* Wadsworth-Duxbury, 1971, 3rd edition, 1978; (editor) *Democracy, Liberalism, and Revolution,* Freel, 1971; *As Orange Goes,* Norton, 1974. Contributor to professional journals.

WORK IN PROGRESS: A book on the attitudes and values of the American political elite, tentatively entitled *Madison's Children.*

L'AMOUR, Louis (Dearborn) 1908-
(Tex Burns)

PERSONAL: Born 1908 in Jamestown, N.D.; son of Louis Charles and Emily (Dearborn) LaMoore; married Katherine Elizabeth Adams, February 19, 1956; children: Beau Dearborn, Angelique Gabrielle. *Education:* Self-educated.

CAREER: Author and lecturer. Has held numerous jobs including positions as longshoreman, lumberjack, miner in the West, elephant handler, hay shocker, professional boxer, flume builder, and fruit picker. Lecturer at many universities including University of Oklahoma, Baylor University, University of Southern California, and University of Redlands. *Military service:* U.S. Army, 1942-46; became first lieutenant. *Member:* Writers Guild of America (West), Western Writers of America, Academy of Motion Picture Arts and Sciences, American Siam Society, California Writers Guild, California Academy of Sciences. *Awards, honors:* LL.D., Jamestown College, 1972; named to Theodore Roosevelt Rough Riders, 1972; American Book Award nomination, 1980, *Bendigo Shafter;* and many other awards.

WRITINGS: Hondo, Gold Medal, 1953, reprinted, Fawcett, 1978; *Showdown at Yellow Butte,* Ace Books, 1953, reprinted, Fawcett, 1978; *Crossfire Trail,* Ace Books, 1954, reprinted, Fawcett, 1978; *Heller with a Gun,* Gold Medal, 1954, reprinted, Fawcett, 1977; *Utah Blaine,* Ace Books, 1954, reprinted, Fawcett, 1978; *Kilkenny,* Ace Books, 1954, reprinted, Fawcett, 1974; *To Tame a Land,* Gold Medal, 1955, reprinted, Fawcett, 1978; *Guns of the Timberland,* Jason, 1955, reprinted, Bantam, in press; *The Burning Hills,* Jason, 1956, reprinted, Bantam, 1980; *Silver Canyon,* Avalon, 1956, reprinted, Bantam, 1978; *Last Stand at Papago Wells,* Gold Medal, 1957, reprinted, Fawcett, 1978; *The Tall Stranger,* Gold Medal, 1957, reprinted, Fawcett, 1978; *Sitka,* Appleton, 1957; *The Man from Skibbereen,* G. K. Hall, 1973; *The Californios,* Dutton, 1974; *Over on the Dry Side,* Saturday Review Press, 1975; *The Man from the Broken Hills,* G. K. Hall, 1975; *To the Far Blue Mountains,* Dutton, 1976; *Westward the Tide,* G. K. Hall, 1977; *Fair Blows the Wind,* Dutton, 1978; *Borden Chantry,* Transworld, 1978; *The Mountain Valley War,* Transworld, 1978; *Bendigo Shafter,* Dutton, 1978.

All published by Bantam, except as indicated: *Radigan,* 1958, reprinted, Fawcett, 1978; *The First Fast Draw,* 1959, reprinted, 1976; *Taggart,* 1959, reprinted, Ulverscroft, 1977;

The Daybreakers, 1960, reprinted, Ulverscroft, 1975; *Flint,* 1960, reprinted, Ulverscroft, 1977; *Sackett,* 1961, reprinted, 1977; *Shalako,* 1962; *Killow,* 1962; *High Lonesome,* 1962, reprinted, 1980; *Lando,* 1962; *How the West Was Won,* 1962; *Fallon,* 1963; *Catlow,* 1963; *Dark Canyon,* 1963; *Mojave Crossing,* 1964; *Hanging Woman Creek,* 1964, reprinted, 1981; *Kiowa Trail,* 1965; *The High Graders,* 1965; *The Sackett Brand,* 1965; *Key-lock Man,* 1965; *Kid Rodelo,* 1966; *Mustang Man,* 1966; *Kilrone,* 1966; *The Broken Gun,* 1966; *The Skyliner,* 1967; *Matagorda,* 1967; *Down the Long Hills,* 1968; *Chancy,* 1968; *Conagher,* 1969; *The Empty Land,* 1969; *The Man Called Noon,* 1970; *Galloway,* 1970; *Reilly's Luck,* 1970; *Brionne,* 1971; *The Lonely Men,* 1971; *Under the Sweetwater Rim,* 1971; *Tucker,* 1971; *North to the Rails,* 1971; *Callaghen,* 1972; *Treasure Mountain,* 1972; *Ride the Dark Trail,* 1972; *The Ferguson Rifle,* 1973; *The Quick and the Dead,* 1973; *Rivers West,* 1975; *The Rider of Lost Creek,* 1976; *Where the Long Grass Blows,* 1976; *Sackett's Gold,* 1977; *War Party,* 1979; *The Iron Marshall,* 1979; *The Proving Trail,* 1979; *Comstock Lode,* 1981.

Under pseudonym Tex Burns; all originally published by Doubleday; all reprinted by Aeonian: *Hopalong Cassidy and the Riders of High Rock,* 1951, reprinted, 1973; *Hopalong Cassidy and the Rustlers of West Fork,* 1951, reprinted, 1976; *Hopalong Cassidy and the Trail to Seven Pines,* 1951, reprinted, 1978; *Hopalong Cassidy, Trouble Shooter,* 1952, reprinted, 1976.

Also author of poetry, *Smoke from This Altar,* 1939. Author of filmscripts and sixty-five television scripts. Has published about four hundred short stories in some eighty magazines in United States and abroad.

SIDELIGHTS: Louis L'Amour is considered by many to be one of the most prolific, bestselling and highly respected writers of Westerns today. Over eighty-two million copies of his novels are now in print, and according to Bantam Books, after the publication of *The Man from the Broken Hills,* L'Amour is their best selling author edging out John Steinbeck and Zane Grey.

Many critics suggest one reason for the great success of his novels is L'Amour's devotion to authenticity and accuracy. Research and special attention paid to details are all trademarks of his works. L'Amour spends a great deal of time researching nearly every situation and placing every scene in the exact location.

Ben Yagoda notes that L'Amour "spends his summers scouting locations and doing research; his books are full of geographical and historical information; a Stanford geology professor is said to assign one of them to his students every year." Also Ned Smith writes that L'Amour "is an encyclopedic researcher. Self-educated, he has acquired an impressive grasp of subjects as diverse as genealogy and cartography. And his books show it; they're an education as well as an entertainment."

L'Amour realizes that many critics do not fully respect writers of Westerns and this he feels is unfair. As he told an interviewer for *Publishers Weekly:* "One of the problems is that we have a few people back East in the literary establishment who eat too much, drink too much, stay up late too many times. And they wake up in the morning and walk into the bathroom, probably in their pajama bottoms, and look at themselves in the mirror . . . and they think 'Oh, the world's going to hell.' Well, out here, across the great body of the country, there are people getting up and going to work every morning, truck drivers, factory workers, ranchers, farmers and whatnot. All kinds of people who're doing a job every

single day. Within their limitations, they're creating, they're building, they're doing, and they don't feel that way at all. And they're the ones making things happen."

L'Amour also objects to the practice of many critics of separating Western novels from other novels. He told Barbara A. Bannon that he does "not distinguish Westerns at all from other kinds of novels. If you are going to characterize my stories I would prefer to have them called stories of the frontier. What is attractive to people reading this kind of a book is the idea of the freedom of the Western man, getting on a horse and moving on somewhere else. We all have dreams of wanting to be this kind of a free agent. To me there is no period in the world's history that is so fascinating as the era in which the American West was opening up. You cannot invent people like the real-life Molly Brown or silver-mining baron Spencer Penrose who built his house in Virginia City, Nevada, with solid silver doorknobs throughout. They were all bigger than life and they did fantastic things."

Ben Yagoda writes in *Esquire* that "the main thing conspiring against [L'Amour] . . . is the dang blasted simplicity of [his] product. . . . So many of L'Amour's heroes are kids because his is a preadult world, where moral problems simply don't exist. A private eye can come to doubt the concept of justice; a space traveler can speculate on the universe; the cowboy simply does what he's got to do and blows the smoke from his gun."

But it is not the praise of critics that motivate him to write, it's his readers. "The important thing to me in my work is my fan mail," L'Amour once wrote. "This is more important to me than what any reviewer or critic says, because these are the people who're reading my books. It not only gives me an idea of what they think about what I'm writing, but also gives me an idea what they're interested in, and where their ideas are. This is one of the things that's helped me realize that I'm writing for a very, very bright bunch of people. And a very special bunch of people, I think."

Approximately thirty of L'Amour's novels have been acquired by motion picture studios and filmed, including *Hondo,* Warner Bros., 1953, *Kilkenny,* Columbia, 1956, *The Burning Hills,* Warner Bros., 1956, *Utah Blaine,* Columbia, 1956, *The Tall Stranger,* Allied Artists, 1957, *Last Stand at Papago Wells,* Columbia, 1958, *Heller with a Gun,* Paramount, 1960, *Guns of the Timberland,* Warner Bros., 1960, *How the West Was Won,* Metro-Goldwyn-Mayer, 1963; *Taggart,* Universal, 1964, *Kid Rodelo,* Paramount, 1966, *Shalako,* Cinerama Releasing Corp., 1968, *Catlow,* Metro-Goldwyn-Mayer, 1971, *The Broken Gun,* Warner Bros., 1972, *The Man Called Noon,* Scotia-Barber, 1973.

Almost all of L'Amour's books have been translated into Japanese, French, German, Spanish, Italian, Norwegian, Swedish, Danish, and Finnish.

AVOCATIONAL INTERESTS: Archaeology and wild life.

BIOGRAPHICAL/CRITICAL SOURCES: Variety, November 25, 1970, June 2, 1971; *New York Times,* October 21, 1971; *Publishers Weekly,* October 8, 1973, November 27, 1978; *Newsweek,* November 10, 1975; *American Way,* April, 1976; *Authors in the News,* Volume II, Gale, 1976; *Detroit News,* March 31, 1978; *Esquire,* March 13, 1979.†

—*Sketch by Margaret Mazurkiewicz*

*   *   *

LARSEN, Egon 1904-

PERSONAL: Surname originally Lehrburger; born July 13, 1904, in Munich, Germany; son of Albert David (a manufacturer) and Beatrice (Koenigsberger) Lehrburger; married second wife, Ursula Lippmann (a translator), July 3, 1940; children: (first marriage) Peter. *Education:* Educated in Munich, Germany. *Home:* 34 Dartmouth Rd., London N.W.2, England. *Agent:* Robert Harben, 3 Church Vale, London N.2, England.

CAREER: Self-employed author and journalist, 1928—. U.S. Office of Strategic Services, civilian staff, London, England, 1944-45; Radio Munich, London correspondent, 1954—; correspondent for *Suddeutsche Zeitung,* Munich, Germany, and for other Central European newspapers. *Member:* P.E.N. (fellow; English Centre, London; Centre of German-Speaking Authors Abroad), Society of Authors (fellow; London). *Awards, honors:* Diesel Silver Medal, 1963.

WRITINGS: Inventor's Cavalcade (originally written in German but published in English), translation by Ernest W. Dickes, Lindsay Drummond, 1943, Transatlantic, 1946; *Inventor's Scrapbook,* Lindsay Drummond, 1947; *Spotlight on Films: A Primer for Film-Lovers,* Parrish, 1950; *Men Who Changed the World: Stories of Invention and Discovery,* Roy, 1952; *Radar Works Like This,* Roy, 1952, 3rd edition, Phoenix House, 1966; *An American in Europe: The Life of Benjamin Thompson, Count Rumford,* Philosophical Library, 1953; *Men Who Shaped the Future: Stories of Invention and Discovery,* Roy, 1954; *The Young Traveller in Germany,* Phoenix House, 1954, Dutton, 1955, 2nd edition, Soccer, 1961; *The True Book about Inventions,* Muller, 1954, published in America as *The Prentice-Hall Book about Inventions,* Prentice-Hall, 1955, 2nd edition (under original title), Soccer, 1961.

The True Book about Firefighting, Muller, 1955, 2nd edition, 1962; *Men under the Sea,* Phoenix House, 1955, Roy, 1956; *You'll See: Report from the Future,* Rider & Co., 1957; *Transistors Work Like This,* Roy, 1957, 2nd edition, Phoenix House, 1963; *Men Who Fought for Freedom,* Roy, 1958; *Atomic Energy: A Layman's Guide to the Nuclear Age,* Hennel Locke, 1958, also published as *Atomic Energy; The First Hundred Years: The Intelligent Layman's Guide to the Nuclear Age,* Pan Books, 1958; (editor) Franklyn M. Branley, *Solar Energy,* English edition, Edmund Ward, 1959; *Transport,* Roy, 1959; *Sir Vivian Fuchs,* Phoenix House, 1959, Roy, 1960.

Power from Atoms, Muller, 1960, Soccer, 1961; *Ideas and Invention,* Spring Books, 1960; *A History of Invention,* Roy, 1961, revised edition, 1969; *The Atom,* Weidenfeld & Nicolson, 1961; *Film Making,* Muller, 1962; *The Cavendish Laboratory: Nursery of Genius,* F. Watts, 1962; (editor with Eric G. Linfield) *England vorwiegend heiter: Kleine Literaturgeschichte des britischen Humors* (originally written in English but published in German; translation by Larsen and wife, Ursula Larsen), Basserman, 1962, reissued as *Laughter in a Damp Climate: 700 Years of British Humour,* Jenkins, 1963, Arc Books, 1965; *Atoms and Atomic Energy* (juvenile), John Day, 1963; (editor) Harry E. Neal, *Communication: From Stone Age to Space Age,* Phoenix House, 1963; (with son, Peter Larsen) *Young Africa,* Roy, 1964.

The Pegasus Book of Inventors, Dobson, 1965: *Munich,* A. S. Barnes, 1966; (with Maurice F. Allward) *Great Inventions of the World,* Hamlyn, 1966; *The Deceivers: Lives of the Great Imposters,* Roy, 1966; *Great Ideas in Engineering,* edited by Patrick Pringle, Robert C. Maxwell, 1967; (editor with Linfield) *Great Humorous Stories of the World,* Arthur Barker, 1967; *First with the Truth: Newspapermen in Action,* Roy, 1968; *Carlo Pozzo di Borgo: One Man against Napoleon,* Dobson, 1968; *Lasers Work Like This,* Roy, 1969.

Hovercraft and Hydrofoils Work Like This, Dent, 1970, Roy, 1971; (editor) Peter Larsen, *The United Nations at Work throughout the World,* Dent, 1970, Lothrop, 1971; *Great Ideas in Industry,* Robert C. Maxwell, 1971; *Strange Sects and Cults,* Arthur Barker, 1971, Hart Publishing, 1972; *Radio and Television,* Dent, 1976; *New Sources of Energy and Power,* Muller, 1976, 2nd edition, 1980; *Telecommunications,* Muller, 1977; *Food: Past, Present and Future,* Muller, 1977; *Weimar Eye-Witness,* Bachman & Turner, 1977; *A Flame in Barbed Wire: The Story of Amnesty International,* Muller, 1978, Norton, 1979; *Wit as a Weapon: The Political Joke in History,* Muller, 1980.

Translator: Erich Weinert, *Stalingrad Diary,* I.N.G. Publications, 1944; *I Escaped from Nazi Germany: A French Deportee's Report,* I.N.G. Publications, 1944; *Free Germans in the French Maquis: The Story of the Committee "Free Germany" in the West,* I.N.G. Publications, 1945; Rene Felix Allendy and Hella Lobstein, *Sex Problems in School,* Staples, 1948; Franz Farga, *Violins and Violinists,* Rockliff, 1950; (with Joseph Avrach) Gustav K. H. Buescher, *The Boys' Book of the Earth,* Burke Publishing, 1960; (with Frank Pickering) Karl Stumpff, *Planet Earth,* University of Michigan Press, 1960. Editor of biographical series, "People from the Past," Dobson, 1963—. Occasional writer for, and director of, documentary films.

SIDELIGHTS: Egon Larsen told *CA:* "The sooner a budding writer discovers what he *can't* write, the sooner he'll start on his career of writing what he can. After doing, early on, a novel, which was for me as hard as mailbag sewing in jail, I came to the conclusion that I was a lousy fiction writer, and that my field was factual books. So far, I've published about fifty of them. When people say I must be a genius to have written so many, I quote Thomas Alva Edison: 'Genius is one per cent inspiration and ninety-nine per cent perspiration.'"

Foreign-language editions of Larsen's books have appeared in over twenty-five countries including Egypt, Thailand, Turkey, Argentina, Ghana, Israel, Japan, and India.

BIOGRAPHICAL/CRITICAL SOURCES: Times Literary Supplement, August 17, 1967.

*   *   *

LAVER, James   1899-1975
(Jacques Reval)

PERSONAL: Born March 14, 1899, in Liverpool, England; died of injuries sustained in a fire in his London apartment, June 3, 1975; son of Arthur James and Florence M. (Barker) Laver; married Veronica Turleigh, 1928; children: Patrick Martin, Brigid Cecilia Laver McEwen. *Education:* Attended Liverpool Institute; Oxford University, B.A. and B.Litt. *Home:* 4/10 The Glebe, London S.E. 3, England. *Agent:* David Higham Associates, 5-8 Lower John St., London W1R 4HA, England.

CAREER: Victoria and Albert Museum, London, England, deputy director of department of engravings, illustration, and design, 1922-59. *Military service:* Served in British Army, Infantry, World War I; received Victory Medal, Allies Medal, Kings Own Royal Regiment (Lancaster). *Member:* International Faculty of Arts (vice-president), Society of International Artists (honorary fellow), P.E.N., Authors Society, Society of Civil Service Authors (vice-president), Society for Theatre Research (vice-president), Royal Academy of Dramatic Arts, Art Worker's Guild (honorary), Beefsteak Club, Chelsea Arts Club (honorary), Saintsbury Club, Dilettanti Club. *Awards, honors:* Newdigate Prize, for *Cer-*

vantes; Commander of the Order of the British Empire, 1951.

WRITINGS: Cervantes (poetry), Basil Blackwell, 1921; *His Last Sebastian,* Simpkin, Marshall, 1922; *Portraits in Oil and Vinegar,* John Castle, 1925; *The Young Man Dances,* John Castle, 1925; (with John Drinkwater, Wilfred Whitten, and W. P. Robins) *The Artist's London,* John Castle, 1925; *A Stitch in Time,* Nonesuch, 1927; (with George Sheringham) *Design in the Theatre,* Studio Books, 1927, reprinted, Arno, 1972; (translator from German) *The Circle of Chalk,* Heinemann, 1928; *A History of British and American Etching,* Benn, 1929; *Love's Progress,* Nonesuch, 1929; *Nineteenth Century Costume,* A. & C. Black, 1929.

Macrocosmos, Heinemann, 1930; *Etchings of Arthur Briscoe,* Halton & Truscott Smith, 1930; *Whistler,* Faber, 1930; *Eighteenth Century Costume,* A. & C. Black, 1931; *Nymph Errant,* Heinemann, 1932; (translator from German) *The Elegant Woman,* Harrap, 1932; *Wesley,* P. Davies, 1932; *Ladies' Mistakes,* Nonesuch, 1933; *Stage Designs by Oliver Messell,* John Lane, 1933; (editor) *Poetical Works of Charles Churchill,* Eyre & Spottiswoode, 1933, published as *Poems of Charles Churchill,* Barnes & Noble, 1970; *Background for Venus,* Heinemann, 1935; *Winter Wedding,* Heinemann, 1935; *Forty Drawings by Horace Brodzky,* Heinemann, 1935; *The Laburnum Tree,* Cresset, 1935; *Tommy Apple,* J. Cape, 1935; *Panic among Puritans,* Heinemann, 1936; *Vulgar Society* (biography of J. J. Tissot), Constable, 1936; *Tommy Apple and Peggy Pear,* J. Cape, 1936; *French Painting and the Nineteenth Century,* Batsford, 1937; *Taste and Fashion,* Harrap, 1937.

Poems of Baudelaire, Limited Editions Club of New York, 1940; *Adventures in Monochrome,* Studio Books, 1941; *Nostradamus: The Future Foretold,* Collins, 1942, reprinted, G. Mann, 1973; *The Ladies of Hampton Court,* Collins, 1942; *Fashion and Fashion Plates,* King Penguin, 1943; *A Letter to a Girl on the Future of Clothes,* Home & Van Thal, 1946; *Hatchards of Piccadilly,* Hatchards, 1947; *Isabella's Pageant,* Faber, 1947; *The Literature of Fashion,* Cambridge University Press, 1947; *Homage to Venus,* Faber, 1948; *British Military Uniforms,* King Penguin, 1948; *Paintings by Michael Ayrton,* Grey Walls Press, 1948; *Style in Costume,* Oxford University Press, 1949.

The Changing Shape of Things: Dress, J. Murray, 1950; *Titian,* Faber, 1950; *Children's Fashions of the 19th Century,* Batsford, 1951; *Tudor Costume,* Harrap, 1951; *Drama: Its Costume and Decor,* Burke Publishing, 1952; *The First Decadent* (biography of J. K. Huysmans), Faber, 1954; *Victorian Vista,* Hulton Press, 1954, Houghton, 1955; *Costume,* Batsford, 1956; *Fragonard,* Faber, 1956; *Edwardian Promenade,* Hulton Press, 1958; *The House of Haig,* John Haig & Co., 1958.

(Author of introduction) Erhard Klepper, *Costume Through the Ages,* Simon & Schuster, 1961; *Between the Wars,* Vista Books, 1961; *Costume,* Cassell, 1963, Hawthorn, 1964; *Museum Piece; Or, the Education of an Iconographer,* Deutsch, 1963, Houghton, 1964; *Costume in Antiquity,* C. N. Potter, 1964; *Costume in the Theatre,* Harrap, 1964, Hill & Wang, 1965; *Manners and Morals in the Age of Optimism,* Harper, 1966 (published in England as *The Age of Optimism: Manners and Morals, 1848-1914,* Wiedenfeld & Nicolson, 1966); (editor) Mila Contini, *Fashion: From Ancient Egypt to the Present Day,* Crescent, 1965; *Victoriana,* Ward, Lock, 1966, Hawthorn, 1967, revised edition, Pyne Press, 1975; *Dandies,* Weidenfeld & Nicolson, 1968; *Modesty in Dress: An Inquiry into the Fundamentals of Fashion,* Houghton,

1969; *A Concise History of Costume and Fashion,* Abrams, 1969.

English Sporting Prints, Ward, Lock, 1970; *The Age of Illusion: Manners and Morals, 1750-1848,* D. McKay, 1972.

Plays: "The Circle of Chalk," 1929; "The Marchioness of Arcis," 1930; (with Romney Brent and Cole Porter) "Nymph Errant," 1935; "The House That Went to Sea," 1938; (with Sir Barry Jackson) "The Swiss Family Robinson," 1938; "The Heart Was Not Burned," 1938; "Mr. Trouhadec," 1939. Contributor to numerous encyclopedias, magazines, and newspapers in England, other European countries, and the United States.

SIDELIGHTS: Many critics felt that James Laver was one of the world's greatest art and fashion historians. Despite the fact that he wrote numerous art books, it appeared that he was especially noted for what the *Washington Post* called "his perceptive and highly amusing comments on the relationship between social history and the clothes people wore at the time."

For example, a reviewer for *New Yorker* once wrote that Laver drew "on psychoanalytic theory, anthropological research, history, sociology, and his own keen aesthetic sense to describe and explain the changes in past styles and to suggest the meaning of the radically changing styles of today. A few readers may find Mr. Laver's cool, expert frankness shocking, but most will find it illuminating, for he effectively tells us some home truths about human beings as well as about their garments."

Laver once explained: "Fashion . . . has a curious coherence. Even when it seems most arbitrary . . . it has a very close relationship to the interior decoration, and even to the architecture, of its period. More than that, it has a symbolic value. . . . Fashion is a very much bigger thing than individual taste or personal convenience. . . . There is something in the story of the clothes we wear which is beyond our comprehension and certainly beyond the control of our conscious minds."

BIOGRAPHICAL/CRITICAL SOURCES: New Yorker, September 27, 1969; *New York Times,* June 4, 1975; *Washington Post,* June 5, 1975; *Time,* June 16, 1975; *Design,* September, 1975.†

*   *   *

LAWRENCE, Jodi   1938-
(Jody Kebin, Jodi Kevin, John Lawrence)

PERSONAL: Born September 7, 1938, in Bristol, Pa.; daughter of Joseph Louis and Beatrice (Crofutt) Vattimo; married Art Kevin (a newscaster); children: Greg, Marc, Ross. *Education:* Attended University of Copenhagen; University of Southern California, A.B. (magna cum laude), 1965, also graduate study. *Religion:* Roman Catholic. *Address:* Box 23, 628 Ave. L., Boulder City, Nev. 89005. *Agent:* Arthur Pine Associates, Inc., 1780 Broadway, New York, N.Y. 10019.

CAREER: Journalist and playwright. Guest lecturer in journalism, University of Southern California, 1968; lecturer in fiction and nonfiction, University of California, Los Angeles, 1969-70. Participating journalist and member of international press corps, Mexico World Film Festival (Acapulco), 1968. West Coast regional editor, Professional Publications, Inc.

MEMBER: Authors Guild of Authors League of America, Society of Magazine Writers of America, American Association of University Women, Actors Studio (member of writers section), Overseas Press Club (associate member), Greater Los Angeles Press Club, Women's University Club. *Awards, honors:* Scandinavian Seminar for Cultural Studies fellowship, 1960; Lowell Prize, Howard F. Lowell Foundation, 1967, for "Sugar Tome Is Dead"; *Writer's Digest* nonfiction award, 1967; international commendation, American Corporation for Public Broadcasting and Radio Nederland, 1971; Temple University English Festival award in two categories; *Mademoiselle* magazine College Board award; Goldey Beacome Award in English literature; AFL-CIO essay award.

WRITINGS—Nonfiction: (Contributor) Howard Seigel and Roger Baedecker, editors, *Survival Kit,* Harper, 1971; *Alpha Brain Waves: Guide to Biofeedback,* Nash Publishing, 1972; *Off the Beaten Track in Hawaii,* Nash Publishing, 1972; *The Search for the Perfect Orgasm,* Nash Publishing, 1973; (contributor) *Writers Yearbook,* Writer's Digest, 1973.

Plays: "Sugar Tome Is Dead" (one-act documentary), produced at Bucks County Playhouse, 1965; "Once a Rebel" (documentary), produced at Actors Studio—West, January-June, 1970.

Screenplays: "Sun Stroke," Madigo Production, 1970; "Year of Action" (documentary), DJM Productions, 1971.

Syndicated columnist, *Cross Country* and *Pro Film.* Contributor of more than three hundred short stories and articles to magazines and newspapers, including *Saga, True, Intermission, Review of the Performing Arts, Today's Film Maker, Show, Reader's Digest, Writer's Digest, Western Literary Review, Stag, Man's World, New York Times,* and *Washington Post.* West coast editor, *Today's Film Maker.*

WORK IN PROGRESS: The biography of a constitutional lawyer; relating twenty years of censorship in America and the ensuing legal battles.†

*   *   *

LAWSON, John   1909-

PERSONAL: Born July 16, 1909, in Leeds, England; came to United States in 1955; son of John (a pharmacist) and Faith Winifred (Clokie) Lawson; married Helen Rosalind Izzett, July 30, 1936; children: Rachel Helen Faith, Stephen Alexander. *Education:* University of London, B.Sc., 1930; Cambridge University, M.A., 1937, B.D., 1945. *Home:* 229 Exwick Rd., Exeter, Devon, England.

CAREER: Methodist minister; pastoral work, England, 1935-55; Candler School of Theology, Emory University, Atlanta, Ga., associate professor, 1955-71, professor of church history, 1971-76. *Member:* International Patristic Conference, Cambridge Union, Friends of Reunion.

WRITINGS—All published by Epworth, except as indicated: *Notes on Wesley's Forty-Four Sermons,* 1946; *The Biblical Theology of S. Irenaeus,* 1948; *Who Joins the Glorious Host?,* 1950; *Full Communion with the Church of England,* 1951; *What Do We Believe?,* S.P.C.K., 1951; *Methodism and Catholicism,* S.P.C.K., 1954; (editor) *Selections from Wesley's Notes on the New Testament,* 1955; *Green and Pleasant Land,* S.C.M. Press, 1955; *Historical and Theological Introduction to the Apostolic Fathers,* Macmillan, 1961; *The Christian Year with Charles Wesley,* 1966; *Comprehensive Handbook of Christian Doctrine,* Prentice-Hall, 1967; *An Evangelical Faith for Today,* Abingdon, 1972; *Introduction to Christian Doctrine,* revised edition, F. Asbury Publishing, 1980.

AVOCATIONAL INTERESTS: Gardening.

BIOGRAPHICAL/CRITICAL SOURCES: Christian Century, March 1, 1967; *Encounter,* winter, 1968.

*   *   *

LAZEROWITZ, Morris   1907-

PERSONAL: Surname originally Laizerowitz; born October 22, 1907, in Lodz, Poland; son of Max (a businessman) and Etta (Plochinsky) Laizerowitz; married Alice Ambrose (a professor of philosophy at Smith College), June 15, 1938. *Education:* Attended University of Nebraska, 1928-30; University of Michigan, A.B., 1933, Ph.D., 1936; Harvard University, postdoctoral study, 1936-37. *Home:* 126 Vernon St., Northampton, Mass. 01060. *Office:* Neilson Library, Smith College, Northampton, Mass. 01060.

CAREER: Smith College, Northampton, Mass., 1938-73, Sophia and Austin Smith Professor of Philosophy, 1964-73. Fulbright Lecturer, Bedford College, University of London, 1951-52; distinguished professor of philosophy, University of Delaware, 1975; taught at Hampshire College, 1977, 1979, 1981; Cowling Professor of Philosophy, Carlton College, 1979. *Member:* American Philosophical Association, Aristotelian Society, Royal Institute of Philosophy. *Awards, honors:* Alfred H. Lloyd postdoctoral fellowship from Horace H. Rackham School of Graduate Studies, University of Michigan, 1937-38.

WRITINGS: (With wife, Alice Ambrose) *Fundamentals of Symbolic Logic,* Rinehart, 1948, revised edition, Holt, 1962; *The Structure of Metaphysics,* Routledge & Kegan Paul, 1955, Humanities, 1963; (with Ambrose) *Logic: The Theory of Formal Inference,* 1961; *Studies in Metaphilosophy,* Humanities, 1964; (editor with William E. Kennick) *Metaphysics: Readings and Reappraisals,* Prentice-Hall, 1966; *Philosophy and Illusion,* Humanities, 1968; (editor and contributor with Ambrose) *G. E. Moore: Essays in Retrospect,* Humanities, 1970; (editor and contributor with Charles Hanly) *Psychoanalysis and Philosophy,* International Universities Press, 1970; (editor with Ambrose) *Ludwig Wittgenstein: Philosophy and Language,* Humanities, 1972; (with Ambrose) *Philosophical Theories,* Mouton, 1976; *The Language of Philosophy,* D. Reidel, 1977; (with Ambrose) *Necesidad y Filosotia,* University of Mexico Press, 1981. Contributor of articles and reviews to philosophical journals.

WORK IN PROGRESS: With Elmer Sprague, editing and contributing to *O.K. Bouwsma: Philosopher-Teacher,* for University of Texas Press.

*   *   *

LAZO, Hector   1899-1965

PERSONAL: Born October 9, 1899, in Guatemala City, Guatemala; came to United States in 1915, naturalized citizen in 1923; died May 3, 1965; son of Luis (a physician) and Emilia (Pena) Lazo; married Susan Bullock, December 25, 1920 (died December, 1939); married Edith Olive Pack (an artist), May 21, 1941; children: (first marriage) Charles R., Susan Belle (Mrs. Reed Moyer). *Education:* Harvard University, A.B. (magna cum laude), 1921; New York University, M.B.A. (highest honors), 1946, Ph.D., 1948. *Politics:* Independent Republican. *Office:* 100 Trinity Place, New York, N.Y. 10006.

CAREER: U.S. Department of Commerce, Washington, D.C., special agent, 1923-27; Dodge Brothers, Detroit, Mich., director of foreign advertising, 1927-28; overseas director of foreign advertising, General Motors Corp., 1928-31; Cooperative Food Distributors, Washington, D.C., executive vice-president, 1931-43; Board of Economic Warfare, Washington, D.C., assistant director, 1943-44; assistant to president and director of public relations, Sunshine Biscuits, Inc., New York City; professor of marketing, Graduate School of Business Administration, New York University, New York City. Chairman of school committee, fire commissioner, and library trustee in Pound Ridge, N.Y. *Military service:* U.S. Marine Corps, 1917. *Member:* American Marketing Association, American Management Association, Industrial Conference Board, New York University Club, Phi Beta Kappa. *Awards, honors:* Named marketing educator of the year, 1964; Medaille France Amerique; American Heritage Award.

WRITINGS: Retail Cooperatives: How to Run Them, Harper, 1937; (with M. H. Bletz) *Who Gets Your Food Dollar?,* Harper, 1938; *Controlled Competition,* Cooperative Food Distributors of America, 1939; *Subsidies as Solution for the Price Squeeze,* privately printed, 1942; *Case Histories of Successful Marketing: Fifty-five Problems—Solutions—Results,* Funk, 1950; *Trail of Inca Gold,* Prentice-Hall, 1955; *Marketing,* Alexander Hamilton Institute, 1961; (with Arnold Corbin) *Management in Marketing,* McGraw, 1961. Also author of *Future of Food Distribution,* 1938. Contributor to numerous books, pamphlets, and professional journals. Editor of quarterly marketing letter.

WORK IN PROGRESS: Research on product planning and development; considerable research completed on Spanish conquest of Peru for historical novel of that period; series of boys' adventure stories.

SIDELIGHTS: Hector Lazo once told *CA* that he "found fiction writing much more difficult than 'professional marketing writing,' but plan to develop fiction." *Avocational interests:* Growing azaleas.†

*   *   *

LEA, F(rank) A(lfred)   1915-1977

PERSONAL: Born August 11, 1915, in Manchester, England; died June 6, 1977; son of Charles Edgar and Dorothy Cadell (Buzzard) Lea. *Education:* Cambridge University, B.A., 1937.

CAREER: Teacher and writer; general secretary, Adelphi School Co., England, 1940-42; Burgess Hill School, Surrey, England, co-headmaster, 1942-46; Cranborne Chase School, Dorset, England, senior history master, 1953; Frensham Heights School, Surrey, senior geography master, 1954-57; International People's College, Elsinore, Denmark, lecturer in history of ideas, beginning 1963.

WRITINGS: Carlyle, Prophet of To-day, Routledge, 1943; *Shelley and the Romantic Revolution,* Routledge, 1945, Folcroft, 1969; *The Wild Knight of Battersea: G. K. Chesterton,* James Clarke, 1945, Richard West, 1973; *The Seed of the Church,* Sheppard Press, 1947; *The Bookworm's Nightmare, and Other Plays for Children,* Jason, 1948; *The Tragic Philosopher: A Study of Frederick Nietzsche,* Philosophical Library, 1957; *The Life of John Middleton Murry,* Methuen, 1959; *A Defence of Philosophy,* Eyre & Spottiswoode, 1962; *Six Short Plays for Schools,* Methuen, 1963; *Uncontemporary Studies,* Brentham Press, Volume I: *The Ethics of Reason: An Essay in Moral Philosophy,* 1975, Volume II: *Voices in the Wilderness: From Poetry to Prophecy in Britain,* 1975. Assistant editor, *Adelphi,* 1937-38, 1941-42; editor, *Peace News,* 1946-49.

AVOCATIONAL INTERESTS: Gardening.†

LEAKE, Chauncey D(epew)   1896-1978

PERSONAL: Born September 5, 1896, in Elizabeth, N.J.; died January 11, 1978, in San Francisco, Calif.; son of Frank Walker and Helen Caroline (Luttgen) Leake; married Elizabeth Nancy Wilson (a microbiologist), October 1, 1921 (died May, 1977); children: Chauncey D., Jr., Wilson Walker. *Education:* Princeton University, Litt.B., 1917; University of Wisconsin, M.S., 1920, Ph.D., 1923. *Office:* Department of Pharmacology, School of Medicine, University of California, San Francisco, Calif. 94143.

CAREER: University of Wisconsin—Madison, assistant professor, 1923-25, associate professor of pharmacology, 1925-28; University of California, San Francisco, 1928-42, became professor of pharmacology, professor of medical history, and librarian in School of Medicine; University of Texas, Medical Branch, Galveston, executive director, 1942-55; Ohio State University, Columbus, professor of pharmacology and lecturer in history and philosophy of medicine, 1955-62; University of California, San Francisco, senior lecturer in history and philosophy of the health professions and senior lecturer in pharmacology, 1962-78, coordinator of medical student research training program, 1962-65. Visiting member of Institute for Advanced Study, Princeton, N.J., 1950, 1952, and 1954; Clendening Lecturer, University of Kansas, 1951; University of Wisconsin, Miller Lecturer, 1952, Waters Lecturer, 1970; Trent Lecturer, Duke University, 1953 and 1969; professor at Hastings College of the Law, 1962-66; special lecturer, Motorola Executive Institute, beginning 1970; Kaufman Lecturer, Ohio University, 1975. Medical research director, wine advisory board, California Department of Agriculture, 1965-68; member of board of directors, Carter-Wallace, Inc., beginning 1970. Consultant to National Research Council and U.S. Public Health Service; honorary consultant, Army Medical Library, 1946-50. *Military service:* U.S. Chemical Warfare Service, 1918-19.

MEMBER: International Academy for the History of Medicine, International Academy for the History of Science, Medical Library Association (honorary member), American Medical Association, American Physiology Society, Society of Experimental History of Medicine (president, 1961-63), American Society for the History of Medicine (president, 1960), History of Science Society (president, 1936-39), American Society of Pharmacology (president, 1958-60), American Academy of Arts and Sciences, National Association of Science Writers (honorary member), Law-Science Academy of America, American Association for the Advancement of Science (fellow; vice-president, 1940; president, 1960), American College of Dentists (honorary fellow), Institute for Biomedical Research (of American Medical Association; member of scientific advisory committee, 1964-69), Hastings Institute Society (honorary fellow), California Academy of Science, Texas Academy of Science, Ohio Academy of Science, Philosophy Society of Texas, Bohemian Club, Cosmos Club, Chit-Chat Club, Kit-Kat Club. *Awards, honors:* Special awards from International Anesthesia Research Society, 1928, and Western Pharmacology Society, 1965; L.H.D., Kenyon College, 1959; D.Sc., Western Medical College of Pennsylvania, 1963, and Ohio State University; LL.D., University of California, 1965; Sc.D., Philadelphia College of Pharmacy and Science, 1969; Distinguished Service Award, Anesthesia Research Society, 1975.

WRITINGS: (Editor) Thomas Percival, *Percival's Medical Ethics,* Williams & Wilkins, 1927, reprinted, AMS Press, 1976; (translator and annotator) William Harvey, *De Motu*

Cordis: Anatomical Studies on the Motion of the Heart and Blood, C. C Thomas, 1928, 6th edition, 1978; *The Opportunity for Pictorial Art in Modern Medicine: An Example in San Francisco,* privately printed, 1937; *Travelogue 1938,* privately printed, 1938; *California's Medical Story in Fresco,* privately printed, 1939.

Allegory 1945, privately printed, 1945; *Letheon: The Cadenced Story of Anesthesia,* University of Texas Press, 1947; (with Patrick Romanell) *Can We Agree?,* University of Texas Press, 1950; *Ashbel Smith and Yellow Fever in Galveston,* University of Texas Press, 1951; *The Old Egyptian Medical Papyri,* University Press of Kansas, 1952; *Tissue Culture Cadences,* privately printed, 1953; *James Blake, M.D.: On the Relation between Chemical Constitution and Biological Action,* [Indianapolis, Ind.], 1955; *Some Founders of Physiology,* American Physiological Society, 1956; *The Amphetamines,* C. C Thomas, 1959.

(With Milton Silverman) *Alcoholic Beverages in Clinical Medicine,* Year Book Medical Publishers, 1966; *What Are We Living For?: Practical Philosophy,* PJD Publications, Volume I: *The Ethics,* 1973, Volume II: *The Logics,* 1974, Volume III: *The Esthetics,* 1976; *An Historical Account of Pharmacology to the 20th Century,* C. C Thomas, 1975.

Contributor of about six hundred articles to medical, scientific, philosophy, and education journals. Founder and editor, *Texas Reports on Biology and Medicine,* 1943-55. Consulting editor, *Excerpta Medica, Current Contents, Perspectives in Biology and Medicine, Archives Internationales de Pharmacodynamie,* and *Research Communications in Chemical Pathology and Pharmacology.*†

*   *   *

LEE, Alfred McClung 1906-

PERSONAL: Born 1906, in Oakmont, Pa.; son of Alfred McClung and Edna (Hamor) Lee; married Elizabeth Riley Briant (a sociologist and writer), 1927; children: Alfred McClung III, Briant Hamor. *Education:* University of Pittsburgh, B.A., 1927, M.A., 1931; Yale University, Ph.D., 1933. *Religion:* Unitarian. *Home:* 100 Hemlock Rd., Short Hills, N.J. 07078. *Office:* Brooklyn College of the City University of New York, Brooklyn, N.Y. 11210.

CAREER: University of Kansas, Lawrence, assistant professor, 1934-35, associate professor, 1935-38; New York University, New York City, lecturer, 1938-39, assistant professor, 1939-42, visiting graduate professor, 1951-55; Wayne University (now Wayne State University), Detroit, Mich., professor, 1942-49, chairman of department of sociology and anthropology, 1942-47; Brooklyn College of the City University of New York, Brooklyn, N.Y., professor of sociology and anthropology, 1949-71, professor emeritus, 1971—, chairman of department of sociology and anthropology, 1950-57, chairman of department of sociology, 1965-66. Sociological Abstracts, Inc., member of advisory council, 1955-65, member of board of directors, 1965—, vice-president, 1966—. Visiting scholar, Drew University, 1975—, and Western Michigan University, 1976-77. Assistant professor, Institute of Human Relations, Yale University, 1937-38; visiting professor, University of Michigan, 1947-48; professor and director, Center for Sociological Research, UNESCO, Milan, Italy, 1957-58; senior Fulbright lecturer, University of Rome, 1960-61. Public affairs specialist, Twentieth Century Fund, 1938-40; executive director, Institute for Propaganda Analysis, 1940-42. Public Affairs Pamphlets, member of board of directors, 1950—, vice-chairman, 1970—. President, National Committee on Fraternities in Education,

1953-60; member of board of directors, Instituto Superiore Internazionale per lo Studio delle Relazioni Pubbliche, 1960-61. Research consultant to Federal Communications Commission, 1941 and Department of Justice, 1943-44. Specialist, lecturer, and consultant, U.S. State Department, 1966-67. Consultant, Metropolitan Applied Research Center, Inc., 1967-75.

MEMBER: American Association for the Advancement of Science (fellow), American Anthropological Association (fellow), American Humanist Association (fellow), American Sociological Association (fellow; president, 1975-76), Association for Humanist Sociology (co-founder; president, 1976-77), American Civil Liberties Union (member of board of directors, New York City, 1949-56), Society for the Study of Social Problems (co-founder; organizing secretary, 1950-51; president, 1953-54), Society for the Psychological Study of Social Issues, American Academy of Political and Social Science, Unitarian Universalist Association (chairman of commission on Unitarian intergroup relations, 1952-54; member of commission on appraisal, 1965-66), Associazione Italiana di Scienze Sociali (fellow), Institut International de Sociologie, Internationale des Etudes et Recherches sur l'-Information, Irish Sociological Association (honorary member), Eastern Sociological Society (president, 1954-55), Irish Texts Society, Sigma Xi (founder of Brooklyn College chapter; chapter president, 1951-55), Omicron Delta Kappa, Alpha Kappa Delta, Sigma Delta Chi, Sigma Chi, Yale Club (New York). *Awards, honors:* Sigma Delta Chi national award for distinguished service in research in journalism, 1937; award of honor, Corriere della Sera Newspapers, 1967; merit award, Eastern Sociological Association, 1974.

WRITINGS: The Daily Newspaper in America, Macmillan, 1937, 3rd edition, Octagon, 1973; (with others) *Studies in the Science of Society,* Yale University Press, 1937; (with Elizabeth Briant Lee) *The Fine Art of Propaganda,* Harcourt, 1939, reprinted, Octagon, 1972; (with N. D. Humphrey) *Race Riot: A First Hand Observation of the 1943 Detroit Riots,* Dryden, 1943, reprinted, Octagon, 1967; (editor and co-author) *Principles of Sociology,* Barnes & Noble, 1946, 3rd edition, 1971; (with E. B. Lee) *Social Problems in America,* Holt, 1949, 2nd edition, 1955.

(Editor and contributor) *Readings in Sociology,* Barnes & Noble, 1951, 2nd edition, 1960; *How to Understand Propaganda,* Rinehart, 1952; (co-editor and contributor) *Public Opinion and Propaganda,* Dryden, 1954; *Fraternities without Brotherhood,* Beacon Press, 1955; (with others) *The Countdown on Segregated Education,* Society for the Advancement of Education, 1960; *La Sociologia delle Comunicazioni* (UNESCO lectures), Taylor (Torino), 1960; (with E. B. Lee) *Marriage and the Family,* Barnes & Noble, 1961, 2nd edition, 1970; *Multivalent Man,* Braziller, 1966; *Toward Humanist Sociology,* Prentice-Hall, 1973; *Sociology for Whom?,* Oxford University Press, 1978.

Contributor to symposia, magazines, and professional journals. Editor, "Major Contributors to Social Science" series, Crowell, 1963-69.

WORK IN PROGRESS: Research on the Northern Irish civil war.

SIDELIGHTS: Alfred McClung Lee told *CA:* "My books have been efforts to work for greater press freedom, for more popular understanding of communication processes (propaganda), for greater equality of opportunity for all racial and religious groups, for a more accurate understanding of motivation and morality, and for broader acceptance of our humanist heritage. . . . I have looked upon [writing] as a way of helping to make life more livable for more people. As a relative principally of lawyers and clergymen, I learned about human deprivation and suffering rather young and rather vividly. It seemed to me that something was to be done on which I might help. I have tried."

Lee originated the national awards for distinguished service in journalism presented annually by the Society of Professional Journalists, Sigma Delta Chi since 1935 while teaching journalism at University of Kansas. More recently, he has become a leader of several movements within established sociological societies to democratize their form of organization, to humanize their annual programs, and to focus attention upon important problems in contemporary society.

AVOCATIONAL INTERESTS: Oil painting and gardening.

BIOGRAPHICAL/CRITICAL SOURCES: Quill, July, 1973; *Journalism History,* spring, 1977; *Bulletin* of the Sociological Association of Ireland, summer, 1978.

*   *   *

LEE, Mark W.   1923-

PERSONAL: Born January 23, 1923, in Akron, Ohio; son of Mark W. and Lura (Oliver) Lee; married Fern Erway, 1943; children: Sharon Anne, Mark, Jr., David, Rachel Jody. *Education:* Attended Nyack College, 1940-43; Wheaton College, B.A., 1946, M.A., 1952; University of Minnesota, graduate study, 1950-56; University of Washington, Ph.D., 1966. *Home:* 881 Silver Ave., San Francisco, Calif. 94134. *Office:* Simpson College, 801 Silver Ave., San Francisco, Calif. 94134.

CAREER: Northwestern College, Minneapolis, Minn., associate professor of speech and drama and chairman of the department, 1948-57; Whitworth College, Spokane, Wash., associate professor, 1957-66, professor of speech and drama, 1967-70, chairman of the department, 1964-70, acting dean of faculty, 1969-70; Simpson College, San Francisco, Calif., president, 1970—. Minister in several churches, 1943—. Public speaker at local, state, and national conventions. Member, Office of Emergency Preparedness. Consultant, Standard Oil of California, credit union leagues, churches, Washington State Board of Health, and Civil Service Commission and Veteran's Administration, 1960—. *Member:* Speech Communication Association of America, American Forensic Association, American Association of Presidents of Universities, Western Speech Association, Pi Kappa Delta (province secretary-treasurer, 1960-62; governor, 1964-66).

WRITINGS: So You Want to Speak: Hints and Helps for Public Speakers, Zondervan, 1951; *The Minister and His Ministry,* Zondervan, 1960; *Our Children Are Our Best Friends: Marriage Is a Family Affair,* Zondervan, 1970; *Creative Christian Marriage,* Regal, 1977; *How to Set Goals and Really Reach Them,* Horizon, 1978; *How to Have a Good Christian Marriage,* Christian Herald, 1978. Editor, *Journal* of the Washington State Speech Association, 1965-66.

WORK IN PROGRESS: A book on counseling.

*   *   *

LEE, Peter H(acksoo)   1929-

PERSONAL: Born January 24, 1929, in Seoul, Korea; son of Chong-guk (an educator and publisher) and Insuk (Hwangbo) Lee; married Catherine Y. Lee, August 25, 1962; children: Caroline, Joseph. *Education:* College St. Thomas, St. Paul, Minn., B.A., 1951; Yale University, M.A., 1953;

University of Munich, Ph.D., 1958. Further study at University of Fribourg (Switzerland), 1954-55, Universities of Milan, Florence, Perugia, 1955-56, Oxford University, 1959. *Office:* Department of East Asian Literature, University of Hawaii, Honolulu, Hawaii 96822.

CAREER: Columbia University, New York, N.Y., assistant professor of Korean and Japanese, 1960-62; University of Hawaii, Honolulu, associate professor, 1962-70, professor of Korean and comparative literature, 1970—. *Member:* Association for Asian Studies, American Oriental Society, American Comparative Literature Association, Chindan Society (Seoul, Korea). *Awards, honors:* Fellowships from American Council of Learned Societies, Bollingen Foundation, Alexander von Humboldt-Stifung, and Guggenheim Foundation.

WRITINGS: Studien zum Saenaennorae: Altkoreanische Dichtung (doctoral dissertation), University of Munich, 1958, enlarged edition published as *Studies in the Saenaennorae: Old Korean Poetry,* Paragon, 1959; (compiler and translator) *Kranich am Meer: Koreanische Gedichte,* Carl Hanser, 1959; *Korean Literary Biographies,* American Council of Learned Societies, 1962; (compiler and translator) *Anthology of Korean Poetry, from the Earliest Era to the Present,* John Day, 1964; *Korean Literature Topics and Themes,* published for Association for Asian Studies by University of Arizona Press, 1965; (compiler and translator) *Lives of Eminent Korean Monks: The Haedong Kosung Chon,* Harvard University Press, 1969; *Flowers of Fire: Twentieth-Century Korean Stories,* University Press of Hawaii, 1974; *Songs of Flying Dragons: A Critical Reading,* Harvard University Press, 1975; *Celebration of Continuity: Themes in Classic East Asian Poetry,* Harvard University Press, 1979; *The Silence of Love: Twentieth-Century Korean Poetry,* University Press of Hawaii, 1980. Contributor to *Dictionary of Oriental Literatures, Encyclopaedia Britannica,* and to journals, including *Hudson Review, Poetry, T'oung Pao, Oriens Extremus, Monumenta Serica, Journal of the American Oriental Society, Harvard Journal of Asiatic Studies,* and *World Literature Today.*

WORK IN PROGRESS: The Rise of Korean Prose Narrative.

SIDELIGHTS: Peter H. Lee told *CA* that it was about him that the late poet Wallace Stevens wrote: "Last week I received a letter, greetings on my seventy-fifth birthday, from a young scholar, a Korean. When he was at New Haven, he used to come up to Hartford and the two of us would go out to Elizabeth Park, in Hartford, and sit on a bench by the pond and talk about poetry. He did not wait for the ducks to bring him ideas but always had in mind questions that disclosed his familiarity with the experience of poetry. He spoke in the most natural English. He is now studying in Switzerland at Fribourg, from where his letter came. It was written in what appeared to be the most natural French. Apparently they prize all-round young men in Korea, too."

Lee is deeply interested in the comparative study of Far Eastern and Western poetry and literary criticism. He is fluent in Chinese, Japanese, Korean, English, German, French, and Italian and can read Spanish and Latin.

BIOGRAPHICAL/CRITICAL SOURCES: Wallace Stevens, *Opus Posthumous,* Knopf, 1957.

*   *   *

LEE, Robert   1929-

PERSONAL: Born April 28, 1929, in San Francisco, Calif.;

son of Frank and Shee (Fong) Lee; married May Gong, February 4, 1951; children: Mellanie, Marcus, Matthew, Wendy, Michelle. *Education:* University of California, Berkeley, A.B., 1951; Pacific School of Religion, M.A., 1953; Union Theological Seminary (New York, N.Y.), B.D., 1954; Columbia University, Ph.D., 1958. *Politics:* Democrat. *Religion:* Presbyterian. *Home:* 18 Kensington Court, San Anselmo, Calif. 94960. *Office:* San Francisco Theological Seminary, 2 Kensington, San Anselmo, Calif. 94960.

CAREER: Lecturer in philosophy, Mills College of Education, 1955-57; Union Theological Seminary, New York, N.Y., assistant professor, 1956-61; San Francisco Theological Seminary, San Francisco, Calif., Margaret Dollar Professor of Social Ethics, 1961—; Graduate Theological Union, Berkeley, Calif., professor of religion and society, 1961—. Visiting professor, International Christian University, Tokyo, 1964-65, University of Hong Kong, 1966; senior fellow, East-West Center, Honolulu, Hawaii, 1972-73; theologian-in-residence, Windward Coalition of Churches, Kailua, Hawaii, 1980. Member of board of directors, Marin Family Service Agency, ISI Trust Fund, ISI Growth Fund, and ISI Income Fund; trustee, Association of South East Asian Seminaries, Singapore; director, Pacific Southwest Student Young Men's Christian Association, Festival Theatre Association, Chinese for Affirmative Action, and Asian Center for Theology and Strategy. *Member:* American Sociological Association, Religious Research Association, American Society of Christian Social Ethics, Society for Scientific Study of Religion, Pacific Sociological Association, Society for Religion in Higher Education. *Awards, honors:* Social Sources of Church Unity selected for Kennedy White House Library; *Religion and Leisure in America* nominated for Best Book of Year Award.

WRITINGS: Social Sources of Church Unity, Abingdon, 1960; (contributor) *Church and the Changing Ministry,* Westminster, 1961; (contributor) *Ethics and Bigness,* Harper, 1962; (editor) *Cities and Churches,* Westminster, 1962; (contributor) *Challenge to Reunion,* McGraw, 1963; (contributor) *The Dilemma of Organizational Society,* Dutton, 1963; *Religion and Leisure in America,* Abingdon, 1964; (with Martin E. Marty) *Religion and Social Conflict,* Oxford University Press, 1964; (contributor) *Evangelism and Social Issues,* Tidings Press, 1964; *The Church and the Exploding Metropolis,* John Knox, 1965; *Inventory of Centers for the Study of Society,* Towne House, 1965; *Stranger in the Land,* Lutterworth, 1966, Friendship Press, 1967; *The Promise of Bennett,* Lippincott, 1969; *The Schizophrenic Church,* Westminster, 1969; *The Spouse Gap,* Abingdon, 1971; *Faith and the Prospects of Economic Collapse,* John Knox Press, 1980; *China Journal: Glimpses of a Nation in Transition,* East-West Publishing, 1980. Editorial consultant, *Dictionary of Christian Ethics;* member of editorial staff, *Masterpieces of Christian Literature;* editor, *Pacific Theological Review.*

*   *   *

LEE, Robert Greene   1886-19(?)

PERSONAL: Born November 11, 1886, in Fort Mill, S.C.; deceased; son of David Ayers and Sarah (Bennett) Lee; married Beulah Gentry, 1913; children: Bula G. Lee King, Roy DeMent. *Education:* Furman University, A.B., 1913; Chicago Law School, Ph.D., 1919. *Religion:* Baptist.

CAREER: Ordained Baptist minister, 1910. Pastor of nine churches in South Carolina, 1909-18; full-time pastorate at Baptist churches in Edgefield, S.C., 1918-20, Chester, S.C., 1921-22, New Orleans, La., 1922-25, and Charleston, S.C.,

1925-27; Bellevue Baptist Church, Memphis, Tenn., pastor, 1927-60, pastor emeritus, beginning 1960. *Awards, honors:* D.D. from Union University, 1929, Furman University, 1937, and Stetson University, 1948; LL.D., from Union University, 1934, Baylor University, 1954, and Howard Payne College, 1956; Litt.D. from Bob Jones University, 1938, and Houghton College, 1952; decreed honorary colonel on the staff of the governor of Louisiana, 1945, the governor of South Carolina, 1947, and the governor of Kentucky, 1962.

WRITINGS—All published by Baptist Sunday School Board, except as indicated: *From Feet to Fathoms,* 1926, reprinted, Zondervan, 1946; *Lord, I Believe,* 1927; *Beds of Pearls,* 1930; *Whirlwinds of God,* 1932; *A Greater Than Solomon,* 1935; *Lee Lines,* 1937; *Pulpit Pleadings,* 1948; *The Sinner's Saviour,* 1950; *The Bible and Prayer,* 1950.

All published by Zondervan, except as indicated: *Pickings,* 1938; *Proximities of Calvary,* 1940; *Glory Today for Conquest Tomorrow,* 1941; *This Critical Hour,* 1942; *Be Ye Also Ready,* 1944; *Rose of Sharon,* 1947; *For the Time of Tears,* 1949; *Yielded Bodies,* 1954; *Modern Illustrations for Public Speakers,* 1955; *Bible Fires,* 1956; *Bought by the Blood,* 1957; *Seven Swords and Other Sermons,* 1958; *A Charge to Keep,* 1959; *Choice Pickings,* 1961; *Salvation in Christ,* 1961; *Quotable Illustrations,* 1961; *God's Answer to Man's Question,* 1962; *Christ above All* (sermons), 1963; *Robert G. Lee's Sourcebook of 500 Illustrations,* 1964; *From Death to Life through Christ* (sermons), 1966; *The Saviour's Seven Statements from the Cross,* 1968; *By Christ Compelled* (sermons), 1969.

Grand Canyon of Resurrection Realities, Eerdmans, 1937, published as *The Wonderful Saviour,* Zondervan, 1965; *The Name Above Every Name,* Revell, 1938; *Bread from Bellevue Oven,* Sword of the Lord, 1947; *Great Is the Lord,* Revell, 1955; *The MUST of the Second Birth,* Revell, 1959; *The Place Called Heaven,* Golden Rule Press, 1959; *If I Were a Jew,* Pepper Publishing, 1960; *The Top Ten of Robert G. Lee* (sermons), Baker Book, 1971; *Talks on Miracles of the Bible,* Baker Book, 1973; *Latest of Lee* (sermons) LeRoi Publishers, 1973; *Payday Everyday,* Broadman, 1974; *Grapes from Gospel Vines* (sermons), Broadman, 1976; *Heart to Heart Messages that Warm the Heart and Exalt the Savior,* Broadman, 1977. Also author of many pamphlets. Contributor to many magazines.†

*   *   *

LEFF, Gordon   1926-

PERSONAL: Born May 9, 1926, in London, England; son of Solomon Elvin (a former company director) and Eva (Gordon) Leff; married Rosemary Kathleen Fox (divorced, 1980); children: Gregory Paul. *Education:* King's College, Cambridge, B.A. (honors), 1951, Ph.D., 1954. *Politics:* None. *Religion:* Agnostic. *Home:* The Sycamores, 12, The Village, Strensall, York Y03 8XS, North Yorkshire, England. *Office:* Department of History, University of York, Hestington, York Y01 500, Yorkshire, England.

CAREER: University of Manchester, Manchester, England, senior lecturer in history, 1956-65; University of York, York, England, reader, 1965-69, professor of history, 1969—. Fellow, King's College, Cambridge University, 1955-59. *Military service:* Royal Artillery, 1945-48; served in India.

WRITINGS: Bradwardine and the Pelagians: A Study of His "De Causa Dei" and Its Opponents, Cambridge University Press, 1957; *Medieval Thought: St. Augustine to Ockham,*

Penguin, 1958; *Gregory of Rimini: Tradition and Innovation in Fourteenth Century Thought*, Barnes & Noble, 1961; *The Tyranny of Concepts: A Critique of Marxism*, Merlin Press, 1961, Dufour, 1963, 2nd edition, University of Alabama Press, 1969; *Richard FitzRalph: Commentator of the Sentences*, Barnes & Noble, 1964; *John Wyclif: The Path to Dissent*, Oxford University Press, 1966; *Heresy in the Middle Ages: The Relation of Heterodoxy to Dissent, c.1250-c.1450*, two volumes, Barnes & Noble, 1967; *Paris and Oxford Universities in the Thirteenth and Fourteenth Centuries: An Institutional and Intellectual History*, Wiley, 1968; *History and Social Theory*, University of Alabama Press, 1969; *William of Ockham: The Metamorphosis of Scholastic Discourse*, Manchester University Press, 1975; *The Dissolution of the Medieval Outlook*, Harper, 1976; *The Concept of Man in the Middle Ages*, Manchester University Press, in press. Contributor of articles to learned journals, and of reviews to *Guardian*, *Spectator*, *Times Literary Supplement*, and *New Statesman*.

AVOCATIONAL INTERESTS: Gardening, watching cricket, walking, reading, and listening to music.

BIOGRAPHICAL/CRITICAL SOURCES: Times Literary Supplement, January 25, 1968, August 29, 1969; *New York Times Book Review*, April 21, 1968; *Virginia Quarterly Review*, autumn, 1968.

*   *   *

LEITH, John H.   1919-

PERSONAL: Born September 10, 1919, in Due West, S.C.; son of William H. (a farmer) and Lucy (Haddon) Leith; married Ann White, September 2, 1943; children: Henry White, Caroline Haddon. *Education:* Erskine College, A.B., 1940; Columbia Theological Seminary, B.D., 1943; Vanderbilt University, M.A., 1946; Yale University, Ph.D., 1949. *Politics:* Democrat. *Home:* 1230 Rennie Ave., Richmond, Va. *Office:* Union Theological Seminary, 3401 Brook Rd., Richmond, Va.

CAREER: Presbyterian minister, Nashville, Tenn., 1944-46, and Auburn, Ala., 1948-59; Auburn University, Auburn, lecturer in religion, 1949-58; Columbia Theological Seminary, Atlanta, Ga., visiting professor, 1955-57; Union Theological Seminary, Richmond, Va., professor of historical theology, 1959—. *Awards, honors:* D.D., Erskine College, 1972, Davidson College, 1978.

WRITINGS: (Contributor) *Reformations Studies: Essays in Honor of Roland H. Bainton*, John Knox, 1962; (editor) *Creeds of Churches*, Doubleday, 1963; *The Church: This Believing Fellowship*, John Knox, 1965, revised edition, 1980; (contributor) *Marburg Revisited*, Augsburg, 1966; (contributor) J. McDowell Richards, editor, *Soli Deo Gloria*, John Knox, 1968; (contributor) Allen O. Miller, editor, *Reconciliation in Today's World*, Eerdmans, 1969; *Assembly at Westminster*, John Knox, 1973; *Introduction to the Reformed Tradition*, John Knox, 1977. Also author of *Greenville Church: The Story of a People 1765-1973*, 1973.

*   *   *

L'ENGLE, Madeleine   1918-

PERSONAL: Name originally Madeleine L'Engle Camp; born November 29, 1918, in New York, N.Y.; daughter of Charles Wadsworth (a foreign correspondent and author) and Madeleine (a pianist; maiden name, Barnett) Camp; married Hugh Franklin (an actor), January 26, 1946; children: Josephine (Mrs. Alan W. Jones), Maria (Mrs. Laurie Franklin), Bion. *Education:* Smith College, A.B. (honors), 1941; Columbia University, graduate study. *Politics:* "New England." *Religion:* Anglican. *Home:* 924 West End Ave., New York, N.Y.; and Crosswicks, Goshen, Conn. 06707.

CAREER: Active career in theater, 1941-47; teacher, Committee for Refugee Education, World War II; currently teaching at St. Hilda's and St. Hugh's School, Morningside Heights, N.Y. Lecturer. *Member:* Authors Guild (vice-president), Authors League, P.E.N. *Awards, honors:* John Newbery Medal, 1963, Hans Christian Andersen Runner-up Award, 1964, Sequoyah Award, 1965, and Lewis Carroll Shelf, 1965, all for *A Wrinkle in Time;* Austrian State Literary Prize, 1969, for *The Moon by Night;* University of Southern Mississippi Medal, 1978; American Book Award, 1980, for *A Swiftly Tilting Planet.*

WRITINGS—All published by Farrar, Straus, except as indicated: *18 Washington Square, South* (one-act play), Baker's Plays, 1945; *The Small Rain*, Vanguard, 1945, published as *Prelude*, 1968; *Ilsa*, Vanguard, 1946; *And Both Were Young*, Lothrop, 1949; *Camilla Dickinson*, Simon & Schuster, 1951, published as *Camilla*, Crowell, 1965; *A Winter's Love*, Lippincott, 1957; *Meet the Austins*, Vanguard, 1960; *A Wrinkle in Time*, 1962; *The Moon by Night*, 1963; *The Twenty-Four Days before Christmas*, 1964; *The Arm of the Starfish*, 1965; *The Love Letters*, 1966; *The Journey with Jonah* (play), 1967; *The Young Unicorns*, 1968; *Dance in the Desert*, 1969; *Lines Scribbled on an Envelope, and Other Poems*, 1969; *The Other Side of the Sun*, 1971; *A Circle of Quiet*, 1972; *A Wind in the Door*, 1973; *The Summer of the Great-Grandmother*, 1974; *Prayers for Sunday*, Morehouse, 1974; *Everyday Prayers*, Morehouse, 1974; *Dragons in the Waters*, 1976; (editor with William B. Green) *Spirit and Light: Essays in Historical Theology*, Seabury, 1976; *The Irrational Season*, Seabury, 1977; *A Swiftly Tilting Planet*, 1978; *The Weather of the Heart*, Shaw, 1978; *Ladder of Angels*, Seabury, 1979; *A Ring of Endless Light*, 1980. Contributor of stories and poems to magazines.

WORK IN PROGRESS: Walking on Water; a novel, *A Severed Wasp.*

SIDELIGHTS: Mary Brinkerhoff has said that Madeleine L'Engle writes "both for children and precocious grown-ups," and that L'Engle deplores "'the tacit assumption that you only write for children if you can't quite make it for adults.'" On the contrary; L'Engle finds "'a child is open to new ideas,' while adults concerned over rent and grocery bills 'are nervous over about anything that might shake the status quo.'"

L'Engle told *CA:* "I never write for children and I don't believe that the 'true' children's writers do. I write for myself, and I am a grownup. To write for children almost always involves writing down to the children, or, just as bad, writing down to your own talent. The techniques of fiction are identical, whether one is writing for adults or children, and I take no whit less care in the novels which are going to be published for children than I do in those which are going to be published for adults."

John Rowe finds her "a curiously-gifted, curiously-learned, curiously-imperfect writer. Her novels for young people seem . . . full of contradictions. They are so often exciting and stylishly written, yet so often complicated beyond endurance or unintentionally comic or embarrassing. . . . And yet I find her an extraordinarily interesting writer. . . . [Her books are] faulty but intriguing, irritating but likeable, unsatisfactory in various ways but stimulating to the mind and the emotions."

Some critics have drawn similarities between L'Engle's Newbery award-winning book, *A Wrinkle in Time,* and books by C. S. Lewis. Such stories, notes Ellen Lewis Buell, "are not for the casual or strictly realistic reader. Imaginative readers with a taste for speculation, a feeling for intricate symbolism, should find it wholly absorbing—for in her highly accelerated spin through space, L'Engle never loses sight of human needs and emotions." The sequel, *A Wind in the Door,* is less effective as noted by Anita Silvey, who writes, "She has forsaken the fantasy to write about her philosophy, and the story . . . lacks the consistency and the believable motivation needed to keep fiction from becoming dogma."

"Few writers are more able to combine the cosmic with the comic," writes Sarah Hayes, "and no one can match L'Engle's treatment of the powers of darkness." Nevertheless, "[L'Engle's] virtues have in the end become her faults: Her wild imagination has overreached itself; her sensuous prose has become purple, and the family life she describes so well suddenly seems rather silly."

The themes of right vs. wrong and good vs. evil—and other matters of conscience—create a bond of continuity among Madeleine L'Engle's books that is often accompanied by suspense. These characteristics frequently compensate for a particular book's shortcomings, for, as Ruth Hill Viguers writes of *The Arm of the Starfish:* "The plot . . . moves with such speed and variety, and emotions are so tautly stretched, that if there are weaknesses, the reader is much too occupied to be aware of them. . . . The story lasts beyond the reading."

"I believe that young readers will let L'Engle know that they are grateful for her having written [*The Young Unicorns*]," affirms Maia Wojciechowska. "What 'critics' will say could hardly matter in her case. . . . Children read her with joy. And the rest of us authors can only wish for the same luck."

Madeleine L'Engle's work has often been received enthusiastically, but with reservations. Of *Dance in the Desert,* one reviewer writes: "The text has a gentle charm, although I could wish that it had been written in the form of a ballad. Verse convinces where prose has a tendency merely to assert." Another writes: "This is truly an exquisite book! Story and words combine to create a mood that is wonderful, exotic, and magical, . . . [one] which is memorable. . . . The writing is tender, exciting, and dramatically moving. . . . Every child should have the opportunity to experience its strange beauty. . . . It's a book of haunting joy and wonder, and may be interpreted in a dozen different ways."

Similarly, Houston Maples calls *The Journey with Jonah* "flawless in construction . . . its freshness and sparkle are irresistible. . . . The beasts are winningly and consistently in character . . . while Jonah is properly irascible and preoccupied as he ponders the frustrating paradox of God's wrath and God's compassion."

L'Engle's largely autobiographical poetry and nonfiction attempt to tell of "the joys and conflicts in being a writer, wife, mother, and struggling human being in these late years of the twentieth century." Polly Longworth comments in her review of *A Circle of Quiet,* "Getting to the core of herself has required admirable honesty, but [the author] has let her artistic self down in the process." Others are disappointed in the outcome of these attempts as well, finding the lushness and intensity of her fiction lacking. Even so, it can be said, as it was of the poems in *Lines Scribbled on an Envelope,* that "they have wry humor, wide understanding, and imagination. Most of all, they have the emotion of a poet's very

personal expression of joy and pain, of facing the inevitable, and discovery that rebellion is not enough."

The film rights to *A Wrinkle in Time* were sold to T.A.T. in 1979.

AVOCATIONAL INTERESTS: Music, the theatre, people, and travel.

BIOGRAPHICAL/CRITICAL SOURCES: New York Times Book Review, March 18, 1962, May 26, 1968, August 10, 1969, February 13, 1972; *Horn Book,* April, 1965, December, 1969, August, 1973; *Book World,* November 5, 1967; *Young Reader's Review,* May, 1969; *Times Literary Supplement,* October 16, 1969, April 4, 1975; *Atlantic,* December, 1969; John Rowe Townsend, *A Sense of Story: Essays on Contemporary Writing for Children,* Lippincott, 1971; *Best Sellers,* April 1, 1971; *Detroit News,* March 19, 1972; *Dallas News,* April 1, 1976; *Authors in the News,* Volume II, Gale, 1976; *Children's Literature Review,* Volume I, Gale, 1976; *New York Times,* November 6, 1979; *Contemporary Literary Criticism,* Volume XII, Gale, 1980; *Los Angeles Times,* May 6, 1980; *Washington Post Book World,* May 11, 1980.

—*Sketch by Penelope S. Gordon*

*   *   *

LENGYEL, Emil 1895-

PERSONAL: Born April 26, 1895, in Budapest, Hungary; came to United States, 1921; naturalized, 1927; son of Joseph (a tradesman) and Johanna (Adam) Lengyel; married· Livia Delej, July 17, 1938; children: Peter. *Education:* Royal Hungarian University, Utriusque Juris Doctor, 1919. *Home:* 239 East 79th St., New York, N.Y. 10021. *Agent:* Bertha Klausner International Literary Agency, 71 Park Ave., New York, N.Y. 10022.

CAREER: Journalist in Vienna, Austria, 1920-21; American correspondent for European newspapers, 1922-30; Brooklyn Polytechnic Institute, Brooklyn, N.Y., adjunct professor of history and economics, 1935-42; New York University, New York City, staff lecturer, 1939-43, assistant professor, 1943-47, associate professor, 1947-51, professor of history, 1951-60, professor emeritus, 1960—; Fairleigh Dickinson University, Rutherford, N.J., professor of history, 1960-75, chairman of social science department, 1963-72, adjunct professor of history, 1972-75; Marymount Manhattan College, New York City, adjunct professor, 1976—. Lecturer, New School for Social Research, New York City, 1950-55. Lecturer to U.S. Armed Forces in World War II; public lecturer throughout America, 1932—. New York State Department of Education, consultant on Middle Eastern subjects. *Military service:* Austro-Hungarian Army, World War I; prisoner of war in Sibera, almost two years. *Member:* American Academy of Political and Social Science, American Historical Association, American-European Friendship Association (president, 1956-62, president emeritus, 1962—), American Association for Middle East Studies, American Association of University Professors, P.E.N., Overseas Press Club, Columbia University Seminar on Pre-Industrial Areas, Mongolian Society. *Awards, honors:* Citation by American-European Friendship Association for distinguished service.

WRITINGS: Cattle Car Express: A Prisoner of War in Siberia, Strassburger Foundation, 1931; *Hitler,* Dial, 1932; *The Cauldron Boils,* Dial, 1932; *The New Deal in Europe,* Funk, 1934; *Millions of Dictators: A Study of Public Opinion,* Funk, 1936; *The Danube,* Random House, 1939; *Turkey,* Random House, 1941; *Dakar: Outpost of Two Hemispheres,* Random House, 1941; *Siberia* (Science Book Club selection), Random House, 1943, revised edition published in England as *Secret Siberia*, R. Hale, 1947; *America's Role in World Affairs*, Harper, 1946, revised and enlarged edition, 1950; *Americans from Hungary*, Lippincott, 1948; *World without End: The Middle East*, John Day, 1953; *Egypt's Role in World Affairs*, Public Affairs Press, 1957; *1000 Years of Hungary*, John Day, 1958.

The Changing Middle East, John Day, 1960; *The Subcontinent of India: An Introduction to the History, Geography, Culture, Politics, and Contemporary Life of India, Pakistan, and Ceylon*, Scholastic Book Services, 1961; *They Called Him Ataturk*, John Day, 1962; *Krishna Menon*, Walker & Co., 1962; *From Prison to Power*, Follett, 1964; *The Land and People of Hungary*, Lippincott, 1965, revised edition, 1972; *Mahatma Gandhi, the Great Soul*, F. Watts, 1966; *Jawaharlal Nehru, the Brahman from Kashmir*, F. Watts, 1968; *Lajos Kossuth, Hungary's Great Patriot*, F. Watts, 1969; *Asoka the Great, India's Royal Missionary*, F. Watts, 1969; *Nationalism: The Last Stage of Communism*, Funk, 1969; *First Book of Turkey*, F. Watts, 1970; *Ignace Paderewski: Musician and Statesman*, F. Watts, 1970; *Pakistan: A First Book*, F. Watts, 1971, new edition, 1972; *Iran: A First Book*, F. Watts, 1972, revised edition, 1979; *Modern Egypt*, F. Watts, 1973; *And All Her Paths Were Peace: The Life of Bertha von Suttner*, Thomas Nelson, 1975.

Foreign Policy Association "Headline Series" publications: (With Joseph C. Harsch) *Eastern Europe Today* [and] *American Policy in Eastern Europe* (the former by Lengyel, the latter by Harsch), 1949; (with Ernest O. Melby) *Israel: Problems of Nation-Building* [and] *Israel: Laboratory of Human Relations* (the former by Lengyel, the latter by Melby), 1951, 2nd edition, 1952; (with Melby) *The Middle East Today*, 1954; (co-author) *Great Decisions*, 1959.

Oxford Book Co. social studies pamphlets: *The Soviet Union: The Land and Its People*, 1951, revised edition, including developments since death of Stalin, 1954, 5th edition, 1962; *The Middle East*, 1951, revised and enlarged edition published as *The Changing Middle East* (not the same as the John Day publication), 1958; *Africa in Ferment*, 1959, revised edition, 1962; *Africa, Past, Present, and Future*, 1966, revised edition, 1967.

Co-author or contributor: *Nazism: An Assault on Civilization*, 1934; *Eye Witness*, Alliance, 1940; *As We See Russia*, published for Overseas Press Club by Dutton, 1948; Arthur Bernard Moehlman and J. S. Roucek, editors, *Comparative Education*, Dryden Press, 1951; Francis James Brown and J. S. Roucek, editors, *One American: The History, Contributions, and Present Problems of Our Racial and National Minorities*, 3rd edition, Prentice-Hall, 1952; (with Thorsten V. Kalijarni and others) *Modern World Politics*, 3rd edition, Crowell, 1953; Charles Angoff, editor, *The Humanities in the Age of Science: In Honor of Peter Sammartino*, Fairleigh Dickinson University Press, 1968. Author of screenplay, "The World in Revolt," produced by 20th Century-Fox in German, and Hungarian, including works of Ferenc Molnar, Erno Szep, Zsigmond Moricz, Sandor Kemeri. Special correspondent and book reviewer for *New York Times*, 1936-46; correspondent of *Toronto Star Weekly*, 1946-56; book reviewer for *Saturday Review;* contributor of articles to *Reporter, Mankind, Asian Student, Annals of the American Academy of Political and Social Science, New York Times Magazine*, and other periodicals.

SIDELIGHTS: Emil Lengyel told *CA:* "[Although] I was writing from my earliest Gymnasium (classical secondary school) days in Budapest, I was 'swept' into writing by my

experience as a prisoner-of-war-in Siberia for two years during World War I. I had been drafted for military service in the Austro-Hungarian army barely out of my teens. As a combatant in the trenches on the eastern front, facing Russians, I had a first-hand view of war and, later, of its consequences. Where it solved one problem it created many others while extinguishing millions of young lives. Then I was taken prisoner and shipped to Siberia. There I contracted a debilitating ailment which qualified me to be exchanged against a Russian prisoner-of-war in Austria-Hungary. As an exchange prisoner, I was dispatched home to Budapest to be with my family at my death, expected shortly. That was sixty-five years ago.

"I did recover, however, at home, and in due time I wrote my first book, a fictionalized account of my two years in Siberia. The book was published—*Cattle Car Express*. Some years later I wrote about my experiences on a larger canvas in my book *Siberia*. That book was published in many versions. While several other books of mine were published in foreign languages, this one had the largest number of translations.

"War for me was a traumatic experience. In nearly all my books, whatever the subject, I have tried to express the view that killing the other fellow across the trenches did not convince him or anyone else of the justice of the cause of the combatants. Some of my books deal with people of peace: Gandhi, Nehru, Asoka, and above all, Betha von Suttner, the first woman Nobel Peace Prize laureate, 1905. Even in books not dealing directly with peace and war, I introduced the subject, where pertinent.

"All my life as a writer and teacher I have been trying to convey the idea that peace comes to the world when people want it. The majority associates war with patriotism, not realizing that it is the opposite of it, bringing our civilizations to collapse by destroying their foundations, youth. While we are encouraged to 'pray for peace,' that's about as far as we go. To advocate it smells of 'subversion.' And our mentality about this problem has not changed even in the face of the threatened global disaster in the nuclear arms age. My contention is that we have no right to call ourselves civilized as long as we are killing the opponent in our final arguments. Indeed, the caveman was more civilized than we are; his slingshot killed one person, a bomb slaughters millions. No matter how unpopular this idea of 'civilization vs. arms race' is, I will keep on trying to employ my typewriter in books in this sense. Provided, of course, I find publishers to propagate this unpopular cause."

BIOGRAPHICAL/CRITICAL SOURCES: New York Times Book Review, March 26, 1967; *Saturday Review*, February 21, 1970.

*   *   *

LEONARD, George B(urr) 1923-

PERSONAL: Born August 9, 1923, in Macon, Ga.; son of George B. (an insurance executive) and Julia (Almand) Leonard; married Emma Jean Clifton, August 1, 1946 (divorced, September 29, 1957); married Lillie Steele Pitts, October 3, 1959 (divorced); children: (first marriage) Ellen, Mimi; (second marriage) Lillie, Jr., Emily. *Education:* Attended Georgia Institute of Technology, 1941-42; University of North Carolina, A.B., 1948. *Home and office address:* Box 509, Mill Valley, Calif. 94941.

CAREER: Look, New York, N.Y., senior editor, 1953-56, San Francisco, Calif., San Francisco editor and senior editor, 1956-62, West Coast editorial manager and senior editor,

1962-70. Member of advisory board, Esalen Institute, Big Sur, Calif. *Military service:* U.S. Army Air Forces, 1943-46, combat pilot in Southwest Pacific theater, 1945; received Air Medal, three battle stars, U.S. Air Force, 1950-53; served in Japan and as managing editor of *Air Training;* became captain. *Member:* Association for Humanistic Psychology (president, 1979-80). *Awards, honors:* Education Writers Association award for articles in *Look,* for three successive years, 1956-58; School Bell Awards for *Look* articles, 1960, 1962, 1964, 1965, 1966; L.H.D., Lewis and Clark College, 1972.

WRITINGS: (With William Attwood and J. Robert Moskin) *The Decline of the American Male,* Random House, 1958; *Shoulder the Sky,* McDowell, Obolensky, 1959; *Education and Ecstasy,* Delacorte, 1968; *The Man and Woman Thing, and Other Provocations,* Delacorte, 1970; *The Transformation: A Guide to the Inevitable Changes in Humankind,* Delacorte, 1972; *The Ultimate Athlete,* Viking, 1975; *The Silent Pulse,* Dutton, 1978.

SIDELIGHTS: George B. Leonard's books deal primarily with the changing aspects of modern life. *Christian Science Monitor's* Neil Millar notes that one of these books, *Education and Ecstasy,* "although ... misguided in parts, ... deals boldly, radically, imaginatively, [and] tenderly with a vital subject. It says magnificent things brilliantly. It also says doubtful things brilliantly, and in such brilliance the doubts loom clear and portentious.... He clearly suspects that 'for all practical purposes' the human spirit knows no walls. This suspicion, implicit in parts of his vivid book, may be its greatest strength." Similarly, Leonard's other books examine the changing relationships between men and women, people and sports, and "humankind" in general, suggesting changes in attitudes and approaches that emphasize emotional and intellectual development and greater human consciousness.

BIOGRAPHICAL/CRITICAL SOURCES: Christian Science Monitor, October 21, 1968; *Book World,* October 27, 1968, November 5, 1972; *National Review,* November 19, 1968; *Saturday Review,* December 21, 1968; *New York Times Book Review,* August 24, 1969; *Library Journal,* March 15, 1970; *New York Times,* August 12, 1975; *Los Angeles Times,* November 26, 1978; *San Francisco Chronicle,* December 24, 1978; *Chicago Tribune,* January 31, 1979.

*　　＊　　＊　　＊*

LEONHARDT, Rudolf Walter　1921-

PERSONAL: Born February 9, 1921, in Altenburg, Thuringia, Germany; son of Rudolf (a soldier) and Paula (Zeiger) Leonhardt; married Ulrike Zoerb (a teacher), June 18, 1949; children: Joachim Rudolf, Doerte Susanne, Timm Christopher. *Education:* Attended Universities of Leipzig, Bonn, London; Cambridge University, Dr. Phil., 1951. *Office: Die Zeit,* 1, Speersort, Hamburg 1, Germany.

CAREER: Cambridge University, Cambridge, England, lecturer in modern German literature, 1948-50; British Broadcasting Corporation, foreign correspondent, 1950-53; *Die Zeit,* Hamburg, Germany, cultural editor, 1955-73, editor-in-chief, 1973—. German correspondent of *The Guardian,* London.

WRITINGS: 77-mal England: Panorama einen Insel, Piper, 1957; *Der Suendenfall der deutschen Germanistik: Vorschlaege zur Wiederbelebung des literarischen Bewustseins in der Bundesrepublik,* Artemis, 1959; *Leben ohne Literatur?,* Keller, 1961; *X-mall, Deutschland,* Piper, 1961, 5th edition, 1962, abridged student edition, edited by Ottomar Rudolf, 1968, translation by Catherine Hutter published as *This*

Germany: The Story since the Third Reich, New York Graphic Society, 1964; *Zeitnotizen: Kritik, Polemik, Feuilleton,* Piper, 1963; *Junge deutsche Dichter fuer Anfaenger,* Diogenes, 1964; (with Marion Doenhoff and Theo Sommer) *Reise in ein fernes Land,* Wegner, 1964; (editor) Erich Kaestner, *Kaestner fuer Erwachsene,* S. Fischer, 1966; *Sylt fuer Anfaenger,* Diogenes, 1969; *Wer wirft den ersten Stein?,* Piper, 1969; *Haschisch-Report,* Piper, 1970; *Drei Wochen und drei Tage: Ein Europaer in Japan,* Hoffmann & Campe, 1970; *Deutschland,* Bucher, 1972; *Argumente pro und contra,* Piper, 1974; *Das Weib, das ich geliebet hab: Heines Maedchen und Frauen,* Hoffmann & Campe, 1975; *Journalismus und Wahrheit,* Reich, 1976. Also author of *Lieder aus dem Krieg,* 1979; and *Sylt 1870-1910,* 1980. Contributor to *Cassell's Encyclopaedia of World Literature,* 1954, and to newspapers, radio, and television in England, Germany, Austria, and Switzerland.

AVOCATIONAL INTERESTS: Sociology of art and literature, people, and "this Germany."

*　　＊　　＊　　＊*

LERNER, Laurence (David)　1925-

PERSONAL: Born December 12, 1925, in Cape Town, South Africa; son of Israel and May (Harrison) Lerner; married Natalie Winch (a teacher), June 15, 1948; children: David Nicholas, Edwin John, Martin Charles, Richard Israel. *Education:* University of Cape Town, M.A.; Pembroke College, Cambridge, B.A. *Home:* 50 Compton Ave., Brighton, Sussex BN1 3PS, England. *Office:* Department of English, University of Sussex, Falmer, Brighton, Sussex, England.

CAREER: Grammar school teacher in Cape Town, South Africa, 1946-47; University College of the Gold Coast (now University of Ghana), Legon, Ghana, lecturer in English, 1949-53; Queen's University of Belfast, Belfast, Northern Ireland, lecturer in English, 1953-62; University of Sussex, Brighton, Sussex, England, lecturer in English, 1962—. Visiting professor of English at Earlham College and University of Connecticut, 1960-61, University of Illinois, 1964, University of Dijon, 1967, and University of Munich, 1968-69 and 1974-75. *Member:* Association of University Teachers, Society of Authors.

WRITINGS: (Editor) John Milton, *Selected Poems,* Penguin, 1953; *English Literature: An Interpretation for Students Abroad,* Oxford University Press, 1954; *The Englishmen,* Hamish Hamilton, 1959; *Domestic Interior, and Other Poems,* Hutchinson, 1959; *The Truest Poetry: An Essay on the Question, What Is Literature?,* Hamish Hamilton, 1960, Horizon, 1964; *The Directions of Memory: Poems, 1958-1962,* Chatto & Windus, 1964; (editor) *Shakespeare's Tragedies: An Anthology of Modern Criticism,* Penguin, 1964; (editor with John Holmstrom) *George Eliot and Her Readers: A Selection of Contemporary Reviews,* Barnes & Noble, 1966; *The Truthtellers: Jane Austen, George Eliot, D. H. Lawrence,* Schocken, 1967; *A Free Man* (novel), Chatto & Windus, 1968; (editor with Holmstrom) *Thomas Hardy and His Readers: A Selection of Contemporary Reviews,* Barnes & Noble, 1968; *Selves* (poems), Routledge & Kegan Paul, 1969.

The Uses of Nostalgia: Studies in Pastoral, Chatto & Windus, 1972; *A.R.T.H.U.R.: The Life and Opinions of a Digital Computer,* Harvester Press, 1974; *An Introduction to English Poetry,* Edward Arnold, 1975; *Love and Marriage: Literature in Its Social Context,* Edward Arnold, 1979; *The Man I Killed* (poems), Secker & Warburg, 1980;

A.R.T.H.U.R. and M.A.R.T.H.A.: Or, the Love of the Computers, Secker & Warburg, 1980. Contributor of poems, reviews, and articles to periodicals, including *New States-man*, *Listener*, *Spectator*, *Times Literary Supplement*, *London Magazine*, *Critical Quarterly*, and *Encounter*.

SIDELIGHTS: Laurence Lerner told *CA:* "I belong to the now large class of academic poets. It's a good thing to be a poet, and a good thing to be a university teacher; it's the combination that's difficult. If you have a voice of your own, you ought to be able to keep it however academic the environment; if you lose it, the fault is likely to lie within, not in circumstances.

"I think poetry ought to be addressed to as wide an audience as is compatible with the poet's integrity; I think it ought to be as comprehensible as is compatible with absorbing the modernist revolution.

"I like travel, and have been to America and to a good lot of Europe as well as Africa; this is itself a subject for poetry, especially when one has four children, who restrict one and whom one loves."

* * *

LERNER, Sharon (Ruth) 1938-

PERSONAL: Born November 9, 1938, in Chicago, Ill.; daughter of Julius N. (a salesman) and Ethel Goldman; married Harry J. Lerner (a publisher), June 25, 1961; children: Adam, Mia, Daniel, Leah. *Education:* University of Minnesota, B.S., 1960. *Home:* 2215 North Willow Lane, Minneapolis, Minn. 55416.

CAREER: Public school art teacher in Minneapolis and White Bear, Minn., 1960-62; Lerner Publications Co., Minneapolis, Minn., art director, 1961—; president, Carolrhoda Books, 1965—; professional jeweler, 1972—. Book illustrator. Art educator and tour guide at Walker Art Center, 1963-65.

WRITINGS—All published by Lerner; author and illustrator, except as indicated: (Author only) *Places of Musical Fame*, 1962; *I Found a Leaf*, 1964; (author only) *The Self-Portrait in Art*, 1965; *I Picked a Flower*, 1966; *I Like Vegetables*, 1966; *Who Will Wake Up Spring?*, 1967; *Straight Is a Line*, 1970; *Orange Is a Color*, 1970; *Square Is a Shape*, 1970; (author only) *Making Jewelry*, 1976; (with Christopher Cerf; author only) *The Prisoner of Vega*, Random House, 1977.

Illustrator; all published by Lerner: Ruth Brin, *Interpretations*, 1965; *I Like Fruit*, 1969; Brin, *Butterflies Are Beautiful*, 1974; Cynthia Overbeck, *The Vegetable Book*, 1977; Overbeck, *The Butterfly Book*, 1977; Anne Orange, *The Flower Book*, 1978; Overbeck, *The Fruit Book*, 1978; Overbeck, *The Fish Book*, 1978; Orange, *The Leaf Book*, 1978.

AVOCATIONAL INTERESTS: Painting, cooking, hiking, biking, traveling, calligraphy.

* * *

Le ROI, David (de Roche) 1905-
(John Roche)

PERSONAL: Born January 28, 1905, in San Francisco, Calif.; son of John (an officer, Indian Army) and Kathleen (Salazar) Le Roi; married Maude Alice Fox, April 23, 1942; children: Jonathan. *Education:* Attended Herriot-Watt College, Edinburgh, Scotland, Church of England Grammar School, Sydney, Australia, and University of Sydney. *Politics:* Conservative Unionist. *Religion:* Church of England.

Home: 12 Kirklees Rd., Thornton Heath, Surrey, England. *Agent:* Richmond Towers & Benson Ltd., 14 Essex St., Strand, London W.C.2, England.

CAREER: Daily Guardian, Sydney, New South Wales, Australia, subeditor, 1923-26; *Daily Chronicle*, London, England, reporter, 1927-28; free-lance correspondent for Australian newspapers, 1929-31; free-lance feature writer for English newspapers, 1932-36; Waverly Educational Book Co., London, assistant technical editor, 1937-39; Fleetway Publications Ltd., London, technical editor in encyclopedia department, 1945-61; science and technical editor, *Look and Learn*, 1961-64. Consultant editor on food technology, processing, and laboratory control, George Newnes Ltd. (publisher), 1954. *Military service:* Royal Air Force, 1939-45. *Member:* International Institute of Arts and Letters (fellow), Institute of Journalists, Society of Authors, National Union of Journalists (life member).

WRITINGS: The Boys' Book of Jets, Thames & Hudson, 1953; *Eagle Book of Modern Wonders*, Hulton Press, 1954; *Invention and Discovery*, Hamish Hamilton, 1955; *Answers to a Thousand Questions*, Hulton Press, 1955; *The Aquarium*, Soccer, 1955; *Hamsters and Guinea Pigs*, Vane, 1955, 2nd edition, 1963; *Pigeons, Doves, and Pigeon-Racing*, Soccer, 1957; *The Scottie Book of Inventions*, Transworld, 1957; *The Boys' Book of Flight*, Iliffe, 1957; *Town Dogs*, Soccer, 1957; *Tortoises, Lizards and Other Reptiles*, Soccer, 1958; *Budgerigars, Canaries and Other Cage Birds*, Soccer, 1958; *Aeronautics*, Educational Book Co., 1958; *All about Radar, Radio and Television*, Wheaton & Co., 1959; *All about Nuclear Power*, Wheaton & Co., 1959; *All about Jet-Propulsion and Rocket Power*, Wheaton & Co., 1959.

Things to Make and Do, Educational Book Co., 1960; *Look at Roads*, Hamish Hamilton, 1960; *Modern Medicine*, Wheaton & Co., 1960; *Modern Agriculture*, Wheaton & Co., 1960; *Man-Made Materials*, Wheaton & Co., 1960; *How We Get and Use Oil*, Routledge & Kegan Paul, 1962; *Land, Sea and Air Weapons*, Educational Book Co., 1962; *Cats*, Vane, 1963; *Aluminum*, Muller, 1964; *Science Today and Tomorrow*, New English Library, 1964; *Towards the Twenty-First Century*, New English Library, 1964; *All about Plastics*, Muller, c.1966; *How Railways Work*, Routledge & Kegan Paul, c.1966; *The Channel Tunnel*, Clifton Books, 1969.

Oceanography, Machinery Publishing Co., 1971; *In the Days of the Dinosaurs*, Idea Books, 1972; *The Physical Sciences: (Mind Alive)*, Marshall Cavendish, 1972; *Prehistoric Life*, Purnell, 1973; *Stars and Planets*, Purnell, 1974; *Rabbits*, Kaye & Ward, 1974; *Rats and Mice*, Kaye & Ward, 1976; *Ponies and Donkeys*, Kaye & Ward, 1976; *Goats*, Kaye & Ward, 1978; *Chickens*, Kaye & Ward, 1980.

Technical editor of *New Universal Encyclopedia*, *Book of Knowledge*, *Children's Encyclopedia*, and *Practical Knowledge for All;* executive editor of *The World of Wonder* and *Outline of Nature*. Contributor of articles on popular science, natural history, biography, and history to some fifty magazines and newspapers in Great Britain, many of the articles syndicated by Express Features and P.A.-Reuter Features. Writer of film and television scripts.

* * *

LeROY, Douglas 1943-

PERSONAL: Born October 27, 1943, in Liberty, S.C.; son of John Thaddeus (in textiles) and Ida (Sluder) LeRoy; married Wanda Thompson, August 31, 1963; children: Dina Kay, Donald Todd, Dara Rae. *Education:* Lee College, Cleveland, Tenn. B.A., 1965. *Politics:* Republican. *Home:*

318 Bahamas Ave., Tampa, Fla. 33617. *Office:* 5606 Nebraska Ave., Tampa, Fla. 33604.

CAREER: Ordained minister of the Church of God; pastor in Fargo, N.D., 1965-66; Northwest Bible College, Minot, N.D., instructor in religion, 1966-68; Church of God, Oklahoma City, Okla., youth and Christian education director, 1968-72; Church of God Publishing House, Cleveland, Tenn., administrative assistant to editor-in-chief and managing editor, *Evangel,* 1972-75; pastor in Louisville, Ky., 1975-78; Church of God, Tampa, Fla., youth and Christian education director, 1978—. Member of executive committee of Cleveland (Tenn.) Community Service Agency, 1974-76. *Member:* International Pentecostal Press Association, International Christian Camping, International Platform Association, Evangelical Press Association, National Fellowship of Christian Educators, Smithsonian Institution (associate), Upsilon Xi, Pi Delta Omicron. *Awards, honors:* Women's Christian Temperance Union Oratorical Award and American Legion Oratorical Award, both 1961; Balfour Award, 1965.

WRITINGS—All published by Pathway Press: *I Didn't Know That,* 1973; *Ministering to Youth,* 1973; *Sons and Daughters Shall Prophesy,* 1974; *We Believe,* 1975; *Basic Bible Study,* 1978. Writer of senior high Sunday School curriculum for Church of God, 1972—. Contributor to religious publications.

WORK IN PROGRESS: Biographies of the general overseers of the Church of God.

AVOCATIONAL INTERESTS: Reading, tennis, softball, football, photography.

*   *   *

LEVERTOV, Denise 1923-

PERSONAL: Born October 24, 1923, in Ilford, Essex, England; came to United States in 1948; naturalized in 1956; daughter of Paul Philip (an Anglican priest) and Beatrice (Spooner-Jones) Levertoff; married Mitchell Goodman (a writer), December 2, 1947 (divorced); children: Nikolai Gregor. *Education:* Privately educated; also studied ballet. *Residence:* New York, N.Y. *Address:* c/o New Directions Press, 333 6th Ave., New York, N.Y. 10014.

CAREER: Poet. After World War II, worked in an antique store and a book store in London, England; taught English in Holland, three months; worked as a nurse at British Hospital, Paris, France, 1943-44; Young Men's Hebrew Association, Poetry Center, New York City, teacher of poetry craft, 1964; City College of the City University of New York, New York City, writer-in-residence, 1965-66; Vassar College, Poughkeepsie, N.Y., visiting lecturer, 1966-67; University of California, Berkeley, visiting professor, 1969; Massachusetts Institute of Technology, Cambridge, visiting professor and poet-in-residence, 1969-70; Kirkland College, Clinton, N.Y., visiting professor, 1970-71; University of Cincinnati, Cincinnati, Ohio, Elliston Lecturer, 1973; Tufts University, Medford, Mass., member of faculty, 1973-79. Initiated the "Writers' and Artists' Protest against the War in Viet Nam," 1965; currently active in the anti-nuclear movement. *Member:* National Academy and Institute of Arts and Letters. *Awards, honors:* Bess Hokins Prize, 1959; Longview Award, 1960; Guggenheim fellowship, 1962; Inez Boulton Prize, 1964; National Institute of Arts and Letters grant, 1965; Morton Dauwen Zabel Memorial Prize, 1965.

WRITINGS—All published by New Directions, except as indicated: *The Double Image,* Cresset, 1946; *Here and Now,*

City Lights, 1957; *Overland to the Islands,* Jargon, 1958; *With Eyes at the Back of Our Heads,* 1959; *The Jacob's Ladder,* 1961; *O Taste and See,* 1964; *The Sorrow Dance,* 1967; (editor and translator with Edward C. Dimock) *In Praise of Krishna: Songs from the Bengali,* Doubleday-Anchor, 1968; (contributor of translations) Jules Supervielle, *Selected Writings,* 1968; (translator) *Selected Poems of Guillevic,* 1969; *Relearning the Alphabet,* 1970; *To Stay Alive,* 1971; *Footprints,* 1972; *The Poet in the World* (essays), 1973; *The Freeing of the Dust,* 1975; *Life in the Forest,* 1978; *Collected Earlier Poems,* 1979. Poetry has also been published in limited editions by small presses. Work has been anthologized in *Penguin Modern Poets IX, The New American Poetry, Poet's Choice, Today's Poets, Poets of Today, New Poets of England and America,* and others. Contributor to magazines and journals. Poetry editor, *Nation,* 1961, 1963-65, *Mother Jones,* 1975-78.

WORK IN PROGRESS: A book about poetry; a second book of essays; new poems; fiction; memoirs.

SIDELIGHTS: "In my opinion Denise Levertov is incomparably the best poet of what is getting to be known as the new avant-garde," Kenneth Rexroth wrote in 1961. "In the first place, she is more civilized [than her contemporaries].... She is securely humane in a way very few people are any more." She is also wiser than most, "far and away the most profound, and what may be more important, the most modest and the most moving." Eve Triem warns readers who might be expecting traditional poetry that Levertov "uses devices, original or in new and disturbing ways." Rexroth suspects that if "all her work of the past ten years were collected, ... she would show as the equal of [Rene] Char and as superior to all but a handful of American poets born in this century."

Levertov's interest in the technique of poetry is centered on the relation between form and content. She wrote in 1959: "I believe content determines form, and yet that content is discovered only *in* form. Like everything living, it is a mystery.... I do not believe that a violent imitation of the horrors of our times is the concern of poetry.... I long for poems of an inner harmony in utter contrast to the chaos in which they exist. Insofar as poetry has a social function it is to awaken sleepers by other means than shock." She also has attempted to define organic poetry, i.e., poetry "based on an intuition of an order, a form beyond forms, in which forms partake, and of which man's creative works are analogies, resemblances, natural allegories. Such a poetry is exploratory."

In *Poetry,* September, 1965, she writes: "How does one go about [organic] poetry? ... First there must be an experience, ... felt by the poet intensely enough to demand of him [an] equivalence in words: he is *brought to speech.* ... [And] the condition of being a poet is that periodically such a cross-section, or constellation, of experiences ... demands, or wakes in him this demand, *the poem.* The beginning of the fulfillment of this demand is to contemplate, to meditate; words which connote a state in which the heat of feeling warms the intellect." In organic poetry "*the form sense* ... is ever present *along with* (yes, paradoxically) fidelity to the revelations of meditation.... A manifestation of form sense is the sense the poet's ear has of some rhythmic norm peculiar to a particular poem, from which the individual lines depart and to which they return...." When Walter Sutton asked Levertov how she came to her idea of organic form, she replied: "I asked myself if there were principles upon which I was working, and I discovered that there were.... I found that I believed in the existence of form in things, and this I would call by Hopkins' word 'inscape'." She told Sutton that she believed that the rhythm of the inner voice controls the rhythm of the poem. Of the inner voice, she said: "What it means to me is that a poet, a verbal kind of person, is constantly talking to himself, inside of himself, constantly approximating and evaluating and trying to grasp his experience in words. And I do it even in dreams. I have many verbal dreams in which I am, as it were, writing the scene as I dream it, and sometimes I don't get it right, and I find myself going back and dreaming the scene over until I've got the words right. That's one example of the inner voice."

Levertov claims a romantic ancestry, on her mother's side, the Welsh mystic Angel Jones of Mold, on her father's, the noted Russian Hasid, Schneour Zalman. Her early poems, written in England, were romantic yet unique. Rexroth said of her then: "In poets like Denise Levertov this tendency (a sort of autumnal-evening *Wienerwald* melancholy) reaches its height.... For the first time, *Schwaermerei* enters English verse."

In 1947, in Geneva, she met her husband. They lived in Paris and Florence, and came to New York late in 1948. She writes: "Marrying an American and coming to live here while still young was very stimulating to me as a writer for it necessitated the finding of new rhythms in which to write, in accordance with new rhythms of life and speech. My reading of William Carlos Williams and Wallace Stevens, which began in Paris in 1948; of [Charles] Olson's essay, 'Projective Verse'; conversations and correspondence with Robert Creely and Robert Duncan," were influential. "[Williams] gave me the use of the American language," she told Walter Sutton. "He showed me how it and the American idiom could be used; and, more than that, he gave me instance after instance of how one's most ordinary experience could be shown in the poem as it was, invested with wonder. From Stevens . . . I think I've gotten, over and over again, a sense of magic."

Soon after her arrival in New York, "she changed her style," says Rexroth, "evolved a style of her own—clear, sparse, immediate and vibrant with a special sensibility and completely feminine." Her language moved into the mainstream of current American English. Rexroth writes: "The *Schwaermerei* and lassitude are gone. Their place has been taken by a kind of animal grace of the word, a pulse like the footfalls of a cat or the wingbeats of a gull. . . . Nothing could be harder, more irreducible, than [her] poems. Like the eggs and birds of Brancusi, they are bezoars shaped and polished in the vitals of a powerful creative sensibility."

In a 1979 interview with Kenneth John Achity, Levertov comments: "People's relationship to language in this time is undeveloped so that poets who are called elitist sometimes are simply using the resources of their own vocabulary. Since that vocabulary is larger than that of the people who are reading them, they are labelled elitist." When asked how she felt about her personal development as a writer, she replied: "In some ways I see myself thematically repeating, . . . when I look back I see that there are certain recurrent themes. I feel two strains, two directions, going on in my poetry currently. One is the development of a fairly tight . . . lyric poem that derives much of its imagery from somewhere close to the unconscious, a kind of dream level of image. And the other is a longer-lined, more discursive poem, with a fictive or narrative element.... They seem to be simultaneous needs in me at present, and I want to push them both a lot further than I have yet." She does not see poetry as having a limited number of forms. "Life is continuously surprising one with its events and its people and you know the unforeseeable is constantly occurring in life. So why not in poetry?"

BIOGRAPHICAL/CRITICAL SOURCES: New York Times Book Review, June 22, 1958, November 19, 1967, November 30, 1975, July 8, 1979; Donald M. Allen, editor, The New American Poetry: 1945-1960, Grove, 1960; Poetry, August, 1960, September, 1965, March, 1968, May, 1968; Kenneth Rexroth, Assays, New Directions, 1961; David Ossman, editor, The Sullen Art, Corinth, 1963; Book Week, August 2, 1964; New York Review of Books, December 31, 1964; M. L. Rosenthal, The Modern Poets, Oxford University Press, 1965; Minnesota Review, index issue, 1965; Times Literary Supplement, January 27, 1966; Linda Wagner, Denise Levertov, Twayne, 1967; Observer Review, July 28, 1968; Jewish Quarterly, winter, 1968-69; Library Journal, March 15, 1970; Nation, June 21, 1971; Choice, June, 1972, April, 1976; Denise Levertov, The Poet in the World, New Directions, 1973; Contemporary Literary Criticism, Gale, Volume I, 1973, Volume II, 1974, Volume III, 1975, Volume V, 1976, Volume VIII, 1978, Volume XV, 1980; James Mersmann, Out of the Vietnam Vortex, University of Kansas Press, 1974; Midwest Quarterly, spring, 1975; San Francisco Review of Books, March, 1979.

*   *   *

LEVIN, Beatrice Schwartz

PERSONAL: Born in Providence, R.I.; daughter of Julius and Sarah (Reganthal) Schwartz; married Franklyn K. Levin (a research geophysicist), September 15, 1946; children: Michael, Alan, Philip. *Education:* Rhode Island College, B.Ed., 1942; University of Wisconsin, M.S., 1947. *Home:* 802 West Forest Dr., Houston, Tex. 77079.

CAREER: Encyclopedia Americana, New York, N.Y., research assistant, 1942-43; Edison High School, Tulsa, Okla., English teacher, 1959-60; Benedictine Heights College, Tulsa, teacher of creative writing, 1960-61; United States Junior Chamber of Commerce, Tulsa, research consultant, 1963-64; Texas Southern University, Houston, assistant professor of English, 1964-69; teacher of creative writing, 1969-80; freelance writer. *Military service:* U.S. Women's Army Corps, 1943-45.

WRITINGS: The Lonely Room, Bobbs-Merrill, 1950; *Eyewitness to Exodus,* Chicago Paperback, 1962; *The Singer and the Summer Song,* Arcadia House, 1964; *Safari Smith, Peace Corps Nurse,* Nova, 1966; *Hidden Treasures* (collected short stories), Lindahl Press, 1980; *Women and Medicine,* Scarecrow, 1980.

WORK IN PROGRESS: Voyages of the Vema, a book on oceanography for boys; *Best School in Town,* a novel about a teacher; *Indian Summer,* a novel about the Southwest; *John Hawk, White Man, Black Man, Indian Chief; Creative Games for Teaching English; Education of a Sentimentalist,* an autobiography; *A Blade of Grass,* a novel about Walt Whitman; *Uncle Fox's Funeral; Bitter Homes and Gardens; Encounter at Entebbe.*

SIDELIGHTS: Beatrice S. Levin told *CA:* "Despite my teaching and regular sales to magazines and newspapers, if I had had to support myself over the years, I would have had to get out the begging bowl. Though I've acquired a certain facility with language, I still find that every new project is like the first book or the first article, feeling my way along, experimenting, wondering if I'm saying what I mean to say. To me, the creative life is the only one worth living, and I find that writing not only adds an extra dimension to everything I experience, but it also makes me both observer and participant in the events, voyages, action and passion of our very exciting era.''

*   *   *

LEVINE, Faye (Iris) 1944-

PERSONAL: Born January 18, 1944, in Stamford, Conn.; daughter of Bernard Harold Shulman and Lillian (Haft) Shulman Levine. *Education:* Radcliffe College, A.B. (cum laude), 1965; Harvard University, Ed.M., 1970. *Home:* 20 East 9th St., No. 8T, New York, N.Y. 10003.

CAREER: Free-lance writer, 1966—. Teacher of English, Kamla Raja Girls' College, Gwalior, Madhya Pradesh, India, 1965-66; reporter, *New York Post*, 1968; teacher in boy's reform school, Shirley, Mass., 1970-71; assignment editor, *Herald* (weekly), 1971-72; consultant, Office de Radiodiffusion-Television Francais, 1973; assistant to the president, Electro-Harmonix, 1975—. *Member:* Authors Guild, American Society of Journalists and Authors, National Press Club, National Young Judaea (corresponding secretary, 1960-61), Redstockings of the Women's Liberation Movement, Bio-Feedback Research Society, Radcliffe Club of New York. *Awards, honors:* Bread Loaf Writers' Conference fellowship, 1967, for four *Atlantic* articles; Radcliffe Institute fellowship, 1973-74.

WRITINGS: The Strange World of the Hare Krishnas, Fawcett, 1974; *The Culture Barons: An Analysis of Power and Money in the Arts*, Crowell, 1976; *Solomon and Sheba*, Putnam, 1980. Contributor to *New Yorker, Ms., Atlantic Monthly, Harper's, Newsday, Newsweek, Penthouse, Ramparts, Rolling Stone, Hierophant, Fusion, New York Ace, Physician's World, Boston Phoenix*, and *Harvard Graduate School of Education News*. Executive editor of *Harvard Crimson*, 1964; consulting editor of *Redstockings Journal/Feminist Revolution*, 1974.

WORK IN PROGRESS: A novel about Harvard University.

SIDELIGHTS: Library Journal reviewer Helen Gregory writes that Faye Levine's second book, *The Culture Barons: An Analysis of Power and Money in the Arts*, is ''a lively and perceptive close-up of the handful of patrons who, through their wealth, dictate to the masses what they will hear and see. The focus is first on New York City, especially the battle for Lincoln Center funding for opera, ballet, and drama as well as the visual arts. Broadway is touched on, but sharper contrast is provided by the discussion of the West Coast scene and the big money-makers: film and rock music.''

BIOGRAPHICAL/CRITICAL SOURCES: New York Times, January 24, 1965, December 6, 1965; *Fusion*, June, 1973; *Publishers Weekly*, January 21, 1974; *Library Journal*, September 15, 1976, May 15, 1980; *Kirkus Reviews*, May, 1980.

*   *   *

LEVITAN, Sar A. 1914-

PERSONAL: Born September 14, 1914, in Shiauliai, Lithuania; son of Osher N. (a rabbi) and JoAnn (Rapoport) Levitan; married Brita Ann Bouchard, October 16, 1946. *Education:* College of the City of New York (now City College of the City University of New York), B.S.S., 1937; Columbia University, M.A., 1939, Ph.D., 1949. *Home:* 1280 21st St. N.W., Washington, D.C. 20036. *Office:* Center for Social Policy Studies, George Washington University, 2000 K St. N.W., Suite 454, Washington, D.C. 20006.

CAREER: State Teachers College (now State University of New York College at Plattsburgh), associate professor of economics, 1946-51; various positions in U.S. Government,

Washington, D.C., 1951-62; George Washington University, Washington, D.C., research professor of labor economics, 1962-64; Upjohn Institute, Washington, D.C., senior economist, 1964-67; George Washington University, research professor of economics and director of Center for Social Policy Studies, 1967—. Chairman of executive committee, National Council on Employment Policy. *Military service:* U.S. Army, 1942-46; became lieutenant colonel. *Member:* American Economic Association, Industrial Relations Research Association (president, Washington chapter, 1958-59), National Economists Club (member, board of governors). *Awards, honors:* Ford Foundation grants, 1962-63, 1967–

WRITINGS: Ingrade Wage-Rate Progression in War and Peace: A Problem in Wage Administration Techniques, Clinton Press, 1950; *Federal Assistance to Labor Surplus Areas*, U.S. Government Printing Office, 1957; *Government Regulation of Internal Union Affairs Affecting the Rights of Members*, U.S. Government Printing Office, 1958; (with Harold L. Sheppard) *Impact of Technological Change upon Communities and Public Policy*, U.S. Department of Commerce, Area Redevelopment Administration, 1960; (with Louise D. Houghteling) *Factors Affecting the Slower Growth of Missouri Population Compared with the U.S.*, revised edition, Legislative Reference Service, U.S. Library of Congress, 1961; *Youth Employment Act*, Upjohn, 1963; *Reducing Worktime as a Means to Combat Unemployment*, Upjohn, 1964; *Federal Manpower Policies and Programs to Combat Unemployment*, Upjohn, 1964; *Federal Aid to Depressed Areas: An Evaluation of the Area Redevelopment Administration*, Johns Hopkins Press, 1964; (with Joseph M. Becker) *Programs to Aid the Unemployed in the 1960's*, Upjohn, 1965; *Programs in Aid of the Poor*, Upjohn, 1965, revised edition published as *Programs in Aid of the Poor for the 1970's*, Johns Hopkins Press, 1969, 4th edition published as *Programs in Aid of the Poor for the 1980's*, 1980.

(Editor with Irving H. Siegel) *Dimensions of Manpower Policy: Programs and Research*, Johns Hopkins Press, 1966; *Antipoverty Work and Training Efforts: Goals and Reality*, Institute of Labor and Industrial Relations (University of Michigan/Wayne State University) and National Manpower Policy Task Force, 1967, 2nd edition, 1970; *The Design of Federal Antipoverty Strategy*, Institute of Labor and Industrial Relations, 1967; (with Garth L. Mangum) *Making Sense of Federal Manpower Policy*, Institute of Labor and Industrial Relations, 1967; (editor with Wilbur J. Cohen and Robert J. Lampman) *Towards Freedom from Want*, Industrial Relations Research Association, 1968; (with Roger H. Davidson) *Antipoverty Housekeeping: The Administration of the Economic Opportunity Act*, Institute of Labor and Industrial Relations, 1968; *The Great Society's Poor Law: A New Approach to Poverty*, Johns Hopkins Press, 1969; (with Mangum) *Federal Training and Work Programs in the Sixties*, Institute of Labor and Industrial Relations, 1969.

(With Mangum and Robert Taggart III) *Economic Opportunity in the Ghetto: The Partnership of Government and Business*, Johns Hopkins Press, 1970; (with Taggart) *Social Experimentation and Manpower Policy: The Rhetoric and the Reality*, Johns Hopkins Press, 1971; (editor) *Blue-Collar Workers: A Symposium on Middle America*, McGraw, 1971; (with Barbara Hetrick) *Big Brother's Indian Programs—With Reservations*, McGraw, 1971; (with Taggart) *Job Crisis for Black Youth: A Report for the Twentieth Century Fund*, Praeger, 1971; (with Mangum and Ray Marshall) *Human Resources and Labor Markets: Labor and Manpower in the American Economy*, Harper, 1972, revised edition, 1980; (with Martin Rein and David Marwick) *Work and*

Welfare Go Together, Johns Hopkins Press, 1972; The Federal Dollar in Its Own Backyard, Bureau of National Affairs, 1973; (with Karen Cleary) Old Wars Remain Unfinished: The Veterans Benefit System, Johns Hopkins University Press, 1973; (with William B. Johnston) Work Is Here to Stay, Alas, Olympus, 1973; (with Taggart) Evaluation of the First 18 Months of the Public Employment Program, Government Printing Office, 1973; (with Taggart) Employment and Earnings Inadequacy, Johns Hopkins University Press, 1974; (with W. B. Johnston and Taggart) Still a Dream: The Changing Status of the Blacks since 1960, Harvard University Press, 1975; (with Karen Cleary Alderman) Child Care and ABC's Too, Johns Hopkins University Press, 1975; (with W. B. Johnston) Indian Giving: The Federal Government and Native Americans, Johns Hopkins University Press, 1975; (with Benjamin H. Johnston) The Job Corps: A Social Experiment that Works, Johns Hopkins University Press, 1975; (with W. B. Johnston and Taggart) Minorities in the United States: Problems, Progress, and Prospects, Public Affairs Press, 1975.

(With Taggart) The Promise of Greatness, Harvard University Press, 1976; (with Joyce K. Zickler) Too Little but not Too Late: Federal Aid to Lagging Areas, Lexington Books, 1976; (with Alderman) Warriors at Work: The Volunteer Armed Force, Sage Publications, 1977; (with Richard S. Belous) More Than Subsistence: Minimum Wages for the Working Poor, Johns Hopkins University Press, 1979; (with Gregory Wurzburg) Evaluating Federal Social Programs: An Uncertain Art, Upjohn Institute, 1979. Contributor to Encyclopaedia Britannica, Encyclopedia of Education, Encyclopedia Americana, and various journals.

WORK IN PROGRESS: The American Family.

BIOGRAPHICAL/CRITICAL SOURCES: Nation, September 8, 1969; Commentary, October, 1969; Library Journal, March 15, 1970; Washington Post Book World, September 5, 1976.

*   *   *

LEWIS, George L. 1916-

PERSONAL: Born December 3, 1916, in Treasureton, Idaho; son of Frederick L. and Inez (Watson) Lewis; married Dorothy McAllister, June 6, 1941; married second wife, Catherine Kalovs; children: (first marriage) Michael D., Terry K., Patrick M. Education: Brigham Young University, B.A., 1941, M.A., 1947; University of Denver, Ph.D., 1954. Home: 3500 Kroehler Dr., Hilliard, Ohio 43026. Office: 239 Arps Hall, 1945 North High St., Columbus, Ohio 43210.

CAREER: High school teacher of speech in Bancroft, Idaho, 1941-42; War Relocation Authority, Topaz, Utah, head educationist, 1942-43; Brigham Young University, Provo, Utah, instructor, 1945-47, assistant professor, 1947-50, associate professor of education, 1950-56; Ohio State University, Columbus, assistant professor, 1956-59, associate professor, 1959-62, professor of speech education and theatre, 1962—. Consultant in education to Jewish religious schools, Columbus, 1960-73. Ohio State University Children's Theatre, director, 1960-73. Advisor, Columbus Children's Theatre of the Arts, 1960—. Military service: U.S. Army Air Forces, 1943-45; served in European theater. Member: National Thespian Society, Speech Communication Association, American Theatre Association, Central States Speech Association, Eastern Speech Association, Ohio Speech Association.

WRITINGS: (Contributor) Keith Brooks, senior author and editor, The Communicative Arts and Sciences of Speech,

C. E. Merrill, 1967; (with Russell Everett, James Gibson, and Kathryn Schoen) Teaching Speech, C. E. Merrill, 1969; Model Lesson Plans, privately printed, 1973; (with Rex Fuller) Story-telling, Dramatization, Creativity, Kendall/ Hunt, 1977. Contributor to Ohio Speech Journal, Central States Speech Journal, Players, Dramatics, and Elementary English. Associate editor, Secondary Speech Educators Central States Speech Journal, 1964-73.

*   *   *

LEWIS, H(ywel) D(avid)   1910-

PERSONAL: Born May 21, 1910, in Llandudno, Caernarvonshire, Wales: son of David John (a minister) and Rebecca (Davies) Lewis; married Megan Elias-Jones, August 17, 1943 (died, 1962); married Megan Pritchard, July 17, 1965. Education: University College of North Wales, B.A. (first class honors in philosophy), 1932, M.A. (with distinction), 1933; Jesus College, Oxford University, B.Litt., 1935. Religion: Presbyterian. Home: 1 Normandy Park, Normandy, near Guilford, Surrey, England.

CAREER: University College of North Wales, Bangor, lecturer, 1936-46, senior lecturer, 1946-47, professor of philosophy, 1947-55; King's College, University of London, London, England, professor of the history and philosophy of religion, 1955-78, fellow, 1963, dean of Faculty of Theology, 1964-68, dean of Faculty of Arts, 1967. Visiting professor at Bryn Mawr College, 1958-59, and Yale University, 1964-65. Wilde Lecturer in natural and comparative religion at Oxford University, 1960-63; Edward Cadbury Lecturer at University of Birmingham, 1962-63; visiting lecturer at Center for the Study of Religions, Harvard University, 1963; Owen Evans Lecturer at University College of Wales, 1964-65; Gifford Lecturer at University of Edinburgh, 1966-67, 1967-68; distinguished lecturer at other colleges and universities in England, Scotland, Northern Ireland, Japan, India, and Canada. External examiner at universities in Nigeria and Ghana, 1957; examiner for Universities of Glasgow, Leeds, Wales, Durham, and for Cambridge University. Member of board, Athlone Press; member of Advisory Council on Education, Wales, 1964-67.

MEMBER: International Society for Metaphysics (president, 1974-80), Royal Institute of Philosophy (chairman of council, 1965—), Society for the Study of Theology (president, 1964-66), Aristotelian Society (president, 1962-63), London Society for the Study of Religion (president, 1970-71), Oxford Society for Historical Theology (president, 1970-71), Mind Association (president, 1948-49), Honourable Society of Cymmrodorion (member of council). Awards, honors: Leverhulme fellow, 1954-55; D.D., University of St. Andrews; D.Litt., Emory University; Energeia Medal, Ateneo Filosofico, Mexico.

WRITINGS: Morals and the New Theology, Harper, 1947; Morals and Revelation, Verry, 1951; (editor and contributor) Contemporary British Philosophy: Personal Statements, Series III, Macmillan, 1956, Series IV, Allen & Unwin, 1976; Our Experience of God, Macmillan, 1959; Freedom and History, Macmillan, 1962; (editor and contributor) Clarity Is Not Enough: Essays in Criticism of Linguistic Philosophy, Humanities, 1963; Philosophy of Religion, English Universities Press, 1965, Barnes & Noble, 1966; (with Robert Lawson Slater) World Religions: Meeting Points and Major Issues, F. Watts, 1966, reissued as The Study of Religions: Meeting Points and Major Issues, Penguin, 1969; Dreaming and Experience (lecture given at London School of Economics and Political Science, May 11, 1967), Athlone Press,

1968; *The Elusive Mind* (Gifford Lectures given at University of Edinburgh, 1966-68), Humanities, 1969.

The Self and Immortality, Macmillan, 1973; (editor) *Philosophy East and West,* Blackie & Son, 1975; (editor with G. R. Damadoran) *The Dynamics of Education,* Ravel, 1975; *Persons and Life after Death,* Macmillan, 1980; *Jesus in the Faith of Christians,* Macmillan, 1981; *The Elusive Self* (second volume of Gifford Lectures), Macmillan, 1981.

Books in Welsh: *Gweriniaeth* (title means "Democracy"), Presbyterian Church of Wales Press, 1940; (with J. A. Thomas) *Y Wladwriaeth a'i Hawdurdod* (title means "The State and Its Authority"), University of Wales Press, 1943; *Ebyrth* (title means "Sacrifices"; poems), Aberystwyth Press, 1943; *Diogelu diwylliant, ac ysgrifian eraill* (title means "In Defense of Culture"), Brython Press, 1945; *Christ a Heddwch,* Gee Press, 1947; *Dilyn Crist* (title means "Christian Discipleship"), Jarvis & Foster, 1951; *Gwybod am Dduw* (title means "Knowledge of God"), University of Wales Press, 1952; *Hen a Newydd* (title means "Old and New"), C. M. Press, 1972; *Pwy yw Iesu Grist?* (title means "Who Is Jesus Christ?"), Gee Press, 1979.

Contributor: Wilfrid Sellars and John Hospers, editors, *Readings in Ethical Theory,* Appleton, 1952, 2nd edition, 1970; Milton K. Munitz, editor, *A Modern Introduction to Ethics,* Free Press, 1958; Victor Gollancz, editor, *The New Year of Grace: An Anthology for Youth and Age,* Doubleday (Toronto), 1961; Ian T. Ramsey, editor, *Prospect for Metaphysics: Essays of Metaphysical Exploration,* Greenwood Press, 1961; Geddes MacGregor and J. Wesley Robb, compilers, *Readings in Religious Philosophy,* Houghton, 1962; Francis George Healey, editor, *Prospect for Theology,* Nisbet, 1966; Rupert Davies, editor, *We Believe in God,* Allen & Unwin, 1968.

Editor: "Muirhead Library of Philosophy," Macmillan, 1948—, including: Radhakrishnan, *The Principal Upanishads;* G. E. Moore, *Some Main Problems of Philosophy;* Moore, *The Common-place Book;* J. N. Findlay, *Values and Intentions;* Brand Blanshard, *Reason and Goodness;* C. A. Campbell, *Selfhood and Godhood.* Also editor of "Religious Studies," Cambridge University Press. Contributor to philosophy and theology journals in England and Wales.

WORK IN PROGRESS: A third volume of Gifford Lectures, sequel to *The Elusive Mind* and *The Elusive Self,* tentatively entitled *The Elusive Self and God.*

SIDELIGHTS: H. D. Lewis told *CA:* "I was brought up in a thoroughly Welsh home, although also bilingual from an early age. I think equally freely in Welsh and English and have been much concerned in efforts to maintain and extend Welsh culture. Beyond this my chief concern has been to show how central religious themes may be sustained in an enlightened age without retreating to simplistic dogmatism or equally simplistic attenuations of faith. The influence of a devout but liberal home has been very great. I owe much in the same way to my Welsh background for my interest in art and poetry, and their affinity with religious insight. At the center of those interests is my main professional concern with problems of the nature of persons and their identity, a central topic for metaphysics and religion.

"My philosophical work has involved a continuous effort, in an adverse philosophical climate, to maintain the place of metaphysical thinking without reverting to the obscurantism that brought it into ill repute earlier this century.

"I have been abroad a great deal, for teaching and other academic purposes, especially in India and America. I am much

attached to both places. I consider Emory University to be as ideal a place to live and teach as we are likely to find."

AVOCATIONAL INTERESTS: Swimming ("which at times makes me feel almost amphibian").

*   *   *

LEWIS, Harry 1942-

PERSONAL: Born November 10, 1942, in Brooklyn, N.Y.; son of Sol (a historian and publisher) and Sylvia (Pincus) Lewis. *Education:* Attended Bard College, 1960; Brooklyn College of the City University of New York, B.A. (cum laude), 1965; New York University, M.A., 1969; University of Massachusetts, graduate study, 1972-73; Fordham University, M.S.W., 1980. *Politics:* Socialist. *Home and office:* 115 Charles St., New York, N.Y. 10014.

CAREER: New York University, New York, N.Y., guest lecturer, 1967-69; Mulch Press, Amherst, Mass., editor and publisher, 1970-76; Mercy College, Dobbs Ferry, N.Y., director of creative writing, 1976—. Instructor in American literature and remedial English, Jersey City State College, 1969-72; University of Massachusetts, part-time instructor in poetry, 1973, director of community writers project at Orchard Hill Residential College, spring, 1974. Practicing psychoanalytic psychotherapist, 1979—. *Member:* Alpha Kappa Delta.

WRITINGS—Poems: Crab Cantos, For Now Press, 1969; *Before and After Abraham,* Loose Change Books, 1971; (translator) Vladimir Mayakovsky, *Brooklyn Bridge,* Broadway Boogie Press, 1974; *Home Cooking,* Mulch Press, 1975; *The Candy Store,* Rootie Tootie Press, 1979; *Babies,* Rootie Tootie Press, 1979; *Hudson (1-16),* Number Books, 1980; *The Wellsprings,* Momo's Press, 1981.

Work is represented in anthologies, including *Ten American Poets,* Euphoria Press, 1968, *Where Is Vietnam?,* edited by Walter Lowenfels, Doubleday, 1968, and *Inside Outer Space,* edited by Robert Vas Dias, Doubleday, 1970.

Contributor of about 160 poems, stories, translations, and reviews to newspapers and magazines, including *Village Voice, New York Times, Penthouse, Harper's Bookletter, Sun, New York, For Now, Mulch, Boston Phoenix, Widening Circle, Promethean,* and *Nation.* Editor, *Landscapes* (of Brooklyn College of the City University of New York), 1963-64, *Pogamoggan* (literary magazine), 1965-66, and "Planet News" poetry column, *East Village Other,* 1969; co-editor, *Mulch,* 1972—; book review editor, *Valley Advocate* (newspaper), 1973-75, and *American Rag,* 1979—; east coast editor, *San Francisco Review of Books.*

WORK IN PROGRESS: A book of poems; a translation of Mayakovsky's poems and journals of his American visit in 1925; a novel, *The Last Stagecoach Robber;* a book-length poem, *A Life in the City.*

*   *   *

LEWIS, Norman 1912-

PERSONAL: Born December 30, 1912, in New York, N.Y. *Education:* City College (now City College of the City University of New York), B.A.; Columbia University, M.A. *Office:* Rio Hondo College, Whittier, Calif. 90608

CAREER: City College (now City College of the City University of New York), New York City, instructor and lecturer, 1942-52; New York University, New York City, 1957-64, began as instructor, became adjunct associate professor of English, 1963; Rio Hondo College, Whittier, Calif., professor of English, 1964—, head of communications department, 1964-75, president of Academic Senate, 1966-68.

WRITINGS: (With others) *Journeys through Wordland,* four books, Amsco School Publications, 1941; *Lessons in Vocabulary and Spelling,* Amsco School Publications, 1941; *Power with Words,* Crowell, 1943, 3rd edition published as *New Power with Words,* 1964; *How to Read Better and Faster,* Crowell, 1944, 4th edition, 1978; *The Lewis English Refresher and Vocabulary Builder: A Six-Weeks Course in the Essentials of Effective English,* Wilfred Funk, 1945, revised and updated edition published as *New Guide to Word Power,* Pyramid Publications, 1963; (with Wilfred John Funk) *Thirty Days to a More Powerful Vocabulary,* Wilfred Funk, 1946, revised edition, 1970; *How to Speak Better English,* Crowell, 1948, revised edition published as *Better English,* 1956; *Word Power Made Easy,* Doubleday, 1949, revised edition, 1978.

The Rapid Vocabulary Builder, Grosset, 1951, revised edition, 1980; *How to Get More Out of Your Reading,* Doubleday, 1951, published as *How to Become a Better Reader,* Macfadden, 1964; *Twenty Days to Better Spelling,* Harper, 1953; *The Comprehensive Word Guide,* Doubleday, 1958, reissued as *The Modern Thesaurus of Synonyms,* 1965; (editor) *The New Roget's Thesaurus of the English Language in Dictionary Form,* revised and enlarged edition, Putnam, 1961, 2nd edition, 1965, abridged version published as *The New Roget's Thesaurus in Dictionary Form,* Washington Square Press, 1961; *Dictionary of Correct Spelling,* Harper, 1962; *Correct Spelling Made Easy,* Random House, 1963; *Dictionary of Modern Pronunciation,* Harper, 1963; *30 Days to Better English,* Doubleday, 1965; *R.S.V.P.* (elementary school textbook on word skills), Books 1, 2, 3, Amsco School Publications, 1967; *See, Say and Write,* Books 1 and 2, Amsco School Publications, 1973; *Instant Speller Power,* Amsco School Publications, 1976; *R.S.V.P. for College English Power,* Amsco School Publications, Book 1, 1977, Book 2, 1978, Book 3, 1979; *R.S.V.P. with Etymology,* Amsco School Publications, Book 1, 1980, Book 2, 1981; *Instant Word Power,* Amsco School Publications, 1980.

Contributor of articles to *Harper's, Reader's Digest, Saturday Evening Post, Cosmopolitan, Scholastic, Pageant,* and to several other magazines and professional journals. Editor, *Correct English,* 1944-47.

*   *   *

LEWIS, (Ernest Michael) Roy 1913-

PERSONAL: Born November 6, 1913, in Felixstowe, England; son of Ernest I. (a teacher) and Susannah (Edmonds) Lewis; married Christine Tew, June 6, 1939; children: Christine Miranda, Elizabeth Rachel. *Education:* University College, Oxford University, B.A., 1934; London School of Economics and Political Science, University of London, graduate study, 1935-36. *Home:* 26 Sydney Rd., Richmond, Surrey, England. *Agent:* David Higham Associates, 5-8 Lower John St., London W.1, England. *Office: Times,* New Printing House Sq., London W.C.1, England.

CAREER: Royal Institute of International Affairs, London, England, economist, 1935-36; *Statist,* London, assistant editor, 1936-39; manager, Pekin Syndicate, 1943-46; *Scope,* feature writer, 1946-48; *Economist,* London, assistant editor and Washington correspondent, 1952-61; *Times,* London, leader writer, 1961—. *Member:* Royal Institute of International Affairs, London Library, Royal Overseas League.

WRITINGS: Shall I Emigrate?, Phoenix House, 1948; (with Angus Maude) *The English Middle Classes,* Phoenix House,

1949, Knopf, 1950, abridged edition, Penguin, 1953, reprint of original edition, Chivers, 1973; (with Harry Ballam) *The Vistors' Book,* Parrish, 1950; (with Maude) *Professional People,* Phoenix House, 1952, published as *Professional People in England,* Harvard University Press, 1953; *Sierra Leone: A Modern Portrait,* H.M.S.O., 1954; (with Rosemary Stewart) *Boss: The Life and Times of the British Business Man,* Phoenix House, 1958, 2nd revised edition, Dent, 1963; *What We Did to Father,* Hutchinson, 1960, published as *The Evolution Man,* Penguin, 1963, published as *Once Upon an Ice Age,* Terra Nova, 1979; (with Stewart) *The Managers,* New American Library, 1961; (with Yvonne Foy) *The British in Africa,* Weidenfeld & Nicolson, 1971, published as *Painting Africa White: The Human Side of British Colonialism,* Universe Books, 1971; *A Force for the Future: The Role of the Police in the Next Ten Years,* Temple Smith, 1976; *Enoch Powell: Principle in Politics,* Cassell, 1979. Contributor to *Encounter, Spectator,* and to British Broadcasting Corp. programs.

SIDELIGHTS: Roy Lewis has traveled over much of the world as a journalist, especially in Africa, India, Australia, China, and the United States. *Avocational interests:* A private press, Keepsake Press, which prints special editions of poetry.

*   *   *

LEWY, Guenter 1923-

PERSONAL: Born August 22, 1923, in Breslau, Germany; son of Henry and Rosel (Leipziger) Lewy; married Ilse Nussbaum (a pediatrician), December 29, 1950; children: Barbara Jean, Peter Ralph. *Education:* City College (now City College of the City University of New York), B.S.S., 1951; Columbia University, M.A., 1952, Ph.D., 1957. *Home:* 64 Harrison Ave., Northampton, Mass. 01060. *Office:* Department of Government, University of Massachusetts, Amherst, Mass. 01003.

CAREER: Columbia University, New York, N.Y., instructor in government, 1953-56; Smith College, Northampton, Mass., assistant professor of government, 1957-63; University of Massachusetts—Amherst, associate professor, 1964-66, professor of government, 1966—. *Military service:* British Army, 1942-46; became sergeant; received Africa Star and Italy Star. *Member:* American Political Science Association, American Society for Political and Legal Philosophy, Phi Beta Kappa. *Awards, honors:* Social Science Research Council fellowship, 1956-57, 1961-62; Rockefeller Foundation fellowship, 1963-64, 1976-77.

WRITINGS: Constitutionalism and Statecraft during the Golden Age of Spain: A Study of the Political Philosophy of Juan de Mariana, S.J., Librairie E. Droz (Geneva), 1960; *The Catholic Church and Nazi Germany,* McGraw, 1964; *Religion and Revolution,* Oxford University Press, 1974; *America in Vietnam,* Oxford University Press, 1978. Also author of several technical reports published by Department of Government, University of Massachusetts.

Contributor: Nils Petter Gleditsch, editor, *Kamp uten Vapen,* Pax Forlag (Oslo), 1965; D. B. Schmidt and E. R. Schmidt, editors, *The Deputy Reader: Studies in Moral Responsibility,* Scott, Foresman, 1965; David Spitz, editor, *Political Theory and Social Change,* Atherton, 1967; Richard A. Wasserstrom, editor, *War and Morality,* Wadsworth, 1970. Contributor of articles and book reviews to *Political Science Quarterly, Church History, Social Research, Western Political Quarterly, Der Staat, Continuum, Comparative Politics,* and other journals.

WORK IN PROGRESS: False Consciousness: An Essay on Mystification.

SIDELIGHTS: In a review of Guenter Lewy's *The Catholic Church and Nazi Germany,* Walter Laqueur of the *New York Review of Books* writes: "The tragic failure of the Catholic Church to live up to its moral canons in the confrontation with Nazism is traced for the first time in shattering detail in this disturbing book, based on painstaking research into hitherto unpublished sources. One specific aspect of this tragedy has recently been widely discussed in the connection with Hochhuth's *The Deputy.* The present book is far wider in scope, less dramatic in presentation, and more authoritative in the description of the real dilemma that faced the Catholic Church.... It tries to be scrupulously fair to the Church, and does not omit mention of those Catholics who fought Nazism." In a *Book Week* article, Telford Taylor notes that "the thrust of Professor Lewy's book is that the Pope's silence was entirely in harmony with Church policies of long standing, which both the Vatican and the German episcopacy had followed since the beginning of the Nazi era, and which are a natural if not inevitable outgrowth of the nature of the Church herself.... Professor Lewy pronounces no judgment, but it is plain that he is deeply critical of the Pope's silence in 1943, and his book must be regarded as a weighty confirmation of Hochhuth's basic thesis."

Christian Century reviewer L. D. Streiker says that "many readers will turn to Lewy's careful study to discover the role of the Catholic hierarchy in Hitler's solution of the 'Jewish question.' ... That the bishops and even the Holy See were indeed aware of the extermination of the Jews, Lewy has extensively documented." And L. L. Snyder of the *Saturday Review* feels that "the author has performed a Herculean task in examining the materials at his disposal." But, Snyder cautions, "at the same time, it ought to be clear to all readers that this book presents one viewpoint of a highly complex situation." The book's weaknesses, he believes, stem from the limits placed on Lewy by the lack of vital records at the Vatican. "Granted that Mr. Lewy cannot force the Vatican to open its archives to him, the fact remains that without this basic source what he can present is only a partial picture instead of his claimed 'treatment in depth.' ... Mr. Lewy is to be commended for his zeal, and there is no doubt about his sincerity. However, he seems to be unaware of the pitfalls of Monday morning quarterbacking or precociously assuming the mantle of wisdom."

Lewy drew a great deal of critical attention with his 1978 book, *America in Vietnam.* Here, according to Malcolm W. Browne, Pulitzer-Prize winning former war correspondent and now *New York Times* reporter, the author "holds that America was justified in involving itself in Vietnam, that essentially the United States observed the rules of war while its enemy did not, and that our side should and probably could have won, if things had worked out differently. America's world image and place in history have been unfairly tarnished by Vietnam, Dr. Lewy asserts, chiefly because ours was the losing side. If Britain had lost to Hitler in 1940, he argues, Britain would have been similarly disadvantaged in the history books but Winston Churchill's struggle would have been no less important and laudable."

Much of Lewy's material is gleaned from declassified military archives, a fact that causes Browne to view the work with some suspicion. "Military archives," he writes, "taken in themselves, as Dr. Lewy has done, can be monstrously misleading.... One senses ... that the author's instinctive scientific skepticism has been dazzled and blunted by gaining access to what were once official secrets. Secrecy in it-self seems somehow to connote truth." As an example Browne cites Lewy's own assertion that through a decade and a half of war, official reporting had become a joke; to say the least, such things as bomb damage assessements, pacification progress reports, and enemy prisoner interrogations transcripts had tended to be highly optimistic. And the reviewer makes the point that "having allowed this, Dr. Lewy then invites the reader to accept these same reports to support his book's sweeping conclusions."

James Webb, an attorney, former Marine infantry officer in Vietnam, and author of the novel *Fields of Fire,* reviewed *America in Vietnam* for the *Washington Post Book World.* He writes: "On one level, Lewy outlines the causes and course of our involvement in Vietnam. On another, he confronts and strips bare many of the sacred cows of the antiwar movement: the moral and legal criticisms of U.S. military tactics; the charges of atrocities and genocide; the often romanticized view of enemy terrorism; and the indignation over U.S. bombing of North Vietnam." Webb feels that Lewy succeeds on both of these levels but that the author is at his best when refuting the pet theories of the antiwar movement. The reviewer lists some of Lewy's often surprising conclusions: "That American bombing was actually more discriminate than bombing in other wars (often at great cost to U.S. aviators); that civilian casualty rates from the fighting were comparable to or less than those of previous conflicts; that the drug and racial problems were imported to Vietnam from home; that minorities did not do a disproportionate share of the dying; and that deserters from South Vietnamese units rarely if ever went over to the Viet Cong." Finally Webb calls *America in Vietnam* "a book rich in detail, valuable for its scholarly insights and documented refutations of those who would have us forever wring our hands in guilt over the conduct of our troops in that failed war."

In a *Chicago Tribune Book World* article, Jack Fuller says that *America in Vietnam* "may mark the first stage of an important national project—the development of a history of the United States' tormented experiences in a land war in Southeast Asia. Until now such a project was probably impossible. Deep political divisions gave the debate over the war the very qualities of a war. Winning was not everything, it was the only thing. Caution and insistence on precision, they were for the peacetime parade field. There were people dying over there. The problem was immediate. Daring seemed to be called for. History became smothered in polemics, propaganda emanating from all sides. Guenter Lewy has attempted in *America in Vietnam* to take a step back from the fray and to examine a number of elements of the rival orthodoxies of the right and left about Vietnam."

Fuller commends Lewy's unbiased scholarship and writes that the author "avoids propounding grand theories about the war. Instead he attempts a careful marshaling of facts concerning specific issues and events. This is the way history begins. If one comes away from *America in Vietnam* with any general sense it is that the United States tragically misjudged the nature of the war it was entering and that the horror of the carnage in Southeast Asia was in the nature of the war more than in maligning American policies for fighting it." Fuller believes that "in this sense, it is an anti-war book. Not because it criticizes the American involvement, which it does. But because it is a detailed evocation of what the work of war inevitably entails." And he concludes that Lewy's book may reopen debate about Vietnam, "but it will be a new kind of debate, carried on increasingly in the academic community and, with luck, under traditions of honesty and scrupulous regard for methods of accuracy that do not apply to harshly contested political struggles.''

BIOGRAPHICAL/CRITICAL SOURCES: New York Post, June 19, 1964; *New York Review of Books,* June 25, 1964; *Saturday Review,* June 27, 1964; *Book Week,* July 5, 1964; *Christian Century,* July 8, 1964; *Chicago Tribune Book World,* November 12, 1978; *New York Times Book Review,* November 19, 1978; *Washington Post Book World,* November 26, 1978.

—*Sketch by Peter M. Gareffa*

*   *   *

LIEBERS, Arthur   1913-

PERSONAL: Born January 7, 1913, in New York, N.Y.; son of Meyer (a merchant) and Marie (Kaplan) Liebers; married Ruth Lampert (a former teacher and writer), December 22, 1951. *Education:* Attended New York University, 1929-31, Columbia University, 1931-33. *Home:* Halsey La., Remsenburg, N.Y. 11960.

CAREER: Free-lance writer, part-time, 1940-52, full-time, 1952—. Member of editorial staff, *Civil Service Leader,* 1942-46, and *Boxoffice* (motion picture trade paper), 1946; head of civil service department, Spadea Schools of New Jersey and New York, 1948-52. Has also been associated with special writing projects for Laird, Bissell & Meeds, New York, N.Y., and for *Scholastic Magazines* and Scholastic Books Services. *Member:* American Newspaper Guild, Dog Fanciers Luncheon Club, Suffolk Dog Obedience Training Club (Long Island). *Awards, honors:* Companion Dogs named book of the year by Dog Writers Association of America, 1960; *Engineers' Handbook Illustrated* named one of the outstanding reference books of the year by American Library Association, 1968; *You Can Be a Carpenter* named one of notable children's trade books in the field of social studies for 1973-74 by *Social Education Magazine; You Can Be a Machinist* and *You Can Be a Mechanic* named books of the year by Child Study Association of America, 1975.

WRITINGS—All published by Arco, except as indicated: *American Foreign Service Tests,* 1947; *Electrician,* 1947; *Engineering Tests: Civil, Mechanical, and Electrical,* 1947; *Librarian,* 1947; *Plumber,* 1947; *Stationary Engineer and Fireman,* 1947; *Careers in Federal Service for the College Trained,* Wilcox & Follett, 1948, published as *Careers in Government for the College Trained,* 1959; *High School Diploma Equivalency Tests,* 1948, 5th edition, 1966; *Postmaster,* 1949; *How to Organize and Run a Club,* Oceana, 1953, published as *Liebers's Guide to Organizing and Running a Club,* Morrow, 1977; *How to Qualify for the U.S. Merchant Marine Academy,* 1954; (with C. Vollmer) *Investigator's Handbook,* 1954, 3rd edition, 1972; *Pharmacist License Tests,* 1955; *Guide to New York City Jobs,* 1956, 2nd edition, 1960; *Oil Burner Installer,* 1956; *Insurance Broker, Fire, Casualty, and Allied Lines,* 1957, 2nd edition, 1962; *Insurance Agent and Broker,* 1957, 2nd edition, 1962; *Life Insurance Agent,* 1957; *Notary Public,* 1957, 5th edition, 1976; *How to Take Tests and Pass Them,* 1958; *Insurance Agent, Accident and Health,* 1958; *Inventor's Complete Guide Book,* Ottenheimer, 1959; *Real Estate Salesman and Broker,* 1959; *How to Get a Civil Service Job,* Ottenheimer, 1959; *Free!,* 1959.

Relax with Yoga, Sterling, 1960; *How to Pass Employment Tests,* Arco, 1960, 6th edition, 1975; *Companion Dogs,* A. S. Barnes, 1960, revised edition, 1972; *Guide to North American Coins,* Arco, 1961; *Refrigeration License,* Arco, 1961;

Encyclopedia of Pleasure Boating, A. S. Barnes, 1961, revised edition, 1972; *Motorboat Owner's Handbook,* Ottenheimer, 1961; *Complete Book of Water Sports,* Coward, 1962, revised edition, 1972; *How to Buy a Used Car,* Charlton, 1963; *Know Your Automobile,* Charlton, 1963; *Key to Success in Business of Your Own,* Key, 1964; *Complete Book of Winter Sports,* Coward, 1964, revised edition, 1971; *United States Coins,* Putnam, 1965; *Engineers' Handbook Illustrated,* Key Publishing, 1968; *Fifty Favorite Hobbies,* Hawthorn, 1968; *Complete Book of Sky Diving,* Coward, 1968; *How to Start a Profitable Retirement Business,* Pilot, 1968; *How to Get the Job You Want Overseas,* Pilot, 1968, 2nd edition, 1976; *Electrical Engineer's Handbook,* Key, 1970; *Starting Your Own Business,* Pilot, 1972; *Complete Book of Cross-Country Skiing and Touring,* Coward, 1973; *Jobs in Construction,* Lothrop, 1973.

Dog training manuals; all published by Sterling: *How to Raise and Train a Dalmatian,* 1958; *How to Raise and Train a German Short-haired Pointer,* 1958; *How to Raise and Train a Maltese,* 1958; *How to Raise and Train a Pedigreed or Mixed Breed Puppy,* 1958; *How to Housebreak and Train Your Dog,* 1958; (with Georgie Sheppard) *How to Raise and Train a Pomeranian,* 1959; (with Paul Jeffries) *How to Raise and Train a Weimaraner,* 1959; (with Dana Miller) *How to Raise and Train a Yorkshire Terrier,* 1959; (with Dorothy Hardy) *How to Raise and Train a Basset Hound,* 1959.

"Vocations in Trade" series; all published by Lothrop: *You Can Be a Carpenter,* 1973; *...a Plumber,* 1973; *...an Electrician,* 1974; *...a Mechanic,* 1975; *...a Machinist,* 1976; *...a Printer,* 1976; *...a Professional Driver,* 1976; *...a Welder,* 1977; *...a Professional Photographer,* 1979.

Editor: *School Daze,* Scholastic, 1958; *Laughs for Teens,* Grosset, 1960; *Wit's End,* Grosset, 1963.

Contributor to *Book of Knowledge, New York Sunday Times, Nation,* and other publications. Former managing editor, *Police and Firemen National Press;* editor, *Legislative Conference News,* 1963-70; editor, hobby and humor section, Scholastic Publishing, *Newstime,* 1965-66.

*   *   *

LILIENTHAL, David E(li)   1899-1981

PERSONAL: Born July 8, 1899, in Morton, Ill; died January 14, 1981, in New York, N.Y.; son of Leo and Minna (Rosenak) Lilienthal; married Helen Marian Lamb, September 4, 1923; children: Nancy Alice, David Eli. *Education:* DePauw University, A.B., 1920; Harvard University, LL.B., 1923. *Home:* 88 Battle Rd., Princeton, N.J. *Office:* 1230 Avenue of the Americas, New York, N.Y.

CAREER: Admitted to Illinois bar, 1923; practicing attorney in Chicago, Ill., 1923-31; member, Wisconsin Public Service Commission, 1931; Tennessee Valley Authority, founding director, and chairman, 1941-46; chairman, U.S Atomic Energy Commission, 1946-50; Development and Resources Corp., New York, N.Y., co-founder, and chairman of the board, 1955-79. Chairman of U.S. State Department Board of Consultants on international control of atomic energy, 1946. Trustee of Twentieth Century Fund, Committee for Economic Development, and Education and World Affairs, Inc. *Member:* American Academy of Arts and Sciences, Century Association, Phi Beta Kappa, Delta Upsilon, Delta Sigma Rho, Sigma Delta Chi. *Awards, honors:* Freedom Award, 1949; Public Welfare Medal of National Academy of Sciences, 1951. Honorary LL.D., DePauw University, 1945, Lehigh University, 1949, Michigan State University of Agriculture and Applied Sciences (now Michigan State University), 1949, Boston University, 1952, Universidad de Los Andes (Colombia), 1954, University of California, 1964, Indiana University, 1965.

WRITINGS: TVA: Democracy on the March, Harper, 1944, revised edition, 1953; *This I Do Believe,* Harper, 1949; *Big Business: A New Era,* Harper, 1953; *Change, Hope, and the Bomb,* Princeton University Press, 1963; *The Journals of David E. Lilienthal,* Harper, Volumes I-II, 1964, Volume III, 1966, Volume IV, 1969, Volume V, 1971, Volume VI, 1976; *Management: A Humanist Art,* Columbia University Press, 1967; (contributor) James MacGregor Burns, editor, *To Heal and to Build: The Programs of President Lyndon B. Johnson,* McGraw, 1968; *Atomic Energy: A New Start,* Harper, 1980. Contributor to *Harper's, New York Times Magazine, Atlantic Monthly, McCall's, Collier's,* and other periodicals.

SIDELIGHTS: The respect which David E. Lilienthal's career as a writer and administrator commanded was strongly evident in the reviews of his books. He was described as "one of the country's most sensitive and reflective public servants" by a *U.S. Quarterly Booklist* reviewer and was frequently commended as a gifted writer who was dedicated to his work. R. L. Duffus of the *New York Times* praised Lilienthal for being "a man who has proved himself a good administrator as well as a good thinker . . . less concerned about institutional frameworks and devices and more concerned with human realities." Lilienthal's 1949 statement of philosophy *This I Do Believe* was cited by a reviewer for *Christian Century* as "a sound, sober and thoughtful book, a testament of faith in the democratic process and in the possibility of attaining good ends by good means—and by no other kind." A *Saturday Review of Literature* critic saw the book as much more than a simple work of sobriety and thoughtfulness. He recommended that it be available "to all of American youth. . . . Young people like affirmation; this book throbs with it. Young people like compassion; this book glows with it. Young people hate defeatism; this book demolishes it." Such positive thinking was welcomed by Duffus who remarked, "The kind of philosophy Mr. Lilienthal expounds may well be a more powerful weapon in our defense than the furious and expanding atom."

After 1964, David Lilienthal's books were limited to the publication of his extensive journals. These had a much greater impact than most people's memoirs. A reviewer for the *New Yorker* explained: "Along with the expected uses of a diary . . . Lilienthal employs his as a whetstone for sharpening his amazing professional skills; he summarizes . . . lessons learned, techniques acquired, and principles defined. Without having planned it . . . he has written a marvellous textbook of public administration." Ten years and four volumes of journals later, *Newsweek's* S. K. Overbeck mused, "One wonders what he didn't commit to his diary; one wants to know more. But the reward of the book lies in its portrait of an American ideal, a man who finds zest and challenge in life's problems, who brushes away anxiety and false emotion, whose roots in realism sustain him."

BIOGRAPHICAL/CRITICAL SOURCES: Saturday Review of Literature, October 8, 1949; *New York Times,* October 9, 1949; *Survey,* January, 1950; *Christian Century,* January 11, 1950; *U.S. Quarterly Booklist,* March, 1950; *The Journals of David E. Lilienthal,* Harper, Volumes I-II, 1964, Volume III, 1966, Volume IV, 1969, Volume V, 1971, Volume VI, 1976; *Saturday Review,* October 17, 1964, January 14, 1967; *New Yorker,* November 21, 1964; *Time,* January 15, 1965, January 26, 1981; *Times Literary Supplement,* August 5, 1965; *New Statesman,* December 31, 1965, July 21, 1967; *New York Times Book Review,* October 16, 1966, March 2, 1969;

Newsweek, October 24, 1966, March 10, 1969, May 24, 1971, January 26, 1981; *Wall Street Journal,* November 17, 1966; *Nation,* April 17, 1967; *Virginia Quarterly Review,* summer, 1967.

*   *   *

LILLINGTON, Kenneth (James)   1916-

PERSONAL: Born September 7, 1916, in Catford, London, England; son of Walter James and Eveline (Jones) Lillington; married Dulcie Elizabeth Lock, September 29, 1942; children: Susan, Elizabeth, Stephen, David. *Education:* Attended St. Dunstan's College and Wandsworth Training College in England. *Religion:* Church of England. *Home:* 90 Wodeland Ave., Guildford, Surrey, England. *Office:* Brooklands Technical College, Weybridge, Surrey, England.

CAREER: Temple Press Ltd., London, England, advertising copywriter, 1938-39; Walton-on-Thames School for Boys, Surrey, England, teacher, 1949-56; Brooklands Technical College, Weybridge, Surrey, England, lecturer in French and English, 1956—. Lecturer on modern literature, Workers' Educational Association, 1950—, on poetry for Poetry Society of London, 1950—. *Military service:* Royal Army Pay Corps, 1941-43, Royal Signals, 1943-46; became sergeant. *Member:* Royal Society of Arts (fellow), International Association of Literature (fellow), Institute of Linguists (associate).

WRITINGS—All published by Heinemann, except as indicated: *The Devil's Grandson* (one-act play), 1954; *Soapy and the Pharaoh's Curse,* 1957; *Conjurer's Alibi,* Nelson, 1960; *The Secret Arrow,* Nelson, 1960; *Blue Murder* (one-act play), 1961; *A Man Called Hughes,* Thomas Nelson, 1962; *My Proud Beauty,* 1963; *The First Book of Classroom Plays* (one-act plays), R. Hale, 1967; *The Fourth Windmill Book of One-Act Plays* (seven plays by Lillington), 1967; *The Second Book of Classroom Plays,* R. Hale, 1968; *The Seventh Windmill Book of One-Act Plays* (eight plays by Lillington), 1972; (editor) *Nine Lives,* Deutsch, 1977; (editor) *For Better for Worse,* Angus Robertson, 1979; *Young Man of Morning* (novel), Faber, 1979. Poems included in *More Comic and Curious Verse* and *Yet More Comic and Curious Verse,* both published by Penguin. Contributor to *Punch* and to education journals.

AVOCATIONAL INTERESTS: Ancient Greece, swimming, professional boxing and its history.

*   *   *

LINDENBERGER, Herbert (Samuel)   1929-

PERSONAL: Born April 4, 1929, in Los Angeles, Calif.; son of Herman (a businessman) and Celia (Weinkrantz) Lindenberger; married Claire Flaherty (a teacher), June 14, 1961. *Education:* Attended Northwestern University, 1946-47; Antioch College, A.B., 1951; University of Vienna, graduate study, 1952-53; University of Washington, Seattle, Ph.D., 1955. *Politics:* Unaffiliated. *Religion:* Jewish. *Home:* 901 Wing Pl., Stanford, Calif. 94305. *Office:* Comparative Literature Program, Stanford University, Stanford, Calif. 94305.

CAREER: University of California, Riverside, instructor, 1954-56, assistant professor, 1956-62, associate professor, 1962-65, professor of comparative literature and English, 1965-66; Washington University, St. Louis, Mo., professor of German and English literature and chairman of program in comparative literature, 1966-69; Stanford University, Stanford, Calif., Avalon Foundation Professor of Humanities in Comparative Literature and English, 1969—, chairman of program in comparative literature, 1969—. *Member:* Modern Language Association of America, American Comparative Literature Association. *Awards, honors:* Guggenheim fellowship, 1968-69.

WRITINGS: On Wordsworth's "Prelude," Princeton University Press, 1963; *Georg Buchner,* Southern Illinois University Press, 1964; *Georg Trakl,* Twayne, 1971; *Historical Drama: The Relation of Literature and Reality,* University of Chicago Press, 1975; *Saul's Fall: A Critical Fiction,* Johns Hopkins University Press, 1979. Also author of "Victims: Five Chamber Plays," serialized in *Players Magazine,* 1965-66. Contributor to numerous reference works, anthologies, and scholarly journals.

WORK IN PROGRESS: Research project on some relationships between opera and literature; research project on institutional bases of literary criticism.

*   *   *

LINK, Arthur S(tanley)   1920-

PERSONAL: Born August 8, 1920, in New Market, Va.; son of John William (a minister) and Helen (Link) Link; married Margaret McDowell Douglas, June 2, 1945; children: Arthur Stanley, Jr., James D., Margaret M., William A. *Education:* University of North Carolina, A.B. (highest honors), 1941, M.A., 1942, Ph.D., 1945; attended Columbia University, 1944-45. *Religion:* Presbyterian. *Home:* 133 Mt. Lucas Rd., Princeton, N.J. 08540. *Office:* Firestone Library, Princeton, N.J. 08540.

CAREER: Princeton University, Princeton, N.J., instructor, 1945-48, assistant professor of history, 1948-49; Northwestern University, Evanston, Ill., associate professor, 1949-54, professor of history, 1954-60; Princeton University, professor of history, 1960-65, Edwards Professor of American History, 1965-76, George H. Davis '86 Professor of American History, 1976—. Albert Shaw Lecturer, Johns Hopkins University, 1956; Harmsworth Professor of American History, Oxford University, 1958-59; Commonwealth Fund lecturer, University of London, 1977. Member, National Historical Publications Commission, 1968-72. Member of board of trustees, Westminster College, 1970—. *Member:* American Historical Association, Organization of American Historians (member of executive committee, 1959-62), Society of American Historians (fellow), American Philosophical Society, American Academy of Arts and Sciences (fellow), Southern Historical Association (vice-president, 1967-68; president, 1968-69; member of executive council, 1969-72). *Awards, honors:* Guggenheim fellow, 1950-51; Bancroft Prize from Columbia University, 1957, for *Wilson: The New Freedom,* and 1961, for *Wilson: The Struggle for Neutrality;* M.A., Oxford University, 1958; Litt.D., Bucknell University, 1961, University of North Carolina, 1962, and Washington and Lee University, 1965; L.H.D., Washington College, 1962; Rockefeller fellow, 1962-63; H.H.D., Davidson College, 1965.

WRITINGS: Wilson, Princeton University Press, Volume I: *The Road to the White House,* 1947, Volume II: *The New Freedom,* 1956, Volume III: *The Struggle for Neutrality: 1914-1915,* 1960, Volume IV: *Confusions and Crises: 1915-1916,* 1964, Volume V: *Campaigns for Progressivism and Peace: 1916-1917,* 1965; (editor with Richard Leopold) *Problems in American History,* Prentice-Hall, 1952, 4th edition (with Leopold and Stanley Coben), 1972; *Woodrow Wilson and the Progressive Era: 1910-1917,* Harper, 1954; *American Epoch: A History of the United States since the 1890s,* Knopf, 1955, 3rd edition (with William Bruce Catton and

William M. Leary, Jr.), 1967, 4th edition (with Catton) published as *American Epoch: A History of the United States since 1900,* Volume I: *The Progressive Era and the First World War: 1900-1920,* 1973, Volume II: *The Age of Franklin D. Roosevelt: 1921-1945,* 1973, Volume III: *The Era of the Cold War: 1946-1973,* 1974, 5th edition (with Catton), two volumes, 1980; *Wilson the Diplomatist: A Look at His Major Foreign Policies,* Johns Hopkins Press, 1957, reprinted, New Viewpoints, 1974.

Woodrow Wilson: A Brief Biography, World Publishing, 1963; (with D. S. Muzzey) *Our American Republic,* Ginn, 1963, new edition, 1966; (with Muzzey) *Our Country's History,* Ginn, 1964, revised edition, 1965; (editor) *The First Presbyterian Church of Princeton: Two Centuries of History,* First Presbyterian Church, 1967; (editor with R. W. Patrick) *Writing Southern History: Essays in Historiography in Honor of Fletcher M. Green,* Louisiana State University Press, 1967; *The Growth of American Democracy: An Interpretive History,* Ginn, 1968; (editor) *Woodrow Wilson: A Profile,* Hill & Wang, 1968; (editor) *The Impact of World War I,* Harper, 1969; (with Leary) *The Progressive Era and the Great War: 1896-1926,* Appleton, 1969; (editor with Leary) *The Diplomacy of World Power: The United States 1889-1920,* St. Martin's, 1970; *The Higher Realism of Woodrow Wilson and Other Essays,* Vanderbilt University Press, 1971; (with Coben) *The Democratic Heritage: A History of the United States,* two volumes, Ginn, 1971; (with others) *Crucial American Elections,* American Philosophical Society, 1973; *Woodrow Wilson: Revolution, War and Peace,* AHM Publishing, 1979; (with Coben, Robert V. Remini, Douglas Greenburg, and Robert McMath) *The American People: A History,* AHM Publishing, 1981. Editor-in-chief, *The Papers of Woodrow Wilson,* 1958—.

Member of board of editors, *Journal of Southern History,* 1955-58, 1963-66, and *Journal of American History,* 1967-70.

SIDELIGHTS: A critic in the *Virginia Quarterly Review* notes that "the publication of 'The Papers of Woodrow Wilson' is doing for late nineteenth- and early twentieth-century American historiography what the publication of 'The Papers of Thomas Jefferson' and of 'The Adams Papers' is doing for an earlier period. Publication of such massive collections of personal documents makes available the source materials from which students of American history can gain insights into the lives of important leaders that even the most carefully researched biographies cannot provide." Though a *Times Literary Supplement* reviewer finds fault with the "poor index" and the occasional lack of explanatory notes (whose main purpose would be to furnish background information on less well-known people and events), he concludes that "the editing of this new series is up to the standard of the other great Princeton series, the Jefferson papers."

AVOCATIONAL INTERESTS: Music, Trollope's novels.

BIOGRAPHICAL/CRITICAL SOURCES: South Atlantic Quarterly, spring, 1967; *Times Literary Supplement,* June 22, 1967; *Virginia Quarterly Review,* summer, 1969.

*   *   *

LITTERER, Joseph A(ugust)   1926-

PERSONAL: Born October 16, 1926, in New York, N.Y.; son of Charles Frank (a printer) and Gladys (Bader) Litterer; married Marie Wilson (a scientific illustrator), October 17, 1953; children: Karin, Susan, David. *Education:* Drexel Institute of Technology, B.S. in E.E., 1950, M.B.A., 1955; University of Illinois, Ph.D., 1959. *Office:* Department of

Management, University of Massachusetts, Amherst, Mass. 01002.

CAREER: Radio Corp. of America, Camden, N.J., supervisor of test equipment, 1952-55; University of Illinois at Urbana-Champaign, 1957-69, began as instructor, became professor of business administration; University of Massachusetts—Amherst, 1969—, currently professor. Consultant to Allis Chalmers, Mobil Oil, Bendix Corp., Corn Products Co., and other business firms. *Military service:* U.S. Army, 1950-52. *Member:* Institute of Management Services (chairman of college on organizations, 1963—), American Economic Association, American Sociological Association, Academy of Management, Society for the Advancement of Management.

WRITINGS—All published by Wiley, except as indicated: (Editor) *Organizations: Structure and Behavior,* 1963, 3rd edition, 1980; *The Analysis of Organizations,* 1965, revised edition, 1978; *Organizations: Systems Control and Growth,* 1969; *Managing for Organizational Effectiveness,* McGraw, 1975; *An Introduction to Management,* 1978; *Management: Concepts and Controversies,* 1980; *Organization by Design: Theory and Practice,* B.P.I., 1981.

WORK IN PROGRESS: Investigating the types and functions of paradigms in management decision making.

AVOCATIONAL INTERESTS: Reading, history, squash, tennis, fishing, sailing, and loafing at the family summer place in Maine.

*   *   *

LITTLE, Lawrence Calvin   1897-1976

PERSONAL: Born May 24, 1897, in Couley, La.; died December 21, 1976, in Westminster, Md.; son of Henry Clay and Minnie (Brett) Little; married Katherine McKenzie, 1922; children: Katherine Taylor, Marjorie Spangler, Betty Morey. *Education:* Davidson College, A.B., 1925; Duke University, M.A., 1929; Adrian College, D.D., 1931; Yale University, Ph.D., 1941. *Religion:* Methodist. *Office:* Department of Education, University of Pittsburgh, Pittsburgh, Pa. 15213.

CAREER: Public school teacher, university instructor, Methodist Church organization official, and pastor, 1916-31; Western Maryland College, Westminster, professor and chairman of department of religious education, 1931-45; University of Pittsburgh, Pittsburgh, Pa., professor of education and chairman of program in religious education, beginning 1945. Member of professors and research section of division of Christian education of National Council of Churches; member, Western Pennsylvania Conference of Methodist Church.

MEMBER: Religious Education Association (member of board of directors), American Academy of Religion, American Educational Research Association, American Association of University Professors, National Society for Study of Education, Society for Scientific Study of Religion, Religious Research Association, National Education Association, Adult Education Association, Philosophical Society, Greater Pittsburgh Council on Adult Education, Phi Delta Kappa, Quiz Club (Pittsburgh). *Awards, honors:* LL.D., Albright College.

WRITINGS: Foundations for a Philosophy of Christian Education, Abingdon, 1962; *A Layman's Appraisal of Christian Adult Education,* Department of Religious Education, University of Pittsburgh, 1964; *Measuring the Effectiveness of Theological Communication,* [Westminster, Md.], 1968;

Religion in Public School Social Studies Curricula, [Westminster, Md.], 1968.

Editor; all published by Department of Religious Education, University of Pittsburgh, except as indicated: *Toward a Better Education in Moral and Spiritual Values,* 1953; *Religion and Education for Professional Responsibility,* 1956; *Formulating the Objectives of Christian Adult Education,* 1958; *The Future Course of Christian Adult Education,* University of Pittsburgh Press, 1959; *Adult Education in the Church of Tomorrow,* 1961; *Guidelines for the Development of Christian Education Curricula for Adults,* 1961; *Abstracts of Selected Doctoral Dissertations on Adult Religious Education,* 1962; *A Bibliography of American Doctoral Dissertations, 1885 to 1959,* 1962; *Wider Horizons for Christian Adult Education,* University of Pittsburgh Press, 1962; *A Bibliography of Doctoral Dissertations in Personality, Character and Religious Education,* University of Pittsburgh Press, 1962; *Bibliography of Doctoral Dissertations on Adults and Adult Education,* University of Pittsburgh Press, 1962, 3rd revised edition, University of Pittsburgh Book Center, 1968; *Toward Understanding Adults and Adult Education,* 1963; *Toward Understanding the Church and the Clergy,* 1963; *Religion and Public Education: A Bibliography,* 1966; *Religion in the Social Studies,* National Conference of Christians and Jews, 1966.

Contributor to religion and education journals.

WORK IN PROGRESS: A Philosophy of Christian Education and *Research Studies on Religion in Public Education.*

AVOCATIONAL INTERESTS: Golf, philately, and gardening.†

*   *   *

LIVINGSTON, William S.   1920-

PERSONAL: Born July 1, 1920, in Ironton, Ohio; son of Samuel George (a civil servant) and Bata Aileen (Elkins) Livingston; married Lana Sanor, July 10, 1943; children: Stepehen, David. *Education:* Ohio State University, B.A., 1943, M.A., 1943; Yale University, Ph.D., 1950. *Politics:* "Objective neutrality." *Religion:* Episcopal. *Home:* 3203 Greenlee Dr., Austin, Tex. 78703. *Office:* Department of Government, University of Texas, Austin, Tex. 78712.

CAREER: University of Texas at Austin, assistant professor, 1949-54, associate professor, 1954-60, professor of government, 1960—, assistant dean of Graduate School, 1954-58, chairman, department of government, 1966-69, chairman of faculty senate, 1973-79, chairman of comparative studies program, 1978-79, vice-president and dean of graduate studies, 1979—. University of Texas System, vice-chancellor for academic programs, 1969-71. Visiting lecturer at Yale University, 1955-56; visiting professor at Duke University, 1961. *Military service:* U.S. Army, Field Artillery, 1943-45; served in Europe; became first lieutenant; received Bronze Star and Purple Heart. *Member:* Canadian Political Science Association, American Political Science Association, Southern Political Science Association (president), Southwestern Political Science Association (president), Southwestern Social Science Association (president), Hansard Society (London), Phi Beta Kappa, Omicron Delta Kappa, Phi Gamma Delta. *Awards, honors:* Ford Foundation faculty fellow, 1952-53; Guggenheim fellow, 1959-60; Teaching Excellence Award, University of Texas, 1959.

WRITINGS: Federalism and Constitutional Change, Clarendon Press, 1956; (editor and co-author) *Federalism in the Commonwealth: A Bibliographical Commentary,* published for Hansard Society by Cassell, 1963; (contributor) Marian D. Irish, editor, *World Pressures on American Foreign Policy*, Prentice-Hall, 1964; (contributor) Robert H. Connery, editor, *Teaching Political Science*, Duke University Press, 1965; (contributor) Valerie Earle, editor, *Federalism: Infinite Variety in Theory and Practice*, Peacock, 1968; (co-editor) *Australia, New Zealand, and the Pacific Islands since the First World War*, University of Texas Press, 1979; (editor) *The Presidency and the Congress: A Shifting Balance of Power?*, L.B.J. School and L.B.J. Library, 1979; (editor and co-author) *A Prospect of Liberal Democracy*, University of Texas Press, 1979; (contributor) Howard Penniman, editor, *Britain at the Polls*, American Enterprise Institute, 1980. Contributor of about fifteen articles to journals.

AVOCATIONAL INTERESTS: Tennis, hunting, philately.

* * *

LOCKRIDGE, Hildegarde (Dolson)   1908-1981
(Hildegarde Dolson)

PERSONAL: Born August 31, 1908, in Franklin, Pa.; daughter of Clifford and Katharine (Brown) Dolson; married Richard Lockridge (a writer), May, 1965. *Education:* Attended Allegheny College, 1926-29. *Home:* 206 Hillside Ct., Tryon, N.C. 28782. *Agent:* James Brown Assos., Inc., 25 West 43rd St., New York, N.Y. 10036.

CAREER: Advertising copywriter in New York, N.Y. at Gimbel's, Macy's, Franklin-Simon, and Bamberger stores, 1933-38; free-lance writer, 1938-81. *Member:* Authors League, American Civil Liberties Union. *Awards, honors:* D.Litt., Allegheny College.

WRITINGS—All under name Hildegarde Dolson; published by Random House, except as indicated: (Self-illustrated) *We Shook the Family Tree* (juvenile), 1946; *The Husband Who Ran Away*, 1948; *The Form Divine*, 1950; *Sorry to Be So Cheerful*, 1955; (with Elizabeth Stevenson Ives) *My Brother Adlai*, Morrow, 1956; *A Growing Wonder*, 1957; *The Great Oildorado*, 1959; *William Penn: Quaker Hero* (juvenile), 1962; *Guess Whose Hair I'm Wearing*, 1963; *Disaster at Johnstown* (juvenile), 1965.

Published by Lippincott: *Open the Door*, 1966; *Heat Lightning*, 1968; *To Spite Her Face* (mystery), 1971; *A Dying Fall* (mystery), 1973; *Please Omit Funeral*, 1975; *Beauty Sleep*, 1978. Contributor of articles to *New Yorker*, *Harper's*, *Ladies Home Journal*, *McCall's*, *Reader's Digest*, and other popular magazines.

(Died January 15, 1981)

* * *

LOFTIS, John (Clyde, Jr.)   1919-

PERSONAL: Born May 16, 1919, in Atlanta, Ga.; son of John Clyde and Marbeth (Brown) Loftis; married Anne Nevins, June 29, 1946; children: Mary, Laura, Lucy. *Education:* Emory University, B.A., 1940; Princeton University, M.A., 1942, Ph.D., 1948. *Home:* 7 Arastradero Rd., Menlo Park, Calif. 94025. *Office:* Department of English, Stanford University, Stanford, Calif. 94305.

CAREER: Princeton University, Princeton, N.J., instructor, 1946-48; University of California, Los Angeles, instructor, 1948-50, assistant professor, 1950-52; Stanford University, Stanford, Calif., associate professor, 1952-58, professor of English, 1958—, Bailey Professor of English, 1977—, chairman of department, 1973-76, director of graduate study, 1960-64. *Military service:* U.S. Naval Reserve, 1942-46; became lieutenant. *Member:* Modern Language Association of America (chairman of Section VII, the Classical Period,

1954), Philological Association of the Pacific Coast, Phi Beta Kappa (secretary of Stanford University chapter, 1957-61), Kappa Alpha. *Awards, honors:* Ford Foundation faculty fellow, 1955-56; Fulbright lecturer, 1959-60; Guggenheim fellow, 1966-67; Folger Shakespeare Library fellow, 1967; National Endowment for the Humanities senior fellow, 1978-79.

WRITINGS: Steele at Drury Lane, University of California Press, 1952; *Comedy and Society from Congreve to Fielding*, Stanford University Press, 1959; *La Independencia de la Literatura Norteamericana*, United States Information Service, 1961; *The Politics of Drama in Augustan England*, Clarendon Press, 1963; *The Spanish Plays of Neoclassical England*, Yale University Press, 1973; (with others) *The Revels History of Drama in English*, Volume V, Methuen, 1976; *Sheridan and the Drama of Georgian England*, Harvard University Press, 1977.

Editor: Richard Steele, *The Theatre*, Clarendon Press, 1962; (compiler with others) *English Literature, 1660-1800: A Bibliography of Modern Studies*, Volume III: *1951-1956*, Princeton University Press, 1962; *Restoration Drama: Modern Essays in Criticism*, Oxford University Press, 1966; Richard Sheridan, *The School for Scandal*, Appleton-Century-Crofts, 1966; Nathaniel Lee, *Lucius Junius Brutus*, University of Nebraska Press, 1967; (with Vinton A. Dearing) *The Works of John Dryden*, University of California Press, Volume IX, 1967, Volume XI (with Dearing and D. S. Rodes), 1978; *The Memoirs of Anne, Lady Halkett, and Ann, Lady Fanshawe*, Clarendon Press, 1979. General editor, Augustan Reprint Society, 1950-52, "Regents Restoration Drama" series, University of Nebraska Press, 1962—; co-editor of annual bibliography of Restoration and eighteenth-century studies for *Philological Quarterly*, 1951-56; member of editorial board, *Studies in English Literature*, 1966—, *Huntington Library Quarterly*, 1969—, and Wesleyan edition of the works of Henry Fielding, 1970—.

* * *

LOGUE, Christopher   1926-
(Count Palmiro Vicarion)

PERSONAL: Born November 23, 1926, in Portsmouth, Hampshire, England. *Home:* 18 Denbigh Close, London W. 11, England.

CAREER: Poet. Has acted in "The Devils," 1970, "Hamlet," 1980, and on television in "The Gadfly," 1977.

WRITINGS—All poetry: *Wand and Quadrant*, [Paris], 1953; *Devil, Maggot and Son*, [Amsterdam], 1954, limited edition, P. Russell, 1956; *The Weekdream Sonnets*, Jack Straw (Paris), 1955; *The Song of the Dead Soldier*, Villiers Publications, c.1956; *The Man Who Told His Love: 20 Poems Based on P. Neruda's "Los Cantos d'amores,"* Scorpion Press, 1958, 2nd edition, 1959; *A Song for Kathleen*, Villiers Publications, 1958; *Memoranda for Marchers*, [London], 1959; *Songs*, Hutchinson, 1959, McDowell, Obolensky, 1960; (compiler) *Count Palmiro Vicarion's Book of Limericks*, Olympia Press (Paris), 1959; *Songs from "The Lily-White Boys,"* Scorpion Press, 1960; (translator and adapter) Homer, *Patrocleia: Book 16 of Homer's Illiad Freely Adapted into English*, Scorpion Press, 1962, published in America as *Patrocleia of Homer: A New Version by Christopher Logue*, University of Michigan Press, 1963; *The Arrival of the Poet in the City: A Treatment for a Film*, Mandarin Books, 1964; *I Shall Vote Labour*, Turret Books, 1966; *Christopher Logue's ABC*, Scorpion Press, 1966; *True Stories*, Four Square Books, 1966; *The Establishment Songs*, Poet & Printer, 1966; (translator and adapter) Homer, *Pax, from*

Book XIX of the Illiad, Turret Books, 1967, also published as *Pax,* Rapp & Carroll, 1967; (with Wallace Southam and Patrick Gower) *Gone Ladies* (contemporary poetry set to music; words by Logue, music by Southam, and arrangement by Gower), Turret Books, 1968; *The Girls,* Turret Books, 1969; *New Numbers,* J. Cape, 1969, Knopf, 1970; (contributor) *The Children's Book of Comic Verse,* Batsford, 1979; (contributor) *The Bumper Book of True Stories,* Private Eye, 1980; *Ode to the Dodo* (selected poems), J. Cape, 1981; *War Music: An Account of Books 16 to 19 of Homer's Iliad,* J. Cape, 1981.

Plays: "Antigone"; "The Trial of Cob and Leach"; "The Lily-White Boys." Author of screenplay for film, "Savage Messiah," 1972. Also author, under pseudonym Count Palmiro Vicarion, of *Lust,* Olympia Press, 1969.

SIDELIGHTS: Recordings of Christopher Logue's poems have been issued in London, under the titles "Red Bird," 1961, "Poets Reading," 1961, and "The Death of Patrocleia," 1962.

BIOGRAPHICAL/CRITICAL SOURCES: Books and Bookmen, May, 1967; *London Magazine,* August, 1968, October, 1969.

*   *   *

LOHF, Kenneth A. 1925-

PERSONAL: Born January 14, 1925, in Milwaukee, Wis.; son of H. A. and Louise (Krause) Lohf. *Education:* Northwestern University, B.A., 1949; Columbia University, M.A., 1950, M.S. in L.S., 1952. *Office:* Rare Book and Manuscript Library, Columbia University Libraries, New York, N.Y. 10027.

CAREER: Columbia University Libraries, New York, N.Y., assistant librarian, department of special collections (Rare Book and Manuscript Library), 1957-67, librarian for rare books and manuscripts, 1967—. *Military service:* U.S. Army Air Forces, 1943-46; served in India, Germany, France, England; became first lieutenant. *Member:* Bibliographical Society of America, Century Association, Grolier Club.

WRITINGS: (With Eugene P. Sheehy) *Joseph Conrad at Mid-Century: Editions and Studies, 1895-1955,* University of Minnesota Press, 1957; (with Sheehy) *The Achievement of Marianne Moore: A Bibliography, 1907-1957,* New York Public Library, 1958; (with Sheehy) *Frank Norris: A Bibliography,* Talisman, 1959; (with Sheehy) *Yvor Winters: A Bibliography,* A. Swallow, 1959; (with Sheehy) *Sherwood Anderson: A Bibliography,* Talisman, 1960; *The Collection of Books, Manuscripts and Autograph Letters in the Library of Jean and Donald Stralem,* privately printed, 1962; (editor and author of preface) Hart Crane, *Seven Lyrics,* Ibex Press, 1966; *XXX for Time* (poems), Humphries, 1966; (compiler) *The Literary Manuscripts of Hart Crane,* Ohio State University Press, 1967; (compiler) *The Engle Collection Presented by Solton and Julia Engle* (catalog), Columbia University Libraries, 1967; (author of afterword) Clement C. Moore, *A Visit from St. Nicholas,* Simon & Schuster, 1971; (author of introduction) Hart Crane, *Ten Unpublished Poems,* Gotham Book Mart, 1972; *The Jack Harris Samuels Library,* Columbia University Libraries, 1974; *The Centenary of John Masefield's Birth,* Columbia University Libraries, 1978; (author of introduction) *The History of Printing from Its Beginnings to 1930,* Kraus International, 1980; *Seasons* (poems), Janus Press, 1980.

Compiler of *An Index to the Little Review, 1914-1929,* New York Public Library, 1961, and *Index to Little Magazines,*

A. Swallow, 1957, 1958, 1960, 1962, 1964. Contributor to *Twentieth Century Literature, Poetry,* and regional literary reviews. Editor, *Columbia Library,* 1981—.

AVOCATIONAL INTERESTS: American poetry, book collecting.

*   *   *

LONG, Howard Rusk 1906-

PERSONAL: Born July 30, 1906, in Columbia, Mo.; son of Connor Melbourne and Carrie (Bramblett) Long; married Margaret Helen Carney, May 3, 1931; children: Nancy Long Bearss, Joseph Carney. *Education:* Attended Purdue University, 1925-26; University of Missouri, B.A. and B.J., 1930, M.A., 1941, Ph.D., 1948. *Religion:* Presbyterian. *Home:* 606 Beadle Dr., Carbondale, Ill. 62901.

CAREER: Worked as reporter on various weekly newspapers; *Chronicle,* Crane, Mo., publisher, 1934-40; University of Missouri—Columbia, 1940-50, began as instructor, professor of journalism, 1948-50; Southern Illinois University at Carbondale, professor of journalism, 1953-74, chairman of department, 1953-70, director of School of Journalism, 1970-74. Visiting professor, Graduate School of Journalism, National Chengchi University, Taipei, Taiwan, 1947-48; visiting specialist in the Philippines for U.S. Information Service, 1958. Manager of Long Ranch livestock farm in Rochester, Ind., 1950-53. *Member:* International Society of Weekly Newspaper Editors (secretary, 1955-72), International Press Institute, American Society of Journalism School Administrators (president, 1960), Association of Education in Journalism, Asia Society, China Academy (academician), English-Speaking Union, British Institute of Journalists, Royal Photographic Society, Missouri Press Association (manager, 1940-50), University of Missouri Journalism Alumni Association (president, 1940), St. Louis Press Club, Kappa Alpha Mu, Kappa Tau Alpha, Alpha Delta Sigma, Sigma Delta Chi, Rotary International, Masons, Elks. *Awards, honors:* Smith-Mundt grant from U.S. State Department, 1957-58; State Department grant to lecture in northern Europe, 1964 and 1976.

WRITINGS: The People of Mushan, University of Missouri Press, 1960; (with H. R. Pratt Boorman) *Recalling the Battle of Britain,* Kent Messenger Press, 1965; *Mainstreet Militants,* Southern Illinois University Press, 1977. Also author of *Swat the Rooster.* Guest editor, *China Post* (Taipei), 1947-48; editor, *Grassroots Editor,* 1960-72.

AVOCATIONAL INTERESTS: Photography and travel.

*   *   *

LONGRIGG, Roger (Erskine) 1929-
(Ivor Drummond, Rosalind Erskine)

PERSONAL: Born May 1, 1929, in Edinburgh, Scotland; son of Stephen Hemsley and Florence (Anderson) Longrigg; married Jane Chichester, June 20, 1957; children: Laura J., Frances A., Clare S. *Education:* Magdalen College, Oxford, B.A., 1952. *Home:* Orchard House, Crookham, Hampshire, England. *Agent:* Curtis Brown Ltd., 1 Craven Hill, London W2 3EW, England.

CAREER: Affiliated with various advertising agencies, 1962-68; currently full-time writer. *Military service:* British Army, 1947-49; became captain. *Member:* Society of Authors, Crime Writers Association, Brooks's Club (London), Pratt's Club, London Library, Greenjackets.

WRITINGS: A High-Pitched Buzz, Faber, 1956; *Switchboard,* Faber, 1957; *Wrong Number,* Faber, 1959; *Daugh-*

ters of Mulberry, Faber, 1961; *The Paper Boats*, Harper, 1963; *The Artless Gambler*, Pelham Books, 1964; *Love among the Bottles*, Faber, 1967; *The Sun on the Water*, Macmillan, 1969; *The Desperate Criminals*, Macmillan, 1971; *The History of Horse Racing*, Stein & Day, 1972; *The Jevington System*, Macmillan, 1973; *Their Pleasing Sport*, Macmillan, 1975; *The Turf: Three Centuries of Horse Racing*, Methuen, 1975; *The History of Foxhunting*, C. N. Potter, 1975; *The Babe in the Wood*, M. Joseph, 1976; *The English Squire and His Sport*, St. Martin's, 1977.

Under pseudonym Ivor Drummond; all published by St. Martin's, except as indicated: *The Man with the Tiny Head*, Harcourt, 1969; *The Priests of the Abomination*, Harcourt, 1970; *The Frog in the Moonflower*, 1972; *The Jaws of the Watchdog*, 1973; *The Power of the Bug*, 1974; *The Tank of Sacred Eels*, 1976; *The Necklace of Skulls*, 1977; *The Stench of Poppies*, 1978; *The Diamonds of Loreta*, 1980.

Under pseudonym Rosalind Erskine: *The Passion Flower Hotel*, Simon & Schuster, 1962; *Passion Flowers in Italy*, J. Cape, 1963, Simon & Schuster, 1964; *Passion Flowers in Business*, J. Cape, 1965.

Also author of radio plays for the BBC, a stage play, "The Platinum Cat," produced in London, 1965, and numerous television plays for BBC-TV and Granada TV, including "Firing Point," 1974, "Bad Connection," 1974, "Arson," 1974, and "Contempt of Court," 1975; author of film scripts for Rank Organization, Metro-Goldwyn-Mayer, Inc., Universal Pictures, and several independent producers. Contributor to magazines and newspapers, including the *London Times*, *Sunday Telegraph*, *Harper's*, *Penthouse*, *Punch*, and *Cosmopolitan*.

BIOGRAPHICAL/CRITICAL SOURCES: New Statesman, March 24, 1967; *Observer*, March 26, 1967; *Times Literary Supplement*, April 6, 1967; *Spectator*, September 13, 1969; *New Yorker*, April 4, 1970; *New York Times Book Review*, February 9, 1975, June 20, 1976; *Listener*, May 6, 1976; *Best Sellers*, November, 1976, September, 1977; *Time*, November 20, 1978.

*   *   *

LOVENSTEIN, Meno 1909-

PERSONAL: Born January 4, 1909, in Durham, N.C.; son of Benjamin (a lawyer) and Rebecca (Greenberg) Lovenstein; married Beatrice Bender (a teacher), February 18, 1930; children: Jonathan Mitchell, Douglas Bender. *Education:* University of Richmond, B.A., 1930; Columbia University, M.A., 1931; Johns Hopkins University, Ph.D., 1935. *Office:* Ohio University, Athens, Ohio 45701.

CAREER: Rockford College, Rockford, Ill., assistant professor, 1938-42; Ohio State University, Columbus, 1946-66, started as associate professor, became professor of economics; Ohio University, Athens, Charles G. O'Bleness Professor of Economics, 1966-79, professor emeritus, 1979—. *Military service:* U.S. Army, instructor at Armed Forces Industrial College, 1942-46. *Member:* American Economic Association, American Association for Advancement of Science, American Association of University Professors. *Awards, honors:* Distinguished teaching award, Ohio State University, 1964, and Ohio University, 1971.

WRITINGS: American Opinion of Soviet Russia, American Council on Public Affairs, 1942; *These* (poems), privately printed, 1942; *Economics and the Educational Administrator*, Ohio State University Press, 1958; (contributor) *The Teaching of Elementary Economics*, Holt, 1962; *Capitalism,*

Communism, Socialism, Curriculum Resources, 1962; (co-editor) *Readings in the Economics of National Security*, U.S. Air Force Academy, 1962; (contributor) Robert Theobold, editor, *Guaranteed Income*, Doubleday, 1966; *The Decade of the University*, Ohio University, 1971; *Against a Garden Wall* (poems), Simmons College Press, 1975.

WORK IN PROGRESS: Economics: A Pathway toward Social Intelligence; poems; fiction.

SIDELIGHTS: Meno Lovenstein told *CA:* "All human effort is make-believe, economics, poems, and short stories, since they confirm man's belief in making a thoughtful response to overwhelming complexity."

*   *   *

LOWENFELS, Walter 1897-1976

PERSONAL: Born May 10, 1897, in New York, N.Y.; died July 7, 1976, in Tarrytown, N.Y.; son of Frederick F. (a dairy owner) and Edith Lowenfels; married Lillian Apotheker, September 28, 1926; children: Michal L. Kane, Manna L. Pertelitt, Judy L. Jacobs, Angela L. Schwartz. *Politics:* Communist.

CAREER: Poet and writer. *Military service:* U.S. Army, private; served during World War I. *Member:* Poetry Society of America, Authors Guild, P.E.N. *Awards, honors:* Richard Aldington Award for American Poets, 1929; *Mainstream* Award, 1957; Longview Foundation Award, 1963.

WRITINGS: U.S.A. with Music (opera), Carrefour (Paris), 1930; *Anonymous: The Need for Anonymity*, Carrefour (Paris), 1960; *To an Imaginary Daughter*, Horizon, 1964; *The Portable Walter: From the Prose and Poetry of Walter Lowenfels*, edited by Robert Gover, International Publishers, 1968; *The Poetry of My Politics* (autobiography), Olivant Press, 1968; (with Howard McCord) *The Life of Fraenkel's Death: A Biographical Inquest*, Washington State University Press, 1970; *The Revolution Is to Be Human*, International Publishers, 1973; *Reality Prime: Pages from a Journal*, Cycle Press, 1974.

Poetry: *Episodes and Epistles*, Thomas Seltzer, 1925; *Finale of Seem: A Lyrical Narrative*, Heinemann, 1929; *Apollinaire: An Elegy*, Hours Press (Paris), 1930; *Elegy for D. H. Lawrence*, Carrefour (Paris), 1932; *The Suicide*, Carrefour (Paris), 1934; *Sonnets of Love and Liberty*, Blue Heron Press, 1955; *American Voices*, Roving Eye Press, 1959; *Some Deaths: Selected Poems, 1929-1962*, Jargon Books, 1964; *Land of Roseberries*, El Corno Emplumado (Mexico City), 1965; *Translations from Scorpius*, Poetry Dimension Press, 1966; *We Are All Poets, Really*, edited by Allen De Loach, Intrepid Press, 1967; *Thou Shalt Not Overkill: Walter Lowenfels' Peace Poems*, edited by wife, Lillian Lowenfels, Hellric Publications, 1968; *Found Poems and Others*, Barlenmir House, 1972.

Editor: (And translator) *Song of Peace: Based on Poems by Paul Eluard, Nicolas Guillen, M. Lukenin, Gabriela Mistral, Viteslave Neyval, Tu Fu*, Roving Eye Press, 1959; *Poets of Today*, Seven Seas Publishers, 1966; *Where Is Vietnam?: American Poets Respond*, Anchor Books, 1967; *In a Time of Revolution: Poems from Our Third World*, Random House, 1969; *The Writing on the Wall: 108 American Poems of Protest*, Doubleday, 1969; *Who Is Lenin?*, Nickel Review, 1970; *The Tenderest Lover: The Erotic Poetry of Walt Whitman*, Delacorte, 1970, published as *The Tenderest Lover: Walt Whitman's Love Poems*, Dell, 1972; *From the Belly of the Shark*, Vintage, 1973; *For Neruda, For Chile: An International Anthology*, Beacon Press, 1975. Also editor of "New Jazz Poets," a poetry recording, Folkways, 1967.

Former associate editor, *Dialogue;* managing editor of Pennsylvania edition, *Daily Worker,* 1940-55.

WORK IN PROGRESS: Autobiography of an Empire, a history of the United States.

SIDELIGHTS: Walter Lowenfels was both poet and social critic and believed that poetry should contain strong social commentary. A Communist for much of his life, Lowenfels' writings are often political.

Lowenfels' early poems, dealing most often with the problems of love, have attracted more critical attention than have his later, more political works. Although advised by other poets, most notably by T. S. Eliot, to concentrate less of his attention on politics, Lowenfels did not change his beliefs. For a number of years, in fact, Lowenfels wrote no poetry, devoting his time to editing the Communist *Daily Worker.*

In 1954, Lowenfels was convicted under the Smith Act for conspiring to teach and advocate the overthrow of the U.S. Government by force. This conviction was based upon Lowenfels' membership in the Communist Party and was later overturned when membership in the party was ruled to not be conspiratorial in nature.

Lowenfels' books have been translated into Spanish, French, and Hungarian. Yale University owns a collection of his manuscripts.

BIOGRAPHICAL/CRITICAL SOURCES: Negro Digest, February, 1965; *Saturday Review,* February 13, 1965, February 25, 1967, January 24, 1970; *Poetry,* July, 1965, September, 1965, March, 1968; *New York Times Book Review,* November 14, 1965, November 9, 1969, September 27, 1970; *Christian Century,* March 22, 1967; *Nation,* April 24, 1967, July 7, 1969; *Book World,* November 9, 1969, April 6, 1975; *Book List,* January 1, 1970; *Top of the News,* April, 1970; *New York Times,* July 8, 1976.†

*   *   *

LUCAS PHILLIPS, C(ecil) E(rnest) 1897-

PERSONAL: Born September 14, 1897, in St. Vincent, British West Indies; son of Miles and Ada Joan (Moon) Lucas Phillips; married Barbara Josephine Hertford, November 24, 1923; children: four daughters. *Education:* Attended St. Lawrence College and King's College, London. *Address:* c/o Barclay's Bank, Esher, Surrey, England.

CAREER: Worked in journalism and public relations, 1922-39. *Military service:* British Army, Royal Artillery, 1914-18, 1939-46; commanded surrendered German Army in Italy, 1945-46; became brigadier general; received Military Cross, Croix de Guerre, Order of British Empire.

WRITINGS—Published by Heinemann, except as indicated: *Cromwell's Captains,* 1938; *The Small Garden,* 1952; *Cockleshell Heroes,* 1956; *Escape of the Amethyst,* Heinemann, 1957, Coward, 1958; (editor) R. Milton Carleton and Marjorie P. Johnson, *Hardy Bulbs and Perennials,* 1957; *The Greatest Raid of All* (Companion Book Club selection), Heinemann, 1958, Little, Brown, 1960.

The Spanish Pimpernel (Companion Book Club selection), 1960; *The Vision Splendid: The Future of the Central African Federation,* 1960; *Alamein,* Heinemann, 1962, Little, Brown, 1963, revised edition, Pan Books, 1965; *Springboard to Victory,* 1966; *Plants for Walls and Gardens,* 1967; (with P. N. Barber) *The Rothschild Rhododendrons,* Cassell, 1967, revised edition, in press; *The Modern Flower Garden,* 1968; *The Design of Small Gardens,* 1969.

The Raiders of Arakan, 1971; *Victoria Cross Battles,* 1973;

The Trees around Us, Follett, 1975; *The New Small Garden,* Collins, 1979. Also author of *Roses for Small Gardens,* published by Pan Books. Editor of "Pan Gardening" series, published by Pan Books. Contributor of numerous articles to newspapers and magazines.

WORK IN PROGRESS: Ornamental Shrubs.

SIDELIGHTS: C. E. Lucas Phillips calls himself a "fanatic" about gardening. Several of his books have appeared in foreign language editions, including French, Danish, Norwegian, Hebrew, and German.

*   *   *

LUNT, James D(oiran) 1917-

PERSONAL: Born November 13, 1917, in Liverpool, England; son of Walter Thomas and Chilli (Dodd) Lunt; married Muriel J. Byrt, 1940; children: Robin James Cameron, Jennifer Lesley. *Education:* Attended King William's College, 1932-35, and Royal Military College, 1936-37. *Home:* Hilltop House, Little Milton, Oxfordshire, England. *Agent:* Bolt & Watson, 8-12 Old Queen St., London S.W.1, England. *Office:* Wadham College, Oxford University, Oxford, England.

CAREER: British Army, Cavalry and Infantry, 1937-72, retired as major general; Oxford University, Wadham College, Oxford, England, bursar, 1972—. *Member:* Royal United Service Institution, Cavalry Club, Flyfishers Club. *Awards, honors:* M.A., Oxford University, 1973; named fellow of the Royal Geographical Society, 1974.

WRITINGS: Charge to Glory, Harcourt, 1960; *Scarlet Lancer,* Harcourt, 1964; *The Barren Rocks of Aden,* Harcourt, 1966; *Bokhara Burnes,* Faber, 1969; *Sepoy to Subedar,* Routledge & Kegan Paul, 1970; *History of the Duke of Wellington's Regiment,* Cooper, 1971; *History of the 16th/5th: The Queen's Royal Lancers,* Cooper, 1973; *John Burgoyne of Saratoga,* Harcourt, 1975; *Imperial Sunset,* MacDonald-Futura, 1981. Contributor to periodicals in the United States and England.

WORK IN PROGRESS: A biography of "Lieutenant-General Sir John Glubb Pasha."

SIDELIGHTS: James D. Lunt spent many years in the Middle East. He is fluent in Arabic. *Avocational interests:* International affairs, music, falconry, fishing.

*   *   *

LYNCH, Kevin 1918-

PERSONAL: Born January 7, 1918, in Chicago, Ill.; son of James J. (a purchasing agent) and Laura (Healy) Lynch; married Anne Borders (a teacher), 1940; children: David, Laura, Catherine, Peter. *Education:* Attended Yale University and Rensselaer Polytechnic Institute, also studied under Frank Lloyd Wright; Massachusetts Institute of Technology, B.C.P., 1948. *Politics:* Socialist. *Home:* 85 Russell Ave., Watertown, Mass. *Office:* Carr, Lynch Associates, 45 Hancock St., Cambridge, Mass.

CAREER: Department of Planning, Greensboro, N.C., planner, 1948-49; Massachusetts Institute of Technology, Cambridge, professor of planning, 1949-79; Carr, Lynch Associates, Cambridge, Mass., partner, 1978—. *Member,* Planning Board, Watertown, Mass., 1962—. Consultant to state of Rhode Island, New England Medical Center, University Circle (Cleveland), Boston Redevelopment Authority, Puerto Rico Industrial Development Corp., M.I.T. Planning Office, Detroit Land Use and Transportation Study, and others. *Member:* American Institute of Planners. *Awards, honors:* Ford Foundation fellowship, 1953; 50th Anniversary Award, American Institute of Planners, 1957; Allied Professions Medal, American Institute of Architects, 1974.

WRITINGS—All published by M.I.T. Press, except as indicated: *The Image of the City,* Massachusetts Institute of Technology, Harvard University Press, 1960; *Site Planning,* 1962, 2nd edition, 1971; (with Donald Appleyard and John R. Myer) *The View from the Road* (monograph), 1963; *What Time Is This Place?,* 1972; *Managing the Sense of a Region,* 1976; *Growing Up in Cities,* 1977; *A Theory of Good City Form,* 1981. Contributor to professional journals.

WORK IN PROGRESS: Research on environmental waste and decline.

*　　*　　*

LYNCH, William F. 1908-

PERSONAL: Born June 16, 1908, in New York, N.Y.; son of Michael J. and Mary (Maloney) Lynch. *Education:* Fordham University, A.B., 1930, Ph.D., 1942. *Home and office:* West Side Jesuit Community, 220 West 98th St., New York, N.Y. 10025.

CAREER: New York Herald-Tribune, New York City, reporter, 1930-31; Fordham University, Bronx, N.Y., instructor, 1931-34; entered Society of Jesus (Jesuits), 1934, ordained Roman Catholic priest, 1946; Fordham University, director of classical theatre, 1940-42; *Thought,* New York City, editor, 1950-56; Georgetown University, Washington, D.C., director of honors program, 1957-61; St. Peter's College, Jersey City, N.J., writer-in-residence, beginning 1961; currently writer-in-residence at West Side Jesuit Community, New York City. Occasional teacher of theology, Woodstock College, 1961—.

WRITINGS: The Image Industries, Sheed, 1959; *An Approach to the Metaphysics of Plato through The Parmenides,* Georgetown University Press, 1959; *Christ and Apollo: The Dimensions of the Literary Imagination,* Sheed, 1960; (co-editor) *The Idea of Catholicism,* Meridian, 1960; *The Integrating Mind,* Sheed, 1962; *Images of Hope: Imagination as Healer of the Hopeless,* Helicon, 1965; *Christ and Prometheus: A New Image of the Secular,* University of Notre Dame Press, 1970; *Images of Faith: An Exploration of the Ironic Imagination,* University of Notre Dame Press, 1973.

WORK IN PROGRESS: A Philosophy of the Theatre.

*　　*　　*

LYNES, (Joseph) Russell (Jr.) 1910-

PERSONAL: Born December 2, 1910, in Great Barrington, Mass.; son of Joseph Russell (a clergyman) and Adelaide (Sparkman) Lynes; married Mildred Akin, May 30, 1934; children: George P., II, Elizabeth Russell. *Education:* Yale University, B.A., 1932. *Home:* 427 East 84th St., New York, N.Y. 10028.

CAREER: Harper & Brothers (publishers), New York City, clerk, 1932-36; Vassar College, Poughkeepsie, N.Y., director of publications, 1936-37; Shipley School, Bryn Mawr, Pa., assistant principal, 1937-40, principal, 1940-44; *Harper's* Magazine, New York City, assistant editor, 1944-47, editor and managing editor, 1947-67, contributing editor, 1967—. Chairman of publications committee, Yale University, 1956-60. Lecturer at universities and museums. Archives of American Art, member of board of directors, 1961—,

president, 1966-71; member, New York City Landmarks Preservation Commission, 1962-69; member, Municipal Art Society, New York; MacDowell Colony, president, 1970-74, trustee; member, New York City Art Commission, 1971-73; member of humanities committee, Whitney Foundation; member of board of directors, Halcyon-Commonwealth Foundation. Associate fellow, Berkeley College, Yale University. Trustee, Collegiate School, 1954-62, and Greenwood Fund, 1960-62. *Wartime service:* Civilian employee of U.S. War Department, 1942-44; served as assistant chief, Pre-induction Training Branch, Army Service Forces. *Member:* Authors League, P.E.N., Society of Architectural Historians, Society of American Historians, New York Historical Society (member of board of trustees), Zeta Psi, Century Association (New York). *Awards, honors:* D.F.A., Union College, 1964; L.H.D., Maryland Institute, 1973; Litt.D., North Adams State College, 1977; L.H.D., City University of New York, 1980.

WRITINGS—All published by Harper, except as indicated: *Highbrow, Lowbrow, Middlebrow,* 1949; *Snobs,* 1950; *Guests,* 1951; *The Tastemakers,* 1954; *A Surfeit of Honey,* 1957, reprinted, Greenwood Press, 1974; (contributor) Eric Larrabee, editor, *American Panorama,* New York University Press, 1957; *Cadwallader: A Diversion,* 1959; *The Domesticated Americans,* 1963; *Confessions of a Dilettante,* 1966; *The Art-Makers of Nineteenth Century America,* Atheneum, 1970; *Good Old Modern,* Atheneum, 1973.

Author of introduction: Nancy Mitford, *Noblesse Oblige,* Harper, 1956; Robert Benton and Harvey Schmidt, *The In and Out Book,* Viking, 1959; Gerard Hoffnung, *Ho, Ho, Hoffnung,* Harper, 1959; Wayne Andrews, *Architecture in America,* Atheneum, 1960; Katherine Tweed, editor, *The Finest Rooms,* Viking, 1964; Alfred Bendiner, *Bendiner's Philadelphia,* A. S. Barnes, 1964; *The Graphic Work of Eugene Berman,* C. N. Potter, 1971; Darwin Payne, *The Man of Only Yesterday,* Harper, 1975. Also author of introductions to several museum catalogues.

Work is represented in numerous anthologies and college textbooks. Author of columns, including "After Hours," for *Harper's,* "The State of Taste," for *Art in America,* 1969-72, and "Russell Lynes Observes," for *Architectural Digest,* 1974—. Contributor to magazines.

WORK IN PROGRESS: A Social History of the Arts in America: 1900-1950, for Harper; *More Than Meets the Eye,* an introduction to the Cooper-Hewitt Museum.

AVOCATIONAL INTERESTS: Liberal and fine arts, tennis.

BIOGRAPHICAL/CRITICAL SOURCES: New York Times, February 21, 1980.

*　　*　　*

LYNN, Kenneth S(chuyler) 1923-

PERSONAL: Born June 17, 1923, in Cleveland, Ohio; son of Ernest Lee (a newspaperman) and Edna (Marcey) Lynn; married Valerie Ann Roemer, September 23, 1948; children: Andrew Schuyler, Elisabeth, Sophia. *Education:* Harvard University, A.B., 1947, M.A., 1950, Ph.D., 1954. *Home:* 1709 Hoban Rd. N.W., Washington, D.C. 20007. *Office:* Department of History, Johns Hopkins University, Baltimore, Md. 21218.

CAREER: Harvard University, Cambridge, Mass., instructor, 1954-55, assistant professor, 1955-59, associate professor, 1959-63, professor of English, 1963-68, chairman of American Civilization Program, 1964-68; Federal City College, Washington, D.C., professor of American studies,

1968-69; Johns Hopkins University, Baltimore, Md., professor of history, 1969—. Fulbright lecturer in Denmark, 1958; visiting professor, University of Madrid, 1963-64. *Military service:* U.S. Army Air Forces, 1943-46; became second lieutenant. *Member:* American Historical Association, American Studies Association, Modern Language Association of America, Massachusetts Historical Society.

WRITINGS: The Dream of Success, Little, Brown, 1955, reprinted, Greenwood Press, 1972; (editor) *The Comic Tradition in America,* Doubleday, 1958; *Mark Twain and Southwestern Humor,* Little, Brown, 1959; (editor) *The American Society,* Braziller, 1963; (editor) *The Professions in America,* Houghton, 1965; *William Dean Howells: An American Life,* Harcourt, 1971; *Visions of America,* Greenwood Press, 1973; *A Divided People,* Greenwood Press, 1977.

General editor, "Riverside Literature" series, Houghton, 1962—. Associate editor, *Daedalus,* 1962-68, and *New England Quarterly,* 1963-68.

BIOGRAPHICAL/CRITICAL SOURCES: Harper's, June, 1971; *New York Times,* June 23, 1971.

*   *   *

LYON, Peyton V(aughan) 1921-

PERSONAL: Born October 2, 1921, in Winnipeg, Manitoba; son of Hebert Redmond and Frederica (Lee) Lyon; married Frances Hazleton, June 26, 1943; children: Russell Vaughan, Stephen Lee, Barbara Jane. *Education:* University of Manitoba, B.A., 1949; Oxford University, M.A., 1953, D.Phil., 1953. *Home:* 17 Apache Crescent, Ottawa, Ontario, Canada K2E 6H8. *Office:* Carleton University, Ottawa, Ontario, Canada.

CAREER: Canadian Fire Insurance Co., Winnipeg, Manitoba, clerk, 1938-40; Canadian Department of External Affairs, Ottawa, Ontario, foreign service officer, 1953-59, serving in Bonn, Germany, four years of that period; University of Western Ontario, London, assistant professor, 1959-61, associate professor, 1961-64, professor of political science, 1964-65; Carleton University, Ottawa, Ontario, professor of political science, 1965—. *Military service:* Royal Canadian Air Force, navigator, 1940-45; served in England and Africa; became flight lieutenant; received King's Commendation. *Member:* Canadian Institute of International Affairs, Canadian Political Science Association.

WRITINGS: The Policy Question: A Critical Appraisal of Canada's Role in World Affairs, McClelland & Stewart, 1963; *Canada in World Affairs, 1961-1963,* Canadian Institute of International Affairs and Oxford University Press, 1968; *NATO as a Diplomatic Instrument,* Atlantic Council of Canada, 1971; (co-editor and contributor) *Continental*

Community: Independence and Integration in North America, McClelland & Stewart, 1974; (editor and contributor) *Canada and the Third World,* Macmillan (Toronto), 1976; (with Brian Tomlin) *Canada As an International Actor,* Macmillan (Toronto), 1979.

Contributor: D.L.B. Hamlin, editor, *The New Europe,* University of Toronto Press, 1962; S. Clarkson, editor, *An Independent Foreign Policy for Canada?,* McClelland & Stewart, 1967; Adam Bromke and Philip E. Uren, editors, *The Communist States and the West,* Praeger, 1967; R. H. Wagenberg, editor, *Canada and the United States in the World of the Seventies,* University of Windsor Press, 1970; Hugh Innis, editor, *International Involvement,* McGraw-Hill Ryerson, 1972; Peter Stringelin, editor, *The European Community and the Outsiders,* Longman, 1973; Michael Fry, editor, *Freedom and Change,* McClelland & Stewart, 1975; H. E. English, editor, *Canada-United States Relations,* Academy of Political Science, 1976; Tomlin, editor, *Canada's Foreign Policy: Analysis and Trends,* Methuen, 1978.

*   *   *

LYONS, Thomas Tolman 1934-

PERSONAL: Born June 21, 1934, in Stoneham, Mass.; son of Louis M. (a journalist) and Margaret (Tolman) Lyons; married Eleanor Coneeney, August 31, 1958; children: John Louis, Kathleen Margaret, David Tolman, Joseph Charles. *Education:* Attended Brown University, 1952-54; Harvard University, B.A., 1957, M.A.T., 1958; postgraduate study at Wesleyan University, Stanford University, and Harvard University. *Politics:* Democrat. *Home and office:* Phillips Academy, Andover, Mass. 01810.

CAREER: Mount Hermon School for Boys, Gill, Mass., teacher of history, 1958-63; Phillips Academy, Andover, Mass., teacher of American history and urban studies, 1963-79, John Mason Kemper Instructor in History, 1979—, chairman of department, 1979—. Visiting fellow, Dartmouth College, 1968-69, Phillips Academy, 1969—. *Awards, honors:* Distinguished Secondary School Teaching Award, Harvard University, 1966.

WRITINGS: (Editor with Edwin C. Rozwenc) *Presidential Power in the New Deal,* Heath, 1963; (editor with Rozwenc) *Realism and Idealism in Wilson's Peace Program,* Heath, 1965; (with Rozwenc) *Reconstruction and the Race Problem,* Heath, 1968; *Black Leadership in American History,* Addison-Wesley, 1971; *The Supreme Court and Individual Liberties in Contemporary America,* Addison-Wesley, 1975; *America,* Addison-Wesley, 1975; *The Expansion of the Federal Republic, 1800-1848,* Independent School Press, 1978; *After Hiroshima: America since 1945,* Independent School Press, 1979.

M

MACAULEY, Robie Mayhew 1919-

PERSONAL: Born May 31, 1919, in Grand Rapids, Mich.; son of George William and Emma (Hobart) Macauley; married Anne Draper, 1948 (died, 1973); married Pamela Painter, 1979; children: (first marriage) Cameron. *Education:* Kenyon College, B.A., 1941; University of Iowa, M.F.A., 1950. *Religion:* Episcopalian. *Agent:* International Creative Management, 40 West 57th St., New York, N.Y. 10019. *Office:* Houghton Mifflin Co., 2 Park St., Boston, Mass. 02107.

CAREER: Bard College, Annandale-on-Hudson, N.Y., instructor in English, 1946-47; University of Iowa, Iowa City, instructor in English, 1947-50; University of North Carolina, Woman's College, Greensboro, assistant professor of English, 1950-53; *Kenyon Review,* Gambier, Ohio, editor, 1959-66; fiction editor, *Playboy,* 1966-77; Houghton Mifflin Co., Boston, Mass., senior editor, 1978—. Kenyon College, associate professor, 1959-61, professor of English, 1961-66; adjunct professor, University of Illinois at Chicago Circle, 1975-78. U.S. Department of State specialist grantee, Australia, 1962. *Military service:* U.S. Army, Counter Intelligence Corps, special agent, 1942-46. *Member:* P.E.N. (U.S. representative to International Congress, Tokyo, 1957, Brazil, 1960), National Council on the Arts. *Awards, honors: Benjamin Franklin* magazine awards citation, 1957; *Kenyon Review* and Rockefeller Foundation fellow, 1958; Guggenheim fellowship, 1964; Fulbright research fellow, University of London, 1964-65; *Furioso* fiction prize.

WRITINGS: The Disguises of Love (novel), Random House, 1951; *The End of Pity* (stories), Lippincott, 1962; *Technique in Fiction,* Harper, 1964; (editor) *Gallery of Modern Fiction,* Salem Press, 1966; (co-editor) *America and Its Discontents,* Xerox College Publishing, 1971; *A Secret History of Time to Come* (novel), Knopf, 1979. Work represented in *O. Henry Memorial Award Prize Stories* and *Best American Short Stories.* Contributor to *New Republic, Esquire, Vogue, Partisan Review, New York Times Book Review, Playboy,* and *Cosmopolitan.*

*   *   *

Mac CAIG, Norman (Alexander) 1910-

PERSONAL: Born November 14, 1910, in Edinburgh, Scotland; son of Robert (a chemist) and Joan (MacLeod) Mac Caig; married Isabel Munro (a school teacher), April 6, 1940; children: Joan Mac Caig Maclean, Ewen. *Education:* Edinburgh University, M.A. (honors in classics), 1932. *Religion:* None. *Home:* 7 Leamington Ter., Edinburgh, Scotland.

CAREER: Teacher in Edinburgh, Scotland, 1934-67, 1969-70; reader in poetry, University of Stirling, 1970-78. Fellow in creative writing, University of Edinburgh, 1967-69. *Member:* Scottish Arts Club (Edinburgh; fellow), Royal Society of Literature (fellow). *Awards, honors;* Arts Council awards, 1954, 1966, 1970, 1971, 1978; Society of Authors awards, 1964, 1967; Heinemann Award, 1967; Order of the British Empire, 1979.

WRITINGS—All poetry; published by Hogarth, except as indicated: *Far Cry,* Routledge, 1943; *The Inward Eye,* Routledge, 1946; *Riding Lights,* 1955, Macmillan, 1956; *The Sinai Sort,* Macmillan, 1957; (editor) *Honor'd Shade: An Anthology of New Scottish Poetry to Mark the Bicentenary of Robert Burns,* W. & R. Chambers, 1959; *A Common Grace,* 1960, Dufour, 1961; *A Round of Applause,* 1962, Dufour, 1963; *Measures,* 1965, Dufour, 1966; *Surroundings,* 1966; *Rings on a Tree,* 1968; *A Man in My Position,* 1969, Wesleyan University Press, 1970; (editor with Alexander Scott) *Contemporary Scottish Verse, 1959-1969,* Calder & Boyars, 1970; *Selected Poems,* 1971; *The White Bird,* 1973; *The World's Room,* 1974; *Tree of Strings,* 1977; *Old Maps and New: Selected Poems,* 1978; *The Equal Skies,* 1980. Contributor of poems and articles to many journals.

SIDELIGHTS: Norman Mac Caig told *CA:* "Of the arts other than poetry, I am most interested in music, of all kinds. I get great pleasure from fishing, particularly in the Highlands. I can read French, Italian, Latin, Greek, and Gaelic. I have visited France, Italy, and the U.S.A."

*   *   *

MACKESY, Piers G(erald) 1924-

PERSONAL: Born September 15, 1924, in Cults, Aberdeenshire, Scotland; son of Pierse Joseph (a major general in the British Army) and Leonora (Cook) Mackesy; married Sarah Davies, December 21, 1957 (divorced, 1978); married Patricia Gore; children: (first marriage) William, Catherine, Serena. *Education:* Christ Church, Oxford, B.A., 1950; Oriel College, Oxford, D.Phil., 1953. *Home:* The Dowerhouse Cottage, Heythrop, Chipping Norton, Oxfordshire, England. *Office:* Pembroke College, Oxford University, Oxford, England.

CAREER: Oxford University, Pembroke College, Oxford,

England, fellow, 1954—. Visiting fellow, Institute for Advanced Study, Princeton, N.J., 1961-62; visiting professor, California Institute of Technology, 1966; lecturer at Clark University, Naval War College, U.S. Military Academy, National War College, and Northeastern University; Lees-Knowles Lecturer, Cambridge University, 1972. Member of Council, Institute of Early American History and Culture, Williamsburg, 1970-73. *Military service:* British Army, 1943-47. *Awards, honors:* Harkness fellow, Harvard University, 1953-54; D.Litt., Oxford University, 1978.

WRITINGS: The War in the Mediterranean, 1803-1810, Harvard University Press, 1957; (contributor) Michael Howard, editor, *Wellingtonian Studies,* Wellington College, 1959; *The War for America, 1775-83,* Harvard University Press, 1964; (contributor) David L. Jacobson, editor, *Essays on the American Revolution,* Holt, 1970; *Statesmen at War,* Longman, Volume I: *The Strategy of Overthrow, 1798-99,* 1974; *The Coward of Minden: The Affair of Lord George Sackville,* Allen Lane, 1979; (contributor) William M. Fowler and Wallace Coyle, editors, *The American Revolution: Changing Perspectives,* Northeastern University Press, 1979. Contributor to *Mariner's Mirror* and to military history journals.

WORK IN PROGRESS: Volume two of *Statesmen at War;* a study of the Narvik operations in 1940.

AVOCATIONAL INTERESTS: Riding, fox hunting, art.

*   *   *

MacLEOD, Ellen Jane (Anderson) 1916-

PERSONAL: Born May 17, 1916, in Glasgow, Scotland; brought to United States by parents in 1925; returned to Scotland in 1951; daughter of Francis (a traffic manager) and Mary Rae (Lawrie) Anderson; married Donald M. MacLeod (a free-lance journalist), December 15, 1953. *Education:* Attended schools in Scotland and United States. *Religion:* Protestant. *Home:* 12 Montgomery Pl., Buchlyvie, Stirlingshire, Scotland FK8 3NF.

CAREER: Early dancing career ended by automobile accident, turned to singing, then library work; County Library, Vancouver, Wash., assistant, 1943-50; author, mainly of youth books, 1955—. *Member:* Society of Authors.

WRITINGS—All published by Pickering & Inglis, except as indicated: *The Seven Wise Owls,* 1956; *Alaska Star,* 1957; *Adventures on the Lazy N,* 1957; *The Ski Lodge Mystery,* Moody, 1957; *The Crooked Signpost,* 1957; *The Hawaiian Lei,* 1958; *Jo-Jo,* 1959; *Mystery Gorge,* 1959; *The Mystery of the Tolling Bell,* 1960; *The Fourth Window,* Cowman, 1961; *The Vanishing Light,* 1961; *The Talking Mountain,* 1962; *Orchids for a Rose* (romantic novel), Arcadia House, 1963; *Island in the Mist,* Bethany, 1965; *Stranger in the Glen,* Arcadia House, 1969; *Trouble at the Circle G,* 1970; *The Broken Melody,* Lenox Hill, 1970; *The Kelpie Ledge,* Lenox Hill, 1972; *Isle of Shadows,* Lenox Hill, 1974.

Also author of scripts for British Broadcasting Corp., including "One Stormy Night" and a play, "Something Fishy"; has novelized picture scripts and written serials.

WORK IN PROGRESS: A twelve-part series for D. C. Thomson.

SIDELIGHTS: Ellen Jane MacLeod told *CA:* "Nothing is so satisfying as one of your readers writing to say, 'Your book was so interesting I couldn't put it down.' For just the space of time [those] persons took to read the book [they] had forgotten all the depressing things that had lowered their spirits. Just for that time, their minds were freed. That's my idea of what writing is all about, especially for the young.

"As I prefer to write fiction and not non-fiction for young readers, I can understand when they write to me saying, 'the story was so exciting, I loved every minute of it.' But to me, the sad part of the current literary scene for youngsters is the lack of adventure. I find so many 'clever' and 'educational' books, which are wonderful in their way, of course, but what happened to the sheer adventure of reading? The young fans, by their letters, agree with me, and who knows better than they what they like?

"One American writer whose books I loved and read over and over was Emilie Loring. Although the first one I read was published in 1925 and the last one in 1945, the first one never appeared dated and was just as fresh, charming and humorous as the last one.

"The German editions of my books have been read with the same enthusiasm and understanding as by the English-speaking fans, which proves that young people are basically the same everywhere. My plays for young people have brought the same responses: 'More adventure and exciting plots, please.' Not one word of how to be 'clever.' Just sheer youthful exuberance. We mustn't let them lose it."

*   *   *

MacLEOD, Jean Sutherland 1908-
(Catherine Airlie)

PERSONAL: Born January 20, 1908, in Glasgow, Scotland; daughter of John (a civil engineer) and Elizabeth (Allen) MacLeod; married Lionel Walton (a land surveyor), January 1, 1935; children: David MacLeod. *Education:* Educated at schools in Glasgow, Scotland, and Swansea, South Wales. *Politics:* Conservative. *Religion:* Presbyterian. *Home:* Tighan-Rudha, Kilmelford, By Oban, Argyllshire, Scotland.

CAREER: British Ministry of Labor, Newcastle upon Tyne, England, secretary, 1930-35; novelist, 1935—. President of Alne and Tollerton area branch, National Society for Prevention of Cruelty to Children. *Member:* Romantic Novelists' Association, Society of Yorkshire Bookmen, Women of Scotland, Clan MacLeod Society (Edinburgh), St. Andrew Society (York). *Awards, honors:* Cartland Historical Novel award, 1962, for *The Dark Fortune; World's Who's Who of Women* plaque for distinguished achievement, 1979.

WRITINGS—All published by Mills & Boon, except as indicated: *Life for Two,* 1936; *Human Sympathy,* 1937; *Summer Rain,* 1938; *Sequel to Youth,* 1938; *Mist Across the Hills,* 1938; *Dangerous Obsession,* 1939; *Run Away from Love,* 1939; *Return to Spring,* 1939, Pocket Books, 1971; *Rainbow Isle,* 1939.

The Whim of Fate, 1940; *Lonely Furrow,* 1940; *Heather-bloom,* 1940; *Reckless Pilgrim,* 1941; *Shadow of a Vow,* 1941; *One Way Out,* 1941; *Forbidden Rapture,* 1941; *Penalty for Living,* 1942; *Blind Journey,* 1942; *Bleak Heritage,* 1942, Pocket Books, 1971; *Reluctant Folly,* 1942; *Unseen Tomorrow,* 1943; *The Rowan Tree,* 1943; *Flower o' the Broom,* 1943; *Circle of Doubt,* 1943; *Lamont of Ardgoyne,* 1944; *Two Paths,* 1944; *Brief Fulfillment,* 1945; *This Much to Give,* 1945; *One Love,* 1945, Pocket Books, 1971; *Tranquil Haven,* 1946; *Sown in the Wind,* 1946, Pocket Books, 1970; *House of Oliver,* 1947; *And We in Dreams,* 1947; *Chalet in the Sun,* 1948; *Ravenscrag,* 1948; *Above the Lattice,* 1949; *Tomorrow's Bargain,* 1949.

Katherine, 1950; *The Valley of Palms,* 1950; *Roadway to the Past,* 1951; *Once to Every Heart,* 1951; *Cameron of Gare,* 1952; *Music at Midnight,* 1952; *The Silent Valley,* 1953; *The Stranger in Their Midst,* 1953; *Dear Doctor Everett,* 1954;

The Man in Authority, 1954; *After Long Journeying*, 1955; *Master of Glenkeith*, 1955, Pocket Books, 1971; *Way in the Dark*, 1956; *My Heart's in the Highlands*, 1956; *Journey in the Sun*, 1957; *The Prisoner of Love*, 1958; *Gated Road*, 1959; *Air Ambulance*, 1959.

The Little Doctor, 1960; *The White Cockade*, 1960; *The Silver Dragon*, 1961; *The Country of the Heart*, 1961; *Slave of the Wind*, 1962, Pocket Books, 1971; *The Dark Fortune*, 1962; *Sugar Island*, 1964; *The Black Cameron*, 1965; *Crane Castle*, 1965; *The Wolf of Heimra*, 1965; *The Drummer of Corrae*, 1966; *The Tender Glory*, 1967; *Lament for a Lover*, 1967; *The Master of Keills*, 1967; *The Bride of Mingulay*, 1967; *The Moonflower*, 1967; *Summer Island*, 1968, Pocket Books, 1971.

The Joshua Tree, 1970; *The Way through the Valley*, 1970, Pocket Books, 1972; *The Fortress*, 1970; *The Scent of Juniper*, 1971; *Light in the Tower*, Pocket Books, 1971; *Moment of Decision*, Pocket Books, 1972; *Adam's Wife*, 1972; *Time Suspended*, 1974; *Rainbow Days*, 1973; *Over the Castle Wall*, 1974; *The Phantom Pipes*, 1975; *Island Stranger*, 1977; *Viking Song*, 1977; *The Ruag Inheritance*, 1978; *Search for Yesterday*, 1978; *Meeting in Madrid*, 1979; *Brief Enchantment*, 1979; *Black Sand, White Sand*, 1980.

Under pseudonym Catherine Airlie: *The Wild Macraes*, 1948; *From Such a Seed*, 1949; *The Restless Years*, 1950; *Fabric of Dreams*, 1951; *Strange Recompense*, 1952; *The Green Rushes*, 1953; *Hidden in the Wind*, 1953; *Wind Sighing*, 1954; *Nobody's Child*, 1954; *The Valley of Desire*, 1955; *The Ways of Love*, 1955; *The Mountain of Stars*, 1956; *Unguarded Hour*, 1956; *Land of Heart's Desire*, 1957; *Red Lotus*, 1958; *The Last of the Kintyres*, 1959; *Shadow on the Sun*, 1960; *One Summer's Day*, 1961; *In the Country of the Heart*, 1961; *The Unlived Year*, 1962; *Passing Strangers*, 1963; *The Wheels of Chance*, 1964; *The Sea Change*, 1965.

Contributor to *Woman's Own, People's Journal, Woman's Weekly, People's Friend*, and other magazines.

WORK IN PROGRESS: Research for a novel about South Africa.

AVOCATIONAL INTERESTS: Sailing, gardening, and photography.

*   *   *

Mac LIAMMOIR, Micheal   1899-1978
(Micheal Mac Liaimmhoir, Micheal Mac Liammhoir)

PERSONAL: Born October 25, 1899, in Cork, Ireland; died March 6, 1978, in Dublin, Ireland; son of Alfred Anthony and Mary Elizabeth (Lawler-Lee) Mac Liammoir. *Education:* Educated privately; studied painting at Slade School of Art, London, England, 1915-16, and on the Continent, 1921-27. *Office:* Dublin Gate Theatre Productions Ltd., 4 Harcourt Ter., Dublin 2, Ireland.

CAREER: Actor, designer, director, and author; identified for over forty years with the Dublin Gate Theatre, Dublin, Ireland, which he founded with Hilton Edwards in 1928, and for which he acted in, directed, and designed some 300 productions. As a child was known on the stage as Alfred Willmore, making his debut in 1911 in London; painted and designed for Irish Theatre and Dublin Drama League, 1918-21; lived abroad, studying painting, until 1927; returned to Ireland and joined Anew McMaster's Shakespeare Company; with Hilton Edwards, in 1928, opened Taibhdheare na Gaillmke (Galway Gaelic Theatre) with his own play, *Diarmuid agus Grainne*, appointed director of the government-subsidized Dublin Gaelic Theatre, 1931; returned to London stage with Dublin Gate Theatre company in 1935, then toured Egypt, 1936-38, and the Balkan states, 1939; made his first appearance in United States at Orson Welles' Woodstock (Ill.) Theatre Festival, 1934; made Broadway debut, 1948, in "John Bull's Other Island"; appeared at Edinburgh Festival, 1957, and Dublin Festivals of 1960, 1962, 1963, 1964; toured four continents with his own one-man show, "The Importance of Being Oscar"; also compiled and performed one-man shows "I Must Be Talking to My Friends," 1963, and "Talking about Yeats," 1965, in Dublin, London, and New York. Other roles included Hamlet, Faust, Othello, Liliom, Marc Antony, Romeo, and leading parts in "Berkeley Square," "Crime and Punishment," "Hedda Gabler," "Mourning Becomes Electra," and in his own adaptation of "The Informer"; television performances include title role in "Othello" and Potemkin in "Great Catherine," both for National Broadcasting Co., 1947; played Iago in Orson Welles' film version of "Othello," produced by United Artists, 1949; appeared in film "What's the Matter with Helen?," 1971.

MEMBER: Gaelic League (Dublin and London), Arts Club (Dublin). *Awards, honors:* Comhar Drama Tochta Silver Award, 1933, Gold Award, 1934; Douglas Hyde Prize, 1952; Kronberg gold medal, 1952, for performance as Hamlet at Eisinore; Lady Gregory Medal from the Irish Academy of Letters, 1960; LL.D., Trinity College, University of Dublin, 1962; Irish Actor's Equity award, 1972, for services to the Irish theatre; honored as Freeman of the City of Dublin, 1973; Chevalier de la Legion d'Honneur, 1973.

WRITINGS—Under name Micheal Mac Liammhoir, except as indicated: *Oidcheanna Sidhe* (short stories), translation by the author published as *Fairy Nights*, both editions, Talbot Press, 1922; *La agus Oiche* (short stories; title means "Day and Night"), Oifig an tSolathair, 1929; *The Ford of the Hurdles* (play), [Dublin], 1929; (illustrator) Padraig O Conaire, *The Woman at the Window and Other Stories*, [Dublin], 1931; *Oidhche Bhealtaine* (play; title means "May Day Eve"), Oifig an tSolathair, 1932; *Diarmuid agus Grainne* (play; produced Galway, Ireland, at Galway Gaelic Theatre, 1928), Oifig diolta Foil-Iseachain Rialtais, 1935; *All for Hecuba: An Irish Theatrical Autobiography*, Methuen, 1946, revised edition, Progress House, 1961, Branden Press, 1967; *Theatre in Ireland*, C. O. Lochlainn, for Cultural Relations Committee of Ireland, 1950, 2nd edition, 1964; (under name Micheal Mac Liammhoir) *Put Money in Thy Purse : The Filming of Orson Welles' "Othello"* (diary), preface by Orson Welles, Methuen, 1952, 2nd edition, revised, 1976; *Ceo Meala la Seaca* (essays; also see below; title means "Honey-Mist on a Frosty Day"), [Dublin], 1952; *Ill Met by Moonlight* (play; first produced in Ireland, 1946), Duffy & Co., 1954; *Aisteori faoi dha Sholas* (memoirs; title means "Actors in Two Lights"), Sairseal argus Dill, 1956, translation by the author published with excerpt from *Ceo Meala la Seaca* as *Each Actor on His Ass*, Routledge & Kegan Paul, 1961; *The Importance of Being Oscar* (one-man entertainment; first produced in Dublin, 1960, produced in New York City, 1961) Dolmen Press, 1963, 2nd edition, revised, 1978; *Blath agus Taibhse: Danta prois* (poems; title means "Flower and Ghost"), Sairseal argus Dill, 1964; (author of introduction under name Micheal Mac Liammhoir) Edwin Smith, *Ireland* (photographs), Viking, 1966; (under name Micheal Mac Liammhoir) *An Oscar of No Importance: Being an Account of the Author's Adventures with His One-Man Show about Oscar Wilde*, Heinemann, 1968; (with Eavan Boland, under name Micheal Mac Liammhoir) *W. B. Yeats and His World,* Thames & Hudson, 1971, Viking, 1972; (under name Micheal Mac Liammoir) *Enter a Goldfish: Memoirs of an Irish Actor, Young and Old,* Thames & Hudson, 1977. Also translator of own play, *Diarmuid and Grainne,* published in Dublin.

Unpublished one-man entertainments: "I Must Be Talking to My Friends," produced in Dublin, 1963, produced in New York City, 1967; "Talking about Yeats," produced in Dublin, 1965.

Also author of numerous unpublished plays, including "Dancing Shadow," 1941, "Where Stars Walk," 1947, "Portrait of Miriam," 1947, "The Mountains Look Different," 1948, "Home for Christmas," 1950, "A Slipper for the Moon," 1952, "The Marvellous History of St. Patrick," 1955, "Prelude on Kazbek Street," 1973, and "Lulu"; author of television plays "The Liar" and "The Speckledy Shawl" (musical). Author of several play adaptations, including *Jane Eyre,* by Charlotte Bronte, *A Tale of Two Cities,* by Charles Dickens, *The Informer,* by Liam O'Flaherty, *Trilby,* by George Du Maurier, and *The Picture of Dorian Grey,* by Oscar Wilde; also author of translations and adaptations of French and Spanish plays, and of three ballets, "The Red Petticoat," "The Enchanted Stream," and "Full Moon for the Bride." Contributor of critical articles to *Irish Statesman, Observer,* and other periodicals.

SIDELIGHTS: Micheal Mac Liammoir once told *CA* that he spoke four languages—Gaelic, English, Spanish, and French—"with equal ease if not total precision." He considered himself to be "brazenly [fluent] and deeply incorrect" in German and Italian. *Avocational interests:* Travel, ballet, comparative religions.

BIOGRAPHICAL/CRITICAL SOURCES: Micheal Mac Liammoir, *All for Hecuba: An Irish Theatrical Autobiography,* Methuen, 1946; *Vogue,* March 15, 1961; Mac Liammoir, *An Oscar of No Importance: Being an Account of the Author's Adventures with His One-Man Show about Oscar Wilde,* Heineman, 1968; *Times Literary Supplement,* November 19, 1971; *Critic,* winter, 1977; Peter Luke, editor, *Enter Certain Players: Edwards—Mac Liammoir and the Gate, 1928-1978,* Dolmen Press, 1978; *Choice,* December, 1978.†

*   *   *

MacSHANE, Frank 1927-

PERSONAL: Born October 19, 1927, in Pittsburgh, Pa.; son of Frank (a journalist) and A. Elizabeth A. (Morse) MacShane; married Virginia Lynn Fry, July 8, 1959; children: Nicholas Morse. *Education:* Harvard University, A.B., 1949; Yale University, M.A., 1951; Oxford University, D.Phil., 1955. *Office:* Writing Division, School of the Arts, Columbia University, New York, N.Y. 10027.

CAREER: McGill University, Montreal, Quebec, lecturer in English, 1955-57; University of California, Berkeley, assistant professor of English, 1959-64; Williams College, Williamstown, Mass., associate professor of English, 1964-67; Columbia University, New York, N.Y., professor of English and chairman of writing division, 1967—. Fulbright professor at University of Chile, 1957, Tribhuvan University, Kathmandu, Nepal, and Centro di Studi Americani, Rome, 1978-79. Visiting lecturer, Vassar College, 1958-59. Director, Poets and Writers, Inc., and The Translation Center. *Member:* National Book Critics Circle, Authors League, P.E.N. American Center, Oxford and Cambridge Club (London); Century Association (New York).

WRITINGS: (Translator) Miguel Seranno, *The Mysteries,* privately printed, 1960; (translator) Miguel Serrano, *The Visits of the Queen of Sheba,* Asia Publishing House, 1960; *Many Golden Ages: Ruins, Temples and Monuments of the Orient,* Tuttle, 1962; (editor) *Impressions of Latin America: Five Centuries of Travel and Adventure by English and North American Writers,* Morrow, 1963; (translator) Miguel Serrano, *The Serpent of Paradise,* Rider & Co., 1963; (editor) *Critical Writings of Ford Madox Ford,* University of Nebraska Press, 1964; (editor) *The American in Europe: A Collection of Impressions Written by Americans from the Seventeenth Century to the Present,* Dutton, 1965; *The Life and Work of Ford Madox Ford,* Horizon Press, 1965; (translator) Miguel Serrano, *C. G. Jung and Hermann Hesse: A Record of Two Friendships,* Schocken, 1966; (translator) Miguel Serrano, *The Ultimate Flower,* Schocken, 1969; *Ford Madox Ford: The Critical Heritage,* Routledge & Kegan Paul, 1972; (translator) Miguel Serrano, *El/Ella,* Harper, 1972; (co-editor) *Borges on Writing,* Dutton, 1973; *The Life of Raymond Chandler,* Dutton, 1976; (editor) *The Notebooks of Raymond Chandler,* Ecco Press, 1976; *The Life of John O'Hara,* Dutton, 1981. Contributor to *New Republic, Nation, London Magazine, Prairie Schooner, New York Times Book Review, Holiday, American Scholar,* and other journals.

SIDELIGHTS: Frank MacShane's *The Life of Raymond Chandler* was the subject of widespread critical attention. Frank Kermode of the *Listener* states: "There is no obvious reason why this should not have been an authoritative biography; and, in a way, it is, though it is a pretty bad book." Kermode pinpoints his dissatisfaction with the work, noting that "one of the main troubles with this book is that Mr. MacShane has gone owlishly all out to make Chandler seem a very great writer. Even if he were, this would not be the way to do it." Kermode concludes, "Chandler was undoubtedly an odd and gifted man, as we see best when MacShane allows him to speak for himself."

Leonard Michaels of the *New York Times Book Review* echoes Kermode's reaction to MacShane's assessment of Chandler's literary status: "Chandler . . . wasn't deceived about the essential quality of his work. There should be no reason now to claim more for him than he claimed for himself. It is, then, surprising to see Frank MacShane compare him to Joyce, Tolstoy, Chaucer, Twain, Conrad and others of the lofty ilk." Despite this concern, however, Michaels approves of MacShane's treatment of Chandler's life: "MacShane gives many other funny events of Chandler's final years in a life that was, all in all, a nauseating, Gothic extravaganza, but he is careful to qualify this impression with sober analyses." The critic concludes that MacShane, "an exceptionally polite biographer," has done "a very good job, but when he inserts his own long critical commentary on Chandler's fiction, it feels as if a good story has been interrupted by a doctoral thesis."

Stefan Kanfer of *Time* notes that MacShane "does little more than apologize for his reticent and rude subject." Kanfer, like other reviewers, also notices MacShane's insistence upon Chandler's literary ability: "Despite [MacShane's] claims for his subject as 'one of the most important writers of his time,' the author saw himself with less extravagance and literary pomp." Kanfer comments that MacShane "offers sheaves of contradictions from Raymond Chandler's long but unprolific career" and questions the need for a Chandler biography, observing that Chandler's life "is hardly the ore of glistening literary biography."

About Frank MacShane's biography, *The Life of John*

O'Hara, James B. Mellow of *Chicago Times Book World* observes that "unintentionally, perhaps, MacShane's life of the irascible writer is a chronicle of the outsized ambitions and bitter defeats of the literary profession in America." Mellow feels that certain of MacShane's arguments in this "brisk and informative biography" are "not altogether" convincing. Alfred Kazin of *New York Times Book Review* comments that "Mr. MacShane's book is so thorough in its recitation of O'Hara's uninspiring life that I suspect that he is less interested in O'Hara than in showing how thorough he can be." Kazin continues that "as a critic trying to summon up appreciation for O'Hara, Mr. MacShane is not accomplished" and concludes that "some of his critical statements are so simplistic that I wondered if Mr. MacShane, as must happen with professional biographers, was not tiring of his subject."

BIOGRAPHICAL/CRITICAL SOURCES: New York Times Book Review, May 16, 1976, January 18, 1981; *Listener*, June 17, 1976; *Time*, June 27, 1976; *Books and Bookmen*, November, 1976, January, 1977; *Chicago Times Book World*, January 11, 1981.

*   *   *

MAHDI, Muhsin S(ayyid) 1926-

PERSONAL: Born June 21, 1926, in Karbala, Iraq; son of Sayyid and Fatima (Hasan) Mahdi; married Cynthia Risner, May 31, 1959; children: Fatima, Nadia. *Education:* American University of Beirut, B.B.A., 1947; University of Chicago, Ph.D., 1954; postdoctoral study at University of Paris, 1954-55, and University of Freiburg im Breisgau, 1954-55. *Home:* 1105 Massachusetts Ave., Cambridge, Mass. 02138. *Office:* Department of Near Eastern Languages, Harvard University, 1737 Cambridge St., Cambridge, Mass. 02138.

CAREER: University of Baghdad, Baghdad, Iraq, instructor, 1955-57; University of Chicago, Chicago, Ill., visiting assistant professor, 1957-58, assistant professor, 1958-62, associate professor, 1962-65, professor of Arabic and Islamic studies, 1965-69, chairman of department of Near Eastern languages and civilizations, 1968-69; Harvard University, Cambridge, Mass., James Richard Jewett Professor of Arabic, 1969—, director of Center for Middle Eastern Studies, 1969—. Visiting professor, University of Freiburg im Breisgau, 1960 and 1965. *Member:* International Society for the Study of Medieval Philosophy, Society for the Study of Islamic Philosophy and Science (president), Academy of Arabic Language, Iraqui Academy, American Research Center in Egypt (president), American Oriental Society. *Awards, honors:* Rockefeller Foundation research fellow, 1960-61; A.M., Harvard University, 1969.

WRITINGS: Ibn Khaldun's Philosophy of History: A Study in the Philosophic Foundation of the Science of Culture, Macmillan, 1957; *Die geistigen und sozialen Wandlungen im Nahen Osten*, Rombach (Freiburg im Bresgau), 1961; (translator and author of introduction) *Al-Farabi's Philosophy of Plato and Aristotle*, Free Press of Glencoe, 1962; (editor with Ralph Lerner) *Medieval Political Philosophy: A Sourcebook*, Free Press of Glencoe, 1963.

Editor and author of introduction and notes: *Al-Farabi's Philosophy of Aristotle*, Dar Majallat Shi'r (Beirut), 1961; *Al-Farabi's Book of Religion and Related Texts*, Dar El-Machreq (Beirut), 1968; *Al-Farabi's Utterances Employed in Logic*, Dar El-Mechreq, 1968; *Al-Farabi's Book of Letters*, Dar El-Mechreq, 1969.

Contributor: William Theodore de Bary, editor, *Approaches to the Oriental Classics*, Columbia University Press, 1959;

Joseph Kitagawa, editor, *Modern Trends in World Religions*, Open Court, 1959; Dieter Oberndoerfer, editor, *Wissenschaftliche Politik: Eine Einfuehrung in Grundfragen ihrer Tradition und Theorie*, Rombach, 1962; Leo Strauss and Joseph Cropsey, editors, *History of Political Philosophy*, Rand McNally, 1963; Cropsey, editor, *Ancients and Moderns: Essays on the Tradition of Political Philosophy in Honor of Leo Strauss*, Basic Books, 1964; G. E. von Grunebaum, editor, *Logic in Classical Islamic Culture*, Otto Harrassowitz (Wiesbaden), 1970. Contributor to *International Encyclopedia of the Social Sciences*. Contributor of numerous articles to *Journal of Near Eastern Studies*.

WORK IN PROGRESS: Al-Farabi's Political Philosophy; The 1001 Nights.

*   *   *

MAINWARING, Marion

PERSONAL: Born in Boston, Mass.; daughter of Herbert James and Marion (Imrie) Mainwaring. *Education:* Simmons College, B.S., 1943; Radcliffe College, Ph.D., 1949. *Mailing address:* 13 Terrane Ave., Natick, Mass.

CAREER: Harvard University, Cambridge, Mass., tutor and teaching fellow, 1947-49; Mount Holyoke College, South Hadley, Mass., instructor in English, 1949-52; Houghton-Mifflin Co., Boston, Mass., reader and editor in Boston, and London, England, 1958—. Newspaper correspondent in ΄ ͎ Balkans, 1962-63; foreign research editor for the Adams Papers, Harvard University Press and Massachusetts Historical Society, 1964-65; survey director, Massachusetts Council on the Arts and Humanities, 1967; foreign correspondent in Paris, France and Athens, Greece for *Boston Herald-Traveler*, 1968—; translator and writer, UNESCO, Paris, 1972—.

WRITINGS: Murder at Midyears, Macmillan, 1953; *Murder in Pastiche*, Macmillan, 1954; *John Quincy Adams and Russia: A Sketch of Early Russian-American Relations*, Quincy Patriot Ledger, 1965; (translator) Ivan Turgenev, *Youth and Age: Three Short Novels by Turgenev*, Hart-Davis, 1968, Farrar, Straus, 1969; *Cultural Needs and Cultural Resources of the Commonwealth of Massachusetts*, Commonwealth of Massachusetts, 1968; (editor) *The Portrait Game*, Chatto & Windus, 1973, Horizon Press, 1974. Contributor to popular magazines and academic journals. Editor, 125th anniversary edition of the *Patriot Ledger*, Quincy, Mass., 1962.

BIOGRAPHICAL/CRITICAL SOURCES: New York Herald Tribune Book Review, October 25, 1953, August 15, 1954; *New York Times*, August 15, 1954; *Christian Science Monitor*, March 4, 1968; *Times Literary Supplement*, August 10, 1968; *National Observer*, September 1, 1969; *New Statesman*, May 25, 1973; *Washington Post*, November 25, 1973.

*   *   *

MALING, Arthur (Gordon) 1923-

PERSONAL: Born June 11, 1923, in Chicago, Ill.; son of Albert (a businessman) and Alma (Gordon) Maling; married Beatrice Goldberg, 1949 (divorced, 1958); children: Michael, Evan Beatrice. *Education:* Harvard University, B.A., 1944. *Home and office:* 111 East Chestnut St., Chicago, Ill. 60611.

CAREER: Maling Bros., Inc. (retail shoe chain), Chicago, Ill., owner, 1946-72. Member of Chicago Art Institute. *Member:* Mystery Writers of America (regional vice-president, 1974-76; director, 1976-80), Authors Guild, Council on Foreign Relations (Chicago), Harvard Alumni Association,

Orchestral Association (Chicago), B'nai B'rith, 210 Associates. *Awards, honors:* Edgar Allen Poe award for best mystery novel published in 1979 from Mystery Writers of America, 1980, and American Book Award nomination, 1980, both for *The Rheingold Route.*

WRITINGS—All mystery novels; all published by Harper: *Decoy,* 1969; *Go-Between,* 1970; *Loophole,* 1971; *The Snowman,* 1973; *Dingdong,* 1974; *Bent Man,* 1975; *Ripoff,* 1976; (editor) *When Last Seen,* 1977; *Schroeder's Game,* 1977; *Lucky Devil,* 1978; *The Rheingold Route,* 1979; *The Koberg Link,* 1979.

WORK IN PROGRESS: Another mystery novel.

*   *   *

MALONEY, Ralph Liston   1927-1973
(Jack Liston)

PERSONAL: Born 1927, in Cambridge, Mass.; died November 22, 1973, in New York, N.Y.; son of Louis Trefflee and Anne (Liston) Maloney; married Joan Wilgus, 1955; children: Deirdre, Liam, Evan Dean. *Education:* Attended Harvard University, 1947-50. *Politics:* Liberal Party. *Agent:* Paul R. Reynolds, Inc., 12 East 41st St., New York, N.Y. 10017.

CAREER: Worked in public relations business for seven years prior to 1959; writer. *Military service:* U.S. Army, two and a half years; became first lieutenant; served as merchant seaman, World War II. *Member:* Authors Guild, Mystery Writers of America, National Maritime Union (retired), American Association of Boxing Managers (honorary member).

WRITINGS: Daily Bread, Houghton, 1960; *Manbait,* Dell, 1960; *The 24-Hour Drink Book: A Guide to Executive Survival,* Obolensky, 1963; *The Great Bonacker Whiskey War,* Little, Brown, 1967; *Fish in a Stream in a Cave* (short stories), Norton, 1972; *The Nixon Recession Caper,* Norton, 1972. Also author of documentary filmscripts for British television. Contributor of short stories to *Atlantic* and other periodicals.

SIDELIGHTS: Commenting on Ralph Maloney's novel *The Nixon Recession Caper* a critic in *Book World* wrote: "This book is a cheerful little diversion about four men who are well-off but broke. They have a lot to eat and drink, especially drink, live in large, comfortable houses, run up good-sized bar bills at their dreary-sounding country club, but they don't have any money [so they decide to rob a bank].... It's a neat, smug, rather thin joke about how crime pays—if you're well-to-do.... The trouble with jokes about the current 'recession,' a euphemism the book quickly scotches, is that the 'recession' just isn't funny, and the ability of white, upper-middle-class men to steal their way around it can't make it funny. Although I suppose it's a consideration irrelevant to the book, you can't help but wonder how all of this easily accomplished criminal frivolity would have turned out had the men been, say, black or *really* poor."

A reviewer in *Time* called Maloney "a light novelist with a heavy hand" who can "write dialogue that gets off the train at Westport. He makes superb use of his country club to write a short history of the decline and fall of the snob in America. But he shows no faith in his material. Just when he should be putting it all together, he takes it all apart, hurrying on to play stand-up comedian in print—and becomes an anything-for-a-laugh gagster.... Like too many American comic novelists, Maloney seems to lack self-respect. The

Nixon Recession Caper is a reasonably funny—and unreasonably tame—piece of what gets called high jinks."

Unlike his colleagues, an *Atlantic* reviewer had no major objections to Maloney's book. "This is a novel of light comedy, decent to read and quite funny, by a writer who whether from experience or observation knows a good deal about the effects of alcohol and the effects of the recession in Eastern suburbia.... How much [the men's] holdup yields, what they do with the money, how they divert themselves against the possibility of detection when it is known that the FBI has been called in are some of the mysteries that make this novel fun. A more unlikely mob of thieves and their molls was never brought together."

AVOCATIONAL INTERESTS: Bird-watching, skiing.

BIOGRAPHICAL/CRITICAL SOURCES: New York Times Book Review, February 5, 1967; *Atlantic,* March, 1972; *Time,* March 7, 1972; *Book World,* April 2, 1972.†

*   *   *

MALPASS, E(ric) L(awson)   1910-

PERSONAL: Born November 14, 1910, in Derby, England; son of Tom Riley and Lilias (Lawson) Malpass; married Muriel Gladys Barnett, October 3, 1936; children: Michael Lawson. *Education:* Attended King Henry VIII School, Coventry, England. *Religion:* Anglican. *Home:* Broadleaves, 216 Breedon St., Long Eaton, Nottingham, England.

CAREER: Barclays Bank Ltd., Long Eaton, Nottingham, England, 1926-66, became first cashier, 1947. *Military service:* Royal Air Force, 1941-46; became flight lieutenant. *Member:* Nottingham Writers' Club (president), Derby Writers' Guild. *Awards, honors:* Winner of *Observer* short story competition, 1955; Palma D'oro for best humorous novel of year in Italy, for *Beefy Jones;* Goldene Leinwand award for most popular film in Germany, 1969, for "Morgens um Sieben," film version of *Morning's at Seven.*

WRITINGS—Novels: *Beefy Jones,* Longmans, Green, 1957; *Operazione Gemelli,* Baldini & Castoldi, 1960; *Morning's at Seven,* Heinemann, 1965, Viking, 1966; *At the Height of the Moon,* Heinemann, 1967; *Oh My Darling Daughter,* Eyre & Spottiswoode, 1970; *Fortinbras Has Escaped,* Transworld, 1970; *Sweet Will,* Macmillan (London), 1973, St. Martin's, 1974; *The Cleopatra Boy,* St. Martin's, 1974; *A House of Women,* St. Martin's, 1975; *The Long Long Dances,* Transworld, 1978; *Summer Awakening,* Transworld, 1978; *The Wind Brings up the Rain,* Heinemann, 1978. Regular contributor of short stories to *Argosy* (London) and to British Broadcasting Corp. programs.

WORK IN PROGRESS: A novel.

SIDELIGHTS: E. L. Malpass's books *Morning's at Seven, At the Height of the Moon,* and *Oh My Darling Daughter* have all been made into films in Germany. *Avocational interests:* Theatre, countryside, church and charity work, and reading.

BIOGRAPHICAL/CRITICAL SOURCES: Book Week, January 30, 1966; *Observer Review,* August 23, 1970; *Times Literary Supplement,* October 2, 1970.

*   *   *

MANCHESTER, William   1922-

PERSONAL: Born April 1, 1922, in Attleboro, Mass.; son of William Raymond and Sallie (Thompson) Manchester; married Julia Brown Marshall, March 27, 1948; children: John Kennerly, Julie Thompson, Laurie. *Education:* Massachusetts State College (now University of Massachusetts), A.B., 1946; University of Missouri, A.M., 1947. *Agent:* Harold Matson Co., Inc., 22 East 40th St., New York, N.Y. 10016.

CAREER: Daily Oklahoman, Oklahoma City, Okla., reporter, 1945-46; *Baltimore Sun,* Baltimore, Md., reporter and foreign correspondent in the Middle East, India, and Southeast Asia, 1947-54; Wesleyan University, Middletown, Conn., managing editor of publications division, 1955-64, member of university faculty, 1968-69, member of faculty of East College, 1968—, writer-in-residence, 1975—, adjunct professor of history, 1979—. Trustee, Friends of the University of Massachusetts Library, 1970-74. Designated historian of President Kennedy's assassination (by Mrs. John F. Kennedy), March 26, 1964. *Military service:* U.S. Marine Corps, 1942-45; became sergeant. *Member:* Authors Guild, American Historical Association, Society of American Historians, Wesleyan University Faculty Club, Williams Club, Century Club. *Awards, honors:* Guggenheim fellow, 1959-60; Wesleyan Center for Advanced Studies fellow, 1959-60; L.H.D., University of Massachusetts, 1965; Dag Hammarskjoeld Prize, 1966; Overseas Press Club Citation for best book on foreign affairs, 1968; University of Missouri honor award for distinguished service in journalism, 1969; Connecticut Book Award, 1975; L.H.D., University of New Haven, 1979; National Book Award nominee, 1980, for *American Caesar.*

WRITINGS: Disturber of the Peace: The Life of H. L. Mencken (first published serially in *Harper's* magazine, July to August, 1950), Harper, 1951; *The City of Anger* (novel), Ballantine, 1953; *Shadow of the Monsoon* (novel), Doubleday, 1956; *Beard the Lion* (novel), Morrow, 1958; *A Rockefeller Family Portrait,* Little, Brown, 1959; (contributor) Bredemier and Toby, editors, *Social Problems in America,* Wiley, 1960; *The Long Gainer* (novel), Little, Brown, 1961; *Portrait of a President,* Little, Brown, 1962, 2nd edition, 1967; (contributor) Don Congdon, editor, *Combat World War I,* Dial, 1964; (contributor) Poyntz Tyler, *Securities Exchanges and the SEC,* Wilson, 1965; *The Death of a President* (Book-of-the-Month Club selection; first published serially in *Look* magazine, January 24, 1967 to March 7, 1967), Harper, 1967; *The Arms of Krupp* (Literary Guild selection; first published serially in *Holiday,* November, 1964 to February, 1965), Little, Brown, 1968; *The Glory and the Dream: A Narrative History of America, 1932-1972* (Literary Guild selection), Little, Brown, 1968; *Controversy and Other Essays in Journalism,* Little, Brown, 1976; *American Caesar: Douglas MacArthur, 1880-1964* (Book-of-the-Month Club selection), Little, Brown, 1978; *Good-bye, Darkness* (memoir of the Pacific war; Book-of-the-Month Club selection), Little, Brown, 1980. Contributor to *Encyclopaedia Britannica.* Contributor to *Atlantic, Harper's, Reporter, Saturday Review, Holiday, Nation, Esquire,* and *Saturday Evening Post.*

SIDELIGHTS: On March 26, 1964, Senator Robert Kennedy announced at a press conference that author William Manchester had been asked by the Kennedy family to write "an extensive account describing the events of and surrounding the death of President Kennedy on November 22, 1963." In addition to this information, reporters in attendance were given a statement explaining that "these arrangements were made with Mr. Manchester in the interest of historical accuracy and to prevent distortion and sensationalism." On the same day this public announcement was made, Manchester and Kennedy privately agreed (in writing) that the Kennedy family must be allowed to approve the text before its publication.

Two years and countless hours of exhaustive research later, Manchester completed his manuscript for Harper & Row Publishers and began to make plans for its magazine serialization. After requesting permission from the Kennedys to proceed with this latter move, Manchester was delighted to receive a telegram from Robert Kennedy which stated, in part, that even though the Kennedys themselves had not read the manuscript, their representative had done so over a period of four months; after recommending a few changes, they unanimously approved publication. At that time, the senator announced that the family would place "no obstacle in the way of publication of [Manchester's] work." Kennedy's only concern, in the event of serialization, was that "incidents would not be taken out of context or summarized in any way which might distort the facts of or the events relating to President Kennedy's death." An identical message was sent to Manchester's publisher from Robert Kennedy.

Interpreting this as an official sign of approval, Manchester instructed his agent to accept a record-setting bid of $665,000 from the publishers of *Look* Magazine for the rights to serialize the book—a decision which pleased Robert Kennedy, according to Manchester. "Great, isn't that a record?," the author quotes the senator as saying when he relayed news of the sale to him. "*Look* has been so nice to the Kennedy family and Henry Luce (then editorial chairman of Time, Inc., publishers of *Life* Magazine, which was also in the running for serialization rights) has been such a bastard."

Not long after this decision was made, however, it became evident that the Kennedys had begun to have second thoughts about the entire project and, assuming that they had control over the manuscript, they decided to withdraw their permission to publish both the book and its serialized version. *Look,* believing that it had purchased a manuscript that the Kennedys had initially approved and then seemed to want to suppress, refused to bow to any family pressure. Though the basic issue appeared to revolve around whether or not the Kennedys had granted permission to publish, the family's real concern centered on certain political passages which, after further consideration, they perceived as being potentially damaging to Lyndon Johnson's presidency as well as to Robert's plans for that same office.

Several months later, with *Look* still determined to publish the original manuscript and the Kennedys requesting the right to delete or change certain information, Jacqueline filed suit against Manchester, Harper & Row, and *Look,* claiming that the publication of the book would cause her "great and irreparable injury" and would result in "sensationalism and commercialism" (despite the fact that most of the profits from the sale of the book had been designated for the Kennedy Memorial Library). All three of the defendants remained firmly opposed to making any changes other than factual corrections, with Gardner Cowles of *Look* stating that "we have gone the limit to try to be fair and thoughtful of everyone's feelings—but yet consistent with accuracy." A little over a month later, in January, 1967, the suit was settled out of court after *Look* and Harper & Row agreed to revise some of the passages that dealt with Jacqueline Kennedy.

Prior to this pre-publication controversy, few people, according to *Time,* foresaw that Manchester's book "would become not only a publishing phenomenon but also an emotional battleground—a book about which other books will be written." Its publication in April, 1967, unleashed a torrent of critical reaction, most of it praising the author's voluminous research but condemning his obvious partiality towards his subject—a partiality most reviewers found inexcusable and highly unprofessional, especially for a man purporting to write "history." As Alistair Cooke comments in *Book Week:* "Mr. Manchester's method is what you might call non-selective documentary, an assembly-line of infinite ingredients whose monotonous movement is teased, for the sake of suspense, by stoppings and starting and flashbacks. . . . As it is, the whole thing bristles with doubts and alarms."

After criticizing Manchester's tendency to revert to the techniques practiced by authors of fictionalized biographies (in which scenes, conversations, and even private thoughts are *reconstructed* in the absence of actual historical proof), Cooke continues: "The trouble—and the triumph—is that there are enough episodes so eerily and circumstantially reported (imagined?) that, all later witnesses to the contrary, this will remain the account that stays in the mind." (In response to these comments, Manchester told *CA* that "all such material [is] on tape or in shorthand.") Furthermore, Cooke adds, "as an attempt at a first-rate piece of journalism, the book offers no insight that goes beneath the surface of the events, the participants, and their reported dialogue. You are left to draw conclusions which may well run counter to Mr. Manchester's intentions. . . . But literature, I take it, is not Mr. Manchester's aim. He is deliberately shoveling at us a mountain of minutiae from which historians fifty or one hundred years from now will trace the true plot, judge the characters fairly, be forever grateful to an author as insatiable as Suetonius for fact and detail, consequence, inconsequence, time, place, smell, rumor, gossip. . . . It is a best seller written for the snooper's world."

Richard Rovere of the *New Yorker* writes: "Manchester has committed an outrage, an indecency. . . . What he has written raises so many questions about his taste, his judgment, his character. . . . [But] one is tempted to put aside questions of taste, and even of complete truthfulness, and say that, whatever its faults, this is a great book. . . . It is a book that provokes extreme responses. Its power is such that the events it describes are more anguishing now, in Manchester's reconstruction of them in words, than when they were actually happening. . . . The prose, though faulted in minor ways, is almost always eloquent, and often poetic. The total effect is shattering, and it seems not at all inconceivable that we have here an American contribution to the great literature of the death of kings. . . . [But] Manchester does not offer *The Death of a President* as poetry or myth. He offers it as history, as scholarship, as verified and verifiable truth. . . . We read this book with the disturbing knowledge that it was compromised from the start, that it was tampered with many times, and that Manchester's insistence, in the *Look* article, that 'the integrity of my work was not negotiable' must be disregarded."

A critic in the *Illustrated London News* notes that "Mr. Manchester seems to have worked on the erroneous principle that if he could stuff in the strict chronology as much as possible about everything that happened to everybody concerned, however ephemerally, . . . he would somehow encompass 'the truth.' The result is an elephantine narrative that has the compulsive readability of the kind of novel conceived, and written as a surefire best-seller. . . . And much of his narrative is full of a breathless mawkishness that would turn one's stomach in a pop novelist or journalist. The unreality of it all is exacerbated by the conflict between the quasi-objective narration and the adulation of Kennedy. . . . The real Kennedy is absent from Mr. Manchester's story: we have instead, a saint martyred, a deity translated."

Joseph Featherstone of the *New Republic,* though he admits that "there are patches of good reporting throughout the 647 pages," generally feels that "*The Death of a President* is an ugly and pointless book, written in a garish style that parodies the New Frontier's own rhetoric. . . . This is history in the sense that the souvenir hunters who put in bids for Lee Oswald's rifle are historians. There is only this ransacking of the past for its artifacts, as though if we picked up enough souvenirs, we could recreate the events and reach the men and women who lived them."

Finally, a *Newsweek* reviewer writes: "Manchester's technique is familiar enough. He calls it 'contemporary history,' but it is actually high-intensity journalism: an often moving, sometimes infuriating blend of meticulously fact-ridden reportage, portentous philosophizing and unabashed emotionalism. . . . His intense involvement is what makes long passages of *The Death of a President* heart-rendingly memorable. But it is also responsible for the book's excesses. . . . The result of all this is to disfigure *The Death of a President*. It was to have been the definitive story of the Kennedy assassination and its aftermath; it is far less than that. Its reportage of the anguish of the New Frontier, of the pageantry and pathos of the funeral, of a world in mourning may never be surpassed. But the enduring chronicle of those days—the distillation of events and emotions into the cadence and perspective of history—remains to be written."

Manchester's biography of General Douglas MacArthur, *American Caesar,* fares somewhat better with the critics, though many of their comments seem reminiscent of the reactions to *The Death of a President*. Burke Wilkinson of the *Christian Science Monitor* writes: "What Manchester has created is not history, despite the prodigious research. It is more like a stage play. . . . Call it history seen through one man's vision and blinders. . . . Call it if you will an enrichment of history. Even in style, the resemblances between Manchester and MacArthur are striking. Both at their worst can be prolix and banal. . . . But like his five-star star of stars [Manchester] can move and stir us too."

Leonard Bushkoff of *Book World* calls the book a "long, highly readable but essentially shallow biography. . . . His is a journalistic, narrative account, entertaining but all surface, facile and fast-moving, with occasional descriptive set-pieces for dramatic effect. Some are quite good . . . but others are superficial, even embarrassingly so. Everything depends on what Manchester has decided to extract from earlier writings. For the footnotes indicate that there is very little original research here. . . . Hence there are some noticeable factual errors, and far too many near misses. . . . Manchester's penchant for dramatizing and personalizing events [also] has its costs."

The question of the author's impartiality is once again mentioned by various reviewers, though it apparently is not quite the problem it was in *The Death of a President*. Eric F. Goldman of the *New York Times Book Review* comments: "Naturally, Mr. Manchester's high opinion of MacArthur affects his interpretations [of major events]. . . . Occasionally Mr. Manchester becomes so involved with his subject that he is swept into MacArthur's overblown or mawkish rhetoric. . . . [But] generally, *American Caesar* is written with taste, grace and verve. Like most of Mr. Manchester's books, it is based on enormous research. In treating all the stormy episodes of General MacArthur's life, . . . he maintains a degree of even-handedness. . . . As a whole, the biography is basically neither pro- nor anti-MacArthur."

Bushkoff, the *Book World* reviewer, is less sure of the author's impartiality. "Certainly Manchester often is critical of MacArthur's personality, of the arrogance, the self-importance, the bizarre exaggerations, the hunger for publicity. But these qualities are treated charitably, are excused by circumstances, by their alleged insignificance, by MacArthur's greatness." The *Christian Science Monitor* critic, Wilkinson, agrees that "Manchester's version of the Pacific War is in very large degree MacArthur's," but he feels that "the author is fully aware of the shortcomings of his hero"; it is simply that "the record was so fine that along with Manchester we quickly forget and forgive the shortcomings."

Forrest McDonald of the *National Review* writes: "William Manchester is a literary craftsman of the first rank.... In a sense this book truly captures the spirit of the man MacArthur.... It inspires and infuriates, it enchants and alienates, but it never leaves one indifferent.... But there is, alas, more art here than history.... In any event, he views MacArthur with a wide-eyed, mouth agape, gee-whiz reverence, and yet manages simultaneously to cling to Truman-Acheson superstitions about the man.... In short, what we have here is splendid entertainment, and little more."

A *Commonweal* reviewer, however, feels that Manchester did an admirable job, considering the complexities of his subject and the world in which he lived. "Such a man [as MacArthur] presents highly difficult challenges to any serious biographer of him, but William Manchester rises to them triumphantly in this meticulously researched work. His psychological interpretations are generally acute and persuasive, his historical judgments generally well-informed and balanced. He is a master of both descriptive and narrative prose—a supreme master, I would say, of what might be called participatory prose, in that the reader is at once caught up in it and carried along by it, as if he himself took part in the events described. He has written a notable book which may well stand up, permanently, as the definitive biography of MacArthur."

From an outside view of World War II in the Pacific, Manchester turned to an inside view—his own. Troubled by the differences he saw between the cocky young Marine sergeant of 1945 and the "portly, balding, Brooks-Brothered man" of 1978, Manchester decided to revisit various battle sites of the Pacific in an attempt to analyze his commitment to the war and to determine what had resulted from his (and, ultimately, our) participation in it. The record of his journey, *Goodbye, Darkness,* alternates personal anecdotes and reflections drawn from the author's own experiences at Okinawa with detailed descriptions of every major Pacific land battle.

Much as in the case of Manchester's previous works, reviewers praise his storytelling ability but are less enthusiastic about his handling of historical fact. Ted Morgan, for example, comments in the *New York Times Book Review* that "Mr. Manchester's combat writing is one of his book's strengths and stands comparison with the best.... The scenes depicted in *Goodbye, Darkness* are models of contained, unemphatic action." But Morgan finds that "the first-hand material ... shores up the stuff that smells of library research. This can be misleading, for I wasn't sure until I'd read the author's note at the end of the book that all the action had taken place on Okinawa." Despite this vagueness, however, Morgan concludes that *Goodbye, Darkness* "is a strong and honest account."

Clay Blair of the *Chicago Tribune Book World* admits that he is "hard-put to describe this intelligent, beautifully crafted but complicated work in a nutshell. It is no simple, straightforward memoir.... [Manchester] vividly—and often lyrically—recreates the battles ..., necessarily drawing heavily

on previously published works." But Blair agrees with Morgan that "the unwary reader [gets] the impression that Manchester fought in every battle he describes." Furthermore, like the *New York Times*'s Anatole Broyard, who believes that Manchester has a penchant for overstatement and "too-grand generalization," Blair notes that the author's stories "are novelistically recreated, with excessive dialog (some of it incredible) and fictitious names. Adding to the organizational confusion, [Manchester] injects current information on the islands he visits and relentless philosophizing and moralizing about the war, the Marine Corps, and mankind in general."

Continues the reviewer: "The end result is an occasionally entertaining, occasionally shocking but ultimately dissatisfying, self-indulgent, and, perhaps unintentionally, self-glorifying book. The reader seldom knows what is fact, what is fiction.... The compulsion to reconcile the cocky 1945 Marine with the troubled 1978 Brooks-Brothered writer seems forced, a gimmick.... Finally, not nearly enough specific credit is given the historians and writers from whom he has so freely borrowed."

"This is a very good book, but for reasons which the author did not intend," writes Josiah Bunting III in his *Washington Post Book World* review of *Goodbye, Darkness.* "It purports to be an organized attempt to make sense of the author's experience in the great adventure and cataclysm of World War II. In this it fails; or, rather, its conclusions are commonplace." Nevertheless, Bunting states, "*Goodbye, Darkness* is a compelling account ... of the war in the Pacific.... Perhaps no other living writer could have gotten it all down so well; but none has looked it over from so many merging or intersecting perspectives." Like Morgan, Bunting finds Manchester's stories "in no way understated"; they are, he says, "movingly rendered and authentic." Thus, he concludes, "as a memoir, [*Goodbye, Darkness*] succeeds superlatively.... [But] as self-conscious autobiography, as an attempt to make sense of the war and his part in it, given the author's and the world's state 35 years later, it is much less accomplished, doomed in the telling by questions ultimately unanswerable."

BIOGRAPHICAL/CRITICAL SOURCES: Saturday Review, January 6, 1951, December 21, 1968, October 14, 1978; *Life,* May 7, 1965; *New York Times,* December 17, 1966, December 18, 1966, December 19, 1966, January 23, 1967, January 30, 1967, August 20, 1968, December 3, 1968, December 6, 1968, September 17, 1980; John Corry, *The Manchester Affair,* Putnam, 1967; *Newsweek,* January 30, 1967, February 13, 1967, March 27, 1967, April 10, 1967, April 24, 1967, July 17, 1967, November 25, 1968, September 11, 1978; *New York Times Book Review,* April, 1967, September 3, 1967, November 24, 1968, November 12, 1978, August 31, 1980; *New Yorker,* April 1, 1967, November 30, 1968; *National Observer,* April 3, 1967, April 24, 1967, December 23, 1978; *Christian Science Monitor,* April 6, 1967, October 23, 1978; *Time,* April 7, 1967, June 28, 1968, August 23, 1968, December 20, 1968, September 11, 1978; *Book Week,* April 9, 1967; *Christian Century,* April 12, 1967; *Observer,* April 16, 1967, January 26, 1969, August 24, 1969; *Nation,* April 17, 1967; *Punch,* April 19, 1967, February 12, 1969; *New York Review of Books,* April 20, 1967, October 12, 1978; *New Statesman,* April 21, 1967, January 31, 1969; *New Republic,* April 22, 1967; *Illustrated London News,* April 29, 1967; *Saturday Night,* May, 1967; *National Review,* May 30, 1967, January 5, 1979; *Books,* June, 1967; *Esquire,* June, 1967, November, 1968; *Books and Bookmen,* June, 1967, November, 1967; *Village Voice,* June 1, 1967; *Ramparts,*

June, 1967; *Commonweal,* June 30, 1967, February 7, 1969, April 27, 1979; *Commentary,* July, 1967; *Washington Post Book World,* January 28, 1968, June 30, 1968, December 1, 1968, September 24, 1978, September 21, 1980; *Atlantic,* December, 1968; *Washington Post,* December 7, 1968, November 25, 1974; *Canadian Forum,* February, 1969; *Spectator,* February 21, 1969, May 20, 1970; *Best Sellers,* September 15, 1970, January, 1979; *Philadelphia Bulletin,* November 17, 1974; *Publishers Weekly,* August 28, 1978; *Miami Herald,* September 24, 1978; *Los Angeles Times Book Review,* October 1, 1978; *Detroit Free Press,* October 29, 1978; *Chicago Tribune Book World,* September 28, 1980.

—*Sketch by Deborah A. Straub*

*   *   *

MANN, Michael   1919-1977

PERSONAL: Born April 21, 1919, in Munich, Germany; died of a heart attack January 1, 1977, in Orinda, Calif.; son of Thomas (the writer) and Katia (Pringsheim) Mann; married Gret Moser, March 6, 1939; children: Frido, Tonio, Raju. *Education:* Duquesne University, M.M., 1957; Harvard University, Ph.D., 1961. *Residence:* Orinda, Calif. *Office:* Department of German, University of California, Berkeley, Calif. 94720.

CAREER: Member of San Francisco Symphony, 1942-49; viola soloist on concert tours, 1950-57; University of California, Berkeley, instructor, 1961-63, assistant professor, 1963-65, associate professor, 1965-70, professor of German literature, 1970-77. *Awards, honors:* Guggenheim fellowship, 1964.

WRITINGS: Heinrich Heines Zeitungsberichte ueber Musik und Malerei, Insel, 1964; (co-author) *Welt Geschichte,* Volume VII: *Die Europaeische Musik von den Anfaengen bis Beethoven,* Propylaen-Weltgesdridte, 1964; *Das Thomas Mann Buch,* Fischer Bucherei, 1965; *Heinrich Heines Musik Kritiken,* Campe, 1971; (with Andrew Oscar Jaszi) *Entzweiung un Vereinigung,* Stiehm, 1973; *Sturm und Drang Drama: Studien und Vorstudien zu Schiller's "Raubern,"* Francke Verlag, 1974; (editor) *Thomas Mann Essays,* Fischer Taschenbuchverlag, 1977.†

*   *   *

MANNES, Marya   1904-

PERSONAL: Born November 14, 1904, in New York, N.Y.; daughter of David (a violinist) and Clara (a pianist; maiden name, Damrosch) Mannes; married Jo Mielziner, 1926 (divorced, 1931); married Richard Blow, 1937 (divorced, 1943); married Christopher Clarkson, April 2, 1948 (divorced, 1966); children: (second marriage) David Jeremy. *Education:* Attended private schools in New York, N.Y. *Agent:* Barbara Rhodes, 140 West End Ave., New York, N.Y. 10023.

CAREER: Vogue, New York City, feature editor, 1933-36; U.S. Government service, 1942-45; *Glamour,* New York City, feature editor, 1946; free-lance writer, 1947-52; *The Reporter,* New York City, staff writer, 1952-63; free-lance writer, 1963—. Host of television program, "I Speak for Myself," 1959; *McCall's,* monthly columnist, 1965-67, movie critic, 1968; monthly columnist, *New York Times,* 1967; television commentator, Channel 13, New York City, 1967-70; columnist, United Features Syndicate, 1971—. Trustee, Mannes College of Music, New York City. Lecturer. *Member:* Authors League, Dramatists Guild, Newspaper Guild, American Federation of Television and Radio Artists. *Awards, honors:* George Polk Memorial Award for

magazine criticism, 1958; L.H.D., Hood College, 1960; achievement award, Federation of Jewish Women's Organization, 1961; award of honor, Theta Sigma Phi, 1962.

WRITINGS: Message from a Stranger (novel), Viking, 1948; *More in Anger* (essays), Lippincott, 1958; *Subverse* (satirical verse), Braziller, 1959; *The New York I Know* (essays), Lippincott, 1961; *But Will It Sell?,* Lippincott, 1964; *They* (novel), Doubleday, 1968; *Out of My Time* (autobiography), Doubleday, 1971; (with Norman Sheresky) *Uncoupling: The Art of Coming Apart,* Dell, 1973; *Last Rights,* Morrow, 1974. Also author of *One Plus One.* Contributor to *New York Times Magazine, Esquire, Harper's, New York Herald Tribune Book Week,* and other magazines.

SIDELIGHTS: In 1968, John Leonard described Marya Mannes as "a good reactionary. She sympathizes with the folk singers and the flower children. She is against war. . . . She believes in the body, the senses, animals, nature, love. But she is not willing to buy righteousness or intolerance from any source. Nor will she cede to any individual organism, if it calls itself human, a presumptive and exclusive license to indulge oneself at the expense of others—barbarism in the guise of identity-search."

Nevertheless, Charles Rolo finds that "her kind of social criticism impresses [one] as somewhat self-indulgent. She has simply voiced the familiar complaints of the civilized mind about the shiny barbarism of the age and has neglected the more taxing job of delving into the why and wherefore of what irks her." A. C. Perta agrees, noting that in *But Will It Sell?,* she is, "to say the least, a trifle condescending. Peering down from the stilts of her incomparable ego, she disdains the stupidity, vulgarity, and barbarism of modern life. . . . At her best, she is crisp, biting, and fluent. At her worst, she suffers from sticky intimacy, convenient generalizations, and reiterated cliches."

Mannes's "best" is more consistently present in her earlier works. In her second book, writes Harry Golden, one becomes aware of her "inherent sense of drama and an abiding respect for words and sentences arranged in rhythmic order." The impact of that drama is clearly felt in her third book, a collection of poems entitled *Subverse.* Of it, S. R. Davis writes: "This is an unhinging book. It is brilliant and dogmatic and partisan and intensely clever. It is devastating and destructive and alarmingly funny. The eye starts down a page dancing in bright meter and comes to a sudden staring stop. A gay and diverting subject is introduced . . . and starts on its merry way and in the second stanza the reader is hit in the stomach." T. F. Houlihan finds that "those seeking some indication of sanity in this world apparently gone mad will find much solace, and many a wry laugh, in Mannes's pungent comments on modern-day business, education, politics, segregation, and sex."

Many critics have noted that it is in the essay that Mannes finds her true strength; in longer works it is harder for her to maintain her characteristic bite. Kenneth Rexroth refers to *They,* her novel, as an "amusing and provoking book that might have been a great one." R. B. Nordberg agrees, writing, "What could have been a very good novel, isn't."

Although her autobiography, *Out of My Time,* is said to be overburdened with excerpts from her early writings and letters, Eileen Kennedy believes it is compelling to watch "an incisive, original mind finding its voice and philosophy." And her early writings are what prompted William Hogan to ask in 1958: "What do you do about someone like this? I think you listen to her, for whether you agree with her or not, her ideas crackle with the energy of an old-fashioned fourth of July celebration."

BIOGRAPHICAL/CRITICAL SOURCES: San Francisco Chronicle, November 3, 1958; *New York Herald Tribune Book Review,* November 9, 1958, September 10, 1961; *Saturday Review,* November 15, 1958, November 2, 1968, September 9, 1972; *Atlantic,* January, 1959; *Christian Science Monitor,* February 12, 1959, September 7, 1961; *Library Journal,* March 1, 1959; *Best Sellers,* June 1, 1964, November 10, 1968, December 1, 1968, November 15, 1971, January 15, 1974; *Commonweal,* August 21, 1964; *New York Times Book Review,* October 20, 1968, November 28, 1971, March 3, 1974; *Time,* November 1, 1968, January 7, 1974; *New York Times,* December 30, 1968; Marya Mannes, *Out of My Time,* Doubleday, 1971.

*   *   *

MANSFIELD, Edwin 1930-

PERSONAL: Born June 8, 1930, in Kingston, N.Y.; son of Raymond and Sara (Haas) Mansfield; married Lucile Howe (a psychologist), 1955; children: Edward, Elizabeth. *Education:* Dartmouth College, A.B., 1951; Duke University, M.A., 1953, Ph.D., 1955; University of London, postgraduate study, 1954-55. *Office:* Department of Economics, University of Pennsylvania, Philadelphia, Pa. 19104.

CAREER: Duke University, Durham, N.C., research associate, 1953-54; Carnegie Institute of Technology (now Carnegie-Mellon University), Pittsburgh, Pa., associate professor of economics, 1955-63; University of Pennsylvania, Wharton School of Finance, Philadelphia, professor of economics, 1963—. Visiting associate professor of economics at Yale University, 1961-62; visiting professor of economics at Harvard University, 1963-64. Chairman, U.S.-U.S.S.R. Working Party on Economics of Science and Technology. Consultant to Federal Power Commission, RAND Corp., National Science Foundation, Small Business Administration, U.S. Army, and U.S. Department of Commerce. *Member:* American Economic Association, American Statistical Association, Econometric Society (fellow), American Academy of Arts and Sciences (fellow), Phi Beta Kappa, Delta Upsilon. *Awards, honors:* Fulbright scholar; Ford Foundation faculty research fellow; fellow, Center for Advanced Study in the Behavioral Sciences; certificate of appreciation from U.S. Secretary of Commerce.

WRITINGS—All published by Norton: (Editor and author of introduction) *Monopoly Power and Economic Performance: The Problem of Industrial Concentration,* 1964, 3rd edition, 1972; (editor) *Managerial Economics and Operations Research: A Non-Mathematical Introduction,* 1966, revised edition, 1970; *The Economics of Technological Change,* 1968; *Industrial Research and Technological Innovation: An Econometric Analysis,* 1968; (compiler) *Defense, Science, and Public Policy,* 1968; *Microeconomics: Theory and Application,* 1970; (compiler) *Elementary Statistics for Economics and Business: Selected Readings,* 1970; *Research and Innovation in the Modern Corporation,* 1971; (editor) *Microeconomics: Selected Readings,* 1971; *Microeconomic Problems,* 1971; *Technological Change: An Introduction to a Vital Area of Modern Economics,* 1971; *The Production and Application of New Industrial Technology,* 1977; *Statistics for Business and Economics,* 1980; *Statistics for Business and Economics: Problems, Exercises, and Case Studies,* 1980; *Statistics for Business and Economics: Readings and Case Studies,* 1980; *Economics: Principles, Problems, Decisions,* 3rd edition (Mansfield was not associated with earlier editions), 1980; *Economics: Readings, Issues, and Cases,* 3rd edition (Mansfield was not associated with earlier editions), 1980; *Study Guide for Economics,* 3rd edition (Mansfield was not associated with earlier editions), 1980. Contributor to half a dozen economics journals. Associate editor, *Journal of the American Statistical Association.*

WORK IN PROGRESS: Several books for Norton.

*   *   *

MARION, John Francis 1922-

PERSONAL: Born February 23, 1922, in Norfolk, Va.; son of Everett Edward and Aileen Frances (McCarthy) Marion. *Education:* Pennsylvania State University, B.A., 1948. *Politics:* Democrat. *Religion:* Roman Catholic. *Home:* 1836 Delancey Pl., Philadelphia, Pa. 19103.

CAREER: Editor, *Commercial America,* 1948-49; *Philadelphia Magazine,* Philadelphia, Pa., editor, 1949-50; J. B. Lippincott Co. (publishers), Philadelphia, publicity director, 1952-53; editor, *Pennsylvania Traveler,* 1959; literary agent and free-lance publicist for five years; Chilton Book Co., Philadelphia, editor-in-chief, 1962-72. *Military service:* U.S. Army, 1943-46. *Member:* Franklin Inn Club, Athenaeum of Philadelphia.

WRITINGS: Lucrezia Bori of the Metropolitan Opera, Kenedy, 1962; *Bicentennial City,* Pyne Press, 1974; *Philadelphia Medica,* Stackpole, 1976; *Famous and Curious Cemeteries,* Crown, 1977; *The Charleston Story,* Stackpole 1978; *The Fine Old House,* Smith-Kline, 1980. Contributor of articles and stories to *New York Times,* Philadelphia *Bulletin, Philadelphia Inquirer, Christian Science Monitor, Philippine-American* (Manila), and *Weekly Post* (Warwickshire, England).

SIDELIGHTS: John Francis Marion told *CA:* "I am now doing what I've always wanted to do. As a young child I was obsessed with books and writing. I've written professionally since I left college, but until 1972 (with one exception) I confined my writing to articles and stories. All of my books have grown from my deep love of history, something which began with the stories my grandmother told me when I squeezed into the chair beside her.

"I owe a great debt to three friends who are or were writers: March Cost, the late British novelist; Doris Langley Moore, the Byron scholar and novelist; and Annette Joelson, the South African writer. During years of friendship they encouraged me and discussed their own problems as writers. This provided a wonderful learning ground for me."

AVOCATIONAL INTERESTS: Music, theater, bicycling, ice skating, dancing, collecting autograph manuscripts and letters.

*   *   *

MARSHALL, John David 1928-

PERSONAL: Born September 7, 1928, in McKenzie, Tenn.; son of Maxwell Cole (a merchant) and Emma (Walpole) Marshall. *Education:* Bethel College, B.A., 1950; Florida State University, M.A., 1951, graduate study, 1951-52. *Politics:* Democrat. *Religion:* Cumberland Presbyterian. *Home:* 802 East Main, Apt. 38, Murfreesboro, Tenn. 37130. *Office:* Andrew L. Todd Library, Middle Tennessee State University, Murfreesboro, Tenn. 37130.

CAREER: Florida State University, Library School, Tallahassee, administrative assistant, Office of Library School Dean, 1951-52; Clemson College (now University) Library, Clemson, S.C., reference librarian, 1952-55; Auburn University Library, Auburn, Ala., head of reference department, 1955-57; University of Georgia Libraries, Athens, head of

Acquisitions Division and assistant professor of libraries, 1957-67; Middle Tennessee State University, Murfreesboro, university librarian and associate professor, 1967-76, professor of library science, 1980—, university bibliographer, 1976—. Consultant, Churchill Memorial and Library, summer, 1979. *Member:* American Library Association (life), Association of College and Research Libraries (publications committee member, 1957-62), Southeastern Library Association (vice-chairman, College and University Libraries Section, 1970-72, chairman, 1972-74; chairman, nominating committee, 1976-78; chairman, honorary membership committee, 1978-80), Southeastern Regional Group of Resources and Technical Services Librarians (vice-chairman, 1966-68; chairman, 1968-70), Tennessee Historical Society, Tennessee Library Association (chairman of intellectual freedom committee, 1968-70), Phi Kappa Phi, Beta Phi Mu (publications committee member, Gamma Chapter, 1963-64).

WRITINGS: (Editor with Wayne Shirley and Louis Shores) *Books, Libraries, Librarians: Contributions to Library Literature,* Shoe String, 1955; *Books in Your Life,* Bethel College, 1959; (editor) *Of, By, and For Librarians: Contributions to Library Literature,* Shoe String, 1960; (editor) *An American Library History Reader: Contributions to Library Literature,* Shoe String, 1961; (editor) *In Pursuit of Library History,* Florida State University Library School, 1961; *Louis Shores: A Bibliography,* Gamma Chapter, Beta Phi Mu, 1964; (editor) Louis Shores, *Mark Hopkins' Log and Other Essays,* Shoe String, 1965; *A Fable of Tomorrow's Library,* Peacock Press, 1965; (editor) *Approaches to Library History,* Florida State University Library School, 1966; (editor) *The Library in the University,* Shoe String, 1967; *Of, By, and For Librarians: Second Series,* Shoe String, 1974; *Louis Shores, Author-Librarian: A Bibliography,* Gamma Chapter, Beta Phi Mu, 1979; *The Southern Books Competition at Twenty-Five,* Howick House, 1980. General editor, "Contributions to Library Literature" series, Shoe String, 1963-78; *Southern Observer,* contributing editor, 1953-1966, contributor of column, "Bibliophile's Notebook," 1954-66; book reviewer, *Library Journal,* 1953-64; book review editor, *Journal of Library History,* 1966-76, *Southeastern Librarian,* 1979—.

WORK IN PROGRESS: Biographical sketches of the 36 honorary members of the Southeastern Library Association for a historical booklet.

SIDELIGHTS: John David Marshall collects the books of three authors: Louis Shores, dean of Florida State University Library School, Lawrence Clark Powell, dean of School of Library Service at the University of California, Los Angeles, and former Prime Minister Sir Winston S. Churchill. His collection of Churchilliana includes some three hundred items either by or about Churchill (in whom he has been interested since about the seventh grade), including a first edition of *Savrola* (Longmans, Green, 1900), Churchill's only novel. Marshall was privileged to hear the famous "iron curtain" speech which Churchill delivered at Westminster College, Fulton, Mo., on March 5, 1946.

BIOGRAPHICAL/CRITICAL SOURCES: New York Times Book Review, May 6, 1956; *Southern Observer,* April, 1960; *College and Research Libraries,* December, 1967.

*　　*　　*

MARSHALL, Michael (Kimbrough) 1948-
(Kim Marshall)

PERSONAL: Born March 11, 1948, in Oakland, Calif.; son of Randolph Laughlin and Anne (Grant) Marshall; married

Rhoda Schneider (a lawyer), May 25, 1973. *Education:* Harvard University, B.A. (magna cum laude), 1969. *Politics:* Independent. *Home:* 222 Clark Rd., Brookline, Mass. 02146. *Agent:* Donald Cutler, Sterling Lord Agency, Inc., 660 Madison Ave., New York, N.Y. 10021. *Office:* Martin Luther King School, 77 Lawrence Ave., Boston, Mass. 02121.

CAREER: Martin Luther King School, Boston, Mass., sixth grade teacher, 1969—. Lecturer, Cambridge Educational Associates, 1974-76. *Member:* Common Cause, Boston Teachers' Union. *Awards, honors:* Calvert Smith Award, *Harvard Magazine,* 1970 and 1971.

WRITINGS—All under name Kim Marshall: *Law and Order in Grade 6-E,* Little, Brown, 1972; *Opening Your Class with Learning Stations,* Education Today, 1974; *The Story of Life: From the Big Bang to You,* Holt, 1980.

Also author of four books in "Kim Marshall" text/workbook series, *Math, English, Vocabulary,* and *Reading,* Educators Publishing Service, 1980-81. Contributor to professional journals. Contributing editor, *Learning.*

SIDELIGHTS: Kim Marshall writes: "The inspiration for my writing has come from my eleven years of work in an inner city Boston public school. I have become fascinated with classroom organization, kids, and curriculum, and have been anxious to share my experiences with others. Recently I have become increasingly interested in desegregation, magnet schools, and in becoming a school principal."

BIOGRAPHICAL/CRITICAL SOURCES: Christian Science Monitor, June 30, 1973.

*　　*　　*

MARTIN, George (Whitney) 1926-

PERSONAL: Born January 25, 1926, in New York, N.Y.; son of George Whitney (a lawyer) and Agnes (Hutchinson) Martin. *Education:* Harvard University, B.A., 1948; attended Trinity College, Cambridge, 1949-50; University of Virginia, LL.B., 1953. *Home and office:* 333 East 68th St., New York, N.Y. 10021.

CAREER: Admitted to bar, 1955; Emmet, Marvin & Martin, Attorneys at Law, New York, N.Y., associate, 1955-58, partner, 1958-59; currently full-time writer. Member of board of directors, Leake & Watts Children's Home, Inc., 1959-67, Metropolitan Opera Guild, 1958-70. *Member:* Century Association, Grolier Club. *Military service:* U.S. Navy, 1944-46; U.S. Army, 1953-54.

WRITINGS: The Opera Companion: A Guide for the Casual Opera-Goer, Dodd, 1961; *The Battle of the Frogs and the Mice: An Homeric Fable,* Dodd, 1962; *Verdi: His Music, Life and Times,* Dodd, 1963, reprinted, DaCapo, 1979; *The Red Shirt and the Cross of Savoy: The Story of Italy's Risorgimento 1748-1871,* Dodd, 1969; *Causes and Conflicts: The Centennial History of the Association of the Bar of the City of New York,* Houghton, 1970; *Madam Secretary: Frances Perkins,* Houghton, 1976; *The Opera Companion to Twentieth Century Opera,* Dodd, 1979. Also author of monographs in *Yale Review.* Contributor of articles to *Opera Annual, Yale Review, Opera News,* and *Bulletin of Instituto de Studi Verdiani,* and of book reviews to *Yale Review* and *Book World.*

WORK IN PROGRESS: Biography of the Damrosch/Mannes family.

SIDELIGHTS: In a review of *Causes and Conflicts: The Centennial History of the Association of the Bar of the City of New York,* a writer for *Virginia Quarterly Review* describes George Martin as "a graceful writer and a discriminating historian . . ." and his book as "a near-model institutional history [which] is perceptive, critical, and judicious. It is also appreciative, interesting, and informative."

Martin's work in the field of opera has been equally well received. *The Opera Companion to Twentieth-Century Opera* has been hailed by *Washington Post's* Joseph McLellan as "an essential reference book, considerably more useful than the standard opera guides that limit themselves to already familiar material." This usefulness is further explained by Donal Henahan, who comments in a *New York Times* review: "Martin has developed a way of guiding the reader through the operatic underbrush that makes up in liveliness and narrative clarity for any scholarly or encyclopedic shortcomings. His prose is straightforward, unadorned and never precious, all rare assets in writing about opera, and if it sometimes seems clipped and lacking in grace, at least one is rarely left wondering what a sentence is supposed to mean."

BIOGRAPHICAL/CRITICAL SOURCES: Book World, May 25, 1969; *Virginia Quarterly Review,* autumn, 1970; *Washington Post,* July 3, 1979; *New York Times,* September 1, 1979.

* * *

MASON, Haydn T(revor) 1929-

PERSONAL: Born January 12, 1929, in Saundersfoot, Pembrokeshire, Wales; son of Herbert Thomas (a blacksmith) and Margaret (Jones) Mason; married Gretchen Reger, February 5, 1955; children: David, Gwyneth. *Education:* University College of Wales, B.A. (honors), 1949; Middlebury College, Middlebury, Vt., A.M., 1951; Jesus College, Oxford, D.Phil., 1960. *Home:* 14 Claremont Rd., Norwich NR4 65H, England. *Office:* School of European Studies, University of East Anglia, Norwich, England.

CAREER: Princeton University, Princeton, N.J., instructor in French, 1954-57; University of Newcastle upon Tyne, Newcastle upon Tyne, England, lecturer in French, 1960-63; University of Reading, Reading, England, lecturer, 1964-65, reader in French, 1965-67; University of East Anglia, Norwich, England, professor of European literature, 1967—. Associate professor of French literature, University of Paris III (Sorbonne-Nouvelle), 1979-81. *Military service:* British Army, 1951-53. *Member:* British Society for Eighteenth-Century Studies, Association of British University Professors of French. *Awards, honors:* Cassell fellow, 1961; Leverhulme award, 1977.

WRITINGS: Pierre Bayle and Voltaire, Oxford University Press, 1963; (editor and author of introduction) Marivaux, *Les Fausses Confidences,* Oxford University Press, 1964, revised edition, 1971; (editor and translator) *The Leibniz-Arnauld Correspondence,* Manchester University Press, 1967; (editor) Voltaire, *Zadig and Other Stories,* Oxford University Press, 1971; *Voltaire,* Hutchinson, 1975; *Voltaire: A Life,* Granada, 1981; *The Writer and His Society: France 1715-1800,* Macmillan, 1981. Contributor to *Times Literary Supplement, French Studies, Modern Language Review, Romantic Review, Modern Language Notes, Notes and Queries, Journal of European Studies,* and *Studies on Voltaire and the Eighteenth Century.*

WORK IN PROGRESS: Critical editions of six of Voltaire's poems, for *Oeuvres completes,* edited by W. H. Barber and others, for the Voltaire Foundation; research for a book on Cyrano de Bergerac, for Grant S. Cutter.

MASON, Philip 1906-
(Philip Woodruff)

PERSONAL: Born March 19, 1906, in London, England; son of H. A. and E. Addison (Woodruff) Mason; married Eileen Mary Hayes, 1935; children: two daughters, two sons. *Education:* Attended Balliol College, Oxford, 1924-28. *Home:* Hither Daggons, Cripplestyle, Alderholt, Near Fordingbridge, Hampshire, England.

CAREER: Indian Civil Service, 1928-47; Institute of Race Relations, London, England, director, 1958-70; writer. Government posts in India included undersecretary, War Department, 1933-36, deputy commissioner, Garhwal, 1936-39, deputy secretary, Defense and War Departments, 1939-42, conference secretary, South-East Asia Command, 1942-44, joint secretary, War Department, 1944-47. *Member:* Travellers Club, Pall Mall Club. *Awards, honors:* Order of the British Empire, 1942; Companion of Indian Empire, 1945; fellow, School of Oriental and African Studies, University of London, 1970; D.Sc., University of Bristol, 1971; D.Litt., Oxford.

WRITINGS: An Essay on Racial Tension, Royal Institute of International Affairs, 1954, Greenwood, 1972; *A New Deal in East Africa,* Royal Institute of International Affairs, 1955; *Christianity and Race,* Lutterworth, 1956, St. Martin's, 1957; *The Birth of a Dilemma: The Conquest and Settlement of Rhodesia,* Oxford University Press for Institute of Race Relations, 1958; (author of introduction and epilogue) *Man, Race and Darwin* (symposium), Oxford University Press, 1960; *Race Relations in Africa Considered against the Background of History and World Opinion,* S.C.M. Press, 1960; *Year of Decision: Rhodesia and Nyasaland in 1960,* Oxford University Press, 1960; *Common Sense about Race,* Macmillan, 1961; *Prospero's Magic: Some Thoughts on Class and Race,* Oxford University Press, 1962; (editor) *India and Ceylon: Unity and Diversity,* Oxford University Press for Institute of Race Relations, 1967; (editor) *Violence in Southern Africa: A Christian Assessment,* S.C.M. Press, 1970; *Patterns of Dominance,* Oxford University Press for Institute of Race Relations, 1970; *Race Relations,* Oxford University Press, 1970; *How People Differ: An Introduction to Race Relations,* Edward Arnold, 1971; *A Matter of Honour,* Holt, 1974; *Kipling: The Glass, the Shadow, and the Fire,* Harper, 1976; *The Dove in Harness,* Harper, 1977; *A Shaft of Sunlight* (autobiography), Scribner, 1978; *Skinner of Skinner's Horse,* Harper, 1979.

Under pseudonym Philip Woodruff: *Call the Next Witness,* J. Cape, 1945, Harcourt, 1946; *The Wild Sweet Witch,* Harcourt, 1947; *Whatever Dies,* J. Cape, 1948; *The Sword of Northumbria,* J. Cape, 1948; *The Island of Chamba,* J. Cape, 1950; *Hernshaw Castle,* J. Cape, 1950; *Colonel of Dragons,* J. Cape, 1951; *The Men Who Ruled India,* Volume I: *The Founders of Modern India,* J. Cape, 1953, St. Martin's, 1954, Volume II: *The Guardians,* St. Martin's, 1954. Contributor to journals and newspapers and to various symposia.

BIOGRAPHICAL/CRITICAL SOURCES: Times Literary Supplement, February 8, 1968; *Virginia Quarterly Review,* summer, 1970; *Christian Century,* September 23, 1970.

* * *

MATHISON, Richard Randolph 1919-1980

PERSONAL: Born October 20, 1919, in Boise, Idaho; died January 31, 1980, in Los Angeles, Calif.; son of Albert Bismarck and Zellah Marie Mathison; married Margaret Kieffer, 1947 (divorced); married Jeanne Hayden, 1973; children: (first marriage) Melinda, Mellisa, Stephanie, Richard, Matthew. *Education:* Attended University of Idaho, 1938-39, George Washington University, 1939-41. *Home:* 8572 Holloway Dr., Los Angeles, Calif. *Office:* Motion Picture Association of America, 8480 Beverly Blvd., Los Angeles, Calif.

CAREER: Writer, Associated Press, 1946; editor, *Fortnight* magazine, 1946-57; religion editor, *Los Angeles Times*, 1957-59; Los Angeles bureau chief, *Newsweek*, 1959-65; Motion Picture Association of America, Los Angeles, Calif., member of Classification and Rating Administration, 1965-80. Appeared in film "The Godfather: Part II." *Military service:* U.S. Marines, 1941-45. U.S. Marine Corps Reserve; retired as major.

WRITINGS: The Eternal Search, Putnam, 1958; *Faiths, Sects and Cults of America*, Bobbs-Merrill, 1960; *Three Cars in Every Garage*, Doubleday, 1968; *His Weird and Wanton Ways: The Secret Life of Howard Hughes*, Morrow, 1977. Ghost writer of a half dozen books. Contributor of articles to magazines.†

* * *

MAULE, Hamilton Bee   1915-
(Tex Maule)

PERSONAL: Born March 19, 1915, in Ojus, Fla.; son of Claude Wendell and Zelita (Bee) Maule; married Dorothy Kaufman, 1959; children: Frederica Kaufman. *Education:* St. Mary's University, San Antonio, B.A., 1936; University of Texas, B.J., 1947. *Home:* 25 Sutton Pl. S., New York, N.Y. 10022. *Agent:* Scott Meredith, 845 Third Ave., New York, N.Y. 10017. *Office:* 551 Fifth Ave., New York, N.Y. 10017.

CAREER: Austin American Statesman, Austin, Tex., reporter, 1946-47; *Dallas Morning News*, Dallas, Tex., reporter, 1948-49; Los Angeles Rams, Los Angeles, Calif., publicity director, 1949-51; Dallas Texans, Dallas, publicity director, 1951-52; *Dallas Morning News*, Dallas, reporter, columnist, 1952-55; *Sports Illustrated*, New York City, senior editor, 1955-75; *Classic* magazine, New York City, senior writer, 1975—. *Wartime service:* U.S. Merchant Marines, 1941-45. *Member:* Authors Guild, Track Writers Association of America, Football Writers Association of America.

WRITINGS—All published by Random House, except as indicated: *Jeremy Todd*, 1959; *Footsteps*, 1960; *Rub-a-Dub-Dub*, 1963; *Running Scared*, Saturday Review Press, 1973.

Under name Tex Maule; all published by McKay, except as indicated: (Author of commentary) Robert Riger, *The Pros* (documentary), Simon & Schuster, 1960; *The Rookie*, 1961; *The Shortstop*, 1962; *The Quarterback*, 1962; *Beatty of the Yankees*, 1963; *Championship Quarterback*, 1963; *The Game*, Random House, 1963, revised edition, 1964; *The Last Out*, 1963; *The Linebacker*, 1965; *The Running Back*, 1966; *The Players*, New American Library, 1972; *Bart Starr: Professional Quarterback*, F. Watts, 1973. Contributor to encyclopedias and *Reader's Digest.* Editor of text, "Spectacle of Sport."

WORK IN PROGRESS: The Long Summer and *The Front Four*, both novels.

AVOCATIONAL INTERESTS: Painting, sculpture.

BIOGRAPHICAL/CRITICAL SOURCES: Best Sellers, July 1, 1968.

MAZURKIEWICZ, Albert J.   1926-

PERSONAL: Born March 1, 1926, in Shenandoah, Pa.; son of Frank A. (a miner) and Pauline (Polunk) Mazurkiewicz; married Helen Lipsett, August 29, 1953; children: Katharine. *Education:* Ursinus College, A.B., 1950; University of Pennsylvania, M.A., 1951; Temple University, Ed.D., 1957. *Home:* 210 Lorraine Dr., Benkeley Heights, N.J. *Office:* Department of Communication Science, Kean College of New Jersey, Union, N.J. 07083.

CAREER: Philadelphia (Pa.) Public Schools, secondary school teacher, 1950-52, elementary school teacher, 1952-53; Temple University, Philadelphia, Pa., room supervisor in laboratory school of reading and study clinic, 1953-55; Lehigh University, Bethlehem, Pa., associate professor of education and director of reading and study clinic, 1955-66; Kean College of New Jersey, Union, N.J. professor of education, 1966—, graduate professor of education, 1969-71, chairman of department of education, 1966-69, chairman of department of communication science, 1971—. Consultant to various schools. *Military service:* U.S. Army Medical Corps; received Bronze Star. *Member:* International Reading Association, American Psychological Association, American Educational Research Association, College Reading Association (former president and member of board of directors), National Council of Teachers of English, Phi Delta Kappa, Kappa Delta Pi. *Awards, honors:* Commonwealth of Pennsylvania leadership in education award; named Outstanding Educator of America, 1971; College Reading Association distinguished service award, 1979; research grants from the Fund for the Advancement of Education, Office of Education and the Initial Teaching Alphabet Foundation.

WRITINGS: (Editor) *Controversial Issues in Reading*, Reading and Study Clinic, Department of Education, Lehigh University, c.1961; (editor) *Explorations in Reading*, Reading and Study Clinic, Department of Education, Lehigh University, 1962; (editor) *Reading, Learning and the Curriculum*, Reading and Study Clinic, Department of Education, Lehigh University, 1963; (with Harold J. Tanyzer) *Early-to-Read I/T/A Program*, seven volumes, Pitman, 1963-65; (with Tanyzer) *The ITA Handbook for Writing and Spelling: Early-to-Read ITA Program*, Initial Teaching Alphabet Publications, 1964; (editor) *New Perspectives in Reading Instruction: A Book of Readings*, Pitman, 1964, 2nd edition, 1969; (editor) *Reading and Child Development*, Reading and Study Clinic, Department of Education, Lehigh University, 1964; *First Grade Reading Using Modified Co-Basal Versus the Initial Teaching Alphabet*, Lehigh University, 1965; (with Tanyzer) *Mie Alfabet Book*, Initial Teaching Alphabet Publications, 1965; (with Tanyzer) *Mie Number Bwk*, Initial Teaching Alphabet Publications, 1965; *The Initial Alphabet and Reading Instruction*, Lehigh University, 1966; (editor) *Wide World of Reading Instruction*, Interstate, 1966; "Growing with Language" series, Pitman, 1968; (co-author) *The Easy-to-Read I.T.A. Program*, Pitman, 1970; *Teaching about Phonics*, St. Martins, 1976. Contributor to *Elementary English, Reading Teacher, Journal of Developmental Reading, Reading World, Spelling Progress Bulletin, Profiles*, and *Educational Leadership.* Editor, *Journal of the Reading Specialist.*

WORK IN PROGRESS: Reading Comprehension.

SIDELIGHTS: Albert J. Mazurkiewicz has traveled around the world, seeing sixty-one countries and all but three states. Currently, Mazurkiewicz is involved in a variety of orthographic research studies. He also serves as an advisor to promote better education through spelling improvement. Mazurkiewicz told *CA,* "I believe that some kind of spelling reform is necessary [in order] to eliminate the difficulties children have in learning to read and write effectively." *Avocational interests:* Swimming, ice skating, orchid growing, and reading.

*   *   *

McCLARY, Ben Harris 1931-

PERSONAL: Born July 8, 1931, in Ocoee, Tenn.; son of Roy Eugene (an engineer) and Arlene (Kimbrough) McClary; married Sandra Carroll Long (divorced January 13, 1977); children: Katherine Elizabeth, Marcus Harris. *Education:* University of Tennessee, B.A., M.A., 1955; University of Sussex, Ph.D., 1966. *Politics:* Democrat, *Religion:* Episcopal. *Home:* 405 Old Chester Rd., Cochran, Ga. 31014. *Office:* Department of English, Middle Georgia College, Cochran, Ga. 31014.

CAREER: Tennessee Wesleyan College, Athens, assistant professor, 1960-64, associate professor of English, 1966-67; Wesleyan College, Macon, Ga., professor of English, 1967-70, Alice Culler Cobb Professor of English Language and Literature, 1970-71, chairman of department, 1967-71; Middle Georgia College, Cochran, professor of English and chairman of Humanities Division, 1971—. Visiting scholar, University of North Carolina at Chapel Hill, 1980-81. *Military service:* U.S. Army, 1955-56. *Member:* Modern Language Association of America, East Tennessee Historical Society (life member), Phi Kappa Phi. *Awards, honors:* Fulbright fellowship, 1964-66; American Philosophical Society grants, 1967, 1970, 1975, 1978; American Council of Learned Societies grant, 1967; National Endowment for the Humanities, summer seminar grant, 1977.

*WRITINGS—*Editor; published by Scholars' Facsimiles & Reprints, except as indicated: (With Richard Beale Davis) *American Cultural History, 1607-1829,* 1961; Benjamin Silliman, *Letters of Shahcoolen,* 1962; *The Lovingood Papers,* University of Tennessee Press, 1962-67; *Washington Irving and the House of Murray: Geoffrey Crayon Charms the British, 1817-1856,* University of Tennessee Press, 1969; *Chinese Novels,* translation by J. F. Davis, 1976; Charles Kelsall, *Horae Viaticae,* 1979. Contributor of articles on Anglo-American literature and culture to periodicals.

WORK IN PROGRESS: A biography of Samuel Rogers; a history of the Willow Pattern design.

BIOGRAPHICAL/CRITICAL SOURCES: Chattanooga Times, January 13, 1963, April 22, 1964; *Macon Telegraph and News,* October 1, 1967; *Wesleyan Alumnae,* May, 1968; *Macon News,* November 30, 1970.

*   *   *

McDONALD, Gregory 1937-

PERSONAL: Born February 15, 1937, in Shrewsbury, Mass.; son of Irving Thomas (an author) and Mae (a painter; maiden name, Haggarty) McDonald; married Susan Aiken, January 13, 1963; children: Christopher Gregory, Douglas Gregory. *Education:* Harvard University, B.A., 1958. *Address:* P.O. Box 193, Lincoln, Mass. 01773. *Agent:* William Morris Agency, 1350 Avenue of the Americas, New York, N.Y. 10019.

CAREER: Former captain of sailing vessels; marine insurance underwriter, 1959-61; Peace Corps volunteer, 1962; teacher, 1963-64; *Boston Globe,* Boston, Mass., critic-at-large columnist and editor of arts and humanities, 1964-73.

Member of visiting committee, Boston Museum of Fine Arts; director, Bach Cantata Singers. *Member:* Mystery Writers of America (vice-president), Harvard Club. *Awards, honors:* Edgar Allen Poe Awards, 1975, for *Fletch,* and 1977, for *Confess, Fletch.*

WRITINGS: Running Scared (novel), Obolensky, 1964; *Fletch* (also see below), Bobbs-Merrill, 1974; *Confess, Fletch* (also see below), Avon, 1976; *Flynn,* Avon, 1977; *Fletch's Fortune* (also see below), Avon, 1978; *Fletch Forever* (anthology; contains excerpts from *Fletch, Confess, Fletch,* and *Fletch's Fortune*), Avon, 1978; *Love among the Mashed Potatoes,* Dutton, 1978; *Who Took Toby Rinaldi?,* Putnam, 1980; *Fletch and the Widow Bradley,* Avon, 1981.

SIDELIGHTS: According to the *Washington Post:* "Seven publishers bid six figures for two new Fletch books; . . . McDonald says, he has turned down three or four movie offers. . . . He says he's leery of what Hollywood might do to his books."

BIOGRAPHICAL/CRITICAL SOURCES: Washington Post, October 11, 1980.

*   *   *

McDONALD, Hugh Dermot 1910-

PERSONAL: Born October 29, 1910, in Dublin, Ireland; married Anne Marion Ball; children: Conagh, Beryl, Neil. *Education:* Attended Wilson's College and Irish Baptist College in Ireland; Kings College, London, B.A., B.D., Ph.D. (all with honours). *Home:* Fairhaven, 43, The Rough, Newick, Sussex, England.

CAREER: Baptist minister; minister of churches in England, 1937-48; London Bible College, London, England, professor of the philosophy of religion, 1948—, vice-principal, 1952—. Visiting professor of philosophy and theology at Northern Baptist Theological Seminary, Chicago, Ill., 1960-61, 1968-69, Trinity Evangelical Divinity School, 1972, Chicago Graduate School of Theology, Regent College, Vancouver, British Columbia, and New College for Advanced Christian Studies, Berkeley, Calif. *Awards, honors:* D.D., University of London.

WRITINGS: Ideas of Revelation: An Historical Study, A.D. 1700 to A.D. 1860, St. Martin's, 1959; (contributor) James Dixon Douglas, editor, *The New Bible Dictionary,* Eerdmans, 1962; (contributor) Carl Henry, editor, *Basic Christian Doctrines,* Holt, 1962; *Theories of Revelation: An Historical Study, 1860-1960,* Allen & Unwin, 1963, Humanities, 1964; *I and He,* Epworth, 1966; *Jesus: Human and Divine,* Zondervan, 1968; *Living Doctrines of the New Testament,* Pickering & Inglis, 1971, Zondervan, 1972; *Freedom in Faith: A Commentary on Paul's Epistle to the Galatians,* Pickering & Inglis, 1973; *The Church and Its Glory: An Exposition of the Epistle to the Ephesians,* Henry E. Walter, 1973; *Commentary on Colossians and Philemon,* Word Books, 1980; *I Want to Know What the Bible Says about the Bible,* Tyndale, 1980. Contributor to *Towards a Theology of the Future,* edited by Clark Pinnock and D. Wells, and to *International Dictionary of the Christian Church* and *Baker Dictionary of Ethics.* Contributor of articles to theological journals.

WORK IN PROGRESS: Books on philosophy and apologetics, Biblical commentary, and Christology.

*   *   *

McLEOD, Raymond, Jr. 1932-

PERSONAL: Born August 19, 1932, in Cameron, Tex.; son

of Raymond Gregg (a railway clerk) and Margaret (a teacher; maiden name, Belcher) McLeod; married Judith Ann Pollock (a teacher), December 17, 1955; married Martha Ann Guenther (an interior designer), May 27, 1978; children: (first marriage) Michael Ray, Gregg Alan, Christopher Robert, Melinda Lee, Suzanne Elaine; (second marriage) Sharlotte Anne. *Education:* Baylor University, B.B.A., 1954; Texas Christian University, M.B.A., 1957; University of Colorado, D.B.A., 1975. *Politics:* Independent. *Religion:* Methodist. *Home:* 1106 Glade, College Station, Tex. 77840. *Office:* College of Business Administration, Texas A & M University, College Station, Tex. 77843.

CAREER: International Business Machines Corp., Dallas, Tex., marketing representative, 1957-65; Lifson, Wilson, Ferguson & Winick, Dallas, consultant, 1965-67; Recognition Equipment, Inc., Dallas, marketing manager, 1967-69; Texas Christian University, Fort Worth, assistant professor of business administration, 1973-80; currently affiliated with College of Business Administration, Texas A & M University, College Station. *Military service:* U.S. Air Force, 1954-56; became captain.

WRITINGS: (With I. H. Forkner) *Computerized Business Systems,* Wiley, 1973; *Management Information Systems,* Science Research Associates, 1979; *Case Book in Management Information Systems,* Science Research Associates, 1979.

* * *

McNEW, Ben(nie) B(anks) 1931-

PERSONAL: Born November 12, 1931, in Greenbrier, Ark.; son of R. H. (a teacher) and Stella (Avery) McNew; married Bonnie Stone, March 31, 1956; children: Bonnie Banks, Mary Kathleen, William Michael. *Education:* Arkansas State Teachers College (now State College of Arkansas), B.S., 1953; University of Arkansas, M.B.A., 1954; University of Texas, Ph.D., 1961. *Religion:* Methodist. *Home address:* Box 568, Middle Tennessee State University, Murfreesboro, Tenn.

CAREER: U.S. Treasury Department, St. Louis, Mo., assistant national bank examiner, 1954-56; Industrial Research and Extension Center, University of Arkansas, Little Rock, industrial specialist, 1956-59; University of Texas, Main University (now University of Texas at Austin), Austin, lecturer in finance, 1959-61; University of Mississippi, University, professor of economics and banking, 1961-68, dean of School of Business Administration, 1968-79; Middle Tennessee State University, Murfreesboro, dean of School of Business, 1980—. *Military service:* U.S. Army, 1950-51. *Member:* American Finance Association, Southern Economic Association, Southwestern Social Science Association, Beta Gamma Sigma, Phi Kappa Phi, Delta Sigma Pi, Omicron Delta Kappa, Lions International (president, Oxford, Miss. chapter, 1964-65).

WRITINGS: (With John M. Peterson) *Average Hourly Earnings in Arkansas Manufacturing,* Industrial Research and Extension Center, University of Arkansas, 1957; *Financial Resources,* Mississippi Economic Council, State Chamber of Commerce, 1962; (with Charles L. Prather) *Fraud Control for Commercial Banks,* Irwin, 1962; (contributor) L. E. Davids, editor, *Money and Banking Casebook,* Irwin, 1966; (contributor) W. H. Baughn and C. E. Walker, editors, *The Bankers' Handbook,* Dow Jones-Irwin, 1966; (contributor) *A History of Mississippi,* College and University Press of Mississippi, 1973; *Banking School Curricula,* School of Banking of the South, 1980. Contributor of articles on finance and economics to professional journals.

MECHANIC, David 1936-

PERSONAL: Born February 21, 1936, in New York, N.Y.; son of Louis and Tillie (Penn) Mechanic; married Margaret Newton (a physician), July 26, 1960; children: Robert Edmund, Michael Alexander. *Education:* City College of New York (now City College of the City University of New York), B.A. (magna cum laude), 1956; Stanford University, M.A., 1957, Ph.D., 1959. *Office:* Graduate School of Social Work, Rutgers University, New Brunswick, N.J. 08903.

CAREER: Institute for Advanced Study in the Behavioral Sciences, Palo Alto, Calif., research assistant, 1956-58; National Institute of Mental Health, Chapel Hill, N.C., postdoctoral fellow, 1959-60; University of Wisconsin— Madison, assistant professor, 1960-62, associate professor of sociology, 1962-65, professor of sociology, 1965-73, John Bascom Professor, 1973-79, chairman of department of sociology, 1968-70, director of Center for Medical Sociology and Health Services Research, 1971-79; Rutgers University, New Brunswick, N.J., professor of social work and sociology, 1979—. Member of panel on health services, President's Science Advisory Committee, 1971-72; coordinator of panel, President's Commission on Mental Health, 1977-78; director of Coordinating Council for Study and Health Care, 1979—. Research fellow, National Institute of Mental Health, 1965-66; fellow of Center for Advanced Study in the Behavioral Sciences, 1974-75. *Member:* American Association for the Advancement of Science (fellow), American Sociology Association (chairman of medical sociology section, 1969-70; member of governing council, 1977-78), Institute of Medicine, National Academy of Science (member of governing council, 1972-74), Phi Beta Kappa. *Awards, honors:* Ford behavioral science fellow, 1956-57; Ward Medal, City College of New York (now City College of the City University of New York); Guggenheim fellowship, 1977-78.

WRITINGS: Students under Stress: A Study in the Social Psychology of Adaptation, Free Press of Glencoe, 1962, 2nd edition, 1978; (co-author) *Social Science of Organizations,* Prentice-Hall, 1963; (contributor) W. W. Cooper, editor, *New Perspectives in Organization Research,* Wiley, 1964; (contributor) L. M. Roberts, editor, *Community Psychiatry,* University of Wisconsin Press, 1966; *Medical Sociology,* Free Press, 1968, revised edition, 1978; *Mental Health and Social Policy,* Prentice-Hall, 1969, 2nd edition, 1980; *Public Expectations and Health Care,* Wiley-Interscience, 1972; *The Concept of Health,* Institute of Society, Ethics, and the Life Sciences, 1973; *Politics, Medicine, and Social Science,* Wiley, 1974; (with Charles E. Lewis and Rashi Fein) *A Right to Health,* Wiley, 1976; *Growth of Bureaucratic Medicine,* Wiley, 1976; (editor with Sol Levine) *Issues in Promoting Health,* Lippincott, 1977; *Future Issues in Health Care,* Free Press, 1979. Contributor to medical, mental hygiene, and sociology journals.

AVOCATIONAL INTERESTS: Political causes concerned with civil liberties, human rights, peace.

* * *

MEE, Charles L., Jr. 1938-

PERSONAL: Born September 15, 1938, in Evanston, Ill.; son of Charles Louis and Sarah (Lowe) Mee; married Claire Lu Thomas (an actress), June, 1959 (divorced, 1962); married Suzi Baker (a poet), November, 1962; children: (second marriage) Erin, Charles. *Education:* Harvard University, B.A. (cum laude), 1960. *Agent:* Lois Wallace, 177 East 70th St., New York, N.Y. 10021.

CAREER: Horizon Magazine, New York, N.Y., editor, 1961-75; full-time writer, 1975—.

WRITINGS: (With editors of *Horizon* Magazine) *Lorenzo de Medici and the Renaissance,* American Heritage Press, 1968; (translator with Edward L. Greenfield) *Dear Prince: The Unexpurgated Counsels of N. Machiavelli to Richard Milhous Nixon,* American Heritage Press, 1969; (editor) *Horizon Bedside Reader,* American Heritage Press, 1971; *White Robe, Black Robe,* Putnam, 1972; *Erasmus: The Eye of the Hurricane,* Coward, 1973; *The Horizon Book of Daily Life in Renaissance Italy,* American Heritage Publishing, 1975; *Meeting at Potsdam,* M. Evans, 1975; (with Ken Munowitz) *Happy Birthday, Baby Jesus,* Harper, 1976; (with Munowitz) *Moses, Moses,* Harper, 1977; *A Visit to Haldeman and Other States of Mind,* M. Evans, 1977; (with Munowitz) *Noah,* Harper, 1978; *Seizure,* M. Evans, 1978; *The End of Order: Versailles, 1919,* Dutton, 1980; *The Ohio Gang,* M. Evans, 1981.

Plays: "Players' Repertoire," first produced in Cambridge, Mass., at Playwrights' Theatre, August, 1960; "Constantinople Smith" (one-act), first produced Off-Broadway at Upstairs at the Downstairs, May, 1961; "The Gate" (one-act), first produced at Upstairs at the Downstairs, May, 1961; "Three by Mee," first produced in New York, N.Y., at Fourth Street Theatre, November, 1962; "Anyone! Anyone!," first produced Off-Broadway at American Place Theatre, 1964. Also author of plays, "God Bless Us Everyone," "The Life of the Party," and "Wedding Night."

SIDELIGHTS: First as the editor of *Horizon* Magazine, then as a free-lance writer, Charles L. Mee, Jr., has more or less made the genre of popular history his specialty. Though his early works in this field focused primarily on Renaissance- and Reformation-era figures and events, his 1975 analysis of the post-war strategy meeting of Truman, Stalin, and Churchill signaled an end to this concentration. A revisionist view of the origins of the Cold War, *Meeting at Potsdam* attempts to demonstrate that the Big Three, each greedy for power and with a perverse love of conflict, deliberately worked out their agreements not to insure peace, but to virtually guarantee war in the years ahead.

Critics have lined up on both sides of Mee's thesis, with one group commending the author for his insight and the other questioning his grasp of history. Walter Clemons, a member of the former group, remarks in *Newsweek* that "sheer pleasure would be low on my list of expectations from a book about the meeting of Truman, Churchill and Stalin in a suburb of Berlin during the summer of 1945 to redraw the map of the world. But Charles Mee . . . treats this unpromising subject with wit and a sharply satirical eye for the discrepancies between public gas and the horse-trading realities of the conference table." Claude Cockburn of the *New York Times Book Review* is equally impressed, asserting that "in this masterpiece of factual research, dramatic narration and vigorous analysis of global realities, Charles L. Mee . . . brilliantly illuminates the width and depth of the gap between what the general public supposed to be happening and what was in fact going on. . . . The nervous reader . . . might indulge in the hope that Mr. Mee is exaggerating. . . . Unfortunately for everyone's peace of mind, Mr. Mee is soon seen to have based his grisly story on irrefutable data and documented it to the point where it is useless to ask anyone to say it wasn't so."

The *National Review*'s Allen G. Weakland, however, *does* insist that it wasn't so. Calling the book a "popular synthesis of scholarly writings" or a "sort of history as pop art,"

Weakland says that it is "not that the facts are not there. Indeed they are—in profusion. . . . [But] anyone desiring to sink his teeth into some good, chewy history had best look elsewhere." In addition, he notes, "it is hard to say exactly what has been added to prior knowledge [in *Meeting at Potsdam*]. . . . Unfortunately, Mee takes the no-footnote route, leaving the reader to plod through bibliographical essays at the rear of the book." The *New Republic*'s James Chace points out that what sources Mee does cite show "he is acquainted with the literature but he has misread the information," resulting in an account which "is absorbing reading but highly misleading because its selective use of scholarly sources seriously distorts the historical realities in order to buttress the author's thesis."

"Here is a book that professes to have, finally, the answer to the question of why the Cold War started," begins Vojtech Mastny in his *New Leader* review of *Meeting at Potsdam*. "It doesn't, really, but the twist it gives to the old controversy is original enough to warrant a close examination. . . . Mee presents his thesis exceedingly well—with force, elegance and a special flair for pertinent and entertaining detail. Although not a professional historian, he knows his sources and treats them with respect. Without doubt, his analysis of the conference is the most serious so far. . . . But he has his . . . shortcomings. He imputes superhuman foresight to the protagonists, and he overrates the importance of a gathering where illustrious men behaved importantly. From these misjudgments it is but a short step to assuming that the participants actually wanted events to turn out the way that they later did. . . . The case is not nearly as clearcut as Mee would have us believe. . . . [His] principal thesis, no matter how alluring in its starkest simplicity, simply fails to do justice to all [the] considerations. At the end of *Meeting at Potsdam*, the author's analytical vigor—the book's greatest asset—gives way to rhetoric concealing a genuine unwillingness to face the issues."

Counters the *Washington Post Book World*'s Thomas G. Paterson: "If [*Meeting at Potsdam*] is at times a bit overstated, oversimplified, or embellished, it is nevertheless informed, authoritative, and grounded in historical record. However brief, Mee's analysis is usually perceptive and persuasive. Impressively interweaving personality sketches and matters of national interest, Mee involves the reader in the frisky give-and-take of the conference through a sprightly writing style. . . . [He] is always frank, stripping away the fluffy rhetoric from power realities. . . . He tends to personalize international issues too much, but he does understand the importance of personal styles and character traits. . . . *Meeting at Potsdam* does not give us much that is new, but Mee tells a familiar story with verve and authority. It is first-rate reading."

BIOGRAPHICAL/CRITICAL SOURCES: Washington Post Book World, May 4, 1969, March 9, 1975, March 27, 1977; *Chicago Tribune Book World,* May 28, 1972; *Saturday Review,* March 8, 1975; *New York Times Book Review,* March 9, 1975; *Newsweek,* March 24, 1975; *New Republic,* April 19, 1975; *Time,* May 5, 1975, May 15, 1978; *New Leader,* June 23, 1975; *Commonweal,* July 18, 1975; *Spectator,* August 2, 1975; *National Review,* March 19, 1976; *Best Sellers,* June, 1977, June, 1978; *Village Voice,* June 27, 1977; *New York Times,* November 16, 1978.

—*Sketch by Deborah A. Straub*

*   *   *

MEIER, August 1923-

PERSONAL: Born April 30, 1923, in New York, N.Y.; son

of Frank A. (a chemist) and Clara L. (a teacher and vice-principal; maiden name, Cohen) Meier. *Education:* Oberlin College, A.B., 1945; Columbia University, A.M., 1949, Ph.D., 1957. *Politics:* Democrat. *Religion:* Unitarian. *Home:* 122 North Prospect St., Kent, Ohio 44240. *Office:* Department of History, Kent State University, Kent, Ohio 44242.

CAREER: Tougaloo College, Tougaloo, Miss., assistant professor of history, 1945-49; Fisk University, Nashville, Tenn., assistant professor of history, 1953-56; Morgan State College, Baltimore, Md., 1957-64, began as assistant professor, became associate professor; Roosevelt University, Chicago, Ill., professor of history, 1964-67; Kent State University, Kent, Ohio, professor, 1967-69, university professor of history, 1969—. Adult adviser, Baltimore chapter of Student Nonviolent Coordinating Committee, 1960-64.

MEMBER: American Historical Association, American Anthropological Association, Association for the Study of Negro Life and History, Organization of American Historians (delegate to American Council of Learned Societies, 1979—), National Association for the Advancement of Colored People (secretary, Newark branch, 1951-52, 1957), Americans for Democratic Action (chairman, Baltimore chapter, 1960-61; member of national board and executive committee, 1960-61) Southern Historical Association. *Awards, honors:* Guggenheim fellowship, 1971-72; Philip Taft Labor History Award for best book on American labor history, 1979, for *Black Detroit and the Rise of the U.A.W.*

WRITINGS: Negro Thought in America, 1880-1915: Racial Ideologies in the Age of Booker T. Washington, University of Michigan Press, 1963; (with Elliot Rudwick) *From Plantation to Ghetto: An Interpretive History of American Negroes,* Hill & Wang, 1966, revised edition, 1970; (with Milton Meltzer) *Time of Trial, Time of Hope: The Negro in America, 1919-1941,* Doubleday, 1966; (with Rudwick) *CORE: A Study in the Civil Rights Movement, 1942-1968,* Oxford University Press, 1973; (with Rudwick) *Along the Color Line,* University of Illinois Press, 1976; (with Rudwick) *Black Detroit and the Rise of the U.A.W.,* Oxford University Press, 1979.

Editor: (With Francis Broderick) *Negro Protest Thought in the Twentieth Century,* Bobbs-Merrill, 1965, 2nd edition (with Broderick and Rudwick) published as *Black Protest Thought in the Twentieth Century,* 1971; (with Rudwick) *The Making of Black America: Essays in Negro Life and History,* Atheneum, 1969; with John H. Bracey and Rudwick) *Black Nationalism in America,* Bobbs-Merrill, 1970; (and author of introduction with Rudwick) *Black Protest in the Sixties,* Quadrangle, 1970; (and author of introduction) *The Transformation of Activism,* Aldine, 1970, 2nd edition published as *Black Experience: The Transformation of Activism,* Transaction Books, 1973; (with Bracey) *American Slavery: The Question of Resistance,* Wadsworth, 1971; (with Bracey) *Black Matriarchy: Myth or Reality?,* Wadsworth, 1971; (with Bracey) *The Black Sociologist: The First Half Century,* Wadsworth, 1971; (with Bracey) *Black Workers and Organized Labor,* Wadsworth, 1971; (with Bracey) *Blacks in the Abolitionist Movement,* Wadsworth, 1971; (with Bracey) *Conflict and Competition: Studies in the Recent Black Protest Movement,* Wadsworth, 1971; (with Bracey) *Free Blacks in America, 1800-1860,* Wadsworth, 1971; (with Bracey) *The Rise of the Ghetto,* Wadsworth, 1971; (with Bracey) *The Afro-Americans,* Allyn & Bacon, 1972.

General editor, "Negro in American Life" series, Atheneum, 1966-74, "Blacks in the New World" series, University of Illinois Press, 1972—. Contributor to *Journal of Negro History, Crisis, Phylon, Journal of Southern History, New Politics,* and other journals. Member of editorial board, *Journal of American History,* 1974-77; member of editorial advisory board, *Civil War History,* Booker T. Washington Papers, and Marcus Garvey Papers.

*   *   *

MEINERS, R(oger) K(eith) 1932-

PERSONAL: Born December 5, 1932, in Forreston, Ill.; son of John H. (a grocer) and Lillian (Buss) Meiners; married Lynn E. Dunn (a painter, etcher, and illustrator), December 12, 1958; children: Katherine Terry, Sally Ann. *Education:* Wheaton College, Wheaton, Ill., B.A., 1954; Westminster Seminary, Philadelphia, Pa., B.D., 1956; University of Denver, M.A., 1957, Ph.D., 1961. *Home:* 435 Kensington Rd., East Lansing, Mich. 48823. *Office:* Department of English, Michigan State University, East Lansing, Mich. 48824.

CAREER: Arizona State University, Tempe, instructor in English, 1959-61, assistant professor, 1961-64, associate professor, 1964; University of Missouri—Columbia, assistant professor, 1964-65, associate professor of English, 1966-69; Michigan State University, East Lansing, professor of English, 1970—.

WRITINGS: The Last Alternatives: A Study of the Works of Allen Tate, A. Swallow, 1963; *Everything to Be Endured: An Essay on Robert Lowell and Modern Poetry,* University of Missouri Press, 1970; *Journeying Back to the World* (poems), University of Missouri Press, 1975. Contributor of poems, essays, and reviews to various journals.

WORK IN PROGRESS: Going Dark (poems); a critical book on contemporary English and American poetry.

SIDELIGHTS: R. K. Meiners told *CA:* "I grew up in a town of 900 people where, to the best of my knowledge, no one ever read a book other than the dog-eared reading and geometry texts they were forced to endure in adolescence. Certainly I never *saw* anyone read a book, and there were few in my house except for a dozen copies of the Bible, a pictorial history of World War I, Foxe's *Book of Martyrs* and (where this came from only God knows) a 19th century edition of the poems of Thomas Moore. I am the only person I know who had read 'Lalla Rookh' at age sixteen and no other poetry save the obligatory Shakespeare play in third-year English and the usual ornaments of the genteel tradition. I smuggled an outlandish assortment of trash magazines to my room, where I usually read by flashlight under the covers. I was a secret reader.

"I never made the connection between those pulps and anthologies and the idea of *writing.* It never occurred to me that one *could* write a book. Writers were people in books; and while I was lost in language as an adolescent, it was always other people's language, and inferior language at that. By the standards of most writers, and especially poets, I began serious writing relatively late, while I was in my mid-twenties. If I had studied literature as an undergraduate it might have speeded the process, but I was wound up in theology, philosophy, and dead languages on the one hand, and ornithology and botany on the other.

"The material occasion for my beginning 'to write' was formed by the late Alan Swallow persuading me that I was denying too much of myself not to attempt to do so. So many American writers of my age or somewhat older owe Alan Swallow so much; me more than most. I never 'studied' with Alan, for he had resigned from the University before I arrived. Fortunately for me, he still lived nearby, running his publishing business from garage and basement. He employed me to package and mail books, and somewhere along the line he persuaded me that they were written by people much like me. Swallow also told me that academic life could do several things to writers (for my early illiteracy did not prevent me from aspiring to the professoriate). The talking and teaching could make [them] want to write in their own language; or they could talk most of their language away and have little left in the evening or the morning for the real work, the writing. He suggested that I was one of the latter. This advice I was too timid to take, and I am still not sure whether I was right or wrong. In any case, academic life has made me an intense but spasmodic writer. I build up the ideas, images, rhythms, an eight line passage here, a paragraph there, in other words, all the material of the writing, in my notebooks during daily reading/thinking/writing sessions. But it is in the gaps and breaks of the university calendar when I can get periods of at least several consecutive days that I do my real writing, for only then can I overcome the fearful inertia of mundane language and develop the required concentration and sustained effort. My relationship to language is too wary, and the language's relationship to me too menacing, for me to slide easily into it at the beginning or the ending of a day largely devoted to language in its various public and historic modes; a more oblique and strategic approach is required.

"All of my obsessions and all of my learnings (some of them arcane) are in my essays and poems in one way or another; my themes in poetry and criticism are much the same. I am, for better or worse, an intellectual in the sense that the texture of an idea is as sensual to me as the texture of granite or old leather or a smooth body; and the path of an idea through language is no less real than the tracks of snails on a wet board in the garden on a summer morning. I am a poet who takes acute pleasure in the sensual movement of ideas, and I have no patience whatever with that sort of dogma which is nearly a contemporary orthodoxy that says that thought, or ideas—the moments and movements of thinking and feeling—are 'abstract' and that something called an 'image' is the poem's only proper reality. Those who think this way do not see that images, the most sensory images, can be as abstract as the most tortuous process of thinking in Hegel. This is forgotten in so much recent poetry and criticism; the mere sensory presence of sensory images, or a myth or autobiography, cannot guarantee the actuality of the poem at all. It is not, for sanity's sake, the *images* which make the *Inferno* the most concretely experiential poem yet imagined. I know it is thought dangerous to say one welcomes ideas in poems; they are regarded like clandestine lovers in rooms where they do not belong.

"It is certainly not only ideas which are important to me, though the way ideas wind themselves in and around these other things, or flee from them, is what lets me know they are important. I couldn't live long without music, for instance; perhaps because it holds out idea and language alike at arm's length. Music winds in and out of my poems like an old dance, a reel or strathspey. Other 'sources' for my poems include all the usual ones: dreams; large and small landscapes, either remembered or immediate; animals; children; all the large and small emotions of love, pain, hate, joy and the absences or presences of those people who have shared in the creation of them."

AVOCATIONAL INTERESTS: Sports, chess, gardening, playing stringed instruments (fiddle, banjo, mandolin, guitar), "omnivorous reading, obsessive brooding."

MELTZER, Allan H. 1928-

PERSONAL: Born February 6, 1928, in Boston, Mass.; son of George B. and Minerva I. (Simons) Meltzer; married Marilyn Ginsburg, August 27, 1950; children: Bruce M., Eric C., Beth D. *Education:* Duke University, A.B., 1948; University of California, Los Angeles, M.A., 1955, Ph.D., 1958. *Home:* 225 Russell Dr., Verona, Pa. *Office:* Graduate School of Industrial Administration, Carnegie-Mellon University, Pittsburgh, Pa. 15213.

CAREER: Hudson Manufacturing Co., Los Angeles, Calif., self-employed, 1948-52; University of Pennsylvania, Wharton School of Finance and Commerce, Philadelphia, lecturer in economics, 1956-57; Carnegie-Mellon University, Graduate School of Industrial Management, Pittsburgh, Pa., assistant professor, 1957-61, associate professor, 1961-64, professor of economics, 1964-69, Ford Distinguished Research Professor, 1969-70, Maurice Falk Professor of Economics and Social Science, 1970—, acting head of department of industrial management, 1960-61 and 1963-64, acting dean of Graduate School of Industrial Management, 1972-73. Ford Foundation visiting professor, University of Chicago, 1964-65; visiting professor of economics, Institute of Economic Research, Belgrade, Yugoslavia, 1968, and Postgraduate School of Economics, Fundacao Getulio Vargas, Rio de Janiero, Brazil, 1976; visiting fellow, Hoover Institution, 1977-78. Carnegie-Mellon University, chairman of Executive Committee of General Faculty, 1965-66, chairman of General Faculty, 1966-67, chairman of Ph.D. Committee, Graduate School of Industrial Management, 1972-73. Consultant to Joint Economic Committee, United States Congress, 1960-61, United States Treasury Department, 1961-62, and House Committee on Banking and Currency, 1963-64. *Member:* American Economic Association, American Finance Association, Phi Beta Kappa. *Awards, honors:* Fulbright scholar, 1955-56; Social Science Research Council fellow, 1955-56; Ford faculty research fellow, 1962-63.

WRITINGS: (With G. Von der Linde) *The Dealer Market for Federal Government Securities,* Joint Economic Committee, U.S. Congress, 1960; (with David Ott) *Federal Tax Treatment of State and Local Government Securities,* Brookings Institution, 1963; (with Karl Brunner) *An Analysis of Federal Reserve Monetary Policymaking,* House Committee on Banking and Currency, U.S. Congress, 1964; (with J. F. Weston) "Wadsworth Series in Finance," Wadsworth, 1966-68; (editor with Brunner) "Carnegie-Rochester" series, North-Holland, 1976—.

Contributor: (With Brunner) T. Bagiotti, editor, *Essays in Honor of Marco Fanno,* Cedam (Padova), 1966; G. Shultz, editor, *Guidelines, Informal Controls and the Market Place,* University of Chicago Press, 1966; (with Brunner) George Horwich, editor, *Monetary Process and Policy: A Symposium,* Irwin, 1967; *Fiscal Policy and Business Capital Formation,* American Enterprise Institute for Public Policy Research, 1967; Henry Manne, editor, *Economic Policy in the Regulation of Corporate Security,* American Enterprise Institute for Public Policy Research, 1969; (with Brunner) Brunner, editor, *Targets and Indicators of Monetary Policy,* Chandler Publishing, 1969; P. Hartland-Thunberg, editor, *Selected Papers on Inflation, Recession, Energy and the International Financial Structure,* Center for Strategic and International Studies, Georgetown University, 1975. Also contributor to proceedings of professional conferences and seminars. Contributor to journals of finance and economics. Member of editorial advisory board, *Journal of Money, Credit and Banking,* 1969-74, *Journal of Economic Litera-*

ture, 1973-75, and *Journal of Monetary Economics,* 1974—; associate editor, *Journal of Finance,* 1974—; member of editorial board, *Policy Review,* 1978—.

*   *   *

MEREDITH, Scott 1923-

PERSONAL: Born November 24, 1923, in New York, N.Y.; son of Henry and Esta Meredith; married Helen Kovet, April 22, 1944; children: Stephen Charles, Randy Beth (Mrs. Larry Sheer). *Education:* Studied privately with tutors. *Office:* Scott Meredith Literary Agency, Inc., 845 Third Ave., New York, N.Y. 10022; and Scott Meredith Literary Agency, 44 Great Russell St., London W.C.1, England.

CAREER: Became magazine writer in early teens and an authors' agent at the age of seventeen; Scott Meredith Literary Agency, Inc., New York, N.Y., president, 1942—, representing almost five hundred authors. Expert witness in copyright cases. Frequent guest on television panel shows. *Military service:* U.S. Army Air Forces, World War II. *Member:* Rare Book Society, Spectator Club, Three Oaks Tennis Club.

WRITINGS: Writing to Sell, Harper, 1950, second revised edition, 1975; *George S. Kaufman and His Friends* (Book of the Month Club selection), Doubleday, 1975 (published in England as *George S. Kaufman and the Algonquin Crowd,* Allen & Unwin, 1979).

Editor: *The Best of Wodehouse,* Pocket Books, 1949; (with P. G. Wodehouse) *The Best of Modern Humor,* McBride, 1951; *Bar Roundup of Best Western Stories,* Dutton, 1952; (with Wodehouse) *The Week-End Book of Humor,* Washburn, 1952, published as *P. G. Wodehouse Selects the Best of Humor,* Grosset, 1965; *Bar Two Round-up of Best Western Stories,* Dutton, 1953; *The Murder of Mr. Malone,* St. John, 1953; *Bar Three Roundup of Best Western Stories,* Dutton, 1954; *Bar Four Roundup of Best Western Stories,* Dutton, 1956; *Bar Five Roundup of Best Western Stories,* Dutton, 1956; (with Ken Murray) *The Ken Murray Book of Humor,* Ace Books, 1957; *Bar Six Roundup of Best Western Stories,* Dutton, 1957; (with Henry Morgan) *The Henry Morgan Book of Humor,* Avon, 1958; (with Sidney Meredith) *The Best from Manhunt,* Pocket Books, 1958; (with Sidney Meredith) *The Bloodhound Anthology,* T.V. Boardman, 1959; *The Fireside Treasury of Modern Humor,* Simon & Schuster, 1963 (published in England as *The Fireside Book of Modern Humour,* Hamish Hamilton, 1964); *Best Western Stories,* Spring Books, 1964; (with Wodehouse) *A Carnival of Modern Humor,* Dial, 1967. Contributor of articles on humor to *Encyclopaedia Britannica,* 1954, 1959, and on fiction writing to *Oxford Encyclopaedia,* 1960. Also contributor of several hundred short stories, articles, novelettes, and serials to magazines.

WORK IN PROGRESS: Louis B. Mayer and His Enemies, for Simon & Schuster.

SIDELIGHTS: Clients of the Scott Meredith Literary Agency have included Norman Mailer, Spiro Agnew, Richard Nixon, and Ellery Queen. Meredith's business style—his aggressive approach toward acquisition of manuscripts, the high prices he exacts for both his authors and himself—has made him famous in the industry. According to Paul D. Zimmerman of *Newsweek,* Meredith solicits partly through mass mailings of publicity material rather than screening all his potential clients, as most agents do, and while most agents read prospective clients' work for free, Meredith charges. Zimmerman also credits Meredith with inventing the auctioning system whereby publishing houses bid on a manuscript rather than waiting for it to be offered, one house at a time, by the author.

Meredith's biography of George S. Kaufman was published both as *George S. Kaufman and His Friends* and *George S. Kaufman and the Algonquin Round Table.* Reviewing the biography, John Lahr of the *Times Literary Supplement* criticizes Meredith's assessment of Kaufman's directorial abilities. Kaufman's direction was "sharp, considered, understated; and effective within a very limited and unadventurous mainstream of modern theatre," he asserts, and "Kaufman never claimed more for himself, but his biographer does. . . . Mr. Meredith's ethic is the Broadway ethic: success excuses all. He sticks to Kaufman's many triumphs and neatly sweeps away the difficulties." Harold Clurman of the *New York Times Review of Books* also questions Meredith's judgement on that point. His reaction to Meredith's title "The Genius" for his chapter on Kaufman's direction is that "Enough is enough: exaggeration does disservice to praise."

At the same time, Clurman praises the scope of the work. He calls it a "veritable encyclopedia of show business and popular literary circles". A reviewer for the *Virginia Quarterly Review* also praises the biography's breadth, writing that "a big, bursting biography just fits the big, rather brash, and bursting talents of George S. Kaufman."

Many of Meredith's books have come out in paperback reprints and in British, Spanish, German, and other foreign-language editions. A number of his stories have been dramatized on television.

BIOGRAPHICAL/CRITICAL SOURCES: New York Times Book Review, November 24, 1974, December 7, 1980; *Newsweek,* December 2, 1974, March 1, 1976; *Virginia Quarterly Review,* spring, 1975; *Times Literary Supplement,* April 7, 1978.

*   *   *

MIDDLETON-MURRY, John (Jr.) 1926-
(Richard Cowper, Colin Middleton-Murry)

PERSONAL: Born May 9, 1926, in Bridport, Dorsetshire, England; son of John (a critic) and Violet (Le Maistre) Middleton-Murry; married Ruth Jezierski (a teacher), July 28, 1950; children: Jacqueline, Helen. *Education:* Oxford University, B.A., 1950. *Politics:* Radical. *Religion:* Humanist. *Home:* 'Landscott,' Lower St., Dittisham, near Dartmouth, Devonshire, England.

CAREER: Whittingehame College, Brighton, England, 1952-67, began as English master, became department head; Atlantic College, South Wales, English department head, 1967-70; free-lance author, 1970—. *Military service:* British Navy, Fleet Air Arm. *Member:* Society of Authors, Science Fiction Writers of America, British Science Fiction Association, West Country Writers Association. *Awards, honors:* British Broadcasting Corp. (B.B.C.) award for radio play, 1965; Hugo Award and Nebula Award nominations, 1977, both for novella "Piper at the Gates of Dawn"; British Fantasy Award nomination, 1979, for *The Road to Corlay.*

WRITINGS—Under pseudonym Richard Cowper; all science fiction: *Breakthrough,* Dobson, 1967, Ballantine, 1969; *Phoenix,* Dobson, 1968, Ballantine, 1970; *Domino,* Dobson, 1971; *Clone,* Doubleday, 1972; *Kaldesak,* Doubleday, 1972; *Time Out of Mind,* Gollancz, 1973; *Worlds Apart,* Gollancz, 1974; *The Twilight of Briareus,* Gollancz, 1974, DAW Books, 1975; *The Custodian, and Other Stories,* Gollancz, 1976; *The Road to Corlay* (Science Fiction Book Club selection), Gollancz, 1978, expanded edition, Pocket Books,

1979; *Profundis*, Gollancz, 1979. Also author of *The Web of the Magi*, Gollancz, and *Out There Where the Big Ships Go*, Pocket Books.

Under pseudonym Colin Middleton-Murry: *The Golden Valley*, Hutchinson, 1958; *Recollections of a Ghost*, Hutchinson, 1960; *A Path to the Sea*, Hutchinson, 1961; *Private View*, Dobson, 1972; *I at the Keyhole*, Stein & Day, 1975 (published in England as *One Hand Clapping: A Memoir of Childhood*, Gollancz, 1975); *Shadows on the Grass*, Gollancz, 1977.

Contributor of articles and short stories to magazines, including *Magazine of Fantasy and Science Fiction*. Fiction reviewer, *Time and Tide*, 1960-62.

WORK IN PROGRESS: A Tapestry of Time, a novel.

SIDELIGHTS: Richard Cowper's *The Road to Corlay* is set in a time after the melting of the ice caps when England has become an archipelago ruled by a totalitarian church. In defiance of the church is the underground Cult of the White Bird led by the boy Thomas, a piper whose music can inspire mystical experiences in his listeners. The first third of the novel, telling the story of Thomas, was previously published as the novella "Piper at the Gates of Dawn." Writing in *Science Fiction and Fantasy Book Review*, Richard L. McKinney believes *The Road to Corlay* "is most effective on the emotional level; it is an easy read, and one does tend to care for the novel's characters, even if their actions are at times mystifying." A reviewer for *Booklist* considers *Corlay* "a well-written, moodily textured novel [that] cuts deep into major questions on the human condition." Charles N. Brown of *Locus* describes it as "a fine book by a seriously underrated writer." In *Analog*, Spider Robinson states, "I loved its opening segment ['Piper at the Gates of Dawn']." The remainder of the book, however, he finds flawed by a sub-plot set in present-day England. "If you keep yanking me back into the present," Robinson writes, "and particularly a clumsily-drawn present . . . and *particularly* a *dull* present . . . you only keep forcefully reminding me that there is no plausible way to get to that colorful and romantic future world. . . . So why, given all this, did I like *Corlay*? Why am I recommending you buy it? . . . Because Richard Cowper is a superb storyteller, and he can write like an enchanted son of a bitch. I stored up objections, yeah, but I kept on turning the pages because I wanted to know *what happened to the people?*"

BIOGRAPHICAL/CRITICAL SOURCES: Science Fiction Reivew, February, 1970, April, 1970; *Contemporary Review*, August, 1970; *Books & Bookmen*, March, 1972, January, 1973, October, 1973, April, 1975, June, 1978; *Observer*, May 28, 1972, December 8, 1974, June 13, 1976, October 16, 1977, July 2, 1978; *New Statesman*, June 16, 1972, March 14, 1975; *Times Literary Supplement*, June 23, 1972, February 2, 1973, November 9, 1973, March 15, 1974, November 21, 1975, November 18, 1977, June 16, 1978; *Psychology Today*, January, 1973, October, 1974, September, 1975; *Book World*, March 16, 1975; *New York Times Book Review*, June 1, 1975; *New Yorker*, September 8, 1975; *Listener*, October 27, 1977; *Spectator*, July 7, 1979; *Science Fiction and Fantasy Book Review*, September, 1979; *Locus*, October, 1979; *Booklist*, November 1, 1979; *Analog*, February, 1980.

*   *   *

MILGROM, Harry 1912-

PERSONAL: Born February 29, 1912, in New York, N.Y.; son of Samuel and Mary (Spector) Milgrom; married Justine Miller (a crafts coordinator for an adult education program),

May 1, 1937; children: Jeffrey, Paul. *Education:* City College (now City College of the City University of New York), B.S., 1932; Columbia University, M.A., 1933. *Home:* 140 Hill Park Ave., Great Neck, N.Y.; and 185 East 85th St., New York, N.Y. 10028. *Office:* Board of Education, 131 Livingston St., Brooklyn, N.Y.

CAREER: City College (now City College of the City University of New York), New York City, instructor in physics, 1947-49; New York City Board of Education, teacher of physics, general science, and radio, 1935-53, supervisor of elementary science, 1953-61, assistant director of science, 1961-67; Hall of Science, New York City, director of education services, 1967-69; New York City Board of Education, director of science, 1969—. Director of summer science institutes at Rutgers University, 1957, Rochester University, 1958, and New Mexico Highlands University, 1961, 1962; director, elementary science project, Manufacturing Chemists Association, 1959-60; director, science honors program for children, School of Engineering, Columbia University, beginning 1962. Science consultant to New York State Education Department and Educational Testing Service. *Wartime service:* Civil Air Patrol, member, 1944-46. *Member:* National Science Supervisors Association, Elementary School Science Association (member of advisory board, beginning 1960), American Association for the Advancement of Science (fellow), National Science Teachers Association, National Association for Research in Science Teaching, Physics Club of New York (treasurer, 1955-56), Phi Beta Kappa.

WRITINGS—Juvenile: *The Adventure Book of Weather*, edited by Alfred D. Beck, Capitol Publishing, 1959, revised edition published as *Understanding Weather*, Collier, 1970; *Matter, Energy and Change: Explorations in Chemistry for Elementary School Children*, Holt, 1960; *Explorations in Science: A Book of Basic Experiments*, Dutton, 1961; (with Hyman Ruchlis) *The Science Book-Lab of Magnets*, Science Materials Center, 1961; (with Ruchlis) *The Science Book of Air Experiments*, Science Materials Center, 1961; (with Ruchlis) *The Science Book-Lab of Mathematical Shapes*, Science Materials Center, 1962; *Further Explorations in Science: A Second Book of Basic Experiments*, Dutton, 1963; *Adventures with a String*, Dutton, 1965; *Adventures with a Ball*, Dutton, 1965; *First Experiments with Gravity*, Dutton, 1966; *Adventures with a Plastic Bag*, Dutton, 1967; *Adventures with a Straw*, Dutton, 1967; (with Ruchlis) *Math Projects: Mathematical Shapes*, Book-Lab, 1968; *Adventures with a Paper Cup*, Dutton, 1968; *Adventures with a Party Plate*, Dutton, 1968.

ABC Science Experiments, Collier, 1970; *The Wonder of Change*, Ginn, 1971; *Adventures with a Cardboard Tube*, Dutton, 1972; *ABC of Ecology*, Macmillan, 1972; *Egg-ventures*, Dutton, 1974; *Paper Science*, Walker & Co., 1978. Also author of "Wonderworld of Science" filmstrips, Bobbs-Merrill, 1957, 1959, and of "Adventure with Weather" (experiment kit), Capitol Publishing, 1959. Contributor to *Book of Popular Science*, *Compton's Pictured Encyclopedia*, and to professional journals. Contributing editor and columnist, *Elementary School Science Bulletin*, 1955-59.

SIDELIGHTS: Harry Milgrom prepared and telecast the first elementary school science series for broadcast in New York City in 1953. *Avocational interests:* Music (especially the violin), crafts, raising wild animals, and collecting scientific curios.

BIOGRAPHICAL/CRITICAL SOURCES: New York Herald Tribune, April 10, 1960.†

MILLS, Ralph J(oseph), Jr. 1931-

PERSONAL: Born December 16, 1931, in Chicago, Ill.; son of Ralph J. (a businessman) and Eileen (McGuire) Mills; married Helen Daggett Harvey (a photographer), November 25, 1959; children: Natalie, Julian, Brett. *Education:* Lake Forest College, B.A., 1954; Northwestern University, M.A., 1956, Ph.D., 1963; Oxford University, student-at-large, 1956-57. *Politics:* Democrat. *Religion:* Roman Catholic. *Home:* 1451 North Astor St., Chicago, Ill. 60610. *Office:* Department of English, University of Illinois at Chicago Circle, Chicago, Ill. 60680.

CAREER: University of Chicago, Chicago, Ill., instructor, 1959-61, assistant professor of English and associate chairman of Committee on Social Thought, 1962-65; University of Illinois at Chicago Circle, associate professor, 1965-67, professor of English, 1967—. *Member:* Phi Beta Kappa, Phi Kappa Phi. *Awards, honors:* English-Speaking Union fellowship, 1956-57; Illinois Arts Council award for poetry, 1979; Society of Midland Authors prize for poetry, 1980.

WRITINGS: Theodore Roethke (pamphlet), University of Minnesota Press, 1963; *Contemporary American Poetry,* Random House, 1965; (editor) *On the Poet and His Craft: Selected Prose of Theodore Roethke,* University of Washington Press, 1965; *Richard Eberhart* (pamphlet), University of Minnesota Press, 1966; *Edith Sitwell: A Critical Essay,* Eerdmans, 1966; *Kathleen Raine: A Critical Essay,* Eerdmans, 1967; (editor and author of introduction) Theodore Roethke, *Selected Letters,* University of Washington Press, 1968; *Creation's Very Self: On the Personal Element in Recent American Poetry,* Texas Christian University Press, 1969; (editor and author of introduction) *The Notebooks of David Ignatow,* Swallow Press, 1973; *Door to the Sun: Poems,* Baleen Press, 1974; *A Man to His Shadow: Poems,* Juniper Books, 1975; *Cry of the Human: Essays on Contemporary American Poetry,* University of Illinois Press, 1975; *Night Road: Poems,* Rook Press, 1978; *Living with Distance: Poems,* Boa Editions, 1979; *With No Answer: Poems,* Juniper Books, 1980; (editor) *Open between Us: Essays, Reviews & Interviews by David Ignatow,* University of Michigan Press, 1980.

Contributor: E. B. Hungerford, editor, *Poets in Progress,* Northwestern University Press, 1962; Marie Borroff, editor. *Wallace Stevens: A Collection of Critical Essays,* Prentice-Hall, 1963; Nathan A. Scott, Jr., editor, *The Climate of Faith in Modern Literature,* Seabury, 1964; Arnold Stein, editor, *Theodore Roethke: Essays on the Poetry,* University of Washington Press, 1965; Scott, editor, *Four Ways of Modern Poetry,* John Knox, 1965; Rosalie Murphy, editor, *Contemporary Poets of the English Language,* St. James Press, 1970; Guy Owen, editor, *Modern American Poetry,* Everett/Edwards, 1972; Daniel Curley, George Scouffas, and Charles Shattuck, editors, *Accent: An Anthology 1940-1960,* University of Illinois Press, 1973; Margaret Stapleton, compiler, *Sir John Betjeman: A Bibliography,* Scarecrow Press, 1974; Denis Donoghue, editor, *Seven American Poets from MacLeish to Nemerov,* University of Minnesota Press, 1975; Lucien Stryk, editor, *Heartland II: Poets of the Midwest,* Northern Illinois University Press, 1975; Lee Bartlett, editor, *Benchmark and Blaze: The Emergence of William Everson,* Scarecrow Press, 1979; Linda Wagner, editor, *Denise Levertov: In Her Own Province,* New Directions, 1979. Contributor of essays on modern poets to *Accent, Poetry, Commentary, Renascence,* and other journals.

SIDELIGHTS: Ralph J. Mills, Jr. aims in his critical studies to bring out the chief qualities of the modern poets in sympathetic interpretation. "I have tried to be on the side of the poets first and foremost," he once commented, "and so have never supported any particular critical doctrine or aesthetic dogma." More recently, Mills told *CA:* "Since 1969 or 1970 I have devoted an increasing amount of time and effort to the writing of poems, with a consequent decrease in my work as a critic and reviewer. I still do write some critical pieces, only now much more occasionally."

BIOGRAPHICAL/CRITICAL SOURCES: Sewanee Review, summer, 1968; *New Republic,* September 21, 1968; *New York Times Book Review,* September 29, 1968; *Virginia Quarterly Review,* autumn, 1968; *New York Times,* January 1, 1969; *Nation,* January 6, 1969; *Poetry,* February, 1969; *London Magazine,* September, 1970.

*   *   *

MINEAR, Paul Sevier 1906-

PERSONAL: Born February 17, 1906, in Mount Pleasant, Iowa; son of George L. (a minister) and Nellie (Sevier) Minear; married Gladys Hoffman, June 14, 1929; children: Paul Lawrence, Richard Hoffman, Anita Sue Fahrni. *Education:* Iowa Wesleyan College, B.A., 1927; Garrett Biblical Institute, B.D., 1930; Northwestern University, M.A., 1930; Yale University, Ph.D., 1932. *Home:* 41 Dolan Dr., Guilford, Conn. 06437.

CAREER: Hawaii School of Religion, Honolulu, assistant professor, 1933-34; Garrett Biblical Institute, Evanston, Ill., 1934-44, began as assistant professor, became professor; Andover Newton Theological School, Newton Centre, Mass., Norris Professor of New Testament, 1944-56; Yale University Divinity School, New Haven, Conn., professor, 1956-71, Winkley Professor of Biblical Theology emeritus, 1971—. Fulbright lecturer, University of Utrecht, 1958-59; vice-rector, Ecumenical Institute for Advanced Theological Studies, Jerusalem, 1970-72; visiting professor at Vancouver School of Religion, 1976, Princeton Theological Seminary, 1977, Brite Divinity School, 1979, and Emory University, 1980. Director of faith and order, World Council of Churches, 1961-63. *Member:* Duodecim, Society for Values in Higher Education, Society of Biblical Literature, Society of New Testament Studies. *Awards, honors:* LL.D., Iowa Wesleyan College, 1942; Dr. theol., University of Utrecht, 1962; LL.D., University of Notre Dame, 1966; D.D., University of Aberdeen, 1975.

WRITINGS: An Introduction to Paul, Abingdon, 1937; *And Great Shall Be Your Reward,* Yale University Press, 1941; *Eyes of Faith,* Westminster, 1946, revised edition, Bethany Press, 1966; *The Choice,* Westminster, 1948; *The Kingdom and the Power,* Westminster, 1950; *Christian Hope and the Second Coming,* Westminster, 1954; *Jesus and His People,* Association Press, 1956; (editor) *The Nature of the Unity We Seek,* Bethany Press, 1958; *Horizons of Christian Community,* Bethany Press, 1959; *Images of the Church in the New Testament,* Westminster, 1960; *Commentary on Mark,* John Knox, 1962; *I Saw a New Earth,* Corpus Books, 1968; *The Obedience of Faith,* S.C.M. Press, 1971; *Commands of Christ,* Abingdon, 1972; *I Pledge Allegiance,* Geneva Press, 1975; *To Heal and to Reveal,* Seabury, 1976; *To Die and to Live,* Seabury, 1977.

*   *   *

MOLDENHAUER, Hans 1906-

PERSONAL: Born December 13, 1906, in Mainz, Germany; son of Richard and Thekla (Weil) Moldenhauer; married Rosaleen Jackman, 1943; children: Margaret, Joseph, Trude,

Myra. *Education:* Altes Humanistisches Gymnasium, abiturum (cum laude), 1925; Whitworth College, B.A., 1945; Chicago Musical College of Roosevelt University, D.F.A., 1951. *Home:* 1011 Comstock Court, Spokane, Wash. 99203.

CAREER: Spokane Junior College and Whitworth College, Spokane, Wash., teacher, 1939-42; Spokane Conservatory, Spokane, founder, 1942, president, 1946—; University of Washington, Seattle, lecturer in music, 1961-64. Active in Webern festivals in Seattle, Wash., 1962, Salzburg/Mittersill, Austria, 1965, Buffalo, N.Y., 1966, Hanover, N.H., 1968, Vienna, Austria, 1972, and Baton Rouge, La., 1978. *Military service:* U.S. Army, 87th Mountain Regiment, 1943. *Member:* International Webern Society (president, 1962—), American Musicological Society (permanent senate member; chairman of Northwestern chapter, 1958-60), American Alpine Club (life member), Masons, Rotary Club (honorary member). *Awards, honors:* Austrian Honor Cross for Science and Art, first class, 1970; Order of Merit First Class, Federal Republic of Germany, 1980.

WRITINGS: Duo-Pianism: A Dissertation, Chicago Musical College Press, 1951; *The Death of Anton Webern: A Drama in Documents,* Philosophical Library, 1961; (compiler) *Anton von Webern: Perspectives,* University of Washington Press, 1966; (with wife, Rosaleen Moldenhauer) *Anton von Webern: A Chronicle of His Life and Work,* Gollancz, 1978, Knopf, 1979. Contributor to professional journals in United States and abroad. Monthly feature column, *Music of the West* magazine.

WORK IN PROGRESS: A catalog of the Moldenhauer Archives, with wife, Rosaleen Moldenhauer; *Music History from Primary Sources,* original music manuscripts, letters, and documents.

SIDELIGHTS: In the *New York Times,* Donal Henahan writes of *Anton von Webern: A Chronicle of His Life and Work:* "We have here not only an exhaustive and probably definitive study of Webern's life and music but an engrossing case history of one man's moral surrender under 20th-century stress. In spite of its scholarly apparatus, this biography can almost be read like a Thomas Mann novel. Hints of *Doctor Faustus* lie all about." Henahan terms the biography "massive" and believes that it is "probably the last word on the composer." Christopher Porterfield of *Time* voices similar praise, "The Moldenhauers ... furnish such extensive extracts from diaries and letters, as well as such detailed 'work histories' of the compositions, that their valuable book adumbrates the shape of many biographies and studies to come."

AVOCATIONAL INTERESTS: Mountaineering.

BIOGRAPHICAL/CRITICAL SOURCES: New York Times, June 10, 1979; *Time,* November 5, 1979; *Spokane Magazine,* October, 1980.

* * *

MOLNAR, Thomas 1921-

PERSONAL: Born June 26, 1921, in Budapest, Hungary; son of Alexander and Aurelie (Blon) Molnar. *Education:* Universite de Bruxelles, M.A. in French literature, 1948, M.A. in philosophy, 1948; Columbia University, Ph.D. in French Literature, 1952. *Home:* 142 West End Ave., New York, N.Y. 10023.

CAREER: Brooklyn College of the City University of New York, Brooklyn, N.Y., professor of French and world literature, 1957—; Long Island University, Greenvale, N.Y., adjunct professor of European intellectual history, 1967—. Vis-

iting professor of political theory, Potchefstroom University, South Africa, 1969; visiting professor of philosophy, Hillsdale College, 1973-74. *Awards, honors:* Relm Foundation grant, 1963-64, for travel and study in French-speaking Africa, 1966, for travel in South America, 1967, for *Sartre: Ideologue of Our Time.*

WRITINGS: Bernanos: His Political Thought and Prophecy, Sheed, 1960; *The Future of Education,* Fleet, 1961, revised edition, 1970; *The Decline of the Intellectual,* Meridian Books, 1962; *The Two Faces of American Foreign Policy,* Bobbs-Merrill, 1962; *Africa: A Political Travelogue,* Fleet, 1965; *South West Africa: The Last Pioneer Country,* Fleet, 1967; *Utopia: The Perennial Heresy,* Sheed, 1967; *Sartre: Ideologue of Our Time,* Funk, 1968; *Ecumenism or New Reformation?,* Funk, 1968; *The Counter-Revolution,* Funk, 1970; *God and the Knowledge of Reality,* Basic Books, 1973; *Authority and Its Enemies,* Arlington House, 1976; *Christian Humanism: A Critique of "The Secular City" and Its Ideology,* Franciscan Herald, 1978; *Theists and Atheists: A Typology of Non-Belief,* Mouton, 1980. Also author of *La Gauche vue d'en face,* 1970, *L'Animal politique,* 1974, *The European Dilemma,* 1974, *Le Socialisme sans visage,* 1976, *Le Modele defigure: L'Amerique de Tocqueville a Carter,* 1978, and *The Catholic Concept of Politics and State,* 1981.

WORK IN PROGRESS: The Pagan Temptation, for Fordham University Press.

BIOGRAPHICAL/CRITICAL SOURCES: Esquire, July, 1965, August, 1973; *New York Review of Books,* July 1, 1965; *New York Times Book Review,* July 18, 1965, December 14, 1969; *Negro Digest,* August, 1965; *Nation,* December 26, 1966; *America,* May 20, 1967; *Catholic World,* August, 1967; *Commonweal,* October 13, 1967; *Saturday Review,* October 26, 1968; *Book World,* October 27, 1968, June 7, 1970; *National Review,* March 7, 1967, August 22, 1967, February 10, 1970, March 28, 1975, October 15, 1976; *Christian Century,* February 20, 1974; *Modern Age,* summer, 1974, spring, 1978; *Choice,* July-August, 1974.

* * *

MONSARRAT, Nicholas (John Turney) 1910-1979

PERSONAL: Born March 22, 1910, in Liverpool, England; died August 8, 1979, in London, England; son of Keith Waldegrave (a surgeon) and Marguerite (Turney) Monsarrat; married Eileen Rowland, September, 1939 (divorced, 1952); married Philippa Crosby, December, 1952 (divorced, 1961); married Ann Griffiths, December, 1961; children: (first marriage) Max; (second marriage) Marc, Anthony. *Education:* Trinity College, Cambridge, B.A. in Law (honors), 1931. *Home:* San Lawrenz, Gozo, Malta. *Agent:* Campbell Thomson & McLaughlin Ltd., 31 Newington Green, London N16 9PU, England; and Curtis Brown, Ltd., 575 Madison Ave., New York, N.Y. 10022.

CAREER: Spent two years in a solicitor's office in Nottingham, England, before giving up law to begin his writing career in London in 1934. For a decade following World War II he was with the British Information Services as chief in South Africa, 1946-52, and chief in Canada, 1953-56. In England he was a borough councillor of Kensington, 1946; in South Africa, chairman of the National War Memorial Health Foundation, 1951-53; in Canada, a member of the board of governors of the Stratford Festival Theatre, 1956-60, and Ottawa Philharmonic Orchestra, 1956. *Military service:* Royal Navy, duty with Atlantic convoys, 1940-46; became lieutenant commander; mentioned in dispatches; Royal Naval Volunteer Reserve. *Member:* Royal Society of Literature (fellow),

Rideau Club (Ottawa), Royal St. Lawrence Yacht Club (Montreal). *Awards, honors:* Heinemann Foundation Prize for Literature, 1951, for *The Cruel Sea;* Coronation Medal, 1953; Chevalier, Sovereign Order of St. John of Jerusalem, 1973.

WRITINGS: Think of Tomorrow, Hurst, 1934; *At First Sight,* Hurst, 1935; *The Whipping Boy,* Jarrolds, 1937; *This Is the Schoolroom,* Cassell, 1939.

H. M. Corvette (also see below), Lippincott, 1943; *East Coast Corvette* (also see below), Lippincott, 1943; *Corvette Command* (also see below), Cassell, 1944; *Leave Cancelled* (also see below), Knopf, 1945; *H. M. Frigate,* Cassell, 1946; *Depends What You Mean by Love* (contains "Heavy Rescue," *Leave Cancelled,* and "H.M.S. Marlborough Will Enter Harbour"), Cassell, 1947, Knopf, 1948; *My Brother Denys,* Cassell, 1948, Knopf, 1949.

The Cruel Sea, Knopf, 1951, reprinted, Bantam, 1979; *The Story of Esther Costello,* Knopf, 1953; *Three Corvettes* (also see below; contains *H. M. Corvette, East Coast Corvette,* and *Corvette Command*), Cassell, 1953; (editor) *The Boys' Book of the Sea,* Cassell, 1954, McGraw, 1955; *Castle Garac,* McClelland, 1955; *The Tribe That Lost Its Head,* William Sloane Associates, 1956; (editor) *The Boys' Book of the Commonwealth,* Cassell, 1957; *The Ship That Died of Shame, and Other Stories,* William Sloane Associates, 1959.

The Nylon Pirate, William Sloane Associates, 1960; *The White Rajah,* William Sloane Associates, 1961; *The Time before This,* William Sloane Associates, 1962; *Smith and Jones,* William Sloane Associates, 1963; *To Stratford with Love,* McClelland, 1963; *A Fair Day's Work,* William Sloane Associates, 1964; *The Pillow Fight,* William Sloane Associates, 1965; *Something to Hide,* Cassell, 1965, Morrow, 1966; *Life Is a Four-Letter Word* (autobiography), Cassell, Volume I: *Breaking In,* 1966, Volume II: *Breaking Out,* 1970, abridged version published in one volume as *Breaking In, Breaking Out,* Morrow, 1970; *Richer Than All His Tribe,* Cassell, 1968, Morrow, 1969.

The Kappillan of Malta, Cassell, 1973, Morrow, 1974; *Monsarrat at Sea* (contains "The Longest Love, the Longest Hate," *Three Corvettes,* "I Was There," "A Ship to Remember," "H.M.S. Marlborough Will Enter Harbour," "It Was Cruel," and "The Ship That Died of Shame"), Cassell, 1975; *The Master Mariner,* Book I: *Running Proud,* Cassell, 1978, Morrow, 1979, Book II: *Darken Ship,* Morrow, 1981.

Also author of play, "The Visitor," produced in London at Daly's Theatre, 1936. Contributor to *Spectator, Atlantic, Saturday Evening Post,* and other periodicals.

WORK IN PROGRESS: The second book of *The Master Mariner.*

SIDELIGHTS: Nicholas Monsarrat described his writing to John Davenport as largely pragmatic: "I'm not a stylist, perhaps, but I want to be read. Every writer wants to be a success, and I think I've got something to say that people want to hear." Although some of Monsarrat's work created a stir among reviewers (of *Leave Cancelled,* Hamilton Basso commented, "I felt damned embarrassed"), he was generally recognized as a talented storyteller whose tales, as characterized by E. W. Foell, are "spare, swift-moving and free of verbal cadenzas." James Kelly suggested the extent of Monsarrat's audience in his review of *The White Rajah:* "It's all good, high-caloried fun and most readers will gladly drop the world they know for a side trip with Mr. Monsarrat to his never-never land."

Some critics have complained that Monsarrat did not main-

tain the high standard established in his bestselling novel, *The Cruel Sea.* Monsarrat commented on this assertion in an interview: "With each book, I like to try something entirely new. You can't go on writing 'Son of the Cruel Sea' for ever. If the critics don't like a new book, they ask why the author doesn't go back to writing what he knows about. But then, if the author does just that, they announce loud and clear that he can only write on one theme, and that it's getting overworked. They've got you, whatever you do. But writing is my life and I wouldn't trade jobs with anyone."

Monsarrat's autobiography, *Life Is a Four-Letter Word,* elicited varied responses. Several reviewers expressed disgust with the quality of the life Monsarrat led. Wilfred De'ath wrote: "I admire Monsarrat for saying that he was . . . a coward, a sensualist, a chauvinist, and an exponent of 'pagan philosophy' which was what Trevor Huddlestone said about him. But I do not admire these qualities in themselves, nor do I admire his sustained non-attempts to improve himself. His treatment of women was often, at the most charitable interpretation, despicable and I would use the same word to describe his attitude to children. . . . His twin preoccupations . . . seem to have been women and social prestige with the sea, writing, and politics vying for a poor third." De'ath concludes that Monsarrat "seems to be someone more deserving of our sympathy than our admiration." "Candour is something," Tom Driberg commented. "This book will enthrall any slightly caddish young man on the make." Conversely, Jean Stubbs found that *Life Is a Four-Letter Word* "breaks out with the force of those seas [Monsarrat] describes so splendidly, allowing us an interior view of both man and writer, each of them larger than life and stranger than fiction. . . . This man lives and writes so generously, and possesses such treasures of character and talent, that he gives his own story a rare perspective. Any criticism the reader may make is said sharper and better by the author himself, and with disarming frankness."

Monsarrat's books have been translated into eighteen languages. Motion pictures have been produced from *The Cruel Sea, The Ship That Died of Shame, The Story of Esther Costello,* and *Something to Hide.*

BIOGRAPHICAL/CRITICAL SOURCES: Saturday Review, November 3, 1956, February 15, 1969; *New York Times Book Review,* November 4, 1956, October 15, 1961; *Christian Science Monitor,* May 2, 1963; *Books and Bookmen,* July, 1968, October, 1968; *Writer's Digest,* August, 1969; *Punch,* August 26, 1970; *Bookseller,* August 29, 1970; *Listener,* September 24, 1970; *Books,* October, 1970; *Washington Post,* March 27, 1979, August 9, 1979.†

*   *   *

MONTGOMERY, Elizabeth Rider

PERSONAL: Born in Huaras, Peru; daughter of Charles Quantrell (a missionary) and Lula (Tralle) Rider; married Norman A. Montgomery, 1930 (divorced); married Arthur Julesberg, 1963; children: Janet Montgomery Small, Robin Athol. *Education:* Attended Washington State Normal School (now Western Washington University), 1924-25, and University of California, Los Angeles, 1927-28. *Religion:* Congregationalist. *Home:* 10203 47th Ave. S.W., D2, Seattle, Wash. 98146.

CAREER: Elementary school teacher, Los Angeles, Calif. and Aberdeen, Wash.; Scott, Foresman & Co., Chicago, Ill., staff writer, 1938-63; free-lance writer of fiction, nonfiction, and drama. *Member:* National League of American Penwomen, Parents and Teachers Association (life member),

Seattle Free Lance Writers, Friends of the Library, Alki Community Club. *Awards, honors:* National Presswomen and Penwomen awards; honored at Matrix Table, 1953; several plays have won national prizes.

WRITINGS—Juvenile fiction: *Sally Does It*, Appleton, 1940; *Bonnie's Baby Brother*, Lippincott, 1942; *Three Miles an Hour*, Dodd, 1952; *Half-Pint Fisherman*, Dodd, 1956; *Second-Fiddle-Sandra*, Dodd, 1958; *Susan and the Storm*, Thomas Nelson, 1960; *The Mystery of Edison Brown*, Scott, Foresman, 1960; *Tide Treasure Camper*, Washburn, 1963; *Two Kinds of Courage*, Washburn, 1966; *Toward Democracy*, Washburn, 1967; *Mystery of the Boy Next Door*, Garrard, 1978.

Non-fiction; published by Dodd, except as indicated: *The Story Behind Great Inventions*, 1944; *The Story Behind Great Medical Discoveries*, 1945; *The Story Behind Great Books*, 1946; *Keys to Nature's Secrets*, 1946; *The Story Behind Great Stories*, 1947; *The Story Behind Modern Books*, 1949; *The Story Behind Musical Instruments*, 1953; *The Story Behind Popular Songs*, 1958; *Till Time Be Conquered*, Alki Church, 1959.

Published by Garrard, except as indicated: *Alexander Graham Bell*, 1963; *Hernando De Soto*, 1964; *Chief Seattle*, 1965; *Lewis and Clark*, 1965; *Old Ben Franklin's Philadelphia*, 1967; *Hans Christian Andersen*, 1968; *When a Ton of Gold Reached Seattle*, 1968; *William C. Handy: Father of the Blues*, 1968; *Chief Joseph*, 1969; *Henry Ford*, 1969; *When Pioneers Pushed West to Oregon*, 1969; *Will Rogers*, 1970; *Gandhi*, 1970; *Albert Schweitzer*, 1971; *Walt Disney*, 1971; *Duke Ellington*, 1972; *Three Jazz Greats* (anthology), 1973; *Dag Hammarskjold*, 1973; *Indian Patriots* (anthology), 1974; *Super Showmen*, 1974; *Founding Fathers*, 1975; *Trouble Is His Name*, 1976; *"Seeing" in the Dark*, 1979; *The Builder Also Grows*, Ashley Books, 1979. Also author of *Wonder Workers in Communication*, 1979.

Textbooks; published by Scott, Foresman: *We Look and See*, 1940; *We Work and Play*, 1940; *We Come and Go*, 1940; *Good Times with Our Friends*, 1941; *Three Friends*, 1944; *Five in the Family*, 1946; *The Girl Next Door*, 1946; *You*, 1948; *Happy Days with Our Friends*, 1948; *Just Like Me*, 1957; *Being Six*, 1957; *Seven Or So*, 1957; *Eight to Nine*, 1957; *Going on Ten*, 1958; *About Yourself*, 1959.

Plays: *All Kinds of People*, Row Peterson, 1950; "Suburb of Heaven," produced by University of Washington, 1960. Author of two juvenile plays, "Old Pipes and the Dryad," 1948, and "Knights of the Silver Shield," 1963; also author of "Noel's Ark," 1951, "Kla-How-Ya" (a symphonic drama of Pacific Northwest history), "Proxy Papa," and "The Klep"; juvenile plays have been produced on radio and television. Contributor of stories and articles to juvenile magazines and papers.

WORK IN PROGRESS: An adult book on speculation.

SIDELIGHTS: Elizabeth Montgomery often speaks informally to beginning writers' groups, telling them it took seven years and more rejection slips than she can count before she sold her first manuscript. Of her methods of writing, she says that she usually keeps two kinds of writing going at once; one acts as a foil for the other. Before actually writing she does a great deal of notebook work. She tries to write a certain number of pages per week, and then she revises a lot.

AVOCATIONAL INTERESTS: Water-color painting, braiding rugs, stamp-collecting, theatre, music and golf. All of the rugs in her apartment and most of the pictures on the walls are her own creations.

BIOGRAPHICAL/CRITICAL SOURCES: Author and Journalist, October, 1945; *Young Wings*, March, 1946; *Wilson Library Bulletin*, May, 1952; *The Baton*, May, 1952; *Seattle Times*, April 10, 1959; *West Seattle Herald*, November 17, 1960.

*   *   *

MONTGOMERY, Herbert J. 1933-

PERSONAL: Born June 26, 1933, in Deer River, Minn.; married; wife's name, Mary A. *Home:* 5309 West 56th St., Edina, Minn. 55436.

CAREER: Editor for Winston Press, Minneapolis, Minn. *Awards, honors:* First prize in *Writer's Digest* contest, 1965, for article co-authored with wife.

WRITINGS—All with wife, Mary A. Montgomery, except as indicated; all published by Winston Press, except as indicated: *Come to Communion: A Program for First Communion Preparation*, 1972; (sole author) *The Apple and the Envelope*, Holt, 1973; *Rodeo Road*, Scholastic Book Services, 1973; *Go in Peace: A Program for Penance Preparation*, 1974; *The Jesus Story*, 1974; *The Chase*, Scholastic Book Services, 1974; *Live This Gift: A Program for Confirmation Preparation*, 1975; *On the Run*, Scholastic Book Services, 1976; *Become This Gift*, 1976; *The Splendor of the Psalms: A Photographic Meditation*, 1977; *Beyond Sorrow: Reflections on Death and Grief*, 1977; *The Two of Us: Reflections on Shared Growth in Marriage*, 1977; *Rejoice! A Child Is Born*, 1977; *The Time of Your Life*, 1977; *Together at the Lord's Supper: Preparation for Holy Communion*, 1977; (sole editor) *Joy One*, revised edition, 1977; *Love and Let Grow: Reflections on Family Living*, 1977; (sole author) *Johnny Appleseed*, new edition, 1979; *The Cooper Contract*, Scholastic Book Services, 1980.

*   *   *

MONTGOMERY, John D(ickey) 1920-

PERSONAL: Born February 15, 1920, in Evanston, Ill.; son of Charles W. (an investment counselor) and Lora (Dickey) Montgomery; married Jane Ireland, December 19, 1954; children: Faith, Patience, John. *Education:* Kalamazoo College, B.A., 1941, M.A., 1942; Harvard University, M.A., 1948, Ph.D., 1951. *Home:* 36 Hyde Ave., Newton, Mass. *Office:* John F. Kennedy School of Government, Harvard University, Cambridge, Mass. 02138.

CAREER: Babson Institute, Wellesley, Mass., chairman of department of government and law, 1946-57, dean of faculty, 1954-57; Michigan State University Vietnam Project, Saigon, Vietnam, chief of academic instruction section, 1957-59; Boston University, Boston, Mass., research professor of government and director of Development Research Center African Studies Program, 1960-63; Harvard University, Cambridge, Mass.; professor of public administration, 1963—, secretary, John F. Kennedy School of Government, 1963-77, chairman of department of government, 1980—. Consultant to operations research office, Johns Hopkins University, 1951-57. Active in civic and community orchestras. *Military service:* U.S. Army, 1941-45. *Member:* American Society of Public Administration, American Society of Political and Legal Philosophy, Society for International Development (chairman of international development research committee, 1965—), Amateur Chamber Music Players. *Awards, honors:* Guggenheim fellowship, 1965; Council on Foreign Relations fellowship, 1959-60; LL.D., Kalamazoo College.

WRITINGS: (Editor and co-author) *The State Versus Socrates: A Case Study in Civic Freedom*, Beacon Press, 1954; *The Purge in Occupied Japan*, Operations Research Office, Johns Hopkins University, 1954; *Forced to Be Free: The Artificial Revolution in Germany and Japan*, University of Chicago Press, 1957; (editor) *Vietnam Government Organization Manual, 1957-58*, National Institute of Administration, Saigon, 1958; *Cases in Vietnamese Administration*, National Institute of Administration, Saigon, 1959; *Aid to Africa: New Test for U.S. Policy*, Foreign Policy Association, 1961; *The Politics of Foreign Aid: American Experience in Southeast Asia*, Praeger, 1962; (co-author) *Rural Improvement and Political Development*, American Society for Public Administration 1965; (co-editor and co-author) *Approaches to Development: Politics, Administration, and Change*, McGraw, 1965; *Foreign Aid in International Politics*, Prentice-Hall, 1967; *Technology and Civic Life: Making and Implementing Development Decisions*, MIT Press, 1974; (editor with Harold D. Lasswell and Daniel Lerner) *Values and Development: Appraising Asian Experience*, MIT Press, 1976; (editor with Lasswell and Joel Migdal) *Patterns of Policy: Comparative and Longitudinal Studies of Population Events*, Transaction Books, 1979.

Editor; all published by John F. Kennedy School of Government, Harvard University: *Public Policy Yearbook*, Volume XIII (with Arthur Smithies), 1964, Volume XIV, 1965, Volume XV (with Smithies), 1966, Volume XVI (with Albert O. Hirschman), 1967, Volume XVII (with Hirschman), 1968.

Contributor: *Tradition, Values, and Socio-Economic Modernization*, Duke University Press, 1961; *Problems in International Relations*, 2nd edition, Prentice-Hall, 1962; *Public Interest*, Atherton, 1962; *Education and Training in the Developing Countries*, Praeger, 1965; Beverly Winikoff, editor, *Nutrition and National Policy*, MIT Press, 1978. Contributor to *World Politics, Contemporary Japan*, and other journals.

*   *   *

MONTGOMERY, Marion H., Jr. 1925-

PERSONAL: Born April 16, 1925, in Thomaston, Ga.; son of M. H. and Lottie Mae (Jenkins) Montgomery; married Dorothy Carlisle, January 20, 1951; children: Priscilla, Deana, Marion III, Heli, Ellyn. *Education:* University of Georgia, 1947-53, A.B., M.A. *Politics:* "Independent conservative." *Religion:* "Anglo Catholic." *Agent:* Dorothy Pittman, Illington Rd., Ossining, N.Y. 10562. *Office:* Department of English, University of Georgia, Athens, Ga. 30602.

CAREER: University of Georgia, Athens, assistant director of university press, 1950-52, business manager of *Georgia Review*, 1951-53, instructor, 1954-60, assistant professor, 1960-67, associate professor, 1967-70, professor of English, 1970—. Instructor, Darlington School for Boys, 1953-54. Writer-in-residence, Converse College, 1963. *Military service:* U.S. Army, 1943-46; became sergeant. *Awards, honors:* Eugene Saxton Memorial Award, Harper, 1960; Georgia Writers Association, award for fiction, 1964, for *Darrell*, award for poetry, 1970, for *The Gull and Other Georgia Scenes;* award for poetry, *Carlton Miscellany*, 1967; Earhart Foundation grant for critical work.

*WRITINGS—*Fiction: *The Wandering of Desire* (novel), Harper, 1962; *Darrell* (novel), Doubleday, 1964; *Ye Olde Bluebird* (novella), New College Press, 1967; *Fugitive* (novel), Harper, 1974.

Poetry: *Dry Lightening*, University of Nebraska Press, 1960;

Stones from the Rubble, Argus Books, 1965; *The Gull and Other Georgia Scenes*, University of Georgia Press, 1969.

Criticism: *Ezra Pound: A Critical Essay*, Eerdmans, 1970; *T. S. Eliot: An Essay on the American Magus*, University of Georgia Press, 1970; *The Reflective Journey toward Order: Essays on Dante, Wordsworth, Eliot, and Others*, University of Georgia Press, 1973; *Eliot's Reflective Journey to the Garden*, Whitston Publishing, 1978; *The Prophetic Poet and the Popular Spirit*, Sherwood Sugden, Volume I: *Why Flannery O'Connor Stayed Home*, 1980, Volume II: *Why Poe Drank Liquor*, in press, Volume III: *Why Hawthorne Was Melancholy*, in press.

Work appears in anthologies, including *Best Poems of 1958* and *Best Short Stories of 1971*. Contributor of poetry and short stories to periodicals. Managing editor, *Western Review*, 1957-58.

SIDELIGHTS: A prominent Southern writer, Marion Montgomery's fiction often contrasts characters who are leaving the rural South for success in the city with those who, having achieved that success, are trying to recapture their rural beginnings. This particular theme comes from Montgomery's interest in the Agrarian writers of the thirties who advocated an artistic return to the land in order to establish a mutually supportive culture and agriculture.

BIOGRAPHICAL/CRITICAL SOURCES: Commonweal, May 11, 1962; *Best Sellers*, May 15, 1964; *Critique*, Volume VIII, number 1, 1965; *Sewanee Review*, spring, 1965; *Poetry*, October, 1966; *Georgia Review*, spring, 1967, summer, 1974; *Writer*, December, 1969; *National Review*, August 11, 1970; *Southern Review*, autumn, 1970, winter, 1975; *American Literature*, January, 1971; *Times Literary Supplement*, January 1, 1971; *New York Times Book Review*, June 9, 1974; *New Republic*, July 27, 1974; *Courier-Journal & Times* (Louisville, Ky.), September 1, 1974; *Recherches Anglaises et Americaines*, IX, 1976; *Contemporary Literary Criticism*, Volume VII, Gale, 1977.

*   *   *

MOONEY, Booth 1912-1977

PERSONAL: Born July 3, 1912, in Decatur, Tex.; died of cancer March 22, 1977, in Sumner, Md.; son of Harvey M. (a farmer) and Eva (Mitchell) Mooney; married Elizabeth Comstock (a free-lance writer), March 9, 1946; children: Edward C., Joan H. *Education:* Attended public schools in Texas. *Politics:* Democrat. *Residence:* Sumner, Md. *Agent:* Paul R. Reynolds, Inc., 12 East 41st St., New York, N.Y. 10017. *Office:* 1625 Eye St. N.W., Washington, D.C. 20006.

CAREER: Texas Weekly, Dallas, associate editor, 1935-41; Mooney & Cullinan (public relations consultants), Dallas, partner, 1946-52; U.S. Senate, Washington, D.C., executive assistant to Senator Lyndon B. Johnson, 1953-58; free-lance writer in Washington, D.C., 1959-77. *Military service:* U.S. Army Air Forces, 1942-45; became captain. *Member:* Metropolitan Club of Washington, Kenwood Country Club.

WRITINGS: The Lyndon Johnson Story, Farrar, Straus, 1956, revised edition, 1964; *Mr. Speaker*, Follett, 1964; *Builders for Progress*, McGraw, 1965; *The Hidden Assassins*, Follett, 1966; *The Politicians: 1945-1960*, Lippincott, 1970; *Roosevelt and Rayburn*, Lippincott, 1971; *LBJ: An Irreverent Chronicle*, Crowell, 1976. Also author of paperback novels, *Here Is My Body* and *The Insiders*.

Biographies for young people; published by Follett: *Sam Houston*, 1966; *Henry Clay*, 1966; *General Billy Mitchell*, 1968; *Woodrow Wilson*, 1968.

SIDELIGHTS: Booth Mooney was a close personal friend of Lyndon B. Johnson and worked for a while as speechwriter and executive assistant to the then-Senator Johnson. Some reviewers have noted that this friendship colored Mooney's biographies of Johnson and his book *The Politicians.* The *Economist's* reviewer wrote that the revised edition of *The Lyndon Johnson Story* gives "little flavour of a highly piquant personality and it is quite uncritical, as befits a man who did two stints on Mr. Johnson's staff." *Book Week's* C. M. Roberts recalled the statement that "'campaign biographies are propaganda'" and commented: "Mooney's book falls into that category, historically.... Nonetheless, this is a most useful book, jampacked as it is with salient facts about LBJ—not all the facts, not even all the salient facts, but the basic facts so necessary to an understanding of the man."

In *The Politicians,* Mooney discussed a number of elected officials from the period following World War II through the presidential election of John F. Kennedy. Gerald W. Johnson commented in the *New York Times Book Review* that the book "could be the opening gun in a pro-Johnson counterattack.... In this volume Lyndon B. Johnson emerges as a hero of the period covered. The book is an estimate of politicians, and in politics, as distinguished from statecraft, Johnson was the master even of Sam Rayburn, while the rest were nowhere." J. J. Flynn, writing in the *Annals of the American Academy of Political and Social Science,* believed that *The Politicians* "should have been subtitled 'Lyndon Johnson's Superb Leadership.' The author has devoted almost half his text to the task of proving that Johnson was the greatest Senate majority leader since Joseph Robinson.... Mooney appears to have taken his previous book, *The Lyndon Johnson Story,* and brought in the rest of the political actors to bolster his star's role."

Some reviewers felt that in his second biography of Johnson, *LBJ: An Irreverent Chronicle,* Mooney managed to achieve some objectivity about his subject. In the *New York Review of Books,* Garry Wills wrote that this book "is especially useful, since it is a corrective to his earlier syncophantic biography. Mooney knew the mushy side of Johnson as well as the mean one. He also knew what a sharp eye he had for people and for character types." William Sternman wrote in *Best Sellers* that although the account is "frankly biased," Mooney presented Johnson as "coarse, crafty, petty, arrogant, and dictatorial, as well as earthy, frank, ingenuous, and warm-hearted.... As far as our understanding of the man is concerned, [this is] a long-delayed corrective to the vicious criticism of LBJ's own final days in office."

BIOGRAPHICAL/CRITICAL SOURCES: Book Week, January 26, 1964; *Economist,* February 15, 1964; *New Republic,* March 14, 1964, June 25, 1966; *New York Times Book Review,* August 23, 1964, June 14, 1970; *Annals of the American Academy of Political and Social Science,* September, 1970; *New York Review of Books,* June 24, 1976; *Best Sellers,* August, 1976.†

*   *   *

MOORE, Charles A(lexander)   1901-1967

PERSONAL: Born March 11, 1901; died, 1967; son of Charles Lee and Lola (Alexander) Moore; married Anne G. Mayo, 1929 (divorced); children: Charles A., Jr. *Office:* Department of Philosophy, University of Hawaii, Honolulu, Hawaii.

CAREER: Yale University, New Haven, Conn., instructor, 1933-36; University of Hawaii, Honolulu, 1936-67, became

senior professor of philosophy. *Member:* American Philosophical Association, American Oriental Society, Association for Asian Studies, Indian Philosophical Congress, Phi Kappa Phi. *Awards, honors:* Watumull Foundation Book Prize, 1959; World Brotherhood (of Hawaii) Award; Pacific and Asian Affairs Council (Hawaii) Citation, 1963; Liberty Bell Award, 1965.

*WRITINGS—*Editor: *Philosophy—East and West,* Princeton University Press, 1944, reprinted, Books for Libraries, 1970; (and author of introduction) *Essays in East-West Philosophy,* University of Hawaii Press, 1951; (with Wing Tsit Chan) Junjiro Takausu, *The Essentials of Buddhist Philosophy,* Asia Publishing House, 1956, reprinted, Greenwood Press, 1973; *Philosophy and Culture—East and West: East-West Philosophy in Practical Perspective,* University of Hawaii Press, 1962; (with S. Radhakrishnan) *A Source Book in Indian Philosophy,* Princeton University Press, 1963; (and contributor) *The Status of the Individual in East and West,* University of Hawaii Press, 1966; *The Indian Mind: Essentials of Indian Philosophy and Culture,* East-West Center Press, 1966; *The Chinese Mind: Essentials of Chinese Philosophy and Culture,* East-West Center Press, 1966; *The Japanese Mind: Essentials of Japanese Philosophy and Culture,* East-West Center Press, 1967. Editor-in-chief, *Philosophy East and West* (quarterly journal).

WORK IN PROGRESS: Two books, *A Source Book in Buddhist Philosophy* and *Idealism in World Perspective.*

BIOGRAPHICAL/CRITICAL SOURCES: Nation, January 1, 1968; *Yale Review,* winter, 1969.†

*   *   *

MOORE, Harry T(hornton)   1908-

PERSONAL: Born August 2, 1908, in Oakland, Calif.; son of Harry T. (an Army lieutenant colonel) and Kathryn W. Moore; married Winifred Sheehan, March 21, 1934; married Beatrice Reynolds Walker, October 12, 1946; children: (first marriage) Brian, Sharon. *Education:* University of Chicago, Ph.B., 1934; Northwestern University, M.A., 1942; Boston University, Ph.D., 1951. *Home:* 922 South Division St., Carterville, Ill. 62918. *Agent:* Laurence Pollinger Ltd., 18 Maddox St., London W. 1, England. *Office:* Department of English, Southern Illinois University, Carbondale, Ill.

CAREER: Illinois Institute of Technology, Chicago, instructor in English, 1940-41; Northwestern University, Evanston, Ill., instructor, 1941-42; Babson Institute, Wellesley Hills, Mass., associate professor and chairman of department of history and literature, 1947-57; Southern Illinois University, Carbondale, professor, 1957-60, research professor of English, 1960-78, professor emeritus, 1978—. Visiting summer professor, University of Colorado, 1959, New York University and Columbia University, 1961. *Military service:* U.S. Army Air Forces, 1942-47; became lieutenant colonel. *Member:* Royal Society of Literature (fellow), Modern Language Association of America, College English Association (president, 1960), National Council of Teachers of English, P.E.N., Sigma Chi, Cliff Dwellers (Chicago). *Awards, honors:* Guggenheim fellowships, 1958, 1960.

WRITINGS: The Novels of John Steinbeck: A First Critical Study, Normandie House, 1939, 2nd edition, Kennikat, 1968; *The Life and Works of D. H. Lawrence,* Twayne, 1951, revised edition, Allen & Unwin, 1963; (co-translator) Karl Jaspers, *Tragedy Is Not Enough,* Beacon Press, 1953; *The Intelligent Heart: The Story of D. H. Lawrence,* Farrar, Straus, 1954, revised edition, Grove, 1960, 2nd revised edition published as *The Priest of Love: A Life of D. H. Law-*

rence, Farrar, Straus, 1974; *Poste Restante: A Lawrence Travel Calendar*, University of California Press, 1956; *D. H. Lawrence: His Life and Works*, Twayne, 1963; *E. M. Forster*, Columbia University Press, 1965; *Twentieth-Century French Literature*, two volumes, Southern Illinois University Press, 1966; (with F. W. Roberts) *D. H. Lawrence and His World*, Studio, 1966; *Twentieth-Century German Literature*, Basic Books, 1967; *Age of the Modern, and Other Literary Essays*, Southern Illinois University Press, 1971; (with Albert Parry) *Twentieth Century Russian Literature*, Southern Illinois University Press, 1974; *Henry James and His World*, Viking, 1974.

Editor: *D. H. Lawrence: Letters to Bertrand Russell*, Gotham, 1948; (with F. J. Hoffman) *The Achievement of D. H. Lawrence*, University of Oklahoma Press, 1953; *D. H. Lawrence, Sex, Literature and Censorship*, Twayne, 1953; (with K. W. Deutsch) Lewis Mumford, *The Human Prospect*, Beacon Press, 1955; *A D. H. Lawrence Miscellany*, Southern Illinois University Press, 1959; *Rainer Maria Rilke: Selected Letters*, Anchor Books, 1960; (and author of introduction) Joshua Sprigg, *Anglia Rediviva: England's Recovery, 1647*, Scholar's Library, 1960; *D. H. Lawrence: The Collected Letters*, Heinemann, 1962; *The World of Lawrence Durrell*, Southern Illinois University Press, 1962; *Contemporary American Novelists*, Southern Illinois University Press, 1964; *Elizabethan Age*, Dell, 1965; (and author of preface) Sergio Pacifici, *The Modern Italian Novel from Manzoni to Svevo*, Southern Illinois University Press, 1967; (with Warren Roberts) *Phoenix II: Uncollected, Unpublished, and Other Prose Works by D. H. Lawrence*, Viking, 1967; Zelda Fitzgerald, *Save Me the Waltz*, Southern Illinois University Press, 1967; (with Ian S. MacNiven) *The Richard Aldington-Lawrence Durrell Letters*, Viking, in press; (with Robert Partlow) *D. H. Lawrence: The Man Who Lived*, Southern Illinois University Press, in press; (with Dale S. Montague) *Frieda Lawrence and Her Circle*, Macmillan, in press. Co-editor, "Crosscurrents/Modern Critiques" series, Southern Illinois University Press, 1961—. Contributor to *Transactions of the Royal Society of Literature of the United Kingdom*, 1962. Contributor to *New York Times*, *Saturday Review*, *Kenyon Review*, and other publications.

SIDELIGHTS: Harry T. Moore's *The Priest of Love* was filmed by Milesian Films in 1980.

BIOGRAPHICAL/CRITICAL SOURCES: Times Literary Supplement, March 7, 1968; *Criticism*, fall, 1968; *Modern Literature Review*, October, 1973; *New Republic*, May 4, 1974; *Christian Science Monitor*, August 7, 1974; *New Statesman*, September 27, 1974; *Hudson Review*, fall, 1974; *Sewanee Review*, January, 1975.

*   *   *

MOORE, John R(obert) 1928-

PERSONAL: Born April 24, 1928, in Kearny, N.J.; son of Edward R. and Pearl (Vannatta) Moore; married Shirley Burr, 1955; children: Linda Elizabeth, Janet Lynn, Karen Joanne. *Education:* Colgate University, A.B., 1949; Cornell University, A.M., 1951, Ph.D., 1956. *Home:* 5208 Pinnacle Lane, Knoxville, Tenn. 37914. *Office:* 716 Stokely Management Center, University of Tennessee, Knoxville, Tenn. 37916.

CAREER: University of Tennessee, Knoxville, 1953—, began as instructor, currently professor of economics, associate dean, College of Business, 1978—. *Member:* American Economic Association, Southern Economic Association, Regional Science Association. *Awards, honors:* Ford Foun-

dation fellow, Harvard University, 1959-60; National Science Foundation fellow, University of California, Berkeley, 1962; National Science Foundation grant, University of Tennessee, 1972-75.

WRITINGS: Economics: Principles, Problems and Perspectives, Allyn & Bacon, 1962, revised edition, 1966; (editor) *The Economic Impact of TVA*, University of Tennessee Press, 1967; (with T. H. Lee) *Regional and Interregional Intersectional Flow Analysis*, University of Tennessee Press, 1972; *The Impact of Foreign Direct Investment on an Underdeveloped Economy: The Venezuelan Case*, Arno, 1976; (with H. W. Henry and others) *Energy Management*, Dekker, 1980.

WORK IN PROGRESS: A book on health and safety in coal mining.

*   *   *

MOORE, John Travers 1908- (John Tripp)

PERSONAL: Born August 24, 1908, in Wellston, Ohio; son of Thomas Emmet (a lawyer and editor) and Mary (Tripp) Moore; married Margaret Rumberger (an author), June 16, 1928. *Education:* University of Dayton, LL.B., 1933. *Home:* 827 North Justice, Hendersonville, N.C. 28739.

CAREER: Poet; in private law practice, 1933-38; associate editor of youth publications, G. A. Pflaum (publisher); managing editor of Army Air Forces technical journal, *Plane Facts*, during World War II; editorial associate and poetry critic, *Writer's Digest.*

WRITINGS: A Child's Book of Psalms, Hobbyhorse House, 1946; *Near Centerville*, privately printed, 1950; *Cincinnati Parks*, Cincinnati Park Board, 1953; *Poems*, Halcyon (London), 1955; *Modern Crusaders*, Farrar, Straus, 1957; *God's Wonderful World*, Augsburg, 1964; (under pseudonym John Tripp) *My Prayer*, Guild-Golden, 1964; *The Story of Silent Night*, Concordia, 1965; *When You Walk Out in Spring*, Helicon, 1965; *Cinnamon Seed*, Houghton, 1967; *Town and Countryside Poems*, Albert Whitman, 1968; *There's Motion Everywhere*, Houghton, 1970; *Poems: On Writing Poetry*, Libra, 1971; *We Are Like Wine*, Droke, 1972. Also author of *All along the Way, The First Moon Landing*, and *Sappho's Poetry.*

With wife, Margaret R. Moore: *Sing-Along Sary*, Harcourt, 1951; *Little Saints*, Grail, 1953; *Big Saints*, Grail, 1954; *The Three Tripps* (Parents' Magazine Book Club selection), Bobbs-Merrill, 1959; *On Cherry Tree Hill*, Bobbs-Merrill, 1960; (editor) *Rhymes and Chimes*, Augsburg, 1966; *The Little Band and the Inaugural Parade*, Albert Whitman, 1968; *Certainly, Carrie, Cut the Cake*, Bobbs-Merrill, 1971; *Pepito's Speech at the United Nations*, Carolrhoda, 1971.

Work appears in anthologies. Contributor of poetry to *New York Times*, *Saturday Evening Post*, *Good Housekeeping*, *Horn Book*, *Child Life*, and other publications.

SIDELIGHTS: John Travers Moore told *CA* that he began his writing career because "I would have fairly burst if I had not walked off a job and devoted full time to writing." *Avocational interests:* Gourmet cooking.

BIOGRAPHICAL/CRITICAL SOURCES: Cincinnati Post and Times-Star, September 24, 1958; *Cincinnati Enquirer*, May 17, 1959, May 24, 1959, May 31, 1959, September 15, 1963; *Hendersonville* (N.C.) *Times-News*, October 17, 1972, June 24, 1975, June 19, 1978; *New York Times*, July 31, 1975; *Asheville* (N.C.) *Times*, December 24, 1975.

MOORE, Marianne (Craig) 1887-1972

PERSONAL: Born November 15, 1887, in Kirkwood, Mo; died February 5, 1972; daughter of John Milton and Mary (Warner) Moore. *Education:* Bryn Mawr College, A.B., 1909; Carlisle Commercial College, graduate, 1910. *Religion:* Presbyterian. *Residence:* New York, N.Y.

CAREER: Author and poet. Teacher, United States Indian School, Carlisle, Pa., 1911-15; assistant, New York Public Library, New York, N.Y., 1921-25. *Member:* National Institute of Arts and Letters, American Academy of Arts and Letters, Bryn Mawr Club.

AWARDS, HONORS: Dial Award, 1924; Helen Haire Levinson Prize, 1932; Ernest Hartsock Memorial Prize, 1935; Shelley Memorial Award, 1941; Contemporary Poetry's Patrons Prize, 1944; Harriet Monroe Poetry Award, 1944; Guggenheim Memorial fellowship, 1945; National Institute of Arts and Letters grant in literature, 1946, gold medal, 1953; National Book Award for poetry and Pulitzer Prize in poetry, 1952, for *Collected Poems;* Bollingen Prize in poetry, Yale University, 1953, for *Collected Poems;* M. Carey Thomas Award, 1953; Poetry Society of America gold medal award, 1960, 1967; Brandeis Award for Poetry, 1963; Academy of American Poets fellowship, 1965, for distinguished poetic achievement over a period of more than four decades; MacDowell medal, 1967; named chevalier of the Legion of Honor, Order of Arts and Letters; named woman of achievement, American Association of University Women, 1968. Honorary degrees: Litt.D. from Wilson College, 1949, Mount Holyoke College, 1950, University of Rochester, 1951, Dickinson College, 1952, Long Island University, 1953, New York University, 1967, St. John's University, 1968, and Princeton University, 1968; L.H.D. from Rutgers University, 1955, Smith College, 1955, and Pratt Institute, 1958.

WRITINGS—Poetry: *Poems,* Egoist Press, 1921, published with additions as *Observations,* Dial, 1924; *Selected Poems,* introduction by T. S. Eliot, Macmillan, 1935; *Pangolin, and Other Verse: Five Poems,* Brendin, 1936; *What Are Years, and Other Poems,* Macmillan, 1941; *Nevertheless,* Macmillan, 1944; *Collected Poems,* Macmillan, 1951; *Like a Bulwark,* Viking, 1956; *O to Be a Dragon,* Viking, 1959; *A Marianne Moore Reader,* Viking, 1961; *The Arctic Ox,* Faber, 1964; *A Talisman,* Adams House, 1965; *Tell Me, Tell Me: Granite, Steel, and Other Topics* (poetry and prose), Viking, 1966; *The Complete Poems of Marianne Moore,* Macmillan, 1967; *Selected Poems,* Faber, 1969; *Unfinished Poems,* P. H. and A.S.W. Rosenbach Foundation, 1972.

Other: (Co-translator) A. Stifter, *Rock Crystal,* Pantheon, 1945; (translator) *Selected Fables of La Fontaine,* Faber, 1955, revised edition, Viking, 1964; *Predilections* (essays and reviews), Viking, 1955; *Letters from and to the Ford Motor Company,* Pierpont Morgan Library, 1958 (first appeared in *New Yorker,* April 13, 1957); (compiler with others) *Riverside Poetry Three: An Anthology of Student Poetry,* Twayne, 1958; *Idiosyncrasy and Technique: Two Lectures,* University of California Press, 1958; *The Absentee: A Comedy in Four Acts* (play; based on Maria Edgeworth's novel of the same name), House of Books, 1962; (contributor) *Poetry in Crystal,* Spiral Press, 1963; *Puss in Boots, The Sleeping Beauty, and Cinderella* (a retelling of three fairy tales based on the French tales of Charles Perrault), illustrated by Eugene Karlin, Macmillan, 1963; (contributor) A. K. Weatherhead, *The Edge of the Image,* University of Washington Press, 1968; *The Accented Syllable,* Albondocani Press, 1969 (first appeared in *The Egoist,* Octo-

ber, 1916); (contributor) *Homage to Henry James,* Appel, 1971.

Poetry; published in limited editions: *Eight Poems,* illustrations by Robert Andrew Parker, New York Museum of Modern Art, 1962; *Occasionem cognosce,* Stinehour Press, 1963; *Dress and Kindred Subjects,* Ibex Press, 1965; *Le mariage . . . ,* Ibex Press, 1965; *Poetry and Criticism,* privately printed, 1965; *Silence,* L. H. Scott, 1965; *Tippoo's Tiger,* Phoenix Book Shop, 1967. Contributor of articles, essays, and verse to numerous magazines. *The Dial,* acting editor, 1926-29, editor, 1929.

SIDELIGHTS: Marianne Moore once told an interviewer for the *New York Times:* "Poetry. I, too, dislike it: There are things that are important beyond all this fiddle. [But,] if you demand on the one hand/the raw material of poetry in/all its rawness and/that which is on the other hand/genuine, then you are interested in poetry."

Moore continued: "I don't call anything I have ever written poetry. In fact, the only reason I know for calling my work poetry at all is that there is no other category in which to put it. I'm a happy hack as a writer.... I never knew anyone with a passion for words who had as much difficulty in saying things as I do. I seldom say them in a manner I like. Each poem I think will be the last. But something always comes up and catches my fancy."

In spite of Moore's rather humble thoughts, many critics believe in the significance of her poetry. For example, John Ashbery glowed: "I am tempted simply to call her our greatest modern poet. This despite the obvious grandeur of her chief competitors, including Wallace Stevens and William Carlos Williams. It seems we can never remind ourselves too often that universality and depth are not the same thing. Marianne Moore has no 'Arma virumque cano' prefacing her work: She even avoids formal beginnings altogether by running the first line in as a continuation of the title. But her work will, I think, continue to be read as poetry when much of the major poetry of our time has become part of the history of literature."

Ashbery isn't alone in his praise of Moore's poetry; James Dickey wrote: "Each of her poems employs items that Ms. Moore similarly encountered and to which she gave a new, Mooreian existence in a new cosmos of consequential relationships. What seems to me to be the most valuable point about Ms. Moore is that such receptivity as hers . . . is not Ms. Moore's exclusive property. Every poem of hers lifts us toward our own discovery-prone lives. It does not state, in effect, that I am more intelligent than you, more creative because I found this item and used it and you didn't. It seems to say, rather, I found this, and what did you find? Or, a better, what can you find?"

Nation critic, Sandra Hochman agreed: "The art of Marianne Moore is not just the valuable art of observation. She is magical. Her poems do have riddles. They can irk us. But they finally carry us forward by the strength of language and, in her own words, the poet's 'burning desire to be explicit.' Nothing is wasted. All is transformed."

It is this desire that underlies Moore's poetry. James Dickey explained that "Ms. Moore tells us that facts make her feel 'profoundly grateful.' This is because knowledge, for her, is not power but love, and in loving it is important to know what you love, as widely and as deeply and as well as possible. In paying so very much attention to the things of this earth that she encounters, or that encounter her, Ms. Moore urges us to do the same, and thus gives us back, in strict syllables, the selves that we had contrived to lose. She persuades us that the human mind is nothing more than an organ for loving things in both complicated and blindingly simple ways, and is organized so as to be able to love in an unlimited number of fashions and for an unlimited number of reasons. This seems to me to constitute the correct poetic attitude, which is essentially a life-attitude, for it stands forever against the notion that the earth is an apathetic limbo lost in space.''

As Ms. Moore herself explained to Howard Nemerov: ''I am . . . much aware of the world's dilemma. People's effect on other people results, it seems to me, in an enforced sense of responsibility—a compulsory obligation to participate in others' problems.''

Marianne Moore is almost as famous for her practice of rewriting her previously published poems as for her poetry itself. This practice has often disturbed many of her followers. Jean Garrigrie explained: ''Poets who revise their poems are apt to incur surprise or weak query (a guise of protest) from those who have long ago fallen in love with that 'one and only,' the original. The poet, patient about perfection, has a right to be impatient with such resistance. But there it is. And a good deal is involved. A line taken out of a poem sparingly built in the first place, that line's removal subtly alters the whole in tone. An 'excess' excised—a qualifying extension or elaboration—complicated one's responses, for one is busy dismissing and it takes time to adjust to the revision. What is being felt is the absence, almost as much as the new presence.''

And Anthony Hecht once wrote that as ''an admiring reader I feel that I have some rights in [this] matter. Her poems are partly mine, now, and I delight in them because they exhibit a mind of great fastidiousness, a delicate and cunning moral sensibility, a tact, a decorum, a rectitude, and finally and most movingly, a capacity for pure praise that has absolutely biblical awe in it. She (and Mr. Auden, too, as it will appear) however much I may wish to take exception to the changes they have made, have provided a field day for Ph.D. candidates for years to come, who can collate versions and come up with theories about why the changes were made.''

AVOCATIONAL INTERESTS: Baseball.

BIOGRAPHICAL/CRITICAL SOURCES: Poetry, April, 1925, May, 1960; Randall Jarrell, *Poetry and the Age,* Knopf, 1953; *New York Times Book Review,* May 16, 1954, October 4, 1959, December 3, 1961, December 25, 1966, March 14, 1967, November 26, 1967; *New Yorker,* February 16, 1957, April 13, 1957, November 28, 1959, January 29, 1966, October 16, 1978; *New Republic,* January 4, 1960; *Atlantic,* February, 1962; *Esquire,* July, 1962; Bernard F. Engel, *Marianne Moore,* Twayne, 1964; *New York Times,* June 3, 1965, July 13, 1965, February 6, 1972; M. L. Rosenthal, *The Modern Poets,* Oxford University Press, 1965; *McCall's,* December, 1965; Howard Nemerov, *Poets on Poetry,* Basic Books, 1966; *Newsweek,* January 2, 1967; *Life,* January 13, 1967; *Nation,* May 8, 1967; *New Leader,* December 4, 1967; *New Republic,* February 24, 1968; *Washington Post,* March 16, 1968, February 7, 1972; *Hudson Review,* spring, 1968; *Detroit News,* February 6, 1972; *Publishers Weekly,* February 14, 1972; *Contemporary Literary Criticism,* Gale, Volume I, 1973, Volume II, 1974, Volume IV, 1975, Volume VIII, 1977, Volume X, 1979, Volume XIII, 1980; *Harper's,* May, 1977; P. W. Hadas, *Marianne Moore: Poet of Affection,* Syracuse University Press, 1977; L. Stapleton, *Marianne Moore,* Princeton University Press, 1978.†

—*Sketch by Margaret Mazurkiewicz*

MOORE, Rosalie (Gertrude) 1910-
(Rosalie Brown)

PERSONAL: Born October 8, 1910, in Oakland, Calif.; daughter of Marvin Alonzo (a railroad man) and Teresa (a teacher; maiden name Woolridge) Moore; married William Louis Brown (a writer), June 30, 1942 (died, September, 1964); children: Deborah Ann Turrietta, Celia Jeanne Barrett, Camas Eve Timmel. *Education:* University of California, A.B. (magna cum laude), 1932, M.A., 1934. *Home:* 476 Cane St., No. 5, Larkspur, Calif. 94939. *Agent:* McIntosh & Otis, Inc., 18 East 41st St., New York, N.Y. 10017.

CAREER: KLX (radio station), Oakland, Calif., copywriter and announcer, 1935-37; Mexico City College, Mexico City, Mexico, lecturer in creative criticism of contemporary literature, 1950; College of Marin, Kentfield, Calif., member of communications department, 1965-76, chairman of department, 1974-75; piano teacher and writer. Founder, with Lawrence Hart and Jeanne McGahey, of Activist Group of poets, under aegis of Lawrence Hart. *Member:* Poetry Society of America, Common Cause, University of California Alumni, Phi Beta Kappa. *Awards, honors:* Charles H. Sergel Drama Prize, University of Chicago, 1938, for poetic drama; award for best poems, New York World's Fair, 1939; Albert Bender Award in literature, 1943; first award, Poetry Society of America, 1944; Yale Series of Younger Poets Award, 1948; Guggenheim fellowships in creative writing (poetry), 1950-51, 1951-52; Vachel Lindsay Award, *Poetry* magazine, 1957; Pulitzer Prize nomination, 1977, for *Year of the Children.*

WRITINGS—Juvenile books with husband under names Bill Brown and Rosalie Brown; published by Coward, except as indicated: *Forest Fireman,* 1956; *Whistle Punk,* 1956; *Boy Who Got Mailed,* 1957; *Big Rig,* 1959; *Department Store Ghost,* 1961; *Tickley and the Fox,* Lantern, 1962; *The Hippopotamus That Wanted to Be a Baby,* Lantern, 1963. Also contributor to school readers.

Poetry under name Rosalie Moore: *The Grasshopper's Man and Other Poems,* with introduction by W. H. Auden, Yale University Press, 1949; *Year of the Children,* Woolmer/Brotherson, 1977; *Of Singles and Doubles: Collected Poems, 1952-1978,* Woolmer/Brotherson, 1979. Poetry anthologized in: *Mark in Time,* Glide Publishers, 1971; *Rising Tides,* Simon & Schuster, 1973; *Woman Poet,* Women-in-Literature, Inc., 1980. Contributor to *New Yorker, Saturday Review, Accent, Poetry, Furioso, Chicago Tribune, American Poetry Review,* and other publications.

WORK IN PROGRESS: The Gutenberg Explosion.

SIDELIGHTS: Rosalie Moore told *CA:* ''I loved writing the children's books in the 1950's when my children were growing up. But after the death of my husband I returned mainly to the writing of poetry, producing another poetic drama and a book-lenghth narrative on a theme to which I had long been committed: the Children's Crusade in Europe in 1212. The crusade brings up the questions: 'How to preserve (or civilize?) the wild child in each of us?' and 'Are children sold out by adults, or even by ourselves as adults?' Teaching for the first time in the Communications Department at the College of Marin in California brought me in touch with hundreds of fast-developing, sometimes idealistic-sometimes 'subversive,' but almost always fast-growing, deeply thinking, young people. And when I went to France on a sabbatical leave in 1972 (finally!) to see the places involved in the thirteenth century events and do research, I began to find many parallels with our 1960's. I don't believe I gave any overt 'answers' in *Year of the Children* (the answers in poetry are built-in, implied, re-experienced if the work is internalized), but I *was* able to identify with the teen-age leader of the French children, Etienne, and show, or try to, what it was like to grow up, to try to change things, in Europe in the Middle Ages during a time of fracture, of breaking away, of discovery and danger. Now that I am expecting a grandchild (Camas and Michael Timmel are the parents) maybe I will get ideas for children's books or poems again.''

*   *   *

MORGAN, Arthur Ernest   1878-1975

PERSONAL: Born June 20, 1878, in Cincinnati, Ohio; died November 16, 1975, in Xenia, Ohio; son of John D. and Anna Frances (Wiley) Morgan; married Urania T. Jones, 1904 (died, 1905); married Lucy Griscom, June 6, 1911; children: (first marriage) Ernest; (second marriage) Griscom, Frances (Mrs. Landrum Bolling), Lucy (deceased), Hilda (Mrs. Bruce Duncan). *Education:* Attended University of Colorado, 1898. *Religion:* Quaker.

CAREER: Civil engineer in private practice, St. Cloud, Minn., 1902-07; supervising engineer of drainage investigations, U.S. Department of Agriculture, 1907-10; Morgan Engineering Co., Memphis, Tenn., president, 1910-15; Dayton Morgan Engineering Co., Dayton, Ohio, president, 1915-35; Antioch College, Yellow Springs, Ohio, president, 1920-36; Tennessee Valley Authority, Washington, D.C., chairman, 1933-38; Community Service, Inc., Yellow Springs, Ohio, president, beginning 1940. Consulting engineer throughout United States, and in India and Africa; planned and directed construction of more than fifty water control projects. American Friends Service Committee representative in Mexico, 1938, and Finland, 1947; member, Government of India Universities Commission, 1947-48; Chairman of Ohio Legislature committee to consolidate the natural resources functions of the state, 1947-48; arbitrator between U.S. Steel Corp. and U.S. Steel workers, 1947-48.

MEMBER: Progressive Education Association (president, 1921), American Unitarian Association (vice-president, 1925), American Society of Civil Engineers (honorary member; vice-president, 1927), American Association for Advancement of Science (fellow). *Awards, honors:* D.Sc., University of Colorado, 1923; D.Eng., Case School of Applied Sciences (now Case Western Reserve University), 1932; D.Sc., University of North Carolina, 1937; LL.D., Antioch College, 1943.

WRITINGS: My World, Kahoe, 1927; *Purpose and Circumstance,* Kahoe, 1928; *Compendium of Antioch Notes,* Kahoe, 1930; *The Seed Man,* Antioch, 1933; *The Long Road,* National Home Library, 1936, 2nd edition, Community Service, 1962; *The Small Community,* Harper, 1942; *Edward Bellamy: A Biography,* Columbia University Press, 1944; *Philosophy of Edward Bellamy,* King's Crown, 1945, reprinted, Hyperion Press (Westport, Conn.), 1979; *Plagiarism in Utopia,* Arthur E. Morgan, 1946; *Nowhere Was Somewhere: How History Makes Utopias and Utopias Make History,* University of North Carolina Press, 1946, reprinted, Greenwood Press, 1976; *A Business of My Own,* Community Service, 1946; *Higher Education in Relation to Rural India,* Hindustani Talami Sangh, 1950; *Industries for Small Communities,* Community Service, 1953; *Search for Purpose,* Antioch, 1955; *The Idea of a Rural University,* Hindustani Talami Sangh, 1955; *The Community of the Future,* Community Service, 1957; *It Can Be Done in Education,* Community Service, 1962; *The Biological Origin of Pleasure and Pain,* Community Service, 1963; *Observations,* Antioch Press, 1968; *Dams and Other Disasters,* Sargent, 1971; *The Making of the T.V.A.,* Prometheus Books, 1974. Editor or director, *Community Service News,* 1944-55, and *Community Comments,* 1955-70.

WORK IN PROGRESS: Collected papers; a philosophy of education.

SIDELIGHTS: Arthur E. Morgan served as the first chairman of the Tennessee Valley Authority.†

*   *   *

MORGAN, Edwin (George)   1920-

PERSONAL: Born April 27, 1920, in Glasgow, Scotland. *Education:* University of Glasgow, M.A., 1947. *Home:* 19 Whittingehame Ct., Glasgow G12 OBG, Scotland.

CAREER: University of Glasgow, Glasgow, Scotland, assistant lecturer, 1947-50, lecturer, 1950-65, senior lecturer, 1965-71, reader, 1971-75, titular professor of English, 1975-80. *Military service:* Royal Army Medical Corps, 1940-46. *Awards, honors:* Cholmondeley Award, 1968; Scottish Arts Council award, 1969, 1973; P.E.N. Memorial Award, 1972.

WRITINGS: Essays, Carcanet Press, 1974; *Hugh MacDiarmid,* Longman, 1976.

Poetry: *The Vision of Cathkin Braes,* Maclellan, 1952; *The Cape of Good Hope,* Peter Russell, 1955; *Starryveldt,* Gomsinger Press (Frauenfeld, Switzerland), 1965; *Scotch Mist,* Renegade Press (Cleveland), 1965; *Sealwear,* Gold Seal Press (Glasgow), 1966; *Emergent Poems,* Hansjorg Mayer (Stuttgart), 1967; *The Second Life,* Edinburgh University Press, 1968; *Gnomes,* Akros Publications, 1968; *Proverbfolder,* Openings Press, 1969; (with Alan Bold and Edward Brathwaite) *Penguin Modern Poets #15,* Penguin, 1969; *The Horseman's Word: A Sequence of Concrete Poems,* Akros Publications, 1970; *Twelve Songs,* Castlelaw Press, 1970; *The Dolphin's Song,* School of English Press, 1971; *Glasgow Sonnets,* Castlelaw Press, 1972; *Instamatic Poems,* Ian McKelvie, 1972; *The Whittrick: A Poem in Eight Dialogues,* Akros Publications, 1973; *From Glasgow to Saturn,* Dufour, 1973; *The New Divan,* Carcanet Press, 1977; *Colour Poems,* Third Eye Centre, 1978; *Star Gate,* Third Eye Centre, 1979.

Translator: *Beowulf: A Verse Translation into Modern English,* Hand & Flower Press, 1952, University of California Press, 1962; *Poems from Eugenio Montale,* University of Reading School of Art, 1959; *Sovpoems: Brecht, Neruda, Pasternak, Tsvetayeva, Mayakowsky, Martynov, Yevtushenko,* Migrant Press, 1961; (with David Wevill) *Sandor Weores and Ferenc Juhasz: Selected Poems,* Penguin, 1970; *Wi the Haill Voice: Poems by Mayakovsky,* Carcanet Press, 1972; *Fifty Renaissance Love Poems,* Whiteknight Press, 1975; *Rites of Passage,* Carcanet Press, 1976; *Platen: Selected Poems,* Castlelaw Press, 1978.

Editor: *Collins Albatross Book of Longer Poems: English and American Poetry from the Fourteenth Century to the Present Day,* Collins, 1963; *New English Dramatists #14,* Penguin, 1970; *Scottish Satirical Verse,* Carcanet Press, 1980. Editor, with George Bruce and Maurice Lindsay, of *Scottish Poetry,* Volumes I-VI, Edinburgh University Press, 1966-72.

WORK IN PROGRESS: An opera libretto about St. Francis of Assisi, with Kenneth Leighton.

SIDELIGHTS: Edwin Morgan has been critically acclaimed for his poetic talent, with several reviewers noting his varied and considerable skills. Writing in *World Literature Today,* Robin Fulton states that Morgan's ''highly various skills amuse, touch, baffle, and surprise us in ways that are very much his own.'' Speaking of the book *Twelve Songs*, John Fuller of *Listener* writes that Morgan's songs ''have great invention and variety, from a word-changing game on the subject of an astronautic disaster to a sexual riddle about an apple.'' A reviewer for the *Times Literary Supplement* notes that Morgan ''writes with a piercing directness and simplicity, or uses . . . mundane material and raises it to rhetoric, though not emptily.'' He also notes that ''Morgan is very much a performer, and when he fails it is through an excess of virtuosity.'' Ian Hamilton echoes this opinion in the *Observer*: ''If Morgan gives the impression of spreading his considerable gifts too wide and thin, he also persuades us that his kind of lively, ranging optimism is unconfinable to any single mode.''

BIOGRAPHICAL/CRITICAL SOURCES: Times Literary Supplement, February 15, 1968, October 14, 1977; *Observer*, May 12, 1968, February 27, 1977; *London Magazine*, July, 1968; *Scottish International*, August, 1968; *Poetry*, October, 1968, July, 1969, April, 1974, January, 1978; *Stand*, Volume X, number 4, 1969; *Listener*, December 24, 1970; *Worlds: Seven Modern Poets*, Penguin, 1974; Robin Fulton, *Contemporary Scottish Poetry*, M. Macdonald, 1974; *Nation*, March 16, 1974; *Punch*, June 8, 1977; *Listener*, August 11, 1977; *New Statesman*, September 30, 1977; *World Literature Today*, autumn, 1978.

* * *

MORGAN, Ted 1932-
(Sanche de Gramont)

PERSONAL: Original name, Sanche de Gramont; pseudonym adopted in 1973 and legalized in 1977; born March 31, 1932, in Geneva, Switzerland; came to United States in 1937, naturalized in February, 1977; son of Gabriel Armand (a diplomat) and Mariette (Negroponte) de Gramont; married second wife, Nancy Ryan (a poet), May 11, 1968 (divorced, 1980); children: (second marriage) Gabriel, Amber. *Education:* Yale University, B.A. (summa cum laude), 1954; Columbia University, M.S., 1955. *Home and office:* 178 East 93rd St., New York, N.Y. 10028. *Agent:* Carl Brandt, 101 Park Ave., New York, N.Y. 10017.

CAREER: Associated Press, New York City, reporter, 1958-59; *New York Herald Tribune*, New York City, reporter and correspondent, 1959-64; free-lance journalist and writer, 1964—. *Military service:* French Army, 1956-57; became lieutenant. *Member:* P.E.N., Authors Guild. *Awards, honors:* Pulitzer Prize, 1961, for local reporting written under pressure of a deadline.

WRITINGS—All under name Sanche de Gramont, except as indicated: *The Secret War: The Story of International Espionage since World War II*, Putnam, 1962; (editor and translator) Louis de Rouvroy, *The Age of Magnificence: Memoirs of the Duc de Saint-Simon*, Putnam, 1963; *U.S.A.*, Editions Recontre (Lausanne), 1966; *Epitaph for Kings*, Putnam, 1968; *The French: Portrait of a People* (Book-of-the-Month Club selection), Putnam, 1969; *Lives to Give*, Putnam, 1971; *The Way Up: The Memoirs of Count Gramont* (novel), Putnam, 1972; *The Strong Brown God: The Story of the Niger River*, Hart-Davis, 1975, Houghton, 1976; (under name Ted Morgan) *On Becoming American*, Houghton, 1978; (under name Ted Morgan) *Maugham*, Simon & Schuster, 1980 (published in England as *Somerset Maugham*, J. Cape, 1980); (under name Ted Morgan) *Rowing toward Eden*, Houghton, 1981. Contributor to newspapers and periodicals.

SIDELIGHTS: In 1973, Sanche de Gramont, a.k.a. Ted

Morgan, a count and a member of one of France's oldest aristocratic families, began to take steps to resolve an identity crisis that had plagued him for many years. The son of a French diplomat stationed in Washington, D.C., de Gramont had spent much of his youth in America and, after a brief stint at the Sorbonne, eventually graduated from Yale University. He then attended the Columbia University School of Journalism and, having obtained his master's degree, went to work for several different American news organizations, including the *New York Herald Tribune*. In 1962, while serving as a foreign correspondent for the *Tribune*, de Gramont was seriously wounded covering a war in Katanga. His employer and the American Embassy in Leopoldville quickly saw to it that he was taken to a London hospital for treatment; the French Embassy, on the other hand, completely ignored him.

While it took fifteen more years for him to make his choice official, de Gramont's experience in Katanga served to tilt the delicate balance between the French and American parts of his psyche squarely in favor of America. But though he subsequently married an American woman and came to feel, speak, and write ''American,'' he remained, in essence, a man without a country, estranged from both his native France and from his family. De Gramont's growing need and desire to ''belong'' to America, in a physical as well as a spiritual sense, culminated in 1973 with a decision to move from his home in Morocco to New York City in order to establish residency and become a U.S. citizen. His break with the past included a name change as well, from the noble French surname to (as he himself describes it) a ''forthright and practical, incisive and balanced'' anagram of de Gramont, Ted Morgan. Why Morgan? As *Time*'s John Skow explains, de Gramont felt that Ted Morgan was ''someone you would lend your car to. Dogs and small children would like him.''

Morgan's account of this entire process, *On Becoming American*, was fairly well-received by the critics, who praised its genial and entertaining style and tone. Writes William Manchester in the *New York Times Book Review*: ''Mr. Morgan—that is the name he prefers, and he has earned it—is a master of his trade. Interwoven with his personal history are skillful digressions: analyses of the successive waves of expatriates to these shores, of resentment of them by those already here, and of American traits, stereotypes and prospects. Although much of the material is familiar, the style is fresh, the narrative compelling.'' However, continues Manchester, ''some of [Morgan's] pledges of allegiance to his adopted country are reminiscent of the annual jingoist parades William Randolph Hearst used to stage. There is a want of discretion in such passages, a suspension of judgment that Mr. Morgan may flaunt but de Gramont would disdain. . . . Talented and ambitious, [Morgan] believes that his $25 naturalization fee was 'the bargain of the century.' It should be added that the transaction was a steal for the United States, too.''

John Skow of *Time* notes: ''Ted Morgan is a man loopy with love for his new country, and the result is a book that is both refreshing and breathless. It has been a long time since anyone serenaded the present reality of the U.S. in such a hyperbolic manner. . . . But passion does not improve the reasoning process, and when the author supports his arguments with windy civics lectures and careless unravelings from U.S. history, he can be more provocative than illuminating. . . . Still, the book is so amiable and loose-jointed, perhaps like the U.S. itself, that the reader is happy to wade through balderdash to the next bit of good storytelling or good sense.''

The *New York Times'* Christopher Lehmann-Haupt calls *On Becoming American* ''a book so full of opinions, anecdotes, gossip, peeves, celebrations, free associations, epiphanies, asides, lists, definitions, prejudices, warnings, and reflections that when you hold it up to your ear and shake it, you can practically hear it rattle.... It is fun. It is flattering. It is crisply written—more concise and punchy, it seems to me, than any of the seven books Mr. Morgan wrote when he was Sanche de Gramont.... I only wish he'd included a bibliography, to tell us where he gleaned so much of his entertaining information. And I wish he'd put a little more emphasis on the advantages of his disadvantage. Having been born and partly raised a foreigner, he is able to see American whole in a way that few who have grown up here can do.''

Some reviewers find Morgan's failure to discuss the advantages of his situation to be an inexcusable flaw rather than just a cause for regret; they consider it presumptuous of him to equate his personal experience with that of all other immigrants. Henry Fairlie, for example, a British writer who has resided in the United States for many years, comments in the *Washington Post Book World* that *On Becoming American* is not only ''shallow and lightweight'' but ''unlikable.'' He writes: ''There is some difference between coming steerage across the Atlantic and coming as people like Gramont and myself, and I am not sure that we can claim to become American when in the last resort we have so little at stake.... From the sunshine of Morocco to the sunshine of California is not the obvious way of knowing what it means to be American. [Morgan] seems to think that changing his name reflects the same experience as a Ukrainian Jew changing his name on arrival at New York harbor. This is not foolish; it is offensive.'' Furthermore, notes Fairlie, though the book contains ''little gobbets of American history,'' there is ''no sense that America is now an old country, and that its historical experience is not easily accessible to the outsider.... [Morgan] has no feel for the rhythm of American life.''

Frederick E. Hoxie of the *Antioch Review* claims that ''Morgan's general observations on American character are superficial and (surprisingly, coming from someone enamored of the country) quite detached.... In addition, descriptions of historical events are not always accurate.... But it is the detached quality of the author's observations that is most striking. The man who has written a book which the dust jacket promises will tell us 'what it means' to be an American doesn't seem to have talked with anyone outside of Palo Alto and New York City's Upper East Side.''

A *Best Sellers* critic characterizes *On Becoming American* as a book that describes a nation ''in which almost everything seems to be perfect or perfectly rationalized.... All in all, there are incisive observations here and there, amusing details and curiosities to pay for the effort of the reader to push through all the balderdash, and there is a definite freshness of approach commonly lacking in most authors who have seen America without the advantage of a foreign perspective.'' Nevertheless, the reviewer concludes, Morgan ''*is not* the typical or average American immigrant.... He is an identity seeker in a bicultural schizophrenia.''

Finally, Jane Larkin Crain of the *Saturday Review* writes: ''With unabashed enthusiasm, Morgan celebrates his adopted country in [*On Becoming American*], although there is enough of the acute and skeptical journalist left in 'Citizen Morgan' to save him from softheadedness or sentimentali-

ty.... Altogether, Morgan's eagerness to defy current conventions of American anti-Americanism, to affirm social progress on numerous fronts, is refreshing, and many of his reflections and assessments are witty, cogent, and engrossing. But there is also about this book a regrettable tendency toward breezy and reductive formulations that undermine its ultimate seriousness.... In these instances and elsewhere—particularly in his recurring and routine denunciations of Richard Nixon, of the history of American anti-communism, of America's involvement in Vietnam, and of the chicanery of the business community—Morgan seems to have borrowed his attitudes and assumptions wholesale from shopworn conventional wisdom, making jejune and facile pronouncements on matters of weight and controversy. Perhaps because Morgan seems not really to have come to terms with his own occasionally contradictory readings of the American experience, his book lacks the consistent focus that would have given it thematic energy and coherence.'' Yet despite these objections, concludes Crain, ''*On Becoming American* is so lively and textured a production that one winds up regretting rather than scorning its shortcomings.''

While spending his morning writing *On Becoming American,* Morgan devoted his afternoons to another major nonfiction project—a biography of W. Somerset Maugham, the popular English novelist who had specifically instructed in his will that no one ever was to have permission to publish his letters or write his biography. While this decree seemed to present a rather formidable obstacle to any potential biographer, Morgan, after discovering that a full-scale study of the author's life did not exist, overcame his initial hesitation and agreed to follow his publisher's suggestion and tackle the Maugham project. Explaining the reason for his acceptance to a *Chicago Tribune Book World* interviewer, Morgan remarked, ''for once in my life, I wanted to do something that would be definitive.''

Morgan, however, did not bargain on the resistance he would encounter in the person of Spencer Curtis Brown, Maugham's agent and literary executor. Though he was already well into the book when he first met Curtis Brown, Morgan was told not to expect any cooperation from the executor or from Maugham's family. Stubbornly committed to continuing the biography, Morgan persisted and eventually got Curtis Brown to at least agree to read the first half of the manuscript when it was ready. Meanwhile, the former newspaperman went ahead with his research, interviewing old associates of Maugham's and visiting twenty libraries from California to England in an attempt to gather information from 5,000 letters the novelist's friends had refused to destroy.

The first half of his manuscript complete, Morgan, as promised, sent a copy to Curtis Brown. In return, Curtis Brown sent a letter to Morgan pointing out errors and offering suggestions, concluding his critique with an expression of his desire to see the second half when it had been completed. Encouraged by this remark, Morgan continued his research with renewed energy, gradually gaining access to more and more material not under Curtis Brown's direct control.

Despite his hard work, however, large gaps remained in Morgan's study of Maugham, especially regarding the elderly novelist's bitter break with his daughter. Submitting a first draft of the biography to the executor, Morgan was pleased to learn that Curtis Brown considered the work to be a ''nonjudgmental'' and scrupulously researched account of Maugham's life. Finally, realizing that it would be impossible to prevent the eventual appearance of a major biography of the author, Curtis Brown decided that it was better to disregard his client's last wishes than to allow an incomplete and inaccurate portrayal to be published. As a result, Morgan was granted estate approval and even received an invitation from Maugham's family to come to England for an interview.

The *Washington Post*'s Michael Kernan calls the resulting biography, *Maugham,* a "compulsively readable" book and "a masterful job of reportage" that "brings into full view a complicated man who went out of his way to distort, conceal and deliberately lie about the facts of his life." *Time* describes it as "by far the most detailed, balanced and tolerant portrait available [of Maugham]" in which Morgan "builds a sound psychological case for Maugham's character and behavior.... The book covers the minutiae of 91 years so thoroughly that a subsequent biography is unlikely."

Christopher Lehmann-Haupt of the *New York Times* writes: "There must be a thousand characters in Ted Morgan's monumental biography of W. Somerset Maugham, and at least 100 meals consumed. So there are moments when you fear the text is about to bog down in trivia. But Mr. Morgan ... never fails to fetch your attention back with some marvelous detail.... So one dare not skip a word of [his] text. And just as well, for it is an amazing account he has put together of all that Maugham was.... It is also an extraordinary job of research Mr. Morgan has done.... Such a wealth of psychological data is presented in this book that it would be reductive to impose one reader's explanation of Maugham. To do so would be to make of a life a diagram. And to Mr. Morgan's great credit, he has made of *Maugham* a life of stature. Quite an ugly life, but heroic nonetheless."

Two British critics, Victoria Glendinning of the *Times Literary Supplement* and Michael Ratcliffe of the *London Times,* basically agree with their American counterparts, but both make the observation that *Maugham* was obviously written by an American for an American audience. For example, though Glendinning finds the biography "extraordinarily compelling," she remarks that the inclusion of vast amounts of trivial detail not directly related to Maugham's life identifies Morgan as a member of "the *Annual Register* school of biography." In addition, she notes, "the index is imperfect, there are misprints or misspellings in proper names, and [the author exhibits an] occasional wild flight of fancy.... Most of the mistakes Mr. Morgan makes are those of innocence and unfamiliarity. He is American, and English social history is a minefield. Behaviour or circumstances that he finds extraordinary or noteworthy are very often, in context, neither." Ratcliffe also tempers his praise with comments about Morgan's exhaustive display of factual information. Claiming such diligence is a typically American characteristic, Ratcliffe criticizes Morgan for not being able to "resist putting every bit of [background research] in—including much information familiar to English readers, some of which is not strictly true ... and some of which is not true at all."

The *New York Times Book Review*'s Margaret Drabble sees other kinds of deficiencies in Morgan's biography. She calls *Maugham* "a sad tale, a Maughamesque story in its own right, rising almost despite itself to a certain tragic dignity. [It] is an extremely interesting biography, but it shares many of the faults as well as the virtues of its subject. Like Maugham, Mr. Morgan is no stylist; he writes inelegantly, relays apocryphal jokes, quotes gossip as though it were fact, is immemsely repetitive and loves to explain the obvious.... When in the mood to defend Maugham as a stylist, he chooses to quote a depressing chunk of prose ... that hardly

makes his point. And when he attempts psychological analysis, the results are disastrous."

Despite these objections, the critic goes on to note that "Mr. Morgan gives us an unexpurgated account of literary life from the turn of the century ... to the 1960s, and he goes to some trouble to fill in background events, to give a sense of historical perspective.... Even the dubious stories have their own interest.... The result is much less distasteful than it might sound, for there is something innocent in Mr. Morgan's omnivorous appetite for gossip.... [He] is not partisan. He is a good raconteur, a curious investigator, and rarely tries to be more." In short, Drabble concludes, "[Morgan] provides enough raw material for us to indulge in our own speculation. And his conclusion, despite the fact that he has during his 700 pages revealed his subject in almost every conceivable attitude of fear, meanness, spite, indignity and rage, is oddly and convincingly respectful."

On the other hand, Harold Acton, writing in the *Washington Post Book World,* feels that Morgan's conclusion is just the opposite. Noting that the author's "moral judgment is implicit in the narrative" and that "it is definitely a harsh one," Acton reports: "Every wrinkle of the dear old crocodile is emphasized with gusto.... In his eagerness to squeeze the juicy orange dry Morgan swamps the reader in irrelevant details and digressions.... He has imparted every scrap he could pick up about Maugham's unhappy marriage and his sexual inclinations.... Having accumulated such a heterogeneous mass of material Morgan could not bear to sift it with his muckrake. Everything is said twice over and heavily underlined. Altogether his anti-hero is depicted as a most unpleasant character."

Daniel J. Cahill of the *Chicago Tribune Book World* attributes most of Morgan's fascination with such information to his background in journalism. He feels that Morgan "brings to the art of literary biography the reporter's eye for catastrophic event and bizarre details. In his hands, Maugham is an admirable subject, with the right degree of scandal and eclat for a far too journalistic rendition of a long and complex life. But Morgan does unfold in a clear, direct narrative the life story that Somerset Maugham desperately hoped would never be written.... Faithful to his plan of comprehensive biography, 'to see a man and all his defects,' Morgan chronicles Maugham's declining years into his 80s and 90s—years of strife and loneliness and bitter recriminations against the memory of his dead wife, closing with a final period of senility. The final impression is that this portrait of Maugham is an extraordinarily ungenerous one. In spite of disclaimers, Morgan concentrates more upon the 'man who suffered' and less upon the 'mind which created.' Morgan's book is not in the tradition of the art of biography that illuminates a life by the power of its perception and psychological understanding. Without a doubt, Morgan's study is a fascinating revelation and will be used for another—more judicious—evaluation of Maugham."

BIOGRAPHICAL/CRITICAL SOURCES: Diacritics, January, 1973; *Saturday Review,* February 4, 1978; *Time,* March 20, 1978, March 10, 1980; *Washington Post Book World,* March 26, 1978, March 2, 1980; *New York Times Book Review,* April 2, 1978, March 9, 1980; *Newsweek,* April 3, 1978; *New Leader,* April 10, 1978; *New York Times,* April 11, 1978, March 9, 1980; *Best Sellers,* July, 1978; *Antioch Review,* fall, 1978; *Los Angeles Times Book Review,* March 30, 1980; *Chicago Tribune Book World,* March 30, 1980; *Washington Post,* April 18, 1980; *London Times,* April 24, 1980; *Times Literary Supplement,* April 25, 1980.

—*Sketch by Deborah A. Straub*

MORRISS, Frank 1923-

PERSONAL: Born March 28, 1923, in Pasadena, Calif.; son of B(un) Gerard (an architect) and Regina (Spann) Morriss; married Mary Rita Moynihan, February 11, 1950; children: Patricia, Mary Ellen, Regina, Gerard. *Education:* Regis College (Denver, Colo.), B.S., 1943; Catholic University, graduate study, 1946; Georgetown University, J.D., 1948; Denver University, graduate study, 1950-52. *Politics:* Conservative. *Religion:* Catholic. *Home:* 3505 Owens St., Wheat Ridge, Colo. *Office:* 1225 Wazee St., Denver, Colo.

CAREER: Register System of Newspapers, Denver, Colo., associate editor, 1949-60; Regis College, Denver, instructor, 1955-61, lecturer in English, 1960-61; Loretto Heights College, Denver, instructor in English and philosophy, 1956-61; St. Michael's College, Winooski Park, Vt., assistant debate coach and instructor in English, 1961-63; *Vermont Catholic Tribune,* Burlington, associate editor, 1961-63; *Register,* Denver, editor of national edition, beginning 1963; free-lance writer, 1967—. *Military service:* U.S. Army, served in South Pacific, Philippine Islands, and Japan, 1943-45; became staff sergeant; received South Pacific campaign ribbons.

WRITINGS—Published by Bruce Publishing, except as indicated: *Boy of Philadelphia,* 1955; *The Adventures of Broken Hand,* 1957; *Alfred of Wessex,* 1959; *Submarine Pioneer: John Philip Holland,* 1961; *Saints for the Small,* 1964; *The Forgotten Revelation,* Franciscan Herald Press, 1964; *The Conservative Imperative,* Catholic Laymen of America, 1965; *The Divine Epic,* Prow Press, 1969; *A Neglected Glory,* Teskey-Sugden, 1976; (with John Gawey) *Catholic Perspectives: Abortion,* Thomas More Press, 1979; *The Catholic as Citizen,* Franciscan Herald, 1979. Contributor to Catholic publications. Founding editor, *Twin Circle,* 1966; contributing editor, *Wanderer.*

WORK IN PROGRESS: The Book of Mary; an anthology of Christmas stories.

SIDELIGHTS: Frank Morriss told *CA:* "Although it sounds stuffy, opinion writing is a way to attempt a more or less permanent contribution to the good of culture or society, or whatever one deems to call it. That contribution, being yours, will be utterly unique—something only you can provide. The vocation or talent to do this was given you, and the failure to use it is to betray that gift. For a writer to write is an obligation, not a compulsion, as so many insist. It can be resisted, as so many resist the use of their abilities. It is not success that should be heralded, but the attempt. Success is usually an accident, but the attempt is one's free choice."

*   *   *

MORSBERGER, Robert Eustis 1929-

PERSONAL: Born September 10, 1929, in Baltimore, Md.; son of Eustis Espey (a printer) and Mary (Burgess) Morsberger; married Katherine Miller, June 17, 1955; children: Grace Anne. *Education:* Johns Hopkins University, B.A., 1950; State University of Iowa, M.A., 1954; Ph.D., 1956. *Politics:* Democrat. *Religion:* Protestant Episcopalian. *Home:* 1530 Berea Ct., Claremont, Calif. 91711. *Office:* Department of English, California State Polytechnic University, Pomona, Calif. 91766.

CAREER: Miami University, Oxford, Ohio, instructor and assistant professor, 1956-59; Utah State University, Logan, assistant professor, 1959-61; Michigan State University, East Lansing, assistant professor, 1961-64, associate professor of American thought and language, 1964-68; Eastern Kentucky University, Richmond, professor of English,

1968-69; California State Polytechnic University, Pomona, professor of English, 1969—, chairman of department, 1974-78. Visiting professor and acting head of English department, University of Nigeria, 1964-66; member of National American Studies faculty, Globeville Project, 1973. Seasonal park ranger at Mount Rainier National Park, 1962, and seasonal ranger and historian at Great Smoky Mountains National Park, 1963, 1964, 1969, 1970, 1971, 1973. *Military service:* U.S. Army, 1951-53.

WRITINGS: How to Improve Your Verbal Skills, Crowell, 1963; *The Language of Composition,* Crowell, 1964; *James Thurber,* Twayne, 1964; *Commonsense Grammar and Style,* Crowell, 1965; *Swordplay and the Elizabethan and Jacobean Stage,* University of Salzburg, 1974; (editor) John Steinbeck, *Viva Zapata!* (screenplay), Viking, 1975; (with Katharine M. Morsberger) *Lew Wallace: Militant Romantic,* McGraw, 1980; (editor) *American Screenwriters,* Volume I, Gale, 1981. Contributor of chapters to books. Contributor of articles to *New England Quarterly, American Literature, Steinbeck Quarterly, Journal of Popular Culture,* and other publications.

WORK IN PROGRESS: A historical novel set in the sixteenth century.

SIDELIGHTS: Robert Eustis Morsberger told *CA:* "Whether writing literary criticism, history, or fiction, I make a special point of writing clear prose and avoiding any sort of jargon, academic or otherwise. To me, the worst fault in writing and in thought is a high degree of abstraction; I like to provide as precise detail as possible. The venerable idea that literature should 'delight and instruct' cannot be improved on; literature is to be enjoyed, and I deplore the sort of criticism that seems joylessly abstract and coldly theoretical. At the same time, a writer must do his homework; *Lew Wallace: Militant Romantic* is the result of thirteen years of research and writing."

AVOCATIONAL INTERESTS: Acting, play-going, old movies, photography, fencing, playing the harmonica and autoharp.

*   *   *

MORTON, Frederic 1924-

PERSONAL: Born October 5, 1924, in Vienna, Austria; came to United States in 1943; son of Frank (a manufacturer of metal goods) and Rose (Ungvary) Morton; married Marcia Colman, 1957; children: one daughter. *Education:* College of the City of New York (now City College of the City University of New York), B.S., 1947; New School for Social Research, M.A., 1949. *Agent:* Sterling Lord Agency, 660 Madison Ave., New York, N.Y. 10021.

CAREER: Lecturer in English and creative writing at University of Utah, New York University, University of Southern California, Johns Hopkins University, and New School for Social Research, 1951-59; free-lance writer, 1959—. *Member:* Authors League, P.E.N. (executive board member). *Awards, honors:* Yaddo residence fellowship, 1951; Columbia University fellowship, 1955; National Book Award nomination, National Institute of Arts and Letters, 1962, and Author of the Year award, National Anti-Defamation League, 1963, both for *The Rothschilds;* American Book Award nomination in general nonfiction, 1980, for *A Nervous Splendor: Vienna, 1888-1889.*

WRITINGS—Novels: *The Hound,* Dodd, 1947; *The Darkness Below,* Crown, 1949; *Asphalt and Desire,* Harcourt, 1952; *The Witching Ship,* Random House, 1960; *The Schat-*

ten Affair, Atheneum, 1965; *Snow Gods*, World Publishing, 1968; *An Unknown Woman*, Atlantic-Little, Brown, 1976.

Nonfiction: *The Rothschilds* (biography), Atheneum, 1962; *A Nervous Splendor: Vienna, 1888-1889* (history), Atlantic-Little, Brown, 1979.

Work anthologized in *Best American Short Stories of 1965*. Contributor of articles and short stories to *Holiday, Atlantic, Esquire, Reporter, Nation,* and *New York Times Book Review*.

SIDELIGHTS: Fleeing Austria after its annexation by Hitler, Frederic Morton lived first in England and then in America. He worked in a bakery and took a B.A. in chemistry with the idea of someday running a bakery. When his first novel won the Dodd Mead Intercollegiate Literary Prize, Morton abandoned a baking career in favor of an academic and literary one. During the fifties, he taught at various colleges while selling his free-lance writing to magazines. In the late fifties, he decided to devote his full time to writing.

About his writing habits, Morton told an interviewer for *Book Week,* "I'm always amazed when I see another book come out." He explained that he belonged to the "Teutonic school of peripatetic procrastination" and, when the weather is nice, he takes "work walks," always remembering pad and pencil "to prove that I'm working." "I have a good alternative for when it rains," he said, "again it's physical, always with the Teutonic school. Somersaults. I do somersaults on the theory I can stimulate myself to greater mental activity. And I chin myself on the molding over my door. It tires me out. To simmer down I nap or clean the typewriter."

Morton's book *The Rothschilds* has been translated into nineteen languages and made into a successful Broadway musical.

BIOGRAPHICAL/CRITICAL SOURCES: Life, September 3, 1965; *Time,* September 10, 1965; *Saturday Review,* October 16, 1965, December 28, 1968; *Harper's,* December, 1965; *New York Times,* January 21, 1966, November 5, 1971, July 13, 1976, October 25, 1979; *Book Week,* February 6, 1966; *Hudson Review,* spring, 1966; *Books & Bookmen,* December, 1966; *Best Sellers,* January 1, 1969; *New York Times Book Review,* January 5, 1969, September 12, 1976, November 18, 1979; *New Yorker,* January 11, 1969; *National Observer,* February 3, 1969; *Book World,* February 23, 1969; *Nation,* March 3, 1969; *Variety,* October 21, 1970; *Newsweek,* November 2, 1970, June 21, 1976; *Christian Science Monitor,* August 4, 1976.

*   *   *

MOW, Anna Beahm 1893-

PERSONAL: Born July 31, 1893, in Daleville, Va.; daughter of I.N.H. and Mary (Buther) Beahm; married Baxter Merrill Mow, 1921; children: Lois (Mrs. Ernest Snavely), Joseph, Merrill. *Education:* Manchester College, B.A., 1918; Bethany Theological Seminary, B.D., 1921, M.R.E., 1941, M.Th. *Home:* 1318 Varnell Ave. N.E., Roanoke, Va. 24012.

CAREER: Church of the Brethren, General Missions Board, Elgin, Ill., missionary in India, 1923-40; Bethany Theological Seminary, Oak Brook, Ill., associate professor of Christian education, 1940-58; now lecturer and leader of retreats and institutes. *Member:* Friends of the Middle East. *Awards, honors:* D.D., Bethany Theological Seminary, 1959; Alumni Award, Manchester College, 1963.

WRITINGS: Say "Yes" to Life!, Zondervan, 1961; *Your Child from Birth to Rebirth: How to Educate a Child to Be*

Ready for Life with God, Zondervan, 1963; *Going Steady with God: Your Life with God Every Day of the Year,* Zondervan, 1965; *Your Teen-ager and You,* Zondervan, 1967; *So Who's Afraid of Birthdays: For Those over Sixty and Those Who Expect to Be,* Lippincott, 1969; *The Secret of Married Love: A Christian Approach,* Lippincott, 1970; *Your Experience and the Bible,* Harper, 1973; *Sensitivity—to What?,* Zondervan, 1975; *Find Your Own Faith,* Zondervan, 1977; *Springs of Love,* Brethren Press, 1979. Contributor to church papers.

BIOGRAPHICAL/CRITICAL SOURCES: Inez Long, *Faces among the Faithful,* Brethren Press, 1962.

*   *   *

MOWITZ, Robert J(ames) 1920-

PERSONAL: Born February 14, 1920, in Tonawanda, N.Y.; son of Benjamin J. (an accountant) and Mae Alice (Linton) Mowitz; married Clara E. MacDonald, March 29, 1942; children: Eric R., Carol J. *Education:* Syracuse University, A.B. (magna cum laude), 1941, Ph.D., 1948. *Home:* 1677 Princeton Dr., State College, Pa. *Office:* Institute of Public Administration, Pennsylvania State University, University Park, Pa.

CAREER: Syracuse University, Syracuse, N.Y., instructor in political science, 1947-48; Wayne State University, Detroit, Mich., 1948-65, began as instructor, became professor of political science; Pennsylvania State University, University Park, director of Institute of Public Administration and professor of political science and public administration, 1965—. Chairman, Governor's Mental Health Inquiry Board, 1959-60; member, Governor's Commission for Modern State Government, 1967-69; consultant, Office of Budget Secretary, 1970-78; member of research advisory board, Committee for Economic Development, 1974-79. Consultant to governmental agencies. *Military service:* U.S. Army, Corps of Engineers, Southwest Pacific Theater; became second lieutenant. *Member:* American Society for Public Administration, Phi Beta Kappa.

WRITINGS: (With Edgar A. Schular and Albert J. Mayer) *Medical Public Relations,* Health Information Foundation, 1952; (contributor) *The States and Subversion,* Cornell University Press, 1952; (with Deil S. Wright) *Profile of a Metropolis,* Wayne State University Press, 1962; (contributor) *Cases in American National Government and Politics,* Prentice-Hall, 1966; *The Design and Implementation of Pennsylvania's Planning, Programming, and Budgeting System,* Commonwealth of Pennsylvania, 1971; (contributor) *Current Practice in Program Budgeting,* Crane, Russak, 1973; *The Design of Public Decision Systems,* University Park Press, 1980.

*   *   *

MUNRO, Thomas 1897-1974

PERSONAL: Born February 15, 1897, in Omaha, Neb.; died April 14, 1974; son of Alexander Allen (a school administrator) and Mary (Spaulding) Munro; married Lucile Nadler, May 18, 1925; children: Eleanor Carroll (Mrs. Alfred Frankfurter), Donald Jacques, Cynthia (Mrs. Olaf H. Prufer), Elizabeth Clerc (Mrs. Patrick Smith). *Education:* Attended Amherst College, 1912-15; Columbia University, A.B., 1916, A.M., 1917, Ph.D., 1920.

CAREER: Columbia University, New York, N.Y., instructor in philosophy, 1918-24; Barnes Foundation, Merion, Pa., associate educational director, 1924-27; University of Pennsylvania, Philadelphia, visiting professor of modern art, 1924-27; Rutgers University, New Brunswick, N.J., professor of philosophy, 1928-31; Cleveland Museum of Art, Cleveland, Ohio, curator of education, 1931-67; Case Western Reserve University, Cleveland, Ohio, professor of art, 1931-67, professor emeritus, 1967-74, chairman of Division of Art, 1933-51. Visiting professor of aesthetics, Sorbonne, University of Paris, 1949-50. *Military service:* U.S. Army, 1918; sergeant in psychological division of Medical Department.

MEMBER: Royal Society of Arts (fellow), American Academy of Arts and Sciences, American Association for Advancement of Science, American Society for Aesthetics (president, 1942-44; honorary president, 1963-74), American Philosophical Association, College Art Association (director, 1957-60), American Museums Association, Union Interalliee (Paris), Century Club (New York). *Awards, honors:* Decorated Chevalier, Legion of Honor, France, 1953, officer, 1961; L.H.D., Coe College, 1955; Cleveland Women's City Club and Ursuline College awards for publications in fine arts.

WRITINGS: Scientific Method in Aesthetics, Norton, 1928; *Great Pictures of Europe,* Tudor, 1930; (editor) *The Future of Aesthetics,* Cleveland Museum of Art, 1942; *The Arts and Their Interrelations,* Liberal Arts Publishing, 1949, revised edition, Press of Western Reserve University, 1967; (with Jane Grimes) *Educational Work at the Cleveland Museum of Art,* 2nd edition, Cleveland Museum of Art, 1952; *Toward Science in Aesthetics,* Liberal Arts Publishing, 1956; *Art Education: Its Philosophy and Psychology,* Liberal Arts Publishing, 1956; *Painting,* Conzett & Huber (Zurich), 1958; (with Catherine M. Wilson) *Mastering Plane Geometry,* Oxford Book Company, 1959; *Evolution in the Arts,* Cleveland Museum of Art, 1963; *Oriental Aesthetics,* Press of Western Reserve University, 1965; *The World of Art: A Study of Painting,* Field Enterprises, 1965; (with P. Guillaume) *Primitive Negro Sculpture,* Hacker Art Books, 1968; *Form and Style in the Arts: An Introduction to Aesthetic Morphology,* Press of Case Western Reserve University, 1970. Contributor to art and philosophy magazines. Editor, *Journal of Aesthetics and Art Criticism,* 1945-63, contributing editor, 1963-74.

AVOCATIONAL INTERESTS: Golf, travel.

BIOGRAPHICAL/CRITICAL SOURCES: Saturday Review, December 7, 1963; *Journal of Aesthetics and Art Criticism,* fall, 1964, summer/fall, 1974; *Journal of Philosophy,* June 3, 1971; *New York Times,* April 15, 1974.†

*   *   *

MUNVES, James (Albert) 1922-

PERSONAL: Born March 23, 1922, in New York, N.Y.; son of Alexander Albert and Helen (Schreiber) Munves; married Barbara Parsons, March 17, 1973; children: (first marriage) Katherine, Emily, Margaret. *Education:* Brown University, A.B., 1943. *Home:* 230 West 78th St., New York, N.Y. 10024. *Agent:* Elaine Markson Literary Agency, 44 Greenwich Ave., New York, N.Y. 10011.

CAREER: New Yorker, New York City, reporter, 1945-48; *Collier's,* New York City, reporter, 1949-50. *Military service:* U.S. Army, Fourth Armored Division, 1943-45; awarded Purple Heart. *Member:* Authors Guild, P.E.N., Linnaen Society.

WRITINGS: We Were There with Lewis and Clark, Grosset, 1959; *We Were There at the Opening of the Atomic Era,*

Grosset, 1960; *A Short Illustrated History of the United States,* Grosset, 1965; *A Day in the Life of the U.N.,* Washington Square Press, 1970; *The F.B.I. and the C.I.A.,* Harcourt, 1975; *Thomas Jefferson and the Declaration of Independence,* Scribner, 1977; *The Treasure of Diogenes Sampuez,* Four Winds Press, 1979; (with Joseph Kelner) *The Kent State Cover-up,* Harper, 1980. Author of motion picture script "War on the Mississippi." Contributor to national magazines, including *New Yorker* and *Nation.*

*   *   *

MURSTEIN, Bernard I(rving) 1929-

PERSONAL: Born April 29, 1929, in Vilna, Lithuania; son of Leon (a taxi fleet owner) and Martha (Schalach) Murstein; married Nelly Kashy (a professor of French and Italian at Connecticut College), August 27, 1954; children: S. Danielle, Colette Anne. *Education:* City College (now City College of the City University of New York), B.S.S., 1950; University of Miami, Miami, Fla., M.S., 1951; University of Texas, Ph.D., 1955. *Politics:* Liberal-independent. *Religion:* Jewish. *Home:* 11 Winchester Rd., New London, Conn. 06320. *Office:* Department of Psychology, Connecticut College, New London, Conn. 06320.

CAREER: University of Texas, Main University (now University of Texas at Austin), Hogg Foundation research fellow at M.D. Anderson Hospital, 1955-56; Louisiana State University, Baton Rouge, assistant professor of psychology and director of psychology clinic, 1956-58; University of Portland, Portland, Ore., associate professor of psychology and coordinator of research, 1958-60; National Institute of Mental Health, Portland, director of research and principal investigator at Interfaith Counseling Center, 1960-62; University of Connecticut, Storrs, associate professor of family relations, 1962-63; Connecticut College, New London, associate professor, 1963-65, professor of psychology, 1965—. Principal investigator, National Institute of Mental Health, 1964-68. Fulbright professor, Universite de Louvain, 1968-69. *Member:* American Psychological Association (fellow), Society for Projective Techniques (fellow), National Council on Family Relations. *Awards, honors:* U.S. Public Health Service fellowship, 1954; National Institute of Mental Health research grants, 1960-63, 1964-68.

WRITINGS: Theory and Research in Projective Techniques, Emphasizing the Thematic Apperception Test, Wiley, 1963; (editor) *Handbook of Projective Techniques,* Basic Books, 1965; *Theories of Attraction and Love,* Springer Publishing, 1971; *Love, Sex, and Marriage through the Ages,* Springer Publishing, 1974; *Who Will Marry Whom: Theories and Research in Marital Choice,* Springer Publishing, 1976; (editor) *Exploring Intimate Life Styles,* Springer Publishing, 1978; *Marriage and Family: A Research Approach,* Brooks-Cole, in press; (with T. Cash and D. Briddel) *Exploring Human Sexualities,* Brooks-Cole, in press.

SIDELIGHTS: Bernard I. Murstein told *CA:* "Some years ago I made a statement after dealing with the contents of our dull, plodding psychological journals. I jocularly referred to it as Murstein's Law: 'The amount of research devoted to a topic on human behavior is inversely related to its importance and interest to mankind.' My research and writing efforts devoted to investigating attraction, love, marital choice and marital functioning have attempted to change the veridicality of that statement and to study what I perceive to be the most important factor in most lives—the quantity and quality of our intimate relationships."

MYERS, Elisabeth P(erkins) 1918-

PERSONAL: Born July 22, 1918, in Grand Rapids, Mich.; daughter of Edward Foote and Lili (Zimmermann) Perkins; married John Holmes Myers (a professor of accounting), August 24, 1940; children: Thomas Perkins. *Education:* Vassar College, A.B., 1940. *Politics:* Republican. *Home:* 1165 Regency Dr., Bloomington, Ind.

CAREER: Wilmette Public Library, Wilmette, Ill., assistant librarian, 1958-60; writer for basic reading series, Science Research Association; writer with Harper & Row educational department. *Member:* Society of Midland Authors, Women's National Press Club, Women in Communications (vice-president, North Shore chapter, 1966-67; president, Bloomington chapter, 1970-71), National Society of Arts and Letters (president, Bloomington chapter, 1979-80), Children's Reading Round Table (president, 1967-68), Women's Press Club of Indiana.

WRITINGS—All juvenile biographies; published by Bobbs-Merrill, except as indicated: *Katharine Lee Bates: Girl Poet,* 1961; *F. W. Woolworth: Five and Ten Boy,* 1962; *George Pullman: Young Sleeping Car Builder,* 1963; *Singer of Six Thousand Songs: A Life of Charles Wesley,* Thomas Nelson, 1965; *Maria Tallchief: America's Prima Ballerina,* Grosset, 1966; *Edward Bok: Young Editor,* 1967; *Angel of Appalachia: Martha Berry,* Messner, 1968; *Jenny Lind: Songbird from Sweden,* Garrard, 1968; *South America's Yankee Genius: Henry Meiggs,* Messner, 1969; *Rutherford B. Hayes,* Reilly & Lee, 1969; *Benjamin Harrison,* Reilly & Lee, 1969; *William Howard Taft,* Reilly & Lee, 1970; *Andrew Jackson,* Reilly & Lee, 1970; *Langston Hughes: Poet of His People,* Garrard, 1970; *Frederick Douglas: Boy Champion of Human Rights,* 1970; *David Sarnoff: Radio and TV Boy,* 1971; *Mary Cassatt,* Reilly & Lee, 1971; *Madam Secretary: Frances Perkins,* Messner, 1972; *John D. Rockefeller: Boy Financier,* 1973; *Pearl S. Buck: Literary Girl,* 1974; *Thomas Paine: Common Sense Boy,* 1976. Contributor of short stories and articles to *Highlights for Children, Jack and Jill, Children's Playmate, Chicago Tribune Magazine, Woman's Day,* and other publications.

WORK IN PROGRESS: An adult novel set in South America; short stories for children; travel articles.

SIDELIGHTS: Elisabeth P. Myers told *CA:* "I seldom go anywhere without pen and notebook because ideas for books and stories are everywhere. I have been writing something everyday since I was nine years old, and now it is almost as important to me as eating." *Avocational interests:* Travel (has visited Europe and South America), volunteer work with local hospital, swimming, tennis, music.

*   *   *

MYRER, Anton 1922-

PERSONAL: Born November 3, 1922, in Worcester, Mass.; married Patricia Schartle, 1970. *Education:* Harvard University, B.A., 1947. *Home:* 3193 Church Rd., Saugerties, N.Y.

CAREER: Novelist. *Military service:* United States Marine Corps, 1942-46. *Member:* Authors Guild, Authors League of America, P.E.N.

WRITINGS: Evil under the Sun, Random House, 1951; *The Big War,* Appleton, 1957; *The Violent Shore,* Little, Brown, 1962; *The Intruder,* Little, Brown, 1965; *Once an Eagle* (Book-of-the-Month Club selection), Holt, 1968; *The Tiger Waits,* Norton, 1973; *The Last Convertible* (Literary Guild selection), Putnam, 1978. Also author of article for the memorial issue on Malcolm Lowry in *Lettres Nouvelles,* summer, 1960. Contributor of articles to periodicals.

SIDELIGHTS: Anton Myer told *CA:* "Shifting American values and the legacies of power, whether civilian or military, have provided the dominant themes of my fiction for the past several years—and of late a deepening sense of alarm over this military-industrial juggernaut we have spawned which can ignore grinding domestic agonies and blandly drop the explosive equivalent of 420 Hiroshimas on a small Southeast Asian nation.

"A native of the Berkshires and Cape Cod, I was influenced deeply by the lives and work of Hawthorne, Melville and Thoreau—that tradition of proud dissent in the face of an encroaching institutional power and indifference which has all but engulfed us as Americans: what concerns me most vitally is a stubborn assertion of individual dignity, the small but essential personal victories which can still be salvaged in a world largely dominated by waste, irresponsibility and violence."

BIOGRAPHICAL/CRITICAL SOURCES: New Yorker, August 24, 1968; *Saturday Review,* Aguust 24, 1968; *New York Times Book Review,* September 15, 1968, April 8, 1973, March 19, 1978, February 25, 1979; *National Review,* June 22, 1973; *Village Voice,* April 3, 1978; *Time,* June 19, 1978.

N

NAGARA, Susumu 1932-

PERSONAL: Born August 21, 1932, in Hiroshima, Japan; son of Masayuki (an artist) and Shizuko (Hatano) Nagara; married Pauline Ryoko Higa (a programmer analyst), August 16, 1963; children: Mie Lynette, Chizu Corliss, Michael Satoshi. *Education:* Hiroshima University, B.A., 1955, M.A., 1959; University of Wisconsin, Ph.D., 1969. *Office:* Department of Far Eastern Languages and Literatures, University of Michigan, 3070 Frieze Bldg., Ann Arbor, Mich. 48104.

CAREER: Hiroshima University High School, Hiroshima, Japan, instructor in English, 1955-57; Kyoto Women's University, Kyoto, Japan, lecturer in English, 1959-61; University of Michigan, Ann Arbor, lecturer, 1966-69, assistant professor, 1969-72, associate professor of Far Eastern languages and literatures, 1972—. Evaluator of language program, Kalamazoo College, Kalamazoo, Mich., 1966—. *Member:* Association of Teachers of Japanese (secretary, 1971—), Linguistics Society of America, Association for Asian Studies, Society for the Teaching of Japanese as a Foreign Language (secretary, 1971—). *Awards, honors:* Social Science Research Council research grant, 1972-73.

WRITINGS: (Contributor) *Working Paper of the DCCS,* University of Michigan, 1970; *Japanese Pidgin English in Hawaii: A Bilingual Description,* University Press of Hawaii, 1972; (co-author) *Handbook to Action English,* World Times of Japan, Book I, 1976, Book II, 1977, Book III, 1978; *The Home Front: Japan,* Silver Burdett, 1979. Editor of *Foreign Language Courier,* 1969.

WORK IN PROGRESS: Research on the history of the Japanese language and bilingualism in Hawaii; research on computer processing of Japanese grammar.†

*   *   *

NEAL, Emily Gardiner

PERSONAL: Born in New York, N.Y.; daughter of John deBarth (an engineer) and Rebekah (McLean) Gardiner; married Alvin W. Neal, March 12, 1930 (deceased); children: Rebekah G. (Mrs. Frank Kennedy), Diana Harrell (Mrs. W. Galbreath). *Education:* Attended David Mannes College of Music. *Politics:* Independent. *Religion:* Episcopalian. *Home:* 655 Albion Ave., Cincinnati, Ohio 45246. *Agent:* Scott Meredith Literary Agency, Inc., 845 Third Ave., New York, N.Y. 10022.

CAREER: Lecturer, writer. Ordained deacon in Episcopal Church, 1978; on staff of St. Thomas Episcopal Church, Cincinnati, Ohio. *Member:* National League of American Penwomen.

WRITINGS: A Reporter Finds God, Morehouse, 1956; *God Can Heal You Now,* Prentice-Hall, 1958; *The Lord Is Our Healer,* Prentice-Hall, 1961; *In the Midst of Life,* Morehouse, 1963; *Father Bob and His Boys,* Bobbs-Merrill, 1963; *Where There's Smoke,* Morehouse, 1966; *The Healing Power of Christ,* Hawthorn, 1972. Contributor to *Redbook, Reader's Digest, McCall's, Look,* and other magazines.

*   *   *

NEATBY, Leslie Hamilton 1902-

PERSONAL: Born May 16, 1902, in Sutton, Surrey, England; son of Andrew Mossforth and Ada Deborah (Fisher) Neatby; married Murdena Thomson Stewart, February 23, 1934; children: Joan Carol (Mrs. A. D. Hudgins). *Education:* University of Saskatchewan, B.A. (honors), 1925, M.A., 1939; attended University of London, 1925-26; Saskatoon Normal School, first class certificate, 1927; University of Toronto, Ph.D., 1950. *Home:* 5D, Latham Place, Saskatoon, Saskatchewan, Canada.

CAREER: Principal of high school in Shellbrook, Saskatchewan, 1930-40; Mount Royal College, Calgary, Alberta, instructor in classics, 1945-47; Acadia University, Wolfville, Nova Scotia, head of department of classics, 1951-67; University of Saskatchewan, Saskatoon, professor of classics, 1967-70. *Military service:* Canadian Army, active duty, 1940-44; became captain. *Member:* Canadian Authors' Association, Canadian Humanities Association (member of national executive committee).

WRITINGS: In Quest of the Northwest Passage, Longmans, Green, 1958; *The Link between the Oceans,* Longmans, Green, 1960; *Conquest of the Last Frontier,* Ohio State University Press, 1966; (editor and translator) J. A. Miertsching, *Frozen Ships: Artic Diary, 1850-1854,* St. Martin's, 1967; *Search for Franklin,* Walker & Co., 1970; *Discovery in Russian and Siberian Waters,* Ohio State University Press, 1973; (editor and translator) Bernhard A. Hantzsch, *My Life among the Eskimos,* Institute for Northern Studies, University of Saskatchewan, 1977; *Chronicle of a Pioneer Prairie Family,* Prairie Books, 1979. Author of chapter in Canadian Centennial volume on Hudson's Bay, issued by Federal Department of Mines and Technical Surveys. Contributor of articles and reviews to *Canadian Historical Review, Beaver, Queen's Quarterly, American Historical Review,* and *Dalhousie Review.*

WORK IN PROGRESS: Translating books.

AVOCATIONAL INTERESTS: Maritime history and discovery, Arctic travel.

*   *   *

NEILL, Thomas Patrick   1915-1970

PERSONAL: Born January 19, 1915, in Telluride, Colo.; died 1970; son of Harry George and Marian (Cuthbertson) Neill; married Agnes Josephine Weber, 1941; children: Thomas, Denis, Catherine, James, Margaret, Mark, John, Joseph, Edward. *Education:* St. Louis University, A.B., 1937, Ph.D., 1943; University of Notre Dame, M.A., 1939. *Religion:* Catholic. *Home:* 6146 Kingsbury Ave., St. Louis, Mo. *Office:* Department of History, St. Louis University, 221 North Grand Blvd., St. Louis, Mo.

CAREER: Aquinas College, Grand Rapids, Mich., instructor, 1941-43; St. Louis University, St. Louis, Mo., instructor, 1943-45, assistant professor, 1945-48, associate professor, 1948-52, professor of modern European history, 1952-70. Lecturer and television speaker. *Member:* American Association of University Professors, Catholic Association for International Peace, American Catholic Association for Intellectual and Cultural Affairs (national chairman, 1954), American Historical Association, American Political Science Association, Missouri Board of Training Schools, Greater St. Louis Historical Society (president, 1948), Alpha Sigma Nu. *Awards, honors:* Knight of St. Gregory; Archbishop Noll Award for outstanding Catholic lay leadership; Cardinal Newman Award.

WRITINGS—Published by Bruce Publishing, except as indicated: *Makers of the Modern Mind,* 1949, 2nd edition, 1963; *They Lived the Faith,* 1951; *Religion and Culture,* 1952; *The Rise and Decline of Liberalism,* 1953; *The Common Good,* Doubleday, 1956, revised edition, Holt, 1962; (editor) *Readings in the History of Western Civilization,* Newman, Volume I, 1957, Volume II, 1958; (with Raymond Schmandt) *History of the Catholic Church,* 1957, 2nd edition, 1965; *1859 in Review,* Newman, 1959; (with others) *A History of Western Civilization,* two volumes, 1959, revised edition, Glencoe Press, 1962; (editor) *The Building of the Human City,* Doubleday, 1960; (with Paul T. Mason) *The Life of Christ in His Church,* Daniel Reardon, 1963; (with James Collins) *Communism,* Sheed, 1964; *Renewing the Face of the Earth: Essays in Contemporary Church-World Relationships,* edited by Harry J. Cargas, 1968; *Modern Europe,* Doubleday, 1970. General editor, "Social Science" series and "College Reading" series, Newman. Contributor to periodicals. Associate editor, *American Catholic Historical Review;* member of advisory editorial board of *Social Order.*†

*   *   *

NELSON, Andrew N(athaniel)   1893-1975

PERSONAL: Born December 23, 1893, in Great Falls, Mont.; died May, 1975; son of Andrew Alexander (a builder) and Gustava (Oberg) Nelson; married Vera Elizabeth Shoff, March 24, 1918; children: Richard Andrew, Donald George, Dorothy Gertrude (Mrs. Kenneth Oster). *Education:* Walla Walla College, B.A.; University of Washington, Seattle, Ph.D. *Home:* 5126 Peacock Lane, La Sierra, Calif. 92505. *Office:* Department of Education, Loma Linda University, La Sierra College, La Sierra, Calif. 92505.

CAREER: Seventh-day Adventist Church, held posts as missionary-educator in Far East, 1918-41, including the presidency of Japan Missionary College, 1925-36, and of Japan Union Mission, 1936-41; Emmanuel Missionary College, Berrien Springs, Mich., dean, 1941-44; U.S. Army, Washington, D.C., civilian research analyst, 1942-46; Philippine Union College, Manila, Republic of the Philippines, president, 1946-52; Mountain View College, Malaybalay, Republic of the Philippines, founder, 1949-52; Japan Union Mission of Seventh-day Adventists, Japan, secretary, 1953-58; Philippine Union College, Manila, dean, 1958-61; Loma Linda University, La Sierra College, La Sierra, Calif., professor of education, beginning 1961. Chaplain to Japanese prisoners in New Bilibid Penitentiary, 1948-52. *Member:* Association of Teachers of Japanese, Association for Asian Studies. *Awards, honors:* U.S. Army civilian commendation for work as Japanese lexicographer during World War II.

WRITINGS: The Supplementary Japanese-English Dictionary, U.S. War Department, 1945; *Japanese-English Technical Terms Dictionary,* U.S. War Department, 1946; *Japanese Language Course,* Japan Publishing House, 1956; *The Modern Reader's Japanese-English Character Dictionary,* Tuttle, 1962, 2nd revised edition, 1971; (with Reuben G. Manalaysay) *The Gist of Christian Education,* La Sierra College Press, 1962, revised edition, 1966; (with Jacob R. Mittleider) *Food for Everyone: The Mittleider Method,* College Press, 1970. Also co-author of *Principles of Christian Education,* 1970.

WORK IN PROGRESS: A book on the origin, history, and present status of the temples of Japan.

BIOGRAPHICAL/CRITICAL SOURCES: Riverside Press-Enterprise, Riverside, Calif., February 27, 1962, May 31, 1963; *Hokubei Mainichi,* San Francisco, Calif., July 6, 1962; *Asia,* January 20, 1963.†

*   *   *

NELSON, J(ohn) Robert   1920-

PERSONAL: Born August 21, 1920, in Winona Lake, Ind.; son of William John (a businessman) and Agnes D. (Soderborg) Nelson; married Dorothy Patricia Mercer (a health educator), August 18, 1945; children: Eric Mercer, William John. *Education:* DePauw University, A.B., 1941; Yale University, B.D., 1944; University of Zurich, D.Theol., 1951. *Politics:* Democrat. *Home:* 480 Jamaicaway, Boston, Mass. 02130. *Office:* 745 Commonwealth Ave., Boston, Mass. 02215.

CAREER: Ordained minister in Methodist Church, 1944; Wesley Foundation, director at Chapel Hill, N.C., 1946-48, associate director in Urbana, Ill., 1950-51; United Student Christian Council, New York, N.Y., study secretary, 1951-53; World Council of Churches, Commission on Faith and Order, Geneva, Switzerland, executive secretary, 1953-57; Vanderbilt University, Nashville, Tenn., professor of theology and dean of Divinity School, 1957-60; Princeton Theological Seminary, Princeton, N.J., visiting professor of ecumenics, 1960-61; United Theological College and Leonard Theological College, India, visiting professor of theology, 1961-62; Oberlin College, Graduate School of Theology, Oberlin, Ohio, Fairchild Professor of Theology, 1962-65; Boston University, School of Theology, Boston, Mass., dean and professor of systematic theology, 1965—. Member of Commission on Faith and Order, National Council of Churches, 1959—; chairman of Commission on Faith and Order, World Council of Churches, 1967-76. Visiting professor, Pontifical Gregorian University, Rome, Italy, 1968;

scholar, Kennedy Institute of Ethics, Georgetown University, 1979-80. Delegate to church conferences in India, 1961, Canada, 1963, Sweden, 1968, and Kenya, 1975; lecturer on Christian unity in thirty-two countries. *Military service:* U.S. Naval Reserve, chaplain, 1944-46; served with Marines in Guam, Japan, and China; became lieutenant.

MEMBER: American Theological Society (former president), American Academy of Arts and Sciences (fellow), Societe Europeenne de Culture (vice-president), North American Academy of Ecumenists (former president), Phi Beta Kappa, Beta Theta Pi, St. Botolph Club (Boston). *Awards, honors:* LL.D., Wilberforce University, 1954; L.H.D., DePauw University, 1960; D.D., Ohio Wesleyan University, 1964; D.H.L., Loyola University, 1969.

WRITINGS: The Realm of Redemption: Studies in the Doctrine of the Nature of the Church in Contemporary Protestant Theology, Epworth, 1951, 4th edition, 1957; (editor) *The Christian Student and the Church,* Association Press, 1952; (editor) *The Christian Student and the University,* Association Press, 1952; (editor) *The Christian Student and the World Struggle,* Association Press, 1952; (editor) *Christian Unity in North America,* Bethany Press, 1958; *A Theology to Match the Church's Opportunity,* Vanderbilt University Press, 1958; *One Lord, One Church,* Association Press, 1958, revised edition published as *Overcoming Christian Divisions,* 1962; *Criterion for the Church,* Abingdon, 1963; (with John E. Skoglund) *Fifty Years of Faith and Order: An Interpretation of the Faith and Order Movement in Contemporary Protestantism,* Committee for Inter-Seminary Movement of National Student Christian Federation, 1963; *Let Us Pray for Unity,* Upper Room, 1963; *Crisis in Unity and Witness,* Westminster Press, 1968; *Church Union in Focus: Guide for Adult Group Study,* United Church Press, 1968; (editor) *No Man Is Alien,* E. J. Brill, 1971; *Doctrines of the Future,* Abingdon, 1978; *Science and Our Troubled Conscience,* Fortress, 1980.

Contributor: Marvin Halverson and Arthur A. Cohen, editors, *Handbook of Christian Theology: Definition Essays on Concepts and Movements of Thought,* Meridian, 1958; Robert McAfee Brown and David H. Scott, editors, *Challenge to Reunion,* McGraw, 1963; Martin Marty and Dean Peerman, editors, *New Theology, Number 9,* Macmillan, 1972; Peter McCord, editor, *A Pope for All Christians,* Paulist/Newman, 1977. Contributor of articles to journals. Editor-at-large, *Christian Century;* associate editor, *Journal of Ecumenical Studies.*

WORK IN PROGRESS: Writing on medical ethics: science and theology; story of modern Christian unity movement.

SIDELIGHTS: J. Robert Nelson told *CA:* "I am astonished to see how the discipline of writing is more like the point of the plow, breaking new soil, than the harrow, smoothing out what has been thought. You cannot know what you know until you accept the discipline of describing and interpreting it." Nelson's works have been translated into several languages.

* * *

NEVILLE, Emily Cheney 1919-

PERSONAL: Born December 28, 1919, in Manchester, Conn.; daughter of Howell (an economist) and Anne (Bunce) Cheney; married Glenn Neville (a newspaperman with Hearst Corp.), December 18, 1948 (died June 1, 1965); children: Emily Tam, Glen H., Dessie, Marcy Ann, Alec. *Education:* Bryn Mawr College, A.B., 1940; Albany Law School, J.D., 1976. *Politics:* Democrat. *Religion:* United Church of Christ. *Residence:* Keene Valley, N.Y. 12943.

CAREER: New York Daily News, New York City, office girl, 1941; *New York Daily Mirror,* New York City, reporter, 1941-43; currently in private law practice. Writer for young people. Active in National Epilepsy Foundation; president of Essex County Health Association; member of Youth Commission of Keene Valley. *Awards, honors:* John Newbery Medal, 1964, for *It's Like This, Cat;* Jane Addams Children's Book Award, 1966, for *Berries Goodman.*

WRITINGS: It's Like This, Cat, Harper, 1963; *Berries Goodman,* Harper, 1965; *The Seventeenth-Street Gang,* Harper, 1966; *Traveler from a Small Kingdom,* Harper, 1968; *Fogarty,* Harper, 1969; *Garden of Broken Glass,* Delacorte, 1975.

SIDELIGHTS: "The new children's literature now deals with all the subjects that were once labeled 'For Adults Only,'" Josh Greenfeld writes in the *New York Times Book Review.* "Emily Cheney Neville is certainly one of the better practitioners of the new children's literature.... She has an honest ear, a penchant for sharp simile ..., the ability to encapsulate an endearing truth simply ..., and, moreover, she knows how to underwrite a dramatic scene so that it reverberates with overtones."

It's Like This, Cat, the story of a young boy and his cat who live in New York City, is perhaps Neville's best-known novel. In their study *Children and Books,* May Hill Arbuthnot and Zena Henderson call it "impressive both for its lightly humorous, easy style and the fidelity with which it portrays a fourteen-year-old boy." "Many stories," Carolyn T. Kingston writes in her *The Tragic Mode in Children's Literature,* "only seem to be realistic. *It's Like This, Cat,* is a realistic story in every sense of the word [and it] rises above the mere presentation of a realistic situation, into the beauty of the tragic realm, because of the author's intense spirit of affirmation. Although loss may occur in life, she seems to say, a balance may be achieved if one can accept the inevitable and go on. Without preachment, she conveys the idea that only spiritual toughness can balance tragedy." Robert Hood, of the *New York Times Book Review,* considers *It's Like This, Cat* to be "the best junior novel I've ever read about big-city life."

Neville told *CA:* "My writing is probably an outgrowth of my childhood in a large, clannish New England family, mingled with my own quite different experiences raising five children in New York City." Currently practicing law, Neville states that she does not plan to incorporate the experience into a future book. "Practicing law and writing books," she says, "almost requires two heads. I hope to get back to writing a book again, but it will be about children and animals and parents, how they talk and why they do what they do with each other. There's no 'bottom line' in my books, while the law is overwhelmingly concerned with just that—the result."

AVOCATIONAL INTERESTS: Travel, reading, animals.

BIOGRAPHICAL/CRITICAL SOURCES: Christian Science Monitor, May 9, 1963; *New York Times Book Review,* May 12, 1963, April 25, 1965, November 6, 1966, January 11, 1970, June 15, 1975; *Saturday Review,* November 12, 1966, November 8, 1969; *Book World,* May 5, 1968; *National Observer,* August 22, 1968; Cornelia Meigs, editor, *A Critical History of Children's Literature,* revised edition, Macmillan, 1969; May Hill Arbuthnot and Zena Henderson, *Children and Books,* 4th edition, Scott, Foresman, 1972; Carolyn T. Kingston, *The Tragic Mode in Children's Literature,* Teachers College Press, 1974; *Contemporary Literary Criticism,* Volume XII, Gale, 1980.

NEWMAN, Peter C(harles)   1929-

PERSONAL: Born May 10, 1929, in Vienna, Austria; moved to Canada, 1940; naturalized Canadian citizen, 1945; son of Oskar and Wanda (Newman) Newman; married Camilla Jane Turner, August 5, 1978; children: (previous marriage) Ashley (daughter). *Education:* University of Toronto, B.A., 1950, M.Com., 1953. *Home:* 64 Admiral Rd., Toronto, Ontario, Canada M5R 2L5. *Office:* 481 University Ave., Toronto, Ontario, Canada M5W 1A7.

CAREER: Financial Post, Toronto, Ontario, assistant editor, 1953-57; *Maclean's* (magazine), Toronto, assistant editor, 1957-59, Ottawa editor, 1959-63, national affairs editor, 1963-64; *Toronto Daily Star,* Toronto, Ottawa editor, 1964-69, editor-in-chief, 1969-71; *Maclean's,* editor, 1971—. Visiting associate professor of political science, McMaster University, 1970, and York University, 1980. *Military service:* Royal Canadian Navy Reserve; became commander. *Member:* International Press Institute (deputy chairman for Canada, 1970-72), Canadian Authors Association, National Press Club (Canada), Rideau Club (Ottawa). *Awards, honors:* National Newspaper Award for feature writing, 1964; Wilderness Award, Canadian Broadcasting Association, 1967; Doctor of Laws, Brock University, 1974; Doctor of Letters, York University, 1975; Officer in Order of Canada, 1978; Knighthood in Order of Saint Lazarus, 1980; Knight of Lippe, 1980.

WRITINGS: Flame of Power: Intimate Profiles of Canada's Greatest Businessmen, Longmans, Green, 1960; *Renegade in Power: The Diefenbacker Years,* McClelland & Stewart, 1963, Bobbs-Merrill, 1964; *The Distemper of Our Times: Canadian Politics in Transition, 1963-1968,* McClelland & Stewart, 1968, published as *A Nation Divided: Canada and the Coming of Pierre Trudeau,* Knopf, 1969; *Home Country,* McClelland & Stewart, 1973; *The Canadian Establishment,* Volume I, McClelland & Stewart, 1975; *King of the Castle,* Atheneum, 1979. Contributor of more than 500 articles on various aspects of Canadian politics and economics to magazines, newspapers, and journals.

BIOGRAPHICAL/CRITICAL SOURCES: Saturday Night, November, 1968; *Canadian Forum,* December, 1968; *Book World,* September 28, 1969; *New York Times Book Review,* November 23, 1969, March 11, 1979; *National Review,* March 10, 1970; *New York Times,* March 20, 1979; *Chicago Tribune Book World,* March 25, 1979.

* * *

NEWMAN, William H(erman)   1909-

PERSONAL: Born October 19, 1909, in Philadelphia, Pa.; son of Herman (a social worker) and Emma (Broomell) Newman; married Clare Berry (a librarian), August 15, 1936; children: Kenneth, Thomas, Roger, Judith. *Education:* Friends University, A.B., 1930; University of Chicago, Ph.D., 1934. *Religion:* Quaker. *Home:* 152 Downey Dr., Tenafly, N.J. 07670. *Office:* 722 Uris Hall, Graduate School of Business, Columbia University, New York, N.Y. 10027.

CAREER: James O. McKinsey & Co., Chicago, Ill., member of staff, 1934-36; Marshall Field & Co., Chicago, assistant to chairman, 1937-38; University of Pennsylvania, Wharton School of Business, Philadelphia, professor of industry, 1939-49; Columbia University, Graduate School of Business, New York, N.Y., Samuel Bronfman Professor of Democratic Business Enterprise, 1951-78, Bronfman Management Scholar, 1978—, director of Strategy Research Center, 1980—. Visiting professor, University of Hawaii, 1964, Robert College, 1964, 1965, London Business School, 1969,

and Claremont Graduate School, 1979, 1980. J. Anderson Fitzgerald Lecturer, University of Texas, 1962. Organization consultant, War Production Board, 1942-43; executive officer, Petroleum Administration for War, 1944-45. Management consultant, 1938—; director of several small companies, 1940—. Member of International Cooperation Administration missions to Chile, 1956, 1957, and to Argentina, 1960, 1961. *Member:* Academy of Management (fellow; president, 1951), American Economic Association, American Society for Public Administration, International Academy of Management (fellow), American Management Association, European Foundation for Management Development. *Awards, honors:* McKinsey Award for one of best management books of 1961-62, for *The Process of Management;* Beta Gamma Sigma Distinguished Scholar, 1978-79.

WRITINGS: The Building Industry and Business Cycles, University of Chicago Press, 1936; *Business Policies and Management,* South-Western, 1940, 5th edition (with James P. Logan), 1965, 6th edition published as *Strategy, Policy, and Central Management,* 1971, 7th edition, 1976; *Administrative Action,* Prentice-Hall, 1951, 2nd edition, 1963; *Cases for Administrative Action,* Prentice-Hall, 1951, 2nd edition, 1963; (with Logan) *Management of Expanding Enterprises,* Columbia University Press, 1953; (with C. E. Summer) *The Process of Management,* Prentice-Hall, 1961, 4th edition (with E. Kirby Warren), 1977; *Constructive Control: Design and Use of Control Systems,* Prentice-Hall, 1975; (editor) *Managers for the Year 2000,* Prentice-Hall, 1978. Contributor of articles to books and professional journals.

* * *

NEWMAN, William S(tein)   1912-

PERSONAL: Born April 6, 1912, in Cleveland, Ohio; married Claire Murray, December 20, 1947; children: Craig William. *Education:* Western Reserve University (now Case Western Reserve University), B.S., 1933, M.A., 1935, Ph.D., 1939; postdoctoral study in Europe, 1939, and at Columbia University, 1940. *Office:* Department of Music, University of North Carolina, Chapel Hill, N.C. 27514.

CAREER: Federal relief administrator, Cleveland, Ohio, 1933-34; high school teacher, Cleveland, 1935-42; University of North Carolina at Chapel Hill, assistant professor, 1945-46, associate professor, 1946-55, professor of music and chairman of piano instruction, 1955-62, Alumni Distinguished Professor of Music, 1962-77, professor emeritus, 1977—, director of graduate studies in music, 1966-77. Summer professor at Columbia University, Juilliard School of Music, University of Montana, University of Colorado, State University of New York at Binghamton, Northwestern University, University of Missouri, and University of Oregon. Private teacher of piano and theory, 1926—; piano soloist with orchestras, including Cleveland Symphony and NBC Symphony Orchestra; concert soloist throughout the country, and soloist with chamber music groups; lecture-recitalist; composer. *Military service:* U.S. Army Air Forces, 1942-45; became major. *Member:* Music Teachers National Association (member of executive board, 1952-56), American Musicological Society (president, 1969-70), Music Library Association, College Music Society, North Carolina Music Educators. *Awards, honors:* Grants from Ford Foundation, 1958-59, University of North Carolina, 1958, Guggenheim Foundation, 1960-61, and American Council of Learned Societies, 1962, 1966-67; National Endowment for the Humanities senior fellow, 1973.

WRITINGS: (Co-author) *The Official Pictorial History of*

the AAF, Duell, Sloan & Pearce, 1947; *The Pianist's Problems,* Harper, 1950, 3rd edition, 1974; *Toward an Understanding of Music,* University of North Carolina Book Exchange, 1952, enlarged version published as *Understanding Music,* Harper, 1953, revised edition, 1967; *A History of the Sonata Idea,* Volume I: *The Sonata in the Baroque Era,* University of North Carolina Press, 1959, 4th edition, Norton, 1981, Volume II: *The Sonata in the Classic Era,* University of North Carolina Press, 1963, 3rd edition, Norton, 1981, Volume III: *The Sonata since Beethoven,* University of North Carolina Press, 1969, 3rd edition, Norton, 1981; *Performance Practices in Beethoven's Piano Sonatas: An Introduction,* Norton, 1971, new edition, Dent, 1972.

Critical editions: *Thirteen Keyboard Sonatas of the 18th and 19th Centuries,* University of North Carolina Press, 1947; *Sons of Bach,* Music Press, 1947; *Two-Part Inventions of J. S. Bach,* Summy-Birchard, 1957; *A Chopin Anthology,* Summy-Birchard, 1957; *Diabelli Variations: 16 Contemporaries of Beethoven on a Waltz Tune,* Summy-Birchard, 1958; *Six Keyboard Sonatas of the Classic Era,* Summy-Birchard, 1965; *Carl Philipp Emanuel Bach's Autobiography,* Fritz Knuf, 1967.

Contributor: *Selections from the "Piano Teacher,"* Summy-Birchard, 1964; *Die Musik in Geschichte und Gegenwart,* Baerenreiter, 1965; M. C. Beardsley and H. M. Schueller, editors, *Aesthetic Inquiry: Essays on Art Criticism and the Philosophy of Art,* Dickinson, 1967; G. Reese and R. J. Snow, editors, *Essays in Musicology, in Honor of Dragan Plamenac on His 70th Birthday,* University of Pittsburgh Press, 1969; J. W. Pruett, editor, *Studies in Musicology, in Memory of Glen Haydon,* University of North Carolina Press, 1969; *Bericht ueber den Internationalen Musikwissenschaftlichen Kongress,* Baerenreiter, 1971; G. Schuhmacher, editor, *Zur Musikalischen Analyse,* Darmstadt, 1974; *Wege der Forschung,* Darmstadt, 1977.

Contributor of articles to *Encyclopaedia Britannica Macropaedia, Grove's Dictionary of Music and Musicians, Colliers Encyclopedia, Enciclopedia della Musica, Grolier's New Book of Knowledge, Jefferson Encyclopedia,* and *New Oxford History of Music.* Contributor of more than 100 articles and reviews to professional publications. Contributing editor, *Piano Quarterly.*

SIDELIGHTS: William S. Newman's private library includes about six thousand sonatas, the musical form on which he has centered much of his research. He has given historical recitals of sonatas at more than one hundred universities, colleges, museums, and other educational centers throughout the country. Newman has also pursued other main research interests, most notably problems of performance practices in the instrumental music of Bach, Mozart, and Beethoven. His own compositions include nocturnes, rhapsodies, operettas, and dance music, as well as sonatas.

AVOCATIONAL INTERESTS: Automotive mechanics, chess, literature.

* * *

NIBLETT, W(illiam) R(oy) 1906-

PERSONAL: Born July 25, 1906, in Keynsham, England; son of William and Ellen (Sage) Niblett; married Sheila Margaret Taylor, 1938; children: Rosalind Mary, Geoffrey Roland. *Education:* University of Bristol, B.A., 1927, D.Ed., 1928; Oxford University, M.Litt., 1930. *Religion:* United Reformed Church. *Home:* Pinfarthings, Amberley, Stroud, Gloucestershire GL5 5JJ, England.

CAREER: University of Durham, Durham, England, lecturer in education, 1934-40, registrar, 1940-44; University of Hull, Hull, England, professor of education, 1945-47; University of Leeds, Leeds, England, professor of education, 1947-59; University of London, London, England, dean of Institute of Education, 1960-68, professor of higher education, 1968-73, professor emeritus, 1973—. Hibbert Lecturer, 1965. Member of University Grants Committee of British Treasury, 1949-59, and National Advisory Council, Training and Supply of Teachers, 1950-61. Trustee of Lucy Cavendish College, Cambridge University, 1978—; chairman of trustees, Higher Education Fund, 1980—. Has lectured in Australia, the Middle East, Japan, New Zealand, United States, and Republic of South Africa. *Member:* Athenaeum Club.

WRITINGS: Essential Education, University of London Press, 1947; *Education and the Modern Mind,* Faber, 1954; *Education, The Lost Dimension,* Morrow, 1955; *Christian Education in a Secular Society,* Oxford University Press, 1960; *The Expanding University,* Faber, 1961; (editor) *Moral Education in a Changing Society,* Faber, 1963; (editor) *Higher Education: Demand and Response,* Jossey-Bass, 1970; (editor) *Universities Facing the Future,* Jossey-Bass, 1972; *Universities between Two Worlds,* Halsted, 1974; (editor) *The Sciences, The Humanities and the Technological Threat,* Halsted, 1975; (with others) *The University Connection,* N.F.E.R. Publishing, 1975.

* * *

NICHOLS, Roy F(ranklin) 1896-1973

PERSONAL: Born March 3, 1896, in Newark, N.J.; died January 11, 1973; son of Franklin C. and Anna (Cairns) Nichols; married Jeannette Paddock, 1920. *Education:* Rutgers, The State University, A.B., 1918, A.M., 1919; Columbia University, Ph.D., 1923. *Religion:* Baptist.

CAREER: Columbia University, New York, N.Y., instructor in history, 1921-25; University of Pennsylvania, Philadelphia, assistant professor, 1925-30, professor of history, 1930-66, dean of Graduate School of Arts and Sciences, 1952-66, vice-provost, 1953-66, professor emeritus, 1966-73. Visiting professor at Columbia University, 1944-45, Cambridge University, 1948-49, and Stanford University, 1952; Fulbright lecturer in India and Japan, 1962. Rutgers, The State University, trustee, 1950-73, member of board of governors, 1956-73. Member, Philadelphia Historical Commission; member, Pennsylvania Historical Commission, 1940-43; president, Association of Graduate Schools of the American Association of Universities, 1963-64; chairman, Council of Graduate Schools in the U.S., 1965.

MEMBER: Social Science Research Council (chairman, 1949-53), American Philosophical Society, American Historical Association (member of council, 1943-47; member of executive committee, 1945-47; vice-president, 1964-65; president, 1965-66), Middle States Association of History Teachers (president, 1932-33), Pennsylvania Federation of Historical Societies (president, 1940-42), Historical Society of Pennsylvania (senator, united chapters), Phi Beta Kappa, Pi Gamma Mu, Phi Alpha Theta, Cosmos Club (Washington, D.C.), Century Club (New York), Authors Club (London, England), Rittenhouse Club (Philadelphia). *Awards, honors:* Pulitzer Prize for history, 1949, for *The Disruption of American Democracy;* Haney Medal for literary excellence, 1961; Silver Medal of Philadelphia Club of Advertising Women; Athenaeum Award, 1962. Honorary degrees: Litt.D., Franklin and Marshall College, 1937, Muhlenberg University,

1956, and University of Chattanooga, 1966; M.A., Cambridge University, 1940; L.H.D., Rutgers, The State University, 1941; LL.D., Moravian College, 1953, Lincoln University, 1959, and Knox College, 1960; S.Sc.D., Lebanon Valley College, 1961; D.Ped., Susquehanna University, 1964.

WRITINGS: The Democratic Machine, 1850-1854, Columbia University Press, 1923; (with others) *Syllabus for History of Civilization,* University of Pennsylvania Press, 1927; *Franklin Pierce,* University of Pennsylvania Press, 1931, 2nd edition, 1958; (with C. A. Beard and W. C. Bagley) *America Yesterday and Today,* Macmillan, 1938; (with wife, Jeannette P. Nichols) *Growth of American Democracy,* Appleton, 1939; (with J. P. Nichols) *Republic of the United States,* two volumes, Appleton, 1942; (with J. P. Nichols) *Short History of American Democracy,* Appleton, 1943; *The Disruption of American Democracy,* Macmillan, 1948; *Advance Agents of American Destiny,* University of Pennsylvania Press, 1956, reprinted, Greenwood Press, 1980; (editor) *Battles and Leaders of the Civil War,* four volumes, A. S. Barnes, 1957; *Religion and American Democracy,* Louisiana State University Press, 1959; *Stakes of Power, 1845-1877,* Hill & Wang, 1961; *Blueprints for Leviathan: American Style,* Atheneum, 1963 (published as *American Leviathans,* Harper, 1966); *The Invention of the American Political Parties,* Macmillan, 1967; *The Pennsylvania Historical and Museum Commission: A History,* Pennsylvania Historical and Museum Commission, 1967; *A Historian's Progress* (autobiography), Knopf, 1968.

SIDELIGHTS: Roy F. Nichols was, as Joseph C. Dougherty wrote in *Best Sellers,* "one of the country's most distinguished American history specialists." Speaking of Nichols' autobiography, *A Historian's Progress,* Henry F. Graff wrote in the *New York Times Book Review:* "Being a humble autobiographer, Nichols does not tell everything he could about himself. Others must bear witness to his commanding gifts as a lecturer, his capacity for generous friendship, and his matchless grace as a racouteur—qualities that inhere in a historian's historian."

In 1969, Nichols and his wife donated their papers and 5,000-volume library to Federal City College in Washington, D.C.

BIOGRAPHICAL/CRITICAL SOURCES: New York Times Book Review, July 23, 1967, July 14, 1968; *Virginia Quarterly Review,* autumn, 1967; *Best Sellers,* July 15, 1968; *New York Times,* January 13, 1973; *Washington Post,* January 13, 1973.†

*   *   *

NICHOLSON, Norman (Cornthwaite) 1914-

PERSONAL: Born January 8, 1914, in Millom, Cumberland, England; son of Joseph (an outfitter) and Edith (Cornthwaite) Nicholson; married Yvonne Gardner (a teacher), July 5, 1956. *Education:* Attended schools in Millom, Cumberland, England. *Religion:* Church of England. *Home:* 14 St. George's Ter., Millom, Cumberland, England. *Agent:* David Higham Associates Ltd., 5-8, Lower John St., Golden Square, London W1R 4HA, England.

CAREER: Author. Public lecturer and broadcaster on modern poetry, the English Lake District, and other subjects. *Member:* Royal Society of Literature, P.E.N. *Awards, honors:* Heineman Prize, 1945, for *Five Rivers;* Cholmondeley Award for Poetry, 1967; M.A., Open University, 1975; Queen's Medal for Poetry, 1977; Litt.D., Liverpool University, 1980.

WRITINGS: (Editor) *An Anthology of Religious Verse, Designed for the Times,* Penguin, 1942; (with John Hall and Keith Douglas) *Selected Poems,* Staples, 1943; *Man and Literature* (criticism), S.C.M. Press, 1943; *Five Rivers* (poetry), Faber, 1944, Dutton, 1945; *The Fire of the Lord* (novel), Nicholson & Watson, 1944, Dutton, 1946; *The Old Man of the Mountains* (three-act verse play; first produced Off-Broadway at Mercury Theatre, 1945), Faber, 1946, revised edition, Macmillan, 1950; *The Green Shore* (novel), Nicholson & Watson, 1947; *Rock Face* (poetry), Faber, 1948; *Cumberland and Westmorland,* R. Hale, 1949; (compiler and author of introduction) *Wordsworth: An Introduction and a Selection by Norman Nicholson,* Transatlantic, 1949.

H. G. Wells (criticism), Arthur Barker, 1950, Alan Swallow, 1951; *Prophesy to the Wind* (verse play in four scenes and prologue), Faber, 1950, Macmillan, 1951; *William Cowper* (criticism), Lehmann, 1951; (compiler and author of introduction) William Cowper, *Poems,* Grey Walls Press, 1951; *The Pot Geranium* (poetry), Faber, 1954; *A Match for the Devil* (verse play in four scenes), Faber, 1955; *The Lakers: Adventures of the First Tourists,* R. Hale, 1955, Dufour, 1964; *Provincial Pleasures,* R. Hale, 1959.

Birth by Drowning (verse play), Faber, 1960; *William Cowper* (pamphlet of criticism), Longmans, Green, 1960; *Portrait of the Lakes* (topography), R. Hale, 1963, Dufour, 1965; *Enjoying It All,* Waltham Forest Books, 1964; (with others) *Writers on Themselves* (radio talks), with introduction by Herbert Read, British Broadcasting Corp., 1964; *Selected Poems,* Faber, 1966; *No Star on the Way Back: Ballads and Carols,* Manchester Institute of Contemporary Arts, 1967; *Greater Lakeland* (topography), R. Hale, 1969, International Publications Service, 1970; *A Local Historian* (poetry), Faber, 1972; *Wednesday Early Closing* (autobiography), Faber, 1975; (editor) *A Choice of Cowper's Verse,* Faber, 1975; *Steel and Stone* (poetry) Ceolfrith Press, 1975; (editor) *The Lake District: An Anthology,* R. Hale, 1977, Penguin, 1978; *The Shadow of Black Combe* (poetry), Mid-Northcumberland Arts Group, 1978. Also author of a television Christmas play, "No Star on the Way Back," 1963. Contributor to *Times Literary Supplement, Church Times, Stand,* and other periodicals.

SIDELIGHTS: Norman Nicholson told *CA:* "I have spent all my life in the house where I was born and in the town where both my parents were born before me. Millom is a small industrial town . . . and most of my poetry takes its imagery from my immediate surroundings—mines, town, the coast, the mountains."

*   *   *

NICHOLSON, Norman L(eon) 1919-

PERSONAL: Born October 14, 1919, in Barking, Essex, England; son of Albert Leon and Dorothy Nicholson; married Helen Smith (a musician), August 15, 1947; children: Charles. *Education:* University of Western Ontario, B.A., 1943, M.Sc., 1947; University of Ottawa, Ph.D., 1951; University of Toronto, M.Ed., 1973, Ed.D., 1975. *Religion:* Anglican. *Office:* Department of Geography, University of Western Ontario, London, Ontario, Canada.

CAREER: Canadian Department of Mines and Technical Surveys, Geographical Branch, Ottawa, Ontario, geographer, 1949-54, director, 1954-64; University of Western Ontario, London, professor of geography, 1964—, chairman of department, 1979—, dean of University College, 1967-69. Chairman of Canadian Permanent Committee on Geographical Names, 1951-61, and of Canadian section of Pan American Institute of Geography and History, 1961-64. *Military service:* Royal Air Force, 1943-46; became flying officer. *Member:* Royal Canadian Geographical Society (fellow; director), Royal Geographical Society (fellow), American Geographical Society (fellow), Canadian Association of Geographers, Association of American Geographers.

WRITINGS: The Boundaries of Canada, Its Provinces and Territories, Queen's Printer (Canada), 1954; (contributor) Gordon East and A.E.F. Moodie, editors, *The Changing World: Studies in Political Geography,* World Book Encyclopedia, 1956; (editor) *Atlas of Canada,* Queen's Printer (Canada), 1958; (contributer) *The World in Which We Live and Work,* de Haan, 1962; *Canada in the American Community,* Van Nostrand, 1963; (contributor) R. R. Krueger and others, editors, *Regional and Resource Planning in Canada,* Holt, 1963; *Breve Geografia Regional de Canada,* Instituto Panamericana de Geografia e Historia (Rio de Janeiro), 1967; (contributor) John Warkentin, editor, *Canada: A Geographical Interpretation,* Methuen, 1968; (contributor) C. A. Fisher, editor, *Essays in Political Geography,* Methuen, 1968; *The Boundaries of the Canadian Confederation,* Macmillan, 1979; (with L. Sebert) *Canadian Maps,* Dawson, 1981. Contributor of more than one hundred articles and reviews to geography journals. Editor, Canadian Association of Geographers, 1951-60.

BIOGRAPHICAL/CRITICAL SOURCES: Times Literary Supplement, December 25, 1969; *Books in Canada,* March, 1980.

*   *   *

NIELSEN, Niels Christian, Jr. 1921-

PERSONAL: Born June 2, 1921, in Long Beach, Calif.; son of Niels Hansen (a merchant) and Frances (Nofziger) Nielsen; married Erika Kreuth (a professor of Germanics), May 10, 1958; children: Camilla Regina, Niels Albrecht. *Education:* Attended University of Southern California, 1938-40; George Pepperdine College (now Pepperdine University), B.A., 1942; Yale University, B.D., 1946, Ph.D., 1951. *Politics:* Democrat. *Religion:* Methodist. *Home:* 2424 Swift, Houston, Tex. 77030. *Office:* Department of Religious Studies, Rice University, Houston, Tex. 77001.

CAREER: Rice University, Houston, Tex. 1951—, professor of philosophy and religious thought, 1959—, chairman of department of religious studies, 1968—. Ordained local elder of Methodist church. *Member:* Society for Values in Higher Education (fellow), American Academy of Religion, American Society for Study of World Religions, American Philosophical Association, Society for Scientific Study of Religion, American Association of University Professors, Metaphysical Society of America, Union for Study of Great Religions (chapter president), Southwest Philosophical Conference (president, 1960), Southern Society for Philosophy of Religion.

WRITINGS: Geistige Landerkunde, USA, Glock & Lutz, 1960; *A Layman Looks at World Religions,* Bethany Press, 1962; *God in Education: A New Opportunity for American Schools,* Sheed & Ward, 1966; *Solzhenitzyn's Religion,* Thomas Nelson, 1976; *The Religion of President Carter,* Thomas Nelson, 1977; *The Crisis of Human Rights,* Thomas Nelson, 1978; (editor) *World Religions,* St. Martin's, 1981. Also author of pamphlet, *Religion and Philosophy in Contemporary Japan,* Rice Institute, 1957. Contributor to *America, Churchman, Monist,* and other religious journals.

NILAND, D'Arcy Francis 1920-1967

PERSONAL: Born 1920, in Glen Innes, New South Wales, Australia; died March 29, 1967; married Ruth Park (a writer), 1942; children: Anne, Rory, Patrick, Deborah, Kilmeny. *Education:* Attended parochial school in Glen Innes, New South Wales, Australia. *Agent:* H. N. Swanson, Inc., 8523 Sunset Blvd., Los Angeles, Calif. 90069.

CAREER: Writer. Worked as magazine editor, special correspondent, and roving journalist. *Awards, honors: Sydney Morning Herald* Literary Competition, first place short story award and second place novel award, 1949; Australian prize winner, First and Second World Short Story Quests, 1950 and 1952; Commonwealth Jubilee Literary Competition, second place novel award, second place short story award, and special short story prize, 1951.

WRITINGS: The Shiralee (Book Society selection), Sloane, 1955, reprinted, Penguin, 1978; *Make Your Stories Sell: Be Your Own Editor,* Angus & Robertson, 1955, published as *Be Your Own Editor: Make Your Stories Sell,* Barrows, 1959; (with wife, Ruth Park) *The Drums Go Bang* (autobiography), Angus & Robertson, 1956; *Call Me When the Cross Turns Over,* Angus & Robertson, 1958, published as *Women from the Country,* Sloane, 1959; *Gold in the Streets,* Horwitz, 1959; *The Big Smoke,* Angus & Robertson, 1959, Sloane, 1961; *The Ballad of the Fat Bushranger,* Horwitz, 1961; *Logan's Girl,* Horwitz, 1961; *Dadda Jumped over Two Elephants,* Sloane, 1963; *The Apprentices,* M. Joseph, 1965; *Pairs and Loners* (short stories), M. Joseph, 1966; *Travelling Songs of Old Australia,* Horwitz, 1966; *Dead Men Running,* M. Joseph, 1969, Penguin, 1978. Also author of radio and television scripts. Contributor of more than five hundred short stories to anthologies and periodicals; contributor of articles to newspapers and magazines.

AVOCATIONAL INTERESTS: Travel.†

*   *   *

NOHL, Frederick 1927-

PERSONAL: Born November 4, 1927, in Chicago, Ill.; son of Herman (a carpenter) and Olga (Wippenbeck) Nohl; married Elisabeth Hannah Strasen, November 25, 1948 (divorced July 19, 1976); married Gail Altman, May 6, 1977; children: (first marriage) Christine Ruth, Lisa Margaret, Constance Marie, Paul Herman, James Frederick. *Education:* Concordia Teachers College, River Forest, Ill., B.S., 1948; attended Olivet Nazarene College, 1950-51; Northwestern University, M.A., 1954; Concordia Theological Seminary, St. Louis, Mo., summer study, 1954-57; attended Washington University, St. Louis, Mo., 1968-69, St. Louis University, 1969, and University of California, San Diego, 1975. *Politics:* Democrat. *Home:* 19 Rock Hill Rd., Apt. 3A, Bala Cynwyd, Pa. 19004. *Office:* Intermed Communications, Inc., 132 Welsh Rd., Horsham, Pa. 19044.

CAREER: St. Paul's Lutheran School, Kankakee, Ill., 1948-54, began as teacher, became principal; St. John's Lutheran School, Forest Park, Ill., principal, 1954-55; Lutheran Church-Missouri Synod, Board of Parish Education, St. Louis, Mo., editor of Lutheran school materials, 1956-69; Concordia Publishing House, St. Louis, Mo., media developer, 1969-75; Lutheran Church in America, Division for Parish Services, special assignments editor, 1975-78; Intermed Communications, Inc., Horsham, Pa., senior editor of *Nursing* (magazine), 1978—. *Member:* American Civil Liberties Union, American Medical Writers Association, Fellowship of Reconciliation, Amnesty International, Common Cause, Lutheran Human Relations Association of

America, National Safety Council (secretary of elementary school section, 1965-66; member of executive committee of section, 1966-67; vice-chairman of section, 1967-68; chairman of section, 1968-69), Concordia Historical Institute (member of board, 1962-79; secretary, 1965-75), St. Louis-St. Louis County White House Conference on Education (member of board, 1959-71; treasurer, 1962-64).

WRITINGS—All published by Concordia: (Editor) *An Instrument for Evaluating Lutheran Elementary Schools*, 1958; (contributor) *Partners in Education*, 1958; (editor with William A. Kramer) *Growing in Faith*, 1958; (contributor) *Your Child and Society*, 1961; *Martin Luther: Hero of Faith*, 1962; (editor with Frederick A. Meyer) *A Curriculum Guide for Lutheran Elementary Schools*, three volumes, 1964; *Race Relations in Christian Perspective*, 1965. Adaptor, "Warner Sex Education Booklets," Concordia, 1963. Editor with Henry C. Niermeier, "Concordia Art Education" series, Concordia, 1968-69. Columnist, *St. Louis Lutheran*, 1966, *St. Louis Journal*, 1967-70, and *Academy*, 1974-75. Editor of audio-visual materials, Fortress Press, 1976-78. Contributor to religious periodicals.

SIDELIGHTS: Frederick Nohl told *CA* that aspiring writers should "write something—anything—every day; it won't make your writing perfect, but it will certainly make your next assignment twice as easy. Inspiration is great, but don't count on it; ultimately, writing is the regular application of the seat of the pants (or skirt) to the seat of a chair. Keep it lean, active, and pointed; remember, humanity's profoundest thoughts are usually only a short, simple sentence long. Feel free to hate your editors, but don't ignore them; they usually know more about quality—and what sells—than you think."

AVOCATIONAL INTERESTS: Swimming, softball, public speaking, travel.

BIOGRAPHICAL/CRITICAL SOURCES: Lutheran Witness, February 28, 1956.

*   *   *

NORTON, Howard Melvin   1911-

PERSONAL: Born May 30, 1911, in Haverhill, Mass.; son of Clarence Alfred and Grace (Eckel) Norton; married Marjorie Anderson, 1940; children: Howard, Jr., Martha (Mrs. C. P. Izzo), Mary Elizabeth, Deborah. *Education:* University of Florida, B.S.J., 1933. *Religion:* Presbyterian. *Home:* 4002 Laird Pl., Chevy Chase, Md. 20015.

CAREER: Whaley-Eaton Service, Japan-China correspondent in Tokyo, Japan, and correspondent for several U.S. newspapers, 1933-40; *Baltimore Sun*, Baltimore, Md., 1940-64, worked as foreign editor, war correspondent in Pacific, chief of London Bureau, 1950-51, chief of Moscow Bureau, 1956-59, national labor and political writer at Washington (D.C.) Bureau, 1959-64; *U.S. News and World Report*, associate editor, 1964-70, White House correspondent, 1970-76; *National Courier*, Washington Bureau chief, 1976-77; National Association for Community Action, Inc., Washington, D.C., editor of publications and editor-writer of monthly newspaper *Network*, 1979—. Radio commentator and panelist in political and labor fields. *Member:* National Press Club (Washington, D.C.), Sigma Delta Chi, Lakewood Country Club (Rockville, Md.). *Awards, honors:* Pulitzer Prize, 1947, for series of articles on unemployment compensation that appeared in the *Baltimore Sun;* first National Mental Health Bell Award was presented to *Baltimore Sun*, 1953, in recognition of expose on Maryland's mental hospitals written by Norton; Centennial Award in Journalism, University of

Florida, 1953; named one of four distinguished alumni of College of Journalism and Communications, University of Florida, 1978.

WRITINGS—Published by Logos International, except as indicated: *Only in Russia*, Van Nostrand, 1961; *The Miracle of Jimmy Carter*, 1977; *Rosalynn: A Portrait*, 1977; *When the Angels Laughed*, 1978; *Good News about Trouble*, 1978. Contributor to *Reader's Digest, Science and Mechanics*, and other magazines.

SIDELIGHTS: Although a non-combatant, Howard Norton was awarded the Pacific-Asiatic ribbon by General Douglas MacArthur for service as a war correspondent in New Guinea and the Central Pacific. He was wounded in landing with the first wave of Marines on Guam in 1944. He also served as war correspondent behind Nazi lines in Italy with Italian Partisan forces and reportedly was the first Allied newsman to report the execution of Mussolini in 1945.

The Miracle of Jimmy Carter has been translated into Japanese, Dutch, German, Swedish, Norwegian, and Spanish.

*   *   *

NOTT, Kathleen Cecilia

PERSONAL: Born in London, England; daughter of Philip and Ellen Nott. *Education:* Attended King's College, London, and Somerville College, Oxford. *Home:* 5 Limpsfield Ave., Thornton, Heath, Surrey, England.

CAREER: Writer. *Member:* P.E.N. (chairman of poetry committee, 1956—; president of English Centre, 1974-75), Progressive League (London; president, 1958-60).

WRITINGS: Mile End (novel), Hogarth, 1938; *The Dry Deluge* (novel), Hogarth, 1947; *Landscapes and Departures* (poetry), Nicholson & Watson, 1947; *The Emperor's Clothes: An Attack on the Dogmatic Orthodoxy of T. S. Eliot, Graham Greene, C. S. Lewis, and Others*, Heinemann, 1953; *Poems from the North*, Hand & Flower, 1956; *Creatures and Emblems* (poetry), Routledge & Kegan Paul, 1960; *Private Fires* (novel), Heinemann, 1960; *A Clean Well-Lighted Place*, Heinemann, 1961; *An Elderly Retired Man* (novel), Faber, 1963; (co-author) *Objections to Humanism*, Constable, 1963; (contributor) *What I Believe*, Allen & Unwin, 1966; *Soul in the Quad: The Use of Language in Philosophy and Literature*, Routledge & Kegan Paul, 1969; *Philosophy and Human Nature*, New York University Press, 1971; *The Good Want Power: An Essay on the Psychological Possibilities of Liberalism*, Basic Books, 1977. Contributor to *Times Literary Supplement, Observer, Spectator, Time and Tide*, and other magazines and journals. Acting editor, *P.E.N. Bulletin of Selected Books*.

WORK IN PROGRESS: A novel, poetry, and an autobiography.

*   *   *

NOURSE, Alan E(dward)   1928-
(Dr. X, Al Edwards)

PERSONAL: Born August 11, 1928, in Des Moines, Iowa; son of Benjamin Chamberlain (an electrical engineer) and Grace (Ogg) Nourse; married Ann Jane Morton, 1952; children: Benjamin, Rebecca, Jonathan, Christopher. *Education:* Rutgers University, B.S., 1951; University of Pennsylvania, M.D., 1955. *Religion:* Episcopalian. *Home address:* Route 1, Box 173, Thorp, Wash. 98946.

CAREER: Virginia Mason Hospital, Seattle, Wash., intern, 1955-56; free-lance writer in North Bend, Wash., 1956-58;

North Bend Medical Clinic, North Bend, partner, 1958-64; free-lance writer, 1964—. *Military service:* U.S. Navy, Hospital Corps, 1946-48. *Member:* American Medical Association, Science Fiction Writers of America (president, 1968-69), Washington State Medical Society, King County Medical Society, Alpha Kappa Kappa. *Awards, honors:* Junior Book Award, Boys Clubs of America, 1963, for *Raiders from the Rings;* Washington State Governor's Award, Governor's Festival of the Arts, 1966, 1974.

WRITINGS—Novels; published by McKay, except as indicated: *Trouble on Titan* (Junior Literary Guild selection), Holt, 1954; *A Man Obsessed,* Ace Books, 1954; *Rocket to Limbo,* 1957; *Scavengers in Space,* 1959; (with J. A. Meyer) *The Invaders Are Coming,* Ace Books, 1959; *Star Surgeon,* 1960; *Raiders from the Rings,* 1962; *The Universe Between,* 1965; *Psi High and Others,* 1967; *The Mercy Men,* 1968; *The Bladerunner,* 1974; *The Practice,* Harper, 1978.

Nonfiction; published by Harper, except as indicated: *So You Want to Be a Doctor,* 1957, revised edition, 1963; (with brother, William B. Nourse) *So You Want to Be a Lawyer,* 1958; *So You Want to Be a Scientist,* 1960; *Nine Planets,* 1960, revised edition, 1970; (with E. Halliday) *So You Want to Be a Nurse,* 1961; (with J. Webbert) *So You Want to Be an Engineer,* 1962; (with Geoffrey Marks) *The Management of a Medical Practice,* Lippincott, 1962; *So You Want to Be a Physicist,* 1964; (with the editors of *Life*) *The Body,* Time, Inc., 1964; *So You Want to Be a Chemist,* 1964; (under pseudonym Dr. X) *Intern,* 1965; *So You Want to Be a Surgeon,* 1966; (with C. Meinhardt) *So You Want to Be an Architect,* 1969; *Universe, Earth and Atom: The Story of Physics,* 1969; *Ladies Home Journal Family Medical Guide,* 1973; *The Outdoorsman's Medical Guide,* 1974; *Vitamins: A Concise Guide,* F. Watts, 1977; *Inside the Mayo Clinic,* McGraw, 1979; *Hormones: An Impact Book,* F. Watts, 1979.

Juveniles; published by F. Watts, except as indicated: *Junior Intern,* Harper, 1957; *Venus and Mercury: A First Book,* 1972; *The Backyard Astronomer,* 1973; *The Giant Planets: A First Book,* 1974; *The Asteroids: A First Book,* 1975; *Viruses: A First Book,* 1976; *Lumps, Bumps and Rashes, A Look at Kids' Diseases: A First Book,* 1976; *Clear Skin, Healthy Skin: A Concise Guide,* 1976; *Fractures, Dislocations and Sprains: A First Book,* 1978; *Hormones: An Impact Book,* 1979; *Menstruation: A First Book,* 1980.

Short story collections: *Tiger by the Tail and Other Science Fiction Stories,* McKay, 1960; *The Counterfeit Man: More Science Fiction Stories,* McKay, 1965; *Rx for Tomorrow: Tales of Science Fiction, Fantasy and Medicine,* McKay, 1971.

Author of column, "Family Doctor," and contributing editor, *Good Housekeeping,* 1976—. Contributor of articles and short stories to numerous periodicals, including *Saturday Evening Post, Argosy, Playboy, Astounding Science Fiction, Better Homes and Gardens,* and *Boys Life;* contributor to medical journals.

AVOCATIONAL INTERESTS: Hunting, fishing, climbing, backpacking.

BIOGRAPHICAL/CRITICAL SOURCES: New York Times Book Review, June 25, 1978; *Los Angeles Times Book Review,* October 7, 1979.

*   *   *

NOVE, Alec 1915-

PERSONAL: Original name, Alexander Novakovsky; surname legally changed in 1936; born November 24, 1915, in Petrograd, Russia (now Leningrad, U.S.S.R.); son of Jacob and Rachel (Zorokhovich) Novakovsky; married Irene MacPherson, 1951; children: David Alexander, Perry Richard, Charles. *Education:* London School of Economics and Political Science, London, B.Sc., 1936. *Office:* Department of International Economic Studies, University of Glasgow, Glasgow G12, Scotland.

CAREER: Held various research posts in London, England, 1936-39; British Civil Service, London, principal, mainly with Board of Trade, 1947-58; University of London, London School of Economics and Political Science, London, reader, 1958-63; University of Glasgow, Glasgow, Scotland, professor of international economic studies, 1963—. Visiting professor, University of Kansas, 1962; and University of Pennsylvania, 1968; lecturer in United States, India, Germany, France, and in other countries. *Military service:* British Army, Royal Signals and Intelligence Corps, 1939-46; became major. *Member:* British Academy (fellow). *Awards, honors:* D.Ag., University of Giessen.

WRITINGS: Communist Economic Strategy: Soviet Growth and Capabilities, National Planning Association, 1959; (with D. Donnelly) *Trade with Communist Countries,* Hutchinson, 1960; *The Soviet Economy,* Praeger, 1961, 2nd edition, 1969; *Economic Rationality and Soviet Politics,* Praeger, 1964; (with J. A. Newth) *The Soviet Middle-East: A Model of Development?,* Praeger, 1967; *Communism at the Crossroads,* Leeds University Press, 1964; *Soviet Jewry and the Fiftieth Anniversary of the Russian Revolution,* World Jewish Congress, 1968; *Economic History of the U.S.S.R.,* Penguin, 1969; (editor with D. M. Nuti) *Socialist Economics,* Penguin, 1972; *Efficiency Criteria for the Nationalized Industries,* Allen & Unwin, 1973; *Planning: What, How, and Why,* Academic Press, 1975; *Stalinism and After,* Allen & Unwin, 1975; *Soviet Economic System,* Allen & Unwin, 1977; *Political Economy and Soviet Socialism,* Allen & Unwin, 1979. Contributor of numerous articles to journals in his field.

AVOCATIONAL INTERESTS: Music, sports, Russian literature, travel, walking.

*   *   *

NUNIS, Doyce B(lackman), Jr. 1924-

PERSONAL: Born May 30, 1924, in Cedartown, Ga.; son of Doyce Blackman and Winnie Ethel (Morris) Nunis. *Education:* University of California, Los Angeles, B.A., 1947; University of Southern California, M.S., 1950, M.Ed., 1952, Ph.D., 1958. *Home:* 4426 Cromwell Ave., Los Angeles, Calif. 90027. *Office* Department of History, University of Southern California, Los Angeles, Calif. 90007.

CAREER: Redondo Beach Elementary School District, Redondo Beach, Calif., teacher, 1948-51; University of Southern California, Los Angeles, lecturer in American history and government, 1951-56; El Camino College, Torrance, Calif., instructor, 1956-59; University of California, Los Angeles, associate professor of education and history and head of Office of Oral History, 1959-65; University of Southern California, Los Angeles, associate professor, 1965-68, professor of history, 1968—.

MEMBER: American Historical Association, American Association of University Professors, Organization of American Historians, California Historical Society, Southern California Historical Society, Phi Alpha Theta, Pi Sigma Alpha. *Awards, honors:* Del Amo Foundation grant for research abroad, 1956; Henry E. Huntington Library grant-in-aid, 1960; joint winner of Louis Knoot Koontz Memorial Award, 1960, for best contribution to *Pacific Historical Review;*

Guggenheim fellow, 1963-64; award of merit, American Association for State and Local History, 1965, 1974; American Philosophical Society fellowship, 1969; award of merit, Los Angeles Westerners, 1971; certificate of merit, Southern California Historical Society, 1972, 1974; award for teaching excellence, University of Southern California Associates, 1975; faculty fellow, University of Southern California, College of Letters, Arts, and Sciences, 1974-78.

WRITINGS—Published by Dawson's Book Shop, except as indicated: *Andrew Sublette, 1808-1853: Rocky Mountain Prince*, 1960; *The Trials of Isaac Graham*, 1967; *The Past Is Prologue: A Centennial Profile of Pacific Mutual Life Insurance Company*, Ritchie, 1968; *History of American Political Thought*, two volumes, Addison-Wesley, 1975; *The Mexican War in Baja California*, 1977.

Editor: *The Golden Frontier: The Recollections of Herman Francis Rinehart, 1851-1869*, University of Texas Press, 1962; *Josiah Belden, 1841 California Overland Pioneer: His Memoir and Early Letters*, Talisman Press, 1962; *The California Diary of Faxon Dean Atherton, 1836-1839*, California Historical Society, 1964; *Letters of a Young Miner*, John Howell Books, 1964; *Journey of James H. Bull: Baja, California, October, 1843-January, 1844*, Dawson's Book Shop, 1966; P. Garrier, *A Medical Journey in California*, Zeitlin & Ver Brugge, 1967; *Hudson's Bay Company's First Fur Brigade to the Sacramento Valley*, Sacramento Book Collectors Club, 1968; *Sketches on a Journey on the Two Oceans*, Dawson's Book Shop, 1971; *San Francisco Vigilante Committee of 1856*, Los Angeles Westerners, 1971; *Drawings of Ignacio Firsch, S.J.*, Dawson's Book Shop, 1972; *Los Angeles and Its Environs in the Twentieth Century: A Bibliography of a Metropolis*, Ritchie, 1973; *Westerners Brand Book #14*, Los Angeles Westerners, 1974; (co-editor) *A Guide to Historic Places in Los Angeles County*, Kendall/Hunt, 1978; *A Frontier Doctor*, R. H. Donnelley, 1979. Also editor of "Santa Barbara Bicentennial Historical Series," six volumes.

Contributor: LeRoy R. Hafen, editor, *The Mountain Men*, Arthur H. Clark, 1966; *University of California Centennial History*, University of California Press, 1968; *Maynard J. Geiger, O.F.M.: Franciscan and Historian—A Seventieth Birthday Tribute*, Friends of Mission Santa Barbara Archive Library, 1971.

Author of introduction: Francis J. Weber, *George Francis Montgomery*, Westernlore, 1966; Weber, *A Bibliography of California Bibliographies*, Ritchie, 1968; Alfred Robinson, *Life in California*, Da Capo Press, 1979.

Contributor of articles to *Pacific Historical Review, Montana Magazine, American West*, and other publications. Editor, *Southern California Quarterly*, 1962—.

BIOGRAPHICAL/CRITICAL SOURCES: *Historical Society of Southern California Newsletter*, Volume I, numbers 3 and 4.

O

OATES, Whitney J(ennings)   1904-1973

PERSONAL: Born March 26, 1904, in Evanston, Ill.; died October 14, 1973, in Sarasota, Fla.; son of James Franklin (an insurance man) and Henrietta (Jennings) Oates; married Virginia Hill, September 1, 1927; children: Henrietta J. (Mrs. Norman W. Kavanaugh). *Education:* Princeton University, A.B., 1926, A.M., 1927, Ph.D., 1931. *Politics:* Democrat. *Religion:* Episcopalian. *Office:* Firestone Library, Princeton University, Princeton, N.J. 08540.

CAREER: Princeton University, Princeton, N.J., instructor, 1927-31, assistant professor, 1931-40, associate professor, 1940-45, professor of classics, 1945-70, West Professor of Classics, 1949-62, Avalon Professor of Humanities, 1962-70. Trustee, Princeton University Press, Rockefeller Brothers Theological Fund, Woodrow Wilson National Fellowship Foundation, and Wenner-Gren Foundation for Anthropological Research; member of board of visitors, Tulane University. Senior fellow, Center for Hellenic Studies, Harvard University; chairman, Council of the Humanities, Princeton University, 1953-70. *Military service:* U.S. Marine Corps Reserve, 1943-53, on active duty 1943-45; became major. *Member:* American Council of Learned Societies (treasurer), American Philological Association, United Chapters of Phi Beta Kappa (senator; vice-president; president), Century Association (New York). *Awards, honors:* L.H.D., Brown University, 1961, and Rockford College, 1961; Litt.D., Middlebury College, 1963.

WRITINGS: The Influence of Simonides of Ceos on Horace, Princeton University Press, 1932, reprinted, Haskell House, 1970; (editor with Eugene O'Neill, Jr.) *The Complete Greek Drama,* Random House, 1938, published as *Seven Famous Greek Plays,* 1961; (editor) *The Stoic and Epicurean Philosopher,* Random House, 1940; (with C. T. Murphy) *Greek Literature in Translation,* Longmans, Green, 1944; (with Murphy and K. Guinagh) *Greek and Roman Classics in Translation,* Longmans, Green, 1946; (editor) *The Basic Writings of St. Augustine,* Random House, 1948; *Aristotle and the Problem of Value,* Princeton University Press, 1963; (editor) Plato, *Lysis,* Heritage Press, 1968; *Plato's View of Art,* Scribner, 1972. Also editor of *From Sophocles to Picasso: The Present-Day Vitality of the Classical Tradition,* 1962. Contributor of articles and reviews to periodicals.

WORK IN PROGRESS: Two books, *Ancient Philosophy* and *Theory of Tragedy.*

SIDELIGHTS: Whitney J. Oates founded the Woodrow Wilson Fellowship program that now aids one thousand students a year. He appeared several times on Columbia Broadcasting System's "Invitation to Learning."†

*   *   *

O'BRADY, Frederic Michel Maurice   1903-

PERSONAL: Original surname, Abel; born December 11, 1903, in Budapest, Hungary; became French citizen, 1947; son of Jules (an expert on cereals and grain) and Anne (Kwaschnofski) Abel; married Edna Lockwood; married Colette Fleuriot, December 13, 1960. *Education:* Attended University of Munich, 1922, and University of Liverpool, 1929. *Religion:* Roman Catholic. *Home:* 1077 East Ave., Rochester, N.Y. 14607.

CAREER: Actor and dancer. Danced with Ballets Russe troupe; member of "Masses," a workers' theatre group, 1932; worked in puppet shows; appeared in plays, including "14 juillet," "Ubu enchaine," "Ninotchka," "The Unthinking Lobster," "Andalousie," and "La Plume de ma tante"; appeared in films, including "Drole de drame," "Blanc comme neige," "Les Amants de Verone," "C'est arrive a Paris," "Foreign Intrigue," "Picnic on the Grass," and "Mr. Arkadin"; has performed on radio and television. Trinity-Pawling School, Pawling, N.Y., French teacher and drama coach, 1963-65; Princeton University, Princeton, N.J., instructor in French, 1965-72. *Military service:* French Foreign Legion, 1939-40. *Member:* Syndicat Francais des Acteurs (former vice-president), Actors' Equity. *Awards, honors:* French Cross, 1949, for artistic merit.

WRITINGS: Exterieurs a Venise (novel), preface by Orson Welles, Gallimard, 1950; *Le Ciel d'en face* (novel), Gallimard, 1954; *Romarin pour le souvenir* (novel), Correa, 1958; *All Told* (autobiography), Simon & Schuster, 1964 (published in England as *All Told: The Memoirs of a Multiple Man,* Bodley Head, 1964); *There's Always a Throgmorton* (novel), Simon & Schuster, 1970; *Propos Pertinents et Impertinents* (textbook), Scribner's, 1973.

Musical works: "L'Object aime" (eleven-minute opera; text by Alfred Jarry), first performed at Paris World Exhibition, 1937; "Rendez-vous a la Trinite" (musical comedy), first produced on French television, 1951; "Le Mecene" (one-act opera), first produced on French television, 1952; "L'Homme oublie," "Yolande," and "Le Generique" (three one-act operas), first broadcast on French radio, 1954; "Concertino en sol" (musical work for two trumpets and strings), 1954; "Fait divers" (oratorio), first broadcast on French radio, 1956. Also composer of incidental music for Cyril Connolly's English translation of "Ubu cocu" by Alfred Jarry, 1963, and for "Fennel and Columbine," 1980.

WORK IN PROGRESS: Pompeii and Circumstance, in Latin.

BIOGRAPHICAL/CRITICAL SOURCES: Andre-Charles Gervais, *Marionettes et marionettistes de France,* Bordas, 1946; *New York Times,* July 13, 1956, October 12, 1960; Frederick Michel Maurice O'Brady, *All Told* (autobiography), Simon & Schuster, 1964 (published in England as *All Told: The Memoirs of a Multiple Man,* Bodley Head, 1964); Ian Cameron, *The Heavies,* Praeger, 1969; Anthony Swerling, *Strindberg's Impact in France,* Trinity Lane Press, 1971; Swerling, *In Quest of Strindberg,* Trinity Lane Press, 1971; Peter Schwed, *Hanging in There,* Houghton, 1977; Maurice Bessy, *Les passagers du souvenir,* Albin Michel (Paris), 1977; Maurice Baquet, *On dirait du veau,* Jacques-Marie Laffont, 1979; Andre Gillois, *Ce siecle avait deux ans,* Belfond (Paris), 1980.

*   *   *

O'CONNOR, (Mary) Flannery   1925-1964

PERSONAL: Born March 25, 1925, in Savannah, Ga.; died August 3, 1964 of lupus in Milledgeville, Ga.; daughter of Edward Francis and Regina (Cline) O'Connor. *Education:* Women's College of Georgia (now Georgia College), A.B., 1945; State University of Iowa, M.F.A., 1947. *Religion:* Roman Catholic. *Home:* Milledgeville, Ga. *Agent:* McIntosh, McKee & Dodds, 22 East 40th St., New York, N.Y. 10016.

CAREER: Author. *Awards, honors:* Kenyon Review fellowship in fiction, 1953; National Institute of Arts and Letters grant in literature, 1957; first prize, O. Henry Memorial Awards, 1957, for "Greenleaf," and 1963 and 1965, for other short stories; Ford Foundation grant, 1959; Litt.D. from St. Mary's College, 1962, and Smith College, 1963; Henry H. Bellaman Foundation special award, 1964; National Book Award, 1972, for *The Complete Short Stories;* Board Award, National Book Critics Circle, 1980, for *The Habit of Being.*

WRITINGS: Wise Blood (novel), Harcourt, 1952, published in *Three by Flannery O'Connor* (see below); *A Good Man Is Hard to Find* (stories; contains "A Good Man Is Hard to Find," "The River," "The Life You Save May Be Your Own," "A Stroke of Good Fortune," "A Temple of the Holy Ghost," "The Artificial Nigger," "A Circle in the Fire," "A Late Encounter with the Enemy," "Good Country People," and "The Displaced Person"; published in *Three by Flannery O'Connor* [see below]), Harcourt, 1955 (published in England as *The Artificial Nigger,* Neville Spearman, 1957); (contributor) Granville Hicks, editor, *The Living Novel,* Macmillan, 1957; *The Violent Bear It Away* (novel), Farrar, Straus, 1960, published in *Three by Flannery O'Connor* (see below); (editor and author of introduction) *A Memoir of Mary Ann,* Farrar, Straus, 1961 (published in England as *Death of a Child,* Burns & Oates, 1961); *Three by Flannery O'Connor* (contains *Wise Blood,* "A Good Man Is Hard to Find," and *The Violent Bear It Away*), Signet, 1964; *Everything That Rises Must Converge* (stories; contains "Everything That Rises Must Converge," "Greenleaf," "A View of the Woods," "The Enduring Chill," "The Comforts of Home," "The Lame Shall Enter First," "Revelation," "Parker's Back," and "Judgment Day"), Farrar, Straus,

1965; *Mystery and Manners: Occasional Prose,* edited by Sally Fitzgerald and Robert Fitzgerald, Farrar, Straus, 1969; *The Complete Short Stories,* Farrar, Straus, 1971; *The Habit of Being* (letters), edited by S. Fitzgerald, Farrar, Straus, 1979. Work in many anthologies including *Eight Great American Short Novels,* edited by Philip Rahv, Berkeley Publishing. Contributor to periodicals, including *Accent, Mademoiselle, Critic,* and *Esquire.*

SIDELIGHTS: A. L. Rowse called Flannery O'Connor "probably the greatest short-story writer of our time," and this opinion was not unique among critics. Though O'Connor's work has been compared frequently with that of Hawthorne, Nathanael West, and Dostoevsky, among others, "as a person and a writer she was a complete original," wrote Josephine Hendin. A religious writer who defined her "subject in fiction" as "the action of grace in territory held largely by the devil," O'Connor nevertheless believed good writing begins in a concrete "experience, not an abstraction." Her writing reflects this by being firmly rooted in her native South. Her Georgian Catholic family has lived in Milledgeville since before the Civil War. "Ours is a real Bible Belt," she once said. "We have a sense of the absolute, ... a sense of Moses' face as he pulverized the idols, ... a sense of time, place and eternity joined." In his book *The Christian Humanism of Flannery O'Connor,* David Eggenschwiler said that "she insisted that the ultimate concerns of her art transcended the natural but that her art was primarily of the concrete world in which the transcendent was manifested.... She sought a more than worldly knowledge, not by knowing the world badly but by knowing it well."

Considering her limited output as a writer, the critical response has been extraordinary. More than a dozen books, chapters in many more, and hundreds of articles have been devoted to O'Connor's work. As Hendin noted in *The World of Flannery O'Connor,* the author produced "a body of work of remarkable uniformity and persistent design." Her themes have been identified by Stanley Edgar Hyman as the "profound equation of the mysteries of sex and religion, ... change of identity, transformation, death-and-rebirth, ... the perverse mother, ... what Walter Allen ... calls a 'world of the God-intoxicated,' ... [and] the transvaluation of values in which progress in the world is retrogression in the spirit."

O'Connor wrote: "I see from the standpoint of Christian orthodoxy. This means that for me the meaning of life is centered in our Redemption by Christ and that what I see in the world I see in relation to that." Andre Bleikasten, however, wrote of the "heresy" of Flannery O'Connor and warned that "O'Connor's public pronouncements on her art—on which most of her commentators have pounced so eagerly—are by no means the best guide to her fiction. As an interpreter, she was just as fallible as anybody else, and in point of fact there is much of what she has said or written about her work that is highly questionable.... The truth of O'Connor's work is the truth of her art, not that of her church. Her fiction does refer to an implicit theology, but if we rely, as we should, on its testimony rather than on the author's comments, we shall have to admit that the Catholic orthodoxy of her work is at least debatable.... Gnawed by old Calvinistic ferments and at the same time corroded by a very modern sense of the absurd, O'Connor's version of Christianity is emphatically and exclusively her own.... Flannery O'Connor was a Catholic. She was not a Catholic writer. She was a writer, and as a writer she belongs to no other parish than literature."

She was, however, a theological writer. As such, Ted R.

Spivey explained, O'Connor dealt with violent and grotesque people because "man has in his soul a powerful destructive element, which often makes him behave in a violent and grotesque manner.... [Her writing is about] the existential struggle with the principle of destruction traditionally called the Devil." Numerous critics see this preoccupation with the demonic as a central characteristic of O'Connor's work. In opposition to this evil force O'Connor places a God whose "grace hits the characters in [her] stories with the force of a mugging," Hendin wrote. The climactic moments of grace in her stories and in her characters' lives have been described by Preston M. Browning, Jr. as "those moments when her characters undergo a traumatic collapse of their illusions of righteousness and self-sufficiency." As *Washington Post* critic William McPherson put it, "the question behind Miss O'Connor's stories is not whether God exists—he's there, all right—but whether men can bear it." Claire Katz summarized, "it is the impulse toward secular autonomy, the smug confidence that human nature is perfectible by its own efforts, that she sets out to destroy, through an act of violence so intense that the character is rendered helpless, ... [thus establishing] the need for absolute submission to the power of Christ." Hermione Lee of *New Statesman* echoed this view when she wrote, "Essentially, O'Connor's subject is acceptance: the point at which her sinners become aware of the awful unavoidability of Grace. All the stories drive towards an appointed end, often of horrifying violence.... The power of the work lies in its suppression of this severely orthodox subject beneath a brilliantly commonplace surface.... Its masterly realism springs from the life in Georgia, but its intellectual energy, and its penetration of grotesque extremes, derives from the faith."

Richard Poirier felt that this outlook contributed to O'Connor's major limitation, namely, "that the direction of her stories tends to be nearly always the same." *Hollins Critic* reviewer Walter Sullivan agreed but added, "what she did well, she did with exquisite competence: her ear for dialogue, her eye for human gestures were as good as anybody's ever were; and her vision was as clear and direct and as annoyingly precious as that of an Old Testament prophet or one of the more irascible Christian saints."

Her stories are not all terror and violence, however. There is also humor here, what Brainerd Cheney called "a brand of humor based on the religious point of view." James Degnan believed that O'Connor's was "a vision that clearly sees the tragedy of a world in which people are hopelessly alienated from each other, but a vision which stresses the comedy of such a world." In the introduction to *Everything That Rises Must Converge,* Robert Fitzgerald wrote, "There is quite a gamut of [comedy,] running from something very like cartooning to an irony dry and refined, especially in the treatment of the most serious matters." Kenneth L. Woodward likened O'Connor's "grimly Gothic humor" to that of William Blake.

In execution O'Connor's work "bears no relation whatever to the so-called 'art novel,'" noted Melvin Friedman. He explained, "her novels and stories are in every sense traditionally constructed and make no use of the experimental suggestions of a Joyce, a Proust, a Faulkner, or even a Styron." He called her characters "almost all fanatics." Another critic, Louise Gossett, observed that "the bold lines of their portraiture ... converge directly on the spiritual errors of the present.... When these lines are too direct, the fiction lapses into preaching." (O'Connor's letters reveal that she was aware of this problem. She wrote, "The novel is an

art form and when you use it for anything other than art, you pervert it.... If you do manage to use it successfully for social, religious, or other purposes, it is because you made it art first.")

It is the author's characters that rivet the attention of readers to her stories; Alice Walker noted that it was for O'Connor's characterizations "that I appreciated her work at first ... these white folks without the magnolia ... and these black folks without melons and superior racial patience, these are like the Southerners that I know." John Idol summed up Flannery O'Connor's fiction as follows: "In the twelve or fifteen of her best stories Miss O'Connor aptly blended satire and reverence, the concrete and the abstract, the comic and the cosmic, earning for herself a secure place among the writers of the Southern Renascence."

O'Connor's posthumously collected nonfiction has also earned praise. Granville Hicks wrote of *Mystery and Manners,* "I had read some of these lectures in one form or another, but until they were brought together I had not realized what an impressive body of literary criticism they constituted." John Leonard wrote that *Mystery and Manners* "should be read by every writer and would-be writer and lover of writing.... [O'Connor] ranks with Mark Twain and Scott Fitzgerald among our finest prose-stylists." Sally and Robert Fitzgerald, who collected and edited *Mystery and Manners* as well as O'Connor's letters, are presently working on a biography of the author.

A two-act play, "The Displaced Person," by Cecil Dawkins (first produced in New York at American Place Theatre, 1966) was based on five stories by Flannery O'Connor. A movie version of *Wise Blood* was directed by John Huston and released in 1980. Her work has been translated into French, Italian, Portuguese, Spanish, Greek, Danish, and Japanese. An annual, *The Flannery O'Connor Bulletin,* started in 1972, is devoted to articles about O'Connor and her work. Her papers are part of the permanent collection of the Georgia College Library.

BIOGRAPHICAL/CRITICAL SOURCES—Books: Joseph J. Waldmier, editor, *Recent American Fiction: Some Critical Views,* Houghton, 1963; Walter Allen, *The Modern Novel,* Dutton, 1964; Louise Y. Gossett, *Violence in Recent Southern Fiction,* Duke University Press, 1965; Robert Fitzgerald, introduction to *Everything That Rises Must Converge* by Flannery O'Connor, Farrar, Straus, 1965; Stanley Edgar Hyman, *Flannery O'Connor,* University of Minnesota Press, 1966; Melvin J. Friedman and Lewis A. Lawson, *The Added Dimension: The Art and Mind of Flannery O'Connor,* Fordham University Press, 1966; Robert Drake, *Flannery O'Connor,* Eerdmans, 1966; Robert E. Reiter, editor, *Flannery O'Connor,* Herder, 1968; C. W. Martin, *The True Country: Themes in the Fiction of Flannery O'Connor,* Vanderbilt University Press, 1969.

Josephine Hendin, *The World of Flannery O'Connor,* Indiana University Press, 1970; Leon V. Driskell and Joan T. Brittain, *The Eternal Crossroads: The Art of Flannery O'Connor,* University Press of Kentucky, 1971; David Eggenschwiler, *The Christian Humanism of Flannery O'Connor,* Wayne State University Press, 1972; K. Feeley, *Flannery O'Connor: Voice of the Peacock,* Rutgers University Press, 1972; Gilbert H. Muller, *Nightmares and Visions: Flannery O'Connor and the Catholic Grotesque,* University of Georgia Press, 1972; Miles Orvell, *Invisible Parade: The Fiction of Flannery O'Connor,* Temple University Press, 1972; *Contemporary Literary Criticism,* Gale, Volume I, 1973, Volume II, 1974, Volume III, 1975, Volume VI, 1976,

Volume X, 1979, Volume XIII, 1980, Volume XV, 1980; Alfred Kazin, *Bright Book of Life: American Novelists and Storytellers from Hemingway to Mailer*, Atlantic-Little, Brown, 1973; Dorothy Walters, *Flannery O'Connor*, Twayne, 1973; Preston M. Browning, Jr., *Flannery O'Connor*, Southern Illinois University Press, 1974; John R. May, *The Pruning Word: The Parables of Flannery O'Connor*, University of Notre Dame Press, 1976; Dorothy Tuck McFarland, *Flannery O'Connor*, Ungar, 1976.

Periodicals: *New York Times Book Review*, June 12, 1955, February 24, 1960, May 30, 1965, November 28, 1971, March 18, 1979; *America*, March 30, 1957, October 17, 1964; *Georgia Review*, summer, 1958; *Censer*, fall, 1960; *Modern Age*, fall, 1960; *English Journal*, April, 1962; *Saturday Review*, May 12, 1962, December 16, 1962, May 29, 1965, May 10, 1969, November 13, 1971; *Sewanee Review*, summer, 1962, autumn, 1963, spring, 1968 (entire issue); *Studies in Short Fiction*, spring, 1964, winter, 1964, winter, 1973, spring, 1975, winter, 1976; *Christian Century*, September 30, 1964, May 19, 1965, July 9, 1969; *Esprit*, winter, 1964 (entire issue); *Renascence*, spring, 1965; *Esquire*, May, 1965; *New York Herald Tribune Book Week*, May 30, 1965; *Southwest Review*, summer, 1965; *Commonweal*, July 9, 1965, December 3, 1965, August 8, 1969; *Hollins Critic*, September, 1965; *Critic*, October-November, 1965; *Catholic Library World*, November, 1967; *Spectator*, August 30, 1968; *Times Literary Supplement*, September 12, 1968; *Contemporary Literature*, winter, 1968; *New York Times*, May 13, 1969, March 9, 1979; *Time*, May 30, 1969, February 14, 1972, March 5, 1979; *Washington Post*, December 1, 1971; *Books and Bookmen*, May, 1972; *Modern Fiction Studies*, spring, 1973; *American Literature*, March 1974, May, 1974; *New Republic*, July 5, 1975, March 10, 1979; *Ms.*, December, 1975; *Arizona Quarterly*, autumn, 1976; *Book World*, February 11, 1979; *Detroit News*, March 25, 1979; *Chicago Tribune*, April 15, 1979; *New Statesman*, December 7, 1979.†

—*Sketch by Catherine Stadelman*

*   *   *

O'CONNOR, John Woolf   1902-1978
(Jack O'Connor)

PERSONAL: Born January 22, 1902, in Nogales, Ariz.; died January 20, 1978, aboard the S.S. *Mariposa* en route to San Francisco, Calif.; son of Andrew John and Ida (Woolf) O'Connor; married Eleanor Bradford Barry, September 10, 1927; children: Gerald, Bradford, Catherine, Caroline. *Education:* Attended Arizona State Teachers College (now Arizona State University), 1921-23, and University of Arizona, 1923-24; University of Arkansas, A.B., 1925; University of Missouri, M.A., 1927. *Home:* 725 Prospect Ave., Lewiston, Idaho.

CAREER: Employed as newspaper reporter, 1924-26; Sul Ross College (now Sul Ross State University), Alpine, Tex., associate professor of English, 1927-31; correspondent for Associated Press and Texas daily newspapers, 1927-30; Arizona State Teachers College (now Arizona State University), Flagstaff, assistant professor of English, 1931-34; University of Arizona, Tucson, associate professor of journalism, 1934-35; *Outdoor Life*, New York, N.Y., editor of arms and ammunition department, 1939-72. *Military service:* U.S. Army, 158th Infantry, 1917-18. *Member:* Tucson Game Protective Association (former president), Sigma Chi. *Awards, honors:* Westherby hunter of the year award, 1957.

WRITINGS—Published by Knopf, except as indicated: *Conquest* (novel), Harper, 1930; *Boom Town* (novel), 1938;

Game in the Desert, Derrydale, 1939; *Hunting in the Southwest*, 1945; *Hunting in the Rockies*, 1947; *The Rifle Book*, 1949, 3rd edition, 1978; *The Big Game Rifle*, 1952; *The Complete Book of Rifles and Shotguns*, Harper, 1961, 2nd edition, Popular Science, 1965; *The Big Game of North America*, Dutton, 1962; *Big Game Hunts*, Dutton, 1963; *The Shotgun Book*, 1965; (with others) *The Complete Book of Shooting*, Harper, 1966; *The Art of Big Game Hunting in North America*, 1967, 2nd edition, 1977; *Horse and Buggy West*, 1969; *The Hunting Rifle*, Winchester Press, 1970; *Sheep and Sheep Hunting*, Winchester Press, 1974. Contributor of articles and stories to national magazines.

SIDELIGHTS: John O'Connor went on hunting trips to many parts of the world, including Africa, Iran, India, Mexico, and Canada.†

*   *   *

O'DONNELL, Lillian Udvardy

PERSONAL: Born in Trieste, Italy; daughter of Zoltan D. and Maria (Busutti) Udvardy; married J. Leonard O'Donnell, 1954. *Residence:* New York, N.Y.

CAREER: Actress on stage and television, stage director for the Schuberts, and director of summer stock packages, 1940-54. *Member:* Actors' Equity Association, Authors League of America, American Federation of Television and Radio Actors, Stage Managers Association, West Side Tennis Club (New York).

WRITINGS: Death on the Grass, Arcadia House, 1959; *Death Blanks the Screen*, Arcadia House, 1960; *Death Schuss*, Abelard, 1963; *Murder under the Sun*, Abelard, 1964; *Death of a Player*, Abelard, 1964; *Babes in the Woods*, Abelard, 1965; *The Sleeping Beauty Murders*, Abelard, 1967; *Tachi Tree*, Abelard, 1968; *Face of the Crime*, Abelard, 1968; *Dive into Darkness*, Abelard, 1971; *The Phone Calls*, Putnam, 1972; *Don't Wear Your Wedding Ring*, Putnam, 1973; *Dial 577-RAPE*, Putnam, 1974; *The Baby Merchants*, Putnam, 1975; *Leisure Dying*, Putnam, 1976; *Aftershock*, Putnam, 1977; *No Business Being a Cop*, Putnam, 1979; *Falling Star*, Putnam, 1979; *Wicked Designs*, Putnam, 1980.

WORK IN PROGRESS: The Children's Zoo.

AVOCATIONAL INTERESTS: Tennis, skiing.

*   *   *

OGBURN, Charlton (Jr.)   1911-

PERSONAL: Born March 15, 1911, in Atlanta, Ga.; son of Charlton (a lawyer) and Dorothy (Stevens) Ogburn; married Mary C. Aldis, June 6, 1945 (divorced, 1951); married Vera Weidman, February 24, 1951; children: (first marriage) Charlton III; (second marriage) Nyssa, Holly. *Education:* Harvard University, S.B., 1932; attended National War College, 1952. *Home and office:* 10710 Vale Road, Oakton, Va. 22124.

CAREER: Viking Press, New York City, publicity writer, 1932-33; Alfred P. Sloan Foundation, New York City, writer, 1936-38; Book-of-the-Month Club, New York City, reviewer, 1940-41; U.S. Department of State, Washington, D.C., division chief, 1946-57; free-lance writer. Vice-president, Fairfax County Park Authority, 1959-61. *Military service:* U.S. Army, 1941-46, served with "Merrill's Marauders" in Burma; became captain; awarded Presidential Unit Citation. *Awards, honors:* Georgia Writers Association award, 1960, for *The Marauders*, 1966, for *The Gold of the River Sea*, and 1967, for *The Winter Beach*; John Burroughs Medal, 1967, for *The Winter Beach*.

WRITINGS: The White Falcon, Houghton, 1955; *The Bridge,* Houghton, 1957; *Big Caesar* (Reader's Digest Condensed Book Club selection), Houghton, 1958; *The Marauders* (Book-of-the-Month Club selection), Harper, 1959; (with mother, Dorothy Ogburn) *Shake-speare: The Man behind the Name,* Morrow, 1962; *The Gold of the River Sea,* Morrow, 1965; *The Winter Beach,* Morrow, 1966; *Down, Boy, Down, Blast You!,* Morrow, 1967; *The Forging of Our Continent: A Geological History of North America,* American Heritage, 1968; *Population and Resources: The Coming Collision* (booklet), Population Reference Bureau, 1970; *The Concrete Invasion: Three Sisters Bridge and the District of Columbia Freeway Crisis* (booklet), D.C. Citizens Referendum Committee, 1970; *The Continent in Our Hands,* Morrow, 1971; *Winespring Mountain,* Morrow, 1973; *The Southern Appalachians: A Wilderness Quest,* Morrow, 1975; *The Adventure of Birds,* Morrow, 1976; *Railroads: The Great American Aventure,* National Geographic Society, 1977. Also author of reports for the Brookings Institution and Ford Foundation. Author of narration for television documentary "The Potomac," WJZ-TV, 1963. Contributor to *Harper's, New Republic, Saturday Evening Post, Reader's Digest, Smithsonian Magazine,* and other periodicals.

SIDELIGHTS: Charlton Ogburn's *The Marauders* was filmed by Warner Brothers in 1962, and *The White Falcon* has been filmed by Walt Disney Studios. *Avocational interests:* "Doing what I should not be doing in an age of servants."

BIOGRAPHICAL/CRITICAL SOURCES: Harper's, November, 1966; *New York Times Book Review,* November 6, 1966, November 14, 1971, July 20, 1975; *National Parks Magazine,* December, 1966; *New Yorker,* January 7, 1967; *Atlantic,* February, 1967; *Christian Science Monitor,* August 15, 1973, December 20, 1976; *New Republic,* September 1, 1973; *Book World,* June 8, 1975, December 12, 1976; *Living Wilderness,* October, 1975; *American Forests,* July, 1977.

*   *   *

OKPEWHO, Isidore 1941-

PERSONAL: Born November 9, 1941, in Nigeria; son of David O. (a laboratory technician) and Regina (Attoh) Okpewho. *Education:* Attended University of Ibadan, 1961-64, and University of Denver, 1972-74. *Religion:* Christian. *Office:* University of Ibadan, Ibadan, Nigeria.

CAREER: Longman Nigeria, Lagos, publisher and editor, 1965-72; University of Ibadan, Ibadan, Nigeria, currently teacher of oral literature and creative writing. *Awards, honors:* African Arts Prize from African Studies Center of University of California, Los Angeles, 1972, for *The Last Duty.*

WRITINGS: The Victims (novel), Longmans, Green, 1970, Doubleday, 1971; *The Last Duty* (novel), Longman, 1976; *The Epic in Africa* (criticism), Columbia University Press, 1979. Editor, *Journal of African and Comparative Literature;* associate editor, *Okike.*

WORK IN PROGRESS: Myth in Africa.

AVOCATIONAL INTERESTS: African art and music, jazz, cinema, swimming, tennis, billiards.

*   *   *

OLDS, Helen Diehl 1895-
(Catherine Young)

PERSONAL: Born April 29, 1895, in Springfield, Ohio; daughter of William Wallace (a hardware merchant) and Henrietta (Zammert) Diehl; married Phelps Olds, January 1,

1918 (deceased); children: Bob Jerry. *Education:* Attended University of Texas, two years; Wittenberg University, B.A., 1921. *Politics:* Democrat. *Religion:* Unity School of Christianity. *Home:* 47-27 Little Neck Pkwy., Apt. 1-E, Little Neck, N.Y. 11363.

CAREER: The Ledger, Little Neck, N.Y., editor, 1927-28; reporter, *Great Neck News,* 1928-30; teacher of creative writing in adult education courses, Great Neck High School, 1948-58; Queens College of the City University of New York, Flushing, N.Y., teacher of juvenile writing, 1954-69. Teacher, Huckleberry Workshop, Hendersonville, N.C., 1950-61, McKendree College writers' workshop, McKendree, Ill., 1959, 1961, Cherryfield Camp, Brevard, N.C., 1962, and Dixie Council of Writers, Young Harris, Ga., 1962. *Member:* Women's National Book Association, Manuscript Club (Long Island; founder; president, 1933-63), Kappa Kappa Gamma.

WRITINGS: Joan of the Journal, D. Appleton, 1930; *Barbara Benton, Editor,* D. Appleton, 1932; *Victoria Clicks,* Messner, 1942; *Jill, Movie Maker,* Messner, 1944; *Lark, Radio Singer,* Messner, 1946; *Come In, Winifred,* Messner, 1947.

You Can't Tell about Love, Messner, 1950; *Fisherman Jody,* Messner, 1951; *Christmas-tree Sam,* Messner, 1952; *Krista and the Frosty Packages,* Messner, 1952; *Sharing Is Fun,* Koinonia Foundation, 1953; *Sara's Lucky Harvest,* Messner, 1953; *Peanut Butter Mascot,* Messner, 1953; *Don and the Book Bus,* Knopf, 1956; *The Silver Button,* Knopf, 1958; *Miss Hattie and the Monkey,* Follett, 1958; *Detour for Meg,* Messner, 1958; *Kate Can Skate,* Knopf, 1960; *What Will I Wear?,* Knopf, 1961; *The Little Ship That Went to Sea,* Reilly & Lee, 1962; *What's a Cousin?,* Knopf, 1962; *Jim Can Swim,* Knopf, 1963; *Christopher Columbus,* Putnam, 1964; *Lyndon Baines Johnson,* Putnam, 1965; *Richard E. Byrd,* Putnam, 1969; *Richard Nixon,* Putnam, 1970. Contributor of articles to magazines, occasionally under pseudonym Catherine Young.

BIOGRAPHICAL/CRITICAL SOURCES: The Ledger, Little Neck, N.Y., August 20, 1959.

*   *   *

OLIEN, Michael D(avid) 1937-

PERSONAL: Born April 16, 1937, in Milwaukee, Wis.; son of Henry Conrad (a chemist) and Hazel (Serles) Olien; married Joan C. Etlinger (a secretary), July 15, 1959; children: Karen Joy. *Education:* Beloit College, B.A., 1959; University of North Carolina, M.A., 1962; University of Oregon, Ph.D., 1967. *Home address:* Route 2, Box 115, Athens, Ga. 30607. *Office:* Department of Anthropology, University of Georgia, Athens, Ga. 30602.

CAREER: Associated Colleges of the Midwest, Central American Field Program, member of anthropological staff in San Jose, Costa Rica, 1964-65; University of Oregon, Eugene, instructor in anthropology, 1965-66; American University, Washington, D.C., assistant professor of anthropology, 1966-67; University of Georgia, Athens, assistant professor, 1967-73, associate professor of anthropology, 1973—. Visiting summer professor at Portland State College (now University), 1966. *Member:* American Anthropological Association (fellow), American Society for Ethnohistory, Latin American Anthropology Group, Southern Anthropological Society (secretary-tresurer, 1968-70).

WRITINGS: The Negro in Costa Rica; The Role of an Ethnic Minority in a Developing Society (monograph), Overseas

Research Center, Wake Forest University, 1970; *Latin Americans: Contemporary Peoples and Their Cultural Traditions*, Holt, 1973; *The Human Myth: An Introduction to Anthropology*, Harper, 1978.

Compiler with Edwin M. Shook and Jorge A. Lines; all published by Tropical Science Center, Associated Colleges of the Midwest: *Anthropological Bibliography of Aboriginal Panama*, 1965; *Anthropological Bibliography of Aboriginal Nicaragua*, 1965; *Anthropological Bibliography of Aboriginal El Salvador*, 1965; *Anthropological Bibliography of Aboriginal Honduras*, 1966.

Contributor: Elizabeth M. Eddy, editor, *Urban Anthropology: Research Perspectives and Strategies*, Southern Anthropological Society, 1968; Fred W. Voget and Robert L. Stephenson, editors, *For the Chief: Essays in Honor of Luther S. Cressman*, University of Oregon Anthropological Papers, 1972; David E. Hunter and Phillip Whitten, editors, *Encyclopedia of Anthropology*, Harper, 1976; Norman E. Whitten, Jr., compiler, *LAAG Contributions to Afro-American Ethnohistory in Latin America and the Caribbean*, Volume I, American Anthropological Association, 1976; Ann Pescatello, editor, *Old Roots in New Lands*, Greenwood Press, 1977. Contributor to professional journals, including *Revista Georgrafica* and *Ethnohistory*.

WORK IN PROGRESS: Cacaoteros and Slaves: The Colonial Costa Rican Cacao Plantations; Colonial Tribe, Republican Kingdom: The Nineteenth-Century Miskito.

*   *   *

OLSEN, Ib Spang 1921-
(Padre Detine, a joint pseudonym)

PERSONAL: Born June 11, 1921, in Denmark; son of Ole Christian (a gardener) and Soffu (Nielsen) Olsen; married Grete Geisler, May 3, 1947 (divorced, 1960); married Nulle Oeigaard (an artist), September 8, 1962; children: (first marriage) Tune, Tine (daughter); (second marriage) Martin, Lasse. *Education:* Blaagaards Seminarium, teacher training, 1939-43; Royal Danish Academy of Art, study of graphic art, 1945-49. *Politics:* Democratic Socialist. *Home:* Slotsparken 64, Bagsvaerd 2880, Denmark. *Agent:* International Children's Book Service, Kildeskovsvej 21, Gentofte 2820, Denmark.

CAREER: Worked as illustrator for Sunday magazine supplements of Danish newspapers, 1942; schoolteacher in Denmark, 1952-60; full-time illustrator and writer, 1960—. Has also designed book covers, murals for schools, posters, and ceramic pieces. Began work in Danish television, 1964, and has done numerous programs for young people.

AWARDS, HONORS: Danish Ministry of Culture Award for best illustrated children's book of the year, 1962, for *Drengen i maanen*, 1963, for *Regnen* and *Blaesten*, 1964, for *Boernerim*, and 1966, for *Mosekonens bryg;* Danish Society of Bookcraft honor list of year's outstanding books included *Kiosken paa torvet*, 1964, *Lars Peters cykel*, 1968, *Hokus Pokus og andre boernerim*, 1969, and *Roegen*, 1971; Hendrixen Medal for outstanding bookcraft, 1967, for *Halfdans abc;* Hans Christian Andersen Medal of International Board on Books for Young People, runner-up, 1968 and 1970, winner, 1972; Storm Petersen Legatet for whole body of work, 1971; has received other awards at Bratislava Biennial, from Organization for Friends of Books, 1966, and from Association of Authors of Juvenile Literature in Finland, 1971.

WRITINGS—Self-illustrated children's books; all published by Gyldendal, except as indicated: *Mosekonens bryg*, Kunst

& Kultur, 1957, translation by Virginia Allen Jensen publised as *The Marsh Crone's Brew*, Abingdon, 1960; *Boernene paa vejen*, Gjellerup, 1958; *Bedstemors vaegtaeppe*, Kunst & Kultur, 1958; *Drengen i maanen*, 1962, translation by Jensen published as *The Boy in the Moon*, Abingdon, 1963; *Regnen* (title means "Rain"), 1963; *Det lille lokomotiv*, Gad, 1963, translation by Jensen published as *The Little Locomotive*, Coward, 1976 (published in England as *The Little Shunting Engine*, World's Work, 1976); *Blaesten* (title means "Wind"), 1963; *Kiosken paa torvet* (title means "The Kiosk on the Square"), 1964; *Kattehuset*, 1968, translation by Jensen published as *Cat Alley*, Coward, 1971; *Marie-hoenen*, 1969; *Hvordan vi fik vores naboer*, 1969; *Roegen*, 1970, translation by Jensen published as *Smoke*, Coward, 1972; *Pjer Brumme: Historier em en lille bjoern*, 1971; *Folkene paa vegen*, 1972; *I Kristoffers spor*, 1973; (adapter) Vilhelm Bergsoe, *Nissen fra Timsgaard*, 1973; *Gamle fru glad*, 1974; *Thors rejse til Udgaard*, 1975; *24 breve til nissen*, Rhodos, 1975; *Min tjeneste hos bjergmanden*, Boernenes Boghandel, 1975; *Thors rejse til Hymer*, 1977; *Thor og Hammeren*, 1978; *Lille dreng paa oesterbro*, 1980.

Other books: (With Erik E. Frederiksen under joint pseudonym Padre Detine) *En Sydamerikaner i Nordsjaelland* (humorous tales), privately printed, 1960; (with Torben Brostroem) *Boern: Det Foerste aar i ord og tegninger*, Hasselbalch, 1962.

Illustrator: *Danish Folk Tales*, J. H. Schultz, 1946; *Danske folkeeventyr*, Kunst & Kultur, 1950; Frank Jaeger, *Hverdaghistorier*, Wivel, 1951; Jaeger, *Tune, det foerste aar*, Branner, 1951; *Fem smaa troldeboern*, Danske Forlag, 1952; *Nissen flytter med*. Gyldendal, 1955; *Abrikosia*, Hoest & Soen, 1958; Virginia Allen Jensen, *Lars Peter's Birthday*, Abingdon, 1959; Jakob J. B. Nygaard, *Tobias tryllemus*, Martins Forlag, 1961, translation by Edith Joan McCormick published as *Tobias, the Magic Mouse*, Harcourt, 1968; Halfdan W. Rasmussen, *Boernerim*, Schoenberg, 1964; Hans Christian Andersen, *Digte*, edited by Bo Groenbech, Dansk Arnkrone, 1966; *Morten poulsens urtehave*, Hoest & Soen, 1967; Rasmussen, *Halfdans abc*, Illustrations-forlaget, 1967; *Molbohistorier*, Schoenberg, 1967; Jensen, *Lars Peters cykel*, Gyldendal, 1968, translation published as *Lars Peter's Bicycle*, Angus & Robertson, 1970; Lise Soerensen, *Da Lyset gik ud*, Gyldendal, 1968; Rasmussen, *Hokus Pokus og andre boernerim*, Schoenberg, 1969; Ole Restrup, *Odin og Tor*, Gad, 1969; Kjeld Elfelt, *Aesop: 50 Fabler*, Schoenberg, 1970; Rasmussen, *Den Lille fraekke Frederick og andre boernerlm*, Branner & Korch, 1971; Rasmussen, *Noget om Nanette*, Schoenberg, 1972; Jensen, *The Nisse from Timsgaard* (adapted from *Nissen fra Timsgaard* by Vilhelm Bergsoe), Coward, 1972; Joergen Lorenzen, *Danske folkeviser: et hundrede udvalgte danske viser*, Gad, 1974; Lennart Hellsing, *Old Mother Hubbard and Her Dog*, translated by Jensen, Coward, 1976; Cecil Boedker, *Da jord en forsvand*, Det Danske Bibelselskab, 1976; Boedker, *Den udgalgte*, Det Danske Bibelselskab, 1977. Also illustrator of *Prinsessen paa glasbjerget*, c. 1945, Boedker's *Barnet i sivkurven*, and a three-volume edition of Danish medieval folksongs.

Television films: "Hvad bliver det naeste?"; "Taarnuret"; "Vitaminerne"; "Den store krage"; "Nikolai"; "Stregen der loeb henad"; "Stregen der loeb opad."

WORK IN PROGRESS: Voksenfaelden.

SIDELIGHTS: Ib Spang Olsen writes: "Almost all of my picture books have been produced as original lithography in photo offset. The original art work is done directly on film, one separate film for each of the four colours to be used in a single picture. In other words, for each illustration I draw four films, and the colours are then mixed for the first time by the printer cooperating closely with me. The finished books are the originals, they are not reproductions. In this way we can produce original lithography of quality at reasonable prices.''

Olsen has given original illustrations for four of his books to the Kerlan Collection at the University of Minnesota.†

*　　*　　*

OLSEN, T(heodore) V(ictor)　1932-
(Joshua Stark, Christopher Storm, Cass Willoughby)

PERSONAL: Born April 25, 1932, in Rhinelander, Wis.; son of Freidolf Victor and Mary (Gross) Olsen; married Beverly Butler, 1976. *Education:* Stevens Point State College (now University of Wisconsin—Stevens Point), B.S., 1955. *Home and office address:* P.O. Box 856, Rhinelander, Wis. 54501. *Agent:* John Payne, Lenniger Literary Agency, Inc., 104 East 40th St., New York, N.Y. 10016.

CAREER: Free-lance writer. *Member:* Western Writers of America, Authors League.

WRITINGS: Haven of the Hunted, Ace Books, 1956; *The Man from Nowhere,* Ace Books, 1959; *McGivern,* Fawcett, 1960; *High Lawless,* Fawcett, 1960; *Gunswift,* Fawcett, 1960; *Ramrod Rider,* Fawcett, 1961; *Brand of the Star,* Fawcett, 1961; *Brothers of the Sword,* Berkley Publishing, 1962; *Savage Sierra,* Fawcett, 1962; (under pseudonym Christopher Storm) *The Young Duke,* Universal, 1963; (under pseudonym Joshua Stark) *Break the Young Land,* Doubleday, 1964; (under pseudonym Christopher Storm) *The Sex Rebels,* Universal, 1964; *A Man Called Brazos,* Fawcett, 1964; *Canyon of the Gun,* Fawcett, 1965; (under pseudonym Christopher Storm) *Campus Motel,* Universal, 1965; *The Stalking Moon,* Doubleday, 1965; *The Hard Men,* Fawcett, 1966; (under pseudonym Cass Willoughby) *Autumn Passion,* Universal, 1966; *Bitter Grass,* Doubleday, 1967; (under pseudonym Joshua Stark) *The Lockhart Breed,* Berkley Publishing, 1967; *Blizzard Pass,* Fawcett, 1968; *Arrow in the Sun,* Doubleday, 1969.

(Under pseudonym Joshua Stark) *Keno,* Berkley Publishing, 1970; *A Man Named Yuma,* Fawcett, 1971; *Eye of the Wolf,* Doubleday, 1971; *There Was a Season,* Doubleday, 1972; *Summer of the Drums,* Doubleday, 1972; *Starbuck's Brand,* Doubleday, 1973; *Mission to the West,* Doubleday, 1973; *Run to the Mountain,* Fawcett, 1974; *Track the Man Down,* Doubleday, 1975; *Day of the Buzzard,* Fawcett, 1976; *Westward They Rode,* Ace Books, 1976; *Bonner's Stallion,* Fawcett, 1977; *Roots of the North,* Pineview, 1979; *Allegories for One Man's Moods,* Pineview, 1979; *Rattlesnake,* Doubleday, 1979.

Contributor: Stephen Payne, editor, *Pick of the Roundup,* Avon, 1963; Betty Baker, editor, *Great Ghost Stories of the Old West,* Four Winds, 1968; Brian Garfield, editor, *War Whoop and Battle Cry,* Scholastic Book Services, 1968; August Derleth, editor, *New Poetry out of Wisconsin,* Stanton & Lee, 1969; Charles N. Heckelmann, editor, *With Guidons Flying,* Doubleday, 1970; Peggy Simpson Curry, editor, *Western Romances,* Fawcett, 1973; August Lenniger, editor, *Western Writers of America Silver Anniversary Anthology,* Ace Books, 1977; Donald Duke, editor, *Water Trails West,* Doubleday, 1978. Contributor of articles to *Roundup* and of more than twenty stories to magazines.

SIDELIGHTS: T. V. Olsen's first published story, ''Backtrail,'' was adapted for the television program, ''Dick Powell's Zane Grey Theater,'' in the spring of 1957. A film version of *The Stalking Moon* was produced by National General Pictures in 1968. *Arrow in the Sun* was adapted to film and produced by Avco Embassy as ''Soldier Blue'' in 1970. *Avocational interests:* Reading.

*　　*　　*

O'MEARA, John J.　1915-

PERSONAL: Born February 18, 1915, in County Galway, Ireland; son of Patrick and Mary (Donelan) O'Meara; married Odile de Barthes de Montfort, 1947; children: Dominique, Catriona, Odile. *Education:* University College, Dublin, M.A., 1939; Oxford University, D.Phil., 1945. *Religion:* Roman Catholic. *Home:* 15 Maple Rd., Dublin 14, Ireland. *Office:* University College, Dublin, Ireland.

CAREER: University College, Dublin, Ireland, professor, 1948—, member, Governing Body of University College, 1956-59, 1962-65; member of senate, National University of Ireland, 1964-72. Governor for Ireland, Foundation Europeenne de la Culture, 1964. Lecturer at universities in Europe and America, including Harvard University and Yale University. Member of Institute for Advanced Study, Princeton, N.J., 1956-57, 1963, 1968, 1975-76. *Member:* Royal Irish Academy (member of council, 1959-60, 1965-68), University Club, Royal Irish Yacht Club. *Awards, honors:* Harvard at Dumbarton Oaks (Washington, D.C.) fellow, 1979—.

WRITINGS: (Translator) Giraldus Cambrensis, *Topography of Ireland,* Dundalgan, 1950; (editor and translator) St. Augustine, *Against the Academics,* Newman, 1950; *The Young Augustine,* Longmans, Green, 1954; (translator) Origen, 'On Prayer' and 'Exhortation to Martyrdom,' Newman, 1954; *Porphyry's Philosophy from Oracles in Augustine,* Etudes Augustiniennes, 1959; *Charter of Christendom,* Macmillan, 1961; *Eriugena,* Mercier Press, 1969; (editor) *The Mind of Eriugena,* Irish Academic Press, 1973; (editor) *An Augustine Reader,* Doubleday, 1973; (translator) *The Voyage of Saint Brendan,* Humanities, 1976. Also editor with B. Naumann of *Latin Script and Letters: A.D. 400-900.* Contributor to *Catholic Youth Encyclopedia.* Contributor to journals. Editor, *Handbook of †[Irish] Association of Classical Teachers,* 1960-61; chairman of editorial board, *European Teacher;* member of editorial board, *University Review* (Dublin).

WORK IN PROGRESS: Saint Augustine on the Creation of Man; Giraldus Cambrensis' Topography of Ireland, for Dolmen Press; an edition of Eriugena's *Periphyseon,* with E. Jeauneau.

AVOCATIONAL INTERESTS: Music.

*　　*　　*

OPPENHEIMER, Evelyn　1907-

PERSONAL: Born October 20, 1907, in Dallas, Tex.; daughter of Louis and Gertrude (Baum) Oppenheimer. *Education:* University of Chicago, Ph.B., 1929. *Home and office:* 7929 Meadow Park, No. 201, Dallas, Tex. 75230.

CAREER: Chicago Evening Post, Chicago, Ill., book reviewer, 1929-30; *Chicago Evening Journal,* Chicago, feature writer and reporter, 1930-31; book reviewer and lecturer, Dallas, Tex., 1936—. Presented book reviews and author interviews on radio stations in Dallas, Houston, Los Angeles, Phoenix, and San Francisco, 1948-77. Instructor in oral book reviewing, Texas Technological College (now Texas

Tech University), 1957, University of Texas at Austin, 1958, 1960, University of California, Los Angeles, 1958, University of Dallas, 1959, Amarillo College, 1960, and Southern Methodist University, 1970-79. Literary agent for a number of southwestern authors. *Member:* Phi Beta Kappa. *Awards, honors:* Awards for broadcasts and feature stories, National Federation of Press Women and Texas Women's Press Association; Southwest Writers Conference award for children's story.

WRITINGS: Legend and Other Poems, Naylor, 1951; *Book Reviewing for an Audience,* Chilton, 1962; (author of introduction) *Heroes of Texas,* Texian Press, 1964; *Red River Dust,* Word, Inc., 1968; *Texas in Color,* Hastings House, 1971; *The Articulate Woman,* Pyramid Publications, 1976; (editor with Bill Porterfield) *The Book of Dallas,* Doubleday, 1977; *Oral Book Reviewing to Stimulate Reading,* Scarecrow, 1980. Contributor to *Denver Post, Chicago Tribune, Dallas Times-Herald,* and other newspapers.

SIDELIGHTS: Evelyn Oppenheimer has traveled in the United States, Canada, and Europe.

*   *   *

OREL, Harold 1926-

PERSONAL: Born March 31, 1926, in Boston, Mass.; son of Saul and Sarah (Wicker) Orel; married Charlyn Hawkins, May 25, 1951; children: Sara Elinor, Timothy Ralston. *Education:* University of New Hampshire, B.A., 1948; University of Michigan, M.A., 1949, Ph.D., 1952. *Home:* 713 Schwarz Rd., Lawrence, Kan. 66044. *Office:* Department of English, University of Kansas, Lawrence, Kan. 66045.

CAREER: University of Maryland, College Park, instructor, 1952-56, instructor in overseas program, 1954-55; General Electric Co., Evendale, Ohio, publications specialist, 1957; University of Kansas, Lawrence, associate professor, 1957-62, professor of English, 1962-74, University Distinguished Professor, 1974—. Lecturer at several universities in Japan and at Westminister Abbey. Consultant, Midwest Research Institute, Kansas City, Mo. *Military service:* U.S. Navy, 1944-46. *Member:* Modern Language Association of America, American Committee on Irish Studies (vice-president, 1960-70; president, 1970-72; member of executive committee, 1972—), Thomas Hardy Society (vice-president, 1968—).

WRITINGS: Thomas Hardy's Epic-Drama: A Study of "The Dynasts," University of Kansas Press, 1963; *The Development of William Butler Yeats, 1885-1900,* University of Kansas Press, 1968; *English Romantic Poets and the Enlightenment: Nine Essays on a Literary Relationship,* Voltaire Foundation, 1973; (contributor) Frank B. Pinion, editor, *Thomas Hardy and the Modern World,* Thomas Hardy Society, 1974; (contributor) Margaret Drabble, editor, *The Genius of Thomas Hardy,* Weidenfeld & Nicolson, 1976; (contributor) Pinion, editor, *Budmouth Essays on Thomas Hardy,* Thomas Hardy Society, 1976; *The Final Years of Thomas Hardy, 1912-1928,* Macmillan, 1976.

Editor: *The World of Victorian Humor,* Appleton, 1961; (with G. J. Worth and contributor) *Six Studies in Nineteenth-Century English Literature and Thought,* University of Kansas Press, 1962; *Thomas Hardy's Personal Writings,* University of Kansas Press, 1966; (with Paul Wiley) *British Poetry, 1880-1920: Edwardian Voices,* Appleton, 1969; (with Worth and contributor) *The Nineteenth-Century Writer and His Audience,* University of Kansas Press, 1969; (and contributor) *Irish History and Culture: Aspects of a People's Heritage,* Regents Press of Kansas, 1976; *Thomas Hardy, The Dynasts,* Macmillan, 1978.

SIDELIGHTS: Harold Orel told *CA:* "I am grateful to the generations of critics and scholars who have gone before me, and who have taught me to read literary texts with greater sensitivity than I could have done unaided. I owe them a debt for which all the books I have written, and am yet to write, can provide only a partial repayment."

BIOGRAPHICAL/CRITICAL SOURCES: Virginia Quarterly Review, spring, 1977; *South Atlantic Quarterly,* summer, 1977; *Hudson Review,* autumn, 1977; *Journal of English and German Philology,* October, 1977; *Victorian Studies,* spring, 1978; *Sewanee Review,* April, 1978; *Modern Fiction Studies,* summer, 1978.

*   *   *

OSBECK, Kenneth W. 1924-

PERSONAL: Born December 13, 1924, in Grand Rapids, Mich.; son of Emil and Hilda Osbeck; married Elizabeth Mary (an assistant professor of drama), August 26, 1950; children: Kathleen, Gregory, Mark, Lisa. *Education:* University of Michigan, B. of Music Ed., 1950, M. of Music Ed., 1956. *Politics:* Republican. *Home:* 107 Ivanhoe N.E., Grand Rapids, Mich. 49506.

CAREER: Grand Rapids School of the Bible and Music, Grand Rapids, Mich., director of music, 1950-66; Grand Rapids Baptist College, Grand Rapids, associate professor of music and fine arts, 1966—; Wealthy St. Baptist Church, Grand Rapids, minister of music, 1969—. Owns custom music publishing company. Consultant, Zondervan Publishing Co.

WRITINGS: A Pocket Guide for the Church Choir Member, Zondervan, 1958, reprinted, Kregel, 1975; *A Junior's Praise,* Kregel, 1959; *Ministry of Music,* Zondervan, 1961; *A Teen-Age Praise,* Kregel, 1962; *Choir Responses,* Kregel, 1962; *Choral Praises,* Kregel, 1963; *My Choir Workbook,* Kregel, 1973; *Singing with Understanding: Including 101 Beloved Hymn Backgrounds,* Kregel, 1978.

*   *   *

OSGOOD, Robert Endicott 1921-

PERSONAL: Born August 14, 1921, in St. Louis, Mo.; son of Harold Alexander and Harriet (Johnson) Osgood; married Gretchen Anderson, 1946. *Education:* Harvard University, B.A., 1943, Ph.D., 1952. *Home:* 5502 Park St., Chevy Chase, Md. 20015. *Office:* School of Advanced International Studies, Johns Hopkins University, 1740 Massachusetts Ave. N.W., Washington, D.C.

CAREER: University of Chicago, Chicago, Ill., Center for the Study of American Foreign and Military Policy, research associate, 1952-61, assistant professor, 1956-58, associate professor, 1958-61, professor of political science, 1961; Johns Hopkins University, School of Advanced International Studies, Washington, D.C., professor of American foreign policy, 1965-73, Christian A. Herter Professor, 1979—, dean 1973-79, Washington Center of Foreign Policy Research, associate director, 1961-65, director, 1965-73, co-director, Security Studies Program, director of studies, Foreign Policy Institute, 1979—. NATO Visiting Professor, University of Manchester, 1959. Lecturer at Army, Navy and Air War Colleges and participant in Salzburg Seminar in American Studies. *Military service:* U.S. Army, 1943-46; became sergeant. *Member:* American Political Science Association, International Institute for Strategic Studies, Council on Foreign Relations.

WRITINGS—All published by Johns Hopkins Press, except

as indicated: *Ideals and Self-Interest in America's Foreign Relations*, University of Chicago Press, 1953; *Limited War: The Challenge to American Strategy*, University of Chicago Press, 1957; *NATO: The Entangling Alliance*, University of Chicago Press, 1962; (with Robert W. Tucker) *Force, Order, and Justice*, 1967; *Alliances and Foreign Policy*, 1968; (with Packard and Badgley) *Japan and the United States in Asia*, 1968; (with Tucker and others) *America and the World*, Volume I: *From the Truman Doctrine to Vietnam*, 1970, Volume II: *Retreat from Empire?: The First Nixon Administration*, 1973; *The Weary and the Wary: United States and Japanese Security Policies in Transition*, 1972; (with Ann L. Hollick) *New Era of Ocean Politics*, 1974; *Limited War Revisited*, Westview, 1979. Contributor to *American Political Science Review, Confluence, New Republic,* and *Social Forces.*

*   *   *

OSTROFF, Anthony J.   1923-1978

PERSONAL: Born November 9, 1923, in Gary, Ind.; died April 9, 1978, in Pacific City, Ore.; son of Anthony Alexander and Anna (Nielsen) Ostroff; married Miriam Virginia Border, May 7, 1948; children: Nicholas Alexander. *Education:* Northwestern University, B.S., 1947; University of Michigan, M.A., 1949; The Sorbonne, University of Paris, and University of Grenoble, postgraduate study, 1950-51. *Home:* 4647 Southwest Dosch Rd., Portland, Ore. 97201.

CAREER: University of California, Berkeley, 1949-69, began as assistant professor, became professor of rhetoric; Lewis and Clark College, Portland, Ore., professor of humanities, 1969-78. Visiting professor, University of Buffalo, 1958; visiting lecturer, Vassar College, 1958-59. Narrator of films for University of California Film Production Service; panelist and performer, KQED television, San Francisco; panelist, lecturer, director, and performer for KPFA radio, Berkeley, Calif., and Pacifica Foundation. Worked with several antiwar organizations. *Military service:* U.S. Army, 1942-45.

MEMBER: American Civil Liberties Union, American Association of University Professors. *Awards, honors:* Avery & Jule Hopwood Award, 1948, 1949; Yaddo Foundation residence fellowship, 1954; Huntington Hartford Foundation fellowship, 1955-56; Borestone Mountain Poetry Award, 1957; Robert Frost fellowship in poetry, 1958; University of California Institute of Creative Arts fellowship, 1963-64; Guggenheim fellowship.

WRITINGS: (With Winfield T. Scott and Galway Kinnell) *Three Self Evaluations*, Beloit, 1953; *Imperatives*, Harcourt, 1962; (editor) *The Contemporary Poet as Artist and Critic*, Little, Brown, 1964; *A Fall in Mexico*, Doubleday, 1977. Work included in *New American Poets II*, Ballantine, 1957, *Best American Short Stories*, Houghton, 1958, *Poetry for Pleasure*, Doubleday, 1960, and *The American Colleges*, Wiley, 1962. Contributor of poetry, fiction, and articles to *Atlantic Monthly, Accent, Epoch, Harper's, Harper's Bazaar, Kenyon Review, Paris Review, Saturday Review,* and other magazines and journals. Guest editor of *Perspective, Berkeley Review,* and *New World Writing.*

WORK IN PROGRESS: A novel, tentatively titled *Letters from a Madman.*

BIOGRAPHICAL/CRITICAL SOURCES: Time, October 5, 1962; *New York Times Book Review*, November 18, 1962; *Christian Science Monitor*, September 8, 1964; *New York Times*, April 14, 1978.†

OTTMAN, Robert W(illiam)   1914-

PERSONAL: Born May 3, 1914, in Fulton, N.Y.; son of Robert Noah and Lillian (Smith) Ottman; married Shirley Johnson, 1976; children (previous marriage) Ruth; stepchildren: Marc Johnson, Miles Johnson, Terese Johnson. *Education:* University of Rochester, B.M., 1938, M.M., 1943; Trinity College of Music, London, England, graduate study, 1945; North Texas State College (now University), Ph.D., 1956. *Home:* 415 Mimosa Dr., Denton, Tex. *Office:* School of Music, North Texas State University, Denton, Tex. 76203.

CAREER: Groveland Public Schools, Groveland, N.Y., supervisor of music, 1938-42; Akron Public Schools, Akron, N.Y., supervisor of music, 1942-43; North Texas State University, Denton, 1946—, currently professor of music, chairman of theory department, and director of Madrigal Singers. *Military service:* U.S. Army, 1943-46. *Member:* Society for Music Theory, Texas Association of College Teachers, Kiwanis.

WRITINGS—All published by Prentice-Hall, except as indicated: *Music for Sight Singing*, 1956, 2nd edition, 1967; *Basic Repertoire for Singers*, Southern Music Company, 1959; *Elementary Harmony: Theory and Practice*, 1961, 2nd edition, 1970; *Advanced Harmony: Theory and Practice*, 1961, 2nd edition, 1972; *The 371 Chorales of Johann Sebastian Bach*, Holt, 1966; *Rudiments of Music*, 1970; *Workbook for Elementary Harmony*, 1974; *Programmed Rudiments of Music*, 1979; *More Music for Sight Singing*, 1981.

*   *   *

OWEN, Guy (Jr.)   1925-

PERSONAL: Born February 24, 1925, in Clarkton, N.C.; son of Guy and Margaret (Elkins) Owen; married Dorothy Jennings, 1952; children: William James, John Leslie. *Education:* Attended Utah State College (now University) and University of Chicago; University of North Carolina, B.A., 1947, M.A., 1949, Ph.D., 1955. *Home:* 107 Montgomery St., Raleigh, N.C. 27607. *Office:* Winston Hall, North Carolina State University, Raleigh, N.C.

CAREER: Davidson College, Davidson, N.C., instructor in English, 1949-51; Elon College, Elon, N.C., assistant professor of English, 1954-55; Stetson University, De Land, Fla., associate professor of English, 1955-62; North Carolina State University at Raleigh, associate professor, 1962-64, professor of English, 1964—. Writer-in-residence, Weymouth Estate, Southern Pines, N.C., 1979. *Military service:* U.S. Army, two years. *Member:* Modern Language Association of America, South Atlantic Modern Language Association. *Awards, honors:* Fellow, Breadloaf Writer's Conference, 1960; Henry Bellamann Foundation Award, 1964; Yaddo grant, 1968; National Endowment for the Arts grant, 1969, for editing *Southern Poetry Review;* Roanoke-Chowan Poetry Cup, Roanoke-Chowan Group, 1969, for *The White Stallion;* Sir Walter Raleigh Award, Historical Book Club of North Carolina, 1970, for *A Journey for Joedel;* North Carolina award for literature, 1972.

WRITINGS—Novels: *Season of Fear*, Random House, 1960; *The Ballad of the Flim-Flam Man*, Macmillan, 1965; *A Journey for Joedel*, Crown, 1970; *The Flim-Flam Man and the Apprentice Grifter*, Crown, 1972; *The Flim-Flam Man and Other Stories*, Moore Publishing, 1980.

Poetry: *Cape Fear Country and Other Poems*, New Athenaeum Press, 1958; *The Guilty and Other Poems*, Goosetree Press, 1962; *The White Stallion and Other Poems*, Blair, 1969.

Editor: (With others) *Southern Poetry Today*, Impetus Press, 1962; (with R. E. Langford and others) *Essays in Modern American Literature*, Stetson University Press, 1962; *Modern American Poetry*, Everett/Edwards, 1972; (with Mary C. Williams) *New Southern Poets*, University of North Carolina Press, 1975; (with Williams) *Contemporary Poetry of North Carolina*, Blair, 1977; (with Williams) *Contemporary Southern Poetry: An Anthology*, Louisiana State University Press, 1979.

Work appears in anthologies. Contributor of short stories and poetry to *Carolina Quarterly*, *South Carolina Review*, *Saturday Review*, *Poetry*, and other periodicals. Founding editor, *Impetus*, 1958-64; contributing editor, *Books Abroad*, 1963-67; editor, *Southern Poetry Review*, 1964-75; co-editor, *North Carolina Folklore*, 1966-72; advisory editor, *Pembroke Magazine*, *Appalachian Journal*, and *Poetry South*.

WORK IN PROGRESS: A novel, *The Apprenticeship of Joel Jarman.*

SIDELIGHTS: Guy Owen's book *The Ballad of the Flim-Flam Man* was filmed by Twentieth Century-Fox in 1966.

BIOGRAPHICAL/CRITICAL SOURCES: Carleton Miscellany, spring, 1965; *New York Times*, March 24, 1965; *National Review*, June 16, 1970; *Book World*, July 5, 1970; *New York Times Book Review*, July 5, 1970, January 7, 1973; *Carolina Quarterly*, fall, 1970; *Virginia Quarterly Review*, fall, 1970, autumn, 1975; *Saturday Review*, September 26, 1970; *Sewanee Review*, July, 1971; *Georgia Review*, spring, 1973; *St. Andrew's Review*, spring-summer, 1975; *Southern Review*, October, 1976; *Choice*, May, 1978; *Pembroke*, spring, 1981.

P

PACIFICI, Sergio 1925-

PERSONAL: Born January 12, 1925, in Leghorn, Italy; son of Angelo (a restauranteur) and Stella (Finzi) Pacifici; married Zlota Grob, June 26, 1974; children: (previous marriage) Tina, Sabrina. *Education:* Los Angeles City College, A.A., 1948; University of California, Los Angeles, B.A., 1949; University of Washington, M.A., 1950; Harvard University, M.A., 1951, Ph.D., 1953. *Home:* 555 Kappock St., 15-L, Riverdale, N.Y. 10463. *Office:* Academic Bldg., Queens College of the City University of New York, Flushing, N.Y. 11367.

CAREER: University of Minnesota, Minneapolis, instructor, 1953-54; Yale University, New Haven, Conn., 1954-63, began as instructor, became assistant professor of Italian, director of summer program in Italian, 1955-58; City University of New York, associate professor of Romance languages at City College, New York, N.Y., 1963-65, professor of Romance languages at Queens College, Flushing, N.Y., 1965—. Member of adult education council, Young Mens Christian Association, New Haven, Conn., 1958—. Consulting editor, George Braziller Inc., 1961, Atlantic Monthly Press, 1963-64. *Member:* American Association of Teachers of Italian, Dante Society of America, Modern Language Association of America, American Association of University Professors. *Awards, honors:* Morse fellow, Yale University, 1958-59; Guggenheim fellow, 1961-62; American Philosophical Society grants, 1958-59, 1962; Yale University faculty grants, 1960, 1961-62, 1963; post-doctoral fellow, Italian Government, summer, 1965; Fulbright travel grant, summer, 1972; City University of New York Research Foundation grants, 1977, 1979.

WRITINGS: A Letter from the King of Portugal, University of Minnesota Press, 1955; (editor) *The Promised Land and Other Poems* (anthology), S. F. Vanni, 1957; *A Guide to Contemporary Italian Literature: From Futurism to Neorealism,* Meridian, 1962; (translator, with Thomas G. Bergin) Salvatore Quasimodo, *The Poet and the Politician,* Southern Illinois University Press, 1964; (co-editor) *A Homage to Dante,* Books Abroad, 1965; *The Modern Italian Novel,* Southern Illinois University Press, Volume I: *From Manzoni to Svevo,* 1967, Volume II: *From Capuana to Tozzi,* 1972, Volume III: *From Pea to Moravia,* 1979; (editor) *From Verismo to Experimentalism: Essays on the Modern Italian Novel,* Indiana University Press, 1969; *Italia: vita e cultura,* Random House, 1970. Contributor of 140 articles on Italian literature to *Grolier International Encyclopedia, World Book Encyclopedia, Encyclopedia Americana,* and *American Academic Encyclopedia.* Contributor of articles and reviews to *Saturday Review, New York Herald Tribune, Italica, Books Abroad,* and to language journals.

WORK IN PROGRESS: From Engagement to Alienation: A Reader's Guide to Contemporary Italian Fiction.

*   *   *

PACK, Robert 1929-

PERSONAL: Born May 19, 1929, in New York, N.Y.; married Isabelle Miller, 1950; married second wife, Patricia Powell, 1961; children: Erik, Pamela, Kevin. *Education:* Dartmouth College, B.A., 1951; Columbia University, M.A., 1953. *Home:* R.D.2, Middlebury, Vt. *Office:* Department of English, Middlebury College, Middlebury, Vt. 05753.

CAREER: Barnard College, New York, N.Y., associate in poetry, 1957-64; Middlebury College, Middlebury, Vt., 1964—, began as assistant professor of English, currently Abernethy Professor of American Literature. Bread Loaf Writers Conference, staff member, director, 1973—. *Awards, honors:* Fulbright fellow in Florence, Italy, 1956-57; National Institute of Arts and Letters award for creative work in literature, 1957; Borestone Mountain Poetry Award, first prize, 1964; National Council of the Arts award.

WRITINGS: The Irony of Joy (poems), Scribner, 1955; *Wallace Stevens: An Approach to His Poetry and Thought,* Rutgers University Press, 1958; *A Stranger's Privilege* (poems), Macmillan, 1959; *The Forgotten Secret,* Macmillan, 1959; *Then What Did You Do?,* Macmillan, 1961; *Guarded by Women* (poems), Random House, 1963; *Selected Poems,* Chatto & Windus, 1964; *How to Catch a Crocodile* (juvenile), Knopf, 1964; *Home from the Cemetery* (poems), Rutgers University Press, 1969; *Nothing but Light* (poems), Rutgers University Press, 1972; *Keeping Watch* (poems), Rutgers University Press, 1976; *Waking to My Name: New and Selected Poems,* Johns Hopkins University Press, 1980.

Editor: (With Donald Hall and Louis Simpson) *New Poems of England and America,* Meridian, 1957, 2nd edition (with Hall), 1962; (and translator, with Marjorie Lelash) *Mozart's Librettos,* Meridian, 1961; (with Tom Driver) *An Anthology of Modern Religious Poetry,* Macmillan, 1963; (with Driver) *Poems of Doubt and Belief* (anthology), Macmillan, 1964;

(and author of introduction) *The Selected Letters of John Keats,* New American Library, 1974. Former poetry editor, *Discovery.*

WORK IN PROGRESS: Affirming Limits, a collection of literary and philosophical essays.

AVOCATIONAL INTERESTS: Music (particularly Italian opera), gardening.

* * *

PACKER, Joy (Petersen) 1905-1977
(Lady Packer)

PERSONAL: Born February 11, 1905, in Cape Town, South Africa; died, 1977; daughter of Julius (a doctor) and Ellen Magdalen (Marais) Petersen; married Sir Herbert Annesley Packer (an admiral in the Royal Navy), 1925 (deceased); children: Peter. *Education:* Attended University of Cape Town. *Religion:* Anglican.

CAREER: Began as a free-lance journalist in Cape Town, South Africa, 1924; *Daily Express,* London, England, news reporter, 1931-32; Hong Kong Radio, Hong Kong, writer of women's features, 1932-35; free-lance correspondent for British publications while living in Balkans, 1936-39; publicity writer for war organizations; broadcaster to South Africa for British Broadcasting Corp., London, 1939-43; affiliated with Ministry of Information, Egypt, 1943, and with Psychological Warfare Branch of Allied Headquarters, Italy, 1944-45. *Member:* International P.E.N., Western Province Sports Club.

WRITINGS—All published by Eyre & Spottiswoode, except as indicated: *Pack and Follow,* 1945, reprinted, Corgi Books, 1974; *Grey Mistress,* 1949, reprinted, Corgi Books, 1974; *Apes and Ivory,* 1953; *Home from Sea,* 1963, Dutton, 1964; *The World Is a Proud Place,* Dutton, 1966; *Valley of the Vines* (Literary Guild selection), Lippincott, 1955, reprinted, Corgi Books, 1977; *The Moon by Night* (Literary Guild selection), Lippincott, 1957; *The High Roof,* Lippincott, 1959; *The Glass Barrier,* Lippincott, 1961; *The Man in the Mews,* 1964, Dutton, 1965; *The Man Out There,* Dutton, 1967; *The Blind Spot,* 1967; *Leopard in the Fold,* 1969; *Veronica,* 1970; *Boomerang,* Corgi Books, 1972; *Deep as the Sea,* Eyre Methuen, 1976; *Dark Curtain,* Eyre Methuen, 1977. Contributor of short stories and articles to magazines.

SIDELIGHTS: Joy Packer's first five books comprise an autobiographical quintette based on her life and travels as the wife of a British naval officer. Her books have been translated into nine languages. *Avocational interests:* Africa, travel, and the study of wildlife.†

* * *

PAINTER, Charlotte

EDUCATION: Stanford University, M.A., 1965. *Home:* 372 63rd St., Oakland, Calif. 94618.

CAREER: Writer. Has taught at Stanford University, 1966-71, University of California, Santa Cruz, 1967, University of California, Berkeley, 1972-73, University of California, Davis, 1977-79, and San Francisco State University, 1978-79. *Awards, honors:* Wallace Stegner writing fellowship, Stanford University, 1961-62; Mary Roberts Rinehart fellowship, 1962; Radcliffe Institute for Independent Study fellowship, 1965-67; National Endowment for the Arts fellowship, 1972; D. H. Lawrence fellowship, 1975.

WRITINGS: Who Made the Lamb, McGraw, 1965; *Confession from the Malaga Madhouse,* Dial, 1971; (co-editor)

Revelations: Diaries of Women, Random House, 1974; *Seeing Things,* Random House, 1976. Contributor to *New Yorker, Redbook, Ladies' Home Journal, Massachusetts Review, Yardbird, Place,* and other periodicals.

* * *

PAKENHAM, Simona Vere 1916-

PERSONAL: Born September 25, 1916, in Taplow, Berkshire, England; daughter of Thomas Compton and Phyllis (Price) Pakenham; married Noel P. D. Iliff, 1938; children: David Anthony. *Education:* Attended Central School of Speech Training and Dramatic Art, 1934, and Old Vic Drama School, 1935-36. *Religion:* Church of England. *Home:* 64 Canonbury Park South, London N.1, England.

CAREER: Writer. Actress and stage designer in repertory, at theaters in London, Dublin, Edinburgh, and elsewhere in British Isles, 1930-52. Regular broadcaster on British Broadcasting Corp. overseas religious programs.

WRITINGS: Ralph Vaughan Williams, A Discovery of His Music, Macmillan (London), 1957; *The First Nowell: A Nativity Play,* Oxford University Press, 1959; *Pigtails and Pernod,* Macmillan (London), 1961; *Sixty Miles from England: A History of the British Colony in Dieppe, 1814-1914,* Macmillan (London), 1967; *In the Absence of the Emperor: London-Paris, 1814-1815,* Cresset Press, 1968; *Cheltenham: A Biography,* Macmillan (London), 1971.

AVOCATIONAL INTERESTS: Music, Biblical studies, gardening.

* * *

PALLAS, Norvin 1918-

PERSONAL: Born April 4, 1918, in Cleveland, Ohio; son of Rudolph and Elsa (Laurence) Pallas. *Education:* Attended public schools in Cleveland, Ohio. *Home:* 3823 Behrwald Ave., Cleveland, Ohio 44109.

CAREER: Free-lance writer. Part-time accountant.

WRITINGS—Published by Washburn, except as indicated: *The Secret of Thunder Mountain,* 1951; *The Locked Safe Mystery,* 1954; *The Star Reporter Mystery,* 1955; *The Singing Trees Mystery,* 1956; *The Empty House Mystery,* 1957; *The Counterfeit Mystery,* 1958; *The Stolen Plans Mystery,* 1959; *The Scarecrow Mystery,* 1960; *The Big Cat Mystery,* 1961; *The Missing Witness Mystery,* 1962; *The Baseball Mystery,* 1963; *The Mystery of Rainbow Gulch,* 1964; *The Abandoned Mine Mystery,* 1965; *The S.S. Shamrock Mystery,* 1966; *Greenhouse Mystery,* 1967; *Code Games,* Sterling, 1971; *Guinness Game Book,* Sterling, 1974; *Calculator Puzzles, Tricks and Games,* Sterling, 1976. Contributor to poetry anthologies. Contributor to newspapers and to puzzle magazines.

AVOCATIONAL INTERESTS: Puzzles.

* * *

PALMER, Bruce (Hamilton) 1932-

PERSONAL: Born December 26, 1932, in Norwood, Mass.; son of Raymond Elsworth (a business executive) and Helen (Collins) Palmer; married Suzanne Ewer, June 26, 1954; children: Mark, Matthew, Maria. *Education:* Williams College, B.A., 1954; attended Ecole d'Etudes Litteraires, 1954-55, and Universidad de Madrid, 1955-56; Brandeis University, M.A., 1958. *Home:* Seabrook Rd., Stockton, N.J. 08559.

CAREER: Choate School, Wallingford, Conn., English teacher, 1956-57; Newark Academy, Newark, N.J., English teacher, 1959-69; Mercer County Community College, Trenton, N.J., assistant professor, 1970-79.

WRITINGS: Blind Man's Mark, Simon & Schuster, 1959; *Flesh and Blood,* Simon & Schuster, 1960; *Many Are the Hearts,* Simon & Schuster, 1961; (with J. C. Giles) *Horseshoe Bend,* Simon & Schuster, 1962; *Hecatomb,* Simon & Schuster, 1965; *First Bull Run* (juvenile), Macmillan, 1965; *Chancellorsville* (juvenile), Macmillan, 1967; *Wine making at Home,* Workman Publishing, 1970; *Making Furniture and Playspaces,* Workman Publishing, 1972; *They Shall Not Pass,* Doubleday, 1972.

WORK IN PROGRESS: A novel.

*   *   *

PALMER, Norman D(unbar)   1909-

PERSONAL: Born June 25, 1909, in Hinckley, Me.; son of Walter Elmer Palmer (a merchant) and Gertrude (Dunbar) Palmer; married Evelyn Florence Kalal, October 28, 1944; children: Patricia Lee. *Education:* Colby College, B.A., 1930; Yale University, M.A., 1932, Ph.D., 1936. *Religion:* Protestant. *Home:* 1110 Signal Hill Lane, Berwyn, Pa. 19312. *Office:* Department of Political Science, University of Pennsylvania, Philadelphia, Pa. 19104.

CAREER: Colby College, Waterville, Me., 1933-42, 1946-47, began as instructor, became associate professor and chairman of department of history and government; University of Pennsylvania, Philadelphia, associate professor, 1947-51, professor of political science, 1951—, chairman of political science department, 1949-52, chairman of international relations department, 1957-65. Fulbright professor, University of Delhi, 1952-53; visiting professor at Columbia University, 1950, School of Advanced International Studies, 1951, Swarthmore College, 1961, University of Hawaii, 1968, Bombay University, 1968, 1973, American University (Cairo), 1971, Duke University, 1974, and U.S. Naval Postgraduate School, 1976. Senior associate, Foreign Policy Research Institute, 1955—; senior specialist, East-West Center (Honolulu), 1966-67; vice-president and director, Philadelphia committee on foreign relations, International Study and Research Institute. Member, Philadelphia Charter Commission, 1951-52; member of steering committee, Global Interdependence Center; director, Philadelphia Transnational Project; trustee, Princeton-in-Asia program. Consultant, Foreign Operations Administration, 1954, and U.S. Department of State, 1954-76. *Military Service:* U.S. Navy, Air Combat Intelligence, 1942-46; became lieutenant commander; awarded Bronze Star Medal.

MEMBER: International Political Science Association, International Study and Research Institute (vice-president; director), International Studies Association (life member; national president, 1970-71), American Political Science Association, American Academy of Political and Social Science (secretary; director), Indian Political Science Association (life member), Association for Asian Studies, National Council of Asian Affairs (president), Friends of India Committee (chairman), American Society for Public Administration, Council on Foreign Relations, (advisor for Asian studies), World Affairs Council of Philadelphia (director), Philadelphia Council for International Visitors (director). *Awards, honors:* L.H.D., Colby College, 1955; Carnegie Endowment for International Peace fellow, 1959-60; American Council of Learned Societies fellow and Guggenheim fellow, both 1961-62; Council on Foreign Relations research fellow, South Asia, 1961-63; American Institute of Indian Studies research fellow, India, 1966-67 and 1971-72.

WRITINGS: The Irish Land League Crisis, Yale University Press, 1940, reprinted, Octagon, 1976; (co-author) *Fundamentals of Political Science,* Prentice-Hall, 1942; (with H. C. Perkins) *International Relations,* Houghton, 1953, 3rd edition, 1969; (co-author) *Major Governments of Asia,* Cornell University Press, 1958, 2nd edition, 1963; (co-author) *Leadership and Political Institutions in India,* Princeton University Press, 1959; (with Shao Chuan Leng) *Sun Yat-sen and Communism,* Praeger, 1961; *The Indian Political System,* Houghton, 1961, 2nd edition, 1971; (co-author) *The United States and the United Nations,* University of Oklahoma Press, 1964; *South Asia and United States Policy,* Houghton, 1966; *Elections and Political Development: The South Asian Experience,* Duke University Press, 1975; (co-author) *Pakistan: The Long View,* Duke University Press, 1978; (co-author) *Dynamics of Development,* Concept Publishing, 1978; (co-author) *The Subcontinent in World Politics,* Duke University Press, 1980; (co-author) *Changing Patterns of Security and Stability in Asia,* Praeger, 1980. Contributor to professional journals. Contributing editor, *Current History;* member of editorial boards, *Orbis* and *Asian Affairs.*

WORK IN PROGRESS: Revision of *The Indian Political System; Philadelphia as a World City; The International Relations of Cities; A Half Century of International Studies: A Critical Analysis.*

SIDELIGHTS: Norman D. Palmer has traveled to four continents, including twelve trips to South Asia. He told *CA:* "Over a period of many years, I have been able to spend a great deal of time and thought both in 'the highlands of the mind' and in many parts of the world, especially South Asia. This opportunity has enabled me to live in several worlds, both literally and figuratively speaking. It has given added dimension to my own life, and has prompted me to write. I write, (1) because I must, (2) because writing forces me to be more thorough in my investigations and to learn more about many things than I otherwise would, (3) because I want to contribute to my major fields of interest, and (4) because I want to project myself into the future."

*   *   *

PALMER, Stuart   1924-

PERSONAL: Born April 29, 1924, in New York, N.Y.; son of Herman and Beatrice (Hunter) Palmer; married Anne Scarborough, 1946; children: Catherine. *Education:* Yale University, B.A., 1949, M.A., 1951, Ph.D., 1955. *Office:* Department of Sociology and Anthropology, University of New Hampshire, Durham, N.H. 03824.

CAREER: Yale University, New Haven, Conn., assistant to dean of Yale College, 1949-51; New Haven College, New Haven, Conn., instructor, 1949-51, 1953-55; University of New Hampshire, Durham, 1955—, currently professor of sociology, chairman of department, 1964-69 and 1979—. Visiting professor of sociology, State University of New York at Albany, 1970-71, University of Sussex, 1976, and University of Georgia, 1977. *Military service:* U.S. Army Air Forces, 1942-45; became first lieutenant; received Air Medal with two oak leaf clusters. U.S. Air Force, active duty, 1951-53. *Member:* American Sociological Association, American Association for the Advancement of Science, American Society of Criminology, American Association of Suicidology, New York Academy of Sciences, Sigma Chi, Alpha Kappa Delta.

WRITINGS: Understanding Other People, Crowell, 1955; *A Study of Murder,* Crowell, 1960; (co-author) *The Challenge of Supervision*, McGraw, 1961; (contributor) J. Gibbs, *Suicide*, Harper, 1968; (contributor) M. Wolfgang, *Studies in Homicide*, Harper, 1968; *Deviance and Conformity*, College and University Press, 1970; *The Violent Society*, College and University Press, 1972; (co-editor) *Rebellion and Retreat*, C.E. Merrill, 1972; *The Prevention of Crime*, Human Sciences Press, 1973; (contributor) S. Steinmetz and M. Straus, *Violence in the Family*, Dodd, 1974; J. Inciardi, *Violent Crime*, Sage Publications, 1978; *Role Stress*, Prentice-Hall, 1980; *Deviant Behavior*, Scott, Foresman, 1981. Contributor of articles to *Nation*, *Journal of Criminal Law*, and sociology journals.

WORK IN PROGRESS: Homocide and Suicide.

*   *   *

PARADIS, Adrian A(lexis) 1912-

PERSONAL: Born November 3, 1912, in Brooklyn, N.Y.; son of Adrian Frederick (a businessman) and Marjorie (Bartholomew) Paradis; married Grace Dennis, October 8, 1938; children: Steven, Joel, Andrea. *Education:* Dartmouth College, A.B., 1934; Columbia University, B.S., 1942. *Politics:* Republican. *Home:* Canaan St., Canaan, N.H. *Agent:* Muriel Fuller, P.O. Box 193, New York, N.Y. 10017. *Office:* Phoenix Publishing, Canaan, N.H.

CAREER: Worked in hotel business, 1935-39; Chadbourne, Wallace, Parke & Whiteside, New York City, law librarian, 1940-42; American Airlines, Inc., New York City, 1942-68, worked as librarian, office manager of department of economic planning, economic analyst, assistant to the secretary, assistant secretary, 1947-68; New England Writing Associates (editorial and public relations firm), Westchester County, N.Y., owner and director, 1968-72; Phoenix Publishing, Canaan, N.H., editor, 1972—. Deputy director of Civil Defense, Westchester County, 1952-56; director and chairman of Ottaquechee (Vt.) Planning and Development Commission, 1969-76.

WRITINGS: 75 Ways for Boys to Earn Money, Greenburg, 1950; *Never Too Young to Earn*, McKay, 1954; *For Immediate Release*, McKay, 1955; *From High School to a Job*, McKay, 1956; *Americans at Work*, McKay, 1958; *Dollars for You*, McKay, 1958; (with wife, Grace D. Paradis) *Grow in Grace*, Abingdon, 1958; *Librarians Wanted*, McKay, 1959; *The New Look in Banking*, McKay, 1961; *Business in Action*, Messner, 1962; (with Betsy Burke) *The Life You Save*, McKay, 1962; *Labor in Action*, Messner, 1963; *The Problem Solvers*, Putnam, 1964; *Gail Borden: Resourceful Boy*, Bobbs-Merrill, 1965; *Government in Action*, Messner, 1965; *You and the Next Decade*, McKay, 1965.

Toward a Better World, McKay, 1966; *The Research Handbook*, Funk, 1966; *Economics in Action Today*, Messner, 1967; *Hungry Years*, Chilton, 1967; *Henry Ford*, Putnam, 1967; *Bulls and Bears*, Hawthorn, 1967; (with G. D. Paradis) *Your Life: Make It Count*, Funk, 1968; *Harvey Firestone*, Bobbs-Merrill, 1968; *Jobs That Take You Places*, McKay, 1968; *Trade: The World's Lifeblood*, Messner, 1969; *Job Opportunities for Young Negroes*, McKay, 1969; *Economics Reference Book*, Chilton, 1970; *Gold: King of Metals*, Hawthorn, 1970; *From Trails to Superhighways*, Messner, 1971; *How Money Works: The Federal Reserve System*, Hawthorn, 1972; *Labor Reference Book*, Chilton, 1972; *International Trade in Action*, Messner, 1973; *Inflation in Action*, Messner, 1974; (with R. Wood) *Social Security in Action*, Messner, 1975; *Opportunities in Banking*, Vocational Guidance Manuals, 1980; *Opportunities in Air Transportation*, Vocational Guidance Manuals, 1981. Contributor of articles to church publications and juvenile periodicals.

PARKER, Elinor Milnor 1906-

PERSONAL: Born March 20, 1906, in Jersey City, N.J.; daughter of Charles Wolcott and Emily (Fuller) Parker. *Education:* Bryn Mawr College, A.B., 1927. *Politics:* Independent. *Religion:* Episcopalian. *Home:* 30 East 72nd St., New York, N.Y. 10021.

CAREER: Affiliated with Bookshop, Morristown, N.J., 1928-38; Scribner Book Store, New York City, head of children's book department, 1938-44, assistant manager, 1944-53; Charles Scribner's Sons, New York City, editor of general trade books, 1953-79, director, 1966-79, editorial consultant, 1979—. *Member:* National Society of Colonial Dames, Cosmopolitan Club (New York).

WRITINGS—Published by Crowell, except as indicated: (Compiler with Natalie Norton) *Reading Is Fun*, Scribner, 1948; *Cooking for One*, 1949, revised edition, 1960; (editor) *A Birthday Garland*, 1949; *Some Dogs*, Pantheon, 1950; (compiler) *100 Story Poems*, 1951; *Entertaining Singlehanded*, 1952; *Most Gracious Majesty*, 1953, revised edition, 1962; (compiler) *100 Poems about People*, 1955; (compiler) *I Was Just Thinking*, 1959; (compiler) *100 More Story Poems*, 1960; (compiler) *The Singing and the Gold*, 1962; (editor) *William Wordsworth*, *Poems*, 1964; (compiler) *Here and There: 100 Poems about Places*, 1967; (compiler) *Four Seasons, Five Senses*, Scribner, 1974; (compiler) *Poets and the English Scene*, Scribner, 1975; (compiler) *Echoes of the Sea*, Scribner, 1977; *Letters and Numbers for Needlepoint*, Scribner, 1978.

AVOCATIONAL INTERESTS: Classical music, bird watching, embroidery, European travel.

*   *   *

PARKINSON, Thomas (Francis) 1920-

PERSONAL: Born February 24, 1920, in San Francisco, Calif.; son of Thomas Francis and Catherine (Green) Parkinson; married Ariel Reynolds, December 23, 1948; children: Katherine, Chrysa. *Education:* University of California, Berkeley, A.B., 1945, M.A., 1946, Ph.D., 1948. *Home:* 1001 Cragmont, Berkeley, Calif. 94708. *Office:* Department of English, University of California, Berkeley, Calif. 94720.

CAREER: University of California, Berkeley, instructor, 1948-50, assistant professor, 1950-53, associate professor, 1953-60, professor of English, 1960—, special assistant to the chancellor, 1979-81. Visiting professor, Wesleyan University, Middletown, Conn., 1951-52, University of Washington, 1968, and University of York (England), 1970; Fulbright professor, Universities of Bordeaux, Toulouse, and Frankfurt, 1953-54, Universities of Grenoble and Nice, 1965-66, and University of Rome, 1970; visiting lecturer, Yeats Summer School, 1965 and 1968. Member of literary panel, National Endowment for the Arts, 1971-74. Honorary fellow, St. Peter's College, Oxford University, 1969-70. *Military service:* U.S. Army Air Forces, 1943. *Member:* Modern Language Association of America, American Association of University Professors, Phi Beta Kappa. *Awards, honors:* Guggenheim fellow and American Philosophical Society grantee in Ireland, England, and Italy, 1957-58; Institute of Creative Art fellow, 1963-64.

WRITINGS: W. B. Yeats, Self-Critic: A Study of His Early Verse (also see below), University of California Press, 1951; *Men, Women, Vines* (poems), Harmon, 1959; (editor) *A Casebook on the Beat*, Crowell, 1961; (editor) *Masterworks of Prose*, Bobbs-Merrill, 1962; *W. B. Yeats: The Later Poetry* (also see below), University of California Press, 1964;

Thanatos (poems), Oyez Press, 1965, 2nd edition, 1976; (editor) *Robert Lowell: A Collection of Critical Essays*, Prentice-Hall, 1968; *Homage to Jack Spicer and Other Poems: Poems 1965-1969*, Ark Press, 1970; *Protect the Earth*, City Light Books, 1970; *W. B. Yeats, Self-Critic: A Study of His Early Verse* [and] *The Later Poetry*, University of California Press, 1971; *What the Blindman Saw; or, Twenty-Five Years of the Endless War* (play), Thorp Springs Press, 1974; *Hart Crane and Yvor Winters: Their Literary Correspondence*, University of California Press, 1978; *From the Grand Chartreuse* (verse), Oyez Press, 1980; *Collected Poems*, Oyez Press, 1980. Also author of two books of poetry, *Letter to a Young Lady*, 1946, and *The Canters of Thomas Parkinson*, 1977. Contributor of articles, poems, and reviews to *Modern Philology, Nation, Poetry, Horizon, Kenyon Review, Listener*, and other periodicals.

WORK IN PROGRESS: Collected Poems; W. B. Yeats: Writing Great Poetry in the Modern World; writing notes and introduction for Yeats' *Michael Robartes and the Dancer; Thorton Wilder as Novelist;* a book of poems, *The Way of the Cross.*

SIDELIGHTS: After spending brief periods in his late teens and early twenties alternately attending college and working at a wide assortment of jobs, Thomas Parkinson reports that he did not settle down and become "what my poetic friends sometimes humorously call an academic square" until the late 1940s. "But how did I become what my academic friends call a bohemian anarchist?," Parkinson continues. "I had been writing verse for years, and while studying at Berkeley met Josephine Miles (this was in 1939) who was just starting her career as instructor. I also met Richard Moore, who still writes but does not publish poetry; he is best known for his films of poets and novelists done for the Public Broadcasting System. In 1944 I met Robert Duncan and got into the habit of attending Kenneth Rexroth's Friday evenings at home. In 1945, a group of us formed a circle that met every week to discuss anarchist theory, but since none of us believed in violence and most of us took a skeptical view of the ballot, we ended up talking about Blake and Yeats and Lawrence and William Morris. Among the people who attended those meetings and went to the anarchist parties thrown by San Francisco's then large group of Italian anarchists were Rexroth, Duncan, Pauline Kael, William Everson, briefly William Stafford, and the founders of the first listener supported radio station, KPFA.

"KPFA gave an audience for poets. Two of its founders, Lewis Hill and Richard Moore, were poets, and a high proportion of the programs were literary. The intellectual ferment off campus at Berkeley during that period was immense. Since English literature in the view of the university ended with the publication of *Jude the Obscure* in 1895, this left us with *our* literature, meaning Yeats, Eliot, Pound, Williams, Stevens, Mann, Proust, Joyce, Lawrence, Brecht, Pirandello, Apollinaire, George, Neruda, Lorca, Valery, Desnos—in short, all the great literature of the twentieth century. So we had weekly seminars on one or another poet.

"We had readings of our own poetry. George Leite had a wonderful modern book store and published *Circle* Magazine, which at one time had a circulation of over 10,000, until George's incapacity for dealing with money forced him into bankruptcy. But by then, the bloom had gone. The Korean War and the Cold War and the loyalty oath at the university chilled everybody. Besides, we had learned from each other what we needed. Everson joined the Catholic Church, I joined the university, Spicer wouldn't sign the loyalty oath and left Berkeley for first Minneapolis then Boston, Robin

Blaser went to Boston (really Cambridge) as a librarian, Rexroth travelled in Europe, Duncan went to Majorca, later I went to Connecticut, then France. We all remained friends, but the party had really broken up.

"In 1955, Allen Ginsberg came to town, and a new party started. All the so-called beat writers came to see me and talk with me, and we became and remained good friends. They didn't all come to see me; I went to see some of them. And I never got along with Kerouac.

"So it has gone. My life is quite simply devoted to two institutions: the tradition of poetry; the greatest institution of higher learning that is, relatively speaking, public and open. . . . My wife and I are what is called responsible citizens (taking critical scholarship to be an art as is poetry; I think it is) with a rewarding past and bright future. I don't even mind working for the chancellor. Maybe my teaching days are past, but I do enjoy being able to do something for the institution that provided a great opportunity to the son of an impoverished artisan."

*   *   *

PARRISH, William E(arl)   1931-

PERSONAL: Born April 7, 1931, in Garden City, Kan.; son of Earl Milton and Anna Maye (Stoker) Parrish; married Helen Sue Stoppel, 1972. *Education:* Kansas State University, B.S., 1952; University of Missouri, M.A., 1953, Ph.D., 1955. *Politics:* Republican. *Religion:* Presbyterian. *Home:* 703 Bonnie Rd., Starkville, Miss. 39759. *Office:* Department of History, Mississippi State University, Mississippi State, Miss. 39762.

CAREER: University of Missouri—Columbia, instructor, 1952-55, visiting associate professor of history, summers, 1956, 1962, Westminster College, Fulton, Mo., associate professor, 1955-63, professor of history, 1966-71, Harry S Truman Professor of American History, 1971-78, chairman of department, 1966-78, dean, 1973-75; Mississippi State University, Mississippi State, head of department of history, 1978—. Chairman of Missouri American Revolution Bicentennial Commission, 1974-76. *Member:* Organization of American Historians, Southern Historical Association, Phi Alpha Theta, Phi Kappa Phi, Pi Delta Epsilon, Alpha Pi Zeta, Phi Gamma Delta. *Awards, honors:* Award of Merit, American Association for State and Local History, 1974.

WRITINGS: David Rice Atchison of Missouri: Border Politician, University of Missouri Press, 1961; *Turbulent Partnership: Missouri and the Union, 1861-1865*, University of Missouri Press, 1963; *Missouri's Struggles Under Radical Rule, 1865-1870*, University of Missouri Press, 1965; (editor) *The Civil War: A Second American Revolution?*, Holt, 1970; *Westminster College: An Informal History, 1851-1969*, Westminster College, 1971; *A History of Missouri*, Volume III: *1860-1875*, University of Missouri Press, 1973; (with Charles T. Jones, Jr. and Lawrence O. Christensen) *Missouri: The Heart of the Nation*, Forum Press, 1980. Contributor to history and religion journals. Member of editorial board, *Historian*, 1968—.

WORK IN PROGRESS: Several books.

*   *   *

PARTRIDGE, Eric (Honeywood)   1894-1979
(Corrie Denison)

PERSONAL: Born February 6, 1894, in Poverty Bay, New Zealand; died June 1, 1979, in Devonshire, England; son of John Thomas (a farmer) and Ethel Annabella (Norris) Partridge; married Agnes Dora Vye-Parmenter, 1925; children: Rosemary Ethel Honeywood Mann. *Education:* University of Queensland, B.A., 1921, M.A., 1923; Oxford University, B.Litt. (with first class honors), 1923.

CAREER: School teacher in Queensland, Australia, 1910-12; lecturer in English at Universities of Manchester and London, England, 1925-27; Scholartis Press, London, founder and managing director, 1927-31; full-time writer and lexicographer, 1932-79. *Military service:* Australian Imperial Forces, Infantry, 1915-19. British Army, 1940-41; became captain. Royal Air Force, 1942-45; became aircraftsman. *Member:* Whitefriars Club, Savile Club, Surrey Cricket Club, Middlesex County Cricket Club.

WRITINGS: (Under pseudonym Corrie Denison) *Glimpses,* Scholartis Press, 1928, reprinted under name Eric Partridge, Books for Libraries, 1971; *Eighteenth Century English Romantic Poetry,* Edouard Champion, 1924, reprinted, Folcroft, 1969; *The French Romantics' Knowledge of English Literature, 1820-1848,* Bibliotheque de la revue de litterature comparee, 1924, reprinted, B. Franklin, 1968; *A Critical Medley: Essays, Studies, and Notes in English, French and Comparative Literature,* Honore Champion, 1926, reprinted, Folcroft, 1969; *Robert Eyres Landor: A Biographical and Critical Sketch,* Fanfrolico Press, 1927, published with *Selections* by R. E. Landor as *Robert Eyres Landor,* Books for Libraries, 1970; *The Old and the New: Christmas and New Year Greetings* (pamphlet), Scholartis Press, 1929.

The First Three Years: An Account and a Bibliography of the Scholartis Press, Scholartis Press, 1930; *Literary Sessions,* Scholartis Press, 1932, reprinted, Folcroft, 1969; *Slang Today and Yesterday,* Routledge & Kegan Paul, 1933, 4th edition, Barnes & Noble, 1970; *Words, Words, Words!,* Methuen, 1933, reprinted, Books for Libraries, 1970; *Name This Child,* Methuen, 1936, 3rd edition, Hamish Hamilton, 1951, abridged edition, 1959, published as *Name Your Child,* Evans Bros., 1968; *A Covey of Partridge,* Routledge & Kegan Paul, 1937, reprinted, Books for Libraries, 1970; *A Dictionary of Slang and Unconventional English,* Macmillan, 1937, 7th edition, 1970, abridged edition published as *A Dictionary of Historical Slang,* edited by Jacqueline Simpson, Penguin, 1972, published as *The Routledge Dictionary of Historical Slang,* Routledge & Kegan Paul, 1973; *The World of Words,* Routledge & Kegan Paul, 1938, 3rd edition, Hamish Hamilton, 1948, reprinted, Books for Libraries, 1970; *An Original Issue of the "Spectator,"* Book Club of California, 1939.

A Dictionary of Cliches, Macmillan, 1940, 5th edition, Routledge & Kegan Paul, 1978; *Slang,* Clarendon Press, 1940; *The Teaching of English to His Majesty's Forces,* privately printed, 1941; *A Dictionary of Abbreviations with Especial Attention to Wartime Abbreviations,* Allen & Unwin, 1942, 3rd edition, 1949; *A Dictionary of R.A.F. Slang,* M. Joseph, 1942; *Usage and Abusage: A Guide to Good English,* Harper, 1942, 6th edition, 1965, published as *A Dictionary of Effective Speech,* Grosset, 1949, abridged edition published as *The Concise Usage and Abusage,* Philosophical Library, 1954, 6th edition, 1965; *Journey to the Edge of Morning: Thoughts upon Books, Love, Life,* Muller, 1946, 2nd edition, 1947, reprinted, Books for Libraries, 1969; *Shakespeare's Bawdy: A Literary and Psychological Essay and Comprehensive Glossary,* Routledge & Kegan Paul, 1947, revised edition, 1968; *Words at War, Words at Peace,* Muller, 1948, reprinted, Books for Libraries, 1970; *English: A Course for Human Beings,* Winchester, 1949, 4th edition, MacDonald, 1962; *Name into Word: Proper Names That Have Become*

Common Property, Secker & Warburg, 1949, 2nd edition, 1950, reprinted, Books for Libraries, 1970.

A Dictionary of the Underworld, British and American, Being the Vocabulary of Crooks, Criminals, Racketeers, Beggars and Tramps, Convicts, the Commercial Underworld, the Drug Traffic, the White Slave Traffic, and Spivs, Macmillan, 1950, 3rd edition, Routledge & Kegan Paul, 1968; *Here, There, and Everywhere: Essays upon Language,* Macmillan, 1950, revised edition, Hamish Hamilton, 1950; (with John W. Clark) *British and American English since 1900,* Philosophical Library, 1951, reprinted, Greenwood Press, 1970; *From Sanskrit to Brazil,* Hamish Hamilton, 1952, published as *From Sanskrit to Brazil: Vignettes and Essays upon Language,* Books for Libraries, 1969; (with Clark) *You Have a Point There: A Guide to Punctuation and Its Allies,* Hamish Hamilton, 1953, 4th edition, 1955, published as *You Have a Point There: A New and Complete Guide to Punctuation,* Routledge & Kegan Paul, 1978; *The "Shaggy Dog" Story,* Faber, 1953, 3rd edition, 1954, reprinted, Books for Libraries, 1970; *Notes on Punctuation,* Basil Blackwell, 1955, 4th edition, 1963; *What's the Meaning?,* Hamish Hamilton, 1956; *English Gone Wrong,* Phoenix House, 1957; *Origins: A Short Etymological Dictionary of Modern English,* Routledge & Kegan Paul, 1958, 4th edition, Macmillan, 1966.

A Charm of Words, Macmillan, 1960; *Adventuring among Words,* Oxford University Press, 1961; *Comic Alphabets,* Routledge & Kegan Paul, 1961; *Smaller Slang Dictionary,* Philosophical Library, 1961, 2nd edition, Routledge & Kegan Paul, 1964; *The Gentle Art of Lexicography as Pursued and Experienced by an Addict,* Macmillan, 1963; *A Dictionary of Catch Phrases, British and American,* Stein & Day, 1977; *Eric Partridge in His Own Words,* Deutsch, 1980.

Editor: The Poems of Cuthbert Shaw and Thomas Russell, Dulau, 1925, reprinted, Books for Libraries, 1970; *A Book of English Prose, 1700-1914,* Arnold, 1926, reprinted, Books for Libraries, 1970; *Pirates, Highwaymen and Adventurers,* Scholartis Press, 1927; William Blake, *Poetical Sketches,* Scholartis Press, 1927; Robert Eyres Landor, *Selections,* Fanfrolico Press, 1927, published with *Robert Eyres Landor: A Biographical and Critical Sketch* as *Robert Eyres Landor,* Books for Libraries, 1970; *The Three Wartons,* Scholartis Press, 1927, reprinted, Books for Libraries, 1970; (with John Brophy) *Songs and Slang of the British Soldier, 1914-1918,* Scholartis Press, 1930, 3rd edition, 1931, published as *The Long Trail: What the British Soldier Sang and Said in the Great War of 1914-1918,* British Book Centre, 1965, revised edition published as *The Long Trail: Soldiers' Songs and Slang, 1914-18,* Sphere Books, 1969; (and author of biographical-critical sketch and commentary) Francis Grose, *A Classical Dictionary of the Vulgar Tongue,* Scholartis Press, 1931, 2nd edition, Barnes & Noble, 1963; *For These Few Minutes: Almost an Anthology,* Barker, 1938; *A New Testament Word Book* (glossary), Routledge & Kegan Paul, 1940, reprinted, Books for Libraries, 1970; *Precis Writing,* Routledge & Kegan Paul, 1940; *A Dictionary of Forces' Slang, 1939-1945,* Secker & Warburg, 1948, reprinted, Books for Libraries, 1970; (with Henry Cecil Wyld) *The Little and Ives Webster Dictionary and Home Reference Library,* Little & Ives, 1957, published as *The Little and Ives Complete Standard Universal Dictionary and Home Reference Library,* Little & Ives, 1957; *A First Book of Quotations,* Hamish Hamilton, 1958, 2nd edition, 1960, published as *A Book of Essential Quotations,* Dutton, 1964; (and author of introduction and commentary) Jonathan Swift, *Polite Conversation,* Oxford University Press, 1963. Also editor of

"Language Library" Series, Oxford University Press. Editor, *The Bakara Bulletin* (Brisbane, Australia), 1919, and *The Window* (periodical), Scholartis Press, 1930.

Contributor: Caroline Clive, *IX Poems by V,* Scholartis Press, 1928; *Three Personal Records of the War, 1914-1919,* Scholartis Press, 1929, published as *Three Men's War,* Harper, 1930; Charles Reece Pemberton, *The Autobiography of Pel. Verjuice,* Scholartis Press, 1929; Godfrey Irwin, *American Tramp and Underworld Slang,* Scholartis Press, 1931; *A Martial Medley,* Scholartis Press, 1931; (author of introduction and contributor of etymologies) Wilfred Granville, *Sea Slang of the Twentieth Century,* Winchester, 1949; Henry Cecil Wyld, editor, *The Universal Dictionary of the English Language,* Routledge & Kegan Paul, 1952; (and author of introduction) *Code Names Dictionary,* Gale, 1963. Contributor to *Quarterly Review* and *Everyman.*

WORK IN PROGRESS: The Quiet Life, an autobiography; *A First Etymological Dictonary of Modern English; The Essential Dictionary of English;* revised and enlarged editions of *A Dictionary of Catch Phrases* and *A Dictionary of Slang.*

SIDELIGHTS: Eric Partridge gave up a promising academic career when, after only two years as a university lecturer, he discovered that he was repeating himself in the classroom. He reasoned that continuing in that vein would only result in a lifetime of boredom for both himself and his students, so he left his position as English instructor to found the small London publishing house, Scholartis Press. The business was fairly successful until the onset of the depression, at which time Partridge was forced to begin working as a free-lance writer.

Some articles which he wrote on the English language and its quirks proved so popular that he was awarded a contract for a book on the subject. His work over the next four decades, almost all of it dealing in some way with language—especially slang, cliches, and jargon—demonstrates that the author had clearly found his niche in life. As he often put it, it was the Great Depression that finally got him into what he really wanted to do all along: write books.

The books he wrote were unquestionably marvels of research. He never used assistants, and if an error was made in research or in writing, he was willing to take responsibility for it. Until his death at age eighty-five he continued the routine of research and scholarship that he had pursued for most of his life. At the height of his writing career he worked an average of eight hours per day, six days per week; and it was only with great reluctance that he reduced this regimen somewhat at the time of a serious operation in 1973.

Eric Partridge once told *CA,* "In all work, whether lexicographical or expository (or even slight and light-hearted), my aim has been to conceal erudition and to be readable to students and general public alike, and to humanize the subjects treated by not forgetting that one's readers are—most of them—human beings."

BIOGRAPHICAL/CRITICAL SOURCES: Time, January 30, 1950; *New Yorker,* August 4, 1951; Eric Partridge, *The Gentle Art of Lexicography,* Macmillan, 1963; *New York Times,* June 1, 1979.

*   *   *

PASSOW, A(aron) Harry 1920-

PERSONAL: Born December 9, 1920, in Liberty, N.Y.; son of Morris and Ida (Weiner) Passow; married Shirley Siegel, 1944; children: Michael Joel, Deborah Miriam, Ruth Ger-

trude. *Education:* New York State College for Teachers (now State University of New York at Albany), B.A. (cum laude), 1942, M.A., 1947; Columbia University, Ed.D., 1951. *Home:* 394 Eton St., Englewood, N.J. *Office:* Teachers College, Columbia University, 525 West 120th St., New York, N.Y. 10027.

CAREER: Science and mathematics teacher in Stony Point, N.Y., and Eden, N.Y., 1942-48; New York State College for Teachers (now State University of New York at Albany), instructor, 1948-50; Columbia University, Teachers College, New York, N.Y., assistant in department of curriculum and teaching, 1950-51, professor of education, 1952-72, Jacob H. Schiff Professor of Education, 1972—, chairman, Committee on Urban Education, and director, Study of District of Columbia Schools, 1966-67, director, Division of Educational Institutions and Programs, 1972-80. Research associate, Horace Mann Institute of School Experimentation, 1952-65. Educational consultant, Mobilization for Youth, Inc., 1962-65; educational consultant and lecturer on education of gifted and on curriculum development. *Military service:* U.S. Army Air Forces, 1943-46; became lieutenant. *Member:* Association for Supervision and Curriculum Development, National Education Association, National Society for Study of Education, American Association of University Professors, American Educational Research Association, Association of Educators of Gifted Children, Council for Exceptional Children, Metropolitan Association for Study of Gifted (president, 1957-58), Phi Delta, Kappa, Kappa Delta Pi.

WRITINGS—Published by Teachers College Press, except as indicated: (With Ronald C. Doll and Stephen M. Corey) *Organizing for Curriculum Improvement,* 1953; (with Miriam L. Goldberg, Abraham Tannenbaum, and Will French) *Planning for Talented Youth: Considerations for Public Schools,* 1955; (with Matthew B. Miles, Dale C. Draper, and Corey) *Training Curriculum Leaders for Cooperative Research,* 1955; (with Florence B. Stratemeyer, Hamden L. Forkner, and Margaret McKim) *Developing a Curriculum for Modern Living,* 1957; (with Harold J. McNally) *Improving the Quality of Public School Programs,* 1960; *Secondary Education for All: The English Approach,* Ohio State University Press, 1961; *The Effects of Ability Grouping,* 1966; (with Goldberg and Tannenbaum) *Education of the Disadvantaged: A Book of Readings,* Holt, 1967; (with Harold J. Noah, Max A. Eckstein, and John R. Mallea) *The National Case Study: An Empirical Comparative Study of Twenty-one Educational Systems,* Wiley, 1976; *Secondary Education Reform: Retrospect and Prospect,* 1976; *American Secondary Education: The Conant Influence,* National Association of Secondary School Principals, 1977; *Education for Gifted Children and Youth: An Old Issue—A New Challenge,* Ventura County Superintendent of Schools, 1980.

Editor: *Education in Depressed Areas,* 1963; *Nourishing Individual Potential,* Association for Supervision and Curriculum Development, 1964; *Intellectual Development: Another Look,* Association for Supervision and Curriculum Development, 1964; *Developing Programs for the Educationally Disadvantaged,* 1968; *Reaching the Disadvantaged Learner,* 1970; *Urban Education in the 1970's,* 1971; *Opening Opportunities for Disadvantaged Learners,* 1972; *Education of the Gifted* (seventy-eighth yearbook of Society for the Study of Education), University of Chicago Press, 1979.

Contributor to bulletins and yearbooks. Contributor of articles and reviews to education journals.

PATCHEN, Kenneth 1911-1972

PERSONAL: Born December 13, 1911, in Niles, Ohio; died January 8, 1972; son of Wayne (a steel mill worker) and Eva Patchen; married Miriam Oikemus, June 28, 1934. *Education:* Attended University of Wisconsin, 1928-29. *Home:* 2340 Sierra Ct., Palo Alto, Calif.

CAREER: Held many jobs in his youth, including working in a steel mill and migratory work in the United States and Canada. Writer of prose and of poetry. Made poetry-jazz appearances across the United States and in Canada, and poetry-recordings for Cadence and Folkways albums. Artist, worked in the graphic arts, and originator of own limited editions books, more than eight hundred issued with individual painted covers. Exhibited paintings in various cities and at universities. *Awards, honors:* Guggenheim fellowship, 1936; Ohioana Book Award in poetry, 1944, for *Cloth of the Tempest,* Shelley Memorial Award, 1954; National Foundation on Arts and Humanities award, 1967, for life-long contribution to American letters.

WRITINGS—Poetry: *Before the Brave,* Random House, 1936, reprinted, Haskell House, 1974; *First Will and Testament,* New Directions, 1939; *Teeth of the Lion,* New Directions, 1942; *The Dark Kingdom,* Harriss & Givens, 1942; *Cloth of the Tempest,* Harper, 1943; *An Astonished Eye Looks Out of the Air,* Untide Press, 1945; *Outlaw of the Lowest Planet,* Grey Walls Press, 1946; *Selected Poems,* New Directions, 1946, revised edition, 1964; *Pictures of Life and Death,* Max Padell, 1947; *They Keep Riding Down All the Time,* Max Padell, 1947; *Panels for the Walls of Heaven,* Bern Porter, 1947; *CCCLXXIV Poems,* Max Padell, 1948; *Red Wine and Yellow Hair,* New Directions, 1949; *To Say If You Love Someone,* Decker Press, 1959; *Orchards, Thrones and Caravans,* Print Workshop, 1952; *Fables and Other Little Tales,* Jonathan Williams, 1953; *The Famous Boating Party and Other Poems in Prose,* New Directions, 1954; *Glory Never Guesses,* privately printed, 1955; *Surprise for the Bagpipe Player,* privately printed, 1956; *When We Were Here Together,* New Directions, 1957; *Hurrah for Anything: Poems and Drawings* (also see below), Jonathan Williams, 1957; *Poemscapes* (also see below), Jonathan Williams, 1958; *Because It Is* (also see below), New Directions, 1960; *Love Poems,* City Lights, 1960, published as *The Love Poems of Kenneth Patchen,* Kraus Reprint, 1973; *Selected Love Poems,* Jargon, 1965; *Poems of Humor and Protest,* City Lights, 1960; *Like Fun I'll Tell You,* Jonathan Williams, 1966; *Hallelujah Anyway* (also see below), New Directions, 1966; *But Even So* (also see below), New Directions, 1968; *Love and War Poems,* Whisper & Shout, 1968; *The Collected Poems of Kenneth Patchen,* New Directions, 1969; *Aflame and Afun of Walking Faces,* New Directions, 1970; *Wonderings,* New Directions, 1971; *In Quest of Candlelighters,* New Directions, 1972; *A Poem for Christmas,* Artichoke, 1976; *The Argument of Innocence,* Scrimshaw Press, 1977.

Novels: *The Journal of Albion Moonlight,* Max Padell, 1941, reprinted, New Directions, 1961; *The Memoirs of a Shy Pornographer: An Amusement,* New Directions, 1945, reprinted, 1965; *Sleepers Awake,* Max Padell, 1946, reprinted, 1969; *See You in the Morning,* Max Padell, 1948.

Plays: "Now You See It (Don't Look Now)," produced Off-off Broadway at Thresholds Theatre, December, 1966; Richard Morgan, editor, *Patchen's Lost Plays,* Capra, 1977.

Omnibus volumes: *Doubleheader* (contains *Poemscapes, Hurrah for Anything,* and *A Letter to God;* also see below), New Directions, 1966; *Out of the World of Patchen,* New Directions, 1970, Volume I: *Because It Is,* Volume II: *But Even So,* Volume III: *Doubleheader,* Volume IV: *Hallelujah Anyway.*

SIDELIGHTS: Largely a self-taught writer, Kenneth Patchen never appeared to win widespread recognition from the professors at universities or many literary critics. As the *New York Times Book Review* noted: "While some critics tended to dismiss his work as naive, romantic, capricious and concerned often with the social problems of the 1930's, others found him a major voice in American poetry.... Even the most generous praise was usually grudging, as if Patchen had somehow won his place through sheer wrong-headed persistence."

The bulk of Patchen's followers were and still are young people. Kenneth Rexroth once pointed out that "during the Second World War and the dark days of reaction afterwards [Patchen] was the most popular poet on college campuses. He is still today an elder statesman of the youth revolt, the counter culture, and still today, he is never mentioned in the literary quarterlies."

One reason for the attraction of recent college-age readers to Patchen may be the quality of timelessness of his beliefs and ideas. An article in the *New York Times* explained that "his anti-war poetry, written nearly four decades ago, has regained popularity in some circles because of sentiment against the war in Vietnam."

A writer for the *New York Times Book Review* once wrote that "there is the voice of anger—outspoken rage against the forces of hypocrisy and injustice in our world. Patchen sees man as a creature of crime and violence, a fallen angel who is haunted by all the horrors of the natural world, and who still continues to kill his own kind: 'Humanity is a good thing. Perhaps we can arrange the murder of a sizable number of people to save it.'"

Beginning in the nineteen-fifties, Kenneth Patchen began reading his poetry to the accompaniment of jazz music. Patchen, in later years, would become famous in poetry circles for pioneering this technique.

BIOGRAPHICAL/CRITICAL SOURCES: Amos N. Wilder, *Spiritual Aspects of the New Poetry,* Harper, 1940; *New York Times Book Review,* February 2, 1958, June 22, 1958, October 20, 1968; *Yale Review,* June, 1958; *Saturday Review,* July 12, 1958; *Poetry,* September, 1958, February, 1965; Kenneth Rexroth, *Assays,* New Directions, 1961; Chad Walsh, *Today's Poets,* Scribner, 1964; Rexroth, *American Poetry in the Twentieth Century,* Herder, 1971; *New York Times,* January 9, 1972, January 10, 1972; *Washington Post,* January 10, 1972; *Newsweek,* January 24, 1972; *Publishers Weekly,* January 24, 1972; *Time,* January 24, 1972; *Contemporary Literary Criticism,* Gale, Volume I, 1973, Volume II, 1974.†

*   *   *

PATCHETT, Mary (Osborne) Elwyn 1897-

PERSONAL: Born December 2, 1897, in Australia; daughter of Herbert Fraser and Jean (Statham) Elwyn; widowed. *Education:* Privately educated. *Politics:* Conservative. *Religion:* Church of England. *Home:* 235 Latymer Ct., London W6 7JZ, England. *Agent:* David Higham Associates Ltd., 5-8 Lower John St., Golden Sq., London W1R 4HA, England; and Harold Ober Associates, Inc., 40 East 49th St., New York, N.Y. 10017.

CAREER: Journalist; full-time writer, mostly of children's books, 1953—. *Member:* Royal Zoological Society (fellow), Society of Australian Writers.

WRITINGS: Space Captives of the Golden Men, Bobbs-Merrill, 1953 (published in England as *Kidnappers of Space: The Story of Two Boys in a Spaceship Abducted by the Golden Men of Mars*, Lutterworth, 1953); *Lee Twins, Beauty Students*, Lane, 1953; *Ajax, the Warrior*, Lutterworth, 1953, published as *Ajax, Golden Dog of the Australian Bush*, Bobbs-Merrill, 1954; *Lost on Venus*, Lutterworth, 1954, published as *Flight to the Misty Planet*, Bobbs-Merrill, 1956; *Tam the Untamed*, Lutterworth, 1954, Bobbs-Merrill, 1955; *Wild Brother*, Collins, 1954; *Evening Star*, Lutterworth, 1954; *Adam Troy, Astroman*, Lutterworth, 1954; *Treasure of the Reef*, Lutterworth, 1955; *Undersea Treasure Hunters*, Lutterworth, 1955; *"Your Call, Miss Gaynor,"* Lutterworth, 1955; *Send for Johnny Danger: The Amazing Adventures of the Sea Pilot, Captain Danger, and His Crew on the Moon*, Lutterworth, 1956, published as *Send for Johnny Danger: The Amazing Adventures of Captain Danger and His Crew on the Moon*, Whittlesey House, 1958; *Return to the Reef*, Lutterworth, 1956; *Cry of the Heart*, Collins, 1956, Abelard, 1957; *Mysterious Pool*, Hamish Hamilton, 1957; *Sally's Zoo*, Hamish Hamilton, 1957; *Outback Adventure*, Lutterworth, 1957; *The Chance of Treasure*, Bobbs-Merrill, 1957; *Caribbean Adventures*, Lutterworth, 1957; *Brumby*, Lutterworth, 1958, published as *Brumby, the Wild White Stallion*, Bobbs-Merrill, 1959; *The Saffron Woman*, Heinemann, 1958; *The Great Barrier Reef*, Bobbs-Merrill, 1958; *Call of the Brush*, Lutterworth, 1959.

The Proud Eagles, Heinemann, 1960, World Publishing, 1961; *The Quest of Ati Manu*, Lutterworth, 1960, Bobbs-Merrill, 1962; *Warrimoo*, Brockhampton Press, 1961, Bobbs-Merrill, 1963; *The End of the Outlaws*, Bobbs-Merrill, 1961; *Brit*, Hodder & Stoughton, 1961; *Come Home, Brumby*, Lutterworth, 1961, published as *Brumby, Come Home*, Bobbs-Merrill, 1962; *The Golden Wolf*, Lutterworth, 1962, Bobbs-Merrill, 1965; *Circus Brumby*, Lutterworth, 1962; *Dangerous Assignment*, Brockhampton Press, 1962, Bobbs-Merrill, 1964; *In a Wilderness*, Hodder & Stoughton, 1962; *Dingo*, Doubleday, 1963; *The Venus Project*, Brockhampton Press, 1963; *Ajax and the Haunted Mountain*, Lutterworth, 1963, Bobbs-Merrill, 1966; *Tiger in the Dark*, Brockhampton Press, 1964, Duell, 1966; *A Budgie Called Fred*, Arthur Barker, 1964; *Ajax and the Drovers*, Lutterworth, 1964; *Stranger in the Herd*, Lutterworth, 1964, Duell, 1966; *The White Dingo*, Lutterworth, 1965; *The Last Warrior* (adult novel), Hodder & Stoughton, 1965, Doubleday, 1966; *Brumby Foal*, Lutterworth, 1965; *Summer on Wildhorse Island*, Brockhampton Press, 1965, Meredith Press, 1967; *The Terror of Manooka*, Lutterworth, 1966; *Summer on Boomerang Beach*, Brockhampton Press, 1967; *Festival of Jewels*, Brockhampton Press, 1968; *Farm beneath the Sea*, Harrap, 1969; *Quarter Horse Boy*, Harrap, 1970; *Rebel Brumby*, Lutterworth, 1972; *Roar of the Lion*, Lutterworth, 1973; *Hunting Cat*, Abelard, 1976.

Also author of *Ark on Horseback, A Moment of Love,* and *Atlanta;* author of radio scripts. Contributor to short story collections and educational books. Contributor to encyclopedias and magazines.

AVOCATIONAL INTERESTS: Children, animals, adventure of every sort, travel.

*   *   *

PAUL, Leslie (Allen) 1905-

PERSONAL: Born April 30, 1905, in Dublin, Ireland; son of Fred and Lottie (Burton) Paul. *Education:* Brockley Central School, M.A. *Home and office:* 6 Church Crott, Madley,

Hereford, England. *Agent:* A. P. Watt & Son, 26/28 Bedford Row, London WC1R 4HL, England; and Willis Kingsley Wing, 24 East 38th St., New York, N.Y. 10016.

CAREER: Began work as journalist at age of 17; *Open Road*, London, England, editor, 1923; *Cambria Daily Leader*, Swansea, Wales, London correspondent, 1925-29; *Plan*, London, editor, 1934-39; tutor in adult education, London, and worker in underground movement in Europe, 1933-40; Ashridge College of Citizenship, Berkhampsted, England, assistant director of studies, 1947-48; Brasted Place (college), Kent, England, director of studies, 1953-57; Leverhulme research fellow, 1957-59; King George's Jubilee Trust and Industrial Welfare Society, London, research fellow, 1959-61; English Church Assembly, London, research director, 1962-64; Kenyon College, Gambier, Ohio, resident fellow, 1964; Queen's College, Birmingham, England, lecturer in ethics and social studies, 1965-70; University of Birmingham, Birmingham, England, lecturer in department of theology, 1965-70. British Council lecturer in Turkey and Israel, 1959; Selwyn Lecturer, St. John's College and Christchurch University, both New Zealand, 1969; lecturer, Townsville University, Australia, 1969; Hale Lecturer, Seabury-Western Theological Seminary, 1970; Lilly Scholar-in-Residence, Eastern College, 1970; Bloemfontein Diocesan Lecturer, South Africa, 1977; Stuart-Asbury Lecturer, University Church, Oxford, 1978; writer-in-residence, St. Paul and St. Mary College, Cheltenham, 1981. Member of Departmental Committee on Youth Services, 1958-60; member of General Synod, Church of England, 1965-70; chairman of Hereford Diocesan Council of Social Action, 1972-78. Regular broadcaster, especially on European and overseas services, British Broadcasting Corp., 1929-65. Adviser to Diocese of Melbourne, Australia, 1969. *Military service:* British Army, Royal Artillery, 1941; Army Education Corps, 1942-46, served as tutor in modern studies at Middle East Forces college in Palestine; became captain. *Member:* Royal Society of Literature (fellow), Society of Authors, Institute of Liturgy and Architecture (honorary fellow). *Awards, honors:* Atlantic Award in literature, 1946; honorary Doctor of Canon Law, Seabury-Western Theological Seminary, 1970; D.Litt., Geneva Theological College, 1974; West Midlands Arts Award, 1977.

WRITINGS: The Pipes of Pan (poems), C. W. Daniel, 1927; *The Folk Trail: An Outline of the Philosophy and Activities of Woodcraft Fellowships*, Noel Douglas, 1929; *The Ashen Stave*, W. C. Boone, 1930; *The Green Company: Pow-wows on Pioneering for Boys and Girls*, C. W. Daniel, 1931; *A Green Love and Other Poems*, privately printed, 1931; *Fugitive Morning* (novel), Denis Archer, 1932; *Two One-Act Plays*, C. W. Daniel, 1933; *Periwake, His Odyssey* (novel), Denis Archer, 1934; *Co-operation in the U.S.S.R.: A Study of the Consumers' Movement*, Gollancz, 1934; *Story without End: The Junior Book of Co-operation*, Co-operative Union, 1935; *Men in May* (novel), Gollancz, 1936; (contributor) *Britain and the Soviets*, Martin Lawrence, 1936; *The Republic of Children*, Allen & Unwin, 1938.

The Annihilation of Man: A Study of the Crisis in the West, Faber, 1944, Harcourt, 1945; *The Living Hedge* (autobiography), Faber, 1946; *The Soviet Union* (bibliography), Ashridge College Press, 1947; *Heron Lake* (autobiography), Batchworth, 1948; *The Meaning of Human Existence*, Faber, 1949, Lippincott, 1950.

The Age of Terror, Faber, 1950, Beacon Press, 1951; *Angry Young Man* (autobiography), Faber, 1951; (author of foreword) Emmanuel Mounier, *Be Not Afraid*, translation by Cynthia Rowland, Rockliff, 1951; *Exile and Other Poems*,

Caravel, 1951; *The English Philosophers,* Faber, 1953; *Sir Thomas More,* Faber, 1953, Books for Libraries Press, 1970; *The Adventure of Man* (geography text), four volumes, Newnes, 1954; *The Jealous God,* Bles, 1955; *The Boy Down Kitchener Street,* Faber, 1957; *Nature into History,* Faber, 1957.

(With others) *The Youth Service in England and Wales,* H.M.S.O., 1960; *Persons and Perceptions,* Faber, 1961; *Son of Man: The Life of Christ,* Dutton, 1961; *The Transition from School to Work,* Industiral Welfare Society, 1962; *Traveller on Sacred Ground,* Hodder & Stoughton, 1963; *Deployment and Payment of the Clergy,* Church Information Office, 1964; *Alternatives to Christian Belief,* Doubleday, 1967; *The Death and Resurrection of the Church,* Hodder & Stoughton, 1968; *Coming to Terms with Sex,* Collins, 1969.

Eros Rediscovered: Restoring Sex to Humanity, Association Press, 1970; (with Donald Swann) *This is the Story of Bontzye Shweig,* Galliard, 1970; *A Patti Col Sesso,* Edizione Paoline, 1971; *Journey to Connemara* (poems), Outposts, 1972; *A Church by Daylight,* Chapman, 1973; *The Waters and the Wild* (novel), St. Martin's, 1975; *First Love,* S.P.C.K., 1977; *The Bulgarian Horse* (novel), Cassell, 1979; *Springs of Good and Evil,* Bible Reading Fellowship, 1979.

Monographs, pamphlets: *The Child and the Race,* Royal Arsenal Co-operative Society, 1926; (editor) *Russia 1931,* Co-operative Union, 1931; *The Training of Pioneers,* National Council of Woodcraft Folk, 1936; *Portrait of an Angry Saint: The Poet Peguy,* Burning Glass Press, 1949; (editor) *Christians and War,* Christian Action, 1951; *The Rebellion of Youth,* Westminster Abbey, 1961; *Hot House,* Newman Neame, 1961; *Values in Modern Society,* Co-operative Union, 1962; *The Church as an Institution,* Prism Pamphlets, 1967; *Colloquium,* [New Zealand], 1969; *Man's Understanding of Himself,* Seabury-Western Theological Seminary, 1971; *Where after Welfare?: The Welfare State Considered,* Hereford Diocesan Council of Social Action, 1976; *Seeking the Christ to Celebrate,* Celebration Council, 1978; *The Early Days of the Woodcraft Folk,* Woodcraft Folk National Council, 1980. Also author of *Blood and Soil,* published by Plan Press, and *Studies in the Sociology of Religion.*

Contributor of stories to anthologies, including *English Story,* Collins, 1941, and *English Country Short Stories,* Elek, 1949; contributor to *Encyclopedia Americana.* Author of scripts for British Broadcasting Corp. and for Associated Television. Contributor to periodicals, including *Kenyon Review, Reporter,* and *Sunday Times* (London).

SIDELIGHTS: At the age of twenty, Leslie Paul founded a youth movement known as The Woodcraft Folk. In 1975, the movement celebrated its fiftieth anniversary with an international camp of 3000 children and young people at Stanford Hall, Loughborough, England. According to Paul, "the youth movements of the twenties are now exciting the interest of historians," and at his suggestion, University College, University of Wales, has established a Youth Movement Archives Department which will publish a series of monographs on the subject.

Paul's best-known book is *Angry Young Man;* published in 1951, the book's title came to symbolize an entire generation of youth. However, *Deployment and Payment of the Clergy,* which came to be known as "The Paul Report," *Alternatives to Christian Belief,* and several of his later works, have made him most famous as a sociologist in the field of religion.

AVOCATIONAL INTERESTS: Photography, bird-watching, making lawns, teaching children chess.

BIOGRAPHICAL/CRITICAL SOURCES: Leslie Paul, *The Living Hedge* (autobiography), Faber, 1946; Paul, *Heron Lake* (autobiography), Batchworth, 1948; Paul, *Angry Young Man* (autobiography), Faber, 1951; *Times Literary Supplement,* September 29, 1961, November, 1961, August 17, 1967; *Best Sellers,* January 1, 1971.

*   *   *

PAUL, Robert S(idney) 1918-

PERSONAL: Born June 10, 1918, in Walton-on-Thames, England; son of Robert James Kingsbury and Florence (Reed) Paul; married Eunice Mary Pickup, 1946; children: Timothy Robert, Lydia Mary, Martin Oliver Kingsbury. *Education:* Attended St. Catherine's College; Mansfield College, Oxford, B.A., M.A., D. Phil. *Office:* Austin Presbyterian Theological Seminary, 100 East 27th St., Austin, Tex. 78705.

CAREER: Ordained minister in Congregational Union of England and Wales, 1945; Christ Church, Leatherhead, Surrey, England, minister, 1945-54; World Council of Churches, Ecumenical Institute, Chateau de Bossey, Celigny, Switzerland, associate director, 1954-58; Hartford Seminary Foundation, Hartford, Conn., Waldo Professor of Church History, 1958-67; Pittsburgh Theological Seminary, Pittsburgh, Pa., professor of modern church history, 1967-77; Austin Presbyterian Theological Seminary, Austin, Tex., professor of ecclesiastical history and Christian thought, 1977—. Chairman, international conference of church historians, Bossey, Switzerland, 1956. *Military service:* Served in British Home Guard during World War II. *Member:* Congregational Historical Society (England), American Society of Church History, Society for the Study of Theology (Great Britain), Oxford Union (Great Britain).

WRITINGS: The Lord Protector, Lutterworth Press, 1955; *The Atonement and the Sacraments,* Abingdon, 1960; (editor) Thomas Goodwin, *An Apologeticall Narration,* United Church, 1963; *Ministry,* Eerdmans, 1965; *The Church in Search of Its Self,* Eerdmans, 1972; *Kingdom Come,* Eerdmans, 1974.

Contributor of chapters to several books, including *Unity in Mid-Career,* edited by Wagoner and Bridston, *Christian Confidence,* edited by Roger Tomes, *From Faith to Faith,* edited by Dikran Y. Hadidian, and *Reformatio Perennis,* edited by Brian Gerrish. Contributor to encyclopedias. Co-editor, *Transactions* of Congregational Historical Society, 1951-54; editor, *Hartford Quarterly,* 1960-67; chairman of faculty editorial committee, *Austin Seminary Bulletin.*

WORK IN PROGRESS: The Assembly of the Lord: Religion and Politics in the Seventeenth Century; several books in the fields of history, theology, and "the theological approach to detective fiction."

SIDELIGHTS: Robert S. Paul writes: "I started out with a biography of Oliver Cromwell in which I set out to make one point that was in danger of being forgotten by other biographers and historians of that Puritan period—the *essential* relationship between religion and politics in the seventeenth century. This subject and this period still remain my academic first-love and primary stimulus, because it was the meeting-place between the ages of faith and the Age of Reason and we are still wrestling culturally with the problems it raised. But in the late 1950s and early 60s, the problem of the Church itself, particularly the ecumenical problem, attracted my attention. At the same time, it appeared that many of the theologians who *ought* to have been helping us on these matters were busy discussing whether God was dead or not, or whether the Kingdom of God was to be exchanged for the secular city, or how theology could be turned to serve the current revolutionary or reactionary fashion. So I decided I had better try to say something about the problems that were affecting the people in the pews, failing anyone more competent. That is how *The Atonement and the Sacraments, Ministry, The Church in Search of Its Self*, and *Kingdom Come* came to be written.

"Now with *The Assembly of the Lord* I am returning to my first love, and looking at how politics and religion were interwoven during the course of the Westminster Assembly. It sounds about as dull as any subject could be, but it is fascinating. Whether I can convey that fascination to others, or whether anyone will be willing to read beyond the subtitle, is of course something to worry me and my publisher."

*   *   *

PAUL, Rodman Wilson 1912-

PERSONAL: Born November 6, 1912, in Villa Nova, Pa.; son of Oglesby and Laura L. (Wilson) Paul; married Anne Thomson, 1951; children: Rodman Wilson, Jr., Deborah Anne, Judith Thomson; (step-daughter) Susan L. Spencer. *Education:* Harvard University, A.B., 1936, A.M., 1937, Ph.D., 1943. *Politics:* Democrat. *Religion:* Episcopalian. *Home:* 480 South Orange Grove Blvd., Apt. 18, Pasadena, Calif. 91105. *Office:* Humanities Division, California Institute of Technology, Pasadena, Calif. 91125.

CAREER: Harvard University, Cambridge, Mass., assistant dean, 1937-38, 1942-43, instructor, 1938-40; Yale University, New Haven, Conn., instructor, 1946-47; California Institute of Technology, Pasadena, associate professor, 1947-51, professor, 1951-72, Edward S. Harkness Professor, 1972—. Chairman, department of college work, Protestant Episcopal Diocese, Los Angeles, 1962-65. *Military service:* U.S. Navy, 1943-46; became lieutenant commander. *Member:* American Historical Association (Pacific Coast branch; president, 1980-81), Organization of American Historians, Society of American Historians (fellow), American Antiquarian Society, Western History Association (president, 1977-78), California Historical Society (fellow). *Awards, honors:* Huntington Library fellow, 1946, 1961; Ford Foundation grant for study in England, 1955-56; Guggenheim fellow, 1967-68; award of merit, American Association for State and Local History.

WRITINGS: The Abrogation of the Gentlemen's Agreement, Harvard University Press, 1936; *California Gold: The Beginning of Mining in the Far West*, Harvard University Press, 1947; (editor) Mark Twain, *Roughing It*, Rinehart, 1952; *Mining Frontiers of the Far West*, Holt, 1963; (editor) C. H. Shinn, *Mining Camps*, Harper, 1965; (editor) *A Victorian Gentlewoman in the Far West: The Reminiscences of Mary Hallock Foote*, Huntington Library, 1972; (editor) W. J. Trimble, *The Mining Advance into the Inland Empire*, Johnson Reprint, 1972; (editor with Richard W. Etulain) *The Frontier and the American West*, A.H.M. Publishing, 1977. Contributor to history journals.

*   *   *

PAUL, Sherman 1920-

PERSONAL: Born August 26, 1920, in Cleveland, Ohio; son of Jacob (a merchant) and Gertrude (Levitt) Paul; married G. McDowell, May 1, 1943; children: Jared, Meredith, Erica, Jeremy. *Education:* University of Iowa, A.B., 1941; Harvard University, A.M., 1948, Ph.D., 1950. *Home:* 903 East College Ave., Iowa City, Iowa. *Office:* Department of English, University of Iowa, Iowa City, Iowa.

CAREER: University of Iowa, Iowa City, instructor in English, 1946; Harvard University, Cambridge, Mass., instructor in English, 1950-52; University of Illinois at Urbana—Champaign, assistant professor, 1952-55, associate professor, 1955-57, professor of English, 1957-67, Center for Advanced Study, began as associate, senior master, 1966-67; University of Iowa, Carpenter Professor, 1967-74, Carver Distinguished Professor, 1974—. Fulbright professor, University of Vienna, 1957-58. *Military service:* U.S. Army Air Forces, 1942-46; became captain. *Member:* Modern Language Association of America, Phi Beta Kappa. *Awards, honors:* Ford Foundation fellow, 1952; Guggenheim fellow, 1963-64.

WRITINGS: Emerson's Angle of Vision: Man and Nature in American Experience, Harvard University Press, 1952; *The Shores of America: Thoreau's Inward Exploration*, University of Illinois Press, 1958; (with Leon Edel, Thomas H. Johnson, and Claude M. Simpson) *Masters of American Literature*, Houghton, 1959; (editor) *Thoreau: A Collection of Critical Essays*, Prentice-Hall, 1962; *Louis Sullivan: An Architect in American Thought*, Prentice-Hall, 1962; *Edmund Wilson: A Study of Literary Vocation in Our Time*, University of Illinois Press, 1965; *Randolph Bourne*, University of Minnesota Press, 1966; *Henry Callahan*, Museum of Modern Art, 1967; *Music of Survival: A Biography of a Poem by William Carlos Williams*, University of Illinois Press, 1968; (editor) *Six Classic American Writers*, University of Minnesota Press, 1970; (editor) *Culture and Criticism*, Midwest Modern Language Association, 1971; *Hart's Bridge*, University of Illinois Press, 1972; *Repossessing and Renewing*, Louisiana State University Press, 1976; *Olson's Push*, Louisiana State University Press, 1978; *The Lost America of Lore*, Louisiana State University Press, 1981.

Member of selection committee, *Literary Classics of the United States*. Contributor to *Encyclopaedia Britannica*. Contributor to magazines and journals, including *Nation*, *Accent*, and *New Leader*. Member of editorial board, *American Literature* and *Boundary 2*; member of advisory board, *PMLA*; editorial advisor, *Studies in Romanticism*.

BIOGRAPHICAL/CRITICAL SOURCES: New York Times Book Review, January 28, 1979.

*   *   *

PAYNE, J(ohn) Barton 1922-

PERSONAL: Born September 12, 1922, in San Francisco, Calif.; son of Philip Francis and Alice (Mould) Payne; married Dorothy Dean Dosker, 1946; children: John Calvin, Philip Barton, Peter Ellis, James Richard, Paula Patience. *Education:* University of California, B.A. (highest honors), 1942, M.A., 1946; San Francisco Theological Seminary, B.D. (summa cum laude), 1945; Princeton Theological Seminary, Th.M., 1948, Th.D., 1949. *Home:* 12270 Conway Rd., Creve Coeur, Mo. 63141. *Office:* Department of Old Testament, Covenant Theological Seminary, St. Louis, Mo.

CAREER: Ordained minister of Reformed Presbyterian Church-Evangelical Synod; Bob Jones University, Greenville, S.C., chairman of department of Old Testament, 1949-54; Trinity Theological Seminary, Chicago, Ill., associate professor of Old Testament, 1954-59; Wheaton College, Graduate School of Theology, Wheaton, Ill., associate professor, 1958-65, professor of Old Testament, 1965-72; Covenant Theological Seminary, St. Louis, Mo., professor of Old Testament and chairman of department, 1972—. Annual professor, Near East School of Archaeological and Biblical Studies, Jerusalem, 1964. *Member:* Evangelical Theological

Society (chairman, Southern section, 1953-54; national secretary, 1955-61; national vice-president, 1965; president, 1966), Near East Archaeological Society, Phi Beta Kappa.

WRITINGS: An Outline of Hebrew History, Baker Book, 1954; *Hebrew Vocabularies*, Baker Book, 1956; *The Imminent Appearing of Christ*, Eerdmans, 1962; *Theology of the Older Testament*, Zondervan, 1962; *New Perspectives on the Old Testament*, Word, Inc., 1969; *Encyclopedia of Biblical Prophecy*, Harper, 1973; *Revelation in Sequence*, Lithocolor, 1973; *The Prophecy Map of Bible History*, Harper, 1974; *Biblical Prophecy for Today*, Baker Book, 1978. Also author of *America's Reformed Presbyterian Bicentennial* and *What Is a Reformed Presbyterian*, both 1974.

Contributor: *Inspiration and Interpretation*, Eerdmans, 1956; *Holy Bible, the Berkeley Version in Modern English*, Zondervan, 1959; *The Biblical Expositor*, Holman, 1960; *The Wycliffe Bible Commentary*, Moody, 1962; *New American Standard Bible*, Lockman Foundation, 1975; *New International Version of the Holy Bible*, Zondervan, 1978. Contributor to encyclopedias, dictionaries, and religion journals.

AVOCATIONAL INTERESTS: Family camping (has camped throughout United States, in Europe, and in Near East).

*   *   *

PAYNE, Stanley G(eorge)   1934-

PERSONAL: Born September 9, 1934, in Denton, Tex.; son of George C. (a carpenter) and E. Margaret (Brown) Payne; married Julia Ann Sherman (a psychologist), June, 1961; children: Michael. *Education:* Pacific Union College, B.A., 1955; Claremont Graduate School, M.A., 1957; Columbia University, Ph.D., 1960. *Home:* 3917 Plymouth Cir., Madison, Wis. 53706. *Office:* Department of History, University of Wisconsin, Madison, Wis. 53706.

CAREER: Columbia University, New York City, lecturer, 1959-60; University of Minnesota, Minneapolis, instructor 1960-62; University of California, Los Angeles, 1962-68, began as assistant professor, became professor of history; University of Wisconsin—Madison, professor of history, 1968—. *Member:* American Historical Association.

WRITINGS: Falange: A History of Spanish Fascism, Stanford University Press, 1961; (with Shepard B. Clough and Otto Pflanze) *A History of the Western World*, Volume III: *Modern Times; 1815 to the Present*, Heath, 1964; *Politics and the Military in Modern Spain*, Stanford University Press, 1967; *Franco's Spain*, Crowell, 1967; *The Spanish Revolution*, Norton, 1970; *A History of Spain and Portugal*, two volumes, University of Wisconsin Press, 1973; *Basque Nationalism*, University of Nevada Press, 1975; *Facism: Comparison and Definition*, University of Wisconsin Press, 1980. Contributor to history journals.

SIDELIGHTS: A New York Times Book Review writer calls *Politics and the Military in Modern Spain* "almost surely the definitive work on how, over the past 150 years, the Spanish Army came to be 'the ultimate arbiter of public affairs in Spain.'" The reviewer finds that Stanley Payne is "generally fair in handling a difficult subject. His research is commanding, his prose style serviceable and his bibliography excellent." At the same time, another of his books, *The Spanish Revolution*, has come to be known as one of the definitive works on that subject. Cecil Eby writes: "[Payne] appears to have read everything and to have forgotten nothing. His book, with its patient attention to details and its careful documentation, will not be popular among the my-

thologizing or activist set, for the author wishes to study revolution, not to make it. But given time and a change of tide, *The Spanish Revolution* ought to work its way close to the head of any five-foot shelf of books about the struggle in Spain. And to be admitted to the company of Orwell, Brenan, and Borkenau is a major achievement."

BIOGRAPHICAL/CRITICAL SOURCES: New York Times Book Review, August 10, 1967; *Virginia Quarterly Review*, autumn, 1967, spring, 1968; *Book World*, March 8, 1970.

*   *   *

PAYSON, Dale   1943-

PERSONAL: Born June 3, 1943, in White Plains, N.Y.; daughter of Henry and Frances T. Payson. *Education:* Endicott Junior College, graduate, 1963; attended School of Visual Arts, summers, 1961 and 1962, and 1963-64. *Home and office:* 149 Franklin St., New York, N.Y. 10013.

CAREER: Sylvox Display Co., New York City, window display designer, 1965; Famous Artists, Westport, Conn., teacher of correspondence course, 1967; Encore Fashions, New York City, fabric designer, 1969-70; Fairfield Co., New York City, colorist, 1970-71.

WRITINGS—For children: *Almost Twins*, Prentice-Hall, 1974; (compiler with Karen Wynant, and illustrator) *The Sleepy Time Treasury*, Prentice-Hall, 1975.

Illustrator: *Ann Aurelia and Dorothy*, Harper, 1967; *The Silver Crown*, Atheneum, 1968; *Next Door to Xanadu*, Harper, 1969; *Amish Boy*, Putnam, 1969; *Amish Wedding*, Putnam, 1970; *If You Listen*, Atheneum, 1971; *Tatu and the Honey Bird*, Putnam, 1972; *The Seven Stone*, Holiday House, 1972; *The Friendship Hedge*, Dutton, 1973; *The Mystery of the Spider Doll*, F. Watts, 1973; *On Reading Palms*, Prentice-Hall, 1973; *The Magic of the Little People*, Messner, 1973; *The Magic Castle Fairy Tale Book*, Random House, 1978.

WORK IN PROGRESS: Writing and illustrating *When Susan Came to My House*, for Dial Press.

*   *   *

PEACOCK, Alan T(urner)   1922-

PERSONAL: Born June 26, 1922, in Ryton-on-Tyne, England; son of Alexander David and Clara (Turner) Peacock; married Margaret Martha Astell Burt, 1944; children: David, Richard, Helen. *Education:* University of St. Andrews, M.A., (with honors), 1947. *Home:* 10 Grange Ct., Edinburgh EH9 1PX, Scotland. *Office:* Office of the Principal, University College, Buckingham MK18 1EG, England.

CAREER: University of St. Andrews, St. Andrews, Scotland, lecturer, 1947-48; University of London, London School of Economics and Political Science, London, England, lecturer, 1948-51, reader in public finance, 1951-56; University of Edinburgh, Edinburgh, Scotland, professor, 1956-62; University of York, York, England, professor of economics, 1962-78; University College, Buckingham, England, professor of economics, 1978—, principal, 1980—. Chief economic adviser, Department of Trade and Industry, government of England, 1973-76. *Military service:* Royal Navy, three years; became lieutenant. *Member:* British Academy (fellow, 1979—), Political Economy Club, Institut International de Finances Publiques (honorary president).

WRITINGS: Economics of National Insurance, Hodge, 1952; (editor) *Income Redistribution and Social Policy*, J. Cape, 1954; (with H. C. Edey) *National Income and Social Accounting*, Hutchinson, 1954; (with R. A. Musgrave) *Clas-*

sics in Public Finance, Macmillan, 1958; (with Jack Wiseman) *Growth of Public Expenditure in the United Kingdom*, Princeton University Press, 1962; (editor with G. Hauser) *Government Finance and Economic Development*, Organization for Economic Cooperation and Development, 1965; (with Wiseman) *Education for Democrats*, Institute for Economic Affairs, 1970; (with Graham K. Shaw) *Economic Theory of Fiscal Policy*, Allen & Unwin, 1971; (with Charles K. Rowley) *Welfare Economics: A Liberal View*, Martin Robertson, 1975; *Credibility of Liberal Economics*, Institute for Economic Affairs, 1977. Also author of *The Composer in the Marketplace*, with R. Weir, 1975, and *Economic Analysis of Government*, 1979; editor of *Structural Economic Policy in the United Kingdom and West Germany*, 1980. Contributor to professional journals and newspapers. Joint editor of *Public Finance* and of *International Economic Papers*.

AVOCATIONAL INTERESTS: Music.

*   *   *

PEAKE, Mervyn   1911-1968

PERSONAL: Born July 9, 1911, in Kuling, Central China; died November 18, 1968, of Parkinson's Disease in Burcot, Oxfordshire, England; moved to England in 1923; son of Ernest Cromwell (a doctor and missionary) and Elizabeth (Powell) Peake; married Maeve Gilmore (a painter), 1937; children: Sebastian, Fabian, Clare. *Education:* Attended Eltham College and Royal Academy Schools. *Home:* 1 Drayton Gardens, London S.W. 10, England. *Agent:* David Higham Associates, 76 Dean St., Soho, London W.1, England.

CAREER: Author, poet, painter. *Military service:* British Army; served as engineer and official military artist during World War II; official illustrator of German concentration camp at Belsen. *Member:* Royal Society of Literature (fellow). *Awards, honors:* Heinemann Award for Literature, 1951, for *Gormenghast* and *The Glassblowers*.

WRITINGS: (Self-illustrated) *Captain Slaughterboard Drops Anchor*, Eyre & Spottiswoode, 1942, Macmillan, 1967; *The Drawings of Mervyn Peake*, Grey Walls Press, 1945; *Titus Groan* (also see below), Eyre & Spottiswoode, 1946; (self-illustrated) *Craft of the Lead Pencil*, Wingate, 1946; (self-illustrated) *Letters from a Lost Uncle*, Eyre & Spottiswoode, 1948; *Gormenghast* (also see below), Eyre & Spottiswoode, 1950; *Mr. Pye*, Heinemann, 1953, reprinted, Allison & Busby, 1970; "The Wit to Woo," first produced at Arts Theatre, London, 1958; *Titus Alone* (also see below), Eyre & Spottiswoode, 1959, new edition, 1970; *The Gormenghast Trilogy* (contains *Titus Groan*, *Gormenghast*, and *Titus Alone*), Weybright & Talley, 1967; (with Brian W. Aldiss and J. G. Ballard) *The Inner Landscape*, Allison & Busby, 1969; *Mervyn Peake: Writings and Drawings*, edited by wife, Maeve Gilmore, and Shelagh Johnson, St. Martin's, 1974; *Boy in Darkness*, Exeter, 1976; *Peake's Progress: Selected Writings and Drawings of Mervyn Peake*, edited by M. Gilmore, Allen Lane, 1979.

Poetry: *Shapes and Sounds*, Chatto & Windus, 1940, reprinted, Village Press, 1974; *The Glassblowers*, Eyre & Spottiswoode, 1945; (self-illustrated) *Rhymes without Reason*, Eyre & Spottiswoode, 1948; (self-illustrated) *Rhyme of the Flying Bomb*, Dent, 1962; *Poems and Drawings*, Keepsake Press, 1965; *A Reverie of Bone, and Other Poems*, Bertram Rota, 1967; *A Book of Nonsense*, Owen, 1972; *Selected Poems of Mervyn Peake*, Faber, 1972; *Twelve Poems: 1939-1960*, Bran's Head Books, 1975. Also illustrator of numerous books.

SIDELIGHTS: Mervyn Peake's most popular work is the *Gormenghast Trilogy*, a singular gothic fantasy of tremendous proportions that is made up of the books *Titus Groan*, *Gormenghast*, and *Titus Alone*. A writer for the *London Times* described the trilogy as "an immensely long and detailed description of a house and its inhabitants who never could have existed, but are presented with such art that the reader cannot doubt their reality." R.G.G. Price of *Punch* thought that the trilogy is "about a closed world set in a vast castle governed by ancient rituals and peopled by eccentrics." Writing in *Critical Quarterly*, Ronald Binns stated that *Titus Groan* is "concerned with [the] lavish description of the decaying world of the castle and its environs, together with the dramatisation of a range of weird and eccentric characters." Speaking of the trilogy as a whole, he wrote: "It belongs to no obvious tradition [and] lacks an ordered structure." In similar terms, Michael Wood wrote in the *Observer* that *Titus Groan* "is impossible to describe and therefore hard to recommend coherently." Ducan Fallowell of *Books and Bookmen* marvelled that Peake "can describe a rafter in two thousand words without introducing anything extraneous such as a pillar or even a beam, or boring you. . . . Two thousand words on a rafter? Which is only *part* of a roof, you know. And Peake describes the whole roof and the castle of which it is a part, a castle five miles long, describes all of it, and what goes on in and around it. Strange."

The trilogy chronicles the life of Titus Groan from his birth to maturity, although, as Robert Ostermann wrote in the *National Observer*, "to speak of these novels as being 'about' anything is as inadequate as saying *The Odyssey* is about a man trying to get home to his wife. Such fiction as this is first and foremost about itself. These novels are not an echo or an imitation of life. Their life is their own—a bizarre, often awe-full life. And it imposes itself with obsessive force on the reader." Wood found that Peake "presents a world which, like Kafka's, demands to be discussed in its own terms—the reverse of an allegory. It is a world of fantasy, . . . a closed, self-sufficient creation." Price echoed this judgment: "The books must be appreciated on their own terms outside the normal categories of fiction as a gigantic feat of sustained invention, a vicarious dream of extraordinary vividness, [and] a triumph of visual writing."

Writing in a lively prose, Peake populated his trilogy with a host of unique and colorful characters. "The people in *Titus Groan*," Lin Carter wrote in *Imaginary Worlds*, "are monstrous caricatures portrayed with the gusto and violent energy of a Dickens." Philip Guerrard of *City of San Francisco* agreed that Peake used "Dickensian caricature." Stephen J. Laut believed that "the characters are as wild a collection of grotesques as one could find." "Mr. Peake's style," Ruth Teiser of the *San Francisco Chronicle* commented, "is marvelous to a degree. . . . His inventiveness, his ingenuity, and his humor are astonishing." Carter praised "the florid richness of the prose," while Ostermann noted Peake's "language and scenes [that] combine the lyrical and the monstrous."

Overall, the Gormenghast Trilogy is highly considered by several critics. Price called it an "odd minor masterpiece," and Ostermann judged it "an eccentric, poetic masterpiece." R. G. Davis of the *New York Times* remarked that "Peake liberates and elevates as well as charms." Writing in the *Spectator*, J.W.M. Thompson stated that Peake has "a secure place among that precious line of originals . . . who resist classification and fashion, and go their own ways."

Titus Groan, *Mr Pye*, and *Rhyme of the Flying Bomb* were adapted as radio plays.

BIOGRAPHICAL/CRITICAL SOURCES: Studio, September, 1946; Best Sellers, November 1, 1967; National Observer, November 6, 1967, December 11, 1967; Saturday Review, December 16, 1967; Spectator, December 29, 1967, January 26, 1968, November 11, 1972; Book World, January 7, 1968; New Statesman, January 26, 1968, November 8, 1974, December 20, 1974, February 16, 1979; Contemporary Review, April, 1968; Observer, April 14, 1968, September 27, 1970, January 28, 1979; New York Times, November 19, 1968; London Times, November 19, 1968, August 5, 1978; Books and Bookmen, February, 1969, March, 1972, April, 1976, April, 1979; Maeve Gilmore, A World Away: A Memoir, Gollancz, 1970; Times Literary Supplement, June 25, 1970, April 21, 1972, January 26, 1973, April 4, 1975; Mervyn Peake, 1911-1968, National Book League, 1972; Lin Carter, Imaginary Worlds, Ballantine, 1973; Cambridge Review, November 23, 1973; John Batchelor, Mervyn Peake: A Biographical and Critical Exploration, Gerald Duckworth, 1974; M. Gilmore and Shelagh Johnson, editors, Mervyn Peake: Writings and Drawings, St. Martin's, 1974; Unisa English Studies, Volume XII, Number 1, 1974; Revue des Langues Vivantes, Number 40, 1974; Listener, December 19, 1974; John Basil Watney, Mervyn Peake, St. Martin's, 1976; Arthur Metzger, A Guide to the Gormenghast Trilogy, T-K Graphics, 1976; City of San Francisco, February 17, 1976; Contemporary Literary Criticism, Volume VII, Gale, 1977; Critical Quarterly, spring, 1979.†

* * *

PEARCE, Roy Harvey 1919-

PERSONAL: Born December 2, 1919, in Chicago, Ill.; son of Walter Leslie and Esther (Bruesch) Pearce; married Marie Vandenberg, 1947; children: Joanna Vandenberg, Robert Elliott. Education: University of California, Los Angeles, B.A., 1940, M.A., 1942; Johns Hopkins University, Ph.D., 1945. Home: 7858 Esterel Dr., La Jolla, Calif. 92037. Office: Department of Literature, University of California, San Diego, La Jolla, Calif. 92093.

CAREER: Ohio State University, Columbus, instructor, 1945-46; University of California, Berkeley, assistant professor, 1946-49; Ohio State University, associate professor, 1949-54, professor, 1954-63; University of California, San Diego, La Jolla, professor of American literature, 1963—. Fulbright professor, University of Bordeaux, 1961-62; visiting professor at Johns Hopkins University, Claremont Graduate School, and Columbia University. Member: International Association of University Professors of English, Modern Language Association of America, American Historical Association, American Studies Association, National Council of Teachers of English, American Academy of Arts and Sciences (fellow), American Anthropological Association (fellow), Tudor and Stuart Club. Awards, honors: Poetry Chap-Book Award, Poetry Society of America, 1961, for The Continuity of American Poetry.

WRITINGS: (Editor with William Matthews) An Annotated Bibliography of American Diaries Written Prior to the Year 1861, University of California Press, 1945; Colonial American Writing, Rinehart, 1951, revised edition, 1968; The Savages of America, Johns Hopkins Press, 1953, revised edition published as Savagism and Civilization, 1965; (with Hoffman and Cady) The Growth of American Literature, American Book Co., 1956; The Continuity of American Poetry, Princeton University Press, 1961; (editor) Walt Whitman, Leaves of Grass, Cornell University Press, 1961; (editor) Henry James, The American, Houghton, 1962; (editor) Whitman: A Collection of Critical Essays, Prentice-Hall, 1962;

(editor) Hawthorne Centenary Essays, Ohio State University Press, 1964; (editor with J. H. Miller) The Act of the Mind: Essays on the Poetry of Wallace Stevens, Johns Hopkins Press, 1965; (editor) Experience in the Novel, Columbia University Press, 1968; Historicism Once More: Problems and Occasions for the American Scholar, Princeton University Press, 1969. General editor, with William Charvat and Claude Simpson, of the Centenary Edition of the Writings of Hawthorne, Ohio State University Press, 1962—. Contributor of articles on American literature and intellectual history, and reviews, to journals.

* * *

PEARCY, G(eorge) Etzel 1905-1980

PERSONAL: Born May 2, 1905, in Greencastle, Ind.; died June 28, 1980, in San Francisco, Calif.; son of George William and Dora (Hodge) Pearcy; married Florence Elizabeth Barili, September 23, 1937. Education: University of California, Los Angeles, B.E., 1931; Clark University, M.A., 1932, Ph.D., 1940. Home: 48 Iran Ship Plaza N., San Francisco, Calif. 94111.

CAREER: University of Pennsylvania, Philadelphia, instructor in geography and economics, 1935-39; University of Alabama, Tuscaloosa, assistant professor of geography, 1939-42; U.S. Army Air Forces, Randolph Field, Tex., supervisor of instruction, 1942-43; Trans-World Airlines, Inc., geographer in Kansas City, Mo., Washington, D.C., and New York, N.Y., 1943-50; U.S. Foreign Service, attache in Bangkok, Thailand, New Delhi, India, London, England, and Paris, France, 1950-57; U.S. Department of State, Washington, D.C., geographer, 1957-69; California State University, Los Angeles, professor of geography and chairman of department, 1969-73. Member: Association of American Geographers (councilor, 1958-61).

WRITINGS: (Co-author) Geopolitics in Principle and Practice, Ginn, 1944; (co-editor) World Political Geography, Crowell, 1948, revised edition, 1957; (with E. A. Stoneman) Handbook of New Nations, Crowell, 1968; (with George P. Stevens) An Introduction to Geography, F. T. Peacock, 1970; Patterns of International Boundaries, Plycon, 1972; A Thirty-eight State U.S.A., Plycon, 1973; Supercounties U.S.A., Plycon, 1976; World Sovereignty, Plycon, 1977; World Food Scene, Plycon, 1980. Editor with George W. Hoffman of Van Nostrand's pocketbook political geographies, "Searchlight" series, and author of Number 26 in the series, The West Indian Scene, 1965, co-author of Number 30, Military Geography. Contributor of articles to Journal of Geography, Economic Geography, Professional Geography, and other professional journals.†

* * *

PEARL, Richard M(axwell) 1913-

PERSONAL: Born May 4, 1913, in New York, N.Y.; son of Morse (an accountant and businessman) and Etta (Stocker) Pearl; married Mignon Wardell (a writer and artist), June 13, 1941. Education: University of Colorado, B.A., 1939, M.A., 1940; Harvard University, M.A., 1946. Politics: Republican. Religion: Unitarian. Home: 16 Valley Pl., Colorado Springs, Colo. 80903. Agent: Paul R. Reynolds, Inc., 12 East 41st St., New York, N.Y. 10017. Office: Department of Geology, Colorado College, Colorado Springs, Colo. 80903.

CAREER: University of Colorado, Boulder, instructor in geology, 1940; operator of mineral supply business, Denver, Colo., 1941; Remington Arms Co., Denver, process engineer, 1941-42; Shell Oil Co., Tulsa, Okla., geologist, 1944;

Colorado College, Colorado Springs, 1946—, currently professor emeritus of geology. Visiting professor, Phoenix College, 1956; extension division professor at three Colorado universities. Adviser in mineralogy and gemology, Denver Public Library, 1949-52. Member of board of advisors, Detroit Concert Band.

MEMBER: American Association for the Advancement of Science (fellow), American Geographical Society (fellow), Gemological Institute of American (certified gemologist), National Association of Geology Teachers (president of Southwest section, 1962-63), American Federation of Mineralogical Societies (co-founder; president, 1948-49), Research Society of America (president of Colorado Springs chapter, 1965-66), Meteoritical Society (fellow), Gemmological Association of Great Britain (fellow with distinction), Gemmological Association of Australia (honorary vice-president), Canadian Gemmological Association (honorary member), Gesellschaft der Freunde der Mineralogie (honorary vice-president), Rocky Mountain Federation of Mineralogical Societies (founder; president, 1941-42), Historical Society of the Pikes Peak Region (president, 1954 and 1966), Council on Abandoned Military Posts, Colorado Mineral Society (co-founder; president, 1948-50), Colorado Scientific Society (honorary member), Colorado Authors' League (vice-president, 1968-69), Phi Beta Kappa, Sigma Xi, Delta Epsilon, Sigma Gamma Epsilon. *Awards, honors:* Books named among *Library Journal's* one hundred best scientific and technical books, 1951, 1961, and 1964; Colorado Authors' League Top Hand awards for best juvenile nonfiction, 1964 and 1967, and for best adult nonfiction, 1965.

WRITINGS: Nature as Sculptor: A Geologic Interpretation of Colorado Scenery, Colorado Museum of Natural History, 1941, revised edition, 1956; (with Henry Carl Dake) *The Art of Gem Cutting,* 3rd edition, Mineralogist Publishing, 1945; *Mineral Collectors Handbook,* Mineral Book Co., 1947; *Popular Gemology,* Wiley, 1948, revised edition, 1965; *Guide to Geologic Literature,* McGraw, 1951; *Colorado Gem Trails,* Sage Books, 1951; *America's Mountain: Pike's Peak and the Pike's Peak Region,* Mineral Book Co., 1954, 3rd edition, Earth Science Publishing, 1976; *How to Know the Minerals and Rocks,* McGraw, 1955; *Rocks and Minerals,* Barnes & Noble, 1956, new edition published as *An Introduction to the Mineral Kingdom,* Blandford, 1966; *Colorado Gem Trails and Mineral Guide,* Sage Books, 1958, 3rd edition, Swallow Press, 1972; *1001 Questions Answered about the Mineral Kingdom,* Dodd, 1959, revised edition, 1968.

Geology: An Introduction to Principles of Physical and Historical Geology, Barnes & Noble, 1960, 4th revised edition, 1975; *Wonders of Rocks and Minerals,* Dodd, 1961; *Successful Mineral Collecting and Prospecting,* McGraw, 1961; *1001 Questions Answered about Earth Science,* Dodd, 1962, published as *1001 Answers to Questions about Earth Science,* Grosset, 1965, revised edition published under original title, Dodd, 1969; *Wonders of Gems,* Dodd, 1963; *American Gem Trails,* McGraw, 1964; *Gems, Minerals, Crystals and Ores: The Collector's Encyclopedia,* Odyssey, 1964; *Colorado Rocks, Minerals, Fossils,* Sage Books, 1964, revised edition published as *Exploring Rocks, Minerals, Fossils in Colorado,* 1969; *The Wonder World of Metals,* Harper, 1966; *Gem Identification Simplified,* Maxwell Publishing, 1968; *Geology Simplified: Keynotes,* Barnes & Noble, 1968; *Seven Keys to the Rocky Mountains,* Maxwell Publishing, 1968.

Cleaning and Preserving Minerals, Maxwell Publishing, 1971, 4th edition, Earth Science Publishing, 1975; *Handbook for Prospectors* (based on *Handbook for Prospectors and Operators of Small Mines* by M. W. von Bernewitz), McGraw, 1973; *Fallen from Heaven: Meteorites and Man,* Earth Science Publishing, 1975; *Garnet: Gem and Mineral,* Earth Science Publishing, 1975; *Nature's Names for Colorado Communities,* Earth Science Publishing, 1975; *Springs of Colorado,* Earth Science Publishing, 1975; *Landforms of Colorado,* Earth Science Publishing, 1975; *Atlas of Crystal Stereograms,* Earth Science Publishing, 1976; *Turquoise,* Earth Science Publishing, 1976.

"Questions and Answers" series; all published by Earth Science Publishing: *The Turn of Time; The Pageant of Life; When Life Began; Vanished Forests; Ancient Invertebrates; The Age of Fishes and Amphibians; Medieval Monsters; Extinct Beasts of the Tertiary; Ice Age Zoo; The Work of Glaciers; Climates of the Past; Patterns of Land and Sea; Waters under the Earth; The Cycle of Streams; Shifting Sands; The Birth and Death of Volcanoes; Our Quaking Earth; Architecture of the Crust; Landscapes in Four Dimensions; The Face of America; Minerals and Crystals; Igneous Rocks; Meteorites; Sedimentary Rocks; Metamorphic Rocks; The Precious Metals; Base Metals; Iron and Ferroalloy Metals; Rare and Unusual Metals; Radioactive Minerals; Gems; Industrial Minerals and Rocks; The Fossil Fuels; Mining and Milling; Water Resources; Mineral Collecting As a Hobby.*

Contributor to eight encyclopedias and yearbooks and four anthologies. Contributor of scientific and non-technical articles and columns to periodicals and newspapers in the United States and England. Member of editorial board, *Achat* (Hamburg, Germany), 1948-50; geologic consultant, *Colorado Wonderland,* 1951-56; editor-in-chief, *Earth Science,* 1947, 1967-68, and 1972—

WORK IN PROGRESS: Books on earth science, history, travel, and related subjects.

* * *

PEASE, William H(enry) 1924-

PERSONAL: Born August 31, 1924, in Winchendon, Mass.; son of Clarence A. G. (a manufacturer) and Arline (a teacher; maiden name, Brooks) Pease; married Jane Hanna (a professor), June 9, 1950. *Education:* Williams College, B.A. (cum laude), 1947; University of Wisconsin, M.A., 1948; University of Rochester, Ph.D., 1955. *Home:* 40 East Summer St., Bangor, Me. 04401. *Office:* Department of History, University of Maine, Orono, Me. 04469.

CAREER: Mount Hermon School, Mount Hermon, Mass., teacher of history and English, 1948-51; Rensselaer Polytechnic Institute, Troy, N.Y., instructor, 1955-56, assistant professor, 1956-58, associate professor of history, 1958-64; University of Calgary, Calgary, Alberta, associate professor of history 1964-66; University of Maine at Orono, associate professor, 1966-68, professor of history, 1968—. Visiting assistant professor of history, Case Institute of Technology (now Case Western Reserve University), 1957-58; Fulbright lecturer, International People's College, Elsinore, Denmark, 1961-62, guest lecturer, University of Lund and University of Goteborg, 1962; associate professor, Tufts University, summer, 1963. *Military service:* U.S. Army, 1943-46. *Member:* American Historical Association, American Studies Association, Organization of American Historians, Society for the History of the Early American Republic, Southern Historical Association, New England Historical Association, South Carolina Historical Society, Phi Beta Kappa. *Awards, honors:* Grants-in-aid from American Council of Learned Societies, American Philosophical Society, National Endowment for the Humanities, Rensselaer Polytechnic Institute, University of Calgary, and University of Maine; President's Research Achievement Award (received jointly with wife), University of Maine, 1977.

WRITINGS—All with wife, Jane H. Pease: *Black Utopia: Negro Communal Experiments in America*, State Historical Society of Wisconsin, 1963; (editor) *The Antislavery Argument*, Bobbs-Merrill, 1965; (editor) *Austin Steward: Twenty-two Years a Slave and Forty Years a Freeman*, Addison-Wesley, 1969; (contributor) August Meier and Elliott Rudwick, editors, *The Making of Black America*, Atheneum, 1969; (contributor) Martin L. Kilson, Nathan Huggins, and Daniel M. Fox, editors, *Key Issues in the Afro-American Experience*, Harcourt, 1971; (contributor) John H. Bracey, Meier, and Rudwick, editors, *Blacks in the Abolitionist Movement*, Wadsworth, 1971; (contributor) Robert V. Haynes, editor, *Blacks in White America before 1865: Issues and Interpretations*, McKay, 1972; *Bound with Them in Chains: A Biographical History of the Antislavery Movement*, Greenwood Press, 1972; *They Who Would Be Free: Blacks' Search for Freedom, 1830-1861*, Atheneum, 1974; *The Fugitive Slave Law and Anthony Burns: A Problem in Law Enforcement*, Lippincott, 1975.

Consultant, "Black Studies" reprint series, Bobbs-Merrill, 1969. Contributor to *Dictionary of Canadian Biography* and *Notable American Women;* contributor of articles and reviews to professional journals, including *Journal of American History, Civil War History, Canadian Historical Review, Midwest Quarterly,* and *Journal of Negro History.*

WORK IN PROGRESS: With Jane H. Pease, a comparative study of Boston, Mass., and Charleston, S.C.; a biography of Samuel Joseph May.

*   *   *

PECK, John 1941-

PERSONAL: Born January 13, 1941, in Pittsburgh, Pa.; son of Clarence Erwin (an engineer) and Louise (Sayenga) Peck; married Ellen McKee, September 2, 1963. *Education:* Allegheny College, A.B., 1962; Stanford University, Ph.D., 1973. *Office:* Mount Holyoke College, South Hadley, Mass. 01075.

CAREER: Princeton University, Princeton, N.J., instructor in English, 1968-70, visiting lecturer, 1972-75; Mount Holyoke College, South Hadley, Mass., assistant professor, 1977-79, associate professor, 1980—. *Awards, honors:* Prix de Rome, 1978.

WRITINGS: Shagbark (poems), Bobbs-Merrill, 1972; *The Broken Blockhouse Wall* (poems), David R. Godine, 1978. Work represented in *American Poets in 1976,* edited by William Heyen, Bobbs-Merrill, 1976, and *Five American Poets,* Carcanet Press, 1979.

SIDELIGHTS: A *Virginia Quarterly Review* critic's assertion that *Shagbark* introduces "a remarkably mature and accomplished writer" is echoed by several reviewers. Donald Davie, writing in *Shenandoah,* finds that in discussing most first books of poetry a reviewer usually speaks of promise, of styles not quite in command, of directions in which the poet ought to explore. Yet, Davie contends, "with [John] Peck this would be impertinent. His several styles are all firmly under control, and he switches from one to another with unflustered tact and decorum and according to no predetermined alignment of himself with this or that 'school.'" And Laurence Lieberman, writing in the *Yale Review,* notes in Peck's poetry the "obvious control, the inobtrusively

handsome glamors of technical firmness." "In Peck's writing . . . ," concludes Lieberman, "the simple mechanics of nature, both animate and inanimate, disclose inexhaustible mysteries. His careful fidelity to the properties of objects in nature carries over into the close-knit mechanics of the poems, both shaggy and polished, intricate and rough-edged as bark."

The Broken Blockhouse Wall has also been well received. In the *New York Times Book Review,* Robert Pinsky contends that Peck's second book combines the "impressive intelligence" of *Shagbark* with "qualities almost as rare." These qualities include "a mastery of traditional prosody," elaborate sentence structure, and a large range of diction. "Moreover," Pinsky continues, "the dense texture and grave, formal idiom present a poetry openly more written than spoken, or more chanted than conversational." Pinsky finds that at times the poetry may be too formal and too scholarly, but he decides that although "some of his poems are hard for me to understand without a lot of work, I have always profited from the work." Similarly, Helen Vendler of the *New Yorker* observes that "Peck's writing is everywhere written; it is not speech transcribed. . . . Peck is acutely alive to the precision of the written." Like Pinsky, Vendler feels that Peck's work is difficult, but she admires the poetry's "beautiful surfaces," and Peck's "patient, intelligent, and curious" inquiry, "the fine uncertainty of his . . . beliefs," and his 'unfailing dialectic.'" Overall, Vendler believes that "Peck has made a distinct advance from his first book, *Shagbark.*"

BIOGRAPHICAL/CRITICAL SOURCES: Shenandoah, fall, 1972; *Virginia Quarterly Review,* spring, 1973; *Yale Review,* winter, 1973; *Contemporary Literary Criticism,* Volume III, Gale, 1975; *New Yorker,* September 18, 1978; *New York Times Book Review,* November 12, 1978; Donald Davie, *Trying to Explain,* University of Michigan Press, 1980; *Salmagundi,* winter-spring, 1980; *Occident,* spring, 1980.

*   *   *

PENFIELD, Wilder (Graves) 1891-1976

PERSONAL: Born January 26, 1891, in Spokane, Wash.; died April 5, 1976, in Montreal, Quebec, Canada; became naturalized Canadian citizen in 1934; son of Charles Samuel (a surgeon) and Jean (a writer and Bible teacher; maiden name, Jefferson) Penfield; married Helen Katherine Kermott, June 6, 1917; children: Wilder, Ruth Mary (Mrs. Crosby Lewis), Priscilla (Mrs. William Chester), Amos Jefferson. *Education:* Princeton University, Litt. B., 1913; Oxford University, B.A., 1916, B.Sc., 1920 (both on Rhodes scholarships), M.A., 1920, D.Sc., 1935; Johns Hopkins University, M.D., 1918; postgraduate study in neurology at medical centers in Germany and Spain, and at Harvard University. *Religion:* Presbyterian. *Home:* 3940 Cote des Neiges, Montreal, Quebec, Canada. *Office:* Montreal Neurological Institute, Department of Neurology and Neurosurgery, 3801 University St., Montreal, Quebec, Canada H3A 2B4.

CAREER: Columbia University, New York City, associate in surgery, 1921-26, assistant professor, 1926-28; neurosurgeon, Presbyterian Hospital, New York City, 1921-28, New York Neurological Institute, New York City, 1925-28, and Royal Victoria and Montreal General Hospitals, Montreal, Quebec, 1928-60; McGill University, Montreal, associate professor of neurosurgery, 1928-33, professor and chairman of department of neurology and neurosurgery, 1933-54; Montreal Neurological Institute, Montreal, founder, 1934, neurosurgeon and director, 1934-60, honorary consultant,

1960-76; writer. Lecturer at numerous universities and other institutions around the world. President, Vanier Institute of the Family, beginning 1965. Member, National Research Council (Canada and the United States). Served as dresser in Hospital V.R. 76, Ris Orangis, France, 1916, and as surgeon at an American Red Cross Hospital in Paris, 1917-18; during World War II developed, with C. H. Best, a cure for seasickness. *Military service:* Royal Canadian Army Medical Corps, 1939-45; became colonel.

MEMBER: International Surgical Association, Royal College of Physicians and Surgeons (Canada; president, 1940-41), Royal Society of Canada, American Neurological Association, National Academy of Sciences, American Surgical Association (fellow), American Academy of Arts and Sciences (honorary fellow), American Philosophical Society, Royal College of Surgeons (England; honorary fellow), Royal College of Physicians (England), Royal Society of Medicine (England), Royal College of Surgeons (Edinburgh), Royal College of Physicians (Edinburgh), Royal Society of London (fellow), and numerous other foreign scientific organizations; Athenaeum Club (London).

AWARDS, HONORS: Beit Memorial research fellow, 1920-21; Companion of Order of St. Michael and St. George, 1943; U.S. Medal of Freedom with silver palm, 1948; Chevalier of the Legion of Honor, 1950; Flavelle Medal, Royal Society of Canada, 1951; Jacoby Award, American Neurological Association, 1953; Order of Merit conferred by Queen Elizabeth II, 1953; Medaille Lannelongue, Academie de Chirurgie, 1958; Lister Medal, Royal College of Surgeons, 1961; Guggenheim fellow, 1961-64; Greek Gold Cross of the Legion of George I, 1964; F.N.G. Starr Award, Canadian Medical Association, 1965; Valentine Prize, Danish Neurological Society, 1966; Otfried Foerster Medal, German neurological Association, 1966; Companion of the Order of Canada, 1967; Golden Brain Award, University of Chicago Brain Research Foundation, 1967; Family of Man Award, Society for the Family, 1967; first recipient of Royal Bank Centennial Award ($50,000), 1967; Triennial Gold Medal, Royal Society of Medicine, 1968; recipient of honorary degrees from more than twenty-five North American and foreign universities, including Yale University, 1954, University of New Delhi, 1957, Royal Military College, 1970, Johns Hopkins University, 1970, and University of Western Ontario, 1972.

WRITINGS: (Editor) *Cytology and Cellular Pathology of the Nervous System,* 3 volumes, Hoeber, 1932, reprinted, Hafner, 1965; (with T. C. Erickson) *Epilepsy and Cerebral Localization,* C. C Thomas, 1941; *Canadian Army Manual of Military Neurosurgery,* Government Printing Office (Ottawa), 1941; (with Theodore B. Rasmussen) *The Cerebral Cortex of Man,* Macmillan, 1950; (with Kristian Kristiansen) *Epileptic Seizure Patterns,* C. C Thomas, 1950; (with Herbert Jasper) *Epilepsy and the Functional Anatomy of the Human Brain,* Little, Brown, 1954; *No Other Gods* (novel), Little, Brown, 1954; *The Excitable Cortex in Conscious Man,* C. C Thomas, 1958; (with Lamar Roberts) *Speech and Brain Mechanisms,* Princeton University Press, 1959; *The Torch* (novel), Little, Brown, 1960; *The Second Career* (essays and addresses), Little, Brown, 1963; *The Difficult Art of Giving: The Epic of Alan Gregg,* Little, Brown, 1967; *Man and His Family* (essays), McClelland & Steward, 1967; *Second Thoughts: Science, the Arts and the Spirit,* McClelland & Stewart, 1970; *The Mystery of the Mind: A Critical Study of Consciousness and the Human Brain,* Princeton University Press, 1975; *No Man Alone: A Surgeon's Story* (autobiography), Little, Brown, 1977.

BIOGRAPHICAL/CRITICAL SOURCES: Viola Whitney

Pratt, *Famous Doctors: Osler, Banting, Penfield,* Clark, Irwin, 1956; Yousaf Karsh, *Portraits of Greatness,* Thomas Nelson, 1959; Wilder Penfield, *No Man Alone: A Surgeon's Story* (autobiography), Little, Brown, 1977.†

* * *

PERCY, Douglas Cecil 1914-

PERSONAL: Born May 5, 1914, in Toronto, Ontario, Canada; son of Douglas and Marie (Turner) Percy; married Betty Willis, 1936; children: Dorothy, Janet. *Education:* Attended Toronto Bible College (now Ontario Bible College), 1933-36. *Home:* 73 Binswood Ave., Toronto, Ontario, Canada M4C 3N8. *Office:* Ontario Bible College, 25 Ballyconnor Ct., Willowdale, Ontario, Canada M2M 4B3.

CAREER: Pastor of country church, 1936-38; Sudan Interior Mission, Nigeria, West Africa, missionary, 1938-58, editorial secretary, 1950-58; Ontario Bible College, Willowdale, missionary counsellor, 1950-58, director of missions, 1958-68, prefessor of missions and director of public relations, 1958-81. Founder, Biliri Bible Training School. *Member:* Association of Professors of Missions, Missionary Health Institute, Authors League of America. *Awards, honors:* Second prize, Zondervan fiction contest, 1950, for *Hidden Valley;* D. Litt., Richmond College, 1979.

WRITINGS: Hidden Valley, Zondervan, 1950; *When the Bamboo Sings,* Zondervan, 1956; *Doctor to Africa,* Sudan Interior Mission, 1959; *Beyond the Tangled Mountain,* Zondervan, 1962; *Flight to Glory,* Zondervan, 1967; *Men with the Heart of a Viking,* Horizon House, 1976; *God on Yonge Street,* Yonge Street Mission, 1978.

Editor: J. W. Sanderson, *Encounter in the Non-Christian Era,* Zondervan, 1970; Walter C. Kaiser, *The Old Testament in Contemporary Preaching,* Baker Book, 1973; Paul Wohlegemuth, *Re-thinking Church Music,* Moody, 1973; F. F. Bruce, *Paul and Jesus,* Baker Book, 1974; Vernon Grounds, *Emotional Problems and the Gospel,* Zondervan, 1976; S. Lewis Johnson, Jr., *The Old Testament in the New,* Zondervan, 1980.

Also author of a two-volume commentary on the Old Testament in the Hausa language for the Sudan Interior Mission, 1946; author of pamphlets. Contributor to magazines. Editor, *Sudan Witness,* 1948-58, and *Evangelical Recorder,* 1953—; associate editor, *Evangelical Christian.*

* * *

PERLE, George 1915-

PERSONAL: Name legally changed, c: 1949; born May 6, 1915, in Bayonne, N.J.; son of Joseph and Mary (Sanders) Perlman; married Barbara Phillips, 1958. *Education:* New York University, Ph.D., 1956. *Home:* 333 Central Park W., New York, N.Y. *Office:* Department of Music, Queens College of the City University of New York, Flushing, N.Y. 11367.

CAREER: University of Louisville, Louisville, Ky., assistant professor, 1949-57; University of California, Davis, associate professor, 1957-61; Queens College of the City University of New York, Flushing, N.Y., associate professor, 1961-65, professor of music, 1966—. Visiting summer professor, University of Southern California, 1965; visiting associate professor, Yale University, 1965-66; visiting professor at State University of New York at Buffalo, 1971-72, University of Pennsylvania, 1976 and 1980, and Columbia University, 1979. *Member:* American Academy and Institute of Arts and Letters, American Musicological Society, International Alban Berg Society.

WRITINGS: Serial Composition and Atonality: An Introduction to the Music of Schoenberg, University of California Press, 1962, 4th edition, 1977; *Twelve-Tone Tonality,* University of California Press, 1977; *The Operas of Alban Berg,* Volume I: *Wozzeck,* University of California Press, 1980. Contributor to *Grove Dictionary of Music* and to numerous American and European music journals.

SIDELIGHTS: George Perle was one of the earliest American composers to identify himself as a creative artist with the revolutionary musical tendencies represented by Schoenberg and his circle. He has had numerous compositions published and recorded.

*   *   *

PERLMAN, Helen Harris 1905-

PERSONAL: Born December 20, 1905, in St. Paul, Minn.; daughter of Lazer and Annie (Schwartz) Harris; married Max. S. Perlman, August 16, 1935; children: Jonathan. *Education:* University of Minnesota, B.A., 1926; Columbia University, M.S., 1943. *Home:* 1321 East 56th St., Chicago, Ill. 60637.

CAREER: Jewish Family Services, social caseworker and supervisor in Chicago, Ill., 1927-35, supervisor and administrator in New York City, 1935-40; Columbia University, School of Social Work, New York City, lecturer, 1940-45; University of Chicago, Chicago, assistant professor, 1945-48, associate professor, 1949-53, professor of social work, 1954-70, Samuel Deutsch Distinguished Service Professor Emeritus, 1970—. Visiting professor at University of California, Berkeley, University of Hawaii, University of Puerto Rico, and other universities, 1950—. *Member:* American Association of University Professors, National Association of Social Workers, Civil Liberties Union, Phi Beta Kappa, Quadrangle Club (University of Chicago). *Awards, honors:* Commonwealth fellowship; D.Litt., Boston University; Regents' Medal for Distinguished Achievement, University of Minnesota.

WRITINGS: Social Casework: A Problem-Solving Process, University of Chicago Press, 1957; *So You Want to Be a Social Worker,* Harper, 1962; *Persona: Social Role and Personality,* University of Chicago Press, 1968; *Helping: Charlotte Towle on Social Work,* University of Chicago Press, 1969; *Perspectives on Social Casework,* Temple University Press, 1971; *Relationship: The Heart of Helping People,* University of Chicago Press, 1979. Contributor of short stories, poetry, and professional articles to periodicals.

SIDELIGHTS: Helen Harris Perlman's book *Social Casework* has been translated into French, German, Swedish, Dutch, Japanese, Italian, Spanish, and several Indian and African dialects. *So You Want to Be a Social Worker* has been translated into Spanish and Portuguese, and *Persona* has been translated into French.

*   *   *

PERLMAN, Mark 1923-

PERSONAL: Born December 23, 1923, in Madison, Wis.; son of Selig and Eva (Shaber) Perlman; married Naomi Waxman, 1953; children: Abigail Ruth. *Education:* University of Wisconsin, B.A., 1947, M.A., 1947; Columbia University, Ph.D., 1950. *Home:* 5622 Bartlett St., Pittsburgh, Pa. 15217. *Office:* Department of Economics, University of Pittsburgh, Pittsburgh, Pa. 15260.

CAREER: Princeton University, Princeton, N.J., instructor, 1947-48; assistant professor at University of Hawaii, Hono-

lulu, 1951-52, and Cornell University, Ithaca, N.Y., 1952-55; Johns Hopkins University, Baltimore, Md., assistant professor, 1955-58, associate professor of political economy, 1958-63; University of Pittsburgh, Pittsburgh, Pa., professor of economics, history, and economics of public health, 1963—, university professor of economics, 1969—. Harvard University, research associate, 1955-57, lecturer, 1957-58; official faculty visitor and visiting fellow, Clare Hall, Cambridge University, 1976-77; visiting lecturer at other universities. Member of Johns Hopkins survey team evaluating public health in Brazil, 1960, and Johns Hopkins medical manpower team in Taiwan, 1962-64. *Member:* American Economic Association, Economic History Association, Economic History Society, Population Association of America, International Union for the Scientific Study of Population, Royal Economic Society, American Jewish Historical Society.

WRITINGS: Judges in Industry: A Study of Labor Arbitration in Australia, Cambridge University Press, 1954; *Labor Union Theories in America: Background and Development,* Row, 1958, new edition, Greenwood Press, 1976; *The Machinists: A New Study in American Trade Unionism,* Harvard University Press, 1961; *Democracy in the International Association of Machinists,* Wiley, 1962; (editor) *Human Resources in the Urban Economy,* Resources for the Future, 1963; (with Timothy D. Baker) *Health Manpower in a Developing Economy,* Johns Hopkins Press, 1967; (editor) *Economics of Health and Medical Care,* Halsted Press, 1974; (editor) *The Organization and Retrieval of Economic Knowledge,* Halsted Press, 1977; (editor with Gordon K. MacLeod) *Health Care Capital: Competition and Control,* Ballinger, 1978.

Contributor: J. Braeman, R. H. Bremmer, and D. Brady, editors, *Twentieth Century America,* Ohio State University Press, 1968; J. P. Nieuwenhuysen and P. J. Drake, editors, *Australian Economic Policy,* Melbourne University Press, 1977; Jacob S. Dreyer, editor, *Breadth and Depth in Economics,* Lexington, 1978; Herbert Giersch, editor, *Capital Shortage and Unemployment in the World Economy: Symposium 1977,* Mohr, 1978; William Fellner, editor, *Contemporary Economic Problems,* American Enterprise Institute, 1979, 2nd edition, 1980.

Co-editor, "Cambridge University Surveys of Current Economics," 1977—. Contributor to journals. Member of editorial board, *Industrial and Labor Relations Review,* 1953-55; managing editor, *Journal of Economic Literature,* 1969-81; founding editor, *Portfolio on International Economic Perspectives* (journal of U.S. Department of State), 1973.

WORK IN PROGRESS: Research in public health, demographic growth and economic development, economic history, history of economic thought, and American industrial productivity measurement.

*   *   *

PEROWNE, Stewart Henry 1901-

PERSONAL: Born June 17, 1901, in Worcester, England; son of Arthur William Thomson (Bishop of Worcester) and Helena Frances (Oldnall-Russell) Perowne; married Freya Stark (a writer), 1947. *Education:* Haileybury College, Cambridge, B.A., 1923, M.A., 1931; additional study at Harvard University. *Home:* 44 Arminger Rd., London, England.

CAREER: Affiliated with British Colonial Administration, 1929-52; served in Palestine, 1929-34, and Malta, 1934-37; post officer, Aden Protectorate, 1937; Arabic program organizer for British Broadcasting Corp., 1938; information officer, Aden, 1939; public relations attache, British Embassy, Bagdad, Iraq, 1941; Oriental counselor, 1944; colonial secretary, Barbados, 1947-49; chief adviser, Cyrenaica. 1949-51. Adviser to United Kingdom delegation to United Nations Assembly, Paris, 1951. Orientalist; recovered sculpture and inscriptions from Imadia and Bethan; discovered ancient city of Aziris, 1951. Helped design stamps for Malta, Aden, Barbados, and Libya; helped design currency notes for West Indies Federation, 1949, and Libya, 1951. *Member:* Society of Antiquaries (fellow), Phoenix-SK Club (Harvard), Travellers' Club (London), Casino Maltese Club. *Awards, honors:* Officer, Order of the British Empire, 1943; Knight of St. John of Jerusalem, 1956.

WRITINGS: The One Remains, Hodder & Stoughton, 1954; *The Life and Times of Herod the Great,* Abingdon, 1956; *The Later Herods,* Abingdon, 1958 (published in England as *The Political Background of the New Testament,* Hodder & Stoughton, 1965); *Hadrian,* Hodder & Stoughton, 1960, Norton, 1961; *Caesars and Saints,* Hodder & Stoughton, 1962, Norton, 1963; *The Pilgrim's Companion in Rome,* Hodder & Stoughton, 1964; *The Pilgrim's Companion in Athens,* Hodder & Stoughton, 1964; *Jerusalem and Bethlehem,* Phoenix House, 1965, A. S. Barnes, 1966; *The End of the Roman World,* Hodder & Stoughton, 1966, Crowell, 1967; *Roman Mythology,* Hamlyn, 1968; *The Siege within the Walls: Malta, 1940-1943,* Hodder & Stoughton, 1970; *Rome: From Its Foundation to the Present Day,* Elek, 1971; *The Journeys of St. Paul,* Hamlyn, 1973; *The Caesars' Wives—Above Suspicion?,* Hodder & Stoughton, 1974; *Archaeology of Greece and the Aegean,* Hamlyn, 1974; *Holy Places of Christendom,* Mowbray, 1976. Contributor to encyclopedias and newspapers.

SIDELIGHTS: Stewart Perowne's books have been published in French and German, and in Braille. *Avocational interests:* Archaeology and the arts.

*   *   *

PERRINE, Laurence 1915-

PERSONAL: Born October 13, 1915, in Toronto, Ontario, Canada; son of Ren Brown and Mary (Dollins) Perrine; married Catherine Stockard, 1949; children: David, Douglas. *Education:* Oberlin College, B.A., 1937, M.A., 1939; Yale University, Ph.D., 1948. *Home:* 7616 Royal Pl., Dallas, Tex. 75230.

CAREER: Southern Methodist University, Dallas, Tex., 1946-81, began as instructor, became Frensley Professor of English. *Military service:* U.S. Army, 1941-45; became master sergeant. *Member:* Modern Language Association of America, National Council of Teachers of English, South Central Modern Language Association (president, 1970-71), Texas Conference of College Teachers of English (president, 1973-74), Texas Institute of Letters.

WRITINGS: Sound and Sense: An Introduction to Poetry, Harcourt, 1956, 5th edition, 1977; *Story and Structure,* Harcourt, 1959, 5th edition, 1978; (editor) *Poetry: Theory and Practice,* Harcourt, 1962; (with James M. Reid and John Ciardi) *Poetry: A Closer Look,* Harcourt, 1963; (with Reid) *100 American Poems of the Twentieth Century,* Harcourt, 1966; *Literature: Structure, Sound, and Sense,* Harcourt, 1970, 3rd edition, 1978; *The Art of Total Relevance: Papers on Poetry,* Newbury House, 1973. Contributor to professional journals.

PERUTZ, Kathrin 1939-

PERSONAL: Born July 1, 1939, in New York, N.Y.; daughter of Tino and Dolly (Hellmann) Perutz; married Michael Studdert-Kennedy, 1966; children: Kostya (son). *Education:* Barnard College, B.A., 1960; New York University, M.A., 1966. *Home:* 16 Avalon Rd., Great Neck, N.Y. 11021.

CAREER: Writer.

WRITINGS: The Garden, Atheneum, 1962; *A House on the Sound,* Heinemann, 1964, Coward, 1965; *The Ghosts,* [England], 1965; *Mother Is a Country,* Harcourt, 1968; *Beyond the Looking Glass: Life in the Beauty Culture,* Morrow, 1970; *Marriage Is Hell,* Morrow, 1972 (published in England as *The Marriage Fallacy,* Hodder & Stoughton, 1972); *Reigning Passions,* Lippincott, 1978.

Work is represented in anthologies, including: *Voices,* M. Joseph, 1965; *New York Spy,* David White, 1967; *America the Beautiful,* David White, 1968. Contributor to *American Scholar, Cosmopolitan, New York Times, Seventeen, Transatlantic Review, Viva, Books and Bookmen,* and numerous other publications in the United States and England.

BIOGRAPHICAL/CRITICAL SOURCES: New York Times Book Review, March 10, 1968; *New Statesman,* June 7, 1968, December 4, 1970; *Hudson Review,* Volume XXI, number 2, 1968.

*   *   *

PETER, John (Desmond) 1921-

PERSONAL: Born October 8, 1921, in Queenstown, South Africa; son of Edward Frederick and Leila (Lehman) Peter; emigrated to Canada in 1950, became naturalized citizen in 1957; married Barbara Mary Girdwood, December 6, 1946 (divorced, 1976); children: Jonathan, Christopher, Katherine, Nicholas, Stephanie. *Education:* University of South Africa, B.A., 1941, LL.B., 1944, D.Litt., 1957; Cambridge University, B.A., 1947, M.A., 1951. *Home:* 9594 Ardmore Dr., Sydney, British Columbia, Canada. *Office:* Department of English, University of Victoria, Victoria, British Columbia, Canada.

CAREER: Cambridge University, Gonville and Caius College, Cambridge, England, supervisor of English studies, 1947-50; University of Manitoba, Winnipeg, associate professor, 1950-56, professor of English, 1956-61; University of Victoria, Victoria, British Columbia, professor of English, 1961—. Visiting professor, University of Wisconsin—Madison, 1964-65; Commonwealth Visiting Professor, Oxford University, 1966-67. *Military service:* South African Artillery, gunner, 1943. *Awards, honors:* Hugh Le May fellow, Rhodes University, 1957-58; Doubleday Canadian Prize Novel Award, 1964, for *Along That Coast;* D.Litt., Rhodes University, 1973.

WRITINGS: Complaint and Satire in Early English Literature, Clarendon, 1956, reprinted, Norwood, 1980; (contributor) *A Book of South African Verse,* Oxford University Press, 1959; *A Critique of "Paradise Lost,"* Columbia University Press, 1960; *Along That Coast* (novel), Doubleday, 1964; *Take Hands at Winter* (novel), Doubleday, 1967; *Runaway* (novel), Doubleday, 1969; *Vallor* (stories), York Press, 1978. Contributor of critical articles, poems, and fiction to Canadian, British, and American journals.

WORK IN PROGRESS: A novel.

*   *   *

PETERS, William 1921-

PERSONAL: Born July 30, 1921, in San Francisco, Calif.;

son of William Ernest (an advertising executive) and Dorothy (Wright) Peters; married Mercy Ann Miller, October 12, 1942 (divorced, 1968); children: Suzanne P. Hilton, Geoffrey W., Jennifer, Gretchen. *Education:* Northwestern University, B.S., 1947. *Politics:* Democrat. *Home:* 1 Lincoln Plaza, Apt. 20T, New York, N.Y. 10023. *Agent:* Curtis Brown Ltd., 575 Madison Ave., New York, N.Y.

CAREER: J. Walter Thompson Co., Chicago, Ill., account executive in public relations, 1947-51; *Ladies' Home Journal*, Philadelphia, Pa., member of fiction staff, 1951-52; *Women's Home Companion*, New York City, article editor, 1952-53; free-lance writer, Pelham, N.Y., 1953-62; Columbia Broadcasting System News, New York City, producer of "CBS Reports," 1962-66; free-lance writer, film director, and television producer, 1966—. Consultant on race relations, 1959—. *Military service:* U.S. Army Air Corps, pilot, 1942-45; became captain; received Air Medal with two oakleaf clusters and Distinguished Flying Cross.

MEMBER: Society of Magazine Writers, Writers Guild of America, East, Directors Guild of America. *Awards, honors:* Two special citations, Benjamin Franklin Magazine awards, Howard W. Blakeslee Award, National Brotherhood Award, and Lincoln University award, for magazine articles; George Foster Peabody Awards, 1963, 1967, 1970; Golden Gavel Award, American Bar Association, 1963; National School Bell Award, National Education Association, 1964; other awards for television documentaries.

WRITINGS: American Memorial Hospital, Reims, France: A History, American Memorial Hospital, 1955; *Passport to Friendship: The Story of the Experiment in International Living,* foreword by Pearl S. Buck, Lippincott, 1957; *The Southern Temper,* foreword by Harry Golden, Doubleday, 1959; (with Mrs. Medgar Evers) *For Us, the Living,* Doubleday, 1967; *A Class Divided,* Doubleday, 1971.

Television documentaries; produced for "CBS Reports," Columbia Broadcasting System: "Mississippi and the 15th Amendment," September 26, 1962; "Storm over the Supreme Court," Part II, March 13, 1963, Part III, June 19, 1963; "The Priest and the Politician," September 18, 1963; "Filibuster: Birth Struggle of a Law," March 18, 1964; "Segregation: Northern Style," December 9, 1964.

Produced for "ABC News," American Broadcasting Co., except as indicated: "Southern Accents—Northern Ghettos," July 6, 1967; "The Eye of the Storm," May 11, 1970; "An Echo of Anger," August 16, 1972; "Suddenly an Eagle," January 7, 1976; "On Camera," July 21, 1977; "Hostage!," January 30, 1978; "Death of a Family," produced for "Bill Moyers' Journal," April 9, 1979; "A Band of Iron," produced for Educational Television Network (South Carolina), 1980.

Contributor to *Good Housekeeping, Interracial Review, Ladies' Home Journal, Look, McCall's, New Republic, Reader's Digest, Redbook, Reporter, Saturday Evening Post, Saturday Review, Sports Illustrated, This Week,* and other periodicals.

*   *   *

PETERSEN, William 1912-

PERSONAL: Born August 3, 1912, in Jersey City, N.J.; son of Henry and Katherine (Gehrhardt) Petersen; married Renee Peller, 1950. *Education:* Columbia University, A.B., 1934, Ph.D., 1954. *Home:* 24900 Pine Hills Dr., Carmel, Calif. 93923.

CAREER: Smith College, Northampton, Mass., visiting lec-

turer, 1953; University of California, Berkeley, assistant professor, 1953-56; University of Colorado, Boulder, associate professor of sociology, 1956-59; University of California, Berkeley, professor of sociology, 1959-66; Boston College, Chestnut Hill, Mass., affiliated with Institute of Human Sciences, 1966-67; Ohio State University, Columbus, Robert Lazarus Professor of Social Demography, 1967-78, professor emeritus, 1978—. *Military service:* U.S. Army Air Forces, four years; became staff sergeant. *Member:* Population Association of America. *Awards, honors:* H. W. van Loon fellow, Amsterdam, 1951-52; National Science Foundation fellow, 1958-59; Ford Foundation fellow, 1973-75; Guggenheim fellow, 1977.

WRITINGS: Some Factors Influencing Postwar Emigration from the Netherlands, Martinus Nijhoff, 1952; *Planned Migration: The Social Determinants of the Dutch-Canadian Movement,* University of California Press, 1955; (editor) *American Social Patterns,* Doubleday-Anchor, 1956; (with Renee Petersen) *University Adult Education: A Guide to Policy,* Harper, 1960; *Population,* Macmillan, 1961, 3rd edition, 1975; (editor) *Social Controversy,* Wadsworth, 1962; (editor) *The Realities of World Communism,* Prentice-Hall, 1963; (with Lionel S. Lewis) *Nevada's Changing Population,* University of Nevada Press, 1963; *The Politics of Population,* Doubleday, 1964; *Japanese Americans: Oppression and Success,* Random House, 1971; (editor) *Readings in Population,* Macmillan, 1972; *Malthus,* Harvard University Press, 1979; *Dictionary of Demography,* Greenwood Press, in press; *Ethnicity,* University of California Press, in press. Contributor of articles on population and social policy to professional journals.

*   *   *

PETERSON, Martin Severin 1897-

PERSONAL: Born April 21, 1897, in Salem, Ore.; son of Axel and Matilda (Collinson) Peterson; married Wilma Mae Loomis, 1926; children: Tom Loomis. *Education:* Reed College, A.B., 1920; University of Chicago, graduate study, 1923-25; University of Nebraska, M.A., 1929, Ph.D., 1932. *Religion:* Episcopalian. *Home:* 15 Lakeview Gardens, Apt. 105, Natick, Mass.

CAREER: University of Nebraska at Lincoln, assistant professor, 1926-45, editor of experiment station publications, 1941-45; Quartermaster Food and Container Institute, Chicago, Ill., chief of technical services office, 1947-62; U.S. Army, Natick Laboratories, Natick, Mass., general physical scientist, 1962-67. *Military service:* U.S. Army, Medical Corps, World War I. *Member:* Institute of Food Technologists, Packaging Institute.

WRITINGS: Joaquin Miller: Literary Frontiersman, Stanford University Press, 1937; (with Wimberly and Owens) *Using Better English,* Ronald, 1937; *Scientific Thinking and Scientific Writing,* Reinhold, 1961; *Food Technology the World Over,* two volumes, Avi, 1963-65; (editor with Arnold Johnson) *Encyclopedia of Food Technology,* Avi, 1974; (editor with Johnson) *Encyclopedia of Food Science,* Avi, 1978; (editor with Edward S. Josephson) *Preservation of Food by Ionizing Radiations,* CRC Press, 1981. Editor of *Food Technology and Food Research,* 1952-60; associate editor, *Prairie Schooner,* 1928-45.

AVOCATIONAL INTERESTS: History of the West, particularly American Indians.

PETERSON, Merrill D(aniel) 1921-

PERSONAL: Born March 31, 1921, in Manhattan, Kan.; son of William Oscar (a minister) and Alice (Merrill) Peterson; married Jean Humphrey, May 24, 1944; children: Jeffrey, Kent. *Education:* Attended Kansas State College (now University), 1939-41; University of Kansas, A.B., 1943; Harvard University, Ph.D., 1950. *Home:* 1817 Yorktown Dr., Charlottesville, Va. 22901. *Office:* Department of History, University of Virginia, Charlottesville, Va. 22903.

CAREER: Brandeis University, Waltham, Mass., 1949-55, began as instructor, became assistant professor; Princeton University, Princeton, N.J., assistant professor and Bicentennial Preceptor in History, 1955-58; Brandeis University, 1958-62, began as associate professor, became professor of history and chairman of School of Social Science; University of Virginia, Charlottesville, Thomas Jefferson Foundation Professor of History, 1962—, chairman of department, 1966-72. Poynter fellow, Indiana University, 1975; lecturer at Mercer University, 1975, Salzburg Seminar in American Studies, 1975, and Louisiana State University, 1980. Member, National Historical Publications and Records Commission, 1973-77. *Military service:* U.S. Navy, 1943-46; became lieutenant junior grade. *Member:* American Historical Association, Organization of American Historians, American Academy of Arts and Sciences (fellow), Society of American Historians (fellow), Southern Historical Association, Phi Beta Kappa. *Awards, honors:* Bancroft Prize of Columbia University, 1961, and Gold Medal of the Jefferson Memorial Association, 1961, both for *The Jefferson Image in the American Mind;* Guggenheim fellowship, 1962-63; Center for Advanced Study in the Behavioral Sciences fellowship, 1968-69; L.H.D., Washington College, 1976; National Endowment for the Humanities fellow and National Humanities Center fellow, both 1980-81.

WRITINGS: The Jefferson Image in the American Mind, Oxford University Press, 1960; (general editor with Leonard Levy) *Major Crises in American History,* two volumes, Harcourt, 1962; (editor) *Democracy, Liberty and Property: State Constitutional Convention Debates of the 1820's,* Bobbs-Merrill, 1966; *Thomas Jefferson: A Profile,* Hill & Wang, 1967; *Thomas Jefferson and the New Nation: A Biography,* Oxford University Press, 1970; *James Madison: A Biography in His Own Words,* Harper, 1975; (editor) *The Portable Thomas Jefferson,* Viking, 1975; *Adams and Jefferson: A Revolutionary Dialogue,* University of Georgia Press, 1976; *Olive Branch and Sword: The Compromise of 1833,* Louisiana State University Press, 1981. Contributor to scholarly journals.

WORK IN PROGRESS: The Great Triumvirate: Webster, Clay, and Calhoun.

SIDELIGHTS: Merrill D. Peterson comments: "I became interested in American history as I was reaching for intellectual maturity at the time of the Second World War. Actually it was less an interest in history than in what American thought and experience could contribute to an understanding of American democracy and its future. Perhaps I was engaged in my own 'search for a usable past,' though the concept was unknown to me. Vernon L. Parrington's *Main Currents in American Thought* was especially important, while the works of Lewis Mumford opened exciting vistas, quite beyond Marx, for the study of American society and culture. Such influences steered me into the special program in the History of American Civilization at Harvard. There Perry Miller was most influential, for he added the scholarly discipline of the history of ideas without in any way diminishing

my intellectual fascination with the subject or my deeper moral commitment. It was probably inevitable that I should, having learned the methods of a Miller, return to the quest of a Parrington; and so it is that my work has focused on Jefferson and the career of American democracy."

AVOCATIONAL INTERESTS: American painting (both historical and contemporary).

*   *   *

PETRIE, Paul J(ames) 1928-

PERSONAL: Born July 1, 1928, in Detroit, Mich.; son of Louis Stuart (a stereotyper) and Mary (Squire) Petrie; married Sylvia Spencer, August 21, 1954; children: Philip Stuart, Emily Ruth, Lisa Evelyn. *Education:* Wayne University (now Wayne State University), B.A., 1950, M.A., 1951; State University of Iowa, Ph.D., 1957. *Politics:* Independent. *Home:* 66 Dendron Rd., Peace Dale, R.I. 02879. *Office:* English Department, University of Rhode Island, Kingston, R.I. 02881.

CAREER: University of Rhode Island, Kingston, instructor, 1959-62, assistant professor, 1962-66, associate professor, 1966-69, professor of English, 1969—. *Military service:* U.S. Army, 1951-53. *Member:* American Association of University Professors.

WRITINGS—Poetry: Confessions of a Non-Conformist (pamphlet), Hillside Press, 1963; *The Race with Time and the Devil,* Golden Quill, 1965; *The Leader: For Martin Luther King, Jr.* (pamphlet), Hellcoal Press, 1968; *From under the Hill of Night,* Vanderbilt University Press, 1969; *The Academy of Goodbye,* University Press of New England, 1974; *Light from the Furnace Rising,* Copper Beech Press, 1978; *Time Songs,* Biscuit City Press, 1979. Poetry is anthologized in *Borestone Mountain Poetry Awards, 1959, 1961, 1967,* edited by Lionel Stevenson and others, Pacific Books, 1960, 1962, 1968, *Midland,* edited by Paul Engle and others, Random House, 1961, and *The Treasury of American Poetry,* Doubleday, 1978. Contributor of two hundred and forty-five poems to sixty journals, including *Atlantic, Commonweal, Massachusetts Review, Michigan Quarterly, Nation, New Republic,* and *New Yorker.*

WORK IN PROGRESS: Two books of poetry, *Glances* and *Strategies in October.*

SIDELIGHTS: Paul J. Petrie writes: "My whole approach to poetry, both thematic and technical, is governed by a hatred of dogmatic theorizing, and since the twentieth century represents the very apotheosis of theorizing, a paradise for half-baked creeds and counter-creeds, I find myself in a 'school' of one. If there is a critical notion which I find appealing, it is that there is nothing that cannot be said in poetry and that there is no limitation on the way it can or should be said. A poem need not be 'new' or 'old,' in 'free verse' or 'meter', 'understated' or 'overstated'—all that it must be is a good poem."

He adds: "As for my own work, I would describe it as lyrical, relatively emotional, dramatic in its inclusion of opposites with a stronger current of movement than is common in verse today, and perhaps an over-indulgence in the doctrine of statement through images. My major strengths are rhythm and organization; my major weaknesses are a lack of exact detail and firm diction. I have a personal notion of the poem as an act of praise (be it positive or negative in theme and tone), and I tend to regard poetry as semi-religious vocation, but I do not demand that others share these attitudes and I can think of excellent poems which would stretch these terms to the breaking point. The poems will remain; the theory will go.''

Petrie's area of major vocational interest is English Romantic poetry. He traveled to Spain and France, 1957-58, and to England and Italy, 1966-67.

AVOCATIONAL INTERESTS: Classical music, tennis.

*   *   *

PETUCHOWSKI, Jakob Josef   1925-

PERSONAL: Born July 30, 1925, in Berlin, Germany; son of Siegmund (a businessman) and Lucie (Loewenthal) Petuchowski; married Elizabeth Rita Mayer, November 28, 1946; children: Samuel Judah, Aaron Mark, Jonathan Mayer. *Education:* University of London, B.A., (with honours), 1947; Hebrew Union College-Jewish Institute of Religion, M.H.L., 1952, Ph.D., 1955. *Home:* 7836 Greenland Pl., Cincinnati, Ohio 45237. *Office:* Hebrew Union College-Jewish Institute of Religion, Cincinnati, Ohio 45220.

CAREER: Ordained rabbi; Temple Emanuel, Welch, W.Va., rabbi, 1949-55; Beth Israel Synagogue, Washington, Pa., rabbi, 1955-56; Hebrew Union College-Jewish Institute of Religion, Cincinnati, Ohio, assistant professor, 1956-59, associate professor, 1959-63, professor of rabbinics, 1963-74, research professor of Jewish theology and liturgy, 1974—. *Member:* American Academy of Religion, American Academy for Jewish Research (fellow). *Awards, honors:* F.H.L., Maimonides College; Dr.Phil.h.c., University of Cologne; D.Litt.h.c., Brown University.

WRITINGS: The Theology of Haham David Nieto, Bloch, 1954, 2nd edition, Ktav, 1970; *Ever Since Sinai—a Modern View of Torah*, Scribe, 1961, 3rd edition, Arbit Books, 1979; *Zion Reconsidered*, Twayne, 1966; *Prayerbook Reform in Europe*, World Union for Progressive Judaism, 1968; *Heirs of the Pharisees*, Basic Books, 1970; *Contributions to the Scientific Study of Jewish Liturgy*, Ktav, 1970; *Understanding Jewish Prayer*, Ktav, 1972; (with Joseph Heinemann) *Literature of the Synagogue*, Behrman House, 1975; *Beten im Judentum*, Katholisches Bibelwerk, 1976; (with Michael Brocke) *The Lord's Prayer and Jewish Liturgy*, Seabury Press, 1978; *Theology and Poetry*, Routledge & Kegan Paul, 1978; *Melchisedech—Urgestalt der Oekumene* (title means ''Melchisedek—Prototype of Ecumenism''), Herder, 1978; *Es Lehrten unsere Meister*, Herder, 1979; *Ferner Lehrten unsere Meister*, Herder, 1980; *Die Stimme vom Sinai*, Herder, 1981. Contributor to *Encyclopaedia Britannica, Grolier's Encyclopedia*, and *Encyclopaedia Judaica;* contributor of more than 475 articles to religious and scholarly journals. Member of editorial board, *Hebrew Union College Annual* and *Judaism—A Quarterly Journal.*

SIDELIGHTS: Jakob Petuchowski told *CA:* ''I had my first article published when I was 16 years old, and writing has been my avocation and my hobby ever since. Much of my writing grows naturally out of my work as teacher and researcher. One aim is to share the fruits of my research with my peers in the scholarly enterprise. Another aim is to bring the fruits of my research to a wider circle of interested and potentially interested circle of readers. That is why I strive for clarity in expression and, as much as possible, for the avoidance of the kind of technical jargon which is all too common in theological publications. . . . In writing my books and articles, I let the ideas germinate inside me for quite some time, without necessarily committing anything to paper, and, once I get down to the actual writing, I do so very rapidly. Depending upon the intended readership, I write in English, German or Hebrew—in that order of linguistic facility. My advice to young writers would be that they should steep themselves in the English classics.''

*   *   *

PEYRE, Henri (Maurice)   1901-

PERSONAL: Born February 21, 1901, in Paris, France; son of Brice Henri and Marie (Tuvien) Peyre; married Marguerite Vanuxem, August 9, 1927 (died, 1962); married Lois Haegert, March 11, 1963. *Education:* University of Paris, Sorbonne and Ecole Normale Superieure, B.A., 1918, Licence, 1922, Agregation, 1924, Doctorat, 1932. *Address:* 290 North Ave., Westport, Conn. 06880.

CAREER: Teacher of French and French literature at Bryn Mawr College, Bryn Mawr, Pa., 1925-28, Yale University, New Haven, Conn., 1928-33, and University of Cairo, Cairo, Egypt, 1933-36; Yale University, Sterling Professor of French, beginning 1938, chairman of department, beginning 1939. Visiting professor or lecturer at University of Lyons, University of Chicago, Cornell University, and Columbia University. *Military service:* French Army, 1924-25. *Member:* American Philosophical Society, American Association of Teachers of French, Modern Language Association of America, American Academy of Arts and Sciences. *Awards, honors:* Officier de la Legion d'Honneur; recipient of honorary degrees from numerous colleges and universities, including Bard College, University of Cincinnati, University of Miami, Middlebury College, Oberlin College, Rutgers University, Tufts University, Boston College, University of Laval, and Kalamazoo College.

WRITINGS: Louis Menard, 1822-1901, Yale University Press, 1932; *Bibliographie critique de Phellenisme en France, 1843-1870*, Yale University Press, 1932; (editor with Joseph Seronde) *Three Classic French Plays*, Heath, 1935; *Shelley et la France*, Paul Barbey, 1935; (editor with Seronde) *Nine Classic French Plays by Corneille, Moliere, Racine*, Heath, 1936; (editor with E. M. Grant) *Seventeenth Century French Prose and Poetry*, Heath, 1937; *Hommes et ouevres du XXe siecle*, R. Correa, 1938.

L'influence des litteratures antiques sur la litterature francaise moderne, Yale University Press, 1941; *Le classicisme francais*, Editions de la Maison Francaise, 1942; (editor) *Essays in Honor of Albert Feuillerat*, Yale University Press, 1943; *Problemes francais de demain: Reflexions a propos d'un livre recent*, Moretus, 1943; *Writers and Their Critics: A Study of Misunderstanding*, Cornell University Press, 1944, revised edition published as *The Failures of Criticism*, 1967; *Les Generations litteraires*, Boivin, 1948.

(Editor) *Pensées de Baudelaire: Recueillies et classees*, J. Corti, 1951; *Connaissance de Baudelaire*, J. Corti, 1951; (with others) *The Cultural Migration*, University of Pennsylvania Press, 1953; *The Contemporary French Novel*, Oxford University Press, 1955, revised edition published as *French Novelists of Today*, 1967; *Observations on Life, Literature and Learning in America* (essays), Southern Illinois University Press, 1961; (editor) *Baudelaire: A Collection of Critical Essays*, Prentice-Hall, 1962; *Literature and Sincerity*, Yale University Press, 1963; (editor) *Contemporary French Literature*, Harper, 1964; *Splendors of Christendom*, Time-Life Books, 1964.

Qu'est-ce que le classicisme?, Nizet, 1965; *The Literature of France*, Prentice-Hall, 1965; (editor) G. Lanson, *Essais de methode de critique et d'histoire*, Hachette, 1965; *The Literature of France*, Volume I, Prentice-Hall, 1966; *Historical and Critical Essays*, University of Nebraska Press, 1968; *Jean Paul Sartre*, Columbia University Press, 1968; (editor)

Fiction in Several Languages, Houghton, 1968; *Qu'est-ce que le romantisme?*, Presses Universitaires de France, 1972; *Qu'est-ce que le symbolisme?*, Presses Universitaires de France, 1976. Contributor to professional journals.

SIDELIGHTS: "There ought to be a word for writers which would serve as the equivalent of 'omnivorous' for readers," observes Victor Howes of the *Christian Science Monitor* in a review of Henri Peyre's *Historical and Critical Essays*. "'Prolific' and 'voluminous' hardly seem adequate to describe the tireless energy of writers, lecturers, culture-transmitters like Henri Peyre. With one foot in academe and one foot in Chautauqua, Professor Peyre has been turning out essays and articles in the 'light classical' repertoire for a generation.... He writes like a pinwheel, ideas flaring out like sparks against the night.... If all this literary productivity sounds too good to be true, let it be said at once that Professor Peyre knows his business.... He has a knack for getting to the heart of the matter, a sense of the crucial issue, a flair for throwing out provocative lines of investigation."

Though the subjects he discusses in *Historical and Critical Essays* range from a French view of Shakespeare's women to the responsibilities of the mass media, Peyre's real specialty is modern French literature. His studies on the topic, most of which are directed at the non-specialist American reader with little or no knowledge of French, have been highly praised for their comprehensiveness as well as for the author's enthusiasm. One book in particular, *The Contemporary French Novel*, and its revised version, *French Novelists of Today*, have been very well-received. Like Howes, J. H. Matthews of *Comparative Literature* finds that the author's work "reveals Henri Peyre as a man of decided opinions, possessed of the courage to express them, and of the ability to organize his material in a volume soundly constructed and cogently argued. Reading this book one is impressed by many qualities, but above all one is struck by the author's integrity. This is a critic who believes in clearly establishing his position, indicating the criteria which oblige him to hold it, and in defending it consistently, with the utmost clarity."

Others, too, have noticed and praised the skill and firmness with which Peyre presents and defends his position. A *Times Literary Supplement* reviewer, for example, finds it stimulating to read the work of a scholar who "has never allowed himself to fall into the pit of pedantry," while the *New York Herald Tribune Book Review*'s Wallace Fowlie notes that "there are many books on French novelists of the 20th century, but Professor Peyre's study is unique in its completeness, in the fullness and detail of its evaluations, [and] in the vigor with which this critic presents his viewpoint and develops his critical theories." Laurent Le Sage of *Saturday Review* is impressed by the fact that although Peyre "does not hesitate to speak out when he thinks the importance of a writer ... is exaggerated," he always "gives his own reasons and recognizes the existence of other points of view." Thomas Bishop, another *Saturday Review* critic, agrees with Le Sage, declaring that "the strength of Mr. Peyre's work is contained in his formidable command of his subject, the precision of his judgments, and his willingness to express definite opinions. Mr. Peyre is not one to throw praise around indiscriminately; he approaches the great names of the modern French novel without awe but rather with refreshing iconoclasm." Though a few reviewers disagree with Bishop and Le Sage, claiming that Peyre is more dogmatic than he is willing to admit, Le Sage points out that "it is hard to quarrel and quibble before such forthrightness."

Among the most common targets of Peyre's wrath are structuralism, the use of computers and card indexes in analyzing

literary works, and the "new novelists" (as Louis Allen reports in *Commonweal*, Peyre endorses Robert Penn Warren's insistence that "experimental writing is an elite word for flop"; Peyre, he says, "refuses to regard [it] as a touchstone of greatness in art"). A staunch moralist, he approves of writers like Malraux, Sartre, and Saint-Exupery who, according to Allen, "carry on the essential moral debate for each generation, on the meaning of life in society, and on individual destiny in a hostile or indifferent universe." Novelists who fail to deal with these concerns in a lucid manner are not worthy of consideration in Peyre's eyes.

But even though some may find his views harsh and uncompromising, few can argue with the extent of Peyre's knowledge of his subject (whatever it may be) or his ability to discuss it with the sparkling vitality, precision, and thoroughness characteristic of almost all his work. "Peyre is a humanist in the richest sense," observes Alfred Owen Aldridge in *Books Abroad*, while Howes, describing his writings as "warm with humanity, scholarship, and the desire to communicate," thanks him for "the way he kindles a learned flame." Concludes Sidney D. Braun of *Criticism*: "A prolific writer, a profound thinker, a universally acclaimed ambassador of good will between America and France, he has, in the opinion of many, done more than any other Frenchman or American in this country to act as friend, mentor and guide to students and scholars."

BIOGRAPHICAL/CRITICAL SOURCES: *New York Times*, May 1, 1955; *Nation*, May 21, 1955; *Saturday Review*, May 28, 1955, September 23, 1961, June 24, 1967; *New York Herald Tribune Book Review*, July 24, 1955; *Commonweal*, July 29, 1955, December 22, 1967; *Spectator*, September 16, 1955; *Times Literary Supplement*, October 7, 1955, October 12, 1967; *Yale Review*, autumn, 1955; *Newsweek*, February 16, 1959; *Yearbook of Comparative and General Literature*, Volume IX, University of North Carolina Press, 1960; *Criticism*, spring, 1967, spring, 1968; *Books Abroad*, spring, 1967, spring, 1968, winter, 1968, spring, 1969; *Christian Science Monitor*, September 19, 1967, November 4, 1968; *Wisconsin Studies in Contemporary Literature*, autumn, 1967; *Virginia Quarterly Review*, autumn, 1967; *New Yorker*, December 2, 1967; *Comparative Literature*, spring, 1969.

*   *   *

PFEFFER, J(ay) Alan   1907-

PERSONAL: Born June 26, 1907, in Brooklyn, N.Y.; son of Isaac (a minister) and Henny (Halpern) Pfeffer; married Bertha Manoff, 1938; children: Robert I., Jo Anne. *Education:* University of Buffalo (now State University of New York at Buffalo), B.A. (magna cum laude), 1935, M.A., 1936; Columbia University, Ph.D., 1946. *Home:* 685 Cowles Rd., Santa Barbara, Calif. 93108. *Office:* Institute for Basic German, Stanford University, Stanford, Calif. 94305.

CAREER: Columbia University, New York, N.Y., extension instructor in German, 1937-39; State University of New York at Buffalo, 1939-62, began as instructor, became professor and director of German studies, director of Institute for Basic German, 1960-62; University of Pittsburgh, Pittsburgh, Pa., professor and chairman of department of Germanic languages, 1962-72, professor emeritus, 1972—, director of Institute for Basic German, 1962-75; Stanford University, Stanford, Calif., consulting professor to department of German studies and director of Institute for Basic German, 1975—. Chairman of advisory language committee, Buffalo (N.Y.) Board of Education, 1958-60. *Member:* American Association of Teachers of German (chapter president, 1949-59), Modern Language Association of America, National Federation of Modern Language Teachers (national president, 1959-60), American Association of University Professors, New York State Federation of Foreign Language Teachers (president, 1949-50), New York State Teachers Association (zone president, 1949-59), Phi Beta Kappa, Delta Phi Alpha (former national first vice-president).

WRITINGS: Military German, Rinehart, 1944; (editor) *Dictionary of Everyday Usage: German-English,* Holt, 1946; *The Proverb in Goethe,* King's Crown Press, 1948; (editor) *Studies in Honor of T. B. Hewitt,* University of Buffalo Press, 1950; (with T. B. Hewitt) *Modern German,* Dryden Press, 1956; *German Review Grammar,* Heath, 1961, 2nd edition, 1969; *A Basic Spoken German Word List,* Level I, Prentice-Hall, 1964; *An Index of English Equivalents,* Level I, Prentice-Hall, 1965; *A Basic (Spoken) German Idiom List,* Level I, Prentice-Hall, 1968; *A Dictionary of Basic (Spoken) German,* Prentice-Hall, 1970; (with Hubert Heinen and others) *Basic (Spoken) German Grammar,* Prentice-Hall, 1974; *Erarbeitung und Wertung dreier Deutscher Korpora,* Gunther Narr, 1975; *Kontexte,* Heath, 1976; *Probleme der Deskriptien Deutschen Grammatik,* Julius Groos, 1981. Contributor to professional journals. Editor, *Modern Language Journal,* 1958-62; associate editor, *German Quarterly;* member of editorial board, *Zielsprache Deutsch.*

WORK IN PROGRESS: A Basic (Spoken) German Idiom List, Level II; *The Structure of Basic (Spoken) German; The Evolution of Basic (Spoken) German; German Loans in English; A Basic German-German Dictionary.*

* * *

PHILIPP, Elliot Elias 1915-
(Philip Embey, Medicus II, Victor Tempest)

PERSONAL: Born July 20, 1915, in London, England; son of Oscar Isaac (a metallurgist) and Clarisse (Weil) Philipp; married Lucy Ruth Hackenbroch, March 22, 1939; children: Anne Susan, Alan Henry. *Education:* St. John's College, Cambridge, B.A., 1936, M.A., 1942, M.B. and B.Ch., 1947; Middlesex Hospital, London, England, M.R.C.O.G., 1947; F.R.C.S., 1951, F.R.C.O.G. 1962. *Politics:* Liberal. *Religion:* Jewish. *Home:* 78 Nottingham Ter., York Gate. London N.W. 1, England. *Office:* 94 Harley St., London W. 1, England.

CAREER: Consultant obstetrician and gynecologist in London, England, 1952—. *Military service:* Royal Air Force Volunteer Reserve; became squadron leader; twice mentioned in dispatches. *Member:* International Society of Psychosomatic Obstetrics and Gynecology, International Psychoprophylactic Society, Royal Society for Medicine, French Society for Psychoprophylaxis, French Society of Gynaecologists, British Society of Authors, Medical Society of London, Hunterian Society, Middle Temple.

WRITINGS: (Under pseudonym Victor Tempest) *Near the Sun: The Impressions of a Medical Officer of Bomber Command,* Crabtree Press, 1946; (editor with E. W. Walls and H.J.B. Atkins) John Hilton, *Rest and Pain,* G. Bell, 1950; (editor under pseudonym Medicus II) John Paterson MacLaren, *Know Your Body,* revised edition, Thorsons, 1955; (under pseudonym Philip Embey) *Woman's Change of Life,* Thorsons, 1956; *From Sterility to Fertility: A Guide to the Causes and Cure of Childlessness,* Philosophical Library, 1957; *Obstetrics and Gynaecology Combined for Students,* H. K. Lewis, 1962, 2nd edition, 1970; (with Eva Crisp) *Midwifery for Nurses,* H. K. Lewis, 1962, 2nd edition, 1964; (with K. L. Gearing) *The Student Nurse in the Operating*

Theatre, E. & S. Livingstone, 1964; (with Erna Wright) *Easy Childbirth,* British Medical Association, 1964; (editor with Josephine Barnes and Michael Newton) *Scientific Foundations of Obstetrics and Gynaecology,* F. A. Davis, 1970, 2nd edition, 1977; *Childlessness,* Arrow Press, 1977; *Childbirth,* Fontana, 1979; *Infertility,* Heinemann Medical Books, 1980. Medical correspondent, *News Chronicle* (London), 1947-56; regular contributor to *Family Doctor,* 1948-63, and *Sunday Times,* 1958-60.

SIDELIGHTS: Elliot Elias Philipp told *CA:* "I write for the rather selfish reason of thinking that I can pass on to others what I have learned from others in a relatively easily absorbable form. I also write because I have the 'bug' which will not let me alone, and which is a form of doodling and polishing the doodles. I write by dictating onto a tape which is faithfully transcribed; then comes the real pleasure of transposing the words, pruning and cutting and slimming to give a better shape to the message. I write to express an admiration for the research of others, the heroism of others, such as in *Near the Sun.* The scientific writing and the reviewing, reporting and editing are all ways of handling on other people's messages to a still broader audience. There is nothing like drudgery in the writing because inspiration always comes from other people, and there seems to be an absolute need to pass it on in some form or another. I suppose it is a way of paying back to medicine what it has given to me; it is a form of digesting and regurgitating and extracting the truth as seen by an observer who must use words as taught by a great educator at St. Paul's School—Eynon Smith, who was killed in the bombing of London in 1941."

* * *

PHILLIPS, Louis 1942-

PERSONAL: Born June 15, 1942, in Lowell, Mass.; son of Louis James and Dorothy (Perkins) Phillips; married Patricia Ranard, August 23, 1972. *Education:* Stetson University, B.A., 1964; University of North Carolina, M.A. (in radio, television, and motion pictures), 1967; City University of New York, M.A. (in English and comparative literature), 1968. *Home:* 447 East 14th St., Apt. 12-D, New York, N.Y. 10009. *Agent:* Charles Hunt, Fifi Oscard Associates, Inc., 19 West 44th St., Suite 1500, New York, N.Y. 10036.

CAREER: State University of New York Maritime College, Fort Schuyler, assistant professor of English, 1967-73; currently teacher of creative writing at School of Visual Arts, New York, N.Y. Playwright-in-residence, University of California, San Diego, 1979, and Colonnades Theatre Lab. Regents fellow, University of California, San Diego, 1979. *Member:* Dramatists Guild, Society of American Magicians. *Awards, honors:* State University of New York Playwright award, 1973, 1975.

WRITINGS: The Man Who Stole the Atlantic Ocean, Prentice-Hall, 1972; *Theodore Jonathan Wainwright Is Going to Bomb the Pentagon,* Prentice-Hall, 1973; *The Film Buff's Calendar,* Drake, 1973; *The Animated Thumb-Tack Railroad Dollhouse and All Round Surprise Book* (juvenile), Lippincott, 1974; (with Karen Markoe) *The Super-Duper American History Fun Book* (juvenile), F. Watts, 1978; *The Brothers Wrong and Wrong Again* (juvenile), McGraw, 1979; *The Handy Book of Baseball Records, Stars, Feats, and Facts,* Harcourt, 1979; (with Arnie Markoe) *The Handy Book of Football Records, Stars, Feats, and Facts,* Harcourt, 1979; (with K. Markoe) *The Handy Book of Women's Sports, Records, Stars, and Feats,* Harcourt, 1979; *Funky Facts* (juvenile), Xerox Books, 1979.

Published by Prologue Press: *The Emancipation of the Encyclopedia Salesman*, 1972; *A Catalogue of Earthly Pleasures* (poems), 1973; *It Takes a Lot of Paper to Gift Wrap an Elephant*, 1973; *Octopus Applause*, 1973; *How Do You Dial a Crocodile?*, 1974; *Become the Touches* (poems), 1975; *Arbuckles Rape* (play), 1978; *Radio Station WGOD Is on the Air* (play), 1979; *All the Natural Cruelty of Things* (poems), 1979. Also author of chapbooks, including *The Insect Trials*, *A Relinquishing of Dreams*, and *Re: Conciliation*.

Unpublished plays: "The Last of the Marx Brothers' Writers," first produced in Waltham, Mass. at Brandeis University, 1973; (with Robert Karmon) "Gulliver" (libretto), first produced at Guthrie Theatre, 1975; "The Ballroom in St. Patrick's Cathedral," produced in New York by Colonnades Theatre Lab, 1978. Also author of "God Have Mercy on the June Bug."

Poems set to music by Thomas Pasatieri and published as *Heloise and Abelard* and *Rites De Passage*, Belwin-Mills. Work anthologized in *West Coast Plays #2*. Contributor to *Modern International Drama*, *Dramatists Guild Quarterly*, *Learning*, *Playbill*, *McCall's*, *Family Circle*, *Grit*, *Humpty Dumpty*, and *Rotarian*.

WORK IN PROGRESS: A short story collection, *Must I Weep for the Dancing Bear?*; poetry, *All That Glows Sees*; a full-length play, *The Dreams of a Pin-Ball Mechanic*.

BIOGRAPHICAL/CRITICAL SOURCES: New York Times, December 2, 1978.

* * *

PHILLIPS, Michael Joseph 1937-

PERSONAL: Born March 2, 1937, in Indianapolis, Ind.; son of Bernice (Farmer) Phillips Hollibaugh. *Education:* Attended Purdue University, 1955-56, University of Edinburgh, 1957-58, 1959-60, and Alliance Francaise, 1958; Wabash College, B.A. (cum laude), 1959; graduate study at New York University, 1960-61, Oxford University, 1969, 1971, and Harvard University, 1970; Indiana University, M.A., 1964, Ph.D., 1971; postdoctoral study at Free University of Indianapolis, 1972-75, Butler University, 1973-75, Indiana University-Purdue University at Indianapolis, 1975, Cambridge University, 1978, and Oxford University, 1978. *Home:* 430 East Wylie, Bloomington, Ind. 47401.

CAREER: Curry's Inc., Bloomington, Ind., bookstore manager, 1961-63; Bobbs-Merrill Co., Inc. (publisher), Indianapolis, Ind., college traveler, 1964-65; University of Wisconsin—Milwaukee, lecturer in English, 1970, 1971; Free University of Indianapolis, Indianapolis, instructor in English, 1973; Indiana University-Purdue University at Indianapolis, instructor in English, 1973-78; Free University of Indianapolis, instructor, 1977-79. Visiting fellow, Harvard University, 1976-77. *Member:* International Comparative Literature Association, Modern Language Association of America, American Comparative Literature Association, Society for the Study of Midwestern Literature, Midwest Modern Language Association, Phi Beta Kappa, Mensa.

*WRITINGS—*Poems, except as indicated: *9 Concrete Poems*, Department of Fine Arts, Indiana University, 1967; *Girls, Girls, Girls*, Bitterroot Press, 1967; *4 Poster Poems*, Department of Fine Arts, Indiana University, 1968; *4 Poems for a Chocolate Princess*, Phillips Publishing, 1968; *7 Poems for Audrey Hepburn*, J. Mark Press, 1968; *Libretto for 23 Poems*, Satori Record Co., 1968; *Kinetics & Concretes*, Department of Fine Arts, Indiana University, 1971; *The Concrete Book*, Terrestial Press, 1971; *8 Page Poems*, De-partment of Fine Arts, Indiana University, 1971; *Love, Love, Love*, Print Center, 1973; *Concrete Sonnets*, Print Center, 1973; *Concrete Haiku*, Peacock Press, 1975; *Visual Sequences*, Peacock Press, 1975; *Abstract Poems*, Print Center, 1978; *Underworld Love Poems*, Frozen Waffles Press, 1979; *31 Erotic Concrete Sonnets for Samantha*, privately printed, 1979; *Edwin Muir* (criticism), Hackett, 1979; *Selected Love Poems*, Hackett, 1980.

Published by Triton Press: *Haiku II*, 1975; *Visual Poems*, 1975; *A Girl*, 1977; *More Women*, 1978; *Movie Star Poems*, 1978; *22 Concrete Poems Written While at Harvard*, 1978.

Published by Free University Press: *Beginnings of Samantha*, 1979; *21 Erotic Haiku for Samantha*, 1979; *3 Visual Waka*, 1979; (editor) *4 Major Visual Poets*, 1980; *35 Boogie Woogie Haiku*, 1980.

Contributor: *America Sings*, Rockwell, 1965; *Indiana Sesquicentennial Poets*, Ball State University, 1968; *Imaged Words/Worded Images*, Outerbridge, 1971; *Poesie in Fusie*, Rook (Belgium), 1972; *Alphabet Anthology*, Writers Workshop, University of Iowa, 1975; *Poetry People*, Ramakrishna-Vivkananda Center, 1976; *20 Jaar de Tafelronde*, Tafelronde, 1977; *Escritura en liber tad*, [Spain], 1978; Kostelanetz, editor, *Texts—Sound Texts*, Morrow, 1980. Also contributor to *Ardestia Verba*, 1971, *Anthology II*, 1972, and *Visual Poetry*, 1975. Contributor of about 800 poems to magazines, newspapers, and journals.

SIDELIGHTS: Michael Joseph Phillips told *CA* that he is greatly interested in writing haiku and waka. "[I] try to take the 'Zen' out of the form and add the content of the Elizabethan sonnet," he explains. "[I also] favor wild, beautiful love poetry celebrating women."

* * *

PIERSON, G(eorge) W(ilson) 1904-

PERSONAL: Born October 22, 1904, in New York, N.Y.; son of Charles Wheeler and Elizabeth G. (Groesbeck) Pierson; married Laetitia Verdery (an artist), September 10, 1936; children: Norah, Laetitia Deems. *Education:* Yale University, B.A., 1926, Ph.D., 1933. *Religion:* Congregational. *Home:* 176 Ives St., Mount Carmel, Conn. 06518. *Office:* 1691 Yale Station, New Haven, Conn. 06020.

CAREER: Yale University, New Haven, Conn., instructor in English, 1926-27, instructor in history, 1929-30, 1933-36, assistant professor, 1936-39, associate professor, 1939-44, professor, 1944-46, Larned Professor of History, 1946-73, Larned Professor of History Emeritus, 1973—, chairman of department, 1956-62, director of Division of Humanities, 1964-70, fellow of Davenport College, executive fellow, 1938-45, chairman, 1946, historian of the university. *Member:* American Historical Association (delegate to American Council of Learned Societies, 1963—), American Studies Association, Society for French Historical Studies, Organization of American Historians, American Academy of Arts and Sciences (fellow), Century Association, National Golf Links. *Awards, honors:* Porter Prize, Yale University, 1933; Guggenheim fellow, 1955-56; W. L. Cross Medal, Yale Graduate School, 1973; De Varre Medal, 1974; Yale Alumni Medal, 1975.

WRITINGS: Tocqueville and Beaumont in America, Oxford University Press, 1938, abridged edition published as *Tocqueville in America*, edited by Dudley C. Lunt, Doubleday, 1959, hardcover edition, Peter Smith, 1960; (contributor) Margaret Clapp, editor, *The Modern University*, Cornell University Press, 1950; *Yale: College and University, 1871-*

1937, Yale University Press, Volume I: *Yale College: An Educational History, 1871-1921*, 1952, Volume II: *Yale: The University College, 1921-1937*, 1955; *The Education of American Leaders: Comparative Contributions of U.S. Colleges and Universities*, Praeger, 1969; *The Moving American*, Knopf, 1973; (co-editor) Gustave de Beaumont, *Lettres d'Amerique*, Presses Universitaires, 1973; *Yale: A Short History*, Office of the Secretary, Yale University, 1976, revised edition, 1979. Contributor of critical essays on the American frontier, regionalism, and American mobility to historical and scholarly journals and of articles on the humanities and higher education in the United States to other publications.

WORK IN PROGRESS: Further research on Yale history, primarily for a book dealing with historical statistics on Yale's development.

SIDELIGHTS: As a graduate student, G. W. Pierson was given what he terms the "happy opportunity" to study the American voyage and experiences of Alexis de Tocqueville through his unpublished letters and diaries. As a result, reports Pierson, "[I] became persuaded that the frontier hypothesis of Frederick Jackson Turner was too narrow, nationalistic, and confusing—and so [I] was led to a critical reappraisal. In 1933 [I] began to try to teach a course on the foreign relations of American civilization which must have been nearly the only one of its kind. In later years [I] became fascinated by the restlessness and mobility of the American experience, which I see as a major factor in our history and an important influence on our national character. Meanwhile, [I also] have been deeply concerned for the liberal arts and the future of independent universities."

*   *   *

PILLING, Arnold R(emington)   1926-

PERSONAL: Born 1926, in Berkeley, Calif.; son of Roy William and Elizabeth (Chambers) Pilling; married Patricia Leslie Marks, 1956; children: Laurie Remington, Leslie Ann, David Harwood, Daniel Gordon. *Education:* Attended University of Colorado, 1945-46; University of California, Berkeley, A.B., 1947, Ph.D., 1958; University College, London, graduate study, 1950-51. *Home:* 590 Lakeview, Birmingham, Mich. 48009. *Office:* Department of Anthropology, Wayne State University, Detroit, Mich. 48202.

CAREER: University of California, Berkeley, assistant archaeologist, 1949-50; Wayne State University, Detroit, Mich., instructor, 1957-59, assistant professor, 1959-62, associate professor, 1962-70, professor of anthropology, 1970—, director of Museum of Anthropology, 1958—. *Military service:* U.S. Navy, 1945-46. *Member:* Royal Anthropological Institute (fellow), American Anthropological Association (fellow), Society of Historical Archaeology (secretary-treasurer, 1967-68) Conference on Michigan Archaeology (vice-chairman, 1967—), Michigan Archaeological Society, Sigma Xi, Algonquin Club (Detroit-Windsor). *Awards, honors:* Fulbright fellowship to Australia, 1953-54.

WRITINGS: (With C.W.M. Hart) *The Tiwi of North Australia*, Holt, 1960, fieldwork edition, 1979; *Aborigine Culture History*, Wayne State University Press, 1962; (editor with Richard A. Waterman) *Diprotodon to Detribalization*, Michigan State University Press, 1970.

Contributor: Robert F. Heizer, editor, *A Manual of Archaeological Field Methods*, National Press, 1949, 3rd edition published as *A Guide to Archaeological Field Methods*, 1958; Heizer, *The Archaeology of the Napa Region*, University of California Press, 1953; Julius Gould and William L.

Kolb, editors, *A Dictionary of the Social Sciences*, Free Press of Glencoe, 1964; Richard B. Lee and I. DeVore, editors, *Man the Hunter*, Aldine, 1968; Americo Paredes and Ellen U. Stekert, editors, *The Urban Experience and Folk Tradition*, University of Texas Press, 1971; Heizer, editor, *Handbook of the North American Indians: California*, Smithsonian Institution Press, 1978; Stevan Harrell and Pamela T. Amoss, editors, *Other Ways of Growing Old*, Stanford University Press, 1979; Robert L. Schuyler, editor, *Urban Archaeology in America*, Baywood, 1981.

WORK IN PROGRESS: Contributor to *Ice Glider Site*, edited by W. Ray Wood, for the National Park Service.

*   *   *

PINDER, John H(umphrey) M(urray)

PERSONAL: Born in London, England; son of Harold Senhouse (a soldier) and Lilian Edith (Murray) Pinder. *Education:* King's College, Cambridge, honors degree in economics, 1949. *Home:* 26 Bloomfield Ter., London S.W. 1, England. *Office:* Policy Studies Institute, 1-2 Castle Lane, London S.W. 1, England.

CAREER: Federal Union (voluntary organization promoting international federation), London, England, press officer, 1950-52; Economist Intelligence Unit (economic and market research), London, 1952-64, became director in charge of international operations; Political and Economic Planning (research institute), London, director, 1964-78; Policy Studies Institute, London, director, 1978—. Member of executive committee of trustees, Federal Trust, 1960—. *Military service:* British Army, West African Artillery, 1943-47; became lieutenant. *Member:* Federal Union (chairman of executive committee, 1956-59) and Brooks's Club (both London).

WRITINGS: U.N. Reform: Proposals for Charter Amendment, Federal Union, 1953; *Britain and the Common Market*, Cresset, 1961; *Europe against De Gaulle*, Praeger, 1963; (with Roy Pryce) *Europe after De Gaulle*, Penguin, 1969; (with others) *The Economics of Europe*, Knight & Co., 1971; (with others) *Reshaping Britain*, Political and Economic Planning, 1974; (with Pauline Pinder) *The European Community's Policy towards Eastern Europe*, Chatham House, 1975. Also author of *The Commonwealth and the Trend towards World and Regional Economic Systems*.

*   *   *

PITCHER, Harvey (John)   1936-

PERSONAL: Born August 26, 1936, in London, England; son of Maurice Albert (a clock specialist) and May (Lapham) Pitcher. *Education:* Oxford University, B.A. (first class honors), 1960. *Home:* 37 Bernard Rd., Cromer, Norfolk, England.

CAREER: University of Glasgow, Glasgow, Scotland, assistant lecturer in Russian, 1961-63; University of St. Andrews, St. Andrews, Fife, Scotland, lecturer in Russian, 1963-71; writer, 1971—. *Member:* British University Association of Slavists, Association of Teachers of Russian.

WRITINGS: Understanding the Russians, Allen & Unwin, 1964; (editor) *Everyday Russian: A Reader*, Bradda Books, 1966; (editor) *Gogol's "Tale of How Ivan Ivanovich Quarrelled with Ivan Nikiforovich,"* Bradda Books, 1970; *The Chekhov Play: A New Interpretation*, Barnes & Noble, 1973; (translator with J. Forsyth) Anton Chekhov, *Chuckle with Chekhov: A Selection of Comic Stories*, Swallow House Books, 1975; *When Miss Emmie Was in Russia: English Governesses Before, During and After the October Revolu-*

tion, J. Murray, 1977; *Chekhov's Leading Lady: A Portrait of the Actress Olga Knipper*, J. Murray, 1979.

WORK IN PROGRESS: Translating Chekhov's early stories (1880-87).

SIDELIGHTS: Reviewing Harvey Pitcher's biography of Chekhov's wife, *Chekhov's Leading Lady: A Portrait of the Actress Olga Knipper*, Patrick Miles comments in the *Times Literary Supplement:* "Meticulously researched and written with great warmth, [the biography] conveys powerfully why of all the women who passed through Chevkhov's life it was Knipper whom he fell in love with most deeply. . . . Pitcher handles the mass of letters and memoirs with an extremely fine touch, and for many the new picture that emerges of Chekhov will seem unflattering. . . . But all this is to experience Chekhov in the process of living, as a real person not always adequately tackling human situations. It is a welcome addition to the efforts of Ronald Hingley, Virginia Llewellyn Smith and others over the years towards dissolving the image of Chekhov conveyed by Soviet hagiography."

BIOGRAPHICAL/CRITICAL SOURCES: Times Literary Supplement, April 25, 1980.

*   *   *

PLATH, David W(illiam)   1930-

PERSONAL: Born December 8, 1930, in Elgin, Ill.; son of Ernest Karl (a furniture retailer) and Laura (Baumgardt) Plath; married Marilyn Ann Lusher, August 25, 1956 (divorced April, 1979); children: Mark Ernest, Gail Christine. *Education:* Northwestern University, B.S., 1952; graduate study at Sophia University, Tokyo, Japan, 1954-55, and University of Michigan, summer, 1956; Harvard University, M.A., 1959, Ph.D., 1962. *Office:* Department of Anthropology, University of Illinois, Urbana, Ill. 61801.

CAREER: University of California, Berkeley, lecturer in anthropology, 1961-63; State University of Iowa, Iowa City, assistant professor, 1963-64, associate professor of anthropology, 1964-66; University of Illinois at Urbana-Champaign, associate professor, 1966-69, professor of anthroplogy and Asian studies, 1969—, head of department of anthropology, 1970-72. Visiting professor, Kyoto University, 1972-73, and Konan University, 1972-73 and 1976. Field researcher in Japan, 1959-61, 1965, and 1972-73; field director, International Honors Program, International School of America, 1969-70; director, Konan-Illinois Center, 1976. Member of joint committee on Japanese studies, American Council of Learned Societies-Social Science Research Council, 1977—. *Military service:* U.S. Naval Reserve, active duty, 1952-55; became lieutenant junior grade. *Member:* American Anthropological Association, American Association for the Advancement of Science, Association for Asian Studies, Gerontological Society.

WRITINGS: The After Hours: Modern Japan and the Search for Enjoyment, University of California Press, 1964; (contributor) June Helm, editor, *Essays on the Visual and Verbal Arts*, University of Washington Press, 1967; (with Yoshie Sugihara) *Sensei and His People: The Building of a Japanese Commune*, University of California Press, 1969; (editor) *Aware of Utopia*, University of Illinois Press, 1971; (contributor) Donald Cowgill and Lowell Holmes, editors, *Aging and Modernization*, Appleton-Century-Crofts, 1972; (contributor) Mary C. Durkin, editor, *People in States*, Addison-Wesley, 1972; (editor) *Adult Episodes in Japan*, E. J. Brill, 1975; (contributor) Thomas R. Williams, editor, *Socialization and Communication in Primary Groups*, Mouton, 1975; (contributor) Paul Baltes and Orville Brim, Jr.,

editors, *Life-Span Development and Behavior III*, Academic Press, 1980; *Long Engagements: Maturity in Modern Japan*, Stanford University Press, 1980. Contributor of articles, reviews, and translations to *Japan Interpreter, American Anthropologist, American Ethnologist, Journal of Asian Studies, Journal of Japanese Studies*, and other professional journals.

WORK IN PROGRESS: Studies of the human life cycle, especially in present-day Japan.

BIOGRAPHICAL/CRITICAL SOURCES: New York Review of Books, September 25, 1969.

*   *   *

PLATT, Eugene Robert   1939-

PERSONAL: Born February 20, 1939, in Charleston, S.C.; son of Paul Calhoun (a machinist) and Estell (Bell) Platt; children: Troye-Suzanne, Paul Calhoun II. *Education:* University of South Carolina, A.B., 1964; Trinity College, Dublin, Diploma in Anglo-Irish Literature, 1970; Clarion State College, M.A., 1973; additional study at Wake Forest University, Catholic University of America, University of South Carolina, and Florida State University. *Religion:* Episcopal. *Home:* 6907 Kincaid Ave., Falls Church, Va. 22042. *Office:* U.S. Commission on Civil Rights, Washington, D.C.

CAREER: Held various administrative posts with U.S. Civil Service in Charleston, S.C., Nashville, Tenn., and Washington, D.C., 1964-69; Clarion State College, Clarion, Pa., assistant to dean of student affairs, 1970-76; affiliated with Bureau of Indian Affairs, 1976-78, and New Orleans Outer Continental Shelf Office, Bureau of Land Management, 1978-79; currently writer-editor at U.S. Commission on Civil Rights, Washington, D.C. Active in the "Poets-in-the-Schools" programs of Alabama, Florida, Pennsylvania, South Carolina, and Virginia; has given poetry readings at numerous colleges, universities, institutes, and societies throughout the United States and in Ireland. *Military service:* U.S. Army, 1957-60; served as paratrooper and chaplain's assistant. *Awards, honors:* Hart Crane and Alice Crane Williams Memorial Fund Award, 1968, for poem "Above and Beyond," and 1969, for poem "Carolina Sands."

*WRITINGS—*Poetry: *coffee and solace* (collection), Commedia Publishing Division (Dublin), 1970; (with John Tomikel) *Six of One/Half Dozen of the Other* (chapbook), Allegheny Press, 1971; *Allegheny Reveries* (chapbook), Commedia Publishing Division, 1972; *an original sin* (collection), Briarpatch Press, 1974; (editor) *A Patrick Kavanagh Anthology*, Commedia Publishing Division, 1973; (editor) *Don't Ask Me Why I Write These Things*, Poets-in-the-Schools Program (Alabama), 1974; (editor) *The Turnings of Autumn*, Poets-in-the-Schools Program (Pennsylvania), 1976; (editor) *Metamorphosis*, Poets-in-the-Schools Program (Virginia), 1977. Guest poet, *Tar River Poets*, Issue XIII; contributor of poems to magazines in the United States and abroad, including *American, Blackbird Circle, Bitterroot, Capella, Crazy Horse, English Record, Icarus, Poet, Poet Lore, Shore Review, South Carolina Review*, and *Woodwind*. Poetry editor, *Sandlapper*, 1974-78; associate editor, *Tinderbox*.

WORK IN PROGRESS: A volume of new and selected poems, *South Carolina State Line;* editing *An Outer Banks Anthology*.

PLUMB, J(ohn) H(arold) 1911-

PERSONAL: Born August 20, 1911, in Leicester, England; son of James and Sarah Ann (Timson) Plumb. *Education:* University of Leicester, B.A. (first class honors), 1933; Christ's College, Cambridge, Ph.D., 1936. *Home:* Christ's College, Cambridge University, Cambridge, England; and The Old Rectory, Westhorpe, Stowmarket, Suffolk, England. *Agent:* Curtis Brown Ltd., 575 Madison Ave., New York, N.Y. 10022.

CAREER: Cambridge University, Cambridge, England, Ehrman Fellow in History at King's College, 1938-46, university lecturer, 1946-62, reader, 1962-65, professor of modern English history, 1966-74, chairman of department of history, 1966-68, director of studies in history, 1946-63, Christ's College, fellow, 1946—, master, 1978—. Visiting professor, Columbia University, 1960; Ford's Lecturer, Oxford University, 1965; Saposnekov Lecturer, City College of the City University of New York, 1968; Guy Stanton Ford Lecturer, University of Minnesota, 1969; Distinguished Visiting Professor, New York University, 1971-72 and 1976, and Washington University, 1977; Cecil and Ida Green Honors Professor, Texas Christian University, 1974; Mellon Lecturer, Folger Library, 1979. Former member of British television team, "Brains Trust." Trustee, National Portrait Gallery, 1960—; syndic, Fitzwilliam Museum, 1960-77. Affiliated with intelligence staff, British Foreign Office, 1940-45. *Member:* Royal Historical Society (fellow), Society of Antiquaries (fellow), British Academy (fellow), Royal Society of Literature (fellow), American Academy of Arts and Sciences (honorary foreign member), Century Club (New York), Brooks's Club, Beefsteak Club. *Awards, honors:* Litt.D., Cambridge University, 1957, University of Leicester, 1968, University of East Anglia, 1973, Bowdoin College, 1974, and University of Southern California, 1978.

WRITINGS: England in the Eighteenth Century, Penguin, 1950, reprinted, 1968; (with C. Howard) *West African Explorers,* Oxford University Press, 1952; *Chatham,* Macmillan, 1953, 2nd edition, Archon Books, 1965; *Sir Robert Walpole,* Volume I: *The Making of a Statesman,* Houghton, 1956, Volume II: *The King's Minister,* Cresset, 1960, Houghton, 1961, both volumes reprinted, Allen Lane, 1972, Augusta M. Kelley, 1973; *The First Four Georges,* Batsford, 1956, Macmillan, 1957, reprinted, Little, Brown, 1975, revised edition, Hamlyn, 1974.

The Horizon Book of the Renaissance (also see below), American Heritage Publishing, 1961, revised edition published as *The Penguin Book of the Renaissance,* Penguin, 1964; *The Golden Book of the Renaissance* (adaptation of *The Horizon Book of the Renaissance*), Golden Press, 1962; *Men and Centuries,* Houghton, 1963; *Men and Places,* Cresset, 1963; *A Pantheistic View of the Universe,* Stockwell, 1964; *The Italian Renaissance* (first published in *The Horizon Book of the Renaissance*), Harper, 1965; *The Origins of Political Stability: England, 1675-1725,* Houghton, 1967 (published in England as *The Growth of Political Stability in England: 1675-1725,* Macmillan, 1967); (with others) *Man versus Society in Eighteenth-Century Britain,* Cambridge University Press, 1968; *The Death of the Past,* Macmillan (London), 1969, Houghton, 1970.

In the Light of History, Allen Lane, 1972, Houghton, 1973; *Royal Heritage: The Treasure of the British Crown,* Harcourt, 1977 (published in England as *Royal Heritage: The Story of Britain's Royal Builders and Collectors,* British Broadcasting Corp., 1977); (with others) *The English Heritage,* Forum Press, 1978; *Georgian Delights,* Little, Brown, 1980.

Editor: *Studies in Social History: A Tribute to G. M. Trevelyan,* Harper, 1955; *The Crisis in the Humanities,* Penguin, 1964; *Renaissance Profiles* (first published in *The Horizon Book of the Renaissance*), Harper, 1965; *The History of Human Society,* Volume I, Knopf, 1965; *The Fontana History of Modern Europe, Volume I,* Harper, 1965. Contributor to history journals and to *Spectator, Listener, Sunday Times, Saturday Review, New York Times, Horizon, American Heritage, Encounter,* and *New York Review of Books.*

WORK IN PROGRESS: The History of British Institutions, for Penguin; *Sir Robert Walpole: The Last Years; Britain: The Sea-borne Empire, 1550-1800.*

SIDELIGHTS: A historian by profession, J. H. Plumb nevertheless holds the rather unusual notion that history, or as he prefers to call it, The Past, deserves to be put to rest once and for all. In his book on the subject, *The Death of the Past,* Plumb argues that not only has technological innovation diminished the past's ability to provide guidance to modern industrial societies, but, more significantly, that people have always tended to rewrite the past to suit their own ends—be it a priest who seeks to confirm a particular religious belief, a king who needs to justify his rule, or a mere "commoner" who wants to add a few illustrious members to an otherwise undistinguished family tree. This "created ideology with a purpose," as the author defines conventional history, is what has made freedom and economic prosperity such rare commodities, for those in power have always manipulated the past at the expense of the "little guy."

Of course, Plumb does not advocate doing away with history and historians altogether. According to William Appleman Williams of the *Nation,* Plumb believes the modern historian should attempt to "defuse" the power of the past "by removing the ideology of the historian and thereby transform what has been an instrument of social control into a tool of human improvement." In order to "cleanse the story of mankind," as Plumb himself states, the historian must "try and understand what happened, purely in its own terms.... [He must] see things as they really were, and from this study ... attempt to formulate processes of social change which are acceptable on historical grounds and none other." But the ideal historian has to do more than just uncover and explain historical events; Williams reports that Plumb also expects him to make "positive statements about human life" while developing "principles about social living" with the ultimate goal of demonstrating that "the condition of mankind has improved" throughout history.

Few observers criticize the spirit behind such a cause, but most doubt that what Plumb proposes is possible. Though a *Times Literary Supplement* critic, for example, calls *The Death of the Past* a "stimulating, courageous, and frequently learned book" which "deserves to be pondered by all who teach or value history," William H. McNeill, himself a historian, comments in the *Saturday Review* that the distinction Plumb makes between "history" (what *really* happened) and "The Past" (what the chroniclers *say* happened) "strikes me as completely false. What Professor Plumb hails as a new genus, history, is merely the onset of a climate of opinion in which he feels at home. Older uses of the past he analyzes, often wittily and well, as self-serving, erroneous, naive.... [But Plumb's] view of man's past ... seems quite as self-serving.... To claim that modern historians have a unique talisman that allows us to know things as they really were—apart, apparently, from the questions we ask and the conceptions we bring to the past—obscures rather than clarifies the real, indisputable advances that have occurred and are occurring in our understanding of mankind's history.

This little book . . . is briskly written, and abounds in arresting turns of phrase. But Plumb's brilliant style cannot really salvage a faulty idea.''

The *New Statesman* reviewer agrees, remarking that "there is not much one can do with [such] a confession of faith except sign it, and with a good deal of mental reservation I should be prepared to sign this one. . . . [But] I have the impression that Plumb is skating on pretty thin ice." The *Nation*'s Williams also sees "much truth in [Plumb's] analysis" but ultimately decides that following his advice "is to start down a path that will change the historian into a kind of superheated lay minister. At best, and by Plumb's own formulation, the historian becomes an advocate who offers one general answer to the questions he has raised. Plumb is trying to keep the crown on Clio's head even as he tells us that the old regime has collapsed.''

Melvin Maddocks of the *Christian Science Monitor*, responding to Plumb's question, "Can man face the future with hope and with resolution without a sense of the past?," concludes that this "is not the final question. The final question must go beyond the morale problem to ask: Can man even function without a sense of the past? . . . Are not the very standards by which historians think bound to be a conscious and subconscious heritage of the past? . . . The Futurist is born with a love of the vacuum. He longs for a brave, new, empty world. What he hates most is the sight of footprints in the sand. But the question-to-end-all-questions he may have to ask himself is: Would I want to live in the kind of world where footprints were not at least a possibility?''

AVOCATIONAL INTERESTS: Collecting French china and English silver; old wines, sailing.

BIOGRAPHICAL/CRITICAL SOURCES: Economist, December 20, 1969; *Christian Science Monitor,* December 24, 1969; *New Statesman,* January 9, 1970; *Times Literary Supplement,* January 22, 1970; *New Republic,* February 7, 1970; *New Yorker,* February 21, 1970; *Saturday Review,* February 21, 1970; *Nation,* March 9, 1970; *Washington Post,* March 20, 1979.

*   *   *

PLUMB, Joseph Charles, Jr. 1942-
(Charlie Plumb)

PERSONAL: Born November 3, 1942, in Gary, Ind.; son of Joseph Charles (a carpenter) and Margery (a secretary; maiden name, Stanford) Plumb. *Education:* U.S. Naval Academy, B.S., 1964. *Religion:* Presbyterian. *Agent:* Midwest Program Service, 208 Lake Quivira, Kansas City, Kan. 66106. *Office address:* Inform, Inc., Box 223, Kansas City, Mo. 64141.

CAREER: President, Inform, Inc., Kansas City, Mo., 1974—, and Midwest Program Service, Kansas City, Kan., 1979—. Director, Empire State Bank, 1974-76; lecturer. *Military service:* U.S. Navy, 1960-74; became lieutenant commander; received Air Medal, Navy Commendation Medal, Combat Action Medal, Vietnam Service Medal, Republic of Vietnam Campaign Medal, Purple Heart, and Silver Star. U.S. Naval Reserves, 1974—; currently commander.

WRITINGS—All under name Charlie Plumb: *I'm No Hero,* Independence Press, 1973; *The Last Domino,* Inform, Inc., 1975; (contributor) *Stand up, Speak out and Win,* Summit Enterprises, 1977; (contributor) *When the Going Gets Tough,* Revell, 1980.

WORK IN PROGRESS: Communicate, a book about letters from prison and analyses by graphologists of those letters;

Response, a book about letters and artwork received from children responding to Plumb's writing and lecturers.

SIDELIGHTS: Charlie Plumb once served as a fighter pilot flying F4-B Phantom jets from the deck of the aircraft carrier *U.S.S. Kitty Hawk.* He flew seventy-five combat missions during the Vietnam war before his plane was shot down. He then spent more than two thousand days in captivity, during which time he served as a specialist in underground communications and as group chaplain. He was repatriated early in 1973 and since then has made more than three hundred public appearances before schools, churches, and professional groups, telling the POW story and secrets of endurance.

*   *   *

PODLECKI, Anthony J(oseph) 1936-

PERSONAL: Born January 25, 1936, in Buffalo, N.Y.; son of Anthony Joseph (a civil servant) and Eugenia (Jendrasiak) Podlecki; married Jennifer Grube, July 28, 1962; children: Christopher, Julia, Antonia. *Education:* College of the Holy Cross, A.B., 1957; Oxford University, B.A., 1960, M.A., 1963; University of Toronto, M.A., 1961, Ph.D., 1963. *Politics:* Democrat. *Religion:* Roman Catholic. *Home:* 4524 West Seventh Ave., Vancouver, British Columbia, Canada. *Office:* Department of Classics, University of British Columbia, Vancouver, British Columbia, Canada.

CAREER: Northwestern University, Evanston, Ill., instructor, 1963-65, assistant professor of classics, 1965-66; Pennsylvania State University, University Park, associate professor, 1966-70, professor of classics, 1970-75, head of department, 1966-75; University of British Columbia, Vancouver, professor of classics and head of department, 1975—. Visiting fellow at Wolfson College, Oxford University, 1970; visiting member, Institute of Greek, University of Strasbourg, 1979.

MEMBER: American Philological Association, Archaeological Institute of America, American Association of University Professors, Classical Association of Canada, Classical Association of Great Britain, Joint Association of Classical Teachers (Great Britain), Classical Association of the Canadian West (member of executive committee), Classical Association of the Pacific Northwest (past president), Cambridge Philological Association (Great Britain), Phi Sigma Iota. *Awards, honors:* Woodrow Wilson fellowship and Fulbright scholarship, both 1957.

WRITINGS: (Editor) Cecil Torr, *Ancient Ships,* Argonaut, 1964; *The Political Background of Aeschylean Tragedy,* University of Michigan Press, 1966; (translator and author of commentary) Aeschylus, *Persians,* Prentice-Hall, 1970; *The Life of Themistocles: A Critical Survey of the Literary and Archaeological Evidence,* McGill-Queen's University Press, 1975; *Age of Glory: Imperial Athens in the Age of Pericles,* Macmillan, 1975.

WORK IN PROGRESS: The Early Greek Poets and Their Times.

*   *   *

POGUE, Forrest Carlisle 1912-

PERSONAL: Born September 17, 1912, in Eddyville, Ky.; son of Forrest C. and Fannye (Carter) Pogue; married Christine Brown, September 4, 1954. *Education:* Murray State Teachers College (now Murray State University), A.B., 1931; University of Kentucky, M.A., 1932; University of Paris, graduate study, 1937-38; Clark University, Ph.D., 1939. *Politics:* Democrat. *Religion:* Presbyterian. *Home:*

Apartment B211, 1111 Army-Navy Dr., Arlington, Va. 22202. *Office:* Apartment B207, 1111 Army-Navy Dr., Arlington, Va. 22202.

CAREER: Western Kentucky State Teachers College (now Western Kentucky University), Bowling Green, instructor in history, 1933; Murray State Teachers College (now Murray State University), Murray, Ky., 1933-42, began as instructor, became associate professor; U.S. Army, civilian historical writer in Paris, France, and Frankfurt, Germany, 1945-46, historian in office of Chief of Military History, Washington, D.C., 1946-52; Johns Hopkins University, Operations Research Office, research analyst at U.S. Army Headquarters, Heidelberg, Germany, 1952-54; Murray State College (now University), professor of history, 1954-56; George C. Marshall Research Library, Lexington, Va., director, 1956-74; executive director, George C. Marshall Research Foundation, 1965-74; Smithsonian Institution, National Museum of History and Technology, Washington, D.C., director of Dwight D. Eisenhower Institute for Historical Research, 1974—. Trustee, Marshall Foundation and Harry S Truman Library Institute. *Military service:* U.S. Army, 1942-45; served in European Theater; received Bronze Star, Croix de Guerre, and five campaign stars, including Normandy invasion arrowhead. *Member:* American Military Institute (past president), Committee on the History of the Second World War (past chairman), Oral History Association (past president), American Historical Association, National Education Association (life member), Organization of American Historians, Southern Historical Association, U.S. Capitol Historical Society (trustee), Senate Historical Office (chairman of advisory committee), American Legion. *Awards, honors:* LL.D., Murray State University, 1970; Litt.D., Washington and Lee University, 1970; L.H.D., Clark University, 1975.

WRITINGS: The Supreme Command, U.S. Government Printing Office, 1954; (co-author) *The Meaning of Yalta,* edited by John Snell, Louisiana State University Press, 1956; (contributor) Kent R. Greenfield, editor, *Command Decisions,* Harcourt, 1959; (contributor) Harry Coles, editor, *Total War and Cold War,* Ohio State University Press, 1962; *George C. Marshall,* Viking, Volume I: *Education of a General: 1880-1939,* 1963, Volume II: *Ordeal and Hope: 1939-1942,* 1966, Volume III: *Organizer of Victory: 1943-1945,* 1973; (contributor) *America's Continuing Revolution,* Doubleday, 1976; (contributor) Michael Carver, editor, *The War Lords,* Little, Brown, 1976. Also contributor to *D-Day: The Normandy Invasion in Retrospect,* 1970, and to *Bicentennial History of the United States,* 1976. Member of advisory committees on the publication of the Marshall papers and the Eisenhower papers.

WORK IN PROGRESS: Volume IV of the biography of George C. Marshall.

SIDELIGHTS: Ever since being chosen in 1956 to collect the personal papers of General George C. Marshall and to conduct a series of interviews with him, Forrest Pogue's life and work have more or less centered around the man who led American armies during World War II and eventually served as Secretary of Defense and Secretary of State. As Marshall's official biographer, Pogue sees his role as the "chance of a lifetime" rather than as the monumental research and writing task it has turned out to be. "Marshall was a unique man," the historian once explained to a *Washington Post* interviewer. "Unlike many of his contemporaries, he never bothered to write his memoirs nor, until very late in his life, would he submit to interviews. So, despite a career in the public eye, he remained a very private per-

son. . . . The interviews [I conducted] were rather difficult at first, because Marshall was never one to volunteer information. But once he became used to me and the tape recorder he really opened up." Contrary to his somewhat cold and aloof public reputation, Marshall, claims Pogue, was a very warm person. "He cared a great deal about his fellow man," his biographer notes, "and I think this was exemplified by his programs to rebuild through the Marshall Plan a Europe he had done so much to defeat during the war. Acts like that personified the man. He was the true blend of militarist and diplomat and that combination is rare."

For the most part, the success of Pogue's massive biographical study has come to depend on how well he manages to break through Marshall's reserve and reveal the "true" statesman. H. S. Hayward of the *Christian Science Monitor,* for example, calls Volume I an "excellent biography" due to its "expert job of synthesis on the man who, as much as anyone, was the architect of the modern American military machine." A *Newsweek* critic, noting that "the years of greatest strife and glory are still ahead as Pogue ends this volume," nevertheless concludes that "not even all the heroics of the war will surpass this cool, meticulous account of how the right man got to the right place at the right time."

"Mr. Pogue, a skilled military historian, has written with compassion, judgment and understanding," remarks H. W. Baldwin of the *New York Times Book Review.* "As any good biographer must, he 'identifies' with his subject. But there is no idolatrous 'worship,' and the general's virtues and weaknesses appear to this reviewer to be objectively—though sympathetically—portrayed." Despite these words of praise, however, Baldwin's overall impression is that "Mr. Pogue casts light, but he does not, for this reviewer, limn the full substance of the man."

The *Saturday Review*'s Walter Millis is somewhat less kind in his assessment of Volume I. "It would be idle to pretend that this . . . is other than a disappointment," he begins. "Whether through want of skill on the part of the biographer, or the resistant nature of his subject matter . . . , little sense either of the man or of what made him emerges. . . . Until [the later volumes] appear, one can return no just verdict either upon Marshall or his biographer."

While the *New York Times Book Review*'s Baldwin believes that Volume I fails to "limn the full substance of the man," Volume II (which covers the early war years), he writes, "is by virtue of the great events it describes and its detailed documentation, more impressive and far more interesting. . . . Well-written, meticulously researched, this portrait of a leader under stress adds corroborative evidence to the histories of World War II that have preceded it, and makes a great figure of that war, who had seemed to most men somewhat distant and frightening, come alive." H. A. DeWeerd of the *Virginia Quarterly Review* shares this opinion, stating: "Dr. Pogue has written a splendid account of the army high command in World War II. It makes an important contribution to the history of our times, and complements previously-published memories and official histories. . . . Marshall appears in this volume, as he did in the previous one, as a selfless man of lofty character and immense integrity."

The *New Republic*'s G. W. Johnson, however, is not so sure that Pogue successfully breaks through Marshall's reserve concerning the events covered in Volume II. He writes: "It is a high tribute to someone, but whether to Pogue or to Marshall no reviewer can determine, that the presentation is always so lucid, credible, calm, and apparently fair-minded, that the inexpert civilian reader is left with the conviction that this must be the truth of the matter.... One is keenly aware that Marshall's restraining hand lay heavily on Pogue. What concerns the General directly is presented with candor that is sometimes startling, but on what concerned others Marshall was grimly silent and imposed silence on his biographer."

A *Choice* critic, noting the amount of detail contained in Volume III, which covers the latter half of the war, calls the book a "basic and indispensable work.... [It] is based on exhaustive research and characterized by balanced judgments." L. E. Spellman of the *Library Journal* asserts that Pogue "knows his subject well, has the facts well in hand, and writes perceptively with a flair that many novelists would envy."

Concludes the *Journal of American History*'s H. L. Coles: "In this, the third volume, scholars see Marshall at his best as soldier and statesman and Pogue at his best as biographer and historian. The product of this happy combination is a basic and indispensable work on World War II.... Not all scholars will agree with [the author's] conclusions, but those who attempt to cover the same ground can ignore his analysis of the evidence only at their peril.... It will be difficult to equal, let alone surpass, the excellence of this volume."

BIOGRAPHICAL/CRITICAL SOURCES: New York Times Book Review, October 13, 1963, January 1, 1967, January 21, 1973; *Newsweek*, October 14, 1963; *Christian Science Monitor*, October 17, 1963; *Saturday Review*, October 19, 1963; *Virginia Quarterly Review*, winter, 1967; *New Republic*, January 14, 1967; *Washington Post*, June 19, 1969; *Library Journal*, September 1, 1972; *Choice*, May, 1973; *Journal of American History*, September, 1973.

—*Sketch by Deborah A. Straub*

*   *   *

POIRIER, Frank E(ugene) 1940-

PERSONAL: Born August 7, 1940, in Paterson, N.J.; son of Alice (Apelian) Poirier; married Darlene Macko, July 6, 1963; children: Alyson, Sevanne. *Education:* Paterson State College (now William Paterson College of New Jersey), B.A., 1962; University of Oregon, M.A., 1964, Ph.D., 1967. *Home:* 420 Greenglade Ave., Worthington, Ohio 43085. *Office:* Department of Anthropology, Ohio State University, Lord Hall, Columbus, Ohio 43210.

CAREER: University of Florida, Gainesville, assistant professor of psychiatry and anthropology, 1967-68; Ohio State University, Columbus, assistant professor, 1968-70, associate professor, 1970-73, professor of anthropology, 1973—. *Member:* International Primatological Society, American Association of Physical Anthropologists, American Anthropological Association, American Association for the Advancement of Science, Current Anthropology, Sigma Xi.

WRITINGS: (Editor) *Primate Socialization*, Random House, 1972; *Fossil Evidence: An Evolutionary Journal*, Mosby, 1973, 3rd edition, 1981; *In Search of Ourselves: Introduction to Physical Anthropology*, Burgess, 1974, 3rd edition, 1981; (co-editor) *Primate Biosocial Development*, Garland Publishing, 1979.

WORK IN PROGRESS: Research on the ecology and social behavior of the Nilgiri Langur.

*   *   *

POIRIER, Richard 1925-

PERSONAL: Born September 9, 1925, in Gloucester,

Mass.; son of Philip (a fisherman) and Annie (Kiley) Poirier. *Education:* Attended University of Paris, 1944-45; Amherst College, B.A., 1949; Yale University, M.A., 1951; postgraduate study, Cambridge University, 1952-53; Harvard University, Ph.D., 1959. *Home:* 16 West 11th St., New York, N.Y. 10011. *Office:* Department of English, Rutgers University, New Brunswick, N.J. 08903.

CAREER: Williams College, Williamstown, Mass., instructor, 1950-52; Harvard University, Cambridge, Mass., instructor, 1958-60, assistant professor of English, 1960-63; Rutgers University, New Brunswick, N.J., Marius Bewley Professor of English, 1963—, chairman of department 1963-72, director of graduate studies, 1970—. Vice-president, Literary Classics of America, Inc., 1979—. *Military service:* U.S. Army, 1943-46. *Member:* American Academy of Arts and Sciences, Phi Beta Kappa, Century Club. *Awards, honors:* Fulbright scholar; Bollingen fellow; Guggenheim fellow; honorary degree from Amherst College, 1978; Achievement Award from Academy of Arts and Letters, 1979.

WRITINGS: (Contributor) *William Faulkner: Two Decades of Criticism*, University of Michigan Press, 1951; *The Comic Sense of Henry James*, Oxford University Press, 1960; *A World Elsewhere*, Oxford University Press, 1966; *The Performing Self*, Oxford University Press, 1970; *Norman Mailer*, Viking, 1974; *Robert Frost: The Work of Knowing*, Oxford University Press, 1978.

Editor: (With Reuben A. Brower) *In Defense of Reading*, Dutton, 1962; (with W. L. Vance) *American Literature*, Little, Brown, 1970; (with Frank Kermode) *The Oxford Reader*, Oxford University Press, 1971. Also editor of *Prize Stories: The O. Henry Awards*, Doubleday, 1961-64; with William Abrahams, 1965-66. Editor, *Partisan Review*, 1963-74. Contributor of essays to various journals.

WORK IN PROGRESS: A study of "genius."

AVOCATIONAL INTERESTS: Travel, film, ballet, New York City.

BIOGRAPHICAL/CRITICAL SOURCES: New York Review, March 9, 1967; *National Review*, March 9, 1967, May 15, 1971; *Yale Review*, spring, 1967; *New Statesman*, May 12, 1967; *Times Literary Supplement*, May 18, 1967; *South Atlantic Quarterly*, autumn, 1967; *Commentary*, October, 1967; *New Republic*, May 1, 1971; *New Leader*, May 17, 1971; *New York Times*, October 16, 1972, October 5, 1977.

*   *   *

POLITZER, Heinrich 1910-1978
(Heinz Politzer)

PERSONAL: Born December 31, 1910, in Vienna, Austria; came to United States in 1947, naturalized citizen; died July 30, 1978, in Berkeley, Calif.; son of Moritz (a lawyer) and Marie H. (Loewenthal) Politzer; married Jane H. Horner, June 12, 1951; children: Maria Bettina Helen, Martin Andrew, David Henry, Stephen Benjamin, Eric Anthony. *Education:* Attended University of Vienna, University of Prague, 1929-34, and University of Pennsylvania, 1948; Bryn Mawr College, Ph.D., 1950. *Politics:* Democrat. *Religion:* Episcopalian. *Home:* 21 Florida Ave., Berkeley, Calif. 94707. *Office:* Department of German, University of California, Berkeley, Calif.

CAREER: Bryn Mawr College, Bryn Mawr, Pa., instructor, 1948-49, assistant professor of German, 1950-52; Oberlin College, Oberlin, Ohio, assistant professor, 1952-54, associate professor of German, 1954-60; University of California, Berkeley, professor of German, 1960-78, professor emeritus,

1978. Visiting summer professor, Middlebury College, 1948; Messenger Lecturer, Cornell University, 1962; lecturer, humanities seminar on the eighteenth century, Johns Hopkins University, 1963; visiting professor, Johann Wolfgang Goethe University, Frankfort am Main, 1965. Constituent member, U.S. Committee for the Study of Austrian Literature, 1968-78; senior fellow, Society for the Humanities, Cornell University, 1971-72. *Member:* International Arthur Schnitzler Research Association, International P.E.N., Modern Language Association of America, American Committee for Austrian Studies (first vice-president, beginning 1972), American Association of University Professors, American Association of Teachers of German, Sigmund Freud Society, Hugo von Hofmannsthal Gesellschaft, Philological Association of the Pacific Coast. *Awards, honors:* American Philosophical Society grants, 1953 and 1954; Guggenheim fellow, 1958-59, 1966-67, and 1974-75; Silver Medal, Commonwealth Club of California, 1963; Commander's Cross of Merit, Federal Republic of Germany, 1964; Austrian Cross of Honor for Arts and Letters, first class, 1966; Golden Goethe Medal, 1969; Grillparzer-Ring, Austrian Ministry of Education and Arts and Letters, 1972.

WRITINGS—All under name Heinz Politzer: (Editor) Franz Kafka, *Vor dem Gesetz,* Schocken, 1934; (co-editor) Kafka, *Gesammelte Schriften,* six volumes, Schocken, 1935; (editor) *Amerika erzaehlt* (American short stories), Volume I, Fischer, 1958, 4th edition, 1962, Volume II, 1971; (with J. W. Kurtz) *German: A Comprehensive Course for College Students,* Norton, 1959, revised edition, 1966; *Die glaeserne Kathedrale* (poems), Bergland, 1959; (editor) Johann Nestroy, *Des wusten Lebens fluecht'ger Reiz* (theater songs), Insel, 1961; (editor) Arthur Schnitzler, *Leutnant Gustl,* Fischer, 1962; *Franz Kafka: Parable and Paradox,* Cornell University Press, 1962, revised edition, 1966; (translator into German) Samuel Taylor Coleridge, *Der Reim von alten Seefahrer,* Insel, 1963; (editor) *Das Kafka-Buch: Eine innere Biographie in Selbstzeugnissen,* Fischer, 1965; (editor) *Grillparzer uber sich selbst: Aus den Tagebuchern,* Insel, 1965; *Das Schweigen der Sirenen: Studien zur deutschen und oesterreichischen Literatur,* Metzler, 1968; *Franz Grillparzer, oder Das abgruendige Biedermeier,* Molden, 1972; *Franz Kafka,* Wissenschaftliche Buchgesellschaft, 1973; *Hatte Oedipus einen Oedipus-Komplex?: Versuche zum Thema Psychoanalyse und Literatur,* Piper, 1974.

Contributor: *Fluegel der Zeit: Deutsche Gedichte, 1900-1950,* Fischer, 1956; *Das deutsche Drama,* August Bagel Verlag, 1958; *Kafka Today,* University of Wisconsin Press, 1958; *Dichter wider Willen,* Rhein-Verlag, 1958; *Museum der modernen Poesie,* Frankfurt-am-Main, 1960; *Panorama moderner Lyrik,* Sigbert Mohn Verlag, 1960; *An den Wind Geschrieben,* Agora, 1960; *Franz Werfel, 1890-1945,* University of Pittsburgh Press, 1961; *Interview mit Amerika,* Hymphenberger, 1962; David M. White and Robert H. Abel, editors, *The Funnies: An American Idiom,* Free Press of Glencoe, 1963; Earl R. Wasserman, editor, *Aspects of the Eighteenth Century,* Johns Hopkins Press, 1965. Also contributor to *Die neue Rundschau* (modern English and American verse), 1949, and to the *Jahrbuch der deutschen Schillergesellschaft,* 1960 and 1965. Contributor of more than eighty articles to professional journals in the United States and Germany.†

*   *   *

POLLAND, Madeleine A(ngela Cahill) 1918-

PERSONAL: Born May 31, 1918, in Kinsale, County Cork, Ireland; daughter of Patrick Richard (a civil servant) and Christina (Culkin) Cahill; married Arthur Joseph Polland (an accountant), June 10, 1946; children: Charlotte Frances, Fergus Adrian. *Politics:* Conservative. *Religion:* Roman Catholic. *Home:* Newstead, 58 Aldenham Ave., Radlett, Hertfordshire, England.

CAREER: Public library, Letchworth, England, assistant librarian, 1938-42; writer, 1958—. *Military service:* Women's Auxiliary Air Force, ground controlled interception division of radar, 1942-45. *Awards, honors:* New York Herald Tribune Honor Book award, 1961, for *Children of the Red King,* and 1962, for *Beorn the Proud.*

WRITINGS: Children of the Red King, Constable, 1960, Holt, 1961; *The Town across the Water,* Constable, 1961, Holt, 1963; *Beorn the Proud,* Constable, 1961, Holt, 1962; *Fingal's Quest,* Doubleday, 1961; *The White Twilight,* Constable, 1962, Holt, 1965; *Chuiraquimba and the Black Robes,* Doubleday, 1962; *The City of the Golden House,* Doubleday, 1963; *The Queen's Blessing,* Constable, 1963, Holt, 1964; *Flame over Tara,* Doubleday, 1964; *Mission to Cathay,* Doubleday, 1965; *Queen without Crown,* Constable, 1965, Holt, 1966; *Thicker Than Water* (adult fiction), Holt, 1966; *Deirdre,* Doubleday, 1967; *The Little Spot of Bother,* Hutchinson, 1967; *Minutes of a Murder,* Holt, 1967; *To Tell My People,* Hutchinson, 1968; *Stranger in the Hills,* Doubleday, 1968; *Random Army,* Hutchinson, 1969.

Shattered Summer, Doubleday, 1970; *Alhambra,* Doubleday, 1970; *Package to Spain,* Walker, 1971; *To Kill a King,* Holt, 1971; *A Family Affair,* Hutchinson, 1971; *Daughter of the Sea,* Doubleday, 1972 (published in England as *Daughter to Poseidon,* Hutchinson, 1972); *Double Shadow,* Fawcett, 1978; *Sabrina,* Delacorte, 1979; *All His Kingdoms,* Delacorte, 1980.

WORK IN PROGRESS: An untitled novel set in Spain, England, and Ireland, 1935-45.

SIDELIGHTS: Best-known as the author of historical novels written with the young reader in mind, Madeleine Polland has been widely praised for her ability to depict realistic and vivid characters with whom her audience can easily identify. "I have always been deeply aware of the reality of history," she explains, "and conscious of the people who made it."

BIOGRAPHICAL/CRITICAL SOURCES: New York Times Book Review, May 9, 1965, October 27, 1968; *Times Literary Supplement,* June 26, 1969; *Best Sellers,* March 15, 1971.

*   *   *

POMFRET, John Edwin 1898-

PERSONAL: Born September 21, 1898; son of Edwin Pomfret (a designer) and Mary (O'Rorke) Pomfret; married Sara Wise, August 28, 1926; children: John Dana. *Education:* University of Pennsylvania, A.B., M.A., Ph.D. *Home:* 1825 St. Julian Pl., 3H, Columbia, S.C. 29204.

CAREER: Princeton University, Princeton, N.J., instructor, 1925-27, assistant professor, 1927-33, associate professor of history, 1933-37; Vanderbilt University, Nashville, Tenn., professor of history and dean, Senior College-Graduate School, 1937-42; College of William and Mary, Williamsburg, Va., president, 1942-51; Huntington Library, San Marino, Calif., director, 1951-66. Associate trustee, University of Pennsylvania, 1946-59; trustee, Virginia Episcopal Theological Seminary, 1946-51, and Southwest Museum, 1952-66; president, Southern University Conference, 1948-49. *Military service:* U.S. Navy, 1918. *Member:* American Antiquarian Society, Massachusetts Historical Society, Phi Beta Kappa (member of senate, 1943-55; vice-president, United

Chapters, 1946-51), Pi Kappa Alpha, Franklin Inn Club (Philadelphia), Sunset Club (Los Angeles), Twilight Club (Pasadena). *Awards, honors:* LL.D. from University of Pennsylvania, 1943, University of Chattanooga (now University of Tennessee at Chattanooga), 1949, Mills College, 1958; Litt.D. from University of Southern California and Claremont Graduate School and University Center, both 1966; Tailteann Award in nonfiction for *The Struggle for Land in Ireland;* Graphic Arts Award for one of fifty best books of the year, for *California Gold Rush Voyages;* State and Local History award for *The Province of East New Jersey.*

WRITINGS: The Struggle for Land in Ireland, Princeton University Press, 1930; *The Geographic Pattern of Mankind,* Appleton, 1935; *The Province of West New Jersey,* Princeton University Press, 1954; *The Province of East New Jersey,* Princeton University Press, 1962; *A History of the Huntington Library and Art Gallery,* Henry E. Huntington, 1969; *Founding the American Colonies,* Harper, 1970; *Colonial New Jersey, a History,* Scribner, 1973.

Editor: *California Gold Rush Voyages,* Huntington Library, 1954; *Twelve Americans Speak,* Huntington Library, 1954; *The New Jersey Proprietors and Their Lands,* Van Nostrand, 1964.

*   *   *

POPPER, Karl R(aimund) 1902-

PERSONAL: Born July 28, 1902, in Vienna, Austria; son of Simon Siegmund Carl (a barrister) and Jenny (Schiff) Popper; married Josefine Anna Henninger, April 11, 1930. *Education:* University of Vienna, Ph.D., 1928; University of New Zealand, M.A., 1938; University of London, D. Lit., 1948. *Home:* Fallowfield, Manor Close, Manor Rd., Penn, Buckinghamshire HP10 8HZ, England. *Office:* London School of Economics and Political Science, University of London, London W.C.2, England.

CAREER: University of Canterbury, Christchurch, New Zealand, senior lecturer in philosophy, 1937-45; University of London, London School of Economics and Political Science, London, England, reader, 1945-49, professor of logic and scientific method, 1949-69, professor emeritus, 1969—. William James Lecturer in Philosophy, Harvard University, 1950; visiting professor, Institute for Advanced Studies, Vienna, 1956, University of California, Berkeley, 1962, University of Minnesota, 1962, Indiana University, 1963, New York University, 1963, Massachusetts Institute of Technology, 1963, and University of Denver, 1966; annual philosophical lecturer, British Academy, 1960; Herbert Spencer Lecturer, Oxford University, 1961 and 1973; Sherman Lecturer, University College, University of London, 1961; Farnum Lecturer, Princeton University, 1963; Arthur Holly Compton Memorial Lecturer, Washington University, St. Louis, 1965; Kenan University Professor, Emory University, 1969; Ziskind Professor, Brandeis University, 1969; Romanes Lecturer, Oxford University, 1972; Henry D. Broadhead Memorial Lecturer, University of Canterbury, 1973; Darwin Lecturer, Cambridge University, 1977; Tanner Lecturer, University of Michigan, 1978; Doubleday Lecturer, Smithsonian Institution, 1979; distinguished lecturer at other institutions in England, Australia, and New Zealand.

MEMBER: International Academy for Philosophy of Science (fellow), Academie Internationale d'Histoire des Sciences, Academie Europeenne des Sciences, des Arts, et des Lettres (member of British delegation), Institut de France, Academie Royale Belgique, American Academy of Arts and Sciences (honorary foreign member), British Academy (fellow), British Society for the History of Science (chairman of philosophy of science group, 1951-53), Aristotelian Society (president, 1958-59), British Society for the Philosophy of Science (president, 1959-61), Association for Symbolic Logic (member of council, 1951-54), Royal Institute of Philosophy (member of board, 1956—), Royal Society of New Zealand (honorary member), Royal Society of London (fellow), Phi Beta Kappa (Harvard chapter; honorary member).

AWARDS, HONORS: Center for Advanced Study in the Behavioral Sciences fellow, 1956-57; LL.D., University of Chicago, 1962, and University of Denver, 1966; knighted by Queen Elizabeth, 1965; Prize of the City of Vienna, 1965, for contributions to the moral and mental sciences; Salk Institute for Biological Studies visiting fellow, 1966-67; Lit.D., University of Warwick, 1971, University of Canterbury, 1973, and Cambridge University, 1980; University of Copenhagen Sonning Prize, 1973; Grand Decoration of Honour in Gold, Austria, 1976; American Political Science Association Lippincott Award, 1976, for *The Open Society and Its Enemies;* D.Litt., University of Salford, 1976, City University, London, 1976, and University of Guelph, 1978; Karl Renner Prize, 1978; Dr. rer. nat. h.c., University of Vienna, 1978; Dr. phil. h.c., University of Mannheim, 1978, and University of Salzburg, 1979; American Museum of Natural History Gold Medal, 1979, for distinguished service to science; Ehrenzeichen fuer Wissenschaft und Kunst, Austria, 1980; Order pour le Merite, German Federal Republic, 1980; Dr. rer. pol. h.c., University of Frankfurt am Main.

WRITINGS: Logik der Forschung: Zur Erkenntnistheorie der modernen Naturwissenschaft, Springer Verlag, 1935, 6th revised and enlarged edition, J.C.B. Mohr, 1976, translation by author of original edition published as *The Logic of Scientific Discovery,* Basic Books, 1959, 6th revised edition, Hutchinson, 1972; *The Open Society and Its Enemies,* Volume I: *The Spell of Plato,* Volume II: *The High Tide of Prophecy: Hegel, Marx, and the Aftermath,* Routledge & Sons, 1945, revised edition, Princeton University Press, 1950, 5th revised edition, 1966; *The Poverty of Historicism,* Beacon Press, 1957, 2nd edition, Routledge & Kegan Paul, 1960; *Conjectures and Refutations: The Growth of Scientific Knowledge,* Basic Books, 1962, 3rd edition, Routledge & Kegan Paul, 1969; *Objective Knowledge: An Evolutionary Approach,* Clarendon Press, 1972, revised edition, Oxford University Press (New York), 1979; *The Philosophy of Karl Popper,* two volumes, edited by Paul A. Schilpp, Open Court, 1974, revised autobiographical section published separately as *Unended Quest: An Intellectual Autobiography,* Fontana, 1976; (with John C. Eccles) *The Self and Its Brain,* Springer International, 1977; *Die beiden Grundprobleme der Erkenntnistheorie,* Volume I, J.C.B. Mohr, 1980.

Contributor: *Gesetz und Wirklichkeit,* [Innsbruck], 1949; *Readings in Philosophy of Science,* Scribner, 1953; *The State versus Socrates,* Beacon Press, 1954; *Contemporary British Philosophy,* Allen & Unwin, 1956; *British Philosophy in the Mid-Century,* Allen & Unwin, 1957; *Observation and Interpretation,* Butterworth & Co., 1957, Dover, 1962; *The Philosophy of History in Our Time,* Anchor Books, 1959, revised edition, 1961; *Philosophy for a Time of Crisis: An Interpretation, with Key Writings by Fifteen Great Modern Thinkers,* Dutton, 1959; *Theories of History,* Free Press of Glencoe, 1959; *Society, Law, and Morality,* Prentice-Hall, 1961; *Der Sinn der Geschichte,* C. H. Beck, 1961; *Geist und Gesicht der Gegenwart,* Europa Verlag, 1962; *Philosophy for a Time of Crisis,* by Albert Einstein, E. M. Forster, Karl R. Popper, and Bertrand Russell, Kinseido, 1962; *Club Vol-*

taire, Szczesny Verlag, 1963; *Plato: Totalitarian or Democrat?*, Prentice-Hall, 1963; *The Philosophy of Rudolf Carnap*, Open Court, 1964; *Theorie und Realitaet*, J.C.B. Mohr, 1964; *Form and Strategy in Science*, D. Reidel, 1964; *The Socratic Enigma*, Bobbs-Merrill, 1964; *Human Understanding: Studies in the Philosophy of David Hume*, Wadsworth, 1965; *Versaeumte Lektionen*, Sigbert Mohn Verlag, 1965; *Philosophical Problems of the Social Sciences*, Macmillan, 1965; *Mind, Matter, and Method: Essays in Honor of Herbert Feigl*, University of Minnesota Press, 1966; *Quantum Theory and Reality*, Springer Verlag, 1967. Also contributor to *Logik der Sozialwissenschaften*, 1965.

Contributor of more than 100 articles to philosophy and science journals. Member of editiorial board, *British Journal for the Philosophy of Science, Ratio, Monist, Dialectica,* and *Erfahrung und Denken.*

WORK IN PROGRESS: Three additional volumes of *Die beiden Grundprobleme der Erkenntnistheorie.*

BIOGRAPHICAL/CRITICAL SOURCES: New Scientist, Volume V, Number 124, 1959; *Archiv fuer Rechts und Sozialphilosophie,* Volume XLVI, Number 3, 1960; *New Society,* September 12, 1963; Mario Bunge, editor, *The Critical Approach to Science and Philosophy: Essays in Honor of Karl R. Popper,* Free Press of Glencoe, 1964; Bryan Magee, *Karl Popper,* Viking, 1973 (published in England as *Popper,* Fontana, 1973); Paul A. Schilpp, editor, *The Philosophy of Karl R. Popper,* two volumes, Open Court, 1974; Karl R. Popper, *Unended Quest: An Intellectual Autobiography,* Fontana, 1976; Robert Ackermann, *The Philosophy of Karl Popper,* University of Massachusetts Press, 1976.

*   *   *

PORTER, Hal 1911-

PERSONAL: Born February 16, 1911, in Albert Park, Victoria, Australia; son of Harold Owen (an engineer) and Ida Violet (Ruff) Porter; married Olivia Parnham, 1939 (divorced, 1943). *Education:* Attended schools in Kensington and Bairnsdale, Victoria, Australia. *Politics:* Liberal-Country Party (Conservative). *Religion:* Church of England. *Home:* Glen Avon, Garvoc, Victoria, Australia.

CAREER: Schoolmaster in Williamstown, Australia, 1927-37, Adelaide, South Australia, 1940-45, Hobart, Tasmania, 1946, Sydney, New South Wales, Australia, 1948, and Ballaarat, Victoria, Australia, 1948-49; George Hotel, St. Kilda, Victoria, manager, 1949; Independents' School, Nijimura, Japan, schoolmaster, 1949-50; Theatre Royal, Hobart, producer, actor, and costume and set designer, 1951-52; Bairnsdale Municipal Library, Bairnsdale, Victoria, chief librarian, 1953-57; Shepparton Regional Library, Shepparton, Victoria, chief regional librarian, 1958-61; currently free-lance writer. Lecturer at Japanese universities under aegis of Australian Department of External Affairs, 1967; lecturer, Ca Foscari University, 1972. Australian representative, Edinburgh Festival, 1962.

AWARDS, HONORS: Short story prize, Sydney Sesquicentenary Literary Competitions, 1938; Commonwealth Literary Fund fellowships, 1956, 1960, 1964, 1968, and 1972; short story prizes, Sydney Journalists' Club award, 1957 and 1959; Commonwealth Literary Fund grants, 1958 and 1960; Adelaide Festival of Arts short story prize, 1962, nonfiction award, 1966, novel award, 1968, and Captain Cook Award, 1970; *Encyclopaedia Britannica* award, 1967; A.N.Z. Bank Local History Award, 1977.

WRITINGS: Short Stories, Adelaide Advertiser, 1943; *The*

Hexagon (poetry), Angus & Robertson, 1956; (editor) *Australian Poetry, 1957,* Angus & Robertson, 1958; *A Handful of Pennies* (novel), Angus & Robertson, 1958; *The Tilted Cross* (novel), Faber, 1961, revised edition, Rigby (Adelaide), 1971; *A Bachelor's Children* (short stories), Angus & Robertson, 1962; (editor) *Coast to Coast: Australian Stories 1961-1962,* Angus & Robertson, 1962; *The Watcher on the Cast-Iron Balcony* (autobiography), Faber, 1963, Transatlantic, 1964; *Stars of Australian Stage and Screen,* Rigby, 1964, Tri-Ocean, 1965; *The Cats of Venice* (short stories), Angus & Robertson, 1965, Tri-Ocean, 1966; *The Paper Chase* (autobiography), Angus & Robertson, 1966; (self-illustrated) *The Actors: An Image of the New Japan,* Angus & Robertson, 1968; *Elijah's Ravens: Poems,* Angus & Robertson, 1968.

Mr. Butterfry and Other Tales of New Japan (short stories), Angus & Robertson, 1970; *Selected Stories,* Angus & Robertson, 1971; *The Right Thing* (novel), Rigby, 1971; (editor) *It Could Be You* (short stories), Rigby, 1972; *In an Australian Country Graveyard and Other Poems,* Thomas Nelson (West Melbourne), 1974; *Fredo Fuss Love Life: Short Stories,* Angus & Robertson, 1974; *The Extra* (autobiography), Thomas Nelson, 1975; *Bairnsdale: Portrait of an Australian Country Town* (history), John Ferguson, 1977; *Seven Cities of Australia* (travel), John Ferguson, 1978; *The Portable Hal Porter* (collected works), University of Queensland Press, 1980; *The Clairvoyant Goat* (short stories), Thomas Nelson, 1980.

Plays: *The Tower* (also see below; three-act; first produced in London at Hampstead Theatre Club, June, 1962), published in *Three Australian Plays,* edited by H. G. Kippax, Penguin, 1963; *The Professor* (three-act; first produced on West End at Royal Court Theatre, May, 1965), Faber, 1966; *Eden House* (also see below; three-act; first produced in Melbourne at St. Martin's Theatre, March 26, 1969; produced as "Home on the Pig's Back" in London at Richmond Theatre, February 28, 1972), Angus & Robertson, 1969; *Parker* (also see below; three-act; first produced in Ballarat at National Theatre, February, 1972), Angus & Robertson, 1971.

Television plays—All networked by Australian Broadcasting Commission: "The Tower" (based on play of same title), 1964; "The Forger," 1965; "Eden House" (based on play of same title), 1971; "Parker" (based on play of same title), 1972. Also author of other television plays for Australian Broadcasting Commission.

Work is represented in anthologies, including *The Penguin Book of Australian Short Stories,* edited by Harry Heseltine, Penguin, 1976, and *An Australian Selection,* edited by John Barnes, Angus & Robertson, 1977. Contributor of stories and articles to magazines and journals, including *Southerly, Vogue, Quadrant, Flame, Australian Letters, London Magazine, Meanjin Quarterly,* and *Texas University.*

WORK IN PROGRESS: Three novellas.

SIDELIGHTS: Commenting on his writing, Hal Porter wrote *CA:* "I have always felt myself a writer, and had works published from the age of ten but did not become a 'professional' writer until I was fifty. I never sit down to write until I've mentally worked out what needs to be written. I write in long hand, and slowly, polishing and perfecting the while, type from this the one and only copy. The sole advice I have to aspiring writers is never *never* to face a blank sheet of paper without having worked out, as scrupulously as possible, what they propose writing.

"Throughout the years I have been influenced by numberless writers but have so absorbed the varicoloured tricks of technique, nuances of style, subtleties of approach, that I can no longer spot the particular influence—but they were a distinguished lot: Tchekov, Katharine Mansfield, V. S. Pritchett, Henry James, Colette, Evelyn Waugh, Harold Nicolson, Jean Stafford, Eudora Welty, Edith Wharton, Vladimir Nabokov, Joseph Conrad, Elizabeth Bowen, Saki, E. M. Forster, Charles Dickens, and others, most of them vividly conscious of words, all of them stylists of the impeccable sort (one could perhaps omit Dickens).

"For an Australian who wants to make Australians clear to the rest of the world, I have had to be both florid and patient, both baroque and meticulous, both cruelly careful and gaudy. There has been the need to superimpose the more sardonic and sophisticated and forthright image on the false image which is still fashionable in the works of such *poseurs* as Sidney Nolan (with his nineteenth-century lies) and Patrick White (with his fictitious, un-Australian suburbia)." Generally, he refuses to comment on the work of other Australians, feeling that "that sort of bloody work can be left to writers *manque*, log-rollers, et al, to the sorts of people who write for the sorts of people who read what is written for them. In a sense I [also] write only for those who read me—there are so many kinds of public. [But] I should die of mortification if a Morris West fan were to become a fan of mine."

As for activities other than writing, Porter notes: "[I] have traveled extensively in the Old World and the East. [I am] particularly fascinated by Japan—intend to live there for several years. [I] have lived in London, Edinburgh, Athens, Venice, and Paris for months at a time, and in other places for shorter periods. [I] have no desire to see South Africa, U.S.A., Canada, or New Zealand. Collect Japanese prints—especially Hokusai. [I] grow old-fashioned roses, but am a particularly perfervid all-round gardener. (I live on cattle property and grow all the flowers from English calendars.) [I] abhor organized sport either as participant or watcher."

BIOGRAPHICAL/CRITICAL SOURCES: Hal Porter, *The Watcher on the Cast-Iron Balcony* (autobiography), Faber, 1963, Transatlantic, 1964; Porter, *The Paper Chase* (autobiography), Angus & Robertson, 1966; *Times Literary Supplement*, May 4, 1967; *Books and Bookmen*, July, 1967; *Variety*, April 16, 1969; *Stage*, March 2, 1972; Mary Lord, *Hal Porter*, Oxford University Press, 1974; Porter, *The Extra* (autobiography), Thomas Nelson, 1975.

*   *   *

POSTGATE, Raymond (William)   1896-1971

PERSONAL: Born November 6, 1896, in Cambridge, England; died March 25, 1971, in England; son of J. P. (professor of Latin at Liverpool University) and Edith (Allen) Postgate; married Daisy Lansbury, November 17, 1918; children: John Raymond, Richard Oliver. *Education:* Attended St. John's College, Oxford. *Politics:* Socialist. *Home:* Red Lion Cottage, Blean, Whitstable, Kent, England. *Agent:* A. P. Watt & Son, 26/28 Bedford Row, London WC1R 4HL, England. *Office:* 14 Buckingham St., London W.C.2, England.

CAREER: Journalist and writer, London, England, 1918-71. Foreign sub-editor, *Daily Herald*, 1919-23; assistant editor, *Lansbury's Weekly*, 1925-27; editor, *Fact*, 1936-39, and *Tribune*, 1940-42. European representative, Alfred A. Knopf, Inc., 1929-49; government servant, Board of Trade and Ministry of Supply, 1942-48. Fellow, Trinity College, Cambridge University. *Member:* National Union of Journalists, Authors' Society, Good Food Club (founder), Savile Club.

WRITINGS: The International during the War, Herald, 1918; *The Bolshevik Theory*, Richards, 1920; *Revolution from 1798 to 1906*, Richards, 1920, reprinted, Harper, 1962; *The Workers' International*, Harcourt, 1920; *Chartism and the "Trades Union,"* [London], 1922; *Out of the Past: Some Revolutionary Sketches*, Labour Publishing Co., 1922, Vanguard, 1926 (published in India as *Revolutionary Biographies*, Arka, 1922); *The Builders' History*, Labour Publishing Co., 1923; (translator) *Eve of Venus*, Houghton, 1924; *Murder, Piracy and Treason: A Selection of Notable English Trials*, Houghton, 1925; *A Short History of the British Workers*, Plebs League, 1926; (with others) *A Worker's History of the Great Strike*, Plebs League, 1927; *That Devil Wilkes*, Vanguard, 1929, revised edition, Dobson, 1956.

(Editor) James Boswell, *The Conversations of Dr. Johnson*, Vanguard, 1930, reprinted, Taplinger, 1970; *Dear Robert Emmet*, Vanguard, 1932 (published in England as *Robert Emmet*, M. Secker, 1931); *No Epitaph* (novel), Hamish Hamilton, 1932, published as *Felix and Anne*, Vanguard, 1933; *Karl Marx*, Hamish Hamilton, 1933; *How to Make a Revolution*, Vanguard, 1934; *What to Do with the B.B.C.*, Hogarth, 1935; (with G. Aylmer Vallance) *England Goes to Press: The English People's Opinion on Foreign Affairs As Reflected in Their Newspapers since Waterloo (1815-1937)*, Bobbs-Merrill, 1937 (published in England as *Those Foreigners: The English People's Opinion on Foreign Affairs As Reflected in Their Newspapers since Waterloo*, Harrap, 1937); *A Pocket History of the British Workers to 1919*, Fact Ltd., 1937; (with G.D.H. Cole) *The British Common People, 1746-1938*, Knopf, 1939 (published in England as *The Common People, 1746-1938*, Methuen, 1939, revised edition published as *The Common People, 1746-1946*, 1956), revised edition published as *The British People, 1746-1946*, Barnes & Noble, 1961.

Verdict of Twelve (novel), Doubleday, 1940, reprinted, Hodder & Stoughton, 1969; (compiler) *Detective Stories of Today*, Faber, 1940; *A Pocket History of the British Working Class*, N.C.L.C. Publishing Society (Scotland), 1942, 3rd edition, 1964; *Let's Talk It Over: An Argument about Socialism for the Unconverted*, Fabian Society, 1942; *Somebody at the Door* (novel), Knopf, 1943, reprinted, Henry Publications Ltd., 1976; (reviser) H. G. Wells, *The Outline of History, Being a Plain History of Life and Mankind*, Garden City Publishing, 1949, revised edition, Doubleday, 1971.

The Plain Man's Guide to Wine, M. Joseph, 1951, Eriksson-Taplinger, 1960, revised edition by John Arlott, Sphere Books, 1978; (translator) Sidonie G. Colette, *Mitsou*, Secker & Warburg, 1951; *The Life of George Lansbury*, Longmans, Green, 1951; *The Ledger Is Kept* (novel), M. Joseph, 1953; *Alphabet of Wine*, Jenkins, 1955; *Story of a Year: 1848*, J. Cape, 1955, Oxford University Press (New York), 1956, reprinted, Greenwood Press, 1975; (editor) Paul Reboux, *Food for the Rich*, Anthony Blond, 1958; *Every Man Is God*, M. Joseph, 1959, Simon & Schuster, 1960.

The Home Wine Cellar, Jenkins, 1960; *The Good Food Guide to London*, Consumers' Association, 1968; *Story of a Year: 1798*, Harcourt, 1969; *Portuguese Wine*, Dent, 1969; (editor and translator) *The Agamemnon of Aeschylus*, Rampant Lions Press, 1969. Also compiler-publisher of *Good Food Guide to Britain* (biennial), beginning 1950. Departmental editor, *Encyclopaedia Britannica*, 14th edition, 1927-28. Contributor to *Holiday, Good Housekeeping, Guardian, Sunday Times*, and other newspapers and magazines.†

POTTLE, Frederick A(lbert) 1897-

PERSONAL: Born August 3, 1897, in Lovell, Me.; son of Fred Leroy and Annette (Kemp) Pottle; married Marion Isabel Starbird (cataloger of the Boswell Papers in the Isham Collection at Yale University), 1920; children: Annette (deceased), Christopher, Samuel (deceased). *Education:* Colby College, A.B. (summa cum laude), 1917; Yale University, M.A., 1921, Ph.D., 1925. *Religion:* Episcopalian. *Home:* 35 Edgehill Rd., New Haven, Conn. *Office:* Department of English, Yale University, Box 1504A Yale Station, New Haven, Conn.

CAREER: University of New Hampshire, Durham, assistant professor, 1921-23; Yale University, New Haven, Conn., instructor, 1925-26, assistant professor, 1926-30, professor, 1930-42, Emily Sanford Professor of English Literature, 1942-44, Sterling Professor of English, 1944-66, professor emeritus, 1966—. *Military service:* U.S. Army, American Expeditionary Forces, 1917-19. *Member:* Modern Language Association of America, Mediaeval Academy of America, Guild of Scholars, American Association of University Professors, American Academy of Arts and Sciences, American Philosophical Society, Provincial Utrechts Genootschap van Kunsten en Wetenschappen, Phi Beta Kappa, Alpha Tau Omega, Grolier Club, Ends of the Earth Club, Elizabethan Club. *Awards, honors:* Litt.D., Colby College, 1941, and Rutgers University, 1951; LL.D., University of Glasgow, 1936; Guggenheim fellow, 1945-46 and 1952-53.

WRITINGS: Stretchers: The Story of a Hospital Unit on the Western Front, Yale University Press, 1929; *The Literary Career of James Boswell,* Clarendon Press, 1929, reprinted, 1965; *The Idiom of Poetry,* Cornell University Press, 1941, revised edition, 1946, reprinted, Indiana University Press, 1963; *Shelley and Browning: A Myth and Some Facts,* Archon Books, 1965; *James Boswell: The Earlier Years 1740-1769,* McGraw, 1966; (with Chauncey Brewster Tinker) *A New Portrait of James Boswell,* Folcroft Library Editions, 1973.

Editor of Boswell Papers; published by McGraw: *Boswell's London Journal, 1762-1763,* 1950; *Boswell in Holland, 1763-1764,* 1952; *Boswell on the Grand Tour: Germany and Switzerland, 1764,* 1953; (with Frank Brady) *Boswell on the Grand Tour: Italy, Corsica, and France, 1765,* 1955; (with Brady) *Boswell in Search of a Wife, 1766-1769,* 1956; (with W. K. Wimsatt) *Boswell for the Defence, 1769-1774,* 1959; *Boswell's Journal of a Tour to the Hebrides,* 1962; (with Charles Ryskamp) *Boswell: The Ominous Years, 1774-1776,* 1963; (with Charles McC. Weis) *Boswell in Extremes, 1776-1778,* 1970; (with Joseph W. Reed) *Boswell, Laird of Auchinleck, 1778-1782,* 1977; (with Irma S. Lustig) *Boswell: The Applause of the Jury, 1782-1785,* 1981. Also editor of private papers of James Boswell, privately printed, 1930-34; chairman of editorial committee, Yale edition (research edition) of the private papers of James Boswell, Volume I: *Correspondence of James Boswell and John Johnston of Grange,* McGraw, 1966.

WORK IN PROGRESS: Copy for the two remaining volumes of the McGraw edition of Boswell's journals and for the first two volumes of the research edition of Boswell's journals; editing further volumes of the Boswell Papers.

SIDELIGHTS: Though he has devoted a great deal of his career to editing the papers of Scottish lawyer and biographer James Boswell, Frederick Pottle admits that the academic life was not his first choice. "From 1917 to 1920 I thought I was a poet and perhaps a writer of fiction," he told *CA.* "At Yale in 1920 I fell deeply in love with scholarship

and shaped my career accordingly. To all but a few writers some assured income apart from publication is necessary. I solved my problem by university teaching. I cannot think of a better solution for all but the giants."

BIOGRAPHICAL/CRITICAL SOURCES: From Sensibility to Romanticism: Essays Presented to Frederick A. Pottle, edited by Frederick Hilles, Oxford University Press, 1965; *New York Times,* February 8, 1966; *Times Literary Supplement,* January 12, 1967; *Carleton Miscellany,* fall, 1967; *Sewanee Review,* autumn, 1968; *Newsweek,* November 16, 1970; *Saturday Review,* February 6, 1971.

*   *   *

PRATT, John Lowell 1906-1968

PERSONAL: Born February 22, 1906, in Montclair, N.J.; died December 25, 1968; son of John Barnes and Mabel (Dodge) Pratt; married first wife, Katharine Warren Jennison, August 15, 1931; married Elizabeth Richmond, November 27, 1952; children: (first marriage) John C., Anthony Barnes, Nancy Jennison (Mrs. Frank Bottero). *Education:* Dartmouth College, A.B., 1929. *Politics:* Republican.

CAREER: A. S. Barnes & Co. (publishers), New York City, president, 1943-59; American Sports Publishing Co., New York City, president, 1959; Thomas Nelson & Sons (publishers), New York City, vice-president 1960-62; J. Lowell Pratt & Co. (sports and recreational publishers), New York City, owner and head, 1962-65. *Military service:* U.S. Navy, three years; became lieutenant commander; received Navy unit citation. *Member:* Coffee House Club and Dutch Treat Club (both New York).

WRITINGS: (Editor) *Sport, Sport, Sport,* F. Watts, 1960; (editor) *More Sport, Sport, Sport,* F. Watts, 1962; *Creative Sports Series,* six volumes, Creative Educational Society, 1962; (editor) *Pro, Pro, Pro,* F. Watts, 1963; (with Jim Benagh) *Official Encyclopedia of Sports,* F. Watts, 1964; (editor) *Baseball's All-Stars,* Doubleday, 1967; (editor) *Currier & Ives Chronicles of America,* Hammond, 1968.†

*   *   *

PREBBLE, John Edward Curtis 1915-
(John Curtis)

PERSONAL: Born June 23, 1915, in Edmonton, Middlesex, England; son of John William (a petty officer in the Royal Navy) and Florence (Wood) Prebble; married Betty Golby, August, 1936; children: John Gade, Simon Christopher, Sarah Brione. *Education:* Attended public school in Saskatchewan, Canada, and Latymer Upper School in London, England. *Home:* Shaw Coign, Alcocks Lane, Burgh Heath, Surrey, England. *Agent:* Curtis Brown Ltd., 1 Craven Hill, London W2 3EP, England.

CAREER: Reporter, columnist, and feature writer for various magazines and newspapers in London, England, 1934-40, 1946-52; free-lance writer, 1952—. *Military service:* British Army, 1940-46; served with Royal Artillery, 1940-45; reporter with Army newspapers in Hamburg, Germany, 1945-46. *Member:* International P.E.N., Royal Society of Literature (fellow), Society of Authors, National Union of Journalists, Writers Guild, Press Club. *Awards, honors:* Western Writers of America Spur Award, 1960, for best western historical novel, *The Buffalo Soldiers,* and 1962, for best western short story; National Association of Independent Schools Award, 1960, for *The Buffalo Soldiers.*

WRITINGS—All published by Secker & Warburg, except as indicated; novels, except as indicated: *Where the Sea*

Breaks, 1944, new edition, 1971; *The Edge of the Night*, Sloane, 1948 (published in England as *The Edge of Darkness*, 1948); *Age without Pity*, Henry Holt, 1950; *The Mather Story*, 1954; *The Brute Streets*, 1954; *My Great-Aunt Appearing Day* (short stories), 1958, enlarged edition published as *Spanish Stirrup*, Holt, 1973; *The Buffalo Soldiers*, Harcourt, 1959, new edition, Secker & Warburg, 1972.

Histories, except as indicated: (With J. A. Jordan) *Elephants and Ivory* (biography), Rinehart, 1956 (published in England as *Mongaso*, Nicholas Kaye, 1956); *Disaster at Dundee*, Harcourt, 1956 (published in England as *The High Girders*, 1956, new edition, 1966); *Culloden*, 1961, Atheneum, 1962; *The Highland Clearances*, 1963; *Glencoe*, Holt, 1966; *The Darien Disaster*, Holt, 1968; *The Lion in the North*, Coward, 1971; *The Massacre at Glencoe*, Viking, 1973; *Mutiny: Highland Regiments in Revolt*, 1975.

Also author of screenplays, including "Zulu," "When the Lion Feeds," "The Killing Season," and "Death Watch," all Avco Embassy, 1968; author of television documentaries and plays, including episodes of "The Six Wives of Henry VIII," "Elizabeth R," "The Borgias," "History of the English Speaking Peoples," and "The Love School," all for the British Broadcasting Corp., and eight episodes of "Churchill: The Wilderness Years," for ITV. Contributor to magazines in Great Britain and the United States.

*   *   *

PRESBERG, Miriam Goldstein 1919-1978 (Miriam Gilbert)

PERSONAL: Born December 1, 1919, in New York, N.Y.; died June 13, 1978; daughter of Charles and Kate (Kinstler) Goldstein; married Abe Presberg, June 18, 1944; children: Karen Laurie, Andrea Claire. *Education:* Hunter College (now Hunter College of the City University of New York), B.A., 1940. *Home:* 146-47 29th Ave., Flushing, N.Y. 11354.

CAREER: Robert M. McBride Co., New York City, secretary to sales manager, 1940-42; Didier Publishing Co., New York City, assistant to president, 1942-43; Arco Publishing Co., New York City, assistant to president, 1943-44; Island Press, New York City, editor, 1944-46; Authors' and Publishers' Service, New York City, director, 1946-78. *Awards, honors:* Brotherhood award for the best magazine fiction of the year, National Conference of Christians and Jews, 1962.

WRITINGS—Under name Miriam Gilbert: *Eli Whitney: Master Craftsman*, Abingdon, 1956; *Jane Addams: World Neighbor*, Abingdon, 1960; *Starting a Terrarium*, Hammond, Inc., 1961, revised edition published as *Science-Hobby Book of Terrariums*, Lerner, 1968; *Starting an Aquarium*, Hammond, Inc., 1961, revised edition published as *Science-Hobby Book of Aquariums*, Lerner, 1968; *Karen Gets a Fever*, Medical Books for Children, 1961; *Cross Country Adventure*, Hammond, Inc., 1961; *Starting a Shell Collection*, Hammond, Inc., 1961, revised edition published as *Science-Hobby Book of Shell Collecting*, Lerner, 1968; *Starting a Rock and Mineral Collection*, Hammond, Inc., 1961, revised edition published as *Science-Hobby Book of Rocks and Minerals*, Lerner, 1968; *Henry Ford: Maker of the Model T*, Houghton, 1962; *The Mighty Voice: Isaiah, Prophet and Poet*, Jewish Publication Society, 1963; *Money and Mud: The Life of John D. Rockefeller*, American Southern Publishing, 1964; *Shy Girl: The Story of Eleanor Roosevelt, First Lady of the World*, Doubleday, 1965; *First Party*, Hastings House, 1966; *Glory Be! The Career of a Young Hair Stylist*, Hastings House, 1967; *Rosie: The Oldest Horse in St. Augustine*, Island Press, 1967; *This Is My Country: A*

Child's Pictorial Guide to the United States, Lion Press, 1968; (with May Guy) *A Doctor Discusses the Care and Development of Your Baby*, Budlong, 1969; (with Marie Pichel Warner) *A Doctor Discusses Breast Feeding*, Budlong, 1970. Contributor of short stories and articles to children's magazines, and author for newspaper syndicates. Copy editor, *Coronet*, 1973.†

*   *   *

PRESS, John (Bryant) 1920-

PERSONAL: Born January 11, 1920, in Norwich, Norfolk, England; son of Edward Kenneth (a businessman) and Gladys (Cooper) Press; married Janet Crompton, December, 20, 1947; children: Roger Crompton, Sara Miranda Judith. *Education:* Corpus Christi College, Cambridge, B.A., 1942, M.A., 1946. *Religion:* Church of England. *Home:* East End Farm, East End, North Leigh, Witney OX8 6PX, England.

CAREER: British Council, lecturer in Athens and Salonika, Greece, 1946-50, administrator in Madras, India, and in Colombo, Ceylon, 1950-52, in Birmingham, England, 1952-54, in Cambridge, England, 1955-63, in London, England, 1963-66, in Paris, France, 1966-71, in London, 1971-72, in Oxford, England, 1972-78, and in London, 1978-79. George Elliston Poetry Foundation Lecturer, University of Cincinnati, 1962. *Military service:* Royal Artillery, 1940-45; became captain. *Member:* Royal Society of Literature (fellow). *Awards, honors:* Heinemann Award of Royal Society of Literature, 1959, for *The Chequer'd Shade*.

WRITINGS: The Fire and the Fountain: An Essay on Poetry, Oxford University Press, 1955, 2nd edition, Barnes & Noble, 1966; *Uncertainties and Other Poems*, Oxford University Press, 1956; (compiler) *Poetic Heritage: A Sunday Times Anthology of English Verse from the 16th to the 20th Century*, Deutsch, 1957, reprinted, Century Bookbindery, 1977; *The Chequer'd Shade: Reflections on Obscurity in Poetry*, Oxford University Press, 1958; *Andrew Marvell* (monograph), Longmans, Green, 1958, revised edition, 1966; *Guy Fawkes Night and Other Poems*, Oxford University Press, 1959; *Robert Herrick* (monograph), Longmans, Green, 1961, revised edition, 1971; *Ice-Storm in Cincinnati*, [Cincinnati], 1962; *Rule and Energy: Trends in British Poetry since the Second World War*, Oxford University Press, 1963, reprinted, Greenwood Press, 1976; (editor) *The Teaching Of English Overseas*, Methuen, 1963; (editor) Francis Turner Palgrave, *The Golden Treasury of the Best Songs and Lyrical Poems in the English Language*, 5th edition, Oxford University Press, 1964; (editor) *Commonwealth Literature: Unity and Diversity in a Common Culture*, Barnes & Noble, 1965; *Louis MacNeice* (monograph), Longmans, Green, 1965; *A Map of Modern English Verse*, Oxford University Press, 1969; *The Lengthening Shadows*, Oxford University Press, 1971; *John Betjeman* (monograph), Longman, 1974; (with Edward Lowbury and Michael Riviere) *Troika* (poems), Daedalus, 1977; (editor) *Essays by Divers Hands*, Volume XXXIX, Oxford University Press, 1977. Also author of English libretto for film production of Bartok's "Bluebeard's Castle." Editor, "Poetic Heritage," *Sunday Times*.

WORK IN PROGRESS: A collection of poetry.

BIOGRAPHICAL/CRITICAL SOURCES: Howard Nemerov, *Poetry and Fiction: Essays*, Rutgers University Press, 1963.

PRESSMAN, Jeffrey L(eonard) 1943-

PERSONAL: Born November 8, 1943, in Los Angeles, Calif.; son of David and Reinie (Epstein) Pressman; married Kate Stith, December 23, 1970. *Education:* Yale University, B.A., 1965; Oxford University, graduate study, 1965-66; University of California, Berkeley, M.A., 1967, Ph.D., 1972. *Politics:* Democrat. *Religion:* Jewish. *Office:* Department of Political Science, Massachusetts Institute of Technology, Cambridge, Mass. 02139.

CAREER: Dartmouth College, Hanover, N.H., instructor, 1971-72, assistant professor of government, 1972-73; Massachusetts Institute of Technology, Cambridge, assistant professor of political science, 1973—. *Member:* American Association for the Advancement of Science, American Political Science Association. *Awards, honors:* Henry fellow at Oxford University, 1965-66.

WRITINGS: House vs. Senate: Conflict in the Appropriations Process, Yale University Press, 1966; *Preconditions of Mayoral Leadership,* Institute of Urban and Regional Development, University of California, 1970; (with Aaron Wildavsky) *Implementation: How Great Expectations in Washington Are Dashed in Oakland, or, Why It's Amazing That Federal Programs Work at All,* University of California Press, 1973, 2nd edition, 1979; (contributor) *Neighborhood Control in the Seventies,* Chandler Publishing, 1973; (with Denis G. Sullivan, Benjamin I. Page, and John J. Lyons) *The Politics of Representation: The Democrat Convention 1972,* St. Martins, 1974; *Federal Programs and City Politics: The Dynamics of the Aid Process in Oakland,* University of California Press, 1975.†

*   *   *

PRESTON, Richard Arthur 1910-

PERSONAL: Born October 4, 1910, in Middlesbrough, England; son of Frank and Florence Rachel (Carter) Preston; married Marjorie Ethel Fishwick, September 2, 1939; children: David Frank, Carol Jane, Peter Eric. *Education:* University of Leeds, B.A. (honors), 1931, M.A., 1932, diploma in education, 1933; Yale University, Ph.D., 1936. *Home:* 1124 Woodburn, Durham, N.C. 27705. *Office:* Department of History, Duke University, Durham, N.C. 27706.

CAREER: University of Toronto, Toronto, Ontario, lecturer in history, 1936-38; University College of South Wales, Cardiff, assistant lecturer in history, 1938-45; University of Toronto, assistant professor of history, 1945-48; Royal Military College of Canada, Kingston, Ontario, professor of history, 1948-65; Duke University, Durham, N.C., William K. Boyd Professor of History, 1965-80, director of Canadian Studies Program, 1973-79. Visiting professor, Duke University, 1962; visiting lecturer and visiting member of Nuffield College, Oxford University, 1963-64. Kingston Centennial of Confederation Committee, co-chairman, 1962-64, chairman, 1964-65; chairman, Canadian National Museum Project, 1963. *Military service:* Royal Air Force, 1940-45; became flight lieutenant; mentioned in dispatches. *Member:* American Historical Association, Association for Canadian Studies in the United States (founder; president, 1969-71), Canadian Historical Association (president, 1961-62), Canadian Institute of International Affairs, English Historical Association, Royal Historical Society (fellow), Ontario Historical Society (vice-president, 1960-61), Kingston Historical Society (honorary life member; vice-president, 1959-65). *Awards, honors:* Commonwealth Fund fellow, 1933-36; Nuffield summer travel award, 1954; Duke University summer research scholar, 1957; City of Kingston Achievement

Award, 1957, for television series and publications on the history of Kingston; Canada Council senior fellow, 1963-64; Social Science Research Council grant, 1963; Canada Confederation Medal, 1967; Guggenheim fellow, 1971-72; named honorary professor of history, Royal Military College of Canada, 1973; Donner Memorial Medal, 1975, for promotion of Canadian studies in the United States; LL.D., Royal Military College of Canada, 1977.

WRITINGS: Gorges of Plymouth Fort: A Life of Sir Ferdinando Gorges, Captain of Plymouth Fort, Governor of New England, and Lord of the Province of Maine, University of Toronto Press, 1953; (with S. F. Wise and H. O. Werner) *Men in Arms: A History of Warfare and Its Interrelationships with Western Society,* Praeger, 1956, 2nd revised edition, 1970; (compiler and translator) L. Lamontagne, *Royal Fort Frontenac,* Champlain Society, 1958; *Kingston before the War of 1812,* Champlain Society, 1958; *Canada in World Affairs, 1959-61,* Oxford University Press, 1965; *Canada and the "Imperial Defense": A Study of the Origins of the British Commonwealth's Defense Organization, 1867-1919,* Duke University Press, 1967; *Canada's RMC: A History of the Royal Military College,* University of Toronto Press, 1969; (editor) *Contemporary Australia: Studies in History, Politics, and Economics,* Duke University Press, 1969; (editor) *The Influence of the United States on Canadian Development: Eleven Case Studies,* Duke University Press, 1972; (editor) *For Friends at Home: A Scottish Emigrant's Letters from Canada, California, and the Cariboo, 1844-1864,* McGill-Queen's University Press, 1974; *The Defence of the Undefended Border: Planning for War in North America, 1867-1939,* McGill-Queen's University Press, 1977.

Contributor: Morris Zaslow, editor, *The Defended Border: Upper Canada and the War of 1812,* Macmillan (Toronto), 1964; W. B. Hamilton, editor, *The Transfer of Institutions,* Duke University Press, 1964; S. F. Wise and Robert C. Brown, *Canada Views the United States: Nineteenth-Century Political Attitudes,* University of Washington Press, 1967; Richard H. Leach, editor, *Contemporary Canada,* Commonwealth Studies Center, Duke University, 1968; M. R. Van Gils, editor, *The Perceived Roles of the Military,* University Press (Rotterdam), 1971; Hector J. Massey, editor, *The Canadian Military: A Profile,* Copp, 1972; D. Rickey and F. Cooling, editors, *Essays in Some Dimensions of Military History,* U.S. Army War College, 1972; Michael Cross and Robert Bothwell, editors, *Policy by Other Means: Essays in Honour of C. P. Stacey,* Clarke, Irwin, 1972; R. B. Byers and Colin S. Grey, editors, *Canadian Military Professionalism: The. Search for Identity,* Canadian Institute of International Affairs, 1973; *To Preserve and Defend,* McGill-Queen's University Press, 1976; Russell F. Weigley, editor, *New Dimensions in Military History,* Presidio Press, 1976.

Also author of television series, "Historic Kingston," 1959, and of several other radio and television scripts on Canadian history. Contributor to proceedings, encyclopedias, and professional journals. Editor of annual report of Canadian Historical Association, 1947-53; editor, *Historic Kingston,* 1951-54.

WORK IN PROGRESS: A study of the problems in teaching about Canada in the United States.

*   *   *

PRICE, Derek (John) de Solla 1922-

PERSONAL: Born January 22, 1922, in London, England; son of Philip (a businessman) and Fanny (de Solla) Price;

married Ellen Hjorth (a jeweler-artist), October 30, 1947; children: Linda Marie, Jeffrey Philip, Mark de Solla. *Education:* University of London, B.Sc., 1942, Ph.D. (physics), 1946; Cambridge University, Ph.D. (history of science), 1954. *Politics:* Left. *Religion:* None. *Home:* 88 Trumbull St., New Haven, Conn. 06520. *Office:* Yale University, 2036 Yale Station, New Haven, Conn. 06520.

CAREER: Southwest Essex Technical College, London, England, assistant, 1938-46; Princeton University, Princeton, N.J., fellow, 1946-47; University of Malaya, Singapore, lecturer, 1947-50; Cambridge University, Cambridge, England, fellow, 1950-56; Smithsonian Institution, Washington, D.C., curator, 1957; Princeton University, Institute for Advanced Study, fellow, 1958-59; Yale University, New Haven, Conn., Avalon Professor of History of Science, 1960—. Consultant to National Science Foundation and on science policy to several nations. *Member:* History of Science Society (member of council), Society for the History of Technology, International Union of the History and Philosophy of Science, American Association for the Advancement of Science. *Awards, honors:* M.A. from Yale University, 1960; Leonardo da Vinci Medal for History of Technology, 1976.

WRITINGS: An Old Palmistry, Heffer, 1953; *The Equatorie of the Planetis,* Cambridge University Press, 1955; (with Needham and Wang) *Heavenly Clockwork,* Cambridge University Press, 1959; *Science since Babylon,* Yale University Press, 1961, enlarged edition, 1975; *Little Science, Big Science,* Columbia University Press, 1963; *Gears from the Greeks,* Science History Publications, 1975; (editor with Ina Spiegel-Roesing) *Science, Technology and Society,* Sage Publications, 1977. Contributor to science journals.

WORK IN PROGRESS: Papers and monographs on the "science of science."

SIDELIGHTS: Derek Price is known for his discovery of the manuscript of a previously unrevealed astronomical work of Chaucer, for the identification of a complicated geared computing machine from Greece, first century B.C., and for his analysis of the exponential growth of science.

*   *   *

PRICE, Jonathan (Reeve)   1941-

PERSONAL: Born October 9, 1941, in Boston, Mass.; son of Robert DeMille (an entrepreneur) and Newell (a teacher; maiden name, Potter) Price. *Education:* Harvard University, B.A. (cum laude), 1963; Yale University, D.F.A., 1968. *Politics:* Radical. *Religion:* "Pagan." *Home:* Newell Farm, Main St., West Newbury, Mass. *Agent:* Georges Borchardt, Inc., 136 East 57th St., New York, N.Y. 10022.

CAREER: New York University, New York City, assistant professor of English, 1968-70; WNET (Channel Thirteen), New York City, video artist-in-residence, beginning 1972.

WRITINGS: On Finnegan's Wake, Grove, 1972; (editor) *Critics on Robert Lowell,* University of Miami Press, 1972; (editor with John Lahr) *Life Show Anthology,* Bantam, 1973; (with Lahr) *Life Show: How to See Theater in Life and Life in Theater,* Viking, 1973; *Video-visions: A Medium Discovers Itself,* New American Library, 1977; *The Best Thing on TV: Commercials,* Viking, 1978; (editor and translator) *Classic Scenes,* New American Library, 1979.

SIDELIGHTS: Jonathan Price told *CA:* "I write concrete poems; that is, the words are shaped on the page so as to suggest the image of the object they refer to. I began with Donne, wanting to make more connections than are possible in a simple down-the-page poem; I imitated Claes Oldenburg

in a series of poems on familiar shapes, notably the Ice Cream Cone; and I have gone on to a number of 'field' poems, in which I take the page as an open field, and scatter the words on it like hunks of snow. I have moved into three-dimensional poems, as with my Word Salad, which uses one-inch plastic cubes with words silk-screened on them, to toss a clatter of thoughts about salad in a clear plastic bowl.''

BIOGRAPHICAL/CRITICAL SOURCES: Washington Post, December 21, 1978.†

*   *   *

PRICE, Richard   1949-

PERSONAL: Born October 12, 1949, in New York, N.Y. *Education:* Cornell University, B.S., 1971; Columbia University, graduate study, 1972-74, M.F.A., 1976; Stanford University, further graduate study, 1973. *Politics:* None. *Religion:* None. *Home and office:* 10 Jones St., New York, N.Y. 10014. *Agent:* Brandt & Brandt, 1501 Broadway, New York, N.Y. 10036.

CAREER: Writer. Lecturer in English as a second language, Hostos Community College, 1973; lecturer in urban affairs, New York University, 1973; lecturer in creative writing, State University of New York at Stony Brook, beginning 1974, New York University, 1974 and 1977, State University of New York at Binghamton, 1976, Hofstra University, 1978-79, and Yale University, 1980. *Awards, honors:* Edith Mirrilees grant in fiction from Stanford University, 1972; Mary Roberts Rinehart Foundation grant, 1973; MacDowell Colony grant, 1973; Yaddo fellow, 1977, 1978, and 1980; *Playboy* Magazine Nonfiction Award, 1979; MacDowell fellow, 1979.

WRITINGS—All novels; all published by Houghton: The Wanderers, 1974; *Bloodbrothers,* 1976; *Ladies' Man,* 1978.

SIDELIGHTS: Despite his desire not to become known as the "Voice of the Bronx," Richard Price has often had his work compared to that of other writers who have focused on the problems of growing up male in various urban centers of the United States—most notably James T. Farrell (Chicago) and Hubert Selby, Jr. (Brooklyn). Price's grittily realistic portrayal of gang life in the Bronx, *The Wanderers* (published when the author was only 24 years old), was hailed as "an extraordinary first novel" by *Newsweek*'s Charles Michener. Continues the critic: "Like the nerviest of the teen-age gang members who give the novel its title, Price prowls the 1960s jungle of a North Bronx housing project and its environs without fear—or shame. His switchblade prose is not interested in shadows but flesh and blood.... His dialogue has the immediacy of overheard subway conversation. His wit is capable of perceiving the dopey pathos behind adolescent swagger and obscenity as well as capturing the surrealistic exhilaration of mass violence."

Rick Kogan of the *Chicago Sun-Times* calls Price's book "one of the few powerful and worthwhile novels of the year.... The language of *The Wanderers* is tough, the gang's actions often crude and vulgar. But it is an important novel for just those reasons. It is real. It is a work that tells its tale in the best possible way—using real characters in a real world.... Richard Price has gathered the pieces to the puzzle of his own youth and the puzzle of growing up in urban America. In *The Wanderers* he has put all the pieces together and they fit like a charm."

"[*The Wanderers*] could be the flip side of 'American Graffiti,'" declares Michael Rogers in *Rolling Stone.* "Price's book chronicles the adventures and depredations of one gang, the Wanderers, during their last year of high school—an amalgam of sex, violence and humor, glued together with superb dialogue and unsentimental sensitivity.... While the book is clearly episodic, and many of the chapters could easily stand on their own as short stories, Price nonetheless manages to blend his humor and horror to create a sense of wholeness."

Hubert Selby himself, writing in the *New York Times Book Review*, feels that "although [*The Wanderers*] is a book specifically about adolescence, and a portion of the Bronx, its scope goes beyond the emotions of teen-agers and the setting of the Big Playground. Richard Price has the empathy and objectivity of a true artist, and so we also experience the adult world outside, struggling with its own inadequacies, ignorance, misconceptions. *The Wanderers* is an outstanding work of art because Mr. Price never imposes himself on the reader. His dialogue is musically true and emotionally correct. He respects his art and his subject, and illuminates our daily world with insights that allow us—at times force us—to feel closer to other human beings whether we like and approve of them or not."

Other critics, however, while willing to regard *The Wanderers* as a good first effort for a young writer, are not quite as eager as some of their colleagues to consider it a masterpiece. Writes Laura Cunningham in the *Village Voice*: "Sexual gropings and lower-class ambience ring true [in *The Wanderers*, but] the action falters. The book resembles 12 related short stories more than it does a novel. There is no real thrust of plot, or even a central character.... The author has much to learn concerning the techniques of building suspense and staging dramatic action." The *New Yorker* critic feels that the twelve stories in *The Wanderers* "provide the reader with a fairly entertaining pop-sociological wallow, but they do not succeed very well as fiction. For one thing, the author shows off his good ear for street talk a bit too indiscriminately.... For another, the stories are very repetitive. It's not always easy to tell one Wanderer from another, chiefly because the boys' individual qualities and histories seem to be less important to Mr. Price than their shared ones."

Finally, Eliot Fremont-Smith of *New York* concludes that *The Wanderers* is "not a bad book; it has moments of insight, some good writing, and a particularly strong and effective portrait of conflict between a muscular, *macho* father and his painfully striving son. But it is not the major work that [some critics] want to claim.... [It] is simply not, in risky conception or sustained powers or horrifying resonance, comparable to *Last Exit to Brooklyn*, much less to the stories of Odysseus. It is more like a contemporary *Studs Lonigan*, an unsentimental *West Side Story*. No great surprises, but ably and honestly done. Good enough should be good enough."

Price's second novel, *Bloodbrothers*, deals with a particularly significant summer in the life of Stony De Coco, the eighteen-year-old son of a successful electrical contractor who must decide whether to go on to college, join his father in the construction business, or work among children as a hospital aide. "In general," remarks William C. Woods of the *Washington Post Book World*, [this is] a bad idea for a novel; not because it isn't a worthwhile story, but because it's been written so often (and sometimes so well) that only the blueprint remains. Any novelist who takes on such familiar stuff will have to have something special going for him. Richard Price does.... [His] material fits the old formula, but it has particular promise. It's about people who haven't often found their way into fiction since James T. Farrell first

put their lives on record many years ago.... For all of its surface violence, blunt language, and brute realism, *Bloodbrothers* is a most subtle book. Its concerns are not limited to the photographic naturalism Price handily achieves, or the presentation of an argument for the group integrity of a mocked majority. It's a novel about brotherhood, family bonds stronger than family hatreds, and ritual initiations on many levels—all of which compose a sharp portrait of a coming-of-age, in sorrow and in strength."

Though *America*'s Gerard C. Reedy reveals that he is "reluctant to admit that my fellow Bronxites realistically and constantly talk, think and act this dirtily," he does feel that "some of Price's episodes [in *Bloodbrothers*] are achingly moving.... [The book] offers powerful writing on almost every page. The author, like his hero, has great story-telling gifts; he also has a good feel for loneliness in the high-rise buildings of New York, or anywhere."

Other reviewers feel that *Bloodbrothers* is a poor follow-up to *The Wanderers*. As *Rolling Stone*'s Greil Marcus notes: "Price's first book.... was not a great novel, but it was a stunning first novel.... Unfortunately, *Bloodbrothers*, a sort of Italian working-class *Catcher in the Rye*, is not even a very good second novel.... Price has dressed up his earlier themes in new clothes, but that's all." Julian Barnes of the *New Statesman* calls it "the Gothic of our time, ... a smart, professional example of the post-Selby genre of lower-depths chic. Perhaps the continuing bankruptcy of New York is behind the flowering of this school, in which your archetypal American family beat and cheat one another, drive each other bananas, and then ensure that the vicious cycle continues into the next generation."

Writes Richard Elman in the *New York Times Book Review*: "Like some proletarian fictions of a few decades back, this story of Stony De Coco, 18, and his clan grinds and blusters from point to point, undeterred by Price's feeling for life or his dramatic gifts.... In *Bloodbrothers*, Price has closed his eyes and stopped up his ears and composed page after page of hostile, insult-laden dialogue interspersed with a hyped-up colloquial narrative through which the reader is bullied to sustain the illusion that the story has been composed by somebody with a background similar to that of the participants.... Most of the time Price isn't content to understate, to let things happen, or even take a chance that the situation of these people is even more ugly or desperate than he knows. If his characters won't cooperate in being utterly unredeemable, he twists their arms or stomps on them a bit.... This sort of stuff is more like a dirty-mouthed Italianate Hyman Kaplan: a few touches aspiring to art, and much of the rest simply kibitzing or commentary."

In his third novel, *Ladies' Man*, Price branches out from his usual themes, moves his Bronx characters to Manhattan, and ages his protagonist somewhat. The story focuses on a traumatic week in the life of Kenny Becker, a thirty-year-old door-to-door salesman who faces a premature mid-life crisis of sorts when his live-in girlfriend's sudden departure leaves him alone and essentially friendless. Terence Winch of the *Washington Post Book World* states that "*Ladies' Man* does not include the panorama of anguish that sweeps through Price's earlier novels. It does, however, offer something better: it is a novel of passion and depth written with great precision and control.... [It] is one of the best novels yet on life in the 1970s.... This is a novel that covers a lot of ground. Solitude and loneliness, sex, work, and life in New York are all part of Price's portrait of Kenny Becker. But more than anything else, *Ladies' Man* is a novel about love and death.... What Kenny learns is hard to say.... Richard

Price does not propose any easy answers to the toughest human questions.''

After noting that Price ''knows the language, mores, herding instincts and hunting habits of the bottom-class urban young just about as well as Margaret Mead got to know those who come of age in Samoa,'' the *New York Times'* Christopher Lehmann-Haupt declares that ''what keeps us reading *Ladies' Man* is not the pain of Kenny Becker's experience, but Mr. Price's inventiveness as a storyteller and the absolute authenticity of the people he creates.... And because Mr. Price doesn't condescend to his characters ... their suffering transcends their narrow circumstances.'' Jerome Charyn of the *New York Times Book Review* agrees that Price ''has an amazing ear and eye for the street'' but feels that ''Kenny gets in the way of the narrative with his 50-cent truths. At times he sounds like a hip Benjamin Franklin in platform shoes.... It's this sort of claptrap that harms the book, because it gives us Richard Price's silliness rather than Kenny Becker's infantile rage. But *Ladies' Man* still has its bite. It's a disturbing, freaky novel about sexual disgust and the pornography of our everyday lives.''

Greil Marcus, commenting once again in *Rolling Stone,* concludes in his review of *Ladies' Man:* ''The force of Price's first two books depended on his freedom to go too far—not simply to be shocking, but really to shock. If he couldn't have crossed into the realm of the forbidden and the unspoken—in terms of lust and violence—his world would have flattened out.... *Ladies' Man* is a step forward.... Kenny's neither so sensitive nor as adventurous as Price's earlier heroes.... Despite the sexual chaos, [the book] never seems to go too far, never shocks. Perhaps it's because Kenny seems so empty we'll easily accept anything that might fill him. And yet he's tougher than he seems; he's never a bore, never without humor, even if it's at his own expense. Like the protagonists of Price's earlier books, he's incomplete as a fictional character, and *Ladies' Man,* like those books, is unsatisfying, perhaps because Price's own life, his achievement, is proof that no-way-out is, for a novelist, an easy way out. But Price is already moving away from the one book so many novelists write over and over again: *Ladies' Man* is more than enough to keep me, and I'd guess a lot of other people, watching the stores for whatever Price does next.''

BIOGRAPHICAL/CRITICAL SOURCES: Chicago Sun-Times, March 31, 1974; *New York,* April 1, 1974; *New York Times Book Review,* April 21, 1974, May 23, 1976, November 12, 1978; *Rolling Stone,* May 9, 1974, May 20, 1976, November 30, 1978; *Newsweek,* May 13, 1974, September 18, 1978; *Village Voice,* May 16, 1974, October 9, 1978; *New Yorker,* May 20, 1974, November 27, 1978; *Contemporary Literary Criticism,* Gale, Volume VI, 1976, Volume XII, 1980; *America,* November 13, 1976; *Saturday Review,* March 20, 1976; *Washington Post Book World,* May 2, 1976, October 15, 1978; *New Statesman,* May 20, 1977; *New York Times,* November 10, 1978, July 22, 1979, August 31, 1979; *New Republic,* January 6, 1979; *New York Review of Books,* January 25, 1979.

—*Sketch by Deborah A. Straub*

*   *   *

PRIME, C(ecil) T(homas)   1909-1979

PERSONAL: Born August 30, 1909, in Cambridge, England; died February 5, 1979, in Carshalton, England; son of Thomas Edgar (a company director) and Edith (Harvey) Prime; married Frances Welby, March 30, 1940; children:

Edith Claire, Helen Frances, Catherine Mary. *Education:* Christ's College, Cambridge, B.A., 1931, M.A., 1934; Chelsea College, London, Ph.D., 1951. *Politics:* None. *Religion:* Church of England. *Home:* Thriplow, 7 Westview Rd., Warlingham, Surrey, England.

CAREER: Whitgift School, South Croydon, England, assistant master, 1931-62, head of science department, 1962-69. *Member:* Institute of Biology (fellow), Botanical Society of the British Isles (member of council), Linnean Society of London (fellow).

WRITINGS: (With R. J. Deacock) *How to Identify Trees and Shrubs from Leaves or Twigs in Summer or Winter,* Heffer, 1935, 6th edition, revised and enlarged, 1970; (with Deacock) *The Shorter British Flora,* Methuen, 1948, 2nd edition, 1953; *Lords and Ladies,* Collins, 1960; (with Maurice Burton) *Nature,* Grolier Society, 1963; *The Young Botanist,* Nelson, 1963; *Investigations in Woodland Ecology,* Heinemann, 1970; *Experiments for Young Botanists,* Bell, 1971; (with Aaron E. Klein) *Seedlings and Soil,* Doubleday, 1973; (translator) John Ray, *Flora of Cambridgeshire,* Wheldon & Wesley, 1975; *Wild Flowers of Europe,* Salamander Books, 1977; *Plant Life,* Collins, 1977.†

*   *   *

PRIOR, A(rthur) N(orman)   1914-1969

PERSONAL: Born December 4, 1914, in Masterton, New Zealand; died October 8, 1969; son of Norman Henry (a doctor) and Elizabeth (Teague) Prior; married Mary Laura Wilkinson, October 22, 1943; children: Martin Hugh, Ann. *Education:* University of Otago, B.A., 1935, M.A., 1937. *Home:* 21 The Paddox, Banbury Rd., Oxford, England. *Office:* Balliol College, Oxford University, Oxford, England.

CAREER: University of Otago, Dunedin, New Zealand, assistant lecturer in philosophy, 1937; University of Canterbury, Christchurch, New Zealand, lecturer, 1946-52, professor of philosophy, 1952-58; University of Manchester, Manchester, England, professor of philosophy, 1959-66; Oxford University, Balliol College, Oxford, England, fellow and tutor in philosophy, 1966-69. John Locke Lecturer, Oxford University, 1956; guest lecturer, Polish Academy of Science, 1961; Dawes Hicks Lecturer, British Academy, 1962; visiting professor, University of Chicago, 1962; Flint Visiting Professor, University of California, Los Angeles, 1965. Participant in international philosophical conferences in Canberra, 1957, Warsaw, 1961, and Helsinki, 1962. *Military service:* Royal New Zealand Air Force, 1942-45. *Member:* British Academy (fellow), Mind Association, Association of Symbolic Logic, Australasian Association of Philosophy (president New Zealand section, 1954), Inland Waterways Association (England).

WRITINGS—Published by Clarendon Press, except as indicated: *Logic and the Basis of Ethics,* 1949; *Formal Logic,* 1955, 2nd edition, 1962; *Time and Modality,* 1957, reprinted, Greenwood Press, 1979; *Past, Present and Future,* 1967; *Papers on Time and Tense,* 1968; *Objects of Thought,* edited by P. T. Geach and A.J.P. Kenny, 1971; *The Doctrine of Propositions and Terms,* edited by Geach and Kenny, University of Massachusetts Press, 1976; *Papers in Logic and Ethics,* edited by Geach and Kenny, University of Massachusetts Press, 1976; *Worlds, Times and Selves,* University of Massachusetts Press, 1977. Contributor to professional journals in England, the United States, Poland, Germany, Australia, India, Belgium, Sweden, and Holland. Member of board of editors, *Journal of Symbolic Logic,* 1960-69.

SIDELIGHTS: A. N. Prior told *CA:* ''My interests are in

time and in imagination—in how to talk sense about what exists no longer or not yet, or is merely thought to exist—and more technically, in medieval logic and in modern logical systems; am indebted here to the 'Polish School' of logicians." *Avocational interests:* Walking, canal cruising.†

* * *

PRITCHETT, C(harles) Herman 1907-

PERSONAL: Born February 9, 1907, in Latham, Ill.; son of Charles and Anna M. (Nottelmann) Pritchett; married Marguerite A. Lentner, 1937; children: Jean, Philip. *Education:* Millikin University, A.B., 1927; University of Chicago, Ph.D., 1937. *Home:* 430 Northridge Rd., Santa Barbara, Calif. 93105. *Office:* Department of Political Science, University of California, Santa Barbara, Calif. 93106.

CAREER: Tennessee Valley Authority, Knoxville, Tenn., research associate, 1934-37; University of London, London School of Economics, London, England, Social Science Research Council fellow, 1937-38; U.S. Department of Labor, Washington, D.C., administrative analyst, 1939; University of Chicago, Chicago, Ill., assistant professor, 1940-46, associate professor, 1946-52, professor of political science, 1952-69, chairman of department, 1948-55, 1958-64; University of California, Santa Barbara, professor of political science, 1969—. Political science advisor, Encyclopaedia Britannica, Inc., 1953-68; Bacon Lecturer, Boston University, 1957; Guy Stanton Ford Lecturer, University of Minnesota, 1959; visiting professor, Stanford University, 1966; member, Commission on Electoral College Reform, American Bar Association, 1966. *Member:* American Political Science Association (president-elect, 1962-63; president, 1963-64), American Association of University Professors (council member, 1959-62), American Society for Public Administration. *Awards, honors:* Ford Foundation faculty fellow, University of Chicago, 1958-59; Litt.D., Millikin University, 1960.

WRITINGS: The Tennessee Valley Authority, University of North Carolina Press, 1943; *The Roosevelt Court: A Study in Judicial Politics and Values, 1937-47,* Macmillan, 1948, reprinted, Quadrangle, 1969; *Civil Liberties and the Vinson Court,* University of Chicago Press, 1954; *The Political Offender and the Warren Court,* Boston University Press, 1958; *The American Constitution,* McGraw, 1959, 3rd edition, 1977; *Congress Versus the Supreme Court,* University of Minnesota Press, 1961; (editor with W. F. Murphy) *Courts, Judges, and Politics,* Random House, 1961, 3rd edition, 1979; *American Constitutional Issues,* McGraw, 1962; (editor with A. F. Westin) *The Third Branch of Government,* Harcourt, 1963; *The American Constitutional System,* McGraw, 1963, 4th edition, 1976; (contributor) *The Revolutionary Theme in Contemporary America,* University Press of Kentucky, 1965; (co-author) *American Government in World Perspective,* Harper, 1967, 4th edition, 1976; *The Federal System in Constitutional Law,* Prentice-Hall, 1978.

* * *

PROCTOR, Samuel 1919-

PERSONAL: Born March 29, 1919, in Jacksonville, Fla.; son of Jack (a merchant) and Celia (Schneider) Proctor; married Bessie Rubin, September 8, 1948; children: Mark Julian, Alan Lowell. *Education:* University of Florida, B.A., 1941, M.A., 1942, Ph.D., 1958; graduate study at University of North Carolina, 1948, and Emory University, 1949. *Politics:* Democrat. *Religion:* Jewish. *Home:* 2235 Northwest Ninth Pl., Gainesville, Fla. 32601. *Office:* Oral History Office,

Florida State Museum, University of Florida, Gainesville, Fla. 32611.

CAREER: University of Florida, Gainesville, instructor, 1946-48, assistant professor, 1948-57, associate professor, 1957-63, professor of history and social sciences, 1963-74, Distinguished Service Professor of History and Social Sciences, 1974, Julian C. Yonge Professor of Florida History, 1976—, university historian, 1953—, director of oral history program, 1968—, curator of Florida State Museum. Visiting professor of history, Jacksonville University, summers, 1963-66. Co-director, Doris Duke Southeastern Indian Oral History Program; director, Center for the Study of Florida History and Humanities. Historian, Florida Civil War Centennial Commission, 1960-65, and Pensacola Preservation Board, 1968; historian and consultant, Florida Public Relations Hall of Fame Commission, 1961—; consultant, Florida Board of Parks and Historic Memorials, 1965—; Florida Division of Archives, History and Records Management, member, 1970—, chairman; member, Florida review committee, National Register for Historic Places, 1971—; chairman of advisory committee, Naming of State Buildings; member of academic advisory council, American Jewish Historical Society. Member of executive committee, Florida Anti-Defamation League, 1957—; member of board of directors, Jacksonville River Garden Home for the Aged. *Military service:* U.S. Army, Engineers, 1943-46. *Member:* American Association for State and Local History (member of council, 1973-77), National Oral History Association (member of council, 1971—; president, 1976), Organization of American Historians, Southern Historical Association, Florida Historical Society (director, 1951-53, 1961—), Florida Anthropological Society, University of Florida Alumni Association (member of executive board), Florida Blue Key, Phi Beta Kappa, Tau Epsilon Phi, Pi Kappa Phi, Alpha Kappa Delta, Phi Alpha Theta, Pi Gamma Mu. *Awards, honors:* Service Award Key, 1953, Michael C. C. Lilienfeld National Distinguished Service Award, 1958, and Outstanding Alumnus Award, 1971, all from Tau Epsilon Phi; named Florida Historian of the Year by Peace River Valley Historical Society, 1967.

WRITINGS: Napoleon Bonaparte Broward: Florida's Fighting Democrat, University of Florida Press, 1950; (contributor) *Future Role and Scope of the University of Florida,* University of Florida, 1962; *Florida Commemorates the Civil War Centennial, 1961-1965: A Manual of the Observance of the Civil War in the Counties and Cities of the State of Florida* (pamphlet), Florida Civil War Centennial Commission, 1962; *Florida a Hundred Years Ago,* Florida Civil War Centennial Commission, 1966; (contributor) *In Search of Gulf Coast Colonial History,* Historic Pensacola Preservation Board, 1970; *Zephaniah Kingsley,* [Jacksonville], 1980.

Editor; all published by University of Florida Press, except as indicated: (And author of introduction) *Dickison and His Men: Reminiscences of the War in Florida,* 1962; *Florida Historic Preservation Planning,* Florida Division of Archives, History and Records, 1971; *Eighteenth Century Florida and Its Borderlands,* 1975; *Eighteenth Century Florida and the Caribbean,* 1976; *Eighteenth Century Florida: Life on the Frontier,* 1976; *Eighteenth Century Florida and the Revolutionary South,* 1978; *Eighteenth Century Florida: Impact of the Revolution,* 1978; (with others) *Tacahale: Essays on the Indians of Florida and Southeastern Georgia during the Historic Period,* 1978.

Also editor of "Bicentennial Floridians" facsimile series, twenty-five volumes, 1973-79. Contributor to encyclopedias;

contributor of more than 70 articles and feature stories to newspapers, magazines, and regional and national history journals, including *Southern Observer, Jacksonville Journal, Southern Jewish Weekly, Mid-America, Canadian Mining Journal, Social Science, Caribbean Quarterly, Civil War Times Illustrated, St. Petersburg Times Sunday Magazine,* and *Florida Historical Quarterly.* Editor, *Florida Historical Quarterly;* member of editorial board, *Oral History Review.*

WORK IN PROGRESS: Editing *Documentary History of Florida, 1821-1971,* and writing *Spain and the United States: A Panorama of Relations Symposium,* both for University of Florida Press; contributing a chapter on Florida governors to *Confederate Governors,* for Louisiana State University Press.

R

RAISTRICK, Arthur 1896-

PERSONAL: Born August 16, 1896, in Saltaire, Yorkshire, England; son of George (an engineer) and Minnie (Bell) Raistrick; married Sarah Elizabeth Chapman, April, 1929 (died, 1972). *Education:* University of Leeds, B.Sc. in C.E., 1922, M.Sc. in C.E., 1923, B.Sc. in Geology (with honors), 1923, Ph.D., 1925. *Politics:* Socialist. *Religion:* Quaker. *Home:* Home Croft, Linton near Skipton, Yorkshire, England.

CAREER: Workers' Educational Association, North of England, tutor-lecturer, 1921-63; University of Durham, Durham, England, tutor in university extra-mural department, and lecturer and reader in applied geology in department of mining and civil engineering, 1929-56; University of Leeds, Leeds, England, tutor in university extra-mural department, 1956-63. National Parks committee, member of Yorkshire Dales group, 1955—, and of national standing committee. *Member:* Institute of Mining Engineers, Geological Society, Newcomen Society, Yorkshire Naturalists Union (former president), Yorkshire Archaeological Society (council member), Ramblers' Association (president, northern section; national vice-president), Holiday Fellowship (national president). *Awards, honors:* Lyell Award of Geological Society; Clough Medal of Edinburgh Geological Society for work on coal; D.Litt. from University of Leeds, 1972, and University of Bradford, 1974; Sorby Medal of Yorkshire Geological Society for work on coal spores.

WRITINGS: Two Centuries of Industrial Welfare: The London (Quaker) Lead Company, 1692-1905, Friends' Historical Society, 1938, reprinted, Moorland, 1968; (with C. E. Marshall) *The Nature and Origin of Coal and Coal Seams,* English Universities Press, 1939; *Teach Yourself Geology,* English Universities Press, 1943, Roy, 1956; *The Story of the Pennine Walls,* Dalesman Publishing Co., 1946; *Malhamdale,* Dalesman Publishing Co., 1946; *Malham and Malham Moor,* Dalesman Publishing Co., 1947, extended edition, 1971; *Grassington and Upper Wharfedale,* Dalesman Publishing Co., 1948; *Silver and Lead: The Story of a Quaker Mining Experiment,* Friends' Home Service Committee, 1948; *The Story of Bolton Priory,* Dalesman Publishing Co., 1949; (with J. L. Illingworth) *The Face of North-West Yorkshire,* Dalesman Publishing Co., 1949, 2nd edition published as *The Face of North-West Yorkshire: Geology and Natural Vegetation,* 1967.

Quakers in Science and Industry: Being an Account of the Quaker Contributions to Science and Industry during the 17th and 18th Centuries, Bannisdale Press, 1950, published with new introduction, Augustus M. Kelley, 1968; *Dynasty of Iron Founders: The Darbys and Coalbrookdale,* Longmans, Green, 1953, reprinted, Augustus M. Kelley, 1970; *The Calamine Mines, Malham, Yorks,* University of Durham Philosophical Society, 1954; *Mines and Miners of Swaledale,* Dalesman Publishing Co., 1955; *The Romans in Yorkshire,* Dalesman Publishing Co., 1960; *Yorkshire and the North-East,* Oliver & Boyd, 1963; *Prehistoric Yorkshire,* Dalesman Publishing Co., 1964; *A History of Lead Mining in the Pennines,* Longmans, Green, 1965; *Vikings, Angles and Danes in Yorkshire,* Dalesman Publishing Co., 1966; (editor and contributor) *North York Moors,* H.M.S.O., 1966; (editor and author of introduction) Charles Hatchett, *The Hatchett Diary: A Tour through the Countries of England and Scotland in 1796, Visiting Their Mines and Manufactories,* Barton, 1967; *The Pennine Dales,* Eyre & Spottiswoode, 1968, Arrow, 1972; *Old Yorkshire Dales,* Augustus M. Kelley, 1968; *Ice Age in Yorkshire,* Dalesman Publishing Co., 1968; *Yorkshire Maps and Map-Makers,* Dalesman Publishing Co., 1969.

West Riding of Yorkshire, Hodder & Stoughton, 1970; (editor) *A Century's Progress: Yorkshire Industry and Commerce,* Brenton Publishing, 1971; *Industrial Archaeology: An Historical Survey,* Eyre & Spottiswoode, 1971, Barnes & Noble, 1972; *Lead Mining in the Mid-Pennines,* Barton, 1973; *The Lead Industry of Wensley Dale and Swaledale,* Moorland, 1975, Volume I: *The Mines,* Volume II: *The Smelting Mills; Buildings in the Yorkshire Dales,* Dalesman Publishing Co., 1975; *Green Roads in the Pennines,* Moorland, 1978.

Contributor: George Sweeting, editor, *The Geology of the Yorkshire Dales,* Geologists' Association (London), 1933; Sweeting, editor, *The Geology of the Country around Harrogate,* Geologists' Association, 1938; H. M. Abrahams, editor, *Britain's National Parks,* Transatlantic, 1959. Contributor of more than one hundred research papers on geology, mining, and archaeology to technical journals.

AVOCATIONAL INTERESTS: Rambling, youth hostelry, music, and natural and industrial history in the north of England.

RALEIGH, John Henry 1920-

PERSONAL: Born 1920, in Springfield, Mass.; son of John Joseph and Theresa (King) Raleigh; married; children: Kingsley, John, Lydia. *Education:* Wesleyan University, B.A., 1943; Princeton University, Ph.D., 1948. *Home:* 1020 Keeler Ave., Berkeley, Calif. *Office:* Department of English, University of California, Berkeley, Calif. 94720.

CAREER: University of California, Berkeley, 1946—, began as instructor, became assistant professor, associate professor, 1954-60, professor of English literature, 1960—, chairman of department, 1969, vice-chancellor for academic affairs, 1969-72. *Member:* Modern Language Association of America. *Awards, honors:* Guggenheim fellow, 1962.

WRITINGS: Matthew Arnold and American Culture, University of California Press, 1957; (editor) *History and the Individual,* Holt, 1962; *The Plays of Eugene O'Neill,* Southern Illinois University Press, 1965; *Time, Place and Idea,* Southern Illinois University Press, 1968; (editor) *Twentieth Century Interpretations of "The Iceman Cometh,"* Prentice-Hall, 1968; *The Chronicle of Leopold and Molly Bloom,* University of California Press, 1977.

AVOCATIONAL INTERESTS: Walking, squash, piano, books.

* * *

RAMQUIST, Grace (Bess) Chapman 1907-

PERSONAL: Born October 8, 1907, in Durant, Okla.; daughter of James Blaine (a minister) and Maud (Frederick) Chapman; married A. E. Ramquist (a publisher's representative), December 25, 1929 (deceased); children: Gloria Ramquist Willingham, John Thomas (deceased). *Education:* William Jewell College, B.A., 1927; graduate study at University of Kansas and Central Missouri State College (now University). *Politics:* Republican. *Religion:* Church of the Nazarene. *Home:* 6555 Holmes St., Kansas City, Mo. 64131.

CAREER: Lillenas Publishing Co., Kansas City, Mo., program editor, 1943-79; Zondervan Publishing House, Grand Rapids, Mich., program editor, 1952—. Kindergarten teacher in Stilwell, Kan., 1960-64, and Kansas City, Mo., 1964-74. *Member:* Missouri State Teachers Association, Kansas City Education Association.

WRITINGS: Skits and Readings for Church and School, Zondervan, Book I, 1946, Book II, 1954, Book III, 1957; (compiler) *The Wit and Wisdom of J. B. Chapman: Unusual Stories Dr. Chapman Told,* Zondervan, 1948; *And Many Believed* (missal study book), Nazarene Publishing, 1951; *Let Us Adore Him* (Christmas service), Lillenas, 1952; *Teen-Age Etiquette,* Zondervan, 1953; *The Conqueror* (Easter service), Lillenas, 1953; *The King Is Coming* (Easter service), Lillenas, 1955; *The Boy of Old Illinois,* Beacon Hill, 1956; *The Boy with the Stam..nering Tongue,* Beacon Hill, 1957; *The Boy Who Made Right Choices,* Beacon Hill, 1958; *The Boy Who Wanted to Preach,* Beacon Hill, 1959; (compiler) *Choice Readings for Banquets and Other Occasions,* Zondervan, 1959.

The Boy with the Singing Heart, Beacon Hill, 1960; *The Boy with Many Problems,* Beacon Hill, 1961; (compiler) *Mother-Daughter Banquets,* Zondervan, 1961; *The Boy Who Moved West,* Beacon Hill, 1962; *No Respector of Persons* (missal study book), Nazarene Publishing, 1962; *The Boy Who Loved School,* Beacon Hill, 1963; (compiler) *Complete Christmas Programs,* Zondervan, Volume I, 1964, Volume II, 1968, Volume III, 1970, Volume IV, 1972, Volume V, 1975, Volume VI, 1980, Volume VII, 1980; *We Seek Only*

Jesus (Easter service), Lillenas, 1969; *Under the Banyan Tree,* Nazarene Publishing, 1969, revised edition, 1977; *A Real Live Missionary,* Nazarene Publishing, 1975; *Digging for Treasures,* Nazarene Publishing, 1976. Compiler of sixty-seven program builders for Christmas, Easter, and for other special days and age groups, Lillenas, 1943-79.

* * *

RANDOLPH, David James 1934-

PERSONAL: Born May 13, 1934, in Elkton, Md.; son of David James and Elsie (Lloyd) Randolph; married Juanita Fenby, June 16, 1957 (divorced, 1977); children: David James III, Tracey Anne. *Education:* University of Delaware, B.A., 1956; Drew University, M.Div., 1959; Boston University, Ph.D., 1962. *Home:* 254 East 68th St., New York, N.Y. 10021. *Office:* Christ Church United Methodist, 520 Park Ave., New York, N.Y. 10021.

CAREER: Methodist minister in Wilmington, Del., 1957-60, Lowell, Mass., 1960-62, and Wilmington, 1962-63; Drew University, School of Theology, Madison, N.J., assistant professor of homiletics and pastoral ministry, 1963-68; United Methodist Church, Nashville, Tenn., director of department of new life ministries, 1968-70, assistant general secretary, 1970-72, assistant general secretary and director of worship and the arts of General Board of Discipleship, 1972-75; Christ Church United Methodist, New York, N.Y., senior minister, 1975—. Visiting lecturer, Princeton Theological Seminary, 1968; lecturer in theology, Vanderbilt University, 1973. U.S. director of Salvation Today study for National Council of Churches. *Member:* Academy of Homiletics (president, 1968-69), Theological Institute (Oxford, England), Metropolitan Club (New York).

WRITINGS: (Author of introduction) Gerhard Ebeling, *On Prayer,* Fortress, 1966; *Baptism: Historical, Theological and Practical Considerations,* Abingdon, 1968; *The Renewal of Preaching,* Fortress, 1969; *God's Party: A Guide to New Forms of Worship,* Abingdon, 1975; (with Jack Kingsbury) *Proclamation: Pentecost I,* Fortress, 1975; *The Happy People* (radio sermons), National Council of Churches, 1976. Also author of study guide and cassette, "Worship: Celebration and Human Experience," Thesis, Inc., 1976.

Editor and contributor: *Faith Alive,* Tidings, 1969; *Ventures in Worship,* Abingdon, Volume I, 1969, Volume II, 1970, Volume III, 1973; (and author of accompanying film script) *The Swinging Church: Christian Mission in Leisure Revolution,* Tidings, 1971; (with Bill Garrett) *Ventures in Song,* Abingdon, 1972; *Peace Plus,* Tidings, 1974. Contributor to denominational and other periodicals.

WORK IN PROGRESS: Ventures in Faith; Festivals for the Future; research projects.

SIDELIGHTS: David James Randolph reports that he is "attempting to develop theology through images, or a theology of the imagination, which will crack the crust of custom and release the living springs of faith. . . . Celebrations—secular and religious—are the nexus for these concerns, and I expect to be at work in this area for time to come. I believe deeply that the basic issue today is not religion, or politics, or education, but life. Can humanity survive with significance?"

His work has been featured on the National Broadcasting Co.'s "Today Show" and in the 1980 U.S. Army film, "He Shall Touch Thy Mouth."

* * *

RANIS, Gustav 1929-

PERSONAL: Born October 24, 1929, in Darmstadt, Germany; came to United States in 1943, naturalized in 1952; son of Max (a lawyer) and Bettina (Goldschmidt) Ranis; married Ray Lee Finkelstein (a college teacher), June 15, 1958; children: Michael Bruce, Alan Jonathan, Bettina Suzanne. *Education:* Brandeis University, B.A., 1952; Yale University, M.A., 1953; Ph.D., 1956. *Home:* 7 Mulberry Rd., Woodbridge, Conn. 06525. *Office:* Economic Growth Center, Yale University, 52 Hillhouse Ave., New Haven, Conn. 06520.

CAREER: Ford Foundation, research economist concerned with India, 1957-58, in Pakistan, 1958-59; Institute of Development Economics, Karachi, Pakistan, joint director of research, 1959-61; Yale University, New Haven, Conn., associate professor, 1961-64, professor of economics, 1964-65; associate director of Economic Growth Center, 1961-64; Agency for International Development, assistant administrator and member of administrator's advisory committee on economic development, 1965-67; Yale University, Economic Growth Center, director, 1967—. Consultant, Office of the Secretary of Treasury, 1957, Committee for Economic Development subcommittee on Japan, 1961, and Ford Foundation, 1962. Organizer, National Academy of Sciences Bicentennial Symposium on the role of science and technology in economic development, 1976. Trustee, Brandeis University, 1968—. *Member:* American Economic Association, Phi Beta Kappa.

WRITINGS: (With John C. H. Fei) *A Study of Planning Methodology with Special Reference to Pakistan's Second Five-Year Plan,* Institute of Development Economics (Karachi), 1960; *Industrial Efficiency and Economic Growth: A Case Study of Karachi,* Institute of Development Economics, 1961; *Urban Consumer Expenditure and the Consumption Function,* Institute of Development Economics, 1961; (with Fei) *Development of the Labor Surplus Economy: Theory and Policy,* Irwin, 1964; (editor and author of introduction) *The United States and the Developing Economies,* Norton, 1964, revised edition, 1973; (with Joan M. Nelson) *Measures to Ensure the Effective Use of Aid,* Office of Program Coordination, Agency for International Development, 1966; (editor) *Government and Economic Development,* Yale University Press, 1971; (editor) *The Gap between Rich and Poor Nations,* St. Martin's, 1972; (editor) *Sharing in Development: A Programme of Employment, Equity and Growth for the Philippines,* International Labor Organization, 1974; (editor with William Beranek) *Science, Technology and Economic Development: A Historical and Comparative Study,* Praeger, 1979; (with S. Kuo and Fei) *Growth with Equity: The Taiwan Case,* Oxford University Press, 1979.

WORK IN PROGRESS: A study of employment, income distribution, and growth in a number of developing countries and a study of technology choice and change in development.

*   *   *

RANSOM, Jay Ellis 1914-

PERSONAL: Born April 12, 1914, in Missoula, Mont.; son of Jay George (a doctor and bookbinder) and Lucy Sophia (a teacher; maiden name, Adams) Ransom; married Barbara Elizabeth Callarman, July 31, 1936; married second wife, Wilhelmina Johanna Buitelaar (an artist and writer), December 28, 1960; children: (first marriage) Jay Frederick, Alix-Gay (Mrs. Ralph DeVito); (second marriage) Scott Pieter, Lisa Johanna (adopted), Stuart Cornelis. *Education:* University of Washington, B.A. (honors), 1935, graduate study,

1936-41; additional graduate study at University of California, 1943-48, and Northrop Institute, 1950-51. *Politics:* "Nominal Democrat." *Religion:* Presbyerian. *Home and office:* 1821 East 9th St., The Dalles, Ore. 97058. *Agent:* Ann Elmo Agency, Inc., 60 East 42nd St., New York, N.Y. 10017.

CAREER: Free-lance writer, 1927-36; U.S. Office of Indian Affairs, Nikolski, Umnak Island, and Stevens Village, Alaska, teacher and community worker, 1936-40; high school and college teacher in Washington, Nevada, and California, 1942-49; Northrop Aircraft, Inc., Hawthorne, Calif., senior technical writer and editor, 1950-52; *Enterprise-Courier,* Oregon City, Ore., farm editor and editorial writer, 1955-56; Valley College, Los Angeles, Calif., chemistry instructor, 1956-57; Aerojet-General Corp., Azusa, Calif., senior technical editor, 1957-59; American Electronics, Inc., El Monte, Calif., publications supervisor and chief technical writer and editor, 1959-60; Hercules Powder Co., Salt Lake City, Utah, chief technical writer, 1962; *Siskiyou Daily News,* Yreka, Calif., city and wire editor, 1965; *Press-Courier,* Oxnard, Calif., photojournalist and Sunday magazine feature specialist, 1966-67; Genge Industries, Inc., Oxnard, chief technical writer and editor, 1967-70; free-lance writer. Director, Western America Institute for Exploration, Inc., 1954-81; West Coast director, Institute for Regional Exploration, 1954-68. Extension Division leader in social sciences and communications, University of California, Los Angeles, 1966-68; teacher of science in secondary schools in Adelaide, South Australia, and MacKay, Queensland, Australia, 1968. Occasional editorial consultant on scientific and technical documentation, 1950-70. Research assistant and assistant director of anthropological/archaeolog;cal expedition to central Aleutian Islands, 1954. Lecturer before civic groups and at colleges and universities.

MEMBER: American Anthropological Association, American Folklore Society, Linguistic Society of America, Pi Gamma Mu, Phi Delta Kappa, Explorers. *Awards, honors:* American Council of Learned Societies grant-in-aid for research in American Indian linguistics, 1945; proclaimed Washington State Author by Washington state librarian, 1965, and Oregon State Author by Oregon state librarian, 1975.

WRITINGS: (Contributor) Dean F. Sherman, editor, *Alaska Cavalcade,* Alaska Life Publishing Co., 1943; *High Tension* (biography), privately printed, 1953; *Arizona Gem Trails and the Colorado Desert of California: A Field Guide for the Gem Hunter, the Mineral Collector, the Uranium Hunter,* Mineralogist Publishing Co., 1955; *Petrified Forest Trials: A Guide to the Petrified Forests of America,* Mineralogist Publishing Co., 1955; *The Rock-Hunter's Range Guide: How and Where to Find Minerals and Gem Stones in the United States,* Harper, 1962; *Fossils in America: Their Nature, Origin Identification and Classification, and a Range Guide to Collecting Sites,* Harper, 1964; *A Range Guide to Mines and Minerals: How and Where to Find Valuable Ores and Minerals in the United States,* Harper, 1964; *Gems and Minerals of America: A Guide to Rock Collecting,* Harper, 1975; *The Gold Hunter's Field Book: How and Where to Prospect for Colors, Nuggets, and Mineable Ores of Gold by Amateur and Serious Followers of Jason and the Golden Fleece,* Harper, 1975, published as *The Gold Hunter's Field Book: How and Where to Find Gold in the United States and Canada,* 1980; *A Complete Field Guide to American Wildlife* (Book-of-the-Month Club selection), Western edition, Harper, 1981.

Poetry is represented in anthologies, including *Full Sails,* edited by Vincent Hill, [Aberdeen, Wash.], 1931, *Younger Poets,* edited by Nellie B. Sergeant, Appleton, 1932, and *The World's Fair Anthology of Verse,* edited by Paul E. Carter, Exposition Press, 1939. Contributor of about 30 scientific papers to research quarterlies, including *American Anthropologist, Southwest Journal of Anthropology, Journal of American Folklore, International Journal of American Linguistics, Explorers Journal,* and *Phi Delta Kappan,* and of about 100 classified scientific and technical papers to missile and aerospace industry company publications; contributor of more than 1000 photo-illustrated feature articles to numerous magazines, including *Better Homes and Gardens, Pageant, American Forests, Catholic Digest, Field and Stream,* and *American West,* and of over 3000 feature articles, spot news, editorials, photo stories, and business articles to newspapers.

WORK IN PROGRESS: Mysteries of the Bighorn Medicine Wheel; research for books in archaeology, space exploration, and natural history.

SIDELIGHTS: Jay Ellis Ransom told *CA* that he has been a compulsive writer since the age of nine and currently averages forty to sixty hours of work in each week of the year. "Although I am retired." he says, "I continue to help beginning authors toward success whenever possible through direct instruction and editing or via voluminous correspondence." Referring to himself as a "word merchant," he estimates that he has some six million words in print.

Intensely interested in all branches of scientific research and development and a former contributor to classified aerospace developmental projects, Ransom keeps abreast of the space age through his journalistic association with NASA. Explains the author: "As director of the Western America Institute for Exploration and the associated Aleutian-Bering Sea Expeditions Research Library, I keep open house for scientifically minded visitors with a bona fide interest in anthropology and archaeology, linguistics, geographic exploration, photography, and educational research, as well as the whole gamut of the earth sciences with rockhounds and gold hunters currently predominating among recent visitations."

Though an author of books on topics in history and even prehistory, Ransom regards himself primarily as a journalist, assisted by photography whenever possible. He has written hundreds of feature articles (illustrated with his own photographs) on the nineteenth-century mining camps of all the Western states, and his many books for gem and mineral collectors are among the most authoritative in the field. States Ransom: "Writing for me is both vocation and avocation and professionalization its primary goal, but whether I write strictly scientific papers or for popular consumption I strive for readability so as to invoke enthusiasm and a deep interest in every potential reader. As a teacher and college instructor long since retired, I have never lost the dream of helping others to learn constructively so that every reader of what I write may feel benefited in some way."

Since 1954, Ransom has assisted scientists and students from American universities and from Great Britain in their expeditions to the central and western Aleutian Islands. For the most part, these expeditions have consisted of investigations into anthropology and archaeology, as well as undersea studies of flora and fauna and the search for Folsom Man's campsites, long since submerged beneath the Bering Sea. In 1980, he contributed anthropological, linguistic, and historical information to the archives of the native Aleut Aleutian/Pribilof Islands Association (headquartered in Anchorage, Alaska), including some previously unknown data which Ransom hopes will help obtain reparations for Attuan Aleuts incarcerated in Japan during World War II.

AVOCATIONAL INTERESTS: Wilderness exploration by canoe and backpack, field archaeology and anthropology, geology, paleontology, mineralogy, history of the American West, travel, and photography.

*   *   *

RASKIN, Edith Lefkowitz 1908-

PERSONAL: Born October 17, 1908, in New York, N.Y.; daughter of Maximillian (in real estate) and Sara (Brown) Lefkowitz; married Joseph Raskin (an artist and writer), October 30, 1936. *Education:* Hunter College (now Hunter College of the City University of New York), B.A., 1930; Cornell University, graduate study, 1939-40; New York University, M.A., 1941; American Museum of Natural History, graduate study. *Home:* 59 West 71st St., New York, N.Y. 10023. *Agent:* Bertha Klausner International Literary Agency, Inc., 71 Park Ave., New York, N.Y. 10016.

CAREER: New York City (N.Y.) Board of Education, teacher of science, 1930-37, biology laboratory teacher, 1937-67. *Member:* United Federation of Teachers, Authors Guild.

WRITINGS: (With Sylvia S. Greenberg) *Home-Made Zoo,* McKay, 1952; *Many Worlds: Seen and Unseen,* McKay, 1954; *Watchers, Pursuers and Masqueraders: Animals and Their Vision,* McGraw, 1964; *The Pyramid of Living Things,* McGraw, 1967; *The Fantastic Cactus: Indoors and in Nature,* Lothrop, 1969; *World Food,* McGraw, 1971.

With husband, Joseph Raskin; all published by Lothrop, except as indicated: *Indian Tales,* Random House, 1969; *Tales Our Settlers Told,* 1972; *Ghosts and Witches Aplenty: More Tales Our Settlers Told,* 1973; *The Newcomers: Ten Tales of American Immigrants,* 1974; *Guilty or Not Guilty: Tales of Justice in Early America,* 1975; *Spies and Traitors: Tales of the Revolutionary and Civil Wars,* 1976; *Strange Shadows: Spirit Tales of Early America,* 1977; *Of Whales and Wolves and Other Adventures in Early America,* 1978; *Tales of Indentured Servants,* 1978.

Work is represented in anthologies, including *Literature: Mythology and Folklore,* edited by James Burl Hogins, Science Research Associates, 1974, *Rhetoric and Literature,* edited by P. Joseph Canavan, McGraw, 1974, and *Expectations 1978,* edited by Betty Kalagian, Braille Institute, 1978.

WORK IN PROGRESS: A historical novel.

SIDELIGHTS: Edith Raskin writes: "I believe that all sciences are inter-related and my books in science attempt to reflect this viewpoint. My interest in American history has been sparked by the many summers my husband and I spent in New England and our many trips to the Southland full of historic sites. . . . Being the woman in our co-authorship, I always make certain that women are included in our tales of early America."

AVOCATIONAL INTERESTS: Plastic arts, theatre, opera, hiking, swimming, and watching baseball.

BIOGRAPHICAL/CRITICAL SOURCES: Best Sellers, March 1, 1968; *Book World,* October 12, 1969.

*   *   *

READ, David Haxton Carswell 1910-

PERSONAL: Born January 2, 1910, in Cupar, Fife, Scotland; son of John Alexander and Catherine (Carswell) Read; married Dorothy Florence Patricia Gilbert, November 23,

1936; children: Rory David. *Education:* University of Edinburgh, M.A. (first class honors), 1932; attended Universities of Montpellier, Strasbourg, and Paris, 1932-33, University of Marburg, 1934; New College, Edinburgh, B.D. (with distinction), 1936. *Home:* 1165 Fifth Ave., New York, N.Y. 10028. *Office:* Madison Avenue Presbyterian Church, 921 Madison Ave., New York, N.Y. 10021.

CAREER: Ordained minister, Church of Scotland, 1936. Minister of churches in Coldstream West and Edinburgh, Scotland, 1936-49; University of Edinburgh, chaplain, 1949-55; chaplain to H.M. the Queen of Scotland, 1952-56; Madison Avenue Presbyterian Church, New York, N.Y., minister, 1956—. Lecturer at theological schools in United States, Australia, Switzerland, and Canada, at colleges, and on radio and television. Croall Lecturer, University of Edinburgh, 1965. Director, Foundation for the Arts, Religion, and Culture. Vice-president, Appeal of Conscience Foundation. Member of board of governors, American-Scottish Foundation; trustee, St. Bernard's School; member of board of ministry, Harvard University. Traveled on Appeal of Conscience Foundation fact-finding missions to Northern Ireland, Irish Republic, U.S.S.R., Czechoslovakia, Rumania, and Hungary. *Military service:* British Army, 1939-45; became chaplain, fourth class; prisoner-of-war, 1940-45; mentioned in dispatches. *Member:* St. Andrew's Society of the State of New York (chaplain), Monday Club, Pilgrims, Century Association (New York City). *Awards, honors:* D.D., Edinburgh University, 1956, Yale University, 1959, Lafayette College, 1965, Hope College, 1969, Knox College, 1979; Litt. D., College of Wooster, 1966; L.H.D., Trinity University, 1972, Hobart and William Smith Colleges, 1972; D.H.L., Japan International Christian University, 1979.

WRITINGS: The Spirit of Life, Hodder & Stoughton, 1939; (translator from the German) *The Church to Come,* Hodder & Stoughton, 1939; *Prisoners' Quest,* S.C.M. Press, 1944; *The Communication of the Gospel,* S.C.M. Press, 1952; *The Christian Faith,* English Universities Press, 1955, Scribner, 1956; *I Am Persuaded* (collected sermons), Clark, 1961, Scribner, 1962; *Sons of Anak: The Gospel and the Modern Giants,* Scribner, 1964; *God's Mobile Family,* Madison Avenue Church Press, 1966; *Whose God Is Dead?,* Forward Movement Publications, 1966; *Holy Common Sense,* Abingdon, 1966; *The Pattern of Christ,* Scribner, 1967; *The Presence of Christ,* Pannonia Press, 1968; *Virginia Woolf Meets Charlie Brown,* Eerdmans, 1968; *Christian Ethics,* Hodder & Stoughton, 1968, Lippincott, 1969; *Giants Cut Down to Size,* Forward Movement Publications, 1970; *Religion without Wrappings,* Eerdmans, 1970; *Overheard,* Abingdon, 1971; *Curious Christians,* Abingdon, 1972; *An Expanding Faith,* Eerdmans, 1973; *Sent from God,* Abingdon, 1974; *Good News in Letters of Paul,* Collins-Fontana, 1975; *Go and Make Disciples,* Abingdon, 1978; *Unfinished Easter,* Harper, 1978; *The Faith Is Still There,* Abingdon, 1981. Contributor of articles on theological topics to *Atlantic, Christian Century, British Weekly,* and a dozen other journals in the United States, Great Britain, and Holland.

*   *   *

REDDING, David A.   1923-

PERSONAL: Born November 24, 1923, in Marietta, Ohio; son of Charles Mitchell (a minister) and Marian (Maxwell) Redding; married Dorothy McCleery, 1951; children: Marian Telford, John Maxwell, David Mitchell, Mark McCleery. *Education:* Attended Western Michigan College, (now University), 1944; U.S. Navy Midshipman's School, Columbia University, commissioned ensign, 1945; College of Wooster,

A.B., 1947; Ohio State University, graduate study, 1950; Oberlin College, B.D., 1952; University of Cincinnati, graduate study, 1961; Vanderbilt University, M. Div., 1973. *Home:* 1262 South State Rd., No. 257, Delaware, Ohio 43015. *Office:* 7080 Olentangy River Rd., Delaware, Ohio 43015.

CAREER: Doylestown High School, Doylestown, Ohio, teacher of English and speech, 1947-49; Evangelical and Reformed Hungarian Church, Cleveland, Ohio, preacher, 1950-52; First Presbyterian Church, Plain City, Ohio, minister, 1952-56; Glendale Presbyterian Church, Cincinnati, Ohio, minister, 1956-63; First Presbyterian Church, East Cleveland, Ohio, minister, 1963-66; Tarkio College, Tarkio, Mo., writer-in-residence, 1966; Flagler Memorial Church, St. Augustine, Fla., minister, 1968-74; Liberty Presbyterian Church, Delaware, Ohio, minister, 1974—. Member of Scioto Valley Presbytery, 1974—. *Military service:* United States Navy, 1943-46. *Awards, honors:* Distinguished alumni award, College of Wooster, 1969.

WRITINGS: The Parables He Told, Revell, 1962; *Psalms of David,* Revell, 1963, published as *Songs in the Night,* Paramount Press, 1970; *The Miracles of Christ,* Revell, 1964; *If I Could Pray Again,* Revell, 1965; *New Immorality,* Revell, 1967; *The Couch and the Altar,* Lippincott, 1968; *What Is the Man?,* Word Books, 1970; *Flagler and His Church,* Paramount Press, 1970; *The Faith of Our Fathers,* Eerdmans, 1971; *Until You Bless Me,* Eerdmans, 1972; *God Is Up to Something,* Word Books, 1972; *Jesus Makes Me Laugh with Him: A Christian Statement on Humor,* Zondervan, 1977; *Lives He Touched: The Relationships of Jesus,* Harper, 1978; (with others) *The Prayers I Love,* Strawberry Hill Press, 1978. Contributor of articles and editorials to *Life, Reader's Digest,* and religious magazines.

AVOCATIONAL INTERESTS: Construction, music, farming, athletics, and the out-of-doors.

BIOGRAPHICAL/CRITICAL SOURCES: Life, June 30, 1961; *Cincinnati Enquirer,* April 7, 1962.

*   *   *

REDGROVE, Peter (William)   1932-

PERSONAL: Born January 2, 1932, in Kingston-on-Thames, England; married; wife's name, Barbara (separated); three children. *Education:* Attended Queen's College, Cambridge.

CAREER: Poet. Has worked as a research chemist and as a journalist for *The Times,* London, England, writing mainly on educational subjects. Taught English language and literature at Academia Britanica in Malaga during stay in Spain, 1957; University of Leeds, Leeds, England, Gregory Fellow in Poetry, 1962-65; Falmouth School of Art, Cornwall, England, resident author and senior lecturer, 1966—. Visiting poet, University of Buffalo, 1961-62; visiting tutor, Bretton Hall College, 1965-66. O'Connor Professor of Literature, Colgate University, 1974-75. Lecturer at numerous universities in England and America; has given poetry recitals in England and the United States. Member of poetry panel, Arts Council. *Awards, honors:* Fulbright grant, 1961-62; Arts Council grant, 1969, 1970, 1973, 1975, 1977; *Guardian* Prize, 1973, for *In the Country of the Skin;* Imperial Tobacco Award for radio drama, 1978, for "The God of Glass."

WRITINGS—Poetry; all published by Routledge & Kegan Paul, except as indicated: The Collector and Other Poems, 1960; *The Nature of Cold Weather* (Poetry Book Society selection), 1961; *At the White Monument,* 1963; *The Force*

and Other Poems (Poetry Book Society selection), 1966; (with D. M. Thomas and D. M. Black) *Penguin Modern Poets 11*, Penguin, 1968; *Work in Progress*, Poet & Printer, 1968; *Dr. Faust's Sea-Spiral Spirit and Other Poems*, 1972; (with Penelope Shuttle) *The Hermaphrodite Album*, Fuller D'Arch Smith, 1973; *Sons of My Skin, 1954-74*, 1975; *From Every Chink of the Ark: New Poems American and English*, 1977; *The Weddings at Nether Powers*, 1979. Also author of poetry pamphlets and broadsides.

Novels; all published by Routledge & Kegan Paul, except as indicated: *In the Country of the Skin*, Sceptre Press, 1972, dramatic adaptation published under same title, Granite Press, 1973; (with P. Shuttle) *The Terrors of Dr. Treviles*, 1974; *The Glass Cottage*, 1976; *The God of Glass*, 1979; *The Sleep of the Great Hypnotist*, 1979; *The Beekeepers*, 1980.

Nonfiction: (With P. Shuttle) *The Wise Wound: Everywoman and Eve's Curse*, R. Marek, 1978.

Plays: *Three Pieces for Voices*, Poet & Printer, 1972; *"Miss Carstairs Dressed for Blooding" and Other Plays*, Marion Boyars, 1976.

Radio scripts; all for British Broadcasting Corp.; "The White Monument," 1963; "The Sermon," 1964; "The Anniversary," 1964; "In the Country of the Skin," 1973; "Dance the Putrefact with Colin Blakely," 1975; (with Yemi Ajibade and Anna Cropper) "The God of Glass," 1977.

Editor: *Poet's Playground*, Leeds Sports Association, 1963; *Universities Poetry 7*, Universities Poetry Management Committee, 1965; (with Harold Pinter and John Fuller) *New Poems 1967: A P.E.N. Anthology*, Hutchinson, 1967; *Lamb and Thundercloud*, Arvon Foundation, 1975.

Recordings: "The Poet Speaks," Argo Gramaphone Records, 1961; "British Poets of Our Time," Argo Gramaphone Records, 1975.

Poetry appears in over thirty anthologies. Contributor to *Times Literary Supplement, Spectator, New Statesman, Observer, Listener,* and other periodicals. Founding editor, *Delta*.

SIDELIGHTS: "There is no poet writing in Britain with a more ebullient imagination," claims Anne Stevenson in the *Times Literary Supplement*, "than Peter Redgrove." Redgrove's poems are of a surrealistic, exuberantly-lush variety that depict, as Douglas Dunn points out, the "imagination allowed to work, on its own principles, to capacity, to a fullness of utterance, [in order] to achieve a necessary condition of expression."

Redgrove's highly-imaginative poetry has a direct effect upon its audience. "You either respond to that imagination and are excited by it," Stevenson notes, "or you reject it altogether. There is little middle ground." The more negative side of this polarization of opinion can be found in Roger Gafitt's judgment that "Redgrove's work [tends] to drown in its own spume" and that "the quality of thought rarely breaks clear of the scrum of boisterous verbiage which comes milling into every poem." In sharp contrast to this view, Ben Howard believes that "admirers of Whitman's expansive line, of Roethke's fluent naturalistic description, and of Ammons's meticulous observation will find much to praise in the work of Redgrove."

Collections of Redgrove's papers are housed at the University of Buffalo's Lockwood Memorial Library, the University of Leeds' Brotherton Library, the University of Texas' Humanities Research Center, and at the University of Indiana Library. He has recorded his poetry for the U.S. Library of Congress, Yale University, the Harvard Poetry Room,

Tokyo University, the British Council, and the Canadian Broadcasting Corp. His books have been translated into French, Russian, Polish, German, and other languages.

BIOGRAPHICAL/CRITICAL SOURCES: London Magazine, April, 1962, December, 1963, October, 1969; *Times Literary Supplement*, December 12, 1963, November 18, 1977, July 25, 1980; *Guardian*, December 16, 1966; *Books & Bookmen*, March, 1967, June, 1973, February, 1975; *Poetry*, May, 1971, February, 1978; Michael Schmidt and Grevel Lindop, editors, *British Poetry since 1960: A Critical Survey*, Carcanet, 1972; *Times Educational Supplement*, March 24, 1972; *New Statesman*, July 21, 1972; *Contemporary Review*, July, 1973; *Midwest Quarterly*, summer, 1974; *Observer*, October 6, 1974, June 24, 1979; *Spectator*, October 12, 1974; *Encounter*, September, 1975; *Listener*, November 20, 1975; *Contemporary Literary Criticism*, Volume VI, Gale, 1976; *Hudson Review*, spring, 1977; *Western Humanities Review*, spring, 1977.

* * *

REEMAN, Douglas Edward 1924-
(Alexander Kent)

PERSONAL: Born October 15, 1924, in Thames Ditton, Surrey, England; son of Charles Percival and Lilian (Waters) Reeman; married Winifred Isabella McGowan Melville, July, 7, 1958. *Education:* Attended local schools in England, 1928-39. *Home:* Blue Posts, Eaton Park Rd., Cobham, Surrey, England.

CAREER: Left school at sixteen and joined the Royal Navy, serving on destroyers and small craft in World War II from 1940-46; became lieutenant; member of Royal Naval Volunteer Reserve for ten years. Began writing short stories while serving from 1946-50 with the London Metropolitan Police, at first on the beat and later as detective in the Criminal Investigation Division. From 1950-60 he was a children's welfare officer for the London County Council, working in the poorer districts of London. He also has done book reviewing and held navigation classes for yachtsmen. Lecturer on juvenile problems and delinquency; script adviser for television and motion pictures. Governor, Foudroyant Trust. Director, Bolitho Maritime Productions Ltd. and Highseas Authors Ltd. *Member:* National Geographic Society, Navy League, Royal Navy Sailing Association, M.T.B. Officers Association, Society for Nautical Research, Maritime Preservation Society, British Sailors Society (president), Royal Society for the Protection of Birds (fellow), Savage Club (London), Officers' Club (London).

WRITINGS: A Prayer for the Ship, Jarrolds, 1958, Putnam, 1973; *High Water*, Jarrolds, 1959; *Send a Gunboat*, Jarrolds, 1960, Putnam, 1961, published as *Escape from Santu*, Hamilton, 1962; *Dive in the Sun*, Putnam, 1961; *The Hostile Shore*, Jarrolds, 1962; *The Last Raider*, Jarrolds, 1963, Putnam, 1964; *With Blood and Iron*, Jarrolds, 1964, Putnam, 1965; *H.M.S. Saracen*, Jarrolds, 1965, Putnam, 1966; *Path of the Storm*, Hutchinson, 1966, Putnam, 1967; *The Deep Silence*, Hutchinson, 1967, Putnam, 1968; *The Pride and the Anguish*, Hutchinson, 1968, Putnam, 1969; *To Risks Unknown*, Hutchinson, 1969, Putnam, 1970; *The Greatest Enemy*, Hutchinson, 1970, Putnam, 1971; *Against the Sea* (nonfiction), Hutchinson, 1971; *Adventures under the Sea*, Walker, 1971; *Rendezvous: South Atlantic*, Putnam, 1972; *Go in and Sink*, Hutchinson, 1973; *The Destroyers*, Putnam, 1974; *Winged Escort*, Putnam, 1975; *Surface with Daring*, Putnam, 1977; *Strike from the Sea*, Morrow, 1978; *A Ship Must Die*, Morrow, 1979.

"Richard Bolitho" series; under pseudonym Alexander Kent: *To Glory We Steer*, Putnam, 1968; *Form Line of Battle!*, Putnam, 1969; *Enemy in Sight!*, Hutchinson, 1970; *The Flag Captain*, Putnam, 1971; *Sloop of War*, Putnam, 1972; *Command a King's Ship*, Putnam, 1973; *Signal: Close Action!*, Putnam, 1974; *Richard Bolitho: Midshipman*, Hutchinson, 1975, Putnam, 1976; *Passage to Mutiny*, Putnam, 1976; *In Gallant Company*, Putnam, 1977; *The Inshore Squadron*, Hutchinson, 1977, Putnam, 1979; *Midshipman Bolitho and the Avenger*, Putnam, 1978; *Stand into Danger*, Putnam, 1980.

SIDELIGHTS: Douglas Reeman's popular character Richard Bolitho is a sea captain in the 18th-century British Navy. His adventures involve many of the major historical events of that period including both the French and American Revolutions. As the series progresses, Bolitho moves up the ranks, eventually attaining the rank of admiral. For avid readers of the series, Hutchinson publishes *The Richard Bolitho Newsletter*.

Reeman told *CA:* "My main interest is in the sea, in ships, and in maritime history. I spend every available moment, when not writing, on travel, research, and seeking out locations and situations for my books. I travel many thousands of miles per year, by sea whenever possible, for as my books are published throughout the world I feel I need to know better the people who read them. My hobbies, too, are connected with the sea: sailing, cruising, and exploring beaches are amongst them—wild birds too, in all forms and of all countries."

Reeman has traveled extensively throughout the world, visiting Australia, Europe, Africa, and the United States. His books have been translated into 22 languages and have sold over 12 million copies.

BIOGRAPHICAL/CRITICAL SOURCES: New York Times, February 16, 1965; *Times Literary Supplement*, May 12, 1966, July 2, 1971; *New York Times Book Review*, March 3, 1968, May 24, 1970; *Top of the News*, June, 1968; *Saturday Review*, November 9, 1968; *Books & Bookmen*, August, 1969; *Observer*, August 13, 1972, November 24, 1974; *Book World*, September 24, 1972; *National Observer*, January 13, 1973; *America*, May 5, 1973; *Christian Science Monitor*, December 3, 1975.

*   *   *

REES, (Morgan) Goronwy 1909-
(R)

PERSONAL: Born November 29, 1909, in Aberystwyth, Cardiganshire, Wales; son of Richard Jenkin (a clergyman) and Apphia Mary (James) Rees; married Margaret Ewing Morris, November 20, 1940; children: Jenny, Lucy (Mrs. Michael Pearson), Daniel, Thomas, Matthew. *Education:* New College, Oxford, first class honors in philosophy, politics, and economics, 1931. *Politics:* Socialist. *Religion:* None. *Home:* 5 Strand-on-the-Green, London W. 4, England. *Agent:* A. D. Peters, 10 Buckingham St., London WC2N 6BU, England.

CAREER: Manchester Guardian (now *Guardian*), Manchester, England, leader writer, 1932-36; *Spectator*, London, England, assistant editor, 1936-39; director of a firm of general engineers and coppersmiths, 1946-51; Oxford University, All Souls College, Oxford, England, estates bursar, 1951-53; University College of Wales, Aberystwyth, principal, 1953-57. *Encounter*, London, contributing editor and author of monthly column under signature "R," 1965—. *Military*

service: British Army, Royal Welch Fusiliers, 1939-45; became lieutenant colonel.

WRITINGS: A Summer Flood (novel), Faber, 1932; *A Bridge to Divide Them* (novel), Faber, 1937; *Where No Wounds Were* (novel), Chatto & Windus, 1950; *A Bundle of Sensations: Sketches in Autobiography*, Chatto & Windus, 1960, Macmillan, 1961; *The Multi-Millionaries: Six Studies in Wealth*, Macmillan, 1961; *The Rhine*, Weidenfeld & Nicholson, 1966, Putnam, 1967; *St. Michael: A History of Marks and Spencer*, Weidenfeld & Nicholson, 1967, revised edition, Pan Books, 1973; *The Great Slump: Capitalism in Crisis, 1929-33*, Weidenfeld & Nicolson, 1970, Harper, 1971; *A Chapter of Accidents*, Library Press, 1972; *Brief Encounters*, Chatto & Windus, 1974; (editor and author of introduction) John McVicar, *McVicar by Himself*, Hutchinson, 1974, revised edition, 1979.

Translator: (With Stephen Spender) Georg Buechner, *Danton's Death*, Faber, 1939; Gustav Janouch, *Conversations with Kafka*, Praeger, 1953, revised edition, New Directions, 1972.

BIOGRAPHICAL/CRITICAL SOURCES: Observer, September 20, 1970; *New Statesman*, September 25, 1970; *Best Sellers*, August 15, 1971.†

*   *   *

REESE, M(ax) M(eredith) 1910-

PERSONAL: Born in August, 1910, in Epsom, Surrey, England; married Clare Campbell, 1950; children: two sons. *Education:* Attended Haileybury College; Merton College, Oxford, M.A. (first class honors in history), 1932. *Home:* 7 Mowatt Rd., Grayshott, Hindhead, Surrey, England.

CAREER: Formerly a teacher, currently a writer, lecturer, and journalist. *Member:* Rotary Club (Haslemere).

WRITINGS: The Tudors and Stuarts, Longmans, Green (New York), 1940, reprinted, Edward Arnold, 1966; *Shakespeare: His World and His Work*, St. Martin's, 1953, revised edition, Edward Arnold, 1980; *The Cease of Majesty: A Study of Shakespeare's History Plays*, Edward Arnold, 1961, St. Martin's, 1962; *William Shakespeare* (juvenile), St. Martin's, 1963; (editor) Shakespeare, *King Henry IV, Part I*, Edward Arnold, 1964; (editor) Shakespeare, *King Henry V*, Edward Arnold, 1966; (editor) *Elizabethan Verse Romances*, Humanities Press, 1968; (editor) Shakespeare, *As You Like It*, Thomas Nelson, 1969; (editor) Shakespeare, *A Midsummer Night's Dream*, Thomas Nelson, 1970; (editor) Edward Gibbon, *Gibbon's Autobiography*, Routledge & Kegan Paul, 1971; *Documents for History Revision*, Edward Arnold, 1971; *The Puritan Impulse: The English Revolution, 1559-1660*, A. & C. Black, 1975; *The Royal Office of Master of the Horse*, Threshold Books, 1976; (contributor) *The British Heritage*, Leisure Arts, 1979; *Oliver Cromwell*, Ward, Lock, 1981.

Also contributor to *The Joy of Knowledge Library*, Mitchell Beazley. Editor, "Offices of State" series, Terence Dalton, 1978. Contributor to *Nelson's Dictionary of World History*.

AVOCATIONAL INTERESTS: Cricket, detective stories.

*   *   *

REID, Alastair 1926-

PERSONAL: Born March 22, 1926, in Whithorn, Scotland; son of William Arnold (a minister) and Marian (Wilson) Reid; children: Jasper. *Education:* St. Andrews University, M.A. (with honors), 1949. *Residence:* Galilea, Mallorca,

Spain. *Office: New Yorker,* 25 West 43rd St., New York, N.Y. 10036.

CAREER: Sarah Lawrence College, Bronxville, N.Y., professor, 1951-55; *New Yorker,* New York, N.Y., staff writer, 1959—. Visiting professor of Latin American studies, Antioch College, 1969-70; summer instructor in Latin American literature, Oxford University and St. Andrew's University, 1972-73; visiting professor, Colorado College, 1977 and 1978, Yale University, 1979, and Dartmouth College, 1979. Lecturer for Association of American Colleges, 1966 and 1969. Translation judge, National Book Awards, 1979. Has given poetry readings at many colleges, universities, and cultural centers in the United States, Great Britain, Spain, and Latin America. *Military service:* Royal Navy, 1943-46. *Awards, honors:* Guggenheim fellow, 1957 and 1958; Columbia University fellow in writing, 1966.

WRITINGS: To Lighten My House (poetry), Morgan, 1953; *I Will Tell You of a Town* (juvenile), Houghton, 1955; *Fairwater* (juvenile), Houghton, 1956; *A Balloon for a Blunderbuss* (juvenile), Harper, 1957; *Allth* (juvenile), Houghton, 1958; *Ounce Dice Trice* (juvenile), Atlantic/Little, Brown, 1958; (with Bob Gill) *The Millionaires,* Simon & Schuster, 1959; *Oddments Inklings Omens Moments* (poetry), Atlantic/Little, Brown, 1959; *Supposing* (juvenile), Atlantic/Little, Brown, 1960; *Passwords: Places Poems Preoccupations* (poetry and prose), Atlantic/Little, Brown, 1963; *To Be Alive* (juvenile), Macmillan, 1966; *Uncle Timothy's Traviata* (juvenile), Dial, 1967; (contributor) Dannie Abse, editor, *Corgi Modern Poets in Focus 3,* Corgi, 1971; *La Isla Azul* (juvenile), Editorial Lumen (Barcelona), 1973; *Weathering: New and Selected Poems,* Dutton, 1978.

Translator: (With others) Jorge Luis Borges, *Ficciones,* Grove, 1965; (with Anthony Kerrigan) *Mother Goose in Spanish,* Crowell, 1967; Pablo Neruda, *We Are Many,* J. Cape, 1967, Grossman, 1968; (with Kerrigan) *Jorge Luis Borges: A Personal Anthology,* Grove, 1967; (with Ben Belitt) Neruda, *A New Decade: Poems 1958-67,* Grove, 1968; (with others) Neruda, *Selected Poems: A Bilingual Edition,* J. Cape, 1970, Delacorte, 1972; Neruda, *Extravagaria,* J. Cape, 1972, Farrar, Straus, 1974; (with others) Borges, *Selected Poems,* Delacorte, 1972; Mario Vargas Llasa, *Sunday Sunday,* Bobbs-Merrill, 1973; Neruda, *Fully Empowered,* Farrar, Straus, 1976; Borges, *Gold of the Tigers,* Dutton, 1977; Jose Emilio Pacheco, *Don't Ask Me How the Time Goes Past,* Columbia University Press, 1977; Neruda, *Isla Negra Notebook,* Farrar, Straus, 1981.

WORK IN PROGRESS: New poems and translations; a collection of essays, *Hispanics.*

SIDELIGHTS: Alastair Reid—poet, translator, essayist, and author of books for children—sees nothing unusual in the fact that he has written in such a variety of genres throughout his career. Switching from one to the other, he told a *Publishers Weekly* interviewer, has "never involved a change of wavelength.... I never *felt* the division between prose and poetry, and now that I'm after writing prose with the same care and intensity that poetry asks for, I'm interested in just writing, putting-into-words-well.... But I am always grateful for the discipline and precision in language that poetry exacts. I'm grateful in a way to translation too, for it keeps the wheels turning.... But I have too many things I want to write myself to do much more translation."

Scottish by birth, Reid has spent much of his life residing everywhere *but* Scotland, including Spain, Latin America, Greece, France, Morocco, Switzerland, and England. His strongest affinity, however, is reserved for the Hispanic countries; as he explains, "there's something in the Scottish attitude I've always rejected, and still do, some leftover Calvinism which frowns on joy, on spontaneity, too cautious for me.... I found something in the Spanish wavelength, in its starkness and spontaneity, that felt like the antidote to Scotland for me.... I would emphatically rather live in a Latin country than any other."

As for his itinerant lifestyle, Reid admits that it is possible only because "writing is the most portable occupation there is.... An itinerant existence has certain strange consequences, however—I have next to no possessions, and I never keep copies of my books or writings once they have come out. I look on my own writing always as something I've left behind, and am only interested in what I'm working on at the moment.... With all this talk about roots ..., I feel somewhat of an odd man out, for I've chosen to cut loose from my roots. It would make no sense at all to call me a Scottish writer. Mid-Atlantic, maybe. But I've elected, for most of my writing life, to live in a limbo, between countries and languages, as interpreters, exiles and displaced persons do. I like the state of being a foreigner. It sharpens the ear and eye, and the kind of alienation it implies is not a bad wavelength for a writer to work on, as long as his nerve and curiosity are up to it, and as long as the mails still go through."

Though Reid has expressed a desire more or less to abandon poetry in favor of writing more prose pieces, this shift in interest cannot be attributed to the reception his work has received through the years. Critics praise virtually all of his books for their light, entertaining style and universal appeal. His very first collection of poems, *To Lighten My House,* was termed "an auspicious debut" by a *Booklist* critic, who went on to state that "he uses the direct and innocent vision of the child to reach the conclusions of the adult." A *San Francisco Chronicle* reviewer, asserting that "it is apparent that this young Scots poet has grown up with Dylan Thomas whispering in his ear," concluded that Reid is "less of a bard and more of a thinker, less original, yet just as lyric" as Thomas.

"Reid's poems happen," noted P. H. Davison in an *Atlantic* review of *Oddments Inklings Omens Moments.* "They do not try to arrange their substance rigidly, but rather in a natural irregularity.... Accordingly, their titles are sometimes too whimsical, and the poems do not often have that finally indestructible quality found in Graves or Yeats. But Reid is a fine poet who takes feeling where he finds it, without categories." Philip Booth of the *Christian Science Monitor* called *Oddments* "a casual (but never random) collection of slant insights, sudden intimations, and sharp portents." Commented the *Yale Review*'s Thom Gunn: "Reid is an extremely pleasant and entirely unpretentious poet.... He knows exactly what he can do, and does it well every time. It is perhaps light verse, but it is excellent light verse."

Reid's books for children have also been very well received, with special attention directed to the fact that adults as well as children will find them thought-provoking and amusing. *I Will Tell You of a Town,* for example, prompted the *Christian Science Monitor* reviewer to remark: "Full of nuance and shading to win the poetry-loving grown-ups, it is generously enough sprinkled with cats, songs and antic-loving children to keep the four-to-eight-year-old set brightly amused." *Fairwater,* described by the *Saturday Review* critic as "a perfect book to read alone, and wonder about," has a "haunting, songlike quality," according to the *New York Times'* Elizabeth Enright. "It is original and poetic and sometimes funny. Its landscape, though gentler and prettier, reminds one of Tolkien's Hobbit country.''

Ounce Dice Trice, a collection of puns and odd-sounding "nonsense" words and names teamed with appropriately whimsical drawings, began as a children's book but, as Lillian Morrison of the *Saturday Review* concluded, "it is for anyone of any age who finds pleasure in words and word sounds." A *San Francisco Chronicle* reviewer agreed, stating that "it got too sophisticated [to be merely a children's book].... It turns out to be a wonderfully engaging, and adult, word book." *Allth,* a fairy tale of sorts, also captured reviewers' attention due to the author's fascination with unusual words and names. The *Christian Science Monitor's* Pamela Marsh wrote that the story is told "with a fine dramatic sense and a joy in ringing words that should enchant the 7-11's and anyone else who gets a look-in." The *Saturday Review* critic noted that *Allth* is written "in mysterious, beautiful language which is perfect for reading aloud." M. S. Libby of the *New York Herald Tribune Book Review* agreed, concluding, "[Reid's] books are treasures to own, to read aloud, to return to, as you do to St. Exupery's *The Little Prince.*"

BIOGRAPHICAL/CRITICAL SOURCES: Booklist, June 1, 1953; *San Francisco Chronicle,* August 23, 1953, September 21, 1958; *Christian Science Monitor,* May 10, 1956, September 29, 1958, October 9, 1958, April 27, 1959, December 5, 1963; *New York Times,* May 13, 1956, August 18, 1957, November 2, 1958; *New York Herald Tribune Book Review,* May 20, 1956, May 12, 1957, September 28, 1958, November 2, 1958, May 8, 1960; *Saturday Review,* June 23, 1956, September 21, 1957, November 1, 1958, July 16, 1960; *Commonweal,* September 26, 1958; *New York Times Book Review,* November 2, 1958; *Christian Century,* February 25, 1959; *Yale Review,* June, 1959; *Atlantic,* July, 1959; *Poetry,* November, 1959; *Chicago Sunday Tribune,* May 8, 1960; *Poetry and Fiction,* Rutgers University Press, 1963; *Time,* September 20, 1963.

—*Sketch by Deborah A. Straub*

*   *   *

REID, John Kelman Sutherland 1910-

PERSONAL: Born March 31, 1910, in Leith, Scotland; son of David and Georgina Thomson (Stuart) Reid; married Margaret Winifrid Brookes, January 3, 1950. *Education:* University of Edinburgh, M.A. (first class honors), 1933, B.D., 1938; attended University of Heidelberg, 1933, University of Marburg, 1937, University of Basel, 1938-39, and University of Strasbourg, 1939. *Home:* 1 Camus Park, Edinburgh EH10 6RY, Scotland.

CAREER: University of Calcutta, Scottish Church College, Calcutta, India, professor of philosophy, 1935-37; ordained in Church of Scotland, 1939; Craigmillar Park Parish Church, Edinburgh, Scotland, minister, 1939-52; University of Leeds, Leeds, England, professor of theology, 1952-61; University of Aberdeen, Aberdeen, Scotland, professor of systematic theology, 1961-76. Kerr Lecturer, University of Glasgow, 1952-54; Montgomery Lecturer, Institute of Christian Education (London), 1960-61; lecturer at Princeton Theological Seminary and at Union Theological Seminary, Richmond, Va., 1960. Honorary secretary, Joint Committee on the New English Bible, Great Britain, 1949—; member of Theological Commission on Faith and Order, World Council of Churches, 1961-76. *Military service:* British Army, chaplain to parachute regiment, 1942-46, 1949-62. *Member:* Society for Study of Theology, Studiorum Novi Testamenti

Societas. *Awards, honors:* D.D., University of Edinburgh, 1957; Territorial Decoration, 1962; Commander of the British Empire, 1970.

WRITINGS: Calvin's Theological Treatises, Westminster, 1954; *Human Destiny,* S.C.M. Press, 1954; *The Biblical Doctrine of the Ministry,* Oliver & Boyd, 1955; *The Authority of Scripture,* Methuen, 1957, 2nd edition, 1970; *Presbyterians and Unity,* Mowbray, 1962; *Our Life in Christ,* Westminster, 1963; *Christian Apologetics,* Hodder & Stoughton, 1969, Eerdmans, 1970.

Translator: Oscar Cullmann, *The Earliest Christian Confessions,* Lutterworth, 1949; Cullmann, *Baptism in the New Testament,* S.C.M. Press, 1950; Jean Bosc, *The Kingly Office of the Lord Jesus Christ,* Oliver & Boyd, 1959; (and author of introduction) Calvin, *Concerning the Eternal Predestination of God,* J. Clarke, 1961. Contributor to religious journals. Assistant editor and co-translator, Barth, *Kirchliche Dogmatik.* Joint editor, *Scottish Journal of Theology,* 1948—.

*   *   *

REIMER, Bennett 1932-

PERSONAL: Surname is pronounced *Reem*-er; born June 19, 1932, in New York, N.Y.; son of George (a businessman) and Sarah (Talkofsky) Reimer; married Sally Harrison, June 17, 1957 (divorced, 1970); married Joyce Bogusky (an instructor in music), March 16, 1973; children: (first marriage) Jan Ellen, Terry. *Education:* State Teachers College (now State University of New York College at Fredonia), B.S., 1954; University of Illinois, M.S., 1955, Ed.D., 1963. *Office:* Department of Music Education, Cleveland Institute of Music, 11021 East Blvd., Cleveland, Ohio 44106.

CAREER: College of William and Mary, Richmond Professional Institute, Richmond, Va., instructor in music and band director, 1955-57; Madison College, Harrisonburg, Pa., assistant professor of music and director of music at Campus Laboratory School, 1958-60; University of Illinois at Urbana-Champaign, 1960-65, began as instructor, became assistant professor of music education; Case Western Reserve University, Cleveland Ohio, professor of music, 1965-73, Kulas Professor of Music, beginning 1973, director of music education, beginning 1965; currently affiliated with Cleveland Institute of Music, Cleveland. Member of Music Education Research Council, 1968-74; member of advisory committee, Council for Research in Music Education, 1963—.

AWARDS, HONORS: Grants from U.S. Office of Education, 1964-67, to develop and test a two-year curriculum in general music for junior and senior high schools, and 1967—, to study an aesthetic education curriculum program for elementary schools.

WRITINGS: (Contributor), *Perspectives in Music Education,* Music Educators National Conference, 1966; (contributor) *Influences in Curriculum Change,* Association for Supervision and Curriculum Development, 1968; *A Philosophy of Music Education,* Prentice-Hall, 1970; (editor with others and contributor) *Toward an Aesthetic Education,* Music Educators National Conference, 1971; (contributor) R. A. Smith, editor, *Aesthetics and Problems of Education,* University of Illinois Press, 1971; (with Edward G. Evans) *The Experience of Music,* Prentice-Hall, 1971; (with Evans) *Developing the Experience of Music,* Prentice-Hall, 1973; (contributor) Justin Belitz, *General Music,* Franciscan Herald Press, 1974.

Author of reports. Contributor to conference reports. Contributor of articles and reviews to music and education journals, including *Music Educators Journal, Journal of Aesthetic Education, Educational Forum, Religious Education, Journal of Research in Music Education,* and *Instrumentalist.* Member of editorial board, *Music Educators Journal,* 1966-70; editorial consultant, *Journal of Aesthetic Education,* 1966—.†

* * *

REINER, William B(uck) 1910-1976

PERSONAL: Born May 23, 1910, in New York, N.Y.; died January 24, 1976, in St. Thomas, Virgin Islands; son of Meyer (a tailor) and Mollie (Silver) Reiner; married Jeannette Ender, October 5, 1935 (died, 1970); married Myrtle Lifland (a professor), January 23, 1971; children: (first marriage) Albey M.; (second marriage) two stepsons. *Education:* City College (now City College of the City University of New York), B.S., 1931, M.S., 1932; New York University, Ph.D., 1942. *Religion:* Jewish. *Home:* 785 Park Ave., New York, N.Y. 10021.

CAREER: New York City public schools, high school teacher of chemistry, 1934-49, Bureau of Educational Research, research assistant, 1949-54, research associate, 1954-63, Bureau of Curriculum Research, assistant director, 1963-65; Hunter College of the City University of New York, New York City, professor of education, beginning 1965, director of Office of Institutional Research, 1966-68. Adjunct professor of research, Long Island University; lecturer at New York University and Brooklyn College of the City University of New York. *Member:* National Education Association, National Science Teachers Association, National Society for the Study of Education, National Council on Measurement in Education, American Educational Research Association, Doctorate Association of New York Educators.

WRITINGS: The Flying Rangers (juvenile science fiction), Messner, 1953; (with Don Wilcox and Helen Olos) *A Child's First Book of Outdoor Adventures,* Grosset, 1954; (with Frederic Shaw) *An Evaluation of the Pedagogic Staff Relations Plan, 1955,* Bureau of Administrative and Budgetary Research, New York (City) Board of Education, 1956; (contributing editor) J. Darrell Barnard, *Teaching High School Science* (pamphlet), American Educational Research Association, 1956; (contributor) Alice Crow and Lester Crow, editors, *Vital Issues in American Education,* Bantam, 1964; (contributor) Alfred de Grazia and David Sohn, editors, *Programs, Teachers, and Machines,* Bantam, 1964; (with Dale Scannell) *Tests of Academic Progress,* Houghton, 1965, revised edition, 1971; (with Charles Spiegler) *What to Do after High School,* Science Research Associates, 1971; (with wife, Myrtle Reiner) *Foundations of Educational Research,* Springer, 1974.

Also author of technical monographs, reports, and tests of academic progress; editor and co-author of "The Research Program in Our Schools," a radio script for WNYE-Radio, 1961. Co-editor, "Problems and Practices in New York City Schools," New York Society for the Experimental Study of Education, 1953, 1955, 1957, and 1959. Author of column "Spotlight on Research," *Science Teacher,* 1959-64. Contributor of more than sixty articles and reviews to education journals, including *Review of Educational Research, School Science and Mathematics, Education, Graduate School Record, Science Education,* and *Journal of Experimental Education.*

AVOCATIONAL INTERESTS: Travel, sports.†

REMAK, Joachim 1920-

PERSONAL: Born December 4, 1920; married Roberta Anne Mattingly, 1948; children: Robert Arthur, Catherine Anne. *Education:* University of California, Berkeley, B.A., 1942, M.A., 1946; attended Columbia University, 1946-47; Stanford University, Ph.D., 1955. *Office:* Department of History, University of California, Santa Barbara, Calif. 93106.

CAREER: U.S. Department of State, Washington, D.C., London, England, and Baden-Baden, Germany, historian, 1947-51; Stanford University, Stanford, Calif., instructor in history, 1954-58; Lewis and Clark College, Portland, Ore., assistant professor, 1958-60, associate professor of history, 1960-65, chairman of department, 1962-63; University of California, Santa Barbara, associate professor, 1965-67, professor of history, 1967—, chairman of department, 1977—. Visiting associate professor, Indiana University, 1963-64. *Military service:* U.S. Navy, 1943-46. *Member:* American Association of University Professors (chapter president, 1961-63), American Historical Association. *Awards, honors:* Co-winner of Borden Award, Hoover Library, 1960; Danforth faculty grant, 1960; Guggenheim fellow, 1965-66; Higby Prize for best article in *Journal of Modern History,* 1970.

WRITINGS: Sarajevo: The Story of a Political Murder, Criterion, 1959; *The Gentle Critic: Theodor Fontane and German Politics,* Syracuse University Press, 1964; *The Origins of World War I, 1871-1914,* Holt, 1967; *The Nazi Years,* Prentice-Hall, 1969; (editor) *The First World War: Causes, Conduct, Consequences,* Wiley, 1971; *The Origins of the Second World War,* Prentice-Hall, 1976. Contributor to United States and German history publications, as well as *Saturday Review, Harper's, Commentary,* and other journals. Co-editor, *Documents on German Foreign Policy, 1918-1945,* Volumes I-IV, U.S. Government Printing Office, 1947-51.

* * *

REMINI, Robert V(incent) 1921-

PERSONAL: Born July 17, 1921; son of William Francis and Lauretta (Tierney) Remini; married Ruth T. Kuhner, 1948; children: Elizabeth Mary, Joan Marie, Robert William. *Education:* Fordham University, B.S., 1943; Columbia University, M.A., 1947, Ph.D., 1951. *Office address:* Department of History, University of Illinois, Box 4348, Chicago, Ill. 60680.

CAREER: Fordham University, New York, N.Y., instructor, 1947-51, assistant professor, 1951-59, associate professor of American history, 1959-65; University of Illinois at Chicago Circle, professor of history, 1965—, chairman of department, 1965-66 and 1967-71. Visiting lecturer, Columbia University, 1959-60. Special editor, Crowell-Collier Educational Corp. *Military service:* U.S. Navy, 1943-46; became lieutenant. *Member:* American Historical Association, Organization of American Historians, American Association of University Professors, Southern Historical Association. *Awards, honors:* Grant-in-aid, American Council of Learned Societies, 1960, and American Philosophical Society, 1964; Encaenia Award, Fordham University, 1963; Friends of American Writers Award of Merit, 1977; Huntington Library fellowship, 1978; Guggenheim fellow, 1978-79.

WRITINGS: Martin Van Buren and the Making of the Democratic Party, Columbia University Press, 1959; *The Election of Andrew Jackson,* Lippincott, 1963; (editor and author of introduction and notes) Dixon Ryan Fox, *The Decline of*

Aristocracy in the Politics of New York, 1801-1840, Harper, 1965; *Andrew Jackson* (biography), Twayne, 1966; (editor and author of introduction) James Parton, *The Presidency of Andrew Jackson,* Harper, 1966; *Andrew Jackson and the Bank War: A Study in the Growth of Presidential Power,* Norton, 1968; (contributor) Arthur Schlesinger, Jr., and Fred L. Israel, editors, *History of American Presidential Elections, 1789-1968,* Volume I, McGraw, 1971; (editor) *The Age of Jackson,* University of South Carolina Press, 1972; (with James I. Clark) *We the People: A History of the United States,* Glencoe Press, 1975; *The Revolutionary Age of Andrew Jackson,* Harper, 1977; *Andrew Jackson and the Course of American Empire, 1767-1821,* Harper, 1977; (with Edwin Miles) *The Era of Good Feelings and the Age of Jackson,* AHM Publishing, 1979.

Consulting editor, *The Papers of Andrew Jackson.* Contributor to *Encyclopaedia Britannica* and to professional journals. Member of editorial board, *Journal of American History,* 1969-72.

WORK IN PROGRESS: A biography of Martin Van Buren.

AVOCATIONAL INTERESTS: Travel, music.

*   *   *

REUBER, Grant L(ouis)   1927-

PERSONAL: Surname is pronounced *Rye*-ber; born November 23, 1927, in Mildmay, Ontario, Canada; son of J. Daniel (a farmer) and Gertrude C. Reuber; married Margaret L. J. Summerhayes (a librarian), October 21, 1951; children: Rebecca, Barbara, Mary. *Education:* University of Western Ontario, B.A. (with honors), 1950; Harvard University, A.M., 1954, Ph.D., 1957; also studied at Sidney Sussex College, Cambridge, 1954-55. *Religion:* Anglican. *Home:* 6 Lakeview Ter., Ottawa, Ontario, Canada K1S 3H4. *Office:* Bank of Montreal, Head Office, 129 St. James St., Montreal, Quebec, Canada.

CAREER: Bank of Canada, Ottawa, Ontario, economist, 1950-52; Canadian Department of Finance, Ottawa, economist, 1955-57; University of Western Ontario, London, assistant professor, 1957-59, associate professor, 1959-62, professor of economics, 1962-78, chairman of department, 1963-69, dean of social sciences, 1969-74, vice-president (academic) and provost, 1974-78; senior vice-president and chief economist, Bank of Montreal, 1978-79; deputy minister of finance, Government of Canada, Ottawa, 1979-80; executive vice-president, Bank of Montreal, 1980—. Member of Royal Commission on Banking and Finance, 1962-63; member of Joint Committee on Economic Policy of the Province of Ontario, 1972-79; chairman of Ontario Economic Council, 1973-78. Consultant to National Council of Applied Economic Research (India), Canadian International Development Agency, Economic Council of Canada, and Organization for Economic Co-operation and Development.

MEMBER: Canadian Economic Association (chairman of founding committee; president, 1967-68), Royal Society of Canada (fellow), American Economic Association, Econometric Society, Economic Study Society, Royal Economic Society, University Club (Toronto). *Awards, honors:* Rockefeller Foundation scholar-in-residence, Bellagio Study and Conference Centre, 1978.

WRITINGS: Britain's Export Trade with Canada, University of Toronto Press, 1960; *Canada-United States Trade: Its Growth and Changing Composition,* Private Planning Association of Canada, 1960; (with R. J. Wonnacott) *The Cost of Capital in Canada,* Resources for the Future, 1961;

Canada's Interest in the Trade Problems of the Less-Developed Countries, Private Planning Association of Canada, 1964; *The Objectives of Monetary Policy,* Queen's Printer, 1964; (with J. V. Graham, S. G. Peitchinis, and others) *The Role of the Trust and Loan Companies in the Canadian Economy,* University of Western Ontario, 1965; (with R. G. Bodkin, E. P. Bond, and T. R. Robinson) *Price Stability and High Employment: The Options for Canadian Economic Policy,* Queen's Printer, 1967; (with Frank Roseman) *The Take-Over of Canadian Firms, 1945-1961: An Empirical Analysis,* Queen's Printer, 1969; (with R. E. Caves) *Canadian Economic Policy and the Impact of International Capital Flows,* University of Toronto Press, 1969.

(With Caves) *Capital Transfers and Economic Policy: Canada, 1951-1962,* Harvard University Press, 1970; *Wage Determination in Canadian Manufacturing: 1953-1966,* Queen's Printer, 1971; *Private Foreign Investment in Development,* Clarendon Press (of Oxford University), 1973; *The Riddle of International Monetary Reform,* Atlantic Council of Canada, 1973; (editor with T. N. Guinsburg) *Perspectives on the Social Sciences in Canada,* University of Toronto Press, 1974; *Canada's Political Economy: Current Issues,* McGraw, 1980.

Contributor: E. P. Neufeld, editor, *Money and Banking in Canada,* McClelland & Stewart, 1964; John H. G. Crispo, editor, *Wages, Prices, Profits, and Economic Policy,* University of Toronto Press, 1968.

R. H. Wagenberg, editor, *Canadian-American Interdependence: How Much?,* University of Windsor Press, 1970; Paul Streeten and Hugh Corbet, editors, *Commonwealth Policy in a Global Context,* Frank Cass, 1971; Fritz Machlup, W. S. Salent, and Lorie Tarshis, editors, *International Mobility and Movement of Capital,* National Bureau of Economic Research, 1972; *Canadian-United States Financial Relationship,* Federal Reserve Bank of Boston, 1972; H. H. Binhammer, J. P. Cairns, and R. W. Broadway, editors, *Canadian Banking and Monetary Policy,* McGraw (Canada), 1972; J. F. Chant, editor, *Canadian Perspectives in Economics,* Collier (Canada), 1972; D.A.L. Auld, editor, *Contemporary Economic Issues in Canada,* Holt, 1972; A.L.K. Acheson, Chant, and M.F.J. Prachowny, editors, *Bretton Woods Revisited,* University of Toronto Press, 1972; L. A. Skeoch, editor, *Canadian Competition Policy,* Queen's University, 1972; *World Trade and Domestic Adjustment* (monograph), Brookings Institution, 1973; L. H. Officer and L. B. Smith, editors, *Issues in Canadian Economics,* McGraw, 1974; *Future Trends in Primary Commodities* (monograph), Brookings Institution, 1974.

S.M.A. Hameed, editor, *Canadian Industrial Relations,* Butterworth & Co., 1975; P. A. Boarman and H. Schollhammer, editors, *Multinational Firms and Governments,* Praeger, 1975; L. V. Castle and F. Holmes, editors, *Co-operation and Development in the Asia/Pacific Region–Relations between Large and Small Countries,* Japan Economic Research Centre (Tokyo), 1976; *Which Way Ahead?,* Fraser Institute (Vancouver), 1977; *Economic Relations between East and West: Prospects and Problems,* Brookings Institution, 1978; *Consultation and Consensus: A New Era in Policy Formulation,* Conference Board in Canada (Ottawa), 1978; J. R. Prichard, W. T. Stanbury, and T. A. Wilson, editors, *Canadian Competition Policy: Essays in Law and Economics,* Butterworth & Co., 1979; R. B. Byers and R. W. Redord, editors, *Canada Challenged: The Viability of Confederation,* Canadian Institute of International Affairs (Toronto), 1979. Contributor of articles and reviews to economics and business journals.

REYES, Carlos 1935-

PERSONAL: Born June 2, 1935, in Marshfield, Mo.; son of Herman Carrol and Alice (Day) King; married second wife, Karen Ann Stoner, May 21, 1978; children: (first marriage) Michael Hollingsworth, Amy Sofia, Nina Heloise, Rachel Kathleen. *Education:* University of Oregon, B.A., 1961; University of Arizona, M.A., 1965. *Home:* 2754 Southeast 27th, Portland, Ore. 97202.

CAREER: University of Maine, Orono, instructor in foreign languages, 1965-66; Portland State University, Portland, Ore., assistant professor of Spanish and Italian, 1966-73; Portland Art Museum School, Portland, instructor in English, 1971-72; restorer and rehabilitator of older homes, 1973—. Member of Oregon Governor's Advisory Committee on the Arts, 1971-72. *Military service:* U.S. Army, 1953-56.

WRITINGS—Poems: *The Windows,* Weed Flower Press, 1967; *Odes for Every Occasion,* Runcible Spoon, 1971; *The Prisoner,* Capra, 1973; *The Orange Letters,* Local Earth, 1976; *The Thought of You,* Isadora, 1978; *The Shingle Weaver's Journal,* Lynx House, 1980.

WORK IN PROGRESS: Two books of poetry, *The Light Keepers* and *Dreaming of Black Birds.*

SIDELIGHTS: Carlos Reyes told *CA:* "After a frustrating career in college teaching I was forced to realize that first and foremost I am a poet (everything else takes second place to that). Poetry writing to me is real and constant in an otherwise chaotic existence."

*   *   *

REYNOLDS, Philip Alan 1920-

PERSONAL: Born May 15, 1920, in Worthing, Sussex, England; son of Harry (a pharmacist) and Ethel (Scott) Reynolds; married December 27, 1946; children: Susan, Anthony John, Michael Scott. *Education:* Queen's College, Oxford University, B.A., 1940, M.A., 1950. *Home:* 8 Castle Park, Lancaster, England.

CAREER: University of London, London School of Economics and Political Science, London, England, 1946-50, began as assistant lecturer, became lecturer in international history; University College of Wales, Aberystwyth, Wilson Professor of International Politics, 1950-64; University of Lancaster, Lancaster, England, professor of politics and pro vice-chancellor, 1964-80, vice-chancellor, 1980—. *Military service:* Royal Artillery, 1940-46; became major. *Member:* Royal Institute of International Affairs, Political Studies Association, British International Studies Association.

WRITINGS: *War in the 20th Century,* University of Wales Press, 1951; *British Foreign Policy in the Inter-War Years,* Longmans, Green, 1954; (contributor) *New Cambridge Modern History,* Volume XII, Cambridge University Press, 1968; *An Introduction to International Relations,* Longman, 1971, revised edition, 1980; (with E. J. Hughes) *The Historian as Diplomat: Charles Kingsley Webster and the United Nations, 1939-1946,* Martin Robertson, 1976; (contributor) K. Goldmann and G. Sjoestedt, editors, *Power, Capabilities, Interdependence,* Sage, 1979. Also contributor to *Studies in Politics,* 1970. Contributor of articles to *Chambers's Encyclopaedia, World Survey,* and to journals, including *Political Studies, International Journal* (Toronto), *International Studies* (New Delhi), and *British Journal of International Studies.*

*   *   *

RHODIN, Eric Nolan 1916-

PERSONAL: Born January 1, 1916, in Niagara Falls, N.Y.;

son of Brodde Erik and Jane (Hyde) Rhodin; married Peg Hollingsworth; children: Victoria, Rebecca, Anthony, William, Susan, Penn, Joanna. *Education:* Lafayette College, B.A., 1938; attended Harvard University, 1940-41; University of Pittsburgh, M.A., 1942. *Politics:* Democrat. *Religion:* Quaker. *Home:* 640 West Lafayette St., Easton, Pa. 18042. *Office:* Department of English, Moravian College, Bethlehem, Pa. 18018.

CAREER: Worked for newspapers in New York and elsewhere, 1938-53; on staff of *Easton Express,* Easton, Pa., 1953-69; Moravian College, Bethlehem, Pa., 1963—, currently professor of English.

WRITINGS: *The Scar,* Harper, 1961; *The Autumn of the Fox,* Doubleday, 1962; *Newspapermen,* Odyssey, 1967; *Winter House,* Westminster, 1970; *The Good Greenwood,* Westminster, 1971; *The Sinister Affair,* Westminster, 1973. Contributor of short stories and poems to magazines and newspapers.

*   *   *

RIASANOVSKY, Nicholas V(alentine) 1923-

PERSONAL: Born December 21, 1923, in Harbin, China; son of Valentine Alexandrovich and Antonina (Podgorinova) Riasanovsky; married Arlene Schlegel, February 15, 1955; children: John, Nicholas, Maria. *Education:* University of Oregon, B.A., 1942; Harvard University, A.M., 1947; Oxford University, D.Phil., 1949. *Religion:* Eastern Orthodox. *Home:* 874 Contra Costa Ave., Berkeley, Calif. 94707. *Office:* Department of History, University of California, Berkeley, Calif. 94720.

CAREER: Taught at State University of Iowa, Iowa City, 1949-57; University of California, Berkeley, 1957—, currently Sidney Hellman Ehrman Professor of European History. Member of board of trustees, National Council for Soviet and East European Research. *Military service:* U.S. Army, became second lieutenant; awarded Bronze Star Medal and four campaign stars. *Member:* American Historical Association, American Association for the Advancement of Slavic Studies (president, 1973-77). *Awards, honors:* Rhodes scholar, 1947-49; Fulbright fellowship, 1954-55; Commonwealth Club of San Francisco Silver Medal for *History of Russia;* grants from Social Science Research Council, American Council of Learned Societies, and Fulbright Foundation, 1964-65, for study in Russia; Guggenheim fellowship, 1969; National Endowment for the Humanities senior fellow, 1975; Fulbright senior scholar, 1979; International Research and Exchanges Board fellow, 1979.

WRITINGS: *Russia and the West in the Teaching of the Slavophiles,* Harvard University Press, 1952; *Nicholas I and Official Nationality in Russia, 1825-1855,* University of California Press, 1959; *A History of Russia,* Oxford University Press, 1963, 3rd edition, 1977; (editor with Gleb Struve) *California Slavic Studies,* University of California Press, Volumes I-XI, 1964-80; *The Teaching of Charles Fourier,* University of California Press, 1969; *A Parting of the Ways: Government and the Educated Public in Russia, 1801-1855,* Clarendon Press, 1976. Contributor to several other books. Member of governing board and editorial board, *The Russian Review.*

WORK IN PROGRESS: A book on the image of Peter the Great in Russian history and thought.

*   *   *

RIBNER, Irving 1921-1972

PERSONAL: Born August 29, 1921, in Brooklyn, N.Y.; died

July 2, 1972; son of Adolph and Helen (Dangler) Ribner; married Roslyn Greenblatt, 1943; children: Clifford Neil, Jonathan Paul. *Education:* Brooklyn College (now Brooklyn College of the City University of New York), A.B., 1941; University of North Carolina, M.A., 1946, Ph.D., 1949. *Home:* Beach Path, Belle Terre, N.Y.

CAREER: Ohio State University, Columbus, instructor, 1949-52; Queens College (now Queens College of the City University of New York), Flushing, N.Y., instructor, 1952-53; Tulane University, New Orleans, La., 1953-64, began as assistant professor, became professor of English, University of Delaware, Newark, H. Rodney Sharp Professor of English, 1964-68; State University of New York at Stony Brook, professor of English, 1968-72, chairman of department, 1968-70. *Military service:* U.S. Army, 1943-46. *Member:* Modern Language Association of America, Shakespeare Association of America, Renaissance Association, Malone Society. *Awards, honors:* Guggenheim, Fulbright, American Council of Learned Societies, and Huntington Library fellowships.

WRITINGS: The English History Play in the Age of Shakespeare, Princeton University Press, 1957, 2nd edition, 1965; *Patterns in Shakespearian Tragedy,* Methuen, 1960, reprinted, Rowman & Littlefield, 1979; *Jacobean Tragedy: The Quest for Moral Order,* Methuen, 1962, reprinted, Rowman & Littlefield, 1979; (editor) *The Complete Plays of Christopher Marlowe,* Odyssey, 1963; (editor) Cyril Tourneur, *The Atheist's Tragedy; Or, the Honest Man's Revenge,* Harvard University Press, 1964; *Tudor and Stuart Drama,* Appleton, 1966, 2nd edition, AHM Publishing, 1978; (reviser) George Lyman Kittredge, editor, *The Complete Works of William Shakespeare,* 2nd edition, thirty-six volumes (Ribner not associated with original edition), Wiley, 1966-69; *William Shakespeare: An Introduction to his Life, Times, and Theatre,* Blaisdell Publishing, 1969. Contributor to learned journals.

BIOGRAPHICAL/CRITICAL SOURCES: New York Times, July 4, 1972.†

*　　*　　*

RICHMOND, H(ugh) M(acrae) 1932-

PERSONAL: Born March 20, 1932, in Burton, England; son of Ronald Jackson (a bank manager) and Isabella (a teacher; maiden name, Macrae) Richmond; married Velma Bourgeois (a professor), August 9, 1958; children: Elizabeth, Claire. *Education:* Emmanuel College, Cambridge, B.A., 1954; Wadham College, Oxford, D.Phil., 1957. *Religion:* Roman Catholic. *Office:* Department of English, University of California, Berkeley, Calif. 94720.

CAREER: Lycee Jean Perrin, Lyons, France, assistant in English, 1954-55; University of California, Berkeley, instructor, 1957-59, assistant professor, 1959-63, associate professor, 1963-68, professor of English, 1968—, director of Shakespeare program, 1973—. *Military service:* British Army, Royal Artillery, 1950-51; became lieutenant. *Member:* Modern Language Association of America, Shakespeare Association of America, Renaissance Society of America, Comparative Literature Association. *Awards, honors:* American Council of Learned Societies fellow for study of European landscape poetry, 1964; National Endowment for the Humanities fellow for study of Shakespeare in performance, 1978; Distinguished Teaching Award, University of California, Berkeley, 1980.

WRITINGS: The School of Love: The Evolution of the Stuart Love Lyric, Princeton University Press, 1964; *Shake-*

speare's Political Plays, Random House, 1967; (editor) Shakespeare, *King Henry IV, Part I,* Bobbs-Merrill, 1967; *Shakespeare's Sexual Comedy: A Mirror for Lovers,* Bobbs-Merrill, 1971; (editor) Shakespeare, *King Henry VIII,* W. C. Brown, 1971; *Renaissance Landscapes,* Mouton, 1973; *The Christian Revolutionary: John Milton,* University of California Press, 1974; *Puritans and Libertines: Anglo-French Literary Relations in the Reformation,* University of California Press, 1981. Contributor of articles to *Comparative Literature, Shakespeare Quarterly, Modern Philology, South Atlantic Quarterly,* and other publications.

WORK IN PROGRESS: Shakespeare and the Novelle, a study of the use of realistic fiction in the theater; a study of the effects of television on Shakespeare.

SIDELIGHTS: H. M. Richmond told *CA:* "My writing and research are chiefly devoted to the study of literature as a subtle documentation of the evolution of human consciousness, and of its expanding potentialities, a study approached through the comparative methodology of historical psychology. Most recently, this study has extended to the investigation of the effect of modern media on classic authors, particularly the impact of cinema, television, and current theatrical techniques on audience responses to Shakespeare. This topic has led to a systematic program of research, teaching, and public productions of Shakespeare plays of all kinds and forms, and it favors a more dynamic social role for literature and its study."

*　　*　　*

RICHTER, Harvena 1919-

PERSONAL: Born March 13, 1919, in Reading, Pa.; daughter of Conrad (the author) and Harvena (Achenbach) Richter. *Education:* University of New Mexico, B.A., 1938; New York University, M.A., 1955, Ph.D., 1967. *Home:* 1932 Candelaria Rd. N.W., Albuquerque, N.M. 87107. *Agent:* Paul R. Reynolds, Inc., 12 East 41st St., New York, N.Y. 10017. *Office:* Department of English, Humanities Bldg., University of New Mexico, Albuquerque, N.M. 87131.

CAREER: Advertising copywriter, copy chief, and advertising director, for Saks Fifth Avenue, Macy's, Elizabeth Arden, and I. Miller, 1941-48; reporter for European edition of *New York Herald Tribune,* North American Newspaper Alliance, Women's National News Service, 1948-49; free-lance writer, 1949-52; New York University, New York, N.Y., instructor in English, 1952-66; University of New Mexico, Albuquerque, assistant professor of English, 1969—. *Member:* Modern Language Association of America, American Association of University Women, Authors Guild of the Authors League of America, Kappa Kappa Gamma.

WRITINGS: The Human Shore, Little, Brown, 1959; *Virginia Woolf: The Inward Voyage,* Princeton University Press, 1970; (editor) Conrad Richter, *The Rawhide Knot and Other Stories,* Knopf, 1978. Contributor of short stories, articles, and poems to magazines, including *New Yorker, Saturday Evening Post, Atlantic Monthly,* and *Glamour.*

WORK IN PROGRESS: Conrad Richter on Writing, for Princeton University Press; a second and third novel; another book on Virginia Woolf.

SIDELIGHTS: Harvena Richter told *CA:* "I grew up in the glow of hearing my father read his writing aloud. Something was absorbed, but diluted into many small streams, from advertising to travel writing, poetry to fiction. I'm especially interested in myth and childhood, that state of personal myth which enchants the more its distance increases." *Avoca-*

tional interests: The sea, far places, music, research into the past, and gardens.

*   *   *

RIDDLE, Maxwell 1907-

PERSONAL: Born July 29, 1907, in Ravenna, Ohio; son of Henry Warner and Mary (Fitz-Gerald) Riddle; married Martha Augusta Hurd, March 31, 1933; children: Betsey (Mrs. Richard Whitmore), Henry Warner III. *Education:* Attended Colgate University, 1925-27, and University of Illinois, 1927-28; University of Arizona, A.B., 1929. *Politics:* Democrat. *Religion:* United Church of Christ. *Home:* 5374 Riddle Rd., P.O. Box 286, Ravenna, Ohio.

CAREER: Free-lance writer, 1929-31; Newspaper Enterprise Association Service, Cleveland, Ohio, turf writer, 1931-38; *Cleveland Press,* Cleveland, reporter, columnist, pets editor, 1938-68. International all-breeds licensed dog judge. *Member:* Dog Writers Association (president, 1948-49, 1980), Sigma Delta Chi, Western Reserve Kennel Club (president, 1950-51), Ravenna Kennel Club. *Awards, honors:* Dog Writer of the Year, 1949, 1961; Kilbon Memorial Award, 1949, 1961; named Dogdom's Man of the Year, 1968; December 14, 1968 was declared "Maxwell Riddle Day" by Cleveland Mayor Carl Stokes; named Dog Journalist of the Year, 1969, 1972.

WRITINGS: The Springer Spaniel, Judy Publishing, 1939, 4th edition published as *Springer for Show and Field,* 1957; *The Lovable Mongrel,* All Pets Publishing, 1954; *This Is the Chihuahua,* Sterling, 1959; *The Complete Book of Puppy Training and Care,* Coward, 1963; *Your Show Dog,* Doubleday, 1968; (chief contributor) *International Dog Encyclopedia,* Howell, 1971, revised edition, 1974; *The Complete Brittany Spaniel,* Howell, 1974; *The New Shetland Sheepdog,* Howell, 1974; (with Seeley) *The Complete Alaskan Malamute,* Howell, 1976; *The Wild Dogs in Life and Legend,* Howell, 1979; *Complete Book of the Family Dog,* Doubleday, 1981. Chief contributor to *The Modern Dog Encyclopedia;* contributor of articles to animal magazines.

BIOGRAPHICAL/CRITICAL SOURCES: Editor and Publisher, March 2, 1957, September 12, 1959; *Time,* May 11, 1959.

*   *   *

RIDLER, Anne Barbara 1912-

PERSONAL: Born July 30, 1912, in Rugby, Warwickshire, England; daughter of Henry Christopher (a master at Rugby School) and Violet Alice (Milford) Bradby; married Vivian Ridler (a printer to Oxford University), 1938; children: Jane, Alison, Benedict, Colin. *Education:* King's College, University of London, diploma in journalism, 1932. *Religion:* Church of England. *Home:* 14 Stanley Rd., Oxford, England.

CAREER: Faber & Faber Ltd., London, England, affiliated with editorial department as secretary and reader, 1935-40. *Awards, honors:* Oscar Blumenthal Prize, 1954, and Union League Civic and Arts Foundation Prize, 1955, both for poems published in *Poetry* (Chicago).

*WRITINGS—*Published by Faber, except as indicated: *Poems,* Oxford University Press, 1939; *A Dream Observed and Other Poems,* [London], 1941; *The Nine Bright Shiners* (poems), 1943; *Cain* (play), Nicholson & Watson, 1943; *The Shadow Factory, A Nativity Play,* 1946; *Henry Bly, and Other Plays,* 1950; *The Golden Bird, and Other Poems,* 1951; *The Trial of Thomas Cranmer* (verse play), 1956; *A Matter of*

Life and Death (poems), 1959; *Selected Poems,* Macmillan, 1961; *Who Is My Neighbor?* (verse play), 1963; *Olive Willis and Downe House* (biography), J. Murray, 1967; *Some Time After* (poems), 1972; *The Jesse Tree,* Lyrebird Press, 1972; (translator of libretto) Monteverdi, *Orfeo,* 1974; (translator of libretto) Cavalli, *Eritrea,* Oxford University Press, 1974; *The Lambton Worm* (libretto), Oxford University Press, 1979. Also translator of several other libretti, as yet unpublished.

Editor or compiler: *The Little Book of Modern Verse,* Faber, 1941, revised and enlarged edition (with Michael Roberts) published under title *Faber Book of Modern Verse,* 1951; *Shakespeare Criticism, 1919-1935,* 2nd edition, Oxford University Press, 1956; *Best Ghost Stories,* 2nd edition, Faber, 1957; Charles Williams, *Image of the City and Other Essays,* Oxford University Press, 1958; *Shakespeare Criticism, 1935-1960,* Oxford University Press, 1963; *Poems and Some Letters of James Thomson,* University of Illinois Press, 1963; Thomas Traherne, *Poems, Centuries and Three Thanksgivings,* Oxford University Press, 1966; (with Christopher Bradby) *Best Stories of Church and Clergy,* Faber, 1966; *Selected Poems of George Darley,* Merrion Press, 1979. Contributor of poetry to periodicals in England and America, including *New Yorker* and *Virginia Quarterly Review;* contributor of reviews to *Manchester Guardian* and *Review of English Studies.*

WORK IN PROGRESS: A Victorian Family Post-Bag.

*   *   *

RIEBER, R(obert) W(olff) 1932-

PERSONAL: Surname is pronounced *Ree*-ber; born March 24, 1932, in Philadelphia, Pa. *Education:* Pennsylvania State University, B.A., 1954; Temple University, M.A., 1955; University of London, Ph.D., 1971.

CAREER: Temple University, Hearing Clinic, Philadelphia, Pa., speech therapist, 1954-55; Mercer County Cerebral Palsy Association, Inc., Mercer County, N.J., speech pathologist, 1955-56; University of Pennsylvania, Graduate Hospital, Philadelphia, speech pathologist, 1956-57; Philadelphia Board of Education, Philadelphia, Pa., speech consultant, 1957-58; New York University, Medical Center, New York City, speech pathologist in Children's Division, 1958-59; director of speech rehabilitation program in schools in Ridgewood, N.J., 1959-60; Rutgers University, New Brunswick, N.J., instructor in speech, 1960-62; Nassau Community College, Garden City, N.Y., assistant professor of speech, 1962-63; Pace College (now University), New York City, assistant professor of speech, 1963-72; John Jay College of Criminal Justice of City University of New York, New York City, adjunct assistant professor, 1970-72, assistant professor of psychology, beginning 1972. Research consultant to New York State Psychiatric Institute.

MEMBER: International Association of Logopedics and Phoniatrics, American Psychological Association, American Speech and Hearing Association, American Anthropological Association (fellow), New York Academy of Sciences, Society for Speech and Voice Therapy of New York City (member of board of directors).

WRITINGS: (Editor and author of introduction) J. C. Amman, *A Dissertation on Speech,* North-Holland Publishing, 1966; (editor with R. S. Brubaker) *Speech Pathology: An International Study of the Science,* Lippincott, 1966; *Communication Disorders: A Historical Essay,* C. C Thomas, 1973; *Historical Roots of Communication Disorders,* Bobbs-Merrill, 1973; (editor with Doris Aaronson) *Developmental*

Psycholinguistics and Communication Disorders, New York Academy of Sciences, 1975; (editor) *The Neuropsychology of Language: Essays in Honor of Eric Lenneberg,* Plenum Press, 1976; (editor with Kurt Salzinger) *The Roots of American Psychology: Historical Influences and Implications for the Future,* New York Academy of Sciences, 1977; (editor) *The Problem of Stuttering: Theory and Therapy,* Elsevier, 1977; (editor with Harold J. Vetter) *The Psychological Foundations of Criminal Justice: Historical Perspectives on Forensic Psychology,* Volume I, John Jay Press, 1978; (editor) *Language Development and Aphasia in Children,* Academic Press, 1980. Editor, ''Language, Man and Society: Foundations of the Behavioral Sciences,'' a series of reprints, AMS Press, 1972—. Contributor to transactions and proceedings. Contributor to *Journal of Psycholinguistics, Folia Phoniatrica, Journal of Psychology,* and *Journal of Speech and Hearing Disorders.* Editor of *Journal of Communication Disorders* and *Journal of Psycholinguistic Research.*†

*   *   *

RINGGREN, (Karl Vilhelm) Helmer   1917-

PERSONAL: Born November 29, 1917, in Ala, Sweden; son of Hugo Vilhelm and Kally Anna Alice (Lyberg) Ringgren; married Ingrid Maria Blom (a teacher); children: Cecilia, Agneta, Viveka. *Education:* University of Uppsala, T.K., 1942, F.K., 1943, T.L., 1945, T.D., 1947, F.L., 1952. *Religion:* Lutheran. *Home:* St. Johannesgatan 41A, Uppsala, Sweden. *Office:* Dekanhuset, Uppsala, Sweden.

CAREER: Abo Akademi, Abo, Finland, assistant professor of Old Testament, 1947-56; University of Uppsala, Uppsala, Sweden, assistant professor of history of religions, 1949-59; Garrett Theological Seminary (now Garrett-Evangelical Theological Seminary), Evanston, Ill., professor of Old Testament, 1960-62; Abo Akademi, professor of history of religions, 1962-65; University of Uppsala, professor of Old Testament, 1965—. *Member:* Society of Biblical Literature, American Oriental Society, Royal Academy of Arts and Sciences (Uppsala), Nathan Soderblom Society (Uppsala; secretary, 1954-59).

WRITINGS: Word and Wisdom: Studies in the Hypostatization of Divine Qualities and Functions in the Ancient Near East, privately printed by H. Ohlsson, 1947; *The Prophetical Conception of Holiness,* Lundequistska Bokhandeln, 1948; *Fatalism in Persian Epics,* Lundequistska Bokhandeln, 1952; *Studies in Arabian Fatalism,* Lundequistska Bokhandeln, 1955; *The Messiah in the Old Testament,* A. R. Allenson (Chicago), 1956; *Handskrifterna fraan Qumran IV-V,* Wretmans Boktryckeri, 1956; *Psaltarens fromhet,* Svenska Kvrkans Diakonistyrelses Bokfoerlag, 1957, translation by Ringgren published as *The Faith of the Psalmists,* Fortress, 1963; (with Ake V. Stroem) *Religionerna i historia och nutid,* Svenska Kvrkans Diakonistyrelses Bokfoerlag, 1957, 6th edition, Verbum, 1974, translation of 3rd edition by Niels L. Jensen, edited by J.C.G. Greig, published as *Religions of Mankind Today and Yesterday,* Fortress, 1967; (editor and translator) *Das Hohe Lied, Klagelieder,* [und] *Das Buch Esther,* Vandenhoeck & Ruprecht, 1958; *Tro och liv enligt doeda-havsrullarna,* Svenska Kvrkans Diakonistyrelses Bokfoerlag, 1961, translation by Emilie T. Sander published as *The Faith of Qumran: Theology of the Dead Sea Scrolls,* Fortress, 1963; (with Walther Zimmerli) *Sprueche: Prediger, uebersetzt und erklaert,* Vandenhoeck & Ruprecht, 1962, revised edition, 1980; *Sacrifice in the Bible,* Lutterworth 1962, Association Press, 1963; *Israelitische Religion,* Kohlhammer, 1963, translation by David E. Green published as *Israelite Religion,* Fortress, 1966; (editor) *Fatalistic Beliefs*

in Religion, Folklore, and Literature, Almqvist & Wiksell (Stockholm), 1967; *Fraemre Orientens religioner i gammal tid,* Svenska Bokfoerlaget, 1967; *Hebreish nyboerjarbok,* C.W.K. Gleerups, 1969; *Religionens form och funktion,* C.W.K. Gleerups, 1970; (editor with G. J. Botterweck) *Theologisches Noerterbuch zum Alten Testament,* W. Kohlhammer, 1970, translation published as *Theological Dictionary of the Old Testament,* Eerdmans, 1977.

WORK IN PROGRESS: A continuation of the Old Testament dictionary.

*   *   *

RIPLEY, Elizabeth Blake   1906-1969

PERSONAL: Born June 9, 1906, in New Haven, Conn.; died June 21, 1969; daughter of James Kingsley and Helen (Putnam) Blake; married Kenneth T. Ripley (divorced). *Education:* Smith College, A.B., 1928; attended Art Students League, 1940-42. *Religion:* Protestant. *Residence:* New London, N.H.

CAREER: Elizabeth Ripley Cards, New London, N.H., owner-manager, 1948-56; Workshop Cards Corp., Concord, N.H., card designer, 1956-62. Writer and illustrator. Nurse's aid, New London Hospital. Worked with Recordings for the Blind, New Haven, Conn. *Member:* League of New Hampshire Arts and Crafts.

WRITINGS—Juvenile biographies: *Leonardo da Vinci,* Oxford University Press, 1952; *Michelangelo,* Oxford University Press, 1953; *Vincent Van Gogh,* Oxford University Press, 1954; *Rembrandt,* Oxford University Press, 1955; *Goya,* Oxford University Press, 1956; *Rubens,* Oxford University Press, 1957; *Durer,* Lippincott, 1958; *Picasso,* Lippincott, 1959; *Botticelli,* Lippincott, 1960; *Raphael,* Lippincott, 1961; *Titian,* Lippincott, 1962; *Winslow Homer,* Lippincott, 1963; *Gainsborough,* Lippincott, 1964; *Velazquez,* Lippincott, 1965; *Rodin,* Lippincott, 1966; *Copley,* Lippincott, 1967; *Hokusai,* Lippincott, 1968.

Compiler and illustrator; all published by Oxford University Press: *Lots of Laughs* (jokes), 1942; *Nothing but Nonsense* (limericks), 1943; *Dopey Doings* (jokes), 1950.

Illustrator; all published by Oxford University Press: *Riddle Me This,* 1940; *Very First Aid,* 1942; *Very First Garden,* 1943; *This Little Boy Went to Kindergarten,* 1944; *Up Goes the House,* 1946; *Counting-out Rhymes,* 1946, reprinted, 1970.

AVOCATIONAL INTERESTS: Making scarecrows for her garden in New London, N.H.

BIOGRAPHICAL/CRITICAL SOURCES: Publishers Weekly, July 28, 1969.†

*   *   *

RIPLEY, Francis Joseph   1912-

PERSONAL: Born 1912, in St. Helens, Lancashire, England; son of Richard D. and Annie (Ranson) Ripley. *Education:* Attended Capuchin College, Birmingham, England, 1930-34, and Upholland College, 1935-39. *Agent:* Messrs. Watt, 10 Norfolk St., London, W.C. 2, England. *Office:* Church of St. Oswald and St. Edmund, Liverpool Rd., Ashton-in-Makerfield, Wigan WN4 9NP, Lancashire, England.

CAREER: Ordained Roman Catholic priest, 1939; Liverpool Archdiocese, Liverpool, England, curate, 1939-44, 1947-50; Catholic Missionary Society, London, England, member, 1950-57, superior, 1957-60; Catholic Information Center,

Liverpool, director, 1961-70; currently chairman of Catholic Truth Society. Created Canon of Archdiocese of Liverpool, 1980. Lectured in United States, 1947. *Military service:* Royal Air Force, chaplain and squadron leader, 1944-47. *Member:* Legion of Mary (laureate member), Society of Authors, Challoner Club (London).

WRITINGS: (With F. S. Mitchell) *Souls at Stake,* Wagner, 1948; *This Is the Faith,* Birchley Hall, 1950, Newman Press, 1952, new edition, Print Organisation, 1974; *Priest of Christ,* Newman Press, 1959; *Your Sunday Gospels,* Catholic Publishing Co., 1959; *A Priest for Ever,* Newman Press, 1960; *One Christ, One Church,* Newman Press, 1960; *The Last Gospel* (Spiritual Book Associates selection), Sheed, 1961; *All Love,* J. S. Burns, 1961; *Selling the Church,* Thomas More, 1962; *African Diary,* J. S. Burns, 1962; *Talks to Legionaries,* J. S. Burns, 1963; *Living for Christ,* St. Paul Publications, 1965; *A Basic Guide to Religious Instruction,* Sands, 1965; *Your Sunday Epistles,* Geoffrey Chapman, 1966; *The Apostolate of the Laity,* Sands, 1967; *More Talks to Legionaries,* J. S. Burns, 1967; (editor) *Pope Paul Says . . . : Translations of Some of Pope Paul's Addresses Issued by the U.S. Catholic Conference,* J. S. Burns, 1968; *Jubilee Talks to Legionaries,* J. S. Burns, 1972; *The St. Peter Catechism of Catholic Doctrine,* 2nd revised edition, Lumen Christi, 1972.

Also author of pamphlets and booklets. Weekly columnist, *Catholic Pictorial;* contributor of articles to religion journals. Editor, *Flarepath,* 1945-47, and *Catholic Truth; Catholic Gazette,* manager, 1952-55, editor, 1955-57.

SIDELIGHTS: Francis Joseph Ripley toured Africa in 1960 and 1962. *Avocational interests:* Playing the organ, music, travel, photography.

*   *   *

RISCHIN, Moses 1925-

PERSONAL: Born October 16, 1925, in New York, N.Y.; son of Meer (a physician) and Rachel (Nelson) Rischin; married Ruth S. Solomon (a specialist in Russian literature); children: Sarah Elizabeth, Abigail Sophia, Rebecca Mira Martha. *Education:* Brooklyn College (now Brooklyn College of the City University of New York), A.B., 1947; Harvard University, A.M., 1948, Ph.D., 1957. *Politics:* Democrat. *Religion:* Jewish. *Home:* 350 Arballo Dr., San Francisco, Calif. 94132. *Office:* History Department, San Francisco State University, 1600 Holloway Ave., San Francisco, Calif. 94132.

CAREER: Brooklyn College (now Brooklyn College of the City University of New York), Brooklyn, N.Y., lecturer, 1949-53; Brandeis University, Waltham, Mass., instructor, 1953-54; New School for Social Research, New York City, lecturer, 1955-58; American Jewish Committee Institute of Human Relations, New York City, research associate, 1956-58; Long Island University, Brooklyn, assistant professor of history, 1958-59; Radcliffe College, Cambridge, Mass., assistant editor, *Notable American Women,* 1959-60; University of California, Los Angeles, lecturer, 1962-64; San Francisco State University, San Francisco, Calif., 1964—, currently professor of history. Fulbright-Hays lecturer, University of Uppsala, 1969. Consultant to Center for the Study of Democratic Institutions, California Council for the Humanities, and *Harvard Encyclopedia for American Ethnic Groups.* Director, Western Jewish History Center of the Magnes Museum.

MEMBER: American Historical Association, American Studies Association, American Jewish Historical Society, Organization of American Historians. *Awards, honors:* Grants-in-aid from American Philosophical Society and American Council of Learned Societies; Tercentenary Fellow in American Jewish History; *The Promised City* was nominated for Pulitzer Prize and received the first non-fiction award of Jewish Book Council of America, 1963; fellowships from American Council of Learned Societies, Guggenheim Foundation, and the National Endowment for the Humanities.

WRITINGS: An Inventory of American Jewish History, foreword by Oscar Handlin, Harvard University Press, 1954; *Our Own Kind: Voting by Race, Creed or National Origin,* Center for the Study of Democratic Institutions, 1960; *The Promised City: New York's Jews, 1870-1914,* Harvard University Press, 1962, 3rd revised edition, 1977; (contributor) *Documentary History of the Jews in the United States, 1790-1840,* three volumes, Columbia University Press, 1963; (editor) *The American Gospel of Success: Individualism and Beyond,* Quadrangle, 1965; (editor and author of introduction) Hutchins Hapgood, *The Spirit of the Ghetto,* Harvard University Press, 1967; (editor with Samuel J. Hurwitz) *A Liberal between Two Worlds: Essays of Solomon F. Bloom,* Public Affairs Press, 1968; (contributor) Charles Wollenberg, editor, *Ethnic Conflict in California,* Tinnon-Brown, 1970; *Immigration and the American Tradition,* Bobbs-Merrill, 1976; (contributor) Richard L. Bushman, editor, *Uprooted Americans,* Little, Brown, 1979; *The Jews of the West: The Metropolitan Years,* American Jewish Historical Society, 1979; *The Jews and Pluralism: Toward an American Freedom Symphony,* Institute on Pluralism and Group Identity, 1980. Editor, "Modern Jewish Experience" series, fifty-nine volumes, Arno Press, 1975. Contributor to *Dictionary of American Biography,* 1977, and *Encyclopedia of American Biography,* 1974. Member of editorial boards of *Journal of American Ethnic History* and *Studies in American Jewish Literature.*

WORK IN PROGRESS: The New Journalism of Abraham Cahan; a biography, *Abraham Cahan.*

*   *   *

RIST, Ray C(harles) 1944-

PERSONAL: Born December 7, 1944, in Carbondale, Ill.; son of Ray C. (a clergyman) and Mildred (Borman) Rist; married Marilee Carol Esala (a professor), 1966; children: Paul. *Education:* Valparaiso University, B.A., 1967; Washington University, St. Louis, Mo., M.A., 1968, Ph.D., 1970. *Office:* College of Human Ecology, Cornell University, Ithaca, N.Y. 14850.

CAREER: Portland State University, Portland, Ore., assistant professor, 1970-72, associate professor of sociology, 1972-74; National Institute of Education, senior policy analyst, 1974-75, head of desegregation studies, 1975, associate director, 1976; Max Planck Institute, West Berlin, Germany, visiting fellow, 1976-77; Cornell University, Ithaca, N.Y., visiting professor, 1977-79, professor, 1979—. Consultant to U.S. Commission on Civil Rights and National Institute of Education. *Member:* American Sociological Association, Society for the Study of Social Problems, Pacific Sociological Association, Midwest Sociological Association, European Group for the Study of Deviance and Social Control. *Awards, honors: American School Board Journal* named *The Urban School* one of nine outstanding education books of 1973; National Science Foundation grant, 1974; Fulbright fellow, 1976-77.

WRITINGS: (Editor) *Restructuring American Education,*

Trans-Action, 1972; *The Quest for Autonomy,* Afro-American Center, University of California, Los Angeles, 1972; *The Urban School: A Factory for Failure,* M.I.T. Press, 1973; (editor) *The Pornography Controversy,* Trans-Action, 1974; *The Invisible Children,* Harvard University Press, 1978; *Guest Workers in Germany,* Praeger, 1978; *Desegregated Schools,* Academic Press, 1979. Contributor of about one hundred articles to journals, including *Harvard Educational Review, Phylon, Daedalus, Journal of International Affairs, Social Problems,* and numerous others. Associate editor of *Northwest Journal of African and Black American Studies, Journal of Black Social Research, Society, Sociology of Education, Urban Education,* and *Children and Youth Services Review.*

WORK IN PROGRESS: A book on west European social policy and another on American youth unemployment.

*   *   *

RIVKIN, Arnold 1919-1968

PERSONAL: Born May 26, 1919, in New York, N.Y.; died, 1968; son of Samuel M. and Ethel (Dubin) Rivkin; married Jeanette Maling, 1953; children: Elizabeth Ann, William Mitchell, Laura Maling. *Education:* Brooklyn College (now Brooklyn College of the City University of New York), B.A. (cum laude), 1941; Harvard University, LL.B. (cum laude), 1948; Salzburg Seminar in American Legal Studies, certificate, 1954.

CAREER: Admitted to the Bar of New York State, 1948, and the Bar of the U.S. Supreme Court, 1956; Anniston Ordnance Depot, Anniston, Ala., director of purchasing and contracting, 1941-42; affiliated with Economic Cooperation Administration, Washington, D.C., 1948-49, and Paris, France, 1949-52; Office of U.S. Special Representative in Europe and permanent representative to North Atlantic Treaty Organization, Paris, assistant general counsel, 1952-53; Mutual Security Agency and Foreign Operations Administration Special Missions, London, England, counsel, 1953-55; International Cooperation Administration, Washington, D.C., associate general counsel, 1955-57; Massachusetts Institute of Technology, Center for International Studies, Cambridge, director of African project and research associate in political economy, 1957-62; International Bank for Reconstruction and Development, Washington, D.C., economic adviser in Africa department, 1962-64, affiliated with Development Advisory Service, beginning 1965. Consultant to U.S. Government agencies, National Academy of Sciences, and private foundations, 1957-62; leader of two economic missions to Nigeria, 1961; economic adviser to prime minister of Sierra Leone, 1964. Lecturer on African affairs in Ghana, Nigeria, Sierra Leone, France, England, Spain, Canada, Israel, and United States; University of California, Los Angeles, visiting professor, 1965, Regents' Professor of African Studies and Economic Development, spring, 1967. *Military service:* U.S. Army, Infantry, 1942-45; received Purple Heart.

MEMBER: Council on Foreign Relations, African Studies Association (fellow), Institute for Differing Civilizations, Society for International Development, International Club of Washington, Harvard Law School Association. *Awards, honors:* International Cooperation Administration Meritorious Service Award, 1958; Brooklyn College Alumni Honors Award, 1963.

WRITINGS: Africa and the West: Elements of Free-World Policy, Praeger, 1962; *The African Presence in World Affairs: National Development and Its Role in Foreign Policy,*

Free Press of Glencoe, 1963; *Africa and the European Common Market: A Perspective,* University of Denver International Affairs Monograph Series, 1964, revised edition, 1966; (editor and author of introduction) *Nations by Design: Institution Building in Africa,* Anchor Books, 1968; *Nation-Building in Africa: Problems and Prospects,* Rutgers University Press, 1969. Author of numerous economic reports. Contributor to professional journals.

AVOCATIONAL INTERESTS: Collects books and Africana.†

*   *   *

ROBBINS, Daniel 1933-

PERSONAL: Born January 15, 1933, in New York, N.Y.; son of David and Ora (Laddon) Robbins; married Eugenia Scandrett (an editor), December 6, 1959; children: Juliette, Miranda, Emily. *Education:* University of Chicago, A.B., 1951; Yale University, M.A., 1956; New York University, graduate study at Institute of Fine Arts, 1956-58, Ph.D., 1974; graduate study at Institute of Art and Archaeology of University of Paris, 1958-59. *Home address:* RD2, Peth Rd., Randolph, Vt. 05060. *Office:* Carpenter Hall, Dartmouth College, Hanover, N.H. 03755.

CAREER: National Gallery of Art, Washington, D.C., curator, 1960-61; Solomon R. Guggenheim Museum, New York, N.Y., curator, 1961-65; Rhode Island School of Design, Museum of Art, Providence, director, 1965-71; Harvard University, Fogg Art Museum, Cambridge, Mass., director, 1971-75, lecturer in fine arts, 1971—; Dartmouth College, Hanover, N.H., visiting research professor, 1975—. Visiting professor at Brown University, 1966-71, Yale University, 1977, and Williams College, 1977. Trustee of American Federation of Arts and Boston Museum of Fine Arts; member of advisory board of National Endowment for the Arts; consultant to Vermont House of Representatives, 1979. *Member:* Association of Art Museum Directors. *Awards, honors:* Fulbright fellowship, 1958-59; French government fellowship, 1959; National Endowment for the Humanities senior fellow, 1976; Guggenheim fellow, 1978.

WRITINGS—Published by Museum of Art, Rhode Island School of Design, except as indicated: *Albert Gleizes,* Solomon R. Guggenheim Museum, 1963; *Painting between the Wars, 1918-1940,* McGraw, 1965; *Walter Murch,* 1966; (author of text) *Edward Mitchell Bannister, 1828-1901,* 1966; (editor with George Downing) *Herbert and Nannette Rothschild Collection,* 1966; (editor with William Seitz) *Exchange Exhibition, Exhibition Exchange,* 1967; (editor) *An American Collection: The Neuberger Collection,* 1968; *Albert Pilavin Collection of Twentieth-Century American Art,* 1969; *George Waterman Collection,* 1969; *Late Works of John Robinson Frazier,* 1969; *Raid the Icebox One with Andy Warhol,* 1969.

Mountain Artisans—Appalachia, 1970; *Joaquin Torres-Garcia, 1874-1949,* 1970; *Vintage Racing Machine: Cars from the Collection of George Waterman, Jr.,* 1970; (author of introduction) *Cleve Gray,* Betty Parsons Gallery, 1971; (author of preface) *New American Graphic Art,* Fogg Art Museum, Harvard University, 1973; (editor) *Jacques Villon,* Fogg Art Museum, Harvard University, 1976; (with others) *Folk Sculpture USA,* edited by Herbert W. Hemphill, Jr., Brooklyn Museum, 1976; *Cubist Drawings,* [Shorewood, N.Y.], 1979; *Villon Drawings,* Goldschmidt, 1979; *Picasso's Vollard Suite,* Dartmouth College Museum and Galleries, 1980; *The Vermont State House: A History and Guide,* Vermont Historical Society, 1980.

ROBERTIELLO, Richard C. 1923-

PERSONAL: Born June 20, 1923, in Brooklyn, N.Y.; son of Attilio and Eleanor (Candela) Robertiello; married Carla Rizzotti, March 11, 1950 (divorced, 1965); married Margery Kerslake, August, 1965 (divorced, 1970); married Roberta Gluck (a psychotherapist), October 28, 1972; children: (first marriage) Elizabeth, Robert. *Education:* Harvard University, B.A., 1943; Columbia University, M.D., 1946. *Home:* 25 East 69th St., New York, N.Y. 10021. *Office:* 49 East 78th St., New York, N.Y. 10021.

CAREER: Practicing psychiatrist and psychoanalyst. Long Island Consultation Center, Forest Hills, N.Y., director of psychiatric services, 1953-75; New York Eye and Ear Infirmary, New York, attending psychiatrist, 1955-70; Manhattan General Hospital, New York City, associate attending psychiatrist, 1955-63; Community Guidance Service, New York City, supervising psychiatrist, 1956—. *Military service:* U.S. Army, 1943-46, 1948-50; became captain. *Member:* American Psychiatric Association (fellow), Academy of Psychoanalysis (fellow), Society of Medical Psychoanalysts, National Psychological Association for Psychoanalysis, Society for the Scientific Study of Sex (member of executive board).

WRITINGS: Voyage from Lesbos: The Psychoanalysis of a Female Homosexual, Citadel, 1959; *A Handbook of Emotional Illness and Treatment: A Contemporary Guide, with Case Histories,* Argonaut, 1961, revised edition, 1962; (with Bertram Pollens and David B. Friedman) *The Analyst's Role,* Citadel, 1963; *Sexual Fulfillment and Self-Affirmation,* Argonaut, 1964; *Hold Them Very Close, Then Let Them Go,* Dial, 1975; (with Grace Kirsten) *Big You, Little You,* Dial, 1977; *Your Own True Love,* Marek, 1978; *A Man in the Making,* Marek, 1979. Editor, *Journal of Contemporary Psychotherapy.* Consulting editor, *Journal of Sex Research.*

WORK IN PROGRESS: A book on psychoanalytic theory and technique.

AVOCATIONAL INTERESTS: Travel, tennis, bridge, and art.

*   *   *

ROBERTS, Willo Davis 1928-

PERSONAL: Born May 29, 1928, in Grand Rapids, Mich.; daughter of Clayton R. and Lealah (Gleason) Davis; married David W. Roberts (a writer and photographer), May 20, 1949; children: Kathleen, David M., Larrilyn (Mrs. Eric Lindquist), Christopher. *Education:* Graduated from high school in Pontiac, Mich., 1946. *Religion:* Lutheran. *Home:* 12020 Engebretson Rd., Granite Falls, Wash. 98252. *Agent:* Curtis Brown Ltd., 575 Madison Ave., New York, N.Y. 10022.

CAREER: Writer of mystery, suspense, gothic, historical, and juvenile novels. Has worked in hospitals and doctors' offices in a paramedical capacity. *Member:* Mystery Writers of America (regional vice-president of Northwest chapter), Science Fiction Writers of America, Authors Guild of Authors League of America, Seattle Freelances. *Awards, honors:* Evansville Book Award, 1979-80, Young Hoosier Award, 1979-80, both for *Don't Hurt Laurie!*

WRITINGS: Murder at Grand Bay, Arcadia House, 1955; *The Girl Who Wasn't There,* Arcadia House, 1957.

Murder Is So Easy, Vega Books, 1961; *The Suspected Four,* Vega Books, 1962; *Nurse Kay's Conquest,* Ace Books, 1966; *Once a Nurse,* Ace Books, 1966; *Nurse at Mystery Villa,* Ace Books, 1967; *Return to Darkness,* Lancer Books, 1969.

Shroud of Fog, Ace Books, 1970; *Devil Boy,* New American Library, 1970; *The Waiting Darkness,* Lancer Books, 1970; *Shadow of a Past Love,* Lancer Books, 1970; *The House at Fern Canyon,* Lancer Books, 1970; *The Tarot Spell,* Lancer Books, 1970; *Invitation to Evil,* Lancer Books, 1970; *The Terror Trap,* Lancer Books, 1971; *King's Pawn,* Lancer Books, 1971; *The Gates of Montrain,* Lancer Books, 1971; *The Watchers,* Lancer Books, 1971; *The Ghosts of Harrel,* Lancer Books, 1971; *Inherit the Darkness,* Lancer Books, 1972; *Nurse in Danger,* Ace Books, 1972; *Becca's Child,* Lancer Books, 1972; *Sing a Dark Song,* Lancer Books, 1972; *The Nurses,* Ace Books, 1972; *The Face of Danger,* Lancer Books, 1972; *Dangerous Legacy,* Lancer Books, 1972; *Sinister Gardens,* Lancer Books, 1972; *The M.D.,* Lancer Books, 1972; *The Evil Children,* Lancer Books, 1973; *The Gods in Green,* Lancer Books, 1973; *Nurse Robin,* Lennox Hill, 1973; *Didn't Anybody Know My Wife?,* Putnam, 1974.

White Jade, Doubleday, 1975; *Key Witness,* Putnam, 1975; *The View from the Cherry Tree,* Atheneum, 1975; *Expendable,* Doubleday, 1976; *The Jaubert Ring,* Doubleday, 1976; *The House of Imposters,* Popular Library, 1977; *Cape of Black Sands,* Popular Library, 1977; *Don't Hurt Laurie!,* Atheneum, 1977; *Act of Fear,* Doubleday, 1977; *The Minden Curse,* Atheneum, 1978.

The Search for Willie, Popular Library, 1980; *Destiny's Women,* Popular Library, 1980; *More Minden Curses,* Atheneum, 1980; *The Girl with the Silver Eyes* (Junior Literary Guild selection), Atheneum, 1980; *A Touch of Frost,* Bantam, 1981.

"The Black Pearl" series, published by Popular Library: *Dark Dowry,* 1978; *The Cade Curse,* 1978; *The Stuart Stain,* 1978; *The Devil's Double,* 1978; *The Radkin Revenge,* 1979; *The Hellfire Heritage,* 1979; *The Macomber Menace,* 1979; *The Gresham Ghost,* 1979.

WORK IN PROGRESS: Three historical novels, for Popular Library.

SIDELIGHTS: Willo Davis Roberts told *CA:* "I feel very fortunate to be able to make a living doing what I love most to do. I began making up stories to tell aloud long before I could write; I think my first written story came at the age of nine, and I've never stopped.

"Reading in the mystery and suspense field was always a pastime, and when I began to write it was natural that a great many of my stories had mystery and suspense themes. The success of my first real historical, *Destiny's Women,* was exciting and has led to contracts to do more of a similar type, a nice change in pace for me. I think a writer needs a change of pace, occasionally; it is very easy to find one's self writing the same book over and over, with different names on the characters, and after a while (even though the readers may not object) the writer begins to go stale. There is no challenge, or fun, in writing the same book you're already done dozens of times.

"One of the brightest spots in my recent career has been the excursion into juveniles. I did not intend to write children's books at all, though I always wrote *about* children. *The View from the Cherry Tree* was originally written as an adult suspense novel; it is about an 11-year-old boy who sees a murder committed, and cannot convince anyone of the truth of this except the murderer. The editors who saw it liked it, but felt it did not fit into any of their categories, and my agent persuaded me to try it as a juvenile. It is now in its fifth printing in hardcover, is in two different paperback editions, has been published overseas and was recently produced on the radio in Germany. And it led me to further juvenile books for several reasons. First, writing for kids turned out to be fun. And second, when the kids like what you write, they write letters to you. Reams of letters. They tell you when they figured out the mystery, they recite the plot back to you as if you'd never heard it, they ask you questions about what happened after your book ended. Since [*The*] *View from the Cherry Tree,* I have done four more children's books.... And the letters continue to come in with gratifying regularity, from kids all over the country.

"In 1977 my husband retired from his 'regular job' and joined me in writing and taking pictures, so we're both freelancing and traveling in search of materials. Our four grown children are also writing, and have begun to sell, and our oldest grandchild—we have three—is beginning to make up his own poems, at the age of three. A writing family makes for a very satisfying life."

*   *   *

ROBINSON, B(asil) W(illiam) 1912-

PERSONAL: Born June 20, 1912, in London, England; son of William and Mabel (Gilbanks) Robinson; married Mary Stewart (died, 1954); married Oriel Steel, 1958; children: (second marriage) William, Alicia. *Education:* Winchester College, exhibitioner, 1926-31; Corpus Christi College, Oxford University, M.A., B.Litt., 1938. *Religion:* Church of England. *Home:* 41 Redcliffe Gardens, London S.W. 10, England.

CAREER: Holyrood School, Bognor Regis, Sussex, England, assistant master, 1936-39; Victoria and Albert Museum, London, England, assistant keeper, 1939-54, deputy keeper, 1954-66, keeper, 1966-72, keeper emeritus, 1972-76. *Military service:* British Army, 1941-46; became captain; received Burma Star. *Member:* Royal Asiatic Society (member of council, 1960-64; president, 1970-73), Japan Society of London (honorary librarian; member of council, 1949-60), Iran Society, Arms and Armour Society (vice-president, 1953—), Meyrick Society, Aldrich Catch Club (founder and chairman).

WRITINGS: A Primer of Japanese Sword Blades, privately printed, 1955; *A Descriptive Catalogue of the Persian Paintings in the Bodleian Library,* Clarendon Press, 1958; (with others) *Chester Beatty Library: Catalogue of the Persian Manuscripts and Miniatures,* Volumes II, III, Hodges, Figgis, 1960, 1962; *The Arts of the Japanese Sword,* Tuttle, 1961; *Kuniyoshi,* H.M.S.O., 1961; *Persian Drawings from the 14th through the 19th Century,* Shorewood, 1965; *Persian Miniature Paintings from Collections in the British Isles,* H.M.S.O., 1967; *Persian Paintings in the India Office Library,* Philip Wilson, 1976; *Islamic Painting and the Arts of the Book,* Faber, 1976. Also author of *Persian Paintings in the John Rylands Library,* 1980, and *Collections Baur: Catalogue of the Japanese Sword-fittings,* 1980. Author of booklets and pamphlets on Japanese and Persian objects of art; contributor of articles and reviews to *Burlington Magazine, Connoisseur,* and similar periodicals.

SIDELIGHTS: B. W. Robinson told *CA:* "From the kind of writing in which I have been engaged it necessarily follows that my object throughout has been *usefulness*—to supply, as clearly and simply as possible, the sort of information anybody in my field would wish to have, in a palatable and readable form." *Avocational interests:* Old English music, cats.

ROBINSON, Frank M(alcolm) 1926-
(Thomas Benji, Robert Courtney, James Walsh)

PERSONAL: Born August 9, 1926, in Chicago, Ill.; son of Raymond (an artist and photographer) and Leona (White) Robinson. *Education:* Beloit College, B.S., 1950; Northwestern University, M.S. (Journalism), 1955. *Politics:* Liberal. *Religion:* Protestant. *Residence:* San Francisco, Calif. *Agent:* Curtis Brown Ltd., 575 Madison Ave., New York, N.Y. 10022.

CAREER: Family Weekly, Chicago, Ill., assistant editor, 1955-56; *Science Digest,* Chicago, assistant editor, 1956-59; *Rogue* (magazine), Chicago, editor, 1959-65; *Cavalier* (magazine), Los Angeles, Calif., managing editor, 1965-66; *Censorship Today,* Los Angeles, editor, 1967; *Playboy,* Chicago, staff writer, 1969-73; freelance writer, 1973—. *Military service:* U.S. Navy, radar technician, 1944-45, 1950-51. *Member:* Phi Beta Kappa, Sigma Delta Chi.

WRITINGS—Fiction, except as indicated: *The Power,* Lippincott, 1956; (editor with Nat Lehrman) *Sex, American Style* (nonfiction), Playboy Press, 1972; (with Thomas N. Scortia) *The Glass Inferno,* Doubleday, 1974; (with Scortia) *The Prometheus Crisis,* Doubleday, 1975; (with Scortia) *The Nightmare Factor,* Doubleday, 1978; (with Scortia) *The Gold Crew,* Warner Books, 1980. Contributor to popular magazines and newspapers, sometimes under pseudonyms Thomas Benji, Robert Courtney, and James Walsh.

WORK IN PROGRESS: A Day in the Life Of; with John Levin, *The Great Divide.*

SIDELIGHTS: The Power was adapted and filmed by Metro-Goldwyn-Mayer in 1968; *The Glass Inferno* was adapted and filmed by Twentieth Century-Fox and Warner Bros.

*   *   *

ROBINSON, William Wheeler 1918-
(Bill Robinson)

PERSONAL: Born October 4, 1918, in Elizabeth, N.J.; son of Henry Pearson (a salesman) and Clare (a journalist; maiden name, Wheeler) Robinson; married Jane Dimock, February 27, 1942; children: William Wheeler, Jr., Martha Jane, Alice Clare. *Education:* Princeton University, A.B., 1939. *Home:* 14 Oyster Bay Dr., Rumson, N.J. *Office: Yachting,* 1 Park Ave., New York, N.Y. 10016.

CAREER: Newark News, Newark, N.J., boating editor, sports writer, 1947-55; *Newark Star-Ledger,* Newark, boating editor, sports writer, 1955-57; *Yachting,* New York, N.Y., associate editor, 1957-64, executive editor, 1964-67, editor, 1967-78, 'editor-at-large, 1979—; covered America's Cup races on radio and television, 1962, 1964, 1967, and 1970. *Military service:* U.S. Naval Reserve, 1941-45; served in South Pacific; became lieutenant commander; received Bronze Star (twice). *Member:* Cruising Club of America, Corinthians (master, 1953-54), New York Yacht Club, Shrewsbury Sailing and Yacht Club (commodore, 1955), Royal Bermuda Yacht Club, Century Association.

WRITINGS—All under name Bill Robinson: (Editor) *Science of Sailing,* Scribner, 1961; *New Boat,* Fleet, 1961; *A Berth to Bermuda,* Van Nostrand, 1961; *Where the Trade Winds Blow,* Scribner, 1963; *Bill Robinson's Book of Expert Sailing,* Scribner, 1964; *Over the Horizon,* Van Nostrand, 1966; *The World of Yachting,* Random House, 1966; (editor) *The Best from "Yachting,"* Scribner, 1967; *Better Sailing for Boys and Girls,* Dodd, 1968; (with H. L. Stone and W. H. Taylor) *America's Cup Races,* Norton, 1970; *Legendary*

Yachts, Macmillan, 1971; *The Sailing Life,* Scribner, 1974; *The Right Boat for You,* Holt, 1974; *Great American Yacht Designers,* Knopf, 1974; *America's Sailing Book,* Scribner, 1976; *A Sailor's Tales,* Norton, 1978; *Cruising: The Boats and the Places,* Norton, 1980. Contributor to magazines and anthologies of sports stories.

AVOCATIONAL INTERESTS: Squash racquets.

* * *

ROGERS, Rosemary 1932-

PERSONAL: Born December 7, 1932, in Panadura, Ceylon; daughter of Cyril Allan (an owner and manager of a private school) and Barbara Jansze; married Summa Navaratnam (divorced); married Leroy Rogers (divorced); children: (first marriage) Rosanne, Sharon; (second marriage) Michael, Adam. *Education:* University of Ceylon, B.A. *Politics:* Democrat. *Religion:* Episcopalian. *Residence:* Carmel, Calif.

CAREER: Associated Newspapers of Ceylon, Colombo, writer of features and public affairs information, 1959-62; Travis Air Force Base, Fairfield, Calif., secretary in billeting office, 1964-69; Solano County Parks Department, Fairfield, secretary, 1969-74; writer. Part-time reporter for *Fairfield Daily Republic.* *Member:* Authors Guild of Authors League of America.

*WRITINGS—*Published by Avon: *Sweet Savage Love,* 1974; *The Wildest Heart,* 1974; *Dark Fires,* 1975; *Wicked Loving Lies,* 1976; *The Crowd Pleasers,* 1978; *The Insiders,* 1979; *Lost Love Last Love,* 1980; *Love Play,* 1981.

WORK IN PROGRESS: A historical novel, a contemporary novel, and a television play.

SIDELIGHTS: Rosemary Rogers wrote her first short story at the age of eight, and as a teenager wrote novels for her own enjoyment. She comments: "I wrote the kind of book I enjoyed reading myself (at various stages I have been an addict of crime, mystery, western, and sloppy love stories!)." As a divorced mother of four trying to eke out a living as a secretary for herself and her children, Rogers returned to her childhood pastime of writing novels, writing at night when her children were asleep. Her first novel, *Sweet Savage Love,* was bought by Avon, the first publisher to which she sent it, and became an instant success selling over one million copies. There are now almost sixteen million copies of her novels in print; her annual income is reported to be one million dollars.

Writing in the *Detroit News,* Paul Hendrickson labels Rogers "the undisputed millionaire superstar of romantic fiction; the Mickey Spillane of passion pulp." Hendrickson points out that Rogers's "literary critics, and they are legion, call her the queen of rape and romance." One of those critics, Joanna Russ of *Book World,* writes that *The Insiders,* which has almost two-and-three-fourths million copies in print, does not possess "any of the usual elements of fiction (characterization, setting, motives, morality, style, plot, even the weather is hardly there)," and calls the book "not a novel at all, but something new: explicit pornography for women."

As quoted by Carol Lawson in the *New York Times Book Review,* Rogers herself describes her novels as "fairy tales. We have to get away from harsh realities. That's why I write escapist fiction with upbeat, happy endings." Rogers' heroines have been criticized as masochistic women with rape fantasies. To which Rogers replies: "Most women *do* have a rape fantasy. But there is a difference between actual rape, which is horrifying, and fantasy. In the rape fantasy, you

pick the man and the circumstances. It's not at all scary." Rogers adds that her heroines "always end up the strong character, the survivor."

Rogers has no illusions that her novels are lasting masterpieces or that she will achieve literary immortality. She told Paul Hendrickson, "If somebody reads me and says they are entertained, if they have escaped from reality for awhile, then that is enough."

AVOCATIONAL INTERESTS: Reading, music, and watching some sports, especially football.

BIOGRAPHICAL/CRITICAL SOURCES: Authors in the News, Volume I, Gale, 1976; *Book World,* January 21, 1979; *New York Times Book Review,* March 18, 1979; *Detroit News,* May 31, 1979.

* * *

ROLLE, Andrew Frank 1922-

PERSONAL: Born April 12, 1922, in Providence, R.I.; son of John B. and Theresa (Maurizio) Rolle; married Frances J. Squires, 1945 (divorced); children: John, Alexander, Julia Elisabeth. *Education:* Occidental College, B.A., 1943; University of California, M.A., 1949, Ph.D., 1952. *Home:* 1244 Glen Oaks, Pasadena, Calif. 91105. *Office:* Department of History, Occidental College, Los Angeles, Calif.

CAREER: U.S. Department of State, Genoa, Italy, vice-consul, 1945-48; Occidental College, Los Angeles, Calif., instructor, 1952-53, assistant professor, 1953-57, associate professor, 1957-62, professor of history, 1962-65, Robert Glass Cleland Professor of History, 1965—. Consultant on Indian land claims, Governor's Committee on California History and Los Angeles Mayor's Committee on History, 1966-68; resident scholar, Rockefeller Foundation Center, Bellagio, Italy, 1971-72; clinical associate, Southern California Psychoanalytic Institute, 1972-76. *Military service:* U.S. Army, Intelligence, 1943-45 and 1951; became first lieutenant.

MEMBER: American Historical Association, American Studies Association (secretary-treasurer of Southern California chapter, 1957; president, 1958), American Council of Learned Societies (regional associate member), Historical Society of Southern California (board member), Phi Beta Kappa. *Awards, honors:* Huntington Library-Rockefeller Foundation fellow, 1953-54; Haynes Foundation fellowship, 1957; award of merit, American Association for State and Local History, 1957, for *An American in California;* Lincoln Sesquicentennial Award, 1959; American Council of Learned Societies grant, 1962; Silver Medal, Italian Ministry of Foreign Affairs, 1963; Cavaliere del Ordine Merito, Republic of Italy, 1975.

WRITINGS: Riviera Path, Mondadori, 1948; *An American in California,* Henry E. Huntington, 1956; (editor) *The Road to Virginia City: The Diary of James Polk Miller,* University of Oklahoma Press, 1960; (with Allan Nevins and Irving Stone) *Lincoln, A Contemporary Portrait,* Doubleday, 1962; *Occidental College: The First 75 Years,* Ward Ritchie, 1962; *California, A History,* Crowell, 1963, 3rd edition, AMH Publishing, 1978; *The Lost Cause,* University of Oklahoma Press, 1965; (editor) Helen Hunt Jackson, *Century of Dishonor: The Early Crusade for Indian Reform,* Harper, 1965; *A Student's Guide to California History,* Columbia University Press, 1965; (with John Gaines) *The Golden State: A History of California,* Crowell, 1965; *A Student's Guide to Los Angeles,* Columbia University Press, 1965; *The American Italians,* Wadsworth, 1972; (contributor) *Essays and*

Assays, California Historical Society, 1973; (contributor) *Los Angeles: Biography of a City,* University of California Press, 1976; *The Italian-Americans: Troubled Roots,* Macmillan, 1980. Also co-author of *Crisis in America,* 1977, and author of booklets. Contributor of articles to encyclopedias, including *Encyclopedia Americana Yearbook* and *Encyclopaedia Britannica.* Contributor of articles and book reviews to historical journals. Editorial associate, *Pacific Historical Review,* 1951-52; member of boards of editors, *The Historian, Pacific Historical Review,* and *California Historical Quarterly.*

WORK IN PROGRESS: A book on the irrational in history, based on seven years of psychiatric training; a book about the explorer, John C. Fremont.

*   *   *

ROLLINS, Wayne G(ilbert) 1929-

PERSONAL: Born August 24, 1929, in Detroit, Mich.; son of Arthur Gilchrist and Ethel (Kamin) Rollins; married Donnalou Myerholtz, August 30, 1953; children: Michael Wayne, Thomas Lawrence, David Mark. *Education:* Capital University, B.A., 1951; Yale University, B.D., 1954, M.A., 1956, Ph.D., 1960. *Politics:* Democrat. *Office:* Assumption College, Worcester, Mass. 01609.

CAREER: Ordained minister in United Church of Christ (Congregational); Princeton University, Princeton, N.J., instructor in religion, 1958-59; Wellesley College, Wellesley, Mass., assistant professor of biblical history, 1959-66; Hartford Seminary Foundation, Hartford, Conn., associate professor of biblical studies, 1966-74; Assumption College, Worcester, Mass., professor of religious studies, director of Ecumenical Institute, and coordinator of graduate program in religious studies, 1974—. Visiting professor, Colgate-Rochester Divinity School, 1968; visiting lecturer, Yale University, 1968-69, Mt. Holyoke College, 1972, and College of the Holy Cross, 1976-77. Researcher at Cambridge University, Cambridge, England, 1970. Member of board of preachers, Wellesley College. *Member:* American Academy of Religion, Societas Novi Testamenti Studiorum, American Association of University Professors, American School of Oriental Research, Society of Biblical Literature and Exegesis.

WRITINGS: The Gospels: Portraits of Christ, Westminster, 1964; (contributor) H. D. Betz, editor, *Plutarch's Theological Writings and Early Christian Literature,* E. J. Brill, 1975; (contributor) Victor Furnish, editor, *Interpreter's Dictionary of the Bible, Supplement,* Abingdon, 1976. Contributor of reviews and articles to religious journals.

WORK IN PROGRESS: Jung and the Bible, for John Knox; contributing to *Christological Perspectives,* edited by R. F. Berkey and S. A. Edwards, for Pilgrim Press.

SIDELIGHTS: Wayne G. Rollins told *CA:* "There are two quotations that help me in my writing: one from Alfred Kazin in the *Atlantic Monthly* (1961), 'The root of bad writing is to be distracted, to be self-conscious, not to keep your eye on the ball, not to confront the subject with entire directness, entire humility, and with concentrated passion.' The second comes from James Hillman in *Revisioning Psychology* (Harper, 1975), 'Why write, if this too easy activity of pushing a pen across paper is not given a certain bull-fighting risk and we do not approach dangerous, agile, and two-horned topics?' To this should be added William Strunk, Jr.'s perennial advice in *The Elements of Style,* 'Clarity, clarity, clarity.'"

AVOCATIONAL INTERESTS: Swimming, singing, bicycle excursions, carpentry, skiing, and tennis.

ROLSTON, Holmes 1900-1977

PERSONAL: Born September 6, 1900, in Staunton, Va.; died November 21, 1977; son of Holmes and Jacqueline (Campbell) Rolston; married Mary Winifred Long, 1930; children: Holmes III, Mary Jacqueline (Mrs. Ernest Trice Thompson, Jr.), Julia Long (Mrs. Gray Watson Hampton, Jr.). *Education:* Washington and Lee University, A.B., 1920, D.D., 1948; Union Theological Seminary, Richmond, Va., B.D., 1927, Th.D., 1932; attended University of Edinburgh, 1928-29. *Politics:* Democrat. *Home:* 1505 West Laburnum Ave., Richmond, Va.

CAREER: Ordained Presbyterian minister, 1927. Bethesda Presbyterian Church, Rockbridge Baths, Va., pastor, 1929-41; West Avenue Presbyterian Church, Charlotte, N.C., pastor, 1942-48; Presbyterian Church in the United States, Board of Christian Education, Richmond, Va., editor-in-chief, 1946-69. Chairman of church extension committee for Hanover Presbytery of Synod of Virginia. Sprunt Lecturer, Union Theological Seminary, Richmond, Va., 1942. *Member:* Fellowship of St. James.

WRITINGS—All published by John Knox, except as indicated: *A Conservative Looks to Barth and Brunner,* Abingdon, 1932; *The Social Message of the Apostle Paul,* 1942; *Stewardship in the New Testament Church,* 1943, revised, 1959; *Consider Paul–Revelation and Inspiration in the Letters of Paul,* 1949; *Personalities around Paul,* 1954; *Faces about the Christ,* 1959; *The Bible in Christian Teaching,* 1962; *The "We Knows" of the Apostle Paul,* 1966; *Personalities around David,* 1968; *John Calvin vs. the Westminster Confession,* 1972; *The Apostle Peter Speaks to Us Today,* 1977. Also author of *Adult Uniform Lessons,* quarterly of Presbyterian Church in the U.S., for twenty-eight years; contributor to periodicals.

AVOCATIONAL INTERESTS: Gardening.†

*   *   *

ROSS, Ian Simpson 1930-

PERSONAL: Born August 9, 1930, in Dundee, Scotland; son of John Gibson (a brass foundry worker) and Agnes (Simpson) Ross; married Marjorie Dudley, 1973; children: Isla, Andrew, David, Marion. *Education:* University of St. Andrews, M.A. (first class honours), 1954; Merton College, Oxford, B.Litt., 1956; University of Texas, Ph.D., 1960. *Home:* 5788 Angus Dr., Vancouver, British Columbia, Canada V6M 3N8. *Office:* Department of English, University of British Columbia, Vancouver, British Columbia, Canada V6T 1W5.

CAREER: University of Texas, Main University (now University of Texas at Austin), special instructor, 1957-58, 1959-60; University of British Columbia, Vancouver, instructor, 1960-62, assistant professor, 1963-65, associate professor, 1965-73, professor of English, 1973—. *Military service:* Royal Air Force, 1948-50. *Member:* Scottish History Society, Scottish Catholic History Association, Association for Scottish Literary Studies, Modern Language Association of America, American Society for Eighteenth-Century Studies, Canadian Society for Eighteenth-Century Studies (former president), Stair Society.

WRITINGS: Lord Kames and the Scotland of His Day, Oxford University Press, 1972; (editor with Ernest C. Mossner) *The Correspondence of Adam Smith,* Oxford University Press, 1977; (editor with W.P.D. Wightman and J. C. Bryce) Adam Smith, *Essays on Philosophical Subjects,* Oxford University Press, 1980; *William Dunbar,* E. J. Brill, 1980.

Member of advisory board, *Texas Studies in Literature and Language.*

WORK IN PROGRESS: A biography of Adam Smith.

AVOCATIONAL INTERESTS: Art history, traveling.

*   *   *

ROTH, Sister Mary Augustine 1926-

PERSONAL: Born January 16, 1926, in Minneapolis, Minn.; daughter of John Albert and Anne (Boies) Roth. *Education:* University of Minnesota, B.A., 1947, M.A., 1948; Catholic University of America, Ph.D., 1961. *Politics:* Republican. *Home:* 1330 Elmhurst Dr. N.E., Cedar Rapids, Iowa 52402. *Office:* Department of English, Mount Mercy College, Cedar Rapids, Iowa 52402.

CAREER: Roman Catholic nun; entered Congregation of the Sisters of Mercy, 1949; Mount Mercy College, Cedar Rapids, Iowa, instructor in English, 1948-56; Sacred Heart High School, Oelwein, Iowa, English teacher, 1956-57; Mount Mercy College, chairman of English department, 1961—, academic dean, 1961-63.

WRITINGS: (Editor and author of critical commentary) Coventry Patmore, *Essay on English Metrical Law: A Critical Edition with a Commentary,* Catholic University of America Press, 1961; *Written in His Hands: The Sisters of Mercy of Cedar Rapids, Iowa–1875-1975,* Laurance Press, 1976; *The McAuley Conference: 1955-65,* Sisters of Mercy, 1978; *With Mercy toward All: Mercy Hospital, Cedar Rapids, Iowa–1900-1978,* Stamats Publishing, 1979; *Courage and Change: Mount Mercy College–The First Fifty Years,* Stamats Publishing, 1980.

*   *   *

ROTHSCHILD, Joseph 1931-

PERSONAL: Born April 5, 1931, in Fulda, Germany; came to the United States in 1940, became citizen in 1945; son of Meinhold and Henrietta (Loewenstein) Rothschild; married Ruth Nachmansohn (an art historian), July 19, 1959; children: Nina, Gerson. *Education:* Columbia University, A.B. (highest honors), 1951, A.M., 1952; Oxford University, D.Phil, 1955. *Religion:* Jewish. *Home:* 445 Riverside Dr., New York, N.Y. 10027. *Office:* Department of Political Science, Columbia University, New York, N.Y. 10027.

CAREER: Columbia University, New York, N.Y., instructor, 1955-58, assistant professor, 1958-62, associate professor, 1962-68, professor of government, 1968—, Class of 1919 Professor of Political Science, 1978—, chairman of department of political science, 1971-75. *Member:* American Association for the Advancement of Slavic Studies, American Professors for Peace in the Middle East (national vice-chairman), Academy of Political Science, Phi Beta Kappa. *Awards, honors:* Social Science Research Council fellow, 1963-64; Guggenheim fellow, 1967-68; American Council of Learned Societies fellow, 1971-72; National Endowment for the Humanities fellow, 1978-79; Lehrman Institute visiting fellow, 1979.

WRITINGS: The Communist Party of Bulgaria: Origins and Development, 1883-1936, Columbia University Press, 1959; (co-editor) *Introduction to Contemporary Civilization in the West,* 3rd edition, Columbia University Press, 1960; (co-editor) *Chapters in Western Civilization,* two volumes, 3rd edition, Columbia University Press, 1961; *Communist Eastern Europe,* Walker & Co., 1964; *Pilsudski's Coup d'Etat,* Columbia University Press, 1966; *East Central Europe between the Two World Wars,* University of Washington Press, 1974.

Contributor: *Studies in Polish Civilization: Selected Papers Presented at the First Congress Convened by the Polish Institute of Arts and Sciences in America, 1966,* Institute on East Central Europe of Columbia University and Polish Institute of Arts and Sciences in America, 1971; Steven L. Spiegel and Kenneth N. Waltz, editors, *Conflict in World Politics,* Winthrop Publishing, 1971; Stanislaus A. Blejwas, editor, *East Central European Studies: A Handbook for Graduate Students,* American Academy for the Advancement of Slavic Studies, 1973; Bela Kiraly and George Barany, editors, *East Central European Perceptions of Early America,* Peter de Ridder Press, 1977; Bogdan Denitch, editor, *Legitimation of Regimes,* Sage Publications, 1979; Edward Allworth, editor, *Ethnic Russia in the USSR: The Dilemma of Dominance,* Pergamon, 1980. Contributor to *Grolier Encyclopedia, Jefferson Encyclopedia, Political Science Quarterly, Problems of Communism, Slavic Review, Massachusetts Review, Columbia Spectator Supplement, Occidente, American Political Science Review, Canadian Slavic Studies, Polish Review, Survey,* and *American Historical Review.*

WORK IN PROGRESS: Ethnopolitics: A Conceptual Framework, for Columbia University Press; east central European history.

*   *   *

ROVERE, Richard H(alworth) 1915-1979

PERSONAL: Surname is pronounced Row-*veer;* born May 5, 1915, in Jersey City, N.J.; died of emphysema, November 23, 1979, in Poughkeepsie, N.Y.; son of Lewis Halworth (an engineer) and Ethel (Roberts) Rovere; married Eleanor Burgess, December 20, 1941; children: Ann Megan, Richard Mark, Elizabeth. *Education:* Columbia University, A.B., 1937. *Politics:* Independent. *Office:* New Yorker, 25 West 43rd St., New York, N.Y. 10036.

CAREER: New Masses, New York City, associate editor, 1938-39; *Nation,* New York City, assistant editor, 1940-43; *Common Sense,* New York City, editor, 1943-44; *New Yorker,* New York City, staff writer, 1944-79. Associate in American civilization, Columbia University, 1957-59; lecturer in history and fellow, Ezra Stiles College, Yale University, 1972-73; visiting professor of English, Vassar College, 1975-76. Trustee, Bard College, 1956-61. *Member:* P.E.N., American Academy of Arts and Sciences (fellow), Council on Foreign Relations, National Press Club (Washington, D.C.), Century Association (New York, N.Y.). *Awards, honors:* Chubb fellow, Yale University, 1951; D.Litt., Bard College, 1962; L.H.D., Grinnell College, 1967.

WRITINGS: Howe and Hummel: Their True and Scandalous History, Farrar, Straus, 1947, reprinted, Publishing Center for Cultural Resources, 1979; (with A. M. Schlesinger, Jr.) *The General and the President,* Farrar, Straus, 1951; *Affairs of State: The Eisenhower Years,* Farrar, Straus, 1956; *Senator Joe McCarthy,* Harcourt, 1959; *The American Establishment and Other Conceits, Enthusiasms, and Hostilities,* Harcourt, 1962; *The Goldwater Caper,* Harcourt, 1965; *Waist Deep in the Big Muddy: Personal Reflections on 1968,* Little, Brown, 1968 (published in England as *Waist Deep in the Big Muddy: Reflections on United States Policy,* Bodley Head, 1968); *Arrivals and Departures: A Journalist's Memoirs,* Macmillan, 1976. *Harper's,* contributing editor, 1949-54, book critic, 1949-50; American correspondent, *Spectator,* 1954-62; member of board of editors, *American Scholar,* 1958-67; chairman of editorial advisory board, *Washington Monthly,* beginning 1969.

WORK IN PROGRESS: Continuing research on American politics, American life, international affairs, and eighteenth century English literature.

SIDELIGHTS: "Richard Rovere was among the fairest, most nearly objective, most brilliant writers on American politics," declared *New Yorker* editor William Shawn at the time of the columnist's death. "He wrote with tremendous skill, with care, with humor, with style.... He brought an extraordinary clarity of mind to bear on complex and confused political situations and made them comprehensible." About once a month for over thirty years, Rovere's "letter from Washington" appeared in the pages of the *New Yorker*. Though only an experiment when it began in 1948 (then-editor Harold Ross wasn't sure whether or not there was anything worth covering "down there"), the column, filled with insightful evaluations and acerbic observations of people and events in Washington, soon established a reputation for Rovere as one of the country's premier political journalists. What made his success even more remarkable was the fact that, unlike most of his colleagues, Rovere lived in New York City, seldom visited the capital, and made a point of not cultivating close friendships with the public figures he was assigned to cover. As he once explained: "My feeling has been that the advantages of acquaintance are often more than offset by the disadvantages and that in general it is best to confine oneself to material that is fixed in the record and cannot be repudiated."

The publication of his autobiography, *Arrivals and Departures,* prompted others to comment on Rovere and his work. Noted the *New York Times Book Review*'s Robert Sherrill: "[Rovere] comes across in these memoirs as totally unpretentious, blithely honest about his life, his work and his era.... He's one of those gentlemen of the press who enjoyed the intimacy of great events but has preferred not to become too familiar with the uncouth left-right bamboozlement that often accompanies them.... [But] he remains something of a mystery because of his belief, I suppose, that 'every man is an island in the only sense that matters,' and he respects his own privacy to such an extent that he has refused to explore with much aggressiveness even that insignificant portion of the universe. A footprint on his beach would not send him madly scurrying in search of a Friday.... [Nevertheless, his memoirs] leave the pleasant feeling that here's a fellow who has seldom used his marvelous talents to bully or pontificate and who has always taken good care of the language."

"*Arrivals and Departures* reveals [Rovere] as that attractive, iconoclastic, mildly eccentric and altogether human figure which those of us who have been reading him for half a lifetime knew that he must be," enthused Harrison Salisbury in the *New Republic*. "[He] is and always has been that best kind of political observer, the man who never lets his heart overcome his mind. He loves politics and politicians. They have for him that irresistible attraction that they must have for any good political analyst.... But Rovere never forgets the con."

Newsweek's Paul D. Zimmerman wrote: "Amid the passionate rhetoric and shrill argument that have dominated the political arena in recent years, the sane, modulated voice of Richard Rovere has often been lost.... [He] has treated such inflammatory issues as Vietnam and Watergate with balance and restraint, not popular qualities in an age of partisanship. So it is with a delight akin to relief that one reads through these rich, tranquil memoirs, so elegantly written, so gracefully balanced between remove and self-revelation, so deliciously edged with the gentle ironies and self-depre-

cation of a truly civilized man.... There aren't many books like this one these days—unhurried, uninsistent, brightened by the kind of humorous profiles that seem to have fallen out of fashion. Nor are there many political writers left like Rovere, a man of letters whose moral compass remains unswayed by the passions of the moment."

In a final tribute to the columnist, a *New Yorker* colleague commented: "Over and over, in odds and ends of confusing and disparate facts that were available to everyone [Rovere] would somehow find a pattern and meaning that had eluded the rest of us. In time, his unshrill and unbullying judgments of people and events often moved into the consciousness of other Americans, including that of academic historians, as the way things had been.... In an era in which some political writers act as if they were part of show business and vie with each other for spots on Hollywood talk programs, Rovere was an old-fashioned figure, going his own quiet way, writing in his own voice.... It seems certain that for a long time to come many of his readers will find themselves looking at a crowded front page and saying, 'I wonder what Rovere would have made of this'; and that those who worked with him, as they round the corner toward his old office, will for a moment expect to see him there, hunched over his typewriter but ready, as ever, to lean back in his chair, light a cigarette, and shoot the breeze."

BIOGRAPHICAL/CRITICAL SOURCES: Richard H. Rovere, *Arrivals and Departures: A Journalist's Memoirs,* Macmillan, 1976; *New York Times Book Review,* November 14, 1976; *Newsweek,* November 29, 1976, December 3, 1979; *New Republic,* January 22, 1977; *Best Sellers,* April, 1977; *New York Times,* November 24, 1979; *Time,* December 3, 1979; *New Yorker,* December 10, 1979.†

—*Sketch by Deborah A. Straub*

*   *   *

ROWEN, Herbert H(arvey) 1916-

PERSONAL: Born October 22, 1916, in Brooklyn, N.Y.; son of Joseph M. (a teacher) and Sarah (Gordon) Rowen; married Mildred Ringel, June 28, 1940; children: Douglas, Amy, Marthe. *Education:* City College (now City College of the City University of New York), B.S.S., 1936; Columbia University, M.A., 1948, Ph.D., 1951. *Home:* 3 Lemore Cir., Rocky Hill, N.J. 08553. *Office:* Department of History, Rutgers University, New Brunswick, N.J. 08903.

CAREER: Converters Paper Co., Newark, N.J., assistant to manager, 1938-42; Random House, Inc., New York, N.Y., editorial assistant, *American College Dictionary,* 1946; Brandeis University, Waltham, Mass., instructor in history, 1950-53; University of Iowa, Iowa City, Iowa, assistant professor, 1953-57; Elmira College, Elmira, N.Y., associate professor, 1957-60; University of Wisconsin—Milwaukee, professor, 1960-64; Rutgers University, New Brunswick, N.J., professor of history, 1964—. Visiting associate professor, University of California, Berkeley, 1959-60. Consulting editor, Free Press. *Military service:* U.S. Army, Signal Corps, 1942-45. *Member:* Royal Netherlands Academy of Arts and Sciences, International Commission for History of Representative and Parliamentary Institutions, American Historical Association, Societe d'Histoire Moderne, Society for French Historical Studies, Nederlands Historisch Genootschap, Phi Beta Kappa. *Awards, honors:* Folger Shakespeare Library grant-in-aid, 1956; Newberry Library fellowship, 1957; Guggenheim fellowship, 1961-62; American Philosophical Society grant-in-aid, 1976; National Endowment for the Humanities fellowship, 1980-81.

WRITINGS: (Translator) Hans Kohn, editor. *German History: Some New German Views,* Beacon Press, 1954; (editor) Simon Nicolas Arnauld de Pomponne, *Pomponne's "Relation de mon ambassade en Hollande" 1669–1671,* Kemink & Zoon, 1955; *The Ambassador Prepares for War: The Dutch Embassy of Arnauld de Pomponne, 1669-1671,* Batsford, 1957; *A History of Early Modern Europe, 1500-1815,* Holt, 1960; (editor) *From Absolutism to Revolution, 1648-1848,* Macmillan, 1963, 2nd edition, 1968; (translator) Jacques Leon Godechot, *France and the Atlantic Revolution of the Eighteenth Century, 1770-1799,* Free Press, 1965; (with Bryce Lyon and Theodore S. Hamerow) *A History of the Western World,* Rand McNally, 1969; (editor) *The Low Countries in Early Modern Times,* Harper, 1972; (translator) Johan Huizinga, *Essays on America,* Harper, 1972; (editor with Carl J. Ekberg) *Early Modern Europe: A Book of Source Readings,* AHM Publishing, 1973; (with De Lamar Jensen) *The Dutch Republic: A Nation in the Making,* Forum, 1976; *John de Witt, Grand Pensionary of Holland, 1625-1672,* Princeton University, Press, 1978; *The King's State: Proprietary Dynasticism in Early Modern France,* Rutgers University Press, 1980. General editor, "Free Press Sources of Western Civilization" series, 1964-65. Contributor of articles and reviews to historical journals.

WORK IN PROGRESS: A study of the stadholders as quasimonarchs in the Dutch Republic; a study of the role of the mob in the politics of the Dutch Republic.

SIDELIGHTS: Herbert H. Rowen told *CA:* "My hope and aim are to match impeccable scholarship—full command of the sources at the service of important ideas—with clear, strong prose. I strive to meet the need of a number of audiences: the broad public, especially through contributions to major encyclopedias . . . ; students, for whom I have written textbooks that I try to make clear, lively, and challenging; and historical scholars, from whom I write (I hope) dense, meaty, significantly new but not faddishly innovative works in a prose stripped of jargon and cliche."

*   *   *

RUBINSTEIN, Alvin Zachary   1927-

PERSONAL: Born April 23, 1927, in New York, N.Y.; son of Max (a storekeeper) and Sylvia (Stone) Rubinstein; married Frankie Kimmelman (a teacher), November 12, 1960. *Education:* City College (now City College of the City University of New York), B.B.A., 1949; University of Pennsylvania, M.A., 1950, Ph.D., 1954. *Office:* Department of Political Science, University of Pennsylvania, Philadelphia, Pa. 19104.

CAREER: University of Pennsylvania, Philadelphia, lecturer, 1957-59, assistant professor, 1959-61, associate professor, 1961-66, professor of political science, 1966—, chairman of graduate program in international relations, 1966-70. Director, Anspach Institute of Foreign Affairs, 1968-70. *Military service:* U.S. Naval Reserve, 1945-47, 1954-56; became lieutenant. *Member:* American Political Science Association, Association of Asian Studies, American Association for the Advancement of Slavic Studies. *Awards, honors:* Ford Foundation international relations fellowship, 1956-57; grants from Inter-University Committee on Travel Grants (for Soviet Union), 1957, American Philosophical Society, 1958, 1959, 1968, Rockefeller Foundation, 1961-62, National Science Foundation, 1970-71, Barra Foundation, 1970-71, Earhart Foundation, 1974, 1979, and Social Science Research Council, 1975; Guggenheim fellowship, 1965-66; NATO fellowship, 1977.

WRITINGS: (Editor and author of introduction and notes) *The Foreign Policy of the Soviet Union,* Random House, 1960, 3rd edition, 1972; (editor with Garold W. Thumm) *The Challenge of Politics: Ideas and Issues,* Prentice-Hall, 1962, 3rd edition, 1970; *The Soviets in International Organizations: Changing Policy toward Developing Countries, 1953-1963,* Princeton University Press, 1964; *Communist Political Systems,* Prentice-Hall, 1966; (with Peter A. M. Berton) *Soviet Works on Southeast Asia: A Bibliography of Non-Periodical Literature, 1946-1965,* University of Southern California Press, 1967; *Yugoslavia and the Nonaligned World,* Princeton University Press, 1970; (editor with George Ginsburgs) *Soviet and American Policies in the United Nations,* New York University Press, 1971; *Soviet and Chinese Influence in the Third World,* Praeger, 1975; *Red Star on the Nile: The Soviet-Egyptian Influence Relationship since the June War,* Princeton University Press, 1977; *Soviet Foreign Policy since World War II: Imperial and Global,* Winthrop Publishing, 1981. Contributor of articles to *American Political Science Review, Reporter, Journal of Asian Studies, Orbis, Bulletin of the Atomic Scientist, Survey,* and other journals. Member of board of editors, *Current History.*

WORK IN PROGRESS: Writing on Soviet policy toward Turkey, Iran, and Afghanistan.

*   *   *

RUDNICK, Milton Leroy   1927-

PERSONAL: Born December 24, 1927, in Fresno, Calif.; son of Edward John and Natalie (Sandler) Rudnick; married Carlene Helmkamp, 1969; children: (previous marriage) Robert A., Deborah J., Richard W. *Education:* Attended California Concordia Junior College, 1945-47; Concordia Seminary, St. Louis, Mo., B.A., 1949, B.D., 1952, M.S.T., 1953, Th.D., 1963; additional study at Washington University, University of Illinois at Urbana-Champaign, and United Theological Seminary. *Home:* 81 West Hoyt Ave., St. Paul, Minn. 55117. *Office:* Concordia College, Hamline and Marshall, St. Paul, Minn. 55104.

CAREER: Minister, Lutheran Church—Missouri Synod; Concordia Seminary, St. Louis, Mo., instructor, 1953-54; Trinity Lutheran Church, New York, N.Y., pastor, 1954-57; St. Paul's Lutheran Church, St. Louis, Mo., pastor, 1957-63; University of Illinois at Urbana-Champaign, Lutheran Chair in Religion, 1963-64; Concordia College, St. Paul, Minn., 1964—, began as assistant professor, currently associate professor of religion. *Member:* American Society of Church History, Academy of Evangelism.

WRITINGS: Christianity Is for You, Concordia, 1961; *Fundamentalism and the Missouri Synod,* Concordia, 1966; *Authority and Obedience in the Church,* Lutheran Education Association, 1977; *Christian Ethics for Today: An Evangelical Approach,* Baker Book, 1979. Also author of *Reason and Religion,* 1965. Contributor to Lutheran publications.

*   *   *

RUMBOLD-GIBBS, Henry St. John Clair   1913-
(Henry Gibbs; pseudonyms: Simon Harvester, John Saxon)

PERSONAL: Born June 28, 1913, in Salisbury, Wiltshire, England; son of Henry John (a farmer, brewer, and race horse owner) and Beatrice Evelyn (a concert pianist; maiden name, Rumbold) Gibbs; married Mary Elizabeth Hutchings. *Education:* Marlborough College.

CAREER: Trained as portrait-painter in London, England,

Paris, France, and Venice, Italy; worked as industrial reporter, film critic, publisher's reader, foreign and war correspondent, and chicken farmer; currently political analyst, traveler, and writer. *Military service:* British Army, Royal Corps of Signals, Royal Intelligence Corps; invalided out, 1941. *Member:* Society of Authors, P.E.N., Mystery Writers of America, Authors Guild, Paternosters. *Awards, honors:* Anisfield-Wolf award for improving racial understanding, 1950 (shared with John Hersey), for *Twilight in South Africa.*

WRITINGS—Under name Henry Gibbs; novels; all published by Jarrolds, except as indicated: *At a Farthing's Rate,* 1943; *Not to the Swift,* 1944; *From All Blindness,* 1944; *Blue Days and Fair,* 1946; *Know Then Thyself,* 1947; *Affectionately Yours, Fanny: Fanny Kemble and the London Theatre,* 1947; *Theatre Tapestry,* 1949; *Ten Thirty Sharp,* 1949; *Withered Garland,* 1950; *Taps, Colonel Roberts,* 1951; *Cream and Cider,* 1952; *Six-Mile Face,* 1952; *Crescent in Shadow,* 1952; *Disputed Barricade,* 1952; *Italy on Borrowed Time,* 1953; *Cape of Shadows,* 1954; *The Masks of Spain,* Muller, 1955; *The Splendor and the Dust,* 1955; *Winds of Time,* 1956; *Thunder at Dawn,* 1957; *The Tumult and Shouting,* 1958; *The Hills of India,* 1961; *The Bamboo Prison,* 1961; *The Crimson Gate,* 1961, Walker, 1963; *The Mortal Fire,* 1963.

Other: (With Cyril Campion) *Man about Town* (a series of romantic episodes based on two radio serials), Rich & Cowan, 1948; *Children's Overture: A Study of Juvenile Delinquency in London Slums,* Jarrolds, 1948; *Twilight in South Africa,* Philosophical Library, 1950; *Background to Bitterness: The Story of South Africa, 1652-1954,* Muller, 1954, Philosophical Library, 1955; *Africa on a Tightrope,* Jarrolds, 1954.

Under pseudonym Simon Harvester; all published by Jarrolds, except as indicated: *Epitaph for Lemmings,* Rich & Cowan, 1943; *Maybe a Trumpet,* Rich & Cowan, 1945; *Lantern for Diogenes,* Rich & Cowan, 1947; *Whatsoever Things Are True,* Rich & Cowan, 1947; *Pawns in Ice,* 1948; *Sequins Lost Their Luster,* Rich & Cowan, 1948; *Breastplate for Aaron,* Rich & Cowan, 1949; *Good Men and True,* Rich & Cowan, 1951; *Obols for Charon: A Mark Blunden Story,* 1951; *Sheep May Safely Graze: A Mark Blunden Story,* Rich & Cowan, 1951; *Vessel May Carry Explosives,* 1951; *Witch Hunt,* 1951; *Cat's Cradle,* 1952; *Traitor's Gate,* 1952; *Lucifer at Sunset,* 1953; *Spiders' Web,* 1953; *The Bamboo Screen,* 1954, Walker, 1968; *Delay in Danger,* 1954; *Arrival in Suspicion,* 1955; *Tiger in the North,* 1955, Walker, 1963; *Dragon Road,* 1956, Walker, 1969; *Paradise Men,* 1956; *The Copper Butterfly,* 1957, Walker, 1962; *Golden Fear,* 1957; *Yesterday Walkers,* 1958; *Hour before Zero,* 1959; *Unsung Road,* 1960, Walker, 1961; *The Chinese Hammer,* 1960, Walker, 1961; *Moonstone Jungle,* 1961; *Silk Road,* 1962, Walker, 1963; *Troika,* 1962; *Red Road,* 1963, Walker, 1964; *Flight In Darkness,* 1964, Walker, 1965; *The Flying Horse,* Walker, 1964; *Assassins Road,* Walker, 1965; *Shadows in a Hidden Land,* Walker, 1966; *Treacherous Road,* 1966, Walker, 1967; *Battle Road,* Walker, 1967; *Zion Road,* Walker, 1968; *The Nameless Road,* 1969, Walker, 1970; *Moscow Road,* 1970, Walker, 1971; *Sahara Road,* Walker, 1972; *A Corner of the Playground,* 1973; *Forgotten Road,* Hutchinson, 1974; *Siberian Road,* Walker, 1976.

SIDELIGHTS: Henry Rumbold-Gibbs has shown himself to be at home with both light and serious subjects. His serious side is most evident in his books on South Africa. Fenner Brockway writes: "His work gives the completest general picture of South Africa now available. The descriptive part of [*Twilight in South Africa*] makes one see and feel and even smell South Africa." John Barkham describes it as "a truth-

ful and courageous book that throws a fierce white light on some very dark places."

The author's skill with lighter subjects is most consistently represented by his mysteries. As a reviewer for the *New Yorker* explains: "[His] affinities are with Eric Ambler rather than with Ian Fleming. Like the former, he moves quietly, plausibly, and with a genuine appreciation of contemporary geopolitics. . . . It is a scene whose look, culture, and current history he apparently knows like the back of his hand. It might be added—and there is no rarer accomplishment in this genre—that he is capable of bringing a thriller not merely to an end but to a thoroughly satisfactory conclusion."

Rumbold-Gibbs knows French, Italian, German, Afrikaans, Arabic, Hindustani, and various dialects.

AVOCATIONAL INTERESTS: International politics, art, music, walking, birdwatching, travel, and athletics.

BIOGRAPHICAL/CRITICAL SOURCES: New Statesman and Nation, July 15, 1950; *New York Times,* December 3, 1950; *New Yorker,* February 17, 1951, April 29, 1961, November 9, 1963, November 20, 1965; *Christian Century,* April, 1951; *New Republic,* April 23, 1951; *Book Week,* January 12, 1964; *New York Times Book Review,* May 31, 1964, January 29, 1967; *Library Journal,* June 1, 1964; *Best Sellers,* December 1, 1965.†

*   *   *

RUNCIMAN, (James Cochran) Steven(son) 1903-

PERSONAL: Born July 7, 1903, in Northumberland, England; son of Walter (viscount of Doxford) and Hilda (Stevenson) Runciman. *Education:* Trinity College, Cambridge, B.A., 1924, M.A., 1928. *Home:* Elshieshields, Lockerbie, Dumfriesshire, Scotland.

CAREER: Cambridge University, Cambridge, England, fellow of Trinity College, 1927-38, university lecturer in history, 1932-38; worked in government service in the Middle East, 1940-42; Istanbul University, Beyazit, Turkey, professor of Byzantine Studies, 1942-45; British Council, Athens, Greece, representative, 1945-47; Oxford University, Magdalen College, Oxford, England, Waynflete Lecturer, 1953-54; University of St. Andrews, St. Andrews, Scotland, Gifford Lecturer, 1960-62; University of Chicago, Chicago, Ill., Alexander White Professor, 1963. Member of advisory council, Victoria and Albert Museum; trustee, British Museum, 1960-66. Frequent lecturer at American universities. *Member:* British Academy (fellow), British Institute of Archaeology (President of Ankara branch, 1962-75), Anglo-Hellenic League (chairman, 1951-67), Athenaeum Club (London). *Awards, honors:* Knighted, 1958; knight commander, Order of the Phoenix, Greece, 1962; Silver Pen Award, British Pen Club, 1968, for *The Great Church in Captivity.* Academic: D. Phil., Salonica University, 1951; LL.D., Glasgow University, 1955; Litt.D., Cambridge University, 1955, Durham University, 1957, Oxford University, 1963, University of London, 1966, University of St. Andrews, 1969, and University of Birmingham, 1973; D.D., Wabash College, 1962; D. Lit. Hum., University of Chicago, 1963, and Ball State University, 1978.

WRITINGS—Published by Cambridge University Press, except as indicated: *The Emperor Romanus Lecapenus,* 1929, reprinted, 1963; *The First Bulgarian Empire,* Bell, 1930; *Byzantine Civilisation,* Arnold & Co., 1933, reprinted, Methuen, 1975; *The Medieval Manichee,* 1947, reprinted, 1963; *A History of the Crusades,* three volumes, 1951-54;

The Eastern Schism, Oxford University Press, 1955; *The Sicilian Vespers,* 1958; *The White Rajahs,* 1960, reprinted, State Mutual Book, 1978; *The Fall of Constantinople,* 1965; *The Great Church in Captivity,* 1968; *Christian Arabs of Palestine,* Longmans, Green, 1970; *The Last Byzantine Renaissance,* 1970; *The Orthodox Churches and the Secular State,* Oxford University Press, 1972; *Byzantine Style and Civilization,* Penguin, 1975; *The Byzantine Theocracy,* 1977; *Mistra: Byzantine Capital of the Peloponnese,* Thames & Hudson, 1980.

Contributor: *Byzantium,* Oxford University Press, 1948; *Golden Age of the Great Cities,* Thames & Hudson, 1952; *Cambridge Economic History,* Volume II, Cambridge University Press, 1952; *A History of the Crusades,* University of Pennsylvania Press, Volume I, 1955, Volume II, 1962. Contributor to history journals.

BIOGRAPHICAL/CRITICAL SOURCES: Times (London), March 10, 1980.

*   *   *

RUNDELL, Walter, Jr. 1928-

PERSONAL: Born November 2, 1928, in Austin, Tex.; son of Walter (a college dean) and Olive (Spillar) Rundell; married Deanna A. Boyd, June 12, 1959; children: Shelley Elizabeth, David Walter, Jennifer Diane. *Education:* Attended Lee College, 1946-48; University of Texas (now University of Texas at Austin), B.J. and B.S. (high honors), 1951; American University, M.A., 1955, Ph.D., 1957. *Politics:* Democrat. *Religion:* Methodist. *Home:* 6817 Pineway St., Hyattsville, Md. 20782 *Office:* Department of History, University of Maryland, College Park, Md. 20742

CAREER: U.S. Army, 1951-57, historical officer in Office of the Chief of Finance, Washington, D.C., 1954-57, became first lieutenant; Del Mar College, Corpus Christi, Tex., instructor in history, 1957-58; Texas Woman's University, Denton, assistant professor of history, 1958-61; American Historical Association, Washington, D.C., assistant executive secretary, 1961-65; director, Survey on the Use of Original Sources in Graduate History Training, National Archives, 1965-67; University of Oklahoma, Norman, professor of history, 1967-69; Iowa State University, Ames, professor of history and chairman of the department, 1969-71; University of Maryland, College Park, professor of history, 1971—, chairman of department, 1971-76. Professorial lecturer, American University, 1962-64, and University of Maryland, 1963-64; visiting professor, Columbia University, 1968, and Emory University, 1970.

MEMBER: American Historical Association, Organization of American Historians, Society of American Archivists (member of council, 1971-1975; president, 1977-1978), Western History Association (member of council, 1962-65), Southern Historical Association, U.S. Capitol Historical Society (vice-president, 1971—), Potomac Corral of Westerners (chuck-wrangler and program chairman, 1962-63). *Awards, honors:* Waldo Gifford Leland Award of Society of American Archivists, 1971, for *In Pursuit of American History: Research and Training in the United States;* Webb-Smith Essay Award of the University of Texas at Arlington, 1975; University of Maryland Student Award for outstanding teaching, 1979.

WRITINGS: (With others) *Probing the American West,* Museum of New Mexico Press, 1962; *Black Market Money: The Collapse of U.S. Military Currency Control in World War II,* Louisiana State University Press, 1964; (editor) *List of Doctoral Dissertations in History in Progress or Completed at Colleges and Universities in the United States since 1961,* American Historical Association, 1964; (with others) *Reflections of Western Historians,* University of Arizona Press, 1969; *In Pursuit of American History: Research and Training in the United States,* University of Oklahoma Press, 1970; (with others) *In Search of Gulf Coast Colonial History,* Historic Pensacola Preservation Board, 1970; *Walter Prescott Webb,* Steck, 1971; *Early Texas Oil: A Photographic History, 1866-1936,* Texas A&M University Press, 1977; *Military Money: A Fiscal History of the U.S. Army Overseas in World War II,* Texas A&M University Press, 1980.

Contributor: Trevor Nevitt Dupuy, editor, *Holidays: Days of Significance for All Americans,* F. Watts, 1965; Dagmar Horna Perman, editor, *Bibliography and the Historian,* American Bibliographical Center-Clio Press, 1968; *Handbook of Texas,* Texas State Historical Association, 1976; *Dictionary of American History,* Scribner, 1976; *Essays on Walter Prescott Webb,* University of Texas Press, 1976; *Concepts of Freedom: 1776-1976, Twelve Essays by American and German Scholars to Commemorate the Bicentennial of the United States,* Ruprecht-Karl-Universitaet, 1977; (with Anne M. Butler) *Agricultural Literature—Proud Heritage—Future Promise,* U.S. Department of Agriculture, 1977; *The Reader's Encyclopedia of the American West,* Crowell, 1977; *Encyclopedia of Southern History,* Louisiana State University Press, 1979; *Dictionary of American Biography,* Supplement VII, Scribner, in press. Also contributor of articles to *Social Studies, American West, Pacific Historical Review, Arizona and the West, Military Affairs, New York History, Business History Review, Western Pennsylvania Historical Magazine, Social Education, American Archivist, Historian, Journal of Southern History,* and other journals. Editor of series of pamphlets for high school teachers published by Service Center for Teachers of History. Member of executive board of *Social Education,* 1962-65; member of advisory board of *America: History and Life,* 1968-76, and *Guide to the Study of United States History Outside the U.S., 1845-1980,* 1978—; member of board of editors of *Historian,* 1972-78, and *Arizona and the West,* 1978-82; *Maryland Historical Magazine,* member of board of editors, 1973-74, member of publications committee, 1974—.

WORK IN PROGRESS: A biography of Walter Prescott Webb; a pictorial history of oil in the Permian Basin (West Texas and New Mexico).

SIDELIGHTS: Walter Rundell, Jr. originally intended to be a music critic (majoring in music literature as well as journalism) but switched to the history field after military assignment as an historian. "Writing," he says, "is the common thread in this switch of vocational aims."

*   *   *

RUNYON, Richard P(orter) 1925-

PERSONAL: Born June 1, 1925, in New York, N.Y.; son of Harold Remson and Fleta (Richardson) Runyon; married Lois Lesinger, September 27, 1947; children: Amy (Mrs. Clark Gaiennie), Richard, Nancy, Thomas, Meribeth. *Education:* Drew University, A.B. (summa cum laude), 1950; Yale University, M.S., 1952, Ph.D., 1954. *Office:* C. W. Post Center, Long Island University, Northern Blvd., Greenvale, N.Y. 11548.

CAREER: Long Island University, C. W. Post Center, Greenvale, N.Y., assistant professor, 1955-57, associate professor, 1957-59, professor of psychology, 1959—, chairman of department, 1955-65, 1968-70, director of research center, 1964-66, dean of Division of Science, 1970—. Member of board of directors, North Nassau Mental Health Clinic. *Member:* American Psychological Association, Eastern Psychological Association, New York State Psychological Association, Sigma Xi.

WRITINGS: (With Audrey Haber) *Fundamentals of Behavioral Statistics,* Addison-Wesley, 1967, 4th edition, 1980, student workbook, 1970; (with Haber) *General Statistics,* Addison-Wesley 1969, 3rd edition, 1977, student workbook, 1969, 3rd edition, 1977; (with Haber and Pietro Badia) *Research Problems in Psychology,* Addison-Wesley, 1970; (editor with Haber and Badia) *Readings in Statistics,* Addison-Wesley, 1970; (with Lawrence Rocks) *The Energy Crisis,* Crown Publishing, 1972; (with Haber) *Fundamentals of Psychology,* Addison-Wesley, 1974; *Descriptive Statistics: A Contemporary Approach,* Addison-Wesley, 1977; *Inferential Statistics: A Contemporary Approach,* Addison-Wesley, 1977; *Nonparametric Statistics: A Contemporary Approach,* Addison-Wesley, 1977; *Winning with Statistics: A Painless First Look at Numbers, Ratios, Percentages, Means, and Inference,* Addison-Wesley, 1977.†

* * *

RUPERT, Hoover 1917-

PERSONAL: Born November 3, 1917, in Madison, N.J.; son of Lynn H. and Hazel (Linabary) Rupert; married Hazel Pearl Senti, 1941; children: Susan, Elizabeth Anne. *Education:* Baker University, A.B., 1938; Boston University, A.M., 1940, S.T.B. (cum laude), 1941; additional study at Union Theological Seminary, New York, N.Y., and Garrett Biblical Institute. *Home:* 4113 Bronson Rd., Kalamazoo, Mich. 49008. *Office:* First United Methodist Church, Kalamazoo, Mich. 49007.

CAREER: Assistant pastor or pastor of Methodist churches in Kansas and Massachusetts, 1936-45; Methodist Church, General Board of Education, Nashville, Tenn., national director of youth department, 1945-50; First Methodist Church, Jackson, Mich., senior minister, 1950-59; First Methodist Church, Ann Arbor, Mich., senior minister, 1959-72; First United Methodist Church, Kalamazoo, Mich., senior minister, 1972—. Leader of American Methodist delegation to World Conference of Christian Youth, Norway, 1947. Lecturer in Methodist pastors' schools in many states; speaker at more than eighty-five college campuses and in forty states. Radio broadcaster. Chairman, ministerial training, Detroit Conference Board; secretary, judicial council of United Methodist Church; trustee of Adrian College and Bronson Methodist Hospital.

MEMBER: World Methodist Council, Michigan Council of Churches, Pi Kappa Delta, Alpha Psi Omega, Rotary Club, Masons. *Awards, honors:* D.D. from Adrian College, 1952 and Baker University, 1966; distinguished alumnus award, Boston University, 1969; L.H.D., Milliken University, 1974.

WRITINGS—Published by Abingdon, except as indicated: (Editor) *Christ above All,* 1948; *Youth and Stewardship,* 1949; *Youth and Evangelism,* 1949; *Handbook of Methodist*

Youth Fellowship, General Board of Education, Methodist Church, 1949; *Your Life Counts,* 1950; *I Belong,* Youth Department, Methodist Church, 1955; *And Jesus Said,* 1960; *Enjoy Your Teen-ager,* 1962; *A Sense of What Is Vital,* 1964; *The Church in Renewal,* privately printed, 1965; *Where Is Thy Sting,* Graded Press, 1969; *What's Good about God,* 1971; *God Will See You Through,* Upper Room, 1976; *Life Demands Answers,* in press. Also author of *Prayer Poems on the Prayer Perfect,* 1943. Contributor to ten other books of sermons, papers, and symposia, and to periodicals. Author of weekly syndicated magazine columns, "Accent on Living" and "Talking to Teens." Regular contributor to daily syndicated newspaper series, "Prayer for Today."

SIDELIGHTS: Hoover Rupert lived for a time in his youth in India, where his parents were missionaries.

* * *

RYRIE, Charles C(aldwell) 1925-

PERSONAL: Born March 2, 1925, in St. Louis, Mo.; son of John Alexander and Elizabeth (Caldwell) Ryrie; married Anne Belden, June 27, 1959; children: Elizabeth, Bruce, Carolyn. *Education:* Haverford College, A.B., 1946; Dallas Theological Seminary, Th.M., 1947, Th.D., 1949; University of Edinburgh, Ph.D., 1954. *Home:* 6719 Velasco Ave., Dallas, Tex. 75214. *Office:* Department of Systematic Theology, Dallas Theological Seminary, Dallas, Tex.

CAREER: Ordained Baptist minister, 1947; Midwest Bible and Missionary Institute, St. Louis, Mo., instructor, 1947; Westmont College, Santa Barbara, Calif., associate professor, 1948-49, professor of Greek and Bible, 1949-53, dean of men, 1950-51, chairman of Division of Biblical Studies and Philosophy, 1950-53; Dallas Theological Seminary, Dallas, Tex., assistant professor, 1954-57, associate professor of systematic theology, 1957-58; Philadelphia College of Bible, Philadelphia, Pa., president, 1958-62; Dallas Theological Seminary, dean of doctoral studies and professor of systematic theology, 1962—. Visiting professor, Dallas Theological Seminary 1953-54. Director of Mosher, Inc., Houston, Word of Life Fellowship, and Central American Mission, Dallas. *Member:* National Institute of Religion, Evangelical Theological Society, Society of Biblical Literature, Phi Beta Kappa.

WRITINGS—Published by Moody, except as indicated: *Easy-to-Get Object Lessons,* Zondervan, 1949; *The Basis of the Premillennial Faith,* Loizeaux Brothers, 1953; *Neo-Orthodoxy: What It Is and What It Does,* 1956; *The Place of Women in the Church,* Macmillan, 1958; *Biblical Theology of the New Testament,* 1959; *The Thessalonian Epistles,* 1959; *The Acts of the Apostles,* 1961; *The Grace of God,* 1963; *Dispensationalism Today,* 1965; *The Holy Spirit,* 1965; *Patterns for Christian Youth,* 1966; *Revelation,* 1968; *Balancing the Christian Life,* 1969; *The Bible and Tomorrow's News: A New Look at Prophecy,* Scripture Press, 1969; *The Bible of the Middle War,* Brite Divinity School, Texas Christian University, 1969; *Easy Object Lessons,* 1970; *A Survey of Bible Doctrine,* 1972; *You Mean the Bible Teaches That?,* 1974; *The Living End,* Revell, 1976; *The Ryrie Study Bible,* 1978.

S

SAHNI, Balbir S. 1934-

PERSONAL: Born July 4, 1934, in Gujarkhan, Pakistan; son of Ishar S. (a businessman) and Mohinder K. (Sethi) Sahni; married Jeanne C. Kerstens, April 13, 1969; children: Isher-Paul S. *Education:* Delhi University, B.A. (honors), 1955, M.A., 1957; New York University, M.B.A., 1959; New School for Social Research, Ph.D., 1965. *Religion:* Sikh. *Home:* 1460 Penfield Dr., Montreal, Quebec, Canada H3G 1B8. *Office:* Department of Economics, Concordia University, Sir George Williams Campus, Montreal, Quebec, Canada H3G 1M8.

CAREER: Government of India, consulate general in New York, N.Y., 1962-65; member of faculty, Sir George Williams Campus, Concordia University, Montreal, Quebec. Consultant, Export Promotions Councils, India. *Member:* American Economic Association, Canadian Economic Association, International Institute of Public Finance, Canadian International Centre of Research on Public Economy (executive secretary, 1966-71), Canadian Tax Foundation, National Tax Association, Tax Institute of America.

WRITINGS: Saving and Economic Development, Scientific Book Agency, 1967; (editor) *Public Expenditure Analysis,* Rotterdam University Press, 1972; (with T. Mathew) *The Shifting and Incidence of the Corporate Income Tax,* Rotterdam University Press, 1976. Co-editor, *Indian Trade Bulletin* and *Canadian CIRIEC Review.*

WORK IN PROGRESS: Public Expenditures and Economic Development, a comparative study; *Growth of Public Sectors: A Comparative Study.*

*   *   *

SAINER, Arthur 1924-

PERSONAL: Born September 12, 1924, in New York, N.Y.; son of Louis and Sadie (Roth) Sainer; married Stefanie Janis, December 23, 1956 (divorced, 1961). *Education:* New York University, B.A., 1946; Columbia University, M.A., 1948. *Religion:* Jewish. *Home:* 565 West End Ave., New York, N.Y. 10024. *Agent:* Ellen Levine, Curtis Brown Ltd., 575 Madison Ave., New York, N.Y. 10022.

CAREER: TV Guide Magazine, New York City, editor, 1956-61; *Village Voice,* New York City, drama and literary critic and book editor, 1961-65; C. W. Post College, Brookline, N.Y., instructor in English, 1963-67; Bennington College, Bennington, Vt., member of drama division, 1967-69;

Village Voice, drama critic, beginning 1969; Wesleyan College, Middletown, Conn., professor of theater, 1977-80; Hunter College of the City University of New York, New York City, professor of theater, 1980—. Lecturer at Sarah Lawrence College, spring, 1964, and Nathaniel Hawthorne College, spring, 1969; associate professor of fiction writing at Staten Island Community College, spring, 1974; instructor at numerous workshops, including Living Theatre playwriting workshop, 1962, and Chautauqua Writers' Workshop, 1969. Conductor of series of radio broadcasts on contemporary theatre, WBAI-FM, 1971-72. Member of academic council, Campus-Free College, Boston, 1971—. *Member:* Playwrights Group (president, 1971—). *Awards, honors:* John Golden playwriting award, 1946, for "Grab Your Hat"; Rockefeller grant, 1967; Ford Foundation grant, 1979.

WRITINGS: The Sleepwalker and the Assassin, Bridgehead Books, 1964; *The Radical Theatre Notebook,* Avon, 1975.

Plays: "The Bitch of Waverly Place," first produced Off-Off-Broadway at Judson Poets' Theatre, March, 1964; "The Game of the Eye," first produced in Bronxville, N.Y., at Sarah Lawrence College, May, 1964; "The Day Speaks but Cannot Weep," first produced Off-Off-Broadway at Cafe La Mama, January, 1965; "The Blind Angel," first produced in New York at Bridge Theatre, February, 1965; "Untitled Chase," first produced in New York at Washington Square Park, September, 1965, produced Off-Broadway at Astor Place Playhouse, November, 1965; "God Wants What Men Want," first produced at Bridge Theatre, May, 1966; "The Bomb Flower," first produced at Bridge Theatre, November, 1966; "The Children's Army Is Late," first produced on Long Island, N.Y., at C. W. Post College, May, 1967, produced in New York at Theater for the New City, March, 1974; "The Thing Itself" (first produced in Minneapolis, Minn., at Firehouse Theatre, July, 1967; produced at Theater for the New City, November, 1972), published in *Playwrights for Tomorrow,* Volume VI, edited by Arthur H. Ballet, University of Minnesota Press, 1969; "Noses," first produced in New York at St. Mark's Church in the Bouwerie, November, 1967; "Boat Sun Cavern," first produced in Bennington, Vt., at Bennington College, May, 1969.

"Van Gogh," first produced Off-Off-Broadway at La Mama Experimental Theatre Club, February, 1970; "I Hear It Kissing Me, Ladies," first produced in New York at Unit Theatre, November, 1970; "Images of the Coming Dead," first produced in New York at Open Space, April, 1971;

"The Celebration: Jooz/Guns/Movies/The Abyss," first produced at Theater for the New City, February, 1972; "Go Children Slowly," first produced Off-Off-Broadway at The Cubiculo, May, 1973; "The Spring Offensive," first produced in New York at Super Nova, June, 1973; "Charlie Chestnut Rides the I.R.T.," first produced at Theater for the New City, 1975; "Day Old Bread," first produced at Theater for the New City, 1976; "The Rich Man, Poor Man Play," first produced in New York, 1976; "Witnesses," first produced at Open Space in Soho, 1977; "Carol in Winter Sunlight," first produced at Theater for the New City, 1977; "After the Baal Shem Tov," first produced at Theater for the New City, 1978; "Sunday Childhood Journeys to Nobody at Home," first produced at Theater for the New City, 1980.

Television plays: "A New Year for Margaret," CBS-TV, 1951; "The Dark Side of the Moon," NBC-TV, 1957; "1 Piece Smash," WGBH (Boston), 1972, published in *The Scene,* Volume II, edited by Stanley Nelson, The Smith, 1974; "A Man Loses His Dog More or Less," WGBH, 1972.

Short fiction anthologized in *American Judaism Reader,* edited by Paul Kresh, Abelard, 1967. Also author of experimental church service produced by OM-Theatre Workshop in Boston, Mass. at Arlington Street Church, May, 1968. Contributor to *Contemporary Dramatists* and to periodicals, including *Bennington Review, Cavalier, Cimaise* (Paris), *yale/theatre,* and *Vogue.* Film critic, *Show Business Illustrated,* 1961; founder and contributing editor, *Ikon,* 1967.

WORK IN PROGRESS: A novel, *Survivals.*

*   *   *

St. JOHN, Patricia Mary   1919-

PERSONAL: Born April 5, 1919, in St. Leonards, Sussex, England; daughter of Harold (a missionary) and Ella Margaret (Swain) St. John. *Education:* Educated at private school in Malvern, England; S.R.N., 1947. *Politics:* Conservative. *Religion:* Protestant. *Home:* 10 Preston Close, Canley, Coventry, England. *Office:* 5 Wigmore St., London W. 1, England.

CAREER: Teacher and school matron in Wales before serving as missionary nurse and sister tutor in North Africa, 1949-61; school work in Wales, 1961-63; returned to Morocco as hospital evangelist. *Awards, honors:* First prize for children's Christian literature, 1948; first prize for "Book of the Month" awarded by "Literature in Schools," Switzerland, 1952.

WRITINGS: Tanglewood Secret, Moody, 1948; *Treasures of the Snow,* Moody, 1952; *Verses,* Children's Special Service Mission, 1954; *Rainbow Garden,* Moody, 1960; *Harold St. John: A Portrait,* Loizeaux, 1961; *Three Go Searching,* Moody, 1966; *R. Hudson Pope: A Biography,* Scripture Union, 1967; *Twice Freed,* Pickering Hughes, 1967; *Breath of Life,* Norfolk Press, 1969; *Mystery of Pheasant Cottage,* Moody, 1978. Also author of *Star of Light* and *The Four Candles,* both published by Moody; author of filmscripts "Tanglewood Secret" and "Treasures in the Snow," both 1980. Contributor to *Christian Herald, Good Housekeeping, Witness,* and other publications.

SIDELIGHTS: Patricia Mary St. John's books for children have been translated into twenty-two languages, including Arabic, Persian, and Hindustani, and transcribed into Braille for the blind.

SALISBURY, Harrison E(vans)   1908-

PERSONAL: Born November 14, 1908, in Minneapolis, Minn.; son of Percy Pritchard and Georgianna (Evans) Salisbury; married Mary Hollis, April 1, 1933 (divorced); married Charlotte Rand, 1964; children: (first marriage) Michael, Stephan. *Education:* University of Minnesota, A.B., 1930. *Home address:* Box 70, Taconic, Conn. 06079. *Agent:* Curtis Brown Ltd., 575 Madison Ave., New York, N.Y. 10022.

CAREER: The Minneapolis Journal, Minneapolis, Minn., reporter, 1928; United Press, reporter, London manager, Moscow manager, and foreign editor, 1930-48; *New York Times,* correspondent in Moscow, 1949-54, reporter in New York, 1955-61, director of national correspondence, 1962-64, assistant managing editor, 1964-71, associate editor, 1971-75, editor of opinion-editorial page, 1971-75. *Member:* National Press Club (Washington, D.C.), Century Association (New York). *Awards, honors:* Pulitzer Prize in international reporting, 1955, for articles on Soviet Union.

WRITINGS: Russia on the Way, Macmillan, 1946; *American in Russia,* Harper, 1955; *Stalin's Russia and After,* Macmillan (London), 1955; *The Shook-up Generation,* Harper, 1958; *To Moscow—and Beyond: A Reporter's Narrative,* Harper, 1960; *Moscow Journal: The End of Stalin,* University of Chicago Press, 1961; *The Northern Palmyra Affair,* Harper, 1962; *A New Russia?,* Harper, 1962; *The Key to Moscow,* Lippincott, 1963; *Russia,* Atheneum, 1965 (published in England as *The Soviet Union,* Encyclopaedia Britannica Educational Corp., 1967); *Orbit of China,* Harper, 1967; (editor and contributor) *The Soviet Union: The First Fifty Years,* Harcourt, 1967 (published in England as *Anatomy of the Soviet Union,* Thomas Nelson, 1967); *Behind the Lines—Hanoi, December 23, 1966-January 7, 1967,* Harper, 1967; (photographer) *Children of Russia,* Oak Tree Press, 1967; (editor) Andrei Sakharov, *Progress, Coexistence, and Intellectual Freedom,* Norton, 1968; *War between Russia and China,* Norton, 1969 (published in England as *The Coming War between Russia and China,* Secker & Warburg, 1969); *The 900 Days: The Siege of Leningrad,* Harper, 1969 (published in England as *The Siege of Leningrad,* Secker & Warburg, 1969); (editor) Georgi K. Zhukov, *Marshal Zhukov's Greatest Battles,* Harper, 1969.

The Many Americas Shall Be One, Norton, 1971; (author of commentary) Emil Schulthess, *Soviet Union,* Harper, 1971; (editor) *The Eloquence of Protest: Voices of the 70's,* Houghton, 1972; (editor and contributor, with James A. Keith and Ida Prince Nelson) *Project WERC Resource Book,* Teacher Assist Center, 1972; (editor with David Schneiderman) *The Indignant Years,* Crown/Arno Press, 1973; *To Peking—and Beyond: A Report on the New Asia,* Quadrangle, 1973; (editor and author of foreword) Sakharov, *Sakharov Speaks,* Knopf, 1974; *The Gates of Hell,* Random House, 1975; *Travels around America,* Walker, 1976; *Black Night, White Snow: Russia's Revolutions, 1905-1917,* Doubleday, 1978; *Russia In Revolution,* Holt, 1979; *Without Fear or Favor,* New York Times Co., 1980.

SIDELIGHTS: W. L. Morin has called Harrison Salisbury "an astute and superbly trained observer." His travels as a reporter have taken him to Russia, Siberia, Central Asia, Outer Mongolia, China, Tibet, North Korea, and Southeast Asia and have given him ample opportunity to become familiar with the varying ways of life and thought. In addition, Salisbury has the distinction of being the first American reporter to go to North Vietnam during the Vietnam conflict. Perhaps as a result of these activities, however, Salisbury may have been on a "watch list" compiled by the National

Security Agency in the late 1960's and early 1970's. As noted in the *Washington Post*, Salisbury was denied access to CIA documents under his name which he requested through the Freedom of Information Act; in April, 1980, he initiated a "$10,000 damage suit ... against the National Security Agency, contending that it illegally intercepted and kept records on his private communications while he was a correspondent. ... The suit asks the court to declare the interceptions illegal and to permit Salisbury access to the records he has requested."

Nevertheless, it is his writings on Russia that have brought Salisbury his widest acclaim, including the Pulitzer Prize for international reporting. One of his few works of fiction, *The Northern Palmyra Affair*, prompted McReady Huston to write: "This could be a book written by a Russian and translated; as to substance, it reveals the author bridging with aplomb the gap between reporting and creation." His extensive research on the siege of Leningrad led C. P. Snow to comment: "Out of it all [Salisbury] has produced something like a non-fiction masterpiece, at the same time realistic, brotherly, and admiring. It is splendid ... that such a work has been written by an American. ... I do not believe that any [other] Westerner could have written this epic so well." Similarly, Robert Conquest finds that in his account of the Russian revolutions, *Black Night, White Snow*, "Salisbury gives an ebullient, impressionistic picture of the whole period. ... Moreover, this goes with considerable—and fascinating—research on details often vital to a general understanding." Conquest continues: "Salisbury is able to show that there can seldom have been events researched in so massive and detailed a fashion; but also that the results, once obtained, were subjected to an equally unprecedented process of suppression and misrepresentation. Of this the author gives a more useful account than [one] usually obtains. ... He is quite at ease with the material, and uses it, or corrects it, to maximum advantage."

BIOGRAPHICAL/CRITICAL SOURCES: New York Times, June 30, 1946, January 27, 1969, January 26, 1978, May 15, 1980; *Political Science Quarterly*, September, 1946; *New York Times Book Review*, March 27, 1960, April 15, 1962, June 4, 1967, November 5, 1967, January 26, 1969, November 30, 1969, January 29, 1978, May 18, 1980; *Saturday Review*, November 18, 1961, May 5, 1962, January 15, 1966, February 1, 1969; *New York Review of Books*, April 10, 1962, August 3, 1967; *San Francisco Chronicle*, April 15, 1962; *Library Journal*, February 1, 1967; *New Statesman*, February 24, 1967; *Esquire*, May, 1967; *Christian Science Monitor*, May 18, 1967, May 25, 1967; *Virginia Quarterly Review*, summer, 1967; *Book World*, November 5, 1967, January 26, 1969; *New Republic*, November 25, 1967; *National Observer*, March 17, 1969; *Best Sellers*, April 15, 1971; *Times Literary Supplement*, August 6, 1976; *Newsweek*, February 13, 1978; *Washington Post*, April 11, 1980.

*   *   *

SALTER, Lionel (Paul)   1914-

PERSONAL: Born September 8, 1914, in London, England; son of Morris and Jeannetta Salter; married Christine Fraser, 1939; children: Graham, Adrian, Brian. *Education:* London Academy of Music, A.L.A.M., 1929; Royal College of Music, L.R.A.M., 1931; St. John's College, Cambridge, B.A., 1935, Mus.B., 1936, M.A., 1939. *Home:* 674 Finchley Rd., London N.W.11, England. *Agent:* David Higham Associates, 5-8 Lower John St., Golden Square, London W1R 4HA, England.

CAREER: British Broadcasting Corp., London, England, began as television music assistant, 1937, conductor and radio producer, 1945-48, European music supervisor, 1948-54, artists' manager, 1954-56, head of television music, 1956-63, head of opera (television and radio), 1963-67, assistant controller of music, 1967-74. Harpsichordist, conductor, and pianist, appearing in more than seventeen countries, and recording for Westminster, Deutsche Grammophon, and other companies; lecturer and broadcaster on musical subjects; composer, editor, and arranger. *Military service:* British Army, Intelligence Corps and Army Education Corps, 1940-44; became lieutenant. *Member:* International Music Centre (Vienna), Critics' Circle.

WRITINGS: Going to a Concert, Phoenix House, 1950; *Going to the Opera*, Phoenix House, 1955; *The Musician and His World*, Gollancz, 1963; (with J. Bornoff) *Music and the 20th Century Media*, Olschki, 1972; *The Gramophone Guide to Classical Composers and Recordings*, Salamander, 1978.

Contributor: *Years of Grace*, Evans, 1950; *The Concerto*, Penguin, 1952; *The Music Masters*, Cassell, 1954; *Music*, Odhams, 1956; *Decca Book of Opera*, Laurie, 1956; *Music and Western Man*, Dent, 1958; *Decca Book of Ballet*, Muller, 1958; *Essays on Music from "The Listener,"* Cassell, 1967; *The Symphony*, Thames & Hudson, 1973; *Building a Library*, Oxford University Press, 1979; *Opera on Record*, Hutchinson, 1979. Translator of over fifty operas for Deutsche Grammophon, Schott, Breitkopf and Hartel, and others. General editor, *BBC Music Guides*, 1967-75. Programme editor, Edinburgh International Festival, 1951-55, and Henry Wood Promenade Concerts, 1967-74. Regular critic for *Gramophone*, 1948—, *Music Teacher*, 1952-79. Contributor of articles on music to *Encyclopaedia Britannica*, *Grove's Dictionary of Music and Musicians*, *International Cyclopedia of Music & Musicians*, *Musical Times*, *Listener*, *Opera*, and other publications.

*   *   *

SAMPSON, Anthony   1926-

PERSONAL: Born August 3, 1926, in Durham, England; son of Michael Trevisky and Phyllis (Seward) Sampson. *Education:* Christ Church, Oxford, M.A., 1950. *Agent:* A. D. Peters, 10 Buckingham St., Adelphi, London W.C.2, England.

CAREER: Drum Magazine, Johannesburg, Republic of South Africa, editor, 1951-55; *Observer*, London, England, member of editorial staff, 1955—. *Military service:* Royal Navy, 1945-47; became sub-lieutenant. *Member:* Beefsteak Club (London).

WRITINGS: Drum, Houghton, 1957; *Treason Cage*, Heinemann, 1958; (with S. Pienaar) *South Africa: Two Views of Separate Development*, Oxford University Press, 1959, *Common Sense about Africa*, Macmillan, 1961; *Anatomy of Britain*, Harper, 1962, revised edition published as *Anatomy of Britain Today*, 1965, 2nd revised edition published as *The New Anatomy of Britain*, 1971; *Macmillan: A Study in Ambiguity*, Simon & Schuster, 1967; *The New Europeans*, Hodder & Stoughton, 1968, published as *Anatomy of Europe*, Harper, 1969; *The Sovereign State of ITT*, Stein & Day, 1973; *The Seven Sisters: The Great Oil Companies and the World They Shaped*, Viking, 1975; *The Arms Bazaar*, Viking, 1977.

SIDELIGHTS: Anthony Sampson writes best-selling guide books as well as books on controversial subjects.

Sampson's guide book *Anatomy of Britain* is for the businessman or tourist who wants to know how the institutions work, how the power is wielded, and how the people act in Britain. The book has been well-received, selling over 10,000 copies in the London Airport bookstore alone.

Sampson's more controversial books include his studies of the conglomerate International Telephone and Telegraph (*The Sovereign State of ITT*), the oil business (*Seven Sisters*), and armament sales (*The Arms Bazaar*). Seymour M. Hersh writes that "Sampson is knowledgeable about and able to effectively report on social, military, and economic problems both in Europe and the United States" and that his books have "presciently isolated major world problems."

BIOGRAPHICAL/CRITICAL SOURCES: *New Republic*, January 27, 1968, November 19, 1977; *New Statesman*, October 11, 1968; *Listener*, November 21, 1968; *Christian Science Monitor*, May 22, 1969; *Observer*, March 21, 1971; *Times Literary Supplement*, September 24, 1971; *Book World*, May 7, 1972; *New York Times Book Review*, June 18, 1972, December 7, 1975, July 24, 1977; *Newsweek*, July 23, 1973; *Time*, August 6, 1973; *Wall Street Journal*, November 12, 1973; *National Review*, December 21, 1973; *Spectator*, October 4, 1975; *New Yorker*, December 8, 1975; *Virginia Quarterly Review*, spring, 1976; *Business Week*, August 8, 1977; *Atlantic*, September, 1977; *New York Review of Books*, September 15, 1977; *Political Science Quarterly*, winter, 1977-78.

* * *

SANDERS, Leonard 1929-
(Dan Thomas)

PERSONAL: Born January 15, 1929, in Denver, Colo.; son of Leonard M. and Jacqueline (Thomas) Sanders; married Florene Cooter, August 21, 1956. *Education:* Attended University of Oklahoma. *Home:* 4200 Clayton Rd. W., Fort Worth, Tex. 76116. *Agent:* Aaron M. Priest Literary Agency, Inc., 150 East 35th St., New York, N.Y. 10016.

CAREER: Newspaperman in Wichita Falls, Tex., and Oklahoma City, Norman, and Enid, Okla.; *Fort Worth Star-Telegram*, Fort Worth, Tex., fine arts editor, 1958-79. *Military service:* U.S. Naval Reserve, two years sea duty.

WRITINGS: *Four-Year Hitch*, Ace Books, 1961; *The Wooden Horseshoe*, Doubleday, 1964; (under pseudonym Dan Thomas) *The Seed* (science fiction), Ballantine, 1968; *The Hamlet Warning*, Scribner, 1976; *The Hamlet Ultimatum*, Scribner, 1979; *Sonoma*, Delacorte, 1981.

WORK IN PROGRESS: Two novels.

* * *

SANDERS, William T(imothy) 1926-

PERSONAL: Born April 19, 1926, in Patchogue, N.Y.; son of William Henry (a chef) and Margaret (Crowley) Sanders; married Lili Chable, May 23, 1953; children: Lili, Kathleen, Theresa. *Education:* Harvard University, B.A., 1949, M.A., 1953, Ph.D., 1957. *Politics:* Non-political. *Religion:* None. *Home:* 2072 North Oak Lane, State College, Pa. 16801. *Office:* Department of Anthropology, Pennsylvania State University, University Park, Pa. 16802.

CAREER: University of Georgia, Athens, field archaeologist, 1956; University of Mississippi, Oxford, assistant professor of sociology and anthropology, 1956-59; Pennsylvania State University, University Park, assistant professor, 1959-62, associate professor, 1962-66, professor of anthropology, 1966—. Fulbright teaching fellow, Cuzco, Peru, 1965. Research associate, Louisiana State University, summer, 1957;

other research and field work in Mexico and Guatemala. *Military service:* U.S. Naval Reserve, active duty, 1943-45. *Member:* American Anthropological Association (fellow), Society for American Archaeology. *Awards, honors:* Pan-American Union fellow, 1960; National Science Foundation research grants, 1961-62, 1963-64, 1968-72.

WRITINGS: (With Barbara J. Price) *Mesoamerica: The Evolution of a Civilization*, Random House, 1968; (with Joseph D. Marino) *New World Pre-History*, Prentice-Hall, 1970; (editor with Joseph W. Michels) *Teotihuacan and Kaminaljuyu: A Study in Culture Contact*, Pennsylvania State University Press, 1978; *The Lowland Huasteca Archaelogical Survey and Excavation: 1957 Field Season*, Department of Anthropology, University of Missouri—Columbia, 1978; (with others) *The Basin of Mexico: Ecological Processes in the Evolution of a Civilization*, Academic Press, 1979. Contributor of articles and reviews to professional journals.†

* * *

SANDERSON, Sabina W(arren) 1931-
(Marion Fawcett)

PERSONAL: Born August 19, 1931, in Upland, Pa.; daughter of Richard and Sabina (Grzybowski) Warren; married Ivan Terence Sanderson (a writer and editor), May 4, 1972 (died February 20, 1973). *Education:* Attended University of Delaware, 1949-52. *Address:* General Delivery, Blairstown, N.J. 07825.

CAREER: Hahnemann Medical College and Hospital, Philadelphia, Pa., secretary in pediatric department, 1953-59; J. B. Lippincott Co. (publishing firm), Philadelphia, associate editor, medical book publishing division, 1959-65; American Philosophical Society Library, Philadelphia, secretarial assistant, 1965-68; Society for Investigation of the Unexplained, Columbia, N.J., executive secretary, assistant to the director, 1968-77.

WRITINGS: *An Index to "Films in Review": 1950-1959*, National Board of Review of Motion Pictures, 1961, *1960-64 Supplement*, 1966; (with Simeon J. Crowther) *Checklist of Pamphlets in the History of Science and Medicine*, American Philosophical Society Library, 1968; (editor) Ivan T. Sanderson, *Green Silence*, McKay, 1974. Contributor to *Films in Review* and to professional journals. *Pursuit*, former executive editor, now consulting editor.

WORK IN PROGRESS: Biography of Ivan T. Sanderson.

SIDELIGHTS: Sabina W. Sanderson told *CA:* "I am an opera addict, enjoy gardening (I grow all my own vegetables), reading, classical music generally, Chinese art, cats, and natural history, but am incurably lazy—my favorite occupation is loafing. I am also an accomplished procrastinator (I have been meaning to join the Procrastinator's Club for years but haven't got round to it yet).

"I'm not sure I really enjoy writing, perhaps because, being a perfectionist, I am a slow writer and worry constantly about finding exactly the right word or phrase. My favorite aphorism is the statement made by the Labour M.P. Philip Snowden: 'Words should convey meaning.'"

* * *

SAYRE, Kenneth Malcolm 1928-

PERSONAL: Born August 13, 1928, in Scottsbluff, Neb.; son of Harry Malcolm (a railroad agent) and Mildred (Potts) Sayre; married Lucille M. Shea, August 19, 1958 (died April 22, 1980); children: Gregory, Christopher, Jeffrey. *Education:* Grinnell College, B.A., 1952; Harvard University,

M.A., 1954, Ph.D., 1958. *Office:* Department of Philosophy, University of Notre Dame, Notre Dame, Ind. 46556.

CAREER: Harvard University, Graduate School of Arts and Sciences, Cambridge, Mass., assistant dean, 1953-56; Massachusetts Institute of Technology, Lincoln Laboratory, Lexington, Mass., systems analyst, 1956-58; University of Notre Dame, Notre Dame, Ind., instructor, 1958-60, assistant professor, 1960-66, associate professor, 1966-71, professor of philosophy, 1971—. Director, Philosophic Institute. *Military service:* U.S. Navy, 1946-48. *Member:* American Philosophical Association.

WRITINGS—Published by University of Notre Dame Press, except as indicated: (Editor with Frederick James Crosson) *The Modeling of Mind: Computers and Intelligence,* 1963; *Recognition: A Study in the Philosophy of Artificial Intelligence,* 1965; (editor with Crosson) *Philosophy and Cybernetics* (essays), 1967; *Plato's Analytic Method,* University of Chicago Press, 1969; *Consciousness: A Philosophic Study of Minds and Machines,* Random House, 1969; *Cybernetics and the Philosophy of Mind,* Routledge & Kegan Paul, 1976; *Moonflight,* 1977; *Starburst,* 1977; (editor) *Values and the Electric Power Industry,* 1977; (editor with Kenneth Goodpaster) *Ethics and Problems of the 21st Century,* 1979; (principal author) *Regulation, Values and the Public Interest,* 1980. Contributor to *Mind, Inquiry Methods, Notre Dame Journal of Formal Logic,* and other periodicals.

* * *

SCHECHTMAN, Joseph B. 1891-1970

PERSONAL: Born September 6, 1891, in Odessa, Russia; came to United States in 1941; died March 1, 1970; son of Boris (a salesman) and Sarah (Faier) Schechtman; married Rachel Davidson (a librarian), May 23, 1936; children: Lea (Mrs. Daniel Behrman), Alexander, Miriam (Mrs. Donald Gottlieb). *Education:* University of Berlin, L.L.D., 1914; University of Novorossiysk, Ph.D., 1915. *Politics:* Zionist. *Religion.* Jewish. *Office:* 515 Park Ave., New York, N.Y. 10022.

CAREER: Institute of Jewish Affairs, New York City, research fellow, 1941-43; Research Bureau on Population Movements, New York City, director, 1943-44; Office of Strategic Services, Washington, D.C., research analyst, 1944-45; Jewish Agency for Palestine, New York City, deputy executive member, 1948-51, executive member, 1965-68. Vice-chairman, American Zionist Council. Member, Middle East Institute. *Member:* American Academy of Political and Social Science, Population Association of America.

WRITINGS: Transjordanien im bereiche des Palaestinamandates, Heinrich Glanz (Vienna), 1937; *European Population Transfers: 1939-1945,* Oxford University Press, 1946, reprinted, Russell & Russell, 1971; *Population Transfers in Asia,* Hallsby Press, 1949; *The Arab Refugee Problem,* Philosophical Library, 1952; *The Vladimir Yabolinsky Story,* Yoseloff, Volume I: *Rebel and Statesman,* 1956, Volume II: *Fighter and Prophet,* 1961; *On Wings of Eagles: The Plight, Exodus and Homecoming of Oriental Jewry,* Yoseloff, 1961; *Star in Eclipse: Russian Jewry Revisited,* Yoseloff, 1961; *Postwar Population Transfers in Europe: 1945-1955,* University of Pennsylvania Press, 1962; *The Refugee in the World: Displacement and Integration,* Yoseloff, 1963; *The Mufti and the Fuehrer: The Rise and Fall of Haj Amin el-Husseini,* Yoseloff, 1965; *The United States and the Jewish State Movement: The Crucial Decade, 1939-1949,* Yoseloff, 1966; *Zionism and Zionists in Soviet Russia: Greatness and Drama,* Zionist Organization of America, 1966; *Jordan: A State*

That Never Was, Cultural Publishing Co., 1968; (with Yehuda Benari) *History of the Revisionist Movement,* Hadar, 1970.

Also author of *The Jews and the Ukranians,* 1917, *Jews and National Movements in Free Russia,* 1917, *Under the Sign of Palestine,* 1918, *Les Pogromes en Ukraine sous les gouvernements ukraniens,* 1927, *Die Juedische Irredenta,* 1929, *The Pogroms of the Volunteer Army,* 1932, and *The Value of Galut Yemen,* 1950. Contributor to professional journals. Co-editor, *Rasswiet,* 1922-24, 1926-34, and *Unser Weg,* 1930-31.

SIDELIGHTS: Joseph B. Schechtman traveled extensively in Europe, the Middle East, and Latin America. He spoke Russian, French, German, and Yiddish.†

* * *

SCHEFLEN, Albert E. 1920-1980

PERSONAL: Born November 15, 1920, in Camden, N.J.; died August 14, 1980, in Chester, Pa.; son of Albert N. (an attorney) and Anne (Weidmann) Scheflen; married Norma K. Adnee, 1956 (divorced, 1966); married Alice K. Rudi (an editor), 1966; children: Linda Scheflen Schwarthey, John, Mark, James, Rhonda Bellon, Nancy Scheflen Winne, Ann. *Education:* Dickinson College, Sc.B., 1942; University of Pennsylvania, M.D., 1945; Philadelphia Psychoanalytic Institute, certification in psychiatry, 1952, and psychoanalysis, 1958. *Politics:* "New Left." *Religion:* Protestant.

CAREER: Researcher in neuropathology, Worcester State Hospital, 1950-51; University of Pennsylvania, School of Medicine, Philadelphia, assistant professor of psychiatry, 1951-55; senior scientist, Eastern Pennsylvania Psychiatric Institute, 1960-66; Albert Einstein College of Medicine, Bronx, N.Y., research professor of psychiatry, 1967-80, researcher, Bronx Psychiatric Center, Jewish Family Services, beginning 1967. Instructor in psychiatry, Medical School, Tufts University, 1950-51; professor, School of Medicine, Temple University, 1963-67. Consultant to Harlem Valley Psychiatric Center and Nathan Ackerman Family Institute. *Military service:* U.S. Navy, Medical Corps, 1945-49. *Member:* American Psychiatric Association, Society for General Systems Research, American Association for the Advancement of Science. *Awards, honors:* Center for Advanced Study in the Behavioral Sciences fellow, 1966; National Institute of Mental Health grant, 1968.

WRITINGS: Direct Analysis, Prentice-Hall, 1960; (editor with Oliver Spurgeon English and others) *Strategy and Structure in Psychotherapy,* Eastern Pennsylvania Psychiatric Institute, 1965; *Body Language and Social Order,* Indiana University Press, 1972; *Communicational Structure,* Prentice-Hall, 1973; *How Behavior Means,* Gordon & Breach, 1973, Anchor Press, 1974; (with Norman Ashcraft) *Human Territories: How We Behave in Space-Time,* Prentice-Hall, 1976; (with Ashcraft) *People Space: The Making and Breaking of Human Boundaries,* Doubleday, 1976. Contributor of articles to scientific journals.

AVOCATIONAL INTERESTS: Travel, gardening, reading.†

* * *

SCHER, Steven Paul 1936-

PERSONAL: Born March 2, 1936, in Budapest, Hungary. *Education:* Yale University, B.A., 1960, M.A., 1963, Ph.D., 1966. *Home:* 102 South Main St., Hanover, N.H. 03755. *Office:* 332 Dartmouth Hall, Dartmouth College, Hanover, N.H. 03755.

CAREER: Columbia University, New York, N.Y., instructor in German, 1965-67; Yale University, New Haven, Conn., assistant professor, 1967-70, associate professor of German, 1970-74; Dartmouth College, Hanover, N.H., professor of German and comparative literature, 1974—, chairman of department of German, 1974-80. *Member:* International P.E.N., Modern Language Association of America, American Comparative Literature Association, American Association of Teachers of German, Thomas Mann Gesellschaft (Zurich), E.T.A. Hoffmann Gesellschaft (Bamberg).

WRITINGS: Verbal Music in German Literature, Yale University Press, 1968; (co-editor) *Post-war German Culture* (anthology), Dutton, 1974, 2nd edition, Institute of German Studies, 1980; (editor) *Literatur und Musik* (anthology), Erich Schmidt Verlag, 1981. Contributor to literary journals.

WORK IN PROGRESS: E.T.A. Hoffmann: A Critical Biography, for University of Chicago Press; *E.T.A. Hoffmann Interpretationen,* an anthology, for Klett-Cotta Verlag.

*   *   *

SCHMEISER, Douglas Albert 1934-

PERSONAL: Born May 22, 1934, in Bruno, Saskatchewan, Canada; son of Charles A. and Elsie (Hazelwanter) Schmeiser; children: Mary Ellen, Douglas Charles, Robert Peter, James Paul, Gary William, Peggy Anne. *Education:* University of Saskatchewan, B.A. (with distinction), 1954, LL.B. (with great distinction), 1956; University of Michigan, LL.M., 1958, S.J.D., 1963. *Religion:* Roman Catholic. *Home:* 22 Simpson Cres., Saskatoon, Saskatchewan, Canada. *Office:* College of Law, University of Saskatchewan, Saskatoon, Saskatchewan, Canada.

CAREER: University of Saskatchewan, Saskatoon, special lecturer in law, 1956-57; private practice of law, Saskatoon, Saskatchewan, 1958-61; University of Saskatchewan, associate professor of law, 1961—, director of graduate legal studies, 1969-74, dean of law, 1974-77. Former president of Catholic Welfare Society and Saskatoon United Appeal; trustee, Saskatoon Separate School Board, 1964-69. Constitutional advisor to various provincial governments. *Member:* Canadian Bar Association, Canadian Association of University Teachers, Canadian Association of Law Teachers (former president), Canada Council (member of advisory academic panel, 1971-74), Canadian Human Rights Foundation, Law Society of Saskatchewan, John Howard Society of Saskatchewan (former director; now director of Saskatoon branch), Saskatoon Bar Association (director; former president).

WRITINGS: Civil Liberties in Canada, Oxford University Press, 1964; *Cases and Comments on Criminal Law,* Butterworths, 1966, 4th edition, 1981; *Cases On Canadian Civil Liberties,* University of Saskatchewan Printing Services, 1971; *The Native Offender and the Law,* Information Canada, 1974.

*   *   *

SCHMITTHOFF, Clive M(acmillan) 1903-

PERSONAL: Born March 24, 1903, in Berlin, Germany; son of Hermann (an advocate) and Anna (Reyersbach) Schmitthoff; married Ilse Auerbach (formerly an advocate), October 25, 1940. *Education:* University of Berlin, Dr. Jur., 1929; Inns of Court School of Law, Barrister-at-Law; University of London, LL.M., 1936, LL.D., 1953. *Address:* 29 Blenheim Rd., Bedford Park, London W4 1ET, England.

CAREER: Barrister-at-Law, London, England, 1936—. City

of London College, London, England, principal lecturer in law, 1948-71, visiting professor of international business law, 1971—, honorary fellow and vice-president, Institute of Export. Visiting professor, Louisiana State University School of Law, 1964, 1965, University of Manitoba School of Law, 1965, 1966, 1978. *Military service:* British Army, 1940-45; became warrant officer. *Member:* Bar Association, Association of Law Teachers (vice-president, 1966—), Mansfield Law Club of the City of London College (chairman, 1948-70). *Awards, honors:* Honorary professor of law, University of Kent, 1971—; Dr. jur. h.c., University of Marburg and University of Berne, 1977; Dr. Litt. h.c., Heriot-Watt, 1978.

WRITINGS: English Conflict of Laws, Pitmans, 1945, 3rd edition, Stevens, 1954; *The Export Trade–The Law and Practice of International Trade,* Stevens, 1948, 7th edition, 1980; *Sale of Goods,* Stevens, 1951, 2nd edition, 1966; *Legal Aspects of Export Sales,* Institute of Export, 1953, revised edition, 1979; (editor) *The Sources of the Law of International Trade,* Praeger, 1964; *The Unification of the Law of International Trade,* Gothenburg School of Economics and Business Administration Publications, 1964; (editor with David A. Godwon Sarre) Charlesworth, *Mercantile Law,* 11th edition, Stevens, 1967, 13th edition, 1977; *Commercial Law in a Changing Economic Climate,* Stevens, 1977. Also editor of *The Harmonisation of European Company Law,* 1973, *European Company Law Texts,* 1974, and, with Peter Curry, *Palmer's Company Law,* 23rd edition, 1981. Regular contributor to legal journals in the United Kingdom and elsewhere. Editor, *Journal of Business Law,* 1957—.

*   *   *

SCHOENBRUN, David (Franz) 1915-

PERSONAL: Born March 15, 1915, in New York, N.Y.; son of Max (a jeweler) and Lucy (Cassirer) Schoenbrun; married Dorothy Scher (a painter), September 23, 1938; children: Lucy (Mrs. Robert Szekely). *Education:* City College (now City College of the City University of New York), B.A., 1934; Columbia University, graduate study, 1965-66. *Politics:* Independent. *Religion:* Jewish. *Agent:* Richard Leibner, N.S. Bienstock, Inc., 10 Columbus Cir., New York, N.Y.

CAREER: High school teacher of French and Spanish in New York City, 1934-36; Dress Manufacturers Association, New York City, labor relations adjustor, 1936-40, editor of trade newspaper, 1937-40; free-lance writer for newspapers and magazines, 1940-41; U.S. Office of War Information, Washington, D.C., chief of European propaganda desk, 1942-43; Overseas News Agency, chief of Paris (France) Bureau, 1945-47; Columbia Broadcasting System (CBS), Inc., chief of Paris Bureau, 1945-60, chief correspondent and chief of Washington, D.C. bureau, 1960-63; Metromedia, New York City, news commentator and chief correspondent, 1964, 1965—. Guest commentator, ABC News, 1967-70; news analyst, WPIX-TV and Independent Network News, 1972—. Senior lecturer at Columbia University, 1968-70, and New School for Social Research, 1970—. *Military service:* U.S. Army, Intelligence, 1943-45; chief of Allied Forces newsroom and commentator for United Nations radio in Algiers, 1943; U.S. intelligence liaison officer with French Army, 1944-45; combat correspondent with U.S. Seventh Army, 1945; received Croix de Guerre.

MEMBER: Overseas Press Club, American Federation of Radio and Television Artists, Association of Radio-Television News Analysts, Anglo-American Press Club (Paris;

past president), Common Cause, Friars Club. *Awards, honors:* Named Chevalier of Legion of Honor, Government of France, 1952; Emmy Award, Academy of Television Arts and Sciences, 1958, for overseas reporting; Overseas Press Club award, 1958, for *As Frances Goes,* and in other years for distinguished reporting and writing; Alfred I. duPont Best Commentator of the Year Award, 1959.

WRITINGS: As Frances Goes, Harper, 1957; *The Three Lives of Charles de Gaulle,* Atheneum, 1965; *Viet Nam: How We Got In, How to Get Out,* Atheneum, 1968; *The New Israelis,* Atheneum, 1973; *Triumph in Paris: The Exploits of Benjamin Franklin,* Harper, 1976; *Soldiers of the Night: The Story of the French Resistance,* Dutton, 1980. Contributor to numerous magazines and newspapers in the United States and Europe.

SIDELIGHTS: In *Soldiers of the Night,* David Schoenbrun recounts the struggle of the French Resistance during World War II. Although Robert Cromie of the *Chicago Tribune Book World* finds that "the book is not easy reading, since it is filled with plots and counterplots, some very intricate," he praises the work for being a "meticulously researched and absorbing account" of the French underground's activities. Schoenbrun details not only the Resistance's fight against the occupying Nazi forces, but also the group's near fatal personal and political infighting. "What makes Mr. Schoenbrun's book a masterful rendering of the Resistance is that he sees clearly both its strengths and weaknesses," according to Philip Hallie of the *New York Times Book Review.* "He sees the youthful valor as well as the terrible self-destructive drive of the Resistance toward chaos." Hallie concludes that "[Schoenbrun's] book is the most complete account of the French Resistance in English, and the most sensitive."

AVOCATIONAL INTERESTS: Reading, travel.

BIOGRAPHICAL/CRITICAL SOURCES: New York Times Book Review, April 28, 1968, June 29, 1980; *Christian Science Monitor,* June 27, 1968; *Chicago Tribune Book World,* June 29, 1980.

*   *   *

SCOTT, Robert Lee 1928-

PERSONAL: Born April 19, 1928, in Fairbury, Neb.; son of Walter E. (a teacher) and Anna (Jensen) Scott; married Betty Foust, September 13, 1947; children: Mark Allen, Janet Lee, Paul Matthew. *Education:* Colorado State College (now University of Northern Colorado), A.B., 1950; University of Nebraska, M.A., 1951; University of Illinois, Ph.D., 1955. *Home:* 7190 Riverview Ter., Minneapolis, Minn. 55432. *Office:* Department of Speech and Communication, University of Minnesota, Minneapolis, Minn. 55455.

CAREER: University of Houston, Houston, Tex., assistant professor of speech, 1953-57; University of Minnesota, Minneapolis, professor of speech, 1957—. *Military service:* U.S. Marine Corps, 1945-46. *Member:* Speech Association of America.

WRITINGS: (With Otis M. Walter) *Thinking and Speaking: A Guide to Intelligent Oral Communication,* Macmillan, 1962, 4th edition, 1979; *Speaker's Reader,* Scott, 1969; (with Wayne Brockriede) *Rhetoric of Black Power,* Harper, 1969; *Moments in the Rhetoric of the Cold War,* Random House, 1970; (with Bernard Brock) *Methods of Rhetorical Criticism,* Harper, 1973, 2nd edition, Wayne State University Press, 1980. Also author of play "Shadows on the Wall," produced in 1962 at Indiana University. *Quarterly Journal of Speech,* contributing editor, 1959-62, editor, 1972-74.

SCUDDER, C(leo) W(ayne) 1915-

PERSONAL: Born April 10, 1915, in Maquon, Ill.; son of James Clement and Leona (Finney) Scudder; married Lyle Mace, November 26, 1938; children: Kathryn L. *Education:* George Peabody College for Teachers, B.S., 1937; Southwestern Baptist Theological Seminary, B.D., 1952, Th.D., 1954; Boston University, postdoctoral study, 1960-61. *Office:* Midwestern Baptist Theological Seminary, 5001 North Oak St. Trafficway, Kansas City, Mo. 64118.

CAREER: Teacher in public schools in Illinois and Georgia; George Peabody College for Teachers, Nashville, Tenn., professor of music education, 1936-37; First Baptist Church, Cordele, Ga., minister of music and education, 1940-48; Southwestern Baptist Theological Seminary, Fort Worth, Tex., professor of Christian ethics, 1954-75; Midwestern Baptist Theological Seminary, Kansas City, Mo., vice-president of business and development, 1975—. *Member:* Seminary Management Association, Southern Baptist Business Officers. *Awards, honors:* Sealantic study grant, American Association of Theological Schools, 1960-61.

WRITINGS: (Contributor) H. C. Brown, editor, *Southwestern Sermons,* Broadman, 1960; *Danger Ahead!,* Broadman, 1961; *The Family in Christian Perspective,* Broadman, 1962; (editor) *Crises in Morality,* Broadman, 1964; (contributor) Brown, editor, *The Cutting Edge: Critical Questions for Contemporary Christians,* Word Books, 1969; (contributor) E. S. West, editor, *Extremism: Left and Right,* Eerdmans, 1972; *Dealing with Moral Problems,* Semway, 1978; (contributor) Pinson, editor, *An Approach to Christian Ethics: The Life, Contributions, and Thought of T. B. Maston,* Broadman, 1979.

*   *   *

SCULLARD, Howard Hayes 1903-

PERSONAL: Born February 9, 1903, in Bedford, England; son of Herbert Hayes (a minister and professor), and Barbara Louise (Dodds) Scullard. *Education:* St. John's College, Cambridge, B.A., 1926; University of London, Ph.D., 1930. *Home:* 6 Foscote Rd., Hendon, London N.W. 4, England.

CAREER: University of London, London, England, New College, classical tutor, 1926-35, King's College, reader, 1935-59, professor of ancient history, 1959-70, professor emeritus, 1970—. Governor, New College. *Member:* British Academy (fellow; member of council, 1962-65), Society of Antiquaries (fellow), Society for the Promotion of Roman Studies (vice-president), Royal Numismatic Society (council member, various periods). *Awards, honors:* Thirlwall Prize, 1929, for *Scipio Africanus in the Second Punic War.*

WRITINGS: Scipio Africanus in the Second Punic War (essay), Cambridge University Press, 1930; *A History of the Roman World from 753 to 146 B.C.,* Methuen, 1935, Macmillan, 1939, 4th edition, Methuen, 1980; (editor with H. E. Butler) *Livy, Book XXX,* Methuen, 1939, 6th edition, 1954; (joint editor and contributor) *The Oxford Classical Dictionary,* Clarendon Press, 1949, 2nd edition (with N.G.L. Hammond), 1970; *Roman Politics, 220-150 B.C.,* Clarendon Press, 1951, 2nd edition, Oxford University Press, 1973; (reviser) Frank B. Marsh, *A History of the Roman World from 146 to 30 B.C.,* 2nd edition, Methuen, 1953, 3rd edition, revised, Barnes & Noble, 1961; *From the Gracchi to Nero: A History of Rome from 133 B.C. to A.D. 68,* Praeger, 1959, 4th edition, Barnes & Noble, 1976; (editor with A.A.M. van der Heyden) *Atlas of the Classical World,* Thomas Nelson, 1960; (reviser with W. S. Maguinnes) John C. Stobart, *The*

Grandeur That Was Rome, 4th edition, Sidgwick & Jackson, 1961, Praeger, 1969; (editor with van der Heyden) *Shorter Atlas of the Classical World*, Thomas Nelson (Edinburgh), 1962, Dutton, 1966; (contributor) Thomas Allen Dorey, editor, *Cicero*, Basic Books, 1965; *The Etruscan Cities and Rome*, Cornell University Press, 1967; *Scipio Africanus, Soldier and Politician*, Cornell University Press, 1970; *The Elephant in the Greek and Roman World*, Thames & Hudson, 1974; (with M. Cary) *A History of Rome*, Macmillan, 1975; *Roman Britain: An Outpost of Empire*, Thames & Hudson, 1979; *Festivals and Ceremonies of the Roman Republic*, Thames & Hudson, 1981. General editor, "Aspects of Greek and Roman Life" series, forty volumes, Thames & Hudson and Cornell University Press, 1967—. Contributor of articles to *Encyclopaedia Britannica*, and of articles and reviews to professional journals.

AVOCATIONAL INTERESTS: Golf.

BIOGRAPHICAL/CRITICAL SOURCES: Times Literary Supplement, September 28, 1967.

*   *   *

SEIFERT, Harvey (J.D.) 1911-

PERSONAL: Born September 25, 1911, in Posey County, Ind.; son of Daniel Frederick (a bookkeeper) and Elfrieda (Ehrhardt) Seifert; married Lois Olive Cummings, August 6, 1942; children: Carolyn, Mary Lois, Linda Jean. *Education:* Evansville College, A.B., 1932; Boston University, M.A., 1934, S.T.B., 1935, Ph.D., 1940; London School of Economics and Political Science, graduate study, 1935-36. *Religion:* Methodist. *Home:* 1527 Bates Pl., Claremont, Calif. 91711.

CAREER: Adrian College, Adrian, Mich., professor of sociology, 1942-45; University of Southern California, Los Angeles, professor of social ethics, 1945-56; School of Theology at Claremont, Claremont, Calif., professor of social ethics, 1956-77, professor emeritus, 1977—. *Member:* American Sociological Association, Religious Research Association, American Society of Christian Social Ethics.

WRITINGS: Fellowships of Concern: A Manual on the Cell Group Process, Abingdon, 1949; *The Church in Community Action*, Abingdon, 1952; *Ethical Resources for International Relations*, Westminster, 1964; *Conquest by Suffering: The Process and Prospects of Non-Violent Resistance*, Westminster, 1965; *Power Where the Action Is*, Westminster, 1968; (with Howard J. Clinebell) *Personal Growth and Social Change: A Guide for Ministers and Laymen as Change Agents*, Westminster, 1969; *Ethical Resources for Political and Economic Decision*, Westminster, 1972; *Reality and Ecstasy: A Religion for the Twenty-First Century*, Westminster, 1974; *New Power for the Church*, Westminster, 1976; *Good News for Rich and Poor*, United Church Press, 1976; (with wife, Lois Seifert) *Liberation of Life*, Upper Room, 1976; (with John Bennett) *U.S. Foreign Policy and Christian Ethics*, Westminster, 1977. Also author of *Decision-Making in World Affairs*, Division of Peace and World Order, Methodist Church. Contributor of articles to professional periodicals.

*   *   *

SELDEN, Samuel 1899-1979

PERSONAL: Born January 2, 1899, in Canton, China; died April 27, 1979; son of Charles Card and Gertrude (Thwing) Selden; married Wautell G. Lambeth, July 19, 1936 (died May, 1948); married Emily Polk Crow, October 25, 1951; children: (first marriage) Priscilla, Samuel. *Education:* Yale

University, A.B., 1922; attended New York School of Fine and Applied Arts, 1929-30, and Columbia University.

CAREER: Provincetown Playhouse, New York, N.Y., assistant technical director, stage manager, and resident actor, 1922-27; University of North Carolina at Chapel Hill, instructor in English, 1927-36, assistant professor, 1936, associate professor, 1937-44, professor of dramatic arts and chairman of department, 1945-59, director of Carolina Playmakers (university theater group), 1944-59; University of California, Los Angeles, professor of theater arts and chairman of department, 1959-66, professor emeritus, 1966-79; Southern Illinois University, Carbondale, distinguished visiting professor of theater, 1966-67; University of North Carolina at Chapel Hill, visiting professor of dramatic arts, 1967-71. State manager, Gladys Klark Players, 1922-27, Greenwich Village Theater, 1925-26, Intimate Opera Co., 1926, and Cape Playhouse, 1927 and 1928. Director of summer theaters in various states, 1937-41, 1946-59, and 1963-64; director of numerous outdoor historical plays. *Military service:* U.S. Army, Medical Corps, 1918. *Member:* American Educational Theatre Association (president, 1960), American National Theatre and Academy (member of board of directors, 1953-58), National Theatre Conference (trustee, 1958-60), Southeastern Theatre Conference (president, 1953-55), Phi Kappa Sigma. *Awards, honors:* Guggenheim fellowship for study in New York and European theaters, 1938-39; Litt.D., Illinois College, 1952; American Educational Theatre Association Award of Merit, 1962; Southeastern Theatre Conference Award for distinguished career, 1963.

WRITINGS: (With Hunton D. Sellman) *Stage Scenery and Lighting* (also see below), Crofts, 1930, 3rd edition, 1959; *A Player's Handbook*, Crofts, 1934; (with Sellman and Hubert C. Heffner) *Modern Theatre Practice*, Crofts, 1935; *The Stage in Action*, Crofts, 1941, reprinted, Southern Illinois University Press, 1967; *Research in Drama and the Theatre in the Universities and Colleges of the United States, 1937-1942*, American Educational Theatre Association, 1944; (editor) *Organizing a Community Theatre*, National Theatre Conference, 1945; *An Introduction to Playwriting*, Crofts, 1946; *First Steps in Acting*, Crofts, 1947, 2nd edition, 1964; *International Folk Plays*, University of North Carolina Press, 1949; (with Mary T. Sphangos) *Frederick Henry Koch: Pioneer Playmaker*, University of North Carolina Library, 1954; *Man in His Theatre*, University of North Carolina Press, 1957; (editor) *Shakespeare: A Player's Handbook of Short Scenes*, Holiday House, 1960; *Theatre Double Game*, University of North Carolina Press, 1969; (with Walter Spearman) *The Carolina Playmakers: The First Fifty Years*, University of North Carolina Press, 1970; (with Tom Rezzuto) *Essentials of Stage Scenery* (based on first part of *Stage Scenery and Lighting*), Appleton, 1972. Contributor of articles to theatre periodicals in the United States and abroad. Editor, *Carolina Play-Book*, 1928-44, *Theatre Annual*, 1944-47, *Revue Internationale de Theatre*, 1947, and *Educational Theatre Journal*, 1955-57.

WORK IN PROGRESS: A volume of satiric animal stories, *Little Fables of University Woods.*†

*   *   *

SELF, Margaret Cabell 1902-

PERSONAL: Born February 12, 1902, in Cincinnati, Ohio; daughter of Hartwell (a lawyer) and Margaret (Logan) Cabell; married Sydney Baldwin Self, June 11, 1921; children: Sydney Baldwin, Jr., Shirley (Mrs. John O. Brotherhood, Jr.), Hartwell C., Virginia Logan (Mrs. Harris Bucklin).

Education: Attended Women's School of Applied Design, 1917-19, and Parson School of Design, 1921. *Home:* Huertas 19, San Miguel de Allende, Guanajuato, Mexico; and Block Island, R.I. 02807 (summer). *Agent:* Lurton Blassingame, Blassingame, McCauley & Wood, 60 East 42nd St., New York, N.Y. 10017.

CAREER: Artist, specializing in portraits, 1923-38; writer, 1935—. Editor, photographer, and reporter, *Block Island Times*, 1970—. Trainer of horses, riding instructor, horse show judge, and founder of New Canaan Mounted Troop (a junior cavalry organization); lecturer on subjects related to riding. Musician (violin, cello, and viola) with Norwalk Symphony, 1948-62; member and concertmistress of Block Island Chamber Ensemble and member of San Miguel Chamber Ensemble, Mexico. *Member:* Authors Guild of Authors League of America, Amateur Chamber Music Association.

WRITINGS: Teaching the Young to Ride, Harper, 1935, enlarged edition, A. S. Barnes, 1946; *Red Clay Country*, Harper, 1936; *Horses: Their Selection, Care and Handling*, A. S. Barnes, 1943; *Those Smith Kids*, Dutton, 1944; *Fun on Horseback*, A. S. Barnes, 1945, revised edition, 1964; *Ponies on Parade*, Dutton, 1945; (editor) *A Treasury of Horse Stories*, A. S. Barnes, 1945, reprinted, 1965; *The Horseman's Encyclopedia*, A. S. Barnes, 1946, revised edition, 1963; *Chitter Chat Stories*, Dutton, 1946; *Come Away* (novel), A. S. Barnes, 1948, reprinted, 1967; *Riding Simplified*, A. S. Barnes, 1948, 2nd edition published as *Horseback Riding Simplified*, Ronald, 1963; *The Horseman's Companion*, A. S. Barnes, 1949; *Your First Pony*, Nicholas Kaye, 1950; *Horsemastership; Methods of Training the Horse and the Rider*, A. S. Barnes, 1952, reprinted, Arco, 1973; *Irish Adventure: A Fox Hunter's Holiday*, A. S. Barnes, 1954, published as *In Ireland with Margaret Cabell Self*, 1967; *Fun on Horseback*, A. S. Barnes, 1954; *The American Horse Show*, A. S. Barnes, 1958; *Jumping Simplified*, Ronald, 1959.

Riding with Mariles, McGraw, 1960; (editor) *A World of Horses*, McGraw, 1961; *The How and Why Wonder Book of Horses*, Grosset, 1962; *The Complete Book of Horses and Ponies*, McGraw, 1963; *The Happy Year*, Channel Press, 1963; *Horses of Today: Arabian, Thoroughbred, Saddle Horse, Standardbred, Western, Pony*, Duell, 1964; *Riding, Step by Step*, A. S. Barnes, 1965; *The Shaggy Little Burro of San Miguel*, Duell, 1965; *Susan and Jane Learn to Ride*, Macrae, 1965; *The Horseman's Almanac and Handbook*, F. Watts, 1965; *At the Horse Show with Margaret Cabell Self*, A. S. Barnes, 1966; *Henrietta*, Vanguard, 1966; *The Morgan Horse in Pictures*, Macrae, 1967; *The American Quarter Horse in Pictures*, Macrae, 1969; *The Young Rider and His First Pony*, A. S. Barnes, 1969; *Sky Rocket: The Story of a Little Bay Horse*, Dodd, 1970; (with Irving Robbin) *Answers about Dogs and Horses*, Grosset, 1970; *The Hunter in Pictures*, Macrae, 1972; *How to Buy the Right Horse*, Farnum, 1972; *The Nature of the Horse*, Arco, 1974; *The Problem Horse and the Problem Horseman*, Arco, 1977. Contributor to encyclopedias, including *Encyclopaedia Britannica* and *Compton's Encyclopedia*.

WORK IN PROGRESS: Children's books; an autobiography, *Many Lives—Many Worlds*.

SIDELIGHTS: Margaret Cabell Self's work with the New Canaan Mounted Troop, a junior cavalry organization, spanned over two decades. The troop, now under the management of some of Self's former students, is a non-profit group whose purpose is to use riding as a means of developing good citizenship qualities—patience, physical fitness, a

sense of responsibility—in young people. Self points to her "long experience with this unit plus the previous eighteen years as an ordinary riding instructor plus a childhood spent with horses" as key factors in her ability to write knowledgeably about riding, training, and showing various breeds of horses. She has also made several documentary films on the same subjects.

AVOCATIONAL INTERESTS: Music; fishing; teaching English to local residents of San Miguel de Allende, Mexico.

*   *   *

SERNA-MAYTORENA, Manuel Antonio   1932-

PERSONAL: Born October 23, 1932, in Empalme, Sonora, Mexico; son of Marcelo and Nieves (Maytorena Trojo) Serna Garcia; married Jane Thomas Norkus, January 25, 1964; children: Mark Ian, Laura Ann. *Education:* Universidad de Guadalajara, B.A., 1952, M.A., 1961; University of Missouri, Ph.D., 1966. *Home:* 8 Lincoln St., Athens, Ohio 45701. *Office:* Department of Modern Languages, Ohio University, Athens, Ohio 45701.

CAREER: Ohio University, Athens, assistant professor, 1966-71, associate professor, 1971-76, professor of Spanish, 1976—. *Member:* Modern Language Association of America, American Association of Teachers of Spanish and Portuguese. *Awards, honors:* Ohio University, research grant, 1968-69, Baker Award, 1973-74.

WRITINGS: Silencio Desnudo (poetry), Imprenta de la Universidad de Guadalajara, 1968; (editor and author of prologue) Guillermo Castillo, *La Multiple* (three-act play), Ediciones Et Caetera, 1970; (translator) Wallace J. Cameron, *El tema del hambre en la novela picaresca espanola: Estudio de su tratamiento*, Editorial Cajica, 1971; *El Hombre y el paisaje del campo jalisciense en la cuesta de la comadres*, Cucadernos, 1971; *Santa: Mexico*, Cucadernos, 1972; *Notas en torno a la estructura de El Hombre*, Ediciones Et Caetera, 1972; *La Exacta pasion: Asedio a la poetica de Raymon Lopez Velarde*, Editorial Cajica, 1973.

WORK IN PROGRESS: Two books of poetry, *Los numeros u los dias* and *Aproximationes al cuento de Rulfo: La Llave y los Pretextos;* a book, *Gamboa y el procese historico-literation.*

AVOCATIONAL INTERESTS: Painting.†

*   *   *

SETTON, Kenneth M(eyer)   1914-

PERSONAL: Born June 17, 1914, in New Bedford, Mass.; son of Ezra (a businessman) and Louise (Crossley) Setton; married Josephine W. Swift, September 11, 1941 (died, 1967); married Margaret T. Henry, January 4, 1969; children: (first marriage) George Whitney Fletcher. *Education:* Boston University, B.A., 1936; Columbia University, M.A., 1938, Ph.D., 1941; also attended University of Chicago, 1936, and Harvard University, 1939-40. *Office:* Institute for Advanced Study, Princeton, N.J. 08540.

CAREER: Boston University, Boston, Mass., instructor in classics and history, 1940-43; University of Manitoba, Winnipeg, associate professor, 1943-45, professor of history and head of department, 1945-50; University of Pennsylvania, Philadelphia, associate professor of medieval history, 1950-53, H. C. Lea Professor of Medieval History, 1953-54, 1955-65, university professor, 1963-65, curator of Lea Library, 1951-54, director of libraries, 1955-65; Columbia University, New York, N.Y., professor of medieval history, 1954-55; University of Wisconsin—Madison, W. F. Vilas Research

Professor of History and director of Institute for Research in the Humanities, 1965-68; Institute for Advanced Study, Princeton, N.J., professor of history, 1968—. Visiting lecturer, Bryn Mawr College, 1952-53. Acting director, Gennadius Library, Athens, Greece, 1960-61; Dumbarton Oaks, member of board of scholars, 1960—, director of symposium, 1968, senior fellow, 1974-79; research fellow, American School of Classical Studies, Athens, 1960-61.

MEMBER: American Philosophical Society (vice-president, 1966-69), Mediaeval Academy of America (fellow; president, 1971-72), American Academy of Arts and Sciences (fellow), American Historical Association, Society of Macedonian Studies (Greece; honorary fellow), Institute of Catalan Studies (Spain; corresponding member), Wistar Association. *Awards, honors:* Guggenheim fellow, Greece, 1949, and Italy, 1950; John Frederick Lewis Prize, American Philosophical Society, 1957, for essay, "The Byzantine Background to the Italian Renaissance"; Litt.D., Boston University, 1957; Gold Cross of the Order of George I (Greece), 1967; Premi Catalonia, Institut d'Estudis Catalans (Barcelona), 1976; Prix Gustave Schlumberger, Academie des Inscriptions et Belles-Lettres (Paris), 1976; John Gilmary Shea Prize, American Catholic Historical Association, 1979; Dr. Phil. h.c., University of Kiel, 1979; Haskins Medal, Mediaeval Academy of America, 1980.

WRITINGS: Christian Attitude towards the Emperor in the Fourth Century, Especially as Shown in Addresses to the Emperor, Columbia University Press, 1941, reprinted, AMS Press, 1967; *Catalan Domination of Athens, 1311-1388,* Mediaeval Academy of America, 1948, revised edition, Variorum, 1975; (editor with Henry R. Winkler) *Great Problems in European Civilization,* Prentice-Hall, 1954, 2nd edition, 1966; (contributor) John Hine Mundy and others, editors, *Essays in Medieval Life and Thought,* Columbia University Press, 1955; (editor-in-chief) *A History of the Crusades,* Volume I: (with M. W. Baldwin) *The First Hundred Years,* University of Pennsylvania Press, 1955, 3rd edition, University of Wisconsin Press, 1969, Volume II: (with R. L. Wolff and H. W. Hazard) *The Later Crusades, 1189-1311,* University of Pennsylvania Press, 1962, 2nd edition, University of Wisconsin Press, 1969, Volume III: (with Hazard) *The Fourteenth and Fifteenth Centuries,* University of Wisconsin Press, 1975, Volume IV: (with Hazard) *The Art and Architecture of the Crusader States,* University of Wisconsin Press, 1977; (author of introduction and bibliography) Henry Osborn Taylor, *Classical Heritage of the Middle Ages,* Harper, 1958.

(Contributor) *Guide to Historical Literature,* American Historical Association, 1961; (with others) *The Age of Chivalry,* National Geographic Society, 1969; (with others) *The Renaissance: Maker of Modern Man,* National Geographic Society, 1970; *Europe and the Levant in the Middle Ages and the Renaissance,* Variorum, 1974; *Athens in the Middle Ages,* Variorum, 1975; *Los Catalanes en Grecia,* Ayma (Barcelona), 1975; (contributor) *Essays in Memory of Basil Laourdas,* [Thessaloniki], 1975; *The Papacy and the Levant, 1204-1571,* American Philosophical Society, Volume I: *The Thirteenth and Fourteenth Centuries,* 1976, Volume II: *The Fifteenth Century,* 1978. Contributor to *Proceedings* of the American Philosophical Society and to professional journals, including *Speculum, American Historical Review, American Journal of Philology,* and *Balkan Studies.*

WORK IN PROGRESS: Volume III of *The Papacy and the Levant,* for the American Philosophical Society; Volumes V and VI of *A History of the Crusades,* for University of Wisconsin Press; editing some correspondence of the Florentine family of the Acciajuoli; various articles for publication in periodicals.

*   *   *

SEXTON, Anne (Harvey)   1928-1974

PERSONAL: Born November 9, 1928, in Newton, Mass.; died October 4, 1974 by her own hand, in Weston, Mass.; daughter of Ralph Churchill (a salesman) and Mary Gray (Staples) Harvey; married Alfred M. Sexton II (a salesman), August 16, 1948 (divorced, 1974); children: Linda Gray, Joyce Ladd. *Education:* Attended Garland Junior College, 1947-48. *Home:* 14 Black Oak Rd., Weston, Mass. 02193. *Agent:* Sterling Lord, 75 East 55th St., New York, N.Y. 10022.

CAREER: Fashion model in Boston, Mass., 1950-51; Wayland High School, Wayland, Mass., teacher, 1967-68; Boston University, Boston, lecturer in creative writing, 1970-71, professor of creative writing, 1972-74; writer. Scholar, Radcliffe Institute for Independent Study, 1961-63; Crawshaw Professor of Literature, Colgate University, 1972. Gave numerous poetry readings at colleges and universities. *Member:* Poetry Society of America, Royal Society of Literature (fellow), New England Poetry Club, Phi Beta Kappa (honorary member). *Awards, honors:* Robert Frost fellowship at Bread Loaf Writers Conference, 1959; *Audience* Poetry Prize, 1958-59; Levinson Prize, *Poetry* Magazine, 1962; American Academy of Arts and Letters traveling fellowship, 1963-64; Ford Foundation grant for year's residence with professional theater, 1964-65; first literary magazine travel grant, Congress for Cultural Freedom, 1965-66; Shelley Memorial Award, 1967; Pulitzer Prize, 1967, for *Live or Die;* Guggenheim fellowship, 1969; Litt.D. from Tufts University, 1970, Regis College, 1971, and Fairfield University, 1971.

WRITINGS—Poetry, except as indicated; published by Houghton, except as indicated: *To Bedlam and Part Way Back,* 1960; *All My Pretty Ones,* 1962; (with Maxine W. Kumin) *Eggs of Things* (juvenile), Putnam, 1963; (with Kumin) *More Eggs of Things* (juvenile), Putnam, 1964; *Selected Poems,* Oxford University Press, 1964; *Live or Die,* 1966; (with Thomas Kinsella and Douglas Livingstone) *Poems,* Oxford University Press, 1968; *Love Poems,* 1969; "Mercy Street" (play), first produced Off-Broadway at American Place Theatre, October 11, 1969; (with Kumin) *Joey and the Birthday Present* (juvenile), McGraw, 1971; *Transformations,* 1971; *The Book of Folly,* 1972; *O Ye Tongues,* Rainbow Press, 1973; *The Death Notebooks,* 1974; *The Awful Rowing toward God,* 1975; (with Kumin) *The Wizard's Tears* (juvenile), McGraw, 1975; *45 Mercy Street,* edited by daughter, Linda Gray Sexton, 1976; *A Self Portrait in Letters* (correspondence), edited by L. G. Sexton and Lois Ames, 1977; *The Heart of Anne Sexton's Poetry* (contains *All My Pretty Ones, Live or Die,* and *Love Poems*), three volumes, 1977; *Words for Dr. Y: Uncollected Poems with Three Stories,* edited by L. G. Sexton, 1978.

Poems represented in numerous anthologies. Contributor to many magazines, including *Harper's, New Yorker, Partisan Review, Saturday Review,* and *Nation.*

SIDELIGHTS: Much of Anne Sexton's poetry is autobiographical and concentrates on her deeply personal feelings, especially anguish. In particular, many of her poems record her battles with mental illness. She spent many years in psychoanalysis, including several long stays in mental hospitals. As she told Beatrice Berg, her writing began, in fact, as therapy, "My analyst told me to write between our sessions about what I was feeling and thinking and dreaming." Her analyst, impressed by her work, encouraged her to keep writing, and then, she told Berg, she saw (on television) "I. A. Richards [a poet and literary critic] describing the form of a sonnet and I thought maybe I could do that. Oh, I was turned on. I wrote two or three a day for about a year." Eventually, Sexton's poems about her psychiatric struggles were gathered in *To Bedlam and Part Way Back* which recounts, as James Dickey writes, the experiences "of madness and near-madness, of the pathetic, well-meaning, necessarily tentative and perilous attempts at cure, and of the patient's slow coming back into the human associations and responsibilities which the old, previous self still demands."

This kind of poetry, which unveils the poet's innermost feelings, is usually termed confessional poetry, and it is the subject of much critical controversy. A *Times Literary Supplement* reviewer, for example, says of *Live or Die* that "many of Mrs. Sexton's new poems are arresting, but such naked psyche-baring makes demands which cannot always be met. Confession may be good for the soul, but absolution is not the poet's job, nor the reader's either." A *Punch* critic adds, "When her artistic control falters the recital of grief and misery becomes embarrassing, the repetitive material starts to grow tedious, the poetic gives way to the clinical and the confessional." Many reviewers raise at least two questions. First, should her poetry be classified as confessional? Second, does her work consistently demonstrate the artistic control which many critics feel is an essential quality of good poetry?

Concerning the first question, Erica Jong objects to the classification: "Whenever Anne Sexton's poems are mentioned, the term 'confessional poetry' is not far behind. It has always seemed a silly and unilluminating term to me; one of those pigeonholing categories critics invent so as not to talk about poetry as poetry.... The mind of the creator is all-important, and the term 'confessional' seems to undercut this, implying that anyone who spilled her guts would be a poet." Sexton also often denigrated the term, but at times she applied it to herself. She told Berg that "for years I railed against being put in this category. Then ... I decided I was the *only* confessional poet." Moreover, in an interview with Patricia Marx, Sexton discussed the effect on her work of another poet often called confessional, W. D. Snodgrass, and acknowledged the confessional quality of her writing: "If anything influenced me it was W. D. Snodgrass' *Heart's Trouble*.... It so changed me, and undoubtedly it must have influenced my poetry. At the same time everyone said, 'You can't write this way. It's too personal; it's confessional; you can't write this, Anne,' and everyone was discouraging me. But then I saw Snodgrass doing what I was doing, and it kind of gave me permission."

The second question is perhaps best answered in critics' specific responses to several of her individual books. Like many of Sexton's volumes, *To Bedlam and Part Way Back* received a mixed response. Dickey praised the subject of the work, but found that "the poems fail to do their subject the kind of justice which I should like to see done.... As they are they lack concentration, and above all the profound, individual linguistic suggestibility and accuracy that poems must have to be good." On the other hand, Melvin Maddocks believes that "Mrs. Sexton's remarkable first book of poems has the personal urgency of a first novel. It is full of the exact flavors of places and peoples remembered, familiar patterns of life recalled and painstakingly puzzled over.... A reader finally judges Mrs. Sexton's success by the extraordinary sense of first-hand experience he too has been enabled to feel." Barbara Howes thinks that many of the

poems are flawed, but overall she judges *Bedlam* "an honest and impressive achievement."

All My Pretty Ones also garnered mixed reviews. Peter Davison finds one poem, "The Operation," "absolutely superb," but he feels that none of the others is nearly as good. Dickey's critique is even stronger: "Miss Sexton's work seems to me very little more than a kind of terribly serious and determinedly outspoken soap-opera." Yet in an essay on both *Bedlam* and *Pretty Ones*, Beverly Fields argues that Sexton's poetry is mostly misread. She contends that the poems are not as autobiographical as they seem, that they are poems not memoirs, and she goes on to analyze many of them in depth in order to show the recurrent symbolic themes and poetic techniques that she feels make Sexton's work impressive.

Dissent among the reviewers continued with the appearance of *Live or Die*, Sexton's best known book. A *Virginia Quarterly Review* critic believes that Sexton is "a very talented poet" who is perhaps too honest: "Confession, while good for the soul, may become tiresome for the reader if not accompanied by the suggestion that something is being held back.... In [*Live or Die*] Miss Sexton's toughness approaches affectation. Like a drunk at a party who corners us with the story of his life, ... the performance is less interesting the third time, despite the poet's high level of technical competence." Joel O. Conarroe, however, has a more positive view of Sexton's candor. "Miss Sexton is an interior voyager," comments Conarroe, "describing in sharp images the difficult discovered landmarks of her own inner landscape.... Poem after poem focuses on the nightmare obsessions of the damned: suicide, crucifixion, the death of others ..., fear, the humiliations of childhood, the boy-child she never had.... It is, though, through facing up to the reality (and implications) of these things that the poet, with her tough honesty, is able to gain a series of victories over them.... All in all, this is a fierce, terrible, beautiful book, well deserving its Pulitzer award."

Transformations, a retelling of Grimm's fairy tales, marked a shift away from the confessional manner of her earlier work, which several commentators found to be a fruitful change. Gail Pool, for example, contends that the tales provided Sexton with "a rich medium for her colorful imagery," a distance from her characters which allowed wit, an eerie realm "where she had always been her sharpest," and "the structure she needed and so often had difficulty imposing on her own work. At last she had found material to which she could bring her intelligence, her wit, all that she knew, and she created, in Stanley Kunitz's words, 'a wild, blood-curdling, astonishing book.'" Christopher Lehmann-Haupt echoes Pool's analysis, arguing that Sexton's earlier work tended to lack control, that perhaps she worked too closely with first-hand experience. In contrast to this, Lehmann-Haupt continues, "by using the artificial as the raw material of *Transformations* and working her way backwards to the immediacy of her personal vision, she draws her readers in more willingly, and thereby makes them more vulnerable to her sudden plunges into personal nightmare." Similarly, Louis Coxe discovers a new objectivity and distance in *Transformations*, which he considers "a growth of the poet's mind and strength."

In *The Death Notebooks, The Awful Rowing toward God*, and *45 Mercy Street*, the last two published posthumously, Sexton returned to the confessional method. While these books have been praised, they have also been more severely criticized than her early writings, many readers detecting a deterioration in quality. William Heyen remarks that Sexton's "poems went almost steadily downhill, became less intense, less dramatic, less interesting as one book followed another.... There were moments, occasional lines or even poems that wept or raged with her old power," but overall her voice became often "maudlin or patently melodramatic or simply silly." Heyen adds that *Awful Rowing* continues the downward trend; it is touching, "but it's not very good." Robert Mazzocco seconds Heyen, commenting that while the early poems "depict intensely introverted states in a highly extroverted style" and are well constructed, the later poems "seem to me less commanding, strike dissonant strains, chromatize the keyboard, or become programmatic." In like manner, Patricia Meyer Spacks argues that Sexton's poems become more and more sentimental in that they overindulge in emotion and fail to evaluate that emotion. The sentimentalism becomes "painfully marked" in *Awful Rowing,* "with its embarrassments of religious pretension.... The problem of internal division, the perception of divinity, the will to rebuild the soul: all alike register unconvincingly. The poetry through which these vast themes are rendered is simply not good enough."

On the other hand, not all critics disparage the later books. In a response to Spacks' critique, Jong comments: "Let's be fair about Sexton's poetry. She was uneven and excessive, but that was because she dared to be a fool and dared to explore the dark side of the unconscious." Moreover, Sandra M. Gilbert believes that *The Death Notebooks* "goes far beyond [the earlier volumes] in making luminous art out of the night thoughts that have haunted this poet for so long." Finally, Jong, in a review of *Notebooks,* assesses Sexton's poetic significance and contends that her artistry is often overlooked: "She is an important poet not only because of her courage in dealing with previously forbidden subjects, but because she can make the language sing. Of what does [her] artistry consist? Not just of her skill in writing traditional poems.... But by artistry, I mean something more subtle than the ability to write formal poems. I mean the artist's sense of where her inspiration lies.... There are many poets of great talent who never take that talent anywhere.... They write poems which any number of people might have written. When Anne Sexton is at the top of her form, she writes a poem which no one else could have written."

BIOGRAPHICAL/CRITICAL SOURCES: Christian Science Monitor, September 1, 1960; *Epoch,* fall, 1960; *Poetry,* February, 1961, May, 1967; *Atlantic,* November, 1962; *Reporter,* January 3, 1963; *Nation,* February 23, 1963; September 14, 1974; *New Yorker,* April 27, 1963; *New York Times Book Review,* April 28, 1963, May 30, 1976, July 25, 1976, November 26, 1978; *Harper's,* September, 1963; *Hudson Review,* winter, 1965-66; *Saturday Review,* December 31, 1966; Edward Hungerford, editor, *Poets in Progress,* Northwestern University Press, 1967; *Observer Review,* May 14, 1967; *Times Literary Supplement,* May 18, 1967; *New Statesman,* June 16, 1967; *Punch,* July 5, 1967; *Shenandoah,* summer, 1967; *Virginia Quarterly Review,* winter, 1967; *New York Review of Books,* June 6, 1968; *New York Times,* March 8, 1969, October 28, 1969, November 2, 1969, November 9, 1969, September 27, 1971; *Village Voice,* November 6, 1969; *New Republic,* November 22, 1969, October 16, 1971; *Paris Review,* spring, 1971; *Ms.,* March, 1974; Robert Phillips, *The Confessional Poets,* Southern Illinois University Press, 1973; *Contemporary Literary Criticism,* Gale, Volume II, 1974, Volume IV, 1975, Volume VI, 1976, Volume VIII, 1978, Volume X, 1979, Volume XV, 1980; *Concerning Poetry,* spring, 1974; *Newsday,* March 23, 1975;

Centennial Review, spring, 1975; *Moons and Lion Tailes,* Volume II, Number 2, 1976; *New Boston Review,* spring, 1978; J. D. McClatchy, editor, *Anne Sexton: The Artist and Her Critics,* Indiana University Press, 1978.†

—*Sketch by David A. Guy*

*   *   *

SHANE, Harold Gray 1914-

PERSONAL: Born August 11, 1914, in Milwaukee, Wis.; son of Ben L. and Grace (Gray) Shane; married Ruth Marion Williams, September 1, 1938 (died, 1964); married June Grant Mulry, 1965; married Catherine McKenzie, 1974; children: (first marriage) Michael Stewart Williams, Patricia Mills, Susan Hatker, Ann Gray. *Education:* Attended University of Wisconsin, 1931-33; Milwaukee State Teachers College (now University of Wisconsin—Milwaukee), B.E., 1935; Ohio State University, M.A., 1939, Ph.D., 1943. *Religion:* Presbyterian. *Home:* 1416 Sare Rd., Bloomington, Ind. 47401. *Office:* Education Building, Indiana University, Bloomington, Ind. 47401.

CAREER: Elementary school teacher and principal in Cincinnati and Toledo, Ohio, 1935-40; Ohio State Department of Education, Columbus, state supervisor of elementary education, 1942-43; Ohio State University, Columbus, assistant professor, 1943-46; Winnetka (Ill.) Public Schools, superintendent, 1946-49; Northwestern University, Evanston, Ill., professor of elementary education and school administration, 1949-59; Indiana University, Bloomington, dean of School of Education, 1959-65, University Professor of Education, 1965—. Visiting professor, University of Hawaii, summer, 1959; visiting lecturer at other universities. Consultant to local school systems in twenty-two states. Member of board of directors, Center for Applied Research in Education, 1961—, and CARE, 1962. Winnetka (Ill.) Public Library, trustee, 1950-57, president, 1951-54. *Military service:* U.S. Navy, line officer, 1943-46.

MEMBER: National Education Association (vice-president of department of elementary school principals, 1939-43), Association for Supervision and Curriculum Development (member of publications committee, 1950-55; president, 1973-74), Association for Childhood Education, John Dewey Society, (member of board of directors, 1954-58, 1959-62; vice-president, 1957-58; member of publications committee, 1959-61), National Society for Study of Education (member of board of directors, 1964-79), National Council for Research in English, American Educational Research Association, American Association of University Professors, Phi Delta Kappa, Kappa Delta Pi, Beta Phi Theta. *Awards, honors:* Enoch Pratt Memorial Library Outstanding Education Book of the Year Award, 1953, for *The American Elementary School,* and 1954, for *Creative School Administration in Elementary and Junior High Schools;* Pi Lambda Theta "Best Book" Award, 1971, for *Guiding Human Development;* Educational Press Association Award for educational journalism, 1974, for article in *Phi Delta Kappan.*

WRITINGS: (Editor) *Nutrition for Health,* Ohio State Department of Education, 1943; (editor) *A Handbook of Inexpensive Resources for the Ohio Elementary Teacher,* Ohio Education Association, 1943; (with Marie Quick) *Working with the Child from Two to Six,* Ohio State Department of Education, 1943; *Living and Learning with the Children of Ohio,* Ohio State Department of Education, 1944; (with others) *The Language Arts in the Ohio Elementary Schools,* Ohio State Department of Education, 1944; (with Ruth Shane) *The New Baby,* Simon & Schuster, 1948, 3rd edition,

1954, school edition, 1950; (contributor) *Basic Reading Instruction in Elementary and High Schools,* University of Chicago Press, 1948.

(With E. T. McSwain) *Evaluation and the Elementary Curriculum,* Holt, 1951, revised edition, 1958; (contributor) *Promoting Growth toward Maturity in Interpreting What Is Read,* University of Chicago Press, 1951; (contributor) *Dealing with Fear and Tension,* Association for Childhood Education, 1952; (editor) *The American Elementary School* (13th yearbook of John Dewey Society), Harper, 1953; (with Wilbur A. Yauch) *Creative School Administration in Elementary and Junior High Schools,* Holt, 1954; (with R. Shane) *The Twins: The Story of Two Little Girls Who Look Alike,* Simon & Schuster, 1955; *Grade Level and Curriculum Chart,* F. Watts, 1956, revised edition, 1957; (contributor) *Social Education of Young Children,* National Council for Social Studies, 1956; (with John R. Lee) *An Evaluative Audit of the Educational Program: An Evaluation and Survey Instrument for the Comprehensive Appraisal of Elementary and Secondary Schools,* revised edition, Field Service and Survey Division, School of Education, Northwestern University, 1959; (with Arnold Gesell, Benjamin Spock, Henry S. Commager, and others) *Guiding Children as They Grow,* National Congress of Parents and Teachers, 1959.

(With Mary Reddin and Margaret Gillespie) *Beginning Language Arts Instruction with Children,* C. E. Merrill, 1961; (contributor) Ellen Lewis Buell, editor, *A Treasury of Little Golden Books* (anthology), Golden Books, 1960; (author of foreword) Charlotte Huck and D. A. Young, *Children's Literature in the Elementary School,* Holt, 1961; (contributor) Leonard Freedman and C. P. Cotter, editors, *Issues of the Sixties,* Wadsworth, 1961; (contributor) Nelson B. Henry, editor, *Individualizing Instruction,* University of Chicago Press, 1962; (with June Grant Mulry, Reddin, and Gillespie) *Improving Language Arts Instruction in the Elementary School,* C. E. Merrill, 1962; (author of foreword) M. E. Bonney and Richard Hampleman, *Personal-Social Evaluation Techniques,* Library of Education, 1962; (with Mulry) *Improving Language Arts Instruction through Research,* Association for Supervision and Curriculum Development, 1963; (with others) *Becoming an Educator,* Houghton, 1963; (contributor) R. J. Corsini and D. D. Howard, editors, *Critical Incidents in Teaching,* Prentice-Hall, 1964; *Our Professional Heritage: Foundations and Principles of Education,* Instructional Systems in Teacher Education, 1966; (senior author) *English,* Books II, III, IV, and V, Laidlaw Brothers, 1967; (with John H. Harris and Georgene Lestina) *Practice for English* (four practice books for grades 3-6), Laidlaw Brothers, 1967; *Linguistics and the Classroom Teacher: Some Implications for Instruction in the Mother Tongue,* Association for Supervision and Curriculum Development, 1967; (with others) *The Arts, the Humanities, and the School Library,* American Association of School Librarians, 1967; (contributor) *Reading Instruction,* Millikin University, 1968; (contributor) *Curriculum Imperative: Survival of Self in Society,* Department of Secondary Education, University of Nebraska, 1968; (with others) *New Approaches to Language and Composition,* Books 7 and 8, Laidlaw Brothers, 1969; (editor and contributor) *The United States and International Education: 68th Yearbook,* Part I, University of Chicago Press, 1969.

(Contributor) Albert H. Marckwardt, editor, *Linguistics in School Programs: 69th Yearbook,* University of Chicago Press, 1970; (with June Grant Shane, Robert Gibson, and Paul Munger) *Guiding Human Development: The Counselor and Teacher in the Elementary School,* Charles A. Jones

Publishing, 1971; (contributor) Robert McClure, editor, *The Curriculum: Past, Present and in Perspective–70th Yearbook,* Part II, University of Chicago Press, 1971; (with Robert H. Anderson) *As the Twig Is Bent: Readings in Early Childhood Education,* Houghton, 1971; (compiler with James Walden and Ronald Green) *Interpreting Language Arts Research for the Teacher,* Association for Supervision and Curriculum Development, 1971; (contributor) Ira Gordon, editor, *Early Childhood Education: 71st Yearbook,* Part II, University of Chicago Press, 1972; (editor and contributor with John I. Goodlad) *The Elementary School in the United States: 72nd Yearbook,* Part II, University of Chicago Press, 1973; (contributor) Anderson, editor, *Education in Anticipation of Tomorrow,* Charles A. Jones, 1973; *The Educational Significance of the Future,* Phi Delta Kappa Foundation, 1973; (with Alvin Toffler and others) *Learning for Tomorrow,* Random House, 1974; (with others) *The Future as an Academic Discipline,* Elsevier-Excerpta Medica, 1975; (with Jonas Salk, Willard Wirtz, and others) *Emerging Moral Dimensions in Society,* Association for Supervision and Curriculum Development, 1975; *Curriculum Change: Toward the 21st Century,* National Education Association, 1977; (contributor) J. K. Phillips, editor, *The Language Connection: From the Classroom to the World,* Association of Classroom Teachers of Foreign Language, 1977; (contributor) Jib Fowles, editor, *Handbook of Futures Research,* Greenwood Press, 1978; (contributor) Donald Orlosky and B. Othanel Smith, editors, *Curriculum Development: Issues and Insights,* Rand McNally, 1978; (with Walden and others) *Classroom-Relevant Research in the Language Arts,* Association for Supervision and Curriculum Development, 1978; (with others) *Alternative Educational Systems,* F. E. Peacock, 1979.

Probable Developments in the Social Sciences: 1980-2000 (monograph), UNESCO, 1980; (contributor) A. Harkins and K. Redd, editors, *Sourcebook II,* World Future Society, 1980; (contributor) K. Ryan and J. Cooper, editors, *Kaleidoscope: Readings in Education,* Houghton, 1980; (contributor) Orlosky, editor, *Introduction to Education,* C. E. Merrill, 1981; *Educating for a New Millenium: The Anticipatory Curriculum,* Phi Delta Kappa Foundation, 1981.

"Gateways to Reading Treasures" series; all with Kathleen Hester; all published by Laidlaw Brothers: *Tales to Read,* 1960; *Stories to Remember,* 1960; *Storyland Favorites,* 1960; *Doorways to Adventure,* 1960; *Magic and Laughter,* 1962; *Words with Wings,* 1963; *Courage and Adventure,* 1963.

Primary urban readers series; with Hester and Barbara Mason; all published by Laidlaw Brothers in 1967: *Happy Days in the City; All Around the City; Good Times in the City; Adventures in the City,* expanded edition, 1968.

Middle school readers series; with Hester and Mason; all published by Laidlaw Brothers in 1970: *Friends from Many Lands; Adventures in Living and Make-Believe; Doorways to Life and Wonder.*

Also author, with York, Ferris, and Keener, of "Using Good English" readers series (grades 2-12), seven books, Laidlaw Brothers, 1961-62, revised editions of Books 7 and 8, 1964.

Film scripts: (With June Grant Shane) "Linguistic Backgrounds of English," Society for Visual Education, Group 1, six filmstrips, 1967, Group 2, six filmstrips, 1969; "Words That Name and Do" (16mm motion picture), Coronet Films, 1969; "Words That Add Meaning" (16mm motion picture), Coronet Films, 1969; (with J. G. Shane) "Understanding Your Language," Group 1, six filmstrips, Society for Visual Education, 1971; "Making English Work for You," six filmstrips, Society for Visual Education, 1975. Also editor and consultant, "Hero Legends of Many Lands" filmstrip series, Society for Visual Education, 1956.

Booklets: *The Solar System* (juvenile), American Education Press, 1939; *The Magic of Electricity* (juvenile), American Education Press, 1939; (with others) *A Wartime Focus for Ohio Elementary Schools*, Ohio Department of Education, 1943; (contributor) *Ohio Schools in Wartime*, Ohio State Department of Education, 1943; (editor) *Books and Materials for Curriculum Workers: An Annual Bibliography*, Association for Supervision and Curriculum Development, 1953; *Oral Aspects of Reading*, University of Chicago Press, 1955; (with others) *Elementary Education in the Chicago Public Schools*, School of Education, Northwestern University, 1959; (with Hollis L. Caswell) *College of Education Semi-centennial Addresses*, Kent State University, 1960; (with others) *Motivation*, Department of Elementary-Kindergarten-Nursery Education, National Education Association, 1968.

Also author of fourteen U.S. Navy textbooks and manuals, including *Skill in the Surf: A Landing Boat Manual* and *The Power Boat Book;* author or editor of numerous educational and administrative reports to universities, school systems, corporations, and government agencies.

Contributor to *Encyclopedia of Educational Research, American Educator Encyclopedia, Compton's Encyclopedia, World Topics Yearbook*, and to yearbooks of educational organizations; also contributor of short stories and articles to *Collier's, Cheshire*, and *Weird Tales*, and of more than 300 articles to educational journals. Member of editorial board, *Childhood Education*, 1947-49, and the *Kappan*, 1961-80; member of editorial advisory board, *Childcraft*, 1964.

WORK IN PROGRESS: Three books; four research reports.

* * *

SHAPIRO, Henry D(avid) 1937-

PERSONAL: Born May 7, 1937, in New York, N.Y.; son of Lawrence Milton (a physician) and Estelle V. (Srebnik) Shapiro; married Nancy Wynne Kasdin, July 14, 1963; children: Lawrence Milton, Elliot Hart, Matthew Joseph. *Education:* Columbia University, A.B., 1958; Cornell University, M.A., 1960; Rutgers University, Ph.D., 1966. *Religion:* Jewish. *Office:* Department of History, University of Cincinnati, Cincinnati, Ohio 45221.

CAREER: Rutgers University, New Brunswick, N.J., assistant instructor in history, 1960-62; Manhattan School of Music, New York, N.Y., lecturer in history of science, 1963; Ohio State University, Columbus, instructor in history, 1963-66; University of Cincinnati, Cincinnati, Ohio, assistant professor, 1966-71, associate professor, 1971-79, professor of history, 1979—. Visiting research fellow, Charles Warren Center, Harvard University, 1971-72; Fulbright senior lecturer, John F. Kennedy Institute, Free University of Berlin, 1977-78. *Member:* American Studies Association. *Awards, honors:* Moses Coit Tyler Prize, Cornell University, 1961, for *Confiscation of Confederate Property in the North;* W. D. Weatherford Prize, Berea College, 1979, for *Appalachia on Our Mind.*

WRITINGS: Confiscation of Confederate Property in the North, Cornell University Press, 1962; (editor and author of introductions with Zane L. Miller) *Physician to the West: Selected Writings of Daniel Drake on Science and Society*, University Press of Kentucky, 1970; (author of introduction)

John C. Campbell, *The Southern Highlander and His Homeland*, University Press of Kentucky, 1969; (contributor) Alexandra Oleson and S. B. Brown, editors, *The Pursuit of Knowledge in the Early American Republic*, Johns Hopkins Press, 1976; (with Miller) *Clifton: Neighborhood and Community in an Urban Setting*, University of Cincinnati, 1976; *Appalachia on Our Mind: The Southern Mountains and Mountaineers in the American Consciousness, 1870-1920*, University of North Carolina Press, 1978. Contributor of articles and reviews to professional journals.

WORK IN PROGRESS: The Sage as Symbol: Harry A. Wolfson and the Usefulness of Philosophy; Country Life in America: Culture Conflict and the Problem of the Past; general research into the idea of culture in America.

* * *

SHARKEY, John Michael 1931-
(Jack Sharkey; pseudonyms: Rick Abbot, Mike Johnson)

PERSONAL: Born May 6, 1931, in Chicago, Ill.; son of John Patrick and Mary (Luckey) Sharkey; married Patricia Walsh, 1962; children: Beth Eileen, Carole Lynn, Susan Kathleen, Michael Joseph. *Education:* St. Mary's College (Winona, Minn.), B.A., 1953. *Religion:* Roman Catholic.

CAREER: Writer, 1952—. *Military service:* U.S. Army, 1955-56. *Member:* Dramatists Guild, Authors League, Alpha Psi Omega.

WRITINGS—All under name Jack Sharkey; novels: *Secret Martians*, Ace, 1960; *Murder, Maestro, Please*, Abelard, 1961; *Death for Auld Lang Syne*, Holt, 1962; *Ultimatum in 2050 A.D.*, Ace, 1965; *The Addams Family*, Pyramid Publications, 1965.

Plays; all published by Samuel French: *Here Lies Jeremy Troy* (three-act; first produced on Broadway, 1965), 1969; *M Is for the Million* (two-act), 1971; *Kiss or Make Up* (three-act), 1972; *How Green Was My Brownie* (three-act), 1972; *A Gentleman and a Scoundrel* (three-act), 1973; *Meanwhile, Back on the Couch* (three-act), 1973; *Roomies!*, 1974; *Spinoff*, 1974; *Who's On First?*, 1975; *The Creature Creeps!*, 1977; *My Son the Astronaut* (musical), 1980; *Par for the Corpse*, 1980; (with David Reiser) *The Picture of Dorian Gray* (musical adaptation), 1980; *Honestly Now!*, 1981; (with Reiser) *Woman Overboard* (musical), 1981; (with Reiser) *Slow Down, Sweet Chariot*, 1981.

Also author or co-author of other plays, all published by Samuel French, including *Saving Grace, The Murder Room, Rich Is Better, Dream Lover, Take a Number, Darling, Missing Link, Once Is Enough, Double Exposure, Turkey in the Straw* (musical), (with Reiser) *What a Spot!* (musical), (with Reiser) *Hope for the Best* (musical), (with Reiser) *Operetta!* (musical), (with Reiser) *Not the "Count of Monte Cristo"?* (musical), *Turnabout*, and *Pushover;* author under pseudonym Rick Abbot of *June Groom, Play On!*, and *A Turn for the Nurse*, and under pseudonym Mike Johnson of *The Clone People* and *Return of the Maniac.*

Contributor of short stories and articles to mystery, science fiction, and men's magazines.

WORK IN PROGRESS: A comedy-farce play, "Don't Tell Mother."

AVOCATIONAL INTERESTS: Charades, chess, playing piano, swimming, handball, reading mystery novels, doing British crossword puzzles.

SHARP, Andrew 1906-1974

PERSONAL: Born November 10, 1906, in Dunedin, New Zealand; died February 8, 1974; son of Andrew and Jane (Smith) Sharp; married Margaret Hope Johnstone, 1945; children: Ian Alexander. *Education:* University of New Zealand, B.A., 1927, M.A., 1928; University of Oxford, Rhodes Scholar, B.A., 1931. *Home:* Unit 2, 17 Selwyn Rd., Epsam, Auckland 3, New Zealand. *Office:* Department of Internal Affairs, Wellington, New Zealand.

CAREER: Indian Civil Service, Burma, assistant commissioner, 1931-32; New Zealand Government Service, at home and overseas as external affairs officer and cultural advisory officer, 1939-74. Senior research fellow in arts, University of Auckland, 1967-70. *Member:* Polynesian Society (member of council and editorial committee, 1958). *Awards, honors:* Litt.D., University of Auckland, 1970.

WRITINGS: (Editor) *The Dillon Letters*, A. H. & A. W. Reed, 1954; *Ancient Voyagers in the Pacific*, Penguin, 1957, revised edition published as *Ancient Voyagers in Polynesia*, University of California Press, 1964; *Crisis at Kerikeri*, A. H. & A. W. Reed, 1958; *The Discovery of the Pacific Islands*, Clarendon Press, 1960; *Adventurous Armada*, Whitcombe & Tombs, 1961; *The Discovery of Australia*, Clarendon Press, 1963; *The New Zealand Colonial Secretary's Office and Department of Internal Affairs*, Government Printer, 1966; *The Voyages of Abel Janszoon Tasman*, Clarendon Press, 1968; (editor and translator) *The Journal of Jacob Roggeveen*, Clarendon Press, 1970; (editor) *Duperrey's Visit to New Zealand in 1824*, Alexander Turnbull Library (Wellington), 1971; (contributor) *New Zealand's Heritage*, Paul Hamlyn, 1971; *The Welfare Tradition*, Heinemann, 1975; (with Frank Rogers) *The Road to Maturity*, Heinemann, 1977. Contributor to *Journal of Pacific History*, *New Zealand Journal of History*, and other history publications.

SIDELIGHTS: Andrew Sharp told *CA*, "My long-time hobby has been research in Pacific studies in the Alexander Turnbull Library, and writing flowing therefrom."†

* * *

SHARP, Harold S(pencer) 1909-

PERSONAL: Born December 23, 1909, in Alameda, Calif.; son of Harold Gibbons (a civil engineer) and Mary (Spencer) Sharp; married Marjorie Barnhill Zehr, June 27, 1958 (died September 9, 1976). *Education:* Indiana University, B.S. in B.A. (with distinction), 1954, M.S. in L.S., 1957. *Home:* 2110 Springfield Ave., Fort Wayne, Ind. 46805.

CAREER: Rosenberg Bros. & Co., San Francisco, Calif., contract administrator, 1928-42; served with Quartermaster Corps, U.S. Army, 1942-52; Farnsworth Electronics Co., Fort Wayne, Ind., chief librarian, 1957-59; General Motors Corp., A.C. Spark Plug Division, Milwaukee, Wis., technical librarian, 1959-63; Lockheed-Georgia Co., Marietta, Ga., engineering information analyst, 1963-64; free-lance library consultant, Berkeley, Calif., 1964-65; University of Hawaii, Honolulu, professor of library science and head of general reference, 1965-68; Indiana State University, Terre Haute, professor of library science, 1968-72. Library consultant sponsored by Special Libraries Association. *Member:* Special Libraries Association (Wisconsin chapter; secretary, 1960-62; vice-president, program chairman, and president-elect, 1962-63), Beta Gamma Sigma, Beta Phi Mu. *Awards, honors:* *Handbook of Pseudonyms and Personal Nicknames* chosen by American Library Association as one of outstanding reference books published in late 1972 and 1973.

WRITINGS—All published by Scarecrow, except as indicated: *The House of a Million Wonders* (booklet), Employee Relations, Inc., 1961; *How To Use Your Library*, Consolidated Book Service, 1963; (editor) *Readings in Special Librarianship*, 1963; (editor) *Readings in Information Retrieval*, 1964; (editor with wife, Marjorie Z. Sharp) *Index to Characters in the Performing Arts*, Volume I: *Non-Musical Plays*, 1966, Volume II: *Operas and Other Musical Productions*, 1969, Volume III: *Ballets A-Z and Symbols*, 1972, Volume IV: *Radio and Television*, 1973; (editor) *Handbook of Pseudonyms and Personal Nicknames*, 1972, supplement, 1975; (editor) *Footnotes to American History*, 1977; (editor) *Footnotes to World History*, 1979; (editor) *Handbook of Geographical Nicknames*, 1980. Contributor of articles on business management and library science to more than twenty-five technical periodicals.

WORK IN PROGRESS: Second supplement to *Handbook of Pseudonyms and Personal Nicknames*, for Scarecrow.

SIDELIGHTS: Harold S. Sharp writes: "[I] play piano (once organized and conducted a college dance orchestra); [I] collect jazz records and have approximately five thousand collector's items. [I] don't care a bit for outdoor life, sports clothes, or open cars, but do like cats, flying, and having two or three books going at once."

* * *

SHAW, Russell B(urnham) 1935-

PERSONAL: Born May 19, 1935, in Washington, D.C.; son of Charles Burnham and Mary (Russell) Shaw; married Carmen Hilda Carbon; children: Mary Hilda, Emily Anne, Janet, Charles, Elizabeth. *Education:* Georgetown University, B.A. (summa cum laude), 1956, M.A., 1960. *Religion:* Catholic. *Home:* 2928 44th Pl. N.W., Washington, D.C. 20016. *Office:* 1312 Massachusetts Ave. N.W., Washington, D.C. 20005.

CAREER: *Catholic Standard*, Washington, D.C., reporter, 1957; National Catholic Welfare Conference News Service, Washington, D.C., staff writer, 1957-66; National Catholic Educational Association, Washington, D.C., director of publications and information, 1966-69; National Catholic Office for Information, Washington, D.C., director, 1969-72; U.S. Catholic Conference, Washington, D.C., associate secretary for communication, 1973-74, secretary for public affairs, 1975—. Director, school public relations workshop, Georgetown University, 1969. Press secretary to U.S. delegation, International Synod of Bishops, 1971, 1974, 1977, and 1980. *Member:* National Press Club, Religious Public Relations Council, Public Relations Society of America.

WRITINGS: *The Dark Disciple*, Doubleday, 1961; *Abortion and Public Policy*, Family Life Bureau, 1966; (co-author) *New Patterns for Catholic Education*, Croft Educational, 1968; *Abortion on Trial*, Pflaum/Standard, 1968; (editor) *Catholic Education Today and Tomorrow*, National Catholic Educational Association, 1968; (editor and contributor) *Trends and Issues in Catholic Education*, Citation, 1969; (with C. A. Koob) *S.O.S. for Catholic Schools*, Holt, 1970; (with G. G. Grisez) *Beyond the New Morality*, University of Notre Dame Press, 1974, revised edition, 1980; *Church and State*, Our Sunday Visitor, 1979. Also author of pamphlets on educational and current affairs topics. Author of syndicated column, "Arts of Leisure," 1966-67. Columnist for *Columbia*, 1966—, *Today's Catholic Teacher*, 1967—, and *Our Sunday Visitor*, 1967-69. Contributor to *Encyclopedia Americana* and *Macmillan Encyclopedia of Education*. Contributor to *America*, *Catholic World*, *Sign*, and other periodicals. Washington correspondent, *St. Louis Review*, 1967-69.

SHELDRICK, Daphne   1934-

PERSONAL: Born June 4, 1934, in Nakuru, Kenya; daughter of Brian (a farmer) and Marjorie (Webb) Jenkins; married Frank William Woodley, June 26, 1953 (divorced, 1959); married David Leslie William Sheldrick (a park warden), October 25, 1960 (died June 13, 1977); children: (first marriage) Gillian Sala Ellen; (second marriage) Angela Mara. *Education:* Attended schools in Kenya. *Politics:* Conservative. *Religion:* Protestant. *Home and office:* Tsavo East National Park, Box 14, Voi, Kenya.

CAREER: Naturalist (has raised orphaned wild animals and rehabilitated them to live in their wild state). Wildlife writer for African Wildlife Leadership Foundation; advisor to Nairobi National Park Orphanage. Active in fund raising for conservation, including launching David Sheldrick Memorial Appeal, 1977. *Awards, honors:* Grand Prix Verite from *Le Parisien,* 1967, for *The Orphans of Tsavo.*

WRITINGS: The Orphans of Tsavo, Collins, 1966; *The Tsavo Story,* Collins, 1973; *My Four Footed Family* (juvenile), Dent, 1979; *An Elephant Called Eleanor* (juvenile), Dent, 1980. Contributor to *Collier's Yearbook,* to magazines, including *Saturday Review* and *Africana,* and to wildlife periodicals in Kenya.

SIDELIGHTS: "Living in the vast Tsavo Park as wife of the warden," Daphne Sheldrick wrote, "it has been my lot to nurture and care for very varied species of wild animal orphans, ranging from elephant and rhino calves to the minute dikdik. These orphans are never penned, but are free to roam where they wish, and finally the objective is to rehabilitate them to their wild environment.

"Some when fully grown sever their ties with their foster parents completely, while others opt to remain in the vicinity of the Park Headquarters and enjoy the best of both worlds. By so doing they can be studied closely, and contribute toward a better understanding of their wild counterparts. Many former orphans have bred and raised families near the headquarters."

Sheldrick adds that since her husband's death, her contribution has become more advisory. "But through my writing," she continues, "I still feel I am doing my bit, even if it is simply helping to generate an awareness and better understanding of animals. Having worked in the field for so long, I can make a valuable contribution by bridging the gap between field wardens and fund raising bodies, knowing the problems as I do."

Because of her late husband's contribution to conservation, the government of Kenya granted her authority to build a house within the Nairobi National Park.

*   *   *

SHEPARD, Odell   1884-1967

PERSONAL: Born July 22, 1884, near Rock Falls, Ill.; died July 19, 1967, in New London, Conn.; son of William Orville (a Methodist bishop) and Emily (Odell) Shepard; married Mary Farwell Record, December 22, 1908; children: Willard Odell. *Education:* Attended Northwestern School of Music, 1900-02, and Northwestern University, 1902-04; University of Chicago, Ph.B., 1907, Ph.M., 1908; Harvard University, Ph.D., 1916. *Politics:* Democrat. *Home:* 4 Jordan Cove Cir., Waterford, Conn. 06385.

CAREER: Newspaper reporter in Chicago, Ill., and St. Louis, Mo., 1906-09; University of Southern California, Los Angeles, professor of English, 1909-14; Harvard University and Radcliffe College, Cambridge, Mass., instructor in En-

glish, 1916-17; Trinity College, Hartford, Conn., Goodwin Professor of English, 1917-46, lecturer, 1946-66. Instructor, Smith Academy, St. Louis, 1908-09; visiting summer professor, University of California, 1920, and Breadloaf School, 1947; visiting professor, Bard College, 1950-51. Organist in Chicago churches, 1905-07. Lieutenant governor of Connecticut, 1940-43.

MEMBER: Thoreau Society of America (co-founder), College English Association (co-founder; past president), Society of American Historians, Civil Liberties Union (Connecticut correspondent), Connecticut Academy of Fine Arts, Delta Tau Delta, Phi Beta Kappa. *Awards, honors:* Guggenheim fellowship for study abroad, 1927-28; Litt.D., Northwestern University, 1932, and Wesleyan University, 1939; Huntington Library international research fellow, 1934-35; Pulitzer Prize in biography (joint award), 1938, and Little, Brown Centennial Contest $5,000 Prize, both for *Pedlar's Progress;* L.H.D., Boston University, 1941.

WRITINGS: Shakespeare Questions (textbook), Houghton 1916; *A Lonely Flute* (verse), Houghton, 1917; *Bliss Carman: A Study of His Poetry,* McClelland & Stewart, 1923; *The Harvest of a Quiet Eye* (prose and verse), Houghton, 1927, reprinted, Books for Libraries, 1971; *The Joys of Forgetting* (essays), Allen & Unwin, 1928, Houghton, 1929, reprinted, Harper, 1979; *The Lore of the Unicorn* (history), Allen & Unwin, 1929, Houghton, 1930, reprinted, Barnes & Noble, 1967; *Thy Rod and Thy Creel* (fishing), Dodd, 1930; *Pedlar's Progress: The Life of Bronson Alcott,* Little, Brown, 1937, reprinted, Greenwood Press, 1968; *Connecticut Past and Present* (history), Knopf, 1939; (with son, Willard Shepard) *Holdfast Gaines* (novel), Macmillan, 1946; (contributor) *The Literary History of the United States,* Macmillan, 1948; (with W. Shepard) *Jenkins' Ear* (novel; Book-of-the-Month Club selection), Macmillan, 1951; (contributor) *The American Story,* Channel, 1956; (contributor) *Unforgettable Americans,* Channel, 1960.

Editor: Henry David Thoreau, *Week on the Concord and Merrimack Rivers,* Scribner, 1921; *Essays of 1925,* Mitchell, 1926; *The Heart of Thoreau's Journals,* Houghton, 1927, 2nd edition, Dover, 1961; (with Robert Hillyer) *Essays of Today: 1926-1927,* Century Co., 1928; *Contemporary Essays,* Scribner, 1929; (with Hillyer) *Prose Masterpieces,* Harcourt, 1931; *Poems of Longfellow,* American Book, 1934, reprinted, Darby, 1980; (with Paul S. Wood) *English Prose and Poetry, 1660-1800,* Houghton, 1934; Amos Bronson Alcott, *Journals,* Little, Brown, 1938; (with Frederick Manchester) *Irving Babbitt, Man and Teacher,* Putnam, 1941, reprinted, Greenwood Press, 1969; *The Best of W. H. Hudson,* Dutton, 1949. Also editor, with others, of *College Survey of English Literature.*

Contributor to *Encyclopaedia Britannica.* Weekly contributor of essays, verse, and reviews to *Christian Science Monitor,* 1922-35; contributor of book reviews to *Nation* and *Yale Review.*

WORK IN PROGRESS: A history, *In Old New London.*

SIDELIGHTS: "It is hard to see how a better book about Bronson Alcott could be written," commented a *New Republic* critic about *Pedlar's Progress,* Odell Shepard's award-winning biography. "Not many readers . . . could have expected it to prove so fruitful a theme for narrative, for picture-making, for the study of personality, as [the author] has shown it to be." Alcott, father of writer Louisa May Alcott (*Little Women*), was a Connecticut farmer's son who began his adult life as an itinerant peddler and eventually became one of America's foremost transcendentalist philosophers and teachers. To prepare a comprehensive study of Alcott's life and work, Shepard read all fifty volumes of his journals and also familiarized himself with his correspondence and other contemporary records. The result, noted the *Chicago Daily Tribune*'s Fanny Butcher, is a book written "with fine enthusiasm. It is the biography of a mind, analyzed, but not psychoanalyzed, an old-fashioned record of a new-fashioned interest in what a man thinks as well as what he does."

Several reviewers admired *Pedlar's Progress* for the author's ability to depict the era as well as the man. Henry Steele Commager, for example, writing in the *New York Times*, found that the book "places Alcott, and all of his fine faith, against the background of American experience; it integrates Alcott and his idealism with American philosophy. It explains the past and the present in terms of a man ... whose life epitomized a whole society." An *American Historical Review* critic agreed, stating that "Professor Shepard's life of Bronson Alcott is not only an admirable biography of a much neglected but important figure in American letters; it is also in itself an important contribution to American letters, notable for the excellence of the writing and still more for a point of view which illuminates its own era as well as that of which it treats."

At least two reviewers, however, held entirely different views of *Pedlar's Progress*. As a *Yale Review* critic observed: "Mr. Shepard, it must be sorrowfully confessed, does not succeed [in producing a good biography]. His book is full and authentic as fact, but once beyond the admirable opening chapters, Alcott's life diffuses itself past the power of Mr. Shepard.... At the end of the story the reader puts down the volume with the vague impression that Alcott was a good, vague sort of man." Concluded H. S. Canby of the *Saturday Review of Literature*: "[Shepard's] book is not perfect. Alcott's unhappy style, sententious, involved, abstract, has had its reaction on Mr. Shepard's own style, which is sometimes inflated, though often also excellent; and the diffuseness of the master is reflected in a diffuseness of the biographer, who is often annoyingly repetitious.... But this is a real biography. Interpretation may differ, but the difficult job has been done."

Shepard himself once told *CA*: "This writer has always had too many 'irons in the fire.' He has never produced two books of the same kind. Throughout his mature life his major interest has been in what he calls 'the history of solitude,' and on that topic he has never published one word. What he considers his best book, *The Lore of the Unicorn*, had a good sale in England and America, but before the first edition was exhausted the plates were destroyed by enemy action in London. He believes he has had as much recognition as he deserves, and certainly he has had a good time."

BIOGRAPHICAL/CRITICAL SOURCES: Saturday Review of Literature, May 8, 1937; *New York Times*, May 9, 1937, July 20, 1967; *Books*, May 9, 1937; *Time*, May 10, 1937; *Chicago Daily Tribune*, May 15, 1937; *Springfield Republican*, May 16, 1937; *New Republic*, June 16, 1937; *Yale Review*, summer, 1937; *American Historical Review*, October, 1937.†

*   *   *

SHERBURNE, Zoa (Morin)   1912-

PERSONAL: Born September 30, 1912, in Seattle, Wash.; daughter of Thomas Joseph and Zoa (Webber) Morin; married Herbert Newton Sherburne, 1935; children: Marie, Norene, Zoey, Herb, Jr., Thomas, Philip, Anne, Robert. *Education:* Attended schools in Seattle, Wash. *Home:* 1131

Fairhaven, Bellingham, Wash. 98225. *Agent:* Ann Elmo Agency, Inc., 52 Vanderbilt Ave., New York, N.Y. 10017.

CAREER: Author. *Member:* National League of American Pen Women (second vice president, Seattle national branch), Seattle Free Lances (president, 1954), Phi Delta Nu (president, 1950). *Awards, honors:* Child Study Award, 1959; Matrix Table Award, 1950; Woman of the Year, Phi Delta Nu.

WRITINGS—All published by Morrow: *Almost April*, 1956; *The High White Wall*, 1957; *Princess in Denim*, 1958; *Jennifer*, 1959; *Evening Star*, 1960; *Ballerina on Skates*, 1961; *Girl in the Shadows*, 1963; *River at Her Feet*, 1965; *Girl in the Mirror*, 1966; *Too Bad about the Haines Girl*, 1967; *The Girl Who Knew Tomorrow*, 1970; *Leslie*, 1972; *Why Have the Birds Stopped Singing?*, 1974. Contributor of over 300 short stories and articles and over 300 verses to periodicals.

WORK IN PROGRESS: The Ghost of Whispering Oaks.

SIDELIGHTS: Zoa Sherburne told *CA*: "Although I had always been interested in writing it was not until I was married and had three and a half children that I thought about trying to write for publication.

"To date, all of my books are contemporary and I confess that I do little research. Except the sort of research a mother is bound to do—overhearing conversations and being on the receiving end of confidences about this or that school chum: 'And do you know, Mother, she hardly ever sees her father ..., and guess what, the boy called her up that same week and even came out to meet her mother!'"

AVOCATIONAL INTERESTS: Bowling.

*   *   *

SHERIDAN, John V.   1915-

PERSONAL: Born December 19, 1915, in Longford, Ireland; son of Farrell (a farmer) and Brigid (Kiernan) Sheridan. *Education:* Attended St. John's College, Waterford, Ireland. *Office:* Our Lady of Malibu Church, 3625 Winter Canyon Rd., Malibu, Calif. 90265.

CAREER: Ordained Roman Catholic priest, 1943; Our Lady Chapel, Los Angeles, Calif., chaplain, 1951-65; assistant pastor in several parishes, including Cathedral of St. Vibiana; Catholic Information Center, Los Angeles, director, 1961-65; currently pastor of Our Lady of Malibu Church, Malibu, Calif., and director of "Rosary Hour" daily broadcasts. Lecturer; has made appearances on television.

WRITINGS: Questions and Answers on the Catholic Faith, foreword by James Francis Cardinal McIntyre, Hawthorn, 1963; *The Church Yesterday and Today*, Our Sunday Visitor, 1975; *Saints in Times of Turmoil*, Paulist Press, 1977.

Pamphlets: *I Believe in God; The Rosary; The Liturgy; Christ in the Home; Christ in the School; Christ in the Office; The Lesson of President Kennedy's Death; The Sacred Liturgy; You Are the Church; Church Is Community; Liturgy: The Church at Prayer; Christ at the Desk; Mary, the Mother of Christ; Tourist in His Footsteps; Loneliness; And When It Is Dawn.*

AVOCATIONAL INTERESTS: Golf; collecting old books and family heirlooms.

*   *   *

SHERLOCK, John   1932-

PERSONAL: Born July 14, 1932, in Manchester, England. *Education:* University of California, Berkeley, B.A., 1956; Columbia University, M.S., 1957; Oxford University, Ph.D.

Agent: Arthur Pine Associates, 1780 Broadway, New York, N.Y. 10019.

CAREER: International Business Machines, New York City, staff writer, 1957; King Publications, San Francisco, Calif., managing editor, 1957-59; *New York Herald Tribune,* New York City, assistant to columnist Joe Hyams, 1960-63; free-lance writer, 1963—. *Military service:* Royal Air Force, 1950-52.

WRITINGS: The Ordeal of Major Grigsby (novel), Morrow, 1964, published as *The Last Grenade,* Dell, 1970; *The Instant Saint,* Morrow, 1965; *The Dream Maker,* Ballantine, 1979; *J.B.'s Daughter,* McGraw, 1980; *The Most Dangerous Gamble,* Coward, 1981; *Maggie Gannon,* McGraw, 1982. Also author of numerous television and feature film scripts. Contributor to British and American magazines, including *Saturday Evening Post, TV Guide, This Week, Today,* and *Travel.*

SIDELIGHTS: In 1969, Josef Shaftel produced motion pictures of *The Ordeal of Major Grigsby* (under the title "The Last Grenade") and *The Instant Saint. Avocational interests:* Travel, skin diving, gliding, collecting and drinking wines, experimenting in foods, and (especially) "just sitting around dusty old squares in southern Europe and waiting for something to happen (it usually does)."

BIOGRAPHICAL/CRITICAL SOURCES: Times Literary Supplement, July 7, 1966.

*   *   *

SHERTZER, Bruce E(ldon) 1928-

PERSONAL: Born January 11, 1928, in Bloomfield, Ind.; son of Edwin F. and Lois B. (Fitzpatrick) Shertzer; married Carol M. Rice, November 24, 1948; children: Sarah, Mark. *Education:* Indiana University, B.S., 1952, M.S., 1953, Ed.D., 1958. *Religion:* Methodist. *Home:* 1620 Western Dr., West Lafayette, Ind. 47906. *Office:* Department of Education, Purdue University, Lafayette, Ind. 46207.

CAREER: Martinsville (Ind.) Metropolitan School District, counselor and teacher, 1951-52, director of testing and guidance, 1954-56; director of division of guidance and pupil instruction, Indiana State Department of Public Instruction, 1956-58; associate director, North Central Association Superior Student Project, 1958-60; Purdue University, Lafayette, Ind., assistant professor, 1960-62, associate professor, 1962-65, professor of education, 1965—, chairman of Counseling and Personnel Services. Visiting professor of educational psychology, University of Hawaii, 1967; Fulbright senior lecturer, University of Reading, 1967-68. *Military service:* U.S. Army, 1946-48; became sergeant. *Member:* American Personnel and Guidance Association (president, 1973-74), Association for Counselor Education and Supervision (president, 1970-71), Indiana Personnel and Guidance Association (president, 1963). *Awards, honors:* Counselor Educator of the Year Award, Indiana Personnel and Guidance Association, 1969.

WRITINGS: (Editor) *Working with Superior Students: Theories and Practices,* Science Research Associates, 1960; (with William Van Hoose) *Guidance in Elementary Schools,* Department of Public Instruction, State of Indiana, 1961; (editor with others) *Counseling: Selected Readings,* C. E. Merrill, 1962; (with Herman J. Peters) *Guidance: Program Development and Management,* C. E. Merrill, 1963, 3rd edition, 1974; (with Harry S. Belman) *My Career Guidebook,* Bruce, 1963, 2nd edition, 1970; (with Richard Knowles) *Teacher's Guide to Group Vocational Guidance,* Bellman

Publishing, 1964, 2nd edition, 1971; (with Peters) *Guidance: Techniques for Individual Appraisal and Development,* Macmillan, 1965; (with Shelley C. Stone) *Fundamentals of Guidance,* Houghton, 1966, 4th edition, 1981; (with Stone) *Fundamentals of Counseling,* Houghton, 1968, 3rd edition, 1980; (editor with Stone) *Introduction to Guidance: Selected Readings,* Houghton, 1970; *Careers in Counseling and Guidance,* Houghton, 1972; *Career Exploration and Planning,* Houghton, 1973, 2nd edition, 1976; *Career Planning,* Houghton, 1977, 2nd edition, 1981; (with J. D. Linden) *Fundamentals of Individual Appraisal,* Houghton, 1979.

Also editor, with Stone, of "Guidance Monograph" series, eighty-eight volumes, Houghton. Contributor of articles to *Personnel and Guidance Journal, Theory into Practice, School Counselor, Vocational Guidance Quarterly, Counselor Education and Supervision,* and other professional journals.

WORK IN PROGRESS: Research on high school counselors' predictive ability and on life-career changes.

*   *   *

SHEW, E(dward) Spencer 1908-1977

PERSONAL: Born November 9, 1908, in Bristol, England; died February 11, 1977; son of William Edward and Laura (Evans) Shew; married Betty Winifred Muriel Fraser (a writer under name Betty Spencer Shew), 1939 (died, 1971). *Education:* Attended Bristol Grammar School. *Agent:* A. P. Watt & Son, 26/28 Bedford Row, London WC1R 4HL, England.

CAREER: Western Daily Press, Bristol, England, reporter, 1927-30; Central News Agency, London, England, law courts reporter, 1930-35, League of Nations correspondent in Geneva, Switzerland, 1935-36, Buckingham Palace court correspondent, 1936-39, diplomatic correspondent, 1939-41; Exchange Telegraph News Agency, London, reporter for press gallery of House of Commons, 1941-45, political correspondent, 1945-65; political correspondent for Press Association, 1966-70. *Member:* Mystery Writers of America, Parliamentary Lobby Journalists (honorary secretary, 1951-68; chairman, 1968-69). *Awards, honors:* Coronation Medal, awarded by King George VI, 1937; Edgar Allan Poe Award from Mystery Writers of America, 1962, for *A Companion to Murder;* Commander of the Order of the British Empire, 1965.

WRITINGS: Miss Proutie (novel), Harrap, 1952; *A Companion to Murder: A Dictionary of Death by Poison, Death by Shooting, Death by Suffocation and Drowning, Death by the Strangler's Hand, 1900-1950,* Cassell, 1960, Knopf, 1961; *A Second Companion to Murder: A Dictionary of Death by the Knife, the Dagger, the Razor; Death by the Axe, the Chopper, the Chisel; Death by the Iron File, the Marline Spike; Death by the Hammer, the Poker, the Bottle; Death by the Jemmy, the Spanner, the Tyre Lever, the Iron Bar, the Starting Handle; Death by the Sandbag, the Sash Weight; Death by the Mallet, the Half-brick, the Stick, the Stone; Death by the Fire Tongs, the Butt End of a Revolver; Death by the Metal Chair, Etc. 1900-1950,* Cassell, 1961, Knopf, 1962; *Hands of the Ripper,* Sphere, 1971. Contributor to newspapers and periodicals.

WORK IN PROGRESS: A history of the M'Naughton Rules governing the plea of insanity in capital trials in the British courts.

SIDELIGHTS: In honor of E. Spencer Shew's long career as a political correspondent, a brass plate has been affixed to the telephone kiosk near the press gallery in the House of Commons from which he frequently used to phone reports.

A Companion to Murder has been translated into Italian; *Hands of the Ripper* has been translated into German and was made into a movie by Hammer Films in 1972.

AVOCATIONAL INTERESTS: The theater, music, the study of crime.†

* * *

SHULEVITZ, Uri 1935-

PERSONAL: Born February 27, 1935, in Warsaw, Poland; came to United States in 1959; naturalized during 1960's; son of Abraham and Szandla (Hermanstat) Shulevitz; married Helene Weiss (an artist), June 11, 1961 (divorced). *Education:* Teacher's College, Israel, Teacher's Degree, 1956; Attended Tel-Aviv Art Institute, evenings, 1953-55, and Brooklyn Museum Art School, 1959-61. *Religion:* Jewish. *Address:* c/o Farrar, Straus & Giroux, Inc., 19 Union Sq. W., New York, N.Y. 10003.

CAREER: Kibbutz Ein-Geddi (collective farm), Israel, member, 1957-58; art director of youth magazine in Israel, 1958-59; illustrator of children's books. Instructor in art, School of Visual Arts, New York City, 1967-68, Pratt Institute, Brooklyn, N.Y., 1970-71, and New School for Social Research, New York City, 1970—. *Military service:* Israeli Army, 1956-59. *Member:* Authors Guild of Authors League of America (member of children's books committee). *Awards, honors:* American Institute of Graphic Arts, Children's Book Awards, 1963-64, 1965-66, 1967-68, and Certificate of Excellence, 1973-74; Certificate of Merit, Society of Illustrators (New York), 1965, for *Charley Sang a Song;* books displayed at Children's Book Exhibition, New York Public Library, 1967, 1968, 1969, 1972, 1973, and 1974, and at International Biennali of Illustrations, Bratislava, Czechoslovakia, 1969; American Library Association, Caldecott Medal, 1969, for *The Fool of the World and the Flying Ship,* Caldecott Honor Book Award, 1980, for *The Treasure;* selected for inclusion in American Booksellers 1969 Gift to the Nation from the Library of the White House; Bronze Medal, International Book Exhibition (Leipzig), 1970, for *Rain Rain Rivers; Dawn* received Christopher Award, 1975, and represented the United States on International Honors List at 1976 Congress of International Board of Books for Young People; Brooklyn Art Books for Children Citation, 1976, for *Dawn,* and 1977; many books selected as American Library Association Notable Books and as *New York Times* Best Books of the Year.

WRITINGS—Self-illustrated: *The Moon in My Room,* Harper, 1963; *One Monday Morning,* Scribner, 1967; *Rain Rain Rivers,* Farrar, Straus, 1969; *The Magician,* Macmillan, 1973; *Dawn,* Farrar, Straus, 1974; *The Treasure,* Farrar, Straus, 1979; *Writings with Pictures: An Introduction to Writing and Illustrating Children's Books,* Watson-Guptill, 1981.

Illustrator: Charlotte Zolotow, *A Rose, A Bridge, and a Wild Black Horse,* Harper, 1964; Mary Stolz, *The Mystery of the Woods,* Harper, 1964; H. R. Hays and Daniel Hays, *Charley Sang a Song,* Harper, 1964; Sulamith Ish-Kishor, *The Carpet of Solomon,* Pantheon, 1964; Jack Sendak, *The Second Witch,* Harper, 1965; Molly Cone, *Who Knows Ten?,* Union of American Hebrew Congregations, 1965; Jacob Grimm and Wilhelm Grimm, *The Twelve Dancing Princesses,* Scribner, 1966; Stolz, *Maximilian's World,* Harper, 1966; Jean Russell Larson, *The Silkspinners,* Scribner, 1967; Dorothy Nathan, *The Month Brothers,* Dutton, 1967; Jan Wahl, *Runaway*

Jonah and Other Tales, Macmillan, 1968; Arthur Ransome, adapter, *The Fool of the World and the Flying Ship,* Farrar, Straus, 1968; Jan Wahl, *The Wonderful Kite,* Delacorte, 1971; Elizabeth Shub, adapter, *Oh What a Noise!* (text adapted from "A Big Noise" by William Brighty Rands), Macmillan, 1971; Afanasyev, *Soldier and Tsar in the Forest,* Farrar, Straus, 1972; Isaac Bashevis Singer, *The Fools of Chelm,* Farrar, Straus, 1973; Robert Louis Stevenson, *The Touchstone,* Greenwillow, 1976; Sholom Aleichem, *Hanukah Money,* Greenwillow, 1978; Richard Kennedy, *The Lost Kingdom of Karnica,* Sierra Club Books, 1979. Designer, with Tom Spain, of film "One Monday Morning." Contributor to *Horn Book.*

SIDELIGHTS: "Drawing has always been with me," Uri Shulevitz once said. "The encouragement of my parents, who were both talented, probably contributed to my early interest in drawing.... Realizing the excess of words in our culture, I followed an Oriental tradition, trying to say more with fewer words. *The Moon in My Room* contains very brief text and suggestive rather than descriptive illustrations, that have the purpose of awakening the child's imagination, leaving him free space to add to his own.

"As far as technique goes: it is best when it is an *organic extension of the content.* This is the way I approach it. Therefore the variety of methods I have used in different books. I am also constantly searching for a new way of illustrating. I use a lot of pen and ink and watercolor. I have used colored inks and tempera in full color illustrations. In some black and white ones, I have also scratched with a razor blade the pen and ink line and then reworked for a long time to achieve a certain effect as in an etching (*The Carpet of Solomon, The Month Brothers, Runaway Jonah*). I have used a Japanese reed pen (*Maximilian's World*) and a Chinese brush (*The Silkspinners*)."

Shulevitz commented in his Caldecott Award acceptance speech: "There is no real distinction between 'art' and illustration, between old art and new art. There is only good art and bad art. While teaching, I have observed that one of the main reasons why students do poor illustration is that they maintain the distinction between 'art' and illustration.

"As a child I loved Rembrandt. I still do. His etchings are sublime illustrations. I have seen a landscape drawing of his at the Fogg Museum that looks like a Chinese painting. In Rembrandt the distinction between East and West, between child and adult, fades away. He was wise. But again, in his day many considered him a fool."

AVOCATIONAL INTERESTS: Art, music, old tales and parables of eastern traditions, yoga and tai-chi-chuan.

BIOGRAPHICAL/CRITICAL SOURCES: The Villager, October 3, 1963; *New York Herald Tribune,* October 6, 1963; *Chicago Tribune,* November 10, 1963; *Christian Science Monitor,* November 19, 1963, November 6, 1969; *Buffalo Evening News,* January 18, 1964; *Book Week* (children's section), May 7, 1967; *Graphis* (Zurich), Number 131, 1967; *School Library Journal,* May, 1969; *Horn Book,* August, 1969, December, 1969, June, 1971; *Commonweal,* November 21, 1969; *New York Times,* December 8, 1969; *New York Times Book Review,* September 21, 1969, September 19, 1970, September 8, 1971, April 15, 1973, November 3, 1974, April 29, 1979; Selma G. Lanes, *Down the Rabbit Hole,* Atheneum, 1971; *Washington Post Book World,* November 7, 1971; *Books of the Times,* December, 1979.

SHUMAN, Samuel I(rving) 1925-

PERSONAL: Born August 7, 1925, in Fall River, Mass.; son of Max (a realtor) and Fannie (Pearlmutter) Shuman; married Maria Barbetsea, March 22, 1964; children: two. *Education:* University of Pennsylvania, A.B., 1947, A.M., 1948, Ph.D., 1951; University of Michigan, J.D., 1954; Harvard University, S.J.D., 1959. *Home:* 3111 Kettering, Houston, Tex. 77027. *Office:* Art Tax Information Center, 1 West Loop S., Suite 703, Houston, Tex. 77027.

CAREER: University of Pennsylvania, Philadelphia, assistant instructor in philosophy, 1949-51; Wayne State University, Detroit, Mich., assistant professor, 1954-55, associate professor, 1955-57, professor of law, 1957-80, professor in department of psychiatry of School of Medicine; C. N. Davidson & Co. (securities brokers), Detroit, partner, 1957-71; Art Tax Information Center, Houston, Tex., president, 1980—. Assistant instructor in philosophy, Temple University, 1949-50; visiting professor of law, University of Michigan, spring, 1961, and University of Rome, springs, 1963 and 1964; lecturer, International Faculty of Comparative Law, Luxembourg, 1964; professor of forensic psychiatry, Lafayette Clinic, Michigan Department of Mental Health, beginning 1967; Franklin Lecturer, 1969. Research assistant, Legislative Research Center, University of Michigan, summers, 1953 and 1954. *Military service:* U.S. Army, 1944. *Member:* International Association for Legal and Political Philosophy, American Law Institute, American Society for Legal and Political Philosophy, Michigan Bar Association, Texas Bar Association. *Awards, honors:* Rockefeller Foundation grants, 1959 and 1961; Fulbright travel grant, 1961; Probus Club Award, 1963, for contribution to humanities.

WRITINGS: Broadcasting and Telecasting of Judicial and Legislative Proceedings, University of Michigan Press, 1956; *Legal Positivism: Its Scope and Limitations,* Wayne State University Press, 1963; (translator with Norbert D. West) *The Austrian Penal Act, 1852 and 1945 as Amended to 1965,* Fred B. Rothman, 1966; (compiler and author of introduction) *The Future of Federalism: The Law Center Dedication Lecture Series,* Wayne State University Press, 1968; (editor and contributor with Gray L. Dorsey) *Validation of New Forms of Social Organization,* Steiner Verlag (Weisbaden), 1968; (editor and contributor) *Law and Disorder: The Legitimation of Direct Action as an Instrument of Social Policy* (lectures), Wayne State University Press, 1971; (general editor with West) *American Law: An Introductory Survey of Some Principles—Cases and Text,* Wayne State University Press, 1971; (contributor) Frank J. Ayd, editor, *Medical, Moral and Legal Issues in Mental Health Care,* Robert E. Krieger, 1974; (contributor) J. C. Schoolar, editor, *Research and the Psychiatric Patient,* Brunner, 1975; (contributor) J. L. Tapp and F. J. Levine, editors, *Law, Justice and the Individual in Society: Psychological and Legal Issues,* Holt, 1977; (contributor) G. Dorsey, editor, *Equality and Freedom: International and Comparative Jurisprudence,* Oceana, 1977; *Psychosurgery and the Medical Control of Violence,* Wayne State University Press, 1977. American editor, *Archiv* (journal of the International Association for Philosophy of Law and Social Philosophy), 1962-79; member of editorial board, *American Journal of Jurisprudence,* 1969—.

*   *   *

SHY, John W(illard) 1931-

PERSONAL: Born March 23, 1931, in Dayton, Ohio; son of Willard Alden and Margaret (Brush) Shy. *Education:* U.S.

Military Academy, B.S., 1952; University of Vermont, M.A., 1957; Princeton University, Ph.D., 1961. *Office:* Department of History, University of Michigan, Ann Arbor, Mich. 48109.

CAREER: U.S. Army, commissioned second lieutenant of Infantry, 1952, served in Japan, 1952-55; Princeton University, Princeton, N.J., instructor, 1959-62, assistant professor, 1962-67, associate professor of history, 1967-68; University of Michigan, Ann Arbor, associate professor, 1968-70, professor of history, 1970—. *Member:* American Historical Association, American Antiquarian Society.

WRITINGS: (With Peter Paret) *Guerrillas in the 1960's,* Praeger, 1962; *Toward Lexington: The Role of the British Army in the Coming of the American Revolution,* Princeton University Press, 1965; (compiler) *The American Revolution,* AHM Publishing, 1973; *A People Numerous and Armed: Reflections on the Military Struggle for American Independence,* Oxford University Press (New York), 1976.

WORK IN PROGRESS: Books on the era of the American Revolution and on the military in Western societies, c. 1740-1850.

*   *   *

SILBERSTANG, Edwin 1930-

PERSONAL: Born January 11, 1930, in New York, N.Y.; son of Louis (a lawyer) and Fay (Berkowitz) Silberstang; divorced; children: Julian, Joyce, Allan. *Education:* University of Michigan, B.A., 1950; Brooklyn Law School, J.D., 1957. *Religion:* Jewish. *Agent:* Mary Yost, 75 East 55th St., New York, N.Y. 10022.

CAREER: Private practice of law in Brooklyn, N.Y., 1958-67; writer, 1967—. *Military service:* U.S. Army, special agent for Counter-Intelligence Corps., 1951-53. *Member:* Authors Guild.

WRITINGS: Rapt in Glory (novel), Pocket Books, 1964; *Nightmare of the Dark* (novel), Knopf, 1967; (editor) Erick Offner, *Worldwide Trademark Protection,* Fieldston, 1968; *Sweet Land of Liberty* (novel), Putnam, 1972; *Playboy's Book of Games,* Playboy Press, 1972; *Insider's Guide to Las Vegas,* John Mechigian, 1973; (editor) Robert Tsay, *Encyclopedia of Chinese Acupuncture,* New Chinese Medicine Association, 1974; *Losers Weepers* (novel), Doubleday, 1974.

Play Chess Tonight, G.B.C. Press, 1976; *Play Pinochle Tonight,* G.B.C. Press, 1976; *Smart Casino Play,* G.B.C. Press, 1977; *Snake Eyes* (novel), Dutton, 1977; *Winning Poker Strategy,* McKay, 1978; *How to Gamble and Win,* F. Watts, 1979; *Winning Casino Craps,* McKay, 1979; *Winner's Guide to Casino Gambling,* Holt, 1980; *Playboy's Guide to Casino Gambling,* four volumes, Seaview, 1980; *Abandoned* (novel), Doubleday, 1981.

SIDELIGHTS: "There is a paradox in my work," Edwin Silberstang writes. "I'm both a serious writer of novels and an author of games books. Beginning with *Playboy's Book of Games,* which was published in 1972, I was recognized as an authority on games and most of my published work has dealt with these games of skill and chance, such as chess and the casino games. However, I consider myself primarily a serious novelist. The reason I write is to express myself through my novels. The locales of my work have been varied, but the theme perhaps remains the same; the outcast from society, either voluntary or forced, and his struggle against that society."

SILVER, Daniel Jeremy 1928-

PERSONAL: Born March 26, 1928, in Cleveland, Ohio; son of Abba Hillel (a rabbi) and Virginia (Horkheimer) Silver; married Adele Zeidman, July 19, 1956; children: Jonathan Moses, Michael Louis, Sarah Jean. *Education:* Harvard University, A.B., 1948; Hebrew Union College, M.H.L. and Rabbi, 1952; University of Chicago, Ph.D., 1962. *Home:* 2841 Weybridge Rd., Cleveland, Ohio. *Office:* The Temple, University Circle and Silver Park, Cleveland, Ohio.

CAREER: Beth Torah Congregation, Chicago, Ill., rabbi, 1954-56; The Temple, Cleveland, Ohio, rabbi, 1956—. Adjunct professor of religion, Case Western Reserve University, 1960—, and Cleveland State University, 1969—. Chairman of academic advisory council, National Foundation for Jewish Culture; chairman of task force on Jewish identity, Central Conference of American Rabbis. Senior fellow, Oxford Post Graduate Center for Hebrew Studies, 1979. Vice-president, Cleveland Museum of Art. *Military service:* U.S. Navy, chaplain in Japan, 1952-54.

WRITINGS: From the Rabbi's Desk, The Temple, 1961; (editor) *In the Time of Harvest* (essays in honor of Silver's father, Abba Hillel Silver), Macmillan, 1963; *The Maimonidean Criticism and the Maimonidean Controversy (1180-1240),* E. J. Brill, 1965; (editor) *Judaism and Ethics,* Ktav, 1970; *A History of Judaism,* Basic Books, 1974. Also author of monographs, *The Retarded Child and Religious Education* and *The Twenty Third Psalm.* Senior editor, *CCAR Journal* (quarterly scholarly publication of Central Conference of American Rabbis), 1964-72.

WORK IN PROGRESS: Why Be a Jew; Moses, the Questionable Hero.

*   *   *

SILVIUS, G(eorge) Harold 1908-

PERSONAL: Born April 4, 1908, in Virdi, Minn.; son of George A. and Mell A. (Goodwin) Silvius; married Josephine O. Edinger, August 29, 1931; children: Diana Faye Gits. *Education:* Stout Institute (now University of Wisconsin—Stout), B.S., 1930; Wayne University (now Wayne State University), M.A., 1937; attended University of Michigan, 1943-44; Pennsylvania State University, Ed.D., 1946. *Home and office:* Art Centre Apartments, 201 East Kirby, Detroit, Mich. 48202.

CAREER: Detroit Public Schools, Detroit, Mich., teacher of industrial arts, 1929-41, assistant supervisor, 1941-45, supervisor of vocational education, 1945-50; Wayne State University, Detroit, assistant professor, 1941-45, associate professor, 1945-50, professor of industrial education and chairman of department, 1950-71, professor of vocational and applied arts, 1971-75, professor emeritus, 1975—. Visiting summer professor, Kent State University, 1938 and 1940, Pennsylvania State University, 1941, 1942, 1953, and 1959, Bradley University, 1949, Washington State University, 1966, and Iowa State University, 1974. Member of Michigan Curriculum Planning Committee for Industrial Arts, 1947-49; member of National Safety Council School Shop Safety Committee, 1948-49; member of national advisory committee, Ford Industrial Arts Award, 1955-58; member of advisory committee on youth employment, City of Detroit Commission on Children and Youth, 1958-71. Director of research projects. Lecturer in and consultant on matters pertaining to industrial, occupational, vocational, and technical education.

MEMBER: Professional Association of Career Education (life member), American Vocational Association (life member; vice-president and member of board of directors, 1962-65), American Industrial Arts Association, American Technical Education Association, American Council on Industrial Arts Teacher Education, American Technical Education Association, Association for Higher Education, National Association of Industrial Teacher Educators (president, 1947-48), National Council of Local Administrators of Vocational Education and Practical Arts, National Education Association, American Association of University Professors, Industrial Teacher Education Conference of the Mississippi Valley, New England Industrial Arts Teachers Association (honorary life member), Michigan Industrial Education Society (honorary life member), Michigan Occupational Education Association, Michigan Council of Local Administrators of Vocational Education and Practical Arts, Michigan Schoolmasters' Club, Detroit Industrial Education Society, Epsilon Pi Tau (laureate member), Iota Lambda Sigma, Phi Delta Kappa, Mu Sigma Pi, Phi Alpha Delta (honorary member). *Awards, honors:* Wayne State University Alumni Association Award, 1966, for twenty-five years of dedicated service in the field of education; University of Wisconsin—Stout Distinguished Alumni Award, 1974; American Vocational Association SHIP Citation, 1975, for outstanding contributions to vocational education.

WRITINGS: (With Gerald B. Baysinger) *Safe Work Practice in Sheet Metal Work,* American Technical Society, 1949; (with Baysinger) *Safe Work Practice in Woodworking,* American Technical Society, 1951, revised and enlarged edition (with Baysinger and K. T. Olsen) published as *Safe Practices in Woodworking and Plastics,* 1955; (with E. H. Curry) *Teaching Successfully the Industrial and Vocational Subjects,* McKnight, 1953, revised and enlarged edition published as *Teaching Successfully in Industrial Education,* 1967; (with Curry) *Teaching Multiple Activities in Industrial Education,* McKnight, 1956, revised and enlarged edition published as *Managing Multiple Activities in Industrial Education,* 1971; (with Baysinger) *The Student Planning Book,* 4th edition, Van Nostrand, 1960; (with Ralph C. Bohn) *Organizing Course Materials for Industrial Education,* McKnight, 1961, revised edition published as *Planning and Organizing Instruction,* 1976. Also author of numerous curriculum guides, syllabi, and brochures published by professional and state associations. Contributor to *Dictionary of Education.* Contributor of over fifty articles to professional journals. Editor-in-chief, *Guild News* (publication of industrial arts department, Wayne State University), 1947-72; member of editorial advisory board, *School Shop,* 1952-56; industrial arts editor, *American Vocational Journal,* 1957-63.

WORK IN PROGRESS: Third editions of *Teaching Successfully in Industrial Education, Managing Multiple Activities in Industrial Education,* and *Planning and Organizing Instruction;* conducting a national study to determine what is needed in the way of professional materials for the preparation and upgrading of teachers for vocational and applied arts education.

*   *   *

SIMMONS, Ernest J(oseph) 1903-1972

PERSONAL: Born December 8, 1903, in Lawrence, Mass.; died May 3, 1972; son of Mark and Annie (McKinnon) Simmons; married Winifred McNamara, June 20, 1940; children: Richard. *Education:* Harvard University, B.A. 1925, M.A., 1926, Ph.D., 1928. *Residence:* Dublin, N.H.

CAREER: Harvard University, Cambridge, Mass., 1929-40,

began as instructor, became assistant professor; Cornell University, Ithaca, N.Y., 1941-45, began as associate professor, became professor of Slavic languages and chairman of department; Columbia University, New York, N.Y., professor of Slavic languages and chairman of department, and professor of Russian literature, 1946-59. Phi Beta Kappa Visiting Scholar in the United States and Europe, 1959-61, 1964-65; Danforth Lecturer in the United States and Europe, 1961-63; Patten Foundation Lecturer, Indiana University, 1964; Wesleyan University, Center for Advanced Studies, senior fellow, 1963-64, 1966, acting director, 1967. Trustee, Sarah Lawrence College, 1955-58. Member of cultural mission to U.S.S.R. for American Council of Learned Societies, 1947. Consultant, Ford Foundation, 1961-63. *Member:* Modern Language Association of America (member of executive council, 1953-54), Century Club (New York), Harvard Club (New York). *Awards, honors:* Grants from Harvard University and from foundations for foreign travel; L.H.D., Northwestern University, 1968.

WRITINGS: English Literature and Culture in Russia, 1553-1840, Harvard University Press, 1935, reprinted, Octagon, 1964; *Pushkin,* Harvard University Press, 1937, reprinted, Peter Smith, 1971; *Dostoevsky: The Making of a Novelist,* Oxford University Press, 1940; *An Outline of Modern Russian Literature, 1880-1940,* Cornell University Press, 1943, reprinted, Greenwood Press, 1971; *Leo Tolstoy,* Little, Brown, 1946; *Russian Fiction and Soviet Ideology,* Columbia University Press, 1958; *Chekhov: A Biography,* Little, Brown, 1962; *Introduction to Russian Realism,* Indiana University Press, 1965; *Introduction to Tolstoy's Writings,* University of Chicago Press, 1968; *Feodor Dostoevsky,* Columbia University Press, 1969; *Tolstoy,* Routledge & Kegan Paul, 1973.

Editor: (With Samuel H. Cross) *Centennial Essays for Pushkin,* Harvard University Press, 1937, reprinted, Russell, 1964; (with Alexander Kaun) *Slavic Studies,* Cornell University Press, 1943, reprinted, Books for Libraries Press, 1972; (with Roman Jakobson) *Russian Epic Studies,* American Folklore Society, 1949; Ivan Turgenev, *Fathers and Children,* Harcourt, 1949; Leo Tolstoy, *War and Peace,* abridged edition, Harcourt, 1972.

Editor and author of introduction: *Through the Glass of Soviet Literature: Views of Russian Society,* Columbia University Press, 1953; *Continuity and Change in Russian and Soviet Thought,* Harvard University Press, 1955; *Pushkin,* Dell, 1961; Tolstoy, *Selected Essays,* Modern Library, 1964; Tolstoy, *Short Stories,* two volumes, Random House, 1964-65; Tolstoy, *Short Novels: Stories of Love, Seduction, and Peasant Life,* Volume I, Modern Library, 1965. Author of approximately two hundred articles, reviews and translations. Contributor to *Atlantic Monthly, Nation,* and *New Republic.* Editor, *American Slavic and East European Review,* 1946-49, and *Columbia Slavic Studies.*

SIDELIGHTS: Ernest J. Simmons travelled extensively for research and conference purposes. His travels included several trips to the Soviet Union and a tour of India.†

* * *

SINGER, Marcus George   1926-

PERSONAL: Born January 4, 1926, in New York, N.Y.; son of David E. and Esther (Kobre) Singer; married Blanche Ladenson, 1947; children: Karen Beth, Debra Ann. *Education:* University of Illinois, A.B., 1948; Cornell University, Ph.D., 1952. *Home:* 5021 Regent St. Madison, Wis. 53705. *Office:* Helen C. White Hall, University of Wisconsin, Madison, Wis. 53706.

CAREER: Cornell University, Ithaca, N.Y., instructor, 1951-52; University of Wisconsin—Madison, instructor, 1952-55, assistant professor, 1955-59, associate professor, 1959-63, professor of philosophy, 1963—, chairman of department, 1963-68. Chairman of philosophy department, University of Wisconsin Center System, 1964-66. Cowling Visiting Professor of Philosophy, Carleton College, fall, 1972; Francis M. Bernardin Distinguished Visiting Professor of Humanities, University of Missouri—Kansas City, spring, 1979. Visiting professor of humanities, University of Florida, 1975; visiting fellow, University of Warwick, 1977. *Military service:* U.S. Army Air Forces, 1944-45. *Member:* American Association of University Professors, American Society for Political and Legal Philosophy, International Association for Philosophy of Law and Social Philosophy, American Association for the Advancement of Science, American Philosophical Association, Royal Institute of Philosophy, Americans for Democratic Action, Aristotelian Society, Mind Association, Phi Beta Kappa, Phi Kappa Phi. *Awards, honors:* American Philosophical Association fellowship, 1956-57; Guggenheim fellow, 1962-63; visiting fellow, Birkbeck College, London, 1962-63.

WRITINGS: (Contributor) *Essays in Moral Philosophy,* edited by A. I. Melden, University of Washington Press, 1958; *Generalization in Ethics,* Knopf, 1961, 2nd edition, Atheneum, 1971; (co-editor) *Introductory Readings in Philosophy,* Scribner, 1962, 2nd edition, 1974; (co-editor) *Reason and the Common Good: Selected Essays of Arthur E. Murphy,* Prentice-Hall, 1963; (co-editor) *Belief, Knowledge, and Truth,* Scribner, 1970; (contributor) *Skepticism and Moral Principles,* New University Press, 1973; (editor) *Morals and Values,* Scribner, 1977. Contributor to encyclopedias and professional journals.

WORK IN PROGRESS: Particularization in Ethics; Justification and Proof in Ethics; Institutional Ethics.

* * *

SISSON, C(harles) H(ubert)   1914-

PERSONAL: Born April 22, 1914, in Bristol, England; son of Richard Percy and Ellen Minnie (Worlock) Sisson; married Nora Gilbertson, 1937; children: Janet, Hilary. *Education:* University of Bristol, B.A., 1934; graduate study at University of Berlin and University of Freiburg, 1934-35, and the Sorbonne, University of. Paris, 1935-36. *Home:* Moorfield Cottage, The Hill, Langport, Somerset TA10 9PU, England.

CAREER: Ministry of Labour, London, England, assistant principal, 1936-42, principal, 1945-53, assistant secretary, 1953-62, under secretary, 1962-68; Department of Employment, London, assistant under secretary of state, 1968-71, director of Occupational Safety and Health, 1971-73. *Military service:* British Army, Intelligence Corps, 1942-45; became sergeant. *Awards, honors:* Senior Simon research fellow, University of Manchester, beginning 1956; D.Litt., University of Bristol, 1980.

WRITINGS: An Asiatic Romance (novel), Gabberbocchus, 1953; *The Spirit of British Administration and Some European Comparisons,* Praeger, 1959, 2nd edition, Faber, 1966; *Christopher Homm* (novel), Methuen, 1965; *Art and Action* (essays), Methuen, 1965; *Essays,* privately printed, 1967; *English Poetry, 1900-1950: An Assessment,* Hart-Davis, 1971; *The Case of Walter Bagehot,* Faber, 1972; *David Hume,* Ramsay Head Press, 1976; *The English Sermon: An Anthology,* Volume II, Carcanet Press, 1976; (editor) David Wright, *South African Album* (poems), Philip Publisher

(Cape Town, South Africa), 1976; (editor) Jonathon Swift, *Selected Poems*, Carcanet New Press, 1977; *The Avoidance of Literature* (collected essays), Carcanet New Press, 1978; (translator) *Some Tales of La Fontaine*, Carcanet New Press, 1979.

Poems: *Versions and Perversions of Heine*, Gaberbocchus, 1955; *Poems*, Peter Russell, 1959; *Twenty-One Poems*, privately printed, 1960; *The London Zoo*, Abelard, 1961; *Numbers*, Methuen, 1965; (translator) *The Poetry of Catullus*, MacGibbon & Kee, 1966, Orion Press, 1967; *The Discarnation: Or, How the Flesh Became Word and Dwelt Among Us*, privately printed, 1967; *Metamorphoses*, Methuen, 1968; *Roman Poems*, privately printed, 1968; *In the Trojan Ditch: Collected Poems and Selected Translations*, Carcanet Press, 1974; *The Corridor*, Mandeville Press, 1975; (translator) *The Poetic Art: A Translation of Horace's "Ars Poetica,"* Carcanet Press, 1975; (translator) Lucretius, *De Rerum Natura: The Poem on Nature*, Carcanet New Press, 1976; *Anchises*, Carcanet New Press, 1976; (translator) *The Divine Comedy of Dante*, Carcanet New Press, 1980; *Exactions*, Carcanet New Press, 1980. Also editor of *The Variorum Edition of the Complete Poems of Thomas Hardy*. Contributor to *New English Weekly*, 1937-49, *X*, 1960-62, *Poetry Nation* and *Poetry Nation Review*, 1973—, and to *Times Literary Supplement*, 1975—. Co-editor, *Poetry Nation Review*, 1976—.

SIDELIGHTS: C. H. Sisson did not begin to publish his poetry until he was well into middle-age. He told *CA:* "I wrote verse as a child and as an adolescent; I gave it up; I started again when I was a soldier during the war; gave it up again; started again; have often resolved to give it up but never quite succeeded." Until his retirement, Sisson was employed as a civil servant in the Ministry of Labor. "It has never occurred to me," he maintains, "that I could earn my living by writing, or that it would be desirable to put myself in a position where I had to do so. Most of my life has been spent in practical affairs, and in a sense all my writing has been occasional." Sisson believes that "ideally, one should speak, whether in prose or verse, because one has something to say, and not otherwise."

Much of what Sisson has to say is politically critical and satirical. His poetry, according to Donald Hall, is "frequently . . . concerned with national spirit and with the mystery of nationhood." At the same time, Hall comments that Sisson's "ideas" can be "religious and moral as well as political." Hall believes that Sisson "detests the present world" and that his work offers "small sense of possible change except for the worse." In his review of *Metamorphoses*, John Press also notes Sisson's "sombre philosophy of life," adding that the "gloom" is "accentuated rather than relieved by an acrid wit." Kenneth Cox writes that Sisson uses "without warning various degrees of irony, from deadpan ambiguity to open derision."

"At his best," writes Roger Garfitt, "Sisson is clearly an important poet, concerned to set the received unit of poetic thought against the disintegration of the modern mind." Sisson has said: "I am recorded as having said in an interview that 'I would judge my prose and poetry as being, in a sense, no more than an ironic contribution to a hopeless situation.' About that there is a touch of the drama which such occasions call for; I would add only that the number of writers who matter, in each generation, is small, and that the number does not increase *pro rata* with the population."

BIOGRAPHICAL/CRITICAL SOURCES: Times Literary Supplement, February 15, 1968, November 29, 1974, January 28, 1977, September 26, 1980; *Punch*, March 27, 1968; *Agenda*, summer-autumn, 1970, autumn, 1974; *Observer*, May 5, 1974; *Listener*, May 9, 1974; *London Magazine*, October-November, 1974; *New Statesman*, April 22, 1977; *New York Times Book Review*, December 18, 1977, April 27, 1980; *Contemporary Literary Criticism*, Volume VIII, Gale, 1978.

*   *   *

SKLAR, Kathryn Kish 1939-

PERSONAL: Born December 26, 1939, in Columbus, Ohio; daughter of William Edward and Elizabeth Sue (Rhodes) Kish; married Robert Sklar (a historian), 1958 (divorced, 1979); children: Leonard, Susan. *Education:* Radcliffe College, A.B., 1965; University of Michigan, Ph.D., 1969. *Office:* Department of History, University of California, Los Angeles, Calif. 90024.

CAREER: University of Michigan, Ann Arbor, assistant professor of history, 1969-74; University of California, Los Angeles, associate professor of history, 1974—. *Member:* American Historical Association, Organization of American Historians, American Studies Association, Conference Group in Women's History, West Coast Association of Women Historians, Berkshire Conference of Women Historians, Phi Beta Kappa. *Awards, honors:* Woodrow Wilson fellowship, 1965-67; Danforth Foundation fellowship, 1967-69; Ford Foundation fellowship for study of the role of women in society, 1973-74; fellow of Radcliffe Institute of Harvard University, 1973-74; National Book Award nomination, 1974, for *Catherine Beecher;* Annual prize, Berkshire Conference of Women Historians, 1975; National Humanities Institute fellowship, 1975-76.

WRITINGS: Catherine Beecher: A Study of American Domesticity, Yale University Press, 1973; (author of introduction) Catherine Beecher, *A Treatise on Domestic Economy*, Schocken, 1977; (contributor) Carol Berkin and Mary Beth Norton, editors, *Women in America: Original Essays and Documents*, Houghton, 1979; (contributor) Cullom Davis and others, editors, *The Public and the Private Lincoln*, Southern Illinois University Press, 1980. Also author of pamphlet, *Recent Scholarship by U.S. Historians on the History of Women*, American Historical Association. Contributor to journals, including *University of Michigan Papers in Women's Studies* and *Feminist Studies*.

WORK IN PROGRESS: A history of urban working-class women from 1870 to 1910.

*   *   *

SLAVIN, Arthur Joseph 1933-

PERSONAL: Born February 15, 1933, in Brooklyn, N.Y.; son of David and Mildred (Eisner) Slavin; married Camille Marie LeBlanc (a registered nurse), June 19, 1954; married second wife, Inger-Johanne Espe, November 30, 1968; children: (first marriage) Ruth, Aaron, Rebecca, Laura; (second marriage) Solveig. *Education:* Attended New York University, 1950-51; Louisiana State University, A.B. (magna cum laude), 1958; University of North Carolina, Ph.D., 1961. *Politics:* Independent Socialist. *Office:* Department of Humanities, University of Louisville, Louisville, Ky.

CAREER: Bucknell University, Lewisburg, Pa., assistant professor of history, 1961-65; University of California, Los Angeles, assistant professor, 1965-66, associate professor of history, 1966-74; University of Louisville, Louisville, Ky., dean of College of Arts and Sciences, 1974-77, Justus Bier

Distinguished Professor, 1977—. Visiting assistant professor of history, Louisiana State University, Baton Rouge, 1963-64; Clark Library lecturer, 1977. Member of board of consultants, National Endowment for the Humanities, 1976—. *Military service:* U.S. Air Force, 1951-55. *Member:* International Commission for the History of Parliamentary and Representative Institutions, American Historical Association, Renaissance Society of America, Conference on British Studies, Royal Historical Society (life fellow), other organizations. *Awards, honors:* Woodrow Wilson fellow, 1958-59; Southern Teaching Fellowship Foundation fellow, 1958-61; grants-in-aid from American Philosophical Society, 1965, and American Council of Learned Societies, 1966 and 1969; Folger Library, fellow, 1965, senior research fellow, 1970-71; University of California Humanities Institute fellow, 1966 and 1968; Guggenheim fellow, 1967-68; Huntington Library fellow, 1975; Danforth Foundation associate, 1979-85; National Endowment for the Humanities fellow, 1980-81.

WRITINGS: Politics and Profit: A Study of Sir Ralph Sadler, 1507-1547, Cambridge University Press, 1966; *The Precarious Balance: England, 1450-1640,* Knopf, 1973; *The Way of the West,* three volumes, Wiley, 1973-75; (contributor) F. Chiappelli, editor, *First Images of America,* two volumes, University of California Press, 1976.

Editor: (And author of introduction) *The New Monarchies and Representative Assemblies: Medieval Constitutionalism or Modern Absolutism?,* Heath, 1964; (and author of introduction) *Henry VIII and the English Reformation,* Heath, 1968; *Humanism, Reform and Reformation in England,* Wiley, 1969; (with Eugene C. Black) *Thomas Cromwell on Church and Commonweath: Selected Letters, 1523-1540,* Harper, 1969; (and contributor) *Tudor Men and Institutions: Studies in English Law and Government,* Louisiana State University, 1972; *The Borzoi History of England,* five volumes, Knopf, 1973-75. Contributor of numerous articles to scholarly journals in England and America.

WORK IN PROGRESS: A book about Lord Chancellor Thomas Wriothesley, *Politics and Power,* as a sequel to the Sadler study; a study of Thomas Cromwell and the revolution of the 1530s in England, for Knopf; a book-length study of aspects of the work of George Orwell; *Norwegian Jews under Nazi Rule.*

SIDELIGHTS: Arthur Joseph Slavin writes: "Since 1975 I have brought my academic and political concerns into closer relationship. Specifically, my interest in politics, government, and the history of both, now focus on twentieth century subjects. As I conclude more than a quarter of a century of writing on England in the crucible of religious revolution, I actively investigate the great crisis of liberty in the 1930s and 1940s, both in its impact on literature (Orwell's fiction and the destruction of memory, personality, history and freedom) and the ideas of citizenship, *egalite* and brotherhood (the Jews under Nazi rule). I anticipate that my writing in the 1980s will concentrate wholly on aspects of twentieth century culture and politics."

AVOCATIONAL INTERESTS: Collecting graphics and recordings of baroque, classical, and modern music.

BIOGRAPHICAL/CRITICAL SOURCES: Times Literary Supplement, February 23, 1967.

*   *   *

SLUSSER, Robert M(elville) 1916-

PERSONAL: Born May 14, 1916, in Downers Grove, Ill.; son of Thomas Harry and Martha (Downer) Slusser; married

Elizabeth A.P. Burbury, 1944; children: Virginia, Paul, James. *Education:* University of Chicago, B.A., 1941; Columbia University, M.A., 1960, Ph.D., 1963. *Home:* 131 Lexington Ave., East Lansing, Mich. 48823. *Office:* Department of History, Michigan State University, East Lansing, Mich. 48824.

CAREER: Johns Hopkins University, Baltimore, Md., associate professor of history, 1963-71; Michigan State University, East Lansing, professor of history, 1971—. *Military service:* U.S. Army, Intelligence, 1943-46; became lieutenant colonel. *Member:* Phi Beta Kappa.

WRITINGS: (With Simon Wolin) *The Soviet Secret Police,* Praeger, 1957; (with Jan F. Triska), *A Calendar of Soviet Treaties, 1917-1957,* Stanford University Press, 1959; (with Triska) *Theory, Law and Policy of Soviet Treaties,* Stanford University Press, 1962; (with Xenia J. Eudin) *Soviet Foreign Policy, 1928-1934,* Pennsylvania State University Press, 1967; *The Berlin Crisis of 1961,* Johns Hopkins University Press, 1973. Editor, *Soviet Economic Policy in Postwar Germany,* Research Program on U.S.S.R., 1953.

WORK IN PROGRESS: Moscow and the Making of a President, 1960, for Johns Hopkins University Press; with George Ginsburgs, *A Calendar of Soviet Treaties, 1958-1973,* for Sijthoff.

*   *   *

SMITH, Anthony (John Francis) 1926-

PERSONAL: Born March 30, 1926, in Maidenhead, England; son of Hubert J. F. (a land agent) and Diana (Watkin) Smith; married Barbara Dorothy Newman (a journalist and economist), September 1, 1956. *Education:* Balliol College, Oxford, M.A., 1951. *Home:* 9 Skeeles Rd., London N.W. 3, England. *Agent:* Curtis Brown Ltd., 1 Craven Hill, London W2 3EP, England.

CAREER: Guardian, Manchester, England, reporter, 1953, 1956-57; general manager, *Drum,* West Africa, 1954-55; *Daily Telegraph,* London, England, science editor, 1957-63; currently free-lance writer. Has appeared on more than 600 radio programs and 50 television programs; presenter of television series, including "Great Zoos," "Great Parks," and "Wilderness," and a radio series, "A Sideways Look At . . . ." *Military service:* Royal Air Force, four years. *Member:* Association of British Science Writers, Explorers Club (New York).

WRITINGS: Blind White Fish in Persia, Dutton, 1953; *Sea Never Dry,* Allen & Unwin, 1958; *High Street Africa,* Allen & Unwin, 1961; *Jambo: African Balloon Safari,* Dutton, 1963 (published in England as *Throw Out Two Hands,* Allen & Unwin, 1963); *The Body,* Walker, 1968, 2nd edition, Allen & Unwin, 1970; *The Seasons: Life and Its Rhythms,* Harcourt, 1970 (published in England as *The Seasons: Rhythms of Life, Cycles of Change,* Weidenfeld & Nicolson, 1970); *The Dangerous Sort: The Story of a Balloon,* Allen & Unwin, 1970; *Mato Grosso: Last Virgin Land,* Dutton, 1971; *Beside the Seaside,* Allen & Unwin, 1972; (with Jill Southam) *Good Beach Guide,* Allen & Unwin, 1973; *The Human Pedigree,* Lippincott, 1975; *Animals on View,* Weidenfeld & Nicolson, 1977; *Wilderness,* Allen & Unwin, 1978; *A Persian Quarter Century,* Hodder & Stoughton, 1979. Also author of commentary for television films, including "Balloon over Africa" series. Contributor of articles to magazines, including *Saturday Evening Post* and *New Scientist.*

SIDELIGHTS: Kestrel Productions produced a film version of *The Body* in 1969.

BIOGRAPHICAL/CRITICAL SOURCES: Book World, June 16, 1968; *New York Times Book Review,* October 20, 1968.

*   *   *

SMITH, Elinor Goulding 1917-

PERSONAL: Born 1917, in New York, N.Y.; daughter of Monroe S. and Laura (Joachim) Goulding; married Robert Paul Smith, 1940; children: Daniel, Joseph. *Education:* Attended Cornell University, 1932-34. *Agent:* McIntosh & Otis, Inc., 475 Fifth Ave., New York, N.Y. 10016.

WRITINGS—All published by Harcourt, except as indicated: *The Complete Book of Absolutely Perfect Housekeeping,* 1956; *The Complete Book of Absolutely Perfect Baby and Child Care,* 1957; *Confessions of Mrs. Smith,* 1958; *The Battered Bride,* 1960; *Elinor Goulding Smith's Great Big Messy Book,* Dial, 1962; *Nobody Really Likes a Nervous Cow,* Doubleday, 1965; *That's Me Always Making History,* Putnam, 1967; *Horses, History, and Havoc,* Collins, World, 1969.†

*   *   *

SMITH, Frederick E(screet) 1922-
(David Farrell)

PERSONAL: Born April 4, 1922, in Hull, Yorkshire, England; son of Harry Sydney and Elma Constance (Escreet) Smith; married Shelagh McGrath, July 7, 1945; children: Raymond Peter, Kevan Frederick. *Education:* Attended high school in Hull, England. *Home:* 3 Hathaway Rd., Southbourne, Bournemouth, Dorsetshire BH6 3HH, England. *Agent:* Deborah Rogers Ltd., 5-11 Mortimer St., London W1N 7RH, England.

CAREER: Hull Corp., Hull, England, local government officer, 1939-40, 1946-47; Premier Steel Products, Cape Town, South Africa, cost accountant, 1948-52; free-lance writer, 1952—. *Military service:* Royal Air Force, served in Britain, Africa, and with South East Asia Command, 1940-46. *Member:* Writers Guild, Pathfinders Association. *Awards, honors:* Mark Twain Literary Award, 1967, for *A Killing for the Hawks.*

WRITINGS: Of Masks and Minds, Hutchinson, 1954; *Laws Be Their Enemy,* Hutchinson, 1955; *633 Squadron,* Hutchinson, 1956, Bantam, 1979; *Lydia Trendennis,* Hutchinson, 1957; *The Sin and the Sinners,* Jarrolds, 1958; *The Grotto of Tiberius,* Hodder & Stoughton, 1961; *The Devil behind Me,* Hoddard & Stoughton, 1962; *The Storm Knight,* Harrap, 1966; *A Killing for the Hawks,* Harrap, 1966, McKay, 1967, reprinted, Cassell, 1980; *Waterloo,* Pan Books, 1969; *The Wider Sea of Love,* Harrap, 1969; *The Tormented,* Cassell, 1974; *633 Squadron: Operation Rhine Maiden,* Cassell, 1975, Bantam, 1979; *Saffron's War,* Futura, 1975; *Saffron's Army,* Futura, 1976; *633 Squadron: Operation Crucible,* Cassell, 1977, Bantam, 1979; *633 Squadron: Operation Valkyrie,* Cassell, 1978, Bantam, 1979; *The War God,* Cassell, 1980. Also author of a play, "The Glass Prison," produced in London, 1953.

Under pseudonym David Farrell; published by Gresham, except as indicated: *Temptation Isle,* 1962; *The Other Cousin,* 1962; *Two Loves,* 1963; *Valley of Conflict,* 1966; *Strange Enemy,* R. Hale, 1966; *Mullion Rock,* Harrap, 1969.

Also author of material for radio and television programs. Contributor of more than eighty short stories and travel articles to magazines in Britain, ten other European countries, South Africa, Canada, Australia, New Zealand, and the Philippines.

WORK IN PROGRESS: Two more books in the "633 Squadron" series.

SIDELIGHTS: Frederick E. Smith has traveled in twenty-two countries and, if necessary, "lives hard" in an effort to make his novels more authentic. For example, he once spent two weeks in Lapland walking over two hundred miles (encountering no other human being for eight days) in order to get the feel of the country before writing *The Devil behind Me.* For *Laws Be Their Enemy,* Smith disguised himself as a colored man and visited shabeens in the crime quarter of Cape Town.

AVOCATIONAL INTERESTS: Sports, conversation.

BIOGRAPHICAL/CRITICAL SOURCES: Bournemouth Evening Echo, September 12, 1963; *Bournemouth Times,* September 13, 1963; *Johannesburg Star,* November 2, 1963; *Best Sellers,* October 1, 1967; *New York Times Book Review,* October 8, 1967.

*   *   *

SMITH, Vian (Crocker) 1920-1969

PERSONAL: Born February 2, 1920, in Totnes, Devon, England; died December 9, 1969; son of Albert George Smith (a carpenter) and Mary Laura (Crocker) Smith; married Susan Spark, August 6, 1942; children: Robert, Stroma, Mark, Penelope, Andrew. *Education:* Attended King Edward VI Grammar School, Totnes, Devon. *Politics:* "No orthodox party—generally radical." *Religion:* Protestant. *Home:* Netherton Farmhouse, Totnes, Devon, England. *Agent:* Winant, Towers Ltd., 14 Clifford's Inn, London EC4A 1DA, England; and Monica McCall, 667 Madison Ave., New York, N.Y.

CAREER: Traveled widely through England, Ireland, and northern France; joined traveling repertory company; worked as free-lance journalist until 1950; feature and news editor of South Devon newspapers until 1963; full-time writer, beginning 1963. *Military service:* British Army, 1939-46.

WRITINGS: Song of the Unsung, Hodder & Stoughton, 1945; *Candles to the Dawn,* Hodder & Stoughton, 1946; *Hungry Waters,* Hodder & Stoughton, 1947; *Hand of the Wind,* Hodder & Stoughton, 1948; *Holiday for Laughter,* Hodder & Stoughton, 1948; *So Many Worlds,* Hodder & Stoughton, 1949.

Press Gang, P. Davies, 1961; *Question Mark,* P. Davies, 1961, published as *Pride of Moor* (Literary Guild selection), Doubleday, 1962; *Genesis Down,* P. Davies, 1962, Doubleday, 1963; *Green Heart* (Literary Guild selection), Doubleday, 1964; *Martin Rides the Moor* (juvenile novel), Constable, 1964, Doubleday, 1965; *The First Thunder,* Doubleday, 1965; *The Horses of Petrock* (juvenile novel), Constable, 1965; *A Second Chance,* Doubleday, 1966; *Tall and Proud* (juvenile), Doubleday, 1966 (published in England as *King Sam,* Constable, 1966); *Portrait of Dartmoor* (nonfiction), R. Hale, 1966; *Come Down the Mountain* (juvenile), Doubleday, 1967; *A Horse Called Freddie,* Stanley Paul, 1967; *Point-to-Point* (nonfiction), Stanley Paul, 1968; *The Wind Blows Free* (adult), Doubleday, 1968; *The Lord Mayor's Show* (juvenile), Longmans Young Books, 1968, Doubleday, 1969; *Moon in the River,* Longmans Young Books, 1969; *The Grand National: A History of the World's Greatest Steeplechase* (nonfiction), Stanley Paul, 1969, A. S. Barnes, 1970; *The Minstrel Boy* (adult), Doubleday, 1970; *Vian Smith's Parade of Horses* (juvenile), Longmans, Green, 1970, published as *Horses in the Green Valley,* Doubleday, 1971.

Radio plays; all produced on BBC radio, London: "Inherit the Earth," "Come Down the Mountain," "The Boy Who Made It," "When Sam Was King," "The White Stallion," "Green Heart," "Three O'Clock on the Sixteenth," "Sunday Morning on the Hill."

Television plays: "Giants on Saturday," for BBC-TV, and "The First Thunder," for ITV.

SIDELIGHTS: Vian Smith was often praised for his ability to create believable characters, especially in his numerous books for children. Commenting on *Tall and Proud,* the story of a handicapped girl who is motivated to learn to walk again as a result of her desire to ride her new horse, a critic in *Young Readers' Review* noted that "basically, it is a story which could be very sticky—[but] it isn't. As he showed in *Martin Rides the Moor,* the author knows children. . . . *Tall and Proud* deserves a wide audience—it's far above the usual horse story. Just as a story of a handicapped girl struggling to overcome her handicap it is well worth reading."

Polly Goodwin of *Book World* called *Come Down the Mountain,* the story of Brenda, a fat, unpopular schoolgirl who finds a new direction in her life after taking responsibility for an abandoned horse, a "thoughtful, well-written, and engrossing novel, . . . which should evoke an eager response from young animal lovers." A reviewer in *New Statesman* considered it a better novel than *National Velvet,* for "in the older book only the horse is treated on a roundly realistic level; the theme is high farce, the lower-class characters lovable, exuberant comics. Mr. Vian Smith's horse is real enough, . . . but no more so than the school-bus load, Evie the come-and-get-it teenager, Brian the school hero, Harold the Drip; no more so than Brenda's relationship with her parents, or with her grandfather, the old huntsman."

Vian Smith's manuscripts and correspondence are preserved in a collection at the Boston University Library.

AVOCATIONAL INTERESTS: The nineteenth century, especially the middle years; horses, steeplechase racing, all sports.

BIOGRAPHICAL/CRITICAL SOURCES: Young Readers' Review, March, 1967; *New Statesman,* November 3, 1967; *Book World,* July 7, 1968; *New York Times Book Review,* July 28, 1968; *Best Sellers,* June 1, 1969; *Books & Bookmen,* December, 1969.†

*   *   *

SNELL, John Leslie, Jr. 1923-1972

PERSONAL: Born June 2, 1923, in Plymouth, N.C.; died May 27, 1972, in Chapel Hill, N.C.; son of John Leslie, Sr. (a federal employee) and Lessie Ann (McLamb) Snell; married Maxine Pybas, December 18, 1943; children: Marcia Ruth, John McCullough, Leslie Ann. *Education:* University of North Carolina, A.B., 1946, M.A., 1947, Ph.D., 1950. *Politics:* Democrat. *Religion:* Methodist.

CAREER: University of North Carolina at Chapel Hill, instructor in social science, 1946-49; University of Wichita, Wichita, Kan., assistant professor of history, 1949-51; Tulane University, New Orleans, La., 1953-66, began as assistant professor, professor of history, 1959-66, dean of Graduate School, 1963-66; University of Pennsylvania, Philadelphia, professor of history, 1966-68; University of North Carolina at Chapel Hill, University Distinguished Professor of History, 1968-72. Visiting summer professor, University of Tennessee, 1947, University of Michigan, 1953, Vanderbilt University, 1954, and Stanford University, 1963. Member, Friends of the Library, University of North Caro-

lina. *Military service:* U.S. Army Air Forces, 1943-45; bomber pilot, European theater; became first lieutenant; received Air Medal, Distinguished Flying Cross. *Member:* American Historical Association, American Association of University Professors, Southern Historical Association, Omicron Delta Kappa, Phi Alpha Theta, University of North Carolina Alumni Association. *Awards, honors:* American Council of Learned Societies Scholar for postdoctoral research at Stanford University, 1951-52, and at Library of Congress and National Archives, 1952-53.

WRITINGS: (Editor and co-author) *The Meaning of Yalta: Big Three Diplomacy and the New Balance of Power,* Louisiana State University Press, 1956; *Wartime Origins of the East-West Dilemma over Germany,* Hauser, 1959; (editor) *The Nazi Revolution: Germany's Guilt or Germany's Fate?,* Heath, 1959, revised edition (with Allan Mitchell) published as *The Nazi Revolution: Hitler's Dictatorship and the German Nation,* 1973; (editor) *European History in the South,* Tulane University, 1960; (editor) *The Outbreak of the Second World War: Design or Blunder?,* Heath, 1962; (with Dexter Perkins) *The Education of Historians in the United States,* McGraw, 1962; *Illusion and Necessity: The Diplomacy of Global War, 1939-1945,* Houghton, 1963; (editor) *War and Totalitarianism, 1870 to the Present,* Heath, 1966; *The Democratic Movement in Germany, 1789-1914,* edited by Hans A. Schmitt, University of North Carolina Press, 1976. Contributor to *Encyclopedia Americana* and to history journals in the United States and Europe.†

*   *   *

SNELLGROVE, L(aurence) E(rnest) 1928-

PERSONAL: Born February 2, 1928, in Woolwich, London, England; son of Ernest George and Emily (Wren) Snellgrove; married Jean Hall, April 5, 1951; children: Peter Laurence. *Education:* Culham College, teacher's certificate, Associate of College of Preceptors, 1953; *Religion:* Church of England. *Home:* 23 Harvest Hill, East Grinstead, Sussex, England.

CAREER: Assistant master of Rose Hill School, Oxford, England, 1950-53, Cheshunt County Secondary School, Hertfordshire, England, 1953-55, and Yaxley School, Huntingdonshire, England, 1955-57; Caterham Valley County Secondary School, Surrey, England, head of history department, 1957-66; de Stafford Comprehensive School, Caterham, Surrey, head of history department, 1966-73; writer and lecturer, 1973—. *Military service:* Royal Air Force, 1945-48; became leading aircraftsman.

WRITINGS—All published by Longmans, Green through 1970 and by Longman after 1970, except as indicated: *From Kitty Hawk to Outer Space,* 1960; *From Steam Carts to Minicars,* 1961; *From Coracles to Cunarders,* 1962; *From "Rocket" to Railcar,* 1963; *Suffragettes and Votes for Women,* 1964; *Franco and the Spanish Civil War,* 1965, McGraw, 1968; *The Modern World since 1870,* 1968; (with Richard J. Cootes) *The Ancient World,* 1970; *Early Modern Age,* 1971; *Hitler,* 1974; *World War II,* 1974; (with J.R.C. Yglesias) *Mainstream English,* five volumes, 1974-75; (with R. Sandford) *Picture the Past,* five volumes, 1974-81; *Wide Range History* (juvenile readers), four volumes, Oliver & Boyd, 1978. Contributor of articles to *Times Educational Supplement* and *New Schoolmaster.*

WORK IN PROGRESS: History around You, in conjunction with a television program.

SIDELIGHTS: L. E. Snellgrove told *CA:* "I started to write when I was very young; the love of words has always been there. My historical writing arose directly out of my teaching. I have always loved history but I think it only fair and honest to say that, although I would and have written for nothing, I do like the idea of earning a living from writing. I hope that my books will give readers a fair, accurate and reasonably up-to-date version of history—a much abused subject. My latest works for younger readers have given me an opportunity to play with words and develop the purely artistic and technical side of telling a story.

"Of the literary scene today I know little and care even less. Writing, at its best, should be about people in relation to the world. 'Literary scenes' are about as real as cardboard cut-outs of people.... I never read reviews of my work and I should think 'incisive' reviews are quite rare. Most reviewers seem to write about themselves although they pretend to be reviewing somebody's book. The only honest reviewer I can think of off-hand was Bernard Shaw. In his musical reviews he did not bother too much about the music if he could explain the uniqueness of himself. Incidentally, Shaw as a stylist was an influence on me.

"My advice to aspiring writers is to work hard, preferably by writing some sort of diary each day. Go back over the work and cut out any word or phrase which could have been expressed more simply. Remember words are about communication to people (not literary poseurs, however talented). Never be a show off. The real failure is not to be understood."

AVOCATIONAL INTERESTS: Music, theatre, swimming, and sitting in a deckchair during the short English summer.

*   *   *

SNEVE, Virginia Driving Hawk   1933-
(Virginia Driving Hawk)

PERSONAL: Surname rhymes with "navy"; born February 21, 1933, in Rosebud, S.D.; daughter of James H. (an Episcopal priest) and Rose (Ross) Driving Hawk; married Vance M. Sneve (a teacher of industrial arts), July 14, 1955; children: Shirley Kay, Paul Marshall, Alan Edward. *Education:* South Dakota State University, B.S., 1954, M.Ed., 1969. *Politics:* Republican. *Religion:* Episcopal. *Residence:* Flandreau, S.D. *Office address:* Brevet Press, Box 1404, Sioux Falls, S.D. 57101.

CAREER: Teacher of English in public schools in White, S.D., 1954-55, and Pierre, S.D., 1955-56; Flandreau Indian School, Flandreau, S.D., teacher of English and speech, 1965-66, guidance counselor, 1966-70; Brevet Press, Sioux Falls, S.D., editor, 1972—. Member of board of directors, Native American consortium, Corporation for Public Broadcasting, 1975-80. Member of Rosebud Sioux Tribe; member of board of directors of United Sioux Tribes Cultural Arts, 1972-73. Historiographer, Episcopal Church of South Dakota, 1976—. *Member:* National League of American Pen Women, South Dakota Press Women. *Awards, honors:* Manuscript award in American Indian category, Interracial Council for Minority Books for Children, 1971, for *Jimmy Yellow Hawk*; Distinguished Alumnus Award, South Dakota State University, 1974; Woman of Achievement Award, National Federation of Press Women, 1975; award for "special contribution to education," South Dakota Indian Education Association, 1975; Doctor of Letters, Dakota Wesleyan University, 1979.

WRITINGS: Jimmy Yellow Hawk (juvenile), Holiday House, 1972; *High Elk's Treasure* (juvenile), Holiday House, 1972; (editor) *South Dakota Geographic Names,* Brevet Press, 1973; *The Dakota's Heritage,* Brevet Press,

1973; *When Thunders Spoke* (juvenile), Holiday House, 1974; *Betrayed* (juvenile), Holiday House, 1974; *The Chichi Hoo-hoo Bogeyman* (juvenile), Holiday House, 1975; *The Twelve Moons* (juvenile), Houghton, 1977; *That They May Have Life: The Episcopal Church in South Dakota, 1859-1976,* Seabury, 1977. Contributor of short stories to anthologies. Contributor of short stories to juvenile magazines and of book reviews and articles to journals.

WORK IN PROGRESS: Two mini-books for Houghton.

SIDELIGHTS: Virginia Sneve told *CA:* "In my writing, both fiction and nonfiction, I try to present an accurate portrayal of American Indian life as I have known it. I also attempt to interpret history from the viewpoint of the American Indian; in so doing, I hope to correct the many misconceptions and untruths which have been too long perpetrated by non-Indian authors who have written about us."

BIOGRAPHICAL/CRITICAL SOURCES: Sioux Falls Argus-Leader, August 5, 1973; *Children's Literature Review,* Volume II, Gale, 1976.

*   *   *

SNOW, Dorothea J(ohnston)   1909-

PERSONAL: Born April 17, 1909, in McMinnville, Tenn.; daughter of Fred Russell and Theresa Ella (Mosher) Johnston; married Clarence A. Snow, 1929; children: Donald M. *Education:* Attended art school in Fort Wayne, Ind., two years. *Religion:* Methodist. *Home:* 1519 Locust Cir. S.E., Huntsville, Ala. 35801.

CAREER: Art teacher in public schools in Tampa, Fla., 1927-28, and Des Moines, Iowa, 1928-29; Art Publishing Co., Chicago, Ill., art director, 1933-36; writer of children's books and illustrator for children's magazines. *Member:* Women's National Book Association, Society of Midland Authors. *Awards, honors:* Friends of American Writers Top Juvenile Award, 1961, for *Sequoyah: Young Cherokee Guide;* Indiana University Hoosier Author Award, 1968, for *Tomahawk Claim.*

WRITINGS: No-Good, the Dancing Donkey, Rand McNally, 1944; *Puddlejumper,* Rand McNally, 1948; *Eli Whitney: Boy Mechanic,* Bobbs-Merrill, 1948; *Goofy,* John Martin, 1948; *John Paul Jones: Salt-Water Boy,* Bobbs-Merrill, 1950; *Raphael Semmes: Tidewater Boy,* Bobbs-Merrill, 1952; *Come, Chucky, Come,* Houghton, 1952; *The Whistling Mountain Mystery,* Bobbs-Merrill, 1954; *Jeb and the Flying Jenny,* Houghton, 1954; *Samuel Morse: Inquisitive Boy,* Bobbs-Merrill, 1955; *The Secret of the Stone Frog,* Bobbs-Merrill, 1959; *Sequoyah: Young Cherokee Guide,* Bobbs-Merrill, 1960; *A Doll for Lily Belle,* Houghton, 1960; *Henry Hudson: Explorer of the North,* Houghton, 1962; *The Mystery of Ghost Burro Canyon,* Bobbs-Merrill, 1962; *A Sight of Everything,* Houghton, 1963; *Benjamin West: Gifted Young Painter,* Bobbs-Merrill, 1967; *Tomahawk Claim,* Bobbs-Merrill, 1968; *Listen to Your Heart,* Bouregy, 1977; *Love's Dream Remembered,* Bouregy, 1979.

All published by Whitman Publishing: *Peter, the Lonesome Hermit,* 1948; *Roy Rogers' Favorite Western Stories,* 1956; *Lassie and the Mystery at Blackberry Bog,* 1956; *Circus Boy under the Big Top,* 1957; *Circus Boy and Captain Jack,* 1957; *Circus Boy and War on Wheels,* 1958; *Lassie and the Secret of the Summer,* 1958; *Indian Chiefs,* 1959; *Donald Duck on Tom Sawyer's Island,* 1960; *The Charmed Circle,* 1962; *That Certain Girl,* 1964. Contributor to *Children's Activities, Child Life, Wee Wisdom,* and other children's magazines.

WORK IN PROGRESS: Two teen-age novels.

SIDELIGHTS: Dorothea J. Snow reports to *CA* that she adheres to an inflexible writing schedule, starting at 9 a.m. daily, and working amid the reference works she finds necessary in writing accurate biographical and historical books. She is no advocate of the tryout method of perfecting manuscripts and finds her family's reactions to her unpublished work confusing. As a result of having grown up in the South, Snow uses southern mountain backgrounds for much of her writing.†

*   *   *

SOLBERG, Richard W. 1917-

PERSONAL: Born May 25, 1917, in Minneapolis, Minn.; son of Carl K. (a clergyman) and Sina (Varland) Solberg; married June Joanne Nelson, August 18, 1942; children: David, John, Mary, Daniel, Lois. *Education:* St. Olaf College, B.A., 1938; University of Wisconsin, M.A., 1939; Luther Theological Seminary, St. Paul, Minn., B.Th., 1943; University of Chicago, Ph.D., 1952. *Politics:* Democrat. *Home:* 30 Waterside Plaza, 15-A, New York, N.Y. 10010. *Office:* 231 Madison Ave., New York, N.Y. 10016.

CAREER: Ordained minister of Lutheran church; St. Olaf College, Northfield, Minn., instructor in history, 1940-41; pastor in Ingleside, Ill., 1943-45; Augustana College, Sioux Falls, S.D., assistant professor, 1945-48, associate professor of history, 1948-53; Lutheran World Federation, Geneva, Switzerland, senior representative in Germany, 1953-56; Augustana College, professor of history and chairman of department, 1956-64; Thiel College, Greenville, Pa., vice-president for academic affairs, 1964-73; Lutheran Church in America, New York, N.Y., director of department for higher education, 1973—. Organization of American States Professor, El Colegio de Mexico, 1963. Advisor on religious affairs, U.S. High Commission in Germany, 1949-50; script adviser for film "Question 7," 1959-60. *Member:* Norwegian-American Historical Association. *Awards, honors:* Officer's Cross, Order of Merit, Federal Republic of Germany, 1956; Inner Mission of Evangelical Church of Germany Johan Hinrich Wichern Award, 1956; Social Science Research Council faculty research grant, 1959; L.H.D., Augustana College, Rock Island, Ill., 1973.

WRITINGS: As between Brothers: The Story of Lutheran Response to World Need, Augsburg, 1957; *Also Sind Wir Viele Ein Leib,* Lutherisches Verlagshaus, 1960; *God and Caesar in East Germany: The Conflicts of Church and State in East Germany since 1945,* Macmillan, 1961; *Kirche in der Anfechtung,* Lutherisches Verlagshaus, 1962; *How Church-Related Are Church-Related Colleges?,* Board of Publications, Lutheran Church in America, 1980. Contributor of articles and reviews to religious periodicals in Germany and the United States.

AVOCATIONAL INTERESTS: Color photography, travel.

*   *   *

SOMAN, Shirley Camper
(Shirley Camper)

PERSONAL: Born March 7, in Boston, Mass.; married second husband, Robert O. Soman (a manufacturer), November 19, 1962; children: (first marriage) Frederic D. Camper, Francie Camper. *Education:* University of Wisconsin, B.A.; Smith College, M.S.S. *Home:* 40 West 77th St., New York, N.Y. 10024.

CAREER: My Baby and *Shaw's Market News,* New York City, associate editor, 1952-53; New York City (N.Y.) Board

of Education, Bureau of Child Guidance, social work and public relations, 1956-57; Family Service Association of America, New York City, editor and consultant, 1957-63. Public relations worker, editor, and social worker for other social agencies and hospitals; free-lance consultant and writer. Former co-owner and vice-president, Associated Film Consultants and Mercury Newsfilms. Member of board, Public Action Coalition for Toys. *Member:* International Psychohistorical Association, American Society of Journalists and Authors, National Association of Science Writers, National Council on Family Relations, Authors League of America, American Medical Writers Association, National Association of Social Workers, Oral History Association.

WRITINGS: (Under name Shirley Camper) *How to Get Along with Your Child,* Belmont Books, 1962; *Let's Stop Destroying Our Children,* Hawthorn, 1974; *The Expectant Parents' Catalogue,* Dell, 1981. Child care columnist, *Redbook,* 1960-62; book columnist for newspaper syndicate. Contributor to newspapers and magazines.

WORK IN PROGRESS: A historical book; a novel; television and video specials and series.

*   *   *

SOMMER, Robert 1929-

PERSONAL: Born April 26, 1929, in New York, N.Y.; son of Robert M. and Margaret Sommer; married Dorothy Twente, 1957 (divorced); married; wife's name Barbara; children: (first marriage) Ted, Kenneth, Margaret. *Education:* University of Kansas, Ph.D., 1956. *Office:* Department of Psychology, University of California, Davis, Calif. 95616.

CAREER: University of Alberta, Edmonton, assistant professor, 1961-63; University of California, Davis, associate professor, 1963-65, professor of psychology, 1965—.

WRITINGS: Expertland, Doubleday, 1963; *The Ecology of Study Areas* (research report), University of California, 1968; *Personal Space: The Behavioral Basis of Design,* Prentice-Hall, 1969; *Design Awareness,* Holt, 1972; *Tight Spaces,* Prentice-Hall, 1974; *Street Art,* Links Books, 1975; *Sidewalk Fossils* (juvenile), Walker, 1975; *The End of Imprisonment,* Oxford University Press, 1976; *The Mind's Eye,* Delta, 1978; (with wife, Barbara A. Sommer) *A Practical Guide to Behavioral Research,* Oxford University Press, 1980; *Farmers Markets of America,* Capra, 1980.

*   *   *

SOMMERFELDT, John R(obert) 1933-

PERSONAL: Born February 4, 1933, in Detroit, Mich.; son of Melvin J. (an engineer) and Virginia (Gruenheck) Sommerfeldt; married Patricia N. Levinske, August 25, 1956; children: Ann, James, John, Elizabeth. *Education:* University of Michigan, A.B., 1954, A.M., 1956, Ph.D., 1960; graduate study at University of Freiburg, 1954-55, and University of Notre Dame, 1955-56; Western Michigan University, postdoctoral study, 1973-77. *Politics:* Republican. *Religion:* Roman Catholic. *Home:* 2809 Warren Cir., Irving, Tex. 75062. *Office:* International Center, University of Dallas, Irving, Tex. 75061.

CAREER: Stanford University, Stanford, Calif., instructor in history, 1958-59; Western Michigan University, Kalamazoo, instructor, 1959-60, assistant professor, 1960-63, associate professor, 1963-65, professor of history, 1965-78, director of Medieval Institute, 1961-78, executive director of Institute of Cistercian Studies, 1973-78; University of Dallas,

Irving, Tex., professor of history, 1978—, president, 1978-80. President, Cistercian Publications.

WRITINGS: (Editor) *Studies in Medieval Culture,* Western Michigan University Press, Volume I, 1964, Volume II, 1966, Volume III, 1970, Volume IV, Part 1, 1973, Parts 2-3, 1974, Volume V, 1975, Volumes VI-X, 1976, Volume XI, 1977, Volume XII, 1978; (editor) *Studies in Medieval Cistercian History,* Cistercian Publications, Volume II, 1977, Volume III, 1978, Volume IV, 1980, Volume V, in press; *Cistercian Ideals and Reality,* Cistercian Publications, 1978; *The Spiritual Master, East and West,* Cistercian Publications, 1980.

WORK IN PROGRESS: An Intellectual History of the Cistercian Order in the Twelfth and Thirteenth Centuries.

* * *

SORRENTINO, Joseph N. 1937-

PERSONAL: Born May 16, 1937, in Brooklyn, N.Y.; son of Nicholas (a street sweeper) and Angelina Sorrentino. *Education:* University of California, Santa Barbara, B.A. (magna cum laude), 1963; Harvard University, J.D. (and valedictorian of Law School), 1967; University of California, Los Angeles, M.A., 1969; Oxford University, further study, 1969. *Religion:* Christianity. *Home:* 12131 Mayfield, Brentwood, Calif. 90291. *Agent:* (Lectures) American Program Bureau, 850 Boyleston St., Chestnut Hill, Mass. 02167. *Office:* Suite 1800, 2049 Century Park E., Los Angeles, Calif. 90067.

CAREER: Went to work at fourteen after flunking out of high school four times; failed at about thirty factory and laboring jobs before enlisting in U.S. Marines, 1955; booted out of Marines with a general discharge (as an incorrigible); attended Erasmus Hall High School nights while working days in a supermarket, graduating with highest honors in the night school's history; after graduating with honors from University of California, reenlisted in Marines, 1963-66, to wipe out the general discharge, became a platoon leader; admitted to California Bar, 1967; practiced law as partner in Olsen & Sorrentino, Los Angeles, Calif., 1967-72; University of California, Santa Barbara, professor of law, beginning 1970. Adjunct professor, University of California, Los Angeles, and University of Southern California, 1972. Juvenile court judge pro tem, 1973-76. Public lecturer, traveling in forty-five states; guest on network television programs, including "Tonight Show," "Merv Griffin Show," "Sixty Minutes," "Good Morning America," "Dinah," and "Mike Douglas Show," and on ABC-TV special, "Youth Terror." Active in Sugar Ray Robinson Youth Foundation. *Awards, honors:* Golden Glove finalist, 1954; American Library Association Notable Book Award, 1971, for *Up from Never;* National University Extension Association Award, 1971, for outstanding creative program; American Academy Achievement Award, 1977.

WRITINGS: Up from Never (autobiography), Prentice-Hall, 1971; *The Moral Revolution,* Nash Publishing, 1972, revised edition, Manor, 1974; *The Concrete Cradle,* Wollstonecraft, 1977; *The Gold Shield,* Dell, 1980. Also author of a book of poems, *The People Who Stopped for You,* 1977.

WORK IN PROGRESS: The Escaping Peril; Court House; The Hemophiles.

SIDELIGHTS: Joseph N. Sorrentino is one of a just a few individuals who has had extensive personal contact with *both* sides of the juvenile court system—first as an offender, and then as a judge. A high school drop-out and tough young member of the Condors, a Brooklyn street gang, the teen-age Sorrentino found himself on the wrong side of the law countless times before deciding to return to high school—for the fifth time—at the age of twenty. An eventual honors graduate of both Erasmus Hall High School and the University of California, he continued his education at Harvard Law School where, at the age of thirty, he gave a valedictory speech on his youth that *Time* magazine referred to as "the year's most moving graduation address."

Since then, Sorrentino has spent a great deal of his spare time talking to high school students and to young men and women in various detention facilities. Attributing many of today's juvenile delinquency problems to the failure of such social institutions as churches, schools, and the family, combined with the state of the economy, the widespread use of drugs, and the lack of a sense of community in most residential areas, he attempts to counteract the effect of these types of failures by helping teen-agers "straighten out their heads." As he once explained to a *Senior Scholastic* interviewer: "I think a lot of them have twisted notions. Some—the hardcore ones—you can't reach at all. But some you can. This notion of being *cool, macho,* grabs kids. I wanted to be cool, too. I dropped out of school and went out there into the job market. Dumb jobs. You get jobs at the bottom of the economic barrel. I tell the kids about the jobs I could get. Busboy. Pin boy. Beach boy. Chicken plucker. Frustration builds up. You try to escape. I tried professional boxing. How many people can become a heavyweight champion? The rest get their faces smashed and their brains pulverized."

In short, says Sorrentino, "I talk about my own experience. I talk about how it was back on the streets, getting into trouble, ending up in reformatories. I talk about the people I liked who got killed." Finally, notes Sorrentino, "[I tell kids that] to be cool is to be a fool. You end up being a loser. It's idiotic. It's insane. You only hurt yourself."

BIOGRAPHICAL/CRITICAL SOURCES: Time, June 30, 1967; Joseph N. Sorrentino, *Up from Never* (autobiography), Prentice-Hall, 1971; *Senior Scholastic,* September 7, 1978.

* * *

SOUTHARD, Samuel 1925-

PERSONAL: Born February 10, 1925, in Lincolnton, N.C.; son of Samuel (a contractor) and Stella (Miller) Southard; married Frances Allen, May 6, 1950; children: Pamela, Melanie. *Education:* George Washington University, A.B., 1948; Southern Baptist Seminary, B.D., 1951, Th.D., 1954; Union Theological Seminary, graduate study, 1953; Georgia State University, M.G.A., 1975. *Home:* 1425 North Mar-Vista Ave., Pasadena, Calif. *Office:* Fuller Theological Seminary, Pasadena, Calif.

CAREER: East Washington Heights Baptist Church, Washington, D.C., assistant pastor, 1946-48; Central State Hospital, Lakeland, Ky., chaplain, 1951-53; Southern Baptist Seminary, Louisville, Ky., instructor in pastoral care, 1953-54; Fort Mitchell Baptist Church, Fort Mitchell, Ky., pastor, 1954-55; Texas Medical Center, Institute of Religion, Houston, Tex., professor, 1955-57; Southern Baptist Theological Seminary, Louisville, 1958-66, began as associate professor, became professor of pastoral care; Presbyterian Church in the U.S., Board of Church Extension, Atlanta, Ga., director of research, 1966-69; Georgia Mental Health Institute, Atlanta, director of professional services and training, 1969-75; pastor, Isle of Hope Baptist Church, 1976-79; Fuller Theological Seminary, Pasadena, Calif., professor of pastoral theology, 1979—. Member of advisory committee, Educational Testing Service, 1955-59; chairman of committee on constitution and standards, Southern Baptist Association for Clinical Pastoral Education; member of committee on clinical pastoral education, American Association of Theological Schools; chairman, Conference on Motivation for the Ministry, 1959. *Military service:* U.S. Army, 1943-46.

WRITINGS: Family and Mental Illness, Westminster, 1957; *Counseling for Church Vocations,* Broadman, 1957; *Religion and Nursing,* Broadman, 1959; (editor) *Conference on Motivation for the Ministry,* Southern Baptist Theological Seminary, 1959; *Pastoral Evangelism,* Broadman, 1962; *Conversion and Christian Character,* Broadman, 1965; *The Imperfect Disciple,* Broadman, 1968; *Family Counseling in East Asia,* East Asian Christian Conference, 1969; *Pastoral Authority in Personal Relationships,* Abingdon, 1969; *People Need People,* Westminster, 1970; *Every Child Has Two Fathers,* Word Books, 1971; *Christians and Mental Health,* Broadman, 1972; *Religious Inquiry,* Abingdon, 1975.

WORK IN PROGRESS: Research on the theology of pastoral care.

* * *

SPEARING, Judith (Mary Harlow) 1922-

PERSONAL: Born November 29, 1922, in Boston, Mass.; daughter of Ralph Volney (a historian and writer) and Judith (Moss) Harlow; married Edward A. Spearing (a chemical engineer), September 21, 1942; children: Peter, Sara, Diana, Janet. *Education:* Attended Syracuse University, 1940-42. *Politics:* Independent. *Religion:* United Church of Christ. *Home:* 18310 Shaw Rd., Auburn Twp., Hiram, Ohio 44234.

CAREER: Free Public Library, Elizabeth, N.J., reference assistant, 1946-51; Chagrin Falls Branch, Cuyahoga County Library, Chagrin Falls, Ohio, adult and children's services assistant, 1961—.

WRITINGS—Children's books: *Ghosts Who Went to School,* Atheneum, 1966; *Museum House Ghosts,* Atheneum, 1969; *A Day with Mrs. Oliver,* Project Learn, 1977; *Ned Stewart's Job,* Project Learn, 1978; *A Garden for You,* Project Learn, 1980. Contributor of short stories to *Episcopalian, New Ingenue,* and *American Girl.*

WORK IN PROGRESS: A horse story for young teens and a biography for adult new readers.

SIDELIGHTS: Judith Spearing told *CA:* "I have enjoyed making up stories almost since I learned to talk. As a girl I brightened the fifteen minute walk to school by telling my younger sister a story that began in September and ended in June and included whatever interested us at the moment. As a young mother I bribed the children to help with the dishes in much the same way and some of my children's stories grew out of stories told over the sink.

"A lot of my recent writing has been done for adult new readers. Writing a real story with real characters while using a severely limited vocabulary is terribly hard work. Sometimes I want to abandon the whole thing but when I get a letter from a teacher that says, 'There are now two more people who know what it feels like to be unable to put a book down, thanks to Judith Spearing,' I decide it's worthwhile in spite of the frustration.

"I still think the most fascinating thing in the world is watching my characters come alive, grapple with their problems, and make decisions. I hope I can go on doing it for a long time."

AVOCATIONAL INTERESTS: Gardening, sewing.

* * *

SPENCE, Eleanor (Rachel) 1928-

PERSONAL: Born October 21, 1928, in Sydney, New South Wales, Australia; daughter of William Charles (a farmer) and Eleanor (Henderson) Kelly; married John A. Spence (a management consultant), June 17, 1952; children: Alister Martin, Nigel Henderson, Lisette Eleanor. *Education:* University of Sydney, B.A., 1949. *Religion:* Roman Catholic. *Home:* 11 Handley Ave., Turramurra, New South Wales 2074, Australia.

CAREER: Author of children's books. Librarian, Commonwealth Public Service Board, Canberra, Australia, 1950-52; children's librarian, Coventry City Libraries, Coventry, England, 1952-54; teaching assistant, Autistic Children's Association of New South Wales, Sydney, Australia, 1974—. *Member:* Australian Society of Authors, Royal Australian Historical Society, Autistic Children's Association of New South Wales. *Awards, honors:* Australian Children's Book of the Year Award, 1964, for *The Green Laurel,* and 1977, for *The October Child;* Facilities for Autistic Handicapped Winston Churchill fellow, 1978; Australian Literature Board writer's fellowship, 1980.

WRITINGS—Children's books; all published by Oxford University Press (Oxford), except as indicated: *Patterson's Track,* 1958; *Summer in Between,* 1959; *Lillipilly Hill,* 1961, Roy, 1963; *The Green Laurel,* 1963, Roy, 1965; *The Year of the Currawong,* Roy, 1965; *The Switherby Pilgrims,* Roy, 1967; *Jamberoo Road,* Roy, 1969; *The Nothing Place,* 1972, Harper, 1973; *Time to Go Home,* 1973; *The Travels of Hermann,* Collins, 1973; *The October Child,* 1976, published as *The Devil Hole,* Lothrop, 1977; *A Candle for St. Anthony,* 1977, Oxford University Press (New York), 1979; *The Seventh Pebble,* Oxford University Press (New York), 1980.

SIDELIGHTS: Eleanor Spence told *CA* that she became interested in writing Australian fiction for children as a result of her work as a librarian in Coventry, where there was a lack of reading matter for children of families intending to move to Australia. She is keeping journals of her work with autistic and handicapped children for possible literary use in the future.

* * *

SPIEGLER, Charles G. 1911-

PERSONAL: Born March 14, 1911, in New York, N.Y.; son of George and Lena (Gang) Spiegler; married Evelyn Weiser (manager of resources development, Lenox Hill Hospital), December, 1948; children: George Benjamin. *Education:* City College (now City College of the City University of New York), B.A., 1932; Columbia University, M.A., 1933. *Politics:* Liberal. *Religion:* Jewish. *Home:* 67-65 Fleet St., Forest Hills, N.Y. 11375.

CAREER: City College (now City College of the City University of New York), New York City, speech examiner, 1933-36; New York City (N.Y.) Board of Education, teacher of English and speech, 1934-54, chairman of academic subjects, 1954-76. Adjunct assistant professor, Bernard M. Baruch College of the City University of New York, 1946-76. Member of staff of Project English (under U.S. Office of Education grant), Hunter College of the City University of New York, 1963-64. Consultant on bibliography of children's books, Scott, Foresman & Co. *Member:* International Reading Association (president of Manhattan chapter, 1957;

member of national commission on lifetime reading, 1963), English Teachers Association, English Association (chairman), Education Writers Association, Kappa Delta Phi, Overseas Press Club.

WRITINGS: (With Martin Hamburger) *If You're Not Going to College,* Science Research Associates, 1959; (with Helen Derrick and Wilbur Schramm) *Adventures for Americans,* Harcourt, 1962, 3rd edition (with Trask Wilkerson and John K. M. McCaffery), 1969; (editor) *Courage under Fire,* C. E. Merrill, 1967; (editor) *Against the Odds,* C. E. Merrill, 1967; (editor) *They Were First,* C. E. Merrill, 1968; (editor) *People Like You,* C. E. Merrill, 1968; (editor) *In New Directions,* C. E. Merrill, 1968; (with William B. Reiner) *What To Do after High School,* Science Research Associates, 1971; (with F. Clifton White) *Yes, We Can,* Abbey Press, 1972; (with Alex McKay and John MacKenzie) *On My Mind,* Addison-Wesley, 1973; (with Roger B. Goodman) *A Matter of Judgment: Stories of Moral Conflict,* Globe Book Co., 1979. Also author of film script, "Museum: Classroom Unlimited," for New York City Board of Education. Contributor of articles to *New York Times Magazine, This Week, Parents' Magazine, Chicago Jewish Forum, T.V. Guide, Scholastic,* and other publications. Writer-editor on educational editions, *Reader's Digest,* 1957-60; New York advisor, *English Record.*

WORK IN PROGRESS: A series of articles on the state of public education in America; anthologies on the theme of moral values aimed at students in various professional disciplines.

SIDELIGHTS: Charles G. Spiegler writes: "The novelist John Gardner through his book *On Moral Fiction* has had a marked influence on my recent writing and has given me the confidence to continue in a direction that my most recent work, *A Matter of Judgment,* began to explore. Because I believe with the character in Sean O'Casey's *Juno and the Paycock* who feels that 'the whole world is in a state of chassis,' I'm devoting much of my time now to help forestall that chaos which the breakdown in morality foreshadows. A psychiatrist friend of mine has predicted that the 21st century will be one of sociopathology. I strive to prove him wrong by exposing my readers to great literature which conveys a wholesome moral message."

AVOCATIONAL INTERESTS: Tennis, reading, the theatre.

*   *   *

SPRING, Joel Henry   1940-

PERSONAL: Born September 24, 1940, in San Diego, Calif.; son of William C. (a naval officer) and Hazel I. (Meachem) Spring; married Deanna D. Demiduk; children: Dawn Persephone, Aaron. *Education:* Roosevelt University, B.A., 1964; University of Wisconsin, M.A., 1965, Ph.D., 1969. *Politics:* Anarchist. *Home:* 3356 Key West, Cincinnati, Ohio 45239. *Office:* College of Education, University of Cincinnati, Cincinnati, Ohio 45221.

CAREER: University of Wisconsin—Madison, instructor in education, 1968-69; Case Western Reserve University, Cleveland, Ohio, associate professor of education, 1969-76; University of Cincinnati, Cincinnati, Ohio, professor of education, 1976—.

WRITINGS: (Editor with Jordan Bishop) *Formative Undercurrents in Compulsory Education,* Centro Intercultural de Documentacion, 1970; *Education and the Rise of the Corporate State,* Beacon Press, 1972; (with Clarence Karier and Paul Violas) *Roots of Crisis,* Rand McNally, 1973; *Primer of*

Libertarian Education, Free Life Editions, 1974; *The Sorting Machine,* Longman, 1976; *American Education,* Longman, 1978; *Educating the Worker-Citizen,* Longman, 1980.

*   *   *

SPUHLER, J(ames) N(orman)   1917-

PERSONAL: Born March 1, 1917, in Tucumcari, N.M.; son of Frank Jacob and Hettie (Aylesworth) Spuhler; married Helen McKaig, September 14, 1946; children: Derek Drake. *Education:* University of New Mexico, B.A., 1940; Harvard University, M.A., 1942, Ph.D., 1946; Oxford University, M.A., 1962. *Home:* 8720 Rio Grande Blvd. N.W., Albuquerque, N.M. 87114. *Office:* Department of Anthropology, University of New Mexico, Albuquerque, N.M. 87131.

CAREER: Ohio State University, Columbus, instructor, 1946-47, assistant professor of anthropology and zoology, 1947-50; University of Michigan, Ann Arbor, research associate and associate biologist, Institute of Human Biology, 1950-55, associate professor, 1953-59, professor of anthropology and human genetics, 1960-68, chairman of department of anthropology, 1959-67; University of New Mexico, Albuquerque, Leslie Spier professor of anthropology, 1967—. Visiting associate professor of anthropology, Northwestern University, summer, 1950; visiting professor of anthropology and zoology, University of Texas, 1965-66. Director, Rockefeller study of the human biology of the Ramah Navaho, summers, 1948-50, and Atomic Bomb Casualty Commission child health survey, 1959. Research fellow, Harvard University, 1949, and Oxford University, 1962-63. Consultant, National Institute of Health, 1955-60, and National Science Foundation, 1965-67. *Military service:* U.S. Naval Reserve, 1942-46, 1951-52; became lieutenant.

MEMBER: American Anthropological Association (fellow; member of executive board, 1958-61), Genetics Society of America, Biometric Society (member of advisory board, Eastern North American Region, 1951-54), American Association for the Advancement of Science (fellow; council member, 1950-54), American Association of Physical Anthropologists (member of executive committee, 1954-55; secretary-treasurer, 1955-58; president, 1975-77), American Society of Human Genetics (member of board of directors, 1951-53; director, 1951-53, 1963-65), Society for the Study of Evolution, American Genetics Association, American Society of Naturalists, Michigan Academy of Science (chairman of anthropology section, 1953-54), Ohio Academy of Science (fellow; vice-president, 1948-49), Ohio Folklore Society (member of executive committee, 1950-51), Japan Society of Human Genetics, Sigma Xi. *Awards, honors:* Center for Advanced Study in the Behavioral Sciences fellowship, 1955-56, 1971-72.

WRITINGS: (Editor) *Yearbook of Physical Anthropology,* Wenner-Gren Foundation, 1952; (editor) James F. Crow and others, *Natural Selection in Man,* Wayne State University Press, 1958; (with others) *The Evolution of Man's Capacity for Culture: Six Essays,* Wayne State University Press, 1959; (editor) *Behavior Consequences of Genetic Differences in Man,* Aldine, 1966; (editor) *Genetic Diversity and Human Behavior,* Aldine, 1967; (with John C. Loehlin and Gardner Lindzey) *Race Differences in Intelligence,* W. H. Freeman, 1975. Editor, *Central States Bulletin,* 1947-49, and *Journal of Anthropological Research,* beginning, 1975; associate editor, *Human Biology,* 1953-74, *American Anthropologist,* 1954-55, *American Journal of Human Genetics,* 1955-58, *Evolution,* 1960-63, and *American Journal of Physical Anthropology,* 1969-73; member of editorial board, *American Naturalist,* 1979—.

SPULBER, Nicolas 1915-

PERSONAL: Born January 1, 1915, in Rumania; son of John (a contractor) and Ana Spulber; married August 5, 1950; wife's name, Pauline; children: Daniel. *Education:* New School for Social Research, M.A., 1950, Ph.D. (magna cum laude), 1952. *Office:* Department of Economics, Indiana University, Bloomington, Ind. 47401.

CAREER: Massachusetts Institute of Technology, Cambridge, research associate at Center for International Studies, 1952-54; Indiana University at Bloomington, lecturer, 1954-55, associate professor, 1955-61, professor of economics, 1961-74, Distinguished Professor, 1974-80, Distinguished Professor Emeritus, 1980—, acting chairman of Institute of East European Studies, 1956-57 and 1958-59. Visiting professor, City University of New York, 1963-64. *Member:* American Economic Association, Royal Economic Society.

WRITINGS: (Editor with Norman J. G. Pounds) *Resources and Planning in Eastern Europe,* Indiana University Press, 1957; (editor with Vratislav Busek) *Czechoslovakia,* Praeger, 1957; *The Economics of Communist Eastern Europe,* M.I.T. Press, 1957, reprinted, Greenwood Press, 1976; (editor) *Study of the Soviet Economy,* Indiana University Press, 1961; *The Soviet Economy: Structure, Principles, Problems,* Norton, 1962, revised edition, 1969; (editor) *Foundations of Soviet Strategy for Economic Growth: Soviet Essays, 1924-1930,* translated by Robert M. Hankin and others, Indiana University Press, 1964; *Soviet Strategy for Economic Growth,* Indiana University Press, 1964; *The State and Economic Development in Eastern Europe,* Random House, 1966; *Socialist Management and Planning: Topics in Comparative Socialist Economics,* Indiana University Press, 1971; (co-author) *Quantitative Economic Policy and Planning: Theory and Models of Economic Control,* Norton, 1976; *Organizational Alternatives in Soviet-Type Economics,* Cambridge University Press, 1979.

* * *

SQUIRE, Norman 1907-

PERSONAL: Born May 9, 1907, in Southsea, Hampshire, England; son of John Henry (a musician) and Mary (Cooper) Squire; married Olivia Walker, September 20, 1947. *Education:* Attended schools in England. *Politics:* Anti-Conservative. *Home:* 51 Neville Ct., London N.W.8, England.

CAREER: Began as errand boy in department store, London, England, at age of thirteen, later salesman; dancer and cabaret artist, 1930-40. *Military service:* British Army, 1940-46; became lieutenant; mentioned in dispatches. *Member:* Imperial Society of Teachers of Dancing (life member; fellow), Lederer's Bridge Club (secretary), Dorset Bridge Club (secretary).

WRITINGS: The Theory of Bidding, Duckworth, 1957, new edition, 1977; *A Guide to Bridge Conventions,* Duckworth, 1958, revised edition, 1978; (with M. Harrison-Gray) *Winning Points at Match-Point Bridge,* Faber, 1959; *Bidding at Bridge,* Penguin, 1964, new edition, Duckworth, 1978; *The Laws of Kalooki,* Crockford, 1964; *How to Win at Roulette,* Pelham Books, 1968, Gamblers Book Club, 1972; *Beginner's Guide to Bridge,* Drake Publishers, 1971; *How to Be a Champion,* Beasley, 1972; *Bidding Today,* Pitman, 1976; *Card-Play Technique,* Pitman, 1976; *Squeeze-Play Simplified,* Duckworth, 1978.

Author of regular bridge column for *Express and Star* and *Bombay Sunday Standard.* Contributor of articles to bridge journals throughout the world. Competition editor, *Bridge,* 1948-64.

WORK IN PROGRESS: Advanced Roulette.

SIDELIGHTS: Norman Squire, winner of many British bridge championships, told *CA:* "I write because I am impelled to do so even if I know that the result will be shelved among the rest of the unpublishable rubbish. I write at high speed, pouring out everything in my mind before placing the material in logical sequence. That is fun. I then start work with the object of saying everything in one-fourth the number of words. An eternal rebel, I am completely uninfluenced by any other writer but have heeded Colette's comment on Simenon's manuscript: 'Take the literature out of it,' and on Q's advice to his students: 'Murder your darlings.'"

* * *

STACK, Herbert James 1893-1967

PERSONAL: Born March 29, 1893, in Orange, Mass; died March 31, 1967; son of William James and Ellen Nellie Stack; married Frances Richmyer, 1922; children: Elizabeth Virginia Stack Duchesne, Robert William. *Education:* Massachusetts Agricultural College (now University of Massachusetts), B.S., 1912; Columbia University, Ph.D., 1929. *Home:* 519 Wyndham Rd., Teaneck, N.J. *Office:* Center for Safety Education, New York University, New York, N.Y.

CAREER: Supervisor in Johnstown, Pa., secondary schools, 1921-27; Columbia University, Teachers College, New York City, lecturer, 1929-36; New York University, Center for Safety Education, New York City, director, 1937-58, program associate, beginning 1958. Part-time instructor for twenty-seven years for Federal Bureau of Investigation and National Police Academy. Member of national health and safety committee, Boy Scouts of America. *Military service:* U.S. Aviation Service, 1919-21; became first lieutenant. *Member:* American Society of Safety Engineers, American Academy of Physical Education, American Association for Health, Physical Education and Recreation. *Awards, honors:* Paul Hoffman Award in traffic safety; Arthur Williams Memorial Medal; Ed.D., University of Massachusetts, 1953.

WRITINGS: (Contributor) *Health Education,* National Education Association and the American Medical Association, 1930, revised edition, 1941; (contributor) *Education for Dynamic Citizenship,* University of Pennsylvania Press, 1939; (with E. Z. Schwartz) *Safety Every Day,* Noble, 1939; (with Don Cash Seaton and Florence Slown Hyde) *Safety in the World of Today,* Beckley-Cardy, 1941, revised edition, 1948; (editor with Elmer B. Siebrecht) *Education for Safe Living,* Prentice-Hall, 1942, 2nd edition (with Siebrecht and J. Duke Elkow), 1949, 3rd edition (with Elkow), 1957, 4th edition, 1966; (with Geraldine Huston) *It's Fun to Be Safe,* Beckley-Cardy, 1942; (with Charles C. Hawkins and Walter A. Cutter) *Careers in Safety: Choosing a Vocation in the Field of Accident Prevention,* Funk, 1945; (editor) *Safety for Greater Adventures: The Contributions of Albert Wurts Whitney,* Center for Safety Education, New York University, 1952; (with Seaton and Hyde) *Safety Challenges You,* Beckley-Cardy, 1953; (editor with Leon Brody) *Highway Safety and Driver Education,* Prentice-Hall, 1954, 2nd edition, 1959; (co-editor) *Man and the Motor Car,* Prentice-Hall, 1957; (with Seaton and Bernard I. Loft) *Administration and Supervision of Safety Education,* Macmillan, 1968. Also contributor of chapters to manuals and pamphlets, and to the "Every Pupil Safety" series, six workbooks, Schulyer-Dobson, 1939. Contributor of articles on safety and safety education to popular magazines and journals.†

STAFFORD, Jean 1915-1979

PERSONAL: Born July 1, 1915, in Covina, Calif.; died in White Plains, N.Y., March 26, 1979; daughter of John Richard (a writer of westerns under pseudonym Jack Wonder) and Mary (McKillop) Stafford; married Robert Lowell (a Pulitzer Prize winning poet), April 2, 1940 (divorced, 1948); married Oliver Jensen (a writer), January 28, 1950 (divorced, 1953); married A. J. Liebling (a columnist for the *New Yorker*), April, 1959 (died, 1963). *Education:* University of Colorado, B.A. and M.A., 1936; Heidelberg University, additional study, 1936-37. *Politics:* Democrat. *Agent:* James Oliver Brown Associates, Inc., 25 West 43rd St., New York, N.Y. 10031.

CAREER: Novelist and short story writer. Instructor, Stephens College, Columbia, Mo., 1937-38; lecturer, Queens College (now Queens College of the City University of New York), 1945; adjunct professor, Columbia University, 1967-69. Secretary, *Southern Review*, 1940-41. Fellow, Center for Advanced Studies, Wesleyan University, 1964-65. *Member:* Cosmopolitan Club (New York). *Awards, honors:* *Mademoiselle*'s merit award, 1944; National Institute of Arts and Letters grant in literature, 1945; Guggenheim fellowships in fiction, 1945, 1948; National Press Club Award, 1948; O. Henry Memorial Award, 1955, for best short story of the year; Ingram-Merrill grant, 1969; Chapelbrook grant, 1969; Pulitzer Prize, 1970, for *The Collected Stories of Jean Stafford*.

WRITINGS: Boston Adventure (novel), Harcourt, 1944, reprinted, 1967; *The Mountain Lion* (novel), Harcourt, 1947, reprinted, University of New Mexico Press, 1977; *The Catherine Wheel* (novel), Harcourt, 1952, reprinted, Manor, 1974; *Children Are Bored on Sunday* (short stories), Harcourt, 1953; (with others) *New Short Novels*, Ballantine, 1954; (with others) *Stories*, Farrar, Straus, 1956; *Elphi: The Cat with the High I.Q.* (juvenile), Farrar, Straus, 1962; (editor and author of introduction) *The Lion and the Carpenter* (juvenile), Macmillan, 1962; *Bad Characters* (short stories), Farrar, Straus, 1966; *A Mother in History* (based on interviews with the mother of Lee Harvey Oswald), Farrar, Straus, 1966; *The Collected Stories of Jean Stafford*, Farrar, Straus, 1969. Contributor of articles and stories to *New Yorker*, *Vogue*, *Harper's*, *Mademoiselle*, *Holiday*, *Horizon*, *Reporter*, *New Republic*, and other magazines.

WORK IN PROGRESS: A novel.

SIDELIGHTS: Jean Stafford was a writer of traditionally structured and painstakingly crafted novels and short stories. H. M. Jones wrote in the *Saturday Review* that "there is no sentence in [*Children Are Bored on Sunday*] which does not have its clean, precise line. Difficult ideas are stated with effortless ease, the difficulty of the idea not being a metaphysical difficulty but a difficulty of conveying to the reader the impression made upon some problematical personality by a particular human situation."

H. M. Jones also appreciated Stafford's neat, crisp style, and he once wrote in a review that "Stafford writes with brilliance. Scene after scene is told with unforgettable care and tenuous entanglements are treated with wise subtlety. She creates a splendid sense of time, of the unending afternoons of youth, and of the actual color of noon and of night." And Thomas Lask wrote in an article in the *New York Times* that he felt "Jean Stafford can teach almost anything one could want to know about swiftly and deftly developing characters balancing them in delicate counterpoint or wrenching conflict, and probing their thoughts and emotions."

Once acknowledging that each novel and short story was a much deliberated literary project, Stafford told an interviewer: "I am a rather slow person, in that experience has to sink in for years before I can use it. . . . I have to let impressions and experience age within me."

Although her first three books were novels and were generally well received, critics seemed much more impressed and enthusiastic with Stafford's short stories. As Jeanette Mann pointed out: "Stafford works within the traditional forms of Chekhov and James in her short fiction. Some critics believe that this form is more compatible to her than is that of the novel. In each story she creates a moment of experience, through the use of realistic settings, characters, and dialogues, so as to present, often through the device of dramatic irony, the sudden illumination of understanding, the symbolic crisis, or the unresolved glimpse into the heart of the situation. She relies heavily upon the use of the symbolic object and often uses it to reflect changes and development within the characters."

It might be this effective use of the short story genre that won Stafford the reputation of being an extremely gifted and sensitive author, reflecting what many readers feel was "a sympathetic yet ultimately bleak vision of alienation and innocence."

However, Eleanor Perry does not agree that Stafford's reputation for sensitivity is well deserved. Illustrating that Stafford's characterization shows a possible lack of sensitivity, and definitely a lack of depth, Perry wrote: "No fault can be found with Miss Stafford's talents, but what happens as one reads one story after another is that a nagging, sometimes boring, similarity surrounds her 'good' characters. They are all weak, defenseless, long-suffering. They rarely act upon or even interact much with their enemies. They suffer from a paralysis of will, they are vitiated by guilt. Their destinies are solved by external characters are always more interesting to create than good ones."

Many critics feel that her reputation of sensitivity also encompasses her reflection of the 'feminine mind.' One such critic, Pete Axthelm felt that "Stafford is one of a group of modern female writers who share an intensely introspective, feminine, sensibility. . . . She has explored obscure and intriguing corners of the feminine mind within the fairly conventional framework of the modern short story."

Several critics have written that this special sensitivity is reflected especially in her book *A Mother in History*, which was the result of a three-day interview with Marguerite Oswald, the mother of Lee Harvey Oswald. Thomas Lask wrote that "the character and psychology of that woman, who sought the spotlight and who felt that not enough had been made of her, were as vividly captured as anything in Miss Stafford's fiction." Marya Mannes wrote in *Book Week* that Stafford let Mrs. Oswald speak for herself. "There Jean Stafford's great skill is manifest in the brief interpolations, between Mrs. Oswald's copious stream, in which [Stafford] manages to convey the trauma of her own involvement with this woman without ever raising her voice. . . . Certainly, *A Mother in History* could be nothing less than a shocking account; an aversion to Marguerite Oswald on the basis of her past behaviour and continuing greediness for attention is understandable. What is disturbing is that so many readers should have construed this report as a tasteless 'expose.' . . . This small book is a triumph of control not only over material but over the writer's emotions."

BIOGRAPHICAL/CRITICAL SOURCES: Saturday Review of Literature, March 1, 1947; *Saturday Review*, May 9, 1953; Harvey Breit, editor, *The Writer Observed*, World Publishing, 1956; *Critique*, spring, 1962; *Book Week*, October 11,

1964; *New York Times Book Review*, October 11, 1964, February 16, 1969; *New Republic*, October 31, 1964; *Contemporary Literary Criticism*, Gale, Volume IV, 1975, Volume VII, 1977; *New York Times*, March 28, 1979; *Washington Post*, March 29, 1979; *Time*, April 9, 1979; *Newsweek*, April 9, 1979.†

—*Sketch by Margaret Mazurkiewicz*

*   *   *

STALLMAN, Robert Wooster 1911-

PERSONAL: Born September 27, 1911, in Milwaukee, Wis.; son of Paul Michael and Hazel (Wooster) Stallman; married Virginia Blume, August 21, 1939; children: William Wooster, Robert Wooster, Jr. *Education:* University of Wisconsin, B.A., 1933, M.A., 1939, Ph.D., 1942. *Home:* One Westwood Rd., Storrs, Conn. 06268. *Office:* Department of English, University of Connecticut, Storrs, Conn. 06268.

CAREER: University of Wisconsin—Madison, instructor, 1939-42; Rhode Island State College (now University of Rhode Island), Kingston, instructor, 1942-43; Yale University, New Haven, Conn., instructor, 1943-44; Katherine Gibbs School, Boston, Mass., lecturer, 1944-46; University of Kansas, Lawrence, assistant professor, 1946-49; University of Connecticut, Storrs, associate professor, 1949-53, professor of English, 1953-74, professor emeritus, 1974—, director of Writers' Conference, 1950-55. Fulbright lecturer in American literature, University of Strasbourg, 1958-59; Bingham Professor in the Humanities, University of Louisville, spring, 1966; Citizen's Professor, University of Hawaii, 1970. Lecturer at University of Minnesota, University of Texas, and other American universities; also lecturer at universities throughout Europe. *Member:* Modern Language Association of America (chairman of various committees, 1951-62), Psi Upsilon. *Awards, honors:* Ford Foundation fellowship to study art in Europe, 1952-53; University of Connecticut Alumni Association award, 1968; La Fondation Camargo fellowship, 1974-75.

WRITINGS: (Contributor) *A Southern Vanguard*, Prentice-Hall, 1947; (contributor) *Forms of Modern Fiction*, University of Minnesota Press, 1948; (contributor) *Critiques and Essays on Modern Fiction*, Ronald, 1952; (contributor) *Southern Renascence*, Johns Hopkins Press, 1953; *The Houses That James Built and Other Literary Studies* (essay collection), Michigan State University Press, 1961, reprinted, Ohio University Press, 1977; *Stephen Crane: A Biography*, Braziller, 1968, revised edition, 1973; *Stephen Crane: A Critical Bibliography*, Iowa State University Press, 1972; *The Figurehead and Other Poems, 1944-1977*, Oolichan Books, 1978.

Editor: (With Ray B. West, Jr., and contributor) *The Art of Modern Fiction*, Rinehart, 1949; (and contributor) *Critiques and Essays in Criticism: 1920-1948*, Ronald, 1949; (and contributor) *The Critic's Notebook*, University of Minnesota Press, 1950, reprinted, Greenwood Press, 1977; *Stephen Crane: The Red Badge of Courage*, Random House, 1951; *Stephen Crane: An Omnibus*, Knopf, 1952; (with R. E. Watters and contributor) *The Creative Reader*, Ronald, 1954, 2nd edition, Wiley, 1962; *Stephen Crane: Stories and Tales*, Knopf, 1955; *Seventeen American Poets*, University of Philippines Press, 1958; (with Lillian Gilkes) *Stephen Crane: Letters*, New York University Press, 1960; *The Art of Joseph Conrad: A Critical Symposium*, Michigan State University Press, 1960, reprinted, Ohio University Press, 1980; *Stephen Crane, "The Red Badge of Courage" and Selected Stories*, New American Library, 1960; *Henry James, The*

Ambassadors, New American Library, 1960; (with Arthur Waldhorn) *American Literature: Readings and Critiques*, Putnam, 1961; (with E. A. Hagemann) *The War Dispatches of Stephen Crane*, New York University Press, 1964; (with E. R. Hagemann) *The New York City Sketches of Stephen Crane*, New York University Press, 1966; *Stephen Crane: Sullivan County Tales and Sketches*, Iowa State University Press, 1968; *The Stephen Crane Reader*, Scott, Foresman, 1972.

Work appears in many anthologies, including Norton Critical Editions of *The Red Badge of Courage* and *Huckleberry Finn*. Contributor to *Collier's Encyclopedia, Encyclopaedia Britannica*, and *Reader's Encyclopedia of American Literature*. Contributor of poems and essays to *New Republic, Kenyon Review, Poetry, Sewanee Review, Southern Review*, and other journals. Associate editor, *Western Review*, 1946-49.

WORK IN PROGRESS: Poems; a novel, *Arsenic*.

SIDELIGHTS: Robert Stallman is a leading scholar of the life and work of Stephen Crane. *Stephen Crane: A Biography* has received critical praise as the first thorough documentation of Crane's life. Lewis Leary, reviewing the book in *Sewanee Review*, praises Stallman's "dedicated and meticulous investigation" and concludes that he "understands as much about Stephen Crane as Stephen Crane ever did." A reviewer for *Prairie Schooner* notes that "some biographies conclude a subject, but this one opens the way to new studies which can be based upon its solid foundation. It is another indispensable book." Daniel Greene, writing in the *National Observer*, calls the book "the definitive critical biography" of Stephen Crane.

Stallman's poetry has been recorded for the Library of Congress.

BIOGRAPHICAL/CRITICAL SOURCES: Antioch Review, summer, 1965; *New York Times*, June 22, 1966; *American Literature*, January, 1967; *Saturday Review*, August 10, 1968; *New York Times Book Review*, August 11, 1968; *Newsweek*, August 12, 1968; *Wall Street Journal*, August 28, 1968; *Times Literary Supplement*, August 29, 1968, October 5, 1973; *Time*, August 30, 1968; *Atlantic*, September, 1968; *Nation*, September 2, 1968; *New Republic*, September 7, 1968; *New Yorker*, September 28, 1968; *National Observer*, September 30, 1968; *Virginia Quarterly Review*, autumn, 1968; *Georgia Review*, spring, 1969; *Sewanee Review*, spring, 1969, July, 1974; *Prairie Schooner*, spring, 1969; *Southwest Review*, summer, 1969.

*   *   *

STANISLAWSKI, Dan 1903-

PERSONAL: Born April 20, 1903, in Bellingham, Wash.; son of Henry and Margaret (Harrington) Stanislawsky; married Doris Barr, May 1, 1934; children: Michael Barr, Anna. *Education:* University of California, Berkeley, A.B., 1937, Ph.D., 1944. *Religion:* Society of Friends. *Home:* 1515 Oxford St., Berkeley, Calif. 94709. *Office:* Department of Geography, University of California, Berkeley, Calif.

CAREER: Clerical and sales work, 1923-34; Syracuse University, Syracuse, N.Y., instructor, 1941-42; University of California, Berkeley lecturer and instructor, 1942-45; University of Washington, Seattle, assistant professor, 1945-47; University of Pennsylvania, Philadelphia, associate professor, 1947-49; University of Texas, Main University (now University of Texas at Austin), professor in department of geography, 1949-62; University of Arizona, Tucson, professor in department of geography and area development, 1963-75; University of California, Berkeley, research associate in department of geography, 1975—. Fulbright professor, University of Brazil, 1961. *Member:* Phi Beta Kappa, Sigma Xi. *Awards, honors:* Guggenheim fellow and Social Science Research Council fellow, 1952-53; Gulbenkian Foundation grant, summer, 1965; citation from Association of American Geographers, 1963, for meritorious contribution to geography (for work on Portugal); Guggenheim fellow, 1968-69.

WRITINGS—All published by University of Texas Press: *The Anatomy of Eleven Towns in Michoacan,* 1950; *The Individuality of Portugal,* 1959; *Portugal's Other Kingdom: The Algarve,* 1963; *Landscapes of Bacchus,* 1970. Contributor of articles to *Geographical Review, Annals of the Association of American Geographers, American Anthropologist,* and other professional journals.

WORK IN PROGRESS: A Ravaged Garden: Nicaragua in the Mid-Sixteenth Century; The Historical Geography of the Wine-vine in the Eastern and Central Mediterranean Areas of Europe.

*   *   *

STARK, Bradford   1948-1979

PERSONAL: Born May 27, 1948, in New York, N.Y.; died October 17, 1979, in Binghamton, N.Y.; son of Bernard (a milliner) and Judith (Glasgow) Stark; married Meryl Payenson, February 4, 1968; children: Kio (daughter). *Education:* City College of the City University of New York, B.A., 1969; Columbia University, M.Sc., 1972.

CAREER: Westermann-Miller Associates, New York, N.Y., urban planner, 1969-70; Crandell Associates, Vestal, N.Y., senior urban planner, beginning 1970. Editor, Loose Change Press, beginning 1970; instructor in writing workshop at Off Campus College, State University of New York at Binghamton, beginning 1973. *Awards, honors:* National Education Association fellowship, 1978.

WRITINGS: An Unlikely but Noble Kingdom (poems), Rainbow Press, 1974; *The Burden of Time* (poems), Bellevue Press, 1976; *A Grade School Grammar* (poems), House of Keys, 1980. Contributor of poems to *Caterpillar, For Now, Gnosis, Endymion, Mulch, World, Mysterious Barricades, Smith, Sun, Choice,* and other little magazines. Editor, *Promethean,* 1968-69.†

*   *   *

STEPHENS, James Charles   1915-

PERSONAL: Born September 15, 1915, in Oakland, Calif.; son of Charles Oliver and Gladys (Hobler) Stephens; married Jean Muriel Smith, August 5, 1943; children: Janet, James, Jr., Jonathan. *Education:* University of California, Berkeley, A.B., 1937, M.A., 1938. *Religion:* Methodist. *Home:* 6513 Jay Miller Dr., Falls Church, Va.

CAREER: Intern, Los Angeles County (Calif.) Civil Service Commission, 1938-39; Home Owners Loan Corp., San Francisco, Calif., classification analyst, 1939-40; U.S. Government, Washington, D.C., classification analyst for Housing Authority, 1940-41, training officer for Federal Public Housing Authority, 1946-47, and for Public Health Service, 1947-50, for Department of the Navy, 1950-55, and for Department of Labor, 1955-70. Professorial lecturer in public administration, George Washington University, 1953-71; professorial lecturer, University of California, Berkeley, 1958-62, and University of Northern Colorado, 1968-72; taught organization and management at Industrial College of the

Armed Forces. *Military service:* U.S. Army, Adjutant General's Office, 1941-46; became colonel. *Member:* Academy of Management, World Future Society.

WRITINGS: (With H. E. Niles and Mary Cushing Niles) *The Office Supervisor,* 3rd edition (Stephens was not associated with earlier editions), Wiley, 1959, 4th edition published as *The Supervisor,* Wiley Eastern Private Ltd. (New Delhi), 1968; *Managing Complexity, Work, Technology, and Human Relations,* University Press of Washington, 1977, revised edition published as *Managing Complexity, Work, Technology, Resources, and Human Relations,* Lomond Systems, 1977.

SIDELIGHTS: James C. Stephens explained to *CA* that "changes in management theory and practice compelled me to write *Managing Complexity, Work, Technology, and Human Relations* after teaching engineers, scientists, military officers, and managers for twenty-five years. Caught in forces over which they have no control, managers must learn to live with them and manage complexity in large, dynamic organizations shaped by technological forces.

"I endeavored to structure *Managing Complexity* to assist readers, hopefully managers, students, and others interested in understanding the transition taking place in management. The book therefore was written to challenge managers in industry and government to re-examine their roles and their management philosophy."

*   *   *

STEPHENS, M(ichael) G(regory)   1946-

PERSONAL: Born March 4, 1946; son of James Stewart (a U.S. customs employee) and Rose (Drew) Stephens. *Education:* Yale University, drama student, 1971-72, M.F.A.; City College of the City University of New York, B.A., M.A. *Home:* 520 West 110th St., No. 9-B, New York, N.Y. 10025. *Office:* Fordham University, Bronx, N.Y. 10458.

CAREER: Novelist, poet, and playwright; has worked in bookstores, on merchant ships, and as a greenskeeper at various times; lecturer, School of General Studies, Columbia University, 1977—; writer-in-residence and assistant professor of communications, Fordham University, 1979—. *Awards, honors:* MacDowell Colony fellowship, 1968; Fletcher Pratt prose fellowship at Breadloaf Writers Conference, 1971; Creative Artists Public Service fiction award, 1978.

WRITINGS: Season at Coole (novel), Dutton, 1972; *Alcohol Poems,* Loose Change Press, 1973; *Paragraphs* (short stories), Mulch Press, 1974; *Still Life* (fiction), Kroesen Books, 1977; *Tangun Legend* (poetry), Seamark Press, 1978; *Shipping Out* (novel), Applewood Press, 1979.

Plays: "A Splendid Occasion in Spring," first produced in New York City at West End Bar, February 9, 1974; "Off-Season Rates," Yale Playwrights Projects, 1978; "Cloud-Dream," Yale Playwrights Projects, 1979; "Our Father," first produced in New York City at The Private Theatre, 1980.

Contributor of articles, stories, poems, and reviews to over 100 literary magazines and newspapers, including *Nation, Rolling Stone, Village Voice, Tri-Quarterly, New Letters, American Pen,* and *Boston Phoenix.*

WORK IN PROGRESS: A novel set in Korea in 1979; a play; an essay on time.

STEPHENSON, Wendell Holmes   1899-1970

PERSONAL: Born March 13, 1899, in Cartersburg, Ind.; died April, 1970; son of Robert W. and Virginia (Rupe) Stephenson; married Hildagarde Voyles; children: Lamar V. *Education:* Attended Earlham College, 1916-17; Indiana University, A.B., 1923, A.M., 1924; University of Michigan, Ph.D., 1928. *Religion:* Society of Friends. *Home:* 2467 University St., Eugene, Ore. *Office:* Department of History, University of Oregon, Eugene, Ore.

CAREER: University of Kentucky, Lexington, instructor, 1924-25, assistant professor, 1925-26, professor, 1945-46; Louisiana State University and Agricultural and Mechanical College, Baton Rouge, associate professor, 1927-31, professor, 1931-45, dean of College of Liberal Arts, 1941-45; Tulane University, New Orleans, La., professor, 1946-53; University of Oregon, Eugene, professor of history, 1953-69, professor emeritus, 1969-70. Fulbright professor in England at University of Birmingham, 1950, and University of Southampton, 1959-60. *Member:* Organization of American Historians, American Historical Association, Agricultural History Society, American Association for State and Local History, Southern Historical Association, Oregon Historical Society, Phi Kappa Phi, Omicron Delta Kappa, Phi Beta Kappa, Phi Delta Kappa, Phi Gamma Mu, Lamda Chi Alpha. *Awards, honors:* D.Litt., Duke University, 1950; LL.D., University of North Carolina, 1953.

WRITINGS: Political Career of General James H. Lane, Kansas Historical Society, 1930; *Alexander Porter, Whig Planter of Old Louisiana,* Louisiana State University Press, 1934, reprinted, Da Capo Press, 1969; *Isaac Franklin, Slave-Trader and Planter of the Old South,* Louisiana State University Press, 1938, reprinted, P. Smith, 1968; *The South Lives in History: Southern Historians and Their Legacy,* Louisiana State University Press, 1955; *A Basic History of the Old South,* Van Nostrand, 1959; *Southern History in the Making: Pioneer Historians of the South,* Louisiana State University Press, 1964; (editor and author of foreword) Charles William Ramsdell, *Behind the Lines in the Southern Confederacy,* Greenwood Press, 1969; *Reconstruction in Texas,* University of Texas, 1970. Co-editor, "Southern Biography" series, nine volumes, 1939-45, and of *A History of the South,* ten volumes, beginning 1938. Managing editor, *Journal of Southern History,* 1934-41, and *Mississippi Valley Historical Review,* 1946-53.

WORK IN PROGRESS: Profiles in Faith.†

*   *   *

STEPTOE, John (Lewis)   1950-

PERSONAL: Born September 14, 1950, in Brooklyn, N.Y.; son of John Oliver (a transit worker) and Elesteen (Hill) Steptoe; children: Bweela (daughter), Javaka (son). *Education:* Attended New York School of Art and Design, 1964-67. *Home:* 840 Monroe St., Brooklyn, N.Y. 11221. *Agent:* Alice Bach, 222 East 75th St., New York, N.Y.

CAREER: Artist and author of children's books. Teacher at Brooklyn Music School, summer, 1970. *Member:* Amnesty International. *Awards, honors:* Gold Medal, Society of Illustrators, 1970, for *Stevie.*

WRITINGS—Children's books; self-illustrated: *Stevie,* Harper, 1969; *Uptown,* Harper, 1970; *Train Ride,* Harper, 1971; *Birthday,* Holt, 1972; *My Special Best Words,* Viking, 1974; *Marcia,* Viking, 1976; *Daddy Is a Monster . . . Sometimes,* Lippincott, 1980.

Illustrator: Lucille B. Clifton, *All Us Come 'cross the Water,*

Holt, 1972; Eloise Greenfield, *She Come Bringing Me That Little Baby Girl,* Lippincott, 1974.

SIDELIGHTS: John Steptoe told *CA:* "One of my incentives for getting into writing children's books was the great and disastrous need for books that black children could honestly relate to. I ignorantly created precedents by writing such a book. I was amazed to find that no one had successfully written a book in the dialogue which black children speak." *Stevie* was written when Steptoe was sixteen.

BIOGRAPHICAL/CRITICAL SOURCES: Life, August 29, 1969; *New York Times Book Review,* November 30, 1969, November 11, 1970; *Children's Literature Review,* Volume II, Gale, 1976.

*   *   *

STERNER, R. Eugene   1912-

PERSONAL: Born July 7, 1912, in Clarion County, Pa.; son of J.C. and Mae (Ashbaugh) Sterner; married Mildred Rabberman (a clerical worker), August 19, 1935; children: Sylvia Waneta Sterner Wilson, Kathy Sue Sterner Hogue, Peggy Loree Sterner Hogue. *Education:* Anderson College, student, 1933-36; Louisiana Polytechnic Institute, B.A., 1941; Alabama Polytechnic Institute (now Auburn University), graduate study, 1942-43; Bonebrake Theological Seminary, theological study, 1947-49. *Politics:* Republican. *Home:* 4545 South Cole Ct., Morrison, Colo. 80465.

CAREER: Minister, Church of God; pastor of churches in Pennsylvania, Louisiana, Alabama, and Ohio, 1936-53, and director of youth work in ten southeastern states, 1944-45; Church of God, Anderson, Ind., director of Radio and Television Commission, 1953-62, director of Church Service, beginning 1962, speaker on "Christian Brotherhood Hour," 1967-77, president of Missionary Board and of commissions on race, social concerns, revision and planning, and world services; currently state minister, Colorado Conference, Church of God. Executive representative for Anderson School of Theology, Anderson College, Anderson, Ind. *Member:* National Religious Broadcasters (member of board of directors), General Commission on Chaplins and Armed Forces Personnel (vice-president), Kiwanis Club (member of board of directors, Anderson).

WRITINGS—All published by Warner Press: *Toward a Christian Fellowship,* 1957; *We Reach Our Hands in Fellowship,* 1960; *You Have a Ministry,* 1963; *Being the Community of Christian Love,* 1971; *Where Are You Going, Jesus?,* 1971; *I Was Thinking about the Church,* 1973; *Freedom's Holy Light,* 1976; *Healing and Wholeness,* 1978. Author of series of twelve booklets, "Steps toward Vital Christian Living," Warner Press, 1955. Contributor to *Vital Christianity* (denominational weekly) and to church school quarterlies.

SIDELIGHTS: R. Eugene Sterner told *CA:* "Writing is to responsibly share worthy thinking. It goes on long after the writer is gone, leaving a legacy for others. For me, there is, first, the gathering of resource material out of broad reading, thinking my subject through and seeing it in its components, outlining my approach and organizing the material before I even start the writing. I live it, think it, reflect upon it for effect and communication. Only then can I write with confidence in my clear objective."

*   *   *

STEVENS, Denis William   1922-

PERSONAL: Born March 2, 1922, in High Wycombe, Buckinghamshire, England; son of William James and Edith

(Driver) Stevens; married Sheila Holloway, June 25, 1949 (divorced); married Leocadia Kwasny, November 21, 1975; children: (first marriage) Anthony Vincent, Daphne Elizabeth, Michael David. *Education:* Jesus College, Oxford, M.A., 1947, graduate study, 1947-49. *Home:* 2203 Las Tunas Rd., Santa Barbara, Calif. 93103.

CAREER: Philharmonia Orchestra, London, England, violinist, 1949; British Broadcasting Corp., London, producer in Music Division, 1949-54; Ambrosian Singers, London, conductor, 1952-69; Columbia University, New York, N.Y., professor of musicology, 1964-75. Distinguished Visiting Professor, Pennsylvania State University, 1962-66; visiting professor, Cornell University, Columbia University, University of California, Berkeley, and University of Washington, 1976. Consultant in musicology, British Broadcasting Corp.; president and artistic director, Accademia Monteverdiana. Lecturer and conductor at principal international festivals. *Military service:* Royal Air Force, 1942-46; served in India and Burma. *Member:* International Musicological Society, Royal Academy of Music (honorary), Society of Antiquaries (fellow), American Musicological Society, Plainsong and Medieval Music Society, Societe Francaise de Musicologie, Worshipful Company of Musicians.

WRITINGS: The Mulliner Book: A Commentary, Stainer & Bell, 1952; *Tudor Church Music,* Merlin Press, 1955, 2nd edition, Norton, 1966; *Thomas Tomkins, 1572-1656,* St. Martin's, 1957; (editor) *A History of Song,* Hutchinson, 1960, Norton, 1961, revised edition, 1970; (with Edward Greenfield and Ivan March) *Stereo Record Guide,* Long Playing Record Library, Volume I, 1960, Volume II, 1961, Volume III, 1963; (editor with Alec Robertson) *The Pelican History of Music,* Penguin, Volume I: *Ancient Forms to Polyphony,* 1960, Volume II: *Renaissance and Baroque,* 1963, Volume III: *Classical and Romantic,* by Hugh Ottaway and Arthur Hutchins, 1968; *Penguin Book of English Madrigals for Four Voices,* Penguin, 1967; (translator and author of foreword) Francois Lesure, *Music and Art in Society,* Pennsylvania State University Press, 1968; *Second Penguin Book of English Madrigals,* Penguin, 1970; *Claudio Monteverdi,* Fairleigh Dickinson University Press, 1978; (editor) *The Letters of Claudio Monteverdi,* Cambridge University Press (New York), 1980; *Musicology: A Practical Guide,* Schirmer Books, 1980.

Also editor of music compositions published by Pennsylvania State University Press, including Handel's *Look Down Harmonious Saint,* 1963, and Thomas Roseingrave's *Compositions for Organ and Harpsichord,* 1964. Associate editor, *Grove's Dictionary of Music and Musicians,* 5th edition, St. Martin's, 1954. Contributor of articles to encyclopedias, dictionaries, popular magazines, and scholarly journals. Music critic, *Gramophone,* 1954-64.

WORK IN PROGRESS: Studies on fourteenth-century English music, Monteverdi, and Italian church music.

AVOCATIONAL INTERESTS: Travel and photography.

BIOGRAPHICAL/CRITICAL SOURCES: Times Literary Supplement, September 21, 1967.

*   *   *

STEWART, George Rippey 1895-1980

PERSONAL: Born May 31, 1895, in Sewickley, Pa.; died August 22, 1980, in San Francisco, Calif.; son of George Rippey and Ella (Wilson) Stewart; married Theodosia Burton, May 17, 1924; children: Jill Stewart Evenson, John Harris. *Education:* Princeton University, A.B., 1917; University

of California, M.A., 1920; Columbia University, Ph.D., 1922. *Home:* 1400 Geary Blvd., Apt. 2509, San Francisco, Calif. 94109.

CAREER: University of Michigan, Ann Arbor, instructor, 1922-23; University of California, Berkeley, 1923-80, professor of English, 1942-62, professor emeritus, 1962-80. Resident fellow in creative writing, Princeton University, 1942-43; Fulbright professor of American literature and civilization, University of Athens, 1952-53. *Military service:* U.S. Army, 1917-19. *Member:* Modern Language Association of America, American Name Society, Bohemian Club (San Francisco), Faculty Club (Berkeley). *Awards, honors:* Silver Medal of Commonwealth Club of California for *Ordeal by Hunger,* 1937, Gold Medal for *East of the Giants,* 1939; International Fantasy Award, 1951, for *Earth Abides;* Award of Merit, American Association for State and Local History, 1963, for *The California Trail;* L.H.D., University of California, 1963.

WRITINGS—Novels: *East of the Giants,* Holt, 1938; *Doctor's Oral,* Random House, 1939; *Storm* (Book of the Month Club selection), Random House, 1941; *Fire,* Random House, 1948; *Earth Abides,* Random House, 1949, 3rd edition, Hermes, 1974; *Sheep Rock,* Random House, 1951; *The Years of the City,* Houghton, 1955.

Nonfiction: *Bret Harte,* Houghton, 1931, reprinted, AMS Press, 1977; *Ordeal by Hunger,* Holt, 1936, reprinted, Houghton, 1960; *Names on the Land,* Random House, 1944; *Man: An Autobiography,* Random House, 1945; (co-author) *The Year of the Oath,* Doubleday, 1950, reprinted, Da Capo Press, 1971; *U.S. 40,* Houghton, 1953, reprinted, Greenwood Press, 1973; *American Ways of Life,* Doubleday, 1954, reprinted, Russell, 1971; *N.A. 1,* Houghton, 1957; *Pickett's Charge,* Houghton, 1960; *The California Trail,* McGraw, 1963; *Committee of Vigilance: Revolution in San Francisco,* Houghton, 1964; *Good Lives,* Houghton, 1967; *Not So Rich as You Think,* Houghton, 1968; *American Place-Names,* Oxford University Press, 1970; *Names on the Globe,* Oxford University Press, 1975; *American Given Names,* Oxford University Press, 1979. Also author of *Technique of English Verse,* 1930, *Bibliography of the Writings of Bret Harte,* 1933, and *John Phoenix Esquire,* 1937.

Juveniles: *To California by Covered Wagon,* Random House, 1954.

WORK IN PROGRESS: A biography of his father-in-law Marion Leroy Burton, a former president of the University of Michigan.

SIDELIGHTS: George Rippey Stewart once told *CA:* "[There are] a number of things that I like to do such as building brick walls, traveling, going to plays, reading, hunting for old trails, doing things with my grandchildren, and fishing. I have traveled over most of Europe, and over nearly all parts of North America. With my family I have lived in France, Mexico, and Greece."

BIOGRAPHICAL/CRITICAL SOURCES: New York Times Book Review, November 23, 1941, February 4, 1968, May 4, 1979; *Book World,* December 10, 1967, January 21, 1968; *Atlantic,* February, 1968; *South Atlantic Quarterly,* autumn, 1968; *New York Times,* September 18, 1970; *Saturday Review,* December 5, 1970; *New Republic,* February 13, 1971; *American Anthropologist,* December, 1971; *American Historical Review,* February, 1972.

*   *   *

STILES, Lindley Joseph 1913-

PERSONAL: Born July 1, 1913, in Tatum, N.M.; son of

David William and Flora (McClain) Stiles; married Marguerite Croonenberghs, July 27, 1935; children: Judith Marguerite Stiles Witmer, Patricia Ann. *Education:* University of Colorado, A.B., 1935, M.A., 1939, Ed.D., 1945. *Religion:* Protestant. *Home:* 3995 Apache Ct. E., Boulder, Colo. 80303.

CAREER: Teacher and principal in Colorado public schools, 1935-45; College of William and Mary, Williamsburg, Va., associate professor of education, 1945-46; University of Illinois at Urbana-Champaign, associate professor and director of student teaching, 1946-47; Ohio State University, Columbus, associate professor of secondary education and director of graduate studies in education, 1947-49; University of Virginia, Charlottesville, dean of School of Education, 1949-55; University of Wisconsin—Madison, dean of School of Education, 1955-66; Northwestern University, Evanston, Ill., professor of education for interdisciplinary studies, professor of sociology, and professor of political science, 1966-79, professor emeritus, 1979—. Summer professor at University of Hawaii, 1960.

MEMBER: National Society of College Teachers of Education (president, 1957-58), Aerospace Education Foundation (president, 1964-66), Air Force Association, American Association of School Administrators, National Education Association (life member), American Association for the Advancement of Science, American Academy of Social and Political Science, National Association of Secondary School Principals, American Association of Colleges for Teacher Education (member of executive committee, 1961-63), American Educational Research Association, American Association of University Professors, Wisconsin Congress of Parents and Teachers (honorary life member), John Dewey Society (member of executive committee, 1951-53), Phi Delta Kappa, Kappa Delta Pi, Phi Mu Sigma, Phi Kappa Pi, Alpha Phi Omega, Phi Eta Sigma. *Awards, honors:* Recognition Medal, University of Colorado, 1958; Distinguished Service in Education Certificate of Recognition, Wisconsin Elementary School Principals Association, 1961; Hoyt Vandenberg Trophy, Air Force Association/Aerospace Education Foundation, 1962; General Muir S. Fairchild Award, Arnold Air Society, 1964; Doctor of Letters, Rider College, 1967; Doctor of Laws, McKendree College, 1969.

WRITINGS: (With Inga Olla Helseth) *Supervision as Guidance,* Virginia Gazette Press, 1946; (with M. F. Dorsey) *Democratic Teaching in Secondary Schools,* Lippincott, 1950; *Moods and Moments* (poetry) Garrett, 1955; (editor) *The Teacher's Role in American Society,* Harper, 1957; (editor) *Teacher Education in the United States,* Ronald, 1960; (co-editor) *Education in Urban Society,* Dodd, 1962; (editor) *Secondary Education in the United States,* Harcourt, 1962; *Ideas and Images for Life with Young People* (poetry), Dembar Educational Research Services, 1964; *The Scholar Teacher,* Illinois State University, 1966; *The Present State of Neglect,* State Department of Public Instruction; *Teacher Certification and Preparation in Massachusetts: Status, Problems, and Proposed Solutions,* Massachusetts Advisory Council on Education, 1968; *Introduction to College: Education,* Putnam, 1969; *Cowboy in the Classroom: A Trilogy of Reflections on a Teaching Career,* Northwestern University Press, 1979.

Contributor of chapters to books. Advisory editor, Ginn's "Studies in Depth" series and Dodd, Mead's college books on education. Contributor to *Encyclopedia of Educational Research* and *Compton's Pictured Encyclopedia;* education advisor, *Random House Dictionary of the English Language.* Contributor of articles to professional journals.

AVOCATIONAL INTERESTS: Research, poetry, boating, golfing, and fishing.

*   *   *

STIRLING, Nora B(romley)   1900-

PERSONAL: Born 1900, in Atlanta, Ga.; daughter of Alexander Williamson (a physician) and Nora (Bromley) Stirling. *Education:* Attended Craigmount in Edinburgh, Scotland, Washington Seminary in Atlanta, Ga., and Madame Alberti's in New York, N.Y. *Home:* 865 United Nations Plaza, New York, N.Y. 10017. *Agent:* Curtis Brown Ltd., 575 Madison Ave., New York, N.Y. 10022.

CAREER: Actress on stage and radio for fifteen years (Broadway plays, stock, road companies, and some 450 radio programs), writing at same time for radio, then television; staff writer, National Broadcasting Co., 1942-45; freelance writer, mainly in field of mental health, 1949—. Consultant, Plays for Living (division of Family Service Association of America). *Member:* Radio Writers Guild (member of council, 1946-49), Authors Guild of Authors League of America, American Federation of Radio and Television Artists, Women's City Club, Query Club, Radio Executives Club.

WRITINGS: Treasure under the Sea, Doubleday, 1957; (contributor) *Reading for Men,* Doubleday, 1958; *Adventures for Today,* Harcourt, 1958, 2nd edition, 1962; *Exploring for Lost Treasure* (Junior Literary Guild selection), Doubleday, 1960; *Family Life Plays,* Association Press, 1961; *Up from the Sea,* Doubleday, 1963; *Who Wrote the Classics?,* John Day, Volume I, 1965, Volume II, 1968; *Wonders of Engineering,* Doubleday, 1966; *You Would If You Loved Me,* M. Evans, 1969; *Who Wrote the Modern Classics?,* John Day, 1970; *Your Money or Your Life,* Bobbs-Merrill, 1974.

Also author, with Nina Ridenour, of play, "My Name Is Legion" (dramatization of Clifford Beers' *A Mind That Found Itself*); author of serials and plays for radio and television and of more than fifty short plays on educational and sociological themes for various private and governmental service organizations. Contributor to Science Research Associates' "Comprehensive Reading" series, 1966. Contributor of articles to magazines and newspapers, including *Argosy, New York Times Magazine, Reader's Digest, True, Christian Science Monitor, Parents' Magazine, New Yorker,* and *Pastoral Psychology.*

WORK IN PROGRESS: A biography of Pearl S. Buck.

SIDELIGHTS: More than 250,000 copies of Nora B. Stirling's plays have been sold in the United States and abroad for production by local groups.

BIOGRAPHICAL/CRITICAL SOURCES: New York World Telegram, June 5, 1944; *New York Times,* October 15, 1944; *Parents' Magazine,* May, 1950; *Independent Woman,* June, 1950; *Life,* June 22, 1953; *Best Sellers,* December 15, 1970.

*   *   *

STOUT, Irving Wright   1903-1972

PERSONAL: Born December 15, 1903, in Fall River, Wis.; died August 9, 1972; son of Thomas Denzil and Etto (Wright) Stout; married Grace Brubaker, January 20, 1934; children: Thomas. *Education:* Platteville State Teachers College (now University of Wisconsin—Platteville), B.Ed., 1936; Northwestern University, M.A., 1944, Ed.D., 1948. *Politics:* Republican. *Religion:* Congregationalist. *Home:* 1303 Mill Ave., Tempe, Ariz. *Office:* Arizona State University, Tempe, Arizona.

CAREER: Milwaukee Public Schools, Milwaukee, Wis., 1928-48, began as teacher, became principal, director of guidance, 1945-47; New York University, New York, N.Y., associate professor of education, 1948-50; Southern Illinois University, Carbondale, Ill., professor of education, 1950-53; Arizona State University, Tempe, professor of education, beginning 1953, dean of Graduate College 1953-63, director of Head Start programs, beginning 1966. Senior partner, Wood & Stout Associates, beginning 1962; senior consultant, Rough Rock demonstration school, beginning 1965. *Member:* American Association of School Administrators, American Academy of Arts and Sciences (fellow), National School Public Relations Association, National Education Association, American Association of University Professors, Newcomen Society, American Association of School Superintendents, Association of Childhood Development, International Society for Research in Child Development, Phoenix Chamber of Commerce, Phi Delta Kappa, Alpha Kappa Delta, Masons.

WRITINGS—All published by John Day, except as indicated: *Well-Adjusted Children,* 1951; *Discipline of Well-Adjusted Children,* 1952; *Teacher-Parent Interviews,* Prentice-Hall, 1954; *Helping Parents Understand Their Child's School,* Prentice-Hall, 1957; *Bringing Up Children,* 1960; *School Public Relations,* Putnam, 1960; *Teaching Moral and Spiritual Values,* 1962; (with Grace Langdon) *Teaching in the Primary Grades,* Macmillan, 1964; (with Langdon) *Homework,* 1969. Co-author, daily newspaper column, "Today's Children," syndicated by King Features. Contributor to professional journals.†

*   *   *

STRAITON, E(dward) C(ornock)   1917-
(Eddie Straiton; pseudonym: T. V. Vet)

PERSONAL: Born March 27, 1917, in Clydebank, Scotland; son of George Ramsay (a farmer) and May (Cornock) Straiton; married Loraine Harrison, March 2, 1943; children: Loraine Mary (Mrs. Philip Channer). *Education:* Glasgow University, M.R.C.V.S., 1940. *Politics:* Conservative. *Religion:* Christian. *Home:* Rock House, New Road, Penkridge, Staffordshire, England. *Office:* Veterinary Hospital, Penkridge, Staffordshire, England.

CAREER: Veterinarian in private practice, Penkridge, Staffordshire, England, 1943—. Television veterinarian for British Broadcasting Corporation, 1956—. Advisor to "All Creatures Great and Small" television series. *Military service:* British Army, 1943-45; became captain. *Member:* British Veterinary Association, British Small Animal Veterinary Association, Institute of Advanced Motorists.

WRITINGS—All under pseudonym T. V. Vet, except as indicated; all published by Farming Press, except as indicated: *The T. V. Vet Book for Stock Farmers,* Volume I: *Recognition and Treatment of Common Cattle Ailments,* 1964, 3rd edition, 1972, Volume II: *Calving the Cow and the Care of the Calf,* 1965, 2nd edition, 1972; *The T. V. Vet Book for Pig Farmers: How to Recognize and Treat Common Pig Ailments,* 1967, 4th edition, 1976; *The T. V. Vet Horse Book: Recognition and Treatment of Common Horse and Pony Ailments,* 1971, 5th edition, 1976, published under real name as *The Horse Owner's Vet Book: Recognition and Treatment of Common Horse and Pony Ailments,* Lippincott, 1973, revised edition, 1979; *The T. V. Vet Sheep Book: Recognition and Treatment of Common Sheep Ailments,* 1972, 3rd edition, 1976; *The T. V. Vet Dog Book: Recognition and Treatment of Common Dog Ailments,* 1974, 2nd edition,

1978; *Cats, Their Health and Care: Owner's Guide to Cat Ailments and Conditions,* 1977; *Junior Book of Pet Care,* 1978; (under name Eddie Straiton) *Animals Are My Life* (autobiography), J. A. Allen, 1979. Contributor to professional journals, including *British Farmer and Stockbreeder* and *Horse and Pony.*

WORK IN PROGRESS: A sequel to *Animals Are My Life.*

*   *   *

STRAND, Kenneth A(lbert)   1927-

PERSONAL: Born September 18, 1927, in Tacoma, Wash.; son of Jens Albrigt and Bertha (Odegaard) Strand; married Lois Marie Lutz (a high school teacher), June 1, 1952. *Education:* Emmanuel Missionary College, B.A., 1952; University of Michigan, M.A., 1955, Ph.D., 1958. *Office:* Department of Church History, Andrews University Theological Seminary, Berrien Springs, Mich. 49104.

CAREER: Emmanuel Missionary College (now undergraduate college of Andrews University), Berrien Springs, Mich., associate professor of religion, 1959-62; Andrews University Theological Seminary, Berrien Springs, associate professor, 1962-66, professor of church history, 1966—. *Member:* International Society for the Comparative Study of Civilizations, Renaissance Society of America, American Society for Reformation Research, American Historical Association, American Society of Church History, American Association of University Professors, Society of Biblical Literature, Phi Beta Kappa.

WRITINGS—All published by Ann Arbor Publishers, except as indicated: *A Reformation Paradox: The Condemned New Testament of the Rostock Brethren of the Common Life,* 1960; *Reformation Bibles in the Crossfire: The Story of Jerome Emser, His Anti-Lutheran Critique and His Catholic Bible Version,* 1961; (editor) *The Reformation and Other Topics Presented to Honor Albert Hyma,* 1962, 2nd edition, 1964; *German Bibles before Luther: The Story of Fourteen High-German Editions,* Eerdmans, 1966; *Early Low-German Bibles: The Story of Four Pre-Lutheran Editions,* Eerdmans, 1967; *Three Essays on Early Church History with Emphasis on the Roman Province of Asia,* Braun-Brumfield, 1967; (editor) *Essays on the Northern Renaissance,* 1968; (editor) *Essays on Luther,* 1969; *Brief Introduction to the Ancient Near East: A Panorama of the Old Testament World,* Braun-Brumfield, 1969; *The Open Gates of Heaven: A Brief Introduction to Literary Analysis of the Book of Revelation,* Braun-Brumfield, 1970; *Reform Appeals of Luther and Calvin,* Braun-Brumfield, 1974; *Perspectives in the Book of Revelation: Essays on Apocalyptic Interpretation,* 1975; *Interpreting the Book of Revelation: Hermeneutical Guidelines, with Brief Introduction to Literary Analysis,* 1976, 2nd edition, 1979; *The Early Christian Sabbath: Selected Essays and a Source Collection,* 1979; (editor and contributor) *The Sabbath in Scripture and History,* Review & Herald, 1981.

Compiler—All published by Ann Arbor Publishers: *Woodcuts from the Earliest Lutheran and Emserian New Testaments,* 1962; *Reformation Bible Pictures: Woodcuts from Early Lutheran and Emserian New Testaments,* 1963; *Woodcuts to the Apocalypse in Duerer's Time,* 1966; *Woodcuts to the Apocalypse from the Early 16th Century,* 1969; *Duerer's Apocalypse: The 1498 German and 1511 Latin Texts in Facsimile Plus Samples of Duerer's Woodcuts and Graeff's Copies,* 1969; *Luther's "September Bible" in Facsimile,* 1972; *Facsimiles from Early Luther Bibles,* two volumes, 1972.

Contributor to scholarly journals, including *Journal of Biblical Literature, New Testament Studies, Archive for Reformation History,* and *Renaissance Quarterly. Andrews University Seminary Studies,* associate editor, 1967-74, editor, 1974—.

WORK IN PROGRESS: Studies on phases of Reformation history, with a book planned on Reformation-era Catholic-German Bibles, for Ann Arbor Publishers.

SIDELIGHTS: Kenneth A. Strand indicates to *CA* that his special interest in writing of the experiences of people in other times, places, and cultures rests on his conviction "that these are both interesting and relevant to us and we see and learn to appreciate the common in the unfamiliar and the unfamiliar in the common." Biblical and historical studies in particular, he feels, have great value as potential sources for the enrichment of human life today. As for his more reference-oriented publications, Strand reports that he enjoys preparing aids for librarians and other researchers "who devote their time so generously to helping others."

*   *   *

STRATHERN, Ann Marilyn   1941-

PERSONAL: Born March 6, 1941, in England; married Andrew J. Strathern. *Education:* Cambridge University, B.A. (honors), 1963, M.A., 1967, Ph.D., 1968. *Office:* Girton College, Cambridge University, Cambridge, England.

CAREER: Cambridge University, Cambridge, England, assistant curator of Museum of Archaeology and Anthropology, 1966-68, director of studies at Girton College, 1968; Australian National University, New Guinea Research Unit, Papua, research fellow, 1970-72, 1974-76; Cambridge University, fellow of Girton College, 1979—. *Member:* Royal Anthropological Society (fellow), Association of Social Anthropologists (England), Association of Social Anthropologists (Australia).

WRITINGS: (With husband, Andrew J. Strathern) *Self-Decoration in Mount Hagen,* Duckworth, 1971; *Women in Between: Female Roles in a Male World,* Mount Hagen, New Guinea, Seminar Press, 1972; (editor) *Nature, Culture and Gender,* Cambridge University Press, 1980; (with Audrey Richards) *Kinship at the Core,* Cambridge University Press, in press. Contributor to *New Guinea Research Bulletin.*

*   *   *

STRICKLAND, Stephen P(arks)   1933-

PERSONAL: Born November 25, 1933, in Birmingham, Ala.; son of Kelly Parks and Alice Winn (Peeples) Strickland; married Tamara Gunsard (an interior decorator), June 15, 1962. *Education:* Emory University, B.A., 1952; Johns Hopkins University, M.A., 1966, Ph.D., 1971. *Home:* 3010 32nd St. N.W., Washington, D.C. 20008.

CAREER: Lycee de Garcons, Mulhouse, France, instructor in English, 1956-57; high school teacher in Alabama, 1957-58; U.S. House of Representatives, Washington, D.C., Congressional staff assistant, 1959-65; American Political Science Association, Washington, D.C., congressional staff fellow, 1965-66; American Council on Education, Washington, D.C., staff associate, 1967-69; President's Commission on White House Fellows, Washington, D.C., associate director, 1967-68, acting director, 1968-69; University of California, San Francisco, Health Policy Program, director of Washington, D.C. office, 1970—. Adjunct professor, University of California, San Francisco, 1970—. President and

treasurer, *The Public Record,* 1970—. Consultant to Office of the Secretary, U.S. Department of Health, Education, and Welfare, 1969-71, Office of Assistant Secretary of Planning and Evaluation, 1971—, Chief Medical Director, Veterans Administration, 1972—, Drug Abuse Council, 1972—, and Citizens Committee on the Population and the American Future, 1972—; senior consultant, Advanced Learning Concepts, Inc., 1971—. Chairman of board of directors, Choral Arts Society of Washington, D.C., 1969-71. *Military service:* U.S. Army Reserve, 1958-67. *Member:* American Political Science Association.

WRITINGS: (Editor and contributor) *Hugo Black and the Supreme Court,* Bobbs-Merrill, 1967; (editor and contributor) *Sponsored Research in American Universities,* American Council on Education, 1968; (editor with John T. Grupenhoff) *Federal Laws: Health and Environment Manpower,* Science and Health Communications Group, 1972; *Politics, Science, and Dread Disease,* Harvard University Press, 1972; *U.S. Health Care: What's Wrong and What's Right,* Potomac Associates, 1972; (with Douglass Cater) *TV Violence and the Child: The Evolution and Fate of the Surgeon General's Report,* Russell Sage Foundation, 1975; (with wife, Tamara G. Strickland) *The Markle Scholars: A Brief History,* Prodist, for John amd Mary Markle Foundation, 1976; *Research and the Health of Americans: Improving the Policy Process,* Heath Lexington, 1978.†

*   *   *

STRYJKOWSKI, Julian   1905-

PERSONAL: Born April 27, 1905, in Stryj, Poland (now in Union of Soviet Socialist Republics). *Education:* University of Lwow, D.Ph., 1932. *Home:* Wyzwolenia 2/47, Warsaw, Poland.

CAREER: Writer. *Tworczsc* (literary monthly), Warsaw, Poland, editor, 1954. *Awards, honors:* Award from Alfred Jurzykowski Foundation (New York), 1980.

WRITINGS—Published by Czytelnik, except as indicated: *Bieg do Fragala* (short stories; title means "Course to Fragala"), 1951; *Pozegnanie z Italia* (title means "Farewell to Italy"), 1954; *Glosy w ciemnosci* (novel; title means "Voices in the Dark"), 1956; *Imie wlasne: Opowiadania* (short stories), 1961; *Czarna roza* (short stories; title means "The Black Rose"), 1962; *Austeria,* 1966, translation by Celina Wieniewska published as *The Inn,* Harcourt, 1971; *Na Wierzbach nasze skrzypce* (short stories; title means "On Willows Our Fiddles"), 1974; *Sen Azrila* (novel; title means "Azril's Dream"), 1975; *Przybysz z Narbony* (novel; title means "The Visitor from Narbona"), 1977; *Wielki Strach* (novel; title means "The Great Fear"), 1980.

Plays: "Dziedzictwo" (title means "Heir"), first produced in 1955; "Sodoma" (title means "Sodom"), first produced in 1963.

SIDELIGHTS: Stryjkowski's books have been translated into fourteen languages.

*   *   *

SUGGS, M(arion) Jack   1924-

PERSONAL: Born June 5, 1924, in Electra, Tex.; son of Claude Frank and Lottie Mae (Gibson) Suggs; married Ruth Barge, 1943; children: Adena Ruth, James Robert, David Nathan. *Education:* University of Texas, B.A., 1946; Texas Christian University, B.D., 1950; Duke University, Ph.D., 1954. *Home:* 5605 Winifred Dr., Fort Worth, Tex. 76133. *Office:* Brite Divinity School, Texas Christian University, Fort Worth, Tex. 76129.

CAREER: First Christian Church, Gladewater, Tex., minister, 1948-50; Wendell Christian Church, Wendell, N.C., minister, 1950-52; Texas Christian University, Brite Divinity School, Fort Worth, Tex., assistant professor, 1952-56, professor of New Testament, 1956-76, dean, 1976—. McFadin Lecturer, Texas Christian University, 1961; convention lecturer in several states. *Member:* Society of Biblical Literature, American Academy of Religion (president, southwestern region, 1959), Phi Beta Kappa, Alpha Kappa Delta, Pi Gamma Mu, Theta Phi. *Awards, honors:* American Council of Learned Societies and American Association of Theological Schools fellowships for research, 1963-64; Christian Research Foundation book award, 1969, for *Wisdom, Christology and Law in Matthew's Gospel;* distinguished alumnus award, Texas Christian University, 1973.

WRITINGS: The Layman Reads His Bible, Bethany, 1957; *The Gospel Story,* Bethany, 1960; (co-editor) *Studies in the History and Text of the New Testament,* University of Utah, 1967; (contributor) W. R. Farmer, C.F.D. Moule, and R. R. Niebuhr, editors, *Christian History and Interpretation,* Cambridge University Press, 1967; *Wisdom, Christology and Law in Matthew's Gospel,* Harvard University Press, 1970; (contributor) D. E. Aune, editor, *Studies in New Testament and Early Christian Literature,* E. J. Brill, 1972; (contributor) Georg Strecker, editor, *Jesus Christus in Historie und Theologie,* J.C.B. Mohr, 1975. New Testament editor, Oxford study edition of the New English Bible, Oxford University Press, 1976. Contributor to scholarly and religious journals.

AVOCATIONAL INTERESTS: Golf, camping, spectator sports.

* * *

SULLIVAN, (Donovan) Michael 1916-

PERSONAL: Born October 29, 1916, in Toronto, Ontario, Canada; son of Alan (an explorer and author) and Elizabeth (Hees) Sullivan; married Ngo Khoan (a biologist), July 20, 1943. *Education:* Cambridge University, B.A. in Architecture, 1939, M.A., 1949, Litt.D., 1966; School of Oriental and African Studies, B.A. (honors in Chinese), 1950; Harvard University, Ph.D. in Fine Arts, 1952. *Office:* Department of Art, Stanford University, Stanford, Calif. 94305.

CAREER: West China Union University, Chengtu, China, lecturer and assistant museum curator, 1942-45; Ginling College, Chengtu, English professor, 1945-46; University of Malaya, Singapore, curator of art museum and lecturer in history of art, 1954-60; University of London, School of Oriental and African Studies, London, England, lecturer in Asian art, 1960-66; Stanford University, Stanford, Calif., professor of Oriental art, 1966—, Christensen Professor of Oriental Art, 1975—. Visiting professor of fine art, University of Michigan, 1964. Slade Professor of Fine Art, Oxford University, 1973-74. Fellow of St. Catherine's College, Oxford University, 1979—. *Member:* American Academy of Arts and Sciences, Royal Society of Arts (fellow). *Awards, honors:* Rockefeller Foundation traveling fellowship in United States, 1950-51; Bollingen Foundation research fellowship in United States, 1952-54; Litt.D. from Cambridge University, 1966, and Oxford University, 1973; Guggenheim fellowship, 1974; National Endowment for the Humanities fellowship, 1976-77; Commonwealth Club's silver medal, 1980.

WRITINGS: Chinese Art in the Twentieth Century, University of California Press, 1959.

An Introduction to Chinese Art, University of California

Press, 1961; *The Birth of Landscape Painting in China,* University of California Press, 1962; *Chinese Ceramics, Bronzes and Jades in the Collection of Sir Alan and Lady Barlow,* [London], 1963; (contributor) Raymond Dawson, editor, *The Legacy of China,* Oxford University Press, 1964; *Chinese and Japanese Art,* Grolier and F. Watts, 1966; *A Short History of Chinese Art,* University of California Press, 1967; *The Cave Temples of Mai-chi-shan,* University of California Press, 1969.

The Meeting of Eastern and Western Art, New York Graphic Society, 1973; *Chinese Art: Recent Discoveries,* Thames & Hudson, 1973; *The Arts of China,* University of California Press, 1973, revised edition, 1980; *The Three Perspectives,* Thames & Hudson, 1974; *Symbols of Eternity: The Art of Landscape Painting in China,* Stanford University Press, 1979; *Chinese Landscaping: Sui and T'ang Dynasties,* University of California Press, 1980. Contributor of articles on Chinese art to *Collier's Encyclopedia, Encyclopaedia Britannica, Chambers's Encyclopedia, Encyclopedia Universale dell 'Arte* and others; contributor to journals and newspapers in United States and England.

WORK IN PROGRESS: Art and the Artist in Chinese Society.

* * *

SUMMERS, Hollis (Spurgeon, Jr.) 1916-
(Jim Hollis, a joint pseudonym)

PERSONAL: Born June 21, 1916, in Eminence, Ky.; son of Hollis Spurgeon and Hazel (Holmes) Summers; married Laura Vimont Clarke, June 30, 1943; children: Hollis Spurgeon III, David Clarke. *Education:* Georgetown College, A.B., 1937; Middlebury College, M.A., 1943; University of Iowa, Ph.D., 1949. *Politics:* Democrat. *Religion:* Baptist. *Home:* 181 North Congress, Athens, Ohio. *Office:* English Department, Ohio University, Athens, Ohio.

CAREER: Holmes High School, Covington, Ky., English teacher, 1937-44; Georgetown College, Georgetown, Ky., professor of English, 1944-49; University of Kentucky, Lexington, professor of English, 1949-59; Ohio University, Athens, professor of English, 1959—. Danforth Lecturer, 1963-64. Fulbright lecturer, University of Canterbury, 1978. Staff member of writers' conferences at such places as Bread Loaf School of English, Antioch, and Morehead. *Awards, honors:* Fund for Advancement of Education grant to visit writing programs in U.S. colleges and universities, 1951-52; College of Arts and Sciences Distinguished Professor of the Year, 1958-59; *Saturday Review* poetry award, 1957, for "Mexico Picnic"; D. Litt., Georgetown College, 1965; National Foundation of Arts grant, 1975.

WRITINGS: City Limit (novel), Houghton, 1948; *Brighten the Corner* (novel), Doubleday, 1952; (editor) *Kentucky Story,* University of Kentucky Press, 1954; (with James Rourke, under joint pseudonym Jim Hollis) *Teach You a Lesson* (novel), Harper, 1956; *The Weather of February* (novel), Harper, 1957; *The Walks Near Athens* (poems), Harper, 1959.

(With Edgar Whan) *Literature: An Introduction,* McGraw, 1960; *Someone Else* (poem for children), Lippincott, 1962; (editor) *Discussions of the Short Story,* Heath, 1963; *Seven Occasions,* Rutgers University Press, 1965; *The Peddler, and Other Domestic Matters,* Rutgers University Press, 1967; *The Day after Sunday,* Harper, 1968.

Start from Home (poems), Rutgers University Press, 1972; *The Garden* (novel), Harper, 1972; *How They Chose the*

Dead (short stories), University of Louisiana Press, 1973; *Occupant Please Forward*, Rutgers University Press, 1976; *Dinosaur* (poems), Rosetta Press, 1977.

SIDELIGHTS: Prairie Schooner reviewer Robert L. Peters writes of Hollis Summers' poetry: "Hollis Summers' dominant trait is a quiet clarity. His effects recall the painter Andrew Wyeth's steady melancholy, his whimsical affection for the mundane, and his strong shadows. . . . Summers allows his forms a full display; their structures glow with vitality."

Miller Williams suggests in his review in *Saturday Review* that Summers' "quiet clarity" reflects the fact that "Summers has an easy hand; he employs the devices of both conventional poetry and contemporary language without awkwardness. . . . More than most poets working now, Summers is given to the abstraction, the direct statement. He cares little for—or, anyway, makes relatively little use of—the submerged metaphor and other indirect ways to meaning, and objects with which he builds his images are usually what he calls them, with nothing hidden inside. This is not to disparage the plainer poems. The direct statement almost always does the job; but it is the lines rich with sense not immediately seen that are strongest."

BIOGRAPHICAL/CRITICAL SOURCES: Prairie Schooner, winter, 1965-66; *Saturday Review*, March 9, 1968; *Contemporary Literary Criticism*, Volume X, Gale, 1979.

*   *   *

SUMMERSELL, Charles Grayson 1908-

PERSONAL: Born February 25, 1908, in Mobile, Ala.; son of Charles Fishweek Gibbs and Sally Rebecca (Grayson) Summersell; married Frances Sharpley, 1934. *Education:* University of Alabama, A.B., 1929, M.A., 1930; Vanderbilt University, Ph.D., 1940. *Religion:* Methodist Episcopal Church. *Home:* 1411 Caplewood Dr., Tuscaloosa, Ala. 35401. *Office:* Department of History, University of Alabama, Tuscaloosa, Ala.

CAREER: University of Alabama, Tuscaloosa, 1935—, began as instructor, professor of history, 1947—, chairman of department, 1954—. Treasurer, Alabama Historical Commission; chairman, Tannehill Furnace and Foundry Commission. *Military service:* U.S. Naval Reserve, 1943-45, 1950-53; became commander; received Letter of Commendation. *Member:* Organization of American Historians, Newcomen Society in North America, U.S. Naval Institute, Sons of the American Revolution (former president, Alabama Society), American Historical Association, American Association of State and Local History, Southern Historical Association, Alabama Historical Association (president, 1956; member of executive committee, 1962—), Phi Beta Kappa (former president, Alpha of Alabama Chapter), Phi Alpha Theta, University Club.

WRITINGS: (With others) *Alabama Past and Future*, Science Research Associates, 1941, revised edition, 1950; *Historical Foundations of Mobile*, Bureau of Educational Research, 1949; *Mobile: History of a Seaport Town*, University of Alabama Press, 1949; *Alabama History for Schools*, Colonial Press, 1957, revised edition, 1961; *Exploring Alabama*, Colonial Press, 1957, 6th edition, 1975; *The Cruise of the C.S.S. Sumter*, Confederate Publishing, 1965; (editor and author of notes) *The Journal of George Townley Fulham*, University of Alabama Press, 1973; (editor, author of introduction, and compiler of bibliography) Peter J. Hamilton, *Colonial Mobile* (originally published in 1910), University of Alabama Press, 1976.

Collaborator on "Alabama History Filmstrips," Associated Educators, 1961, "Florida History Filmstrips," 1963, 1964, and "Texas History Filmstrips," Associated Educators, 1965. Contributor to major encyclopedias and to professional journals. Member of editorial advisory board, *American Neptune, A Quarterly Journal of Maritime History;* member of editorial board, *Alabama Review.*

WORK IN PROGRESS: Rivers of Alabama—A History.

AVOCATIONAL INTERESTS: Photography, including microphotography and audio-visual devices, boating and swimming.

*   *   *

SUPER, Donald E(dwin) 1910-

PERSONAL: Born July 10, 1910, in Honolulu, Hawaii; son of Paul and Margaret-Louise (Stump) Super; married Anne-Margaret Baker, 1936; children: Robert Marion, Charles McAfee. *Education:* University of Oxford, B.A., 1932, M.A., 1936; Columbia University, Ph.D., 1940. *Home:* 124 Stonebridge Rd., Montclair, N.J.

CAREER: Young Men's Christian Association, Cleveland, Ohio, secretary, 1932-36; Columbia University, Teachers College, New York, N.Y., research assistant, 1936-38; Clark University, Worcester, Mass., assistant professor, 1938-42; Columbia University, Teachers College, associate professor of education, 1945-49, professor of psychology and education, 1949-75, professor emeritus, 1975—; Cambridge University, Wolfson College, Cambridge, England, fellow, 1975-79. University of Paris, Fulbright lecturer, 1958-59, visiting professor, 1976-79. American specialist in Japan, 1961. President, Montclair Board of Education, Montclair, N.J., beginning 1965. *Military service:* U.S. Army Air Forces, 1942-45; became major. *Member:* American Personnel and Guidance Association (president, 1953-54), American Psychological Association (president of division of counseling psychology, 1952-53), American Educational Research Association, American Association for the Advancement of Science, International Association for Educational and Vocational Guidance (vice-president, 1960—). *Awards, honors:* Ford fellow in Poland, 1960.

WRITINGS: Avocational Interest Patterns, Stanford University Press, 1940; *Dynamics of Vocational Adjustment*, Harper, 1942; (with John O. Crites) *Appraising Vocational Fitness*, Harper, 1949, 2nd edition, 1962; *Opportunities in Psychology*, Vocational Guidance Manuals, 1955, 2nd edition published as *Opportunities in Psychology Careers*, 1968, 3rd edition published as *Opportunities in Psychology Careers Today*, 1976; *Psychology of Careers*, Harper, 1957; *Vocational Development*, Teachers College, Columbia University, 1957; *Scientific Careers and Vocational Development Theory*, Teachers College, Columbia University, 1957; (with Phoebe L. Overstreet) *Vocational Maturity of Ninth-Grade Boys*, Teachers College, Columbia University, 1960; *Career Development: Self-Concept Theory*, College Entrance Examination Board, 1963; *La Psychologie des Interets*, Presses Universitaires de France, 1964; (compiler) *Computer-Assisted Counseling*, Teachers College Press, 1970; *Occupational Psychology*, Wadsworth, 1970; *Measuring Vocational Maturity for Counseling and Evaluation*, National Vocational Guidance Association, 1974; *Work Values Inventory* (booklet), Riverside Press, 1976. Consulting editor, *Journal of Vocational Behavior* and *British Journal of Guidance and Counselling.*

WORK IN PROGRESS: The Career Pattern Study, a twenty-year study of vocational development; two monographs.

SYMONS, Julian (Gustave) 1912-

PERSONAL: Born May 30, 1912, in London, England; son of Morris Albert (an auctioneer) and Minnie Louise (Bull) Symons; married Kathleen Clark, October 25, 1941; children: Marcus Richard Julian. *Education:* Educated in state schools in England. *Politics:* "Left wing, with no specific party allegiance." *Home:* Groton House, 330 Dover Rd., Walmer, Deal, Kent, England. *Agent:* Curtis Brown, Ltd., 1 Craven Hill, London W2 3EP, England.

CAREER: Shorthand typist and secretary in London, England, 1929-41; advertising copywriter in London, 1944-47; full-time writer, 1947—. Member of council, Westfield College, University of London, 1972—. *Military service:* British Army, Royal Armoured Corps, 1942-44. *Member:* Crime Writers Association (chairman, 1958-59), Society of Authors (chairman of committee of management, 1970-71), Mystery Writers of America, P.E.N., Detective's Club (president, 1976—), Royal Society of Literature (fellow). *Awards, honors:* Crime Writers Association, award for best crime story of the year, 1957, for *The Color of Murder,* special award, 1966, for *Crime and Detection;* Mystery Writers of America, Edgar Allan Poe Award for best crime story of the year, 1961, for *The Progress of a Crime,* special award, 1973, for *Bloody Murder;* Grand Master of Swedish Academy of Detection, 1977, and Danish Poe-Kluhben, 1979.

WRITINGS—Poems: *Confusions about X,* Fortune Press, 1939; *The Second Man,* Routledge & Kegan Paul, 1943; *A Reflection on Auden,* Poem-of-the-Month Club, 1973; *The Object of an Affair,* Tragara Press, 1974.

Novels; published by Harper, except as indicated: *The Immaterial Murder Case,* Gollancz, 1945, Macmillan, 1957; *A Man Called Jones,* Gollancz, 1947, reprinted, Collins, 1963; *Bland Beginning,* 1949 (published in England as *Bland Beginning: A Detective Story,* Gollancz, 1949); *The 31st of February* (also see below), 1950 (published in England as *The Thirtyfirst of February: A Mystery Novel,* Gollancz, 1950); *The Broken Penny,* Gollancz, 1952, 1953; *The Narrowing Circle,* 1954 (published in England as *The Narrowing Circle: A Crime Novel,* Gollancz, 1954); *The Paper Chase,* Collins, 1956, published as *Bogue's Fortune,* 1957; *The Color of Murder,* 1957; *The Gigantic Shadow,* Collins, 1958, published as *The Pipe Dream,* 1959; *The Progress of a Crime* (also see below), 1960; *The Plain Man,* 1962 (published in England as *The Killing of Francie Lake,* Collins, 1962); *The End of Solomon Grundy* (also see below), 1964; *The Belting Inheritance,* 1965; *The Julian Symons Omnibus* (contains "The 31st of February," "The Progress of a Crime," and "The End of Solomon Grundy"), Collins, 1966; *The Man Who Killed Himself,* 1967; *The Man Whose Dreams Came True,* 1968; *The Man Who Lost His Wife,* 1970; *The Players and the Game,* 1972; *The Plot against Roger Rider,* 1973; *A Three-Pipe Problem,* 1975; *The Blackheath Poisonings,* 1978; *Sweet Adelaide,* 1980.

Other works: (Editor) *An Anthology of War Poetry,* Penguin, 1942; (editor and author of introduction) Samuel Johnson, *Selected Writings,* Grey Walls Press, 1949, British Book Centre (New York), 1950; *A.J.A. Symons: His Life and Speculations,* Eyre & Spottiswoode, 1950; *Charles Dickens,* Roy, 1951, 2nd edition, Arthur Barker, 1969; *Thomas Carlyle: The Life and Ideas of a Prophet,* Oxford University Press (New York), 1952, reprinted, Books for Libraries, 1970; *Horatio Bottomley: A Biography,* Cresset Press, 1955; (editor) Thomas Carlyle, *Selected Works, Reminiscences and Letters,* Clarke, Irwin & Co., 1956, Harvard University Press, 1957; *The General Strike: A Historical*

Portrait, Cresset Press, 1957, Dufour, 1963; *The Hundred Best Crime Stories,* Sunday Times, 1959.

A Reasonable Doubt: Some Criminal Cases Re-examined, Cresset Press, 1960; *The Thirties: A Dream Revolved,* Cresset Press, 1960, Greenwood Press, 1973, revised edition, Faber, 1975; *Murder, Murder* (short story collection) Fontana Books, 1961; *The Detective Story in Britain,* Longmans, Green, 1962; *Buller's Campaign,* Cresset Press, 1963; *Francis Quarles Investigates* (short story collection), Panther Books, 1965; *England's Pride: The Story of the Gordon Relief Expedition,* Hamish Hamilton, 1965; *Critical Occasions,* Hamish Hamilton, 1966; *A Pictorial History of Crime,* Crown, 1966 (published in England, as *Crime and Detection: An Illustrated History from 1840,* Studio Vista, 1966); (editor) A.J.A. Symons, *Essays and Biographies,* Cassell, 1969; *Mortal Consequences: A History—from the Detective Story to the Crime Novel,* Harper, 1972 (published in England as *Bloody Murder; from the Detective Story to the Crime Novel: A History,* Faber, 1972); (editor and author of introduction) *Between the Wars: Britain in Photo,* Batsford, 1972; *Notes from Another Country,* Alan Ross, 1972; (editor and author of introduction) Wilkie Collins, *The Woman Who Wore White,* Penguin, 1974; (editor) *The Angry Thirties,* Eyre & Spottiswoode, 1976; *The Tell-Tale Heart: The Life and Works of Edgar Allan Poe,* Harper, 1978; *Portrait of an Artist: Conan Doyle,* Whizzard/Deutsch, 1980; (editor) Edgar Allan Poe, *Selected Tales,* Oxford University Press, 1980.

Also author of radio plays "Affection Unlimited," 1968, and "Night Rider to Dover," 1969, and of television plays "Miranda and a Salesman," 1963, "The Witnesses," 1964, "The Finishing Touch," 1965, "Curtains for Sheila," 1965, "Tigers of Subtopia," 1968, "The Pretenders," 1970, and "Whatever's Peter Playing At?," 1974. Editor, "Penguin Mystery" series, beginning 1974. Contributor to *Times Literary Supplement, New York Times,* and other newspapers and magazines. Editor, *Twentieth Century Verse,* 1937-39; reviewer, *Manchester Evening News,* 1947-56, and *Sunday Times,* 1958—.

WORK IN PROGRESS: A new crime story; an anthology of crime short stories; a collection of critical essays.

SIDELIGHTS: Although a respected poet, critic, biographer, and historian, Julian Symons is also well-known for his crime novels. These works have been widely acclaimed for their psychological insight and complexity and for the variety of forms and techniques they display. In the *Armchair Detective,* Steven R. Carter notes that Symons's novels extend from the "conventional detective" to "acute social satires" and remarks that "Symons has helped to increase the range and worth of crime fiction in many ways." Carter elaborates: "His crime novels . . . combine ingenious plotting with psychological and social probing. In addition, he has a gift . . . for wry humor and satire." The critic states that while Symons is not the only writer to possess such talents, "The variety of his forms and techniques goes beyond that of any other crime writer." In the same publication, Allen J. Huben contends: "Symons does not repeat himself: Each novel stands alone on its own credentials, which are usually impressive."

Symons uses the structure of the crime novel to examine contemporary problems and concerns, such as political corruption, moral instability, and, most importantly, "the violence behind respectable faces." In his introduction to *The Julian Symons Omnibus,* the author reflects: "Why put such ideas . . . into the form of crime stories, rather than 'straight' novels? The thing that absorbs me most in our age is the violence behind respectable faces, the civil servant planning how to kill Jews most efficiently, the judge speaking with passion about the need for capital punishment, the quiet obedient boy who kills for fun. These are extreme cases, but if you want to show the violence that lives behind the bland faces most of us present to the world, what better vehicle can you have than the crime novel?''

Leo Harris of *Books and Bookmen* calls Symons "one of the few truly professional crime writers of the day who do not content themselves with merely entertaining, with merely purveying wish-fulfillment or timepassing puzzles. His books have always the rebarbative surface of warts-and-all truthfulness." And Carter, in discussing the scope of Symon's novels, comments: "The success of many of his experiments in the form has shown that the mystery need not constrain a talented writer either technically or thematically. His main contribution to the crime novel is that he has proven how flexible a vehicle it is for presenting a personal vision of the stresses of modern western civilization."

Symons's manuscript collection is housed at the University of Texas at Austin.

AVOCATIONAL INTERESTS: Cricket and football.

BIOGRAPHICAL/CRITICAL SOURCES: Francis Scarfe, *Auden and After: The Liberation of Poetry, 1930-1941*, Routledge & Kegan Paul, 1942; *New York Times*, October 23, 1949, November 9, 1952, April 24, 1955, June 29, 1958, July 3, 1978; *Spectator*, October 26, 1951, January 19, 1980; *New York Herald Tribune Book Review*, June 22, 1958, November 4, 1962; *Times Literary Supplement*, April 8, 1965, February 1, 1975, August 11, 1978, May 9, 1980; *The Julian Symons Omnibus*, Collins, 1966; *New Statesman*, December 23, 1966, October 20, 1978; *New York Times Book Review*, January 8, 1967, December 9, 1973, July 9, 1978, February 4, 1979; *New Yorker*, April 1, 1972; *Best Sellers*, April 15, 1972; *Book World*, May 28, 1972; *Books and Bookmen*, October, 1972; *Contemporary Literary Criticism*, Gale, Volume II, 1974, Volume XIV, 1980; *Washington Post Book World*, July 9, 1978; *Observer*, July 23, 1978; *New Republic*, August 26, 1978; *Washington Post*, December 26, 1978; *Armchair Detective*, Volume XII, number 1, 1979.

* * *

SYPHER, Wylie 1905-

PERSONAL: Born December 12, 1905, in Mt. Kisco, N.Y.; son of Harry Wylie and Martha (Berry) Sypher; married Lucy Johnston (a writer and educator), August 31, 1929; children: G. Wylie, Gale (Mrs. Charles Jacob). *Education:* Amherst College, A.B., 1927; Tufts University, A.M., 1929; Harvard University, A.M., 1932, Ph.D., 1937. *Home:* 60 Williston Rd., Auburndale, Mass. 02166. *Office:* Department of English, Simmons College, Boston, Mass. 02115.

CAREER: Simmons College, Boston, Mass., instructor, 1929-36, assistant professor, 1936-41, associate professor, 1941-45, professor, 1945-66, alumnae professor of English, 1966-72, professor emeritus, 1973—, lecturer in English, 1973—, chairman, Division of Language, Literature, and Arts, 1945-66, dean of graduate division, 1950-67, chairman of department of English, 1966-72, coordinator of graduate programs, 1973—. Summer lecturer, University of Minnesota, 1945, University of Wisconsin, 1948 and 1951, and Bread Loaf School of English, 1957-75. *Member:* P.E.N. *Awards, honors:* Guggenheim fellowships, 1949-50, 1958-59; Litt.D., Middlebury College, 1969; L.H.D., Simmons College, 1973, Amherst College, 1977.

WRITINGS: Guinea's Captive Kings, University of North Carolina Press, 1942; *Enlightened England*, Norton, 1947; *Four Stages of Renaissance Style*, Doubleday, 1955; "The New Meanings of Comedy" in *Comedy*, Doubleday, 1956; *Rococo to Cubism in Art and Literature*, Random House, 1960; *Loss of the Self*, Random House, 1962; *Art History*, Random House, 1963; *Literature and Technology*, Random House, 1968; *The Ethic of Time*, Seabury, 1976.

* * *

SZASZ, Suzanne (Shorr) 1919-

PERSONAL: Born October 20, 1919, in Budapest, Hungary; daughter of Joseph (a doctor) and Maria (Baron) Szekely; married Ray Shorr (a photographer), December 22, 1956. *Education:* Pazmany Peter University, Budapest, Staatsprufung, 1937. *Home:* 37 East 63rd St., New York, N.Y.

CAREER: Photographer for magazines, advertising, and other media. *Member:* American Society of Magazine Photographers, National Press Photographers. *Awards, honors:* Encyclopaedia Britannica-University of Missouri School of Journalism Awards, 1953-62; Art Directors Award, 1960.

WRITINGS—Photographic books: (Text by Anna W. Wolf) *Helping Your Child's Emotional Growth*, Doubleday, 1952; *Guide to Photographing Children*, Chilton, 1957; (text by Susan Lyman) *Young Folks' New York*, Crown, 1960; (text by Clara and Morey Appell) *Glenn Learns to Read*, Duell, 1964; (text by Paul Gallico) *The Silent Miaow*, Crown, 1964; *Child Photography Simplified*, Amphoto, 1966, 2nd edition, 1978; *Modern Wedding Photography*, Amphoto, 1977; *The Body Language of Children*, foreword by Benjamin Spock, Norton, 1978.

SIDELIGHTS: Suzanne Szasz's work has been included in many photographic shows, including the "Family of Man" at the Museum of Modern Art, and a one-person show at the Camera Club of New York, January, 1981.

* * *

SZAZ, Zoltan Michael 1930-

PERSONAL: Born January 3, 1930, in Budapest, Hungary; came to United States in 1950, naturalized in 1955; son of Geza and Magda (Nagy) Szaz; married Jayne Anne Davis, September 7, 1957; children: Claire A., Anna M., Mary C., Christopher M. *Education:* Attended Philosophical-Theological College, Dillingen, West Germany, 1948-49, and University of Munich, 1949-50; St. John's University, Collegeville, Minn., B.A. (cum laude), 1951; Catholic University of America, M.A., 1952, Ph.D., 1956. *Politics:* Republican. *Religion:* Catholic.

CAREER: Washington correspondent for Radio Free Europe, 1953-55; *Free World Review*, Washington, D.C., associate editor, 1956-58; editor, *Free World Forum*, 1958-62; St. John's University, Graduate School, Jamaica, N.Y., public relations consultant, 1960, instructor, 1960-62, assistant professor, 1962-64; Seton Hall University, South Orange, N.J., lecturer, 1965-66, associate professor of government, 1966-68; American Institute on Problems of European Unity, Washington, D.C., 1968—, began as executive director, currently vice-president. Lecturer in West Germany, 1958, 1961, 1963, and at five southern universities, 1960; associate professor of political science, Troy State University, 1971-72. Executive director, Council for Hungarians in Rumania, 1965—. Vice-president, Everett McKinley Dirksen Forum, 1969-71. *Member:* International Political Science Association, American Political Science Association, American

Hungarian Federation (secretary for international affairs, 1965—), Young Republican National Federation (member of foreign affairs committee), New York Association of Young Republican Clubs (chairman of 11th Judicial District), Young Republicans Club of District of Columbia (chairman of foreign affairs committee, 1954-59), Pi Gamma Mu. *Awards, honors:* Arpad Academy of Arts and Sciences Gold Medal, 1973.

WRITINGS: Germany's Eastern Frontiers: The Problem of the Oder-Neisse Line, Regnery, 1960; (editor) *Die nationale Frage in der oesterreichisch-ungarischen Monarchie, 1900-1918,* Ungarischen Akademie der Wissenschaften, 1966; (editor) *MBFR at the Crossroads,* American Institute on Problems of European Unity, 1974. Contributor of more than twenty articles in English, German, and Spanish to professional journals.

WORK IN PROGRESS: The Great Power Conflict since 1945.†

*   *   *

SZERLIP, Barbara   1949-

PERSONAL: Born November 28, 1949, in New Jersey; daughter of Stewart S. (an insurance broker) and Ziril (Weinstein) Szerlip. *Education:* Attended University of Miami, 1967-69, and University of California, Santa Barbara, 1969-71. *Home:* 532B Lombard St., San Francisco, Calif. 94133; and c/o 879 Northeast 195th St., No. 223, North Miami Beach, Fla. 33179.

CAREER: Sivananda Yoga Ashram, Val Morin, Quebec, instructor in Hatha Yoga and Kirtan Mantras, cook, and baker, 1969; leather craftsman in Montreal, Quebec, 1969; *Tractor* (literary magazine), San Francisco, Calif., founder and editor, 1971-75; writer. Professional masseuse in San Francisco, 1973; assistant technical director, actress, dancer, and singer with summer stock theaters in White Lake, N.Y., and East Monticello, N.Y., various years. *Awards, honors:* Coordinating Council of Literary Magazines grant, 1973, for continued publication of *Tractor,* and 1975; Fels Award, 1975; National Endowment for the Arts writing fellowship, 1976-77; Pushcart Prize, 1977.

WRITINGS: Teopantiahuac, Water Table Press, 1971; *Sympathetic Alphabet,* Mother's Hen Press, 1975; (editor) *California Treasures: An Exploration in Museum Education for Children,* Museums Affiliated with Public Schools, 1978; *The Ugliest Woman in the World and Other Histories,* Gallimanfry Press, 1978.

Work is represented in anthologies, including *Four Young Women: Poems,* edited by Kenneth Rexroth, McGraw, 1973, *Contemporary Women Poets,* Merlin Press, 1977, *The California Poetry,* edited by Ishmael Reed, Y'Bird, 1979, *Wonders,* Summit Books, 1980, *Blood of Their Blood,* New Rivers Press, 1980, and *For Rexroth,* 1980.

WORK IN PROGRESS: A novella, tentatively entitled *Journals of a Sea Animal.*

T

TABORSKY, Edward (Joseph) 1910-

PERSONAL: Born March 18, 1910, in Praha, Czechoslovakia; son of Edward and Oldra (Nekvasilova) Taborsky; married Edith Calder, 1943; children: Ivan, Sonia, Helen Louise. *Education:* Charles University, Doctor of Law and Political Science, 1934. *Home:* 4503 Parkwood, Austin, Tex. 78722. *Office:* Department of Government, University of Texas, Austin, Tex. 78712.

CAREER: Secretary to Czechoslovakia's Minister for Foreign Affairs, 1937-39; personal aide to President of Czechoslovakia, 1939-45; envoy extraordinary and minister plenipotentiary of Czechoslovakia to Sweden, 1945-48; Charles University, Praha, Czechoslovakia, lecturer, 1946; University of Stockholm, Stockholm, Sweden, lecturer, 1948-49; University of Texas at Austin, 1949—, began as lecturer, currently professor of government. Summer professorships at several universities. *Member:* American Association for the Advancement of Slavic Studies, Southwestern Social Science Association, Slavonic Benevolent Order of Texas. *Awards, honors:* Guggenheim fellow, 1959-60.

WRITINGS: (Co-editor) *Czechoslovak Yearbook of International Law,* Czechoslovak Economic Service in the U.S.A., 1942; *The Czechoslovak Cause,* Witherby, 1944; *Czechoslovak Democracy at Work,* Allen & Unwin, 1945; *O novou demokracii* (title means "For a New Democracy"), Fr. Borovy, 1945; *Pravda Zvitezila* (title means "The Truth Has Prevailed"), Druzstevni Prace, 1947; *Nase nova ustava* (title means "Our New Constitution"), Cin, 1948; *Conformity under Communism,* Public Affairs Press, 1958; *Communism in Czechoslovakia, 1948-1960,* Princeton University Press, 1961; *Communist Penetration of the Third World,* Robert Speller, 1973; *Presidentuv sekretar vypovida* (title means "The President's Secretary Tells His Story"), Konfrontation S.A., 1978; *President Edvard Benes between the East and the West,* Hoover Institution, 1980. Contributor to British and American journals.

*   *   *

TAYLOR, Richard W(arren) 1924-

PERSONAL: Born December 8, 1924, in Hollywood, Calif.; son of Herbert S. and Bonnie (Snoke) Taylor; married Mary Lyon Seasholes, August 20, 1948; children: George Frederic II, Brooks Arnold, Woodman Lyon, Bradbury Warren, Nathan Haller. *Education:* University of California, Los Angeles, A.B., 1947; Boston University, S.T.B., 1950; University of Southern California, A.M., 1951; graduate study at University of Chicago, 1951-54, and Harvard University, 1960-61. *Politics:* Democrat. *Home address:* Christian Institute for the Study of Religion and Society, P.O. Box 4600, 17 Miller's Rd., Bangalore 560 046, India. *Office:* c/o United Methodist Division of World Missions, 475 Riverside Dr., New York, N.Y. 10115.

CAREER: Ordained elder in United Methodist Church, working under Division of World Missions, 1954—. Lecturer and head of department of sociology, Hislop College and Nagpur University, Nagpur, India, 1955-58; director, Christian Retreat and Study Centre, Rajpur, India, 1958-60; Christian Institute for the Study of Religion and Society, Bangalore, India, research secretary, 1961-74, senior associate director of research, 1974—; adjunct professor of social ethics and Christian social thought, Serampore College, Serampore, India, 1961-69; missionary-in-residence, Missionary Orientation Center, Stony Point, N.Y., 1966-67. Fellow, Institute for Ecumenical and Cultural Research, Collegeville, Minn., 1972-73, and Institute for Philosophy and Religion, Boston University, 1977-78. *Military service:* U.S. Army Air Forces, 1943-46; became lieutenant.

WRITINGS: (With H.F.J. Daniel and others) *Revolution and Reconstruction,* S.C.M. Press (Bangalore), 1957; (with James P. Alter and others) *Community Development in India's Industrial Urban Areas,* Committee for Literature on Social Concerns, 1958; (with M. M. Thomas) *Mud Walls and Steel Mills,* Friendship, 1963; (contributor) H. Buerkle, editor, *Indische Beitraege zur Theologie der Gegenwart,* Evangelisches Verlagswerk (Stuttgart), 1966, translation published as *Indian Voices in Today's Theological Debate,* Lucknow Publishing House, 1972; (contributor) D. B. Robertson, editor, *Voluntary Associations: Essays in Honor of James Luther Adams,* John Knox, 1966; (contributor) S. K. Chatterji, editor, *The Asian Meaning of Modernization,* East Asia Christian Conference (Delhi), 1972.

Published by Christian Institute for the Study of Religion and Society: (With C. M. Abraham and others) *The Changing Pattern of Family in India,* 1960, revised edition, 1966; (editor with Thomas) *Tribal Awakening,* 1965; (contributor) H. Jai Singh, editor, *Inter-Religious Dialogue,* 1967; (contributor) Chatterji, editor, *Legalisation of Abortion,* 1971; (contributor) T. S. Wilkinson and Thomas, editors, *Ambedkar and the Neo-Buddhist Movement,* 1972; *The Contribution of*

E. Stanley Jones, 1973; *Jesus in Indian Paintings,* 1975; (editor) *Society and Religion: Essays in Honour of M. M. Thomas,* 1976; (editor) *Religion and Society: The First Twenty-Five Years,* 1980. Editor with Thomas, *Religion and Society* (quarterly journal), 1962—.

WORK IN PROGRESS: A book on modern Indian ashrams; a study of the early thought of Verrier Elwin; a survey of religious shrines in southern India.

AVOCATIONAL INTERESTS: Indian art history.

* * *

TAYLOR, Robert Lewis 1912-

PERSONAL: Born September 24, 1912, in Carbondale, Ill.; son of Roscoe Aaron (in real estate) and Mabel (Bowyer) Taylor; married Judith Martin, February 3, 1945; children: Martin Lewis, Elizabeth Ann. *Education:* Attended Southern Illinois University; University of Illinois, A.B., 1933. *Politics:* Republican. *Home:* Bulls Bridge Rd., South Kent, Conn.

CAREER: First job was on a weekly newspaper in Carbondale, Ill., 1934, but after a year there he sailed for Tahiti and remained in the South Seas until 1936, financing himself by serving as a correspondent for *American Boy.* Reporter for *St. Louis Post Dispatch,* St. Louis, Mo., 1936-39; *New Yorker,* New York, N.Y., profile writer, 1939—. *Military service:* U.S. Naval Reserve, 1942-46; became lieutenant commander. *Member:* Club Nautico, Club Monte Carlo, Down East Yacht Club (Boothbay Harbor, Me.), Oceans Racquet and Tennis Club (Daytona Beach, Fla.). *Awards, honors:* Sigma Delta Chi runner-up award in general reporting division, 1939; Pulitzer Prize in fiction, 1959, for *The Travels of Jaimie McPheeters.*

WRITINGS—All published by Doubleday, except as indicated: *Adrift in a Boneyard* (fantasy novel), 1947; *Doctor, Lawyer, Merchant, Chief* (collection), 1948; *W. C. Fields: His Follies and Fortunes,* 1949, reprinted, New American Library, 1967; *The Running Pianist,* 1950; *Professor Fodorski,* 1950; *Winston Churchill: An Informal Study of Greatness,* 1952; *The Bright Sands* (novel), 1954; *Center Ring: The People of the Circus,* 1956; *The Travels of Jaimie McPheeters,* 1958, reprinted, Ace Books, 1979; *A Journey to Matecumbe,* McGraw, 1961, published as *Treasure of Matecumbe,* Pocket Books, 1976; *Two Roads to Guadalupe,* 1964; *Vessel of Wrath: The Life and Times of Carry Nation,* New American Library, 1966; *A Roaring in the Wind: Being a History of Alder Gulch, Montana,* Putnam, 1977; *Niagara,* Putnam, 1980. Contributor to *Saturday Evening Post, Life, Collier's, Esquire, Redbook, Reader's Digest,* and other periodicals.

SIDELIGHTS: Robert Taylor told *CA:* "I have never been interested in writing books or pieces with a high moral lesson; my goal has been to provide entertainment of as high a literary quality as I can. For this reason, I always felt at home in the style of the *New Yorker* magazine as it used to be, when it had real humor. Because I very much enjoy traveling, and history, I've found that historical novels are fun to do. I'm proud to say that mine are represented on many a school reading list these days."

The Travels of Jaimie McPheeters was adapted into a television series in 1960; *Professor Fodorski* was adapted into a musical play entitled "All American" in 1963; *W. C. Fields: His Follies and Fortunes* was adapted into a musical play entitled "W. C." in 1971; *A Journey to Matecumbe* was adapted into a film entitled "The Treasure of Matecumbe" in 1976.

AVOCATIONAL INTERESTS: Boating, fishing, traveling.

BIOGRAPHICAL/CRITICAL SOURCES: New York Times Book Review, March 16, 1958, February 5, 1978; *Saturday Review,* February 14, 1948, April 19, 1958; *New York Times,* May 5, 1959; *Commonweal,* February 3, 1967; *Book Week,* February 26, 1967; *West Coast Review of Books,* March, 1978; *Christian Science Monitor,* March 1, 1978; *Contemporary Literary Criticism,* Volume XIV, Gale, 1980.

* * *

TELEKI, Geza 1943-

PERSONAL: Born December 7, 1943, in Kolozsvar, Hungary; naturalized U.S. citizen; son of Geza (a politician and scientist) and Hanna (Mikes) Teleki. *Education:* George Washington University, B.A., 1967; Pennsylvania State University, M.A., 1970, Ph.D., 1977. *Politics:* None. *Religion:* None. *Home address:* P.O. Box 467, Lemont, Pa. 16851. *Office:* Department of Anthropology, George Washington University, Washington, D.C. 20052.

CAREER: University of New Mexico, Albuquerque, field assistant in archaeology at Sapawe (a Pueblo Indian site), 1966; Smithsonian Institution, Washington, D.C., laboratory assistant in physical anthropology, 1967; Gombe Stream Research Centre, Gombe National Park, Tanzania, field research assistant, 1968-69, senior field researcher in primatology, 1970-71; Hall's Island Gibbon Colony, Hall's Island, Bermuda, senior research assistant in primatology, 1971; George Washington University, Washington, D.C., assistant professorial lecturer, 1978-79, associate professorial lecturer, 1980—. Field assistant in ethology at Ngorongoro Crater, Tanzania, 1968, and Serengeti National Park, 1970; director, Wildlife Survey Project, Sierra Leone, 1979-80. Consultant for Survival Service Commission of the International Union for the Conservation of Nature, 1979—; research consultant on gibbon behavior. *Member:* International Primate Protection League, Audubon Society, American Society of Primatologists, American Anthropological Association, American Museum of Natural History.

WRITINGS: The Predatory Behavior of Wild Chimpanzees, Bucknell University Press, 1973; (contributor) D. M. Rumbaugh, editor, *Gibbon and Siamang,* S. Karger, 1974; (with Karen Steffy) *Goblin: A Wild Chimpanzee,* Dutton, 1977; *Chimpanzee Behavior* (slide and study guide set), Educational Images, 1979; (with Lori Baldwin and Meredith Rucks) *Aerial Apes: Gibbons of Asia,* Coward, 1979; *Ecology of Gombe National Park* (slide and study guide set), Educational Images, 1979; (with Steffy and Baldwin) *Leakey the Elder: A Chimpanzee and His Community,* Dutton, 1980.

Contributor of photographs: Pierre Rossion, *Science et vie* (title means "Science and Life"), Excelsior (Paris), 1973; R. S. Lazarus, *The Riddle of Man,* Prentice-Hall, 1974; *Animals in Action,* Reader's Digest Books, 1974; *East African Wildlife,* Time-Life, 1974; *Our Vanishing Wildlife,* Reader's Digest Books, 1974; John Alcock, *An Evolutionary Approach to Animal Behavior,* Sinauer, 1974; Helena Curtis, *Biology,* Worth Publishers, 1974; S. I. Rosen, *Introduction to Physical Anthropology,* McGraw, 1974. Has also made films of his field research on gibbons.

Author of research reports. Contributor of photographs to *Il Libro Del Anno* and *Encyclopaedia Britannica Yearbook.* Contributor of articles to journals, including *Scientific American, Primates, Journal of Human Evolution,* and *Folia Primatologica.* Editor of *Matrix* (interscience journal of George Washington University), 1965-67.

WORK IN PROGRESS: Editing a book on predatory behavior in human evolution, with R.S.O. Harding.

*   *   *

TESSIER, (Ernst) M(aurice)   1885-1973
(Maurice Dekobra)

PERSONAL: Born May 28, 1885, in Paris, France; died June 2, 1973. *Education:* Attended College Rollin; University of Paris, B.A. *Religion:* Catholic. *Home:* 12 rue Beaujon, Paris 8, France. *Agent:* Odette Arnaud, II rue Teheran, Paris 8, France.

CAREER: Writer, beginning 1920; special foreign correspondent for French newspapers and magazines, 1920-45. Film director. *Military service:* French Army, 1914-18; liaison officer with British, Indian, and American armies; received Legion of Honour. *Member:* National Union of French Writers and Composers (vice-president, beginning 1955), International Academy (Washington, D.C.). *Awards, honors:* Literary Gold Medal of City of Paris for literature, 1954; Grand Cross of Temple of Jerusalem; Grand Cross of St. John the Baptist; Doctor of Letters, Andrah University, Waltair, India; Prix du Quai des Orfevres.

WRITINGS—All under pseudonym Maurice Dekobra, except as indicated: *Messieurs les Tommies*, La Renaissance du Livre, 1917; *Sammy, volontaire americain*, L'Edition Francaise Illustree, 1918; *Grain de' Cachou*, La Renaissance du Livre, 1918; *Le Voyage sentimental de Lord Littlebird*, L'Edition Francaise Illustree, 1919; *Les Liaisons tranquilles*, La Renaissance du Livre, 1920; *Mon coeur au ralenti*, Baudiniere, 1924, reprinted, Presses de la Cite, 1974, translation by Neal Wainwright published as *Wings of Desire*, Macaulay, 1925; *La Madone des sleepings*, Baudiniere, 1925, reprinted, Presses de la Cite, 1974, translation by Wainwright published as *The Madonna of the Sleeping Cars*, Payson & Clarke, 1927; *Flammes de velours*, Baudiniere, 1927, translation by F. M. Atkinson published as *The Love Clinic*, Payson & Clarke, 1929 (published in England as *Flames of Velvet*, Laurie, 1931); *La Gondole aux chimeres*, Baudiniere, 1927, reprinted, Presses de la Cite, 1974, translation by Wainwright published as *The 13th Lover*, Payson & Clarke, 1928 (published in England as *Phantom Gondola*, Laurie, 1930); *Serenade au bourreau*, Baudiniere, 1928, translation by Wainwright published as *Serenade to the Hangman*, Payson & Clarke, 1929 (translation by Sheila O'Callaghan published in England as *The Hangman Never Waits*, W. H. Allen, 1960); *Le Tigres parfumes*, Editions de France, 1929, translation by Wainwright published as *The Perfumed Tigers*, Brewer & Warren, 1930.

Le Sphinx a parle, Baudiniere, 1930, reprinted, J'ai lu, 1968, translation by Metcalfe Wood published as *The Sphinx Has Spoken*, Brewer & Warren, 1930; *L'Archange aux pieds fourchus*, Baudiniere, 1931, translation by Samuel Sloan published as *The Cloven-Footed Angel*, Macaulay, 1932; *Aux cent mille sourires*, Baudiniere, 1932; *La Volupte eclairant le monde*, Baudiniere, 1932, translation by Wainwright published as *Passion Lighting the World*, Macaulay, 1933 (translation by Wood published in England as *Love Calling*, Laurie, 1934); (editor with R. W. Hartland) *Ma princesse cherie*, Oxford University Press, 1932, reprinted, 1962; *La Prison des reves*, Baudiniere, 1933, translation by Wood published as *Princess Brinda*, Laurie, 1936; *Madame joli-supplice*, Baudiniere, 1934, translation by Wainwright published as *His Chinese Concubine*, Laurie, 1936; *Mimi Broadway* [and] *Les Mousquetaires d'Ellis island*, Baudiniere, 1936.

Emigres de luxe, Brentano's 1941, published as *Casanova a Manhattan*, Valmont, 1960, translation published as *Emigrants de Luxe*, Laurie, 1942; *Le Roman d'un lache*, Brentano's, 1942, translation published as *The Romance of a Coward*, Laurie, 1943; *Lune de miel a Shanghai*, Brentano's, 1943, translation published as *Shanghai Honeymoon*, Philosophical Library, 1946 (published in England as *Honeymoon in Shanghai*, Laurie, 1946); *La Madone a Hollywood*, Didier, 1943, translation published as *The Madonna in Hollywood*, Laurie, 1945; *Fusille a l'aube: Ou, l'etonnante aventure d'une espionne anglaise a Vienne en 1914*, Baudiniere, 1944, reprinted, J'ai lu, 1967; *La Perruche bleue: Journal d'une courtisane sous la terreur nazie*, Brentano's, 1945, translation by R. Spodhem published as *The Blue Parrot*, Laurie, 1948; *A Paris tout les deux*, Didier, 1945, translation by Henry Noble Hall published as *Paradise in Montparnasse*, Ackerman, 1946; *Sept Ans chez les hommes libres: Journal d'un francais aux Etats-Unis, 1939-1946*, SFELT (Paris), 1946, translation by Warre Bradley Wells published as *Seven Years among Free Men*, Laurie, 1948; *La Pagode des amours mortes*, S.E.P.E. (Paris), 1948; *La Rose qui saigne* [and] *Le Fou Bassan*, La Technique du Livre, 1948.

Operation Magali, Hachette, 1951, translation by Phillippa Kaye published under same title, W. H. Allen, 1952; *Sous le signe du cobra: Mes souvenirs de globe-trotter*, Baudiniere, 1952; *L'Armee rouge est a New-York*, Editions du Scorpion, 1954; *La Pagode des amours*, Tallandier, 1955; *La Veuve aux gants roses: Roman americain*, Editions du Scorpion, 1956, translation published as *Widow with Pink Gloves*, Laurie, 1939, translation by O'Callaghan published as *She Wore Pink Gloves*, W. H. Allen, 1958; *Minuit, l'heure galante*, Editions du Scorpion, 1956; *Monsieur Lambers mourra ce soir*, Librairie des Champs-Elysees, 1956; *Un Soir sur le Danube: Le Roman d'un traitre*, Tallandier, 1957; *Ferocement votre*, Editions du Scorpion, 1957; (editor, under name M. Tessier, with H. Nicholas) *Les Fabliaux*, F. Lanore, 1958; *Le Lis dans la tempete: Le Roman d'une reine de beaute*, Valmont, 1959; *Passeport diplomatique*, Tallandier, 1959; *Les Sept Femmes du prince Hassan*, Valmont, 1959, translation by Frances Fleetwood published as *The Seventh Wife of Prince Hassan*, W. H. Allen, 1961.

L'Homme qu'elles aimaient trop, Valmont, 1960; *Le Pacha de Brooklyn*, Valmont, 1960; *Dalila, sirene du desert*, Livre Artistique, 1961; *La Venus aux yeux d'or*, Editions Karolus, 1962, translation by O'Callaghan published as *The Golden-Eyed Venus*, W. H. Allen, 1963; (with Anne Mariel) *L'Amazone de Pretoria: Un Episode de la guerre du Transvaal*, Presses de la Cite, 1963, translation by Peter J. Sinclair published as *Diamond Queen*, Doubleday, 1965; (with Mariel) *Anicia, l'espionne de Moukden*, Presses de la Cite, 1964; *Le Vengeur de Mayerling*, Presses de la Cite, 1965; (with Mariel) *Veronica, qui etes-vous?: Le Journal d'un play boy*, Presses de la Cite, 1965; *L'Espion qui faisait rire*, Presses de la Cite, 1966; (with Mariel) *Anicia et le sultan rouge*, Presses de la Cite, 1966; (with Mariel) *Anicia et le tigre royal*, Presses de la Cite, 1967; (with Mariel) *Fascinante Veronica*, Presses de la Cite, 1968; *Les Turquoises meurent aussi*, Presses de la Cite, 1969; *Le Salon de Madame Ublo: La Menagerie des gens de lettres*, A. Michel, 1969; (with Mariel) *Rendez-vous chez Maxim's*, Presses de la Cite, 1970; *Un Banco de deux milliards*, Presses de la Cite, 1971; *La Madame des Boeings*, Presses de la Cite, 1972.

Also author of *La Rire dans la steppe*, translation published as *Crimson Smile*, Laurie, 1929, *La Venus a roulettes*, translation by Wood published as *Venus on Wheels*, Macaulay,

1930, *Phryne*, translation by Wood published as *Love as a Fine Art*, Laurie, 1932, *Samourai et cylindres*, 1935, translation by Wood published as *My Japanese Holiday*, Greenberg, 1936 (published in England as *A Frenchman in Japan*, Laurie, 1936), *Confucius en pullover*, translation by Wood published as *Confucius in a Tail-Coat*, Laurie, 1935, *Hamydal le philosophie*, translation by Wood published as *Hamydal, the Vagabond Philosopher*, Laurie, 1937, and *Bouddha le terrible*, translation by Fleetwood published as *Double or Quits*, W. H. Allen, 1962.

Other translations include: *The Clown Prince*, translated by Wainwright, Payson & Clarke, 1928; *Midnight on the Place Pigalle*, translated by Wood, Laurie, 1933; *The Street of Painted Lips*, translated by Wainwright, Macaulay, 1934; *Bedroom Eyes*, translated by Maverick Terrell, Macaulay, 1935; *Blood and Caviare*, translated by Wood, Laurie, 1937; *Written with Lipstick*, Hutchinson, 1938; *Stars and Strips*, translated by Wood, Laurie, 1939; *Death Requests the Pleasure*, translated by Wood, Laurie, 1940; *Twenty-one Nights in Paris*, Laurie, 1940; (with Leyla George) *Mata Hari's Daughter*, Kitabistan, 1943; *Hell Is Sold Out*, translated by Alan French, Laurie, 1948, published as *The Bachelor's Widow*, Ace, 1954; *Poison at Plessis*, W. H. Allen, 1953; *Man Who Died Twice*, W. H. Allen, 1954; *Chinese Puzzle*, W. H. Allen, 1956; *The Widow's Might*, translated by O'Callaghan, W. H. Allen, 1957; *Lady Is a Vamp*, translated by O'Callaghan, W. H. Allen, 1958.†

*   *   *

TEUNE, Henry 1936-

PERSONAL: Born March 19, 1936, in Chicago, Ill,; son of Julius (a printer) and Grace (Vander Veen) Teune; married Elaine Meltz (a teacher), February 10, 1962; children: Elana. *Education:* Central University of Iowa, B.A., 1957; University of Illinois, M.A., 1958; Indiana University, Ph.D., 1961. *Home:* 8201 Henry Ave., G-11, Philadelphia, Pa. 19118. *Office:* Department of Political Science, University of Pennsylvania, Philadelphia, Pa. 19104.

CAREER: University of Pennsylvania, Philadelphia, assistant professor, 1961-65, associate professor, 1965-72, professor of political science, 1972—, vice-dean of Graduate School of Arts and Sciences, 1967-69, acting chairman of department of political sciences, 1970-71, chairman, 1975-80. Visiting associate professor and fellow at Cornell University, Center for International Studies, 1969. Research exchange scholar, National Academy of Science (Yugoslavia), 1975. *Member:* International Studies Association (president, 1980), American Political Science Association, American Sociological Association. *Awards, honors:* American Council of Learned Societies grant, Yugoslavia, 1969-70; Fulbright research grant, 1972; LL.D., Central University of Iowa, 1974.

WRITINGS: (Contributor) P. E. Jacobs and J. V. Toscano, editors, *The Integration of Political Communities*, Lippincott, 1964; (with A. Przeworski) *The Logic of Comparative Social Inquiry*, Wiley, 1970; (contributor) *Values and the Active Community*, Free Press, 1971; (contributor) G. Zaltman, editor, *Perspectives on Social Change*, Wiley, 1973; (with F. Riggs and G. Sartori) *The Tower of Babel*, University Center for International Studies (Pittsburgh), 1975; (contributor) A. Szali and R. Petrella, editors, *Cross National Comparative Research*, Pergamon, 1977; (contributor) D. Ashford, editor, *Comparing Public Policies*, Sage Publications, Inc., 1977; (with Z. Mlinar) *The Developmental Logic of Social Systems*, Sage Publications, Inc., 1978; (editor with

Mlinar, and contributor) *The Social Ecology of Change*, Sage Publications (London), 1978. Contributor to professional journals.

WORK IN PROGRESS: The Future of American Democracy; Theories of Political Systems; research on methodology, comparative politics, political development, political systems, and local politics.

SIDELIGHTS: Teune has travelled and conducted research in several countries in Asia and Europe, especially Poland and Yugoslavia.

*   *   *

THAYER, Lee (Osborne) 1927-

PERSONAL: Born December 18, 1927, in Greenfield, Kan.; son of Garret O. (an oil operator) and Ruth (Ray) Thayer; married Nancy Lee Wright (a writer), August 14, 1964; children: Cassandra Lee, Stephanie Lynn, Joshua Lee, Jessica Sam. *Education:* University of Wichita (now Wichita State University), B.A. (cum laude), 1953, M.A., 1956; University of Oklahoma, Ph.D., 1963. *Home:* 1711 South Wisconsin Ave., Racine, Wis. 53403. *Office:* Humanities Division, University of Wisconsin—Parkside, Kenosha, Wis. 53141.

CAREER: University of Oklahoma, Norman, instructor in College of Business Administration, 1956-58; University of Wichita (now Wichita State University), Wichita, Kan., assistant professor, 1958-61, associate professor of administration and psychology, 1961-64; University of Missouri at Kansas City, professor of administration and director of research, 1964-68; University of Iowa, Iowa City, Gallup Professor of Communication and director of Center for the Advanced Study of Communication, 1968-73; Simon Fraser University, Burnaby, B.C., professor of communication studies, 1973-76; University of Massachusetts—Amherst, 1976-77; University of Helsinki, Helsinki, Finland, Fulbright professor, 1977-78; University of Houston, Houston, Tex., Distinguished Visiting Professor, 1978; University of Wisconsin—Parkside, Kenosha, professor of communication, 1978—. Visiting professor at Harvard University, 1961, Institut de l'Environment, Paris, 1970, and University of Amsterdam, 1972. Member of board, Institute of General Semantics and Instituto de Comunicacion Social (Mexico). Consultant to U.S. Government and to industry. *Military service:* U.S. Naval Reserve, 1953-56; became lieutenant.

MEMBER: International Society for General Semantics, International Association for Cybernetics, Academy of Management, American Association for the Advancement of Science, Creative Education Foundation, Society for General Systems Research, American Society for Information Sciences, National Society for the Study of Communication (president, 1968-69), New York Academy of Sciences, Alpha Kappa Psi, Psi Chi. *Awards, honors:* Foundation for Economic Education fellow, 1964, 1966; research grants from National Science Foundation, National Aeronautics and Space Administration, Ford Foundation, Marketing Science Institute, U.S. Office of Education, and others.

*WRITINGS—*Occasionally under name Lee O. Thayer: (With George E. Harris) *Sales and Engineering Representation*, McGraw, 1958; *Administrative Communication*, Irwin, 1961; *Communication and Communication Systems in Organization, Management, and Interpersonal Relations*, Irwin, 1968.

Editor: *Communication: Theory and Research*, C. C Thomas, 1967; *Communication: Concepts and Perspectives*, Spartan, 1967; *Communication-Spectrum '7: Proceedings of the*

15th Annual Conference of the National Society for the Study of Communication, Allen Press, 1968; *Communication: General Semantics Perspectives,* Spartan, 1969; (and contributor) *Communication: Ethical and Moral Issues,* Gordon & Breach, 1974; *Ethics, Morality, and the Media: Reflections on American Culture,* Hastings House, 1980.

Contributor: F. W. Wilson, editor, *Numerical Control in Manufacturing,* McGraw, 1963; J. G. Longenecker, editor, *Principles of Management and Organizational Behavior,* C. E. Merrill, 1964; *Occasional Papers in Advertising,* University of Illinois Press, 1966; F.E.X. Dance, editor, *Human Communication Theory: Original Essays,* Holt, 1967; Frank Greenwood, editor, *Casebook for Management and Business Policy: A System Approach,* International Textbook Co., 1968; D. L. Arm, editor, *Vistas in Science,* University of New Mexico Press, 1968.

Johnnye Akin and others, editors, *Language Behavior: A Book of Readings in Communication,* Mouton, 1970; D. E. Costello, editor, *Communication: On Being Human,* Simon & Schuster, 1971; Rubin Gotesky and Ervin Laszlo, editors, *Evolution-Revolution: Patterns of Development in Nature, Society, Man, and Knowledge,* Gordon & Breach, 1971; Laszlo, editor, *The Relevance of General Systems Theory,* Braziller, 1972; Laszlo and J. B. Wilbur, editors, *Values and the Man-Made Man,* Gordon & Breach, 1972; Costello, editor, *Learning and Communication Education,* Simon & Schuster, 1972; B. D. Ruben and J. Y. Kim, editors, *General Systems and Human Communication Theory,* Hayden, 1975; Laszlo and Emily B. Sellon, editors, *Vistas in Physical Reality: A Festschrift for Henry Margenau,* Plenum, 1976; John B. Calhoun, editor, *Perspectives on Adaptation, Environment, and Population,* National Institute of Mental Health, 1977; Leif Aberg and Eija Erholm, editors, *Viestinnan Virtauksia,* Otava (Helsinki), 1978; Ruben, editor, *Communication Yearbook II,* Transaction Books, 1978; R. W. Budd and Ruben, editors, *Approaches to Human Communication,* 2nd edition, Hayden, 1978.

Also author of numerous invited papers and published reports. Contributor to journals. Editor, *Communication.*

WORK IN PROGRESS: Three books, *Towards a Philosophy for the Social Sciences, The Idea of Communication,* and *People and Communication: Paradoxes, Perplexities, Perversities;* articles and research projects on communication and social change, managerial competence, and other aspects of communication, organization, and human nature.

SIDELIGHTS: Lee Thayer told *CA:* "What continues to surface in the range of my work is this: *As we communicate, so shall we be*—whether as individuals in everyday life, or as a civilization. In our pursuit of freedom *from* this or that imagined constraint in our contemporary culture, we have lost our grasp of what it is we *should* be. How, Eliot said, can we know what we are if we do not know what we should be?

"Communication—and I'm thinking here mainly of how we understand others, of what we 'consume' in our information-rich civilization—can serve us ill as readily as well. We are enchanted by the means, and have lost sight of the ends. Since, as Blake told us, everything that can be believed is an image of the truth, and since we are producing far more truths today than any one of us can possibly consume—the key question becomes this: What truths do we want/need in order to mature, finally, as a civilization—or as individuals?

"We have come to understand *communication* in ways which obscure us from the fact that what is problematic is not communication, not society, but us. The key question in the study of communication is not 'How does communication work?' but 'What are people *for?*' At all levels, this is what concerns me when I write."

*   *   *

THOMAS, Lowell (Jackson) 1892-

PERSONAL: Born April 6, 1892, in Woodington, Ohio; son of Harry George (a physician) and Harriet (a school teacher; maiden name, Wagner) Thomas; married Frances Ryan, August 4, 1917 (died, 1975); married Mariana Munn, January 5, 1977; children: (first marriage) Lowell Jackson, Jr. *Education:* University of Northern Indiana, B.S., 1911; University of Denver, B.A., M.A., 1912; attended Kent College of Law, 1912-14; Princeton University, M.A., 1916. *Home:* Hammersley Hill, Pawling, N.Y. 12564.

CAREER: Radio and television commentator, producer, and writer. Reporter and editor on newspapers in Cripple Creek and Denver, Colo., 1911-12; reporter for several newspapers, including *Chicago Journal,* Chicago, Ill., 1912-14; instructor in oratory, Kent College of Law, Chicago, 1912-14; began lecturing on travel, 1915—; named by President Woodrow Wilson to head commission to study World War I and to report to Versailles Peace Conference; appointed by U.S. War Department as historian for the first flight around the world, 1924; began nightly network radio news broadcast on CBS, 1930-32, NBC, 1932-47, and returned to CBS, 1947-76. Began a network television news broadcast for NBC in 1939; host of television series "High Adventure," 1957-59; producer of television series for BBC, "The World of Lowell Thomas." Narrator-commentator for Twentieth Century-Fox "Movietone" newsreels, 1935-52; originator of "Cinerama" film concept, 1952, and produced several "Cinerama" films, including "Seven Wonders of the World" and "Search for Paradise." President of board of directors, American School for Boys (Baghdad); head of various fund-raising organizations, including Tibetan Relief and Goddard Space Center.

MEMBER: American Geographic Society (fellow; member of council, beginning 1963), Royal Geographic Society (fellow), Association of Radio News Analysts, English Speaking Union (honorary life member), Explorers Club (honorary president, 1961—), Overseas Press Club (New York; past president), American Museum of Natural History (life member), Marco Polo Club (past president), Kappa Sigma, Tau Kappa Alpha, Phi Delta Phi, Sigma Delta Chi, Alpha Epsilon, Princeton Players Club, Royal and Ancient St. Andrews Golf Club, Dutch Treat Club, Bohemian Club (San Francisco), Advertising Club (New York), Pine Valley Golf Club (New York).

AWARDS, HONORS: duPont radio award, 1945, for best news broadcasting; Chauncey M. Depew Medal, Sons of the American Revolution, 1964; Distinguished Service award, National Association of Broadcasters, 1968; Personality of the Year award, International Radio and Television Society, 1968; Horatio Alger award, 1970; George Washington Award, Freedoms Foundation, 1978; Chevalier of French Legion of Honor. Litt.D. from Grove City College, 1933, St. Bonaventure University, 1938, Franklin and Marshall College, 1942, Rider College, 1948, and Ohio Wesleyan University, 1949; LL.D from Albright College, 1934, Lafayette College, 1937, Washington and Jefferson College, 1942, and Olivet College, 1950; L.H.D. from Clark University, 1941, Boston University, 1943, Union College, 1944, and University of Tampa, 1949; H.H.D. from Temple University, 1942.

WRITINGS: With Lawrence in Arabia, photographs by

H. A. Chase and the author, Century Company, 1924, enlarged edition, Doubleday, 1967; *Beyond Khyber Pass*, photographs by Chase and the author, Century Company, 1925; (editor) *The First World Flight: Being the Personal Narratives of Lowell Smith, Erik Nelson, Leigh Wade, Leslie Arnold, Henry Ogden, John Harding*, Houghton, 1925; *The Boys' Life of Colonel Lawrence*, Century Company, 1927, revised edition, Appleton, 1938; *Count Luckner: The Sea Devil*, Doubleday, 1927, reprinted, Popular Library, 1964; *European Skyways: The Story of a Tour of Europe by Airplane*, Houghton, 1927; *Raiders of the Deep*, Doubleday, 1928; *Adventures in Afghanistan for Boys*, Century Company, 1928; *Woodfill of the Regulars: A True Story of Adventure from the Arctic to the Argonne*, Doubleday, 1929; *The Hero of Vincennes: The Story of George Rogers Clark*, Houghton, 1929; *The Sea Devil's Fo'c'sle*, Doubleday, 1929.

The Wreck of the Dumaru: A Story of Cannibalism in an Open Boat, Doubleday, 1930; *India: Land of the Black Pagoda*, photographs by H. A. Chase and the author, Century Company, 1930; *Lauterbach of the China Sea: The Escapes and Adventures of a Seagoing Falstaff*, Doubleday, 1930; *Rolling Stone: The Life and Adventures of Arthur Radclyffe Dugmore*, Doubleday, 1931; *Tall Stories: The Rise and Triumph of the Great American Whopper*, Funk, 1931; *This Side of Hell: Dan Edwards, Adventurer*, Doubleday, 1932; *Kabluk of the Eskimo*, Little, Brown, 1932; (with Frank Shoonmaker) *The American Travelers' Guide Book: Spain*, Simon & Schuster, 1932; (with Smedley D. Butler) *Old Gimlet Eye: The Adventures of Smedley D. Butler*, Farrar, Rinehart, 1933; *Thrills*, Towner & Buranelli; 1933; *Fan Mail*, Dodge Publishing, 1935; *The Untold Story of Exploration*, Dodd, 1935; *A Trip to New York with Bobby and Betty*, Dodge Publishing, 1936; *Thrilling Moments in Thrilling Lives* (pamphlet), Sun Oil Company, 1936; *Seeing Canada with Lowell Thomas*, Saalfield, 1936; *Seeing India with Lowell Thomas*, Saalfield, 1936; *Men of Danger*, Frederick A. Stokes, 1936; (with Tex O'Reilly) *Born to Raise Hell: The Life Story of Tex O'Reilly, Soldier of Fortune*, Doubleday, 1936; (with Percy Burton) *Adventures Among Immortals*, Dodd, 1937; *Hungry Waters: The Story of the Great Flood, Together with an Account of Famous Floods of History and Plans for Flood Prevention and Control*, John C. Winston, 1937, illustrated edition, 1938; *Seeing Mexico with Lowell Thomas*, Saalfield, 1937; *Seeing Japan with Lowell Thomas*, Saalfield, 1937; (with Rexford W. Barton) *Wings Over Asia: A Geographic Journey by Airplane*, John C. Winston, 1937; *With Allenby in the Holy Land*, Cassell, 1938; (with Barton) *In New Brunswick We'll Find It*, Appleton, 1939; *Magic Dials: The Story of Radio and Television*, Polygraphic Company, 1939.

How to Keep Mentally Fit, Howell, Soskin & Company, 1940; *Pageant of Adventure*, Funk, 1940; (with Ted Shane) *Softball! So What?*, Frederick A. Stokes, 1940; (with Berton Braley) *Stand Fast for Freedom*, John C. Winston, 1940; *Pageant of Life*, Funk, 1941; (with wife, Frances R. Thomas) *Pageant of Romance*, Dutton, 1943; *These Men Shall Never Die*, John C. Winston, 1943, reprinted, Books for Libraries, 1971.

Back to Mandalay, Greystone, 1951; *The New York Thruway Story* (pamphlet), Stewart, 1955; (editor) *Great True Adventures*, Hawthorn, 1955; (contributor) Norman Vincent Peale, editor, *Faith Made Them Champions*, Prentice-Hall, 1955; *Seven Wonders of the World*, Hannover House, 1956; *The St. Lawrence Seaway Story*, Stewart, 1957; *History as You Heard It*, Doubleday, 1957; *The Vital Spark: 101 Out-*

standing Lives, Doubleday, 1959.

(Editor with Charles Hurd) *Cavalcade of Europe: A Handbook of Information on 22 Countries by 14 Noted Overseas Correspondents*, Doubleday, 1960; *Sir Hubert Wilkins: His World of Adventure: A Biography*, McGraw, 1961 (published in England as *Sir Hubert Wilkins: His World of Adventure: An Autobiography Recounted*, Arthur Barker, 1962); (editor with son, Lowell Thomas, Jr.) *More Great True Adventures*, Hawthorn, 1963; *Lowell Thomas' Book of the High Mountains*, Messner, 1964; (with son, Lowell Thomas, Jr.) *Famous First Flights That Changed History*, Doubleday, 1969; (with Jack Girsham) *Burma Jack*, Norton, 1971; (with Edward Jablonski) *Doolittle: A Biography*, Doubleday, 1976 (published in England as *Bomber Commander: The Life of James H. Doolittle*, Sidgwick & Jackson, 1977); *Good Evening Everybody: From Cripple Creek to Samarkand*, Morrow, 1976; *So Long Until Tomorrow: From Quaker Hill to Kathmandu*, Morrow, 1977. Also editor and author of biography, *Kipling Stories, and a Life of Kipling*, 1936. Contributor to numerous periodicals, including *Life*. Associate editor, *Asia*, 1919-23; member of editorial board, *Writer*.

SIDELIGHTS: "I think we're just now entering the golden era of exploration," Lowell Thomas recently commented. "First of all, a large part of the earth's surface has not been explored in detail. In the second place, three-fourths of the planet is covered with water, and we're just beginning to explore underseas. And third—space. During my lifetime, we are told, aside from the field of human relations and philosophy and so on, the world has made greater advances than in the previous 5,000 years. So I think the opportunities for adventure are greater now than ever before."

Lowell Thomas should know about "opportunities for adventure." Now a well-known world traveler and foreign correspondent, Thomas first gained world recognition as the exclusive biographer of T. E. Lawrence, known as Lawrence of Arabia. It was toward the end of the First World War, while traveling with the Allied forces as an observer and correspondent, that he first met Lawrence. An unknown English-born archaeologist, Lawrence at that time was the leader of a unified force of Arab tribes fighting Turkish domination in the Middle East. It became Thomas's ambition to bring the story of Lawrence of Arabia to the world; he assembled a show, including films and his own narration, and went on tour. It was hugely successful, with Thomas repeating the show to over 4,000 separate audiences. The subsequent book, *With Lawrence in Arabia*, established Thomas's reputation and secured his financial fortune.

In 1930, Thomas began his distinguished career as a radio broadcast journalist. He became known and recognized for his distinctive voice, described by William T. Noble of the *Detroit News* as "a voice so resonant and musical it is unforgettable." His nightly broadcast ran 46 years, the longest continuous run in the history of network broadcasting. At the same time to he continued his lectures and world travels, and wrote voraciously. Because he was traveling so much of the time, he recorded such feats as being the first to broadcast from a ship, from an airplane, from a coal mine, and from a submarine. In his many travels around the world, Thomas witnessed wars and revolutions, visited pigmies in Southeast Asia and ate with cannibals in New Guinea, traveled in the company of the Prince of Wales, and journeyed to exotic world spots rarely or never seen before by the eye or camera lens of the Western world. In 1949, Thomas was invited by the Dalai Lama to visit the forbidden city of Lhasa in Tibet. The journey nearly cost him his life; traveling along a pass in the Himalayas, he fell from his horse, broke his leg and hip, and would have slid off into a precipice had it not been for his son's intervention. To get medical attention, he had to be carried 200 miles by litter to the nearest airstrip.

Despite this and other near escapes from death, Thomas has maintained the belief that life is a lot of fun and is meant to be enjoyed to the fullest. "It seems to me that the day-by-day exploits and adventures of mankind are fantastic, fabulous," he explains. "I consider giving birth one of life's greatest adventures. A clergyman saving a soul, if he can, is another of life's great adventurers. Surgeons, schoolteachers, they're all adventurers." Thomas says that the one thing he hasn't done that he would like to do is travel to another planet. "I've told our space people at NASA that I want to go on one of the space trips. They've put me down as number two. First is the head of NASA. What I'd really like to do is get outside our own solar system, where there'd be a possibility of visiting a planet that might be inhabited." Thomas comments that he'd "like to find some people as delightful as the Tibetans, or the English. I admire both." Although he doesn't believe travel to inhabited planets will occur in his lifetime, Thomas is characteristically optimistic. "It seems to me that nothing is impossible. I do believe the time will come—when human beings from our planet will get to other planets."

AVOCATIONAL INTERESTS: Skiing, riding, golf.

BIOGRAPHICAL/CRITICAL SOURCES: Mildred Houghton Comfort, *Lowell Thomas, Adventurer*, Denison, 1965; N. R. Bowen, editor, *Lowell Thomas: The Stranger Everyone Knows*, Doubleday, 1968; *Dallas News*, September 1, 1974; *Authors in the News*, Gale, Volume I, 1976, Volume II, 1976; *Detroit News*, February 1, 1976; *People*, May 24, 1976; *Saturday Review*, August 21, 1976; *New York Times Book Review*, August 22, 1976, February 5, 1978; *Christian Science Monitor*, September 1, 1976, December 14, 1977; *America*, October 9, 1976; Irving E. Fong, *Those Radio Commentators*, Iowa State University Press, 1977.†

*   *   *

THOMPSON, Charles Lowell 1937-

PERSONAL: Born February 25, 1937, in Columbus, Ohio; son of Charles Hollington (a physician) and Naomi (Jones) Thompson; married Harriet Wolstenholme, June 21, 1957; children: Charles, Cynthia, Marcia. *Education:* Attended Ohio Wesleyan University, 1955-58; University of Tennessee, B.S., 1959, M.S., 1961; Ohio State University, Ph.D., 1967. *Politics:* Conservative. *Religion:* Methodist. *Home:* 7817 Luxmore Dr., Knoxville, Tenn. 37919. *Office:* Department of Educational and Counseling Psychology, University of Tennessee, 108 CEB, Knoxville, Tenn. 37916

CAREER: University of Tennessee, Knoxville, assistant professor, 1967-70, associate professor, 1970-73, professor of educational psychology and guidance, 1973—. *Member:* American Psychological Association, American Personnel and Guidance Association, East Tennessee Personnel and Guidance Association (president, 1971-72), Phi Delta Theta, Phi Delta Kappa. *Awards, honors:* East Tennessee Personnel and Guidance Association publications award, 1973.

*WRITINGS—*All with William A. Poppen, except as indicated: *For Those Who Care: Ways of Relating to Youth*, C. E. Merrill, 1972; *School Counseling: Theories and Concepts*, Professional Educators Publications, 1974; *Guidance for the Elementary School*, Robertson County Board of Education (Springfield, Tenn.), Brooks/Cole, 1975; *Guidance Activities for Counselors and Teachers*, Brooks/Cole, 1979; (with Linda Rudolph) *Counseling Children*,

Brooks/Cole, 1981. Contributor of over forty articles on guidance, counseling, and educational psychology to various journals. Editor of the "Idea Exchange" column in *Elementary School Guidance and Counseling*, 1979-81.

WORK IN PROGRESS: Researching methods for teaching discipline to children and youth and developing guides for parents and teachers.

*   *   *

THORP, Willard 1899-

PERSONAL: Born April 20, 1899, in Sidney, N.Y.; son of William and Harriet (Willard) Thorp; married Margaret Farrand (a writer), June 12, 1930 (died October 2, 1970). *Education:* Hamilton College, A.B., 1920; Harvard University, A.M., 1921; Princeton University, Ph.D., 1926. *Home:* 428 Nassau St., Princeton, N.J. 08540. *Office:* Department of English, Princeton University, Princeton, N.J.

CAREER: Smith College, Northampton, Mass., 1921-24, began as instructor, became assistant professor of English; Princeton University, Princeton, N.J., instructor, 1926-28, assistant professor, 1928-39, associate professor, 1939-44, professor of English, 1944-67, professor emeritus, 1967—, Holmes Professor of Belles Lettres, 1952-67, chairman of department, 1958-63. M. D. Anderson Visiting Professor, Rice Institute (now University), 1952-53; summer professor, Harvard University, University of Minnesota, University of Virginia, University of Hawaii, University of Washington, Seattle, Duke University, and University of Miami, Coral Gables.

MEMBER: American Studies Association (president, 1958-59), Modern Language Association of America (member of executive council, 1954-57), American Antiquarian Society, Melville Society (past president), Association of Princeton Graduate Alumni (past president), Phi Beta Kappa, Psi Upsilon. *Awards, honors:* American Council of Learned Societies fellow, 1931-32; Library of Congress fellow in American letters, 1944-49; Guggenheim fellow, 1966-67; Litt.D., Hamilton College, 1947, and Princeton University, 1978; L.H.D., Kalamazoo College, 1960; American Literature Group J. B. Hubbell Medal.

WRITINGS: *Triumph of Realism in Elizabethan Drama*, Princeton University Press, 1928; *American Writing in the Twentieth Century*, Harvard University Press, 1960; *American Humorists*, University of Minnesota Press, 1964; (with others) *The Princeton Graduate School: A History*, Princeton University Press, 1978; *Catholic Novelists in Defense of Their Faith, 1829-1865*, Arno, 1978.

Editor: (With Thomas M. Parrott) *Poetry of the Transition, 1850-1914*, Oxford University Press, 1932; *Songs from the Restoration Theater*, Princeton University Press, 1934, reprinted, Da Capo Press, 1970; (with Howard Lowry) *An Oxford Anthology of English Poetry*, Oxford University Press, 1935, 2nd edition, 1956; *Herman Melville: Representative Selections*, American Book, 1938; (with others) *American Issues*, Volume I: *The Social Record*, Volume II: *The Literary Record*, Lippincott, 1941, 4th edition, 1960, enlarged edition of Volume II published as *The American Literary Record*, 1961; (with wife, Margaret Farrand Thorp) *Modern Writing*, American Book, 1944; *Lives of Eighteen from Princeton*, Princeton University Press, 1946, reprinted, Books for Libraries, 1968; (with others) *Literary History of the United States*, three volumes, Macmillan, 1948, 4th revised edition published in two volumes, 1974; *Herman Melville, Moby Dick*, Oxford University Press, 1948; *A Southern Reader*, Knopf, 1955; (and author of introduction) Elizabeth

Maddox Roberts, *The Great Meadow*, New American Library, 1961; Melville, *Billy Budd and Other Tales*, New American Library, 1961; Theodore Dreiser, *Sister Carrie*, Signet, 1962; Henry James, *The Madonna of the Future and Other Early Stories*, Signet, 1962; Nathaniel Hawthorne, *The Scarlet Letter*, Collier, 1962; *Great Short Works of the American Renaissance*, Harper, 1968; *Great Short Works of American Realism*, Harper, 1968; *Four Classic American Novels*, New American Library, 1969; Henry David Thoreau, *Walden*, C. E. Merrill, 1969. Contributor to philological journals and literary reviews. Member of editorial board, *American Literature*, 1950-57; member of editorial committee, *PMLA*, 1958-70.

SIDELIGHTS: Willard Thorp is largely responsible for the development of Princeton University's special program in American civilization, a program which draws faculty and undergraduate students from twelve cooperating departments and seeks to treat American civilization as an "organic whole." He told *CA:* "As a teacher, literary scholar, and critic, I have tried to remember that it was my duty to make an author's work more accessible to readers. With me, the creative writer comes first. Too many in my profession condescend to their authors, so it seems, and use them as stalking horses for their theories of literature. It is our business to show how the work of art may yield instruction or delight or both, as Horace said many years ago."

AVOCATIONAL INTERESTS: Music, art history, nature.

* * *

TINKER, Hugh (Russell) 1921-

PERSONAL: Born July 20, 1921, in Westcliff, England; son of Clement Hugh and Gertrude Tinker; married Elisabeth Willis, August 23, 1947; children: Jonathan, Mark, David. *Education:* Sidney Sussex College, Cambridge, B.A., 1948, M.A., 1951; University of London, diploma in public administration, 1948, Ph.D., 1951. *Politics:* Liberal. *Religion:* Baptist. *Home:* Montbegon, Hornby, Lancaster, England; and Aspen Lea, Little Hampden, Great Missenden, Bucks, England. *Office:* Department of Politics, University of Lancaster, Lancaster, England.

CAREER: Affiliated with Indian Civil Service, 1945-46; University of London, London, England, professor, 1948-69; Institute of Race Relations, London, director, 1969-72; University of London, Institute of Commonwealth Studies, senior research fellow, 1972-77; University of Lancaster, Lancaster, England, professor of politics, 1977—. Visiting professor, University of Rangoon, Burma, 1954-55, and Cornell University, 1959. Member of council, Minority Rights Group. *Military service:* Indian Armored Corps, 1941-45.

WRITINGS: Foundations of Local Self-Government in India, Pakistan, and Burma, Athlone Press, 1954, 2nd edition, 1967; *The Union of Burma*, Oxford University Press, 1957, 4th edition, 1967; *India and Pakistan: A Political Analysis*, Praeger, 1962, 2nd edition, 1968; *Ballot Box and Bayonet*, Oxford University Press, 1964, 2nd edition 1966; *Reorientations: Essays on Asia in Transition*, Praeger, 1965; *South Asia: A Short History*, Praeger, 1966; *Experiment with Freedom: India and Pakistan, 1947*, Oxford University Press, 1967; *A New System of Slavery: The Export of Indian Labour Overseas, 1830-1920*, Oxford University Press, 1974; *Separate and Unequal: India and the Indian in the British Commonwealth, 1920-1950*, Hurst & Blackett, 1976; *The Banyan Tree: Overseas Emigrants from India, Pakistan and Bangladesh*, Oxford University Press, 1977; *Race, Conflict,*

and the International Order, Macmillan, 1977; *The Ordeal of Love: C. F. Andrews and India*, Oxford University Press, 1979.

WORK IN PROGRESS: A two-volume study, *The Transfer of Power in Burma*.

SIDELIGHTS: C. F. Andrews, one of the members of a small group of now-forgotten Britons who actively supported the move towards India's independence, became the subject of Hugh Tinker's first biographical study more by chance than by design. During the course of his research on the history of Indian migration and indentured labor, Tinker read Andrews's letters to the viceroy of India and soon became fascinated by the maddeningly eccentric man the *Times Literary Supplement*'s Eric Stokes calls "a sort of white Ghandi." The resulting biography, *The Ordeal of Love*, prompted Stokes to comment: "In the lengthening line of books that now stands to Hugh Tinker's credit, this is one of his best. . . . It is a piece of remarkable scholarship infused with an underlying warmth unusual in a historian whose professional duties have lain with the dryasdust records of the British-Indian bureaucracy. . . . Although Tinker's book was undertaken as a labour of love, biography remains the cruellest of the arts. Andrews, who was a compulsive correspondent and fond of self-display, lays himself bare. Tinker has deliberately rejected the method of analysis in order to allow the record to speak for itself. . . . [He] has succeeded in reminding hard-faced historians that the British decolonizing process in India possessed a moral dimension and, in Andrews, threw up a tumultuous personality whose disturbing presence persists long after history has pensioned off the white officials who worked the levers of power."

BIOGRAPHICAL/CRITICAL SOURCES: Times Literary Supplement, June 13, 1980.

* * *

TOLBERT, E(lias) L(ake) 1915-

PERSONAL: Born December 11, 1915, in Middletown, Va.; son of Robert and Lillian (Horne) Tolbert; married Frances Thornton Miller, 1947; children: Jane Thornton, Margaret Ross. *Education:* University of Virginia, B.S., 1938; Ohio State University, M.A., 1947; Columbia University, Ed.D., 1952. *Religion:* Episcopalian. *Home:* 326 Southwest 27th St., Gainesville, Fla. 32601. *Office:* Department of Education, University of Florida, Gainesville, Fla.

CAREER: Teacher in Orange, Va., 1939-40, and Fairfax, Va., 1940-41; State Department of Education, Danville, Va., vocational and educational counselor, 1948-49, 1951-52; North Carolina State College of Agriculture and Engineering of the University of North Carolina (now North Carolina State University at Raleigh), assistant professor of occupational information and guidance, 1952-57; Madison College, Harrisonburg, Va., professor of guidance counselling and dean of students, 1957-67; University of Florida, Gainesville, associate professor of education, beginning 1967. Adviser to church youth group, beginning 1957. *Military service:* U.S. Army, Corps of Engineers, 1941-45; participated in campaigns in Rhineland, Northern France, and Germany; became major; awarded Bronze Star, Silver Star. *Member:* American Personnel and Guidance Association, National Vocational Guidance Association, American College Personnel Association, Association of Counselor Educators and Supervisors, American Psychological Association, Phi Delta Kappa, Kappa Delta Pi, Phi Delta Theta.

WRITINGS: Introduction to Counseling, McGraw, 1959, 2nd edition, 1971; *Research for Teachers and Counselors*,

Burgess, 1967; *Counseling for Career Development,* Houghton, 1974, 2nd edition, 1980; *An Introduction to Guidance,* Little, Brown, 1978.

AVOCATIONAL INTERESTS: Travel and photography.†

* * *

TOMLIN, E(ric) W(alter) F(rederick) 1913-

PERSONAL: Born January 30, 1913, in London, England; son of Edgar Herbert and Mary (Dexter) Tomlin; married, 1947 (divorced); children: Walter Stuart. *Education:* Oxford University, B.A., 1935, M.A., 1936. *Religion:* Church of England. *Home:* Tall Trees, Morwenstow, Bude, Cornwall EX23 9PQ, England; and 31 Redan St., London W14, England. *Agent:* Howard Moorepark, 444 East 82nd St., New York, N.Y. 10028.

CAREER: Sloane School, London, England, assistant master, 1936-38; Marlborough College, Wiltshire, England, assistant master, 1938-39; journalist in United Kingdom and Europe, 1939-40; member of Home Guard, 1940; Staff College, Baghdad, Iraq, British advisor, 1940; British Council Service (Britain's foreign cultural service), posts in Iraq, Turkey, France, and Japan, 1941-71, cultural counsellor, 1956-71. Visiting professor of philosophy, University of Southern California, Los Angeles, 1960; visiting fellow, Wolfson College, Cambridge University, 1971; professor of literature and philosophy, University of Nice, 1972-74. *Member:* Society of Authors, British Association of Orientalists, Turco-British Association, Japan-British Society (council), Royal Asian Society (fellow), Philosophical Society of England (fellow), Royal Society of Literature (fellow), Athenaeum Club (London), Oxford Union Society. *Awards, honors:* Order of the British Empire, officer, 1959, commander, 1965; Bollingen fellowship, 1960-61; M.A., Cambridge University, 1971.

WRITINGS: Turkey: The Modern Miracle, F. Watts, 1940; *Life in Modern Turkey,* Thomas Nelson, 1946; *The Approach to Metaphysics,* Routledge & Kegan Paul, 1947; *The Great Philosophers: The Western World,* Hutchinson, 1948, published as *Western Philosophers,* Harper, 1963; *The Great Philosophers: The Eastern World,* Hutchinson, 1950, published as *Oriental Philosophers,* Harper, 1963; *Simone Weil,* Yale University Press, 1954; *Living and Knowing,* Harper, 1955; (contributor) *A New Outline of Modern Knowledge,* Simon & Schuster, 1957.

R. G. Collingwood, Longmans, Green, 1960; *Wyndham Lewis,* Longmans, Green, 1960; (contributor) *The Modern Age,* Penguin, 1960; *La Vie et l'oeuvre de Bertrand Russell,* Editions Prix Nobel, 1963; (editor with Masao Hirai) *T. S. Eliot: A Tribute from Japan,* Kenkyusha, 1965; *Tokyo Essays,* Hokuseido, 1967; (editor and author of introduction) *Wyndham Lewis: An Anthology of His Prose,* Methuen, 1969; (editor) *Charles Dickens, 1812-1870: A Centennial Volume,* Simon & Schuster, 1969 (published in England as *Charles Dickens, 1812-1870: A Centenary Volume,* Weidenfeld & Nicolson, 1969); *The Last Country: My Years in Japan,* Faber, 1972, Merrimack Book Service, 1974; *Japan,* Thames & Hudson, 1972, Walker, 1973; *Man, Time and the New Science,* Rebel Press, 1973; (editor) *Arnold Toynbee: A Selection from His Works,* Oxford University Press, 1979; *The World of St. Boniface,* Paternoster Press, 1980.

Contributor of articles to *Criterion, Scrutiny, Spectator, Time and Tide, Economist, Now!, New Universities Quarterly,* and other journals, and of reviews to journals in France, Germany, Italy, Israel, and Japan.

WORK IN PROGRESS: The Concept of Life; a novel, a volume of short stories.

AVOCATIONAL INTERESTS: Music.

* * *

TORRANCE, E. Paul 1915-

PERSONAL: Born October 8, 1915, in Milledgeville, Ga.; son of Ellis Watson and Jimmie Pearl (Ennis) Torrance; married J. Pansy Nigh, 1959. *Education:* Georgia Military College, associate in arts, 1936; Mercer University, B.A. (summa cum laude), 1940; University of Minnesota, M.A., 1944; University of Michigan, Ph.D., 1951. *Religion:* Baptist. *Home:* 185 Riverhill Dr., Athens, Ga. 30606. *Office:* Aderhald Hall, University of Georgia, Athens, Ga. 30602.

CAREER: Midway Vocational High School, Milledgeville, Ga., teacher, 1936-37; Georgia Military College, Milledgeville, teacher, counselor, and principal, 1937-44; Kansas State College of Agriculture and Applied Science (now Kansas State University), Manhattan, counselor, 1946-48, director of Counseling Bureau, 1949-51; U.S. Air Force, Survival Research Field Unit, Stead Air Force Base, Nev., director, 1951-57; University of Minnesota, Minneapolis, professor of educational psychology, 1958-66; University of Georgia, Athens, professor of educational psychology, 1966-73, Alumni Distinguished Professor, 1973—, chairman of department, 1966-78. Member of board of trustees, Creative Education Foundation, 1975-79.

MEMBER: American Educational Research Association, American Psychological Association, National Association for Gifted Children, American Sociological Society, Phi Delta Kappa, Psi Chi. *Awards, honors:* Award of American Personnel and Guidance Association for *Guiding Creative Talent; Booklist* award for outstanding education book of the year, 1970-71, for *Creative Learning and Teaching;* distinguished alumnus award, Georgia Military College, 1972; Association for the Gifted award for distinguished contribution to the understanding and education of gifted children, 1973; Kappa Delta Pi award for excellence as a teacher educator, 1975; National Association for Gifted Children award for outstanding pioneering work in identifying and developing creative talent; Psi Chi award for outstanding contribution to psychology; Educational Press Association of America distinguished achievement award for excellence in educational journalism; Georgia College distinguished service award; Sertoma Clubs of Hawaii Service to Mankind Award.

WRITINGS: (Editor) *Education and Talent,* University of Minnesota Press, 1960; *Guiding Creative Talent,* Prentice-Hall, 1962; *Education and the Creative Potential,* University of Minnesota Press, 1963; *Constructive Behavior: Stress, Personality, and Mental Health,* Wadsworth, 1965; *Gifted Children in the Classroom,* Macmillan, 1965; *Rewarding Creative Behavior: Experiments in Classroom Creativity,* Prentice-Hall, 1965; (with Cunnington) *Sounds and Images,* Ginn, 1965; (with Myers) *Invitations to Thinking and Doing,* Ginn, 1965; *Invitations to Speaking and Writing Creatively,* Ginn, 1965; (editor with R. D. Strom) *Mental Health and Achievement,* Wiley, 1965; (with Myers) *Can You Imagine?,* Ginn, 1965; *Torrance Tests of Creative Thinking,* Personnel Press, 1966; *Dimensions of Early Learning: Creativity,* Adapt Press, 1969.

(With Myers) *Creative Learning and Teaching,* Harper, 1970; (with W. F. White) *Issues and Advances in Educational Psychology,* F. E. Peacock, 1970, revised edition, 1975; *Encouraging Creativity in the Classroom,* National

Education Association, 1970; (with J. C. Gowan and Joe Khatena) *Educating the Ablest*, F. E. Peacock, 1971, revised edition, 1979; (with wife, J. Pansy Torrance) *Is Creativity Teachable?*, Phi Delta Kappa, 1973; (with Khatena) *Thinking Creatively with Sounds and Words*, Ginn, 1973; *What Research Says to the Teacher: Creativity in the Classroom*, National Education Association, 1977; (with Khatena) *Khatena-Torrance Creative Perception Inventory*, Charles Stoelting, 1977; *Discovery and Nurturance of Giftedness in the Culturally Different*, Council for Exceptional Children, 1977; *Search for Creativity*, Creative Education Foundation, 1979. Author of "Imagi/Craft" series, Ginn, 1965; also author of *Thinking Creatively in Action and Movement* and *Your Style of Learning and Thinking*, both 1979.

Contributor: A. P. Hare, E. F. Borgatta and R. F. Bales, *Small Groups*, Knopf, 1955; J. L. Moreno, *Sociometry and the Science of Man*, Beacon House, 1956; A. H. Rubinstein and C. J. Haberstroh, *Some Theories of Organization*, Dorsey Press, 1960; L. Petrullo and B. M. Bass, *Leadership and Interpersonal Behavior*, Holt, 1961; S. J. Parnes and H. F. Harding, *A Source Book for Creative Thinking*, Scribner, 1962; G.Z.F. Bereday and J. A. Lauwreys, *The Gifted Child*, Harcourt, 1962; L. D. Crow and Alice Crow, editors, *Readings in Human Learning*, McKay, 1963; L. D. Crow and Alice Crow, *Mental Hygiene for Teachers*, Macmillan, 1963; W. W. Charters, Jr. and N. L. Gage, editors, *Readings in the Social Psychology of Education*, Allyn & Bacon, 1963; J. M. Seidman, *Educating for Mental Health*, Crowell, 1963; C. W. Taylor and F. Barron, *Scientific Creativity: Its Recognition and Development*, Wiley, 1963; Taylor, *Creativity: Progress and Potential*, McGraw, 1964; Taylor, *Widening Horizons in Creativity*, Wiley, 1964; J. S. Roucek, *The Difficult Child*, Philosophical Library, 1964; R. D. Strom, *Inner-City Teacher*, Merrill, 1966; Taylor and F. E. Williams, *Instructional Media and Creativity*, Wiley, 1966; Roucek, *Programmed Instruction*, Philosophical Library, 1966; J. C. Gowan and G. D. Demos, *The Disadvantaged and Potential Dropout*, C. C Thomas, 1966. Contributor to professional journals.

WORK IN PROGRESS: Predicting Creative Behavior; Images of the Future of Gifted Children; Uses of Tests in Understanding and Predicting Creative Behavior; Longitudinal Studies of Creative Achievement.

SIDELIGHTS: Torrance Tests of Creative Thinking has been translated into over forty languages; *Guiding Creative Talent* has been published in Japanese and Spanish; *Creative Learning and Teaching* has been published in Spanish and Portuguese; *Gifted Children in the Classroom* has been published in Japanese and Spanish; and *Is Creativity Teachable?* has been published in Portuguese. *Avocational interests:* Photography.

*   *   *

TORREGIAN, Sotere 1941-

PERSONAL: Born June 25, 1941, in Newark, N.J.; son of Sam (a laborer) and Mary (Giuseffina) Torregian; married Kathleen Brummal (a poet and writer), December, 1966 (divorced); children: Tatyana, Janaina. *Education:* Attended Rutgers University, 1960-63. *Politics:* "Overall, politics= peace." *Religion:* "Raised as Greek Catholic." *Home and office:* 2405 Alpine Rd., Menlo Park, Calif. 94025.

CAREER: Stanford Bookstore, Stanford, Calif., clerk, 1967-69; Stanford University, Stanford, Calif., assistant in department of anthropology, 1970-73; University of Santa Clara, Santa Clara, Calif., visiting lecturer, 1970-72, currently fac-

ulty member. *Awards, honors:* Frank O'Hara award from Poet's Foundation, 1968.

WRITINGS: Golden Palomino Bites the Clock, Angel Hair Books, 1966; *The Wounded Mattress*, Oyez, 1968; (editor) *Bibliography of Francophone Caribbean Culture and Literature with Annotations*, privately printed, 1971; *The Age of Gold: Poems, 1968-1970*, Kulchur Foundation, 1976; *AMTRAK Trek*, New York Telephone Books, 1979.

WORK IN PROGRESS: A book of poems, *The Age of Gold That Can Fit into Anyone's Pocket; Song for Woman, II;* surrealist essays; *Theatres,* "poem-plays"; a novel, *A Nestorian Monument in Cathay.*

*   *   *

TOURNIER, Michel 1924-

PERSONAL: Born December 19, 1924, in Paris, France; son of Alphonse and Marie-Madeleine (Fournier) Tournier. *Education:* Attended University of Paris and University of Tuebingen. *Home:* Le Presbytere, Choisel, 78460 Chevreuse, France. *Office:* Editions Plon, 8 rue Garanciere, Paris 6, France.

CAREER: Producer and director, R.T.F., 1949-54; newspaper work, 1955-58; Editions Plon, Paris, France, director of literary services, 1958-68; writer. *Member:* Academie Goncourt. *Awards, honors:* Grand Prix du Roman from Academie Francaise, 1967, for *Vendredi; ou, Les Limbes du Pacifique;* Prix Goncourt, 1970, for *Le Roi des aulnes;* Chevalier de la Legion d'honneur.

WRITINGS: Vendredi; ou, Les Limbes du Pacifique (novel), Gallimard, 1967, revised edition, 1978, translation by Norman Denny published as *Friday*, Doubleday, 1969 (published in England as *Friday; or, The Other Island*, Collins, 1969), juvenile edition published as *Vendredi; ou, La Vie sauvage*, Flammarion, 1971, translation by Ralph Manheim published as *Friday and Robinson: Life on Esperanza Island*, Knopf, 1972; *Le Roi des aulnes* (novel), Gallimard, 1970, translation by Barbara Bray published as *The Ogre*, Doubleday, 1972 (published in England as *The Erlking*, Collins, 1972); *Les Meteores* (novel), Gallimard, 1975; *Le Vent paraclet* (essays), Gallimard, 1977; *Canada: Journal de voyage* (nonfiction), La Presse, 1977; *Le Coq de bruyere* (short stories), Gallimard, 1978; *Des clefs et des serrures* (essays), Editions du Chene, 1979; *Gaspard, Melchior et Balthazar* (novel), Gallimard, 1980.

SIDELIGHTS: Winner of two prestigious French literary prizes, Michel Tournier, as a *Times Literary Supplement* critic once observed, "writes slowly but successfully." After completing three novels he declined to submit to publishers because he judged them unworthy of publication, Tournier wrote two more novels, *Friday* and *The Ogre*, which quickly established him as one of the most remarkable writers to appear on the postwar French literary scene. Unmistakably the products of a highly imaginative mind, his novels—consisting primarily of philosophical speculation—are not for the casual reader; densely packed with a complex network of symbols and allusions, they have been criticized for their pretentiousness and, on occasion, for their somewhat disturbing and even frightening themes. Yet virtually no one regards Tournier as anything less than a writer of the highest intellectual order.

Friday, described by the *New Statesman*'s Gillian Tindall as "an idiosyncratic Frenchman's reconstruction of our petrified classic [*Robinson Crusoe*], with 20th century insights," was the first of Tournier's novels to appear in print. Beginning with the traditional Robinson Crusoe formula (which views man as a rational, tool-using creature who seeks to control his world through the imposition of physical and social order), Tournier deviates from the Daniel Defoe version somewhat to stress the existence of other alternatives—mainly non-rational and non-technical ones—that man has at his disposal to deal with the environment. While both Defoe and Tournier's castaways at first strive to "civilize" life on their little island, Tournier, unlike Defoe, has his Crusoe gradually become less and less interested in imposing his will on nature as he grows mystically closer to his surroundings. By the time his would-be savior Friday arrives, Crusoe is ready to go completely "native"; with Friday as his teacher, he learns to abandon the old European conventions as he sheds his clothes, worships the sun, and eats, sleeps, and works only when he feels like it. In a particularly ironic twist, Tournier has Friday, not Crusoe, join the crew of a rescue ship upon its departure for Europe; Crusoe chooses instead to remain on the island. Thus, as opposed to the rationalism espoused by the eighteenth-century Defoe, Tournier, using the same basic material, suggests another, more "modern" approach to determining one's place in the natural world—an approach that is more sensual and spontaneous.

At first glance, the *New Yorker* critic found all of this philosophizing to be "not a particularly attractive prospect" for a novel. Yet, he concludes, "Tournier is a cultivated and disciplined writer, and his Robinson . . . is most likable." The *New Statesman*'s Tindall also admits that the story of Crusoe "as a microcosm of Man everywhere is not a symbolism with immediate appeal to me," but, she insists, "do try the book. There is much more in it. . . . A French critic apparently described the work as 'Crusoe seen through the eyes of Freud, Jung and Claude Levi-Strauss'; while this encapsulation sounds glib, it does sum up usefully the author's overall approach."

T. J. Fleming of the *New York Times Book Review* reports that there is "a remarkable heady French wine in the old English bottle. . . . [Tournier] has attempted nothing less than an exploration of the soul of modern man [in *Friday*]. . . . Again and again, he finds fresh and original ways of viewing primary experiences such as time and work and religious faith, the relationship of men to animals and trees and their own shadowy selves, to civilization and the essential earth. The telling is intensely French. The focus is on thinking, and thinking about feeling. . . . [*Friday*] works, because the framework of the classic makes this abracadabra of believability convincing."

With the publication of his second novel, a fable-like tale called *The Ogre,* Tournier received world-wide attention. Based in part on Goethe's poem "The Erl King" and often compared to Guenter Grass's *The Tin Drum, The Ogre* is set in Germany between 1938 and 1945, where an imprisoned giant of a Frenchman, Abel Tiffauges, serves his Nazi captors as a procurer of young boys for an elite Hitler youth camp. Haunted by the symbolic nature of his own actions and of the destructive actions of mankind in general, the brooding Tiffauges views his role in life as that of a "beast of burden," a man who will save himself by saving others. Readers, however, find his role difficult to determine, for while Tiffauges seems to be a somewhat shadowy symbol of resistance (he dies after marching into a bog while carrying a Jewish child he rescued from a concentration camp), he can also—as the author suggests when someone attempts to assassinate him on July 20, 1944—be regarded as an embodiment of Hitler as well. As the *Times Literary Supplement*

reviewer explains: "The book as a whole is a journey from a contrived surrealism to, as it were, the real thing. The novel is so charged with symbols that it is hard to tell whether it is intended to have one meaning or many, or just how menacing an ogre Tiffauges is. . . . He is no simple monster."

Other critics, too, have been baffled by the multiplicity of ideas and interpretations present in the story, yet they still regard it as a worthwhile literary experience. *Newsweek*'s Peter Prescott calls it a "fine novel" that is "more likely to be praised than read. A good demanding fable, a meditative story of unaccustomed viscosity that rewards a second reading, it also seems curiously old-fashioned. . . . *The Ogre* is built in the way Bach built his fugues; themes and statements are introduced, inverted, tangled and marched past each other, all to be resolved in loud, majestic chords. . . . And yet the symbols and correspondences of this story, which are far more complex than I have been able to indicate, would be insufficient to sustain it as fiction. Tournier's achievement rests in his remarkable blend of myth with realism. . . . He offers a succession of scenes . . . which, as Abel says, not only decipher the essence of existence, but exalt it."

On the other hand, the *New York Review of Books*'s Karl Miller writes: "*The Ogre* is a very clever book in its belletristic way. . . . It may not be a likely story, but it is an absorbing one. Tiffauges's obsessions . . . are conveyed in an alliterative rhetoric of rare words and allusions. . . . There is clearly some renewal here of the profundities and affirmations of [*Friday*], and I imagine that it wouldn't be easy to say why one should be dazzled by the first book and repelled by its successor." Miller claims that his main objection to *The Ogre* lies in "the weakness of the distinction it draws between the malignity of the Nazis and the comparative benignity of this creature who achieves an apotheosis in the Nazi heartland. And its picture of the malignity of the Nazis is very dubious anyway. . . . Tournier documents [their] behavior . . . with reference to the evidence obtained for the Nuremburg Trials. . . . But it would appear that he has misrepresented that history while using it as a setting for an account of a fairly exotic psychological state." In short, Miller states, *The Ogre* "is all too mysterious and magical for me. . . . Tournier's imaginings come no closer to the condition of life in Nazi Germany than his Academician's prose does to the delusions of a supposedly ignorant obsessional."

"Like a good Hegelian, Tournier presents his thesis and antithesis," admits R. Z. Sheppard of *Time.* "But he is also a good Jungian. Signs, symbols and archetypes are pried from every incident and lofted chaotically into the mythological vacuum of the modern world. The presumption is that these fragments are awaiting a supersign that will unify them into some sort of new mythic order. When this in fact occurs in Tournier's book, the effect is one not of artistic revelation but of melodramatic kitsch." In apparent agreement with Miller, Sheppard goes on to note that unlike *Friday, The Ogre* seems to render the author "incapable of expressing an idea without sacrificing art to pedagogy." Thus, he concludes, "without at least a mail-order course in triadic dialectics, it is best to forgo analysis of Tournier's synthesis."

Marian Engel's reaction to *The Ogre* is almost exactly opposite that of her colleagues at *Time* and the *New York Review of Books.* As she notes in her *New York Times Book Review* article: "There are passages of great descriptive beauty [in *The Ogre*], and Tournier does not artistically shy away from fact. . . . [His book] can be taken as an explication of the German role in World War II and as a hundred other things as well. The book's French title was that of Goethe's poem the Erl-King—and, though I have also tied it to the Childe Harold legend, it is capable of other interpretations. In its richness and strangeness it encompasses also that other French anarchic misfit, Big Meaulnes, incorporating his loneliness in the Wagnerian web of Goetterdaemmerung. As you read the book, you, too, are drawn into that web, an experience that is dangerous and purging. . . . Abel Tiffauges is as complex and dangerous in English as in French; his themes are eternal and disturbing. To follow his dark path is a magnificent experience.''

As he reveals in the essay collection *Le Vent paraclet*, Tournier makes a conscious effort to include "eternal and disturbing" elements in novels that are otherwise conventional (as opposed to experimental) in form. According to a *Times Literary Supplement* reviewer, Tournier confesses to adhering to an orthodox structure "partly as bait, in order to get people to read what they might otherwise refuse. Deception is needed because he is a metaphysical novelist, more likely to find charm and inspiration in Leibniz or Spinoza than in the work of other novelists. . . . He adapts the supposedly safe conventions of realism to fantastic, transcendent ends.''

Even among Tournier's fans, though, there are those who wonder where all of his intellectual games will eventually lead him. A *French Review* critic, for example, fears that "Tournier, despite his great gifts and some admirable and durable achievements, is moving closer and closer towards turning his mind into a fun-house where he manipulates those jets of air which amuse some and scandalize others and which, unfortunately, are not to be taken very seriously.''

Not so, insists a *World Literature Today* reviewer. "Tournier's tales in their symbolic significance are more convincing than realistic fiction," she declares. "They represent a poetic rendering of his relationship to the world. Concretizing arcane reality through delusion or enchantment, Tournier is a magician who gives us the reassurance that there is a secret garden next to our backyard, that there is another world behind the mirror and that there is a small island in the Pacific Ocean where we lived happily once upon a time.'' Concludes an *Antioch Review* critic: "Tournier's imagination is flamboyant, his interests in minutia obsessive . . . , and his narrative power immense. . . . [If] he has not yet hit on the truly great novel, he . . . is aiming in exactly the right direction.''

BIOGRAPHICAL/CRITICAL SOURCES: New Statesman, February 7, 1969; *New York Times Book Review,* April 13, 1969, October 3, 1972; *New Yorker,* June 14, 1969; *Times Literary Supplement,* October 23, 1970, October 7, 1977, October 13, 1978; *Time,* August 21, 1972; *Newsweek,* October 4, 1972; *New York Review of Books,* November 30, 1972, December 14, 1972; *Books and Bookmen,* January, 1973; *Antioch Review,* June, 1973; *Journal of Popular Culture,* summer, 1974; *Contemporary Literary Criticism,* Volume VI, Gale, 1976; *French Review,* May, 1978, April, 1979; *World Literature Today,* spring, 1979.

—*Sketch by Deborah A. Straub*

*   *   *

TRASLER, Gordon (Blair) 1929-

PERSONAL: Born 1929, in Bournemouth, England; son of Frank Ferrier and Marian (Blair) Trasler; married Kathleen Patricia Fegan, 1953. *Education:* University of London, B.Sc., 1952, Ph.D., 1955; University of Exeter, M.A., 1960. *Home:* 2 White Shute Lane, St. Cross, Winchester, Hampshire, England. *Office:* Department of Psychology, University of Southampton, Southampton, England.

CAREER: Wandsworth Prison, London, England, psychologist, 1955-56; Winchester Prison, Hampshire, England, psychologist, 1956-57; University of Southampton, Southampton, England, lecturer in social psychology, 1957-64, professor of psychology, 1964—, dean of social sciences, 1970-73. Justice of the Peace for the county of Hampshire, 1978—. *Military service:* British Army, 1945-47. *Member:* British Psychological Society (fellow; chairman of division of legal and criminological psychology, 1980—), British Society of Criminology, Institute for the Study and Treatment of Delinquency, American Society of Criminology, Howard League for Penal Reform, Magistrates' Association.

WRITINGS: In Place of Parents: A Study of Foster Care, Humanities, 1960; *The Explanation of Criminality,* Humanities, 1962; *The Shaping of Social Behaviour,* University of Southampton Press, 1967; (with others) *The Formative Years,* British Broadcasting Corp., 1968, published as *The Formative Years: How Children Become Members of Their Society,* Schocken, 1970; (editor with D. P. Farrington) *Behaviour Modification with Offenders,* Cambridge Institute of Criminology, 1979.

Contributor: P. Halmos, editor, *Sociological Studies in the British Penal Services,* University of Keele, 1965; R.J.N. Tod, editor, *Children in Care,* Longmans, Green, 1968; H. J. Butcher and H. B. Pont, editors, *Educational Research in Britain-II,* University of London, 1969; H. J. Eysenck, W. Arnold, and R. Meili, editors, *Encyclopedia of Psychology,* Search Press, 1972; R. M. Carter, D. Glaser, and L. T. Watkins, editors, *Correctional Institutions,* Lippincott, 1972; J. B. Mays, editor, *Juvenile Delinquency, the Family and the Social Group,* Longmans, 1972; Eysenck, editor, *Handbook of Abnormal Psychology,* 2nd edition (Trasler was not associated with earlier edition), Pitman Medical, 1973; L. Blom-Cooper, editor, *Progress in Penal Reform,* Oxford University Press, 1974; R. D. Hare and D. Schalling, editors, *Psychopathic Behaviour: Approaches to Research,* Wiley, 1978; E. A. Wenk, editor, *Theoretical Perspectives on School Crime-III,* National Council on Crime and Delinquency (Hackensack, N.J.), 1978; G. D. Mitchell, editor, *A New Dictionary of Sociology,* Routledge & Kegan Paul, 1979; *Youth Custody,* British Association of Social Workers, 1979; *Young Adult Offenders,* Institute for the Study and Treatment of Delinquency, 1979; P. G. Hollowell, editor, *Property and Social Relations,* Heinemann, 1980; *Foundations of Psychosomatics,* Wiley, 1981. Editor, *British Journal of Criminology,* 1979—; review editor, *Criminal Justice and Behavior,* 1980—.

*   *   *

TRENT, William 1919-

PERSONAL: Born March 30, 1919, in Montreal, Quebec, Canada; son of Horace and Mabel (Blake) Trent; married Dawn McGlaughlin, 1952; children: William Blake, Shelley Elizabeth. *Education:* Attended Sir George Williams University, three years. *Residence:* Lanark, Ontario, Canada.

CAREER: The Herald, Montreal, Quebec, reporter, 1940-43; *Montreal Daily Star,* Montreal, assistant city editor, 1943-54; *Weekend Magazine,* Montreal, writer, 1959-75.

WRITINGS: Northwoods Doctor, Lippincott, 1962; *The Alvin Karpis Story,* Coward, 1970; *The Steven Truscott Story,* Simon & Schuster, 1971; *How to Live with Your Heart,* Quadrangle, 1975.

TRETHOWAN, K(enneth) Illtyd 1907-

PERSONAL: Born May 12, 1907, in Salisbury, Wiltshire, England; son of William James and Emma (van Kempen) Trethowan. *Education:* Brasenose College, Oxford, M.A. *Home:* Downside Abbey, Bath, Somerset, England.

CAREER: Ordained Roman Catholic priest; became monk of Benedictine Order, Downside Abbey, Bath, Somerset, England; member of staff of Downside School, Downside Abbey, 1936—.

WRITINGS: Certainty, Dacre Press, 1948; *Christ in the Liturgy,* Sheed, 1950; (with Dom Mark Pontifex) *The Meaning of Existence,* Longmans, Green, 1954; *An Essay in Christian Philosophy,* Longmans, Green, 1954; *The Basis of Belief,* Hawthorn, 1961; (contributor) *Prospect for Metaphysics,* Allen & Unwin, 1961; (contributor) *Theology and the University,* Darton, Longman & Todd, 1964; (with Alexander Dru) *Maurice Blondel,* Holt, 1966; *Absolute Value,* Allen & Unwin, 1970; *The Absolute and the Atonement,* Allen & Unwin, 1971; *Mysticism and Theology,* Geoffrey Chapman, 1975. Editor of *Downside Review,* 1946-52, 1960-65.

* * *

TRIFFIN, Robert 1911-

PERSONAL: Born October 5, 1911, in Flobecq, Belgium; came to the United States in 1939, naturalized citizen in 1942; son of François and Céline (van Hooland) Triffin; married Lois Brandt, May 30, 1940; children: Nicholas, Marc-Kerry, Eric. *Education:* Catholic University of Louvain, LL.D., 1934, M.A. (in economics), 1935; Harvard University, Ph.D., 1939. *Home:* 10 Ave. Hennebel, 1348 Louvain la Neuve, Belgium. *Office:* Louvain University, IRES, 1348 Louvain la Neuve, Belgium.

CAREER: Harvard University, Cambridge, Mass., instructor, 1939-42; Federal Reserve Board, Washington, D.C., chief of Latin American section, 1942-46; International Monetary Fund, Washington, D.C., Exchange Control Division, chief, 1946-47, director of European office, 1948-49; European Recovery Administration, Paris, France, adviser on monetary policy, 1949-51; Yale University, New Haven, Conn., Pelatiah Perit Professor of Political and Social Science, 1951-58, Frederick William Beinecke Professor of Economics, 1958-80, master of Berkeley College, 1969-77. Currently teaching spring terms at Louvain University (Louvain la Neuve, Belgium). Served as director of six monetary missions to Latin America, 1942-48; negotiator and U.S. alternate representative on managing board, European Payments Union, 1950-51; member of President Kennedy's task force on the balance of payments, 1961; member of board of economists, *Time* magazine. Consultant to European Economic Community, 1959—, Council of Economic Advisors, United Nations, Organization for European Cooperation, several U.S Government agencies, the Congolese Government, and various Latin American central banks.

MEMBER: American Economic Association (member of executive committee, 1961-62; vice-president, 1967-68), Societe d'Economie Politique (Paris), Council on Foreign Relations, World Academy of Art and Science, American Academy of Arts and Sciences, European Academy, Academie Royale de Belgique, Yale Club. *Awards, honors:* Wells Prize in economics, Harvard University, 1940, for *Monopolistic Competition and General Equilibrium Theory;* commandor, Orden del Merito (Paraguay), 1944; Emile de Laveleye Prize, 1963-68; Gouverneur Emile Cornez Prize, 1969; honorary doctorate, Catholic University of Louvain, 1970; commandor, Orden del Quetzal (Guatemala), 1971; com-

mandor, Ordre de la Couronne (Belgium), 1973; LL.D., University of New Haven, 1976; Merrill Foundation and Ford Foundation research grants.

WRITINGS: Monopolistic Competition and General Equilibrium Theory, Harvard University Press, 1940, reprinted, 1968; *Monetary and Banking Reform in Paraguay,* [Washington, D.C.], 1946; *Europe and the Money Muddle,* Yale University Press, 1957; *Gold and the Dollar Crisis,* Yale University Press, 1960, revised edition, 1966; (with Geer Stuvel and others) *Statistics of Sources and Uses of Finance, 1948-58,* Organization for Economic Cooperation and Development, 1960; *The Evolution of the International Monetary System: Historical Reappraisal and Future Perspectives,* Yale University Press, 1964; *The World Money Maze: National Currencies in International Payments,* Yale University Press, 1966; *Our International Monetary System: Yesterday, Today and Tomorrow,* Random House, 1968; *The Fate of the Pound,* Atlantic Institute (Paris), 1969; (contributor) *International Finance,* Princeton University Press, 1979. Author of numerous articles, lectures, and papers published in the United States, Europe, South America, Asia, and Africa.

SIDELIGHTS: Robert Triffin is a noted economist who, according to Harry G. Johnson, "enjoys the universal respect of experts on international monetary affairs, by virtue of his having been the first to analyze with powerful logic and clear detail the inherent instability of the present international monetary system. . . ." Triffin told *CA* that his "major economic interests and activity" are the result of his "early and persistent concern for international peace and understanding." Triffin added that these concerns particularly influenced his proposals for "worldwide monetary reform (the 'Triffin Plan') and regional monetary integration in Europe, Asia, Latin America, and Africa."

BIOGRAPHICAL/CRITICAL SOURCES: National Review, October 4, 1966; *Economist,* October 29, 1966; *Yale Review,* June, 1967; *Book World,* August 11, 1968.

* * *

TRIMINGHAM, J(ohn) Spencer 1904-

PERSONAL: Born November 17, 1904, in Thorne, England; son of Charles and Alice (Ventress) Trimingham; married Wardeh Salameh, 1932. *Education:* University of Birmingham, diploma in social science, 1930; Oxford University, M.A., 1934; attended Wells Theological College, 1935-36. *Home:* 72 Exmoor Dr., Worthing, West Sussex, England.

CAREER: Church Missionary Society, secretary of missions in North Sudan, 1937-49, Egypt, 1949-51, and West Africa, 1951-52; University of Glasgow, Glasgow, Scotland, lecturer in Islamic studies, 1953-56, head of department of Arabic and Islamic studies, 1956-64; American University of Beirut, Beirut, Lebanon, part-time professor in history department, 1964-70; Near East School of Theology, Beirut, associate professor of Islamic studies, 1970-77. *Member:* Royal Asiatic Society (fellow). *Awards, honors:* D.Litt., University of Glasgow, 1959; Carnegie travel research award, 1960; Leverhulme research grant, 1961.

WRITINGS: Sudan Colloquial Arabic, Clarendon Press (of Oxford University), 1946; *The Christian Approach to Islam in the Sudan,* Oxford University Press, 1948; *Islam in the Sudan,* Oxford University Press, 1949; *The Christian Church in Post-War Sudan,* World Dominion Press, 1949; *Church and Mission in Ethiopia,* World Dominion Press, 1950; *Islam in Ethiopia,* Oxford University Press, 1952; *Islam in West Africa,* Clarendon Press (of Oxford University),

1959; *A History of Islam in West Africa,* Oxford University Press, 1962; *Islam in East Africa,* Clarendon Press (of Oxford University), 1964; *The Influence of Islam upon Africa,* Longmans, Green, 1968, 2nd edition, 1979; *The Sufi Orders in Islam,* Clarendon Press (of Oxford University), 1971, Oxford University Press (New York), 1973; *Two Worlds Are Ours,* Librairie du Liban, 1971; *Christianity among the Arabs in Pre-Islamic Times,* Longman, 1979. Also author of research pamphlets.

WORK IN PROGRESS: Studies in Christian Mysticism.

* * *

TROY, Una 1913-

PERSONAL: Born May 21, 1913, in Fermoy, County Cork, Ireland; daughter of John and Bridget (Hayes) Troy; married J. C. Walsh (deceased); children: Janet Helleris. *Home:* 6 Osborne Ter., Bonmahon, County Waterford, Ireland. *Agent:* David Higham Associates, Ltd., 5-8 Lower John St., London W1R 4HA, England.

CAREER: Writer. *Member:* Society of Authors, Playwrights and Composers, P.E.N., Soroptimist. *Awards, honors:* Shaw First Prize, play competition, Abbey Theatre, Dublin.

WRITINGS—All published by Dutton: *We Are Seven,* 1957; *Miss Maggie and the Doctor,* 1958; *The Graces of Ballykeen,* 1960; *The Other End of the Bridge,* 1961; *Esmond,* 1962; *The Prodigal Father,* 1965.

All published by R. Hale: *The Benefactors,* 1969; *Tiger Puss,* 1970; *Stop Press,* 1971; *The Castle That Nobody Wanted,* 1972; *Doctor Go Home,* 1973; *Out of the Everywhere,* 1976; *Caught in the Furze,* 1977; *A Sack of Gold,* 1979.

Also author of four plays, "Mount Prospect," "Swans and Geese," "An Apple a Day," and "The Old Road," all produced at Abbey Theatre, Dublin; co-author of motion picture "She Didn't Say No," based on her book, *We Are Seven.* Contributor of short stories to Irish and American magazines.

WORK IN PROGRESS: A novel.

AVOCATIONAL INTERESTS: Theater, cinema, television, reading, swimming, and rock-climbing.

BIOGRAPHICAL/CRITICAL SOURCES: Times Literary Supplement, April 11, 1958, September 25, 1959; *New York Times Book Review,* June 29, 1958, January 3, 1960; *Spectator,* October 2, 1959; *Commonweal,* February 26, 1960; *Saturday Review,* April 10, 1965.

* * *

TRUDEAU, (Joseph Philippe) Pierre (Yves) Elliott 1919-

PERSONAL: Born October 18, 1919, in Montreal, Quebec, Canada; son of Charles-Emile (a lawyer and businessman) and Grace (Elliott) Trudeau; married Margaret Sinclair, March 4, 1971 (separated, 1977); children: Justin Pierre, Alexandre Emmanuel, Michel Charles-Emile. *Education:* Jean de Brebeuf College, B.A. (with honors), 1940; University of Montreal, LL.L. (with honors), 1943; Harvard University, M.A. (political economy), 1945; graduate study at Ecole des Sciences Politiques (Paris) and London School of Economics and Political Science. *Religion:* Roman Catholic. *Home:* Prime Minister's Residence, 24 Sussex Dr., Ottawa, Ontario, Canada K1M 1M4. *Office:* Office of the Prime Minister, Parliamentary Bldgs., Ottawa, Ontario, Canada K1A 0A2.

CAREER: Called to the Bar of Quebec, 1943, and to the Bar

of Ontario, created Queen's counsel, 1969; Government of Canada, Privy Council, Ottawa, Ontario, desk officer, 1949-51; established private law practice in Montreal, Quebec, 1951; University of Montreal, Montreal, associate professor of constitutional law and staff member of Institute of Public Law, 1961-65; Government of Canada, Liberal Party representative in House of Commons, 1965—, parliamentary secretary to the Prime Minister, 1966-67, Minister of Justice and Attorney General, 1967-68, member of Privy Council, 1967—, leader of Liberal Party and Prime Minister, 1968-79, 1980—, leader of official opposition in Parliament, 1979-80. Co-founder and member of political organization, Le Rassemblement, 1956-59. Delegate to France-Canada Interparliamentary Association meetings in Paris, 1966; Canadian delegate to twenty-first session of U.N. General Assembly, 1966; toured French-speaking African countries on behalf of Canadian Government, 1967. *Member:* Royal Society of Canada, Canadian Bar Association, Ontario Bar Association, Quebec Bar Association, Montreal Civil Liberties Union (founding member). *Awards, honors:* President's Medal for best scholarly article from University of Western Ontario, 1959, for "Some Obstacles to Democracy in Quebec"; recipient of numerous honorary degrees, including LL.D., University of Alberta, 1968, Queen's University, 1968, and Duke University, 1974; honorary fellow, London School of Economics and Political Science, 1969.

WRITINGS: (Editor and contributor) *La Greve de l'amiante* (title means "The Asbestos Strike"), Editions Cite Libre, 1956, illustrated version, International Scholarly Book Services, 1971, translation by James Boake published as *The Asbestos Strike,* James Lewis & Samuel, 1974; (contributor) Mason Wade, editor, *Canadian Dualism,* University of Toronto Press, 1960; (with Jacques Hebert) *Deux Innocents en Chine* (travel diary), Les Editions de l'Homme, 1961, translation by I. M. Owen published as *Two Innocents in Red China,* Oxford University Press, 1968; (contributor) Michael Oliver, editor, *Social Purpose for Canada,* University of Toronto Press, 1961; (contributor) Paul-Andre Crepeau and C. B. MacPherson, editors, *The Future of Canadian Federalism,* University of Toronto Press, 1965; (contributor) Paul Fox, editor, *Politics: Canada,* McGraw, 1966; *Le Federalisme et la societe canadienne-francaise* (essays), Editions H.M.H., 1967, translation published as *Federalism and the French Canadians,* St. Martin's, 1968; *Responses de Pierre Elliott Trudeau,* Editions du Jour, 1968, 2nd edition, 1968; *The Gospel According to Saint Pierre,* compiled by Brian Shaw, Pocket Books (Canada), 1969; *The Constitution and the People of Canada/La Constitution eanadienne et le citoyen: An Approach to the Objectives of Confederation, the Rights of People, and the Institutions of Government* (working paper from the 1969 Canadian Constitutional Conference; in English and French), The Queen's Printer, 1969; *Federal-Provincial Grants and the Spending Power of Parliament/Les Subventions federales-provinciales et le pouvoir de depenser du Parlement canadien* (working paper from the 1969 Constitutional Conference; in English and French), [Ottawa], 1969.

Les Cheminements de la politique (addresses, essays, and lectures), Editions du Jour, 1970, translation by Owen published as *Approaches to Politics,* Oxford University Press, 1970; (contributor) Allan Ezra Gotlieb, editor, *Human Rights, Federalism, and Minorities/Les Droits de l'homme, le federalisme, et les minorites* (in English and French), Canadian Institute of International Affairs, 1970; *Conversation with Canadians* (collected remarks), University of Toronto Press, 1972; *The Best of Trudeau; A Compendium of*

Whimsical Wit and Querulous Quip by Canada's Putative Prince, Modern Canadian Library, 1972; *Trudeau en direct* (speeches), Editions du Jour, 1972; *PM/Dialogue,* High Hill Publishing House, 1972; *Pierre Elliott Trudeau* (quotations), compiled by Charles Bordeleau, Editions Heritage, 1978.

Contributor to *Cite Libre, Canadian Journal of Economics and Political Science, Maclean's, Canadian Forum, Revue de Notariat,* and other periodicals. Co-founder and co-director, *Cite Libre* (monthly political review), beginning 1950.

SIDELIGHTS: Born into a wealthy and politically conservative Montreal family and educated at an elite French-Canadian Jesuit prep school, Pierre Elliott Trudeau has been in conflict with tradition and the status quo throughout virtually his entire life. Classmates and teachers at his primary school remember him as headstrong and individualistic, frequently involved in fights and practical jokes, but almost always at the top of his class academically. As he revealed to Edith Iglauer in an extensive *New Yorker* profile, Trudeau himself recalls being "impertinent to my father, to my teachers, to everybody. It got me into trouble, but when I was intimidated I had to have the last word. As I became more mature, I would state my case and sit back, which is a form of answering."

Despite the disruption caused by his behavior problems, Trudeau regards his prep school years as an extremely influential period in his life. He credits one of his teachers, Father Robert Bernier, with being the first person to make him "study the right works" and to talk politics with him. Under the tutelage of Father Bernier, the young Trudeau discovered the world of art, music, philosophy, history, and literature. In the course of his career, he has often used this knowledge to his advantage, quoting from the works of Plato, de Tocqueville, and Montesquieu to illustrate or defend a point. Yet Trudeau hesitates to single out any one of these men as a major influence on his current political philosophy. Claiming his taste can best be described as "eclectic," he insists that "many people in my position have read more than I have in the field of history and economics. I have probably read more of Dostoevski, Stendhal, and Tolstoy than the average statesman, and less of Keynes, Mill, and Marx. . . . I am not a scholar of any of these disciplines. . . . [But] I have done a lot of other reading and travelling."

Much of this travelling occurred in the late 1940s after Trudeau abandoned his Ph.D. studies and embarked on a trip around the world, by motorcycle where possible and with a knapsack on his back. Eager for adventure, he deliberately sought out forbidden, out-of-the-way places; he illegally entered Poland, Hungary, and Yugoslavia (from which he was expelled), was arrested as an Israeli spy by Arabs in Jerusalem, crossed the Khyber Pass during border skirmishes between the recently-partitioned nations of India and Pakistan, arrived in Shanghai in the midst of a Maoist-Nationalist confrontation, witnessed some of the street fighting resulting from a civil war in Burma, and rode with a military convoy across Vietnam and Cambodia. It was a somewhat tamer pastime, however—attending an international economic conference in Moscow—that earned him a spot on a 1950s McCarthy blacklist, preventing his entry into the United States and eventually helping to make it more difficult for him to obtain a teaching position at the University of Montreal.

Upon his return to Canada, Trudeau became interested in an asbestos miners' strike in Quebec, serving as a legal aide to the labor side of the dispute in its struggle against the Ameri-

can owners of the company and the corrupt and authoritarian provincial government of Maurice Duplessis and his supporters among reactionary members of the local clergy. His experiences during the bitter strike (described in *La Greve de l'amiante*), combined with the insight gained from his travels abroad, convinced him of the need for extensive political and social reform in Canada, especially in Quebec, which Trudeau felt was stagnating under the repressive Duplessis regime. Determined to see Duplessis ousted, Trudeau and others who felt as he did founded a left-of-center intellectual quarterly, *Cite Libre,* to serve as a forum for the discussion of their ideas, and formed a multi-party political group known as "Le Rassemblement" to offer an alternative to Duplessis.

During this same period of political activism, Trudeau worked briefly in Ottawa for the Canadian government, then set up a law office in Montreal which specialized in handling "interesting" cases for clients who could not afford to pay. But it was not until after Duplessis's death in the late 1950s that he was finally able to secure a position on the University of Montreal faculty. A controversial figure on campus due to his provocative lectures, Trudeau gradually abandoned his involvement with left-wing politics while at the university, citing a difference of opinion on the matter of Quebec as a major factor in his decision. "In those days," he recalls, "the N.D.P. [New Democratic Party, a prominent socialist group] didn't think it was important to do anything in Quebec. . . . So we disagreed." Trudeau then began to consider the possibility of joining the Liberal Party. At first, party leaders resisted his overtures, refusing to back him in a parliamentary election; their resistance hardened as Trudeau grew more and more critical of Liberal Prime Minister Lester Pearson's policy of allowing American nuclear warheads on Canadian soil. Nevertheless, Trudeau reports, "in time he and I put our differences aside. We both felt that now he was taking me and I was taking him for better or worse. This was true of the Liberal Party, too." In 1965, he officially joined the party and was elected representative from a well-to-do suburb of Montreal.

More accurately described as a catapult than as an ascent to power, Trudeau's subsequent campaign for the position of prime minister began in December, 1967, when Pearson announced his intention to resign. Because conditions in Quebec were worsening, party leaders decided that their best choice for Pearson's replacement would be a French-Canadian capable of unifying the country. Attention centered on Jean Marchand, a prominent, well-respected Quebec labor leader and personal friend of Trudeau's who had also been elected as a Liberal Party representative in the 1965 elections. He declined to run, however, and urged Trudeau, who had already made a name for himself in Parliament, to try instead. Party leaders hesitated at first, but a "Draft Trudeau" movement was gaining momentum and the time seemed right for a Liberal victory at the polls.

It was during this 1968 campaign that Trudeau's image as a swinger emerged. To make the most of the candidate's charismatic effect on crowds, especially women and young people, a team of media experts was called in and "Trudeaumania" (a term coined by Canadian journalists) was born. That he slid down bannisters in the House of Commons while carrying legislation, wore sandals to diplomatic functions, walked on his hands while waiting to meet officials, and performed yoga headstands at parties were among the most widely circulated stories; in addition, he became the subject of a rock recording, "Go, Go Trudeau," and of a best-selling poster in which he was shown clenching a rose between his teeth. Less widely circulated, however, were the personal observations of colleagues and friends, one of whom described Trudeau as a basically shy and hard-working man who adopts flamboyance and off-beat mannerisms as a counterbalance to seriousness. Another told the *New Yorker*'s Iglauer: "The playboy image of Pierre reflects one-tenth of one percent of his activity. Pierre is always challenging, provoking, shocking, so that no one can see what he's really like. He keeps us guessing all the time, which is what he wants. He is arrogant with people who don't know anything, and he himself has a passionate eagerness to know, to see and learn. He respects competence. He is an individualist who is always challenging himself, and who will always be lonely. He has one consistent personality trait, and this may be what some people don't like: to go through with anything he starts, and through to the end."

Though most of that first successful campaign was based on image rather than substance, Trudeau did and still does have one goal which has remained of tantamount importance to his political philosophy—the integration of Quebec into the structure of the federal government without the destruction of its cultural and linguistic differences. Understandably sympathetic to the problems of the French-Canadian minority in Canada, Trudeau is nevertheless a staunch federalist who believes that separatism would be disastrous for both Quebec and for Canada as a whole. In fact, much of the governmental reorganization and reform he has proposed while in office has worked towards this ultimate goal of creating a "Just Society" in which individuality is protected and cooperation between disparate groups is the rule of the day.

Trudeau survived two attempts to oust him and his government, once in 1972, when the Liberals fell from a position of dominance to a shaky minority government, and again in 1974, when the Liberals regained a surprisingly hefty majority in Parliament. In 1979, however, he was not so lucky. In this election, Trudeau faced Joe Clark, a folksy Tory conservative from the western province of Alberta who referred to the prime minister as "the prince of broken promises." Consciously patterning himself after Jimmy Carter, Clark came virtually out of nowhere and took the country by surprise, searching for and finding a great deal of support among those relatively affluent, right-of-center Canadians who were eager for a change and who were suspicious of pinstriped suits, Ph.D.'s, and eastern dominance. During the course of the campaign, he offered his own set of promises, including tax relief, reductions in the size and power of the bureaucracy, relaxation of certain rules governing bilingual labelling, legislation designed to encourage the expansion of private enterprise, and a resumption of discussion on such topics as capital punishment and defense spending. Aware that their man was no match for Trudeau as far as charismatic appeal was concerned, Canadian conservatives relied on their party platform to pull in the votes, and it did. While they failed to gain enough seats to constitute a majority government, they at least managed to outnumber the Liberals in the final tally, 136 to 114, making Clark the new prime minister. Trudeau sadly but graciously conceded defeat, hinting at his intention to withdraw from active politics after seeing his party through the upcoming referendum on Quebec's future in the Canadian federation.

A mere six months later, however, Clark's government was in a shambles after a parliamentary vote of no confidence forced him to call for new elections. A victim of a foreign policy fiasco—a promise to move the Canadian Embassy in Israel from Tel Aviv to Jerusalem (an announcement that enraged the Arab world)—and an extremely unpopular aus-

terity budget, which included an immediate increase in domestic oil prices as well as an 18-cent-per-gallon increase in gasoline taxes, Clark was quickly perceived as an incompetent who made unreasonable demands. Though he had already announced his desire to retire from politics, Trudeau declared that it was his duty to accept the draft of his party to run for re-election; cynical observers attributed his sudden interest in the job to a desire not to go down in history as a loser. In any case, conducting an amazingly subdued campaign, Trudeau once again offered himself and his party to the voters as the only reasonable alternative to the bumbling Clark, caustically pointing out to Canadians that "you don't have to sit through three and four reels to see it's going to be a grade C movie."

In late February of 1980, Trudeau and the Liberals scored an astonishing victory at the polls, gaining thirty-two seats in Parliament, enough to constitute a majority government. Greeting his supporters and members of the media at a post-election celebration, a moist-eyed but jubilant Trudeau grinned and declared, "Welcome to the 1980s!"

Unlike the long-haired, liberal "swinger" who took Canada by storm in 1968, the 1980 version of Pierre Trudeau, though still as debonair and as vigorous as ever, has mellowed considerably. Marriage and children, followed by a highly-publicized separation instigated by his free-spirited wife, Margaret, have considerably lessened the impact of his reputation as a playboy. A serious and conscientious leader of his country, he is a far cry from the liberal dilettante some feared he would be. As Gerald Clark of the *New York Times Magazine* remarks, "Trudeau proved to be neither a swinger nor insensitive to the problems of people less well endowed intellectually or financially than himself. What he was—and remains—is an intricate individualist who cannot really be categorized."

As prime minister, Trudeau still faces many of the same problems he grappled with in the previous decade—Quebec, the economy, and Canada's role in world affairs—plus a few new ones, especially those resulting from the western provinces' burgeoning oil industry (Trudeau's policy of less private and more government control is not at all popular in the West, as evidenced by the fact that only two of the thirty-two seats won by the Liberals in the 1980 election came from provinces west of Ontario). Though his most conspicuous campaign promise involved not these issues but his oft-repeated intention to step down in a few years in order to spend more time with his sons "before I become too decrepit," Trudeau nevertheless left the door open to speculation about his future plans when he remarked just prior to the 1980 campaign that "Gladstone didn't quit until he was 84." But as *Time* quoted from a *Montreal Gazette* editorial written shortly after the election: "Canadians have given Mr. Trudeau a rare chance to end his career on a high note of accomplishment, rather than the sour anti-climax of last spring's defeat. It is his last and perhaps his greatest challenge."

AVOCATIONAL INTERESTS: Swimming, skiing, flying, scuba diving, and canoeing.

BIOGRAPHICAL/CRITICAL SOURCES—Books: John D. Harbron, *This Is Trudeau*, Longmans, Green, 1968; D. Steubing and others, *Trudeau: A Man for Tomorrow*, Clarke, Irwin, 1968; Martin Sullivan, *Mandate '68*, Doubleday, 1968; Petjo Maltest, editor, *Citations de P.E.T.*, Inter-Distribution (Montreal), 1968; Peter C. Newman, *A Nation Divided: Canada and the Coming of Pierre Trudeau*, Knopf, 1969; Walter Stewart, *Trudeau in Power*, Outerbridge &

Dienstfrey, 1972; George Radwanski, *Trudeau*, Macmillan, 1979; Richard Gwen, *Northern Magus*, McLelland & Stewart, 1980.

Periodicals: *New York Times*, April 8, 1968; *Wall Street Journal*, April 17, 1968; *Life*, April 19, 1968; *Washington Post*, April 28, 1968, October 3, 1973; *New York Times Magazine*, June 16, 1968, November 3, 1974; *Economist*, June 29, 1968; *Newsweek*, September 2, 1968, February 18, 1980, March 3, 1980; *New York Times Book Review*, November 17, 1968; *Detroit Free Press*, March 23, 1969; *New Yorker*, July 5, 1969; *Look*, February 24, 1970; *Christian Century*, April 19, 1972; *Maclean's*, June 4, 1979; *Time*, March 3, 1980.

—*Sketch by Deborah A. Straub*

* * *

TSCHUMI, Raymond Robert 1924-

PERSONAL: Born November 27, 1924, in Saint-Imier, Switzerland; son of Robert Louis (a correspondent) and Marguerite (Romy) Tschumi; married Julia Lozano, September 21, 1952; children: Jean-Raymond, Laurent. *Education:* University of Geneva, Licence-es-lettres, 1946, Doctorat-es-lettres, 1951. *Religion:* Protestant. *Home:* Flurhofstrasse 88, St. Gallen, Switzerland. *Office:* Hochschule St. Gallen, Dufourstrasse 50, St. Gallen, Switzerland.

CAREER: Brown University, Providence, R.I., assistant in French, 1947-48; University of Geneva, Geneva, Switzerland, privat-docent, 1951, charge de cours for American literature, 1957—; Hochschule St. Gallen, St. Gallen, Switzerland, professor of English language and literature, 1956—. *Member:* Anglo-Swiss Club (president, 1956—), IAUPE, Institut Jurassien. *Awards, honors:* Prix Hentsch de Litterature (Geneva), 1946 and 1950.

WRITINGS: L'Arche (poetry), Editions du Chandelier, 1950; *Thought in Twentieth Century English Poetry*, Routledge & Kegan Paul, 1951, reprinted, Norwood, 1978; *Regards voraces* (poetry), La Galere, 1952; *Renouveau* (poetry), Delfica, 1953; *A Philosophy of Literature*, Linden Press (London), 1961, Dufour, 1962; *Science, Philosophy and Literary Criticism: Notes on Their Interaction in England and America*, Polygraphischer Verlag (Zurich), 1961; *Jean-Vincent Verdonnet*, Formes et Langages, 1973; *Signal de Cime*, Saint Germain, 1973; *Theorie de la culture*, L'Age d'Homme, 1975, translation published as *Theory of Culture*, NOK Publishers, 1978. Also author of *Concert d'ouvertures*, 1967, *De Dante a Milton*, 1967, *De la Pensee continue*, 1968, and *Poemes choisis*, 1973.

WORK IN PROGRESS: Research on American literature and on the cultural crisis since the Renaissance; poetical parodies in French; essays; poetry; *Les Aventures de Pequignot*, a novel.

SIDELIGHTS: Raymond Tschumi believes in the unity of culture through the imagination. "Whether literature is expression or communication," he writes, "it is the link between the soul, which is ours, and the universe, which is strange or hostile. A society of specialists needs the all-embracing imagination."

* * *

TSUZUKI, Chushichi 1926-

PERSONAL: Born September 18, 1926, in Aichi, Japan; son of Kinosuke and Sato (Takeuchi) Tsuzuki; married Haruko Matsumura, 1961. *Education:* Hitotsubashi University, B.A., 1950; Princeton University, graduate study, 1952-53;

University of Wisconsin, M.A., 1954; Oxford University, D.Phil., 1959. *Home:* 201 Meguro-Mita Park Mansion, 10-45, 2-chome Mita, Meguro, Tokyo, Japan. *Office:* Hitotsubashi University, Kunitachi, Tokyo, Japan.

CAREER: Hitotsubashi University, Tokyo, Japan, 1959—, began as assistant professor, professor of social thought, 1970—. Overseas fellow, St. John's College, Cambridge University, 1976-77. *Member:* Society for the Study of Labour History.

WRITINGS: H. M. Hyndman and British Socialism, Oxford University Press, 1961; *The Life of Eleanor Marx: A Socialist Tragedy*, Oxford University Press, 1967; *Edward Carpenter: Prophet of Human Fellowship*, Cambridge University Press, 1980.

* * *

TUCHMAN, Barbara (Wertheim) 1912-

PERSONAL: Born January 30, 1912, in New York, N.Y.; daughter of Maurice (a banker) and Alma (Morgenthau) Wertheim; married Lester R. Tuchman (a physician), 1940; children: Lucy, Jessica, Alma. *Education:* Radcliffe College, B.A., 1933. *Home:* 875 Park Ave., New York, N.Y. *Agent:* Henry Volkening, 551 Fifth Ave., New York, N.Y. 10017.

CAREER: Institute of Pacific Relations, New York City, research and editorial assistant, 1933-35; *Nation*, New York City, staff writer and foreign correspondent, 1935-37, correspondent in Madrid, 1937, correspondent in United States, 1939; Office of War Information, New York City, editor, 1943-45. Trustee, Radcliffe College, 1960-72. Appointed Jefferson Lecturer by the National Endowment for the Humanities, 1980. Lecturer at Harvard University, University of California, U.S. Naval War College, and other institutions. Member of council, Smithsonian Institution. *Member:* Society of American Historians (president, 1970-73), Authors Guild (treasurer), Authors League (member of council), American Academy of Arts and Letters (president, 1979—), American Academy of Arts and Sciences, Cosmopolitan Club. *Awards, honors:* Pulitzer Prize, 1963, for *The Guns of August*, and 1972, for *Stilwell and the American Experience in China, 1911-1945*; gold medal for history, American Academy of Arts and Sciences, 1978; received Order of Leopold; D.Litt. from Yale University, Columbia University, New York University, Williams College, University of Massachusetts, Smith College, Hamilton College, Mount Holyoke College, Boston University, and others.

WRITINGS: The Lost British Policy: Britain and Spain since 1700, United Editorial, 1938; *Bible and Sword: England and Palestine from the Bronze Age to Balfour*, New York University Press, 1956; *The Zimmermann Telegram*, Viking, 1958, new edition, Macmillan, 1966; *The Guns of August* (Book-of-the-Month Club selection), Macmillan, 1962 (published in England as *August 1914*, Constable, 1962); *The Proud Tower: A Portrait of the World before the War, 1890-1914* (Book-of-the-Month Club selection), Macmillan, 1966; *Stilwell and the American Experience in China, 1911-1945* (Book-of-the-Month Club selection), Macmillan, 1971 (published in England as *Sand against the Wind: Stilwell and the American Experience in China, 1911-1945*, Macmillan, [London], 1971); *Notes from China*, Collier Books, 1972; *A Distant Mirror: The Calamitous Fourteenth Century*, Knopf, 1978. Contributor to *Harper's*, *Atlantic*, *New York Times*, *American Scholar*, *Foreign Affairs*, and others.

SIDELIGHTS: Barbara Tuchman writes narrative histories that are strongly literary in nature, believing the work of most historians to be too scholarly for the average reader.

"Historians who put in everything plus countless footnotes aren't thinking of their readers," she says. "Subsequently, they're not readable." Tuchman favors the literary approach. "There should be a beginning, a middle, and an end," she states, "plus an element of suspense to keep a reader turning the pages."

Although not trained as a historian, Tuchman does not see that as a disadvantage. "I never took a Ph.D.," she explains. "It's what saved me, I think. If I had taken a doctoral degree, it would have stifled any writing capacity." To prepare for her books, Tuchman first researches the available information and then visits the appropriate historical sites. For *The Guns of August*, she walked the battlefields of World War I; for *A Distant Mirror*, she crossed the same mountains the Crusaders of the fourteenth century crossed.

Tuchman's books have been awarded two Pulitzer Prizes and received high praise from the critics. O. Edmond Clubb calls *Stilwell and the American Experience in China* "an admirably structured work that is excellent as narrative and fascinating as history." Allen S. Whiting describes it as "the most interesting and informative book on U.S.-China relations to appear since World War II." Christopher Lehmann-Haupt praises Tuchman's ability "to organize her material coherently [and] to trace bright narrative threads without sacrificing complexities." He concludes that Tuchman writes "popular history, to be sure, but it is popular history that doesn't conceal the voids beyond."

In 1979, Tuchman was the first woman to be selected for the National Endowment for the Humanities' Jefferson Lectureship. A biographical statement distributed by the Endowment at that time summarizes Tuchman's approach to her craft: "Barbara Tuchman believes in the writing of history as it actually occurred, in a narrative style which elicits the variety and complexity of the specific periods in which she immerses herself, and she prides herself on being 'a good storyteller.' She considers herself a writer first and historian second. 'I am a writer whose subject is history' is her self-description. She is a non-academic historian with a journalist's instincts for people and events, and a firm believer in standards of excellence in her craft. The complexity of life, the hopes and upheavals of people and nations, the interweaving of history and current social and political questions—all have been hallmarks of Barbara Tuchman's contributions to public understanding through her writing and her lectures, and all have reached their zenith in the best-selling *A Distant Mirror*."

Tuchman's books have been translated into thirteen languages including Hebrew, Japanese, and Rumanian. *The Guns of August* was filmed in 1964.

BIOGRAPHICAL/CRITICAL SOURCES: Saturday Review, January 27, 1962, January 15, 1966, February 20, 1971; *New York Times Book Review*, January 28, 1962, November 12, 1978; *Christian Science Monitor*, February 1, 1962, March 24, 1971, September 18, 1978; *Time*, February 9, 1962, January 14, 1966, February 15, 1971; *New Yorker*, April 14, 1962, February 5, 1966, November 13, 1978; *Times Literary Supplement*, June 8, 1962, December 10, 1971; *New Statesman*, June 22, 1962; *Wall Street Journal*, January 14, 1966; *Atlantic*, February, 1966, October, 1978; *Harper's*, February, 1966; *America*, February 5, 1966; *National Review*, February 8, 1966; *Nation*, February 14, 1966, April 26, 1971; *Economist*, February 26, 1966; *Punch*, March 9, 1966; *Critic*, April-May, 1966; *Current History*, May, 1966; *Virginia Quarterly Review*, summer, 1966; *American Historical Review*, July, 1966; *Journal of American History*, Septem-

ber, 1966, December, 1971; *Cosmopolitan*, January, 1967; *Newsweek*, February 15, 1971; *New York Times*, February 15, 1971, February 27, 1979; *Life*, February 19, 1971; *Book World*, February 28, 1971, October 8, 1978; *New Republic*, March 27, 1971; *Esquire*, June, 1971; *Progressive*, June, 1971; *New York Review of Books*, July 22, 1971, August 9, 1973, September 28, 1978; *Listener*, January 6, 1972, March 29, 1979; *American Political Science Review*, June, 1972; *Christian Century*, May 14, 1975; Kathleen Bowman, *New Women in Social Sciences*, Creative Education Press, 1976; *Village Voice*, June 19, 1978; *Business Week*, September 25, 1978; *Washington Post*, October 5, 1978; *New Leader*, October 9, 1978; *Commentary*, December, 1978; *Spectator*, March 31, 1979; *Books & Bookmen*, May, 1979; *Ms.*, July, 1979; *Observer*, July 15, 1979.

*   *   *

TUCKER, Robert C(harles)   1918-

PERSONAL: Born May 29, 1918, in Kansas City, Mo.; son of Charles and Adele (Steinfels) Tucker; married Evgenia Pestretsova, 1946; children: Elizabeth A. *Education:* Attended University of Michigan, 1935-37; Harvard University, B.A., 1939, M.A., 1941, Ph.D., 1958. *Office:* Department of Politics, Princeton University, Princeton, N.J. 08540.

CAREER: Member of staff of Office of Strategic Services, 1942-44, U.S. Foreign Service at U.S. Embassy in Moscow, U.S.S.R., 1944-53, and Social Science Division of RAND Corp., 1954-58; Indiana University at Bloomington, professor of government, 1958-62; Princeton University, Princeton, N.J., professor of politics, 1962—. Visiting member, Institute for Advanced Study. *Member:* American Political Science Association, American Association for the Advancement of Slavic Studies. *Awards, honors:* Center for Advanced Study in the Behavioral Sciences fellow, 1964-65; Guggenheim fellow, 1968-69; National Book Award nomination, 1974, for *Stalin as Revolutionary;* American Academy of Arts and Sciences fellow, 1975—; National Endowment for the Humanities fellow, 1975-76.

WRITINGS—Published by Norton, except as indicated: *Philosophy and Myth in Karl Marx*, Cambridge University Press, 1961; *The Soviet Political Mind*, Praeger, 1963, 2nd edition, Norton, 1972; (co-editor and author of introduction) *The Great Purge Trial*, Grosset, 1965; *The Marxian Revolutionary Idea*, 1969; *Stalin as Revolutionary*, 1973; (editor) *The Marx-Engels Reader*, 1973; (editor) *The Lenin Anthology*, 1975; (editor) *Stalinism: Essays in Historical Interpretation*, 1977. Contributor to professional journals, including *Chronicle of Higher Education* and to *New Leader* and *New Republic*.

*   *   *

TUCKER, William E(dward)   1932-

PERSONAL: Born June 22, 1932, in Charlotte, N.C.; son of Cecil Edward and Ethel (Godley) Tucker; married Ruby Jean Jones, April 8, 1955; children: Janet Sue, William Edward, Jr., Gordon Vance. *Education:* Atlantic Christian College, A.B., 1953; Texas Christian University, B.D., 1956; Yale University, M.A., 1958, Ph.D., 1960. *Politics:* Democrat. *Religion:* Christian Church (Disciples of Christ). *Home:* 2900 Simondale Dr., Fort Worth, Tex. 76109. *Office:* Office of the Chancellor, Texas Christian University, Fort Worth, Tex. 76129.

CAREER: Atlantic Christian College, Wilson, N.C., associate professor, 1959-63, professor of religion, 1963-66, chairman of department of religion and philosophy, 1962-66;

Texas Christian University, Brite Divinity School, Fort Worth, associate professor and assistant dean, 1966-69, professor of church history and associate dean, 1969-71, dean, 1971-76; Bethany College, Bethany, W. Va., president, 1976-79; Texas Christian University, chancellor, 1979—. *Member:* American Society of Church History, Disciples of Christ Historical Society, American Historical Association, American Academy of Religion.

WRITINGS: J. H. Garrison and Disciples of Christ, Bethany Press, 1964; (with Lester G. McAllister) *Journey in Faith: A History of the Christian Church (Disciples of Christ),* Bethany Press, 1975.

Contributor: P. Hunter Beckelhymer, editor, *The Word We Preach,* Texas Christian University Press, 1970; Jerald C. Brauer, editor, *The Westminster Dictionary of Church History,* Westminster, 1971; Edward T. James, editor, *Dictionary of American Biography, Supplement Three, 1941-45,* Scribner, 1973; David C. Roller and Robert W. Twyman, editors, *The Encyclopedia of Southern History,* Louisiana State University Press, 1979.

*   *   *

TULLOCK, Gordon   1922-

PERSONAL: Born February 13, 1922, in Rockford, Ill.: son of George Duncan and Helen Tullock. *Education:* University of Chicago, student, 1939-43, D.J., 1947; special studies in Chinese at Yale University and Cornell University, 1950-53. *Home:* 4 West Ridge Dr., Blacksburg, Va. 24060. *Office:* Center for Study of Public Choice, Virginia Polytechnic Institute and State University, Blacksburg, Va. 24061.

CAREER: U.S. Department of State, Washington, D.C., Foreign Service officer, 1947-56; University of Virginia, Charlottesville, postdoctoral fellow at Thomas Jefferson Center, 1958-59; University of South Carolina, Columbia, 1959-62, began as assistant professor, became associate professor in department of international studies; University of Virginia, associate professor in department of economics, 1962-67; Rice University, Houston, Tex., professor of economics and political science, 1967-68; Virginia Polytechnic Institute and State University, Center for Study of Public Choice, Blacksburg, University Distinguished Professor, 1968—. *Military service:* U.S. Army, 1943-45. *Member:* Cosmos club, Colonnade club.

WRITINGS: (Editor) *A Practical Guide for the Ambitious Politician,* University of South Carolina Press, 1961; (with James Buchanan) *The Calculus of Consent,* University of Michigan Press, 1962; *The Politics of Bureaucracy,* Public Affairs Press, 1965; *The Organization of Inquiry,* Duke University Press, 1966; *Toward a Mathematics of Politics,* University of Michigan Press, 1967; *Private Wants, Public Means: An Economic Analysis of the Desirable Scope of Government,* Basic Books, 1970; *The Logic of the Law,* Basic Books, 1971; *The Social Dilemma: The Economics of War and Revolution,* Center for Study of Public Choice, 1974; (with Richard B. McKenzie) *The New World of Economics: Explorations into the Human Experience,* Irwin, 1975; (with McKenzie) *Economics: A Way of Understanding Social Order,* McGraw, 1978. Contributor to professional journals. Editor, *Public Choice Journal,* 1968—.

WORK IN PROGRESS: Numerous economic applications.

SIDELIGHTS: A Practical Guide for the Ambitious Politician is a new printing of a book written in 1616 by Du Refuge. *Avocational interests:* Biology, military history.

TUOHY, John Francis   1925-
(Frank Tuohy)

PERSONAL: Born May 2, 1925, in Uckfield, England; son of Patrick Gerald and Dorothy (Annandale) Tuohy. *Education:* King's College, Cambridge, B.A. (first class honors), 1946. *Address:* c/o Lloyd's Bank Ltd., Uckfield, Sussex, England. *Agent:* A. D. Peters & Co. Ltd., 10 Buckingham St., London WC2N 6BU, England.

CAREER: University of Turku, Turku, Finland, lecturer, 1947-48; University of Sao Paulo, Sao Paulo, Brazil, professor of English language and literature, 1950-56; Jagiellonian University, Krakow, Poland, contract professor, 1958-60; Waseda University, Tokyo, Japan, visiting professor, 1964-67; Purdue University, Lafayette, Ind., writer-in-residence, 1970-71, 1976, and 1980. *Member:* P.E.N. Club, Royal Society of Literature (London; fellow), Society of Authors. *Awards, honors:* Katherine Mansfield Prize, 1960, and Society of Authors travelling scholarship, 1963, both for *The Admiral and the Nuns;* Geoffrey Faber Memorial Prize, 1963-64, and James Tait Black Memorial Prize, 1964, both for *The Ice Saints;* E. M. Forster Memorial Award, 1971; William Heinemann Award, 1979, for *Live Bait.*

WRITINGS—Under name Frank Tuohy: *The Animal Game* (novel), Scribner, 1957; *The Warm Nights of January* (novel), Macmillan (London), 1960; *The Admiral and the Nuns* (stories), Scribner, 1962; *The Ice Saints* (novel), Scribner, 1964; *Portugal,* Thames & Hudson, 1969, Viking, 1970; *Fingers in the Door* (stories), Scribner, 1970; (contributor) *Winter's Tales,* Macmillan, Number 17, 1971, Number 18, 1972, Number 20, 1974; *W. B. Yeats* (biography), Macmillan (New York), 1976; *Live Bait* (stories), Holt, 1979. Also author of television play "The Japanese Student," 1973. Contributor of stories to *Encounter.*

SIDELIGHTS: In a style that the *Observer*'s Paul Bailey terms "economical and telling," Frank Tuohy's work explores the ways in which social, sexual, and cultural distinctions serve to alienate human beings from one another. In a critique of *Live Bait* for the *New York Times Book Review,* Julia O'Faolain comments: "Hierarchical social systems—Japanese, Communist, British—interest [Tuohy], and he enjoys moving characters conditioned by one code into areas in which another prevails. Signals are then misread, susceptibilities offended, and in one case the result is a suicide. The codes, held against one another like transparencies, reveal not only their own limitations but those of the human condition." Kingsley Shorter of the *New Leader* offers similar remarks concerning *Fingers in the Door.* Shorter notes that Tuohy evokes "the deadly art of social classification" and adds: "Tuohy knows that class, like race or creed, is only one of the grosser and more visible ways we 'classify in order to deal with one another,' he recognizes that classification is a never-ending process pursued at every level of consciousness down to the very minutiae of existence. . . . In the mute agony of his characters, Tuohy reveals the *reducto ad absurdum* of the class system: The dreadful discovery that one is all alone, the solitary member of a class of one."

BIOGRAPHICAL/CRITICAL SOURCES: Observer, May 17, 1970; *New Leader,* October 5, 1970; *New York Times,* January 6, 1979; *Washington Post Book World,* February 11, 1979; *Los Angeles Times Book Review,* February 18, 1979; *New York Times Book Review,* February 25, 1979.

*   *   *

TURGEON, Charlotte Snyder   1912-
PERSONAL: Born June 21, 1912, in Marblehead, Mass.;

daughter of Frederick Sylvester and Anne T. (Wills) Snyder; married Frederick King Turgeon (a professor), November 28, 1934; children: Charles F., Thomas S., Charlotte Anne. *Education:* Smith College, B.A. *Politics:* Independent. *Religion:* Episcopalian. *Home:* Blake Field, Amherst, Mass. *Agent:* McIntosh & Otis, Inc., 475 Fifth Ave., New York, N.Y. 10017.

WRITINGS: (Editor and translator) *Tante Marie's French Kitchen,* Oxford University Press, 1942; *Cooking for Christmas,* Oxford University Press, 1950; (translator) H. P. Pellaprat, *Good Food from France,* Barrows, 1951; (editor) M. Hill and I. Radcliffe, *Food to Make You Famous,* Farrar, Straus, 1953; (translator) *Tante Marie's French Pastry,* Oxford University Press, 1954, published as *French Cakes and Pastries,* Kaye, 1954; *Time to Entertain,* Little, Brown, 1954, revised edition (with others) published as *Saturday Evening Post's Time to Entertain Cookbook,* Curtis Publishing, 1979.

(American editor) P. Montagne, *Larousse Gastronomique,* Crown, 1961, new edition published as *The New Larousse Gastronomique,* Crown, 1977; *Charlotte Turgeon's Summer Cookbook,* Crowell, 1961; (translator) *The Complete Tante Marie Cookery Book,* Kaye, 1961; *Cooking for Many on Holidays and Other Festive Occasions,* Crown, 1962; (with Donn Pierce) *The Master in the Kitchen,* Knopf, 1964; (editor and translator) Contesse de Toulouse-Lautrec, *La Cuisine de France* (in English), Orion, 1964 (published in England as *Good French Cooking,* Hamlyn, 1966); (editor and translator) Michel Oliver, *Cooking Is Child's Play,* preface by Jean Cocteau, Random House, 1965; (editor and translator) Michel Oliver, *Making French Desserts* [and] *Pastry Is Child's Play,* Random House, 1966; (co-editor and co-translator) *The Great Scandinavian Cook Book,* Crown, 1967; (translator) Christine Ripault, *Children's Gastronomique,* Crown, 1968.

(Contributor of recipes) Jeanine Larner, *Murder on the Menu,* Scribner, 1972; *Charlotte Turgeon's Creative Cooking Course,* Ottenheimer, 1975; (editor) *Holiday Magazine Award Cookbook,* Curtis Publishing, 1976; *Saturday Evening Post's All American Cookbook,* Curtis Publishing, 1977; (with others) *Saturday Evening Post's of Cabbages and Kings Cookbook,* Curtis Publishing, 1977; (with others) *Saturday Evening Post's Fiber and Bran Better Health Cookbook,* Curtis Publishing, 1977; *Saturday Evening Post's Small Batch Canning and Freezing Cookbook,* Curtis Publishing, 1978; (American editor) *Mitchell Beaseley's Cookbook,* Crown, 1980.

BIOGRAPHICAL/CRITICAL SOURCES: Life, October 22, 1961; *Christian Science Monitor,* December, 1961.

* * *

TURNBULL, Andrew Winchester 1921-1970

PERSONAL: Born February 2, 1921, in Baltimore, Md.; died by his own hand, January 10, 1970, in Cambridge, Mass.; son of Bayard (an architect) and Margaret Carroll (Jones) Turnbull; married Joanne Tudhope Johnson, December 18, 1954; children: Joanne, Frances. *Education:* Princeton University, B.A., 1942; Harvard University, M.A., 1947, Ph.D., 1954. *Religion:* Presbyterian. *Home:* 167 Brattle St., Cambridge, Mass. *Agent:* Harold Ober Associates, Inc., 40 East 49th St., New York, N.Y.

CAREER: Massachusetts Institute of Technology, Cambridge, instructor in humanities, 1954-58; free-lance writer, 1958-67; University of Bordeaux, Bordeaux, France, Fulbright lecturer in American literature, 1967-68; visiting professor, Brandeis University and Trinity College, Hartford, Conn., 1969, and Brown University, 1969-70. *Military service:* U.S. Naval Reserve, 1942-46; became lieutenant. *Awards, honors:* Guggenheim fellowship, 1964-65.

WRITINGS: Scott Fitzgerald, Scribner, 1962; (editor) *The Letters of F. Scott Fitzgerald,* Scribner, 1963; (editor) *Scott Fitzgerald: Letters to His Daughter,* Scribner, 1965; *Thomas Wolfe,* Scribner, 1967. Contributor to *New Yorker* and *Esquire.*

SIDELIGHTS: According to William Barrett, Andrew Winchester Turnbull's biography of F. Scott Fitzgerald "displaces every work before it." It is one that, noted Paul West, "intensifies the F. Scott image while noting how he transposes himself, which he did without pride or mercy." John Brooks predicted that the biography would be "the one that his warmest admirers will take most closely to their hearts."

Brooks continued: "Turnbull, putting his emphasis on Fitzgerald's personal, emotional life as reconstructed from interviews with hundreds of people, adds no new critical insights but presents a hero who lives on every page." A *Time* reviewer noted that in these interviews, Turnbull "apparently sought out every friend and enemy that Fitzgerald ever had," concluding that such "zealous reportage has produced a portrait that makes vividly comprehensible both Fitzgerald's failure as a man and his success as a writer."

David Littlejohn praised Turnbull's last book, *Thomas Wolfe.* He wrote: "Andrew Turnbull has brought Thomas Wolfe to life. By an ingenious use of others' memories and reminiscences, woven together with a discreet selection of the *honest* materials from Wolfe's own store, he has written a kind of objective 'novel.' . . . He allows us not only to see and hear Thomas Wolfe, talking, teaching, eating, walking, gesturing, sleeping; but even, gradually, to move inside him, to feel the inner pressures and compulsions, to share the activity of his creative mind at work." C. Hugh Holman agreed that Turnbull "has succeeded magnificently in giving us a comprehension of Wolfe's vitality, gusto, curiosity, egotism, and humanity through a record of representative days and hours in his lonely, tormented, and very messy life. . . . To have brought such a man persuasively before us in this relatively brief and graceful book is a major triumph of the biographer's art."

BIOGRAPHICAL/CRITICAL SOURCES: New York Herald Tribune Book Review, March 11, 1962; *New York Times Book Review,* March 11, 1962, February 11, 1968; *Time,* March 30, 1962; *Atlantic,* April, 1962; *Canadian Forum,* June, 1962; *New Republic,* February 24, 1968; *National Observer,* February 26, 1968; *Virginia Quarterly Review,* spring, 1968; *Harper's,* March, 1968, April, 1968; *Saturday Night,* May, 1968; *New York Review,* May 6, 1968; *Reporter,* May 30, 1968; *Carleton Miscellany,* summer, 1968; *Times Literary Supplement,* September 12, 1968.†

* * *

TURNBULL, Colin M(acmillan) 1924-

PERSONAL: Born November 23, 1924, in Harrow, England; naturalized U.S. citizen; son of John R(utherford) and Dorothy (Chapman) Turnbull. *Education:* Magdalen College, Oxford, B.A. (honors), 1947, M.A., 1949; University of London, attended School of Oriental and African Studies, 1948-49, diploma in education, 1949; attended Banaras Hindu University, 1949-51; Oxford University, diploma in social anthropology, 1956, B.Litt., 1957, D.Phil., 1964. *Residence:* Lancaster, Va. 22503. *Office:* Department of Anthropology, George Washington University, Washington, D.C. 20052.

CAREER: Anthropological field research in Ituri Forest, Congo, 1951, 1954-55, 1957-59; American Museum of Natural History, New York, N.Y., assistant curator, 1959-65, associate curator, 1965-69; Hofstra University, Hempstead, N.Y., professor of anthropology, 1969-73; Virginia Commonwealth University, Richmond, professor of anthropology, 1973-75; George Washington University, Washington, D.C., visiting professor, 1976—. Adjunct associate professor at Hunter College of the City University of New York, 1966-67, New York University, 1967-69, and Vassar College, 1968-69. Former consultant to U.S. State Department, American University, and Agency for International Development. Editor, Wenner-Gren Foundation, 1968-73. *Military service:* Royal Navy Volunteer Reserve, 1942-45; became lieutenant. *Member:* Royal Anthropological Institute of London (fellow), International African Institute, Musee Royal de l'Afrique Centrale (Tervuren, Belgium; corresponding member). *Awards, honors:* Voss Fund research grant from American Museum of Natural History for research in northern Uganda, 1964-66; Wenner-Gren Foundation grant for field research in Central African Republic, 1967; National Science Foundation grant for field research in Republic of Zaire, 1970-72; National Academy of Arts and Letters Award, 1975.

WRITINGS: The Forest People, Simon & Schuster, 1961; *The Lonely African,* Simon & Schuster, 1962; *The Peoples of Africa,* World Publishing, 1962; *The Mbuti Pygmies: An Ethnographic Survey,* American Museum of Natural History, 1965; *Wayward Servants: The Two Worlds of the African Pygmies,* Natural History Press, 1965; (contributor) James Gibbs, editor, *Peoples of Africa,* Holt, 1965; *Tradition and Change in African Tribal Life,* World Publishing, 1966; (with Thubten Jigme Norbu) *Tibet,* Simon & Schuster, 1968; (photographic illustrator) Elizabeth Shepherd, *In a Pygmy Camp,* Lothrop, 1969.

The Mountain People, Simon & Schuster, 1972; (compiler) *Africa and Change,* Knopf, 1973; *Man in Africa,* Anchor Press, 1976. Also co-author with Peter Brook of play, "Les Iks." Contributor of articles to *Man, Natural History,* and *Journal of the Royal Anthropological Institute.*

WORK IN PROGRESS: The Quest; Stress and Society; Anthropologist Self.

SIDELIGHTS: Colin M. Turnbull writes that he is "interested as an anthropologist in the ways different people live and think; and, as an individual, interested in the apparent deterioration in human relationships, interpersonal and intergroup." Turnbull's writing, the result of his field research in Africa, reflects this interest in different people. David Hopgood recommends *Tradition and Change in African Tribal Life* because it contains "more wisdom about the way most people live in Africa ... than any other book I know.... [Turnbull] refuses to let the reader follow the all-too-natural inclination to measure Africa by how it differs from our own society.... With Turnbull as guide, you can live for a few hours in the African tribal community. If you do, you may come away with a new outlook on the differing ways men meet their problems and a more modest view of our position in the world."

Two other books, *The Forest People* and *The Mountain People,* reflect Turnbull's thoughts on two vastly different groups of people. *The Forest People* is about the years he spent with the Pygmies of the Congo. According to Horace Judson, Turnbull found the Pygmies "'infinitely wise' and 'without evil,' [a people] who confirmed ... 'how the qualities of truth, goodness and beauty can be found wherever we

care to look for them.'" *The Mountain People* tells of Turnbull's time with the Ik of northern Uganda. A generation ago, the Ik were valley hunters, but the creation of a game reserve forced them into the mountains and farming. Afflicted by lack of technical knowledge, drought, isolation, and finally starvation, the Ik give precedence to those of childbearing age, ignoring the needs of the very young and the very old. According to Turnbull, well-fed parents would gorge themselves until they vomited rather than share food with their own infants. Unfortunately, Turnbull, as Judson describes, "in an enormous magnification, projects his ghostly pictures of Ik guilt onto the future of Western technological society.... The Ik in their desolation are no longer a tribal society, as Turnbull must know: they lack the social structure to bear the weight of the thesis he tries to lay upon them." Although agreeing on Turnbull's over-magnification, Christopher Lehmann-Haupt is impressed with the book, calling it an "agonized, despairing account.... One may resist the apocalyptic tones of his conclusions; one may seek comfort in the fact that the Ik represent an isolated case ...; one may even accuse Turnbull of being as subjective in the lessons he draws as he was in his initial dislike of the Ik. But even stripped of its implications, the story is shocking and depressing.... And Turnbull has described it with hideous power."

BIOGRAPHICAL/CRITICAL SOURCES: Book Week, April 9, 1967; *Books,* October, 1967; *Saturday Review,* January 25, 1969; *New York Times,* February 6, 1969, October 30, 1972; *Book World,* February 16, 1969; *Time,* November 20, 1972; *Milwaukee Journal,* May 6, 1973; *Authors in the News,* Volume I, Gale, 1976.

*   *   *

TURNER, John Elliot 1917-

PERSONAL: Born September 25, 1917, in Amble, England; son of George Murray (a clergyman) and Helen (Elliot) Turner; married Elsie Reinschmidt, July 7, 1944; children: Debra Marlene, Noel Sean. *Education:* Yankton College, B.A., 1939; University of Minnesota, M.A., 1949, Ph.D., 1950. *Home:* 1576 Vincent St., St. Paul, Minn. 55108. *Office:* 1425 B Social Science Tower (WB), University of Minnesota, Minneapolis, Minn. 55455.

CAREER: University of Minnesota, Minneapolis, instructor, 1947-49, 1950-52, assistant professor, 1952-57, associate professor, 1957-59, professor of political science, 1959-74, regents' professor, 1974—. Member of review panel on research projects, National Endowment for the Humanities, 1969-74, and U.S. Office of Education, 1973. Member of board of trustees, Yankton College, 1971-74. Consultant to numerous colleges and universities. *Military service:* U.S. Army, 1942-46. *Member:* International Studies Association (executive director, 1970-73; member of governing council, 1973-74; chairperson, Resources Committee, 1973-74), American Political Science Association (member of editorial board, 1965-70; member of council, 1974-76; chairperson of Elections Committee, 1975, 1976), Midwest Political Science Association. *Awards, honors:* Hill Family travel grant to U.S.S.R., 1958; Fulbright research scholar, 1961-62; LL.D. from Yankton College, 1967; Northwest Area Foundation traveling fellowship, summers, 1968, 1976, and 1978.

WRITINGS: (With Harold S. Quigley) *The New Japan,* University of Minnesota Press, 1956; (with Herbert McCloskey) *The Soviet Dictatorship,* McGraw, 1960; (editor with Robert T. Holt) *The Soviet Union: Paradox and Change,* Holt, 1962; (contributor) *Cases in Comparative*

Politics, edited by J. B. Christoph, Little, Brown, 1965; (with Holt) *The Political Basis of Economic Development,* Van Nostrand, 1966; (with Holt) *Political Parties in Action: The Battle of Baron's Court,* Free Press, 1967; (with Holt) *Methodology of Comparative Research,* Free Press, 1970; *Labour's Doorstep Politics in London,* Macmillan, 1978; (with Harold W. Chase) *American Government in Comparative Perspective,* F. Watts, 1980. Co-editor, *Comparative Studies in Behavioral Science,* Wiley, 1969-76; member of editorial board, "Professional Papers in International Studies" series, Sage Publications, 1971-78. Contributing editor, *Minneapolis Star,* 1978—. Contributor of articles and reviews to professional journals. Member of editorial board, *Georgia Political Science Journal,* 1973—.

* * *

TURNER, John Frayn 1923-

PERSONAL: Born August 9, 1923, in Portsmouth, England; son of George Francis and Daisy Louise (Frayn) Turner; married Joyce Isabelle Howson, August 9, 1945; children: Francesca Lynn. *Education:* Educated in English schools. *Home:* 9 Southbury, Lawn Rd., Guildford, Surrey, England. *Agent:* London Authors, 8 Upper Brook St., London W.1, England. *Office:* Central Office of Information, Hercules Rd., London S.E.1, England.

CAREER: Ideal Home, London, England, feature writer, 1951-55; *House Beautiful,* London, editor, 1956-57; *News Chronicle,* London, columnist, 1958-59; *Weekend Magazine,* London, feature writer, 1962-63; Royal Air Force, Publicity Branch, London, editor, 1963-73; Central Office of Information, London, senior editor, 1973—. *Military service:* Royal Navy.

WRITINGS: Service Most Silent: The Navy's Fight against Enemy Mines, Harrap, 1955; *V.C.s of the Royal Navy,* Harrap, 1956; *Prisoner at Large,* Staples Press, 1957; *Periscope Patrol: The Saga of Malta Submarines,* Harrap, 1957; *Hovering Angels: The Record of the Royal Navy's Helicopters,* Harrap, 1957; *Invasion '44: The Full Story of D-Day in Normandy,* Putnam, 1959; *Battle Stations: The U.S. Navy's War,* Putnam, 1960; *V.C.s of the Air,* Harrap, 1960; *Highly Explosive: The Exploits of Major "Bill" Hartley, M.B.E., G.M. of Bomb Disposal,* Harrap, 1961; *The Blinding Flash: The Remarkable Story of Ken Revis and His Struggle to Overcome Blindness,* Harrap, 1962; *V.C.s of the Army, 1939-1951,* Harrap, 1962; *A Girl Called Johnnie: Three Weeks in an Open Boat,* Harrap, 1963; *Famous Air Battles,* Arthur Barker, 1963; *Destination Berchtesgaden: The U.S. Seventh Army Story,* Ian Allan, 1975; *British Aircraft of World War II,* Sidgwick & Jackson, 1975; *Famous Flights,* Arthur Barker, 1978. Also author of *World War II: An American Epic* and *American Aircraft of World War II.* Contributor of special research for Douglas Bader's *Fight for the Sky,* Sidgwick & Jackson, 1973. Contributor to newspapers and magazines.

* * *

TURNER, Victor Witter 1920-

PERSONAL: Born May 28, 1920, in Glasgow, Scotland; son of Norman (an engineer) and Violet (Witter) Turner; married Edith Lucy Brocklesby Davis, January 30, 1943; children: Frederick, Robert, Irene Helen, Alexander Lewis Charles, Rory Peter Benedict. *Education:* University College, London, B.A. (honors), 1949; Victoria University of Manchester, Ph.D., 1955. *Religion:* Roman Catholic. *Home:* 107 Carrsbrook Dr., Charlottesville, Va. *Office:* Department of Anthropology, 303 Brooks Hall, University of Virginia, Charlottesville, Va.

CAREER: Rhodes-Livingstone Institute, Lusaka, Northern Rhodesia, research officer, 1950-54; Victoria University of Manchester, Manchester, England 1954-63, began as lecturer, became senior lecturer; Cornell University, Ithaca, N.Y., professor of anthropology, 1963-68, chairman of Committee on African Studies, 1964-68; University of Chicago, Chicago, Ill., professor of anthropology and social thought, 1968-77; University of Virginia, Charlottesville, William R. Kenan Professor of Anthropology, 1977—, member of Center for Advanced Studies, 1977-80. Simon Research Fellow, University of Manchester, 1956-58; fellow, Center for Advanced Study in the Behavioral Sciences, Stanford, Calif., 1961-62; Princeton University, chairman of advisory council to Department of Anthropology, 1975-77, member of council, 1977. *Military service:* British Army, 1941-46. *Member:* Association of Social Anthropologists of Great Britain and Commonwealth, Royal Anthropological Institute, International African Institute, African Studies Association of United Kingdom, American Anthropological Association, Rhodes-Livingstone Institute.

WRITINGS: Schism and Continuity in an African Society, Manchester University Press, 1957; *Ndembu Divination: Its Symbolism and Techniques,* Manchester University Press, 1961; *Chihamba the White Spirit,* Manchester University Press, 1962; (with D. Forde, M. Fortes, and M. Gluckman) *Essays in the Ritual of Social Relations,* Manchester University Press, 1963; *Lunda Medicines and the Treatment of Disease,* Rhodes-Livingstone Museum, 1964; *The Drums of Affliction,* Oxford University Press, 1965; *The Forest of Symbols: Essays on African Religion,* Cornell University Press, 1966; (editor with M. Swartz and A. Tuden) *Political Anthropology,* Aldine, 1966; *Ritual Process,* Aldine, 1969.

(Editor) *Profiles of Change: African Society and Colonial Rule,* Cambridge University Press, 1970; *Dramas, Fields, and Metaphors,* Cornell University Press, 1974; *Revelation and Divination in Ndembu Ritual,* Cornell University Press, 1975; (with Edith Turner) *Image and Pilgrimage in Christian Culture: Anthropological Perspectives,* Columbia University Press, 1978; *Process, Performance, and Pilgrimage,* Concept Publishing, 1979. General editor, "Symbol, Myth, and Ritual" series, Cornell University Press. Contributor to *Times Literary Supplement, Africa, Man, Wiseman Review,* and other publications.

* * *

TURNER, William O(liver) 1914-

PERSONAL: Born September 19, 1914, in Tacoma, Wash.; son of William Paddock and Ava (Oliver) Turner. *Education:* Knox College, B.A., 1936. *Religion:* Presbyterian. *Residence:* Tacoma, Wash. *Agent:* Harold Matson Co., Inc., 22 East 40th St., New York, N.Y. 10017.

CAREER: North Shore Publishing Co., Evanston, Ill., reporter, 1937-40; Stamats Publishing Co., Cedar Rapids, Iowa, editor, 1950-55; free lance fiction writer. *Military service:* U.S. Army, 1942-46. *Member:* Western Writers of America (president, 1963-64), Phi Delta Theta.

WRITINGS: The Proud Diggers, Houghton, 1954; *The Settler,* Houghton, 1956; *War Country,* Houghton, 1957; *The Long Rope,* Doubleday, 1959; *The Treasure of Fan Fan Flat,* Doubleday, 1961; *Throttle the Hawk,* Ward, Lock, 1961, Berkley Publishing, 1966; *The High-Hander,* Ace Books, 1963 (published in England as *Troublebuster,* Ward, Lock, 1963); *Gunpoint,* Berkley Publishing, 1964 (published in England as *The Snare,* Ward, Lock, 1964); *Destination Doubtful,* Ballantine, 1965; *Five Days to Salt Lake,* Ballantine, 1966; *Blood Dance,* Berkley Publishing, 1967; *Thief Hunt,* Doubleday, 1968; *Mayberly's Kill,* Doubleday, 1969; *A Man Called Jeff,* Berkley Publishing, 1969; *Place of the Trap,* Doubleday, 1970; *Call the Beast Thy Brother,* Doubleday, 1973; *Medicine Creek,* Doubleday, 1975; *Shortcut to Devil's Claw,* Berkley Publishing, 1977; *The Man in the Yellow Mercedes,* Berkley Publishing, 1979.

WORK IN PROGRESS: Kill Call.

SIDELIGHTS: Many of William O. Turner's books have been translated into German, Norwegian, Danish, Italian, and Spanish. *Mayberly's Kill* was made into a motion picture starring Robert Redford.

BIOGRAPHICAL/CRITICAL SOURCES: Seattle Post-Intelligencer, March 10, 1974; *Authors in the News,* Volume I, Gale, 1976.

U

ULLMAN, James Ramsey 1907-1971

PERSONAL: Born November 24, 1907, in New York, N.Y.; died June 20, 1971, in Boston, Mass.; son of Alexander F. and Eunice (Ramsey) Ullman; married Ruth Fishman, June 27, 1930 (divorced, 1945); married Elaine Luria, January 25, 1946; married Marian Blinn, March 18, 1961; children: (first marriage) James R., Jr., William A. *Education:* Princeton University, B.A., 1929. *Home:* 168 Marlborough St., Boston, Mass. 02116. *Agent:* Harold Matson Co., 22 East 40th St., New York, N.Y. 10016.

CAREER: Newspaper reporter and feature writer, 1929-32; theatrical producer in New York, N.Y., 1933-37; executive of Works Progress Administration Federal Theater Project in New York and California, 1938-39; full-time writer, 1939-71. As a theatrical producer, worked with twelve Broadway plays, including co-production of Sidney Kingsley's Pulitzer Prize winning "Men in White," 1934. *Wartime service:* American Field Service, Volunteer Ambulance Corps, 1942-43; attached to British 8th Army in Africa; became lieutenant; received African Star. *Member:* Authors Guild, Authors League of America, P.E.N., Overseas Press Club, American Alpine Club, Explorers Club, Princeton Club of New York, St. Botolph Club (Boston). *Awards, honors:* The manuscripts and personal papers of James Ramsey Ullman have been collected by the Princeton University Library.

WRITINGS: Mad Shelley, Princeton University Press, 1930, reprinted, Gordian, 1975; *The Other Side of the Mountain,* Carrick, 1938; *High Conquest,* Lippincott, 1941; *The White Tower,* Lippincott, 1945, reprinted, Collins, 1973; (editor) *Kingdom of Adventure: Everest,* Sloane, 1947; *River of the Sun,* Lippincott, 1950, reprinted, White Lion Publishers, 1974; *Windom's Way,* Lippincott, 1952; *Island of the Blue Macaws,* Lippincott, 1953; *The Sands of Karakorum,* Lippincott, 1953, reprinted, White Lion Publishers, 1976; *Banner in the Sky: The Story of a Boy and a Mountain,* Lippincott, 1954, reprinted, Archway, 1980; *The Age of Mountaineering,* Lippincott, 1954, revised edition, 1964; (with Tenzing Norgay) *Tiger of the Snows,* Putnam, 1955 (published in England as *Tenzing: Man of Everest,* Harrap, 1955, revised edition published as *Man of Everest: The Autobiography of Tenzing as Told to James Ramsey Ullman,* Severn House, 1975); *The Day on Fire: A Novel Suggested by the Life of Arthur Rimbaud,* World Publishing, 1958, reprinted, Avon, 1978; *Down the Colorado with Major Powell,* Houghton, 1960; *Fia Fia,* World Publishing, 1962 (published

in England as *Island below the World,* Collins, 1962, reprinted, White Lion Publishers, 1975); *Where the Bong Tree Grows: The Log of One Man's Journey in the South Pacific,* World Publishing, 1963; (with others) *Americans on Everest: The Official Account of the Ascent Led by Norman Dyherenfurth,* Lippincott, 1964; *Straight Up: The Life and Death of John Harlin,* Doubleday, 1968; (with Al Dinhofer) *Caribbean Here and Now: The Complete Vacation Guide to Fifty-two Sunny Islands in the Caribbean Sea,* Macmillan, 1968, 3rd edition, 1970; *And Not to Yield,* Doubleday, 1970. Contributor of fiction and nonfiction to national periodicals, including *Holiday, Saturday Evening Post, Life, Sports Illustrated, Horizon,* and *Saturday Review.*

SIDELIGHTS: A world traveler, adventurer, and mountaineer, James Ramsey Ullman climbed many of the world's most challenging mountains, including Mt. Olympus, Ixtacihuatl (the Mexican volcano), the Jungfrau, the Matterhorn, the foothills of the Andes (which reach sixteen and seventeen thousand feet in height), as well as many peaks of the Tetons and Rockies. In 1963 he fulfilled a lifelong ambition by participating in the first American expedition to climb Mt. Everest. Ullman took part in the 1965 Montgomery, Alabama civil rights freedom march.

Many of his books have been published in England and many have appeared in foreign translation. *High ·Conquest, The White Tower, River of the Sun, Windom's Way,* and *Banner in the Sky* have been sold to motion picture companies.†

*   *   *

ULLMAN, Richard Henry 1933-

PERSONAL: Born December 12, 1933, in Baltimore, Md.; son of Jerome E. and Frances (Oppenheimer) Ullman; married Margaret Yoma Crosfield, 1959 (divorced, 1975); married Susan Sorrell, 1977; children: (first marriage) Claire, Jennifer. *Education:* Harvard University, A.B., 1955; Oxford University, B.Phil, 1957, D.Phil., 1960. *Office:* Woodrow Wilson School of Public and International Affairs, Princeton University, Princeton, N.J. 08544.

CAREER: Harvard University, Cambridge, Mass., instructor, 1960-63, assistant professor of government, 1963-65; Princeton University, Woodrow Wilson School of Public and International Affairs, Princeton, N.J., associate professor, 1965-69, professor of politics and international affairs, 1969-77, professor of international affairs, 1977—. Member of staff of National Security Council, Executive Office of the President, 1967, and policy planning staff, Office of the Secretary of Defense, 1967-68; Council on Foreign Relations, director of studies, 1973-76, director of 1980's project, 1974-77. *Awards, honors:* Rhodes scholarship, Oxford University, 1955-58; George Louis Beer Prize, American Historical Association, 1969, for *Britain and the Russian Civil War.*

WRITINGS: *Anglo-Soviet Relations, 1917-1921,* Princeton University Press, Volume I: *Intervention and the War,* 1961, Volume II: *Britain and the Russian Civil War,* 1968, Volume III: *The Anglo-Soviet Accord,* 1973; (co-editor) *Theory and Policy in International Relations,* Princeton University Press, 1972. Author of numerous articles. Member of editorial board, *New York Times,* 1977-78; editor, *Foreign Policy,* 1978-80.

WORK IN PROGRESS: A book-length essay on international security, for the 1980's project of the Council on Foreign Relations.

* * *

UNDERHILL, Ruth Murray 1884-

PERSONAL: Born August 22, 1884, in Ossining, N.Y.; daughter of Abram (a lawyer) and Anna Taber (Murray) Underhill. *Education:* Vassar College, A.B., 1905; attended London School of Economics, and University of Munich, 1908; Columbia University, Ph.D., 1937. *Politics:* Democrat. *Religion:* Quaker. *Home and office:* 2623 South Clayton St., Denver, Colo. 80210.

CAREER: Social worker in New York City with Charity Organization Society, American Red Cross, and other agencies, 1909-30; Columbia University, New York City, research fellow and assistant in anthropology, 1930-35; U.S. Bureau of Indian Affairs, Washington, D.C., and in field, consultant in anthropology, 1936-47; University of Denver, Denver, Colo., professor of anthropology, 1947-52, professor emeritus, 1952—. Teacher of anthropology at State Teachers College (now State University of New York College at New Platz), 1955-56, and Colorado Woman's College (now Temple Buell College); frequent lecturer at University of Denver and Iliff Theological Seminary, Denver. Lecturer on Indians for series of thirty educational television programs; interviewer of Indians for radio series. Member of board of directors, International House, Denver, 1958—.

MEMBER: American Anthropological Society, American Association for the Advancement of Science, American Folklore Society, American Ethnological Society (president, 1961), Colorado-Wyoming Academy of Sciences, Colorado Authors League (member of board of directors), Colorado Folklore Society (past president), Denver Womens Press Club, Phi Beta Kappa, Kappa Gamma Delta. *Awards, honors:* LL.D., University of Denver, 1962; Nancy Bloch Intercultural Award, Library of Downtown Community School, 1962; received citation for public service, Colorado Woman's College (now Temple Buell College), 1963; D.Sc., University of Colorado, 1965; Top Hand Awards, Colorado Authors League.

WRITINGS: *The Autobiography of a Papago Woman,* American Anthropological Association, 1936, revised edition published as *Papago Woman,* Holt, 1979; (translator) *Singing for Power: The Song Magic of the Papago Indians of Southern Arizona,* University of California Press, 1938, reprinted, 1976; *First Penthouse Dwellers of America,* J. J. Augustin, 1938, reprinted, Gannon, 1976; *Indians of Southern California,* Haskell Institute, 1938, reprinted, AMS Press, 1980; *Social Organization of Papago Indians,* Colum-

bia University Press, 1939, reprinted, AMS Press, 1969; *Hawk Over Whirlpools* (novel), J. J. Augustin, 1940; *The Papago Indians and Their Relatives, the Pima,* U.S. Indian Service, 1940, reprinted, AMS Press, 1977; *Pueblo Crafts,* Haskell Institute, 1944, reprinted, AMS Press, 1977; *The Northern Paiute Indian,* Haskell Institute, 1945, reprinted, AMS Press, 1980; *Workaday Life in the Pueblos,* Haskell Institute, 1945; *Papago Indian Religion,* Columbia University Press, 1946, reprinted, AMS Press, 1969; *Red Man's America,* University of Chicago Press, 1953, revised edition, 1971; *The Navajos,* University of Oklahoma Press, 1956, reprinted, University of Oklahoma Press, 1971; *First Came the Family,* Morrow, 1958; *Beaverbird,* Coward, 1959; *Antelope Singer,* Coward, 1961; *Red Man's Religion,* University of Chicago Press, 1965; *So Many Kinds of Navajos,* [Gallup, New Mexico], 1971; (contributor) *Papago Indians I,* Garland Publishing, 1974. Author of a series of pamphlets on Indians, for Doubleday; contributor of articles to professional journals.

SIDELIGHTS: Ruth Murray Underhill told *CA:* "After graduation from college, I spent some years in travel, social work and desultory writing. . . . [I] took up anthropology for further understanding of human problems and found the Papago Indians of Arizona, whom I was sent to visit, a most interesting and poetic people. My research thus became centered on Indians, and I joined the Indian Service."

Underhill speaks five languages, including Papago. She has enjoyed mountain climbing and travel, including a world tour from 1952 to 1953.

* * *

UNGER, Maurice Albert 1917-
(Al Munger)

PERSONAL: Born June 18, 1917, in Brooklyn, N.Y.; son of Harry and Augusta (Hoormann) Unger; married Ruth Mann, 1945 (divorced, 1965); children: H. Stephen, Douglas, John. *Education:* Duke University, A.B., 1940, LL.B., 1946, J.D., 1970; Harvard University, graduate study in business administration, 1941. *Home:* 1810 Alpine, Boulder, Colo. 80302.

CAREER: Private practice of law, Patchogue, N.Y., 1946-50; National Technological Institute, New York, N.Y., instructor in real estate, 1950-51; University of Idaho, Moscow, assistant professor of real estate, 1951-56; University of Massachusetts, Amherst, associate professor of finance, 1956-57; University of Florida, Gainesville, associate professor of real estate, 1957-62; University of Colorado, Boulder, 1962-80, became professor of real estate. *Military service:* U.S. Navy, 1941-45; became lieutenant. *Member:* American Society of Appraisers, American Finance Association, American Arbitration Association (panel member), New York Bar Association, Rocky Mountain Charolais Association, Rocky Mountain Business Law Association.

WRITINGS: *Questions and Answers for the Real Estate Broker's and Salesmen's Examinations,* Oceana, 1951, 3rd edition, revised by Oceana editorial staff, 1966; *Real Estate: Principles and Practices,* South-Western, 1954, 6th edition, 1979; *The Green Fuse* (novel), Pageant, 1954; (with Harold A. Wolf) *Personal Finance,* Allyn & Bacon, 1964, 3rd edition, 1972; *Elements of Business Law,* Prentice-Hall, 1968; *How to Invest in Real Estate,* McGraw, 1975; *Financial Planning for Retirement,* South-Western, 1978; (with Roland Molicher) *Real Estate Finance,* South-Western, 1978. Contributor of articles to popular magazines and to professional periodicals.

WORK IN PROGRESS: Elements of Real Estate Appraisal; The Last Resort.

* * *

UNTERMEYER, Bryna Ivens 1909-

PERSONAL: Born April 27, 1909, in New York, N.Y.; daughter of Benjamin F. (a lawyer) and Millie (Drescher) Isaacs; married Louis Untermeyer (author and editor), July 23, 1948 (died December 19, 1977); married Emanuel E. Raices, June 9, 1979. *Education:* Hunter College (now Hunter College of the City University of New York), B.A., 1930. *Home and office:* Great Hill Rd., Newtown, Conn. 06470. *Agent:* McIntosh & Otis, Inc., 475 Fifth Ave., New York, N.Y. 10017.

CAREER: Old Mr. Boston Liquors, New York City, house organ editor, 1941; *She,* New York City, editor, 1942-46; *Seventeen,* New York City, fiction editor, 1946-57; freelance writer and editor, 1957—.

WRITINGS: (Editor) *The Seventeen Reader,* Lippincott, 1951; (editor) *Nineteen from Seventeen,* Lippincott, 1952; (editor) *Stories from Seventeen,* Lippincott, 1955; (editor with husband, Louis Untermeyer) *Grimm's Fairy Tales,* Limited Editions Club, 1962; *Memoir for Mrs. Sullavan,* Simon & Schuster, 1966; (editor) *Sorry, Dear,* Golden Press, 1968; (editor with L. Untermeyer) *A Galaxy of Verse,* M. Evans, 1978.

Editor with L. Untermeyer of books in "Golden Treasury of Children's Literature" series; published by Golden Press, including: *Big and Little Creatures,* 1961; *Beloved Tales,* 1962; *Fun and Fancy,* 1962; *Old Friends and Lasting Favorites,* 1962; *Wonderlands,* 1962; *Unfamiliar Marvels,* 1963; *Creatures Wild and Tame,* 1963; *Adventurers All,* 1963; *Legendary Animals,* 1963; *Tall Tales,* 1963; *The Golden Treasury of Children's Literature,* 1966 (published in England as *The Children's Treasury of Literature in Colour,* Hamlyn, 1966).

WORK IN PROGRESS: Cats as Cats Can; a novel, *Comedy of Eros.*

SIDELIGHTS: Bryna Untermeyer told *CA:* "Although my ambition to work in some editorial or writing capacity goes as far back as grammar school days, the break into publishing was the result of the Second World War. Women finally were getting a chance at men's jobs: I became editor of a large liquor company's external house organ. From there, it was an easy transition to *She* and then *Seventeen.* When I left *Seventeen,* I began the exciting, active editorial collaboration with my late husband, Louis Untermeyer.

AVOCATIONAL INTERESTS: Raising orchids, cats, and dogs, travel.

* * *

USHERWOOD, Stephen Dean 1907-

PERSONAL: Born September 14, 1907, in London, England; son of John Frederick (a school headmaster) and Grace Ellen (a college headmistress; maiden name, Crush) Usherwood; married Hazel Doreen Weston (teacher of crafts and author of children's books), July 27, 1935 (died, 1968); married Elizabeth Ada Beavington (a bank official), October 24, 1970; children: (first marriage) Susan Clare, Nicholas John. *Education:* Oriel College, Oxford, M.A. (with honors in classics), 1928, M.A. in modern history, 1930, diploma in education, 1931. *Politics:* Conservative. *Religion:* Roman Catholic. *Home and office:* 24 St. Mary's Grove, London N1 2NT, England.

CAREER: Teacher of history and religion at various schools, Hampshire and Surrey, England, 1931-41; British Broadcasting Corporation, London, England, foreign news reporter, 1946-55, liaison officer with U.S. Intelligence units in United States, Japan, and Okinawa, 1951-52, producer, school broadcasting department, 1955-68. Lecturer and broadcaster on history, religion, and travel. Producer of Festival of Britain Pageant, Basingstoke, Hampshire, England, 1951. *Military service:* Royal Air Force, Air Sea Rescue Service, 1941-42; became flight lieutenant; staff intelligence duties attached to Foreign Office, 1943-46. *Member:* Oxford Union, Oriel Society.

WRITINGS: Reign by Reign, Norton, 1960; *The Bible: Book by Book,* Norton, 1962; *Shakespeare: Play by Play,* Hill & Wang, 1968; *History from Familiar Things,* five volumes, Ginn, 1968-72; *Britain: Century by Century,* David & Charles, 1972; *Food, Drink and History,* David & Charles, 1972; *Europe: Century by Century,* David & Charles, 1972; *The Great Enterprise,* Folio Society, 1979. Contributor of articles on Soviet radio propaganda to *World Today,* on lacrosse to *Country Life* and *Oxford Junior Encyclopedia,* on history to *History Today, International History, Port of London Authority,* and others. Writer of radio scripts on history, art, religion, and sports, and of historical teaching notes accompanying forty-two educational filmstrips, issued by the Rank Organisation Film Library.

V

VALBUENA-BRIONES, Angel (Julian) 1928-

PERSONAL: Born January 11, 1928, in Madrid, Spain; naturalized U.S. citizen in 1963; son of Angel and Francisca (Briones) Valbuena-Prat; married Barbara Northrup Hobart, November 9, 1957; children: Teresa, Vivian. *Education:* University of Murcia, Licenciado (summa cum laude), 1949; University of Madrid, Ph.D. (cum laude), 1952. *Home:* 203 Nottingham Rd., Newark, Del. 19711. *Office:* Department of Languages, Smith Hall, University of Delaware, Newark, Del. 19711.

CAREER: Murcia University, Murcia, Spain, Professor Ayudante, 1949-51; Oxford University, Oxford, England, lecturer in Spanish, 1953-55; Madrid University, Madrid, Spain, Professor Ayudante, 1955-56; Yale University, New Haven, Conn., assistant professor of Spanish, 1958-60; University of Delaware, Newark, Elias Ahuja Professor of Spanish Literature, 1960—. Visiting lecturer, University of Wisconsin, 1956-58; conducted lecture tour of South America, summer, 1957; visiting professor, New York University, summers, 1960 and 1961, and University of Madrid, 1965, 1970-71, and summer, 1977. *Member:* International Association of Hispanists, International Federation for Modern Languages, American Association of Teachers of Spanish and Portuguese, Modern Language Association of America, Renaissance Society of America, Hispanic Society of America, Sigma Delta Pi (honorary member; vice-president of Northeast section and Delaware State director, 1971-73), Delaware Art Museum, Greenville Country Club. *Awards, honors:* Instituto de Cultura Hispanica fellow, 1951-52; University of Wisconsin Alumnae research grant, 1957; Consejo Superior de Investigaciones Cientificas research grants, 1951 and 1970-71.

WRITINGS: Nueva poesia de Puerto Rico, Instituto de Cultura Hispanica, 1952; (editor and author of notes) Pedro Calderon de la Barca, *Las Comedias de capa y espada de Calderon: La Dama duenda* (also see below) [and] *No hay casa como callar,* Clasicos Castellanos, 1954, reprinted, Espase-Calpe, 1973; (editor) Calderon de la Barca, *Dramas de honor de Calderon,* two volumes, Clasicos Castellanos, 1956, 2nd edition, 1965; (editor) Calderon de la Barca, *Obras completas de Calderon,* Aguilar, Volume II: *Comedias,* 1956, Volume I: *Dramas,* 1959, 2nd edition, 1966; *Literature Hispanoamericana,* G. Gili, 1962, 4th edition, 1969; *Perspectiva critica de los dramas de Calderon,* Rialp, 1965; *Ideas y Palabras,* Eliseo Torres, 1968; (editor and author of

introduction and notes) Calderon de la Barca, *El Garrote mas bien dado o el alcalde de Zalamea de Calderon,* Anaya, 1971; (editor) Calderon de la Barca, *Primera parte de comedias. de don Pedro Calderon de la Barca,* Volume I, Consejo Superior de Investigaciones Cientificas, 1974; (editor) Calderon de la Barca, *La Dama duende,* Ediciones Catedra, 1976. Also editor of *Ensayo sobre la obra de Calderon,* 1954, and *Calderon y la comedia nueva,* 1977. Contributor to professional journals, including *Arbor, Thesaurus, Cuadernos Americanso,* and *Norte.* Member of editorial board, *Arbor,* 1970.†

* * *

VALENS, E(vans) G., Jr. 1920-

PERSONAL: Born April 17, 1920, in State College, Pa.; son of Evans G. (in sales) and Mabel (Grazier) Valens; married Winifred A. Crary, October, 1941 (divorced, 1975); children: Tom, Marc John, Dan Malcolm, Jo Anne. *Education:* Amherst College, B.A., 1941. *Residence:* Mill Valley, Calif. 94941. *Agent:* Curtis Brown Ltd., 575 Madison Ave., New York, N.Y. 10022.

CAREER: El Paso Herald-Post, El Paso, Tex., reporter, 1942-43; United Press Association, correspondent in San Francisco, Calif., Salt Lake City, Utah, Helena, Mont., Honolulu, Hawaii, New York City, Guam, Okinawa, and Germany, 1943-48; Station KQED (educational television), San Francisco, producer, writer, and director, 1954-61, 1970-71; currently full-time writer. Television writer-producer, National Broadcasting Co., New York City, 1957, and Johns Hopkins University, Baltimore, Md., 1957. Producer and director of various film series for National Educational Television, including "The Atom," "The Elements," "Virus," and "The Measure of Man." *Awards, honors:* Received Purple Heart while serving as correspondent in Okinawa, 1945; Thomas Alva Edison Foundation National Mass Media Award for best science book for youth, 1959, for *Elements of the Universe.*

WRITINGS: (With Glenn Theodore Seaborg) *Elements of the Universe,* Dutton, 1958; *Me and Frumpet,* Dutton, 1958; (with Wendell M. Stanley and others) *Viruses and the Nature of Life,* Dutton, 1961; *Wingfin and Topple* (children's fantasy), World Publishing, 1962; *Wildfire* (juvenile), World Publishing, 1963; *Magnet* (juvenile), World Publishing, 1964; *The Number of Things: Pythagoras, Geometry and Humming Strings,* Dutton, 1964; *Motion* (juvenile), World Publishing, 1965; *A Long Way Up: The Story of Jill Kinmont*, Harper, 1966, revised edition published as *The Other Side of the Mountain*, Warner Books, 1975; *Cybernaut* (poem), Viking, 1968; *The Attractive Universe: Gravity and the Shape of Space*, World Publishing, 1969; (with Ernest G. Beier) *People Reading: How We Control Others, How They Control Us*, Stein & Day, 1975; *The Other Side of the Mountain: Part II*, Warner Books, 1978.

Also author of television scripts, including "The Silver Lieutenant," produced in San Francisco at KPIX, 1954, "The Red Myth" (semi-dramatic documentary series), 1957, "A Small Planet Takes a Look at Itself" (ten-part live documentary series), NBC, 1957, "Johns Hopkins File 7" (seven half-hour live shows), ABC, 1957, and of narration for "Moonwalk One" (feature-length documentary on Apollo 11).

WORK IN PROGRESS: A nonfiction book, *Dream,* completion expected in 1982.

SIDELIGHTS: E. G. Valens writes *CA:* "Late in 1957, we aired a series of live television shows about the International Geophysical Year. We called it 'A Small Planet Takes a Look at Itself.' In our imagination, with the help of star backgrounds, a six-foot relief model of Earth, and a meticulously sculptured 19-inch moon, we backed-off into space and surveyed our planet with fresh eyes. The view was a surprise, like hearing your own voice for the first time. It was exciting to see the planet whole, and it was humbling to realize how neatly man was trapped, like color in an apple, within the skin.

"I wanted to know more and to write more, and I gathered information for some years. However, the material refused to fit in a single frame. So in 1965 I began writing two very different books about the same subject: the Earth in space—the force that holds it in orbit, the problems (psychological as well as technical) of getting away from it and then back to it again. The end result was a long poem, *Cybernaut,* and a straight, expository 'science book,' *The Attractive Universe.* These two books were written concurrently, which is to say in alternate months, weeks, even days. They borrowed constantly from each other.

"The poem is about a lone man's return from a long, sterile journey into space. The book is a factual account of gravitation, relativity, and the nature of weight and weightlessness. They were finished at the same time and published within a year of each other.

"Some ideas and images began in one book and jumped to the other, seemingly for reasons of their own. The idea of a man launching himself (by legpower) into orbit around an asteroid would not fit in the poem, but it grew to become a chapter in *The Attractive Universe.* On the other hand, the example of weightlessness originally presented in the gravity book changed form somewhat and moved over to the poem.

"The moral of all this? A reminder that science, as well as art, has to do with discovering, feeling, experiencing, sensing, realizing; and that neither art nor science has an intention of remaining in its proper pigeonhole. Both these subjects are sensitive to promising analogies, both are concerned with seeing beyond the surface and getting at the root of things. The poem, of course, is more personal. It embodies my concern with what we are up against today on this sad planet, with what we are doing to ourselves so efficiently, with our dialogues between child and parent, individual and his scientifically sophisticated master, and why these dialogues are often heavy with concern but barren of understanding. I revere science as an art and fear it as an

implement. The poem describes the weightlessness, the blocking of perception and other deprivations of sense and spirit, which faces each of us today in his own space as progress rolls forward, flattening us."

Several of Valens's books have been translated into Russian, Japanese, Italian, German, Swedish, Danish, Iranian, and Czechoslovakian. Universal released "The Other Side of the Mountain" in 1975 and "The Other Side of the Mountain: Part II" in 1978, both of which are film adaptations of Valens's books of the same titles.

*   *   *

VALI, Ferenc Albert 1905-

PERSONAL: Born May 25, 1905, in Budapest, Hungary; came to United States in 1957; naturalized citizen; son of Martin and Elza (Philipp) Vali; married Rose Nagel (an artist), March 22, 1949. *Education:* University of Budapest, Doctor Juris, 1927; London School of Economics and Political Science, Ph.D., 1932; Academy of International Law, The Hague, Netherlands, diploma, 1932. *Home:* 12 Wildwood Lane, Amherst, Mass. *Office:* Department of Political Science, University of Massachusetts, Amherst, Mass. 01002.

CAREER: Member of Hungarian Bar, 1932-43, 1946-47; attorney in Budapest, Hungary, 1932-43; University of Budapest, Budapest, professorial lecturer, Faculty of Law and Political Science, 1935-43, professor, 1946-49; University of Istanbul, Istanbul, Turkey, visiting professor, 1943-46; adviser on international law to Hungarian Ministry of Finance, 1947-49; legal adviser to Hungarian branch office of International Business Machines Corp. (IBM), 1949-51; Rockefeller Foundation, New York, N.Y., fellow, 1957-58; Harvard University, Center for International Affairs, Cambridge, Mass., research associate, 1958-61; University of Massachusetts—Amherst, professor of political science, 1961-75, professor emeritus, 1975—. Visiting professor of International law, Cornell Law School, spring, 1959. *Member:* American Political Science Association, American Society of International Law, American Academy of Political and Social Science. *Awards, honors:* LL.D., Wayne State University, 1962.

WRITINGS: The Clause of Public Order, University of Budapest Press, 1928; *Die Deutsch-Oesterreichische Zollunion,* Manz, 1932; *Servitudes of International Law,* P. S. King & Son, 1933, 2nd edition, Stevens & Son, 1958; *Rift and Revolt in Hungary,* Harvard University Press, 1961; *The Quest for a United Germany,* Johns Hopkins Press, 1967; *Bridge across the Bosporus: The Foreign Policy of Turkey,* Johns Hopkins Press, 1971; *The Turkish Straits and NATO,* Hoover Institution Press, 1972; *Politics of the Indian Ocean Region: The Balances of Power,* Free Press, 1976.

Contributor: Adam Bromke, editor, *The Communist States at the Crossroads between Moscow and Peking,* Praeger, 1965; Tamas Aczel, editor, *Ten Years After,* MacGibbon & Kee, 1966; Franklin L. Burdette and William G. Andrews, editors, *Issues of World Communism,* Van Nostrand, 1966; Andrew Gyorgy, Hubert S. Gibbs, and Robert S. Jordan, editors, *Problems of International Relations,* Prentice-Hall, 1970; Bromke and Teresa Rakowska-Harmstone, editors, *The Communist States in Disarray,* University of Minnesota Press, 1972. Contributor of articles on international law and international relations to American, Hungarian, and British journals.

SIDELIGHTS: Arrested by the Hungarian Security Police with his wife, in August, 1951, Ferenc Vali was condemned and sentenced to fifteen years for high treason (espionage). He was provisionally released in October, 1956, and after the first successful days of the Revolution, was recalled to the University of Budapest and participated in an attempt to reorganize the Hungarian Ministry of Foreign Affairs. After the downfall of the Revolution in November, the Valis decided to leave the country in order to avoid reimprisonment.

At the Center for International Affairs at Harvard University, Vali worked with Henry Kissinger and Zbigniew Brzezinski. He has made numerous research trips, and he says that the "most outstanding among them was a journey around the periphery of the Indian Ocean." In 1977 Vali was invited by the Australian National University at Canberra to work on a project concerning the strategic problems of the Indian Ocean. His *Servitudes of International Law* is an internationally-used textbook.

*   *   *

VANCE, Stanley   1915-

PERSONAL: Born May 5, 1915, in Minersville, Pa. *Education:* St. Charles Seminary, A.B., 1937; attended McCann School of Business, 1941-43; University of Pennsylvania, M.A., 1944, Ph.D., 1951. *Home:* 1701 Cherokee Blvd., Knoxville, Tenn. *Office:* Department of Personnel and Industrial Management, University of Tennessee, Knoxville, Tenn. 37916.

CAREER: University of Pennsylvania, Wharton School of Finance and Commerce, Philadelphia, instructor, 1945-47; University of Connecticut, Storrs, assistant professor, 1947-52; University of Massachusetts—Amherst, professor, 1952-56; Kent State University, Kent, Ohio, dean, 1956-60; University of Oregon, Eugene, H. T. Miner Professor of Business Administration, 1960-74, head of Personnel and Industrial Management Department, 1963-74; University of Tennessee, Knoxville, William B. Stokely Professor of Management, 1975—. President, Foundation for Administrative Research, 1973—. *Member:* Academy of Management (fellow; president, 1975-76), American Society of Personnel Administration, Association for Business Simulation and Experiential Learning (president, 1975-76), International Academy of Management (fellow).

WRITINGS: American Industries, Prentice-Hall, 1955; *Industrial Administration*, McGraw, 1959; *Management Decision Simulation*, McGraw, 1960; *Industrial Structure and Policy*, Prentice-Hall, 1961; *Elements of Linear Programming: A Case Approach*, University of Oregon, 1963; *Boards of Directors: Structure and Performance*, University of Oregon, 1964; (contributor) H. B. Maynard, editor, *Handbook of Business Administration*, McGraw, 1967; *The Corporate Director*, Dow Jones-Irwin, 1968; *Managers in the Conglomerate Era*, Wiley, 1971; (contributor) J. W. McGuire, editor, *Contemporary Management*, Prentice-Hall, 1974.

*   *   *

VANDERBILT, Amy   1908-1974

PERSONAL: Born July 22, 1908, in New York, N.Y.; died December 27, 1974, from injuries sustained in a fall from the second floor of her New York City townhouse; daughter of Joseph Mortimer (an insurance broker) and Mary Estelle (Brooks) Vanderbilt; married Robert S. Brinkerhoff, 1929 (divorced); married Morton G. Clark, 1935; married Hans Knopf, 1945 (divorced, 1954); married Curtis Kellar, March 1, 1968; children: (second marriage) Lincoln Gill Clark; (third marriage) Paul Vanderbilt Knopf, Stephan John

Knopf. *Education:* Attended New York University, 1926-28. *Politics:* Democrat. *Religion:* Episcopalian. *Home and office:* 438 East 87th St., New York, N.Y. 10028.

CAREER: Staten Island Advance, Staten Island, N.Y., society feature writer, 1927-29; assistant advertising publicity director, H. R. Mallison Co., 1929-30; advertising account executive, New York City, 1930-33; columnist, International News Service, 1933-34; home service director of magazines, Tower Publications, 1934; Publicity Associations, New York City, vice-president, 1937-40, president, 1940-45; Royal Crest Sterling, Newark, N.J., entertaining-etiquette consultant, 1940-64. Lecturer, Keedick Lecture Bureau, 1953-64; dress designer, Bristol, Inc., 1960-65; director, "Amy Vanderbilt Success Program for Women," 1963-74. Host of television etiquette program, "It's Good Taste," 1954-60, and radio program, "The Right Thing to Do," 1960-62. Advisor on etiquette for New York Transit Authority, 1961; consultant on wines, Classic Imports, Inc., 1964-74. *Member:* American Federation of Television and Radio Artists, Overseas Press Club, Screen Actors Guild, National Association for Mental Health (member of board of directors), New York Academy of Sciences, Richmond Historical Society (member of board of trustees, Staten Island chapter).

WRITINGS: Amy Vanderbilt's Complete Book of Etiquette, Doubleday, 1952, revised edition, 1978; *Amy Vanderbilt's Everyday Etiquette*, Hanover House, 1956, revised and expanded by Lettitia Baldrige, Doubleday, 1978; *Amy Vanderbilt's Complete Cookbook*, Doubleday, 1961. Author of syndicated column, "Amy Vanderbilt's Etiquette," 1954-74. Monthly contributor to *McCall's*, 1963, and *Ladies' Home Hournal*, 1965-74. Also contributor to magazines and newspapers. Consultant to *World Book Encyclopedia* and *World Almanac*.

WORK IN PROGRESS: Two books in the field of etiquette.

SIDELIGHTS: Robert McFadden wrote: "To Amy Vanderbilt, etiquette was more than a set of social rules or a guide to gracious living. It was, rather, a panoramic view of the world that enabled her to see—and comment extensively upon the greatness and smallness of people.... Miss Vanderbilt never talked of etiquette as mere rules, but, rather as the basis of kindnesses among people. In recent years, she called traditional etiquette out of place in an era of social, philosophical and economic upheaval and war atrocities."

Vanderbilt often described her first book of etiquette as a "guide to gracious living rather than a rulebook." A reporter for *Time* wrote: "Vanderbilt continually revised her book to reflect society's increasing informality." A reporter for *Newsweek* agreed, "Vanderbilt admitted that changing times were forcing her to modify her views: 'I try to find out what the most genteel people regularly do, what traditions they have discarded, and what compromises they have made.'" But no matter what changes occurred, Vanderbilt believed strongly that "only a great fool or a great genius is likely to flout all social grace with impunity."

Vanderbilt was fluent in French and had working knowledge of Spanish, Italian, German, Portuguese and Dutch. A rose was named for her by Jackson and Perkins, rose growers.

AVOCATIONAL INTERESTS: Cooking, walking, Latin dancing, gardening, decorating, and antique collecting.

BIOGRAPHICAL/CRITICAL SOURCES: Family Circle, March, 1959; *Reader's Digest*, September, 1959; *Time*, March 1, 1963, January 6, 1975; *New Republic*, April 29, 1972; *New York Times*, December 28, 1974; *Newsweek*, January 6, 1975; *Ladies' Home Journal*, March, 1975.†

VAN DOOREN, Leonard Alfred Theophile 1912-

PERSONAL: Born December 29, 1912, in London, England; son of Louis and Ada E. Van Dooren. *Home and office:* Locka Old Hall, Arkholme, Carnforth LA6 1BD, England.

CAREER: Land agent and surveyor in London, England, prior to World War II; Capernwray Bible School, Carnforth, England, director of school's conference centre, 1947-77, principal of school, 1948-75, currently president of Capernwray Bible Schools International. Worldwide Bible teaching minister.

WRITINGS—All published by Latimer Publishing: *Pressing On*, 1951; *Maintain the Spiritual Glow*, 1956; *Prayer: The Christian's Vital Breath*, 1962; *Come See the Place*, 1962; *The Challenge of the Macedonian Call*, 1963; *Introducing the Old Testament*, 1967; *Jesus Is Alive*, 1967; *Becoming Fishers of Men*, 1967; *Letters to Francisco*, 1967; *Introducing the New Testament*, 1972; *The Life I Now Live*, 1974; *Men Alive! Church Aflame!*, 1976; *Stepping In and Stepping Out*, 1978; *Pentecost: Day of God's Power*, 1979. Author of more than 100 booklets and evangelistic tracts.

WORK IN PROGRESS: A general introduction to the Bible.

*   *   *

VAN DOREN, Mark 1894-1972

PERSONAL: Born June 13, 1894, in Hope, Ill.; died December 10, 1972, in Torrington, Conn.; buried in Cornwall Hollow, Conn.; son of Charles Lucius (a physician) and Dora (Butz) Van Doren; married Dorothy Graffe (a writer), September 1, 1922; children: Charles, John. *Education:* University of Illinois at Urbana-Champaign, A.B., 1914, A.M., 1915; Columbia University, Ph.D., 1920. *Residence:* Falls Village, Conn. 06031.

CAREER: Columbia University, New York, N.Y., instructor, 1920-24, assistant professor, 1924-35, associate professor, 1935-42, professor of English, 1942-59. Lecturer at St. John's College (Maryland), 1937-57; visiting professor of English at Harvard University, 1963. Participant in "Invitation to Learning," CBS radio talk show, 1940-42. *Military service:* Served in U.S. Army, Infantry, during World War I.

MEMBER: National Institute of Arts and Letters, American Academy of Arts and Letters. *Awards, honors:* Pulitzer Prize for poetry, 1940, for *Collected Poems;* Litt.D. from Bowdoin College, 1944, University of Illinois, 1958, Columbia University, 1960, Knox College, 1966, Harvard University, 1966, and Jewish Theological Seminary of America, 1970; L.H.D. from Adelphi University, 1957, and Mount Mary College, 1965; St. John's College fellowship, 1959; M.D., Connecticut State Medical Society, 1966; Alexander Hamilton Medal, Columbia College, 1959; Sarah Josepha Hale Award, Richards Free Library (Newport, New Hampshire), 1960; Golden Rose Award, New England Poetry Society, 1960; brotherhood award, National Conference of Christians and Jews, 1960; creativity award, Huntington Hartford Foundation, 1962; Emerson-Thoreau Award, American Academy of Arts and Sciences, 1963; Academy of American Poets fellowship, 1967.

WRITINGS—Poems: *Spring Thunder and Other Poems*, Seltzer, 1924; *7 P.M. and Other Poems*, Boni, 1926; *Now the Sky and Other Poems*, Boni, 1928; *Jonathan Gentry*, Boni, 1931; *A Winter Diary and Other Poems*, Macmillan, 1935; *The Last Look and Other Poems*, Holt, 1937; *Collected Poems, 1922-1928*, Holt, 1939; *The Mayfield Deer*, Holt, 1941; *Our Lady Peace and Other War Poems*, New Directions, 1942; *The Seven Sleepers and Other Poems*, Holt,

1942; *The Country Year*, Morrow, 1946; *The Careless Clock: Poems about Children in the Family*, Sloane, 1947; *New Poems*, Sloane, 1948; *Humanity Unlimited: Twelve Sonnets*, College of William and Mary Press, 1950; *In That Far Land*, Prairie Press, 1951; *Mortal Summer*, Prairie Press, 1953; *Spring Birth and Other Poems*, Holt, 1953; *Selected Poems*, Holt, 1954; *Morning Worship and Other Poems*, Harcourt, 1960; *Collected and New Poems, 1924-1963*, Hill & Wang, 1963; (with Archibald MacLeish) *Narrative Poems*, Hill & Wang, 1964; *John Bradford*, Hayloft Press, 1966; *100 Poems*, Hill & Wang, 1967; *The Stove I Worship*, Hayloft Press, 1967; *Winter Calligraphy*, Hill & Wang, 1968; *That Shining Place*, Hill & Wang, 1969; *In Winter Sing Summer*, Bridge & Bryon, Inc., 1970; *Good Morning: Last Poems*, Hill & Wang, 1973. Also author of *Parents' Recompense*, 1965.

Fiction: *Dick and Tom: Tales of Two Ponies* (juvenile), Macmillan, 1931; *Dick and Tom in Town* (juvenile), Macmillan, 1932; *The Transients*, Morrow, 1935; *Windless Cabins*, Holt, 1940; *The Transparent Tree* (juvenile), Holt, 1940; *Tilda*, Holt, 1943; *The Witch of Ramoth and Other Tales*, Maple Press, 1950; *The Short Stories of Mark Van Doren*, Abelard, 1950; *Nobody Say a Word and Other Stories*, Holt, 1953; *Home with Hazel and Other Stories*, Harcourt, 1957; *Collected Stories*, Hill & Wang, Volume I, 1962, Volume II, 1965, Volume III, 1968; (author of introduction) Richard Henry Dana, *Two Years before the Mast*, Bantam, 1963; *Somebody Came* (juvenile), Quist, 1966.

Nonfiction: *Henry David Thoreau*, Houghton, 1916, reprinted, Russell & Russell, 1961; *The Poetry of John Dryden*, Harcourt, 1920, revised edition, Minority Press, 1931, published as *John Dryden: A Study of His Poetry*, Holt, 1946, first edition reprinted, Haskell House, 1969; (with brother, Carl Van Doren) *American and British Literature since 1890*, Century Co., 1925, 2nd revised edition, Appleton, 1967; *Edwin Arlington Robinson*, Literary Guild, 1927, reprinted, Norwood, 1976; *Shakespeare*, Holt, 1939; (with Theodore Spencer) *Studies in Metaphysical Poetry*, Columbia University Press, 1939, reprinted, Kennikat Press, 1964; (with Huntington Cairns and Allen Tate) *Invitation to Learning*, Random House, 1941; (with others) *The New Invitation to Learning*, Random House, 1942; *The Private Reader*, Holt, 1942, reprinted, Kraus Reprint, 1968; *Liberal Education*, Holt, 1943, published with new introduction, Beacon Press, 1959; *The Noble Voice: A Study of Ten Great Poems*, Holt, 1946, published as *Great Poems of Western Literature*, Collier Books, 1962; *Nathaniel Hawthorne*, Sloane, 1949, reprinted, Greenwood Press, 1972; *Man's Right to Knowledge and the Free Use Thereof*, Columbia University Press, 1954; *The Autobiography of Mark Van Doren*, Harcourt, 1958; *Don Quixote's Profession*, Columbia University Press, 1958; (author of introduction) Francis Parkman, *The Oregon Trail*, Holt, 1959; *The Happy Critic*, Hill & Wang, 1961; *The Dialogues of Archibald MacLeish and Mark Van Doren*, edited by Warren V. Bush, Dutton, 1964; (with others) *Insights into Literature*, Houghton, 1965; *Carl Sandburg*, U.S. Government Printing Office, 1969; (with Maurice Samuel) *In the Beginning, Love: Dialogues on the Bible*, edited by Edith Samuel, John Day, 1973. Also contributor to *The Letters of Robinson Jeffers*, Ann N. Ridgeway, editor, 1966.

Editor: *An American Bookshelf*, five volumes, Macy Masius, 1927-28; *Samuel Sewell's Diary*, Macy Masius, 1927; Mason Locke Weems, *A History of the Life and Death, Virtues and Exploits of General George Washington*, Macy Masius, 1927; *The Travels of William Bartram*, Macy Masius, 1928; Robert Montgomery Bird, *Nick of the Woods, or,*

Jibbenainosay: A Tale of Kentucky, Macy Masius, 1928; William Byrd, *A Journey to the Land of Eden and Other Papers,* Macy Masius, 1928; *An Anthology of World Poetry,* Boni, 1928, 2nd revised edition, Harcourt, 1963; (with Garibaldi M. Lapolla) *A Junior Anthology of World Poetry,* Boni, 1929; *An Autobiography of America,* Boni, 1929; *Correspondence of Aaron Burr and His Daughter Theodosia,* Covici-Friede, 1929; Cotton Mather, *The Life of Sir William Phips,* Covici-Friede, 1930, reprinted, AMS Press, 1971; *American Poets, 1630-1930,* Little, Brown, 1932; *The Oxford Book of American Prose,* Oxford University Press, 1932; (with Lapolla) *The World's Best Poems,* Boni, 1932.

(With John W. Cunliffe and Karl Young) *Century Readings in English Literature,* 5th edition (Van Doren was not associated with earlier editions), Appleton-Century-Crofts, 1940; *A Listener's Guide to "Invitation to Learning,"* Columbia Broadcasting System, Volume I: *1940-41,* 1940, Volume II: *1941-42,* 1942; *The Night of the Summer Solstice and Other Stories of the Russian War,* Holt, 1943; *Walt Whitman,* Viking, 1945, revised edition by Malcolm Cowley, 1973; *The Portable Emerson,* Viking, 1946, reprinted, Penguin, 1977; William Wordsworth, *Selected Poetry,* Random House, 1950; *The Best of Hawthorne,* Ronald, 1951; *Introduction to Poetry,* Sloane, 1951, also published as *Enjoying Poetry,* Sloane, 1951; *Selected Letters of William Cowper,* Farrar, Straus, 1951; (with others) *Riverside Poetry: 48 New Poems by 27 Poets,* Twayne, 1956.

Plays: *The Last Days of Lincoln* (produced in Tallahassee at Florida State University, October 18, 1961), Hill & Wang, 1959; "Never, Never Ask His Name" (also see below), produced in Tallahassee at Florida State University, 1965; *Three Plays* (contains "Never, Never Ask His Name," "A Little Night Music," and "The Weekend That Was"), Hill & Wang, 1966.

SIDELIGHTS: Mark Van Doren's interest in poetry began with his introduction to Wordsworth. "No poetry had made any great difference to me," he told Archibald MacLeish, "until suddenly I found myself reading Wordsworth.... It was music."

During his 39 years of teaching at Columbia University, Van Doren had many opportunities to advise students interested in becoming writers. "My advice to an ambitious young writer," he told Roy Newquist, "is to get the best education he can.... And never should he get too far from the soul of man, which is the basic concern of all art." He considered the question of a student's eventual success as a writer to be an impossible one to answer and recalled: "One day when I was talking to such a student, I said, 'Oh dear, let's see. Do you like coffee?' And he said, 'I'm crazy about coffee.' Well, he got the point right away. That's all the point I had." Included among Van Doren's former students are Thomas Merton, Lionel Trilling, Louis Zukofsky, Whittaker Chambers, Jack Kerouac, and Allen Ginsberg.

Van Doren's work is a studied application of his theories of knowledge, poetry, and teaching. He told MacLeish: "The subject [of a poem] is something that has struck you very deeply just because it's there, and because it's beautiful and important." Philip Booth found that "Van Doren's poems are seemingly simply talk made music; he deals with universal themes in the most specific terms, but he risks abstractions where nothing else will reach, and love is a word he is unafraid to write out." Although Paul Engle thought that "now and then one wishes that [Van Doren] would commit some wildness to the page," Theodore Roethke saw him as "a careful craftsman with a sharp eye for the homely and a mind aware of the profound implications of the casual."

Van Doren never considered himself a part of New York's literary world, nor did he establish friendships with writers simply because they were such. As Van Doren himself remained outside of literary circles, so his work stands apart from the mainstream of contemporary American letters. *Poetry* editors commented: "Van Doren has not received, nor will he evoke, applause from the avant garde; he is solidly entrenched in the tradition of definite purpose framed in strict patterns. There is nothing spectacular about his style.... He avoids either extreme of the obsessively confessional and the unemotionally unaffected.... Van Doren has never been a slave to a vogue, and never having been in fashion will never be out of it."

Van Doren's place among the critics is also characterized by non-extremism. "Among good critics," wrote Alfred Kazin, "Mr. Van Doren has always stood out as The Great Neutral, and that neutrality is the secret and condition of his quality. For if he has an ardent mind, it is also a tidy one; and if it is never aloof, it always lives on its own track; a mind exact and generous and often piercing in its intuitions, but very careful never to overreach, to say too much; ambitious only to stop on the necessary point made, the observation perfectly seen."

In an interview with Melvin Maddocks, Van Doren stated: "The job of the poet is to render the world—to see it and report it without loss, without perversion. No poet ever talks about feelings. Only sentimental people do. Feelings aren't pleasant. No one ever enjoyed real feelings—fear, pity, jealously, all the feelings connected with love. Feelings mean suffering. Writing poems is a way of getting rid of feelings. You have to think to do anything well.... You finally express what you have to express in cold blood."

Van Doren did not turn his talents to writing plays until the middle 1950's, when he composed *The Last Days of Lincoln.* Of this work he told MacLeish: "Having become utterly enthralled by this person, I just had to do something about it. I had to get him talking." The play is wholly in verse except for Lincoln's speeches. "This play scores high as poetic drama," noted critic John Holmes, "and as a distinguished addition to Civil War literature."

BIOGRAPHICAL/CRITICAL SOURCES: Alfred Kreymbourg, *Our Singing Strength,* Coward, 1924; *Saturday Review,* November 17, 1937; *New York Herald Tribune,* March 29, 1942; Dorothy Van Doren, *The Country Wife,* Morrow, 1950; *Library Journal,* October 15, 1958; *New York Times,* October 26, 1958, January 31, 1965, January 11, 1969, June 13, 1969; Mark Van Doren, *The Autobiography of Mark Van Doren,* Harcourt, 1958; D. Van Doren, *The Professor and I,* Appleton, 1959; *New York Herald Tribune Book Review,* February 15, 1959; *Newsweek,* February 23, 1959; *Christian Science Monitor,* February 25, 1960; *Poetry,* November, 1960, March, 1964; Dorothy Nyren, editor, *Library of Literary Criticism,* 2nd edition, Ungar, 1961; Warren V. Bush, editor, *The Dialogues of Archibald MacLeish and Mark Van Doren,* Dutton, 1964; Roy Newquist, *Counterpoint,* Rand McNally, 1964; *New York Times Book Review,* November 10, 1968; *Washington Post,* June 11, 1969; *Life,* June 30, 1969; *Contemporary Literary Criticism,* Gale, Volume VI, 1976, Volume X, 1979.†

*   *   *

VAN DUSEN, Albert E(dward) 1916-

PERSONAL: Born May 14, 1916, in Vilas, N.C.; son of Albert P. (a professor) and Chloe (Lewis) Van Dusen; married Wilda E. Reep (a researcher) May 3, 1946. *Education:* Wesleyan University, B.A., 1938; University of Pennsylvania, M.A., 1940, Ph.D., 1948. *Home:* Ball Hill Rd., Storrs, Conn. 06268. *Office:* Department of History, University of Connecticut, Storrs, Conn. 06268.

CAREER: Duke University, Durham, N.C., instructor, 1941-46; Wesleyan University, Middletown, Conn., instructor, 1946-48; Department of the Army, Pentagon, Washington, D.C., historian, 1948-49; University of Connecticut, Storrs, 1949—, began as assistant professor, currently professor of history. Connecticut state historian, 1952—. Member of Connecticut Historical Commission, 1957—, archives and education committee, Museum of the American China Trade, 1967—, educational advisors committee, Old Sturbridge Village, 1970—, Connecticut American Revolution Bicentennial Commission, 1971-78, advisory board, Connecticut Historical Records, 1976—, advisory board, Connecticut Trust for Historic Preservation, 1977—, and Connecticut committee, National Coordinating Committee for the Promotion of History, 1978—. Trustee, Stowe-Day Foundation, 1963—. *Military service:* U.S. Army, 1945.

MEMBER: American Historical Association, Organization of American Historians, Marine Historical Association, American Association for State and Local History (chairman of awards committee, New England section, 1967—; member of council, 1970-74), New England Historical Association, Antiquarian and Landmarks Society of Connecticut (vice-president, 1971—), Connecticut Historical Society (chairman of publications committee, 1954-78), Association for the Study of Connecticut History (member of council, 1970-72, 1974-76, and 1977—; president, 1972-74; member of publications committee, 1976-77), Mansfield Historical Society (president, 1963-65), Acorn Club (president, 1974-76).

Awards, honors: Research grants from American Philosophical Society, 1963, National Endowment for the Humanities, 1970-74, Howard and Bush Foundation, 1971, 1975, Hartford Foundation for Public Giving, 1971, 1978, National Historical Publications and Records Commission, 1973—, and American Revolution Bicentennial Commission, 1975. Selected one of the five best teachers at the University of Connecticut, 1964; Directors' Award, Connecticut League of Historical Societies, 1977, for "outstanding service in the field of state and local history over a period of many years."

WRITINGS: Middletown and the American Revolution (booklet), Rockfall Corporation and Middlesex Historical Society, 1950; (editor) *The Public Records of the State of Connecticut,* Connecticut State Library, Volume IX: *1797-1799,* 1953, Volume X (with wife, Wilda E. Van Dusen): *1800-1801,* 1965; *Connecticut,* Random House, 1961; (with Frances Humphreville) *This Is Connecticut,* L. W. Singer, 1963; *Puritans against the Wilderness,* Pequot Press, 1975. Also author of *A History of Wesleyan University, 1831-1887,* 1981. Contributor to several encyclopedias, including *World Book, Collier's Year Book, Encyclopedia Americana,* and *Encyclopaedia Britannica;* contributor of numerous articles and book reviews to history journals.

WORK IN PROGRESS: Editing *The Papers of Jonathan Trumbull, Sr.*

SIDELIGHTS: Albert E. Van Dusen told *CA:* "My major book, *Connecticut,* was prepared over the years 1953-1960 in response to a request by the Connecticut State library committee for a modern, scholarly survey of Connecticut's history. It was a challenging task to try to delineate what was distinctive about this little state. I attempted to combine a scholarly and comprehensive text with a highly illustrated format. At the time, it appeared to be the only state history

of its type. Since my book was published, the interest shown by scholars in local and state history has burgeoned—a trend which has been strong in Connecticut and which delights me greatly."

AVOCATIONAL INTERESTS: Travel, gardening, and mountain climbing.

* * *

VAN DUSEN, Henry P(itney) 1897-1975

PERSONAL: Born December 11, 1897; died February 13, 1975; son of George Richstein (a lawyer) and Katharine James (Pitney) Van Dusen; married Elizabeth Bartholomew, June 19, 1931 (died January 29, 1975); children: John George, Henry Hugh, Derek Bartholomew. *Education:* Princeton University, A.B., 1919; New College (Edinburgh), graduate study, 1921-22; Union Theological Seminary, B.D., 1924; Edinburgh University, Ph.D., 1932.

CAREER: Princeton University, Princeton, N.J., Philadelphian Society, secretary, 1919-21; ordained Presbyterian minister, 1924; independent work in colleges, 1924-26; Union Theological Seminary, New York City, instructor, 1926-28, assistant professor, 1928-31, associate professor of systematic theology and philosophy of religion, 1931-36, Roosevelt Professor of Systematic Theology, 1936-59, professor of Christian theology, 1959-61, Lamont Professor of Christian Theology, 1961-63, Lamont Professor of Christian Theology emeritus and traveling professor, 1963-75, dean of students, 1931-39, president, 1945-63, president emeritus, 1963-75; Auburn Theological Seminary, New York City, president, 1945-63, president emeritus, 1963-75. Associate executive secretary, Young Men's Christian Association, student division, 1927-28; World Council of Churches, member of provisional committee and administrative committee, 1939-48, chairman of study committee, 1939-54, chairman of study committee, U.S.A. member churches, 1940-48, chairman of joint committee of World Council of Churches and International Missionary Council, 1954-61. Fellow, National Council on Values in Higher Education. Member of board of appointments, Harvard University Divinity School, 1953-55; chairman, Board of Interseminary Movement, 1940-48; vice-president, Board of Foreign Missions, Presbyterian Church, 1949-52; Commission on Ecumenical Mission and Relations, United Presbyterian Church, 1957-63; Federal Council of Churches, member of department of research and education, joint committee on religious liberty of Federal Council of Churches and Foreign Missions Conference, and comissions on evangelism and on religion and health, 1938-49; National Council of Churches, member of general board and of division of foreign mission, chairman, 1956-63; Council for Clinical Training of Theological Students. member of board of governors, secretary, 1933-42, vice-president, 1942-48. Delegate to numerous religious conferences, national and international.

Member of board of trustees: Princeton University, Rockefeller Foundation, General Education Board, Fund for the Republic, Vassar College, 1937-41, Millbrook School, 1939-48, Freedom House, 1941-48, Smith College, 1945-50, Elizabeth Morrow School, United Board for Christian Higher Education in Asia (president, 1946-49, 1953-64), Morningside Heights, Inc. (vice-president; chairman, public safety committee, 1952-63), Missionary Research Library, Nanking Theological Seminary (chairman, beginning 1953), Interdenominational Theological Center (Atlanta, Ga.; chairman, 1962), Fund for Theological Education (chairman, executive committee, beginning 1953), Theological Education Fund,

Church Peace Union, 1954-57, St. Vladimir's Russian Orthodox Seminary, Windham House, 1963-66, Interchurch Center (New York City; vice-president, beginning 1964).

MEMBER: Phi Beta Kappa, Young Men's Christian Association (national council and national board, 1936-48; student department committee, 1924-46; national student advisory council). *Awards, honors:* S.T.D., New York University, 1945, Westminster Theological Seminary, 1956, Columbia University, 1956; D.D., Amherst College, 1946, Edinburgh University, 1946, Oberlin College, 1947, Yale University, 1947, Heidelberg College, 1950, Queen's University, Kingston, Ontario, 1952, Harvard University, 1954, Dartmouth College, 1956, Colgate University, 1960, Virginia Theological Seminary, 1963, Pacific School of Religion, 1963, Bucknell University, 1964, Assumption College, 1968; Litt.D., Jewish Theological Seminary, 1958; L.H.D., Bates College, 1959.

WRITINGS: In Quest of Life's Meaning, Association Press, 1926; *The Plain Man Seeks for God,* Scribner, 1933; *God in These Times,* Scribner, 1935; *For the Healing of the Nations: Impressions of Christianity around the World,* Scribner, 1940; *Reality and Religion,* Association Press, 1940; *Methodism's World Mission,* Methodist Publishing, 1940; *What IS the Church Doing?,* Scribner, 1943; *East Indies Discoveries,* Friendship, 1944; *They Found the Church There,* Scribner, 1945; *World Christianity: Yesterday, Today, and Tomorrow,* Abingdon, 1947; *God in Education,* Scribner, 1951; *Life's Meaning,* Association Press, 1951; *Spirit, Son and Father: Christian Faith in the Light of the Holy Spirit,* Scribner, 1958; *One Great Ground of Hope: Christian Missions and Christian Unity,* Westminster, 1961; *The Vindication of Liberal Theology,* Scribner, 1963; *Dag Hammarskjold: The Statesman and His Faith,* Harper, 1967, revised edition published as *Dag Hammerskjold: The Man and His Faith,* 1969 (first edition published in England as *Dag Hammerskjold: A Biographical Interpretation of "Markings,"* Faber, 1967).

Contributor: *Dynamic Faith,* Association Press, 1927; *The Christian Message for the World Today,* Round Table Press, 1934; *The Vitality of the Christian Tradition,* Scribner, 1944; *Protestantism,* Methodist Church, 1944; *Religion and World Order,* Harper, 1944; *This Ministry: The Contribution of Henry Sloane Coffin,* Scribner, 1945; *Christian World Mission,* Methodist Church, 1946; *Modern Education and Human Values,* University of Pittsburgh Press, 1947; *Renewal and Advance* (volume of Whitby Conference addresses), Edinburgh House Press, 1948; *Education for Professional Responsibility,* Carnegie Press, 1948; *The Enduring Gospel,* S.C.M. Press, 1950; Sir James Marchant, editor, *The Coming-of-Age of Christianity,* Canterbury Press, 1950; *A Guide to the Religions of America,* Simon & Schuster, 1955, revised edition, 1962; *A Handbook of Christian Theology,* Meridian, 1958; *Unity at Mid-Career,* Macmillan, 1963; *Paths to World Order,* Columbia University Press, 1967.

Editor: (With Thomas W. Graham) *The Story of Jesus,* Association Press, 1925; *Ventures in Belief,* Scribner, 1930; (with S. M. Cavert) *The Church through Half a Century,* Scribner, 1936; *Church and State in the Modern World,* Harper, 1937; (with D. E. Roberts) *Liberal Theology: An Appraisal,* Scribner, 1942; *The Christian Answer,* Scribner, 1945; (with John T. McNeil and John Baillie) *The Library of Christian Classics* (twenty-six volume series), Westminster, beginning 1953; *The Spiritual Legacy of John Foster Dulles,* Westminster, 1960; *Christianity on the March,* Harper, 1963. Member of editorial board, *Religion in Life,* beginning 1934,

Christianity and Crises, Christendom, 1945-48, and *Ecumenical Review.*

SIDELIGHTS: Henry Van Dusen was one of the first leaders of the modern ecumenical movement. He was a delegate to almost every major ecumenical conference from the Oxford Conference on Church, Community, and State, in 1937, to the time of his death in 1975. *Avocational interests:* Sailing.

BIOGRAPHICAL/CRITICAL SOURCES: Saturday Review, January 4, 1964; *New York Times Book Review,* January 15, 1967; *Christian Science Monitor,* January 26, 1967; *New York Times,* February 14, 1975; *Washington Post,* February 15, 1975.†

*   *   *

VAN EVERY, Dale   1896-1976

PERSONAL: Born July 23, 1896, in Levering, Mich.; died May 28, 1976, in Santa Barbara, Calif.; son of Wilbert Maurice and Estella (Palmer) Van Every; married Ellen Calhoun, 1922; married Florence Mason, 1937 (died, 1969); married Frances R. Francis, April 22, 1972; children: (first marriage) David, Joan. *Education:* Stanford University, A.B., 1920. *Home and office:* 1521 Laguna St., Apt. 107, Santa Barbara, Calif. 93101. *Agent:* Paul R. Reynolds, Inc., 12 East 41st St., New York, N.Y. 10017; and William Morris Agency, 1350 Avenue of the Americas, New York, N.Y. 10019.

CAREER: United Press International, New York, N.Y., and Washington, D.C., correspondent and editor, 1920-28; writer and producer for various motion picture studios in Hollywood, Calif., 1928-43; free-lance writer, 1943-76. *Military service:* U.S. Army Ambulance Service, 1917-19; became second lieutenant. *Awards, honors:* Commonwealth Club of California Awards for *The Shining Mountains, Bridal Journey, Forth to the Wilderness, Ark of Empire,* and *The Final Challenge;* Colonial Dames of America Award for contribution of outstanding excellence to the field of American colonial history, 1962, for *Forth to the Wilderness.*

WRITINGS: The A.E.F. in Battle, Appleton, 1928; *Westward the River,* Putnam, 1945; *The Shining Mountains,* Messner, 1948; *Bridal Journey,* Messner, 1950, reprinted, Bantam, 1976; *The Captive Witch,* Messner, 1951; *The Trembling Earth,* Messner, 1953, reprinted, Popular Library, 1975; *Men of the Western Waters,* Houghton, 1956; *The Voyagers,* Holt, 1957; *Our Country Then* (anthology), Holt, 1958; *The Scarlet Feather,* Holt, 1959; *The Frontier People of America,* Morrow, Volume I: *Forth to the Wilderness: 1754-1774,* 1961, reprinted, Arno, 1977, Volume II: *A Company of Heroes: 1775-1783,* 1962, reprinted, Arno, 1977, Volume III: *Ark of Empire: 1784-1803,* 1963, Volume IV: *The Final Challenge: 1804-1845,* 1964; *Disinherited: The Lost Birthright of the American Indian,* Morrow, 1966; *The Day the Sun Died,* Little, Brown, 1971. Also editor of *The First American Frontier.*

WORK IN PROGRESS: Another novel on the American frontiersman; a story on Indian-white interaction during the life of Mohawk leader Joseph Brant.

SIDELIGHTS: One of Dale Van Every's most ambitious projects, a four-volume survey of early American history entitled *The Frontier People of America,* was very well-received by the critics. Commenting on the first volume in the series, a reviewer for the *Annals* of the American Academy of Political and Social Science, wrote: "Mr. Van Every has succeeded in sifting a mass of controversial and confusing data, and has prepared a narrative that is as clear and simple to follow as it is vivid, challenging, and suggestive.'' J. C. Miller of *New York Herald Tribune Books* felt that ''[the author's] style will bear comparison with the best contemporary writers in the field of American history'' and that he easily conveyed the feeling that ''history is made by human beings rather than by political and economic forces.'' In his review of the third volume in the series, a *Best Sellers* critic simply states: ''Students of early American history . . . will bless the author for [such] a readable and authoritative investigation.''

The publication of the fourth and final volume of the series led critics to reflect on the overall merits of Van Every's work. R. A. Billington of *Book Week* wrote: ''The trail that [Mr. Van Every] follows is wide, and paved with hundreds of books and monographs that he has used intelligently. Yet he has not been guilty of just another narrative, for he brings to his task certain virtues. . . . One is a remarkable literary skill. . . . [But] even more significant is [his] broad philosophical insight.'' Finally, a *Virginia Quarterly Review* critic noted: ''As in the earlier volumes, Van Every's great contribution is his impressionistic approach to the pioneers, a form of collective biography which catches the spirit of the frontiersmen as few writers have done. . . . [The volumes] are ably written syntheses, Turnerian in their theses, romantic in their themes, and forthright in their assertion that men, not forces, make history.''

BIOGRAPHICAL/CRITICAL SOURCES: San Francisco Chronicle, July 9, 1961; *Christian Science Monitor*, August 11, 1961; *New York Herald Tribune Books*, September 3, 1961; *Annals* of the American Academy of Political and Social Science, March, 1962, March, 1963; *Saturday Review*, April 20, 1963, April 2, 1966; *Best Sellers*, October 15, 1963, April 1, 1975; *Book Week*, November 17, 1963, January 10, 1965; *Virginia Quarterly Review*, winter, 1965; *New York Times Book Review*, March 27, 1966.†

*   *   *

van GULIK, Robert Hans   1910-1967

PERSONAL: Born August 9, 1910, in Zutphen, Netherlands; died September 24, 1967, of cancer, in The Hague, Netherlands; son of William Jacobus and Bertha (de Ruyter) van Gulik; married Shui Shih-fang (Frances Shui), 1943; children: Willem Robert, Pieter Anton, Pauline Frances, Thomas Mathys. *Education:* Attended University of Leyden; University of Utrecht, Ph.D. (with honors), 1935. *Home:* Louis Davidsstraat 379, Waldeck, The Hague, Netherlands.

CAREER: Joined Netherlands Foreign Service in 1935, posted in China, Japan, and India, interned in Japan during World War II, released through diplomatic exchange in 1942, served as first secretary to Netherlands Embassy in Chungking, China, 1943-46, counsellor of Netherlands Embassy and political delegate to Far Eastern Commission in Washington, D.C., 1946-47, counsellor of Netherlands Embassy in Tokyo, Japan, 1948-52, director of the Middle East with Netherlands Ministry of Foreign Affairs, 1953-56, minister to Lebanon and Syria, 1956-59, ambassador to the Federation of Malaya, 1959-62, director of research with Ministry of Foreign Affairs in The Hague, Netherlands, 1962-65, and ambassador to Japan and the Republic of Korea, 1965-67. Lecturer in ancient Chinese history, University of Malaya, 1960-61. *Wartime service:* Seconded to Allied Headquarters in Cairo and New Delhi, 1942. *Member:* Royal Netherlands Academy of Arts and Sciences, Mystery Writers of America (corresponding member), British Crime Writers' Associa-

tion. *Awards, honors:* Grand Cross, Order of the Cedars of Lebanon; Officer, Order of Orange Nassau; Knight of the Netherlands Lion; Order of Merit of Syria; commander, Order of Menelik, Ethiopia; Grand Cross, Order of the Rising Sun, Japan; Order of Culture, Republic of Korea.

WRITINGS—Nonfiction: (With C. C. Uhlenbeck) *An English-Blackfoot Vocabulary*, Royal Netherlands Academy of Arts and Sciences, 1930, reprinted, AMS Press, 1977; (translator from the Sanskrit) *Urvaci*, [The Hague], 1932; (with Uhlenbeck) *A Blackfoot-English Vocabulary*, Royal Netherlands Academy of Arts and Sciences, 1934, reprinted, AMS Press, 1977; *Hayagriva, the Mantrayanic Aspect of Horse-Cult in China and Japan* (doctoral thesis), E. J. Brill, 1935; (translator) Mi Fei, *On Ink Stones*, Kelly & Walsh, 1938; *The Lore of the Chinese Lute*, Monumenta Nipponica Monographs, 1940, revised edition, Tuttle, 1969; *Hsi K'ang and His Poetical Essay on the Lute*, Monumenta Nipponica Monographs, 1941, revised edition, Tuttle, 1968; (translator from the Chinese into Japanese) *Shukai-hen*, [Tokyo], 1941; (editor) *Tung-kao chan-shih chi-kan*, Commercial Press, 1944; (editor) *Trifling Tale of a Spring Dream*, [Tokyo], 1950; *Erotic Colour Prints of the Ming Period*, three volumes, privately printed, 1951; *Siddham*, [Nagpur, India], 1956; (translator from the Chinese) Wan-jung Kuei, *Parallel Cases from under the Pear Tree*, E. J. Brill, 1956; (translator from the Chinese) Shih-hua Lu, *Scrapbook for Chinese Collectors*, [Beirut], 1958; *Chinese Pictorial Art as Viewed by the Connoisseur*, Istituto Italiano per il Medio ed l'Estremo Oriente, 1958; *Sexual Life in Ancient China*, E. J. Brill, 1961; *The Gibbon in China*, E. J. Brill, 1967.

Fiction: (Self-illustrated) *Een Gegeven Dag: Amsterdams Mysterie*, W. van Hoeve, 1963; *De Nacht van de Tijger: Een Rechter Tie Verhaal*, W. van Hoeve, 1963; *Vier Vingers: Een Rechter Tie Verhaal*, [Amsterdam], 1964.

''Judge Dee Mystery'' series; self-illustrated: (Translator) *Dee Goong An*, limited edition, [Tokyo], 1949, reprinted, Arno, 1976; *The Chinese Maze Murders* (also see below), W. van Hoeve, 1956; *New Year's Eve in Lan-fang*, [Beirut], 1958; *The Chinese Bell Murders*, M. Joseph, 1958, Harper, 1959; *The Chinese Gold Murders*, M. Joseph, 1959, Harper, 1961; *The Chinese Lake Murders*, Harper, 1960; *The Chinese Nail Murders*, Harper, 1961; *The Red Pavilion*, Art Printing Works (Kuala Lumpur, Malaya), 1961; *The Haunted Monastery* (also see below), Art Printing Works, 1962; *The Lacquer Screen*, Art Printing Works, 1962, Scribner, 1970; *The Emperor's Pearl*, Scribner, 1963; *The Willow Pattern*, Scribner, 1965; *The Monkey and the Tiger*, Heinemann, 1965, Scribner, 1966; *The Phantom of the Temple*, Scribner, 1966; *Murder in Canton*, Heinemann, 1966, Scribner, 1967; *Judge Dee at Work*, Heinemann, 1967, Scribner, 1971; *Poets and Murder*, Heinemann, 1968, Scribner, 1972 (published in England as *The Fox-Magic Murders*, Panther Books, 1973); *The Haunted Monastery and The Chinese Maze Murders: Two Chinese Detective Novels*, Dover, 1976.

Contributor of articles and reviews to Orientalist journals. Co-editor, *Monumenta Nipponica* (Tokyo), beginning 1938.

SIDELIGHTS: An ambassador and noted Orientalist, Robert Hans van Gulik's interest in Eastern culture and language began with his first glimpse of the Chinese script on his father's porcelain collection. He began studying the Chinese language in the Chinatown section of Batavia (in the Dutch East Indies), where his father was stationed with the Army. Later, at the University of Leyden, van Gulik expanded his studies to include Japanese and Tibetan. In addition, he privately studied Sanskrit, Russian, and comparative philology.

In 1940, van Gulik discovered *Dee Goong An,* an eighteenth-century Chinese detective novel. While translating this novel into English, van Gulik wondered why Oriental readers were so fond of poorly translated, third-rate thrillers from the West when their own ancient literature contained so many interesting characters and plots. With this question in mind, he began to write mysteries for modern Eastern audiences. Van Gulik based these stories on authentic, ancient Chinese literature, largely retaining the puzzle-plot form of these originals. Apparently, his method was quite successful; a *Time* critic once commented that although van Gulik's "writing lacks somewhat in professional sheen," he more than compensated for this shortcoming with "rich and accurate historical detail." Allen J. Hubin wrote that "the China of old, in Mr. van Gulik's skilled hands, comes vividly alive again."

Judge Dee, van Gulik's fictional detective, was based on the celebrated Chinese judge and detective of the seventh-century Tang Dynasty, Jen-chieh. All of the Judge Dee mysteries have been translated into Dutch; the earlier stories were translated into French, Swedish, Spanish, Finnish, Yugoslavian, Japanese, Italian, and German.

BIOGRAPHICAL/CRITICAL SOURCES: New York Times Book Review, October 14, 1962, May 23, 1965, April 24, 1966, March 12, 1967, February 9, 1969; *Times Literary Supplement,* March 31, 1963, May 17, 1964; *Time,* August 18, 1967.†

* * *

VANSITTART, Peter   1920-

PERSONAL: Born August 27, 1920, in Bedford, England; son of Edward and Mignon (Clemence) Vansittart. *Education:* Attended Haileybury College, and Worcester College, Oxford. *Home:* 9 Upper Park Rd., Hampstead, London NW3, England. *Agent:* Anthony Sheil Associates, 2/3 Morwell St., London WC1B 3AR, England.

CAREER: Novelist, 1942—. Director of Burgess Hill School, Hampstead, England, 1947-59. *Awards, honors:* Society of Authors traveling scholarship, 1970.

WRITINGS: I Am the World, Chatto & Windus, 1942; *Enemies,* Chapman & Hall, 1947; *The Overseer,* Chapman & Hall, 1948; *Broken Canes,* Bodley Head, 1950; *A Verdict of Treason,* Bodley Head, 1951; *A Little Madness,* Bodley Head, 1953; *The Game and the Ground,* Abelard, 1955; *Orders of Chivalry,* Abelard, 1956; *The Tournament,* Walker & Co., 1958.

A Sort of Forgetting, Bodley Head, 1960; *Carolina,* Ace Books, 1961; *Sources of Unrest,* Bodley Head, 1962; *The Siege,* Walker & Co., 1962; *The Friends of God,* Macmillan, 1963; *The Lost Lands,* Walker & Co., 1964; *The Dark Tower,* Macdonald & Co., 1965; *The Shadow Land,* Macdonald & Co., 1967; *The Story Teller,* P. Owen, 1968; *Green Knights, Black Angels: A Mosaic of History,* Macmillan, 1969; *Pastimes of a Red Summer,* P. Owen, 1969; *Landlord,* P. Owen, 1970; *Vladivostok,* Covent Garden Press, 1972; *Dictators,* Studio Vista, 1973; *Worlds and Underworlds,* P. Owen, 1974; *Quintet,* P. Owen, 1976; *Flakes of History,* Park Editions, 1978; *Lancelot,* P. Owen, 1978; *The Death of Robin Hood,* P. Owen, 1981; *When This Bloody War Is Ended,* J. Cape, in press.

WORK IN PROGRESS: John Paul Jones; The Conjurers.

SIDELIGHTS: In a review of *Green Knights, Black Angels,* a *Times Literary Supplement* critic writes: "Provocative, stimulating, maddening, exciting, disjointed, brilliant, compressed, illuminating—these are a few of the adjectives that flood into the mind as one reads (and re-reads, for this is a book which could not be absorbed even at a hundred sittings) Peter Vansittart's *Green Knights, Black Angels: A Mosaic of History.* Who will read and re-read it? The dedicated adolescent historian who thrills to fresh aspects of his subject, and the adult who perhaps teaches history, art, civics, philology, literature, or religion and enjoys being given a shot in the arm. These will survive Mr. Vansittart's primary (and flattering) assumption that all of us can follow him anywhere—up and down the centuries, in and out of cultures, the world over—then read on and become first filled with amazement at the author's rich scholarship, then fascinated by his startling ability to draw illuminating conclusions from his evidence. Every paragraph, every sentence on some pages is a challenge to the intellect. And some passages are pure poetry."

Benedict Nightingale finds that *Pastimes of a Red Summer* "isn't a historical novel in any inhibiting sense of the phrase, though [Vansittart's] allusive, impressionistic prose does evoke his chosen period more vividly than many writers with that aim alone." But the reviewer notes that "there are times when—as tends to happen with authors who haven't had the recognition they deserve—Mr. Vansittart lets his imagery become too private. It presumably means something to him that a fop has a smile 'like tea made of fingernails,' but not much to me. There are times, too, when his palpably fine intelligence seems over-interested in effects that beg to be described as 'beautiful' or 'exquisite.' But be that as it may, both adjectives aptly and unironically describe the effect of the novel as a whole."

Peter Vansittart told *CA* that each of his books "really has its own motives, some contradictory, difficult to express. It is not important. One's yearning to communicate, from out of a very private life, has many interpretations, none of them lies, yet none wholly truthful. But by setting myself to explore different people, different relationships, in different layers of time, trying to fuse the apparently bizarre with the apparently commonplace, I keep myself in movement. For me, remote pasts, surviving in myth, dream, and a certain obstinant intractibility in human nature, remain very much a power in our contemporary world. Here is the basic theme of my novels, whether 'historical' or 'contemporary.' For me, the novel is a form certainly as poetic as most verse and I try to make my own work a kind of poetry. On the whole I have succeeded more with fellow writers than with the reading public. I have had many failures. One of my own favorite books, *Harry,* may never be published. But Dorothy Parker described one novel as 'as glittering a work of satire as we have had for many long years, and I think that it is safe to say will not have again for many more.'"

AVOCATIONAL INTERESTS: Sports, music.

BIOGRAPHICAL/CRITICAL SOURCES: Spectator, March 22, 1968, September 27, 1969; *Punch,* March 27, 1968; *Times Literary Supplement,* June 26, 1969; *Observer Review,* September 12, 1969; *Books and Bookmen,* March, 1971.

* * *

Van TIL, Cornelius   1895-

PERSONAL: Born May 3, 1895, in the Netherlands; came to United States in 1905, naturalized in 1911; son of Ite and Klazina (Van der Veen) Van Til; married Rena Klooster, September 15, 1925; children: Earl Calvin. *Education:* Calvin College, A.B., 1922; Princeton University, A.M., 1924,

Ph.D., 1927; Princeton Theological Seminary, Th.B., 1924, Th.M., 1925. *Home:* 16 Rich Ave., Philadelphia, Pa. 19118. *Office:* Westminster Theological Seminary, Chestnut Hill, Philadelphia, Pa. 19118.

CAREER: Minister of the Christian Reformed Church. Christian Reformed Church, Spring Lake, Mich., pastor, 1927-28; Princeton Theological Seminary, Princeton, N.J., instructor in apologetics, 1928-29; Westminster Theological Seminary, Philadelphia, Pa., professor of apologetics, 1929-72, professor emeritus, 1972—. Lecturer at the University of Tapei, Kobe Theological Seminary, and National University of Korea, 1960. *Awards, honors:* Professor, honoris causa, Debrecen, Hungary.

WRITINGS—All published by Presbyterian & Reformed, except as indicated: *Paul at Athens,* J. Grotenhuis Lewis; *The New Modernism,* 1946, 2nd edition, 1947; *Common Grace,* 1947, 2nd edition, 1954; (author of introduction) Benjamin Warfield, *The Inspiration and Authority of the Bible,* 1948; *Christianity and Idealism,* 1955; *The Defense of the Faith,* 1955, 2nd edition, 1963; *The Dilemma of Education,* 2nd edition, 1956; *Apologetics,* Westminster Theological Seminary, 1956; *Christian Theistic Ethics,* Westminster Theological Seminary, 1958; *The Theology of James Daane,* 1959; *An Introduction to Systematic Theology,* Westminster Theological Seminary, 1961; *Psychology of Religion,* Westminster Theological Seminary, 1961; *The New Evangelicalism,* Westminster Theological Seminary, 1961; *Christianity and Barthianism,* Baker Book, 1962; *Karl Barth and Evangelicalism,* 1964; *The Case for Calvinism,* 1964; *The Confession of 1967: Its Theological Background and Ecumenical Significance,* 1967; *A Christian Theory of Knowledge,* 1969; *The Sovereignty of Grace: An Appraisal of G. C. Berkoouwer's View of Dordt,* 1969; *The Great Debate Today,* 1970; *The Reformed Pastor and Modern Thought,* 1971; *The New Hermeneutics,* 1974. Also author of *The Triumph of Grace: The Heidelberg Catechism,* 1958—. Joint editor, *Philosophia Reformata.* Contributor to theological journals.

* * *

VARTANIAN, Aram 1922-

PERSONAL: Born November 14, 1922, in New York, N.Y.; married Irka Eitingon, 1948 (divorced, 1961); married Anne Darrow, 1979; children: Michael. *Education:* Columbia College, B.A., 1944; Columbia University, M.A., 1947, Ph.D., 1951. *Home:* 37 Washington Sq. West, New York, N.Y. 10011. *Office:* Department of French and Italian, New York University, New York, N.Y. 10003.

CAREER: Tulane University, New Orleans, La., assistant professor of French, 1951-52; Harvard University, Cambridge, Mass., assistant professor of French, 1952-57; University of Minnesota, Minneapolis, associate professor, 1957-62, professor of French, 1962-64; New York University, New York, N.Y., professor of French, 1964—. *Military service:* U.S. Army, Intelligence, 1943-46. *Member:* Modern Language Association of America, Phi Beta Kappa. *Awards, honors:* Ford Foundation fellow, 1951-52; Fulbright research grant in France, 1962-63; Guggenheim fellow, 1962-63.

WRITINGS: Diderot and Descartes: A Study of Scientific Naturalism in the Enlightenment, Princeton University Press, 1953, reprinted, Greenwood Press, 1975; *La Mettrie's l'Homme Machine: A Study in the Origins of an Idea,* Princeton University Press, 1960; (editor and author of introduction and notes) Diderot, *Les Bijoux indiscrets,* Hermann (Paris), 1978.

Contributor: *Diderot Studies,* Syracuse University Press,

1949; P. Wiener and A. Noland, *Roots of Scientific Thought: A Cultural Perspective,* Basic Books, 1957; *Studies in Eighteenth Century Culture,* Volume I, Case Western Reserve Press, 1971, Volume VII, University of Wisconsin Press, 1978; *Essays on Diderot and the Enlightenment in Honor of Otis Fellows,* Droz, 1974; *Studies on Voltaire and the Eighteenth Century,* Voltaire Foundation, 1976; *Essays on the Age of Enlightenment in Honor of Ira O. Wade,* Droz, 1977; *Enlightenment Studies in Honor of Lester G. Crocker,* Voltaire Foundation, 1979. Also contributor to *Encyclopedia of Philosophy,* 1967, *Dictionary of Scientific Biography,* 1972-73, and *Dictionary of the History of Ideas,* 1973.

* * *

VERBA, Sidney 1932-

PERSONAL: Born May 26, 1932, in Brooklyn, N.Y.; son of Morris Harry and Recci (Salman) Verba; married Esther Cynthia Winston, 1954; children: Margaret Lynn, Erica Kim. *Education:* Harvard University, B.A., 1953; Princeton University, M.P.A., 1955, Ph.D., 1959. *Office:* Department of Government, Harvard University, Cambridge, Mass. 02138.

CAREER: Princeton University, Princeton, N.J., assistant professor of political science, 1959-62, associate professor of politics, 1962-64; Stanford University, Stanford, Calif., professor of political science, 1964-69; University of Chicago, Chicago, Ill., professor, 1969-72; Harvard University, Cambridge, Mass., professor of government, 1972—. Member of committee on comparative politics, Social Science Research Council. *Member:* American Political Science Association, American Association of University Professors. *Awards, honors:* Fulbright fellowship, 1955-56; Center for Advanced Study in the Behavioral Sciences fellow, 1963-64.

WRITINGS—Published by Princeton University Press, except as indicated: *Small Groups and Political Behavior: A Study of Leadership,* 1961; (co-editor) *The International System,* 1961; (co-author) *The Civic Culture: Political Attitudes and Democracy in Five Nations,* 1963; (co-author and co-editor) *Political Culture and Political Development,* 1965: *The Modes of Democratic Participation,* Sage Publications, 1971; (with Norman Nie) *Participation in America,* Harper, 1972; (co-author) *The Changing American Voter,* Harvard University Press, 1976; (with others) *Participation and Political Equality,* Cambridge University Press, 1978.

* * *

VICKERY, Olga W(estland) 1925-1970

PERSONAL: Born August 22, 1925, in Temerowce, Poland; died October 4, 1970; daughter of Paul and Anna (Dobelowska) Wasylchuck; married John Britton Vickery, August 5, 1950; children: Anne Elizabeth (Mrs. William H. Floto). *Education:* University of Toronto, B.A., 1947; Bryn Mawr College, M.A., 1948; University of Wisconsin, Ph.D., 1953.

CAREER: Mount Holyoke College, South Hadley, Mass., instructor, 1951-53; Lake Forest College, Lake Forrest, Ill., instructor, 1956-59; Purdue University, West Lafayette, Ind., assistant professor of English, 1959-64; University of California, Riverside, associate professor of English, 1964-65; University of Southern California, Los Angeles, professor of English, 1966-70. *Member:* Modern Language Association of America, American Association of University Professors.

WRITINGS: The Novels of William Faulkner, Louisiana State University Press, 1959, revised edition, 1964; (editor with F. J. Hoffman) *William Faulkner: Three Decades of Criticism*, Michigan State University Press, 1960; (editor with husband, John B. Vickery) *"Light in August" and the Critical Spectrum*, Wadsworth, 1971. Contributor of articles to professional journals.

WORK IN PROGRESS: Jean Stafford, for Twayne's "U.S. Authors" series.†

*   *   *

VICTOR, Edward 1914-

PERSONAL: Born March 4, 1914, in Boston, Mass.; son of Maurice and Anna (Silbert) Victor; married Jeannette R. Drucker, December 28, 1936; children: Amy Paula. *Education:* Harvard University, A.B., 1935, Ed.D., 1957; Boston University, A.M., 1936, Ed.M. 1941. *Home:* 9819 Calico Dr., Sun City, Ariz. *Office:* School of Education, Arizona State University, Tempe, Ariz. 85281.

CAREER: Boston University, Boston, Mass., instructor, 1943-44; Westbrook Junior College, Portland, Me., head of science department, 1944-51; science supervisor in public schools, Newport, R.I., 1951-57; University of Virginia, Charlottesville, assistant professor, 1957-58; Northwestern University, Evanston, Ill., professor of science education, 1958-78. Adjunct professor, Arizona State University, 1958—. Science consultant for Cenco educational films, Encyclopaedia Britannica Films, and Illinois Bell Telephone Co. *Member:* National Science Teachers Association, American Association for the Advancement of Science, National Association for Research in Science Teaching, Association for the Education of Teachers of Science, Central Association of Science and Mathematic Teachers, Illinois Academy of Science. *Awards, honors:* Received teaching recognition award, National Science Teachers Association.

WRITINGS—Published by Follett, except as indicated: *Friction*, 1961; *Machines*, 1962; *Magnets*, 1962; (with E. Hone and A. Joseph) *A Sourcebook for Elementary Science*, Harcourt, 1962, revised edition, 1971; *Molecules and Atoms*, 1963; *Science for the Elementary School*, Macmillan, 1965, 4th edition, 1980; *Planes and Rockets*, 1965; *Heat*, 1967; *Electricity*, 1967; *Airplanes*, 1967; (editor) *Readings in Science Education for the Elementary School*, Macmillan, 1967, 3rd edition, 1975; *Magnets and Electro-magnets*, Benefic, 1967; *Sound*, Benefic, 1969; *Living Things*, Benefic, 1969.

WORK IN PROGRESS: Revising *Science for the Elementary School*, for Macmillan.

SIDELIGHTS: Edward Victor told *CA:* "I came to write all of these books because I felt that there was a great need to teach better science in the elementary school. Consequently, the books published by Macmillan and Harcourt are designed for the elementary schoolteacher.... I really love writing these books, take great pleasure in the way they are received, and honestly feel that I am making a small contribution towards the better teaching and learning of elementary science."

*   *   *

VINE, Louis L(loyd) 1922-

PERSONAL: Born May 19, 1922, in Brooklyn, N.Y.; married Florence Levine, December 25, 1947; children: Joan, James, Sandra. *Education:* Attended Cornell University, 1939-40; Middlesex University, D.V.M., 1944. *Religion:* Jewish. *Home:* Hidden Hills, Chapel Hill, N.C. *Agent:* George Scheer, Chapel Hill, N.C. *Office:* Vine Veterinary Hospital, Chapel Hill, N.C.

CAREER: Vine Veterinary Hospital, Chapel Hill, N.C., owner, 1944—. Director, Chapel Hill Children's Museum and Zoo; director, Chapel Hill Dog Show and Obedience Trials. Lecturer at veterinary symposiums. *Member:* American Veterinary Medical Association, North Carolina Veterinary Medical Association, Central North Carolina Veterinary Medical Association, Junior Chamber of Commerce, Exchange Club, Masonic Lodge, Shriner.

WRITINGS: Dogs in My Life, Appleton, 1961; *Dogs Are My Patients*, Hammond-Hammond, 1962; *Your Dog, His Health and Happiness: The Breeder's and Pet Owners Guide to Better Dog Care*, Arco, 1973; *The Total Dog Book*, Popular Library, 1977; *Behavior and Training of Dogs and Puppies*, Arco, 1977; *Breeding, Whelping and Natal Care of Dogs*, Arco, 1977; *Common Sense Book of Complete Cat Care*, Morrow, 1978. Contributor to professional journals.

AVOCATIONAL INTERESTS: Sports.

*   *   *

VODOLA, Thomas M(ichael) 1925-

PERSONAL: Born July 11, 1925, in New York, N.Y.; son of Thomas (a musician) and Mae (Grindstaff) Vodola; married Theresa H. Volponi, December 22, 1946; children: Thomas A., Anthony F., Lilimaria, Theresa. *Education:* New York University, B.S., 1950, M.A., 1958; Temple University, Ed.D., 1970. *Politics:* Independent. *Religion:* Roman Catholic. *Home:* 3213 Sharpe Rd., Wall, N.J. 07719. *Office:* Township of Ocean School District, 163 Monmouth Rd., Oakhurst, N.J. 07755.

CAREER: Elementary and high school teacher of health and physical education in Wall Township, N.J., 1955-65; Township of Ocean School District, Oakhurst, N.J., high school teacher of health, physical education, and driver education, 1965-71, district director of health, physical education, and program for the handicapped, 1971—. Part-time instructor, Montclair State College; adjunct professor, Monmouth College. Chairman, New Jersey Youth Fitness Committee, 1964—; co-chairman of subcommittee on the handicapped, New Jersey Governor's Committee on Children and Youth, 1970—; games director, New Jersey Special Olympics, 1971-72, and New Jersey Office of Champion Games, 1972—. *Military service:* U.S. Army Air Forces, 1943-46.

MEMBER: American Association for Health, Physical Education and Recreation, National Education Association, National Council on Measurement, New Jersey Association for Health, Physical Education and Recreation (president, 1969-71), New Jersey Education Association, New Jersey Association for Retarded Children, Phi Delta Kappa. *Awards, honors:* Dr. Thomas M. Vodola Day proclaimed by governor of state of New Jersey, 1975; Humanitarian Award, New Jersey Association for Children with Learning Disabilities, 1976; Dedicated Leadership Award, American Academy of Physical Education, 1977, for developing outstanding physical education program for the handicapped; Professional Achievement Award, New Jersey Association for Health, Physical Education and Recreation, 1979; Honor Award, American Association for Health, Physical Education and Recreation, 1980.

WRITINGS: Individualized Physical Education Program for the Handicapped Child, Prentice-Hall, 1973; *Statistics Made Easy for the Classroom Teacher*, C. F. Wood, 1974; (contributor) Robert E. Weber, editor, *Handbook on Learning Disabilities: A Prognosis for the Child, the Adolescent, the Adult*, Prentice-Hall, 1974; *Diagnostic-Prescriptive Motor Ability and Physical Fitness Tasks and Activities for the*

Normal and Atypical Individual, C. F. Wood, 1978; *How to Establish School, District, or Agency Norms,* C. F. Wood, 1980; *How to Write and Process a Competitive Grant Proposal,* C. F. Wood, 1981. Contributor to publications of American Association for Health, Physical Education and Recreation.

SIDELIGHTS: Thomas M. Vodola told *CA:* "My publications reflect factors that have motivated me throughout my educational career: a sincere belief that all instruction should be *student-centered* and *completely individualized,* an all-consuming desire to help handicapped individuals, and a desire to document the values derived from education through tests, measurements, and research. I started writing because I wanted to express my personal feelings. I felt (and still feel) that there is an inconsistency between what educators say should be done and what we actually put into practice.

"The intent of all my texts is the same: to provide the reader with skills and strategies which can be immediately applied to education. I make every effort to blend theory into practice. My personal pet peeve: most texts are too theory-laden, with little implications for the practitioner."

*　　*　　*

VOGEL, Victor H(ugh)　1905-1978

PERSONAL: Born March 17, 1905, in Kiowa, Kan.; died June 18, 1978; son of Conrad (a building contractor) and Nettie (Hooper) Vogel; married Virginia Evelyn Tinker, June 2, 1931; children: Victor Conrad (deceased), Robert Lance, Albert Vance. *Education:* University of Colorado, M.D., 1929; Johns Hopkins University, M.P.H., 1940. *Home:* 12401 Alba Rd., Ben Lomond, Calif. 95005.

CAREER: U.S. Public Health Service, intern in San Francisco, Calif., 1929-30, ship surgeon, 1930-31, commissioned officer, 1931-59, including various assignments as executive officer of Lexington Hospital, Lexington, Ky., 1935-37, 1943-44, and of Fort Worth Hospital, Fort Worth, Tex., 1938-39, assistant chief of Mental Hygiene Division, Washington, D.C., 1940-41, chief medical officer in Office of Vocational Rehabilitation, Washington, D.C., 1944-46, medical officer in charge of Lexington Hospital, 1946-52, and of activities in Europe, Paris, France, 1952-54, chief quarantine officer of Los Angeles Harbor and Airport, Los Angeles, Calif., 1954-59; ship surgeon, *S.S. Mariposa,* 1959-63; chairman, State of California Narcotic Addict Evaluation Authority, 1963-70; Sylvania Electronics Co., Santa Cruz, Calif., part-time medical director, beginning 1964. Diplomate, American Board of Psychiatry and Neurology. *Member:* American Medical Association, American Psychiatric Association (fellow), American Academy of Forensic Sciences (fellow), American Association of Public Health Physicians.

WRITINGS: (Contributor) *Principles of Physical Rehabilitation,* Lea & Febiger, 1946; (with wife, Virginia Vogel) *Facts about Narcotics* (pamphlet), Science Research Associates, 1952, revised edition published as *Facts about Narcotics and Other Dangerous Drugs,* 1966; (with David Maurer) *Narcotics and Narcotic Addiction,* C. C Thomas, 1954, 4th edition, 1973; (contributor) *Traumatic Medicine for the Attorney,* Butterfield, 1963; (with Virginia Vogel) *Facts about Venereal Disease,* Science Research Associates, 1969. Contributor to professional and other journals. Editorial consultant, *Journal of the American Medical Association.*†

*　　*　　*

von GRUNEBAUM, G(ustave) E(dmund)　1909-1972

PERSONAL: Born September 1, 1909, in Vienna, Austria; came to United States in 1938, naturalized in 1944; died February 27, 1972; buried in Westwood, Calif.; son of Egon and Edith (Weissel) von Grunebaum; married Giselle Eugenie Steuerman, September 9, 1941; children: Tessa Jennifer, Claudia Constance. *Education:* University of Vienna, Dr.Phil., 1931; University of Berlin, post-doctoral fellowship, 1932-33. *Home:* 251 Veteran Ave., Los Angeles, Calif.

CAREER: Oriental Institute, Vienna, Austria, leader of extension institute, 1936-38; Asia Institute, New York, N.Y., assistant professor of Arabic and Islamic studies, 1938-42, chairman of department of Arabic, 1942-43; University of Chicago, Chicago, Ill., assistant professor, 1943-46, associate professor, 1946-49, professor of Arabic, 1949-57; University of California, Los Angeles, professor of history and director of Near Eastern Center, beginning 1957. Visiting professor, University of Frankfurt, 1952, 1956, and 1957. International Symposium of Islamists, chairman in Mainz, 1952, Spa, 1953, and Royaumont, 1962, co-chairman in Bordeaux, 1956, and Brussels, 1961; chairman of international committee, biennial Levi Della Vida conferences. President, American Research Center in Egypt, 1966-72; member of board of governors, American Research Institute in Turkey and Center for Arabic Studies Abroad; fellow, Middle East Institute. Member of joint committee on Near East and Middle East, American Council of Learned Societies and Social Science Research Council. Member of advisory committee, National Undergraduate Program for the Overseas Study of Arabic. Lecturer to university affiliates, religious organizations, and student groups.

MEMBER: International Federation for Modern Languages and Literatures, Centro Scambi e Studi Internazionali (member of international committee), American Oriental Society (vice-president, 1954-55), American Society for the Study of Religion (charter member), American Association for Middle East Studies (member of board of trustees; vice-president, 1963-64, 1964-65), American Historical Association (member of advisory committees of Islamic section and conference on Asian history), American Academy of Arts and Sciences (fellow), American Philosophical Society, Islamic Research Association (Bombay, India; honorary member), Accademia Leonardo da Vinci, Accademia Nazionale dei Lincei, Accademia del Mediterraneo (Palermo, Italy). *Awards, honors:* Dr.h.c., University of Frankfurt, 1964, and Hebrew Union College, 1969.

WRITINGS: Die Wirklichkeitweite der frueharabischen Dichtung: Eine literaturwissenschaftliche Unterschung, Selbstverlag des Orientalischen Institutes der Universitaet (Vienna), 1937; *Medieval Islam: A Study in Cultural Orientation,* University of Chicago Press, 1946, 2nd edition, 1953; (translator with Theodora M. Abel) Burhan al-Din, *Instruction of the Student: The Method of Learning,* King's Crown Press, 1947; *Muhammadan Festivals,* Schuman, 1951, reprinted, Curzon Press, 1976; (editor and translator) Muhammad ibn al-Tayyib al-Baqillani, *A Tenth-Century Document of Arabic Literary Theory and Criticism,* University of Chicago Press, 1950, reprinted, 1975; *Islam: Essays in the Nature and Growth of a Cultural Tradition,* American Anthropological Association, 1955, 2nd edition, Barnes & Noble, 1961; *Kritik und Dichtkunst: Studien zur arabischen Literaturgeschichte,* Harrassowitz (Wiesbaden), 1955; (editor) *Unity and Variety in Muslim Civilization,* University of Chicago Press, 1955.

(Editor with Willy Hartner) *Klassizismus und Kulturverfall,* Klostermann, 1960; *Modern Islam: The Search for Cultural Identity,* University of California Press, 1962; *Der Islam im Mittelalter,* Artemis (Zurich), 1963; *Der Islam: Seine Expan-*

sion im nahen und mittleren Osten, Afrika, und Spanien, Propylaen Verlag (Berlin), 1963, revised edition published as *Der Islam in seiner klassischen Epoche: 622-1258,* Artemis, 1967, translation by Katherine Watson published as *Classical Islam: A History, 600-1258,* Aldine, 1970; *French African Literature: Some Cultural Implications,* Mouton, 1964; (editor with Roger Caillois) *The Dream and Human Societies,* University of California Press, 1966; *Studien zum Kulturbild und Selbstverstaendnis des Islam,* Artemis, 1969.

(Editor with Aziz Ahmad) *Muslim Self-Statement in India and Pakistan: 1857-1968,* Harrassowitz, 1970; (editor) *Logic in Classical Islamic Culture,* Harrassowitz, 1970; *Der Islam: Die islamischen Reiche nach dem Fall von Konstantinopel,* Fischer (Frankfurt), 1971; (editor) *Theology and Law in Islam,* International Publications Service, 1971; (editor) *Arabic Poetry: Theory and Development,* Harrassowitz, 1973; *Islam and Medieval Hellenism: Social and Cultural Perspectives,* Variorum Reprints, 1976. Also author, with others, of *Palestine: A Study of Jewish, Arab and British Policies,* 1947, and of *Dirasat fi 'l-adab al-'arabi,* 1959. Contributor to *Cambridge Medieval History.*

Editor-in-chief, *Bibliothek des Morgenlandes* and *The Islamic World.* Co-founder and member of board of editors, *Comparative Studies in Society and History* and *Journal for the Economic and Social History of the Orient;* consulting editor, *Journal of Near Eastern Studies.* Contributor of articles and translations to professional journals in the United States and abroad.

WORK IN PROGRESS: History of the Muslim World; a history of Islam for a series on world religions; chapters on Islam for a world history.

SIDELIGHTS: G. E. von Grunebaum traveled extensively in the Near East throughout the 1950s and 1960s. *Avocational interests:* Philately.

BIOGRAPHICAL/CRITICAL SOURCES: New York Times Book Review, October 29, 1967; Girdhari L. Tikku, editor, *Islam and Its Cultural Divergence: Studies in Honor of Gustave E. von Grunebaum,* University of Illinois Press, 1971.†

*   *   *

Von LEYDEN, Wolfgang Marius 1911-

PERSONAL: Born December 28, 1911, in Berlin, Germany; son of Victor Ernst and Luise Anna (Reichenheim) Von Leyden; married Iris Edith Sharwood-Smith, 1953; children: Lucie-Marion, Victor-James. *Education:* Attended University of Berlin, 1931-32, and University of Goettingen, 1932-33; University of Florence, Ph.D., 1936; Oxford University, Ph.D., 1944. *Home:* 5 Pimlico, Durham, England.

CAREER: Oxford University, Oxford, England, tutor, 1946; University of Durham, Durham, England, lecturer, 1946-56, senior lecturer, 1956-62, reader, 1962-77. Visiting professor, State University of New York at Binghamton, 1966-67; distinguished visiting scholar in political philosophy, department of government, London School of Economics and Political Science, 1978-81. Librarian and member of governing body, Hatfield College, Durham, 1947-54. Conducted lecture tours to Germany, 1949, 1955, and adult education tutorial classes, 1947-52. Examiner of Ph.D. theses at Oxford and Cambridge Universities. Broadcast on BBC, 1946. *Awards, honors:* Grants from Rockefeller Foundation and Jowett Copyright Fund.

WRITINGS: John Locke: Essays on the Law of Nature, Clarendon Press, 1954, revised edition, 1958; *Remembering: A Philosophical Problem,* Duckworth, 1961; (contributor)

The New Cambridge Modern History, Cambridge University Press, 1961; (contributor) W. Marg, editor, *Herodot,* Wissenschaftliche Buchgesellschaft, 1962; *Seventeenth Century Metaphysics,* Duckworth, 1968, Barnes & Noble, 1969; (contributor) L. W. Lolton, editor, *John Locke: Problems and Perspectives,* Cambridge University Press, 1969; (contributor) G. J. Shochet, editor, *Life, Liberty, and Property,* University of California Press, 1971; (contributor) M. Krausz, editor, *Critical Essays on the Philosophy of R. G. Collingwood,* Oxford University Press, 1972; *Hobbes and Locke: The Politics of Freedom and Obligation,* Macmillan (London), 1981. Also author of *Aristotle on Equality and Justice,* 1981. Member of editorial board of "John Locke's Collected Works," Clarendon Press; compiled original calendar of, and report on, the Lovelace Collection of John Locke's unpublished papers at Bodleian Library, Oxford, 1946. Contributor to philosophical journals in Europe and the United States.

AVOCATIONAL INTERESTS: Music, art history, traveling, languages.

*   *   *

VUGTEVEEN, Verna Aardema 1911-
(Verna Aardema)

PERSONAL: Born June 6, 1911, in New Era, Mich.; daughter of Alfred Eric (a businessman) and Dorothy (VanderVen) Norberg; married Albert Aardema, May 29, 1936 (died, 1974); married Joel Vugteveen, 1975; children: (first marriage) Austin, Paula. *Education:* Michigan State College of Agriculture and Applied Science (now Michigan State University), B.A., 1934. *Politics:* Republican. *Religion:* Church of the Open Door. *Home:* 1423 Forest Park Rd., Muskegon, Mich. 49441.

CAREER: Grade school teacher in Pentwater, Mich., 1934-35, and in Muskegon, Mich., 1935-36, 1945-46, 1951-73, most recently at Lincoln School, Mona Shores; *Muskegon Chronicle,* Muskegon, staff correspondent, 1951-72. Sunday school teacher for twelve years. *Member:* National Education Association, Juvenile Writers' Workshop (publicity chairman, 1955-65), Michigan Education Association, Mona Shores Education Association (corresponding secretary, 1965-70). *Awards, honors:* Caldecott Award, 1976, for *Why Mosquitoes Buzz in People's Ears.*

WRITINGS—Under name Verna Aardema: *Tales from the Story Hat,* Coward, 1960; *Otwe,* Coward, 1960; *The Sky-God Stories,* Coward, 1960; *The Na of Wa,* Coward, 1960; *More Tales from the Story Hat,* Coward, 1966; *Tales for the Third Ear,* Dutton, 1969; *Behind the Back of the Mountain,* Dial, 1973; *Why Mosquitoes Buzz in People's Ears,* Dial, 1975; *Who's in Rabbit's House,* Dial, 1977; *Ji-Nongo-Nongo Means Riddles,* Four Winds Press, 1978; *The Riddle of the Drum, a Tale from Tizapan, Mexico,* Four Winds Press, 1979; *Half-a-Ball-of-Kenki,* Warne, 1979.

WORK IN PROGRESS: How Kipat Shot the Rain on Kapiti Plain and *What's So Funny, Ketu?,* both for Dial; *The Vingananee and the Tree Toad,* for Warne.

SIDELIGHTS: Verna Aardema reports that she "retired from teaching in order to have more time for writing and speaking and storytelling in schools, colleges, and at state and national conventions." She gave *CA* this third-person account of the start of her writing career: "Verna Aardema . . . decided to become a writer at the age of 11. Verna was a bookworm. But in her household, reading was considered a form of laziness. In her case it really was. Because in order to get her to help with the housework, they first had to get her away from whatever book she happened to be reading. She was always in trouble over that.

"Then one day she got an 'A' on a poem she had written at school. When her mother read it, she said, 'Why, Verna, you're going to be a writer just like my grandfather.' That was the first time Verna had been noticed for any *good* reason. And she decided to make a career of being like her great-grandfather!

"At Michigan State College, Verna took every writing course in the catalogue, and in her senior year won three writing contests. She got into the field of folktales sort of by default. The first story she submitted to Coward-McCann, the editor wanted to use as chapter one of a juvenile novel. By return mail, Verna couldn't think of chapter *two*. So she suggested doing a collection of African tales which had not been done for children in America. The editor told her to go ahead. She's been doing folk tales ever since."

BIOGRAPHICAL/CRITICAL SOURCES: Muskegon Chronicle, April 12, 1960, June 20, 1979; *Grand Rapids Press,* April 17, 1960; *Junior Libraries,* November, 1960; *Cleveland Press,* November 8, 1960; *Michigan State University Magazine,* October, 1961.

W

WAGAR, W(alter) Warren 1932-

PERSONAL: Born June 5, 1932, in Baltimore, Md.; son of Walter Warren and Laura (Stoner) Wagar; married Dorothy Bowers, 1953; children: John Alden, Bruce Alan, Steven Lawrence, Jennifer Lynne. *Education:* Franklin and Marshall College, A.B., 1953; Indiana University, M.A., 1954; Yale University, Ph.D., 1959; studied at Queen Mary College, London, 1957-58. *Home:* 724 Pickwick Dr., Vestal, N.Y. *Office:* Department of History, State University of New York, Binghamton, N.Y.

CAREER: Wellesley College, Wellesley, Mass., history instructor, 1958-61, assistant professor, 1961-65, associate professor of history, 1965-66; University of New Mexico, Albuquerque, associate professor, 1966-69, professor of history, 1969-70; State University of New York at Binghamton, professor of history, 1970—, chairperson of department, 1977-80. *Member:* American Historical Association, World Future Society, Conference on Utopian Studies, Middle Atlantic Radical Historians Organizations, New York State Association of European Historians (president, 1977-78), Phi Beta Kappa. *Awards, honors:* Fulbright grant, 1957-58; American Council of Learned Societies Fellowship, 1963-64; National Endowment for the Humanities senior fellowship, 1974-75.

WRITINGS: H. G. Wells and the World State, Yale University Press, 1961; *The City of Man: Prophecies of a World Civilization in Twentieth-Century Thought,* Houghton, 1963; (editor) *H. G. Wells: Journalism and Prophecy,* Houghton, 1964, revised edition, Bodley Head, 1966; (editor) *European Intellectual History since Darwin and Marx,* Harper, 1967; (editor) *Science, Faith and Man,* Walker, 1968; (editor) *The Idea of Progress since the Renaissance,* Wiley, 1969; (editor) *History and the Idea of Mankind,* University of New Mexico Press, 1971; *Building the City of Man: Outlines of a World Civilization,* Grossman, 1971; *Good Tidings: The Belief in Progress from Darwin to Marcuse,* Indiana University Press, 1972; *Books in World History,* Indiana University Press, 1973; *World Views: A Study in Comparative History,* Dryden, 1977. Contributor of numerous articles to journals.

WORK IN PROGRESS: Terminal Visions: The Literature of Last Things, a study of eschatological themes in modern fiction.

SIDELIGHTS: W. Warren Wagar wrote *CA:* "The focus of nearly all my work is the only thing that we can do a damned thing about: the future. I have studied anticipations of the future in modern thought and literature, and I have tried to help shape the future, through advocacy of the replacement of our obsolescent local orders by a democratic and socialist world civilization."

* * *

WAGNER, Karl Edward 1945-

PERSONAL: Born December 12, 1945, in Knoxville, Tenn.; son of Aubrey Joseph (chairman of board of directors of Tennessee Valley Authority) and Dorothea Johanna (Huber) Wagner. *Education:* Kenyon College, A.B., 1967; University of North Carolina, M.D., 1974. *Politics:* Independent. *Residence:* Chapel Hill, N.C. *Agent:* Kirby McCauley, 60 East 42nd St., New York, N.Y. 10017.

CAREER: Carcosa (publishing house), Chapel Hill, N.C., founder and editor, 1972—; John Umstead Hospital, Butner, N.C., resident in psychiatry, 1974; free-lance writer, 1975—. Member of judging panel, World Fantasy Award, 1978. *Member:* Science Fiction Writers of America, North Carolina Writers Conference. *Awards, honors:* August Derleth Award, 1974, for short story "Sticks," and 1977, for short story "Two Suns Setting."

WRITINGS—Fantasy novels, except as indicated; published by Warner Paperback, except as indicated: *Darkness Weaves with Many Shades . . . ,* Powell Publications, 1970, revised edition, Warner Paperback, 1978; *Death Angel's Shadow,* 1973; *Midnight Sun* (story collection), Gary Hoppenstand, 1974; *Bloodstone,* 1975; *Dark Crusade,* 1976; *Legion from the Shadows,* Zebra Publications, 1976; *Night Winds,* 1978; *The Road of Kings: Conan,* Bantam, 1979; (editor) *The Year's Best Horror Stories* (anthology), DAW Books, 1980.

Editor; all story collections by Robert E. Howard; all published by Berkley: *The Hour of the Dragon,* 1977; *The People of the Black Circle,* 1977; *Red Nails,* 1977.

WORK IN PROGRESS: Four novels: *In the Wake of Night, Satan's Gun, Blue Lady, Come Back,* and *Queen of the Night;* two story collections: *In a Lonely Place* and *Silver Dagger.*

SIDELIGHTS: Writing in *Fantasy Newsletter,* Karl Edward Wagner notes: "Ready or not, we're about to live in the age our science fiction prophets warned us about. That's as good an excuse to turn to a fantasy world as you could ask."

Wagner's own fantasy writings often feature the swashbuckling character Kane. As Don Herron writes in *Nyctalops*, "you're not going to do better than Wagner for rousing, old-time S[word] and S[orcery] among today's writers."

BIOGRAPHICAL/CRITICAL SOURCES: Science Fiction Review, February, 1978; *Nyctalops,* March, 1978; *Fantasy Newsletter,* March, 1980.

* * *

WAGNER, Linda Welshimer 1936-

PERSONAL: Born August 18, 1936, in St. Marys, Ohio; daughter of Sam A. (a merchant) And Esther (Scheffler) Welshimer; married Paul V. Wagner January 22, 1957 (divorced, 1975); children: Paul Douglas, Thomas Anderson, Andrea Townsend. *Education:* Bowling Green State University, B.A. (magna cum laude), 1957, B.S. (magna cum laude), 1957, M.A., 1959, licentiate, 1961, Ph.D., 1963. *Office:* Morrill Hall, Michigan State University, East Lansing, Mich. 48823.

CAREER: High school teacher for three years; Bowling Green State University, Bowling Green, Ohio, instructor in English, 1960-64; Wayne State University, Detroit, Mich., assistant professor of English, 1966-68; Michigan State University, East Lansing, associate professor, 1968-71, professor of English, 1971—, associate dean, College of Arts and Letters, 1979—. *Member:* Modern Language Association of America.

WRITINGS: The Poems of William Carlos Williams: A Critical Study, Wesleyan University Press, 1964; *Denise Levertov,* Twayne, 1967; *Intaglios: Poems,* South & West, 1967; *The Prose of William Carlos Williams,* Wesleyan University Press, 1970; *Phyllis McGinley,* Twayne, 1970; *William Faulkner: Four Decades of Criticism,* Michigan State University Press, 1973; *Ernest Hemingway: Five Decades of Criticism,* Michigan State University Press, 1974; *T. S. Eliot,* McGraw, 1974; *Hemingway and Faulkner: Inventors/Masters,* Scarecrow, 1975; (with C. David Mead) *Introducing Poems,* Harper, 1976; *"Speaking Straight Ahead": Interviews with William Carlos Williams,* New Directions, 1976; *Ernest Hemingway: A Reference Guide,* G. K. Hall, 1977; *Robert Frost: The Critical Heritage,* Burt Franklin, 1977; *William Carlos Williams: A Reference Guide,* G. K. Hall, 1978; *Edgar Lee Masters,* Scribner, 1979; *Denise Levertov: In Her Own Province,* New Directions, 1979; *Dos Passos: Artist as American,* University of Texas Press, 1979; *Joyce Carol Oates: Critical Essays,* G. K. Hall, 1979; *American Modern Selected Essays in Poetry and Fiction,* Kennikat, 1980. Contributor of over 130 essays and poems to scholarly and poetry periodicals, including *Kenyon Review, Shakespeare Quarterly,* and *Minnesota Review.*

WORK IN PROGRESS: Critical studies of Ellen Glasgow and E. E. Cummings.

BIOGRAPHICAL/CRITICAL SOURCES: New York Times Book Review, July 1, 1979.

* * *

WAGNER, Ray(mond) David 1924-

PERSONAL: Born February 29, 1924, in Philadelphia, Pa.; son of James and Ethel (Shreiber) Wagner; married Beatrice Walsh, January, 1952 (divorced, 1965); married Mary Davidson, 1967; children (first marriage): Roger; (second marriage): Wendy, David. *Education:* University of Pennsylvania, B.S., 1953, M.S., 1955; San Diego State College (now University), postgraduate study. *Home:* 5865 Estelle St.,

San Diego, Calif. 92115. *Office:* Crawford High School, 55th and Orange Ave., San Diego, Calif.

CAREER: Crawford High School, San Diego, Calif., history teacher, 1957—. *Member:* American Aviation Historical Society, National Education Association, California Teachers Association, San Diego Teachers Association.

WRITINGS: American Combat Planes, Hanover House, 1960, revised edition, Doubleday, 1968; *North American Sabre,* Macdonald & Co., 1963; (with Heinz Nowarra) *German Combat Planes,* Doubleday, 1971; (editor) *Soviet Air Force in World War II,* Doubleday, 1973; *American Combat Planes since 1917,* Doubleday, 1980.

WORK IN PROGRESS: Research on military aircraft history in America and abroad.

BIOGRAPHICAL/CRITICAL SOURCES: San Diego Evening Tribune, February 21, 1961.

* * *

WALCUTT, Charles Child 1908-

PERSONAL: Born December 22, 1908, in Montclair, N.J.; son of Henry Leeds and Clara (Child) Walcutt; married Sue Grundy Bonner, 1934 (divorced); married Jeanne H. Bocca, 1962; children: (first marriage) Margaret Campbell, Philip Lowell. *Education:* University of Arizona, B.A., 1930; University of Michigan, M.A., 1932, Ph.D., 1937. *Home:* 18 Knightsbridge Rd., Great Neck, N.Y. 11021. *Office:* Graduate School and University Center, City University of New York, 33 East 42nd St., New York, N.Y. 10036.

CAREER: University of Oklahoma, Norman, 1938-44, began as assistant professor, became associate professor; Michigan State Normal College (now Eastern Michigan University), Ypsilanti, professor 1944-47; Washington and Jefferson College, Washington, Pa., professor, 1947-48, Wallace Professor of Rhetoric, 1948-51; Queens College of the City University of New York, Flushing, N.Y., associate professor, 1951-58, professor of English, beginning 1958; Graduate School and University Center of the City University of New York, New York, N.Y., professor, 1964—. Fulbright director of American Institute, University of Oslo, 1957-58; Fulbright professor, University of Lyon, 1965-66; summer professor at University of Arizona, University of New Mexico, and Columbia University. Chairman of selection committee for Explicator Prize, beginning 1955. Reading consultant, Council for Basic Education. *Member:* English Institute, Modern Language Association of America, National Council of Teachers of English (member of national advisory council, 1940-44), Reading Reform Foundation (member of advisory committee), American Association of University Professors (chairman, 1946-47), Alpha Tau Omega, Phi Kappa Phi, Phi Beta Kappa, Alpha Kappa Psi, Pi Delta Epsilon, Andiron Club, Fireside Club. *Awards, honors:* Fulbright award, 1957; American Council of Learned Societies grant, 1959; Council for Basic Education research award, 1960-61.

WRITINGS: (Editor) *The Mind in the Making,* Harper, 1939; *The Romantic Compromise in the Novels of Winston Churchill,* University of Michigan Press, 1951; *American Literary Naturalism,* University of Minnesota Press, 1956; (with Sibyl Terman) *Reading: Chaos and Cure,* McGraw, 1958; *Tomorrow's Illiterates,* Little, Brown, 1961; *An Anatomy of Prose,* Macmillan, 1962; *Your Child's Reading,* Cornerstone Library, 1963; (editor with J. E. Whitesell) *The Explicator Cyclopedia,* Quadrangle, Volume I, 1966, Volume II, 1968, Volume III, 1968; *Man's Changing Mask: Modes and Methods of Characterization in Fiction,* University of Minnesota

Press, 1966; (with Glenn McCracken) *Lippincott's Basic Reading*, Lippincott, 1963, 4th edition, 1981; (with Mc-Cracken) *Reading Goals: The Blue Book*, Lippincott, 1966; (with McCracken) *Reading Goals: The Red Book*, Lippincott, 1966; *Jack London*, University of Minnesota Press, 1966; (with McCracken) *The Orange Book*, Lippincott, 1968; (editor) *Seven Novelists in the American Naturalist Tradition*, University of Minnesota Press, 1974; (with McCracken and Joan Lamport) *Teaching Reading: A Phonic-Linguistic Approach to Developmental Reading*, Macmillan, 1974. Also author of *The Dilemma of Private Economy and Public Waste*, 1979. Contributor to literary journals. Editor, *Explicator Checklist*, 1945-58.

WORK IN PROGRESS: A study of the language of the social sciences, tentatively entitled, *Language, Abstraction, and Truth.*

SIDELIGHTS: Charles Child Walcutt told *CA:* "My initial interest in American literature (particularly the novel) has continued unabated, as my many books and articles demonstrate. Beginning in the 1940's, however, I became profoundly involved with the mis-teaching of reading in America and the consequent growth of actual and 'functional' illiteracy. This interest has provoked several books and an important series of reading texts, *Basic Reading.*"

Walcutt says that *The Dilemma of Private Economy and Public Waste* explores "the role of government waste, regulation, and spending in our economy. My plea for less government at every level makes me look very conservative," he explains, "but I am still at heart an Emersonian idealist, rooted in what I believe are the fundamental strengths of the American Dream."

BIOGRAPHICAL/CRITICAL SOURCES: Times Literary Supplement, May 11, 1967; *Criticism*, summer, 1967; *Wisconsin Studies in Contemporary Literature*, summer, 1967.

*   *   *

WALDHORN, Arthur   1918-

PERSONAL: Born September 30, 1918, in New York, N.Y.; son of David M. and Carolyn (Barnett) Waldhorn; married Hilda Kurland, 1942; children: Valerie, Stephen. *Education:* New York University, B.A., 1940, Ph.D., 1950. *Home:* 7 Stuyvesant Oval, New York, N.Y. 10003.

CAREER: Colby Academy, Brooklyn, N.Y., teacher 1939-41; Sewanhaka High School, Floral Park, N.Y., teacher, 1939-41; City College of the City University of New York, New York City, professor of English, 1946-76, professor emeritus, 1976—; New York University, New York City, adjunct professor, 1978-80. Fulbright Professor of American Literature in Milan, Italy, 1958-59, Hull, England, 1965-66, and Tokyo and Kyoto, Japan; lecturer throughout Italy, India, and Germany. *Military service:* U.S. Army Air Forces, 1942-45; became sergeant. *Member:* College English Association, National Council of Teachers of English, American Association of University Professors, New York College English Association (president, 1955-56), New York University English Graduate Association (president, 1956-57).

WRITINGS: (With Arthur Zeiger) *English Made Simple*, Garden City, 1954; (with Zeiger) *Word Mastery Made Simple*, Garden City, 1954; (co-editor) *A Bible for the Humanities*, Harper, 1954; *Concise Dictionary of the American Language*, Philosophical Library, 1956; (co-author) *From Homer to Joyce*, Holt, 1959; (assistant editor) *Good Reading*, New American Library, 1959, revised edition, Bowker, 1978; (co-editor) *American Literature: Readings and Cri-*

tiques, Putnam, 1961; (co-editor) *The Rite of Becoming*, New American Library, 1966; *Ernest Hemingway: A Reader's Guide*, Farrar, Straus, 1972; (editor) *Ernest Hemingway: Critical Essays*, McGraw, 1973.

AVOCATIONAL INTERESTS: Travel, music.

*   *   *

WALKER, (Addison) Mort   1923-
(Addison Walker)

PERSONAL: Born September 3, 1923, in El Dorado, Kan.; son of Robin A. (an architect) and Carolyn (a designer and illustrator; maiden name, Richards) Walker; married Jean Suffill, March 12, 1949; children: Greg, Brian, Polly, Morgan, Marjorie, Neal, Roger. *Education:* University of Missouri, B.A., 1948. *Residence:* Greenwich, Conn.

CAREER: Hallmark Greeting Cards, Kansas City, Mo., designer, 1942-43; Dell Publishing Co., New York City, editor, 1948-50; King Features Syndicate, New York City, creator of comic strips, "Beetle Bailey," 1950—, (with Dik Browne) "Hi and Lois," 1954—, "Sam's Strip," 1961-63, (under name Addison Walker) "Boner's Ark," 1969—, and "Sam and Silo," 1977—. Founder, Museum of Cartoon Art. Former member of President's Committee for Employing the Handicapped. Has given public lectures. *Military service:* U.S. Army, 1943-46; served in Europe; became first lieutenant. *Member:* National Cartoonists Society (former president), Artists and Writers Association, Newspaper Comic Council. *Awards, honors:* Reuben Award for best cartoonist, National Cartoonists Society, 1954; Banshee Award, 1955; National Cartoonists Society plaque for best comic strip, 1966, 1969; I1 Secolo XIX, 1972; Adamson Award, 1975; Power of Printing Award, 1977; Elzie Segar Award, 1977; Fourth Estate Award, American Legion, 1978; Jester Award, 1979.

WRITINGS: (With Dik Browne) *Most* (juvenile), Windmill Books, 1971; (with Browne) *Land of Lost Things* (juvenile), Windmill Books, 1972; *Backstage at the Strips*, Mason/Charter, 1975. Also author of *The Lexicon of Comicana*, 1980.

Cartoon books; published by Grosset, except as indicated: *Beetle Bailey and Sarge*, Dell, 1958; (with Browne) *Trixie*, Avon, 1960; *Beetle Bailey*, 1968; *Fall Out Laughing, Beetle Bailey*, 1969; *At Ease, Beetle Bailey*, 1970; (with Browne) *Hi and Lois*, 1970; *I Don't Want to Be Out Here Any More than You Do, Beetle Bailey*, 1970; *Sam's Strip Lives*, Carriage House, 1970; *What Is It Now, Beetle Bailey?*, 1971; (with Browne) *Hi and Lois in Darkest Suburbia*, 1971; *Beetle Bailey on Parade*, 1972; *I'll Throw the Book at You, Beetle Bailey*, 1973; *We're All in the Same Boat, Beetle Bailey*, 1973; *Shape Up or Ship Out, Beetle Bailey*, 1974.

Take Ten, Beetle Bailey, 1975; *I've Got You on My List, Beetle Bailey*, 1975; *Take a Walk, Beetle Bailey*, 1975; *I Thought You Brought the Compass, Beetle Bailey*, 1975; *Is That All, Beetle Bailey?*, 1976; *About Face, Beetle Bailey*, 1976; *I'll Flip You for It, Beetle Bailey*, 1976; *I Just Want to Talk to You, Beetle Bailey*, 1978; *Looking Good, Beetle Bailey*, 1978; *Give Us a Smile, Beetle Bailey*, 1979; *Up, Up and Away, Beetle Bailey*, 1980; (with Browne) *Hi and Lois Family Ties*, 1980.

Work is widely anthologized in the United States and abroad. Contributor of cartoons to popular magazines, including *New Yorker* and *Saturday Evening Post*. Co-editor of *National Cartoonists Society Album.*

SIDELIGHTS: Mort Walker began his career in the 1940's

as a free-lance cartoonist. Although he was successful as a free-lancer (he was the most widely published cartoonist in the country) he decided in 1950 to try his hand at a syndicated comic strip. He based the strip on a character he had been using in cartoons for the *Saturday Evening Post,* a college student named Spider who habitually wore his hat down over his eyes. King Features Syndicate liked the idea and character but insisted on two changes. First, they wanted the locale to be changed from a college campus to a military base. Second, they wanted the character's name changed because another character in a King Features comic strip already had the name Spider. Walker agreed to the changes. The result was "Beetle Bailey," a comic strip about a reluctant army draftee, similar to Spider in his hat-wearing preference, who lives on a military base called Camp Swampy.

"Beetle Bailey" debuted on September 3, 1950—Walker's 27th birthday—and was an immediate success. Revolving around the activities of Beetle, whose primary activity is avoiding work, the strip features a host of unique characters whose interrelationships provide the fuel for the strip's humor. Some of these characters are Sarge, whose job it is to force Beetle to work, Plato, the local intellectual, and Zero, who is well-meaning but inept. Very little action occurs outside of Camp Swampy or involves anyone but the regular cast of characters. Unlike some other comic strips, "Beetle Bailey" does not make comments on current events or issues. Walker has said: "I try to make people laugh, and keep my own views out of it. People don't want ideas pressed on them. They get plenty of that on the editorial page. I wouldn't want a clown in a circus to deliver an ecology speech. I wouldn't want to find anti-war messages on my golf balls. The papers are full enough of tragedy. The comic pages should be a relief from that other stuff." Over 1,500 newspapers around the world now carry "Beetle Bailey," making it one of the top three comic strips in the field. Toys, games, comic books, and many other products have been inspired by the strip.

After the success of "Beetle," Walker branched off with another strip, "Hi and Lois," which he does in collaboration with Dik Browne. Lois is Beetle's sister and was first introduced in "Beetle Bailey" during Beetle's visits back home. After being introduced, Lois settled down to comic strip life in suburbia with her husband Hi and their four children Chip, Trixie, Dot, and Ditto. Other characters include Thirsty Thurston, their alcohol-loving neighbor, and Abercrombie and Fitch, their philosophical garbagemen. Dealing with the problems of family life in modern America, the strip has grown in popularity until it is now carried in over 600 newspapers throughout the world.

Other strips Walker has been involved with include "Sam's Strip," in which characters from old comic strips make guest appearances and periodical "Comics Character Conventions" would be held, and "Boner's Ark," which features an arkful of animals who sail the seven seas in search of land.

In 1974, Walker founded the Museum of Cartoon Art in Port Chester, New York. The museum collects and maintains examples of comic strips, original artwork, animated films, and other related cartoon works. It now houses over fifty thousand cartoons, making it the world's largest collection. Many thousands of people have visited the museum. As Walker writes in an article for *Horizon:* "Many viewers [of the cartoon collection] enjoy the simple nostalgia of seeing all the old comics characters from their childhood. . . . Other visitors see the historic value of the exhibits, the political cartoon treatment of various presidents, for instance, or the way the average citizen lived in the 1920's or 1930's." The

museum, housed in the architecturally-unique Ward Castle, also includes a library and research center for scholars in the field.

Speaking of the cartooning art, Walker has written: "The comic-strip creator must be a prolific author, as well as an artist, set designer, humorist, casting director, sociologist, and producer. It is one of the few creative areas left where the individual is personally in complete control of his product."

BIOGRAPHICAL/CRITICAL SOURCES: Editor & Publisher, August 12, 1950, October 26, 1968, September 20, 1980; *Greenwich Review,* October 12, 1972; *Christian Science Monitor,* May 2, 1973; *Horizon,* July, 1980.

* * *

WALKER, Warren S(tanley) 1921-

PERSONAL: Born March 19, 1921, in Brooklyn, N.Y.; son of Harold S. and Althea (Loescher) Walker; married Barbara Kerlin (a writer), December 9, 1943; children: Brian, Theresa. *Education:* New York College for Teachers (now State University of New York at Albany), A.B., 1947, M.A., 1948; Cornell University, Ph.D., 1951. *Office:* Texas Tech University, Lubbock, Tex. 79409.

CAREER: Blackburn College, Carlinville, Ill., 1951-59, began as faculty member, became chairman of English department; Parsons College, Fairfield, Iowa, professor and dean, 1959-64; Texas Tech University, Lubbock, professor of English, 1964-71, Horn Professor of English and director of Archive of Turkish Oral Narrative, 1971—. Fulbright lecturer in American literature at University of Ankara, Ankara, Turkey, 1961-62. Visiting summer professor at New York College for Teachers (now State University of New York at Albany), 1957, State University College of Education (now State University of New York College at Cortland), 1959, and State University of New York College at Oneonta, 1980. Director, Fairfield (Iowa) Community Fund, 1963-64. Member of advisory board of Texas Cultural Alliance, 1976—. *Military service:* U.S. Army Air Forces, 1942-45; served in Italy. *Member:* Modern Language Association of America, American Folklore Society, American Association of University Professors, National Council of Teachers of English, Middle East Studies Association, International Society for Folk Narrative Research, New York Folklore Society. *Awards, honors:* Citation from Turkish Ministry of Education for contribution to study of Turkish culture, 1967; citation from Turkish Ministry of State for contributions to study of Turkish folklore, 1973.

WRITINGS: James Fenimore Cooper: An Introduction and Interpretation, Barnes & Noble, 1962, revised edition, Holt, 1966; (with Ahmet Uysal) *Tales Alive in Turkey,* Harvard University Press, 1966; *Plots & Characters in the Fiction of James Fenimore Cooper,* Shoe String, 1978.

Editor: *Whatever Makes Papa Laugh: A Folklore Sheaf Honoring Harold W. Thompson,* New York Folklore Society, 1958; (and author of introduction) James Fenimore Cooper, *The Spy,* Hafner, 1960; (with wife, Barbara K. Walker) *Nigerian Folk Tales* (as told by Olawale Idewu and Omotayo Adu), Rutgers University Press, 1961, 2nd edition, Shoe String, 1980; *Twentieth-Century Short Story Explication: Interpretations, 1900-1960 Inclusive, of Short Fiction since 1800,* Shoe String, 1961, Supplement I, 1963, Supplement II, 1965, 3rd edition, 1977, Supplement I (to 3rd edition), 1980; (with B. K. Walker) *The Erie Canal: Gateway to Empire,* Heath, 1963; (and author of introduction) Cooper, *The Red Rover,* University of Nebraska Press, 1963; *Prose Lyrics: A*

Collection of Familiar Essays, Odyssey, 1964; (and author of introduction) Cooper, *The Sea Lions,* University of Nebraska Press, 1965; *Leatherstocking and the Critics,* Scott, Foresman, 1965; (with Ahmet Uysal) *Turkish Folktales,* Folkways Records, 1965; (with Faruk Sumer and Uysal) *The Book of Dede Korkut: A Turkish Epic,* University of Texas Press, 1972; *Archive of Turkish Oral Narrative; Preliminary Catalogue No. 1,* Texas Tech Press, 1975.

Contributor: Clay Perry, *Underground Empire: Wonders and Tales of New York Caves,* S. Daye, 1948; Mary Cunningham, editor, *James Fenimore Cooper: A Reappraisal,* New York Historical Association, 1954. Contributor of more than twenty articles and reviews to professional and folklore journals. Member of editorial board, Center for Editions of American Authors, Cooper Edition. Member of editorial board, "The Works of Joseph Conrad," Cambridge University Press. Bibliographer for *Studies in Short Fiction,* 1973—.

WORK IN PROGRESS: Twentieth-Century Short Story Explication, Supplement II to 3rd edition; *Archive of Turkish Oral Narrative: Preliminary Catalogue No. 2.*

SIDELIGHTS: Warren S. Walker spends summers at his home, self-built with hand tools, on an island in Georgian Bay, writing, fishing, boating and swimming. He reads French and German and has some facility in spoken Turkish.

* * *

WALSH, Donald Devenish 1903-1980

PERSONAL: Born October 31, 1903, in Providence, R.I.; died May 23, 1980, in Madison, Conn.; son of John Francis and Catherine (Devenish) Walsh; married Donna Rowell (an editor), May 22, 1954. *Education:* Harvard University, S.B. (magna cum laude), 1925. *Politics:* Democrat. *Religion:* None. *Home:* Bushnell Lane, Madison, Conn. 06443.

CAREER: Choate School, Wallingford, Conn., teacher of French and Spanish, 1928-53, 1955-59, director of studies, 1952-53, 1955-59; Modern Language Association of America, New York, N.Y., assistant secretary, 1953-55, director of foreign language program, 1959-65; Northeast Conference on the Teaching of Foreign Languages, Madison, Conn., secretary-treasurer, 1964-73. Trustee of Hammonasset School and The Country School, both in Madison. *Member:* American Association of Teachers of Spanish and Portuguese (president, 1959), Modern Language Association of America, American Association of Teachers of French (honorary member), American Translators Association, P.E.N. American Center. *Awards, honors:* L.H.D., Middlebury College, 1968; Northeast Conference Award, 1974.

WRITINGS: Introductory Spanish: Reading, Writing, Speaking, privately printed, 1944, Norton, 1946, revised edition published as *A Brief Introduction to Spanish,* Norton, 1950; (with Harlan Sturm) *Repaso: Lectura, explicacion, practica,* Norton, 1948, revised edition, 1971; *What's What: A List of Useful Terms for the Teacher of Modern Languages* (booklet), Modern Language Association of America, 1963, 3rd edition, 1965; (with Oscar Cargill and William Charvat) *The Publication of Academic Writing* (booklet), Modern Language Association of America, 1966; *A Handbook for Teachers of Spanish and Portuguese,* Heath, 1969.

Editor: *Seis relatos americanos,* Norton, 1943; *Cuentos y versos americanos,* Norton, 1942, revised edition published as *Cuentos americanos con algunos versos,* 1948, 3rd edition (with Lawrence Bayard Kiddle), 1970; (and author of introduction and notes) Arturo Uslar Pietri, *Las Lanzas colora-*

das, Norton, 1944; (and author of introduction and notes) Jesus Goytortua Santos, *Pensativa,* Crofts, 1947; Goytortua Santos, *Lluvia roja,* Appleton, 1949; Gregorio Martinez Sierra, *Sueno de una noche de agosto,* Norton, 1952.

Translator: Pablo Neruda, *The Captain's Verses,* New Directions, 1972; Neruda, *Residence on Earth,* New Directions, 1973; Julio Alvarez Del Vayo, *Give Me Combat,* Little, Brown, 1973; Ernesto Cardenal, *In Cuba,* New Directions, 1974; Cardenal, *The Gospel in Solentiname,* Orbis Books, Volume I, 1976, Volume II, 1978, Volume III, 1979; (with Robert Pring-Mill) Cardenal, *Apocalypse and Other Poems,* New Directions, 1977; Angel Gonzalez, *Harsh World and Other Poems,* Princeton University Press, 1977; Angel Cuadra, *Poemas en correspondencia,* Solar, 1979; Juana Rosa Pita, *Mar entre rejas,* Solar, 1979. Editor, *Hispania,* 1949-57.

WORK IN PROGRESS: Translating Ernesto Cardenal's *Zero Hour and Other Documentary Poems.*

* * *

WALTON, Clarence C. 1915-

PERSONAL: Born June 22, 1915, in Scranton, Pa.; son of Leo A. and Mary (Southard) Walton; married Elizabeth Kennedy, June 1, 1946; children: Thomas Michael, Mary Elizabeth. *Education:* University of Scranton, B.A., 1937; Syracuse University, M.A., 1938; Catholic University of America, Ph.D., 1951. *Home:* American College, Bryn Mawr, Pa. 19010. *Agent:* Richard Irwin, Homewood, Ill. *Office:* 703 Uris Hall, Columbia University, New York, N.Y. 10027.

CAREER: Duquesne University, Pittsburgh, Pa., instructor in social science, 1940; University of Scranton, Scranton, Pa., professor and chairman of department of history and political science, 1946-53; Duquesne University, dean of School of Business Administration, 1953-58; Columbia University, New York, N.Y., professor and associate dean of Graduate School of Business, 1958-64, dean of School of General Studies, 1964-69; Catholic University of America, Washington, D.C., president, 1969-79; Columbia University, professor of business, 1979—. Visiting professor, University of Helsinki, 1959, University of Buenos Aires, 1961, University of California, Berkeley, 1963-64, and Oregon State University, 1969. Board member, Geico Corp. and Peavey Co. *Military service:* U.S. Naval Reserve, Naval Intelligence, 1942-46; served as communications officer; became lieutenant. *Member:* American Academy of Political and Social Science, Academy of Political Science, American Economic Association, Western Political Science Association. *Awards, honors:* Penfield fellow, Institute of Advanced International Studies, Geneva, 1951-52.

WRITINGS: (With Richard Eells) *Conceptual Foundations of Business,* Irwin, 1961; (with F. Cleveland) *Corporations in Crisis: The Electrical Cases,* Wadsworth, 1964; (editor with Eells) *Readings in Business,* Macmillan, 1964; *Ethics and Ethos in American Business,* Prentice-Hall, 1965; *Corporate Social Responsibility,* Wadsworth, 1966; *The Business System,* three volumes, Free Press, 1967; (editor) *Business and Social Progress,* Committee for Economic Development, 1970; *Ethics of Corporate Conduct,* Prentice-Hall, 1977; *Old Foundations for a New Society,* Pennsylvania State University Press, 1977; *Inflation and National Survival,* Academy of Political Science, 1979; (with F. de Bolman) *Disorders in Higher Education,* Prentice-Hall, 1979. Contributor to professional journals.

WORK IN PROGRESS: Ethics of the Professions.

WALWORTH, Nancy Zinsser 1917-

PERSONAL: Born October 29, 1917, in New York, N.Y.; daughter of William H. and Joyce (Knowlton) Zinsser; married Edward H. Walworth, Jr., February 5, 1944; children: Edward Z., Joyce K., Seth, Cornelia J. *Education:* Smith College, A.B., 1938; Radcliffe College, A.M., 1940. *Home:* 25 Lamberr Rd., New Canaan, Conn.

CAREER: War Department, Washington, D.C., secretary to John J. McCloy, Assistant Secretary of War, 1941-44; Potomac School, Washington, D.C., teacher of English and social studies, 1944-45; Dwight School, Englewood, N.J., teacher of English and social studies, 1947-50. Town of New Canaan, New Canaan Citizens School Council, co-chairman of educational objectives committee, 1955-57, democratic selectman, 1971-74, member of Park and Recreation Commission, 1977—. Trustee of Country Day School, 1958-60, and New Canaan Library, 1960-64.

WRITINGS—All with Polly Schoyer Brooks; all published by Lippincott: *The World Awakes: The Renaissance in Western Europe,* 1962; *The World of Walls: The Middle Ages in Western Europe,* 1966; *When the World Was Rome,* 1972. Contributor of numerous articles to *Junior Encyclopedia Britannica,* 1965-67.

SIDELIGHTS: Nancy Zinsser Walworth wrote *CA:* "Mrs. Brooks and I started writing history books for young people when we found ourselves on a parents' committee to investigate social studies curricula of the local public schools. We were dismayed to find a gap in reference material at the junior high level, particularly in history. Since our children were heading for the junior high at that time, we decided to try to plug the gap.

"We felt that young people would respond to biographies more than to straight chronological history, and so in our three books (covering about a 2300-year span from the beginnings of the Roman Empire to the end of the Renaissance) we tried to write in lively language about a wide mix of people: artists, soldiers, writers, priests, kings, and queens, set against the important events of the time. Our publishers allowed us about eighty illustrations per book and we selected the most vivid contemporary art we could find. We used our children as critics; one of them, by then an architect, did some diagrams and drawings for our book on Rome.

"We have done much traveling to help us recreate historical scenes—to battlefields, walled cities, abbeys and castles, aqueducts, countless museums and innumerable ruins, accompanied by our enthusiastic husbands."

*   *   *

WAMSLEY, Gary L(ee) 1935-

PERSONAL: Born August 18, 1935, in Falls City, Neb.; son of William Charles (a plant engineer) and Jacqueline (Callahan) Wamsley; married Diane M. Stevenson, September 28, 1956; married Susan B. Gauthier, March 5, 1971; children: (first marriage) Christina Marie, Carrie Lynn, Maria Alissa, Alissa Ann; (second marriage) David Bradley, Jonathan Asbury. *Education:* Attended El Camino College, 1953-54; University of California, Los Angeles, B.A., 1958, M.A., 1961; University of Pittsburgh, Ph.D., 1968. *Home:* 57 Indian Meadow Dr., Blacksburg, Va. 24060. *Office:* Center for Public Administration and Policy, Virginia Polytechnic Institute and State University, Blacksburg, Va. 24061.

CAREER: State of California, Department of Finance, Sacramento, assistant budget analyst, 1963-64, research assistant, 1964-65; San Diego State College (now University), San

Diego, Calif., assistant professor of political science, 1966-67; Vanderbilt University, Nashville, Tenn., assistant professor of political science, 1967-72, co-director of Robert A. Taft Seminars on Politics and Government, 1967-70; University of Kansas, Lawrence, associate professor of political science, and director of Institute of Public Affairs and Community Development, 1972-77; Virginia Polytechnic Institute and State University, Blacksburg, professor and director of Center for Public Administration and Policy, 1977—. Director of reorganization study of the Selective Service System for the President's Reorganization Project, 1978-80. Member of Inter-University Seminar on the Armed Forces and Society, 1968—. Participant, National Science Foundation Institute on Mass Political Communications, Ohio University, 1971. *Military service:* U.S. Air Force, 1959-63; became captain. *Member:* International Studies Association, American Society for Public Administration, American Political Science Association.

WRITINGS: Selective Service and a Changing America, C. E. Merrill, 1969; (contributor) Roger Little, editor, *Selective Service and American Society,* Russell Sage, 1969; (contributor) Mayer N. Zald, editor, *Power in Organizations,* Vanderbilt University Press, 1970; (contributor) *Southern Metropolis: Aspects of Development in Nashville,* Vanderbilt University Press, 1975; (with Zald) *The Political Economy of Public Organizations,* Indiana University Press, 1975; (contributor) LeRoy Rieselbach, editor, *People vs. Government: The Responsiveness of American Institutions,* Indiana University Press, 1976.

Also author of several government reports. Contributor of book reviews to *American Journal of International Law, Administrative Science Quarterly,* and *American Political Science Review;* contributor of articles to *Americana Annual,* and to journals, including *American Journal of Sociology, Journalism Quarterly, Business and Government Review,* and *Social Science Quarterly.* Member of editorial board, *Administrative Science Quarterly,* 1972-73; editor, *Administration and Policy,* 1977—.

*   *   *

WARNER, Denis Ashton 1917-

PERSONAL: Born December 12, 1917, in Hobart, Tasmania, Australia; son of Hugh Ashton and Nelly (Callan) Warner; married Peggy Strafford Hick, June 12, 1945; children: Shelley, Nicholas, Annabel. *Education:* Attended Harvard University. *Home:* Ramslade, Nepean Highway, Mt. Eliza, Victoria, Australia.

CAREER: The Mercury, Hobart, Tasmania, Australia, reporter, 1937-39; *Melbourne Herald,* Melbourne, Australia, reporter, 1939-40, war correspondent with U.S. forces in Central Pacific, 1944-46, and with the British Pacific fleet in Central Pacific, 1945; Reuter-Australian Associated Press, Tokyo, Japan, bureau chief, 1947-48; *London Daily Telegraph–Melbourne Herald,* Far Eastern correspondent, 1949-55; *Melbourne Herald,* and other Australian and New Zealand papers, specialist in Far Eastern affairs, 1956-65; *Reporter* magazine, staff correspondent in Southeast Asia, 1965—. Asian correspondent, *Look* magazine, 1968-72. Associate Nieman fellow, Harvard University, 1956-57. *Military service:* Australian Imperial Forces, 1940-43. *Awards, honors:* Cited by Overseas Press Club, New York, for excellence in reporting on Southeast Asia for *Reporter* magazine, 1965 and 1968.

WRITINGS: Written in Sand, Angus & Robertson, 1944; (co-author and co-editor) *Near North,* Angus & Robertson,

1947; *Out of the Gun*, Hutchinson, 1956; *Australia's Northern Neighbors*, Longmans, Green, 1957; *Hurricane from China*, Macmillan, 1961; *The Last Confucian*, Macmillan, 1964; *Reporting Southeast Asia*, Tri-Ocean, 1966; (co-author) *The Tide at Sunrise: A History of the Russo-Japanese War, 1904-1905*, Charterhouse, 1974; *Certain Victory: How Hanoi Won the War*, Hutchinson, 1978; *The Great Road: Japan's March to the Twentieth Century*, Hutchinson, 1980. Contributor to leading Australian and American newspapers and to periodicals.

*   *   *

WARNER, Gertrude Chandler   1890-1979

PERSONAL: Born April 16, 1890, in Putnam, Conn.; died August 30, 1979; daughter of Edgar Morris and Jane Elizabeth (Carpenter) Warner. *Education:* Attended Yale University. *Politics:* Republican. *Religion:* Congregationalist. *Home:* 22 Ring St., Putnam, Conn. 06260.

CAREER: Grade school teacher in Putnam, Conn., 1918-50. Free-lance writer, 1919-79. Involved in publicity work, American Red Cross, beginning 1917; service chairman, Connecticut Cancer Society, beginning 1950. *Awards, honors:* Named woman of the year, Emblem Club, 1965; received 50-year pin and citation, American National Red Cross.

WRITINGS—Juveniles: *The House of Delight*, Pilgrim Press, 1916; *Star Stories*, Pilgrim Press, 1918; *The Boxcar Children*, Rand McNally, 1924, revised edition, Scott, Foresman, 1942; *The World in a Barn*, Friendship, 1927; *Windows into Alaska*, Friendship, 1928; *The World on a Farm*, Friendship, 1931; *Children of the Harvest*, Friendship, 1940; *Surprise Island*, Scott, Foresman, 1949; *1001 Nights* (revision of *Arabian Nights*), Scott, Foresman, 1954; *Peter Piper: A Missionary Parakeet*, Zondervan, 1967.

Juvenile mysteries; all published by Albert Whitman: *The Yellow House Mystery*, 1953; *Mystery Ranch*, 1958; *Mike's Mystery*, 1960; *Blue Bay Mystery*, 1961; *Woodshed Mystery*, 1962; *The Lighthouse Mystery*, 1963; *The Mountain Top Mystery*, 1964; *The Schoolhouse Mystery*, 1965; *The Caboose Mystery*, 1966; *Houseboat Mystery*, 1967; *Snowbound Mystery*, 1968; *Treehouse Mystery*, 1969; *Bicycle Mystery*, 1970; *Mystery in the Sand*, 1971; *Mystery Behind the Wall*, 1973; *Bus Station Mystery*, 1974; *Benny Uncovers a Mystery*, edited by Caroline Rubin, 1976.

Adult: (With Frances Warner) *Life's Minor Collisions*, Houghton, 1921; (with F. Warner) *Pleasures and Palaces*, Houghton, 1933, reprinted, Books for Libraries, 1968; *Henry Barnard: An Introduction*, Connecticut State Teachers Association, 1937; *History of Connecticut*, Connecticut State Teachers Association, 1948. Contributor of essays and articles to magazines.

SIDELIGHTS: Gertrude Warner once told *CA:* "I am telling the exact truth when I say that my sister and I began to write when we were just able to hold a pencil. (She later was known as an essay writer, author of *Endicott and I*, and more than once was compared favorably with a renowned essayist.) As children, we received from our mother a ten-cent blank book to prevent the house from being littered with scraps of paper containing a 'good word' or a full sentence, or even a whole article."

AVOCATIONAL INTERESTS: Engrossing, crewel embroidery.†

WARNER, Oliver (Martin Wilson)   1903-1976

PERSONAL: Born February 28, 1903, in London, England; died August 14, 1976, in England; son of Richard Cromwell and Grace Rankin (Wilson) Warner; married Dorothea Blanchard, 1925 (died, 1937); married Elizabeth Strahan, 1937; children: Charles, Olivia. *Education:* Attended Denstone College; Gonville and Caius College, Cambridge, B.A., 1925, M.A., 1946. *Religion:* Church of England. *Home:* Old Manor Cottage, Haslemere, Surrey, England.

CAREER: Chatto & Windus Ltd. (book publisher), London, England, reader, 1926-41; British Admiralty, London, civilian officer, 1941-47; British Council, London, deputy director of publications, 1947-63. Writer. Member of advisory board, Buckler's Hard Maritime Museum, 1964-70. *Member:* Royal Society of Literature (fellow), Society for Nautical Research (member of council, 1955-63, 1970-71; president, 1973), Navy Records Society (member of council, 1960-64, 1967-68, 1970-72), Royal Automobile Club (London), Three Counties Club (Haselmere). *Awards, honors:* Royal Asiatic Society gold medal, 1920.

WRITINGS: *A Secret of the Marsh*, Dutton, 1927; *Hero of the Restoration*, Jarrolds, 1936; *Uncle Lawrence*, Random House, 1939; *Captains and Kings*, Allen & Unwin, 1947; *An Introduction to British Marine Painting*, Batsford, 1948.

Joseph Conrad, Longmans, Green, 1951, reprinted, Folcroft Library Editions, 1969; *Captain Marryat: A Rediscovery*, Constable, 1953, reprinted, Hyperion Press (Westport, Conn.), 1979; *Lord Nelson: Guide to Reading*, Caravel, 1955; *Battle Honours of the Royal Navy*, George Philip, 1956; *English Maritime Writing: Hakluyt to Cook*, Longmans, Green, 1958; *Sailing Ships*, De Graff, 1958; *Victory: The Life of Lord Nelson* (U.S. History Book Club selection), Little, Brown, 1958 (published in England as *A Portrait of Lord Nelson*, Chatto & Windus, 1958, reprinted, 1979); *Trafalgar*, Macmillan, 1959.

The Battle of the Nile, Macmillan, 1960; *Emma Hamilton and Sir William*, Chatto & Windus, 1960; *The Glorious First of June*, Macmillan, 1961; *The Crown Jewels*, Penguin, 1961; *Great Seamen*, G. Bell, 1961; *William Wilberforce and His Times*, Batsford, 1962, Arco, 1963; (with J. C. Beaglehole) *Captain Cook and the South Pacific*, American Heritage Publishing, 1963; *Great Sea Battles*, Macmillan, 1963; (with Chester W. Nimitz) *Nelson and the Age of Fighting Sail*, American Heritage Publishing, 1963; *English Literature: A Portrait Gallery*, Chatto & Windus, 1964; *The Sea and the Sword: The Baltic, 1630-1945*, Morrow, 1965; *Nelson's Battle*, Macmillan, 1965; (author of introduction) Charles H. Gibbs-Smith, *Balloons and Ships*, Van Nostrand, 1965; (with Margaret Meade-Fetherstonhaugh) *Uppark and Its People*, Allen & Unwin, 1965; (editor) *Best Sea Stories*, Faber, 1965; *Marshall Mannerheim and the Finns*, Weidenfeld & Nicolson, 1967; (author of introduction) Captain Marryat, *Mr. Midshipman Easy*, Pan Books, 1967; *Cunningham of Hyndehope: Admiral of the Fleet*, Ohio University Press, 1967; *A Journey to the Northern Capitals*, Allen & Unwin, 1968; *The Life and Letters of Vice-Admiral Lord Collingwood*, Oxford University Press, 1968.

Admiral of the Fleet: The Life of Sir Charles Lambe, Sidgwick & Jackson, 1970; (editor) *Nelson's Last Diary*, Kent State University Press, 1971; *With Wolfe to Quebec: The Path to Glory*, Collins, 1972; *Great Battle Fleets*, Hamlyn Publishing, 1973; *The Life-Boat Service: A History of the Royal National Life-Boat Institution, 1824-1974*, Cassell, 1974; *Nelson*, Follett, 1975; *The British Navy: A Concise History*, Thames & Hudson, 1975; *Command at Sea: Great*

Fighting Admirals from Hawke to Nimitz, St. Martin's Press, 1976; *Great Naval Actions of the British Navy,* David & Charles, 1976; *Fighting Sail,* Cassell, 1979.

Also author of *The Battle of Jutland, An Account of the Discovery of Tahiti from the Journal of George Robertson,* and *Warfare Under Sails.* Book reviewer, *The Tatler,* 1964-65.

AVOCATIONAL INTERESTS: Numismatics.†

* * *

WARNER, Wayne E(arl) 1933-

PERSONAL: Born June 4, 1933, in Wendling, Ore.; son of Harry E. (a mill worker) and Ethel (Bowers) Warner; married Evangeline Joy Mitchell, May 3, 1958 (died August 28, 1973); children: Lori Lee, Avonna Marie, Lolisa Joy. *Education:* Attended Eugene Technical School, 1956-58; Eugene Bible College, ministerial diploma, 1961; Drury College, graduate study, 1969 and 1970. *Politics:* Republican. *Home:* 1712 West McGee, Springfield, Mo. 65807. *Office:* Assemblies of God, 1445 Boonville, Springfield, Mo. 65802.

CAREER: Ordained minister of the Assemblies of God, 1963; pastor in Yacolt, Wash., 1962 and 1963, Perryton, Tex., 1963 and 1964, and Hopedale, Ill., 1964-68; *Mackinaw Valley News,* Minier, Ill., editor, 1964-68; Gospel Publishing House, Springfield, Mo., book editor, 1968-80; Assemblies of God, Springfield, director of archives, 1980—. *Military service:* U.S. Army, 1953-55; became sergeant. *Member:* Missouri Writer's Guild.

WRITINGS: Good Morning, Lord: Devotions for Servicemen, Baker Book, 1971; *1000 Stories and Quotations of Famous People,* Baker Book, 1972; *Faith, Hope, Love,* Concordia, 1974; *Letters to Tony,* Gospel Publishing, 1975; *Touched by the Fire,* Logos International, 1978.

WORK IN PROGRESS: A biography of evangelist Maria B. Woodworth-Etter (1824-1924).

* * *

WASHBURN, (Henry) Bradford (Jr.) 1910-

PERSONAL: Born June 7, 1910, in Cambridge, Mass.; son of Henry Bradford (a clergyman) and Edith (Hall) Washburn; married Barbara T. Polk, April 27, 1940; children: Dorothy Polk, Edward Hall, Elizabeth Bradford. *Education:* Harvard University, A.B. (cum laude), 1933, graduate work at Institute of Geographical Exploration, 1934-35, A.M., 1960. *Home:* 220 Somerset St., Belmont, Mass. 02178. *Office:* Museum of Science, Science Park, Boston, Mass. 02114.

CAREER: Museum director, mountaineer, and explorer, who began Alpine ascents at age sixteen and Alaska climbs in 1930; Harvard University, Cambridge, Mass., instructor at Institute of Geographical Explorations, 1935-42; Museum of Science, Boston, Mass., director, 1939-80, chairman of the corporation, 1980—. Leader of National Geographic Society expeditions in Yukon, 1935, and over Mount McKinley (photographic flights), 1936-38; consultant on cold climate equipment to U.S. Army Air Forces and director of Alaskan test projects, 1942-45; leader or co-leader of other Alaskan expeditions, mainly on Mount McKinley, 1947, 1949, 1951, 1955, 1965; his first ascents of Alaska peaks include Mount Lucania, 1937, Mount Sanford and Mount Marcus Baker, 1938, Mount Bertha, 1940, Mount Hayes, 1941, west ridge of Mount McKinley, 1951. Director or trustee of John Hancock Mutual Life Insurance Co., New England Telephone & Telegraph Co., National Rowing Foundation, Inc., and WGBH Educational Foundation, Inc.

Member of advisory bodies to National Armed Forces Museum, 1964-68, U.S. Commissioner of Education, 1965-66, and Secretary of the Interior (on national parks), 1966—. Member of board of overseers, Harvard College, 1955-61; member of Massachusetts Rhodes Scholars Committee, 1959-64; trustee of Smith College, 1962-68. Consultant to American Heritage Press.

MEMBER: American Academy of Arts and Sciences (fellow), Arctic Institute of North America (honorary fellow), Royal Geographical Society (London; fellow), American Geographical Society (honorary fellow), California Academy of Sciences (honorary fellow), American Association for the Advancement of Science (fellow), Association of Science Technology Centers (honorary fellow), Groupe de Haute Montagne (France; honorary member), Explorers Club (New York), Harvard Travellers Club (honorary fellow), Tavern Club (Boston); honorary member of other mountaineering, naturalist, and camera clubs in United States, England, and Canada.

AWARDS, HONORS: Cuthbert Peek Award of Royal Geographical Society, 1938, for Alaskan exploration and glacier studies; Franklin L. Burr Prize of National Geographic Society for Alaskan exploration, 1940, and Yukon exploration, 1965; Exceptional Civilian Service Award from Secretary of War, 1946; Ph.D. from University of Alaska, 1951, University of Suffolk, 1965, Boston College, 1974, Harvard University, 1975, and Babson College, 1980; Sc.D. from Tufts University and Colby College, 1957, Northeastern University, 1958, and University of Massachusetts, 1972; Gold Medal of Harvard Travellers Club, 1959; Bradford Washburn Gold Medal and Award was established in his honor by trustees of Museum of Science, 1964; Richard Hopper Day Medal of Philadelphia Academy of Arts and Sciences, 1966; Julius Adams Stratton Prize of Friends of Switzerland, 1970; Certificate of Honor, National Conference on the Humanities, 1971; blue ribbons from U.S. Congress of Surveying and Mapping, 1975, for Squam Range map, and 1979, for Heart of the Grand Canyon map; Gold Research Medal of Royal Scottish Geographical Society, 1979.

WRITINGS: The Trails and Peaks of the Presidential Range of the White Mountains (guide book), Davis Press, 1926; *Among the Alps with Bradford,* Putnam, 1927; *Bradford on Mt. Washington,* Putnam, 1928; *Bradford on Mt. Fairweather,* Putnam, 1930; *Mount McKinley and the Alaska Range in Literature* (descriptive bibliography), Museum of Science (Boston), 1951; (with Caroline Harrison) *Allan and Trisha Visit Science Park* (juvenile), Little, Brown, 1953; *A Tourist Guide to Mount McKinley,* Northwest Publishing, 1971. Editor, "Mount McKinley, Alaska: A Reconnaissance Map," published under auspices of Museum of Science, Swiss Foundation for Alpine Research, and American Academy of Arts and Sciences, 1960. Contributor of features to *National Geographic, Life, Mountain World,* and articles or photographs to *Look, Sports Illustrated, Illustrated London News, Scientific American, Polar Record, New England Journal of Medicine,* and other periodicals in United States, England, Japan, and Germany.

SIDELIGHTS: Before he was out of school Bradford Washburn had climbed the Matterhorn and Mount Rosa as well as most of the major peaks in the Mont Blanc chain, and had photographed the ascent of Mont Blanc and the Grepon for Burton Holmes. Aerial photography work outside of Alaska includes Bermuda in 1938, and ten flights in Switzerland to photograph the Mont Blanc, Matterhorn, and Bernese Oberland areas in 1958. His photographs have been exhibited at the Museum of Modern Art and in "The World from the

Air'' show at Kodak Pavilion, New York World's Fair. In 1971 Washburn did field work preliminary to a mapping project covering 170 square miles in the heart of the Grand Canyon, work financed by a grant from the National Geographic Society. In 1978 he started field work for a new large-scale map of Mount Washington in New Hampshire.

*   *   *

WATERS, Frank 1902-

PERSONAL: Born July 25, 1902, in Colorado Springs, Colo.; son of Frank Jonathan and May Ione (Dozier) Waters; married Rose Marie Woodell, November 11, 1961 (divorced December, 1965); married Barbara A. Hayes, December 12, 1979. *Education:* Attended Colorado College, 1922-25. *Residence:* Taos, N.M. 87571. *Agent:* Joan Daves, 59 East 54th St., New York, N.Y. 10022.

CAREER: Southern California Telephone Co., engineer in Los Angeles, Riverside, and Imperial Valley, Calif., 1926-35; U.S. Government, Office of Coordinator of Inter-American Affairs, Washington, D.C., chief content officer, 1943-46; *El Crepusculo* (Spanish-English newspaper), Taos, N.M., editor, 1949-51; Los Alamos Scientific Laboratory, Los Alamos, N.M., information consultant, 1953-56; C. V. Whitney Motion Picture Co., Los Angeles, writer, 1957. Writer-in-residence, Colorado State University, Fort Collins, Colo., winter, 1966; vice-chairman, New Mexico Arts Commission, 1965. *Military service:* U.S. Army, 1942-43; prepared training films on weapons. *Member:* Phi Kappa Phi. *Awards, honors:* Received silver medal from Commonwealth Club of California, 1942, for *The Man Who Killed the Deer;* received award for achievement in literature, New Mexico Arts Commission, 1975. Academic: Received honorary doctorates from University of Albuquerque, 1973, Colorado State University, 1973, New Mexico State University, 1976, University of New Mexico, 1978, and Colorado College, 1978.

WRITINGS—Novels: *The Wild Earth's Nobility,* Liveright, 1935; *Below Grass Roots,* Liveright, 1937; *Dust within the Rock,* Liveright, 1940; *People of the Valley,* Swallow Press, 1941; *The Man Who Killed the Deer,* Swallow Press, 1942; (with Houston Branch) *River Lady,* Swallow Press, 1942; *The Yogi of Cockroach Court,* Swallow Press, 1947; (with Branch) *Diamond Head,* Farrar, Straus, 1948; *The Woman of Otowi Crossing,* Swallow Press, 1966; *Pike's Peak,* Swallow Press, 1971.

Nonfiction: *Midas of the Rockies: The Story of Winfield Scott Stratton,* Covici-Friede, 1937, reprinted, Swallow Press, 1971; *The Colorado,* Farrar & Rinehart, 1946; *Masked Gods: Navajo and Pueblo Cermonialism,* University of New Mexico Press, 1950, reprinted, Ballantine, 1975; *The Brothers of Tombstone,* C. N. Potter, 1960, reprinted, University of Nebraska Press, 1976; *Book of the Hopi,* Viking, 1963; *Leon Gaspard* (monograph), Northland Press, 1964; *Pumpkin Seed Point,* Swallow Press, 1969; *To Possess the Land,* Swallow Press, 1973; *Mexico Mystique,* Swallow Press, 1975. Contributor of book reviews to *Saturday Review,* 1950-56; contributor of articles to *Yale Review, Holiday,* and other periodicals.

SIDELIGHTS: Frank Waters's books have been published in French, Dutch, Swedish, Japanese, and German. *River Lady* was made into a motion picture by Universal-International, 1949; the film rights to *The Man Who Killed the Deer* were purchased by Sagittarius Productions, Inc. in 1970.

WATSON, Burton (DeWitt) 1925-

PERSONAL: Born June 13, 1925, in New Rochelle, N.Y.; son of Arthur James (a hotel manager) and Carolyn LeHentz (Bass) Watson. *Education:* Columbia University, B.A., 1949, M.A., 1951, Ph.D., 1956; Kyoto University, additional study, 1952-55. *Politics:* Democrat. *Mailing address:* c/o J. P. Dundon, Box 165, North Branch, N.J. *Office:* 507 Sankyu Bldg., 2-6 Jinai-cho, Moriguchi-shi, Osaka-fu, Japan 570.

CAREER: Columbia University, New York, N.Y., research assistant in Chinese studies, on leave in Japan, 1956-61, assistant professor of Chinese and Japanese, 1961-62, 1964-65, assistant professor, on leave in Japan, 1962-67, professor of Chinese, 1967-73; currently free-lance translator. Lecturer in English and Chinese, Kyoto University, Kyoto, Japan, 1959-61, 1962—. Visiting professor of Chinese, Stanford University, 1965-66. *Military service:* U.S. Navy, 1943-46. *Member:* Phi Beta Kappa. *Awards, honors:* Cutting fellowship, 1956-57; received gold medal award from Columbia University, 1979.

WRITINGS—All published by Columbia University Press, except as indicated: *Ssu-ma Ch'ien: Grand Historian of China,* 1958; (with William Theodore deBarry and Wing-tsit Chan) *Sources of Chinese Tradition,* 1960; *Early Chinese Literature,* 1962; *Great Historical Figures of Japan,* Japan Culture Institute, 1978; Michael C. Tobias and Harold Drasdo, editors, *The Mountain Spirit,* Overlook Press, 1979.

Translator: Ssu-ma, *Records of the Grand Historian of China,* two volumes, 1961; *Cold Mountain: A Hundred Poems by the T'ang Poet Han-shan,* Grove, 1962; *Mo Tzu: Basic Writings* (also see below), 1963; *Hsuen Tzu: Basic Writings* (also see below), 1963; *Han Fei Tzu: Basic Writings* (also see below), 1964; *Chuang Tzu: Basic Writings,* 1964, revised edition published as *The Complete Works of Chuang Tzu,* 1968; (and editor) *Su Tung-p'o: Selections from a Sung Dynasty Poet,* 1965; K. Yoshikawa, *Introduction to Sung Poetry,* Harvard University Press, 1966; (and editor) Yuzo Sugimura, *Chinese Sculpture, Bronzes, and Jades in Japanese Collections,* East-West Center Press, 1966; (and editor) *Basic Writings of Mo Tzu, Hsuen Tzu, and Han Fei Tzu* (contains *Mo Tzu: Basic Writings, Hsuen Tzu: Basic Writings,* and *Han Fei Tzu: Basic Writings*), 1967; *Chinese Lyricism: Shih Poetry from the Second to Twelfth Century,* 1971; (and author of introduction) *Chinese Rhyme-Prose: Poems in the Fu Form from the Han and Six Dynasties Period,* 1971; *The Old Man Who Does As He Pleases,* 1973; *Courtier and Commoner in Ancient China: Selections from the History of Former Han by Pan Ku,* 1974; *Japanese Literature in Chinese: Poetry and Prose in Chinese by Japanese Writers,* Volume I, 1975, Volume II, 1976; (with others) *Biographical Dictionary of Japanese Literature,* Kodansha International, 1976-78; *Ryokan: Zen Monk Poet of Japan,* 1977; *Meng Ch'iu: Famous Episodes from Chinese History,* Kodansha International, 1979.

Contributor to *Anthology of Japanese Literature, Modern Japanese Literature,* 1955, and *Anthology of Chinese Literature,* 1965.

WORK IN PROGRESS: Translating with Hiroaki Sato, an anthology of Japanese poetry.

*   *   *

WATSON, Sally (Lou) 1924-

PERSONAL: Born January 28, 1924, in Seattle, Wash.; daughter of William Harris (an electronics engineer) and

Dorothy (an educator; maiden name, Taft) Watson. *Education:* Reed College, B.A., 1950. *Home:* "Sutemi," Fairview Rd., Headley Down, Bordon, Hampshire, England. *Agent:* McIntosh and Otis, Inc., 475 Fifth Ave., New York, N.Y. 10017.

CAREER: Great Books Foundation, Los Angeles, Calif., area representative, 1953-56; Listen and Learn With Phonics (basic reading instruction), Oakland, Calif., executive secretary, writer, and artist, 1957-63. Member of juvenile panel, Pacific Northwest Writers Conference, Seattle, Wash., 1962. Judo instructor, referee, and examiner, 1969-80. Copper enamelist, 1976—. *Military service:* U.S. Navy, 1944-46. *Member:* International Platform Association, Writer's Guild, Mensa, Reed College Alumni Association. *Awards, honors:* Brooklyn Community Woodward School's annual book award, 1959, for *To Build a Land;* named to *Hornbook* honor list, 1963, for *Witch of the Glens.*

WRITINGS—Published by Holt, except as indicated: *Highland Rebel,* 1954; *Mistress Malapert,* 1955; *To Build a Land,* 1957; *Poor Felicity,* Doubleday, 1961; *Witch of the Glens,* Viking, 1962; *Lark,* 1964; *Other Sandals,* 1966; *Hornet's Nest,* 1967; *The Mukhtar's Children,* 1968; *Jade,* 1969; *Magic at Wychwood,* Knopf, 1970; *Linnet,* Dutton, 1971. Also author of a serial, "Heroes of Bet Haverim," published in *World Over.*

WORK IN PROGRESS: Writing science-fiction literature; two judo books, *Judo for Fun* and *No Blood on the Mat.*

SIDELIGHTS: Sally Watson wrote *CA:* "Mother says I wrote my first book at four. It had four pages, was lavishly illustrated, and began 'The sun roze up,' after which she encouraged me to go on writing books for children. But I wasn't having it. By that time I had read *Emily of New Moon* and knew perfectly well that no ordinary type like me could possibly get published. Until I was 28 and re-met an old school friend who *had.* The result was miraculous. All the unused reading, word-collecting, even research flowed forth; I went home that night and started *Highland Rebel,* finished the first draft in six weeks, sold it at first submission without revision—all of which gave me an altogether erroneous idea of how easy it was. Every one I write since is harder than the one before.

"I suppose I write for young people because it's what I still like to read—with girls having adventures, too. I noticed very young that even she-authors tended to write boys for all their heroes, and I was expected to identify with boys —and it was girls who did most of the reading—and even adventurous girls like Caddie Woodlawn tended to sell out for tame domesticity at the end. (*My* heroines may ultimately marry, but they don't get tame; and one of them even sails off into the sunset for a short but active future harassing slave ships.)

"Mainly I tell a story. But my characters have real and complex problems: they have to think about things, they always grow and develop. Not moralizing: just the result of confronting life.

"I tell aspiring writers to read their heads off and experiment. Study the bits you like (or hate) most, to see why. Don't be afraid to imitate styles you like: clearly there's something—an affinity—an I-wish-I'd-written-that! that will eventually turn into your own style. Even quite minor writers can help. (I'm always far too lavish with descriptive words; put them all down at first draft—long strings of them in parentheses, to be sorted and weeded out—or changed altogether later, when I've a bit more perspective, . . . after which my editors weed some more. I do love words!)"

AVOCATIONAL INTERESTS: Scottish dancing, both Highland and eighteenth-century ballroom dancing; Mensa conferences and activities; lecturing, gardening, various handcrafts, including knitting and decoupage.

*　　*　　*

WATTERS, Barbara H(unt) 1907-
(Barbara Hunt)

PERSONAL: Born October 17, 1907, in Chicago, Ill.; daughter of Anthony Charles (a bond broker) and Margaret (Paddock) Hunt; married James William Watters (a research chemist), December 28, 1940 (died, 1968). *Education:* Attended University of Chicago, 1923-25, Art Institute of Chicago, 1925-27, and Brown University, 1954-57. *Home:* 1331 21st St. N.W., Washington, D.C. 20036. *Agent:* Curtis Brown Ltd., 575 Madison Ave., New York, N.Y. 10022.

CAREER: Ran knitting shop, raised chickens in Florida, worked in art gallery and as comparison shopper, and told fortunes while becoming established as free-lance writer. *Member:* Authors Guild of America.

WRITINGS—Under name Barbara Hunt: *Sea Change,* Rinehart, 1946; *A Little Night Music,* Rinehart, 1947; *The Villa and the Horde,* Macdonald & Co., 1957; *Cotton Web,* Macdonald & Co., 1958. Contributor of short stories and articles under name Barbara Hunt to *Coronet, Collier's,* and *Saturday Evening Post,* and reviews to *Providence Journal.*

Under name Barbara H. Watters; all published by Valhalla: *The Astrologer Looks at Murder,* 1969; *What's Wrong with Your Sun Sign?,* 1970; *Sex and the Outer Planets,* 1971; *Horary Astrology and the Judgment of Events,* 1973.

WORK IN PROGRESS: A nonfiction book based on a study of social development from a relativistic and psychological point of view.

AVOCATIONAL INTERESTS: Oil painting, dressmaking, leatherwork, gardening.

*　　*　　*

WATTS, Mabel Pizzey 1906-
(Patricia Lynn)

PERSONAL: Born May 20, 1906, in London, England; daughter of Ernest Henry and Edith (Elias) Pizzey; married William Watts; children: Stanley David McEtchin, Robert Lloyd McEtchin, Mrs. John F. Babcock. *Education:* Attended schools in London, England, and in Edmonton and Vancouver, Canada. *Home:* 1520 Ralston Ave., Burlingame, Calif. 94010.

CAREER: Writer of children's books. Worked in an office in Vancouver, British Columbia. *Member:* Burlingame Writers Club (president, 1962—).

WRITINGS: Dozens of Cousins, McGraw, 1950; (adapter) *Woody Woodpecker's Peck of Troubles,* Whitman Publishing, 1950; *Over the Hills to Ballybog,* Dutton, 1954; *The Patchwork Kilt,* Dutton, 1954; *Bedtime Stories,* Rand McNally, 1955; *Daniel, the Cocker Spaniel,* Rand McNally, 1955; *Goody-Naughty Book,* Rand McNally, 1956; *A Cow in the House* (Junior Literary Guild selection), Follett, 1956; *Hideaway Animals,* Rand McNally, 1957; *Feathered Friends,* Rand McNally, 1957; *Everyone Waits* (Junior Literary Guild selection), Abelard, 1959; *Helpful Henrietta,* Rand McNally, 1959; *Mailman Mike,* Rand McNally, 1959.

My Truck Book, Rand McNally, 1960; *Something for You, Something for Me,* Abelard, 1960; *Weeks and Weeks* (Junior Literary Guild selection), Abelard, 1961; *Famous Folk Tales to Read Aloud,* Grosset, 1961; *Tales of Mystery and Magic,* Grosset, 1961; *Read Aloud Horse Stories,* Grosset, 1961; *Where Is the Keeper,* Whitman Publishing, 1961; *The Little Horseman,* Rand McNally, 1961; *Hildy's Hideaway,* Whitman Publishing, 1961; *The Lion and the Mouse,* Whitman Publishing, 1961; *Little Raccoon,* Rand McNally, 1961; *Funtime: To Read Aloud,* Grosset, 1961; *Little Fox,* Rand McNally, 1962; *Little Tiger,* Rand McNally, 1962; *A Little from Here, A Little for There,* Abelard, 1962; *The Bed of Thistledown,* Abelard, 1962; *Henrietta and the Hat,* Parents Magazine Press, 1962; *The Boy Who Listened to Everyone,* Parents Magazine Press, 1963; *Come Play with Me,* Whitman Publishing, 1963; *A New Suit for Henry,* Guild Books, 1963; *Little Campers,* Rand McNally, 1963; *Little Cub Scout,* Rand McNally, 1964; *The Day It Rained Watermelons,* Lantern Press, 1964; *The Light Across Piney Valley,* Abelard, 1965; *A Visit to Disneyland,* Whitman Publishing, 1965; *Read Aloud Storytime,* Grosset, 1965; *My Father Can Fix Anything,* Whitman Publishing, 1965; *Casey, the Clumsy Colt,* Whitman Publishing, 1965; *Douting Tomas,* Initial Teaching Alphabet Publishing (I.T.A.), 1965; *The Narrow Escapes of Solomon Smart,* Parents Magazine Press, 1966; *The Story of Zachary Zween,* Parents Magazine Press, 1967; *I'm for You, and You're for Me,* Abelard, 1967; *Yin Sun and the Lucky Dragon,* Westminster, 1969; *The King and the Whirlybird,* Parents Magazine Press, 1969.

While the Horses Galloped to London, Parents Magazine Press, 1971; *The Elephant that Became a Ferryboat,* Lantern Press, 1971; *Little Red Riding Hood,* Western Publishing, 1972; *The Basket That Flew over the Mountain,* Lantern Press, 1972; (with Kurt Werth) *Molly and the Giant,* Parents Magazine Press, 1973; *Knights of the Square Table,* Lantern Press, 1973; *Where Is the Keeper?,* Western Publishing, 1979; *Zoo Friends Are at Our School Today,* Western Publishing, 1979. Contributor to *Rand McNally Book of Favorite Pastimes,* 1963.

Under pseudonym Patricia Lynn; all published by Albert Whitman: *Around and About on Buttercup Farm,* 1951; *Digger Dan,* 1953; *Handy Andy,* 1953; *Trumpet,* 1953; *Nobody's Puppy,* 1953; *Busy Bill,* 1954; *Farm A.B.C.,* 1954; *Getting Ready for Roddy,* 1955; *Ho-Hum!,* 1957.

*   *   *

WEALES, Gerald (Clifford) 1925-

PERSONAL: Born June 12, 1925, in Connersville, Ind.; son of Frank and Mary (Burton) Weales. *Education:* Columbia University, A.B., 1948, A.M., 1949, Ph.D., 1958. *Office:* Department of English, University of Pennsylvania, Philadelphia, Pa. 19104.

CAREER: Georgia Institute of Technology, Atlanta, Ga., instructor in English, 1951-53; Newark College of Engineering (now New Jersey Institute of Technology), Newark, N.J., instructor in English, 1953-55; Wayne State University, Detroit, Mich., instructor in English, 1955-56; Brown University, Providence, R.I., assistant professor of English, 1957-58; University of Pennsylvania, Philadelphia, 1958—, currently professor of English. *Military service:* U.S. Army, 1943-46, became sergeant; received Bronze Star and Purple Heart. *Awards, honors:* George Jean Nathan award for drama criticism, 1965.

WRITINGS: Miss Grimsbee Is a Witch (juvenile), Little, Brown, 1957; *Tale for a Bluebird* (novel), Harcourt, 1960; *Religion in Modern English Drama,* University of Pennsylvania Press, 1961; *American Drama Since World War II,* Harcourt, 1962; (editor) *Five Edwardian Plays,* Hill &

Wang, 1962; (editor) *Eleven Plays,* Norton, 1964; *A Play and Its Parts,* Basic Books, 1964; *Miss Grimsbee Takes a Vacation* (juvenile), Little, Brown, 1965; *Tennessee Williams,* University of Minnesota Press, 1965; (editor) *The Plays of William Wycherley,* Doubleday, 1966; (editor) Arthur Miller, *Death of a Salesman,* Viking, 1967; *The Jumping-Off Place: American Drama in the 1960s,* Macmillan, 1969; *Clifford Odets, Playwright,* Bobbs-Merrill, 1971; (editor) Arthur Miller, *The Crucible,* Viking, 1971; (editor with R. J. Nelson) *Revolution* (play collection), McKay, 1975; (editor with Nelson) *Enclosure* (play collection), McKay, 1975. Drama critic for *Commonweal.* Contributor of numerous chapters to books; contributor to magazines and newspapers.

WORK IN PROGRESS: A study of American film comedy of the 1930s.

*   *   *

WEATHERHEAD, A(ndrew) Kingsley 1923-

PERSONAL: Born October 8, 1923, in Manchester, England; son of Leslie Dixon (a minister and writer) and Evelyn (Triggs) Weatherhead; married Ingrid Lien, 1952; children: Lyn Kristin, Leslie Richard, Andrea Kathryn. *Education:* University of Cambridge, B.A., 1944, M.A., 1949; University of Edinburgh, M.A., 1946; University of Washington, Seattle, Ph.D., 1958. *Home:* 2698 Fairmount Blvd., Eugene, Ore. 97403. *Office:* Department of English, University of Oregon, Eugene, Ore. 97403.

CAREER: University of Puget Sound, Tacoma, Wash., 1951-58, began as instructor, became assistant professor; Louisana State University (now University of New Orleans), New Orleans, associate professor, 1958-60; University of Oregon, Eugene, professor of English, 1960—. *Member:* Modern Language Association of America, American Association of University Professors.

WRITINGS: A Reading of Henry Green, University of Washington Press, 1961; *The Edge of the Image: Marianne Moore, William Carlos Williams, and Some Other Poets,* University of Washington Press, 1967; (editor with Stanley Greenfield) *The Poem,* Appleton-Century-Crofts, 1967; *Stephen Spender and the Thirties,* Bucknell University Press, 1975; *Leslie Weatherhead: A Personal Portrait,* Abingdon, 1975. Contributor to *Modern Fiction Studies, Accent, Twentieth Century Literature,* and other periodicals.

SIDELIGHTS: Poetry reviewer, Ralph J. Mills, Jr. writes that A. Kingsley Weatherhead's *The Edge of the Image* "is a close examination of the poems of W. C. Williams and Marianne Moore. But the author goes even further in exploring the nature of that modernist poetry whose stress is on the primacy of the image and 'the practice of presenting an object apparently for itself'; an important chapter discusses crucial differences in theory and practice between 'imagination and fancy' as they determine poetic structure. The concluding portion of this admirable essay is devoted to some of the inheritors of the William-Pound tradition, notably, Charles Olson, Denise Levertov, and Robert Duncan."

BIOGRAPHICAL/CRITICAL SOURCES: Poetry, January, 1969.

*   *   *

WEBB, Wilse B(ernard) 1920-

PERSONAL: Born October 13, 1920, in Hollandale, Miss.; son of Wilse Lent and Estelle (Bernard) Webb; married Mary Hayward, 1942; children: Ann, Jean, Thomas, Molly. *Education:* Louisiana State University, B.A., 1941; University of Iowa, M.A., 1943, Ph.D., 1947. *Religion:* Episcopalian. *Home:* 405 Northeast 4th Ave., Gainesville, Fla. *Office:* Department of Psychology, University of Florida, Gainesville, Fla. 32601.

CAREER: University of Tennessee, Knoxville, assistant professor, 1947-48; Washington University, St. Louis, Mo., assistant professor, 1948-53; U.S. Naval School of Aviation Medicine, Pensacola, Fla., head of aviation psychology laboratory, 1953-58; University of Florida, Gainesville, head professor, department of psychology, 1958-69, graduate research professor, 1969—. *Military service:* U.S. Air Force, four years; became first lieutenant; awarded four battle stars. *Member:* American Psychological Association, American Association for the Advancement of Science, Southern Society for Philosophy and Psychology (president, 1959-60), Sigma Xi, Sigma Alpha Epsilon.

WRITINGS: Profession of Psychology, Holt, 1962; (with Robert L. Williams) *Sleep Therapy*, C. C Thomas, 1966; *Sleep: An Active Process*, Scott, Foresman, 1973; *Sleep: The Gentle Tyrant*, Prentice-Hall, 1975; *Current Sleep Research: Methods and Findings*, American Psychological Association, in press. Contributor of over one hundred articles to professional journals.

* * *

WEBER, Carl J(efferson) 1894-1966

PERSONAL: Born January 20, 1894, in Baltimore, Md.; died December 20, 1966; son of A. S. (a clergyman) and Lora (Jefferson) Weber; married Clara W. Carter, June 23, 1921; children: David C., Dorothy C. (Mrs. William H. Trogdon). *Education:* Attended Baltimore Junior College, 1908-1910; Johns Hopkins University, B.A., 1914; Oxford University, B.A., 1916, M.A., 1920. *Home:* 42 Burleigh St., Waterville, Me.

CAREER: Colby College, Waterville, Me., 1919-59, became Roberts Professor of English Literature, curator of rare books and manuscripts, Colby College Library, 1940-59. Visiting professor at Gonzaga University, 1965-66; visiting summer professor at Johns Hopkins University, University of Maine, West Virginia University, University of Southern California, New York University, University of North Carolina, University of Colorado, and University of California, Los Angeles. *Military service:* U.S. Army, 69th Field Artillery, adjutant, 1918; became captain in Field Artillery Reserve Corps. *Member:* Modern Langauge Association of America (secretary, Victorian Group, 1938-41), Phi Beta Kappa. *Awards, honors:* Rhodes Scholar to Queen's College, Oxford University, 1914-17; Guggenheim fellow, 1944-45; American Council of Learned Societies awards, 1962 and 1964; D.Litt. from Franklin and Marshall College, 1938; D.H.L. from Colby College, 1959.

WRITINGS: Rebekah Owen and Thomas Hardy, Colby College Press, 1939; *Hardy of Wessex: A Centennial Biography*, Columbia University Press, 1940, revised edition, 1965; *Thomas Hardy in Maine*, Richard West, 1942, reprinted, Haskell House, 1975; (compiler) *The First Hundred Years of Thomas Hardy*, Russell, 1942, reprinted, 1965; *Hardy in America*, Colby College Press, 1946, reprinted, Russell, 1966; *A Bibliography of Jacob Abbott*, Colby College Press, 1948; *A Thousand and One Fore-Edge Paintings*, Colby College Press, 1949; *The Tragedy of Little Hintock*, Richard West, 1950; *Hardy and the Lady from Madison Square*, Colby College Press, 1952, reprinted, Kennikat, 1973; (editor of centennial edition) *FitzGerald's Rubaiyat*, Colby College Press, 1959; (editor) Hardy, *Far from the Madding*

Crowd, Rinehart, 1959; *The Rise and Fall of James Ripley Osgood*, Colby College Press, 1959; (editor) Hardy, *Dearest Emmie*, Macmillan (London), 1963; (editor) Hardy, *Love Poems*, Macmillan (London), 1963; *The First Hundred Years of Thomas Hardy*, Russell, 1965; (editor) Hardy, *An Indiscretion in the Life of an Heiress*, Russell, 1965; *Fore-Edge Painting*, Harvey House, 1966; (editor with wife, Clara C. Weber) *Max Gate Letters*, Anthoensen Press, 1967. Contributor of articles to literary journals. Editor, *Colby Mercury*, 1929-42, and *Colby Library Quarterly*, 1943-59.

BIOGRAPHICAL/CRITICAL SOURCES: Colby Library Quarterly, June, 1959; *New York Times*, December 21, 1966.†

* * *

WEES, Frances Shelley 1902-
(Frances Shelley)

PERSONAL: Born April 29, 1902, in Gresham, Ore.; daughter of Ralph Eaton and Rose Emily (Shelley) Johnson; married W. R. Wees, 1924; children: Margarita Josephine Wees Smith, Timothy John. *Education:* Saskatoon Normal School, teacher's certificate, 1923. *Home and office:* R.R. 3, Stouffville, Ontario, Canada. *Agent:* Curtis Brown Ltd., 575 Madison Ave., New York, N.Y. 10022.

CAREER: Director, Canadian Chautauquas, 1924-31; Company of Public Relations, Toronto, Ontario, account executive, 1941-45; United Nations Relief and Rehabilitation Administration, Ottawa, Ontario, executive director of national clothing collection, 1946. Public relations consultant for Toronto Art Gallery, Lever Brothers, other companies and organizations. Lecturer to Canadian women's organizations. *Member:* Canadian Women's Press Club, Daughters of the American Revolution, Canadian Authors' Association, Mystery Writers of America, National Genealogical Society, British Genealogical Society, New England Historical and Genealogical Society, Heliconian Club (Toronto).

WRITINGS: The Maestro Murders, Mystery League, 1931; *The Mystery of the Creeping Man*, Macrae Smith, 1931; *Detectives Ltd.*, Eyre & Spottiswoode, 1933; *Romance Island*, Macrae Smith, 1933; *Honeymoon Mountain*, Macrae Smith, 1934; *It Began in Eden*, Macrae Smith, 1936; *Untravelled World*, Eyre & Spottiswoode, 1936; "Pathways to Reading" series, Gage, 1937-38; Volume I: *Baby, Sally, and Joe*, Volume II: *Home and Round About*, Volume III: *The Open Door*, Volume IV: *Storyland*, Volume X: *Golden Windows; Lost House*, Macrae Smith, 1938; (with J. E. Poirier) "J'Apprends a Lire" series, Gage, 1939.

A Star for Susan, Macrae Smith, 1940; *Someone Called Maggie Lane*, Macrae Smith, 1947; *Under the Quiet Water*, Macrae Smith, 1949; *Melody Unheard*, Macrae Smith, 1950; *M'Lord, I Am Not Guilty*, Doubleday, 1954; *The Keys of My Prison*, Doubleday, 1956; *This Necessary Murder*, Jenkins, 1957; *Where Is Jenny Now?*, Doubleday, 1958; *The Country of the Strangers*, Doubleday, 1960; *Dangerous Deadline*, Ward, Lock, 1961; *The Treasure of Echo Valley*, Abelard, 1964; *Mystery in Newfoundland*, Abelard, 1965; *Faceless Enemy*, Doubleday, 1966; *The Last Concubine*, Abelard, 1970; *The Mystery of the Secret Tunnel*, Scholastic Book Services, 1977, revised edition, 1979. Contributor to Canadian, British, and American periodicals including *MacLean's*, *Saturday Night*, *Chatelaine*, *Woman's Home Companion*, *Argosy*, and *Ladies' Home Journal*.

SIDELIGHTS: Frances Shelley Wees wrote *CA:* "My mystery story, *Lost House*, published in 1938, is the first novel published about marihuana. It was published in 1938 after having been written four or five years earlier, and rejected by my agent because 'nobody will ready a book about an unknown drug.' I had got my information about marihuana from a book on Central America by W. Lavallin Puxley, published by Dodd, Mead in 1928. When marihuana became known, my agent wrote and asked what I had done with my old script. I had kept it—all but the past eleven pages, which I rewrote. Our present country place, now a permanent home, was bought with the proceeds [of the sale]—and is called 'Lost House.'

"My genealogical studies have proved completely engrossing, and I am only now trying to collect my material into one book. Since I live away out in the country and am not socially-minded, I have had time to proceed. I joined all the genealogical societies I could find, and got in touch with genealogical publishers. It was necessary for me to buy the very expensive books I needed—but they are a good investment. . . . The results to me are slightly astounding. I have found my premise to be absolutely true—we are all much more closely related than we dream. My basic family name is Johnson: my father's family descend from Captain John Johnson of Roxbury, Mass. in 1630. He has no English ancestry, but the mothers of the Johnson line do. . . . My problem is how to make the final report interesting to everyone, not just members of this family complex. I hope I can."

Wees visited the Soviet Union in 1957, and Red China in 1959, traveling on a Canadian passport (she has dual nationality). Many of her mystery novels have been translated into German and Scandinavian.

AVOCATIONAL INTERESTS: Genealogical research.

* * *

WEHEN, Joy DeWeese
(Jennifer Wade)

PERSONAL: Born in Penang, Malaya; daughter of Stanley (a financial consultant) and Dorothy (a former newspaper writer; maiden name DeWeese) Wehen. *Education:* Educated at private schools in British Columbia, California, Connecticut, and Switzerland; also studied in England. *Religion:* Episcopalian. *Residence:* San Francisco, Calif.

CAREER: Writer of suspense fiction for young people and adults. Life governor of the Royal Hospital for Incurables. *Member:* Authors League of America, English-Speaking Union (founder, first chairman, Younger Members Group of California), DeYoung Museum Society. *Awards, honors:* Second prize in *Writer's Digest* international short story contest, for "Gift Wrap with Love," 1965; $1,000 national award from English-Speaking Union for best essay on ways of promoting Anglo-American solidarity and friendship.

WRITINGS: Stairway to a Secret (Junior Literary Guild selection), Dutton, 1953, included in *Best Loved Girls' Books,* Doubleday, 1961; *The Tower in the Sky* (Junior Literary Guild selection), Dutton, 1955; *Stranger at Golden Hill,* Duell, Sloan & Pearce, 1961; *The Silver Cricket* (Junior Literary Guild selection), Duell, Sloan & Pearce, 1966; *So Far from Malabar,* Hawthorn, 1970; (under pseudonym Jennifer Wade) *The Singing Wind,* Coward, 1977. Contributor to *New Streets and Roads;* contributor to *Gourmet, Time and Tide* (Great Britian), *Detective Book* magazine, *American Girl, Jack and Jill, Christian Science Monitor, Opera and Concert, Diplomat, Design, Horizon,* and other publications. California editor of *Antique Monthly,* 1976.

SIDELIGHTS: Joy DeWeese Wehen wrote *CA:* "With my last book, written under the pseudonym of Jennifer Wade, I

changed from writing educational adventure books for teenagers to that of romantic suspense fiction for adults. One of the main reasons was the continual lowering of the age definition of 'young adult' by today's publishers. When I first began writing for teenagers, the field was considered for 16-up; my heroine would be in her late teens, the hero in his early 20's: I was really writing about adults. But gradually, my editors began asking me to consider my audience as younger and younger until 'young adult' became 12 years old! They still wanted adult plots, but much shorter books, and with vocabulary limitations. I decided it was time to switch to writing romantic suspense for real adults and judging by the reception of *The Singing Wind* by both readers and critics, I made the right decision. But even in my adult fiction, I try to lift it a little out of the rut of a run-of-the-mill Gothic by adding historical color and information (carefully researched) details of food, costume, architecture and especially furniture, as well as having one particular and little-known theme running through the book.

"My advice to any young writer is a variation on the familiar 'write about what you know.' To me that misses the entire point of why one writes at all. What is far more important is: 'Write about what you *love.*' It doesn't matter whether it's Salt Lake City or Samarkand, Renaissance painting or New England recipes, if you love it, that passion will communicate itself to your readers and what better definition is there of good writing than *passion on paper?*"

* * *

WEINBERG, Gerhard L(udwig) 1928-

PERSONAL: Born January 1, 1928, in Hanover, Germany; son of Max B. (an accountant) and Kathe (Grunebaum) Weinberg; married Wilma Jeffrey, March 29, 1958. *Education:* New York College for Teachers (now State University of New York at Albany), B.A., 1948; University of Chicago, M.A., 1949, Ph.D., 1951. *Politics:* Democratic. *Religion:* Jewish. *Home:* 331 Azalea Dr., Chapel Hill, N.C. 27514. *Office:* Department of History, University of North Carolina, Chapel Hill, N.C. 27514.

CAREER: Columbia University, research analyst in war documentation project in Alexandria, Va., 1951-54; University of Chicago, Chicago, Ill., lecturer in modern European history, 1954-55; University of Kentucky, Lexington, visiting lecturer, 1955-56, assistant professor of modern European history, 1957-59; American Historical Association, Alexandria, Va., director of microfilm project, 1956-57; University of Michigan, Ann Arbor, associate professor, 1959-63, professor of modern European history, 1963-74; University of North Carolina at Chapel Hill, William Rand Kenan, Jr. Professor of History, 1974—. Consultant on German documents microfilming, American Historical Association, 1957-60. Chairman, Ann Arbor City Democratic party, 1961-63; member, Democratic State Central Committee of Michigan, 1963-67. *Military Service:* U.S. Army, 1946-47. *Member:* American Historical Association, American Committee on the History of the Second World War, Conference Group for Central European History, Coordinating Committee on Women in the Historical Profession. *Awards, honors:* Rockefeller Foundation and Social Science Research Council fellow, 1962-63; American Council of Learned Societies fellow, 1965-66; Guggenheim fellow, 1971-72; George Louis Beer Prize from American Historical Association, 1972, for *The Foreign Policy of Hitler's Germany;* National Endowment for the Humanities fellow, 1978-79.

WRITINGS: (With others) *Guide to Captured German Documents,* Maxwell Air Force Base, 1952; *Germany and the Soviet Union, 1939-41,* E. J. Brill, 1954, Humanities, 1972; (editor) *Hitlers Zweites Buch: Ein Dokument aus dem Jahre 1928,* Deutsche Verlags-Anstalt, 1961; (with John Armstrong and others) *Soviet Partisans in World War II,* University of Wisconsin Press, 1964; *The Foreign Policy of Hitler's Germany, 1933-36: Diplomatic Revolution in Europe,* University of Chicago Press, 1969; (editor) *Transformation of a Continent: Europe in the Twentieth Century,* Burgess, 1975; *The Foreign Policy of Hitler's Germany: Starting World War II, 1937-1939,* University of Chicago Press, 1980. Also author of guides to German records for National Archives. Contributor of articles and reviews to professional journals.

WORK IN PROGRESS: "A political, military, and diplomatic history of World War II including both sides and covering Europe and the Pacific."

*   *   *

WEINTRAUB, Wiktor   1908-

PERSONAL: Born April 10, 1908, in Zawiercie, Poland; son of Maurycy and Eugenia Rebeka (Dobrzynski) Weintraub; married Anna Tenenbaum, 1934 (died, 1967); married Maria Evelina Zoltowska, 1974. *Education:* Crakow University, M.A., 1929, Ph.D., 1930. *Home:* 383 Broadway, Cambridge, Mass. 02139. *Office:* Harvard University, 171 Widener, Cambridge, Mass. 02138.

CAREER: Literary critic in Warsaw, Poland, 1932-39; editor of a Polish fortnightly in Jerusalem, Palestine, 1942-45; freelance writer in London, England, 1945-50; Harvard University, Cambridge, Mass., visiting lecturer, 1950-54, associate professor, 1954-59, professor of Slavic languages and literature, 1959-71, Alfred Jurzykowski Professor of Polish Language and Literature, 1971-78, professor emeritus, 1978—. *Member:* American Association for Advancement of Slavic Studies. *Awards, honors:* Guggenheim fellowship, 1954.

WRITINGS: The Style of Jan Kochanowski (in Polish), Kasa im Mianowskiego, 1923; *The Poetry of Adam Mickiewicz,* Mouton, 1954; *Literature as Prophecy,* Mouton, 1959; *Profecja i Profesura: Mickiewicz, Michelet i Quinet* (title means "Prophecy and Professorship: Mickiewicz, Michelet, and Quinet"), Panstwowy Instytut Wydawniczy, 1975; *Rzecz Czarnoleska* (title means "The Poetry of Jan Kochanowski"), Wydawnictuo Literackie, 1977; *Od Rej do Boya* (title means "From Rej to Boy"), Panstwowy Instytut Wydawniczy, 1977. Contributor to journals of Slavic studies.

WORK IN PROGRESS: Mickiewicz's Mystical Poetics.

*   *   *

WEISS, Paul   1901-

PERSONAL: Born May 19, 1901, in New York, N.Y.; son of Samuel (a laborer) and Emma (Rothschild) Weiss; married Victoria Brodkin, October 27, 1928 (died, 1953); children: Judith, Jonathan. *Education:* City College (now City College of the City University of New York), B.A. (cum laude), 1927; Harvard University (studied under Alfred North Whitehead), M.A., 1928, Ph.D., 1929. *Religion:* Jewish. *Office:* Department of Philosophy, Catholic University of America, Washington, D.C. 20007.

CAREER: Harvard University, Cambridge, Mass., instructor and tutor in philosophy, 1930-31; Radcliffe College, Cambridge, instructor in philosophy, 1930-31; Bryn Mawr College, Bryn Mawr, Pa., associate in philosophy, 1931-33, associate professor, 1933-40, professor of philosophy, 1940-

46, chairman of department, 1944-46; Yale University, New Haven, Conn., professor of philosophy, 1946-63, Sterling Professor of Philosophy, 1963-69, fellow of Ezra Stiles College; Catholic University of America, Washington, D.C., Heffer Professor of Philosophy, 1969—. Hebrew University, Jerusalem, Israel, visiting professor of philosophy, 1951, Orde Wingate Lecturer, 1954; visiting professor at Yale University, 1945-46, and University of Southern California, 1964. Lecturer, Aspen Institute and University of Denver, both 1952; Powell Lecturer, University of Indiana, 1958; Gates Lecturer, Grinnell College, 1960; Matchette Lecturer, Purdue University, 1961, and Wesleyan College, 1963; Aquinas Lecturer, University of Marquette, 1963, and St. Mary's College, 1971; Rhodes Lecturer, Haverford College, 1964; Phi Beta Kappa Lecturer, 1968-69. Lecturer at numerous other universities and colleges. Member of board of governors, Hebrew University, 1970—; member of board of directors, Luce Foundation.

MEMBER: American Philosophical Association, Conference of Science, Philosophy and Religion (founding member), C. S. Peirce Society (founding member; president, 1952), Philosophy of Education Society (founder; vice-president), Philosophical Society for the Study of Sport (founder; president, 1973), Metaphysical Society of America (founder; president, 1951-52; councillor, 1953-56), Societe Europeanne de Culture, American Association for Middle East Studies, American Association of University Professors, Phi Beta Kappa, New York Philosophic Club, Aurelian Club, Morys Club, Elizabethan Club. *Awards, honors:* Guggenheim fellowship, 1938; Townsend Harris Medalist, 1964; Rockefeller grant to India and Israel, 1954; De Vane Medalist, Yale University, 1972; City College of the City University of New York Medalist, 1973; National Endowment for the Humanities study grant, 1973; Hofstra Medalist, 1974. Academic: L.H.D. from Grinnell College, 1960 and Pace College, 1969; L.L.D. from Bellarmine College, 1973 and Haverford College, 1974.

WRITINGS: Reality, Princeton University Press, 1938, reprinted, Southern Illinois University Press, 1967; *Nature and Man,* Holt, 1947, reprinted, Southern Illinois University Press, 1965; *Man's Freedom,* Yale University Press, 1950, reprinted, Southern Illinois University Press, 1967; *Modes of Being,* Southern Illinois University Press, 1958; *Our Public Life,* Indiana University Press, 1959; *Nine Basic Arts,* Southern Illinois University Press, 1961; *World of Art,* Southern Illinois University Press, 1961; *History: Written and Lived,* Southern Illinois University Press, 1962; *Religion and Art,* Marquette University Press, 1963; *Philosophy in Process,* Southern Illinois University Press, Volume I, 1964, Volume II, 1966, Volume III, 1968, Volume IV, 1969, Volume V, 1971, Volume VI, 1975, Volume VII, 1978; *The God We Seek,* Southern Illinois University Press, 1964; *The Making of Men,* Southern Illinois University Press, 1967; (with son, Jonathan Weiss) *Right and Wrong: A Philosophical Dialogue between Father and Son,* Basic Books, 1967; *Sport: A Philosophic Inquiry,* Southern Illinois University Press, 1969; *Beyond All Appearances,* Southern Illinois University Press, 1974; *Cinematics,* Southern Illinois University Press, 1975; *First Considerations: An Examination of Philosophical Evidence,* Southern Illinois University Press, 1967; *You, I, and the Others,* Southern Illinois University Press, 1980.

Contributor: *Ninth International Congress of Philosophy,* Cambridge University Press, 1930; *American Philosophy Today and Tomorrow,* Furman University Press, 1935; *Approaches to World Peace,* Harper, 1944; *Perspectives on a*

Troubled Decade, Harper, 1949; *Moral Principles of Action* Harper, 1952; *Personal Moments of Discovery*, 1953; *Philosophy and History*, New York University Press, 1962. Also contributor to numerous other books.

Editor with Charles Hartshorne, *Collected Papers of Charles Sanders Peirce*, six volumes, Harvard University Press, 1931-35. Founder and editor, *Review of Metaphysics*, 1947-64; member of editorial board of *Judaism*. Contributor to professional journals.

SIDELIGHTS: Paul Weiss wrote *CA:* "To see if you really mean to be a creative person, ask yourself whether or not you would be willing to be given the opportunity to produce the greatest work in the world on condition that no one will ever know you did it. If you can say that you would not, you reveal that you are concerned, not with being a creative person, but with achieving fame, fortune, or a reputation."

BIOGRAPHICAL/CRITICAL SOURCES: Criticism, winter, 1967.

*   *   *

WEISS, Peter 1916-

PERSONAL: Born November 8, 1916, in Nowawes, Germany; emigrated to Sweden in 1939; son of Eugene (a textile manufacturer) and Frieda (Hummel) Weiss; married second wife, Gunilla Palmstierna (a ceramist and designer), 1964. *Education:* Attended Art Academy, Prague, Czechoslovakia, 1937-38. *Residence:* Stockholm, Sweden. *Address:* c/o Suhrkamp Verlag, Lindenstrasse 29-35, 6 Frankfurt-am-Main, West Germany.

CAREER: Writer, painter, and filmmaker. Has designed stage sets and done book covers and illustrations for his own works. *Awards, honors:* Charles-Veillon-Literaturpreis, 1963, for *Fluchtpunkt;* Lessing-Preis, 1965, Antoinette Perry (Tony) Award, 1966, and Drama Critics Circle Award, 1966, all for "Marat/Sade"; Heinrich-Mann-Preis from Akademie der Kuenste, East Berlin, 1966, for "Die Ermittlung" ("The Investigation").

WRITINGS: Duellen, Tryckeri Bjoerkmans (Stockholm), 1953; *Avantgardefilm*, Walstroem & Widstrand (Stockholm), 1956; *Der Schatten des Koerpers des Kutschers* (self-illustrated; title means "The Shadow of the Coachman's Body"; also see below), Suhrkamp (Frankfurt), 1960, 3rd edition, 1966; *Abschied von den Eltern: Erzaehlung* (autobiographical novel), Suhrkamp, 1961, 3rd edition, 1966, translation by Christopher Levenson published as *The Leavetaking* (also see below), Harcourt, 1962; *Fluchpunkt: Roman* (autobiographical novel), Suhrkamp, 1962, translation to *Vanishing Point* and bound with *The Leavetaking*, Calder & Boyars, 1966, translation by Levenson, E. B. Garside, and Alastair Hamilton of *The Leavetaking* and *Vanishing Point* published jointly as *Exile: A Novel*, Delacorte, 1968; (translator) August Strindberg, *Ein Traumspiel*, Suhrkamp, 1963; *Das Gespraech der drei Gehenden*, Suhrkamp, 1963, 4th edition, 1968, translation by Garside and Rosemarie Waldrop published as *Conversation of the Three Wayfarers* in *Bodies and Shadows: Two Short Novels* (also see below), Delacorte, 1970, translation by S. M. Cupitt published as *The Conversation of the Three Walkers* and bound with *The Shadow of the Coachman's Body*, Calder & Boyars, 1972.

Notizen zum kulturellen Leben in der Democratische Republik Viet Nam, Suhrkamp, 1968, translation published as *Notes on the Cultural Life of the Democratic Republic of Vietnam*, Dell, 1970; (editor with Peter Limqueco) *Russell-*

tribunalen, PAN/Norstedt (Stockholm), 1968, translation published as *Prevent the Crime of Silence: Reports from the Sessions of the International War Crimes Tribunal Founded by Bertrand Russell*, Allen Lane, 1971; *Bodies and Shadows: Two Short Novels* (contains *The Shadow of the Coachman's Body* and *Conversation of the Three Wayfarers*), translation by Garside and Waldrop, Delacorte, 1970; *American Presence in South East Asia*, Island Publishers (Singapore), 1971; (illustrator and author of foreword) Hermann Hesse, *Kindheit des Zauberers: Ein Autobiograph*, Insel Verlag, 1974; *Die Aesthetik des Widerstands Roman*, three volumes, Suhrkamp, 1975-81; (illustrator) Hesse, *Der verbannte Ehemann oder Anton Schievelbeyn's ohnfreywillige Reisse nacher Ost-Indien*, Insel Verlag, 1977.

Also author of pamphlets and reports on various aspects of the war in Vietnam.

Plays: *Die Verfolgung und Ermordung Jean Paul Marats, dargestellt durch die Schauspielgruppe des Hospizes zu Charenton unter Anleitung des Herrn de Sade: Drama in Zwei Akten* (two-act; often called "Marat/Sade" [also see below]; first produced in West Berlin at Schiller Theater, April 29, 1964, produced on Broadway at Martin Beck Theatre, December 27, 1965), Suhrkamp, 1964, 8th edition, 1967, translation by Geoffrey Skelton with verse adaptation by Adrian Mitchell published in England as *The Persecution and Assassination of Marat as Performed by the Inmates of the Asylum of Charenton under the Direction of the Marquis de Sade: A Play*, J. Calder, 1965, 4th edition, Calder & Boyars, 1969, published as *The Persecution and Assassination of Jean-Paul Marat as Performed by the Inmates of the Asylum of Charenton under the Direction of the Marquis de Sade: A Play*, Atheneum, 1966.

Die Ermittlung: Oratorium in Elf Gesaengen (also see below; first produced simultaneously in about twenty theaters in West and East Germany, October 19, 1965), Suhrkamp, 1965, English version by Jon Swan and Ulu Grosbard published as *The Investigation: A Play* (produced on Broadway at Ambassador Theatre, October 4, 1966), Atheneum, 1966 (published in England as *The Investigation: Oratorio in Eleven Cantos*, Calder & Boyars, 1966).

Sangen om Skrapuken (musical verse drama; first produced with music by Bengt-Arne Wallin in Stockholm at Scala Theater, January 20, 1967), Seelig, 1967, German version by Weiss published as *Gesang vom Lusitanischen Popanz* (also see below), Ruetten & Loening, 1968, 2nd edition published with other plays by Weiss as *Gesang vom Lusitanischen Popanz und andere Stuecke* (contains "Gesang vom Lusitanischen Popanz," "Nacht mit Gaesten" [also see below], and "Die Versicherung"), Deutscher Taschenbuch Verlag, 1971, translation from the German by Lee Baxandall published as *Song of the Lusitanian Bogey* in *Two Plays* (also see below; produced Off-Broadway at St. Mark's Playhouse, July 30, 1968).

Diskurs ueber die Vorgeschichte und den Verlauf des lang andauernden Befreiungskrieges in Viet Nam als Beispiel fuer die Notwendigkeit des bewaffneten Kampfes der Unterdrueckten gegen ihre Unterdruecker, sowie ueber die Versuche der Vereinigten Staaten Von Amerika die Grundlagen der Revolution zu vernichten (also see below; first produced in Frankfurt, 1968), Suhrkamp, 1967, translation by Skelton published in England as *Discourse on Vietnam*, Calder & Boyars, 1970, published as *Discourse on the Progress of the Prolonged War of Liberation in Viet Nam . . .* in *Two Plays* (also see below); *Der Turm* (also see below; title means "The Tower"; produced in New York City by Actors' Experimental Unit, April 24, 1974), Reclam, 1968.

Nacht mit Gaesten (also see below) [and] *Wie dem Herrn Mockinpott das Leiden ausgetrieben wird* (also see below; two one-acts; "Nacht mit Gaesten" [title means "Night with Guests"] first produced in Berlin at Schiller Theater, October, 1963; "Wie dem Herrn Mockinpott das Leiden ausgetrieben wird" [title means "How Mr. Mockinpott Was Cured of His Sufferings"] first produced in Hanover, Germany, at Hanover State Theater, 1967, produced Off-Broadway at Greenwich Mews Playhouse, May 31, 1973), Suhrkamp, 1969; *Trotzki im Exil: Stueck in Zwei Akten* (two-act; first produced in Dusseldorf, January, 1970), Suhrkamp, 1970, translation by Skelton published as *Trotsky in Exile: A Play*, Atheneum, 1972; *Hoelderlin: Stueck in Zwei Akten* (two-act; first produced in Stuttgart at Staats Theater, September 15, 1971), Suhrkamp, 1971; (adapter) Franz Kafka, "The Trial," produced in Bremen, Germany, 1974.

Collections: *Dramen,* two volumes (contains "Der Turm," "Die Versicherung," "Nacht mit Gaesten," "Mockinpott," "Marat/Sade," "Die Ermittlung," "Lusitanischer Popanz," and "Viet Nam Diskurs"), Suhrkamp, 1968; *Rapporte,* two volumes, Suhrkamp, 1968-71; *Two Plays* (contains "Song of the Lusitanian Bogey" translated by Lee Baxandall and "Discourse on the Progress of the Prolonged War of Liberation in Viet Nam ..." translated by Skelton), Atheneum, 1970.

Also author of "The Insurance," as yet neither published nor produced; wrote, directed, and helped film "Hallucinations," 1953, "Faces in the Shadow," 1956, "The Mirage," 1958, and "The Studio of Dr. Faust."

SIDELIGHTS: "My plays do not have conventional lead roles," Peter Weiss once declared. "The lead roles are played by history and ideas." His two best-known works, "Marat/Sade" and "The Investigation," certainly seem to bear out this self-assessment. The basis of "Marat/Sade," for example, is a fierce (but imaginary) dialectical battle between the Marquis de Sade (Weiss's embodiment of the spirit of individualism, anarchy, and self-indulgence) and Jean-Paul Marat (a fanatical populist, idealist, and Marxist-like revolutionary convinced that the end justifies the means). Their debate takes place in the bath house of the Charenton insane asylum as de Sade, at the suggestion of the warden, directs a company of his fellow inmates in a play depicting Marat's assassination. Weiss's other major work, "The Investigation," is based on transcripts from the 1964-65 trial of several minor German officials who participated in the murders of millions of prisoners at Auschwitz; the play is essentially an unadorned recital of Nazi atrocities presented in a detached, documentary style.

While basing a play on historical fact is by no means a new technique, in Weiss's case, the existence of many transla-tions, many productions, and many interpretations has com-plicated attempts to judge his work. For the most part, criti-cism regarding "Marat/Sade" and "The Investigation" has centered around the question of whether or not they consti-tute true drama. Pointing out the readily apparent influence of Brecht and Artaud on his work, most reviewers have con-cluded that his plays fall within the bounds of the theatre of absurdity or the theatre of cruelty, but that they also contain elements of both which seem diametrically opposed and therefore mutually exclusive. This is especially true of "Marat/Sade"; as Robert Brustein remarks in his book *The Third Theatre*, this particular play "is a compound of . . . the cool alienation techniques of Brecht and the boiling 'total theatre' of Artaud—and we may speculate that each ap-proach proceeds from a different side of the author's na-ture." This perception of two contradictory natures in one

individual has led Brustein and other critics to believe that the ultimate success of a Weiss play depends on how well the playwright manages to resolve the duality and ambiguity in himself as it reveals itself in his work.

In "Marat/Sade," an example of this duality occurs in the radically differing philosophies espoused by Marat and de Sade during the course of their debate. Because Weiss de-votes virtually equal time to each man's argument, reviewers have often had a great deal of difficulty deciding just who *really* speaks for the playwright. (Weiss subsequently re-vealed that his purpose in writing the play was to clarify the various positions in his *own* mind and that he personally fa-vors productions which tilt the scales rather heavily toward Marat's viewpoint). Admitting that "[Weiss] has an uncanny instinct for seizing upon central modern obsessions and transforming them, through a process of symbolic compres-sion, into visual art," Brustein nevertheless concludes that "ultimately, the play proves too rich for its own blood and fails to realize its extraordinary promise. . . . One of the weaknesses of Weiss's design is that in stating and restating his two positions he never lets them engage each other fully. . . . They exist in separate compartments of his brain, and never lock in significant combat. Instead of developing his theme, Weiss concentrates on his spectacle—the intellec-tual debate tends to get swallowed up in theatrical deliri-um. . . . [He] is subtly suggesting (a suggestion which seems to invalidate his own politics) that human activity is insane, and that human history takes place in a madhouse."

Other critics also believe that Weiss's preoccupation with the theme of insanity tends to overshadow what he has to say via Marat and de Sade. Noting that his play-within-a-play structure has "a baffling angle"—namely, that "it is dif-ficult to distinguish the contemporary play [Weiss's] from its antecedent [de Sade's]," an *America* reviewer states that "the audience is never sure when Marat and de Sade are speaking for themselves—or for Peter Weiss. It is evident that Mr. Weiss intended his play to have some kind of perti-nence to the human condition, either contemporary or his-torical. He seems to be saying that the Charenton asylum is a microcosm of a larger madhouse, the world. But so many other inferences can be drawn from his play that his meaning remains obscure."

Expressing his agreement with this last remark, John Simon declares in the *Hudson Review* that Weiss's play "is a house of mirrors, a fun palace, a many-bottomed valise whose final bottom is infinity. It is highly sophisticated theatre, but only a slender addition to the drama." Determining that the basic dilemma in "Marat/Sade" appears to boil down to "who is mad and who is sane, or what is reality and what illusion," Simon concludes that "even anecdotally the play is an ambi-guity: in the final chaos, it is impossible to assess who or what triumphs, if anything does. And formally, the play fluc-tuates between the doggerel of the medieval morality and the free verse of contemporary looseness. The raucous song in-terludes contribute yet another disturbing dimension. In ev-ery possible labyrinthine way, the implicated spectators are confounded and disordered. . . . 'Marat/Sade' begins at the confluence of Brechtian alienation, Pirandellian illusionism, and Artaudian shock treatment, and follows them to where they conjointly debouch into the sea of the absurd."

Despite their reservations about the success of Weiss's en-deavors, however, most reviewers agree that the mere theat-rical experience of "Marat/Sade" should not be missed. The *America* critic, for example, declares that "aside from what-ever dramatic importance it has, 'Marat/Sade' is spectacular theatre." He explains: "From the moment the house lights are darkened, director Peter Brook takes charge and the play's intellectual content is lost in the phantasmagoria of horror theatre.... While 'Marat/Sade' may be run-of-the-mill cerebral drama, Peter Brook's direction lifts it to the pinnacle of sensational showmanship.''

Insisting that the play is ''no freak show'' but conceding that its very structure defies conventional production, *Harper's* Robert Kotlowitz calls director Brook and his company ''remarkable new performers. Their asylum never goes false for a moment, nor does their projection of de Sade's malicious therapeutic exercise. They play, it seems, only to and for each other, as though we were not even in the theatre, ringing a chilling series of visual shocks at us.''

The *Commentary* critic agrees, stating: ''No one can deny that watching two dozen or so skillfully individualized lunatics drift about a stage, trying to adapt themselves to the exigencies of political drama is harrowing and fascinating. Peter Brook, the director, has artfully seen to it that not a corner of his platform goes to waste, and wherever the eye gazes, a whole history of horror is waiting for it. Behind the dialogue there is always the threatening murmur of derangement, the convulsive twitches of madness. In such a setting, every didactic word uttered is charged with some form of drama.... Granted the work is not so completely satisfying as it would have been had madness and its asylum been more pertinent to Weiss's subject, but I would not object to a playwright arranging automobile accidents on stage if he could get his audience to listen to him.... Weiss may be occasionally faulty in presenting such a large area of argument, but there is no doubt that one is watching the product of an intelligent mind.''

Brustein concludes: ''['Marat/Sade' makes for] an intoxicating evening of theatre.... [It] is a play that touches on the borders of our secret being. If it doesn't touch our core, then this may be because Peter Weiss has not yet learned to marshal his abundant energies toward a consistent goal, to choose a single artistic commitment from a wealth of possibilities. But if this brilliantly theatrical play finally fails to achieve dramatic art, we can be grateful for once that its defects stem not from an author's poverty of imagination but rather from his excess of it.''

In response to criticism about the confusing multiplicity of interpretations possible for ''Marat/Sade,'' Weiss told interviewer Michael Roloff of the *Partisan Review:* ''Every director has the right to interpret the subject matter of a play according to his own point of view. According to his temperament and to a great extent, of course, according to his situation in a particular society he will emphasize one or another of the play's features. For a director in Western society—in which, on the whole, the concept of class struggle is viewed as no longer having any bearing on reality, and in which, in all artistic endeavor, the belief flourishes that our problems are insoluble anyway and that everything is basically absurd and mad—it will be almost natural to let the madhouse atmosphere in 'Marat/Sade' predominate.

''However, if a director believes that Marxism has not lost its efficacy and that the central points in the argument proffered by Marat (which, of course, in many instances prefigured Marx's theses) are still pertinent, he will emphasize these statements in the play and he will use them to allude to the present....

''For the playwright, naturally, it is most important that a production should express a play's dualism, the ambivalence of its situation—in 'Marat/Sade,' the confrontation of individualism and Socialism/Collectivism.... So far as I am

concerned the essence of the play is not the chaos that develops towards the end but the constant pull and tug of the arguments, which are intended to see through the humbug of society and to provoke the audience to think.... I was primarily interested in representing a never-ending dialogue and . . . the purpose of the dialogue is to clarify the situation. Everything irrational and absurd is foreign to me.''

''The Investigation,'' another highly unconventional and therefore controversial Weiss play, has also generated some confusion among theatre critics, primarily due to its ambiguous relationship to reality. Basically, the entire play consists of excerpts from the transcript of a trial held in Germany in 1964 and 1965 during which twenty-one men who operated the Auschwitz concentration camp were tried for the murders of some four million people. Weiss condenses the cast to twenty-three characters (representing the defendants, witnesses, attorneys, and judge) and assembles them on a stage which is virtually bare except for a courtroom-like seating arrangement; unlike ''Marat/Sade'''s graphic visual depictions of violence and insanity, however, the ''action'' in ''The Investigation'' essentially involves a static, unemotional reading of the testimony from the trial. But in a deliberate break from reality (a break regarded by most observers as an attempt to ''universalize'' the events in question), Weiss does not use the words Nazi, German, or Jew during the course of the entire play.

Critics were puzzled as to how they were supposed to react to such a ''non-play,'' as several described it; how, they wondered, could a playwright transcribe court testimony as free verse and call it a play? Was ''The Investigation'' to be taken as fiction or as an abstract version of reality? Why did Weiss omit all specific references to the perpetrators and victims of the crimes at Auschwitz?

Describing himself as a man in exile who has no emotional attachments to Germany and who, having spent the war years in relative comfort in Sweden, could not relate to the horrors of Auschwitz, Weiss has insisted all along that his play ''is not to be taken as a limited portrayal of Nazi inhumanity to Jews.... I simply identify myself with the oppressed of the world.'' Yet many critics feel that Weiss's decision to exclude all mention of specifics in his adaptation of the facts has once again created a different, but unmistakable atmosphere of ambiguity and irresolution in his work; dramatic impact is lessened, they claim, by making the subject so abstract and remote that the events fail to move us as they should. As a *Time* reviewer notes: ''Many of the vignettes claw at the skin without reaching the heart.... Emotionally, Weiss fails by being emetic rather than tragically cathartic. Intellectually, he appears to embrace the fallacy of universal guilt.... As the victims, the Jews merit the epitaph of being named. As the perpetrators of the crime, the Germans deserve to be indicted.... To arouse the conscience of man is admirable but in this non-play Weiss mainly succeeds in raising the gorge.''

'''The Investigation' is not art,'' declares the *Nation's* Harold Clurman. ''Still it probably functions as a shattering event where it is presented to an audience which in one way or another has been intimately involved with its horizon.... 'The Investigation' may prove a 'shocker' but not a truly meaningful occasion. It will not get under the audience's skin, it will not 'teach them a lesson.' ... Weiss intended to make his documentary as factual as possible but it ends by seeming abstract. It is not the abstraction of art. On the contrary, it neutralizes the effect of the performance. That is why I can say very little about the production.... We are neither in a real courtroom of real people nor within an original and self-justifying stage form.''

Jack Richardson of *Commentary* agrees with Clurman's views on "The Investigation." He writes: "Art as it generally appears is completely absent in 'The Investigation.' We are given a work appearing to abstain from a personal vision, image, or interpretation of that time in history.... On the face of it, it would seem that Weiss simply decided to export the proceedings at Frankfurt.... The solution that the semidocumentary method of 'The Investigation' offers is successful neither as a substitute for art nor as a moral alternative to silence. In fact, it seems infected with the worst excesses of both.... Placed in the theater, these transcripts, partly from being enmeshed in faulty theatrics, but more importantly from never having been intended as cohesive dramatic moments, drift by without ever achieving more than the status of minor evidence of what everyone who has had the shape an estimate of life which included the madness of an Auschwitz knew already. The words, originally used to articulate a description of brutality that was to be legally judged, become, on the stage, a type of naive shock propaganda—a demeaning metamorphosis.''

Richardson also objects to Weiss's lack of concern for the particulars of the story, calling it "a strange practice for one purporting a documentary method." Concludes the critic: "If Weiss wants to free 'The Investigation' from the specifics of the history that produced it, he should have to earn that right as a dramatist by taking the risks of one. If he wants to hint that Auschwitz is more than a German creation, that the soil of any country would be hospitable to its like, then a great deal more is demanded of him than the excision of proper nouns. As it is, this use of the trial to support conclusions of its editor is what is most objectionable about 'The Investigation.'''

As in the case of "Marat/Sade," however, there are those (such as the *New Yorker* reviewer) who feel that if "Mr. Weiss hasn't given us a drama, he has assuredly given us a compelling theatrical entity." Remarking that "criticism of 'The Investigation' is in a way, irrelevant," the *New York Times'* Walter Kerr describes it as "disturbing in its implications, repetitive in its method, wearing as an experience, yet incontestably an experience of some sort." Comparing it to "Marat/Sade," R. J. Schroeder of *Commonweal* calls "The Investigation" a "landmark play" that "succeeds in every way that 'Marat/Sade' ... fails." Explains the critic: "'Marat/Sade' has become an intellectually interesting, cognitively shocking, but emotionally uninvolving theatrical experience that is therefore forgettable.... [On the other hand,] whether it is stylized or simply spoken, ['The Investigation'] is often intellectually boring, and is rarely cerebrally stimulating, but is it emotionally (or should I say humanly?) stunning and utterly memorable.... During its course, its audience becomes a congregation, and at its close files silently from its presence as from a religious service. For the play is not 'enjoyed'; it is experienced. It is not 'analyzed'; it is absorbed. Here we deal, not with Marat's embroidered intellectualizations about one aspect of ourselves, or with de Sade's about another, but rather with the unintellectualized essence of our selves and our kind—with those unmagnified (if only they were!) ambiguities and ambivalences which made, and continue to make, Auschwitz possible.''

Despite the controversy surrounding the dramatic value of his work, Peter Weiss remains a passionate Marxist, convinced that a writer's duty is not merely to entertain, but to attempt to change the world through his writing. In a 1966 speech at Princeton University, Weiss explained, in part, the reasons leading up to his decision to discuss volatile political and historical questions such as the ones he raises in "Marat/Sade" and "The Investigation": "Since the beginning of my work my attitude toward commitment has steadily changed. In my first attempts to write I had only my own existence in mind. It was the time of emigration and war. I didn't belong anywhere and I made a virtue out of the nonbelonging. My commitment was not to be engaged in a struggle which in my view was insane.... My commitment was not to myself.... Then suddenly it was all over. Nothing was damaged in my room, there was food in the kitchen, outside there were millions and millions of dead.... Now my commitment led me to a search for the reasons for this dying, which seemed so meaningless. In the beginning I could still identify myself with either the murdered or the murderers. I no longer thought of myself as different or better than they were and I thought it would just depend on which side I had been put.... There were some years when I suffered an atavistic and petrified guilt that I too should have gone the way which had been staked out for me and that I was a traitor toward all these millions who were caught....

"I could have gone on, deeply committed to my art, writing, painting, making films about this doomed state, expressing despair and distortion, and even some rebellion and shouts that it should be all different, and that there should be, somewhere, some hope.... [But] as long as I felt I could go on with my art without bothering about the rest, I was part of the corruption.... Very belatedly I explored the facts of politics and economics which made the hallucinative machinery run.... The more I understood the signs of injustice, the treachery and violence around, the better became my spirits.... I examined the view that the author should keep out of political participation, that he should be the one who keeps objectivity alive, that he should see both the positive and negative aspects in the forces involved in their universal struggle. But was not life too short for this objectivity? Wasn't it just another lie in order not to get oneself burned? ...

"[In short,] it was not enough to establish empathy with the suppressed and exploited. I also had to stand up for them in my writing. I could not longer believe in an independent circle of art.... I do not think this is an exceptional situation for a writer. There are many who work out of both needs: to express human individualism and radical political change. The conflicts which arise out of this commitment will be part of our work, we will have to live with them, often they will furnish the very problems we try to solve in writing.''

BIOGRAPHICAL/CRITICAL SOURCES: Partisan Review, spring, 1965; *America,* January 29, 1966, October 29, 1966; *Look,* February 22, 1966; *Commentary,* March, 1966, December, 1966; *Commonweal,* March 4, 1966, November 4, 1966; *Hudson Review,* spring, 1966; *Harper's,* April, 1966; *Nation,* May 30, 1966, October 17, 1966; *New York Times Magazine,* October 2, 1966; *New York Times,* October 5, 1966, May 15, 1980; *Time,* October 14, 1966; *New Yorker,* October 15, 1966; *Newsweek,* October 17, 1966; *Saturday Review,* October 22, 1966; *New Republic,* November 20, 1966; *Christian Century,* December 14, 1966; Frederich Lumley, *New Trends in Twentieth-Century Drama,* Oxford University Press, 1967; Walter Wager, *The Playwrights Speak,* Delacorte, 1967; *Contemporary Literature,* Volume IX, Number 1, 1968; Robert Brustein, *The Third Theatre,* Knopf, 1969; Ian Hilton, *Peter Weiss: A Search for Affinities,* O. Wolff, 1970; *Contemporary Literary Criticism,*

Gale, Volume III, 1975, Volume XV, 1980; Otto F. Best, *Peter Weiss,* translated by Ursula Molinaro, Ungar, 1976.

—*Sketch by Deborah A. Straub*

* * *

WELCH, Ann Courtenay (Edmonds) 1917-
(Ann C. Douglas, Ann C. Edmonds)

PERSONAL: Born May 20, 1917, in London, England; daughter of Courtenay Harold Wish (an engineer) and Edith Maud (Austin) Edmonds; married Graham Douglas, 1939 (divorced, 1950); married Lorne Elphinstone Welch (an engineer), June 25, 1953; children: Vivien Ann Douglas, Elizabeth Ann Douglas, Janet. *Education:* Attended a private school in England. *Home:* 14 Upper Old Park Lane, Farnham, Surrey, England.

CAREER: Pilot, and holder of British women's national glider goal flight record of 328 miles (1961); manager of British team in World Gliding Championships, 1948-68; chairman of organizing committee for England's National Gliding Championships, 1948-63, and for World Gliding Championships, 1965; vice-president, Commission Internationale Vol a Voile, 1971. Lecturer on gliding. Artist and illustrator. *Military service:* Air Transport Auxiliary, ferry pilot, World War II; became first officer. *Member:* Royal Aeronautical Society (associate fellow), British Hang Gliding Association (president), Federation Aeronalitique Internationale (vice-president), Royal Meteorological Society (fellow), Bosham Sailing Club. *Awards, honors:* Member of Order of the British Empire, 1953; Officer of the British Empire, 1966; Royal Aero Club silver medal, 1958; FAI bronze medal, 1969; Lilienthal Medal, 1973.

WRITINGS: (With husband, Lorne Welch) *Manual for Elementary Flying Instruction in Two-Seater Gliders,* British Gliding Association, 1952, 2nd edition published as *Flying Training in Gliders,* 1956; (with L. Welch and F. G. Irving) *The Soaring Pilot,* J. Murray, 1955, 3rd edition published as *The New Soaring Pilot,* 1968; *Go Gliding,* illustrations by Gabor Denes, Faber, 1960; *Glider Flying,* Constable, 1963; *John Goes Gliding* (juvenile novel), J. Cape, 1964; *The Woolacombe Bird* (historical novel for young people), J. Cape, 1964, World Publishing, 1965; (with L. Welch) *The Story of Gliding,* J. Murray, 1965, 2nd edition, 1980; *Pilots Weather,* J. Murray, 1973; (with G. Breen) *Hang Glider Pilot,* J. Murray, 1977; *Accidents Happen,* J. Murray, 1979; *The Book of Airports,* Batsford, 1979. Also author of *Soaring and Hang Gliders,* with R. Hill.

Under name Ann C. Douglas: *Clouds Reading for Pilots,* Transatlantic, 1943; (with P. A. Wills and A. E. Slater) *Gliding and Advanced Soaring,* J. Murray, 1947, Transatlantic, 1949.

Under name Ann C. Edmonds: (Editor with Norman Macmillan) *Let Experts Tell You—How We Fly,* Virture, 1939; *Silent Flight,* Country Life, 1939; *Come Gliding with Me,* Muller, 1955, Soccer, 1956.

WORK IN PROGRESS: An autobiography.

SIDELIGHTS: As manager of a British gliding team, chairman of an international gliding jury, or international commission representative, Ann Courtenay Welch has been to world championships in Switzerland, Sweden, Spain, France, Poland, Germany, Argentina, Yugoslavia, Australia, Finland, Austria, and the United States. She intends to spend her retiring years ocean sailing. *Avocational interests:* Skiing, scuba diving, photography, modern houses, and sailing with her grandchildren.

WELLARD, James (Howard) 1909-

PERSONAL: Born January 12, 1909, in London, England; son of James Hitchen and Frances (Massey) Wellard; married Mary Higgins, June 3, 1944; children: John, Julia. *Education:* University College, London, B.A. (honors), 1932; University of Chicago, Ph.D., 1934. *Home and office:* 14 The Pryors, East Heath Rd., London N.W.3, England. *Agent:* William Morris Agency, 1350 Ave. of the Americas, New York, N.Y. 10019.

CAREER: Journalist on American and British newspapers, 1940-56; war correspondent in European Theater, 1941-45; free-lance writer. Visiting lecturer, University of Illinois at Urbana-Champaign, 1955-56; assistant professor, Longwood College, Farmville, Va., 1957-61; Fulbright lecturer, University of Tehran, Tehran, Iran, 1959-60. *Member:* Society of Authors, Writers Guild of Great Britain, Royal Geographical Society.

WRITINGS: Understanding the English, McGraw, 1937; *Book Selection: Its Principles and Practice,* Grafton & Co., 1937; *The Public Library Comes of Age,* Grafton & Co., 1940; *The Snake in the Grass,* Dodd, 1942; *General George S. Patton, Jr., Man under Mars,* Dodd, 1946; *A Moment in Time,* Dodd, 1947; *The Ancient Way,* Laurie, 1949; *Spotlight on Murder,* Foulsham, 1949; *Journey to a High Mountain,* Dodd, 1950; *Woman Returning,* Laurie, 1951; *Summer at the Castle,* St. Martin's, 1953; *Night in Babylon,* St. Martin's, 1953; *Deep Is the Night,* Farrar, Straus, 1953; *Action of the Tiger,* St. Martin's, 1955; *Memoirs of a Cross-Eyed Man,* St. Martin's, 1956; *Conversations with a Witch,* Macmillan, 1958; *The Affair in Arcady,* Reynal, 1959.

A Sound of Trumpets, Little, Brown, 1960; *A Man and His Journey,* Hutchinson, 1962; *The Great Sahara,* Hutchinson, 1964, Dutton, 1965; *Lost Worlds of Africa,* Dutton, 1967; *The Sun-gazers,* Hutchinson, 1968; *Desert Pilgrimage,* Hutchinson, 1970; *Babylon,* Saturday Review Press, 1972 (published in England as *By the Waters of Babylon,* Hutchinson, 1972); *The Search for the Etruscans,* Thomas Nelson, 1973; *The French Foreign Legion,* Little, Brown, 1974; *The Search for Lost Worlds,* Pan Books, 1975; *Samarkand and Beyond: History of Desert Caravans,* Constable, 1977; *The Search for Lost Cities,* Constable, 1980. Contributor of stories and articles to magazines.

SIDELIGHTS: A *Choice* reviewer writes that "there is drama and romance in [*Babylon,*] this historic narrative with which the history undergraduate can identify. James Wellard successfully separates myth from truth and legend from archaeological facts. The book reads like an incredible adventure story which can be read in one day." A. Bakshian of the *National Review* agrees and feels Wellard "writes an engaging narrative, and the casual reader will enjoy following the downward winding history of the greatest city of antiquity through two thousand turbulent years."

AVOCATIONAL INTERESTS: Sailing.

BIOGRAPHICAL/CRITICAL SOURCES: Choice, June, 1973; *Best Sellers,* November 1, 1973; *National Review,* December 8, 1973.

* * *

WELLWARTH, George E(manuel) 1932-

PERSONAL: Born June 6, 1932, in Vienna, Austria; son of Erwin (a theater owner) and Martha (Sobotka) Wellwarth. *Education:* New York University, B.A. (summa cum laude), 1953; Columbia University, M.A., 1954; University of Chicago, Ph.D., 1957. *Office:* Theatre Department, State University of New York, Binghamton, N.Y. 13901.

CAREER: Wilson Junior College, Chicago, Ill., instructor in English, 1955-58; University of Chicago, Chicago, Ill., lecturer in English, 1958; City College (now City College of the City University of New York), New York, N.Y., instructor in English, 1959-60; Staten Island Community College (now College of Staten Island of the City University of New York), Staten Island, N.Y., assistant professor, 1960-63, associate professor of English, 1963-64; Pennsylvania State University, University Park, assistant professor, 1964-66, associate professor of English, 1966-70; State University of New York at Binghamton, Binghamton, N.Y., professor of theatre and comparative literature, 1970—. One-time professional actor in Chicago, Ill., San Diego, Calif., and in Off-Broadway theaters. *Member:* Modern Language Association of America, American Educational Theatre Association, American Comparative Literature Association, Phi Beta Kappa.

WRITINGS: The Theatre of Protest and Paradox: Developments in the Avant-Garde Drama, New York University Press, 1964, 2nd edition, 1971; (editor and translator with Michael Benedikt) *Modern French Theatre: An Anthology of Plays–The Avant-Garde, Dada, and Surrealism,* Dutton, 1964 (published in England as *Modern French Plays: An Anthology from Jarry to Ionesco,* Faber, 1965); (translator) Siegfried Melchinger, *The Concise Encyclopedia of Modern Drama,* foreword by Eric Bentley, Horizon Press, 1964; (editor and translator with Benedikt) *Postwar German Theatre: An Anthology of Plays,* Dutton, 1967; (editor with Benedikt) *Modern Spanish Theatre: An Anthology of Plays,* Dutton, 1968.

(Editor) *The New Wave Spanish Drama: An Anthology,* New York University Press, 1970; *German Drama between the Wars,* Dutton, 1971; (editor) *Spanish Underground Drama,* Pennsylvania State University Press, 1972; *Themes of Drama,* Crowell, 1972; *New Generation Spanish Drama,* Engendra Press, 1976; *Three Catalan Dramatists,* Engendra Press, 1976. Translator of plays of Jean Tardieu, produced Off-Broadway, January, 1962. Contributor of forty-five articles to learned journals. Co-editor and co-founder, *Modern International Drama* (magazine).

WORK IN PROGRESS: A study of the relationship between dramatic form and subject matter and political and social conditions; a study of philosophical themes in modern drama.

SIDELIGHTS: George E. Wellwarth has traveled and observed theatre in all countries of western Europe except Finland; he is fluent in French, German, Spanish, and Catalan.

BIOGRAPHICAL/CRITICAL SOURCES: Nation, September 4, 1967; *Poetry,* February, 1969; *Books Abroad,* spring, 1971.

*   *   *

WERTENBAKER, Lael (Tucker) 1909-
(Lael Tucker)

PERSONAL: Born March 28, 1909, in Bradford, Pa.; daughter of Royal K. and Juliet (Luttrell) Tucker; married Charles Christian Wertenbaker (a writer, editor; deceased); children: Christian Tucker, Lael Louisiana Timberlake. *Education:* Attended University of Louisville. *Politics:* Independent. *Religion:* Episcopalian. *Home:* R.D., Marlborough, N.H. *Agent:* Don Congdon, Harold Matson Inc., 22 East 40th St., New York, N.Y. 10016.

CAREER: Theatre Guild, Inc., New York City, treasurer and road agent, 1928-38; *Time,* New York City, reporter,

foreign correspondent, and war correspondent, 1938-47. Vice-president, History in Sound and Light Corp. Trustee, National Repertory Theatre Foundation and Monadnock Music. Director of the board, MacDowell Colony and Ossabaw Island Foundation. *Member:* Overseas Press Club, P.E.N.

WRITINGS—Published by Little, Brown, except as indicated: *The Eye of the Lion,* 1965; *The Afternoon Women,* 1966; (with the editors of Time-Life Books) *The World of Picasso,* Time-Life, 1967; *Unbidden Guests,* 1970; (with Jean Rosenthal) *The Magic of Light,* 1972; *Perilous Voyage,* 1975; *To Mend the Heart,* Viking, 1980.

All with Suzanne Gleaves: *Tip and Dip* (juvenile), Lippincott, 1960; *Mercy Percy* (juvenile), Lippincott, 1961; *You and the Armed Services,* Simon & Schuster, 1961; *Rhyming Word Games,* Simon & Schuster, 1964.

Under name Lael Tucker: *Lament for Four Virgins,* Random House, 1952; *Festival,* Random House, 1954 (published in England as *The Deeper Strings,* Heinemann, 1956); *Death of a Man,* Random House, 1957; *Mister Junior,* Pageant, 1958.

Also author of scripts for Columbia Broadcasting System programs on Attaturk, Goering, Wilkie, and Pierre Laval, 1959-63; author of scripts for series, "Around the World with Orson Welles."

SIDELIGHTS: Lael Tucker Wertenbaker wrote *CA:* "Writers' brief biographies often display startling similarity. They did curious jobs such as oiler on seagoing tankers (I was a road agent for the Theatre Guild among others). They read as if print was food from an early age (I did, too, but can't pretend I understood what I read, just ate WORDS). They began writing early on (at nine, I was sole writer and editor of 'The Tucker Weekly,' a family newsletter). They establish fierce self-disciplines since it rarely happens that anyone else cares whether they write or not (I arise at dawn and write early, because that is my best time of day). Advice to young writers: Always give your writing your best time of day. And remember that not-writing is mighty easy.

"My chief and only open boast is that for forty years I have earned a living by writing. When I was supporting two children, I had a sign on my desk which read: 'I will write anything for cash money!' Easy to say, but I found it impossible to write anything in which I did not believe or which I did not really like. The competition is tough in all forms and fields.

"Each book becomes my favorite. *To Mend the Heart,* a non-fiction one, the story of cardiac surgery, was one of the most exciting. Interviewing the pioneers—all but two still alive—was tremendously rewarding. In fiction you create characters and when they come alive it is most extraordinary. In non-fiction you meet them with the privilege of prying which is fascinating."

Death of a Man was adapted for the theatre by Garson Kanin and was produced on Broadway.

*   *   *

WESSON, Robert G(ale) 1920-

PERSONAL: Born March 11, 1920, in Washington, D.C.; son of Laurence G. (a chemist) and Elizabeth (Matthews) Wesson; married Deborah Tarsier, April 24, 1958 (divorced, 1978); children: Laura Helen, Carol Ann, Richard M., Eric A. *Education:* University of Arizona, A.B., 1940; Fletcher School of Law and Diplomacy, M.A., 1941; Columbia University, additional study, 1946-47, Ph.D., 1961. *Home:* 984 Memorial Dr., Cambridge, Mass. 02138.

CAREER: Self-employed in private business in Costa Rica and Brazil, 1948-58; Bates College, Lewiston, Me., visiting assistant professor, 1961-62, 1963-64; University of California, Santa Barbara, Calif., assistant professor, 1964-66, associate professor, 1966-71, professor of political science, 1971—, senior research fellow, Hoover Institution, 1978—.

WRITINGS: Soviet Communes, Rutgers University Press, 1963; *The American Problem: The Cold War in Perspective,* Abelard, 1963; *The Imperial Order,* University of California Press, 1967; *Soviet Foreign Policy in Perspective,* Dorsey, 1969.

The Soviet Russian State, Wiley, 1972; *The Soviet State: An Aging Revolution,* Wiley, 1972; *The Russian Dilemma,* Rutgers University Press, 1974; *Why Marxism?,* Basic Books, 1976; *Foreign Policy for a New Age,* Houghton, 1977; *Communism and Communist Systems,* Prentice-Hall, 1978; *Lenin's Legacy,* Hoover Institution, 1978; *State Systems,* Free Press, 1978; *The Aging of Communism,* Praeger, 1980; *Modern Government: Three Worlds of Politics,* Prentice-Hall, 1981; *The United States and Brazil: Limits of Influence,* Praeger, 1981. Also editor and contributor, *The Soviet Union: Looking to the 1980s,* 1980. Contributor of articles to *Current History, Soviet Studies, Orbis, Survey, Natural History,* and other periodicals.

SIDELIGHTS: Robert Wesson wrote *CA:* "Writing is something of a necessity for me, probably because I can speak a good deal less well than I can think. Consequently, having wearied of a somewhat desultory business career, I tried my hand at fiction, short stories and the beginnings of a melodramatic novel. Of course, I collected nothing but rejections and couldn't even get my friends to read my works. So I set out to learn about something to write about and to get a position from which one could publish, that is, went into the academic profession. Hence for the past twenty years, most of my children have been books. Of course, the biological children are more challenging than the literary, but the latter do not rebel, and if they turn out poorly, one can just forget them and proceed to produce another."

* * *

WEST, Anthony (Panther) 1914-

PERSONAL: Born August 4, 1914, in Hunstanton, Norfolk, England; came to United States in 1950; son of authors H. G. Wells and Rebecca West; married second wife, Lily Dulaney Emmet, December 20, 1952; children: (first marriage) Caroline, Edmund. *Education:* Educated in England. *Agent:* Wallace and Shiel Agency, Inc., 177 East 70th St., New York, N.Y. 10021. *Office: New Yorker,* 25 West 43rd St., New York, N.Y. 10036.

CAREER: Roamed the world for about four years before resettling in England; worked as a dairy farmer and breeder of Guernsey cattle, 1937-43; spent the war years with British Broadcasting Corp., working with Far Eastern Division, 1943-45, and Japanese Service, 1945-47; writer in England, 1947-50; member of staff of *New Yorker,* New York, N.Y., 1950—. *Member:* Century Association (New York). *Awards, honors;* Houghton Mifflin literary fellowship, 1950, for *The Vintage.*

WRITINGS: Gloucestershire (guidebook), Faber, 1939, revised edition, 1952; *On a Dark Night* (novel), Eyre & Spottiswoode, 1949, published as *The Vintage,* Houghton, 1950; *Another Kind* (novel), Eyre & Spottiswoode, 1951, Houghton, 1952; *D. H. Lawrence* (critical biography), Arthur Barker, 1951, 2nd edition, 1966; *The Crusades* (juvenile), Random House, 1954 (published in England as *All about the*

Crusades, W. H. Allen, 1967); *Heritage* (novel), Random House, 1955; *Principles and Persuasions* (literary essays), Harcourt, 1957; *The Trend Is Up* (novel), Random House, 1960; *Elizabethan England,* Odyssey, 1965; (editor) John Galsworthy, *The Galsworthy Reader,* Scribner, 1968; *David Rees among Others* (novel), Random House, 1970; *Mortal Wounds,* McGraw, 1973; *John Piper,* Secker & Warburg, 1979. Regular reviewer for *New Statesman* and *Nation* in the late 1930's; more recently reviewer for *Time* and *New Yorker.*

SIDELIGHTS: Anthony West's *Heritage* is an autobiographical novel about a lonely young boy who, like West, is the son of two famous and unmarried authors. C. J. Rolo comments in *Atlantic:* "This is a story which might easily have slipped into the familiar dispirited key, but Mr. West has given it a spirited individuality.... What is best about it, perhaps, is the maturity of feeling—the ability of the narrator to write movingly about his hurts and disappointments without relapsing into self-pity." The *Chicago Sunday Tribune's* Fanny Butcher calls the novel "a penetrating, amusing, often satirical, often affectionate picture of highly individualistic human beings, and a fascinating and penetrating study of the effect of an uncommon heritage." The *Time* reviewer echoes this opinion, "In other hands this could have been a sour book; instead, it is intelligent, witty, and tolerant toward the childishness of the great."

Another autobiographical novel by West is *David Rees among Others,* which S. K. Oberbeck calls in *Book World* "the sort of traditional story one has read before but reads again with pleasure—especially when it's done by a fictional pro. It's almost the kind of book that used to be written, that authors today, stuck with Robbins, Portnoy or John Fowles, would be afraid to write. It resolves something. It makes the pieces fit. That's reassuring—or gently deceptive—in this skeptical, one-up age, but it's still satisfying." The *Time* critic calls the novel a "sometimes fascinating and occasionally excruciating little chronicle about a lonely boy growing up in England just after World War II" but feels that because the novel's subject matter so closely parallels West's own life "one inevitably begins to wonder what is, and what is not, literally true. The result is profoundly corrosive to that suspension of literal belief that allows a novel to work upon the imagination." Similarly, Robert Maurer comments in *Saturday Review:* "One might expect that by now the familiarity of this story would breed critical contempt.... And yet it is West's peculiar insistence on reality that keeps his novel from being either patly derivative or sentimental. Like David, he has obviously himself learned how every happy moment is mixed with illusion, how memory and imagination tend to prettify past experiences.... His vision, therefore, is tough, sharply etched."

BIOGRAPHICAL/CRITICAL SOURCES: Saturday Review, October 1, 1955, October 3, 1970, November 20, 1973; *New York Times,* October 2, 1955; *Chicago Sunday Tribune,* October 2, 1955; *Time,* October 10, 1955, November 16, 1970; *New Yorker,* October 29, 1955; *Atlantic,* November, 1955; *Book World,* November 8, 1970; *New York Times Book Review,* November 8, 1970; *Best Sellers,* February 1, 1974; *Virginia Quarterly Review,* summer, 1974.†

* * *

WEST, Francis (James) 1927-

PERSONAL: Born June 26, 1927, in East Yorkshire, England; son of George Henry (a builder) and Florence Caroline (Selby) West; married Katharine Ogilvie White (a university teacher), May 24, 1963 (divorced October, 1976). *Education:* University of Leeds, B.A., 1947, Ph.D., 1951; Trinity College, Cambridge, Ph.D., 1956. *Politics:* Conservative. *Religion:* Church of England. *Home:* 6 Sylvan Ct., Newtown, Victoria, Australia. *Office:* Department of History, Deakin University, Geelong, Victoria 3216, Australia.

CAREER: Australian National University, Canberra, research fellow in history, 1952-55; Victoria University, Wellington, New Zealand, senior lecturer in history, 1955-59; Australian National University, senior research fellow and senior fellow in Pacific history and government, 1959-64, professorial fellow in Pacific history, 1964-76; Independent University, Buckingham, England, professor of history and dean of arts, 1973-75; Deakin University, Geelong, Australia, professor of history and government and planning dean of social sciences, 1976—. Professor of comparative government, University of Adelaide, 1964-65. Fellow under cultural relations program, Southeast Asia Treaty Organization, 1958-59; fellow and steward, University House, Canberra, 1960. Academic assistant to director, Research School of Pacific Studies, Canberra, 1962—. Member, Australian Humanities Research Council, 1966—. *Member:* Royal Historical Society (London; fellow), Institute of International Affairs, British Academy (fellow), Australian Academy of the Humanities (fellow), Australia and New Zealand Association for Advancement of Science, New Guinea Society of Canberra (committee member, 1960-63; president, 1962-63), Selden Society (London), Cambridge Historical Society. *Awards, honors:* Carnegie Commonwealth award, 1965; Ford Foundation travel and study grant, 1972-73.

WRITINGS: Political Advancement in the South Pacific, Oxford University Press, 1961; *Hubert Murray,* Oxford University Press, 1962; (with others) *The Independence of Papua-New Guinea,* Angus & Robertson, 1962; *The Justiciarship in England, 1066-1232,* Cambridge University Press, 1966; (with others) *New Guinea on the Threshold,* Australian National University Press, 1966; (with others) *Social Change: The Colonial Situation,* Wiley, 1966; *Hubert Murray: Australian Pro-Consul,* Oxford University Press, 1968; (editor) *Selected Letters of Hubert Murray,* Oxford University Press, 1970; *Biography as History,* Sydney University Press, 1973; (with others) *The Changing Pacific,* Oxford University Press, 1979; W. H. Morris-Jones and F. A. Madden, editors, *Australia and Britain,* Sydney University Press, 1980; *University House,* Australian National University Press, 1980. Contributor to *Encyclopaedia Britannica, Speculum, Pacific Affairs,* and to political and historical journals; contributor of art criticism to *Canberra Times* and book reviews to newspapers.

WORK IN PROGRESS: Classic Liberal: A Life of Gilbert Murray O.M.

SIDELIGHTS: Francis West's extensive travels in the Pacific includes trips to New Guinea, Fiji, Samoa, and Tahiti. *Avocational interests:* Cricket, tennis, bridge.

BIOGRAPHICAL/CRITICAL SOURCES: Foreign Affairs, South Pacific Commission Technical Paper 127, [Noumea], 1959.

*   *   *

WEST, Ray B(enedict), Jr.   1908-

PERSONAL: Born July 30, 1908, in Logan, Utah; son of Ray Benedict and Mary (Morrell) West; married Lucille McMullin, 1934; children: Lelia West Schoenberg, Julie West Staheli. *Education:* Utah State University, B.S., 1933; University of Utah, M.A., 1935; State University of Iowa,

Ph.D., 1945. *Home address:* P.O. Box 487, Santaquin, Utah. *Agent:* Curtis Brown Ltd., 575 Madison Ave., New York, N.Y. 10022. *Office:* Department of English, San Francisco State University, San Francisco, Calif. 94132.

CAREER: Weber College (now Weber State College), Ogden, Utah, instructor, 1941-43; University of Montana, Missoula, instructor, 1943-44; Utah State University, Logan, associate professor, 1945-46; University of Kansas, Lawrence, associate professor and director of creative writing, 1946-49; State University of Iowa, Iowa City, 1949-59, began as associate professor, became professor of English; San Francisco State University, San Francisco, Calif., professor of English, 1959-75, professor emeritus, 1975—, chairman of department of creative writing, 1969-73. Visiting professor at University of Innsbrook, 1951-52, and University of Ankara (Turkey), 1957-58. *Member:* Modern Language Association of America, Philological Association of the Pacific Coast. *Awards, honors:* Fulbright fellowship (Austria), 1951-52; Rockefeller Foundation scholarship (Turkey), 1957-58.

WRITINGS: (Editor) *Rocky Mountain Stories,* Big Mountain Press, 1941; (editor) *Rocky Mountain Reader,* Dutton, 1946; *Rocky Mountain Cities,* Norton, 1947; *Writing in the Rocky Mountains,* University of Nebraska Press, 1947; (editor with R. W. Stallman) *The Art of Modern Fiction,* Holt, 1949, 2nd edition, 1956; (editor) *Essays in Modern Literary Criticism,* Holt, 1952; *The Short Story in America,* Regnery, 1952; *Kingdom of the Saints,* Viking, 1957; (editor) *American Short Stories,* Crowell, 1960; (editor) *Country in the Mind,* Angel Island Publications, 1962; *Katherine Anne Porter,* University of Minnesota Press, 1963; *The Art of Writing Fiction,* Crowell, 1968; *The Writer in the Room,* Michigan State University Press, 1968; *Reading the Short Story,* Crowell, 1968. Short Stories anthologized in *O. Henry Prize Short Stories,* 1948, and *Best American Short Stories,* 1951. Contributor of articles, short stories, and poetry to professional journals and literary magazines. Editor, *Western Review,* 1936-59; advisory editor, *Contact,* 1959—.

WORK IN PROGRESS: A study of tragedy and comedy in modern literature.

SIDELIGHTS: Ray B. West, Jr. has made radio appearances on "The Chicago Roundtable" and "Invitation to Learning." Some of his writings have been translated into Japanese, Korean, Italian, German, Chinese, and Turkish.

*   *   *

WHEATON, William L. C.   1913-1978

PERSONAL: Born April 10, 1913, in Cleveland, Ohio; died February 19, 1978, in Berkeley, Calif.; son of William Arthur and Gertrude (Cody) Wheaton; married Katherine Fruend, August 20, 1935 (divorced, 1963); married Margaret Eyles Fry, November 9, 1963; children: (first marriage) William, Martha; (second marriage) Edward Fry. *Education:* Princeton University, A.B., 1934; Harvard University, graduate study, 1945-46; University of Chicago, Ph.D., 1952. *Home:* 1512 La Loma, Berkeley, Calif. 94708. *Office:* University of California, Berkeley, Calif. 94720.

CAREER: Assistant director of parks in Cleveland, Ohio, 1937-40; National Housing Agency, Washington, D.C., officer, 1943-45; Housing and Home Finance Agency, Washington, D.C., special assistant to the administrator, 1946-48; Harvard University, Cambridge, Mass., associate professor of regional planning, 1948-53, chairman of department, 1951-53; University of Pennsylvania, Philadelphia, professor of city planning, 1952, director of Institute for Urban Studies, 1954-63; University of California, Berkeley, professor of city planning, 1963-78, director of Institute of Urban and Regional Development, 1963-68, dean of College of Environmental Design, 1967-76. United Nations, U.S. representative to Committee on Housing, Building, and Planning, 1963-65, senior representative to Nagoya Development Center, 1968-71. Member of board of directors, San Francisco Planning and Urban Renewal, 1963-69, California Tomorrow, 1963-78, Planning and Development Corp., 1965-74, Regional Science Research Institute, 1965-78, and Lasker Trust, 1968-78. Chairman of California Council on Intergovernmental Relations, 1967-68; member of economic council, Philadelphia Chamber of Commerce. Member of Democratic Advisory Council, 1959-61; consultant in the field of planning and urban development, 1960-78.

MEMBER: American Institute of Planners (member of board of governors, 1958-61), Planning Foundation of America (member of board of directors, 1965-78), National Housing Conference (chairman, 1956-58, president, 1958-60, member of board of directors, 1948-78), National Association of Housing and Renewal Officials, American Society of Planning Officials (member of board of governors, 1970-74), American Political Science Association, Regional Science Association, Lambda Alpha, Princeton Club. *Awards, honors:* Distinguished Service Medal, American Society of Planning Officials, 1974.

WRITINGS: (With M. J. Schussheim) *The Cost of Municipal Services in Residential Areas,* Housing and Home Finance Agency, 1955; (with Martin Myerson) *Housing, People and Cities,* McGraw, 1961; *Explorations into Urban Structure,* University of Pennsylvania Press, 1963; *Integration of Political Communities,* Lippincott, 1964; (editor with Grace Milgram and Mary Ellin Meyerson) *Urban Housing,* Free Press, 1966; (with Warren W. Jones and Warren H. Fox) *Adapting Professional Manpower from Aerospace to Urban Government,* College of Environmental Design, University of California, 1972. Contributor of about twenty study reports and articles to professional journals.

WORK IN PROGRESS: With Clyde Roseman, *Planning in the Philadelphia Metropolitan Region,* for University of California Press.†

*   *   *

WHISTLER, Laurence 1912-

PERSONAL: Born January 21, 1912, in Eltham, Kent, England; son of Henry (a building contractor) and Helen (Ward) Whistler; married Jill Furse (an actress), September 12, 1939 (died 1944); married Theresa Furse (an author), August 15, 1950; children: (first marriage) Simon, Caroline; (second marriage) Daniel, Frances. *Education:* Balliol College, Oxford, B.A. (with 2nd class honors in English literature), 1934. *Religion:* Church of England. *Home:* Alton Barnes, Marlborough, Wiltshire, England.

CAREER: Poet and author. Engraver of glass, chiefly steelpoint or drill, 1935—. *Military service:* British Army, 1940-45, serving in Royal Corps of Signals, 1940-41, and Rifle Brigade, 1941-45; became captain. *Member:* Royal Society of Literature (fellow), Society of Authors, Guild of Glass Engravers (first president, 1975-80), Glass Circle. *Awards, honors:* Chancellor's English Essay Prize, Oxford University, 1934; Royal Medal for Poetry, 1935; Atlantic Award in Literature, 1945; Commander, Order of the British Empire, 1970.

WRITINGS: Children of Hertha, and Other Poems, Holywell Press, 1929; *Proletaria, en avant!: A Poem of Socialism,* Alden Press, 1932; *Armed October, and Other Poems,*

Cobden-Sanderson, 1932; *Four Walls,* (poems), Heinemann, 1934, Macmillan, 1935; *The Emperor Heart* (poems), Heinemann, 1936, Macmillan, 1937; *Sir John Vanbrugh, Architect and Dramatist, 1664-1726,* Cobden-Sanderson, 1938, Macmillan, 1939; *In Time of Suspense* (poems), Heinemann, 1940; *The Burning Glass,* privately printed, 1941; *Ode to the Sun, and Other Poems,* Heinemann, 1942; *Who Live in Unity* (poems), Heinemann, 1944; *Jill Furse: Her Nature and Her Poems, 1915-1944,* Chiswick Press, 1945; (with brother, Rex Whistler) *Oho!: Certain Two-Faced Individuals Now Exposed by the Bodley Head,* John Lane, 1946; *The Masque of Christmas: Dramatic Joys of the Festival, Old and New,* Curtain Press, 1947; *The English Festivals,* Heinemann, 1947; *Rex Whistler: His Life and His Drawings,* Art & Technics, 1948, Pellegrini & Cudahy, 1949; *The World's Room* (collected poems), Heinemann, 1949.

(Editor and author of introduction) *Selected Poems of John Keats,* Grey Walls Press, 1950; (editor and author of introduction) R. Whistler, *The Koenigsmark Drawings,* Richards Press, 1952; *The Engraved Glass of Laurence Whistler,* Hart-Davis, 1952; *The Kissing Bough: A Christmas Custom,* Heinemann, 1953; *The Imagination of Vanbrugh, and His Fellow Artists,* Art & Technics, 1954; *Stowe: A Guide to the Gardens,* published for Stowe School by Country Life, 1956; *The View from This Window* (poems), Hart-Davis, 1956; *Engraved Glass, 1952-1958,* Hart-Davis, 1959; (with Ronald Fuller) *The Work of Rex Whistler,* Batsford, 1960; *Audible Silence* (poems), Hart-Davis, 1961; *Fingal's Cave* (poem), privately printed, 1963; *The Initials in the Heart,* Houghton, 1964, 2nd edition, Hart-Davis, 1966; *To Celebrate Her Living* (poems), Hart-Davis, 1967; *For Example: Ten Sonnets in Sequence to a New Pattern* (poems), privately printed, 1969; *Way: Two Affirmations, in Glass and Verse,* Golden Head Press, 1969; *Pictures on Glass,* Cupid Press, 1972; *The Image on the Glass,* J. Murray, 1975; *AHA,* illustrations by Rex Whistler, Houghton, 1979. Occasional contributor to *Connoisseur, Country Life,* and *Times Literary Supplement.*

WORK IN PROGRESS: A biography of his brother, Rex Whistler, tentatively entitled *The Laughter and the Urn.*

SIDELIGHTS: Laurence Whistler told *CA* he began the revival of diamond point engraving on glass in Britain in 1935. He engraves goblets, decanters, window-panes, and also large-scale works like office panels and church windows. His books are chiefly concerned with architecture and with the work of his elder brother, the artist Rex Whistler, killed in action with the Welsh Guards in Normandy in 1944. (Several of Whistler's books of poetry are also illustrated with his brother's artwork.) *The Initials in the Heart* is the story of Laurence Whistler's first marriage.

BIOGRAPHICAL/CRITICAL SOURCES: Punch, July 5, 1967; *Books and Bookmen,* November, 1967.

*   *   *

WHITE, Alan
(James Fraser, Alec Whitney)

PERSONAL: Born in Yorkshire, England. *Agent:* John Cushman Associates, Inc., 25 West 43rd St., New York, N.Y. 10036.

WRITINGS: Death Finds the Day, Harcourt, 1965 (published in England as *The Long Day's Dying,* Hodder & Stoughton, 1965); *The Wheel,* Hodder & Stoughton, 1966, Harcourt, 1967; *The Long Night's Walk,* Hodder & Stoughton, 1968, Harcourt, 1969; *The Long Drop,* Barrie & Jenkins, 1969, Harcourt, 1970; *Possess the Land,* Harcourt, 1970 (published in England as *Kibbutz,* Barrie & Jenkins,

1970); *The Long Watch*, Harcourt, 1971; *The Long Midnight*, Barrie & Jenkins, 1972, Harcourt, 1974; *The Long Fuse*, Barrie & Jenkins, 1973, Harcourt, 1974; *The Long Summer*, Barrie & Jenkins, 1974, Harcourt, 1975; *The Long Hand of Death*, Barrie & Jenkins, 1977; *The Long Silence*, Mason/Charter, 1977; *Ravenswycke*, Houghton, 1980.

Under pseudonym James Fraser: *The Evergreen Death*, Jenkins, 1968, Harcourt, 1969; *A Cock-Pit of Roses*, Jenkins, 1969, Harcourt, 1970; *Deadly Nightshade*, Harcourt, 1970; *Death in a Pheasant's Eye*, Barrie & Jenkins, 1971; *The Five-Leafed Clover*, Barrie & Jenkins, 1973; *A Wreath of Lords and Ladies*, Barrie & Jenkins, 1974, Doubleday, 1975; *Who Steals My Name . . .?*, Doubleday, 1976; *Heart's Ease in Death*, Doubleday, 1977.

Under pseudonym Alec Whitney: *Armstrong*, Barrie & Jenkins, 1973, Doubleday, 1977; *Death in Darkness*, Barrie & Jenkins, 1975, Doubleday, 1977.†

*   *   *

WHITE, Edmund III 1940-

PERSONAL: Born January 13, 1940, in Cincinnati, Ohio; son of Edmund Valentine II (an engineer) and Delilah (a psychologist; maiden name, Teddlie) White. *Education:* University of Michigan, B.A., 1962. *Agent:* Helen Brann, Helen Brann Agency, Inc., 14 Sutton Pl. S., New York, N.Y. 10022.

CAREER: Time, Inc., Book Division, New York City, staff writer, 1962-70; *Saturday Review*, New York City, senior editor, 1972-73; writer. *Awards, honors:* Hopwood Awards, 1961 and 1962, for fiction and drama; Ingram Merrill grant, 1973, in support of work on novel.

WRITINGS—Nonfiction, except as indicated: (With Peter Wood) *When Zeppelins Flew*, Time-Life, 1969; *Forgetting Elena* (novel), Random House, 1973; (with Dale Browne) *The First Men*, Time-Life, 1973; (with Charles Silverstein) *The Joy of Gay Sex: An Intimate Guide for Gay Men to the Pleasures of a Gay Lifestyle*, Crown, 1977; *Nocturnes for the King of Naples* (novel), St. Martin's, 1978; *States of Desire: Travels in Gay America*, Dutton, 1980. Also author of *Argument for a Myth* and "The Blue Boy in Black," a play, first performed in New York City at Masque Theater, April, 1963.

WORK IN PROGRESS: A novel, tentatively entitled *Woman Reading Pascal*.

SIDELIGHTS: Edmund White's first novel, *Forgetting Elena*, has been widely praised for its satiric and insightful look at social interaction. A mystery novel, the book concerns a young man (the narrator) who suddenly wakes not knowing who or where he is. As he seeks his identity, as well as the identities of those around him, he becomes enmeshed in a game of social survival. He finds that he has awakened in an artistically elite society; in the dark as to the systems of social hierarchy and etiquette, he struggles to avoid humiliation and to gain social acceptance. In *Library Journal*, White states that the novel's premise illustrates "how sinister" life would be in an artistically obsessed society. He explains: "Every word and gesture would be governed by a subtle etiquette and would convey a symbolic meaning. Ordinary morality would be obscured or forgotten. People would seek the beautiful and not the good—and perhaps, cut free from ethics, the beautiful would turn out to be merely pretty."

Critics, however, believe that *Forgetting Elena* has greater implications than those noted above. "Edmund White seems to be engaging in a satirical examination of a specific subcul-

ture in a definite geographical location [Fire Island, N.Y.]," according to the *Nation's* Simon Karlinsky, "but before he is done he has produced a parable about the nature of social interaction that transcends any given period and applies to the human predicament at large." Karlinsky adds that "White's analysis of the drives and pressures common to *all* groupings, cliques and coteries which are based on the presumption of the members' superiority to the rest of mankind . . . is revealing and thorough." Alan Friedman calls *Forgetting Elena* "a masterful piece of work" and an "astonishing first novel." He continues: "Its poetic brilliance is more precious and more devious than the precious deviousness it scrutinizes. Moreover, it precisely strives for that effect from the start, the effect of a 'charade or hieroglyph.' When it ends, my private eye tells me that the young man knew himself better before he found out who he was. That may be a virtue in a detective story as far-reaching as this one, the tale of a sleuth who strives to detect the mystery of the self."

Nocturnes for the King of Naples, White's second novel, has won similar acclaim for its discerning treatment of human values and relationships. As John Yohalem explains in the *New York Times Book Review*, "*Nocturnes* is a series of apostrophes to a nameless, evidently famous dead lover, a man who awakened the much younger, also nameless narrator . . . to the possibility of sexual friendship. It was an experience that the narrator feels he did not justly appreciate," Yohalem continues, "and that he has long and passionately—and fruitlessly—sought to replace on his own terms." David Shields of the *Chicago Tribune* offers this assessment of the novel's impact: "Because of the speaker's final realization of the impossibility of ever finding a ground for satisfaction, a home, this book is more than a chronicle of sorrow and regret. It becomes, rather, a true elegy in which sorrow and self-knowledge combine and transform into a higher form of insight. This higher insight is the artistic intuition of the mortality of human things and ways."

Reaction to *States of Desire: Travels in Gay America*, White's "guide" to homosexual communities across America, has been widespread and generally favorable, although some critics have expressed indignation at the book's militant tone. *Newsweek's* Walter Clemons finds *States of Desire* "consistently entertaining and often funny," but also "troubling" because of "White's militant stance [which] is calculated to ruffle many gays as well as most straights." Clemons notes that White's "novelistic gifts—curiosity about character (his own as well as others), an alert ear and eye for revelatory detail—make this book absorbing."

Not all critics, however, have reviewed the book with such enthusiasm. The *New York Times'* John Leonard, for example, criticizes White for raising then failing to answer several "interesting questions" concerning "the modern homosexual subculture." Moreover, Leonard states that he was annoyed by White's apparent "disdain" toward heterosexuals and his willingness "to forgive the preposterous in a homosexual [more readily] than in a heterosexual." Paul Cowan of the *New York Times Book Review* chides White for producing "an aimless, shapeless narrative that sometimes borders on pornography," instead of "a fine, revealing book" that may have enabled heterosexuals to better understand homosexual lifestyles and problems. Cowan elaborates: "Though his book is partly autobiographical, he never tries to help readers who don't share his sexual preference to understand his assumptions or the assumptions of the people he describes. . . . Though he seems to like the promiscuous America he portrays, he never makes it seem even remotely attractive to an outsider."

Despite such criticism, the response to *States of Desire,* has been generally favorable. Ned Rorem of the *Washington Post Book World* remarks that in spite of its flaws, "this book tenders its subject without apology and with the cultural clarity of an address to peers." And Leonard concludes: "Mr White comes out of the closet with a brass band and a Moog synthesizer. He acquaints us with terror and qualm. Simply as anthropology, *States of Desire* commands attention and respect."

BIOGRAPHICAL/CRITICAL SOURCES: New York Times Book Review, March 25, 1973, February 3, 1980; *Newsweek,* April 30, 1973, February 11, 1980; *Nation,* January 5, 1974, March 1, 1980; *Washington Post Book World,* November 12, 1978, December 10, 1978, January 27, 1980; *Chicago Tribune,* December 10, 1978, April 6, 1980; *Harper's,* March, 1979; *New York Times,* January 21, 1980; *Times Literary Supplement,* September 5, 1980.†

—*Sketch by Denise Gottis*

*   *   *

WHITE, Leslie A(lvin)   1900-1975

PERSONAL: Born January 19, 1900, in Salida, Colo.; died March 31, 1975, in Lone Pine, Calif.; son of Alvin Lincoln and Mildred (Millard) White; married Mary A. Pattison, February 9, 1931 (deceased). *Education:* Attended Louisiana State University, 1919-21, and New School for Social Research, 1922-24; Columbia University, A.B., 1923, A.M., 1924; University of Chicago, Ph.D., 1927.

CAREER: University of Buffalo (now State University of New York at Buffalo), instructor, 1927-28, assistant professor of sociology and anthropology, 1928-30; University of Michigan, Ann Arbor, assistant professor, 1930-32, associate professor, 1932-43, professor of anthropology, beginning 1943, chairman of department, 1945-47. Curator of anthropology, Buffalo Museum of Science, 1927-30; instructor, summer session, University of Chicago, 1931, and Columbia University, 1948; lecturer, Yenching University (China), 1936; visiting professor at Yale University, 1947, Harvard University, 1949, University of California, Berkeley, 1957, Rice University, 1970, San Francisco State College (now University), 1970-71, and University of California, Santa Barbara, beginning 1971. Fellow, Center for Advance Study in the Behavioral Sciences, Stanford University, 1960-61. *Military service:* U.S. Navy, 1918-19; became petty officer third class. *Member:* American Anthropological Association (member of executive board, 1959-61; president, 1963-64), American Folk-Lore Society (treasurer, 1931), American Association for Advancement of Science (vice-president, chairman, Section H, 1958), Research Club (University of Michigan), Phi Beta Kappa. *Awards, honors:* Distinguished Faculty Service Award, University of Michigan, 1957; Viking Medal and Award, 1959; Sc.D., University of Buffalo, 1962; L.L.D., University of California, 1970.

WRITINGS: The Acoma Indians, U.S. Bureau of American Ethnology, 1929-30, reprinted, Rio Grande, 1973; *The Pueblo of Santo Domingo, New Mexico,* American Anthropological Association, 1935, reprinted, Kraus Reprint, 1969; (editor) *Pioneers in American Anthropology: The Bandelier-Morgan Letters, 1873-1883,* University of New Mexico Press, 1940, reprinted, AMS Press, 1978; *The Pueblo of Santa Ana, New Mexico,* American Anthropological Association, 1942, reprinted, Kraus Reprint, 1969; *The Science of Culture: A Study of Man and Civilization,* Farrar, Straus, 1949, 2nd edition, 1969; *The Evolution of Culture: The Development of Civilization to the Fall of Rome,* McGraw,

1959; (editor and author of introduction) Lewis Henry Morgan, *The Indian Journals, 1859-62,* University of Michigan Press, 1959; (contributor) Adolph Francis Alphonse Bandelier, *Correspondencia de Adolfo F. Bandelier,* Instituto Nacional de Antropologia e Historia (Mexico), 1960; *The Pueblo of Sia, New Mexico,* U.S. Government Printing Office, 1962, published as *Zia, the Sun Symbol Pueblo,* Calvin Horn, 1974; *The Ethnography and Ethnology of Franz Boas,* Texas Memorial Museum, University of Texas at Austin, 1963; (editor) Lewis Henry Morgan, *Ancient Society,* Harvard University Press, 1964; (with Beth Dillingham) *The Concept of Culture,* Burgess, 1973; *Journal of a Trip to the Orient,* Tourmaline Press, 1973; *The Concept of Cultural Systems: A Key to Understanding Tribes and Nations,* Columbia University Press, 1975. Also author of anthropological monographs, including *The Pueblo of San Felipe,* American Anthropological Association, 1932, and *The Social Organization of Ethnological Theory,* Rice University, 1966. Contributor of articles to professional journals. Also editor of *Extracts from the Travel Journals of Lewis Henry Morgan,* 1937.

BIOGRAPHICAL/CRITICAL SOURCES: G. E. Dole and R. L. Carneiro, editors, *Essays in the Science of Culture in Honor of Leslie A. White,* Crowell, 1960.†

*   *   *

WHITE, Terence de Vere   1912-

PERSONAL: Born April 29, 1912, in Dublin, Ireland; son of Frederick S. D. de Vere (a doctor of law) and Ethel (Perry) White; married Elizabeth Mary O'Farrell (a potter), 1941; children: Deborah White Singmaster, Ralph, John. *Education:* Trinity College, Dublin, B.A. (with honors), 1931, LL.B., 1933. *Religion:* Roman Catholic. *Agent:* R. S. Simon, 32 College Cross, London N.1., England.

CAREER: Called to the Bar, 1933; former solicitor and senior partner, McCann, Fitzgerald, Roche & Dudley; Incorporated Law Society, Dublin, Ireland, member of council, 1954-61; *Irish Times,* Dublin, literary editor, 1961-77; author. Member of board of trustees, National Library of Ireland, 1949-78, and Chester Beatty Library, 1968-79; vice-chairman, National Gallery of Ireland, 1967—; member of board of directors, Gate Theatre, 1970—; professor of literature, Royal Hibernian Academy, 1973—. *Member:* Irish Academy of Letters, Royal Hibernian Academy (honorary member), Kildare Street Club.

WRITINGS: The Road of Excess (biography), Brown & Nolan, 1946; *Kevin O'Higgins* (biography), Methuen, 1948; *The Story of the Royal Dublin Society,* Kerryman, 1955; *A Fretful Midge,* Routledge & Kegan Paul, 1957; (editor) George Egerton, *A Leaf from the Yellow Book: Letters and Diaries of George Egerton,* Richards Press, 1958; *An Affair with the Moon* (novel), Gollancz, 1959; *Prenez Garde* (novel), Gollancz, 1966; *The Remainder Man* (novel), Gollancz, 1963; *Lucifer Falling* (novel), Gollancz, 1966, World Publishing, 1967; *The Parents of Oscar Wilde: Sir William and Lady Wilde* (biography), Hodder & Stoughton, 1967; *Tara* (novel), Gollancz, 1967; *Ireland,* Walker & Co., 1968; *Leinster,* Faber, 1968; *The Lambert Mile* (novel), Gollancz, 1969, published as *The Lambert Revels,* Little, Brown, 1970.

The March Hare (novel), Gollancz, 1970; *The Minister for Justice* (novel), Gambit, 1971 (published in England as *Mr. Stephen,* Gollancz, 1971); *The Anglo-Irish,* Gollancz, 1972; *The Distance and the Dark* (novel), Gambit, 1973; *The Radish Memoirs,* Gollancz, 1974; *Big Fleas as Little Fleas,* Gollancz, 1976; *Tom Moore,* Hamish Hamilton, 1977; *Chimes at*

Midnight, Gollancz, 1977; *My Name Is Norval,* Gollancz, 1978, Harper, 1979; *Birds of Prey,* Gollancz, 1980. Contributor to *Horizon, Cambridge Review, Sunday Times,* and *Observer.*

* * *

WHITE, Theodore H(arold) 1915-

PERSONAL: Born May 6, 1915, in Boston, Mass.; son of David and Mary (Winkeller) White; married Nancy Ariana Van Der Heyden Bean, March 29, 1947 (divorced, 1971); married Beatrice Kevitt Hofstadter, March, 1974; children: (first marriage) Ariana Van der Heyden, David Fairbank. *Education:* Harvard University, A.B. (summa cum laude), 1938. *Home:* Old Route 67, Bridgewater, Conn. 06752. *Office:* 168 East 64th St., New York, N.Y. 10021. *Agent:* Julian Bach Literary Agency, Inc., 3 East 48th St., New York, N.Y. 10017.

CAREER: Time Magazine, New York City, Far East correspondent and chief of China bureau, 1939-45; *New Republic* Magazine, New York City, editor, 1947; Overseas News Agency, New York City, chief European correspondent, 1948-50; *Reporter* Magazine, New York City, chief European correspondent, 1950-53, national correspondent, 1955-56; free-lance writer and correspondent, 1956—. Covered China war front, Indian uprising, and Honan famine during World War II; present at Japanese surrender aboard U.S.S. Missouri, 1945; covered post-World War II European events, including administration of Marshall Plan and North Atlantic Treaty Organization. Member of board of overseers, Harvard University, 1968-74. *Member:* Council on Foreign Relations, Foreign Correspondents Club (president, 1944-45), National Press Club (Washington, D.C.), Phi Beta Kappa, Century Club, Harvard Club. *Awards, honors:* Sidney Hillman Foundation Award, 1954, and National Association of Independent Schools Award, 1954, both for *Fire in the Ashes;* Benjamin Franklin Magazine Award, 1956, for article in *Collier's,* "Germany—Friend or Foe?"; Ted V. Rodgers Award, 1956; Pulitzer Prize for general nonfiction, 1962, and National Association of Independent Schools Award, 1962, both for *The Making of the President: 1960;* Emmy Award of National Academy of Television Arts and Sciences, 1964, for best television film in all categories, "The Making of the President: 1960," and 1967, for best documentary television writing, "China: The Roots of Madness"; Fourth Estate Award, National Press Club; Journalist of the Year Award, Columbia School of Journalism.

WRITINGS: (With Annalee Jacoby) *Thunder Out of China* (Book-of-the-Month Club selection), Sloane, 1946, reprinted, Da Capo Press, 1980; (editor) Joseph Warren Stilwell, *The Stillwell Papers,* Sloane, 1948, reprinted, Schocken, 1972; *Fire in the Ashes* (Book-of-the-Month Club selection), Sloane, 1953, reprinted, 1968; *The Mountain Road* (Book-of-the-Month Club selection), Sloane, 1958; *The View From the Fortieth Floor* (Literary Guild selection), Sloane, 1960; *The Making of the President: 1960,* Atheneum, 1961; *The Making of the President: 1964,* Atheneum, 1965; *Caesar at the Rubicon: A Play about Politics,* Atheneum, 1968, published as *Caesar at the Rubicon: A Play in Three Acts,* Samuel French, 1971; *China: The Roots of Madness* (revision of television documentary script; also see below), Norton, 1968; *The Making of the President: 1968,* Atheneum, 1969; *The Making of the President: 1972* (Literary Guild selection), Atheneum, 1973; *Breach of Faith: The Fall of Richard Nixon* (Book-of-the-Month Club selection), Atheneum, 1975; *In Search of History: A Personal Adventure,* Harper, 1978.

Also author of television documentary scripts, including "The Making of the President: 1960," "China: The Roots of Madness," and "The Making of the President: 1968."

Contributor to *Life, Time, Fortune, Reporter, Holiday, Harper's, Saturday Review, Collier's, New York,* and other magazines and newspapers.

SIDELIGHTS: With the publication of *The Making of the President: 1960,* his Pulitzer Prize-winning report on the 1960 presidential campaign and election, Theodore White established a tradition of excellence that not only himself but others have found difficult to live up to. Considered by many to be a classic in political journalism, it was, as a *National Observer* critic notes, "a ground-breaking achievement," for "no one before had thought to bring a whole presidential campaign together in a single, lucid, anecdotal, and timely volume." A *San Francisco Chronicle* reviewer calls it "the most exhilarating non-fiction of the season. . . . It is both exciting and revealing Americana. . . . A familiar story . . . appears to be new and fresh as White reconstructs it. He does so with brilliance, intelligence and for the most part scrupulous objectivity." Bernard Levin of the *Spectator* comments: "Not since Mencken has there been American political reporting of this quality, and Mencken had little of Mr. White's thoroughness and none of his stunningly persuasive objectivity. . . . He produces one of the most exciting and significant pieces of socio-political analysis for years. . . . As journalism [the book] is unsurpassed; as a record and textbook it is invaluable."

James MacGregor Burns, writing in the *New York Times Book Review,* states: "No book that I know of has caught the heartbeat of a campaign as strikingly as Theodore White has done in *The Making of the President: 1960.* . . . By artistic rearrangement of his materials he has gained space for long, hard appraisals of American politics. . . . If this book were merely a campaign report, it could be recommended glowingly on its own terms. But it is more than this." A *Saturday Review* critic sees it as "an extraordinary performance by a shrewd interpreter of the American scene. . . . It launches what I hope will be a new genre in American political literature. It is sensitive and brilliant reporting, and an invaluable document for history."

Several other critics, however, question White's objectivity. Though most have high praise for his overall achievement in reporting on such a complex chain of events, they feel that his partiality towards certain political figures (as well as an accompanying touch of sentimentality about American politics in general) detracts from the book's impact. "Author White strives for objectivity," reports *Time,* "but there is no question whose campaign button adorned his lapel. . . . His coverage of Kennedy is more complete, more successful than his picture of Nixon. . . . A complete analysis of the 1960 campaign will have to await a later day and more penetrating research. As reporting, the book is a notable achievement. White has written a fascinating story of a fascinating campaign." A *Christian Science Monitor* critic agrees that "never has there been as competent, penetrating, and complete account of an American presidential election as this." But, after noting that White was "warmly received" by the Kennedy group while Nixon's "held [him] at arm's length," the reviewer concludes: "[White] struggles manfully to clarify the Nixon character and only partly succeeds. . . . The book is written in the emotional mood of the correspondents traveling with Mr. Kennedy in the last weeks of the campaign, when they expected a landslide. This is a serious flaw, since the meaning of the outcome is greatly overstated."

The Making of the President: 1964 was not as successful as its predecessor, perhaps, as the *National Observer* critic points out, "because the campaign itself was less interesting.... [White] found no heroes in 1964; like so many others, he saw no romance in Lyndon Johnson or Barry Goldwater." In the *New York Review of Books,* I. F. Stone admits that "Theodore H. White has become the poet laureate of American presidential campaigns." Nevertheless, he concludes, *The Making of the President: 1964* "is on a lower level" than its predecessor. "The wonder and zest of the first often decline into a schoolgirlish gushiness in the second. The first is muscular, the second mawkish.... [Yet] no one could feel a candidate's pulse more sympathetically [than White]." The *New Yorker* notes that "[Mr. White] does quite a good job of it.... His method is a compound of diary-keeping, daily journalism, weekly journalism, editorial writing, and extrasensory perception. It is an entertaining mixture, and some of the microscopic details are priceless, but on the whole, it is more White than history." A *Times Literary Supplement* reviewer writes: "Alas, the 1964 version has all and much more than all the faults of the first book and hardly any of its merits. It is a depressing failure.... The *aficionados* of American politics will find a little new information here, some, if too infrequent, patches of Mr. White at his brilliant reporter's best ... and a good deal of unimpressive political cogitation."

On the other hand, an *Atlantic* reviewer notes: "In *The Making of the President: 1960* Theodore H. White had almost a classical plot with a single action and a single hero.... By comparison, 1964 presented a more diffuse and less focused drama. Yet *The Making of the President: 1964* is in many ways a more exciting book, if only because his earlier triumph has sharpened Mr. White's skill at a style of reporting that he seems to have made all his own.... His politicians ... emerge as three-dimensional characters in a way not usual in political reporting."

It was not, however, until the appearance of *The Making of the President: 1968* that critics began to take a long, hard look at White's approach. What had only been mentioned more or less in passing by a few reviewers in 1960 and 1964—namely, White's occasional lack of objectivity as well as his patriotic sentimentality about America and the American political system—became a major problem in the eyes of the 1968 reviewers. A *Commonweal* critic writes: "Like Harold Stassen, T. H. White is ruining a good thing with his quadrennial lustings after the presidency.... This third *Making* book is the plain *reductio ad absurdum* of the first, which—for all its fascination and birth of genre—was conspicuously sanguine on issues and soft on politicians.... While White's coziness with the candidates may not have hurt his books all that much in 1960 and 1964 when the old politics still had some kick, he is terribly guilty by his associations in *Making 1968....* The unhappiest feature of *Making 1968* is the reporter's undisguised sympathy for the establishment.... Except for the Wallace campaign and the peace movement, basely equated in their extremism, White is all heroes and worship.... [But] apart from internal criticism, *Making 1968* fails for large reasons. A single reporter is simply incommensurate with a presidential campaign.... 'This is the most dramatic confrontation of America and its problems in over 100 years,' White mused in *Newsweek* before publication. 'It's just a question of whether I'm good enough to write the story for what it's really worth.' He wasn't."

Bill Moyers, writing in *Saturday Review,* notes: "If Theodore White did not exist, the Ford Foundation would have to award Harvard University a grant to create him. How else would the Establishment tell its story? *The Making of the President: 1968* is essentially that: the authorized version, the view through the official keyhole. For Teddy White, the most successful entrepreneur of political detail and perception in American journalism today, tells the story of 1968 as he did four and eight years ago.... But times have changed.... 1968 was the Year of Decay.... Under such circumstances no single author, not even a Teddy White, could chart the shifting boundaries of our political terrain. That he has tried, against impossible odds, is a tribute to the man's intrepid will. Certainly his is the most coherent and the most eloquent account we are likely to get from any reporter's notes.... But there is a tone in it that we are not accustomed to hearing in Teddy White."

"Most of what [he] reports is interesting," continues Moyers, "much of what he does *not* report is significant. Something is missing because interpreting politics at the top so completely and so officially for eight years had finally caught up with Theodore White.... He could not, in honest loyalty as well as by instinct, completely separate himself from the beseiged.... He could never achieve total freedom from his prejudices.... And so White is left with this splendid story, not wholly true.... [He] told us what happened at the top, and told it as no one else can. But the top was no longer that important."

A *Time* reviewer writes: "In two previous chronicles of President-making, Theodore H. White's talents were more than equal to the task.... This time the odds were against him. White's best reportage delineates character; portraiture is his forte. In 1968, events overshadowed individuals.... White's reconstruction of these events often bears the paste-pot smell of newspaper clippings.... His reaction is detached and too concerned with the pattern of the old politics.... There are nuggets of anecdotage along the way.... [But] after eight years and three elections, White has established his own political system. He has a vast network of friendly power brokers, government aides, trend watchers, reporters, poll takers and precinct vigilantes. This book is almost overwhelmed by his efforts to preserve—and not to offend—this intricate organization."

White's *The Making of the President: 1972* was criticized for virtually the same excesses and deficiencies as the 1968 version. "The rambling chronicle offers few new insights into either the Nixon victory or the McGovern defeat," writes a *New Republic* reviewer. "Watergate aside, White willingly accepts most of the Nixon rationale—even on the war.... But if the analysis is disappointing, the level of characterization is more gratifying, reflecting the legwork, extensive interviews and careful research involved." Garry Wills of the *New York Review of Books,* noting the author's "indiscriminate celebration of the ruler" (Nixon), concludes that "the 'Whitiad,' now in its second decade, gets worse stanza by stanza.... White conducts his old civics lesson without having learned a thing." Finally, Anthony Lewis of the *New York Times* offers this summary of *The Making of the President: 1972:* "Theodore H. White is so awesomely diligent a reporter, so accomplished a political analyst, so engaging a person that criticizing him seems like sacrilege.... But ... it is time for someone to say that White has written a bad book. *The Making of the President: 1972* is as impressive as its predecessors in its eye for both the revealing detail and the sweep of events. But White naturally does more than describe. He gives his own judgment on larger historical issues, and there I think he has gone profoundly wrong.... Alas, one [also] detects in Theodore White some of that unfortunate pleasure in curling up with the powerful. . . . [As a result,] winners take all in the White universe; and losers get no mercy.''

In 1976, restless and unable to apply himself to the task of preparing for and writing *The Making of the President: 1976,* White broke with tradition and turned to writing about himself instead. The result, *In Search of History,* is called ''a minor classic of American biography'' by the *New Leader.* ''It vibrates with the themes most characteristic of national self-discovery,'' continues the reviewer, ''recording the passage from obscurity and poverty to the close observation of power,' from facts to ideas, from promise to fulfillment and then to perplexity.'' But even in his autobiography White comes under fire for his lack of objectivity. ''The special insignia of White's writing has long been the evocation of sympathy,'' reports the *New Leader.* ''The autobiography is similarly free of rancor. Almost everyone . . . is washed in authorial good will.'' Furthermore, the reviewer writes, White's ''own sense of politics remains rooted in camaraderie rather than causes, and in attributing to politicians ideas that are really only mental gestures, White once again exaggerates the importance of the men he has covered.''

Richard Rovere of the *New York Times Book Review* calls *In Search of History* ''by far [White's] finest, most affecting work. . . . It has all the pace and energy of the earlier work and more of many other things; more insight, more reflection, more candor, more intimacy, more humor, more humility, surer and sharper judgments of those he writes about, including himself.'' On the other hand, Christopher Lehmann-Haupt feels that ''somewhere in this public autobiography Mr. White seems to lose his way. The first half is extremely strong—the sections covering his youth, his education, and his adventures in China. Here personal experience very nearly equals history. . . . But somehow in the second half, the momentum of White's narrative falters. This isn't to say that vivid close-up portraits of historical figures don't continue to appear. . . . It is simply that when White moves on from China to Europe to witness that continent's post-war recovery, and then back to the United States to report on domestic politics, the center of the action moves away from him. He is no longer really part of the story he is covering, as he was in China. So when he writes about himself he neglects history, and vice versa.'' Lehmann-Haupt, in addition to several other reviewers, finds White's occasional use of the third person when referring to himself to be somewhat distracting. ''Nowhere do these passages stop reminding us by their lack of irony and humor how much more successfully this device fares in the hands of Norman Mailer,'' he concludes.

William Greider of *Book World* states that, as a reflective memoir, *In Search of History* simply ''doesn't work. [White] begins bravely, announcing self-doubts and confusion, but after traveling through many continents and interesting events, glimpsing famous men from Mao to Eisenhower, one is left at the conclusion with the same questions. Readers who loved the powerful narrative line of White's other books will find this one strangely disjointed and unthematic. . . . The memoir ends lamely, acknowledging that he has not really sorted out the fundamental confusions about politics and the nation.'' Unlike other reviewers, however, Greider does not particularly find the first part of the book to be much better than the last half, noting that ''even [White's] memories of wartime China and *Time* are seen through a murky lens,'' as if he is ''unable to address them directly.''

Finally, Eric F. Goldman of *Saturday Review* writes that *In Search of History* ''has its less than felicitous moments. It has long been noted that White is a man much given to heroes. . . . Moreover, White, like a number of journalists, throws a special aura around 'history.' . . . In this volume, [the author], anxious to escape what he considers the confines of journalism, at times pauses for a passage that can be disconcerting. . . . Happily, neither White's search for history, nor his proneness for heroes—nor his occasional splashes of neon prose—are major aspects of the book. For the most part, it is a work in the high tradition of American memoirs, written with power and grace of style, many an astute perception, and an attitude toward his country that is at once deeply affectionate, unhesitatingly critical, and engagingly quizzical. . . . White's treatment of his Chinese and European years in this book of memoirs is mellower, [and] more balanced, [than his earlier *Thunder out of China* and *Fire in the Ashes*] and it provides a constant flow of absorbing personal material. More strikingly, *In Search of History* includes frequent incisive, richly human vignettes of the great and not-so-great figures White came to know. . . . White indicates that a second and perhaps third volume of memoirs will follow. . . . If the future volume or volumes maintain the vivid, probing, questing 'storytelling' of the first, and White does not search too hard for 'history,' his total memoirs may well prove one the bench-mark books . . . of our generation.''

AVOCATIONAL INTERESTS: Woodworking, gardening, and painting.

BIOGRAPHICAL/CRITICAL SOURCES: Saturday Review, May 10, 1958, May 21, 1960, July 8, 1961, July 10, 1965, August 9, 1969, October 9, 1973, September 2, 1978; *New York Times Book Review,* May 11, 1958, May 22, 1960, July 9, 1961, July 11, 1965, April 14, 1968, September 22, 1968, August 6, 1978, December 24, 1978; *New York Herald Tribune Book Review,* May 11, 1958, May 22, 1960, July 9, 1961; *Atlantic,* June, 1958, August, 1961, August, 1965, May, 1968; *Time,* May 23, 1960, July 21, 1961, March 29, 1968, August 1, 1969, July 3, 1978; *New Yorker,* June 4, 1960, July 22, 1961, August 7, 1965, September 20, 1969; *Times Literary Supplement,* December 2, 1960, November 4, 1965; *San Francisco Chronicle,* July 5, 1961, July 6, 1961; *Christian Science Monitor,* July 6, 1961, September 4, 1969; *New Republic,* July 10, 1961, July 10, 1965, August 16, 1969, August 11, 1973, September 9, 1978; *Commonweal,* December 8, 1961, August 22, 1969; *New Statesman,* April 6, 1962; *Spectator,* April 6, 1962, December 6, 1969, May 2, 1970.

Life, June 18, 1965; *Book Week,* July 11, 1965; *National Observer,* July 12, 1965, August 18, 1969; *America,* July 17, 1965; *Harper's,* August, 1965; *New York Review of Books,* August 5, 1965, October 4, 1973, November 9, 1978; *Playboy,* May, 1968; *Best Sellers,* May 15, 1968, September 15, 1969, January, 1979; *Book World,* July 14, 1968, July 27, 1969, October 12, 1969, August 27, 1978; *New York Times,* January 2, 1969, July 9, 1969, July 23, 1969, February 21, 1971, August 30, 1973; *Newsweek,* January 13, 1969, July 28, 1969, August 13, 1973, August 14, 1978; *New York Post,* July 22, 1969; *Washington Post,* August 11, 1969; *Virginia Quarterly Review,* autumn, 1969; *New York,* September 8, 1969; *Christian Century,* October 1, 1969; *Observer,* November 23, 1969; *Newsday,* June 6, 1978; *People,* July 31, 1978; *Books of the Times,* August, 1978; *Nation,* October 14, 1978; *Los Angeles Times Book Review,* October 15, 1978; *Us,* October 17, 1978; *New Leader,* October 23, 1978; Theodore H. White, *In Search of History* (autobiography), Harper, 1978.

—*Sketch by Deborah A. Straub*

WHITEHOUSE, W(alter) A(lexander) 1915-

PERSONAL: Born February 27, 1915, in Huddersfield, England; son of Walter and Clara (Berry) Whitehouse; married Beatrice Mary Kent Smith, 1946 (died, 1971); married Audrey Ethel Lemmon, 1974. *Education:* St. John's College, Cambridge, M.A., 1936; Balliol College, Oxford, B.Litt. and M.A., 1940. *Office:* The Manse, Ravenstonedale, Cumbria, England.

CAREER: Minister of Elland Congregational Church, 1940-44; Oxford University, Mansfield College, Oxford, England, chaplain, and tutor, 1944-47; University of Durham, Durham, England, reader in divinity, 1947-65, principal of St. Cuthbert's Society, 1955-60, pro-vice-chancellor and sub-warden, 1961-64; University of Kent at Canterbury, Canterbury, England, professor of theology and master of Eliot College, 1965-77. *Awards, honors:* D.D., University of Edinburgh, 1960.

WRITINGS: (Contributor) *Reformation Old and New,* Lutterworth, 1947; *Christian Faith and the Scientific Attitude,* Philosophical Library, 1952; (contributor) *Essays in Christology for Karl Barth,* Lutterworth, 1956; *Order, Goodness, Glory,* Oxford University Press, 1960; (contributor) Daniel Thomas Jenkins, editor, *The Scope of Theology,* World Publishing, 1965; (with others) *Christian Confidence,* edited by Roger Tomes, S.P.C.K., 1970; *Authority of Grace,* T. & T. Clark, 1980.

*   *   *

WHITIN, Thomson McLintock 1923-

PERSONAL: Born January 12, 1923, in Worcester, Mass.; son of Richard Courtenay and Ina (Watson) Whitin; married Edith Osborn Sherer; children: Charles, Sonia, Holly, Richard. *Education:* Princeton University, A.B., 1943, M.A., 1949, Ph.D., 1952. *Home:* Jacoby Rd., Higgenum, Conn. *Office:* Wesleyan University, Middletown, Conn. 06457.

CAREER: Princeton University, Princeton, N.J., research associate, 1950-53; Massachusetts Institute of Technology, Cambridge, 1953-60, began as assistant professor, became associate professor; U.S. Atomic Energy Commission, Washington, D.C., chief economist, 1956-57; University of California, Berkeley, professor, 1960-63; Wesleyan University, Middletown, Conn., professor, 1963—. *Military service:* U.S. Navy, 1943-46; became lieutenant junior grade; awarded Atlantic and Pacific ribbons, two battle stars. *Member:* American Economic Association, The Institute of Management Sciences (secretary-treasurer, 1956-58; chairman of education committee, 1961), Operations Research Society of America (member of education committee, 1955; co-auditor, 1955; member of finance committee, 1960), Econometric Society (fellow).

WRITINGS: Theory of Inventory Management, Princeton University Press, 1953, revised edition, 1957; (with George Hadley) *Analysis of Inventory Systems,* Prentice-Hall, 1963.

Contributor: *Economic Activity Analysis,* Wiley, 1954; (with Hadley) H. Scarf and others, editors, *Multistage Inventory Models and Techniques,* Stanford University Press, 1963; (with H. M. Wagner) A. F. Veinott, editor, *Mathematical Studies in Management Science,* Macmillan, 1965; McShubik, editor, *Essays in Mathematical Economics,* Princeton University Press, 1967; Cavan and Bochove, editors, *Modelling for Government and Business,* Nijoff, 1977. Contributor to professional journals.

WHITING, Thomas A. 1917-

PERSONAL: Born June 21, 1917, in Camilla, Ga.; married Martha Page, November 21, 1944 (deceased); married Helen Knarr Thurmond; children: Peggy, Linda. *Education:* Emory University, A.B., 1941; Yale University, M. Div., 1944. *Home:* 1370 North Decatur Rd. N.E., Atlanta, Ga. 30306. *Office:* 159 Ralph McGill Ave., Atlanta, Ga. 30308.

CAREER: Minister of South Georgia Conference of the Methodist Church, 1944—; First Methodist Church, Valdosta, Ga., senior minister, 1957-63; Wesley Monumental Methodist Church, Savannah, Ga., senior minister, 1963-65; Peachtree Road Methodist Church, Atlanta, Ga., senior minister, 1965-76; First United Methodist Church, Decatur, Ga., senior minister, 1976-80, superintendent of Atlanta-Emory district, 1980—. Superintendent of Macon district, Macon, Ga., for one year. Preacher for Methodist series on radio program, "The Protestant Hour." *Member:* Omicron Delta Kappa, Kappa Alpha, Kiwanis. *Awards, honors:* D.D., Lambuth College, 1963.

WRITINGS: Sermons on the Prodigal Son, Abingdon, 1960; *Don't Be Afraid of the Dark,* Bethany Press, 1969. Also contributor to *I Heard the Call to Preach,* 1948. Contributor to religious publications.

WORK IN PROGRESS: Publication of his sermon series on "The Protestant Hour," tentatively entitled, *Be Good to Yourself,* for Abingdon.

AVOCATIONAL INTERESTS: Golf, music.

*   *   *

WHITNEY, J(ohn) D(enison) 1940-

PERSONAL: Born September 23, 1940, in Pasadena, Calif.; son of John K. and Nathalie A. (Crane) Whitney; married Judy A. Weyenberg, January 30, 1971; children: Barbara, Joanne, David, Roger, Douglas, Suzanne, Michael. *Education:* University of Michigan, B.A., 1962, M.A., 1966. *Home:* 3851 Henry St., Wausau, Wis. 54401. *Office:* Department of English, University of Wisconsin, Marathon Center, Wausau, Wis. 54401.

CAREER: Teacher of English in public schools of Allen Park, Mich., 1962-66; University of Wisconsin—Platteville, instructor in English, 1966-69; University of Wisconsin, Marathon Center, Wausau, 1969—, began as assistant professor, currently associate professor of English. *Awards, honors:* Wisconsin Arts Board writing fellowship, 1976.

WRITINGS—Poems: Hello, Artists Workshop Press, 1965, 2nd edition, 1967; *Tracks,* Elizabeth Press, 1969; *The Nabisco Warehouse,* Elizabeth Press, 1971; *sd,* Elizabeth Press, 1973; *Tongues,* Elizabeth Press, 1976; *Some,* Never Dismount Press, 1976; *Mother,* Chapbook Press, 1981.

Work is represented in anthologies, including *New Voices in American Poetry,* edited by D. A. Evans, Winthrop Publishing, 1973, *My Music Bent,* edited by James L. Weil, Elizabeth Press, 1973, and *Bear Crossings,* edited by Anne Newman and Julie Suk, New South Co., 1978. Editor and publisher, *It,* 1965-72.

WORK IN PROGRESS: A Text: A Commonplace Book of the New American Writing.

SIDELIGHTS: J. D. Whitney told *CA:* "When I write, I participate in the synergy of the process: the energy from which the poem springs, the energy I have in the act of writing (particularity, ear, attention, intelligence, specificity), the energy the writing itself generates when in process, the energy in language (the language we're alive in is alive). Poetry as oral/aural choreography: the dance of language in mouth and ear. Poet as vehicle, poet as cargo."

* * *

WHITNEY, Phyllis A(yame) 1903-

PERSONAL: Born September 9, 1903, in Yokohama, Japan; daughter of Charles Joseph and Lillian (Mandeville) Whitney; married George A. Gardner, 1925 (divorced); married Lovell F. Jahnke (a businessman), 1950; children: (first marriage) Georgia. *Education:* Attended public schools in Chicago, Ill. *Agent:* Patricia Myrer, McIntosh & Otis, 475 Fifth Ave., New York, N.Y. 10017.

CAREER: Author. Former children's book editor with the *Chicago Sun* and *Philadelphia Inquirer.* Taught juvenile writing at Northwestern University, New York University, and at writers' conferences. *Member:* Authors League of America, Mystery Writers of America (member of board of directors, 1959-62; president, 1975) Midland Authors, Children's Reading Round Table. *Awards, honors:* Youth Today contest winner, 1947, for *Willow Hill;* Edgar Allan Poe Award for best juvenile mystery, Mystery Writers of America, 1960, for *Mystery of the Haunted Pool,* and 1964, for *Mystery of the Hidden Hand;* Sequoyah Children's Book Award, 1963, for *Mystery of the Haunted Pool.*

WRITINGS—Novels for young people: *A Place for Ann,* Houghton, 1941; *A Star for Ginny,* Houghton, 1942; *A Window for Julie,* Houghton, 1943; *The Silver Inkwell,* Houghton, 1945; *Willow Hill,* McKay, 1947; *Ever After,* Houghton, 1948; *Linda's Homecoming,* McKay, 1950; *Love Me, Love Me Not,* Houghton, 1952; *Step to the Music,* Crowell, 1953; *A Long Time Coming,* McKay, 1954; *The Fire and the Gold,* Crowell, 1956; *The Highest Dream,* McKay, 1956; *Creole Holiday,* Westminster, 1959; *Nobody Likes Trina,* Westminster, 1972.

Mysteries for young people; all published by Westminster: *Mystery of the Gulls,* 1949; *The Island of Dark Woods,* 1951; *Mystery of the Black Diamonds,* 1954; *Mystery on the Isle of Skye,* 1955; *Mystery of the Green Cat,* 1957; *Secret of the Samurai Sword,* 1958; *Mystery of the Haunted Pool,* 1960; *Secret of the Tiger's Eye,* 1961; *Mystery of the Golden Horn,* 1962; *Mystery of the Hidden Hand,* 1963; *Secret of the Emerald Star,* 1964; *Mystery of the Angry Idol,* 1965; *Secret of the Spotted Shell,* 1967; *Secret of Goblin Glen,* 1968; *Mystery of the Crimson Ghost,* 1969; *Secret of the Missing Footprint,* 1970; *The Vanishing Scarecrow,* 1971; *Mystery of the Scowling Boy,* 1973; *Secret of Haunted Mesa,* 1975; *Secret of the Stone Face,* 1977.

Adult novels; published by Appleton-Century-Crofts, except as indicated: *Red Is for Murder,* Ziff-Davis, 1943; *The Quicksilver Pool,* 1955; *The Trembling Hills,* 1956; *Skye Cameron,* 1957; *The Moonflower,* 1958; *Thunder Heights,* 1960; *Blue Fire,* 1961; *Window on the Square,* 1962; *Seven Tears for Apollo,* 1963; *Black Amber,* 1964; *Sea Jade,* 1965.

Published by Doubleday: *Columbella,* 1966; *Silverhill,* 1967; *Hunter's Green,* 1968; *The Winter People,* 1969; *Lost Island,* 1970; *Listen for the Whisperer,* 1972; *Snowfire,* 1973; *The Turquoise Mask,* 1974; *Spindrift,* 1975; *The Golden Unicorn,* 1976; *The Stone Bull,* 1977; *The Glass Flame,* 1978; *Domino,* 1979; *Poinciana,* 1980. Author of numerous short stories; contributor of articles to *Writer.*

SIDELIGHTS: Phyllis A. Whitney told *CA:* "I have always written because I couldn't help it. From the age of twelve on I loved to make-up stories, and I've been doing it ever since. I believe in entertaining my readers, and I also hope to make them think and feel. I have great respect and admiration for fellow writers in the mystery-suspense field, and I read both to enjoy and to learn. I seem to have been born with a hunger for stories."

Whitney travels extensively to collect background material for her books' exotic settings. Her works have been published in twenty countries outside of the United States. *The Glass Flame* has sold over one million copies.

BIOGRAPHICAL/CRITICAL SOURCES: Christian Science Monitor, May 4, 1967; *New York Times Book Review,* July 2, 1967, November 22, 1970.

* * *

WHITROW, Gerald James 1912-

PERSONAL: Born June 9, 1912, in Kimmeridge, Dorset, England; son of George William (an editor) and Emily (Watkins) Whitrow; married Magda Mostel, 1946. *Education:* Christ Church, Oxford, B.A., 1933, M.A., 1937, D.Phil., 1939. *Religion:* Church of England. *Home:* 41, Home Park Rd., Wimbledon, London SW19 7HS, England. *Office:* Department of Mathematics, Imperial College of Science, London SW7 2BZ, England.

CAREER: Oxford University, Christ Church, Oxford, England, research lecturer, 1936-40; University of London, Imperial College, London, England, lecturer in mathematics, 1945-51, reader in applied mathematics, 1951-72, professor of the history and applications of mathematics, 1972-79, senior research fellow and emeritus professor, 1979—. Visiting professor, University of Hamburg, Hamburg, Germany, 1960. *Military service:* British Army, 1940-45; became experimental officer. *Member:* Royal Astronomical Society of London (fellow; member of council, 1950-54 and 1963-67; vice-president, 1966-67), British Society for the Philosophy of Science (a founder; president, 1955-57 and 1967-68), British Society for the History of Science (president, 1968-70), British Society for the History of Mathematics (founder; president, 1971-73), International Society for the Study of Time (founder; president, 1966-69), Athenaeum Club (London).

WRITINGS: Structure of the Universe, Hutchinson, 1949; (with Jones and Rotblat) *Atoms and the Universe,* Eyre & Spottiswoode, 1956, reprinted, Penguin, 1973; *Structure and Evolution of the Universe,* Hutchinson, 1959; (with Bondi, Bonnor and Lyttleton) *Rival Theories of Cosmology,* Oxford University Press, 1960; *The Natural Philosophy of Time,* Nelson, 1961, reprinted, Oxford University Press, 1980; *Einstein: The Man and His Achievement,* British Broadcasting Corp. Publications, 1967; *What Is Time?,* Thames & Hudson, 1972; (contributor) *Time and the Sciences,* Unesco, 1979. Contributor to professional journals. Editor, *Observatory* magazine, 1948-50, and the Royal Astronomical Society of London's "Monthly Notices," 1949-51.

WORK IN PROGRESS: Papers on relativity, cosmology, history of mathematics, and the philosophy of science.

SIDELIGHTS: Gerald James Whitrow makes frequent radio and television broadcasts. *Avocational interests:* Physical and astronomical cosmology, history of mathematics, astronomy, and physics, and philosophy of science.

* * *

WHYTE, Henry Malcolm 1920-

PERSONAL: Born October 26, 1920, in Jammalamadorgu, India; son of Henry William (a clergyman) and Ruby (Flower) Whyte; married Marguerite Mary Lamont, July 18,

1946; married second wife, Judith Phyllis Angus, October 10, 1974; children: (first marriage) Bruce Macgregor, Christine. *Education:* University of Queensland, B.Sc., 1942, M.B., 1944; Oxford University, D.Phil., 1951; F.R.A.C.P., 1956; F.R.C.P., 1971. *Home:* 5 Scarborough St., Red Hill, Australian Capital Territory, Australia. *Office:* Health Promotion Centre, Childers St., Canberra, Australian Capital Territory, Australia.

CAREER: University of Queensland, Queensland, Australia, senior lecturer, department of physiology, 1946-47; Oxford University, Oxford, England, assistant to Nuffield Professor of Clinical Medicine, 1948-51; Sydney Hospital, Sydney, Australia, Kanematsu Memorial Institute, senior clinical research fellow, 1952-56, director of clinical research department, 1956-60, director of medical research, 1960-66; Australian National University, Canberra, Foundation Professor of Clinical Science, John Curtin School of Medical Research, 1966-77; Capital Territory Health Commission, Canberra, specialist, Alcohol and Drug Dependence Unit, 1977—. Visiting scientist, National Heart Institute, Bethesda, Md., 1961-62. Life Insurance Medical Research Fund of Australia and New Zealand, medical director, 1960-66, chairman of advisory council, 1966—. *Military service:* Royal Australian Army Medical Corps, 1945-46. *Member:* Royal Australasian College of Physicians, Royal College of Physicians.

WRITINGS: The Fats of Life, Ure Smith, 1961, published in America as *Eat to Your Heart's Content,* Hawthorn, 1962; (editor with R. G. Brown) *Medical Practice and the Community,* Australian National University Press, 1970. Contributor to medical and scientific journals.

*　*　*

WHYTE, William Foote 1914-

PERSONAL: Born June 27, 1914, in Springfield, Mass.; son of John and Isabel (Van Sickle) Whyte; married Kathleen King, 1938; children: Joyce, Martin, Lucy, John. *Education:* Swarthmore College, A.B., 1936; Harvard University, Society of Fellows, 1936-40; University of Chicago, Ph.D., 1943. *Religion:* Presbyterian. *Home:* 1 Sundowns Rd., Ithaca, N.Y. 14850. *Office:* New York State School of Industrial and Labor Relations, Cornell University, P.O. Box 1000, Ithaca, N.Y. 14853.

CAREER: University of Oklahoma, Norman, assistant professor, 1942-43; University of Chicago, Chicago, Ill., 1944-48, began as assistant professor, became associate professor; Cornell University, New York State School of Industrial and Labor Relations, Ithaca, N.Y., professor, 1948-79, professor emeritus, 1979—, director of Social Science Research Center, 1956-61. *Member:* American Anthropological Association (fellow), Society for Applied Anthropology (president, 1964), American Sociological Association (fellow), Industrial Relations Research Association (president, 1963, 1980), American Academy of Arts and Sciences, Latin American Studies Association, Phi Beta Kappa. *Awards, honors:* Career research award, National Institute of Mental Health, 1964-79.

WRITINGS: Street Corner Society, University of Chicago Press, 1943, revised edition, 1955; *Human Relations in the Restaurant Industry,* McGraw, 1948; *Pattern for Industrial Peace,* Harper, 1951; *Money and Motivation,* Harper, 1955; *Man and Organization,* Irwin, 1959; *Men at Work,* Irwin, 1961; *Action Research for Management,* Irwin, 1965; *Organizational Behavior,* Irwin, 1969; *Organizing for Agricultural Development,* Transaction Books, 1975; *Power, Poli-*

tics, and Progress, Elsevier (North Holland), 1977. Co-editor, "Sociology and Anthropology" series, Dorsey, 1959-63, and "Behavioral Science in Business" series, Irwin, 1960-63. Contributor of articles to professional journals. Editor, *Human Organization* (journal of The Society for Applied Anthropology), 1956-61, 1962-63.

WORK IN PROGRESS: Research on worker participation in management and employee ownership, and on organizational aspects of agricultural research and development in Latin America; his autobiography.

SIDELIGHTS: William Foote Whyte told *CA:* "My best known book is *Street Corner Society,* which more than thirty-five years after its initial publication is still widely used in college sociology courses. In dropping out of active teaching, . . . I expect to push ahead with articles and books on the topics noted above, and I have also written drafts of the first part of an autobiography."

*　*　*

WIBBERLEY, Leonard (Patrick O'Connor) 1915-
(Leonard Holton, Patrick O'Connor, Christopher Webb)

PERSONAL: Born April 9, 1915, in Dublin, Ireland; came to U.S. in 1943; son of Thomas (a professor of agriculture) and Sinaid (O'Connor) Wibberley; married Katherine Hazel Holton; six children. *Education:* Attended schools in Ireland and England. *Politics:* Liberal. *Religion:* Christian. *Address:* Box 522, Hermosa Beach, Calif.

CAREER: Author. Was an apprentice to a London publisher; at sixteen became a copy boy on the *Sunday Dispatch;* during depression, worked as street fiddler, ditchdigger, dishwasher, and cook; reporter for the *London Daily Mirror* and assistant London editor for *Malayan Straits Times* and *Singapore Free Press,* 1932-36; editor of *Trinidad Evening News,* Trinidad, West Indies, 1936-38; worked for oil company in Trinidad, 1939-41; came to U.S. in 1943 to work for Walsh Kaiser Shipyards; also served as cable editor for Associated Press, New York, N.Y., U.S. correspondent for *London Evening News,* and member of staff, *Los Angeles Times,* Los Angeles, Calif. *Military service:* Trinidad Artillery Volunteers; served as lance bombardier.

WRITINGS—Juveniles; all published by Farrar, Straus, except as indicated: The King's Beard, Pelligrini & Cudahy, 1952; *The Secret of the Hawk,* Ariel Books, 1952; *The Coronation Book,* 1953; *Deadman's Cave,* 1954; *The Spies of Everest,* 1954; *The Wound of Peter Wayne,* 1955; *The Life of Winston Churchill,* 1956; *John Barry: Father of the Navy,* 1957; *Kevin O'Connor and the Light Brigade,* 1957; *Wes Powell: Conqueror of the Grand Canyon,* 1958; *John Treegate's Musket,* 1959; *Peter Treegate's War,* 1960; *Sea Captain from Salem,* 1961; *Treegate's Raiders,* 1962; "Thomas Jefferson" series, Volume I: *Young Man from the Piedmont,* 1963, Volume II: *A Dawn in the Trees,* 1964, Volume III: *The Gales of Spring,* 1965, Volume IV: *The Time of the Harvest,* 1966, series published in one volume as *Man of Liberty,* 1969; *Encounter Near Venus,* 1967; *Attar of the Ice Valley,* 1969; *Leopard's Prey,* 1971; *The Red Pawns,* 1973; *Flint's Island,* 1974; *Guarneri: Story of a Genius,* 1975; *The Last Battle,* 1976; *Perilous Gold,* 1978; *Little League Family,* Doubleday, 1978; *The Crime of Martin Coverly,* 1980.

Adult fiction: *Mrs. Searwood's Secret Weapon,* Little, Brown, 1954; *The Mouse that Roared,* Little, Brown, 1955; *McGillicudy McGotham,* Little, Brown, 1956; *Beware of the Mouse,* Putnam, 1957; *Take Me to Your President,* Putnam,

1957; *The Quest of Excalibur,* Putnam, 1959; *The Hands of Cormac Joyce,* Putnam, 1960; *Stranger at Killknock,* Putnam, 1961; *The Mouse on the Moon,* Morrow, 1962; *A Feast of Freedom,* Morrow, 1963; *The Island of the Angels,* Morrow, 1965; *The Centurion,* Morrow, 1966; *The Road from Toomi,* Morrow, 1967; *Adventures of an Elephant Boy,* Morrow, 1968; *The Mouse on Wall Street,* Morrow, 1969; *Meeting with a Great Beast,* Morrow, 1971; *The Testament of Theophilus,* Morrow, 1973; *The Last Stand of Father Felix,* Morrow, 1974; *1776—And All That,* Morrow, 1975; *One in Four,* Morrow, 1976; *The Mouse that Poured,* Morrow, 1981.

Adult nonfiction; all published by Ives Washburn, except as indicated: *The Trouble with the Irish,* Holt, 1956; *The Coming of the Green,* Holt, 1958; *The Land that Isn't There,* 1959; *No Garlic in the Soup,* 1959; *Yesterday's Land,* 1961; *Ventures into the Deep,* 1962; *Ah Julian: A Memoir of Julian Brodetsky,* 1963; *Fiji: Islands of the Dawn,* 1964; *Towards a Distant Island,* 1966; *Something to Read,* 1967; *Hound of the Sea,* 1969; *Voyage by Bus,* Morrow, 1971; *The Shannon Sailors,* Morrow, 1972; *The Good Natured Man: A Portrait of Liver Goldsmith,* Morrow, 1979.

Plays; all published by Dramatic Publishing: *The Heavenly Quarterback,* 1968; *Gift of a Star* (one act), 1969; *Black Jack Rides Again,* 1971; *Once, in a Garden,* 1975; *The Vicar of Wakefield* (based on novel by Oliver Goldsmith), 1976.

Other; all published by Ives Washburn: *The Time of the Lamb,* 1961; *The Ballad of the Pilgrim Cat,* 1962; *The Shepherd's Reward,* 1963.

Under pseudonym Leonard Holton; all detective fiction; all published by Dodd, except as indicated: *Saint Maker,* 1959; *A Pact with Satan,* 1960; *Secret of the Doubting Saint,* 1961; *Deliver Us from Wolves,* 1963; *Flowers by Request,* 1964; *Out of the Depths,* 1966; *A Touch of Jonah,* 1968; *A Problem in Angels,* 1970; *The Mirror of Hell,* 1972; *The Devil to Play,* 1974; *A Corner of Paradise,* St. Martin's, 1976.

Under pseudonym Patrick O'Connor; all juveniles; all published by Ives Washburn: *Flight of the Peacock,* 1954; *The Society of Foxes,* 1954; *The Watermelon Mystery,* 1955; *Gunpowder for Washington,* 1956; "The Black Tiger" series: *The Black Tiger,* 1956, *The Black Tiger at Le Mans,* 1958, . . . *at Bonneville,* 1960, . . . *at Indianapolis,* 1962; *The Lost Harpooner,* 1957; *Mexican Road Race,* 1957; *The Five-Dollar Watch Mystery,* 1959; *Treasure at Twenty Fathoms,* 1961; *The Raising of the Dubhe,* 1964; *Seawind from Hawaii,* 1965; *South Swell,* 1967; *Beyond Hawaii,* 1969; *A Car Called Camellia,* 1970.

Under pseudonym Christopher Webb; all juveniles; all published by Funk: *Matt Tyler's Chronicles,* 1958; *Mark Toyman's Inheritance,* 1960; *Zebulon Pike: Soldier and Explorer,* 1961; *The River of Pee Dee Jack,* 1962; *Quest of the Otter,* 1963; *The Ann and Hope Mutiny,* 1966; *Eusebius the Phoenician,* 1967.

SIDELIGHTS: Leonard Wibberley wrote *CA:* "When I was young I never read any books which were published specifically for children, and I would have been offended if I had been offered one. I did of course read Grimm's Fairy Tales but Heavens, the brothers Grimm collected those from grown-up people and never for a moment thought of them as being intended only for children. I still read them although I am quite hoary now, but then I feel that if you don't read works of pure imagination part of your mind goes dead. Such works are essential for food for adults as well as children, and movies like 'Star Wars,' 'Close Encounters of the Third Kind,' and 'Jaws' are actually fairy stories—the big shark in 'Jaws' taking the place of the dragon that the young boy has to kill when everybody else has failed.

"Good children's books then, are excellent reading for both children and adults, and a great many parents would get as much joy out of *Treasure Island, Black Beauty,* and *Heidi* as their children do if the parents would just stop being stuffy and busy and pick them up and read them.

"Mediocre or poor children's books adults cannot abide nor children either. So what I am saying is that it takes just as much skill and talent to write a good book for children as it does to write a good novel for adults—and perhaps a little more. Perhaps a little more because a child gets bored more quickly than an adult. You can't counteract the boredom by having something exciting happen on every page. That in itself gets boring. You must keep the characters real and interesting—even when the characters themselves are bored, their boredom has to be interesting.

"The story has gone around that children don't like descriptive passages but that is not true. They love descriptive passages as much as adults, provided there is something striking about the description—striking in the sense that it goes home. It is passable to say 'The slate roofs were wet with rain.' It is much better to say 'The slate roofs of the village gleamed with a quiet sadness from the falling of the rain.' There's music in that and there should always be music in words.

"Many people think of me as a writer of children's books, but I think of myself as a novelist who also likes to write children's books—that is books in which the plot is a bit more exciting, the colors touch more vivid, the action faster and more direct, than in the adult novel. But I love most of all writing novels. What are my favorite novels of my own production? I think the African trilogy—*The Road from Toomi, Meeting with a Great Beast,* and *The Last Stand of Father Felix.*

"What do I think of myself as a novelist? I think I'm good—not brilliant but not mediocre either."

The Mouse that Roared was made into a motion picture with the same title, by Columbia in 1958. It's sequel, *The Mouse on the Moon,* was filmed with the same title by Lopert in 1963. *The Hands of Cormac Joyce* was made into a television movie.

AVOCATIONAL INTERESTS: Scuba diving, sailing, painting, music, and violin making.

BIOGRAPHICAL/CRITICAL SOURCES: New York Times Book Review, July 12, 1959; *Book Week,* November 1, 1964; *Best Sellers,* February 15, 1968, October, 1976; *Books,* November, 1969; *Christian Science Monitor,* November 6, 1974; *Children's Book Review,* October, 1976; *Children's Literature Review,* Volume III, Gale, 1978.

*   *   *

WIDMER, Kingsley 1925-

PERSONAL: Born July 17, 1925, in Minneapolis, Minn.; married Eleanor Rackow; children: Matthew August, Jonah Lawrence. *Education:* Attended University of Wisconsin; University of Minnesota, B.A., 1949, M.A., 1951; University of Washington, Ph.D., 1957. *Office:* School of Literature, San Diego State University, 5402 College Ave., San Diego, Calif. 92115.

CAREER: Reed College, Portland, Ore., Ford Foundation intern in humanities, 1955, instructor, 1955-56; San Diego State University, San Diego, Calif., 1956—, professor of

English, 1967—. Visiting professor at University of California, Berkeley, 1960-61, Simon Fraser University (British Columbia), 1967, University of Nice, 1970, State University of New York at Buffalo, 1974, and University of Tulsa, 1975, 1976, and 1978; Fulbright senior lecturer in American literature, Tel Aviv University, 1963-64. *Military service:* U.S. Army, Infantry, during World War II. *Member:* Phi Beta Kappa.

WRITINGS: (Editor with wife, Eleanor Widmer) *Literary Censorship,* Wadsworth, 1961; *The Art of Perversity: D. H. Lawrence,* University of Washington Press, 1962; *Henry Miller: A Critical Study,* Twayne, 1963; *The Literary Rebel,* Southern Illinois University Press, 1965; *The Experience of Freedom: Censorship and the Teacher,* American Federation of Teachers, 1966; *The Ways of Nihilism: Herman Melville's Short Novels,* Ritchie, 1970; *The End of Culture: Essays on Sensibility in Contemporary Society,* San Diego State University Press, 1975; *Paul Goodman,* Twayne, 1979; *Edges of Extremity: Ideologies in Literary Modernism* (monograph), University of Tulsa, 1980. Also author of *Curses, Selected Verses,* in press. Author of numerous essays, articles, and reviews.

* * *

WILGUS, A(lva) Curtis 1897-

PERSONAL: Born April 2, 1897, in Platteville, Wis.; son of James Alva (a historian) and Alberta (McGurer) Wilgus; married Karna Steelquist; children: Robert. *Education:* Wisconsin State Teachers College, graduate, 1916; University of Wisconsin, A.B., 1920, A.M., 1921, Ph.D., 1925; University of California, Berkeley, additional study, 1921-22. *Residence:* North Miami Beach, Fla.; and New York, N.Y.

CAREER: High school teacher and principal, 1916-18; University of Wisconsin (now University of Wisconsin—Madison), Madison, assistant instructor in history, 1922-24; University of South Carolina, Columbia, associate professor of history, 1924-30; George Washington University, Washington, D.C., chair of Hispanic-American history, 1930-51, acting dean of Columbian College, 1932-34, director of Center of Inter-American Studies, 1932-37; University of Florida, Gainesville, director of School of Inter-American Studies and professor of history, 1951-63, director of Caribbean Conferences, 1951-67. Visiting summer professor or lecturer at more than fifty colleges and universities. Latin American expert, U.S. Office of Education, 1942; program officer, Division of Education and Teacher Aides, Office of Coordinator of Inter-American Affairs, 1943-44. Chairman of advisory committee for restoration of city of St. Augustine, Florida Board of Parks and Historic Memorials, 1958; member of board of directors and secretary-treasurer, Colonial St. Augustine, Inc., 1951-61; Pan-American Foundation, organizing member, 1938, director, 1939-67; secretary-general, Inter-American Academy, 1960-67; member of President's Board of Foreign Scholarships, 1963-66. Consultant to Nystrom Map Co., Time/Life Books, Scholastic Book Services, and other publishers. *Military service:* U.S. Army, 1918.

MEMBER: Geographical and Historical Society of the Americas, Inter-American Bibliographical and Library Association (organizing member, 1930; president, 1936—), American Historical Association, Educational Research Bureau, American Council on Public Relations, Conference on Latin American History, Institute of International Education, American Council on Education, American Library

Institute, National Council for Social Studies, Society for Advancement of Education (organizing member, 1939), American Association of University Professors, Academy of World Economics, South Carolina Historical Association (co-founder, 1929), corresponding member of eight Latin-American historical associations, Pi Gamma Mu, Delta Phi Epsilon, Omicron Delta Kappa, and numerous other associations and organizations.

AWARDS, HONORS: Medalla de Honor de la Instrucion Publica de Venezuela, 1934; Cervantes Medal, Hispanic Institute of Florida, 1953; Knight Grand Cross of Military Order of St. Brigida of Sweden, 1954; Chevalier et Compagnon Honoraire, Les Chevaliers de la Croix de Lorraine et Compagnons de la Resistance, 1954; Bi-Centennial Medal, Columbia University, 1954.

WRITINGS: An Outline of Hispanic-American History, McKinley Publishing, 1927; *A History of Hispanic America,* Mimeo-Form Service, 1931; *An Atlas of Hispanic-American History,* George Washington University Press, 1932; *The Histories of Hispanic America,* Pan American Union, 1932; *Histories and Historians of Hispanic America,* Cooper Square, 1936, revised edition, 1965; *A Caravan Tour to Argentina and Brazil,* World Travel Guild, 1936; *A Syllabus for Teaching Latin-American History in High Schools,* Pan American Union, 1936, revised edition, 1940; (co-author) *The Other Americans,* American Association of University Women, 1937; (co-author) *Outline History of Latin America,* Barnes & Noble, 1939; *The Development of Hispanic America,* Farrar and Rinehart, 1941, revised edition published as *Latin America, 1492-1942: A Guide to Historical and Cultural Development before World War II,* Scarecrow, 1973; *Latin America in Maps,* Barnes & Noble, 1943, revised edition published as *Historical Atlas of Latin America: Political, Geographic, Economic, Cultural,* Cooper Square, 1967; *Latin America in the Nineteenth Century: A Selected Bibliography of Books of Travel and Description Published in English,* Scarecrow, 1973; *Historiography of Latin America: A Guide to Historical Writing, 1500-1800,* Scarecrow, 1975; *Latin America, Spain and Portugal: A Selected and Annotated Bibliographical Guide to Books Published 1954-1974,* Scarecrow, 1977.

Editor: *Modern Hispanic America,* George Washington University Press, 1933, reprinted, Kennikat, 1971; *The Caribbean Area,* George Washington University Press, 1934; *Argentina, Brazil and Chile since Independence,* George Washington University Press, 1935, reprinted, Russell, 1963; *Colonial Hispanic America,* George Washington University Press, 1936, reprinted, Russell, 1963; *South American Dictators,* George Washington University Press, 1937, reprinted, Russell, 1963; *Readings in Hispanic-American History,* two volumes, George Washington University Press, 1938; *Hispanic-American Essays,* University of North Carolina Press, 1942, reprinted, Arno, 1972; *Readings in Latin-American Civilization,* Barnes & Noble, 1946.

Editor of series: "The Caribbean Conference" series, seventeen volumes, University of Florida Press, 1951-68; "Latin American Gateway" series, four volumes, University of Florida Press, 1964-65; "Library of Latin American History and Culture" series, thirty-two volumes, Cooper Square, 1964-72; "Source Books and Studies on Latin America" series, eight volumes, Praeger, 1969; "Historical Dictionaries of Latin America" series, twenty-three volumes, Scarecrow, 1970-81.

Present or former Latin-American advisory editor or consultant to *World Book Encyclopedia, Grolier Encyclopedia,*

American People's Encyclopedia, Encyclopedia Americana, Pan-American Year Book, and *Worldmark Encyclopedia.* Contributor of over 300 articles to more than 100 periodicals in the United States, Latin America, and Europe. Editor-in-chief, *World Affairs,* 1941-51; compiler and editor, *Doors to Latin America,* 1954—; founder, associate editor, and chairman of editorial board, *Journal of Inter-American Studies,* 1958—; editorial advisory board, *Luso-Brazilian Review,* 1964.

SIDELIGHTS: A. Curtis Wilgus wrote *CA:* "I have been interested in Latin America since 1916 when I took a course in Latin American geography by one of the greatest authorities in this country. But my interest soon turned to history (my father was a historian), and since then I have traveled in all parts of Latin America and have studied and written about the area. I consider myself a 'Latiamericanologist' rather than just a 'Latinamericanist.'

"My interests and publications have been in the fields of history, geography, international relations, biography, bibliography, and historiography. Since all of my work has been play I have lived an intellectually satisfying life. For many years I looked forward to retirement and I kept a retirement file for there were so many things I wanted to do.

"Most of my life I have been a hedonist, a pragmatist, an optimist, and an opportunist. I believe thoroughly in timing and good luck. A rule that I have always followed is: give a little time to thinking and a little thought to timing. And usually when I am in doubt I don't.

"History is a subject which deals with the thoughts, actions, creations, and relationships of people. Teaching history has not always been satisfying for me although it has been a living and I like teaching. Perhaps 95% of the facts of history have disappeared so that the historian tries to find and use some of these even though some of these 'facts' might not stand up in a court of law. Unfortunately very few people seem to learn anything from history—certainly our State Department often does not. History is being pushed back into the past and this helps better to understand the present. But the mystery of history is always with us."

* * *

WILHELMSEN, Frederick D(aniel) 1923-

PERSONAL: Born May 18, 1923, in Detroit, Mich.; son of Edward Daniel and Claire (Perso) Wilhelmsen; divorced; children: Alexandra Leonora, Elizabeth Cristina, Francesca Juliana. *Education:* Attended University of Detroit, 1941-43; University of San Francisco, A.B., 1947; University of Notre Dame, M.A., 1948; University of Madrid, Spain, Ph. et Litt.D., 1958. *Religion:* Roman Catholic. *Office:* Department of Philosophy and Politics, University of Dallas, Irving, Tex.

CAREER: Art Instruction Inc., Pasadena, Calif., representative, 1948-50; University of Santa Clara, Santa Clara, Calif., professor of philosophy, 1950-60; Al-Hikma University, Baghdad, Iraq, professor, 1960-61; Catholic University of Navarra, Pamplona, Spain, professor, beginning 1961; has taught in department of philosophy and politics, University of Dallas, Irving, Tex. *Military service:* U.S. Army, 1944-46. *Member:* Catholic Philosophical Society of America (western division), Asociacion de Menendez-Pelayo (Spain), Royal Stuart Society (London). *Awards, honors:* Guggenheim fellow; grants from Relm and Foreign Affairs Foundations; Smith-Mundt Professor in Iraq; Fulbright Professor in Spain; Knight of the Grand Cross of the Order of the Outlawed Legitimacy.

WRITINGS: Hilaire Belloc: No Alienated Man, Sheed, 1953; *Man's Knowledge of Reality,* Prentice-Hall, 1956; *Omega: Last of the Barques,* Newman, 1956; *The Metaphysics of Love,* Sheed, 1962; *El Problema de la Trascendencia en la Metafisica Actual,* Ediciones Rialp, 1963; *La Ortodoxia Publica y los Poderes de la Irracionalidad,* Ediciones Rialp, 1965; (editor and author of introduction) Romano Guardini, *The End of the Modern World: A Search for Orientation,* translation by Joseph Theman and Herbert Burke, Regnery, 1968; (editor) *Seeds of Anarchy: A Study of Campus Revolution,* Argus Academic Press, 1969.

(With Jane Bret) *The War in Man: Media and Machines,* University of Georgia Press, 1970; *The Paradoxical Structure of Existence,* University of Dallas Press, 1970, 2nd edition, 1973; (with Bret) *Telepolitics: The Politics of Neuronic Man,* Tundra Books, 1972; *Christianity and Political Philosophy,* University of Georgia Press, 1978; *Citizen of Rome: Reflections from the Life of a Roman Catholic,* Sherwood Sugden & Co., 1980. Contributor to *National Review, America, Commonweal,* and other periodicals in the United States, Spain, and Austria. Senior editor, *Triumph* (magazine), 1976.

BIOGRAPHICAL/CRITICAL SOURCES: National Review, July 26, 1969, February 25, 1971.

* * *

WILKINSON, Ernest Leroy 1899-1978

PERSONAL: Born May 4, 1899, in Ogden, Utah; died, 1978; son of Robert Brown and Annie Cecilia (Andersen) Wilkinson; married Alice Valera Ludlow, August 15, 1923; children: Ernest Ludlow, Marian (Mrs. Gordon Jensen), Alice Ann (Mrs. John K. Mangum), David Lawrence, Douglas Dwight. *Education:* Attended Weber College (now Weber State College), 1917-18; Brigham Young University, A.B., 1921; George Washington University, J.D., 1926; Harvard University, S.J.D., 1927. *Politics:* "Jeffersonian Republican." *Religion:* Church of Jesus Christ of Latter-day Saints. *Home:* 2745 North University Ave., Provo, Utah 84601. *Office:* Brigham Young University, Provo, Utah 84601.

CAREER: Admitted to Washington State Bar, 1926, Utah State Bar, 1927, and New York State Bar, 1928; Weber College (now Weber State College), Ogden, Utah, member of faculty, 1921-23; Business High School, Washington, D.C., member of faculty, 1923-26; New Jersey Law School, Newark, professor of law, 1927-33; Hughes, Schurman & Dwight, New York, N.Y., associate, 1928-35; Moyle & Wilkinson, Washington, D.C., partner, 1935-40; head of Ernest L. Wilkinson, Washington, D.C., 1940-51, and Wilkinson, Cragun & Barker, Washington, D.C., beginning 1951; Brigham Young University, Provo, Utah, president, 1950-64 and 1965-71, director and editor of *Centennial History,* beginning 1971. Member of board of directors, Deseret News Publishing Co., beginning 1954, Beneficial Life Insurance Co., 1957-60, KSL, Inc., Radio Service Corp. of Utah, beginning 1960, Rolling Hills Orchard, 1961-71, and Ellison Ranching Co., beginning 1962. President, Manhattan and Queens branches, Bishop Queens Ward, New York Stake, Church of Jesus Christ of Latter-day Saints, 1930-35, member of presidency, Washington Stake, 1940-49; member, National Committee of Army and Navy Chaplains, 1947-50; chancellor, Unified School System of Church of Jesus Christ of Latter-day Saints, 1953-64; member of governor's commission representing Utah, White House Conference on Education, 1955; delegate to Republican National Convention, 1956, 1960, 1968, and 1972, Republican nominee for senator from Utah, 1964, Republican committeeman from Utah, 1972-75; president, National Right to Work Legal Defense and Education Foundation, 1969-73. Trustee, Utah Foundation, beginning 1960, and Foundation for Economic Freedom, 1960-71. Fellow, American Bar Foundation. *Military service:* U.S. Army, 1918.

MEMBER: International Platform Association, Provo Chamber of Commerce, Salt Lake City Chamber of Commerce, Order of the Coif, Phi Kappa Phi. *Awards, honors:* LL.D., Brigham Young University, 1957, and Grove City College, 1971; Freedoms Foundation of America George Washington Medal, 1961, for speech on free enterprise, 1971, for speech on student riots, and 1973; American Coalition of Patriotic Societies Award, 1963; D.P.S., Fort Lauderdale University, 1970; Religious Heritage of America, Inc., Business Man of the Year in Education Award, 1971.

WRITINGS: Earnestly Yours (collected speeches), Deseret, 1971; (editor) *Brigham Young University: The First One Hundred Years,* four volumes, Brigham Young University Press, 1975; (with W. Cleon Skousen) *Brigham Young University: A School of Destiny,* Brigham Young University Press, 1976. Contributor to *American Bar Association Journal.*†

*   *   *

WILKINSON, Lancelot Patrick 1907-

PERSONAL: Born June 1, 1907, in Broughty Ferry, Scotland; son of Lancelot George William (a schoolmaster) and Kate (Howland) Wilkinson; married Sydney Alix Eason, February 16, 1944; children: Richard Murray, Stephen Patrick (both adopted). *Education:* Attended Charterhouse, Surrey, England; King's College, Cambridge, B.A., 1930, M.A., 1933. *Home:* 9 Huntingdon Rd., Cambridge, England. *Office:* King's College, Cambridge University, Cambridge, England.

CAREER: Cambridge University, Cambridge, England, King's College, fellow and lecturer in classics, 1932—, dean, 1934-45, assistant tutor, 1945-46, senior tutor, 1946-56, vice-provost, 1961-65, university lecturer in classics, 1936-67, university reader in classics, 1967-74, orator of the university, 1958-74. Temporary senior assistant, Foreign Office, 1939-45; governor, Queen Mary College, University of London, 1954-57; member of governing body, Charterhouse, Surrey, England. *Member:* Royal Society of Literature (fellow), Horatian Society, Virgil Society.

WRITINGS—All published by Cambridge University Press, except as indicated: *Horace and His Lyric Poetry,* 1945; *Letters of Cicero,* Bles, 1949; *Ovid Recalled,* 1955, abridged edition published as *Ovid Surveyed,* 1962; *Golden Latin Artistry,* 1963; (with R. H. Bulmer) *Register of Members of King's College, Cambridge, 1919-58,* 1963; *The Georgics of Virgil: A Critical Survey,* 1969; *The Roman Experience,* Elek, 1974; *Classical Attitudes to Modern Issues,* 1978. Also author of the Latin text for Benjamin Britten's *Cantata Misericordium,* 1963.

AVOCATIONAL INTERESTS: Travel, especially to Italy and Greece.

*   *   *

WILLCOX, William Bradford 1907-

PERSONAL: Born October 29, 1907, in Ithaca, N.Y.; son of Walter Francis and Alice (Work) Willcox; married Faith Mellen, October 31, 1936 (died July 5, 1978); children: Alanson Francis, Ellen Willcox Ham, Faith Marian. *Education:*

Attended Cambridge University, 1927; Cornell University, A.B., 1928; Yale University, B.F.A. (architecture), 1932, Ph.D., 1936. *Home:* Jackson Rd., Higganum, Conn. *Office:* 1603A Yale Station, New Haven, Conn.

CAREER: Williams College, Williamstown, Mass., instructor in history, 1936-41; University of Michigan, Ann Arbor, assistant professor, 1941-46, associate professor, 1946-50, professor of history, 1950-70, acting chairman of department, 1958-60, 1963-64, chairman, 1965-70; Yale University, New Haven, Conn., professor of history, 1970—. Member, Institute for Advanced Study, Princeton, N.J., 1946-47; Fulbright lecturer, Balliol College, Oxford University, 1957-58. Phi Beta Kappa visiting scholar, 1975-76, and 1977-78. Member of council, Institute of Early American History and Culture, 1955-58; member of screening committee, Senior Fulbright Awards in History, 1960-63; member of council, Conference on British Studies, 1965-67. *Member:* American Historical Association (member of council, 1965-70), Midwest Conference on British Historical Studies (chairman, 1959-61), Phi Beta Kappa, Phi Kappa Phi, Elizabethan Club, Century Association. *Awards, honors:* Porter Prize, Yale University, 1936; Russel Award, University of Michigan, 1945; Bancroft Prize, Columbia University, 1965.

WRITINGS: Gloucestershire: A Study in Local Government, 1590-1640, Yale University Press, 1940; *Star of Empire: A Study of Britain as a World Power, 1485-1945,* Knopf, 1950; (editor) *The American Rebellion: Sir Henry Clinton's Narrative of His Campaigns, 1775-1782,* Yale University Press, 1954; *Portrait of a General: Sir Henry Clinton in the War of Independence,* Knopf, 1964; *The Age of Oligarchy, 1688-1830,* Heath, 1966; (editor) *Papers of Benjamin Franklin,* twenty-one volumes, Yale University Press, 1970—. Contributor to history journals.

AVOCATIONAL INTERESTS: Travel.

*   *   *

WILLIAMS, Dorian 1914-

PERSONAL: Born July 1, 1914, in London, England; son of Vivian D. S. and Violet (Wood) Williams; married Jennifer Neale, April 4, 1957; children: Piers Dorian, Carola Dawn. *Education:* Attended Harrow School. *Home:* Pendley Manor, Tring, Hertfordshire, England. *Agent:* John Farquharson Ltd., Bell House, 8 Bell Yard, London WC2A 2JU, England.

CAREER: Schoolmaster in England, 1936-45; Pendley Center of Adult Education, Hertfordshire, England, founder and director, 1945—; British Broadcasting Corp., London, England, equestrian commentator, 1951—. Lecturer on communications in industry. Director and producer, Pendley Shakespeare Festival, 1949—. Master of foxhounds, Whaddon Chase, 1951—. Chairman, National Equestrian Centre, 1967-74; master, Farriers' Co., 1977-78. *Awards, honors:* Gold Medal, British Horse Society, 1962; officer, Order of the British Empire, 1978.

WRITINGS: Poems for the People, Stockwell, 1943; *Peace Weapon: A Treatise on Education,* Stockwell, 1943; *Clear Round: The Story of Show Jumping,* Hodder & Stoughton, 1957; *Pendley and a Pack of Hounds,* Hodder & Stoughton, 1959.

Horses in Color, Batsford, 1959, Viking, 1960; (with wife, Jennifer Williams) *Every Child's Book of Riding,* Burke Publishing, 1960; (with J. Williams) *The Girls' Book of Horses and Riding,* Roy, 1961, 3rd edition, Burke Publishing, 1968; (with J. Williams) *Show Pony: A Practical Guide to Pony*

Care and Showing, Brockhampton Press, 1961, Dutton, 1965; *Wendy Wins a Pony,* Burke Publishing, 1961; *Wendy Wins Her Spurs,* Burke Publishing, 1962; *Wendy at Wembley,* Burke Publishing, 1963; *A Gallery of Riders,* Burke Publishing, 1963; *Work with Horses as a Career,* Batsford, 1963; *Pony to Jump,* Stephen Greene, 1963; *Learning to Ride,* Collins, 1964; *The Vanguard Book of Ponies and Riding,* Collins, 1966; *Showing Horse Sense,* Arthur Barker, 1967; *Pancho: The Story of a Horse,* Dent, 1967, Walker & Co., 1968; *The Vanguard Book of Horses,* Collins, 1967; (editor) *The Horseman's Companion,* Eyre & Spottiswoode, 1967; *Show Jumping,* Faber, 1968, published as *Show Jumper,* A. S. Barnes, 1970; (editor) *My Favourite Horse Stories,* Lutterworth, 1968, revised edition, Hamlyn, 1976.

Show Jumping: The Great Ones, Pelham, 1970, Arco, 1972; *Dorian Williams' World of Show Jumping,* Purnell, 1970; *Kingdom for a Horse,* Dent, 1971; *The Book of Horses,* Lippincott, 1971; *Great Moments in Sports: Show Jumping,* Transatlantic, 1974; *Lost* (novel), Standfast Press, 1975; *Great Riding Schools of the World,* Macmillan, 1975; *Horse of the Year: The Story of a Unique Horse Show,* David & Charles, 1976; (editor) *Horseman's Companion,* Eyre Methuen, 1978; *Master of One* (autobiography), Dent, 1978.

BIOGRAPHICAL/CRITICAL SOURCES: Times Literary Supplement, April 13, 1967, May 25, 1967; *Books and Bookmen,* December, 1967.

* * *

WILLIAMS, T(homas) Harry 1909-1979

PERSONAL: Born May 19, 1909, in Vinegar Hill, Ill.; died July 6, 1979; son of William Dwight (a farmer) and Emeline Louisa (Collins) Williams; married Estelle Skolfield, December 27, 1952; children: May Frances (Mrs. John Doles, Jr.). *Education:* Platteville State Teachers College (now University of Wisconsin—Platteville), Ed.B., 1931; University of Wisconsin, Ph.M., 1932, Ph.D., 1937. *Home:* 353 Nelson Dr., Baton Rouge, La. 70808. *Office:* Department of History, Louisiana State University, Baton Rouge, La.

CAREER: Instructor, University of Wisconsin Extension Division, 1936-38; Municipal University of Omaha (now University of Nebraska at Omaha), 1938-41, began as instructor, became assistant professor; Louisiana State University, Baton Rouge, 1941-79, professor of history, 1948-55, Boyd Professor of History, 1953-79. Visiting summer professor at various universities, including West Virginia University, Tulane University, University of Colorado, and University of Rhode Island; Harmsworth Professor of American History, Queen's College, Oxford University, 1966-67. Member of history advisory committee, Department of the Army, 1955-60; vice-chairman, Louisiana Civil War Centennial Commission, 1961-65. *Member:* American Association of University Professors, Society of American Historians, Civil War Centennial Association (director), American Historical Association, Organization of American Historians (vice-president, 1971-72; president, 1972-73), American Military Institute, Southern Historical Association (vice-president, 1957-58; president, 1958-59). *Awards, honors:* LL.D., Northland College, 1953; Lincoln Diploma of Honor, Lincoln Memorial University, 1956; Guggenheim fellow, 1957; Doctor of Letters, Bradley University, 1959; Harry S Truman Award in Civil War History, 1963; Pulitzer Prize and National Book Award, both 1970, both for *Huey Long.*

WRITINGS: Lincoln and the Radicals, University of Wisconsin Press, 1941, reprinted, 1960; (editor) *Selected Writings and Speeches of Abraham Lincoln,* Packard, 1943; *Lincoln and His Generals* (Book-of-the-Month Club selection), Knopf, 1952; *P.G.T. Beauregard: Napoleon in Gray,* Louisiana State University Press, 1955; (editor) *With Beauregard in Mexico: The Mexican War Reminiscences of P.G.T. Beauregard,* Louisiana State University Press, 1956; (editor) *Abraham Lincoln: Selected Speeches, Messages, and Letters,* Rinehart, 1957; (with Richard Nelson Current and Frank Freidel) *A History of the United States* (also see below), Knopf, 1959.

Americans at War: The Development of the American Military System, Louisiana State University Press, 1960, new edition, Collier, 1962; *Romance and Realism in Southern Politics,* University of Georgia Press, 1961; (with Current and Freidel) *American History: A Survey* (also see below; based on *A History of the United States*), Knopf, 1961, 5th revised edition, 1979; (editor) Edward Porter Alexander, *Military Memoirs of a Confederate,* Indiana University Press, 1962; *McClellan, Sherman, and Grant,* Rutgers University Press, 1962, reprinted, Greenwood Press, 1976; *The Union Sundered,* Time-Life Books, 1963; *The Union Restored,* Time-Life Books, 1963; (editor) *Hayes: The Diary of a President,* McKay, 1964; *Hayes of the Twenty-Third: The Civil War Volunteer Officer,* Knopf, 1965; (with Hazel C. Wolf) *Our American Nation,* C. E. Merrill, 1966; *Huey Long,* Knopf, 1969; (with Current and Freidel) *Essentials of American History* (condensation of *American History: A Survey*), Knopf, 1972, 2nd edition, 1976, revised edition published in two volumes, 1977. Editor, "Southern Biography" series, Louisiana State University Press.

WORK IN PROGRESS: A history of U.S. wars; a biography of Lyndon Baines Johnson.

SIDELIGHTS: In 1969, after some thirteen years of research and writing, historian T. Harry Williams published his massive biography of the flamboyant Depression-era politician Huey Long. Already highly regarded as an authority on the Civil War, Williams first became interested in the idea of a biography of Long in the early 1950's after reviewing the methods developed by scholars involved in the Columbia University Oral History Project. According to the *New York Times Book Review,* the aim of the project was to preserve, "through tape-recorded recollections of the participants, details of recent history that might otherwise disappear in an age when the telephone and rapid travel have displaced the voluminous letters, diaries and papers that politicians of an earlier century left behind."

With the help of Huey's son, Senator Russell Long of Louisiana, Williams contacted dozens of Huey's friends and associates. "I got more testimony than I was ever able to use," reported Williams. "Once [his friends] agreed to see me, they were sometimes shy to start with. The trick was to get them going. Usually, all it took was to ask if they remembered the first time they ever met Huey. *Everybody* remembered that!" By the time Williams actually began writing the biography in 1962, he had transcripts of nearly three hundred interviews with which to work.

As a result of his pioneering work, Williams received both a Pulitzer Prize and a National Book Award. Critical reaction to the biography was overwhelmingly favorable. A *Book World* reviewer, for example, called *Huey Long* "a brilliant, bawdy and unforgettable picture of the most colorful, as well as the most dangerous, man ever to engage in American politics. . . . I know of no other biography of a twentieth-century American figure that is so vividly revealing. . . . [It] is a triumphant demonstration of the value of oral history." Yet despite this endorsement of the new procedure, the reviewer brought to light two of its possible drawbacks as reflected in Williams' book—namely, that Long's friends talked "more fully and freely" than his enemies and that few of them were able to offer much insight into the workings of Long's mind (perhaps due to his own fear of forming close personal relationships). Aside from such problems, however, the reviewer concluded that "Williams has written what is clearly one of the major biographies of our time, a work that combines superb scholarship and brilliant writing. As literature, this factual portrait of the Kingfish [Long] can stand comparison with the fictional version in Robert Penn Warren's *All the King's Men* [a novel based on Long's life]."

Walter Clemons of *Life* commented: "In 876 pages without a skippable paragraph, T. Harry Williams makes good his claim that genius is not too strong a word [to describe Huey Long].... Williams is an expert guide to the bizarre [world of] Louisiana politics." Clemons also praised Williams' oral history method, noting that "the buzz of conflicting testimony, weighed and evaluated, gives the book a rare freshness and vernacular immediacy." In short, he wrote, *Huey Long* is "a great biography—the portrait of a boisterous extrovert who was also 'a remarkably introspective politician,' a vulnerable man haunted and obsessed by time, who went tragically wrong as he slouched toward greatness."

A *Washington Post* critic described *Huey Long* as "a carefully rounded portrait of a fascinating, occasionally ridiculous, and finally frightening man. It is hard to imagine that a more complete study of Huey Long, his career, his state and his times could be achieved. The facts are there in copious abundance from ancestors to death.... [Williams] bends over backward to present every side of every issue, demythologizing Huey Long as he produces a three-dimensional view of this complex man. The biography is a tribute to Williams's skill as a writer and competence as a historian. [But] this is not to say that Williams is not a partisan. His sympathies are clearly on the side of Long's reforms and against Long's opponents.... [In] trying to see all aspects of every situation, he too often falls into the trap of coming up squarely on every side of the question. This leads occasionally to confused and sometimes contradictory judgments."

Christopher Lehmann-Haupt of the *New York Times*, after having noted that the author admitted from the beginning that he considered Huey Long to be a "great man," concluded that "I'm not sure if Mr. Williams proves his thesis.... [But] it doesn't matter. The theory forces one to focus on the man. By consulting the oral history, ... Mr. Williams has found out more about the man than any other historian has ever known. And in this case the man is interesting enough to sustain any thesis, even one a thousand pages long. Actually, the book seems much shorter than it is.... [The author] is as natural a storyteller as Huey was an orator and filibusterer.... [A mere summary of Long's life] leaves out the color and scope of Mr. Williams's epic—the outrageousness of Long's personality, the brashness of his behavior and the incredible limits to which he went to accumulate perhaps more power than any American political figure has controlled before or since.... [The author] cuts at that reputation. He concedes that Long outdid himself, rotted in his greed for power.... But Mr. Williams holds to the theory of Robert Penn Warren's *All the King's Men*—'that the politician who wishes to do good may have to do some evil to achieve his goal.'"

Only a few reviewers were unimpressed by *Huey Long.* Describing it as "laborious," the *Newsweek* critic wrote: "T. Harry Williams's truths are no match for Warren's fictions [in *All the King's Men*]. It is no fun to watch the great

myth of the Kingfish systematically dismantled in the interest of an accurate record.... It is a week's unrelieved work to read this book, and its refusal to distort or mythologize—or dramatize—makes the reading unexciting." A *Nation* reviewer, admitting that the book "is not totally without revelations," nevertheless concluded that Williams "has achieved the impossible. He has written an incredibly tedious and, before the last of the 906 pages has fallen, an excruciatingly boring book about Louisiana's famous Kingfish.... The author's vices as a biographer would be virtues if he were an archaeologist. He is endlessly patient in digging.... This Germanic researching is quite all right as long as you don't unload all your debris on the reader. But Williams seems to have done just that.... [In addition,] Williams has made little effort to lead the reader to any broader conclusion than the conclusion of one tarnished political career.... Even less forgivable, Williams does not entertain the reader."

Finally, a *New Republic* reviewer, while commending Williams for his "years of invaluable research," ultimately found the book to be "disappointing." As he explained: "In the book the facts often overwhelm the framework, and the reader is engulfed in a maze of details that often do little to clarify or illuminate the admitted complexities of Long's career and character.... Time and time again he defends Huey's controversial tactics.... Like many biographers, Williams often overestimates his subject's importance in events.... Also weakening the whole book is a writing style sometimes reminiscent of old *Time* style.... In view of the book's virtues—it is the fullest, most 'objective' portrait of the Kingfish yet produced—one has to be disappointed over its faults.... Professor Williams' book is no tragedy, nor has he abused his obvious talents. Yet I cannot avoid a feeling of regret that the book did not match its potentiality."

BIOGRAPHICAL/CRITICAL SOURCES: University Bookman, autumn, 1967; *New York Times,* October 27, 1969; *New York Times Book Review,* November 2, 1969; *Newsweek,* November 3, 1969; *Nation,* November 3, 1969; *Life,* November 7, 1969; *Book World,* November 9, 1969; *Washington Post,* November 24, 1969; *New Republic,* December 13, 1969; *Best Sellers,* December 15, 1969; *New Leader,* December 22, 1969; *Virginia Quarterly Review,* winter, 1970; *New York Review of Books,* February 26, 1970; *Listener,* April 9, 1970; *Writer's Digest,* September, 1970.

—*Sketch by Deborah A. Straub*

*   *   *

WILLIAMS, (Margaret) Wetherby (Margaret Erskine)

PERSONAL: Born in Kingston, Ontario, Canada; British subject; daughter of Thomas and Elizabeth (Erskine) Williams. *Education:* Privately educated. *Politics:* Conservative. *Religion:* Church of England. *Home:* Flat 18, 58 Rutland Gate, London S.W.7, England. *Agent:* A. M. Heath & Co. Ltd., 40-42 William IV St., London WC2N 4DD, England.

CAREER: Free-lance writer, 1947—. Does volunteer work for Women's Royal Voluntary Services, Friends of Guy's Hospital, and Harrison Homes. *Member:* International P.E.N., Crime Writers Association.

WRITINGS—Crime novels; all under pseudonym Margaret Erskine; all published by Doubleday, except as indicated: *And Being Dead,* Bles, 1938; *The Limping Man,* 1939, published as *The Painted Mask,* Ace Books, 1972; *The Voice of the House,* 1947, reprinted, Ace Books, 1972 (published in

England as *Whispering House,* Hammond, 1947); *I Knew MacBean,* 1948; *Give up the Ghost,* 1949, reprinted, Ian Henry Publications, 1976.

The Disappearing Bridegroom, Hammond, 1950; *The Silver Ladies,* 1951, reprinted, Ace Books, 1973; *Look behind You, Lady,* 1952 (published in England as *Death of Our Dear One,* Hammond, 1952, reprinted, White Lion Publishers, 1973); *Dead by Now,* Hammond, 1953, Doubleday, 1954, revised edition, Ace Books, 1972; *Old Mrs. Ommanney Is Dead,* 1955 (published in England as *Fatal Relations,* Hammond, 1955, reprinted, White Lion Publishers, 1973); *The Voice of Murder,* 1956, reprinted, Ian Henry Publications, 1976; *Sleep No More,* Hodder & Stoughton, 1958; *A Graveyard Plot,* 1959; *The House of the Enchantress,* Hodder & Stoughton, 1959.

The Woman at Belguardo, 1961; *No. 9 Belmont Square,* 1963 (published in England as *The House in Belmont Square,* Hodder & Stoughton, 1963); *Take a Dark Journey,* Hodder & Stoughton, 1965; *The Family at Tammerton,* 1966; *Case with Three Husbands,* 1967; *The Ewe Lamb,* 1968.

The Case of Mary Fielding, 1970; *The Brood of Folly,* 1971; *Don't Look behind You,* Ace Books, 1972; *Caravan of Night,* Ace Books, 1972; *Besides the Wench Is Dead,* 1973; *Harriet, Farewell,* 1975; *The House in Hook Street,* 1977.

SIDELIGHTS: Margaret Wetherby Williams told *CA:* "I was brought up in an old country house in Devonshire, complete with ghost who had his being in the nursery wing. I was educated by a governess but, like the mock turtle in Alice 'with extras.'"†

*   *   *

WILLIAMS, William Appleman 1921-

PERSONAL: Born June 12, 1921, in Atlantic, Iowa; son of William Carleton and Mildrede (Appleman) Williams; married; five children. *Education:* U.S. Naval Academy, B.S. in Electrical and Thermodynamic Engineering, 1944; University of Wisconsin, M.A., 1948, Ph.D., 1950; University of Leeds, postgraduate study, 1948. *Office:* History Department, Oregon State University, Corvallis, Ore. 97331.

CAREER: Teacher of history courses at Washington and Jefferson College, Bard College, Ohio State University, and University of Oregon; University of Wisconsin—Madison, faculty member, 1957-68, professor of history, 1960-68; Oregon State University, Corvallis, professor of history, 1968—. James Pinckney Harrison Distinguished Visiting Professor, College of William and Mary, 1980. *Member:* Organization of American Historians (president, 1980-81). *Military service:* U.S. Navy, 1944-47. *Awards, honors:* Grants from Ford Foundation for study in sociology, and grants from Fund for Social Analysis, Louis B. Rabinowitz Foundation, University of Wisconsin Graduate Research Committee, American Council of Learned Societies, Social Science Research Council, and American Philosophical Society; distinguished Fulbright scholar at University of Melbourne, 1977.

WRITINGS: *American-Russian Relations, 1781-1947,* Rinehart, 1952, reprinted, Octagon Books, 1971; (editor) *The Shaping of American History: Readings and Documents in American Foreign Relations, 1750-1955,* Rand McNally, 1956, 2nd edition published as *The Shaping of American Diplomacy,* 1970; (contributor) *American Radicals ... Some Problems and Personalities,* Monthly Review Press, 1957; *America and the Middle East: Open Door Imperialism or Enlightened Leadership?,* Rinehart, 1958; *The Tragedy of American Diplomacy,* World Publishing, 1959, 2nd revised edition, Dell, 1972.

The Contours of American History, World Publishing, 1961, published with a new foreword by author, Quadrangle, 1966; *The United States, Cuba, and Castro: An Essay on the Dynamics of Revolution and the Dissolution of Empire,* Monthly Review Press, 1962; *The Great Evasion: An Essay on the Contemporary Relevance of Karl Marx and on the Wisdom of Admitting the Heretic into the Dialogue about America's Future,* New Viewpoints, 1968; *The Roots of the Modern American Empire: A Study of the Growth and Shaping of a Social Consciousness in a Marketplace Society,* Random House, 1969.

(Editor) *From Colony to Empire: Essays in the History of American Foreign Relations,* Wiley, 1972; *Some Presidents: Wilson to Nixon,* Vintage Books, 1972; *History as a Way of Learning: Articles, Excerpts and Essays,* New Viewpoints, 1973, new edition, 1974; *America Confronts a Revolutionary World, 1776-1976,* Morrow, 1976; *Americans in a Changing World: A History of the United States in the Twentieth Century,* Harper, 1978; *Empire as a Way of Life: An Essay on the Causes and Character of America's Present Predicament,* Oxford University Press, 1980.

BIOGRAPHICAL/CRITICAL SOURCES: *Saturday Review,* February 21, 1970; *New York Times Book Review,* February 22, 1970; *Nation,* February 23, 1970.

*   *   *

WILLIAMSON, Audrey (May) 1913-

PERSONAL: Born May 29, 1913, in Thornton Heath, Surrey, England; daughter of Herbert and May (Tester) Williamson. *Education:* Attended English schools. *Home:* 1 Landseer House, John Islip St., London S.W.1., England. *Agent:* James Brown Associates, Inc., 25 West 43rd St., New York, N.Y. 10036.

CAREER: Author, journalist, and lecturer to historical and literary societies. Ballet critic, *Tribune,* 1951-53; London theatre correspondent, *Age,* 1952-66; assistant drama critic, *Times,* 1956-64; New York Theatre correspondent, *Scotsman,* 1963-64; New York opera and ballet correspondent, *Guardian,* 1963-64; book reviewer, *Tribune,* 1973—. *Member:* Society of the Study of Labour History, Thomas Paine Society, Richard III Society, Crime Writers Association. *Awards, honors:* Crime Writers Association's Gold Dagger, 1978, for *The Mystery of the Princes: An Investigation into a Supposed Murder.*

WRITINGS: *Contemporary Ballet,* Rockliff, 1946, Macmillan, 1950; *Ballet Renaissance,* Golden Galley Press (London), 1948; *Old Vic Drama: A Twelve Years' Study of Plays and Players,* Rockliff, 1948, Macmillan, 1949.

The Art of Ballet, Macmillan, 1950, revised edition, 1953; *Theatre of Two Decades,* Rockliff, 1951, Macmillan, 1952; *Gilbert and Sullivan Opera: A New Assessment,* Macmillan, 1953, second edition, Rockliff, 1955; *Contemporary Theatre, 1953-56,* Macmillan, 1956; *Paul Rogers,* Rockliff, 1956; *Old Vic Drama 2: 1947-1957,* Macmillan, 1957; (with Charles Landstone) *The Bristol Old Vic: The First Ten Years,* Miller, 1957; *Ballet of Three Decades,* Macmillan, 1958.

Wagner Opera, J. Calder, 1962; *Bernard Shaw: Man & Writer,* Crowell, 1963.

Thomas Paine: His Life, Work, and Times, St. Martin's, 1973; *Wilkes: A Friend to Liberty,* Reader's Digest Services, 1974; *Artists and Writers in Revolt: The Pre-Raphaelites,* David & Charles, 1976; *The Mystery of the Princes: An Investigation into a Supposed Murder,* Allan Sutton, 1978; *Funeral March for Siegfried,* Elek, 1979; *Death of a Theatre*

Filly, Elek, 1980. Contributor to *Enciclopedia Della Spetta-cola, Dictionary of Literary Biography,* and to *Theatre Arts, Opera News, Drama, Music America,* and other periodicals.

WORK IN PROGRESS: A third detective novel, *Dances and Songs of Death.*

*   *   *

WILLINGHAM, Calder (Baynard, Jr.)   1922-

PERSONAL: Born December 23, 1922, in Atlanta, Ga.; son of Calder Baynard (a hotel manager) and Eleanor Churchill (Willcox) Willingham; married Helene Rothenberg, 1945; married second wife, Jane Marie Bennett, September 15, 1953; children: (first marriage) Paul Thomas; (second marriage) Frederick Calder, Sara Jane, Mark Osgood, Pamela, Christopher. *Education:* Attended The Citadel, 1940-41, and University of Virginia, 1941-43. *Home:* 1 Shingle Camp Hill Rd., New Hampton, N.H. 03256.

CAREER: Novelist, playwright, screen writer. *Awards, honors:* British Film Academy Award for best screenplay, 1969, for "The Graduate."

WRITINGS: End as a Man, Vanguard, 1947; *Geraldine Bradshaw,* Vanguard, 1950; *Reach to the Stars,* Vanguard, 1951; *The Gates of Hell* (short stories), Vanguard, 1951; *Natural Child,* Dial, 1952; *To Eat a Peach,* Dial, 1955; *Eternal Fire,* Vanguard, 1963; *Providence Island,* Vanguard, 1969; *Rambling Rose,* Delacorte, 1972; *The Big Nickel,* Dial, 1975; *The Building of Venus Four,* Manor, 1977.

Films: "The Strange One" (based on his novel *End as a Man*), Columbia, 1957; (with Stanley Kubrick and Tim Thompson) "Paths of Glory" (based on the novel of the same title by Humphrey Cobb), United Artists, 1957; "The Vikings," United Artists, 1958; "One-Eyed Jacks," Paramount, 1961; (with Buck Henry) "The Graduate" (based on the novel of the same title by Charles Webb), Embassy Pictures, 1967; "Little Big Man" (based on the novel of the same title by Thomas Berger), CBS Films, 1972; "Thieves Like Us," United Artists, 1975.

Also author of a play, "End as a Man," based on his novel of the same title.

SIDELIGHTS: Calder Willingham's work has sparked a good deal of controversy among literary critics. To some he is, as Jack Kroll of *Newsweek* puts it, "perhaps the outstanding talent of that generation" of authors which includes Norman Mailer, William Styron, and James Jones, "the most original, the real, although perhaps subtlest, innovator, and the one writer who has achieved what used to be called mastery over the craft of his art." But to others he is a verbose smut writer. An *Atlantic* reviewer says that "Willingham has a mind for the hallucinated, the perverse, the psychopathic, and the unillusioned and unlovely in human being and human situation. He also has a fine, clear ear for speech, and some disturbingly independent notions on what is fit for telling and how to tell it. The results are not ingratiating." Willingham responds: "The charge made by some that I am 'a verbose smut writer' and that my work is 'pornographic' amazes me. I see in my writing virtually none of the sadism of pornography or the nasty and jejune neuroticism of smut. On the contrary, the erotic power of my writing seems to me to derive from love and respect for humanity's better half. My best characters by no coincidence are girls and women. This is a cheap, cowardly, and lying criticism. These people fear the erotic for reasons of their own. Beyond such disgusting cowardice, they reflect and express the spiritual sickness of our time."

Willingham's first novel, *End as a Man* was written when he was twenty-three years old. Critically, it has remained the best received of his novels, and it is the one to which his later work is most often compared. John Woodburn of the *Saturday Review* calls it "a fearful book, a hard and angry book, filled with a contempt that is close to loathing; but the contempt is made valid and mature because it is balanced with understanding and pity, and the restless, ranging imagination, creative and often brilliant is laid like a montage upon the flat surface of the setting.... Calder Willingham is a good and sharply arresting writer, ... someone to watch steadily." In a *New Yorker* article, J. M. Lalley writes, "With all its technical crudities and philosophic immaturity, this is a novel capable of evoking, even in a seasoned reader, something like cathartic terror." And J. T. Farrell of the *New York Times* says that "this first novel is the work of an artist, written with power, honesty and courage; it carries its own conviction on every page. Its complete realism may shock the tender-minded; yet few of those who read *End as a Man* are ever likely to forget it.... I consider it a permanent contribution to American literature."

In a *New York Times* review of *Geraldine Bradshaw,* John Barkham makes the point that "none of the characters in this story is in the least likable, yet," he feels, "even the most subsidiary of them is pinpointed with clarity and economy.... In its way the book is a dazzling performance." Barkham concludes that *Geraldine Bradshaw* is "remarkable enough to establish Mr. Willingham among the foremost of our realistic novelists." A *San Francisco Chronicle* writer says that Willingham "does not exercise his undeniable talent sufficiently. It is possible that his reflection of the monotony of single-minded sex-pursuit comes close to the truth. But the four-letter monotone in which it is here related defeats what may have been the author's purpose." Kelsey Guilfoil of the *Chicago Sunday Tribune* states that "this novel will have no serious competitors for the title of the filthiest book of the year."

The mixed reviews continue with *Eternal Fire,* published in 1963. *Library Journal*'s J. C. Pine writes that "Willingham has been the *enfant terrible* of American fiction.... [Yet] he is a serious and in many ways a talented writer." Saul Maloff, in a *Commonweal* article, expresses contempt for Willingham's work: "Stripped down to what it essentially is, we have nothing but melodrama of the grand guignol variety, advanced soap-opera against a background of Southern Gothic.... Obviously, the stage is set for pornography; and if that is what we are looking for, Willingham is not one to disappoint us." But a *Newsweek* writer gives the book high praise: "*Eternal Fire* deserves a place among the dozen or so novels that must be mentioned if one is to speak of greatness in American fiction.... Willingham sustains a broad, pitiless, and savagely serious burlesque of all men who presume to call themselves virtuous and civilized."

Providence Island appears to have evoked even more criticism than most of Willingham's novels. There is disapproval of the eroticism in the book. Guy Davenport of the *National Review,* for instance, asks "who reads such trash? A Victorian would have said, 'The Cook.' But there are no more cooks, or very few, and the ones I know are too intelligent to follow the doings of Mr. Willingham's paper-doll characters, even into their fornications, which have the same relation to sex as screaming does to a Rossini aria." Thomas Lask, in a *New York Times* review, criticizes Willingham's use of dialogue in this novel. He writes: "There is enough talk in it to drive a totally deaf man to sign on as a lighthouse keeper off the Cape of Good Hope.... If all the blather were pumped out of this novel, it could be reduced to the size of a restaurant menu without a loss of a single vital ingredient." *Life*'s Melvin Maddocks says that *Providence Island* is "a poor book in cruelly obvious ways. The style wanders erratically from New York satirical to Southern pastoral. Scenes ramble on and on, slightly out of focus, like a home movie. Worst of all, the plot seems borrowed from a bad *Playboy* cartoon." Even Jack Kroll, who normally has great praise for Willingham, writes that "it is the sad and deliberate anticlimax of this review to report that his new book will not help him to gain the belated recognition which is more than his due. . . . For the first time in his career this brilliant original sounds old-fashioned—it is as if he were really writing, disguised as the kind of big book that is making it these days, a tract against that kind of book and all the moral and esthetic implications of the culture that produces it."

In his *Best Sellers* review of *Rambling Rose*, Fred Rotondaro writes: "In the hands of a writer less talented than Willingham, Rambling Rose would have become just another girl on the make. In this volume though she becomes much more than that. She is a very uninhibited woman trying to find happiness as she lives her crazy and sometimes tragic life. Eventually, she does find happiness and Willingham, excellent artist that he is, simply touches that portion of her life leaving the reader to draw his own conclusions." But a *Virginia Quarterly Review* writer notes that "the book must be criticized for its change in viewpoint and direction at midpoint, when emphasis is shifted away from a nubile young girl for whom sex is a constant preoccupation to the even younger lad who tells the story, and to his imperceptive family. As a yarn about female concupiscence the volume has some pornographic interest; when it wanders on the other hand into a pseudo-serious analysis of situation and character it becomes tiresome."

Of *The Big Nickel*, published in 1975, *Library Journal*'s Eric Moon writes: "The old, old plot—a novelist whose first book has been a critical success can't get started on opus no. 2—is given a little livelier treatment here than in dozens of other novels which have used it. . . . Willingham is never uninteresting but there's no doubt that he's batting well below his average this time." And Jonathan Yardley of the *New Republic* calls the author "one of the most skilled, observant and purely funny satirists of the post-war generation. . . . Even at his least successful, Willingham is fun to read—which is about all that can be said on behalf of *The Big Nickel*. . . . Nobody, but nobody, writes about sex with such irreverence, such outrageous imagery. The utter astonishment with which man can view woman is rarely depicted so humorously—or so knowingly. That's Willingham at his best." But Yardley concludes that this book is "more tantalizing than satisfying."

Although Willingham has become a very well-known novelist, he has also been extremely successful in the field of screen writing. One of his most famous scripts is "The Graduate," produced in 1967 by Embassy Pictures, starring Dustin Hoffman, Katherine Ross, and Anne Bancroft. Bosley Crowther of the *New York Times* calls it "a film that is not only one of the best of the year, but also one of the best seriocomic social satires we've had from Hollywood since Preston Sturges was making them. . . . In telling a pungent story of the sudden confusions and dismays of a bland young man fresh out of college who is plunged headlong into the intellectual vacuum of his affluent parents' circle of friends, it fashions a scarifying picture of the raw vulgarity of the swimming-pool rich, and it does so with a lively and exciting expressiveness through vivid cinema." Another well-known

screenplay by Willingham is "Little Big Man," a 1972 CBS Films production which also starred Dustin Hoffman. The film proved extremely popular, although critics gave it a rather lukewarm reception. A *Time* reviewer, for instance, says that the author "has provided a scenario that begins with robust rawhide humor, turns to profundity—then collapses into petulant editorial. In the era of occupied Alcatraz, surely it is no news that the white man spoke with forked tongue, that the first Americans were maltreated as the last savages." John Simon says that the film "does not come off as a whole because it is too episodic, which could work better in a book where the author can take his time." Simon does, however, find that "if you look at the film as a series of cavalierly tacked together vignettes, an estimable number of these work, either in part or even as a whole." And the *Newsweek* critic, after denouncing some parts of the movie, decides that it is a "rambunctious triumph" because it "has contrived to lampoon, revere or revile the length and breadth of the entire frontier. . . . [It] accomplishes that rarest achievement, the breathing of life into an ossified art form. . . . Blood brother to the 1903 one-reeler, 'The Great Train Robbery,' 'Little Big Man' is the new western to begin all westerns."

Willingham says that he writes in the dramatic media for money and for recreation, and that his "serious work has been done in the novel." He told *CA:* "I today regard narrative as the most important quality of the novel; I believe that a good story is more than merely entertaining, that characterization, style, philosophical depth, even poetry flow from the story. I believe a novel should have plot, suspense, dramatic development, and I strive to achieve same."

BIOGRAPHICAL/CRITICAL SOURCES: New York Times Book Review, February 16, 1947, February 26, 1950, October 29, 1972, March 23, 1975; *New York Herald Tribune Book Review*, February 16, 1947, June 17, 1951, December 2, 1951, November 30, 1952; *New Yorker*, March 8, 1947, March 18, 1950; *New Republic*, March 24, 1947, December 26, 1970, April 5, 1975; *Saturday Review*, April 5, 1947, April 30, 1955; *New York Times*, February 26, 1950, July 22, 1951, December 16, 1951, November 2, 1952, February 27, 1955, December 22, 1967, April 1, 1969; *San Francisco Chronicle*, March 5, 1950; *Chicago Sunday Tribune*, March 19, 1950; *Nation*, June 4, 1955, March 31, 1969; *Library Journal*, December 1, 1962, February 15, 1975; *Commonweal*, February 1, 1963, January 22, 1971; *Life*, February 14, 1969; *Newsweek*, March 10, 1969; *Best Sellers*, March 15, 1969, November 1, 1972; *National Review*, May 20, 1969; *Books and Bookmen*, December, 1969; *Time*, December 21, 1970; *New Leader*, December 28, 1971; *Times Literary Supplement*, July 6, 1973; *Virginia Quarterly Review*, winter, 1973; *Choice*, June, 1975; *Contemporary Literary Criticism*, Volume V, Gale, 1976.

—*Sketch by Peter M. Gareffa*

*   *   *

WILLIS, Margaret 1899-

PERSONAL: Born January 16, 1899, in Clinton, N.Y.; daughter of Herbert Leland and May (Smith) Willis. *Education:* Wellesley College, B.A., 1919; Columbia University, M.A., 1925, additional study, 1931-32 and 1946; also attended Johns Hopkins University, 1926-27, and Zimmern School for International Studies, Geneva, Switzerland, 1928. *Home:* 1612 McLean Rd., Mount Vernon, Wash. 98273.

CAREER: Teacher of American children in Tokyo, Japan, 1919-21; high school history teacher in Mount Vernon,

Wash., 1921-24 and in Towson, Md., 1925-27; American College for Girls, Istanbul, Turkey, teacher of history, economics, and international relations, 1927-31; Bennett School, Millbrook, N.J., teacher of history and economics, 1931-32; Ohio State University, University School, Columbus, teacher of core and social studies, 1932-46; Cairo School for American Children, Cairo, Egypt, principal, 1946-48; Ohio State University, University School, teacher of core, social studies, and guidance, 1948-67, associate emeritus professor, 1967—. *Member:* American Association of University Professors, Foreign Policy Association, National Education Association, National Council for the Social Studies (delegate to representative assembly, 1960), Association for Supervision and Curriculum Development, American Association for the United Nations, American Civil Liberties Union, National Retired Teachers Association, Ohio Council for the Social Studies (president, 1962-63), Social Studies Association of Central Ohio (president, 1950-51), Wellesley Club.

WRITINGS: (Contributor) *Programs for the Gifted,* Harper, 1961; *The Guinea Pigs after Twenty Years,* Ohio State University Press, 1961; *Three Dozen Years: A Report on the University School, 1932-68,* Ohio State University Bookstore, 1968; (editor) Martin Sampson, *Indians of Skagit County,* Skagit County Historical Society, 1972; (compiler and contributor) *Chechacos All: The Pioneering of Skagit,* Skagit County Historical Society, 1973; (compiler and contributor) *Skagit Settlers: Trials and Triumphs,* Skagit County Historical Society, 1975. Also author of *Buildings of Old Skagit County: Ten Self-Guided Tours,* 1977, and of pamphlet, *Secondary Education for Veterans of World War II,* 1945. Contributor of articles to historical journals.

* * *

WILNER, Herbert 1925-1977

PERSONAL: Born December 12, 1925, in Brooklyn, N.Y.; died May 6, 1977; son of Beny (a jeweler) and Sarah (Mokotoff) Wilner; married Nancy Ruben (a researcher in psychiatry), August 22, 1946; children: Steven, Sarah, Amy. *Education:* Brooklyn College (now Brooklyn College of the City University of New York), B.A., 1946; Columbia University, M.A., 1948; State University of Iowa, Ph.D., 1954. *Politics:* Democrat. *Religion:* Jewish. *Agent:* James O. Brown, James Brown Associates, Inc., 25 West 43rd St., New York, N.Y. 10036.

CAREER: University of Kansas, Lawrence, instructor in English, 1948-50; Southern Connecticut State College, New Haven, instructor, 1954-55; Yale University, New Haven, instructor in English, 1955-57; San Francisco State University, San Francisco, Calif., beginning 1957, became professor of English; Fulbright guest professor, Innsbruck University, 1964-65; writer-in-residence, University of Kansas, 1971. *Member:* American Federation of Teachers, Authors League. *Awards, honors:* Gold medal in fiction for best novel by a California writer, Commonwealth Club, 1966, for *All the Little Heroes.*

WRITINGS: (Co-author) *The Seven Years,* Dutton, 1957; *All the Little Heroes,* Bobbs-Merrill, 1966; *Aspects of American Fiction,* Americana-Austriaca, 1966; *Dovisch in the Wilderness and Other Stories,* Bobbs-Merrill, 1969; (with Leo Litwak) *College Days in Earthquake Country,* Random House, 1972. Work represented in anthologies. Contributor of articles and short stories to national publications, including *Esquire* and *Saturday Evening Post.*

WORK IN PROGRESS: A novel.†

WILSON, Bryan R(onald) 1926-

PERSONAL: Born June 25, 1926, in Leeds, England. *Education:* University College of Leicester, B.Sc., 1952; London School of Economics, Ph.D., 1955. *Office:* All Souls College, Oxford University, Oxford, England.

CAREER: University of Leeds, Leeds, England, lecturer in sociology, 1955-62, warden of Sadler Hall, 1959-62; Oxford University, Oxford, England, reader in sociology, 1962—, fellow of All Souls College, 1963—. Visiting professor at University of Ghana, 1964, University of Leuven, 1976, and University of Toronto, 1978. *Military service:* British Army, 1944-47. *Member:* Society for the Scientific Study of Religion (member of council, 1977-80), British Sociological Association. *Awards, honors:* Commonwealth Fund fellow at University of California, Berkeley, 1957-58; American Council of Learned Societies fellow at University of California, Berkeley, 1966-67; Japan Society fellow, 1975.

WRITINGS: Sects and Society, University of California Press, 1961, reprinted, Greenwood Press, 1978; (contributor) A. T. Welford, editor, *Society: Problems and Methods of Study,* Routledge & Kegan Paul, 1962; (contributor) Marjorie Reeves, editor, *Eighteen Plus Unity and Diversity in Higher Education,* Faber, 1965; *Religion in Secular Society,* New Thinkers' Library, Watts, 1966; (editor and contributor) *Patterns of Sectarianism,* Heinemann, 1967; (editor and contributor) *Rationality,* Harper, 1970; *The Youth Culture and the Universities,* Faber, 1970, *Religious Sects,* McGraw, 1970; *Magic and the Millennium,* Harper, 1973; *The Noble Savages,* University of California Press, 1975; (editor and contributor) *Education, Equality and Society,* Allen & Unwin, 1975; *Contemporary Transformations of Religion,* Oxford University Press, 1976. Contributor to numerous periodicals, including *Twentieth Century, Sunday Times, Observer, Spectator, Texas Quarterly, Archives de Sociologie des Religions, Criminal Law Review, Education Today,* and to sociology journals in England and America. Joint founding editor, *Annual Review of the Social Sciences of Religion,* 1977—; associate European editor, *Journal for the Scientific Study of Religion,* 1977—.

WORK IN PROGRESS: Comparative studies of sectarianism; a dictionary of minority religious movements in contemporary Britain, essays in the sociology of religion; new religious movements.

AVOCATIONAL INTERESTS: Music, graphic arts, oriental porcelain, herbaceous borders.

* * *

WILSON, Mitchell 1913-1973

PERSONAL: Born July 17, 1913, in New York, N.Y.; died February 25, 1973, in New York, N.Y.; son of Philip and Regina (Reiman) Wilson; married Helen Weinberg, 1941 (divorced); married Stella Adler (an actress); children: (first marriage) Erica Spellman, Victoria Wilson; (stepchild) Ellen Oppenheim. *Education:* New York University, B.A., 1934; Columbia University, M.A., 1938. *Home:* 1016 Fifth Ave., New York, N.Y.

CAREER: Columbia University, New York City, tutor in physics, 1938-40; City College of New York (now City College of the City University of New York), New York City, instructor in physics, 1940; Columbian Carbon Co., New York City, physics research director, 1941-45; free lance writer, 1945-73.

WRITINGS—Novels; published by Simon & Schuster, except as indicated: *Stalk the Hunter,* 1942; *Footsteps Behind*

Her, 1943; *None So Blind,* 1944; *The Panic Stricken,* 1945; *The Kimballs,* 1947; *Live with Lightning,* Little, Brown, 1949; *My Brother, My Enemy,* Little, Brown, 1952; *The Lovers,* Doubleday, 1954; *Meeting at a Far Meridian,* Doubleday, 1961; *The Huntress,* Doubleday, 1966; *Passion to Know,* Doubleday, 1972.

Nonfiction: *American Science and Invention,* Simon & Schuster, 1954; *The Human Body,* Western Publishing, 1959, revised edition (with Ann Reit) published as *The Body in Action,* 1962; (with the editors of *Life*), *Energy,* Time-Life, 1963, revised edition, Silver Burdett, 1969; *See-Saws and Cosmic Rays: A First View of Physics,* Lothrup, 1967.

Contributor to *Observer, Nation,* and other periodicals.

SIDELIGHTS: Although not ideological, many of Mitchell Wilson's novels were very popular in the Soviet Union. Beginning with *Live with Lightning,* the Russian editions of his books were bestsellers. Unlike most Western authors who are published in the Soviet Union, Wilson received royalty payments for his work.

Wilson's early novels are suspense stories, but it was his later works, dealing with scientists and the strains they feel between their ideals and the uses to which their work is put, that became so popular in the Soviet Union. "My heroes care," Wilson once said. "They are deeply concerned and committed people."

Wilson's collected manuscripts are housed at Boston University.

BIOGRAPHICAL/CRITICAL SOURCES: New York Times Book Review, January 11, 1959, October 2, 1966; *Nation,* September 10, 1960; *New Yorker,* January 6, 1962; *New York Times,* April 3, 1962, February 27, 1973; *Saturday Review,* May 13, 1967; *Science Books,* September, 1967; *Books & Bookmen,* October, 1969; *Scientific American,* October, 1972.†

* * *

WILSON, Thomas Williams, Jr. 1912-

PERSONAL: Born September 1, 1912, in Baltimore, Md.; son of Thomas Williams (a businessman) and Helen (Hines) Wilson; married second wife (a public relations director), 1958; children (first marriage) Thomas Williams III, Sally Bird (Mrs. Robert T. Hall), Ann Remington. *Education:* Attended Princeton University, 1931-34. *Politics:* Democrat. *Home:* 3317 Q. St. N.W., Washington, D.C. *Agent:* Theron Raines, Raines & Raines, 475 Fifth Ave., New York, N.Y. 10017. *Office:* U.S. Department of State, Washington, D.C.

CAREER: Reporter and correspondent for *Baltimore Evening Sun,* European edition of *New York Herald Tribune* in Paris, France, International News Service in Paris, and *Wall Street Journal* in Washington, D.C., 1934-40; affiliated with U.S. War Production Board and Board of Economic Warfare, 1940-45; affiliated with educational films, 1946-48, and with U.S. Economic Cooperation Administration, 1948-53; did public relations work, 1953-61; affiliated with U.S. Department of State, 1961—.

WRITINGS: Cold War and Common Sense, New York Graphic Society, 1962; *The Great Weapons Heresy,* Houghton, 1970; *Science, Technology and Development: The Politics of Modernization,* Foreign Policy, 1979. Contributor of articles to *Harper's, Reporter,* and other magazines. Columnist, *Baltimore Sun,* 1938. Editor, *Economic World,* 1959-61.

WORK IN PROGRESS: A history of the Marshall Plan.

SIDELIGHTS: Thomas Wilson, Jr.'s book *The Great Weapons Heresy* was one of several books written about the Oppenheimer affair of the early 1950's. J. Robert Oppenheimer, often referred to as the "Father of the Atomic Bomb," was a well-respected scientist and government adviser, who after several policy disagreements concerning the use and build up of nuclear weapons fell out of favor with an extremely small but at the time, very influential group of U.S. government officials. In 1953, a former Air Force Security officer accused Oppenheimer of having been a Soviet espionage agent for more than fourteen years. Although the evidence the Air Force officer offered to substantiate his claims was considered by many to be ridiculous, when President Eisenhower was notified of the accusation he ordered a security hearing to investigate. As a result of the hearing, Oppenheimer was denied security clearance, meaning he no longer had access to restricted materials on atomic energy.

Wilson's book views the Oppenheimer case within the arena of the strategic arms race between the United States and the Soviet Union. Allen Weinstein writes in the *Nation* that *The Great Weapons Heresy* "summarized the arguments over nuclear strategy that formed one of several grounds upon which Oppenheimer lost his security clearance.... However, Wilson is less concerned with offering a balanced presentation of the complex set of factors that led to the AFC's decision to revoke Oppenheimer's clearance than he is with producing an admirable lawyer's brief for arms control agreements. Oppenheimer serves as the author's convenient symbol of scientific support for such agreements, and as an eloquent polemic for arms control negotiations, the book fulfills a useful function."

Washington Post reviewer George Thayer writes that "Wilson makes one valid point. Oppenheimer, [Wilson] writes, was one of the first and surely one of the most prominent and influential Americans to recognize that 5,000 nuclear bombs would not necessarily make a nation militarily superior to one with only 1,000 nuclear bombs. If Soviet society can be effectively destroyed with only 1,000 A- or H- bombs (taking into account duds and those destroyed before reaching target), what is the point of having 5,000?"

Thayer continues: "The attitude that somehow the United States is more secure by 'staying ahead' of the Soviet Union, when either country has the capacity virtually to destroy the other with only a small fraction of the total bombs in its personal arsenal, is still with us today."

BIOGRAPHICAL/CRITICAL SOURCES: Washington Post, February 12, 1970; *Life,* February 27, 1970; *Nation,* April 27, 1970; *National Review,* June 2, 1970; *New York Times Book Review,* June 28, 1970; *New York Review of Books,* July 2, 1970.

* * *

WILTSE, Charles M(aurice) 1907-

PERSONAL: Born April 4, 1907, in San Francisco, Calif.; son of Herbert Alphonso and Mary (Blake) Wiltse; married Kelly Tollolah Tooks, December 24, 1952. *Education:* Attended Marshall University, 1924-26; West Virginia University, A.B., 1929; Cornell University, Ph.D., 1932. *Home:* 17 Haskins Rd., Hanover, N.H. 03755. *Office:* Baker Library, Dartmouth College, Hanover, N.H. 03755.

CAREER: U.S. Government, Washington, D.C., 1935-67. Researcher, National Resources Committee, 1935-38; assistant to director of education, National Youth Administration, 1938-40; special assistant to executive secretary, War Production Board, 1943-47; consultant on industrial mobilization, National Security Resources Board, 1948-49; deputy executive secretary, National Production Authority and Defense Production Administration, 1951-53; U.S. Army Medical Service, historian, 1954-60, chief historian, 1960-67; Dartmouth College, Hanover, N.H., professor of history, 1967-72. *Military service:* U.S. Army, 1943. *Member:* American Historical Association, Society of American Historians, Organization of American Historians, Society of American Archivists, Western History Association. *Awards, honors:* Guggenheim fellowship, 1949-51; Litt.D., Marshall University, 1952.

WRITINGS: The Jeffersonian Tradition in American Democracy, University of North Carolina Press, 1935, reprinted, Hill & Wang, 1960; *Life of John C. Calhoun,* Bobbs-Merrill, Volume I: *Nationalist, 1782-1828,* 1944, Volume II: *Nullifier, 1829-1839,* 1949, Volume III: *Sectionalist, 1840-1850,* 1951; *Aluminum Policies of the War Production Board and Predecessor Agencies, May 1940 to November 1945,* War Production Board, 1946; *Lead and Zinc Policies of the War Production Board and Predecessor Agencies, May 1940 to March 1944,* War Production Board, 1946; (co-author) *Industrial Mobilization for War,* U.S. Government Printing Office, 1947; *The New Nation, 1800-1845,* Hill & Wang, 1961; (editor with John Boyd Coates) *The Medical Department: Personnel in World War II,* Office of the Surgeon General, 1963; *The Medical Department: Medical Service in the Mediterranean and Minor Theaters,* Office of the Chief of Military History, 1965; (editor) *David Walker's Appeal,* Hill & Wang, 1965; (editor) *Expansion and Reform, 1815-1850,* Free Press, 1967; (editor) *Medical Supply in World War II,* U.S. Government Printing Office, 1968; (editor) *The Papers of Daniel Webster: Correspondence,* University Press of New England, Volume I: (with Harold Moser) *1798-1824,* 1974, Volume II: (with Moser) *1825-1829,* 1976, Volume III: (with David G. Allen) *1830-1834,* 1977, Volume IV: (with Moser) *1835-1839,* 1980. Also author of numerous other government publications. Contributor to anthologies and journals.†

*   *   *

WIMSATT, W(illiam) K(urtz), Jr.   1907-1975

PERSONAL: Born November 17, 1907, in Washington, D.C.; died December 17, 1975, in New Haven, Conn.; son of William Kurtz and Bertha (McSherry) Wimsatt; married Margaret Elizabeth Hecht, September, 1944; children: William Alexander (deceased), James Christopher. *Education:* Georgetown University, A.B. (summa cum laude), 1928, A.M., 1929; Yale University, Ph.D., 1939. *Home:* 80 Cold Spring St., New Haven, Conn. 06511. *Office:* 1882 Yale Station, New Haven, Conn.

CAREER: Portsmouth Priory School, Portsmouth, R.I., head of English department, 1930-35; Yale University, New Haven, Conn., instructor, 1939-43, assistant professor, 1943-49, associate professor, 1949-55, professor of English, 1955-75, Frederick Clifford Ford Professor of English, 1965-74, Sterling Professor of English, 1974-75, fellow of Silliman College, 1941-75. *Member:* Modern Language Association of America (member of executive committee, 1955-58), English Institute (supervising committee chairman, 1954), Connecticut Academy of Arts and Sciences (former president). *Awards, honors:* Guggenheim fellowship, 1947; Ford Foundation Fund for Advancement of Education fellowship, 1953-54; Yale University senior faculty fellowship, 1960-61; Litt.D., Villanova University, 1962, University of Notre Dame, 1963, Le Moyne College, 1965, and Kenyon College, 1970; LL.D., St. Louis University, 1964.

WRITINGS: The Prose Style of Samuel Johnson, Yale University Press, 1941, reprinted, Shoe String, 1972; *Philosophic Words,* Yale University Press, 1948, reprinted, Shoe String, 1968; (editor) *Alexander Pope, Selected Poetry and Prose,* Rinehart, 1951, 2nd edition, 1972; *The Verbal Icon,* University of Kentucky Press, 1954; (editor) *English Stage Comedy: English Institute Essays, 1954,* Columbia University Press, 1955; (with Cleanth Brooks) *Literary Criticism: A Short History,* two volumes, Knopf, 1957, reprinted, University of Chicago Press, 1978; (editor with F. A. Pottle) *Boswell for the Defense,* McGraw, 1959; (editor) *Samuel Johnson on Shakespeare,* Hill & Wang, 1960, published as *Dr. Johnson On Shakespeare,* Penguin, 1969; (editor) *Explication as Criticism: Selected Papers from the English Institute,* Columbia University Press, 1963; *Hateful Contraries,* University of Kentucky Press, 1965; *The Portraits of Alexander Pope,* Yale University Press, 1965; (editor) *The Idea of Comedy,* Prentice-Hall, 1969; (editor and author of foreword) *Versification: Major Language Types,* New York University Press, 1972; (editor and author of introduction) *Literary Criticism: Idea and Act,* University of California Press, 1974; *Day of the Leopards: Essays in Defense of Poems,* Yale University Press, 1976; (editor with Frank Brady) *Samuel Johnson: Selected Poetry and Prose,* University of California Press, 1978.

SIDELIGHTS: W. K. Wimsatt, Jr. was a prominent literary theorist. He sought to isolate poetry from both the intentions of the poet and the emotional reactions of the reader, turning poetry into what he called "a verbal icon." Since his ideas were contrary to those of many of his contemporaries, Wimsatt was compelled to argue and defend his views in much of his writing, which he did with great scholarship. His *Literary Criticism: A Short History,* described by a reviewer for the *New York Times Book Review* as "the standard work on the subject," contains many of his theories.

AVOCATIONAL INTERESTS: Chess, painting, collecting Indian artifacts.

BIOGRAPHICAL/CRITICAL SOURCES: Comparative Literature, fall, 1955, fall, 1974; *Archaeology,* summer, 1958; *PMLA,* December, 1958; *Times Literary Supplement,* February 20, 1959, December 9, 1965; *Yale Review,* spring, 1966, summer, 1967; *Modern Language Review,* October, 1966, January, 1977; *Review of Metaphysics,* March, 1967; *Journal of Aesthetics,* spring, 1967, summer, 1975; *Modern Philology,* May, 1967; *Criticism,* winter, 1968; *New York Times Book Review,* February 25, 1968; *New Statesman,* June 19, 1970; Frank Bradly, John Palmer, and Martin Price, editors, *Literary Theory and Structure: Essays in Honor of William K. Wimsatt,* Yale University Press, 1973; *Virginia Quarterly Review,* spring, 1975; *Commonweal,* May 21, 1976; *New Republic,* November 27, 1976; *Review of English Studies,* February, 1978.†

*   *   *

WINKS, Robin William   1930-

PERSONAL: Born December 5, 1930, in West Lafayette, Ind.; married Avril Flockton, 1952; children: Honor Leigh, Eliot Myles. *Education:* University of Colorado, B.A. (magna cum laude), 1952, M.A., 1953; University of New Zealand, graduate study, 1952; Johns Hopkins University, Ph.D. (with distinction), 1957. *Office:* Department of History, Yale University, New Haven, Conn.

CAREER: University of Colorado, Boulder, instructor, 1953; Connecticut College for Women (now Connecticut College), New London, instructor, 1956-57; Yale University, New Haven, Conn., 1957—, began as instructor, associate professor, 1957-67, professor of history, 1967—, master of Berkeley College, 1977—. Visiting professor, University of Alberta, Edmonton, University of Malaya, Kuala Lumpur, University of London, University of Washington, American University, Beirut, and University of Sydney. Cultural attache, American Embassy, London, England, 1969-71. Director of Yale conference on the teaching of the social studies. *Member:* American Historical Association, Organization of American Historians, Canadian Historical Association, Royal Historical Society, Asia Society, Athenaeum Reform Club, Royal Commonwealth Society, Yale Club. *Awards, honors:* Fulbright award; Morse fellow, 1959-60; Social Science Research Council award, 1959-60; Smith-Mundt fellow, 1962-63; senior faculty fellowship, Yale University, 1965-66; Guggenheim fellowship, 1976-77; has also received numerous honorary degrees.

WRITINGS: These New Zealanders!, Whitcombe, 1953, 2nd edition, 1966; *New Trends and Recent Literature in Canadian History,* American Historical Association, 1959, revised edition, 1966; *Marshall Plan and the American Economy,* Holt, 1960; *Canada and the United States: The Civil War Years,* Johns Hopkins University Press, 1960, revised edition, 1972; (general editor) "The Modern Nations in Historical Perspective" series, Prentice-Hall, 1963; *British Imperialism: Gold, God or Glory?,* Holt, 1963; *The Cold War,* Macmillan, 1964, revised edition (with Dan Yergin), 1978; (editor) *British Empire-Commonwealth: Historiographical Re-Assessments,* Duke University Press, 1966; (compiler with John Bastin) *Malaysia: Selected Historical Readings,* Oxford University Press, 1967, revised edition, 1979; *The Historian as Detective,* Harper, 1969; (with Marcus Cunliffe) *Pastmasters,* Harper, 1969; *Canadian-West Indian Union,* Athlone, 1970; *Blacks in Canada,* Yale University Press, 1971; *Slavery: A Comparative Perspective,* New York University Press, 1972; (with others) *The American Experience,* Addison-Wesley, 1972, 3rd edition, 1979; (editor) *Other Voices, Other Views,* Greenwood Press, 1978; *The Relevance of Canadian History,* Macmillan, 1979; *An American's Guide to Britain,* Scribner, 1979; *Western Civilization,* Prentice-Hall, 1979; *Detective Fiction,* Prentice-Hall, 1980.

WORK IN PROGRESS: The Idea of an American Imperialism; a general history of the British Empire; a biography of W.F.D. Jervois.

AVOCATIONAL INTERESTS: Travel, wine, and old maps.

*   *   *

WINSLOW, Ola Elizabeth   1885(?)-1977

PERSONAL: Born 1885(?), in Grant City, Mo.; died September 27, 1977, in Damariscotta, Me.; daughter of William Delos and Hattie Elizabeth (Colby) Winslow. *Education:* Stanford University, A.B., 1906, A.M., 1914; University of Chicago, Ph.D., 1922; special studies at Johns Hopkins University. *Residence:* Sheepscot, Me.

CAREER: College of the Pacific (now University of the Pacific), San Jose, Calif., instructor, 1909-14; Goucher College, Baltimore, Md., professor of English and head of department, 1914-44, assistant dean, 1919-21; Wellesley College, Wellesley, Mass., professor, 1944-50, professor emeritus, 1950-77; Radcliffe College, Cambridge, Mass., professor of English, 1950-62. *Awards, honors:* Pulitzer Prize in biography, 1941, for *Jonathan Edwards, 1703-1758;* D.Litt., Goucher College, 1951.

WRITINGS: Low Comedy as a Structural Element in English Drama from the Beginnings to 1642, George Banta,

1926, reprinted, Richard West, 1977; (compiler) *Harper's Literary Museum,* Harper, 1927, reprinted, Arno, 1972; (compiler) *American Broadside Verse,* Yale University Press, 1930, reprinted, AMS Press, 1974; *Jonathan Edwards, 1703-1758,* Macmillan, 1940, reprinted, Octagon, 1972; *Meetinghouse Hill, 1630-1783,* Macmillan, 1952, reprinted, Norton, 1972; *Master Roger Williams,* Macmillan, 1957, reprinted, Octagon, 1973; *John Bunyan,* Macmillan, 1961; *Samuel Sewall of Boston,* Macmillan, 1964; *Portsmouth, the Life of a Town,* Macmillan, 1966; (editor) Jonathan Edwards, *Basic Writings,* New American Library, 1966; *John Eliot: Apostle to the Indians,* Houghton, 1968; *'And Plead for the Rights of All': Old South Church in Boston, 1669-1969,* Nimrod Press, 1970; *A Destroying Angel: The Conquest of Smallpox in Colonial Boston,* Houghton, 1974. Contributor of reviews and articles to magazines.

SIDELIGHTS: Ola Elizabeth Winslow was a highly-regarded expert in the field of Colonial religious history. To research her biography of John Bunyon, Winslow spent four months in England examining the Bunyon materials in the British Museum. Similar research efforts mark her other works, including the Pulitzer Prize-winning *Jonathan Edwards.*

BIOGRAPHICAL/CRITICAL SOURCES: New York Times Book Review, May 8, 1966; *Christian Century,* September 11, 1968; *Wall Street Journal,* September 17, 1968; *Christian Science Monitor,* October 9, 1968; *Virginia Quarterly Review,* summer, 1974; *New England Quarterly,* September, 1974.†

*   *   *

WINT, Guy   1910-1969

PERSONAL: Born 1910, in London, England; died January, 1969; son of Frank John and Gertrude (Hoe) Wint; married Freda Mettam, 1947; children: Benedick, Allegra. *Education:* Attended Dulwich College; Oriel College, Oxford, B.A., 1931; additional study at University of Berlin. *Home:* 50 Park Town, Oxford, England.

CAREER: League of Nations, Geneva, Switzerland, research secretary, 1932-36; officer on special duty, Government of India, External Affairs Department, 1940-46; political advisor, Control Commission for Germany, 1947-49; *Manchester Guardian and Observer,* Manchester, England, staff member. Affiliated with St. Anthony's College, Oxford University, Oxford, England, beginning 1957. *Awards, honors:* Leverhulme research fellowship, 1937-40.

WRITINGS: (With Sir George Schuster) *India and Democracy,* Macmillan, 1941; *British in Asia,* Faber, 1947, reprinted, Russell, 1971; *Spotlight on Asia,* Penguin, 1955; (with Peter Calvocoressi) *Middle East Crisis,* Penguin, 1957; *Dragon and Sickle,* Pall Mall Press, 1958, revised edition published as *Communist China's Crusade,* Praeger, 1965; *Common Sense about China,* Macmillan, 1960; *The Third Killer,* Chatto & Windus, 1965; (editor) *Asia: A Handbook,* Praeger, 1966 (revised edition published in England as *Asia Handbook,* Penguin, 1969); (editor) Joseph Wolff, *Mission to Bokhara,* Routledge & Kegan Paul, 1969; (with Calvocoressi) *Total War: The Story of World War II,* Pantheon, 1972 (published in England as *Total War: Causes and Courses of the Second World War,* Penguin, 1972). Also author of *What Happened in Korea,* 1954.†

*   *   *

WISH, Harvey   1909-1968

PERSONAL: Born September 4, 1909, in Chicago, Ill.; died

March 8, 1968; son of Samuel and Rebecca Wish; married Anne Kruger, May 16, 1932; children: Dorothy. *Education:* Illinois Institute of Technology, B.S., 1931; University of Chicago, M.A., 1933; Northwestern University, Ph.D., 1936; post-doctoral study at Harvard University, 1943-44. *Home:* 2625 Euclid Heights Blvd., Cleveland Heights, Ohio. *Office:* Case Western Reserve University, Cleveland, Ohio.

CAREER: De Paul University, Chicago, Ill., assistant professor, 1936-42; Smith College, Northampton, Mass., associate professor, 1943-45; Case Western Reserve University, Cleveland, Ohio, professor of history, 1945-63, Elbert Jay Benton Distinguished Professor of History, 1963-68. Summer lecturer at University of Southern California, 1948, San Diego State College (now University), 1949, University of Michigan, 1951, and Columbia University, 1958; Fulbright lecturer, Universities of Munich, Vienna, Copenhagen, Nice, and Uppsala, 1954; Carnegie Distinguished Professor, University of Hawaii, 1956; John G. Winant Distinguished Lectureship, Great Britain, 1961. *Member:* American Historical Association, American Association of University Professors, Organization of American Historians (member of executive committee), Ohio Academy of History (president). *Awards, honors:* A. J. Beveridge Award; Ohio Academy of History annual award, for *The American Historian.*

WRITINGS: George Fitzhugh: Propagandist of the Old South (biography), Louisiana State University Press, 1943; *Contemporary America: The National Scene Since 1900,* Harper, 1945, 4th edition, 1966; *Society and Thought in America* (History Club Book of the Month selection), two volumes, McKay, 1950-52, 2nd edition, 1962; *The American Historian,* Oxford University Press, 1960.

Editor: F. L. Olmstead, *The Slave States,* Putnam, 1959; *Ante-bellum Writings of George Fitzhugh and Hinton Rowan Helper on Slavery,* Putnam, 1960; William Bradford, *Of Plymouth Plantation,* Putnam, 1962; *American Historians: A Selection,* Oxford University Press, 1962; *Slavery in the South,* Farrar, Straus, 1964; *The Negro since Emancipation,* Prentice-Hall, 1965; James Harvey Robinson, *The New History,* Free Press of Glencoe, 1965; *Reconstruction in the South 1865-1877,* Farrar, Straus, 1965; *Readings in Society and Thought in Modern America,* McKay, 1966; Samuel Sewell, *The Diary of Samuel Sewell,* Putnam, 1967. Also editor of Theodore Roosevelt, *Winning of the West* (original paperback), Putnam.

WORK IN PROGRESS: The Era of John Dewey, for Oxford University Press.†

*   *   *

WITTLIN, Jozef 1896-1976

PERSONAL: Born August 17, 1896, in Dmytrow, Poland; came to United States in 1941, naturalized in 1949; died February 29, 1976, in New York, N.Y.; son of Karol and Eliza (Rosenfeld) Wittlin; married Halina Anna Handelsman (a librarian), July 6, 1924; children: Elizabeth (Mrs. Michel Lipton). *Education:* Attended University of Vienna, 1915-16, and University of Lwow, 1918-19. *Home:* 5400 Fieldston Rd., New York, N.Y. 10471.

CAREER: High school and college teacher of Polish language and literature in Lwow, Poland, 1919-21; Municipal Theater, Lodz, Poland, literary director, 1922-23; School of Drama, Lodz, founder and professor, 1922-23; writer, 1923-76. Scriptwriter and broadcaster, Radio Free Europe, 1952-72. *Military service:* Polish Eastern Legion, 1914-15; Austro-Hungarian Army, 1916-18. *Member:* P.E.N. American Center, P.E.N.-in-exile (chairman of American branch, 1960-63;

honorary member of executive board), Polish Institute of Arts and Sciences in America, Deutsche Akademie fuer Dichtung und Sprache (corresponding member). *Awards, honors:* Polish P.E.N. Club award, 1935, for translation of Homer's *Odyssey* from Greek into Polish hexameter; awards from "Academy of the Independents" and from readers of *Wiadomosci Literackie* (literary magazine; Warsaw), 1936, for *Sol ziemi;* Golden Laurel from Polish Academy of Literature, 1937; awards from American Academy of Arts and Letters and National Institute of Arts and Letters, 1943, for *The Salt of the Earth;* Alfred Jurzykowski Foundation prize, 1965, for entire literary work.

WRITINGS: Hymny (poems; title means "Hymns"), [Poznan, Poland], 1920; (translator) Homer, *Odyseja,* [Lwow, Poland], 1924, 3rd edition, Veritas (London), 1957; *Wojna, pokoj, i dusza poety* (essays; title means "War, Peace, and a Poet's Soul"), Z. Pomaranski (Zamosc, Poland), 1925; *Sol ziemi* (novel), Roj (Warsaw), 1935, translation by Pauline de Chary published as *The Salt of the Earth,* Methuen, 1939, Sheridan, 1941, new edition with postscript, Stackpole, 1970, new Polish edition with two additional texts, Panstwowy Instytut Wydawniczy (Warsaw), 1979; (editor with Manfred Kridl and Wladyslaw Malinowski) *For Your Freedom and Ours: Polish Progressive Spirit through the Centuries* (anthology), translated by Ludwik Krzyzanowski and revised by Sidney Sulkin and Edith Sulkin, Ungar, 1943 (published in England as *The Democratic Heritage of Poland: "For Your Freedom and Ours,"* Allen & Unwin, 1944); *Moj Lwow* (title means "My Lwow"), Biblioteka Polska (New York), 1947, reprinted, Polska Fundacja Kulturalna, 1976; *Etapy* (title means "Stages"), Roj, 1952; *Orfeusz w piekle XX wieku* (essays; title means "Orpheus in the Hell of the Twentieth Century"), Instytut Literacki (Paris), 1963; *Poezje* (title means "Poems"), Panstwowy Instytut Wydawniczy, 1978.

Contributor: Emil Ludwig and Henry B. Kranz, editors, *The Torch of Freedom: Twenty Exiles of History,* Farrar-Rinehart, 1943; Kridl, editor, *Adam Mickiewicz, Poet of Poland,* Columbia University Press, 1951; Leopold Tyrmand, editor, *Explorations in Freedom: Prose, Narrative and Poetry from Kultura,* Free Press, 1970.

Work is represented in numerous anthologies in the United States and abroad, including *Heart of Europe,* edited by Klaus Mann and Hermann Kesten, L. B. Fischer, 1943, *Poetry of Freedom,* edited by William Rose Benet and Norman Cousins, Random House, 1945, *A World of Great Stories,* edited by Hiram Haydn and John Curnos, Crown, 1947, *An Anthology of Polish Literature,* edited by Kridl, Columbia University Press, 1947, *Poeti polacchi contemporanei,* edited and translated by Carlo Verdiani, Silva Editore (Genoa), 1961, *Introduction to Modern Polish Literature: An Anthology,* edited by Adam Gillon and Ludwik Krzyzanowski, Twayne, 1964, *Polnische Poesie des 20. Jahrhunderts,* edited and translated by Karl Dedecius, Carl Hanser Verlag, 1964, *Neue Polische Lyrik,* edited and translated by Dedecius, Moderner Buchclub, 1965, and *Anthologie de la poesie polonaise,* edited by Constantin Jelenski, Editions du Seuil, 1965.

Also translator into Polish of *Steppenwolf,* by Hermann Hesse, *Hiroshima,* by John Hersey, *Pinocchio,* by Carlos Collodi, five novels by Joseph Roth, and various works by Wilfred Owen, W. H. Auden, Robinson Jeffers, William Carlos Williams, e. e. cummings, Langston Hughes, Stephen Vincent Benet, Richard Dehmel, R. M. Rilke, Hermann Kesten, Salvatore Quasimodo, Umberto Saba, Alphonso

Gatto, Miguel Hernandez, Jose Hierro, and Francisco Brines.

SIDELIGHTS: A ten-year effort intended as the first volume in a trilogy that was never completed, *The Salt of the Earth* is a World War I novel based on author Jozef Wittlin's own experiences in the infantry. An epic treatment of the theme of the ordinary, unknown soldier, the book focuses on the story of Peter Neviadomski, an uneducated peasant called upon to serve in the army of Austrian emperor Franz Josef. Covering only the first six weeks of the conflict, *The Salt of the Earth* contrasts the nobility of the human spirit with the degradation and brutality of war and contemporary life. S. E. Hyman of the *New Republic* called it "an intimate and always ironic picture of the war, not on a canvas of titanic battles and vast strategic movements, but on the smallest canvas imaginable—Peter Neviadomski."

Noted *Books* critic Marianne Hauser: "Reading Wittlin's novel some years ago in French, it impressed me as a work of exceptional power. Because of the statuesque simplicity of its style it did not seem like a translation.... And now, having reread the novel in the American edition, I find that the story of Peter Neviadomski seems quite as much at home in English."

"The esteem this novel has won from critics abroad may be readily understood," declared John Cournos of the *New York Times*. "It has three qualities, rare enough in combination: a deep sympathy for the humble and downtrodden, a passionate sincerity in the expression of this sympathy and, what is very important, a competent craftsmanship."

Finally, N. L. Rothman of the *Saturday Review of Literature* wrote: "Wittlin's work does not lack for distinctive qualities of its own; he brings to it some irony, much pity, a studious objectivity, and a remarkable absence of hate or passion. It is this last absence which, almost like a presence, suffuses all of his pages with a cool light. There is no fuming and bitterness to destroy focus. Every character who appears ... is outlined with an imperturbable clarity.... The result is clearly to be seen, an atmosphere of unmistakable truth."

BIOGRAPHICAL/CRITICAL SOURCES: Saturday Review of Literature, August 2, 1941, October 4, 1941; *New Yorker*, October 4, 1941; *New York Times*, October 5, 1941; *Books*, October 5, 1941; *New York Herald Tribune*, October 25, 1941; *New Republic*, October 27, 1941; *Polish Review IX*, Number 1, 1964; Zoya Yurieff, *Joseph Wittlin*, Twayne, 1973.†

*   *   *

WODEHOUSE, P(elham) G(renville)   1881-1975
(P. Brooke-Haven, Pelham Grenville, J. Plum, C. P. West, J. Walker Williams, Basil Windham)

PERSONAL: Surname is pronounced *Wood*-house; born October 15, 1881, in Guildford, Surrey, England; naturalized U.S. citizen, 1955; died of a heart attack, February 14, 1975, in Southampton, N.Y.; son of Henry Ernest (a civil servant and judge) and Eleanor (Deane) Wodehouse; married Ethel Rowley, September 30, 1914; children: Leonora (stepdaughter; deceased). *Education:* Attended Dulwich College, 1894-1900. *Home:* Basket Neck Lane, Remsenburg, Long Island, N.Y. 11960.

CAREER: Novelist, short story writer, and playwright. Hong Kong & Shanghai Bank, London, England, clerk, 1901-03; *London Globe*, London, assistant on "By the Way" column, 1902-03, writer of column, 1903-09; writer, under various pseudonyms, and drama critic for *Vanity Fair*,

1915-19. *Member:* Dramatists Guild, Authors League of America, Old Alleynian Association (New York; president), Coffee House (New York). *Awards, honors:* Litt.D., Oxford University, 1939; named Knight Commander, Order of the British Empire, 1975.

WRITINGS—Novels: *The Pothunters*, A & C Black, 1902, Macmillan, 1924, reprinted, Souvenir Press, 1972, International Scholarly Book, 1977; *A Prefect's Uncle*, A & C Black, 1903, Macmillan, 1924, reprinted, Souvenir Press, 1972, International Scholarly Book, 1977; *The Gold Bat*, A & C Black, 1904, Macmillan, 1923, reprinted, Souvenir Press, 1974, International Scholarly Book, 1977; *The Head of Kay's*, A & C Black, 1905, Macmillan, 1922, reprinted, Souvenir Press, 1974, International Scholarly Book, 1977; *Love among the Chickens*, George Newnes, 1906, Circle Publishing, 1909, revised edition, Jenkins, 1921, autograph edition, 1963; *The White Feather*, A & C Black, 1907, Macmillan, 1922, reprinted, Souvenir Press, 1972, International Scholarly Book, 1977; (with A. W. Westbrook) *Not George Washington*, Cassell, 1907; *The Swoop!; or, How Clarence Saved England: A Tale of the Great Invasion* (also see below), Alston Rivers, 1909; *Mike: A Public School Story*, two parts, A & C Black, 1909, Macmillan, 1924, revised edition of second part published as *Enter Psmith*, Macmillan, 1935, entire book published in two volumes as *Mike at Wrykyn*, Jenkins, 1953, reprinted, Barrie & Jenkins, 1976, and *Mike and Psmith*, Jenkins, 1953, reprinted, Meredith Press, 1969.

The Intrusion of Jimmy, W. J. Watt, 1910 (published in England as *A Gentleman of Leisure*, Alston Rivers, 1910, abridged edition, George Newnes, 1920, autograph edition, Jenkins, 1962, reprinted, Star Books, 1978); *Psmith in the City*, A & C Black, 1910, reprinted, Penguin, 1970; *The Prince and Betty*, W. J. Watt, 1912 (published in England as *Psmith, Journalist*, A & C Black, 1915, reprinted, Penguin, 1970); *The Prince and Betty* (different book from above title), Mills & Boon, 1912; *The Little Nugget*, Methuen, 1913, W. J. Watt, 1914, reprinted with a new preface by the author, Barrie & Jenkins, 1972, Penguin, 1978; *Something New*, Appleton, 1915, reprinted, Beagle Books, 1972 (published in England as *Something Fresh*, Methuen, 1915, reprinted, Jenkins, 1969); *Uneasy Money*, Appleton, 1916, reprinted, Penguin, 1978; *Piccadilly Jim*, Dodd, 1917, revised edition, 1931, autograph edition, Jenkins, 1966, reprinted, Penguin, 1969; *A Damsel in Distress*, Doran, 1919, autograph edition, Jenkins, 1956, reprinted, Star Books, 1978; *Their Mutual Child*, Boni & Liveright, 1919 (published in England as *The Coming of Bill*, Jenkins, 1920, autograph edition, 1966, reprinted, Barrie & Jenkins, 1976).

The Little Warrior, Doran, 1920 (published in England as *Jill the Reckless*, Jenkins, 1921, autograph edition, 1958); *Three Men and a Maid*, Doran, 1922 (published in England as *The Girl on the Boat*, Jenkins, 1922, autograph edition, 1956); *The Adventures of Sally*, Jenkins, 1922, reprinted, Barrie & Jenkins, 1973, published as *Mostly Sally*, Doran, 1923; *Leave It to Psmith* (also see below), Jenkins, 1923, autograph edition, 1961, reprinted, 1976, Doran, 1924; *Bill the Conqueror: His Invasion of England in the Springtime*, Methuen, 1924, Doran, 1925, reprinted, British Book Center, 1975; *Sam in the Suburbs*, Doran, 1925 (published in England as *Sam the Sudden*, Methuen, 1925, reprinted with a new preface by the author, Barrie & Jenkins, 1972, Penguin, 1978); *The Small Bachelor* (based on his play, "Oh! Lady, Lady!"; also see below), Doran, 1927, reprinted, Ballantine, 1977; *Money for Nothing*, Doubleday, Doran, 1928, autograph edition, Jenkins, 1959, reprinted, Barrie & Jenkins, 1976; *Fish Preferred* (also see below), Doubleday, Doran,

1929, reprinted, Simon & Schuster, 1969 (published in England as *Summer Lightning,* Jenkins, 1929, autograph edition, 1964).

Big Money, Doubleday, Doran, 1931, autograph edition, Jenkins, 1965; *If I Were You,* Doubleday, Doran, 1931, autograph edition, Jenkins, 1958, reprinted, Barrie & Jenkins, 1976; *Doctor Sally,* Methuen, 1932, reprinted, Thomas Nelson, 1966; *Hot Water,* Doubleday, Doran, 1932, autograph edition, Jenkins, 1956, reprinted, Penguin, 1978; *Heavy Weather,* Little, Brown, 1933, autograph edition, Jenkins, 1960, reprinted, Penguin, 1973; *Thank You, Jeeves,* Little, Brown, 1934, autograph edition, Jenkins, 1956, reprinted, Coronet Books, 1977; *Brinkley Manor,* Little, Brown, 1934 (published in England as *Right Ho, Jeeves* [also see below], Jenkins, 1934, autograph edition, 1957, reprinted, Penguin, 1975); *Trouble Down at Tudsleigh* (also see below), International Magazine Co., 1935; *The Luck of the Bodkins,* Jenkins, 1935, Little, Brown, 1936, autograph edition, Jenkins, 1956, reprinted, Penguin, 1975; *Laughing Gas,* Doubleday, Doran, 1936, autograph edition, Jenkins, 1959, reprinted, Ballantine, 1977; *Summer Moonshine,* Doubleday, Doran, 1937, autograph edition, Jenkins, 1956, reprinted, Penguin, 1976; *The Code of the Woosters,* Doubleday, Doran, 1938, autograph edition, Jenkins, 1962, reprinted, Penguin, 1975; *Uncle Fred in the Springtime,* Doubleday, Doran, 1939, autograph edition, Jenkins, 1962, reprinted, Penguin, 1976.

Quick Service, Doubleday, Doran, 1940, autograph edition, Jenkins, 1960, reprinted, Penguin, 1972; *Money in the Bank,* Doubleday, Doran, 1942, reprinted, Penguin, 1978; *Joy in the Morning,* Doubleday, 1946, reprinted with a new preface by the author, Jenkins, 1974; *Full Moon,* Doubleday, 1947; *Spring Fever,* Doubleday, 1948, reprinted, Jenkins, 1976; *Uncle Dynamite,* Jenkins, 1948, reprinted, Star Books, 1978; *The Mating Season,* Didier, 1949, reprinted, Penguin, 1971.

The Old Reliable, Doubleday, 1951, reprinted, Pan Books, 1968; *Angel Cake* (based on the play, "The Butter and Egg Man," by George F. Kaufman), Doubleday, 1952 (published in England as *Barmy in Wonderland,* Jenkins, 1952, autograph edition, 1958); *Pigs Have Wings* Doubleday, 1952, reprinted with a new preface by the author, Barrie & Jenkins, 1974, Ballantine, 1977; *Ring for Jeeves,* Jenkins, 1953, autograph edition, 1963, reprinted, Sphere Books, 1977, published as *The Return of Jeeves,* Simon & Schuster, 1954; *Jeeves and the Feudal Spirit,* Jenkins, 1954, reprinted, Coronet Books, 1977, published as *Bertie Wooster Sees It Through,* Simon & Schuster, 1955; *French Leave,* Jenkins, 1956, Simon & Schuster, 1959, reprinted with a new preface by the author, Barrie & Jenkins, 1974; *The Butler Did It,* Simon & Schuster, 1957 (published in England as *Something Fishy,* Jenkins, 1957, reprinted, Star Books, 1978); *Cocktail Time,* Simon & Schuster, 1958.

How Right You Are, Jeeves, Simon & Schuster, 1960 (published in England as *Jeeves in the Offing,* Jenkins, 1960); *Ice in the Bedroom,* Simon & Schuster, 1961; *Service with a Smile,* Simon & Schuster, 1961, reprinted, Penguin, 1975; *Stiff Upper Lip, Jeeves,* Simon & Schuster, 1963; *Biffen's Millions,* Simon & Schuster, 1964 (published in England as *Frozen Assets,* Jenkins, 1964, reprinted, Barrie & Jenkins, 1976); *The Brinkmanship of Galahad Threepwood: A Blandings Castle Novel,* Simon & Schuster, 1965 (published in England as *Galahad at Blandings,* Jenkins, 1965); *The Purloined Paperweight,* Simon & Schuster, 1967 (published in England as *Company for Henry,* Jenkins, 1967); *Do Butlers Burgle Banks?,* Simon & Schuster, 1968; *A Pelican at Blandings,* Jenkins, 1969, published as *No Nudes Is Good Nudes,* Simon & Schuster, 1970.

The Girl in Blue, Barrie & Jenkins, 1970, Simon & Schuster, 1971; *Jeeves and the Tie That Binds,* Simon & Schuster, 1971 (published in England as *Much Obliged, Jeeves,* autograph edition, Barrie & Jenkins, 1971); *Pearls, Girls, and Monty Bodkins,* Barrie & Jenkins, 1972, published as *The Plot That Thickened,* Simon & Schuster, 1973; *Bachelors Anonymous,* Barrie & Jenkins, 1973, Simon & Schuster, 1974; *The Cat-Nappers: A Jeeves and Bertie Story,* Simon & Schuster, 1974 (published in England as *Aunts Aren't Gentlemen: A Jeeves and Bertie Story,* Barrie & Jenkins, 1974); *Sunset at Blandings,* Chatto & Windus, 1977, Simon & Schuster, 1978.

Stories: *Tales of St. Austin's,* A & C Black, 1903, Macmillan, 1923, reprinted, Penguin, 1978; *The Man Upstairs and Other Stories,* Methuen, 1914, reprinted with a new preface by the author, Barrie & Jenkins, 1971; *The Man with Two Left Feet and Other Stories,* Methuen, 1917, A. L. Burt, 1933, reprinted, Penguin, 1978; *My Man Jeeves* (also see below), George Newnes, 1919, published as *Carry On, Jeeves* (also see below), Jenkins, 1925, autograph edition, 1960, reprinted, Penguin, 1975; *The Indiscretions of Archie,* Doran, 1921, reprinted, Jenkins, 1965; *The Clicking of Cuthbert* (also see below), Jenkins, 1922, autograph edition, 1956, published as *Golf without Tears,* Doran, 1924; *Jeeves,* Doran, 1923 (published in England as *The Inimitable Jeeves,* Jenkins, 1923, autograph edition, 1956, reprinted, Penguin, 1975); *Ukridge,* Jenkins, 1924, autograph edition, 1960, reprinted, Penguin, 1973, published as *He Rather Enjoyed It,* Doran, 1926; *The Heart of a Goof,* Jenkins, 1926, autograph edition, 1956, reprinted, Penguin, 1978, published as *Divots,* Doran, 1927; *Meet Mr. Mulliner,* Jenkins, 1927, Doubleday, Doran, 1928, autograph edition, Jenkins, 1956.

Mr. Mulliner Speaking, Jenkins, 1929, Doubleday, Doran, 1930, autograph edition, Jenkins, 1961; *Very Good, Jeeves,* Doubleday, Doran, 1930, autograph edition, Jenkins, 1958, reprinted, Penguin, 1975; *Mulliner Nights,* Doubleday, Doran, 1933, autograph edition, Jenkins, 1966, reprinted, Vintage Books, 1975; *The Great Sermon Handicap* (short story, first published in *Jeeves;* also see above), Hodder & Stoughton, 1933; *Blandings Castle,* Doubleday, Doran, 1935 (published in England as *Blandings Castle and Elsewhere,* Jenkins, 1935, autograph edition, 1957); *Young Men in Spats,* Doubleday, Doran, 1936, autograph edition, Jenkins, 1957; *The Crime Wave at Blandings* (also see below), Doubleday, Doran, 1937 (published in England as *Lord Emsworth and Others,* Jenkins, 1937, autograph edition, 1956, reprinted, 1976); *Eggs, Beans and Crumpets,* Doubleday, Doran, 1940, autograph edition, Jenkins, 1963, reprinted, Penguin, 1976; *Dudley Is Back to Normal,* Doubleday, Doran, 1940; *Nothing Serious,* Jenkins, 1950, Doubleday, 1951, autograph edition, Jenkins, 1964; *Selected Stories,* introduction by John W. Aldridge, Modern Library, 1958; *A Few Quick Ones,* Simon & Schuster, 1959, reprinted, Coronet Books, 1978; *Plum Pie,* Jenkins, 1966, Simon & Schuster, 1967; *Jeeves, Jeeves, Jeeves,* Avon, 1976; David A. Jasen, editor, *The Swoop and Other Stories,* with an appreciation by Malcolm Muggeridge, Seabury, 1979.

Omnibus volumes: *Jeeves Omnibus,* Jenkins, 1931; *Nothing but Wodehouse* (includes selections from *Jeeves, Very Good, Jeeves, He Rather Enjoyed It, Meet Mr. Mulliner, Mr. Mulliner Speaking,* and the complete novel, *Leave It to Psmith*), edited by Ogden Nash, Doubleday, Doran, 1932; *P. G. Wodehouse* (anthology), edited by E. V. Knox, Methuen, 1934; *Mulliner Omnibus,* Jenkins, 1935, published as *The World of Mr. Mulliner,* 1972, Taplinger, 1974; *The Week-end Wodehouse* (includes Part 1: "Mulliner Stories,"

Part 2: "Jeeves Stories," Part 3: "Drones and Others," and Part 4: "Fish Preferred"), Doubleday, Doran, 1939, revised edition, Jenkins, 1951; *Wodehouse on Golf* (includes "Divots," "Golf without Tears," "The Medicine Girl," "There's Always Golf!," "The Letter of the Law," and "Archibald's Benefit"), Doubleday, Doran, 1940; *The Best of Wodehouse* (includes "Jeeves and the Yuletide Spirit," "Trouble Down at Tudsleigh," "Good-bye to Butlers," "Strychnine in the Soup," "The Level Business Head," "The Crime Wave at Blandings," "Sonny Boy," "The Letter of the Law," "Tried in the Furnace," and "Freddie, Oofy and the Beef Trust"), selected and introduced by Scott Meredith, Pocket Books, 1949.

The Most of P. G. Wodehouse, Simon & Schuster, 1960; *The World of Jeeves*, Jenkins, 1967, published in two volumes, Manor Books, 1976, Volume I: *The World of Jeeves*, Volume II: *All about Jeeves; Right Ho, Jeeves* [and] *Carry On, Jeeves* (two novels published together; also see above), introduction by Malcolm Muggeridge, Heron Books, 1970; *The Golf Omnibus: Thirty-one Golfing Short Stories*, Barrie & Jenkins, 1973, Simon & Schuster, 1974; *The World of Psmith* (includes "Mike and Psmith," "Psmith in the City," "Psmith, Journalist," and "Leave It to Psmith"), Barrie & Jenkins, 1974; *The World of Ukridge*, Barrie & Jenkins, 1975; *The World of Blandings* (includes "Something Fresh," "The Custody of the Pumpkin," "Lord Emsworth Acts for the Best," "Pig-Hoo-o-o-o-ey," and "Summer Lightning"), Barrie & Jenkins, 1976; *The Uncollected Wodehouse*, edited by David A. Jasen, foreword by Malcolm Muggeridge, Seabury, 1976; *Vintage Wodehouse*, edited by Richard Usborne, Barrie & Jenkins, 1977; *Wodehouse at Work to the End*, edited by Usborne, Barrie & Jenkins, 1977.

Other books: (Adapter) *William Tell Told Again* (based on the classic tale), A & C Black, 1904; (with H. W. Westbrook) *The Globe "By the Way" Book: A Literary Quick-Lunch for People Who Have Only Got Five Minutes to Spare*, Globe, 1908; *Louder and Funnier* (essays), Faber, 1932, autograph edition, Jenkins, 1963, reprinted, Barrie & Jenkins, 1976; (editor) *A Century of Humour*, Hutchinson, 1934; (contributor) Peter Wait, editor, *Stories by Modern Masters: P. G. Wodehouse, George A. Birmingham, Arnold Bennett, H. C. Bailey, Ernest Bramah, A. A. Milne*, Methuen, 1936; (editor with Scott Meredith and author of introduction) *The Week-End Book of Humour*, Washburn, 1952, published as *P. G. Wodehouse Selects the Best of Humor*, Grosset, 1965; (editor with Meredith and author of introduction) *The Best of Modern Humour*, Metcalf, 1952, reprinted, Books for Libraries, 1971; *Performing Flea: A Self-Portrait in Letters* (letters written by Wodehouse to William Townsend; also see below), introduction by Townsend, Jenkins, 1953, published as *Author! Author!*, Simon & Schuster, 1962; (with Guy Bolton) *Bring On the Girls!: The Improbable Story of Our Life in Musical Comedy with Pictures to Prove It* (also see below), Simon & Schuster, 1953; *America, I Like You*, Simon & Schuster, 1956, revised edition published as *Over Seventy: An Autobiography with Digressions* (also see below), Jenkins, 1957; (editor with Meredith and author of introduction) *A Carnival of Modern Humor*, Delacorte, 1967; *Wodehouse on Wodehouse* (contains *Performing Flea, Bring On the Girls!*, and *Over Seventy*), Hutchinson, 1980.

Plays: (With John Stapleton) "A Gentleman of Leisure" (comedy; based on Wodehouse's novel of the same title), first produced on Broadway at Playhouse Theatre, August 24, 1911; (with Stapleton) "A Thief for the Night," first produced on Broadway at Playhouse Theatre, 1913; (with H. W. Westbrook) "Brother Alfred," first produced on West End

at Savoy Theatre, 1913; *The Play's the Thing* (three-act drama; based on *Spiel in Schloss* by Ferenc Molnar; first produced on Broadway at Henry Miller's Theatre, November 3, 1926), Brentano's, 1927; (with Valerie Wyngate) "Her Cardboard Lover" (based on a play by Jacques Deval), first produced in New York at Empire Theatre, March 21, 1927; *Good Morning, Bill* (three-act comedy; based on a play by Ladislaus Fodor; first produced on West End at Duke of York's Theatre, November 28, 1927), Methuen, 1928; (with Ian Hay) *A Damsel in Distress* (three-act comedy; based on Wodehouse's novel of the same title; first produced Off-Broadway at New Theatre, August 13, 1928), Samuel French, 1930; (with Hay) *Baa, Baa, Black Sheep* (three-act comedy; first produced Off-Broadway at New Theatre, April 22, 1929), Samuel French, 1930; *Candlelight* (three-act drama; based on "Kleine Komodie" by Siegfried Geyer; first produced in New York at Empire Theatre, September 30, 1929), Samuel French, 1934; (with Hay) *Leave It to Psmith* (three-act comedy; based on Wodehouse's novel of the same title; first produced in London at Shaftesbury Theatre, September 29, 1930), Samuel French, 1932; (with Guy Bolton) "Who's Who" (three-act comedy), first produced on West End at Duke of York's Theatre, September 20, 1934; "The Inside Stand" (three-act farce), first produced in London at Saville Theatre, November 20, 1935; (with Bolton) "Don't Listen, Ladies" (two-act comedy; based on the play "N'ecoutez pas, mesdames," by Sacha Guitry), first produced on Broadway at Booth Theatre, December 28, 1948; (with Bolton) *Carry On, Jeeves* (three-act comedy; based on Wodehouse's novel of the same title), Evans Brothers, 1956.

Musicals: (Author of lyrics with others) "The Gay Gordons," book by Seymour Hicks, music by Guy Jones, first produced in London at Aldwych Theatre, 1913; (with C. H. Bovill and F. Tours) "Nuts and Wine," first produced in London at Empire Theatre, 1914; (with Guy Bolton and H. Reynolds) "Miss Springtime," music by Emmerich Kalman and Jerome Kern, first produced in New York at New Amsterdam Theatre, September 25, 1916; (with Bolton) "Ringtime," first produced in New York, 1917; (author of book and lyrics with Bolton) "Have a Heart," music by Kern, first produced in New York at Liberty Theatre, January 11, 1917; (author of book and lyrics with Bolton) "Oh, Boy," first produced in New York at Princess Theatre, February 20, 1917, produced in London as "Oh, Joy," 1919; (author of book and lyrics with Bolton) "Leave It to Jane" (musical version of "The College Widow" by George Ade), music by Kern, first produced in Albany, N.Y., July, 1917, produced on Broadway at Longacre Theatre, August 28, 1917; (author of book and lyrics with Bolton) "The Riviera Girl," music by Kalman, first produced in New York at New Amsterdam Theatre, September 24, 1917; (author of book and lyrics with Bolton) "Miss 1917," music by Victor Herbert and Kern, first produced Off-Broadway at Century Theatre, November 5, 1917; (with Bolton) "The Second Century Show," first produced in New York, 1917; (author of book and lyrics with Bolton) "Oh! Lady, Lady!," music by Kern, first produced in New York at Princess Theatre, February 1, 1918; (with Bolton) "See You Later," music by J. Szule, first produced in Baltimore at Academy of Music, April 15, 1918; (author of book and lyrics with Bolton) "The Girl behind the Gun" (based on play "Madame et son filleul," by Hennequin and Weber), music by Ivan Caryll, first produced in New York at New Amsterdam Theatre, September 16, 1918, produced in London as "Kissing Time" at Winter Garden Theatre, 1918; (author of book and lyrics with Bolton) "Oh My Dear," music by Louis Hirsch, first produced in New York at Princess Theatre, November 27, 1918, produced in Toronto as "Ask Dad," 1918; (with Bolton) "The Rose of China," music by Armand Vecsey, first produced in New York at Lyric Theatre, November 25, 1919.

(Author of lyrics with Clifford Grey) "Sally," music by Jerome Kern, first produced in New York by Flo Ziegfeld, 1920; (author of book and lyrics with Fred Thompson) "The Golden Moth," music by Ivor Novello, first produced in London at Adelphi Theatre, October 5, 1921; (author of book and lyrics with George Grossmith) "The Cabaret Girl," music by Kern, first produced in London at Winter Garden Theatre, 1922; (author of book and lyrics with Grossmith) "The Beauty Prize," music by Kern, first produced in London at Aldwych Theatre, September 5, 1923; (author of book and lyrics with Bolton) "Sitting Pretty," music by Kern, first produced in New York at Fulton Theatre, April 8, 1924; (adapter with Laurie Wylie) *Hearts and Diamonds* (light opera; based on *The Orlov* by Bruno Granichstaedten and Ernest Marischka; first produced in London at Strand Theatre, June 1, 1926), English lyrics by Graham John, Keith Prowse & Co., 1926; (with others) "Showboat," music by Oscar Hammerstein, first produced on Broadway at Ziegfeld Theatre, December 27, 1927; (author of book with Bolton) "Oh Kay!," lyrics by Ira Gershwin, music by George Gershwin, first produced on Broadway at Imperial Theatre, November 8, 1926; (author of book and lyrics with Bolton) "The Nightingale," music by Vecsey, first produced on Broadway at Al Jolson's Theatre, January 3, 1927; (author of lyrics with Ira Gershwin) "Rosalie," book by Bolton and Bill McGuire, music by George Gershwin and Sigmund Romberg, first produced in New York at New Amsterdam Theatre, January 10, 1928; (author of book with George Grossmith; author of lyrics with Grey) *The Three Musketeers* (based on the novel by Alexandre Dumas; first produced in New York at Lyric Theatre, March 13, 1928), music by Rudolph Friml, Harms Inc., 1937; (author of book with Bolton, Howard Lindsay, and Russel Crouse) *Anything Goes* (first produced on Broadway at Alvin Theatre, November 21, 1934), music and lyrics by Cole Porter, Samuel French, 1936.

Films: (With others) "A Damsel in Distress" (based on his novel of the same title), RKO General, Inc., 1920; "Rosalie" (based on his play of the same title), Metro-Goldwyn-Mayer, Inc., 1930. Also author of "Summer Lightning" (based on his novel of the same title) and "Three French Girls."

SIDELIGHTS: Pelham Grenville Wodehouse—known almost from the start as "Plum" to those closest to him—was born into a family of British government employees with a tradition of service in the Far Eastern colonies. His father was a judge in Hong Kong, and two of his uncles and all three of his brothers were engaged in administrative or educational occupations in the Orient. Even though his parents lived in Hong Kong, Wodehouse was born in England when his mother was visiting her sister there. After spending the first two years of his life in the Far East, he was sent back to England with his two older brothers for what was considered a proper British education.

During their early school years, the boys lived with a variety of relatives and family friends and then, when they were old enough, entered the appropriate preparatory schools. It had been decided that young Plum would be embarking upon a career in the Royal Navy, so he was routed to Malvern House, a school that specialized in nautical training. He was, however, not very well suited to the career chosen by his father. Knowing that his substandard eyesight would pre-

vent him from passing the naval examination anyway, he was not very enthusiastic toward his studies. His brother Armine had, in the meantime, been sent to Dulwich College in southeast London. On a visit there, Plum fell in love with the school and, after considerable pleading with his father, was allowed to transfer. On May 2, 1894, Wodehouse first entered the prep school which was to be his home for the next six years and which was to form the basis for a life-long enchantment with the English public-school system.

Plum did very well at Dulwich, both scholastically and athletically. He played cricket and rugby, excelling at both, and in 1897 was awarded one of four annual academic scholarships to Oxford University. Unfortunately his father's failing health forced him into an early retirement, and the family was unable to subsidize two sons at the university. It was decided that the elder son, Armine, would study at Oxford, while Plum would finish his education at Dulwich and enter the world of business.

Wodehouse had long entertained thoughts of becoming a writer—he told interviewer Gerald Clarke of the *Paris Review:* "I was writing stories when I was five. I don't remember what I did before that. Just loafed, I suppose."—and he had published his first story in the February, 1900, issue of *Public School Magazine.* His father, however, would hear nothing of the boy trying to earn a living as a writer. He felt that his son should be gainfully employed in a field offering a regular salary, job security, and a good pension. Using his connections in the Far East, he secured for the boy the position of clerk in the Hong Kong and Shanghai Bank. The bank trained young men in London and then shipped them to the Orient as branch managers. Plum, although not happy with the position, and even less happy with the thought of being sent to the East, made a half-hearted attempt at becoming a banker.

It quickly became apparent that the young Wodehouse was not going to be a great success in the world of finance. The bank's training scheme called for apprentices to be transferred through a succession of departments so that they would be familiar with the various phases of branch operation when they eventually became managers. Wodehouse would no sooner learn one task than he would find himself suddenly assigned to a new, and invariably more complicated, department. As David A. Jasen says in his *P. G. Wodehouse: Portrait of a Master:* "It was during these final stages that he knew he had met his match. The whole scheme revealed itself as being absolutely incomprehensible. That much was crystal clear. He was completely baffled."

While working at the bank, Wodehouse wrote steadily, contributing pieces to several publications, including *Public School Magazine, The Captain, Tit-Bits,* and *Answers;* these contributions totalled eighty published items during his two-year tenure at the Hong Kong and Shanghai Bank. In the summer of 1901, he learned that one of his old Dulwich masters, William Beach-Thomas, had given up teaching and was currently employed at the *Globe,* London's oldest evening newspaper, as an assistant to Harold Begbie who edited the paper's "By the Way" column. Wodehouse asked if Beach-Thomas could possibly find him some work as a writer. It was agreed that, should the two journalists wish to take some time off, Wodehouse would write the column for them. But it wasn't until March of 1902 that he was called upon to do so. At that time Beach-Thomas and Begbie informed him that he could write the column daily from March 27 until April 2, an assignment that would necessitate Wodehouse's prolonged absence from the bank. He called in sick for a week.

Meanwhile he had been working on his first serial, *The Pothunters,* for publication in *Public School Magazine.* In 1902, A & C Black decided to publish the work as a novel and told the young author that he would receive a ten percent royalty on each copy sold. The bank appeared less appealing all the time.

When Beach-Thomas took his annual five-week vacation in 1902, Wodehouse was asked to replace him temporarily. On September 9 of that year, he quit his bank job and became a full-time writer. That same month saw the publication of *The Pothunters* as well as the appearance of his first article in *Punch,* the leading British humor magazine. After Beach-Thomas's return, Wodehouse continued to work quite successfully as a freelance, contributing stories, articles, and verse to many of the popular magazines and newspapers of the day. In August, 1903, Beach-Thomas resigned from the *Globe,* and P. G. Wodehouse accepted his position as Begbie's assistant on "By the Way."

In 1904, with five weeks holiday due him, Wodehouse decided to fulfill his long-held ambition to see the United States. Since trans-Atlantic travel was fairly inexpensive in those days, he was easily able to book second-class passage on the steamer *St. Louis* for the nine-day trip to New York. America was everything he expected; he found New York to be tremendously exciting, and he was given the opportunity of visiting the training camp of boxer Kid McCoy. Wodehouse, a great fan of the fights, was especially impressed with this part of his trip, and he later used the experience as the basis for a series of stories about a young boxer whom he called Kid Brady. Soon after Wodehouse's return to England, Harold Begbie resigned as editor of the "By the Way" column, and Wodehouse assumed the position. At the same time Wodehouse introduced his friend Herbert W. Westbrook to the *Globe*'s owner, Sir George Armstrong, and succeeded in getting him a job as assistant on the column. The two collaborated on "By the Way" while sharing living quarters in London, and Wodehouse continued publishing short stories, articles, and novels.

In December, 1904, Owen Hall, well-known musical comedy playwright, asked Wodehouse to write the lyrics for a song in his new play, "Sergeant Brue." For writing "Put Me in My Little Cell," Wodehouse was paid the equivalent of a week's salary at the *Globe.* He attended the opening night performance of the play and then returned to the Strand Theatre the next week to see it again. Jasen quotes the author's diary entry on the show; "Encored both times. Audience laughed several times during each verse. This is fame." It also proved to be the beginning of a long and profitable infatuation with the theatre. His musical career was furthered when, in 1906, he was given the task of writing encores for "The Beauty of Bath" at the Aldwych Theatre. There he was introduced to a young songwriter named Jerome Kern, and together they wrote a topical song, "Mr. Chamberlain," for Seymour Hicks.

Wodehouse took a second trip to the United States in 1909, this time bringing with him two short stories, both of which he sold on the morning of his arrival. *Cosmopolitan* bought one for two hundred dollars, and *Collier's* took the other for three hundred. The British magazines were paying only a fraction of these amounts at the time, so Wodehouse, excited at the prospect of a steady stream of sales of this magnitude, wired his resignation to the *Globe.* He sold a few more pieces, but by early 1910 it was becoming obvious that the big New York publications were not going to buy everything he sent them. Somewhat dejectedly, he returned to England and resumed his position on "By the Way."

But he went to New York again in 1914. Having been very successful writing a few songs, several novels, and a large number of stories and articles in England, he felt that he was ready to try once again to make a living in the United States. After being excused from military service in World War I due to poor eyesight, Wodehouse spent the war years in New York. The day after his arrival he met Ethel Rowley, a widow and fellow Briton, who was in America visiting friends. They were married on September 30, 1914, two months after their introduction by a mutual friend. True to the Wodehouse *oeuvre,* the courtship and wedding had their moments of hysteria: the prospective groom succumbed to a violent sneezing fit in the middle of the marriage proposal; and the minister arrived quite late to the wedding ceremony, explaining that he had just made a killing in the stock market.

It was not long after the wedding that Wodehouse sold his first story to the *Saturday Evening Post,* the pinnacle of the magazine world at the time. The *Post* bought his novel *Something New* for publication as a serial and paid him thirty-five hundred dollars (eventually twenty-one of his novels would be serialized by the *Post,* the last twelve bringing him forty thousand dollars apiece). Wodehouse's fortunes as a writer took a dramatic upward turn. The prestige of publication in the *Post,* as well as an improvement in the quality of his writing due to his association with the magazine's editor, George Horace Lorimer, brought offers from numerous other sources.

Wodehouse was working as a drama critic for *Vanity Fair* when he ran into his old friend Jerome Kern on the opening night of "Very Good, Eddie" which Kern had written with Guy Bolton. Kern invited Wodehouse to his apartment, and it was there, on December 24, 1915, that he first met Bolton. The three men discussed musical comedy and were delighted to find that they shared many of the same opinions. They formed a partnership and were soon working on "Pom Pom," a musical that was already in production but in need of extensive revision. Soon after the completion of that project, they were engaged by Abraham Lincoln Erlanger, who, with his partner Marc Klaw, was a dominant force in the New York theatre, to rewrite a Viennese operetta into a musical comedy. "Miss Springtime" opened September 25, 1916, at the New Amsterdam Theatre and immediately drew rave reviews. The show ran for 227 performances in New York and then toured the country for five years. Thus began a collaboration that became legendary in the field of musical comedy. With Bolton writing the book, Wodehouse the lyrics, and Kern the music, the trio produced some of the most popular Broadway hits of the early twentieth century. In addition to his work with Bolton and Kern, Wodehouse's talents as a lyricist resulted in productions, over the course of fifty years, with such theatrical figures as Victor Herbert, Armand Vecsey, Florenz Ziegfeld, George and Ira Gershwin, Oscar Hammerstein, and Cole Porter.

No discussion of Wodehouse's life would be complete without mention of the infamous broadcasts, made from Germany during World War II, that for a time threatened his reputation and his work. At the zenith of his career, Wodehouse was staying at his home in Le Touquet, France, when the German army invaded that country. There was an RAF squadron stationed in the area, and a small colony of English and other non-French people were living there at the time. In early May of 1940, they became aware of a possible invasion but were not officially warned until the last minute. By the time word came for them to evacuate, all that remained of the RAF squadron was a single fighter plane. Although its pilot offered the single vacant seat to Wodehouse, he would not abandon his wife in France and decided, instead, that they would pack a few belongings and drive to the coast where they could take a boat across the channel. Unfortunately the car broke down before they had traveled two miles, forcing them to return to Le Touquet where they and several other stranded foreigners awaited the Germans.

Le Touquet was occupied on May 22, 1940. At first the Germans did nothing but keep an eye on things. Each morning Wodehouse was required to report to the local Kommandatur, but other than this relatively minor inconvenience, he was not severely restricted. The group was, however, at the mercy of the Nazis when it came to outside information. As a result, they were unaware of the evacuation at Dunkirk and the subsequent Franco-German armistice. But on July 21, the war caught up with them. All of the male residents of Le Touquet were ordered to ready themselves for immediate transportation to an internment camp. They were stuffed into a bus and taken on a seven-hour trip to the prison at Loos. Wodehouse and two other men were locked in a twelve-by-eight-foot cell that contained only one bed, assigned to the oldest man in the cell; Wodehouse and the remaining man had to share the floor. At the end of a week, it was announced that prisoners over the age of sixty would be released. The rest were to prepare for another transfer.

Wodehouse, age fifty-eight, was packed into the cattle car of a train with forty-nine other men and taken on a nineteen-hour journey to Liege, Belgium. There the S.S. took over and marched them for several miles to a former Belgian Army barracks. They were held there for a week and then moved to a citadel just outside of the town of Huy. The citadel was built of stone, its walls fourteen feet thick, and was originally intended to house two hundred. The Germans crammed eight hundred men into it. They were kept at Huy for five weeks before being moved once more, this time to their final destination, the insane asylum at Tost in Upper Silesia. Compared to their previous prisons, the camp at Tost proved to be fairly tolerable. It was relatively spacious, and the prisoners were given the freedom to form an orchestra, put on shows, and conduct church services. The atmosphere was relaxed enough for Wodehouse to complete a novel, *Money in the Bank,* during his internment there.

An Associated Press reporter was permitted to visit Tost in December of 1940. He interviewed Wodehouse and reported, among other things, that the author had refused special privileges offered by his captors. The article was the first news the outside world had heard about Wodehouse since his capture. His readers went wild; prominent figures in the publishing world and the theatrical business put pressure on the German authorities to release him; Guy Bolton circulated a petition to have Wodehouse released to the United States which was not, as yet, at war with Germany. But the Germans would not let him go. In June, however, because he was nearing his sixtieth birthday, or perhaps because of the publicity, Wodehouse was taken from Tost to Berlin where he was given conditional freedom. His wife was allowed to join him, and they were assigned a suite at the Hotel Adlon where, although kept under careful observation, they were comparatively comfortable.

Soon after his arrival in Berlin, representatives of several American companies came to ask Wodehouse if he would be interested in taping some talks for broadcast to the still-neutral United States. Thinking this might be a good way to keep in touch with his fans, he readily agreed, and between June 26 and July 2, 1941, he taped five programs which were broadcast primarily to the United States, but which were also picked up in England. The talks dealt mostly with

Wodehouse's experiences as a prisoner, and, always the optimist, he told how he and his fellow captives had made the best of a horrible situation. He also ridiculed the Germans by making some rather humorous observations which, having been written in Wodehouse's peculiar style of idiomatic English, were surprisingly allowed to pass uncensored. Jasen writes: "That the Germans allowed him to broadcast those talks exactly as he had written them leaves their motive very much in doubt. It is difficult to see what they could have hoped to gain from them, for Plum did not gloss over the miseries of internment. If they were intended merely as a sop to the many important Americans who had urged for Plum's release and were therefore regarded as just so much worthless nonsense, then the Germans obviously did not understand the subtleties of the Wodehouse brand of humour." This is further evidenced by the report that at one point during the war, the Germans, having gotten their information on contemporary English dress from a recent Wodehouse novel, parachuted a spy wearing *spats* into the Fen country. He was, of course, very quickly captured.

Taken on context alone, according to Jasen, the end result of the broadcasts was that Wodehouse, "in his inimitable way, made the Nazis look particularly stupid in their handling of the internment camps." There were, however, several factors that affected the publicity surrounding the talks which Wodehouse had failed to anticipate. Foremost among these was the fact that even though the United States, his adopted country, was not yet involved in the war, England was locked in a bitter struggle with Germany. The British still felt the sting of Dunkirk, and London was being assaulted daily by Luftwaffe bombers. Wodehouse may have been addressing the talks to his American fans, but he was still a British citizen; and, although he might not have been aware of the legal technicalities, English law considered it a treasonable act to use an enemy's broadcast facilities for any purpose in time of war.

Further trouble developed from the fact that very few Englishmen actually heard the broadcasts themselves. They had to rely on the news media to tell them what Wodehouse had said, and the media, from all indications, were apparently less concerned with the truth than they were with trying to stir up public indignation with the story of the rich writer who had "abandoned" his native country years earlier for the French Riviera and the lights of Broadway and who was now collaborating with the enemy. The most vicious of the journalistic attacks came over the British Broadcasting Corp. radio network from William Connor, a writer for the *Daily Mirror* under the name "Cassandra." Reading from a script he had prepared himself, Connor began, "I have come to tell you tonight of the story of a rich man trying to make his last and greatest sale—that of his own country. It is a sombre story of honour pawned to the Nazis for the price of a soft bed." With rising melodrama, Connor fabricated an incident in which Goebbels "said unto him: 'All this power will I give thee if thou wilt worship the Fuehrer.' Pelham fell on his knees." The broadcast concluded with an account of the bombing of Wodehouse's beloved Dulwich; Connor said, "*You* should have been there, Mr. Wodehouse—you with your impartiality, your reasonableness and perhaps even one of your famous little jokes."

There was, throughout Connor's entire broadcast, no mention of what Wodehouse had said in his talks. Jasen adds: "That the BBC should have warranted an attack of this nature on a man who was in no position to defend himself against the charges seems very much out of character. But the truth is that the BBC's Board of Governors was strongly opposed to it. The Board was overruled, however, by the then Minister of Information, Mr. Duff Cooper, on whose insistence Connor went on the air.'' As a result of this and attacks by other journalists, the British people were led to believe that P. G. Wodehouse had been broadcasting propaganda from inside Germany. The reaction, as reported by Richard Voorhees in his *P. G. Wodehouse,* was illogical but bitter: ''Certain British libraries withdrew Wodehouse's books from circulation; the BBC put a ban of his lyrics for at least two years; the Beefsteak Club cancelled his membership; still worse, Dulwich struck his name from the rolls. A number of readers suddenly discovered that the novels proved Wodehouse to have been a Fascist even before Hitler. As long as three years after Connor's talk there were demands from members of Parliament that Wodehouse be tried for treason.''

Not everyone had abandoned him, however. Many friends and readers, as well as most people who had actually heard the broadcasts, realized that the accusations against him were absurd. Malcolm Muggeridge, in *Homage to P. G. Wodehouse,* edited by Thelma Cazalet-Keir, wrote that ''Wodehouse is ill-fitted to live in an age of ideological conflict. He just does not react to human beings in that sort of way, and never seems to hate anyone—not even old friends who turned on him. . . . Of the various indignities heaped upon him at the time of his disgrace—like being expelled from the Beefsteak Club—the only one he really grieved over was being expunged from some alleged roll of honour at his old school, Dulwich. Such a temperment unfits him to be a good citizen in the mid-twentieth century.'' Those who knew Wodehouse best agreed with Muggeridge. The author's easy-going nature was legendary, and his naivete (indeed total disinterest) in things of a political nature would easily verify his innocent motive for agreeing to do the broadcasts.

Muggeridge, who was a British liaison officer serving with a French unit at the time of the liberation of Paris, became involved with Wodehouse's case when he was asked to look into the matter of the British writer who was being held in a French hotel. The Wodehouses had been sent to Paris while it was still held by the Nazis (who had apparently lost interest in Wodehouse as the war turned against them and probably wanted him as far out of the way as possible). When the Allies retook Paris, the retreating Germans left their two civilian prisoners behind. The French authorities, realizing that Wodehouse was wanted by the British, kept him confined to his suite in the Bristol Hotel. Muggeridge thoroughly investigated the case and reported his findings to his superiors. His conclusion: ''In the broadcasts there is not one phrase or word which can possibly be regarded as treasonable.'' He adds that, ironically, the broadcasts ''were subsequently used at an American political warfare school as an example of how anti-German propaganda could subtly be put across by a skilful writer in the form of seemingly innocuous, light-hearted descriptive material.''

Wodehouse, completely cleared of all charges by both the French and British governments, finally commented publically on the broadcasts when, on May 8, 1946, *Variety* printed a letter in which he insisted that his intention was merely to amuse the American public with a ''humorous description of camp life.'' Wodehouse quoted a letter sent to him by a man, a former prisoner of war, who wrote: ''I would like to tell you that having read your broadcasts I cannot see how anyone could possibly see anything in the slightest pro-German or anti-British in them. But I will not give you my own opinion, I will tell you that of the late Air Mar-

shal Boyd. I was his personal assistant and we were prisoners together in Italy. He read your broadcasts and gave them to me saying, 'Why the Germans ever let him say all this I cannot think. They have either got more sense of humour than I credited them with or it has just slipped past the censor. There is some stuff about being packed in cattle trucks and a thing about Loos jail that you would think would send a Hun crazy. Wodehouse has probably been shot by now.'" As Wodehouse said in the *Variety* letter, ''the opinion of a British Air Marshal who knew what was in the talks ought to carry more weight than that of British newspaper men who didn't.'' Many years later, just a few months before he died, Wodehouse made his last statement on the broadcasts. When asked by *Paris Review* interviewer Clarke if he regretted taping the talks, he replied: ''Oh, yes. Oh, rather. I wish I hadn't. It never occurred to me that there was anything wrong in the broadcasts. They altered my whole life. I suppose I would have gone back to England and so on if it hadn't been for them.''

In May of 1946, *Money in the Bank,* written during his internment, was published in London by Jenkins; it was the first Wodehouse book to see print in England since 1940. If there was any doubt about his continuing popularity as a result of the broadcasts, it was dispelled when the book sold 26,000 copies.

On April 18, 1947, the Wodehouses once again departed for the United States, this time to stay for good. They lived in a variety of places in or near New York City for several years while Wodehouse resumed his writing career. In 1951 they purchased a home situated on twelve acres in Remsenburg, Long Island, three-quarters of a mile from the Guy Boltons' house. Here Wodehouse found the solitude of life in the country which he had loved since childhood, and he spent his remaining years in the midst of fresh air and greenery. His daily routine varied little during that time. He would get up early, spend forty-five minutes doing his ''daily dozen'' exercises, write for the rest of the morning, watch ''The Edge of Night'' on television, eat lunch, walk three miles to the post office to collect the mail, work until five p.m., bathe, eat dinner, read until ten, take the dogs for a walk, then retire. When, well into his eighties, he was asked the secret of long life, Wodehouse stressed regular exercise—long walks and calisthenics—and cold martinis, two before lunch and two before dinner. He died Friday, February 14, 1975, of an apparent heart attack, in Southampton Hospital, having been admitted for treatment of a skin rash. He was ninety-three years and four months old at the time.

The world P. G. Wodehouse created in his writings may, at times, seem strange and somewhat dated to the modern reader. Wodehouse, it must be remembered, was born in Victorian England. He was a member of the Beefsteak Club while Rudyard Kipling was still a member (he became a correspondent of Kipling's), and as a boy he read the works of many of the great nineteenth-century writers as they were published. Richard Voorhees points out that ''Since Wodehouse wrote his first fourteen books during the reign of Edward VII, they are bound to date in many ways.'' But why, then, are his later books, those written in the fifties and sixties, also full of outdated manners and customs? Sometimes, according to Voorhees, the anachronisms are accidental, as when 1948 model cars are equipped with running boards, or when a character is found to be smoking a brand of cigarette that has long since disappeared from the market. But he maintains that, more often, ''the anachronisms are clearly deliberate. Wodehouse perpetrates some of them because they appeal to his sense of the absurd, because they have an antiquarian smack.... Wodehouse commits other anachronisms because they are part of his equipment as a professional novelist, because he has used them successfully for so many years. Thus he continues to write of village concerts at which baritones sing 'The Yeoman's Wedding Song,' of village fetes with bun-eating contests and egg-and-spoon races; thus he writes as though people wore pince-nez and men wore spats.'' But Voorhees concludes that the most important reason for the anachronisms is that Wodehouse is ''repelled by much of the modern world and is taking refuge from it.''

That Wodehouse's world is far removed from the realities of modern life is without doubt. The question is, did this world of his *ever* exist? Many critics unhesitatingly state that Wodehouse made the whole thing up, that he created a time and place that never were. He responded to this idea in the interview with Clarke, saying that, although anachronisms may come up occasionally in his books, they are the result of his difficulty in remembering details, that his stories may seem out-of-date, but the time in which they are set did exist. ''It was going strong between the wars,'' he insisted.

Wodehouse wrote of life among the upper classes, but it is difficult to determine whether he meant to glorify the titled and the idle rich or to satirize their pomposity and snobbery. Voorhees believes that he did a bit of both, offering as an example of the former his obvious ''love of country houses and castles. He became acquainted with them when, as a boy on holidays from school, he accompanied a clerical uncle on his rounds. Later he visited some of them for longer periods, and still later—when he became rich from his writing—he often leased one of them for part of a year or more.... Castles, of course, are not only impressive physical objects; they represent a way of life, and Wodehouse finds that way attractive.'' Regarding satire, most critics agree that Wodehouse engages in it very mildly, if at all. Richard Ingrams in Cazalet-Keir's *Homage to P. G. Wodehouse,* writes that he ''is definitely not a satirist. Savage indignation, of the type which lacerated the heart of Swift and others, is an emotion totally foreign to him.... If there is any satire in Wodehouse ... it is of a basic and rather schoolboyish kind.'' And according to Alden Whitman of the *New York Times,* George Orwell pointed out, in a 1945 essay, that Wodehouse was able to accept establishment figures while exploiting their comic possibilities, making them ''ridiculous, not immoral or contemptible.''

The characters in Wodehouse's world are thoroughly unique. One of his earliest, Stanley Featherstonehaugh Ukridge, who appeared in the author's first humorous adult novel, *Love among the Chickens,* was one of the few Wodehouse characters to be based on a real person. The inspiration for Ukridge came from Wodehouse's friend William Townend who apparently knew a man who had started a chicken farm in Devonshire. As David A. Jasen tells it, ''the man in question had run through an inheritance, quarrelled with a rich aunt, was an inveterate drinker, and habitually sponged on every likely acquaintance.'' Wodehouse immediately saw the comic possibilities there and set to work on a story. ''To round out the character,'' Jasen says, ''Plum added some of the more eccentric characteristics of his part-time boarder, Herbert Westbrook, whose often startling antics were to provide grist for Plum's mill in future stories.'' The result was a novel in which, as R.B.D. French says in his book *P. G. Wodehouse,* ''Jeremy Garnet, a young author of Wodehouse's own standing, falls in love with a girl he meets in the train on his way to help Ukridge with the chickens at Lyme Regis. His efforts to cut out his rival, a dashing

naval officer, and win over the girl's father ... are much impeded by the well-intended but catastrophic interventions of Ukridge, who, however, remains for the most part against the background of his poultry farm as it totters to financial ruin.'' As French notes, Wodehouse had, ''as commonly happens with authors, ... come upon a major character'' without perceiving his stature. When *Love among the Chickens* was revised in 1921, Ukridge was brought into greater prominence, and the character eventually became the basis for a number of future stories.

Three years after Ukridge's premiere in *Love among the Chickens,* Wodehouse introduced another character who began life in the background of a novel but was destined to become famous in his own right. The novel was *Mike,* and the title character's best friend was Psmith (pronounced Smith; ''the 'P' is silent as in pshrimp''). Psmith is the exact opposite of Ukridge in almost every way: where Ukridge is friendly, outgoing, and prone to familiarity, Psmith is extremely proper and formal; Ukridge is something of a slob, while Psmith is always impeccably groomed; Ukridge is very energetic and a bit inclined to panic, Psmith is noted for his cool-headedness. Voorhees writes that Psmith ''has already gone beyond the school world'' even though the novel is set at Sedleigh where he and Mike are students. Psmith is above the childish behavior of the other pupils; he talks about his youth as though it were long past. He is politically aware, having embraced socialism (''It's a great scheme. You work for the equal distribution of property and start by collaring all you can and sitting on it.''), and to prove he is serious about it goes around calling everyone ''comrade.'' Voorhees calls him ''one of Wodehouse's nonstop talkers.... Sometimes his constant chitchat has a strategic purpose, for Psmith, though a decent enough cricket player and tough enough fighter when obliged to brawl, prefers to dominate groups and to get his way with words.'' As a character who appears in Wodehouse's last public school novel and then turns up again as an adult, Psmith may be seen as something of a transition between the author's earliest work and the bulk of his fiction. But he was featured in only a few stories before disappearing. Wodehouse explained to Clarke why he dropped one of his most interesting characters: ''I don't think that the things that made him funny as a very young man would be funny in an older man.... I couldn't go on with him. I don't think he'd have worked as a maturer character.''

In poking fun at the upper classes, Wodehouse included among his comic characters a good many titled persons. According to his *New York Times* obituary, he was once charged with being unduly fond of earls; his reply: ''In the course of my literary career, I have featured quite a number of these fauna, but as I often say—well perhaps once a month—why not? Show me the Hon. who by pluck and determination has raised himself from the depths, step by step, and I will show you a man of whom any author might be proud.'' Foremost among Wodehouse's earls are Lords Emsworth, Ickenham, and Marshmoreton. Emsworth, the owner of Blandings Castle, is an absentminded old geezer who is plagued with a roguish son, a nagging sister, and an overly-virtuous secretary. He is supposed to be working on a family history, as his sister, Lady Constance, is always reminding him, but he usually manages to get out of it. Marshmoreton, as Voorhees puts it, ''is simply Lord Emsworth under another name. Wodehouse gives him different obsessions (gardening in corduroy trousers, squirting whale oil on insects), but the differences are insignificant, and the resemblances are marked: a family history to write, a sister as chatelaine, a blockhead of a son." Ickenham, however, is a totally different character. He is supposedly around sixty years old but acts like an adolescent, occasionally, Voorhees says, "regressing to the age of the schoolboy and taking up with delight such old weapons as the slingshot and the peashooter." French calls him "a kind of elderly Psmith, but without Psmith's quality of repose," and mentions his "genius for intrigue and impersonation." Ickenham has been known to pass himself off as the noted nerve specialist Sir Roderick Glossop, famous explorer Major Brabazon-Plank, and Inspector Jarvis of Scotland Yard, as well as a host of lesser personalities that he makes up to suit various occasions.

But Wodehouse's most famous characters are Bertram Wilberforce Wooster and his incredible valet Jeeves. They first appeared in a story entitled "Extricating Young Gussie" which Wodehouse wrote for the *Saturday Evening Post.* While Bertie was a main character in the story, Jeeves was relegated to a minor part. As Wodehouse explained to Clarke: "I only intended to use him once. His first entrance was: 'Mrs. Gregson to see you, Sir'.... He only had one other line: 'Very good, Sir. Which suit will you wear?' But then I was writing a story, 'The Artistic Career of Corky,' about two young men, Bertie Wooster and his friend Corky, getting into a lot of trouble. I thought: Well, how can I get them out? And I thought: 'Suppose one of them had an omniscient valet?' I wrote a short story about him, then another short story, then several more short stories and novels." In the introduction to his *Jeeves Omnibus,* Wodehouse wrote, "I still blush to think of the off-hand way I treated him at our first encounter."

Contrary to the assumptions of many readers and critics, Jeeves is no mere butler; he is a valet or, as he puts it, a gentleman's personal gentleman. In addition to the duties normally performed by a butler, a gentleman's gentleman is responsible for the running of the entire household as well as such things as his employer's dress and daily schedule. Jeeves, unlike most valets, is also entrusted with the task of saving the lives of Bertie and his numerous scheming accomplices from time to time.

In his book *The Comic Style of P. G. Wodehouse,* Robert A. Hall calls Jeeves "one of the most memorable characters invented in twentieth-century English-language fiction. His head sticks out at the back, and he eats a great deal of fish, which to Bertie's way of thinking makes him so brainy. His favorite reading is Spinoza, or else the great Russian novelists. His range of knowledge is encyclopaedic, so that he can furnish information or give an extempore lecture on almost every subject.... His speech is an exaggeratedly ultra-formal, ultra-standard English. In the stories, his function is to get Bertie (and often others as well) out of jams, through his analysis of the 'psychology of the individual' (one of his favorite expressions) and through the measures he takes, often when Bertie, through his own bungling, is *in extremis.* Jeeves is an intellectual *deus ex machina,* to rescue Bertie from the scrapes the latter gets into through his presumption unsupported by intellectual strength."

Bertie, for his part, may be seen as the most outstanding example of a long line of irresponsible young gentlemen characterized by Wodehouse, or, as Voorhees phrases it, the "crowning achievement in the creation of the silly young ass," and "one of literature's idiots." While there can be little doubt as to Bertie's lack of intelligence (he readily admits it; in one of the stories in *My Man Jeeves,* when Bertie says, "We must think, sir," Bertie replies, "You do it. I don't have the equipment."), he remains one of Wodehouse's

most personable and engaging characters. He is extremely good natured and gregarious, always ready for a dinner party or a weekend at one of his aunts' country houses. Although he is presumably in his late twenties, he persists in childish schemes that invariably backfire leaving his salvation, time and again, in the hands of Jeeves. Bertie lives by the strict "Code of the Woosters" which compels him never to let a pal down. As a result he is at the mercy of an endless supply of old school chums and girl friends who entreat him to rescue them from a variety of sticky situations. French surmises that "if the Duke of Wellington had asked the Wooster of that day to charge the Old Guard, you would not have heard that Wooster saying that he had to run into Brussels for a moment and was afraid he would not be able to manage it. He would have been where Bertie is to be found—in the thick of the grape-shot, or purloining a policeman's helmet to get young Stephanie Byng out of a jam, as the case may be."

In the early short stories featuring Jeeves and Bertie, the young master gets himself into a variety of scrapes from which it becomes necessary for the wise valet to extricate him, including a few accidental engagements to young ladies to whom he is particularly unsuited. But beginning with the first novel in which they are the main characters, Hall points out, "the emphasis changes, and Bertie's efforts to avoid marriage become the main-spring of the plot. Florence Craye appears (in *Joy in the Morning*) as one of the threats to his bachelordom; but there are others as well. In *Right Ho, Jeeves* the droopy, soupy, sentimental Madeline Bassett misunderstands Bertie's pleas on behalf of his newt-fancier friend Gussie Fink-Nottle, and thinks he is pleading his own cause. From then on, every time that she feels disappointed in her love for someone else, she tells Bertie she will marry him; his naive code of being a *preux chevalier* forbids him to spurn her love.... This essential situation is repeated in each one of the later Bertie-Jeeves novels, with marriage to either Pauline Stoker (in *Thank You, Jeeves),* Madeline Bassett, or the red-haired hellion Bobbie Wickham (in *Jeeves in the Offing)* as a major threat."

It isn't that Bertie is anti-marriage, it's just that—as Jeeves puts it—he is "one of nature's bachelors." Besides, none of the heroines in the stories, even though they are all very attractive and many are quite charming, are quite right for him. They fall, Voorhees finds, into three distinct categories. The first includes the wild ones like Bobbie Wickham and Stephanie ("Stiffy") Byng who "compel young men to puncture people's hot water bottles, push constables in ponds, steal, kidnap, and so on." The second is the serious type who "wishes to reform Bertie, to make him drink and smoke less, for instance. Because she is intelligent, she wishes to educate him, to make him read Bergson and go to serious plays instead of musical comedies. Because she is athletic, she wishes to get him into condition.... Such a girl has too much virtue for Bertie"; this is the category which includes Honoria Glossop, daughter of the nerve specialist (or loony doctor, as he is more often called). And the third type of heroine, of which Madeline Basset is an example, is what Voorhees calls "sappy." Madeline, for instance, "believes that the stars are God's daisy chain and that the mists over the meadow are the bridal veils of the elves." Another example of this type, Phyllis Mills, "speaks in baby talk, asking Bertie if he does not think that the dachshund Poppet is a sweet little doggie and asserting that Bertie's friend Kipper Herring is a lambkin." Bertie might be said to be a dedicated moderate: fun-loving, but not wild; an avid reader and theatregoer, but one who prefers mysteries and musicals to the weightier works; and, although he certainly cannot be accused of being overly-mature, his childishness draws up somewhat short of the infant stage, causing him to frown upon the use of baby talk. He is, thus, unable to settle down with any of the women who turn up in the novels, and, thanks to the intervention of Jeeves, he is consistently delivered from their grasp.

Aunts, in a variety of forms, are widely scattered throughout Wodehouse's works, but they are particularly prevalent in the Jeeves stories. Bertie's two aunts, Agatha and Dahlia, both own large country estates which Bertie is fond of visiting, and it is there that some of the most hilarious action in the novels takes place. Agatha is an evil-tempered tyrant who, Bertie claims, "kills rats with her teeth and wears barbed wire next to the skin." Voorhees refers to her as "an older Honoria Glossop, a woman who wants to turn Bertie into a serious and responsible man, failing to see that the operation is painful and the change in any case, impossible." It is Agatha who introduces him to a number of fine young ladies, all of whom prove to be dreadful burdens of one kind or another. Dahlia, a former fox hunter who still speaks as though she were trying to project her voice across several meadows, is a gruff but lovable individual of whom Bertie is very fond. She occasionally has tantrums during which she has been known to throw an assortment of fragile objects at walls, floors, and servants, and many times Bertie is forced to censor her saltier epithets for the benefit of his sensitive readers. Dahlia may be a sort of grown-up Stiffy Byng, constantly involving Bertie in plots and schemes, often illegal, usually unethical, which eventually require the resources of Jeeves to be carried out successfully. She generally blackmails Bertie into submission by threatening to banish him from her dinner table, thus depriving him of the fruits of the culinary labors of her renowned French chef Anatole. Since Bertie is dedicated to the cause of eating well, he always complies.

The inspiration for the aunts in Wodehouse's stories undoubtedly came from his own life. R.B.D. French explains that "while his parents were in the East, Wodehouse was looked after by relatives at home, and in his own phrase passed from aunt to aunt. That is the simple explanation of the regiment of aunts in his books. . . . Aunts in the leisured classes had plenty of time to give unwanted attention to nephews and nieces." According to Jasen, Wodehouse had two particular aunts who served as models for those in the Jeeves and Bertie stories. His aunt Louisa, eldest of his mother's sisters, was one of his favorites, and she became Aunt Dahlia. Another sister, Mary, was a writer and a bit of a tyrant whose overbearing nature "made an indelible impression on her young nephew that was to manifest itself in Bertie Wooster's unsympathetic Aunt Agatha."

As a result of his distinctive writing style—a style that has served as the inspiration for a number of contemporary humorists—many critics have labeled Wodehouse the dominant force in the establishment of modern humorous fiction technique. But Robert A. Hall, who notes that the author has been hailed as "the greatest master of twentieth-century prose," says that "despite general recognition of Wodehouse's merits as a stylist . . . there has been relatively little detailed analysis of the features that have contributed to his almost unparalleled success in humorous writing." Hall's book *The Comic Style of P. G. Wodehouse* is a thorough study of the stylistic devices Wodehouse used for comic effect. "Humor," says Hall, "has two essential ingredients. For us to laugh at something, it must contain some kind of incongruity, and we must be emotionally neutral, without our personal feelings being involved." He finds that "Wode-

house makes use of just about every resource available in standard English plus a few from non-standard English, to obtain his effects."

Hall mentions Wodehouse's inventive word formations, adding and subtracting prefixes and suffixes, as an example. He writes: "To *de-dog the premises* is not too great a variation on the pattern of *de-louse* or *de-bunk;* but Wodehouse obtains a greater humorous effect by prefixing *de-* to proper names, as when Pongo Twistleton brings the housemaid Elsie Bean out of a cupboard [in *Uncle Dynamite*]: 'His manner as he de-Beaned the cupboard was somewhat distrait,' or when 'Kipper' Herring, after Bobbie Wickham has left his company, is described as 'finding himself de-Wickhamed' [in *Jeeves in the Offing*]. On the analogy of such formations as *homeward, northward, inward,* Wodehouse obtains a special effect when he says of Lord Emsworth [in *Summer Lightning*], 'He pottered off pigward.'" Hall also cites several instances in which Wodehouse stretches the patterns of word formations and meanings beyond their normal limits. In *Heavy Weather* he fashions a verb *to huss* from the noun hussy: "I regard the entire personnel of the ensemble of our musical comedy theatres as—if you will pardon me being Victorian for a moment—painted hussies." "They've got to paint." 'Well, they needn't huss.'" In Wodehouse's parlance, a cowpuncher punches cows and corn-chandler chandles corn. He is also prone to separate some words, such as *hobnob,* into their constituent elements. Thus in *Uncle Dynamite* a character says, "To offer a housemaid a cigarette is not hobbing. Nor, when you light it for her, does that constitute nobbing."

As a master craftsman Wodehouse would never overuse any single stylistic device, but one that comes up, Hall points out, about twice in any given story, is what is called the transferred epithet, "especially an adjective modifying a noun instead of the corresponding adverb modifying the verb of the sentence." In the story "Jeeves and the Impending Doom," this phenomenon is evidenced by the sentence, "He uncovered the fragrant eggs and I pronged a moody forkful." In *Joy in the Morning* we have, "I balanced a thoughtful lump of sugar on the teaspoon." And in *Jeeves and the Feudal Spirit,* "He waved a concerned cigar."

Misunderstandings of many kinds abound in Wodehouse stories. These often are the result of syntactic or lexicographic confusion, as in a scene from "Jeeves and the Yuletide Spirit" in which Sir Roderick Glossop misunderstands Bertie Wooster's use of the nickname *Tuppy:* "'Awfully sorry about all this,' I said in a hearty sort of voice. 'The fact is, I thought you were Tuppy.'" "'Kindly refrain from inflicting your idiotic slang on me. What do you mean by the adjective "tuppy"?'" "'It isn't so much an adjective, don't you know. More of a noun, I should think, if you examine it squarely. What I'mean to say is, I thought you were your nephew.'" Hall cites one more case of this type of misunderstanding which occurs in *Uncle Dynamite* when Constable Potter confuses two meanings of the word *by:* "'I was assaulted by the duck pond.'" "'By the duck pond?' Sir Aylmer asked, his eyes widening." "'Yes, sir.'" "'How the devil can you be assaulted by a duck pond?' Constable Potter saw where the misunderstanding had arisen. The English language is full of these pitfalls. 'When I say "by the duck pond," I didn't mean "by the duck pond," I meant "by the duck pond." That is to say,' proceeded Constable Potter, speaking just in time, 'near or adjacent to, in fact on the edge of.'"

Another good example of Wodehouse's unique use of language to evoke humor can be found running throughout the

Jeeves and Bertie stories. Even though Bertie is supposedly a graduate of Eton and Oxford, his vocabulary is extremely limited, and he spends a good deal of time groping for the right word, or, as Wodehouse so often says, the *mot juste*. In *Stiff Upper Lip, Jeeves* he says, "I suppose Stiffy's sore about this . . . what's the word? . . . Not vaseline . . . Vacillation, that's it." In *Jeeves and the Feudal Spirit* Hall finds one of the many instances in which Bertie depends on Jeeves to fill in the blank: "Let a pluggily like young Thos loose in the community with a cosh, and you are inviting disaster and . . . what's the word? Something about cats." Jeeves replies, "Cataclysms, sir?"

Jeeve's vocabulary is, in fact, so broad that Bertie, who is at least somewhat accustomed to it, is often forced to translate for his friends. Hall refers to a scene in "The Artistic Career of Corky" as an example; Jeeves says, "The scheme I would suggest cannot fail of success, but it has what may seem to you a drawback, sir, in that it requires a certain financial outlay." "He means," Bertie explains to Corky, "that he has got a pippin of an idea, but it's going to cost a lot."

Puns also make frequent appearances in Wodehouse's work. In *Thank You, Jeeves,* a Mr. Stoker says, "Reminds me of that thing about Lo somebody's name led all the rest." Jeeves refreshes his memory, "Abou ben Adhem, sir." And the puzzled Stoker asks, "Have I *what?*" When, in *Jeeves and the Feudal Spirit,* Bertie is released from jail and is asked, "Are you all right, now?" he replies, "Well, I have a pinched look." And in *The Mating Season* Bertie asks, "I look like something the cat found in Tutankhamen's tomb, do I not?" Jeeves answers, "I would not go as far as that, sir, but I have unquestionably seen you more *soigne*." Bertie notes that "it crossed my mind for an instant that with a little thought one might throw together something rather clever about 'Way down upon the soigne river,' but I was too listless to follow up."

But Hall identifies Wodehouse's best-known stylistic device as "his imagery involving similes, metaphors, and other types of comparison. The chief characteristic of his imagery is the wide range from which he draws his comparisons, using them in every instance to emphasize resemblances which at first glance seem highly incongruous (and hence provide the reader's laughter), but which at the same time are highly appropriate to the particular person or situation described. His imagery—carefully planned, of course, like all the rest of his writing—is therefore particularly vivid and apposite." An example from *Leave It to Psmith:* "A sound like two or three pigs feeding rather noisily in the middle of a thunderstorm interrupted his meditation." In *The Mating Season* Wodehouse used, "That 'ha, ha,' so like the expiring quack of a duck dying of a broken heart." And finally in *The Code of the Woosters* we find: "Have you ever heard Sir Watkyn Bassett dealing with a bowl of soup? It's not unlike the Scottish express going through a tunnel." As Hall says, "such a list could be continued almost indefinitely; a whole volume could be compiled simply by excerpting all the imagery which Wodehouse uses in his stories."

Wodehouse's brilliance in utilizing these various stylistic devices, his deft handling of the English language, and his humorous observations on human nature combined to make him one of the most popular writers of the twentieth century. David A. Jasen, who calls Wodehouse the "funniest writer in the world," believes that the author built up a large following through the use of repetition. "It is always a delight to welcome an old friend," he writes, "for old friends recall happily shared experiences, and this is the sense of intimacy gotten when reading the works of Wodehouse." Jasen says

that Wodehouse "took pieces of his childhood, blended with snatches of the quickly altering world of the Edwardians and the early Georgians, and added his own abundantly creative imagination. His plots fit his people, who are consistent not with reality but with themselves and the world of his conception. He attempted to be realistic only in this way and achieved a timelessness in his world which makes his writings universally appealing. His humor depends mainly on exaggeration and understatement, the incongruous, the inappropriate phrase, and the use of the literal interpretation of an idiomatic expression out of context for effect. He developed a new vocabulary, mixing slang along with classical phrases, and fashioning supremely inventive as well as highly diverting hyperboles. He is extremely serious about his work and took tremendous trouble with its construction. He polished his sentences as meticulously as one of his Drones would choose a tie. His only object in writing was purely and simply to amuse." Wodehouse confirmed this in his autobiographical *Over Seventy* when he wrote: "My books may not be the sort of books the cognoscenti feel justified in blowing the twelve and a half shillings on, but I do work at them. When in due course Charon ferries me across the Styx and everyone is telling everyone else what a rotten writer I was, I hope at least one voice will be heard piping up: 'But he did take trouble.'"

Some of Wodehouse's short stories were produced by the BBC under the title "Wodehouse Playhouse."

BIOGRAPHICAL/CRITICAL SOURCES: George Orwell, *The Orwell Reader,* Harcourt, 1933; P. G. Wodehouse, *Performing Flea: A Self-Portrait in Letters,* Jenkins, 1953; Wodehouse and Guy Bolton, *Bring On the Girls!: The Improbable Story of Our Life in Musical Comedy with Pictures to Prove It,* Simon & Schuster, 1953; Wodehouse, *Over Seventy: An Autobiography with Digressions,* Jenkins, 1957; Richard Usborne, *Wodehouse at Work,* Jenkins, 1961; John W. Aldridge, *Time to Murder and Create,* McKay, 1966; Richard Voorhees, *P. G. Wodehouse,* Twayne, 1966; R.B.D. French, *P. G. Wodehouse,* Oliver & Boyd, 1966, Barnes & Noble, 1967; Geoffrey W. Jaggard, *Wooster's World,* Macdonald & Co., 1967; Geoffrey W. Jaggard, *Blandings the Blest and the Blue Blood,* Macdonald & Co., 1968; David A. Jasen, *A Bibliography and Reader's Guide to the First Editions of P. G. Wodehouse,* Archon, 1970; *Writers Digest,* October, 1971; H. W. Wind, *The World of P. G. Wodehouse,* Praeger, 1972; Thelma Cazalet-Keir, editor, *Homage to P. G. Wodehouse,* Barrie & Jenkins, 1973; *Contemporary Literary Criticism,* Gale, Volume I, 1973, Volume II, 1974, Volume V, 1976, Volume X, 1979; Jasen, *P. G. Wodehouse: A Portrait of a Master,* Mason & Lipscomb, 1974; Robert A. Hall, Jr., *The Comic Style of P. G. Wodehouse,* Archon, 1974; *New York Times,* February 15, 1975; *Paris Review,* winter, 1975; *Authors in the News,* Volume II, Gale, 1976.†

—*Sketch by Peter M. Gareffa*

*   *   *

WOHLRABE, Raymond A. 1900-1977

PERSONAL: Born April 25, 1900, in Superior, Wis.; died June 23, 1977; son of Adolph Gustav and Flora (McCallum) Wohlrabe. *Education:* University of Washington, B.S., 1922; additional study at Purdue University, 1923-24, University of Southern California, University of Washington, and University of British Columbia.

CAREER: Science teacher in public schools, Burlington, Wash., 1922-23, Port Townsend, Wash., 1924-25, Portland,

Ore., 1925-26, and Seattle, Wash., 1926-66. *Member:* National Retired Teachers Association, Phi Lambda Upsilon.

WRITINGS—All published by World Publishing, except as indicated: *Crystals,* Lippincott, 1962; *Metals,* Lippincott, 1964; *Exploring Electrostatics,* 1965; *Exploring Solar Energy,* 1966; *The Pacific Northwest,* 1968; *High Desert and Canyon Country,* 1969; *Fundamental Physical Forces,* Lippincott, 1969; *Exploring Giant Molecules,* 1969; *Exploring the World of Leaves,* Crowell, 1976.

With Werner Krusch, except as indicated; all published by Lippincott: *The Land and People of Austria,* 1956, revised edition, 1972; *The Land and People of Germany,* 1957, revised edition, 1972; *The Land and People of Venezuela,* 1959, revised edition, 1963; *The Land and People of Portugal,* 1960, revised edition, 1963; *The Land and People of Denmark,* 1961, revised edition, 1972; *The Key to Vienna,* 1961; *Picture Map Geography of Western Europe,* 1967; (with Adriaan J. Barnouw) *The Land and People of Holland,* revised edition, 1972. Contributor of travel articles to magazines and newspapers; also contributor of articles to juvenile publications.

WORK IN PROGRESS: More travel and science books.

SIDELIGHTS: Raymond Wohlrabe once wrote *CA:* "My interest in photography and in travel as a hobby led to my becoming an author. After teaching photography in high school and adult evening school I was selected to serve as a Seattle exchange teacher for a year in one of the Los Angeles high schools. While there, I took advantage of the opportunity to study photography under Ansel Adams at the Art Center School. My first writing was for the Eastman Kodak Company's little magazine, *Kodakery,* which was discontinued quite a number of years ago.

"Eventually I became interested in making use of my years of experience in teaching science in high school in writing books about science that would be popular with young people. Experiments that youngsters could do were worked into the text of each science book. All of these were tried out on students in my own classes to make certain youngsters would be able to do them at home or in the school laboratory. An effort was made to use purely scientific terms only where these were absolutely necessary and where scientific terminology had to be used, to include simple explanations that could be easily understood. This made factual science books far more interesting to the young reader than the regular textbooks normally used in their class activities."

AVOCATIONAL INTERESTS: Photography, hiking, travel, art.†

*   *   *

WOLF, Leonard 1923-

PERSONAL: Born March 1, 1923, in Vulcan, Romania; son of Joseph and Rose (Engel) Wolf; married Patricia Evans, December 2, 1944; married Deborah Goleman (a cultural anthropologist), April 10, 1960; children: Sarah, Aaron, Naomi. *Education:* Attended Ohio State University, 1941-43; University of California, Berkeley, A.B., 1945, M.A., 1950; University of Iowa, Ph.D., 1954. *Religion:* Jewish. *Home:* 36 Farnsworth Lane, San Francisco, Calif. 94117. *Agent:* Julian Bach, Jr., 747 Third Ave., New York, N.Y. 10017. *Office:* Department of English, San Francisco State University, San Francisco, Calif. 94132.

CAREER: Instructor in English at Coe College, Cedar Rapids, Iowa, and University of Iowa, Iowa City, both 1952-54; University of Minnesota, Duluth, lecturer in English, 1954-

55; St. Mary's College, Moraga, Calif., assistant professor of English, 1955-57; San Francisco State University, San Francisco, Calif., 1957—, currently professor of English. Visiting professor at Columbia University, New York University, University of Shiraz, Ben Gurion University, and University of Hawaii. *Military service:* U.S. Army. *Awards, honors:* Recipient of James Phelan Poetry Award from University of California and O. Henry Fiction Award.

WRITINGS: Hamadryad Hunted (poems), Bern Porter, 1945; (translator) Itzik Manger, *The Book of Paradise,* Hill & Wang, 1964; (editor with wife, Deborah Wolf) *Voices from the Love Generation,* Little, Brown, 1968; (editor) *The Uses of the Present,* McGraw, 1969; *The Passion of Israel,* Little, Brown, 1970; *A Dream of Dracula: In Search of the Living Dead,* Little, Brown, 1972; *The Annotated Dracula,* C. N. Potter, 1974; *Monsters,* Straight Arrow, 1974; *The Annotated Frankenstein,* C. N. Potter, 1976; *Wolf's Complete Book of Terror,* C. N. Potter, 1979; *Bluebeard: The Life and Crimes of Gilles de Rais,* C. N. Potter, 1980. Contributor of poems and short fiction magazines.

SIDELIGHTS: Leonard Wolf writes: "My interests seem to be polymorphous. They are saved from being perverse by my admiration of the power of history on the present. I admire Hellenism with a Hebrew passion."

Besides Hellenism, another "Hebrew passion" of Wolf's concerns ghosts, vampires, monsters, and various other horrible creatures and "things that go bump in the night." *Wolf's Complete Book of Terror* is described by the *Washington Post Book World*'s Jack Sullivan as not only "the largest anthology of scary stories to appear in over 30 years," but also as "one of the most resolutely gruesome, unpleasant collections ever published. [The author] . . . has chosen exceptionally violent and obsessive stories even from writers normally associated with a more civilized, understated aesthetic. . . . [He] reprints a number of stories which reflect the current fetish for pornographic violence and cruelty." Nevertheless, the critic concludes, "there are enough well-written tales in this huge book . . . to hook the uninitiated reader onto this strangely seductive literature."

Nick B. Williams of the *Los Angeles Times Book Review* agrees that a little bit of grossness goes a long way ("for horror, like love, in overdoses blows the fuses"), but promises that "you name it and you'll find it in this [book]—monsters, demons, blood lust, the living dead, snakes, worms, werewolves, ambulant skeletons, and the demented. . . . For those who will risk damage to fathom the arcane, know that these tales burst open the gates to the unbearable."

BIOGRAPHICAL/CRITICAL SOURCES: Atlantic, January, 1973; *Time,* January 15, 1973; *Los Angeles Times Book Review,* July 1, 1979; *New York Times Book Review,* July 22, 1979; *Washington Post Book World,* July 29, 1979.

*   *   *

WOLFE, Bernard 1915-

PERSONAL: Born August 28, 1915, in New Haven, Conn.; son of Robert and Ida (Gordon) Wolfe. *Education:* Yale University, B.A., 1935, graduate study, 1935-36. *Address:* c/o Eliot Gordon Co., 8888 Olympic Blvd., Beverly Hills, Calif. *Agent:* Harold Matson Co., Inc., 22 East 40th St., New York, N.Y. 10016.

CAREER: Free-lance writer, primarily of novels and short stories; screenwriter, Universal-International Pictures, Tony Curtis Productions, and other film producers. *Member:* Phi Beta Kappa, Sigma Xi.

WRITINGS: Plastics: What Everyone Should Know, Bobbs-Merrill, 1945; (with Milton "Mezz" Mezzrow) *Really the Blues* (novel), Random House, 1946, reprinted, Anchor Books, 1972; (with Raymond Rosenthal) *Hypnotism Comes of Age: Its Progress from Mesmer to Psychoanalysis*, Bobbs-Merrill, 1948; *Limbo* (novel), Random House, 1952 (published in England as *Limbo 90*, Secker & Warburg, 1953); *The Late Risers, Their Masquerade* (novel), Random House, 1954; *In Deep* (novel), Knopf, 1957; *The Great Prince Died* (novel), Scribner, 1959, published as *Trotsky Dead*, Wollstonecraft, 1975; *The Magic of Their Singing* (novel), Scribner, 1961; *Come On Out, Daddy* (novel), Scribner, 1963; *Move Up, Dress Up, Drink Up, Burn Up* (short story collection), Doubleday, 1968; *Memoirs of a Not Altogether Shy Pornographer* (novel), Doubleday, 1972; *Logan's Gone* (novel), Nash Publishing, 1974; *Lies* (novel), Wollstonecraft, 1975; *Full Disclosure*, Wollstonecraft, 1975. Contributor of short stories and essays to *Nation, Pageant, Playboy, Temps Modernes, Esquire*, and other magazines.†

* * *

WOLFE, Louis 1905-

PERSONAL: Born June 29, 1905, in Bound Brook, N.J.; son of William (a merchant) and Charlotte (Kasnetz) Wolfe; married 1958; wife's name, Adele (a teacher). *Education:* Rutgers University, B.Litt.; graduate work at Columbia University, New York University, New School for Social Research, City College (now City College of the City University of New York), and Colorado University. *Home and office:* 160 East 89th St., New York, N.Y.

CAREER: Free-lance author. Teacher and radio broadcaster in New York City; professional storyteller at camps, recreation centers, and on the air; editor, Bureau of Curriculum Research, New York City Board of Education; editor, G. P. Putnam's Sons. *Member:* Authors Guild.

WRITINGS—Published by Putnam, except as indicated: *Clear the Track*, Lippincott, 1951; *Adventures on Horseback*, Dodd, 1952; *Indians Courageous*, Dodd, 1953; *Stories of Our American Past*, Globe, 1954; *Let's Go to a Planetarium*, 1958; *Let's Go to a City Hall*, 1958; *Let's Go to a Weather Station*, 1959.

Probing the Atmosphere, 1961; *Wonders of the Atmosphere*, 1962; *Let's Go to the Louisiana Purchase*, 1963; *The Deepest Hole in the World*, 1963; *Ifrikya*, 1964; *Let's Go with Paul Revere*, 1964; *Let's Go on the Klondike Gold Rush*, 1964; *Let's Go with Drake to Discover Oil*, 1966; *United States History: A Simplified Outline*, American R.O.M. Corp., 1967; *Journey of the Oceanauts: Across the Bottom of the Atlantic Ocean on Foot*, Norton, 1968.

Ships that Explore the Deep, 1971; *Aquaculture: Farming in Water*, 1972; *Disease Detectives*, F. Watts, 1979. Also author of radio scripts and of stories for comics. Contributor to *Reader's Digest, Woman's Home Companion, Coronet, Pageant, True, Children's Digest, Parade*, and other magazines.

WORK IN PROGRESS: Disaster Detectives, for Messner.

AVOCATIONAL INTERESTS: Golf, travel.

* * *

WOLTERS, Richard A. 1920-

PERSONAL: Born February 8, 1920, in Philadelphia, Pa.; married Olive Myers (a special education teacher), August 1, 1943; children: Roger Mansfield, Gretchen Olive. *Education:* Pennsylvania State University, B.A., 1942. *Home:* 12

Susquehanna Rd., Ossining, N.Y. 10562. *Office:* Studio 202, 119 Fifth Ave., New York, N.Y. 10003.

CAREER: Chemist in rocket and atomic research, 1942-47; free-lance photographer for magazines, including *Science Illustrated* and *Business Week* and free-lance writer. Former picture editor for *Sports Illustrated;* former illustrations editor, *Business Week*. Photography has been shown at one man show in New York. *Member:* Midtown Turf, Yachting and Pool Association (president, 1957-68), Westchester Retriever Club (president, 1962-67).

WRITINGS: Gun Dog, Dutton, 1961; (editor) *The World of Wood, Field and Stream*, Holt, 1962; *Family Dog*, Dutton, 1963; *Water Dog*, Dutton, 1964; (contributor) *American Trout Fishing*, Knopf, 1965; *Beau from Both Ends of His Leash*, Dutton, 1966; *Instant Dog*, Dutton, 1968; *Art and Technique of Soaring*, McGraw, 1971; *Living on Wheels*, Dutton, 1973; *Once upon a Thermal*, Crown, 1975; *City Dog*, Dutton, 1976; *Kid's Dog*, Doubleday, 1977; *The World of Silent Flight*, McGraw, 1979. Contributor to *Parade, True, Guns and Hunting, Argosy*, and numerous other magazines.

WORK IN PROGRESS: Born to Swim, juvenile fiction; a book on the history and sociology of the Labrador retriever, for Petersen Publishing.

BIOGRAPHICAL/CRITICAL SOURCES: True, July, 1961; *Sports Illustrated*, August, 1968; *Signature*, May, 1979; *Christian Science Monitor*, March 7, 1980.

* * *

WOOD, A(rthur) Skevington 1916-

PERSONAL: Born April 21, 1916, in Ashbourne, Derbyshire, England; son of William Arthur (a school headmaster) and May (Cooper) Wood; married Mary Fearnley, January 1, 1943. *Education:* Attended Wesley Theological College, Leeds, 1936-40; University of London, B.A., 1939; New College, Edinburgh, Ph.D., 1951. *Home:* Clift House, Calver, Sheffield 530 1XG, England.

CAREER: Methodist circuit minister, 1940-62; Movement for World Evangelization, West Croydon, Surrey, England, lecturer, 1962-70; Cliff College, Derbyshire, England, senior tutor in theology, 1970-77, principal, 1977—. Vice-president, National Young Life Campaign. *Member:* Royal Historical Society (fellow), British Christian Endeavour Union (president, 1959-60), Society for Ecclesiastical History (founder member), Church Historical Society, Wesley Historical Society (life member), Evangelical Alliance, Evangelization Society, Victory Tract Club.

WRITINGS: Thomas Haweis, 1734-1820, S.P.C.K., for Church Historical Society, 1957; *And with Fire: Messages on Revival*, Pickering & Inglis, 1958; *Luther's Principles of Biblical Interpretation*, Tyndale Press, 1960; *The Inextinguishable Blaze: Spiritual Renewal and Advance in the Eighteenth Century*, Eerdmans, 1960; *The Bible Is History*, Bible Testimony Fellowship, 1960; *Life by the Spirit*, Zondervan, 1963 (published in England as *Paul's Pentecost: Studies in the Life of the Spirit from Romans 8*, Paternoster Press, 1963); *Designed by Love: Short Studies in the Plan of Salvation*, Christian Endeavour Union, 1963; *Heralds of the Gospel: Message, Method and Motive in Preaching*, Marshall, Morgan & Scott, 1963, published as *The Art of Preaching: Message, Method, and Motive in Preaching*, Zondervan, 1964; *Prophecy in the Space Age: Studies in Prophetic Themes*, Zondervan, 1963; *William Grimshaw of Haworth*, Evangelical Library, 1963; *Evangelism: Its Theology and Practice*, Zondervan, 1966; *The Principles of Biblical Inter-*

pretation as Enunciated by Irenaeus, Origen, Augustine, Luther, and Calvin, Zondervan, 1967; *The Burning Heart: John Wesley, Evangelist,* Paternoster Press, 1967, Eerdmans, 1968; *Captive to the Word: Martin Luther, Doctor of Sacred Scripture,* Eerdmans, 1969; *Signs of the Times: Biblical Prophecy and Current Events,* Lakeland Paperbacks, 1970, Baker Book, 1971; *The Evangelical Understanding of the Gospel,* CEIM, 1974; *The Nature of Man,* Scripture Union, 1978; *For All Seasons: Sermons for the Christian Year,* Hodder & Stoughton, 1979; *What the Bible Teaches about God,* Kingsway, 1980.

Contributor: Tom Allan, editor, *Crusade in Scotland,* Pickering & Inglis, 1955; G. W. Kirby, editor, *Remember I Am Coming Soon: A Symposium on the Second Advent,* Victory Press, 1964; Stanley Banks, editor, *The Right Way: A Symposium of Teaching on the Way of Holiness,* Oliphants, 1964; A. H. Chapple, editor, *Sermons for Today,* Marshall, Morgan & Scott, 1968; Clark H. Pinnock, editor, *Grace Unlimited,* Bethany Fellowship, 1975. Contributor to *Baker's Dictionary of Theology, New Bible Dictionary, International Standard Bible Encyclopedia, Zondervan Pictorial Encyclopedia of the Bible, Baker's Dictionary of Christian Ethics, The Expositor's Bible Commentary, Christianity Today* and *The Hour.*

WORK IN PROGRESS: Research on the rise of Anglican evangelicalism in the London area and the expansion of Methodism after the death of Wesley.

BIOGRAPHICAL/CRITICAL SOURCES: Encounter, autumn, 1968.

*   *   *

WOOD, E(dward) Rudolf   1907-

PERSONAL: Born February 26, 1907, in Keighley, Yorkshire, England; son of John (a hairdresser) and Kate (Hartley) Wood; married Margaret Bellamy (a playwright), April 27, 1937; children: Margaret Helen, Caroline. *Education:* University of Manchester, B.A. *Politics:* Socialist. *Religion:* Agnostic. *Home:* White House, Much Birch, Hereford, Herefordshire, England.

CAREER: High School for Boys, Hereford, England, deputy headmaster, 1950-67. *Military service:* Royal Air Force, education officer, 1941-46; became flight lieutenant; received Czechoslovak Medal of Merit, first class. *Member:* British Theatre Association.

WRITINGS: (With Edward Loring Black) *First Year English,* Blackie & Son, 1961-63.

Editor: *Short Historical Plays by Modern Authors,* Macmillan, 1938; (and author of introduction and notes) *Seven Short Plays,* Heinemann, 1956; *Specimens of Contemporary Drama,* Heinemann, 1957; *Contemporary Short Stories,* Blackie & Son, 1958; (and author of introduction) *The Windmill Book of One Act Plays,* eleven books, Heinemann, 1960—.

General editor, "Hereford Plays" series, published by Heinemann, 1960—, thirty volumes, including: John Synge, *Riders to the Sea;* Robert Bolt, *A Man for All Seasons;* Arthur Miller, *The Crucible;* Bolt, *Vivat Vivat Regina,* 1974; J. B. Priestly, *Eden End,* 1974; Miller, *A View from the Bridge,* 1975; Priestly, *The Linden Tree,* 1976; David Storey, *The Changing Room,* 1977; Terence Rattigan, *The Browning Version,* 1980; Clifford Odets, *Golden Boy,* 1980; Rattigan, *Harlequinade,* 1980.

WORK IN PROGRESS: Plays, for Cambridge University Press.

WOOD, James Playsted   1905-
(Playsted Wood)

PERSONAL: Born December 11, 1905, in Brooklyn, N.Y.; son of William Thomas and Olive Padbury (Hicks) Wood; married Elizabeth Craig (teacher of French, Latin, and Greek), August 14, 1943. *Education:* Columbia University, A.B., 1927, M.A., 1933. *Religion:* Protestant. *Home:* 103 Atwater Rd., Springfield, Mass. 01107.

CAREER: Du Pont Manual Training High School, Louisville, Ky., teacher of English, 1930-37; Amherst College, Amherst, Mass., began as instructor, became assistant professor of English, 1937-46; Curtis Publishing Co., Philadelphia, Pa., assistant to director of research, 1946-62, managing editor, *Jack and Jill,* 1954-55, contributing editor, 1959-64; full-time writer, 1966—. Instructor, Southern Writers Workshop, University of Georgia, 1957-65. Contributing editor, Limited Editions Club, 1974-76. *Military service:* U.S. Army Air Forces, served in Office of Chief of Staff, General Marshall, in Pentagon, Washington, D.C., 1943-46; became major; received army commendation medal.

WRITINGS: The Presence of Everett Marsh, Bobbs-Merrill, 1937; *Magazines in the United States: Their Social and Economic Influence,* Ronald, 1949, 3rd edition, revised and enlarged, 1971; (with D. M. Hobart) *Selling Forces,* Ronald, 1952; *The Beckoning Hill,* Longmans, Green, 1954; *An Elephant in the Family,* Thomas Nelson, 1957; *Of Lasting Interest: The Story of the Reader's Digest,* Doubleday, 1958, revised edition, 1967; *The Story of Advertising,* Ronald, 1958.

Advertising and the Soul's Belly: Repetition and Memory in Advertising, University of Georgia Press, 1961; *The Queen's Most Honorable Pirate,* Harper, 1961; *The Elephant in the Barn,* Harper, 1961; *A Hound, a Bay Horse, and a Turtle-Dove: A Life of Thoreau for the Young Reader,* Pantheon, 1963; *Trust Thyself: A Life of Ralph Waldo Emerson for the Young Reader,* Pantheon, 1964; *The Life and Words of John F. Kennedy: A Thorough Narrative of the Late President's Life,* Doubleday, 1964; *The Man Who Hated Sherlock Holmes: A Life of Sir Arthur Conan Doyle,* Random House, 1965; *Very Wild Animal Stories,* Pantheon, 1965; *The Lantern Bearer: A Life of Robert Louis Stevenson,* Pantheon, 1965; *The Elephant-on Ice,* Seabury, 1965; *The Golden Swan,* Seabury, 1965; *The Snark Was a Boojum: A Life of Lewis Carroll,* Pantheon, 1966; *Washington, D.C.,* Seabury, 1966; *What's the Market?: The Story of Stock Exchanges,* Duell, Sloan & Pearce, 1966; *Sunnyside: A Life of Washington Irving,* Pantheon, 1967; *When I Was Jersey,* Pantheon, 1967; *Boston,* Seabury, 1967; *The Man With Two Countries,* Seabury, 1967; *Alaska: The Great Land,* Meredith Corp., 1967; *Spunkwater, Spunkwater: A Life of Mark Twain,* Pantheon, 1968; *Mr. Jonathan Edwards,* Seabury, 1968; *The Elephant Tells,* Reilly & Lee, 1968; *This Is Advertising,* Crown, 1968; *I Told You So!: A Life of H. G. Wells,* Pantheon, 1969; *The Mammoth Parade,* Pantheon, 1969; *Colonial Massachusetts,* Thomas Nelson, 1969.

The Unpardonable Sin: A Life of Nathaniel Hawthorne, Pantheon, 1970; *The People of Concord,* Seabury, 1970; *Scotland Yard,* Hawthorn, 1970; *The Admirable Cotton Mather,* Seabury, 1971; *The Curtis Magazines, 1883-1970,* Ronald, 1971; *This Little Pig: The Story of Marketing,* Thomas Nelson, 1971; *New England Academy: Wilbraham to Wilbraham & Monson,* R. L. Dothard Associates, 1971; *Poetry Is,* Houghton, 1972; *Emily Elizabeth Dickinson,* Thomas Nelson, 1972; *The Great Glut,* Thomas Nelson, 1973; *Kentucky Time,* Addison-Wesley, 1977; *Chase Scene,* Elsevier/Nelson, 1979.

Contributor of articles and verse to *Reader's Digest, Ladies' Home Journal, Georgia Review, Saturday Review, Book World, New England Quarterly,* and *American Scholar,* and contributor of hundreds of stories, articles, and poems to *Jack and Jill.* Editor, with Kenneth Roberts, of *One Hundred Years Ago: American Writing,* Funk, 1947-48.

SIDELIGHTS: James Playsted Wood wrote *CA:* "I learned to read from Horatio Alger, Jr. and Winston Churchill. An aged grandfather devoured an Alger book every day, and I puzzled over it after he had finished it. At night my father was reading Churchill's novels to him. I listened and during the day picked up *Richard Carvel* and hunted for the printed words and sentences I had heard. Even then I was aware of the authors behind the books and filled with wonder that a man could write a whole bookfull of words.

"In high school I edited the school paper and at fifteen was reporting the school news for the Holyoke (Mass.) *Transcript.* My first job after school was in the *Herald-Sun* Syndicate in New York which I left for the editorial library ('morgue') of Horace Greeley's *New York Tribune.* I seem always to have had to do with the printed word. It pursued me even into the army where at one point I edited an ordnance magazine, *Firepower,* and later was officer-in-charge of *War Times,* weekly newspaper of the War Department.

"An odd way to say it perhaps, but I write because I would not know how not to write. I have had various jobs, but they were always peripheral. I worked at them to eat but wrote to stay alive. Despite or because of its inescapable demand for intense concentration writing has long seemed to me central and become as natural as the movement of my legs when I walk or the rhythm of my pulse."

AVOCATIONAL INTERESTS: Collecting jade, growing hollies, and ice skating.

BIOGRAPHICAL/CRITICAL SOURCES: Book Week, June 25, 1967; *Book World,* March 17, 1968; *Young Readers Review,* October, 1969.

*   *   *

WOODBRIDGE, Hensley Charles 1923-

PERSONAL: Born February 6, 1923, in Champaign, Ill.; son of Dudley Warner (a professor) and Ruby Belle (Mendenhall) Woodbridge; married Annie Emma Smith (a teacher), August 28, 1953; children: Ruby Susan Jung. *Education:* College of William and Mary, A.B., 1943; Universidad Nacional Autonoma de Mexico, summer study, 1941, 1945; Harvard University, M.A., 1946; University of Illinois, Ph.D., 1950, M.S. in L.S., 1951. *Politics:* Democrat. *Home:* 1804 West Freeman, Carbondale, Ill. 62901. *Office:* Department of Foreign Languages, Southern Illinois University, Carbondale, Ill. 62901.

CAREER: Mexican correspondent for Worldover Press, 1945; University of Richmond, Richmond, Va., instructor in French and Spanish, 1946-47; Auburn University, Auburn, Ala., reference librarian, 1951-53; Murray State College (now Murray State University), Murray, Ky., librarian, 1953-65; Southern Illinois University at Carbondale, associate professor, 1965-71, professor of modern languages, 1971—, Latin American bibliographer, 1965-74. *Member:* Mediaeval Academy of America, Bibliographical Society of America, American Association of Teachers of Spanish and Portuguese, Modern Language Association of America, Immigration History Society, Instituto de Estudios Madrilenos, Kentucky Folklore Society, Kentucky Historical Society, Filson Club. *Awards, honors:* Lincoln Memorial University, D.A., 1976.

WRITINGS: (Compiler) *A List of the Catalan, Italian, Portuguese and Rumanian Periodicals in the Library of the University of Illinois,* Library of the University of Illinois, 1949; (with Paul Olson) *A Tentative Bibliography of Hispanic Linguistics,* Department of Spanish and Italian, University of Illinois, 1952; (editor and translator) F.H.A. von Humboldt, *Political Essay on the Kingdom of New Spain,* Book 1, University of Kentucky Library, 1957; (contributor) Harold B. Allen, *Minor Dialect Areas of the Upper Midwest,* University of Alabama Press, 1958; (contributor) *Jesse Stuart: A Bibliography,* Lincoln Memorial University Press, 1960; (with Hunter M. Hancock) *A Bibliography of the Striped Bass or Rockfish Roccus Saxatilis (Walbaum),* Sport Fishing Institute, 1964, revised edition (with William Massmann), 1967; (with Gerald M. Moser) *Ruben Dario y "El Cojo Ilustrado,"* Hispanic Institute, Columbia University, 1964; (compiler with John London and George H. Tweney) *Jack London: A Bibliography,* Talisman Press, 1966, 2nd edition, KTO Press, 1973; (compiler) *Jesse and Jane Stuart: A Bibliography,* Murray State University, 1969, 2nd edition, 1979; (compiler) *Ruben Dario: A Selective and Annotated Bibliography,* Scarecrow, 1975; (compiler) *Benito Perez Galdos: A Selective Bibliography,* Scarecrow, 1975; (with L. S. Thompson) *Printing in Colonial Spanish America,* Whitston Publishing, 1976; (compiler with wife, Annie Woodbridge) *Collected Short Stories of Mary Johnston,* Whitston Publishing, 1981.

Contributor of reviews, bibliographies, articles, and translations to some four dozen journals in the United States and to periodicals in Great Britain, India, Belgium, Spain, and Mexico. Editor, *Kentucky Library Association Bulletin,* 1959-60 and *Kentucky Folklore Record,* 1963-64; contributing editor, *American Book Collector,* 1965-73; associate editor, *Hispania,* 1967—; editor and publisher, *Jack London Newsletter,* 1967—; member of editorial board, *Modern Language Journal,* 1971-73.

WORK IN PROGRESS: Third edition of *Jesse and Jane Stuart: A Bibliography;* compiling *Clarin: An Annotated Bibliography.*

BIOGRAPHICAL/CRITICAL SOURCES: Times Literary Supplement, May 11, 1967; *Jack London Newsletter,* May, 1972.

*   *   *

WOODRESS, James (Leslie, Jr.) 1916-

PERSONAL: Born July 7, 1916, in Webster Groves, Mo.; son of James Leslie (electrical engineer) and Jessie (Smith) Woodress; married Roberta Wilson, September 28, 1940. *Education:* Amherst College, A.B., 1938; New York University, M.A., 1943; Duke University, Ph.D., 1950. *Politics:* Democrat. *Religion:* Protestant. *Home:* 824 Sycamore Lane, Davis, Calif. 95616. *Office:* Department of English, University of California, Davis, Calif. 95616.

CAREER: Radio Station KWK, St. Louis, Mo., assistant news editor, 1939-40; United Press International, New York, N.Y., rewrite man, 1941-43; Grinnell College, Grinnell, Iowa, instructor in English, 1949-50; Butler University, Indianapolis, Ind., 1950-58, began as assistant professor, became associate professor; California State University, Northridge, Los Angeles, 1958-66, began as associate professor, became professor of English, chairman of department, 1958-63, dean of School of Letters and Science, 1963-65; University of California, Davis, professor of English, 1966—. Fulbright lecturer in France, 1962-63 and Italy, 1965-66. Visiting professor, Sorbonne, University of Paris. *Military service:* U.S.

Army, Field Artillery, 1943-46; became lieutenant. *Member:* Modern Language Association of America, American Studies Association, National Council of Teachers of English, American Association of University Professors, Phi Beta Kappa. *Awards, honors:* Ford fellowship, 1952-53; Huntington Library summer grant, 1955; Guggenheim fellowship, 1957-58.

WRITINGS: Howells and Italy, Duke University Press, 1952, reprinted, Greenwood Press, 1969; *Booth Tarkington: Gentleman from Indiana,* Lippincott, 1955; *Dissertations in American Literature, 1891-1955,* Duke University Press, 1957, 3rd edition, 1967; *A Yankee's Odyssey: The Life of Joel Barlow,* Lippincott, 1958; *Willa Cather: Her Life and Art,* Pegasus, 1970; (editor) *Eight American Authors,* Norton, 1971, revised edition, 1972; *American Fiction: 1900-1950,* Gale, 1974. Also editor, *Essays Mostly on Periodical Publishing in America,* 1973. Editor, with Richard B. Morris, of the McGraw-Hill and E. P. Dutton series, "Voices from America's Past," 1962-63, revised edition, 1976; editor of *American Literary Scholarship: An Annual,* Duke University Press, 1965-69, 1975-77, 1979, and 1981. Contributor to professional journals. Advisory editor, *College English,* 1961-63, and *Resources for American Literary Study,* 1970—.

SIDELIGHTS: American Literature reviewer Terence Martin writes in his review of *Willa Cather: Her Life and Art* that James Woodress "portrays a writer whose religion was art, who valued struggle more than achievement, who dealt less effectively with immediate materials than with those which had haunted her for years. He places Willa Cather in a tradition of American romanticism coming from Emerson and Whitman."

BIOGRAPHICAL/CRITICAL SOURCES: American Literature, November, 1971.

*   *   *

WOODWARD, G(eorge) W(illiam) O(tway) 1924-

PERSONAL: Born January 28, 1924, in Belfast, Northern Ireland; son of Henry Greville (a stockbroker) and Alice Mary (Foster) Woodward; married Elizabeth Farnworth (a teacher), July 1, 1950; children: Helen, Catherine, Margaret. *Education:* Trinity College, Dublin, B.A., 1950, Ph.D., 1955. *Politics:* Floating voter. *Religion:* Church of Ireland. *Office:* Department of History, University of Canterbury, Christchurch 1, New Zealand.

CAREER: University of Nottingham, Nottingham, England, senior lecturer in history, 1952-66; University of Canterbury, Christchurch, New Zealand, professor of history, 1967—. *Military service:* Royal Air Force, 1943-46; flying officer. *Member:* College Historical Society (Trinity College branch).

WRITINGS: A Short History of 16th Century England, New American Library, 1963 (published in England as *Reformation and Resurgence, 1485-1603,* Blandford, 1963, published under same title, Humanities, 1968); *The Dissolution of the Monasteries,* Blandford, 1966, Walker, 1967; *Queen Elizabeth I: An Illustrated Biography,* Pitkin Pictorials, 1967, British Book Center, 1974; *Henry VIII: An Illustrated Biography,* Pitkin Pictorials, 1967, published as *King Henry VIII,* British Book Center, 1978; *Mary, Queen of Scots,* Pitkin Pictorials, 1971, British Book Center, 1978; *The Six Wives of Henry VIII,* Pitkin Pictorials, 1971, British Book Center, 1974; *Richard III,* Pitkin Pictorials, 1972, British Book Center, 1978. Contributor to history journals in Britain, Belgium, Germany, the Netherlands, and Switzerland.

WORK IN PROGRESS: An examination of the finances of the dissolution of the English monasteries.

*   *   *

WOODY, Regina Jones 1894-
(Nila Devi)

PERSONAL: Born January 4, 1894, in Boston, Mass.; daughter of Lewis Llewellyn and Regina (Lichtenstein) Jones; married McIver Woody, May 1, 1918 (died, 1970); children: McIver Wallace, Regina L., Emma McIver (Mrs. James M. Sowa). *Education:* Educated in Wellesley, Mass. *Politics:* Republican. *Religion:* Presbyterian. *Home:* 440 Westminster Ave., Elizabeth, N.J.

CAREER: Former professional dancer under stage name, Nila Devi; featured in Keith Orpheum vaudeville, 1913-17; also appeared as Danseuse Etoile, at Folies Bergere and Moulin Rouge, Paris, and at Winter Garden, Budapest. Teacher of juvenile writing, New York University, 1946-50. *Member:* American Library Association, Authors League, Society of Descendants of Colonial Clergy, Daughters of the American Revolution, Camellia Society. *Awards, honors:* Author Award, New Jersey Association of English Teachers, 1964.

WRITINGS: The Stars Came Down, Harcourt, 1945; *Starlight,* Morrow, 1946; *Boarding School,* Houghton, 1949; *Student Dancer,* Houghton, 1951; *Ballet in the Barn,* Ariel, 1952; *Almena's Dogs,* Ariel, 1954; *Young Dancer's Career Book,* Dutton, 1958; *Dancing for Joy,* Dutton, 1959; *A Time to Dance,* Chilton, 1963; *Wisdom to Know,* Funk, 1964; *TV Dancer,* Doubleday, 1967; *The Young Medics,* Messner, 1968; *One Day at a Time,* Westminster, 1968; *Dance to a Lonely Tune,* Westminster, 1970; *Second Sight for Tommy,* Westminster, 1972. Contributor of articles and short stories to magazines; contributor of a serial, "Schoolgirl Ballerina," to *American Girl.* Editor of "Young Dancer" section, *Dance,* 1951-61.

WORK IN PROGRESS: Teenage Dancers.

SIDELIGHTS: Regina Jones Woody wrote *CA:* "My autobiography, *Dancing for Joy,* is an account of my early career. I started out as a star in Paris at seventeen, danced in Budapest, and Algiers, came back to the USA and danced on Broadway. Later headlined the Keith and Orpheum circuits with Madame Eva Gauthier.

"Writing has always been a joy. It's hard work, it's lonely. What one believes is one's best work is often ignored or deprecated, while a casual piece receives undue acclaim. But one carries on and tries again. I sold my first piece at seven for one dollar to *Dumb Animals,* a small magazine. It was about my St. Bernard dog and my champagne-colored cat. My first book was a fairy story, *The Stars Came Down.* The second, *Starlight,* was the half-way true story of my own golden palomino. From there on everything that I experienced went into a book.

"Like everything in life one thing leads to another, and all that has gone before makes a background of ever deepening understanding of human beings which I hope seeps into every story as written. As long as one is working, trying and striving, happiness is within the reach of every human being, however small he is or how minute his contribution. I don't mean 'fun' happiness which makes whoopee Al Jolson fashion, or happiness in euphoria which is drug-induced, but the kind of happiness in which one is working to the best of one's ability in a field one deems well worth working in. It is an unsentimental kind of happiness and has nothing much to do with success, or money or fame. Instead, it is happiness which causes one to light a candle instead of cursing the dark. No one need to stand and wait. Light a match and count the ways you can help. There's always room for one more helping hand in every field of endeavor, be it the chorus of a Broadway show, your neighbor next door, or the emergency room at a nearby hospital.''

*   *   *

WORMINGTON, H(annah) M(arie) 1914-
(Hannah Marie Volk)

PERSONAL: Born September 5, 1914, in Denver, Colo.; daughter of Charles Watkins (a realtor) and Adrienne (Roucolle) Wormington; married George D. Volk (a petroleum geologist), September 6, 1940. *Education:* University of Denver, B.A., 1935; studied in France, England, and Spain, 1935; Radcliffe College, M.A., 1950, Ph.D., 1954. *Address:* 4600 East 17th Ave., Denver, Colo. 80020.

CAREER: Denver Museum of Natural History, Denver, Colo., staff archaeologist, 1935-37, curator of archaeology, 1937-68; University of Colorado Museum, Boulder, research associate in Paleo-Indian studies, beginning 1968. Assistant professor, University of Denver, 1947-49; visiting lecturer, University of Colorado, 1950-53; visiting professor, Arizona State University, 1968-69, and Colorado College, 1969-70; adjunct professor, Colorado College, 1972—; visiting professor, University of Minnesota, 1973. Has conducted field research in France, 1935, in the western United States, 1936-41, 1947, 1951-52, 1963, 1966-67, 1968, in Mexico, 1952, in Alberta, Canada, 1955, 1956, and in Alaska, 1965. Has attended international congresses.

MEMBER: American Anthropological Association (fellow), Society for American Archaeology (first vice-president, 1950-51, 1955-56; president, 1968-69), Society of Vertebrate Paleontology, American Association of Physical Anthropologists, Phi Beta Kappa. *Awards, honors:* Wenner-Gren research grant, 1969-70; Guggenheim fellowship, 1970-71.

WRITINGS: Ancient Man in North America, Denver Museum of Natural History, 1939, 5th edition, 1964; *Prehistoric Indians of the Southwest,* Denver Museum of Natural History, 1947; *Origins,* Instituto Panamericano de Geografía e Historia (Mexico), 1953; *A Reappraisal of the Fremont Culture with a Summary of the Archaeology of the Northern Periphery,* Denver Museum of Natural History, 1955; (with Robert H. Lister) *Archaeological Investigations on the Uncompahgre Plateau in West Central Colorado,* Denver Museum of Natural History, 1956; *Prehistoric Hunters and Gatherers,* U.S. National Park Service, 1960; (with Richard G. Forbis) *An Introduction to the Archaeology of Alberta, Canada,* Denver Museum of Natural History, 1965; (contributor) Malcolm Rogers, editor, *Ancient Hungers of the Far West,* Cropley Press, 1966; (senior editor) *Pleistocene Studies in Southern Nevada,* Nevada State Museum, 1967; *Ancient Man in the Americas,* Seminar Press, 1974; (with Arminta Neal) *The Story of Pueblo Pottery,* 4th edition (Wormington was not associated with earlier editions), Denver Museum of Natural History, 1974.

Contributor to symposia, proceedings, and memorial volumes, and to *Handbook of North American Indians.* Contributor to *American Antiquity, American Scientists,* and *Arctic Anthropology.* Editor of museum series in *American Anthropologist.*

WORK IN PROGRESS: Prehistoric Latin America; The Frazier Agate Basin Site: Weld County, Colo., with Frank Frazier.

SIDELIGHTS: Hannah Marie Wormington has traveled in the Soviet Union, Latin America, Europe, Africa, and Japan.†

*   *   *

WRIGHT, D(onald) I(an) 1934-

PERSONAL: Born October 22, 1934, in Aldgate, South Australia; son of Cyril Noel (a farmer) and Florence (Lemaitre) Wright; married Janice Gambling (a librarian), January 9, 1960; children: David Arthur, Alan Michael, Ian Mark. *Education:* University of Adelaide, B.A., 1956; Australian National University, Ph.D., 1968. *Politics:* Agnostic. *Religion:* Atheist. *Home:* 9 Murrakin St., Kahibah, New South Wales, 2290 Australia. *Office:* Department of History, University of Newcastle, Newcastle, New South Wales, 2308 Australia.

CAREER: University of Newcastle, Newcastle, New South Wales, Australia, lecturer, 1968-70, senior lecturer in history, 1970—. *Military service:* Australian Army, 1953. *Member:* Australian Historical Association, South Asian Studies Association of Australia and New Zealand, Asian Studies Association (United States), Specific Learning Difficulties Association of New South Wales (president).

WRITINGS: Shadow of Dispute: Aspects of Commonwealth-State Relations, 1901-1910, Australian National University Press, 1970; (editor and translator) *The French Revolution: Introductory Documents* Queensland University Press, 1974; (with B. W. Hodgins and W. Heick) *Federalism in Canada and Australia: The Early Years,* Australian National University Press, 1978; (co-author) *The River Murray in Transport and Trade,* Royal Australian Historical Society, 1980. Contributor to Australian history journals, including *Journal of the Royal Australian Historical Society, South Australiana, Queensland Heritage, Historical Studies of Australia and New Zealand, Tasmanian Historical Research Association Journal,* and *Australian National University Historical Journal.*

WORK IN PROGRESS: A group of articles on late eighteenth-century missionary activity in southern India; a book on the history of the Methodist Central Mission in Sydney, Australia.

*   *   *

WRIGHT, David (John Murray) 1920-

PERSONAL: Born February 23, 1920, in Johannesburg, South Africa; son of Gordon Alfred (a stockbroker) and Jean (Murray) Wright; married Phillipa Reid (an actress), October 6, 1951. *Education:* Oriel College, Oxford, B.A., 1942. *Religion:* Church of England. *Agent:* A.D. Peters, 10 Buckingham St., Adelphi, London WC2N 6BU, England.

CAREER: Sunday Times, London, England, member of staff, 1942-47; free-lance writer, 1947—. Gregory Fellow in Poetry, University of Leeds, 1965-67. *Member:* Royal Society of Literature (fellow, 1967), Caves de France, Mandrake Club. *Awards, honors:* Atlantic Award for Literature, 1950; third Guinness poetry award, 1958, for "A Thanksgiving"; second Guinness poetry award, 1960, for "Adam at Evening."

WRITINGS: Poems, Editions Poetry, 1947; (with John Heath-Stubbs) *The Forsaken Garden,* Lehmann, 1950; (with Heath-Stubbs) *The Faber Book of 20th Century Verse,* Faber, 1953, 2nd revised edition, 1965; *Moral Stories,* Verschoyle, 1954; (translator) *Beowulf,* Penguin, 1957; *Monologue of a Deaf Man* (poems), Deutsch, 1958.

Roy Campbell (biography), published for the British Council by Longmans, Green, 1961; (translator into prose) Geoffrey Chaucer, *The Canterbury Tales,* Barrie & Rockliff, 1964, Random House, 1965; *The Mid-Century: English Poetry, 1940-1960,* Penguin, 1964; *Adam at Evening* (poems), Hodder & Stoughton, 1965; (with Patrick Swift) *Algarve,* Barrie & Rockliff, 1965, International Publications Service, 1965, 2nd edition, Barrie & Jenkins, 1971; (compiler and author of introduction) *Longer Contemporary Poems,* Penguin, 1966; (with Swift) *Minho and North Portugal: A Portrait and a Guide,* Barrie & Rockliff, 1968; *Nerve Ends* (poems), Hodder & Stoughton, 1969; *Deafness: A Personal Account,* Allen Lane, 1969, published as *Deafness,* Stein & Day, 1970; (with Swift) *Lisbon: A Portrait and a Guide,* Barrie & Jenkins, 1971, Scribner, 1972; *A View of the North* (poems), Carcanet Press, 1976; *A South African Album,* (poems), David Philip, 1976; *To the Gods the Shades: New and Collected Poems,* Carcanet Press, 1976; *Selected Poems,* Ad Donker (Johannesburg), 1980; *Metrical Observations* (poems), Carcanet Press, 1980.

Editor: *South African Stories,* Faber, 1960; (and author of introduction and commentary) *Seven Victorian Poets,* Heinemann, 1964, Barnes & Noble, 1966; (and author of introduction) *The Penguin Book of English Romantic Verse,* Penguin, 1968; Thomas De Quincey, *Recollections of the Lakes and the Lake Poets,* Penguin, 1970; Edward Trelawny, *Records of Shelley, Bryon, and the Author,* Penguin, 1973; *Penguin Book of Everyday Verse,* Allen Lane, 1976; Thomas Hardy, *Under the Greenwood Tree,* Penguin, 1978; Hardy, *Selected Poems,* Penguin, 1978; Edward Thomas, *Selected Poems and Prose,* Penguin, 1981.

Contributor to numerous periodicals including *Aquarius, Bloody Horse, Encounter, Times Literary Supplement, Time and Time, Listener, New Yorker, Paris Review,* and *Hudson Review.* Co-editor, *Nimbus,* 1956-57 and *X* (quarterly review), 1959-62.

SIDELIGHTS: David Wright wrote *CA:* "I am a South African poet who lives in England; or to put it in another way, an English poet who was born in South Africa." *Avocational interests:* South African history (pursued on travels in Africa).

BIOGRAPHICAL/CRITICAL SOURCES: Poetry, June, 1967; *London Magazine,* October, 1969; *Book World,* March 8, 1970; *Times Literary Supplement,* February 25, 1977, April 4, 1980.

*   *   *

WRIGHT, Howard Wilson 1915-

PERSONAL: Born September 30, 1915, in Glen Olden, Pa.; son of Milton Stanley (employed in railroad operation) and Mabel (Farra) Wright; married Marian Jane Lybbert, April 9, 1941; children: Craig M., Constance M., Brian E. *Education:* Temple University, B.S.C., 1937; University of Iowa, M.A., 1940, Ph.D., 1947. *Home:* 7109 Eversfield Dr., Hyattsville, Md. *Office:* Cost Accounting Principles Research Institute, 7100 Baltimore Ave., Suite 303, College Park, Md.

CAREER: Arthur Andersen & Co. (public accountants), New York, N.Y., staff accountant, 1937-38; University of Iowa, Iowa City, instructor in accounting, 1938-39, 1940-41, 1946; University of Maryland, College Park, associate pro-

fessor, 1946-50, professor of accounting, 1952-76, professor emeritus, 1976—; Cost Accounting Principles Research Institute, College Park, director, 1975—. Assistant to controller, Economic Cooperation Administration, Washington, D.C., 1950-51 and Department of Defense, Washington, D.C., 1951-52. Consultant to Economic Cooperation Administration, Office of Secretary of Defense, Army Audit Agency, Auditor-General of U.S. Air Force, Department of Health, Education, and Welfare, Internal Revenue Service, Department of Justice, and various business corporations. *Military service:* U.S. Army, Field Artillery, 1942-46; became captain. *Member:* American Institute of Certified Public Accountants, American Accounting Association, Financial Executives Institute (associate member).

WRITINGS: (With E. L. Kohler) *Accounting in the Federal Government,* Prentice-Hall, 1956; *Accounting for Defense Contracts,* Prentice-Hall, 1962; *Accounting for Government Contracts,* Federal Publications, Inc., 1979. Contributor to professional journals.

*   *   *

WRIGHTSON, Patricia 1921-

PERSONAL: Born June 19, 1921, in Lismore, New South Wales, Australia; daughter of Charles Radcliff and Alice (Dyer) Furlonger; married, 1943 (divorced, 1953); children: Jennifer Mary (Mrs. Donald Ireland), Peter Radcliff. *Education:* Educated in Australia. *Address:* P.O. Box 91, Maclean 2463, New South Wales, Australia.

CAREER: Hospital administrator; *School Magazine,* Sydney, New South Wales, Australia, editor, 1970-75. Writer. *Member:* Australian Society of Authors, Authors Guild of America. *Awards, honors:* Book of the Year Award from Children's Book Council of Australia, 1956, for *The Crooked Snake;* Notable Books of the Year Award from American Library Association, 1963, for *The Feather Star;* Spring Award from *Book World,* 1968, and Hans Christian Andersen Honors List award, 1970, both for *A Racecourse for Andy;* Book of the Year Award from Children's Book Council of Australia, 1974, for *The Nargun and the Stars,* and 1978, for *The Ice Is Coming.*

WRITINGS: The Crooked Snake, Angus & Robertson, 1955, reprinted, Hutchinson, 1972; *The Bunyip Hole,* Angus & Robertson, 1957, reprinted, Hutchinson, 1973; *The Rocks of Honey,* Angus & Robertson, 1960, reprinted, Penguin, 1977; *The Feather Star,* Harcourt, 1962; *Down to Earth,* Harcourt, 1965; *A Racecourse for Andy,* Harcourt, 1968 (published in England as *I Own the Racecourse,* Hutchinson, 1968); *An Older Kind of Magic,* Harcourt, 1972; (editor) *Beneath the Sun: An Australian Collection for Children,* Collins, 1972; *The Nargun and the Stars,* Hutchinson, 1973, Atheneum, 1974; *The Ice Is Coming,* Atheneum, 1977; (editor) *Emu Stew: A Collection of Stories and Poems for Children,* Kestrel, 1977; *The Dark Bright Water,* Atheneum, 1979.

WORK IN PROGRESS: Behind the Wind, for Hutchinson.

BIOGRAPHICAL/CRITICAL SOURCES: School Librarian, March, 1969; *Newsletter,* May, 1970; H. M. Saxby, *A History of Australian Children's Literature,* Volume II, Wentworth Books (Sydney), 1971; John Rowe Townsend, *A Sense of Story,* Lippincott, 1971; *New Statesman,* November 9, 1973; *Best Sellers,* December, 1977; *New York Times Book Review,* January 29, 1978.

Y

YAMAUCHI, Edwin M(asao) 1937-

PERSONAL: Surname is pronounced Ya-ma-*u*-chi; born February 1, 1937, in Hilo, Hawaii; son of Shokyo and Haruko (Owan) Yamauchi; married Kimie Honda (a secretary), August 31, 1962; children: Brian, Gail. *Education:* Attended Columbia Bible College, 1955-56, and University of Hawaii, 1957-58; Shelton College, B.A., 1960; Harvard University, additional study, 1962; Brandeis University, M.A., 1962, Ph.D., 1964. *Politics:* Independent. *Religion:* Evangelical. *Home:* 807 Erin Dr., Oxford, Ohio 45056. *Office:* Department of History, Miami University, Oxford, Ohio 45056.

CAREER: Shelton College, Ringwood (now in Cape May), N.J., instructor in Greek, 1960-61; Rutgers University, New Brunswick, N.J., assistant professor of history, 1964-69; Miami University, Oxford, Ohio, associate professor, 1969-73, professor of history, 1973—, director of graduate studies, 1978—. Has participated in archaeological excavations in Jerusalem and Tel Anafa, Israel.

MEMBER: American Oriental Society, American Schools of Oriental Research, American Scientific Affiliation (fellow), Archaeological Institute of America (president, Oxford chapter, 1973-74), Association of Ancient Historians, Evangelical Theological Society (chairman, Eastern section, 1965-66), Society of Biblical Literature, Conference on Faith and History (president, 1974-76), Near East Archaeological Society (member of board of directors, 1973—; vice-president, 1978-79), Society of Mithraic Studies, Israel Exploration Society. *Awards, honors:* National Endowment for the Humanities fellowship, 1968; American Institute of Holy Land Studies research fellowship, 1968; American Philosophical Society grant for research in England, 1970; Institute for Advanced Christian Studies fellowship, 1974-75.

WRITINGS: Composition and Corroboration in Classical and Biblical Studies, Presbyterian & Reformed, 1966; *Greece and Babylon: Early Contacts between the Aegean and the Near East,* Baker Book, 1967; *Mandaic Incantation Texts,* American Oriental Society, 1967; *Gnostic Ethics and Mandaean Origins,* Harvard University Press, 1970; *The Stones and the Scriptures,* Lippincott, 1972, revised edition, Inter-Varsity Press, 1973; *Pre-Christian Gnosticism,* Eerdmans, 1973; (with D. J. Wiseman) *Archaeology and the Bible,* Zondervan, 1979; *World of the First Christian,* Eerdmans, 1979; *The Archaeology of New Testament Cities in Western Asia Minor,* Baker Book, 1980.

Contributor of chapters to books. Contributor to dictionaries and encyclopedias, including *Biblical World: A Dictionary of Biblical Archaeology, Wycliffe Bible Encyclopedia, New Illustrated Encyclopaedia of the Bible, Pictorial Bible Encyclopedia, Dictionary of the Christian Church, Dictionary of Christian Ethics, New Perspectives on the Old Testament,* and *Dictionary of Biblical Archaeology,* and to festschrifts and journals. Editor-at-large, *Christianity Today,* 1972-80; consulting editor in history, *Journal of the American Scientific Affiliation.*

*　　*　　*

YATES, A(lan) G(eoffrey) 1923-
(Carter Brown, Alan Yates)

PERSONAL: Born August 1, 1923, in London, England; son of Henry Thomas and Linda (Willingale) Yates; married Denise Sinclair Mackellar; children: Priscilla, Jeremy, Andrew, Christopher. *Education:* Attended public schools in Essex, England. *Agent:* Scott Meredith Literary Agency, 845 Third Ave., New York, N.Y. 10022.

CAREER: Gaumont-British Films, London, England, sound recordist, 1946-48; salesman in Sydney, Australia, 1948-51; Qantas Empire Airways, Sydney, editor of public relations section, 1951-53; writer, beginning 1953. *Military service:* Royal Navy, 1942-46; became lieutenant. *Member:* Authors Guild, Authors League of America.

WRITINGS—All under pseudonym Carter Brown, except as indicated; published by Horwitz (Sydney, Australia), many published in United States by New American Library: *Venus Unarmed,* 1953; *My Mermaid Murmurs Murder,* 1953; *The Frame Is Beautiful,* 1953; *The Fraulein Is Feline,* 1953; *Shady Lady,* 1954; *Trouble Is a Dame,* 1954; *Homicide Hoyden,* 1954; *Murder—Paris Fashion,* 1954; *Nemesis Wore Nylons,* 1954; *Maid for Murder,* 1954; *A Morgue Amour,* 1954; *The Killer Is Kissable,* 1954; *Curtains for a Chorine,* 1955; *Shamus, Your Slip Is Showing,* 1955; *Honey, Here's Your Hearse,* 1955; *The Two-timing Blonde,* 1955; *Sob-Sister Cries Murder,* 1955; *Curves for the Coroner,* 1955; *Miss Called Murder,* 1955; *Swan Song for a Siren,* 1955; *Bullet for My Baby,* 1955; *Kiss and Kill,* 1955; *The Wench Is Wicked,* 1955; *Lead Astray,* 1955; *The Hoodlum Is a Honey,* 1955; *Murder by Misdemeanor,* 1955; *Lipstick Larceny,* 1955.

No Halo for Hedy, 1956; *Strictly for Felony,* 1956; *Delilah Was Deadly,* 1956; *The Lady Has No Convictions,* 1956;

Baby, You're Guilt-edged, 1956; *No Harp for My Angel,* 1956; *Bid the Babe By-By,* 1956; *Meet Murder,* 1956; *Caress before Killing,* 1957; *Sweetheart, This Is Homicide,* 1957; *Model of No Virtue,* 1957; *Donna Died Laughing,* 1957; *Madame, You're Mayhem,* 1957; *Sinner, You Slay Me,* 1957; *Wreath for a Redhead,* 1957; *Eve, It's Extortion,* 1957; *Bella Donna Was Poison,* 1957; *Chorine Makes a Killing,* 1957; (under name A. G. Yates) *The Cold Dark Hours,* 1958; *Ice-Cold in Ermine,* 1958; *No Body She Knows,* 1958; *No Future Fair Lady,* 1958; *Widow Bewitched,* 1958; *High Fashion in Homicide,* 1958; *The Body,* 1958; *The Blonde* (also see below), 1958; *The Corpse,* 1958; *The Lover,* 1959; *The Mistress,* 1959; *The Victim,* 1959; *The Loving and the Dead,* 1959; *Walk Softly Witch,* 1959; *The Passionate,* 1959; *None but the Lethal Heart,* 1959; *The Wanton,* 1959; *Suddenly by Violence,* 1959; *The Dame,* 1959; *Terror Comes Creeping,* 1959.

The Desired, 1960; *The Bombshell,* 1960; *The Wayward Wahine,* 1960; *Graves, I Dig,* 1960; *Tomorrow Is Murder,* 1960; *The Temptress,* 1960; *The Brazen,* 1960; *The Dream Is Deadly,* 1960; *Lament for a Lousy Lover,* 1960; *The Savage Salome,* 1961; *The Million Dollar Babe,* 1961; *The Ever-loving Blues,* 1961; *The Unorthodox Corpse,* 1961; *The Myopic Mermaid,* 1961; *The Stripper,* 1961; *The Tigress,* 1961; *The Exotic,* 1961; *The Sad-eyed Seductress,* 1961; *Zelda,* 1961; *Angel,* 1962; *Murder Wears a Mantilla,* 1962; *Ice-Cold Nude,* 1962; *Hellcat,* 1962; *Murder in the Keyclub,* 1962; *The Lady Is Transparent,* 1962; *The Hong Kong Caper,* 1962; *The Dumdum Murder,* 1962; *The Gilt-edged Cage,* 1962; *Lover Don't Come Back,* 1962; *A Murderer among Us,* 1962; *Blonde on the Rocks,* 1963; *Girl in a Shroud* (also see below), 1963; *The Girl Who Was Possessed,* 1963; *The Jade-eyed Jungle,* 1963; *Lady Is Available,* 1963; *Nymph to the Slaughter* (also see below), 1963; *The Passionate Pagan,* 1963; *The White Bikini,* 1963; *Charlie Sent Me!,* 1963; *The Scarlet Flush,* 1963; *The Dance of Death,* 1964; *The Never-Was Girl,* 1964; *The Silken Nightmare,* 1964; *The Velvet Vixen,* 1964; *The Wind-up Doll,* 1964; *The Bump and Grind Murders,* 1964; *Who Killed Dr. Sex?,* 1964; *Catch Me a Phoenix!* (also see below), 1965; *A Corpse for Christmas,* 1965; *Murder Is a Package Deal,* 1965; *No Blonde Is an Island,* 1965; *Nude—with a View,* 1965; *The Girl from Outer Space,* 1965; *The Sometime Wife,* 1965; *The Hammer of Thor,* 1965; *Blonde on a Broomstick,* 1966; *So What Killed the Vampire?,* 1966; *Play Now . . . Kill Later,* 1966; *Until Temptation Do Us Part,* 1967; *House of Sorcery,* 1967; *The Mini-Murders,* 1968.

The Clown, 1972; *Negative in Blue,* 1974; *The Pipes Are Calling,* 1976; *The Coven* [and] *The Creative Murders,* 1978; *Sex Clinic* [and] *W.H.O.R.E.,* 1978; *Catch Me a Phoenix* [and] *Nymph to the Slaughter,* 1979; *The Asceptic Murders* [and] *Night Wheeler,* 1979; *The Blonde* [and] *Girl in a Shroud,* 1979. Also author of *Chinese Donovan* and *The Savage Sisters.*

Published by New English Library, except as indicated: *Target for Their Dark Desire,* 1968; *The Plush-lined Coffin,* 1968; *The Super Spy,* 1969; *The Witches,* 1969; *The Black Lace Hangover,* 1969; (under name Alan Yates) *Catalan,* Hodder & Stoughton, 1975; (under name Alan Yates) *Coriolanus, the Chariot,* Ace Books, 1978.

Published by Belmont-Tower: *Busted Wheeler,* 1979; *Donovan's Delight,* 1979; *See It Again, Sam,* 1979; *The Spanking Girls,* 1979; *The Strawberry Blonde Jungle,* 1979; *The Rip-off,* 1979; *Model for Murder,* 1980; *The Phantom Lady,* 1980.

SIDELIGHTS: Several of Alan Yates' books have been pub-

lished in as many as twelve languages and twenty countries. *The Body* and *Curtains for Chorine* have been sold to French film companies. The "Carter Brown Mystery Theater," an Australian radio series that ran from 1956 to 1958, was devoted to Yates' works. Yates told *CA* that he "won the 'thirstiest' award, an annual award for the hardest drinking protagonist in the year's crop of mysteries," in Paris, France, for a translation of one of his books, *A Palir La Nuit,* published by Gallimard.

AVOCATIONAL INTERESTS: Tennis and car racing.†

*　　*　　*

YOST, Charles W(oodruff) 1907-

PERSONAL: Born November 6, 1907, in Watertown, N.Y.; son of Nicholas Doxtater and Gertrude (Cooper) Yost; married Irena Oldakowska, September 8, 1934; children: Nicholas Churchill, Casimir Anthony, Felicity. *Education:* Princeton University, A.B., 1928; Ecole des Hautes Etudes Internationales, University of Paris, graduate study, 1928-29. *Politics:* Democrat. *Religion:* Presbyterian. *Home:* 2801 Massachusetts Ave. N.W., Washington, D.C. 20007. *Office:* Aspen Institute, 2010 Massachusetts Ave. N.W., Washington, D.C. 20036.

CAREER: U.S. Department of State, Washington, D.C., foreign service officer, 1930-33, 1935-71, serving as deputy U.S. representative to United Nations, 1961-66, chief U.S. representative to United Nations, 1969-71, and counselor to United Nations Association, 1971; president of National Committee on U.S.-China Relations, United Nations Plaza, New York, N.Y., 1972-75; Aspen Institute, Washington, D.C., special advisor, 1976—. Principal posts also include vice-consul in Alexandria, Egypt, 1931-32, and Warsaw, Poland, 1932-33; secretary-general of U.S. delegation to Potsdam Conference, 1945; diplomatic posts in Thailand, 1945-46, Vienna, Austria, 1948-49, and Athens, Greece, 1950-53; deputy U.S. high commissioner for Austria, 1953-54; ambassador to Laos, 1954-56; minister, U.S. Embassy, Paris, France, 1956-57; ambassador to Syria, 1957-58, and Morocco, 1958-61. Distinguished Lecturer, School of International Affairs, Columbia University, 1971-73. *Member:* Council on Foreign Relations (senior fellow, 1966-69), American Philosophical Society, American Association for the Advancement of Science. *Awards, honors:* Rockefeller Public Service Award, 1964; LL.D. from St. Lawrence University, Princeton University, Hamilton College, and University of Louisville.

WRITINGS: The Age of Triumph and Frustration: Modern Dialogues, Speller, 1964; *The Insecurity of Nations: International Relations in the Twentieth Century,* published for the Council on Foreign Relations by Praeger, 1968; *The Pursuit of World Order* (inaugural lecturer of World Order Research Institute), Villanova University Press, 1969; *The Conduct and Misconduct of Foreign Affairs,* Random House, 1972; *History and Memory,* Norton, 1980.

SIDELIGHTS: Charles W. Yost told *CA:* "My latest book, *History and Memory,* distills my observations and conclusions about the checkered history of the half century of my adult life, illustrated by personal reminiscences from my diplomatic experience around the world."

Harry Schwartz of the *New York Times Book Review* calls *History and Memory* "an interesting alternative to the conventional autobiographies and memoirs of his diplomatic predecessors." According to Schwartz, "*History and Memory* is only about 10 percent autobiography, and the apparent function of that part is to lend authority and credibility to the remainder of the volume, which is nothing less than an attempt to sketch the troubled history of this century, to spotlight the causes of the world's chief current discontents and dangers, and to outline, at least in part, what the world, and particularly the United States, should do to avert any of the numerous catastrophes that now threaten humanity.''

BIOGRAPHICAL/CRITICAL SOURCES: New York Times, February 9, 1968; *New York Review of Books,* September 12, 1968; *Times Literary Supplement,* June 12, 1969; *New York Times Book Review,* September 14, 1980.

* * *

YOUNG, Kenneth 1916-

PERSONAL: Born November 27, 1916, in Middlestown, Yorkshire, England; son of Robert William (an ironfounder) and Alice Jane (Ramsden) Young; married Phyllis Dicker, May 2, 1952; children: Milena, Julian, Christian, Phyllida, Quentin. *Education:* University of Leeds, B.A. (first class honors). *Politics:* Conservative. *Religion:* Church of England. *Home:* The Little House, Oxenden St., Herne Bay, Kent, England.

CAREER: British Broadcasting Corp., London, England, sub-editor, 1948-49; *Daily Mirror,* London, sub-editor, 1949-50; *Daily Telegraph,* London, book critic and leader writer, 1951-60; *Yorkshire Post,* Leeds, England, editor-in-chief, 1961-65; Beaverbrook Newspapers Ltd., London, political and literary adviser, 1965—. Governor, Welbeck College. *Member:* Royal Society of Literature (fellow). *Military service:* Intelligence Corps, 1940-45; served in Algeria, Italy, and Greece; became major. Second secretary, British Foreign Office, 1945-48.

WRITINGS: D. H. Lawrence, Longmans, Green, 1952, revised edition, 1960; *John Dryden: A Critical Biography,* Sylvan Press, 1954, Russell, 1969; *Ford Madox Ford,* Longmans, Green, 1956, revised edition, 1970; (editor) *The Bed Post: A Miscellany of the Yorkshire Post,* Macdonald & Co., 1962; *Arthur James Balfour: The Happy Life of the Politician, Prime Minister, Statesman, and Philosopher, 1848-1930,* G. Bell, 1963; *The Press and the Universities* (lecture), University of Hull, 1964; (editor) *The Second Bed Post: A Miscellany of the Yorkshire Post,* Macdonald & Co., 1964; *Churchill and Beaverbrook: A Study in Friendship and Politics,* Eyre & Spottiswoode, 1966, James Heineman, 1967; *Rhodesia and Independence: A Study in British Colonial Policy,* James Heineman, 1967, new edition, Dent, 1969; *Music's Great Days in the Spas and Watering-Places,* Macmillan, 1968; *Compton Mackenzie,* Longmans, Green, 1968; *The Greek Passion: A Study in People and Politics,* Dent, 1969; *Sir Alec Douglas-Home,* Dent, 1970, Fairleigh Dickinson University Press, 1971; *Chapel,* Eyre Methuen, 1972; (editor) *The Journals of Sir Robert Bruce Lockhart,* Macmillan, 1973; *Stanley Baldwin,* Weidenfeld & Nicolson, 1976. Contributor of articles to *Spectator, Encounter,* and other periodicals. Contributor to British Broadcasting Corp. and Independent Television programs.

WORK IN PROGRESS: A Neighbourhood of Writers: Stephen Crane, Henry James, Ford Madox Ford, and H. G. Wells.

AVOCATIONAL INTERESTS: Politics and music.

BIOGRAPHICAL/CRITICAL SOURCES: Times Literary Supplement, March 9, 1967; *New Statesman,* March 31, 1967; *Books and Bookmen,* May, 1967, October, 1969; *Observer Review,* January 19, 1969; *Spectator,* September 27, 1969; *Punch,* October 7, 1970.

* * *

YOUNG, Paul Thomas 1892-1978

PERSONAL: Born May 26, 1892, in Los Angeles, Calif.; died June 17, 1978; son of William Stewart and Cynthia Adele (Nichols) Young; married Josephine Kennedy, 1929 (died, 1962); married Marvyle Davis, October 29, 1963 (died March 2, 1978); children: (first marriage) Rosemary Adele (Mrs. L. L. Mitchell), Stewart Adams. *Education:* Occidental College, A.B., 1914; Princeton University, A.M., 1915; Cornell University, Ph.D., 1918. *Religion:* Congregationalist. *Home:* 573 South Boyle Ave., Los Angeles, Calif. 90033. *Office:* Department of Psychology, University of Illinois, Urbana, Ill. 61801.

CAREER: Cornell University, Ithaca, N.Y., assistant in psychology, 1917; University of Minnesota, Minneapolis, instructor, 1919-21; University of Illinois at Urbana-Champaign, assistant professor, 1921-34, professor of psychology, 1934-60, professor emeritus, beginning 1960. *Member:* American Psychological Association (fellow), American Association for the Advancement of Science (fellow), Psychonomic Society, Midwestern Psychological Association (life member), Illinois Psychological Association (life member), Phi Beta Kappa, Sigma Xi, University Club (Urbana). *Awards, honors:* National Research Council fellow, 1926-27; D.Sc., Occidental College, 1961; National Science Foundation grant.

WRITINGS—All published by Wiley, except as indicated: *Motivation of Behavior,* 1936; *Emotion in Man and Animal: Its Nature and Dynamic Basis,* 1943, 2nd revised edition, Robert E. Krieger, 1973; *Motivation and Emotion,* 1961; *Understanding Your Feelings and Emotions,* Prentice-Hall, 1975. Contributor of numerous articles on motivation to encyclopedias; contributor of about eighty papers to technical journals.

WORK IN PROGRESS: Continuing research and writing.

SIDELIGHTS: Paul Thomas Young retired officially in September, 1960, after thirty-nine years on the Illinois faculty; he worked for several more years on his laboratory tests under a $21,900 grant from the National Science Foundation. His writing was mainly in the field of comparative and experimental psychology. *Avocational interests:* Music and travel.†

Z

ZACK, Arnold M(arshall) 1931-

PERSONAL: Born October 7, 1931, in Lynn, Mass.; son of Samuel George (an attorney) and Bess (Freedman) Zack; married Norma Wilner, August 10, 1969; children: Jonathan, Rachel. *Education:* Tufts University, A.B., 1953; Yale University, LL.B., 1956; Harvard University, M.P.A., 1961, M.A., 1963. *Home and office:* 170 West Canton St., Boston, Mass. 02118.

CAREER: Attorney, arbitrator, and manpower consultant in Boston, Mass., 1956—. Lecturer in labor economics, Northeastern University; Fulbright professor, Haile Selassie I University, 1963-64. Director, Labor Management Institute. Consultant to United Nations Congo Operation, U.S. Peace Corps, Department of Labor, Ethiopian Ministry of National Community Development, and to other agencies. *Member:* National Academy of Arbitrators (member of board of governors, 1976-79; vice-president, 1980-83), African Studies Association (fellow), Industrial Relations Research Association (chapter officer and program chairman at 1959 national meeting), Society for International Development, International Society for Labor Law and Social Legislation, Harvard Club of Boston, Yale Club of New York.

WRITINGS: Trade Unions and the Development of Middle Level Manpower, University of Ghana, 1962; *The New Labor Relations in Ethiopia,* Department of Economics, Haile Selassie I University, 1964; *Labor Training in Developing Countries: A Challenge in Responsible Democracy,* Praeger, 1964; *Understanding Fact Finding in the Public Sector,* U.S. Government Printing Office, 1974; *Understanding Grievance Arbitration in the Public Sector,* U.S. Government Printing Office, 1974; *Grievance Arbitration: A Practical Guide,* International Labor Office, 1977; *Arbitration of Discipline and Discharge Cases,* American Arbitration Association, 1979.

Contributor: Colin Legum, editor, *Africa: A Handbook to the Continent,* Praeger, 1962; William Y. Elliot, editor, *Education and Training in Developing Countries: The Role of U.S. Foreign Aid,* Praeger, 1966; Jeffrey Butler, editor, *Boston University Papers on Africa,* Praeger, 1967; Thomas Christensen, editor, *Proceedings of Annual Conference of New York University Conference on Labor,* Matthew Bender, 1968, 1970; Sam Zageria, editor, *Public Workers and Public Unions,* Prentice-Hall, 1972. Contributor of articles to reports and journals.

ZEFF, Stephen A(ddam) 1933-

PERSONAL: Born July 26, 1933, in Chicago, Ill.; son of Roy David (an advertising man) and Hazel (Sex) Zeff. *Education:* University of Colorado, B.S., 1955, M.S., 1957; University of Michigan, M.B.A., 1960, Ph.D., 1962. *Office:* Jesse H. Jones Graduate School of Administration, Rice University, Houston, Tex. 77001.

CAREER: University of Colorado, Boulder, instructor in accounting, 1955-57; University of Michigan, Ann Arbor, lecturer in accounting, 1960-61; Tulane University, New Orleans, La., assistant professor, 1961-63, associate professor, 1963-67, professor of accounting, 1967-78; Rice University, Houston, Tex., professor of accounting, 1978-79, Herbert S. Autrey Professor, 1979—. Arthur Andersen & Co. Lecturer, University of Edinburgh, 1970; Australian Society of Accountants Research Lecturer, 1972; Distinguished International Lecturer, American Accounting Association, 1977; Stanford University Lecturer in Accounting, 1978. Honorary senior Fulbright scholar, Monash University, 1972. *Member:* American Accounting Association, American Economic Association, National Association of Accountants, Financial Executives Institute, Accounting Association of Australia and New Zealand, Beta Alpha Psi, Beta Gamma Sigma. *Awards, honors:* Certificate of merit from National Association of Accountants, 1958-59; U.S. Steel Foundation fellow, 1960-61; Wissner Award for Teaching Excellence, 1968-69.

WRITINGS: Uses of Accounting for Small Business, Bureau of Business Research, University of Michigan, 1962; (editor with Thomas F. Keller) *Financial Accounting Theory: Issues and Controversies,* McGraw, Volume I, 1964, 2nd edition, 1973, Volume II, 1969; *The American Accounting Association: Its First Fifty Years,* Prentice-Hall, 1966; (editor) *Business Schools and the Challenge of International Business,* Graduate School of Business Administration, Tulane University, 1968; (editor with Alfred Rappaport and Peter A. Firmin) *Public Reporting by Conglomerates: The Issues, the Problems, and Some Possible Solutions,* Prentice-Hall, 1968; *Forging Accounting Principles in Five Countries: A History and an Analysis of Trends,* Stipes, 1972; *Forging Accounting Principles in Australia,* Australian Society of Accountants, 1973; (editor) *Asset Appreciation, Business Income and Price-Level Accounting, 1918-1935,* Arno, 1976; *Forging Accounting Principles in New Zealand,* Victoria University Press, 1979; (editor with Joel Demski and Nicholas Dopuch) *Essays in Honor of William A. Paton: Pioneer Accounting Theorist,* Division of Research, Graduate School of Business Administration, University of Michigan, 1979. Contributor of articles to professional and academic periodicals. *Accounting Review,* book review editor, 1962-66, editor, 1977—.

WORK IN PROGRESS: A history of the Accounting Principles Board; a biographical study of the late Henry Rand Hatfield of the University of California, Berkeley.

* * *

ZIEGLER, Alan 1947-
(Mercy Bona)

PERSONAL: Born August 21, 1947, in Brooklyn, N.Y.; son of Matthew and Pearl (Popowsky) Ziegler. *Education:* Union College and University, Schenectady, N.Y., B.S., 1970; City College of the City University of New York, M.A., 1974. *Home:* 309 West 104th St., New York, N.Y. 10025. *Office:* Teachers and Writers Collaborative, 84 Fifth Ave., New York, N.Y. 10011.

CAREER: Press-Enterprise (daily newspaper), Riverside, Calif., reporter, 1969; *Evening Press* (daily newspaper), Binghamton, N.Y., reporter, 1970; Consolidated Computer Corp., New York City, machine operator, 1971-72; Environment Information Center (publisher), New York City, associate editor, 1972-74; Bronx Community College of the City University of New York, New York City, faculty member, English Department, 1974-76; resident in poetry writing, New York State Poets-in-the-School, 1974-78; creative writing resident, Teachers and Writers Collaborative, New York City, 1974—; field representative to literature program, New York State Arts Council, 1979—. *Member:* Coordinating Council of Literary Magazines. *Awards, honors:* Newspaper Fund award, 1969.

WRITINGS—All published by Release Press, except as indicated: *Planning Escape* (poems), 1973; (under pseudonym Mercy Bona; with Harry Greenberg and Larry Zirlin) *Sleeping Obsessions* (poetry), 1976; (editor) *Poets on Stage* (essays), 1978; (with Joseph Szabo) *Almost Grown* (poems), Harmony, 1978; *The Writing Workshop: How to Teach Creative Writing,* Teachers and Writers Collaborative, 1981; *So Much to Do* (poems), 1981. Contributor of poems, fiction, and articles to literary magazines and other periodicals. Editor of *Paper Highway,* 1968-69; former associate editor of *Environment Information Access;* co-editor of *Some,* 1972—.

WORK IN PROGRESS: The Friend Song, and Other Stories; "Joy," a screenplay.

SIDELIGHTS: Alan Ziegler wrote *CA:* "I have been told my poetry is very readable, even when the content is 'strange.' Often, I take common experiences and perceptions and twist them into new shapes; sometimes I elongate them past their borderlines, while other times I try to compress them into a flash. Hopefully, the result is a shedding of light. I am less interested in where a poem is going than in how it gets there. I write a lot of what has been called 'prose poetry.' A prose poem is easier to recognize than to define. The obvious difference is that verse poems utilize linebreaks and prose poems don't. Beyond that, it is a question of individual style. For the last few years I have also been writing fiction. My chief concern is telling a story, both to the reader and myself. Many contemporary fiction writers have eschewed 'plots' in their writing; I think it's important that, even if there is not a conventional plot structure, some kind of a story be told.

"I work very hard to make my writing simple and flowing (it needs to be *both*). After a college reading, a student came up to me at the reception and said, 'Oh, so you just sit down and write that stuff.' He was correct that I do sit down, and I do write that stuff, but he left out a lot that goes on in between.

"I have written a movie treatment, which essentially means writing the skeleton of the story. This is particularly careful writing, because each sentence is a commitment—perhaps leading to several pages of screenplay. I also write song lyrics—where rhyme and meter still reign, and where you can spurt out direct, emotional statements (as long as the melody is good).

"For the last six years I have taught creative writing workshops to students ranging from 7 to 75, with all stops in between. Most of my work has been for Teachers and Writers Collaborative, a marvelous organization which sends writers and other artists into New York schools.

"I have written articles about the phenomenon of teaching writing, culminating in a book, *The Writing Workshop: How to Teach Creative Writing,* in which I try to offer an approach to teaching writing in the classroom which emphasizes the experience and imagination of each individual student. Much of what I say to students has been culled from my own and others' writing experiences."

* * *

ZIM, Sonia Bleeker 1909-1971
(Sonia Bleeker)

PERSONAL: Born November 28, 1909, in Starchevicvhi, White Russia; died November 13, 1971, of cancer; daughter of Ivan and Yedlia Bleeker; married Herbert S. Zim (an author), January 16, 1934; children: Aldwin Herbert, Roger Spencer. *Education:* Hunter College (now Hunter College of the City University of New York), B.A., 1933; Columbia University, graduate study in anthropology. *Religion:* Society of Friends. *Address:* Box 34, Tavernier, Fla. 33070.

CAREER: Simon & Schuster, Inc., New York, N.Y., editor, 1931-46; full-time writer of youth books, 1950-71. *Member:* American Anthropological Association, Delta Kappa Gamma (honorary member). *Awards, honors:* D.S., Beloit College, 1967.

WRITINGS—Under name Sonia Bleeker, except as indicated: (Editor of Russian translation) Wanda Wasilewska, *The Rainbow,* Simon & Schuster, 1945; (with Margarita Madrigal) *An Invitation to Russian,* Simon & Schuster, 1949.

All published by Morrow, except as indicated: *Indians of the Longhouse,* 1950; *The Apache Indians: Raiders of the Southwest,* 1951; *The Sea Hunters: Indians of the Northwestern Coast,* 1951; *The Cherokee: Indians of the Mountains,* 1952; *The Crow Indians,* 1953; *The Delaware Indians: Eastern Fishermen and Farmers,* 1953; *The Golden Play Book of Indian Stamps,* Simon & Schuster, 1954; *The Seminole Indians,* Morrow, 1954; *The Pueblo Indians: Farmers of the Rio Grande,* 1955; *The Chippewa Indians: Rice Gatherers of the Great Lakes,* 1955; *The Mission Indians of California,* 1956; *Horsemen of the Western Plateaus: The Nez Perce Indians,* 1957; *The Navajo: Herders, Weavers, and Silversmiths,* 1958; *The Eskimo: Arctic Hunters and Trappers,* 1959.

The Inca: Indians of the Andes, 1960; *The Maya, Indians of Central America,* 1961; *The Sioux Indians: Hunters and Warriors of the Plains,* 1962; *The Aztec: Indians of Mexico,* 1963; *The Masai: Herders of East Africa,* 1964; *The Tuareg: Nomads and Warriors of the Sahara,* 1964; *The Ashanti of*

Ghana, 1966; *The Pygmies: Africans of the Congo Forest,* 1968; *The Ibo of Biafra,* 1969; *Indians,* Golden Press, 1969; (with husband, Herbert S. Zim; under name Sonia Bleeker Zim) *Mexico: A Regional Guide,* Golden Press, 1969.

The Zulu of South Africa: Cattlemen, Farmers, and Warriors, 1970; (with H. S. Zim) *Life and Death,* 1970. Contributor of short stories to magazines.

SIDELIGHTS: When she and her husband traveled, Sonia Bleeker Zim usually concentrated on research for books. In addition to their trips in North America, they traveled in Europe and in 1961 went around the world; in 1962 they visited Mexico, in 1963, Africa, in 1964, Russia, the Near East, and Europe, and in 1965, Guatemala, Mexico, and the American southwest. In addition to periodic visits to Mexico, they made another round-the-world trip in 1969-70 and visited Mexico, Colombia, Peru, and Brazil in the fall of 1970. Her last book, *Life and Death,* was written during her struggle with terminal cancer.†

*   *   *

ZINK, David D(aniel) 1927-

PERSONAL: Born September 17, 1927, in Kansas City, Mo.; son of David Daniel and Virginia (Taylor) Zink; married Joan Wilson (a poet and free-lance writer), February 5, 1948; children: Laurie Wilson, David Paul. *Education:* University of Texas, B.Journalism, 1952; University of Colorado, M.A., 1957, Ph.D., 1962. *Office:* Department of English, Lamar University, P.O. Box 10023, Beaumont, Tex. 77710.

CAREER: U.S. Army Air Forces, 1946-49, and career officer, 1952-65; served in Korea; U.S. Air Force Academy, Colorado Springs, Colo., instructor, 1957-59, assistant professor, 1961-64, associate professor of English, 1964-65; left service as captain; Lamar University, Beaumont, Tex., associate professor, 1965-72, professor of English, 1972—. Adviser to Texas Navy on maritime history of Texas. *Member:* International Oceanographic Foundation, Modern Humanities Research Association, American Association of University Professors, U.S. Naval Institute, Melville Society, Daedalus Research Institute, Jung Foundation. *Awards, honors*—Military: Received battle star and presidential unit citation.

WRITINGS: Leslie Stephen, Twayne, 1972; (with wife, Joan Zink) *You Are the Mystery,* CSA Press, 1976; *The Stones of Atlantis,* Prentice-Hall, 1978; *The Ancient Stones Speak: A Journey to the World's Most Mysterious Megalithic Sites,* Dutton, 1979. Contributor of articles and reviews to *New England Review, Forum, Conradiana, American Neptune,* and other journals. Former editor, *Icarus.*†

*   *   *

ZOLOTOW, Charlotte S. 1915-

PERSONAL: Born June 26, 1915, in Norfolk, Va.; daughter of Louis J. and Ella (Bernstein) Shapiro; married Maurice Zolotow (a writer), April 14, 1938 (divorced); children: Stephen, Ellen. *Education:* Attended University of Wisconsin for three years. *Religion:* Jewish. *Home:* 29 Elm Pl., Hastings-on-Hudson, N.Y. 10706. *Office:* Harper & Row, 10 East 53rd St., New York, N.Y. 10022.

CAREER: Harper & Row, New York, N.Y., senior editor of children's book department, 1940-44, 1962-70, editorial director, Junior Books Department, 1970—, vice-president and associate publisher of Junior Books Department, 1976—. Lecturer, University of Indiana Writers' Conference, 1961, 1962. *Awards, honors: New York Herald Tribune*

honorable mention for book, *Indian, Indian;* Harper Gold Medal Award, 1974.

WRITINGS: The Park Book, Harper, 1944; *But Not Billy,* Harper, 1947; *Storm Book,* Harper, 1952; *The City Boy and the Country Horse,* Wonder Books, 1952; *Magic Word,* Grosset, 1952; *Indian, Indian,* Golden Books, 1952; *The Quiet Mother and the Noisy Little Boy* (Junior Literary Guild selection), Lothrop, 1953; *One Step, Two,* Lothrop, 1955; *Over and Over,* Harper, 1957; *Not a Little Monkey,* Lothrop, 1957; *Do You Know What I'll Do?,* Harper, 1958; *Sleepy Book,* Lothrop, 1958; *The Night Mother Went Away,* Lothrop, 1958, revised edition published as *The Summer Night,* Harper 1974; *The Bunny Who Found Easter,* Parnassus, 1959.

Big Brother, Harper, 1960; *Aren't You Glad?,* Golden Books, 1960; *In My Garden,* Lothrop, 1960; *Little Black Puppy,* Golden Books, 1960; *Three Funny Friends,* Harper, 1961; *The Man with Purple Eyes,* Abelard, 1961; *When the Wind Stops,* Abelard, 1962, new edition, Harper, 1975; *Mr. Rabbit and the Little Girl* (Parents Magazine Book Club selection), Harper, 1962; *Thomas the Tiger,* Lothrop, 1963; *The Sky Was Blue,* Harper, 1963; *The Quarreling Book,* Harper, 1963; *The White Marble,* Abelard, 1963; *A Rose, a Bridge and a Wild Black Horse,* Harper, 1964; *I Have a Horse of My Own,* Abelard, 1964; *The Poodle Who Barked at the Wind,* Lothrop, 1964; *Someday,* Harper, 1965; *When I Have a Little Girl,* Harper, 1965; *Flocks of Birds,* Abelard, 1965; *If It Weren't for You,* Harper, 1966; *I Want to Be Little,* Abelard, 1966; *Big Sister and Little Sister,* Harper, 1966; *When I Have a Son,* Harper, 1967; *All That Sunlight,* Harper, 1967; *Summer Is . . . ,* Abelard, 1967; *The Hating Book,* Harper, 1967; *My Friend John,* Harper, 1968; *The New Friend,* Abelard, 1968; *Mr. Rabbit and the Lovely Present,* Bodley Head, 1968; *The Sleepy Book,* Lothrop, 1968; *A Father Like That,* Harper, 1968; *A Day in the Life of Yani,* Crowell, 1969; *The Old Dog,* Coward, 1969.

A Day in the Life of Latef, Crowell, 1970; *Where I Begin,* Coward, 1970; *Flocks of Birds,* Abelard, 1970; *River Winding,* Abelard, 1970; *Wake Up and Goodnight,* Harper, 1971; *You and Me,* Macmillan, 1971; *The Beautiful Christmas Tree,* Parnassus, 1972; *William's Doll,* Harper, 1972; *Hold My Hand,* Harper, 1972; *Janey,* Harper, 1973; (editor) *Overpraised Season* (anthology), Harper, 1973; *My Grandson Lew,* Harper, 1974; *The Unfriendly Book,* Harper, 1975; *It's Not Fair,* Harper, 1976; *May I Visit,* Harper, 1976; *If You Listen,* Harper, 1980; *Say It!,* Greenwillow, 1980.

SIDELIGHTS: Most critics agree that Zolotow's empathy is what attracts the large number of readers to her books. Marcus Crouch of *School Librarian* remarks that Zolotow "writes the kind of poetry that children write. She catches the fleeting moment as it passes and imprisons it in words. Her verses are frail and delicate. One readily acknowledges her sensitivity. . . ." May Hill Arbuthnot and Zena Sutherland agree with Crouch and explain in their book, *Children and Books,* that "few writers for small children so empathize with them as does Charlotte Zolotow, whose books—with some exceptions—are really explorations of relationships cast in story form and given vitality by perfected simplicity of style and by the humor and tenderness of the stories. . . . [Her] understanding of children's emotional needs and problems, and her ability to express them with candor have made her one of the major contemporary writers of realistic books for small children."

A reviewer for *Junior Bookshelf* also senses the strong bond between Zolotow and the young people who read her books.

The reviewer writes that Zolotow "has an astute perception of what the small child knows instinctively is important to him in that quickening moment when he awakens or at the end of the day when he slips into sleep and dreams. The poetry of the words and pictures will make any preschool child wriggle his toes with delight and wonder at this perfect mirror of domestic bliss."

In publicity material released by Harper & Row, Zolotow seems to answer the question of why she is so successful in relating to children: "My children and their friends often remind me of feelings from my childhood which become the theme of a book. It is a kind of double-exposure—the adult awareness of a phenomenon and the memory of what it seemed as a child. A good picture book must be unpretentious and direct. There should be some universal truth or feeling in it, and what Margaret Wise Brown called the 'unexpected inevitable.' I love children's books because they are part of the freshness and originality of children, qualities that open to infinite variety in theme and treatment."

Also a successful editor for Harper & Row, Zolotow expresses her position on editing to Jean Mercier for *Publishers Weekly:* "We have to allow authors to put in their books all the information that's valid. We have to allow them to write about abortion, sex encounters, death, divorce and all kinds of problems if these are vital to the story. I don't believe any subject should be taboo if it's handled with taste. We have to tell young people the truth. I don't see how this position can be altered."

In a *Los Angeles Times* article discussing what many people feel is the new trend in of realism in youth books, Zolotow tells Dolores Barclay: "What's called the new reality is just common respect for the child. Young people today are a great deal more sophisticated. Books we used to publish for 14-year olds are now being read by 10-year olds. In picture books for younger readers there was a time when death or divorce were never treated and everything worked out well. There's a general implication now that publishers are looking for problem books.... We are not seeking controversial books. We are seeking good books."

Many observers feel one reason for Zolotow's success as an editor is her talent for linking the right artist with the right children's author. For example, Neil Millar in his review of *River Winding,* writes in *Christian Science Monitor:* "This is a near-perfect match of poet and illustrator. [The] poems, free verse or formal, are gems, glimpses of a gentle—most rustic—world seen through a gentle child's perception."

As Zolotow tells Jean Mercier: "We look for those who don't follow the text slavishly; they put in their own individual touches, their own viewpoints. Often the illustrators' work means that some of the text or dialogue can be eliminated. But it has to be there in the first place, so they can 'see' what's happening and get ideas."

BIOGRAPHICAL/CRITICAL SOURCES: School Librarian, September, 1971; May Hill Arbuthnot and Zena Sutherland, *Children and Books,* 4th edition, Scott, Foresman, 1972; *Junior Bookshelf,* December, 1972; *Publishers Weekly,* June 10, 1974; *Children's Literature Review,* Volume II, Gale, 1976; *Christian Science Monitor,* November 13, 1978; *Los Angeles Times,* February 29, 1980.